T

THE VIRGIN BOOK OF BRITISH HIT SINGLES

THE VIRGIN BOOK OF BRITISH HIT SINGLES

Edited by Martin Roach

OFFICIAL

Published by Virgin Books 2008
2 4 6 8 10 9 7 5 3 1

Based on data compiled by Graham Betts

First published in Great Britain in 2008 by
Virgin Books
Random House, 20 Vauxhall Bridge Road,
London SW1V 2SA

www.virginbooks.com
www.rbooks.co.uk

Addresses for companies within The Random House Group Limited can be found at:
www.randomhouse.co.uk/offices.htm

The Random House Group Limited Reg. No. 954009

A CIP catalogue record for this book is available from the British Library

ISBN 9780753515372

How to Use this Book

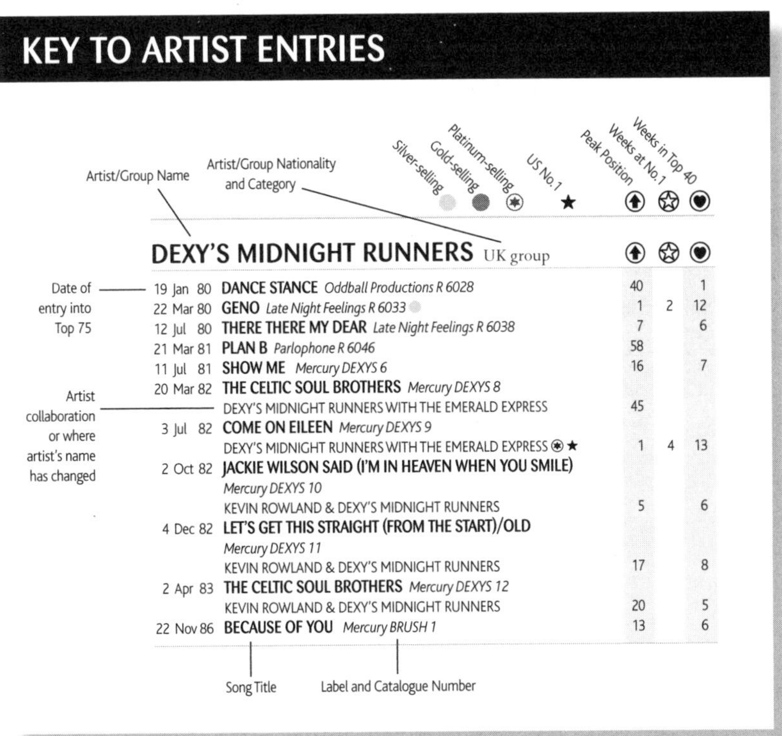
KEY TO ARTIST ENTRIES
Artist/Group Name
Artist/Group Nationality and Category
Silver-selling
Gold-selling
Platinum-selling
US No.1
Peak Position
Weeks at No.1
Weeks in Top 40
DEXY'S MIDNIGHT RUNNERS UK group
Date of entry into Top 75
19 Jan 80 DANCE STANCE Oddball Productions R 6028 40 1
22 Mar 80 GENO Late Night Feelings R 6033 1 2 12
12 Jul 80 THERE THERE MY DEAR Late Night Feelings R 6038 7 6
21 Mar 81 PLAN B Parlophone R 6046 58
11 Jul 81 SHOW ME Mercury DEXYS 6 16 7
20 Mar 82 THE CELTIC SOUL BROTHERS Mercury DEXYS 8
DEXY'S MIDNIGHT RUNNERS WITH THE EMERALD EXPRESS 45
Artist collaboration or where artist's name has changed
3 Jul 82 COME ON EILEEN Mercury DEXYS 9
DEXY'S MIDNIGHT RUNNERS WITH THE EMERALD EXPRESS ★ 1 4 13
2 Oct 82 JACKIE WILSON SAID (I'M IN HEAVEN WHEN YOU SMILE)
Mercury DEXYS 10
KEVIN ROWLAND & DEXY'S MIDNIGHT RUNNERS 5 6
4 Dec 82 LET'S GET THIS STRAIGHT (FROM THE START)/OLD
Mercury DEXYS 11
KEVIN ROWLAND & DEXY'S MIDNIGHT RUNNERS 17 8
2 Apr 83 THE CELTIC SOUL BROTHERS Mercury DEXYS 12
KEVIN ROWLAND & DEXY'S MIDNIGHT RUNNERS 20 5
22 Nov 86 BECAUSE OF YOU Mercury BRUSH 1 13 6
Song Title
Label and Catalogue Number

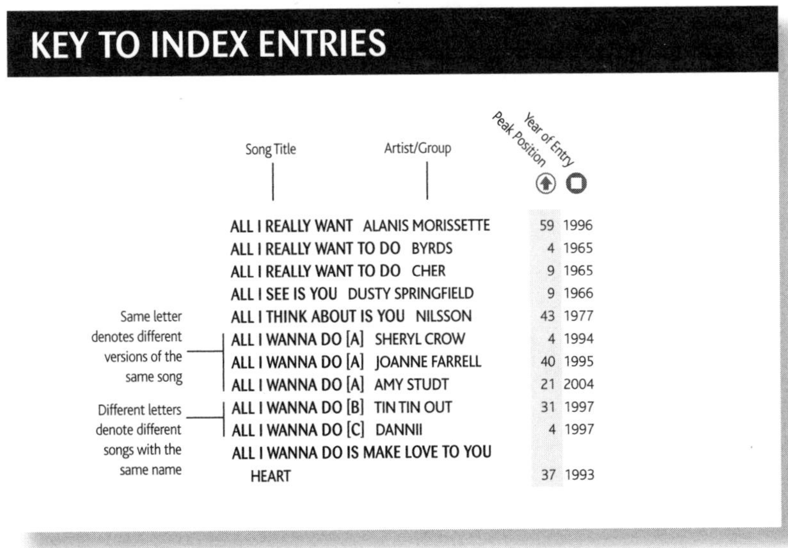
KEY TO INDEX ENTRIES
Song Title
Artist/Group
Peak Position
Year of Entry
ALL I REALLY WANT ALANIS MORISSETTE 59 1996
ALL I REALLY WANT TO DO BYRDS 4 1965
ALL I REALLY WANT TO DO CHER 9 1965
ALL I SEE IS YOU DUSTY SPRINGFIELD 9 1966
ALL I THINK ABOUT IS YOU NILSSON 43 1977
ALL I WANNA DO [A] SHERYL CROW 4 1994
ALL I WANNA DO [A] JOANNE FARRELL 40 1995
ALL I WANNA DO [A] AMY STUDT 21 2004
ALL I WANNA DO [B] TIN TIN OUT 31 1997
ALL I WANNA DO [C] DANNII 4 1997
ALL I WANNA DO IS MAKE LOVE TO YOU
HEART 37 1993
Same letter denotes different versions of the same song
Different letters denote different songs with the same name

Acknowledgements

Martin Roach would like to thank Westlife, Liam Howlett, Harriet Pearson at Sony BMG, Korda Marshall, Craig Jennings, Kaye, Alfie and Korda, Dave Hanley, Phil Robinson and everyone who has worked so hard on this title at Virgin Books. Special thanks to Richard Cable for championing the idea with me; likewise to Martin Talbot, Jonathan Woods and Phil Matcham at the Official Charts Company. Thanks also for additional research to Joe Shooman (Quincy Jones, Bruce Dickinson, Burt Bacharach), Ben Myers (Green Day, PJ Harvey), Ben Welch (Mark Ronson) and David Nolan (ABBA, Tony Wilson).

Contents

Editor's Note

In this edition of *The Virgin Book of British Hit Singles*, I have featured some key examples of when the charts reflected a major shift or moment in British society. Although the majority of the pages in this book contain statistical data, the thousands of facts presented here are actually a genuinely potent document of our time, a numerical catalogue of fashions, political crises, musical genres and trends, social divisions and national unity. Flick to any single page and select a chart hit – chances are you will recognise a moment in your own life, which will be inextricably linked to a period in time, perhaps a flashpoint in British history or maybe something more simple, like a childhood friend or a family memory. By telling the tale of the Sex Pistols' controversial peak, the 'Battle of Britain' when Blur and Oasis ruled the (Britpop) world, the omnipresence of reality TV talent shows, the colossal impact of grunge and the confrontational sexuality of 'Relax', I am also recounting episodes in British life, chapters of a story that can be told without reference to the social soundtrack, but are infinitely less entertaining, emotional and memorable with the volume turned down.

Introduction

In the 1970s and 1980s, a whole generation of music fans used to sit in their bedrooms on a Sunday night, BBC Radio 1 blaring out, a cassette recorder plugged in to the radio and a blank C-60 tape at the ready. It was a rite of passage, a teenage essential. It felt contraband. The sound of the DJ's voice being crudely cut off at the start of a song (because the 'Record' button was pressed too late) seemed to serve as a reminder of the illicit copying. Home taping was killing music, apparently, and those pesky cheapskate kids were the worst offenders. The record business and Musicians' Union were appalled – the entire chart Top 40, plundered on to magnetic tape without a single penny being paid to the artists. This was piracy, copyright theft, stealing. Bad things would happen to these young pirates.

Rewind another two decades or so and there is another precedent. In the 1960s you will find a fascinating precursor to the institutional panic of the post-millennial music business with the so-called 'non-needle time' era. The hundreds of radio stations of the present day were but a distant whim of the future and the BBC provided most people's only access to music, other than actual concerts. The airwaves were usually filled with covers of old songs and orchestral music, both performed live by musicians belonging to the Musicians' Union. With the advent of more vinyl, records began being played more often and the Union was petrified at the prospect of their members becoming redundant. Similarly, the record companies feared that too much airtime devoted to vinyl spins would dilute actual sales of new songs. So, the concept of 'non-needle time' was proposed, whereby each day's programming had a maximum amount of vinyl spins, thereby guaranteeing certain quantities of live music and, by definition, work for the MU members. In fact, the early origins of the seminal John Peel Sessions were rooted in the need for 'stylus on vinyl' not taking over the airwaves. A backlash against this non-needle-time culture sprang up in the form of pirate radio stations, usually anchored off the British coast in international waters, broadcasting music played from vinyl, all day long. The record labels dabbled with Radio Luxembourg on occasion, though only usually in the form of 'info-mercials' about certain acts.

The system seems archaic now; the record companies' myopic stance on vinyl getting airtime is almost comically at odds with today's focus on getting on to radio stations, holy-grail play lists. Radio is king and all that. Yet, back then, needle time was seen as a very real threat to working musicians, their income and the future creation of new music.

Sounds familiar?

Of course, home taping and vinyl on the airwaves didn't kill music. No one was arrested. As far as the history books tell us, the musicians of those decades didn't starve and the record companies certainly didn't seem to lose too many profits.

So, fast forward to 2008, and the music world into which this first edition of *The Virgin Book of British Hit Singles* is published is so far removed from its predecessors of twenty, ten, even five years ago, as to be unrecognisable. Home taping has been replaced by the digital download, both legal and illegal, but this time, as a result, *everything* has changed.

Artists are releasing albums for 'free', record companies' equities are in freefall, shops have stopped selling CD singles, what is going on? And to paraphrase David Byrne of Talking Heads, how did we get here?

There have been many watershed moments, but perhaps if we start at the point when the record business started suing its own customers. Never a good development. Why? To be fair to the much-maligned record companies, because the Beelzebub of the music business – Napster – and its band of jolly little demons were sharing songs and albums for free. The advent of digital technology had reduced the sweat and blood of an artist's inspiration down to a small file, a series of 1s and 0s, embedded in a computer that could – and this was the worst bit, the Armageddon moment – *share* it with other users.

The market leader in this so-called 'peer-to-peer' file sharing was indeed Napster. Its history has been written a thousand times, but suffice to say, Napster was so appealing to the general public that it was the then-fastest software adoption in history; at one point, numerous American universities had to ban the service because it was taking up so much bandwidth that people weren't able to do research on the socio-economic divergence of the major corn producers from the two sub-continents and other culturally vital works of academia. As long as we could get a free copy of 'Crazy Frog', we didn't care.

All joking aside, that rapid adoption was symptomatic of a seismic fault in the record business. It may be hard to sympathise with multi-billion-pound corporations, but imagine if the product you make every day and is the core of your business is suddenly, overnight it seems, being giving away for free. And you can't do anything about it.

That's why the record business sued its own customers. It had to be stopped, they said. Napster's founder, Shawn Fanning, eventually saw his service closed down by the courts, only for it to be re-launched as a legal site; meanwhile, like those ants round the edges of your garden, you squash one but three more turn up in their place. But it was too late. *Blender* magazine even suggested that the Napster debacle was the 'Biggest Record Company Screw Up of All Time', likening it to 'trying to cork a hurricane'.

In retrospect, we shouldn't have been surprised by the pace of change. In 1877, Thomas Edison successfully recovered 'Mary's Little Lamb' from a strip of tin foil wrapped around a spinning cylinder and in doing so invented the phonograph. A mere century later, The Sex Pistols were born. No future? Plenty. The revolution accelerated exponentially when digital technology exploded. Radio had taken forty years to get a global audience of 50 million people; television took fifteen years to do the same; the Internet achieved the same in less than thirty-six months.

So this is how it came to pass, but *why* was it so? The key causes are manifold. First, the technology was – speaking objectively – quite brilliant. The digital option was cheaper, faster and more convenient than buying a physical CD; when broadband turned a twelve-minute download into a twenty-second exercise, the problem exploded (Interestingly, digital radio means that you can record a single played on air to exceptionally high standards, but the industry wasn't worried about that innovation). Don't even start on how good iTunes is ...

Second, the high prices of CDs had started to drive many people to seek out cheaper forms of accessing music. When that technology was first introduced, a CD cost approximately the equivalent of thirty of today's pounds – not since the days of 12-inch mixes boosting record company coffers was a cash injection like this available. Why the CD revolution was, quite literally, pennies from heaven, was because people wanted to replace their entire record collection. In other words, they bought the identical product *twice*. Then, when the record companies repackaged countless artists' back catalogues into a single Greatest Hits, we bought it again. That's three bites of the same cherry. They even said you could spread jam on the CD, throw it across the room and it would still play. So we bought it, and the shiny new expensive CD player. And Walkman. Etc., etc.

Third, the power balance between record labels and artists was shifting, again as a consequence of technological advances. The signs were there and pre-cursors to this are plentiful. Here's an example, one of many: in 1990, a young Essex rave head called Liam Howlett handed a tape of original tunes to XL Records. He'd written the tunes in his bedroom on a Roland W30 keyboard and an Akai 950; the recordings were ready for the charts. Liam didn't need a £5,000-a-day studio, a producer on royalties and a record label with a bottomless chequebook to finance the recording of his tunes. He called himself Prodigy and 20 million album sales later, is the biggest selling hard-dance act of all time with Number 1 albums in over twenty-five countries (we know all about the Firestarter). Liam is one of the earliest and most successful examples of talent adopting the new technology for creative reasons, but in the process cracks started to emerge in the record business model that nearly two decades later are chasms. He wasn't a sole prodigy either. The tide had turned. Back then, Liam's records were distributed through conventional channels using retail stores and physical CDs and vinyl. It wouldn't be long, however before pioneers like Liam began to question this route to market. The creative part of the process could suddenly be done quickly and cheaply; before long, for many, the manufacture of the CD was, in theory, redundant. Other parts of the production chain would also be affected – only recently, a huge mastering facility in central London closed down because software advances meant this previously exacting part of the process could now also be done at home.

Fourth, people started adding, poking and googling each other. The birth of social network sites (see separate feature) is a historically important technological and social revolution touched on elsewhere in this book, but suffice to say here that – in addition to Napster *et al.* – it was a further conduit for the mass distribution of these digital music files. MySpace is perhaps the daddy, Facebook and Bebo the offspring, and there will be many more. The relevance here is that people, bands, songwriters could now showcase their music to an audience of millions free of charge – enter Arctic Monkeys, Belle & Sebastian, Kate Nash *et al.* The record labels shuddered once more. The revolution was here.

Let me quote you the words of industry legend and technology seer, the late Maurice Oberstein – at an industry event in the early 1990s designed to discuss the impact of digital files and CD culture, he asked his profit-rich colleagues, 'Do you realise we are giving away our master tapes here?'

The advent of the digital file was like a tremor at the earth's core; by the time it had risen to the surface, its effects were off the Richter scale. The most direct repercussion was that a band was now able to make a song themselves and, via social network sites or destinations such as iTunes, sell it to the public without any need for recourse to the conventional record business.

In theory.

In practice, this hasn't happened perhaps as much as people at first feared. The most obvious high profile example is Radiohead's 2007 album *In Rainbows*. The new album was offered on their own site at a price the buyer thought was fair, even if that figure was £0.00. On the first day of its release, *In Rainbows* was downloaded a staggering 1.2 million times – stats tell us that only a third of those paid nothing; the average price was £4 and a substantial number paid the equivalent full album price. The band's experiment effectively disqualified their seventh album from the charts but it would have easily been a Number 1 record. When it was subsequently released as a physical album late in 2007, it shifted over 45,000 copies in a week in retail outlets and hit the top spot after all. One unsung irony is that the band's enigmatic and brilliantly gifted singer, Thom Yorke, is by all accounts a vinyl junkie.

In a sense, this was nothing new. For years, record companies gave away CDs free of charge as so-called cover-mounts on magazines; did this devalue the core product? Unlikely. Admittedly, these were usually compilations or very old albums, but how many of those free CDs have you still got and still play?

Of course, seven albums into a globally successful career, such risks are altogether manageable. While admiring Radiohead's innovation – and, let's be frank, nerve – the strategy will do little to assist new bands. After selling 40,000 copies of their 2005 debut album, *Tragedy Rocks*, on Warners, Camden-based band The Crimea opted to offer their follow-up, *Secrets Of The Witching Hour*, for free via their own site. Their theory was by distributing their album more widely, more people would come to their live shows. The free album was downloaded 60,000 times, a 50 per cent increase on the conventionally released predecessor. However, none of these copies were paid for and the exercise was seen by many as a career downturn.

In March 2008, The Charlatans offered their new album, *You Cross My Path*, as a free download from the website of alternative radio station XFM – a full month before the new album's eventual physical release. Prince glued his new opus to the front of the *Daily Mail*, as a way of promoting his twenty-one-date near-residency at the O2 Arena, where he also gave away the album to ticket holders. McFly also released their July 2008 album, *Radio Active*, with copies of the *Mail on Sunday* (an audience of nearly three million).

But this phenomenon is not taking over the industry (yet). The Charlatans album only landed at Number 39 – previous albums were often chart-toppers. And for every Thom Yorke there is a Noel Gallagher, that most savage wit of the pop biz, who is not so keen. In July 2008, he said on BBC Radio 1 that, 'I'm not going to spend a year in the most expensive recording studio in London, with one of the most expensive producers in the world, and use one of the most expensive artists for the cover and then give it away for free.'

A second major repercussion of the download era is the absolute renaissance of the live circuit. The gig, concert, show, spectacular, call it what you will, rules again. In the 'good old days', bands toured an album to fuel record sales; record companies often offered 'tour support', namely money, to keep the band out on the road longer and therefore sell more records. Not any more.

While CD sales have been in freefall and record companies' nails are bitten to the quick, the live circuit has never been healthier. You buy a chart album for £8 with your weekly shop, but the only way you can get to hear the same artists is to pay good money for a live ticket. The tables have turned ('scuse the pun) because a front-row seat for a show can cost more than double what the artists' entire back-catalogue will set you back. It is perfectly commonplace to pay ten times more for your seat in a venue than for the album the artist is performing from.

Has this put us off?

Far from it.

Revenues from live shows are said to be up 50 per cent over the past decade. This at a time when record companies revenues are barely enough to pay for a sandwich, never mind an executive lunch. The live show is now, some say, a rare example of like-minded individuals coming together, away from their MySpace accounts and Facebook profiles, to socialise in real life once more. You can't enjoy the primal excitement of a brilliant live show via a download; a great live band is a unique chemistry of individuals and songs that cannot be replicated easily; so the live show has that most awfully termed managerial asset – a USP.

So much so, that the new emperors of the music business are to be found elsewhere than the hallowed record company headquarters – in 2007, Madonna signed a new deal with the promoter and live entertainment behemoth, Live Nation (giving them involvement with all aspects of her income except music publishing). U2 have done a similar deal (albeit with physical CDs still going through Universal Records). Remember in 1965 when Bob Dylan was berated for 'going electric'? Well, now his records are distributed by a coffee company. (As late as July 2008, indie band Hamfatter even secured funding via the BBC2 entrepreneurial TV show *Dragons' Den.*)

Unfortunately, the same cannot be said for physical sales of CD singles, the third and perhaps most extreme repercussion of the download age. There were very early warning signs. The dissemination of infant CD-burning technology saw the collapse of legitimate markets in the Far East where in some countries black-market copies can account for upwards of 80 per cent of all sales. Although this is as much a piracy issue as a technological one, it was inevitable that similar problems would spread west. Since 1997, sales in the UK have dropped from 77.6 million in that year to a low of 23.2 million in 2004. In 2008, Woolworths announced it was to stop selling actual CD singles altogether – that store had long been a bastion of the Monday morning rush to get a new band's single, yet now it couldn't wash its hands of its old favourite fast enough. Others followed suit. By the time this book is updated in 2010, industry insiders suggest that, in America at least, physical CD singles will no longer exist. The download doesn't offer that comfort to the back-catalogue of these labels either – like when we bought replacement CDs for all our vinyl – because any CDs already owned are transferred in a few minutes.

The statistics are stark: in the year of the download chart being launched, 5.8 million legal downloads were sold compared to 26.5 million physical singles sold – a ratio of approximately one in five. By the end of 2007, downloads accounted for 78 million out of a total of 86.6 million, with the balance very much reversed, representing a figure of 90 per cent.

With sales of their physical formats imploding, the record companies have been forced to find new ways to generate income. This cataclysmic impact has penetrated so deeply into the roots of the industry that it has rapidly changed the strategies and policies for record companies and new bands – and therefore the type and number of artists who will be appearing in future editions of this book. Labels are now looking to strike what is known as '360 deals' (David Brent would call them 'multi-platform') namely where they advance monies against a share of an artist's music, but also a slice of touring, sponsorship, publishing rights, TV appearances, merchandising, ringtones, multi-media etc. Bands are understandably baulking at this, but the climate has changed and the labels cannot exist on CD sales alone. Especially if that CD is now considered a cut-price commodity.

Robbie Williams won few friends when he cheered, 'I'm rich beyond my wildest dreams!' after signing with EMI for £80 million in 2002, but the whispers about the vast advance did not highlight the all-inclusive nature of his deal. The naysayers questioned how an artist who had not broken the USA could recoup such a vast sum; insiders pointed to the 360-style deal as justification. The money markets remain doubtful; when EMI was recently sold to private equity firm Terra Firma, it was a figure that was a third of the sum mentioned when Universal had mooted buying it rival ten years' previously.

As a consumer, we cannot lose. Music is cheaper than ever before to access; the variety, speed and convenience of accessing that music is staggering; live shows have never been so well funded and therefore spectacular and festivals are enjoying a complete revival (in 2007 there were 450 in the UK alone). We've never had it so good.

For the record companies, well, let's just say it's been better. The global record industry has effectively been told that its core product is of little or no value. In 2008, we can get most chart albums for around eight or nine pounds, some for less (the online retailers like CD WOW opened the floodgates). This figure is actually slightly lower than record companies were getting for *dealer* price not so long ago. The days of a net profit per album CD of £5 are but a happy memory; a record label earning more than £2 per unit in 2008 would pat itself on the back. When shifting over a million copies of a big artist, that drop in revenue is staggering.

Record companies hope that downloads will replace physical format sales, but they are also not so recklessly optimistic to rely on this. What the download phenomenon has seen in recent years is an industry, if not complacent, then certainly comfortable, that was wrenched into a whole new scary place – the best record labels with the best executives will rise to the challenge and morph into something new and hungry; the worst will implode at a frightening pace.

Did they deserve it? Some argue yes. But there is an element of user honesty needed here – you hear complaints of declining music standards and albums with two singles and ten filler songs. Downloading allows selective purchasing, take the two classics, leave the rest, spend £1.98 instead of £10. But let's face it, there are an awful lot of peer-to-peer swaps made of entire albums, never mind just singles. In its purest form, it is copyright theft: take the analogy of walking into an art gallery and helping yourself to your favourite painting then strolling out. The police are gonna come calling and you can't take that lovely painting with you to the cell. Plus, regardless of the critics who scorn excessive profiteering and cry justice has been done, making an album can be an extremely expensive and high-risk venture. It's common knowledge that most 'pop' acts will need a chequebook that's good for at least £1 million to break them. User-friendly programming and songwriting software, such as Cubase and Logic – which can be used at home – make such expenses less vital, yes, but certain acts will always need massive marketing budgets.

For a while, it wasn't just the music behemoths that were worried. Initially, smaller independent record labels were fearful – providing the digital product to a still-evolving download industry and countless sites was beyond the financial and logistical capabilities of many smaller labels. In 2004 when iTunes launched in the UK, it had no independent music content. Some observers feared the download would be the domain of the fat bank-balances of the majors. There was even talk of heaving the Office of Fair Trading into the argument. As it transpired, thankfully, this was a false prophecy of doom for the independent sector. With independent record label presence on Napster and iTunes now secured, the panic has dissipated and the impact of downloads – with cutting irony – has hit the four biggest labels hardest.

Another extremely positive facet of the download culture is the breadth of music being accessed. These songs might not make it into this book by charting in the singles lists, but with over 130,000 different songs being downloaded in the UK each and every week, no one can complain that the technology has limited choice. People are listening to more music and discovering more bands than ever before browsing in the sanctuary of their own home rather than in a megastore or an independent Nick Hornby-style record shop. Further, singles have greater longevity of sales, with downloads bringing revenues in months after a song has left the traditional chart lists. Bands have seen much more active downloading of back-catalogue too, which can only be a good thing.

There is also possibly an erroneous assumption being made that every song downloaded would have been purchased in its physical equivalent form. Highly unlikely. And if a 'pirate' copies a CD that they would never have actually bought over the counter, is that a sale lost? Or is someone who downloaded a band now more familiar with that artist and therefore more likely to buy in the future?

It was inevitable that the new technology would have to impact on the charts. In September 2004, the Official Charts Company announced the first ever download chart, compiled using online sales only. Hit Singles giants Westlife were the first Number 1 with 'Flying Without Wings'. (See Westlife biography – coincidentally, that same band hold the record for making the most versions of a song to download – namely 60 takes on 'You Raise Me Up/Flying Without Wings'. The band personalised each version with a spoken word intro saying 'This is for ...' and listed 60 different girls' names.)

The compilation of the charts themselves has evolved too. Initially, downloads were allowed to count towards a singles chart position provided that a physical single was also available in shops; later, downloads were counted in the charts one week prior to the physical copy being sold; finally, in January 2007, downloads counted in the charts regardless of whether a physical format was available or not. Thus, we had songs charting without a physical copy ever being available in shops. 'Crazy' by Gnarls Barkley was the most downloaded song ever (before being toppled by Leona Lewis' 'Bleeding Love') and the most obvious example. After spending nine weeks at the top, it is rightly highlighted as the watershed moment when the download went mainstream. If something's on the *Six O'Clock News*, you know times are a-changin'.

The physical collation of the singles charts will necessarily continue to change. With subscription services beginning to filter through and numerous websites now offering nearly 1,000 albums for legitimate, band-approved free download, the OCC is challenged with keeping pace with a beast that is evolving almost by the day. The doom-mongers who trumpet the end of the charts are misguided because the singles chart is made of sterner stuff. When Led Zeppelin chose not to release singles in the 1970s, the charts didn't crumble overnight. They just didn't include many Led Zeppelin songs.

The most oft-quoted change to the content of the singles charts since the advent of the download is the way songs enter lower and work their way up the list, like in the 'good ol' days'. Uncles in bad shirts across the land have been tutting across Sunday lunches for years about how 'in their day, a band had to work for their Number 1, none of these straight-in-at-number-1-Johnny-come-Latelys ... ' etc. Now, hit singles can chart low, reach the top and even after stick around for weeks.

Notable singles in this vein include 'Numb/Encore' by Jay-Z and Linkin Park, which at the end of March 2008 had been in the charts for 174 weeks. Also the classic song 'Chasing Cars' by Snow Patrol initially entered at Number 25 and rose to 7, but then re-entered the charts when eligibility rules were changed to allow downloads to count, and has remained in the charts ever since – at the time of writing, it sells 2,000 downloads a week.

It's easy to see the argument that downloads have revitalised the charts. The single as a physical format was dying out long before downloads; so you can easily argue that downloads actually gave the genre a new lease of life. And how many times have you heard a song on the radio but never got around to buying the CD single? Now, for 99p and less than five minutes on your computer, it's yours. For every CD single that was sold, the artist might typically earn 50p; from a download at 99p, that figure is now more like 10p to the musician. A smaller slice of a bigger pie then? Not yet; downloads are increasing at a huge rate, but are yet to reach the highs of physical format sales. In simple terms, a download single would have to sell five times the quantity to earn the artist the same amount as a physical format except for the fact that CD singles have plummeted from the all-time high of £4 and now sell for somewhere around £1.50. A balance is being reached.

So it's not all making hay for the artists. They have to rethink as well. Some artists now use technology to sell you a CD of that night's live show as you leave the venue. Others look to more traditional ideas to raise income. Band merchandise has never been so profitable or popular, with T-shirts often taking precedence over a new album at a gig. You sell a CD for £10 and a T-shirt for £20. Some bands – even big bands – fear CD sales at gigs will cut into valuable T-shirt sales.

The statistics are easy to read but look behind them and you still need to mobilise an awful lot of people to have a big single. If you do sell 250,000 copies in a week, it will make headlines in the music media. But what does that actually mean? Well, there are 6,500 retail outlets that contribute sales to the OCC's network. So that would mean an average of thirty-eight people coming into a store and buying that single. In one week. That's five people a day. Downloads can do that without a single person visiting a single shop. And, let's face it, we are a lazy species by nature, and if we can download a song we will; if we go to a record store, they don't have it, we end up buying a DVD of *Gavin & Stacey* or phone credits instead, then before we know it, it's six months later and we're saying, 'Ah, I never did buy that.' By now it's deleted from stores so, if we really love it, back to iTunes it is.

Conversely, there is now a whole revival school of 7- inch singles, some releases *only* being made available in this format – this appeals to the record collector, the DJs, huge chunks of the dance scene and others who remain unconvinced that a digital file – something you can't hold and feel – isn't the only way forward and simply sounds too clinical. 'Five Minutes With The Arctic Monkeys' for example, was limited to 500 copies only and sold for £3.99 – put that on eBay now and you will probably get around £100.

It's a case of recognising the seismic shift in culture. Years ago, CD supporters would take great satisfaction going to the house of a vinyl collector to scoff at their gate-fold sleeves and box sets strewn all over the house – noting that they in fact live alone but need a three-bedroom house to fit in all the 'classics'. Smugly, they'd think of their nice neat little CD collection back at home, a thousand albums spread across a few square metres of wall. Twenty years later, they were destined to meet a teenage music fan who would walk in, look in bemusement at the wall plastered with CDs and wave an iPod the size of a matchbox at them with 345,678 songs on it.

So, what you hold in your hands is a book of data that is a record of phenomenal change, evolution, creative advancement and absolute cutting edge technology; yet, at the same time, there remains a core appeal to any band to break into the Top 40 charts. It might be by downloads, by physical sales – although not yet ringtones – but a Top 40 chart hit is still the Holy Grail for most acts. And Top 40 hits still make those sales because they appeal on an altogether more base level than discussions groups about peer-to-peer transference and Direct-to-consumer marketing strategies. They are great songs. You don't walk down a street and hear a song blaring out of a car radio and think, *Yes, I bet that has a healthy proportion of download sales versus physical* ... You think, That's a great tune.

It is my opinion that the state of the music industry is undeniably fragile; however, the state of *music* has never been better. Despite having fifty-plus years of precedent to compete with, new artists are still providing classic tunes, sounds, gigs and videos. How this new talent is recorded and sold has to be seen as side dishes to the main feast which will always be how good is the music. That's a luxury you can ill afford to enjoy if you have a staff of 3,000 and a plummeting stock value, but to the lucky outsider, we've never had it so good.

And downloads have helped these emerging bands, without a doubt. As has been mentioned, they can post their tunes – without a record deal – on sites such as Myspace and reach a global audience instantly; if that online presence creates interest, when a record label approaches them, the power balance is no longer all one way, they do have options; smaller independent labels can take more of a risk with a new artists as their costs are smaller. This can only be a positive development.

And downloading has raised the bar – in a book such as this, the singles are often the rare highlights taken from an otherwise underwhelming album. Who hasn't peeled off the cellophane on the way home from a shop to listen to a new album, then by the time you pull up at home, you realise you already knew the best tunes and have just wasted £10?

Remember this core truth – people won't download a song if it's rubbish. Even if the band themselves deliver it in person with a 12-inch pizza, people aren't gonna want it. The pessimists tell us that the core product has become worth less than the peripheral products it first created. But this isn't true. The music is still the most valuable asset, it is how it is sold – or distributed – that has changed. So the central commandment about the music business and the charts still remains. In time, when the industry and the bands, managers and business brains have caught up and settled on a island of stability amidst this sea of change and uncertainty, the song will still rule the charts. And, more excitingly, if a band now produces a song that slices into popular culture, they can hit the charts without taking the head buyer of a high street outlet for lunch, without having to buy window space, without having to have 'retail clout'. Downloading has re-energised the charts and has offered a lifeline to a generation of musicians who can now release their material on a scale never before possible. Downloading has made music a meritocracy again, pure and simple.

So what does the future hold? If I knew that, I'd be too rich to spend time writing books. Subscription services are a hot topic, whereby a customer pays either a site and/or a record label an annual fee for all the music they want; how this will impact on the charts remains to be seen. Part of the mass appeal of downloading is convenience/speed and cost – once the music industry finds a way to offer these twin deities of pricing and convenience, those precious net profits will start to climb once more. Illegal sites will exist – regardless of lawyers with double-barrelled surnames and expensive court cases – as long as there are naughty people who want things for free; artists will continue to experiment with their music and how it is presented to the public; but one thing remains unchanged – the song is king.

Long live the king.

A–D

KEY TO ARTIST ENTRIES

Artist/Group Name

Artist/Group Nationality and Category

Silver-selling ● Gold-selling ● Platinum-selling ⊛ US No.1 ★ Peak Position Weeks at No.1 Weeks in Top 40

DEXY'S MIDNIGHT RUNNERS UK group

Date	Title / Label	Peak Position	Weeks at No.1	Weeks in Top 40
19 Jan 80	**DANCE STANCE** *Oddball Productions R 6028*	40		1
22 Mar 80	**GENO** *Late Night Feelings R 6033* ●	1	2	12
12 Jul 80	**THERE THERE MY DEAR** *Late Night Feelings R 6038*	7		6
21 Mar 81	**PLAN B** *Parlophone R 6046*	58		
11 Jul 81	**SHOW ME** *Mercury DEXYS 6*	16		7
20 Mar 82	**THE CELTIC SOUL BROTHERS** *Mercury DEXYS 8* DEXY'S MIDNIGHT RUNNERS WITH THE EMERALD EXPRESS	45		
3 Jul 82	**COME ON EILEEN** *Mercury DEXYS 9* DEXY'S MIDNIGHT RUNNERS WITH THE EMERALD EXPRESS ⊛ ★	1	4	13
2 Oct 82	**JACKIE WILSON SAID (I'M IN HEAVEN WHEN YOU SMILE)** *Mercury DEXYS 10* KEVIN ROWLAND & DEXY'S MIDNIGHT RUNNERS	5		6
4 Dec 82	**LET'S GET THIS STRAIGHT (FROM THE START)/OLD** *Mercury DEXYS 11* KEVIN ROWLAND & DEXY'S MIDNIGHT RUNNERS	17		8
2 Apr 83	**THE CELTIC SOUL BROTHERS** *Mercury DEXYS 12* KEVIN ROWLAND & DEXY'S MIDNIGHT RUNNERS	20		5
22 Nov 86	**BECAUSE OF YOU** *Mercury BRUSH 1*	13		6

Date of entry into Top 75

Artist collaboration or where artist's name has changed

Song Title

Label and Catalogue Number

Silver-selling ○ · Gold-selling ● · Platinum-selling · US No.1 ★ · Peak Position · Weeks at No.1 · Weeks in Top 40

A UK group

Date	Title / Label	Peak Position	Weeks at No.1	Weeks in Top 40
7 Feb 98	**FOGHORN** *Tycoon TYCD 5*	63		
11 Apr 98	**NUMBER ONE** *Tycoon TYCD 6*	47		
27 Jun 98	**SING-A-LONG** *Tycoon TYCD 7*	57		
24 Oct 98	**SUMMER ON THE UNDERGROUND** *Tycoon TYCD 8*	72		
5 Jun 99	**OLD FOLKS** *Tycoon TYCD 9*	54		
21 Aug 99	**I LOVE LAKE TAHOE** *Tycoon TYCD 10*	59		
2 Mar 02	**NOTHING** *London LONCD 463*	9		4
1 Jun 02	**STARBUCKS** *London LONCD 467*	20		2
30 Nov 02	**SOMETHING'S GOING ON** *London LONCD 471*	51		
13 Sep 03	**GOOD TIME** *London LONCD 480*	23		1
14 May 05	**RUSH SONG** *London LONCDP487*	35		1
30 Jul 05	**BETTER OFF WITH HIM** *London LONCD488*	52		

A-STUDIO Russian production group

Date	Title / Label	Peak Position	Weeks at No.1	Weeks in Top 40
8 Jul 06	**SOS** *Absolution CXABSOL7* A-STUDIO FEATURING POLINA	64		

A*TEENS Swedish group

Date	Title / Label	Peak Position	Weeks at No.1	Weeks in Top 40
4 Sep 99	**MAMMA MIA** *Stockholm 5613432*	12		3
11 Dec 99	**SUPER TROUPER** *Stockholm 5615002*	21		1
26 May 01	**UPSIDE DOWN** *Stockholm 1588492*	10		4
27 Oct 01	**HALFWAY AROUND THE WORLD** *Stockholm 0153612*	30		1

A VS B UK production duo

Date	Title / Label	Peak Position	Weeks at No.1	Weeks in Top 40
9 May 98	**RIPPED IN 2 MINUTES** *Positiva CDTIV 89*	49		

AALIYAH US singer

Date	Title / Label	Peak Position	Weeks at No.1	Weeks in Top 40
2 Jul 94	**BACK AND FORTH** *Jive JIVECD 357*	16		2
15 Oct 94	**(AT YOUR BEST) YOU ARE LOVE** *Jive JIVECD 359*	27		1
11 Mar 95	**AGE AIN'T NOTHING BUT A NUMBER** *Jive JIVECD 369*	32		1
13 May 95	**DOWN WITH THE CLIQUE** *Jive JIVECD 377*	33		1
9 Sep 95	**THE THING I LIKE** *Jive JIVECD 382*	33		1
3 Feb 96	**I NEED YOU TONIGHT** *Big Beat A 8130CD* JUNIOR M.A.F.I.A. FEATURING AALIYAH	66		
24 Aug 96	**IF YOUR GIRL ONLY KNEW** *Atlantic A 5669CD*	21		1
23 Nov 96	**GOT TO GIVE IT UP** *Atlantic A 5632CD*	37		1
24 May 97	**IF YOUR GIRL ONLY KNEW/ONE IN A MILLION** *Atlantic A 5610CD*	15		2
30 Aug 97	**4 PAGE LETTER** *Atlantic AT 0010CD1*	24		1
22 Nov 97	**THE ONE I GAVE MY HEART TO/HOT LIKE FIRE** *Atlantic AT 0017CD*	30		1
18 Apr 98	**JOURNEY TO THE PAST** *Atlantic AT 0026CD*	22		2
12 Sep 98	**ARE YOU THAT SOMEBODY?** *Atlantic AT 0047CD*	11		3
22 Jul 00	**TRY AGAIN** *Virgin VUSCD 167* ★	5		8
21 Jul 01	**WE NEED A RESOLUTION** *Blackground VUSCD 206* AALIYAH FEATURING TIMBALAND	20		2
19 Jan 02	**MORE THAN A WOMAN** *Blackground VUSCD 230*	1	1	7
18 May 02	**ROCK THE BOAT** *Blackground VUSCD 243*	12		2
26 Apr 03	**DON'T KNOW WHAT TO TELL YA** *Independiente/Blackground/Unique ISOM 73MS*	22		2

ABBA Swedish/Norwegian group

Date	Title / Label	Peak Position	Weeks at No.1	Weeks in Top 40
20 Apr 74	**WATERLOO** *Epic EPC 2240*	1	2	9
13 Jul 74	**RING RING** *Epic EPC 2452*	32		3
12 Jul 75	**I DO I DO I DO I DO I DO** *Epic EPC 3229*	38		1
20 Sep 75	**S.O.S.** *Epic EPC 3576*	6		9
13 Dec 75	**MAMMA MIA** *Epic EPC 3790* ○	1	2	13
27 Mar 76	**FERNANDO** *Epic EPC 4036* ●	1	4	14
21 Aug 76	**DANCING QUEEN** *Epic EPC 4499* ● ★	1	6	15
20 Nov 76	**MONEY MONEY MONEY** *Epic EPC 4713* ●	3		12
26 Feb 77	**KNOWING ME KNOWING YOU** *Epic EPC 4955* ●	1	5	12
22 Oct 77	**THE NAME OF THE GAME** *Epic EPC 5750* ●	1	4	12
4 Feb 78	**TAKE A CHANCE ON ME** *Epic EPC 5950* ●	1	3	10
16 Sep 78	**SUMMER NIGHT CITY** *Epic EPC 6395* ○	5		7
3 Feb 79	**CHIQUITITA** *Epic EPC 7030* ●	2		8
5 May 79	**DOES YOUR MOTHER KNOW** *Epic EPC 7316* ○	4		7
21 Jul 79	**ANGELEYES/VOULEZ-VOUS** *Epic EPC 7499* ○	3		9
20 Oct 79	**GIMME GIMME GIMME (A MAN AFTER MIDNIGHT)** *Epic EPC 7914* ○	3		8
15 Dec 79	**I HAVE A DREAM** *Epic EPC 8088* ●	2		8
2 Aug 80	**THE WINNER TAKES IT ALL** *Epic EPC 8835*	1	2	8
15 Nov 80	**SUPER TROUPER** *Epic EPC 9089* ●	1	3	10
18 Jul 81	**LAY ALL YOUR LOVE ON ME** *Epic EPC A 1314*	7		5
12 Dec 81	**ONE OF US** *Epic EPC A 1740* ●	3		9
20 Feb 82	**HEAD OVER HEELS** *Epic EPC A 2037*	25		5
23 Oct 82	**THE DAY BEFORE YOU CAME** *Epic EPC A 2847*	32		4
11 Dec 82	**UNDER ATTACK** *Epic EPC A 2971*	26		5
12 Nov 83	**THANK YOU FOR THE MUSIC** *CBS A 3894*	33		2
5 Sep 92	**DANCING QUEEN** *Polydor PO231*	16		4
29 May 04	**WATERLOO** *Polydor 9820539*	20		1

ABBACADABRA UK group

Date	Title / Label	Peak Position	Weeks at No.1	Weeks in Top 40
5 Sep 92	**DANCING QUEEN** *PWL International PWL 246*	57		

RUSS ABBOT UK comedian/singer

Date	Title / Label	Peak Position	Weeks at No.1	Weeks in Top 40
6 Feb 82	**A DAY IN THE LIFE OF VINCE PRINCE** *EMI 5249*	61		
29 Dec 84	**ATMOSPHERE** *Spirit FIRE 4* ○	7		9
13 Jul 85	**ALL NIGHT HOLIDAY** *Spirit FIRE 6*	20		5

GREGORY ABBOTT US singer

Date	Title / Label	Peak Position	Weeks at No.1	Weeks in Top 40
22 Nov 86	**SHAKE YOU DOWN** *CBS A 7326* ○ ★	6		10

ABC UK group

Date	Title / Label	Peak Position	Weeks at No.1	Weeks in Top 40
31 Oct 81	**TEARS ARE NOT ENOUGH** *Neutron NT 101*	19		6
20 Feb 82	**POISON ARROW** *Neutron NT 102* ○	6		8
15 May 82	**THE LOOK OF LOVE** *Neutron NT 103* ○	4		9
4 Sep 82	**ALL OF MY HEART** *Neutron NT 104*	5		7
5 Nov 83	**THAT WAS THEN BUT THIS IS NOW** *Neutron NT 105*	18		3
21 Jan 84	**S.O.S.** *Neutron NT 106*	39		2
10 Nov 84	**HOW TO BE A MILLIONAIRE** *Neutron NT 107*	49		
6 Apr 85	**BE NEAR ME** *Neutron NT 108*	26		3
15 Jun 85	**VANITY KILLS** *Neutron NT 109*	70		
18 Jan 86	**OCEAN BLUE** *Neutron NT 110*	51		
6 Jun 87	**WHEN SMOKEY SINGS** *Neutron NT 111*	11		8
5 Sep 87	**THE NIGHT YOU MURDERED LOVE** *Neutron NT 112*	31		4
28 Nov 87	**KING WITHOUT A CROWN** *Neutron NT 113*	44		
27 May 89	**ONE BETTER WORLD** *Neutron NT 114*	32		2
23 Sep 89	**THE REAL THING** *Neutron NT 115*	68		
14 Apr 90	**THE LOOK OF LOVE (REMIX)** *Neutron NT 116*	68		
27 Jul 91	**LOVE CONQUERS ALL** *Parlophone R 6292*	47		
11 Jan 92	**SAY IT** *Parlophone R 6298*	42		
22 Mar 97	**STRANGER THINGS** *Blatant/Deconstruction 453632*	57		

PAULA ABDUL US singer

Date	Title / Label	Peak Position	Weeks at No.1	Weeks in Top 40
4 Mar 89	**STRAIGHT UP** *Siren SRN 111* ○ ★	3		11
3 Jun 89	**FOREVER YOUR GIRL** *Siren SRN 112* ★	24		4
19 Aug 89	**KNOCKED OUT** *Siren SRN 92*	45		
2 Dec 89	**(IT'S JUST) THE WAY THAT YOU LOVE ME** *Siren SRN 101*	74		
7 Apr 90	**OPPOSITES ATTRACT** *Siren SRN 124* PAULA ABDUL & THE WILD PAIR ○ ★	2		11
21 Jul 90	**KNOCKED OUT (REMIX)** *Virgin America VUS 23*	21		3
29 Sep 90	**COLD HEARTED** *Virgin America VUS 27* ★	46		
22 Jun 91	**RUSH RUSH** *Virgin America VUS 38* ★	6		9
31 Aug 91	**THE PROMISE OF A NEW DAY** *Virgin America VUS 44* ★	52		
18 Jan 92	**VIBEOLOGY** *Virgin America VUS 53*	19		4
8 Aug 92	**WILL YOU MARRY ME** *Virgin America VUS 58*	73		
17 Jun 95	**MY LOVE IS FOR REAL** *Virgin VUSCD 91* PAULA ABDUL FEATURING OFRA HAZA	28		2

ABERFELDY UK group

Date	Title / Label	Peak Position	Weeks at No.1	Weeks in Top 40
28 Aug 04	**HELIOPOLIS BY NIGHT** *Rough Trade RTRADSCD192*	66		
26 Feb 05	**LOVE IS AN ARROW** *Rough Trade RTRADSCD218*	60		

ABI UK singer

Date	Title / Label	Peak Position	Weeks at No.1	Weeks in Top 40
13 Jun 98	**COUNTING THE DAYS** *Kuku CDKUKU 1*	44		

ABIGAIL UK singer

Date	Title / Label	Peak Position	Weeks at No.1	Weeks in Top 40
16 Jul 94	**SMELLS LIKE TEEN SPIRIT** *Klone CDKLONE 25*	29		3

ANDY ABRAHAM UK singer

Date	Title / Label	Peak Position	Weeks at No.1	Weeks in Top 40
8 Apr 06	**HANG UP** *Sony BMG 82876816722*	63		
23 Dec 06	**DECEMBER BRINGS ME BACK TO YOU** *Sony BMG 88697045072* ANDY ABRAHAM & MICHAEL UNDERWOOD	18		2

ABBA

It's hard to imagine now, but there have been times when the UK chart has fallen out of love with ABBA. Initially, however, they started where they intended to go on – at the top. Pop rocker Benny Andersson and his friend and folk-skiffle fan Björn Ulvaeus had previously recorded together before they teamed up in the early 1970s with Agnetha Fältskog (who'd enjoyed a chart-topper in Sweden aged only seventeen and was already renowned as a singer-songwriter) and Anni-Frid Lyngstad (also a Swedish chart-topper). So collectively, they clearly had individual and collaborative chart pedigree going, but it was the Eurovision Song Contest, staged in Brighton that year, that would galvanise the quartet's combined prowess, initially known in 1973 as Björn & Benny, Agnetha & Anni-Frid, changing their name to the more user-friendly acronym of ABBA in 1974 with the song 'Waterloo' (the monicker is actually that of a well-known fish-canning company in Sweden). This glam-rock stomper was the hands-down winner of the contest, also becoming their debut hit at the top of the UK singles charts.

The key to any Eurovision act's longevity, however, is whether they can muster a follow-up to the initial winning tune. In ABBA's case the answer appeared to be a resounding ... no, they can't. Their second UK single, the forgettable 'Ring Ring' only managed to scrape up to Number 32 (it was in fact a re-release of a song that the foursome had put forward as a potential Swedish Eurovision song in 1973). Their next, 'I Do, I Do, I Do, I Do, I Do' climbed to the even less dizzy heights of Number 38. These spangly Swedes were surely just another Euro-flash in the pan?

Then 1975's 'S.O.S.' turned things around. With its kitchen-sink production and emotionally wracked lyrics and vocals, the song tested human resistance to melodic catchiness to the limit. Its chorus was so tempting, even being borrowed by Sex Pistol Glen Matlock for the Top Ten hit 'Pretty Vacant' in 1977. 'S.O.S.' put ABBA back in the UK Top Ten and began a blitzkreig of hits for the group that transformed them from Eurovision has-beens to one of the biggest pop bands ever to grace the charts. 'Mamma Mia' was Number 1 by December 1975, swiftly followed by 'Fernando' and 'Dancing Queen'. Characteristic multi-layered female vocals became part of an easily distinguishable ABBA sound that the record-buying public adored. A relentless wave of Top Fives followed until 1982, notching up nine chart-toppers in all. At one point, they were officially Sweden's biggest export business – overseas territories such as Australia seemed particularly enamoured with their charms.

They set up their own state-of-the-art studio in a vacant theatre in 1978, and hired it out to a diverse range of bands, including Led Zeppelin who recorded much of their *In Through The Outdoor* opus there (the studio eventually closed down and is now a gym). They always provided a spectacular show when touring, but life on the road was not especially popular with certain group members. Then, as personal tensions rose within the group – Ulvaeus and Fältskog split up in 1979; Andersson and Lyngstad divorced in 1981 – the group's UK chart profile declined and their last clutch of singles struggled to make the Top 30. Their final release 'Thank You For The Music' only reached Number 33. They never actually announced a split, they simply bowed out. A stunning achievement topped off by a graceful exit. With rather more low-key musicals and solo projects for the individual members, ABBA dropped off the radar.

They had the record sales, but there was one thing ABBA never had: the cachet of credibility. But that was to change over the following decade. A turning point was 'Abbaesque', the 1992 EP by synth-pop duo Erasure. The four-track release of ABBA cover versions was accompanied by a series of videos that were camper than an entire row of gold lamé tents. 'Take A Chance On Me' was the standout track as a dragged-up Vince Clarke and Andy Bell spoofed the original ABBA video. The EP was the start of a cultural shift in the perception of ABBA that gained momentum during the 1990s with ABBA music featuring in films like *Muriel's Wedding* in 1994, ABBA songs being covered by everyone from Evan Dando of The Lemonheads to Boyzone, plus the musical *Mamma Mia!*, featuring a storyline built around ABBA songs, which premiered in 1999. When Madonna had one of the biggest hits of her career in 2006 with 'Hung Up' – featuring a sanctioned sample of 'Gimme, Gimme, Gimme (A Man After Midnight)', the final veil of doubt was lifted. ABBA were cool. And they couldn't half shift records – annual global record sales rarely dip below two million.

In 2008, 'Mamma Mia' the song and the show became *Mamma Mia!* the movie, starring Meryl Streep and – unbelievably – former James Bond Pierce Brosnan. At the film's Swedish premiere the four members of the group were fleetingly together in public for the first time in more than two decades. There was the inevitable talk of reunions. Björn Ulvaeus didn't mince his words when the possibility was put to him. 'We will never appear on stage again', he stated in news reports. 'There is simply no motivation to regroup. Money is not a factor.' With 400 million worldwide records sales he's probably not lying.

In taking this approach, what ABBA have cleverly done is preserve their memory and ensure that they retain the affection of their fans as well as constantly recruiting new converts to their music. Despite their famous extravagant 1970s and 1980s costumes, in record collections and videos, they will never age. They remain forever in their ceremonial pomp yet, rather brilliantly, seem to be able to pierce the popular culture of any year since their prime. The masters of pop? Don't bet against it.

Silver-selling ○ Gold-selling ● Platinum-selling ⊛ US No.1 ★ | Peak Position | Weeks at No.1 | Weeks in Top 40

COLONEL ABRAMS US singer

Date	Title	Peak Position	Weeks at No.1	Weeks in Top 40
17 Aug 85	**TRAPPED** *MCA 997* ●	3		13
7 Dec 85	**THE TRUTH** *MCA 1022*	53		
8 Feb 86	**I'M NOT GONNA LET YOU (GET THE BEST OF ME)** *MCA 1031*	24		5
15 Aug 87	**HOW SOON WE FORGET** *MCA 1179*	75		

ABS UK singer

Date	Title	Peak Position	Weeks at No.1	Weeks in Top 40
31 Aug 02	**WHAT YOU GOT** *S 74321957192*	4		5
7 Jun 03	**STOP SIGN** *BMG 82876530392*	10		4
6 Sep 03	**MISS PERFECT** *BMG 82876556742* ABS FEATURING NODESHA	5		5

ABSOLUTE US production duo

Date	Title	Peak Position	Weeks at No.1	Weeks in Top 40
18 Jan 97	**I BELIEVE** *AM:PM 5820752* ABSOLUTE FEATURING SUZANNE PALMER	38		1
14 Mar 98	**CATCH ME** *AM:PM 5825032*	69		

AC/DC Australian group

Date	Title	Peak Position	Weeks at No.1	Weeks in Top 40
10 Jun 78	**ROCK 'N' ROLL DAMNATION** *Atlantic K 11142*	24		7
1 Sep 79	**HIGHWAY TO HELL** *Atlantic K 11321*	56		
2 Feb 80	**TOUCH TOO MUCH** *Atlantic K 11435*	29		4
28 Jun 80	**DIRTY DEEDS DONE DIRT CHEAP** *Atlantic HM2*	47		
28 Jun 80	**HIGH VOLTAGE (LIVE VERSION)** *Atlantic HM1*	48		
28 Jun 80	**IT'S A LONG WAY TO THE TOP (IF YOU WANNA ROCK 'N' ROLL)** *Atlantic HM3*	55		
28 Jun 80	**WHOLE LOTTA ROSIE** *Atlantic HM4*	36		3
13 Sep 80	**YOU SHOOK ME ALL NIGHT LONG** *Atlantic K 11600*	38		2
29 Nov 80	**ROCK 'N' ROLL AIN'T NOISE POLLUTION** *Atlantic K 11630*	15		6
6 Feb 82	**LET'S GET IT UP** *Atlantic K 11706*	13		5
3 Jul 82	**FOR THOSE ABOUT TO ROCK (WE SALUTE YOU)** *Atlantic K 11721*	15		5
29 Oct 83	**GUNS FOR HIRE** *Atlantic A 9774*	37		2
4 Aug 84	**NERVOUS SHAKEDOWN** *Atlantic A 9651*	35		3
6 Jul 85	**DANGER** *Atlantic A 9532*	48		
18 Jan 86	**SHAKE YOUR FOUNDATIONS** *Atlantic A 9474*	24		3
24 May 86	**WHO MADE WHO** *Atlantic A 9425*	16		4
30 Aug 86	**YOU SHOOK ME ALL NIGHT LONG** *Atlantic A 9377*	46		
16 Jan 88	**HEATSEEKER** *Atlantic A 9136*	12		5
2 Apr 88	**THAT'S THE WAY I WANNA ROCK 'N' ROLL** *Atlantic A 9098*	22		4
22 Sep 90	**THUNDERSTRUCK** *Atco B 8907*	13		4
24 Nov 90	**MONEYTALKS** *Atco B 8886*	36		1
27 Apr 91	**ARE YOU READY** *Atco B 8830*	34		2
17 Oct 92	**HIGHWAY TO HELL (LIVE)** *Atco B 8479*	14		3
6 Mar 93	**DIRTY DEEDS DONE DIRT CHEAP (LIVE)** *Atco B 6073CD*	68		
10 Jul 93	**BIG GUN** *Atco B 8396CD*	23		2
30 Sep 95	**HARD AS A ROCK** *Atlantic A 4368CD*	33		1
11 May 96	**HAIL CAESAR** *East West 7559660512*	56		
15 Apr 00	**STIFF UPPER LIP** *EMI CDSTIFF 100*	65		

ACE UK group

Date	Title	Peak Position	Weeks at No.1	Weeks in Top 40
9 Nov 74	**HOW LONG** *Anchor ANC 1002*	20		8

RICHARD ACE Jamaican singer

Date	Title	Peak Position	Weeks at No.1	Weeks in Top 40
2 Dec 78	**STAYIN' ALIVE** *Blue Inc. INC 2*	66		

ACE OF BASE Swedish group

Date	Title	Peak Position	Weeks at No.1	Weeks in Top 40
8 May 93	**ALL THAT SHE WANTS** *London 8612702* ⊛	1	3	14
28 Aug 93	**WHEEL OF FORTUNE** *London 8615452*	20		4
13 Nov 93	**HAPPY NATION** *London 8619272*	42		
26 Feb 94	**THE SIGN** *London ACECD 1* ● ★	2		12
11 Jun 94	**DON'T TURN AROUND** *London ACECD 2*	5		9
15 Oct 94	**HAPPY NATION** *London 8610972*	40		1
14 Jan 95	**LIVING IN DANGER** *Metronome ACECD 3*	18		2
11 Nov 95	**LUCKY LOVE** *London ACCDP 4*	20		3
27 Jan 96	**BEAUTIFUL LIFE** *Metronome ACECD 5*	15		4
25 Jul 98	**LIFE IS A FLOWER** *London ACECD 7* ○	5		8
10 Oct 98	**CRUEL SUMMER** *London ACECD 8*	8		3
19 Dec 98	**ALWAYS HAVE, ALWAYS WILL** *London ACECD 9*	12		7
17 Apr 99	**EVERY TIME IT RAINS** *London ACECD 10*	22		2

ACEN UK producer

Date	Title	Peak Position	Weeks at No.1	Weeks in Top 40
8 Aug 92	**TRIP II THE MOON** *Production House PNT 042*	38		1
10 Oct 92	**TRIP II THE MOON (REMIX)** *Production House PNT 042RX*	71		

ACT UK/German group

Date	Title	Peak Position	Weeks at No.1	Weeks in Top 40
23 May 87	**SNOBBERY AND DECAY** *ZTT ZTAS 28*	60		

ACT ONE US group

Date	Title	Peak Position	Weeks at No.1	Weeks in Top 40
18 May 74	**TOM THE PEEPER** *Mercury 6008 005*	40		1

ACZESS UK producer

Date	Title	Peak Position	Weeks at No.1	Weeks in Top 40
27 Oct 01	**DO WHAT WE WOULD** *INCredible 6719782*	65		

ADAM & THE ANTS UK group

Date	Title	Peak Position	Weeks at No.1	Weeks in Top 40
2 Aug 80	**KINGS OF THE WILD FRONTIER** *CBS 8877*	48		
11 Oct 80	**DOG EAT DOG** *CBS 9039* ○	4		8
6 Dec 80	**ANTMUSIC** *CBS 9352* ●	2		16
27 Dec 80	**YOUNG PARISIANS** *Decca F 13803* ○	9		9
24 Jan 81	**CARTROUBLE** *Do It DUN 10*	33		3
24 Jan 81	**ZEROX** *Do It DUN 8*	45		
21 Feb 81	**KINGS OF THE WILD FRONTIER** *CBS 8877*	2		11
9 May 81	**STAND AND DELIVER** *CBS A 1065* ●	1	5	11
12 Sep 81	**PRINCE CHARMING** *CBS A 1408* ●	1	4	9
12 Dec 81	**ANT RAP** *CBS A 1738* ●	3		9
27 Feb 82	**DEUTSCHER GIRLS** *Ego 5*	13		5
13 Mar 82	**THE ANTMUSIC EP (THE B-SIDES)** *Do It DUN 20*	46		
22 May 82	**GOODY TWO SHOES** *CBS A 2367* ○	1	2	8
18 Sep 82	**FRIEND OR FOE** *CBS A 2736*	9		7
27 Nov 82	**DESPERATE BUT NOT SERIOUS** *CBS A 2892*	33		1
29 Oct 83	**PUSS 'N' BOOTS** *CBS A 3614* ○	5		7
10 Dec 83	**STRIP** *CBS A 3589*	41		
22 Sep 84	**APOLLO 9** *CBS A 4719*	13		6
13 Jul 85	**VIVE LE ROCK** *CBS A 6367*	50		
17 Feb 90	**ROOM AT THE TOP** *MCA 1387*	13		5
28 Apr 90	**CAN'T SET THE RULES ABOUT LOVE** *MCA 1404*	47		
11 Feb 95	**WONDERFUL** *EMI CDEMS 366*	32		2
3 Jun 95	**GOTTA BE A SIN** *EMI CDEMS 379*	48		

A.D.A.M. French duo

Date	Title	Peak Position	Weeks at No.1	Weeks in Top 40
1 Jul 95	**ZOMBIE** *Eternal YZ 951CD* A.D.A.M. FEATURING AMY	16		9

ARTHUR ADAMS US singer

Date	Title	Peak Position	Weeks at No.1	Weeks in Top 40
24 Oct 81	**YOU GOT THE FLOOR** *RCA 146*	38		1

BEN ADAMS UK singer

Date	Title	Peak Position	Weeks at No.1	Weeks in Top 40
11 Jun 05	**SORRY** *Phonogenic 82876699392*	18		2

BRYAN ADAMS Canadian singer/guitarist

Date	Title	Peak Position	Weeks at No.1	Weeks in Top 40
12 Jan 85	**RUN TO YOU** *A&M AM 224*	11		9
16 Mar 85	**SOMEBODY** *A&M AM 236*	35		4
25 May 85	**HEAVEN** *A&M AM 256* ★	38		2
10 Aug 85	**SUMMER OF 69** *A&M AM 267*	42		
2 Nov 85	**IT'S ONLY LOVE** *A&M AM 285* BRYAN ADAMS & TINA TURNER	29		4
21 Dec 85	**CHRISTMAS TIME** *A&M AM 297*	55		
22 Feb 86	**THIS TIME** *A&M AM 295*	41		
12 Jul 86	**STRAIGHT FROM THE HEART** *A&M AM 322*	51		
28 Mar 87	**HEAT OF THE NIGHT** *A&M ADAM 2*	50		
20 Jun 87	**HEARTS ON FIRE** *A&M ADAM 3*	57		
17 Oct 87	**VICTIM OF LOVE** *A&M AM 407*	68		
29 Jun 91	**(EVERYTHING I DO) I DO IT FOR YOU** *A&M AM 789* ⊛ ★	1	16	23
14 Sep 91	**CAN'T STOP THIS THING WE STARTED** *A&M AM 612*	12		5
23 Nov 91	**THERE WILL NEVER BE ANOTHER TONIGHT** *A&M AM 838*	32		2
22 Feb 92	**THOUGHT I'D DIED AND GONE TO HEAVEN** *A&M AM 848*	8		5
18 Jul 92	**ALL I WANT IS YOU** *A&M AM 879*	22		3
26 Sep 92	**DO I HAVE TO SAY THE WORDS** *A&M AM 0068*	30		2
30 Oct 93	**PLEASE FORGIVE ME** *A&M 5804232* ●	2		13
15 Jan 94	**ALL FOR LOVE** *A&M 5804772* BRYAN ADAMS, ROD STEWART & STING ○ ★	2		11
22 Apr 95	**HAVE YOU EVER REALLY LOVED A WOMAN?** *A&M 5810282* ○ ★	4		8
11 Nov 95	**ROCK STEADY** *Capitol CDCL 763* BONNIE RAITT & BRYAN ADAMS	50		
1 Jun 96	**THE ONLY THING THAT LOOKS GOOD ON ME IS YOU** *A&M 5813692*	6		4
24 Aug 96	**LET'S MAKE A NIGHT TO REMEMBER** *A&M 5815672*	10		5
23 Nov 96	**STAR** *A&M 5820252*	13		2

Key: Silver-selling ○ · Gold-selling ● · Platinum-selling ⊛ · US No.1 ★ · Peak Position · Weeks at No.1 · Weeks in Top 40

Date	Title / Label	Peak Position	Weeks at No.1	Weeks in Top 40
8 Feb 97	**I FINALLY FOUND SOMEONE** *A&M 5820832* BARBRA STREISAND & BRYAN ADAMS	10		5
19 Apr 97	**18 TIL I DIE** *A&M 5821852*	22		1
20 Dec 97	**BACK TO YOU** *A&M 5824752*	18		3
21 Mar 98	**I'M READY** *A&M 5825352*	20		2
10 Oct 98	**ON A DAY LIKE TODAY** *Mercury MERCD 516*	13		2
12 Dec 98	**WHEN YOU'RE GONE** *A&M 5828212* BRYAN ADAMS FEATURING MELANIE C ⊛	3		15
15 May 99	**CLOUD NUMBER 9** *A&M 5828492*	6		4
18 Dec 99	**THE BEST OF ME** *Mercury/A&M 4971952*	47		
18 Mar 00	**DON'T GIVE UP** *Xtravaganza XTRAV 9CDS* CHICANE FEATURING BRYAN ADAMS ○	1	1	7
20 Jul 02	**HERE I AM** *A&M 4977442*	5		6
25 Sep 04	**OPEN ROAD** *Polydor 9868053*	21		1
11 Dec 04	**FLYING** *Polydor 9869276*	39		1

CLIFF ADAMS ORCHESTRA UK orchestra

Date	Title / Label	Peak Position	Weeks at No.1	Weeks in Top 40
28 Apr 60	**LONELY MAN THEME** *Pye International 7N 25056*	39		1

GAYLE ADAMS US singer

Date	Title / Label	Peak Position	Weeks at No.1	Weeks in Top 40
26 Jul 80	**STRETCHIN' OUT** *Epic EPC 8791*	64		

OLETA ADAMS US singer

Date	Title / Label	Peak Position	Weeks at No.1	Weeks in Top 40
24 Mar 90	**RHYTHM OF LIFE** *Fontana OLETA 1*	52		
3 Nov 90	**RHYTHM OF LIFE** *Fontana OLETA 1*	56		
12 Jan 91	**GET HERE** *Fontana OLETA 3*	4		10
13 Apr 91	**YOU'VE GOT TO GIVE ME ROOM/RHYTHM OF LIFE** *Fontana OLETA 4*	49		
29 Jun 91	**CIRCLE OF ONE** *Fontana OLETA 5*	73		
28 Sep 91	**DON'T LET THE SUN GO DOWN ON ME** *Fontana TRIBO 1*	33		3
25 Apr 92	**WOMAN IN CHAINS** *Fontana IDEA 16* TEARS FOR FEARS FEATURING OLETA ADAMS	57		
10 Jul 93	**I JUST HAD TO HEAR YOUR VOICE** *Fontana OLETA 6*	42		
7 Oct 95	**NEVER KNEW LOVE** *Fontana OLECD 9*	22		2
16 Dec 95	**RHYTHM OF LIFE (REMIX)** *Fontana OLECD 10*	38		1
10 Feb 96	**WE WILL MEET AGAIN** *Mercury OLECD 11*	51		

RYAN ADAMS US singer

Date	Title / Label	Peak Position	Weeks at No.1	Weeks in Top 40
8 Dec 01	**NEW YORK NEW YORK** *Mercury 1722232*	53		
20 Apr 02	**ANSWERING BELL** *Lost Highway 1722402*	39		1
28 Sep 02	**NUCLEAR** *Lost Highway 1722592*	37		1
31 Jan 04	**SO ALIVE** *Lost Highway 9861611*	21		1
10 Jul 04	**WONDERWALL** *Lost Highway 9863098*	27		1

ADAMSKI UK producer

Date	Title / Label	Peak Position	Weeks at No.1	Weeks in Top 40
20 Jan 90	**N-R-G** *MCA 1386*	12		4
7 Apr 90	**KILLER** *MCA 1400* ●	1	4	16
8 Sep 90	**THE SPACE JUNGLE** *MCA 1435*	7		6
17 Nov 90	**FLASHBACK JACK** *MCA 1459*	46		
9 Nov 91	**NEVER GOIN' DOWN/BORN TO BE ALIVE** *MCA MCS 1578* ADAMSKI FEATURING JIMI POLO/ADAMSKI FEATURING SOHO	51		
4 Apr 92	**GET YOUR BODY** *MCA MCS 1613* ADAMSKI FEATURING NINA HAGEN	68		
4 Jul 92	**BACK TO FRONT** *MCA MCS 1644*	63		
11 Jul 98	**ONE OF THE PEOPLE** *ZTT 101CD* ADAMSKI'S THING	56		

ADDAMS & GEE UK duo

Date	Title / Label	Peak Position	Weeks at No.1	Weeks in Top 40
20 Apr 91	**CHUNG KUO (REVISITED)** *Debut DEBT 3108*	72		

ADDICTIVE UK duo

Date	Title / Label	Peak Position	Weeks at No.1	Weeks in Top 40
22 Mar 08	**GONNA BE MINE** *Gusto/2NV CDGUST59* ADDICTIVE FEATURING T2	47		

ADDIS BLACK WIDOW US duo

Date	Title / Label	Peak Position	Weeks at No.1	Weeks in Top 40
3 Feb 96	**INNOCENT** *Mercury Black Vinyl MBVCD 1*	42		

ADDRISI BROTHERS US duo

Date	Title / Label	Peak Position	Weeks at No.1	Weeks in Top 40
6 Oct 79	**GHOST DANCER** *Scotti Brothers K 11361*	57		

ADELE UK singer

Date	Title / Label	Peak Position	Weeks at No.1	Weeks in Top 40
26 Jan 08	**CHASING PAVEMENTS** *XL Recordings XLS321CD*	2		10
9 Feb 08	**HOMETOWN GLORY** *XL Recordings Pacemaker1*	32		2

ADEMA US group

Date	Title / Label	Peak Position	Weeks at No.1	Weeks in Top 40
16 Mar 02	**GIVING IN** *Arista 74321924022*	62		
10 Aug 02	**THE WAY YOU LIKE IT** *Arista 74321954712*	61		
23 Aug 03	**UNSTABLE** *Arista 82876550862*	46		

ADEVA US singer

Date	Title / Label	Peak Position	Weeks at No.1	Weeks in Top 40
14 Jan 89	**RESPECT** *Cooltempo COOL 179*	17		7
25 Mar 89	**MUSICAL FREEDOM (MOVING ON UP)** *Cooltempo COOL 182* PAUL SIMPSON FEATURING ADEVA	22		6
12 Aug 89	**WARNING** *Cooltempo COOL 185*	17		6
21 Oct 89	**I THANK YOU** *Cooltempo COOL 192*	17		5
16 Dec 89	**BEAUTIFUL LOVE** *Cooltempo COOL 195*	57		
28 Apr 90	**TREAT ME RIGHT** *Cooltempo COOL 200*	62		
6 Apr 91	**RING MY BELL** *Cooltempo COOL 224* MONIE LOVE Vs ADEVA	20		4
19 Oct 91	**IT SHOULD'VE BEEN ME** *Cooltempo COOL 236*	48		
29 Feb 92	**DON'T LET IT SHOW ON YOUR FACE** *Cooltempo COOL 248*	34		2
6 Jun 92	**UNTIL YOU COME BACK TO ME** *Cooltempo COOL 254*	45		
17 Oct 92	**I'M THE ONE FOR YOU** *Cooltempo COOL 264*	51		
11 Dec 93	**RESPECT (REMIX)** *Network NWKCD 79*	65		
27 May 95	**TOO MANY FISH** *Virgin VUSCD 89* FRANKIE KNUCKLES FEATURING ADEVA	34		1
18 Nov 95	**WHADDA U WANT (FROM ME)** *Virgin VUSCD 98* FRANKIE KNUCKLES FEATURING ADEVA	36		1
6 Apr 96	**DO WATCHA DO** *Avex UK AVEXCD 24* HYPER GO GO & ADEVA	54		
4 May 96	**I THANK YOU (REMIX)** *Cooltempo CDCOOLS 318*	37		1
12 Apr 97	**DO WATCHA DO (REMIX)** *Distinctive DISNCD 28* HYPER GO GO & ADEVA	60		
26 Jul 97	**WHERE IS THE LOVE/THE WAY THAT YOU FEEL** *Distinctive DISNCD 31*	54		

ADICTS UK group

Date	Title / Label	Peak Position	Weeks at No.1	Weeks in Top 40
14 May 83	**BAD BOY** *Razor RZS 104*	75		

ADIEMUS UK duo

Date	Title / Label	Peak Position	Weeks at No.1	Weeks in Top 40
14 Oct 95	**ADIEMUS** *Venture VEND 4*	48		

ADONIS US production duo

Date	Title / Label	Peak Position	Weeks at No.1	Weeks in Top 40
13 Jun 87	**DO IT PROPERLY ('NO WAY BACK')/NO WAY BACK** *London LON 136* ADONIS FEATURING 2 PUERTO RICANS, A BLACK MAN & A DOMINICAN	47		

ADRENALIN M.O.D. UK production group

Date	Title / Label	Peak Position	Weeks at No.1	Weeks in Top 40
8 Oct 88	**O-O-O** *MCA RAGAT 2*	49		

ADULT NET UK/US group

Date	Title / Label	Peak Position	Weeks at No.1	Weeks in Top 40
10 Jun 89	**WHERE WERE YOU** *Fontana BRX 2*	66		

ADVENTURES UK group

Date	Title / Label	Peak Position	Weeks at No.1	Weeks in Top 40
15 Sep 84	**ANOTHER SILENT DAY** *Chrysalis CHS 2000*	71		
1 Dec 84	**SEND MY HEART** *Chrysalis CHS 2001*	62		
13 Jul 85	**FEEL THE RAINDROPS** *Chrysalis AD 1*	58		
9 Apr 88	**BROKEN LAND** *Elektra EKR 69*	20		5
2 Jul 88	**DROWNING THE THE SEA OF LOVE** *Elektra EKR 76*	44		
13 Jun 92	**RAINING ALL OVER THE WORLD** *Polydor PO 211*	68		

ADVENTURES OF STEVIE V UK/US group

Date	Title / Label	Peak Position	Weeks at No.1	Weeks in Top 40
21 Apr 90	**DIRTY CASH** *Mercury MER 311*	2		12
29 Sep 90	**BODY LANGUAGE** *Mercury MER 331*	29		3
2 Mar 91	**JEALOUSY** *Mercury MER 337*	58		
27 Sep 97	**DIRTY CASH (REMIX)** *Avex Trax AVEXCDX 57*	69		

Silver-selling ○ · Gold-selling ● · Platinum-selling ⊛ · US No.1 ★ · Peak Position · Weeks at No.1 · Weeks in Top 40

ADVERTS UK group

Date	Title / Label	Peak Position	Weeks at No.1	Weeks in Top 40
27 Aug 77	**GARY GILMORE'S EYES** *Anchor ANC 1043*	18		7
4 Feb 78	**NO TIME TO BE 21** *Bright BR1*	34		2

AEROSMITH US group

Date	Title / Label	Peak Position	Weeks at No.1	Weeks in Top 40
17 Oct 87	**DUDE (LOOKS LIKE A LADY)** *Geffen GEF 29*	45		
16 Apr 88	**ANGEL** *Geffen GEF 34*	69		
9 Sep 89	**LOVE IN AN ELEVATOR** *Geffen GEF 63*	13		7
24 Feb 90	**DUDE (LOOKS LIKE A LADY)** *Geffen GEF 72*	20		4
14 Apr 90	**RAG DOLL** *Geffen GEF 76*	42		
1 Sep 90	**THE OTHER SIDE** *Geffen GEF 79*	46		
10 Apr 93	**LIVIN' ON THE EDGE** *Geffen GFSTD 35*	19		3
3 Jul 93	**EAT THE RICH** *Geffen GFSTD 46*	34		1
30 Oct 93	**CRYIN'** *Geffen GFSTD 56*	17		4
18 Dec 93	**AMAZING** *Geffen GFSTD 63*	57		
2 Jul 94	**SHUT UP AND DANCE** *Geffen GFSTD 75*	24		2
20 Aug 94	**SWEET EMOTION** *Columbia 6604492*	74		
5 Nov 94	**CRAZY/BLIND MAN** *Geffen GFSTD 80*	23		2
8 Mar 97	**FALLING IN LOVE (IS HARD ON THE KNEES)** *Columbia 6640752*	22		2
21 Jun 97	**HOLE IN MY SOUL** *Columbia 6645012*	29		1
27 Dec 97	**PINK** *Columbia 6648722*	38		1
12 Sep 98	**I DON'T WANT TO MISS A THING** *Columbia 6664082* ● ★	4		18
26 Jun 99	**PINK** *Columbia 6675342*	13		3
17 Mar 01	**JADED** *Columbia 6709312*	13		3

AFI US group

Date	Title / Label	Peak Position	Weeks at No.1	Weeks in Top 40
21 Jun 03	**GIRL'S NOT GREY** *DreamWorks 4504601*	22		1
20 Sep 03	**THE LEAVING SONG PART 2** *DreamWorks 4504625*	43		
24 Jun 06	**MISS MURDER** *Interscope 9859439*	44		

AFRICAN BUSINESS Italian group

Date	Title / Label	Peak Position	Weeks at No.1	Weeks in Top 40
17 Nov 90	**IN ZAIRE** *Urban URB 64*	73		

AFRO CELT SOUND SYSTEM UK/Irish/African group

Date	Title / Label	Peak Position	Weeks at No.1	Weeks in Top 40
29 Apr 00	**RELEASE** *Realworld RWSCD 10*	71		

AFRO MEDUSA UK group

Date	Title / Label	Peak Position	Weeks at No.1	Weeks in Top 40
28 Oct 00	**PASILDA** *Rulin 6CDS*	31		1

AFTER 7 US group

Date	Title / Label	Peak Position	Weeks at No.1	Weeks in Top 40
3 Nov 90	**CAN'T STOP** *Virgin America VUS 31*	54		

AFROMAN US rapper

Date	Title / Label	Peak Position	Weeks at No.1	Weeks in Top 40
6 Oct 01	**BECAUSE I GOT HIGH (IMPORT)** *Universal 0152822*	45		
27 Oct 01	**BECAUSE I GOT HIGH** *Universal MCSTD 40266* ●	1	3	12
2 Feb 02	**CRAZY RAP** *Universal MCSTD 40273*	10		5

AFTER THE FIRE UK group

Date	Title / Label	Peak Position	Weeks at No.1	Weeks in Top 40
9 Jun 79	**ONE RULE FOR YOU** *CBS 7025*	40		1
8 Sep 79	**LASER LOVE** *CBS 7769*	62		
9 Apr 83	**DER KOMMISSAR** *CBS A 2399*	47		

AFTERSHOCK US duo

Date	Title / Label	Peak Position	Weeks at No.1	Weeks in Top 40
21 Aug 93	**SLAVE TO THE VIBE** *Virgin America VUSCD 75*	11		6

AFX UK producer

Date	Title / Label	Peak Position	Weeks at No.1	Weeks in Top 40
11 Aug 01	**2 REMIXES BY AFX** *MEN 1 MEN1CD*	69		

AGE OF CHANCE UK group

Date	Title / Label	Peak Position	Weeks at No.1	Weeks in Top 40
17 Jan 87	**KISS** *Fon AGE 5*	50		
30 May 87	**WHO'S AFRAID OF THE BIG BAD NOISE?** *Fon VS 962*	65		
20 Jan 90	**HIGHER THAN HEAVEN** *Virgin VS 1228*	53		

AGE OF LOVE Belgian/Italian group

Date	Title / Label	Peak Position	Weeks at No.1	Weeks in Top 40
5 Jul 97	**AGE OF LOVE - THE REMIXES** *React CDREACT 100*	17		2
19 Sep 98	**AGE OF LOVE** *React CDREACT 135*	38		1

AGENT BLUE UK producer

Date	Title / Label	Peak Position	Weeks at No.1	Weeks in Top 40
29 May 04	**SEX DRUGS AND ROCKS THROUGH YOUR WINDOW** *Fierce Panda NING153CD*	71		
21 Aug 04	**SOMETHING ELSE** *Island TEMPTCD011*	59		
19 Mar 05	**CHILDREN'S CHILDREN** *Universal MCSTD40401*	62		

AGENT OO UK production duo

Date	Title / Label	Peak Position	Weeks at No.1	Weeks in Top 40
7 Mar 98	**THE MAGNIFICENT** *Inferno CDFERN 002*	65		

AGENT PROVOCATEUR UK production group

Date	Title / Label	Peak Position	Weeks at No.1	Weeks in Top 40
22 Mar 97	**AGENT DAN** *Epic AGENT 3CD*	49		

AGENT SUMO UK production duo

Date	Title / Label	Peak Position	Weeks at No.1	Weeks in Top 40
9 Jun 01	**24 HOURS** *Virgin VSCDT 1806*	44		
20 Apr 02	**WHY** *Virgin VSCDT 1819*	40		1

AGNELLI & NELSON Irish duo

Date	Title / Label	Peak Position	Weeks at No.1	Weeks in Top 40
15 Aug 98	**EL NINO** *Xtravaganza 0091575 EXT*	21		1
11 Sep 99	**EVERYDAY** *Xtravaganza XTRAV 2CDS*	17		2
17 Jun 00	**EMBRACE** *Xtravaganza XTRAV 11CDS*	35		1
9 Sep 00	**HUDSON STREET** *Xtravaganza XTRAV 13CDS*	29		1
7 Apr 01	**VEGAS** *Xtravaganza XTRAV 23CDS*	48		
15 Jun 02	**EVERYDAY (ALEX GOLD 2002 MIXES)** *Xtravaganza XTRAV 31CDS*	33		1
3 Apr 04	**HOLDING ON TO NOTHING** *Xtravaganza XTRAV 43CX* AGNELLI & NELSON FEATURING AUREUS	41		

CHRISTINA AGUILERA US singer

Date	Title / Label	Peak Position	Weeks at No.1	Weeks in Top 40
11 Sep 99	**GENIE IN A BOTTLE (IMPORT)** *RCA 701062*	50		
16 Oct 99	**GENIE IN A BOTTLE** *RCA 74321705482* ★	1	2	15
26 Feb 00	**WHAT A GIRL WANTS** *RCA 74321737522* ★	3		7
22 Jul 00	**I TURN TO YOU** *RCA 74321765472*	19		4
11 Nov 00	**COME ON OVER BABY (ALL I WANT IS YOU)** *RCA 74321799912* ★	8		4
10 Mar 01	**NOBODY WANTS TO BE LONELY** *Columbia 6709462* RICKY MARTIN WITH CHRISTINA AGUILERA	4		6
30 Jun 01	**LADY MARMALADE** *Interscope 4975612* CHRISTINA AGUILERA/LIL' KIM/MYA/PINK ● ★	1	1	13
23 Nov 02	**DIRRTY** *RCA 74321962722* CHRISTINA AGUILERA FEATURING REDMAN	1	2	7
22 Feb 03	**BEAUTIFUL (IMPORT)** *RCA 74321983652*	51		
8 Mar 03	**BEAUTIFUL** *RCA 82876502462*	1	1	8
21 Jun 03	**FIGHTER** *RCA 82876524292*	3		8
20 Sep 03	**CAN'T HOLD US DOWN** *RCA 82876556332* CHRISTINA AGUILERA FEATURING LIL' KIM	6		6
20 Dec 03	**THE VOICE WITHIN** *RCA 82876584292*	9		7
13 Nov 04	**CAR WASH** *DreamWorks 9864630* CHRISTINA AGUILERA & MISSY ELLIOTT	4		10
4 Dec 04	**TILT YA HEAD BACK** *Universal MCSTD40396* NELLY & CHRISTINA AGUILERA	5		9
29 Jul 06	**AIN'T NO OTHER MAN** *RCA 82876860722*	2		10
18 Nov 06	**HURT** *RCA 88697013962*	11		7
16 Dec 06	**TELL ME** *Atlantic AT0268CD* P DIDDY FEATURING CHRISTINA AGUILERA	8		13
10 Mar 07	**CANDYMAN** *Download*	17		10
8 Dec 07	**HURT** *RCA 88697013962*	39		1

A-HA Norwegian group

Date	Title / Label	Peak Position	Weeks at No.1	Weeks in Top 40
28 Sep 85	**TAKE ON ME** *Warner Brothers W 9006* ● ★	2		16
28 Dec 85	**THE SUN ALWAYS SHINES ON TV** *Warner Brothers W 8846* ○	1	2	10
5 Apr 86	**TRAIN OF THOUGHT** *Warner Brothers W 8736*	8		6
14 Jun 86	**HUNTING HIGH AND LOW** *Warner Brothers W 6663*	5		5
4 Oct 86	**I'VE BEEN LOSING YOU** *Warner Brothers W 8594*	8		8
6 Dec 86	**CRY WOLF** *Warner Brothers W 8500* ○	5		5
28 Feb 87	**MANHATTAN SKYLINE** *Warner Brothers W 8405*	13		8
4 Jul 87	**THE LIVING DAYLIGHTS** *Warner Brothers W 8305*	5		5
26 Mar 88	**STAY ON THESE ROADS** *Warner Brothers W 7936*	5		7
18 Jun 88	**THE BLOOD THAT MOVES THE BODY** *Warner Brothers W 7840*	25		2
27 Aug 88	**TOUCHY!** *Warner Brothers W 7749*	11		5
3 Dec 88	**YOU ARE THE ONE** *Warner Brothers W 7636*	13		8

Silver-selling ● Gold-selling ● Platinum-selling ● US No.1 ★ | Peak Position | Weeks at No.1 | Weeks in Top 40

Date	Title / Label	Peak Position	Weeks at No.1	Weeks in Top 40
13 Oct 90	**CRYING IN THE RAIN** *Warner Brothers W9547*	13		6
15 Dec 90	**I CALL YOUR NAME** *Warner Brothers W9462*	44		
26 Oct 91	**MOVE TO MEMPHIS** *Warner Brothers W0070*	47		
5 Jun 93	**DARK IS THE NIGHT** *Warner Brothers W0175CD*	19		3
18 Sep 93	**ANGEL** *Warner Brothers W0195CD*	41		
26 Mar 94	**SHAPES THAT GO TOGETHER** *Warner Brothers W0236CD*	27		2
3 Jun 00	**SUMMER MOVED ON** *WEA 275CD*	33		1
4 Feb 06	**ANALOGUE (ALL I WANT)** *Polydor 9876840*	10		3
29 Apr 06	**COSY PRISONS** *Polydor 9856227*	39		1

AHMAD US rapper

Date	Title / Label	Peak Position	Weeks at No.1	Weeks in Top 40
9 Jul 94	**BACK IN THE DAY** *Giant 74321212942*	64		

AIDA Dutch production duo

Date	Title / Label	Peak Position	Weeks at No.1	Weeks in Top 40
19 Feb 00	**FAR AND AWAY** *48K/Perfecto SPECT 03CDS*	58		

AIR French production duo

Date	Title / Label	Peak Position	Weeks at No.1	Weeks in Top 40
21 Feb 98	**SEXY BOY** *Virgin VSCDT 1672*	13		2
16 May 98	**KELLY WATCH THE STARS** *Virgin VSCDT 1690*	18		2
21 Nov 98	**ALL I NEED** *Virgin VSCDT 1702*	29		1
26 Feb 00	**PLAYGROUND LOVE** *Virgin VSCDT 1764*	25		1
2 Jun 01	**RADIO #1** *Virgin VSCDT 1803*	31		1
21 Aug 04	**ALPHA BETA GAGA** *Source VSCDX1880*	44		

AIR SUPPLY Australian duo

Date	Title / Label	Peak Position	Weeks at No.1	Weeks in Top 40
27 Sep 80	**ALL OUT OF LOVE** *Arista ARIST 362*	11		8
2 Oct 82	**EVEN THE NIGHTS ARE BETTER** *Arista ARIST 474*	44		
20 Nov 93	**GOODBYE** *Giant 74321153462*	66		

AIR TRAFFIC UK group

Date	Title / Label	Peak Position	Weeks at No.1	Weeks in Top 40
7 Apr 07	**CHARLOTTE** *EMI CDEM720*	33		1
30 Jun 07	**SHOOTING STAR** *EMI CDEM724*	30		1
6 Oct 07	**NO MORE RUNNING AWAY** *EMI CDEM729*	45		

AIRHEAD UK group

Date	Title / Label	Peak Position	Weeks at No.1	Weeks in Top 40
5 Oct 91	**FUNNY HOW** *Korova KOW 47*	57		
28 Dec 91	**COUNTING SHEEP** *Korova KOW 48*	35		2
7 Mar 92	**RIGHT NOW** *Korova KOW 49*	50		

AIRHEADZ UK production duo

Date	Title / Label	Peak Position	Weeks at No.1	Weeks in Top 40
28 Apr 01	**STANLEY (HERE I AM)** *AM:PM CDAMPM 145*	36		1

AIRSCAPE Belgian production group

Date	Title / Label	Peak Position	Weeks at No.1	Weeks in Top 40
9 Aug 97	**PACIFIC MELODY** *Xtravaganza 0091165*	27		1
29 Aug 98	**AMAZON CHANT** *Xtravaganza 0091605 EXT*	46		
4 Dec 99	**L'ESPERANZA** *Xtravaganza XTRAV 7CD*	33		1

LAUREL AITKEN & THE UNITONE Jamaican singer

Date	Title / Label	Peak Position	Weeks at No.1	Weeks in Top 40
17 May 80	**RUDI GOT MARRIED** *I-Spy SEE 6*	60		

AKA UK group

Date	Title / Label	Peak Position	Weeks at No.1	Weeks in Top 40
12 Oct 96	**WARNING** *RCA 74321360662*	43		

AKABU UK producer

Date	Title / Label	Peak Position	Weeks at No.1	Weeks in Top 40
15 Sep 01	**RIDE THE STORM** *NRK Sound Division NRKCD 053*			
	AKABU FEATURING LINDA CLIFFORD	69		

AKALA UK rapper

Date	Title / Label	Peak Position	Weeks at No.1	Weeks in Top 40
28 May 05	**ROLL WID US** *Illa State ILLA001CD2*	72		

JEWEL AKENS US singer

Date	Title / Label	Peak Position	Weeks at No.1	Weeks in Top 40
25 Mar 65	**THE BIRDS AND THE BEES** *London HLN 9954*	29		7

AKIN UK duo

Date	Title / Label	Peak Position	Weeks at No.1	Weeks in Top 40
14 Jun 97	**STAY RIGHT HERE** *WEA 117CD*	60		

AKON US singer

Date	Title / Label	Peak Position	Weeks at No.1	Weeks in Top 40
25 Dec 04	**LOCKED UP** *Universal E9864569*			
	AKON FEATURING STYLES P	61		
5 Mar 05	**LOCKED UP** *Universal 9864570CD*	5		10
14 May 05	**LONELY** *Universal MCSTD40415*	1	2	14
20 Aug 05	**BELLY DANCER (BANANZA)** *Universal MCSXD40426*	5		5
4 Feb 06	**SOUL SURVIVOR** *Def Jam 9889047*			
	YOUNG JEEZY FEATURING AKON	16		3
19 Aug 06	**GIRLS** *Virgin VUSCD328*			
	BEENIE FEATURING AKON	47		
16 Sep 06	**SNITCH** *Interscope 1705438*			
	OBIE TRICE FEATURING AKON	44		
18 Nov 06	**SMACK THAT** *Universal 1714412*			
	AKON FEATURING EMINEM	1	1	16
13 Jan 07	**I WANNA LOVE YOU** *Universal 1722994*			
	AKON FEATURING SNOOP DOGGY DOGG	3		14
3 Feb 07	**THE SWEET ESCAPE** *Interscope 1724450*			
	GWEN STEFANI FEATURING AKON	2		19
14 Apr 07	**DON'T MATTER** *Universal 1734175* ★	3		12
2 Jun 07	**I TRIED** *Download*			
	BONE THUGS-N-HARMONY FEATURING AKON	69		
11 Aug 07	**MAMA AFRICA** *Universal 1743396*	47		
15 Sep 07	**SORRY BLAME IT ON ME** *Universal 1752178*	22		10
1 Dec 07	**SWEETEST GIRL (DOLLAR BILL)** *Download*			
	WYCLEF JEAN FEATURING AKON, LIL WAYNE & NIIA	66		
1 Mar 08	**WANNA BE STARTIN' SOMETHING 2008** *Download*			
	MICHAEL JACKSON WITH AKON	69		

ALABAMA 3 UK group

Date	Title / Label	Peak Position	Weeks at No.1	Weeks in Top 40
22 Nov 97	**SPEED AT THE SOUND OF LONELINESS** *Elemental ELM 42CDS*	72		
11 Apr 98	**AIN'T GOIN' TO GOA** *Elemental ELM 45CDS1*	40		1

ALARM UK group

Date	Title / Label	Peak Position	Weeks at No.1	Weeks in Top 40
24 Sep 83	**68 GUNS** *IRS PFP 1023*	17		5
21 Jan 84	**WHERE WERE YOU HIDING WHEN THE STORM BROKE** *IRS 101*	22		4
31 Mar 84	**THE DECEIVER** *IRS 103*	51		
3 Nov 84	**THE CHANT HAS JUST BEGUN** *IRS 104*	48		
2 Mar 85	**ABSOLUTE REALITY** *IRS ALARM 1*	35		2
28 Sep 85	**STRENGTH** *IRS IRM 104*	40		1
18 Jan 86	**SPIRIT OF '76** *IRS IRM 109*	22		3
26 Apr 86	**KNIFE EDGE** *IRS IRM 112*	43		
17 Oct 87	**RAIN IN THE SUMMERTIME** *IRS IRM 144*	18		3
12 Dec 87	**RESCUE ME** *IRS IRM 150*	48		
20 Feb 88	**PRESENCE OF LOVE (LAUGHERNE)** *IRS IRM 155*	44		
16 Sep 89	**SOLD ME DOWN THE RIVER** *IRS EIRS 123*	43		
4 Nov 89	**A NEW SOUTH WALES/THE ROCK** *IRS EIRS 129*			
	ALARM FEATURING THE MORRISTON ORPHEUS MALE VOICE CHOIR	31		3
3 Feb 90	**LOVE DON'T COME EASY** *IRS EIRS 134*	48		
27 Oct 90	**UNSAFE BUILDING 1990** *IRS ALARM 2*	54		
13 Apr 91	**RAW** *IRS ALARM 3*	51		
3 Jul 04	**NEW HOME NEW LIFE** *Snapper Music SMASCD062*	45		
18 Feb 06	**SUPERCHANNEL** *Liberty 3535112*			
	ALARM MMVI	24		1

MORRIS ALBERT Brazilian singer

Date	Title / Label	Peak Position	Weeks at No.1	Weeks in Top 40
27 Sep 75	**FEELINGS** *Decca F 13591* ●	4		9

ALBERTA Sierra Leonean singer

Date	Title / Label	Peak Position	Weeks at No.1	Weeks in Top 40
26 Dec 98	**YOYO BOY** *RCA 74321640602*	48		

ALBERTO Y LOS TRIOS PARANOIAS UK comedy group

Date	Title / Label	Peak Position	Weeks at No.1	Weeks in Top 40
23 Sep 78	**HEADS DOWN NO NONSENSE MINDLESS BOOGIE** *Logo GO 323*	47		

ALBION Dutch producer

Date	Title / Label	Peak Position	Weeks at No.1	Weeks in Top 40
3 Jun 00	**AIR 2000** *Platipus PLATCD 73*	59		

ALCATRAZZ US production duo

Date	Title / Label	Peak Position	Weeks at No.1	Weeks in Top 40
17 Feb 96	**GIV ME LUV** *AM:PM 5814332*	12		2

ALCAZAR Swedish group

Date	Title / Label	Peak Position	Weeks at No.1	Weeks in Top 40
8 Dec 01	**CRYING AT THE DISCOTEQUE** *Arista 74321893432*	13		6
16 Mar 02	**SEXUAL GUARANTEE** *Arista 74321920252*	30		1
2 Oct 04	**THIS IS THE WORLD WE LIVE IN** *RCA 82876652372*	15		2

ALDA Icelandic singer

Date	Title / Label	Peak Position	Weeks at No.1	Weeks in Top 40
29 Aug 98	**REAL GOOD TIME** *Wildstar CDWILD 7*	7		5
26 Dec 98	**GIRLS NIGHT OUT** *Wildstar CDWILD 10*	20		5

ALENA Jamaican singer

Date	Title / Label	Peak Position	Weeks at No.1	Weeks in Top 40
13 Nov 99	**TURN IT AROUND** *Wonderboy WBOYD 16*	14		3

ALESHA UK singer

Date	Title / Label	Peak Position	Weeks at No.1	Weeks in Top 40
26 Aug 06	**LIPSTICK** *Polydor 1705458*	14		2
4 Nov 06	**KNOCKDOWN** *Polydor 1713036*	45		

ALESSI US duo

Date	Title / Label	Peak Position	Weeks at No.1	Weeks in Top 40
11 Jun 77	**OH LORI** *A&M AMS 7289*	8		11

ALEX PARTY Italian group

Date	Title / Label	Peak Position	Weeks at No.1	Weeks in Top 40
18 Dec 93	**SATURDAY NIGHT PARTY (READ MY LIPS)** *Cleveland City Imports CCICD 17000*	49		
28 May 94	**SATURDAY NIGHT PARTY (READ MY LIPS)** *Cleveland City Imports CCICD 17000*	29		2
18 Feb 95	**DON'T GIVE ME YOUR LIFE** *Systematic SYSCD 7* ●	2		11
18 Nov 95	**WRAP ME UP** *Systematic SYSCD 22*	17		2
19 Oct 96	**READ MY LIPS (REMIX)** *Systematic SYSCD 30*	28		1

ALEXIA Italian singer

Date	Title / Label	Peak Position	Weeks at No.1	Weeks in Top 40
21 Mar 98	**UH LA LA LA** *Dance Pool ALEX 1CD*	10		7
13 Jun 98	**GIMME LOVE** *Dance Pool ALEX 2CDZ*	17		3
10 Oct 98	**THE MUSIC I LIKE** *Dance Pool ALEX 3CD*	31		1
22 Feb 03	**RING** *Virgin VSCDT 1836*	48		

ALFI & HARRY US singer

Date	Title / Label	Peak Position	Weeks at No.1	Weeks in Top 40
23 Mar 56	**THE TROUBLE WITH HARRY** *London HLU 8242*	15		5

ALFIE UK group

Date	Title / Label	Peak Position	Weeks at No.1	Weeks in Top 40
8 Sep 01	**YOU MAKE NO BONES** *Twisted Nerve TN 033CD*	61		
16 Mar 02	**A WORD IN YOUR EAR** *Twisted Nerve TN 037CD*	66		
21 Jun 03	**PEOPLE** *Regal Recordings REG 84CD*	53		
13 Sep 03	**STUNTMAN** *Regal Recordings REG 87CDS*	51		
28 Feb 04	**NO NEED** *Regal Recordings REG 99CD*	66		
13 Aug 05	**YOUR OWN RELIGION** *Regal REG124CD*	61		

JOHN ALFORD UK actor/singer

Date	Title / Label	Peak Position	Weeks at No.1	Weeks in Top 40
17 Feb 96	**SMOKE GETS IN YOUR EYES** *Love This LUVTHIS CD7*	13		4
25 May 96	**BLUE MOON/ONLY YOU** *Love This LUVTHISCDX 9*	9		3
23 Nov 96	**IF/KEEP ON RUNNING** *Love This LUVTHISCD 15*	24		2

ALI UK singer

Date	Title / Label	Peak Position	Weeks at No.1	Weeks in Top 40
23 May 98	**LOVE LETTERS** *Wild Card 5698092*	63		
24 Oct 98	**FEELIN' YOU** *Wild Card 5676992*	63		

TATYANA ALI US singer

Date	Title / Label	Peak Position	Weeks at No.1	Weeks in Top 40
14 Nov 98	**DAYDREAMIN'** *Epic 6669372*	6		3
13 Feb 99	**BOY YOU KNOCK ME OUT** *MJJ 6674742* TATYANA ALI FEATURING WILL SMITH ●	3		5
19 Jun 99	**EVERYTIME** *Epic 6665462*	20		2

ALI & FRAZIER UK duo

Date	Title / Label	Peak Position	Weeks at No.1	Weeks in Top 40
7 Aug 93	**UPTOWN TOP RANKING** *Arista 74321158842*	33		3

ALIBI UK duo

Date	Title / Label	Peak Position	Weeks at No.1	Weeks in Top 40
15 Feb 97	**I'M NOT TO BLAME** *Urgent 74321434762*	51		
7 Feb 98	**HOW MUCH I FEEL** *Urgent 74321548472*	58		
7 Jul 07	**SEXUAL HEALING** *Gusto CDGUS48* ALIBI VS ROCKEFELLER	34		1

ALICE BAND UK/Irish/US group

Date	Title / Label	Peak Position	Weeks at No.1	Weeks in Top 40
23 Jun 01	**ONE DAY AT A TIME** *Instant Karma KARMA 5CD*	52		
27 Apr 02	**NOW THAT YOU LOVE ME** *Instant Karma KARMA 17CD*	44		

ALICE DEEJAY Dutch group

Date	Title / Label	Peak Position	Weeks at No.1	Weeks in Top 40
31 Jul 99	**BETTER OFF ALONE** *Positiva CDTIV 113* DJ JURGEN PRESENTS ALICE DEEJAY .	2		13
4 Dec 99	**BACK IN MY LIFE** *Positiva CDTIV 121* ●	4		13
15 Jul 00	**WILL I EVER** *Positiva CDTIV 134*	7		7
21 Oct 00	**THE LONELY ONE** *Positiva CDTIV 145*	16		3
10 Feb 01	**CELEBRATE OUR LOVE** *Positiva CDTIV 149*	17		3

ALICE IN CHAINS US group

Date	Title / Label	Peak Position	Weeks at No.1	Weeks in Top 40
23 Jan 93	**WOULD** *Columbia 6588882*	19		1
20 Mar 93	**THEM BONES** *Columbia 6590902*	26		2
5 Jun 93	**ANGRY CHAIR** *Columbia 6593652*	33		1
23 Oct 93	**DOWN IN A HOLE** *Columbia 6597512*	36		1
11 Nov 95	**GRIND** *Columbia 6626232*	23		1
10 Feb 96	**HEAVEN BESIDE YOU** *Columbia 6628935*	35		1

ALIEN ANT FARM US group

Date	Title / Label	Peak Position	Weeks at No.1	Weeks in Top 40
30 Jun 01	**MOVIES** *DreamWorks 4508992*	53		
8 Sep 01	**SMOOTH CRIMINAL (IMPORT)** *DreamWorks 4508852CD*	74		
29 Sep 01	**SMOOTH CRIMINAL** *DreamWorks DRMDM 50887*	3		10
16 Feb 02	**MOVIES** *DreamWorks 4508492*	5		4
25 May 02	**ATTITUDE** *DreamWorks 4508292*	66		

ALIEN VOICES UK producer

Date	Title / Label	Peak Position	Weeks at No.1	Weeks in Top 40
26 Dec 98	**LAST CHRISTMAS** *Wildstar CDWILD 15* ALIEN VOICES FEATURING THE THREE DEGREES	54		

ALISHA US singer

Date	Title / Label	Peak Position	Weeks at No.1	Weeks in Top 40
25 Jan 86	**BABY TALK** *Total Control TOCO 6*	67		

ALISHA'S ATTIC UK duo

Date	Title / Label	Peak Position	Weeks at No.1	Weeks in Top 40
3 Aug 96	**I AM, I FEEL** *Mercury AATDD 1*	14		8
2 Nov 96	**ALISHA RULES THE WORLD** *Mercury AATCD 2*	12		4
15 Mar 97	**INDESTRUCTIBLE** *Mercury AATCD 3*	12		4
12 Jul 97	**AIR WE BREATHE** *Mercury AATCD 4*	12		2
19 Sep 98	**THE INCIDENTALS** *Mercury AATCD 5*	13		5
9 Jan 99	**WISH I WERE YOU** *Mercury AATDD 6*	29		3
17 Apr 99	**BARBARELLA** *Mercury AATCD 7*	34		1
24 Mar 01	**PUSH IT ALL ASIDE** *Mercury AATDD 8*	24		2
28 Jul 01	**PRETENDER GOT MY HEART** *Mercury AATDD 9*	43		

ALIVE Italian production group

Date	Title / Label	Peak Position	Weeks at No.1	Weeks in Top 40
27 Jul 02	**ALIVE** *Serious CDAMPM 153* ALIVE FEATURING D D KLEIN	49		

ALIZEE French singer

Date	Title / Label	Peak Position	Weeks at No.1	Weeks in Top 40
23 Feb 02	**MOI LOLITA** *Polydor 5705952*	9		5

ALKALINE TRIO UK group

Date	Title / Label	Peak Position	Weeks at No.1	Weeks in Top 40
2 Feb 02	**PRIVATE EYE** *B Unique/Vagrant BUN 013CDX*	51		
30 Mar 02	**STUPID KID** *B Unique/Vagrant BUN 016CD*	53		
26 Jul 03	**WE'VE HAD ENOUGH** *Vagrant 9809023*	50		
18 Oct 03	**ALL ON BLACK** *Interscope 9811506*	60		

Silver-selling ○ Gold-selling ● Platinum-selling ◉ US No.1 ★ | Peak Position | Weeks at No.1 | Weeks in Top 40

Date	Title / Label	Peak Position	Weeks at No.1	Weeks in Top 40
9 Jul 05	**TIME TO WASTE** *Vagrant VRUK013CDS*	32		1
3 Dec 05	**MERCY ME** *Vagrant VRUK024CDS*	30		1
4 Mar 06	**BURN** *Vagrant VRUK029CDS*	34		1

ALL ABOUT EVE UK group

Date	Title / Label	Peak Position	Weeks at No.1	Weeks in Top 40
31 Oct 87	**IN THE CLOUDS** *Mercury EVEN 5*	47		
23 Jan 88	**WILD HEARTED WOMAN** *Mercury EVEN 6*	33		4
9 Apr 88	**EVERY ANGEL** *Mercury EVEN 7*	30		3
30 Jul 88	**MARTHA'S HARBOUR** *Mercury EVEN 8*	10		6
12 Nov 88	**WHAT KIND OF FOOL** *Mercury EVEN 9*	29		3
30 Sep 89	**ROAD TO YOUR SOUL** *Mercury EVEN 10*	37		2
16 Dec 89	**DECEMBER** *Mercury EVEN 11*	34		2
28 Apr 90	**SCARLET** *Mercury EVEN 12*	34		1
15 Jun 91	**FAREWELL MR SORROW** *Mercury EVEN 14*	36		1
10 Aug 91	**STRANGE WAY** *Vertigo EVEN 15*	51		
19 Oct 91	**THE DREAMER** *Vertigo EVEN 16*	41		
10 Oct 92	**PHASED (EP)** *MCA MCS 1688*	38		1
28 Nov 92	**SOME FINER DAY** *MCA MCS 1706*	57		
5 Jun 04	**LET ME GO HOME** *Voiceprint AAEVP 10CD2*	52		

ALL-AMERICAN REJECTS US group

Date	Title / Label	Peak Position	Weeks at No.1	Weeks in Top 40
2 Aug 03	**SWING SWING** *DreamWorks 4504616*	13		3
22 Nov 03	**THE LAST SONG** *DreamWorks 4504641*	69		
11 Mar 06	**MOVE ALONG** *Interscope 9853100*	42		
17 Jun 06	**DIRTY LITTLE SECRET** *DreamWorks 9858254*	18		3
7 Oct 06	**IT ENDS TONIGHT** *Interscope 1708086*	66		

ALL ANGELS UK group

Date	Title / Label	Peak Position	Weeks at No.1	Weeks in Top 40
30 Dec 06	**ANGELS** *UCJ 1717439*	48		

ALL BLUE UK duo

Date	Title / Label	Peak Position	Weeks at No.1	Weeks in Top 40
21 Aug 99	**PRISONER** *WEA 213CD1*	73		

ALL EYES UK group

Date	Title / Label	Peak Position	Weeks at No.1	Weeks in Top 40
13 Nov 04	**SHE'S A VISION** *Specsavers CXSPECS1*	65		

ALL-4-ONE US group

Date	Title / Label	Peak Position	Weeks at No.1	Weeks in Top 40
2 Apr 94	**SO MUCH IN LOVE** *Atlantic A 7261CD*	60		
18 Jun 94	**I SWEAR** *Atlantic A 7255CD* ◉ ★	2		17
19 Nov 94	**SO MUCH IN LOVE (REMIX)** *Atlantic A 7216CD*	49		
15 Jul 95	**I CAN LOVE YOU LIKE THAT** *Atlantic A 8193CD*	33		1

ALL SAINTS UK/Canadian group

Date	Title / Label	Peak Position	Weeks at No.1	Weeks in Top 40
6 Sep 97	**I KNOW WHERE IT'S AT** *London LONCD 398*	4		6
22 Nov 97	**NEVER EVER** *London LONCD 407*	1	1	20
9 May 98	**UNDER THE BRIDGE/LADY MARMALADE** *London LONCD 408* ●	1	2	9
12 Sep 98	**BOOTIE CALL** *London LONCD 415*	1	1	5
5 Dec 98	**WAR OF NERVES** *London LONCD 421* ○	7		7
26 Feb 00	**PURE SHORES** *London LONCD 444*	1	2	11
14 Oct 00	**BLACK COFFEE** *London LONCD 454* ○	1	1	8
27 Jan 01	**ALL HOOKED UP** *London LONCD 456*	7		2
11 Nov 06	**ROCK STEADY** *Parlophone CDR6726*	3		6

ALL SEEING I UK production group

Date	Title / Label	Peak Position	Weeks at No.1	Weeks in Top 40
28 Mar 98	**BEAT GOES ON** *ffrr FCD 334*	11		5
23 Jan 99	**WALK LIKE A PANTHER '98** *ffrr FCDP 351* ALL SEEING I FEATURING TONY CHRISTIE	10		5
18 Sep 99	**1ST MAN IN SPACE** *ffrr FCDP 370*	28		1

ALL SYSTEMS GO UK group

Date	Title / Label	Peak Position	Weeks at No.1	Weeks in Top 40
18 Jun 88	**POP MUZIK** *Unique NIQ 03*	63		

RICHARD ALLAN US actor/singer

Date	Title / Label	Peak Position	Weeks at No.1	Weeks in Top 40
24 Mar 60	**AS TIME GOES BY** *Parlophone R 4634*	43		

STEVE ALLAN UK singer

Date	Title / Label	Peak Position	Weeks at No.1	Weeks in Top 40
27 Jan 79	**TOGETHER WE ARE BEAUTIFUL** *Creole CR 164*	67		

DONNA ALLEN US singer

Date	Title / Label	Peak Position	Weeks at No.1	Weeks in Top 40
18 Apr 87	**SERIOUS** *Portrait PRT 6507447*	8		7
3 Jun 89	**JOY AND PAIN** *BCM 257*	10		7
21 Jan 95	**REAL** *Epic 6610882*	34		1
11 Oct 97	**SATURDAY** *AM:PM 5823752* EAST 57TH STREET FEATURING DONNA ALLEN	29		1

LILY ALLEN UK singer

Date	Title / Label	Peak Position	Weeks at No.1	Weeks in Top 40
8 Jul 06	**SMILE** *Regal REG135*	1	1	14
30 Sep 06	**LDN** *Regal CDREG137*	6		6
16 Dec 06	**LITTLEST THINGS** *Regal CDREG140*	21		3
17 Feb 07	**ALFIE** *Regal CDREG141*	15		6
7 Jul 07	**OH MY GOD** *Columbia 88697113172* MARK RONSON FEATURING LILY ALLEN	8		8
27 Oct 07	**DRIVIN' ME WILD** *Geffen 1750856* COMMON FEATURING LILY ALLEN	56		

DOT ALLISON UK singer

Date	Title / Label	Peak Position	Weeks at No.1	Weeks in Top 40
17 Aug 02	**STRUNG OUT** *Mantra MNT 74CD*	67		

ALLISONS UK duo

Date	Title / Label	Peak Position	Weeks at No.1	Weeks in Top 40
23 Feb 61	**ARE YOU SURE** *Fontana H 294*	2		16
18 May 61	**WORDS** *Fontana H 304*	34		4
15 Feb 62	**LESSONS IN LOVE** *Fontana H 362*	30		5

ALLNIGHT BAND UK group

Date	Title / Label	Peak Position	Weeks at No.1	Weeks in Top 40
3 Feb 79	**THE JOKER (THE WIGAN JOKER)** *Casino Classics CC 6*	50		

ALLSTARS UK group

Date	Title / Label	Peak Position	Weeks at No.1	Weeks in Top 40
23 Jun 01	**BEST FRIENDS** *Island CID 775*	20		3
22 Sep 01	**THINGS THAT GO BUMP IN THE NIGHT/ IS THERE SOMETHING I SHOULD KNOW** *Island CID 783*	12		3
26 Jan 02	**THE LAND OF MAKE BELIEVE** *Island CID 791*	9		5
11 May 02	**BACK WHEN/GOING ALL THE WAY** *Island CID 796*	19		1

ALLURE US group

Date	Title / Label	Peak Position	Weeks at No.1	Weeks in Top 40
14 Jun 97	**HEAD OVER HEELS** *Epic 6645942* ALLURE FEATURING NAS	18		1
10 Jan 98	**ALL CRIED OUT** *Epic 6652715* ALLURE FEATURING 112	12		4

ALMIGHTY UK group

Date	Title / Label	Peak Position	Weeks at No.1	Weeks in Top 40
30 Jun 90	**WILD AND WONDERFUL** *Polydor PO 75*	50		
2 Mar 91	**FREE 'N' EASY** *Polydor PO 127*	35		1
11 May 91	**DEVIL'S TOY** *Polydor PO 144*	36		1
29 Jun 91	**LITTLE LOST SOMETIMES** *Polydor PO 151*	42		
3 Apr 93	**ADDICTION** *Polydor PZCD 261*	38		1
29 May 93	**OUT OF SEASON** *Polydor PZCD 266*	41		
30 Oct 93	**OVER THE EDGE** *Polydor PZCD 298*	38		1
24 Sep 94	**WRENCH** *Chrysalis CDCHS 5014*	26		1
14 Jan 95	**JONESTOWN MIND** *Chrysalis CDCHSS 5017*	26		1
16 Mar 96	**ALL SUSSED OUT** *Chrysalis CDCHS 5030*	28		1
25 May 96	**DO YOU UNDERSTAND** *Raw Power RAWX 1022*	38		1

MARC ALMOND UK singer

Date	Title / Label	Peak Position	Weeks at No.1	Weeks in Top 40
2 Jul 83	**BLACK HEART** *Some Bizzare BZS 19* MARC & THE MAMBAS	49		
2 Jun 84	**THE BOY WHO CAME BACK** *Some Bizzare BZS 23*	52		
1 Sep 84	**YOU HAVE** *Some Bizzare BZS 24*	57		
20 Apr 85	**I FEEL LOVE (MEDLEY)** *Forbidden Fruit BITE 4* BRONSKI BEAT & MARC ALMOND ○	3		10
24 Aug 85	**STORIES OF JOHNNY** *Some Bizzare BONK 1*	23		4
26 Oct 85	**LOVE LETTER** *Some Bizzare BONK 2*	68		
4 Jan 86	**THE HOUSE IS HAUNTED (BY THE ECHO OF YOUR LAST GOODBYE)** *Some Bizzare GLOW 1*	55		
7 Jun 86	**A WOMAN'S STORY** *Some Bizzare GLOW 2* MARC ALMOND & THE WILLING SINNERS	41		
18 Oct 86	**RUBY RED** *Some Bizzare GLOW 3*	47		
14 Feb 87	**MELANCHOLY ROSE** *Some Bizzare GLOW 4*	71		
3 Sep 88	**TEARS RUN RINGS** *Parlophone R 6186*	26		6
5 Nov 88	**BITTER SWEET** *Some Bizzare R 6194*	40		1

Date	Title	Peak Position	Weeks at No.1	Weeks in Top 40
14 Jan 89	**SOMETHING'S GOTTEN HOLD OF MY HEART** *Parlophone R 6201* MARC ALMOND FEATURING SPECIAL GUEST STAR GENE PITNEY	1	4	10
8 Apr 89	**ONLY THE MOMENT** *Parlophone R 6210*	45		
3 Mar 90	**A LOVER SPURNED** *Some Bizzare R 6229*	29		2
19 May 90	**THE DESPERATE HOURS** *Some Bizzare R 6252*	45		
23 Mar 91	**SAY HELLO WAVE GOODBYE** *Mercury SOFT 1* SOFT CELL/MARC ALMOND	38		2
18 May 91	**TAINTED LOVE** *Mercury SOFT 2* SOFT CELL/MARC ALMOND	5		7
28 Sep 91	**JACKY** *Some Bizzare YZ 610*	17		5
11 Jan 92	**MY HAND OVER MY HEART** *Some Bizzare YZ 633*	33		2
25 Apr 92	**THE DAYS OF PEARLY SPENCER** *Some Bizzare YZ 638*	4		6
27 Mar 93	**WHAT MAKES A MAN A MAN (LIVE)** *Some Bizzare YZ 720CD*	60		
13 May 95	**ADORED AND EXPLORED** *Some Bizzare MERCD 431*	25		2
29 Jul 95	**THE IDOL** *Some Bizzare MERCD 437*	44		
30 Dec 95	**CHILD STAR** *Some Bizzare MERCD 450*	41		
28 Dec 96	**YESTERDAY HAS GONE** *EMI Premier CDPRESX 13* PJ PROBY & MARC ALMOND FEATURING THE MY LIFE STORY ORCHESTRA	58		

ALOOF UK group

Date	Title	Peak Position	Weeks at No.1	Weeks in Top 40
19 Sep 92	**ON A MISSION** *Cowboy RODEO 5*	64		
18 May 96	**WISH YOU WERE HERE** *East West EW 038CD*	61		
30 Nov 96	**ONE NIGHT STAND** *East West EW 067CD*	30		1
1 Mar 97	**WISH YOU WERE HERE (REMIX)** *East West EW 083CD1*	43		
29 Aug 98	**WHAT I MISS THE MOST** *East West EW 179CD1*	70		

HERB ALPERT US trumpeter/singer

Date	Title	Peak Position	Weeks at No.1	Weeks in Top 40
3 Jan 63	**THE LONELY BULL** *Stateside SS 138*	22		5
9 Dec 65	**SPANISH FLEA** *Pye International 7N 25335* HERB ALPERT & THE TIJUANA BRASS	3		19
24 Mar 66	**TIJUANA TAXI** *Pye International 7N 25352* HERB ALPERT & THE TIJUANA BRASS	37		3
27 Apr 67	**CASINO ROYALE** *A&M AMS 700* HERB ALPERT & THE TIJUANA BRASS	27		8
3 Jul 68	**THIS GUY'S IN LOVE WITH YOU** *A&M AMS 727* ★	3		14
18 Jun 69	**WITHOUT HER** *A&M AMS 755* HERB ALPERT & THE TIJUANA BRASS	36		3
12 Dec 70	**JERUSALEM** *A&M AMS 810* HERB ALPERT & THE TIJUANA BRASS	42		
13 Oct 79	**RISE** *A&M AMS 7465* ★	13		7
19 Jan 80	**ROTATION** *A&M AMS 7500*	46		
21 Mar 87	**KEEP YOUR EYE ON ME** *Breakout USA 602*	19		7
6 Jun 87	**DIAMONDS** *Breakout USA 605*	27		4

ALPHABEAT Danish group

Date	Title	Peak Position	Weeks at No.1	Weeks in Top 40
1 Mar 08	**FASCINATION** *Charisma CASDX18*	6		4

ALPHAVILLE German group

Date	Title	Peak Position	Weeks at No.1	Weeks in Top 40
18 Aug 84	**BIG IN JAPAN** *WEA International X9505*	8		9

ALPINESTARS UK production duo

Date	Title	Peak Position	Weeks at No.1	Weeks in Top 40
22 Jun 02	**CARBON KID** *Riverman RMR 11VS* ALPINE STARS FEATURING BRIAN MOLKO	63		

ALSOU Russian singer

Date	Title	Peak Position	Weeks at No.1	Weeks in Top 40
12 May 01	**BEFORE YOU LOVE ME** *Mercury 1589142*	27		1

GERALD ALSTON US singer

Date	Title	Peak Position	Weeks at No.1	Weeks in Top 40
15 Apr 89	**ACTIVATED** *RCA ZB 42681*	73		

ALTER EGO German production duo

Date	Title	Peak Position	Weeks at No.1	Weeks in Top 40
11 Dec 04	**ROCKER** *Skint SKINT103CD*	32		1

ALTERED IMAGES UK group

Date	Title	Peak Position	Weeks at No.1	Weeks in Top 40
28 Mar 81	**DEAD POP STARS** *Epic EPC A 1023*	67		
26 Sep 81	**HAPPY BIRTHDAY** *Epic EPC A 1522*	2		9
12 Dec 81	**I COULD BE HAPPY** *Epic EPC A 1834*	7		10
27 Mar 82	**SEE THOSE EYES** *Epic EPC A 2198*	11		5
22 May 82	**PINKY BLUE** *Epic EPC A 2426*	35		3
19 Mar 83	**DON'T TALK TO ME ABOUT LOVE** *Epic EPC A 3083*	7		6
28 May 83	**BRING ME CLOSER** *Epic EPC A 3398*	29		3
16 Jul 83	**LOVE TO STAY** *Epic EPC A 3582*	46		

ALTERKICKS UK group

Date	Title	Peak Position	Weeks at No.1	Weeks in Top 40
26 Mar 05	**DO EVERYTHING I TAUGHT YOU** *XL Recordings XLS212CD*	71		

ALTERN 8 UK duo

Date	Title	Peak Position	Weeks at No.1	Weeks in Top 40
13 Jul 91	**INFILTRATE 202** *Network NWK 24*	28		4
16 Nov 91	**ACTIV 8 (COME WITH ME)** *Network NWK 34*	3		8
8 Feb 92	**FREQUENCY** *Network NWK 37*	41		
11 Apr 92	**EVAPOR 8** *Network NWK 38*	6		5
4 Jul 92	**HYPNOTIC ST-8** *Network NWK 49*	16		3
10 Oct 92	**SHAME** *Network NWKTEN 56* ALTERN 8 VS EVELYN KING	74		
12 Dec 92	**BRUTAL-8-E** *Network NWK 59*	43		
3 Jul 93	**EVERYBODY** *Network NWKCD 73*	58		

ALTHIA & DONNA Jamaican duo

Date	Title	Peak Position	Weeks at No.1	Weeks in Top 40
24 Dec 77	**UP TOWN TOP RANKING** *Lightning LIG 506*	1	1	11

ALY & AJ US duo

Date	Title	Peak Position	Weeks at No.1	Weeks in Top 40
13 Oct 07	**POTENTIAL BREAK UP SONG** *Hollywood/Angel CASD10*	22		3

ALY-US US group

Date	Title	Peak Position	Weeks at No.1	Weeks in Top 40
21 Nov 92	**FOLLOW ME** *Cooltempo COOL 266*	43		
25 May 02	**FOLLOW ME (REMIX)** *Strictly Rhythm SRUKCD 05*	54		

SADIE AMA UK singer

Date	Title	Peak Position	Weeks at No.1	Weeks in Top 40
10 Feb 07	**FALLIN'** *Download*	68		

SHOLA AMA UK singer

Date	Title	Peak Position	Weeks at No.1	Weeks in Top 40
19 Apr 97	**YOU MIGHT NEED SOMEBODY** *WEA 097CD*	4		11
30 Aug 97	**YOU'RE THE ONE I LOVE** *Freakstreet WEA 121CD1*	3		6
29 Nov 97	**WHO'S LOVING MY BABY** *Freakstreet WEA 145 CD1*	13		2
21 Feb 98	**MUCH LOVE** *WEA 154CD1*	17		2
11 Apr 98	**SOMEDAY I'LL FIND YOU/I'VE BEEN TO A MARVELLOUS PARTY** *EMI CDTCB 001* SHOLA AMA & CRAIG ARMSTRONG/DIVINE COMEDY	28		1
17 Apr 99	**TABOO** *WEA 203CD* GLAMMA KID FEATURING SHOLA AMA	10		5
6 Nov 99	**STILL BELIEVE** *WEA 239CD1*	26		1
29 Apr 00	**IMAGINE** *WEA 252CD*	24		1
11 Sep 04	**YOU SHOULD READILY KNOW** *Relentless RELCD9* PIRATES FEATURING ENYA, SHOLA AMA, NAILA BOSS & ISHANI	8		6

EDDIE AMADOR US producer

Date	Title	Peak Position	Weeks at No.1	Weeks in Top 40
24 Oct 98	**HOUSE MUSIC** *Pukka CDPUKKA 18*	37		1
22 Jan 00	**RISE** *Defected DEFECT 9CDS*	19		2

RUBY AMANFU Ghanaian singer

Date	Title	Peak Position	Weeks at No.1	Weeks in Top 40
15 Mar 03	**SUGAH** *Polydor 0658302*	32		1

AMAR UK singer

Date	Title	Peak Position	Weeks at No.1	Weeks in Top 40
9 Sep 00	**SOMETIMES (IT SNOWS IN APRIL)** *Blanco Y Negro NEG 129CD*	48		

AMAZULU UK group

Date	Title	Peak Position	Weeks at No.1	Weeks in Top 40
6 Jul 85	**EXCITABLE** *Island IS 201*	12		7
23 Nov 85	**DON'T YOU JUST KNOW IT** *Island IS 233*	15		9
15 Mar 86	**THE THINGS THE LONELY DO** *Island IS 267*	43		
31 May 86	**TOO GOOD TO BE FORGOTTEN** *Island IS 284*	5		10
13 Sep 86	**MONTEGO BAY** *Island IS 293*	16		6
10 Oct 87	**MONY MONY** *EMI EM 32*	38		2

Silver-selling ● Gold-selling ● Platinum-selling ⊛ US No.1 ★ | Peak Position | Weeks at No.1 | Weeks in Top 40

AMBASSADOR Dutch producer

Date	Title / Label	Peak Position	Weeks at No.1	Weeks in Top 40
12 Feb 00	**ONE OF THESE DAYS** *Platipus PLATCD 69*	67		

AMBASSADORS OF FUNK UK group

Date	Title / Label	Peak Position	Weeks at No.1	Weeks in Top 40
31 Oct 92	**SUPERMARIOLAND** *Living Beat SMASH 23* AMBASSADORS OF FUNK FEATURING MC MARIO	8		6

AMBER Dutch singer

Date	Title / Label	Peak Position	Weeks at No.1	Weeks in Top 40
24 Jun 00	**SEXUAL** *Substance SUBS 2CDS*	34		1

AMBULANCE LTD US group

Date	Title / Label	Peak Position	Weeks at No.1	Weeks in Top 40
12 Mar 05	**STAY WHERE YOU ARE** *TVT TVTUKCD5*	67		
25 Jun 05	**PRIMITIVE (THE WAY I TREAT YOU)** *TVT TVTUKCD10*	72		

AMEN US group

Date	Title / Label	Peak Position	Weeks at No.1	Weeks in Top 40
17 Feb 01	**TOO HARD TO BE FREE** *Virgin VUSCD 191*	72		
21 Jul 01	**THE WAITING 18** *Virgin VUSCD 207*	61		
3 Apr 04	**CALIFORNIA'S BLEEDING** *Columbia 6746162*	52		

AMEN CORNER UK group

Date	Title / Label	Peak Position	Weeks at No.1	Weeks in Top 40
26 Jul 67	**GIN HOUSE BLUES** *Deram DM 136*	12		7
11 Oct 67	**WORLD OF BROKEN HEARTS** *Deram DM 151*	24		5
17 Jan 68	**BEND ME SHAPE ME** *Deram DM 172*	3		12
31 Jul 68	**HIGH IN THE SKY** *Deram DM 197*	6		11
29 Jan 69	**(IF PARADISE IS) HALF AS NICE** *Immediate IM 073*	1	2	10
25 Jun 69	**HELLO SUZIE** *Immediate IM 081*	4		10
14 Feb 76	**(IF PARADISE IS) HALF AS NICE** *Immediate IMS 103*	34		2

AMEN! UK UK group

Date	Title / Label	Peak Position	Weeks at No.1	Weeks in Top 40
8 Feb 97	**PASSION** *Feverpitch CDFVR 1015*	15		3
28 Jun 97	**PEOPLE OF LOVE** *Feverpitch CDFVR 18*	36		1
6 Sep 03	**PASSION** *Positiva CDTIV 195*	40		1

AMERICA US group

Date	Title / Label	Peak Position	Weeks at No.1	Weeks in Top 40
18 Dec 71	**HORSE WITH NO NAME/EVERYONE I MEET IS FROM CALIFORNIA** *Warner Brothers K 16128* ★	3		11
25 Nov 72	**VENTURA HIGHWAY** *Warner Brothers K 16219*	43		
6 Nov 82	**YOU CAN DO MAGIC** *Capitol CL 264*	59		

AMERICAN BREED US group

Date	Title / Label	Peak Position	Weeks at No.1	Weeks in Top 40
7 Feb 68	**BEND ME SHAPE ME** *Stateside SS 2078*	24		5

AMERICAN HEAD CHARGE US group

Date	Title / Label	Peak Position	Weeks at No.1	Weeks in Top 40
8 Jun 02	**JUST SO YOU KNOW** *Mercury 5829622*	52		

AMERICAN HI-FI US group

Date	Title / Label	Peak Position	Weeks at No.1	Weeks in Top 40
8 Sep 01	**FLAVOR OF THE WEAK** *Mercury 5886722*	31		2
26 Apr 03	**THE ART OF LOSING** *Mercury 0779152*	75		

AMERICAN MUSIC CLUB US group

Date	Title / Label	Peak Position	Weeks at No.1	Weeks in Top 40
24 Apr 93	**JOHNNY MATHIS' FEET** *Virgin VSCDG 1445*	58		
10 Sep 94	**WISH THE WORLD AWAY** *Virgin VSCDX 1512*	46		

AMERIE US singer

Date	Title / Label	Peak Position	Weeks at No.1	Weeks in Top 40
9 Nov 02	**WHY DON'T WE FALL IN LOVE** *Columbia 6732212* AMERIE FEATURING LUDACRIS	40		1
22 Feb 03	**PARADISE** *Def Jam 0637242* LL COOL J FEATURING AMERIE	18		3
4 Jun 05	**1 THING** *Columbia 6759402*	4		9
3 Sep 05	**TOUCH** *Columbia 6760612*	19		2
5 May 07	**TAKE CONTROL** *Columbia 88697085182*	10		6
21 Jul 07	**GOTTA WORK** *Columbia 88697138472*	21		4

AMES BROTHERS US group

Date	Title / Label	Peak Position	Weeks at No.1	Weeks in Top 40
4 Feb 55	**NAUGHTY LADY OF SHADY LANE** *HMV 10800*	6		6

AMILLIONSONS UK production group

Date	Title / Label	Peak Position	Weeks at No.1	Weeks in Top 40
24 Aug 02	**MISTI BLU** *London LONCD 468*	39		1

AMIRA US singer

Date	Title / Label	Peak Position	Weeks at No.1	Weeks in Top 40
13 Dec 97	**MY DESIRE** *VC Recordings VCRD 27*	51		
8 Aug 98	**MY DESIRE (REMIX)** *VC Recordings VCRD 36*	46		
10 Feb 01	**MY DESIRE (2nd REMIX)** *VC Recordings VCRD 71*	20		2

CHERIE AMORE French singer

Date	Title / Label	Peak Position	Weeks at No.1	Weeks in Top 40
15 Apr 00	**I DON'T WANT NOBODY (TELLIN' ME WHAT TO DO)** *Eternal WEA 262CD*	33		1

VANESSA AMOROSI Australian vocalist

Date	Title / Label	Peak Position	Weeks at No.1	Weeks in Top 40
23 Sep 00	**ABSOLUTELY EVERYBODY** *Mercury 1582972*	7		6

AMOS UK producer

Date	Title / Label	Peak Position	Weeks at No.1	Weeks in Top 40
3 Sep 94	**ONLY SAW TODAY - INSTANT KARMA** *Positiva CDTIV 16*	48		
25 Mar 95	**LET LOVE SHINE** *Positiva CDTIV 24*	31		1
7 Oct 95	**CHURCH OF FREEDOM** *Positiva CDTIV 38*	54		
12 Oct 96	**STAMP!** *Positiva CDTIV 65* JEREMY HEALY & AMOS	11		3
31 May 97	**ARGENTINA** *Positiva CDTIV 74* JEREMY HEALY & AMOS	30		1

TORI AMOS US singer/pianist

Date	Title / Label	Peak Position	Weeks at No.1	Weeks in Top 40
23 Nov 91	**SILENT ALL THESE YEARS** *East West YZ 618*	51		
1 Feb 92	**CHINA** *East West YZ 7531*	51		
21 Mar 92	**WINTER** *East West A 7504*	25		2
20 Jun 92	**CRUCIFY** *East West A 7479*	15		4
22 Aug 92	**SILENT ALL THESE YEARS** *East West A 7433*	26		3
22 Jan 94	**CORNFLAKE GIRL** *East West A 7281CD*	4		5
19 Mar 94	**PRETTY GOOD YEAR** *East West A 7263CD*	7		2
28 May 94	**PAST THE MISSION** *East West YZ 7257CD*	31		2
15 Oct 94	**GOD** *East West A 7251CD*	44		
13 Jan 96	**CAUGHT A LITE SNEEZE** *East West A 5524CD2*	20		2
23 Mar 96	**TALULA** *East West A 8512CD*	22		1
3 Aug 96	**HEY JUPITER/PROFESSIONAL WIDOW (IT'S GOT TO BE BIG)** *East West A 5494CD*	20		3
9 Nov 96	**BLUE SKIES** *Perfecto PERF 130CD1* BT FEATURING TORI AMOS	26		1
11 Jan 97	**PROFESSIONAL WIDOW (IT'S GOT TO BE BIG)** *East West A 5450CD* ●	1	1	7
2 May 98	**SPARK** *East West AT 0031CD*	16		2
13 Nov 99	**GLORY OF THE 80'S** *Atlantic AT 0077CD1*	46		
26 Oct 02	**A SORTA FAIRYTALE** *Epic 6730432*	41		

AMOURE UK production duo

Date	Title / Label	Peak Position	Weeks at No.1	Weeks in Top 40
27 May 00	**IS THAT YOUR FINAL ANSWER? (WHO WANTS TO BE A MILLIONAIRE - THE SINGLE)** *Celador MILLION 2*	33		1

AMP FIDDLER US keyboard player

Date	Title / Label	Peak Position	Weeks at No.1	Weeks in Top 40
20 Mar 04	**I BELIEVE IN YOU** *Genuine GEN022CD*	72		
19 Jun 04	**DREAMIN'** *Genuine GEN025CDM*	71		

AMPS US group

Date	Title / Label	Peak Position	Weeks at No.1	Weeks in Top 40
21 Oct 95	**TIPP CITY** *4AD BAD 5015CD*	61		

AMSTERDAM UK group

Date	Title / Label	Peak Position	Weeks at No.1	Weeks in Top 40
5 Feb 05	**THE JOURNEY/STOP KNOCKING THE WALLS DOWN** *Beat Crazy BEAT001CD* AMSTERDAM/RICKY	32		1
11 Jun 05	**DOES THIS TRAIN STOP ON MERSEYSIDE** *Beat Crazy BEAT002CD1*	53		

ANASTACIA US singer

Date	Title / Label	Peak Position	Weeks at No.1	Weeks in Top 40
30 Sep 00	**I'M OUTTA LOVE** *Epic 6695782*	6		12
3 Feb 01	**NOT THAT KIND** *Epic 6707632*	11		6
2 Jun 01	**COWBOYS & KISSES** *Epic 6712622*	28		1
25 Aug 01	**MADE FOR LOVIN' YOU** *Epic 6717172*	27		1
1 Dec 01	**PAID MY DUES** *Epic 6721252*	14		6
6 Apr 02	**ONE DAY IN YOUR LIFE** *Epic 6724562*	11		7
21 Sep 02	**WHY'D YOU LIE TO ME** *Epic 6731112*	25		1
7 Dec 02	**YOU'LL NEVER BE ALONE** *Epic 6733802*	31		1
3 Apr 04	**LEFT OUTSIDE ALONE** *Epic 6746482*	3		18
14 Aug 04	**SICK AND TIRED** *Epic 6751092*	4		8
27 Nov 04	**WELCOME TO MY TRUTH** *Epic 6754922*	25		1
23 Apr 05	**HEAVY ON MY HEART** *Epic 6758402*	21		1
3 Dec 05	**PIECES OF A DREAM** *Epic 82876738082*	48		

AND WHY NOT? UK group

Date	Title / Label	Peak Position	Weeks at No.1	Weeks in Top 40
14 Oct 89	**RESTLESS DAYS (SHE CRIES OUT LOUD)** *Island IS 426*	38		2
13 Jan 90	**THE FACE** *Island IS 444*	13		6
21 Apr 90	**SOMETHING YOU GOT** *Island 452*	39		1

... AND YOU WILL KNOW US BY THE TRAIL OF THE DEAD US group

Date	Title / Label	Peak Position	Weeks at No.1	Weeks in Top 40
11 Nov 00	**MISTAKES AND REGRETS** *Domino RUG 114CD*	69		
11 May 02	**ANOTHER MORNING STONER** *Interscope 4977162*	54		

ANGRY ANDERSON Australian singer

Date	Title / Label	Peak Position	Weeks at No.1	Weeks in Top 40
19 Nov 88	**SUDDENLY** *Food For Thought YUM 113*	3		11

BRETT ANDERSON UK singer

Date	Title / Label	Peak Position	Weeks at No.1	Weeks in Top 40
31 Mar 07	**LOVE IS DEAD** *Drowned In Sound DISOO22CD2*	42		

CARL ANDERSON US singer

Date	Title / Label	Peak Position	Weeks at No.1	Weeks in Top 40
8 Jun 85	**BUTTERCUP** *Streetwave KHAN 45*	49		

CARLEEN ANDERSON US singer

Date	Title / Label	Peak Position	Weeks at No.1	Weeks in Top 40
12 Feb 94	**NERVOUS BREAKDOWN** *Circa YRCDG 112*	27		2
28 May 94	**MAMA SAID** *Circa YRCD 114*	26		2
13 Aug 94	**TRUE SPIRIT** *Circa YRCD 118*	24		2
14 Jan 95	**LET IT LAST** *Circa YRCDG 119*	16		2
7 Feb 98	**MAYBE I'M AMAZED** *Circa YRCD 128*	24		1
25 Apr 98	**WOMAN IN ME** *Circa YRCD 129*	74		

LAURIE ANDERSON US singer/violinist

Date	Title / Label	Peak Position	Weeks at No.1	Weeks in Top 40
17 Oct 81	**O SUPERMAN** *Warner Brothers K 17870*	2		5

LC ANDERSON VS PSYCHO RADIO UK singer with Italian production group

Date	Title / Label	Peak Position	Weeks at No.1	Weeks in Top 40
26 Jul 03	**RIGHT STUFF** *Faith & Hope FHCD039*	45		

LYNN ANDERSON US singer

Date	Title / Label	Peak Position	Weeks at No.1	Weeks in Top 40
20 Feb 71	**ROSE GARDEN** *CBS 5360*	3		4

MOIRA ANDERSON UK singer

Date	Title / Label	Peak Position	Weeks at No.1	Weeks in Top 40
27 Dec 69	**THE HOLY CITY** *Decca F 12989*	43		

SUNSHINE ANDERSON US singer

Date	Title / Label	Peak Position	Weeks at No.1	Weeks in Top 40
2 Jun 01	**HEARD IT ALL BEFORE** *Atlantic AT 0100CD*	9		19
22 Sep 01	**LUNCH OR DINNER** *Atlantic AT 0109CD*	57		

JOHN ANDERSON BIG BAND UK big band

Date	Title / Label	Peak Position	Weeks at No.1	Weeks in Top 40
21 Dec 85	**GLENN MILLER MEDLEY** *Modern GLEN 1*	61		

LEROY ANDERSON & HIS POPS CONCERT ORCHESTRA US orchestra

Date	Title / Label	Peak Position	Weeks at No.1	Weeks in Top 40
28 Jun 57	**FORGOTTEN DREAMS** *Brunswick 05485*	24		3

ANDERSON BRUFORD WAKEMAN HOWE UK group

Date	Title / Label	Peak Position	Weeks at No.1	Weeks in Top 40
24 Jun 89	**BROTHER OF MINE** *Arista 112379*	63		

PETER ANDRE UK singer

Date	Title / Label	Peak Position	Weeks at No.1	Weeks in Top 40
10 Jun 95	**TURN IT UP** *Mushroom D 1000*	64		
16 Sep 95	**MYSTERIOUS GIRL** *Mushroom D 1192*	53		
16 Mar 96	**ONLY ONE** *Mushroom D 1307*	16		2
1 Jun 96	**MYSTERIOUS GIRL** *Mushroom DX 2000* PETER ANDRE FEATURING BUBBLER RANX .	2		15
14 Sep 96	**FLAVA** *Mushroom DX 2003*	1	1	8
7 Dec 96	**I FEEL YOU** *Mushroom D 1521*	1	1	6
8 Mar 97	**NATURAL** *Mushroom DX 1577*	6		3
9 Aug 97	**ALL ABOUT US** *Mushroom MUSH 5CD*	3		5
8 Nov 97	**LONELY** *Mushroom MUSH 16CD*	6		3
24 Jan 98	**ALL NIGHT ALL RIGHT** *Mushroom MUSH 21CD* PETER ANDRE FEATURING WARREN G	16		3
25 Jul 98	**KISS THE GIRL** *Mushroom MUSH 34CDSX*	9		3
6 Mar 04	**MYSTERIOUS GIRL** *Mushroom PA001CDX* PETER ANDRE FEATURING BUBBLER RANX	1	1	8
12 Jun 04	**INSANIA** *East West PA002CD*	3		4
18 Sep 04	**THE RIGHT WAY** *Atlantic ATUK001CD1*	14		2
16 Dec 06	**A WHOLE NEW WORLD** *K&P Recordings CDKANDP1* KATIE PRICE & PETER ANDRE	12		3

CHRIS ANDREWS UK singer

Date	Title / Label	Peak Position	Weeks at No.1	Weeks in Top 40
7 Oct 65	**YESTERDAY MAN** *Decca F 12236*	3		14
2 Dec 65	**TO WHOM IT CONCERNS** *Decca F 22285*	13		9
14 Apr 66	**SOMETHING ON MY MIND** *Decca F 22365*	41		
2 Jun 66	**WHATCHA GONNA DO NOW** *Decca F 22404*	40		1
25 Aug 66	**STOP THAT GIRL** *Decca F 22472*	36		2

EAMONN ANDREWS Irish TV/radio presenter

Date	Title / Label	Peak Position	Weeks at No.1	Weeks in Top 40
20 Jan 56	**SHIFTING WHISPERING SANDS (PARTS 1 & 2)** *Parlophone R 4106* EAMONN ANDREWS WITH RON GOODWIN & HIS ORCHESTRA	18		3

MICHAEL ANDREWS US instrumentalist

Date	Title / Label	Peak Position	Weeks at No.1	Weeks in Top 40
27 Dec 03	**MAD WORLD** *Adventure/Sanctuary SANXD 250X* MICHAEL ANDREWS FEATURING GARY JULES	1	3	11

ANDROIDS Australian group

Date	Title / Label	Peak Position	Weeks at No.1	Weeks in Top 40
17 May 03	**DO IT WITH MADONNA** *Universal MCSTD 40321*	15		4

ANEKA UK singer

Date	Title / Label	Peak Position	Weeks at No.1	Weeks in Top 40
8 Aug 81	**JAPANESE BOY** *Hansa 5*	1	1	9
7 Nov 81	**LITTLE LADY** *Hansa 8*	50		

DAVE ANGEL UK producer

Date	Title / Label	Peak Position	Weeks at No.1	Weeks in Top 40
2 Aug 97	**TOKYO STEALTH FIGHTER** *Fourth & Broadway BRCD 355*	58		

SIMONE ANGEL Dutch singer

Date	Title / Label	Peak Position	Weeks at No.1	Weeks in Top 40
13 Nov 93	**LET THIS FEELING** *A&M 5803652*	60		

ANGEL CITY Dutch production duo

Date	Title / Label	Peak Position	Weeks at No.1	Weeks in Top 40
8 Nov 03	**LOVE ME RIGHT (OH SHEILA)** *Data 59CDS* ANGEL CITY FEATURING LARA McALLEN	11		5
3 Jul 04	**TOUCH ME** *Data 73CDX*	18		3
16 Oct 04	**DO YOU KNOW (I GO CRAZY)** *Data 76CDS*	8		6
26 Feb 05	**SUNRISE** *Data 84CDS*	9		3

Silver-selling ● Gold-selling ● Platinum-selling ⊛ US No.1 ★ | Peak Position | Weeks at No.1 | Weeks in Top 40

ANGELETTES UK group

Date	Title / Label	Peak Position	Weeks at No.1	Weeks in Top 40
13 May 72	**DON'T LET HIM TOUCH YOU** *Decca F 13284*	35		3

ANGELHEART UK producer

Date	Title / Label	Peak Position	Weeks at No.1	Weeks in Top 40
6 Apr 96	**COME BACK TO ME** *Hi-Life 5776312* ANGELHEART FEATURING ROCHELLE HARRIS	68		
22 Mar 97	**I'M STILL WAITING** *Hi-Life 5735452* ANGELHEART FEATURING ALETIA BOURNE	74		

ANGELIC UK production group

Date	Title / Label	Peak Position	Weeks at No.1	Weeks in Top 40
17 Jun 00	**IT'S MY TURN** *Serious MCSTD 40235*	11		3
24 Feb 01	**CAN'T KEEP ME SILENT** *Serious SERR 023CD*	12		2
10 Nov 01	**STAY WITH ME** *Serious SERR 35CD*	36		1

ANGELIC UPSTARTS UK group

Date	Title / Label	Peak Position	Weeks at No.1	Weeks in Top 40
21 Apr 79	**I'M AN UPSTART** *Warner Brothers K 17354*	31		4
11 Aug 79	**TEENAGE WARNING** *Warner Brothers K 17426*	29		4
3 Nov 79	**NEVER 'AD NOTHIN'** *Warner Brothers K 17476*	52		
9 Feb 80	**OUT OF CONTROL** *Warner Brothers K 17558*	58		
22 Mar 80	**WE GOTTA GET OUT OF THIS PLACE** *Warner Brothers K 17576*	65		
2 Aug 80	**LAST NIGHT ANOTHER SOLDIER** *Zonophone Z 7*	51		
7 Feb 81	**KIDS ON THE STREET** *Zonophone Z 16*	57		

ANGELLE UK singer

Date	Title / Label	Peak Position	Weeks at No.1	Weeks in Top 40
17 Aug 02	**JOY AND PAIN** *Innovation CXINNOV 1*	43		

BOBBY ANGELO & THE TUXEDOS UK group

Date	Title / Label	Peak Position	Weeks at No.1	Weeks in Top 40
10 Aug 61	**BABY SITTIN'** *HMV POP 892*	30		2

ANGELS US group

Date	Title / Label	Peak Position	Weeks at No.1	Weeks in Top 40
3 Oct 63	**MY BOYFRIEND'S BACK** *Mercury AMT 1211* ★	50		

ANGELS AND AIRWAVES US group

Date	Title / Label	Peak Position	Weeks at No.1	Weeks in Top 40
27 May 06	**THE ADVENTURE** *Geffen MCSTD40461*	20		1
5 Aug 06	**IT HURTS** *Geffen 1702863*	59		

ANGELS REVERSE Dutch group

Date	Title / Label	Peak Position	Weeks at No.1	Weeks in Top 40
31 Aug 02	**DON'T CARE** *Inferno CDFERN 46*	71		

ANGELWITCH UK group

Date	Title / Label	Peak Position	Weeks at No.1	Weeks in Top 40
7 Jun 80	**SWEET DANGER** *EMI 5064*	75		

ANIMAL US puppet/drummer

Date	Title / Label	Peak Position	Weeks at No.1	Weeks in Top 40
23 Jul 94	**WIPE OUT** *BMG Kidz 74321219532*	38		2

ANIMAL NIGHTLIFE UK group

Date	Title / Label	Peak Position	Weeks at No.1	Weeks in Top 40
13 Aug 83	**NATIVE BOY (UPTOWN)** *Innervision A 3584*	60		
18 Aug 84	**MR SOLITAIRE** *Island IS 193*	25		7
6 Jul 85	**LOVE IS JUST THE GREAT PRETENDER** *Island IS 200*	28		3
5 Oct 85	**PREACHER PREACHER** *Island IS 245*	67		

ANIMALHOUSE UK group

Date	Title / Label	Peak Position	Weeks at No.1	Weeks in Top 40
15 Jul 00	**READY TO RECEIVE** *Boiler House! 74321771072*	61		

ANIMALS UK group

Date	Title / Label	Peak Position	Weeks at No.1	Weeks in Top 40
16 Apr 64	**BABY LET ME TAKE YOU HOME** *Columbia DB 7247*	21		8
25 Jun 64	**HOUSE OF THE RISING SUN** *Columbia DB 7301* ★	1	1	12
17 Sep 64	**I'M CRYING** *Columbia DB 7354*	8		10
4 Feb 65	**DON'T LET ME BE MISUNDERSTOOD** *Columbia DB 7445*	3		9
8 Apr 65	**BRING IT ON HOME TO ME** *Columbia DB 7539*	7		10
15 Jul 65	**WE GOTTA GET OUT OF THIS PLACE** *Columbia DB 7639*	2		9
28 Oct 65	**IT'S MY LIFE** *Columbia DB 7741*	7		10
17 Feb 66	**INSIDE LOOKING OUT** *Decca F 12332*	12		8
2 Jun 66	**DON'T BRING ME DOWN** *Decca F 12407*	6		8
27 Oct 66	**HELP ME GIRL** *Decca F 12502* ERIC BURDON & THE ANIMALS	14		8
15 Jun 67	**WHEN I WAS YOUNG** *MGM 1340* ERIC BURDON & THE ANIMALS	45		
6 Sep 67	**GOOD TIMES** *MGM 1344* ERIC BURDON & THE ANIMALS	20		7
18 Oct 67	**SAN FRANCISCAN NIGHTS** *MGM 1359* ERIC BURDON & THE ANIMALS	7		9
14 Feb 68	**SKY PILOT** *MGM 1373* ERIC BURDON & THE ANIMALS	40		1
15 Jan 69	**RING OF FIRE** *MGM 1461* ERIC BURDON & THE ANIMALS	35		3
7 Oct 72	**HOUSE OF THE RISING SUN** *RAK RR 1*	25		4
18 Sep 82	**HOUSE OF THE RISING SUN** *RAK RR 1*	11		8

ANIMOTION US group

Date	Title / Label	Peak Position	Weeks at No.1	Weeks in Top 40
11 May 85	**OBSESSION** *Mercury PH 34*	5		10

PAUL ANKA Canadian singer

Date	Title / Label	Peak Position	Weeks at No.1	Weeks in Top 40
9 Aug 57	**DIANA** *Columbia DB 3980* ★	1	9	25
8 Nov 57	**I LOVE YOU BABY** *Columbia DB 4022*	3		15
8 Nov 57	**TELL ME THAT YOU LOVE ME** *Columbia DB 4022*	25		2
31 Jan 58	**YOU ARE MY DESTINY** *Columbia DB 4063*	6		13
30 May 58	**CRAZY LOVE** *Columbia DB 4110*	26		1
26 Sep 58	**MIDNIGHT** *Columbia DB 4172*	26		1
30 Jan 59	**(ALL OF A SUDDEN) MY HEART SINGS** *Columbia DB 4241*	10		13
10 Jul 59	**LONELY BOY** *Columbia DB 4324* ★	3		17
30 Oct 59	**PUT YOUR HEAD ON MY SHOULDER** *Columbia DB 4355*	7		12
26 Feb 60	**IT'S TIME TO CRY** *Columbia DB 4390*	28		1
21 Apr 60	**PUPPY LOVE** *Columbia DB 4434*	33		1
15 Sep 60	**HELLO YOUNG LOVERS** *Columbia DB 4504*	44		
15 Mar 62	**LOVE ME WARM AND TENDER** *RCA 1276*	19		10
26 Jul 62	**A STEEL GUITAR AND A GLASS OF WINE** *RCA 1292*	41		
28 Sep 74	**(YOU'RE) HAVING MY BABY** *United Artists UP 35713* PAUL ANKA FEATURING ODIA COATES ★	6		8

ANA ANN UK singer

Date	Title / Label	Peak Position	Weeks at No.1	Weeks in Top 40
23 Feb 02	**RIDE** *LL RIDELLR 100*	24		1
6 Mar 04	**CHILDREN OF THE WORLD** *Century Vista LLR104* ANA ANN & THE LONDON COMMUNITY CHOIR	44		

ANNIE Norwegian singer

Date	Title / Label	Peak Position	Weeks at No.1	Weeks in Top 40
25 Sep 04	**CHEWING GUM** *679 679L075CD1*	25		1
12 Mar 05	**HEARTBEAT** *679 679L091CD2*	50		

ANOTHER CHANCE UK production duo

Date	Title / Label	Peak Position	Weeks at No.1	Weeks in Top 40
28 Apr 07	**EVERYTIME I SEE HER (SOUND OF EDEN)** *Positiva CDTIVS253*	62		

ANOTHER LEVEL UK group

Date	Title / Label	Peak Position	Weeks at No.1	Weeks in Top 40
28 Feb 98	**BE ALONE NO MORE** *Northwestside 74321551982* ANOTHER LEVEL FEATURING JAY-Z	6		6
18 Jul 98	**FREAK ME** *Northwestside 74321582362* ●	1	1	10
7 Nov 98	**GUESS I WAS A FOOL** *Northwestside 74321621202*	5		4
23 Jan 99	**I WANT YOU FOR MYSELF** *Northwestside 74321643632* ANOTHER LEVEL/GHOSTFACE KILLAH	2		6
10 Apr 99	**BE ALONE NO MORE** *Northwestside 74321658482* ANOTHER LEVEL FEATURING JAY-Z	11		5
12 Jun 99	**FROM THE HEART** *Northwestside 74321673012*	6		7
4 Sep 99	**SUMMERTIME** *Northwestside 74321694672* ANOTHER LEVEL FEATURING TQ	7		4
13 Nov 99	**BOMB DIGGY** *Northwestside 74321712212*	6		5

ANOTHERSIDE UK duo

Date	Title / Label	Peak Position	Weeks at No.1	Weeks in Top 40
5 Jul 03	**THIS IS YOUR NIGHT** *J-Did/V2 JAD 5023293*	41		

ANT & DEC UK duo

Date	Title / Label	Peak Position	Weeks at No.1	Weeks in Top 40
18 Dec 93	**TONIGHT I'M FREE** *Telstar CDSTAS 2706* PJ & DUNCAN	62		
23 Apr 94	**WHY ME** *Telstar CDSTAS 2719* PJ & DUNCAN	27		2

Silver-selling | Gold-selling | Platinum-selling | US No.1 ★ | Peak Position | Weeks at No.1 | Weeks in Top 40

Date	Title / Label	Peak Position	Weeks at No.1	Weeks in Top 40
23 Jul 94	**LET'S GET READY TO RHUMBLE** *XSrhythm CDDEC 1* PJ & DUNCAN	9		9
8 Oct 94	**IF I GIVE YOU MY NUMBER** *XSrhythm CDDEC 2* PJ & DUNCAN	15		5
3 Dec 94	**ETERNAL LOVE** *XSrhythm CDDEC 3* PJ & DUNCAN	12		8
25 Feb 95	**OUR RADIO ROCKS** *XSrhythm CDANT 4* PJ & DUNCAN	15		3
29 Jul 95	**STUCK ON U** *Telstar CDDEC 5* PJ & DUNCAN	12		4
14 Oct 95	**U KRAZY KATZ** *XSrhythm CDDEC 6* PJ & DUNCAN	15		3
2 Dec 95	**PERFECT** *Telstar CDANT 7* PJ & DUNCAN	16		3
30 Mar 96	**STEPPING STONE** *Telstar CDANT 8* PJ & DUNCAN	11		4
24 Aug 96	**BETTER WATCH OUT** *Telstar CDDEC 9*	10		3
23 Nov 96	**WHEN I FALL IN LOVE** *Telstar CDDEC 10*	12		5
15 Mar 97	**SHOUT** *Telstar CDDEC 11*	10		3
10 May 97	**FALLING** *Telstar CDDEC 12*	14		2
8 Jun 02	**WE'RE ON THE BALL** *Columbia 6727312*	3		6

ANTARCTICA Australian producer

Date	Title / Label	Peak Position	Weeks at No.1	Weeks in Top 40
29 Jan 00	**RETURN TO REALITY** *React CDREACT 173*	53		
8 Jul 00	**ADRIFT (CAST YOUR MIND)** *React CDREACT 172*	72		

BILLE ANTHONY UK singer

Date	Title / Label	Peak Position	Weeks at No.1	Weeks in Top 40
15 Oct 54	**THIS OLE HOUSE** *Columbia DB 3519* BILLIE ANTHONY WITH ERIC JUPP & HIS ORCHESTRA	4		16

MARC ANTHONY US singer

Date	Title / Label	Peak Position	Weeks at No.1	Weeks in Top 40
5 Oct 91	**RIDE ON THE RHYTHM** *Atlantic A 7602* LITTLE LOUIE VEGA & MARC ANTHONY	71		
31 Jan 98	**RIDE ON THE RHYTHM** *Perfecto PERF 151CD1*	36		1
13 Nov 99	**I NEED TO KNOW** *Columbia 6683612*	28		1

MIKI ANTHONY UK singer

Date	Title / Label	Peak Position	Weeks at No.1	Weeks in Top 40
3 Feb 73	**IF IT WASN'T FOR THE REASON THAT I LOVE YOU** *Bell 1275*	27		5

RAY ANTHONY & HIS ORCHESTRA

US bandleader/trumpeter and orchestra

Date	Title / Label	Peak Position	Weeks at No.1	Weeks in Top 40
4 Dec 53	**DRAGNET** *Capitol CL 13983*	7		2

RICHARD ANTHONY French singer

Date	Title / Label	Peak Position	Weeks at No.1	Weeks in Top 40
12 Dec 63	**WALKING ALONE** *Columbia DB 7133*	37		1
23 Apr 64	**IF I LOVED YOU** *Columbia DB 7235*	18		9

ANTHRAX US group

Date	Title / Label	Peak Position	Weeks at No.1	Weeks in Top 40
28 Feb 87	**I AM THE LAW** *Island IS LAW 1*	32		3
27 Jun 87	**INDIANS** *Island IS 325*	44		
5 Dec 87	**I'M THE MAN** *Island IS 338*	20		4
10 Sep 88	**MAKE ME LAUGH** *Island IS 379*	26		2
18 Mar 89	**ANTI-SOCIAL** *Island IS 409*	44		
1 Sep 90	**IN MY WORLD** *Island IS 470*	29		1
5 Jan 91	**GOT THE TIME** *Island IS 476*	16		3
6 Jul 91	**BRING THE NOISE** *Island IS 490* ANTHRAX FEATURING CHUCK D	14		3
8 May 93	**ONLY** *Elektra EKR 166CD*	36		2
11 Sep 93	**BLACK LODGE** *Elektra EKR 171CD*	53		

ANTI-NOWHERE LEAGUE UK group

Date	Title / Label	Peak Position	Weeks at No.1	Weeks in Top 40
23 Jan 82	**STREETS OF LONDON** *WXYZ ABCD 1*	48		
20 Mar 82	**I HATE...PEOPLE** *WXYZ ABCD 2*	46		
3 Jul 82	**WOMAN** *WXYZ ABCD 4*	72		

ANTICAPPELLA UK/Italian group

Date	Title / Label	Peak Position	Weeks at No.1	Weeks in Top 40
16 Nov 91	**2√231** *PWL Continental PWL 205*	24		3
18 Apr 92	**EVERY DAY** *PWL Continental PWL 220*	45		
25 Jun 94	**MOVE YOUR BODY** *Media MCSTD 1980* ANTICAPPELLA FEATURING MC FIXX IT	21		2
1 Apr 95	**EXPRESS YOUR FREEDOM** *Media MCSTD 2048*	31		1
25 May 96	**21231/MOVE YOUR BODY (REMIX)** *Media MCSTD 40037*	54		

ANTONY & THE JOHNSONS US group

Date	Title / Label	Peak Position	Weeks at No.1	Weeks in Top 40
28 May 05	**HOPE THERE'S SOMEONE** *Rough Trade RTRADSCD229*	44		
3 Dec 05	**YOU ARE MY SISTER** *Rough Trade RTRADSCDX276*	39		1

A1 UK/Norwegian group

Date	Title / Label	Peak Position	Weeks at No.1	Weeks in Top 40
3 Jul 99	**BE THE FIRST TO BELIEVE** *Columbia 6674222*	6		5
11 Sep 99	**SUMMERTIME OF OUR LIVES** *Columbia 6678322*	5		3
20 Nov 99	**EVERYTIME/READY OR NOT** *Columbia 6681872*	3		4
4 Mar 00	**LIKE A ROSE** *Columbia 6689032*	6		4
9 Sep 00	**TAKE ON ME** *Columbia 6695902*	1	1	6
18 Nov 00	**SAME OLD BRAND NEW YOU** *Columbia 6705202*	1	1	9
3 Mar 01	**NO MORE** *Columbia 6708742*	6		3
2 Feb 02	**CAUGHT IN THE MIDDLE** *Columbia 6722322*	2		6
25 May 02	**MAKE IT GOOD** *Columbia 6726182*	11		2

APACHE INDIAN UK singer

Date	Title / Label	Peak Position	Weeks at No.1	Weeks in Top 40
28 Nov 92	**JUST WANNA KNOW/FE' REAL** *10 TEN 416* MAXI PRIEST/MAXI PRIEST FEATURING APACHE INDIAN	33		2
2 Jan 93	**ARRANGED MARRIAGE** *Island CID 544*	16		5
27 Mar 93	**CHOK THERE** *Island CID 555*	30		2
14 Aug 93	**NUFF VIBES EP** *Island CID 560*	5		8
23 Oct 93	**MOVIN' ON** *Island CID 580*	48		
7 May 94	**WRECKX SHOP** *MCA MCSTD 1969* WRECKX-N-EFFECT FEATURING APACHE INDIAN	26		1
11 Feb 95	**MAKE WAY FOR THE INDIAN** *Island CID 586* APACHE INDIAN & TIM DOG	29		1
22 Apr 95	**RAGGAMUFFIN GIRL** *Island CID 606* APACHE INDIAN FEATURING FRANKIE PAUL	31		1
29 Mar 97	**LOVIN' (LET ME LOVE YOU)** *Coalition COLA 002CD*	53		
18 Oct 97	**REAL PEOPLE** *Coalition COLA 019CD*	66		

APARTMENT UK group

Date	Title / Label	Peak Position	Weeks at No.1	Weeks in Top 40
19 Feb 05	**EVERYONE SAYS I'M PARANOID/JUNE JULY** *Fierce Panda NING160CD*	67		

APHEX TWIN UK producer

Date	Title / Label	Peak Position	Weeks at No.1	Weeks in Top 40
9 May 92	**DIGERIDOO** *R&S RSUK 12*	55		
27 Nov 93	**ON** *Warp WAP 39CD*	32		1
8 Apr 95	**VENTOLIN** *Warp WAP 60CD*	49		
26 Oct 96	**GIRL/BOY (EP)** *Warp WAP 78CD*	64		
18 Oct 97	**COME TO DADDY** *Warp WAP 94CD*	36		1
3 Apr 99	**WINDOWLICKER** *Warp WAP 105CD*	16		1

APHRODITE UK producer

Date	Title / Label	Peak Position	Weeks at No.1	Weeks in Top 40
16 Nov 02	**SEE THRU IT** *V2 VVR 5020983* APHRODITE FEATURING WILDFLOWER	68		

APHRODITE'S CHILD Greek group

Date	Title / Label	Peak Position	Weeks at No.1	Weeks in Top 40
6 Nov 68	**RAIN AND TEARS** *Mercury MF 1039*	29		5

A+ US rapper

Date	Title / Label	Peak Position	Weeks at No.1	Weeks in Top 40
13 Feb 99	**ENJOY YOURSELF** *Universal UND 56230*	5		6

APOLLO FOURFORTY UK production/group

Date	Title / Label	Peak Position	Weeks at No.1	Weeks in Top 40
22 Jan 94	**ASTRAL AMERICA** *Stealth Sonic SSXCD 2*	36		1
5 Nov 94	**LIQUID COOL** *Stealth Sonic SSXCD 3*	35		1
25 Mar 95	**(DON'T FEAR) THE REAPER** *Stealth Sonic SSXCD 4*	35		1
27 Jul 96	**KRUPA** *Epic SSXCD 5*	23		2
28 Sep 96	**KRUPA** *Epic SSXCD 5*	24		2
15 Feb 97	**AIN'T TALKIN' 'BOUT NO DUB** *Stealth Sonic SSXCDX 6*	7		5
5 Jul 97	**RAW POWER** *Stealth Sonic SSXCD 7*	32		1
11 Jul 98	**RENDEZ-VOUS 98** *Epic 6661102* JEAN-MICHEL JARRE & APOLLO 440	12		4
8 Aug 98	**LOST IN SPACE** *Stealth Sonic SSX 9CD*	4		6
28 Aug 99	**STOP THE ROCK** *Epic SSX 10CD*	10		4
27 Nov 99	**HEART GO BOOM** *Epic SSX 11CD*	57		
9 Dec 00	**CHARLIE'S ANGELS 2000** *Epic SSX 13CD*	29		1

Silver-selling ● | Gold-selling ● | Platinum-selling | US No.1 ★ | Peak Position | Weeks at No.1 | Weeks in Top 40

Date	Title / Label	Peak	Wks No.1	Wks Top 40
21 Jun 03	**DUDE DESCENDING A STAIRCASE** *Sony Music SSX 14CDX* APOLLO FOUR FORTY FEATURING THE BEATNUTS	58		

APOLLO Swedish instrumentalist

Date	Title / Label	Peak	Wks No.1	Wks Top 40
17 Feb 96	**EXCLUSIVE** *Logic 74321324102* APOLLO PRESENTS HOUSE OF VIRGINISM	67		

FIONA APPLE US singer

Date	Title / Label	Peak	Wks No.1	Wks Top 40
26 Feb 00	**FAST AS YOU CAN** *Columbia 6689962*	33		1

KIM APPLEBY UK singer

Date	Title / Label	Peak	Wks No.1	Wks Top 40
3 Nov 90	**DON'T WORRY** *Parlophone R 6272* ●	2		9
9 Feb 91	**G.L.A.D.** *Parlophone R 6281*	10		5
29 Jun 91	**MAMA** *Parlophone R 6291*	19		6
19 Oct 91	**IF YOU CARED** *Parlophone R 6297*	44		
31 Jul 93	**LIGHT OF THE WORLD** *Parlophone CDR 6352*	41		
13 Nov 93	**BREAKAWAY** *Parlophone CDR 6362*	56		
12 Nov 94	**FREE SPIRIT** *Parlophone CDR 6397*	51		

APPLEJACKS UK group

Date	Title / Label	Peak	Wks No.1	Wks Top 40
5 Mar 64	**TELL ME WHEN** *Decca F 11833*	7		11
11 Jun 64	**LIKE DREAMERS DO** *Decca F 11916*	20		9
15 Oct 64	**THREE LITTLE WORDS (I LOVE YOU)** *Decca F 11981*	23		5

APPLES UK group

Date	Title / Label	Peak	Wks No.1	Wks Top 40
23 Mar 91	**EYE WONDER** *Epic 6566717*	75		

APPLETON Canadian duo

Date	Title / Label	Peak	Wks No.1	Wks Top 40
14 Sep 02	**FANTASY** *Polydor 5709852*	2		5
22 Feb 03	**DON'T WORRY** *Polydor 0658192*	5		5
26 Jul 03	**EVERYTHING EVENTUALLY** *Polydor 9808278*	38		1

CHARLIE APPLEWHITE US singer

Date	Title / Label	Peak	Wks No.1	Wks Top 40
23 Sep 55	**BLUE STAR (THE MEDIC THEME)** *Brunswick 05416* CHARLIE APPLEWHITE WITH VICTOR YOUNG & HIS ORCHESTRA & CHORUS	20		1

APRIL WINE Canadian group

Date	Title / Label	Peak	Wks No.1	Wks Top 40
15 Mar 80	**I LIKE TO ROCK** *Capitol CL 16121*	41		
11 Apr 81	**JUST BETWEEN YOU AND ME** *Capitol CL 16184*	52		

AQUA Danish group

Date	Title / Label	Peak	Wks No.1	Wks Top 40
25 Oct 97	**BARBIE GIRL** *Universal UMD 80413*	1	4	18
7 Feb 98	**DOCTOR JONES** *Universal UMD 80457* ●	1	2	12
16 May 98	**TURN BACK TIME** *Universal UMD 80490*	1	1	7
1 Aug 98	**MY OH MY** *Universal UMD 85058*	6		3
26 Dec 98	**GOOD MORNING SUNSHINE** *Universal UMD 85086*	18		4
26 Feb 00	**CARTOON HEROES** *Universal MCSTD 40226*	7		5
10 Jun 00	**AROUND THE WORLD** *Universal MCSXD 40234*	26		1

AQUAGEN German production duo

Date	Title / Label	Peak	Wks No.1	Wks Top 40
9 Dec 00	**PHATT BASS** *NuLife 74321817102* WARP BROTHERS VERSUS AQUAGEN	9		6
1 Mar 03	**HARD TO SAY I'M SORRY** *All Around The World CXGLOBE 265*	33		1

AQUALUNG UK singer

Date	Title / Label	Peak	Wks No.1	Wks Top 40
28 Sep 02	**STRANGE AND BEAUTIFUL** *B Unique BUN 032CDX*	7		4
14 Dec 02	**GOOD TIMES GONNA COME** *B Unique BUN 043CDX*	71		
25 Oct 03	**BRIGHTER THAN SUNSHINE** *B Unique BUN 072CDX*	37		1
27 Mar 04	**EASIER TO LIE** *B Unique WEA373CD2*	60		

AQUANUTS US/Argentinian production group

Date	Title / Label	Peak	Wks No.1	Wks Top 40
4 May 02	**DEEP SEA** *Data 34T*	75		

AQUARIAN DREAM US group

Date	Title / Label	Peak	Wks No.1	Wks Top 40
24 Feb 79	**YOU'RE A STAR** *Elektra LV 7*	67		

ARAB STRAP UK group

Date	Title / Label	Peak	Wks No.1	Wks Top 40
13 Sep 97	**THE GIRLS OF SUMMER (EP)** *Chemikal Underground CHEM 017CD*	74		
4 Apr 98	**HERE WE GO/TRIPPY** *Chemikal Underground CHEM 20CD*	48		
10 Oct 98	**(AFTERNOON) SOAPS** *Chemikal Underground CHEM 27CD*	74		
10 Feb 01	**LOVE DETECTIVE** *Chemikal Underground CHEM 049CD*	66		

ARCADE FIRE Canadian group

Date	Title / Label	Peak	Wks No.1	Wks Top 40
9 Apr 05	**NEIGHBOURHOOD #2 (LAIKA)** *Rough Trade RTRADSCD225*	30		1
4 Jun 05	**POWER OUT** *Rough Trade RTRADSCD232*	26		1
13 Aug 05	**COLD WIND** *Rough Trade RTRADS254*	52		
17 Sep 05	**REBELLION (LIES)** *Rough Trade RTRADSCD252*	19		1
26 Nov 05	**WAKE UP** *Rough Trade RTRADSCD286*	29		1
17 Mar 07	**KEEP THE CAR RUNNING** *Download*	56		

ARCADIA UK group

Date	Title / Label	Peak	Wks No.1	Wks Top 40
26 Oct 85	**ELECTION DAY** *Odeon NSR 1*	7		5
25 Jan 86	**THE PROMISE** *Odeon NSR 2*	37		2
26 Jul 86	**THE FLAME** *Odeon NSR 3*	58		

TASMIN ARCHER UK singer

Date	Title / Label	Peak	Wks No.1	Wks Top 40
12 Sep 92	**SLEEPING SATELLITE** *EMI EM 233* ●	1	2	11
20 Feb 93	**IN YOUR CARE** *EMI CDEMS 260*	16		4
29 May 93	**LORDS OF THE NEW CHURCH** *EMI CDEM 266*	26		3
21 Aug 93	**ARIENNE** *EMI CDEM 275*	30		2
8 Jan 94	**SHIPBUILDING** *EMI CDEM 302*	40		1
23 Mar 96	**ONE MORE GOOD NIGHT WITH THE BOYS** *EMI CDEM 401*	45		

ARCHIES US cartoon/characters

Date	Title / Label	Peak	Wks No.1	Wks Top 40
11 Oct 69	**SUGAR SUGAR** *RCA 1872* ★	1	8	22

ARCHITECHS UK duo

Date	Title / Label	Peak	Wks No.1	Wks Top 40
7 Oct 00	**BODY GROOVE** *Go! Beat GOBCD 33* ARCHITECHS FEATURING NANA ●	3		9
7 Apr 01	**SHOW ME THE MONEY** *Go! Beat GOBCD 38*	20		2

ARCTIC MONKEYS UK group

Date	Title / Label	Peak	Wks No.1	Wks Top 40
29 Oct 05	**I BET YOU LOOK GOOD ON THE DANCEFLOOR** *Domino RUG212CD*	1	1	16
28 Jan 06	**WHEN THE SUN GOES DOWN** *Domino RUG216CD*	1	1	9
26 Aug 06	**LEAVE BEFORE THE LIGHTS COME ON** *Domino RUG236CD*	4		6
14 Apr 07	**BRAINSTORM** *Domino RUG254CD*	2		6
5 May 07	**FLUORESCENT ADOLESCENT** *Domino RUG261CD*	5		8
5 May 07	**505** *Download*	74		
15 Dec 07	**TEDDY PICKER** *Domino RUG279CD*	20		1

JANN ARDEN Canadian singer

Date	Title / Label	Peak	Wks No.1	Wks Top 40
13 Jul 96	**INSENSITIVE** *A&M 5812652*	40		1

A.R.E. WEAPONS US group

Date	Title / Label	Peak	Wks No.1	Wks Top 40
4 Aug 01	**STREET GANG** *Rough Trade RTRADESCD 022*	72		

TINA ARENA Australian singer

Date	Title / Label	Peak	Wks No.1	Wks Top 40
15 Apr 95	**CHAINS** *Columbia 6611255*	6		9
12 Aug 95	**HEAVEN HELP MY HEART** *Columbia 6620975*	25		3
2 Dec 95	**SHOW ME HEAVEN** *Columbia 6626975*	29		1
3 Aug 96	**SORRENTO MOON (I REMEMBER)** *Columbia 6635435*	22		3
27 Jun 98	**WHISTLE DOWN THE WIND** *Really Useful 5672192*	24		2
24 Oct 98	**IF I WAS A RIVER** *Columbia 6665605*	43		
13 Mar 99	**BURN** *Columbia 6667442*	47		
20 May 00	**LIVE FOR THE ONE I LOVE** *Columbia 6691332*	63		
12 Apr 03	**NEVER (PAST TENSE)** *Illustrious CDILL 010* ROC PROFECT FEATURING TINA ARENA	42		

Silver-selling ● Gold-selling ● Platinum-selling ⊛ US No.1 ★ | Peak Position | Weeks at No.1 | Weeks in Top 40

ARGENT UK group

Date	Title	Peak Position	Weeks at No.1	Weeks in Top 40
4 Mar 72	**HOLD YOUR HEAD UP** *Epic EPC 7786*	5		9
10 Jun 72	**TRAGEDY** *Epic EPC 8115*	34		4
24 Mar 73	**GOD GAVE ROCK AND ROLL TO YOU** *Epic EPC 1243*	18		6

INDIA.ARIE US singer

Date	Title	Peak Position	Weeks at No.1	Weeks in Top 40
30 Jun 01	**VIDEO** *Motown TMGCD 1505*	32		1
20 Oct 01	**BROWN SKIN** *Motown TMGCD 1507*	29		1
12 Apr 03	**LITTLE THINGS** *Motown TMGCD 1509*	62		
24 Jun 06	**I AM NOT MY HAIR** *Motown/Uni-Island TMGCD1514*	65		

ARIEL UK production group

Date	Title	Peak Position	Weeks at No.1	Weeks in Top 40
27 Mar 93	**LET IT SLIDE** *Deconstruction 74321134512*	57		
21 Jun 97	**DEEP (I'M FALLING DEEPER)** *Wonderboy WBOYD 005*	47		
17 Jun 00	**A9** *Essential Recordings ESCD 15*	28		1

ARIZONA UK group

Date	Title	Peak Position	Weeks at No.1	Weeks in Top 40
12 Mar 94	**I SPECIALIZE IN LOVE** *Union City UCRCD 27* ARIZONA FEATURING ZEITIA	74		

SHIP'S COMPANY & ROYAL MARINE BAND OF HMS ARK ROYAL UK choir and marine band

Date	Title	Peak Position	Weeks at No.1	Weeks in Top 40
23 Dec 78	**THE LAST FAREWELL** *BBC RESL 61*	46		

ARKARNA UK group

Date	Title	Peak Position	Weeks at No.1	Weeks in Top 40
25 Jan 97	**HOUSE ON FIRE** *WEA 088CD1*	33		1
2 Aug 97	**SO LITTLE TIME** *WEA 108CD1*	46		

JOAN ARMATRADING UK singer/guitarist

Date	Title	Peak Position	Weeks at No.1	Weeks in Top 40
16 Oct 76	**LOVE AND AFFECTION** *A&M AMS 7249*	10		9
23 Feb 80	**ROSIE** *A&M AMS 7506*	49		
14 Jun 80	**ME MYSELF I** *A&M AMS 7527*	21		7
6 Sep 80	**ALL THE WAY FROM AMERICA** *A&M AMS 7552*	54		
12 Sep 81	**I'M LUCKY** *A&M AMS 8163*	46		
16 Jan 82	**NO LOVE** *A&M AMS 8179*	50		
19 Feb 83	**DROP THE PILOT** *A&M AMS 8306*	11		7
16 Mar 85	**TEMPTATION** *A&M AM 238*	65		
26 May 90	**MORE THAN ONE KIND OF LOVE** *A&M AM 561*	75		
23 May 92	**WRAPPED AROUND HER** *A&M AM 877*	56		

ARMOURY SHOW UK group

Date	Title	Peak Position	Weeks at No.1	Weeks in Top 40
25 Aug 84	**CASTLES IN SPAIN** *Parlophone R 6079*	69		
26 Jan 85	**WE CAN BE BRAVE AGAIN** *Parlophone R 6087*	66		
17 Jan 87	**LOVE IN ANGER** *Parlophone R 6149*	63		

DAVE ARMSTRONG & REDROCHE Canadian duo

Date	Title	Peak Position	Weeks at No.1	Weeks in Top 40
19 Jan 08	**LOVE HAS GONE** *Hed Kandi HK50CDS* DAVE ARMSTRONG & REDROCHE FEATURING H-BOOGIE	43		

LOUIS ARMSTRONG US trumpeter/singer

Date	Title	Peak Position	Weeks at No.1	Weeks in Top 40
19 Dec 52	**TAKES TWO TO TANGO** *Brunswick 04995*	6		10
13 Apr 56	**THEME FROM *THE THREEPENNY OPERA*** *Philips PB 574* LOUIS ARMSTRONG WITH HIS ALL-STARS	8		11
15 Jun 56	**TAKE IT SATCH EP** *Philips BBE 12035* LOUIS ARMSTRONG WITH HIS ALL-STARS	29		1
13 Jul 56	**THE FAITHFUL HUSSAR** *Philips PB 604* LOUIS ARMSTRONG WITH HIS ALL-STARS	27		2
6 Nov 59	**MACK THE KNIFE** *Philips PB 967* LOUIS ARMSTRONG WITH HIS ALL-STARS	24		1
4 Jun 64	**HELLO DOLLY** *London HLR 9878* ★	4		12
7 Feb 68	**WHAT A WONDERFUL WORLD/CABARET** *HMV POP 1615*	1	4	24
26 Jun 68	**THE SUNSHINE OF LOVE** *Stateside SS 2116*	41		
16 Apr 88	**WHAT A WONDERFUL WORLD** *A&M AM 435*	53		
19 Nov 94	**WE HAVE ALL THE TIME IN THE WORLD** *EMI CDEM 357* ●	3		9

ARMY OF LOVERS Swedish group

Date	Title	Peak Position	Weeks at No.1	Weeks in Top 40
17 Aug 91	**CRUCIFIED** *Ton Son Ton WOK 2007*	47		
28 Dec 91	**OBSESSION** *Ton Son Ton WOK 2009*	67		
15 Feb 92	**CRUCIFIED** *Ton Son Ton WOK 2017*	31		3
18 Apr 92	**RIDE THE BULLET** *Ton Son Ton WOK 2018*	67		

ARNEE & THE TERMINATORS UK group

Date	Title	Peak Position	Weeks at No.1	Weeks in Top 40
24 Aug 91	**I'LL BE BACK** *Epic 6574177*	5		6

ARNIE'S LOVE US group

Date	Title	Peak Position	Weeks at No.1	Weeks in Top 40
26 Nov 83	**I'M OUT OF YOUR LIFE** *Streetwave WAVE 9*	67		

DAVID ARNOLD UK pianist/composer

Date	Title	Peak Position	Weeks at No.1	Weeks in Top 40
23 Oct 93	**PLAY DEAD** *Island CID 573* BJORK & DAVID ARNOLD	12		5
18 Oct 97	**ON HER MAJESTY'S SECRET SERVICE** *East West EW 136CD* PROPELLERHEADS & DAVID ARNOLD	7		3
22 Nov 97	**DIAMONDS ARE FOREVER** *East West EW 141CD* DAVID McALMONT & DAVID ARNOLD	39		1
29 Apr 00	**THEME FROM *RANDALL & HOPKIRK (DECEASED)*** *Island CID 762* NINA PERSSON & DAVID ARNOLD	49		

EDDY ARNOLD US singer

Date	Title	Peak Position	Weeks at No.1	Weeks in Top 40
17 Feb 66	**MAKE THE WORLD GO AWAY** *RCA 1496*	8		15
26 May 66	**I WANT TO GO WITH YOU** *RCA 1519*	46		
28 Jul 66	**IF YOU WERE MINE MARY** *RCA 1529*	49		

PP ARNOLD US singer

Date	Title	Peak Position	Weeks at No.1	Weeks in Top 40
4 May 67	**FIRST CUT IS THE DEEPEST** *Immediate IM 047*	18		8
2 Aug 67	**THE TIME HAS COME** *Immediate IM 055*	47		
24 Jan 68	**(IF YOU THINK YOU'RE) GROOVY** *Immediate IM 061*	41		
10 Jul 68	**ANGEL OF THE MORNING** *Immediate IM 067*	29		6
24 Sep 88	**BURN IT UP** *Rhythm King LEFT 27* BEATMASTERS WITH PP ARNOLD	14		6

ARPEGGIO US group

Date	Title	Peak Position	Weeks at No.1	Weeks in Top 40
31 Mar 79	**LOVE AND DESIRE (PART 1)** *Polydor POSP 40*	63		

ARRESTED DEVELOPMENT US group

Date	Title	Peak Position	Weeks at No.1	Weeks in Top 40
16 May 92	**TENNESSEE** *Cooltempo COOL 253*	46		
24 Oct 92	**PEOPLE EVERYDAY** *Cooltempo COOL 265* ●	2		13
9 Jan 93	**MR WENDAL/REVOLUTION** *Cooltempo CDCOOL 268*	4		7
3 Apr 93	**TENNESSEE** *Cooltempo CDCOOL 270*	18		4
28 May 94	**EASE MY MIND** *Cooltempo CDCOOL 293*	33		2

STEVE ARRINGTON US singer

Date	Title	Peak Position	Weeks at No.1	Weeks in Top 40
27 Apr 85	**FEEL SO REAL** *Atlantic A 9576*	5		8
6 Jul 85	**DANCIN' IN THE KEY OF LIFE** *Atlantic A 9534*	21		5

ARRIVAL UK group

Date	Title	Peak Position	Weeks at No.1	Weeks in Top 40
10 Jan 70	**FRIENDS** *Decca F 12986*	8		7
6 Jun 70	**I WILL SURVIVE** *Decca F 13026*	16		10

ARROW Montserrat singer

Date	Title	Peak Position	Weeks at No.1	Weeks in Top 40
28 Jul 84	**HOT HOT HOT** *Cooltempo ARROW 1*	59		
13 Jul 85	**LONG TIME** *London LON 70*	30		3
3 Sep 94	**HOT HOT HOT (REMIX)** *The Hit Label HLC 7*	38		1

ARROWS US/UK group

Date	Title	Peak Position	Weeks at No.1	Weeks in Top 40
25 May 74	**A TOUCH TOO MUCH** *RAK 171*	8		8
1 Feb 75	**MY LAST NIGHT WITH YOU** *RAK 189*	25		6

Silver-selling ● Gold-selling ● Platinum-selling ⊛ US No.1 ★ — Peak Position / Weeks at No.1 / Weeks in Top 40

ARSENAL FC UK football club

Date	Title / Label	Peak Position	Weeks at No.1	Weeks in Top 40
8 May 71	**GOOD OLD ARSENAL** *Pye 7N 45067* ARSENAL F.C. FIRST TEAM SQUAD	16		5
15 May 93	**SHOUTING FOR THE GUNNERS** *London LONCD 342* ARSENAL FA CUP SQUAD FEATURING TIPPA IRIE & PETER HUNNIGALE	34		2
23 May 98	**HOT STUFF** *Grapevine AFCCD 1*	9		3
3 Jun 00	**ARSENAL NUMBER ONE/OUR GOAL** *Grapevine CDGPS 280*	46		

ART BRUT UK group

Date	Title / Label	Peak Position	Weeks at No.1	Weeks in Top 40
10 Apr 04	**FORMED A BAND** *Rough Trade RTRADSCD174*	52		
18 Dec 04	**MODERN ART/MY LITTLE BROTHER** *Fierce Panda NING164CD*	49		
14 May 05	**EMILY KANE** *Fierce Panda NING167CD*	41		
8 Oct 05	**GOOD WEEKEND** *Fierce Panda NING173CD*	56		

ART COMPANY Dutch group

Date	Title / Label	Peak Position	Weeks at No.1	Weeks in Top 40
26 May 84	**SUSANNA** *Epic A 4174*	12		7

ART OF NOISE UK group

Date	Title / Label	Peak Position	Weeks at No.1	Weeks in Top 40
24 Nov 84	**CLOSE (TO THE EDIT)** *ZTT ZTPS 01*	8		9
13 Apr 85	**MOMENTS IN LOVE/BEAT BOX** *ZTT ZTPS 02*	51		
9 Nov 85	**LEGS** *China WOK 5*	69		
22 Mar 86	**PETER GUNN** *China WOK 6* ART OF NOISE FEATURING DUANE EDDY	8		7
21 Jun 86	**PARANOIMIA** *China WOK 9* ART OF NOISE FEATURING MAX HEADROOM	12		7
18 Jul 87	**DRAGNET** *China WOK 14*	60		
29 Oct 88	**KISS** *China 11* ART OF NOISE FEATURING TOM JONES	5		5
12 Aug 89	**YEBO** *China 18*	63		
16 Jun 90	**ART OF LOVE** *China 23*	67		
11 Jan 92	**INSTRUMENTS OF DARKNESS (ALL OF US ARE ONE PEOPLE)** *China WOK 2012*	45		
29 Feb 92	**SHADES OF PARANOIMIA** *China WOK 2014*	53		
26 Jun 99	**METAFORCE** *ZTT 129CD*	53		

ART OF TRANCE UK producer

Date	Title / Label	Peak Position	Weeks at No.1	Weeks in Top 40
31 Oct 98	**MADAGASCAR** *Platipus PLAT 43CD*	69		
7 Aug 99	**MADAGASCAR (REMIX)** *Platipus PLAT 58CD*	48		
15 Jun 02	**MADAGASCAR (2nd REMIX)** *Platipus PLATCD 0102*	41		
10 Aug 02	**LOVE WASHES OVER** *Platipus PLATCD 98*	60		

ARTEMESIA Dutch producer

Date	Title / Label	Peak Position	Weeks at No.1	Weeks in Top 40
15 Apr 95	**BITS + PIECES** *Hooj Choons HOOJ 31CD*	46		
23 Sep 95	**BITS + PIECES** *Hooj Choons HOOJ 31CD*	75		
12 Aug 00	**BITS + PIECES** *Tidy Trax TIDT 141CD* MOVIN' MELODIES PRESENTS ARTEMISIA	51		

ARTFUL DODGER UK production duo

Date	Title / Label	Peak Position	Weeks at No.1	Weeks in Top 40
11 Dec 99	**RE-REWIND THE CROWD SAY BO SELECTA** *Public Demand/Relentless RELENT 1CDS* ARTFUL DODGER FEATURING CRAIG DAVID .	2		13
4 Mar 00	**MOVIN TOO FAST** *Locked On/XL Recordings LUX 117CD* ARTFUL DODGER & ROMINA JOHNSON ●	2		8
15 Jul 00	**WOMAN TROUBLE** *Public Demand/ffrr FCDP 380* ARTFUL DODGER FEATURING ROBBIE CRAIG & CRAIG DAVID	6		7
25 Nov 00	**PLEASE DON'T TURN ME ON** *ffrr FCD 388* ARTFUL DODGER FEATURING LIFFORD	4		8
17 Mar 01	**THINK ABOUT ME** *ffrr FCD 394* ARTFUL DODGER FEATURING MICHELLE ESCOFFERY	11		5
15 Sep 01	**TWENTYFOURSEVEN** *ffrr FCDP 400* ARTFUL DODGER FEATURING MELANIE BLATT	6		5
15 Dec 01	**IT AIN'T ENOUGH** *ffrr/Public Demand FCD 401* DREEM TEEM VERSUS ARTFUL DODGER	20		2

NEIL ARTHUR UK singer

Date	Title / Label	Peak Position	Weeks at No.1	Weeks in Top 40
5 Feb 94	**I LOVE I HATE** *Chrysalis CDCHSS 5005*	50		

ARTIFICIAL FUNK Danish duo

Date	Title / Label	Peak Position	Weeks at No.1	Weeks in Top 40
22 Mar 03	**TOGETHER** *Skint 82CD* ARTIFICIAL FUNK FEATURING NELLIE ETTISON	40		1

ARTIFICIAL INTELLIGENCE German production duo

Date	Title / Label	Peak Position	Weeks at No.1	Weeks in Top 40
21 Aug 04	**UPRISING/THROUGH THE GATE** *V Recordings VRECS001UK*	73		

ARTISTS AGAINST AIDS WORLDWIDE

Multinational charity ensemble

Date	Title / Label	Peak Position	Weeks at No.1	Weeks in Top 40
17 Nov 01	**WHAT'S GOING ON** *Columbia 6721172*	6		4

ARTISTS UNITED AGAINST APARTHEID

Multinational protest group

Date	Title / Label	Peak Position	Weeks at No.1	Weeks in Top 40
23 Nov 85	**SUN CITY** *Manhattan MT 7*	21		4

ASAP UK group

Date	Title / Label	Peak Position	Weeks at No.1	Weeks in Top 40
14 Oct 89	**SILVER AND GOLD** *EMI EM 107*	60		
3 Feb 90	**DOWN THE WIRE** *EMI EM 131*	67		

ASCENSION UK production duo

Date	Title / Label	Peak Position	Weeks at No.1	Weeks in Top 40
5 Jul 97	**SOMEONE** *Perfecto PERF 141CD*	55		
15 Jul 00	**SOMEONE (REMIX)** *Code Blue BLU 011CD1*	43		
23 Mar 02	**FOR A LIFETIME** *Xtravaganza XTRAV 20CDS* ASCENSION FEATURING ERIN LORDAN	45		

ASH UK group

Date	Title / Label	Peak Position	Weeks at No.1	Weeks in Top 40
1 Apr 95	**KUNG FU** *Infectious INFECT 21CD*	57		
12 Aug 95	**GIRL FROM MARS** *Infectious INFECT 24CD*	11		3
21 Oct 95	**ANGEL INTERCEPTOR** *Infectious INFECT 27CD*	14		2
27 Apr 96	**GOLDFINGER** *Infectious INFECT 39CD*	5		3
6 Jul 96	**OH YEAH** *Infectious INFECT 41CD*	6		3
25 Oct 97	**A LIFE LESS ORDINARY** *Infectious INFECT 50CD*	10		3
3 Oct 98	**JESUS SAYS** *Infectious INFECT 59CD*	15		2
5 Dec 98	**WILD SURF** *Infectious INFECT 61CDS*	31		1
10 Feb 01	**SHINING LIGHT** *Infectious INFECT 98CDSX*	8		3
14 Apr 01	**BURN BABY BURN** *Infectious INFECT 99CDS*	13		3
21 Jul 01	**SOMETIMES** *Infectious INFEC 101CDS*	21		2
13 Oct 01	**CANDY** *Infectious INFEC 106CDSX*	20		2
12 Jan 02	**THERE'S A STAR** *Infectious INFEC 112CDS*	13		1
7 Sep 02	**ENVY** *Infectious INFECT 119CDSX*	21		1
15 May 04	**ORPHEUS** *Infectious ASH01CD*	13		2
31 Jul 04	**STARCROSSED** *Infectious ASH02CD*	22		2
18 Dec 04	**RENEGADE CAVALCADE** *Atlantic ASH03CD*	33		1
28 Apr 07	**YOU CAN'T HAVE IT ALL** *Infectious ASH05CD*	16		1
30 Jun 07	**POLARIS** *Infectious ASH06CD*	32		1
22 Sep 07	**END OF THE WORLD** *Infectious ASH07CD*	62		

ASHA Italian singer

Date	Title / Label	Peak Position	Weeks at No.1	Weeks in Top 40
8 Jul 95	**JJ TRIBUTE** *ffrreedom TABCD 228*	38		1

ASHANTI US singer

Date	Title / Label	Peak Position	Weeks at No.1	Weeks in Top 40
2 Feb 02	**ALWAYS ON TIME** *Def Jam 5889462* JA RULE FEATURING ASHANTI ★	6		10
25 May 02	**WHAT'S LUV** *Atlantic AT 0128CD* FAT JOE FEATURING ASHANTI	4		5
8 Jun 02	**FOOLISH (IMPORT)** *Mercury 5829372*	68		
20 Jul 02	**FOOLISH** *Murder Inc 0639942* ★	4		8
12 Oct 02	**DOWN 4 U** *Murder Inc 0639002* IRV GOTTI PRESENTS JA RULE, ASHANTI, CHARLI BALTIMORE & VITA	4		5
23 Nov 02	**HAPPY** *Def Jam 0638242*	13		4
29 Mar 03	**MESMERIZE** *Murder Inc 0779582* JA RULE FEATURING ASHANTI	12		6
28 Jun 03	**ROCK WIT U (AWWW BABY)** *Murder Inc 9808432*	7		6
1 Nov 03	**RAIN ON ME** *Murder Inc 9813177*	19		3
6 Nov 04	**WONDERFUL** *Def Jam 9864606* JA RULE FEATURING R KELLY & ASHANTI	1	1	5
5 Feb 05	**ONLY U** *The Inc 2103786*	2		5
18 Jun 05	**DON'T LET THEM** *The Inc 9882726*	38		1
27 Jan 07	**PAC'S LIFE** *Interscope 1723503* 2PAC FEATURING TI & ASHANTI	21		2

ASHAYE UK singer

Date	Title / Label	Peak Position	Weeks at No.1	Weeks in Top 40
15 Oct 83	**MICHAEL JACKSON MEDLEY** *Record Shack SOHO 10*	45		

RICHARD ASHCROFT UK singer

Date	Title	Label	Peak Position	Weeks at No.1	Weeks in Top 40
15 Apr 00	A SONG FOR LOVERS	*Hut HUTCD 128*	3		6
24 Jun 00	MONEY TO BURN	*Hut HUTCD 136*	17		2
23 Sep 00	C'MON PEOPLE (WE'RE MAKING IT NOW)	*Hut HUTCD 138*	21		1
19 Oct 02	CHECK THE MEANING	*Hut HUTCD 161*	11		2
18 Jan 03	SCIENCE OF SILENCE	*Hut HUTCD 163*	14		3
19 Apr 03	BUY IT IN BOTTLES	*Hut HUTCD 167*	26		1
21 Jan 06	BREAK THE NIGHT WITH COLOUR	*Parlophone CDR6680*	3		6
29 Apr 06	MUSIC IS POWER	*Parlophone CDR6688*	20		2
22 Jul 06	WORDS JUST GET IN THE WAY	*Parlophone CDR6700*	40		1

JOHN ASHER UK singer

Date	Title	Label	Peak Position	Weeks at No.1	Weeks in Top 40
15 Nov 75	LET'S TWIST AGAIN	*Creole CR 112*	14		5

ASHFORD & SIMPSON US duo

Date	Title	Label	Peak Position	Weeks at No.1	Weeks in Top 40
18 Nov 78	IT SEEMS TO HANG ON	*Warner Brothers K 17237*	48		
5 Jan 85	SOLID	*Capitol CL 345* ●	3		11
20 Apr 85	BABIES	*Capitol CL 355*	56		

ASHTON, GARDNER & DYKE UK group

Date	Title	Label	Peak Position	Weeks at No.1	Weeks in Top 40
16 Jan 71	RESURRECTION SHUFFLE	*Capitol CL 15665*	3		12

ASIA UK group

Date	Title	Label	Peak Position	Weeks at No.1	Weeks in Top 40
3 Jul 82	HEAT OF THE MOMENT	*Geffen GEF A 2494*	46		
18 Sep 82	ONLY TIME WILL TELL	*Geffen GEF A 2228*	54		
13 Aug 83	DON'T CRY	*Geffen A 3580*	33		2

ASIA BLUE UK group

Date	Title	Label	Peak Position	Weeks at No.1	Weeks in Top 40
27 Jun 92	ESCAPING	*Atomic WNR 882*	50		

ASIAN DUB FOUNDATION UK group

Date	Title	Label	Peak Position	Weeks at No.1	Weeks in Top 40
21 Feb 98	FREE SATPAL RAM	*ffrr FCD 326*	56		
2 May 98	BUZZIN'	*ffrr FCDP 335*	31		1
4 Jul 98	BLACK WHITE	*ffrr FCD 337*	52		
18 Mar 00	REAL GREAT BRITAIN	*ffrr FCD 376*	41		
3 Jun 00	NEW WAY, NEW LIFE	*ffrr FCD 378*	49		
1 Feb 03	FORTRESS EUROPE	*Virgin DINSDY 253*	57		

ASSEMBLY UK group

Date	Title	Label	Peak Position	Weeks at No.1	Weeks in Top 40
12 Nov 83	NEVER NEVER	*Mute TINY 1* ○	4		8

ASSOCIATES UK duo

Date	Title	Label	Peak Position	Weeks at No.1	Weeks in Top 40
20 Feb 82	PARTY FEARS TWO	*Associates ASC 1*	9		7
8 May 82	CLUB COUNTRY	*Associates ASC 2*	13		9
7 Aug 82	LOVE HANGOVER/18 CARAT LOVE AFFAIR	*Associates ASC 3*	21		7
16 Jun 84	THOSE FIRST IMPRESSIONS	*WEA YZ 6*	43		
1 Sep 84	WAITING FOR THE LOVEBOAT	*WEA YZ 16*	53		
19 Jan 85	BREAKFAST	*WEA YX 28*	49		
17 Sep 88	HEART OF GLASS	*WEA YZ 310*	56		

ASSOCIATION US group

Date	Title	Label	Peak Position	Weeks at No.1	Weeks in Top 40
22 May 68	TIME FOR LIVING	*Warner Brothers WB 7195*	23		7

RICK ASTLEY UK singer

Date	Title	Label	Peak Position	Weeks at No.1	Weeks in Top 40
8 Aug 87	NEVER GONNA GIVE YOU UP	*RCA PB 41447* ● ★	1	5	14
31 Oct 87	WHENEVER YOU NEED SOMEBODY	*RCA PB 41567*	3		8
12 Dec 87	WHEN I FALL IN LOVE/MY ARMS KEEP MISSING YOU	*RCA PB 41683* ○	2		8
27 Feb 88	TOGETHER FOREVER	*RCA PB 41817* ★	2		7
24 Sep 88	SHE WANTS TO DANCE WITH ME	*RCA PB 42189*	6		8
26 Nov 88	TAKE ME TO YOUR HEART	*RCA PB 42573*	8		8
11 Feb 89	HOLD ME IN YOUR ARMS	*RCA PB 42615*	10		6
26 Jan 91	CRY FOR HELP	*RCA PB 44247*	7		6
30 Mar 91	MOVE RIGHT OUT	*RCA PB 44407*	58		
29 Jun 91	NEVER KNEW LOVE	*RCA PB 44737*	70		
4 Sep 93	THE ONES YOU LOVE	*RCA 74321160142*	48		
13 Nov 93	HOPELESSLY	*RCA 74321175642*	33		1

ASTRO TRAX UK production group

Date	Title	Label	Peak Position	Weeks at No.1	Weeks in Top 40
24 Oct 98	THE ENERGY (FEEL THE VIBE)	*Satellite 74321622052*	74		

ASWAD UK group

Date	Title	Label	Peak Position	Weeks at No.1	Weeks in Top 40
3 Mar 84	CHASING FOR THE BREEZE	*Island IS 160*	51		
6 Oct 84	54-66 (WAS MY NUMBER)	*Island IS 170*	70		
27 Feb 88	DON'T TURN AROUND	*Mango IS 341* ○	1	2	9
21 May 88	GIVE A LITTLE LOVE	*Mango IS 358*	11		6
24 Sep 88	SET THEM FREE	*Mango IS 383*	70		
1 Apr 89	BEAUTY'S ONLY SKIN DEEP	*Mango MNG 105*	31		3
22 Jul 89	ON AND ON	*Mango MNG 708*	25		5
18 Aug 90	NEXT TO YOU	*Mango MNG 753*	24		4
17 Nov 90	SMILE — ASWAD FEATURING SWEETIE IRIE	*Mango MNG 767*	53		
30 Mar 91	TOO WICKED (EP)	*Mango MNG 771*	61		
31 Jul 93	HOW LONG — YAZZ & ASWAD	*Polydor PZCD 252*	31		4
9 Oct 93	DANCEHALL MOOD	*Bubblin' CDBUBB 1*	48		
18 Jun 94	SHINE	*Bubblin' CDBUBB 3* ○	5		12
17 Sep 94	WARRIORS	*Bubblin' CDBUBB 4*	33		2
18 Feb 95	YOU'RE NO GOOD	*Bubblin' CDBUBB 5*	35		2
5 Aug 95	IF I WAS	*Bubblin' CDBUBB 6*	58		
31 Aug 02	SHY GUY	*Universal Music TV 0192632*	62		

AT THE DRIVE-IN US group

Date	Title	Label	Peak Position	Weeks at No.1	Weeks in Top 40
19 Aug 00	ONE ARMED SCISSOR	*Grand Royal GR 091CD*	64		
16 Dec 00	ROLODEX PROPAGANDA	*Grand Royal/Virgin VUSCD 189*	54		
24 Mar 01	INVALID LITTER DEPT	*Grand Royal/Virgin VUSCD 193*	50		

ATARIS US group

Date	Title	Label	Peak Position	Weeks at No.1	Weeks in Top 40
11 Oct 03	THE BOYS OF SUMMER	*Columbia 6743402*	49		

ATB German producer

Date	Title	Label	Peak Position	Weeks at No.1	Weeks in Top 40
13 Mar 99	9PM (TILL I COME)	*Ministry Of Sound DATA 1*	68		
22 May 99	9PM (TILL I COME) (GERMAN IMPORT)	*Club Tools CLU 66066*	47		
19 Jun 99	9PM (TILL I COME) (AUSTRALIAN IMPORT)	*Dancenet DNET 131*	63		
3 Jul 99	9PM (TILL I COME)	*Sound Of Ministry MOSCDS 132*	1	2	11
9 Oct 99	DON'T STOP (IMPORT)	*Club Tools CLU 66406*	61		
23 Oct 99	DON'T STOP	*Sound Of Ministry MOSCDS 134* ○	3		6
25 Mar 00	KILLER	*Sound Of Ministry MOSCDS 138*	4		5
27 Jan 01	THE FIELDS OF LOVE — ATB FEATURING YORK	*Club Tools 0124095 CLU*	16		2
30 Jun 01	LET U GO	*Kontour 0117335 KTR*	34		1

ATC Multinational group

Date	Title	Label	Peak Position	Weeks at No.1	Weeks in Top 40
17 Aug 02	AROUND THE WORLD (LA LA LA LA)	*Liberty CDATC 001*	15		3

ATEED German singer

Date	Title	Label	Peak Position	Weeks at No.1	Weeks in Top 40
4 Oct 03	COME TO ME	*Better The Devil BTD 4CD*	56		

A.T.F.C. UK producer

Date	Title	Label	Peak Position	Weeks at No.1	Weeks in Top 40
16 Sep 00	BAD HABIT — A.T.F.C. PRESENTS ONEPHATDEEVA FEATURING LISA MILLETT	*Defected DEFECT 8CDS*	17		2
30 Oct 99	IN AND OUT OF MY LIFE — A.T.F.C. PRESENTS ONEPHATDEEVA	*Defected DFECT 19CDX*	11		3
9 Feb 02	SLEEP TALK — A.T.F.C. FEATURING LISA MILLETT	*Defected DFECT 43CDS*	33		1

ATGOC Italian producer

Date	Title	Label	Peak Position	Weeks at No.1	Weeks in Top 40
21 Nov 98	REPEATED LOVE	*Wonderboy WBOYD 012*	38		1

ATHLETE UK group

Date	Title	Label	Peak Position	Weeks at No.1	Weeks in Top 40
29 Jun 02	YOU GOT THE STYLE	*Parlophone CDATH 001*	37		1
16 Nov 02	BEAUTIFUL	*Parlophone CDATH 002*	41		
5 Apr 03	EL SALVADOR	*Parlophone CDATHS 003*	31		1
5 Jul 03	WESTSIDE	*Parlophone CDATHS 005*	42		
4 Oct 03	YOU GOT THE STYLE	*Parlophone CDATH 006*	42		
29 Jan 05	WIRES	*Parlophone CDATHS007*	4		7
7 May 05	HALF LIGHT	*Parlophone CDATHS008*	16		3

Silver-selling ○ Gold-selling ● Platinum-selling ⊛ US No.1 ★ | Peak Position | Weeks at No.1 | Weeks in Top 40

Date	Title / Label	Peak Position	Weeks at No.1	Weeks in Top 40
27 Aug 05	**TOURIST** *Parlophone CDATH009*	43		
26 Nov 05	**TWENTY FOUR HOURS** *Parlophone CDATH010*	42		
25 Aug 07	**HURRICANE** *Parlophone CDATH011*	31		3

CHET ATKINS US guitarist

Date	Title / Label	Peak Position	Weeks at No.1	Weeks in Top 40
17 Mar 60	**TEENSVILLE** *RCA 1174*	46		

ATL US group

Date	Title / Label	Peak Position	Weeks at No.1	Weeks in Top 40
29 May 04	**CALLING ALL GIRLS** *Epic 6748272*	12		3
28 Aug 04	**MAKE IT UP WITH LOVE** *Epic 6751102*	21		2

ATLANTA RHYTHM SECTION US group

Date	Title / Label	Peak Position	Weeks at No.1	Weeks in Top 40
27 Oct 79	**SPOOKY** *Polydor POSP 74*	48		

ATLANTIC OCEAN Dutch production duo

Date	Title / Label	Peak Position	Weeks at No.1	Weeks in Top 40
19 Feb 94	**WATERFALL** *Eastern Bloc BLOCCD 001*	22		4
2 Jul 94	**BODY IN MOTION** *Eastern Bloc BLOCCD 009*	15		2
26 Nov 94	**MUSIC IS A PASSION** *Eastern Bloc BLOCCDX 017*	59		
30 Nov 96	**WATERFALL (REMIX)** *Eastern Bloc BLOC 104CD*	21		2

ATLANTIC STARR US group

Date	Title / Label	Peak Position	Weeks at No.1	Weeks in Top 40
9 Sep 78	**GIMME YOUR LOVIN'** *A&M AMS 7380*	66		
29 Jun 85	**SILVER SHADOW** *A&M AM 260*	41		
7 Sep 85	**ONE LOVE** *A&M AM 273*	58		
15 Mar 86	**SECRET LOVERS** *A&M AM 307*	10		10
24 May 86	**IF YOUR HEART ISN'T IN IT** *A&M AM 319*	48		
13 Jun 87	**ALWAYS** *Warner Brothers W 8455* ○ ★	3		12
12 Sep 87	**ONE LOVER AT A TIME** *Warner Brothers W 8327*	57		
27 Aug 94	**EVERYBODY'S GOT SUMMER** *Arista 74321228072*	36		1

ATLANTIS VS AVATAR UK production group

Date	Title / Label	Peak Position	Weeks at No.1	Weeks in Top 40
28 Oct 00	**FIJI** *Inferno CDFERN 34*	52		

ATMOSFEAR UK group

Date	Title / Label	Peak Position	Weeks at No.1	Weeks in Top 40
17 Nov 79	**DANCING IN OUTER SPACE** *MCA 543*	46		

ATOMIC KITTEN UK group

Date	Title / Label	Peak Position	Weeks at No.1	Weeks in Top 40
11 Dec 99	**RIGHT NOW** *Innocent SINCD 15*	10		7
8 Apr 00	**SEE YA** *Innocent SINCD 17*	6		4
15 Jul 00	**I WANT YOUR LOVE** *Innocent SINDX 18*	10		3
21 Oct 00	**FOLLOW ME** *Innocent SINDX 22*	20		2
10 Feb 01	**WHOLE AGAIN** *Innocent SINDX 24* .	1	4	20
4 Aug 01	**ETERNAL FLAME** *Innocent SINCD 27* ●	1	2	10
1 Jun 02	**IT'S OK** *Innocent SINCD 36* ○	3		11
7 Sep 02	**THE TIDE IS HIGH (GET THE FEELING)** *Innocent SINDX 38* ●	1	3	12
7 Dec 02	**LAST GOODBYE/BE WITH YOU** *Innocent SINDX 42*	2		9
12 Apr 03	**LOVE DOESN'T HAVE TO HURT** *Innocent SINDX 45*	4		6
8 Nov 03	**IF YOU COME TO ME** *Innocent SINDX 50*	3		6
27 Dec 03	**LADIES NIGHT** *Innocent SINDX 53* ATOMIC KITTEN FEATURING KOOL & THE GANG	8		8
10 Apr 04	**SOMEONE LIKE ME/RIGHT NOW 2004** *Innocent SINDX 60*	8		5
26 Feb 05	**CRADLE** *Innocent SINDX72*	10		2

ATOMIC ROOSTER UK band

Date	Title / Label	Peak Position	Weeks at No.1	Weeks in Top 40
6 Feb 71	**TOMORROW NIGHT** *B&C CB 131*	11		11
10 Jul 71	**THE DEVIL'S ANSWER** *B&C CB 157*	4		12

WINIFRED ATWELL UK pianist

Date	Title / Label	Peak Position	Weeks at No.1	Weeks in Top 40
12 Dec 52	**BRITANNIA RAG** *Decca F 10015*	5		6
15 May 53	**CORONATION RAG** *Decca F 10110*	5		6
25 Sep 53	**FLIRTATION WALTZ** *Decca F 10161*	10		3
4 Dec 53	**LET'S HAVE A PARTY** *Philips PB 213*	2		9
26 Nov 54	**LET'S HAVE A PARTY** *Philips PB 213*	14		6
23 Jul 54	**RACHMANINOFF'S 18TH VARIATION ON A THEME BY PAGANINI (THE STORY OF THREE LOVES)** *Philips PB 234*	9		9
26 Nov 54	**LET'S HAVE ANOTHER PARTY** *Philips PB 268*	1	5	8
4 Nov 55	**LET'S HAVE A DING DONG** *Decca F 10634*	3		10
16 Mar 56	**POOR PEOPLE OF PARIS** *Decca F 10681*	1	3	16
18 May 56	**PORT AU PRINCE** *Decca F 10727* WINIFRED ATWELL & FRANK CHACKSFIELD	18		6
20 Jul 56	**LEFT BANK** *Decca F 10762*	14		7
26 Oct 56	**MAKE IT A PARTY** *Decca F 10796*	7		12
22 Feb 57	**LET'S ROCK 'N' ROLL** *Decca F 10852*	24		4
6 Dec 57	**LET'S HAVE A BALL** *Decca F 10956*	4		6
7 Aug 59	**THE SUMMER OF SEVENTEENTH DOLL** *Decca F 11143*	24		2
27 Nov 59	**PIANO PARTY** *Decca F 11183*	10		7

AUDIO BULLYS UK production duo

Date	Title / Label	Peak Position	Weeks at No.1	Weeks in Top 40
18 Jan 03	**WE DON'T CARE** *Source SOURCD 061*	15		2
31 May 03	**THE THINGS/TURNED AWAY** *Source SOURCDX 084*	22		1
26 Jun 04	**BREAK DOWN THE DOORS** *Subliminal SUB124CD* MORILLO FEATURING THE AUDIO BULLYS	44		
4 Jun 05	**SHOT YOU DOWN** *Source SOURCDX111* AUDIO BULLYS FEATURING NANCY SINATRA	3		14
5 Nov 05	**I'M IN LOVE** *Source SOURCD113*	27		2

AUDIOSLAVE US group

Date	Title / Label	Peak Position	Weeks at No.1	Weeks in Top 40
1 Feb 03	**COCHISE** *Epic/Interscope 6732762*	24		1
18 Jun 05	**BE YOURSELF** *Epic/Interscope 9882599*	40		1

AUDIOWEB UK group

Date	Title / Label	Peak Position	Weeks at No.1	Weeks in Top 40
14 Oct 95	**SLEEPER** *Mother MUMCD 69*	74		
9 Mar 96	**YEAH** *Mother MUMCD 72*	73		
15 Jun 96	**INTO MY WORLD** *Mother MUMCD 76*	42		
19 Oct 96	**SLEEPER (REMIX)** *Mother MUMCD 78*	50		
15 Feb 97	**BANKROBBER** *Mother MUMCD 85*	19		1
24 May 97	**FAKER** *Mother MUMCD 91*	70		
25 Apr 98	**POLICEMAN SKANK...(THE STORY OF MY LIFE)** *Mother MUMCD 100*	21		1
4 Jul 98	**PERSONAL FEELING** *Mother MUMCD 104*	65		
20 Feb 99	**TEST THE THEORY** *Mother MUMCD 110*	56		

AUF DER MAUR Canadian singer/guitarist

Date	Title / Label	Peak Position	Weeks at No.1	Weeks in Top 40
28 Feb 04	**FOLLOWED THE WAVES** *EMI CDEM 635*	35		1
15 May 04	**REAL A LIE** *EMI CDEMS 642*	33		1
9 Oct 04	**TASTE YOU** *EMI CDEM 650*	51		

AURORA UK production duo

Date	Title / Label	Peak Position	Weeks at No.1	Weeks in Top 40
5 Jun 99	**HEAR YOU CALLING** *Addictive 12AD 040*	71		
5 Feb 00	**HEAR YOU CALLING** *Positiva CDTIV 124*	17		2
23 Sep 00	**ORDINARY WORLD** *Positiva CDTIV 139* AURORA FEATURING NAIMEE COLEMAN	5		4
13 Apr 02	**DREAMING** *EMI CDEM 611*	24		2
6 Jul 02	**THE DAY IT RAINED FOREVER** *EMI CDEMS 613*	29		1

AURRA US group

Date	Title / Label	Peak Position	Weeks at No.1	Weeks in Top 40
4 May 85	**LIKE I LIKE IT** *10 TEN 45*	51		
19 Apr 86	**YOU AND ME TONIGHT** *10 TEN 71*	12		7
21 Jun 86	**LIKE I LIKE IT** *10 TEN 126*	43		

ADAM AUSTIN UK singer

Date	Title / Label	Peak Position	Weeks at No.1	Weeks in Top 40
13 Feb 99	**CENTERFOLD** *Media PSRCA 0107*	41		

DAVID AUSTIN UK singer

Date	Title / Label	Peak Position	Weeks at No.1	Weeks in Top 40
21 Jul 84	**TURN TO GOLD** *Parlophone R 6068*	68		

PATTI AUSTIN US singer

Date	Title / Label	Peak Position	Weeks at No.1	Weeks in Top 40
20 Jun 81	**RAZZAMATAZZ** *A&M 8140* QUINCY JONES FEATURING PATTI AUSTIN	11		6
12 Feb 83	**BABY COME TO ME** *Qwest K 15005* PATTI AUSTIN & JAMES INGRAM ★	11		9
5 Sep 92	**I'LL KEEP YOUR DREAMS ALIVE** *Ammi 101* GEORGE BENSON & PATTI AUSTIN	68		

AUTECHRE UK duo

Date	Title / Label	Peak Position	Weeks at No.1	Weeks in Top 40
7 May 94	**BASSCAD** *Warp WAP 44CD*	56		

AUTEURS UK group

Date	Title / Label	Peak Position	Weeks at No.1	Weeks in Top 40
27 Nov 93	LENNY VALENTINO *Hut HUTCD 36*	41		
23 Apr 94	CHINESE BAKERY *Hut HUTDX 41*	42		
6 Jan 96	BACK WITH THE KILLER AGAIN *Hut HUTCD 65*	45		
24 Feb 96	LIGHT AIRCRAFT ON FIRE *Hut HUTCD 66*	58		
3 Jul 99	THE RUBETTES *Hut HUTCD 113*	66		

AUTOMATIC UK group

Date	Title / Label	Peak Position	Weeks at No.1	Weeks in Top 40
8 Apr 06	RAOUL *B Unique/Polydor BUN104CD*	32		1
10 Jun 06	MONSTER *B Unique/Polydor BUN106CD*	4		11
30 Sep 06	RECOVER *B Unique/Polydor BUN110CDX*	25		1
20 Jan 07	RAOUL *B Unique/Polydor BUN117CDX*	30		2

AUTUMN UK group

Date	Title / Label	Peak Position	Weeks at No.1	Weeks in Top 40
16 Oct 71	MY LITTLE GIRL *Pye 7N 45090*	37		2

PETER AUTY & THE SINFONIA OF LONDON UK boy soprano and orchestra

Date	Title / Label	Peak Position	Weeks at No.1	Weeks in Top 40
14 Dec 85	WALKING IN THE AIR *Stiff LAD 1*	42		
19 Dec 87	WALKING IN THE AIR *CBS GA 3950*	37		1

AVALANCHES Australian group

Date	Title / Label	Peak Position	Weeks at No.1	Weeks in Top 40
7 Apr 01	SINCE I LEFT YOU *XL Recordings XLS 128CD*	16		2
21 Jul 01	FRONTIER PSYCHIATRIST *XL Recordings XLS 134CD1*	18		3

FRANKIE AVALON US singer

Date	Title / Label	Peak Position	Weeks at No.1	Weeks in Top 40
10 Oct 58	GINGERBREAD *HMV POP 517*	30		1
24 Apr 59	VENUS *HMV POP 603* ★	16		6
22 Jan 60	WHY *HMV POP 688* ★	20		4
28 Apr 60	DON'T THROW AWAY ALL THOSE TEARDROPS *HMV POP 727*	37		1

AVENGED SEVENFOLD US group

Date	Title / Label	Peak Position	Weeks at No.1	Weeks in Top 40
18 Mar 06	BEAST AND THE HARLOT *Warner Brothers W705CD1*	47		
27 Oct 07	ALMOST EASY *Warner Brothers W785CD*	67		

AVERAGE WHITE BAND UK group

Date	Title / Label	Peak Position	Weeks at No.1	Weeks in Top 40
22 Feb 75	PICK UP THE PIECES *Atlantic K 10489* ★	6		8
26 Apr 75	CUT THE CAKE *Atlantic K 10605*	31		1
9 Oct 76	QUEEN OF MY SOUL *Atlantic K 10825*	23		6
28 Apr 79	WALK ON BY *RCA XC 1087*	46		
25 Aug 79	WHEN WILL YOU BE MINE *RCA XB 1096*	49		
26 Apr 80	LET'S GO ROUND AGAIN PART 1 *RCA AWB 1*	12		8
26 Jul 80	FOR YOU FOR LOVE *RCA AWB 2*	46		
26 Mar 94	LET'S GO ROUND AGAIN (REMIX) *The Hit Label HLC 5*	56		

KEVIN AVIANCE US singer

Date	Title / Label	Peak Position	Weeks at No.1	Weeks in Top 40
13 Jun 98	DIN DA DA *Distinctive DISNCD 42*	65		

AVONS UK trio

Date	Title / Label	Peak Position	Weeks at No.1	Weeks in Top 40
13 Nov 59	SEVEN LITTLE GIRLS SITTING IN THE BACK SEAT *Columbia DB 4363*	3		13
7 Jul 60	WE'RE ONLY YOUNG ONCE *Columbia DB 4461*	45		
27 Oct 60	FOUR LITTLE HEELS *Columbia DB 4522*	45		
26 Jan 61	RUBBER BALL *Columbia DB 4569*	30		2

AWESOME UK group

Date	Title / Label	Peak Position	Weeks at No.1	Weeks in Top 40
8 Nov 97	RUMOURS *Universal MCSTD 40145*	58		
21 Mar 98	CRAZY *Universal MCSTD 40195*	63		

AWESOME 3 UK group

Date	Title / Label	Peak Position	Weeks at No.1	Weeks in Top 40
8 Sep 90	HARD UP *A&M AM 591*	55		
3 Oct 92	DON'T GO *Citybeat CBE 1271*	75		
4 Jun 94	DON'T GO (REMIX) *Citybeat CBX 771CD*	45		
26 Oct 96	DON'T GO (2ND REMIX) *XL Recordings XLS 78CD* AWESOME 3 FEATURING JULIE McDERMOTT	27		1

HOYT AXTON US singer

Date	Title / Label	Peak Position	Weeks at No.1	Weeks in Top 40
7 Jun 80	DELLA AND THE DEALER *Young Blood YB 82*	48		

AXUS UK producer

Date	Title / Label	Peak Position	Weeks at No.1	Weeks in Top 40
26 Sep 98	ABACUS (WHEN I FELL IN LOVE) *INCredible INCRL 8CD*	62		

AXWELL Swedish producer

Date	Title / Label	Peak Position	Weeks at No.1	Weeks in Top 40
20 Aug 05	FEEL THE VIBE (TIL THE MORNING COMES) *Data DATA85CDS*	16		2
30 Sep 06	WATCH THE SUNRISE *Positiva CDTIV243* AXWELL FEATURING STEVE EDWARDS	70		
18 Aug 07	I FOUND U *Positiva CDTIV261* AXWELL FEATURING MAX C	6		6

ROY AYERS US vibraphonist/singer

Date	Title / Label	Peak Position	Weeks at No.1	Weeks in Top 40
21 Oct 78	GET ON UP, GET ON DOWN *Polydor AYERS 7*	41		
13 Jan 79	HEAT OF THE BEAT *Polydor POSP 16* ROY AYERS & WAYNE HENDERSON	43		
2 Feb 80	DON'T STOP THE FEELING *Polydor STEP 6*	56		
16 May 98	EXPANSIONS *Soma Recordings SOMA 65CDS* SCOTT GROOVES FEATURING ROY AYERS	68		

AYLA German producer

Date	Title / Label	Peak Position	Weeks at No.1	Weeks in Top 40
4 Sep 99	AYLA *Positiva CDTIV 117*	22		1

AZ US rapper

Date	Title / Label	Peak Position	Weeks at No.1	Weeks in Top 40
30 Mar 96	SUGARHILL *Cooltempo CDCOOL 315*	67		

AZ YET US group

Date	Title / Label	Peak Position	Weeks at No.1	Weeks in Top 40
1 Mar 97	LAST NIGHT *LaFace 74321423202*	21		1
21 Jun 97	HARD TO SAY I'M SORRY *LaFace 74321481482* AZ YET FEATURING PETER CETERA	7		5

CHARLES AZNAVOUR French singer

Date	Title / Label	Peak Position	Weeks at No.1	Weeks in Top 40
22 Sep 73	THE OLD FASHIONED WAY *Barclay BAR 20*	38		2
22 Jun 74	SHE *Barclay BAR 26* ●	1	4	12

AZTEC CAMERA UK group

Date	Title / Label	Peak Position	Weeks at No.1	Weeks in Top 40
19 Feb 83	OBLIVIOUS *Rough Trade RT 122*	47		
4 Jun 83	WALK OUT TO WINTER *Rough Trade RT 132*	64		
5 Nov 83	OBLIVIOUS *WEA AZTEC 1*	18		8
1 Sep 84	ALL I NEED IS EVERYTHING/JUMP *WEA AC 1*	34		3
13 Feb 88	HOW MEN ARE *WEA YZ 168*	25		4
23 Apr 88	SOMEWHERE IN MY HEART *WEA YZ 181*	3		9
6 Aug 88	WORKING IN A GOLDMINE *WEA YZ 199*	31		3
8 Oct 88	DEEP AND WIDE AND TALL *WEA YZ 154*	55		
7 Jul 90	THE CRYING SCENE *WEA YZ 492*	70		
6 Oct 90	GOOD MORNING BRITAIN *WEA YZ 521* AZTEC CAMERA & MICK JONES	19		6
18 Jul 92	SPANISH HORSES *WEA YZ 688*	52		
1 May 93	DREAM SWEET DREAMS *WEA YZ 740CD1*	67		

AZURE Italian/US duo

Date	Title / Label	Peak Position	Weeks at No.1	Weeks in Top 40
25 Apr 98	MAMA USED TO SAY *Inferno CDFERN 005*	56		

AZYMUTH Brazilian group

Date	Title / Label	Peak Position	Weeks at No.1	Weeks in Top 40
12 Jan 80	JAZZ CARNIVAL *Milestone MRC 101*	19		5

BOB AZZAM & HIS ORCHESTRA Egyptian orchestra

Date	Title / Label	Peak Position	Weeks at No.1	Weeks in Top 40
26 May 60	MUSTAPHA *Decca F 21235*	23		9

Silver-selling ○ Gold-selling ● Platinum-selling ⊛ US No.1 ★ — Peak Position · Weeks at No.1 · Weeks in Top 40

B

DEREK B UK rapper

Date	Title / Label	Peak Position	Weeks at No.1	Weeks in Top 40
27 Feb 88	**GOODGROOVE** *Music Of Life 7NOTE 12*	16		5
7 May 88	**BAD YOUNG BROTHER** *Tuff Audio DRKB 1*	16		5
2 Jul 88	**WE'VE GOT THE JUICE** *Tuff Audio DRKB 2*	56		

ERIC B & RAKIM US duo

Date	Title / Label	Peak Position	Weeks at No.1	Weeks in Top 40
7 Nov 87	**PAID IN FULL** *Fourth & Broadway BRW 78*	15		5
20 Feb 88	**MOVE THE CROWD** *Fourth & Broadway BRW 88*	53		
12 Mar 88	**I KNOW YOU GOT SOUL** *Cooltempo COOL 146*	13		4
2 Jul 88	**FOLLOW THE LEADER** *MCA 1256*	21		4
19 Nov 88	**THE MICROPHONE FIEND** *MCA 1300*	74		
12 Aug 89	**FRIENDS** *MCA 1352* JODY WATLEY WITH ERIC B & RAKIM	21		3

HOWIE B UK singer

Date	Title / Label	Peak Position	Weeks at No.1	Weeks in Top 40
19 Jul 97	**ANGELS GO BALD: TOO** *Polydor 5711672*	36		1
18 Oct 97	**SWITCH** *Polydor 5717112*	62		
11 Apr 98	**TAKE YOUR PARTNER BY THE HAND** *Polydor 5693272* HOWIE B FEATURING ROBBIE ROBERTSON	74		

JOHN B UK producer

Date	Title / Label	Peak Position	Weeks at No.1	Weeks in Top 40
22 Jun 02	**UP ALL NIGHT/TAKE CONTROL** *Metalheadz METH 041CD*	58		

JON B US singer

Date	Title / Label	Peak Position	Weeks at No.1	Weeks in Top 40
17 Oct 98	**THEY DON'T KNOW** *Epic 6663975*	32		1
26 May 01	**DON'T TALK** *Epic 6712792*	29		1
19 Mar 05	**LATELY** *Sanctuary Urban SANXS357*	68		

LISA B US singer

Date	Title / Label	Peak Position	Weeks at No.1	Weeks in Top 40
12 Jun 93	**GLAM** *ffrr FCD 210*	49		
25 Sep 93	**FASCINATED** *ffrr FCD 218*	35		1
8 Jan 94	**YOU AND ME** *ffrr FCD 226*	39		1

LORNA B UK singer

Date	Title / Label	Peak Position	Weeks at No.1	Weeks in Top 40
28 Jan 95	**DO YOU WANNA PARTY** *Steppin' Out SPONCD 2* DJ SCOTT FEATURING LORNA B	36		1
1 Apr 95	**SWEET DREAMS** *Steppin' Out SPONCD 3* DJ SCOTT FEATURING LORNA B	37		1
15 Mar 97	**FEELS SO GOOD** *Avex UK AVEXCD 53* ZERO VU FEATURING LORNA B	69		

MARK B UK producer

Date	Title / Label	Peak Position	Weeks at No.1	Weeks in Top 40
10 Feb 01	**THE UNKNOWN** *Wordplay WORDCDS 011* MARK B & BLADE	49		
26 May 01	**YA DON'T SEE THE SIGNS** *Wordplay WORDCDSE 019* MARK B & BLADE	23		1
25 Sep 04	**MOVE NOW** *Genuine GEN033CD* MARK B FEATURING TOMMY EVANS	61		

MELANIE B UK singer

Date	Title / Label	Peak Position	Weeks at No.1	Weeks in Top 40
26 Sep 98	**I WANT YOU BACK** *Virgin VSCDT 1716* MELANIE B FEATURING MISSY 'MISDEMEANOR' ELLIOTT ○	1	1	6
10 Jul 99	**WORD UP** *Virgin VSCDT 1748 (MELANIE C)*	14		3
7 Oct 00	**TELL ME** *Virgin VSCDX 1777*	4		4
3 Mar 01	**FEELS SO GOOD** *Virgin VSCDT 1787*	5		5
16 Jun 01	**LULLABY** *Virgin VSCDT 1798*	13		2
25 Jun 05	**TODAY** *Amber Cafe AMBER003* MELANIE BROWN	41		

SANDY B US singer

Date	Title / Label	Peak Position	Weeks at No.1	Weeks in Top 40
20 Feb 93	**FEEL LIKE SINGIN'** *Nervous SANCD 1*	60		
18 May 96	**MAKE THE WORLD GO ROUND** *Champion CHAMPCD 322*	73		
24 May 97	**MAKE THE WORLD GO ROUND (REMIX)** *Champion CHAMPCD 327*	35		1
8 Nov 97	**AIN'T NO NEED TO HIDE** *Champion CHAMPCD 331*	60		
28 Feb 98	**MAKE THE WORLD GO ROUND (REMIX)** *Champion CHAMPCD 333*	20		2
1 May 04	**MAKE THE WORLD GO ROUND 2004** *Champion CHAMPCD 780*	51		

STEVIE B US singer

Date	Title / Label	Peak Position	Weeks at No.1	Weeks in Top 40
23 Feb 91	**BECAUSE I LOVE YOU (THE POSTMAN SONG)** *Polydor PO 126* ★	6		7

TAIRRIE B US rapper

Date	Title / Label	Peak Position	Weeks at No.1	Weeks in Top 40
1 Dec 90	**MURDER SHE WROTE** *MCA 1455*	71		

B B & Q BAND US group

Date	Title / Label	Peak Position	Weeks at No.1	Weeks in Top 40
18 Jul 81	**ON THE BEAT** *Capitol CL 202*	41		
6 Jul 85	**GENIE** *Cooltempo COOL 110* BROOKLYN BRONX & QUEENS	40		1
20 Sep 86	**(I'M A) DREAMER** *Cooltempo COOL 132*	35		2
17 Oct 87	**RICHOCHET** *Cooltempo COOL 154*	71		

B. BUMBLE & THE STINGERS US group

Date	Title / Label	Peak Position	Weeks at No.1	Weeks in Top 40
19 Apr 62	**NUT ROCKER** *Top Rank JAR 611*	1	1	14
3 Jun 72	**NUT ROCKER** *Stateside SS 2203*	19		8

B-CREW US group

Date	Title / Label	Peak Position	Weeks at No.1	Weeks in Top 40
20 Sep 97	**PARTAY FEELING** *Positiva CDTIV 78*	45		

B-15 PROJECT UK group

Date	Title / Label	Peak Position	Weeks at No.1	Weeks in Top 40
17 Jun 00	**GIRLS LIKE US** *Ministry Of Sound RELENT 3CDS* B-15 PROJECT FEATURING CHRISSY D & LADY G	7		4

B-52's US group

Date	Title / Label	Peak Position	Weeks at No.1	Weeks in Top 40
11 Aug 79	**ROCK LOBSTER** *Island WIP 6506*	37		2
9 Aug 80	**GIVE ME BACK MY MAN** *Island WIP 6579*	61		
7 May 83	**(SONG FOR A) FUTURE GENERATION** *Island IS 107*	63		
10 May 86	**ROCK LOBSTER/PLANET CLAIRE** *Island BFT 1*	12		5
3 Mar 90	**LOVE SHACK** *Reprise W 9917* ○	2		11
19 May 90	**ROAM** *Reprise W 9827*	17		6
18 Aug 90	**CHANNEL Z** *Reprise W 9737*	61		
20 Jun 92	**GOOD STUFF** *Reprise W 0109*	21		4
12 Sep 92	**TELL IT LIKE IT T-I-IS** *Reprise W 0130*	61		
9 Jul 94	**(MEET) THE FLINTSTONES** *MCA MCSTD 1986*	3		10
30 Jan 99	**LOVE SHACK 99** *Reprise W 0461CD*	66		

B-MOVIE UK group

Date	Title / Label	Peak Position	Weeks at No.1	Weeks in Top 40
18 Apr 81	**REMEMBRANCE DAY** *Deram DM 437*	61		
27 Mar 82	**NOWHERE GIRL** *Some Bizzare BZZ 8*	67		

B REAL US rapper

Date	Title / Label	Peak Position	Weeks at No.1	Weeks in Top 40
5 Apr 97	**HIT 'EM HIGH (THE MONSTARS' ANTHEM)** *Atlantic A 5449CD* *B REAL/BUSTA RHYMES/COOLIO/LL COOL J/METHOD MAN*	8		4

B-TRIBE German instrumentalist

Date	Title / Label	Peak Position	Weeks at No.1	Weeks in Top 40
25 Sep 93	**!FIESTA FATAL!** *East West YZ 770CD*	64		

B*WITCHED Irish group

Date	Title / Label	Peak Position	Weeks at No.1	Weeks in Top 40
6 Jun 98	**C'EST LA VIE** *Glow Worm 6660532* .	1	2	16
3 Oct 98	**ROLLERCOASTER** *Glow Worm 6664752* ●	1	2	9
19 Dec 98	**TO YOU I BELONG** *Glow Worm 6667712* ●	1	1	8
27 Mar 99	**BLAME IT ON THE WEATHERMAN** *Glow Worm 6670335* ○	1	1	6
10 Apr 99	**THANK ABBA FOR THE MUSIC** *Epic ABCD1* STEPS, TINA COUSINS, CLEOPATRA, B*WITCHED, BILLIE	4		11
16 Oct 99	**JESSE HOLD ON** *Glow Worm 6679612*	4		5
18 Dec 99	**I SHALL BE THERE** *Glow Worm 6683332* B*WITCHED FEATURING LADYSMITH BLACK MAMBAZO	13		5
8 Apr 00	**JUMP DOWN** *Glow Worm 6691285*	16		2

Silver-selling ○ Gold-selling ● Platinum-selling ⊛ US No.1 ★
Peak Position · Weeks at No.1 · Weeks in Top 40

BABE INSTINCT UK duo

Date	Title	Label	Peak Position	Weeks at No.1	Weeks in Top 40
16 Jan 99	DISCO BABES FROM OUTER SPACE	Positiva CDTIV 103	21		1

BABE TEAM UK group

Date	Title	Label	Peak Position	Weeks at No.1	Weeks in Top 40
8 Jun 02	OVER THERE	Blacklist 0140695 ERE	45		

ALICE BABS Swedish singer

Date	Title	Label	Peak Position	Weeks at No.1	Weeks in Top 40
15 Aug 63	AFTER YOU'VE GONE	Fontana TF 409	43		

BABY BUMPS UK duo

Date	Title	Label	Peak Position	Weeks at No.1	Weeks in Top 40
8 Aug 98	BURNING	Delirious DELICD 10	17		2
26 Feb 00	I GOT THIS FEELING	Sound Of Ministry MOSCDS 137	22		1

BABY D UK/Maltese group

Date	Title	Label	Peak Position	Weeks at No.1	Weeks in Top 40
18 Dec 93	DESTINY	Production House PNC 057	69		
23 Jul 94	CASANOVA	Production House PNC 065	67		
19 Nov 94	LET ME BE YOUR FANTASY	Systematic SYSCD 4 ●	1	2	10
3 Jun 95	(EVERYBODY'S GOT TO LEARN SOMETIME) I NEED YOUR LOVING	Systematic SYSCD 11 ○	3		9
13 Jan 96	SO PURE	Systematic SYSCD 21	3		5
6 Apr 96	TAKE ME TO HEAVEN	Systematic SYSCD 26	15		3
2 Sep 00	LET ME BE YOUR FANTASY (REMIX)	Systematic SYSCD 35	16		3

BABY DC US rapper

Date	Title	Label	Peak Position	Weeks at No.1	Weeks in Top 40
24 Apr 99	BOUNCE, ROCK, SKATE, ROLL BABY DC FEATURING IMAJIN	Jive 0522142	45		

BABY FORD UK producer

Date	Title	Label	Peak Position	Weeks at No.1	Weeks in Top 40
10 Sep 88	OOCHY KOOCHY (F.U. BABY YEAH YEAH)	Rhythm King 7BFORD 1	58		
24 Dec 88	CHIKKI CHIKKI AHH AHH	Rhythm King 7BFORD 2	54		
17 Jun 89	CHILDREN OF THE REVOLUTION	Rhythm King 7BFORD 4	53		
17 Feb 90	BEACH BUMP	Rhythm King 7BFORD 6	68		

BABY JUNE UK singer

Date	Title	Label	Peak Position	Weeks at No.1	Weeks in Top 40
15 Aug 92	HEY! WHAT'S YOUR NAME	Arista 115271	75		

BABY O US group

Date	Title	Label	Peak Position	Weeks at No.1	Weeks in Top 40
26 Jul 80	IN THE FOREST	Calibre CAB 505	46		

BABY ROOTS UK group

Date	Title	Label	Peak Position	Weeks at No.1	Weeks in Top 40
1 Aug 92	ROCK ME BABY	ZYX 68027	71		

BABYBIRD UK group

Date	Title	Label	Peak Position	Weeks at No.1	Weeks in Top 40
10 Aug 96	GOODNIGHT	Echo ECSCD 24	28		1
12 Oct 96	YOU'RE GORGEOUS	Echo ECSCD 26 ●	3		14
1 Feb 97	CANDY GIRL	Echo ECSCD 31	14		2
17 May 97	CORNERSHOP	Echo ECSCD 33	37		1
9 May 98	BAD OLD MAN	Echo ECSCD 60	31		1
22 Aug 98	IF YOU'LL BE MINE	Echo ECSCX 65	28		2
27 Feb 99	BACK TOGETHER	Echo ECSCD 73	22		1
25 Mar 00	THE F-WORD	Echo ECSCD 92	35		1
3 Jun 00	OUT OF SIGHT	Echo ECSCD 97	58		

BABYFACE US singer

Date	Title	Label	Peak Position	Weeks at No.1	Weeks in Top 40
9 Jul 94	ROCK BOTTOM	Epic 6601832	50		
1 Oct 94	WHEN CAN I SEE YOU	Epic 6606592	35		1
9 Nov 96	THIS IS FOR THE LOVER IN YOU	Epic 6639352	12		3
8 Mar 97	EVERYTIME I CLOSE MY EYES	Epic 6642492	13		3
19 Jul 97	HOW COME, HOW LONG BABYFACE FEATURING STEVIE WONDER	Epic 6646202	10		3
25 Oct 97	SUNSHINE JAY-Z FEATURING BABYFACE & FOXY BROWN	Northwestside 74321528702	25		1

BABYLON ZOO UK group

Date	Title	Label	Peak Position	Weeks at No.1	Weeks in Top 40
27 Jan 96	SPACEMAN	EMI CDEM 416 ⊛	1	5	9
27 Apr 96	ANIMAL ARMY	EMI CDEM 425	17		2
5 Oct 96	THE BOY WITH X-RAY EYES	EMI CDEMS 440	32		1
6 Feb 99	ALL THE MONEY'S GONE	EMI CDEM 519	46		

BABYS UK group

Date	Title	Label	Peak Position	Weeks at No.1	Weeks in Top 40
21 Jan 78	ISN'T IT TIME	Chrysalis CHS 2173	45		

BABYSHAMBLES UK group

Date	Title	Label	Peak Position	Weeks at No.1	Weeks in Top 40
11 Dec 04	KILLAMANGIRO	Rough Trade RTRADSCD201	8		5
27 Aug 05	FUCK FOREVER	Rough Trade RTRADSCDX210	4		4
10 Dec 05	ALBION	Rough Trade TRADSCD260	8		2
11 Nov 06	JANIE JONES (STRUMMERVILLE) BABYSHAMBLES & FRIENDS	B Unique BUN116CD	17		1
29 Sep 07	DELIVERY	Parlophone CDRS6747	6		2
15 Dec 07	YOU TALK	Parlophone CDRS6750	54		

BACCARA Spanish duo

Date	Title	Label	Peak Position	Weeks at No.1	Weeks in Top 40
17 Sep 77	YES SIR I CAN BOOGIE	RCA PB 5526 ●	1	1	14
14 Jan 78	SORRY I'M A LADY	RCA PB 5555 ○	8		8

BURT BACHARACH US pianist

Date	Title	Label	Peak Position	Weeks at No.1	Weeks in Top 40
20 May 65	TRAINS AND BOATS AND PLANES	London HL 9968	4		10
1 May 99	TOLEDO ELVIS COSTELLO/BURT BACHARACH	Mercury 8709652	72		

BACHELORS Irish group

Date	Title	Label	Peak Position	Weeks at No.1	Weeks in Top 40
24 Jan 63	CHARMAINE	Decca F 11559	6		19
4 Jul 63	FARAWAY PLACES	Decca F 11666	36		2
29 Aug 63	WHISPERING	Decca F 11712	18		9
23 Jan 64	DIANE	Decca F 11799	1	1	17
19 Mar 64	I BELIEVE	Decca F 11857	2		15
4 Jun 64	RAMONA	Decca F 11910	4		12
13 Aug 64	I WOULDN'T TRADE YOU FOR THE WORLD	Decca F 11949	4		15
3 Dec 64	NO ARMS CAN EVER HOLD YOU	Decca F 12034	7		10
1 Apr 65	TRUE LOVE FOR EVER MORE	Decca F 12108	34		3
20 May 65	MARIE	Decca F 12156	9		10
28 Oct 65	IN THE CHAPEL IN THE MOONLIGHT	Decca F 12256	27		4
6 Jan 66	HELLO DOLLY	Decca F 12309	38		2
17 Mar 66	THE SOUND OF SILENCE	Decca F 12351	3		12
7 Jul 66	CAN I TRUST YOU	Decca F 12417	26		6
1 Dec 66	WALK WITH FAITH IN YOUR HEART	Decca F 22523	21		8
6 Apr 67	OH HOW I MISS YOU	Decca F 22592	30		5
5 Jul 67	MARTA	Decca F 22634	20		7

TAL BACHMAN Canadian singer/guitarist

Date	Title	Label	Peak Position	Weeks at No.1	Weeks in Top 40
30 Oct 99	SHE'S SO HIGH	Columbia 6679932	30		1

BACHMAN-TURNER OVERDRIVE Canadian group

Date	Title	Label	Peak Position	Weeks at No.1	Weeks in Top 40
16 Nov 74	YOU AIN'T SEEN NOTHIN' YET	Mercury 6167 025 ○ ★	2		12
1 Feb 75	ROLL ON DOWN THE HIGHWAY	Mercury 6167 071	22		4

BACK TO THE PLANET UK group

Date	Title	Label	Peak Position	Weeks at No.1	Weeks in Top 40
10 Apr 93	TEENAGE TURTLES	Parallel LLLCD 3	52		
4 Sep 93	DAYDREAM	Parallel LLLCD 8	52		

BACKBEAT BAND US group

Date	Title	Label	Peak Position	Weeks at No.1	Weeks in Top 40
26 Mar 94	MONEY	Virgin VSCDX 1489	48		
14 May 94	PLEASE MR POSTMAN	Virgin VSCDX 1502	69		

BACKSTREET BOYS US group

Date	Title	Label	Peak Position	Weeks at No.1	Weeks in Top 40
28 Oct 95	WE'VE GOT IT GOIN' ON	Jive JIVECD 386	54		
16 Dec 95	I'LL NEVER BREAK YOUR HEART	Jive JIVECD 389	42		
1 Jun 96	GET DOWN (YOU'RE THE ONE FOR ME)	Jive JIVECD 394	14		4
24 Aug 96	WE'VE GOT IT GOIN' ON	Jive JIVECD 400	3		5
16 Nov 96	I'LL NEVER BREAK YOUR HEART	Jive JIVERCD 406	8		4

BURT BACHARACH

The charts are home to a multitude of obvious celebrity performers, some of them songwriters, some of them singers, some both. At the opposite end of the spectrum are the largely anonymous songwriters who craft huge hits for stars, yet are never known by the public. Somewhere in the middle are rarities such as Burt Bacharach, whose impact on the singles charts both in the UK and America is almost without comparison. In the history of popular music, rarely has there been a more influential figure, with Bacharach boasting a total of fifty-two UK hit singles over the course of half a century.

It's important to digest what his thankfully long life means in terms of his musical longevity – he was born in Missouri, May 1928, just over six months after the world's first ever talking movie, *The Jazz Singer*, was released. The Great Depression was just around the corner and the Second World War was over a decade into the future; yet this is a man who in the twenty-first century has a legion of celebrity fans – such as Rod Stewart, Noel Gallagher and Faith No More – which defies belief.

His impressive musical education at three music universities and academies was followed by a stint in the army before his powerful muse was unleashed on to the public. Like McCartney/Lennon, Jagger/Richards, Leiber/Stoller and a host of others, Bacharach's talent was at first a shared genius. He met his musical partner, lyricist Hal David, in 1957 at New York City's Brill Building. The pair almost immediately scored back to back UK Number 1 singles in 1958 with Marty Robbins' 'The Story Of My Life' then 'Magic Moments' by Perry Como. Bacharach was not a studio wallflower hiding from reality, however. Around this time he spent several years on the road as Marlene Dietrich's pianist and arranger.

Inevitably, any feature on Bacharach will read like a list of achievements because, essentially, that is the nature and extent of his prolific talent. Perhaps the most noted relationship he enjoyed with a singer was that with Dionne Warwick, who was initially a session vocalist brought in to demo tracks he'd written. She quickly moved to centre stage when Bacharach suggested Warwick was singing better than any of the so-called 'stars' she was demoing for. Once established as a performer in her own right, Warwick scored a string of chart hits including arguably her most famous moment, 1964's 'Walk On By', that hit Number 9 and has since been covered by a varied range of artists, from Isaac Hayes to The Stranglers.

Another singer whose career has been boosted by the songs of Bacharach/David is Gene Pitney, whose boyish good looks and uniquely high-register singing brought him a hit with 'Twenty Four Hours From Tulsa'.

The 1960s saw everyone from The Beatles to Elvis Presley record Bacharach/David songs, and Presley's great friend, Tom Jones, came into his own with 'What's New Pussycat?', taken from the movie of the same name. That song not only became one of Jones's signature performances over the course of his career, but also was nominated for an Academy Award in 1964 for 'Best Original Song'. The who's who continues with artists such as Johnny Mathis, Jack Jones, Sandie Shaw, The Walker Brothers, Herb Alpert, Luther Vandross, Cilla Black and Dusty Springfield, with the poignant and powerful Number 3 hit 'I Just Don't Know What To Do With Myself'. This last song is perhaps symptomatic of Bacharach's ability to write music that straddles the decades and eras, with the most recent version coming from the gnarly blues-rock duo The White Stripes, who included it on their successful 2003 album, *Elephant*.

Outside the hit singles realm, Bacharach/David composed scores for several film and Broadway productions, including *Butch Cassidy And The Sundance Kid*, the track 'Raindrops Keep Fallin' On My Head' earning yet another Grammy nomination.

Sadly, a disastrous movie project, 1973's *Lost Horizon*, led to a rift so strong with Hal David that lawsuits between the pair erupted. The 1970s were a difficult time for Bacharach, with a problematic personal life and stuttering commercial profile, but fortunes took an upturn during the next decade as he and his new partner (lyricist and wife) Carole Bayer Sager produced 'Heartlight', sung by Neil Diamond and featured on the soundtrack *E.T.: The Extra-Terrestrial*, as well as 'Making Love' by Roberta Flack, both hits in the States. Drawn back to orchestral appearances and collaborations, Bacharach's career continued to be artistically successful, and he followed up his 1998 Grammy Award-winning work with Elvis Costello with a series of jazz collaborations and an intriguing project with hip hop heavyweight, Dr Dre. Who else born before the Second World War could work with a hip-hop legend?

Tragically, the four-times-married Bacharach outlived his daughter, Nikki, a sufferer from Asperger's syndrome and of chronic ill health since her premature birth – she killed herself in 2007, aged just forty. His 1969 instrumental named after her will thus for ever be his most poignant piece. The huge number of successful versions of Bacharach's songs is testament to the lasting nature of the work of this genuine songwriting legend and his quite breathtaking impact on the UK singles charts.

Date	Title / Label	Peak Position	Weeks at No.1	Weeks in Top 40
18 Jan 97	**QUIT PLAYING GAMES (WITH MY HEART)** *Jive JIVECD 409* ○	2		8
29 Mar 97	**ANYWHERE FOR YOU** *Jive JIVECD 416*	4		3
2 Aug 97	**EVERYBODY (BACKSTREET'S BACK)** *Jive JIVECD 426* ○	3		10
11 Oct 97	**AS LONG AS YOU LOVE ME** *Jive JIVECD 434* ●	3		15
14 Feb 98	**ALL I HAVE TO GIVE** *Jive JIVECD 445* ○	2		6
15 May 99	**I WANT IT THAT WAY** *Jive 0523392* ●	1	1	12
30 Oct 99	**LARGER THAN LIFE** *Jive 0550562*	5		6
26 Feb 00	**SHOW ME THE MEANING OF BEING LONELY (IMPORT)** *Jive 9250002*	66		
4 Mar 00	**SHOW ME THE MEANING OF BEING LONELY** *Jive 9250002* ○	3		6
24 Jun 00	**THE ONE** *Jive 9250662*	8		3
18 Nov 00	**SHAPE OF MY HEART** *Jive 9251442*	4		5
24 Feb 01	**THE CALL** *Jive 9251702*	8		3
7 Jul 01	**MORE THAN THAT** *Jive 9252342*	12		3
12 Jan 02	**DROWNING** *Jive 9253082*	4		3
9 Jul 05	**INCOMPLETE** *Jive 82876699282*	8		4
5 Nov 05	**JUST WANT YOU TO KNOW** *Jive 82876734282*	8		2
3 Nov 07	**INCONSOLABLE** *Jive 88697106602*	24		1

BACKYARD DOG UK production group

Date	Title / Label	Peak Position	Weeks at No.1	Weeks in Top 40
7 Jul 01	**BADDEST RUFFEST** *East West W 233CD*	15		3

BAD BOYS INC UK group

Date	Title / Label	Peak Position	Weeks at No.1	Weeks in Top 40
14 Aug 93	**DON'T TALK ABOUT LOVE** *A&M 5803412*	19		4
2 Oct 93	**WHENEVER YOU NEED SOMEONE** *A&M 5804032*	26		2
11 Dec 93	**WALKING ON AIR** *A&M 5804692*	24		5
21 May 94	**MORE TO THIS WORLD** *A&M 5806072*	8		4
23 Jul 94	**TAKE ME AWAY (I'LL FOLLOW YOU)** *A&M 5806912*	15		3
17 Sep 94	**LOVE HERE I COME** *A&M 5807752*	26		2

BAD COMPANY UK group

Date	Title / Label	Peak Position	Weeks at No.1	Weeks in Top 40
1 Jun 74	**CAN'T GET ENOUGH** *Island WIP 6191*	15		6
22 Mar 75	**GOOD LOVIN' GONE BAD** *Island WIP 6223*	31		4
30 Aug 75	**FEEL LIKE MAKIN' LOVE** *Island WIP 6242*	20		8

BAD COMPANY UK group

Date	Title / Label	Peak Position	Weeks at No.1	Weeks in Top 40
9 Mar 02	**SPACEHOPPER/TONIGHT** *Ram RAMM 37*	56		
4 May 02	**RUSH HOUR/BLIND** *BC Recordings BCRUK 002CD*	59		
15 Mar 03	**MO' FIRE** *BC Recordings BCRUK 003CD* BAD COMPANY UK/RAWHILL CRU	24		1

BAD ENGLISH UK/US group

Date	Title / Label	Peak Position	Weeks at No.1	Weeks in Top 40
25 Nov 89	**WHEN I SEE YOU SMILE** *Epic 6553471* ★	61		

BAD HABIT BOYS German production group

Date	Title / Label	Peak Position	Weeks at No.1	Weeks in Top 40
1 Jul 00	**WEEKEND** *Inferno CDFERN 28*	41		

BAD MANNERS UK group

Date	Title / Label	Peak Position	Weeks at No.1	Weeks in Top 40
1 Mar 80	**NE-NE-NA-NA-NA-NA-NU-NU** *Magnet MAG 164*	28		9
14 Jun 80	**LIP UP FATTY** *Magnet MAG 175*	15		10
27 Sep 80	**SPECIAL BREW** *Magnet MAG 180* ○	3		9
6 Dec 80	**LORRAINE** *Magnet MAG 181*	21		10
28 Mar 81	**JUST A FEELING** *Magnet MAG 187*	13		7
27 Jun 81	**CAN CAN** *Magnet MAG 190* ○	3		10
26 Sep 81	**WALKING IN THE SUNSHINE** *Magnet MAG 197*	10		7
21 Nov 81	**BUONA SERA** *Magnet MAG 211*	34		7
1 May 82	**GOT NO BRAINS** *Magnet MAG 216*	44		
31 Jul 82	**MY GIRL LOLLIPOP (MY BOY LOLLIPOP)** *Magnet MAG 232*	9		5
30 Oct 82	**SAMSON AND DELILAH** *Magnet MAG 236*	58		
14 May 83	**THAT'LL DO NICELY** *Magnet MAG 243*	49		

BAD MEETS EVIL US producer

Date	Title / Label	Peak Position	Weeks at No.1	Weeks in Top 40
1 Sep 01	**SCARY MOVIES** *Mole UK MOLEUK 045* BAD MEETS EVIL FEATURING EMINEM & ROYCE DA59	63		

BAD NEWS UK group

Date	Title / Label	Peak Position	Weeks at No.1	Weeks in Top 40
12 Sep 87	**BOHEMIAN RHAPSODY** *EMI EM 24*	44		

BAD RELIGION US group

Date	Title / Label	Peak Position	Weeks at No.1	Weeks in Top 40
11 Feb 95	**21ST CENTURY (DIGITAL BOY)** *Columbia 6611435*	41		
21 Aug 04	**LOS ANGELES IS BURNING** *Epitaph 11692*	67		

WALLY BADAROU French producer

Date	Title / Label	Peak Position	Weeks at No.1	Weeks in Top 40
19 Oct 85	**CHIEF INSPECTOR** *Fourth & Broadway BRW 37*	46		

BADDIEL & SKINNER UK comedians

Date	Title / Label	Peak Position	Weeks at No.1	Weeks in Top 40
1 Jun 96	**THREE LIONS (THE OFFICIAL SONG OF THE ENGLAND FOOTBALL TEAM)** *Epic 6632732* BADDIEL & SKINNER & LIGHTNING SEEDS ⊛	1	2	13
20 Jun 98	**THREE LIONS (THE OFFICIAL SONG OF THE ENGLAND FOOTBALL TEAM)** *Epic 6660982* BADDIEL & SKINNER & LIGHTNING SEEDS ⊛	1	3	9
15 Jun 02	**THREE LIONS** *Epic 6728152* BADDIEL & SKINNER & LIGHTNING SEEDS	16		3
10 Jun 06	**THREE LIONS** *Epic 82876856672* BADDIEL & SKINNER & LIGHTNING SEEDS	9		4

KLAUS BADELT German composer

Date	Title / Label	Peak Position	Weeks at No.1	Weeks in Top 40
29 Jul 06	**HE'S A PIRATE** *Nebula NEBCD090*	40		1

BADFELLAS UK/Kenyan duo

Date	Title / Label	Peak Position	Weeks at No.1	Weeks in Top 40
15 Feb 03	**SOC IT TO ME** *Serious SER 053CD* BADFELLAS FEATURING CK	55		

BADFINGER UK group

Date	Title / Label	Peak Position	Weeks at No.1	Weeks in Top 40
10 Jan 70	**COME AND GET IT** *Apple 20*	4		10
9 Jan 71	**NO MATTER WHAT** *Apple 31*	5		12
29 Jan 72	**DAY AFTER DAY** *Apple 40*	10		8

BADLY DRAWN BOY UK singer

Date	Title / Label	Peak Position	Weeks at No.1	Weeks in Top 40
4 Sep 99	**ONCE AROUND THE BLOCK** *Twisted Nerve TNXL 003CD*	46		
17 Jun 00	**ANOTHER PEARL** *Twisted Nerve TNXL 004CD*	41		
16 Sep 00	**DISILLUSION** *Twisted Nerve TNXL 005CD*	26		1
25 Nov 00	**ONCE AROUND THE BLOCK** *Twisted Nerve TNXL 009CD*	27		1
19 May 01	**PISSING IN THE WIND** *Twisted Nerve TNXL 010CD*	22		1
6 Apr 02	**SILENT SIGH** *Twisted Nerve TNXL 012CD1*	16		2
22 Jun 02	**SOMETHING TO TALK ABOUT** *Twisted Nerve TNXL 014CD*	28		1
26 Oct 02	**YOU WERE RIGHT** *Twisted Nerve TNXL 015CD*	9		2
18 Jan 03	**BORN AGAIN** *Twisted Nerve TNXL 016CD*	16		1
3 May 03	**ALL POSSIBILITIES** *Twisted Nerve TNXL 017CD*	24		1
31 Jul 04	**YEAR OF THE RAT** *XL Recordings TNXL018CD*	38		1
21 Oct 06	**NOTHING'S GONNA CHANGE YOUR MIND** *EMI CDEM701*	38		1

BADMAN UK producer

Date	Title / Label	Peak Position	Weeks at No.1	Weeks in Top 40
2 Feb 91	**MAGIC STYLE** *Citybeat CBE 759*	61		

ERYKAH BADU US singer

Date	Title / Label	Peak Position	Weeks at No.1	Weeks in Top 40
19 Apr 97	**ON & ON** *Universal UND 56117*	12		2
14 Jun 97	**NEXT LIFETIME** *Universal UND 56132*	30		1
29 Nov 97	**APPLE TREE** *Universal UND 56150*	47		
11 Jul 98	**ONE** *Elektra E 3833CD1* BUSTA RHYMES FEATURING ERYKAH BADU	23		1
6 Mar 99	**YOU GOT ME** *MCA MCSTD 48110* ROOTS FEATURING ERYKAH BADU	31		1
15 Sep 01	**SWEET BABY** *Epic 6718822* MACY GRAY FEATURING ERYKAH BADU	23		2

JOAN BAEZ US singer

Date	Title / Label	Peak Position	Weeks at No.1	Weeks in Top 40
6 May 65	**WE SHALL OVERCOME** *Fontana TF 564*	26		7
8 Jul 65	**THERE BUT FOR FORTUNE** *Fontana TF 587*	8		10
2 Sep 65	**IT'S ALL OVER NOW BABY BLUE** *Fontana TF 604*	22		6
23 Dec 65	**FAREWELL ANGELINA** *Fontana TF 639*	35		1
28 Jul 66	**PACK UP YOUR SORROWS** *Fontana TF 727*	50		
9 Oct 71	**THE NIGHT THEY DROVE OLD DIXIE DOWN** *Vanguard VS 35138*	6		10

Silver-selling ● Gold-selling ● Platinum-selling ⊛ US No.1 ★ | Peak Position | Weeks at No.1 | Weeks in Top 40

BAHA MEN Bahamian group

Date	Title	Peak Position	Weeks at No.1	Weeks in Top 40
14 Oct 00	**WHO LET THE DOGS OUT** *Edel 0115425 ERE* ⊛	2		18
3 Feb 01	**YOU ALL DAT** *Edel 0124855 ERE* BAHA MEN: GUEST VOCAL IMANI COPPOLA	14		3
13 Jul 02	**MOVE IT LIKE THIS** *EMI CDEM 615*	16		4

ABIGAIL BAILEY UK singer

Date	Title	Peak Position	Weeks at No.1	Weeks in Top 40
17 Dec 05	**I JUST CAN'T GET ENOUGH** *All Around The World CDGLOBE473* HERD & FITZ FEATURING ABIGAIL BAILEY	11		6
22 Jul 06	**SOMETHING ON YOUR MIND** *Island APOLLO103CD* MYNC PROJECT FEATURING ABIGAIL BAILEY	71		

CAROL BAILEY UK singer

Date	Title	Peak Position	Weeks at No.1	Weeks in Top 40
25 Feb 95	**FEEL IT** *Multiply CDMULTY 3*	41		

PHILIP BAILEY US singer

Date	Title	Peak Position	Weeks at No.1	Weeks in Top 40
9 Mar 85	**EASY LOVER** *CBS A 4915* PHILIP BAILEY (DUET WITH PHIL COLLINS) ●	1	4	10
18 May 85	**WALKING ON THE CHINESE WALL** *CBS A 6202*	34		4

MERRIL BAINBRIDGE Australian singer

Date	Title	Peak Position	Weeks at No.1	Weeks in Top 40
7 Dec 96	**MOUTH** *Gotham 74321431012*	51		

ADRIAN BAKER UK singer/multi-instrumentalist

Date	Title	Peak Position	Weeks at No.1	Weeks in Top 40
19 Jul 75	**SHERRY** *Magnet MAG 34*	10		7

ANITA BAKER US singer

Date	Title	Peak Position	Weeks at No.1	Weeks in Top 40
15 Nov 86	**SWEET LOVE** *Elektra EKR 44*	13		9
31 Jan 87	**CAUGHT UP IN THE RAPTURE** *Elektra EKR 49*	51		
8 Oct 88	**GIVING YOU THE BEST THAT I GOT** *Elektra EKR 79*	55		
30 Jun 90	**TALK TO ME** *Elektra EKR 111*	68		
17 Sep 94	**BODY AND SOUL** *Elektra EKR 190CD*	48		

ARTHUR BAKER US producer

Date	Title	Peak Position	Weeks at No.1	Weeks in Top 40
20 May 89	**IT'S YOUR TIME** *Breakout USA 654* ARTHUR BAKER FEATURING SHIRLEY LEWIS	64		
21 Oct 89	**THE MESSAGE IS LOVE** *Breakout USA 668* ARTHUR BAKER & THE BACKSTREET DISCIPLES FEATURING AL GREEN	38		2
30 Nov 02	**CONFUSION** *Whacked WACKT 002CD* ARTHUR BAKER VS NEW ORDER	64		

HYLDA BAKER & ARTHUR MULLARD UK comedians

Date	Title	Peak Position	Weeks at No.1	Weeks in Top 40
9 Sep 78	**YOU'RE THE ONE THAT I WANT** *Pye 7N 46121*	22		5

GEORGE BAKER SELECTION Dutch group

Date	Title	Peak Position	Weeks at No.1	Weeks in Top 40
6 Sep 75	**PALOMA BLANCA** *Warner Brothers K 16541*	10		9

BAKSHELF DOG UK puppet

Date	Title	Peak Position	Weeks at No.1	Weeks in Top 40
21 Dec 02	**NO LIMITS** *WVC CDCHURCH 1*	51		

BALAAM AND THE ANGEL UK group

Date	Title	Peak Position	Weeks at No.1	Weeks in Top 40
29 Mar 86	**SHE KNOWS** *Virgin VS 842*	70		

LONG JOHN BALDRY UK singer

Date	Title	Peak Position	Weeks at No.1	Weeks in Top 40
8 Nov 67	**LET THE HEARTACHES BEGIN** *Pye 7N 17385*	1	5	13
28 Aug 68	**WHEN THE SUN COMES SHINING THRU'** *Pye 7N 17593*	29		3
23 Oct 68	**MEXICO** *Pye 7N 17563*	15		7
29 Jan 69	**IT'S TOO LATE NOW** *Pye 7N 17664*	21		5

BALEARIC BILL Belgian production group

Date	Title	Peak Position	Weeks at No.1	Weeks in Top 40
2 Oct 99	**DESTINATION SUNSHINE** *Xtravaganza XTRAV 3CDS*	36		1

EDWARD BALL UK singer

Date	Title	Peak Position	Weeks at No.1	Weeks in Top 40
20 Jul 96	**THE MILL HILL SELF HATE CLUB** *Creation CRESCD 233*	57		
22 Feb 97	**LOVE IS BLUE** *Creation CRESCD 244*	59		

KENNY BALL & HIS JAZZMEN

UK trumpeter and backing group

Date	Title	Peak Position	Weeks at No.1	Weeks in Top 40
23 Feb 61	**SAMANTHA** *Pye Jazz Today 7NJ 2040*	13		14
11 May 61	**I STILL LOVE YOU ALL** *Pye Jazz 7NJ 2042*	24		5
31 Aug 61	**SOMEDAY (YOU'LL BE SORRY)** *Pye Jazz 7NJ 2047*	28		6
9 Nov 61	**MIDNIGHT IN MOSCOW** *Pye Jazz 7NJ 2049*	2		20
15 Feb 62	**MARCH OF THE SIAMESE CHILDREN** *Pye Jazz 7NJ 2051*	4		12
17 May 62	**THE GREEN LEAVES OF SUMMER** *Pye Jazz 7NJ 2054*	7		13
23 Aug 62	**SO DO I** *Pye Jazz 7NJ 2056*	14		7
18 Oct 62	**THE PAY OFF (AMOI DE PAYER)** *Pye Jazz 7NJ 2061*	23		6
17 Jan 63	**SUKIYAKI** *Pye Jazz 7NJ 2062*	10		10
25 Apr 63	**CASABLANCA** *Pye Jazz 7NJ 2064*	21		8
13 Jun 63	**RONDO** *Pye Jazz 7NJ 2065*	24		6
22 Aug 63	**ACAPULCO 1922** *Pye Jazz 7NJ 2067*	27		4
11 Jun 64	**HELLO DOLLY** *Pye Jazz 7NJ 2071*	30		5
19 Jul 67	**WHEN I'M SIXTY FOUR** *Pye 7N 17348*	43		

MICHAEL BALL UK singer/actor

Date	Title	Peak Position	Weeks at No.1	Weeks in Top 40
28 Jan 89	**LOVE CHANGES EVERYTHING** *Really Useful RUR 3* ●	2		10
28 Oct 89	**THE FIRST MAN YOU REMEMBER** *Really Useful RUR 6* MICHAEL BALL & DIANA MORRISON	68		
10 Aug 91	**IT'S STILL YOU** *Polydor PO 160*	58		
25 Apr 92	**ONE STEP OUT OF TIME** *Polydor PO 206*	20		1
12 Dec 92	**IF I CAN DREAM (EP)** *Polydor PO 248*	51		
11 Sep 93	**SUNSET BOULEVARD** *Polydor PZCD 293*	72		
30 Jul 94	**FROM HERE TO ETERNITY** *Columbia 6606905*	36		1
17 Sep 94	**THE LOVERS WE WERE** *Columbia 6607972*	63		
9 Dec 95	**THE ROSE** *Columbia 6614535*	42		
17 Feb 96	**SOMETHING INSIDE SO STRONG** *Columbia 6629005*	40		1

STEVE BALSAMO UK singer

Date	Title	Peak Position	Weeks at No.1	Weeks in Top 40
16 Mar 02	**SUGAR FOR THE SOUL** *Columbia 6718552*	32		1

BALTIMORA Irish singer

Date	Title	Peak Position	Weeks at No.1	Weeks in Top 40
10 Aug 85	**TARZAN BOY** *Columbia DB 9102* ●	3		9

CHARLI BALTIMORE US rapper

Date	Title	Peak Position	Weeks at No.1	Weeks in Top 40
1 Aug 98	**MONEY** *Epic 6662272*	12		3
12 Oct 02	**DOWN 4 U** *Murder Inc 0639002* IRV GOTTI PRESENTS JA RULE, ASHANTI, CHARLI BALTIMORE & VITA	4		5

BAM BAM US singer/drummer

Date	Title	Peak Position	Weeks at No.1	Weeks in Top 40
19 Mar 88	**GIVE IT TO ME** *Serious 7OUS 10*	65		

AFRIKA BAMBAATAA US singer

Date	Title	Peak Position	Weeks at No.1	Weeks in Top 40
28 Aug 82	**PLANET ROCK** *Polydor POSP 497* AFRIKA BAMBAATAA & THE SONIC SOUL FORCE	53		
10 Mar 84	**RENEGADES OF FUNK** *Tommy Boy AFR 1* AFRIKA BAMBAATAA & THE SONIC SOUL FORCE	30		3
1 Sep 84	**UNITY (PART 1 - THE THIRD COMING)** *Tommy Boy AFR 2* AFRIKA BAMBAATAA & JAMES BROWN	49		
27 Feb 88	**RECKLESS** *EMI EM 41* AFRIKA BAMBAATAA FEATURING UB40 & FAMILY	17		6
12 Oct 91	**JUST GET UP AND DANCE** *EMI USA MT 100*	45		
17 Oct 98	**GOT TO GET UP** *Multiply CDMULTY 42*	22		2
18 Sep 99	**AFRIKA SHOX** *Hard Hands HAND 057CD1* LEFTFIELD/BAMBAATAA	7		3
25 Aug 01	**PLANET ROCK** *Tommy Boy TBCD 2266* PAUL OAKENFOLD PRESENTS AFRIKA BAMBAATAA	47		
13 Mar 04	**D-FUNKTIONAL** *Wall Of Sound WALLD092* MEKON FEATURING AFRIKA BAMBAATAA	72		

BAMBOO UK producer

Date	Title	Peak Position	Weeks at No.1	Weeks in Top 40
17 Jan 98	**BAMBOOGIE** *VC Recordings VCRD 29* ●	2		8
4 Jul 98	**THE STRUTT** *VC Recordings VCRD 35*	36		1

BANANARAMA UK group

Date	Title / Label	Peak Position	Weeks at No.1	Weeks in Top 40
13 Feb 82	**IT AIN'T WHAT YOU DO IT'S THE WAY THAT YOU DO IT** *Chrysalis CHS 2570* FUN BOY THREE & BANANARAMA ○	4		7
10 Apr 82	**REALLY SAYING SOMETHING** *Deram NANA 1* BANANARAMA WITH FUN BOY THREE ○	5		9
3 Jul 82	**SHY BOY** *London NANA 2* ○	4		8
4 Dec 82	**CHEERS THEN** *London NANA 3*	45		
26 Feb 83	**NA NA HEY HEY KISS HIM GOODBYE** *London NANA 4*	5		9
9 Jul 83	**CRUEL SUMMER** *London NANA 5*	8		8
3 Mar 84	**ROBERT DE NIRO'S WAITING** *London NANA 6* ○	3		9
26 May 84	**ROUGH JUSTICE** *London NANA 7*	23		3
24 Nov 84	**HOTLINE TO HEAVEN** *London NANA 8*	58		
24 Aug 85	**DO NOT DISTURB** *London NANA 9*	31		3
31 May 86	**VENUS** *London NANA 10* ★	8		11
16 Aug 86	**MORE THAN PHYSICAL** *London NANA 11*	41		
14 Feb 87	**TRICK OF THE NIGHT** *London NANA 12*	32		3
11 Jul 87	**I HEARD A RUMOUR** *London NANA 13*	14		7
10 Oct 87	**LOVE IN THE FIRST DEGREE** *London NANA 14* ○	3		9
9 Jan 88	**I CAN'T HELP IT** *London NANA 15*	20		4
9 Apr 88	**I WANT YOU BACK** *London NANA 16*	5		9
24 Sep 88	**LOVE, TRUTH AND HONESTY** *London NANA 17*	23		6
19 Nov 88	**NATHAN JONES** *London NANA 18*	15		8
25 Feb 89	**HELP!** *London LON 222* BANANARAMA/LA NA NEE NEE NOO NOO ○	3		8
10 Jun 89	**CRUEL SUMMER (REMIX)** *London NANA 19*	19		4
28 Jul 90	**ONLY YOUR LOVE** *London NANA 21*	27		3
5 Jan 91	**PREACHER MAN** *London NANA 23*	20		4
20 Apr 91	**LONG TRAIN RUNNING** *London NANA 24*	30		4
29 Aug 92	**MOVIN' ON** *London NANA 25*	24		3
28 Nov 92	**LAST THING ON MY MIND** *London NANA 26*	71		
20 Mar 93	**MORE MORE MORE** *London NACPD 27*	24		3
6 Aug 05	**MOVE IN MY DIRECTION** *A & G Productions CXAG003*	14		2
19 Nov 05	**LOOK ON THE FLOOR (HYPNOTIC TANGO)** *A & G Productions CXAG004*	26		1

BAND Canadian group

Date	Title / Label	Peak Position	Weeks at No.1	Weeks in Top 40
18 Sep 68	**THE WEIGHT** *Capitol CL 15559*	21		7
4 Apr 70	**RAG MAMA RAG** *Capitol CL 15629*	16		7

BAND AID Multinational charity ensemble

Date	Title / Label	Peak Position	Weeks at No.1	Weeks in Top 40
15 Dec 84	**DO THEY KNOW IT'S CHRISTMAS?** *Mercury FEED 1* ⊛	1	5	11
7 Dec 85	**DO THEY KNOW IT'S CHRISTMAS?** *Mercury FEED 1*	3		6
23 Dec 89	**DO THEY KNOW IT'S CHRISTMAS?** *PWL/Polydor FEED 2* BAND AID II ⊛	1	3	5
11 Dec 04	**DO THEY KNOW IT'S CHRISTMAS?** *Mercury 9869413* BAND AID 20 ⊛	1	4	7
10 Dec 05	**DO THEY KNOW IT'S CHRISTMAS?** *Mercury 9869413* BAND AID 20	52		
15 Dec 07	**DO THEY KNOW IT'S CHRISTMAS?** *Download*	24		3

BAND AKA US group

Date	Title / Label	Peak Position	Weeks at No.1	Weeks in Top 40
15 May 82	**GRACE** *Epic EPC A 2376*	41		
5 Mar 83	**JOY** *Epic EPC A 3145*	24		5

BAND OF GOLD Dutch group

Date	Title / Label	Peak Position	Weeks at No.1	Weeks in Top 40
14 Jul 84	**LOVE SONGS ARE BACK AGAIN (MEDLEY)** *RCA 428*	24		6

BANDA SONORA UK producer

Date	Title / Label	Peak Position	Weeks at No.1	Weeks in Top 40
6 Oct 01	**GUITARRA G** *Defected DFECT 36CDS*	50		
19 Oct 02	**PRESSURE COOKER** *Defected DFTD 060CDS* G CLUB PRESENTS BANDA SONORA	46		

BANDERAS UK duo

Date	Title / Label	Peak Position	Weeks at No.1	Weeks in Top 40
23 Feb 91	**THIS IS YOUR LIFE** *London LON 290*	16		6
15 Jun 91	**SHE SELLS** *London LON 298*	41		

BANDITS UK group

Date	Title / Label	Peak Position	Weeks at No.1	Weeks in Top 40
28 Jun 03	**TAKE IT AND RUN** *B Unique BUN 055CDX*	32		1
20 Sep 03	**2 STEP ROCK** *B Unique BUN 065CDX*	35		1

HONEY BANE UK singer

Date	Title / Label	Peak Position	Weeks at No.1	Weeks in Top 40
24 Jan 81	**TURN ME ON TURN ME OFF** *Zonophone Z 15*	37		2
18 Apr 81	**BABY LOVE** *Zonophone Z 19*	58		

BANG UK duo

Date	Title / Label	Peak Position	Weeks at No.1	Weeks in Top 40
6 May 89	**YOU'RE THE ONE** *RCA PB 42715*	74		

THOMAS BANGALTER & DJ FALCON French duo

Date	Title / Label	Peak Position	Weeks at No.1	Weeks in Top 40
4 Jan 03	**SO MUCH LOVE TO GIVE (IMPORT)** *Roule TOGETHER 2*	71		

BANGLES US group

Date	Title / Label	Peak Position	Weeks at No.1	Weeks in Top 40
15 Feb 86	**MANIC MONDAY** *CBS A 6796* ○	2		9
26 Apr 86	**IF SHE KNEW WHAT SHE WANTS** *CBS A 7062*	31		2
5 Jul 86	**GOING DOWN TO LIVERPOOL** *CBS A 7255*	56		
13 Sep 86	**WALK LIKE AN EGYPTIAN** *CBS 6500717* ○ ★	3		15
10 Jan 87	**WALKING DOWN YOUR STREET** *CBS BANGS 1*	16		3
18 Apr 87	**FOLLOWING** *CBS BANGS 2*	55		
6 Feb 88	**HAZY SHADE OF WINTER** *Def Jam BANGS 3*	11		6
5 Nov 88	**IN YOUR ROOM** *CBS BANGS 4*	35		3
18 Feb 89	**ETERNAL FLAME** *CBS BANGS 5* ● ★	1	4	13
10 Jun 89	**BE WITH YOU** *CBS BANGS 6*	23		6
14 Oct 89	**I'LL SET YOU FREE** *CBS BANGS 7*	74		
9 Jun 90	**WALK LIKE AN EGYPTIAN** *CBS BANGS 8*	73		
15 Mar 03	**SOMETHING THAT YOU SAID** *Liberty BANGLES 003*	38		1

DEVENDRA BANHART US singer

Date	Title / Label	Peak Position	Weeks at No.1	Weeks in Top 40
17 Sep 05	**I FEEL JUST LIKE A CHILD** *XL Recordings XLS217CD*	68		

LLOYD BANKS US rapper

Date	Title / Label	Peak Position	Weeks at No.1	Weeks in Top 40
21 Aug 04	**ON FIRE** *Interscope 9863485*	19		3
21 Oct 06	**HANDS UP** *Atlantic AT0253CD* LLOYD BANKS FEATURING 50 CENT	43		

BANNED UK group

Date	Title / Label	Peak Position	Weeks at No.1	Weeks in Top 40
17 Dec 77	**LITTLE GIRL** *Harvest HAR 5145*	36		2

BUJU BANTON Jamaican singer

Date	Title / Label	Peak Position	Weeks at No.1	Weeks in Top 40
7 Aug 93	**MAKE MY DAY** *Mercury BUJCD 2*	72		

PATO BANTON UK singer

Date	Title / Label	Peak Position	Weeks at No.1	Weeks in Top 40
1 Oct 94	**BABY COME BACK** *Virgin VSCDT 1522* ⊛	1	4	16
11 Feb 95	**THIS COWBOY SONG** *A&M 5809652* STING FEATURING PATO BANTON	15		4
8 Apr 95	**BUBBLING HOT** *Virgin VSCDT 1530* PATO BANTON WITH RANKING ROGER	15		5
20 Jan 96	**SPIRITS IN THE MATERIAL WORLD** *MCA MCSTD 2113* PATO BANTON WITH STING	36		1
27 Jul 96	**GROOVIN'** *IRS CDEIRS 195* PATO BANTON & THE REGGAE REVOLUTION	14		3

BAR CODES UK group

Date	Title / Label	Peak Position	Weeks at No.1	Weeks in Top 40
17 Dec 94	**SUPERMARKET SWEEP (WILL YOU DANCE WITH ME)** *Blanca Casa BC 101CD* BAR CODES FEATURING ALISON BROWN	72		

BAR-KAYS US group

Date	Title / Label	Peak Position	Weeks at No.1	Weeks in Top 40
23 Aug 67	**SOUL FINGER** *Stax 601 014*	33		3
22 Jan 77	**SHAKE YOUR RUMP TO THE FUNK** *Mercury 6167 417*	41		
12 Jan 85	**SEXOMATIC** *Club JAB 10*	51		

CHRIS BARBER'S JAZZ BAND UK trombonist

Date	Title / Label	Peak Position	Weeks at No.1	Weeks in Top 40
13 Feb 59	**PETITE FLEUR** *Pye Nixa 2026*	3		24
9 Oct 59	**LONESOME (SI TU VOIS MA MERE)** *Columbia DB 4333* CHRIS BARBER FEATURING MONTY SUNSHINE	27		2
4 Jan 62	**REVIVAL** *Columbia SCD 2166*	43		

Silver-selling ○ · Gold-selling ● · Platinum-selling · US No.1 ★ · Peak Position · Weeks at No.1 · Weeks in Top 40

BARCLAY JAMES HARVEST UK group

Date	Title / Label	Peak Position	Weeks at No.1	Weeks in Top 40
2 Apr 77	**LIVE (EP)** *Polydor 2229 198*	49		
26 Jan 80	**LOVE ON THE LINE** *Polydor POSP 97*	63		
22 Nov 80	**LIFE IS FOR LIVING** *Polydor POSP 195*	61		
21 May 83	**JUST A DAY AWAY** *Polydor POSP 585*	68		

BARDO UK duo

Date	Title / Label	Peak Position	Weeks at No.1	Weeks in Top 40
10 Apr 82	**ONE STEP FURTHER** *Epic EPC A 2265* ○	2		6

BARDOT Australian group

Date	Title / Label	Peak Position	Weeks at No.1	Weeks in Top 40
14 Apr 01	**POISON** *East West EW 229CD*	45		

BAREFOOT MAN German singer

Date	Title / Label	Peak Position	Weeks at No.1	Weeks in Top 40
5 Dec 98	**BIG PANTY WOMAN** *Plaza PZACD 082*	21		5

BARENAKED LADIES Canadian group

Date	Title / Label	Peak Position	Weeks at No.1	Weeks in Top 40
20 Feb 99	**ONE WEEK** *Reprise W 468CD* ★	5		5
15 May 99	**IT'S ALL BEEN DONE BEFORE** *Reprise W 476CD*	28		1
24 Jul 99	**CALL AND ANSWER** *Reprise W 498CD1*	52		
11 Dec 99	**BRIAN WILSON** *Reprise W 511CD1*	73		

BARKIN BROTHERS UK production group

Date	Title / Label	Peak Position	Weeks at No.1	Weeks in Top 40
15 Apr 00	**GONNA CATCH YOU** *Brothers Organisation BRUVCD 15* BARKIN BROTHERS FEATURING JOHNNIE FIORI	51		

GARY BARLOW UK singer/pianist

Date	Title / Label	Peak Position	Weeks at No.1	Weeks in Top 40
20 Jul 96	**FOREVER LOVE** *RCA 74321397922* ●	1	1	6
10 May 97	**LOVE WON'T WAIT** *RCA 74321470842* ○	1	1	5
26 Jul 97	**SO HELP ME GIRL** *RCA 74321501202*	11		2
15 Nov 97	**OPEN ROAD** *RCA 74321518292*	7		3
17 Jul 99	**STRONGER** *RCA 74321682012*	16		2
9 Oct 99	**FOR ALL THAT YOU WANT** *RCA 74321701012*	24		1

BARNBRACK UK group

Date	Title / Label	Peak Position	Weeks at No.1	Weeks in Top 40
16 Mar 85	**BELFAST** *Homespun HS 092*	45		

BARNDANCE BOYS UK group

Date	Title / Label	Peak Position	Weeks at No.1	Weeks in Top 40
13 Sep 03	**YIPPIE I OH** *Concept CDCON 41*	32		1

RICHARD BARNES UK singer/guitarist

Date	Title / Label	Peak Position	Weeks at No.1	Weeks in Top 40
23 May 70	**TAKE TO THE MOUNTAINS** *Philips BF 1840*	35		3
24 Oct 70	**GO NORTH** *Philips 6006 039*	38		1

BARON UK DJ

Date	Title / Label	Peak Position	Weeks at No.1	Weeks in Top 40
7 Feb 04	**THE WAY IT WAS/REDHEAD** *Virus VRS012*	71		
12 Feb 05	**SUPERNATURE** *Breakbeat Kaos BBK006* BARON & FRESH	59		
30 Apr 05	**GUNS AT DAWN** *Breakbeat Kaos BBK008* DJ BARON FEATURING PENDULUM	71		

BARRACUDAS UK/US group

Date	Title / Label	Peak Position	Weeks at No.1	Weeks in Top 40
16 Aug 80	**SUMMER FUN** *EMI-Wipe Out Z 5*	37		3

AMANDA BARRIE UK actress

Date	Title / Label	Peak Position	Weeks at No.1	Weeks in Top 40
16 Dec 95	**SOMETHING STUPID** *EMI Premier CDEMS 411* AMANDA BARRIE & JOHNNIE BRIGGS	35		1

J.J. BARRIE Canadian singer

Date	Title / Label	Peak Position	Weeks at No.1	Weeks in Top 40
24 Apr 76	**NO CHARGE** *Power Exchange PX 209* ○	1	1	10

KEN BARRIE UK singer

Date	Title / Label	Peak Position	Weeks at No.1	Weeks in Top 40
10 Jul 82	**POSTMAN PAT** *Post Music PP 001*	44		
25 Dec 82	**POSTMAN PAT** *Post Music PP 001*	54		
24 Dec 83	**POSTMAN PAT** *Post Music PP 001*	59		

BARRON KNIGHTS UK comedy group

Date	Title / Label	Peak Position	Weeks at No.1	Weeks in Top 40
9 Jul 64	**CALL UP THE GROUPS** *Columbia DB 7317* BARRON KNIGHTS WITH DUKE D'MOND	3		12
22 Oct 64	**COME TO THE DANCE** *Columbia DB 7375* BARRON KNIGHTS WITH DUKE D'MOND	42		
25 Mar 65	**POP GO THE WORKERS** *Columbia DB 7525* BARRON KNIGHTS WITH DUKE D'MOND	5		11
16 Dec 65	**MERRY GENTLE POPS** *Columbia DB 7780* BARRON KNIGHTS WITH DUKE D'MOND	9		7
1 Dec 66	**UNDER NEW MANAGEMENT** *Columbia DB 8071* BARRON KNIGHTS WITH DUKE D'MOND	15		7
23 Oct 68	**AN OLYMPIC RECORD** *Columbia DB 8485*	35		3
29 Oct 77	**LIVE IN TROUBLE** *Epic EPC 5752* ○	7		9
2 Dec 78	**A TASTE OF AGGRO** *Epic EPC 6829* ●	3		9
8 Dec 79	**FOOD FOR THOUGHT** *Epic EPC 8011*	46		
4 Oct 80	**THE SIT SONG** *Epic EPC 8994*	44		
6 Dec 80	**NEVER MIND THE PRESENTS** *Epic EPC 9070*	17		6
5 Dec 81	**BLACKBOARD JUMBLE** *CBS A 1795*	52		
19 Mar 83	**BUFFALO BILL'S LAST SCRATCH** *Epic EPC A 3208*	49		

JOE BARRY US singer

Date	Title / Label	Peak Position	Weeks at No.1	Weeks in Top 40
24 Aug 61	**I'M A FOOL TO CARE** *Mercury AMT 1149*	49		

LEN BARRY US singer

Date	Title / Label	Peak Position	Weeks at No.1	Weeks in Top 40
4 Nov 65	**1-2-3-** *Brunswick 05942*	3		14
13 Jan 66	**LIKE A BABY** *Brunswick 05949*	10		8

JOHN BARRY UK bandleader

Date	Title / Label	Peak Position	Weeks at No.1	Weeks in Top 40
5 Mar 60	**HIT AND MISS** *Columbia DB 4414* JOHN BARRY SEVEN	10		11
28 Apr 60	**BEAT FOR BEATNIKS** *Columbia DB 4446* JOHN BARRY ORCHESTRA	40		1
14 Jul 60	**NEVER LET GO** *Columbia DB 4480* JOHN BARRY ORCHESTRA	49		
18 Aug 60	**BLUEBERRY HILL** *Columbia DB 4480* JOHN BARRY ORCHESTRA	34		1
8 Sep 60	**WALK DON'T RUN** *Columbia DB 4505* JOHN BARRY SEVEN	11		12
8 Dec 60	**BLACK STOCKINGS** *Columbia DB 4554* JOHN BARRY SEVEN	27		6
2 Mar 61	**THE MAGNIFICENT SEVEN** *Columbia DB 4598* JOHN BARRY SEVEN	45		
26 Apr 62	**CUTTY SARK** *Columbia DB 4806* JOHN BARRY SEVEN	35		2
1 Nov 62	**THE JAMES BOND THEME** *Columbia DB 4898* JOHN BARRY ORCHESTRA	13		8
21 Nov 63	**FROM RUSSIA WITH LOVE** *Ember S 181* JOHN BARRY ORCHESTRA	39		1
11 Dec 71	**THE THEME FROM *THE PERSUADERS*** *CBS 7469*	13		14

MICHAEL BARRYMORE UK comedian

Date	Title / Label	Peak Position	Weeks at No.1	Weeks in Top 40
16 Dec 95	**TOO MUCH FOR ONE HEART** *EMI CDEM 412*	25		3

LIONEL BART UK composer/singer

Date	Title / Label	Peak Position	Weeks at No.1	Weeks in Top 40
25 Nov 89	**HAPPY ENDINGS (GIVE YOURSELF A PINCH)** *EMI EM 121*	68		

BARTHEZZ Dutch DJ

Date	Title / Label	Peak Position	Weeks at No.1	Weeks in Top 40
22 Sep 01	**ON THE MOVE** *Positiva CDTIV 158*	18		2
20 Apr 02	**INFECTED** *Positiva CDTIVS 168*	25		2

BAS NOIR US duo

Date	Title / Label	Peak Position	Weeks at No.1	Weeks in Top 40
11 Feb 89	**MY LOVE IS MAGIC** *10 TEN 257*	73		

Silver-selling · Gold-selling · Platinum-selling · US No.1 ★ · Peak Position · Weeks at No.1 · Weeks in Top 40

ROB BASE & DJ E-Z ROCK US duo

Date	Title / Label	Peak Position	Weeks at No.1	Weeks in Top 40
16 Apr 88	**IT TAKES TWO** *Citybeat CBE 724*	24		3
14 Jan 89	**GET ON THE DANCE FLOOR** *Supreme SUPE 139*	14		5
4 Mar 89	**IT TAKES TWO** *Citybeat CBE 724*	49		
22 Apr 89	**JOY AND PAIN** *Supreme SUPE 143*	47		

BASEMENT UK group

Date	Title / Label	Peak Position	Weeks at No.1	Weeks in Top 40
14 Jun 03	**SLAIN THE TRUTH (AT THE ROADHOUSE)** *Deltasonic DLTCD 012*	48		

BASEMENT BOYS US production group

Date	Title / Label	Peak Position	Weeks at No.1	Weeks in Top 40
23 Feb 91	**IS IT LOVE** *Eternal YZ 509* BASEMENT BOYS PRESENT ULTRA NATE	71		

BASEMENT JAXX UK production duo

Date	Title / Label	Peak Position	Weeks at No.1	Weeks in Top 40
31 May 97	**FLY LIFE** *Multiply CDMULTY 21*	19		1
1 May 99	**RED ALERT** *XL Recordings XLS 100CD*	5		8
14 Aug 99	**RENDEZ-VU** *XL Recordings XLS 110CD*	4		5
6 Nov 99	**JUMP N' SHOUT** *XL Recordings XLS 116CD*	12		3
15 Apr 00	**BINGO BANGO** *XL Recordings XLS 120CD*	13		2
16 Jun 01	**ROMEO** *XL Recordings XLS 132CD*	6		7
6 Oct 01	**JUS 1 KISS** *XL Recordings XLS 136CD1*	23		1
8 Dec 01	**WHERE'S YOUR HEAD AT** *XL Recordings XLS 140CD*	9		5
29 Jun 02	**GET ME OFF** *XL Recordings XLS 146CD*	22		2
22 Nov 03	**LUCKY STAR** *XL Recordings XLS 172CD* BASEMENT JAXX FEATURING DIZZEE RASCAL	23		1
17 Jan 04	**GOOD LUCK** *XL Recordings XLS 178CD* BASEMENT JAXX FEATURING LISA KEKAULA	12		5
10 Apr 04	**PLUG IT IN** *XL Recordings XLS 180CD* BASEMENT JAXX FEATURING JC CHASEZ	22		1
10 Jul 04	**GOOD LUCK** *XL Recordings XLS 190CD* BASEMENT JAXX FEATURING LISA KEKAULA	14		4
26 Mar 05	**OH MY GOSH** *XL Recordings XLS209CD1*	8		7
25 Jun 05	**U DON'T KNOW ME** *XL Recordings XLS215CD2* BASEMENT JAXX FEATURING LISA KEKAULA	26		1
8 Oct 05	**DO YOUR THING** *XL Recordings XLS220CD*	32		1
9 Sep 06	**HUSH BOY** *XL Recordings XLS241CD*	27		2
11 Nov 06	**TAKE ME BACK TO YOUR HOUSE** *XL Recordings XLS253CD1*	42		

BASIA Polish singer

Date	Title / Label	Peak Position	Weeks at No.1	Weeks in Top 40
23 Jan 88	**PROMISES** *Epic BASH 4*	48		
28 May 88	**TIME AND TIDE** *Epic BASH 5*	61		
14 Jan 95	**DRUNK ON LOVE** *Epic 6611582*	41		

TONI BASIL US singer

Date	Title / Label	Peak Position	Weeks at No.1	Weeks in Top 40
6 Feb 82	**MICKEY** *Radialchoice TIC 4* ● ★	2		10
1 May 82	**NOBODY** *Radialchoice TIC 2*	52		

OLAV BASOSKI Dutch producer

Date	Title / Label	Peak Position	Weeks at No.1	Weeks in Top 40
26 Aug 00	**OPIUM SCUMBAGZ** *Defected DFECT 20CDS*	56		
29 Oct 05	**WATERMAN** *Positiva CDTIVS224* OLAV BASOSKI FEATURING MICHIE ONE	45		

FONTELLA BASS US singer

Date	Title / Label	Peak Position	Weeks at No.1	Weeks in Top 40
2 Dec 65	**RESCUE ME** *Chess CRS 8023*	11		10
20 Jan 66	**RECOVERY** *Chess CRS 8027*	32		3

NORMAN BASS German producer

Date	Title / Label	Peak Position	Weeks at No.1	Weeks in Top 40
21 Apr 01	**HOW U LIKE BASS** *Substance SUBS 10CDS*	17		3

BASS BOYZ UK producer

Date	Title / Label	Peak Position	Weeks at No.1	Weeks in Top 40
28 Sep 96	**GUNZ AND PIANOZ** *Polydor 5753432*	74		

BASS BUMPERS UK/German group

Date	Title / Label	Peak Position	Weeks at No.1	Weeks in Top 40
25 Sep 93	**RUNNIN'** *Vertigo VERCD 78*	68		
5 Feb 94	**THE MUSIC'S GOT ME** *Vertigo VERCD 84*	25		2

BASS JUMPERS Dutch production duo

Date	Title / Label	Peak Position	Weeks at No.1	Weeks in Top 40
13 Feb 99	**MAKE UP YOUR MIND** *Pepper 0530112*	44		

BASS-O-MATIC UK producer

Date	Title / Label	Peak Position	Weeks at No.1	Weeks in Top 40
12 May 90	**IN THE REALM OF THE SENSES** *Virgin VS 1265*	66		
1 Sep 90	**FASCINATING RHYTHM** *Virgin VS 1274*	9		9
22 Dec 90	**EASE ON BY** *Virgin VS 1295*	61		
3 Aug 91	**FUNKY LOVE VIBRATIONS** *Virgin VS 1355*	71		

SHIRLEY BASSEY UK singer

Date	Title / Label	Peak Position	Weeks at No.1	Weeks in Top 40
15 Feb 57	**BANANA BOAT SONG** *Philips PB 668*	8		10
23 Aug 57	**FIRE DOWN BELOW** *Philips PB 723*	30		2
6 Sep 57	**YOU YOU ROMEO** *Philips PB 723*	29		1
19 Dec 58	**AS I LOVE YOU** *Philips PB 845*	1	4	19
26 Dec 58	**KISS ME HONEY HONEY KISS ME** *Philips PB 860*	3		17
31 Mar 60	**WITH THESE HANDS** *Columbia DB 4421*	38		1
4 Aug 60	**AS LONG AS HE NEEDS ME** *Columbia DB 4490*	2		26
11 May 61	**YOU'LL NEVER KNOW** *Columbia DB 4643*	6		14
27 Jul 61	**REACH FOR THE STARS/CLIMB EV'RY MOUNTAIN** *Columbia DB 4685*	1	1	17
23 Nov 61	**I'LL GET BY** *Columbia DB 4737*	10		8
15 Feb 62	**TONIGHT** *Columbia DB 4777*	21		7
26 Apr 62	**AVE MARIA** *Columbia DB 4816*	31		4
31 May 62	**FAR AWAY** *Columbia DB 4836*	24		10
30 Aug 62	**WHAT NOW MY LOVE** *Columbia DB 4882*	5		16
28 Feb 63	**WHAT KIND OF FOOL AM I?** *Columbia DB 4974*	47		
26 Sep 63	**I (WHO HAVE NOTHING)** *Columbia DB 7113*	6		17
23 Jan 64	**MY SPECIAL DREAM** *Columbia DB 7185*	32		5
9 Apr 64	**GONE** *Columbia DB 7248*	36		3
15 Oct 64	**GOLDFINGER** *Columbia DB 7360*	21		8
20 May 65	**NO REGRETS (NON JE NE REGRETTE RIEN)** *Columbia DB 7535*	39		1
11 Oct 67	**BIG SPENDER** *United Artists UP 1192*	21		15
20 Jun 70	**SOMETHING** *United Artists UP 35125*	4		18
2 Jan 71	**THE FOOL ON THE HILL** *United Artists UP 35156*	48		
27 Mar 71	**(WHERE DO I BEGIN) LOVE STORY** *United Artists UP 35194*	34		6
7 Aug 71	**FOR ALL WE KNOW** *United Artists UP 35267*	6		21
15 Jan 72	**DIAMONDS ARE FOREVER** *United Artists UP 35293*	38		2
3 Mar 73	**NEVER NEVER NEVER** *United Artists UP 35490*	8		16
22 Aug 87	**THE RHYTHM DIVINE** *Mercury MER 253* YELLO FEATURING SHIRLEY BASSEY	54		
16 Nov 96	**DISCO LA PASSIONE** *East West EW072CD* CHRIS REA & SHIRLEY BASSEY	41		
20 Dec 97	**HISTORY REPEATING** *Wall Of Sound WALLD 036* PROPELLERHEADS & SHIRLEY BASSEY	19		4
23 Oct 99	**WORLD IN UNION** *Universal TV 4669402* SHIRLEY BASSEY/BRYN TERFEL	35		1
5 May 07	**THE LIVING TREE** *Lock Stock & Barrel LSBRCD003*	37		1
4 Aug 07	**GET THE PARTY STARTED** *Lock Stock & Barrel LSBRCD006*	47		

BASSHEADS UK group

Date	Title / Label	Peak Position	Weeks at No.1	Weeks in Top 40
16 Nov 91	**IS THERE ANYBODY OUT THERE** *Deconstruction R 6303*	5		5
30 May 92	**BACK TO THE OLD SCHOOL** *Deconstruction R 6310*	12		3
28 Nov 92	**WHO CAN MAKE ME FEEL GOOD** *Deconstruction R 6326*	38		1
28 Aug 93	**START A BRAND NEW LIFE (SAVE ME)** *Deconstruction CDR 6353*	49		
15 Jul 95	**IS THERE ANYBODY OUT THERE (REMIX)** *Deconstruction 74321293882*	24		2

BASSHUNTER Swedish producer

Date	Title / Label	Peak Position	Weeks at No.1	Weeks in Top 40
12 Jan 08	**NOW YOU'RE GONE** *Hard2Beat H2B01CDS* BASSHUNTER FEATURING DJ MENTAL THEOS	1	5	12

BASSTOY US DJ

Date	Title / Label	Peak Position	Weeks at No.1	Weeks in Top 40
27 May 00	**RUNNIN** *Neo NEOCD 029*	62		
19 Jan 02	**RUNNIN'(REMIX)** *Black & Blue NEOCD 073* MARK PICCHIOTTI PRESENTS BASSTOY FEATURING DANA	13		2

BATES German group

Date	Title / Label	Peak Position	Weeks at No.1	Weeks in Top 40
3 Feb 96	**BILLIE JEAN** *Virgin International DINSD 151*	67		

MIKE BATT WITH THE NEW EDITION UK group

Date	Title / Label	Peak Position	Weeks at No.1	Weeks in Top 40
16 Aug 75	**SUMMERTIME CITY** *Epic EPC 3460*	4		7

Silver-selling ● Gold-selling ● Platinum-selling ⊛ US No.1 ★ — Peak Position | Weeks at No.1 | Weeks in Top 40

BATTLE UK duo

Date	Title / Label	Peak Position	Weeks at No.1	Weeks in Top 40
25 Mar 06	**TENDENCY** *Transgressive TRANS022CD*	37		1
24 Jun 06	**CHILDREN** *Transgressive TRANS030CD*	60		

BAUHAUS UK group

Date	Title / Label	Peak Position	Weeks at No.1	Weeks in Top 40
18 Apr 81	**KICK IN THE EYE** *Beggars Banquet BEG 54*	59		
4 Jul 81	**THE PASSION OF LOVERS** *Beggars Banquet BEG 59*	56		
6 Mar 82	**KICK IN THE EYE (EP)** *Beggars Banquet BEG 74*	45		
19 Jun 82	**SPIRIT** *Beggars Banquet BEG 79*	42		
9 Oct 82	**ZIGGY STARDUST** *Beggars Banquet BEG 83*	15		5
22 Jan 83	**LAGARTIJA NICK** *Beggars Banquet BEG 88*	44		
9 Apr 83	**SHE'S IN PARTIES** *Beggars Banquet BEG 91*	26		4
29 Oct 83	**THE SINGLES 1981-83** *Beggars Banquet BEG 100E*	52		

LES BAXTER US singer

Date	Title / Label	Peak Position	Weeks at No.1	Weeks in Top 40
13 May 55	**UNCHAINED MELODY** *Capitol CL 14257* ★	10		9

TOM BAXTER UK singer

Date	Title / Label	Peak Position	Weeks at No.1	Weeks in Top 40
31 Jul 04	**THIS BOY** *Sony Music 6751692*	65		
15 Dec 07	**BETTER** *Charisma CASD8*	67		

BAY CITY ROLLERS UK group

Date	Title / Label	Peak Position	Weeks at No.1	Weeks in Top 40
18 Sep 71	**KEEP ON DANCING** *Bell 1164*	9		12
9 Feb 74	**REMEMBER (SHA-LA-LA)** *Bell 1338*	6		9
27 Apr 74	**SHANG-A-LANG** *Bell 1355*	2		9
27 Jul 74	**SUMMERLOVE SENSATION** *Bell 1369*	3		10
12 Oct 74	**ALL OF ME LOVES ALL OF YOU** *Bell 1382*	4		9
8 Mar 75	**BYE BYE BABY** *Bell 1409*	1	6	14
12 Jul 75	**GIVE A LITTLE LOVE** *Bell 1425*	1	3	9
22 Nov 75	**MONEY HONEY** *Bell 1461*	3		9
10 Apr 76	**LOVE ME LIKE I LOVE YOU** *Bell 1477*	4		9
11 Sep 76	**I ONLY WANNA BE WITH YOU** *Bell 1493*	4		9
7 May 77	**IT'S A GAME** *Arista 108*	16		5
30 Jul 77	**YOU MADE ME BELIEVE IN MAGIC** *Arista 127*	34		1

DUKE BAYSEE UK singer

Date	Title / Label	Peak Position	Weeks at No.1	Weeks in Top 40
3 Sep 94	**SUGAR SUGAR** *Bell 74321228702*	30		3
21 Jan 95	**DO YOU LOVE ME** *Double Dekker CDDEK 1*	46		

BAZ UK singer

Date	Title / Label	Peak Position	Weeks at No.1	Weeks in Top 40
15 Dec 01	**BELIEVERS** *One Little Indian 313 TP7CD*	36		1
30 Mar 02	**SMILE TO SHINE** *One Little Indian 316 TP7CD*	58		

BBC CONCERT ORCHESTRA
UK orchestra and chorus

Date	Title / Label	Peak Position	Weeks at No.1	Weeks in Top 40
22 Jun 96	**ODE TO JOY (FROM BEETHOVEN'S SYMPHONY NO 9)** *Virgin VSCDT 1591* BBC CONCERT ORCHESTRA/BBC SYMPHONY CHORUS/ STEPHEN JACKSON	36		1

BBE Italian/French group

Date	Title / Label	Peak Position	Weeks at No.1	Weeks in Top 40
28 Sep 96	**SEVEN DAYS AND ONE WEEK** *Positiva CDTIV 67*	3		7
29 Mar 97	**FLASH** *Positiva CDTIV 73*	5		3
14 Feb 98	**DESIRE** *Positiva CDTIV 87*	19		2
30 May 98	**DEEPER LOVE (SYMPHONIC PARADISE)** *Positiva CDTIV 93*	19		1

BBG UK group

Date	Title / Label	Peak Position	Weeks at No.1	Weeks in Top 40
28 Apr 90	**SNAPPINESS** *Urban URB 54* BBG FEATURING DINA TAYLOR	28		3
11 Aug 90	**SOME KIND OF HEAVEN** *Urban URB 59*	65		
23 Mar 96	**LET THE MUSIC PLAY** *MCA MCSTD 40029* BBG FEATURING ERIN	46		
18 May 96	**SNAPPINESS (REMIX)** *Hi-Life 5762972*	50		
5 Jul 97	**JUST BE TONIGHT** *Hi-Life 5738972*	45		

BBM UK group

Date	Title / Label	Peak Position	Weeks at No.1	Weeks in Top 40
6 Aug 94	**WHERE IN THE WORLD** *Virgin VSCD 1495*	57		

BBMAK UK group

Date	Title / Label	Peak Position	Weeks at No.1	Weeks in Top 40
28 Aug 99	**BACK HERE** *Telstar CDSTAS 3053*	37		1
24 Feb 01	**BACK HERE** *Telstar CDSTAS 3166*	5		5
26 May 01	**STILL ON YOUR SIDE** *Telstar CXSTAS 3185*	8		3
16 Nov 02	**OUT OF MY HEART** *Telstar CDSTAS 3281*	36		1

BE BOP DELUXE UK group

Date	Title / Label	Peak Position	Weeks at No.1	Weeks in Top 40
21 Feb 76	**SHIPS IN THE NIGHT** *Harvest HAR 5104*	23		6
13 Nov 76	**HOT VALVES EP** *Harvest HAR 5117*	36		2

BE YOUR OWN PET US group

Date	Title / Label	Peak Position	Weeks at No.1	Weeks in Top 40
26 Mar 05	**DAMN DAMN LEASH** *XL Recordings XLS212CD*	68		
2 Jul 05	**FIRE DEPARTMENT** *Rough Trade RTRADSCD238*	59		
4 Feb 06	**LET'S GET SANDY** *XL Recordings XLS224CD*	51		
25 Mar 06	**ADVENTURE** *XL Recordings XLS225CD*	36		1

BEACH BOYS US group

Date	Title / Label	Peak Position	Weeks at No.1	Weeks in Top 40
1 Aug 63	**SURFIN' USA** *Capitol CL 15305*	34		5
9 Jul 64	**I GET AROUND** *Capitol CL 15350* ★	7		12
29 Oct 64	**WHEN I GROW UP TO BE A MAN** *Capitol CL 15361*	27		4
21 Jan 65	**DANCE DANCE DANCE** *Capitol CL 15370*	24		6
3 Jun 65	**HELP ME RHONDA** *Capitol CL 15392* ★	27		10
2 Sep 65	**CALIFORNIA GIRLS** *Capitol CL 15409*	26		7
17 Feb 66	**BARBARA ANN** *Capitol CL 15432*	3		10
21 Apr 66	**SLOOP JOHN B** *Capitol CL 15441*	2		15
28 Jul 66	**GOD ONLY KNOWS** *Capitol CL 15459*	2		13
3 Nov 66	**GOOD VIBRATIONS** *Capitol CL 15475* ★	1	2	13
4 May 67	**THEN I KISSED HER** *Capitol CL 15502*	4		11
23 Aug 67	**HEROES AND VILLAINS** *Capitol CL 15510*	8		9
22 Nov 67	**WILD HONEY** *Capitol CL 15521*	29		3
17 Jan 68	**DARLIN'** *Capitol CL 15527*	11		14
8 May 68	**FRIENDS** *Capitol CL 15545*	25		6
24 Jul 68	**DO IT AGAIN** *Capitol CL 15554*	1	1	13
25 Dec 68	**BLUEBIRDS OVER THE MOUNTAIN** *Capitol CL 15572*	33		2
26 Feb 69	**I CAN HEAR MUSIC** *Capitol CL 15584*	10		11
11 Jun 69	**BREAK AWAY** *Capitol CL 15598*	6		11
16 May 70	**COTTONFIELDS** *Capitol CL 15640*	5		16
3 Mar 73	**CALIFORNIA SAGA-CALIFORNIA** *Reprise K 14232*	37		1
3 Jul 76	**GOOD VIBRATIONS** *Capitol CL 15875*	18		5
10 Jul 76	**ROCK AND ROLL MUSIC** *Reprise K 14440*	36		2
31 Mar 79	**HERE COMES THE NIGHT** *Caribou CRB 7204*	37		2
16 Jun 79	**LADY LYNDA** *Caribou CRB 7427*	6		8
29 Sep 79	**SUMAHAMA** *Caribou CRB 7846*	45		
29 Aug 81	**BEACH BOYS MEDLEY** *Capitol CL 213*	47		
22 Aug 87	**WIPEOUT** *Urban URB 5* FAT BOYS & THE BEACH BOYS	2		8
19 Nov 88	**KOKOMO** *Elektra EKR 85* ★	25		5
2 Jun 90	**WOULDN'T IT BE NICE** *Capitol CL 579*	58		
29 Jun 91	**DO IT AGAIN** *Capitol EMCT 1*	61		
2 Mar 96	**FUN FUN FUN** *Polygram TV 5762972* STATUS QUO WITH THE BEACH BOYS	24		1

WALTER BEASLEY US singer/saxophonist

Date	Title / Label	Peak Position	Weeks at No.1	Weeks in Top 40
23 Jan 88	**I'M SO HAPPY** *Urban URB 14*	70		

BEASTIE BOYS US group

Date	Title / Label	Peak Position	Weeks at No.1	Weeks in Top 40
28 Feb 87	**(YOU GOTTA) FIGHT FOR YOUR RIGHT TO PARTY** *Def Jam 6504187*	11		9
30 May 87	**NO SLEEP TILL BROOKLYN** *Def Jam BEAST 1*	14		5
18 Jul 87	**SHE'S ON IT** *Def Jam BEAST 2*	10		5
3 Oct 87	**GIRLS/SHE'S CRAFTY** *Def Jam BEAST 3*	34		2
11 Apr 92	**PASS THE MIC** *Capitol 12CL 653*	47		
4 Jul 92	**FROZEN METAL HEAD (EP)** *Capitol 12CL 665*	55		
9 Jul 94	**GET IT TOGETHER/SABOTAGE** *Capitol CDCL 716*	19		2
26 Nov 94	**SURE SHOT** *Capitol CDCLS 726*	27		2
4 Jul 98	**INTERGALACTIC** *Grand Royal CDCL 803*	5		5
7 Nov 98	**BODY MOVIN'** *Grand Royal CDCLS 809*	15		2
29 May 99	**REMOTE CONTROL/3 MCS AND 1 DJ** *Grand Royal CDCLS 812*	21		1
18 Dec 99	**ALIVE** *Grand Royal CDCL 818*	28		1
12 Jun 04	**CH-CHECK IT OUT** *Capitol CDCLS 857*	8		3
25 Sep 04	**TRIPLE TROUBLE** *Capitol CDCLS 859*	37		1
18 Dec 04	**AN OPEN LETTER TO NYC** *Capitol CDCLS867*	38		1

Key: ○ Silver-selling · ● Gold-selling · ⊛ Platinum-selling · ★ US No.1 · Peak Position · Weeks at No.1 · Weeks in Top 40

BEAT UK group

Date	Title	Peak	Wks No.1	Wks Top 40
8 Dec 79	TEARS OF A CLOWN/RANKING FULL STOP *2 Tone CHSTT 6* ○	6		9
23 Feb 80	HANDS OFF – SHE'S MINE *Go Feet FEET 1*	9		7
3 May 80	MIRROR IN THE BATHROOM *Go Feet FEET 2*	4		6
16 Aug 80	BEST FRIEND/STAND DOWN MARGARET (DUB) *Go Feet FEET 3*	22		7
13 Dec 80	TOO NICE TO TALK TO *Go Feet FEET 4* ○	7		8
18 Apr 81	DROWNING/ALL OUT TO GET YOU *Go Feet FEET 6*	22		3
20 Jun 81	DOORS OF YOUR HEART *Go Feet FEET 9*	33		3
5 Dec 81	HIT IT *Go Feet FEET 11*	70		
17 Apr 82	SAVE IT FOR LATER *Go Feet FEET 333*	47		
18 Sep 82	JEANETTE *Go Feet FEET 15*	45		
4 Dec 82	I CONFESS *Go Feet FEET 16*	54		
30 Apr 83	CAN'T GET USED TO LOSING YOU *Go Feet FEET 17* ○	3		9
2 Jul 83	ACKEE 1-2-3 *Go Feet FEET 18*	54		
27 Jan 96	MIRROR IN THE BATHROOM (REMIX) *Go Feet 74321232062*	44		

BEAT RENEGADES UK production duo

Date	Title	Peak	Wks No.1	Wks Top 40
19 May 01	AUTOMATIK *Slinky Music SLINKY014CD*	73		

BEAT SYSTEM UK producer

Date	Title	Peak	Wks No.1	Wks Top 40
3 Mar 90	WALK ON THE WILD SIDE *Fourth & Broadway BRW 163*	63		
18 Sep 93	TO A BRIGHTER DAY (O' HAPPY DAY) *ffrr FCD 217*	70		

BEAT UP UK group

Date	Title	Peak	Wks No.1	Wks Top 40
4 Dec 04	MESSED UP *Fantastic Plastic FPS043*	62		
5 Mar 05	ALRIGHT *Fantastic Plastic FPS045*	58		

BEATCHUGGERS Danish producer

Date	Title	Peak	Wks No.1	Wks Top 40
18 Nov 00	FOREVER MAN (HOW MANY TIMES) *ffrr FCD 386* BEATCHUGGERS FEATURING ERIC CLAPTON	26		1

BEATFREAKZ Dutch production group

Date	Title	Peak	Wks No.1	Wks Top 40
6 May 06	SOMEBODY'S WATCHING ME *Data DATA113CDS*	3		12
14 Oct 06	SUPERFREAK *Data DATA135CDS*	7		4

BEATINGS UK group

Date	Title	Peak	Wks No.1	Wks Top 40
26 Oct 02	BAD FEELINGS *Fantastic Plastic FPS 034*	68		

BEATLES UK group

Date	Title	Peak	Wks No.1	Wks Top 40
11 Oct 62	LOVE ME DO *Parlophone R 4949*	17		14
17 Jan 63	PLEASE PLEASE ME *Parlophone R 4983*	2		15
18 Apr 63	FROM ME TO YOU *Parlophone R 5015*	1	7	19
6 Jun 63	MY BONNIE *Polydor NH 66833* TONY SHERIDAN & THE BEATLES	48		
29 Aug 63	SHE LOVES YOU *Parlophone R 5055* ★	1	6	29
5 Dec 63	I WANT TO HOLD YOUR HAND *Parlophone R 5084* ★	1	5	18
26 Mar 64	CAN'T BUY ME LOVE *Parlophone R 5114* ★	1	3	13
11 Jun 64	AIN'T SHE SWEET *Polydor 52 317*	29		4
16 Jul 64	A HARD DAY'S NIGHT *Parlophone R 5160* ★	1	3	13
3 Dec 64	I FEEL FINE *Parlophone R 5200* ★	1	5	12
15 Apr 65	TICKET TO RIDE *Parlophone R 5265* ★	1	3	11
29 Jul 65	HELP! *Parlophone R 5305* ★	1	3	14
9 Dec 65	DAY TRIPPER/WE CAN WORK IT OUT *Parlophone R 5389*	1	5	11
16 Jun 66	PAPERBACK WRITER *Parlophone R 5452* ★	1	2	10
11 Aug 66	YELLOW SUBMARINE/ELEANOR RIGBY *Parlophone R 5493*	1	4	12
23 Feb 67	PENNY LANE/STRAWBERRY FIELDS FOREVER *Parlophone R 5570* ★	2		10
12 Jul 67	ALL YOU NEED IS LOVE *Parlophone R 5620* ★	1	3	13
29 Nov 67	HELLO GOODBYE *Parlophone R 5655* ★	1	7	11
13 Dec 67	MAGICAL MYSTERY TOUR (DOUBLE EP) *Parlophone SMMT/MMT 1*	2		12
20 Mar 68	LADY MADONNA *Parlophone R 5675*	1	2	8
4 Sep 68	HEY JUDE *Apple R 5722* ★	1	2	14
23 Apr 69	GET BACK *Apple R 5777* BEATLES WITH BILLY PRESTON ★	1	6	15
4 Jun 69	THE BALLAD OF JOHN AND YOKO *Apple R 5786*	1	3	12
8 Nov 69	SOMETHING/COME TOGETHER *Apple R 5814*	4		8
14 Mar 70	LET IT BE *Apple R 5833* ★	2		9
13 Mar 76	YESTERDAY *Apple R 6013* ★	8		6
27 Mar 76	HEY JUDE *Apple R 5722*	12		6
27 Mar 76	PAPERBACK WRITER *Parlophone R 5452*	23		4
3 Apr 76	STRAWBERRY FIELDS FOREVER *Parlophone R 5570*	32		2
3 Apr 76	GET BACK *Apple R 5777* BEATLES WITH BILLY PRESTON	28		4
10 Apr 76	HELP! *Parlophone R 5305*	37		1
10 Jul 76	BACK IN THE U.S.S.R. *Parlophone R 6016*	19		6
7 Oct 78	SGT PEPPER'S LONELY HEARTS CLUB BAND - WITH A LITTLE HELP FROM MY FRIENDS *Parlophone R 6022*	63		
5 Jun 82	BEATLES MOVIE MEDLEY *Parlophone R 6055*	10		7
16 Oct 82	LOVE ME DO *Parlophone R 4949*	4		6
22 Jan 83	PLEASE PLEASE ME *Parlophone R 4983*	29		3
23 Apr 83	FROM ME TO YOU *Parlophone R 5015*	40		1
3 Sep 83	SHE LOVES YOU *Parlophone R 5055*	45		
26 Nov 83	I WANT TO HOLD YOUR HAND *Parlophone R 5084*	62		
31 Mar 84	CAN'T BUY ME LOVE *Parlophone R 5114*	53		
21 Jul 84	A HARD DAY'S NIGHT *Parlophone R 5160*	52		
8 Dec 84	I FEEL FINE *Parlophone R 5200*	65		
20 Apr 85	TICKET TO RIDE *Parlophone R 5265*	70		
30 Aug 86	YELLOW SUBMARINE/ELEANOR RIGBY *Parlophone R 5493*	63		
28 Feb 87	PENNY LANE/STRAWBERRY FIELDS FOREVER *Parlophone R 5570*	65		
18 Jul 87	ALL YOU NEED IS LOVE *Parlophone R 5620*	47		
5 Dec 87	HELLO GOODBYE *Parlophone R 5655*	63		
26 Mar 88	LADY MADONNA *Parlophone R 5675*	67		
10 Sep 88	HEY JUDE *Apple R 5722*	52		
22 Apr 89	GET BACK *Apple R 5777* BEATLES WITH BILLY PRESTON	74		
17 Oct 92	LOVE ME DO *Parlophone R 4949*	53		
1 Apr 95	BABY IT'S YOU *Apple CDR 6406*	7		3
16 Dec 95	FREE AS A BIRD *Apple CDR 6422*	2		5
16 Mar 96	REAL LOVE *Apple CDR 6425*	4		3

BEATMASTERS UK group

Date	Title	Peak	Wks No.1	Wks Top 40
9 Jan 88	ROK DA HOUSE *Rhythm King LEFT 11* BEATMASTERS FEATURING THE COOKIE CREW	5		7
24 Sep 88	BURN IT UP *Rhythm King LEFT 27* BEATMASTERS WITH PP ARNOLD	14		6
22 Apr 89	WHO'S IN THE HOUSE *Rhythm King LEFT 31* BEATMASTERS FEATURING MERLIN	8		7
12 Aug 89	HEY DJ I CAN'T DANCE TO THAT MUSIC YOU'RE PLAYING/ SKA TRAIN *Rhythm King LEFT 34* BEATMASTERS FEATURING BETTY BOO	7		9
2 Dec 89	WARM LOVE *Rhythm King LEFT 37* BEATMASTERS FEATURING CLAUDIA FONTAINE	51		
21 Sep 91	BOULEVARD OF BROKEN DREAMS *Rhythm King 6573617*	62		
16 May 92	DUNNO WHAT IT IS (ABOUT YOU) *Rhythm King 6580017* BEATMASTERS FEATURING ELAINE VASSELL	43		

BEATNUTS US group

Date	Title	Peak	Wks No.1	Wks Top 40
14 Jul 01	NO ESCAPIN' THIS *Epic 6713412*	47		
21 Jun 03	DUDE DESCENDING A STAIRCASE *Sony Music SSX 14CDX* APOLLO FOUR FORTY FEATURING THE BEATNUTS	58		

BEATS INTERNATIONAL UK group

Date	Title	Peak	Wks No.1	Wks Top 40
10 Feb 90	DUB BE GOOD TO ME *Go! Beat GOD 39* BEATS INTERNATIONAL FEATURING LINDY LAYTON ●	1	4	12
12 May 90	WON'T TALK ABOUT IT *Go! Beat GOD 43*	9		6
15 Sep 90	BURUNDI BLUES *Go! Beat GOD 45*	51		
2 Mar 91	ECHO CHAMBER *Go! Beat GOD 51*	60		
21 Sep 91	THE SUN DOESN'T SHINE *Go! Beat GOD 59*	66		
23 Nov 91	IN THE GHETTO *Go! Beat GOD 64*	44		

BEAUTIFUL PEOPLE UK production group

Date	Title	Peak	Wks No.1	Wks Top 40
28 May 94	IF 60S WERE 90S *Essential ESSX 2037*	74		

BEAUTIFUL SOUTH UK group

Date	Title	Peak	Wks No.1	Wks Top 40
3 Jun 89	SONG FOR WHOEVER *Go! Discs GOD 32* ○	2		10
23 Sep 89	YOU KEEP IT ALL IN *Go! Discs GOD 35*	8		7
2 Dec 89	I'LL SAIL THIS SHIP ALONE *Go! Discs GOD 38*	31		3
6 Oct 90	A LITTLE TIME *Go! Discs GOD 47* ●	1	1	10
8 Dec 90	MY BOOK *Go! Discs GOD 48*	43		
16 Mar 91	LET LOVE SPEAK UP ITSELF *Go! Discs GOD 53*	51		
11 Jan 92	OLD RED EYES IS BACK *Go! Discs GOD 66*	22		4
14 Mar 92	WE ARE EACH OTHER *Go! Discs GOD 71*	30		2
13 Jun 92	BELL BOTTOMED TEAR *Go! Discs GOD 78*	16		4
26 Sep 92	36D *Go! Discs GOD 88*	46		
12 Mar 94	GOOD AS GOLD *Go! Discs GODCD 110*	23		4
4 Jun 94	EVERYBODY'S TALKIN' *Go! Discs GODCD 113*	12		6
3 Sep 94	PRETTIEST EYES *Go! Discs GODCD 119*	37		1
12 Nov 94	ONE LAST LOVE SONG *Go! Discs GODCD 122*	14		3
18 Nov 95	PRETENDERS TO THE THRONE *Go! Discs GODCD 134*	18		3
12 Oct 96	ROTTERDAM *Go! Discs GODCD 155*	6		8
14 Dec 96	DON'T MARRY HER *Go! Discs GOLCD 158*	8		8

Legend: Silver-selling ○ · Gold-selling ● · Platinum-selling ✱ · US No.1 ★ · Peak Position · Weeks at No.1 · Weeks in Top 40

Date	Title / Label	Peak Position	Weeks at No.1	Weeks in Top 40
29 Mar 97	**BLACKBIRD ON THE WIRE** *Go! Discs 5821252*	23		1
5 Jul 97	**LIARS' BAR** *Go! Discs 5822492*	43		
3 Oct 98	**PERFECT 10** *Go! Discs 5664832* ○	2		10
19 Dec 98	**DUMB** *Go! Discs 5667532*	16		4
20 Mar 99	**HOW LONG'S A TEAR TAKE TO DRY?** *Go! Discs 8708232*	12		3
10 Jul 99	**THE TABLE** *Go! Discs 5621652*	47		
7 Oct 00	**CLOSER THAN MOST** *Go! Discs 5629682*	22		1
23 Dec 00	**THE RIVER/JUST CHECKIN'** *Go! Discs 5727552*	59		
17 Nov 01	**THE ROOT OF ALL EVIL** *Go! Discs 5888712*	50		
25 Oct 03	**JUST A FEW THINGS THAT I AIN'T** *Go! Discs 9813039*	30		1
13 Dec 03	**LET GO WITH THE FLOW** *Go! Discs 9815084*	47		
23 Oct 04	**LIVIN' THING** *Sony Music 6753712*	24		1
18 Dec 04	**THIS OLD SKIN** *Sony Music 6756842*	43		
19 Feb 05	**THIS WILL BE OUR YEAR** *Sony Music 6757462*	36		1
20 May 06	**MANCHESTER** *Sony Music 82876831132*	41		

GILBERT BECAUD French singer

Date	Title / Label	Peak Position	Weeks at No.1	Weeks in Top 40
29 Mar 75	**A LITTLE LOVE AND UNDERSTANDING** *Decca F 13537*	10		10

BECK US singer

Date	Title / Label	Peak Position	Weeks at No.1	Weeks in Top 40
5 Mar 94	**LOSER** *Geffen GFSTD 67*	15		4
29 Jun 96	**WHERE IT'S AT** *Geffen GFSTD 22156*	35		1
16 Nov 96	**DEVILS HAIRCUT** *Geffen GFSTD 22183*	22		1
8 Mar 97	**THE NEW POLLUTION** *Geffen GFSTD 22205*	14		3
24 May 97	**SISSYNECK** *Geffen GFSTD 22253*	30		1
8 Nov 97	**DEADWEIGHT** *Geffen GFSTD 22293*	23		1
19 Dec 98	**TROPICALIA** *Geffen GFSTD 22365*	39		1
20 Nov 99	**SEXX LAWS** *Geffen 4971822*	27		1
8 Apr 00	**MIXED BIZNESS** *Geffen 4973012*	34		1
26 Mar 05	**E-PRO** *Interscope 9880052*	38		1
16 Jul 05	**GIRL** *Interscope 9882469*	45		

JEFF BECK UK singer/guitarist

Date	Title / Label	Peak Position	Weeks at No.1	Weeks in Top 40
23 Mar 67	**HI-HO SILVER LINING** *Columbia DB 8151*	14		10
2 Aug 67	**TALLYMAN** *Columbia DB 8227*	30		2
28 Feb 68	**LOVE IS BLUE** *Columbia DB 8359*	23		6
9 Jul 69	**GOO GOO BARABAJAGAL (LOVE IS HOT)** *Pye 7N 17778* DONOVAN WITH THE JEFF BECK GROUP	12		6
4 Nov 72	**HI-HO SILVER LINING** *RAK RR3*	17		9
5 May 73	**I'VE BEEN DRINKING** *RAK RR4* JEFF BECK & ROD STEWART	27		5
9 Oct 82	**HI-HO SILVER LINING** *RAK RR3*	62		
7 Mar 92	**PEOPLE GET READY** *Epic 6577567* JEFF BECK & ROD STEWART	49		

ROBIN BECK Canadian singer

Date	Title / Label	Peak Position	Weeks at No.1	Weeks in Top 40
22 Oct 88	**THE FIRST TIME** *Mercury MER 270* ○	1	3	11

VICTORIA BECKHAM UK singer

Date	Title / Label	Peak Position	Weeks at No.1	Weeks in Top 40
26 Aug 00	**OUT OF YOUR MIND** *NuLife 74321782942* TRUE STEPPERS & DANE BOWERS FEATURING VICTORIA BECKHAM ●	2		8
29 Sep 01	**NOT SUCH AN INNOCENT GIRL** *Virgin VSCDT 1816*	6		3
23 Feb 02	**A MIND OF ITS OWN** *Virgin VSCDT 1824*	6		4
10 Jan 04	**THIS GROOVE/LET YOUR HEAD GO** *19 Recordings/Moody CXVB 1*	3		6

BEDAZZLED UK group

Date	Title / Label	Peak Position	Weeks at No.1	Weeks in Top 40
4 Jul 92	**SUMMER SONG** *Columbia 6581627*	73		

DANIEL BEDINGFIELD UK singer

Date	Title / Label	Peak Position	Weeks at No.1	Weeks in Top 40
8 Dec 01	**GOTTA GET THRU THIS** *Relentless RELENT 27CD* ●	1	3	14
24 Aug 02	**JAMES DEAN (I WANNA KNOW)** *Polydor 5709342*	4		5
7 Dec 02	**IF YOU'RE NOT THE ONE** *Polydor 0658632* ●	1	1	18
19 Apr 03	**I CAN'T READ YOU** *Polydor 0657132*	6		5
2 Aug 03	**NEVER GONNA LEAVE YOUR SIDE** *Polydor 9809362*	1	1	8
1 Nov 03	**FRIDAY** *Polydor 9812920*	28		1
6 Nov 04	**NOTHING HURTS LIKE LOVE** *Polydor 9868820*	3		4
19 Feb 05	**WRAP MY WORDS AROUND YOU** *Polydor 9870179*	12		3
4 Jun 05	**THE WAY** *Polydor 9871535*	41		

NATASHA BEDINGFIELD UK singer

Date	Title / Label	Peak Position	Weeks at No.1	Weeks in Top 40
15 May 04	**SINGLE** *Phonogenic 82876615232*	3		7
28 Aug 04	**THESE WORDS** *Phonogenic 82876639182*	1	2	10
11 Dec 04	**UNWRITTEN** *Phonogenic 82876663542* ★	6		8
16 Apr 05	**I BRUISE EASILY** *Phonogenic 82876681532*	12		4
14 Apr 07	**I WANNA HAVE YOUR BABIES** *Phonogenic 82876886422*	7		7
23 Jun 07	**SOULMATE** *Phonogenic 88697111992*	7		8
29 Mar 08	**LOVE LIKE THIS** *Phonogenic 88697287252* NATASHA BEDINGFIELD FEATURING SEAN KINGSTON	27		1

BEDLAM UK production duo

Date	Title / Label	Peak Position	Weeks at No.1	Weeks in Top 40
6 Feb 99	**DA-FORCE** *Playola 0091695 PLA*	68		

BEDLAM AGO GO UK group

Date	Title / Label	Peak Position	Weeks at No.1	Weeks in Top 40
4 Apr 98	**SEASON NO. 5** *Sony S2 BDLM 2CD*	57		

BEDOUIN SOUNDCLASH Canadian group

Date	Title / Label	Peak Position	Weeks at No.1	Weeks in Top 40
8 Oct 05	**WHEN THE NIGHT FEELS MY SONG** *B Unique/Polydor BUN098CD*	24		7

BEDROCK UK group

Date	Title / Label	Peak Position	Weeks at No.1	Weeks in Top 40
1 Jun 96	**FOR WHAT YOU DREAM OF** *Stress CDSTR 23* BEDROCK FEATURING KYO	25		1
12 Jul 97	**SET IN STONE/FORBIDDEN ZONE** *Stress CDSTR 80*	71		
6 Nov 99	**HEAVEN SCENT** *Bedrock BEDRCDS 001*	35		1
8 Jul 00	**VOICES** *Bedrock BEDRCDS 005*	44		
18 Dec 68	**OB-LA-DI OB-LA-DA** *Columbia DB 8516*	20		6

CELI BEE & THE BUZZY BUNCH US group

Date	Title / Label	Peak Position	Weeks at No.1	Weeks in Top 40
17 Jun 78	**HOLD YOUR HORSES BABE** *TK TKR 6032*	72		

BEE GEES UK group

Date	Title / Label	Peak Position	Weeks at No.1	Weeks in Top 40
27 Apr 67	**NEW YORK MINING DISASTER 1941** *Polydor 56 161*	12		7
12 Jul 67	**TO LOVE SOMEBODY** *Polydor 56 178*	41		
20 Sep 67	**MASSACHUSETTS** *Polydor 56 192*	1	4	16
22 Nov 67	**WORLD** *Polydor 56 220*	9		13
31 Jan 68	**WORDS** *Polydor 56 229*	8		9
27 Mar 68	**JUMBO/THE SINGER SANG HIS SONG** *Polydor 56 242*	25		5
7 Aug 68	**I'VE GOTTA GET A MESSAGE TO YOU** *Polydor 56 273*	1	1	13
19 Feb 69	**FIRST OF MAY** *Polydor 56 304*	6		10
4 Jun 69	**TOMORROW TOMORROW** *Polydor 56 331*	23		5
16 Aug 69	**DON'T FORGET TO REMEMBER** *Polydor 56 343*	2		13
28 Mar 70	**I.O.I.O.** *Polydor 56 377*	49		
5 Dec 70	**LONELY DAYS** *Polydor 2001 104*	33		7
29 Jan 72	**MY WORLD** *Polydor 2058 105*	16		9
22 Jul 72	**RUN TO ME** *Polydor 2058 255*	9		9
28 Jun 75	**JIVE TALKIN'** *RSO 2090 160* ○ ★	5		10
31 Jul 76	**YOU SHOULD BE DANCING** *RSO 2090 195* ★	5		9
13 Nov 76	**LOVE SO RIGHT** *RSO 2090 207*	41		
29 Oct 77	**HOW DEEP IS YOUR LOVE** *RSO 2090 259* ● ★	3		15
4 Feb 78	**STAYIN' ALIVE** *RSO 2090 267* ○ ★	4		12
15 Apr 78	**NIGHT FEVER** *RSO 002* ● ★	1	2	17
25 Nov 78	**TOO MUCH HEAVEN** *RSO 25* ● ★	3		11
17 Feb 79	**TRAGEDY** *RSO 27* ● ★	1	2	8
14 Apr 79	**LOVE YOU INSIDE OUT** *RSO 31* ★	13		6
5 Jan 80	**SPIRITS (HAVING FLOWN)** *RSO 52*	16		6
17 Sep 83	**SOMEONE BELONGING TO SOMEONE** *RSO 96*	49		
26 Sep 87	**YOU WIN AGAIN** *Warner Brothers W 8351* ●	1	4	10
12 Dec 87	**E.S.P.** *Warner Brothers W 8139*	51		
15 Apr 89	**ORDINARY LIVES** *Warner Brothers W 7523*	54		
24 Jun 89	**ONE** *Warner Brothers W 2916*	71		
2 Mar 91	**SECRET LOVE** *Warner Brothers W 0014*	5		9
21 Aug 93	**PAYING THE PRICE OF LOVE** *Polydor PZCD 284*	23		4
27 Nov 93	**FOR WHOM THE BELL TOLLS** *Polydor PZCD 299* ○	4		12
16 Apr 94	**HOW TO FALL IN LOVE PART 1** *Polydor PZCD 311*	30		1
1 Mar 97	**ALONE** *Polydor 5735272* ○	5		7
21 Jun 97	**I COULD NOT LOVE YOU MORE** *Polydor 5712232*	14		1
8 Nov 97	**STILL WATERS (RUN DEEP)** *Polydor 5718892*	18		2
18 Jul 98	**IMMORTALITY** *Epic 6661682* CELINE DION WITH THE BEE GEES ○	5		7
7 Apr 01	**THIS IS WHERE I CAME IN** *Polydor 5879772*	18		3

BEENIE MAN Jamaican rapper

Date	Title / Label	Peak Position	Weeks at No.1	Weeks in Top 40
20 Sep 97	**DANCEHALL QUEEN** *Island Jamaica IJCD 2018* CHEVELLE FRANKLYN/BEENIE MAN	70		
7 Mar 98	**WHO AM I** *Greensleeves GRECD 588*	10		3

Silver-selling ● Gold-selling ● Platinum-selling ⊛ US No.1 ★ | Peak Position | Weeks at No.1 | Weeks in Top 40

Date	Title / Label	Peak Position	Weeks at No.1	Weeks in Top 40
8 Aug 98	**FOUNDATION** *Shocking Vibes SVJCDS1* BEENIE MAN AND THE TAXI GANG	69		
4 Mar 00	**MONEY** *Parlophone Rhythm CDRHYTHM 27* JAMELIA FEATURING BEENIE MAN	5		5
24 Mar 01	**GIRLS DEM SUGAR** *Virgin VUSCD 173* BEENIE MAN FEATURING MYA	13		4
28 Sep 02	**FEEL IT BOY** *Virgin VUSCD 258* BEENIE MAN FEATURING JANET JACKSON	9		4
14 Dec 02	**DIRTY HARRY'S REVENGE** *Kaos 004P* ADAM F FEATURING BEENIE MAN	50		
8 Feb 03	**STREET LIFE** *Virgin VUSDX 260*	13		3
13 Mar 04	**DUDE** *Virgin VUSCDX 282* BEENIE MAN FEATURING MS THING	7		5
21 Aug 04	**KING OF THE DANCEHALL** *Virgin VUSCD 293*	14		3
19 Aug 06	**GIRLS** *Virgin VUSCD328* BEENIE FEATURING AKON	47		

BEES UK duo

Date	Title / Label	Peak Position	Weeks at No.1	Weeks in Top 40
1 May 04	**WASH IN THE RAIN** *Virgin VSCDT 1868*	31		1
26 Jun 04	**HORSEMEN** *Virgin VSCDX 1869*	41		
16 Apr 05	**CHICKEN PAYBACK** *Virgin VSCDX1884*	28		1

B.E.F. UK group

Date	Title / Label	Peak Position	Weeks at No.1	Weeks in Top 40
27 Jul 91	**FAMILY AFFAIR** *10 TEN 369* B.E.F. FEATURING LALAH HATHAWAY	37		1

LOU BEGA German singer

Date	Title / Label	Peak Position	Weeks at No.1	Weeks in Top 40
7 Aug 99	**MAMBO NO. 5 (A LITTLE BIT OF…) (IMPORT)** *Ariola 74321658012*	31		3
4 Sep 99	**MAMBO NO. 5 (A LITTLE BIT OF…)** *RCA 74321696722* ⊛	1	2	11
18 Dec 99	**I GOT A GIRL** *RCA 74321720642*	55		

BEGGAR & CO UK group

Date	Title / Label	Peak Position	Weeks at No.1	Weeks in Top 40
7 Feb 81	**(SOMEBODY) HELP ME OUT** *Ensign ENY 201*	15		6
12 Sep 81	**MULE (CHANT NO. 2)** *RCA 130*	37		1

BEGINERZ UK duo

Date	Title / Label	Peak Position	Weeks at No.1	Weeks in Top 40
13 Jul 02	**RECKLESS GIRL** *Cheeky 74321942232*	28		1

BEGINNING OF THE END Bahamian quartet

Date	Title / Label	Peak Position	Weeks at No.1	Weeks in Top 40
23 Feb 74	**FUNKY NASSAU** *Atlantic K 10021*	31		3

BEIJING SPRING UK duo

Date	Title / Label	Peak Position	Weeks at No.1	Weeks in Top 40
23 Jan 93	**I WANNA BE IN LOVE AGAIN** *MCA MCSTD 1709*	43		
8 May 93	**SUMMERLANDS** *MCA MCSTD 1761*	53		

BEL AMOUR French production group

Date	Title / Label	Peak Position	Weeks at No.1	Weeks in Top 40
12 May 01	**BEL AMOUR** *Credence CDCRED 010*	23		1

BEL CANTO Norwegian group

Date	Title / Label	Peak Position	Weeks at No.1	Weeks in Top 40
14 Oct 95	**WE'VE GOT TO WORK IT OUT** *Good Groove CDGG 2*	65		

HARRY BELAFONTE US singer

Date	Title / Label	Peak Position	Weeks at No.1	Weeks in Top 40
1 Mar 57	**BANANA BOAT SONG** *HMV POP 308* HARRY BELAFONTE WITH TONY SCOTT'S ORCHESTRA & CHORUS & MILLARD THOMAS, GUITAR	2		18
14 Jun 57	**ISLAND IN THE SUN** *RCA 1007*	3		25
6 Sep 57	**SCARLET RIBBONS** *HMV POP 360* HARRY BELAFONTE & MILLARD THOMAS	18		6
1 Nov 57	**MARY'S BOY CHILD** *RCA 1022*	1	7	12
22 Aug 58	**LITTLE BERNADETTE** *RCA 1072*	16		7
28 Nov 58	**MARY'S BOY CHILD** *RCA 1022*	10		6
12 Dec 58	**SON OF MARY** *RCA 1084*	18		4
11 Dec 59	**MARY'S BOY CHILD** *RCA 1022*	30		1
28 Sep 61	**HOLE IN THE BUCKET** *RCA 1247* HARRY BELAFONTE & ODETTA	32		3

BELL & JAMES US duo

Date	Title / Label	Peak Position	Weeks at No.1	Weeks in Top 40
31 Mar 79	**LIVIN' IT UP (FRIDAY NIGHT)** *A&M AMS 7424*	59		

BELL & SPURLING UK duo

Date	Title / Label	Peak Position	Weeks at No.1	Weeks in Top 40
13 Oct 01	**SVEN SVEN SVEN** *Eternal WEA 336CD*	7		4
8 Jun 02	**GOLDENBALLS (MR BECKHAM TO YOU)** *Eternal WEA 350CD*	25		3

ANDY BELL UK singer

Date	Title / Label	Peak Position	Weeks at No.1	Weeks in Top 40
8 Oct 05	**CRAZY** *Sanctuary SANXS396*	35		1

ARCHIE BELL & THE DRELLS US singer

Date	Title / Label	Peak Position	Weeks at No.1	Weeks in Top 40
7 Oct 72	**HERE I GO AGAIN** *Atlantic K 10210*	11		8
27 Jan 73	**THERE'S GONNA BE A SHOWDOWN** *Atlantic K 10263*	36		1
8 May 76	**SOUL CITY WALK** *Philadelphia International PIR 4250*	13		9
11 Jun 77	**EVERYBODY HAVE A GOOD TIME** *Philadelphia International PIR 5179*	43		
28 Jun 86	**DON'T LET LOVE GET YOU DOWN** *Portrait A 7254*	49		

BELL BIV DEVOE US group

Date	Title / Label	Peak Position	Weeks at No.1	Weeks in Top 40
30 Jun 90	**POISON** *MCA 1414*	19		6
22 Sep 90	**DO ME** *MCA 1440*	56		
15 Aug 92	**THE BEST THINGS IN LIFE ARE FREE** *Perspective PERSS 7400* LUTHER VANDROSS & JANET JACKSON WITH SPECIAL GUESTS BBD & RALPH TRESVANT ●	2		11
9 Oct 93	**SOMETHING IN YOUR EYES** *MCA MCSTD 1934*	60		
16 Dec 95	**THE BEST THINGS IN LIFE ARE FREE (REMIX)** *A&M 5813092* LUTHER VANDROSS & JANET JACKSON WITH SPECIAL GUESTS BBD & RALPH TRESVANT	7		5

BELL BOOK & CANDLE German group

Date	Title / Label	Peak Position	Weeks at No.1	Weeks in Top 40
17 Oct 98	**RESCUE ME** *Logic 74321616882*	63		

BELL X1 Irish group

Date	Title / Label	Peak Position	Weeks at No.1	Weeks in Top 40
26 Jun 04	**EVE THE APPLE OF MY EYE** *Island CID 856*	65		
25 Mar 06	**FLAME** *Island CID919*	65		

FREDDIE BELL & THE BELLBOYS US group

Date	Title / Label	Peak Position	Weeks at No.1	Weeks in Top 40
28 Sep 56	**GIDDY-UP-A-DING-DONG** *Mercury MT 122*	4		10

BELLAMY BROTHERS US duo

Date	Title / Label	Peak Position	Weeks at No.1	Weeks in Top 40
17 Apr 76	**LET YOUR LOVE FLOW** *Warner Brothers K 16690* ★	7		11
21 Aug 76	**SATIN SHEETS** *Warner Brothers K 16775*	43		
11 Aug 79	**IF I SAID YOU HAD A BEAUTIFUL BODY WOULD YOU HOLD IT AGAINST ME** *Warner Brothers K 17405* ●	3		12

MAGGIE BELL UK singer

Date	Title / Label	Peak Position	Weeks at No.1	Weeks in Top 40
15 Apr 78	**HAZELL** *Swansong SSK 19412*	37		2
17 Oct 81	**HOLD ME** *Swansong BAM 1* B.A. ROBERTSON & MAGGIE BELL	11		7

WILLIAM BELL US singer

Date	Title / Label	Peak Position	Weeks at No.1	Weeks in Top 40
29 May 68	**TRIBUTE TO A KING** *Stax 601 038*	31		5
20 Nov 68	**PRIVATE NUMBER** *Stax 101* JUDY CLAY & WILLIAM BELL	8		13
26 Apr 86	**HEADLINE NEWS** *Absolute LUTE 1*	70		

BELLATRIX Icelandic group

Date	Title / Label	Peak Position	Weeks at No.1	Weeks in Top 40
16 Sep 00	**JEDI WANNABE** *Fierce Panda NING 101CD*	65		

BELLE & SEBASTIAN UK group

Date	Title / Label	Peak Position	Weeks at No.1	Weeks in Top 40
24 May 97	**DOG ON WHEELS** *Jeepster JPRCDS 001*	59		
9 Aug 97	**LADY LINE PAINTER JANE** *Jeepster JPRCDS 002*	41		
25 Oct 97	**3..6..9 SECONDS OF LIGHT (EP)** *Jeepster JPRCDS 003*	32		1
3 Jun 00	**LEGAL MAN** *Jeepster JPRCDS 018*	15		2
30 Jun 01	**JONATHAN DAVID** *Jeepster JPRCDS 022*	31		1
8 Dec 01	**I'M WAKING UP TO US** *Jeepster JPRCDS 023*	39		1

Silver-selling · Gold-selling · Platinum-selling · US No.1 ★ · Peak Position · Weeks at No.1 · Weeks in Top 40

Date	Title	Label	Peak Position	Weeks at No.1	Weeks in Top 40
29 Nov 03	STEP INTO MY OFFICE BABY	Rough Trade RTRADESCD 128	32		1
28 Feb 04	I'M A CUCKOO	Rough Trade RTRADSCD 157	14		2
3 Jul 04	BOOKS	Rough Trade RTRADSCD 180	20		1
28 Jan 06	FUNNY LITTLE FROG	Rough Trade RTRADSCD283	13		2
15 Apr 06	THE BLUES ARE STILL BLUE	Rough Trade RTRADSCD313	25		1
8 Jul 06	THE WHITE COLLAR BOY	Rough Trade RTRADSCD355	45		

BELLE & THE DEVOTIONS UK group

Date	Title	Label	Peak Position	Weeks at No.1	Weeks in Top 40
21 Apr 84	LOVE GAMES	CBS A 4332	11		5

REGINA BELLE US singer

Date	Title	Label	Peak Position	Weeks at No.1	Weeks in Top 40
21 Oct 89	GOOD LOVIN'	CBS 6552307	73		
11 Dec 93	A WHOLE NEW WORLD (ALADDIN'S THEME) PEABO BRYSON & REGINA BELLE ★	Columbia 6599002	12		9

BELLE STARS UK group

Date	Title	Label	Peak Position	Weeks at No.1	Weeks in Top 40
5 Jun 82	IKO IKO	Stiff BUY 150	35		1
17 Jul 82	THE CLAPPING SONG	Stiff BUY 155	11		7
16 Oct 82	MOCKINGBIRD	Stiff BUY 159	51		
15 Jan 83	SIGN OF THE TIMES	Stiff BUY 167	3		8
16 Apr 83	SWEET MEMORY	Stiff BUY 174	22		4
13 Aug 83	INDIAN SUMMER	Stiff BUY 185	52		
14 Jul 84	80S ROMANCE	Stiff BUY 200	71		

BELLEFIRE Irish group

Date	Title	Label	Peak Position	Weeks at No.1	Weeks in Top 40
14 Jul 01	PERFECT BLISS	Virgin VSCDT 1807	18		3
18 May 02	ALL I WANT IS YOU	Virgin VSCDT 1820	18		2
24 Apr 04	SAY SOMETHING ANYWAY	East West EW 287CD	26		1
16 Oct 04	SPIN THE WHEEL	East West EW293CD	67		

BELLINI German production group

Date	Title	Label	Peak Position	Weeks at No.1	Weeks in Top 40
27 Sep 97	SAMBA DE JANIERO	Virgin DINSD 165	8		5

BELLRAYS US group

Date	Title	Label	Peak Position	Weeks at No.1	Weeks in Top 40
20 Jul 02	THEY GLUED YOUR HEAD ON UPSIDE DOWN	Poptones MC 5073SCD	75		

BELLY US group

Date	Title	Label	Peak Position	Weeks at No.1	Weeks in Top 40
23 Jan 93	FEED THE TREE	4AD BAD 3001CD	32		1
10 Apr 93	GEPETTO	4AD BAD 2018CD	49		
4 Feb 95	NOW THEY'LL SLEEP	4AD BAD 5003CD	28		1
22 Jul 95	SEAL MY FATE	4AD BADD 5007CD	35		1

BELOVED UK group

Date	Title	Label	Peak Position	Weeks at No.1	Weeks in Top 40
21 Oct 89	THE SUN RISING	WEA YZ 414	26		4
27 Jan 90	HELLO	WEA YZ 426	19		5
24 Mar 90	YOUR LOVE TAKES ME HIGHER	East West YZ 463	39		2
9 Jun 90	TIME AFTER TIME	East West YZ 482	46		
10 Nov 90	IT'S ALRIGHT NOW	East West YZ 541	48		
23 Jan 93	SWEET HARMONY	East West YZ 709CD	8		7
10 Apr 93	YOU'VE GOT ME THINKING	East West YZ 738CD	23		3
14 Aug 93	OUTERSPACE GIRL	East West YZ 726CD	38		1
30 Mar 96	SATELLITE	East West EW 034CD	19		2
10 Aug 96	EASE THE PRESSURE	East West EW 058CD	43		
30 Aug 97	THE SUN RISING	East West EW 122CD1	31		1

BELTRAM US producer

Date	Title	Label	Peak Position	Weeks at No.1	Weeks in Top 40
28 Sep 91	ENERGY FLASH (EP)	R&S RSUK 3	52		
7 Dec 91	THE OMEN PROGRAM 2 BELTRAM	R&S RSUK 7	53		

BEN'S BROTHER UK group

Date	Title	Label	Peak Position	Weeks at No.1	Weeks in Top 40
18 Aug 07	LET ME OUT	Relentless RELCD39	38		1

BENNY BENASSI PRESENTS THE BIZ French producer

Date	Title	Label	Peak Position	Weeks at No.1	Weeks in Top 40
26 Jul 03	SATISFACTION	Data 58CDS	2		7
14 Feb 04	NO MATTER WHAT YOU DO	Data 66CDS	40		1

PAT BENATAR US singer

Date	Title	Label	Peak Position	Weeks at No.1	Weeks in Top 40
21 Jan 84	LOVE IS A BATTLEFIELD	Chrysalis CHS 2747	49		
12 Jan 85	WE BELONG	Chrysalis CHS 2821	22		6
23 Mar 85	LOVE IS A BATTLEFIELD	Chrysalis PAT 1	17		7
15 Jun 85	SHADOWS OF THE NIGHT	Chrysalis PAT 2	50		
19 Oct 85	INVINCIBLE (THEME FROM *THE LEGEND OF BILLIE JEAN*)	Chrysalis PAT 3	53		
15 Feb 86	SEX AS A WEAPON	Chrysalis PAT 4	67		
2 Jul 88	ALL FIRED UP	Chrysalis PAT 5	19		7
1 Oct 88	DON'T WALK AWAY	Chrysalis PAT 6	42		
14 Jan 89	ONE LOVE	Chrysalis PAT 7	59		
30 Oct 93	SOMEBODY'S BABY	Chrysalis CDCHS 5001	48		

DAVID BENDETH UK singer

Date	Title	Label	Peak Position	Weeks at No.1	Weeks in Top 40
8 Sep 79	FEEL THE REAL	Sidewalk SID 113	44		

BENELUX & NANCY DEE Belgian/Dutch/Luxembourgish group

Date	Title	Label	Peak Position	Weeks at No.1	Weeks in Top 40
25 Aug 79	SWITCH	Scope SC 4	52		

ERIC BENET US singer

Date	Title	Label	Peak Position	Weeks at No.1	Weeks in Top 40
22 Mar 97	SPIRITUAL THANG	Warner Brothers W 0390CD	62		
1 May 99	GEORGY PORGY ERIC BENET FEATURING FAITH EVANS	Warner Brothers W 478CD1	28		1
5 Feb 00	WHY YOU FOLLOW ME	Warner Brothers W 491CD	48		

BENNETT US singer

Date	Title	Label	Peak Position	Weeks at No.1	Weeks in Top 40
22 Feb 97	MUM'S GONE TO ICELAND	Roadrunner RR 22853	34		1
3 May 97	SOMEONE ALWAYS GETS THERE FIRST	Roadrunner RR 22983	69		

BOYD BENNETT & HIS ROCKETS US singer

Date	Title	Label	Peak Position	Weeks at No.1	Weeks in Top 40
23 Dec 55	SEVENTEEN	Parlophone R 4063	16		2

CLIFF BENNETT & THE REBEL ROUSERS UK singer

Date	Title	Label	Peak Position	Weeks at No.1	Weeks in Top 40
1 Oct 64	ONE WAY LOVE	Parlophone R 5173	9		8
4 Feb 65	I'LL TAKE YOU HOME	Parlophone R 5229	42		
11 Aug 66	GOT TO GET YOU INTO MY LIFE	Parlophone R 5489	6		10

PETER E BENNETT WITH THE CO-OPERATION CHOIR UK singer with choir

Date	Title	Label	Peak Position	Weeks at No.1	Weeks in Top 40
7 Nov 70	THE SEAGULL'S NAME WAS NELSON	RCA 1991	45		

TONY BENNETT US singer

Date	Title	Label	Peak Position	Weeks at No.1	Weeks in Top 40
15 Apr 55	STRANGER IN PARADISE	Philips PB 420	1	2	16
16 Sep 55	CLOSE YOUR EYES	Philips PB 445	18		1
13 Apr 56	COME NEXT SPRING	Philips PB 537	29		1
5 Jan 61	TILL	Philips PB 1079	35		1
18 Jul 63	THE GOOD LIFE	CBS AAG 153	27		11
6 May 65	IF I RULED THE WORLD	CBS 201735	40		1
27 May 65	I LEFT MY HEART IN SAN FRANCISCO	CBS 201730	46		
30 Sep 65	I LEFT MY HEART IN SAN FRANCISCO	CBS 201730	25		9
23 Dec 65	THE VERY THOUGHT OF YOU	CBS 202021	21		7

BRENDAN BENSON US singer

Date	Title	Label	Peak Position	Weeks at No.1	Weeks in Top 40
9 Apr 05	SPIT IT OUT	V2 VVR5031203	75		

GARY BENSON UK singer

Date	Title	Label	Peak Position	Weeks at No.1	Weeks in Top 40
9 Aug 75	DON'T THROW IT ALL AWAY	State STAT 10	20		7

GEORGE BENSON US singer/guitarist

Date	Title / Label	Peak Position	Weeks at No.1	Weeks in Top 40
25 Oct 75	**SUPERSHIP** *CTI CTSP 002*	30		5
4 Jun 77	**NATURE BOY** *Warner Brothers K 16921*	26		5
24 Sep 77	**THE GREATEST LOVE OF ALL** *Arista 133*	27		6
31 Mar 79	**LOVE BALLAD** *Warner Brothers K 17333*	29		5
26 Jul 80	**GIVE ME THE NIGHT** *Warner Brothers K 17673*	7		8
4 Oct 80	**LOVE X LOVE** *Warner Brothers K 17699*	10		6
7 Feb 81	**WHAT'S ON YOUR MIND** *Warner Brothers K 17748*	45		
19 Sep 81	**LOVE ALL THE HURT AWAY** *Arista ARIST 428* ARETHA FRANKLIN & GEORGE BENSON	49		
14 Nov 81	**TURN YOUR LOVE AROUND** *Warner Brothers K 17877*	29		5
23 Jan 82	**NEVER GIVE UP ON A GOOD THING** *Warner Brothers K 17902*	14		8
21 May 83	**LADY LOVE ME (ONE MORE TIME)** *Warner Brothers W 9614*	11		8
16 Jul 83	**FEEL LIKE MAKIN' LOVE** *Warner Brothers W 9551*	28		4
24 Sep 83	**IN YOUR EYES** *Warner Brothers W 9487*	7		8
17 Dec 83	**INSIDE LOVE (SO PERSONAL)** *Warner Brothers W 9427*	57		
19 Jan 85	**20/20** *Warner Brothers W 9120*	29		5
20 Apr 85	**BEYOND THE SEA (LA MER)** *Warner Brothers W 9014*	60		
16 Aug 86	**KISSES IN THE MOONLIGHT** *Warner Brothers W 8640*	60		
29 Nov 86	**SHIVER** *Warner Brothers W 8523*	19		7
14 Feb 87	**TEASER** *Warner Brothers W 8437*	45		
27 Aug 88	**LET'S DO IT AGAIN** *Warner Brothers W 7780*	56		
5 Sep 92	**I'LL KEEP YOUR DREAMS ALIVE** *Ammi 101* GEORGE BENSON & PATTI AUSTIN	68		
11 Jul 98	**SEVEN DAYS** *MCA MCSTD 48083* MARY J BLIGE FEATURING GEORGE BENSON	22		1

RHIAN BENSON UK singer

Date	Title / Label	Peak Position	Weeks at No.1	Weeks in Top 40
23 Oct 04	**SAY HOW I FEEL** *DKG DKG710071002*	27		1

BENT UK duo

Date	Title / Label	Peak Position	Weeks at No.1	Weeks in Top 40
12 Jul 03	**STAY THE SAME** *Sport 9CDX*	59		

BENTLEY RHYTHM ACE UK group

Date	Title / Label	Peak Position	Weeks at No.1	Weeks in Top 40
6 Sep 97	**BENTLEY'S GONNA SORT YOU OUT!** *Skint CDRS 6476*	17		2
27 May 00	**THEME FROM GUTBUSTER** *Parlophone CDRS 6537*	29		1
2 Sep 00	**HOW'D I DO DAT** *Parlophone CDRS 6543*	57		

BROOK BENTON US singer

Date	Title / Label	Peak Position	Weeks at No.1	Weeks in Top 40
10 Jul 59	**ENDLESSLY** *Mercury AMT 1043*	28		2
6 Oct 60	**KIDDIO** *Mercury AMT 1109*	41		
16 Feb 61	**FOOLS RUSH IN** *Mercury AMT 1121*	50		
13 Jul 61	**BOLL WEEVIL SONG** *Mercury AMT 1148*	30		8

BENZ UK group

Date	Title / Label	Peak Position	Weeks at No.1	Weeks in Top 40
16 Dec 95	**BOOM ROCK SOUL** *Hacktown 74321329652*	62		
16 Mar 96	**URBAN CITY GIRL** *Hacktown 74321348732*	31		1
25 May 96	**MISS PARKER** *Hacktown 74321377292*	35		1
29 Mar 97	**IF I REMEMBER** *Hendricks CDBENZ 1*	59		
9 Aug 97	**ON A SUN-DAY** *Hendricks CDBENZ 2*	73		

BERLIN US group

Date	Title / Label	Peak Position	Weeks at No.1	Weeks in Top 40
25 Oct 86	**TAKE MY BREATH AWAY (LOVE THEME FROM *TOP GUN*)** *CBS A 7320* ● ★	1	4	13
17 Jan 87	**YOU DON'T KNOW** *Mercury MER 237*	39		2
14 Mar 87	**LIKE FLAMES** *Mercury MER 240*	47		
20 Feb 88	**TAKE MY BREATH AWAY (LOVE THEME FROM *TOP GUN*)** *CBS A 7320*	52		
13 Oct 90	**TAKE MY BREATH AWAY (LOVE THEME FROM *TOP GUN*)** *CBS 6563617*	3		8

FRANCESCA BERLIN UK singer

Date	Title / Label	Peak Position	Weeks at No.1	Weeks in Top 40
19 Aug 06	**COLOURS FADED** *Moon MNR001*	60		

ELMER BERNSTEIN US orchestra leader

Date	Title / Label	Peak Position	Weeks at No.1	Weeks in Top 40
18 Dec 59	**STACCATO'S THEME** *Capitol CL 15101*	4		11

LEONARD BERNSTEIN, ORCHESTRA & CHORUS US conductor/orchestra and chorus

Date	Title / Label	Peak Position	Weeks at No.1	Weeks in Top 40
2 Jul 94	**AMERICA - WORLD CUP THEME 1994** *Deutsche Grammophon USACD 1*	44		

BERRI UK singer

Date	Title / Label	Peak Position	Weeks at No.1	Weeks in Top 40
26 Nov 94	**THE SUNSHINE AFTER THE RAIN** *3 Beat TABCD 223* NEW ATLANTIC/U4EA FEATURING BERRI	26		4
2 Sep 95	**THE SUNSHINE AFTER THE RAIN** *ffrreedom TABCD 232* ○	4		9
2 Dec 95	**SHINE LIKE A STAR** *3 Beat TABCD 239*	20		2

LaKIESHA BERRI US singer

Date	Title / Label	Peak Position	Weeks at No.1	Weeks in Top 40
5 Jul 97	**LIKE THIS AND LIKE THAT** *Adept ADPTCD 7*	54		

CHUCK BERRY US singer/guitarist

Date	Title / Label	Peak Position	Weeks at No.1	Weeks in Top 40
21 Jun 57	**SCHOOL DAY** *Columbia DB 3951*	24		4
25 Apr 58	**SWEET LITTLE SIXTEEN** *London HLM 8585*	16		5
11 Jul 63	**GO GO GO** *Pye International 7N 25209*	38		1
10 Oct 63	**LET IT ROCK/MEMPHIS TENNESSEE** *Pye International 7N 25218*	6		10
19 Dec 63	**RUN RUDOLPH RUN** *Pye International 7N 25228*	36		2
13 Feb 64	**NADINE (IS IT YOU)** *Pye International 7N 25236*	27		4
7 May 64	**NO PARTICULAR PLACE TO GO** *Pye International 7N 25242*	3		9
20 Aug 64	**YOU NEVER CAN TELL** *Pye International 7N 25257*	23		7
14 Jan 65	**PROMISED LAND** *Pye International 7N 25285*	26		5
28 Oct 72	**MY DING-A-LING** *Chess 6145 019* ★	1	4	17
3 Feb 73	**REELIN' AND ROCKIN'** *Chess 6145 020*	18		6

DAVE BERRY UK singer

Date	Title / Label	Peak Position	Weeks at No.1	Weeks in Top 40
19 Sep 63	**MEMPHIS TENNESSEE** *Decca F 11734* DAVE BERRY & THE CRUISERS	19		9
9 Jan 64	**MY BABY LEFT ME** *Decca F 11803* DAVE BERRY & THE CRUISERS	37		1
30 Apr 64	**BABY IT'S YOU** *Decca F 11876*	24		5
6 Aug 64	**THE CRYING GAME** *Decca F 11937*	5		11
26 Nov 64	**ONE HEART BETWEEN TWO** *Decca F 12020*	41		
25 Mar 65	**LITTLE THINGS** *Decca F 12103*	5		10
22 Jul 65	**THIS STRANGE EFFECT** *Decca F 12188*	37		5
30 Jun 66	**MAMA** *Decca F 12435*	5		15

MIKE BERRY WITH THE OUTLAWS UK singer

Date	Title / Label	Peak Position	Weeks at No.1	Weeks in Top 40
12 Oct 61	**TRIBUTE TO BUDDY HOLLY** *HMV POP 912* MIKE BERRY WITH THE OUTLAWS	24		5
3 Jan 63	**DON'T YOU THINK IT'S TIME** *HMV POP 1105* MIKE BERRY WITH THE OUTLAWS	6		11
11 Apr 63	**MY LITTLE BABY** *HMV POP 1142* MIKE BERRY WITH THE OUTLAWS	34		5
2 Aug 80	**THE SUNSHINE OF YOUR SMILE** *Polydor 2059 261* ○	9		9
29 Nov 80	**IF I COULD ONLY MAKE YOU CARE** *Polydor POSP 202*	37		4
5 Sep 81	**MEMORIES** *Polydor POSP 287*	55		

NICK BERRY UK actor/singer

Date	Title / Label	Peak Position	Weeks at No.1	Weeks in Top 40
4 Oct 86	**EVERY LOSER WINS** *BBC RESL 204*	1	3	8
13 Jun 92	**HEARTBEAT** *Columbia 6581517*	2		7
31 Oct 92	**LONG LIVE LOVE** *Columbia 6587597*	47		

BEST COMPANY UK duo

Date	Title / Label	Peak Position	Weeks at No.1	Weeks in Top 40
27 Mar 93	**DON'T YOU FORGET ABOUT ME** *ZYX 69468*	65		

BEST SHOT UK group

Date	Title / Label	Peak Position	Weeks at No.1	Weeks in Top 40
5 Feb 94	**UNITED COLOURS** *East West YZ 795CD*	64		

BETA BAND UK group

Date	Title / Label	Peak Position	Weeks at No.1	Weeks in Top 40
14 Jul 01	**BROKE/WON** *Regal Recordings REG 60CDDJ*	30		1
27 Oct 01	**HUMAN BEING** *Regal Recordings REG 65CD*	57		
16 Feb 02	**SQUARES** *Regal Recordings REG 69CD*	42		
24 Apr 04	**ASSESSMENT** *Regal Recordings REG 102CDS*	31		1
24 Jul 04	**OUT-SIDE** *Regal Recordings REG 110CDS*	54		

Silver-selling · Gold-selling · Platinum-selling · US No.1 · Peak Position · Weeks at No.1 · Weeks in Top 40

BEVERLEY SISTERS UK group

Date	Title / Label	Peak Position	Weeks at No.1	Weeks in Top 40
27 Nov 53	**I SAW MOMMY KISSING SANTA CLAUS** *Philips PB 188*	6		5
13 Apr 56	**WILLIE CAN** *Decca F 10705*	23		4
1 Feb 57	**I DREAMED** *Decca F 10832*	24		2
13 Feb 59	**LITTLE DRUMMER BOY** *Decca F 11107*	6		13
20 Nov 59	**LITTLE DONKEY** *Decca F 11172*	14		7
23 Jun 60	**GREEN FIELDS** *Columbia DB 4444*	29		2

BEYOND UK group

Date	Title / Label	Peak Position	Weeks at No.1	Weeks in Top 40
21 Sep 91	**RAGING EP** *Harvest HARS 530*	68		

BG THE PRINCE OF RAP US rapper

Date	Title / Label	Peak Position	Weeks at No.1	Weeks in Top 40
18 Jan 92	**TAKE CONTROL OF THE PARTY** *Columbia 6576330*	71		

BHANGRA KNIGHTS VS HUSAN UK duo

Date	Title / Label	Peak Position	Weeks at No.1	Weeks in Top 40
17 May 03	**HUSAN** *Positiva CDTIV 188*	7		5

BHOYS OF PARADISE UK group

Date	Title / Label	Peak Position	Weeks at No.1	Weeks in Top 40
3 Jul 04	**DIRTY OLD TOWN/THE ROAD TO PARADISE** *Lord Of The Wing LWSP7*	46		

BIBLE UK group

Date	Title / Label	Peak Position	Weeks at No.1	Weeks in Top 40
20 May 89	**GRACELAND** *Chrysalis BIB 4*	51		
26 Aug 89	**HONEY BE GOOD** *Chrysalis BIB 5*	54		

BIDDU ORCHESTRA Indian producer

Date	Title / Label	Peak Position	Weeks at No.1	Weeks in Top 40
2 Aug 75	**SUMMER OF '42** *Epic EPC 3318*	14		7
17 Apr 76	**RAIN FOREST** *Epic EPC 4084*	39		1
11 Feb 78	**JOURNEY TO THE MOON** *Epic EPC 5910*	41		

BIFFY CLYRO UK group

Date	Title / Label	Peak Position	Weeks at No.1	Weeks in Top 40
16 Feb 02	**57** *Beggars Banquet BBQ 358CD*	61		
5 Apr 03	**THE IDEAL HEIGHT** *Beggars Banquet BBQ 365CD*	46		
7 Jun 03	**QUESTIONS AND ANSWERS** *Beggars Banquet BBQ 368CD*	26		1
21 Aug 04	**GLITTER AND TRAUMA** *Beggars Banquet BBQ 377CD*	21		1
2 Oct 04	**MY RECOVERY INJECTION** *Beggars Banquet BBQ 379CD*	24		1
26 Feb 05	**ONLY ONE WORD COMES TO MIND** *Beggars Banquet BBQ384CD*	27		1
17 Mar 07	**SATURDAY SUPERHOUSE** *14th Floor 14FLR19CD*	13		2
19 May 07	**LIVING IS A PROBLEM BECAUSE EVERYTHING DIES** *Warner Brothers 14FLR21CD*	19		2
28 Jul 07	**FOLDING STARS** *14th Floor 14FLR24CD*	18		1
13 Oct 07	**MACHINES** *14th Floor 14FLR27CD*	29		1
9 Feb 08	**WHO'S GOT A MATCH** *14th Floor 14FLR29CD*	27		1

BIG ANG UK producer

Date	Title / Label	Peak Position	Weeks at No.1	Weeks in Top 40
10 Sep 05	**IT'S OVER NOW** *All Around The World CDGLOBE298* BIG ANG FEATURING SIOBHAN	29		2

BIG AUDIO DYNAMITE UK group

Date	Title / Label	Peak Position	Weeks at No.1	Weeks in Top 40
22 Mar 86	**E=MC2** *CBS A 6963*	11		6
7 Jun 86	**MEDICINE SHOW** *CBS 7181*	29		3
18 Oct 86	**C'MON EVERY BEATBOX** *CBS 6501477*	51		
21 Feb 87	**V THIRTEEN** *CBS BAAD 2*	49		
28 May 88	**JUST PLAY MUSIC** *CBS BAAD 4*	51		
12 Nov 94	**LOOKING FOR A SONG** *Columbia 6610182* BIG AUDIO	68		

BIG BAM BOO UK/Canadian duo

Date	Title / Label	Peak Position	Weeks at No.1	Weeks in Top 40
28 Jan 89	**SHOOTING FROM MY HEART** *MCA 1281*	61		

BIG BANG THEORY UK producer

Date	Title / Label	Peak Position	Weeks at No.1	Weeks in Top 40
2 Mar 02	**GOD'S CHILD** *Defected DFECT 45CDS*	51		

BIG BASS VS MICHELLE NARINE Canadian production group and singer

Date	Title / Label	Peak Position	Weeks at No.1	Weeks in Top 40
2 Sep 00	**WHAT YOU DO** *Stonebridge/Edel 0110965 ERE*	67		
6 Jan 07	**WHAT YOU DO (PLAYING WITH STONES) (REMIX)** *Apollo Recordings APOLLO106CDS*	27		2

BIG BEN UK clock

Date	Title / Label	Peak Position	Weeks at No.1	Weeks in Top 40
1 Jan 00	**MILLENNIUM CHIMES** *London BIGONE 2000*	53		

BIG BEN BANJO BAND UK group

Date	Title / Label	Peak Position	Weeks at No.1	Weeks in Top 40
10 Dec 54	**LET'S GET TOGETHER NO. 1** *Columbia DB 3549*	6		4
9 Dec 55	**LET'S GET TOGETHER AGAIN** *Columbia DB 3676*	18		2

BIG BOI US rapper

Date	Title / Label	Peak Position	Weeks at No.1	Weeks in Top 40
10 May 03	**A.D.I.D.A.S.** *Columbia 6738652* KILLER MIKE FEATURING BIG BOI	22		1
16 Jul 05	**GIRLFIGHT** *Virgin VUSDX301* BROOKE VALENTINE FEATURING BIG BOI & LIL' JON	35		1

BIG BOPPER US singer

Date	Title / Label	Peak Position	Weeks at No.1	Weeks in Top 40
26 Dec 58	**CHANTILLY LACE** *Mercury AMT 1002*	12		8

BIG BOSS STYLUS UK production duo

Date	Title / Label	Peak Position	Weeks at No.1	Weeks in Top 40
31 Jul 99	**LET'S GET IT ON** *All Around The World CDGLOBE 195* BIG BOSS STYLUS PRESENTS RED VENOM	72		

BIG BROVAZ UK group

Date	Title / Label	Peak Position	Weeks at No.1	Weeks in Top 40
26 Oct 02	**NU FLOW** *Epic 6730282*	3		13
15 Feb 03	**OK** *Epic 6735212*	7		5
17 May 03	**FAVOURITE THINGS** *Epic 6738075*	2		8
13 Sep 03	**BABY BOY** *Epic 6743092*	4		10
20 Dec 03	**AIN'T WHAT YOU DO** *Epic 6745105*	15		3
17 Apr 04	**WE WANNA THANK YOU (THE THINGS YOU DO)** *Epic 6748602*	17		2
9 Oct 04	**YOURS FATALLY** *Epic 6753542*	15		2
13 May 06	**HANGIN' AROUND** *Genetic GENE500033*	57		

BIG COUNTRY UK group

Date	Title / Label	Peak Position	Weeks at No.1	Weeks in Top 40
26 Feb 83	**FIELDS OF FIRE (400 MILES)** *Mercury COUNT 2*	10		8
28 May 83	**IN A BIG COUNTRY** *Mercury COUNT 3*	17		6
3 Sep 83	**CHANCE** *Mercury COUNT 4*	9		8
21 Jan 84	**WONDERLAND** *Mercury COUNT 5*	8		6
29 Sep 84	**EAST OF EDEN** *Mercury MER 175*	17		4
1 Dec 84	**WHERE THE ROSE IS SOWN** *Mercury MER 185*	29		4
19 Jan 85	**JUST A SHADOW** *Mercury BCO 8*	26		3
12 Apr 86	**LOOK AWAY** *Mercury BIGC 1*	7		7
21 Jun 86	**THE TEACHER** *Mercury BIGC 2*	28		3
20 Sep 86	**ONE GREAT THING** *Mercury BIGC 3*	19		4
29 Nov 86	**HOLD THE HEART** *Mercury BIGC 4*	55		
20 Aug 88	**KING OF EMOTION** *Mercury BIGC 5*	16		4
5 Nov 88	**BROKEN HEART (THIRTEEN VALLEYS)** *Mercury BIGC 6*	47		
4 Feb 89	**PEACE IN OUR TIME** *Mercury BIGC 7*	39		2
12 May 90	**SAVE ME** *Mercury BIGC 8*	41		
21 Jul 90	**HEART OF THE WORLD** *Mercury BIGC 9*	50		
31 Aug 91	**REPUBLICAN PARTY REPTILE (EP)** *Vertigo BIC 1*	37		1
19 Oct 91	**BEAUTIFUL PEOPLE** *Vertigo BIC 2*	72		
13 Mar 93	**ALONE** *Compulsion CDPULSS 4*	24		2
1 May 93	**SHIPS (WHERE WERE YOU)** *Compulsion CDPULSS 6*	29		2
10 Jun 95	**I'M NOT ASHAMED** *Transatlantic TRAX 1009*	69		
9 Sep 95	**YOU DREAMER** *Transatlantic TRAX 1012*	68		
21 Aug 99	**FRAGILE THING** *Track 0004A* BIG COUNTRY FEATURING EDDI READER	69		

BIG DADDY US group

Date	Title / Label	Peak Position	Weeks at No.1	Weeks in Top 40
9 Mar 85	**DANCING IN THE DARK EP** *Making Waves SURF 1033*	21		4

BIG DADDY KANE US rapper

Date	Title / Label	Peak Position	Weeks at No.1	Weeks in Top 40
13 May 89	**RAP SUMMARY/WRATH OF KANE** *Cold Chillin' W 2973*	52		
26 Aug 89	**SMOOTHER OPERATOR** *Cold Chillin' W 2804*	65		
13 Jan 90	**AIN'T NO STOPPIN' US NOW** *Cold Chillin' W 2605*	44		

BIG DISH UK group

Date	Title	Peak Position	Weeks at No.1	Weeks in Top 40
12 Jan 91	**MISS AMERICA** *East West YZ 529*	37		2

BIG FUN UK group

Date	Title	Peak Position	Weeks at No.1	Weeks in Top 40
12 Aug 89	**BLAME IT ON THE BOOGIE** *Jive 217*	4		9
25 Nov 89	**CAN'T SHAKE THE FEELING** *Jive 234*	8		7
17 Mar 90	**HANDFUL OF PROMISES** *Jive 243*	21		4
23 Jun 90	**YOU'VE GOT A FRIEND** *Jive CHILD 90* BIG FUN & SONIA FEATURING GARY BARNACLE	14		5
4 Aug 90	**HEY THERE LONELY GIRL** *Jive 251*	62		

BIG MOUNTAIN US group

Date	Title	Peak Position	Weeks at No.1	Weeks in Top 40
4 Jun 94	**BABY I LOVE YOUR WAY** *RCA 74321198062* ●	2		12
24 Sep 94	**SWEET SENSUAL LOVE** *Giant 74321234642*	51		

BIG RON UK producer

Date	Title	Peak Position	Weeks at No.1	Weeks in Top 40
11 Mar 00	**LET THE FREAK** *48K SPECT 06CDS*	57		

BIG ROOM GIRL UK production duo

Date	Title	Peak Position	Weeks at No.1	Weeks in Top 40
20 Feb 99	**RAISE YOUR HANDS** *VC Recordings VCRD 44* BIG ROOM GIRL FEATURING DARRYL PANDY	40		1

BIG SOUND AUTHORITY UK group

Date	Title	Peak Position	Weeks at No.1	Weeks in Top 40
19 Jan 85	**THIS HOUSE (IS WHERE YOUR LOVE STANDS)** *Source BSA 1*	21		6
8 Jun 85	**A BAD TOWN** *Source BSA 2*	54		

BIG SUPREME UK singer

Date	Title	Peak Position	Weeks at No.1	Weeks in Top 40
20 Sep 86	**DON'T WALK** *Polydor POSP 809*	58		
14 Mar 87	**PLEASE YOURSELF** *Polydor POSP 840*	64		

BIG THREE UK group

Date	Title	Peak Position	Weeks at No.1	Weeks in Top 40
11 Apr 63	**SOME OTHER GUY** *Decca F 11614*	37		2
11 Jul 63	**BY THE WAY** *Decca F 11689*	22		9

BIG TIME CHARLIE UK production duo

Date	Title	Peak Position	Weeks at No.1	Weeks in Top 40
23 Oct 99	**ON THE RUN** *Inferno CDFERN 18*	22		1
18 Mar 00	**MR DEVIL** *Inferno CDFERN 24* BIG TIME CHARLIE FEATURING SOOZY Q	39		1

BIGFELLA UK production duo

Date	Title	Peak Position	Weeks at No.1	Weeks in Top 40
17 Aug 02	**BEAUTIFUL** *NuLife 74321954381* BIGFELLA FEATURING NOEL McCALLA	52		

BARRY BIGGS Jamaican singer

Date	Title	Peak Position	Weeks at No.1	Weeks in Top 40
28 Aug 76	**WORK ALL DAY** *Dynamic DYN 101*	38		2
4 Dec 76	**SIDESHOW** *Dynamic DYN 118* ●	3		14
23 Apr 77	**YOU'RE MY LIFE** *Dynamic DYN 127*	36		3
9 Jul 77	**THREE RING CIRCUS** *Dynamic DYN 128*	22		7
15 Dec 79	**WHAT'S YOUR SIGN GIRL** *Dynamic DYN 150*	55		
20 Jun 81	**WIDE AWAKE IN A DREAM** *Dynamic DYN 10*	44		

IVOR BIGGUN UK comedian/singer

Date	Title	Peak Position	Weeks at No.1	Weeks in Top 40
2 Sep 78	**WINKER'S SONG (MISPRINT)** *Beggars Banquet BOP 1* IVOR BIGGUN & THE RED NOSE BURGLARS	22		8
12 Sep 81	**BRAS ON 45 (FAMILY VERSION)** *Beggars Banquet BOP 6* IVOR BIGGUN & THE D CUPS	50		

BILBO UK group

Date	Title	Peak Position	Weeks at No.1	Weeks in Top 40
26 Aug 78	**SHE'S GONNA WIN** *Lightning LIG 548*	42		

MR ACKER BILK UK clarinettist/singer

Date	Title	Peak Position	Weeks at No.1	Weeks in Top 40
22 Jan 60	**SUMMER SET** *Columbia DB 4382* MR ACKER BILK & HIS PARAMOUNT JAZZ BAND	5		16
9 Jun 60	**GOODNIGHT SWEET PRINCE** *Melodisc MEL 1547* MR ACKER BILK & HIS PARAMOUNT JAZZ BAND	50		
18 Aug 60	**WHITE CLIFFS OF DOVER** *Columbia DB 4492* MR ACKER BILK & HIS PARAMOUNT JAZZ BAND	30		6
8 Dec 60	**BUONA SERA** *Columbia DB 4544* MR ACKER BILK & HIS PARAMOUNT JAZZ BAND	7		15
13 Jul 61	**THAT'S MY HOME** *Columbia DB 4673* MR ACKER BILK & HIS PARAMOUNT JAZZ BAND	7		15
2 Nov 61	**STARS AND STRIPES FOREVER/CREOLE JAZZ** *Columbia SCD 2155* MR ACKER BILK & HIS PARAMOUNT JAZZ BAND	22		10
30 Nov 61	**STRANGER ON THE SHORE** *Columbia DB 4750* MR ACKER BILK WITH THE LEON YOUNG STRING CHORALE ★	2		52
15 Mar 62	**FRANKIE AND JOHNNY** *Columbia DB 4795* MR ACKER BILK & HIS PARAMOUNT JAZZ BAND	42		
26 Jul 62	**GOTTA SEE BABY TONIGHT** *Columbia SCD 2176* MR ACKER BILK & HIS PARAMOUNT JAZZ BAND	24		7
27 Sep 62	**LONELY** *Columbia DB 4897* MR ACKER BILK WITH THE LEON YOUNG STRING CHORALE	14		11
24 Jan 63	**A TASTE OF HONEY** *Columbia DB 4949* MR ACKER BILK WITH THE LEON YOUNG STRING CHORALE	16		8
21 Aug 76	**ARIA** *Pye 7N 45607* ACKER BILK, HIS CLARINET AND STRINGS	5		10

BILL UK singer

Date	Title	Peak Position	Weeks at No.1	Weeks in Top 40
23 Oct 93	**CAR BOOT SALE** *Mercury MINCD 1*	73		

BILL & BEN UK puppet duo

Date	Title	Peak Position	Weeks at No.1	Weeks in Top 40
13 Jul 02	**FLOBBADANCE** *BBC WMSS 60552*	23		2

BILLIAM UK group

Date	Title	Peak Position	Weeks at No.1	Weeks in Top 40
29 Sep 07	**BEAUTIFUL ONES** *Nightingale 2*	32		1

BILLY TALENT Canadian group

Date	Title	Peak Position	Weeks at No.1	Weeks in Top 40
13 Sep 03	**TRY HONESTY** *Atlantic AT 0160CD*	68		
10 Apr 04	**THE EX** *Atlantic AT 0173CD*	61		
17 Jul 04	**RIVER BELOW** *Atlantic AT 0178CD*	70		
24 Jun 06	**DEVIL IN A MIDNIGHT MASS** *Atlantic AT0245CD*	66		
23 Sep 06	**RED FLAG** *Atlantic AT0256CD*	49		

BIMBO JET French group

Date	Title	Peak Position	Weeks at No.1	Weeks in Top 40
26 Jul 75	**EL BIMBO** *EMI 2317*	12		9

BINARY FINARY UK production duo

Date	Title	Peak Position	Weeks at No.1	Weeks in Top 40
10 Oct 98	**1998** *Positiva CDTIV 98*	24		1
28 Aug 99	**1999** *Positiva CDTIV 118*	11		5

UMBERTO BINDI Italian singer

Date	Title	Peak Position	Weeks at No.1	Weeks in Top 40
10 Nov 60	**IL NOSTRO CONCERTO** *Oriole CD 1577*	47		

BINI & MARTINI Italian production duo

Date	Title	Peak Position	Weeks at No.1	Weeks in Top 40
4 Mar 00	**HAPPINESS (MY VISION IS CLEAR)** *Azuli AZNYCDX 113*	53		
10 Mar 01	**BURNING UP** *Azuli AZNY 137*	65		

BIOHAZARD US group

Date	Title	Peak Position	Weeks at No.1	Weeks in Top 40
9 Jul 94	**TALES FROM THE HARD SIDE** *Warner Brothers W0254CD*	47		
20 Aug 94	**HOW IT IS** *Warner Brothers W0259CD*	62		

BIOSPHERE Norwegian instrumentalist

Date	Title	Peak Position	Weeks at No.1	Weeks in Top 40
29 Apr 95	**NOVELTY WAVES** *Apollo 20CDX*	51		

BIRDLAND UK group

Date	Title	Peak Position	Weeks at No.1	Weeks in Top 40
1 Apr 89	**HOLLOW HEART** *Lazy 13*	70		
8 Jul 89	**PARADISE** *Lazy 14*	70		

Platinum-selling ⊛ Gold-selling ● Silver-selling ● US No.1 ★ — Peak Position · Weeks at No.1 · Weeks in Top 40

Date	Title / Label	Peak Position	Weeks at No.1	Weeks in Top 40
3 Feb 90	**SLEEP WITH ME** *Lazy 17*	32		1
22 Sep 90	**ROCK 'N' ROLL NIGGER** *Lazy 20*	47		
2 Feb 91	**EVERYBODY NEEDS SOMEBODY** *Lazy 24*	44		

BIRDS UK group

Date	Title / Label	Peak Position	Weeks at No.1	Weeks in Top 40
27 May 65	**LEAVING HERE** *Decca F 12140*	45		

ZOE BIRKETT UK singer

Date	Title / Label	Peak Position	Weeks at No.1	Weeks in Top 40
25 Jan 03	**TREAT ME LIKE A LADY** *10/Universal 0196832*	12		3

JANE BIRKIN & SERGE GAINSBOURG

UK/French duo

Date	Title / Label	Peak Position	Weeks at No.1	Weeks in Top 40
30 Jul 69	**JE T'AIME...MOI NON PLUS** *Fontana TF 1042*	2		9
4 Oct 69	**JE T'AIME...MOI NON PLUS** *Major Minor MM 645*	1	1	9
7 Dec 74	**JE T'AIME...MOI NON PLUS** *Antic K 11511*	31		7

BIS UK group

Date	Title / Label	Peak Position	Weeks at No.1	Weeks in Top 40
30 Mar 96	**THE SECRET VAMPIRE SOUNDTRACK EP** *Chemikal Underground CHEM 003CD*	25		1
22 Jun 96	**BIS VS THE DIY CORPS (EP)** *Teen-C SKETCH 001CD*	45		
9 Nov 96	**ATOM POWERED ACTION (EP)** *Wiiija WIJ 55CD*	54		
15 Mar 97	**SWEET SHOP AVENGERZ** *Wiiija WIJ 67CD*	46		
10 May 97	**EVERYBODY THINKS THEY'RE GOING TO GET THEIRS** *Wiiija WIJ 69CD*	64		
14 Nov 98	**EURODISCO** *Wiiija WIJ 86CD*	37		1
27 Feb 99	**ACTION AND DRAMA** *Wiiija WIJ 95CD*	50		

BISCUIT BOY UK group

Date	Title / Label	Peak Position	Weeks at No.1	Weeks in Top 40
15 Sep 01	**MITCH** *Mercury 5887592*	75		

ELVIN BISHOP US guitarist

Date	Title / Label	Peak Position	Weeks at No.1	Weeks in Top 40
15 May 76	**FOOLED AROUND AND FELL IN LOVE** *Capricorn 2089 024*	34		2

BIZARRE US rapper

Date	Title / Label	Peak Position	Weeks at No.1	Weeks in Top 40
2 Jul 05	**ROCKSTAR** *Sanctuary Urban SANXS379*	17		2

BIZARRE INC UK production group

Date	Title / Label	Peak Position	Weeks at No.1	Weeks in Top 40
16 Mar 91	**PLAYING WITH KNIVES** *Vinyl Solution STORM 25R*	43		
14 Sep 91	**SUCH A FEELING** *Vinyl Solution STORM 32S*	13		8
23 Nov 91	**PLAYING WITH KNIVES (REMIX)** *Vinyl Solution STORM 38S*	4		6
3 Oct 92	**I'M GONNA GET YOU** *Vinyl Solution STORM 46S* BIZARRE INC FEATURING ANGIE BROWN	3		9
27 Feb 93	**TOOK MY LOVE** *Vinyl Solution STORM 60CD* BIZARRE INC FEATURING ANGIE BROWN	19		3
23 Mar 96	**KEEP THE MUSIC STRONG** *Some Bizzare MERCD 451*	33		1
6 Jul 96	**SURPRISE** *Some Bizzare MERCD 462*	21		2
14 Sep 96	**GET UP SUNSHINE SREET** *Some Bizzare MERCD 471*	45		
13 Mar 99	**PLAYING WITH KNIVES (2ND REMIX)** *Vinyl Solution VC 01CD1*	30		1

BIZZ NIZZ US/Belgian group

Date	Title / Label	Peak Position	Weeks at No.1	Weeks in Top 40
31 Mar 90	**DON'T MISS THE PARTY LINE** *Cooltempo COOL 203*	7		9

BIZZI UK singer

Date	Title / Label	Peak Position	Weeks at No.1	Weeks in Top 40
6 Dec 97	**BIZZI'S PARTY** *Parlophone Rhythm CDRHYTHM 7*	62		

BJORK Icelandic singer

Date	Title / Label	Peak Position	Weeks at No.1	Weeks in Top 40
27 Apr 91	**OOOPS** *ZTT ZANG 19* 808 STATE FEATURING BJORK	42		
19 Jun 93	**HUMAN BEHAVIOUR** *One Little Indian 112 TP7CD*	36		1
4 Sep 93	**VENUS AS A BOY** *One Little Indian 122 TP7CD*	29		2
23 Oct 93	**PLAY DEAD** *Island CID 573* BJORK & DAVID ARNOLD	12		5
4 Dec 93	**BIG TIME SENSUALITY** *One Little Indian 132 TP7CD*	17		6
19 Mar 94	**VIOLENTLY HAPPY** *One Little Indian 142 TP7CD*	13		3
6 May 95	**ARMY OF ME** *One Little Indian 162 TP7CD*	10		3
26 Aug 95	**ISOBEL** *One Little Indian 172 TP7CD*	23		1
25 Nov 95	**IT'S OH SO QUIET** *One Little Indian 182 TP7CD*	4		11
24 Feb 96	**HYPERBALLAD** *One Little Indian 192 TP7CD*	8		2
9 Nov 96	**POSSIBLY MAYBE** *One Little Indian 193 TP7CD*	13		2
1 Mar 97	**I MISS YOU** *One Little Indian 194 TP7CDL*	36		1
20 Dec 97	**BACHELORETTE** *One Little Indian 212 TP7CD*	21		1
17 Oct 98	**HUNTER** *One Little Indian 222 TP7CD*	44		
12 Dec 98	**ALARM CALL** *One Little Indian 232 TP7CDL*	33		1
19 Jun 99	**ALL IS FULL OF LOVE** *One Little Indian 242 TP7CD*	24		1
18 Aug 01	**HIDDEN PLACE** *One Little Indian 332 TP7CD*	21		1
17 Nov 01	**PAGAN POETRY** *One Little Indian 352 TP7CD*	38		1
23 Mar 02	**COCOON** *One Little Indian 322 TP7CD*	35		1
7 Dec 02	**IT'S IN OUR HANDS** *One Little Indian 366 TP7CD*	37		1
30 Oct 04	**WHO IS IT** *One Little Indian 446 TP7CD*	26		1
12 Mar 05	**TRIUMPH OF A HEART** *One Little Indian 447TP7CD2*	31		1

BJORN AGAIN Australian tribute group

Date	Title / Label	Peak Position	Weeks at No.1	Weeks in Top 40
24 Oct 92	**ERASURE-ISH (A LITTLE RESPECT/STOP!)** *M&G MAGS 32*	25		2
12 Dec 92	**SANTA CLAUS IS COMING TO TOWN** *M&G MAGS 35*	55		
27 Nov 93	**FLASHDANCE...WHAT A FEELING** *M&G MAGCD 50*	65		

BK UK producer

Date	Title / Label	Peak Position	Weeks at No.1	Weeks in Top 40
25 Nov 00	**HOOVERS & HORNS** *Nukleuz NUKC 0185* FERGIE & BK	57		
10 Nov 01	**TRAGIC/PLEASE FUNK ME/DON'T GIVE UP** *Nukleuz NUKP*	??		
8 Dec 01	**FLASH** *Nukleuz NUKPA 0361* BK & NICK SENTIENCE	67		
26 Jan 02	**ERECTION (TAKE IT TO THE TOP)** *Nukleuz NUKCD 0352* CORTINA FEATURING BK & MADAM FRICTION	48		
9 Feb 02	**FLASH** *Nukleuz NUKC 0361* BK & NICK SENTIENCE	61		
7 Dec 02	**REVOLUTION** *Nukleuz NUKFB 0437*	42		
16 Aug 03	**KLUB KOLLABORATIONS EP** *Nukleuz 0524 FNUK*	43		
17 Jan 04	**KLUB KOLLABORATIONS EP** *Nukleuz 0524 FNUK*	59		

BLACK UK group

Date	Title / Label	Peak Position	Weeks at No.1	Weeks in Top 40
27 Sep 86	**WONDERFUL LIFE** *Ugly Man JACK 71*	72		
27 Jun 87	**SWEETEST SMILE** *A&M AM 394*	8		7
22 Aug 87	**WONDERFUL LIFE** *A&M AM 402*	8		7
16 Jan 88	**PARADISE** *A&M AM 422*	38		2
24 Sep 88	**THE BIG ONE** *A&M AM 468*	54		
21 Jan 89	**NOW YOU'RE GONE** *A&M AM 491*	66		
4 May 91	**FEEL LIKE CHANGE** *A&M AM 780*	56		
15 Jun 91	**HERE IT COMES AGAIN** *A&M AM 753*	70		
5 Mar 94	**WONDERFUL LIFE** *Polygram TV 5805552*	42		

CILLA BLACK UK singer

Date	Title / Label	Peak Position	Weeks at No.1	Weeks in Top 40
17 Oct 63	**LOVE OF THE LOVED** *Parlophone R 5065*	35		3
6 Feb 64	**ANYONE WHO HAD A HEART** *Parlophone R 5101*	1	3	14
7 May 64	**YOU'RE MY WORLD** *Parlophone R 5133*	1	4	14
6 Aug 64	**IT'S FOR YOU** *Parlophone R 5162*	7		10
14 Jan 65	**YOU'VE LOST THAT LOVIN' FEELIN'** *Parlophone R 5225*	2		9
22 Apr 65	**I'VE BEEN WRONG BEFORE** *Parlophone R 5269*	17		6
13 Jan 66	**LOVE'S JUST A BROKEN HEART** *Parlophone R 5395*	5		9
31 Mar 66	**ALFIE** *Parlophone R 5427*	9		10
9 Jun 66	**DON'T ANSWER ME** *Parlophone R 5463*	6		10
20 Oct 66	**A FOOL AM I** *Parlophone R 5515*	13		9
8 Jun 67	**WHAT GOOD AM I** *Parlophone R 5608*	24		5
29 Nov 67	**I ONLY LIVE TO LOVE YOU** *Parlophone R 5652*	26		7
13 Mar 68	**STEP INSIDE LOVE** *Parlophone R 5674*	8		9
12 Jun 68	**WHERE IS TOMORROW** *Parlophone R 5706*	39		2
12 Feb 69	**SURROUND YOURSELF WITH SORROW** *Parlophone R 5759*	3		9
9 Jul 69	**CONVERSATIONS** *Parlophone R 5785*	7		12
13 Dec 69	**IF I THOUGHT YOU'D EVER CHANGE YOUR MIND** *Parlophone R 5820*	20		7
20 Nov 71	**SOMETHING TELLS ME (SOMETHING IS GONNA HAPPEN TONIGHT)** *Parlophone R 5924*	3		12
2 Feb 74	**BABY WE CAN'T GO WRONG** *EMI 2107*	36		4
18 Sep 93	**THROUGH THE YEARS** *Columbia 6596982*	54		
30 Oct 93	**HEART AND SOUL** *Columbia 6598562* CILLA BLACK WITH DUSTY SPRINGFIELD	75		

FRANK BLACK US singer

Date	Title / Label	Peak Position	Weeks at No.1	Weeks in Top 40
21 May 94	**HEADACHE** *4AD BAD 4007CD*	53		
20 Jan 96	**MEN IN BLACK** *Dragnet 6627862*	37		1
27 Jul 96	**I DON'T WANT TO HURT YOU (EVERY SINGLE TIME)** *Dragnet 6634635*	63		

Key: Silver-selling ○ · Gold-selling ● · Platinum-selling ⊛ · US No.1 ★ · Peak Position · Weeks at No.1 · Weeks in Top 40

JEANNE BLACK *US singer*

Date	Title	Peak Position	Weeks at No.1	Weeks in Top 40
23 Jun 60	**HE'LL HAVE TO STAY** *Capitol CL 15131*	41		

BLACK & WHITE ARMY *UK football supporters' group*

Date	Title	Peak Position	Weeks at No.1	Weeks in Top 40
23 May 98	**BLACK & WHITE ARMY** *Toon 1CD*	26		1

BLACK BOX *Italian production group*

Date	Title	Peak Position	Weeks at No.1	Weeks in Top 40
12 Aug 89	**RIDE ON TIME** *Deconstruction PB 43055* ⊛	1	6	17
17 Feb 90	**I DON'T KNOW ANYBODY ELSE** *Deconstruction PB 43479*	4		7
2 Jun 90	**EVERYBODY EVERYBODY** *Deconstruction PB 43715*	16		3
3 Nov 90	**FANTASY** *Deconstruction PB 43895* ○	5		10
15 Dec 90	**THE TOTAL MIX** *Deconstruction PB 44235*	12		7
6 Apr 91	**STRIKE IT UP/RIDE ON TIME (REMIX)** *Deconstruction PB 44459*	16		5
14 Dec 91	**OPEN YOUR EYES** *Deconstruction PB 45053*	48		
14 Aug 93	**ROCKIN' TO THE MUSIC** *Deconstruction 74321158122*	39		1
24 Jun 95	**NOT ANYONE** *Mercury MERCD 434*	31		1
20 Apr 96	**I GOT THE VIBRATION/A POSITIVE VIBRATION** *Manifesto MERCD 459*	21		2
22 Feb 97	**NATIVE NEW YORKER** *Manifesto FESCD 18*	46		

BLACK BOX RECORDER *UK group*

Date	Title	Peak Position	Weeks at No.1	Weeks in Top 40
22 Apr 00	**THE FACTS OF LIFE** *Nude NUD 48CD1*	20		1
15 Jul 00	**THE ART OF DRIVING** *Nude NUD 51CD1*	53		

BLACK CONNECTION *Italian production group*

Date	Title	Peak Position	Weeks at No.1	Weeks in Top 40
14 Mar 98	**GIVE ME RHYTHM** *Xtravaganza 0091465 EXT*	32		1
24 Oct 98	**I'M GONNA GET YA BABY** *Xtravaganza 0091615 EXT*	62		

BLACK CROWES *US group*

Date	Title	Peak Position	Weeks at No.1	Weeks in Top 40
1 Sep 90	**HARD TO HANDLE** *Def American DEFA 6*	45		
12 Jan 91	**TWICE AS HARD** *Def American DEFA 7*	47		
22 Jun 91	**JEALOUS AGAIN/SHE TALKS TO ANGELS** *Def American DEFA 8*	70		
24 Aug 91	**HARD TO HANDLE** *Def American DEFA 10*	39		1
26 Oct 91	**SEEING THINGS** *Def American DEFA 13*	72		
2 May 92	**REMEDY** *Def American DEFA 16*	24		2
26 Sep 92	**STING ME** *Def American DEFA 21*	42		
28 Nov 92	**HOTEL ILLNESS** *Def American DEFA 23*	47		
11 Feb 95	**HIGH HEAD BLUES/A CONSPIRACY** *American Recordings 74321258492*	25		1
22 Jul 95	**WISER TIME** *American Recordings 74321298272*	34		1
27 Jul 96	**ONE MIRROR TO MANY** *American Recordings 74321398572*	51		
7 Nov 98	**KICKING MY HEART AROUND** *American Recordings 6666665*	55		

BLACK DIAMOND *US singer*

Date	Title	Peak Position	Weeks at No.1	Weeks in Top 40
17 Sep 94	**LET ME BE** *Systematic SYSCD 1*	56		

BLACK DOG *UK producer*

Date	Title	Peak Position	Weeks at No.1	Weeks in Top 40
3 Apr 99	**BABYLON** *warner.esp WESP 006 CD1* BLACK DOG FEATURING OFRA HAZA	65		

BLACK DUCK *UK rapper*

Date	Title	Peak Position	Weeks at No.1	Weeks in Top 40
17 Dec 94	**WHIGGLE IN LINE** *Flying South CDDUCK 1*	33		4

BLACK EYED PEAS *US group*

Date	Title	Peak Position	Weeks at No.1	Weeks in Top 40
10 Oct 98	**JOINTS & JAMS** *Interscope IND 95604*	53		
12 May 01	**REQUEST & LINE** *Interscope 4975032* BLACK EYED PEAS FEATURING MACY GRAY	31		1
13 Sep 03	**WHERE IS THE LOVE** *A&M 9810996* ⊛	1	6	13
13 Dec 03	**SHUT UP** *A&M 9814501* ○	2		10
20 Mar 04	**HEY MAMA** *A&M 9861976*	6		7
10 Jul 04	**LET'S GET IT STARTED** *A&M 9863032*	11		8
28 May 05	**DON'T PHUNK WITH MY HEART** *Interscope 9882331*	3		13
3 Sep 05	**DON'T LIE** *A&M 9884438*	6		7
26 Nov 05	**MY HUMPS** *A&M 9887259*	3		16
18 Mar 06	**PUMP IT** *A&M 9850564*	3		12
24 Jun 06	**MAS QUE NADA** *Concord/UCJ 9859631* SERGIO MENDES & THE BLACK EYED PEAS	6		8

BLACK GORILLA *UK group*

Date	Title	Peak Position	Weeks at No.1	Weeks in Top 40
27 Aug 77	**GIMME DAT BANANA** *Response SR 502*	29		5

BLACK GRAPE *UK group*

Date	Title	Peak Position	Weeks at No.1	Weeks in Top 40
10 Jun 95	**REVEREND BLACK GRAPE** *Radioactive RAXTD 16*	9		3
5 Aug 95	**IN THE NAME OF THE FATHER** *Radioactive RAXTD 19*	8		3
2 Dec 95	**KELLY'S HEROES** *Radioactive RAXDT 22*	17		2
25 May 96	**FAT NECK** *Radioactive RAXTD 24*	10		2
29 Jun 96	**ENGLAND'S IRIE** *Radioactive RAXTD 25* BLACK GRAPE FEATURING JOE STRUMMER & KEITH ALLEN	6		3
1 Nov 97	**GET HIGHER** *Radioactive RAXTD 32*	24		1
7 Mar 98	**MARBLES** *Radioactive RAXTD 33*	46		

BLACK KEYS *US duo*

Date	Title	Peak Position	Weeks at No.1	Weeks in Top 40
11 Sep 04	**10AM AUTOMATIC** *Epitah 11732*	66		
11 Dec 04	**TILL I GET MY WAY/GIRL IS ON MY MIND** *Fat Possum 11832*	62		

BLACK LACE *UK group*

Date	Title	Peak Position	Weeks at No.1	Weeks in Top 40
31 Mar 79	**MARY ANN** *EMI 2919*	42		
24 Sep 83	**SUPERMAN (GIOCA JOUER)** *Flair FLA 105* ○	9		8
30 Jun 84	**AGADOO** *Flair FLA 107* ●	2		18
24 Nov 84	**DO THE CONGA** *Flair FLA 108*	10		7
1 Jun 85	**EL VINO COLLAPSO** *Flair LACE 1*	42		
7 Sep 85	**I SPEAKA DA LINGO** *Flair LACE 2*	49		
7 Dec 85	**HOKEY COKEY** *Flair LACE 3*	31		3
20 Sep 86	**WIG WAM BAM** *Flair LACE 5*	63		
26 Aug 89	**I AM THE MUSIC MAN** *Flair LACE 10*	52		
22 Aug 98	**AGADOO** *Now CDWAG 260*	64		

BLACK LEGEND *Italian group*

Date	Title	Peak Position	Weeks at No.1	Weeks in Top 40
20 May 00	**YOU SEE THE TROUBLE WITH ME (IMPORT)** *Rise RISECD 072*	52		
24 Jun 00	**YOU SEE THE TROUBLE WITH ME** *Eternal WEA 282CD* ○	1	1	8
4 Aug 01	**SOMEBODY** *WEA 328CDX* SHORTIE VS BLACK LEGEND	37		1

BLACK MACHINE *French/Nigerian duo*

Date	Title	Peak Position	Weeks at No.1	Weeks in Top 40
9 Apr 94	**HOW GEE** *London LONCD 348*	17		4

BLACK MAGIC *US producer*

Date	Title	Peak Position	Weeks at No.1	Weeks in Top 40
1 Jun 96	**FREEDOM (MAKE IT FUNKY)** *Positiva CDTIV 51*	41		

BLACK REBEL MOTORCYCLE CLUB *US group*

Date	Title	Peak Position	Weeks at No.1	Weeks in Top 40
2 Feb 02	**LOVE BURNS** *Virgin VUSCD 234*	37		1
1 Jun 02	**SPREAD YOUR LOVE** *Virgin VUSCD 245*	27		1
28 Sep 02	**WHATEVER HAPPENED TO MY ROCK AND ROLL** *Virgin VUSCD 257*	46		
30 Aug 03	**STOP** *Virgin VUSCD 273*	19		1
29 Nov 03	**WE'RE ALL IN LOVE** *Virgin VUSCDX 279*	45		
27 Aug 05	**AIN'T NO EASY WAY** *Echo ECSCX175*	21		1
28 Apr 07	**WEAPON OF CHOICE** *Universal 1732965*	35		1

BLACK RIOT *US producer*

Date	Title	Peak Position	Weeks at No.1	Weeks in Top 40
3 Dec 88	**WARLOCK/A DAY IN THE LIFE** *Champion CHAMP 75*	68		

BLACK ROB *US rapper*

Date	Title	Peak Position	Weeks at No.1	Weeks in Top 40
12 Aug 00	**WHOA** *Puff Daddy 74321782732*	44		
6 Oct 01	**BAD BOY FOR LIFE** *Arista 74321889982* P DIDDY FEATURING BLACK ROB & MARK CURRY	13		5

BLACK ROCK *German duo*

Date	Title	Peak Position	Weeks at No.1	Weeks in Top 40
7 May 05	**BLUE WATER** *Positiva CDTIVS217* BLACK ROCK FEATURING DEBRA ANDREW	36		1

BLACK SABBATH *UK group*

Date	Title	Peak Position	Weeks at No.1	Weeks in Top 40
29 Aug 70	**PARANOID** *Vertigo 6059 010*	4		14
3 Jun 78	**NEVER SAY DIE** *Vertigo SAB 001*	21		6
14 Oct 78	**HARD ROAD** *Vertigo SAB 002*	33		2

Silver-selling · Gold-selling · Platinum-selling · US No.1 ★ · Peak Position · Weeks at No.1 · Weeks in Top 40

Date	Title / Label	Peak Position	Weeks at No.1	Weeks in Top 40
5 Jul 80	**NEON KNIGHTS** *Vertigo SAB 3*	22		6
16 Aug 80	**PARANOID** *Nems BSS 101*	14		9
6 Dec 80	**DIE YOUNG** *Vertigo SAB 4*	41		
7 Nov 81	**MOB RULES** *Vertigo SAB 5*	46		
13 Feb 82	**TURN UP THE NIGHT** *Vertigo SAB 6*	37		2
15 Apr 89	**HEADLESS CROSS** *IRS EIRS 107*	62		
13 Jun 92	**TV CRIMES** *IRS EIRSP 178*	33		1

BLACK SHEEP US duo

Date	Title / Label	Peak Position	Weeks at No.1	Weeks in Top 40
19 Nov 94	**WITHOUT A DOUBT** *Mercury MERCD 417*	60		

BLACK SLATE UK/Jamaican group

Date	Title / Label	Peak Position	Weeks at No.1	Weeks in Top 40
20 Sep 80	**AMIGO** *Ensign ENY 42*	9		7
6 Dec 80	**BOOM BOOM** *Ensign ENY 47*	51		

BLACK UHURU Jamaican group

Date	Title / Label	Peak Position	Weeks at No.1	Weeks in Top 40
8 Sep 84	**WHAT IS LIFE?** *Island IS 150*	56		
31 May 86	**THE GREAT TRAIN ROBBERY** *Real Authentic Sound RAS 7018*	62		

BLACK VELVETS UK group

Date	Title / Label	Peak Position	Weeks at No.1	Weeks in Top 40
26 Mar 05	**3345** *Vertigo 9870472*	34		1
17 Sep 05	**ONCE IN A WHILE** *Vertigo 9873237*	75		

BAND OF THE BLACK WATCH UK bagpipe band

Date	Title / Label	Peak Position	Weeks at No.1	Weeks in Top 40
30 Aug 75	**SCOTCH ON THE ROCKS** *Spark SRL 1128*	8		12
13 Dec 75	**DANCE OF THE CUCKOOS (THE LAUREL AND HARDY THEME)** *Spark SRL 1135*	37		3

TONY BLACKBURN UK radio DJ

Date	Title / Label	Peak Position	Weeks at No.1	Weeks in Top 40
24 Jan 68	**SO MUCH LOVE** *MGM 1375*	31		3
26 Mar 69	**IT'S ONLY LOVE** *MGM 1467*	40		1
5 May 07	**I AM A CIDER DRINKER 2007** *EMI Gold 3926532* WURZELS FEATURING TONY BLACKBURN	57		

BLACKBYRDS US group

Date	Title / Label	Peak Position	Weeks at No.1	Weeks in Top 40
31 May 75	**WALKING IN RHYTHM** *Fantasy FTC 114*	23		5

BLACKFOOT US group

Date	Title / Label	Peak Position	Weeks at No.1	Weeks in Top 40
6 Mar 82	**DRY COUNTY** *Atco K 11686*	43		
18 Jun 83	**SEND ME AN ANGEL** *Atco B 9880*	66		

J BLACKFOOT US singer

Date	Title / Label	Peak Position	Weeks at No.1	Weeks in Top 40
17 Mar 84	**TAXI** *Allegiance ALES 2*	48		

BLACKFOOT SUE UK band

Date	Title / Label	Peak Position	Weeks at No.1	Weeks in Top 40
12 Aug 72	**STANDING IN THE ROAD** *Jam 13*	4		9
16 Dec 72	**SING DON'T SPEAK** *Jam 29*	36		1

BLACKGIRL US trio

Date	Title / Label	Peak Position	Weeks at No.1	Weeks in Top 40
16 Jul 94	**90S GIRL** *RCA 74321217882*	23		2

BLACKNUSS Swedish group

Date	Title / Label	Peak Position	Weeks at No.1	Weeks in Top 40
28 Jun 97	**DINAH** *Arista 74321479762*	56		

BLACKOUT UK production duo

Date	Title / Label	Peak Position	Weeks at No.1	Weeks in Top 40
27 Mar 99	**GOTTA HAVE HOPE** *Multiply CDMULTY 47*	46		
31 Mar 01	**MR DJ** *Independiente ISOM 48MS*	19		3
6 Oct 01	**GET UP** *Independiente ISOM 52MS*	67		

BILL BLACK'S COMBO US bass player

Date	Title / Label	Peak Position	Weeks at No.1	Weeks in Top 40
8 Sep 60	**WHITE SILVER SANDS** *London HLU 9090*	50		
3 Nov 60	**DON'T BE CRUEL** *London HLU 9212*	32		3

BLACKstreet US group

Date	Title / Label	Peak Position	Weeks at No.1	Weeks in Top 40
19 Jun 93	**BABY BE MINE** *MCA MCSTD 1772* BLACKstreet FEATURING TEDDY RILEY	37		1
13 Aug 94	**BOOTI CALL** *Interscope A 8250CD*	56		
11 Feb 95	**U BLOW MY MIND** *Interscope A 8222CD*	39		1
27 May 95	**JOY** *Interscope A 8195CD*	56		
19 Oct 96	**NO DIGGITY** *Interscope IND 95003* BLACKstreet FEATURING DR DRE ★	9		6
8 Mar 97	**GET ME HOME** *Def Jam DEFCD 32* FOXY BROWN FEATURING BLACKstreet	11		3
26 Apr 97	**DON'T LEAVE ME** *Interscope IND 95534*	6		8
27 Sep 97	**FIX** *Interscope IND 97521*	7		3
13 Dec 97	**(MONEY CAN'T) BUY ME LOVE** *Interscope IND 95563*	18		4
27 Jun 98	**THE CITY IS MINE** *Northwestside 74321588012* JAY-Z FEATURING BLACKstreet	38		1
12 Dec 98	**TAKE ME THERE** *Interscope IND 95620* BLACKstreet & MYA FEATURING MASE & BLINKY BLINK	7		7
17 Apr 99	**GIRLFRIEND/BOYFRIEND** *Interscope IND 95640* BLACKstreet FEATURING JANET	11		4
10 Jul 99	**GET READY** *Puff Daddy 74321682612* MASE FEATURING BLACKstreet	32		2
8 Feb 03	**WIZZY WOW** *DreamWorks 4507902*	37		1

BLACKWELLS US group

Date	Title / Label	Peak Position	Weeks at No.1	Weeks in Top 40
18 May 61	**LOVE OR MONEY** *London HLW 9334*	46		

RICHARD BLACKWOOD UK comedian

Date	Title / Label	Peak Position	Weeks at No.1	Weeks in Top 40
17 Jun 00	**MAMA - WHO DA MAN?** *East West MICKY 01CD1*	3		5
16 Sep 00	**1-2-3-4 GET WITH THE WICKED** *East West MICKY 05CD1*	10		4
25 Nov 00	**SOMEONE THERE FOR ME** *Hopefield MICKY 06CD*	23		1

BLAGGERS I.T.A. UK group

Date	Title / Label	Peak Position	Weeks at No.1	Weeks in Top 40
12 Jun 93	**STRESS** *Parlophone CDITA 1*	56		
9 Oct 93	**OXYGEN** *Parlophone CDITA 2*	51		
8 Jan 94	**ABANDON SHIP** *Parlophone CDITA 3*	48		

BLAHZAY BLAHZAY US duo

Date	Title / Label	Peak Position	Weeks at No.1	Weeks in Top 40
2 Mar 96	**DANGER** *Mercury Black Vinyl MBVCD 2*	56		

VIVIAN BLAINE US singer

Date	Title / Label	Peak Position	Weeks at No.1	Weeks in Top 40
10 Jul 53	**BUSHEL AND A PECK** *Brunswick 05100*	12		1

BLAIR UK singer

Date	Title / Label	Peak Position	Weeks at No.1	Weeks in Top 40
2 Sep 95	**HAVE FUN, GO MAD!** *Mercury MERCD 443*	37		1
6 Jan 96	**LIFE** *Mercury MERCD 447*	44		

BLAK TWANG UK singer

Date	Title / Label	Peak Position	Weeks at No.1	Weeks in Top 40
29 Jun 02	**TRIXSTAR** *Bad Magic MAGIC24* BLAK TWANG FEATURING ESTELLE	54		
26 Oct 02	**SO ROTTEN** *Bad Magic MAGICD 25* BLAK TWANG FEATURING JAHMALI	48		

PETER BLAKE UK singer

Date	Title / Label	Peak Position	Weeks at No.1	Weeks in Top 40
8 Oct 77	**LIPSMACKIN' ROCK 'N' ROLLIN'** *Pepper UP 36295*	40		1

BLAME UK production duo

Date	Title / Label	Peak Position	Weeks at No.1	Weeks in Top 40
11 Apr 92	**MUSIC TAKES YOU** *Moving Shadow SHADOW 11*	48		

BLAMELESS UK group

Date	Title / Label	Peak Position	Weeks at No.1	Weeks in Top 40
4 Nov 95	**TOWN CLOWNS** *China WOKCD 2046*	56		
23 Mar 96	**BREATHE (A LITTLE DEEPER)** *China WOKCD 2070*	27		1
1 Jun 96	**SIGNS...** *China WOKCD 2077*	49		

BLANCMANGE UK duo

Date	Title / Label	Peak Position	Weeks at No.1	Weeks in Top 40
17 Apr 82	**GOD'S KITCHEN/I'VE SEEN THE WORD** *London BLANC 1*	65		
31 Jul 82	**FEEL ME** *London BLANC 2*	46		
30 Oct 82	**LIVING ON THE CEILING** *London BLANC 3* (Silver-selling)	7		12
19 Feb 83	**WAVES** *London BLANC 4*	19		7
7 May 83	**BLIND VISION** *London BLANC 5*	10		6
26 Nov 83	**THAT'S LOVE, THAT IS** *London BLANC 6*	33		3
14 Apr 84	**DON'T TELL ME** *London BLANC 7*	8		9
21 Jul 84	**THE DAY BEFORE YOU CAME** *London BLANC 8*	22		6
7 Sep 85	**WHAT'S YOUR PROBLEM?** *London BLANC 9*	40		2
10 May 86	**I CAN SEE IT** *London BLANC 11*	71		

BOBBY BLANCO & MIKKI MOTO US duo

Date	Title / Label	Peak Position	Weeks at No.1	Weeks in Top 40
29 May 04	**3AM** *Defected DFTD088*	70		

BILLY BLAND US singer

Date	Title / Label	Peak Position	Weeks at No.1	Weeks in Top 40
19 May 60	**LET THE LITTLE GIRL DANCE** *London HL 9096*	15		9

BLANK & JONES German production duo

Date	Title / Label	Peak Position	Weeks at No.1	Weeks in Top 40
26 Jun 99	**CREAM** *Deviant DVNT 31CDS*	24		2
27 May 00	**AFTER LOVE** *Nebula NEBCDS 3*	57		
30 Sep 00	**THE NIGHTFLY** *Nebula NEBCDS 010*	55		
3 Mar 01	**BEYOND TIME** *Gang Go/Edel 01245115 GAG*	53		
29 Jun 02	**DJS FANS AND FREAKS** *Incentive CENT 42CDS*	45		

BLAQUE IVORY US group

Date	Title / Label	Peak Position	Weeks at No.1	Weeks in Top 40
3 Jul 99	**808** *Columbia 6674962*	31		1

BLAST Italian group

Date	Title / Label	Peak Position	Weeks at No.1	Weeks in Top 40
18 Jun 94	**CRAYZY MAN** *UMM MCSTD 1982* BLAST FEATURING VDC	22		1
12 Nov 94	**PRINCES OF THE NIGHT** *UMM MCSTD 2011* BLAST FEATURING VDC	40		1

MELANIE BLATT UK singer

Date	Title / Label	Peak Position	Weeks at No.1	Weeks in Top 40
15 Sep 01	**TWENTYFOURSEVEN** *ffrr FCDP 400* ARTFUL DODGER FEATURING MELANIE BLATT	6		5
2 Mar 02	**I'M LEAVIN'** *Rufflife RLCDM 03* OUTSIDAZ FEATURING RAH DIGGA & MELANIE BLATT	41		
6 Sep 03	**DO ME WRONG** *London LONCD 479* MEL BLATT	18		1

BLAZE US group

Date	Title / Label	Peak Position	Weeks at No.1	Weeks in Top 40
10 Mar 01	**MY BEAT** *Black & Blue/Kickin NEOCD 053* BLAZE FEATURING PALMER BROWN	53		
21 Sep 02	**DO YOU REMEMBER HOUSE** *Slip N Slide SLIPCD 151* BLAZE FEATURING PALMER BROWN	55		
14 May 05	**MOST PRECIOUS LOVE** *Defected DFTD100CDS* BLAZE PRESENTS UDA FEATURING BARBARA TUCKER	44		
29 Apr 06	**MOST PRECIOUS LOVE** *Defected DFTD125CDX* BLAZE FEATURING BARBARA TUCKER	17		2

BLAZIN' SQUAD UK group

Date	Title / Label	Peak Position	Weeks at No.1	Weeks in Top 40
31 Aug 02	**CROSSROADS** *East West SQUAD 01CD*	1	1	8
23 Nov 02	**LOVE ON THE LINE** *East West SQUAD 02CD*	6		8
22 Feb 03	**REMINISCE/WHERE THE STORY ENDS** *East West SQUAD 03CD*	8		3
5 Jul 03	**WE JUST BE DREAMIN'** *East West SQUAD 04CD*	3		6
15 Nov 03	**FLIP REVERSE** *East West SQUAD 05CD*	2		6
14 Feb 04	**HERE 4 ONE** *East West SQUAD 06CD*	6		3
21 Oct 06	**ALL NIGHT LONG** *Peach Records PRL106*	54		

BLEACHIN' UK group

Date	Title / Label	Peak Position	Weeks at No.1	Weeks in Top 40
22 Jul 00	**PEAKIN'** *Boiler House! 74321774822*	32		1

BLESSID UNION OF SOULS US group

Date	Title / Label	Peak Position	Weeks at No.1	Weeks in Top 40
27 May 95	**I BELIEVE** *EMI CDEM 374*	29		3
23 Mar 96	**LET ME BE THE ONE** *EMI CDEM 387*	74		

BLESSING UK group

Date	Title / Label	Peak Position	Weeks at No.1	Weeks in Top 40
11 May 91	**HIGHWAY 5** *MCA MCS 1509*	42		
18 Jan 92	**HIGHWAY 5 (REMIX)** *MCA MCS 1603*	30		3
19 Feb 94	**SOUL LOVE** *MCA MCSTD 1940*	73		

MARY J. BLIGE US singer

Date	Title / Label	Peak Position	Weeks at No.1	Weeks in Top 40
28 Nov 92	**REAL LOVE** *Uptown MCSTD 1721*	68		
27 Feb 93	**REMINISCE** *Uptown MCSTD 1731*	31		1
12 Jun 93	**YOU REMIND ME** *Uptown MCSTD 1770*	48		
28 Aug 93	**REAL LOVE (REMIX)** *Uptown MCSTD 1922*	26		3
4 Dec 93	**YOU DON'T HAVE TO WORRY** *Uptown MCSTD 1948*	36		1
14 May 94	**MY LOVE** *Uptown MCSTD 1972*	29		1
10 Dec 94	**BE HAPPY** *Uptown MCSTD 2033*	30		1
15 Apr 95	**I'M GOIN' DOWN** *Uptown MCSTD 2053*	12		3
29 Jul 95	**I'LL BE THERE FOR YOU-YOU'RE ALL I NEED TO GET BY** *Def Jam DEFDX11* METHOD MAN FEATURING MARY J BLIGE	10		3
30 Sep 95	**MARY JANE (ALL NIGHT LONG)** *Uptown MCSTD 2088*	17		3
16 Dec 95	**(YOU MAKE ME FEEL LIKE A) NATURAL WOMAN** *Uptown MCSTD 2108*	23		1
30 Mar 96	**NOT GON' CRY** *Arista 74321358252*	39		1
1 Mar 97	**CAN'T KNOCK THE HUSTLE** *Northwestside 74321447192* JAY-Z FEATURING MARY J BLIGE	30		1
17 May 97	**LOVE IS ALL WE NEED** *Uptown MCSTD 48053*	15		3
16 Aug 97	**EVERYTHING** *MCA MCSTD 48059*	6		6
29 Nov 97	**MISSING YOU** *MCA MCSTD 48071*	19		1
11 Jul 98	**SEVEN DAYS** *MCA MCSTD 48083* MARY J. BLIGE FEATURING GEORGE BENSON	22		1
13 Mar 99	**AS** *Epic 6670122* GEORGE MICHAEL & MARY J BLIGE (Silver-selling)	4		7
21 Aug 99	**ALL THAT I CAN SAY** *MCA MCSTD 40215*	29		1
11 Dec 99	**DEEP INSIDE** *MCA MCSTD 40224*	42		
29 Apr 00	**GIVE ME YOU** *MCA MCSTD 40230*	19		3
16 Dec 00	**911** *Columbia 6706122* WYCLEF FEATURING MARY J BLIGE	9		7
6 Oct 01	**FAMILY AFFAIR** *MCA MCSTD 40267* ★	8		11
9 Feb 02	**DANCE FOR ME** *MCA MCSXD 40274* MARY J BLIGE FEATURING COMMON	13		3
11 May 02	**NO MORE DRAMA** *MCA MCSXD 40281*	9		4
24 Aug 02	**RAINY DAYZ** *MCA MCSXD 40288* MARY J BLIGE FEATURING JA RULE	17		3
27 Sep 03	**LOVE @ 1ST SIGHT** *MCA MCSTD 40338* MARY J BLIGE FEATURING METHOD MAN	18		3
6 Dec 03	**NOT TODAY** *Geffen MCSTD 40349* MARY J BLIGE FEATURING EVE	40		1
20 Dec 03	**WHENEVER I SAY YOUR NAME** *A&M 9815304* STING & MARY J BLIGE	60		
18 Dec 04	**I TRY** *Island MCSTD40390* TALIB KWELI FEATURING MARY J BLIGE	59		
31 Dec 05	**BE WITHOUT YOU** *Geffen MCSTD40445*	32		3
8 Apr 06	**ONE** *Geffen MCSTD40458* MARY J BLIGE & U2	2		10
8 Jul 06	**ENOUGH CRYIN'** *Geffen MCSXD40465* MARY J BLIGE FEATURING BROOK-LYNN	46		
30 Dec 06	**MJB DA MVP** *Geffen 1720304*	33		2
27 Jan 07	**RUNAWAY LOVE** *Def Jam 1723705* LUDACRIS FEATURING MARY J. BLIGE	52		
26 Jan 08	**JUST FINE** *Geffen 1761580*	16		5

BLIND MELON US group

Date	Title / Label	Peak Position	Weeks at No.1	Weeks in Top 40
12 Jun 93	**TONES OF HOME** *Capitol CDCL 687*	62		
11 Dec 93	**NO RAIN** *Capitol CDCL 699*	17		3
9 Jul 94	**CHANGE** *Capitol CDCL 717*	35		1
5 Aug 95	**GALAXIE** *Capitol CDCLS 755*	37		1

BLINK Irish group

Date	Title / Label	Peak Position	Weeks at No.1	Weeks in Top 40
16 Jul 94	**HAPPY DAY** *Lime CDR 6385*	57		

BLINK 182 US group

Date	Title / Label	Peak Position	Weeks at No.1	Weeks in Top 40
2 Oct 99	**WHAT'S MY AGE AGAIN?** *MCA MCSTD 40219*	38		1
25 Mar 00	**ALL THE SMALL THINGS** *MCA MCSTD 40223*	2		8
8 Jul 00	**WHAT'S MY AGE AGAIN?** *MCA MCSZD 40219*	17		2
14 Jul 01	**THE ROCK SHOW** *MCA MCSTD 40259*	14		4
6 Oct 01	**FIRST DATE** *MCA MCSTD 40264*	31		1
6 Dec 03	**FEELING THIS** *Geffen MCSTD 40347*	15		2
13 Mar 04	**I MISS YOU** *Geffen MCSTD 40359*	8		5
3 Jul 04	**DOWN** *Geffen MCSTD 40366*	24		1

Date	Title / Label	Peak Position	Weeks at No.1	Weeks in Top 40
25 Dec 04	**ALWAYS** *Geffen MCSTD 40400*	36		1
10 Dec 05	**NOT NOW** *Geffen MCSTD40440*	30		1

BLOC PARTY UK group

Date	Title / Label	Peak Position	Weeks at No.1	Weeks in Top 40
15 May 04	**BANQUET/STAYING FAT** *Moshi Moshi MOSHI10CD*	51		
24 Jul 04	**LITTLE THOUGHT/TULIPS** *Wichita WEBB067SCD*	38		1
6 Nov 04	**HELICOPTER** *Wichita WEBB070SCD*	26		1
12 Feb 05	**SO HERE WE ARE/POSITIVE TENSION** *Wichita WEBB076SCD*	5		3
7 May 05	**BANQUET** *Wichita WEBB078SCD*	13		1
30 Jul 05	**THE PIONEERS** *Wichita WEBB088SCD*	18		1
15 Oct 05	**TWO MORE YEARS** *Wichita WEBB095SCD*	7		5
3 Feb 07	**THE PRAYER** *Wichita WEBB118SCD*	4		5
14 Apr 07	**I STILL REMEMBER** *Wichita WEBB125SCD*	20		2
21 Jul 07	**HUNTING FOR WITCHES** *Wichita WEBB130SCD*	22		1
24 Nov 07	**FLUX** *Wichita WEBB135SCD*	8		10

BLOCKSTER UK producer

Date	Title / Label	Peak Position	Weeks at No.1	Weeks in Top 40
16 Jan 99	**YOU SHOULD BE...** *Sound Of Ministry MOSCDS 128*	3		6
24 Jul 99	**GROOVELINE** *Sound Of Ministry MOSCDS 131*	18		1

KRISTINE BLOND Danish singer

Date	Title / Label	Peak Position	Weeks at No.1	Weeks in Top 40
11 Apr 98	**LOVE SHY** *Reverb BNOISE 1CD*	22		1
11 Nov 00	**LOVE SHY (REMIX)** *Relentless RELENT 4CDS*	28		1
4 May 02	**YOU MAKE ME GO OOH** *WEA 343CD1*	35		1

BLONDIE US group

Date	Title / Label	Peak Position	Weeks at No.1	Weeks in Top 40
18 Feb 78	**DENIS** *Chrysalis CHS 2204* ●	2		11
6 May 78	**(I'M ALWAYS TOUCHED BY YOUR) PRESENCE DEAR** *Chrysalis CHS 2217*	10		7
26 Aug 78	**PICTURE THIS** *Chrysalis CHS 2242* ○	12		8
11 Nov 78	**HANGING ON THE TELEPHONE** *Chrysalis CHS 2266* ○	5		9
27 Jan 79	**HEART OF GLASS** *Chrysalis CHS 2275* ⊛ ★	1	4	10
19 May 79	**SUNDAY GIRL** *Chrysalis CHS 2320* ●	1	3	10
29 Sep 79	**DREAMING** *Chrysalis CHS 2350* ○	2		7
24 Nov 79	**UNION CITY BLUE** *Chrysalis CHS 2400* ○	13		9
23 Feb 80	**ATOMIC** *Chrysalis CHS 2410* ●	1	2	7
12 Apr 80	**CALL ME** *Chrysalis CHS 2414* ○ ★	1	1	7
8 Nov 80	**THE TIDE IS HIGH** *Chrysalis CHS 2465* ● ★	1	2	10
24 Jan 81	**RAPTURE** *Chrysalis CHS 2485* ○ ★	5		7
8 May 82	**ISLAND OF LOST SOULS** *Chrysalis CHS 2608*	11		8
24 Jul 82	**WAR CHILD** *Chrysalis CHS 2624*	39		1
3 Dec 88	**DENIS (REMIX)** *Chrysalis CHS 3328*	50		
11 Feb 89	**CALL ME (REMIX)** *Chrysalis CHS 3342*	61		
10 Sep 94	**ATOMIC (REMIX)** *Chrysalis CDCHS 5013*	19		3
8 Jul 95	**HEART OF GLASS (REMIX)** *Chrysalis CDCHS 5023*	15		2
28 Oct 95	**UNION CITY BLUE (REMIX)** *Chrysalis CDCHSS 5027*	31		1
13 Feb 99	**MARIA** *Beyond 74321645632* ●	1	1	8
12 Jun 99	**NOTHING IS REAL BUT THE GIRL** *Beyond 74321669472*	26		1
18 Oct 03	**GOOD BOYS** *Epic 6743995*	12		2

NIKKI BLONSKY, ZAC EFRON & AMANDA BYNES US group

Date	Title / Label	Peak Position	Weeks at No.1	Weeks in Top 40
18 Aug 07	**YOU CANT STOP THE BEAT (HAIRSPRAY)** *Download*	71		

BLOOD ARM US group

Date	Title / Label	Peak Position	Weeks at No.1	Weeks in Top 40
11 Jun 05	**SAY YES** *City Rockers ROCKERS29CD*	52		
7 Oct 06	**SUSPICIOUS CHARACTER** *City Rockers ROCKERS34CD*	62		

BLOOD RED SHOES UK duo

Date	Title / Label	Peak Position	Weeks at No.1	Weeks in Top 40
16 Feb 08	**YOU BRING ME DOWN** *V2 1756838*	64		

BLOOD SWEAT & TEARS US group

Date	Title / Label	Peak Position	Weeks at No.1	Weeks in Top 40
30 Apr 69	**YOU'VE MADE ME SO VERY HAPPY** *CBS 4116*	35		2

BLOODHOUND GANG US group

Date	Title / Label	Peak Position	Weeks at No.1	Weeks in Top 40
23 Aug 97	**WHY'S EVERYBODY ALWAYS PICKIN' ON ME?** *Geffen GFSTD 22252*	56		
15 Apr 00	**THE BAD TOUCH** *Geffen 4972682* ●	4		13
2 Sep 00	**THE BALLAD OF CHASEY LAIN** *Geffen 4973822*	15		3
1 Oct 05	**FOXTROT UNIFORM CHARLIE KILO** *Geffen 9885038*	47		

BLOODSTONE US group

Date	Title / Label	Peak Position	Weeks at No.1	Weeks in Top 40
18 Aug 73	**NATURAL HIGH** *Decca F 13382*	40		1

BOBBY BLOOM US singer

Date	Title / Label	Peak Position	Weeks at No.1	Weeks in Top 40
29 Aug 70	**MONTEGO BAY** *Polydor 2058 051*	3		12
9 Jan 71	**HEAVY MAKES YOU HAPPY** *Polydor 2001 122*	31		4

BLOOMSBURY SET UK group

Date	Title / Label	Peak Position	Weeks at No.1	Weeks in Top 40
25 Jun 83	**HANGING AROUND WITH THE BIG BOYS** *Stiletto STL 13*	56		

TANYA BLOUNT US singer

Date	Title / Label	Peak Position	Weeks at No.1	Weeks in Top 40
11 Jun 94	**I'M GONNA MAKE YOU MINE** *Polydor OZCD 315*	69		

KURTIS BLOW US rapper

Date	Title / Label	Peak Position	Weeks at No.1	Weeks in Top 40
15 Dec 79	**CHRISTMAS RAPPIN'** *Mercury BLOW 7*	30		3
11 Oct 80	**THE BREAKS** *Mercury BLOW 8*	47		
16 Mar 85	**PARTY TIME (THE GO-GO EDIT)** *Club JAB 12*	67		
15 Jun 85	**SAVE YOUR LOVE (FOR NUMBER 1)** *Club JAB 14* RENE & ANGELA FEATURING KURTIS BLOW	66		
18 Jan 86	**IF I RULED THE WORLD** *Club JAB 26*	24		5
8 Nov 86	**I'M CHILLIN'** *Club JAB 42*	64		

BLOW MONKEYS UK group

Date	Title / Label	Peak Position	Weeks at No.1	Weeks in Top 40
1 Mar 86	**DIGGING YOUR SCENE** *RCA PB 40599*	12		7
17 May 86	**WICKED WAYS** *RCA MONK 2*	60		
31 Jan 87	**IT DOESN'T HAVE TO BE THIS WAY** *RCA MONK 4*	5		7
28 Mar 87	**OUT WITH HER** *RCA MONK 5*	30		3
30 May 87	**(CELEBRATE) THE DAY AFTER YOU** *RCA MONK 6* BLOW MONKEYS WITH CURTIS MAYFIELD	52		
15 Aug 87	**SOME KIND OF WONDERFUL** *RCA MONK 7*	67		
6 Aug 88	**THIS IS YOUR LIFE** *RCA PB 42149*	70		
8 Apr 89	**THIS IS YOUR LIFE (REMIX)** *RCA PB 42695*	32		3
15 Jul 89	**CHOICE?** *RCA PB 42885* BLOW MONKEYS FEATURING SYLVIA TELLA	22		5
14 Oct 89	**SLAVES NO MORE** *RCA PB 43201* BLOW MONKEYS FEATURING SYLVIA TELLA	73		
26 May 90	**SPRINGTIME FOR THE WORLD** *RCA PB 43623*	69		

BLU PETER UK producer

Date	Title / Label	Peak Position	Weeks at No.1	Weeks in Top 40
21 Mar 98	**TELL ME WHAT YOU WANT/JAMES HAS KITTENS** *React CDREACT 285*	70		

BLUE UK group

Date	Title / Label	Peak Position	Weeks at No.1	Weeks in Top 40
30 Apr 77	**GONNA CAPTURE YOUR HEART** *Rocket ROKN 522*	18		7

BLUE UK group

Date	Title / Label	Peak Position	Weeks at No.1	Weeks in Top 40
2 Jun 01	**ALL RISE** *Innocent SINCD 28* ○	4		11
8 Sep 01	**TOO CLOSE** *Innocent SINCD 30* ○	1	1	8
24 Nov 01	**IF YOU COME BACK** *Innocent SINCD 32* ○	1	1	8
30 Mar 02	**FLY BY II** *Innocent SINCD 33*	6		9
2 Nov 02	**ONE LOVE** *Innocent SINCD 41* ○	3		10
21 Dec 02	**SORRY SEEMS TO BE THE HARDEST WORD** *Innocent SINCD 43* BLUE FEATURING ELTON JOHN ○	1	1	12
29 Mar 03	**U MAKE ME WANNA** *Innocent SINCD 44*	4		6
1 Nov 03	**GUILTY** *Innocent SINCD 51*	2		7
27 Dec 03	**SIGNED SEALED DELIVERED I'M YOURS** *Innocent SINCD 54* BLUE FEATURING STEVIE WONDER & ANGIE STONE	11		6
3 Apr 04	**BREATHE EASY** *Innocent SINDX 58*	4		8
10 Jul 04	**BUBBLIN'** *Innocent SINDX 64*	9		6
20 Nov 04	**CURTAIN FALLS** *Innocent SINDX 67*	4		9

BABBITY BLUE UK singer

Date	Title / Label	Peak Position	Weeks at No.1	Weeks in Top 40
11 Feb 65	**DON'T MAKE ME (FALL IN LOVE WITH YOU)** *Decca F 12053*	48		

BARRY BLUE UK singer

Date	Title / Label	Peak Position	Weeks at No.1	Weeks in Top 40
28 Jul 73	**(DANCING) ON A SATURDAY NIGHT** *Bell 1295* ○	2		12
3 Nov 73	**DO YOU WANNA DANCE** *Bell 1336*	7		11

Date	Title / Label	Peak Position	Weeks at No.1	Weeks in Top 40
2 Mar 74	**SCHOOL LOVE** *Bell 1345*	11		7
3 Aug 74	**MISS HIT AND RUN** *Bell 1364*	26		5
26 Oct 74	**HOT SHOT** *Bell 1379*	23		5

BLUE ADONIS Belgian production group

Date	Title / Label	Peak Position	Weeks at No.1	Weeks in Top 40
17 Oct 98	**DISCO COP** *Serious SERR 002CD* BLUE ADONIS FEATURING LIL' MISS MAX	27		1

BLUE AEROPLANES UK group

Date	Title / Label	Peak Position	Weeks at No.1	Weeks in Top 40
17 Feb 90	**JACKET HANGS** *Ensign ENY 628*	72		
26 May 90	**...AND STONES** *Ensign ENY 632*	63		

BLUE AMAZON UK production duo

Date	Title / Label	Peak Position	Weeks at No.1	Weeks in Top 40
17 May 97	**AND THEN THE RAIN FALLS** *Sony S2 BAS 301 CD*	53		
1 Jul 00	**BREATHE** *Subversive SUB 61D*	73		

BLUE BAMBOO Belgian producer

Date	Title / Label	Peak Position	Weeks at No.1	Weeks in Top 40
3 Dec 94	**ABC AND D...** *Escapade CDJAPE 6*	23		2

BLUE BOY UK producer

Date	Title / Label	Peak Position	Weeks at No.1	Weeks in Top 40
1 Feb 97	**REMEMBER ME** *Pharm CDPHARM 1*	8		12
23 Aug 97	**SANDMAN** *Sidewalk CDSWALK 001*	25		1

BLUE FEATHERS Dutch group

Date	Title / Label	Peak Position	Weeks at No.1	Weeks in Top 40
3 Jul 82	**LET'S FUNK TONIGHT** *Mercury MER 109*	50		

BLUE HAZE UK group

Date	Title / Label	Peak Position	Weeks at No.1	Weeks in Top 40
18 Mar 72	**SMOKE GETS IN YOUR EYES** *A&M AMS 891*	32		3

BLUE MELONS UK group

Date	Title / Label	Peak Position	Weeks at No.1	Weeks in Top 40
8 Jun 96	**DO WAH DIDDY DIDDY** *Fundamental FUNDCD 1*	70		

BLUE MERCEDES UK duo

Date	Title / Label	Peak Position	Weeks at No.1	Weeks in Top 40
10 Oct 87	**I WANT TO BE YOUR PROPERTY** *RCA BONA 1*	23		4
13 Feb 88	**SEE WANT MUST HAVE** *RCA BONA 2*	57		
23 Jul 88	**LOVE IS THE GUN** *RCA BONA 3*	46		

BLUE MINK UK/US group

Date	Title / Label	Peak Position	Weeks at No.1	Weeks in Top 40
15 Nov 69	**MELTING POT** *Philips BF 1818*	3		12
28 Mar 70	**GOOD MORNING FREEDOM** *Philips BF 1838*	10		9
19 Sep 70	**OUR WORLD** *Philips 6006 042*	17		7
29 May 71	**THE BANNER MAN** *Regal Zonophone RZ 3034*	3		13
11 Nov 72	**STAY WITH ME** *Regal Zonophone RZ 3064*	11		11
3 Mar 73	**BY THE DEVIL (I WAS TEMPTED)** *EMI 2007*	26		7
23 Jun 73	**RANDY** *EMI 2028*	9		10

BLUE NILE UK group

Date	Title / Label	Peak Position	Weeks at No.1	Weeks in Top 40
30 Sep 89	**THE DOWNTOWN LIGHTS** *Linn LKS 3*	67		
29 Sep 90	**HEADLIGHTS ON PARADE** *Linn LKS 4*	72		
19 Jan 91	**SATURDAY NIGHT** *Linn LKS 5*	50		
4 Sep 04	**I WOULD NEVER** *Sanctuary SANXD305*	52		

BLUE OYSTER CULT US group

Date	Title / Label	Peak Position	Weeks at No.1	Weeks in Top 40
20 May 78	**(DON'T FEAR) THE REAPER** *CBS 6333*	16		11

BLUE PEARL UK/US group

Date	Title / Label	Peak Position	Weeks at No.1	Weeks in Top 40
7 Jul 90	**NAKED IN THE RAIN** *Big Life BLR 23*	4		11
3 Nov 90	**LITTLE BROTHER** *Big Life BLR 32*	31		3
11 Jan 92	**(CAN YOU) FEEL THE PASSION** *Big Life BLR 67*	14		5
25 Jul 92	**MOTHER DAWN** *Big Life BLR 73*	50		
27 Nov 93	**FIRE OF LOVE** *Logic 74321170292* JUNGLE HIGH WITH BLUE PEARL	71		
4 Jul 98	**NAKED IN THE RAIN (REMIX)** *Malarky MLKD 7*	22		1

BLUE RONDO A LA TURK UK group

Date	Title / Label	Peak Position	Weeks at No.1	Weeks in Top 40
14 Nov 81	**ME AND MR SANCHEZ** *Virgin VS 463*	40		1
13 Mar 82	**KLACTOVEESEDSTEIN** *Diable Noir VS 476*	50		

BLUE ZOO UK group

Date	Title / Label	Peak Position	Weeks at No.1	Weeks in Top 40
12 Jun 82	**I'M YOUR MAN** *Magnet MAG 224*	55		
16 Oct 82	**CRY BOY CRY** *Magnet MAG 234*	13		8
28 May 83	**I JUST CAN'T (FORGIVE AND FORGET)** *Magnet MAG 241*	60		

BLUEBELLS UK group

Date	Title / Label	Peak Position	Weeks at No.1	Weeks in Top 40
12 Mar 83	**CATH/WILL SHE ALWAYS BE WAITING** *London LON 20*	62		
9 Jul 83	**SUGAR BRIDGE (IT WILL STAND)** *London LON 27*	72		
24 Mar 84	**I'M FALLING** *London LON 45*	11		7
23 Jun 84	**YOUNG AT HEART** *London LON 49*	8		9
1 Sep 84	**CATH** *London LON 54*	38		2
9 Feb 85	**ALL I AM (IS LOVING YOU)** *London LON 58*	58		
27 Mar 93	**YOUNG AT HEART** *London LONCD 338*	1	4	10

BLUES BAND UK group

Date	Title / Label	Peak Position	Weeks at No.1	Weeks in Top 40
12 Jul 80	**BLUES BAND (EP)** *Arista BOOT 2*	68		

BLUES BROTHERS US group

Date	Title / Label	Peak Position	Weeks at No.1	Weeks in Top 40
7 Apr 90	**EVERYBODY NEEDS SOMEBODY TO LOVE** *East West A 7591*	12		6

BLUESKINS UK group

Date	Title / Label	Peak Position	Weeks at No.1	Weeks in Top 40
21 Feb 04	**CHANGE MY MIND/I WANNA KNOW** *Domino RUG174CD*	56		
5 Jun 04	**THE STUPID ONES** *Domino RUG 175CD*	61		

BLUETONES UK group

Date	Title / Label	Peak Position	Weeks at No.1	Weeks in Top 40
17 Jun 95	**ARE YOU BLUE OR ARE YOU BLIND?** *Superior Quality BLUE 001CD*	31		1
14 Oct 95	**BLUETONIC** *Superior Quality BLUE 002CD*	19		1
3 Feb 96	**SLIGHT RETURN** *Superior Quality BLUE 003CD*	2		6
11 May 96	**CUT SOME RUG/CASTLE ROCK** *Superior Quality BLUE 005CD*	7		2
28 Sep 96	**MARBLEHEAD JOHNSON** *Superior Quality BLUE 006CD*	7		4
21 Feb 98	**SOLOMON BITES THE WORM** *Superior Quality BLUE 007CD*	10		2
9 May 98	**IF...** *Superior Quality BLUED 009*	13		4
8 Aug 98	**SLEAZY BED TRACK** *Superior Quality BLUED 010*	35		1
4 Mar 00	**KEEP THE HOME FIRES BURNING** *Superior Quality BLUED 012*	13		2
20 May 00	**AUTOPHILIA** *Superior Quality BLUEDD 013*	18		2
6 Apr 02	**AFTER HOURS** *Mercury BLUED 016*	26		1
3 May 03	**FAST BOY/LIQUID LIPS** *Superior Quality BLUE 18CDS*	25		1
23 Aug 03	**NEVER GOING NOWHERE** *Superior Quality BLUE 020CDS2*	40		1
30 Sep 06	**MY NEIGHBOUR'S HOUSE** *Cooking Vinyl FRYCD280*	68		

COLIN BLUNSTONE UK singer

Date	Title / Label	Peak Position	Weeks at No.1	Weeks in Top 40
12 Feb 72	**SAY YOU DON'T MIND** *Epic EPC 7765*	15		7
11 Nov 72	**I DON'T BELIEVE IN MIRACLES** *Epic EPC 8434*	31		3
17 Feb 73	**HOW COULD WE DARE TO BE WRONG** *Epic EPC 1197*	45		
14 Mar 81	**WHAT BECOMES OF THE BROKENHEARTED** *Stiff BROKEN 1* DAVE STEWART, GUEST VOCALS: COLIN BLUNSTONE	13		7
29 May 82	**TRACKS OF MY TEARS** *PRT 7P 236*	60		

JAMES BLUNT UK singer

Date	Title / Label	Peak Position	Weeks at No.1	Weeks in Top 40
19 Mar 05	**WISEMEN** *Atlantic AT0198CD*	44		
11 Jun 05	**YOU'RE BEAUTIFUL** *Atlantic AT0207CD*	1	5	28
8 Oct 05	**HIGH** *Atlantic AT0184CD*	74		
15 Oct 05	**HIGH** *Atlantic AT0222CDX*	16		5
31 Dec 05	**GOODBYE MY LOVER** *Atlantic AT0230CDX*	9		13
18 Mar 06	**WISEMEN** *Atlantic AT0236CD*	23		5
8 Sep 07	**1973** *Atlantic AT0285CDX*	4		10
15 Dec 07	**SAME MISTAKE** *Atlantic AT0294CD2*	57		
29 Mar 08	**CARRY YOU HOME** *Atlantic AT0300CD*	65		

BLUR UK group

Date	Title / Label	Peak Position	Weeks at No.1	Weeks in Top 40
27 Oct 90	**SHE'S SO HIGH/I KNOW** *Food 26*	48		
27 Apr 91	**THERE'S NO OTHER WAY** *Food 29*	8		7
10 Aug 91	**BANG** *Food 31*	24		3
11 Apr 92	**POPSCENE** *Food 37*	32		1
1 May 93	**FOR TOMORROW** *Food CDFOODS 40*	28		3

Silver-selling ○ Gold-selling ● Platinum-selling ⊛ US No.1 ★ — Peak Position / Weeks at No.1 / Weeks in Top 40

Date	Title	Label	Peak Position	Weeks at No.1	Weeks in Top 40
10 Jul 93	CHEMICAL WORLD	Food CDFOODS 45	28		3
16 Oct 93	SUNDAY SUNDAY	Food CDFOODS 46	26		1
19 Mar 94	GIRLS AND BOYS	Food CDFOODS 47	5		5
11 Jun 94	TO THE END	Food CDFOODS 50	16		3
3 Sep 94	PARKLIFE	Food CDFOODS 53	10		4
19 Nov 94	END OF A CENTURY	Food CDFOODS 56	19		2
26 Aug 95	COUNTRY HOUSE	Food CDFOODS 63 ●	1	2	9
9 Sep 95	COUNTRY HOUSE	Food 63	57		
25 Nov 95	THE UNIVERSAL	Food CDFOODS 69 ○	5		7
24 Feb 96	STEREOTYPES	Food CDFOOD 73	7		3
11 May 96	CHARMLESS MAN	Food CDFOOD 77	5		4
1 Feb 97	BEETLEBUM	Food CDFOODS 89	1	1	3
19 Apr 97	SONG 2	Food CDFOODS 93	2		3
28 Jun 97	ON YOUR OWN	Food CDFOOD 98	5		3
27 Sep 97	MOR	Food CDFOOD 107	15		1
6 Mar 99	TENDER	Food CDFOODS 117 ○	2		8
10 Jul 99	COFFEE + TEA	Food CDFOODS 122	11		4
27 Nov 99	NO DISTANCE LEFT TO RUN	Food CDFOOD 123	14		1
28 Oct 00	MUSIC IS MY RADAR	Food CDFOODS 135	10		2
26 Apr 03	OUT OF TIME	Parlophone CDR 6606	5		4
19 Jul 03	CRAZY BEAT	Parlophone CDR 6610	18		1
18 Oct 03	GOOD SONG	Parlophone CDR 6619	22		1

BM DUBS UK production group

Date	Title	Label	Peak Position	Weeks at No.1	Weeks in Top 40
17 Mar 01	WHOOMP THERE IT IS BM DUBS PRESENT MR RUMBLE FEATURING BRASSTOOTH & KEE	Incentive CENT 16CDS	32		1

BMR German producer

Date	Title	Label	Peak Position	Weeks at No.1	Weeks in Top 40
1 May 99	CHECK IT OUT (EVERYBODY) BMR FEATURING FELICIA	AM:PM CDAMPM 120	29		1

BMU US/UK group

Date	Title	Label	Peak Position	Weeks at No.1	Weeks in Top 40
18 Feb 95	U WILL KNOW	Mercury MERCD 420	23		1

BO SELECTA UK comedian

Date	Title	Label	Peak Position	Weeks at No.1	Weeks in Top 40
27 Dec 03	PROPER CRIMBO	BMG 82876581412	4		5

STAN BOARDMAN UK comedian

Date	Title	Label	Peak Position	Weeks at No.1	Weeks in Top 40
10 Jun 06	STAN'S WORLD CUP SONG	Harkit HRKCD8155	15		4

BOB & EARL US duo

Date	Title	Label	Peak Position	Weeks at No.1	Weeks in Top 40
12 Mar 69	HARLEM SHUFFLE	Island WIP 6053	7		12

BOB & MARCIA Jamaican duo

Date	Title	Label	Peak Position	Weeks at No.1	Weeks in Top 40
14 Mar 70	YOUNG GIFTED AND BLACK	Harry J HJ 6605	5		12
5 Jun 71	PIED PIPER	Trojan TR 7818	11		9

BOB THE BUILDER UK animated TV character

Date	Title	Label	Peak Position	Weeks at No.1	Weeks in Top 40
16 Dec 00	CAN WE FIX IT	BBC Music WMSS 60372 ⊛	1	3	11
15 Sep 01	MAMBO NO 5	BBC Music WMSS 60442 ●	1	1	9

BOBBYSOCKS Norwegian/Swedish duo

Date	Title	Label	Peak Position	Weeks at No.1	Weeks in Top 40
25 May 85	LET IT SWING	RCA PB 40127	44		

ANDREA BOCELLI Italian tenor

Date	Title	Label	Peak Position	Weeks at No.1	Weeks in Top 40
24 May 97	TIME TO SAY GOODBYE SARAH BRIGHTMAN/ANDREA BOCELLI ●	Coalition COLA 003CD	2		11
25 Sep 99	CANTO DELLA TERRA	Sugar 5613192	25		2
18 Dec 99	AVE MARIA	Philips 4644852	65		
1 Jul 00	CANTO DELLA TERRA	Sugar 5613192	24		2
3 Nov 07	CON TE PARTIRO	Download	69		

KAREN BODINGTON & MARK WILLIAMS
Australian duo

Date	Title	Label	Peak Position	Weeks at No.1	Weeks in Top 40
2 Sep 89	HOME AND AWAY	First Night SCORE 19	73		

BODY COUNT US group

Date	Title	Label	Peak Position	Weeks at No.1	Weeks in Top 40
8 Oct 94	BORN DEAD	Rhyme Syndicate SYNDG 4	28		1
17 Dec 94	NECESSARY EVIL	Virgin VSCDX 1529	45		

BODYROCKERS UK/Australian duo

Date	Title	Label	Peak Position	Weeks at No.1	Weeks in Top 40
30 Apr 05	I LIKE THE WAY	Mercury 9871115	3		21

BODYROX UK production duo

Date	Title	Label	Peak Position	Weeks at No.1	Weeks in Top 40
14 Oct 06	YEAH YEAH	Eye Industries/UMTV 1702567	45		
4 Nov 06	YEAH YEAH (REMIX) BODYROX FEATURING LUCIANA	Eye Industries/UMTV 1712693	2		14
19 Jan 08	WHAT PLANET YOU ON BODYROX FEATURING LUCIANA	Phonetic 1754549	54		

BODYSNATCHERS UK group

Date	Title	Label	Peak Position	Weeks at No.1	Weeks in Top 40
15 Mar 80	LET'S DO ROCK STEADY	2 Tone CHSTT 9	22		7
19 Jul 80	EASY LIFE	2 Tone CHSTT 12	50		

HAMILTON BOHANNON
US drummer/singer

Date	Title	Label	Peak Position	Weeks at No.1	Weeks in Top 40
15 Feb 75	SOUTH AFRICAN MAN	Brunswick BR 16	22		7
24 May 75	DISCO STOMP	Brunswick BR 19	6		11
5 Jul 75	FOOT STOMPIN' MUSIC	Brunswick BR 21	23		5
6 Sep 75	HAPPY FEELING	Brunswick BR 24	49		
26 Aug 78	LET'S START THE DANCE	Mercury 6167 700	56		
13 Feb 82	LET'S START TO DANCE AGAIN	London HL 10582	49		

BOILING POINT US group

Date	Title	Label	Peak Position	Weeks at No.1	Weeks in Top 40
27 May 78	LET'S GET FUNKTIFIED	Bang 1312	41		

C.J. BOLLAND UK producer

Date	Title	Label	Peak Position	Weeks at No.1	Weeks in Top 40
5 Oct 96	SUGAR IS SWEETER	Internal LIECD 35	11		3
17 May 97	THE PROPHET	ffrr FCD 300	19		1
3 Jul 99	IT AIN'T GONNA BE ME	Essential Recordings ESCDP 5	35		1

MICHAEL BOLTON US singer

Date	Title	Label	Peak Position	Weeks at No.1	Weeks in Top 40
17 Feb 90	HOW AM I SUPPOSED TO LIVE WITHOUT YOU	CBS 6553977 ★	3		8
28 Apr 90	HOW CAN WE BE LOVERS	CBS 6559187	10		8
21 Jul 90	WHEN I'M BACK ON MY FEET AGAIN	CBS 6560777	44		
20 Apr 91	LOVE IS A WONDERFUL THING	Columbia 6567717	23		6
27 Jul 91	TIME LOVE AND TENDERNESS	Columbia 6569897	28		3
9 Nov 91	WHEN A MAN LOVES A WOMAN	Columbia 6574887 ★	8		5
8 Feb 92	STEEL BARS	Columbia 6577257	17		4
9 May 92	MISSING YOU NOW MICHAEL BOLTON FEATURING KENNY G	Columbia 6579917	28		2
31 Oct 92	TO LOVE SOMEBODY	Columbia 6584557	16		5
26 Dec 92	DRIFT AWAY	Columbia 6588657	18		3
13 Mar 93	REACH OUT I'LL BE THERE	Columbia 6588972	37		2
13 Nov 93	SAID I LOVED YOU BUT I LIED	Columbia 6598762	15		5
26 Feb 94	SOUL OF MY SOUL	Columbia 6601772	32		1
14 May 94	LEAN ON ME	Columbia 6604132	14		5
9 Sep 95	CAN I TOUCH YOU...THERE?	Columbia 6624385	6		7
2 Dec 95	A LOVE SO BEAUTIFUL	Columbia 6627092	27		1
16 Mar 96	SOUL PROVIDER	Columbia 6629812	35		1
8 Nov 97	THE BEST OF LOVE/GO THE DISTANCE	Columbia 6652802	14		2

BOMB THE BASS UK group

Date	Title	Label	Peak Position	Weeks at No.1	Weeks in Top 40
20 Feb 88	BEAT DIS	Mister-ron DOOD 1 ○	2		7
27 Aug 88	MEGABLAST/DON'T MAKE ME WAIT BOMB THE BASS FEATURING MERLIN & ANTONIA/BOMB THE BASS FEATURING LORRAINE	Mister-ron DOOD 2	6		8
26 Nov 88	SAY A LITTLE PRAYER BOMB THE BASS FEATURING MAUREEN	Rhythm King DOOD 3	10		8
27 Jul 91	WINTER IN JULY	Rhythm King 6572757	7		8
9 Nov 91	THE AIR YOU BREATHE	Rhythm King 6575387	52		
2 May 92	KEEP GIVING ME LOVE	Rhythm King 6579887	62		
1 Oct 94	BUG POWDER DUST BOMB THE BASS FEATURING JUSTIN WARFIELD	Stoned Heights BRCD 300	24		1
17 Dec 94	DARKHEART BOMB THE BASS FEATURING SPIKEY TEE	Stoned Heights BRCD 305	35		1

Silver-selling ○ · Gold-selling ● · Platinum-selling ⊛ · US No.1 ★ · Peak Position · Weeks at No.1 · Weeks in Top 40

Date	Title / Label	Peak Position	Weeks at No.1	Weeks in Top 40
1 Apr 95	**1 TO 1 RELIGION** *Stoned Heights BRCD 313* BOMB THE BASS FEATURING CARLTON	53		
16 Sep 95	**SANDCASTLES** *Fourth & Broadway BRCD 324* BOMB THE BASS FEATURING BERNARD FOWLER	54		

BOMBALURINA UK group

Date	Title / Label	Peak Position	Weeks at No.1	Weeks in Top 40
28 Jul 90	**ITSY BITSY TEENY WEENY YELLOW POLKA DOT BIKINI** *Carpet CRPT 1* BOMBALURINA FEATURING TIMMY MALLETT ○	1	3	10
24 Nov 90	**SEVEN LITTLE GIRLS SITTING IN THE BACKSEAT** *Carpet CRPT 2*	18		4

BOMBERS Canadian group

Date	Title / Label	Peak Position	Weeks at No.1	Weeks in Top 40
5 May 79	**(EVERYBODY) GET DANCIN'** *Flamingo FM 1*	37		1
18 Aug 79	**LET'S DANCE** *Flamingo FM 4*	58		

BOMFUNK MC'S UK/Finnish group

Date	Title / Label	Peak Position	Weeks at No.1	Weeks in Top 40
5 Aug 00	**FREESTYLER** *Dancepool DPS 2CD*	2		11
2 Dec 00	**UP ROCKING BEATS** *INCredible 6706132*	11		7

B.O.N. German duo

Date	Title / Label	Peak Position	Weeks at No.1	Weeks in Top 40
3 Feb 01	**BOYS** *Epic 6707092*	15		3

BON GARCON UK duo

Date	Title / Label	Peak Position	Weeks at No.1	Weeks in Top 40
18 Jun 05	**FREEK U** *Eye Industries/UMTV 9871395*	42		

BON JOVI US group

Date	Title / Label	Peak Position	Weeks at No.1	Weeks in Top 40
31 Aug 85	**HARDEST PART IS THE NIGHT** *Vertigo VER 22*	68		
9 Aug 86	**YOU GIVE LOVE A BAD NAME** *Vertigo VER 26* ★	14		7
25 Oct 86	**LIVIN' ON A PRAYER** *Vertigo VER 28* ★	4		14
11 Apr 87	**WANTED DEAD OR ALIVE** *Vertigo JOV 1*	13		5
15 Aug 87	**NEVER SAY GOODBYE** *Vertigo JOV 2*	21		4
24 Sep 88	**BAD MEDICINE** *Vertigo JOV 3* ★	17		5
10 Dec 88	**BORN TO BE MY BABY** *Vertigo JOV 4*	22		5
29 Apr 89	**I'LL BE THERE FOR YOU** *Vertigo JOV 5* ★	18		5
26 Aug 89	**LAY YOUR HANDS ON ME** *Vertigo JOV 6*	18		5
9 Dec 89	**LIVING IN SIN** *Vertigo JOV 7*	35		2
4 Aug 90	**BLAZE OF GLORY** *Vertigo JBJ 1* JON BON JOVI ★	13		6
10 Nov 90	**MIRACLE** *Vertigo JBJ 2* JON BON JOVI	29		3
24 Oct 92	**KEEP THE FAITH** *Jambco JOV 8*	5		5
23 Jan 93	**BED OF ROSES** *Jambco JOVCD 9*	13		4
15 May 93	**IN THESE ARMS** *Jambco JOVCD 10*	9		6
7 Aug 93	**I'LL SLEEP WHEN I'M DEAD** *Jambco JOVCD 11*	17		3
2 Oct 93	**I BELIEVE** *Jambco JOVCD 12*	11		3
26 Mar 94	**DRY COUNTY** *Jambco JOVCD 13*	9		4
24 Sep 94	**ALWAYS** *Jambco JOVCD 14*	2		16
17 Dec 94	**PLEASE COME HOME FOR CHRISTMAS** *Jambco JOVCD 16*	7		4
25 Feb 95	**SOMEDAY I'LL BE SATURDAY NIGHT** *Jambco JOVDD 15*	7		4
10 Jun 95	**THIS AIN'T A LOVE SONG** *Mercury JOVCX 17*	6		6
30 Sep 95	**SOMETHING FOR THE PAIN** *Mercury JOVCX 18*	8		5
25 Nov 95	**LIE TO ME** *Mercury JOVCD 19*	10		4
9 Mar 96	**THESE DAYS** *Mercury JOVCD 20*	7		3
6 Jul 96	**HEY GOD** *Mercury JOVCX 21*	13		3
14 Jun 97	**MIDNIGHT IN CHELSEA** *Mercury MERCD 488* JON BON JOVI	4		3
30 Aug 97	**QUEEN OF NEW ORLEANS** *Mercury MERCD 493* JON BON JOVI	10		2
15 Nov 97	**JANIE, DON'T TAKE YOUR LOVE TO TOWN** *Mercury 5749872* JON BON JOVI	13		2
10 Apr 99	**REAL LIFE** *Reprise W 479CD*	21		2
3 Jun 00	**IT'S MY LIFE** *Mercury 5627682*	3		9
9 Sep 00	**SAY IT ISN'T SO** *Mercury 5688982*	10		2
9 Dec 00	**THANK YOU FOR LOVING ME** *Mercury 5727312*	12		4
19 May 01	**ONE WILD NIGHT** *Mercury 5729502*	10		2
28 Sep 02	**EVERYDAY** *Mercury 0639372*	5		3
21 Dec 02	**MISUNDERSTOOD** *Mercury 0638162*	21		1
24 May 03	**ALL ABOUT LOVIN' YOU** *Mercury 9800242*	9		3
24 Sep 05	**HAVE A NICE DAY** *Mercury 9885841*	6		3
11 Feb 06	**WELCOME TO WHEREVER YOU ARE** *Mercury 9879526*	19		1
24 Jun 06	**WHO SAYS YOU CAN'T GO HOME** *Mercury 9858248*	5		2
7 Jul 07	**(YOU WANT TO) MAKE A MEMORY** *Mercury 1737482*	33		1
22 Mar 08	**LIVIN' ON A PRAYER** *Download*	70		

RONNIE BOND UK singer/drummer

Date	Title / Label	Peak Position	Weeks at No.1	Weeks in Top 40
31 May 80	**IT'S WRITTEN ON YOUR BODY** *Mercury MER 13*	52		

BONDE DO ROLE Brazilian group

Date	Title / Label	Peak Position	Weeks at No.1	Weeks in Top 40
2 Jun 07	**OFFICE BOY** *Domino RUG255CD*	75		

GARY U.S. BONDS US singer

Date	Title / Label	Peak Position	Weeks at No.1	Weeks in Top 40
19 Jan 61	**NEW ORLEANS** *Top Rank JAR 527* U.S. BONDS	16		9
20 Jul 61	**QUARTER TO THREE** *Top Rank JAR 575* ★ U.S. BONDS	7		11
30 May 81	**THIS LITTLE GIRL** *EMI America EA 122*	43		
22 Aug 81	**JOLE BLON** *EMI America EA 127*	51		
31 Oct 81	**IT'S ONLY LOVE** *EMI America EA 128*	43		
17 Jul 82	**SOUL DEEP** *EMI America EA 140*	59		

BONE UK duo

Date	Title / Label	Peak Position	Weeks at No.1	Weeks in Top 40
2 Apr 94	**WINGS OF LOVE** *Deconstruction 74321176282*	55		

BONE THUGS-N-HARMONY US group

Date	Title / Label	Peak Position	Weeks at No.1	Weeks in Top 40
4 Nov 95	**1ST OF THA MONTH** *Epic 6625172*	32		1
10 Aug 96	**THA CROSSROADS** *Epic 6635502* ★	8		9
9 Nov 96	**1ST OF THA MONTH** *Epic 6638505*	15		2
15 Feb 97	**DAYS OF OUR LIVEZ** *East West A 3982CD*	37		1
26 Jul 97	**LOOK INTO MY EYES** *Epic 6647862*	16		2
24 May 03	**HOME** *Epic 6738305* BONE THUGS-N-HARMONY FEATURING PHIL COLLINS	19		2
2 Jun 07	**I TRIED** *Download* BONE THUGS-N-HARMONY FEATURING AKON	69		

ELBOW BONES & THE RACKETEERS US group

Date	Title / Label	Peak Position	Weeks at No.1	Weeks in Top 40
14 Jan 84	**A NIGHT IN NEW YORK** *EMI America EA 165*	33		5

BONEY M Jamaican/Antilles/Montserrat group

Date	Title / Label	Peak Position	Weeks at No.1	Weeks in Top 40
18 Dec 76	**DADDY COOL** *Atlantic K 10827* ○	6		12
12 Mar 77	**SUNNY** *Atlantic K 10892*	3		9
25 Jun 77	**MA BAKER** *Atlantic K 10965*	2		13
29 Oct 77	**BELFAST** *Atlantic K 11020*	8		12
29 Apr 78	**RIVERS OF BABYLON/BROWN GIRL IN THE RING** *Atlantic/Hansa K 11120* ⊛	1	5	26
7 Oct 78	**RASPUTIN** *Atlantic/Hansa K 11192* ●	2		8
2 Dec 78	**MARY'S BOY CHILD - OH MY LORD** *Atlantic/Hansa K 11221* ⊛	1	4	8
3 Mar 79	**PAINTER MAN** *Atlantic/Hansa K 11255* ○	10		5
28 Apr 79	**HOORAY HOORAY IT'S A HOLI-HOLIDAY** *Atlantic/Hansa K 11279* ○	3		7
11 Aug 79	**GOTTA GO HOME/EL LUTE** *Atlantic/Hansa K 11351* ○	12		10
15 Dec 79	**I'M BORN AGAIN** *Atlantic/Hansa K 11410*	35		4
26 Apr 80	**MY FRIEND JACK** *Atlantic/Hansa K 11463*	57		
14 Feb 81	**CHILDREN OF PARADISE** *Atlantic/Hansa K 11637*	66		
21 Nov 81	**WE KILL THE WORLD (DON'T KILL THE WORLD)** *Atlantic/Hansa K 11689*	39		3
24 Dec 88	**MEGAMIX/MARY'S BOY CHILD (REMIX)** *Ariola 111947*	52		
5 Dec 92	**BONEY M MEGAMIX** *Arista 74321125127*	7		7
17 Apr 93	**BROWN GIRL IN THE RING (REMIX)** *Arista 74321137052*	38		1
8 May 99	**MA BAKER - SOMEBODY SCREAM** *Logic 74321653872* BONEY M VS HORNY UNITED	22		1
29 Dec 01	**DADDY COOL 2001** *BMG 74321913512*	47		
22 Dec 07	**MARY'S BOY CHILD - OH MY LORD** *Download*	47		

BONIFACE UK singer

Date	Title / Label	Peak Position	Weeks at No.1	Weeks in Top 40
31 Aug 02	**CHEEKY** *Columbia 6729902*	25		1

GRAHAM BONNET UK singer

Date	Title / Label	Peak Position	Weeks at No.1	Weeks in Top 40
21 Mar 81	**NIGHT GAMES** *Vertigo VER 1* ○	6		8
13 Jun 81	**LIAR** *Vertigo VER 2*	51		

GRAHAM BONNEY UK singer

Date	Title / Label	Peak Position	Weeks at No.1	Weeks in Top 40
24 Mar 66	**SUPERGIRL** *Columbia DB 7843*	19		7

Silver-selling ○ Gold-selling ● Platinum-selling ⊛ US No.1 ★ | Peak Position | Weeks at No.1 | Weeks in Top 40

BONNIE PRINCE BILLY US singer

Date	Title / Label	Peak Position	Weeks at No.1	Weeks in Top 40
4 Sep 04	AGNES QUEEN OF SORROW *Domino RUG185CD*	69		

BONO Irish singer

Date	Title / Label	Peak Position	Weeks at No.1	Weeks in Top 40
25 Jan 86	IN A LIFETIME *RCA PB 40535* CLANNAD FEATURING BONO	20		4
10 Jun 89	IN A LIFETIME *RCA PB 42873* CLANNAD FEATURING BONO	17		5
4 Dec 93	I'VE GOT YOU UNDER MY SKIN *Island CID 578* FRANK SINATRA WITH BONO	4		6
9 Apr 94	IN THE NAME OF THE FATHER *Island CID 593* BONO & GAVIN FRIDAY	46		
23 Oct 99	NEW DAY *Columbia 6682122* WYCLEF JEAN FEATURING BONO	23		1

BONZO DOG DOO-DAH BAND UK group

Date	Title / Label	Peak Position	Weeks at No.1	Weeks in Top 40
6 Nov 68	I'M THE URBAN SPACEMAN *Liberty LBF 15144*	5		12

BETTY BOO UK rapper

Date	Title / Label	Peak Position	Weeks at No.1	Weeks in Top 40
12 Aug 89	HEY DJ I CAN'T DANCE TO THAT MUSIC YOU'RE PLAYING/ SKA TRAIN *Rhythm King LEFT 34* BEATMASTERS FEATURING BETTY BOO	7		9
19 May 90	DOIN' THE DO *Rhythm King LEFT 39*	7		10
11 Aug 90	WHERE ARE YOU BABY *Rhythm King LEFT 43* ○	3		9
1 Dec 90	24 HOURS *Rhythm King LEFT 45*	25		6
8 Aug 92	LET ME TAKE YOU THERE *WEA YZ 677*	12		6
3 Oct 92	I'M ON MY WAY *WEA YZ 693*	44		
10 Apr 93	HANGOVER *WEA YZ 719CD*	50		

BOO RADLEYS UK group

Date	Title / Label	Peak Position	Weeks at No.1	Weeks in Top 40
20 Jun 92	DOES THIS HURT/BOO! FOREVER *Creation CRE 128*	67		
23 Oct 93	WISH I WAS SKINNY *Creation CRESCD 169*	75		
12 Feb 94	BARNEY (...& ME) *Creation CRESCD 178*	48		
11 Jun 94	LAZARUS *Creation CRESCD 187*	50		
11 Mar 95	WAKE UP BOO! *Creation CRESCD 191*	9		6
13 May 95	FIND THE ANSWER WITHIN *Creation CRESCD 202*	37		1
29 Jul 95	IT'S LULU *Creation CRESCD 211*	25		1
7 Oct 95	FROM THE BENCH AT BELVIDERE *Creation CRESCD 214*	24		1
17 Aug 96	WHAT'S IN THE BOX? (SEE WHATCHA GOT) *Creation CRESCD 220*	25		1
19 Oct 96	C'MON KIDS *Creation CRESCD 236*	18		1
1 Feb 97	RIDE THE TIGER *Creation CRESCD 248X*	38		1
17 Oct 98	FREE HUEY *Creation CRESCD 299X*	54		

BOO-YAA T.R.I.B.E. US group

Date	Title / Label	Peak Position	Weeks at No.1	Weeks in Top 40
30 Jun 90	PSYKO FUNK *Fourth & Broadway BRW 179*	43		
6 Nov 93	ANOTHER BODY MURDERED *Epic 6597942* FAITH NO MORE & BOO-YAA T.R.I.B.E.	26		2

BOOGIE BOX HIGH UK group

Date	Title / Label	Peak Position	Weeks at No.1	Weeks in Top 40
4 Jul 87	JIVE TALKIN' *Hardback 7BOSS 4*	7		8

BOOGIE DOWN PRODUCTIONS US duo

Date	Title / Label	Peak Position	Weeks at No.1	Weeks in Top 40
4 Jun 88	MY PHILOSOPHY/STOP THE VIOLENCE *Jive JIVEX 170*	69		

BOOGIE PIMPS German production duo

Date	Title / Label	Peak Position	Weeks at No.1	Weeks in Top 40
17 Jan 04	SOMEBODY TO LOVE *Data 61CDS*	3		13
8 May 04	SUNNY *Data 67CDX*	10		4

BOOKER T. & THE M.G.s US group

Date	Title / Label	Peak Position	Weeks at No.1	Weeks in Top 40
11 Dec 68	SOUL LIMBO *Stax 102*	30		5
7 May 69	TIME IS TIGHT *Stax 119*	4		16
30 Aug 69	SOUL CLAP '69 *Stax 127*	35		3
15 Dec 79	GREEN ONIONS *Atlantic K 10109* ○	7		8

BOOM! UK group

Date	Title / Label	Peak Position	Weeks at No.1	Weeks in Top 40
27 Jan 01	FALLING *London LONCD 458*	11		3

TAKA BOOM US singer

Date	Title / Label	Peak Position	Weeks at No.1	Weeks in Top 40
19 Feb 00	MUST BE THE MUSIC *Incentive CENT 4CDS* JOEY NEGRO FEATURING TAKA BOOM	8		3
16 Sep 00	SATURDAY *Yola CDX03* JOEY NEGRO FEATURING TAKA BOOM	41		
9 Jun 01	JUST CAN'T GET ENOUGH (NO NO NO NO) *Xtravaganza XTRAV 25CD* EYE TO EYE FEATURING TAKA BOOM	36		1

BOOM BOOM ROOM UK group

Date	Title / Label	Peak Position	Weeks at No.1	Weeks in Top 40
8 Mar 86	HERE COMES THE MAN *Fun After All FUN 101*	74		

BOOMKAT US duo

Date	Title / Label	Peak Position	Weeks at No.1	Weeks in Top 40
31 May 03	THE WRECKONING *DreamWorks 4504580*	37		1

BOOMTOWN RATS Irish group

Date	Title / Label	Peak Position	Weeks at No.1	Weeks in Top 40
27 Aug 77	LOOKING AFTER NO. 1 *Ensign ENY 4*	11		8
19 Nov 77	MARY OF THE FOURTH FORM *Ensign ENY 9*	15		8
15 Apr 78	SHE'S SO MODERN *Ensign ENY 13*	12		9
17 Jun 78	LIKE CLOCKWORK *Ensign ENY 14* ○	6		10
14 Oct 78	RAT TRAP *Ensign ENY 16* ●	1	2	13
21 Jul 79	I DON'T LIKE MONDAYS *Ensign ENY 30* ●	1	4	10
17 Nov 79	DIAMOND SMILES *Ensign ENY 33*	13		7
26 Jan 80	SOMEONE'S LOOKING AT YOU *Ensign ENY 34*	4		6
22 Nov 80	BANANA REPUBLIC *Ensign BONGO 1* ○	3		9
31 Jan 81	THE ELEPHANT'S GRAVEYARD (GUILTY) *Ensign BONGO 2*	26		4
12 Dec 81	NEVER IN A MILLION YEARS *Mercury MER 87*	62		
20 Mar 82	HOUSE ON FIRE *Mercury MER 91*	24		4
18 Feb 84	TONIGHT *Mercury MER 154*	73		
19 May 84	DRAG ME DOWN *Mercury MER 163*	50		
2 Jul 94	I DON'T LIKE MONDAYS *Vertigo VERCD 87*	38		1

CLINT BOON EXPERIENCE UK group

Date	Title / Label	Peak Position	Weeks at No.1	Weeks in Top 40
6 Nov 99	WHITE NO SUGAR *Artful CDARTFUL 32*	61		
5 Feb 00	BIGGEST HORIZON *Artful CDARTFUL 33*	70		
5 Aug 00	DO WHAT YOU DO (EARWORM SONG) *Artful CDARTFUL 34*	63		

DANIEL BOONE UK singer

Date	Title / Label	Peak Position	Weeks at No.1	Weeks in Top 40
14 Aug 71	DADDY DON'T YOU WALK SO FAST *Penny Farthing PEN 764*	17		12
1 Apr 72	BEAUTIFUL SUNDAY *Penny Farthing PEN 781*	21		9

DEBBY BOONE US singer

Date	Title / Label	Peak Position	Weeks at No.1	Weeks in Top 40
24 Dec 77	YOU LIGHT UP MY LIFE *Warner Brothers K 17043* ★	48		

PAT BOONE US singer

Date	Title / Label	Peak Position	Weeks at No.1	Weeks in Top 40
18 Nov 55	AIN'T THAT A SHAME *London HLD 8172*	7		9
27 Apr 56	I'LL BE HOME *London HLD 8253*	1	5	22
27 Jul 56	LONG TALL SALLY *London HLD 8291*	18		7
17 Aug 56	I ALMOST LOST MY MIND *London HLD 8303* ★	14		7
7 Dec 56	FRIENDLY PERSUASION *London HLD 8346*	3		21
11 Jan 57	AIN'T THAT A SHAME *London HLD 8172* ★	22		2
11 Jan 57	I'LL BE HOME *London HLD 8253*	19		2
1 Feb 57	DON'T FORBID ME *London HLD 8370* ★	2		16
26 Apr 57	WHY BABY WHY *London HLD 8404*	17		7
5 Jul 57	LOVE LETTERS IN THE SAND *London HLD 8445* ★	2		21
27 Sep 57	REMEMBER YOU'RE MINE/THERE'S A GOLDMINE IN THE SKY *London HLD 8479*	5		18
6 Dec 57	APRIL LOVE *London HLD 8512* ★	7		23
13 Dec 57	WHITE CHRISTMAS *London HLD 8520*	29		1
4 Apr 58	A WONDERFUL TIME UP THERE *London HLD 8574*	2		17
11 Apr 58	IT'S TOO SOON TO KNOW *London HLD 8574*	7		12
27 Jun 58	SUGAR MOON *London HLD 8640*	6		12
29 Aug 58	IF DREAMS CAME TRUE *London HLD 8675*	16		11
5 Dec 58	GEE BUT IT'S LONELY *London HLD 8739*	30		1
6 Feb 59	I'LL REMEMBER TONIGHT *London HLD 8775*	18		9
10 Apr 59	WITH THE WIND AND THE RAIN IN YOUR HAIR *London HLD 8824*	21		3
22 May 59	FOR A PENNY *London HLD 8855*	19		9
31 Jul 59	'TWIXT TWELVE AND TWENTY *London HLD 8910*	18		7
23 Jun 60	WALKING THE FLOOR OVER YOU *London HLD 9138*	39		2
6 Jul 61	MOODY RIVER *London HLD 9350* ★	18		10
7 Dec 61	JOHNNY WILL *London HLD 9461*	4		11
15 Feb 62	I'LL SEE YOU IN MY DREAMS *London HLD 9504*	27		8

Date	Title	Label	Peak Position	Weeks at No.1	Weeks in Top 40
24 May 62	QUANDO QUANDO QUANDO	London HLD 9543	41		
12 Jul 62	SPEEDY GONZALES	London HLD 9573	2		15
15 Nov 62	THE MAIN ATTRACTION	London HLD 9620	12		9

BOOTH & THE BAD ANGEL UK/US duo

Date	Title	Label	Peak Position	Weeks at No.1	Weeks in Top 40
22 Jun 96	I BELIEVE	Fontana BBDD 1	25		1
11 Jul 98	FALL IN LOVE WITH ME	Mercury MERCD 503	57		

TIM BOOTH UK singer

Date	Title	Label	Peak Position	Weeks at No.1	Weeks in Top 40
10 Jul 04	DOWN TO THE SEA	Sanctuary SANXS279	68		

KEN BOOTHE Jamaican singer

Date	Title	Label	Peak Position	Weeks at No.1	Weeks in Top 40
21 Sep 74	EVERYTHING I OWN	Trojan TR 7920	1	3	11
14 Dec 74	CRYING OVER YOU	Trojan TR 7944	11		6

BOOTHILL FOOT-TAPPERS UK group

Date	Title	Label	Peak Position	Weeks at No.1	Weeks in Top 40
14 Jul 84	GET YOUR FEET OUT OF MY SHOES	Go! Discs TAP 1	64		

BOOTSY'S RUBBER BAND US group

Date	Title	Label	Peak Position	Weeks at No.1	Weeks in Top 40
8 Jul 78	BOOTZILLA	Warner Brothers K 17196	43		

BOOTY LUV UK production group

Date	Title	Label	Peak Position	Weeks at No.1	Weeks in Top 40
2 Dec 06	BOOGIE 2NITE	Hed Kandi HK27CDS	3		16
19 May 07	SHINE	Hed Kandi HK33CDX	10		7
15 Sep 07	DON'T MESS WITH MY MAN	Hed Kandi HK38CDS	11		4
8 Dec 07	SOME KINDA RUSH	Data HK46CDX	19		7

BOSS US producer

Date	Title	Label	Peak Position	Weeks at No.1	Weeks in Top 40
27 Aug 94	CONGO	Cooltempo CDCOOL 296	54		

NAILA BOSS UK singer

Date	Title	Label	Peak Position	Weeks at No.1	Weeks in Top 40
22 May 04	IT CAN'T BE RIGHT 2PLAY FEATURING RAGHAV & NAILA BOSS	2PSL/inferno 2PSLCD04	8		4
10 Jul 04	LA LA LA	La Boss NBCD1	65		
11 Sep 04	YOU SHOULD READILY KNOW PIRATES FEATURING ENYA, SHOLA AMA, NAILA BOSS & ISHANI	Relentless RELCD9	8		6

BOSTON US group

Date	Title	Label	Peak Position	Weeks at No.1	Weeks in Top 40
29 Jan 77	MORE THAN A FEELING	Epic EPC 4658	22		7
7 Oct 78	DON'T LOOK BACK	Epic EPC 6653	43		

EVE BOSWELL Hungarian singer

Date	Title	Label	Peak Position	Weeks at No.1	Weeks in Top 40
30 Dec 55	PICKIN' A CHICKEN	Parlophone R 4082	9		13

JUDY BOUCHER UK singer

Date	Title	Label	Peak Position	Weeks at No.1	Weeks in Top 40
4 Apr 87	CAN'T BE WITH YOU TONIGHT	Orbitone OR 721	2		12
4 Jul 87	YOU CAUGHT MY EYE	Orbitone OR 722	18		4

BOUNCING CZECKS UK group

Date	Title	Label	Peak Position	Weeks at No.1	Weeks in Top 40
29 Dec 84	I'M A LITTLE CHRISTMAS CRACKER	RCA 463	72		

BOUNTY KILLER Jamaican rapper

Date	Title	Label	Peak Position	Weeks at No.1	Weeks in Top 40
27 Feb 99	IT'S A PARTY	Edel 0066135 BLA	65		

BOURGEOIS TAGG US group

Date	Title	Label	Peak Position	Weeks at No.1	Weeks in Top 40
6 Feb 88	I DON'T MIND AT ALL	Island IS 353	35		2

BOURGIE BOURGIE UK group

Date	Title	Label	Peak Position	Weeks at No.1	Weeks in Top 40
3 Mar 84	BREAKING POINT	MCA BOU 1	48		

TOBY BOURKE UK singer

Date	Title	Label	Peak Position	Weeks at No.1	Weeks in Top 40
7 Jun 97	WALTZ AWAY DREAMING TOBY BOURKE/GEORGE MICHAEL	Aegean AECD 01	10		3

BOW WOW WOW UK group

Date	Title	Label	Peak Position	Weeks at No.1	Weeks in Top 40
26 Jul 80	C30, C60, C90, GO	EMI 5088	34		2
6 Dec 80	YOUR CASSETTE PET	EMI WOW 1	58		
28 Mar 81	W.O.R.K. (N.O. NAH NO NO MY DADDY DON'T)	EMI 5153	62		
15 Aug 81	PRINCE OF DARKNESS	RCA 100	58		
7 Nov 81	CHIHUAHUA	RCA 144	51		
30 Jan 82	GO WILD IN THE COUNTRY	RCA 175	7		8
1 May 82	SEE JUNGLE (JUNGLE BOY)/TV SAVAGE	RCA 220	45		
5 Jun 82	I WANT CANDY	RCA 238	9		7
31 Jul 82	LOUIS QUATORZE	RCA 263	66		
12 Mar 83	DO YOU WANNA HOLD ME?	RCA 314	47		

BOWA US duo

Date	Title	Label	Peak Position	Weeks at No.1	Weeks in Top 40
7 Dec 91	DIFFERENT STORY BOWA FEATURING MALA	Dead Dead Good 8	64		

DANE BOWERS UK singer

Date	Title	Label	Peak Position	Weeks at No.1	Weeks in Top 40
29 Apr 00	BUGGIN' TRUE STEPPERS FEATURING DANE BOWERS	NuLife 74321753342	6		6
26 Aug 00	OUT OF YOUR MIND TRUE STEPPERS & DANE BOWERS FEATURING VICTORIA BECKHAM	NuLife 74321782942	2		8
3 Mar 01	SHUT UP AND FORGET ABOUT IT	Arista 74321835342	9		3
7 Jul 01	ANOTHER LOVER	Arista 74321863412	9		3

DAVID BOWIE UK singer

Date	Title	Label	Peak Position	Weeks at No.1	Weeks in Top 40
6 Sep 69	SPACE ODDITY	Philips BF 1801	5		12
24 Jun 72	STARMAN	RCA 2199	10		8
16 Sep 72	JOHN I'M ONLY DANCING	RCA 2263	12		9
9 Dec 72	THE JEAN GENIE	RCA 2302	2		13
14 Apr 73	DRIVE-IN SATURDAY	RCA 2352	3		10
30 Jun 73	LIFE ON MARS	RCA 2316	3		12
15 Sep 73	THE LAUGHING GNOME	Deram DM 123	6		10
20 Oct 73	SORROW	RCA 2424	3		14
23 Feb 74	REBEL REBEL	RCA LPBO 5009	5		6
20 Apr 74	ROCK 'N' ROLL SUICIDE	RCA LPBO 5021	22		6
22 Jun 74	DIAMOND DOGS	RCA APBO 0293	21		6
28 Sep 74	KNOCK ON WOOD	RCA 2466	10		5
1 Mar 75	YOUNG AMERICANS	RCA 2523	18		6
2 Aug 75	FAME	RCA 2579 ★	17		7
11 Oct 75	SPACE ODDITY	RCA 2593	1	2	10
29 Nov 75	GOLDEN YEARS	RCA 2640	8		10
22 May 76	TVC 15	RCA 2682	33		3
19 Feb 77	SOUND AND VISION	RCA PB 0905	3		10
15 Oct 77	HEROES	RCA PB 1121	24		8
21 Jan 78	BEAUTY AND THE BEAST	RCA PB 1190	39		2
2 Dec 78	BREAKING GLASS (EP)	RCA BOW 1	54		
5 May 79	BOYS KEEP SWINGIN'	RCA BOW 2	7		8
21 Jul 79	D.J.	RCA BOW 3	29		3
15 Dec 79	JOHN I'M ONLY DANCING (AGAIN) (1975)/ JOHN I'M ONLY DANCING (1972)	RCA BOW 4	12		6
1 Mar 80	ALABAMA SONG	RCA BOW 5	23		4
16 Aug 80	ASHES TO ASHES	RCA BOW 6	1	2	8
1 Nov 80	FASHION	RCA BOW 7	5		7
10 Jan 81	SCARY MONSTERS (AND SUPER CREEPS)	RCA BOW 8	20		4
28 Mar 81	UP THE HILL BACKWARDS	RCA BOW 9	32		3
14 Nov 81	UNDER PRESSURE QUEEN & DAVID BOWIE	EMI 5250	1	2	9
28 Nov 81	WILD IS THE WIND	RCA BOW 10	24		8
6 Mar 82	BAAL'S HYMN (EP)	RCA BOW 11	29		2
10 Apr 82	CAT PEOPLE (PUTTING OUT THE FIRE)	MCA 770	26		5
27 Nov 82	PEACE ON EARTH - LITTLE DRUMMER BOY DAVID BOWIE & BING CROSBY	RCA BOW 12	3		6
26 Mar 83	LET'S DANCE	EMI America EA 152 ★	1	3	10
11 Jun 83	CHINA GIRL	EMI America EA 157	2		6
24 Sep 83	MODERN LOVE	EMI America EA 158	2		7
5 Nov 83	WHITE LIGHT, WHITE HEAT	RCA 372	46		
22 Sep 84	BLUE JEAN	EMI America EA 181	6		6
8 Dec 84	TONIGHT	EMI America EA 187	53		
9 Feb 85	THIS IS NOT AMERICA DAVID BOWIE & THE PAT METHENY GROUP	EMI America EA 190	14		5
8 Jun 85	LOVING THE ALIEN	EMI America EA 195	19		4
7 Sep 85	DANCING IN THE STREET DAVID BOWIE & MICK JAGGER	EMI America EA 204	1	4	9

Date	Title / Label	Peak Position	Weeks at No.1	Weeks in Top 40
15 Mar 86	**ABSOLUTE BEGINNERS** *Virgin VS 838*	2		7
21 Jun 86	**UNDERGROUND** *EMI America EA 216*	21		4
8 Nov 86	**WHEN THE WIND BLOWS** *Virgin VS 906*	44		
4 Apr 87	**DAY-IN DAY-OUT** *EMI America EA 230*	17		4
27 Jun 87	**TIME WILL CRAWL** *EMI America EA 237*	33		2
29 Aug 87	**NEVER LET ME DOWN** *EMI America EA 239*	34		3
7 Apr 90	**FAME (REMIX)** *EMI-USA FAME 90*	28		3
22 Aug 92	**REAL COOL WORLD** *Warner Brothers W 0127*	53		
27 Mar 93	**JUMP THEY SAY** *Arista 74321139422*	9		4
12 Jun 93	**BLACK TIE WHITE NOISE** *Arista 74321148682* DAVID BOWIE FEATURING AL B. SURE!	36		1
23 Oct 93	**MIRACLE GOODNIGHT** *Arista 74321162262*	40		1
4 Dec 93	**BUDDHA OF SUBURBIA** *Arista 74321177052* DAVID BOWIE FEATURING LENNY KRAVITZ	35		2
23 Sep 95	**THE HEART'S FILTHY LESSON** *RCA 74321307032*	35		1
2 Dec 95	**STRANGERS WHEN WE MEET/THE MAN WHO SOLD THE WORLD (LIVE)** *RCA 74321329402*	39		1
2 Mar 96	**HALLO SPACEBOY** *RCA 74321353842*	12		3
8 Feb 97	**LITTLE WONDER** *RCA 74321452072*	14		2
26 Apr 97	**DEAD MAN WALKING** *RCA 74321475852*	32		1
30 Aug 97	**SEVEN YEARS IN TIBET** *RCA 74321512542*	61		
21 Feb 98	**I CAN'T READ** *Velvet ZYX 87578*	73		
2 Oct 99	**THURSDAY'S CHILD** *Virgin VSCDT 1753*	16		2
18 Dec 99	**UNDER PRESSURE (REMIX)** *Parlophone CDQUEEN 28* QUEEN & DAVID BOWIE	14		3
5 Feb 00	**SURVIVE** *Virgin VSCDT 1767*	28		1
29 Jul 00	**SEVEN** *Virgin VSCDT 1776*	32		1
11 May 02	**LOVING THE ALIEN** *Positiva CDTIV 172* SCUMFROG VS BOWIE	41		
28 Sep 02	**EVERYONE SAYS 'HI'** *Columbia 6731342*	20		1
12 Jul 03	**JUST FOR ONE DAY (HEROES)** *Virgin DINST 263* DAVID GUETTA VS DAVID BOWIE	73		
26 Jun 04	**REBEL NEVER GETS OLD** *Columbia 6750406*	47		
21 Apr 07	**LIFE ON MARS** *Download*	55		
29 Dec 07	**PEACE ON EARTH - LITTLE DRUMMER BOY** *Download* DAVID BOWIE & BING CROSBY	73		

BOWLING FOR SOUP US group

Date	Title / Label	Peak Position	Weeks at No.1	Weeks in Top 40
17 Aug 02	**GIRL ALL THE BAD GUYS WANT** *Music For Nations CDXKUT 194*	8		4
16 Nov 02	**EMILY** *Music For Nations CDXKUT 198*	67		
6 Sep 03	**PUNK ROCK 101** *Music For Nations CDKUT 203*	43		
16 Oct 04	**1985** *Jive 82876647652*	35		1
3 Feb 07	**HIGH SCHOOL NEVER ENDS** *A & G Productions CDAG009*	40		1

GEORGE BOWYER UK singer

Date	Title / Label	Peak Position	Weeks at No.1	Weeks in Top 40
22 Aug 98	**GUARDIANS OF THE LAND** *Boys BYSCD 01*	33		1

BOX CAR RACER US group

Date	Title / Label	Peak Position	Weeks at No.1	Weeks in Top 40
6 Jul 02	**I FEEL SO** *MCA MCSTD 40290*	41		

BOX TOPS US group

Date	Title / Label	Peak Position	Weeks at No.1	Weeks in Top 40
13 Sep 67	**THE LETTER** *Stateside SS 2044* ★	5		11
20 Mar 68	**CRY LIKE A BABY** *Bell 1001*	15		10
23 Aug 69	**SOUL DEEP** *Bell 1068*	22		8

BOXER REBELLION UK group

Date	Title / Label	Peak Position	Weeks at No.1	Weeks in Top 40
10 Apr 04	**IN PURSUIT** *Poptones MC5088SCD*	57		
9 Oct 04	**CODE RED** *Vertigo 9867001*	61		

BOY GEORGE UK singer

Date	Title / Label	Peak Position	Weeks at No.1	Weeks in Top 40
7 Mar 87	**EVERYTHING I OWN** *Virgin BOY 100*	1	2	8
6 Jun 87	**KEEP ME IN MIND** *Virgin BOY 101*	29		3
18 Jul 87	**SOLD** *Virgin BOY 102*	24		4
21 Nov 87	**TO BE REBORN** *Virgin BOY 103*	13		5
5 Mar 88	**LIVE MY LIFE** *Virgin BOY 105*	62		
18 Jun 88	**NO CLAUSE 28** *Virgin BOY 106*	57		
8 Oct 88	**DON'T CRY** *Virgin BOY 107*	60		
4 Mar 89	**DON'T TAKE MY MIND ON A TRIP** *Virgin BOY 108*	68		
19 Sep 92	**THE CRYING GAME** *Spaghetti CIAO 6*	22		3
12 Jun 93	**MORE THAN LIKELY** *Gee Street GESCD 49* PM DAWN FEATURING BOY GEORGE	40		1
1 Apr 95	**FUNTIME** *Virgin VSCDG 1538*	45		
1 Jul 95	**IL ADORE** *Virgin VSCDX 1543*	50		
21 Oct 95	**SAME THING IN REVERSE** *Virgin VSCDT 1561*	56		

BOY KILL BOY UK group

Date	Title / Label	Peak Position	Weeks at No.1	Weeks in Top 40
25 Feb 06	**BACK AGAIN** *Vertigo 9876834*	26		1
20 May 06	**SUZIE** *Vertigo 9856256*	17		2
12 Aug 06	**CIVIL SIN** *Vertigo 1702238*	44		
25 Nov 06	**SHOOT ME DOWN** *Vertigo 1709308*	63		

BOY LEAST LIKELY TO UK duo

Date	Title / Label	Peak Position	Weeks at No.1	Weeks in Top 40
6 May 06	**BE GENTLE WITH ME** *Too Young To Die TYTD006CD*	62		

BOY MEETS GIRL US duo

Date	Title / Label	Peak Position	Weeks at No.1	Weeks in Top 40
3 Dec 88	**WAITING FOR A STAR TO FALL** *RCA PB 49519*	9		8

JIMMY BOYD US singer

Date	Title / Label	Peak Position	Weeks at No.1	Weeks in Top 40
8 May 53	**TELL ME A STORY** *Philips PB 126* FRANKIE LAINE & JIMMY BOYD	5		16
27 Nov 53	**I SAW MOMMY KISSING SANTA CLAUS** *Columbia DB 3365* ★	3		6

JACQUELINE BOYER French singer

Date	Title / Label	Peak Position	Weeks at No.1	Weeks in Top 40
28 Apr 60	**TOM PILLIBI** *Columbia DB 4452*	33		2

BOYS US group

Date	Title / Label	Peak Position	Weeks at No.1	Weeks in Top 40
12 Nov 88	**DIAL MY HEART** *Motown ZB 42245*	61		
29 Sep 90	**CRAZY** *Motown ZB 44037*	57		

BOYSTEROUS UK group

Date	Title / Label	Peak Position	Weeks at No.1	Weeks in Top 40
22 Nov 03	**UP AND DOWN** *Square Biz SBR4*	53		

BOYSTOWN GANG US group

Date	Title / Label	Peak Position	Weeks at No.1	Weeks in Top 40
22 Aug 81	**AIN'T NO MOUNTAIN HIGH ENOUGH - REMEMBER ME (MEDLEY)** *WEA DICK 1*	46		
31 Jul 82	**CAN'T TAKE MY EYES OFF YOU** *ERC 101*	4		8
9 Oct 82	**SIGNED SEALED DELIVERED (I'M YOURS)** *ERC 102*	50		

BOYZ II MEN US group

Date	Title / Label	Peak Position	Weeks at No.1	Weeks in Top 40
5 Sep 92	**END OF THE ROAD** *Motown TMG 1411* ★	1	3	19
19 Dec 92	**MOTOWNPHILLY** *Motown TMG 1402*	23		4
27 Feb 93	**IN THE STILL OF THE NITE (I'LL REMEMBER)** *Motown TMGCD 1415*	27		3
3 Sep 94	**I'LL MAKE LOVE TO YOU** *Motown TMGCD 1431* ★	5		10
26 Nov 94	**ON BENDED KNEE** *Motown TMGCD 1433* ★	20		2
22 Apr 95	**THANK YOU** *Motown TMGCD 1438*	26		2
8 Jul 95	**WATER RUNS DRY** *Motown TMGCD 1443*	24		1
9 Dec 95	**ONE SWEET DAY** *Columbia 6626035* MARIAH CAREY & BOYZ II MEN ★	6		8
20 Jan 96	**HEY LOVER** *Def Jam DEFCD 14* LL COOL J FEATURING BOYZ II MEN	17		2
20 Sep 97	**4 SEASONS OF LONELINESS** *Motown 8606992* ★	10		4
6 Dec 97	**A SONG FOR MAMA** *Motown 8607372*	34		1
25 Jul 98	**CAN'T LET HER GO** *Motown 8607952*	23		1
17 Nov 07	**END OF THE ROAD** *Download*	43		

BOYZONE Irish group

Date	Title / Label	Peak Position	Weeks at No.1	Weeks in Top 40
10 Dec 94	**LOVE ME FOR A REASON** *Polydor 8512802*	2		10
29 Apr 95	**KEY TO MY LIFE** *Polydor PZCD 342*	3		7
12 Aug 95	**SO GOOD** *Polydor 5797732*	3		4
25 Nov 95	**FATHER AND SON** *Polydor 5775762*	2		15
9 Mar 96	**COMING HOME NOW** *Polydor 5775722*	4		7
19 Oct 96	**WORDS** *Polydor 5755372*	1	1	9
14 Dec 96	**A DIFFERENT BEAT** *Polydor 5732072*	1	1	6
22 Mar 97	**ISN'T IT A WONDER** *Polydor 5735472*	2		5
2 Aug 97	**PICTURE OF YOU** *Polydor 5713112*	2		7
6 Dec 97	**BABY CAN I HOLD YOU/SHOOTING STAR** *Polydor 5691652*	2		11
2 May 98	**ALL THAT I NEED** *Polydor 5698732*	1	1	5
15 Aug 98	**NO MATTER WHAT** *Polydor 5675672*	1	3	15
5 Dec 98	**I LOVE THE WAY YOU LOVE ME** *Polydor 5631992*	2		10
13 Mar 99	**WHEN THE GOING GETS TOUGH** *Polydor 5699132*	1	2	9
22 May 99	**YOU NEEDED ME** *Polydor 5639332*	1	1	7
4 Dec 99	**EVERY DAY I LOVE YOU** *Polydor 5615802*	3		9

BRAD US group

Date	Title	Peak Position	Weeks at No.1	Weeks in Top 40
26 Jun 93	**20TH CENTURY** *Epic 6592482*	64		

JAMES DEAN BRADFIELD UK singer/guitarist

Date	Title	Peak Position	Weeks at No.1	Weeks in Top 40
22 Jul 06	**THAT'S NO WAY TO TELL A LIE** *Columbia 82876861592*	18		1
7 Oct 06	**AN ENGLISH GENTLEMAN** *Columbia 88697003182*	31		1

SCOTT BRADLEY UK singer

Date	Title	Peak Position	Weeks at No.1	Weeks in Top 40
15 Oct 94	**ZOOM** *Hidden Agenda HIDDCD 1*	61		

PAUL BRADY Irish singer/guitarist

Date	Title	Peak Position	Weeks at No.1	Weeks in Top 40
13 Jan 96	**THE WORLD IS WHAT YOU MAKE IT** *Mercury PBCD 1*	67		

BILLY BRAGG UK singer

Date	Title	Peak Position	Weeks at No.1	Weeks in Top 40
16 Mar 85	**BETWEEN THE WARS (EP)** *Go! Discs AGOEP 1*	15		5
28 Dec 85	**DAYS LIKE THESE** *Go! Discs GOD 8*	43		
28 Jun 86	**LEVI STUBBS TEARS** *Go! Discs GOD 12*	29		3
15 Nov 86	**GREETINGS TO THE NEW BRUNETTE** *Go! Discs GOD 15* BILLY BRAGG WITH JOHNNY MARR & KIRSTY MacCOLL	58		
14 May 88	**SHE'S LEAVING HOME** *Childline CHILD 1* BILLY BRAGG WITH CARA TIVEY ●	1	4	10
10 Sep 88	**WAITING FOR THE GREAT LEAP FORWARDS** *Go! Discs GOD 23*	52		
8 Jul 89	**WON'T TALK ABOUT IT/BLAME IT ON THE BASSLINE** *Go! Beat GOD 33* NORMAN COOK FEATURING BILLY BRAGG/NORMAN COOK FEATURING MC WILDSKI	29		4
6 Jul 91	**SEXUALITY** *Go! Discs GOD 56*	27		3
7 Sep 91	**YOU WOKE UP MY NEIGHBOURHOOD** *Go! Discs GOD 60*	54		
29 Feb 92	**ACCIDENT WAITING TO HAPPEN (EP)** *Go! Discs GOD 67*	33		2
31 Aug 96	**UPFIELD** *Cooking Vinyl FRYCD 051*	46		
17 May 97	**THE BOY DONE GOOD** *Cooking Vinyl FRYCD 064*	55		
1 Jun 02	**TAKE DOWN THE UNION JACK** *Cooking Vinyl FRYCD 131XX* BILLY BRAGG & THE BLOKES	22		1
12 Nov 05	**WE LAUGHED** *Cooking Vinyl FRYCD252* ROSETTA LIFE FEATURING BILLY BRAGG	11		3

BRAIDS US duo

Date	Title	Peak Position	Weeks at No.1	Weeks in Top 40
2 Nov 96	**BOHEMIAN RHAPSODY** *Atlantic A 5640CD*	21		2

BRAINBASHERS UK production duo

Date	Title	Peak Position	Weeks at No.1	Weeks in Top 40
1 Jul 00	**DO IT NOW** *Tidy Trax TIDY 137CD*	64		

BRAINBUG Italian producer

Date	Title	Peak Position	Weeks at No.1	Weeks in Top 40
3 May 97	**NIGHTMARE** *Positiva CDTIV 76*	11		3
22 Nov 97	**BENEDICTUS/NIGHTMARE** *Positiva CDTIV 86*	24		1
4 Sep 04	**NIGHTMARE** *Positiva 12TIV 200*	63		

BRAINCHILD German producer

Date	Title	Peak Position	Weeks at No.1	Weeks in Top 40
30 Oct 99	**SYMMETRY C** *Multiply CDMULTY 55*	31		1

BRAKES UK group

Date	Title	Peak Position	Weeks at No.1	Weeks in Top 40
25 Jun 05	**ALL NIGHT DISCO PARTY** *Rough Trade RTRADSCD241*	67		

WILFRID BRAMBELL & HARRY H. CORBETT UK comedy actors

Date	Title	Peak Position	Weeks at No.1	Weeks in Top 40
28 Nov 63	**AT THE PALACE (PARTS 1 & 2)** *Pye 7N 15588*	25		9

BRAN VAN 3000 Canadian group

Date	Title	Peak Position	Weeks at No.1	Weeks in Top 40
6 Jun 98	**DRINKING IN LA** *Capitol CDCL 802*	34		1
21 Aug 99	**DRINKING IN LA** *Capitol CDCL 811* ●	3		7
16 Jun 01	**ASTOUNDED** *Virgin VUSCD 194* BRAN VAN 3000 FEATURING CURTIS MAYFIELD	40		1

BRANCACCIO & AISHER UK production duo

Date	Title	Peak Position	Weeks at No.1	Weeks in Top 40
16 Mar 02	**IT'S GONNA BE (A LOVELY DAY)** *Credence CDCRED 017*	40		1

MICHELLE BRANCH US singer

Date	Title	Peak Position	Weeks at No.1	Weeks in Top 40
13 Apr 02	**EVERYWHERE** *Maverick W 577CD*	18		4
3 Aug 02	**ALL YOU WANTED** *Maverick W 585CDX*	33		1
23 Nov 02	**THE GAME OF LOVE** *Arista 74321959442* SANTANA FEATURING MICHELLE BRANCH	16		3
12 Jul 03	**ARE YOU HAPPY NOW?** *Maverick W 613CD*	31		1

BRAND NEW US group

Date	Title	Peak Position	Weeks at No.1	Weeks in Top 40
14 Feb 04	**SIC TRANSIT GLORIA GLORY FADES** *Sore Point SORE011CDS*	37		1
29 May 04	**THE QUIET THINGS THAT NO ONE EVER KNOWS** *Sore Point SORE014CDS*	39		1

BRAND NEW HEAVIES UK/US group

Date	Title	Peak Position	Weeks at No.1	Weeks in Top 40
5 Oct 91	**NEVER STOP** *ffrr F 165* BRAND NEW HEAVIES FEATURING N'DEA DAVENPORT	43		
15 Feb 92	**DREAM COME TRUE** *ffrr F 180* BRAND NEW HEAVIES FEATURING N'DEA DAVENPORT	24		3
18 Apr 92	**ULTIMATE TRUNK FUNK EP** *ffrr F 185* BRAND NEW HEAVIES FEATURING N'DEA DAVENPORT	19		4
1 Aug 92	**DON'T LET IT GO TO YOUR HEAD** *ffrr BNH 1* BRAND NEW HEAVIES FEATURING N'DEA DAVENPORT	24		2
19 Dec 92	**STAY THIS WAY** *ffrr BNH 2* BRAND NEW HEAVIES FEATURING N'DEA DAVENPORT	40		1
26 Mar 94	**DREAM ON DREAMER** *ffrr BNHCD 3* BRAND NEW HEAVIES FEATURING N'DEA DAVENPORT	15		2
11 Jun 94	**BACK TO LOVE** *ffrr BNHCD 4* BRAND NEW HEAVIES FEATURING N'DEA DAVENPORT	23		3
13 Aug 94	**MIDNIGHT AT THE OASIS** *ffrr BNHCDP 5* BRAND NEW HEAVIES FEATURING N'DEA DAVENPORT	13		5
5 Nov 94	**SPEND SOME TIME** *ffrr BNHCD 6* BRAND NEW HEAVIES FEATURING N'DEA DAVENPORT	26		2
11 Mar 95	**CLOSE TO YOU** *ffrr BNCDP 7* BRAND NEW HEAVIES FEATURING N'DEA DAVENPORT	38		2
12 Apr 97	**SOMETIMES** *ffrr BNHCD 8* ●	11		4
28 Jun 97	**YOU ARE THE UNIVERSE** *ffrr BNHCD 9*	21		1
18 Oct 97	**YOU'VE GOT A FRIEND** *ffrr BNHCD 10*	9		6
10 Jan 98	**SHELTER** *London BNHCD 11*	31		2
11 Sep 99	**SATURDAY NITE** *ffrr BNHCD 12*	35		1
29 Jan 00	**APPARENTLY NOTHING** *ffrr BNHCD 13*	32		1
23 Oct 04	**BOOGIE** *Onetwo TBNHCDS001* BRAND NEW HEAVIES FEATURING NICOLE	66		

JOHNNY BRANDON UK singer

Date	Title	Peak Position	Weeks at No.1	Weeks in Top 40
11 Mar 55	**TOMORROW** *Polygon P 1131* JOHNNY BRANDON & THE PHANTOMS & THE NORMAN WARREN MUSIC	8		8
1 Jul 55	**DON'T WORRY** *Polygon P 1163*	18		4

BRANDY US singer

Date	Title	Peak Position	Weeks at No.1	Weeks in Top 40
10 Dec 94	**I WANNA BE DOWN** *Atlantic A 7217CD*	44		
3 Jun 95	**I WANNA BE DOWN (REMIX)** *Atlantic A 7186CD*	36		1
3 Feb 96	**SITTIN' UP IN MY ROOM** *Arista 74321344012*	30		2
6 Jun 98	**THE BOY IS MINE** *Atlantic AT 0036CD* BRANDY & MONICA ● ★	2		18
10 Oct 98	**TOP OF THE WORLD** *Atlantic AT 0046CD* BRANDY FEATURING MASE ●	2		5
12 Dec 98	**HAVE YOU EVER?** *Atlantic AT 0058CD* ★	13		5
19 Jun 99	**ALMOST DOESN'T COUNT** *Atlantic AT 0068CD1*	15		3
16 Jun 01	**ANOTHER DAY IN PARADISE** *WEA 327CD1* BRANDY & RAY J	5		8
23 Feb 02	**WHAT ABOUT US** *Atlantic AT 0125CD*	4		6
15 Jun 02	**FULL MOON (IMPORT)** *Atlantic 7567853092*	72		
29 Jun 02	**FULL MOON** *Atlantic AT 0130CD*	15		4
26 Jun 04	**TALK ABOUT OUR LOVE** *Atlantic AT 0177CD* BRANDY FEATURING KANYE WEST	6		5
16 Oct 04	**AFRODISIAC** *Atlantic AT0183CD*	11		4
2 Apr 05	**WHO IS SHE 2 U** *Atlantic AT0192CD*	50		

LAURA BRANIGAN US singer

Date	Title	Peak Position	Weeks at No.1	Weeks in Top 40
18 Dec 82	**GLORIA** *Atlantic K 11759*	6		8
7 Jul 84	**SELF CONTROL** *Atlantic A 9676* ●	5		12
6 Oct 84	**THE LUCKY ONE** *Atlantic A 9636*	56		

Silver-selling ● Gold-selling ● Platinum-selling ⊛ US No.1 ★ — Peak Position | Weeks at No.1 | Weeks in Top 40

BRASS CONSTRUCTION US group

Date	Title / Label	Peak Position	Weeks at No.1	Weeks in Top 40
3 Apr 76	**MOVIN'** *United Artists UP 36090*	23		6
5 Feb 77	**HA CHA CHA (FUNKTION)** *United Artists UP 36205*	37		1
26 Jan 80	**MUSIC MAKES YOU FEEL LIKE DANCING** *United Artists UP 615*	39		1
28 May 83	**WALKIN' THE LINE** *Capitol CL 292*	47		
16 Jul 83	**WE CAN WORK IT OUT** *Capitol CL 299*	70		
7 Jul 84	**PARTYLINE** *Capitol CL 335*	56		
27 Oct 84	**INTERNATIONAL** *Capitol CL 341*	70		
9 Nov 85	**GIVE AND TAKE** *Capitol CL 377*	62		
28 May 88	**MOVIN' 1988 (REMIX)** *Syncopate SY 11*	24		3

BRAT UK singer

Date	Title / Label	Peak Position	Weeks at No.1	Weeks in Top 40
10 Jul 82	**CHALK DUST-THE UMPIRE STRIKES BACK** *Hansa SMASH 1*	19		7

BRATZ ROCK ANGELZ US toy group

Date	Title / Label	Peak Position	Weeks at No.1	Weeks in Top 40
15 Oct 05	**SO GOOD** *Universal 9885281*	23		3

BRAUND REYNOLDS UK production duo

Date	Title / Label	Peak Position	Weeks at No.1	Weeks in Top 40
17 Dec 05	**ROCKET (A NATURAL GAMBLER)** *Virgin TENCDX504*	27		2

BRAVADO UK group

Date	Title / Label	Peak Position	Weeks at No.1	Weeks in Top 40
18 Jun 94	**HARMONICA MAN** *Peach PEACHCD 5*	37		1

BRAVERY US group

Date	Title / Label	Peak Position	Weeks at No.1	Weeks in Top 40
12 Mar 05	**AN HONEST MISTAKE** *Loog 9880300*	7		3
4 Jun 05	**FEARLESS** *Loog 9882338*	43		
10 Sep 05	**UNCONDITIONAL** *Loog 9885197*	49		

BRAVO ALL STARS UK/German/US group

Date	Title / Label	Peak Position	Weeks at No.1	Weeks in Top 40
29 Aug 98	**LET THE MUSIC HEAL YOUR SOUL** *Edel 0039335 ERE*	36		1

ALAN BRAXE & FRED FALKE French production duo

Date	Title / Label	Peak Position	Weeks at No.1	Weeks in Top 40
25 Nov 00	**INTRO** *Vulture/Credence CDCRED 006*	35		1

DHAR BRAXTON US singer

Date	Title / Label	Peak Position	Weeks at No.1	Weeks in Top 40
31 May 86	**JUMP BACK (SET ME FREE)** *Fourth & Broadway BRW 47*	32		4

TONI BRAXTON US singer

Date	Title / Label	Peak Position	Weeks at No.1	Weeks in Top 40
18 Sep 93	**ANOTHER SAD LOVE SONG** *LaFace 74321163502*	51		
15 Jan 94	**BREATHE AGAIN** *LaFace 74321163502* ●	2		11
2 Apr 94	**ANOTHER SAD LOVE SONG** *LaFace 74321196682*	15		6
9 Jul 94	**YOU MEAN THE WORLD TO ME** *LaFace 74321214702*	30		3
3 Dec 94	**LOVE SHOULDA BROUGHT YOU HOME** *LaFace 74321249412*	33		1
13 Jul 96	**YOU'RE MAKIN ME HIGH** *LaFace 74321395402* ★	7		9
2 Nov 96	**UN-BREAK MY HEART** *LaFace 74321410632* ⊛ ★	2		17
24 May 97	**I DON'T WANT TO** *LaFace 74321468612*	9		6
8 Nov 97	**HOW COULD AN ANGEL BREAK MY HEART** *LaFace 74321531982* TONI BRAXTON WITH KENNY G	22		3
29 Apr 00	**HE WASN'T MAN ENOUGH** *LaFace 74321757852*	5		7
8 Mar 03	**HIT THE FREEWAY** *Arista 82876506372* TONI BRAXTON FEATURING LOON	29		1

BRAXTONS US group

Date	Title / Label	Peak Position	Weeks at No.1	Weeks in Top 40
1 Feb 97	**SO MANY WAYS** *Atlantic A 5469CD*	32		1
29 Mar 97	**THE BOSS** *Atlantic A 5441CD*	31		1
19 Jul 97	**SLOW FLOW** *Atlantic AT 0001CD*	26		1

BREAD US group

Date	Title / Label	Peak Position	Weeks at No.1	Weeks in Top 40
1 Aug 70	**MAKE IT WITH YOU** *Elektra 2101 010* ★	5		13
15 Jan 72	**BABY I'M A-WANT YOU** *Elektra K 12033*	14		9
29 Apr 72	**EVERYTHING I OWN** *Elektra K 12041*	32		4
30 Sep 72	**THE GUITAR MAN** *Elektra K 12066*	16		8
25 Dec 76	**LOST WITHOUT YOUR LOVE** *Elektra K 12241*	27		4

BREAK MACHINE US group

Date	Title / Label	Peak Position	Weeks at No.1	Weeks in Top 40
4 Feb 84	**STREET DANCE** *Record Shack SOHO 13*	3		11
12 May 84	**BREAKDANCE PARTY** *Record Shack SOHO 20*	9		7
11 Aug 84	**ARE YOU READY?** *Record Shack SOHO 24*	27		4

BREAKBEAT ERA UK group

Date	Title / Label	Peak Position	Weeks at No.1	Weeks in Top 40
18 Jul 98	**BREAKBEAT ERA** *XL Recordings XLS 95CD*	38		1
21 Aug 99	**ULTRA-OBSCENE** *XL Recordings XLS 107CD*	48		
11 Mar 00	**BULLITPROOF** *XL Recordings XLS 115CD*	65		

BREAKFAST CLUB US group

Date	Title / Label	Peak Position	Weeks at No.1	Weeks in Top 40
27 Jun 87	**RIGHT ON TRACK** *MCA 1146*	54		

BREAKS CO-OP New Zealand/UK group

Date	Title / Label	Peak Position	Weeks at No.1	Weeks in Top 40
3 Jun 06	**THE OTHERSIDE** *Parlophone CDRS6689*	43		

BREATHE UK group

Date	Title / Label	Peak Position	Weeks at No.1	Weeks in Top 40
30 Jul 88	**HANDS TO HEAVEN** *Siren SRN 68*	4		9
22 Oct 88	**JONAH** *Siren SRN 95*	60		
3 Dec 88	**HOW CAN I FALL** *Siren SRN 102*	48		
11 Mar 89	**DON'T TELL ME LIES** *Siren SRN 109*	45		

FREDDY BRECK German singer

Date	Title / Label	Peak Position	Weeks at No.1	Weeks in Top 40
13 Apr 74	**SO IN LOVE WITH YOU** *Decca F 13481*	44		

BRECKER BROTHERS US duo

Date	Title / Label	Peak Position	Weeks at No.1	Weeks in Top 40
4 Nov 78	**EAST RIVER** *Arista ARIST 211*	34		1

BREED 77 Gibraltairian group

Date	Title / Label	Peak Position	Weeks at No.1	Weeks in Top 40
1 May 04	**THE RIVER** *Albert Productions JASCDUKL007*	39		1
7 Aug 04	**WORLD'S ON FIRE** *Albert Productions JASCDUK011*	43		
5 Feb 05	**SHADOWS** *Albert Productions JASCDVUK013*	42		

BREEDERS US/UK group

Date	Title / Label	Peak Position	Weeks at No.1	Weeks in Top 40
18 Apr 92	**SAFARI (EP)** *4AD BAD 2003*	69		
21 Aug 93	**CANNONBALL (EP)** *4AD BAD 3011CD*	40		1
6 Nov 93	**DIVINE HAMMER** *4AD BAD 3017CD*	59		
23 Jul 94	**HEAD TO TOE (EP)** *4AD BAD 4012CD*	68		
14 Sep 02	**SON OF THREE** *4AD BAD 2213CD*	72		

BREEKOUT CREW US duo

Date	Title / Label	Peak Position	Weeks at No.1	Weeks in Top 40
24 Nov 84	**MATT'S MOOD** *London LON 59*	51		

ANN BREEN Irish singer

Date	Title / Label	Peak Position	Weeks at No.1	Weeks in Top 40
19 Mar 83	**PAL OF MY CRADLE DAYS** *Homespun HS 052*	69		
7 Jan 84	**PAL OF MY CRADLE DAYS** *Homespun HS 052*	74		

JO BREEZER UK singer

Date	Title / Label	Peak Position	Weeks at No.1	Weeks in Top 40
13 Oct 01	**VENUS AND MARS** *Columbia 6717612*	27		1

BRENDON UK singer

Date	Title / Label	Peak Position	Weeks at No.1	Weeks in Top 40
19 Mar 77	**GIMME SOME** *Magnet MAG 80*	14		8

MAIRE BRENNAN Irish singer

Date	Title / Label	Peak Position	Weeks at No.1	Weeks in Top 40
16 May 92	**AGAINST THE WIND** *RCA PB 45399*	64		
5 Jun 99	**SALTWATER** *Xtravaganza XTRAV 1CDS* CHICANE FEATURING MAIRE BRENNAN OF CLANNAD	6		7

ROSE BRENNAN Irish singer

Date	Title / Label	Peak Position	Weeks at No.1	Weeks in Top 40
7 Dec 61	**TALL DARK STRANGER** *Philips PB 1193*	31		7

Key: Silver-selling ○ · Gold-selling ● · Platinum-selling ⊛ · US No.1 ★ · Peak Position · Weeks at No.1 · Weeks in Top 40

WALTER BRENNAN US singer

Date	Title / Label	Peak Position	Weeks at No.1	Weeks in Top 40
28 Jun 62	**OLD RIVERS** *Liberty LIB 55436*	38		2

TONY BRENT UK singer

Date	Title / Label	Peak Position	Weeks at No.1	Weeks in Top 40
19 Dec 52	**WALKIN' TO MISSOURI** *Columbia DB 3147*	7		5
2 Jan 53	**MAKE IT SOON** *Columbia DB 3187*	9		9
23 Jan 53	**GOT YOU ON MY MIND** *Columbia DB 3226*	12		1
30 Nov 56	**CINDY OH CINDY** *Columbia DB 3844*	16		7
28 Jun 57	**DARK MOON** *Columbia DB 3950*	17		14
28 Feb 58	**THE CLOUDS WILL SOON ROLL BY** *Columbia DB 4066*	20		5
5 Sep 58	**GIRL OF MY DREAMS** *Columbia DB 4177*	16		7
24 Jul 59	**WHY SHOULD I BE LONELY** *Columbia DB 4304*	24		4

BERNARD BRESSLAW UK singer/actor

Date	Title / Label	Peak Position	Weeks at No.1	Weeks in Top 40
5 Sep 58	**MAD PASSIONATE LOVE** *HMV POP 522*	6		11

TERESA BREWER US singer

Date	Title / Label	Peak Position	Weeks at No.1	Weeks in Top 40
11 Feb 55	**LET ME GO LOVER** *Vogue Coral Q 72043* TERESA BREWER WITH THE LANCERS	9		10
13 Apr 56	**A TEAR FELL** *Vogue Coral Q 72146*	2		15
13 Jul 56	**SWEET OLD-FASHIONED GIRL** *Vogue Coral Q 72172*	3		15
10 May 57	**NORA MALONE** *Vogue Coral Q 72224*	26		2
23 Jun 60	**HOW DO YOU KNOW IT'S LOVE** *Coral Q 72396*	21		9

BRIAN & MICHAEL UK duo

Date	Title / Label	Peak Position	Weeks at No.1	Weeks in Top 40
25 Feb 78	**MATCHSTALK MEN AND MATCHSTALK CATS AND DOGS** *Pye 7N 46035* ●	1	3	14

BRICK US group

Date	Title / Label	Peak Position	Weeks at No.1	Weeks in Top 40
5 Feb 77	**DAZZ** *Bang 004*	36		2

EDIE BRICKELL US singer

Date	Title / Label	Peak Position	Weeks at No.1	Weeks in Top 40
4 Feb 89	**WHAT I AM** *Geffen GEF 49* EDIE BRICKELL & THE NEW BOHEMIANS	31		4
27 May 89	**CIRCLE** *Geffen GEF 51* EDIE BRICKELL & THE NEW BOHEMIANS	74		
1 Oct 94	**GOOD TIMES** *Geffen GFSTD 78*	40		1

ALICIA BRIDGES US singer

Date	Title / Label	Peak Position	Weeks at No.1	Weeks in Top 40
11 Nov 78	**I LOVE THE NIGHTLIFE (DISCO ROUND)** *Polydor 2066 936*	32		4
8 Oct 94	**I LOVE THE NIGHTLIFE (DISCO ROUND) (REMIX)** *Mother MUMCD 57*	61		

BRIGHOUSE & RASTRICK BRASS BAND
UK brass band

Date	Title / Label	Peak Position	Weeks at No.1	Weeks in Top 40
12 Nov 77	**THE FLORAL DANCE** *Transatlantic BIG 548* ●	2		12

BETTE BRIGHT UK singer

Date	Title / Label	Peak Position	Weeks at No.1	Weeks in Top 40
8 Mar 80	**HELLO I AM YOUR HEART** *Korova KOW 3*	50		

BRIGHT EYES US group

Date	Title / Label	Peak Position	Weeks at No.1	Weeks in Top 40
2 Apr 05	**FIRST DAY OF MY LIFE** *Saddle Creek SCE79CD*	37		1
6 Aug 05	**EASY/LUCKY/FREE** *Saddle Creek SCE84CD*	42		
14 Apr 07	**FOUR WINDS** *Polydor 1725984*	57		

SARAH BRIGHTMAN UK singer

Date	Title / Label	Peak Position	Weeks at No.1	Weeks in Top 40
11 Nov 78	**I LOST MY HEART TO A STARSHIP TROOPER** *Ariola/Hansa AHA 527* SARAH BRIGHTMAN & HOT GOSSIP ●	6		11
7 Apr 79	**THE ADVENTURES OF THE LOVE CRUSADER** *Ariola/Hansa AHA 538* SARAH BRIGHTMAN & THE STARSHIP TROOPERS	53		
30 Jul 83	**HIM** *Polydor POSP 625* SARAH BRIGHTMAN & THE LONDON PHILHARMONIC	55		
23 Mar 85	**PIE JESU** *HMV WEBBER 1* SARAH BRIGHTMAN & PAUL MILES-KINGSTON ○	3		7
11 Jan 86	**THE PHANTOM OF THE OPERA** *Polydor POSP 800* SARAH BRIGHTMAN & STEVE HARLEY	7		7
4 Oct 86	**ALL I ASK OF YOU** *Polydor POSP 802* CLIFF RICHARD & SARAH BRIGHTMAN ○	3		14
10 Jan 87	**WISHING YOU WERE SOMEHOW HERE AGAIN** *Polydor POSP 803*	7		6
11 Jul 92	**AMIGOS PARA SIEMPRE (FRIENDS FOR LIFE)** *Really Useful RUR 10* JOSE CARRERAS & SARAH BRIGHTMAN	11		9
24 May 97	**TIME TO SAY GOODBYE** *Coalition COLA 003CD* SARAH BRIGHTMAN/ANDREA BOCELLI ●	2		11
23 Aug 97	**WHO WANTS TO LIVE FOREVER** *Coalition COLA 014CD*	45		
6 Dec 97	**JUST SHOW ME HOW TO LOVE YOU** *Coalition COLA 035CD* SARAH BRIGHTMAN & THE LSO FEATURING JOSE CURA	54		
14 Feb 98	**STARSHIP TROOPERS** *Coalition COLA 040CD* UNITED CITIZEN FEDERATION FEATURING SARAH BRIGHTMAN	58		
13 Feb 99	**EDEN** *Coalition COLA 065CD*	68		

BRIGHTON & HOVE ALBION FC
UK football club

Date	Title / Label	Peak Position	Weeks at No.1	Weeks in Top 40
28 May 83	**THE BOYS IN THE OLD BRIGHTON BLUE** *Energy NRG 2*	65		

BRILLIANT UK group

Date	Title / Label	Peak Position	Weeks at No.1	Weeks in Top 40
19 Oct 85	**IT'S A MAN'S MAN'S MAN'S WORLD** *Food 5*	58		
22 Mar 86	**LOVE IS WAR** *Food 6*	64		
2 Aug 86	**SOMEBODY** *Food 7*	67		

DANIELLE BRISEBOIS US singer

Date	Title / Label	Peak Position	Weeks at No.1	Weeks in Top 40
9 Sep 95	**GIMME LITTLE SIGN** *Epic 6610782*	75		

JOHNNY BRISTOL US singer

Date	Title / Label	Peak Position	Weeks at No.1	Weeks in Top 40
24 Aug 74	**HANG ON IN THERE BABY** *MGM 2006 443*	3		10
19 Jul 80	**MY GUY – MY GIRL (MEDLEY)** *Atlantic/Hansa K 11550* AMII STEWART & JOHNNY BRISTOL	39		1

BRISTOL CITY & THE WURZELS
UK football club with UK comedy group

Date	Title / Label	Peak Position	Weeks at No.1	Weeks in Top 40
6 Oct 07	**ONE FOR THE BRISTOL CITY** *CIA CIA004*	66		

BRIT PACK UK/Irish group

Date	Title / Label	Peak Position	Weeks at No.1	Weeks in Top 40
12 Feb 00	**SET ME FREE** *When! WENX 2000*	41		

BRITISH SEA POWER UK group

Date	Title / Label	Peak Position	Weeks at No.1	Weeks in Top 40
12 Jul 03	**CARRION/APOLOGIES TO INSECT LIFE** *Rough Trade RTRADESCD 92X*	36		1
1 Nov 03	**REMEMBER ME** *Rough Trade RTRADESCD 126*	30		1
2 Apr 05	**IT ENDED ON AN OILY STAGE** *Rough Trade RTRADSCDX220*	18		1
4 Jun 05	**PLEASE STAND UP** *Rough Trade RTRADSCDX242*	34		1
19 Jan 08	**WAVING FLAGS** *Rough Trade RTRADESCD416*	31		1

BRITISH WHALE UK singer/guitarist

Date	Title / Label	Peak Position	Weeks at No.1	Weeks in Top 40
27 Aug 05	**THIS TOWN AIN'T BIG ENOUGH FOR BOTH OF US** *Atlantic ATUK011CD*	6		2

ANDREA BRITTON UK singer

Date	Title / Label	Peak Position	Weeks at No.1	Weeks in Top 40
11 Jan 03	**AM I ON YOUR MIND** *Innocent SINCD 40* OXYGEN FEATURING ANDREA BRITTON	30		1
19 Jun 04	**TAKE MY HAND** *Direction 6749932* JURGEN VRIES FEATURING ANDREA BRITTON	23		2
5 Mar 05	**WINTER** *Data 80CDS* DT8 PROJECT FEATURING ANDREA BRITTON	35		1
28 Jul 07	**COUNTING DOWN THE DAYS** *Positiva CDTIVS245* SUNFREAKZ FEATURING ANDREA BRITTON	37		1

BROCK LANDARS UK production duo

Date	Title / Label	Peak Position	Weeks at No.1	Weeks in Top 40
11 Jul 98	**S.M.D.U.** *Parlophone CDBLUE 001*	49		

BROCKIE/ED SOLO UK production duo

Date	Title / Label	Peak Position	Weeks at No.1	Weeks in Top 40
24 Apr 04	**SYSTEM CHECK** *Undiluted UD010*	68		

Silver-selling ○ | Gold-selling ● | Platinum-selling ⊛ | US No.1 ★ | Peak Position | Weeks at No.1 | Weeks in Top 40

BROKEN ENGLISH UK group

Date	Title / Label	Peak Position	Weeks at No.1	Weeks in Top 40
30 May 87	COMIN' ON STRONG *EMI EM 5*	18		7
3 Oct 87	LOVE ON THE SIDE *EMI EM 55*	69		

BRONSKI BEAT UK group

Date	Title / Label	Peak Position	Weeks at No.1	Weeks in Top 40
2 Jun 84	SMALLTOWN BOY *Forbidden Fruit BITE 1* ○	3		11
22 Sep 84	WHY? *Forbidden Fruit BITE 2* ○	6		8
1 Dec 84	IT AIN'T NECESSARILY SO *Forbidden Fruit BITE 3*	16		8
20 Apr 85	I FEEL LOVE (MEDLEY) *Forbidden Fruit BITE 4* BRONSKI BEAT & MARC ALMOND ○	3		10
30 Nov 85	HIT THAT PERFECT BEAT *Forbidden Fruit BITE 6* ○	3		11
29 Mar 86	COME ON, COME ON *Forbidden Fruit BITE 7*	20		6
1 Jul 89	CHA CHA HEELS *Arista 112331* EARTHA KITT & BRONSKI BEAT	32		3
2 Feb 91	SMALLTOWN BOY (REMIX) *London LON 287* JIMMY SOMERVILLE WITH BRONSKI BEAT	32		2

BRONX US group

Date	Title / Label	Peak Position	Weeks at No.1	Weeks in Top 40
24 Apr 04	THEY WILL KILL US ALL (WITHOUT MERCY) *Wichita WEBB060SCD*	65		
17 Jul 04	FALSE ALARM *Wichita WEBB062SCD*	73		

JET BRONX & THE FORBIDDEN UK group

Date	Title / Label	Peak Position	Weeks at No.1	Weeks in Top 40
17 Dec 77	AIN'T DOIN' NOTHIN' *Lightning LIG 50*	49		

BROOK BROTHERS UK duo

Date	Title / Label	Peak Position	Weeks at No.1	Weeks in Top 40
30 Mar 61	WARPAINT *Pye 7N 15333*	5		13
24 Aug 61	AIN'T GONNA WASH FOR A WEEK *Pye 7N 15369*	13		8
25 Jan 62	HE'S OLD ENOUGH TO KNOW BETTER *Pye 7N 15409*	37		1
16 Aug 62	WELCOME HOME BABY *Pye 7N 15453*	33		3
21 Feb 63	TROUBLE IS MY MIDDLE NAME *Pye 7N 15498*	38		1

BROOKLYN BOUNCE German production group

Date	Title / Label	Peak Position	Weeks at No.1	Weeks in Top 40
30 May 98	THE MUSIC'S GOT ME *Club Tools 0064795 CLU*	67		

ELKIE BROOKS UK singer

Date	Title / Label	Peak Position	Weeks at No.1	Weeks in Top 40
2 Apr 77	PEARL'S A SINGER *A&M AMS 7275*	8		8
20 Aug 77	SUNSHINE AFTER THE RAIN *A&M AMS 7306*	10		8
25 Feb 78	LILAC WINE *A&M AMS 7333*	16		6
3 Jun 78	ONLY LOVE CAN BREAK YOUR HEART *A&M AMS 7353*	43		
11 Nov 78	DON'T CRY OUT LOUD *A&M AMS 7395*	12		8
5 May 79	THE RUNAWAY *A&M AMS 7428*	50		
16 Jan 82	FOOL IF YOU THINK IT'S OVER *A&M AMS 8187*	17		7
1 May 82	OUR LOVE *A&M AMS 8214*	43		
17 Jul 82	NIGHTS IN WHITE SATIN *A&M AMS 8235*	33		3
22 Jan 83	GASOLINE ALLEY *A&M AMS 8305*	52		
22 Nov 86	NO MORE THE FOOL *Legend LM 4*	5		11
4 Apr 87	BREAK THE CHAIN *Legend LM 8*	55		
11 Jul 87	WE'VE GOT TONIGHT *Legend LM 9*	69		

GARTH BROOKS US singer

Date	Title / Label	Peak Position	Weeks at No.1	Weeks in Top 40
1 Feb 92	SHAMELESS *Capitol CL 646*	71		
22 Jan 94	THE RED STROKES/AIN'T GOING DOWN (TILL THE SUN COMES UP) *Liberty CDCLS 704*	13		4
16 Apr 94	STANDING OUTSIDE THE FIRE *Liberty CDCL 712*	28		1
18 Feb 95	THE DANCE/FRIENDS IN LOW PLACES *Capitol CDCL 735*	36		2
17 Feb 96	SHE'S EVERY WOMAN *Capitol CDCL 767*	55		
13 Nov 99	LOST IN YOU *Capitol CDCL 814*	70		

MEL BROOKS US film director

Date	Title / Label	Peak Position	Weeks at No.1	Weeks in Top 40
18 Feb 84	TO BE OR NOT TO BE (THE HITLER RAP) *Island IS 158*	12		6

MEREDITH BROOKS US singer

Date	Title / Label	Peak Position	Weeks at No.1	Weeks in Top 40
2 Aug 97	BITCH *Capitol CDCL 790* ○	6		9
6 Dec 97	I NEED *Capitol CDCLS 794*	28		1
7 Mar 98	WHAT WOULD HAPPEN *Capitol CDCL 798*	49		

NORMAN BROOKS Canadian singer

Date	Title / Label	Peak Position	Weeks at No.1	Weeks in Top 40
12 Nov 54	A SKY BLUE SHIRT AND A RAINBOW TIE *London L 1228*	17		1

STEVE BROOKSTEIN UK singer

Date	Title / Label	Peak Position	Weeks at No.1	Weeks in Top 40
1 Jan 05	AGAINST ALL ODDS *Syco Music 82876672732*	1	1	8

BROS UK group

Date	Title / Label	Peak Position	Weeks at No.1	Weeks in Top 40
5 Dec 87	WHEN WILL I BE FAMOUS *CBS ATOM 2*	2		9
19 Mar 88	DROP THE BOY *CBS ATOM 3* ○	2		8
18 Jun 88	I OWE YOU NOTHING *CBS ATOM 4*	1	2	9
17 Sep 88	I QUIT *CBS ATOM 5*	4		5
3 Dec 88	CAT AMONG THE PIGEONS/SILENT NIGHT *CBS ATOM 6* ○	2		7
29 Jul 89	TOO MUCH *CBS ATOM 7* ○	2		6
7 Oct 89	CHOCOLATE BOX *CBS ATOM 8*	9		4
16 Dec 89	SISTER *CBS ATOM 9*	10		5
10 Mar 90	MADLY IN LOVE *CBS ATOM 10*	14		3
13 Jul 91	ARE YOU MINE *Columbia 6568707*	12		4
21 Sep 91	TRY *Columbia 6574047*	27		4

BROTHER BEYOND UK group

Date	Title / Label	Peak Position	Weeks at No.1	Weeks in Top 40
4 Apr 87	HOW MANY TIMES *EMI 5591*	62		
8 Aug 87	CHAIN-GANG SMILE *Parlophone R 6160*	57		
23 Jan 88	CAN YOU KEEP A SECRET *Parlophone R 6174*	56		
30 Jul 88	THE HARDER I TRY *Parlophone R 6184* ○	2		11
5 Nov 88	HE AIN'T NO COMPETITION *Parlophone R 6193*	6		6
21 Jan 89	BE MY TWIN *Parlophone R 6195*	14		5
1 Apr 89	CAN YOU KEEP A SECRET (REMIX) *Parlophone R 6197*	22		3
28 Oct 89	DRIVE ON *Parlophone R 6233*	39		2
9 Dec 89	WHEN WILL I SEE YOU AGAIN *Parlophone R 6239*	43		
10 Mar 90	TRUST *Parlophone R 6245*	53		
19 Jan 91	THE GIRL I USED TO KNOW *Parlophone R 6265*	48		

BROTHER BROWN Danish DJ/production duo

Date	Title / Label	Peak Position	Weeks at No.1	Weeks in Top 40
2 Oct 99	UNDER THE WATER *ffrr FCD 367* BROTHER BROWN FEATURING FRANK'EE	18		2
24 Nov 01	STAR CATCHING GIRL *Rulin 21CDS* BROTHER BROWN FEATURING FRANK'EE	51		

BROTHERHOOD UK group

Date	Title / Label	Peak Position	Weeks at No.1	Weeks in Top 40
27 Jan 96	ONE SHOT/NOTHING IN PARTICULAR *Bite It BHOODD 3*	55		

BROTHERHOOD OF MAN UK group

Date	Title / Label	Peak Position	Weeks at No.1	Weeks in Top 40
14 Feb 70	UNITED WE STAND *Deram DM 284*	10		9
4 Jul 70	WHERE ARE YOU GOING TO MY LOVE *Deram DM 298*	22		7
13 Mar 76	SAVE YOUR KISSES FOR ME *Pye 7N 45569* ⊛	1	6	16
19 Jun 76	MY SWEET ROSALIE *Pye 7N 45602*	30		5
26 Feb 77	OH BOY (THE MOOD I'M IN) *Pye 7N 45656*	8		11
9 Jul 77	ANGELO *Pye 7N 45699* ●	1	1	12
14 Jan 78	FIGARO *Pye 7N 46037* ●	1	1	10
27 May 78	BEAUTIFUL LOVER *Pye 7N 46071*	15		8
30 Sep 78	MIDDLE OF THE NIGHT *Pye 7N 46117*	41		
3 Jul 82	LIGHTNING FLASH *EMI 5309*	67		

BROTHERS UK group

Date	Title / Label	Peak Position	Weeks at No.1	Weeks in Top 40
29 Jan 77	SING ME *Bus Stop Bus 1054*	8		9

BROTHERS FOUR US group

Date	Title / Label	Peak Position	Weeks at No.1	Weeks in Top 40
23 Jun 60	GREENFIELDS *Philips PB 1009*	40		1

BROTHERS IN RHYTHM UK production duo

Date	Title / Label	Peak Position	Weeks at No.1	Weeks in Top 40
16 Mar 91	SUCH A GOOD FEELING *Fourth & Broadway BRW 228*	64		
14 Sep 91	SUCH A GOOD FEELING *Fourth & Broadway BRW 228*	14		7
30 Apr 94	FOREVER AND A DAY *Stress CDSTR 36* BROTHERS IN RHYTHM PRESENT CHARVONI	51		

BROTHERS JOHNSON US duo

Date	Title / Label	Peak Position	Weeks at No.1	Weeks in Top 40
9 Jul 77	STRAWBERRY LETTER 23 *A&M AMS 7297*	35		1
2 Sep 78	AIN'T WE FUNKIN' NOW *A&M AMS 7379*	43		

Date	Title	Label	Peak Position	Weeks at No.1	Weeks in Top 40
4 Nov 78	**RIDE-O-ROCKET**	*A&M AMS 7400*	50		
23 Feb 80	**STOMP**	*A&M AMS 7509*	6		8
31 May 80	**LIGHT UP THE NIGHT**	*A&M AMS 7526*	47		
25 Jul 81	**THE REAL THING**	*A&M AMS 8149*	50		

BROTHERS LIKE OUTLAW UK group

Date	Title	Label	Peak Position	Weeks at No.1	Weeks in Top 40
23 Jan 93	**GOOD VIBRATIONS** BROTHERS LIKE OUTLAW FEATURING ALISON EVELYN	*Gee Street GESCD 44*	74		

EDGAR BROUGHTON BAND UK group

Date	Title	Label	Peak Position	Weeks at No.1	Weeks in Top 40
18 Apr 70	**OUT DEMONS OUT**	*Harvest HAR 5015*	39		1
23 Jan 71	**APACHE DROPOUT**	*Harvest HAR 5032*	33		4

BOBBY BROWN US singer

Date	Title	Label	Peak Position	Weeks at No.1	Weeks in Top 40
6 Aug 88	**DON'T BE CRUEL**	*MCA 1268*	42		
17 Dec 88	**MY PREROGATIVE**	*MCA 1299* ★	6		10
25 Mar 89	**DON'T BE CRUEL (REMIX)**	*MCA 1310*	13		6
20 May 89	**EVERY LITTLE STEP**	*MCA 1338*	6		6
15 Jul 89	**ON OUR OWN (FROM GHOSTBUSTERS II)**	*MCA 1350* ●	4		8
23 Sep 89	**ROCK WIT'CHA**	*MCA 1367*	33		3
25 Nov 89	**RONI**	*MCA 1384*	21		3
9 Jun 90	**THE FREE STYLE MEGA-MIX**	*MCA 1421*	14		6
30 Jun 90	**SHE AIN'T WORTH IT** GLENN MEDEIROS FEATURING BOBBY BROWN ★	*London LON 265*	12		7
22 Aug 92	**HUMPIN' AROUND**	*MCA MCS 1680*	19		4
17 Oct 92	**GOOD ENOUGH**	*MCA MCS 1704*	41		
19 Jun 93	**THAT'S THE WAY LOVE IS**	*MCA MCSTD 1783*	56		
22 Jan 94	**SOMETHING IN COMMON** BOBBY BROWN & WHITNEY HOUSTON	*MCA MCSTD 1957*	16		3
25 Jun 94	**TWO CAN PLAY THAT GAME**	*MCA MCSTD 1973*	38		10
1 Apr 95	**TWO CAN PLAY THAT GAME**	*MCA MCSTD 1973* ●	3		1
8 Jul 95	**HUMPIN' AROUND (REMIX)**	*MCA MCSTD 2073*	8		4
14 Oct 95	**MY PREROGATIVE (REMIX)**	*MCA MCSTD 2094*	17		1
3 Feb 96	**EVERY LITTLE STEP (REMIX)**	*MCA MCSTD 48004*	25		1
22 Nov 97	**FEELIN' INSIDE**	*MCA MCSTD 48067*	40		1
21 Dec 02	**THUG LOVIN'** JA RULE FEATURING BOBBY BROWN	*Def Jam 637872*	15		6

CRAZY WORLD OF ARTHUR BROWN UK singer

Date	Title	Label	Peak Position	Weeks at No.1	Weeks in Top 40
26 Jun 68	**FIRE**	*Track 604 022*	1	1	14

CHRIS BROWN US singer

Date	Title	Label	Peak Position	Weeks at No.1	Weeks in Top 40
11 Feb 06	**RUN IT!** CHRIS BROWN FEATURING JUELZ SANTANA ★	*Jive 82876780532*	2		9
29 Apr 06	**YO! (EXCUSE ME MISS)**	*Jive 82876832192*	13		5
22 Jul 06	**GIMME THAT REMIX** CHRIS BROWN FEATURING LIL' WAYNE	*Jive 82876880762*	23		3
1 Sep 07	**WALL TO WALL**	*Download*	75		
3 Nov 07	**KISS KISS** CHRIS BROWN FEATURING T-PAIN ★	*Download*	38		3
16 Feb 08	**WITH YOU**	*RCA 88697269362*	14		5

DENNIS BROWN Jamaican singer

Date	Title	Label	Peak Position	Weeks at No.1	Weeks in Top 40
3 Mar 79	**MONEY IN MY POCKET**	*Lightning LV 5*	14		8
3 Jul 82	**LOVE HAS FOUND ITS WAY**	*A&M AMS 8226*	47		
11 Sep 82	**HALFWAY UP HALFWAY DOWN**	*A&M AMS 8250*	56		

DIANA BROWN & BARRIE K. SHARPE UK duo

Date	Title	Label	Peak Position	Weeks at No.1	Weeks in Top 40
2 Jun 90	**THE MASTERPLAN**	*ffrr F 133*	39		2
1 Sep 90	**SUN WORSHIPPERS (POSITIVE THINKING)**	*ffrr F 144*	61		
23 Mar 91	**LOVE OR NOTHING**	*ffrr F 152*	71		
27 Jun 92	**EATING ME ALIVE**	*ffrr F 190*	53		

ERROL BROWN UK singer

Date	Title	Label	Peak Position	Weeks at No.1	Weeks in Top 40
4 Jul 87	**PERSONAL TOUCH**	*WEA YZ 130*	25		4
28 Nov 87	**BODY ROCKIN'**	*WEA YZ 162*	51		
14 Feb 98	**IT STARTED WITH A KISS** HOT CHOCOLATE FEATURING ERROL BROWN	*EMI CDHOT 101*	18		2

FOXY BROWN US singer

Date	Title	Label	Peak Position	Weeks at No.1	Weeks in Top 40
21 Sep 96	**TOUCH ME TEASE ME** CASE FEATURING FOXY BROWN	*Def Jam DEFCD 18*	26		1
8 Mar 97	**GET ME HOME** FOXY BROWN FEATURING BLACKstreet	*Def Jam DEFCD 32*	11		3
10 May 97	**AIN'T NO PLAYA** JAY-Z FEATURING FOXY BROWN	*Northwestside 74321474842*	31		1
21 Jun 97	**I'LL BE** FOXY BROWN FEATURING JAY-Z	*Def Jam 5710432*	9		2
11 Oct 97	**BIG BAD MAMMA** FOXY BROWN FEATURING DRU HILL	*Def Jam 5749792*	12		2
25 Oct 97	**SUNSHINE** JAY-Z FEATURING BABYFACE & FOXY BROWN	*Northwestside 74321528702*	25		1
13 Mar 99	**HOT SPOT**	*Def Jam 8708352*	31		1
8 Sep 01	**OH YEAH**	*Def Jam 5887312*	27		1

GLORIA D BROWN US singer

Date	Title	Label	Peak Position	Weeks at No.1	Weeks in Top 40
8 Jun 85	**THE MORE THEY KNOCK, THE MORE I LOVE YOU**	*10 TEN 52*	57		

HORACE BROWN US singer

Date	Title	Label	Peak Position	Weeks at No.1	Weeks in Top 40
25 Feb 95	**TASTE YOUR LOVE**	*Uptown MCSTD 2026*	58		
18 May 96	**ONE FOR THE MONEY**	*Motown 8605232*	12		3
12 Oct 96	**THINGS WE DO FOR LOVE**	*Motown 8605712*	27		1

HOWARD BROWN UK singer

Date	Title	Label	Peak Position	Weeks at No.1	Weeks in Top 40
19 Mar 05	**YOU'RE THE FIRST THE LAST MY EVERYTHING**	*HBOS CDHALIFAX1*	13		2

IAN BROWN UK singer

Date	Title	Label	Peak Position	Weeks at No.1	Weeks in Top 40
24 Jan 98	**MY STAR**	*Polydor 5719872*	5		3
4 Apr 98	**CORPSES**	*Polydor 5696552*	14		2
20 Jun 98	**CAN'T SEE ME**	*Polydor 5440452*	21		1
20 Feb 99	**BE THERE** UNKLE FEATURING IAN BROWN	*Mo Wax MW 108CD1*	8		3
6 Nov 99	**LOVE LIKE A FOUNTAIN**	*Polydor 5615162*	23		1
19 Feb 00	**DOLPHINS WERE MONKEYS**	*Polydor 5616372*	5		3
17 Jun 00	**GOLDEN GAZE**	*Polydor 5618452*	29		1
29 Sep 01	**F.E.A.R.**	*Polydor 5872842*	13		2
23 Feb 02	**WHISPERS**	*Polydor 5705382*	33		1
2 Oct 04	**KEEP WHAT YA GOT**	*Fiction 9868284*	18		2
27 Nov 04	**REIGN** UNKLE FEATURING IAN BROWN	*Mo Wax GUSIN007CDS*	40		1
29 Jan 05	**TIME IS MY EVERYTHING**	*Fiction 9869961*	15		2
17 Sep 05	**ALL ABLAZE**	*Polydor 9873252*	20		1
29 Sep 07	**ILLEGAL ATTACKS** IAN BROWN FEATURING SINEAD O'CONNOR	*Fiction 1724668*	16		1

JAMES BROWN US singer

Date	Title	Label	Peak Position	Weeks at No.1	Weeks in Top 40
23 Sep 65	**PAPA'S GOT A BRAND NEW BAG**	*London HL 9990*	25		6
24 Feb 66	**I GOT YOU (I FEEL GOOD)**	*Pye International 7N 25350*	29		3
16 Jun 66	**IT'S A MAN'S MAN'S MAN'S WORLD**	*Pye International 7N 25371*	13		8
10 Oct 70	**GET UP I FEEL LIKE BEING A SEX MACHINE**	*Polydor 2001 071*	32		3
27 Nov 71	**HEY AMERICA**	*Mojo 2093 006*	47		
18 Sep 76	**GET UP OFFA THAT THING**	*Polydor 2066 687*	22		5
29 Jan 77	**BODY HEAT**	*Polydor 2066 763*	36		2
10 Jan 81	**RAPP PAYBACK (WHERE IZ MOSES?)**	*RCA 28*	39		2
2 Jul 83	**BRING IT ON...BRING IT ON**	*Sonet SON 2258*	45		
1 Sep 84	**UNITY (PART 1 - THE THIRD COMING)** AFRIKA BAAMBAATAA & JAMES BROWN	*Tommy Boy AFR 2*	49		
27 Apr 85	**FROGGY MIX**	*Boiling Point FROG 1*	50		
1 Jun 85	**GET UP I FEEL LIKE BEING A SEX MACHINE**	*Boiling Point POSP 751*	47		
25 Jan 86	**LIVING IN AMERICA**	*Scotti Brothers A 6701*	5		8
1 Mar 86	**GET UP I FEEL LIKE BEING A SEX MACHINE**	*Boiling Point POSP 751*	46		
18 Oct 86	**GRAVITY**	*Scotti Brothers 6500597*	65		
30 Jan 88	**SHE'S THE ONE**	*Urban URB 13*	45		
23 Apr 88	**THE PAYBACK MIX**	*Urban URB 17*	12		5
4 Jun 88	**I'M REAL** JAMES BROWN FEATURING FULL FORCE	*Scotti Brothers JSB 1*	31		3
23 Jul 88	**I GOT YOU (I FEEL GOOD)**	*A&M AM 444*	52		
16 Nov 91	**GET UP I FEEL LIKE BEING A SEX MACHINE**	*Polydor PO 185*	69		
24 Oct 92	**I GOT YOU (I FEEL GOOD) (REMIX)** JAMES BROWN VS DAKEYNE	*FBI 9*	72		
17 Apr 93	**CAN'T GET ANY HARDER**	*Polydor PZCD 262*	59		
17 Apr 99	**FUNK ON AH ROLL**	*Inferno/Eagle EAGXA 073*	40		1
22 Apr 00	**FUNK ON AH ROLL (REMIX)**	*Eagle EAGXS 127*	63		

Silver-selling ● Gold-selling ● Platinum-selling ✱ US No.1 ★ — Peak Position · Weeks at No.1 · Weeks in Top 40

JENNIFER BROWN Swedish singer

Date	Title	Peak	Wks at No.1	Wks in Top 40
1 May 99	**TUESDAY AFTERNOON** *RCA 74321604092*	57		

JOCELYN BROWN US singer

Date	Title	Peak	Wks at No.1	Wks in Top 40
21 Apr 84	**SOMEBODY ELSE'S GUY** *Fourth & Broadway BRW 5*	13		7
22 Sep 84	**I WISH YOU WOULD** *Fourth & Broadway BRW 14*	51		
15 Mar 86	**LOVE'S GONNA GET YOU** *Warner Brothers W 8889*	70		
29 Jun 91	**ALWAYS THERE** *Talkin Loud TLK 10* INCOGNITO FEATURING JOCELYN BROWN	6		7
14 Sep 91	**SHE'S GOT SOUL** *A&M AM 819* JAMESTOWN FEATURING JOCELYN BROWN	57		
7 Dec 91	**DON'T TALK JUST KISS** *Tug SNOG 2* RIGHT SAID FRED. GUEST VOCALS: JOCELYN BROWN	3		9
20 Mar 93	**TAKE ME UP** *A&M AMCD 210* SONIC SURFERS FEATURING JOCELYN BROWN	61		
11 Jun 94	**NO MORE TEARS (ENOUGH IS ENOUGH)** *Ding Dong 74321209032* KYM MAZELLE & JOCELYN BROWN	13		4
8 Oct 94	**GIMME ALL YOUR LOVIN'** *Ding Dong 74321231322* KYM MAZELLE & JOCELYN BROWN	22		2
13 Jul 96	**KEEP ON JUMPIN'** *Manifesto FESCD 11* TODD TERRY FEATURING MARTHA WASH & JOCELYN BROWN	8		5
10 May 97	**IT'S ALRIGHT, I FEEL IT!** *Talkin Loud TLCD 22* NUYORICAN SOUL FEATURING JOCELYN BROWN	26		1
12 Jul 97	**SOMETHING GOIN' ON** *Manifesto FESCD 25* TODD TERRY FEATURING MARTHA WASH & JOCELYN BROWN	5		7
25 Oct 97	**I AM THE BLACK GOLD OF THE SUN** *Talkin Loud TLCD 26* NUYORICAN SOUL FEATURING JOCELYN BROWN	31		1
22 Nov 97	**HAPPINESS** *Sony S3 KAMCD 2* KAMASUTRA FEATURING JOCELYN BROWN	45		
2 May 98	**FUN** *INCredible INCRL 2CD* DA MOB FEATURING JOCELYN BROWN	33		1
29 Aug 98	**AIN'T NO MOUNTAIN HIGH ENOUGH** *INCredible INCRL 7CD*	35		1
27 Mar 99	**I BELIEVE** *Playola 0091705 PLA* JAMESTOWN FEATURING JOCELYN BROWN	62		
3 Jul 99	**IT'S ALL GOOD** *INCredible INCRL 14CD* DA MOB FEATURING JOCELYN BROWN	54		
11 Mar 00	**BELIEVE** *Defected DFECT 14CDS* MINISTERS DE LA FUNK FEATURING JOCELYN BROWN	45		
27 Jan 01	**BELIEVE (REMIX)** *Defected DFECT 26CDS* MINISTERS DE LA FUNK FEATURING JOCELYN BROWN	42		
7 Sep 02	**THAT'S HOW GOOD YOUR LOVE IS** *Defected DFTD 057CDS* IL PADRINOS FEATURING JOCELYN BROWN	54		

JOE BROWN UK singer

Date	Title	Peak	Wks at No.1	Wks in Top 40
17 Mar 60	**DARKTOWN STRUTTERS BALL** *Decca F 11207*	34		3
26 Jan 61	**SHINE** *Pye 7N 15322*	33		4
11 Jan 62	**WHAT A CRAZY WORLD WE'RE LIVING IN** *Piccadilly 7N 35024*	37		1
17 May 62	**A PICTURE OF YOU** *Piccadilly 7N 35047*	2		17
13 Sep 62	**YOUR TENDER LOOK** *Piccadilly 7N 35058*	31		5
15 Nov 62	**IT ONLY TOOK A MINUTE** *Piccadilly 7N 35082*	6		12
7 Feb 63	**THAT'S WHAT LOVE WILL DO** *Piccadilly 7N 35106*	3		12
27 Jun 63	**NATURE'S TIME FOR LOVE** *Piccadilly 7N 35129*	26		4
26 Sep 63	**SALLY ANN** *Piccadilly 7N 35138*	28		5
29 Jun 67	**WITH A LITTLE HELP FROM MY FRIENDS** *Pye 7N 17339*	32		2
14 Apr 73	**HEY MAMA** *Ammo AMO 101*	33		4

KATHY BROWN US singer

Date	Title	Peak	Wks at No.1	Wks in Top 40
25 Nov 95	**TURN ME OUT** *Stress CDSTR 40*	44		
20 Sep 97	**TURN ME OUT (TURN TO SUGAR) (REMIX)** *ffrr FCD 314* PRAXIS FEATURING KATHY BROWN	35		1
10 Apr 99	**JOY** *Azuli AZNYCDX 094*	63		
5 May 01	**LOVE IS NOT A GAME** *Defected DFECT 31CDS* J MAJIK FEATURING KATHY BROWN	34		1
2 Jun 01	**OVER YOU** *Defected DFECT 28CDS* WARREN CLARKE FEATURING KATHY BROWN	42		
22 Jan 05	**STRINGS OF LIFE (STRONGER ON MY OWN)** *Defected DFTD094CDS* SOUL CENTRAL FEATURING KATHY BROWN	6		4

MARK BROWN US singer

Date	Title	Peak	Wks at No.1	Wks in Top 40
9 Feb 08	**THE JOURNEY CONTINUES** *Download* MARK BROWN FEATURING SARAH CRACKNELL	11		4

MIQUEL BROWN US singer

Date	Title	Peak	Wks at No.1	Wks in Top 40
18 Feb 84	**HE'S A SAINT, HE'S A SINNER** *Record Shack SOHO 15*	68		
24 Aug 85	**CLOSE TO PERFECTION** *Record Shack SOHO 48*	63		

PETER BROWN US singer

Date	Title	Peak	Wks at No.1	Wks in Top 40
11 Feb 78	**DO YA WANNA GET FUNKY WITH ME** *TK TKR 6009*	43		
17 Jun 78	**DANCE WITH ME** *TK TKR 6027*	57		

POLLY BROWN UK singer

Date	Title	Peak	Wks at No.1	Wks in Top 40
14 Sep 74	**UP IN A PUFF OF SMOKE** *GTO GT 2*	43		

ROY CHUBBY BROWN UK comedian

Date	Title	Peak	Wks at No.1	Wks in Top 40
13 May 95	**LIVING NEXT DOOR TO ALICE (WHO THE F**K IS ALICE)** *NOW CDWAG 245* SMOKIE FEATURING ROY CHUBBY BROWN	64		
26 Aug 95	**LIVING NEXT DOOR TO ALICE (WHO THE F**K IS ALICE)** *NOW CDWAG 245* SMOKIE FEATURING ROY CHUBBY BROWN ●	3		14
21 Dec 96	**ROCKIN' GOOD CHRISTMAS** *Polystar 5732612*	51		

SAM BROWN UK singer

Date	Title	Peak	Wks at No.1	Wks in Top 40
11 Jun 88	**STOP** *A&M AM 440*	52		
4 Feb 89	**STOP** *A&M AM 440* ●	4		9
13 May 89	**CAN I GET A WITNESS** *A&M AM 509*	15		5
3 Mar 90	**WITH A LITTLE LOVE** *A&M AM 539*	44		
5 May 90	**KISSING GATE** *A&M AM 549*	23		6
26 Aug 95	**JUST GOOD FRIENDS** *Dick Bros. DDICK 014CD1* FISH FEATURING SAM BROWN	63		

SHARON BROWN US singer

Date	Title	Peak	Wks at No.1	Wks in Top 40
17 Apr 82	**I SPECIALIZE IN LOVE** *Virgin VS 494*	38		3
26 Feb 94	**I SPECIALIZE IN LOVE (REMIX)** *Deep Distraxion OILYCD 025*	62		

BROWN SAUCE UK group

Date	Title	Peak	Wks at No.1	Wks in Top 40
12 Dec 81	**I WANNA BE A WINNER** *BBC RESL 101*	15		9

DUNCAN BROWNE UK singer

Date	Title	Peak	Wks at No.1	Wks in Top 40
19 Aug 72	**JOURNEY** *RAK 135*	23		6
22 Dec 84	**THEME FROM THE TRAVELLING MAN** *Towerbell TOW 54*	68		

JACKSON BROWNE US singer

Date	Title	Peak	Wks at No.1	Wks in Top 40
1 Jul 78	**STAY** *Asylum K 13128*	12		8
18 Oct 86	**IN THE SHAPE OF A HEART** *Elektra EKR 42*	66		
25 Jun 94	**EVERYWHERE I GO** *Elektra EKR 184CD1*	67		

TOM BROWNE US trumpeter

Date	Title	Peak	Wks at No.1	Wks in Top 40
19 Jul 80	**FUNKIN' FOR JAMAICA (N.Y.)** *Arista ARIST 357*	10		8
25 Oct 80	**THIGHS HIGH (GRIP YOUR HIPS AND MOVE)** *Arista ARIST 367*	45		
30 Jan 82	**FUNGI MAMA (BEBOPAFUNKADISCOLYPSO)** *Arista ARIST 450*	58		
11 Jan 92	**FUNKIN' FOR JAMAICA (REMIX)** *Arista 114998*	45		

BROWNS US group

Date	Title	Peak	Wks at No.1	Wks in Top 40
18 Sep 59	**THE THREE BELLS** *RCA 1140* ★	6		13

BROWNSTONE US group

Date	Title	Peak	Wks at No.1	Wks in Top 40
1 Apr 95	**IF YOU LOVE ME** *MJJ 6614135*	8		9
15 Jul 95	**GRAPEVYNE** *MJJ 6620942*	16		2
23 Sep 95	**I CAN'T TELL YOU WHY** *MJJ 6623775*	27		1
17 May 97	**5 MILES TO EMPTY** *MJJ 6640962*	12		3
27 Sep 97	**KISS AND TELL** *Epic 6649852*	21		1

BROWNSVILLE STATION US group

Date	Title	Peak	Wks at No.1	Wks in Top 40
2 Mar 74	**SMOKIN' IN THE BOYS' ROOM** *Philips 6073 834*	27		5

DAVE BRUBECK QUARTET US group

Date	Title	Peak	Wks at No.1	Wks in Top 40
26 Oct 61	**TAKE FIVE** *Fontana H 339*	6		14
8 Feb 62	**IT'S A RAGGY WALTZ** *Fontana H 352*	36		2
17 May 62	**UNSQUARE DANCE** *CBS AAG 102*	14		11

Silver-selling ○ Gold-selling ● Platinum-selling ✪ US No.1 ★ — Peak Position / Weeks at No.1 / Weeks in Top 40

TOMMY BRUCE UK singer

Date	Title	Peak Position	Weeks at No.1	Weeks in Top 40
26 May 60	**AIN'T MISBEHAVIN'** *Columbia DB 4453* TOMMY BRUCE AND THE BRUISERS	3		14
8 Sep 60	**BROKEN DOLL** *Columbia DB 4498* TOMMY BRUCE AND THE BRUISERS	36		2
22 Feb 62	**BABETTE** *Columbia DB 4776*	50		

CLAUDIA BRUCKEN German singer

Date	Title	Peak Position	Weeks at No.1	Weeks in Top 40
11 Aug 90	**ABSOLUT(E)** *Island IS 471*	71		
16 Feb 91	**KISS LIKE ETHER** *Island IS 479*	63		

BRUISERS UK group

Date	Title	Peak Position	Weeks at No.1	Weeks in Top 40
8 Aug 63	**BLUE GIRL** *Parlophone R 5042*	31		4

FRANK BRUNO UK boxer

Date	Title	Peak Position	Weeks at No.1	Weeks in Top 40
23 Dec 95	**EYE OF THE TIGER** *RCA 74321336282*	28		3

TYRONE BRUNSON US singer/bass player

Date	Title	Peak Position	Weeks at No.1	Weeks in Top 40
25 Dec 82	**THE SMURF** *Epic EPC A 3024*	52		

BASIL BRUSH UK puppet

Date	Title	Peak Position	Weeks at No.1	Weeks in Top 40
27 Dec 03	**BOOM BOOM/CHRISTMAS SLIDE** *Right RRBB001* BASIL BRUSH FEATURING INDIA BEAU	44		

DORA BRYAN UK actress/singer

Date	Title	Peak Position	Weeks at No.1	Weeks in Top 40
5 Dec 63	**ALL I WANT FOR CHRISTMAS IS A BEATLE** *Fontana TF 427*	20		5

KELLE BRYAN UK singer

Date	Title	Peak Position	Weeks at No.1	Weeks in Top 40
2 Oct 99	**HIGHER THAN HEAVEN** *1st Avenue MERCD 522*	14		2

ANITA BRYANT US singer

Date	Title	Peak Position	Weeks at No.1	Weeks in Top 40
26 May 60	**PAPER ROSES** *London HLL 9144*	24		1
6 Oct 60	**MY LITTLE CORNER OF THE WORLD** *London HLL 9171*	48		

PEABO BRYSON US singer

Date	Title	Peak Position	Weeks at No.1	Weeks in Top 40
20 Aug 83	**TONIGHT I CELEBRATE MY LOVE** *Capitol CL 302* PEABO BRYSON & ROBERTA FLACK ○	2		10
16 May 92	**BEAUTY AND THE BEAST** *Epic 6576607* CELINE DION & PEABO BRYSON	9		4
17 Jul 93	**BY THE TIME THIS NIGHT IS OVER** *Arista 74321157142* KENNY G WITH PEABO BRYSON	56		
11 Dec 93	**A WHOLE NEW WORLD (ALADDIN'S THEME)** *Columbia 6599002* PEABO BRYSON & REGINA BELLE ★	12		9

BT US producer

Date	Title	Peak Position	Weeks at No.1	Weeks in Top 40
18 Mar 95	**EMBRACING THE SUNSHINE** *Perfecto YZ 895CD*	34		1
16 Sep 95	**LOVING YOU MORE** *Perfecto PERF 110CD* BT FEATURING VINCENT COVELLO	28		1
10 Feb 96	**LOVING YOU MORE (REMIX)** *Perfecto PERF 117CD* BT FEATURING VINCENT COVELLO	14		2
9 Nov 96	**BLUE SKIES** *Perfecto PERF 130CD1* BT FEATURING TORI AMOS	26		1
19 Jul 97	**FLAMING JUNE** *Perfecto PERF 145CD1*	19		2
29 Nov 97	**LOVE, PEACE & GREASE** *Perfecto PERF 153CD1*	41		
10 Jan 98	**FLAMING JUNE** *Perfecto PERF 157CD1*	28		2
18 Apr 98	**REMEMBER** *Perfecto PERF 160CD1*	27		1
21 Nov 98	**GODSPEED** *Renaissance RENCD 002*	54		
9 Oct 99	**MERCURY AND SOLACE** *Headspace HEDSCD 001*	38		1
24 Jun 00	**DREAMING** *Headspace HEDSCD 002* BT FEATURING KIRSTY HAWKSHAW	38		1
23 Jun 01	**NEVER GONNA COME BACK DOWN** *Ministry Of Sound MOSBT CDS1*	51		
15 May 04	**LOVE COMES AGAIN** *Nebula NEBCD 058* TIESTO FEATURING BT	30		1

B.T. EXPRESS US group

Date	Title	Peak Position	Weeks at No.1	Weeks in Top 40
29 Mar 75	**EXPRESS** *Pye International 7N 25674*	34		3
26 Jul 80	**DOES IT FEEL GOOD/GIVE UP THE FUNK (LET'S DANCE)** *Calibre CAB 503*	52		
23 Apr 94	**EXPRESS (REMIX)** *PWL International PWCD 285*	67		

B2K US group

Date	Title	Peak Position	Weeks at No.1	Weeks in Top 40
24 Aug 02	**UH HUH** *Epic 6729512*	35		1
29 Mar 03	**BUMP BUMP BUMP** *Epic 6736452* B2K FEATURING P DIDDY	11		6
21 Jun 03	**GIRLFRIEND** *Epic 6739335*	10		4
18 Oct 03	**UH HUH 2003** *Epic 6744012*	31		1
20 Mar 04	**BADABOOM** *Epic 6747512* B2K FEATURING FABOLOUS	26		2

MICHAEL BUBLE Canadian singer

Date	Title	Peak Position	Weeks at No.1	Weeks in Top 40
9 Apr 05	**HOME/SONG FOR YOU** *Reprise W668CD1*	31		2
3 Dec 05	**HOME/SONG FOR YOU** *Reprise W693CD*	63		
28 Apr 07	**EVERYTHING** *Reprise W761CD1*	38		2
20 Oct 07	**EVERYTHING** *Reprise W761CD1*	52		
27 Oct 07	**HOME/SONG FOR YOU** *Reprise W693CD*	45		
1 Dec 07	**LOST** *Reprise W789CD*	19		3

BUBBLEROCK UK singer

Date	Title	Peak Position	Weeks at No.1	Weeks in Top 40
26 Jan 74	**(I CAN'T GET NO) SATISFACTION** *UK 53*	29		3

ROY BUCHANAN US singer

Date	Title	Peak Position	Weeks at No.1	Weeks in Top 40
31 Mar 73	**SWEET DREAMS** *Polydor 2066 307*	40		2

BUCKETHEADS US producer

Date	Title	Peak Position	Weeks at No.1	Weeks in Top 40
4 Mar 95	**THE BOMB! (THESE SOUNDS FALL INTO MY MIND)** *Positiva CDTIV 33* ○	5		10
20 Jan 96	**GOT MYSELF TOGETHER** *Positiva CDTIV 48*	12		2

LINDSEY BUCKINGHAM US singer/guitarist

Date	Title	Peak Position	Weeks at No.1	Weeks in Top 40
16 Jan 82	**TROUBLE** *Mercury MER 85*	31		3

JEFF BUCKLEY US singer/guitarist

Date	Title	Peak Position	Weeks at No.1	Weeks in Top 40
27 May 95	**LAST GOODBYE** *Columbia 6620422*	54		
6 Jun 98	**EVERYBODY HERE WANTS YOU** *Columbia 6657912*	43		
9 Jun 07	**HALLELUJAH** *Columbia 88697098847*	65		

BUCKS FIZZ UK group

Date	Title	Peak Position	Weeks at No.1	Weeks in Top 40
28 Mar 81	**MAKING YOUR MIND UP** *RCA 56* ●	1	3	11
6 Jun 81	**PIECE OF THE ACTION** *RCA 88* ○	12		7
15 Aug 81	**ONE OF THOSE NIGHTS** *RCA 114*	20		7
28 Nov 81	**THE LAND OF MAKE BELIEVE** *RCA 163*	1	2	13
27 Mar 82	**MY CAMERA NEVER LIES** *RCA 202* ○	1	2	7
19 Jun 82	**NOW THOSE DAYS ARE GONE** *RCA 241* ○	8		8
27 Nov 82	**IF YOU CAN'T STAND THE HEAT** *RCA 300* ○	10		9
12 Mar 83	**RUN FOR YOUR LIFE** *RCA FIZ 1*	14		6
18 Jun 83	**WHEN WE WERE YOUNG** *RCA 342*	10		5
1 Oct 83	**LONDON TOWN** *RCA 363*	34		4
17 Dec 83	**RULES OF THE GAME** *RCA 380*	57		
25 Aug 84	**TALKING IN YOUR SLEEP** *RCA FIZ 2*	15		6
27 Oct 84	**GOLDEN DAYS** *RCA FIZ 3*	42		
29 Dec 84	**I HEAR TALK** *RCA FIZ 4*	34		4
22 Jun 85	**YOU AND YOUR HEART SO BLUE** *RCA PB 40233*	43		
14 Sep 85	**MAGICAL** *RCA PB 40367*	57		
7 Jun 86	**NEW BEGINNING (MAMBA SEYRA)** *Polydor POSP 794*	8		8
30 Aug 86	**LOVE THE ONE YOU'RE WITH** *Polydor POSP 813*	47		
15 Nov 86	**KEEP EACH OTHER WARM** *Polydor POSP 835*	45		
5 Nov 88	**HEART OF STONE** *RCA PB 42035*	50		

BUCKSHOT LEFONQUE US group

Date	Title	Peak Position	Weeks at No.1	Weeks in Top 40
6 Dec 97	**ANOTHER DAY** *Columbia 6653762*	65		

Silver-selling ○ · Gold-selling ● · Platinum-selling · US No.1 ★ · Peak Position · Weeks at No.1 · Weeks in Top 40

ROY BUDD UK composer

Date	Title	Label	Peak Position	Weeks at No.1	Weeks in Top 40
10 Jul 99	GET CARTER	*Cinephile CINX 1003*	68		

JOE BUDDEN US rapper

Date	Title	Label	Peak Position	Weeks at No.1	Weeks in Top 40
19 Jul 03	PUMP IT UP	*Def Jam 9808879*	13		5
16 Oct 04	WHATEVER U WANT	*Def Jam 9864266* CHRISTINA MILIAN FEATURING JOE BUDDEN	9		4

BUDGIE UK group

Date	Title	Label	Peak Position	Weeks at No.1	Weeks in Top 40
3 Oct 81	KEEPING A RENDEZVIUS	*RCA BUDGIE 3*	71		

MUTYA BUENA UK singer

Date	Title	Label	Peak Position	Weeks at No.1	Weeks in Top 40
18 Nov 06	THIS IS NOT REAL LOVE	*Aegean/Sony 88697019792* GEORGE MICHAEL & MUTYA	15		3
26 May 07	REAL GIRL	*Fourth & Broadway 1734395*	2		11
3 Nov 07	JUST A LITTLE BIT	*Fourth & Broadway 1748789*	65		
12 Jan 08	B BOY BABY	*Fourth & Broadway 1756344*	73		

BUFFALO G Irish duo

Date	Title	Label	Peak Position	Weeks at No.1	Weeks in Top 40
10 Jun 00	WE'RE REALLY SAYING SOMETHING	*Epic 6694182*	17		2

BUFFALO TOM US group

Date	Title	Label	Peak Position	Weeks at No.1	Weeks in Top 40
23 Oct 99	GOING UNDERGROUND	*Ignition IGNSCD 16*	6		3

BUG KANN & PLASTIC JAM UK group

Date	Title	Label	Peak Position	Weeks at No.1	Weeks in Top 40
31 Aug 91	MADE IN TWO MINUTES	*Optimum Dance BKPJ 1S* BUG KANN & PLASTIC JAM FEATURING PATTI LOW & DOOGIE	70		
26 Feb 94	MADE IN TWO MINUTES (REMIX)	*PWL International PWCD 286*	64		

BUGGLES UK duo

Date	Title	Label	Peak Position	Weeks at No.1	Weeks in Top 40
22 Sep 79	VIDEO KILLED THE RADIO STAR	*Island WIP 6524* ●	1	1	8
26 Jan 80	THE PLASTIC AGE	*Island WIP 6540*	16		7
5 Apr 80	CLEAN CLEAN	*Island WIP 6584*	38		2
8 Nov 80	ELSTREE	*Island WIP 6624*	55		

BUGZ IN THE ATTIC UK group

Date	Title	Label	Peak Position	Weeks at No.1	Weeks in Top 40
22 Jan 05	BOOTY LA LA	*V2 VVR5030093*	44		

JAMES BULLER UK singer/actor

Date	Title	Label	Peak Position	Weeks at No.1	Weeks in Top 40
6 Mar 99	CAN'T SMILE WITHOUT YOU	*BBC Music WMSS 60092*	51		

BULLET FOR MY VALENTINE UK group

Date	Title	Label	Peak Position	Weeks at No.1	Weeks in Top 40
9 Apr 05	4 WORDS (TO CHOKE UPON)	*Visible Noise TORMENT51*	40		1
1 Oct 05	SUFFOCATING UNDER WORDS OF SORROW	*Visible Noise TORMENT58CD*	37		1
18 Feb 06	ALL THESE THINGS I HATE	*Visible Noise TORMENT64CD*	29		1
29 Jul 06	TEARS DON'T FALL	*Visible Noise TORMENT69CD*	37		1
2 Feb 08	SCREAM AIM FIRE	*20-20 Recordings 88697222602*	34		1

BULLETPROOF UK producer

Date	Title	Label	Peak Position	Weeks at No.1	Weeks in Top 40
10 Mar 01	SAY YEAH/DANCE TO THE RHYTHM	*Tidy Trax TIDY 148CD*	62		

BUMP UK production duo

Date	Title	Label	Peak Position	Weeks at No.1	Weeks in Top 40
4 Jul 92	I'M RUSHING	*Good Boy EDGE7 1*	40		1
11 Nov 95	I'M RUSHING (REMIX)	*Deconstruction 74321320692*	45		

BUMP & FLEX UK production duo

Date	Title	Label	Peak Position	Weeks at No.1	Weeks in Top 40
23 May 98	LONG TIME COMING	*Heat Recordings HEATCD 014*	73		

EMMA BUNTON UK singer

Date	Title	Label	Peak Position	Weeks at No.1	Weeks in Top 40
13 Nov 99	WHAT I AM	*VC Recordings VCRD 53* TIN TIN OUT FEATURING EMMA BUNTON ○	2		7
14 Apr 01	WHAT TOOK YOU SO LONG	*Virgin VSCDT 1796* ○	1	2	9
8 Sep 01	TAKE MY BREATH AWAY	*Virgin VSCDT 1814*	5		4
22 Dec 01	WE'RE NOT GONNA SLEEP TONIGHT	*Virgin VSCDT 1821*	20		4
7 Jun 03	FREE ME	*19/Universal 9807473*	5		6
25 Oct 03	MAYBE	*19/Universal 9812785*	6		6
7 Feb 04	I'LL BE THERE	*19/Universal 9816268*	7		4
12 Jun 04	CRICKETS SING FOR ANAMARIA	*19 9866856*	15		3
25 Nov 06	DOWNTOWN	*19 1717347*	3		6
24 Feb 07	ALL I NEED TO KNOW	*19 1723657*	60		

TIM BURGESS UK singer

Date	Title	Label	Peak Position	Weeks at No.1	Weeks in Top 40
18 Dec 93	I WAS BORN ON CHRISTMAS DAY	*Heavenly HVN 36CD* SAINT ETIENNE CO STARRING TIM BURGESS	37		2
6 Sep 03	I BELIEVE IN THE SPIRIT	*PIAS PIASB109CD*	44		
15 Nov 03	ONLY A BOY	*PIAS PIASB119CD*	54		

GEOFFREY BURGON UK orchestra leader

Date	Title	Label	Peak Position	Weeks at No.1	Weeks in Top 40
26 Dec 81	BRIDESHEAD THEME	*Chrysalis CHS 2562*	48		

KENI BURKE US singer

Date	Title	Label	Peak Position	Weeks at No.1	Weeks in Top 40
27 Jun 81	LET SOMEBODY LOVE YOU	*RCA 93*	59		
18 Apr 92	RISIN' TO THE TOP	*RCA PB 49103*	70		

BURN UK group

Date	Title	Label	Peak Position	Weeks at No.1	Weeks in Top 40
8 Jun 02	THE SMILING FACE	*Hut HUTCD 155*	72		
29 Mar 03	DRUNKEN FOOL	*Hut HUTCD 166*	54		

HANK C. BURNETTE Swedish multi-instrumentalist

Date	Title	Label	Peak Position	Weeks at No.1	Weeks in Top 40
30 Oct 76	SPINNING ROCK BOOGIE	*Sonet SON 2094*	21		7

JOHNNY BURNETTE US singer

Date	Title	Label	Peak Position	Weeks at No.1	Weeks in Top 40
29 Sep 60	DREAMIN'	*London HLG 9172*	5		15
12 Jan 61	YOU'RE SIXTEEN	*London HLG 9254*	3		12
13 Apr 61	LITTLE BOY SAD	*London HLG 9315*	12		10
10 Aug 61	GIRLS	*London HLG 9388*	37		2
17 May 62	CLOWN SHOES	*Liberty LIB 55416*	35		3

ROCKY BURNETTE US singer

Date	Title	Label	Peak Position	Weeks at No.1	Weeks in Top 40
17 Nov 79	TIRED OF TOEIN' THE LINE	*EMI 2992*	58		

JERRY BURNS UK singer

Date	Title	Label	Peak Position	Weeks at No.1	Weeks in Top 40
25 Apr 92	PALE RED	*Columbia 6579467*	64		

PETE BURNS UK singer

Date	Title	Label	Peak Position	Weeks at No.1	Weeks in Top 40
19 Jun 04	JACK AND JILL PARTY	*Olde English LKCD02*	75		

RAY BURNS UK singer

Date	Title	Label	Peak Position	Weeks at No.1	Weeks in Top 40
11 Feb 55	MOBILE	*Columbia DB 3563*	4		13
26 Aug 55	THAT'S HOW A LOVE SONG WAS BORN	*Columbia DB 3640* RAY BURNS WITH THE CORONETS	14		6

MALANDRA BURROWS UK singer

Date	Title	Label	Peak Position	Weeks at No.1	Weeks in Top 40
1 Dec 90	JUST THIS SIDE OF LOVE	*Yorkshire Television DALE 1*	11		6
18 Oct 97	CARNIVAL IN HEAVEN	*warner.esp WESP 001CD*	49		
29 Aug 98	DON'T LEAVE ME	*warner.esp WESP 004CD*	54		

JENNY BURTON US singer

Date	Title	Label	Peak Position	Weeks at No.1	Weeks in Top 40
30 Mar 85	BAD HABITS	*Atlantic A 9583*	68		

BURUNDI STEIPHENSON BLACK
Burundan tribal drummers with French producer

Date	Title / Label	Peak Position	Weeks at No.1	Weeks in Top 40
13 Nov 71	**BURUNDI BLACK** *Barclay BAR 3*	31		11

BUS STOP UK/Canadian production group

Date	Title / Label	Peak Position	Weeks at No.1	Weeks in Top 40
23 May 98	**KUNG FU FIGHTING** *All Around The World CDGLOBE 173* BUS STOP FEATURING CARL DOUGLAS	8		9
24 Oct 98	**YOU AIN'T SEEN NOTHIN' YET** *All Around The World CDGLOBE 187* BUS STOP FEATURING RANDY BACHMAN	22		2
10 Apr 99	**JUMP** *All Around The World CXGLOBE 186*	23		1
7 Oct 00	**GET IT ON** *All Around The World CDGLOBE 225* BUS STOP FEATURING T REX	59		

LOU BUSCH US orchestra leader/pianist

Date	Title / Label	Peak Position	Weeks at No.1	Weeks in Top 40
27 Jan 56	**ZAMBESI** *Capitol CL 14504*	2		17

BUSH UK group

Date	Title / Label	Peak Position	Weeks at No.1	Weeks in Top 40
8 Jun 96	**MACHINEHEAD** *Interscope IND 95505*	48		
1 Mar 97	**SWALLOWED** *Interscope IND 95528*	7		3
7 Jun 97	**GREEDY FLY** *Interscope IND 95536*	22		1
1 Nov 97	**BONE DRIVEN** *Interscope IND 95553*	49		
4 Dec 99	**THE CHEMICALS BETWEEN US** *Trauma/Polydor 4972222*	46		
18 Mar 00	**WARM MACHINE** *Trauma/Polydor 4972752*	45		
3 Jun 00	**LETTING THE CABLES SLEEP** *Trauma/Polydor 4973352*	51		

KATE BUSH UK singer

Date	Title / Label	Peak Position	Weeks at No.1	Weeks in Top 40
11 Feb 78	**WUTHERING HEIGHTS** *EMI 2719* ●	1	4	11
10 Jun 78	**MAN WITH THE CHILD IN HIS EYES** *EMI 2806*	6		9
11 Nov 78	**HAMMER HORROR** *EMI 2887*	44		
17 Mar 79	**WOW** *EMI 2911*	14		7
15 Sep 79	**KATE BUSH ON STAGE EP** *EMI MIEP 2991*	10		7
26 Apr 80	**BREATHING** *EMI 5058*	16		6
5 Jul 80	**BABOOSHKA** *EMI 5085* ○	5		7
4 Oct 80	**ARMY DREAMERS** *EMI 5106*	16		7
6 Dec 80	**DECEMBER WILL BE MAGIC AGAIN** *EMI 5121*	29		6
11 Jul 81	**SAT IN YOUR LAP** *EMI 5201*	11		7
7 Aug 82	**THE DREAMING** *EMI 5296*	48		
17 Aug 85	**RUNNING UP THAT HILL** *EMI KB 1* ○	3		8
26 Oct 85	**CLOUDBUSTING** *EMI KB 2*	20		4
1 Mar 86	**HOUNDS OF LOVE** *EMI KB 3*	18		4
10 May 86	**THE BIG SKY** *EMI KB 4*	37		2
1 Nov 86	**DON'T GIVE UP** *Virgin PGS 2* PETER GABRIEL & KATE BUSH	9		7
8 Nov 86	**EXPERIMENT IV** *EMI KB 5*	23		3
30 Sep 89	**THE SENSUAL WORLD** *EMI EM 102*	12		3
2 Dec 89	**THIS WOMAN'S WORK** *EMI EM 119*	25		3
10 Mar 90	**LOVE AND ANGER** *EMI EM 134*	38		2
7 Dec 91	**ROCKET MAN (I THINK IT'S GOING TO BE A LONG LONG TIME)** *Mercury TRIBO 2*	12		5
18 Sep 93	**RUBBERBAND GIRL** *EMI CDEM 280*	12		3
27 Nov 93	**MOMENTS OF PLEASURE** *EMI CDEM 297*	26		2
16 Apr 94	**THE RED SHOES** *EMI CDEMS 316*	21		2
30 Jul 94	**THE MAN I LOVE** *Mercury MERCD 408* KATE BUSH & LARRY ADLER	27		1
19 Nov 94	**AND SO IS LOVE** *EMI CDEMS 355*	26		1
5 Nov 05	**KING OF THE MOUNTAIN** *EMI CDEM674*	4		4

BUSTED UK group

Date	Title / Label	Peak Position	Weeks at No.1	Weeks in Top 40
28 Sep 02	**WHAT I GO TO SCHOOL FOR** *Universal MCSXD 40294*	3		8
25 Jan 03	**YEAR 3000** *Universal MCSXD 40306*	2		12
3 May 03	**YOU SAID NO** *Universal MCSXD 40318*	1	1	7
23 Aug 03	**SLEEPING WITH THE LIGHT ON** *Universal MCSXD 40327*	3		8
22 Nov 03	**CRASHED THE WEDDING** *Universal MCSTD 40345*	1	1	7
28 Feb 04	**WHO'S DAVID** *Universal MCSXD 40355*	1	1	7
8 May 04	**AIR HOSTESS** *Universal MCSXD 40361*	2		4
7 Aug 04	**THUNDERBIRDS/3 AM** *Universal MCSXD 40375*	1	2	10

BUSTER UK group

Date	Title / Label	Peak Position	Weeks at No.1	Weeks in Top 40
19 Jun 76	**SUNDAY** *RCA 2678*	49		

BERNARD BUTLER UK guitarist

Date	Title / Label	Peak Position	Weeks at No.1	Weeks in Top 40
27 May 95	**YES** *Hut HUTCD 53* McALMONT & BUTLER	8		6
4 Nov 95	**YOU DO** *Hut HUTDG 57* McALMONT & BUTLER	17		2
17 Jan 98	**STAY** *Creation CRESCD 281*	12		2
28 Mar 98	**NOT ALONE** *Creation CRESCD 289*	27		1
27 Jun 98	**A CHANGE OF HEART** *Creation CRESCD 297*	45		
23 Oct 99	**YOU MUST GO ON** *Creation CRESCD 324*	44		
10 Aug 02	**FALLING** *Chrysalis CDCHS 5141* McALMONT & BUTLER	23		2
9 Nov 02	**BRING IT BACK** *Chrysalis CDCHSS 5145* McALMONT & BUTLER	36		1

JONATHAN BUTLER South African singer

Date	Title / Label	Peak Position	Weeks at No.1	Weeks in Top 40
25 Jan 86	**IF YOU'RE READY (COME GO WITH ME)** *Jive 109* RUBY TURNER FEATURING JONATHAN BUTLER	30		4
8 Aug 87	**LIES** *Jive 141*	18		6

BUTTERSCOTCH UK group

Date	Title / Label	Peak Position	Weeks at No.1	Weeks in Top 40
2 May 70	**DON'T YOU KNOW** *RCA 1937*	17		9

BUTTHOLE SURFERS US group

Date	Title / Label	Peak Position	Weeks at No.1	Weeks in Top 40
5 Oct 96	**PEPPER** *Capitol CDCL 778*	59		

BUZZCOCKS UK group

Date	Title / Label	Peak Position	Weeks at No.1	Weeks in Top 40
18 Feb 78	**WHAT DO I GET** *United Artists UP 36348*	37		1
13 May 78	**I DON'T MIND** *United Artists UP 36386*	55		
15 Jul 78	**LOVE YOU MORE** *United Artists UP 36433*	34		3
23 Sep 78	**EVER FALLEN IN LOVE (WITH SOMEONE YOU SHOULDN'T'VE)** *United Artists UP 36455*	12		8
25 Nov 78	**PROMISES** *United Artists UP 36471*	20		7
10 Mar 79	**EVERYBODY'S HAPPY NOWADAYS** *United Artists UP 36499*	29		4
21 Jul 79	**HARMONY IN MY HEAD** *United Artists UP 36541*	32		3
25 Aug 79	**SPIRAL SCRATCH EP** *New Hormones ORG 1*	31		3
6 Sep 80	**ARE EVERYTHING/WHY SHE'S A GIRL FROM THE CHAINSTORE** *United Artists BP 365*	61		

B.V.S.M.P. US trio

Date	Title / Label	Peak Position	Weeks at No.1	Weeks in Top 40
23 Jul 88	**I NEED YOU** *Debut DEBT 3044*	3		9

BWO Swedish group

Date	Title / Label	Peak Position	Weeks at No.1	Weeks in Top 40
8 Mar 08	**SUNSHINE IN THE RAIN** *Shell GET11CDX*	69		

BY ALL MEANS US group

Date	Title / Label	Peak Position	Weeks at No.1	Weeks in Top 40
18 Jun 88	**I SURRENDER TO YOUR LOVE** *Fourth & Broadway BRW 102*	65		

MAX BYGRAVES UK singer

Date	Title / Label	Peak Position	Weeks at No.1	Weeks in Top 40
14 Nov 52	**COWPUNCHER'S CANTATA** *HMV B 10250*	6		8
14 May 54	**HEART OF MY HEART** *HMV B 10654*	7		8
10 Sep 54	**GILLY GILLY OSSENFEFFER KATZENELLEN BOGEN BY THE SEA** *HMV B 10734*	7		8
21 Jan 55	**MR SANDMAN** *HMV B 10801*	16		1
18 Nov 55	**MEET ME ON THE CORNER** *HMV POP 116*	2		11
17 Feb 56	**BALLAD OF DAVY CROCKETT** *HMV POP 153*	20		1
25 May 56	**OUT OF TOWN** *HMV POP 164*	18		7
5 Apr 57	**HEART** *Decca F 10862*	14		8
2 May 58	**YOU NEED HANDS/TULIPS FROM AMSTERDAM** *Decca F 11004*	3		25
22 Aug 58	**LITTLE TRAIN/GOTTA HAVE RAIN** *Decca F 11046*	28		2
2 Jan 59	**MY UKELELE** *Decca F 11077*	19		4
18 Dec 59	**JINGLE BELL ROCK** *Decca F 11176*	7		4
10 Mar 60	**FINGS AIN'T WOT THEY USED T'BE** *Decca F 11214*	5		13
28 Jul 60	**CONSIDER YOURSELF** *Decca F 11251*	50		
1 Jun 61	**BELLS OF AVIGNON** *Decca F 11350*	36		2
19 Feb 69	**YOU'RE MY EVERYTHING** *Pye 7N 17705*	34		1
6 Oct 73	**DECK OF CARDS** *Pye 7N 45276*	13		10
9 Dec 89	**WHITE CHRISTMAS** *Parkfield PMS 5012*	71		

Silver-selling ○ Gold-selling ● Platinum-selling ⊛ US No.1 ★ | Peak Position | Weeks at No.1 | Weeks in Top 40

BYKER GROOOVE! UK group

Date	Title / Label	Peak Position	Weeks at No.1	Weeks in Top 40
24 Dec 94	**LOVE YOUR SEXY…!!** *Groove GROVD 01*	48		

DONALD BYRD US trumpeter

Date	Title / Label	Peak Position	Weeks at No.1	Weeks in Top 40
26 Sep 81	**LOVING YOU/LOVE HAS COME AROUND** *Elektra K 12559*	41		

GARY BYRD & THE GB EXPERIENCE US group

Date	Title / Label	Peak Position	Weeks at No.1	Weeks in Top 40
23 Jul 83	**THE CROWN** *Motown TMGT 1312*	6		8

BYRDS US group

Date	Title / Label	Peak Position	Weeks at No.1	Weeks in Top 40
17 Jun 65	**MR TAMBOURINE MAN** *CBS 201765* ★	1	2	14
12 Aug 65	**ALL I REALLY WANT TO DO** *CBS 201796*	4		9
11 Nov 65	**TURN! TURN! TURN! (TO EVERYTHING THERE IS A SEASON)** *CBS 202008* ★	26		5
5 May 66	**EIGHT MILES HIGH** *CBS 202067*	24		5
5 Jun 68	**YOU AIN'T GOIN' NOWHERE** *CBS 3411*	45		
13 Feb 71	**CHESTNUT MARE** *CBS 5322*	19		8

EDWARD BYRNES & CONNIE STEVENS US actors

Date	Title / Label	Peak Position	Weeks at No.1	Weeks in Top 40
5 May 60	**KOOKIE KOOKIE (LEND ME YOUR COMB)** *Warner Brothers WB 5*	27		6

BYSTANDERS UK group

Date	Title / Label	Peak Position	Weeks at No.1	Weeks in Top 40
9 Feb 67	**98.6** *Piccadilly 7N 35363*	45		

C

MELANIE C UK singer

Date	Title / Label	Peak Position	Weeks at No.1	Weeks in Top 40
12 Dec 98	**WHEN YOU'RE GONE** *A&M 5828212* BRYAN ADAMS FEATURING MELANIE C ⊛	3		15
9 Oct 99	**GOIN' DOWN** *Virgin VSCDT 1744*	4		9
4 Dec 99	**NORTHERN STAR** *Virgin VSCDT 1762*	4		7
1 Apr 00	**NEVER BE THE SAME AGAIN** *Virgin VSCDT 1786* MELANIE C & LISA LEFT EYE LOPES ●	1	1	10
19 Aug 00	**I TURN TO YOU** *Virgin VSCDT 1772* ○	1	1	3
9 Dec 00	**IF THAT WERE ME** *Virgin VSCDT 1786*	18		4
8 Mar 03	**HERE IT COMES AGAIN** *Virgin VSCDT 1842*	7		3
14 Jun 03	**ON THE HORIZON** *Virgin VSCDT 1851*	14		2
22 Nov 03	**MELT/YEH YEH YEH** *Virgin VSCDY 1858*	27		1
16 Apr 05	**NEXT BEST SUPERSTAR** *Red Girl CXREDG1*	10		2
7 Apr 07	**I WANT CANDY** *Red Girl CDREDG3*	24		1
30 Jun 07	**CAROLYNA** *Red Girl CDREDG4*	49		

ROY C US singer

Date	Title / Label	Peak Position	Weeks at No.1	Weeks in Top 40
21 Apr 66	**SHOTGUN WEDDING** *Island WI 273*	6		9
25 Nov 72	**SHOTGUN WEDDING** *UK 19*	8		11

C & C MUSIC FACTORY US production duo

Date	Title / Label	Peak Position	Weeks at No.1	Weeks in Top 40
15 Dec 90	**GONNA MAKE YOU SWEAT (EVERYBODY DANCE NOW)** *CBS 6564540* C & C MUSIC FACTORY (FEATURING FREEDOM WILLIAMS) ★	3		11
30 Mar 91	**HERE WE GO** *Columbia 6567557* C & C MUSIC FACTORY (FEATURING FREEDOM WILLIAMS)	20		5
6 Jul 91	**THINGS THAT MAKE YOU GO HMMM** *Columbia 6566907* C & C MUSIC FACTORY (FEATURING FREEDOM WILLIAMS)	4		10
23 Nov 91	**JUST A TOUCH OF LOVE EVERYDAY** *Columbia 6575247* C & C MUSIC FACTORY FEATURING ZELMA DAVIS	31		2
18 Jan 92	**PRIDE (IN THE NAME OF LOVE)** *Columbia 6577017* CLIVILLES & COLE	15		4
14 Mar 92	**A DEEPER LOVE** *Columbia 6578497* CLIVILLES & COLE	15		4
3 Oct 92	**KEEP IT COMIN' (DANCE TILL YOU CAN'T DANCE NO MORE)** *Columbia 6584307* C & C MUSIC FACTORY FEATURING Q UNIQUE & DEBORAH COOPER	34		2
27 Aug 94	**DO YOU WANNA GET FUNKY** *Columbia 6607622*	27		1
18 Feb 95	**I FOUND LOVE/TAKE A TOKE** *Columbia 6612112* C & C MUSIC FACTORY/C & C MUSIC FACTORY FEATURING MARTHA WASH	26		1
11 Nov 95	**I'LL ALWAYS BE AROUND** *MCA MCSTD 40001*	42		

C.J. & CO US group

Date	Title / Label	Peak Position	Weeks at No.1	Weeks in Top 40
30 Jul 77	**DEVIL'S GUN** *Atlantic K 10956*	43		

C-SIXTY FOUR UK duo

Date	Title / Label	Peak Position	Weeks at No.1	Weeks in Top 40
19 Mar 05	**ON A GOOD THING** *Manifesto 9870564*	54		

CA VA CA VA UK group

Date	Title / Label	Peak Position	Weeks at No.1	Weeks in Top 40
18 Sep 82	**WHERE'S ROMEO** *Regard RG 103*	49		
19 Feb 83	**BROTHER BRIGHT** *Regard RG 105*	65		

MONTSERRAT CABALLE Spanish soprano

Date	Title / Label	Peak Position	Weeks at No.1	Weeks in Top 40
7 Nov 87	**BARCELONA** *Polydor POSP 887* FREDDIE MERCURY & MONTSERRAT CABALLE	8		5
8 Aug 92	**BARCELONA** *Polydor PO 221* FREDDIE MERCURY & MONTSERRAT CABALLE	2		6

CABANA Brazilian duo

Date	Title / Label	Peak Position	Weeks at No.1	Weeks in Top 40
15 Jul 95	**BAILANDO CON LOBOS** *Hi-Life 5792512*	65		

CABARET VOLTAIRE UK group

Date	Title / Label	Peak Position	Weeks at No.1	Weeks in Top 40
18 Jul 87	**DON'T ARGUE** *Parlophone R 6157*	69		
4 Nov 89	**HYPNOTISED** *Parlophone R 6227*	66		
12 May 90	**KEEP ON** *Parlophone R 6250*	55		
18 Aug 90	**EASY LIFE** *Parlophone R 6261*	61		

CABIN CREW Australian production duo

Date	Title / Label	Peak Position	Weeks at No.1	Weeks in Top 40
12 Mar 05	**STAR TO FALL** *Data DATA87CDX*	4		6

CABLE US group

Date	Title / Label	Peak Position	Weeks at No.1	Weeks in Top 40
14 Jun 97	**FREEZE THE ATLANTIC** *Infectious INFECT 38CD*	44		

CACIQUE UK group

Date	Title / Label	Peak Position	Weeks at No.1	Weeks in Top 40
1 Jun 85	**DEVOTED TO YOU** *Diamond Duel DISC 1*	69		

CACTUS WORLD NEWS Irish group

Date	Title / Label	Peak Position	Weeks at No.1	Weeks in Top 40
8 Feb 86	**YEARS LATER** *MCA 1024*	59		
26 Apr 86	**WORLDS APART** *MCA 1040*	58		
20 Sep 86	**THE BRIDGE** *MCA 1080*	74		

CADETS WITH EILEEN READ Irish group

Date	Title / Label	Peak Position	Weeks at No.1	Weeks in Top 40
3 Jun 65	**JEALOUS HEART** *Pye 7N 15852*	42		

SUSAN CADOGAN UK singer

Date	Title / Label	Peak Position	Weeks at No.1	Weeks in Top 40
5 Apr 75	**HURT SO GOOD** *Magnet MAG 23* ○	4		9
19 Jul 75	**LOVE ME BABY** *Magnet MAG 36*	22		6

CAESARS Swedish group

Date	Title / Label	Peak Position	Weeks at No.1	Weeks in Top 40
19 Apr 03	**JERK IT OUT** *Virgin DINSD 244*	60		
30 Apr 05	**JERK IT OUT** *Virgin DINSD274*	8		5

COLBIE CAILLAT US singer

Date	Title / Label	Peak Position	Weeks at No.1	Weeks in Top 40
6 Oct 07	**BUBBLY** *Island 1747525*	72		

AL CAIOLA US orchestra leader/guitarist

Date	Title / Label	Peak Position	Weeks at No.1	Weeks in Top 40
15 Jun 61	**THE MAGNIFICENT SEVEN** *HMV POP 889*	34		4

Silver-selling ● Gold-selling ● Platinum-selling ● US No.1 ★ | Peak Position | Weeks at No.1 | Weeks in Top 40

CAKE US group

Date	Title / Label	Peak Position	Weeks at No.1	Weeks in Top 40
22 Mar 97	**THE DISTANCE** *Capricorn 5742212*	22		2
31 May 97	**I WILL SURVIVE** *Capricorn 5744712*	29		1
1 May 99	**NEVER THERE** *Capricorn 8708112*	66		
3 Nov 01	**SHORT SKIRT LONG JACKET** *Columbia 6720402*	63		

CALIFORNIA SUNSHINE
Israeli/Italian production group

Date	Title / Label	Peak Position	Weeks at No.1	Weeks in Top 40
16 Aug 97	**SUMMER '89** *Perfecto PERF 143CD*	56		

CALL US group

Date	Title / Label	Peak Position	Weeks at No.1	Weeks in Top 40
30 Sep 89	**LET THE DAY BEGIN** *MCA 1362*	42		

TERRY CALLIER US singer/guitarist

Date	Title / Label	Peak Position	Weeks at No.1	Weeks in Top 40
13 Dec 97	**BEST BIT EP** *Heavenly HVN 72CD*			
	BETH ORTON FEATURING TERRY CALLIER	36		1
23 May 98	**LOVE THEME FROM SPARTACUS** *Talkin Loud TLCD 32*	57		

CALLING US group

Date	Title / Label	Peak Position	Weeks at No.1	Weeks in Top 40
29 Jun 02	**WHEREVER YOU WILL GO (IMPORT)** *RCA 74321912242*	64		
6 Jul 02	**WHEREVER YOU WILL GO** *RCA 74321947652*	3		9
2 Nov 02	**ADRIENNE** *RCA 74321968352*	18		2
29 May 04	**OUR LIVES** *RCA 82876618652*	13		3
28 Aug 04	**THINGS WILL GO MY WAY** *RCA 82876637372*	34		1

EDDIE CALVERT UK trumpeter

Date	Title / Label	Peak Position	Weeks at No.1	Weeks in Top 40
18 Dec 53	**OH MEIN PAPA** *Columbia DB 3337*	1	9	21
8 Apr 55	**CHERRY PINK AND APPLE BLOSSOM WHITE** *Columbia DB 3581*	1	4	21
13 May 55	**STRANGER IN PARADISE** *Columbia DB 3594*	14		4
29 Jul 55	**JOHN AND JULIE** *Columbia DB 3624*	6		11
9 Mar 56	**ZAMBESI** *Columbia DB 3747*	13		7
7 Feb 58	**MANDY (LA PANSE)** *Columbia DB 3956*	9		14
20 Jun 58	**LITTLE SERENADE** *Columbia DB 4105*	28		2

CAMEO US group

Date	Title / Label	Peak Position	Weeks at No.1	Weeks in Top 40
31 Mar 84	**SHE'S STRANGE** *Club JAB 2*	37		1
13 Jul 85	**ATTACK ME WITH YOUR LOVE** *Club JAB 16*	65		
14 Sep 85	**SINGLE LIFE** *Club JAB 21*	15		7
7 Dec 85	**SHE'S STRANGE** *Club JAB 25*	22		6
22 Mar 86	**A GOODBYE** *Club JAB 28*	65		
30 Aug 86	**WORD UP** *Club JAB 38* ●	3		9
29 Nov 86	**CANDY** *Club JAB 43*	27		7
25 Apr 87	**BACK AND FORTH** *Club JAB 49*	11		7
17 Oct 87	**SHE'S MINE** *Club JAB 57*	35		1
29 Oct 88	**YOU MAKE ME WORK** *Club JAB 70*	74		
28 Jul 01	**LOVERBOY** *Virgin VUSCD 211*			
	MARIAH CAREY FEATURING CAMEO	12		2

ANDY CAMERON UK singer/Scottish football fanatic

Date	Title / Label	Peak Position	Weeks at No.1	Weeks in Top 40
4 Mar 78	**ALLY'S TARTAN ARMY** *Klub 03*	6		8

CAM'RON US rapper

Date	Title / Label	Peak Position	Weeks at No.1	Weeks in Top 40
19 Sep 98	**HORSE AND CARRIAGE** *Epic 6662612*			
	CAM'RON FEATURING MASE	12		3
17 Aug 02	**OH BOY** *Roc-A-Fella 0639642*			
	CAM'RON FEATURING JUELZ SANTANA	13		5
8 Feb 03	**HEY MA** *Roc-A-Fella 0637242*			
	CAM'RON FEATURING JUELZ SANTANA	8		8
5 Apr 03	**BOY (I NEED YOU)** *Def Jam 0779282*			
	MARIAH CAREY FEATURING CAM'RON	17		3
12 Feb 05	**GIRLS** *Roc-A-Fella 2103990*			
	CAM'RON FEATURING MONA LISA	25		2

TONY CAMILLO'S BAZUKA US producer

Date	Title / Label	Peak Position	Weeks at No.1	Weeks in Top 40
31 May 75	**DYNOMITE (PART 1)** *A&M AMS 7168*	28		4

CAMISRA UK group

Date	Title / Label	Peak Position	Weeks at No.1	Weeks in Top 40
21 Feb 98	**LET ME SHOW YOU** *VC Recordings VCRD 31*	5		5
11 Jul 98	**FEEL THE BEAT** *VC Recordings VCRD 39*	32		1
22 May 99	**CLAP YOUR HANDS** *VC Recordings VCRD 49*	34		1

CAMOUFLAGE US group

Date	Title / Label	Peak Position	Weeks at No.1	Weeks in Top 40
24 Sep 77	**BEE STING** *State STAT 58*			
	CAMOUFLAGE FEATURING MYSTI	48		

A CAMP Swedish group

Date	Title / Label	Peak Position	Weeks at No.1	Weeks in Top 40
1 Sep 01	**I CAN BUY YOU** *Stockholm 0152162*	46		

CAMP LO US duo

Date	Title / Label	Peak Position	Weeks at No.1	Weeks in Top 40
16 Aug 97	**LUCHINI AKA (THIS IS IT)** *ffrr FCD 305*	74		

CAMPAG VELOCET UK group

Date	Title / Label	Peak Position	Weeks at No.1	Weeks in Top 40
19 Feb 00	**VITO SATAN** *Pias Recordings PIASX 010CD*	75		

ALI CAMPBELL UK singer

Date	Title / Label	Peak Position	Weeks at No.1	Weeks in Top 40
20 May 95	**THAT LOOK IN YOUR EYE** *Kuff KUFFDG 1*	5		8
26 Aug 95	**LET YOUR YEAH BE YEAH** *Kuff KUFFD 2*	25		2
9 Dec 95	**SOMETHIN' STUPID** *Kuff KUFFDG 5*			
	ALI & KIBIBI CAMPBELL	30		1

DANNY CAMPBELL & SASHA
UK singer and producer

Date	Title / Label	Peak Position	Weeks at No.1	Weeks in Top 40
31 Jul 93	**TOGETHER** *ffrr FCD 212*	57		

ELLIE CAMPBELL UK singer

Date	Title / Label	Peak Position	Weeks at No.1	Weeks in Top 40
3 Apr 99	**SWEET LIES** *Eastern Bloc 0519222*	42		
14 Aug 99	**SO MANY WAYS** *Eastern Bloc 0519362*	26		1
9 Jun 01	**DON'T WANT YOU BACK** *Jive 9201302*	50		

ETHNA CAMPBELL UK singer

Date	Title / Label	Peak Position	Weeks at No.1	Weeks in Top 40
27 Dec 75	**THE OLD RUGGED CROSS** *Philips 6006 475*	33		3

IAN CAMPBELL FOLK GROUP UK group

Date	Title / Label	Peak Position	Weeks at No.1	Weeks in Top 40
11 Mar 65	**THE TIMES THEY ARE A-CHANGIN'** *Transatlantic SP 5*	42		

GLEN CAMPBELL US singer

Date	Title / Label	Peak Position	Weeks at No.1	Weeks in Top 40
29 Jan 69	**WICHITA LINEMAN** *Ember EMBS 261*	7		11
7 May 69	**GALVESTON** *Ember EMBS 263*	14		10
6 Dec 69	**ALL I HAVE TO DO IS DREAM** *Capitol CL 15619*			
	BOBBIE GENTRY & GLEN CAMPBELL	3		13
7 Feb 70	**TRY A LITTLE KINDNESS** *Capitol CL 15622*	45		
9 May 70	**HONEY COME BACK** *Capitol CL 15638*	4		16
26 Sep 70	**EVERYTHING A MAN COULD EVER NEED** *Capitol CL 15653*	32		3
21 Nov 70	**IT'S ONLY MAKE BELIEVE** *Capitol CL 15663*	4		13
27 Mar 71	**DREAM BABY** *Capitol CL 15674*	39		1
4 Oct 75	**RHINESTONE COWBOY** *Capitol CL 15824* ● ★	4		11
26 Mar 77	**SOUTHERN NIGHTS** *Capitol CL 15907* ★	28		5
30 Nov 02	**RHINESTONE COWBOY (GIDDY UP GIDDY UP)** *Serious SER 059CD*			
	RIKKI & DAZ FEATURING GLEN CAMPBELL	12		3

JO ANN CAMPBELL US singer

Date	Title / Label	Peak Position	Weeks at No.1	Weeks in Top 40
8 Jun 61	**MOTORCYCLE MICHAEL** *HMV POP 873*	41		

JUNIOR CAMPBELL UK singer

Date	Title / Label	Peak Position	Weeks at No.1	Weeks in Top 40
14 Oct 72	**HALLELUJAH FREEDOM** *Deram DM 364*	10		8
2 Jun 73	**SWEET ILLUSION** *Deram DM 387*	15		8

Silver-selling · Gold-selling · Platinum-selling · US No.1 · Peak Position · Weeks at No.1 · Weeks in Top 40

NAOMI CAMPBELL UK model/singer

Date	Title	Label	Peak Position	Weeks at No.1	Weeks in Top 40
24 Sep 94	LOVE AND TEARS	Epic 6608352	40		1

PAT CAMPBELL Irish singer

Date	Title	Label	Peak Position	Weeks at No.1	Weeks in Top 40
15 Nov 69	THE DEAL	Major Minor MM 648	31		2

STAN CAMPBELL UK singer

Date	Title	Label	Peak Position	Weeks at No.1	Weeks in Top 40
6 Jun 87	YEARS GO BY	WEA YZ 127	65		

TEVIN CAMPBELL US singer

Date	Title	Label	Peak Position	Weeks at No.1	Weeks in Top 40
18 Apr 92	TELL ME WHAT YOU WANT ME TO DO	Qwest W 0102	63		

CAN German group

Date	Title	Label	Peak Position	Weeks at No.1	Weeks in Top 40
28 Aug 76	I WANT MORE	Virgin VS 153	26		8

CANDIDO Cuban percussionist

Date	Title	Label	Peak Position	Weeks at No.1	Weeks in Top 40
18 Jul 81	JINGO	Excalibur EXC 102	55		

CANDLEWICK GREEN UK group

Date	Title	Label	Peak Position	Weeks at No.1	Weeks in Top 40
23 Feb 74	WHO DO YOU THINK YOU ARE	Decca F 13480	21		5

CANDY FLIP UK duo

Date	Title	Label	Peak Position	Weeks at No.1	Weeks in Top 40
17 Mar 90	STRAWBERRY FIELDS FOREVER	Debut DEBT 3092	3		8
14 Jul 90	THIS CAN BE REAL	Debut DEBT 3099	60		

CANDY GIRLS UK group

Date	Title	Label	Peak Position	Weeks at No.1	Weeks in Top 40
30 Sep 95	FEE FI FO FUM CANDY GIRLS FEATURING SWEET PUSSY PAULINE	VC Recordings VCRD 1	23		2
24 Feb 96	WHAM BAM CANDY GIRLS FEATURING SWEET PUSSY PAULINE	VC Recordings VCRD 6	20		2
7 Dec 96	I WANT CANDY CANDY GIRLS FEATURING VALERIE MALCOLM	Feverpitch CDFVR 1013	30		1

CANDYLAND UK group

Date	Title	Label	Peak Position	Weeks at No.1	Weeks in Top 40
9 Mar 91	FOUNTAIN O' YOUTH	Non Fiction YES 4	72		

CANDYSKINS UK group

Date	Title	Label	Peak Position	Weeks at No.1	Weeks in Top 40
19 Oct 96	MRS HOOVER	Ultimate TOPP 051CD	65		
8 Feb 97	MONDAY MORNING	Ultimate TOPP 055CD	34		1
3 May 97	HANG MYSELF ON YOU	Ultimate TOPP 059CD	65		

CANIBUS US rapper

Date	Title	Label	Peak Position	Weeks at No.1	Weeks in Top 40
27 Jun 98	SECOND ROUND KO	Universal UND 56198	35		1
10 Oct 98	HOW COME YOUSSOU N'DOUR & CANIBUS	Interscope IND 95598	52		

CANNED HEAT US group

Date	Title	Label	Peak Position	Weeks at No.1	Weeks in Top 40
24 Jul 68	ON THE ROAD AGAIN	Liberty LBS 15090	8		13
1 Jan 69	GOING UP THE COUNTRY	Liberty LBF 15169	19		8
17 Jan 70	LET'S WORK TOGETHER	Liberty LBF 15302	2		12
11 Jul 70	SUGAR BEE	Liberty LBF 15350	49		

FREDDY CANNON US singer

Date	Title	Label	Peak Position	Weeks at No.1	Weeks in Top 40
14 Aug 59	TALLAHASSEE LASSIE	Top Rank JAR 135	17		8
1 Jan 60	WAY DOWN YONDER IN NEW ORLEANS	Top Rank JAR 247	3		16
5 Mar 60	CALIFORNIA HERE I COME	Top Rank JAR 309	25		2
17 Mar 60	INDIANA	Top Rank JAR 309	42		
19 May 60	THE URGE	Top Rank JAR 369	18		7
20 Apr 61	MUSKRAT RAMBLE	Top Rank JAR 548	32		2
28 Jun 62	PALISADES PARK	Stateside SS 101	20		6

CANTAMUS GIRLS CHOIR UK choir

Date	Title	Label	Peak Position	Weeks at No.1	Weeks in Top 40
31 Dec 05	EVERYBODY'S GOTTA LEARN SOMETIME	EMI Classics 3497582	73		

BLU CANTRELL US singer

Date	Title	Label	Peak Position	Weeks at No.1	Weeks in Top 40
24 Nov 01	HIT 'EM UP STYLE (OOPS)	Arista 74321891632	12		3
19 Jul 03	BREATHE (IMPORT) BLU CANTRELL FEATURING SEAN PAUL	Arista 82876534002	59		
9 Aug 03	BREATHE BLU CANTRELL FEATURING SEAN PAUL	Arista 82876545722	1	4	15
13 Dec 03	MAKE ME WANNA SCREAM	Arista 82876583432	24		1

JIM CAPALDI UK singer/drummer

Date	Title	Label	Peak Position	Weeks at No.1	Weeks in Top 40
27 Jul 74	IT'S ALL UP TO YOU	Island WIP 6198	27		5
25 Oct 75	LOVE HURTS	Island WIP 6246	4		10

CAPERCAILLIE UK/Canadian/Irish group

Date	Title	Label	Peak Position	Weeks at No.1	Weeks in Top 40
23 May 92	A PRINCE AMONG ISLANDS EP	Survival ZB 45393	39		1
17 Jun 95	DARK ALAN (AILEIN DUNN)	Survival SURCD 55	65		

CAPPELLA Italian producer

Date	Title	Label	Peak Position	Weeks at No.1	Weeks in Top 40
9 Apr 88	PUSH THE BEAT/BAUHAUS	Fast Globe FGL 1	60		
6 May 89	HELYOM HALIB	Music Man MMPS 7004	11		6
23 Sep 89	HOUSE ENGERY REVENGE	Music Man MMPS 7009	73		
27 Apr 91	EVERYBODY	ffrr F 158	66		
18 Jan 92	TAKE ME AWAY CAPPELLA FEATURING LOLEATTA HOLLOWAY	PWL Continental PWL 210	25		3
3 Apr 93	U GOT 2 KNOW	Internal Dance IDC 1	6		9
14 Aug 93	U GOT 2 KNOW (REMIX)	Internal Dance IDCR 2	43		
23 Oct 93	U GOT 2 LET THE MUSIC	Internal Dance IDC 3	2		8
19 Feb 94	MOVE ON BABY	Internal Dance IDC 4	7		6
18 Jun 94	U & ME	Internal Dance IDCC 6	10		6
15 Oct 94	MOVE IT UP/BIG BEAT	Internal Dance IDC 7	16		4
16 Sep 95	TELL ME THE WAY	Systematic SYSCD 17	17		2
6 Sep 97	BE MY BABY	Nukleuz PSNC 0072	53		

CAPRICCIO UK production duo

Date	Title	Label	Peak Position	Weeks at No.1	Weeks in Top 40
27 Mar 99	EVERYBODY GET UP	Defected DFECT 2CDS	44		

CAPRICE US singer

Date	Title	Label	Peak Position	Weeks at No.1	Weeks in Top 40
4 Sep 99	OH YEAH	Virgin VSCDT 1745	24		1
10 Mar 01	ONCE AROUND THE SUN	Virgin VSCDT 1750	24		1

CAPRICORN Belgian producer

Date	Title	Label	Peak Position	Weeks at No.1	Weeks in Top 40
29 Nov 97	20 HZ (NEW FREQUENCIES)	R&S RS 97126CD	73		

TONY CAPSTICK & THE CARLTON MAIN/FRICKLEY COLLIERY BAND

UK radio DJ/folk singer/comedian and brass band

Date	Title	Label	Peak Position	Weeks at No.1	Weeks in Top 40
21 Mar 81	THE SHEFFIELD GRINDER/CAPSTICK COMES HOME TONY CAPSTICK & THE CARLTON MAIN/FRICKLEY COLLIERY BAND	Dingles SID 27	3		5

CAPTAIN UK group

Date	Title	Label	Peak Position	Weeks at No.1	Weeks in Top 40
13 May 06	BROKE	EMI CDEM689	34		1
5 Aug 06	GLORIOUS	EMI CDEM700	30		1
25 Nov 06	FRONTLINE	EMI CDEM708	62		

CAPTAIN HOLLYWOOD PROJECT US group

Date	Title	Label	Peak Position	Weeks at No.1	Weeks in Top 40
22 Sep 90	I CAN'T STAND IT TWENTY 4 SEVEN FEATURING CAPTAIN HOLLYWOOD	BCM BCMR 395	7		9
24 Nov 90	ARE YOU DREAMING TWENTY 4 SEVEN FEATURING CAPTAIN HOLLYWOOD	BCM 07504	17		9
27 Mar 93	ONLY WITH YOU	Pulse 8 CDLOSE 40	67		
6 Nov 93	MORE AND MORE	Pulse 8 CDLOSE 50	23		4
5 Feb 94	IMPOSSIBLE	Pulse 8 CDLOSE 54	29		2
11 Jun 94	ONLY WITH YOU	Pulse 8 CDLOSE 62	61		
1 Apr 95	FLYING HIGH	Pulse 8 CDLOSE 82	58		

CAPTAIN SENSIBLE UK singer

Date	Title	Peak Position	Weeks at No.1	Weeks in Top 40
26 Jun 82	**HAPPY TALK** *A&M CAP 1* ○	1	2	6
14 Aug 82	**WOT** *A&M CAP 2*	26		4
24 Mar 84	**GLAD IT'S ALL OVER/DAMNED ON 45** *A&M CAP 6*	6		8
28 Jul 84	**THERE ARE MORE SNAKES THAN LADDERS** *A&M CAP 7*	57		
10 Dec 94	**THE HOKEY COKEY** *Have A Nice Day CDHOKEY 1*	71		

CAPTAIN & TENNILLE US duo

Date	Title	Peak Position	Weeks at No.1	Weeks in Top 40
2 Aug 75	**LOVE WILL KEEP US TOGETHER** *A&M AMS 7165* ★	32		4
24 Jan 76	**THE WAY I WANT TO TOUCH YOU** *A&M AMS 7203*	28		4
4 Nov 78	**YOU NEVER DONE IT LIKE THAT** *A&M AMS 7384*	63		
16 Feb 80	**DO THAT TO ME ONE MORE TIME** *Casablanca CAN 175* ★	7		8

IRENE CARA US singer

Date	Title	Peak Position	Weeks at No.1	Weeks in Top 40
3 Jul 82	**FAME** *RSO 90* ●	1	3	13
4 Sep 82	**OUT HERE ON MY OWN** *RSO 66*	58		
4 Jun 83	**FLASHDANCE...WHAT A FEELING** *Casablanca CAN 1016* ○ ★	2		12

CARAMBA Swedish singer

Date	Title	Peak Position	Weeks at No.1	Weeks in Top 40
12 Nov 83	**FEDORA (I'LL BE YOUR DAWG)** *Billco BILL 101*	56		

CARAVELLES UK duo

Date	Title	Peak Position	Weeks at No.1	Weeks in Top 40
8 Aug 63	**YOU DON'T HAVE TO BE A BABY TO CRY** *Decca F 11697*	6		11

CARBON/SILICON UK duo

Date	Title	Peak Position	Weeks at No.1	Weeks in Top 40
16 Jun 07	**THE NEWS** *Carbon Silicon CS1001*	59		

CARDIGANS Swedish group

Date	Title	Peak Position	Weeks at No.1	Weeks in Top 40
17 Jun 95	**CARNIVAL** *Trampolene PZCD 345*	72		
30 Sep 95	**SICK & TIRED** *Stockholm 5773112*	34		2
2 Dec 95	**CARNIVAL** *Trampolene PZCD 345*	35		1
17 Feb 96	**RISE & SHINE** *Trampolene 5778252*	29		1
21 Sep 96	**LOVEFOOL** *Stockholm 5752952*	21		3
7 Dec 96	**BEEN IT** *Stockholm 5759672*	56		
3 May 97	**LOVEFOOL** *Stockholm 5710502* ●	2		9
6 Sep 97	**YOUR NEW CUCKOO** *Stockholm 5716632*	35		1
17 Oct 98	**MY FAVOURITE GAME** *Stockholm 5679912*	14		9
6 Mar 99	**ERASE/REWIND** *Stockholm 5635352*	7		5
24 Jul 99	**HANGING AROUND** *Stockholm 5612692*	17		2
25 Sep 99	**BURNING DOWN THE HOUSE** *Gut CDGUT 26* TOM JONES & THE CARDIGANS	7		5
22 Mar 03	**FOR WHAT IT'S WORTH** *Stockholm 0657232*	31		1
26 Jul 03	**YOU'RE THE STORM** *Stockholm 9809673*	74		
15 Oct 05	**I NEED SOME FINE WINE AND YOU, YOU NEED TO BE NICER** *Stockholm 9874124*	59		

CARE UK duo

Date	Title	Peak Position	Weeks at No.1	Weeks in Top 40
12 Nov 83	**FLAMING SWORD** *Arista KBIRD 2*	48		

MARIAH CAREY US singer

Date	Title	Peak Position	Weeks at No.1	Weeks in Top 40
4 Aug 90	**VISION OF LOVE** *CBS 6559320* ★	9		9
10 Nov 90	**LOVE TAKES TIME** *CBS 6563647* ★	37		2
26 Jan 91	**SOMEDAY** *Columbia 6565837* ★	38		2
1 Jun 91	**THERE'S GOT TO BE A WAY** *Columbia 6569317*	54		
5 Oct 91	**EMOTIONS** *Columbia 6574037* ★	17		6
11 Jan 92	**CAN'T LET GO** *Columbia 6576627*	20		5
18 Apr 92	**MAKE IT HAPPEN** *Columbia 6579417*	17		3
27 Jun 92	**I'LL BE THERE** *Columbia 6581377* ★	2		7
21 Aug 93	**DREAMLOVER** *Columbia 6594445* ★	9		8
6 Nov 93	**HERO** *Columbia 6598122* ★	7		11
19 Feb 94	**WITHOUT YOU** *Columbia 6599192* ●	1	4	11
18 Jun 94	**ANYTIME YOU NEED A FRIEND** *Columbia 6603542*	8		4
17 Sep 94	**ENDLESS LOVE** *Epic 6608062* LUTHER VANDROSS & MARIAH CAREY	3		7
10 Dec 94	**ALL I WANT FOR CHRISTMAS IS YOU** *Columbia 6610702* ●	2		6
23 Sep 95	**FANTASY** *Columbia 6624952* ○ ★	4		9
9 Dec 95	**ONE SWEET DAY** *Columbia 6626035* MARIAH CAREY & BOYZ II MEN ○ ★	6		8
17 Feb 96	**OPEN ARMS** *Columbia 6629772*	4		4
22 Jun 96	**ALWAYS BE MY BABY** *Columbia 6633345* ★	3		8
6 Sep 97	**HONEY** *Columbia 6650192* ★	3		6
13 Dec 97	**BUTTERFLY** *Columbia 6653365*	22		3
13 Jun 98	**MY ALL** *Columbia 6660592* ★	4		6
19 Dec 98	**WHEN YOU BELIEVE (FROM THE PRINCE OF EGYPT)** *Columbia 6667522* MARIAH CAREY & WHITNEY HOUSTON	4		7
10 Apr 99	**I STILL BELIEVE** *Columbia 6670735*	16		3
6 Nov 99	**HEARTBREAKER** *Columbia 6683012* MARIAH CAREY FEATURING JAY-Z ★	5		6
11 Mar 00	**THANK GOD I FOUND YOU** *Columbia 6690582* MARIAH CAREY FEATURING JOE & 98°	10		4
30 Sep 00	**AGAINST ALL ODDS (TAKE A LOOK AT ME NOW)** *Columbia 6698872* MARIAH CAREY FEATURING WESTLIFE ○	1	2	8
28 Jul 01	**LOVERBOY** *Virgin VUSCD 211* MARIAH CAREY FEATURING CAMEO	12		2
29 Dec 01	**NEVER TOO FAR/DON'T STOP (FUNKIN' 4 JAMAICA)** *Virgin VUSCD 228* MARIAH CAREY/MARIAH CAREY FEATURING MYSTIKAL	32		2
30 Nov 02	**THROUGH THE RAIN** *Mercury 0638072*	8		4
5 Apr 03	**BOY (I NEED YOU)** *Def Jam 0779282* MARIAH CAREY FEATURING CAM'RON	17		3
7 Jun 03	**I KNOW WHAT YOU WANT** *J Records 82876528292* BUSTA RHYMES & MARIAH CAREY	3		11
9 Apr 05	**IT'S LIKE THAT** *Def Jam 9881337*	4		7
16 Jul 05	**WE BELONG TOGETHER** *Def Jam 9883483* ★	2		12
15 Oct 05	**GET YOUR NUMBER/SHAKE IT OFF** *Def Jam 9886375*	9		6
24 Dec 05	**DON'T FORGET ABOUT US** *Def Jam/Island 9889761* ★	11		4
10 Jun 06	**SAY SOMETHIN'** *Mercury 9885446*	27		1
1 Dec 07	**ALL I WANT FOR CHRISTMAS IS YOU** *Columbia 6610702*	4		5
29 Dec 07	**WHEN YOU BELIEVE (FROM THE PRINCE OF EGYPT)** *Columbia 6667522* MARIAH CAREY & WHITNEY HOUSTON	65		

BELINDA CARLISLE US singer

Date	Title	Peak Position	Weeks at No.1	Weeks in Top 40
12 Dec 87	**HEAVEN IS A PLACE ON EARTH** *Virgin VS 1036* ○ ★	1	2	11
27 Feb 88	**I GET WEAK** *Virgin VS 1046*	10		7
7 May 88	**CIRCLE IN THE SAND** *Virgin VS 1074*	4		8
6 Aug 88	**MAD ABOUT YOU** *IRS IRM 118*	67		
10 Sep 88	**WORLD WITHOUT YOU** *Virgin VS 1114*	34		3
10 Dec 88	**LOVE NEVER DIES...** *Virgin VS 1150*	54		
7 Oct 89	**LEAVE A LIGHT ON** *Virgin VS 1210* ○	4		9
9 Dec 89	**LA LUNA** *Virgin VS 1230*	38		1
24 Feb 90	**RUNAWAY HORSES** *Virgin VS 1244*	40		1
26 May 90	**VISION OF YOU** *Virgin VS 1264*	41		
13 Oct 90	**(WE WANT) THE SAME THING** *Virgin VS 1219*	6		7
22 Dec 90	**SUMMER RAIN** *Virgin VS 1323*	23		5
20 Apr 91	**VISION OF YOU** *Virgin VS 1264*	71		
28 Sep 91	**LIVE YOUR LIFE BE FREE** *Virgin VS 1370*	12		6
16 Nov 91	**DO YOU FEEL LIKE I FEEL** *Virgin VS 1383*	29		2
11 Jan 92	**HALF THE WORLD** *Virgin VS 1388*	35		1
29 Aug 92	**LITTLE BLACK BOOK** *Virgin VS 1428*	28		2
25 Sep 93	**BIG SCARY ANIMAL** *Virgin VSCDT 1472*	12		4
27 Nov 93	**LAY DOWN YOUR ARMS** *Virgin VSDG 1476*	27		2
13 Jul 96	**IN TOO DEEP** *Chrysalis CDCHS 5033*	6		4
21 Sep 96	**ALWAYS BREAKING MY HEART** *Chrysalis CDCHS 5037*	8		4
30 Nov 96	**LOVE IN THE KEY OF C** *Chrysalis CDCHS 5044*	20		1
1 Mar 97	**CALIFORNIA** *Chrysalis CDCHSS 5047*	31		1
27 Nov 99	**ALL GOD'S CHILDREN** *Virgin VSCDT 1756*	66		

BOB CARLISLE US singer

Date	Title	Peak Position	Weeks at No.1	Weeks in Top 40
30 Aug 97	**BUTTERFLY KISSES** *Jive JIVECD 249*	56		

CARLTON UK singer

Date	Title	Peak Position	Weeks at No.1	Weeks in Top 40
16 Feb 91	**LOVE AND PAIN** *Smith & Mighty SNM 4*	56		
1 Apr 95	**1 TO 1 RELIGION** *Stoned Heights BRCD 313* BOMB THE BASS FEATURING CARLTON	53		

CARL CARLTON US singer

Date	Title	Peak Position	Weeks at No.1	Weeks in Top 40
18 Jul 81	**SHE'S A BAD MAMA JAMA (SHE'S BUILT, SHE'S STACKED)** *20th Century TC 2488*	34		5

VANESSA CARLTON US singer

Date	Title	Peak Position	Weeks at No.1	Weeks in Top 40
3 Aug 02	**A THOUSAND MILES** *A&M 4977542*	6		10
30 Nov 02	**ORDINARY DAY** *A&M 4978132*	53		
15 Feb 03	**BIG YELLOW TAXI** *Geffen 4978492* COUNTING CROWS FEATURING VANESSA CARLTON	16		5

Silver-selling ● Gold-selling ● Platinum-selling ● US No.1 ★ | Peak Position | Weeks at No.1 | Weeks in Top 40

CARMEL UK group

Date	Title / Label	Peak Position	Weeks at No.1	Weeks in Top 40
6 Aug 83	**BAD DAY** *London LON 29*	15		6
11 Feb 84	**MORE, MORE, MORE** *London LON 44*	23		4
14 Jun 86	**SALLY** *London LON 90*	60		

ERIC CARMEN US singer

Date	Title / Label	Peak Position	Weeks at No.1	Weeks in Top 40
10 Apr 76	**ALL BY MYSELF** *Arista 42*	12		6

KIM CARNEGIE UK singer

Date	Title / Label	Peak Position	Weeks at No.1	Weeks in Top 40
19 Jan 91	**JAZZ RAP** *Best ZB 44085*	73		

KIM CARNES US singer

Date	Title / Label	Peak Position	Weeks at No.1	Weeks in Top 40
9 May 81	**BETTE DAVIS' EYES** *EMI America EA 121* ★	10		6
8 Aug 81	**DRAW OF THE CARDS** *EMI America EA 125*	49		
9 Oct 82	**VOYEUR** *EMI America EA 143*	68		

CARNIVAL UK production group

Date	Title / Label	Peak Position	Weeks at No.1	Weeks in Top 40
12 Sep 98	**ALL OF THE GIRLS (ALL AI-DI-GIRL DEM)** *Pepper 0530072* CARNIVAL FEATURING RIP VS RED RAT	51		

RENATO CAROSONE & HIS SEXTET

Italian singer

Date	Title / Label	Peak Position	Weeks at No.1	Weeks in Top 40
4 Jul 58	**TORERO - CHA CHA CHA** *Parlophone R 4433*	25		1

MARY CHAPIN CARPENTER US singer

Date	Title / Label	Peak Position	Weeks at No.1	Weeks in Top 40
20 Nov 93	**HE THINKS HE'LL KEEP HER** *Columbia 6598632*	71		
7 Jan 95	**ONE COOL REMOVE** *Columbia 6611342* SHAWN COLVIN WITH MARY CHAPIN CARPENTER	40		1
3 Jun 95	**SHUT UP AND KISS ME** *Columbia 6613675*	35		1

CARPENTERS US duo

Date	Title / Label	Peak Position	Weeks at No.1	Weeks in Top 40
5 Sep 70	**(THEY LONG TO BE) CLOSE TO YOU** *A&M AMS 800* ★	6		13
9 Jan 71	**WE'VE ONLY JUST BEGUN** *A&M AMS 813*	28		6
18 Sep 71	**SUPERSTAR/FOR ALL WE KNOW** *A&M AMS 864*	18		10
1 Jan 72	**MERRY CHRISTMAS DARLING** *A&M AME 601*	45		
23 Sep 72	**I WON'T LAST A DAY WITHOUT YOU/GOODBYE TO LOVE** *A&M AMS 7023*	9		11
7 Jul 73	**YESTERDAY ONCE MORE** *A&M AMS 7073* ●	2		14
20 Oct 73	**TOP OF THE WORLD** *A&M AMS 7086* ● ★	5		16
2 Mar 74	**JAMBALAYA (ON THE BAYOU)/MR GUDER** *A&M AMS 7098*	12		9
8 Jun 74	**I WON'T LAST A DAY WITHOUT YOU** *A&M AMS 7111*	32		3
18 Jan 75	**PLEASE MR. POSTMAN** *A&M AMS 7141* ● ★	2		11
19 Apr 75	**ONLY YESTERDAY** *A&M AMS 7159*	7		9
30 Aug 75	**SOLITAIRE** *A&M AMS 7187*	32		3
20 Dec 75	**SANTA CLAUS IS COMIN' TO TOWN** *A&M AMS 7144*	37		2
27 Mar 76	**THERE'S A KIND OF HUSH (ALL OVER THE WORLD)** *A&M AMS 7219*	22		5
3 Jul 76	**I NEED TO BE IN LOVE** *A&M AMS 7238*	36		2
8 Oct 77	**CALLING OCCUPANTS OF INTERPLANETARY CRAFT (THE RECOGNISED ANTHEM OF WORLD CONTACT DAY)** *A&M AMS 7318*	9		8
11 Feb 78	**SWEET SWEET SMILE** *A&M AMS 7327*	40		1
22 Oct 83	**MAKE BELIEVE IT'S YOUR FIRST TIME** *A&M AM 147*	60		
8 Dec 90	**MERRY CHRISTMAS DARLING/(THEY LONG TO BE) CLOSE TO YOU** *A&M AM 716*	25		4
13 Feb 93	**RAINY DAYS AND MONDAYS** *A&M AMCD 0180*	63		
24 Dec 94	**TRYIN' TO GET THE FEELING AGAIN** *A&M 5807612*	44		

CARPET BOMBERS FOR PEACE

Multinational group

Date	Title / Label	Peak Position	Weeks at No.1	Weeks in Top 40
5 Apr 03	**SALT IN THE WOUND** *Jungle JUNG 066CD*	67		

JOE 'FINGERS' CARR US orchestra leader/pianist

Date	Title / Label	Peak Position	Weeks at No.1	Weeks in Top 40
29 Jun 56	**PORTUGUESE WASHERWOMAN** *Capitol CL 14587*	20		8

LINDA CARR US singer

Date	Title / Label	Peak Position	Weeks at No.1	Weeks in Top 40
12 Jul 75	**HIGHWIRE** *Chelsea 2005 025* *LINDA CARR & THE LOVE SQUAD*	15		8
5 Jun 76	**SOLD MY ROCK 'N' ROLL (GAVE IT FOR FUNKY SOUL)** *Spark SRL 1139* *LINDA CARR & THE FUNKY BOYS*	36		5

LUCY CARR UK singer

Date	Title / Label	Peak Position	Weeks at No.1	Weeks in Top 40
25 Jan 03	**MISSING YOU** *Lickin LICKINCD 001*	28		7
9 Aug 03	**THIS IS GOODBYE** *Lickin LICKINCX 002*	41		

PEARL CARR & TEDDY JOHNSON UK duo

Date	Title / Label	Peak Position	Weeks at No.1	Weeks in Top 40
20 Mar 59	**SING LITTLE BIRDIE** *Columbia DB 4275*	12		1
6 Apr 61	**HOW WONDERFUL TO KNOW** *Columbia DB 4603*	23		1

SUZI CARR US singer

Date	Title / Label	Peak Position	Weeks at No.1	Weeks in Top 40
8 Oct 94	**ALL OVER ME** *Cowboy RODEO 947CD*	45		

VALERIE CARR US singer

Date	Title / Label	Peak Position	Weeks at No.1	Weeks in Top 40
4 Jul 58	**WHEN THE BOYS TALK ABOUT THE GIRLS** *Columbia DB 4131*	29		2

VIKKI CARR US singer

Date	Title / Label	Peak Position	Weeks at No.1	Weeks in Top 40
1 Jun 67	**IT MUST BE HIM (SEUL SUR SON ETOILE)** *Liberty LIB 55917*	2		16
30 Aug 67	**THERE I GO** *Liberty LBF 15022*	50		
12 Mar 69	**WITH PEN IN HAND** *Liberty LBF 15166*	39		2

RAFFAELLA CARRA Italian singer

Date	Title / Label	Peak Position	Weeks at No.1	Weeks in Top 40
15 Apr 78	**DO IT DO IT AGAIN** *Epic EPC 6094*	9		9

PAUL CARRACK UK singer

Date	Title / Label	Peak Position	Weeks at No.1	Weeks in Top 40
16 May 87	**WHEN YOU WALK IN THE ROOM** *Chrysalis CHS 3109*	48		
18 Mar 89	**DON'T SHED A TEAR** *Chrysalis CHS 3166*	60		
6 Jan 96	**EYES OF BLUE** *IRS CDEIRS 192*	40		1
6 Apr 96	**HOW LONG?** *IRS CDEIRS 193*	32		2
24 Aug 96	**EYES OF BLUE (REMIX)** *IRS CDEIRS 194*	45		

JOSE CARRERAS Spanish tenor

Date	Title / Label	Peak Position	Weeks at No.1	Weeks in Top 40
11 Jul 92	**AMIGOS PARA SIEMPRE (FRIENDS FOR LIFE)** *Really Useful RUR 10* JOSE CARRERAS & SARAH BRIGHTMAN	11		9
30 Jul 94	**LIBIAMO/LA DONNA E MOBILE** *Teldec YZ 843CD* JOSE CARRERAS, PLACIDO DOMINGO & LUCIANO PAVAROTTI	21		2
25 Jul 98	**YOU'LL NEVER WALK ALONE** *Decca 4607982* CARRERAS/DOMINGO/PAVAROTTI WITH MEHTA	35		1

TIA CARRERE US singer

Date	Title / Label	Peak Position	Weeks at No.1	Weeks in Top 40
30 May 92	**BALLROOM BLITZ** *Reprise W 0105*	26		4

JIM CARREY Canadian actor/singer

Date	Title / Label	Peak Position	Weeks at No.1	Weeks in Top 40
21 Jan 95	**CUBAN PETE** *Columbia 6606625*	31		1

CARRIE UK/US group

Date	Title / Label	Peak Position	Weeks at No.1	Weeks in Top 40
14 Mar 98	**MOLLY** *Island CID 687*	56		
9 May 98	**CALIFORNIA SCREAMIN'** *Island CID 694*	55		

DINA CARROLL UK singer

Date	Title / Label	Peak Position	Weeks at No.1	Weeks in Top 40
2 Feb 91	**IT'S TOO LATE** *Mercury ITM 3* QUARTZ INTRODUCING DINA CARROLL	8		9
15 Jun 91	**NAKED LOVE (JUST SAY YOU WANT ME)** *Mercury ITM 4* QUARTZ & DINA CARROLL	39		1
11 Jul 92	**AIN'T NO MAN** *A&M AM 0001*	16		6
10 Oct 92	**SPECIAL KIND OF LOVE** *A&M AM 0088*	16		4
5 Dec 92	**SO CLOSE** *A&M AM 0101*	20		6
27 Feb 93	**THIS TIME** *A&M AMCD 0184*	23		4
15 May 93	**EXPRESS** *A&M 5802632*	12		4
16 Oct 93	**DON'T BE A STRANGER** *A&M 5803892* ●	3		11
11 Dec 93	**THE PERFECT YEAR** *A&M 5804812* ●	5		9
28 Sep 96	**ESCAPING** *Mercury DCCD 1*	3		6
21 Dec 96	**ONLY HUMAN** *Mercury DCCD 2*	33		1

Date	Title	Label	Peak Position	Weeks at No.1	Weeks in Top 40
24 Oct 98	ONE, TWO, THREE	*1st Avenue MERCD 514*	16		2
24 Jul 99	WITHOUT LOVE	*1st Avenue FESCDD 57*	13		4
16 Jun 01	SOMEONE LIKE YOU	*1st Avenue 5689072*	38		1

RON CARROLL US singer

Date	Title	Label	Peak Position	Weeks at No.1	Weeks in Top 40
4 Mar 00	LUCKY STAR SUPERFUNK FEATURING RON CARROLL	*Virgin DINSD 198*	42		
28 Apr 01	MY LOVE KLUSTER FEATURING RON CARROLL	*Scorpio Music 1928112*	73		

RONNIE CARROLL UK singer

Date	Title	Label	Peak Position	Weeks at No.1	Weeks in Top 40
27 Jul 56	WALK HAND IN HAND *RONNIE CARROLL WITH WALLY SCOTT AND HIS ORCHESTRA*	*Philips PB 605*	13		8
29 Mar 57	THE WISDOM OF A FOOL *RONNIE CARROLL WITH WALLY SCOTT AND HIS ORCHESTRA*	*Philips PB 667*	20		2
31 Mar 60	FOOTSTEPS *RONNIE CARROLL WITH WALLY SCOTT AND HIS ORCHESTRA*	*Philips PB 1004*	36		2
22 Feb 62	RING A DING GIRL *RONNIE CARROLL WITH WALLY SCOTT AND HIS ORCHESTRA*	*Philips PB 1222*	46		
2 Aug 62	ROSES ARE RED (MY LOVE) *RONNIE CARROLL WITH WALLY SCOTT AND HIS ORCHESTRA*	*Philips 326532 BF*	3		14
15 Nov 62	IF ONLY TOMORROW (COULD BE LIKE TODAY) *RONNIE CARROLL WITH WALLY SCOTT AND HIS ORCHESTRA*	*Philips 326550 BF*	33		2
7 Mar 63	SAY WONDERFUL THINGS *RONNIE CARROLL WITH WALLY SCOTT AND HIS ORCHESTRA*	*Philips 326574 BF*	6		13

JASPER CARROTT UK comedian

Date	Title	Label	Peak Position	Weeks at No.1	Weeks in Top 40
16 Aug 75	FUNKY MOPED/MAGIC ROUNDABOUT	*DJM DJS 388* ○	5		13

CARS US group

Date	Title	Label	Peak Position	Weeks at No.1	Weeks in Top 40
11 Nov 78	MY BEST FRIEND'S GIRL	*Elektra K 12301*	3		6
17 Feb 79	JUST WHAT I NEEDED	*Elektra K 12312*	17		8
28 Jul 79	LET'S GO	*Elektra K 12371*	51		
5 Jun 82	SINCE YOU'RE GONE	*Elektra K 13177*	37		1
29 Sep 84	DRIVE	*Elektra E 9706* ○	5		9
3 Aug 85	DRIVE	*Elektra E 9706* ●	4		9

ALEX CARTANA UK singer

Date	Title	Label	Peak Position	Weeks at No.1	Weeks in Top 40
6 Sep 03	SHAKE IT (MOVE A LITTLE CLOSER) LEE CABRERA FEATURING ALEX CARTANA	*Credence CDCRED 039*	16		3
8 May 04	HEY PAPI	*EMI PAP1CDS*	34		1

AARON CARTER US singer

Date	Title	Label	Peak Position	Weeks at No.1	Weeks in Top 40
29 Nov 97	CRUSH ON YOU	*Ultra Pop 6099605 ULT*	9		4
7 Feb 98	CRAZY LITTLE PARTY GIRL	*Ultra Pop 0099645 ULT*	7		4
28 Mar 98	I'M GONNA MISS YOU FOREVER	*Ultra Pop 0099725 ULT*	24		2
4 Jul 98	SURFIN' USA	*Ultra Pop 0099805 ULT*	18		3
16 Sep 00	I WANT CANDY	*Jive 9250892*	31		1
28 Oct 00	AARON'S PARTY (COME GET IT)	*Jive 9251272*	51		
13 Apr 02	LEAVE IT UP TO ME	*Jive 9253262*	22		2

BRAD CARTER UK producer

Date	Title	Label	Peak Position	Weeks at No.1	Weeks in Top 40
23 Oct 04	MORNING ALWAYS COMES TOO SOON	*Positiva CDTIVS210*	48		

CLARENCE CARTER US singer

Date	Title	Label	Peak Position	Weeks at No.1	Weeks in Top 40
10 Oct 70	PATCHES	*Atlantic 2091 030*	2		12

NICK CARTER US singer

Date	Title	Label	Peak Position	Weeks at No.1	Weeks in Top 40
19 Oct 02	HELP ME	*Jive 9254332*	17		2

CARTER - THE UNSTOPPABLE SEX MACHINE UK group

Date	Title	Label	Peak Position	Weeks at No.1	Weeks in Top 40
26 Jan 91	BLOODSPORTS FOR ALL	*Rough Trade R 20112687*	48		
22 Jun 91	SHERIFF FATMAN	*Big Cat USM 1*	23		5
26 Oct 91	AFTER THE WATERSHED	*Big Cat USM 2*	11		4
11 Jan 92	RUBBISH	*Big Cat USM 3*	14		3
25 Apr 92	THE ONLY LIVING BOY IN NEW CROSS	*Big Cat USM 4*	7		3
4 Jul 92	DO RE ME SO FAR SO GOOD	*Chrysalis USM 5*	22		2
28 Nov 92	THE IMPOSSIBLE DREAM	*Chrysalis USM 6*	21		2
4 Sep 93	LEAN ON ME I WON'T FALL OVER	*Chrysalis CDUSM 7*	16		2
16 Oct 93	LENNY AND TERENCE	*Chrysalis CDUSM 8*	40		1
12 Mar 94	GLAM ROCK COPS	*Chrysalis CDUSMS 10*	24		2
19 Nov 94	LET'S GET TATTOOS	*Chrysalis CDUSMS 30*	30		2
4 Feb 95	THE YOUNG OFFENDER'S MUM	*Chrysalis CDUSMS 12*	34		2
30 Sep 95	BORN ON THE 5TH OF NOVEMBER	*Chrysalis CDUSM 13*	35		1

CARTER TWINS Irish vocal duo

Date	Title	Label	Peak Position	Weeks at No.1	Weeks in Top 40
8 Mar 97	THE TWELFTH OF NEVER/TOO RIGHT TO BE WRONG	*RCA 74321453082*	61		

JUNIOR CARTIER UK producer

Date	Title	Label	Peak Position	Weeks at No.1	Weeks in Top 40
6 Nov 99	WOMEN BEAT THEIR MEN	*Nucamp CAMPD 3X*	70		

CARTOONS Danish group

Date	Title	Label	Peak Position	Weeks at No.1	Weeks in Top 40
3 Apr 99	WITCH DOCTOR	*Flex TOONCD 1* ●	2		11
19 Jun 99	DOODAH	*Flex CDTOON 002*	7		6
4 Sep 99	AISY WAISY	*Flex CDTOONS 003*	16		2

RICHARD CARTRIDGE UK singer

Date	Title	Label	Peak Position	Weeks at No.1	Weeks in Top 40
25 Sep 04	I'VE FOUND LOVE AGAIN	*Springboard Media SMCDSRC001*	50		

CARVELLS UK singer/multi-instrumentalist

Date	Title	Label	Peak Position	Weeks at No.1	Weeks in Top 40
26 Nov 77	THE L.A. RUN	*Creole CR 143*	31		2

CASCADA German group

Date	Title	Label	Peak Position	Weeks at No.1	Weeks in Top 40
5 Aug 06	EVERYTIME WE TOUCH	*All Around The World CDGLOBE537*	2		18
16 Dec 06	TRULY MADLY DEEPLY	*All Around The World CDGLOBE622*	4		12
17 Feb 07	I NEED A MIRACLE	*Ministry Of Sound PDT20CDS*	8		6
7 Jul 07	NEVER ENDING DREAM	*All Around The World CDGLOBE70*	46		
15 Dec 07	WHAT HURTS THE MOST	*All Around The World CDGLOBE790*	10		11

CASCADES US group

Date	Title	Label	Peak Position	Weeks at No.1	Weeks in Top 40
28 Feb 63	RHYTHM OF THE RAIN	*Warner Brothers WB 88*	5		14

CASE US singer

Date	Title	Label	Peak Position	Weeks at No.1	Weeks in Top 40
21 Sep 96	TOUCH ME TEASE ME CASE FEATURING FOXY BROWN	*Def Jam DEFCD 18*	26		1
10 Nov 01	LIVIN' IT UP JA RULE FEATURING CASE	*Def Jam 5888142*	27		2
3 Aug 02	LIVIN' IT UP JA RULE FEATURING CASE	*Def Jam 0639782*	5		6

ED CASE UK producer

Date	Title	Label	Peak Position	Weeks at No.1	Weeks in Top 40
21 Oct 00	SOMETHING IN YOUR EYES	*Red Rose CDROSE 003*	38		1
15 Sep 01	WHO? ED CASE & SWEETIE IRIE	*Columbia 6718302*	29		1
20 Jul 02	GOOD TIMES ED CASE & SKIN	*Columbia 6727672*	49		

NATALIE CASEY UK singer/actress

Date	Title	Label	Peak Position	Weeks at No.1	Weeks in Top 40
7 Jan 84	CHICK CHICK CHICKEN	*Polydor CHICK 1*	72		

JOHNNY CASH US singer

Date	Title	Label	Peak Position	Weeks at No.1	Weeks in Top 40
3 Jun 65	IT AIN'T ME, BABE	*CBS 201760*	28		6
6 Sep 69	A BOY NAMED SUE	*CBS 4460*	4		13
23 May 70	WHAT IS TRUTH	*CBS 4934*	21		9
15 Apr 72	A THING CALLED LOVE JOHNNY CASH WITH THE EVANGEL TEMPLE CHOIR	*CBS 7797*	4		12
3 Jul 76	ONE PIECE AT A TIME JOHNNY CASH WITH THE TENNESSEE THREE	*CBS 4087*	32		5
10 May 03	HURT/PERSONAL JESUS	*American/Lost Highway 0779982*	42		
15 Nov 03	HURT/PERSONAL JESUS	*American/Lost Highway 0779982*	39		1

CA$HFLOW US group

Date	Title	Label	Peak Position	Weeks at No.1	Weeks in Top 40
24 May 86	MINE ALL MINE/PARTY FREAK	*Club JAB 30*	15		6

Silver-selling ● Gold-selling ● Platinum-selling ✪ US No.1 ★ | Peak Position · Weeks at No.1 · Weeks in Top 40

CASHMERE US group

Date	Title / Label	Peak Position	Weeks at No.1	Weeks in Top 40
19 Jan 85	**CAN I** *Fourth & Broadway BRW 19*	29		6
23 Mar 85	**WE NEED LOVE** *Fourth & Broadway BRW 22*	52		

CASINO UK production group

Date	Title / Label	Peak Position	Weeks at No.1	Weeks in Top 40
17 May 97	**SOUND OF EDEN** *Worx WORXCD 006*	52		
10 Jul 99	**ONLY YOU** *Pow! CDPOW 006*	72		
23 Feb 67	**THEN YOU CAN TELL ME GOODBYE** *President PT 123*	28		5

CASSIDY US singer

Date	Title / Label	Peak Position	Weeks at No.1	Weeks in Top 40
29 May 04	**HOTEL** *J Records 82876618612* CASSIDY FEATURING R KELLY	3		12
25 Sep 04	**GET NO BETTER** *J Records 82876649282* CASSIDY FEATURING MASHONDA	24		2

DAVID CASSIDY US singer/actor

Date	Title / Label	Peak Position	Weeks at No.1	Weeks in Top 40
8 Apr 72	**COULD IT BE FOREVER/CHERISH** *Bell 1224*	2		14
16 Sep 72	**HOW CAN I BE SURE** *Bell 1258*	1	2	9
25 Nov 72	**ROCK ME BABY** *Bell 1268*	11		8
24 Mar 73	**I'M A CLOWN/SOME KIND OF A SUMMER** *Bell MABEL 4*	3		10
13 Oct 73	**DAYDREAMER/THE PUPPY SONG** *Bell 1334*	1	3	14
11 May 74	**IF I DIDN'T CARE** *Bell 1350*	9		7
27 Jul 74	**PLEASE PLEASE ME** *Bell 1371*	16		5
5 Jul 75	**I WRITE THE SONGS/GET IT UP FOR LOVE** *RCA 2571*	11		8
25 Oct 75	**DARLIN'** *RCA 2622*	16		7
23 Feb 85	**THE LAST KISS** *Arista ARIST 589*	6		7
11 May 85	**ROMANCE (LET YOUR HEART GO)** *Arista ARIST 620*	54		

EVA CASSIDY US singer

Date	Title / Label	Peak Position	Weeks at No.1	Weeks in Top 40
21 Apr 01	**OVER THE RAINBOW** *Blix Street/Hot HIT 16*	42		
11 Oct 03	**YOU TAKE MY BREATH AWAY** *Blix Street/Hot HIT 27*	54		
22 Dec 07	**WHAT A WONDERFUL WORLD** *Dramatico TD001* EVA CASSIDY & KATIE MELUA	1	1	3

CASSIE US singer

Date	Title / Label	Peak Position	Weeks at No.1	Weeks in Top 40
19 Aug 06	**ME & U** *Bad Boy AT0251CD*	6		12
28 Oct 06	**LONG WAY 2 GO** *Bad Boy AT0262CD*	12		7

CASSIUS French production duo

Date	Title / Label	Peak Position	Weeks at No.1	Weeks in Top 40
23 Jan 99	**CASSIUS 1999** *Virgin DINSD 177*	7		4
15 May 99	**FEELING FOR YOU** *Virgin DINSD 181*	16		2
20 Nov 99	**LA MOUCHE** *Virgin DINSD 188*	53		
5 Oct 02	**THE SOUND OF VIOLENCE** *Virgin DINSD 241*	49		

CAST UK group

Date	Title / Label	Peak Position	Weeks at No.1	Weeks in Top 40
15 Jul 95	**FINETIME** *Polydor 5795072*	17		3
30 Sep 95	**ALRIGHT** *Polydor 5799272*	13		3
20 Jan 96	**SANDSTORM** *Polydor 5778732*	8		4
30 Mar 96	**WALKAWAY** *Polydor 5762852*	9		5
26 Oct 96	**FLYING** *Polydor 5754772*	4		3
5 Apr 97	**FREE ME** *Polydor 5736512*	7		4
28 Jun 97	**GUIDING STAR** *Polydor 5711732*	9		3
13 Sep 97	**LIVE THE DREAM** *Polydor 5716852*	7		3
15 Nov 97	**I'M SO LONELY** *Polydor 5690592*	14		2
8 May 99	**BEAT MAMA** *Polydor 5635952*	9		2
7 Aug 99	**MAGIC HOUR** *Polydor 5612272*	28		1
28 Jul 01	**DESERT DROUGHT** *Polydor 5871762*	45		

CAST OF CASUALTY UK group

Date	Title / Label	Peak Position	Weeks at No.1	Weeks in Top 40
14 Mar 98	**EVERLASTING LOVE** *warner.esp WESP 003CD*	5		3

CAST OF HIGH SCHOOL MUSICAL US group

Date	Title / Label	Peak Position	Weeks at No.1	Weeks in Top 40
30 Sep 06	**BREAKING FREE** *Walt Disney HSMCD01*	9		10
9 Dec 06	**WE'RE ALL IN THIS TOGETHER** *Walt Disney 3814510*	40		1
13 Jan 07	**STICK TO THE STATUS QUO** *Download*	74		

CAST OF HIGH SCHOOL MUSICAL 2 US group

Date	Title / Label	Peak Position	Weeks at No.1	Weeks in Top 40
28 Jul 07	**WHAT TIME IS IT** *Walt Disney 5016470*	20		4
6 Oct 07	**YOU ARE THE MUSIC IN ME** *Walt Disney 5075640*	26		2
6 Oct 07	**EVERYDAY** *Download*	59		

CAST OF THE NEW ROCKY HORROR SHOW UK group

Date	Title / Label	Peak Position	Weeks at No.1	Weeks in Top 40
12 Dec 98	**THE TIMEWARP** *Damn It Janet DAMJAN 1CD*	57		

ROY CASTLE UK singer/trumpeter

Date	Title / Label	Peak Position	Weeks at No.1	Weeks in Top 40
22 Dec 60	**LITTLE WHITE BERRY** *Philips PB 1087*	40		1

CASUALS UK group

Date	Title / Label	Peak Position	Weeks at No.1	Weeks in Top 40
14 Aug 68	**JESAMINE** *Decca F 22784*	2		15
4 Dec 68	**TOY** *Decca F 22852*	30		6

CAT UK singer

Date	Title / Label	Peak Position	Weeks at No.1	Weeks in Top 40
23 Oct 93	**TONGUE TIED** *EMI CDEM 286*	17		3

CATATONIA UK group

Date	Title / Label	Peak Position	Weeks at No.1	Weeks in Top 40
3 Feb 96	**SWEET CATATONIA** *Blanco Y Negro NEG 85CD*	61		
4 May 96	**LOST CAT** *Blanco Y Negro NEG 88CD1*	41		
7 Sep 96	**YOU'VE GOT A LOT TO ANSWER FOR** *Blanco Y Negro NEG 93CD1*	35		1
30 Nov 96	**BLEED** *Blanco Y Negro NEG 97CD1*	46		
18 Oct 97	**I AM THE MOB** *Blanco Y Negro NEG 107CD*	40		1
31 Jan 98	**MULDER AND SCULLY** *Blanco Y Negro NEG 109CD*	3		7
7 Mar 98	**THE BALLAD OF TOM JONES** *Gut CDGUT 18* SPACE WITH CERYS OF CATATONIA	4		6
2 May 98	**ROAD RAGE** *Blanco Y Negro NEG 112CD*	5		5
1 Aug 98	**STRANGE GLUE** *Blanco Y Negro NEG 113CD*	11		3
7 Nov 98	**GAME ON** *WEA NEG 114CD*	33		1
10 Apr 99	**DEAD FROM THE WAIST DOWN** *Blanco Y Negro NEG 115CD*	7		5
24 Jul 99	**LONDINIUM** *Blanco Y Negro NEG 117CD*	20		1
13 Nov 99	**KARAOKE QUEEN** *Blanco Y Negro NEG 119CD*	36		1
4 Aug 01	**STONE BY STONE** *Blanco Y Negro NEG 134CD*	19		1

CATCH UK group

Date	Title / Label	Peak Position	Weeks at No.1	Weeks in Top 40
17 Nov 90	**FREE (C'MON)** *ffrr F 147*	70		
11 Oct 97	**BINGO** *Virgin VSCDT 1656*	23		2
21 Feb 98	**DIVE IN** *Virgin VSCDT 1665*	44		

CATHERINE WHEEL UK group

Date	Title / Label	Peak Position	Weeks at No.1	Weeks in Top 40
23 Nov 91	**BLACK METALLIC (EP)** *Fontana CW 1*	68		
8 Feb 92	**BALLOON** *Fontana CW 2*	59		
18 Apr 92	**I WANT TO TOUCH YOU** *Fontana CW 3*	35		1
9 Jan 93	**30TH CENTURY MAN** *Fontana CWCD 4*	47		
10 Jul 93	**CRANK** *Fontana CWCD 5*	66		
16 Oct 93	**SHOW ME MARY** *Fontana CWCDA 6*	62		
5 Aug 95	**WAYDOWN** *Fontana CWCD 7*	67		
13 Dec 97	**DELICIOUS** *Chrysalis CDCHS 5071*	53		
28 Feb 98	**MA SOLITUDA** *Chrysalis CDCHS 5077*	53		
2 May 98	**BROKEN NOSE** *Chrysalis CDCHS 5086*	48		

LORRAINE CATO UK singer

Date	Title / Label	Peak Position	Weeks at No.1	Weeks in Top 40
6 Feb 93	**HOW CAN YOU TELL ME IT'S OVER** *Columbia 6587662*	46		
3 Aug 96	**I WAS MADE TO LOVE YOU** *MCA MCSTD 40055*	41		

CATS UK group

Date	Title / Label	Peak Position	Weeks at No.1	Weeks in Top 40
9 Apr 69	**SWAN LAKE** *BAF 1*	48		

CATS U.K. UK group

Date	Title / Label	Peak Position	Weeks at No.1	Weeks in Top 40
6 Oct 79	**LUTON AIRPORT** *WEA K 18075*	22		6

NICK CAVE & THE BAD SEEDS
Australian singer and group

Date	Title	Peak Position	Weeks at No.1	Weeks in Top 40
11 Apr 92	**STRAIGHT TO YOU/JACK THE RIPPER** *Mute 140*	68		
12 Dec 92	**WHAT A WONDERFUL WORLD** *Mute 151* NICK CAVE & SHANE McGOWAN	72		
9 Apr 94	**DO YOU LOVE ME** *Mute CDMUTE 160*	68		
14 Oct 95	**WHERE THE WILD ROSES GROW** *Mute CDMUTE 185* NICK CAVE + KYLIE MINOGUE	11		3
9 Mar 96	**HENRY LEE** *Mute CDMUTE 189* NICK CAVE & THE BAD SEEDS & PJ HARVEY	36		1
22 Feb 97	**INTO MY ARMS** *Mute CDMUTE 192*	53		
31 May 97	**(ARE YOU) THE ONE THAT I'VE BEEN…** *Mute CDMUTE 206*	67		
31 Mar 01	**AS I SAT SADLY BY HER SIDE** *Mute CDMUTE 249*	42		
2 Jun 01	**FIFTEEN FEET OF PURE WHITE SNOW** *Mute CDMUTE 262*	52		
8 Mar 03	**BRING IT ON** *Mute CDMUTE 265*	58		
18 Sep 04	**NATURE BOY** *Mute CDMUTE 324*	37		1
27 Nov 04	**BREATHLESS/THERE SHE GOES MY BEAUTIFUL WORLD** *Mute CDMUTE329*	45		
26 Mar 05	**GET READY FOR LOVE** *Atlantic AT0196CD*	62		
1 Mar 08	**DIG, LAZARUS, DIG** *Mute CDMUTE377*	66		

CAVE IN US group

Date	Title	Peak Position	Weeks at No.1	Weeks in Top 40
31 May 03	**ANCHOR** *RCA 82876522992*	53		

CAVEMAN UK duo

Date	Title	Peak Position	Weeks at No.1	Weeks in Top 40
9 Mar 91	**I'M READY** *Profile PROF 330*	65		

C.C.S. UK group

Date	Title	Peak Position	Weeks at No.1	Weeks in Top 40
31 Oct 70	**WHOLE LOTTA LOVE** *RAK 104*	13		11
27 Feb 71	**WALKIN'** *RAK 109*	7		13
4 Sep 71	**TAP TURNS ON THE WATER** *RAK 119*	5		11
4 Mar 72	**BROTHER** *RAK 126*	25		6
4 Aug 73	**THE BAND PLAYED THE BOOGIE** *RAK 154*	36		4

CECIL UK group

Date	Title	Peak Position	Weeks at No.1	Weeks in Top 40
25 Oct 97	**HOSTAGE IN A FROCK** *Parlophone CDRS 6471*	68		
28 Mar 98	**THE MOST TIRING DAY** *Parlophone CDRS 6490*	69		

CELEDA US singer

Date	Title	Peak Position	Weeks at No.1	Weeks in Top 40
5 Sep 98	**MUSIC IS THE ANSWER (DANCIN' & PRANCIN')** *Twisted UK TWCD 10038* DANNY TENAGLIA & CELEDA	36		1
12 Jun 99	**BE YOURSELF** *Twisted UK TWCD 10049*	61		
23 Oct 99	**MUSIC IS THE ANSWER (REMIX)** *Twisted UK TWCD 10052*	50		

CELETIA UK singer

Date	Title	Peak Position	Weeks at No.1	Weeks in Top 40
11 Apr 98	**REWIND** *Big Life BLRD 142*	29		1
8 Aug 98	**RUNAWAY SKIES** *Big Life BLRD 144*	66		

CENOGINERZ Dutch producer

Date	Title	Peak Position	Weeks at No.1	Weeks in Top 40
2 Feb 02	**GIT DOWN** *Tripoli Trax TTRAX 081CD*	75		

CENTORY US group

Date	Title	Peak Position	Weeks at No.1	Weeks in Top 40
17 Dec 94	**POINT OF NO RETURN** *EMI CDEM 354*	67		

CENTRAL LINE UK group

Date	Title	Peak Position	Weeks at No.1	Weeks in Top 40
31 Jan 81	**(YOU KNOW) YOU CAN DO IT** *Mercury LINE 7*	67		
15 Aug 81	**WALKING INTO SUNSHINE** *Mercury MER 78*	42		
30 Jan 82	**DON'T TELL ME** *Mercury MER 90*	55		
20 Nov 82	**YOU'VE SAID ENOUGH** *Mercury MER 117*	58		
22 Jan 83	**NATURE BOY** *Mercury MER 131*	21		5
11 Jun 83	**SURPRISE SURPRISE** *Mercury MER 133*	48		

CERRONE French producer

Date	Title	Peak Position	Weeks at No.1	Weeks in Top 40
5 Mar 77	**LOVE IN C MINOR** *Atlantic K 10895*	31		3
29 Jul 78	**SUPERNATURE** *Atlantic K 11089* ●	8		9
13 Jan 79	**JE SUIS MUSIC** *CBS 6918*	39		1
10 Aug 96	**SUPERNATURE (REMIX)** *Encore CDCOR 013*	66		

A CERTAIN RATIO UK group

Date	Title	Peak Position	Weeks at No.1	Weeks in Top 40
16 Jun 90	**WON'T STOP LOVING YOU** *A&M ACR 540*	55		

PETER CETERA US singer

Date	Title	Peak Position	Weeks at No.1	Weeks in Top 40
2 Aug 86	**GLORY OF LOVE** *Full Moon W 8662* ● ★	3		10
21 Jun 97	**HARD TO SAY I'M SORRY** *LaFace 74321481482* AZ YET FEATURING PETER CETERA	7		5

FRANK CHACKSFIELD UK orchestra leader

Date	Title	Peak Position	Weeks at No.1	Weeks in Top 40
3 Apr 53	**LITTLE RED MONKEY** *Parlophone R 3658* FRANK CHACKSFIELD'S TUNESMITHS, FEATURING JACK JORDAN - CLAVIOLINE	10		3
22 May 53	**TERRY'S THEME FROM *LIMELIGHT*** *Decca F 10106*	2		24
12 Feb 54	**EBB TIDE** *Decca F 10122*	9		2
24 Feb 56	**IN OLD LISBON** *Decca F 10689*	15		4
18 May 56	**PORT AU PRINCE** *Decca F 10727* WINIFRED ATWELL & FRANK CHACKSFIELD	18		6
31 Aug 56	**DONKEY CART** *Decca F 10743*	26		2

CHAD & RYAN US duo

Date	Title	Peak Position	Weeks at No.1	Weeks in Top 40
6 Oct 07	**I DON'T DANCE** *Download*	57		

CHAIRMEN OF THE BOARD US group

Date	Title	Peak Position	Weeks at No.1	Weeks in Top 40
22 Aug 70	**GIVE ME JUST A LITTLE MORE TIME** *Invictus INV 501*	3		11
14 Nov 70	**YOU'VE GOT ME DANGLING ON A STRING** *Invictus INV 504*	5		12
20 Feb 71	**EVERYTHING'S TUESDAY** *Invictus INV 507*	12		9
15 May 71	**PAY TO THE PIPER** *Invictus INV 511*	34		5
4 Sep 71	**CHAIRMAN OF THE BOARD** *Invictus INV 516*	48		
15 Jul 72	**WORKING ON A BUILDING OF LOVE** *Invictus INV 519*	20		7
7 Oct 72	**ELMO JAMES** *Invictus INV 524*	21		6
16 Dec 72	**I'M ON MY WAY TO A BETTER PLACE** *Invictus INV 527*	30		5
23 Jun 73	**FINDERS KEEPERS** *Invictus INV 530*	21		7
13 Sep 86	**LOVERBOY** *EMI EM 5585* CHAIRMEN OF THE BOARD FEATURING GENERAL JOHNSON	56		

CHAKACHAS Belgian group

Date	Title	Peak Position	Weeks at No.1	Weeks in Top 40
11 Jan 62	**TWIST TWIST** *RCA 1264*	48		
27 May 72	**JUNGLE FEVER** *Polydor 2121 064*	29		3

GEORGE CHAKIRIS US singer/actor

Date	Title	Peak Position	Weeks at No.1	Weeks in Top 40
2 Jun 60	**HEART OF A SINGLE GIRL** *Triumph ROM 1010*	49		

CHAKKA BOOM BANG
Dutch production group

Date	Title	Peak Position	Weeks at No.1	Weeks in Top 40
20 Jan 96	**TOSSING AND TURNING** *Hooj Choons HOOJCD 39*	57		

CHAKRA UK production duo

Date	Title	Peak Position	Weeks at No.1	Weeks in Top 40
18 Jan 97	**I AM** *WEA 091CD*	24		1
23 Aug 97	**HOME** *WEA 116CD2*	46		
23 Oct 99	**LOVE SHINES THROUGH** *WEA 227CD*	67		
26 Aug 00	**HOME (REMIX)** *WEA 266CD*	47		

SUE CHALONER UK singer

Date	Title	Peak Position	Weeks at No.1	Weeks in Top 40
22 May 93	**MOVE ON UP** *Pulse 8 CDLOSE 41*	64		

CHAM Jamaican singer

Date	Title	Peak Position	Weeks at No.1	Weeks in Top 40
9 Sep 06	**GHETTO STORY** *Atlantic AT0254CD*	62		

RICHARD CHAMBERLAIN US singer/actor

Date	Title / Label	Peak Position	Weeks at No.1	Weeks in Top 40
7 Jun 62	**THEME FROM *DR KILDARE* (THREE STARS WILL SHINE TONIGHT)** *MGM 1160*	12		8
1 Nov 62	**LOVE ME TENDER** *MGM 1173*	15		10
21 Feb 63	**HI-LILI HI-LO** *MGM 1189*	20		9
18 Jul 63	**TRUE LOVE** *MGM 1205*	30		4

CHAMELEON UK duo

Date	Title / Label	Peak Position	Weeks at No.1	Weeks in Top 40
18 May 96	**THE WAY IT IS** *Stress CDSTR 65*	34		1

CHAMILLIONAIRE US duo

Date	Title / Label	Peak Position	Weeks at No.1	Weeks in Top 40
19 Aug 06	**RIDIN'** *Universal 1705043* CHAMILLIONAIRE FEATURING KRAYZIE BONE	2		11
2 Dec 06	**GROWN AND SEXY** *Universal 1713495*	35		1
6 Oct 07	**HIP HOP POLICE** *Universal 1751125* CHAMILLIONAIRE FEATURING SLICK RICK	50		

CHAMPAIGN US group

Date	Title / Label	Peak Position	Weeks at No.1	Weeks in Top 40
9 May 81	**HOW 'BOUT US** *CBS A 1046*	5		9

CHAMPS US group

Date	Title / Label	Peak Position	Weeks at No.1	Weeks in Top 40
4 Apr 58	**TEQUILA** *London HLU 8580* ★	5		9
17 Mar 60	**TOO MUCH TEQUILA** *London HLH 9052*	49		

CHAMPS BOYS French group

Date	Title / Label	Peak Position	Weeks at No.1	Weeks in Top 40
19 Jun 76	**TUBULAR BELLS** *Philips 6006 519*	41		

GENE CHANDLER US singer

Date	Title / Label	Peak Position	Weeks at No.1	Weeks in Top 40
5 Jun 68	**NOTHING CAN STOP ME** *Soul City SC 102*	41		
3 Feb 79	**GET DOWN** *20th Century BTC 1040*	11		8
1 Sep 79	**WHEN YOU'RE NUMBER 1** *20th Century TC 2411*	43		
28 Jun 80	**DOES SHE HAVE A FRIEND** *20th Century TC 2451*	28		5

CHANEL US singer

Date	Title / Label	Peak Position	Weeks at No.1	Weeks in Top 40
30 Sep 06	**MY LIFE** *Hed Kandi HK22CDS*	39		1

CHANELLE US singer

Date	Title / Label	Peak Position	Weeks at No.1	Weeks in Top 40
11 Mar 89	**ONE MAN** *Cooltempo COOL 183*	16		6
10 Dec 94	**ONE MAN (REMIX)** *Deep Distraxion OILYCD 031*	50		

CHANGE US group

Date	Title / Label	Peak Position	Weeks at No.1	Weeks in Top 40
28 Jun 80	**A LOVER'S HOLIDAY/GLOW OF LOVE** *WEA K 79141*	14		6
6 Sep 80	**SEARCHING** *WEA K 79156*	11		8
2 Jun 84	**CHANGE OF HEART** *WEA YZ 7*	17		7
11 Aug 84	**YOU ARE MY MELODY** *WEA YZ 14*	48		
16 Mar 85	**LET'S GO TOGETHER** *Cooltempo COOL 107*	37		3
25 May 85	**OH WHAT A FEELING** *Cooltempo COOL 109*	56		
13 Jul 85	**MUTUAL ATTRACTION** *Cooltempo COOL 111*	60		

CHANGING FACES US duo

Date	Title / Label	Peak Position	Weeks at No.1	Weeks in Top 40
24 Sep 94	**STROKE YOU UP** *Big Beat A 8251CD*	43		
26 Jul 97	**G.H.E.T.T.O.U.T.** *Atlantic AT 0003CD*	10		3
1 Nov 97	**I GOT SOMEBODY ELSE** *Atlantic AT 0014CD*	42		
4 Apr 98	**TIME AFTER TIME** *Atlantic AT 0027CD*	35		1
1 Aug 98	**SAME TEMPO** *Atlantic 5826952*	53		

BRUCE CHANNEL US singer

Date	Title / Label	Peak Position	Weeks at No.1	Weeks in Top 40
22 Mar 62	**HEY! BABY** *Mercury AMT 1171* ★	2		12
26 Jun 68	**KEEP ON** *Bell 1010*	12		14

CHANNEL X Belgian group

Date	Title / Label	Peak Position	Weeks at No.1	Weeks in Top 40
14 Dec 91	**GROOVE TO MOVE** *PWL Continental 209*	67		

CHANSON US group

Date	Title / Label	Peak Position	Weeks at No.1	Weeks in Top 40
13 Jan 79	**DON'T HOLD BACK** *Ariola ARO 140*	33		3

CHANTAYS US group

Date	Title / Label	Peak Position	Weeks at No.1	Weeks in Top 40
18 Apr 63	**PIPELINE** *London HLD 9696*	16		11

CHANTER SISTERS UK group

Date	Title / Label	Peak Position	Weeks at No.1	Weeks in Top 40
17 Jul 76	**SIDE SHOW** *Polydor 2058 735*	43		

CHAOS UK group

Date	Title / Label	Peak Position	Weeks at No.1	Weeks in Top 40
3 Oct 92	**FAREWELL MY SUMMER LOVE** *Arista 74321116397*	55		

HARRY CHAPIN US singer

Date	Title / Label	Peak Position	Weeks at No.1	Weeks in Top 40
11 May 74	**W.O.L.D.** *Elektra K 12133*	34		3

TRACY CHAPMAN US singer

Date	Title / Label	Peak Position	Weeks at No.1	Weeks in Top 40
11 Jun 88	**FAST CAR** *Elektra EKR 73*	5		8
30 Sep 89	**CROSSROADS** *Elektra EKR 95*	61		

CHAPTERHOUSE UK group

Date	Title / Label	Peak Position	Weeks at No.1	Weeks in Top 40
30 Mar 91	**PEARL** *Dedicated STONE 003*	67		
12 Oct 91	**MESMERISE** *Dedicated HOUSE 001*	60		

CHAQUITO UK orchestra

Date	Title / Label	Peak Position	Weeks at No.1	Weeks in Top 40
27 Oct 60	**NEVER ON SUNDAY** *Fontana H 265*	50		

CHARLATANS UK group

Date	Title / Label	Peak Position	Weeks at No.1	Weeks in Top 40
2 Jun 90	**THE ONLY ONE I KNOW** *Situation Two SIT 70T*	9		7
22 Sep 90	**THEN** *Situation Two SIT 74T*	12		4
9 Mar 91	**OVER RISING** *Situation Two SIT 76*	15		3
17 Aug 91	**INDIAN ROPE** *Dead Dead Good GOOD 1T*	57		
9 Nov 91	**ME. IN TIME** *Situation Two SIT 84*	28		2
7 Mar 92	**WEIRDO** *Situation Two SIT 88*	19		2
18 Jul 92	**TREMELO SONG (EP)** *Situation Two SIT 97T*	44		
5 Feb 94	**CAN'T GET OUT OF BED** *Beggars Banquet BBQ 27CD*	24		2
19 Mar 94	**I NEVER WANT AN EASY LIFE IF ME AND HE WERE EVER TO GET THERE** *Beggars Banquet BBQ 31CD*	38		1
2 Jul 94	**JESUS HAIRDO** *Beggars Banquet BBQ 32CD*	48		
7 Jan 95	**CRASHIN' IN** *Beggars Banquet BBQ 44CD*	31		1
27 May 95	**JUST LOOKIN'/BULLET COMES** *Beggars Banquet BBQ 55CD*	32		1
26 Aug 95	**JUST WHEN YOU'RE THINKING THINGS OVER** *Beggars Banquet BBQ 60CD*	12		2
7 Sep 96	**ONE TO ANOTHER** *Beggars Banquet BBQ 301CD*	3		5
5 Apr 97	**NORTH COUNTRY BOY** *Beggars Banquet BBQ 309CD*	4		4
21 Jun 97	**HOW HIGH** *Beggars Banquet BBQ 312CD*	6		3
1 Nov 97	**TELLIN' STORIES** *Beggars Banquet BBQ 318CD*	16		1
16 Oct 99	**FOREVER** *Universal MCSTD 40220*	12		2
18 Dec 99	**MY BEAUTIFUL FRIEND** *Universal MCSTD 40225*	31		1
27 May 00	**IMPOSSIBLE** *Universal MCSTXD 40231*	15		2
8 Sep 01	**LOVE IS THE KEY** *Universal MCSTD 40262*	16		1
1 Dec 01	**A MAN NEEDS TO BE TOLD** *Universal MCSTD 40271*	31		1
22 May 04	**UP AT THE LAKE** *Universal MCSTD 40363*	23		1
7 Aug 04	**TRY AGAIN TODAY** *Universal MCSTD 40370*	24		1
15 Apr 06	**BLACKENED BLUE EYES** *Creole SANXS421*	28		1
15 Jul 06	**NYC (THERE'S NO NEED TO STOP)** *Creole SANXS427*	53		
25 Nov 06	**YOU'RE SO PRETTY WE'RE SO PRETTY** *Universal 1712414*	56		

CHARLENE US singer

Date	Title / Label	Peak Position	Weeks at No.1	Weeks in Top 40
15 May 82	**I'VE NEVER BEEN TO ME** *Motown TMG 1260*	1	1	10

DON CHARLES UK singer

Date	Title / Label	Peak Position	Weeks at No.1	Weeks in Top 40
22 Feb 62	**WALK WITH ME MY ANGEL** *Decca F 11424*	39		1

RAY CHARLES US singer

Date	Title / Label	Peak Position	Weeks at No.1	Weeks in Top 40
1 Dec 60	**GEORGIA ON MY MIND** *HMV POP 792* ★	24		5
19 Oct 61	**HIT THE ROAD JACK** *HMV POP 935* ★	6		10

Date	Title / Label	Peak Position	Weeks at No.1	Weeks in Top 40
14 Jun 62	**I CAN'T STOP LOVING YOU** *HMV POP 1034* ★	1	2	16
13 Sep 62	**YOU DON'T KNOW ME** *HMV POP 1064*	9		11
13 Dec 62	**YOUR CHEATING HEART** *HMV POP 1099*	13		7
28 Mar 63	**DON'T SET ME FREE** *HMV POP 1133*	37		1
16 May 63	**TAKE THESE CHAINS FROM MY HEART** *HMV POP 1161*	5		16
12 Sep 63	**NO ONE** *HMV POP 1202*	35		4
31 Oct 63	**BUSTED** *HMV POP 1221*	21		8
24 Sep 64	**NO ONE TO CRY TO** *HMV POP 1333*	38		1
21 Jan 65	**MAKIN' WHOOPEE** *HMV POP 1383*	42		
10 Feb 66	**CRYIN' TIME** *HMV POP 1502*	50		
21 Apr 66	**TOGETHER AGAIN** *HMV POP 1519*	48		
5 Jul 67	**HERE WE GO AGAIN** *HMV POP 1595*	38		1
20 Dec 67	**YESTERDAY** *Stateside SS 2071*	44		
31 Jul 68	**ELEANOR RIGBY** *Stateside SS 2170*	36		5
13 Jan 90	**I'LL BE GOOD TO YOU** *Qwest W 2697* QUINCY JONES FEATURING RAY CHARLES & CHAKA KHAN	21		5

SUZETTE CHARLES US singer

Date	Title / Label	Peak Position	Weeks at No.1	Weeks in Top 40
21 Aug 93	**FREE TO LOVE AGAIN** *RCA 74321158372*	58		

TINA CHARLES UK singer

Date	Title / Label	Peak Position	Weeks at No.1	Weeks in Top 40
7 Feb 76	**I LOVE TO LOVE (BUT MY BABY LOVES TO DANCE)** *CBS 3937* ●	1	3	11
1 May 76	**LOVE ME LIKE A LOVER** *CBS 4237*	31		2
21 Aug 76	**DANCE LITTLE LADY DANCE** *CBS 4480* ○	6		12
4 Dec 76	**DR LOVE** *CBS 4779* ○	4		9
14 May 77	**RENDEZVOUS** *CBS 5174*	27		4
29 Oct 77	**LOVE BUG - SWEETS FOR MY SWEET (MEDLEY)** *CBS 5680*	26		4
11 Mar 78	**I'LL GO WHERE YOUR MUSIC TAKES ME** *CBS 6062*	27		6
30 Aug 86	**I LOVE TO LOVE (REMIX)** *DMC DECK 1*	67		

CHARLES & EDDIE US duo

Date	Title / Label	Peak Position	Weeks at No.1	Weeks in Top 40
31 Oct 92	**WOULD I LIE TO YOU** *Capitol CL 673* ⊛	1	2	15
20 Feb 93	**N.Y.C. (CAN YOU BELIEVE THIS CITY)** *Capitol CDCL 681*	33		3
22 May 93	**HOUSE IS NOT A HOME** *Capitol CDCLS 688*	29		2
13 May 95	**24-7-365** *Capitol CDCLS 747*	38		2

DICK CHARLESWORTH & HIS CITY GENTS UK group

Date	Title / Label	Peak Position	Weeks at No.1	Weeks in Top 40
4 May 61	**BILLY BOY** *Top Rank JAR 558*	43		

CHARLOTTE UK singer

Date	Title / Label	Peak Position	Weeks at No.1	Weeks in Top 40
12 Mar 94	**QUEEN OF HEARTS** *Big Life BLRD 106*	54		
2 May 98	**BE MINE** *Parlophone Rhythm CDRHYTHM 10*	59		
29 May 99	**SKIN** *Parlophone Rhythm CDRHYTHM 20*	56		
4 Sep 99	**SOMEDAY** *Parlophone Rhythm CDRHYTHM 23*	74		

CHARME US group

Date	Title / Label	Peak Position	Weeks at No.1	Weeks in Top 40
17 Nov 84	**GEORGY PORGY** *RCA 464*	68		

CHARO & THE SALSOUL ORCHESTRA US singer and orchestra

Date	Title / Label	Peak Position	Weeks at No.1	Weeks in Top 40
29 Apr 78	**DANCE A LITTLE BIT CLOSER** *Salsoul SSOL 101*	44		

CHAS & DAVE UK duo

Date	Title / Label	Peak Position	Weeks at No.1	Weeks in Top 40
11 Nov 78	**STRUMMIN'** *EMI 2874* CHAS & DAVE WITH ROCKNEY	52		
26 May 79	**GERTCHA** *EMI 2947*	20		6
1 Sep 79	**THE SIDEBOARD SONG (GOT MY BEER IN THE SIDEBOARD HERE)** *EMI 2986*	55		
29 Nov 80	**RABBIT** *Rockney 9* ○	8		8
12 Dec 81	**STARS OVER 45** *Rockney KOR 12*	21		6
13 Mar 82	**AIN'T NO PLEASING YOU** *Rockney KOR 14* ○	2		9
17 Jul 82	**MARGATE** *Rockney KOR 15*	46		
19 Mar 83	**LONDON GIRLS** *Rockney KOR 17*	63		
3 Dec 83	**MY MELANCHOLY BABY** *Rockney KOR 21*	51		
3 May 86	**SNOOKER LOOPY** *Rockney POT 147* MATCHROOM MOB WITH CHAS & DAVE	6		7

JC CHASEZ US singer

Date	Title / Label	Peak Position	Weeks at No.1	Weeks in Top 40
10 Apr 04	**PLUG IT IN** *XL Recordings XLS 180CD* BASEMENT JAXX FEATURING JC CHASEZ	22		1
24 Apr 04	**SOME GIRLS/BLOWIN' ME UP** *Jive 82876605442*	13		4

CHEAP TRICK US group

Date	Title / Label	Peak Position	Weeks at No.1	Weeks in Top 40
5 May 79	**I WANT YOU TO WANT ME** *Epic EPC 7258*	29		6
2 Feb 80	**WAY OF THE WORLD** *Epic EPC 8114*	73		
31 Jul 82	**IF YOU WANT MY LOVE** *Epic EPC A 2406*	57		

OLIVER CHEATHAM US singer

Date	Title / Label	Peak Position	Weeks at No.1	Weeks in Top 40
2 Jul 83	**GET DOWN SATURDAY NIGHT** *MCA 828*	38		1
5 Apr 03	**MAKE LUV** *Positiva CDTIV 187* ROOM 5 FEATURING OLIVER CHEATHAM ○	1	4	10
6 Dec 03	**MUSIC AND YOU** *Positiva CDTIVS 197* ROOM 5 FEATURING OLIVER CHEATHAM	38		1

CHUBBY CHECKER US singer

Date	Title / Label	Peak Position	Weeks at No.1	Weeks in Top 40
22 Sep 60	**THE TWIST** *Columbia DB 4503*	44		
30 Mar 61	**PONY TIME** *Columbia DB 4591* ★	27		5
17 Aug 61	**LET'S TWIST AGAIN** *Columbia DB 4691*	37		1
28 Dec 61	**LET'S TWIST AGAIN** *Columbia DB 4691*	2		23
11 Jan 62	**THE TWIST** *Columbia DB 4503*	14		9
5 Apr 62	**SLOW TWISTIN'** *Columbia DB 4808*	23		5
19 Apr 62	**TEACH ME TO TWIST** *Columbia DB 4802* CHUBBY CHECKER & BOBBY RYDELL	45		
9 Aug 62	**DANCIN' PARTY** *Columbia DB 4876*	19		11
1 Nov 62	**LIMBO ROCK** *Cameo Parkway P 849*	32		7
20 Dec 62	**JINGLE BELL ROCK** *Cameo Parkway C 205* CHUBBY CHECKER & BOBBY RYDELL	40		1
31 Oct 63	**WHAT DO YA SAY** *Cameo Parkway P 806*	37		1
29 Nov 75	**LET'S TWIST AGAIN/THE TWIST** *London HL 10512* ○	5		9
18 Jun 88	**THE TWIST (YO, TWIST)** *Urban URB 20* FAT BOYS & CHUBBY CHECKER	2		9

CHECKMATES LTD. US group

Date	Title / Label	Peak Position	Weeks at No.1	Weeks in Top 40
15 Nov 69	**PROUD MARY** *A&M AMS 769*	30		3

JUDY CHEEKS US singer

Date	Title / Label	Peak Position	Weeks at No.1	Weeks in Top 40
13 Nov 93	**SO IN LOVE (THE REAL DEAL)** *Positiva CDTIV 6*	27		1
7 May 94	**REACH** *Positiva CDTIV 12*	17		2
4 Mar 95	**THIS TIME/RESPECT** *Positiva CDTIV 28*	23		1
17 Jun 95	**YOU'RE THE STORY OF MY LIFE/AS LONG AS YOU'RE GOOD TO ME** *Positiva CDTIV 34*	30		1
13 Jan 96	**REACH** *Positiva CDTIV 42*	22		2

CHEEKY GIRLS Romanian duo

Date	Title / Label	Peak Position	Weeks at No.1	Weeks in Top 40
14 Dec 02	**CHEEKY SONG (TOUCH MY BUM)** *Multiply CDMULTY 97* ○	2		11
17 May 03	**TAKE YOUR SHOES OFF** *Multiply CXMULTY 101*	3		6
16 Aug 03	**HOORAY HOORAY (IT'S A CHEEKY HOLIDAY)** *Multiply CXMULTY 106*	3		5
20 Dec 03	**HAVE A CHEEKY CHRISTMAS** *Multiply CXMULTY 110*	10		3
9 Oct 04	**CHEEKY FLAMENCO** *XBN XBNCD1*	29		1
18 Dec 04	**BOYS AND GIRLS** *XBN XBNCDS3*	50		

CHEETAH GIRLS US group

Date	Title / Label	Peak Position	Weeks at No.1	Weeks in Top 40
20 Jan 07	**THE PARTY'S JUST BEGUN** *Walt Disney 3844312*	53		

CHEETAHS UK group

Date	Title / Label	Peak Position	Weeks at No.1	Weeks in Top 40
1 Oct 64	**MECCA** *Philips BF 1362*	36		1
21 Jan 65	**SOLDIER BOY** *Philips BF 1383*	39		1

CHEF US cartoon character

Date	Title / Label	Peak Position	Weeks at No.1	Weeks in Top 40
26 Dec 98	**CHOCOLATE SALTY BALLS (PS I LOVE YOU)** *Columbia 6667985* ⊛	1	1	11

CHELSEA F.C. UK football club

Date	Title / Label	Peak Position	Weeks at No.1	Weeks in Top 40
26 Feb 72	**BLUE IS THE COLOUR** *Penny Farthing PEN 782*	5		11
14 May 94	**NO ONE CAN STOP US NOW** *RCA 74321210452*	23		2

Key: Silver-selling ○ · Gold-selling ● · Platinum-selling ⊛ · US No.1 ★ · Peak Position · Weeks at No.1 · Weeks in Top 40

Date	Title / Label	Peak Position	Weeks at No.1	Weeks in Top 40
17 May 97	**BLUE DAY** *WEA 112CD* SUGGS & CO FEATURING CHELSEA TEAM	22		3
27 May 00	**BLUE TOMORROW** *Telstar TV CFCCD 2000* CHELSEA FOOTBALL CLUB	22		1

CHEMICAL BROTHERS UK duo

Date	Title / Label	Peak Position	Weeks at No.1	Weeks in Top 40
17 Jun 95	**LEAVE HOME** *Junior Boy's Own CHEMSD 1*	17		2
9 Sep 95	**LIFE IS SWEET** *Junior Boy's Own CHEMSDX 2*	25		2
27 Jan 96	**LOOPS OF FURY EP** *Freestyle Dust CHEMSD 3*	13		1
12 Oct 96	**SETTING SUN** *Virgin CHEMSD 4* ○	1	1	5
5 Apr 97	**BLOCK ROCKIN' BEATS** *Virgin CHEMSD 5*	1	1	4
20 Sep 97	**ELEKTROBANK** *Virgin CHEMSD 6*	17		1
12 Jun 99	**HEY BOY HEY GIRL** *Virgin CHEMSD 8* ○	3		7
14 Aug 99	**LET FOREVER BE** *Virgin CHEMSD 9*	9		3
23 Oct 99	**OUT OF CONTROL** *Virgin CHEMSD 10*	21		2
22 Sep 01	**IT BEGAN IN AFRIKA** *Virgin CHEMSD 12*	8		2
26 Jan 02	**STAR GUITAR** *Virgin CHEMSD 14*	8		4
4 May 02	**COME WITH US/THE TEST** *Virgin CHEMSD 15*	14		2
27 Sep 03	**THE GOLDEN PATH** *Virgin CHEMSD 18* CHEMICAL BROTHERS FEATURING THE FLAMING LIPS	17		2
29 Jan 05	**GALVANIZE** *Virgin CHEMSD21*	3		7
14 May 05	**BELIEVE** *Virgin CHEMSDX22*	18		2
23 Jul 05	**THE BOXER** *Freestyle Dust CHEMSDX23*	41		
16 Jun 07	**DO IT AGAIN** *Virgin CHEMSD25*	12		7
15 Sep 07	**SALMON DANCE** *Virgin CHEMSD26*	27		2

CHEQUERS UK group

Date	Title / Label	Peak Position	Weeks at No.1	Weeks in Top 40
18 Oct 75	**ROCK ON BROTHER** *Creole CR 111*	21		5
28 Feb 76	**HEY MISS PAYNE** *Creole CR 116*	32		3

CHER US singer

Date	Title / Label	Peak Position	Weeks at No.1	Weeks in Top 40
19 Aug 65	**ALL I REALLY WANT TO DO** *Liberty LIB 66114*	9		9
31 Mar 66	**BANG BANG (MY BABY SHOT ME DOWN)** *Liberty LIB 66160*	3		11
4 Aug 66	**I FEEL SOMETHING IN THE AIR** *Liberty LIB 12034*	43		
22 Sep 66	**SUNNY** *Liberty LIB 12083*	32		3
6 Nov 71	**GYPSYS TRAMPS AND THIEVES** *MCA MU 1142* ★	4		12
16 Feb 74	**DARK LADY** *MCA 101* ★	36		1
19 Dec 87	**I FOUND SOMEONE** *Geffen GEF 31*	5		8
2 Apr 88	**WE ALL SLEEP ALONE** *Geffen GEF 35*	47		
2 Sep 89	**IF I COULD TURN BACK TIME** *Geffen GEF 59*	6		9
13 Jan 90	**JUST LIKE JESSE JAMES** *Geffen GEF 69*	11		7
7 Apr 90	**HEART OF STONE** *Geffen GEF 75*	43		
11 Aug 90	**YOU WOULDN'T KNOW LOVE** *Geffen GEF 77*	55		
13 Apr 91	**THE SHOOP SHOOP SONG (IT'S IN HIS KISS)** *Epic 6566737* ●	1	5	13
13 Jul 91	**LOVE AND UNDERSTANDING** *Geffen GFS 5*	10		7
12 Oct 91	**SAVE UP ALL YOUR TEARS** *Geffen GFS 11*	37		2
7 Dec 91	**LOVE HURTS** *Geffen GFS 16*	43		
18 Apr 92	**COULD'VE BEEN YOU** *Geffen GFS 19*	31		2
14 Nov 92	**OH NO NOT MY BABY** *Geffen GFS 29*	33		3
16 Jan 93	**MANY RIVERS TO CROSS** *Geffen GFSTD 31*	37		2
6 Mar 93	**WHENEVER YOU'RE NEAR** *Geffen GFSTD 32*	72		
15 Jan 94	**I GOT YOU BABE** *Geffen GFSTD 64* CHER WITH BEAVIS & BUTT-HEAD	35		1
18 Mar 95	**LOVE CAN BUILD A BRIDGE** *London COCD 1* CHER, CHRISSIE HYNDE & NENEH CHERRY WITH ERIC CLAPTON ○	1	1	6
28 Oct 95	**WALKING IN MEMPHIS** *WEA 021CD1*	11		4
20 Jan 96	**ONE BY ONE** *WEA 032CD*	7		7
27 Apr 96	**NOT ENOUGH LOVE IN THE WORLD** *WEA 052CD*	31		1
17 Aug 96	**THE SUN AIN'T GONNA SHINE ANYMORE** *WEA 071CD*	26		1
31 Oct 98	**BELIEVE** *WEA 175CD* ⊛ ★	1	7	21
6 Mar 99	**STRONG ENOUGH** *WEA 201CD* ○	5		8
19 Jun 99	**ALL OR NOTHING** *WEA 212CD1*	12		4
6 Nov 99	**DOV'E L'AMORE** *WEA 230CD1*	21		1
17 Nov 01	**THE MUSIC'S NO GOOD WITHOUT YOU** *WEA 337CD*	8		4

CHERI Canadian duo

Date	Title / Label	Peak Position	Weeks at No.1	Weeks in Top 40
19 Jun 82	**MURPHY'S LAW** *Polydor POSP 459*	13		8

CHERISH US group

Date	Title / Label	Peak Position	Weeks at No.1	Weeks in Top 40
23 Sep 06	**DO IT TO IT** *Capitol CDCL878* CHERISH FEATURING SEAN PAUL	30		2

CHEROKEES UK group

Date	Title / Label	Peak Position	Weeks at No.1	Weeks in Top 40
3 Sep 64	**SEVEN DAFFODILS** *Columbia DB 7341*	33		2

CHERELLE US singer

Date	Title / Label	Peak Position	Weeks at No.1	Weeks in Top 40
28 Dec 85	**SATURDAY LOVE** *Tabu A 6829* CHERRELLE WITH ALEXANDER O'NEAL	6		9
1 Mar 86	**WILL YOU SATISFY?** *Tabu A 6927*	57		
6 Feb 88	**NEVER KNEW LOVE LIKE THIS** *Tabu 6513827* ALEXANDER O'NEAL FEATURING CHERRELLE	26		5
6 May 89	**AFFAIR** *Tabu 6546737*	67		
24 Mar 90	**SATURDAY LOVE (REMIX)** *Tabu 6558007* CHERRELLE WITH ALEXANDER O'NEAL	55		
2 Aug 97	**BABY COME TO ME** *One World Entertainment OWECD 1* ALEXANDER O'NEAL FEATURING CHERRELLE	56		

DON CHERRY US singer

Date	Title / Label	Peak Position	Weeks at No.1	Weeks in Top 40
10 Feb 56	**BAND OF GOLD** *Philips PB 549*	6		11

EAGLE-EYE CHERRY US/Swedish singer

Date	Title / Label	Peak Position	Weeks at No.1	Weeks in Top 40
4 Jul 98	**SAVE TONIGHT** *Polydor 5695952* ○	6		11
14 Nov 98	**FALLING IN LOVE AGAIN** *Polydor 5630252*	8		4
20 Mar 99	**PERMANENT YEARS** *Polydor 5636752*	43		
29 Apr 00	**ARE YOU STILL HAVING FUN?** *Polydor 5618032*	21		3
11 Nov 00	**LONG WAY AROUND** *Polydor 5677812* EAGLE-EYE CHERRY FEATURING NENEH CHERRY	48		

NENEH CHERRY US/Swedish singer

Date	Title / Label	Peak Position	Weeks at No.1	Weeks in Top 40
10 Dec 88	**BUFFALO STANCE** *Circa YR 21* ○	3		10
20 May 89	**MANCHILD** *Circa YR 30*	5		8
12 Aug 89	**KISSES ON THE WIND** *Circa YR 33*	20		4
23 Dec 89	**INNA CITY MAMMA** *Circa YR 42*	31		4
29 Sep 90	**I'VE GOT YOU UNDER MY SKIN** *Circa YR 53*	25		3
3 Oct 92	**MONEY LOVE** *Circa YR 83*	23		2
19 Jun 93	**BUDDY X** *Circa YRCD 98*	35		2
25 Jun 94	**7 SECONDS** *Columbia 6605082* YOUSSOU N'DOUR (FEATURING NENEH CHERRY) ○	3		18
18 Mar 95	**LOVE CAN BUILD A BRIDGE** *London COCD 1* CHER, CHRISSIE HYNDE & NENEH CHERRY WITH ERIC CLAPTON ○	1	1	6
3 Aug 96	**WOMAN** *Hut HUTD 70*	9		4
14 Dec 96	**KOOTCHI** *Hut HUTCD 75*	38		1
22 Feb 97	**FEEL IT** *Hut HUTCD 79*	68		
6 Nov 99	**BUDDY X 99** *4 Liberty LIBTCD33* DREEM TEEM Vs NENEH CHERRY	15		3
11 Nov 00	**LONG WAY AROUND** *Polydor 5677812* EAGLE-EYE CHERRY FEATURING NENEH CHERRY	48		

CHERRY GHOST UK group

Date	Title / Label	Peak Position	Weeks at No.1	Weeks in Top 40
21 Apr 07	**MATHEMATICS** *Heavenly HVN167CD*	57		
23 Jun 07	**PEOPLE HELP THE PEOPLE** *EMI HVN168CD*	27		1

CHERRYFALLS UK group

Date	Title / Label	Peak Position	Weeks at No.1	Weeks in Top 40
14 Aug 04	**STANDING WATCHING** *Island CID 868*	64		
9 Apr 05	**MY DRUG** *Island CID881*	71		

CHI-LITES US group

Date	Title / Label	Peak Position	Weeks at No.1	Weeks in Top 40
28 Aug 71	**(FOR GOD'S SAKE) GIVE MORE POWER TO THE PEOPLE** *MCA MU 1138*	32		2
15 Jan 72	**HAVE YOU SEEN HER** *MCA MU 1146*	3		11
27 May 72	**OH GIRL** *MCA MU 1156* ★	14		8
23 Mar 74	**HOMELY GIRL** *Brunswick BR 9*	5		11
20 Jul 74	**I FOUND SUNSHINE** *Brunswick BR 12*	35		3
2 Nov 74	**TOO GOOD TO BE FORGOTTEN** *Brunswick BR 13*	10		10
21 Jun 75	**HAVE YOU SEEN HER/OH GIRL** *Brunswick BR 20*	5		9
13 Sep 75	**IT'S TIME FOR LOVE** *Brunswick BR 25*	5		9
31 Jul 76	**YOU DON'T HAVE TO GO** *Brunswick BR 34*	3		10
13 Aug 83	**CHANGING FOR YOU** *R&B RBS 215*	61		

CHIC US group

Date	Title / Label	Peak Position	Weeks at No.1	Weeks in Top 40
26 Nov 77	**DANCE DANCE DANCE (YOWSAH YOWSAH YOWSAH)** *Atlantic K 11038* ○	6		11
1 Apr 78	**EVERYBODY DANCE** *Atlantic K 11097*	9		9
18 Nov 78	**LE FREAK** *Atlantic K 11209* ● ★	7		14
24 Feb 79	**I WANT YOUR LOVE** *Atlantic LV 16*	4		10
30 Jun 79	**GOOD TIMES** *Atlantic K 11310* ★	5		7
13 Oct 79	**MY FORBIDDEN LOVER** *Atlantic K 11385*	15		5

Date	Title / Label	Peak Position	Weeks at No.1	Weeks in Top 40
8 Dec 79	**MY FEET KEEP DANCING** *Atlantic K 11415*	21		7
12 Mar 83	**HANGIN'** *Atlantic A 9898*	64		
19 Sep 87	**JACK LE FREAK** *Atlantic A 9198*	19		5
14 Jul 90	**MEGACHIC - CHIC MEDLEY** *East West A 7949*	58		
15 Feb 92	**CHIC MYSTIQUE** *Warner Brothers W 0083*	48		
5 Aug 06	**SENSITIVITY** *Positiva CDTIV238*			
	SHAPESHIFTERS & CHIC	40		1

CHICAGO US group

Date	Title / Label	Peak Position	Weeks at No.1	Weeks in Top 40
10 Jan 70	**I'M A MAN** *CBS 4715*	8		10
18 Jul 70	**25 OR 6 TO 4** *CBS 5076*	7		11
9 Oct 76	**IF YOU LEAVE ME NOW** *CBS 4603* ★	1	3	16
5 Nov 77	**BABY WHAT A BIG SURPRISE** *CBS 5672*	41		
21 Aug 82	**HARD TO SAY I'M SORRY** *Full Moon K 79301* ★	4		10
27 Oct 84	**HARD HABIT TO BREAK** *Full Moon W 9214*	8		10
26 Jan 85	**YOU'RE THE INSPIRATION** *Warner Brothers W 9126*	14		6

CHICANE UK producer

Date	Title / Label	Peak Position	Weeks at No.1	Weeks in Top 40
21 Dec 96	**OFFSHORE** *Xtravaganza 0091005 EXT*	14		5
14 Jun 97	**SUNSTROKE** *Xtravaganza 0091125 EXT*	21		1
13 Sep 97	**OFFSHORE** *Xtravaganza 0091255 EXT*	17		2
20 Dec 97	**LOST YOU SOMEWHERE** *Xtravaganza 0091415 EXT*	35		1
10 Oct 98	**STRONG IN LOVE** *Xtravaganza 0091675 EXT*			
	CHICANE FEATURING MASON	32		1
5 Jun 99	**SALTWATER** *Xtravaganza XTRAV 1CDS*			
	CHICANE FEATURING MAIRE BRENNAN OF CLANNAD	6		7
18 Mar 00	**DON'T GIVE UP** *Xtravaganza XTRAV 9CDS*			
	CHICANE FEATURING BRYAN ADAMS	1	1	7
22 Jul 00	**NO ORDINARY MORNING/HALCYON** *Xtravaganza XTRAV 12CDS*	28		1
28 Oct 00	**AUTUMN TACTICS** *Xtravaganza XTRAV 17CDS*	44		
8 Feb 03	**SALTWATER** *Xtravaganza XTRAV 35CDS*	43		
8 Mar 03	**LOVE ON THE RUN** *WEA 361CD1*			
	CHICANE FEATURING PETER CUNNAH	33		1
14 Feb 04	**DON'T GIVE UP 2004** *Xtravaganza XTRAV 44CDS*	43		
29 Apr 06	**STONED IN LOVE** *Universal TV 9878360*			
	CHICANE FEATURING TOM JONES	7		6

CHICKEN SHACK UK group

Date	Title / Label	Peak Position	Weeks at No.1	Weeks in Top 40
7 May 69	**I'D RATHER GO BLIND** *Blue Horizon 57-3153*	14		10
6 Sep 69	**TEARS IN THE WIND** *Blue Horizon 57-3160*	29		4

CHICKEN SHED THEATRE UK group

Date	Title / Label	Peak Position	Weeks at No.1	Weeks in Top 40
27 Dec 97	**I AM IN LOVE WITH THE WORLD** *Columbia 6654172*	15		3

CHICKS ON SPEED Multinational group

Date	Title / Label	Peak Position	Weeks at No.1	Weeks in Top 40
21 Feb 04	**WHAT WAS HER NAME** *Skint 94CD*			
	DAVE CLARKE FEATURING CHICKS ON SPEED	50		
13 Mar 04	**WORDY RAPPINGHOOD** *Labels 5478360*	66		

CHICO UK singer

Date	Title / Label	Peak Position	Weeks at No.1	Weeks in Top 40
11 Mar 06	**IT'S CHICO TIME** *Sony BMG 82876812132*	1	1	8
26 Aug 06	**DISCO** *Sony BMG 82876892752*	24		1
20 Oct 07	**CURVY COLA BOTTLE BODY** *Chico Enterprises CDCHIENT1*	45		

CHICORY TIP UK group

Date	Title / Label	Peak Position	Weeks at No.1	Weeks in Top 40
29 Jan 72	**SON OF MY FATHER** *CBS 7737*	1	3	13
20 May 72	**WHAT'S YOUR NAME** *CBS 8021*	13		7
31 Mar 73	**GOOD GRIEF CHRISTINA** *CBS 1258*	17		10

CHIEFTAINS Irish group

Date	Title / Label	Peak Position	Weeks at No.1	Weeks in Top 40
18 Mar 95	**HAVE I TOLD YOU LATELY THAT I LOVE YOU** *RCA 74321271702*			
	CHIEFTAINS WITH VAN MORRISON	71		
12 Jun 99	**I KNOW MY LOVE** *RCA Victor 74321670622*			
	CHIEFTAINS FEATURING THE CORRS	37		1

CHIFFONS US group

Date	Title / Label	Peak Position	Weeks at No.1	Weeks in Top 40
11 Apr 63	**HE'S SO FINE** *Stateside SS 172* ★	16		11
18 Jul 63	**ONE FINE DAY** *Stateside SS 202*	29		3
26 May 66	**SWEET TALKIN' GUY** *Stateside SS 512*	31		5
18 Mar 72	**SWEET TALKIN' GUY** *London HL 10271*	4		12

CHIKINKI UK group

Date	Title / Label	Peak Position	Weeks at No.1	Weeks in Top 40
29 Nov 03	**ASSASSINATOR 13** *Island CID 834*	72		
27 Mar 04	**LIKE IT OR LEAVE IT** *Island CID 848*	65		
19 Jun 04	**ETHER RADIO** *Island CID 860*	50		
6 Nov 04	**ALL EYES** *Island CIDX 875*	74		

CHILD UK group

Date	Title / Label	Peak Position	Weeks at No.1	Weeks in Top 40
29 Apr 78	**WHEN YOU WALK IN THE ROOM** *Ariola Hansa AHA 511*	38		1
22 Jul 78	**IT'S ONLY MAKE BELIEVE** *Ariola Hansa AHA 522*	10		9
28 Apr 79	**ONLY YOU (AND YOU ALONE)** *Ariola Hansa AHA 536*	33		4

JANE CHILD Canadian singer

Date	Title / Label	Peak Position	Weeks at No.1	Weeks in Top 40
12 May 90	**DON'T WANNA FALL IN LOVE** *Warner Brothers W 9817*	22		5

CHILDLINERS Multinational charity ensemble

Date	Title / Label	Peak Position	Weeks at No.1	Weeks in Top 40
16 Dec 95	**THE GIFT OF CHRISTMAS** *London LONCD 376*	9		5

CHILDREN FOR RWANDA UK choir

Date	Title / Label	Peak Position	Weeks at No.1	Weeks in Top 40
10 Sep 94	**LOVE CAN BUILD A BRIDGE** *East West YZ 849CD*	57		

CHILDREN OF THE NIGHT UK producer

Date	Title / Label	Peak Position	Weeks at No.1	Weeks in Top 40
26 Nov 88	**IT'S A TRIP (TUNE IN, TURN ON, DROP OUT)** *Jive 189*	52		

TONI CHILDS US singer

Date	Title / Label	Peak Position	Weeks at No.1	Weeks in Top 40
25 Mar 89	**DON'T WALK AWAY** *A&M AM 462*	53		

CHILI HI FLY Australian group

Date	Title / Label	Peak Position	Weeks at No.1	Weeks in Top 40
18 Mar 00	**IS IT LOVE?** *Ministry Of Sound MOSCDS 141*	37		1

CHILL FAC-TORR US group

Date	Title / Label	Peak Position	Weeks at No.1	Weeks in Top 40
2 Apr 83	**TWIST (ROUND 'N' ROUND)** *Phillyworld PWS 109*	37		3

CHILLI US/Ghanaian/Brazilian group

Date	Title / Label	Peak Position	Weeks at No.1	Weeks in Top 40
20 Sep 97	**TIC, TIC TAC** *Arista 74321511332*			
	CHILLI FEATURING CARRAPICHO	59		

CHIMES UK group

Date	Title / Label	Peak Position	Weeks at No.1	Weeks in Top 40
19 Aug 89	**1-2-3-** *CBS 6551667*	60		
2 Dec 89	**HEAVEN** *CBS 6554327*	66		
19 May 90	**STILL HAVEN'T FOUND WHAT I'M LOOKING FOR** *CBS CHIM 1*	6		7
28 Jul 90	**TRUE LOVE** *CBS CHIM 2*	48		
29 Sep 90	**HEAVEN** *CBS CHIM 3*	24		5
1 Dec 90	**LOVE COMES TO MIND** *CBS CHIM 4*	49		

CHIMIRA South African singer

Date	Title / Label	Peak Position	Weeks at No.1	Weeks in Top 40
6 Dec 97	**SHOW ME HEAVEN** *Neoteric NRDCD 11*	70		

CHINA BLACK UK duo

Date	Title / Label	Peak Position	Weeks at No.1	Weeks in Top 40
16 Jul 94	**SEARCHING** *Wild Card CARDD 7*	4		13
29 Oct 94	**STARS** *Wild Card CARDD 9*	19		5
11 Feb 95	**ALMOST SEE YOU (SOMEWHERE)** *Wild Card CARDW 15*	31		1
3 Jun 95	**SWING LOW SWEET CHARIOT** *Polygram TV SWLDW 2*			
	LADYSMITH BLACK MAMBAZO FEATURING CHINA BLACK	15		5

CHINA CRISIS UK group

Date	Title / Label	Peak Position	Weeks at No.1	Weeks in Top 40
7 Aug 82	**AFRICAN AND WHITE** *Inevitable INEV 011*	45		
22 Jan 83	**CHRISTIAN** *Virgin VS 562*	12		6
21 May 83	**TRAGEDY AND MYSTERY** *Virgin VS 587*	46		
15 Oct 83	**WORKING WITH FIRE AND STEEL** *Virgin VS 620*	48		
14 Jan 84	**WISHFUL THINKING** *Virgin VS 647*	9		6
10 Mar 84	**HANNA HANNA** *Virgin VS 665*	44		
30 Mar 85	**BLACK MAN RAY** *Virgin VS 752*	14		6
1 Jun 85	**KING IN A CATHOLIC STYLE (WAKE UP)** *Virgin VS 765*	19		5

Silver-selling ● Gold-selling ● Platinum-selling ⊛ US No.1 ★ — Peak Position · Weeks at No.1 · Weeks in Top 40

Date	Title / Label	Peak Position	Weeks at No.1	Weeks in Top 40
7 Sep 85	**YOU DID CUT ME** *Virgin VS 799*	54		
8 Nov 86	**ARIZONA SKY** *Virgin VS 898*	47		
24 Jan 87	**BEST KEPT SECRET** *Virgin VS 926*	36		2

CHINA DRUM UK group

Date	Title / Label	Peak Position	Weeks at No.1	Weeks in Top 40
2 Mar 96	**CAN'T STOP THESE THINGS** *Mantra MNT 8CD*	65		
20 Apr 96	**LAST CHANCE** *Mantra MNT 10CD*	60		
9 Aug 97	**FICTION OF LIFE** *Mantra MNT 21CD*	65		
27 Sep 97	**SOMEWHERE ELSE** *Mantra MNT022CD1*	74		

JONNY CHINGAS US keyboard player

Date	Title / Label	Peak Position	Weeks at No.1	Weeks in Top 40
19 Feb 83	**PHONE HOME** *CBS A 3121*	43		

CHINGY US rapper

Date	Title / Label	Peak Position	Weeks at No.1	Weeks in Top 40
25 Oct 03	**RIGHT THURR** *Capitol CDCLS 849*	17		3
21 Feb 04	**HOLIDAE INN** *Capitol CDCLS 852*	35		1
29 May 04	**ONE CALL AWAY** *Capitol CDCL 856*			
	CHINGY FEATURING J WEAV	26		2
13 Nov 04	**BALLA BABY** *Parlophone CDCLS865*	34		1
23 Sep 06	**PULLIN' ME BACK** *Capitol CDR6710*			
	CHINGY FEATURING TYRESE	44		

CHIPMUNKS US cartoon characters

Date	Title / Label	Peak Position	Weeks at No.1	Weeks in Top 40
24 Jul 59	**RAGTIME COWBOY JOE** *London HLU 8916*			
	DAVID SEVILLE & THE CHIPMUNKS	11		8
19 Dec 92	**ACHY BREAKY HEART** *Epic 6588837*			
	ALVIN & THE CHIPMUNKS FEATURING BILLY RAY CYRUS	53		
14 Dec 96	**MACARENA** *Sony Wonder 6639981*			
	LOS DEL CHIPMUNKS	65		

CHIPPENDALES US/UK dancers

Date	Title / Label	Peak Position	Weeks at No.1	Weeks in Top 40
31 Oct 92	**GIVE ME YOUR BODY** *XSrhythm XSR 3*	28		2

CHIPZ Dutch group

Date	Title / Label	Peak Position	Weeks at No.1	Weeks in Top 40
24 Feb 07	**COWBOY** *Sony BMG 88697060862*	44		

CHOCOLATE MONDAY UK group

Date	Title / Label	Peak Position	Weeks at No.1	Weeks in Top 40
12 Feb 05	**YOUR PLACE OR MINE** *DPI DPIBD1*	49		
29 Oct 05	**MODEL LIFE** *DPI CDDPIBD2*	61		

CHOCOLATE PUMA Dutch group

Date	Title / Label	Peak Position	Weeks at No.1	Weeks in Top 40
24 Mar 01	**I WANNA BE U** *Cream 13CD*	6		6
19 Aug 06	**ALWAYS AND FOREVER** *Positiva CDTIV241*	43		

CHOIRBOYS UK group

Date	Title / Label	Peak Position	Weeks at No.1	Weeks in Top 40
31 Dec 05	**TEARS IN HEAVEN** *UCJ 4763116*	22		1

CHOO CHOO PROJECT US duo

Date	Title / Label	Peak Position	Weeks at No.1	Weeks in Top 40
15 Jan 00	**HAZIN' & PHAZIN'** *Defected DEFECT 10CDS*	21		2

CHOONG FAMILY UK group

Date	Title / Label	Peak Position	Weeks at No.1	Weeks in Top 40
11 Feb 06	**MEMORY LANE** *Grizlockaz GRICDSMF1001*	57		

CHOPS-EMC+EXTENSIVE UK group

Date	Title / Label	Peak Position	Weeks at No.1	Weeks in Top 40
8 Aug 92	**ME ISRAELITES** *Faze 2 FAZE 6*	60		

CHORDETTES US group

Date	Title / Label	Peak Position	Weeks at No.1	Weeks in Top 40
17 Dec 54	**MR SANDMAN** *Columbia DB 3553* ★	11		8
31 Aug 56	**BORN TO BE WITH YOU** *London HLA 8302*	8		9
18 Apr 58	**LOLLIPOP** *London HLD 8584*	6		8

CHORDS UK group

Date	Title / Label	Peak Position	Weeks at No.1	Weeks in Top 40
6 Oct 79	**NOW IT'S GONE** *Polydor 2059 141*	63		
2 Feb 80	**MAYBE TOMORROW** *Polydor POSP 101*	40		1
26 Apr 80	**SOMETHING'S MISSING** *Polydor POSP 146*	55		
12 Jul 80	**THE BRITISH WAY OF LIFE** *Polydor 2059 258*	54		
18 Oct 80	**IN MY STREET** *Polydor POSP 185*	50		

CHRIS & JAMES UK duo

Date	Title / Label	Peak Position	Weeks at No.1	Weeks in Top 40
17 Sep 94	**CALM DOWN (BASS KEEPS PUMPIN')** *Stress 12STR 38*	74		
4 Nov 95	**FOX FORCE FIVE** *Stress CDSTR 61*	71		
7 Nov 98	**CLUB FOR LIFE '98** *Stress CDSTR 85*	66		

NEIL CHRISTIAN UK singer

Date	Title / Label	Peak Position	Weeks at No.1	Weeks in Top 40
7 Apr 66	**THAT'S NICE** *Strike JH 301*	14		8

ROGER CHRISTIAN UK singer

Date	Title / Label	Peak Position	Weeks at No.1	Weeks in Top 40
30 Sep 89	**TAKE IT FROM ME** *Island IS 427*	63		

CHRISTIANS UK group

Date	Title / Label	Peak Position	Weeks at No.1	Weeks in Top 40
31 Jan 87	**FORGOTTEN TOWN** *Island IS 291*	22		8
13 Jun 87	**HOOVERVILLE (THEY PROMISED US THE WORLD)** *Island IS 326*	21		5
26 Sep 87	**WHEN THE FINGERS POINT** *Island IS 335*	34		2
5 Dec 87	**IDEAL WORLD** *Island IS 347*	14		10
23 Apr 88	**BORN AGAIN** *Island IS 365*	25		4
15 Oct 88	**HARVEST FOR THE WORLD** *Island IS 395*	8		6
20 May 89	**FERRY 'CROSS THE MERSEY** *PWL 41*			
	CHRISTIANS, HOLLY JOHNSON, PAUL McCARTNEY, GERRY MARSDEN & STOCK AITKEN WATERMAN	1	3	6
23 Dec 89	**WORDS** *Island IS 450*	18		5
7 Apr 90	**I FOUND OUT** *Island IS 453*	56		
15 Sep 90	**GREENBANK DRIVE** *Island IS 466*	63		
5 Sep 92	**WHAT'S IN A WORD** *Island IS 536*	33		3
14 Nov 92	**FATHER** *Island IS 543*	55		
6 Mar 93	**THE BOTTLE** *Island CID 549*	39		1

CHRISTIE UK group

Date	Title / Label	Peak Position	Weeks at No.1	Weeks in Top 40
2 May 70	**YELLOW RIVER** *CBS 4911*	1	1	21
10 Oct 70	**SAN BERNADINO** *CBS 5169*	7		10
25 Mar 72	**IRON HORSE** *CBS 7747*	47		

DAVID CHRISTIE French singer

Date	Title / Label	Peak Position	Weeks at No.1	Weeks in Top 40
14 Aug 82	**SADDLE UP** *KR 9*	9		7

JOHN CHRISTIE Australian singer/pianist

Date	Title / Label	Peak Position	Weeks at No.1	Weeks in Top 40
25 Dec 76	**HERE'S TO LOVE (AULD LANG SYNE)** *EMI 2554*	24		4

LOU CHRISTIE US singer

Date	Title / Label	Peak Position	Weeks at No.1	Weeks in Top 40
24 Feb 66	**LIGHTNIN' STRIKES** *MGM 1297* ★	11		8
28 Apr 66	**RHAPSODY IN THE RAIN** *MGM 1308*	37		1
13 Sep 69	**I'M GONNA MAKE YOU MINE** *Buddah 201 057*	2		15
27 Dec 69	**SHE SOLD ME MAGIC** *Buddah 201 073*	25		6

TONY CHRISTIE UK singer

Date	Title / Label	Peak Position	Weeks at No.1	Weeks in Top 40
9 Jan 71	**LAS VEGAS** *MCA MK 5058*	21		8
8 May 71	**I DID WHAT I DID FOR MARIA** *MCA MK 5064*	2		14
20 Nov 71	**IS THIS THE WAY TO AMARILLO** *MCA MKS 5073*	18		11
10 Feb 73	**AVENUES AND ALLEYWAYS** *MCA MKS 5101*	37		2
17 Jan 76	**DRIVE SAFELY DARLIN'** *MCA 219*	35		2
23 Jan 99	**WALK LIKE A PANTHER '98** *ffrr FCDP 351*			
	ALL SEEING I FEATURING TONY CHRISTIE	10		5
26 Mar 05	**(IS THIS THE WAY TO) AMARILLO?** *Universal TV 9828606*			
	TONY CHRISTIE FEATURING PETER KAY ⊛	1	7	21
6 Aug 05	**AVENUES AND ALLEYWAYS** *Universal TV 9831670*	26		1
17 Dec 05	**MERRY XMAS EVERYBODY** *Amarillo AMARILLOCD1*	49		
31 Dec 05	**(IS THIS THE WAY TO) AMARILLO?** *Universal TV 9828606*			
	TONY CHRISTIE FEATURING PETER KAY	58		
10 Jun 06	**(IS THIS THE WAY TO) THE WORLD CUP?** *Tug CDSNOG16*	8		5

Key: ○ Silver-selling · ● Gold-selling · ⊛ Platinum-selling · ★ US No.1 · Peak Position · Weeks at No.1 · Weeks in Top 40

SHAWN CHRISTOPHER US singer

Date	Title	Peak Position	Weeks at No.1	Weeks in Top 40
22 Sep 90	**ANOTHER SLEEPLESS NIGHT** *Arista 113506* MIKE 'HITMAN' WILSON FEATURING SHAWN CHRISTOPHER	50		
4 May 91	**ANOTHER SLEEPLESS NIGHT** *Arista 114186*	50		
21 Mar 92	**DON'T LOSE THE MAGIC** *Arista 115097*	30		3
2 Jul 94	**MAKE MY LOVE** *BTB BTBCD 502*	57		

CHUCKS UK group

Date	Title	Peak Position	Weeks at No.1	Weeks in Top 40
24 Jan 63	**LOO-BE-LOO** *Decca F 11569*	22		6

CHUMBAWHUMBA UK group

Date	Title	Peak Position	Weeks at No.1	Weeks in Top 40
18 Sep 93	**ENOUGH IS ENOUGH** *One Little Indian 79 TP7CD* CHUMBAWAMBA & CREDIT TO THE NATION	56		
4 Dec 93	**TIMEBOMB** *One Little Indian 89 TP7CD*	59		
23 Aug 97	**TUBTHUMPING** *EMI CDEM 486* ⊛	2		17
31 Jan 98	**AMNESIA** *EMI CDEM 498*	10		4
13 Jun 98	**TOP OF THE WORLD (OLÉ OLÉ OLÉ)** *EMI CDEM 511*	21		2

CHUBBY CHUNKS UK producer

Date	Title	Peak Position	Weeks at No.1	Weeks in Top 40
4 Jun 94	**TESTAMENT 4** *Cleveland City CLECD 13017* CHUBBY CHUNKS VOLUME II	52		
29 May 99	**I'M TELLIN' YOU** *Cleveland City CLECD 13052* CHUBBY CHUNKS FEATURING KIM RUFFIN	61		

CHUPITO Spanish singer

Date	Title	Peak Position	Weeks at No.1	Weeks in Top 40
23 Sep 95	**AMERICAN PIE** *Eternal WEA 018CD*	54		

CHARLOTTE CHURCH UK singer

Date	Title	Peak Position	Weeks at No.1	Weeks in Top 40
25 Dec 99	**JUST WAVE HELLO** *Sony Classical 6685312*	34		2
1 Feb 03	**THE OPERA SONG (BRAVE NEW WORLD)** *Direction 6734642* JURGEN VRIES FEATURING CMC	3		7
9 Jul 05	**CRAZY CHICK** *Sony BMG 6759542*	2		9
8 Oct 05	**CALL MY NAME** *Sony BMG 82876727642*	10		5
17 Dec 05	**EVEN GOD CAN'T CHANGE THE PAST** *Sony BMG 82876767052*	17		2
11 Mar 06	**MOODSWINGS (TO COME AT ME LIKE THAT)** *Sony BMG 82876804482*	14		3

CIARA US singer

Date	Title	Peak Position	Weeks at No.1	Weeks in Top 40
15 Jan 05	**GOODIES (IMPORT)** *Jive 82876648252* CIARA FEATURING PETEY PABLO ★	68		
29 Jan 05	**GOODIES** *LaFace 82876673132* CIARA FEATURING PETEY PABLO ★	1	1	6
23 Apr 05	**1 2 STEP** *LaFace 82876688342* CIARA FEATURING MISSY ELLIOTT	3		8
13 Aug 05	**OH** *LaFace 82876711372* CIARA FEATURING LUDACRIS	4		7
18 Mar 06	**LIKE YOU** *Columbia 82876779522* BOW WOW FEATURING CIARA	17		3
26 Aug 06	**SO WHAT** *Geffen 1705382* FIELD MOBB FEATURING CIARA	56		
31 Mar 07	**LIKE A BOY** *LaFace 88697082882*	16		7

CICERO UK singer

Date	Title	Peak Position	Weeks at No.1	Weeks in Top 40
18 Jan 92	**LOVE IS EVERYWHERE** *Spaghetti CIAO 3*	19		5
18 Apr 92	**THAT LOVING FEELING** *Spaghetti CIAO 4*	46		
1 Aug 92	**HEAVEN MUST HAVE SENT YOU BACK** *Spaghetti CIAO 5*	70		

GABRIELLA CILMI Australian singer

Date	Title	Peak Position	Weeks at No.1	Weeks in Top 40
15 Mar 08	**SWEET ABOUT ME** *Island 1764472*	38		1

CINDERELLA US group

Date	Title	Peak Position	Weeks at No.1	Weeks in Top 40
6 Aug 88	**GYPSY ROAD** *Vertigo VER 40*	54		
4 Mar 89	**DON'T KNOW WHAT YOU GOT** *Vertigo VER 43*	54		
17 Nov 90	**SHELTER ME** *Vertigo VER 51*	55		
27 Apr 91	**HEARTBREAK STATION** *Vertigo VER 53*	63		

CINDY & THE SAFFRONS UK group

Date	Title	Peak Position	Weeks at No.1	Weeks in Top 40
15 Jan 83	**PAST, PRESENT AND FUTURE** *Stiletto STL 9*	56		

CINERAMA UK duo

Date	Title	Peak Position	Weeks at No.1	Weeks in Top 40
18 Jul 98	**KERRY KERRY** *Cooking Vinyl FRYCD 072*	71		

GIGLIOLA CINQUETTI Italian singer

Date	Title	Peak Position	Weeks at No.1	Weeks in Top 40
23 Apr 64	**NON HO L'ETA PER AMARTI** *Decca F 21882*	17		13
4 May 74	**GO (BEFORE YOU BREAK MY HEART)** *CBS 2294*	8		8

CIRCA UK production group

Date	Title	Peak Position	Weeks at No.1	Weeks in Top 40
27 Nov 99	**SUN SHINING DOWN** *Inferno CDFERN 22* CIRCA FEATURING DESTRY	70		

CIRCUIT UK group

Date	Title	Peak Position	Weeks at No.1	Weeks in Top 40
20 Jul 91	**SHELTER ME** *Cooltempo COOL 237*	44		
1 Apr 95	**SHELTER ME (REMIX)** *Pukka CDPUKA 2*	50		

CIRCULATION UK production duo

Date	Title	Peak Position	Weeks at No.1	Weeks in Top 40
1 Sep 01	**TURQUOISE** *Hooj Choons HOOJ 109CD*	64		

CIRRUS UK group

Date	Title	Peak Position	Weeks at No.1	Weeks in Top 40
30 Sep 78	**ROLLIN' ON** *Jet 123*	62		

CITIZEN CANED UK producer

Date	Title	Peak Position	Weeks at No.1	Weeks in Top 40
7 Apr 01	**THE JOURNEY** *Serious SERR 029CD*	41		

CITY BOY UK group

Date	Title	Peak Position	Weeks at No.1	Weeks in Top 40
8 Jul 78	**5-7-0-5** *Vertigo 6059 207* ○	8		10
28 Oct 78	**WHAT A NIGHT** *Vertigo 6059 211*	39		1
15 Sep 79	**THE DAY THE EARTH CAUGHT FIRE** *Vertigo 6059 238*	67		

CITY HIGH US group

Date	Title	Peak Position	Weeks at No.1	Weeks in Top 40
6 Oct 01	**WHAT WOULD YOU DO** *Interscope IND 97617*	3		12
16 Mar 02	**CARAMEL** *Interscope 4976742* CITY HIGH FEATURING EVE	9		5

CK & SUPREME DREAM TEAM Dutch production group

Date	Title	Peak Position	Weeks at No.1	Weeks in Top 40
11 Jan 03	**DREAMER** *Multiply CDMULTY 96*	23		2

GARY CLAIL ON-U SOUND SYSTEM UK singer/producer

Date	Title	Peak Position	Weeks at No.1	Weeks in Top 40
14 Jul 90	**BEEF** *RCA PB 49265*	64		
30 Mar 91	**HUMAN NATURE** *Perfecto PB 44401*	10		8
8 Jun 91	**ESCAPE** *Perfecto PB 44563*	44		
14 Nov 92	**WHO PAYS THE PIPER** *Perfecto 74321117017*	31		2
22 May 93	**THESE THINGS ARE WORTH FIGHTING FOR** *Perfecto 74321147222*	45		

CLAIRE & FRIENDS UK singer

Date	Title	Peak Position	Weeks at No.1	Weeks in Top 40
7 Jun 86	**IT'S 'ORRIBLE BEING IN LOVE (WHEN YOU'RE 8)** *BBC RESL 189*	13		7

CLANNAD Irish band

Date	Title	Peak Position	Weeks at No.1	Weeks in Top 40
6 Nov 82	**THEME FROM HARRY'S GAME** *RCA 292* ○	5		5
2 Jul 83	**NEW GRANGE** *RCA 340*	65		
12 May 84	**ROBIN (THE HOODED MAN)** *RCA HOOD 1*	42		
25 Jan 86	**IN A LIFETIME** *RCA PB 40535* CLANNAD FEATURING BONO	20		4
10 Jun 89	**IN A LIFETIME** *RCA PB 42873* CLANNAD FEATURING BONO	17		5
10 Aug 91	**BOTH SIDES NOW** *MCA MCS 1546*	74		
5 Jun 99	**SALTWATER** *Xtravaganza XTRAV 1CDS* CHICANE FEATURING MAIRE BRENNAN OF CLANNAD	6		7

Silver-selling ● Gold-selling ● Platinum-selling ● US No.1 ★ — Peak Position / Weeks at No.1 / Weeks in Top 40

JIMMY CLANTON US singer

Date	Title	Peak	Wks No.1	Wks Top 40
21 Jul 60	ANOTHER SLEEPLESS NIGHT *Top Rank JAR 382*	50		

CLAP YOUR HANDS SAY YEAH US group

Date	Title	Peak	Wks No.1	Wks Top 40
17 Dec 05	IS THIS LOVE *Wichita WEBB101S*	74		
11 Mar 06	IN THIS HOME ON ICE *Wichita WEBB102SCD*	68		

ERIC CLAPTON UK singer/guitarist

Date	Title	Peak	Wks No.1	Wks Top 40
20 Dec 69	COMIN' HOME *Atlantic 584 308* DELANEY & BONNIE & FRIENDS FEATURING ERIC CLAPTON	16		7
12 Aug 72	LAYLA *Polydor 2058 130* DEREK & THE DOMINOES	7		8
27 Jul 74	I SHOT THE SHERIFF *RSO 2090 132* ★	9		8
10 May 75	SWING LOW SWEET CHARIOT *RSO 2090 158*	19		8
16 Aug 75	KNOCKIN' ON HEAVEN'S DOOR *RSO 2090 166*	38		2
24 Dec 77	LAY DOWN SALLY *RSO 2090 264*	39		1
21 Oct 78	PROMISES *RSO 21*	37		2
6 Mar 82	LAYLA *RSO 87* DEREK & THE DOMINOES	4		7
5 Jun 82	I SHOT THE SHERIFF *RSO 88*	64		
23 Apr 83	THE SHAPE YOU'RE IN *Duck W 9701*	75		
16 Mar 85	FOREVER MAN *Warner Brothers W 9069*	51		
4 Jan 86	EDGE OF DARKNESS *BBC RESL 178* ERIC CLAPTON FEATURING MICHAEL KAMEN	65		
17 Jan 87	BEHIND THE MASK *Duck W 8461*	15		8
20 Jun 87	TEARING US APART *Duck W 8299* ERIC CLAPTON & TINA TURNER	56		
27 Jan 90	BAD LOVE *Duck W 2644*	25		4
14 Apr 90	NO ALIBIS *Duck W 3644*	53		
16 Nov 91	WONDERFUL TONIGHT (LIVE) *Duck W 0069*	30		4
8 Feb 92	TEARS IN HEAVEN *Reprise W 0081*	5		8
1 Aug 92	RUNAWAY TRAIN *Rocket EJS 29* ELTON JOHN & ERIC CLAPTON	31		2
29 Aug 92	IT'S PROBABLY ME *A&M AM 883* STING WITH ERIC CLAPTON	30		4
3 Oct 92	LAYLA (ACOUSTIC) *Duck W 0134*	45		
15 Oct 94	MOTHERLESS CHILD *Duck W 0271CD*	63		
18 Mar 95	LOVE CAN BUILD A BRIDGE *London COCD 1* CHER, CHRISSIE HYNDE & NENEH CHERRY WITH ERIC CLAPTON ●	1	1	6
20 Jul 96	CHANGE THE WORLD *Reprise W 0358CD*	18		3
4 Apr 98	MY FATHER'S EYES *Duck W 0443CD*	33		1
4 Jul 98	CIRCUS *Duck W 0447CD*	39		1
18 Nov 00	FOREVER MAN (HOW MANY TIMES) *ffrr FCD 386* BEATCHUGGERS FEATURING ERIC CLAPTON	26		1

DAVE CLARK FIVE UK group

Date	Title	Peak	Wks No.1	Wks Top 40
3 Oct 63	DO YOU LOVE ME *Columbia DB 7112*	30		3
21 Nov 63	GLAD ALL OVER *Columbia DB 7154*	1	2	18
20 Feb 64	BITS AND PIECES *Columbia DB 7210*	2		11
28 May 64	CAN'T YOU SEE THAT SHE'S MINE *Columbia DB 7291*	10		11
13 Aug 64	THINKING OF YOU BABY *Columbia DB 7335*	26		3
22 Oct 64	ANYWAY YOU WANT IT *Columbia DB 7377*	25		4
14 Jan 65	EVERYBODY KNOWS *Columbia DB 7453*	37		2
11 Mar 65	REELIN' AND ROCKIN' *Columbia DB 7503*	24		6
27 May 65	COME HOME *Columbia DB 7580*	16		8
15 Jul 65	CATCH US IF YOU CAN *Columbia DB 7625*	5		11
11 Nov 65	OVER AND OVER *Columbia DB 7744* ★	45		
19 May 66	LOOK BEFORE YOU LEAP *Columbia DB 7909*	50		
16 Mar 67	YOU GOT WHAT IT TAKES *Columbia DB 8152*	28		7
1 Nov 67	EVERYBODY KNOWS *Columbia DB 8286*	2		12
28 Feb 68	NO ONE CAN BREAK A HEART LIKE YOU *Columbia DB 8342*	28		4
18 Sep 68	RED BALLOON *Columbia DB 8465*	7		10
27 Nov 68	LIVE IN THE SKY *Columbia DB 8505*	39		2
25 Oct 69	PUT A LITTLE LOVE IN YOUR HEART *Columbia DB 8624*	31		3
6 Dec 69	GOOD OLD ROCK 'N ROLL *Columbia DB 8638*	7		11
7 Mar 70	EVERYBODY GET TOGETHER *Columbia DB 8660*	8		8
4 Jul 70	HERE COMES SUMMER *Columbia DB 8689*	44		
7 Nov 70	MORE GOOD OLD ROCK 'N ROLL *Columbia DB 8724*	34		4
1 May 93	GLAD ALL OVER *EMI CDEMCT 8*	37		1

DEE CLARK US singer

Date	Title	Peak	Wks No.1	Wks Top 40
2 Oct 59	JUST KEEP IT UP *London HL 8915*	26		1
11 Oct 75	RIDE A WILD HORSE *Chelsea 2005 037*	16		7

GARY CLARK UK singer

Date	Title	Peak	Wks No.1	Wks Top 40
30 Jan 93	WE SAIL ON THE STORMY WATERS *Circa YRCDX 93*	34		1
3 Apr 93	FREEFLOATING *Circa YRCDX 94*	50		
19 Jun 93	MAKE A FAMILY *Circa YRCDX 105*	70		

LONI CLARK US singer

Date	Title	Peak	Wks No.1	Wks Top 40
5 Jun 93	RUSHING *A&M 5802862*	37		1
22 Jan 94	U *A&M 5804752*	28		2
17 Dec 94	LOVE'S GOT ME ON A TRIP SO HIGH *A&M 5808872*	59		

PETULA CLARK UK singer

Date	Title	Peak	Wks No.1	Wks Top 40
11 Jun 54	THE LITTLE SHOEMAKER *Polygon P 1117*	7		10
18 Feb 55	MAJORCA *Polygon P 1146*	12		5
25 Nov 55	SUDDENLY THERE'S A VALLEY *Pye Nixa N 15013*	7		10
26 Jul 57	WITH ALL MY HEART *Pye Nixa N 15096*	4		18
15 Nov 57	ALONE *Pye Nixa N 15112*	8		12
28 Feb 58	BABY LOVER *Pye Nixa N 15126*	12		7
26 Jan 61	SAILOR *Pye 7N 15324*	1	1	14
13 Apr 61	SOMETHING MISSING *Pye 7N 15337*	44		
13 Jul 61	ROMEO *Pye 7N 15361*	3		14
16 Nov 61	MY FRIEND THE SEA *Pye 7N 15389*	7		9
8 Feb 62	I'M COUNTING ON YOU *Pye 7N 15407*	41		
28 Jun 62	YA YA TWIST *Pye 7N 15448*	14		10
2 May 63	CASANOVA/CHARIOT *Pye 7N 15522*	39		1
12 Nov 64	DOWNTOWN *Pye 7N 15722* ★	2		14
11 Mar 65	I KNOW A PLACE *Pye 7N 15772*	17		8
12 Aug 65	YOU BETTER COME HOME *Pye 7N 15864*	44		
14 Oct 65	ROUND EVERY CORNER *Pye 7N 15945*	43		
4 Nov 65	YOU'RE THE ONE *Pye 7N 15991*	23		9
10 Feb 66	MY LOVE *Pye 7N 17038* ★	4		9
21 Apr 66	A SIGN OF THE TIMES *Pye 7N 17071*	49		
30 Jun 66	I COULDN'T LIVE WITHOUT YOUR LOVE *Pye 7N 17133*	6		10
2 Feb 67	THIS IS MY SONG *Pye 7N 17258*	1	2	12
25 May 67	DON'T SLEEP IN THE SUBWAY *Pye 7N 17325*	12		9
13 Dec 67	THE OTHER MAN'S GRASS (IS ALWAYS GREENER) *Pye 7N 17416*	20		7
6 Mar 68	KISS ME GOODBYE *Pye 7N 17466*	50		
30 Jan 71	THE SONG OF MY LIFE *Pye 7N 45026*	32		8
15 Jan 72	I DON'T KNOW HOW TO LOVE HIM *Pye 7N 45112*	47		
19 Nov 88	DOWNTOWN *PRT PYS 19*	10		8

ROLAND CLARK US singer

Date	Title	Peak	Wks No.1	Wks Top 40
1 May 99	FLOWERZ *ffrr FCD 361* ARMAND VAN HELDEN FEATURING ROLAND CLARK	18		3
23 Mar 02	SPEED (CAN YOU FEEL IT?) *Club Tools 0135815 CLU* AZZIDO DA BASS FEATURING ROLAND CLARK	68		

DAVE CLARKE UK producer

Date	Title	Peak	Wks No.1	Wks Top 40
30 Sep 95	RED THREE, THUNDER/STORM *Deconstruction 74321306992*	45		
3 Feb 96	SOUTHSIDE *Bush 74321335382*	34		1
15 Jun 96	NO ONE'S DRIVING *Bush 74321380162*	37		1
8 Dec 01	THE COMPASS *Skint 73CD*	46		
28 Dec 02	THE WOLF *Skint 78*	66		
25 Oct 03	WAY OF LIFE *Skint 93CD*	59		
21 Feb 04	WHAT WAS HER NAME *Skint 94CD* DAVE CLARKE FEATURING CHICKS ON SPEED	50		

JOHN COOPER CLARKE UK poet

Date	Title	Peak	Wks No.1	Wks Top 40
10 Mar 79	GIMMIX! PLAY LOUD *Epic EPC 7009*	39		1

RICK CLARKE UK singer

Date	Title	Peak	Wks No.1	Wks Top 40
30 Apr 88	I'LL SEE YOU ALONG THE WAY *WA 1*	63		

WARREN CLARKE UK producer

Date	Title	Peak	Wks No.1	Wks Top 40
2 Jun 01	OVER YOU *Defected DFECT 28CDS* WARREN CLARKE FEATURING KATHY BROWN	42		

KELLY CLARKSON US singer

Date	Title	Peak	Wks No.1	Wks Top 40
6 Sep 03	MISS INDEPENDENT *S 82876553642*	6		6
29 Nov 03	LOW/THE TROUBLE WITH LOVE IS *S 82876570702*	35		1
16 Jul 05	SINCE U BEEN GONE *RCA 82876700852*	5		13
1 Oct 05	BEHIND THESE HAZEL EYES *RCA 82876730302*	9		10

Silver-selling | Gold-selling | Platinum-selling | US No.1 | Peak Position | Weeks at No.1 | Weeks in Top 40

Date	Title / Label	Peak Position	Weeks at No.1	Weeks in Top 40
10 Dec 05	**BECAUSE OF YOU** *RCA 82876764542*	7		16
25 Mar 06	**WALK AWAY** *RCA 82876809832*	21		5
1 Jul 06	**BREAKAWAY** *RCA 82876845702*	22		3
23 Jun 07	**NEVER AGAIN** *RCA 88697110252*	9		4

CLARKSVILLE UK singer

Date	Title / Label	Peak Position	Weeks at No.1	Weeks in Top 40
7 Feb 04	**SPINNING** *Wildstar CDWILD 53*	72		

CLASH UK group

Date	Title / Label	Peak Position	Weeks at No.1	Weeks in Top 40
2 Apr 77	**WHITE RIOT** *CBS 5058*	38		1
8 Oct 77	**COMPLETE CONTROL** *CBS 5664*	28		2
4 Mar 78	**CLASH CITY ROCKERS** *CBS 5834*	35		3
24 Jun 78	**(WHITE MAN) IN HAMMERSMITH PALAIS** *CBS 6383*	32		3
2 Dec 78	**TOMMY GUN** *CBS 6788*	19		8
3 Mar 79	**ENGLISH CIVIL WAR (JOHNNY COMES MARCHING HOME)** *CBS 7082*	25		6
19 May 79	**THE COST OF LIVING EP** *CBS 7324*	22		7
15 Dec 79	**LONDON CALLING** *CBS 8087*	11		8
9 Aug 80	**BANKROBBER** *CBS 8323*	12		7
6 Dec 80	**THE CALL UP** *CBS 9339*	40		1
24 Jan 81	**HITSVILLE UK** *CBS 9480*	56		
25 Apr 81	**THE MAGNIFICENT SEVEN** *CBS 1133*	34		2
28 Nov 81	**THIS IS RADIO CLASH** *CBS A 1797*	47		
1 May 82	**KNOW YOUR RIGHTS** *CBS A 2309*	43		
26 Jun 82	**ROCK THE CASBAH** *CBS A 2429*	30		7
25 Sep 82	**SHOULD I STAY OR SHOULD I GO/STRAIGHT TO HELL** *CBS A 2646*	17		7
12 Oct 85	**THIS IS ENGLAND** *CBS A 6122*	24		3
12 Mar 88	**I FOUGHT THE LAW** *CBS CLASH 1*	29		3
7 May 88	**LONDON CALLING** *CBS CLASH 2*	46		
21 Jul 90	**RETURN TO BRIXTON** *CBS 6560727*	57		
2 Mar 91	**SHOULD I STAY OR SHOULD I GO** *Columbia 6566677*	1	2	7
13 Apr 91	**ROCK THE CASBAH** *Columbia 6568147*	15		5
8 Jun 91	**LONDON CALLING** *Columbia 6569467*	64		

CLASS ACTION US group

Date	Title / Label	Peak Position	Weeks at No.1	Weeks in Top 40
7 May 83	**WEEKEND** *Jive 35* CLASS ACTION FEATURING CHRIS WILTSHIRE	49		

CLASSICS IV US group

Date	Title / Label	Peak Position	Weeks at No.1	Weeks in Top 40
28 Feb 68	**SPOOKY** *Liberty LBS 15051*	46		

CLASSIX NOUVEAUX UK group

Date	Title / Label	Peak Position	Weeks at No.1	Weeks in Top 40
28 Feb 81	**GUILTY** *Liberty BP 388*	43		
16 May 81	**TOKYO** *Liberty BP 397*	67		
8 Aug 81	**INSIDE OUTSIDE** *Liberty BP 403*	45		
7 Nov 81	**NEVER AGAIN (THE DAYS TIME ERASED)** *Liberty BP 406*	44		
13 Mar 82	**IS IT A DREAM** *Liberty BP 409*	11		7
29 May 82	**BECAUSE YOU'RE YOUNG** *Liberty BP 411*	43		
30 Oct 82	**THE END...OR THE BEGINNING** *Liberty BP 414*	60		

CLAWFINGER Swedish/Norwegian group

Date	Title / Label	Peak Position	Weeks at No.1	Weeks in Top 40
19 Mar 94	**WARFAIR** *East West YZ 804CD1*	54		

ADAM CLAYTON & LARRY MULLEN Irish duo

Date	Title / Label	Peak Position	Weeks at No.1	Weeks in Top 40
15 Jun 96	**THEME FROM *MISSION: IMPOSSIBLE*** *Mother MUMCD 75*	7		10

MERRY CLAYTON US singer

Date	Title / Label	Peak Position	Weeks at No.1	Weeks in Top 40
21 May 88	**YES** *RCA PB 49563*	70		

CLAYTOWN TROUPE UK group

Date	Title / Label	Peak Position	Weeks at No.1	Weeks in Top 40
16 Jun 90	**WAYS OF LOVE** *Island IS 464*	57		
14 Mar 92	**WANTED IT ALL** *EMI USA MT 102*	74		

CLEA UK group

Date	Title / Label	Peak Position	Weeks at No.1	Weeks in Top 40
4 Oct 03	**DOWNLOAD IT** *1967 CLEA01CD*	21		2
28 Feb 04	**STUCK IN THE MIDDLE** *1967 CLEA02CD*	23		1
29 Oct 05	**WE DON'T HAVE TO TAKE OUR CLOTHES OFF** *Upside UPSIDECD02* DA PLAYAZ VS CLEA	35		1

Date	Title / Label	Peak Position	Weeks at No.1	Weeks in Top 40
24 Apr 06	**LUCKY LIKE THAT** *Upside UPSIDECD04*	55		

JOHNNY CLEGG & SAVUKA UK/South African group

Date	Title / Label	Peak Position	Weeks at No.1	Weeks in Top 40
16 May 87	**SCATTERLINGS OF AFRICA** *EMI 5605*	75		

CLEOPATRA UK group

Date	Title / Label	Peak Position	Weeks at No.1	Weeks in Top 40
14 Feb 98	**CLEOPATRA'S THEME** *WEA 133CD*	3		6
16 May 98	**LIFE AIN'T EASY** *WEA 159CD1*	4		5
22 Aug 98	**I WANT YOU BACK** *WEA 172CD1*	4		5
6 Mar 99	**A TOUCH OF LOVE** *WEA 199CD*	24		1
10 Apr 99	**THANK ABBA FOR THE MUSIC** *Epic ABCD1* STEPS, TINA COUSINS, CLEOPATRA, B*WITCHED, BILLIE	4		11
29 Jul 00	**COME AND GET ME** *WEA 261CD1*	29		1

CLEPTOMANIACS UK production group

Date	Title / Label	Peak Position	Weeks at No.1	Weeks in Top 40
3 Feb 01	**ALL I DO** *Defected DFECT 27CDS* CLEPTOMANIACS FEATURING BRYAN CHAMBERS	23		1

CLERGY UK production duo

Date	Title / Label	Peak Position	Weeks at No.1	Weeks in Top 40
20 Jul 02	**THE OBOE SONG** *ffrr DFCD 005*	50		

CLICK US group

Date	Title / Label	Peak Position	Weeks at No.1	Weeks in Top 40
29 Jun 96	**SCANDALOUS** *Jive JIVECD 393*	54		

CLIENT UK duo

Date	Title / Label	Peak Position	Weeks at No.1	Weeks in Top 40
26 Jun 04	**IN IT FOR THE MONEY** *Toast Hawaii CDTH005*	51		
2 Oct 04	**RADIO** *Toast Hawaii CDTH006*	68		
22 Jan 05	**PORNOGRAPHY** *Toast Hawaii LCDTH008*	22		1

JIMMY CLIFF Jamaican singer

Date	Title / Label	Peak Position	Weeks at No.1	Weeks in Top 40
25 Oct 69	**WONDERFUL WORLD BEAUTIFUL PEOPLE** *Trojan TR 690*	6		11
14 Feb 70	**VIETNAM** *Trojan TR 7722*	46		
8 Aug 70	**WILD WORLD** *Island WIP 6087*	8		11
19 Mar 94	**I CAN SEE CLEARLY NOW** *Columbia 6601982*	23		4

BUZZ CLIFFORD US singer

Date	Title / Label	Peak Position	Weeks at No.1	Weeks in Top 40
2 Mar 61	**BABY SITTIN' BOOGIE** *Fontana H 297*	17		11

LINDA CLIFFORD US singer

Date	Title / Label	Peak Position	Weeks at No.1	Weeks in Top 40
10 Jun 78	**IF MY FRIENDS COULD SEE ME NOW** *Curtom K 17163*	50		
5 May 79	**BRIDGE OVER TROUBLED WATER** *RSO 30*	28		5
15 Sep 01	**RIDE THE STORM** *NRK Sound Division NRKCD 053* AKABU FEATURING LINDA CLIFFORD	69		

CLIMAX BLUES BAND UK group

Date	Title / Label	Peak Position	Weeks at No.1	Weeks in Top 40
9 Oct 76	**COULDN'T GET IT RIGHT** *BTM SBT 105*	10		8

CLIMIE FISHER UK duo

Date	Title / Label	Peak Position	Weeks at No.1	Weeks in Top 40
5 Sep 87	**LOVE CHANGES (EVERYTHING)** *EMI EM 15*	67		
12 Dec 87	**RISE TO THE OCCASION** *EMI EM 33*	10		8
12 Mar 88	**LOVE CHANGES EVERYTHING** *EMI EM 47*	2		9
21 May 88	**THIS IS ME** *EMI EM 58*	22		3
20 Aug 88	**I WON'T BLEED FOR YOU** *EMI EM 66*	35		1
24 Dec 88	**LOVE LIKE A RIVER** *EMI EM 81*	22		3
23 Sep 89	**FACTS OF LOVE** *EMI EM 103*	50		

SIMON CLIMIE UK singer

Date	Title / Label	Peak Position	Weeks at No.1	Weeks in Top 40
19 Sep 92	**SOUL INSPIRATION** *Epic 6582837*	60		

PATSY CLINE US singer

Date	Title / Label	Peak Position	Weeks at No.1	Weeks in Top 40
26 Apr 62	**SHE'S GOT YOU** *Brunswick 05866*	43		
29 Nov 62	**HEARTACHES** *Brunswick 05878*	31		4
8 Dec 90	**CRAZY** *MCA 1465*	14		7

Silver-selling ○ Gold-selling ● Platinum-selling ⊛ US No.1 ★ — Peak Position · Weeks at No.1 · Weeks in Top 40

CLINIC UK group

Date	Title / Label	Peak Position	Weeks at No.1	Weeks in Top 40
22 Apr 00	**THE RETURN OF EVIL BILL** *Domino RUG 093CD*	70		
4 Nov 00	**THE SECOND LINE** *Domino RUG 116CD*	56		
2 Mar 02	**WALKING WITH THEE** *Domino Recordings RUG 134CD*	65		

GEORGE CLINTON US singer

Date	Title / Label	Peak Position	Weeks at No.1	Weeks in Top 40
4 Dec 82	**LOOPZILLA** *Capitol CL 271*	57		
26 Apr 86	**DO FRIES GO WITH THAT SHAKE** *Capitol CL 402*	57		
27 Aug 94	**BOP GUN (ONE NATION)** *Fourth & Broadway BRCD 308* ICE CUBE FEATURING GEORGE CLINTON	22		2

CLIPSE US duo

Date	Title / Label	Peak Position	Weeks at No.1	Weeks in Top 40
22 Feb 03	**WHEN THE LAST TIME** *Arista 82876502212*	41		
24 May 03	**MA I DON'T LOVE HER** *Arista 82876526482* CLIPSE FEATURING FAITH EVANS	38		1

CLIPZ UK producer

Date	Title / Label	Peak Position	Weeks at No.1	Weeks in Top 40
6 Mar 04	**COCOA/JIGGY** *Full Cycle FCY064*	71		
5 Mar 05	**SLIPPERY SLOPES/NASTY BREAKS** *Full Cycle FCY075*	72		

CLOCK UK group

Date	Title / Label	Peak Position	Weeks at No.1	Weeks in Top 40
30 Oct 93	**HOLDING ON** *Media MRLCD 007*	66		
21 May 94	**THE RHYTHM** *Media MCSTD 1971*	28		1
10 Sep 94	**KEEP THE FIRES BURNING** *Media MCSTD 1998*	36		1
4 Mar 95	**AXEL F/KEEP PUSHIN'** *Media MCSXD 2041*	7		7
1 Jul 95	**WHOOMPH! (THERE IT IS)** *Media MCSTD 2059*	4		6
26 Aug 95	**EVERYBODY** *Media MCSTD 2077*	6		4
18 Nov 95	**IN THE HOUSE** *Media MCSTD 40005*	23		1
24 Feb 96	**HOLDING ON 4 U** *Media MCSTD 40019*	27		1
7 Sep 96	**OH WHAT A NIGHT** *Power Station MCSTD 40057*	13		9
22 Mar 97	**IT'S OVER** *Media MCSTD 40100*	10		3
18 Oct 97	**U SEXY THING** *Media MCSTD 40138*	11		7
17 Jan 98	**THAT'S THE WAY (I LIKE IT)** *Media MCSTD 40148*	11		3
11 Jul 98	**ROCK YOUR BODY** *Media MCSTD 40160*	30		1
28 Nov 98	**BLAME IT ON THE BOOGIE** *Media MCSTD 40191*	16		2
31 Jul 99	**SUNSHINE DAY** *Media MCSTD 40208*	58		

ROSEMARY CLOONEY US singer

Date	Title / Label	Peak Position	Weeks at No.1	Weeks in Top 40
14 Nov 52	**HALF AS MUCH** *Columbia DB 3129* ★	3		9
5 Feb 54	**MAN (UH-HUH)** *Philips PB 220*	7		5
8 Oct 54	**THIS OLE HOUSE** *Philips PB 336* ★	1	1	18
17 Dec 54	**MAMBO ITALIANO** *Philips PB 382* ROSEMARY CLOONEY WITH THE MELLOMEN	1	3	16
20 May 55	**WHERE WILL THE BABY'S DIMPLE BE** *Philips PB 428* ROSEMARY CLOONEY WITH THE MELLOMEN	6		13
30 Sep 55	**HEY THERE** *Philips PB 494* ★	4		11
29 Mar 57	**MANGOS** *Philips PB 671*	17		9

CLOR UK group

Date	Title / Label	Peak Position	Weeks at No.1	Weeks in Top 40
7 May 05	**LOVE & PAIN** *Regal REG120CD*	48		
23 Jul 05	**OUTLINES** *Regal REG121CDS*	43		
22 Oct 05	**GOOD STUFF** *Regal REG128CD*	50		

CLOUD UK instrumental group

Date	Title / Label	Peak Position	Weeks at No.1	Weeks in Top 40
31 Jan 81	**ALL NIGHT LONG/TAKE IT TO THE TOP** *UK Champagne FUNK 1*	72		

CLOUT South African group

Date	Title / Label	Peak Position	Weeks at No.1	Weeks in Top 40
17 Jun 78	**SUBSTITUTE** *Carrere EMI 2788* ●	2		13

CLS US production duo

Date	Title / Label	Peak Position	Weeks at No.1	Weeks in Top 40
30 May 98	**CAN YOU FEEL IT** *Satellite 74321580162*	46		

CLUB NOUVEAU US group

Date	Title / Label	Peak Position	Weeks at No.1	Weeks in Top 40
21 Mar 87	**LEAN ON ME** *King Jay W 8430* ○ ★	3		9

CLUB 69 Austrian/US duo

Date	Title / Label	Peak Position	Weeks at No.1	Weeks in Top 40
5 Dec 92	**LET ME BE YOUR UNDERWEAR** *ffrr F 204*	33		2
14 Nov 98	**ALRIGHT** *Twisted UK TWCD 10039* CLUB 69 FEATURING SUZANNE PALMER	70		

CLUBHOUSE Italian production group

Date	Title / Label	Peak Position	Weeks at No.1	Weeks in Top 40
23 Jul 83	**DO IT AGAIN-BILLIE JEAN (MEDLEY)** *Island IS 132*	11		5
3 Dec 83	**SUPERSTITION - GOOD TIMES (MEDLEY)** *Island IS 147*	59		
1 Jul 89	**I'M A MAN - YE KE YE KE (MEDLEY)** *Music Man MMPS 7003*	69		
20 Apr 91	**DEEP IN MY HEART** *ffrr F 157*	55		
4 Sep 93	**LIGHT MY FIRE** *PWL Continental PWCD 272* CLUBHOUSE FEATURING CARL	45		
30 Apr 94	**LIGHT MY FIRE (REMIX)** *PWL Continental PWCD 288* CLUBHOUSE FEATURING CARL	7		6
23 Jul 94	**LIVING IN THE SUNSHINE** *PWL Continental PWCD 309* CLUBHOUSE FEATURING CARL	21		2
11 Mar 95	**NOWHERE LAND** *PWL International PWCD 318* CLUBHOUSE FEATURING CARL	56		

CLUBZONE UK/German group

Date	Title / Label	Peak Position	Weeks at No.1	Weeks in Top 40
19 Nov 94	**HANDS UP** *Logic 74321236982*	50		

CLUELESS US production group

Date	Title / Label	Peak Position	Weeks at No.1	Weeks in Top 40
5 Apr 97	**DON'T SPEAK** *ZYX 660738*	61		

CLYDE VALLEY STOMPERS UK group

Date	Title / Label	Peak Position	Weeks at No.1	Weeks in Top 40
9 Aug 62	**PETER AND THE WOLF** *Parlophone R 4928*	25		7

CM2 UK group

Date	Title / Label	Peak Position	Weeks at No.1	Weeks in Top 40
18 Jan 03	**FALL AT YOUR FEET** *INCredible 6732532* CM2 FEATURING LISA LAW	66		

CO-CO UK group

Date	Title / Label	Peak Position	Weeks at No.1	Weeks in Top 40
22 Apr 78	**BAD OLD DAYS** *Ariola Hansa AHA 513*	13		6

COAST TO COAST UK group

Date	Title / Label	Peak Position	Weeks at No.1	Weeks in Top 40
31 Jan 81	**(DO) THE HUCKLEBUCK** *Polydor POSP 214* ○	5		11
23 May 81	**LET'S JUMP THE BROOMSTICK** *Polydor POSP 249*	28		5

COAST 2 COAST Irish production duo

Date	Title / Label	Peak Position	Weeks at No.1	Weeks in Top 40
16 Jun 01	**HOME** *Religion 0126955 RLG* COAST 2 COAST FEATURING DISCOVERY	44		

COASTERS US group

Date	Title / Label	Peak Position	Weeks at No.1	Weeks in Top 40
27 Sep 57	**SEARCHIN'** *London HLE 8450*	30		1
15 Aug 58	**YAKETY YAK** *London HLE 8665* ★	12		8
27 Mar 59	**CHARLIE BROWN** *London HLE 8819*	6		12
30 Oct 59	**POISON IVY** *London HLE 8938*	15		7
9 Apr 94	**SORRY BUT I'M GONNA HAVE TO PASS** *Rhino A 4519CD*	41		

LUIS COBOS Spanish orchestra leader

Date	Title / Label	Peak Position	Weeks at No.1	Weeks in Top 40
16 Jun 90	**NESSUN DORMA FROM 'TURANDOT'** *Epic 6560057* LUIS COBOS FEATURING PLACIDO DOMINGO	59		

EDDIE COCHRAN US singer/guitarist

Date	Title / Label	Peak Position	Weeks at No.1	Weeks in Top 40
7 Nov 58	**SUMMERTIME BLUES** *London HLU 8702*	18		6
13 Mar 59	**C'MON EVERYBODY** *London HLU 8792*	6		13
16 Oct 59	**SOMETHIN' ELSE** *London HLU 8944*	22		3
22 Jan 60	**HALLELUJAH I LOVE HER SO** *London HLW 9022*	22		4
12 May 60	**THREE STEPS TO HEAVEN** *London HLG 9115*	1	2	15
6 Oct 60	**SWEETIE PIE** *London HLG 9196*	38		2
3 Nov 60	**LONELY** *London HLG 9196*	41		
15 Jun 61	**WEEKEND** *London HLG 9362*	15		15
30 Nov 61	**JEANNIE, JEANNIE, JEANNIE** *London HLG 9460*	31		1
25 Apr 63	**MY WAY** *Liberty LIB 10088*	23		9
24 Apr 68	**SUMMERTIME BLUES** *Liberty LBF 15071*	34		6

Silver-selling | Gold-selling | Platinum-selling | US No.1 ★ | Peak Position | Weeks at No.1 | Weeks in Top 40

Date	Title	Peak Position	Weeks at No.1	Weeks in Top 40
13 Feb 88	**C'MON EVERYBODY** *Liberty EDDIE 501*	14		5

TOM COCHRANE Canadian singer

Date	Title	Peak Position	Weeks at No.1	Weeks in Top 40
27 Jun 92	**LIFE IS A HIGHWAY** *Capitol CL 660*	62		

COCK ROBIN US group

Date	Title	Peak Position	Weeks at No.1	Weeks in Top 40
31 May 86	**THE PROMISE YOU MADE** *CBS A 6764*	28		6

JARVIS COCKER UK singer

Date	Title	Peak Position	Weeks at No.1	Weeks in Top 40
20 Jan 07	**DON'T LET HIM WASTE YOUR TIME** *Rough Trade RTRADSCD385*	36		1

JOE COCKER UK singer

Date	Title	Peak Position	Weeks at No.1	Weeks in Top 40
22 May 68	**MARJORINE** *Regal Zonophone RZ 3006*	48		
2 Oct 68	**WITH A LITTLE HELP FROM MY FRIENDS** *Regal Zonophone RZ 3013*	1	1	12
27 Sep 69	**DELTA LADY** *Regal Zonophone RZ 3024*	10		10
4 Jul 70	**THE LETTER** *Regal Zonophone RZ 3027*	39		2
26 Sep 81	**I'M SO GLAD I'M STANDING HERE TODAY** *MCA 741* CRUSADERS, FEATURED VOCALIST JOE COCKER	61		
15 Jan 83	**UP WHERE WE BELONG** *Island WIP 6830* JOE COCKER & JENNIFER WARNES ● ★	7		10
14 Nov 87	**UNCHAIN MY HEART** *Capitol CL 465*	46		
13 Jan 90	**WHEN THE NIGHT COMES** *Capitol CL 535*	65		
7 Mar 92	**(ALL I KNOW) FEELS LIKE FOREVER** *Capitol CL 645*	25		4
9 May 92	**NOW THAT THE MAGIC HAS GONE** *Capitol CL 657*	28		3
4 Jul 92	**UNCHAIN MY HEART** *Capitol CL 664*	17		4
21 Nov 92	**WHEN THE NIGHT COMES** *Capitol CL 674*	61		
13 Aug 94	**THE SIMPLE THINGS** *Capitol CDCLS 722*	17		2
22 Oct 94	**TAKE ME HOME** *Capitol CDCLS 729* JOE COCKER FEATURING BEKKA BRAMLETT	41		
17 Dec 94	**LET THE HEALING BEGIN** *Capitol CDCLS 727*	32		2
23 Sep 95	**HAVE A LITTLE FAITH** *Capitol CDCLS 744*	67		
12 Oct 96	**DON'T LET ME BE MISUNDERSTOOD** *Parlophone CDCLS 779*	53		

COCKEREL CHORUS UK group

Date	Title	Peak Position	Weeks at No.1	Weeks in Top 40
24 Feb 73	**NICE ONE CYRIL** *Young Blood YB 1017*	14		9

COCKNEY REJECTS UK group

Date	Title	Peak Position	Weeks at No.1	Weeks in Top 40
1 Dec 79	**I'M NOT A FOOL** *EMI 5008*	65		
16 Feb 80	**BADMAN** *EMI 5035*	65		
26 Apr 80	**THE GREATEST COCKNEY RIPOFF** *Zonophone Z 2*	21		4
17 May 80	**I'M FOREVER BLOWING BUBBLES** *Zonophone Z 4*	35		1
12 Jul 80	**WE CAN DO ANYTHING** *Zonophone Z 6*	65		
25 Oct 80	**WE ARE THE FIRM** *Zonophone Z 10*	54		

COCO UK group

Date	Title	Peak Position	Weeks at No.1	Weeks in Top 40
8 Nov 97	**I NEED A MIRACLE** *Positiva CDTIV 81*	39		1

COCONUTS US group

Date	Title	Peak Position	Weeks at No.1	Weeks in Top 40
11 Jun 83	**DID YOU HAVE TO LOVE ME LIKE YOU DID** *EMI America EA 156*	60		

COCTEAU TWINS UK group

Date	Title	Peak Position	Weeks at No.1	Weeks in Top 40
28 Apr 84	**PEARLY-DEWDROPS' DROPS** *4AD 405*	29		4
30 Mar 85	**AIKEA-GUINEA** *4AD AD 501*	41		
23 Nov 85	**TINY DYNAMITE (EP)** *4AD BAD 510*	52		
7 Dec 85	**ECHOES IN A SHALLOW BAY (EP)** *4AD BAD 511*	65		
25 Oct 86	**LOVE'S EASY TEARS** *4AD BAD 610*	53		
8 Sep 90	**ICEBLINK LUCK** *4AD AD 0011*	38		2
2 Oct 93	**EVANGELINE** *Fontana CTCD 1*	34		1
18 Dec 93	**WINTER WONDERLAND/FROSTY THE SNOWMAN** *Fontana COCCD 1*	58		
26 Feb 94	**BLUEBEARD** *Fontana CTCD 2*	33		1
7 Oct 95	**TWINLIGHTS (EP)** *Fontana CTCD 3*	59		
4 Nov 95	**OTHERNESS (EP)** *Fontana CTCD 4*	59		
30 Mar 96	**TISHBITE** *Fontana CTCD 5*	34		1
20 Jul 96	**VIOLAINE** *Fontana CTCD 6*	56		

C.O.D. US group

Date	Title	Peak Position	Weeks at No.1	Weeks in Top 40
14 May 83	**IN THE BOTTLE** *Streetwave WAVE 2*	54		

CODE RED UK group

Date	Title	Peak Position	Weeks at No.1	Weeks in Top 40
6 Jul 96	**I GAVE YOU EVERYTHING** *Polydor 5763992*	50		
16 Nov 96	**THIS IS OUR SONG** *Polydor 5766332*	59		
14 Jun 97	**CAN WE TALK...** *Polydor 5710992*	29		1
9 Aug 97	**IS THERE SOMEONE OUT THERE?** *Polydor 5714652*	34		1
4 Jul 98	**WHAT WOULD YOU DO IF...?** *Polydor 5673312*	55		

COFFEE US group

Date	Title	Peak Position	Weeks at No.1	Weeks in Top 40
27 Sep 80	**CASANOVA** *De-Lite MER 38*	13		7
6 Dec 80	**SLIP AND DIP/I WANNA BE WITH YOU** *De-Lite DE 1*	57		

ALMA COGAN UK singer

Date	Title	Peak Position	Weeks at No.1	Weeks in Top 40
19 Mar 54	**BELL BOTTOM BLUES** *HMV B 10653*	4		9
27 Aug 54	**LITTLE THINGS MEAN A LOT** *HMV B 10717*	11		5
3 Dec 54	**I CAN'T TELL A WALTZ FROM A TANGO** *HMV B 10786*	6		11
27 May 55	**DREAMBOAT** *HMV B 10872*	1	2	16
23 Sep 55	**BANJO'S BACK IN TOWN** *HMV B 10917*	17		4
14 Oct 55	**GO ON BY** *HMV B 10917*	16		1
16 Dec 55	**TWENTY TINY FINGERS** *HMV POP 129*	17		5
23 Dec 55	**NEVER DO A TANGO WITH AN ESKIMO** *HMV POP 129*	6		1
30 Mar 56	**WILLIE CAN** *HMV POP 187* ALMA COGAN WITH DESMOND LANE - PENNY WHISTLE	13		8
13 Jul 56	**THE BIRDS AND THE BEES** *HMV POP 223*	25		3
10 Aug 56	**WHY DO FOOLS FALL IN LOVE** *HMV POP 223*	22		4
2 Nov 56	**IN THE MIDDLE OF THE HOUSE** *HMV POP 261*	20		4
18 Jan 57	**YOU ME AND US** *HMV POP 284*	18		6
29 Mar 57	**WHATEVER LOLA WANTS** *HMV POP 317*	26		2
31 Jan 58	**THE STORY OF MY LIFE** *HMV POP 433*	25		2
14 Feb 58	**SUGARTIME** *HMV POP 450*	16		11
23 Jan 59	**LAST NIGHT ON THE BACK PORCH** *HMV POP 573*	27		2
18 Dec 59	**WE GOT LOVE** *HMV POP 670*	26		4
12 May 60	**DREAM TALK** *HMV POP 728*	48		
11 Aug 60	**TRAIN OF LOVE** *HMV POP 760*	27		2
20 Apr 61	**COWBOY JIMMY JOE** *Columbia DB 4607*	37		2

SHAYE COGAN US singer

Date	Title	Peak Position	Weeks at No.1	Weeks in Top 40
24 Mar 60	**MEAN TO ME** *MGM 1063*	40		1

COHEED AND CAMBRIA US group

Date	Title	Peak Position	Weeks at No.1	Weeks in Top 40
18 Feb 06	**THE SUFFERING** *Columbia 82876766672*	60		

COHEN VS DELUXE Brazilian/UK duo

Date	Title	Peak Position	Weeks at No.1	Weeks in Top 40
13 Mar 04	**JUST KICK** *Intec INTEC024*	70		

IZHAR COHEN & ALPHABETA Israeli group

Date	Title	Peak Position	Weeks at No.1	Weeks in Top 40
13 May 78	**A BA NI BI** *Polydor 2001 781*	20		6

MARC COHN US singer/pianist

Date	Title	Peak Position	Weeks at No.1	Weeks in Top 40
25 May 91	**WALKING IN MEMPHIS** *Atlantic A 7747*	66		
10 Aug 91	**SILVER THUNDERBIRD** *Atlantic A 7657*	54		
12 Oct 91	**WALKING IN MEMPHIS** *Atlantic A 7585*	22		4
29 May 93	**WALK THROUGH THE WORLD** *Atlantic A 7340CD*	37		2

COLA BOY UK duo

Date	Title	Peak Position	Weeks at No.1	Weeks in Top 40
6 Jul 91	**7 WAYS TO LOVE** *Arista 114526*	8		5

COLD JAM US group

Date	Title	Peak Position	Weeks at No.1	Weeks in Top 40
28 Jul 90	**LAST NIGHT A DJ SAVED MY LIFE** *Big Wave BWR 39* COLD JAM FEATURING GRACE	64		

COLD WAR KIDS US group

Date	Title	Peak Position	Weeks at No.1	Weeks in Top 40
10 Feb 07	**HANG ME UP TO DRY** *V2 VVR5044633*	57		

COLDCUT UK duo

Date	Title	Peak Position	Weeks at No.1	Weeks in Top 40
20 Feb 88	**DOCTORIN' THE HOUSE** *Ahead Of Our Time CCUT 2* COLDCUT FEATURING YAZZ & THE PLASTIC POPULATION	6		7

Date	Title / Label	Peak Position	Weeks at No.1	Weeks in Top 40
10 Sep 88	**STOP THIS CRAZY THING** *Ahead Of Our Time CCUT 4* COLDCUT FEATURING JUNIOR REID & THE AHEAD OF OUR TIME ORCHESTRA	21		5
25 Mar 89	**PEOPLE HOLD ON** *Ahead Of Our Time CCUT 5* COLDCUT FEATURING LISA STANSFIELD	11		7
3 Jun 89	**MY TELEPHONE** *Ahead Of Our Time CCUT 6*	52		
16 Dec 89	**COLDCUT'S CHRISTMAS BREAK** *Ahead Of Our Time CCUT 7*	67		
26 May 90	**FIND A WAY** *Ahead Of Our Time CCUT 8* COLDCUT FEATURING QUEEN LATIFAH	52		
4 Sep 93	**DREAMER** *Arista 74321156642*	54		
22 Jan 94	**AUTUMN LEAVES** *Arista 74321171052*	50		
16 Aug 97	**MORE BEATS & PIECES** *Ninja Tune ZENCDS 58*	37		1
16 Jun 01	**REVOLUTION** *Ninja Tune ZENCDS 88*	67		
29 Apr 06	**TRUE SKOOL** *Ninja Tune ZENCDS178* COLDCUT FEATURING ROOTS MANUVA	61		

COLDPLAY UK group

Date	Title / Label	Peak Position	Weeks at No.1	Weeks in Top 40
18 Mar 00	**SHIVER** *Parlophone CDR 6536*	35		1
8 Jul 00	**YELLOW** *Parlophone CDR 6538*	4		9
4 Nov 00	**TROUBLE** *Parlophone CDRS 6549*	10		5
17 Aug 02	**IN MY PLACE** *Parlophone CDR 6579*	2		5
23 Nov 02	**THE SCIENTIST** *Parlophone CDR 6588*	10		4
5 Apr 03	**CLOCKS** *Parlophone CDR 6594*	9		4
4 Jun 05	**SPEED OF SOUND** *Parlophone CDR6664*	2		11
17 Sep 05	**FIX YOU** *Parlophone CDRS6671*	4		11
31 Dec 05	**TALK** *Parlophone CDR6679*	10		7

ANDY COLE UK footballer/singer

Date	Title / Label	Peak Position	Weeks at No.1	Weeks in Top 40
18 Sep 99	**OUTSTANDING** *WEA 224CD*	68		

COZY COLE US drummer

Date	Title / Label	Peak Position	Weeks at No.1	Weeks in Top 40
5 Dec 58	**TOPSY (PARTS 1 AND 2)** *London HL 8750*	29		1

KEYSHIA COLE US singer

Date	Title / Label	Peak Position	Weeks at No.1	Weeks in Top 40
15 Apr 06	**I SHOULD HAVE CHEATED/I CHANGED MY MIND** *A&M/Polydor 9855074*	48		
4 Nov 06	**(WHEN YOU GONNA) GIVE IT UP TO ME** *VP/Atlantic AT0265CD* SEAN PAUL FEATURING KEYSHIA COLE	31		1
3 Mar 07	**LAST NIGHT** *Atlantic AT0273CD* P DIDDY FEATURING KEYSHIA COLE	14		10

LLOYD COLE & THE COMMOTIONS UK group

Date	Title / Label	Peak Position	Weeks at No.1	Weeks in Top 40
26 May 84	**PERFECT SKIN** *Polydor COLE 1*	26		4
25 Aug 84	**FOREST FIRE** *Polydor COLE 2*	41		
17 Nov 84	**RATTLESNAKES** *Polydor COLE 3*	65		
14 Sep 85	**BRAND NEW FRIEND** *Polydor COLE 4*	19		6
9 Nov 85	**LOST WEEKEND** *Polydor COLE 5*	17		5
18 Jan 86	**CUT ME DOWN** *Polydor COLE 6*	38		2
3 Oct 87	**MY BAG** *Polydor COLE 7*	46		
9 Jan 88	**JENNIFER SHE SAID** *Polydor COLE 8*	31		2
23 Apr 88	**FROM THE HIP (EP)** *Polydor COLE 9*	59		
3 Feb 90	**NO BLUE SKIES** *Polydor COLE 11*	42		
7 Apr 90	**DON'T LOOK BACK** *Polydor COLE 12*	59		
31 Aug 91	**SHE'S A GIRL AND I'M A MAN** *Polydor COLE 14*	55		
25 Sep 93	**SO YOU'D LIKE TO SAVE THE WORLD** *Fontana VIBE D1*	72		
16 Sep 95	**LIKE LOVERS DO** *Fontana LCDD 1*	24		2
2 Dec 95	**SENTIMENTAL FOOL** *Fontana LCDD 2*	73		

MJ COLE UK producer

Date	Title / Label	Peak Position	Weeks at No.1	Weeks in Top 40
23 May 98	**SINCERE** *AM:PM 5826912*	38		1
6 May 00	**CRAZY LOVE** *Talkin Loud TLCD 59*	10		5
12 Aug 00	**SINCERE** *Talkin Loud TLCD 60*	13		3
2 Dec 00	**HOLD ON TO ME** *Talkin Loud TLCD 62* MJ COLE FEATURING ELISABETH TROY	35		1
29 Mar 03	**WONDERING WHY** *Talkin Loud 0779522*	30		1

NAT 'KING' COLE US singer/pianist

Date	Title / Label	Peak Position	Weeks at No.1	Weeks in Top 40
14 Nov 52	**SOMEWHERE ALONG THE WAY** *Capitol CL 13774*	3		7
19 Dec 52	**BECAUSE YOU'RE MINE** *Capitol CL 13811*	6		4
2 Jan 53	**FAITH CAN MOVE MOUNTAINS** *Capitol CL 13811*	10		4
24 Apr 53	**PRETEND** *Capitol CL 13878*	2		18
14 Aug 53	**CAN'T I?** *Capitol CL 13937*	6		8
18 Sep 53	**MOTHER NATURE AND FATHER TIME** *Capitol CL 13912*	7		7
16 Apr 54	**TENDERLY** *Capitol CL 14061*	10		1
10 Sep 54	**SMILE** *Capitol CL 14149*	2		14
8 Oct 54	**MAKE HER MINE** *Capitol CL 14149*	11		2
25 Feb 55	**A BLOSSOM FELL** *Capitol CL 14235*	3		10
26 Aug 55	**MY ONE SIN** *Capitol CL 14327*	17		2
27 Jan 56	**DREAMS CAN TELL A LIE** *Capitol CL 14513*	10		9
11 May 56	**TOO YOUNG TO GO STEADY** *Capitol CL 14573*	8		14
14 Sep 56	**LOVE ME AS THOUGH THERE WERE NO TOMORROW** *Capitol CL 14621*	11		15
19 Apr 57	**WHEN I FALL IN LOVE** *Capitol CL 14709*	2		20
5 Jul 57	**WHEN ROCK 'N ROLL CAME TO TRINIDAD** *Capitol CL 14733*	28		1
18 Oct 57	**MY PERSONAL POSSESSION** *Capitol CL 14765* NAT 'KING' COLE & THE FOUR KNIGHTS	21		2
25 Oct 57	**STARDUST** *Capitol CL 14787*	24		2
29 May 59	**YOU MADE ME LOVE YOU** *Capitol CL 15017*	22		3
4 Sep 59	**MIDNIGHT FLYER** *Capitol CL 15056*	23		4
12 Feb 60	**TIME AND THE RIVER** *Capitol CL 15111*	23		3
26 May 60	**THAT'S YOU** *Capitol CL 15129*	10		8
10 Nov 60	**JUST AS MUCH AS EVER** *Capitol CL 15163*	18		9
2 Feb 61	**THE WORLD IN MY ARMS** *Capitol CL 15178*	36		2
16 Nov 61	**LET TRUE LOVE BEGIN** *Capitol CL 15224*	29		5
22 Mar 62	**BRAZILIAN LOVE SONG** *Capitol CL 15241*	34		1
31 May 62	**THE RIGHT THING TO SAY** *Capitol CL 15250*	42		
19 Jul 62	**LET THERE BE LOVE** *Capitol CL 15257* NAT 'KING' COLE WITH GEORGE SHEARING	11		12
27 Sep 62	**RAMBLIN' ROSE** *Capitol CL 15270*	5		13
20 Dec 62	**DEAR LONELY HEARTS** *Capitol CL 15280*	37		2
12 Dec 87	**WHEN I FALL IN LOVE** *Capitol CL 15975*	4		5
22 Jun 91	**UNFORGETTABLE** *Elektra EKR 128* NATALIE COLE WITH NAT 'KING' COLE	19		6
14 Dec 91	**THE CHRISTMAS SONG** *Capitol CL 641*	69		
19 Mar 94	**LET'S FACE THE MUSIC AND DANCE** *EMI CDEM 312*	30		2
29 Dec 07	**THE CHRISTMAS SONG** *Download*	51		

NATALIE COLE US singer

Date	Title / Label	Peak Position	Weeks at No.1	Weeks in Top 40
11 Oct 75	**THIS WILL BE** *Capitol CL 15834*	32		4
8 Aug 87	**JUMP START** *Manhattan MT 22*	44		
26 Mar 88	**PINK CADILLAC** *Manhattan MT 35*	5		9
25 Jun 88	**EVERLASTING** *Manhattan MT 46*	28		4
20 Aug 88	**JUMP START** *Manhattan MT 50*	36		3
26 Nov 88	**I LIVE FOR YOUR LOVE** *Manhattan MT 57*	23		8
15 Apr 89	**MISS YOU LIKE CRAZY** *EMI-USA MT 63* ●	2		12
22 Jul 89	**REST OF THE NIGHT** *EMI-USA MT 69*	56		
16 Dec 89	**STARTING OVER AGAIN** *EMI-USA MT 77*	56		
21 Apr 90	**WILD WOMEN DO** *EMI-USA MT 81*	16		5
22 Jun 91	**UNFORGETTABLE** *Elektra EKR 128* NATALIE COLE WITH NAT 'KING' COLE	19		6
16 May 92	**THE VERY THOUGHT OF YOU** *Elektra EKR 147*	71		

PAULA COLE US singer

Date	Title / Label	Peak Position	Weeks at No.1	Weeks in Top 40
28 Jun 97	**WHERE HAVE ALL THE COWBOYS GONE?** *Warner Brothers W 0406CD*	15		6
1 Aug 98	**I DON'T WANT TO WAIT** *Warner Brothers W 0422CD*	43		

COLLAGE US group

Date	Title / Label	Peak Position	Weeks at No.1	Weeks in Top 40
21 Sep 85	**ROMEO WHERE'S JULIET** *MCA 1006*	46		

COLLAPSED LUNG UK group

Date	Title / Label	Peak Position	Weeks at No.1	Weeks in Top 40
22 Jun 96	**LONDON TONIGHT/EAT MY GOAL** *Deceptive BLUFF 029CD*	31		2
30 May 98	**EAT MY GOAL** *Deceptive BLUFF 060CD*	18		2

DAVE & ANSIL COLLINS Jamaican duo

Date	Title / Label	Peak Position	Weeks at No.1	Weeks in Top 40
27 Mar 71	**DOUBLE BARREL** *Technique TE 901*	1	2	13
26 Jun 71	**MONKEY SPANNER** *Technique TE 914*	7		10

EDWYN COLLINS UK singer

Date	Title / Label	Peak Position	Weeks at No.1	Weeks in Top 40
11 Aug 84	**PALE BLUE EYES** *Swamplands SWP 1* PAUL QUINN & EDWYYN COLLINS	72		
12 Nov 94	**EXPRESSLY (EP)** *Setanta ZOP 001CD1*	42		
17 Jun 95	**A GIRL LIKE YOU** *Setanta ZOP 003CD* ●	4		11
2 Mar 96	**KEEP ON BURNING** *Setanta ZOP 004CD1*	45		
2 Aug 97	**THE MAGIC PIPER (OF LOVE)** *Setanta SETCDA 041*	32		1
18 Oct 97	**ADIDAS WORLD** *Setanta SETCDA 045*	71		

Silver-selling ○ · Gold-selling ● · Platinum-selling · US No.1 ★ · Peak Position · Weeks at No.1 · Weeks in Top 40

JEFF COLLINS UK singer

Date	Title / Label	Peak Position	Weeks at No.1	Weeks in Top 40
18 Nov 72	**ONLY YOU** *Polydor 2058 287*	40		1

JUDY COLLINS US singer

Date	Title / Label	Peak Position	Weeks at No.1	Weeks in Top 40
17 Jan 70	**BOTH SIDES NOW** *Elektra EKSN 45043*	14		8
5 Dec 70	**AMAZING GRACE** *Elektra 2101 020*	5		41
17 May 75	**SEND IN THE CLOWNS** *Elektra K 12177*	6		8

MICHELLE COLLINS UK singer/actress

Date	Title / Label	Peak Position	Weeks at No.1	Weeks in Top 40
27 Feb 99	**SUNBURN** *BBC Music WMSS 60082*	28		2

PHIL COLLINS UK singer/drummer

Date	Title / Label	Peak Position	Weeks at No.1	Weeks in Top 40
17 Jan 81	**IN THE AIR TONIGHT** *Virgin VSK 102* ●	2		8
7 Mar 81	**I MISSED AGAIN** *Virgin VS 402*	14		5
30 May 81	**IF LEAVING ME IS EASY** *Virgin VS 423*	17		6
23 Oct 82	**THRU' THESE WALLS** *Virgin VS 524*	56		
4 Dec 82	**YOU CAN'T HURRY LOVE** *Virgin VS 531* ●	1	2	13
19 Mar 83	**DON'T LET HIM STEAL YOUR HEART AWAY** *Virgin VS 572*	45		
7 Apr 84	**AGAINST ALL ODDS (TAKE A LOOK AT ME NOW)** *Virgin VS 674* ● ★	2		12
26 Jan 85	**SUSSUDIO** *Virgin VS 736* ★	12		7
9 Mar 85	**EASY LOVER** *CBS A 4915* PHILIP BAILEY (DUET WITH PHIL COLLINS) ●	1	4	10
13 Apr 85	**ONE MORE NIGHT** *Virgin VS 755* ★	4		7
27 Jul 85	**TAKE ME HOME** *Virgin VS 777*	19		6
23 Nov 85	**SEPARATE LIVES** *Virgin VS 818* PHIL COLLINS & MARILYN MARTIN ○ ★	4		11
18 Jun 88	**IN THE AIR TONIGHT (REMIX)** *Virgin VS 102*	4		7
3 Sep 88	**A GROOVY KIND OF LOVE** *Virgin VS 1117* ○ ★	1	2	12
26 Nov 88	**TWO HEARTS** *Virgin VS 1141* ○ ★	6		9
4 Nov 89	**ANOTHER DAY IN PARADISE** *Virgin VS 1234* ○ ★	2		9
27 Jan 90	**I WISH IT WOULD RAIN DOWN** *Virgin VS 1240*	7		7
28 Apr 90	**SOMETHING HAPPENED ON THE WAY TO HEAVEN** *Virgin VS 1251*	15		5
28 Jul 90	**THAT'S JUST THE WAY IT IS** *Virgin VS 1277*	26		2
6 Oct 90	**HANG IN LONG ENOUGH** *Virgin VS 1300*	34		1
8 Dec 90	**DO YOU REMEMBER (LIVE)** *Virgin VS 1305*	57		
15 May 93	**HERO** *Atlantic A 7360* DAVID CROSBY FEATURING PHIL COLLINS	56		
30 Oct 93	**BOTH SIDES OF THE STORY** *Virgin VSCDT 1500*	7		3
15 Jan 94	**EVERYDAY** *Virgin VSCDT 1505*	15		4
7 May 94	**WE WAIT AND WE WONDER** *Virgin VSCDT 1510*	45		
5 Oct 96	**DANCE INTO THE LIGHT** *Face Value EW 066CD*	9		3
14 Dec 96	**IT'S IN YOUR EYES** *Face Value EW 076CD1*	30		1
12 Jul 97	**WEAR MY HAT** *Face Value EW 113CD*	43		
7 Nov 98	**TRUE COLOURS** *Virgin VSCDT 1715*	26		1
6 Nov 99	**YOU'LL BE IN MY HEART** *Walt Disney 0100735 DNY*	17		3
22 Sep 01	**IN THE AIR TONITE** *WEA 331CD* LIL' KIM FEATURING PHIL COLLINS	26		1
16 Nov 02	**CAN'T STOP LOVING YOU** *Face Value EW 254CD*	28		1
24 May 03	**HOME** *Epic 6738305* BONE THUGS-N-HARMONY FEATURING PHIL COLLINS	19		2
29 Nov 03	**LOOK THROUGH MY EYES** *Walt Disney DISNEY001*	61		
15 Sep 07	**IN THE AIR TONIGHT** *Virgin VS102*	14		13

RODGER COLLINS US singer

Date	Title / Label	Peak Position	Weeks at No.1	Weeks in Top 40
3 Apr 76	**YOU SEXY SUGAR PLUM (BUT I LIKE IT)** *Fantasy FTC 132*	22		5

WILLIE COLLINS US singer

Date	Title / Label	Peak Position	Weeks at No.1	Weeks in Top 40
28 Jun 86	**WHERE YOU GONNA BE TONIGHT?** *Capitol CL 410*	46		

WILLIE COLON US singer/trombonist

Date	Title / Label	Peak Position	Weeks at No.1	Weeks in Top 40
28 Jun 86	**SET FIRE TO ME** *A&M AM 330*	41		

COLOR ME BADD US group

Date	Title / Label	Peak Position	Weeks at No.1	Weeks in Top 40
18 May 91	**I WANNA SEX YOU UP** *Giant W 0036* ○	1	3	12
3 Aug 91	**ALL 4 LOVE** *Giant W 0053* ★	5		8
12 Oct 91	**I ADORE MI AMOR** *Giant W 0067* ★	44		
22 Feb 92	**HEARTBREAKER** *Giant W 0078*	58		
20 Nov 93	**TIME AND CHANCE** *Giant 74321168992*	62		
16 Apr 94	**CHOOSE** *Giant 74321199432*	65		

COLORADO UK group

Date	Title / Label	Peak Position	Weeks at No.1	Weeks in Top 40
21 Oct 78	**CALIFORNIA DREAMIN'** *Pinnacle PIN 67*	45		

COLOUR FIELD UK group

Date	Title / Label	Peak Position	Weeks at No.1	Weeks in Top 40
21 Jan 84	**THE COLOUR FIELD** *Chrysalis COLF 1*	43		
28 Jul 84	**TAKE** *Chrysalis COLF 2*	70		
26 Jan 85	**THINKING OF YOU** *Chrysalis COLF 3*	12		7
13 Apr 85	**CASTLES IN THE AIR** *Chrysalis COLF 4*	51		

COLOUR GIRL UK singer

Date	Title / Label	Peak Position	Weeks at No.1	Weeks in Top 40
11 Mar 00	**CAN'T GET USED TO LOSING YOU** *4 Liberty LIBTCD 037*	31		1
9 Sep 00	**JOYRIDER (YOU'RE PLAYING WITH FIRE)** *4 Liberty LIBTCD 039*	51		
3 Feb 01	**MAS QUE NADA** *4 Liberty LIBTCD 040* COLOUR GIRL FEATURING PSG	57		

COLOURS UK producer

Date	Title / Label	Peak Position	Weeks at No.1	Weeks in Top 40
27 Feb 99	**WHAT U DO** *Inferno CDFERN 12* COLOURS FEATURING EMMANUEL & ESKA	51		

COLOURSOUND UK group

Date	Title / Label	Peak Position	Weeks at No.1	Weeks in Top 40
28 Sep 02	**FLY WITH ME** *City Rockers ROCKERS 20CD*	49		

COLUMBO UK production duo

Date	Title / Label	Peak Position	Weeks at No.1	Weeks in Top 40
15 May 99	**ROCKABILLY BOB** *V2/Milkgems VVR 5006903* COLUMBO FEATURING OOE	59		

SHAWN COLVIN US singer/guitarist

Date	Title / Label	Peak Position	Weeks at No.1	Weeks in Top 40
27 Nov 93	**I DON'T KNOW WHY** *Columbia 6598272*	62		
12 Feb 94	**ROUND OF BLUES** *Columbia 6594282*	73		
3 Sep 94	**EVERY LITTLE THING HE DOES IS MAGIC** *Columbia 6607742*	65		
7 Jan 95	**ONE COOL REMOVE** *Columbia 6611342* SHAWN COLVIN WITH MARY CHAPIN CARPENTER	40		1
12 Aug 95	**I DON'T KNOW WHY** *Columbia 6622725*	52		
15 Mar 97	**GET OUT OF THIS HOUSE** *Columbia 6638522*	70		
30 May 98	**SUNNY CAME HOME** *Columbia 6648022*	29		1

COMING OUT CREW US duo

Date	Title / Label	Peak Position	Weeks at No.1	Weeks in Top 40
18 Mar 95	**FREE, GAY AND HAPPY** *Out On Vinyl CDOOV 002*	50		

COMMANDER TOM German producer

Date	Title / Label	Peak Position	Weeks at No.1	Weeks in Top 40
23 Dec 00	**EYE BEE M** *Tripoli Trax TTRAX 069CD*	75		
5 Feb 05	**ATTENTION!** *Data 81CDS*	23		1

COMMENTATORS UK impersonator

Date	Title / Label	Peak Position	Weeks at No.1	Weeks in Top 40
22 Jun 85	**N-N-NINETEEN NOT OUT** *Oval 100*	13		4

COMMITMENTS Irish group

Date	Title / Label	Peak Position	Weeks at No.1	Weeks in Top 40
30 Nov 91	**MUSTANG SALLY** *MCA MCS 1598*	63		

COMMODORES US group

Date	Title / Label	Peak Position	Weeks at No.1	Weeks in Top 40
24 Aug 74	**MACHINE GUN** *Tamla Motown TMG 902*	20		8
23 Nov 74	**THE ZOO (THE HUMAN ZOO)** *Tamla Motown TMG 924*	44		
2 Jul 77	**EASY** *Motown TMG 1073*	9		9
8 Oct 77	**SWEET LOVE/BRICK HOUSE** *Motown TMG 1086*	32		5
11 Mar 78	**TOO HOT TO TROT/ZOOM** *Motown TMG 1096*	38		1
24 Jun 78	**FLYING HIGH** *Motown TMG 1111*	37		1
5 Aug 78	**THREE TIMES A LADY** *Motown TMG 1113* ● ★	1	5	11
25 Nov 78	**JUST TO BE CLOSE TO YOU** *Motown TMG 1127*	62		
25 Aug 79	**SAIL ON** *Motown TMG 1155*	8		7
3 Nov 79	**STILL** *Motown TMG 1166* ○ ★	4		7
19 Jan 80	**WONDERLAND** *Motown TMG 1172*	40		1
2 Aug 80	**LADY (YOU BRING ME UP)** *Motown TMG 1238*	56		
21 Nov 81	**OH NO** *Motown TMG 1245*	44		
26 Jan 85	**NIGHTSHIFT** *Motown TMG 1371* ○	3		11
11 May 85	**ANIMAL INSTINCT** *Motown ZB 40097*	74		
25 Oct 86	**GOIN' TO THE BANK** *Polydor POSPA 826*	43		
13 Aug 88	**EASY** *Motown ZB 41793*	15		7

COMMON US rapper

Date	Title	Peak Position	Weeks at No.1	Weeks in Top 40
8 Nov 97	**REMINDING ME (OF SEF)** *Relativity 6560762* COMMON FEATURING CHANTAY SAVAGE	59		
14 Oct 00	**THE LIGHT/THE 6TH SENSE** *MCA MCSTD 40237*	56		
28 Apr 01	**GETO HEAVEN** *MCA MCSTD 40246* COMMON FEATURING MACY GRAY	48		
9 Feb 02	**DANCE FOR ME** *MCA MCSXD 40274* MARY J BLIGE FEATURING COMMON	13		3
27 Oct 07	**DRIVIN' ME WILD** *Geffen 1750856* COMMON FEATURING LILY ALLEN	56		

COMMUNARDS UK duo

Date	Title	Peak Position	Weeks at No.1	Weeks in Top 40
12 Oct 85	**YOU ARE MY WORLD** *London LON 77*	30		4
24 May 86	**DISENCHANTED** *London LON 89*	29		3
23 Aug 86	**DON'T LEAVE ME THIS WAY** *London LON 103* COMMUNARDS WITH SARAH-JANE MORRIS ●	1	4	12
29 Nov 86	**SO COLD THE NIGHT** *London LON 110*	8		9
21 Feb 87	**YOU ARE MY WORLD** *London LON 123*	21		5
12 Sep 87	**TOMORROW** *London LON 143*	23		5
7 Nov 87	**NEVER CAN SAY GOODBYE** *London LON 158* ○	4		10
20 Feb 88	**FOR A FRIEND** *London LON 166*	28		3
11 Jun 88	**THERE'S MORE TO LOVE** *London LON 173*	20		6

PERRY COMO US singer

Date	Title	Peak Position	Weeks at No.1	Weeks in Top 40
16 Jan 53	**DON'T LET THE STARS GET IN YOUR EYES** *HMV B 10400* PERRY COMO WITH THE RAMBLERS ★	1	5	15
4 Jun 54	**WANTED** *HMV B 10667* ★	4		15
25 Jun 54	**IDLE GOSSIP** *HMV B 10710*	3		15
10 Dec 54	**PAPA LOVES MAMBO** *HMV B 10776*	16		1
30 Dec 55	**TINA MARIE** *HMV POP 103*	24		1
27 Apr 56	**JUKE BOX BABY** *HMV POP 191*	22		6
25 May 56	**HOT DIGGITY (DOG ZIGGITY BOOM)** *HMV POP 212* ★	4		13
21 Sep 56	**MORE** *HMV POP 240*	10		6
28 Sep 56	**GLENDORA** *HMV POP 240*	18		12
7 Feb 58	**MAGIC MOMENTS** *RCA 1036*	1	8	17
7 Mar 58	**CATCH A FALLING STAR** *RCA 1036* ★	9		10
9 May 58	**KEWPIE DOLL** *RCA 1055*	9		7
30 May 58	**I MAY NEVER PASS THIS WAY AGAIN** *RCA 1062*	15		8
5 Sep 58	**MOON TALK** *RCA 1071*	17		11
7 Nov 58	**LOVE MAKES THE WORLD GO ROUND** *RCA 1086*	6		14
21 Nov 58	**MANDOLINS IN THE MOONLIGHT** *RCA 1086*	13		12
27 Feb 59	**TOMBOY** *RCA 1111*	10		12
10 Jul 59	**I KNOW** *RCA 1126*	13		16
26 Feb 60	**DELAWARE** *RCA 1170*	3		12
10 May 62	**CATERINA** *RCA 1283*	37		1
30 Jan 71	**IT'S IMPOSSIBLE** *RCA 2043*	4		21
15 May 71	**I THINK OF YOU** *RCA 2075*	14		10
21 Apr 73	**AND I LOVE YOU SO** *RCA 2346*	3		23
25 Aug 73	**FOR THE GOOD TIMES** *RCA 2402* ○	7		25
8 Dec 73	**WALK RIGHT BACK** *RCA 2432*	33		8
25 May 74	**I WANT TO GIVE** *RCA LPBO 7518*	31		5
15 Dec 07	**IT'S BEGINNING TO LOOK A LOT LIKE CHRISTMAS** *Download*	49		

COMPAGNONS DE LA CHANSON French group

Date	Title	Peak Position	Weeks at No.1	Weeks in Top 40
9 Oct 59	**THE THREE BELLS (THE JIMMY BROWN SONG)** *Columbia DB 4358*	21		3

COMSAT ANGELS UK group

Date	Title	Peak Position	Weeks at No.1	Weeks in Top 40
21 Jan 84	**INDEPENDENCE DAY** *Jive 54*	71		

CON FUNK SHUN US group

Date	Title	Peak Position	Weeks at No.1	Weeks in Top 40
19 Jul 86	**BURNIN' LOVE** *Club JAB 32*	68		

CONCEPT US singer

Date	Title	Peak Position	Weeks at No.1	Weeks in Top 40
14 Dec 85	**MR DJ** *Fourth & Broadway BRW 40*	27		5

CONCRETES Swedish group

Date	Title	Peak Position	Weeks at No.1	Weeks in Top 40
26 Jun 04	**YOU CAN'T HURRY LOVE** *EMI LFS011*	55		
2 Oct 04	**SEEMS FINE** *EMI LFSX013*	52		
18 Mar 06	**CHOSEN ONE** *EMI LFCD019*	54		

CONDUCTOR & THE COWBOY UK production/duo

Date	Title	Peak Position	Weeks at No.1	Weeks in Top 40
20 May 00	**FEELING THIS WAY** *Serious SERR 016CD*	35		1

CONGREGATION UK group

Date	Title	Peak Position	Weeks at No.1	Weeks in Top 40
27 Nov 71	**SOFTLY WHISPERING I LOVE YOU** *Columbia DB 8830*	4		13

CONGRESS UK production duo

Date	Title	Peak Position	Weeks at No.1	Weeks in Top 40
26 Oct 91	**40 MILES** *Inner Rhythm 7HEART 01*	26		3

CONJURE ONE Canadian producer

Date	Title	Peak Position	Weeks at No.1	Weeks in Top 40
15 Feb 03	**SLEEP/TEARS FROM THE MOON** *Nettwerk 331792*	42		

ARTHUR CONLEY US singer

Date	Title	Peak Position	Weeks at No.1	Weeks in Top 40
27 Apr 67	**SWEET SOUL MUSIC** *Atlantic 584 083*	7		13
10 Apr 68	**FUNKY STREET** *Atlantic 583 175*	46		

CONNELLS US group

Date	Title	Peak Position	Weeks at No.1	Weeks in Top 40
12 Aug 95	**'74-'75** *TNT LONCD 369*	14		7
16 Mar 96	**'74-'75** *TNT LONCD 369*	21		2

HARRY CONNICK US singer

Date	Title	Peak Position	Weeks at No.1	Weeks in Top 40
25 May 91	**RECIPE FOR LOVE/IT HAD TO BE YOU** *Columbia 6568907*	32		4
3 Aug 91	**WE ARE IN LOVE** *Columbia 6572847*	62		
23 Nov 91	**BLUE LIGHT RED LIGHT (SOMEONE'S THERE)** *Columbia 6575367*	54		

BILLY CONNOLLY UK singer/comedian

Date	Title	Peak Position	Weeks at No.1	Weeks in Top 40
1 Nov 75	**D.I.V.O.R.C.E.** *Polydor 2058 652* ○	1	1	10
17 Jul 76	**NO CHANCE (NO CHARGE)** *Polydor 2058 748*	24		5
25 Aug 79	**IN THE BROWNIES** *Polydor 2059 160*	38		2
9 Mar 85	**SUPER GRAN** *Stiff BUY 218*	32		4

SARAH CONNOR German singer

Date	Title	Peak Position	Weeks at No.1	Weeks in Top 40
13 Oct 01	**LET'S GET BACK TO BED...BOY** *Epic 6718662* SARAH CONNOR FEATURING TQ	16		3
5 Jun 04	**BOUNCE** *Epic 6749001*	14		3

CONQUERING LION UK rapper

Date	Title	Peak Position	Weeks at No.1	Weeks in Top 40
8 Oct 94	**CODE RED** *Mango CIDM 821*	53		

LEENA CONQUEST & HIP HOP FINGER US singer

Date	Title	Peak Position	Weeks at No.1	Weeks in Top 40
18 Jun 94	**BOUNDARIES** *Naturalresponse 74321208522*	67		

JESS CONRAD UK singer

Date	Title	Peak Position	Weeks at No.1	Weeks in Top 40
30 Jun 60	**CHERRY PIE** *Decca F 11236*	39		1
26 Jan 61	**MYSTERY GIRL** *Decca F 11315*	18		6
11 Oct 62	**PRETTY JENNY** *Decca F 11511*	50		

CONSORTIUM UK group

Date	Title	Peak Position	Weeks at No.1	Weeks in Top 40
12 Feb 69	**ALL THE LOVE IN THE WORLD** *Pye 7N 17635*	22		7

BILL CONTI US film musical director

Date	Title	Peak Position	Weeks at No.1	Weeks in Top 40
27 Jan 07	**GONNA FLY NOW (THEME FROM *ROCKY*)** *Download* ★	52		

CONTOURS US group

Date	Title	Peak Position	Weeks at No.1	Weeks in Top 40
24 Jan 70	**JUST A LITTLE MISUNDERSTANDING** *Tamla Motown TMG 723*	31		5

CONTRABAND German/US group

Date	Title	Peak Position	Weeks at No.1	Weeks in Top 40
20 Jul 91	**ALL THE WAY FROM MEMPHIS** *Impact American EM 195*	65		

CONTROL UK group

Date	Title	Peak Position	Weeks at No.1	Weeks in Top 40
2 Nov 91	**DANCE WITH ME (I'M YOUR ECSTASY)** *All Around The World GLOBE 105*	17		4

CONVERT Belgian production duo

Date	Title	Peak Position	Weeks at No.1	Weeks in Top 40
11 Jan 92	**NIGHTBIRD** *A&M AM 845*	39		1
29 May 93	**ROCKIN' TO THE RHYTHM** *A&M 5802532*	42		
31 Jan 98	**NIGHTBIRD** *Wonderboy WBOYD 008*	45		

CONWAY BROTHERS US group

Date	Title	Peak Position	Weeks at No.1	Weeks in Top 40
22 Jun 85	**TURN IT UP** *10 TEN 57*	11		7

RUSS CONWAY UK pianist

Date	Title	Peak Position	Weeks at No.1	Weeks in Top 40
29 Nov 57	**PARTY POPS** *Columbia DB 4031*	24		5
29 Aug 58	**GOT A MATCH** *Columbia DB 4166*	30		1
28 Nov 58	**MORE PARTY POPS** *Columbia DB 4204*	10		7
23 Jan 59	**THE WORLD OUTSIDE** *Columbia DB 4234*	24		1
20 Feb 59	**SIDE SADDLE** *Columbia DB 4256*	1	4	30
6 Mar 59	**THE WORLD OUTSIDE** *Columbia DB 4234*	24		3
15 May 59	**ROULETTE** *Columbia DB 4298*	1	2	19
21 Aug 59	**CHINA TEA** *Columbia DB 4337*	5		13
13 Nov 59	**SNOW COACH** *Columbia DB 4368*	7		9
20 Nov 59	**MORE AND MORE PARTY POPS** *Columbia DB 4373*	5		8
5 Mar 60	**ROYAL EVENT** *Columbia DB 4418*	15		4
21 Apr 60	**FINGS AIN'T WOT THEY USED TO BE** *Columbia DB 4422*	47		
19 May 60	**LUCKY FIVE** *Columbia DB 4457*	14		7
29 Sep 60	**PASSING BREEZE** *Columbia DB 4508*	16		8
24 Nov 60	**EVEN MORE PARTY POPS** *Columbia DB 4535*	27		7
19 Jan 61	**PEPE** *Columbia DB 4564*	19		9
25 May 61	**PABLO** *Columbia DB 4649*	45		
24 Aug 61	**SAY IT WITH FLOWERS** *Columbia DB 4665* DOROTHY SQUIRES & RUSS CONWAY	23		7
30 Nov 61	**TOY BALLOONS** *Columbia DB 4738*	7		10
22 Feb 62	**LESSON ONE** *Columbia DB 4784*	21		6
29 Nov 62	**ALWAYS YOU AND ME** *Columbia DB 4934*	33		3

NORMAN COOK UK producer/DJ

Date	Title	Peak Position	Weeks at No.1	Weeks in Top 40
8 Jul 89	**WON'T TALK ABOUT IT/BLAME IT ON THE BASSLINE** *Go! Beat GOD 33* NORMAN COOK FEATURING BILLY BRAGG/NORMAN COOK FEATURING MC WILDSKI	29		4
21 Oct 89	**FOR SPACIOUS LIES** *Go! Beat GOD 37* NORMAN COOK FEATURING LESTER	48		

PETER COOK UK comedian

Date	Title	Peak Position	Weeks at No.1	Weeks in Top 40
17 Jun 65	**GOODBYE-EE** *Decca F 12158* PETER COOK & DUDLEY MOORE	18		8
15 Jul 65	**THE BALLAD OF SPOTTY MULDOON** *Decca F 12182*	34		4

BRANDON COOKE US producer

Date	Title	Peak Position	Weeks at No.1	Weeks in Top 40
29 Oct 88	**SHARP AS A KNIFE** *Club JAB 73* BRANDON COOKE FEATURING ROXANNE SHANTE	45		

SAM COOKE US singer

Date	Title	Peak Position	Weeks at No.1	Weeks in Top 40
17 Jan 58	**YOU SEND ME** *London HLU 8506* ★	29		1
14 Aug 59	**ONLY SIXTEEN** *HMV POP 642*	23		4
7 Jul 60	**WONDERFUL WORLD** *HMV POP 754*	27		5
29 Sep 60	**CHAIN GANG** *RCA 1202*	9		11
27 Jul 61	**CUPID** *RCA 1242*	7		13
8 Mar 62	**TWISTIN' THE NIGHT AWAY** *RCA 1277*	6		14
16 May 63	**ANOTHER SATURDAY NIGHT** *RCA 1341*	23		9
5 Sep 63	**FRANKIE AND JOHNNY** *RCA 1361*	30		5
22 Mar 86	**WONDERFUL WORLD** *RCA PB 49871* ●	2		9
10 May 86	**ANOTHER SATURDAY NIGHT** *RCA PB 49849*	75		

COOKIE UK group

Date	Title	Peak Position	Weeks at No.1	Weeks in Top 40
16 Jul 05	**DO IT AGAIN** *The Bakery CXBAKERY1*	52		

COOKIE CREW UK group

Date	Title	Peak Position	Weeks at No.1	Weeks in Top 40
9 Jan 88	**ROK DA HOUSE** *Rhythm King LEFT 11* BEATMASTERS FEATURING THE COOKIE CREW	5		7
7 Jan 89	**BORN THIS WAY (LET'S DANCE)** *ffrr FFR 19*	23		3
1 Apr 89	**GOT TO KEEP ON** *ffrr FFR 25*	17		6
15 Jul 89	**COME AND GET SOME** *ffrr F 110*	42		
27 Jul 91	**SECRETS (OF SUCCESS)** *ffrr F 159* COOKIE CREW FEATURING DANNY D	53		

COOKIES US group

Date	Title	Peak Position	Weeks at No.1	Weeks in Top 40
10 Jan 63	**CHAINS** *London HLU 9634*	50		

COOL DOWN ZONE UK group

Date	Title	Peak Position	Weeks at No.1	Weeks in Top 40
30 Jun 90	**HEAVEN KNOWS** *10 TEN 309*	52		

COOL JACK Italian production duo

Date	Title	Peak Position	Weeks at No.1	Weeks in Top 40
9 Nov 96	**JUS' COME** *AM:PM 5819892*	44		

COOL, THE FAB & THE GROOVY UK production duo

Date	Title	Peak Position	Weeks at No.1	Weeks in Top 40
1 Aug 98	**SOUL BOSSA NOVA** *Manifesto FESCD 48* COOL, THE FAB & THE GROOVY PRESENT QUINCY JONES	47		

RITA COOLIDGE US singer

Date	Title	Peak Position	Weeks at No.1	Weeks in Top 40
25 Jun 77	**WE'RE ALL ALONE** *A&M AMS 7295*	6		12
15 Oct 77	**(YOUR LOVE HAS LIFTED ME) HIGHER AND HIGHER** *A&M AMS 7315*	48		
4 Feb 78	**WORDS** *A&M AMS 7330*	25		6
25 Jun 83	**ALL TIME HIGH** *A&M AM 007*	75		

COOLIO US rapper

Date	Title	Peak Position	Weeks at No.1	Weeks in Top 40
23 Jul 94	**FANTASTIC VOYAGE** *Tommy Boy TB 0617CD*	41		
15 Oct 94	**I REMEMBER** *Tommy Boy TBXCD 635*	73		
28 Oct 95	**GANGSTA'S PARADISE** *Tommy Boy MCSTD 2104* COOLIO FEATURING LV ⊛ ★	1	2	18
20 Jan 96	**TOO HOT** *Tommy Boy TBCD 718*	9		4
6 Apr 96	**1,2,3,4 (SUMPIN' NEW)** *Tommy Boy TBCD 7721*	13		5
17 Aug 96	**IT'S ALL THE WAY LIVE (NOW)** *Tommy Boy TBCD 7731*	34		1
14 Sep 96	**STOMP - THE REMIXES** *Qwest W 0372CD* QUINCY JONES FEATURING MELLE MEL, COOLIO, YO-YO, SHAQUILLE O'NEAL & THE LUNIZ	28		1
5 Apr 97	**HIT 'EM HIGH (THE MONSTARS' ANTHEM)** *Atlantic A 5449CD* B REAL/BUSTA RHYMES/COOLIO/LL COOL J/METHOD MAN	8		4
7 Jun 97	**THE WINNER** *Atlantic A 5433CD*	53		
19 Jul 97	**C U WHEN U GET THERE** *Tommy Boy TBCD 785* COOLIO FEATURING 40 THEVZ ●	3		10
11 Oct 97	**OOH LA LA** *Tommy Boy TBCD 799*	14		3
28 Oct 06	**GANGSTA WALK** *All Around The World CDGLOBE565* COOLIO FEATURING SNOOP DOGG	67		

COOLNOTES UK group

Date	Title	Peak Position	Weeks at No.1	Weeks in Top 40
18 Aug 84	**YOU'RE NEVER TOO YOUNG** *Abstract Dance AD 1*	42		
17 Nov 84	**I FORGOT** *Abstract Dance AD 2*	63		
23 Mar 85	**SPEND THE NIGHT** *Abstract Dance AD 3*	11		8
13 Jul 85	**IN YOUR CAR** *Abstract Dance AD 4*	13		7
19 Oct 85	**HAVE A GOOD FOREVER** *Abstract Dance AD 5*	73		
17 May 86	**INTO THE MOTION** *Abstract Dance AD 8*	66		

COOPER Dutch production group

Date	Title	Peak Position	Weeks at No.1	Weeks in Top 40
11 Jan 03	**I BELIEVE IN LOVE** *Incentive PDT 05CDS*	50		

ALICE COOPER US singer

Date	Title	Peak Position	Weeks at No.1	Weeks in Top 40
15 Jul 72	**SCHOOL'S OUT** *Warner Brothers K 16188*	1	3	10
7 Oct 72	**ELECTED** *Warner Brothers K 16214*	4		10
10 Feb 73	**HELLO HURRAY** *Warner Brothers K 16248*	6		10
21 Apr 73	**NO MORE MR. NICE GUY** *Warner Brothers K 16262*	10		8
19 Jan 74	**TEENAGE LAMENT '74** *Warner Brothers K 16345*	12		7
21 May 77	**(NO MORE) LOVE AT YOUR CONVENIENCE** *Warner Brothers K 16935*	44		

Silver-selling ○ Gold-selling ● Platinum-selling ⊛ US No.1 ★

Date	Title	Label	Peak Position	Weeks at No.1	Weeks in Top 40
23 Dec 78	**HOW YOU GONNA SEE ME NOW**	*Warner Brothers K 17270*	61		
6 Mar 82	**SEVEN AND SEVEN IS (LIVE)**	*Warner Brothers K 17924*	62		
8 May 82	**FOR BRITAIN ONLY/UNDER MY WHEELS**	*Warner Brothers K 17940*	66		
18 Oct 86	**HE'S BACK (THE MAN BEHIND THE MASK)**	*MCA 1090*	61		
9 Apr 88	**FREEDOM**	*MCA 1241*	50		
29 Jul 89	**POISON**	*Epic 6550617*	2		10
7 Oct 89	**BED OF NAILS**	*Epic ALICE 3*	38		2
2 Dec 89	**HOUSE OF FIRE**	*Epic ALICE 4*	65		
22 Jun 91	**HEY STOOPID**	*Epic 6569837*	21		3
5 Oct 91	**LOVE'S A LOADED GUN**	*Epic 6574387*	38		2
6 Jun 92	**FEED MY FRANKENSTEIN**	*Epic 6580927*	27		2
28 May 94	**LOST IN AMERICA**	*Epic 6603472*	22		2
23 Jul 94	**IT'S ME**	*Epic 6605632*	34		1

TOMMY COOPER UK comedian

Date	Title	Label	Peak Position	Weeks at No.1	Weeks in Top 40
29 Jun 61	**DON'T JUMP OFF THE ROOF DAD**	*Palette PG 9019*	40		1

COOPER TEMPLE CLAUSE UK group

Date	Title	Label	Peak Position	Weeks at No.1	Weeks in Top 40
29 Sep 01	**LET'S KILL MUSIC**	*Morning 9*	41		
9 Feb 02	**FILM MAKER/BEEN TRAINING DOGS**	*Morning 16*	20		2
18 May 02	**WHO NEEDS ENEMIES**	*Morning 25*	22		1
13 Sep 03	**PROMISES PROMISES**	*Morning 30*	19		1
22 Nov 03	**BLIND PILOTS**	*Morning 38*	37		1
4 Nov 06	**HOMO SAPIENS**	*Sequel SEQXS002*	36		1
20 Jan 07	**WAITING GAME**	*Sequel SEQXD004*	41		

JULIAN COPE UK singer

Date	Title	Label	Peak Position	Weeks at No.1	Weeks in Top 40
19 Nov 83	**SUNSHINE PLAYROOM**	*Mercury COPE 1*	64		
31 Mar 84	**THE GREATNESS AND PERFECTION OF LOVE**	*Mercury MER 155*	52		
27 Sep 86	**WORLD SHUT YOUR MOUTH**	*Island IS 290*	19		5
17 Jan 87	**TRAMPOLENE**	*Island IS 305*	31		4
11 Apr 87	**EVE'S VOLCANO (COVERED IN SIN)**	*Island IS 318*	41		
24 Sep 88	**CHARLOTTE ANNE**	*Island IS 380*	35		3
21 Jan 89	**5 O'CLOCK WORLD**	*Island IS 399*	42		
24 Jun 89	**CHINA DOLL**	*Island IS 406*	53		
9 Feb 91	**BEAUTIFUL LOVE**	*Island IS 483*	32		3
20 Apr 91	**EAST EASY RIDER**	*Island IS 492*	51		
3 Aug 91	**HEAD**	*Island IS 497*	57		
8 Aug 92	**WORLD SHUT YOUR MOUTH**	*Island IS 534*	44		
17 Oct 92	**FEAR LOVES THIS PLACE**	*Island IS 545*	42		
12 Aug 95	**TRY TRY TRY**	*Echo ECSCD 11*	24		1
27 Jul 96	**I COME FROM ANOTHER PLANET, BABY**	*Echo ECSCD 22*	34		1
5 Oct 96	**PLANETARY SIT-IN (EVERY GIRL HAS YOUR NAME)**	*Echo ECSCD 25*	34		1

ROSS COPPERMAN US singer

Date	Title	Label	Peak Position	Weeks at No.1	Weeks in Top 40
12 May 07	**ALL SHE WROTE**	*Phonogenic 88697048572*	39		1
25 Aug 07	**FOUND YOU**	*Phonogenic 88697137592*	68		

IMANI COPPOLA US singer

Date	Title	Label	Peak Position	Weeks at No.1	Weeks in Top 40
28 Feb 98	**LEGEND OF A COWGIRL**	*Columbia 6656015*	32		1
3 Feb 01	**YOU ALL DAT** — BAHA MEN: GUEST VOCAL IMANI COPPOLA	*Edel 0124855 ERE*	14		3

CORAL UK group

Date	Title	Label	Peak Position	Weeks at No.1	Weeks in Top 40
27 Jul 02	**GOODBYE**	*Deltasonic DLTCD 2005*	21		1
19 Oct 02	**DREAMING OF YOU**	*Deltasonic DLTCD 2008*	13		3
15 Mar 03	**DON'T THINK YOU'RE THE FIRST**	*Deltasonic DLTCDC 2010*	10		2
26 Jul 03	**PASS IT ON**	*Deltasonic DLTCD 2013*	5		3
18 Oct 03	**SECRET KISS**	*Deltasonic DLTCD 2015*	25		1
6 Dec 03	**BILL MCCAI**	*Deltasonic DLTCD 2017*	23		1
21 May 05	**IN THE MORNING**	*Deltasonic DLTCD2033*	6		6
3 Sep 05	**SOMETHING INSIDE OF ME**	*Deltasonic DLTCD2039*	41		
11 Aug 07	**WHO'S GONNA FIND ME**	*Deltasonic DLTCD068*	25		1
13 Oct 07	**JACQUELINE**	*Deltasonic DLTCD072*	44		
23 Feb 08	**PUT THE SUN BACK**	*Deltasonic DLTCD074*	64		

CORD UK group

Date	Title	Label	Peak Position	Weeks at No.1	Weeks in Top 40
8 Jul 06	**WINTER**	*Island CORDCD007*	34		1
30 Sep 06	**SEA OF TROUBLE**	*Island CORDCD009*	50		

FRANK CORDELL UK orchestra leader

Date	Title	Label	Peak Position	Weeks at No.1	Weeks in Top 40
24 Aug 56	**SADIE'S SHAWL**	*HMV POP 229*	29		2
16 Feb 61	**BLACK BEAR**	*HMV POP 824*	44		

LOUISE CORDET French singer

Date	Title	Label	Peak Position	Weeks at No.1	Weeks in Top 40
5 Jul 62	**I'M JUST A BABY**	*Decca F 11476*	13		11

CORENELL German producer

Date	Title	Label	Peak Position	Weeks at No.1	Weeks in Top 40
16 Jun 07	**KEEP ON JUMPIN'** — CORENELL & LISA MARIE EXPERIENCE	*Gusto CDGUS46*	37		1

BILLY CORGAN US singer/guitarist

Date	Title	Label	Peak Position	Weeks at No.1	Weeks in Top 40
18 Jun 05	**WALKING SHADE**	*Reprise W673DVD*	74		

CHRIS CORNELL US singer

Date	Title	Label	Peak Position	Weeks at No.1	Weeks in Top 40
23 Oct 99	**CAN'T CHANGE ME**	*A&M 4971732*	62		
16 Dec 06	**YOU KNOW MY NAME**	*Interscope 1718880*	7		8

DON CORNELL US singer

Date	Title	Label	Peak Position	Weeks at No.1	Weeks in Top 40
3 Sep 54	**HOLD MY HAND**	*Vogue Q 2013*	1	5	21
22 Apr 55	**STRANGER IN PARADISE**	*Vogue Q 72073*	19		2

LYNN CORNELL UK singer

Date	Title	Label	Peak Position	Weeks at No.1	Weeks in Top 40
20 Oct 60	**NEVER ON SUNDAY**	*Decca F 11277*	30		7

CORNERSHOP UK group

Date	Title	Label	Peak Position	Weeks at No.1	Weeks in Top 40
30 Aug 97	**BRIMFUL OF ASHA**	*Wiiija WIJ 75CD*	60		
28 Feb 98	**BRIMFUL OF ASHA (REMIX)**	*Wiiija WIJ 81CD* ●	1	1	9
16 May 98	**SLEEP ON THE LEFT SIDE**	*Wiiija WIJ 80CD*	23		1
16 Mar 02	**LESSONS LEARNT FROM ROCK I TO ROCKY III**	*Wiiija WIJ 129CD*	37		1
7 Aug 04	**TOPKNOT**	*Rough Trade RTRADSCD168*	53		

HUGH CORNWELL UK singer/guitarist

Date	Title	Label	Peak Position	Weeks at No.1	Weeks in Top 40
24 Jan 87	**FACTS + FIGURES**	*Virgin VS 922*	61		
7 May 88	**ANOTHER KIND OF LOVE**	*Virgin VS 945*	71		
12 Feb 05	**(UNDER HER) SPELL**	*Track TRACK00013B*	62		

CO-RO German production group

Date	Title	Label	Peak Position	Weeks at No.1	Weeks in Top 40
12 Dec 92	**BECAUSE THE NIGHT** — CO-RO FEATURING TARLISA	*ZYX 68227*	61		

CORONA Italian singer

Date	Title	Label	Peak Position	Weeks at No.1	Weeks in Top 40
10 Sep 94	**THE RHYTHM OF THE NIGHT**	*WEA YZ 837CD1* ○	2		10
8 Apr 95	**BABY BABY**	*Eternal YZ 919CD*	5		6
22 Jul 95	**TRY ME OUT**	*Eternal YZ 955CD* ○	6		9
23 Dec 95	**I DON'T WANNA BE A STAR**	*Eternal 029CD*	22		4
22 Feb 97	**MEGAMIX**	*Eternal 092CD*	36		1

CORONATION STREET CAST

UK's longest-running TV soap opera

Date	Title	Label	Peak Position	Weeks at No.1	Weeks in Top 40
16 Dec 95	**ALWAYS LOOK ON THE BRIGHT SIDE OF LIFE** — CORONATION STREET CAST FEATURING BILL WADDINGTON	*EMI Premier CDEMS 411*	35		1

CORONETS UK group

Date	Title	Label	Peak Position	Weeks at No.1	Weeks in Top 40
26 Aug 55	**THAT'S HOW A LOVE SONG WAS BORN** — RAY BURNS WITH THE CORONETS	*Columbia DB 3640*	14		6
25 Nov 55	**TWENTY TINY FINGERS**	*Columbia DB 3671*	20		1

BRIANA CORRIGAN UK singer

Date	Title	Label	Peak Position	Weeks at No.1	Weeks in Top 40
11 May 96	**LOVE ME NOW**	*East West EW041CD1*	48		

CORRS Irish group

Date	Title / Label	Peak Position	Weeks at No.1	Weeks in Top 40
17 Feb 96	**RUNAWAY** *Atlantic A 5727CD*	49		
7 Dec 96	**RUNAWAY** *Atlantic A 5727CD*	60		
1 Feb 97	**LOVE TO LOVE YOU/RUNAWAY** *Atlantic A 5621CD*	62		
25 Oct 97	**ONLY WHEN I SLEEP** *Atlantic AT 0015CD*	58		
20 Dec 97	**I NEVER LOVED YOU ANYWAY** *Atlantic AT 0018CD*	43		
28 Mar 98	**WHAT CAN I DO** *Atlantic AT 0029CD*	53		
16 May 98	**DREAMS** *Atlantic AT 0032CD* ○	6		8
29 Aug 98	**WHAT CAN I DO (REMIX)** *Atlantic AT 0044CD* ○	3		7
28 Nov 98	**SO YOUNG** *Atlantic AT 0057CD1*	6		8
27 Feb 99	**RUNAWAY (REMIX)** *Atlantic AT 0062CD* ●	2		9
12 Jun 99	**I KNOW MY LOVE** *RCA Victor 74321670622* CHIEFTAINS FEATURING THE CORRS	37		1
11 Dec 99	**RADIO** *Atlantic AT 0079CD*	18		1
15 Jul 00	**BREATHLESS** *Atlantic AT 0084CD* ○	1	1	9
11 Nov 00	**IRRESISTIBLE** *Atlantic AT 0089CD*	20		1
28 Apr 01	**GIVE ME A REASON** *Atlantic AT 0097CD*	27		1
10 Nov 01	**WOULD YOU BE HAPPIER** *Atlantic AT 0115CD*	14		2
29 May 04	**SUMMER SUNSHINE** *Atlantic AT 0179CD1*	6		5
25 Sep 04	**ANGEL** *Atlantic AT 0182CD*	16		2
18 Dec 04	**LONG NIGHT** *Atlantic AT 0190CD1*	31		1
5 Nov 05	**HEART LIKE A WHEEL/OLD TOWN** *Atlantic ATUK016CD*	68		

CORRUPTED CRU UK group

Date	Title / Label	Peak Position	Weeks at No.1	Weeks in Top 40
2 Mar 02	**GARAGE** *Red Rose CDRROSE 011* CORRUPTED CRU FEATURING MC NEAT	59		

FERRY CORSTEN Dutch DJ/singer

Date	Title / Label	Peak Position	Weeks at No.1	Weeks in Top 40
8 Jun 02	**PUNK** *Positiva CDTIV 173*	29		1
21 Feb 04	**ROCK YOUR BODY ROCK** *Positiva CDTIVS 202*	11		4
10 Jul 04	**IT'S TIME** *Positiva CDTIVS 206*	51		
4 Feb 06	**FIRE** *Positiva CDTIVS229*	40		1
15 Jul 06	**WATCH OUT** *Positiva CDTIVS239*	57		

CORTINA UK producer

Date	Title / Label	Peak Position	Weeks at No.1	Weeks in Top 40
24 Mar 01	**MUSIC IS MOVING** *Nukleuz NUKC 0159*	42		
26 Jan 02	**ERECTION (TAKE IT TO THE TOP)** *Nukleuz NUKCD 0352* CORTINA FEATURING BK & MADAM FRICTION	48		

VLADIMIR COSMA Hungarian orchestra leader

Date	Title / Label	Peak Position	Weeks at No.1	Weeks in Top 40
14 Jul 79	**DAVID'S SONG (MAIN THEME FROM *KIDNAPPED*)** *Decca FR 13841*	64		

COSMIC BABY German producer

Date	Title / Label	Peak Position	Weeks at No.1	Weeks in Top 40
26 Feb 94	**LOOPS OF INFINITY** *Logic 74321191432*	70		

COSMIC GATE German production/remix duo

Date	Title / Label	Peak Position	Weeks at No.1	Weeks in Top 40
4 Aug 01	**FIREWIRE** *Data 24CDS*	9		5
11 May 02	**EXPLORATION OF SPACE** *Data 30CDS*	29		1
25 Jan 03	**THE WAVE/RAGING** *Nebula NEBCD 036*	48		

COSMIC ROUGH RIDERS UK group

Date	Title / Label	Peak Position	Weeks at No.1	Weeks in Top 40
4 Aug 01	**REVOLUTION (IN THE SUMMERTIME)** *Poptones MC 5047SCX*	35		1
29 Sep 01	**THE PAIN INSIDE** *Poptones MC 5052SCX*	36		1
5 Jul 03	**BECAUSE YOU** *Measured MRCOSMIC 002SCX*	34		1
20 Sep 03	**JUSTIFY THE RAIN** *Measured MRCOSMIC 3SC*	39		1

COSMOS US producer

Date	Title / Label	Peak Position	Weeks at No.1	Weeks in Top 40
18 Sep 99	**SUMMER IN SPACE** *Island Blue PFACD 3*	49		
5 Oct 02	**TAKE ME WITH YOU** *Polydor 0659952*	32		1

ANTONY COSTA UK singer

Date	Title / Label	Peak Position	Weeks at No.1	Weeks in Top 40
18 Feb 06	**DO YOU EVER THINK OF ME?** *Globe Records 9877410*	19		1

DON COSTA US orchestra leader

Date	Title / Label	Peak Position	Weeks at No.1	Weeks in Top 40
13 Oct 60	**NEVER ON SUNDAY** *London HLT 9195*	27		4

NIKKA COSTA US singer

Date	Title / Label	Peak Position	Weeks at No.1	Weeks in Top 40
11 Aug 01	**LIKE A FEATHER** *Virgin VUSCD 199*	53		

ELVIS COSTELLO UK singer

Date	Title / Label	Peak Position	Weeks at No.1	Weeks in Top 40
5 Nov 77	**WATCHING THE DETECTIVES** *Stiff BUY 20*	15		10
11 Mar 78	**(I DON'T WANNA GO TO) CHELSEA** *Radar ADA 3* ELVIS COSTELLO & THE ATTRACTIONS	16		8
13 May 78	**PUMP IT UP** *Radar ADA 10* ELVIS COSTELLO & THE ATTRACTIONS	24		7
28 Oct 78	**RADIO RADIO** *Radar ADA 24* ELVIS COSTELLO & THE ATTRACTIONS	29		4
10 Feb 79	**OLIVER'S ARMY** *Radar ADA 31* ELVIS COSTELLO & THE ATTRACTIONS ●	2		10
12 May 79	**ACCIDENTS WILL HAPPEN** *Radar ADA 35* ELVIS COSTELLO & THE ATTRACTIONS	28		4
16 Feb 80	**I CAN'T STAND UP FOR FALLING DOWN** *F. Beat XX 1*	4		6
12 Apr 80	**HI FIDELITY** *F. Beat XX 3*	30		2
7 Jun 80	**NEW AMSTERDAM** *F. Beat XX 5*	36		2
20 Dec 80	**CLUBLAND** *F. Beat XX 12* ELVIS COSTELLO & THE ATTRACTIONS	60		
3 Oct 81	**A GOOD YEAR FOR THE ROSES** *F. Beat XX 17*	6		8
12 Dec 81	**SWEET DREAMS** *F. Beat XX 19*	42		
10 Apr 82	**I'M YOUR TOY** *F. Beat XX 21* ELVIS COSTELLO & THE ATTRACTIONS WITH THE ROYAL PHILHARMONIC ORCHESTRA	51		
19 Jun 82	**YOU LITTLE FOOL** *F. Beat XX 26*	52		
31 Jul 82	**MAN OUT OF TIME** *F. Beat XX 28*	58		
25 Sep 82	**FROM HEAD TO TOE** *F. Beat XX 30*	43		
11 Dec 82	**PARTY PARTY** *A&M AMS 8267* ELVIS COSTELLO & THE ATTRACTIONS WITH THE ROYAL HORN GUARDS	48		
11 Jun 83	**PILLS AND SOAP** *Imp 001* IMPOSTER	16		3
9 Jul 83	**EVERYDAY I WRITE THE BOOK** *F. Beat XX 32*	28		6
17 Sep 83	**LET THEM ALL TALK** *F. Beat XX 33*	59		
28 Apr 84	**PEACE IN OUR TIME** *Imposter TRUCE 1* IMPOSTER	48		
16 Jun 84	**I WANNA BE LOVED/TURNING THE TOWN RED** *F. Beat XX 35*	25		5
25 Aug 84	**THE ONLY FLAME IN TOWN** *F. Beat XX 37*	71		
4 May 85	**GREEN SHIRT** *F. Beat ZB 40085*	68		
1 Feb 86	**DON'T LET ME BE MISUNDERSTOOD** *F. Beat ZB 40555* COSTELLO SHOW FEATURING THE CONFEDERATES	33		3
30 Aug 86	**TOKYO STORM WARNING** *Imp 007*	73		
4 Mar 89	**VERONICA** *Warner Brothers W 7558*	31		3
20 May 89	**BABY PLAYS AROUND (EP)** *Warner Brothers W 2949*	65		
4 May 91	**THE OTHER SIDE OF SUMMER** *Warner Brothers W 0025*	43		
5 Mar 94	**SULKY GIRL** *Warner Brothers W 0234CD* ELVIS COSTELLO & THE ATTRACTIONS	22		2
30 Apr 94	**13 STEPS LEAD DOWN** *Warner Brothers W 0245CD* ELVIS COSTELLO & THE ATTRACTIONS	59		
26 Nov 94	**LONDON'S BRILLIANT PARADE** *Warner Brothers W 0270CD1* ELVIS COSTELLO & THE ATTRACTIONS	48		
11 May 96	**IT'S TIME** *Warner Brothers W 0348CD* ELVIS COSTELLO & THE ATTRACTIONS	58		
1 May 99	**TOLEDO** *Mercury 8709652* ELVIS COSTELLO/BURT BACHARACH	72		
31 Jul 99	**SHE** *Mercury MERDD 521*	19		2
20 Apr 02	**TEAR OFF YOUR OWN HEAD** *Mercury 5828872*	58		

BILLY COTTON & HIS BAND UK orchestra leader

Date	Title / Label	Peak Position	Weeks at No.1	Weeks in Top 40
1 May 53	**IN A GOLDEN COACH** *Decca F 10058* BILLY COTTON & HIS BAND, VOCALS BY DOREEN STEPHENS	3		10
18 Dec 53	**I SAW MOMMY KISSING SANTA CLAUS** *Decca F 10206* BILLY COTTON & HIS BAND, VOCALS BY THE MILL GIRLS & THE BANDITS	11		3
30 Apr 54	**FRIENDS AND NEIGHBOURS** *Decca F 10299* BILLY COTTON & HIS BAND, VOCALS BY THE BANDITS	3		12

MIKE COTTON'S JAZZMEN UK group

Date	Title / Label	Peak Position	Weeks at No.1	Weeks in Top 40
20 Jun 63	**SWING THAT HAMMER** *Columbia DB 7029*	36		2

COUGARS UK instrumental group

Date	Title / Label	Peak Position	Weeks at No.1	Weeks in Top 40
28 Feb 63	**SATURDAY NITE AT THE DUCK POND** *Parlophone R 4989*	33		3

COUNCIL COLLECTIVE UK/US charity ensemble

Date	Title / Label	Peak Position	Weeks at No.1	Weeks in Top 40
22 Dec 84	**SOUL DEEP (PART 1)** *Polydor MINE 1*	24		4

Silver-selling · Gold-selling · Platinum-selling · US No.1 ★ · Peak Position · Weeks at No.1 · Weeks in Top 40

COUNT INDIGO UK singer

Date	Title / Label	Peak Position	Weeks at No.1	Weeks in Top 40
9 Mar 96	**MY UNKNOWN LOVE** *Cowboy RODEO 952CD*	59		

COUNTING CROWS US group

Date	Title / Label	Peak Position	Weeks at No.1	Weeks in Top 40
30 Apr 94	**MR JONES** *Geffen GFSTD 69*	28		1
9 Jul 94	**ROUND HERE** *Geffen GFSTD 74*	70		
15 Oct 94	**RAIN KING** *Geffen GFSTD 82*	49		
19 Oct 96	**ANGELS OF THE SILENCES** *Geffen GFSTD 22182*	41		
14 Dec 96	**A LONG DECEMBER** *Geffen GFSTD 22190*	62		
31 May 97	**DAYLIGHT FADING** *Geffen GFSTD 22247*	54		
20 Dec 97	**A LONG DECEMBER** *Geffen GFSTD 22190*	68		
30 Oct 99	**HANGINAROUND** *Geffen 4971842*	46		
29 Jun 02	**AMERICAN GIRLS** *Geffen 4977452*	33		1
15 Feb 03	**BIG YELLOW TAXI** *Geffen 4978492* COUNTING CROWS FEATURING VANESSA CARLTON	16		5
21 Jun 03	**IF I COULD GIVE YOU ALL MY LOVE** *Geffen GED 9806831*	50		
27 Mar 04	**HANGINAROUND** *Geffen 9861994*	68		
24 Jul 04	**ACCIDENTLY IN LOVE** *DreamWorks 9862881*	28		2

COUNTRYMEN UK group

Date	Title / Label	Peak Position	Weeks at No.1	Weeks in Top 40
3 May 62	**I KNOW WHERE I'M GOING** *Piccadilly 7N 35029*	45		

COURSE Dutch production group

Date	Title / Label	Peak Position	Weeks at No.1	Weeks in Top 40
19 Apr 97	**READY OR NOT** *The Brothers Organisation CDBRUV 2*	5		5
5 Jul 97	**AIN'T NOBODY** *The Brothers Organisation CDBRUV 3*	8		4
20 Dec 97	**BEST LOVE** *The Brothers Organisation CDBRUV 6*	51		

COURTEENERS UK group

Date	Title / Label	Peak Position	Weeks at No.1	Weeks in Top 40
3 Nov 07	**ACRYLIC** *A&M 1749715*	44		
26 Jan 08	**WHAT TOOK YOU SO LONG** *A&M 1756917*	20		1

MICHAEL COURTNEY UK singer

Date	Title / Label	Peak Position	Weeks at No.1	Weeks in Top 40
4 May 02	**CHIRPY CHIRPY CHEEP CHEEP/JAGGED EDGE** *Nap Music SLCPCD 001*	64		

TINA COUSINS UK singer

Date	Title / Label	Peak Position	Weeks at No.1	Weeks in Top 40
15 Aug 98	**MYSTERIOUS TIMES** *Multiply CDMULTY 40* SASH! FEATURING TINA COUSINS	2		8
21 Nov 98	**PRAY** *Jive 0519162*	20		2
27 Mar 99	**KILLIN' TIME** *Jive/Eastern Bloc 0519232*	15		3
10 Apr 99	**THANK ABBA FOR THE MUSIC** *Epic ABCD1* STEPS, TINA COUSINS, CLEOPATRA, B*WITCHED, BILLIE	4		11
10 Jul 99	**FOREVER** *Jive 0519332*	45		
9 Oct 99	**ANGEL** *Ebul/Jive 0519432*	46		
10 Dec 05	**WONDERFUL LIFE** *All Around The World CDGLOBE472*	58		

DON COVAY US singer

Date	Title / Label	Peak Position	Weeks at No.1	Weeks in Top 40
7 Sep 74	**IT'S BETTER TO HAVE (AND DON'T NEED)** *Mercury 6052 634*	29		4

COVENTRY CITY CUP FINAL SQUAD

UK football club

Date	Title / Label	Peak Position	Weeks at No.1	Weeks in Top 40
23 May 87	**GO FOR IT!** *Sky Blue SKB 1*	61		

COVER GIRLS US group

Date	Title / Label	Peak Position	Weeks at No.1	Weeks in Top 40
1 Aug 92	**WISHING ON A STAR** *Epic 6581437*	38		1

DAVID COVERDALE & WHITESNAKE

UK group

Date	Title / Label	Peak Position	Weeks at No.1	Weeks in Top 40
7 Jun 97	**TOO MANY TEARS** *EMI CDEM 471*	46		

COVERDALE PAGE UK duo

Date	Title / Label	Peak Position	Weeks at No.1	Weeks in Top 40
3 Jul 93	**TAKE ME FOR A LITTLE WHILE** *EMI CDEM 270*	29		1
23 Oct 93	**TAKE A LOOK AT YOURSELF** *EMI CDEM 279*	43		

JULIE COVINGTON UK singer

Date	Title / Label	Peak Position	Weeks at No.1	Weeks in Top 40
25 Dec 76	**DON'T CRY FOR ME ARGENTINA** *MCA 260*	1	1	15
3 Dec 77	**ONLY WOMEN BLEED** *Virgin VS 196*	12		10
15 Jul 78	**DON'T CRY FOR ME ARGENTINA** *MCA 260*	63		
21 May 77	**O.K.?** *Polydor 2001 714* JULIE COVINGTON, RULA LENSKA, CHARLOTTE CORNWELL & SUE JONES-DAVIES	10		5

CARL COX UK producer

Date	Title / Label	Peak Position	Weeks at No.1	Weeks in Top 40
28 Sep 91	**I WANT YOU (FOREVER)** *Perfecto PB 44885* DJ CARL COX	23		4
8 Aug 92	**DOES IT FEEL GOOD TO YOU** *Perfecto 74321102877* DJ CARL COX	35		1
6 Nov 93	**THE PLANET OF LOVE** *Perfecto 74321161772* CARL COX CONCEPT	44		
9 Mar 96	**TWO PAINTINGS AND A DRUM** *Edel 0090715 COX*	24		1
8 Jun 96	**SENSUAL SOPHIS-TI-CAT/THE PLAYER** *Ultimatum 0090875 COX*	25		1
12 Dec 98	**THE LATIN THEME** *Edel 0091685 COX*	52		
22 May 99	**PHUTURE 2000** *Worldwide Ultimatum 0091715 COX*	40		1

DEBORAH COX Canadian singer

Date	Title / Label	Peak Position	Weeks at No.1	Weeks in Top 40
11 Nov 95	**SENTIMENTAL** *Arista 74321324962*	34		1
24 Feb 96	**WHO DO U LOVE** *Arista 74321337942*	31		1
31 Jul 99	**IT'S OVER NOW** *Arista 74321686942*	49		
9 Oct 99	**NOBODY'S SUPPOSED TO BE HERE** *Arista 74321702102*	55		

MICHAEL COX UK singer

Date	Title / Label	Peak Position	Weeks at No.1	Weeks in Top 40
9 Jun 60	**ANGELA JONES** *Triumph RGM 1011*	7		13
20 Oct 60	**ALONG CAME CAROLINE** *HMV POP 789*	41		

PETER COX UK singer

Date	Title / Label	Peak Position	Weeks at No.1	Weeks in Top 40
2 Aug 97	**AIN'T GONNA CRY AGAIN** *Chrysalis CDCHS 5056*	37		1
15 Nov 97	**IF YOU WALK AWAY** *Chrysalis CDCHSS 5069*	24		1
20 Jun 98	**WHAT A FOOL BELIEVES** *Chrysalis CDCHS 5089*	39		1

GRAHAM COXON UK guitarist/singer

Date	Title / Label	Peak Position	Weeks at No.1	Weeks in Top 40
20 Mar 04	**FREAKIN' OUT** *Transcopic R 6632*	37		1
15 May 04	**BITTERSWEET BUNDLE OF MAN** *Transcopic CDRS 6637*	22		1
7 Aug 04	**SPECTACULAR** *Transcopic CDRS 6643*	32		1
6 Nov 04	**FREAKIN' OUT/ALL OVER ME** *Transcopic CDRS6652*	19		2
11 Mar 06	**STANDING ON MY OWN AGAIN** *Parlophone CDR6681*	20		1
20 May 06	**YOU & I** *Parlophone CDRS6691*	39		1
21 Jul 07	**THIS OLD TOWN** *Download* PAUL WELLER & GRAHAM COXON	39		1

CRACKER US group

Date	Title / Label	Peak Position	Weeks at No.1	Weeks in Top 40
28 May 94	**LOW** *Virgin America VUSDG 80*	43		
23 Jul 94	**GET OFF THIS** *Virgin America VUSCD 83*	41		
3 Dec 94	**LOW** *Virgin America VUSDG 80*	54		

SARAH CRACKNELL UK singer

Date	Title / Label	Peak Position	Weeks at No.1	Weeks in Top 40
14 Sep 96	**ANYMORE** *Gut CDGUT 3*	39		1
9 Feb 08	**THE JOURNEY CONTINUES** *Download* MARK BROWN FEATURING SARAH CRACKNELL	11		4

CRACKOUT UK group

Date	Title / Label	Peak Position	Weeks at No.1	Weeks in Top 40
22 Jun 02	**I AM THE ONE** *Hut HUTCD 156*	72		
9 Aug 03	**OUT OF OUR MINDS** *Hut HUTCD 170*	63		
13 Mar 04	**THIS IS WHAT WE DO** *Hut HUTCD174*	65		

CRADLE OF FILTH UK group

Date	Title / Label	Peak Position	Weeks at No.1	Weeks in Top 40
15 Mar 03	**BABYLON A.D. (SO GLAD FOR THE MADNESS)** *Epic 6735549*	35		1

CRAIG UK singer

Date	Title / Label	Peak Position	Weeks at No.1	Weeks in Top 40
23 Dec 00	**AT THIS TIME OF YEAR** *WEA 321CD*	14		3

SIMON COWELL

If reality TV audition shows have peeled back the mystique of the music business, then they have also given us a new generation of stars who might previously have been 'behind the scenes': enter Simon Cowell, one of the most powerful and recognisable faces in entertainment.

Of course, before the global fame, Simon Cowell was initially simply an A&R (artist-and-repertoire) man at a major record label. He was born into a family regarded as part of the social elite in the wealthy commuter belt of Elstree, Hertfordshire. His mother was a former ballet dancer and his father a successful property developer and music business executive (Cowell's younger brother is also now a millionaire developer).

Cowell did not go to university, instead choosing a series of odd jobs before landing in the mail room at EMI, where his father was an executive. He quickly bagged a junior position in the A&R department as an assistant and that, looking back, was the moment the UK record industry changed.

In the early 1980s, he set up his own independent record label, but that came to an end after only a year. Undeterred, following a further spell at EMI, he became involved with Fanfare Records and enjoyed several pop hits including the half-million selling 'So Macho' by Sinitta. Huge collaborations with the production team of Stock Aitken Waterman further boosted his success. But due to circumstances entirely beyond his control, this label also began to limp when a parent company ran into financial difficulties, and suddenly Cowell landed with a bump back at his parents' home, virtually broke and effectively back to square one.

Once more he clocked on in the record industry, this time as an A&R consultant for BMG and this is when he began his inexorable rise towards being ranked twenty-first on the 2007 *Forbes* Celebrity 100 Power List. Over time, Cowell clawed his way up the ranks via a combination of gruelling work hours and genuine hit-making, bringing the public an endless list of pop hits by artists such as Curiosity Killed The Cat, Sonia, 5ive, Robson & Jerome and, the biggest of them all, Westlife. He is often criticised for his role in the creation of novelty hits – such the Teletubbies, the World Wrestling Federation and Mighty Morphin Power Rangers – but Cowell was being paid to make his label money and children's songs such as these certainly did that.

However, it is perhaps for his role as a judge on various talent shows that Cowell will for ever be remembered. Initially, it was *Pop Idol* in 2001 where his caustic wit and cutting (yet usually correct) observations regularly reduced young hopefuls to tears. It's pure pantomime every time he says his signature phrase, 'I don't mean to be rude, but ...'; however, an objective critic will usually back up his comments with alarming regularity.

After this, Cowell produced his own show, *The X Factor*, then began a love affair with the US when he launched *American Idol*, becoming a household name from the very first season. His white-toothed smile and immaculate clothes play up to his reputation – when he appeared on BBC Radio 4's *Desert Island Discs* in 2006, he was allowed to pick a book and a luxury item along with his eight records – he asked for *Hollywood Wives* by Jackie Collins and a mirror.

His UK-based media and entertainment company, Syco Records, has become one of the most powerful businesses in world media, courtesy of several factors: Cowell's involvement with the artists he finds on his reality TV shows (whose debut releases invariably sell many millions of copies); new acts such as the multi-platinum selling Il Divo, the logical fusion of pop and opera; and other successful audition show franchises such as *Britain/America's Got Talent* (now in over 100 countries); *American Inventor*, *Cupid*; *Grease Is The Word*; and *Celebrity Duets*.

It's all too easy to mock and say that the higher the waistband, the lower the standard, but if you actually look at the facts, that just isn't true. Simon Cowell undeniably has an ear for a hit; he *knows* what the public wants to buy. He has been involved with seventy Number 1 hits in the US and UK and sold over 150 million records. For every Zig And Zag there is a Leona Lewis; for every Robson & Jerome there's an Il Divo.

Known to be supremely astute with people, Cowell relentlessly charms the bands he wants to work with. Insiders tell us that during a meeting he will look each and every person in the room in the eye, making each individual feel special – watch the next series of *The X Factor* and you will see a little nod, a quiet wink, some warm gesture to keep the spirits lifted and his connection with the artist alive.

Cowell is a true modern icon: in 2006, he was voted the tenth most terrifying celebrity on television; he has mansions in the UK and US; he adores fast and luxurious cars – the highlight of his extensive collection is the $1 million Bugatti Veyron (the fastest production car ever built) and for many months he was the fastest celebrity on *Top Gear*'s 'Star in a Reasonably Priced Car' segment. On a more subdued note, Cowell is a prodigious charity fundraiser and frequently invites sick children backstage to the screenings of *The X Factor*.

He is often parodied in the media and has appeared in such shows as *The Simpsons* and *Scary Movie 3* (where he judges a rap battle and gets shot), and the figures about his worth and fortune just keep getting more staggering. His wealth is said to stand at around £150 million with an annual salary likely to be in the region of £60 million – we know this because in 2006 his tax bill was reported to be over £20 million. *American Idol* alone is said to pay him £20 million per season ...

Not bad for a former mailboy who once ran a record label out of a converted gentleman's washroom in an NCP car park in London.

Silver-selling ○ Gold-selling ● Platinum-selling US No.1 ★

FLOYD CRAMER US pianist

Date	Title	Label	Peak Position	Weeks at No.1	Weeks in Top 40
13 Apr 61	**ON THE REBOUND**	*RCA 1231*	1	1	13
20 Jul 61	**SAN ANTONIO ROSE**	*RCA 1241*	36		3
23 Aug 62	**HOT PEPPER**	*RCA 1301*	46		

CRAMPS US group

Date	Title	Label	Peak Position	Weeks at No.1	Weeks in Top 40
9 Nov 85	**CAN YOUR PUSSY DO THE DOG?**	*Big Beat NS 110*	68		
10 Feb 90	**BIKINI GIRLS WITH MACHINE GUNS**	*Enigma ENV 17*	35		1

CRANBERRIES Irish group

Date	Title	Label	Peak Position	Weeks at No.1	Weeks in Top 40
27 Feb 93	**LINGER**	*Island CID 556*	74		
12 Feb 94	**LINGER**	*Island CID 559*	14		10
7 May 94	**DREAMS**	*Island CIDX 594*	27		4
1 Oct 94	**ZOMBIE**	*Island CID 600*	14		5
3 Dec 94	**ODE TO MY FAMILY**	*Island CIDX 601*	26		1
11 Mar 95	**I CAN'T BE WITH YOU**	*Island CIDX 605*	23		3
12 Aug 95	**RIDICULOUS THOUGHTS**	*Island CID 616*	20		1
20 Apr 96	**SALVATION**	*Island CID 633*	13		2
13 Jul 96	**FREE TO DECIDE**	*Instant CIDX 637*	33		2
17 Apr 99	**PROMISES**	*Island US 5725912*	13		3
17 Jul 99	**ANIMAL INSTINCT**	*Island US 5621972*	54		

LES CRANE US singer

Date	Title	Label	Peak Position	Weeks at No.1	Weeks in Top 40
19 Feb 72	**DESIDERATA**	*Warner Brothers K 16119*	7		11

CRANES UK group

Date	Title	Label	Peak Position	Weeks at No.1	Weeks in Top 40
25 Sep 93	**JEWEL**	*Dedicated CRANE 007CD*	29		1
3 Sep 94	**SHINING ROAD**	*Dedicated CRANE 008CD1*	57		

CRASH TEST DUMMIES Canadian group

Date	Title	Label	Peak Position	Weeks at No.1	Weeks in Top 40
23 Apr 94	**MMM MMM MMM MMM**	*RCA 74321201512* ○	2		8
16 Jul 94	**AFTERNOONS & COFFEESPOONS**	*RCA 74321219622*	23		3
15 Apr 95	**THE BALLAD OF PETER PUMPKINHEAD**	*RCA 74321276772*			
	CRASH TEST DUMMIES FEATURING ELLEN REID		30		2

BEVERLEY CRAVEN UK singer/pianist

Date	Title	Label	Peak Position	Weeks at No.1	Weeks in Top 40
20 Apr 91	**PROMISE ME**	*Epic 6559437* ○	3		10
20 Jul 91	**HOLDING ON**	*Epic 6565507*	32		4
5 Oct 91	**WOMAN TO WOMAN**	*Epic 6574647*	40		1
7 Dec 91	**MEMORIES**	*Epic 6576617*	68		
25 Sep 93	**LOVE SCENES**	*Epic 6595952*	34		1
20 Nov 93	**MOLLIE'S SONG**	*Epic 6598132*	61		

BILLY CRAWFORD US singer

Date	Title	Label	Peak Position	Weeks at No.1	Weeks in Top 40
10 Oct 98	**URGENTLY IN LOVE**	*V2 VVR 5003063*	48		
3 May 03	**YOU DIDN'T EXPECT THAT**	*V2 VVR 5022083*	35		1
30 Aug 03	**TRACKIN'**	*V2 VVR 5023108*	32		1

JIMMY CRAWFORD UK singer

Date	Title	Label	Peak Position	Weeks at No.1	Weeks in Top 40
8 Jun 61	**LOVE OR MONEY**	*Columbia DB 4633*	49		
16 Nov 61	**I LOVE HOW YOU LOVE ME**	*Columbia DB 4717*	18		7

MICHAEL CRAWFORD UK actor

Date	Title	Label	Peak Position	Weeks at No.1	Weeks in Top 40
10 Jan 87	**THE MUSIC OF THE NIGHT**	*Polydor POSP 803*	7		6
15 Jan 94	**THE MUSIC OF THE NIGHT**	*Columbia 6597382*			
	BARBRA STREISAND (DUET WITH MICHAEL CRAWFORD)		54		

RANDY CRAWFORD US singer

Date	Title	Label	Peak Position	Weeks at No.1	Weeks in Top 40
21 Jun 80	**LAST NIGHT AT DANCELAND**	*Warner Brothers K 17631*	61		
30 Aug 80	**ONE DAY I'LL FLY AWAY**	*Warner Brothers K 17680* ○	2		8
20 May 81	**YOU MIGHT NEED SOMEBODY**	*Warner Brothers K 17803*	11		9
8 Aug 81	**RAINY NIGHT IN GEORGIA**	*Warner Brothers K 17840*	18		8
31 Oct 81	**SECRET COMBINATION**	*Warner Brothers K 17872*	48		
30 Jan 82	**IMAGINE**	*Warner Brothers K 17906*	60		
5 Jun 82	**ONE HELLO**	*Warner Brothers K 17948*	48		
19 Feb 83	**HE REMINDS ME**	*Warner Brothers K 17970*	65		
8 Oct 83	**NIGHT LINE**	*Warner Brothers W 9530*	51		
29 Nov 86	**ALMAZ**	*Warner Brothers W 8583*	4		8
18 Jan 92	**DIAMANTE**	*London LON 313*			
	ZUCCHERO WITH RANDY CRAWFORD		44		
15 Nov 97	**GIVE ME THE NIGHT**	*WEA 142CD*	60		

ROBERT CRAY US blues guitarist

Date	Title	Label	Peak Position	Weeks at No.1	Weeks in Top 40
20 Jun 87	**RIGHT NEXT DOOR (BECAUSE OF ME)**	*Mercury CRAY 3*			
	ROBERT CRAY BAND		50		
20 Apr 96	**BABY LEE**	*Silvertone ORECD 81*			
	JOHN LEE HOOKER WITH ROBERT CRAY		65		

CRAZY ELEPHANT US group

Date	Title	Label	Peak Position	Weeks at No.1	Weeks in Top 40
21 May 69	**GIMME GIMME GOOD LOVIN'**	*Major Minor MM 609*	12		13

CRAZY FROG US group

Date	Title	Label	Peak Position	Weeks at No.1	Weeks in Top 40
4 Jun 05	**AXEL F**	*Gusto CDGUS17* ●	1	4	13
3 Sep 05	**POPCORN**	*Gusto CDGUS21*	12		4
24 Dec 05	**JINGLE BELLS/U CAN'T TOUCH THIS**	*Gut CDGUS27*	5		4
10 Jun 06	**WE ARE THE CHAMPIONS**	*Gut CDGUS41*	11		3
23 Dec 06	**LAST CHRISTMAS**	*Tug CDSNOG17*	16		2

CRAZY TOWN US group

Date	Title	Label	Peak Position	Weeks at No.1	Weeks in Top 40
7 Apr 01	**BUTTERFLY**	*Columbia 6710012* ○ ★	3		11
11 Aug 01	**REVOLVING DOOR**	*Columbia 6714942*	23		3
30 Nov 02	**DROWNING**	*Columbia 6733262*	50		

CRAZYHEAD UK group

Date	Title	Label	Peak Position	Weeks at No.1	Weeks in Top 40
16 Jul 88	**TIME HAS TAKEN ITS TOLL ON YOU**	*Food 12*	65		
25 Feb 89	**HAVE LOVE WILL TRAVEL (EP)**	*Food SGE 2025*	68		

CREAM UK group

Date	Title	Label	Peak Position	Weeks at No.1	Weeks in Top 40
20 Oct 66	**WRAPPING PAPER**	*Reaction 591 007*	34		3
15 Dec 66	**I FEEL FREE**	*Reaction 591 011*	11		10
8 Jun 67	**STRANGE BREW**	*Reaction 591 015*	17		8
5 Jun 68	**ANYONE FOR TENNIS (THE SAVAGE SEVEN THEME)**	*Polydor 56 258*	40		1
9 Oct 68	**SUNSHINE OF YOUR LOVE**	*Polydor 56 286*	25		6
15 Jan 69	**WHITE ROOM**	*Polydor 56 300*	28		6
9 Apr 69	**BADGE**	*Polydor 56 315*	18		9
28 Oct 72	**BADGE**	*Polydor 2058 285*	42		
26 Nov 05	**SUNSHINE OF YOUR LOVE**	*Manifesto 9874942*			
	CREAM VS HOXTONS		46		

CREATION UK group

Date	Title	Label	Peak Position	Weeks at No.1	Weeks in Top 40
7 Jul 66	**MAKING TIME**	*Planet PLF 116*	49		
3 Nov 66	**PAINTER MAN**	*Planet PLF 119*	36		2

CREATURES UK duo

Date	Title	Label	Peak Position	Weeks at No.1	Weeks in Top 40
3 Oct 81	**MAD EYED SCREAMER**	*Polydor POSPD 354*	24		6
23 Apr 83	**MISS THE GIRL**	*Wonderland SHE 1*	21		4
16 Jul 83	**RIGHT NOW**	*Wonderland SHE 2*	14		7
14 Oct 89	**STANDING HERE**	*Wonderland SHE 17*	53		
27 Mar 99	**SAY**	*Sioux 6CD*	72		
25 Oct 03	**GODZILLA**	*Sioux 14CD3*	53		

CREDIT TO THE NATION UK group

Date	Title	Label	Peak Position	Weeks at No.1	Weeks in Top 40
22 May 93	**CALL IT WHAT YOU WANT**	*One Little Indian 94 TP7CD*	57		
18 Sep 93	**ENOUGH IS ENOUGH**	*One Little Indian 79 TP7CD*			
	CHUMBAWAMBA & CREDIT TO THE NATION		56		
12 Mar 94	**TEENAGE SENSATION**	*One Little Indian 124 TP7DC*	24		1
14 May 94	**SOWING THE SEEDS OF HATRED**	*One Little Indian 134 TP7DC*	72		
22 Jul 95	**LIAR LIAR**	*One Little Indian 144 TP7DC*	60		
12 Sep 98	**TACKY LOVE SONG**	*Chrysalis CDCHS 5097*	60		

CREED US group

Date	Title	Label	Peak Position	Weeks at No.1	Weeks in Top 40
15 Jan 00	**HIGHER**	*Epic 6683152*	47		
20 Jan 01	**WITH ARMS WIDE OPEN**	*Epic 6706952* ★	13		3
29 Sep 01	**HIGHER**	*Epic 6710642*	64		
16 Mar 02	**MY SACRIFICE**	*Epic 6723162*	18		3
3 Aug 02	**ONE LAST BREATH/BULLETS**	*Epic 6728262*	47		

CREEDENCE CLEARWATER REVIVAL
US group

Date	Title / Label	Peak Position	Weeks at No.1	Weeks in Top 40
28 May 69	**PROUD MARY** *Liberty LBF 15223*	8		13
16 Aug 69	**BAD MOON RISING** *Liberty LBF 15230*	1	3	13
15 Nov 69	**GREEN RIVER** *Liberty LBF 15250*	19		9
14 Feb 70	**DOWN ON THE CORNER** *Liberty LBF 15283*	31		5
4 Apr 70	**TRAVELLIN' BAND** *Liberty LBF 15310*	8		11
20 Jun 70	**UP AROUND THE BEND** *Liberty LBF 15354*	3		10
5 Sep 70	**LONG AS I CAN SEE THE LIGHT** *Liberty LBF 15384*	20		8
20 Mar 71	**HAVE YOU EVER SEEN THE RAIN** *Liberty LBF 15440*	36		3
24 Jul 71	**SWEET HITCH-HIKER** *United Artists UP 35261*	36		4
2 May 92	**BAD MOON RISING** *Epic 6580047*	71		

KID CREOLE & THE COCONUTS
US group

Date	Title / Label	Peak Position	Weeks at No.1	Weeks in Top 40
13 Jun 81	**ME NO POP I** *Ze WIP 6711* KID CREOLE & THE COCONUTS PRESENTS COATI MUNDI	32		3
15 May 82	**I'M A WONDERFUL THING, BABY** *Ze WIP 6756*	4		8
24 Jul 82	**STOOL PIGEON** *Ze WIP 6793*	7		7
9 Oct 82	**ANNIE I'M NOT YOUR DADDY** *Ze WIP 6801*	2		7
11 Dec 82	**DEAR ADDY** *Ze WIP 6840*	29		5
10 Sep 83	**THERE'S SOMETHING WRONG IN PARADISE** *Island IS 130*	35		3
19 Nov 83	**THE LIFEBOAT PARTY** *Island IS 142*	49		
14 Apr 90	**THE SEX OF IT** *CBS 6556987*	29		2
10 Apr 93	**I'M A WONDERFUL THING, BABY (REMIX)** *Island CID 551*	60		

CRESCENDO
UK/US duo

Date	Title / Label	Peak Position	Weeks at No.1	Weeks in Top 40
23 Dec 95	**ARE YOU OUT THERE** *ffrr FCD 270*	20		3

CRESCENT
UK group

Date	Title / Label	Peak Position	Weeks at No.1	Weeks in Top 40
18 May 02	**ON THE RUN** *Hut HUTCD 153*	49		
27 Jul 02	**TEST OF TIME** *Hut HUTCD 157*	60		
28 Sep 02	**SPINNIN' WHEELS** *Hut HUTDX 160*	61		

CREW CUTS
Canadian group

Date	Title / Label	Peak Position	Weeks at No.1	Weeks in Top 40
1 Oct 54	**SH-BOOM** *Mercury MB 3140* ★	12		9
15 Apr 55	**EARTH ANGEL** *Mercury MB 3202*	4		20

BERNARD CRIBBINS
UK comedian

Date	Title / Label	Peak Position	Weeks at No.1	Weeks in Top 40
15 Feb 62	**HOLE IN THE GROUND** *Parlophone R 4869*	9		13
5 Jul 62	**RIGHT SAID FRED** *Parlophone R 4923*	10		8
13 Dec 62	**GOSSIP CALYPSO** *Parlophone R 4961*	25		5

CRIBS
UK group

Date	Title / Label	Peak Position	Weeks at No.1	Weeks in Top 40
6 Mar 04	**YOU WERE ALWAYS THE ONE** *Wichita WEBB059SCD*	66		
29 May 04	**WHAT ABOUT ME** *Wichita WEBB061SCD*	75		
30 Apr 05	**HEY SCENESTERS!** *Wichita WEBB074SCD*	27		1
25 Jun 05	**MIRROR KISSERS** *Wichita WEBB080SCD*	27		1
3 Sep 05	**MARTELL** *Wichita WEBB092SCD*	39		1
17 Dec 05	**YOU'RE GONNA LOSE US** *Wichita WEBB097SCD*	30		1
26 May 07	**MEN'S NEEDS** *Wichita WEBB124SCD*	17		2
11 Aug 07	**MOVING PICTURES** *Wichita WEBB128SCD*	38		1
10 Nov 07	**DON'T YOU WANNA BE RELEVANT?** *Wichita WEBB156SCD*	39		1

CRICKETS
US group

Date	Title / Label	Peak Position	Weeks at No.1	Weeks in Top 40
27 Sep 57	**THAT'LL BE THE DAY** *Vogue Coral Q 72279* ★	1	3	15
27 Dec 57	**OH BOY** *Coral Q 72298*	3		15
14 Mar 58	**MAYBE BABY** *Coral Q 72307*	4		10
25 Jul 58	**THINK IT OVER** *Coral Q 72329*	11		7
24 Apr 59	**LOVE'S MADE A FOOL OF YOU** *Coral Q 72365*	26		2
15 Jan 60	**WHEN YOU ASK ABOUT LOVE** *Coral Q 72382*	27		1
12 May 60	**MORE THAN I CAN SAY** *Coral Q 72395*	42		
26 May 60	**BABY MY HEART** *Coral Q 72395*	33		2
21 Jun 62	**DON'T EVER CHANGE** *Liberty LIB 55441*	5		13
24 Jan 63	**MY LITTLE GIRL** *Liberty LIB 10067*	17		8
6 Jun 63	**DON'T TRY TO CHANGE ME** *Liberty LIB 10092*	37		1
14 May 64	**YOU'VE GOT LOVE** *Coral Q 72472* BUDDY HOLLY & THE CRICKETS	40		1
2 Jul 64	**(THEY CALL HER) LA BAMBA** *Liberty LIB 55696*	21		6

CRIMEA
Irish group

Date	Title / Label	Peak Position	Weeks at No.1	Weeks in Top 40
21 Jan 06	**LOTTERY WINNERS ON ACID** *Warner Brothers W698CD1*	31		1
22 Apr 06	**WHITE RUSSIAN GALAXY** *Warner Brothers W708CD1*	51		

CRISPY & COMPANY
US group

Date	Title / Label	Peak Position	Weeks at No.1	Weeks in Top 40
16 Aug 75	**BRAZIL** *Creole CR 109*	26		4
27 Dec 75	**GET IT TOGETHER** *Creole CR 114*	21		6

CRITTERS
US group

Date	Title / Label	Peak Position	Weeks at No.1	Weeks in Top 40
30 Jun 66	**YOUNGER GIRL** *London HL 10047*	38		1

TONY CROMBIE & HIS ROCKETS
UK drummer

Date	Title / Label	Peak Position	Weeks at No.1	Weeks in Top 40
19 Oct 56	**TEACH YOU TO ROCK/SHORT'NIN' BREAD** *Columbia DB 3822*	25		2

BING CROSBY
US singer/actor

Date	Title / Label	Peak Position	Weeks at No.1	Weeks in Top 40
14 Nov 52	**ISLE OF INNISFREE** *Brunswick 04900*	3		12
5 Dec 52	**ZING A LITTLE ZONG** *Brunswick 04981* BING CROSBY & JANE WYMAN	10		2
19 Dec 52	**SILENT NIGHT** *Brunswick 03929*	8		2
19 Mar 54	**CHANGING PARTNERS** *Brunswick 05244*	9		3
7 Jan 55	**COUNT YOUR BLESSINGS** *Brunswick 05339*	11		3
29 Apr 55	**STRANGER IN PARADISE** *Brunswick 05410*	17		2
27 Apr 56	**IN A LITTLE SPANISH TOWN** *Brunswick 05543*	22		3
23 Nov 56	**TRUE LOVE** *Capitol CL 14645* BING CROSBY & GRACE KELLY	4		27
24 May 57	**AROUND THE WORLD** *Brunswick 05674*	5		15
9 Aug 75	**THAT'S WHAT LIFE IS ALL ABOUT** *United Artists UP 35852*	41		
3 Dec 77	**WHITE CHRISTMAS** *MCA 111*	5		6
27 Nov 82	**PEACE ON EARTH - LITTLE DRUMMER BOY** *RCA BOW 12* DAVID BOWIE & BING CROSBY	3		6
17 Dec 83	**TRUE LOVE** *Capitol CL 315* BING CROSBY & GRACE KELLY	70		
21 Dec 85	**WHITE CHRISTMAS** *MCA BING 1*	69		
19 Dec 98	**WHITE CHRISTMAS** *MCA MCSTD 48105*	29		3
15 Dec 07	**WHITE CHRISTMAS** *MCA MCSTD 48105*	42		
29 Dec 07	**PEACE ON EARTH - LITTLE DRUMMER BOY** *Download* DAVID BOWIE & BING CROSBY	73		

DAVID CROSBY
US singer/guitarist

Date	Title / Label	Peak Position	Weeks at No.1	Weeks in Top 40
15 May 93	**HERO** *Atlantic A 7360* DAVID CROSBY FEATURING PHIL COLLINS	56		

CROSBY, STILLS & NASH
US/UK group

Date	Title / Label	Peak Position	Weeks at No.1	Weeks in Top 40
16 Aug 69	**MARRAKESH EXPRESS** *Atlantic 584 283*	17		6
21 Jan 89	**AMERICAN DREAM** *Atlantic A 9003* CROSBY, STILLS, NASH & YOUNG	55		

CHRISTOPHER CROSS
US singer

Date	Title / Label	Peak Position	Weeks at No.1	Weeks in Top 40
19 Apr 80	**RIDE LIKE THE WIND** *Warner Brothers K 17582*	69		
14 Feb 81	**SAILING** *Warner Brothers K 17695* ★	48		
17 Oct 81	**ARTHUR'S THEME (BEST THAT YOU CAN DO)** *Warner Brothers K 17847*	56		
9 Jan 82	**ARTHUR'S THEME (BEST THAT YOU CAN DO)** *Warner Brothers K 17847* ★	7		8
5 Feb 83	**ALL RIGHT** *Warner Brothers W 9843*	51		

CROSS
UK group

Date	Title / Label	Peak Position	Weeks at No.1	Weeks in Top 40
17 Oct 87	**COWBOYS AND INDIANS** *Virgin VS 1007*	74		

CROW
German production duo

Date	Title / Label	Peak Position	Weeks at No.1	Weeks in Top 40
19 May 01	**WHAT YA LOOKIN' AT** *Tidy Trax TIDY 153CD*	60		

SHERYL CROW
US singer

Date	Title / Label	Peak Position	Weeks at No.1	Weeks in Top 40
18 Jun 94	**LEAVING LAS VEGAS** *A&M 5806472*	66		
5 Nov 94	**ALL I WANNA DO** *A&M 5808452*	4		10
11 Feb 95	**STRONG ENOUGH** *A&M 5809212*	33		2
27 May 95	**CAN'T CRY ANYMORE** *A&M 5810552*	33		1
29 Jul 95	**RUN, BABY, RUN** *A&M 5811492*	24		1

Silver-selling ○ Gold-selling ● Platinum-selling ✪ US No.1 ★ | Peak Position | Weeks at No.1 | Weeks in Top 40

Date	Title / Label	Peak Position	Weeks at No.1	Weeks in Top 40
11 Nov 95	WHAT I CAN DO FOR YOU *A&M 5812292*	43		
21 Sep 96	IF IT MAKES YOU HAPPY *A&M 5819032*	9		4
30 Nov 96	EVERYDAY IS A WINDING ROAD *A&M 5820232*	12		3
29 Mar 97	HARD TO MAKE A STAND *A&M 5821492*	22		1
12 Jul 97	A CHANGE WOULD DO YOU GOOD *A&M 5822092*	8		3
18 Oct 97	HOME *A&M 5823992*	25		1
13 Dec 97	TOMORROW NEVER DIES *A&M 5824572*	12		7
12 Sep 98	MY FAVORITE MISTAKE *A&M 5827632*	9		3
5 Dec 98	THERE GOES THE NEIGHBORHOOD *A&M 5828092*	19		2
6 Mar 99	ANYTHING BUT DOWN *A&M 5828292*	19		1
11 Sep 99	SWEET CHILD O' MINE *Columbia 6678882*	30		1
13 Apr 02	SOAK UP THE SUN *A&M 4977052*	16		3
13 Jul 02	STEVE McQUEEN *A&M 4977422*	44		
1 Nov 03	FIRST CUT IS THE DEEPEST *A&M 9813556*	37		1
3 Jul 04	LIGHT IN YOUR EYES *A&M 9862700*	73		
1 Oct 05	GOOD IS GOOD *A&M 9885348*	75		

CROWD Multinational group

Date	Title / Label	Peak Position	Weeks at No.1	Weeks in Top 40
1 Jun 85	YOU'LL NEVER WALK ALONE *Spartan BRAD 1* ●	1	2	7

CROWDED HOUSE Australian/New Zealand group

Date	Title / Label	Peak Position	Weeks at No.1	Weeks in Top 40
6 Jun 87	DON'T DREAM IT'S OVER *Capitol CL 438*	27		5
22 Jun 91	CHOCOLATE CAKE *Capitol CL 618*	69		
2 Nov 91	FALL AT YOUR FEET *Capitol CL 626*	17		4
29 Feb 92	WEATHER WITH YOU *Capitol CL 643*	7		7
20 Jun 92	FOUR SEASONS IN ONE DAY *Capitol CL 655*	26		3
26 Sep 92	IT'S ONLY NATURAL *Capitol CL 661*	24		2
2 Oct 93	DISTANT SUN *Capitol CDCLS 697*	19		3
20 Nov 93	NAILS IN MY FEET *Capitol CDCLS 701*	22		3
19 Feb 94	LOCKED OUT *Capitol CDCLS 707*	12		3
11 Jun 94	FINGERS OF LOVE *Capitol CDCL 715*	25		2
24 Sep 94	PINEAPPLE HEAD *Capitol CDCL 723*	27		1
22 Jun 96	INSTINCT *Capitol CDCLS 774*	12		2
17 Aug 96	NOT THE GIRL YOU THINK YOU ARE *Capitol CDCLS 776*	20		1
9 Nov 96	DON'T DREAM IT'S OVER *Capitol CDCL 780*	25		1
7 Jul 07	DON'T STOP NOW *Parlophone CDR6743*	41		
22 Dec 07	POUR LE MONDE *Download*	51		

CROWN HEIGHTS AFFAIR US group

Date	Title / Label	Peak Position	Weeks at No.1	Weeks in Top 40
19 Aug 78	GALAXY OF LOVE *Mercury 6168 801*	24		7
11 Nov 78	I'M GONNA LOVE YOU FOREVER *Mercury 6168 803*	47		
14 Apr 79	DANCE LADY DANCE *Mercury 6168 804*	44		
3 May 80	YOU GAVE ME LOVE *De-Lite MER 9*	10		10
9 Aug 80	YOU'VE BEEN GONE *De-Lite MER 28*	44		

JULEE CRUISE US singer

Date	Title / Label	Peak Position	Weeks at No.1	Weeks in Top 40
10 Nov 90	FALLING *Warner Brothers W 9544*	7		8
2 Mar 91	ROCKIN' BACK INSIDE MY HEART *Warner Brothers W 0004*	66		
11 Sep 99	IF I SURVIVE *Distinctive DISNCD 55* HYBRID FEATURING JULEE CRUISE	52		

CRUSADERS US group

Date	Title / Label	Peak Position	Weeks at No.1	Weeks in Top 40
18 Aug 79	STREET LIFE *MCA 513*	5		8
26 Sep 81	I'M SO GLAD I'M STANDING HERE TODAY *MCA 741* CRUSADERS, FEATURED VOCALIST JOE COCKER	61		
7 Apr 84	NIGHT LADIES *MCA 853*	55		

CRUSH UK duo

Date	Title / Label	Peak Position	Weeks at No.1	Weeks in Top 40
24 Feb 96	JELLYHEAD *Telstar CDSTAS 2809*	50		
3 Aug 96	LUV'D UP *Telstar CDSTAS 2833*	45		

BOBBY CRUSH UK pianist

Date	Title / Label	Peak Position	Weeks at No.1	Weeks in Top 40
4 Nov 72	BORSALINO *Philips 6006 248*	37		2

TAIO CRUZ UK singer

Date	Title / Label	Peak Position	Weeks at No.1	Weeks in Top 40
11 Nov 06	I JUST WANNA KNOW *Universal 1713178*	29		2
15 Sep 07	MOVING ON *Island 1746784*	26		2
23 Feb 08	COME ON GIRL *Fourth & Broadway 1764408* TAIO CRUZ FEATURING LUCIANA	5		5

CRW Italian group

Date	Title / Label	Peak Position	Weeks at No.1	Weeks in Top 40
26 Feb 00	I FEEL LOVE *VC Recordings VRCD 63*	15		2
25 Nov 00	LOVIN' *VC Recordings VRCD 77*	49		
27 Apr 02	LIKE A CAT *BXR BXRC 0397* CRW FEATURING VERONIKA	57		
26 Oct 02	PRECIOUS LIFE *BXR BXRC 0395* CRW PRESENTS VERONIKA	57		

CRY BEFORE DAWN Irish group

Date	Title / Label	Peak Position	Weeks at No.1	Weeks in Top 40
17 Jun 89	WITNESS FOR THE WORLD *Epic GONE 3*	67		

CRY OF LOVE US group

Date	Title / Label	Peak Position	Weeks at No.1	Weeks in Top 40
15 Jan 94	BAD THING *Columbia 6600462*	60		

CRY SISCO! UK singer

Date	Title / Label	Peak Position	Weeks at No.1	Weeks in Top 40
2 Sep 89	AFRO DIZZI ACT *Escape AWOL 1*	42		

CRYIN' SHAMES UK group

Date	Title / Label	Peak Position	Weeks at No.1	Weeks in Top 40
31 Mar 66	PLEASE STAY *Decca F 12340*	26		4

CRYSTAL METHOD US instrumental duo

Date	Title / Label	Peak Position	Weeks at No.1	Weeks in Top 40
11 Oct 97	(CAN'T YOU) TRIP LIKE I DO *Epic 6650862* FILTER & THE CRYSTAL METHOD	39		1
7 Mar 98	KEEP HOPE ALIVE *Sony S2 CM 3CD*	71		
8 Aug 98	COMIN' BACK *Sony S2 CM 4CD*	73		

CRYSTAL PALACE UK football club

Date	Title / Label	Peak Position	Weeks at No.1	Weeks in Top 40
12 May 90	GLAD ALL OVER/WHERE EAGLES FLY *Parkfield PMS 5019*	50		

CRYSTALS US group

Date	Title / Label	Peak Position	Weeks at No.1	Weeks in Top 40
22 Nov 62	HE'S A REBEL *London HLU 9611* ★	19		8
20 Jun 63	DA DOO RON RON *London HLU 9732*	5		14
19 Sep 63	THEN HE KISSED ME *London HLU 9773*	2		12
5 Mar 64	I WONDER *London HLU 9852*	36		1
19 Oct 74	DA DOO RON RON *Warner Brothers K 19010*	15		7

CSILLA Hungarian singer

Date	Title / Label	Peak Position	Weeks at No.1	Weeks in Top 40
13 Jul 96	MAN IN THE MOON *Worx WORXCD 001*	69		

CSS Brazilian group

Date	Title / Label	Peak Position	Weeks at No.1	Weeks in Top 40
10 Mar 07	OFF THE HOOK *Warner Brothers WEA416CD*	43		
19 May 07	LET'S MAKE LOVE AND LISTEN TO DEATH FROM ABOVE *Sire WEA418CD*	39		1

ALEX CUBA BAND Cuban group

Date	Title / Label	Peak Position	Weeks at No.1	Weeks in Top 40
6 Nov 04	LO MISMO QUE YO (IF ONLY) *Shell GET2CD* ALEX CUBA BAND FEATURING RON SEXSMITH	52		

CUBAN BOYS UK group

Date	Title / Label	Peak Position	Weeks at No.1	Weeks in Top 40
25 Dec 99	COGNOSCENTI VERSUS THE INTELLIGENTSIA *EMI CDCUBAN 001* ○	4		5

CUBAN HEELS UK group

Date	Title / Label	Peak Position	Weeks at No.1	Weeks in Top 40
19 Mar 05	SHE'S ON FIRE *Sugar Shack FOD062*	72		

CUBIC 22 Belgian production group

Date	Title / Label	Peak Position	Weeks at No.1	Weeks in Top 40
22 Jun 91	NIGHT IN MOTION *XL Recordings XLS 20*	15		5

CUD UK group

Date	Title / Label	Peak Position	Weeks at No.1	Weeks in Top 40
19 Oct 91	OH NO WON'T DO *A&M AMB 829*	49		
28 Mar 92	THROUGH THE ROOF *A&M AM 857*	44		

Column key: ○ Silver-selling · ● Gold-selling · ⊛ Platinum-selling · ★ US No.1 · Peak Position · Weeks at No.1 · Weeks in Top 40

Date	Title	Label	Peak Position	Weeks at No.1	Weeks in Top 40
30 May 92	**RICH AND STRANGE**	*A&M AM 871*	24		1
15 Aug 92	**PURPLE LOVE BALLOON**	*A&M AM 0024*	27		1
10 Oct 92	**ONCE AGAIN**	*A&M AM 0081*	45		
12 Feb 94	**NEUROTICA**	*A&M 5805172*	37		1
2 Apr 94	**STICKS AND STONES**	*A&M 5805472*	68		
3 Sep 94	**ONE GIANT LOVE**	*A&M 5807292*	52		

CUFF LINKS US group

Date	Title	Label	Peak Position	Weeks at No.1	Weeks in Top 40
29 Nov 69	**TRACY**	*MCA MU 1101*	4		14
14 Mar 70	**WHEN JULIE COMES AROUND**	*MCA MU 1112*	10		11

JAMIE CULLUM UK singer/pianist

Date	Title	Label	Peak Position	Weeks at No.1	Weeks in Top 40
20 Mar 04	**THESE ARE THE DAYS/FRONTIN'**	*UCJ 9866211*	12		3
20 Nov 04	**EVERLASTING LOVE**	*UCJ 9868834*	20		3
1 Oct 05	**GET YOUR WAY**	*UCJ 9873425*	44		
10 Dec 05	**MIND TRICK**	*UCJ 9875047*	32		1

CULT UK group

Date	Title	Label	Peak Position	Weeks at No.1	Weeks in Top 40
22 Dec 84	**RESURRECTION JOE**	*Beggars Banquet BEG 122*	74		
25 May 85	**SHE SELLS SANCTUARY**	*Beggars Banquet BEG 135*	15		9
5 Oct 85	**RAIN**	*Beggars Banquet BEG 147*	17		6
30 Nov 85	**REVOLUTION**	*Beggars Banquet BEG 152*	30		2
28 Feb 87	**LOVE REMOVAL MACHINE**	*Beggars Banquet BEG 182*	18		4
2 May 87	**LIL' DEVIL**	*Beggars Banquet BEG 188*	11		6
22 Aug 87	**WILD FLOWER (DOUBLE SINGLE)**	*Beggars Banquet BEG 195D*	24		1
29 Aug 87	**WILD FLOWER**	*Beggars Banquet BEG 195*	30		2
1 Apr 89	**FIRE WOMAN**	*Beggars Banquet BEG 228*	15		3
8 Jul 89	**EDIE (CIAO BABY)**	*Beggars Banquet BEG 230*	32		3
18 Nov 89	**SUN KING/EDIE (CIAO BABY)**	*Beggars Banquet BEG 235*	39		1
10 Mar 90	**SWEET SOUL SISTER**	*Beggars Banquet BEG 241*	42		
14 Sep 91	**WILD HEARTED SON**	*Beggars Banquet BEG 255*	40		1
29 Feb 92	**HEART OF SOUL**	*Beggars Banquet BEG 260*	51		
30 Jan 93	**SHE SELLS SANCTUARY (REMIX)**	*Beggars Banquet BEG 253CD*	15		3
8 Oct 94	**COMING DOWN**	*Beggars Banquet BBQ 40CD*	50		
7 Jan 95	**STAR**	*Beggars Banquet BBQ 45CD*	65		

CULTURE BEAT UK/US/German group

Date	Title	Label	Peak Position	Weeks at No.1	Weeks in Top 40
3 Feb 90	**CHERRY LIPS (DER ERDBEERMUND)**	*Epic 6556337*	55		
7 Aug 93	**MR VAIN**	*Epic 6594682* ●	1	4	13
6 Nov 93	**GOT TO GET IT**	*Epic 6597212*	4		7
15 Jan 94	**ANYTHING**	*Epic 6600252*	5		6
2 Apr 94	**WORLD IN YOUR HANDS**	*Epic 6602292*	20		2
27 Jan 96	**INSIDE OUT**	*Epic 6626562*	32		1
15 Jun 96	**CRYING IN THE RAIN**	*Epic 6633582*	29		1
28 Sep 96	**TAKE ME AWAY**	*Epic 6637552*	52		
20 Sep 03	**MR VAIN RECALL**	*East West EW 270CD*	51		

CULTURE CLUB UK group

Date	Title	Label	Peak Position	Weeks at No.1	Weeks in Top 40
18 Sep 82	**DO YOU REALLY WANT TO HURT ME**	*Virgin VS 518* ●	1	3	11
27 Nov 82	**TIME (CLOCK OF THE HEART)**	*Virgin VS 558* ●	3		10
9 Apr 83	**CHURCH OF THE POISON MIND**	*Virgin VS 571* ○	2		7
17 Sep 83	**KARMA CHAMELEON**	*Virgin VS 612* ⊛ ★	1	6	18
10 Dec 83	**VICTIMS**	*Virgin VS 641* ●	3		8
24 Mar 84	**IT'S A MIRACLE**	*Virgin VS 662*	4		6
6 Oct 84	**THE WAR SONG**	*Virgin VS 694* ○	2		7
1 Dec 84	**THE MEDAL SONG**	*Virgin VS 730*	32		2
15 Mar 86	**MOVE AWAY**	*Virgin VS 845*	7		6
31 May 86	**GOD THANK YOU WOMAN**	*Virgin VS 861*	31		3
31 Oct 98	**I JUST WANNA BE LOVED**	*Virgin VSCDT 1710*	4		6
7 Aug 99	**YOUR KISSES ARE CHARITY**	*Virgin VSCDT 1736*	25		2
27 Nov 99	**COLD SHOULDER/STARMAN**	*Virgin VSCDT 1758*	43		

SMILEY CULTURE UK singer

Date	Title	Label	Peak Position	Weeks at No.1	Weeks in Top 40
15 Dec 84	**POLICE OFFICER**	*Fashion FAD 7012*	12		7
6 Apr 85	**COCKNEY TRANSLATION**	*Fashion FAD 7028*	71		
13 Sep 86	**SCHOOLTIME CHRONICLE**	*Polydor POSP 815*	59		

LARRY CUNNINGHAM & THE MIGHTY AVONS Irish group

Date	Title	Label	Peak Position	Weeks at No.1	Weeks in Top 40
10 Dec 64	**TRIBUTE TO JIM REEVES**	*King KG 1016*	40		2

CUPID'S INSPIRATION UK group

Date	Title	Label	Peak Position	Weeks at No.1	Weeks in Top 40
19 Jun 68	**YESTERDAY HAS GONE**	*Nems 56 3500*	4		10
2 Oct 68	**MY WORLD**	*Nems 56 3702*	33		4

CURE UK group

Date	Title	Label	Peak Position	Weeks at No.1	Weeks in Top 40
12 Apr 80	**A FOREST**	*Fiction FICS 10*	31		3
4 Apr 81	**PRIMARY**	*Fiction FICS 12*	43		
17 Oct 81	**CHARLOTTE SOMETIMES**	*Fiction FICS 14*	44		
24 Jul 82	**HANGING GARDEN**	*Fiction FICS 15*	34		1
27 Nov 82	**LET'S GO TO BED**	*Fiction FICS 17*	44		
9 Jul 83	**THE WALK**	*Fiction FICS 18*	12		6
29 Oct 83	**THE LOVE CATS**	*Fiction FICS 19*	7		8
7 Apr 84	**THE CATERPILLAR**	*Fiction FICS 20*	14		6
27 Jul 85	**IN BETWEEN DAYS**	*Fiction FICS 22*	15		7
21 Sep 85	**CLOSE TO ME**	*Fiction FICS 23*	24		5
3 May 86	**BOYS DON'T CRY**	*Fiction FICS 24*	22		5
18 Apr 87	**WHY CAN'T I BE YOU**	*Fiction FICS 25*	21		4
4 Jul 87	**CATCH**	*Fiction FICS 26*	27		3
17 Oct 87	**JUST LIKE HEAVEN**	*Fiction FICS 27*	29		3
20 Feb 88	**HOT HOT HOT!!!**	*Fiction FICSX 28*	45		
22 Apr 89	**LULLABY**	*Fiction FICS 29*	5		4
2 Sep 89	**LOVESONG**	*Fiction FICS 30*	18		4
31 Mar 90	**PICTURES OF YOU**	*Fiction FICS 34*	24		4
29 Sep 90	**NEVER ENOUGH**	*Fiction FICS 35*	13		3
3 Nov 90	**CLOSE TO ME (REMIX)**	*Fiction FICS 36*	13		4
28 Mar 92	**HIGH**	*Fiction FICS 39*	8		2
11 Apr 92	**HIGH (REMIX)**	*Fiction FICSX 41*	44		
23 May 92	**FRIDAY I'M IN LOVE**	*Fiction FICS 42*	6		6
17 Oct 92	**A LETTER TO ELSIE**	*Fiction FICS 46*	28		1
4 May 96	**THE 13TH**	*Fiction 5764692*	15		1
29 Jun 96	**MINT CAR**	*Fiction FICSD 52*	31		1
14 Dec 96	**GONE**	*Fiction FICD 53*	60		
29 Nov 97	**WRONG NUMBER**	*Fiction FICD 54*	62		
10 Nov 01	**CUT HERE**	*Fiction 5873892*	54		
31 Jul 04	**THE END OF THE WORLD**	*Geffen 9862976*	25		1
30 Oct 04	**TAKING OFF**	*Geffen 9864491*	39		1

CURIOSITY KILLED THE CAT UK group

Date	Title	Label	Peak Position	Weeks at No.1	Weeks in Top 40
13 Dec 86	**DOWN TO EARTH** CURIOSITY KILLED THE CAT	*Mercury CAT 2*	3		11
4 Apr 87	**ORDINARY DAY** CURIOSITY KILLED THE CAT	*Mercury CAT 3*	11		6
20 Jun 87	**MISFIT** CURIOSITY KILLED THE CAT	*Mercury CAT 4*	7		7
19 Sep 87	**FREE** CURIOSITY KILLED THE CAT	*Mercury CAT 5*	56		
16 Sep 89	**NAME AND NUMBER** CURIOSITY	*Mercury CAT 6*	14		7
25 Apr 92	**HANG ON IN THERE BABY** CURIOSITY	*RCA PB 45377*	3		8
29 Aug 92	**I NEED YOUR LOVIN'** CURIOSITY	*RCA 74321111377*	47		
30 Oct 93	**GIMME THE SUNSHINE** CURIOSITY	*RCA 74321168602*	73		

CHANTAL CURTIS French singer

Date	Title	Label	Peak Position	Weeks at No.1	Weeks in Top 40
14 Jul 79	**GET ANOTHER LOVE**	*Pye 7P 5003*	51		

TC CURTIS Jamaican singer

Date	Title	Label	Peak Position	Weeks at No.1	Weeks in Top 40
23 Feb 85	**YOU SHOULD HAVE KNOWN BETTER**	*Hot Melt VS 754*	50		

CURVE UK group

Date	Title	Label	Peak Position	Weeks at No.1	Weeks in Top 40
16 Mar 91	**THE BLINDFOLD (EP)**	*AnXious ANX 27*	68		
25 May 91	**COAST IS CLEAR**	*AnXious ANX 30*	34		1
9 Nov 91	**CLIPPED**	*AnXious ANX 35*	36		1
7 Mar 92	**FAIT ACCOMPLI**	*AnXious ANX 36*	22		2
18 Jul 92	**HORROR HEAD (EP)**	*AnXious ANXT 38*	31		1
4 Sep 93	**BLACKERTHREETRACKER EP**	*AnXious ANXCD 42*	39		1
16 May 98	**COMING UP ROSES**	*Universal UND 80489*	51		

CURVED AIR UK group

Date	Title	Label	Peak Position	Weeks at No.1	Weeks in Top 40
7 Aug 71	**BACK STREET LUV**	*Warner Brothers K 16092*	4		10

Silver-selling ● Gold-selling ● Platinum-selling ⊛ US No.1 ★ | Peak Position | Weeks at No.1 | Weeks in Top 40

MALACHI CUSH Irish singer

Date	Title / Label	Peak Position	Weeks at No.1	Weeks in Top 40
19 Apr 03	**JUST SAY YOU LOVE ME** *Mercury 0779072*	49		

CUSHH Danish group

Date	Title / Label	Peak Position	Weeks at No.1	Weeks in Top 40
10 Mar 07	**DO IT 2 ME** *Download*	31		1

CUT 'N' MOVE Danish group

Date	Title / Label	Peak Position	Weeks at No.1	Weeks in Top 40
2 Oct 93	**GIVE IT UP** *EMI CDEM 273*	61		
9 Sep 95	**I'M ALIVE** *EMI CDEM 375*	49		

FRANKIE CUTLASS US rapper

Date	Title / Label	Peak Position	Weeks at No.1	Weeks in Top 40
5 Apr 97	**THE CYPHER: PART 3** *Epic 6641445*	59		

JON CUTLER US producer

Date	Title / Label	Peak Position	Weeks at No.1	Weeks in Top 40
19 Jan 02	**IT'S YOURS** *Direction 6720537* JOHN CUTLER FEATURING E-MAN	38		1

CUTTING CREW UK group

Date	Title / Label	Peak Position	Weeks at No.1	Weeks in Top 40
16 Aug 86	**(I JUST) DIED IN YOUR ARMS** *Siren 21* ● ★	4		9
25 Oct 86	**I'VE BEEN IN LOVE BEFORE** *Siren 29*	31		3
7 Mar 87	**ONE FOR THE MOCKINGBIRD** *Siren 40*	52		
21 Nov 87	**I'VE BEEN IN LOVE BEFORE** *Siren SRN 29*	24		5
22 Jul 89	**(BETWEEN A) ROCK AND A HARD PLACE** *Siren SRN 108*	66		

CYBERSONIK US production group

Date	Title / Label	Peak Position	Weeks at No.1	Weeks in Top 40
10 Nov 90	**TECHNARCHY** *Champion CHAMP 264*	73		

CYCLEFLY Irish group

Date	Title / Label	Peak Position	Weeks at No.1	Weeks in Top 40
6 Apr 02	**NO STRESS** *Radioactive RAXTD 41*	68		

CYGNUS X German producer

Date	Title / Label	Peak Position	Weeks at No.1	Weeks in Top 40
11 Mar 00	**THE ORANGE THEME** *Hooj Choons HOOJ 88CD*	43		
18 Aug 01	**SUPERSTRING** *Xtravaganza XTRAV 28CDS*	33		1

JOHNNY CYMBAL UK singer

Date	Title / Label	Peak Position	Weeks at No.1	Weeks in Top 40
14 Mar 63	**MR BASS MAN** *London HLR 9682*	24		7

CYPRESS HILL US group

Date	Title / Label	Peak Position	Weeks at No.1	Weeks in Top 40
31 Jul 93	**INSANE IN THE BRAIN** *Ruffhouse 6595332*	32		2
2 Oct 93	**WHEN THE SH.. GOES DOWN** *Ruffhouse 6596702*	19		3
11 Dec 93	**I AIN'T GOIN' OUT LIKE THAT** *Ruffhouse 6596902*	15		5
26 Feb 94	**INSANE IN THE BRAIN** *Ruffhouse 6601762*	21		2
7 May 94	**LICK A SHOT** *Ruffhouse 6603192*	20		2
7 Oct 95	**THROW YOUR SET IN THE AIR** *Ruffhouse 6623542*	15		2
17 Feb 96	**ILLUSIONS** *Columbia 6629052*	23		1
10 Oct 98	**TEQUILA SUNRISE** *Columbia 6664935*	23		1
10 Apr 99	**DR GREENTHUMB** *Columbia 6671202*	34		1
26 Jun 99	**INSANE IN THE BRAIN** *INCredible INCRL 17CD* JASON NEVINS VERSUS CYPRESS HILL	19		2
29 Apr 00	**RAP SUPERSTAR/ROCK SUPERSTAR** *Columbia 6692645*	13		3
16 Sep 00	**HIGHLIFE/CAN'T GET THE BEST OF ME** *Columbia 6697895*	35		1
8 Dec 01	**LOWRIDER/TROUBLE** *Columbia 6721662*	33		1
27 Mar 04	**WHAT'S YOUR NUMBER?** *Columbia 6746172*	44		

BILLY RAY CYRUS US singer

Date	Title / Label	Peak Position	Weeks at No.1	Weeks in Top 40
25 Jul 92	**ACHY BREAKY HEART** *Mercury MER 373* ●	3		9
10 Oct 92	**COULD'VE BEEN ME** *Mercury MER 378*	24		3
28 Nov 92	**THESE BOOTS ARE MADE FOR WALKIN'** *Mercury MER 384*	63		
19 Dec 92	**ACHY BREAKY HEART** *Epic 6588837* ALVIN & THE CHIPMUNKS FEATURING BILLY RAY CYRUS	53		

CZR US production group

Date	Title / Label	Peak Position	Weeks at No.1	Weeks in Top 40
30 Sep 00	**I WANT YOU** *Credence CDCRED 002* CZR FEATURING DELANO	57		

D

ASHER D UK singer

Date	Title / Label	Peak Position	Weeks at No.1	Weeks in Top 40
4 Aug 01	**BABY, CAN I GET YOUR NUMBER** *East West EW 235CD* OBI PROJECT FEATURING HARRY, ASHER D & DJ WHAT?	75		
8 Jun 02	**BACK IN THE DAY/WHY ME** *Independiente ISOM 57MS*	43		

CHUCK D US rapper

Date	Title / Label	Peak Position	Weeks at No.1	Weeks in Top 40
6 Jul 91	**BRING THE NOISE** *Island IS 490* ANTHRAX FEATURING CHUCK D	14		3
26 Oct 96	**NO** *Mercury MERCD 476*	55		
23 Jun 01	**ROCK DA FUNKY BEATS** *Xtrahard X2H3 CDS* PUBLIC DOMAIN FEATURING CHUCK D	19		2

DIMPLES D US rapper

Date	Title / Label	Peak Position	Weeks at No.1	Weeks in Top 40
17 Nov 90	**SUCKER DJ** *FBI 11*	17		7

LONGSY D'S HOUSE SOUND UK producer

Date	Title / Label	Peak Position	Weeks at No.1	Weeks in Top 40
4 Mar 89	**THIS IS SKA** *Big One VBIG 13*	56		

MAXWELL D UK DJ

Date	Title / Label	Peak Position	Weeks at No.1	Weeks in Top 40
15 Sep 01	**SERIOUS** *4 Liberty LIBTCD 046*	38		1

NIKKI D US rapper

Date	Title / Label	Peak Position	Weeks at No.1	Weeks in Top 40
6 May 89	**MY LOVE IS SO RAW** *Def Jam 6548987* ALYSON WILLIAMS FEATURING NIKKI D	34		2
30 Mar 91	**DADDY'S LITTLE GIRL** *Def Jam 6567347*	75		

VICKY D US singer

Date	Title / Label	Peak Position	Weeks at No.1	Weeks in Top 40
13 Mar 82	**THIS BEAT IS MINE** *Virgin VS 486*	42		

D KAY & EPSILION Austrian duo

Date	Title / Label	Peak Position	Weeks at No.1	Weeks in Top 40
30 Aug 03	**BARCELONA** *Alphamagic/BC/BMG BCAU001C* D KAY & EPSILON FEATURING STAMINA MC	14		3

D'MENACE UK production duo

Date	Title / Label	Peak Position	Weeks at No.1	Weeks in Top 40
8 Aug 98	**DEEP MENACE (SPANK)** *Inferno CDFERN 8*	20		2

D MOB UK group

Date	Title / Label	Peak Position	Weeks at No.1	Weeks in Top 40
15 Oct 88	**WE CALL IT ACIEED** *ffrr FFR 13* D MOB FEATURING GARY HAISMAN	3		8
3 Jun 89	**IT IS TIME TO GET FUNKY** *ffrr F 107* D MOB FEATURING LRS	9		8
21 Oct 89	**C'MON AND GET MY LOVE** *ffrr F 117* D MOB WITH CATHY DENNIS	15		8
6 Jan 90	**PUT YOUR HANDS TOGETHER** *ffrr F 124* D MOB FEATURING NUFF JUICE	7		6
7 Apr 90	**THAT'S THE WAY OF THE WORLD** *ffrr F 132* D MOB WITH CATHY DENNIS	48		
12 Feb 94	**WHY** *ffrr FCD 227* D MOB WITH CATHY DENNIS	23		2
3 Sep 94	**ONE DAY** *ffrr FCDP 239*	41		

D*NOTE UK producer

Date	Title / Label	Peak Position	Weeks at No.1	Weeks in Top 40
12 Jul 97	**WAITING HOPEFULLY** *VC Recordings VCRD 21*	46		
15 Nov 97	**LOST AND FOUND** *VC Recordings VCRD 25*	59		
27 Apr 02	**SHED MY SKIN** *Channel 4 Music C4M 00182*	73		

D.O.S.E. UK production group

Date	Title / Label	Peak Position	Weeks at No.1	Weeks in Top 40
23 Mar 96	**PLUG MYSELF IN** *Coliseum TOGA 001CD1* D.O.S.E. FEATURING MARK E SMITH	50		

Silver-selling ● Gold-selling ● Platinum-selling ✪ US No.1 ★ Peak Position Weeks at No.1 Weeks in Top 40

D-RAIL UK group

Date	Title / Label	Peak Position	Weeks at No.1	Weeks in Top 40
5 Feb 05	**HOW DO I SAY GOODBYE?** *Silverword ECPCDS1*	63		

D:REAM UK duo

Date	Title / Label	Peak Position	Weeks at No.1	Weeks in Top 40
4 Jul 92	**U R THE BEST THING** *FXU 3*	72		
30 Jan 93	**THINGS CAN ONLY GET BETTER** *Magnet MAG 1010CD*	24		3
24 Apr 93	**U R THE BEST THING (REMIX)** *Magnet MAG 1011CD*	19		6
31 Jul 93	**UNFORGIVEN** *Magnet MAG 1016CD*	29		2
2 Oct 93	**STAR/I LIKE IT** *Magnet MAG 1019CD*	26		3
8 Jan 94	**THINGS CAN ONLY GET BETTER (REMIX)** *Magnet MAG 1020CD* ●	1	4	14
26 Mar 94	**U R THE BEST THING (2ND REMIX)** *Magnet MAG 1021CD*	4		7
18 Jun 94	**TAKE ME AWAY** *Magnet MAG 1025CD*	18		3
10 Sep 94	**BLAME IT ON ME** *Magnet MAG 1027CD*	25		3
8 Jul 95	**SHOOT ME WITH YOUR LOVE** *Magnet MAG 1034CD*	7		4
9 Sep 95	**PARTY UP THE WORLD** *Magnet MAG 1037CD*	20		4
11 Nov 95	**THE POWER (OF ALL THE LOVE IN THE WORLD)** *Magnet MAG 1039CD* D:REAM FEATURING TJ DAVIS	40		1
3 May 97	**THINGS CAN ONLY GET BETTER (REMIX)** *Magnet MAG 1050CD*	19		2

D-SHAKE Dutch producer

Date	Title / Label	Peak Position	Weeks at No.1	Weeks in Top 40
2 Jun 90	**YAAH/TECHNO TRANCE** *Cooltempo COOL 213*	20		4
2 Feb 91	**MY HEART THE BEAT** *Cooltempo COOL 228*	42		

D-SIDE Irish group

Date	Title / Label	Peak Position	Weeks at No.1	Weeks in Top 40
26 Apr 03	**SPEECHLESS** *WEA 366CD*	9		4
26 Jul 03	**INVISIBLE** *WEA 369CD*	7		4
13 Dec 03	**REAL WORLD** *Blacklist/Edel 9814017*	9		3
12 Jun 04	**PUSHIN' ME OUT** *Blacklist/Edel 0155826ERE*	21		1

D-TEK UK production group

Date	Title / Label	Peak Position	Weeks at No.1	Weeks in Top 40
6 Nov 93	**DROP THE ROCK (EP)** *Positiva 12TIV 5*	70		

D TRAIN US singer

Date	Title / Label	Peak Position	Weeks at No.1	Weeks in Top 40
6 Feb 82	**YOU'RE THE ONE FOR ME** *Epic EPC A 2016*	30		5
8 May 82	**WALK ON BY** *Epic EPC A 2298*	44		
7 May 83	**MUSIC PART 1** *Prelude A 3332*	23		4
16 Jul 83	**KEEP GIVING ME LOVE** *Prelude A 3497*	65		
27 Jul 85	**YOU'RE THE ONE FOR ME** *Prelude ZB 40302*	15		7
12 Oct 85	**MUSIC (REMIX)** *Prelude ZB 40431*	62		

AZZIDO DA BASS German producer

Date	Title / Label	Peak Position	Weeks at No.1	Weeks in Top 40
4 Mar 00	**DOOMS NIGHT** *Club Tools 0067285 CLU*	58		
24 Jun 00	**DOOMS NIGHT** *Club Tools 0067285 CLU*	46		
21 Oct 00	**DOOMS NIGHT (REMIX)** *Club Tools 0120285 CLU*	8		4
23 Mar 02	**SPEED (CAN YOU FEEL IT?)** *Club Tools 0135815 CLU* AZZIDO DA BASS FEATURING ROLAND CLARK	68		

DA BRAT US rapper

Date	Title / Label	Peak Position	Weeks at No.1	Weeks in Top 40
22 Oct 94	**FUNKDAFIED** *Columbia 6609212*	65		

DA CLICK UK group

Date	Title / Label	Peak Position	Weeks at No.1	Weeks in Top 40
16 Jan 99	**GOOD RHYMES** *ffrr FCD 353*	14		4
29 May 99	**WE ARE DA CLICK** *ffrr FCD 363*	38		1

DA FOOL US producer

Date	Title / Label	Peak Position	Weeks at No.1	Weeks in Top 40
16 Jan 99	**NO GOOD** *ffrr FCD 352*	38		1

RICARDO DA FORCE UK rapper

Date	Title / Label	Peak Position	Weeks at No.1	Weeks in Top 40
18 Mar 95	**PUMP UP THE VOLUME** *Stress CDSTR 49* GREED FEATURING RICARDO DA FORCE	51		
16 Sep 95	**STAYIN' ALIVE** *All Around The World CDGLOBE 131* N-TRANCE FEATURING RICARDO DA FORCE ●	2		8
31 Aug 96	**WHY** *ffrr FCD 280*	58		

DA HOOL German rapper

Date	Title / Label	Peak Position	Weeks at No.1	Weeks in Top 40
14 Feb 98	**MEET HER AT THE LOVE PARADE** *Manifesto FESCD 39*	15		2
22 Aug 98	**BORA BORA** *Manifesto FESCD 47*	35		1
28 Jul 01	**MEET HER AT THE LOVE PARADE 2001 (REMIX)** *Manifesto FESCD 85*	11		3

DA LENCH MOB US group

Date	Title / Label	Peak Position	Weeks at No.1	Weeks in Top 40
20 Mar 93	**FREEDOM GOT AN A.K.** *East West America A 8431CD*	51		

DA MOB US group

Date	Title / Label	Peak Position	Weeks at No.1	Weeks in Top 40
2 May 98	**FUN** *INCredible INCRL 2CD* DA MOB FEATURING JOCELYN BROWN	33		1
3 Jul 99	**IT'S ALL GOOD** *INCredible INCRL 14CD* DA MOB FEATURING JOCELYN BROWN	54		

DA MUTTZ UK production duo

Date	Title / Label	Peak Position	Weeks at No.1	Weeks in Top 40
9 Dec 00	**WASSUUP** *Eternal WEA 319CD*	11		6

DA PLAYAZ VS CLEA Swedish production group

Date	Title / Label	Peak Position	Weeks at No.1	Weeks in Top 40
29 Oct 05	**WE DON'T HAVE TO TAKE OUR CLOTHES OFF** *Upside UPSIDECD02*	35		1

DA SLAMMIN' PHROGZ French production duo

Date	Title / Label	Peak Position	Weeks at No.1	Weeks in Top 40
29 Apr 00	**SOMETHING ABOUT THE MUSIC** *WEA 251CD*	53		

RUI DA SILVA Portuguese producer

Date	Title / Label	Peak Position	Weeks at No.1	Weeks in Top 40
13 Jan 01	**TOUCH ME** *Kismet 74321823992* RUI DA SILVA FEATURING CASSANDRA ●	1	1	9

DA TECHNO BOHEMIAN Dutch production group

Date	Title / Label	Peak Position	Weeks at No.1	Weeks in Top 40
25 Jan 97	**BANGIN' BASS** *Hi-Life 5731772*	63		

PAUL DA VINCI UK singer

Date	Title / Label	Peak Position	Weeks at No.1	Weeks in Top 40
20 Jul 74	**YOUR BABY AIN'T YOUR BABY ANYMORE** *Penny Farthing PEN 843*	20		7

TERRY DACTYL & THE DINOSAURS UK group

Date	Title / Label	Peak Position	Weeks at No.1	Weeks in Top 40
15 Jul 72	**SEASIDE SHUFFLE** *UK 5*	2		11
13 Jan 73	**ON A SATURDAY NIGHT** *UK 21*	45		

DADA US group

Date	Title / Label	Peak Position	Weeks at No.1	Weeks in Top 40
4 Dec 93	**DOG** *IRS CDEIRSS 185*	71		
5 May 07	**LOLLIPOP** *Data DATA158CDS* DADA FEATURING SANDY RIVERA & TRIX	18		2

DADDY YANKEE Puerto Rican singer

Date	Title / Label	Peak Position	Weeks at No.1	Weeks in Top 40
30 Jul 05	**GASOLINA** *Machete 9883426*	5		6

DADDY'S FAVOURITE UK producer

Date	Title / Label	Peak Position	Weeks at No.1	Weeks in Top 40
21 Nov 98	**I FEEL GOOD THINGS FOR YOU** *Go! Beat GONCD 12*	44		
9 Oct 99	**I FEEL GOOD THINGS FOR YOU** *Go! Beat GONCD 22*	50		

DAFFY DUCK German production group

Date	Title / Label	Peak Position	Weeks at No.1	Weeks in Top 40
6 Jul 91	**PARTY ZONE** *East West YZ 592* DAFFY DUCK FEATURING THE GROOVE GANG	58		

DAFT PUNK French production duo

Date	Title / Label	Peak Position	Weeks at No.1	Weeks in Top 40
22 Feb 97	**DA FUNK/MUSIQUE** *Soma VSCDT 1625*	7		4
26 Apr 97	**AROUND THE WORLD** *Virgin VSCDT 1633*	5		3
4 Oct 97	**BURNIN'** *Virgin VSCDT 1649*	30		1
28 Feb 98	**REVOLUTION 909** *Virgin VSCDT 1682*	47		
25 Nov 00	**ONE MORE TIME** *Virgin VSCDT 1791*	2		9
23 Jun 01	**DIGITAL LOVE** *Virgin VSCDT 1810*	14		3
17 Nov 01	**HARDER BETTER FASTER STRONGER** *Virgin VSCDT 1822*	25		2

Silver-selling ● Gold-selling ● Platinum-selling ● US No.1 ★ — Peak Position · Weeks at No.1 · Weeks in Top 40

Date	Title / Label	Peak Position	Weeks at No.1	Weeks in Top 40
23 Apr 05	**ROBOT ROCK** *Virgin VSCDX1897*	32		1
16 Jul 05	**TECHNOLOGIC** *Virgin VSCDX1900*	40		1

DAISY CHAINSAW UK group

Date	Title / Label	Peak Position	Weeks at No.1	Weeks in Top 40
18 Jan 92	**LOVE YOUR MONEY** *Deva 001*	26		3
28 Mar 92	**PINK FLOWER/ROOM ELEVEN** *Deva 82 TP7*	65		

DAKOTAS UK group

Date	Title / Label	Peak Position	Weeks at No.1	Weeks in Top 40
11 Jul 63	**THE CRUEL SEA** *Parlophone R 5044*	18		12

JIM DALE UK singer

Date	Title / Label	Peak Position	Weeks at No.1	Weeks in Top 40
11 Oct 57	**BE MY GIRL** *Parlophone R 4343*	2		16
10 Jan 58	**JUST BORN** *Parlophone R 4376*	27		2
17 Jan 58	**CRAZY DREAM** *Parlophone R 4376*	24		1
7 Mar 58	**SUGARTIME** *Parlophone R 4402*	25		3

DALE & GRACE US duo

Date	Title / Label	Peak Position	Weeks at No.1	Weeks in Top 40
9 Jan 64	**I'M LEAVING IT UP TO YOU** *London HL 9807* ★	42		

DALE SISTERS US group

Date	Title / Label	Peak Position	Weeks at No.1	Weeks in Top 40
23 Nov 61	**MY SUNDAY BABY** *Ember S 140*	36		3

DALI'S CAR UK group

Date	Title / Label	Peak Position	Weeks at No.1	Weeks in Top 40
3 Nov 84	**THE JUDGEMENT IS THE MIRROR** *Paradox DOX 1*	66		

DALLAS SUPERSTARS Finnish production duo

Date	Title / Label	Peak Position	Weeks at No.1	Weeks in Top 40
27 Sep 03	**HELIUM** *All Around The World CDGLOBE 289*	64		

ROGER DALTREY UK singer

Date	Title / Label	Peak Position	Weeks at No.1	Weeks in Top 40
14 Apr 73	**GIVING IT ALL AWAY** *Track 2094 110*	5		11
4 Aug 73	**I'M FREE** *Ode ODS 66302*	13		9
14 May 77	**WRITTEN ON THE WIND** *Polydor 2121 319*	46		
2 Aug 80	**FREE ME** *Polydor 2001 980*	39		2
11 Oct 80	**WITHOUT YOUR LOVE** *Polydor POSP 181*	55		
3 Mar 84	**WALKING IN MY SLEEP** *WEA U 9686*	56		
5 Oct 85	**AFTER THE FIRE** *10 TEN 69*	50		
8 Mar 86	**UNDER A RAGING MOON** *10 TEN 81*	43		

DAMAGE UK group

Date	Title / Label	Peak Position	Weeks at No.1	Weeks in Top 40
20 Jul 96	**ANYTHING** *Big Life BLRD 129*	68		
12 Oct 96	**LOVE II LOVE** *Big Life BLRD 131*	12		5
14 Dec 96	**FOREVER** *Big Life BLRDB 132* ●	6		7
22 Mar 97	**LOVE GUARANTEED** *Big Life BLRDA 133*	7		4
17 May 97	**WONDERFUL TONIGHT** *Big Life BLRDA 134*	3		6
9 Aug 97	**LOVE LADY** *Big Life BLRDB 137*	33		1
1 Jul 00	**GHETTO ROMANCE** *Cooltempo CDCOOL 347*	7		5
28 Oct 00	**RUMOURS** *Cooltempo CDCOOLS 352*	22		2
31 Mar 01	**STILL BE LOVIN' YOU** *Cooltempo CDCOOLS 355*	11		4
14 Jul 01	**SO WHAT IF I** *Cooltempo CDCOOLS 357*	12		3
15 Dec 01	**AFTER THE LOVE HAS GONE** *Cooltempo CDCOOLS 360*	42		

BOBBY D'AMBROSIO US producer

Date	Title / Label	Peak Position	Weeks at No.1	Weeks in Top 40
2 Aug 97	**MOMENT OF MY LIFE** *Ministry Of Sound MOSCDS 1* BOBBY D'AMBROSIO FEATURING MICHELLE WEEKS	23		1

DAMIAN UK singer/actor

Date	Title / Label	Peak Position	Weeks at No.1	Weeks in Top 40
26 Dec 87	**THE TIME WARP 2** *Jive 160*	51		
27 Aug 88	**THE TIME WARP 2** *Jive 182*	64		
19 Aug 89	**THE TIME WARP 2 (REMIX)** *Jive 209*	7		10
16 Dec 89	**WIG WAM BAM** *Jive 236*	49		

DAMNED UK group

Date	Title / Label	Peak Position	Weeks at No.1	Weeks in Top 40
5 May 79	**LOVE SONG** *Chiswick CHIS 112*	20		5
20 Oct 79	**SMASH IT UP** *Chiswick CHIS 116*	35		1
1 Dec 79	**I JUST CAN'T BE HAPPY TODAY** *Chiswick CHIS 120*	46		
4 Oct 80	**HISTORY OF THE WORLD (PART 1)** *Chiswick CHIS 135*	51		
28 Nov 81	**FRIDAY 13TH (EP)** *Stale One TRY 1*	50		
10 Jul 82	**LOVELY MONEY** *Bronze BRO 149*	42		
9 Jun 84	**THANKS FOR THE NIGHT** *Damned 1*	43		
30 Mar 85	**GRIMLY FIENDISH** *MCA GRIM 1*	21		5
22 Jun 85	**THE SHADOW OF LOVE (EDITION PREMIERE)** *MCA GRIM 2*	25		6
21 Sep 85	**IS IT A DREAM** *MCA GRIM 3*	34		3
8 Feb 86	**ELOISE** *MCA GRIM 4* ●	3		7
22 Nov 86	**ANYTHING** *MCA GRIM 5*	32		2
7 Feb 87	**GIGOLO** *MCA GRIM 6*	29		2
25 Apr 87	**ALONE AGAIN OR** *MCA GRIM 7*	27		5
28 Nov 87	**IN DULCE DECORUM** *MCA GRIM 8*	72		

KENNY DAMON US singer

Date	Title / Label	Peak Position	Weeks at No.1	Weeks in Top 40
19 May 66	**WHILE I LIVE** *Mercury MF 907*	48		

VIC DAMONE US singer

Date	Title / Label	Peak Position	Weeks at No.1	Weeks in Top 40
6 Dec 57	**AN AFFAIR TO REMEMBER** *Philips PB 745*	29		2
9 May 58	**ON THE STREET WHERE YOU LIVE** *Philips PB 819*	1	2	17
1 Aug 58	**THE ONLY MAN ON THE ISLAND** *Philips PB 837*	24		3

DAN-I UK singer

Date	Title / Label	Peak Position	Weeks at No.1	Weeks in Top 40
10 Nov 79	**MONKEY CHOP** *Island WIP 6520*	30		4

RICHIE DAN UK producer

Date	Title / Label	Peak Position	Weeks at No.1	Weeks in Top 40
12 Aug 00	**CALL IT FATE** *Pure Silk CDPSR 1*	34		1

DANA UK singer

Date	Title / Label	Peak Position	Weeks at No.1	Weeks in Top 40
4 Apr 70	**ALL KINDS OF EVERYTHING** *Rex R 11054*	1	2	14
13 Feb 71	**WHO PUT THE LIGHTS OUT** *Rex R 11062*	14		10
25 Jan 75	**PLEASE TELL HIM I SAID HELLO** *GTO GT 6*	8		12
13 Dec 75	**IT'S GONNA BE A COLD COLD CHRISTMAS** *GTO GT 45*	4		5
6 Mar 76	**NEVER GONNA FALL IN LOVE AGAIN** *GTO GT 55*	31		3
16 Oct 76	**FAIRYTALE** *GTO GT 66*	13		15
31 Mar 79	**SOMETHING'S COOKIN' IN THE KITCHEN** *GTO GT 243*	44		
15 May 82	**I FEEL LOVE COMIN' ON** *Creole CR 32*	66		

DANA INTERNATIONAL Israeli singer

Date	Title / Label	Peak Position	Weeks at No.1	Weeks in Top 40
27 Jun 98	**DIVA** *Dance Pool DANA 1CD*	11		2

CHARLEAN DANCE UK singer

Date	Title / Label	Peak Position	Weeks at No.1	Weeks in Top 40
22 Sep 07	**MR DJ** *Positiva CDTIVS260*	51		

DANCE CONSPIRACY UK production duo

Date	Title / Label	Peak Position	Weeks at No.1	Weeks in Top 40
3 Oct 92	**DUB WAR** *XL Recordings XLT 34*	72		

DANCE FLOOR VIRUS Italian group

Date	Title / Label	Peak Position	Weeks at No.1	Weeks in Top 40
21 Oct 95	**MESSAGE IN A BOTTLE** *Epic 6623742*	49		

DANCE TO TIPPERARY Irish group

Date	Title / Label	Peak Position	Weeks at No.1	Weeks in Top 40
24 May 03	**THE BHOYS ARE BACK IN TOWN** *Nede NRCD 2105*	44		

DANCE 2 TRANCE German production duo

Date	Title / Label	Peak Position	Weeks at No.1	Weeks in Top 40
24 Apr 93	**P.OWER OF A.MERICAN N.ATIVES** *Logic 74321139582*	25		3
24 Jul 93	**TAKE A FREE FALL** *Logic 74321153602*	36		1
4 Feb 95	**WARRIOR** *Logic 74321257722*	56		

DANCING DJS UK production duo

Date	Title / Label	Peak Position	Weeks at No.1	Weeks in Top 40
6 Aug 05	**FADING LIKE A FLOWER** *All Around The World CDGLOBE426* DANCING DJS VS ROXETTE	18		4

EVAN DANDO US singer/guitarist

Date	Title / Label	Peak Position	Weeks at No.1	Weeks in Top 40
24 Jun 95	**PERFECT DAY** *Virgin VSCDT 1552* KIRSTY MacCOLL & EVAN DANDO	75		

Silver-selling · Gold-selling · Platinum-selling · US No.1 ★ · Peak Position · Weeks at No.1 · Weeks in Top 40

Date	Title	Peak Position	Weeks at No.1	Weeks in Top 40
31 May 03	**STOP MY HEAD** *Setanta SETCDB 127*	38		1
13 Dec 03	**IT LOOKS LIKE YOU** *Setanta SETCDA 130*	68		

DANDY WARHOLS US group

Date	Title	Peak Position	Weeks at No.1	Weeks in Top 40
28 Feb 98	**EVERY DAY SHOULD BE A HOLIDAY** *Capitol CDCL 797*	29		1
2 May 98	**NOT IF YOU WERE THE LAST JUNKIE ON EARTH** *Capitol CDCL 800*	13		2
8 Aug 98	**BOYS BETTER** *Capitol CDCLS 805*	36		1
10 Jun 00	**GET OFF** *Capitol CDCLS 821*	38		1
9 Sep 00	**BOHEMIAN LIKE YOU** *Capitol CDCLS 823*	42		
7 Jul 01	**GODLESS** *Capitol CDCL 829*	66		
10 Nov 01	**BOHEMIAN LIKE YOU** *Capitol CDCLX 823*	5		5
16 Mar 02	**GET OFF** *Capitol CDCL 835*	34		1
17 May 03	**WE USED TO BE FRIENDS** *Capitol CDCL 843*	18		1
9 Aug 03	**YOU WERE THE LAST HIGH** *Parlophone CDCLX 845*	34		1
6 Dec 03	**PLAN A** *Parlophone CDCLS 851*	66		
10 Sep 05	**SMOKE IT** *Parlophone CDCLS871*	59		
12 Aug 06	**HORNY AS A DANDY** *Feverpitch/Free2air CDFEV14* MOUSSE T VS DANDY WARHOLS	17		2

DANDYS UK group

Date	Title	Peak Position	Weeks at No.1	Weeks in Top 40
14 Mar 98	**YOU MAKE ME WANT TO SCREAM** *Artificial ATFCD 3*	71		
30 May 98	**ENGLISH COUNTRY GARDEN** *Artificial ATFCD 4*	57		

D'ANGELO US singer

Date	Title	Peak Position	Weeks at No.1	Weeks in Top 40
28 Oct 95	**BROWN SUGAR** *Cooltempo CDCOOL 307*	24		2
2 Mar 96	**COLD WORLD** *Geffen GFSTD 22114* GENIUS/GZA FEATURING D'ANGELO	40		1
2 Mar 96	**CRUISIN'** *Cooltempo CDCOOL 316*	31		1
15 Jun 96	**LADY** *Cooltempo CDCOOLS 323*	21		1
22 May 99	**BREAK UPS 2 MAKE UPS** *Def Jam 8709272* METHOD MAN FEATURING D'ANGELO	33		1

DANGER DANGER US group

Date	Title	Peak Position	Weeks at No.1	Weeks in Top 40
8 Feb 92	**MONKEY BUSINESS** *Epic 6577517*	42		
28 Mar 92	**I STILL THINK ABOUT YOU** *Epic 6578387*	46		
13 Jun 92	**COMIN' HOME** *Epic 6581337*	75		

CHARLIE DANIELS BAND US group

Date	Title	Peak Position	Weeks at No.1	Weeks in Top 40
22 Sep 79	**THE DEVIL WENT DOWN TO GEORGIA** *Epic EPC 7737*	14		7

JOHNNY DANKWORTH UK bandleader/saxophonist

Date	Title	Peak Position	Weeks at No.1	Weeks in Top 40
22 Jun 56	**EXPERIMENTS WITH MICE** *Parlophone R 4185*	7		12
23 Feb 61	**AFRICAN WALTZ** *Columbia DB 4590*	9		18

DANNY & THE JUNIORS US group

Date	Title	Peak Position	Weeks at No.1	Weeks in Top 40
17 Jan 58	**AT THE HOP** *HMV POP 436* ★	3		14
10 Jul 76	**AT THE HOP** *ABC 4123*	39		2

DANNY WILSON UK group

Date	Title	Peak Position	Weeks at No.1	Weeks in Top 40
22 Aug 87	**MARY'S PRAYER** *Virgin VS 934*	42		
2 Apr 88	**MARY'S PRAYER** *Virgin VS 934*	3		8
17 Jun 89	**THE SECOND SUMMER OF LOVE** *Virgin VS 1186*	23		5
16 Sep 89	**NEVER GONNA BE THE SAME** *Virgin VS 1203*	69		

DANSE SOCIETY UK group

Date	Title	Peak Position	Weeks at No.1	Weeks in Top 40
27 Aug 83	**WAKE UP** *Society SOC 5*	61		
5 Nov 83	**HEAVEN IS WAITING** *Society SOC 6*	60		

STEVEN DANTE UK singer

Date	Title	Peak Position	Weeks at No.1	Weeks in Top 40
26 Sep 87	**THE REAL THING** *Chrysalis CHS 3167* JELLYBEAN FEATURING STEVEN DANTE	13		8
9 Jul 88	**I'M TOO SCARED** *Cooltempo DANTE 1*	34		3

TONJA DANTZLER US singer

Date	Title	Peak Position	Weeks at No.1	Weeks in Top 40
17 Dec 94	**IN AND OUT OF MY LIFE** *ffrr FCD 246*	66		

DANZEL Belgian singer

Date	Title	Peak Position	Weeks at No.1	Weeks in Top 40
6 Nov 04	**PUMP IT UP** *Data 75CDS*	11		3

DANZIG US group

Date	Title	Peak Position	Weeks at No.1	Weeks in Top 40
14 May 94	**MOTHER** *American Recordings MOMDD 1*	62		

DAPHNE US singer

Date	Title	Peak Position	Weeks at No.1	Weeks in Top 40
9 Dec 95	**CHANGE** *Stress CDSTR 54*	71		

DAPHNE & CELESTE US duo

Date	Title	Peak Position	Weeks at No.1	Weeks in Top 40
5 Feb 00	**OOH STICK YOU!** *Universal MCSTD 40209*	8		9
17 Jun 00	**UGLY** *Universal MCSTD 40232*	18		4
2 Sep 00	**SCHOOL'S OUT** *Universal MCSTD 40238*	12		2

TERENCE TRENT D'ARBY US singer

Date	Title	Peak Position	Weeks at No.1	Weeks in Top 40
14 Mar 87	**IF YOU LET ME STAY** *CBS TRENT 1*	7		10
20 Jun 87	**WISHING WELL** *CBS TRENT 2* ★	4		9
10 Oct 87	**DANCE LITTLE SISTER (PART ONE)** *CBS TRENT 3*	20		5
9 Jan 88	**SIGN YOUR NAME** *CBS TRENT 4*	2		8
20 Jan 90	**TO KNOW SOMEONE DEEPLY IS TO KNOW SOMEONE SOFTLY** *CBS TRENT 6*	55		
17 Apr 93	**DO YOU LOVE ME LIKE YOU SAY** *Columbia 6590732*	14		4
19 Jun 93	**DELICATE** *Columbia 6593312* TERENCE TRENT D'ARBY FEATURING DES'REE	14		4
28 Aug 93	**SHE KISSED ME** *Columbia 6595922*	16		5
20 Nov 93	**LET HER DOWN EASY** *Columbia 6598642*	18		4
8 Apr 95	**HOLDING ON TO YOU** *Columbia 6614235*	20		5
5 Aug 95	**VIBRATOR** *Columbia 6622585*	57		

RICHARD DARBYSHIRE UK singer

Date	Title	Peak Position	Weeks at No.1	Weeks in Top 40
20 Aug 88	**COMING BACK FOR MORE** *Chrysalis JEL 4* JELLYBEAN FEATURING RICHARD DARBYSHIRE	41		
24 Jul 93	**THIS I SWEAR** *Dome CDDOME 1003*	50		
12 Feb 94	**WHEN ONLY LOVE WILL DO** *Dome CDDOME 1008*	54		

DARE UK group

Date	Title	Peak Position	Weeks at No.1	Weeks in Top 40
29 Apr 89	**THE RAINDANCE** *A&M AM 483*	62		
29 Jul 89	**ABANDON** *A&M AM 519*	71		
10 Aug 91	**WE DON'T NEED A REASON** *A&M AM 775*	52		
5 Oct 91	**REAL LOVE** *A&M AM 824*	67		
13 Sep 03	**CHIHUAHUA** *All Around The World CDGLOBE 311*	45		

MATT DAREY UK producer

Date	Title	Peak Position	Weeks at No.1	Weeks in Top 40
9 Oct 99	**LIBERATION (TEMPTATION – FLY LIKE AN EAGLE)** *Incentive CENT 1CDS* MATT DAREY PRESENTS MASH UP	19		2
22 Apr 00	**FROM RUSSIA WITH LOVE** *Liquid Asset ASSETCD 003* MATT DAREY PRESENTS DSP	40		1
15 Jul 00	**BEAUTIFUL** *Incentive CENT 7CDS* MATT DAREY'S MASH UP PRESENTS MARCELLA WOODS	21		2
20 Apr 02	**BEAUTIFUL** *Incentive CENT 38CDS* MATT DAREY FEATURING MARCELLA WOODS	10		4
14 Dec 02	**U SHINE ON** *Incentive CENT 50CDS* MATT DAREY & MARCELLA WOODS	34		1

BOBBY DARIN US singer

Date	Title	Peak Position	Weeks at No.1	Weeks in Top 40
1 Aug 58	**SPLISH SPLASH** *London HLE 8666*	18		7
9 Jan 59	**QUEEN OF THE HOP** *London HLE 8737*	24		2
29 May 59	**DREAM LOVER** *London HLE 8867*	1	4	19
25 Sep 59	**MACK THE KNIFE** *London HLK 8939* ★	1	2	17
29 Jan 60	**LA MER (BEYOND THE SEA)** *London HLK 9034*	8		10
31 Mar 60	**CLEMENTINE** *London HLK 9086*	8		12
30 Jun 60	**BILL BAILEY** *London HLK 9142*	34		2
16 Mar 61	**LAZY RIVER** *London HLK 9303*	2		11
6 Jul 61	**NATURE BOY** *London HLK 9375*	24		6
12 Oct 61	**YOU MUST HAVE BEEN A BEAUTIFUL BABY** *London HLK 9429*	10		9
26 Oct 61	**THEME FROM COME SEPTEMBER** *London HLK 9407* BOBBY DARIN ORCHESTRA	50		
21 Dec 61	**MULTIPLICATION** *London HLK 9474*	5		12
19 Jul 62	**THINGS** *London HLK 9575*	2		16
4 Oct 62	**IF A MAN ANSWERS** *Capitol CL 15272*	24		5

Silver-selling · Gold-selling · Platinum-selling · US No.1 ★ · Peak Position · Weeks at No.1 · Weeks in Top 40

Date	Title / Label	Peak Position	Weeks at No.1	Weeks in Top 40
29 Nov 62	**BABY FACE** *London HLK 9624*	40		1
25 Jul 63	**EIGHTEEN YELLOW ROSES** *Capitol CL 15306*	37		1
13 Oct 66	**IF I WERE A CARPENTER** *Atlantic 584 051*	9		11
14 Apr 79	**DREAM LOVER/MACK THE KNIFE** *Lightning LIG 9017*	64		

DARIO G UK group

Date	Title / Label	Peak Position	Weeks at No.1	Weeks in Top 40
27 Sep 97	**SUNCHYME** *Eternal 130CD*	2		10
20 Jun 98	**CARNAVAL DE PARIS** *Eternal 162CD*	5		6
12 Sep 98	**SUNMACHINE** *Eternal 173CD*	17		2
25 Mar 00	**VOICES** *Eternal 256CD1*	37		1
3 Feb 01	**DREAM TO ME** *Manifesto FESCD 79*	9		4
8 Jun 02	**CARNAVAL 2002** *Eternal WEA 349CD*	34		1
25 Jan 03	**HEAVEN IS CLOSER (FEELS LIKE HEAVEN)** *Serious SER 61CD*	39		1

DARIUS UK singer

Date	Title / Label	Peak Position	Weeks at No.1	Weeks in Top 40
10 Aug 02	**COLOURBLIND** *Mercury 639662*	1	2	11
7 Dec 02	**RUSHES** *Mercury 0638052*	5		6
15 Mar 03	**INCREDIBLE (WHAT I MEANT TO SAY)** *Mercury 0779782*	9		3
21 Jun 03	**GIRL IN THE MOON** *Mercury 9808234*	21		1
30 Oct 04	**KINDA LOVE** *Mercury 9868350*	8		2
22 Jan 05	**LIVE TWICE** *Mercury 9869470*	7		3

DARK GLOBE UK production duo

Date	Title / Label	Peak Position	Weeks at No.1	Weeks in Top 40
1 May 04	**BREAK MY WORLD** *Island CID 853* DARK GLOBE FEATURING AMANDA GHOST	52		

DARK MONKS UK production duo

Date	Title / Label	Peak Position	Weeks at No.1	Weeks in Top 40
14 Sep 02	**INSANE** *Incentive CENT 45CDS*	62		

DARK STAR UK group

Date	Title / Label	Peak Position	Weeks at No.1	Weeks in Top 40
26 Jun 99	**ABOUT 3AM** *Harvest CDEM 545*	50		
15 Jan 00	**GRACEADELICA** *Harvest CDEMS 556*	25		1
13 May 00	**I AM THE SUN** *Harvest CDEMS 566*	31		1

DARKMAN UK rapper

Date	Title / Label	Peak Position	Weeks at No.1	Weeks in Top 40
14 May 94	**YABBA DABBA DOO** *Wild Card CARDD 6*	49		
20 Aug 94	**WHO'S THE DARKMAN** *Wild Card CARDD 8*	46		
3 Dec 94	**YABBA DABBA DOO** *Wild Card CARDD 11*	37		1
21 Oct 95	**BRAND NEW DAY** *Wild Card 5771892*	74		

DARKNESS UK group

Date	Title / Label	Peak Position	Weeks at No.1	Weeks in Top 40
8 Mar 03	**GET YOUR HANDS OFF MY WOMAN** *Must Destory DUSTY 006CD*	43		
28 Jun 03	**GROWING ON ME** *Must Destory DUSTY 010CD*	11		3
4 Oct 03	**I BELIEVE IN A THING CALLED LOVE** *Must Destroy DARK 01CD*	2		11
27 Dec 03	**CHRISTMAS TIME (DON'T LET THE BELLS END)** *Must Destroy DARK 02CD*	2		5
3 Apr 04	**LOVE IS ONLY A FEELING** *Must Destroy DARK 03CD*	5		5
1 Jan 05	**CHRISTMAS TIME (DON'T LET THE BELLS END)** *Must Destroy DARK 01CD*	58		
26 Nov 05	**ONE WAY TICKET** *Atlantic DARK04CD*	8		4
4 Mar 06	**IS IT JUST ME?** *Atlantic DARK05CD*	8		2
3 Jun 06	**GIRLFRIEND** *Atlantic DARK06CD*	39		1

DARLING BUDS UK group

Date	Title / Label	Peak Position	Weeks at No.1	Weeks in Top 40
8 Oct 88	**BURST** *Epic BLOND 1*	50		
7 Jan 89	**HIT THE GROUND** *CBS BLOND 2*	27		3
25 Mar 89	**LET'S GO ROUND THERE** *CBS BLOND 3*	49		
22 Jul 89	**YOU'VE GOT TO CHOOSE** *CBS BLOND 4*	45		
2 Jun 90	**TINY MACHINE** *CBS BLOND 5*	60		
12 Sep 92	**SURE THING** *Epic 6582157*	71		

GUY DARRELL UK singer

Date	Title / Label	Peak Position	Weeks at No.1	Weeks in Top 40
18 Aug 73	**I'VE BEEN HURT** *Santa Ponsa PNS 4*	12		10

JAMES DARREN US singer/actor

Date	Title / Label	Peak Position	Weeks at No.1	Weeks in Top 40
11 Aug 60	**BECAUSE THEY'RE YOUNG** *Pye International 7N 25059*	29		4
14 Dec 61	**GOODBYE CRUEL WORLD** *Pye International 7N 25116*	28		5
29 Mar 62	**HER ROYAL MAJESTY** *Pye International 7N 25125*	36		2
21 Jun 62	**CONSCIENCE** *Pye International 7N 25138*	30		3

DARTS UK group

Date	Title / Label	Peak Position	Weeks at No.1	Weeks in Top 40
5 Nov 77	**DADDY COOL/THE GIRL CAN'T HELP IT** *Magnet MAG 100*	6		13
28 Jan 78	**COME BACK MY LOVE** *Magnet MAG 110*	2		11
6 May 78	**BOY FROM NEW YORK CITY** *Magnet MAG 116*	2		10
5 Aug 78	**IT'S RAINING** *Magnet MAG 126*	2		9
11 Nov 78	**DON'T LET IT FADE AWAY** *Magnet MAG 134*	18		8
10 Feb 79	**GET IT** *Magnet MAG 140*	10		6
21 Jul 79	**DUKE OF EARL** *Magnet MAG 147*	6		8
20 Oct 79	**CAN'T GET ENOUGH OF YOUR LOVE** *Magnet MAG 156*	43		
1 Dec 79	**REET PETITE** *Magnet MAG 160*	51		
31 May 80	**LET'S HANG ON** *Magnet MAG 174*	11		9
6 Sep 80	**PEACHES** *Magnet MAG 179*	66		
29 Nov 80	**WHITE CHRISTMAS/SH-BOOM (LIFE COULD BE A DREAM)** *Magnet MAG 184*	48		

DARUDE Finnish producer

Date	Title / Label	Peak Position	Weeks at No.1	Weeks in Top 40
24 Jun 00	**SANDSTORM** *Neo NEOCD 033*	3		13
25 Nov 00	**FEEL THE BEAT** *Neo NEOCD 045*	5		8
15 Sep 01	**OUT OF CONTROL (BACK FOR MORE)** *Neo NEOCD 067*	13		3

DAS EFX US duo

Date	Title / Label	Peak Position	Weeks at No.1	Weeks in Top 40
7 Aug 93	**CHECK YO SELF** *Fourth & Broadway BRCD 283* ICE CUBE FEATURING DAS EFX	36		3
25 Apr 98	**RAP SCHOLAR** *East West E 3853CD* DAS EFX FEATURING REDMAN	42		

DASHBOARD CONFESSIONAL US group

Date	Title / Label	Peak Position	Weeks at No.1	Weeks in Top 40
22 Nov 03	**HANDS DOWN** *Interscope 9813790*	60		
27 Mar 04	**RAPID HOPE LOSS** *Vagrant 9861991*	75		
2 Sep 06	**DON'T WAIT** *Vagrant VRUK037CDS*	68		

DATSUNS New Zealand group

Date	Title / Label	Peak Position	Weeks at No.1	Weeks in Top 40
5 Oct 02	**IN LOVE** *V2 VVR 5020953*	25		1
22 Feb 03	**HARMONIC GENERATOR** *V2 VVR 5021228*	33		1
6 Sep 03	**MF FROM HELL** *V2 VVR 5021753*	55		
12 Jun 04	**BLACKEN MY THUMB** *V2 VVR 5026953*	48		
23 Oct 04	**GIRLS BEST FRIEND** *V2 VVR 5028893*	71		

N'DEA DAVENPORT US singer

Date	Title / Label	Peak Position	Weeks at No.1	Weeks in Top 40
5 Oct 91	**NEVER STOP** *ffrr F 165* BRAND NEW HEAVIES FEATURING N'DEA DAVENPORT	43		
15 Feb 92	**DREAM COME TRUE** *ffrr F 180* BRAND NEW HEAVIES FEATURING N'DEA DAVENPORT	24		3
18 Apr 92	**ULTIMATE TRUNK FUNK EP** *ffrr F 185* BRAND NEW HEAVIES FEATURING N'DEA DAVENPORT	19		4
1 Aug 92	**DON'T LET IT GO TO YOUR HEAD** *ffrr BNH 1* BRAND NEW HEAVIES FEATURING N'DEA DAVENPORT	24		2
19 Dec 92	**STAY THIS WAY** *ffrr BNH 2* BRAND NEW HEAVIES FEATURING N'DEA DAVENPORT	40		1
11 Sep 93	**TRUST ME** *Cooltempo CDCOOL 278* GURU FEATURING N'DEA DAVENPORT	34		1
26 Mar 94	**DREAM ON DREAMER** *ffrr BNHCD 3* BRAND NEW HEAVIES FEATURING N'DEA DAVENPORT	15		2
11 Jun 94	**BACK TO LOVE** *ffrr BNHCD 4* BRAND NEW HEAVIES FEATURING N'DEA DAVENPORT	23		3
13 Aug 94	**MIDNIGHT AT THE OASIS** *ffrr BNHCDP 5* BRAND NEW HEAVIES FEATURING N'DEA DAVENPORT	13		5
5 Nov 94	**SPEND SOME TIME** *ffrr BNHCD 6* BRAND NEW HEAVIES FEATURING N'DEA DAVENPORT	26		2
11 Mar 95	**CLOSE TO YOU** *ffrr BNCDP 7* BRAND NEW HEAVIES FEATURING N'DEA DAVENPORT	38		2
20 Jun 98	**BRING IT ON** *Gee Street VVR 5002033*	52		
15 Dec 01	**YOU CAN'T CHANGE ME** *Defected DFECT 41CDS* ROGER SANCHEZ FEATURING ARMAND VAN HELDEN AND N'DEA DAVENPORT	25		1

ANNE-MARIE DAVID French singer

Date	Title / Label	Peak Position	Weeks at No.1	Weeks in Top 40
28 Apr 73	**WONDERFUL DREAM** *Epic EPC 1446*	13		9

CRAIG DAVID UK singer

Date	Title / Label	Peak Position	Weeks at No.1	Weeks in Top 40
11 Dec 99	**RE-REWIND THE CROWD SAY BO SELECTA** *Public Demand/Relentless RELENT 1CDS* ARTFUL DODGER FEATURING CRAIG DAVID ⊛	2		13
15 Apr 00	**FILL ME IN** *Wildstar CDWILD 28* ●	1	1	10
15 Jul 00	**WOMAN TROUBLE** *Public Demand/ffrr FCDP 380* ARTFUL DODGER FEATURING ROBBIE CRAIG & CRAIG DAVID	6		7
5 Aug 00	**7 DAYS** *Wildstar CDWILD 30*	1	1	9
2 Dec 00	**WALKING AWAY** *Wildstar CDWILD 35* ○	3		8
31 Mar 01	**RENDEZVOUS** *Wildstar CDWILD 36*	8		6
9 Nov 02	**WHAT'S YOUR FLAVA?** *Wildstar CDWILD 43*	8		4
1 Feb 03	**HIDDEN AGENDA** *Wildstar CDWILD 44*	10		3
10 May 03	**RISE & FALL** *Wildstar CDWILD 45* CRAIG DAVID & STING	2		7
9 Aug 03	**SPANISH** *Wildstar CXWILD 49*	8		3
25 Oct 03	**WORLD FILLED WITH LOVE** *Wildstar CDWILD 51*	15		2
10 Jan 04	**YOU DON'T MISS YOUR WATER** *Wildstar CDWILD 52*	43		
20 Aug 05	**ALL THE WAY** *Warner Brothers WEA393CD1*	3		5
12 Nov 05	**DON'T LOVE YOU NO MORE** *Warner Brothers WEA396CD2*	4		10
18 Mar 06	**UNBELIEVABLE** *Warner Brothers WEA402CD1*	18		3
1 Sep 07	**THIS IS THE GIRL** *679 679L148CD* KANO FEATURING CRAIG DAVID	18		6
10 Nov 07	**HOT STUFF** *Warner Brothers WEA434CD2*	7		7
9 Feb 08	**6 OF 1 THING** *Warner Brothers WEA440CD*	39		1

F.R. DAVID French singer

Date	Title / Label	Peak Position	Weeks at No.1	Weeks in Top 40
2 Apr 83	**WORDS** *Carrere CAR 248*	2		11
18 Jun 83	**MUSIC** *Carrere CAR 282*	71		

TERRA DEVA US singer

Date	Title / Label	Peak Position	Weeks at No.1	Weeks in Top 40
15 Feb 03	**STING ME RED (YOU THINK YOU'RE SO)** *Cream 19CDS* WHO DA FUNK FEATURING TERRA DEVA	32		1
12 Feb 05	**WHAT DO YOU WANT?** *Subliminal SUB138CD* MORILLO FEATURING TERRA DEVA	61		

DAVID DEVANT & HIS SPIRIT WIFE UK group

Date	Title / Label	Peak Position	Weeks at No.1	Weeks in Top 40
5 Apr 97	**GINGER** *Rhythm King KIND 4CD*	54		
21 Jun 97	**THIS IS FOR REAL** *Rhythm King KIND 5CD*	61		

DAVID & JONATHAN UK duo

Date	Title / Label	Peak Position	Weeks at No.1	Weeks in Top 40
13 Jan 66	**MICHELLE** *Columbia DB 7800*	11		6
7 Jul 66	**LOVERS OF THE WORLD UNITE** *Columbia DB 7950*	7		13

JIM DAVIDSON UK comedian

Date	Title / Label	Peak Position	Weeks at No.1	Weeks in Top 40
27 Dec 80	**WHITE CHRISTMAS/TOO RISKY** *Scratch SCR 001*	52		

PAUL DAVIDSON Jamaican singer

Date	Title / Label	Peak Position	Weeks at No.1	Weeks in Top 40
27 Dec 75	**MIDNIGHT RIDER** *Tropical ALO 56*	10		8

DAVE DAVIES UK singer/guitarist

Date	Title / Label	Peak Position	Weeks at No.1	Weeks in Top 40
19 Jul 67	**DEATH OF A CLOWN** *Pye 7N 17356*	3		10
6 Dec 67	**SUSANNAH'S STILL ALIVE** *Pye 7N 17429*	20		6

WINDSOR DAVIES & DON ESTELLE UK actors/comedians

Date	Title / Label	Peak Position	Weeks at No.1	Weeks in Top 40
17 May 75	**WHISPERING GRASS** *EMI 2290* ●	1	3	12
25 Oct 75	**PAPER DOLL** *EMI 2361*	41		

BILLIE DAVIS UK singer

Date	Title / Label	Peak Position	Weeks at No.1	Weeks in Top 40
30 Aug 62	**WILL I WHAT** *Parlophone R 4932* MIKE SARNE WITH BILLIE DAVIS	18		10
7 Feb 63	**TELL HIM** *Decca F 11572*	10		11
30 May 63	**HE'S THE ONE** *Decca F 11658*	40		1
9 Oct 68	**I WANT YOU TO BE MY BABY** *Decca F 12823*	33		6

DARLENE DAVIS US singer

Date	Title / Label	Peak Position	Weeks at No.1	Weeks in Top 40
7 Feb 87	**I FOUND LOVE** *Serious 7OUS 1*	55		

JOHN DAVIS & THE MONSTER ORCHESTRA US group

Date	Title / Label	Peak Position	Weeks at No.1	Weeks in Top 40
10 Feb 79	**AIN'T THAT ENOUGH FOR YOU** *Miracle M 2*	70		

MAC DAVIS US singer

Date	Title / Label	Peak Position	Weeks at No.1	Weeks in Top 40
4 Nov 72	**BABY DON'T GET HOOKED ON ME** *CBS 8250* ★	29		5
15 Nov 80	**IT'S HARD TO BE HUMBLE** *Casablanca CAN 210*	27		7

ROY DAVIS Jr US producer

Date	Title / Label	Peak Position	Weeks at No.1	Weeks in Top 40
1 Nov 97	**GABRIEL** *XL Recordings XLS 88CD* ROY DAVIS Jr FEATURING PEVEN EVERETT	22		2
31 Jan 04	**ABOUT LOVE** *Classic CMC21*	70		

SAMMY DAVIS Jr US singer/actor

Date	Title / Label	Peak Position	Weeks at No.1	Weeks in Top 40
29 Jul 55	**SOMETHING'S GOTTA GIVE** *Brunswick 05428*	11		7
9 Sep 55	**LOVE ME OR LEAVE ME** *Brunswick 05428*	8		8
30 Sep 55	**THAT OLD BLACK MAGIC** *Brunswick 05450*	16		1
7 Oct 55	**HEY THERE** *Brunswick 05469*	19		1
20 Apr 56	**IN A PERSIAN MARKET** *Brunswick 05518*	28		1
28 Dec 56	**ALL OF YOU** *Brunswick 05629*	28		1
16 Jun 60	**HAPPY TO MAKE YOUR ACQUAINTANCE** *Brunswick 05830* SAMMY DAVIS Jr & CARMEN McRAE	46		
22 Mar 62	**WHAT KIND OF FOOL AM I?/GONNA BUILD A MOUNTAIN** *Reprise R 20048*	26		5
13 Dec 62	**ME AND MY SHADOW** *Reprise R 20128* SAMMY DAVIS Jr FEATURING FRANK SINATRA	20		5

SKEETER DAVIS US singer

Date	Title / Label	Peak Position	Weeks at No.1	Weeks in Top 40
14 Mar 63	**END OF THE WORLD** *RCA 1328*	18		12

SPENCER DAVIS GROUP UK group

Date	Title / Label	Peak Position	Weeks at No.1	Weeks in Top 40
5 Nov 64	**I CAN'T STAND IT** *Fontana TF 499*	47		
25 Feb 65	**EVERY LITTLE BIT HURTS** *Fontana TF 530*	41		
10 Jun 65	**STRONG LOVE** *Fontana TF 571*	44		
2 Dec 65	**KEEP ON RUNNING** *Fontana TF 632*	1	1	12
24 Mar 66	**SOMEBODY HELP ME** *Fontana TF 679*	1	2	10
1 Sep 66	**WHEN I COME HOME** *Fontana TF 739*	12		8
3 Nov 66	**GIMME SOME LOVING** *Fontana TF 762*	2		11
26 Jan 67	**I'M A MAN** *Fontana TF 785*	9		6
9 Aug 67	**TIME SELLER** *Fontana TF 854*	30		5
10 Jan 68	**MR SECOND CLASS** *United Artists UP 1203*	35		3

TJ DAVIS UK singer

Date	Title / Label	Peak Position	Weeks at No.1	Weeks in Top 40
27 Jul 96	**BRILLIANT FEELING** *Arista 74321380902* FULL MONTY ALLSTARS FEATURING TJ DAVIS	72		
29 Dec 01	**WONDERFUL LIFE** *Melting Pot MPRCD 20*	42		

DAWN US group

Date	Title / Label	Peak Position	Weeks at No.1	Weeks in Top 40
16 Jan 71	**CANDIDA** *Bell 1118*	9		10
10 Apr 71	**KNOCK THREE TIMES** *Bell 1146* ★	1	5	24
31 Jul 71	**WHAT ARE YOU DOING SUNDAY** *Bell 1169* DAWN FEATURING TONY ORLANDO	3		12
10 Mar 73	**TIE A YELLOW RIBBON ROUND THE OLD OAK TREE** *Bell 1287* DAWN FEATURING TONY ORLANDO ★	1	4	35
4 Aug 73	**SAY, HAS ANYBODY SEEN MY SWEET GYPSY ROSE** *Bell 1322* DAWN FEATURING TONY ORLANDO	12		12
9 Mar 74	**WHO'S IN THE STRAWBERRY PATCH WITH SALLY** *Bell 1343*	37		2

DAWN OF THE REPLICANTS UK group

Date	Title / Label	Peak Position	Weeks at No.1	Weeks in Top 40
7 Feb 98	**CANDLEFIRE** *East West EW 147CD1*	52		
4 Apr 98	**HOGWASH FARM (THE DIESEL HANDS EP)** *East West EW 157CD*	65		

DANA DAWSON US singer

Date	Title / Label	Peak Position	Weeks at No.1	Weeks in Top 40
15 Jul 95	**3 IS FAMILY** *EMI CDEM 378*	9		6
28 Oct 95	**GOT TO GIVE ME LOVE** *EMI CDEM 392*	27		1
4 May 96	**SHOW ME** *EMI CDEMS 423*	28		1
20 Jul 96	**HOW I WANNA BE LOVED** *EMI CDEMS 432*	42		

Silver-selling ● Gold-selling ● Platinum-selling ● US No.1 ★ — Peak Position · Weeks at No.1 · Weeks in Top 40

BOBBY DAY US singer

Date	Title / Label	Peak Position	Weeks at No.1	Weeks in Top 40
7 Nov 58	**ROCKIN' ROBIN** *London HL 8726*	29		2

DARREN DAY UK singer/actor

Date	Title / Label	Peak Position	Weeks at No.1	Weeks in Top 40
8 Oct 94	**YOUNG GIRL** *Bell 74321231082*	42		
8 Jun 96	**SUMMER HOLIDAY MEDLEY** *RCA 74321384472*	17		2
9 May 98	**HOW CAN I BE SURE?** *Eastcoast DDCD 001*	71		

DORIS DAY US singer

Date	Title / Label	Peak Position	Weeks at No.1	Weeks in Top 40
14 Nov 52	**SUGARBUSH** *Columbia DB 3123* DORIS DAY & FRANKIE LAINE	8		8
21 Nov 52	**MY LOVE AND DEVOTION** *Columbia DB 3157* DORIS DAY WITH PERCY FAITH & HIS ORCHESTRA	10		2
3 Apr 53	**MA SAYS PA SAYS** *Columbia DB 3242* DORIS DAY & JOHNNIE RAY	12		1
17 Apr 53	**FULL TIME JOB** *Columbia DB 3242* DORIS DAY & JOHNNIE RAY	11		1
24 Jul 53	**LET'S WALK THATA-WAY** *Philips PB 157* DORIS DAY & JOHNNIE RAY	4		14
2 Apr 54	**SECRET LOVE** *Philips PB 230* ★	1	9	29
27 Aug 54	**BLACK HILLS OF DAKOTA** *Philips PB 287*	7		8
1 Oct 54	**IF I GIVE MY HEART TO YOU** *Philips PB 325* DORIS DAY WITH THE MELLOMAN	4		11
8 Apr 55	**READY WILLING AND ABLE** *Philips PB 402* DORIS DAY WITH BUDDY COLE & HIS ORCHESTRA	7		9
9 Sep 55	**LOVE ME OR LEAVE ME** *Philips PB 479*	20		1
21 Oct 55	**I'LL NEVER STOP LOVING YOU** *Philips PB 497* DORIS DAY WITH PERCY FAITH & HIS ORCHESTRA	17		3
29 Jun 56	**WHATEVER WILL BE WILL BE (QUE SERA SERA)** *Philips PB 586* DORIS DAY WITH FRANK DE VOL & HIS ORCHESTRA	1	6	22
13 Jun 58	**A VERY PRECIOUS LOVE** *Philips PB 799* DORIS DAY WITH FRANK DE VOL & HIS ORCHESTRA	16		11
15 Aug 58	**EVERYBODY LOVES A LOVER** *Philips PB 843* DORIS DAY WITH FRANK DE VOL & HIS ORCHESTRA	25		4
12 Mar 64	**MOVE OVER DARLING** *CBS AAG 183*	8		14
18 Apr 87	**MOVE OVER DARLING** *CBS LEGS 1*	45		

INAYA DAY US singer

Date	Title / Label	Peak Position	Weeks at No.1	Weeks in Top 40
22 May 99	**JUST CAN'T GET ENOUGH** *AM:PM CDAMPM 121* HARRY 'CHOO CHOO' ROMERO PRESENTS INAYA DAY	39		1
7 Oct 00	**FEEL IT** *Positiva CDTIV 141*	51		
23 Jul 05	**NASTY GIRL** *All Around The World CDGLOBE449*	9		5

DAY ONE UK duo

Date	Title / Label	Peak Position	Weeks at No.1	Weeks in Top 40
13 Nov 99	**I'M DOIN' FINE** *Melankolic/Virgin SADD6*	68		

PATTI DAY US singer

Date	Title / Label	Peak Position	Weeks at No.1	Weeks in Top 40
9 Dec 89	**RIGHT BEFORE MY EYES** *Debut DEBT 3080*	69		

DAYEENE Swedish duo

Date	Title / Label	Peak Position	Weeks at No.1	Weeks in Top 40
17 Jul 99	**AND IT HURTS** *Pukka CDPUKKA 20*	63		

TAYLOR DAYNE US singer

Date	Title / Label	Peak Position	Weeks at No.1	Weeks in Top 40
23 Jan 88	**TELL IT TO MY HEART** *Arista 109616*	3		9
19 Mar 88	**PROVE YOUR LOVE** *Arista 109830*	8		7
11 Jun 88	**I'LL ALWAYS LOVE YOU** *Arista 111536*	41		
18 Nov 89	**WITH EVERY BEAT OF MY HEART** *Arista 112760*	53		
14 Apr 90	**I'LL BE YOUR SHELTER** *Arista 112996*	43		
4 Aug 90	**LOVE WILL LEAD YOU BACK** *Arista 113277* ★	69		
3 Jul 93	**CAN'T GET ENOUGH OF YOUR LOVE** *Arista 74321147852*	14		6
16 Apr 94	**I'LL WAIT** *Arista 74321203472*	29		2
4 Feb 95	**ORIGINAL SIN (THEME FROM *THE SHADOW*)** *Arista 74321223462*	63		
18 Nov 95	**SAY A PRAYER** *Arista 74321324292*	58		
13 Jan 96	**TELL IT TO MY HEART (REMIX)** *Arista 74321335962*	23		2

DAYTON US group

Date	Title / Label	Peak Position	Weeks at No.1	Weeks in Top 40
10 Dec 83	**THE SOUND OF MUSIC** *Capitol CL 318*	75		

DAZZ BAND US group

Date	Title / Label	Peak Position	Weeks at No.1	Weeks in Top 40
3 Nov 84	**LET IT ALL BLOW** *Motown TMG 1361*	12		10

DB BOULEVARD Italian production group

Date	Title / Label	Peak Position	Weeks at No.1	Weeks in Top 40
23 Feb 02	**POINT OF VIEW** *Illustrious CDILL 002*	3		8

DBM German group

Date	Title / Label	Peak Position	Weeks at No.1	Weeks in Top 40
12 Nov 77	**DISCO BEATLEMANIA** *Atlantic K 11027*	45		

D, B, M & T UK group

Date	Title / Label	Peak Position	Weeks at No.1	Weeks in Top 40
1 Aug 70	**MR PRESIDENT** *Fontana 6007 022*	33		4

D'BORA US singer

Date	Title / Label	Peak Position	Weeks at No.1	Weeks in Top 40
14 Sep 91	**DREAM ABOUT YOU** *Polydor PO 161*	75		
1 Jul 95	**GOING ROUND** *Vibe MCSTD 2055*	40		1
30 Mar 96	**GOOD LOVE REAL LOVE** *Music Plant MCSTD 40023*	58		

NINO DE ANGELO German singer

Date	Title / Label	Peak Position	Weeks at No.1	Weeks in Top 40
21 Jul 84	**GUARDIAN ANGEL** *Carrere CAR 335*	57		

DE BOS Dutch producer

Date	Title / Label	Peak Position	Weeks at No.1	Weeks in Top 40
25 Oct 97	**ON THE RUN** *Jive JIVECD 433*	51		

CHRIS DE BURGH UK singer

Date	Title / Label	Peak Position	Weeks at No.1	Weeks in Top 40
23 Oct 82	**DON'T PAY THE FERRYMAN** *A&M AMS 8256*	48		
12 May 84	**HIGH ON EMOTION** *A&M AM 190*	44		
12 Jul 86	**THE LADY IN RED** *A&M AM 331* ●	1	3	12
20 Sep 86	**FATAL HESITATION** *A&M AM 346*	44		
13 Dec 86	**A SPACEMAN CAME TRAVELLING/THE BALLROOM OF ROMANCE** *A&M AM 365*	40		1
12 Dec 87	**THE SIMPLE TRUTH (A CHILD IS BORN)** *A&M AM 427*	55		
29 Oct 88	**MISSING YOU** *A&M AM 474*	3		9
7 Jan 89	**TENDER HANDS** *A&M AM 486*	43		
14 Oct 89	**THIS WAITING HEART** *A&M AM 528*	59		
25 May 91	**THE SIMPLE TRUTH (A CHILD IS BORN)** *A&M RELF 1*	36		1
11 Apr 92	**SEPARATE TABLES** *A&M AM 863*	30		2
21 May 94	**BLONDE HAIR BLUE JEANS** *A&M 5805932*	51		
9 Dec 95	**THE SNOWS OF NEW YORK** *A&M 5813132*	60		
27 Sep 97	**SO BEAUTIFUL** *A&M 5823932*	29		2
18 Sep 99	**WHEN I THINK OF YOU** *A&M 4971302*	59		

DE CASTRO SISTERS US group

Date	Title / Label	Peak Position	Weeks at No.1	Weeks in Top 40
11 Feb 55	**TEACH ME TONIGHT** *London HL 8104*	20		1

DE-CODE UK group

Date	Title / Label	Peak Position	Weeks at No.1	Weeks in Top 40
18 May 96	**WONDERWALL/SOME MIGHT SAY** *Neoteric NRCD 2* DE-CODE FEATURING BEVERLI SKEETE	69		

ETIENNE DE CRECY French producer

Date	Title / Label	Peak Position	Weeks at No.1	Weeks in Top 40
28 Mar 98	**PRIX CHOC REMIXES** *Different DIF 007CD*	60		
20 Jan 01	**AM I WRONG** *XL Recordings XLS 127CD*	44		

DE FUNK UK/Italian production group

Date	Title / Label	Peak Position	Weeks at No.1	Weeks in Top 40
25 Sep 99	**PLEASURE LOVE** *INCredible INCS 3CD* DE FUNK FEATURING F45	49		

LENNIE DE ICE UK producer

Date	Title / Label	Peak Position	Weeks at No.1	Weeks in Top 40
17 Apr 99	**WE ARE I. E.** *Distinctive DISNCD 50*	61		

DE LA SOUL US group

Date	Title / Label	Peak Position	Weeks at No.1	Weeks in Top 40
8 Apr 89	**ME MYSELF AND I** *Big Life BLR 7*	22		6
8 Jul 89	**SAY NO GO** *Big Life BLR 10*	18		5
21 Oct 89	**EYE KNOW** *Big Life BLR 13*	14		6

Silver-selling ● Gold-selling ● Platinum-selling ● US No.1 ★ | Peak Position | Weeks at No.1 | Weeks in Top 40

Date	Title / Label	Peak Position	Weeks at No.1	Weeks in Top 40
23 Dec 89	**THE MAGIC NUMBER/BUDDY** *Big Life BLR 14*	7		7
24 Mar 90	**MAMA GAVE BIRTH TO THE SOUL CHILDREN** *Gee Street GEE 26* QUEEN LATIFAH + DE LA SOUL	14		6
27 Apr 91	**RING RING RING (HA HA HEY)** *Big Life BLR 42*	10		5
3 Aug 91	**A ROLLER SKATING JAM NAMED 'SATURDAYS'** *Big Life BLR 55*	22		4
23 Nov 91	**KEEPIN' THE FAITH** *Big Life BLR 64*	50		
18 Sep 93	**BREAKADAWN** *Big Life BLRD 103*	39		1
2 Apr 94	**FALLIN'** *Epic 6602622* TEENAGE FANCLUB & DE LA SOUL	59		
29 Jun 96	**STAKES IS HIGH** *Tommy Boy TBCD 7730*	55		
8 Mar 97	**4 MORE** *Tommy Boy TBCD 7779A* DE LA SOUL FEATURING ZHANE	52		
22 Jul 00	**OOOH** *Tommy Boy TBCD 2102B* DE LA SOUL FEATURING REDMAN	29		1
11 Nov 00	**ALL GOOD** *Tommy Boy TBCD 2154B* DE LA SOUL FEATURING CHAKA KHAN	33		1
2 Mar 02	**BABY PHAT** *Tommy Boy TBCD 2359B*	55		

DONNA DE LORY US singer

Date	Title / Label	Peak Position	Weeks at No.1	Weeks in Top 40
24 Jul 93	**JUST A DREAM** *MCA MCSTD 1750*	71		

WALDO DE LOS RIOS Argentinian orchestra leader

Date	Title / Label	Peak Position	Weeks at No.1	Weeks in Top 40
10 Apr 71	**MOZART SYMPHONY NO. 40 IN G MINOR K550 1ST MOVEMENT (ALLEGRO MOLTO)** *A&M AMS 836*	5		15

VINCENT DE MOOR Dutch producer

Date	Title / Label	Peak Position	Weeks at No.1	Weeks in Top 40
16 Aug 97	**FLOWTATION** *XL Recordings XLS 89CD*	54		
7 Apr 01	**FLY AWAY** *VC Recordings VCRD 87*	30		1

DE NADA UK group

Date	Title / Label	Peak Position	Weeks at No.1	Weeks in Top 40
25 Aug 01	**LOVE YOU ANYWAY** *Wildstar CDWILD 37*	15		3
9 Feb 02	**BRING IT ON TO MY LOVE** *Wildstar CDWILD 39*	24		2

DE NUIT Italian production duo

Date	Title / Label	Peak Position	Weeks at No.1	Weeks in Top 40
23 Nov 02	**ALL THAT MATTERED (LOVE YOU DOWN)** *Credence CDCRED 029*	38		1

LYNSEY DE PAUL UK singer/pianist

Date	Title / Label	Peak Position	Weeks at No.1	Weeks in Top 40
19 Aug 72	**SUGAR ME** *MAM 81*	5		8
2 Dec 72	**GETTING A DRAG** *MAM 88*	18		7
27 Oct 73	**WON'T SOMEBODY DANCE WITH ME** *MAM 109*	14		7
8 Jun 74	**OOH I DO** *Warner Brothers K 16401*	25		6
2 Nov 74	**NO HONESTLY** *Jet 747*	7		8
22 Mar 75	**MY MAN AND ME** *Jet 750*	40		1
26 Mar 77	**ROCK BOTTOM** *Polydor 2058 859* LYNSEY DE PAUL & MIKE MORAN	19		6

TULLIO DE PISCOPO Italian singer/drummer

Date	Title / Label	Peak Position	Weeks at No.1	Weeks in Top 40
28 Feb 87	**STOP BAJON...PRIMAVERA** *Greyhound GREY 9*	58		

REBECCA DE RUVO Swedish singer

Date	Title / Label	Peak Position	Weeks at No.1	Weeks in Top 40
1 Oct 94	**I CAUGHT YOU OUT** *Arista 74321230782*	72		

TERI DE SARIO US singer

Date	Title / Label	Peak Position	Weeks at No.1	Weeks in Top 40
2 Sep 78	**AIN'T NOTHING GONNA KEEP ME FROM YOU** *Casablanca CAN 128*	52		

DE SOUZA UK production group

Date	Title / Label	Peak Position	Weeks at No.1	Weeks in Top 40
14 Apr 07	**GUILTY** *Hed Kandi HK32CDS* DE SOUZA FEATURING SHENA	46		

STEPHANIE DE SYKES UK singer

Date	Title / Label	Peak Position	Weeks at No.1	Weeks in Top 40
20 Jul 74	**BORN WITH A SMILE ON MY FACE** *Bradley's BRAD 7409* STEPHANIE DE SYKES WITH RAIN ●	2		9
19 Apr 75	**WE'LL FIND OUR DAY** *Bradley's BRAD 7509*	17		7

WILLIAM DE VAUGHN US singer

Date	Title / Label	Peak Position	Weeks at No.1	Weeks in Top 40
6 Jul 74	**BE THANKFUL FOR WHAT YOU'VE GOT** *Chelsea 2005 002*	31		3
20 Sep 80	**BE THANKFUL FOR WHAT YOU'VE GOT** *EMI 5101*	44		

TONY DE VIT UK singer

Date	Title / Label	Peak Position	Weeks at No.1	Weeks in Top 40
4 Mar 95	**BURNING UP** *Icon ICONCD 001*	25		2
12 Aug 95	**HOOKED** *Labello Dance LAD 18CD* 99TH FLOOR ELEVATORS FEATURING TONY DE VIT	28		1
9 Sep 95	**TO THE LIMIT** *X:Plode BANG 1CD*	44		
30 Mar 96	**I'LL BE THERE** *Labello Dance LAD 25CD2* 99TH FLOOR ELEVATORS FEATURING TONY DE VIT	37		1
28 Oct 00	**DAWN** *Tidy Trax TIDY 140CD*	56		
21 Dec 02	**I DON'T CARE** *Tidy Trax TIDY 181T*	65		
12 Jul 03	**GIVE ME A REASON** *Tidy Two 123C* TONY DE VIT FEATURING NIKI MAK	53		

DEACON BLUE UK group

Date	Title / Label	Peak Position	Weeks at No.1	Weeks in Top 40
23 Jan 88	**DIGNITY** *CBS DEAC 4*	31		4
9 Apr 88	**WHEN WILL YOU MAKE MY TELEPHONE RING** *CBS DEAC 5*	34		3
16 Jul 88	**CHOCOLATE GIRL** *CBS DEAC 6*	43		
15 Oct 88	**REAL GONE KID** *CBS DEAC 7*	8		9
4 Mar 89	**WAGES DAY** *CBS DEAC 8*	18		4
20 May 89	**FERGUS SINGS THE BLUES** *CBS DEAC 9*	14		4
16 Sep 89	**LOVE AND REGRET** *CBS DEAC 10*	28		2
6 Jan 90	**QUEEN OF THE NEW YEAR** *CBS DEAC 11*	21		3
25 Aug 90	**FOUR BACHARACH AND DAVID SONGS EP** *CBS DEAC 12*	2		7
25 May 91	**YOUR SWAYING ARMS** *Columbia 6568937*	23		3
27 Jul 91	**TWIST AND SHOUT** *Columbia 6573027*	10		7
12 Oct 91	**CLOSING TIME** *Columbia 6575027*	42		
14 Dec 91	**COVER FROM THE SKY** *Columbia 6576737*	31		2
28 Nov 92	**YOUR TOWN** *Columbia 6587867*	14		3
13 Feb 93	**WILL WE BE LOVERS** *Columbia 6589732*	31		2
24 Apr 93	**ONLY TENDER LOVE** *Columbia 6591842*	22		2
17 Jul 93	**HANG YOUR HEAD** *Columbia 6594602*	21		2
2 Apr 94	**I WAS RIGHT AND YOU WERE WRONG** *Columbia 6602222*	32		2
28 May 94	**DIGNITY** *Columbia 6604485*	20		1
28 Apr 01	**EVERYTIME YOU SLEEP** *Papillon BTFLY 0011*	64		

DEAD DRED UK production duo

Date	Title / Label	Peak Position	Weeks at No.1	Weeks in Top 40
5 Nov 94	**DRED BASS** *Moving Shadow SHADOW 50CD*	60		

DEAD END KIDS UK group

Date	Title / Label	Peak Position	Weeks at No.1	Weeks in Top 40
26 Mar 77	**HAVE I THE RIGHT** *CBS 4972*	6		9

DEAD KENNEDYS US group

Date	Title / Label	Peak Position	Weeks at No.1	Weeks in Top 40
1 Nov 80	**KILL THE POOR** *Cherry Red CHERRY 16*	49		
30 May 81	**TOO DRUNK TO FUCK** *Cherry Red CHERRY 24*	36		1

DEAD OR ALIVE UK group

Date	Title / Label	Peak Position	Weeks at No.1	Weeks in Top 40
24 Mar 84	**THAT'S THE WAY (I LIKE IT)** *Epic A 4271*	22		6
1 Dec 84	**YOU SPIN ME ROUND (LIKE A RECORD)** *Epic A 4861* ●	1	2	11
20 Apr 85	**LOVER COME BACK TO ME** *Epic A 6086*	11		6
29 Jun 85	**IN TOO DEEP** *Epic A 6360*	14		6
21 Sep 85	**MY HEART GOES BANG (GET ME TO THE DOCTOR)** *Epic A 6571*	23		3
20 Sep 86	**BRAND NEW LOVER** *Epic 6500757*	31		3
10 Jan 87	**SOMETHING IN MY HOUSE** *Epic BURNS 1*	12		5
4 Apr 87	**HOOKED ON LOVE** *Epic BURNS 2*	69		
3 Sep 88	**TURN AROUND AND COUNT 2 TEN** *Epic BURNS 4*	70		
22 Jul 89	**COME HOME WITH ME BABY** *Epic BURNS 5*	62		
17 May 03	**YOU SPIN ME ROUND (LIKE A RECORD)** *Epic 6735785*	23		2
11 Feb 06	**YOU SPIN ME ROUND (LIKE A RECORD)** *Epic 82876806212*	5		6

DEAD PREZ US duo

Date	Title / Label	Peak Position	Weeks at No.1	Weeks in Top 40
11 Mar 00	**HIP HOP** *Epic 6689862*	41		

DEAD 60'S UK group

Date	Title / Label	Peak Position	Weeks at No.1	Weeks in Top 40
16 Oct 04	**RIOT RADIO** *Deltasonic DLTCD025*	30		1
9 Apr 05	**THE LAST RESORT** *Deltasonic DLTCD2032*	24		1
25 Jun 05	**LOADED GUN** *Deltasonic DLTCD2037*	28		1
24 Sep 05	**RIOT RADIO** *Deltasonic DLTCD2041*	30		1
3 Dec 05	**GHOSTFACED KILLER** *Deltasonic DLTCD042*	25		1
22 Sep 07	**STAND UP** *Deltasonic DLTCD067*	54		

Silver-selling ○ Gold-selling ● Platinum-selling ⊛ US No.1 ★ | Peak Position | Weeks at No.1 | Weeks in Top 40

DEADLY SINS UK/Italian duo

Date	Title / Label	Peak Position	Weeks at No.1	Weeks in Top 40
30 Apr 94	WE ARE GOING ON DOWN *ffreedom TABCD 220*	45		

HAZELL DEAN UK singer

Date	Title / Label	Peak Position	Weeks at No.1	Weeks in Top 40
18 Feb 84	EVERGREEN/JEALOUS LOVE *Proto ENA 114*	63		
21 Apr 84	SEARCHIN' (I GOTTA FIND A MAN) *Proto ENA 109*	6		9
28 Jul 84	WHATEVER I DO (WHEREVER I GO) *Proto ENA 119*	4		10
3 Nov 84	BACK IN MY ARMS (ONCE AGAIN *Proto ENA 122*	41		
2 Mar 85	NO FOOL (FOR LOVE) *Proto ENA 123*	41		
12 Oct 85	THEY SAY IT'S GONNA RAIN *Parlophone R 6107*	58		
2 Apr 88	WHO'S LEAVING WHO *EMI EM 45*	4		9
25 Jun 88	MAYBE (WE SHOULD CALL IT A DAY) *EMI EM 62*	15		5
24 Sep 88	TURN IT INTO LOVE *EMI EM 71*	21		6
26 Aug 89	LOVE PAINS *Lisson DOLE 12*	48		
23 Mar 91	BETTER OFF WITHOUT YOU *Lisson DOLE 19*	72		

JIMMY DEAN US singer

Date	Title / Label	Peak Position	Weeks at No.1	Weeks in Top 40
26 Oct 61	BIG BAD JOHN *Philips PB 1187* ★	2		12
8 Nov 62	LITTLE BLACK BOOK *CBS AAG 122*	33		3

LETITIA DEAN & PAUL MEDFORD UK actors

Date	Title / Label	Peak Position	Weeks at No.1	Weeks in Top 40
25 Oct 86	SOMETHING OUTA NOTHING *BBC RESL 203*	12		4

DEAR JON UK group

Date	Title / Label	Peak Position	Weeks at No.1	Weeks in Top 40
22 Apr 95	ONE GIFT OF LOVE *MDMC DEVCS 2*	68		

DEARS Canadian group

Date	Title / Label	Peak Position	Weeks at No.1	Weeks in Top 40
20 Nov 04	LOST IN THE PLOT *Bella Union BELLACD86*	49		
14 May 05	22 - THE DEATH OF ALL THE ROMANCE *Bella Union BELLACD100*	53		

DEATH CAB FOR CUTIE US group

Date	Title / Label	Peak Position	Weeks at No.1	Weeks in Top 40
22 Apr 06	CROOKED TEETH *Atlantic AT0232CD*	69		
29 Jul 06	I WILL FOLLOW YOU INTO THE DARK *Atlantic AT0246CD*	66		

DEATH FROM ABOVE 1979 Canadian duo

Date	Title / Label	Peak Position	Weeks at No.1	Weeks in Top 40
13 Nov 04	ROMANTIC RIGHTS *679 679L090CD*	57		
26 Feb 05	BLOOD ON OUR HANDS *679 679L078CD*	33		1
25 Jun 05	BLACK HISTORY MONTH *679 679L106CD*	48		

DEATH IN VEGAS UK production duo

Date	Title / Label	Peak Position	Weeks at No.1	Weeks in Top 40
2 Aug 97	DIRT *Concrete HARD 27CD*	61		
1 Nov 97	ROCCO *Concrete HARD 29CD*	51		
12 Feb 00	AISHA *Concrete HARD 43CD*	9		3
6 May 00	DIRGE *Concrete HARD 44CD*	24		1
21 Sep 02	HANDS AROUND MY THROAT *Concrete HARD 48CD*	36		1
28 Dec 02	SCORPIO RISING *Concrete HARD 54CD* DEATH IN VEGAS FEATURING LIAM GALLAGHER	14		4

DeBARGE US group

Date	Title / Label	Peak Position	Weeks at No.1	Weeks in Top 40
6 Apr 85	RHYTHM OF THE NIGHT *Gordy TMG 1376*	4		10
21 Sep 85	YOU WEAR IT WELL *Gordy ZB 40345* EL DeBARGE WITH DeBARGE	54		

CHICO DeBARGE US singer

Date	Title / Label	Peak Position	Weeks at No.1	Weeks in Top 40
14 Mar 98	IGGIN' ME *Universal UND 56170*	50		

EL DeBARGE US singer

Date	Title / Label	Peak Position	Weeks at No.1	Weeks in Top 40
21 Sep 85	YOU WEAR IT WELL *Gordy ZB 40345* EL DeBARGE WITH DeBARGE	54		
28 Jun 86	WHO'S JOHNNY ('SHORT CIRCUIT' THEME) *Gordy ELD 1*	60		
31 Mar 90	SECRET GARDEN *Qwest W 9992* QUINCY JONES FEATURING AL B SURE!, JAMES INGRAM, EL DeBARGE & BARRY WHITE	67		

DIANA DECKER US singer

Date	Title / Label	Peak Position	Weeks at No.1	Weeks in Top 40
23 Oct 53	POPPA PICCOLINO *Columbia DB 3325*	2		10

DECLAN US singer

Date	Title / Label	Peak Position	Weeks at No.1	Weeks in Top 40
21 Dec 02	TELL ME WHY *Liberty CDDECS 004* DECLAN FEATURING THE YOUNG VOICES CHOIR	29		1

DECOY AND ROY Belgian group

Date	Title / Label	Peak Position	Weeks at No.1	Weeks in Top 40
1 Feb 03	INNER LIFE *Data/Ministry Of Sound/Heat DATA 43CDS*	45		

DAVE DEE UK singer

Date	Title / Label	Peak Position	Weeks at No.1	Weeks in Top 40
14 Mar 70	MY WOMAN'S MAN *Fontana TF 1074*	42		

DAVE DEE, DOZY, BEAKY, MICK & TICH UK group

Date	Title / Label	Peak Position	Weeks at No.1	Weeks in Top 40
23 Dec 65	YOU MAKE IT MOVE *Fontana TF 630*	26		4
3 Mar 66	HOLD TIGHT *Fontana TF 671*	4		15
9 Jun 66	HIDEAWAY *Fontana TF 711*	10		10
15 Sep 66	BEND IT *Fontana TF 746*	2		12
8 Dec 66	SAVE ME *Fontana TF 775*	3		10
9 Mar 67	TOUCH ME TOUCH ME *Fontana TF 798*	13		7
18 May 67	OKAY! *Fontana TF 830*	4		9
11 Oct 67	ZABADAK! *Fontana TF 873*	3		13
14 Feb 68	THE LEGEND OF XANADU *Fontana TF 903*	1	1	11
3 Jul 68	LAST NIGHT IN SOHO *Fontana TF 953*	8		10
2 Oct 68	WRECK OF THE ANTOINETTE *Fontana TF 971*	14		8
5 Mar 69	DON JUAN *Fontana TF 1000*	23		6
14 May 69	SNAKE IN THE GRASS *Fontana TF 1020*	23		7

DEE DEE Belgian singer

Date	Title / Label	Peak Position	Weeks at No.1	Weeks in Top 40
20 Jul 02	FOREVER *Incentive CENT 43CDS*	12		5
1 Mar 03	THE ONE *Incentive CENT 52CDX*	28		1

JAZZY DEE US rapper

Date	Title / Label	Peak Position	Weeks at No.1	Weeks in Top 40
5 Mar 83	GET ON UP *Laurie LRS 101*	53		

JOEY DEE & THE STARLITERS US singer

Date	Title / Label	Peak Position	Weeks at No.1	Weeks in Top 40
8 Feb 62	PEPPERMINT TWIST *Columbia DB 4758* ★	33		6

KIKI DEE UK singer

Date	Title / Label	Peak Position	Weeks at No.1	Weeks in Top 40
10 Nov 73	AMOUREUSE *Rocket PIG 4*	13		11
7 Sep 74	I GOT THE MUSIC IN ME *Rocket PIG 12* KIKI DEE BAND	19		6
12 Apr 75	(YOU DON'T KNOW) HOW GLAD I AM *Rocket PIG 16* KIKI DEE BAND	33		2
3 Jul 76	DON'T GO BREAKING MY HEART *Rocket ROKN 512* ELTON JOHN & KIKI DEE ● ★	1	6	13
11 Sep 76	LOVING AND FREE/AMOUREUSE *Rocket ROKN 515*	13		7
19 Feb 77	FIRST THING IN THE MORNING *Rocket ROKN 520*	32		4
11 Jun 77	CHICAGO *Rocket ROKN 526*	28		3
21 Feb 81	STAR *Ariola ARO 251*	13		7
23 May 81	PERFECT TIMING *Ariola ARO 257*	66		
20 Nov 93	TRUE LOVE *Rocket EJSCX 32* ELTON JOHN & KIKI DEE ○	2		8

DEEE-LITE US/Russian/Japanese group

Date	Title / Label	Peak Position	Weeks at No.1	Weeks in Top 40
18 Aug 90	GROOVE IS IN THE HEART/WHAT IS LOVE *Elektra EKR 114*	2		10
24 Nov 90	DEEE-LITE THEME/POWER OF LOVE *Elektra EKR 117*	25		3
23 Feb 91	HOW DO YOU SAY...LOVE/GROOVE IS IN THE HEART (REMIX) *Elektra EKR 118*	52		
27 Apr 91	GOOD BEAT *Elektra EKR 122*	53		
13 Jun 92	RUNAWAY *Elektra EKR 148*	45		
30 Jul 94	PICNIC IN THE SUMMERTIME *Elektra EKR 186CD1*	43		

DEEJAY PUNK-ROC US DJ

Date	Title / Label	Peak Position	Weeks at No.1	Weeks in Top 40
21 Mar 98	DEAD HUSBAND *Independiente ISOM 9MS*	71		
9 May 98	MY BEATBOX *Independiente ISOM 12MS*	43		
8 Aug 98	FAR OUT *Independiente ISOM 17MS*	43		

Silver-selling ● Gold-selling ● Platinum-selling ● US No.1 ★ | Peak Position | Weeks at No.1 | Weeks in Top 40

Date	Title / Label	Peak Position	Weeks at No.1	Weeks in Top 40
20 Feb 99	**ROC-IN-IT** *Independiente ISOM 21MS* DEEJAY PUNK-ROC VS ONYX	59		

CAROL DEENE UK singer

Date	Title / Label	Peak Position	Weeks at No.1	Weeks in Top 40
26 Oct 61	**SAD MOVIES (MAKE ME CRY)** *HMV POP 922*	44		
25 Jan 62	**NORMAN** *HMV POP 973*	24		5
5 Jul 62	**JOHNNY GET ANGRY** *HMV POP 1027*	32		2
23 Aug 62	**SOME PEOPLE** *HMV POP 1058*	25		9

DEEP BLUE UK producer

Date	Title / Label	Peak Position	Weeks at No.1	Weeks in Top 40
16 Apr 94	**HELICOPTER TUNE** *Moving Shadow SHADOW 41CD*	68		

DEEP BLUE SOMETHING US group

Date	Title / Label	Peak Position	Weeks at No.1	Weeks in Top 40
6 Jul 96	**BREAKFAST AT TIFFANY'S** *Interscope IND 80032*	55		
21 Sep 96	**BREAKFAST AT TIFFANY'S** *Interscope IND 80032*	1	1	11
7 Dec 96	**JOSEY** *Interscope IND 95518*	27		1

DEEP C UK group

Date	Title / Label	Peak Position	Weeks at No.1	Weeks in Top 40
19 Jan 91	**AFRICAN REIGN** *M&G MAGS 4*	75		
8 Jun 91	**CHILL TO THE PANIC** *M&G MAGS 10*	73		

DEEP COVER UK production duo

Date	Title / Label	Peak Position	Weeks at No.1	Weeks in Top 40
11 May 02	**SOUNDS OF EDEN (EVERYTIME I SEE THE GIRL)** *Attitude 0158392*	63		

DEEP CREED '94 US producer

Date	Title / Label	Peak Position	Weeks at No.1	Weeks in Top 40
7 May 94	**CAN U FEEL IT** *Eastern Bloc BLOCCD 005*	59		

DEEP DISH US production duo

Date	Title / Label	Peak Position	Weeks at No.1	Weeks in Top 40
26 Oct 96	**STAY GOLD** *Deconstruction 74321418222*	41		
1 Nov 97	**STRANDED** *Deconstruction 74321512232*	60		
3 Oct 98	**THE FUTURE OF THE FUTURE (STAY GOLD)** *Deconstruction 74321616252* DEEP DISH WITH EVERYTHING BUT THE GIRL	31		1
9 Oct 04	**FLASHDANCE** *Positiva CDTIVS211*	3		11
23 Jul 05	**SAY HELLO** *Positiva CDTIVS220*	14		4
29 Apr 06	**DREAMS** *Positiva CDTIV232* DEEP DISH FEATURING STEVIE NICKS	14		3

DEEP FEELING UK group

Date	Title / Label	Peak Position	Weeks at No.1	Weeks in Top 40
25 Apr 70	**DO YOU LOVE ME** *Page One POF 165*	34		2

DEEP FOREST French instrumental duo

Date	Title / Label	Peak Position	Weeks at No.1	Weeks in Top 40
5 Feb 94	**SWEET LULLABY** *Columbia 6599242*	10		5
21 May 94	**DEEP FOREST** *Columbia 6604115*	20		2
23 Jul 94	**SAVANNA DANCE** *Columbia 6606355*	28		1
24 Jun 95	**MARTA'S SONG** *Columbia 6621402*	26		1

DEEP PURPLE UK group

Date	Title / Label	Peak Position	Weeks at No.1	Weeks in Top 40
15 Aug 70	**BLACK NIGHT** *Harvest HAR 5020*	2		14
27 Feb 71	**STRANGE KIND OF WOMAN** *Harvest HAR 5033*	8		11
13 Nov 71	**FIREBALL** *Harvest HAR 5045*	15		11
1 Apr 72	**NEVER BEFORE** *Purple PUR 102*	35		3
16 Apr 77	**SMOKE ON THE WATER** *Purple PUR 132*	21		6
15 Oct 77	**NEW LIVE AND RARE EP** *Purple PUR 135*	31		2
7 Oct 78	**NEW LIVE AND RARE II (EP)** *Purple PUR 137*	45		
2 Aug 80	**BLACK NIGHT** *Harvest PUR 5210*	43		
1 Nov 80	**NEW LIVE AND RARE VOLUME 3 EP** *Harvest SHEP 101*	48		
26 Jan 85	**PERFECT STRANGERS** *Polydor POSP 719*	48		
15 Jun 85	**KNOCKING AT YOUR BACK DOOR/PERFECT STRANGERS** *Polydor POSP 749*	68		
18 Jun 88	**HUSH** *Polydor PO 4*	62		
20 Oct 90	**KING OF DREAMS** *RCA PB 49247*	70		
2 Mar 91	**LOVE CONQUERS ALL** *RCA PB 49225*	57		
24 Jun 95	**BLACK NIGHT (REMIX)** *EMI CDEM 382*	66		

DEEP RIVER BOYS US group

Date	Title / Label	Peak Position	Weeks at No.1	Weeks in Top 40
7 Dec 56	**THAT'S RIGHT** *HMV POP 263*	29		1

DEEP SENSATION UK duo

Date	Title / Label	Peak Position	Weeks at No.1	Weeks in Top 40
4 Sep 04	**SOMEHOW SOMEWHERE** *In The House INTHS 07*	74		

SCOTTI DEEP US producer

Date	Title / Label	Peak Position	Weeks at No.1	Weeks in Top 40
15 Mar 97	**BROOKLYN BEATS** *Xtravaganza 0090095*	67		

DEEPEST BLUE Israeli producer

Date	Title / Label	Peak Position	Weeks at No.1	Weeks in Top 40
2 Aug 03	**DEEPEST BLUE** *Data 55CDS*	7		5
28 Feb 04	**GIVE IT AWAY** *Data 65CDS*	9		4
5 Jun 04	**IS IT A SIN?** *Open OPEN3CDX*	24		1
4 Sep 04	**SHOOTING STAR** *Open OPEN05CDS*	57		

RICK DEES & HIS CAST OF IDIOTS US radio DJ

Date	Title / Label	Peak Position	Weeks at No.1	Weeks in Top 40
18 Sep 76	**DISCO DUCK (PART ONE)** *RSO 2090 204* ★	6		9

DEETAH Chilean singer

Date	Title / Label	Peak Position	Weeks at No.1	Weeks in Top 40
26 Sep 98	**RELAX** *ffrr FCDP 345*	11		6
1 May 99	**EL PARAISO RICO** *ffrr FCD 356*	39		1

DEEYAH Norwegian singer

Date	Title / Label	Peak Position	Weeks at No.1	Weeks in Top 40
12 Feb 05	**PLAN OF MY OWN** *Brainwash BRNWSHCDXS1*	37		1

DEF LEPPARD UK group

Date	Title / Label	Peak Position	Weeks at No.1	Weeks in Top 40
17 Nov 79	**WASTES** *Vertigo 6059 247*	61		
23 Feb 80	**HELLO AMERICA** *Vertigo LEPP 1*	45		
5 Feb 83	**PHOTOGRAPH** *Vertigo VER 5*	66		
27 Aug 83	**ROCK OF AGES** *Vertigo VER 6*	41		
1 Aug 87	**ANIMAL** *Bludgeon Riffola LEP 1*	6		8
19 Sep 87	**POUR SOME SUGAR ON ME** *Bludgeon Riffola LEP 2*	18		4
28 Nov 87	**HYSTERIA** *Bludgeon Riffola LEP 3*	26		3
9 Apr 88	**ARMAGEDDON IT** *Bludgeon Riffola LEP 4*	20		4
16 Jul 88	**LOVE BITES** *Bludgeon Riffola LEP 5* ★	11		6
11 Feb 89	**ROCKET** *Bludgeon Riffola LEP 6*	15		5
28 Mar 92	**LET'S GET ROCKED** *Bludgeon Riffola DEF 7*	2		6
27 Jun 92	**MAKE LOVE LIKE A MAN** *Bludgeon Riffola LEP 7*	12		4
12 Sep 92	**HAVE YOU EVER NEEDED SOMEONE SO BAD** *Bludgeon Riffola LEP 8*	16		3
30 Jan 93	**HEAVEN IS** *Bludgeon Riffola LEPCD 9*	13		3
1 May 93	**TONIGHT** *Bludgeon Riffola LEPCD 10*	34		2
18 Sep 93	**TWO STEPS BEHIND** *Bludgeon Riffola LEPCD 12*	32		2
15 Jan 94	**ACTION** *Bludgeon Riffola LEPCD 13*	14		3
14 Oct 95	**WHEN LOVE & HATE COLLIDE** *Bludgeon Riffola LEPCD 14* ●	2		8
4 May 96	**SLANG** *Bludgeon Riffola LEPDD 15*	17		3
13 Jul 96	**WORK IT OUT** *Bludgeon Riffola LEPCD 16*	22		1
28 Sep 96	**ALL I WANT IS EVERYTHING** *Bludgeon Riffola LEPDD 17*	38		1
30 Nov 96	**BREATHE A SIGH** *Bludgeon Riffola LEPCD 18*	43		
24 Jul 99	**PROMISES** *Bludgeon Riffola 5621362*	41		
9 Oct 99	**GOODBYE** *Bludgeon Riffola 5622892*	54		
17 Aug 02	**NOW** *Bludgeon Riffola 0639692*	23		1
26 Apr 03	**LONG LONG WAY TO GO** *Bludgeon Riffola 9800024*	40		1

DEFAULT Canadian group

Date	Title / Label	Peak Position	Weeks at No.1	Weeks in Top 40
8 Feb 03	**WASTING MY TIME** *Island CID 809*	73		

DEFINITION OF SOUND UK duo

Date	Title / Label	Peak Position	Weeks at No.1	Weeks in Top 40
9 Mar 91	**WEAR YOUR LOVE LIKE HEAVEN** *Circa YR 61*	17		6
1 Jun 91	**NOW IS TOMORROW** *Circa YR 66*	46		
8 Feb 92	**MOIRA JANE'S CAFE** *Circa YR 80*	34		2
19 Sep 92	**WHAT ARE YOU UNDER** *Circa YR 95*	68		
14 Nov 92	**CAN I GET OVER** *Circa YR 97*	61		
20 May 95	**BOOM BOOM** *Fontana DOSCD 1*	59		
2 Dec 95	**PASS THE VIBES** *Fontana DOSCD 2*	23		2
24 Feb 96	**CHILD** *Fontana DOSCD 3*	48		

DEFTONES US group

Date	Title / Label	Peak Position	Weeks at No.1	Weeks in Top 40
21 Mar 98	**MY OWN SUMMER (SHOVE IT)** *Maverick W 0432CD*	29		1
11 Jul 98	**BE QUIET AND DRIVE (FAR AWAY)** *Maverick W 0445CD*	50		
26 Aug 00	**CHANGE (IN THE HOUSE OF FLIES)** *Maverick W 531CD*	53		
24 May 03	**MINERVA** *Maverick W 605CD*	15		1
4 Oct 03	**HEXAGRAM** *Maverick W 623CD*	68		
28 Oct 06	**HOLE IN THE EARTH** *Maverick W741CD1*	69		

Silver-selling · Gold-selling · Platinum-selling · US No.1 ★ · Peak Position · Weeks at No.1 · Weeks in Top 40

GAVIN DEGRAW US singer

Date	Title / Label	Peak Position	Weeks at No.1	Weeks in Top 40
2 Jul 05	**I DON'T WANT TO BE** *J Records 82876702222*	38		1

DEGREES OF MOTION US group

Date	Title / Label	Peak Position	Weeks at No.1	Weeks in Top 40
25 Apr 92	**DO YOU WANT IT RIGHT NOW** *ffrr F 184* DEGREES OF MOTION FEATURING BITI	31		4
18 Jul 92	**SHINE ON** *ffrr F 192* DEGREES OF MOTION FEATURING BITI WITH KIT WEST	43		
7 Nov 92	**SOUL FREEDOM – FREE YOUR SOUL** *ffrr FX 201* DEGREES OF MOTION FEATURING BITI	64		
19 Mar 94	**SHINE ON (REMIX)** *ffrr FCD 229* DEGREES OF MOTION FEATURING BITI	8		6
25 Jun 94	**DO YOU WANT IT RIGHT NOW (REMIX)** *ffrr FCD 236* DEGREES OF MOTION FEATURING BITI	26		2

DEJA US duo

Date	Title / Label	Peak Position	Weeks at No.1	Weeks in Top 40
29 Aug 87	**SERIOUS** *10 TEN 132*	75		

DÉJÀ VU UK group

Date	Title / Label	Peak Position	Weeks at No.1	Weeks in Top 40
5 Feb 94	**WHY WHY WHY** *Cowboy CDRODEO 941*	57		

DEJURE UK production duo

Date	Title / Label	Peak Position	Weeks at No.1	Weeks in Top 40
23 Aug 03	**SANCTUARY** *Nebula NEBT 032*	62		

DESMOND DEKKER Jamaican singer

Date	Title / Label	Peak Position	Weeks at No.1	Weeks in Top 40
12 Jul 67	**007 (SHANTY TOWN)** *Pyramid PYR 6004* DESMOND DEKKER & THE ACES	14		9
19 Mar 69	**THE ISRAELITES** *Pyramid PYR 6058* DESMOND DEKKER & THE ACES	1	1	12
25 Jun 69	**IT MEK** *Pyramid PYR 6068* DESMOND DEKKER & THE ACES	7		10
10 Jan 70	**PICKNEY GAL** *Pyramid PYR 6078* DESMOND DEKKER & THE ACES	42		
22 Aug 70	**YOU CAN GET IT IF YOU REALLY WANT** *Trojan TR 7777*	2		14
10 May 75	**THE ISRAELITES** *Cactus CT 57*	10		8
30 Aug 75	**SING A LITTLE SONG** *Cactus CT 73*	16		7

DEL AMITRI UK group

Date	Title / Label	Peak Position	Weeks at No.1	Weeks in Top 40
19 Aug 89	**KISS THIS THING GOODBYE** *A&M AM 515*	59		
13 Jan 90	**NOTHING EVER HAPPENS** *A&M AM 536*	11		6
24 Mar 90	**KISS THIS THING GOODBYE** *A&M AM 551*	43		
16 Jun 90	**MOVE AWAY JIMMY BLUE** *A&M AM 555*	36		2
3 Nov 90	**SPIT IN THE RAIN** *A&M AM 589*	21		4
9 May 92	**ALWAYS THE LAST TO KNOW** *A&M AM 870*	13		5
11 Jul 92	**BE MY DOWNFALL** *A&M AM 884*	30		2
12 Sep 92	**JUST LIKE A MAN** *A&M AM 0057*	25		3
23 Jan 93	**WHEN YOU WERE YOUNG** *A&M AMCD 0132*	20		1
18 Feb 95	**HERE AND NOW** *A&M 5809692*	21		3
29 Apr 95	**DRIVING WITH THE BRAKES ON** *A&M 5810072*	18		2
8 Jul 95	**ROLL TO ME** *A&M 5811312*	22		2
28 Oct 95	**TELL HER THIS** *A&M 5812172*	32		1
21 Jun 97	**NOT WHERE IT'S AT** *A&M 5822532*	21		1
6 Dec 97	**SOME OTHER SUCKER'S PARADE** *A&M 5824352*	46		
13 Jun 98	**DON'T COME HOME TOO SOON** *A&M 5827052*	15		3
5 Sep 98	**CRY TO BE FOUND** *A&M MERCD 513*	40		1
13 Apr 02	**JUST BEFORE YOU LEAVE** *Mercury 4976972*	37		1

DE'LACY US group

Date	Title / Label	Peak Position	Weeks at No.1	Weeks in Top 40
2 Sep 95	**HIDEAWAY** *Slip 'N' Slide 74321310472*	9		8
31 Aug 96	**THAT LOOK** *Slip 'N' Slide 74321398322*	19		2
14 Feb 98	**HIDEAWAY 1998 (REMIX)** *Slip 'N' Slide 74321561052*	21		1

DELAGE UK group

Date	Title / Label	Peak Position	Weeks at No.1	Weeks in Top 40
15 Dec 90	**ROCK THE BOAT** *PWL/Polydor PO 113*	63		

DELAKOTA UK duo

Date	Title / Label	Peak Position	Weeks at No.1	Weeks in Top 40
18 Jul 98	**THE ROCK** *Go! Beat GOBCD 10*	60		
19 Sep 98	**C'MON CINCINNATI** *Go! Beat GOBCD 11* DELAKOTA FEATURING ROSE SMITH	55		
13 Feb 99	**555** *Go! Beat GOBCD 14*	42		

DELANEY & BONNIE US duo

Date	Title / Label	Peak Position	Weeks at No.1	Weeks in Top 40
20 Dec 69	**COMIN' HOME** *Atlantic 584 308* DELANEY & BONNIE & FRIENDS FEATURING ERIC CLAPTON	16		7

DELAYS UK group

Date	Title / Label	Peak Position	Weeks at No.1	Weeks in Top 40
2 Aug 03	**HEY GIRL** *Rough Trade RTRADESCD103*	40		1
31 Jan 04	**LONG TIME COMING** *Rough Trade RTRADESCD136*	16		2
3 Apr 04	**NEARER THAN HEAVEN** *Rough Trade RTRADSCD175*	21		2
4 Dec 04	**LOST IN A MELODY/WANDERLUST** *Rough Trade RTRADSCD197*	28		1
4 Mar 06	**VALENTINE** *Rough Trade RTRADSCD265*	23		1
20 May 06	**HIDEAWAY** *Rough Trade RTRADSCDX336*	35		1

DELEGATION UK group

Date	Title / Label	Peak Position	Weeks at No.1	Weeks in Top 40
23 Apr 77	**WHERE IS THE LOVE (WE USED TO KNOW)** *State STAT 40*	22		5
20 Aug 77	**YOU'VE BEEN DOING ME WRONG** *State STAT 55*	49		

DELERIUM Canadian production duo

Date	Title / Label	Peak Position	Weeks at No.1	Weeks in Top 40
12 Jun 99	**SILENCE** *Nettwerk 398152*	73		
5 Feb 00	**HEAVEN'S EARTH** *Nettwerk 331032*	44		
14 Oct 00	**SILENCE (REMIX)** *Nettwerk 331082* DELERIUM FEATURING SARAH McLACHLAN	3		10
7 Jul 01	**INNOCENTE (FALLING IN LOVE)** *Nettwerk 331182* DELERIUM FEATURING LEIGH NASH	32		1
24 Nov 01	**UNDERWATER** *Nettwerk 331432* DELERIUM FEATURING RANI	33		1
12 Jul 03	**AFTER ALL** *Nettwerk 332012* DELERIUM FEATURING JAEL	46		
28 Feb 04	**TRULY** *Nettwerk 332202*	54		
27 Nov 04	**SILENCE 2004 (2ND REMIX)** *Nettwerk 332422* DELERIUM FEATURING SARAH McLACHLAN	38		1

DELFONICS US group

Date	Title / Label	Peak Position	Weeks at No.1	Weeks in Top 40
10 Apr 71	**DIDN'T I (BLOW YOUR MIND THIS TIME)** *Bell 1099*	22		6
10 Jul 71	**LA-LA MEANS I LOVE YOU** *Bell 1165*	19		9
16 Oct 71	**READY OR NOT HERE I COME** *Bell 1175*	41		

DELGADOS UK group

Date	Title / Label	Peak Position	Weeks at No.1	Weeks in Top 40
23 May 98	**PULL THE WIRES FROM THE WALL** *Chemikal Underground CHEM 023CD*	69		
3 Jun 00	**AMERICAN TRILOGY** *Chemikal UnDerground CHEM 039CD*	61		
1 Mar 03	**ALL YOU NEED IS HATE** *Mantra MNT 79CD*	72		
18 Sep 04	**EVERYBODY COME DOWN** *Chemikal Underground CHEM073CD*	67		

DELINQUENT UK production duo

Date	Title / Label	Peak Position	Weeks at No.1	Weeks in Top 40
8 Mar 08	**MY DESTINY** *M&B/AATW CDGLOBE823* DELINQUENT FEATURING K-CAT	19		4

DELIRIOUS? UK group

Date	Title / Label	Peak Position	Weeks at No.1	Weeks in Top 40
1 Mar 97	**WHITE RIBBON DAY** *Furious? CDFURY 1*	41		
17 May 97	**DEEPER** *Furious? CDFURY 2*	20		2
26 Jul 97	**PROMISE** *Furious? CDFURY 3*	20		1
15 Nov 97	**DEEPER (EP)** *Furious? CXFURY 4*	36		1
27 Mar 99	**SEE THE STAR** *Furious? CDFURY 5*	16		1
4 Mar 00	**IT'S OK** *Furious? CDFURY 6*	18		1
16 Jun 01	**WAITING FOR THE SUMMER** *Furious? CDFURY 7*	26		1
22 Dec 01	**I COULD SING OF YOUR LOVE FOREVER** *Furious? CDFURY 9*	40		1
22 Oct 05	**PAINT THE TOWN RED** *Furious? CDFURY10*	56		

DELIVERANCE SOUNDTRACK US duo

Date	Title / Label	Peak Position	Weeks at No.1	Weeks in Top 40
31 Mar 73	**DUELLING BANJOS** *Warner Brothers K 16223*	17		7

DELLS US R&B group

Date	Title / Label	Peak Position	Weeks at No.1	Weeks in Top 40
16 Jul 69	**I CAN SING A RAINBOW – LOVE IS BLUE (MEDLEY)** *Chess CRS 8099*	15		7

DELUXE US singer

Date	Title / Label	Peak Position	Weeks at No.1	Weeks in Top 40
18 Mar 89	**JUST A LITTLE MORE** *Unyque UNQ 5*	74		

TIM DELUXE UK producer

Date	Title / Label	Peak	Wks No.1	Wks Top 40
20 Jul 02	IT JUST WON'T DO *Underwater H2O 016CD* TIM DELUXE FEATURING SAM OBERNIK	14		4
4 Oct 03	LESS TALK MORE ACTION *Underwater H2O 028CD*	45		
7 Feb 04	MUNDAYA (THE BOY) *Underwater H2O 040CD* TIM DELUXE FEATURING SHAHIN BADAR	61		
13 Mar 04	JUST KICK *Intec INTEC024* COHEN VS DELUXE	70		
2 Jun 07	LET THE BEATS ROLL *Skint SKINT133* TIM DELUXE FEATURING SIMON FRANKS	71		

DEM FRANCHIZE BOYZ US group

Date	Title / Label	Peak	Wks No.1	Wks Top 40
25 Mar 06	I THINK THEY LIKE ME *Virgin VUSDX321*	66		

DEM 2 UK production duo

Date	Title / Label	Peak	Wks No.1	Wks Top 40
24 Oct 98	DESTINY *Locked On LOX 101CD*	58		

MARCO DEMARK Italian producer

Date	Title / Label	Peak	Wks No.1	Wks Top 40
8 Mar 08	TINY DANCER *All Around The World CDGLOBE808* MARCO DENMARK FEATURING CASEY BARNES	54		

DEMON VS HEARTBREAKER French production group

Date	Title / Label	Peak	Wks No.1	Wks Top 40
19 May 01	YOU ARE MY HIGH *Source SOURCDSE 1032*	70		

CHAKA DEMUS & PLIERS Jamaican duo

Date	Title / Label	Peak	Wks No.1	Wks Top 40
12 Jun 93	TEASE ME *Mango CIDM 806*	3		14
18 Sep 93	SHE DON'T LET NOBODY *Mango CIDM 810*	4		8
18 Dec 93	TWIST AND SHOUT *Mango CIDM 814* CHAKA DEMUS & PLIERS FEATURING JACK RADICS & TAXI GANG	1	2	11
12 Mar 94	MURDER SHE WROTE *Mango CIDM 812*	27		2
18 Jun 94	I WANNA BE YOUR MAN *Mango CIDM 817*	19		4
27 Aug 94	GAL WINE *Mango CIDM 818*	20		3
1 Apr 95	TWIST AND SHOUT *Mango CIDM 814* CHAKA DEMUS & PLIERS FEATURING JACK RADICS & TAXI GANG	67		
31 Aug 96	EVERY KINDA PEOPLE *Island Jamaica IJCD 2005*	47		
30 Aug 97	EVERY LITTLE THING SHE DOES IS MAGIC *Virgin VSCDT 1654*	51		

TERRY DENE UK singer

Date	Title / Label	Peak	Wks No.1	Wks Top 40
7 Jun 57	A WHITE SPORT COAT *Decca F 10895*	18		7
19 Jul 57	START MOVIN' *Decca F 10914*	15		8
16 May 58	STAIRWAY OF LOVE *Decca F 11016*	16		5

CATHY DENNIS UK singer

Date	Title / Label	Peak	Wks No.1	Wks Top 40
21 Oct 89	C'MON AND GET MY LOVE *ffrr F 117* D MOB WITH CATHY DENNIS	15		8
7 Apr 90	THAT'S THE WAY OF THE WORLD *ffrr F 132* D MOB WITH CATHY DENNIS	48		
4 May 91	TOUCH ME (ALL NIGHT LONG) *Polydor CATH 3*	5		9
20 Jul 91	JUST ANOTHER DREAM *Polydor CATH 2*	13		6
5 Oct 91	TOO MANY WALLS *Polydor CATH 4*	17		6
7 Dec 91	EVERYBODY MOVE *Polydor CATH 5*	25		5
29 Aug 92	YOU LIED TO ME *Polydor CATH 6*	34		2
21 Nov 92	IRRESISTIBLE *Polydor CATH 7*	24		3
6 Feb 93	FALLING *Polydor CATHD 8*	32		1
12 Feb 94	WHY *ffrr FCD 227* D MOB WITH CATHY DENNIS	23		2
10 Aug 96	WEST END PAD *Polydor 5752812*	25		1
1 Mar 97	WATERLOO SUNSET *Polydor 5759612*	11		3
21 Jun 97	WHEN DREAMS TURN TO DUST *Polydor 5711852*	43		

JACKIE DENNIS UK singer

Date	Title / Label	Peak	Wks No.1	Wks Top 40
14 Mar 58	LA DEE DAH *Decca F 10992*	4		9
27 Jun 58	PURPLE PEOPLE EATER *Decca F 11033*	29		1

STEFAN DENNIS Australian actor

Date	Title / Label	Peak	Wks No.1	Wks Top 40
6 May 89	DON'T IT MAKE YOU FEEL GOOD *Sublime LIME 105*	16		6
7 Oct 89	THIS LOVE AFFAIR *Sublime LIME 113*	67		

DENNISONS UK group

Date	Title / Label	Peak	Wks No.1	Wks Top 40
15 Aug 63	BE MY GIRL *Decca F 11691*	46		
7 May 64	WALKIN' THE DOG *Decca F 11880*	36		2

RICHARD DENTON & MARTIN COOK UK instrumental duo

Date	Title / Label	Peak	Wks No.1	Wks Top 40
15 Apr 78	THEME FROM THE HONG KONG BEAT *BBC RESL 52*	25		3

JOHN DENVER US singer

Date	Title / Label	Peak	Wks No.1	Wks Top 40
17 Aug 74	ANNIE'S SONG *RCA APBO 0295* ★	1	1	13
12 Dec 81	PERHAPS LOVE *CBS A 1905* PLACIDO DOMINGO WITH JOHN DENVER	46		

KARL DENVER UK singer/guitarist

Date	Title / Label	Peak	Wks No.1	Wks Top 40
22 Jun 61	MARCHETA *Decca F 11360*	8		16
19 Oct 61	MEXICALI ROSE *Decca F 11395*	8		10
25 Jan 62	WIMOWEH *Decca F 11420*	4		15
22 Feb 62	NEVER GOODBYE *Decca F 11431*	9		15
7 Jun 62	A LITTLE LOVE A LITTLE KISS *Decca F 11470*	19		9
20 Sep 62	BLUE WEEKEND *Decca F 11505*	33		3
21 Mar 63	CAN YOU FORGIVE ME *Decca F 11608*	32		5
13 Jun 63	INDIAN LOVE CALL *Decca F 11674*	32		5
22 Aug 63	STILL *Decca F 11720*	13		13
5 Mar 64	MY WORLD OF BLUE *Decca F 11828*	29		5
4 Jun 64	LOVE ME WITH ALL YOUR HEART *Decca F 11905*	37		2
9 Jun 90	LAZYITIS - ONE ARMED BOXER *Factory FAC 2227* HAPPY MONDAYS & KARL DENVER	46		

DEODATO Brazilian keyboard player

Date	Title / Label	Peak	Wks No.1	Wks Top 40
5 May 73	ALSO SPRACH ZARATHUSTRA (2001) *CTI 4000*	7		7

DEPARTMENT S UK group

Date	Title / Label	Peak	Wks No.1	Wks Top 40
4 Apr 81	IS VIC THERE? *Demon D 1003*	22		8
11 Jul 81	GOING LEFT RIGHT *Stiff BUY 118*	55		

DEPARTURE UK group

Date	Title / Label	Peak	Wks No.1	Wks Top 40
14 Aug 04	ALL MAPPED OUT *Parlophone CDR 6642*	30		1
30 Oct 04	BE MY ENEMY *Parlophone CDRS 6653*	41		
16 Apr 05	LUMP IN MY THROAT *Parlophone CDRS6659*	30		1
18 Jun 05	ALL MAPPED OUT *Parlophone CDRS6665*	33		1

DEPECHE MODE UK group

Date	Title / Label	Peak	Wks No.1	Wks Top 40
4 Apr 81	DREAMING OF ME *Mute 013*	57		
13 Jun 81	NEW LIFE *Mute 014*	11		9
19 Sep 81	JUST CAN'T GET ENOUGH *Mute 016*	8		8
13 Feb 82	SEE YOU *Mute 018*	6		8
8 May 82	THE MEANING OF LOVE *Mute 022*	12		6
28 Aug 82	LEAVE IN SILENCE *Mute BONG 1*	18		7
12 Feb 83	GET THE BALANCE RIGHT *Mute 7BONG 2*	13		7
23 Jul 83	EVERYTHING COUNTS *Mute 7BONG 3*	6		8
1 Oct 83	LOVE IN ITSELF.2 *Mute 7BONG 4*	21		6
24 Mar 84	PEOPLE ARE PEOPLE *Mute 7BONG 5*	4		8
1 Sep 84	MASTER AND SERVANT *Mute 7BONG 6*	9		7
10 Nov 84	SOMEBODY/BLASPHEMOUS RUMOURS *Mute 7BONG 7*	16		4
11 May 85	SHAKE THE DISEASE *Mute BONG 8*	18		7
28 Sep 85	IT'S CALLED A HEART *Mute BONG 9*	18		3
22 Feb 86	STRIPPED *Mute BONG 10*	15		4
26 Apr 86	A QUESTION OF LUST *Mute BONG 11*	28		3
23 Aug 86	A QUESTION OF TIME *Mute BONG 12*	17		4
9 May 87	STRANGELOVE *Mute BONG 13*	16		4
5 Sep 87	NEVER LET ME DOWN AGAIN *Mute BONG 14*	22		3
9 Jan 88	BEHIND THE WHEEL *Mute BONG 15*	21		3
28 May 88	LITTLE 15 (IMPORT) *Mute LITTLE 15*	60		
25 Feb 89	EVERYTHING COUNTS (LIVE) *Mute BONG 16*	22		5
9 Sep 89	PERSONAL JESUS *Mute BONG 17*	13		5
17 Feb 90	ENJOY THE SILENCE *Mute BONG 18*	6		7
19 May 90	POLICY OF TRUTH *Mute BONG 19*	16		4
29 Sep 90	WORLD IN MY EYES *Mute BONG 20*	17		4
27 Feb 93	I FEEL YOU *Mute CDBONG 21*	8		4
8 May 93	WALKING IN MY SHOES *Mute CDBONG 22*	14		2
25 Sep 93	CONDEMNATION *Mute CDBONG 23*	9		2
22 Jan 94	IN YOUR ROOM *Mute CDBONG 24*	8		3
15 Feb 97	BARREL OF A GUN *Mute CDBONG 25*	4		2

Silver-selling ○ Gold-selling ● Platinum-selling ✪ US No.1 ★ — Peak Position | Weeks at No.1 | Weeks in Top 40

Date	Title	Peak Position	Weeks at No.1	Weeks in Top 40
12 Apr 97	**IT'S NO GOOD** *Mute CDBONG 26*	5		3
28 Jun 97	**HOME** *Mute CDBONG 27*	23		2
1 Nov 97	**USELESS** *Mute CDBONG 28*	28		1
19 Sep 98	**ONLY WHEN I LOSE MYSELF** *Mute CDBONG 29*	17		2
5 May 01	**DREAM ON** *Mute LCDBONG 30*	6		2
11 Aug 01	**I FEEL LOVED** *Mute LCDBONG 31*	12		2
17 Nov 01	**FREELOVE** *Mute LCDBONG 32*	19		2
30 Oct 04	**ENJOY THE SILENCE (REMIX)** *Mute LCDBONG 34*	7		3
4 Dec 04	**SOMETHING TO DO** *Mute L12BONG34*	75		
15 Oct 05	**PRECIOUS** *Mute LCDBONG35*	4		3
24 Dec 05	**A PAIN THAT I'M USED TO** *Mute LCDBONG36*	15		1
8 Apr 06	**SUFFER WELL** *Mute LCDBONG37*	12		2
17 Jun 06	**JOHN THE REVELATOR/LILIAN** *Mute LCDBONG38*	18		1
11 Nov 06	**MARTYR** *Mute CDBONG39*	13		1

DEPTH CHARGE UK producer

Date	Title	Peak Position	Weeks at No.1	Weeks in Top 40
29 Jul 95	**LEGEND OF THE GOLDEN SNAKE** *DC 01CD*	75		

DER DRITTE RAUM German producer

Date	Title	Peak Position	Weeks at No.1	Weeks in Top 40
4 Sep 99	**HALE BOPP** *Addictive 12AD 042*	75		

YVES DERUYTER Belgian producer

Date	Title	Peak Position	Weeks at No.1	Weeks in Top 40
14 Apr 01	**BACK TO EARTH** *UK Bonzai UKBONZAICD 01*	63		
19 Jan 02	**BACK TO EARTH (REMIX)** *UK Bonzai UKBONZA 109CD*	56		

DESERT UK production duo

Date	Title	Peak Position	Weeks at No.1	Weeks in Top 40
20 Oct 01	**LETTIN' YA MIND GO** *Future Groove CDFGR 017*	74		

DESERT EAGLE DISCS UK production duo

Date	Title	Peak Position	Weeks at No.1	Weeks in Top 40
1 Mar 03	**BIGGER BETTER DEAL** *Echo ECSCD 129* DESERT EAGLE DISCS FEATURING KEISHA	67		

DESERT SESSIONS US group

Date	Title	Peak Position	Weeks at No.1	Weeks in Top 40
15 Nov 03	**CRAWL HOME** *Island CID 835*	41		

DESIDERIO UK/Dutch production duo

Date	Title	Peak Position	Weeks at No.1	Weeks in Top 40
3 Jun 00	**STARLIGHT** *Code Blue BLU 010CD*	57		

DESIRELESS French singer

Date	Title	Peak Position	Weeks at No.1	Weeks in Top 40
31 Oct 87	**VOYAGE VOYAGE** *CBS DESI 1*	53		
14 May 88	**VOYAGE VOYAGE (REMIX)** *CBS DESI 2*	5		9

DESIYA UK duo

Date	Title	Peak Position	Weeks at No.1	Weeks in Top 40
1 Feb 92	**COMIN' ON STRONG** *Black Market 12MKT 2* DESIYA FEATURING MELISSA YIANNAKOU	74		

DESKEE UK/German production group

Date	Title	Peak Position	Weeks at No.1	Weeks in Top 40
3 Feb 90	**LET THERE BE HOUSE** *Big One VBIG 19*	52		
8 Sep 90	**DANCE DANCE** *Big One VBIG 22*	74		

DES'REE UK singer

Date	Title	Peak Position	Weeks at No.1	Weeks in Top 40
31 Aug 91	**FEEL SO HIGH** *Dusted Sound 6573667*	51		
11 Jan 92	**FEEL SO HIGH** *Dusted Sound 6576897*	13		5
21 Mar 92	**MIND ADVENTURES** *Dusted Sound 6578637*	43		
27 Jun 92	**WHY SHOULD I LOVE YOU** *Dusted Sound 6580917*	44		
19 Jun 93	**DELICATE** *Columbia 6593312* TERENCE TRENT D'ARBY FEATURING DES'REE	14		4
9 Apr 94	**YOU GOTTA BE** *Dusted Sound 6601342*	20		5
18 Jun 94	**I AN'T MOVIN'** *Dusted Sound 6604672*	44		
3 Sep 94	**LITTLE CHILD** *Dusted Sound 6604515*	69		
11 Mar 95	**YOU GOTTA BE** *Dusted Sound 6613215*	14		5
20 Jun 98	**LIFE** *Sony S2 6659302*	8		11
7 Nov 98	**WHAT'S YOUR SIGN** *Sony S2 6665165*	19		2
3 Apr 99	**YOU GOTTA BE (REMIX)** *Dusted Sound S2 6668935*	10		4
16 Oct 99	**AIN'T NO SUNSHINE** *Universal Music TV 1564332* LADYSMITH BLACK MAMBAZO FEATURING DES'REE	42		
5 Apr 03	**IT'S OKAY** *Sony Music 6736495*	69		

DESTINY'S CHILD US group

Date	Title	Peak Position	Weeks at No.1	Weeks in Top 40
28 Mar 98	**NO NO NO** *Columbia 6656592* DESTINY'S CHILD FEATURING WYCLEF JEAN	5		6
11 Jul 98	**WITH ME** *Columbia 6661472*	19		2
7 Nov 98	**SHE'S GONE** *Columbia 6664915* MATTHEW MARSDEN FEATURING DESTINY'S CHILD	24		1
23 Jan 99	**GET ON THE BUS** *East West E 3780CD* DESTINY'S CHILD FEATURING TIMBALAND	15		3
24 Jul 99	**BILLS, BILLS, BILLS** *Columbia 6676902* ★	6		7
30 Oct 99	**BUG A BOO** *Columbia 6681882*	9		4
8 Apr 00	**SAY MY NAME** *Columbia 6691882* ★	3		8
29 Jul 00	**JUMPIN' JUMPIN'** *Columbia 6696292*	5		8
2 Dec 00	**INDEPENDENT WOMEN PART 1** *Columbia 6705932* ● ★	1	1	11
28 Apr 01	**SURVIVOR** *Columbia 6711732* ○	1	1	8
4 Aug 01	**BOOTYLICIOUS** *Columbia 6717382* ★	2		8
24 Nov 01	**EMOTION** *Columbia 6721112*	3		8
13 Nov 04	**LOSE MY BREATH** *Columbia 6754912*	2		10
19 Feb 05	**SOLDIER** *Columbia 6757622* DESTINY'S CHILD FEATURING TI & LIL' WAYNE	4		5
7 May 05	**GIRL** *Columbia 6758952*	6		5

MARCELLA DETROIT US singer

Date	Title	Peak Position	Weeks at No.1	Weeks in Top 40
12 Mar 94	**I BELIEVE** *London LONCD 347*	11		6
14 May 94	**AIN'T NOTHING LIKE THE REAL THING** *London LONCD 350* MARCELLA DETROIT & ELTON JOHN	24		3
16 Jul 94	**I'M NO ANGEL** *London LOCDP 351*	33		1

DETROIT COBRAS US group

Date	Title	Peak Position	Weeks at No.1	Weeks in Top 40
25 Sep 04	**CHA CHA TWIST** *Rough Trade RTRADSCD189*	59		

DETROIT EMERALDS US group

Date	Title	Peak Position	Weeks at No.1	Weeks in Top 40
10 Feb 73	**FEEL THE NEED IN ME** *Janus 6146 020*	4		13
5 May 73	**YOU WANT IT YOU GOT IT** *Westbound 6146 103*	12		7
11 Aug 73	**I THINK OF YOU** *Westbound 6146 104*	27		6
18 Jun 77	**FEEL THE NEED IN ME** *Atlantic K 10945*	12		10

DETROIT GRAND PU BAHS US group

Date	Title	Peak Position	Weeks at No.1	Weeks in Top 40
8 Jul 00	**SANDWICHES** *Jive Electro 9230252*	29		1

DETROIT SPINNERS US group

Date	Title	Peak Position	Weeks at No.1	Weeks in Top 40
21 Apr 73	**COULD IT BE I'M FALLING IN LOVE** *Atlantic K 10283*	11		10
29 Sep 73	**GHETTO CHILD** *Atlantic K 10359*	7		10
19 Oct 74	**THEN CAME YOU** *Atlantic K 10495* DIONNE WARWICK & THE DETROIT SPINNERS ★	29		4
11 Sep 76	**THE RUBBERBAND MAN** *Atlantic K 10807*	16		9
29 Jan 77	**WAKE UP SUSAN** *Atlantic K 10799*	29		3
7 May 77	**COULD IT BE I'M FALLING IN LOVE EP** *Atlantic K 10935*	32		3
23 Feb 80	**WORKING MY WAY BACK TO YOU - FORGIVE ME GIRL (MEDLEY)** *Atlantic K 11432* ○	1	2	10
10 May 80	**BODY LANGUAGE** *Atlantic K 11392*	40		1
28 Jun 80	**CUPID-I'VE LOVED YOU FOR A LONG TIME (MEDLEY)** *Atlantic K 11498*	4		7
24 Jun 95	**I'LL BE AROUND** *Cooltempo CDCOOL 306* RAPPIN' 4-TAY FEATURING THE SPINNERS	30		2
14 Nov 70	**IT'S A SHAME** *Tamla Motown TMG 755* DETROIT SPINNERS & MOTOWN SPINNERS	20		9

DEUCE UK group

Date	Title	Peak Position	Weeks at No.1	Weeks in Top 40
21 Jan 95	**CALL IT LOVE** *London LONCD 355*	11		9
22 Apr 95	**I NEED YOU** *London LONCD 365*	10		3
19 Aug 95	**ON THE BIBLE** *London LONCD 368*	13		4
29 Jun 96	**NO SURRENDER** *Love This LUVTHISCD 10*	29		1

dEUS Belgian group

Date	Title	Peak Position	Weeks at No.1	Weeks in Top 40
11 Feb 95	**HOTEL LOUNGE (BE THE DEATH OF ME)** *Island CID 603*	55		
13 Jul 96	**THEME FROM TURNPIKE (EP)** *Island CID 630*	68		
19 Oct 96	**LITTLE ARITHMETICS** *Island CID 643*	44		
15 Mar 97	**ROSES** *Island CID 645*	56		
24 Apr 99	**INSTANT STREET** *Island CID 742*	49		
3 Jul 99	**SISTER DEW** *Island CID 750*	62		

SIDNEY DEVINE UK singer

Date	Title / Label	Peak	Wks at No.1	Wks in Top 40
1 Apr 78	**SCOTLAND FOREVER** *Philips SCOT 1*	48		

DEVO US group

Date	Title / Label	Peak	Wks at No.1	Wks in Top 40
22 Apr 78	**(I CAN'T GET ME NO) SATISFACTION** *Stiff BOY 1*	41		
13 May 78	**JOCKO HOMO** *Stiff DEV 1*	62		
12 Aug 78	**BE STIFF** *Stiff BOY 2*	71		
2 Sep 78	**COME BACK JONEE** *Virgin VS 223*	60		
22 Nov 80	**WHIP IT** *Virgin VS 383*	51		

SHEILA B. DEVOTION French singer

Date	Title / Label	Peak	Wks at No.1	Wks in Top 40
11 Mar 78	**SINGIN' IN THE RAIN PART 1** *Carrere EMI 2751*	11		9
22 Jul 78	**YOU LIGHT MY FIRE** *Carrere EMI 2828*	44		
24 Nov 79	**SPACER** *Carrere CAR 128* SHEILA AND B. DEVOTION	18		11

DEXY'S MIDNIGHT RUNNERS UK group

Date	Title / Label	Peak	Wks at No.1	Wks in Top 40
19 Jan 80	**DANCE STANCE** *Oddball Productions R 6028*	40		1
22 Mar 80	**GENO** *Late Night Feelings R 6033* ○	1	2	12
12 Jul 80	**THERE THERE MY DEAR** *Late Night Feelings R 6038*	7		6
21 Mar 81	**PLAN B** *Parlophone R 6046*	58		
11 Jul 81	**SHOW ME** *Mercury DEXYS 6*	16		7
20 Mar 82	**THE CELTIC SOUL BROTHERS** *Mercury DEXYS 8* DEXY'S MIDNIGHT RUNNERS WITH THE EMERALD EXPRESS	45		
3 Jul 82	**COME ON EILEEN** *Mercury DEXYS 9* DEXY'S MIDNIGHT RUNNERS WITH THE EMERALD EXPRESS ⊛ ★	1	4	13
2 Oct 82	**JACKIE WILSON SAID (I'M IN HEAVEN WHEN YOU SMILE)** *Mercury DEXYS 10* KEVIN ROWLAND & DEXY'S MIDNIGHT RUNNERS	5		6
4 Dec 82	**LET'S GET THIS STRAIGHT (FROM THE START)/OLD** *Mercury DEXYS 11* KEVIN ROWLAND & DEXY'S MIDNIGHT RUNNERS	17		8
2 Apr 83	**THE CELTIC SOUL BROTHERS** *Mercury DEXYS 12* KEVIN ROWLAND & DEXY'S MIDNIGHT RUNNERS	20		5
22 Nov 86	**BECAUSE OF YOU** *Mercury BRUSH 1*	13		6

D4 New Zealand group

Date	Title / Label	Peak	Wks at No.1	Wks in Top 40
28 Sep 02	**GET LOOSE** *Infectious INFEC 117CDSX*	64		
7 Dec 02	**COME ON** *Infectious INFEC 121CDSX*	50		
29 Mar 03	**LADIES MAN** *Infectious INFEC 122CDSX*	41		

D4L US group

Date	Title / Label	Peak	Wks at No.1	Wks in Top 40
15 Apr 06	**LAFFY TAFFY** *Asylum AT0237CD*	29		1

DHS UK producer

Date	Title / Label	Peak	Wks at No.1	Wks in Top 40
9 Feb 02	**HOUSE OF GOD** *Club Tools 0135825 CLU*	72		

DHT Belgian production group

Date	Title / Label	Peak	Wks at No.1	Wks in Top 40
17 Dec 05	**LISTEN TO YOUR HEART** *Ministry Of Sound DATA109CDS* DHT FEATURING EDMEE	7		10

TONY DI BART UK singer

Date	Title / Label	Peak	Wks at No.1	Wks in Top 40
9 Apr 94	**THE REAL THING** *Cleveland City Blues CCBCD 15001* ○	1	1	10
20 Aug 94	**DO IT** *Cleveland City Blues CCBCD 15003*	21		2
20 May 95	**WHY DID YA** *Cleveland City Blues CCBCD 15004*	46		
2 Mar 96	**TURN YOUR LOVE AROUND** *Cleveland City Blues CCBCD 15006*	66		
17 Oct 98	**THE REAL THING (REMIX)** *Cleveland City CLECD 13050*	51		

GREGG DIAMOND BIONIC BOOGIE US instrumentalist

Date	Title / Label	Peak	Wks at No.1	Wks in Top 40
20 Jan 79	**CREAM (ALWAYS RISES TO THE TOP)** *Polydor POSP 18*	61		

JIM DIAMOND UK singer

Date	Title / Label	Peak	Wks at No.1	Wks in Top 40
3 Nov 84	**I SHOULD HAVE KNOWN BETTER** *A&M AM 220*	1	1	11
2 Feb 85	**I SLEEP ALONE AT NIGHT** *A&M AM 229*	72		
18 May 85	**REMEMBER I LOVE YOU** *A&M AM 247*	42		
22 Feb 86	**HI HO SILVER** *A&M AM 296* ○	5		9

NEIL DIAMOND US singer

Date	Title / Label	Peak	Wks at No.1	Wks in Top 40
7 Nov 70	**CRACKLIN' ROSIE** *Uni UN 529* ★	3		16
20 Feb 71	**SWEET CAROLINE** *Uni UN 531*	8		10
8 May 71	**I AM...I SAID** *Uni UN 532*	4		11
13 May 72	**SONG SUNG BLUE** *Uni UN 538* ★	14		11
14 Aug 76	**IF YOU KNOW WHAT I MEAN** *CBS 4398*	35		1
23 Oct 76	**BEAUTIFUL NOISE** *CBS 4601*	13		8
24 Dec 77	**DESIREE** *CBS 5869*	39		2
25 Nov 78	**YOU DON'T BRING ME FLOWERS** *CBS 6803* BARBRA (Streisand) & NEIL (Diamond) ● ★	5		9
3 Mar 79	**FOREVER IN BLUE JEANS** *CBS 7047*	16		10
15 Nov 80	**LOVE ON THE ROCKS** *Capitol CL 16173*	17		9
14 Feb 81	**HELLO AGAIN** *Capitol CL 16176*	51		
20 Nov 82	**HEARTLIGHT** *CBS A 2814*	47		
21 Nov 92	**MORNING HAS BROKEN** *Columbia 6588267*	36		1

DIAMOND HEAD UK group

Date	Title / Label	Peak	Wks at No.1	Wks in Top 40
11 Sep 82	**IN THE HEAT OF THE NIGHT** *MCA DHM 102*	67		

DIAMONDS Canadian group

Date	Title / Label	Peak	Wks at No.1	Wks in Top 40
31 May 57	**LITTLE DARLIN'** *Mercury MT 148*	3		17

DICK & DEEDEE US duo

Date	Title / Label	Peak	Wks at No.1	Wks in Top 40
26 Oct 61	**THE MOUNTAIN'S HIGH** *London HLG 9408*	37		2

CHARLES DICKENS UK singer

Date	Title / Label	Peak	Wks at No.1	Wks in Top 40
1 Jul 65	**THAT'S THE WAY LOVE GOES** *Pye 7N 15887*	37		3

GWEN DICKEY US singer

Date	Title / Label	Peak	Wks at No.1	Wks in Top 40
27 Jan 90	**CAR WASH** *Swanyard SYR 7*	72		
2 Jul 94	**AIN'T NOBODY (LOVES ME BETTER)** *X-clusive XCLU 010CD* KWS & GWEN DICKEY	21		3
14 Feb 98	**WISHING ON A STAR** *Northwestside 74321554632* JAY-Z FEATURING GWEN DICKEY	13		3
31 Oct 98	**CAR WASH** *MCA MCSTD 48096* ROSE ROYCE FEATURING GWEN DICKEY	18		1

NEVILLE DICKIE UK pianist

Date	Title / Label	Peak	Wks at No.1	Wks in Top 40
25 Oct 69	**ROBIN'S RETURN** *Major Minor MM 644*	33		4

DICKIES US group

Date	Title / Label	Peak	Wks at No.1	Wks in Top 40
16 Dec 78	**SILENT NIGHT** *A&M AMS 7403*	47		
21 Apr 79	**BANANA SPLITS (TRA LA LA SONG)** *A&M AMS 7431*	7		7
21 Jul 79	**PARANOID** *A&M AMS 7368*	45		
15 Sep 79	**NIGHTS IN WHITE SATIN** *A&M AMS 7469*	39		2
16 Feb 80	**FAN MAIL** *A&M AMS 7504*	57		
19 Jul 80	**GIGANTOR** *A&M AMS 7544*	72		

BRUCE DICKINSON UK singer

Date	Title / Label	Peak	Wks at No.1	Wks in Top 40
28 Apr 90	**TATTOOED MILLIONAIRE** *EMI EM 138*	18		3
23 Jun 90	**ALL THE YOUNG DUDES** *EMI EM 142*	23		4
25 Aug 90	**DIVE! DIVE! DIVE!** *EMI EM 151*	45		
4 Apr 92	**(I WANT TO BE) ELECTED** *London LON 319* MR BEAN & SMEAR CAMPAIGN FEATURING BRUCE DICKINSON	9		4
28 May 94	**TEARS OF THE DRAGON** *EMI CDEM 322*	28		1
8 Oct 94	**SHOOT ALL THE CLOWNS** *EMI CDEMS 341*	37		1
13 Apr 96	**BACK FROM THE EDGE** *Raw Power RAWX 1012*	68		
3 May 97	**ACCIDENT OF BIRTH** *Raw Power RAWX 1042*	54		

BARBARA DICKSON UK singer

Date	Title / Label	Peak	Wks at No.1	Wks in Top 40
17 Jan 76	**ANSWER ME** *RSO 2090 174*	9		6
26 Feb 77	**ANOTHER SUITCASE IN ANOTHER HALL** *MCA 266*	18		6
19 Jan 80	**CARAVAN SONG** *Epic EPC 8103*	41		
15 Mar 80	**JANUARY FEBRUARY** *Epic EPC 8115*	11		7
14 Jun 80	**IN THE NIGHT** *Epic EPC 8593*	48		
5 Jan 85	**I KNOW HIM SO WELL** *RCA CHESS 3* ELAINE PAIGE & BARBARA DICKSON ●	1	4	13

Key: Silver-selling · Gold-selling · Platinum-selling · US No.1 ★ · Peak Position · Weeks at No.1 · Weeks in Top 40

DICTATORS US group

Date	Title	Label	Peak Position	Weeks at No.1	Weeks in Top 40
17 Sep 77	SEARCH AND DESTORY	Asylum K 13091	49		

BO DIDDLEY US singer/guitarist

Date	Title	Label	Peak Position	Weeks at No.1	Weeks in Top 40
10 Oct 63	PRETTY THING	Pye International 7N 25217	34		1
18 Mar 65	HEY GOOD LOOKIN'	Chess 8000	39		1

DIDDY UK producer

Date	Title	Label	Peak Position	Weeks at No.1	Weeks in Top 40
19 Feb 94	GIVE ME LOVE	Positiva CDTIV 8	52		
12 Jul 97	GIVE ME LOVE (REMIX)	Feverpitch CDFVR 19	23		1

DIDO UK singer

Date	Title	Label	Peak Position	Weeks at No.1	Weeks in Top 40
24 Feb 01	HERE WITH ME	Cheeky 74321832732 (silver)	4		9
2 Jun 01	THANK YOU	Cheeky 74321853042	3		7
22 Sep 01	HUNTER	Cheeky 74321885722	17		4
20 Apr 02	ONE STEP TOO FAR (FAITHLESS FEATURING DIDO)	Cheeky 74321926412	6		2
4 May 02	ONE STEP TOO FAR (FAITHLESS FEATURING DIDO)	Cheeky 74321936742	68		
13 Sep 03	WHITE FLAG	Cheeky 82876546022	2		13
13 Dec 03	LIFE FOR RENT	Cheeky 82876579472	8		7
24 Apr 04	DON'T LEAVE HOME	Cheeky 82876611722	25		3
25 Sep 04	SAND IN MY SHOES	Cheeky 82876626922	29		1

DIESEL PARK WEST UK group

Date	Title	Label	Peak Position	Weeks at No.1	Weeks in Top 40
4 Feb 89	ALL THE MYTHS ON SUNDAY	Food 17	66		
1 Apr 89	LIKE PRINCES DO	Food 19	58		
5 Aug 89	WHEN THE HOODOO COMES	Food 20	62		
18 Jan 92	FALL TO LOVE	Food 35	48		
21 Mar 92	BOY ON TOP OF THE NEWS	Food 36	58		
5 Sep 92	GOD ONLY KNOWS	Food 39	57		

DIFFERENT GEAR VERSUS THE POLICE Italian production group

Date	Title	Label	Peak Position	Weeks at No.1	Weeks in Top 40
5 Aug 00	WHEN THE WORLD IS RUNNING DOWN (YOU CAN'T GO WRONG)	Pagan 039CDS	28		1

DIFFORD & TILBROOK UK duo

Date	Title	Label	Peak Position	Weeks at No.1	Weeks in Top 40
30 Jun 84	LOVE'S CRASHING WAVES	A&M AM 193	57		

DIFF'RENT DARKNESS UK group

Date	Title	Label	Peak Position	Weeks at No.1	Weeks in Top 40
27 Dec 03	ORCHESTRAL MANOEUVRES IN THE DARKNESS	Guided Missile GUIDE49CD	66		

DIGABLE PLANETS US group

Date	Title	Label	Peak Position	Weeks at No.1	Weeks in Top 40
13 Feb 93	REBIRTH OF SLICK (COOL LIKE DAT)	Pendulum EKR 159CD	67		

RAH DIGGA US rapper

Date	Title	Label	Peak Position	Weeks at No.1	Weeks in Top 40
2 Mar 02	I'M LEAVIN' (OUTSIDAZ FEATURING RAH DIGGA & MELANIE BLATT)	Rufflife RLCDM 03	41		
21 Jun 03	BOUT (JAMELIA FEATURING RAH DIGGA)	Parlophone CDRS 6597	37		1

DIGITAL DREAM BABY UK producer

Date	Title	Label	Peak Position	Weeks at No.1	Weeks in Top 40
14 Dec 91	WALKING IN THE AIR	Columbia 6576067	49		

DIGITAL EXCITATION Belgian producer

Date	Title	Label	Peak Position	Weeks at No.1	Weeks in Top 40
29 Feb 92	PURE PLEASURE	R&S RSUK 10	37		1

DIGITAL ORGASM Belgian group

Date	Title	Label	Peak Position	Weeks at No.1	Weeks in Top 40
7 Dec 91	RUNNING OUT OF TIME	Dead Dead Good GOOD 009	16		7
18 Apr 92	STARTOUCHERS	DDG International GOOD 13	31		2
25 Jul 92	MOOG ERUPTION	DDG International GOOD 17	62		

DIGITAL UNDERGROUND US group

Date	Title	Label	Peak Position	Weeks at No.1	Weeks in Top 40
16 Mar 91	SAME SONG	Big Life BLR 40	52		

DILATED PEOPLES US group

Date	Title	Label	Peak Position	Weeks at No.1	Weeks in Top 40
23 Feb 02	WORST COMES TO THE WORST	Capitol CDCL 834	29		2
10 Apr 04	THIS WAY	Capitol CDCL 854	35		1

DILEMMA Italian production group

Date	Title	Label	Peak Position	Weeks at No.1	Weeks in Top 40
6 Apr 96	IN SPIRIT	ffrr FCDE 274	42		

DILLINJA UK producer

Date	Title	Label	Peak Position	Weeks at No.1	Weeks in Top 40
9 Nov 02	TWIST 'EM OUT	Renegade Hardware RH40	50		
21 Dec 02	LIVE OR DIE/SOUTH MANZ	Valve VLV007	53		
10 May 03	THIS IS A WARNING/SUPER DJ	Valve VLV008	47		
28 Jun 03	TWIST 'EM OUT (DILLINJA FEATURING SKIBADEE)	Trouble On Vinyl TOV 56CD	35		1
27 Sep 03	FAST CAR	Valve VLV011	56		
12 Jun 04	ALL THE THINGS/FORSAKEN DREAMS	Valve VLV012	71		
10 Jul 04	IN THE GRIND/ACID TRAK	Valve VLV013	71		
8 Jan 05	THUGGED OUT BITCH/RAINFOREST	Valve VLV014	54		

DIMESTARS UK group

Date	Title	Label	Peak Position	Weeks at No.1	Weeks in Top 40
16 Jun 01	MY SUPERSTAR	Polydor 5870912	72		

D-INFLUENCE UK production group

Date	Title	Label	Peak Position	Weeks at No.1	Weeks in Top 40
20 Jun 92	GOOD LOVER	East West A 8573	46		
27 Mar 93	GOOD LOVER (REMIX)	East West America A 8439CD	61		
24 Jun 95	MIDNITE	East West A 4418CD	58		
16 Aug 97	HYPNOTIZE	Echo ECSCD 41	33		1
11 Oct 97	MAGIC	Echo ECSCD 45	45		
5 Sep 98	ROCK WITH YOU	Echo ECSCD 56	30		1

MARK DINNING US singer

Date	Title	Label	Peak Position	Weeks at No.1	Weeks in Top 40
10 Mar 60	TEEN ANGEL	MGM 1053 ★	37		2

DINOSAUR Jr US group

Date	Title	Label	Peak Position	Weeks at No.1	Weeks in Top 40
2 Feb 91	THE WAGON	Blanco Y Negro NEG 48	49		
14 Nov 92	GET ME	Blanco Y Negro NEG 60	44		
30 Jan 93	START CHOPPIN	Blanco Y Negro NEG 61CD	20		2
12 Jun 93	OUT THERE	Blanco Y Negro NEG 63CD	44		
27 Aug 94	FEEL THE PAIN	Blanco Y Negro NEG 74CD	25		1
11 Feb 95	I DON'T THINK SO	Blanco Y Negro NEG 77CD	67		
5 Apr 97	TAKE A RUN AT THE SUN	Blanco Y Negro NEG 103CD	53		

DIO US group

Date	Title	Label	Peak Position	Weeks at No.1	Weeks in Top 40
20 Aug 83	HOLY DIVER	Vertigo DIO 1	72		
29 Oct 83	RAINBOW IN THE DARK	Vertigo DIO 2	46		
11 Aug 84	WE ROCK	Vertigo DIO 3	42		
29 Sep 84	MYSTERY	Vertigo DIO 4	34		2
10 Aug 85	ROCK 'N' ROLL CHILDREN	Vertigo DIO 5	26		4
2 Nov 85	HUNGRY FOR HEAVEN	Vertigo DIO 6	72		
17 May 86	HUNGRY FOR HEAVEN	Vertigo DIO 7	56		
1 Aug 87	I COULD HAVE BEEN A DREAMER	Vertigo DIO 8	69		

DION US singer

Date	Title	Label	Peak Position	Weeks at No.1	Weeks in Top 40
26 Jun 59	A TEENAGER IN LOVE (DION & THE BELMONTS)	London HLU 8874	28		2
19 Jan 61	LONELY TEENAGER	Top Rank JAR 521	47		
2 Nov 61	RUNAROUND SUE	Top Rank JAR 586 ★	11		9
15 Feb 62	THE WANDERER	HMV POP 971	10		10
22 May 76	THE WANDERER	Philips 6146 700	16		8
19 Aug 89	KING OF THE NEW YORK STREET	Arista 112556	74		

CELINE DION Canadian singer

Date	Title	Label	Peak Position	Weeks at No.1	Weeks in Top 40
16 May 92	BEAUTY AND THE BEAST (CELINE DION & PEABO BRYSON)	Epic 6576607	9		4
4 Jul 92	IF YOU ASKED ME TO	Epic 6581927	60		
14 Nov 92	LOVE CAN MOVE MOUNTAINS	Epic 6587787	46		

BRUCE DICKINSON

Paul Bruce Dickinson is a best-selling author, screenplay writer, airline pilot, train enthusiast and Olympic-standard fencer. Oh, and he also happens to be the singer in gargantuan Heavy Metal legend, Iron Maiden. His inclusion here might be surprising in the sense that Iron Maiden have enjoyed almost twice as many singles *outside* the Top Ten as they have inside that elite cluster; yet their impact on the UK singles charts cannot be underestimated, not just because of their own success but also because of the legion of other bands they have influenced.

Bruce's own story is suitably colourful. His early childhood was transient and left him feeling like an outsider – an outlook on life that he carried with him into adulthood and served him well in his rock career. After being expelled from Oundle school for an incident with urine and a teacher's dinner, he cut his teeth in a succession of groups beginning with the letter S: Styx, Speed, Shots and most significantly Samson, featuring the blues/guitar talents of Paul Samson, all of which were instrumental in forging Dickinson's trademark operatic vocals. He was soon at the forefront of the New Wave Of British Heavy Metal (NWOBHM). After a final gig with Samson at 1981's Reading Festival, he was snapped up by Iron Maiden who had parted ways with enigmatic vocalist, Paul Di'Anno.

Interestingly, due to litigation between Samson and their ex-management at the time, Dickinson was unable to write officially for his debut Maiden LP, the career-defining *Number Of The Beast*. It has been hinted that he had 'a moral contribution' to several tracks, including breakthrough single, 'Run To The Hills', released on 12 February 1982 and peaking at Number 7 in the UK charts. Despite Maiden's growing worldwide fanbase, it was to be their only Top Ten hit for an astounding six years. The group's success was never reliant on the triple assault of MTV-type music shows, radio support and mainstream magazine features but rather on a gruelling gigging schedule. By the end of the globe-straddling, seemingly endless 'World Slavery' tour to support the *Powerslave* album in 1986, Dickinson was so burned out he came close to leaving the group who had snagged eight top twenty singles between 1982 and 1986.

The last two years of the 1980s were better. The release of the prog-rock tinted *Seventh Son Of A Seventh Son* album brought a succession of top ten singles, beginning with 'Can I Play With Madness?', a poppy number (for Maiden) co-written between Dickinson, guitarist Adrian Smith and bassist and stalwart Steve Harris (peaking at Number 3, Maiden's biggest hit at that point) and continuing with 'The Evil That Men Do' (Number 5, 1 August 1988) and 'The Clairvoyant' (Number 6, 7 November). Meanwhile, Bruce had been invited to contribute to the soundtrack of *A Nightmare On Elm Street IV*; collaborating with long-time friend and ex-Gillan guitarist Janick Gers, the pair came up with the delightfully titled 'Bring Your Daughter ... To The Slaughter'. This remains a classic example of meticulous chart timing: its release in the traditionally quiet first chart of January, mixed with clever multi-formatting and a mass mobilisation of Maiden fans led to the band's first – and only – Number 1 in the first month of 1991.

After the dubious honour of guesting alongside Mr Bean on the Number 9 charity single, 'I Wanna Be Elected', Bruce shocked the rock world by leaving Maiden to pursue a solo career that had already kicked off with the title track from his *Tattooed Millionaire* album, the song reaching Number 18 in 1990 (on the same album, the song 'Born In '58' references his early years in the small mining town of Worksop). It was a productive time artistically for the Sheffield-raised singer, but a fallow period in terms of actual chart placings, as a succession of singles failed to make any impact, a fact that was mirrored by Iron Maiden's relative decline in this period too, partly down to the new line-up and partly because of the rise of grunge – suddenly, old heavy metal bands were seen as painfully passé, even though many grunge bands openly cited them as key influences.

Dickinson rejoined Maiden in 2000, and their dual fortunes reversed: return album *The Wicker Man* reached Number 9 in May 2000, and since then Maiden and Bruce have snagged six Top Ten singles and continue to tour the world, releasing a series of new albums and retrospectives that bring their work to new generations of metal fans.

Perhaps equally impressive, though, are Bruce's extra-curricular activities. He is indeed an Olympic-standard fencer; he flies commercial 757s for the airline Astraeus and even captained a mercy mission flying 200 British citizens out of the Lebanon during the Hezbollah conflict with Israel during 2006; his novels were naughtily crude in the vein of many great British ribald farces; his radio shows display the staggering depth of his musical expertise, and his knowledge of all things locomotive would put even pop's famed trainspotter, Pete Waterman, to the test. The title of one of Maiden's singles, 'Infinite Dreams' doesn't just seem to be the name of a song but, for Bruce Dickinson, a way of life.

Legend: ○ Silver-selling · ● Gold-selling · ⊛ Platinum-selling · ★ US No.1 · Peak Position · Weeks at No.1 · Weeks in Top 40

Date	Title / Label	Peak Position	Weeks at No.1	Weeks in Top 40
26 Dec 92	**IF YOU ASKED ME TO** *Epic 6581927*	57		
3 Apr 93	**WHERE DOES MY HEART BEAT NOW** *Epic 6563265*	72		
29 Jan 94	**THE POWER OF LOVE** *Epic 6597992* ★	4		8
23 Apr 94	**MISLED** *Epic 6602922*	40		1
22 Oct 94	**THINK TWICE** *Epic 6606422* ⊛	1	6	25
20 May 95	**ONLY ONE ROAD** *Epic 6613535*	8		5
9 Sep 95	**TU M'AIMES ENCORE (TO LOVE ME AGAIN)** *Epic 6624255*	7		6
2 Dec 95	**MISLED** *Epic 6626495*	15		2
2 Mar 96	**FALLING INTO YOU** *Epic 6629795*	10		7
1 Jun 96	**BECAUSE YOU LOVED ME (THEME FROM UP CLOSE AND PERSONAL)** *Epic 6632382* ○ ★	5		14
5 Oct 96	**IT'S ALL COMING BACK TO ME NOW** *Epic 6637112* ○	3		10
21 Dec 96	**ALL BY MYSELF** *Epic 6640622* ○	6		5
28 Jun 97	**CALL THE MAN** *Epic 6646922*	11		4
15 Nov 97	**TELL HIM** *Epic 6653052* BARBRA STREISAND & CELINE DION ●	3		10
20 Dec 97	**THE REASON** *Epic 6653812*	11		6
21 Feb 98	**MY HEART WILL GO ON** *Epic 6655472* ⊛ ★	1	2	17
18 Jul 98	**IMMORTALITY** *Epic 6661682* CELINE DION WITH THE BEE GEES ○	5		7
28 Nov 98	**I'M YOUR ANGEL** *Epic 6666282* CELINE DION & R KELLY ○ ★	3		9
10 Jul 99	**TREAT HER LIKE A LADY** *Epic 6675525*	29		1
11 Dec 99	**THAT'S THE WAY IT IS** *Epic 6684622*	12		8
8 Apr 00	**THE FIRST TIME EVER I SAW YOUR FACE** *Epic 6691942*	19		2
23 Mar 02	**A NEW DAY HAS COME** *Epic 6725032*	7		8
31 Aug 02	**I'M ALIVE** *Epic 6730652*	17		4
7 Dec 02	**GOODBYE'S (THE SADDEST WORD)** *Epic 6733732*	38		1
20 Sep 03	**ONE HEART** *Epic 6743482*	27		1
10 Nov 07	**TAKING CHANCES** *Columbia 88697170002*	40		1

DIONNE Canadian singer

Date	Title / Label	Peak Position	Weeks at No.1	Weeks in Top 40
23 Sep 89	**COME GET MY LOVIN'** *Citybeat CBC 745*	69		

WASIS DIOP Senegalese producer

Date	Title / Label	Peak Position	Weeks at No.1	Weeks in Top 40
10 Feb 96	**AFRICAN DREAM** *Mercury MERCD 453* WASIS DIOP FEATURING LENA FIAGBE	44		

DIRE STRAITS UK group

Date	Title / Label	Peak Position	Weeks at No.1	Weeks in Top 40
10 Mar 79	**SULTANS OF SWING** *Vertigo 6059 206* ○	8		8
28 Jul 79	**LADY WRITER** *Vertigo 6059 230*	51		
17 Jan 81	**ROMEO AND JULIET** *Vertigo MOVIE 1*	8		8
4 Apr 81	**SKATEAWAY** *Vertigo MOVIE 2*	37		2
10 Oct 81	**TUNNEL OF LOVE** *Vertigo MUSIC 3*	54		
4 Sep 82	**PRIVATE INVESTIGATIONS** *Vertigo DSTR 1* ○	2		7
22 Jan 83	**TWISTING BY THE POOL** *Vertigo DSTR 2*	14		6
18 Feb 84	**LOVE OVER GOLD (LIVE)/SOLID ROCK (LIVE)** *Vertigo DSTR 6*	50		
20 Apr 85	**SO FAR AWAY** *Vertigo DSTR 9*	20		4
6 Jul 85	**MONEY FOR NOTHING** *Vertigo DSTR 10* ○ ★	4		12
26 Oct 85	**BROTHERS IN ARMS** *Vertigo DSTR 11*	16		7
11 Jan 86	**WALK OF LIFE** *Vertigo DSTR 12*	2		9
3 May 86	**YOUR LATEST TRICK** *Vertigo DSTR 13*	26		4
5 Nov 88	**SULTANS OF SWING** *Vertigo DSTR 15*	62		
31 Aug 91	**CALLING ELVIS** *Vertigo DSTR 16*	21		2
2 Nov 91	**HEAVY FUEL** *Vertigo DSTR 17*	55		
29 Feb 92	**ON EVERY STREET** *Vertigo DSTR 18*	42		
27 Jun 92	**THE BUG** *Vertigo DSTR 19*	67		
22 May 93	**ENCORES EP** *Vertigo DSCD 20*	31		1

DIRECKT UK production duo

Date	Title / Label	Peak Position	Weeks at No.1	Weeks in Top 40
13 Aug 94	**TWO FATT GUITARS (REVISITED)** *UFG 7CD*	36		1

DIRECT DRIVE UK group

Date	Title / Label	Peak Position	Weeks at No.1	Weeks in Top 40
26 Jan 85	**ANYTHING** *Polydor POSP 728*	67		
4 May 85	**A.B.C. (FALLING IN LOVE'S NOT EASY)** *Boiling Point POSP 742*	75		

DIRT DEVILS UK/Finnish production duo

Date	Title / Label	Peak Position	Weeks at No.1	Weeks in Top 40
2 Feb 02	**THE DRILL** *NuLife 74321915262*	15		3
6 Dec 03	**MUSIC IS LIFE** *NuLife 82876571412*	53		

DIRTY PRETTY THINGS UK group

Date	Title / Label	Peak Position	Weeks at No.1	Weeks in Top 40
29 Apr 06	**BANG BANG YOU'RE DEAD** *Vertigo 9854376*	5		5
22 Jul 06	**DEADWOOD** *Vertigo 1703653*	20		1
7 Oct 06	**WONDERING** *Vertigo 1705365*	34		1

DIRTY VEGAS UK production group

Date	Title / Label	Peak Position	Weeks at No.1	Weeks in Top 40
19 May 01	**DAYS GO BY** *Credence CDCRED 011*	27		2
3 Aug 02	**GHOSTS** *Credence CDCRED 028*	31		1
12 Oct 02	**DAYS GO BY** *Credence CDCREDS 030*	16		3
23 Oct 04	**WALK INTO THE SUN** *Parlophone CDRS6647*	54		

DISCHARGE UK group

Date	Title / Label	Peak Position	Weeks at No.1	Weeks in Top 40
24 Oct 81	**NEVER AGAIN** *Clay 6*	64		

DISCO ANTHEM Dutch producer

Date	Title / Label	Peak Position	Weeks at No.1	Weeks in Top 40
18 Jun 94	**SCREAM** *Sweat MCSTD 1977*	47		

DISCO CITIZENS UK producer

Date	Title / Label	Peak Position	Weeks at No.1	Weeks in Top 40
22 Jul 95	**RIGHT HERE RIGHT NOW** *Deconstruction 74321293872*	40		1
12 Apr 97	**FOOTPRINT** *Xtravaganza 0091115*	34		1
4 Jul 98	**NAGASAKI BADGER** *Xtravaganza 0091595 EXT*	56		

DISCO EVANGELISTS UK production group

Date	Title / Label	Peak Position	Weeks at No.1	Weeks in Top 40
8 May 93	**DE NIRO** *Positiva CDTIV 2*	59		

DISCO TEX & THE SEX-O-LETTES US group

Date	Title / Label	Peak Position	Weeks at No.1	Weeks in Top 40
23 Nov 74	**GET DANCING** *Chelsea 2005 013* ○	8		11
26 Apr 75	**I WANNA DANCE WIT CHOO** *Chelsea 2005 024* DISCO TEX & THE SEX-O-LETTES FEATURING SIR MONTI ROCK III	6		9

DISCO TEX UK group

Date	Title / Label	Peak Position	Weeks at No.1	Weeks in Top 40
24 Mar 01	**I CAN CAST A SPELL** *Absolution CDABSOL 1* DISCO TEX PRESENTS CLOUDBURST	35		1

DISPOSABLE HEROES OF HIPHOPRISY US duo

Date	Title / Label	Peak Position	Weeks at No.1	Weeks in Top 40
4 Apr 92	**TELEVISION THE DRUG OF THE NATION** *Fourth & Broadway BRW 241*	57		
30 May 92	**LANGUAGE OF VIOLENCE** *Fourth & Broadway 12BRW 248*	68		
19 Dec 92	**TELEVISION THE DRUG OF THE NATION** *Fourth & Broadway BRW 241*	44		

DISTANT SOUNDZ UK group

Date	Title / Label	Peak Position	Weeks at No.1	Weeks in Top 40
9 Mar 02	**TIME AFTER TIME** *W10/Incentive CENT 36CDS*	20		3

SACHA DISTEL French singer

Date	Title / Label	Peak Position	Weeks at No.1	Weeks in Top 40
10 Jan 70	**RAINDROPS KEEP FALLING ON MY HEAD** *Warner Brothers WB 7345*	10		13

DISTILLERS US/Australian group

Date	Title / Label	Peak Position	Weeks at No.1	Weeks in Top 40
15 Nov 03	**DRAIN THE BLOOD** *Sire W 628CD*	51		
10 Apr 04	**THE HUNGER** *Sire W 636CD*	48		
19 Jun 04	**BEAT YOUR HEART OUT** *Sire W 644CD*	74		

DISTORTED MINDS UK production duo

Date	Title / Label	Peak Position	Weeks at No.1	Weeks in Top 40
29 Mar 03	**T-10/THE TENTH PLANET** *Kaos 006P*	43		
24 Jan 04	**T-10/THE TENTH PLANET (REMIX)** *Kaos KAOS006*	45		

DISTURBED US group

Date	Title / Label	Peak Position	Weeks at No.1	Weeks in Top 40
7 Apr 01	**VOICES** *Giant 74321848962*	52		
28 Sep 02	**PRAYER** *Reprise W 591CD*	31		1
14 Dec 02	**REMEMBER** *Reprise W 596CD*	56		

DIVA Norwegian duo

Date	Title / Label	Peak Position	Weeks at No.1	Weeks in Top 40
7 Oct 95	**THE SUN ALWAYS SHINES ON TV** *East West YZ 947CD*	53		
20 Jul 96	**EVERYBODY (MOVE YOUR BODY)** *East West YZ 035CD*	44		

DIVA SURPRISE US/Spanish production duo

Date	Title / Label	Peak Position	Weeks at No.1	Weeks in Top 40
14 Nov 98	**ON THE TOP OF THE WORLD** *Positiva CDTIV 100* DIVA SURPRISE FEATURING GEORGIA JONES	29		1

DIVE UK production duo

Date	Title / Label	Peak Position	Weeks at No.1	Weeks in Top 40
21 Feb 98	**BOOGIE** *WEA 147CD1*	35		1

DIVE DIVE UK group

Date	Title / Label	Peak Position	Weeks at No.1	Weeks in Top 40
12 Mar 05	**555 FOR FILMSTARS** *Diablo DIACD006*	48		
18 Jun 05	**THE SORRY SUITOR** *Diablo DIACD007*	54		

DIVERSIONS UK group

Date	Title / Label	Peak Position	Weeks at No.1	Weeks in Top 40
20 Sep 75	**FATTIE BUM BUM** *Gull GULS 18*	34		2

DIVINE US singer

Date	Title / Label	Peak Position	Weeks at No.1	Weeks in Top 40
15 Oct 83	**LOVE REACTION** *Design Communication DES 4*	65		
14 Jul 84	**YOU THINK YOU'RE A MAN** *Proto ENA 118*	16		8
20 Oct 84	**I'M SO BEAUTIFUL** *Proto ENA 121*	52		
27 Apr 85	**WALK LIKE A MAN** *Proto ENA 125*	23		5
20 Jul 85	**TWISTIN' THE NIGHT AWAY** *Proto ENA 127*	47		

DIVINE US group

Date	Title / Label	Peak Position	Weeks at No.1	Weeks in Top 40
16 Oct 99	**LATELY** *Mushroom/Red Ant RA 002CDS* ★	52		

DIVINE COMEDY UK group

Date	Title / Label	Peak Position	Weeks at No.1	Weeks in Top 40
29 Jun 96	**SOMETHING FOR THE WEEKEND** *Setanta SETCD 26*	14		4
24 Aug 96	**BECOMING MORE LIKE ALFIE** *Setanta SETCD 27*	27		1
16 Nov 96	**THE FROG PRINCESS** *Setanta SETCD 32*	15		1
22 Mar 97	**EVERYBODY KNOWS (EXCEPT YOU)** *Setanta SETCDA 038*	14		2
11 Apr 98	**I'VE BEEN TO A MARVELLOUS PARTY** *EMI CDTCB 001*	28		1
26 Sep 98	**GENERATION SEX** *Setanta SETCDA 050*	19		1
28 Nov 98	**THE CERTAINTY OF CHANCE** *Setanta SETCDA 067*	49		
6 Feb 99	**NATIONAL EXPRESS** *Setanta SETCDB 069*	8		5
21 Aug 99	**THE POP SINGER'S FEAR OF THE POLLEN COUNT** *Setanta SETCDB 070*	17		2
13 Nov 99	**GIN SOAKED BOY** *Setanta SETCD 071*	38		1
10 Mar 01	**LOVE WHAT YOU DO** *Parlophone CDRS 6554*	26		1
26 May 01	**BAD AMBASSADOR** *Parlophone CDRS 6558*	34		1
10 Nov 01	**PERFECT LOVESONG** *Parlophone CDRS 6561*	42		
3 Apr 04	**COME HOME BILLY BIRD** *Parlophone CDRS 6630*	25		1
26 Jun 04	**ABSENT FRIENDS** *Parlophone CDRS 6641*	38		1
24 Jun 06	**DIVA LADY** *Parlophone CDRS6698*	52		
26 Aug 06	**TO DIE A VIRGIN** *Parlophone CDRS6712*	67		

DIVINE INSPIRATION UK production group

Date	Title / Label	Peak Position	Weeks at No.1	Weeks in Top 40
18 Jan 03	**THE WAY (PUT YOUR HAND IN MY HAND)** *Data/Ministry Of Sound/Heat DATA 42CDS*	5		5
15 Nov 03	**WHAT WILL BE WILL BE (DESTINY)** *Heat Recordings HEATCD036*	55		

DIVINYLS Australian group

Date	Title / Label	Peak Position	Weeks at No.1	Weeks in Top 40
18 May 91	**I TOUCH MYSELF** *Virgin America VUS 36*	10		7

DIXIE CHICKS US group

Date	Title / Label	Peak Position	Weeks at No.1	Weeks in Top 40
3 Jul 99	**THERE'S YOUR TROUBLE** *Epic 6675165*	26		1
6 Nov 99	**READY TO RUN** *Epic 6682472*	53		
19 Apr 03	**LANDSLIDE** *Epic 6737392*	55		
17 Jun 06	**NOT READY TO MAKE NICE** *Open Wide 82876861242*	70		

DIXIE CUPS US group

Date	Title / Label	Peak Position	Weeks at No.1	Weeks in Top 40
18 Jun 64	**CHAPEL OF LOVE** *Pye International 7N 25245* ★	22		7
13 May 65	**IKO IKO** *Red Bird RB 10024*	23		7

DIZZY HEIGHTS UK rapper

Date	Title / Label	Peak Position	Weeks at No.1	Weeks in Top 40
18 Dec 82	**CHRISTMAS RAPPING** *Polydor WRAP 1*	49		

DJ ALIGATOR PROJECT Danish DJ/producer

Date	Title / Label	Peak Position	Weeks at No.1	Weeks in Top 40
7 Oct 00	**THE WHISTLE SONG** *EMI CDBLOW 001*	57		
19 Jan 02	**THE WHISTLE SONG (BLOW MY WHISTLE BITCH) (REMIX)** *All Around The World CDGLOBE 247*	5		7

DJ AMS & KHIZA UK duo

Date	Title / Label	Peak Position	Weeks at No.1	Weeks in Top 40
12 Mar 05	**HOT LIKE FIRE** *Goldmind GM008CD* – DJ AMS & KHIZA FEATURING BINNS & TAFARI	72		

DJ BADMARSH & SHRI UK/Indian duo

Date	Title / Label	Peak Position	Weeks at No.1	Weeks in Top 40
28 Jul 01	**SIGNS** *Outcaste OUT 38CD1* – DJ BADMARSH & SHRI FEATURING UK APACHE	63		

DJ BOBO Swiss DJ/producer

Date	Title / Label	Peak Position	Weeks at No.1	Weeks in Top 40
24 Sep 94	**EVERYBODY** *PWL Continental PWCD 312*	47		
17 Jun 95	**LOVE IS ALL AROUND** *Avex UK AVEXCD 7*	49		
25 Oct 03	**CHIHUAHUA** *Fuelin 82876559422*	36		1

DJ CASPER US DJ/producer

Date	Title / Label	Peak Position	Weeks at No.1	Weeks in Top 40
13 Mar 04	**CHA CHA SLIDE** *All Around The World CDGLOBE329*	1	1	14
16 Oct 04	**OOPS UPSIDE YOUR HEAD** *All Around The World CDGLOBE376* – DJ CASPER FEATURING THE GAP BAND	16		3

DJ CHUS Spanish DJ/producer

Date	Title / Label	Peak Position	Weeks at No.1	Weeks in Top 40
2 Nov 02	**THAT FEELING** *Defected DFTD 055R2* – DJ CHUS PRESENTS GROOVE FOUNDATION	65		

DJ DADO Italian DJ/producer

Date	Title / Label	Peak Position	Weeks at No.1	Weeks in Top 40
6 Apr 96	**X-FILES** *ZYX 8065R8*	8		4
14 Mar 98	**COMING BACK** *ffrr TABCD 247*	63		
11 Jul 98	**GIVE ME LOVE** *VC Recordings VCRD 37* – DJ DADO VS MICHELLE WEEKS	59		
8 May 99	**READY OR NOT** *Chemistry CDKEM 006* – DJ DADO & SIMONE JAY	51		

DJ DAN US DJ/producer

Date	Title / Label	Peak Position	Weeks at No.1	Weeks in Top 40
5 May 01	**THAT ZIPPER TRACK** *Duty Free DF 213CD* – DJ DAN PRESENTS NEEDLE DAMAGE	53		

DJ DEE KLINE UK DJ/producer

Date	Title / Label	Peak Position	Weeks at No.1	Weeks in Top 40
3 Jun 00	**I DON'T SMOKE** *East West EW 213CD*	11		3

DJ DISCIPLE US DJ/producer

Date	Title / Label	Peak Position	Weeks at No.1	Weeks in Top 40
12 Nov 94	**ON THE DANCEFLOOR** *Mother MUMCD 55*	67		

DJ DUKE US DJ/producer

Date	Title / Label	Peak Position	Weeks at No.1	Weeks in Top 40
8 Jan 94	**BLOW YOUR WHISTLE** *ffrr FCD 228*	15		3
16 Jul 94	**TURN IT UP (SAY YEAH)** *ffrr FCD 235*	31		1

DJ EMPIRE German producers

Date	Title / Label	Peak Position	Weeks at No.1	Weeks in Top 40
12 Feb 00	**THE CHASE** *Logic 74321732112* – DJ EMPIRE PRESENTS GIORGIO MORODER	46		

DJ ERIC UK production duo

Date	Title / Label	Peak Position	Weeks at No.1	Weeks in Top 40
13 Feb 99	**WE ARE LOVE** *Distinctive DISNCD 49*	37		1
10 Jun 00	**DESIRE** *Distinctive DISNCD 56*	67		

DJ 'FAST' EDDIE US DJ/producer

Date	Title / Label	Peak Position	Weeks at No.1	Weeks in Top 40
11 Apr 87	**CAN U DANCE** *Champion CHAMP 41* – KENNY 'JAMMIN' JASON & 'FAST' EDDIE SMITH	71		
14 Nov 87	**CAN U DANCE** *Champion CHAMP 41* – KENNY 'JAMMIN' JASON & 'FAST' EDDIE SMITH	67		
21 Jan 89	**HIP HOUSE/I CAN DANCE** *DJInternational DJIN 5*	47		
11 Mar 89	**YO YO GET FUNKY** *DJInternational DJIN 7*	54		
28 Oct 89	**GIT ON UP** *DJInternational 6553667* – DJ 'FAST' EDDIE FEATURING SUNDANCE	49		

Silver-selling ○ Gold-selling ● Platinum-selling ⊛ US No.1 ★ — Peak Position · Weeks at No.1 · Weeks in Top 40

DJ FLAVOURS UK DJ/producer

Date	Title / Label	Peak Position	Weeks at No.1	Weeks in Top 40
11 Oct 97	**YOUR CARESS (ALL I NEED)** *All Around The World CDGLOBE 160*	19		2

DJ FORMAT UK DJ/producer

Date	Title / Label	Peak Position	Weeks at No.1	Weeks in Top 40
22 Mar 03	**WE KNOW SOMETHING YOU DON'T KNOW** *Genuine GEN 004CDX* DJ FORMAT FEATURING CHARLI 2NA & AKIL	73		

DJ FRESH UK DJ/producer

Date	Title / Label	Peak Position	Weeks at No.1	Weeks in Top 40
1 Nov 03	**DA LICKS/TEMPLE OF DOOM** *Breakbeat Kaos BBK001P*	60		
31 Jul 04	**SUBMARINES** *Breakbeat Kaos BBK004*	73		
30 Oct 04	**WHEN THE SUN GOES DOWN** *Breakbeat Kaos BBK005SCD* DJ FRESH FEATURING ADAM F	68		
12 Feb 05	**SUPERNATURE** *Breakbeat Kaos BBK006* BARON & FRESH	59		
9 Jul 05	**TARANTULA/FASTEN YOUR SEATBELT** *Breakbeat Kaos BBK009SCD* PENDULUM & FRESH FEATURING SPYDA	60		

DJ GARRY Belgian DJ/producer

Date	Title / Label	Peak Position	Weeks at No.1	Weeks in Top 40
19 Jan 02	**DREAM UNIVERSE** *Xtravaganza XTRAV 32CDS*	36		1

DJ GERT Belgian DJ/producer

Date	Title / Label	Peak Position	Weeks at No.1	Weeks in Top 40
26 May 01	**GIVE ME SOME MORE** *Mostika 23200253*	50		

DJ GREGORY French DJ/producer

Date	Title / Label	Peak Position	Weeks at No.1	Weeks in Top 40
9 Nov 02	**TROPICAL SOUNDCLASH** *Defected DFTD 061CDS*	59		
11 Oct 03	**ELLE/TROPICAL SOUNDCLASH** *Defected DFTD 077CDX*	73		

DJ HYPE UK DJ/producer

Date	Title / Label	Peak Position	Weeks at No.1	Weeks in Top 40
20 Mar 93	**SHOT IN THE DARK** *Suburban Base SUBBASE 20CD*	63		
2 Jun 01	**CASINO ROYALE/DEAD A'S** *True Playaz TPRCD 004* DJ ZINC/DJ HYPE	58		

DJ INNOCENCE UK DJ/producer

Date	Title / Label	Peak Position	Weeks at No.1	Weeks in Top 40
6 Apr 02	**SO BEAUTIFUL** *Echo ECSCD 119* DJ INNOCENCE FEATURING ALEX CHARLES	51		

DJ JEAN Dutch DJ/producer

Date	Title / Label	Peak Position	Weeks at No.1	Weeks in Top 40
11 Sep 99	**THE LAUNCH** *AM:PM CDAMPM 123* ○	2		8

DJ JURGEN Dutch group

Date	Title / Label	Peak Position	Weeks at No.1	Weeks in Top 40
31 Jul 99	**BETTER OFF ALONE** *Positiva CDTIV 113* DJ JURGEN PRESENTS ALICE DEEJAY ⊛	2		13

DJ KOOL US DJ/rapper

Date	Title / Label	Peak Position	Weeks at No.1	Weeks in Top 40
22 Feb 97	**LET ME CLEAR MY THROAT** *American Recordings 74321452092*	8		5

DJ KRUSH US DJ/producer

Date	Title / Label	Peak Position	Weeks at No.1	Weeks in Top 40
16 Mar 96	**MEISO** *Mo Wax MW 042CD*	52		
12 Oct 96	**ONLY THE STRONG SURVIVE** *Mo Wax MW 060CD*	71		

DJ LUCK & MC NEAT UK duo

Date	Title / Label	Peak Position	Weeks at No.1	Weeks in Top 40
25 Dec 99	**A LITTLE BIT OF LUCK** *Red Rose CDRROSE 1*	9		12
27 May 00	**MASTERBLASTER 2000** *Red Rose RROSE 002CD* DJ LUCK & MC NEAT FEATURING JJ	5		5
7 Oct 00	**AIN'T NO STOPPIN US** *Red Rose CDRROSE 004* DJ LUCK & MC NEAT FEATURING JJ	8		3
17 Mar 01	**PIANO LOCO** *Island CID 773*	12		4
8 Sep 01	**I'M ALL ABOUT YOU** *Island CID 781* DJ LUCK & MC NEAT FEATURING ARI GOLD	18		2
25 May 02	**IRIE** *Island CID 795*	31		1

DJ MANTA Dutch production duo

Date	Title / Label	Peak Position	Weeks at No.1	Weeks in Top 40
9 Oct 99	**HOLDING ON** *AM:PM CDAMPM 125*	47		

DJ MARKY & XRS Brazilian production duo

Date	Title / Label	Peak Position	Weeks at No.1	Weeks in Top 40
20 Jul 02	**LK (CAROLINA CAROL BELA)** *V Recordings V 035* DJ MARKY & XRS FEATURING STAMINA MC	17		4
16 Nov 02	**LK (REMIX)** *V Recordings V 038* DJ MARKY & XRS FEATURING STAMINA MC	45		

DJ MIKO Italian producer

Date	Title / Label	Peak Position	Weeks at No.1	Weeks in Top 40
13 Aug 94	**WHAT'S UP** *Systematic SYSCD 2*	6		8

DJ MILANO Italian DJ/producer

Date	Title / Label	Peak Position	Weeks at No.1	Weeks in Top 40
28 Mar 98	**SANTA MARIA** *All Around The World CDGLOBE 163* DJ MILANO FEATURING SAMANTHA FOX	31		1

DJ MISJAH & DJ TIM Italian production duo

Date	Title / Label	Peak Position	Weeks at No.1	Weeks in Top 40
23 Mar 96	**ACCESS** *ffrreedom TABCD 240*	16		2
27 May 00	**ACCESS (REMIX)** *Tripoli Trax TTRAXCD 063*	45		

DJ ÖTZI Austrian DJ/producer

Date	Title / Label	Peak Position	Weeks at No.1	Weeks in Top 40
18 Aug 01	**HEY BABY (IMPORT)** *EMI 8892462*	41		
22 Sep 01	**HEY BABY** *EMI CDOTZI 001* ⊛	1	1	18
1 Dec 01	**DO WAH DIDDY** *EMI CDOTZI 002*	9		7
29 Dec 01	**X-MAS TIME** *EMI CDOTZI 003*	51		
8 Jun 02	**HEY BABY (UNOFFICIAL WORLD CUP REMIX)** *EMI CDOTZI 004*	10		3
28 Dec 02	**LIVE IS LIFE** *Liberty CDLIVE001* HERMES HOUSE BAND & DJ OTZI	50		

DJ PIED PIPER UK production group

Date	Title / Label	Peak Position	Weeks at No.1	Weeks in Top 40
2 Jun 01	**DO YOU REALLY LIKE IT** *Relentless RELMOS 1* DJ PIED PIPER & THE MASTERS OF CEREMONIES ●	1	1	12

DJ POWER Italian DJ/producer

Date	Title / Label	Peak Position	Weeks at No.1	Weeks in Top 40
7 Mar 92	**EVERYBODY PUMP** *Cooltempo COOL 252*	46		

DJ PROFESSOR Italian DJ/producer

Date	Title / Label	Peak Position	Weeks at No.1	Weeks in Top 40
10 Aug 91	**WE GOTTA DO IT** *Fourth & Broadway BRW 225* DJ PROFESSOR FEATURING FRANCESCO ZAPPALA	57		
28 Mar 92	**ROCK ME STEADY** *PWL Continental PWL 219*	49		
8 Oct 94	**ROCKIN' ME** *Citra 1CD*	56		
1 Mar 97	**WALKIN' ON UP** *Nukleuz MCSTD 40098* DJ PROF-X-OR	64		

DJ QUICKSILVER Belgian/Turkish production duo

Date	Title / Label	Peak Position	Weeks at No.1	Weeks in Top 40
5 Apr 97	**BELLISSIMA** *Positiva CDTIV 72* ●	4		15
6 Sep 97	**FREE** *Positiva CDTIVS 77*	7		5
21 Feb 98	**PLANET LOVE** *Positiva CDTIV 88*	12		3

DJ RAP UK DJ/singer

Date	Title / Label	Peak Position	Weeks at No.1	Weeks in Top 40
4 Jul 98	**BAD GIRL** *Higher Ground HIGHS 8CD*	32		1
17 Oct 98	**GOOD TO BE ALIVE** *Higher Ground HIGHS 14CD*	36		1
3 Apr 99	**EVERYDAY GIRL** *Higher Ground HIGHS 19CD*	47		

DJ ROLANDO AKA AZTEC MYSTIC US DJ/producer

Date	Title / Label	Peak Position	Weeks at No.1	Weeks in Top 40
21 Oct 00	**JAGUAR** *430 West 430 WUKTCD1*	43		

DJ SAKIN & FRIENDS German DJ/producer

Date	Title / Label	Peak Position	Weeks at No.1	Weeks in Top 40
20 Feb 99	**PROTECT YOUR MIND (FOR THE LOVE OF A PRINCESS)** *Positiva CDTIV 107* ○	4		7
5 Jun 99	**NOMANSLAND (DAVID'S SONG)** *Positiva CDTIV 112*	14		4

DJ SAMMY Spanish DJ/producer

Date	Title / Label	Peak Position	Weeks at No.1	Weeks in Top 40
9 Nov 02	**HEAVEN** *Data 45CDS* DJ SAMMY & YANOU FEATURING DO ○	1	1	14
8 Mar 03	**THE BOYS OF SUMMER** *Data 49CDS*	2		8
21 Jun 03	**SUNLIGHT** *Data 54CDS*	8		7

Date	Title / Label	Peak Position	Weeks at No.1	Weeks in Top 40
25 Jun 05	**WHY** *Data 89CDS*	7		4
17 Nov 07	**HEAVEN** *Download* DJ SAMMY & YANOU FEATURING DO	69		

DJ SANDY German DJ/producer

Date	Title / Label	Peak Position	Weeks at No.1	Weeks in Top 40
1 Jul 00	**OVERDRIVE** *Positiva CDTIV 133* DJ SANDY VS HOUSETRAP	32		1

DJ SCOT PROJECT German DJ/producer

Date	Title / Label	Peak Position	Weeks at No.1	Weeks in Top 40
27 Jul 96	**U (I GOT THE FEELING)** *Positiva CDTIV 55*	66		
14 Feb 98	**Y (HOW DEEP IS YOUR LOVE)** *Perfecto PERF 158CD1*	57		

DJ SCOTT UK DJ/producer

Date	Title / Label	Peak Position	Weeks at No.1	Weeks in Top 40
28 Jan 95	**DO YOU WANNA PARTY** *Steppin' Out SPONCD 2* DJ SCOTT FEATURING LORNA B	36		1
1 Apr 95	**SWEET DREAMS** *Steppin' Out SPONCD 3* DJ SCOTT FEATURING LORNA B	37		1

DJ DOC SCOTT UK DJ/producer

Date	Title / Label	Peak Position	Weeks at No.1	Weeks in Top 40
1 Feb 92	**NHS (EP)** *Absolute 2 ABS 001DJ*	64		

DJ SEDUCTION UK DJ/producer

Date	Title / Label	Peak Position	Weeks at No.1	Weeks in Top 40
22 Feb 92	**HARDCORE HEAVEN/YOU AND ME** *ffreedom TAB 103*	26		3
11 Jul 92	**COME ON** *ffreedom TAB 111*	37		2

DJ SHADOW US DJ/producer

Date	Title / Label	Peak Position	Weeks at No.1	Weeks in Top 40
25 Mar 95	**WHAT DOES YOUR SOUL LOOK LIKE** *Mo Wax MW 027CD*	59		
14 Sep 96	**MIDNIGHT IN A PERFECT WORLD** *Mo Wax MW 057CD*	54		
9 Nov 96	**STEM** *Mo Wax MW 058CD*	74		
11 Oct 97	**HIGH NOON** *Mo Wax MW 063CD*	22		1
20 Dec 97	**CAMEL BOBSLED RACE** *Mo Wax MW 084CD*	62		
24 Jan 98	**WHAT DOES YOUR SOUL LOOK LIKE? (PART 1)** *Mo Wax MW 087*	54		
1 Jun 02	**YOU CAN'T GO HOME AGAIN** *Island CID 797*	30		1
2 Nov 02	**SIX DAYS** *Island CID 807*	28		2
20 Jan 07	**THIS TIME (I'M GONNA TRY IT MY WAY)** *Island 1716789*	54		

DJ SHOG German DJ/producer

Date	Title / Label	Peak Position	Weeks at No.1	Weeks in Top 40
20 Jul 02	**THIS IS MY SOUND** *NuLife 74321942272*	40		1

DJ SNEAK US DJ/producer

Date	Title / Label	Peak Position	Weeks at No.1	Weeks in Top 40
1 Feb 03	**FIX MY SINK** *Credence CDCREDS 033* DJ SNEAK FEATURING BEAR WHO	26		1

DJ SS UK DJ/producer

Date	Title / Label	Peak Position	Weeks at No.1	Weeks in Top 40
20 Apr 02	**THE LIGHTER** *Formation FORM 12093*	63		

DJ SUPREME UK DJ/producer

Date	Title / Label	Peak Position	Weeks at No.1	Weeks in Top 40
5 Oct 96	**THA WILD STYLE** *Distinctive DISNCD 19*	39		1
3 May 97	**THA WILD STYLE (REMIX)** *Distinctive DISNCD 29*	24		1
6 Dec 97	**ENTER THE SCENE** *Distinctive DISNCD 40* DJ SUPREME VS THE RHYTHM MASTERS	49		
21 Feb 98	**THA HORNS OF JERICHO** *All Around The World CDGLOBE 164*	29		1
16 Jan 99	**UP TO THE WILDSTYLE** *All Around The World CDGLOBE 170* PORN KINGS VERSUS DJ SUPREME	10		3

DJ TAUCHER German DJ/producer

Date	Title / Label	Peak Position	Weeks at No.1	Weeks in Top 40
8 May 99	**CHILD OF THE UNIVERSE** *Addictive 12AD 037*	74		

DJ TIESTO Dutch DJ/producer

Date	Title / Label	Peak Position	Weeks at No.1	Weeks in Top 40
12 May 01	**FLIGHT 643** *Nebula NEBCD 016*	56		
29 Sep 01	**URBAN TRAIN** *VC Recordings/Nebula VCRD 95* DJ TIESTO FEATURING KIRSTY HAWKSHAW	22		2
13 Apr 02	**LETHAL INDUSTRY** *Nebula VCRD 103*	25		1
29 Jun 02	**643 (LOVE'S ON FIRE)** *Nebula VCRD 106* DJ TIESTO FEATURING SUZANNE PALMER	36		1
30 Nov 02	**OBSESSION** *Nebula NEBCD 029* TIESTO & JUNKIE XL	56		
11 Oct 03	**TRAFFIC** *Nebula NEBCD 052*	48		
15 May 04	**LOVE COMES AGAIN** *Nebula NEBCD 058* TIESTO FEATURING BT	30		1
23 Oct 04	**JUST BE** *Nebula NEBCD062* TIESTO FEATURING KIRSTY HAWKSHAW	43		
23 Apr 05	**ADAGIO FOR STRINGS** *Nebula NEBCD068*	37		1
11 Nov 06	**DANCE4LIFE** *Nebula NEBCD100* TIESTO FEATURING MAXI JAZZ	67		

DJ TOUCHE UK DJ/producer

Date	Title / Label	Peak Position	Weeks at No.1	Weeks in Top 40
31 Jan 04	**THE PADDLE/THE GIRL'S A FREAK** *Southern Fried ECB60*	65		

DJ VISAGE Danish DJ/producer

Date	Title / Label	Peak Position	Weeks at No.1	Weeks in Top 40
10 Jun 00	**THE RETURN (TIME TO SAY GOODBYE)** *One Step Music OSMCDS 13* DJ VISAGE FEATURING CLARISSSA	58		

DJ ZINC UK DJ/producer

Date	Title / Label	Peak Position	Weeks at No.1	Weeks in Top 40
18 Nov 00	**138 TREK** *Phaze One CDX033*	27		1
2 Jun 01	**CASINO ROYALE/DEAD A'S** *True Playaz TPRCD 004* DJ ZINC/DJ HYPE	58		
13 Apr 02	**REACHOUT** *True Playaz TPR 12039*	73		
21 Sep 02	**FAIR FIGHT/AS WE DO** *BinGo! Beats BINGO 008*	72		
13 Mar 04	**SKA** *True Playaz TPR12051*	54		
15 May 04	**STEPPIN STONES/SOUTH PACIFIC** *BinGo! Beats BINGO 012*	62		
8 Jan 05	**DRIVE BY CAR/INS** *BinGo! Beats BINGO023* DJ ZINC FEATURING EKSMAN	66		

DJAIMIN Swiss producer

Date	Title / Label	Peak Position	Weeks at No.1	Weeks in Top 40
19 Sep 92	**GIVE YOU** *Cooltempo COOL 262*	45		

DJD UK producer

Date	Title / Label	Peak Position	Weeks at No.1	Weeks in Top 40
8 Jun 02	**SHAKE IT BABY** *Direction 6721812* DJD PRESENTS HYDRAULIC DOGS	56		

DJH Italian production group

Date	Title / Label	Peak Position	Weeks at No.1	Weeks in Top 40
16 Feb 91	**THINK ABOUT...** *RCA PB 44385* DJH FEATURING STEFY	22		4
13 Jul 91	**I LIKE IT** *RCA PB 44741* DJH FEATURING STEFY	16		6
19 Oct 91	**MOVE YOUR LOVE** *RCA PB 44965* DJH FEATURING STEFY	73		

DJPC Belgian producer

Date	Title / Label	Peak Position	Weeks at No.1	Weeks in Top 40
26 Oct 91	**INSSOMNIAK** *Hype 7PUM 005*	62		
29 Feb 92	**INSSOMNIAK (REMIX)** *Hype PUMR 005*	64		

DJ'S RULE Canadian duo

Date	Title / Label	Peak Position	Weeks at No.1	Weeks in Top 40
2 Mar 96	**GET INTO THE MUSIC** *Distinctive DISNCD 9*	72		
5 Apr 97	**GET INTO THE MUSIC (REMIX)** *Distinctive DISNCDD 27* DJ'S RULE FEATURING KAREN BROWN	65		

BORIS DLUGOSCH German/US producer

Date	Title / Label	Peak Position	Weeks at No.1	Weeks in Top 40
7 Dec 96	**KEEP PUSHIN'** *Manifesto FESCD 17* BORIS DLUGOSCH PRESENTS BOOOM!	41		
13 Sep 97	**HOLD YOUR HEAD UP HIGH** *Positiva CDTIV 79* BORIS DLUGOSCH PRESENTS BOOOM!	23		1
16 Jun 01	**NEVER ENOUGH** *Positiva CDTIV 156* BORIS DLUGOSCH FEATURING ROISIN MURPHY	16		3

D'LUX UK group

Date	Title / Label	Peak Position	Weeks at No.1	Weeks in Top 40
22 Jun 96	**LOVE RESURRECTION** *Logic 74321371012*	58		

DMAC UK singer

Date	Title / Label	Peak Position	Weeks at No.1	Weeks in Top 40
27 Jul 02	**THE WORLD SHE KNOWS** *Chrysalis CDCHS 5140*	33		1

Silver-selling ○ · Gold-selling ● · Platinum-selling · US No.1 ★ · Peak Position · Weeks at No.1 · Weeks in Top 40

DMX US rapper

Date	Title	Peak Position	Weeks at No.1	Weeks in Top 40
15 May 99	**SLIPPIN'** *Def Jam 8707552*	30		1
15 Dec 01	**WHO WE BE** *Def Jam 5888512*	34		1
3 May 03	**X GON GIVE IT TO YA** *Def Jam 0779042*	6		10
11 Oct 03	**WHERE THE HOOD AT?** *Def Jam 9811251*	16		3
10 Jan 04	**GET IT ON THE FLOOR** *Def Jam 9815206* DMX FEATURING SWIZZ BEATZ	34		1
22 Apr 06	**INNOCENT MAN** *Mona MONASP5CDS* MARK MORRISON FEATURING DMX	46		

DNA UK production duo

Date	Title	Peak Position	Weeks at No.1	Weeks in Top 40
28 Jul 90	**TOM'S DINER** *A&M AM 592* DNA FEATURING SUZANNE VEGA ○	2		9
18 Aug 90	**LA SERENISSIMA** *Raw Bass RBASS 006*	34		4
3 Aug 91	**REBEL WOMAN** *DNA 7DNA 001* DNA FEATURING JAZZI P	42		
1 Feb 92	**CAN YOU HANDLE IT** *EMI EM 219* DNA FEATURING SHARON REDD	17		3
9 May 92	**BLUE LOVE (CALL MY NAME)** *EMI EM 226* DNA FEATURING JOE NYE	66		

DO ME BAD THINGS UK group

Date	Title	Peak Position	Weeks at No.1	Weeks in Top 40
6 Nov 04	**TIME FOR DELIVERANCE** *Must Destroy MDA002CD*	57		
9 Apr 05	**WHAT'S HIDEOUS** *Must Destroy MDA003CD*	33		1
25 Jun 05	**MOVE IN STEREO (LIV ULLMAN ON DRUMS)** *Must Destroy MDA004CD*	49		

CARL DOBKINS US singer

Date	Title	Peak Position	Weeks at No.1	Weeks in Top 40
31 Mar 60	**LUCKY DEVIL** *Brunswick 05817*	44		

ANITA DOBSON UK actress

Date	Title	Peak Position	Weeks at No.1	Weeks in Top 40
9 Aug 86	**ANYONE CAN FALL IN LOVE** *BBC RESL 191* ANITA DOBSON FEATURING THE SIMON MAY ORCHESTRA ○	4		7
18 Jul 87	**TALKING OF LOVE** *Parlophone R 6159*	43		

FEFE DOBSON Canadian singer

Date	Title	Peak Position	Weeks at No.1	Weeks in Top 40
8 May 04	**EVERYTHING** *Mercury 9862501*	42		

DR ALBAN Nigerian producer

Date	Title	Peak Position	Weeks at No.1	Weeks in Top 40
5 Sep 92	**IT'S MY LIFE** *Logic 74321153307*	2		11
14 Nov 92	**ONE LOVE** *Logic 74321108727*	45		
10 Apr 93	**SING HALLELUJAH!** *Logic 74321136202*	16		7
26 Mar 94	**LOOK WHO'S TALKING** *Logic 74321195342*	55		
13 Aug 94	**AWAY FROM HOME** *Logic 74321222682*	42		
29 Apr 95	**SWEET DREAMS** *Logic 74321251552* SWING FEATURING DR ALBAN	59		

DOCTOR & THE MEDICS UK group

Date	Title	Peak Position	Weeks at No.1	Weeks in Top 40
10 May 86	**SPIRIT IN THE SKY** *IRS IRM 113* ○	1	3	13
9 Aug 86	**BURN** *IRS IRM 119*	29		4
22 Nov 86	**WATERLOO** *IRS IRM 125* DOCTOR & THE MEDICS FEATURING ROY WOOD	45		

DR DRE US rapper

Date	Title	Peak Position	Weeks at No.1	Weeks in Top 40
22 Jan 94	**NUTHIN' BUT A 'G' THANG/LET ME RIDE** *Death Row A 8328CD*	31		2
3 Sep 94	**DRE DAY** *Death Row A 8292CD*	59		
15 Apr 95	**NATURAL BORN KILLAZ** *Death Row A 8197CD* DR DRE & ICE CUBE	45		
10 Jun 95	**KEEP THEIR HEADS RINGIN'** *Priority PTYCD 103*	25		2
13 Apr 96	**CALIFORNIA LOVE** *Death Row DRWCD 3* 2PAC FEATURING DR DRE	6		5
19 Oct 96	**NO DIGGITY** *Interscope IND 95003* BLACKstreet FEATURING DR DRE ★	9		6
11 Jul 98	**ZOOM** *Interscope IND 95594* DR DRE & LL COOL J	15		2
14 Aug 99	**GUILTY CONSCIENCE** *Interscope IND 4971282* EMINEM FEATURING DR DRE	5		6
25 Mar 00	**STILL DRE** *Interscope 4972862* DR DRE FEATURING SNOOP DOGGY DOGG	6		6
10 Jun 00	**FORGOT ABOUT DRE** *Interscope 4973422* DR DRE FEATURING EMINEM	7		6
3 Feb 01	**THE NEXT EPISODE** *Interscope 4974762* DR DRE FEATURING SNOOP DOGGY DOGG	3		7
19 Jan 02	**BAD INTENTIONS** *Interscope 4973932* DR DRE FEATURING KNOC-TURN'AL	4		7
14 Feb 04	**THE NEXT EPISODE** *Interscope 4974762* DR DRE FEATURING SNOOP DOGGY DOGG	58		
14 Feb 04	**BAD INTENTIONS** *Interscope 4973932* DR DRE FEATURING KNOC-TURN'AL	67		

DR FEELGOOD UK group

Date	Title	Peak Position	Weeks at No.1	Weeks in Top 40
11 Jun 77	**SNEAKIN' SUSPICION** *United Artists UP 36255*	47		
24 Sep 77	**SHE'S A WIND UP** *United Artists UP 36304*	34		3
30 Sep 78	**DOWN AT THE DOCTOR'S** *United Artists UP 36444*	48		
20 Jan 79	**MILK AND ALCOHOL** *United Artists UP 36468* ○	9		7
5 May 79	**AS LONG AS THE PRICE IS RIGHT** *United Artists YUP 36506*	40		1
8 Dec 79	**PUT HIM OUT OF YOUR MIND** *United Artists BP 306*	73		

DR HOOK US group

Date	Title	Peak Position	Weeks at No.1	Weeks in Top 40
24 Jun 72	**SYLVIA'S MOTHER** *CBS 7929* DR HOOK & THE MEDICINE SHOW	2		11
26 Jun 76	**A LITTLE BIT MORE** *Capitol CL 15871* ●	2		13
30 Oct 76	**IF NOT YOU** *Capitol CL 15885*	5		9
25 Mar 78	**MORE LIKE THE MOVIES** *Capitol CL 15967*	14		8
22 Sep 79	**WHEN YOU'RE IN LOVE WITH A BEAUTIFUL WOMAN** *Capitol CL 16039* ●	1	3	14
5 Jan 80	**BETTER LOVE NEXT TIME** *Capitol CL 16112*	8		6
29 Mar 80	**SEXY EYES** *Capitol CL 16127*	4		8
23 Aug 80	**YEARS FROM NOW** *Capitol CL 16154*	47		
8 Nov 80	**SHARING THE NIGHT TOGETHER** *Capitol CL 16171*	43		
22 Nov 80	**GIRLS CAN GET IT** *Mercury MER 51*	40		1
1 Feb 92	**WHEN YOU'RE IN LOVE WITH A BEAUTIFUL WOMAN** *Capitol EMCT 4*	44		
6 Jun 92	**A LITTLE BIT MORE** *EMI EMCT 6*	47		

DR OCTAGON US producer

Date	Title	Peak Position	Weeks at No.1	Weeks in Top 40
7 Sep 96	**BLUE FLOWERS** *Mo Wax MW055CD*	66		

DOCTOR SPIN UK production duo

Date	Title	Peak Position	Weeks at No.1	Weeks in Top 40
3 Oct 92	**TETRIS** *Carpet CRPT 4*	6		7

KEN DODD UK singer

Date	Title	Peak Position	Weeks at No.1	Weeks in Top 40
7 Jul 60	**LOVE IS LIKE A VIOLIN** *Decca F 11248*	8		17
15 Jun 61	**ONCE IN EVERY LIFETIME** *Decca F 11355*	28		11
1 Feb 62	**PIANISSIMO** *Decca F 11422*	21		12
29 Aug 63	**STILL** *Columbia DB 7094*	35		7
6 Feb 64	**EIGHT BY TEN** *Columbia DB 7191*	22		11
23 Jul 64	**HAPPINESS** *Columbia DB 7325*	31		11
26 Nov 64	**SO DEEP IS THE NIGHT** *Columbia DB 7398*	31		6
2 Sep 65	**TEARS** *Columbia DB 7659*	1	5	24
18 Nov 65	**THE RIVER (LE COLLINE SONO IN FIORO)** *Columbia DB 7750*	3		13
12 May 66	**PROMISES** *Columbia DB 7914*	6		13
4 Aug 66	**MORE THAN LOVE** *Columbia DB 7976*	14		9
27 Oct 66	**IT'S LOVE** *Columbia DB 8031*	36		4
19 Jan 67	**LET ME CRY ON YOUR SHOULDER** *Columbia DB 8101*	11		6
30 Jul 69	**TEARS WON'T WASH AWAY THESE HEARTACHES** *Columbia DB 8600*	22		8
5 Dec 70	**BROKEN HEARTED** *Columbia DB 8725*	15		9
10 Jul 71	**WHEN LOVE COMES ROUND AGAIN (L'ARCA DI NOE)** *Columbia DB 8796*	19		12
18 Nov 72	**JUST OUT OF REACH (OF MY TWO EMPTY ARMS)** *Columbia DB 8947*	29		5
29 Nov 75	**(THINK OF ME) WHEREVER YOU ARE** *EMI 2342*	21		6
26 Dec 81	**HOLD MY HAND** *Images IMGS 0002*	44		

DODGY UK group

Date	Title	Peak Position	Weeks at No.1	Weeks in Top 40
8 May 93	**LOVEBIRDS** *A&M AMCD 0177*	65		
3 Jul 93	**I NEED ANOTHER (EP)** *A&M 5803172*	67		
6 Aug 94	**THE MELOD-EP** *Bostin 5806772*	53		
1 Oct 94	**STAYING OUT FOR THE SUMMER** *Bostin 5807972*	38		1
7 Jan 95	**SO LET ME GO FAR** *Bostin 5809032*	30		2
11 Mar 95	**MAKING THE MOST OF** *Bostin 5809892* DODGY WITH THE KICK HORNS	22		1
10 Jun 95	**STAYING OUT FOR THE SUMMER (REMIX)** *Bostin 5810952*	19		2
8 Jun 96	**IN A ROOM** *A&M 5816252*	12		3
10 Aug 96	**GOOD ENOUGH** *A&M 5818152*	4		7

Silver-selling · Gold-selling · Platinum-selling · US No.1 · Peak Position · Weeks at No.1 · Weeks in Top 40

Date	Title	Peak Position	Weeks at No.1	Weeks in Top 40
16 Nov 96	**IF YOU'RE THINKING OF ME** *A&M 5819992*	11		2
15 Mar 97	**FOUND YOU** *A&M 5821332*	19		2
26 Sep 98	**EVERY SINGLE DAY** *A&M MERCD 512*	32		1

TIM DOG US rapper

Date	Title	Peak Position	Weeks at No.1	Weeks in Top 40
29 Oct 94	**BITCH WITH A PERM** *Dis-stress DISCD 1*	49		
11 Feb 95	**MAKE WAY FOR THE INDIAN** *Island CID 586* APACHE INDIAN & TIM DOG	29		1

DOG EAT DOG US group

Date	Title	Peak Position	Weeks at No.1	Weeks in Top 40
19 Aug 95	**NO FRONTS** *Roadrunner RR 23312*	64		
3 Feb 96	**NO FRONTS - THE REMIXES** *Roadrunner RR 23313*	9		3
13 Jul 96	**ISMS** *Roadrunner RR 23083*	43		

NATE DOGG US rapper

Date	Title	Peak Position	Weeks at No.1	Weeks in Top 40
23 Jul 94	**REGULATE** *Death Row A 8290CD* WARREN G & NATE DOGG	5		12
3 Feb 01	**OH NO** *Rawkus RWK 302* MOS DEF & NATE DOGG FEATURING PHAROAHE MONCH	24		3
25 Aug 01	**WHERE I WANNA BE** *London LONCD 461* SHADE SHEIST FEATURING NATE DOGG & KURUPT	14		3
29 Sep 01	**AREA CODES** *Def Jam 5887722* LUDACRIS FEATURING NATE DOGG	25		2
1 Mar 03	**THE STREETS** *Def Jam 0779852* WC FEATURING SNOOP DOGG & NATE DOGG	48		
12 Jul 03	**21 QUESTIONS** *Interscope 9807195* 50 CENT FEATURING NATE DOGG	6		7
14 Feb 04	**THE SET UP (YOU DON'T KNOW)** *Interscope 9815333* OBIE TRICE FEATURING NATE DOGG	32		1

DOGS UK group

Date	Title	Peak Position	Weeks at No.1	Weeks in Top 40
5 Mar 05	**SHE'S GOT A REASON** *Island/Uni-Island CID882*	36		1
14 May 05	**TUNED TO A DIFFERENT STATION** *Island CID891*	29		1
30 Jul 05	**SELFISH WAYS** *Island CID901*	45		
10 Dec 05	**TARRED & FEATHERED (WHAT A BAD BOY)** *Island CID908*	64		

DOGS D'AMOUR UK group

Date	Title	Peak Position	Weeks at No.1	Weeks in Top 40
4 Feb 89	**HOW COME IT NEVER RAINS** *China 13*	44		
5 Aug 89	**SATELLITE KID** *China 17*	26		2
14 Oct 89	**TRAIL OF TEARS** *China 20*	47		
23 Jun 90	**VICTIMS OF SUCCESS** *China 24*	36		2
15 Sep 90	**EMPTY WORLD** *China 27*	61		
19 Jun 93	**ALL OR NOTHING** *China WOKCD 2033*	53		

DOGS DIE IN HOT CARS UK group

Date	Title	Peak Position	Weeks at No.1	Weeks in Top 40
8 May 04	**GODHOPPING** *V2 VVR 5025868*	24		1
17 Jul 04	**I LOVE YOU 'CAUSE I HAVE TO** *V2 VVR 5025878*	32		1
16 Oct 04	**LOUNGER** *V2 VVR5028213*	43		

KEN DOH UK producer

Date	Title	Peak Position	Weeks at No.1	Weeks in Top 40
30 Mar 96	**NAKASAKI EP (I NEED A LOVER TONIGHT)** *ffrr FCD 272*	7		5

PETE DOHERTY UK singer

Date	Title	Peak Position	Weeks at No.1	Weeks in Top 40
24 Apr 04	**FOR LOVERS** *Rough Trade RTRADSCD177* WOLFMAN FEATURING PETE DOHERTY	7		4
22 May 04	**BABYSHAMBLES** *High Society HSCDS003*	32		1
29 Oct 05	**THEIR WAY** *Rough Trade RTRADSCD267* LITTL'ANS FEATURING PETER DOHERTY	22		1
30 Sep 06	**PRANGIN' OUT** *Locked On/679 679L141CD1* STREETS FEATURING PETE DOHERTY	25		2

JOE DOLAN Irish singer

Date	Title	Peak Position	Weeks at No.1	Weeks in Top 40
25 Jun 69	**MAKE ME AN ISLAND** *Pye 7N 17738*	3		17
1 Nov 69	**TERESA** *Pye 7N 17833*	20		6
28 Feb 70	**YOU'RE SUCH A GOOD LOOKING WOMAN** *Pye 7N 17891*	17		11
17 Sep 77	**I NEED YOU** *Pye 7N 45702*	43		

THOMAS DOLBY UK singer

Date	Title	Peak Position	Weeks at No.1	Weeks in Top 40
3 Oct 81	**EUROPA AND THE PIRATE TWINS** *Parlophone R 6051*	48		
14 Aug 82	**WINDPOWER** *Venice In Peril VIPS 103*	31		4
6 Nov 82	**SHE BLINDED ME WITH SCIENCE** *Venice In Peril VIPS 104*	49		
16 Jul 83	**SHE BLINDED ME WITH SCIENCE** *Venice In Peril VIPS 105*	56		
21 Jan 84	**HYPERACTIVE** *Parlophone Odeon R 6065*	17		6
31 Mar 84	**I SCARE MYSELF** *Parlophone Odeon R 6067*	46		
16 Apr 88	**AIRHEAD** *Manhattan MT 38*	53		
9 May 92	**CLOSE BUT NO CIGAR** *Virgin VS 1410*	22		3
11 Jul 92	**I LOVE YOU GOODBYE** *Virgin VS 1417*	36		2
26 Sep 92	**SILK PYJAMAS** *Virgin VS 1430*	62		
22 Jan 94	**HYPERACTIVE** *Parlophone CDEMCTS 10*	23		2

JOE DOLCE MUSIC THEATRE US singer

Date	Title	Peak Position	Weeks at No.1	Weeks in Top 40
7 Feb 81	**SHADDAP YOU FACE** *Epic EPC 9518*	1	3	9

DOLL UK group

Date	Title	Peak Position	Weeks at No.1	Weeks in Top 40
13 Jan 79	**DESIRE ME** *Beggars Banquet BEG 11*	28		5

DOLLAR UK duo

Date	Title	Peak Position	Weeks at No.1	Weeks in Top 40
11 Nov 78	**SHOOTING STAR** *Carrere 2871*	14		10
19 May 79	**WHO WERE YOU WITH IN THE MOONLIGHT** *Carrere CAR 110*	14		9
18 Aug 79	**LOVE'S GOTTA HOLD ON ME** *Carrere CAR 122*	4		9
24 Nov 79	**I WANNA HOLD YOUR HAND** *Carrere CAR 131*	9		8
25 Oct 80	**TAKIN' A CHANCE ON YOU** *WEA K 18353*	62		
15 Aug 81	**HAND HELD IN BLACK AND WHITE** *WEA BUCK 1*	19		8
14 Nov 81	**MIRROR MIRROR (MON AMOUR)** *WEA BUCK 2*	4		12
20 Mar 82	**RING RING** *Carrere CAR 225*	61		
27 Mar 82	**GIVE ME BACK MY HEART** *WEA BUCK 3*	4		8
19 Jun 82	**VIDEOTHEQUE** *WEA BUCK 4*	17		8
18 Sep 82	**GIVE ME SOME KINDA MAGIC** *WEA BUCK 5*	34		3
16 Aug 86	**WE WALKED IN LOVE** *Arista DIME 1*	61		
26 Dec 87	**O L'AMOUR** *London LON 146*	7		6
16 Jul 88	**IT'S NATURE'S WAY (NO PROBLEM)** *London LON 179*	58		

PLACIDO DOMINGO Spanish tenor

Date	Title	Peak Position	Weeks at No.1	Weeks in Top 40
12 Dec 81	**PERHAPS LOVE** *CBS A 1905* PLACIDO DOMINGO WITH JOHN DENVER	46		
27 May 89	**TILL I LOVED YOU** *CBS 6548437* PLACIDO DOMINGO & JENNIFER RUSH	24		4
16 Jun 90	**NESSUN DORMA FROM 'TURANDOT'** *Epic 6560057* LUIS COBOS FEATURING PLACIDO DOMINGO	59		
30 Jul 94	**LIBIAMO/LA DONNA E MOBILE** *Teldec YZ 843CD* JOSE CARRERAS, PLACIDO DOMINGO & LUCIANO PAVAROTTI	21		2
25 Jul 98	**YOU'LL NEVER WALK ALONE** *Decca 4607982* CARRERAS/DOMINGO/PAVAROTTI WITH MEHTA	35		1

DOMINO US rapper

Date	Title	Peak Position	Weeks at No.1	Weeks in Top 40
22 Jan 94	**GETTO JAM** *Chaos 6600402*	33		2
14 May 94	**SWEET POTATO PIE** *Chaos 6603292*	42		

FATS DOMINO US singer

Date	Title	Peak Position	Weeks at No.1	Weeks in Top 40
27 Jul 56	**I'M IN LOVE AGAIN** *London HLU 8280*	12		14
30 Nov 56	**BLUEBERRY HILL** *London HLU 8330*	6		15
25 Jan 57	**AIN'T THAT A SHAME** *London HLU 8173*	23		2
1 Feb 57	**HONEY CHILE** *London HLU 8356*	29		1
29 Mar 57	**BLUE MONDAY** *London HLP 8377*	23		2
19 Apr 57	**I'M WALKIN'** *London HLP 8407*	19		7
19 Jul 57	**VALLEY OF TEARS** *London HLP 8449*	25		1
28 Mar 58	**THE BIG BEAT** *London HLP 8575*	20		4
4 Jul 58	**SICK AND TIRED** *London HLP 8628*	26		1
22 May 59	**MARGIE** *London HLP 8865*	18		5
16 Oct 59	**I WANT TO WALK YOU HOME** *London HLP 8942*	14		5
18 Dec 59	**BE MY GUEST** *London HLP 9005*	11		11
17 Mar 60	**COUNTRY BOY** *London HLP 9073*	19		7
21 Jul 60	**WALKING TO NEW ORLEANS** *London HLP 9163*	19		7
10 Nov 60	**THREE NIGHTS A WEEK** *London HLP 9198*	45		
5 Jan 61	**MY GIRL JOSEPHINE** *London HLP 9244*	32		2
27 Jul 61	**IT KEEPS RAININ** *London HLP 9374*	49		
30 Nov 61	**WHAT A PARTY** *London HLP 9456*	43		
29 Mar 62	**JAMBALAYA** *London HLP 9520*	41		
31 Oct 63	**RED SAILS IN THE SUNSET** *HMV POP 1219*	34		3
24 Apr 76	**BLUEBERRY HILL** *United Artists UP 35797*	41		

Silver-selling ○ · Gold-selling ● · Platinum-selling · US No.1 ★ · Peak Position · Weeks at No.1 · Weeks in Top 40

DON PABLO'S ANIMALS Italian group

Date	Title / Label	Peak Position	Weeks at No.1	Weeks in Top 40
19 May 90	**VENUS** *Rumour RUMA 18*	4		8

DON-E UK singer

Date	Title / Label	Peak Position	Weeks at No.1	Weeks in Top 40
9 May 92	**LOVE MAKES THE WORLD GO ROUND** *Fourth & Broadway BRW 242*	18		5
25 Jul 92	**PEACE IN THE WORLD** *Fourth & Broadway BRW 256*	41		
28 Feb 98	**DELICIOUS** *Mushroom MUSH 20CD* DENI HINES FEATURING DON-E	52		

SIOBHAN DONAGHY UK singer

Date	Title / Label	Peak Position	Weeks at No.1	Weeks in Top 40
5 Jul 03	**OVERRATED** *London LONCD 476*	19		1
27 Sep 03	**TWIST OF FATE** *London LONCD 481*	52		
21 Apr 07	**DON'T GIVE IT UP** *Parlophone CDR6729*	45		

LONNIE DONEGAN UK singer

Date	Title / Label	Peak Position	Weeks at No.1	Weeks in Top 40
6 Jan 56	**ROCK ISLAND LINE** *Decca F 10647*	8		18
20 Apr 56	**STEWBALL** *Pye Nixa N 15036*	27		1
27 Apr 56	**LOST JOHN** *Pye Nixa N 15036*	2		17
6 Jul 56	**SKIFFLE SESSION EP** *Pye Nixa NJE 1017*	20		2
7 Sep 56	**BRING A LITTLE WATER SYLVIE/DEAD OR ALIVE** *Pye Nixa N 15071*	7		13
21 Dec 56	**LONNIE DONEGAN SHOWCASE (LP)** *Pye Nixa NPT 19012*	26		3
18 Jan 57	**DON'T YOU ROCK ME DADDY-O** *Pye Nixa N 15080*	4		17
5 Apr 57	**CUMBERLAND GAP** *Pye Nixa N 15087*	1	5	12
7 Jun 57	**GAMBLIN' MAN/PUTTING ON THE STYLE** *Pye Nixa N 15093*	1	2	19
11 Oct 57	**MY DIXIE DARLING** *Pye Nixa N 15108*	10		15
20 Dec 57	**JACK O' DIAMONDS** *Pye Nixa 7N 15116*	14		15
11 Apr 58	**GRAND COOLIE DAM** *Pye Nixa 7N 15129*	6		15
11 Jul 58	**SALLY DON'T YOU GRIEVE/BETTY BETTY BETTY** *Pye Nixa 7N 15148*	11		7
26 Sep 58	**LONESOME TRAVELLER** *Pye Nixa 7N 15158*	28		1
14 Nov 58	**LONNIE'S SKIFFLE PARTY** *Pye Nixa 7N 15165*	23		5
21 Nov 58	**TOM DOOLEY** *Pye Nixa 7N 15172*	3		14
6 Feb 59	**DOES YOUR CHEWING GUM LOSE IT'S FLAVOUR** *Pye 7N 15181*	3		12
8 May 59	**FORT WORTH JAIL** *Pye Nixa 7N 15198*	14		5
26 Jun 59	**THE BATTLE OF NEW ORLEANS** *Pye 7N 15206*	2		16
11 Sep 59	**SAL'S GOT A SUGAR LIP** *Pye 7N 15223*	13		4
4 Dec 59	**SAN MIGUEL** *Pye 7N 15237*	19		4
24 Mar 60	**MY OLD MAN'S A DUSTMAN** *Pye 7N 15256*	1	4	13
26 May 60	**I WANNA GO HOME** *Pye 7N 15267*	5		17
25 Aug 60	**LORELEI** *Pye 7N 15275*	10		8
24 Nov 60	**LIVELY** *Pye 7N 15312*	13		8
8 Dec 60	**VIRGIN MARY** *Pye 7N 15315*	27		4
11 May 61	**HAVE A DRINK ON ME** *Pye 7N 15354*	8		13
31 Aug 61	**MICHAEL ROW THE BOAT/LUMBERED** *Pye 7N 15371*	6		10
18 Jan 62	**THE COMANCHEROS** *Pye 7N 15410*	14		10
5 Apr 62	**THE PARTY'S OVER** *Pye 7N 15424*	9		11
16 Aug 62	**PICK A BALE OF COTTON** *Pye 7N 15455*	11		8

TANYA DONELLY US singer/guitarist

Date	Title / Label	Peak Position	Weeks at No.1	Weeks in Top 40
30 Aug 97	**PRETTY DEEP** *4AD BAD 7007CD*	55		
6 Dec 97	**THE BRIGHT LIGHT** *4AD BAD 7012CD*	64		

DONNAS US group

Date	Title / Label	Peak Position	Weeks at No.1	Weeks in Top 40
12 Apr 03	**TAKE IT OFF** *Atlantic AT0148CD*	38		1
5 Jul 03	**WHO INVITED YOU** *Atlantic AT0156CD*	61		
23 Oct 04	**FALL BEHIND ME** *Atlantic AT0186CD*	55		
19 Mar 05	**I DON'T WANT TO KNOW** *Atlantic AT0197CD*	55		

RAL DONNER US singer

Date	Title / Label	Peak Position	Weeks at No.1	Weeks in Top 40
21 Sep 61	**YOU DON'T KNOW WHAT YOU'VE GOT** *Parlophone R 4820*	25		9

DONOVAN UK singer

Date	Title / Label	Peak Position	Weeks at No.1	Weeks in Top 40
25 Mar 65	**CATCH THE WIND** *Pye 7N 15801*	4		11
3 Jun 65	**COLOURS** *Pye 7N 15866*	4		10
11 Nov 65	**TURQUOISE** *Pye 7N 15984*	30		4
8 Dec 66	**SUNSHINE SUPERMAN** *Pye 7N 17241* ★	2		11
9 Feb 67	**MELLOW YELLOW** *Pye 7N 17267*	8		8
25 Oct 67	**THERE IS A MOUNTAIN** *Pye 7N 17403*	8		9
21 Feb 68	**JENNIFER JUNIPER** *Pye 7N 17457*	5		10
29 May 68	**HURDY GURDY MAN** *Pye 7N 17537*	4		10
4 Dec 68	**ATLANTIS** *Pye 7N 17660*	23		5
9 Jul 69	**GOO GOO BARABAJAGAL (LOVE IS HOT)** *Pye 7N 17778* DONOVAN WITH THE JEFF BECK GROUP	12		6
1 Dec 90	**JENNIFER JUNIPER** *Fontana SYP 1* SINGING CORNER MEETS DONOVAN	68		

JASON DONOVAN Australian singer

Date	Title / Label	Peak Position	Weeks at No.1	Weeks in Top 40
10 Sep 88	**NOTHING CAN DIVIDE US** *PWL 17* ○	5		10
10 Dec 88	**ESPECIALLY FOR YOU** *PWL 24* KYLIE MINOGUE & JASON DONOVAN ●	1	3	12
4 Mar 89	**TOO MANY BROKEN HEARTS** *PWL 32* ●	1	2	11
10 Jun 89	**SEALED WITH A KISS** *PWL 39*	1	2	8
9 Sep 89	**EVERY DAY (I LOVE YOU MORE)** *PWL 43*	2		6
9 Dec 89	**WHEN YOU COME BACK TO ME** *PWL 46* ●	2		9
7 Apr 90	**HANG ON TO YOUR LOVE** *PWL 51*	8		5
30 Jun 90	**ANOTHER NIGHT** *PWL 58*	18		4
1 Sep 90	**RHYTHM OF THE RAIN** *PWL 60*	9		5
27 Oct 90	**I'M DOING FINE** *PWL 69*	22		5
18 May 91	**RSVP** *PWL 80*	17		4
22 Jun 91	**ANY DREAM WILL DO** *Really Useful RUR 7* ●	1	2	10
24 Aug 91	**HAPPY TOGETHER** *PWL 203*	10		5
7 Dec 91	**JOSEPH MEGA REMIX** *Really Useful RUR 9* JASON DONOVAN & ORIGINAL LONDON CAST FEATURING LINZI HATELY, DAVID EASTER & JOHNNY AMOBI	13		6
18 Jul 92	**MISSION OF LOVE** *Polydor PO 222*	26		3
28 Nov 92	**AS TIME GOES BY** *Polydor PO 245*	26		2
7 Aug 93	**ALL AROUND THE WORLD** *Polydor PZCD 278*	41		

DONS German/Belgian production duo

Date	Title / Label	Peak Position	Weeks at No.1	Weeks in Top 40
5 Nov 05	**PUMP UP THE JAM** *Data DATA94CDS* DONS FEATURING TECHNOTRONIC	22		2

DOOBIE BROTHERS US group

Date	Title / Label	Peak Position	Weeks at No.1	Weeks in Top 40
9 Mar 74	**LISTEN TO THE MUSIC** *Warner Brothers K 16208*	29		6
7 Jun 75	**TAKE ME IN YOUR ARMS** *Warner Brothers K 16559*	29		4
17 Feb 79	**WHAT A FOOL BELIEVES** *Warner Brothers K 17314* ★	31		5
14 Jul 79	**MINUTE BY MINUTE** *Warner Brothers K 17411*	47		
24 Jan 87	**WHAT A FOOL BELIEVES** *Warner Brothers W 8451* DOOBIE BROTHERS FEATURING MICHAEL McDONALD	57		
29 Jul 89	**THE DOCTOR** *Capitol CL 536*	73		
27 Nov 93	**LONG TRAIN RUNNIN' (REMIX)** *Warner Brothers W 0217CD*	7		7
14 May 94	**LISTEN TO THE MUSIC (REMIX)** *Warner Brothers W 0228CD*	37		2

DOOLALLY UK production duo

Date	Title / Label	Peak Position	Weeks at No.1	Weeks in Top 40
14 Nov 98	**STRAIGHT FROM THE HEART** *Locked On LOX 104CD*	20		2
7 Aug 99	**STRAIGHT FROM THE HEART** *Chocolate Boy LOX 112CD*	9		4

DOOLEYS UK group

Date	Title / Label	Peak Position	Weeks at No.1	Weeks in Top 40
13 Aug 77	**THINK I'M GONNA FALL IN LOVE WITH YOU** *GTO GT 95*	13		9
12 Nov 77	**LOVE OF MY LIFE** *GTO GT 110* ○	9		10
13 May 78	**DON'T TAKE IT LYIN' DOWN** *GTO GT 220*	60		
2 Sep 78	**A ROSE HAS TO DIE** *GTO GT 229*	11		9
10 Feb 79	**HONEY I'M LOST** *GTO GT 242*	24		5
16 Jun 79	**WANTED** *GTO GT 249* ○	3		11
22 Sep 79	**THE CHOSEN FEW** *GTO GT 258* ○	7		8
8 Mar 80	**LOVE PATROL** *GTO GT 260*	29		5
6 Sep 80	**BODY LANGUAGE** *GTO GT 276*	46		
10 Oct 81	**AND I WISH** *GTO GT 300*	52		

VAL DOONICAN Irish singer

Date	Title / Label	Peak Position	Weeks at No.1	Weeks in Top 40
15 Oct 64	**WALK TALL** *Decca F 11982*	3		20
21 Jan 65	**THE SPECIAL YEARS** *Decca F 12049*	7		12
8 Apr 65	**I'M GONNA GET THERE SOMEHOW** *Decca F 12118*	25		4
17 Mar 66	**ELUSIVE BUTTERFLY** *Decca F 12358*	5		11
3 Nov 66	**WHAT WOULD I BE** *Decca F 12505*	2		15
23 Feb 67	**MEMORIES ARE MADE OF THIS** *Decca F 12566*	11		10
25 May 67	**TWO STREETS** *Decca F 12608*	39		1
18 Oct 67	**IF THE WHOLE WORLD STOPPED LOVING** *Pye 7N 17396*	3		16
21 Feb 68	**YOU'RE THE ONLY ONE** *Pye 7N 17465*	37		1
12 Jun 68	**NOW** *Pye 7N 17534*	43		
23 Oct 68	**IF I KNEW THEN WHAT I KNOW NOW** *Pye 7N 17616*	14		11
23 Apr 69	**RING OF BRIGHT WATER** *Pye 7N 17713*	48		
4 Dec 71	**MORNING** *Philips 6006 177*	12		10
10 Mar 73	**HEAVEN IS MY WOMAN'S LOVE** *Philips 6028 031*	34		3

DOOP Dutch production duo

Date	Title / Label	Peak Position	Weeks at No.1	Weeks in Top 40
12 Mar 94	**DOOP** *Citybeat CBE 774CD* ●	1	3	9

DOORS US group

Date	Title / Label	Peak Position	Weeks at No.1	Weeks in Top 40
16 Aug 67	**LIGHT MY FIRE** *Elektra EKSN 45014* ★	49		
28 Aug 68	**HELLO I LOVE YOU** *Elektra EKSN 45037*	15		9
16 Oct 71	**RIDERS ON THE STORM** *Elektra K 12021*	22		8
20 Mar 76	**RIDERS ON THE STORM** *Elektra K 12203*	33		4
3 Feb 79	**HELLO I LOVE YOU** *Elektra K 12215* ★	71		
27 Apr 91	**BREAK ON THROUGH** *Elektra EKR 121*	64		
1 Jun 91	**LIGHT MY FIRE** *Elektra EKR 125*	7		6
10 Aug 91	**RIDERS ON THE STORM** *Elektra EKR 131*	68		

D.O.P. UK production duo

Date	Title / Label	Peak Position	Weeks at No.1	Weeks in Top 40
3 Feb 96	**STOP STARTING TO START STOPPING (EP)** *Hi-Life 5779472*	58		
13 Jul 96	**GROOVY BEAT** *Hi-Life 5750652*	54		

DOPE SMUGGLAZ UK production duo

Date	Title / Label	Peak Position	Weeks at No.1	Weeks in Top 40
5 Dec 98	**THE WORD** *Mushroom PERFCDS 1*	62		
7 Aug 99	**DOUBLE DOUBLE DUTCH** *Perfecto PERF 2CDS*	15		3

CHARLIE DORE UK singer

Date	Title / Label	Peak Position	Weeks at No.1	Weeks in Top 40
17 Nov 79	**PILOT OF THE AIRWAVES** *Island WIP 6526*	66		

ANDREA DORIA Italian producer

Date	Title / Label	Peak Position	Weeks at No.1	Weeks in Top 40
26 Apr 03	**BUCCI BAG** *Southern Fried ECB 38CDS*	57		

DOROTHY UK instrumental duo

Date	Title / Label	Peak Position	Weeks at No.1	Weeks in Top 40
9 Dec 95	**WHAT'S THAT TUNE (DOO-DOO-DOO-DOO-DOO-DOO-DOO-DOO-DOO)** *RCA 74321330912*	31		1

LEE DORSEY US singer

Date	Title / Label	Peak Position	Weeks at No.1	Weeks in Top 40
3 Feb 66	**GET OUT OF MY LIFE WOMAN** *Stateside SS 485*	22		6
5 May 66	**CONFUSION** *Stateside SS 506*	38		3
11 Aug 66	**WORKING IN THE COALMINE** *Stateside SS 528*	8		10
27 Oct 66	**HOLY COW** *Stateside SS 552*	6		11

MARC DORSEY US singer

Date	Title / Label	Peak Position	Weeks at No.1	Weeks in Top 40
19 Jun 99	**IF YOU REALLY WANNA KNOW** *Jive 0522592*	58		

TOMMY DORSEY US bandleader/trombonist

Date	Title / Label	Peak Position	Weeks at No.1	Weeks in Top 40
17 Oct 58	**TEA FOR TWO CHA CHA** *Brunswick 05757* TOMMY DORSEY ORCHESTRA STARRING WARREN COVINGTON	3		19

DOUBLE Swiss duo

Date	Title / Label	Peak Position	Weeks at No.1	Weeks in Top 40
25 Jan 86	**THE CAPTAIN OF HER HEART** *Polydor POSP 779*	8		6
5 Dec 87	**DEVIL'S BALL** *Polydor POSP 888*	71		

DOUBLE DEE Italian duo

Date	Title / Label	Peak Position	Weeks at No.1	Weeks in Top 40
1 Dec 90	**FOUND LOVE** *Epic 6563766* DOUBLE DEE FEATURING DANY	63		
25 Nov 95	**FOUND LOVE (REMIX)** *Sony S2 DANUCD 1* DOUBLE DEE FEATURING DANY	33		1
27 Sep 03	**SHINING** *Positiva CDTIV 194*	58		

DOUBLE 99 UK production duo

Date	Title / Label	Peak Position	Weeks at No.1	Weeks in Top 40
31 May 97	**RIPGROOVE** *Satellite 74321485132*	31		1
1 Nov 97	**RIPGROOVE (REMIX)** *Satellite 74321529322*	14		4

DOUBLE SIX UK group

Date	Title / Label	Peak Position	Weeks at No.1	Weeks in Top 40
19 Sep 98	**REAL GOOD** *Multiply CDMULTY 39*	66		
12 Jun 99	**BREAKDOWN** *Multiply CDMULTY 50*	59		

DOUBLE TROUBLE UK production duo

Date	Title / Label	Peak Position	Weeks at No.1	Weeks in Top 40
27 May 89	**JUST KEEP ROCKIN'** *Desire WANT 9* DOUBLE TROUBLE & THE REBEL MC	11		10
7 Oct 89	**STREET TUFF** *Desire WANT 18* DOUBLE TROUBLE & THE REBEL MC	3		10
12 May 90	**TALK BACK** *Desire WANT 27* DOUBLE TROUBLE FEATURING JANETTE SEWELL	71		
30 Jun 90	**LOVE DON'T LIVE HERE ANYMORE** *Desire WANT 32* DOUBLE TROUBLE FEATURING JANETTE SEWELL & CARL BROWN	21		5
15 Jun 91	**RUB-A-DUB** *Desire WANT 41*	66		

DOUBLE YOU? Italian singer

Date	Title / Label	Peak Position	Weeks at No.1	Weeks in Top 40
2 May 92	**PLEASE DON'T GO** *ZYX 67488*	41		

ROB DOUGAN UK singer

Date	Title / Label	Peak Position	Weeks at No.1	Weeks in Top 40
4 Apr 98	**FURIOUS ANGELS** *Cheeky CHEKCD 025*	42		
6 Jul 02	**CLUBBED TO DEATH** *Cheeky 74321941702*	24		2

CARL DOUGLAS Jamaican singer

Date	Title / Label	Peak Position	Weeks at No.1	Weeks in Top 40
17 Aug 74	**KUNG FU FIGHTING** *Pye 7N 45377* ● ★	1	3	11
30 Nov 74	**DANCE THE KUNG FU** *Pye 7N 45418*	35		2
3 Dec 77	**RUN BACK** *Pye 7N 46018*	25		9
23 May 98	**KUNG FU FIGHTING** *All Around The World CDGLOBE 173* BUS STOP FEATURING CARL DOUGLAS	8		9

CAROL DOUGLAS US singer

Date	Title / Label	Peak Position	Weeks at No.1	Weeks in Top 40
22 Jul 78	**NIGHT FEVER** *Gull GULS 61*	66		

CRAIG DOUGLAS UK singer

Date	Title / Label	Peak Position	Weeks at No.1	Weeks in Top 40
12 Jun 59	**A TEENAGER IN LOVE** *Top Rank JAR 133*	13		11
7 Aug 59	**ONLY SIXTEEN** *Top Rank JAR 159*	1	4	15
22 Jan 60	**PRETTY BLUE EYES** *Top Rank JAR 268*	4		14
28 Apr 60	**THE HEART OF A TEENAGE GIRL** *Top Rank JAR 340*	10		8
11 Aug 60	**OH! WHAT A DAY** *Top Rank JAR 406*	43		
20 Apr 61	**A HUNDRED POUNDS OF CLAY** *Top Rank JAR 555*	9		9
29 Jun 61	**TIME** *Top Rank JAR 569*	9		13
22 Mar 62	**WHEN MY LITTLE GIRL IS SMILING** *Top Rank JAR 610*	9		10
28 Jun 62	**OUR FAVOURITE MELODIES** *Columbia DB 4854*	9		9
18 Oct 62	**OH LONESOME ME** *Decca F 11523*	15		8
28 Feb 63	**TOWN CRIER** *Decca F 11575*	36		3

DOVE Irish group

Date	Title / Label	Peak Position	Weeks at No.1	Weeks in Top 40
11 Sep 99	**DON'T DREAM** *ZTT 135CD*	37		1

DOVES UK group

Date	Title / Label	Peak Position	Weeks at No.1	Weeks in Top 40
14 Aug 99	**HERE IT COMES** *Casino CHIP 003CD*	73		
1 Apr 00	**THE CEDAR ROOM** *Heavenly HVN 95CD*	33		1
10 Jun 00	**CATCH THE SUN** *Heavenly HVN 96CDS*	32		1
11 Nov 00	**THE MAN WHO TOLD EVERYTHING** *Heavenly HVN 98CDS*	32		1
27 Apr 02	**THERE GOES THE FEAR** *Heavenly HVN 111CD*	3		2
3 Aug 02	**POUNDING** *Heavenly HVN 116CD*	21		2
26 Oct 02	**CAUGHT BY THE RIVER** *Heavenly HVN 126CDS*	29		1
19 Feb 05	**BLACK AND WHITE TOWN** *Heavenly HVN145CDS*	6		3
21 May 05	**SNOWDEN** *Heavenly HVN150CDS*	17		1
24 Sep 05	**SKY STARTS FALLING** *Heavenly HVN152CD*	45		

DOWLANDS UK duo

Date	Title / Label	Peak Position	Weeks at No.1	Weeks in Top 40
9 Jan 64	**ALL MY LOVING** *Oriole CB 1897*	33		5

ROBERT DOWNEY Jr US actor/singer

Date	Title / Label	Peak Position	Weeks at No.1	Weeks in Top 40
30 Jan 93	**SMILE** *Epic 6589052*	68		

DON DOWNING US singer

Date	Title / Label	Peak Position	Weeks at No.1	Weeks in Top 40
10 Nov 73	**LONELY DAYS, LONELY NIGHTS** *People PEO 102*	32		5

WILL DOWNING US singer

Date	Title / Label	Peak Position	Weeks at No.1	Weeks in Top 40
2 Apr 88	**A LOVE SUPREME** *Fourth & Broadway BRW 90*	14		6
25 Jun 88	**IN MY DREAMS** *Fourth & Broadway BRW 104*	34		3
1 Oct 88	**FREE** *Fourth & Broadway BRW 112*	58		
21 Jan 89	**WHERE IS THE LOVE** *Fourth & Broadway BRW 122* MICA PARIS & WILL DOWNING	19		4
28 Oct 89	**TEST OF TIME** *Fourth & Broadway BRW 146*	67		
24 Feb 90	**COME TOGETHER AS ONE** *Fourth & Broadway BRW 159*	48		
18 Sep 93	**THERE'S NO LIVING WITHOUT YOU** *Fourth & Broadway BRCD 278*	67		

JASON DOWNS US singer

Date	Title / Label	Peak Position	Weeks at No.1	Weeks in Top 40
12 May 01	**WHITE BOY WITH A FEATHER** *Pepper 9230412* JASON DOWNS FEATURING MILK	19		4
14 Jul 01	**CAT'S IN THE CRADLE** *Pepper 9230442* JASON DOWNS FEATURING MILK	65		

DRAGONHEART UK group

Date	Title / Label	Peak Position	Weeks at No.1	Weeks in Top 40
27 Nov 04	**VIDEO KILLED THE RADIO STAR** *Lipstick 6150304*	74		

CHARLIE DRAKE UK comedian/singer

Date	Title / Label	Peak Position	Weeks at No.1	Weeks in Top 40
8 Aug 58	**SPLISH SPLASH** *Parlophone R 4461*	7		11
24 Oct 58	**VOLARE** *Parlophone R 4478*	28		2
27 Oct 60	**MR CUSTER** *Parlophone R 4701*	12		11
5 Oct 61	**MY BOOMERANG WON'T COME BACK** *Parlophone R 4824*	14		11
1 Jan 72	**PUCKWUDGIE** *Columbia DB 8829*	47		

NICK DRAKE UK singer

Date	Title / Label	Peak Position	Weeks at No.1	Weeks in Top 40
29 May 04	**MAGIC** *Island CID 854*	32		1
25 Sep 04	**RIVER MAN** *Island CID 871*	48		

DRAMATIS UK group

Date	Title / Label	Peak Position	Weeks at No.1	Weeks in Top 40
5 Dec 81	**LOVE NEEDS NO DISGUISE** *Beggars Banquet BEG 33* GARY NUMAN & DRAMATIS	33		2
13 Nov 82	**I CAN SEE HER NOW** *Rocket XPRES 83*	57		

RUSTY DRAPER US country singer

Date	Title / Label	Peak Position	Weeks at No.1	Weeks in Top 40
11 Aug 60	**MULE SKINNER BLUES** *Mercury AMT 1101*	39		2

DREAD FLIMSTONE & THE NEW TONE AGE FAMILY US group

Date	Title / Label	Peak Position	Weeks at No.1	Weeks in Top 40
30 Nov 91	**FROM THE GHETTO** *Urban URB 87*	66		

DREAD ZEPPELIN US tribute band

Date	Title / Label	Peak Position	Weeks at No.1	Weeks in Top 40
1 Dec 90	**YOUR TIME IS GONNA COME** *IRS DREAD 1*	59		
13 Jul 91	**STAIRWAY TO HEAVEN** *IRS DREAD 2*	62		

DREADZONE UK group

Date	Title / Label	Peak Position	Weeks at No.1	Weeks in Top 40
6 May 95	**ZION YOUTH** *Virgin VSCDG 1537*	49		
29 Jul 95	**CAPTAIN DREAD** *Virgin VSCDG 1541*	49		
23 Sep 95	**MAXIMUM (EP)** *Virgin VSCDT 1555*	56		
6 Jan 96	**LITTLE BRITAIN** *Virgin VSCDG 1565*	20		5
30 Mar 96	**LIFE LOVE AND UNITY** *Virgin VSCDT 1583*	56		
10 May 97	**EARTH ANGEL** *Virgin VSCDT 1593*	51		
26 Jul 97	**MOVING ON** *Virgin VSCDT 1635*	58		

DREAM US group

Date	Title / Label	Peak Position	Weeks at No.1	Weeks in Top 40
17 Mar 01	**HE LOVES U NOT** *Bad Boy 74321823542*	17		4

DREAM ACADEMY UK group

Date	Title / Label	Peak Position	Weeks at No.1	Weeks in Top 40
30 Mar 85	**LIFE IN A NORTHERN TOWN** *Blanco Y Negro NEG 10*	15		6
14 Sep 85	**THE LOVE PARADE** *Blanco Y Negro NEG 16*	68		

DREAM FREQUENCY UK producer

Date	Title / Label	Peak Position	Weeks at No.1	Weeks in Top 40
12 Jan 91	**LOVE PEACE AND UNDERSTANDING** *Citybeat CBE 756*	71		
25 Jan 92	**FEEL SO REAL** *Citybeat CBE 763* DREAM FREQUENCY FEATURING DEBBIE SHARP	23		4
25 Apr 92	**TAKE ME** *Citybeat CBE 768*	39		2
21 May 94	**GOOD TIMES/THE DREAM** *Citybeat CBE 773CD*	67		
10 Sep 94	**YOU MAKE ME FEEL MIGHTY REAL** *Citybeat CBE 775CD*	65		

DREAM WARRIORS Canadian group

Date	Title / Label	Peak Position	Weeks at No.1	Weeks in Top 40
14 Jul 90	**WASH YOUR FACE IN MY SINK** *Fourth & Broadway BRW 183*	16		5
24 Nov 90	**MY DEFINITION OF A BOOMBASTIC JAZZ STYLE** *Fourth & Broadway BRW 197*	13		7
2 Mar 91	**LUDI** *Fourth & Broadway BRW 206*	39		1

DREAMCATCHER UK group

Date	Title / Label	Peak Position	Weeks at No.1	Weeks in Top 40
12 Jan 02	**I DON'T WANT TO LOSE MY WAY** *Positiva CDTIVS 157*	14		2

DREAMHOUSE UK group

Date	Title / Label	Peak Position	Weeks at No.1	Weeks in Top 40
3 Jun 95	**STAY** *Chase CDPALACE 1*	62		

DREAMWEAVERS US group

Date	Title / Label	Peak Position	Weeks at No.1	Weeks in Top 40
10 Feb 56	**IT'S ALMOST TOMORROW** *Brunswick 05515*	1	2	18

DREEM TEEM UK production group

Date	Title / Label	Peak Position	Weeks at No.1	Weeks in Top 40
13 Dec 97	**THE THEME** *4 Liberty 74321542032*	34		1
6 Nov 99	**BUDDY X 99** *4 Liberty LIBTCD33* DREEM TEEM Vs NENEH CHERRY	15		3
15 Dec 01	**IT AIN'T ENOUGH** *ffrr/Public Demand FCD 401* DREEM TEEM VERSUS ARTFUL DODGER	20		2

EDDIE DRENNON AND B.B.S. UNLIMITED US Group

Date	Title / Label	Peak Position	Weeks at No.1	Weeks in Top 40
28 Feb 76	**LET'S DO THE LATIN HUSTLE** *Pye International 7N 25702*	20		4

ALAN DREW UK singer

Date	Title / Label	Peak Position	Weeks at No.1	Weeks in Top 40
26 Sep 63	**ALWAYS THE LONELY ONE** *Columbia DB 7090*	48		

DRIFTERS US group

Date	Title / Label	Peak Position	Weeks at No.1	Weeks in Top 40
8 Jan 60	**DANCE WITH ME** *London HLE 8988*	17		5
3 Nov 60	**SAVE THE LAST DANCE FOR ME** *London HLK 9201* ★	2		17
16 Mar 61	**I COUNT THE TEARS** *London HLK 9287*	28		3
5 Apr 62	**WHEN MY LITTLE GIRL IS SMILING** *London HLK 9522*	31		3
10 Oct 63	**I'LL TAKE YOU HOME** *London HLK 9785*	37		3
24 Sep 64	**UNDER THE BOARDWALK** *Atlantic AT 9785*	45		
8 Apr 65	**AT THE CLUB** *Atlantic AT 4019*	35		3
29 Apr 65	**COME ON OVER TO MY PLACE** *Atlantic AT 4023*	40		1
2 Feb 67	**BABY WHAT I MEAN** *Atlantic 584 065*	49		
25 Mar 72	**AT THE CLUB/SATURDAY NIGHT AT THE MOVIES** *Atlantic K 10148*	3		17
26 Aug 72	**COME ON OVER TO MY PLACE** *Atlantic K 10216*	9		10
4 Aug 73	**LIKE SISTER AND BROTHER** *Bell 1313*	7		11
15 Jun 74	**KISSIN' IN THE BACK ROW OF THE MOVIES** *Bell 1358* ○	2		12
12 Oct 74	**DOWN ON THE BEACH TONIGHT** *Bell 1381*	7		8
8 Feb 75	**LOVE GAMES** *Bell 1396*	33		4
6 Sep 75	**THERE GOES MY FIRST LOVE** *Bell 1433* ○	3		11
29 Nov 75	**CAN I TAKE YOU HOME LITTLE GIRL** *Bell 1462*	10		9
13 Mar 76	**HELLO HAPPINESS** *Bell 1469*	12		6
11 Sep 76	**EVERY NITE'S A SATURDAY NIGHT WITH YOU** *Bell 1491*	29		4
18 Dec 76	**YOU'RE MORE THAN A NUMBER IN MY LITTLE RED BOOK** *Arista 78* ○	5		11
14 Apr 79	**SAVE THE LAST DANCE FOR ME/WHEN MY LITTLE GIRL IS SMILING** *Lightning LIG 9014*	69		

DRIFTWOOD Dutch production group

Date	Title / Label	Peak Position	Weeks at No.1	Weeks in Top 40
1 Feb 03	**FREELOADER** *Positiva CDTIV 185*	32		1

JULIE DRISCOLL UK singer

Date	Title / Label	Peak Position	Weeks at No.1	Weeks in Top 40
17 Apr 68	**THIS WHEEL'S ON FIRE** *Marmalade 598 006* JULIE DRISCOLL, BRIAN AUGER & THE TRINITY	5		14

MINNIE DRIVER UK actress/singer

Date	Title / Label	Peak Position	Weeks at No.1	Weeks in Top 40
9 Oct 04	**EVERYTHING I'VE GOT IN MY POCKET** *Liberty 8674202*	34		1
22 Jan 05	**INVISIBLE GIRL** *Liberty 8703422*	68		

DRIVER 67 UK singer

Date	Title / Label	Peak Position	Weeks at No.1	Weeks in Top 40
23 Dec 78	**CAR 67** *Logo GO 336* ○	7		8

DRIZABONE UK production group

Date	Title / Label	Peak Position	Weeks at No.1	Weeks in Top 40
22 Jun 91	**REAL LOVE** *Fourth & Broadway BRW 223*	16		5
26 Oct 91	**CATCH THE FIRE** *Fourth & Broadway BRW 232*	54		
23 Apr 94	**PRESSURE** *Fourth & Broadway BRCD 264*	33		1
15 Oct 94	**BRIGHTEST STAR** *Fourth & Broadway BRCD 293*	45		
4 Mar 95	**REAL LOVE** *Fourth & Broadway BRCD 311*	24		3

FRANK D'RONE US singer

Date	Title / Label	Peak Position	Weeks at No.1	Weeks in Top 40
22 Dec 60	**STRAWBERRY BLONDE (THE BAND PLAYED ON)** *Mercury AMT 1123*	24		6

DROWNING POOL US group

Date	Title / Label	Peak Position	Weeks at No.1	Weeks in Top 40
27 Apr 02	**BODIES** *Epic 6723172*	34		1
10 Aug 02	**TEAR AWAY** *Epic 6729832*	65		

DRU HILL US group

Date	Title / Label	Peak Position	Weeks at No.1	Weeks in Top 40
15 Feb 97	**TELL ME** *Fourth & Broadway BRCD 342*	30		1
10 May 97	**IN MY BED** *Fourth & Broadway BRCD 353*	16		1
11 Oct 97	**BIG BAD MAMMA** *Def Jam 5749792* FOXY BROWN FEATURING DRU HILL	12		2
6 Dec 97	**5 STEPS** *Island Black Music CID 675*	22		1
24 Oct 98	**HOW DEEP IS YOUR LOVE** *Island Black Music CID 725* DRU HILL FEATURING REDMAN	9		4
6 Feb 99	**THESE ARE THE TIMES** *Island Black Music CID 733*	4		4
10 Jul 99	**WILD WILD WEST** *Columbia 6675962* WILL SMITH FEATURING DRU HILL ● ★	2		12

DRUGSTORE UK/US/Brazilian group

Date	Title / Label	Peak Position	Weeks at No.1	Weeks in Top 40
10 Jun 95	**FADER** *Honey HONCD 7*	72		
2 May 98	**EL PRESIDENT** *Roadrunner RR 22369*	20		2
4 Jul 98	**SOBER** *Roadrunner RR 22303*	68		

DRUM CLUB UK duo

Date	Title / Label	Peak Position	Weeks at No.1	Weeks in Top 40
6 Nov 93	**SOUND SYSTEM** *Butterfly BFLD 10*	62		

DRUM THEATRE UK group

Date	Title / Label	Peak Position	Weeks at No.1	Weeks in Top 40
15 Feb 86	**LIVING IN THE PAST** *Epic A 6798*	67		
17 Jan 87	**ELDORADO** *Epic EMU 1*	44		

DRUMSOUND/SIMON BASSLINE SMITH UK production duo

Date	Title / Label	Peak Position	Weeks at No.1	Weeks in Top 40
26 Jul 03	**JUNGLIST** *Technique TECH021*	67		
12 Jun 04	**THE ODYSSEY/BODY MOVIN** *Prototype PROUK004*	66		

DRUNKENMUNKY Dutch production group

Date	Title / Label	Peak Position	Weeks at No.1	Weeks in Top 40
4 Oct 03	**E** *All Around The World CDGLOBE 285*	41		

DRUPI Italian singer

Date	Title / Label	Peak Position	Weeks at No.1	Weeks in Top 40
1 Dec 73	**VADO VIA** *A&M AMS 7083*	17		10

DSK UK production group

Date	Title / Label	Peak Position	Weeks at No.1	Weeks in Top 40
31 Aug 91	**WHAT WOULD WE DO/READ MY LIPS** *Boy's Own BOI 6*	46		
22 Nov 97	**WHAT WOULD WE DO (REMIX)** *Fresh FRSHD 63*	55		

DSM US group

Date	Title / Label	Peak Position	Weeks at No.1	Weeks in Top 40
7 Dec 85	**WARRIOR GROOVE** *10 DAZZ 45-7*	68		

DT8 PROJECT UK duo

Date	Title / Label	Peak Position	Weeks at No.1	Weeks in Top 40
3 May 03	**DESTINATION** *ffrr DFCD 007* DT8 FEATURING ROXANNE WILDE	23		2
14 Aug 04	**THE SUN IS SHINING (DOWN ON ME)** *Mondo MND019CD*	17		2
5 Mar 05	**WINTER** *Data 80CDS* DT8 PROJECT FEATURING ANDREA BRITTON	35		1

DTI US group

Date	Title / Label	Peak Position	Weeks at No.1	Weeks in Top 40
16 Apr 88	**KEEP THIS FREQUENCY CLEAR** *Premiere UK ERE 501*	73		

DTOX UK group

Date	Title / Label	Peak Position	Weeks at No.1	Weeks in Top 40
21 Nov 92	**SHATTERED GLASS** *Vitality VITal 1*	75		

D12 US group

Date	Title / Label	Peak Position	Weeks at No.1	Weeks in Top 40
17 Mar 01	**SHIT ON YOU** *Interscope 4974962*	10		5
21 Jul 01	**PURPLE PILLS** *Interscope 4975692* ○	2		10
17 Nov 01	**FIGHT MUSIC** *Shady/Interscope 4976522*	11		3
14 Feb 04	**SHIT ON YOU** *Interscope 4974962*	71		
24 Apr 04	**MY BAND** *Interscope 9862352*	2		9
7 Aug 04	**HOW COME** *Interscope 9863318*	4		6

JOHN DU CANN UK singer

Date	Title / Label	Peak Position	Weeks at No.1	Weeks in Top 40
22 Sep 79	**DON'T BE A DUMMY** *Vertigo 6059 241*	33		2

DUALERS UK duo

Date	Title / Label	Peak Position	Weeks at No.1	Weeks in Top 40
30 Oct 04	**KISS ON THE LIPS** *Galley Music GALLEY10003*	21		2
19 Nov 05	**TRULY MADLY DEEPLY** *Gut CDGUT73*	23		1
24 Jun 06	**DON'T GO** *Galley Music GALLEY104CDX*	61		

DUB PISTOLS UK group

Date	Title / Label	Peak Position	Weeks at No.1	Weeks in Top 40
10 Oct 98	**CYCLONE** *Concrete HARD 36CD*	63		
18 Oct 03	**PROBLEM IS** *Distinctive DISNCD 107* DUB PISTOLS FEATURING TERRY HALL	66		

DUB WAR UK group

Date	Title / Label	Peak Position	Weeks at No.1	Weeks in Top 40
3 Jun 95	**STRIKE IT** *Earache MOSH 138CD*	70		
27 Jan 96	**ENEMY MAKER** *Earache MOSH 147CD*	41		
24 Aug 96	**CRY DIGNITY** *Earache MOSH 163CD*	59		
29 Mar 97	**MILLION DOLLAR LOVE** *Earache MOSH 170CD1*	73		

DUBLINERS Irish group

Date	Title / Label	Peak Position	Weeks at No.1	Weeks in Top 40
30 Mar 67	**SEVEN DRUNKEN NIGHTS** *Major Minor MM 506*	7		17
30 Aug 67	**BLACK VELVET BAND** *Major Minor MM 530*	15		11
20 Dec 67	**MAIDS WHEN YOU'RE YOUNG NEVER WED AN OLD MAN** *Major Minor MM 551*	43		
28 Mar 87	**THE IRISH ROVER** *Stiff BUY 258* POGUES & THE DUBLINERS	8		6
16 Jun 90	**JACK'S HEROES/WHISKEY IN THE JAR** *Pogue Mahone YZ 500* POGUES & THE DUBLINERS	63		

DUBSTAR UK group

Date	Title / Label	Peak Position	Weeks at No.1	Weeks in Top 40
8 Jul 95	**STARS** *Food CDFOOD 61*	40		1
30 Sep 95	**ANYWHERE** *Food CDFOOD 67*	37		1
6 Jan 96	**NOT SO MANIC NOW** *Food CDFOODS 71*	18		4
30 Mar 96	**STARS** *Food CDFOODS 75*	15		5
3 Aug 96	**ELEVATOR SONG** *Food CDFOOD 80*	25		1
19 Jul 97	**NO MORE TALK** *Food CDFOOD 96*	20		2
20 Sep 97	**CATHEDRAL PARK** *Food CDFOOD 104*	41		
7 Feb 98	**I WILL BE YOUR GIRLFRIEND** *Food CDFOODS 108*	28		1
27 May 00	**I (FRIDAY NIGHT)** *Food CDFOODS 128*	37		1

DUELS UK group

Date	Title / Label	Peak Position	Weeks at No.1	Weeks in Top 40
22 Apr 06	**ANIMAL** *Nude NUDCDS62*	47		

Silver-selling ○ · Gold-selling ● · Platinum-selling ⊛ · US No.1 ★ · Peak Position · Weeks at No.1 · Weeks in Top 40

HILARY DUFF US singer/actress

Date	Title / Label	Peak Position	Weeks at No.1	Weeks in Top 40
1 Nov 03	**SO YESTERDAY** *Hollywood HOL003CD1*	9		4
24 Apr 04	**COME CLEAN** *Hollywood HOL005CD1*	18		3
5 Nov 05	**WAKE UP** *Angel ANGEDX5*	7		6
25 Mar 06	**FLY** *Angel ANGEDX13*	20		2
24 Mar 07	**WITH LOVE** *Angel ANGECD32*	29		2

MARY DUFF Irish singer

Date	Title / Label	Peak Position	Weeks at No.1	Weeks in Top 40
10 Jun 95	**SECRET LOVE** *Ritz RITZCD 285* DANIEL O'DONNELL & MARY DUFF	28		1
9 Mar 96	**TIMELESS** *Ritz RITZCD 293* DANIEL O'DONNELL & MARY DUFF	32		1

DUFFO Australian singer

Date	Title / Label	Peak Position	Weeks at No.1	Weeks in Top 40
24 Mar 79	**GIVE ME BACK ME BRAIN** *Beggars Banquet BEG 15*	60		

DUFFY UK singer

Date	Title / Label	Peak Position	Weeks at No.1	Weeks in Top 40
19 Jan 08	**ROCKFERRY** *A&M 1754106*	45		
23 Feb 08	**MERCY** *A&M 1761794*	1	5	6

STEPHEN 'TIN TIN' DUFFY UK singer

Date	Title / Label	Peak Position	Weeks at No.1	Weeks in Top 40
9 Jul 83	**HOLD IT** *Curve X 9763*	55		
2 Mar 85	**KISS ME** *10 TIN 2* ○	4		9
18 May 85	**ICING ON THE CAKE** *10 TIN 3*	14		7

DUKE UK singer

Date	Title / Label	Peak Position	Weeks at No.1	Weeks in Top 40
25 May 96	**SO IN LOVE WITH YOU** *Encore CDCOR 009*	66		
26 Oct 96	**SO IN LOVE WITH YOU** *Pukka CDPUKKA 11*	22		2
11 Nov 00	**SO IN LOVE WITH YOU (REMIX)** *48k/Perfecto SPECT 08CDS*	65		

GEORGE DUKE US singer/keyboard player

Date	Title / Label	Peak Position	Weeks at No.1	Weeks in Top 40
12 Jul 80	**BRAZILIAN LOVE AFFAIR** *Epic EPC 8751*	36		2

DUKE SPIRIT UK group

Date	Title / Label	Peak Position	Weeks at No.1	Weeks in Top 40
12 Jun 04	**DARK IS LIGHT ENOUGH** *Loog 9866673*	55		
16 Oct 04	**CUTS ACROSS THE LAND** *Loog 9868119*	45		
19 Feb 05	**LION RIP** *Loog 9870092*	25		1
14 May 05	**LOVE IS AN UNFAMILIAR NAME** *Loog 9871175*	33		1
1 Oct 05	**CUTS ACROSS THE LAND** *Loog 9873986*	66		

DUKES UK duo

Date	Title / Label	Peak Position	Weeks at No.1	Weeks in Top 40
17 Oct 81	**MYSTERY GIRL** *WEA K 18867*	47		
1 May 82	**THANK YOU FOR THE PARTY** *WEA K 19136*	53		

CANDY DULFER Dutch saxophonist

Date	Title / Label	Peak Position	Weeks at No.1	Weeks in Top 40
24 Feb 90	**LILY WAS HERE** *RCA ZB 43045* DAVID A STEWART FEATURING CANDY DULFER	6		10
4 Aug 90	**SAXUALITY** *RCA PB 43769*	60		

DUM DUMS UK group

Date	Title / Label	Peak Position	Weeks at No.1	Weeks in Top 40
11 Mar 00	**EVERYTHING** *Good Behaviour CDGOOD1*	21		3
8 Jul 00	**CAN'T GET YOU OUT OF MY THOUGHTS** *Good Behaviour CDGOOD2*	18		2
23 Sep 00	**YOU DO SOMETHING TO ME** *Good Behaviour CXGOOD3*	27		1
17 Feb 01	**ARMY OF TWO** *Good Behaviour CXGOOD5*	27		1

THULI DUMAKUDE South African singer

Date	Title / Label	Peak Position	Weeks at No.1	Weeks in Top 40
2 Jan 88	**THE FUNERAL (SEPTEMBER 25TH, 1977)** *MCA 1228*	75		

JOHN DUMMER & HELEN APRIL UK duo

Date	Title / Label	Peak Position	Weeks at No.1	Weeks in Top 40
28 Aug 82	**BLUE SKIES** *Speed 8*	54		

DUMONDE German production duo

Date	Title / Label	Peak Position	Weeks at No.1	Weeks in Top 40
27 Jan 01	**TOMORROW** *Variation VART 6*	60		
19 May 01	**NEVER LOOK BACK** *Manifesto FESCD 83*	36		1

DUNBLANE UK group

Date	Title / Label	Peak Position	Weeks at No.1	Weeks in Top 40
21 Dec 96	**KNOCKIN' ON HEAVEN'S DOOR/THROW THESE GUNS AWAY** *BMG 74321442182* ●	1	1	4

JOHNNY DUNCAN & THE BLUE GRASS BOYS US group

Date	Title / Label	Peak Position	Weeks at No.1	Weeks in Top 40
26 Jul 57	**LAST TRAIN TO SAN FERNANDO** *Columbia DB 3959*	2		17
25 Oct 57	**BLUE BLUE HEARTACHES** *Columbia DB 3996*	27		1
29 Nov 57	**FOOTPRINTS IN THE SNOW** *Columbia DB 4029*	27		2

DAVID DUNDAS UK singer

Date	Title / Label	Peak Position	Weeks at No.1	Weeks in Top 40
24 Jul 76	**JEANS ON** *Air CHS 2094* ○	3		9
9 Apr 77	**ANOTHER FUNNY HONEYMOON** *Air CHS 2136*	29		3

ERROLL DUNKLEY Jamaican singer

Date	Title / Label	Peak Position	Weeks at No.1	Weeks in Top 40
22 Sep 79	**O.K. FRED** *Scope SC 6*	11		8
2 Feb 80	**SIT DOWN AND CRY** *Scope SC 11*	52		

CLIVE DUNN UK actor

Date	Title / Label	Peak Position	Weeks at No.1	Weeks in Top 40
28 Nov 70	**GRANDAD** *Columbia DB 8726*	1	3	21

SIMON DUPREE & THE BIG SOUND UK group

Date	Title / Label	Peak Position	Weeks at No.1	Weeks in Top 40
22 Nov 67	**KITES** *Parlophone R 5646*	9		12
3 Apr 68	**FOR WHOM THE BELL TOLLS** *Parlophone R 5670*	43		

JERMAINE DUPRI US singer

Date	Title / Label	Peak Position	Weeks at No.1	Weeks in Top 40
1 Oct 05	**GOTTA GETCHA** *Virgin VUSDX309*	54		

DURAN DURAN UK group

Date	Title / Label	Peak Position	Weeks at No.1	Weeks in Top 40
21 Feb 81	**PLANET EARTH** *EMI 5137*	12		7
16 May 81	**CARELESS MEMORIES** *EMI 5168*	37		4
25 Jul 81	**GIRLS ON FILM** *EMI 5206*	5		9
28 Nov 81	**MY OWN WAY** *EMI 5254*	14		9
15 May 82	**HUNGRY LIKE THE WOLF** *EMI 5295* ○	5		10
21 Aug 82	**SAVE A PRAYER** *EMI 5327* ○	2		8
13 Nov 82	**RIO** *EMI 5346* ○	9		10
26 Mar 83	**IS THERE SOMETHING I SHOULD KNOW** *EMI 5371* ●	1	2	7
29 Oct 83	**UNION OF THE SNAKE** *EMI 5429* ○	3		5
4 Feb 84	**NEW MOON ON MONDAY** *EMI DURAN 1*	9		5
28 Apr 84	**THE REFLEX** *EMI DURAN 2* ○ ★	1	4	11
3 Nov 84	**WILD BOYS** *EMI DURAN 3* ○	2		12
18 May 85	**A VIEW TO A KILL** *EMI DURAN 007* ○ ★	2		11
1 Nov 86	**NOTORIOUS** *EMI DDN 45*	7		5
21 Feb 87	**SKIN TRADE** *EMI TRADE 1*	22		5
25 Apr 87	**MEET EL PRESIDENTE** *EMI TOUR 1*	24		3
1 Oct 88	**I DON'T WANT YOUR LOVE** *EMI YOUR 1*	14		4
7 Jan 89	**ALL SHE WANTS IS** *EMI DD 11*	9		4
22 Apr 89	**DO YOU BELIEVE IN SHAME** *EMI DD 12*	30		3
16 Dec 89	**BURNING THE GROUND** *EMI DD 13*	31		3
4 Aug 90	**VIOLENCE OF SUMMER (LOVE'S TAKING OVER)** *Parlophone DD 14*	20		3
17 Nov 90	**SERIOUS** *Parlophone DD 15*	48		
30 Jan 93	**ORDINARY WORLD** *Parlophone CDDDS 16*	6		7
10 Apr 93	**COME UNDONE** *Parlophone CDDDS 17*	13		6
4 Sep 93	**TOO MUCH INFORMATION** *Parlophone CDDDS 18*	35		1
25 Mar 95	**PERFECT DAY** *Parlophone CDDDS 20*	28		2
17 Jun 95	**WHITE LINES (DON'T DO IT)** *Parlophone CDDD 19* DURAN DURAN FEATURING MELLE MEL & GRANDMASTER FLASH & THE FURIOUS FIVE	17		4
24 May 97	**OUT OF MY MIND** *Virgin VSCDT 1639*	21		1
30 Jan 99	**ELECTRIC BARBARELLA** *EMI CDELEC 2000*	23		1
10 Jun 00	**SOMEONE ELSE NOT ME** *Hollywood 0108845 HWR*	53		
16 Oct 04	**(REACH UP FOR THE) SUNRISE** *Epic 6753532*	5		3
12 Feb 05	**WHAT HAPPENS TOMORROW** *Epic 6756502*	11		2
24 Nov 07	**FALLING DOWN** *Epic 88697191302*	52		

JIMMY DURANTE US singer/comedian

Date	Title / Label	Peak Position	Weeks at No.1	Weeks in Top 40
14 Dec 96	**MAKE SOMEONE HAPPY** *Warner Brothers W0385CD*	69		

JUDITH DURHAM Australian singer

Date	Title / Label	Peak Position	Weeks at No.1	Weeks in Top 40
15 Jun 67	**OLIVE TREE** *Columbia DB 8207*	33		3

IAN DURY & THE BLOCKHEADS UK group

Date	Title / Label	Peak Position	Weeks at No.1	Weeks in Top 40
29 Apr 78	**WHAT A WASTE** *Stiff BUY 27*	9		8
9 Dec 78	**HIT ME WITH YOUR RHYTHM STICK** *Stiff BUY 38* ●	1	1	12
11 Aug 79	**REASONS TO BE CHEERFUL (PART 3)** *Stiff BUY 50* ○	3		6
30 Aug 80	**I WANT TO BE STRAIGHT** *Stiff BUY 90*	22		6
15 Nov 80	**SUPERMAN'S BIG SISTER** *Stiff BUY 100*	51		
25 May 85	**HIT ME WITH YOUR RHYTHM STICK (REMIX)** *Stiff BUY 214*	55		
26 Oct 85	**PROFOUNDLY IN LOVE WITH PANDORA** *EMI EM 5534*	45		
27 Jul 91	**HIT ME WITH YOU RHYTHM STICK (2ND REMIX)** *Flying FLYR 1*	73		
11 Mar 00	**DRIP FED FRED** *Virgin VSCDT 1768* MADNESS FEATURING IAN DURY	55		

DUST BROTHERS US production duo

Date	Title / Label	Peak Position	Weeks at No.1	Weeks in Top 40
11 Dec 99	**THIS IS YOUR LIFE** *Restless 74321713962*	60		

DUST JUNKYS UK group

Date	Title / Label	Peak Position	Weeks at No.1	Weeks in Top 40
15 Nov 97	**(NONSTOPOPERATION)** *Polydor 5719732*	47		
28 Feb 98	**WHAT TIME IS IT?** *Polydor 5694912*	39		1
16 May 98	**NOTHIN' PERSONAL** *Polydor 5699092*	62		

DUSTED UK group

Date	Title / Label	Peak Position	Weeks at No.1	Weeks in Top 40
20 Jan 01	**ALWAYS REMEMBER TO RESPECT AND HONOUR YOUR MOTHER** *Go! Beat GOLCD 36*	31		1

SLIM DUSTY Australian singer/guitarist

Date	Title / Label	Peak Position	Weeks at No.1	Weeks in Top 40
30 Jan 59	**A PUB WITH NO BEER** *Columbia DB 4212* SLIM DUSTY WITH DICK CARR & HIS BUSHLANDERS	3		15

DUTCH Dutch producer

Date	Title / Label	Peak Position	Weeks at No.1	Weeks in Top 40
20 Sep 03	**MY TIME** *Illustrious/Epic CDILL 018* DUTCH FEATURING CRYSTAL WATERS	22		1

DUTCH FORCE Dutch producer

Date	Title / Label	Peak Position	Weeks at No.1	Weeks in Top 40
6 May 00	**DEADLINE** *Inferno CDFERN 27*	35		1

DWEEB UK group

Date	Title / Label	Peak Position	Weeks at No.1	Weeks in Top 40
22 Feb 97	**SCOOBY DOO** *Blanco Y Negro NEG 100CD*	63		
7 Jun 97	**OH YEAH, BABY** *Blanco Y Negro NEG 102CD*	70		

DYKEENIES UK group

Date	Title / Label	Peak Position	Weeks at No.1	Weeks in Top 40
21 Apr 07	**NEW IDEAS** *Lavolta LAVOLTA012*	54		
21 Jul 07	**CLEAN UP YOUR EYES** *Lavolta LAVOLTA015*	53		
22 Sep 07	**STITCHES** *Lavolta LAVOLTA016*	61		

BOB DYLAN US singer/guitarist

Date	Title / Label	Peak Position	Weeks at No.1	Weeks in Top 40
25 Mar 65	**TIMES THEY ARE A-CHANGIN'** *CBS 201751*	9		10
29 Apr 65	**SUBTERRANEAN HOMESICK BLUES** *CBS 201753*	9		9
17 Jun 65	**MAGGIE'S FARM** *CBS 201781*	22		6
19 Aug 65	**LIKE A ROLLING STONE** *CBS 201811*	4		10
28 Oct 65	**POSITIVELY FOURTH STREET** *CBS 201824*	8		12
27 Jan 66	**CAN YOU PLEASE CRAWL OUT YOUR WINDOW** *CBS 201900*	17		5
14 Apr 66	**ONE OF US MUST KNOW (SOONER OR LATER)** *CBS 202053*	33		2
12 May 66	**RAINY DAY WOMEN NOS. 12 & 35** *CBS 202307*	7		8
21 Jul 66	**I WANT YOU** *CBS 202258*	16		8
14 May 69	**I THREW IT ALL AWAY** *CBS 4219*	30		5
13 Sep 69	**LAY LADY LAY** *CBS 4434*	5		11
10 Jul 71	**WATCHING THE RIVER FLOW** *CBS 7329*	24		7
6 Oct 73	**KNOCKIN' ON HEAVEN'S DOOR** *CBS 1762*	14		9
7 Feb 76	**HURRICANE** *CBS 3878*	43		
29 Jul 78	**BABY STOP CRYING** *CBS 6499*	13		9
28 Oct 78	**IS YOUR LOVE IN VAIN** *CBS 6718*	56		
20 May 95	**DIGNITY** *Columbia 6620762*	33		1
11 Jul 98	**LOVE SICK** *Columbia 6659972*	64		
14 Oct 00	**THINGS HAVE CHANGED** *Columbia 6693792*	58		
6 Oct 07	**MOST LIKELY YOU GO YOUR OWN WAY** *Columbia 88697163192*	51		

DYNAMITE MC UK producer

Date	Title / Label	Peak Position	Weeks at No.1	Weeks in Top 40
20 Sep 03	**HOTNESS** *Ram RAMM 45* DYNAMITE MC & ORIGIN UNKNOWN	66		
5 Jun 04	**RIDE** *Utlimate Dilemma EW 288CD*	54		

DYNAMIX II US duo

Date	Title / Label	Peak Position	Weeks at No.1	Weeks in Top 40
8 Aug 87	**JUST GIVE THE DJ A BREAK** *Cooltempo COOL 151* DYNAMIX II FEATURING TOO TOUGH TEE	50		

DYNASTY US group

Date	Title / Label	Peak Position	Weeks at No.1	Weeks in Top 40
13 Oct 79	**I DON'T WANT TO BE A FREAK (BUT I CAN'T HELP MYSELF)** *Solar FB 1694*	20		5
9 Aug 80	**I'VE JUST BEGUN TO LOVE YOU** *Solar SO 10*	51		
21 May 83	**DOES THAT RING A BELL** *Solar E 9911*	53		

DYVERSE UK group

Date	Title / Label	Peak Position	Weeks at No.1	Weeks in Top 40
31 Jan 04	**MISGUIDED** *Chilli Discs CCHIL 002*	71		

DYSFUNCTIONAL PSYCHEDELIC WALTONS UK production duo

Date	Title / Label	Peak Position	Weeks at No.1	Weeks in Top 40
12 Apr 03	**PAYBACK TIME** *Sony Music 6737622*	48		

RONNIE DYSON US singer

Date	Title / Label	Peak Position	Weeks at No.1	Weeks in Top 40
4 Dec 71	**WHEN YOU GET RIGHT DOWN TO IT** *CBS 7449*	34		5

E–H

KEY TO ARTIST ENTRIES

Artist/Group Name — Artist/Group Nationality and Category — Silver-selling — Gold-selling — Platinum-selling — US No.1 ★ — Peak Position — Weeks at No.1 — Weeks in Top 40

DEXY'S MIDNIGHT RUNNERS UK group

		Peak Position	Weeks at No.1	Weeks in Top 40
19 Jan 80	**DANCE STANCE** *Oddball Productions R 6028*	40		1
22 Mar 80	**GENO** *Late Night Feelings R 6033*	1	2	12
12 Jul 80	**THERE THERE MY DEAR** *Late Night Feelings R 6038*	7		6
21 Mar 81	**PLAN B** *Parlophone R 6046*	58		
11 Jul 81	**SHOW ME** *Mercury DEXYS 6*	16		7
20 Mar 82	**THE CELTIC SOUL BROTHERS** *Mercury DEXYS 8* DEXY'S MIDNIGHT RUNNERS WITH THE EMERALD EXPRESS	45		
3 Jul 82	**COME ON EILEEN** *Mercury DEXYS 9* DEXY'S MIDNIGHT RUNNERS WITH THE EMERALD EXPRESS ★	1	4	13
2 Oct 82	**JACKIE WILSON SAID (I'M IN HEAVEN WHEN YOU SMILE)** *Mercury DEXYS 10* KEVIN ROWLAND & DEXY'S MIDNIGHT RUNNERS	5		6
4 Dec 82	**LET'S GET THIS STRAIGHT (FROM THE START)/OLD** *Mercury DEXYS 11* KEVIN ROWLAND & DEXY'S MIDNIGHT RUNNERS	17		8
2 Apr 83	**THE CELTIC SOUL BROTHERS** *Mercury DEXYS 12* KEVIN ROWLAND & DEXY'S MIDNIGHT RUNNERS	20		5
22 Nov 86	**BECAUSE OF YOU** *Mercury BRUSH 1*	13		6

Date of entry into Top 75

Artist collaboration or where artist's name has changed

Song Title

Label and Catalogue Number

KATHERINE E US singer

Date	Title / Label	Peak Position	Weeks at No.1	Weeks in Top 40
6 Apr 91	**I'M ALRIGHT** *Dead Dead Good GOOD 2*	41		
18 Jan 92	**THEN I FEEL GOOD** *PWL Continental PWL 13*	56		
29 Jan 05	**SALTY** *Kingsize KS093D1* DYLAN RHYMES FEATURING KATHERINE ELLIS	70		

SHEILA E US singer/percussionist

Date	Title / Label	Peak Position	Weeks at No.1	Weeks in Top 40
23 Feb 85	**THE BELLE OF ST MARK** *Warner Brothers W 9180*	18		5

E-LUSTRIOUS UK production duo

Date	Title / Label	Peak Position	Weeks at No.1	Weeks in Top 40
15 Feb 92	**DANCE NO MORE** *MOS 001T* E-LUSTRIOUS FEATURING DEBORAH FRENCH	58		
2 Jul 94	**IN YOUR DANCE** *UFG 6CD*	69		

E-MALE UK group

Date	Title / Label	Peak Position	Weeks at No.1	Weeks in Top 40
31 Jan 98	**WE ARE E-MALE** *East West EW 137CD*	44		

E-MOTION UK duo

Date	Title / Label	Peak Position	Weeks at No.1	Weeks in Top 40
3 Feb 96	**THE NAUGHTY NORTH & THE SEXY SOUTH** *Soundproof MCSTD 40017*	20		2
17 Aug 96	**I STAND ALONE** *Soundproof MCSTD 40061*	60		
26 Oct 96	**THE NAUGHTY NORTH & THE SEXY SOUTH** *Soundproof MCSTD 40076*	17		2

E-ROTIC German/US group

Date	Title / Label	Peak Position	Weeks at No.1	Weeks in Top 40
3 Jun 95	**MAX DON'T HAVE SEX WITH YOUR EX** *Stip CDSTIP 2*	45		

E-SMOOVE US producer

Date	Title / Label	Peak Position	Weeks at No.1	Weeks in Top 40
15 Aug 98	**DÉJÀ VU** *AM:PM 5827671* E-SMOOVE FEATURING LATANZA WATERS	63		

E-TRAX German production duo

Date	Title / Label	Peak Position	Weeks at No.1	Weeks in Top 40
9 Jun 01	**LET'S ROCK** *Tidy Trax TIDY 155CD*	60		

E-TYPE Swedish singer

Date	Title / Label	Peak Position	Weeks at No.1	Weeks in Top 40
23 Sep 95	**THIS IS THE WAY** *ffrreedom TABCD 237*	53		
24 Jun 00	**CAMPIONE 2000** *Polydor 1580822*	58		

E-Z ROLLERS UK group

Date	Title / Label	Peak Position	Weeks at No.1	Weeks in Top 40
24 Apr 99	**WALK THIS LAND** *Moving Shadow 130CD1*	18		2
8 Feb 03	**BACK TO LOVE** *Moving Shadow 159CD*	61		

E-ZEE POSSEE UK group

Date	Title / Label	Peak Position	Weeks at No.1	Weeks in Top 40
26 Aug 89	**EVERYTHING STARTS WITH AN 'E'** *More Protein PROT 1*	69		
20 Jan 90	**LOVE ON LOVE** *More Protein PROT 3*	59		
17 Mar 90	**EVERYTHING STARTS WITH AN 'E'** *More Protein PROT 1*	15		6
30 Jun 90	**THE SUN MACHINE** *More Protein PROT 4*	62		
21 Sep 91	**BREATHING IS E-ZEE** *More Protein PROT 12* E-ZEE POSSEE FEATURING TARA NEWLEY	72		

EAGLES US group

Date	Title / Label	Peak Position	Weeks at No.1	Weeks in Top 40
9 Aug 75	**ONE OF THESE NIGHTS** *Asylum AYM 543* ★	23		6
1 Nov 75	**LYIN' EYES** *Asylum AYM 548*	23		6
6 Mar 76	**TAKE IT TO THE LIMIT** *Asylum K 13029*	12		6
15 Jan 77	**NEW KID IN TOWN** *Asylum K 13069* ★	20		6
16 Apr 77	**HOTEL CALIFORNIA** *Asylum K 13079* ★	8		10
16 Dec 78	**PLEASE COME HOME FOR CHRISTMAS** *Asylum K 13145*	30		2
13 Oct 79	**HEARTACHE TONIGHT** *Asylum K 12394* ★	40		1
1 Dec 79	**THE LONG RUN** *Elektra K 12404*	66		
13 Jul 96	**LOVE WILL KEEP US ALIVE** *Geffen GFSTD 21980*	52		
25 Oct 03	**HOLE IN THE WORLD** *Eagles 8122745472*	69		

EAGLES OF DEATH METAL US group

Date	Title / Label	Peak Position	Weeks at No.1	Weeks in Top 40
9 Sep 06	**I WANT YOU SO HARD (BOY'S BAD NEWS)** *20-20 Recordings 82876886682*	73		

EAMON US singer

Date	Title / Label	Peak Position	Weeks at No.1	Weeks in Top 40
3 Apr 04	**F**K IT (I DON'T WANT YOU BACK) (IMPORT)** *Jive 82876604852*	46		
24 Apr 04	**F**K IT (I DON'T WANT YOU BACK)** *Jive 82876608522* (Silver)	1	4	17
16 Oct 04	**LOVE THEM** *Jive 82876639212* EAMON FEATURING GHOSTFACE	27		2
25 Aug 07	**(HOW COULD YOU) BRING HIM HOME** *Download*	61		

ROBERT EARL UK singer

Date	Title / Label	Peak Position	Weeks at No.1	Weeks in Top 40
25 Apr 58	**I MAY NEVER PASS THIS WAY AGAIN** *Philips PB 805*	14		13
24 Oct 58	**MORE THAN EVER (COME PRIMA)** *Philips PB 867*	26		4
13 Feb 59	**WONDERFUL SECRET LOVE** *Philips PB 891*	17		10

CHARLES EARLAND US instrumentalist

Date	Title / Label	Peak Position	Weeks at No.1	Weeks in Top 40
19 Aug 78	**LET THE MUSIC PLAY** *Mercury 6167 703*	46		

STEVE EARLE US guitarist/singer

Date	Title / Label	Peak Position	Weeks at No.1	Weeks in Top 40
15 Oct 88	**COPPERHEAD ROAD** *MCA 1280*	45		
31 Dec 88	**JOHNNY COME LATELY** *MCA 1301*	75		

EARLIES UK/US group

Date	Title / Label	Peak Position	Weeks at No.1	Weeks in Top 40
6 Nov 04	**MORNING WONDER** *WEA IAMNAMES07*	67		
12 Mar 05	**BRING IT BACK AGAIN** *WEA IAMNAMES09*	61		

EARLY MUSIC CONSORT UK instrumental group

Date	Title / Label	Peak Position	Weeks at No.1	Weeks in Top 40
3 Apr 71	**HENRY VIII SUITE (EP)** *BBC RESL 1* EARLY MUSIC CONSORT DIRECTED BY DAVID MUNROW	49		

EARTH WIND & FIRE US group

Date	Title / Label	Peak Position	Weeks at No.1	Weeks in Top 40
12 Feb 77	**SATURDAY NITE** *CBS 4835*	17		8
11 Feb 78	**FANTASY** *CBS 6056*	14		9
13 May 78	**JUPITER** *CBS 6267*	41		
29 Jul 78	**MAGIC MIND** *CBS 6490*	54		
7 Oct 78	**GOT TO GET YOU INTO MY LIFE** *CBS 6553*	33		4
9 Dec 78	**SEPTEMBER** *CBS 6922* (Silver)	3		11
12 May 79	**BOOGIE WONDERLAND** *CBS 7292* EARTH WIND & FIRE WITH THE EMOTIONS (Gold)	4		11
28 Jul 79	**AFTER THE LOVE HAS GONE** *CBS 7721* (Silver)	4		8
6 Oct 79	**STAR** *CBS 7092*	16		6
15 Dec 79	**CAN'T LET GO** *CBS 8077*	46		
8 Mar 80	**IN THE STONE** *CBS 8252*	53		
11 Oct 80	**LET ME TALK** *CBS 8982*	29		3
20 Dec 80	**BACK ON THE ROAD** *CBS 9377*	63		
7 Nov 81	**LET'S GROOVE** *CBS A 1679* (Silver)	3		11
6 Feb 82	**I'VE HAD ENOUGH** *CBS A 1959*	29		1
5 Feb 83	**FALL IN LOVE WITH ME** *CBS A 2927*	47		
7 Nov 87	**SYSTEM OF SURVIVAL** *CBS EWF 1*	54		
31 Jul 99	**SEPTEMBER 99 (REMIX)** *INCredible INCR 24CD*	25		2

EARTHLING UK production duo

Date	Title / Label	Peak Position	Weeks at No.1	Weeks in Top 40
14 Oct 95	**ECHO ON MY MIND PART II** *Cooltempo CDCOOL 312*	61		
1 Jun 96	**BLOOD MUSIC (EP)** *Cooltempo CDCOOL 319*	69		

EAST 57TH STREET US group

Date	Title / Label	Peak Position	Weeks at No.1	Weeks in Top 40
11 Oct 97	**SATURDAY** *AM:PM 5823752* EAST 57TH STREET FEATURING DONNA ALLEN	29		1

EAST OF EDEN UK group

Date	Title / Label	Peak Position	Weeks at No.1	Weeks in Top 40
17 Apr 71	**JIG A JIG** *Deram DM 297*	7		11

EAST 17 UK group

Date	Title / Label	Peak Position	Weeks at No.1	Weeks in Top 40
29 Aug 92	**HOUSE OF LOVE** *London LON 325*	10		7
14 Nov 92	**GOLD** *London LON 331*	28		2
30 Jan 93	**DEEP** *London LOCDP 334* (Silver)	5		9
10 Apr 93	**SLOW IT DOWN** *London LONCD 339*	13		5
26 Jun 93	**WEST END GIRLS** *London LONCD 344*	11		4
4 Dec 93	**IT'S ALRIGHT** *London LONCD 345* (Silver)	3		12
14 May 94	**AROUND THE WORLD** *London LONCD 349* (Silver)	3		10
1 Oct 94	**STEAM** *London LONCD 353*	7		6

Key: Silver-selling ○ · Gold-selling ● · Platinum-selling ⊛ · US No.1 ★ · Peak Position · Weeks at No.1 · Weeks in Top 40

Date	Title	Label	Peak Position	Weeks at No.1	Weeks in Top 40
3 Dec 94	STAY ANOTHER DAY ⊛	London LONCD 354	1	5	10
25 Mar 95	LET IT RAIN	London LOCDP 363	10		5
17 Jun 95	HOLD MY BODY TIGHT	London LOCDP 367	12		4
4 Nov 95	THUNDER ○	London LOCDP 373	4		11
10 Feb 96	DO U STILL?	London LOCDP 379	7		5
10 Aug 96	SOMEONE TO LOVE	London LONCD 385	16		4
2 Nov 96	IF YOU EVER (EAST 17 FEATURING GABRIELLE) ●	London LONCD 388	2		11
18 Jan 97	HEY CHILD	London LONCD 390	3		3
14 Nov 98	EACH TIME	Telstar CDSTAS 3017	2		5
13 Mar 99	BETCHA CAN'T WAIT	Telstar CDSTAS 3031	12		3

EAST SIDE BEAT Italian production duo

Date	Title	Label	Peak Position	Weeks at No.1	Weeks in Top 40
30 Nov 91	RIDE LIKE THE WIND	ffrr F 176	3		8
19 Dec 92	ALIVE AND KICKING	ffrr F 206	26		4
29 May 93	YOU'RE MY EVERYTHING	ffrr FCD 207	65		

EASTERN LANE UK group

Date	Title	Label	Peak Position	Weeks at No.1	Weeks in Top 40
15 Nov 03	FEED YOUR ADDICTION	Rough Trade RTRADESCD132	72		
13 Mar 04	SAFFRON	Rough Trade RTRADSCD156	55		
6 Nov 04	I SAID PIG ON FRIDAY	Rough Trade RTRADSCD199	65		

SHEENA EASTON UK singer

Date	Title	Label	Peak Position	Weeks at No.1	Weeks in Top 40
5 Apr 80	MODERN GIRL	EMI 5042	56		
19 Jul 80	9 TO 5 ●	EMI 5066	3		12
9 Aug 80	MODERN GIRL ○ ★	EMI 5042	8		10
25 Oct 80	ONE MAN WOMAN	EMI 5114	14		6
14 Feb 81	TAKE MY TIME	EMI 5135	44		
2 May 81	WHEN HE SHINES	EMI 5166	12		6
27 Jun 81	FOR YOUR EYES ONLY	EMI 5195	8		10
12 Sep 81	JUST ANOTHER BROKEN HEART	EMI 5232	33		4
5 Dec 81	YOU COULD HAVE BEEN WITH ME	EMI 5252	54		
31 Jul 82	MACHINERY	EMI 5326	38		3
12 Feb 83	WE'VE GOT TONIGHT (KENNY ROGERS & SHEENA EASTON)	Liberty UP 658	28		3
21 Jan 89	THE LOVER IN ME	MCA 1289	15		6
18 Mar 89	DAYS LIKE THIS	MCA 1325	43		
15 Jul 89	101	MCA 1348	54		
18 Nov 89	THE ARMS OF ORION (PRINCE WITH SHEENA EASTON)	Warner Brothers W 2757	27		4
9 Dec 00	GIVING UP GIVING IN	Universal MCSTD 40244	54		

EASTSIDE CONNECTION US group

Date	Title	Label	Peak Position	Weeks at No.1	Weeks in Top 40
8 Apr 78	YOU'RE SO RIGHT FOR ME	Creole CR 149	44		

CLINT EASTWOOD US actor

Date	Title	Label	Peak Position	Weeks at No.1	Weeks in Top 40
7 Feb 70	I TALK TO THE TREES	Paramount PARA 3004	18		2
29 Sep 84	LAST PLANE (ONE WAY TICKET)	MCA 910	51		

CLINT EASTWOOD & GENERAL SAINT UK duo

Date	Title	Label	Peak Position	Weeks at No.1	Weeks in Top 40
2 Apr 94	OH CAROL!	Copasetic COPCD 0009	54		

EASYBEATS Australian group

Date	Title	Label	Peak Position	Weeks at No.1	Weeks in Top 40
27 Oct 66	FRIDAY ON MY MIND	United Artists UP 1157	6		13
10 Apr 68	HELLO, HOW ARE YOU	United Artists UP 2209	20		8

EASYWORLD UK group

Date	Title	Label	Peak Position	Weeks at No.1	Weeks in Top 40
1 Jun 02	BLEACH	Jive 9253552	67		
21 Sep 02	YOU AND ME	Jive 9254102	57		
8 Feb 03	JUNKIES	Jive 9254522	40		1
18 Oct 03	2ND AMENDMENT	Jive 82876554692	42		
31 Jan 04	TIL THE DAY	Jive 82876585372	27		1
11 Sep 04	HOW DID IT EVER COME TO THIS?	Jive 82876632102	50		

EAT UK/US group

Date	Title	Label	Peak Position	Weeks at No.1	Weeks in Top 40
12 Jun 93	BLEED ME WHITE	Fiction FICCD 48	73		

EAT STATIC UK production duo

Date	Title	Label	Peak Position	Weeks at No.1	Weeks in Top 40
22 Feb 97	HYBRID	Planet Dog BARK 024CD	41		
27 Sep 97	INTERCEPTOR	Planet Dog BARK 030CD	44		
27 Jun 98	CONTACT...	Planet Dog BARK 033CD	67		

CLEVELAND EATON US singer/bass player

Date	Title	Label	Peak Position	Weeks at No.1	Weeks in Top 40
23 Sep 78	BAMA BOOGIE WOOGIE	Gull GULS 63	35		2

EAV Austrian group

Date	Title	Label	Peak Position	Weeks at No.1	Weeks in Top 40
27 Sep 86	BA-BA-BANKROBERRY (ENGLISH VERSION)	Columbia DB 9139	63		

EAZY-E US rapper

Date	Title	Label	Peak Position	Weeks at No.1	Weeks in Top 40
6 Jan 96	JUST TAH LET U KNOW	Ruthless 6628162	30		2

EBONY DUBSTERS UK production duo

Date	Title	Label	Peak Position	Weeks at No.1	Weeks in Top 40
24 Jan 04	MURDERATION	Ebony EBR029	59		
22 May 04	NUMBER 1/THE RITUAL	Ebony EBR030	58		

ECHELON UK group

Date	Title	Label	Peak Position	Weeks at No.1	Weeks in Top 40
20 Nov 04	PLUS	Poptones MC5095SCD	57		

ECHO & THE BUNNYMEN UK group

Date	Title	Label	Peak Position	Weeks at No.1	Weeks in Top 40
17 May 80	RESCUE	Korova KOW 1	62		
18 Apr 81	SHINE SO HARD (EP)	Korova ECHO 1	37		2
18 Jul 81	A PROMISE	Korova KOW 15	49		
29 May 82	THE BACK OF LOVE	Korova KOW 24	19		6
22 Jan 83	THE CUTTER	Korova KOW 26	8		6
16 Jul 83	NEVER STOP	Korova KOW 28	15		5
28 Jan 84	THE KILLING MOON	Korova KOW 32	9		5
21 Apr 84	SILVER	Korova KOW 34	30		4
14 Jul 84	SEVEN SEAS	Korova KOW 35	16		5
19 Oct 85	BRING ON THE DANCING HORSES	Korova KOW 43	21		5
13 Jun 87	THE GAME	WEA YZ 134	28		3
1 Aug 87	LIPS LIKE SUGAR	WEA YZ 144	36		2
20 Feb 88	PEOPLE ARE STRANGE	WEA YZ 175	29		3
2 Mar 91	PEOPLE ARE STRANGE	East West YZ 567	34		2
28 Jun 97	NOTHING LASTS FOREVER	London LOCDP 396	8		4
13 Sep 97	I WANT TO BE THERE WHEN YOU COME	London LONCD 399	30		1
8 Nov 97	DON'T LET IT GET YOU DOWN	London LOCDP 406	50		
27 Mar 99	RUST	London LONCD 424	22		1
5 May 01	IT'S ALRIGHT	Cooking Vinyl FRY CD104	41		
17 Sep 05	STORMY WEATHER	Cooking Vinyl FRYCD246	55		

ECHOBASS UK producer

Date	Title	Label	Peak Position	Weeks at No.1	Weeks in Top 40
14 Jul 01	YOU ARE THE WEAKEST LINK	House Of Bush CDANNE 001	53		

ECHOBEATZ UK production duo

Date	Title	Label	Peak Position	Weeks at No.1	Weeks in Top 40
25 Jul 98	MAS QUE NADA	Eternal WEA 176CD	10		4

ECHOBELLY UK group

Date	Title	Label	Peak Position	Weeks at No.1	Weeks in Top 40
2 Apr 94	INSOMNIAC	Fauve FAUV 1CS	47		
2 Jul 94	I CAN'T IMAGINE THE WORLD WITHOUT ME	Fauve FAUV 2CD	39		1
5 Nov 94	CLOSE...BUT	Fauve FAUV 4CD	59		
2 Sep 95	GREAT THINGS	Fauve FAUV 5CD	13		2
4 Nov 95	KING OF THE KERB	Fauve FAUV 7CD	25		1
2 Mar 96	DARK THERAPY	Fauve FAUV 8CD	20		2
23 Aug 97	THE WORLD IS FLAT	Epic 6648152	31		1
8 Nov 97	HERE COMES THE BIG RUSH	Epic 6652452	56		

BILLY ECKSTINE US singer

Date	Title	Label	Peak Position	Weeks at No.1	Weeks in Top 40
12 Nov 54	NO ONE BUT YOU	MGM 763	3		17
27 Sep 57	PASSING STRANGERS (BILLY ECKSTINE & SARAH VAUGHAN)	Mercury MT 164	22		2
13 Feb 59	GIGI	Mercury AMT 1018	8		14
12 Mar 69	PASSING STRANGERS (BILLY ECKSTINE & SARAH VAUGHAN)	Mercury MF 1082	20		13

ECLIPSE Italian producer

Date	Title / Label	Peak Position	Weeks at No.1	Weeks in Top 40
14 Aug 99	**MAKES ME LOVE YOU** *Azuli AZNYCDX 100*	25		2

SILVIO ECOMO Dutch producer

Date	Title / Label	Peak Position	Weeks at No.1	Weeks in Top 40
15 Jul 00	**STANDING** *Hooj Choons HOOJ 098CD*	70		

EDDIE & THE HOT RODS UK group

Date	Title / Label	Peak Position	Weeks at No.1	Weeks in Top 40
11 Sep 76	**LIVE AT THE MARQUEE (EP)** *Island IEP 2*	43		
13 Nov 76	**TEENAGE DEPRESSION** *Island WIP 6354*	35		2
23 Apr 77	**I MIGHT BE LYING** *Island WIP 6388*	44		
13 Aug 77	**DO ANYTHING YOU WANT TO DO** *Island WIP 6401*	9		10
21 Jan 78	**QUIT THIS TOWN** *Island WIP 6411*	36		2

EDDY UK singer

Date	Title / Label	Peak Position	Weeks at No.1	Weeks in Top 40
9 Jul 94	**SOMEDAY** *Positiva CDTIV 14*	49		

DUANE EDDY US singer/guitarist

Date	Title / Label	Peak Position	Weeks at No.1	Weeks in Top 40
5 Sep 58	**REBEL ROUSER** *London HL 8669*	19		10
2 Jan 59	**CANNONBALL** *London HL 8764*	22		4
19 Jun 59	**PETER GUNN THEME** *London HLW 8879*	6		11
24 Jul 59	**YEP** *London HLW 8879*	17		5
4 Sep 59	**FORTY MILES OF BAD ROAD** *London HLW 8929*	11		9
18 Dec 59	**SOME KINDA EARTHQUAKE** *London HLW 9007*	12		5
19 Feb 60	**BONNIE CAME BACK** *London HLW 9050*	12		10
28 Apr 60	**SHAZAM!** *London HLW 9104*	4		13
21 Jul 60	**BECAUSE THEY'RE YOUNG** *London HLW 9162*	2		17
10 Nov 60	**KOMMOTION** *London HLW 9225*	13		8
12 Jan 61	**PEPE** *London HLW 9257*	2		13
20 Apr 61	**THEME FROM DIXIE** *London HLW 9324*	7		9
22 Jun 61	**RING OF FIRE** *London HLW 9370*	17		10
14 Sep 61	**DRIVIN' HOME** *London HLW 9406* DUANE EDDY & THE REBELS	30		3
5 Oct 61	**CARAVAN** *Parlophone R 4826*	42		
24 May 62	**DEEP IN THE HEART OF TEXAS** *RCA 1288*	19		5
23 Aug 62	**BALLAD OF PALADIN** *RCA 1300*	10		9
8 Nov 62	**DANCE WITH THE GUITAR MAN** *RCA 1316*	4		14
14 Feb 63	**BOSS GUITAR** *RCA 1329*	27		7
30 May 63	**LONELY BOY LONELY GUITAR** *RCA 1344*	35		2
29 Aug 63	**YOUR BABY'S GONE SURFIN'** *RCA 1357*	49		
8 Mar 75	**PLAY ME LIKE YOU PLAY YOUR GUITAR** *GTO GT 11* DUANE EDDY & THE REBELETTES	9		8
22 Mar 86	**PETER GUNN** *China WOK 6* ART OF NOISE FEATURING DUANE EDDY	8		7

EDDY & THE SOUL BAND US percussionist

Date	Title / Label	Peak Position	Weeks at No.1	Weeks in Top 40
23 Feb 85	**THE THEME FROM *SHAFT*** *Club JAB 11*	13		5

RANDY EDELMAN US singer/pianist

Date	Title / Label	Peak Position	Weeks at No.1	Weeks in Top 40
6 Mar 76	**CONCRETE AND CLAY** *20th Century BTC 2261*	11		7
18 Sep 76	**UPTOWN UPTEMPO WOMAN** *20th Century BTC 2225*	25		6
15 Jan 77	**YOU** *20th Century BTC 2253*	49		
17 Jul 82	**NOBODY MADE ME** *Rocket XPRES 81*	60		

EDELWEISS Austrian group

Date	Title / Label	Peak Position	Weeks at No.1	Weeks in Top 40
29 Apr 89	**BRING ME EDELWEISS** *WEA YZ 353*	5		7

EDEN UK/Australian group

Date	Title / Label	Peak Position	Weeks at No.1	Weeks in Top 40
6 Mar 93	**DO U FEEL 4 ME** *Logic 74321135422*	51		

EDISON LIGHTHOUSE UK group

Date	Title / Label	Peak Position	Weeks at No.1	Weeks in Top 40
24 Jan 70	**LOVE GROWS (WHERE MY ROSEMARY GOES)** *Bell 1091*	1	5	12
30 Jan 71	**IT'S UP TO YOU PETULA** *Bell 1136*	49		

EDITORS UK group

Date	Title / Label	Peak Position	Weeks at No.1	Weeks in Top 40
5 Feb 05	**BULLETS** *Kitchenware SKCD77*	54		
30 Apr 05	**MUNICH** *Kitchenware SKCD782*	22		1
23 Jul 05	**BLOOD** *Kitchenware SKCD792*	18		1
8 Oct 05	**BULLETS** *Kitchenware SKCD802*	27		1
14 Jan 06	**MUNICH** *Kitchenware SKCD832*	10		5
8 Apr 06	**ALL SPARKS** *Kitchenware SKCD84*	21		2
1 Jul 06	**BLOOD** *Kitchenware SKCD87*	39		1
23 Jun 07	**SMOKERS OUTSIDE THE HOSPITAL DOORS** *Columbia SKCD93*	7		4
8 Sep 07	**THE END HAS A START** *Kitchenware SKCD952*	27		1
8 Dec 07	**THE RACING RATS** *Kitchenware SKCD97*	26		1

DAVE EDMUNDS UK singer/guitarist

Date	Title / Label	Peak Position	Weeks at No.1	Weeks in Top 40
21 Nov 70	**I HEAR YOU KNOCKING** *MAM 1* DAVE EDMUNDS' ROCKPILE	1	6	13
20 Jan 73	**BABY I LOVE YOU** *Rockfield ROC 1*	8		11
9 Jun 73	**BORN TO BE WITH YOU** *Rockfield ROC 2*	5		10
2 Jul 77	**I KNEW THE BRIDE** *Swansong SSK 19411*	26		7
30 Jun 79	**GIRLS TALK** *Swansong SSK 19418* (silver-selling)	4		9
22 Sep 79	**QUEEN OF HEARTS** *Swansong SSK 19419*	11		7
24 Nov 79	**CRAWLING FROM THE WRECKAGE** *Swansong SSK 19420*	59		
9 Feb 80	**SINGING THE BLUES** *Swansong SSK 19422*	28		5
28 Mar 81	**ALMOST SATURDAY NIGHT** *Swansong SSK 19424*	58		
20 Jun 81	**THE RACE IS ON** *Swansong SSK 19425* DAVE EDMUNDS & THE STRAY CATS	34		3
26 Mar 83	**SLIPPING AWAY** *Arista ARIST 522*	60		
7 Apr 90	**KING OF LOVE** *Capitol CL 568*	68		

ALTON EDWARDS Zimbabwean singer

Date	Title / Label	Peak Position	Weeks at No.1	Weeks in Top 40
9 Jan 82	**I JUST WANNA (SPEND SOME TIME WITH YOU)** *Streetwave STRA 1897*	20		6

DENNIS EDWARDS US singer

Date	Title / Label	Peak Position	Weeks at No.1	Weeks in Top 40
24 Mar 84	**DON'T LOOK ANY FURTHER** *Gordy TMG 1334* DENNIS EDWARDS FEATURING SIEDAH GARRETT	45		
20 Jun 87	**DON'T LOOK ANY FURTHER** *Gordy TMG 1334* DENNIS EDWARDS FEATURING SIEDAH GARRETT	55		

RUPIE EDWARDS Jamaican singer

Date	Title / Label	Peak Position	Weeks at No.1	Weeks in Top 40
23 Nov 74	**IRE FEELINGS (SKANGA)** *Cactus CT 38*	9		9
8 Feb 75	**LEGO SKANGA** *Cactus CT 51*	32		2

STEVE EDWARDS UK singer

Date	Title / Label	Peak Position	Weeks at No.1	Weeks in Top 40
15 Jul 06	**WORLD, HOLD ON (CHILDREN OF THE SKY)** *Defected DFTD132CDX* BOB SINCLAR FEATURING STEVE EDWARDS	9		9
30 Sep 06	**WATCH THE SUNRISE** *Positiva CDTIV243* AXWELL FEATURING STEVE EDWARDS	70		

TOMMY EDWARDS US singer

Date	Title / Label	Peak Position	Weeks at No.1	Weeks in Top 40
3 Oct 58	**IT'S ALL IN THE GAME** *MGM 989* ★	1	3	17
7 Aug 59	**MY MELANCHOLY BABY** *MGM 1020*	29		1

EELS US group

Date	Title / Label	Peak Position	Weeks at No.1	Weeks in Top 40
15 Feb 97	**NOVOCAINE FOR THE SOUL** *DreamWorks DRMCD 22174*	10		4
17 May 97	**SUSAN'S HOUSE** *DreamWorks DRMCD 22238*	9		4
13 Sep 97	**YOUR LUCKY DAY IN HELL** *DreamWorks DRMCD 22277*	35		1
26 Sep 98	**LAST STOP THIS TOWN** *DreamWorks DRMCD 22346*	23		1
12 Dec 98	**CANCER FOR THE CURE** *DreamWorks DRMCD 22373*	60		
26 Feb 00	**MR E'S BEAUTIFUL BLUES** *DreamWorks DRMCD 4509772*	11		2
24 Jun 00	**FLYSWATER** *DreamWorks DRMCD 4509462*	55		
22 Sep 01	**SOULJACKER PART 1** *DreamWorks 4508932*	30		1
28 May 05	**HEY MAN (NOW YOU'RE REALLY LIVING)** *Vagrant 9881879*	45		

EFUA UK singer

Date	Title / Label	Peak Position	Weeks at No.1	Weeks in Top 40
3 Jul 93	**SOMEWHERE** *Virgin VSCDT 1463*	42		

EGG UK group

Date	Title / Label	Peak Position	Weeks at No.1	Weeks in Top 40
30 Jan 99	**GETTING AWAY WITH IT** *Indochina ID 079CD*	58		
15 Jul 06	**WALKING AWAY** *Gusto CDGUS37* THE EGG VERSUS DAVID GUETTA	56		
19 Aug 06	**LOVE DON'T LET ME GO (WALKING AWAY)** *Gusto CDGUS42* DAVID GUETTA VS THE EGG	3		12

Silver-selling ○ · Gold-selling ● · Platinum-selling ✪ · US No.1 ★ · Peak Position · Weeks at No.1 · Weeks in Top 40

EGGS ON LEGS UK singer

Date	Title	Label	Peak Position	Weeks at No.1	Weeks in Top 40
23 Sep 95	COCK A DOODLE DO IT	Avex UKAVEXCD 18	42		

EGYPTIAN EMPIRE UK producer

Date	Title	Label	Peak Position	Weeks at No.1	Weeks in Top 40
24 Oct 92	THE HORN TRACK	ffrreedom TAB 115	61		

EIFFEL 65 Italian group

Date	Title	Label	Peak Position	Weeks at No.1	Weeks in Top 40
21 Aug 99	BLUE (DA BA DEE) (IMPORT)	Logic 74321688212	39		1
25 Sep 99	BLUE (DA BA DEE)	Eternal WEA 226CD1 ●	1	3	17
19 Feb 00	MOVE YOUR BODY	Eternal WEA 255CD1	3		7

808 STATE UK group

Date	Title	Label	Peak Position	Weeks at No.1	Weeks in Top 40
18 Nov 89	PACIFIC	ZTT ZANG 1	10		5
31 Mar 90	THE EXTENDED PLEASURE OF DANCE (EP)	ZTT ZANG 2T	56		
2 Jun 90	THE ONLY RHYME THAT BITES	ZTT ZANG 3	10		8
15 Sep 90	TUNES SPLITS THE ATOM	ZTT ZANG 6			
	MC TUNES VERSUS 808 STATE		18		5
10 Nov 90	CUBIK/OLYMPIC	ZTT ZANG 5	10		5
16 Feb 91	IN YER FACE	ZTT ZANG 14	9		5
27 Apr 91	OOOPS	ZTT ZANG 19			
	808 STATE FEATURING BJORK		42		
17 Aug 91	LIFT/OPEN YOUR MIND	ZTT ZANG 20	38		2
29 Aug 92	TIMB BOMB/NIMBUS	ZTT ZANG 33	59		
12 Dec 92	ONE IN TEN	ZTT ZANG 39			
	808 STATE Vs UB40		17		7
30 Jan 93	PLAN 9	ZTT ZANG 38CD	50		
26 Jun 93	10 X 10	ZTT ZANG 42CD	67		
13 Aug 94	BOMBADIN	ZTT ZANG 54CD	67		
29 Jun 96	BOND	ZTT ZANG 80CD	57		
8 Feb 97	LOPEZ	ZTT ZANG 87CD	20		1
16 May 98	PACIFIC (REMIX)/CUBIK	ZTT ZANG 98CD1	21		1
6 Mar 99	THE ONLY RHYME THAT BITES 99	ZTT 125CD			
	MC TUNES VERSUS 808 STATE		53		

18 WHEELER UK group

Date	Title	Label	Peak Position	Weeks at No.1	Weeks in Top 40
15 Mar 97	STAY	Creation CRESCD 249	59		

EIGHTH WONDER UK group

Date	Title	Label	Peak Position	Weeks at No.1	Weeks in Top 40
2 Nov 85	STAY WITH ME	CBS A 6594	65		
20 Feb 88	I'M NOT SCARED	CBS SCARE 1	7		9
25 Jun 88	CROSS MY HEART	CBS 6515527	13		6
1 Oct 88	BABY BABY	CBS BABE 1	65		

EIGHTIES MATCHBOX B-LINE DISASTER UK group

Date	Title	Label	Peak Position	Weeks at No.1	Weeks in Top 40
28 Sep 02	CELEBRATE YOUR MOTHER	Universal MCSTD 40296	66		
18 Jan 03	PSYCHOSIS SAFARI	Universal MCSTD 40308	26		1
24 May 03	CHICKEN	Island MCSXD 40317	30		1
24 Jan 04	MISTER MENTAL	Universal MCSXD 40353	25		1
10 Jul 04	I COULD BE AN ANGLE	Island MCSTD 40368	35		1
23 Oct 04	RISE OF THE EAGLES	Universal MCSTD 40382	40		1

EINSTEIN UK rapper

Date	Title	Label	Peak Position	Weeks at No.1	Weeks in Top 40
18 Nov 89	ANOTHER MONSTERJAM	ffrr F 116			
	SIMON HARRIS FEATURING EINSTEIN		65		
15 Dec 90	TURN IT UP	Swanyard SYD 9			
	TECHNOTRONIC FEATURING MELISSA & EINSTEIN		42		
24 Aug 96	THE POWER 96	Arista 74321398672			
	SNAP FEATURING EINSTEIN		42		

EL CHOMBO Panamanian singer

Date	Title	Label	Peak Position	Weeks at No.1	Weeks in Top 40
16 Dec 06	CHACARRON	Substance SUBS21CDX	20		2

EL COCO US group

Date	Title	Label	Peak Position	Weeks at No.1	Weeks in Top 40
14 Jan 78	COCOMOTION	Pye International 7N 25761	31		2

EL MARIACHI US producer

Date	Title	Label	Peak Position	Weeks at No.1	Weeks in Top 40
9 Nov 96	CUBA	ffrr FCD 286	38		1

EL PRESIDENTE UK group

Date	Title	Label	Peak Position	Weeks at No.1	Weeks in Top 40
14 May 05	100MPH	One 82876692142	37		1
6 Aug 05	WITHOUT YOU	One 82876710782	30		1
22 Oct 05	ROCKET	One 82876743032	48		
18 Feb 06	TURN THIS THING AROUND	One 82876781382	39		1

ELASTICA UK group

Date	Title	Label	Peak Position	Weeks at No.1	Weeks in Top 40
12 Feb 94	LINE UP	Deceptive BLUFF 004CD	20		1
22 Oct 94	CONNECTION	Deceptive BLUFF 010CD	17		2
25 Feb 95	WAKING UP	Deceptive BLUFF 011CD	13		3
24 Jun 00	MAD DOG	Deceptive BLUFF 077CD	44		

ELATE UK group

Date	Title	Label	Peak Position	Weeks at No.1	Weeks in Top 40
26 Jul 97	SOMEBODY LIKE YOU	VC Recordings VCRD 22	38		1

DONNIE ELBERT US singer

Date	Title	Label	Peak Position	Weeks at No.1	Weeks in Top 40
8 Jan 72	WHERE DID OUR LOVE GO	London HL 10352	8		8
26 Feb 72	I CAN'T HELP MYSELF	Avco 6105 009	11		9
29 Apr 72	LITTLE PIECE OF LEATHER	London HL 10370	27		8

ELBOW UK group

Date	Title	Label	Peak Position	Weeks at No.1	Weeks in Top 40
5 May 01	RED	V2 VVR 5016158	36		1
21 Jul 01	POWDER BLUE	V2 VVR 5016163	41		
20 Oct 01	NEWBORN	V2 VVR 5016173	42		
16 Feb 02	ASLEEP IN THE BACK	V2 VVR 5018703	19		1
16 Aug 03	FALLEN ANGEL	V2 VVR 5021808	19		1
8 Nov 03	FUGITIVE MOTEL	V2 VVR 5021828	44		
6 Mar 04	NOT A JOB	V2 VVR 5024678	26		1
10 Sep 05	FORGET MYSELF	V2 VVR5032548	22		1
19 Nov 05	LEADERS OF THE FREE WORLD	V2 VVR5035628	53		
22 Mar 08	GROUNDS FOR DIVORCE	Fiction 1761656	19		2

ELECTRA UK group

Date	Title	Label	Peak Position	Weeks at No.1	Weeks in Top 40
6 Aug 88	JIBARO	ffrr F 9	54		
30 Dec 89	IT'S YOUR DESTINY/AUTUMN LOVE	London F 121	51		

ELECTRAFIXION UK group

Date	Title	Label	Peak Position	Weeks at No.1	Weeks in Top 40
19 Nov 94	ZEPHYR	WEA YZ 865CD	47		
9 Sep 95	LOWDOWN	WEA YZ 977CD	54		
4 Nov 95	NEVER	Spacejunk 022CD	58		
16 Mar 96	SISTER PAIN	Spacejunk 037CD	27		1

ELECTRASY UK group

Date	Title	Label	Peak Position	Weeks at No.1	Weeks in Top 40
13 Jun 98	LOST IN SPACE	MCA MCSTD 40171	60		
5 Sep 98	MORNING AFTERGLOW	MCA MCSTD 40184	19		3
28 Nov 98	BEST FRIEND'S GIRL	MCA MCSXD 40195	41		

ELECTRIBE 101 UK group

Date	Title	Label	Peak Position	Weeks at No.1	Weeks in Top 40
28 Oct 89	TELL ME WHEN THE FEVER ENDED	Mercury MER 310	32		2
24 Feb 90	TALKING WITH MYSELF	Mercury MER 316	23		4
22 Sep 90	YOU'RE WALKING	Mercury MER 328	50		
10 Oct 98	TALKING WITH MYSELF '98 (REMIX)	Manifesto FESDD 49	39		1

ELECTRIC LIGHT ORCHESTRA UK group

Date	Title	Label	Peak Position	Weeks at No.1	Weeks in Top 40
29 Jul 72	10538 OVERTURE	Harvest HAR 5053	9		7
27 Jan 73	ROLL OVER BEETHOVEN	Harvest HAR 5063	6		8
6 Oct 73	SHOWDOWN	Harvest HAR 5077	12		8
9 Mar 74	MA-MA-MA-BELLE	Warner Brothers K 16349	22		5
10 Jan 76	EVIL WOMAN	Jet 764	10		7
3 Jul 76	STRANGE MAGIC	Jet 779	38		1
13 Nov 76	LIVIN' THING	Jet UP 36184 ○	4		11
19 Feb 77	ROCKARIA!	Jet UP 36209	9		9
21 May 77	TELEPHONE LINE	Jet UP 36254	8		9
29 Oct 77	TURN TO STONE	Jet UP 36313	18		11
28 Jan 78	MR BLUE SKY	Jet UP 36342 ○	6		11
10 Jun 78	WILD WEST HERO	Jet 109 ○	6		10
7 Oct 78	SWEET TALKIN' WOMAN	Jet 121 ○	6		8
9 Dec 78	ELO EP	Jet ELO 1	34		5
19 May 79	SHINE A LITTLE LOVE	Jet 144 ○	6		8

Key: Silver-selling ● Gold-selling ● Platinum-selling ● US No.1 ★ — Peak Position · Weeks at No.1 · Weeks in Top 40

Date	Title / Label	Peak Position	Weeks at No.1	Weeks in Top 40
21 Jul 79	THE DIARY OF HORACE WIMP *Jet 150*	8		7
1 Sep 79	DON'T BRING ME DOWN *Jet 153*	3		8
17 Nov 79	CONFUSION/LAST TRAIN TO LONDON *Jet 166*	8		8
24 May 80	I'M ALIVE *Jet 179*	20		6
21 Jun 80	XANADU *Jet 185* OLIVIA NEWTON-JOHN & ELECTRIC LIGHT ORCHESTRA	1	2	10
2 Aug 80	ALL OVER THE WORLD *Jet 195*	11		6
22 Nov 80	DON'T WALK AWAY *Jet 7004*	21		8
1 Aug 81	HOLD ON TIGHT *Jet 7011*	4		11
24 Oct 81	TWILIGHT *Jet 7015*	30		4
9 Jan 82	TICKET TO THE MOON/HERE IS THE NEWS *Jet 7018*	24		5
18 Jun 83	ROCK 'N' ROLL IS KING *Jet A 3500*	13		7
3 Sep 83	SECRET MESSAGES *Jet A 3720*	48		
1 Mar 86	CALLING AMERICA *Epic A 6844*	28		5
11 May 91	HONEST MEN *Telstar ELO 100* ELECTRIC LIGHT ORCHESTRA PART 2	60		

ELECTRIC PRUNES US group

Date	Title / Label	Peak Position	Weeks at No.1	Weeks in Top 40
9 Feb 67	I HAD TOO MUCH TO DREAM LAST NIGHT *Reprise RS 20532*	49		
11 May 67	GET ME TO THE WORLD ON TIME *Reprise RS 20564*	42		

ELECTRIC SIX US group

Date	Title / Label	Peak Position	Weeks at No.1	Weeks in Top 40
18 Jan 03	DANGER HIGH VOLTAGE *XL Recordings XLS 151CD*	2		7
14 Jun 03	GAY BAR *XL Recordings XLS 158CD*	5		5
25 Oct 03	DANCE COMMANDER *XL Recordings XLS 170CD*	40		1
25 Dec 04	RADIO GAGA *WEA WEA381CD1*	21		3

ELECTRIC SOFT PARADE UK group

Date	Title / Label	Peak Position	Weeks at No.1	Weeks in Top 40
4 Aug 01	EMPTY AT THE END/SUMATRAN *DB 0067JC* SOFT PARADE	65		
10 Nov 01	THERE'S A SILENCE *DB 007CD7JC*	52		
16 Mar 02	SILENT TO THE DARK II *DB DB008 CDE7*	23		1
1 Jun 02	EMPTY AT THE END *DB DB009 ECD7*	39		1

ELECTRIQUE BOUTIQUE UK/French production group

Date	Title / Label	Peak Position	Weeks at No.1	Weeks in Top 40
26 Aug 00	REVELATION *Data 14CDS*	37		1

ELECTRONIC UK group

Date	Title / Label	Peak Position	Weeks at No.1	Weeks in Top 40
16 Dec 89	GETTING AWAY WITH IT *Factory FAC 2577*	12		7
27 Apr 91	GET THE MESSAGE *Factory FAC 2877*	8		6
21 Sep 91	FEEL EVERY BEAT *Factory FAC 3287*	39		2
4 Jul 92	DISAPPOINTED *Parlophone R 6311*	6		4
6 Jul 96	FORBIDDEN CITY *Parlophone CDR 6436*	14		2
28 Sep 96	FOR YOU *Parlophone CDR 6445*	16		1
15 Feb 97	SECOND NATURE *Parlophone CDR 6455*	35		1
24 Apr 99	VIVID *Parlophone CDR 6514*	17		1

ELECTRONICAS Dutch instrumental group

Date	Title / Label	Peak Position	Weeks at No.1	Weeks in Top 40
19 Sep 81	ORIGINAL BIRD DANCE *Polydor POSP 360*	22		5

ELECTROSET UK production group

Date	Title / Label	Peak Position	Weeks at No.1	Weeks in Top 40
21 Nov 92	HOW DOES IT FEEL *ffrr F 203*	27		2
15 Jul 95	SENSATION *ffrreedom TABCD 231*	69		

ELEGANTS US group

Date	Title / Label	Peak Position	Weeks at No.1	Weeks in Top 40
26 Sep 58	LITTLE STAR *HMV POP 520* ★	25		2

ELEMENT FOUR UK group

Date	Title / Label	Peak Position	Weeks at No.1	Weeks in Top 40
9 Sep 00	*BIG BROTHER* UK TV THEME *Channel 4 Music C4M 00072*	4		6
4 Aug 01	*BIG BROTHER* UK TV THEME *Channel 4 Music C4M 00072*	63		

ELEPHANT MAN Jamaican singer

Date	Title / Label	Peak Position	Weeks at No.1	Weeks in Top 40
22 Nov 03	PON DE RIVER, PON DE BANK *Atlantic AT 0168CD*	29		1
4 Sep 04	JOOK GAL *VP VPCD6416*	41		

ELEVATION UK production duo

Date	Title / Label	Peak Position	Weeks at No.1	Weeks in Top 40
23 May 92	CAN YOU FEEL IT *Nova Mute 12NOMU 3*	62		

ELEVATOR SUITE UK production trio

Date	Title / Label	Peak Position	Weeks at No.1	Weeks in Top 40
12 Aug 00	BACK AROUND *Infectious INFECT 85CDS*	71		

ELEVATORMAN UK production group

Date	Title / Label	Peak Position	Weeks at No.1	Weeks in Top 40
14 Jan 95	FUNK AND DRIVE *Wired 211*	37		2
1 Jul 95	FIRED UP *Wired 216*	44		

ELGINS US group

Date	Title / Label	Peak Position	Weeks at No.1	Weeks in Top 40
1 May 71	HEAVEN MUST HAVE SENT YOU *Tamla Motown TMG 771*	3		12
9 Oct 71	PUT YOURSELF IN MY PLACE *Tamla Motown TMG 787*	28		6

ELIAS & HIS ZIGZAG JIVE FLUTES

South African instrumental group

Date	Title / Label	Peak Position	Weeks at No.1	Weeks in Top 40
25 Apr 58	TOM HARK *Columbia DB 4109*	2		14

YVONNE ELLIMAN US singer

Date	Title / Label	Peak Position	Weeks at No.1	Weeks in Top 40
29 Jan 72	I DON'T KNOW HOW TO LOVE HIM *MCA MMKS 5077*	47		
6 Nov 76	LOVE ME *RSO 2090 205*	6		11
7 May 77	HELLO STRANGER *RSO 2090 236*	26		4
13 Aug 77	I CAN'T GET YOU OUT OF MY MIND *RSO 2090 251*	17		11
6 May 78	IF I CAN'T HAVE YOU *RSO 2090 266* ★	4		9

DUKE ELLINGTON US orchestra leader

Date	Title / Label	Peak Position	Weeks at No.1	Weeks in Top 40
5 Mar 54	SKIN DEEP *Philips PB 243* DUKE ELLINGTON WITH LOUIS BELLSON (DRUMS)	7		4

LANCE ELLINGTON UK singer

Date	Title / Label	Peak Position	Weeks at No.1	Weeks in Top 40
21 Aug 93	LONELY (HAVE WE LOST OUR LOVE) *RCA 74321158332*	57		

RAY ELLINGTON UK band leader

Date	Title / Label	Peak Position	Weeks at No.1	Weeks in Top 40
15 Nov 62	THE MADISON *Ember S 102*	36		1

ELLIOT MINOR UK group

Date	Title / Label	Peak Position	Weeks at No.1	Weeks in Top 40
21 Apr 07	PARALLEL WORLDS *Repossession REPO5CDS*	31		1
18 Aug 07	JESSICA *Repossession REPO7CDS*	19		1
10 Nov 07	WHITE ONE IS EVIL *Warner Brothers WEA432CD2*	27		1
9 Feb 08	STILL FIGURING OUT *Repossession WEA468CD*	17		2

BERN ELLIOTT & THE FENMEN UK group

Date	Title / Label	Peak Position	Weeks at No.1	Weeks in Top 40
21 Nov 63	MONEY *Decca F 11770*	14		10
19 Mar 64	NEW ORLEANS *Decca F 11852*	24		6

MISSY 'MISDEMEANOUR' ELLIOTT US rapper

Date	Title / Label	Peak Position	Weeks at No.1	Weeks in Top 40
30 Aug 97	THE RAIN (SUPA DUPA FLY) *East West E 3919CD*	16		2
29 Nov 97	SOCK IT 2 ME *East West E 3890CD*	33		1
25 Apr 98	BEEP ME 911 *East West E 3859CD*	14		2
22 Aug 98	HIT 'EM WIT DA HEE *East West E 3824CD1* MISSY 'MISDEMEANOR' ELLIOTT FEATURING LIL' KIM	25		1
22 Aug 98	MAKE IT HOT *East West E 3821CD* NICOLE FEATURING MISSY 'MISDEMEANOR' ELLIOTT	22		2
26 Sep 98	I WANT YOU BACK *Virgin VSCDT 1716* MELANIE B FEATURING MISSY 'MISDEMEANOR' ELLIOTT	1	1	6
21 Nov 98	5 MINUTES *Elektra E 3803CD* LIL' MO FEATURING MISSY 'MISDEMEANOR' ELLIOTT	72		
13 Mar 99	HERE WE COME *Virgin DINSD 179* TIMBALAND/MISSY ELLIOTT & MAGOO	43		
25 Sep 99	ALL N MY GRILL *Elektra E 3742CD* MISSY 'MISDEMEANOR' ELLIOTT FEATURING MC SOLAAR	20		2
22 Jan 00	HOT BOYZ *Elektra E 7002CD* MISSY MISDEMEANOR ELLIOTT FEATURING NAS, EVE & Q-TIP	18		2
28 Apr 01	GET UR FREAK ON *Elektra E 7206CD*	4		8
18 Aug 01	ONE MINUTE MAN *The Gold Mind/Elektra E 7245CD* MISSY ELLIOTT FEATURING LUDACRIS	10		4
13 Oct 01	SUPERFREAKON *Elektra 7559672550*	72		
22 Dec 01	SON OF A GUN (BETCHA THINK THIS SONG IS ABOUT YOU) *Virgin VUSCDX 232* JANET JACKSON WITH CARLY SIMON FEATURING MISSY ELLIOTT	13		5

Key: ○ Silver-selling · ● Gold-selling · ⊛ Platinum-selling · ★ US No.1 · Peak Position · Weeks at No.1 · Weeks in Top 40

Date	Title / Label	Peak Position	Weeks at No.1	Weeks in Top 40
6 Apr 02	**4 MY PEOPLE** *Elektra E 7286CD*	5		9
16 Nov 02	**WORK IT** *Elektra E 7344CD*	6		6
22 Mar 03	**GOSSIP FOLKS** *Elektra E 7380CD* MISSY ELLIOTT FEATURING LUDACRIS	9		7
22 Nov 03	**PASS THAT DUTCH** *Elektra E 7509CD*	10		4
13 Mar 04	**COP THAT SHIT** *Unique Corp TIMBACD001* TIMBALAND/MAGOO/MISSY ELLIOTT	22		2
3 Apr 04	**I'M REALLY HOT** *Elektra E 7552CD*	22		2
17 Jul 04	**PUSH** *Def Jam 9862837* GHOSTFACE FEATURING MISSY ELLIOTT	34		1
13 Nov 04	**CAR WASH** *DreamWorks 9864630* CHRISTINA AGUILERA & MISSY ELLIOTT	4		10
19 Mar 05	**TURN DA LIGHTS OFF** *Atlantic AT0200CD* TWEET FEATURING MISSY ELLIOTT	29		1
23 Apr 05	**1 2 STEP** *LaFace 82876688342* CIARA FEATURING MISSY ELLIOTT	3		8
2 Jul 05	**LOSE CONTROL** *Atlantic AT0209CD*	7		9
8 Oct 05	**TEARY EYED** *Atlantic AT0215CD*	47		
26 Aug 06	**WE RUN THIS** *Atlantic AT0255CD*	38		1

JOEY B ELLIS US rapper

Date	Title / Label	Peak Position	Weeks at No.1	Weeks in Top 40
16 Feb 91	**GO FOR IT (HEART AND SOUL)** *Capitol CL 601* ROCKY V FEATURING JOEY B ELLIS & TYNETTA HARE	20		5
18 May 91	**THOUGHT U WERE THE ONE FOR ME** *Capitol CL 614*	58		

SHIRLEY ELLIS US singer

Date	Title / Label	Peak Position	Weeks at No.1	Weeks in Top 40
6 May 65	**THE CLAPPING SONG** *London HLR 9961*	6		12
8 Jul 78	**THE CLAPPING SONG (EP)** *MCA MCEP 1*	59		

SOPHIE ELLIS-BEXTOR UK singer

Date	Title / Label	Peak Position	Weeks at No.1	Weeks in Top 40
25 Aug 01	**TAKE ME HOME (A GIRL LIKE ME)** *Polydor 5872312* ○	2		8
15 Dec 01	**MURDER ON THE DANCEFLOOR** *Polydor 5704942*	2		13
22 Jun 02	**GET OVER YOU/MOVE THIS MOUNTAIN** *Polydor 5708342*	3		6
16 Nov 02	**MUSIC GETS THE BEST OF ME** *Polydor 0659232*	14		2
25 Oct 03	**MIXED UP WORLD** *Polydor 9812108*	7		4
10 Jan 04	**I WON'T CHANGE YOU** *Polydor 9815124*	9		4
10 Feb 07	**CATCH YOU** *Fascination 1724021*	8		6
26 May 07	**ME AND MY IMAGINATION** *Fascination 1733077*	23		2
25 Aug 07	**TODAY THE SUN'S ON US** *Fascination 1741966*	64		

ELLIS, BEGGS & HOWARD UK group

Date	Title / Label	Peak Position	Weeks at No.1	Weeks in Top 40
2 Jul 88	**BIG BUBBLES, NO TROUBLES** *RCA PB 42089*	59		
11 Mar 89	**BIG BUBBLES, NO TROUBLES** *RCA PB 42089*	41		

JENNIFER ELLISON UK singer/actress

Date	Title / Label	Peak Position	Weeks at No.1	Weeks in Top 40
28 Jun 03	**BABY I DON'T CARE** *East West EW 268CD*	6		7
7 Aug 04	**BYE BYE BOY** *Sky-rocket CDSKYCON1*	13		3

ELWOOD US rapper

Date	Title / Label	Peak Position	Weeks at No.1	Weeks in Top 40
26 Aug 00	**SUNDOWN** *Palm Pictures PPCD 70342*	72		

EMBRACE UK group

Date	Title / Label	Peak Position	Weeks at No.1	Weeks in Top 40
17 May 97	**FIREWORKS EP** *Hut HUTCD 84*	34		1
19 Jul 97	**ONE BIG FAMILY EP** *Hut HUTCD 86*	21		1
8 Nov 97	**ALL YOU GOOD GOOD PEOPLE EP** *Hut HUTCD 90*	8		2
6 Jun 98	**COME BACK TO WHAT YOU KNOW** *Hut HUTCD 93*	6		3
29 Aug 98	**MY WEAKNESS IS NONE OF YOUR BUSINESS** *Hut HUTCD 103*	9		1
13 Nov 99	**HOOLIGAN** *Hut HUTCD 123*	18		1
25 Mar 00	**YOU'RE NOT ALONE** *Hut HUTCD 126*	14		2
10 Jun 00	**SAVE ME** *Hut HUTCD 133*	29		1
19 Aug 00	**I WOULDN'T WANNA HAPPEN TO YOU** *Hut HUTDX 137*	23		1
1 Sep 01	**WONDER** *Hut HUTDX 142*	14		2
17 Nov 01	**MAKE IT LAST** *Hut HUTCD 144*	35		1
11 Sep 04	**GRAVITY** *Independiente ISOM87SMS*	7		5
27 Nov 04	**ASHES** *Independiente ISOM89SMS*	11		3
26 Feb 05	**LOOKING AS YOU ARE** *Independiente ISOM91SMS*	11		2
11 Jun 05	**A GLORIOUS DAY** *Independiente ISOM94SMS*	28		1
1 Apr 06	**NATURE'S LAW** *Independiente ISOM103SMS*	2		7
10 Jun 06	**WORLD AT YOUR FEET** *Independiente ISOM107SMS*	3		5
23 Sep 06	**TARGET** *Independiente ISOM110MSST*	29		1
16 Dec 06	**I CAN'T COME DOWN** *Independiente ISOM115MS*	54		

KEITH EMERSON UK keyboard player

Date	Title / Label	Peak Position	Weeks at No.1	Weeks in Top 40
10 Apr 76	**HONKY TONK TRAIN BLUES** *Manticore K 13513*	21		4

EMERSON, LAKE & PALMER UK group

Date	Title / Label	Peak Position	Weeks at No.1	Weeks in Top 40
4 Jun 77	**FANFARE FOR THE COMMON MAN** *Atlantic K 10946* ○	2		12

DICK EMERY UK comedian

Date	Title / Label	Peak Position	Weeks at No.1	Weeks in Top 40
26 Feb 69	**IF YOU LOVE HER** *Pye 7N 17644*	32		3
13 Jan 73	**YOU ARE AWFUL** *Pye 7N 45202*	43		

EMF UK group

Date	Title / Label	Peak Position	Weeks at No.1	Weeks in Top 40
3 Nov 90	**UNBELIEVABLE** *Parlophone R 6273* ○ ★	3		10
2 Feb 91	**I BELIEVE** *Parlophone R 6279*	6		5
27 Apr 91	**CHILDREN** *Parlophone R 6288*	19		4
31 Aug 91	**LIES** *Parlophone R 6295*	28		2
2 May 92	**UNEXPLAINED EP** *Parlophone SGE 2026*	18		2
19 Sep 92	**THEY'RE HERE** *Parlophone R 6321*	29		2
21 Nov 92	**IT'S YOU** *Parlophone R 6327*	23		2
25 Feb 95	**PERFECT DAY** *Parlophone CDRS 6401*	27		1
8 Jul 95	**I'M A BELIEVER** *Parlophone CDR 6412* EMF/REEVES & MORTIMER	3		5
28 Oct 95	**AFRO KING** *Parlophone CDRS 6416*	51		

EMILIA Swedish singer

Date	Title / Label	Peak Position	Weeks at No.1	Weeks in Top 40
12 Dec 98	**BIG BIG WORLD** *Universal UMD 87190* ○	5		11
1 May 99	**GOOD SIGN** *Universal UMD 87206*	54		

EMINEM US rapper

Date	Title / Label	Peak Position	Weeks at No.1	Weeks in Top 40
10 Apr 99	**MY NAME IS** *Interscope IND 95639*	2		8
14 Aug 99	**GUILTY CONSCIENCE** *Interscope IND 4971282* EMINEM FEATURING DR DRE	5		6
10 Jun 00	**FORGOT ABOUT DRE** *Interscope 4973422* DR DRE FEATURING EMINEM	7		6
8 Jul 00	**THE REAL SLIM SHADY** *Interscope 4973792* ○	1	1	13
14 Oct 00	**THE WAY I AM** *Interscope 4974252*	8		7
16 Dec 00	**STAN** *Interscope 4974702* ⊛	1	1	14
1 Sep 01	**SCARY MOVIES** *Mole UK MOLEUK 045* BAD MEETS EVIL FEATURING EMINEM & ROCE DA 5' 9	63		
1 Jun 02	**WITHOUT ME** *Interscope 4977282* ●	1	1	13
28 Sep 02	**CLEANIN' OUT MY CLOSET** *Interscope 4973942*	4		9
14 Dec 02	**LOSE YOURSELF** *Interscope 4978282* ○ ★	1	1	18
15 Mar 03	**SING FOR THE MOMENT** *Interscope 4978612*	6		6
19 Jul 03	**BUSINESS** *Interscope 9809382*	6		6
14 Feb 04	**THE REAL SLIM SHADY** *Interscope 4973792*	72		
13 Nov 04	**JUST LOSE IT** *Interscope 2103242*	1	1	10
12 Feb 05	**LIKE TOY SOLDIERS** *Aftermath 2103964*	1	1	7
14 May 05	**MOCKINGBIRD** *Interscope9882073*	4		7
6 Aug 05	**ASS LIKE THAT** *Interscope 9883904*	4		6
31 Dec 05	**WHEN I'M GONE** *Interscope 9889581*	5		7
18 Nov 06	**SMACK THAT** *Universal 1714412* AKON FEATURING EMINEM	1	1	16

EMMA UK singer

Date	Title / Label	Peak Position	Weeks at No.1	Weeks in Top 40
28 Apr 90	**GIVE A LITTLE LOVE BACK TO THE WORLD** *Big Wave BWR 33*	33		3

EMMIE UK singer

Date	Title / Label	Peak Position	Weeks at No.1	Weeks in Top 40
23 Jan 99	**MORE THAN THIS** *Indirect FESCD 52*	5		5

AN EMOTIONAL FISH Irish group

Date	Title / Label	Peak Position	Weeks at No.1	Weeks in Top 40
23 Jun 90	**CELEBRATE** *East West YZ 489*	46		

EMOTIONS US group

Date	Title / Label	Peak Position	Weeks at No.1	Weeks in Top 40
10 Sep 77	**BEST OF MY LOVE** *CBS 5555* ○ ★	4		10
24 Dec 77	**I DON'T WANNA TO LOSE YOUR LOVE** *CBS 5819*	40		3
12 May 79	**BOOGIE WONDERLAND** *CBS 7292* EARTH WIND & FIRE WITH THE EMOTIONS ●	4		11

ALEC EMPIRE German producer

Date	Title / Label	Peak Position	Weeks at No.1	Weeks in Top 40
13 Apr 02	**ADDICTED TO YOU** *Digital Empire DHRMCD 38CD1*	64		

EMPIRION UK production group

Date	Title / Label	Peak Position	Weeks at No.1	Weeks in Top 40
6 Jul 96	**NARCOTIC INFLUENCE** *XL Recordings XLS 72CD*	64		
21 Jun 97	**BETA** *XL Recordings XLS 77CD*	75		

EN VOGUE US group

Date	Title / Label	Peak Position	Weeks at No.1	Weeks in Top 40
5 May 90	**HOLD ON** *East West America 7908*	5		9
21 Jul 90	**LIES** *East West America 7893*	44		
4 Apr 92	**MY LOVIN'** *East West America A 8578*	4		8
15 Aug 92	**GIVING HIM SOMETHING HE CAN FEEL** *East West America A 8524*	44		
7 Nov 92	**FREE YOUR MIND/GIVING HIM SOMETHING HE CAN FEEL** *East West America A 8524*	16		5
16 Jan 93	**GIVE IT UP TURN IT LOOSE** *East West America A 8445CD*	22		2
10 Apr 93	**LOVE DON'T LOVE YOU** *East West America A 8424CD*	64		
9 Oct 93	**RUNAWAY LOVE** *East West America A 8359CD*	36		2
19 Mar 94	**WHATTA MAN** *ffrr FCD 222* SALT-N-PEPA WITH EN VOGUE	7		8
11 Jan 97	**DON'T LET GO (LOVE)** *East West A 3976CD* ○	5		13
14 Jun 97	**WHATEVER** *East West E 3642CD*	14		3
6 Sep 97	**TOO GONE, TOO LONG** *East West E 3908CD*	20		1
28 Nov 98	**HOLD ON (REMIX)** *East West E 3796CD*	53		
1 Jul 00	**RIDDLE** *Elektra E7053CD*	33		1

EN-CORE UK producer

Date	Title / Label	Peak Position	Weeks at No.1	Weeks in Top 40
9 Sep 00	**COOCHY COO** *VC Recordings VCRD 72* EN-CORE FEATURING STEPHEN EMMANUEL & ESKA	32		1

ENCORE UK producer

Date	Title / Label	Peak Position	Weeks at No.1	Weeks in Top 40
14 Feb 98	**LE DISC JOCKEY** *Sum CDSUM 2*	12		2

ENEMY UK group

Date	Title / Label	Peak Position	Weeks at No.1	Weeks in Top 40
21 Apr 07	**AWAY FROM HERE** *Warner Brothers WEA419CD*	8		6
30 Jun 07	**HAD ENOUGH** *Warner Brothers WEA423CD*	4		5
29 Sep 07	**YOU'RE NOT ALONE** *Warner Brothers WEA427CD*	18		1
15 Dec 07	**WE'LL LIVE AND DIE IN THESE TOWNS** *Warner Brothers WEA437CD*	21		1
29 Mar 08	**THIS SONG IS ABOUT YOU** *Warner Brothers WEA442CD*	41		

ENERGISE UK group

Date	Title / Label	Peak Position	Weeks at No.1	Weeks in Top 40
16 Feb 91	**REPORT TO THE DANCEFLOOR** *Network NWKT 16*	69		

ENERGY 52 German DJ/producer

Date	Title / Label	Peak Position	Weeks at No.1	Weeks in Top 40
8 Mar 97	**CAFÉ DEL MAR** *Hooj Choons HOOJCD 51*	51		
25 Jul 98	**CAFE DEL MAR '98 (REMIX)** *Hooj Choons HOOJ 64CD*	12		4
12 Oct 02	**CAFÉ DEL MAR (2ND REMIX)** *Lost Language LOST 019CD*	24		2

ENERGY ORCHARD Irish group

Date	Title / Label	Peak Position	Weeks at No.1	Weeks in Top 40
27 Jan 90	**BELFAST** *MCA 1392*	52		
7 Apr 90	**SAILORTOWN** *MCA 1402*	73		

HARRY ENFIELD UK comedian

Date	Title / Label	Peak Position	Weeks at No.1	Weeks in Top 40
7 May 88	**LOADSAMONEY (DOIN' UP THE HOUSE)** *Mercury DOSH 1*	4		6

ENGINEERS UK group

Date	Title / Label	Peak Position	Weeks at No.1	Weeks in Top 40
5 Mar 05	**FORGIVENESS** *Echo ECSCD159*	48		

ENGLAND DAN & JOHN FORD COLEY US duo

Date	Title / Label	Peak Position	Weeks at No.1	Weeks in Top 40
25 Sep 76	**I'D REALLY LOVE TO SEE YOU TONIGHT** *Atlantic K 10810*	26		5
23 Jun 79	**LOVE IS THE ANSWER** *Big Tree K 11296*	45		

ENGLAND BOYS UK group

Date	Title / Label	Peak Position	Weeks at No.1	Weeks in Top 40
8 Jun 02	**GO ENGLAND** *Mercury 5829592*	26		1

ENGLAND SISTERS US group

Date	Title / Label	Peak Position	Weeks at No.1	Weeks in Top 40
17 Mar 60	**HEARTBEAT** *HMV POP 710*	33		1

ENGLAND SUPPORTERS' BAND

UK soccer supporters' band

Date	Title / Label	Peak Position	Weeks at No.1	Weeks in Top 40
27 Jun 98	**THE GREAT ESCAPE** *V2 VVR 5002163*	46		
24 Jun 00	**THE GREAT ESCAPE 2000** *V2 VVR 5014293*	26		1

ENGLAND UNITED Amalgamation of UK stars

Date	Title / Label	Peak Position	Weeks at No.1	Weeks in Top 40
13 Jun 98	**(HOW DOES IT FEEL TO BE) ON TOP OF THE WORLD?** *London LONCD 414*	9		3

ENGLAND WORLD CUP SQUAD

The England football team

Date	Title / Label	Peak Position	Weeks at No.1	Weeks in Top 40
18 Apr 70	**BACK HOME** *Pye 7N 17920*	1	3	14
10 Apr 82	**THIS TIME (WE'LL GET IT RIGHT)/ENGLAND WE'LL FLY THE FLAG** *England ER 1*	2		9
19 Apr 86	**WE'VE GOT THE WHOLE WORLD AT OUR FEET/WHEN WE ARE FAR FROM HOME** *Columbia DB 9128*	66		
21 May 88	**ALL THE WAY** *MCA GOAL 1* ENGLAND FOOTBALL TEAM & THE SOUND OF STOCK, AITKEN & WATERMAN	64		
2 Jun 90	**WORLD IN MOTION** *Factory/MCA FAC 2937* ENGLANDNEWORDER ●	1	2	10
15 Jun 02	**WORLD IN MOTION** *London NUOCD 12* ENGLANDNEWORDER	43		

ENGLAND'S BARMY ARMY UK group

Date	Title / Label	Peak Position	Weeks at No.1	Weeks in Top 40
12 Jun 99	**COME ON ENGLAND!** *Wildstar CDWILD 20*	45		

KIM ENGLISH US singer

Date	Title / Label	Peak Position	Weeks at No.1	Weeks in Top 40
23 Jul 94	**NITE LIFE** *Hi-Life PZCD 323*	35		1
4 Mar 95	**TIME FOR LOVE** *Hi-Life HICD 8*	48		
9 Sep 95	**I KNOW A PLACE** *Hi-Life 5798072*	52		
30 Nov 96	**NITE LIFE (REMIX)** *Hi-Life 5755332*	35		1
26 Apr 97	**SUPERNATURAL** *Hi-Life 5736972*	50		

SCOTT ENGLISH US singer

Date	Title / Label	Peak Position	Weeks at No.1	Weeks in Top 40
9 Oct 71	**BRANDY** *Horse HOSS 7*	12		8

ENIGMA UK group

Date	Title / Label	Peak Position	Weeks at No.1	Weeks in Top 40
23 May 81	**AIN'T NO STOPPING** *Creole CR 9*	11		6
8 Aug 81	**I LOVE MUSIC** *Creole CR 14*	25		6
15 Dec 90	**SADNESS PART 1** *Virgin International DINS 101* ○	1	1	11
30 Mar 91	**MEA CULPA PART II** *Virgin International DINS 104*	55		
10 Aug 91	**PRINCIPLES OF LUST** *Virgin International DINS 110*	59		
11 Jan 92	**THE RIVERS OF BELIEF** *Virgin International DINS 112*	68		
29 Jan 94	**RETURN TO INNOCENCE** *Virgin International DINSD 123* ○	3		12
14 May 94	**THE EYES OF TRUTH** *Virgin International DINSD 126*	21		2
20 Aug 94	**AGE OF LONELINESS** *Virgin International DINSD 135*	21		3
25 Jan 97	**BEYOND THE INVISIBLE** *Virgin International DINSD 155*	26		1
19 Apr 97	**TNT FOR THE BRAIN** *Virgin International DINSD 161*	60		

ENTER SHIKARI UK group

Date	Title / Label	Peak Position	Weeks at No.1	Weeks in Top 40
10 Mar 07	**ANYTHING CAN HAPPEN IN THE NEXT HALF HOUR** *Ambush Reality AMBR003CD*	27		1
30 Jun 07	**JONNY SNIPER** *Ambush Reality AMBR004CD*	75		

ENVY & OTHER SINS UK group

Date	Title / Label	Peak Position	Weeks at No.1	Weeks in Top 40
15 Mar 08	**HIGHNESS** *A&M 1762714*	65		

ENYA Irish singer/pianist

Date	Title / Label	Peak Position	Weeks at No.1	Weeks in Top 40
15 Oct 88	**ORINOCO FLOW** *WEA YZ 312* ○	1	3	8
24 Dec 88	**EVENING FALLS...** *WEA YZ 356*	20		3
10 Jun 89	**STORMS IN AFRICA (PART II)** *WEA YZ 368*	41		
19 Oct 91	**CARIBBEAN BLUE** *WEA YZ 604*	13		6
7 Dec 91	**HOW CAN I KEEP FROM SINGING** *WEA YZ 365*	32		3
1 Aug 92	**BOOK OF DAYS** *WEA YZ 640*	10		4

Silver-selling · Gold-selling · Platinum-selling · US No.1 ★ · Peak Position · Weeks at No.1 · Weeks in Top 40

Date	Title / Label	Peak Position	Weeks at No.1	Weeks in Top 40
14 Nov 92	**THE CELTS** *WEA YZ 705*	29		2
18 Nov 95	**ANYWHERE IS** *WEA 023CD*	7		9
7 Dec 96	**ON MY WAY HOME** *WEA 047CD*	26		1
13 Dec 97	**ONLY IF…** *WEA 143CD*	43		
25 Nov 00	**ONLY TIME** *WEA 316CD*	32		2
31 Mar 01	**WILD CHILD** *WEA 324CD*	72		
2 Feb 02	**MAY IT BE** *WEA W 578CD*	50		
5 Jun 04	**I DON'T WANNA KNOW (IMPORT)** *Universal 9862372PMI* MARIO WINANS FEATURING ENYA & P DIDDY	71		
12 Jun 04	**I DON'T WANNA KNOW** *Bad Boy MCSTD40369* MARIO WINANS FEATURING ENYA & P DIDDY	1	1	12
11 Sep 04	**YOU SHOULD READILY KNOW** *Relentless RELCD9* PIRATES FEATURING ENYA, SHOLA AMA, NAILA BOSS & ISHANI	8		6
17 Dec 05	**AMARANTINE** *Warner Brothers WEA397CD1*	53		

EON UK producer

Date	Title / Label	Peak Position	Weeks at No.1	Weeks in Top 40
17 Aug 91	**FEAR, THE MINDKILLER** *Vinyl Solution STORM 33*	63		

MANTRONIK VS EPMD US rap duo

Date	Title / Label	Peak Position	Weeks at No.1	Weeks in Top 40
15 Aug 98	**STRICTLY BUSINESS** *Parlophone CDR 6502*	43		

EQUALS UK/Guyanese pop group

Date	Title / Label	Peak Position	Weeks at No.1	Weeks in Top 40
21 Feb 68	**I GET SO EXCITED** *President PT 180*	44		
1 May 68	**BABY COME BACK** *President PT 135*	1	3	17
21 Aug 68	**LAUREL AND HARDY** *President PT 200*	35		4
27 Nov 68	**SOFTLY SOFTLY** *President PT 222*	48		
2 Apr 69	**MICHAEL AND THE SLIPPER TREE** *President PT 240*	24		6
30 Jul 69	**VIVA BOBBY JOE** *President PT 260*	6		13
27 Dec 69	**RUB A DUB DUB** *President PT 275*	34		3
19 Dec 70	**BLACK SKIN BLUE EYED BOYS** *President PT 325*	9		8

ERASURE UK duo

Date	Title / Label	Peak Position	Weeks at No.1	Weeks in Top 40
5 Oct 85	**WHO NEEDS LOVE LIKE THAT** *Mute 40*	55		
25 Oct 86	**SOMETIMES** *Mute 51*	2		12
28 Feb 87	**IT DOESN'T HAVE TO BE** *Mute 56*	12		7
30 May 87	**VICTIM OF LOVE** *Mute 61*	7		7
3 Oct 87	**THE CIRCUS** *Mute 66*	6		8
5 Mar 88	**SHIP OF FOOLS** *Mute 74*	6		6
11 Jun 88	**CHAINS OF LOVE** *Mute 83*	11		6
1 Oct 88	**A LITTLE RESPECT** *Mute 85*	4		9
10 Dec 88	**CRACKERS INTERNATIONAL EP** *Mute 93*	2		12
30 Sep 89	**DRAMA!** *Mute 89*	4		6
9 Dec 89	**YOU SURROUND ME** *Mute 99*	15		7
10 Mar 90	**BLUE SAVANNAH** *Mute 109*	3		9
2 Jun 90	**STAR** *Mute 111*	11		5
29 Jun 91	**CHORUS** *Mute 125*	3		7
21 Sep 91	**LOVE TO HATE YOU** *Mute 131*	4		8
7 Dec 91	**AM I RIGHT (EP)** *Mute 134*	15		5
11 Jan 92	**AM I RIGHT (EP) (REMIX)** *Mute L12MUTE 134*	22		1
28 Mar 92	**BREATH OF LIFE** *Mute 142*	8		5
13 Jun 92	**ABBA-ESQUE EP** *Mute 144*	1	5	10
7 Nov 92	**WHO NEEDS LOVE LIKE THAT** *Mute 150*	10		3
23 Apr 94	**ALWAYS** *Mute CDMUTE 152*	4		6
30 Jul 94	**RUN TO THE SUN** *Mute CDMUTE 153*	6		3
3 Dec 94	**I LOVE SATURDAY** *Mute CDMUTE 166*	20		4
23 Sep 95	**STAY WITH ME** *Mute LDMUTE 174*	15		3
9 Dec 95	**FINGERS AND THUMBS (COLD SUMMER'S DAY)** *Mute CDMUTE 178*	20		1
18 Jan 97	**IN MY ARMS** *Mute CDMUTE 190*	13		2
8 Mar 97	**DON'T SAY YOUR LOVE IS KILLING ME** *Mute CDMUTE 195*	23		1
21 Oct 00	**FREEDOM** *Mute LCDMUTE 244*	27		1
18 Jan 03	**SOLSBURY HILL** *Mute LCDMUTE 275*	10		2
19 Apr 03	**MAKE ME SMILE (COME UP AND SEE ME)** *Mute LCDMUTE 292*	14		1
25 Oct 03	**OH L'AMOUR** *Mute LCDMUTE 213*	13		2
15 Jan 05	**BREATHE** *Mute LCDMUTE 330*	4		4
2 Apr 05	**DON'T SAY YOU LOVE ME** *Mute LCDMUTE337*	15		1
2 Jul 05	**HERE I GO IMPOSSIBLE AGAIN** *Mute LCDMUTE344*	25		1
14 Apr 07	**I COULD FALL IN LOVE WITH YOU** *Mute LCDMUTE366*	21		1
23 Jun 07	**SUNDAY GIRL** *Mute LCDMUTE376*	33		1

ERIC & THE GOOD GOOD FEELING UK group

Date	Title / Label	Peak Position	Weeks at No.1	Weeks in Top 40
3 Jun 89	**GOOD GOOD FEELING** *Equinox EQN 1*	73		

ERICKE Dutch producer

Date	Title / Label	Peak Position	Weeks at No.1	Weeks in Top 40
10 Feb 07	**THE BEAT IS ROCKIN'** *Gusto CDGUS44*	25		3

ERIK UK singer

Date	Title / Label	Peak Position	Weeks at No.1	Weeks in Top 40
10 Apr 93	**LOOKS LIKE I'M IN LOVE AGAIN** *PWL Sanctuary PWCD 252* KEY WEST FEATURING ERIK	46		
29 Jan 94	**GOT TO BE REAL** *PWL International PWCD 278*	42		
1 Oct 94	**WE GOT THE LOVE** *PWL International PWCD 305*	55		

ERIN UK singer

Date	Title / Label	Peak Position	Weeks at No.1	Weeks in Top 40
15 Aug 92	**THE ART OF MOVING BUTTS** *Shut Up And Dance SUAD 34S* SHUT UP & DANCE FEATURING ERIN	69		
23 Mar 96	**LET THE MUSIC PLAY** *MCA MCSTD 40029* BBG FEATURING ERIN	46		
23 Mar 02	**FOR A LIFETIME** *Xtravaganza XTRAV 20CDS* ASCENSION FEATURING ERIN LORDAN	45		

ERNESTO VS BASTIAN Dutch duo

Date	Title / Label	Peak Position	Weeks at No.1	Weeks in Top 40
24 Sep 05	**DARK SIDE OF THE MOON** *Nebula NEBCD080*	48		

EROTIC DRUM BAND Canadian group

Date	Title / Label	Peak Position	Weeks at No.1	Weeks in Top 40
9 Jun 79	**LOVE DISCO STYLE** *Scope SC 1*	47		

ERUPTION US group

Date	Title / Label	Peak Position	Weeks at No.1	Weeks in Top 40
18 Feb 78	**I CAN'T STAND THE RAIN** *Atlantic K 11068* ERUPTION FEATURING PRECIOUS WILSON	5		11
21 Apr 79	**ONE WAY TICKET** *Atlantic/Hansa K 11266*	9		8

SHAUN ESCOFFERY UK singer

Date	Title / Label	Peak Position	Weeks at No.1	Weeks in Top 40
10 Mar 01	**SPACE RIDER** *Oyster Music OYSCD 4*	52		
20 Jul 02	**DAYS LIKE THIS** *Oyster Music OYSCDS 8*	53		

ESCORTS UK group

Date	Title / Label	Peak Position	Weeks at No.1	Weeks in Top 40
2 Jul 64	**THE ONE TO CRY** *Fontana TF 474*	49		

ESCRIMA UK group

Date	Title / Label	Peak Position	Weeks at No.1	Weeks in Top 40
11 Feb 95	**TRAIN OF THOUGHT** *ffrreedom TABCD 225*	36		1
7 Oct 95	**DEEPER** *Hooj Choons TABCD 236*	27		1

ESKA UK singer

Date	Title / Label	Peak Position	Weeks at No.1	Weeks in Top 40
27 Feb 99	**WHAT U DO** *Inferno CDFERN 12* COLOURS FEATURING EMMANUEL & ESKA	51		
9 Sep 00	**COOCHY COO** *VC Recordings VCRD 72* EN-CORE FEATURING STEPHEN EMMANUEL & ESKA	32		1
28 Jul 01	**SUNSET** *V2 VVR 5016768* NITIN SAWHNEY FEATURING ESKA	65		

ESKIMOS & EGYPT UK group

Date	Title / Label	Peak Position	Weeks at No.1	Weeks in Top 40
13 Feb 93	**FALL FROM GRACE** *One Little Indian EEF 96CD*	51		
29 May 93	**UK-USA** *One Little Indian 99 TP7CD*	52		

ESPIRITU UK/French duo

Date	Title / Label	Peak Position	Weeks at No.1	Weeks in Top 40
6 Mar 93	**CONQUISTADOR** *Heavenly HVN 28CD*	47		
7 Aug 93	**LOS AMERICANOS** *Heavenly HVN 33CD*	45		
20 Aug 94	**BONITA MANANA** *Columbia 6606925*	50		
25 Mar 95	**ALWAYS SOMETHING THERE TO REMIND ME** *WEA YZ 911CD* TIN TIN OUT FEATURING ESPIRITU	14		3

ESSENCE UK production group

Date	Title / Label	Peak Position	Weeks at No.1	Weeks in Top 40
21 Mar 98	**THE PROMISE** *Innocent SINCD 1*	27		1

ESSEX US group

Date	Title / Label	Peak Position	Weeks at No.1	Weeks in Top 40
8 Aug 63	**EASIER SAID THAN DONE** *Columbia DB 7077* ★	41		

DAVID ESSEX UK singer

Date	Title / Label	Peak Position	Weeks at No.1	Weeks in Top 40
18 Aug 73	**ROCK ON** *CBS 1693* ○	3		10
10 Nov 73	**LAMPLIGHT** *CBS 1902*	7		15
11 May 74	**AMERICA** *CBS 2176*	32		3
12 Oct 74	**GONNA MAKE YOU A STAR** *CBS 2492* ●	1	3	14
14 Dec 74	**STARDUST** *CBS 2828*	7		9
5 Jul 75	**ROLLIN' STONE** *CBS 3425*	5		6
13 Sep 75	**HOLD ME CLOSE** *CBS 3572* ●	1	3	9
6 Dec 75	**IF I COULD** *CBS 3776*	13		7
20 Mar 76	**CITY LIGHTS** *CBS 4050*	24		4
16 Oct 76	**COMING HOME** *CBS 4486*	24		5
17 Sep 77	**COOL OUT TONIGHT** *CBS 5495*	23		5
11 Mar 78	**STAY WITH ME BABY** *CBS 6063*	45		
19 Aug 78	**OH WHAT A CIRCUS** *Mercury 6007 185* ●	3		9
21 Oct 78	**BRAVE NEW WORLD** *CBS 6705*	55		
3 Mar 79	**IMPERIAL WIZARD** *Mercury 6007 202*	32		5
5 Apr 80	**SILVER DREAM MACHINE (PART 1)** *Mercury BIKE 1* ○	4		10
14 Jun 80	**HOT LOVE** *Mercury HOT 11*	57		
26 Jun 82	**ME AND MY GIRL (NIGHT-CLUBBING)** *Mercury MER 107*	13		8
11 Dec 82	**A WINTER'S TALE** *Mercury MER 127* ○	2		8
4 Jun 83	**THE SMILE** *Mercury ESSEX 1*	52		
27 Aug 83	**TAHITI** *Mercury BOUNT 1*	8		7
26 Nov 83	**YOU'RE IN MY HEART** *Mercury ESSEX 2*	59		
23 Feb 85	**FALLING ANGELS RIDING (MUTINY)** *Mercury ESSEX 5*	29		3
18 Apr 87	**MYFANWY** *Arista RIS 11*	41		
26 Nov 94	**TRUE LOVE WAYS** *Polygram TV TLWCD 2* DAVID ESSEX & CATHERINE ZETA JONES	38		1

GLORIA ESTEFAN US singer

Date	Title / Label	Peak Position	Weeks at No.1	Weeks in Top 40
16 Jul 88	**ANYTHING FOR YOU** *Epic 65167377* GLORIA ESTEFAN & MIAMI SOUND MACHINE ★	10		10
22 Oct 88	**1-2-3-** *Epic 6529587* GLORIA ESTEFAN & MIAMI SOUND MACHINE	9		6
17 Dec 88	**RHYTHM IS GONNA GET YOU** *Epic 6545147* GLORIA ESTEFAN & MIAMI SOUND MACHINE	16		6
11 Feb 89	**CAN'T STAY AWAY FROM YOU** *Epic 6514447* GLORIA ESTEFAN & MIAMI SOUND MACHINE	7		9
15 Jul 89	**DON'T WANNA LOSE YOU** *Epic 6550540* ★	6		9
16 Sep 89	**OYE MI CANTO (HEAR MY VOICE)** *Epic 6552877*	16		6
25 Nov 89	**GET ON YOUR FEET** *Epic 6554507*	23		4
3 Mar 90	**HERE WE ARE** *Epic 6554737*	23		5
26 May 90	**CUTS BOTH WAYS** *Epic 6559827*	49		
26 Jan 91	**COMING OUT OF THE DARK** *Epic 6565747* ★	25		4
6 Apr 91	**SEAL OUR FATE** *Epic 6567737*	24		4
8 Jun 91	**REMEMBER ME WITH LOVE** *Epic 6569687*	22		4
21 Sep 91	**LIVE FOR LOVING YOU** *Epic 6573837*	33		2
24 Oct 92	**ALWAYS TOMORROW** *Epic 6583977*	24		3
12 Dec 92	**MIAMI HIT MIX/CHRISTMAS THROUGH YOUR EYES** *Epic 6588377*	8		7
13 Feb 93	**I SEE YOUR SMILE** *Epic 6589612*	48		
3 Apr 93	**GO AWAY** *Epic 6590952*	13		5
3 Jul 93	**MI TIERRA** *Epic 6593512*	36		1
14 Aug 93	**IF WE WERE LOVERS/CON LOS ANOS QUE ME QUEDAN** *Epic 6595702*	40		1
18 Dec 93	**MONTUNO** *Epic 6599972*	55		
15 Oct 94	**TURN THE BEAT AROUND** *Epic 6606822*	21		5
3 Dec 94	**HOLD ME THRILL ME KISS ME** *Epic 6610802* ○	11		7
18 Feb 95	**EVERLASTING LOVE** *Epic 6611595*	19		3
25 May 96	**REACH** *Epic 6632642*	15		4
24 Aug 96	**YOU'LL BE MINE (PARTY TIME)** *Epic 6636505*	18		2
14 Dec 96	**I'M NOT GIVING YOU UP** *Epic 6640225*	28		1
6 Jun 98	**HEAVEN'S WHAT I FEEL** *Epic 6660042*	17		3
10 Oct 98	**OYE** *Epic 6664645*	33		1
16 Jan 99	**DON'T LET THIS MOMENT END** *Epic 6667472*	28		1
8 Jan 00	**MUSIC OF MY HEART** *Epic 6678052* N SYNC & GLORIA ESTEFAN	34		2

ESTELLE UK singer

Date	Title / Label	Peak Position	Weeks at No.1	Weeks in Top 40
29 Jun 02	**TRIXSTAR** *Bad Magic MAGIC24* BLAK TWANG FEATURING ESTELLE	54		
31 Jul 04	**1980** *V2/J-Did JAD5027813*	14		4
16 Oct 04	**FREE** *V2/J-Did JAD5027848*	15		4
12 Feb 05	**OUTSPOKEN – PART 1** *Buzzin Fly 010BUZZCD* BEN WATT FEATURING ESTELLE & BABY BLAK	74		
9 Apr 05	**GO GONE** *V2 JAD5030948*	32		1
11 Jun 05	**WHY GO?** *Cheeky 82876699292* FAITHLESS FEATURING ESTELLE	49		
15 Mar 08	**AMERICAN BOY** *Atlantic AT0304CD* ESTELLE FEATURING KANYE WEST	1	1	1

DEON ESTUS US singer/bass player

Date	Title / Label	Peak Position	Weeks at No.1	Weeks in Top 40
25 Jan 86	**MY GUY – MY GIRL (MEDLEY)** *Sedition EDIT 3310* AMII STEWART & DEON ESTUS	63		
29 Apr 89	**HEAVEN HELP ME** *Mika 2*	41		

ETA Danish instrumental group

Date	Title / Label	Peak Position	Weeks at No.1	Weeks in Top 40
28 Jun 97	**CASUAL SUB (BURNING SPEAR)** *East West EW 110CD*	28		1
31 Jan 98	**CASUAL SUB (BURNING SPEAR) (REMIX)** *East West Dance EW 145CD*	28		1

ETERNAL UK group

Date	Title / Label	Peak Position	Weeks at No.1	Weeks in Top 40
2 Oct 93	**STAY** *EMI CDEM 284*	4		8
15 Jan 94	**SAVE OUR LOVE** *EMI CDEM 296*	8		5
30 Apr 94	**JUST A STEP FROM HEAVEN** *EMI CDEM 311*	8		8
20 Aug 94	**SO GOOD** *EMI CDEMS 339*	13		5
5 Nov 94	**OH BABY I...** *EMI CDEM 353* ○	4		10
24 Dec 94	**CRAZY** *EMI CDEMX 364*	15		5
21 Oct 95	**POWER OF A WOMAN** *EMI CDEM 396*	5		5
9 Dec 95	**I AM BLESSED** *EMI CDEMS 408*	7		10
9 Mar 96	**GOOD THING** *EMI CDEM 419*	8		3
17 Aug 96	**SOMEDAY** *EMI CDEMS 439*	4		4
7 Dec 96	**SECRETS** *EMI CDEM 459*	9		3
8 Mar 97	**DON'T YOU LOVE ME** *EMI CDEMS 465*	3		5
31 May 97	**I WANNA BE THE ONLY ONE** *EMI CDEM 472* ETERNAL FEATURING BEBE WINANS ●	1	1	12
11 Oct 97	**ANGEL OF MINE** *EMI CDEM 493* ○	4		8
30 Oct 99	**WHAT'CHA GONNA DO** *EMI CDEM 552*	16		2

ETHAN UK singer

Date	Title / Label	Peak Position	Weeks at No.1	Weeks in Top 40
12 Mar 05	**IN MY HEART** *Back Yard BACK13CSCO1*	49		

ETHER UK group

Date	Title / Label	Peak Position	Weeks at No.1	Weeks in Top 40
28 Mar 98	**WATCHING YOU** *Parlophone CDR 6491*	74		

ETHICS Dutch producer

Date	Title / Label	Peak Position	Weeks at No.1	Weeks in Top 40
25 Nov 95	**TO THE BEAT OF THE DRUM (LA LUNA)** *VC Recordings VCRD 5*	13		3

ETHIOPIANS Jamaican group

Date	Title / Label	Peak Position	Weeks at No.1	Weeks in Top 40
13 Sep 67	**TRAIN TO SKAVILLE** *Rio 130*	40		1

TONY ETORIA UK singer

Date	Title / Label	Peak Position	Weeks at No.1	Weeks in Top 40
4 Jun 77	**I CAN PROVE IT** *GTO GT 89*	21		6

EUROGROOVE UK group

Date	Title / Label	Peak Position	Weeks at No.1	Weeks in Top 40
20 May 95	**MOVE YOUR BODY** *Avex UK AVEXCD 4*	29		1
5 Aug 95	**DIVE TO PARADISE** *Avex UK AVEXCD 10*	31		1
21 Oct 95	**IT'S ON YOU (SCAN ME)** *Avex UK AVEXCD 17*	25		1
3 Feb 96	**MOVE YOUR BODY (REMIX)** *Avex UK AVEXCD 22*	44		

EUROPE Swedish group

Date	Title / Label	Peak Position	Weeks at No.1	Weeks in Top 40
1 Nov 86	**THE FINAL COUNTDOWN** *Epic A 7127* ●	1	2	12
31 Jan 87	**ROCK THE NIGHT** *Epic EUR 1*	12		7
18 Apr 87	**CARRIE** *Epic EUR 2*	22		6
20 Aug 88	**SUPERSTITIOUS** *Epic EUR 3*	34		2
1 Feb 92	**I'LL CRY FOR YOU** *Epic 6576977*	28		3
21 Mar 92	**HALFWAY TO HEAVEN** *Epic 6578517*	42		
25 Dec 99	**THE FINAL COUNTDOWN** *Epic 6685042*	36		2

EURYTHMICS UK group

Date	Title / Label	Peak Position	Weeks at No.1	Weeks in Top 40
4 Jul 81	**NEVER GONNA CRY AGAIN** *RCA 68*	63		
20 Nov 82	**LOVE IS A STRANGER** *RCA DA 1*	54		
12 Feb 83	**SWEET DREAMS (ARE MADE OF THIS)** *RCA DA 2* ○ ★	2		11
9 Apr 83	**LOVE IS A STRANGER** *RCA DA 1*	6		6
9 Jul 83	**WHO'S THAT GIRL?** *RCA DA 3*	3		9
5 Nov 83	**RIGHT BY YOUR SIDE** *RCA DA 4*	10		9
21 Jan 84	**HERE COMES THE RAIN AGAIN** *RCA DA 5* ○	8		7
3 Nov 84	**SEXCRIME (NINETEEN EIGHTY FOUR)** *Virgin VS 728* ○	4		9
19 Jan 85	**JULIA** *Virgin VS 734*	44		

Silver-selling ○ Gold-selling ● Platinum-selling ⊛ US No.1 ★ — Peak Position, Weeks at No.1, Weeks in Top 40

Date	Title / Label	Peak Position	Weeks at No.1	Weeks in Top 40
20 Apr 85	**WOULD I LIE TO YOU?** *RCA PB 40101*	17		5
6 Jul 85	**THERE MUST BE AN ANGEL (PLAYING WITH MY HEART)** *RCA PB 40247*	1	1	11
2 Nov 85	**SISTERS ARE DOING IT FOR THEMSELVES** *RCA PB 40339* EURYTHMICS & ARETHA FRANKLIN	9		8
11 Jan 86	**IT'S ALRIGHT (BABY'S COMING BACK)** *RCA PB 40375*	12		7
14 Jun 86	**WHEN TOMORROW COMES** *RCA DA 7*	30		3
6 Sep 86	**THORN IN MY SIDE** *RCA DA 8*	5		9
29 Nov 86	**THE MIRACLE OF LOVE** *RCA DA 9*	23		7
28 Feb 87	**MISSIONARY MAN** *RCA DA 10*	31		3
24 Oct 87	**BEETHOVEN (I LOVE TO LISTEN TO)** *RCA DA 11*	25		3
26 Dec 87	**SHAME** *RCA DA 12*	41		
9 Apr 88	**I NEED A MAN** *RCA DA 15*	26		3
11 Jun 88	**YOU HAVE PLACED A CHILL IN MY HEART** *RCA DA 16*	16		6
26 Aug 89	**REVIVAL** *RCA DA 17*	26		4
4 Nov 89	**DON'T ASK ME WHY** *RCA DA 19*	25		4
3 Feb 90	**THE KING AND QUEEN OF AMERICA** *RCA DA 20*	29		3
12 May 90	**ANGEL** *RCA DA 21*	23		3
9 Mar 91	**LOVE IS A STRANGER** *RCA PB 44265*	46		
16 Nov 91	**SWEET DREAMS (ARE MADE OF THIS) (REMIX)** *RCA PB 45031*	48		
16 Oct 99	**I SAVED THE WORLD TODAY** *RCA 74321695632*	11		3
5 Feb 00	**17 AGAIN** *RCA 74321726262*	27		1
12 Nov 05	**I'VE GOT A LIFE** *RCA 82876748352*	14		2

EUSEBE UK group

Date	Title / Label	Peak Position	Weeks at No.1	Weeks in Top 40
26 Aug 95	**SUMMERTIME HEALING** *Mama's Yard CDMAMA 4*	32		1

EVANESCENCE US group

Date	Title / Label	Peak Position	Weeks at No.1	Weeks in Top 40
31 May 03	**BRING ME TO LIFE (IMPORT)** *Epic 8734881CD*	60		
14 Jun 03	**BRING ME TO LIFE** *Epic 6739762*	1	4	14
4 Oct 03	**GOING UNDER** *Epic 6743522*	8		4
20 Dec 03	**MY IMMORTAL** *Epic 6745422*	7		7
12 Jun 04	**EVERYBODY'S FOOL** *Epic 6747992*	24		2
30 Sep 06	**CALL ME WHEN YOU'RE SOBER** *Columbia 82876894152*	4		6
20 Jan 07	**LITHIUM** *Wind Up 88697042082*	32		1

FAITH EVANS US rapper

Date	Title / Label	Peak Position	Weeks at No.1	Weeks in Top 40
14 Oct 95	**YOU USED TO LOVE ME** *Puff Daddy 74321299812*	42		
23 Nov 96	**STRESSED OUT** *Jive JIVECD 404* A TRIBE CALLED QUEST FEATURING FAITH EVANS & RAPHAEL SAADIQ	33		1
28 Jun 97	**I'LL BE MISSING YOU** *Puff Daddy 74321499102* PUFF DADDY & FAITH EVANS FEATURING 112 ⊛ ★	1	6	18
14 Nov 98	**LOVE LIKE THIS** *Puff Daddy 74321665692*	24		2
1 May 99	**ALL NIGHT LONG** *Puff Daddy 74321625592* FAITH EVANS FEATURING PUFF DADDY	23		2
1 May 99	**GEORGY PORGY** *Warner Brothers W 478CD1* ERIC BENET FEATURING FAITH EVANS	28		1
30 Dec 00	**HEARTBREAK HOTEL** *Arista 74321820572* WHITNEY HOUSTON FEATURING FAITH EVANS & KELLY PRICE	25		3
24 May 03	**MA I DON'T LOVE HER** *Arista 82876526482* CLIPSE FEATURING FAITH EVANS	38		1
9 Apr 05	**HOPE** *Capitol 8694660* TWISTA FEATURING FAITH EVANS	25		3
14 May 05	**AGAIN** *EMI CDEMS658*	12		4
20 Aug 05	**MESMERIZED** *EMI CDEMS665*	48		
14 Jul 07	**I'LL BE MISSING YOU** *Download* PUFF DADDY FEATURING FAITH EVANS	32		1

MAUREEN EVANS UK singer

Date	Title / Label	Peak Position	Weeks at No.1	Weeks in Top 40
22 Jan 60	**THE BIG HURT** *Oriole CB 1533*	26		2
17 Mar 60	**LOVE KISSES AND HEARTACHES** *Oriole CB 1540*	44		
2 Jun 60	**PAPER ROSES** *Oriole CB 1550*	40		1
29 Nov 62	**LIKE I DO** *Oriole CB 1763*	3		17
27 Feb 64	**I LOVE HOW YOU LOVE ME** *Oriole CB 1906*	34		5

PAUL EVANS US singer

Date	Title / Label	Peak Position	Weeks at No.1	Weeks in Top 40
27 Nov 59	**SEVEN LITTLE GIRLS SITTING IN THE BACK SEAT** *London HLL 8968* PAUL EVANS & THE CURLS	25		1
31 Mar 60	**MIDNITE SPECIAL** *London HLL 9045*	41		
16 Dec 78	**HELLO THIS IS JOANNIE (THE TELEPHONE ANSWERING MACHINE SONG)** *Spring 2066 932* ○	6		9

EVASIONS UK group

Date	Title / Label	Peak Position	Weeks at No.1	Weeks in Top 40
13 Jun 81	**WIKKA WRAP** *Groove GP 107*	20		6

E.V.E. UK/US group

Date	Title / Label	Peak Position	Weeks at No.1	Weeks in Top 40
1 Oct 94	**GROOVE OF LOVE** *Gasoline Alley MCSTD 2007*	30		1
28 Jan 95	**GOOD LIFE** *Gasoline Alley MCSTD 2038*	39		1

EVE US rapper

Date	Title / Label	Peak Position	Weeks at No.1	Weeks in Top 40
22 Jan 00	**HOT BOYZ** *Elektra E 7002CD* MISSY MISDEMEANOR ELLIOTT FEATURING NAS, EVE & Q-TIP	18		2
19 May 01	**WHO'S THAT GIRL** *Interscope 4975572*	6		5
25 Aug 01	**LET ME BLOW YA MIND** *Interscope 4976052* EVE FEATURING GWEN STEFANI	4		10
9 Mar 02	**BROTHA PART II** *J Records 74321922142* ANGIE STONE FEATURING ALICIA KEYS & EVE	37		1
16 Mar 02	**CARAMEL** *Interscope 4976742* CITY HIGH FEATURING EVE	9		5
5 Oct 02	**GANGSTA LOVIN'** *Interscope 4978042* EVE FEATURING ALICIA KEYS	6		6
12 Apr 03	**SATISFACTION** *Interscope 4978262*	20		2
6 Dec 03	**NOT TODAY** *Geffen MCSTD 40349* MARY J BLIGE FEATURING EVE	40		1
26 Mar 05	**RICH GIRL** *Interscope 9880219* GWEN STEFANI FEATURING EVE	4		9
16 Jun 07	**LIKE THIS** *Columbia 88697110322* KELLY ROWLAND FEATURING EVE	4		10
18 Aug 07	**TAMBOURINE** *Interscope 1745307*	19		5

EVERCLEAR US group

Date	Title / Label	Peak Position	Weeks at No.1	Weeks in Top 40
1 Jun 96	**HEARTSPARK DOLLARSIGN** *Capitol CDCLS 773*	48		
31 Aug 96	**SANTA MONICA (WATCH THE WORLD DIE)** *Capitol CDCL 775*	40		1
9 May 98	**EVERYTHING TO EVERYONE** *Capitol CDCL 799*	41		
14 Oct 00	**WONDERFUL** *Capitol CDCLS 824*	36		1

BETTY EVERETT US singer

Date	Title / Label	Peak Position	Weeks at No.1	Weeks in Top 40
14 Jan 65	**GETTING MIGHTY CROWDED** *Fontana TF 520*	29		6
30 Oct 68	**IT'S IN HIS KISS** *President PT 215*	34		4

KENNY EVERETT
UK comedian/radio DJ/TV personality

Date	Title / Label	Peak Position	Weeks at No.1	Weeks in Top 40
12 Nov 77	**CAPTAIN KREMMEN (RETRIBUTION)** *DJM DJS 10810* KENNY EVERETT & MIKE VICKERS	32		3
26 Mar 83	**SNOT RAP** *RCA KEN 1*	9		5

EVERLAST US rapper

Date	Title / Label	Peak Position	Weeks at No.1	Weeks in Top 40
27 Feb 99	**WHAT IT'S LIKE** *Tommy Boy TBCD 7470*	34		1
3 Jul 99	**ENDS** *Tommy Boy TBCD 346*	47		
20 Jan 01	**BLACK JESUS** *Tommy Boy TBCD 2180B*	37		1

EVERLY BROTHERS US duo

Date	Title / Label	Peak Position	Weeks at No.1	Weeks in Top 40
12 Jul 57	**BYE BYE LOVE** *London HLA 8440*	6		16
8 Nov 57	**WAKE UP LITTLE SUSIE** *London HLA 8498* ★	2		13
23 May 58	**ALL I HAVE TO DO IS DREAM/CLAUDETTE** *London HLA 8618* ★	1	7	21
12 Sep 58	**BIRD DOG** *London HLA 8685* ★	2		16
23 Jan 59	**PROBLEMS** *London HLA 8781*	6		12
22 May 59	**TAKE A MESSAGE TO MARY** *London HLA 8863*	20		10
29 May 59	**POOR JENNY** *London HLA 8863*	14		11
11 Sep 59	**('TIL) I KISSED YOU** *London HLA 8934*	2		15
12 Feb 60	**LET IT BE ME** *London HLA 9039*	13		7
14 Apr 60	**CATHY'S CLOWN** *Warner Brothers WB 1* ★	1	7	18
14 Jul 60	**WHEN WILL I BE LOVED** *London HLA 9157*	4		16
22 Sep 60	**LUCILLE/SO SAD (TO WATCH GOOD LOVE GO BAD)** *Warner Brothers WB 19*	4		13
15 Dec 60	**LIKE STRANGERS** *London HLA 9250*	11		10
9 Feb 61	**WALK RIGHT BACK/EBONY EYES** *Warner Brothers WB 33*	1	3	16
15 Jun 61	**TEMPTATION** *Warner Brothers WB 42*	1	2	14
5 Oct 61	**MUSKRAT/DON'T BLAME ME** *Warner Brothers WB 50*	20		5
18 Jan 62	**CRYIN' IN THE RAIN** *Warner Brothers WB 56*	6		14
17 May 62	**HOW CAN I MEET HER** *Warner Brothers WB 67*	12		8
25 Oct 62	**NO ONE CAN MAKE MY SUNSHINE SMILE** *Warner Brothers WB 79*	11		9
21 Mar 63	**SO IT WILL ALWAYS BE** *Warner Brothers WB 94*	23		9
13 Jun 63	**IT'S BEEN NICE** *Warner Brothers WB 99*	26		4
17 Oct 63	**THE GIRL SANG THE BLUES** *Warner Brothers WB 109*	25		7
16 Jul 64	**FERRIS WHEEL** *Warner Brothers WB 135*	22		7
3 Dec 64	**GONE GONE GONE** *Warner Brothers WB 146*	36		4
6 May 65	**THAT'LL BE THE DAY** *Warner Brothers WB 158*	30		2
20 May 65	**THE PRICE OF LOVE** *Warner Brothers WB 161*	2		13

Silver-selling ○ Gold-selling ● Platinum-selling ⊛ US No.1 ★ | Peak Position | Weeks at No.1 | Weeks in Top 40

Date	Title / Label	Peak Position	Weeks at No.1	Weeks in Top 40
26 Aug 65	**I'LL NEVER GET OVER YOU** *Warner Brothers WB 5639*	35		2
21 Oct 65	**LOVE IS STRANGE** *Warner Brothers WB 5649*	11		8
8 May 68	**IT'S MY TIME** *Warner Brothers WB 7192*	39		2
22 Sep 84	**ON THE WINGS OF A NIGHTINGALE** *Mercury MER 170*	41		

PHIL EVERLY US singer

Date	Title / Label	Peak Position	Weeks at No.1	Weeks in Top 40
6 Nov 82	**LOUISE** *Capitol CL 266*	47		
19 Feb 83	**SHE MEANS NOTHING TO ME** *Capitol CL 276* PHIL EVERLY & CLIFF RICHARD	9		7
10 Dec 94	**ALL I HAVE TO DO IS DREAM/MISS YOU NIGHTS** *EMI CDEMS 359* PHIL EVERLY & CLIFF RICHARD/CLIFF RICHARD	14		4

EVERSTRONG UK group

Date	Title / Label	Peak Position	Weeks at No.1	Weeks in Top 40
23 Apr 05	**TAKE ME HOME (WOMBLE 'TIL I DIE)** *Cornish Blue Music CBMCD02*	73		

EVERTON FC UK football club

Date	Title / Label	Peak Position	Weeks at No.1	Weeks in Top 40
11 May 85	**HERE WE GO** *Columbia DB 9106*	14		3
20 May 95	**ALL TOGETHER NOW** *MDMC DEVCS 3*	24		2

EVERYTHING BUT THE GIRL UK duo

Date	Title / Label	Peak Position	Weeks at No.1	Weeks in Top 40
12 May 84	**EACH AND EVERYONE** *Blanco Y Negro NEG 1*	28		4
21 Jul 84	**MINE** *Blanco Y Negro NEG 3*	58		
6 Oct 84	**NATIVE LAND** *Blanco Y Negro NEG 6*	73		
2 Aug 86	**COME ON HOME** *Blanco Y Negro NEG 21*	44		
11 Oct 86	**DON'T LEAVE ME BEHIND** *Blanco Y Negro NEG 23*	72		
13 Feb 88	**THESE EARLY DAYS** *Blanco Y Negro NEG 30*	75		
9 Jul 88	**I DON'T WANT TO TALK ABOUT IT** *Blanco Y Negro NEG 34*	3		8
27 Jan 90	**DRIVING** *Blanco Y Negro NEG 40*	54		
22 Feb 92	**COVERS EP** *Blanco Y Negro NEG 54*	13		5
24 Apr 93	**THE ONLY LIVING BOY IN NEW YORK (EP)** *Blanco Y Negro NEG 62CD*	42		
19 Jun 93	**I DIDN'T KNOW I WAS LOOKING FOR LOVE (EP)** *Blanco Y Negro NEG 64CD*	72		
4 Jun 94	**ROLLERCOASTER (EP)** *Blanco Y Negro NEG 69CD*	65		
20 Aug 94	**MISSING** *Blanco Y Negro NEG 71CD*	69		
28 Oct 95	**MISSING (REMIX)** *Blanco Y Negro NEG 84CD* ⊛	3		19
20 Apr 96	**WALKING WOUNDED** *Virgin VSCDT 1577*	6		3
29 Jun 96	**WRONG** *Virgin VSCDT 1589*	8		5
5 Oct 96	**SINGLE** *Virgin VSCDT 1600*	20		2
7 Dec 96	**DRIVING (REMIX)** *Blanco Y Negro NEG 99CD1*	36		1
1 Mar 97	**BEFORE TODAY** *Virgin VSCDT 1624*	25		1
3 Oct 98	**THE FUTURE OF THE FUTURE (STAY GOLD)** *Deconstruction 74321616252* DEEP DISH WITH EVERYTHING BUT THE GIRL	31		1
25 Sep 99	**FIVE FATHOMS** *Virgin VSCDT 1742*	27		1
4 Mar 00	**TEMPERAMENTAL** *Virgin VSCDT 1761*	72		
27 Jan 01	**TRACEY IN MY ROOM** *VC Recordings VCRD 78* EBTG VS SOUL VISION	34		1

E'VOKE UK duo

Date	Title / Label	Peak Position	Weeks at No.1	Weeks in Top 40
25 Nov 95	**RUNAWAY** *ffrreedom TABCD 238*	30		1
24 Aug 96	**ARMS OF LOREN** *Manifesto FESCD 10*	25		2
2 Feb 02	**ARMS OF LOREN 2001** *Inferno CDFERN 001*	31		1

EVOLUTION UK production duo

Date	Title / Label	Peak Position	Weeks at No.1	Weeks in Top 40
20 Mar 93	**LOVE THING** *Deconstruction 74321134272*	32		1
3 Jul 93	**EVERYBODY DANCE** *Deconstruction 74321152012*	19		3
8 Jan 94	**EVOLUTIONDANCE PART ONE (EP)** *Deconstruction 74321171912*	52		
4 Nov 95	**LOOK UP TO THE LIGHT** *Deconstruction 74321318042*	55		
19 Oct 96	**YOUR LOVE IS CALLING** *Deconstruction 74321422872*	60		

EX PISTOLS UK group

Date	Title / Label	Peak Position	Weeks at No.1	Weeks in Top 40
2 Feb 85	**LAND OF HOPE AND GLORY** *Virginia PISTOL 76*	69		

EXCITERS US group

Date	Title / Label	Peak Position	Weeks at No.1	Weeks in Top 40
21 Feb 63	**TELL HIM** *United Artists UP 1011*	46		
4 Oct 75	**REACHING FOR THE BEST** *20th Century BTC 1005*	31		4

!!! US group

Date	Title / Label	Peak Position	Weeks at No.1	Weeks in Top 40
21 Aug 04	**HELLO? IS THIS THING ON?** *Warp WAP176CD*	74		

EXETER BRAMDEAN BOYS' CHOIR
UK choir

Date	Title / Label	Peak Position	Weeks at No.1	Weeks in Top 40
18 Dec 93	**REMEMBERING CHRISTMAS** *Golden Sounds DSCC 1*	46		

EXILE US group

Date	Title / Label	Peak Position	Weeks at No.1	Weeks in Top 40
19 Aug 78	**KISS YOU ALL OVER** *RAK 279* ○ ★	6		9
12 May 79	**HOW COULD THIS GO WRONG** *RAK 293*	67		
12 Sep 81	**HEART AND SOUL** *RAK 333*	54		

EXOTERIX UK producer

Date	Title / Label	Peak Position	Weeks at No.1	Weeks in Top 40
24 Apr 93	**VOID** *Positiva CDTIV 1*	58		
5 Feb 94	**SATISFY MY LOVE** *Union City UCRCD 26*	62		

EXOTICA UK/Italian group

Date	Title / Label	Peak Position	Weeks at No.1	Weeks in Top 40
16 Sep 95	**THE SUMMER IS MAGIC** *Polydor 5798392* EXOTICA FEATURING ITSY FOSTER	68		

EXPLOSION US group

Date	Title / Label	Peak Position	Weeks at No.1	Weeks in Top 40
26 Mar 05	**HERE I AM** *Virgin VUSDX298*	75		

EXPLOITED UK group

Date	Title / Label	Peak Position	Weeks at No.1	Weeks in Top 40
18 Apr 81	**DOGS OF WAR** *Secret SHH 110*	63		
17 Oct 81	**DEAD CITIES** *Secret SHH 120*	31		3
5 Dec 81	**DON'T LET 'EM GRIND YOU DOWN** *Superville EXP 1003* EXPLOITED & ANTI-PASTI	70		
8 May 82	**ATTACK** *Secret SHH 130*	50		

EXPOSE US group

Date	Title / Label	Peak Position	Weeks at No.1	Weeks in Top 40
28 Aug 93	**I'LL NEVER GET OVER YOU (GETTING OVER ME)** *Arista 74321158962*	75		

EXPRESS OF SOUND Italian production group

Date	Title / Label	Peak Position	Weeks at No.1	Weeks in Top 40
2 Nov 96	**REAL VIBRATION** *Positiva CDTIV 66*	45		

EXPRESSOS UK group

Date	Title / Label	Peak Position	Weeks at No.1	Weeks in Top 40
21 Jun 80	**HEY GIRL** *WEA K 18246*	60		
14 Mar 81	**TANGO IN MONO** *WEA K 18431*	70		

EXTREME US group

Date	Title / Label	Peak Position	Weeks at No.1	Weeks in Top 40
8 Jun 91	**GET THE FUNK OUT** *A&M AM 737*	19		5
27 Jul 91	**MORE THAN WORDS** *A&M AM 792* ○ ★	2		10
12 Oct 91	**DECADENCE DANCE** *A&M AM 773*	36		1
23 Nov 91	**HOLE HEARTED** *A&M AM 839*	12		3
2 May 92	**SONG FOR LOVE** *A&M AM 698*	12		5
5 Sep 92	**REST IN PEACE** *A&M AM 0055*	13		4
14 Nov 92	**STOP THE WORLD** *A&M AM 0096*	22		1
6 Feb 93	**TRAGIC COMIC** *A&M AMCD 0156*	15		2
11 Mar 95	**HIP TODAY** *A&M 5809932*	44		

E.Y.C. US group

Date	Title / Label	Peak Position	Weeks at No.1	Weeks in Top 40
11 Dec 93	**FEELIN' ALRIGHT** *MCA MCSTD 1952*	16		6
5 Mar 94	**THE WAY YOU WORK IT** *MCA MCSTD 1963*	14		7
14 May 94	**NUMBER ONE** *MCA MCSTD 1976*	27		3
30 Jul 94	**BLACK BOOK** *MCA MCSTD 1987*	13		4
10 Dec 94	**ONE MORE CHANCE** *MCA MCSTD 2025*	25		5
23 Sep 95	**OOH-AH-AA (I FEEL IT)** *Gasoline Alley MCSTD 2096*	33		1
2 Dec 95	**IN THE BEGINNING** *Gasoline Alley MCSTD 2107*	41		

EYE TO EYE UK production duo

Date	Title / Label	Peak Position	Weeks at No.1	Weeks in Top 40
9 Jun 01	**JUST CAN'T GET ENOUGH (NO NO NO NO)** *Xtravaganza XTRAV 25CD* EYE TO EYE FEATURING TAKA BOOM	36		1

Silver-selling ● Gold-selling ● Platinum-selling ✪ US No.1 ★ | Peak Position | Weeks at No.1 | Weeks in Top 40

EYEOPENER UK group

Date	Title	Peak Position	Weeks at No.1	Weeks in Top 40
20 Nov 04	**HUNGRY EYES** *All Around The World CDGLOBE362*	16		4

EYES CREAM Italian producer

Date	Title	Peak Position	Weeks at No.1	Weeks in Top 40
16 Oct 99	**FLY AWAY (BYE BYE)** *Accolade CDAC 001*	53		

F

ADAM F UK producer

Date	Title	Peak Position	Weeks at No.1	Weeks in Top 40
27 Sep 97	**CIRCLES** *Positiva CDFJ 002*	20		2
7 Mar 98	**MUSIC IN MY MIND** *Positiva CDFJ 003*	27		1
15 Sep 01	**SMASH SUMTHIN'** *Def Jam 5886932* REDMAN FEATURING ADAM F	11		3
1 Dec 01	**STAND CLEAR** *Chrysalis CDEM 597* ADAM F FEATURING M.O.P.	43		
6 Apr 02	**WHERE'S MY** *EMI CDEMS 598* ADAM F FEATURING LIL' MO	37		1
27 Apr 02	**METROSOUND** *Kaos 001P* ADAM F & J MAJIK	54		
8 Jun 02	**STAND CLEAR (REMIX)** *Kaos KAOSCD 002* ADAM F FEATURING M.O.P.	50		
31 Aug 02	**SMASH SUMTHIN' (REMIX)** *Kaos KOASCD 003* ADAM F FEATURING REDMAN	47		
14 Dec 02	**DIRTY HARRY'S REVENGE** *Kaos 004P* ADAM F FEATURING BEENIE MAN	50		
30 Oct 04	**WHEN THE SUN GOES DOWN** *Breakbeat Kaos BBK005SCD* DJ FRESH FEATURING ADAM F	68		

FAB UK production group

Date	Title	Peak Position	Weeks at No.1	Weeks in Top 40
7 Jul 90	**THUNDERBIRDS ARE GO** *Brothers Organisation FAB 1* FAB FEATURING MC PARKER	5		6
20 Oct 90	**THE PRISONER** *Brothers Organisation FAB 6* FAB FEATURING MC NUMBER 6	56		
1 Dec 90	**THE STINGRAY MEGAMIX** *Brothers Organisation FAB 2* FAB FEATURING AQUA MARINA	66		

FAB! Irish group

Date	Title	Peak Position	Weeks at No.1	Weeks in Top 40
1 Aug 98	**TURN AROUND** *Break Records BRCX 107*	59		

FAB FOR German/US group

Date	Title	Peak Position	Weeks at No.1	Weeks in Top 40
15 Feb 03	**LAST NIGHT A DJ BLEW MY MIND** *Illustrious CDILL 013* FAB FOR FEATURING ROBERT OWENS	34		1

SHELLEY FABARES US singer

Date	Title	Peak Position	Weeks at No.1	Weeks in Top 40
26 Apr 62	**JOHNNY ANGEL** *Pye International 7N 25132* ★	41		

FABIAN US singer

Date	Title	Peak Position	Weeks at No.1	Weeks in Top 40
10 Mar 60	**HOUND DOG MAN** *HMV POP 695*	46		

LARA FABIAN Belgian singer

Date	Title	Peak Position	Weeks at No.1	Weeks in Top 40
28 Oct 00	**I WILL LOVE AGAIN** *Columbia 6694062*	63		

FABOLOUS US rapper

Date	Title	Peak Position	Weeks at No.1	Weeks in Top 40
16 Aug 03	**CAN'T LET YOU GO** *Elektra E 7408CD* FABOLOUS FEATURING MIKE SHOREY & LIL' MO	14		3
1 Nov 03	**INTO YOU** *Elektra E 7470CD* FABOLOUS FEATURING TAMIA	18		3
20 Mar 04	**BADABOOM** *Epic 6747512* B2K FEATURING FABOLOUS	26		2
27 Nov 04	**BREATHE** *Atlantic AT0189CD*	28		2
2 Apr 05	**BABY** *Atlantic AT0199CDX* FABOLOUS FEATURING MIKE SHOREY	41		

FABULOUS BAKER BOYS UK production duo

Date	Title	Peak Position	Weeks at No.1	Weeks in Top 40
15 Nov 97	**OH BOY** *Multiply CDMULTY 28*	34		1

FACES UK group

Date	Title	Peak Position	Weeks at No.1	Weeks in Top 40
18 Dec 71	**STAY WITH ME** *Warner Brothers K 16136*	6		9
17 Feb 73	**CINDY INCIDENTALLY** *Warner Brothers K 16247*	2		8
8 Dec 73	**POOL HALL RICHARD/I WISH IT WOULD RAIN** *Warner Brothers K 16341*	8		10
7 Dec 74	**YOU CAN MAKE ME DANCE SING OR ANYTHING (EVEN TAKE THE DOG FOR A WALK, MEND A FUSE, FOLD AWAY THE IRONING BOARD, OR ANY OTHER DOMESTIC SHORTCOMINGS)** *Warner Brothers K 16494* ROD STEWART & THE FACES	12		8
4 Jun 77	**THE FACES (EP)** *Riva 8*	41		

FACTORY OF UNLIMITED RHYTHM Jamaican group

Date	Title	Peak Position	Weeks at No.1	Weeks in Top 40
1 Jun 96	**THE SWEETEST SURRENDER** *Kuff KUFFD 6*	59		

FADERS UK group

Date	Title	Peak Position	Weeks at No.1	Weeks in Top 40
2 Apr 05	**NO SLEEP TONIGHT** *Polydor 9870597*	13		4
9 Jul 05	**JUMP** *Polydor 9872017*	21		1

DONALD FAGEN US singer

Date	Title	Peak Position	Weeks at No.1	Weeks in Top 40
3 Jul 93	**TOMORROW'S GIRLS** *Reprise W0180CDX*	46		

JOE FAGIN UK singer

Date	Title	Peak Position	Weeks at No.1	Weeks in Top 40
7 Jan 84	**THAT'S LIVIN' ALRIGHT** *Towerbell TOW 46* ●	3		8
5 Apr 86	**BACK WITH THE BOYS AGAIN/GET IT RIGHT** *Towerbell TOW 84*	53		

YVONNE FAIR US singer

Date	Title	Peak Position	Weeks at No.1	Weeks in Top 40
24 Jan 76	**IT SHOULD HAVE BEEN ME** *Tamla Motown TMG 1013*	5		10

FAIR WEATHER UK group

Date	Title	Peak Position	Weeks at No.1	Weeks in Top 40
18 Jul 70	**NATURAL SINNER** *RCA 1977*	6		11

FAIRGROUND ATTRACTION UK group

Date	Title	Peak Position	Weeks at No.1	Weeks in Top 40
16 Apr 88	**PERFECT** *RCA PB 41845* ●	1	1	10
30 Jul 88	**FIND MY LOVE** *RCA PB 42079*	7		8
19 Nov 88	**A SMILE IN A WHISPER** *RCA PB 42249*	75		
28 Jan 89	**CLARE** *RCA PB 42607*	49		

FAIRPORT CONVENTION UK group

Date	Title	Peak Position	Weeks at No.1	Weeks in Top 40
23 Jul 69	**SI TU DOIS PARTIR** *Island WIP 6064*	21		6

ANDY FAIRWEATHER-LOW UK singer

Date	Title	Peak Position	Weeks at No.1	Weeks in Top 40
21 Sep 74	**REGGAE TUNE** *A&M AMS 7129*	10		7
6 Dec 75	**WIDE EYED AND LEGLESS** *A&M AMS 7202*	6		9

ADAM FAITH UK singer

Date	Title	Peak Position	Weeks at No.1	Weeks in Top 40
20 Nov 59	**WHAT DO YOU WANT** *Parlophone R 4591*	1	3	19
22 Jan 60	**POOR ME** *Parlophone R 4623*	1	1	17
14 Apr 60	**SOMEONE ELSE'S BABY** *Parlophone R 4643*	2		11
30 Jun 60	**WHEN JOHNNY COMES MARCHING HOME/MADE YOU** *Parlophone R 4665*	5		12
15 Sep 60	**HOW ABOUT THAT** *Parlophone R 4689*	4		11
17 Nov 60	**LONELY PUP (IN A CHRISTMAS SHOP)** *Parlophone R 4708*	4		11
9 Feb 61	**WHO AM I/THIS IS IT!** *Parlophone R 4735*	5		13
27 Apr 61	**EASY GOING ME** *Parlophone R 4766*	12		10
20 Jul 61	**DON'T YOU KNOW IT** *Parlophone R 4807*	12		9
26 Oct 61	**THE TIME HAS COME** *Parlophone R 4837*	4		12
18 Jan 62	**LONESOME** *Parlophone R 4864*	12		9
3 May 62	**AS YOU LIKE IT** *Parlophone R 4896*	5		13
30 Aug 62	**DON'T THAT BEAT ALL** *Parlophone R 4930* ADAM FAITH WITH JOHNNY KEATING & HIS ORCHESTRA	8		10
13 Dec 62	**BABY TAKE A BOW** *Parlophone R 4964*	22		5

Silver-selling ○ · Gold-selling ● · Platinum-selling ⊛ · US No.1 ★ · Peak Position · Weeks at No.1 · Weeks in Top 40

Date	Title	Peak Position	Weeks at No.1	Weeks in Top 40
31 Jan 63	**WHAT NOW** *Parlophone R 4990* ADAM FAITH WITH JOHNNY KEATING & HIS ORCHESTRA	31		5
11 Jul 63	**WALKIN' TALL** *Parlophone R 5039*	23		5
19 Sep 63	**THE FIRST TIME** *Parlophone R 5061* ADAM FAITH & THE ROULETTES	5		10
12 Dec 63	**WE ARE IN LOVE** *Parlophone R 5091* ADAM FAITH & THE ROULETTES	11		11
12 Mar 64	**IF HE TELLS YOU** *Parlophone R 5109* ADAM FAITH & THE ROULETTES	25		6
28 May 64	**I LOVE BEING IN LOVE WITH YOU** *Parlophone R 5138* ADAM FAITH & THE ROULETTES	33		5
26 Nov 64	**MESSAGE TO MARTHA (KENTUCKY BLUEBIRD)** *Parlophone R 5201*	12		10
11 Feb 65	**STOP FEELING SORRY FOR YOURSELF** *Parlophone R 5235*	23		5
17 Jun 65	**SOMEONE'S TAKEN MARIA AWAY** *Parlophone R 5289*	34		1
20 Oct 66	**CHERYL'S GOIN' HOME** *Parlophone R 5516*	46		

HORACE FAITH Jamaican singer

Date	Title	Peak Position	Weeks at No.1	Weeks in Top 40
12 Sep 70	**BLACK PEARL** *Trojan TR 7790*	13		9

PERCY FAITH Canadian orchestra leader

Date	Title	Peak Position	Weeks at No.1	Weeks in Top 40
5 Mar 60	**THEME FROM *A SUMMER PLACE*** *Philips PB 989* ★	2		28

FAITH BROTHERS UK group

Date	Title	Peak Position	Weeks at No.1	Weeks in Top 40
13 Apr 85	**THE COUNTRY OF THE BLIND** *Siren 2*	63		
6 Jul 85	**A STRANGER ON HOME GROUND** *Siren 4*	69		

FAITH, HOPE & CHARITY US group

Date	Title	Peak Position	Weeks at No.1	Weeks in Top 40
31 Jan 76	**JUST ONE LOOK** *RCA 2632*	38		2
23 Jun 90	**BATTLE OF THE SEXES** *WEA YZ 4801*	53		

FAITH NO MORE US group

Date	Title	Peak Position	Weeks at No.1	Weeks in Top 40
6 Feb 88	**WE CARE A LOT** *Slash LASH 17*	53		
10 Feb 90	**EPIC** *Slash LASH 21*	37		2
14 Apr 90	**FROM OUT OF NOWHERE** *Slash LASH 24*	23		4
14 Jul 90	**FALLING TO PIECES** *Slash LASH 25*	41		
8 Sep 90	**EPIC** *Slash LASH 26*	25		4
6 Jun 92	**MIDLIFE CRISIS** *Slash LASH 37*	10		3
15 Aug 92	**A SMALL VICTORY** *Slash LASH 39*	29		3
12 Sep 92	**A SMALL VICTORY (REMIX)** *Slash LASHX 40*	55		
21 Nov 92	**EVERYTHING'S RUINED** *Slash LASH 43*	28		2
16 Jan 93	**I'M EASY/BE AGGRESSIVE** *Slash LACDP 44*	3		6
6 Nov 93	**ANOTHER BODY MURDERED** *Epic 6597942* FAITH NO MORE & BOO-YAA T.R.I.B.E.	26		2
11 Mar 95	**DIGGING THE GRAVE** *Slash LACDP 51*	16		3
27 May 95	**RICOCHET** *Slash LASCD 53*	27		1
29 Jul 95	**EVIDENCE** *Slash LACDP 54*	32		2
31 May 97	**ASHES TO ASHES** *Slash LASCD 61*	15		2
16 Aug 97	**LAST CUP OF SORROW** *Slash LASCD 62*	51		
13 Dec 97	**THIS TOWN AIN'T BIG ENOUGH FOR THE BOTH OF US** *Roadrunner RR 22513* SPARKS VERSUS FAITH NO MORE	40		1
17 Jan 98	**ASHES TO ASHES** *Slash LASCD 63*	29		1
7 Nov 98	**I STARTED A JOKE** *Slash LASCD 65*	49		

MARIANNE FAITHFULL UK singer

Date	Title	Peak Position	Weeks at No.1	Weeks in Top 40
13 Aug 64	**AS TEARS GO BY** *Decca F 11923*	9		12
18 Feb 65	**COME AND STAY WITH ME** *Decca F 12075*	4		12
6 May 65	**THIS LITTLE BIRD** *Decca F 12162*	6		10
22 Jul 65	**SUMMER NIGHTS** *Decca F 12193*	10		8
4 Nov 65	**YESTERDAY** *Decca F 12268*	36		2
9 Mar 67	**IS THIS WHAT I GET FOR LOVING YOU** *Decca F 22524*	43		
24 Nov 79	**THE BALLAD OF LUCY JORDAN** *Island WIP 6491*	48		

FAITHLESS UK group

Date	Title	Peak Position	Weeks at No.1	Weeks in Top 40
5 Aug 95	**SALVA MEA (SAVE ME)** *Cheeky CHEKCD 008*	30		1
9 Dec 95	**INSOMNIA** *Cheeky CHEKCD 010*	27		1
23 Mar 96	**DON'T LEAVE** *Cheeky CHEKCD 012*	34		1
26 Oct 96	**INSOMNIA** *Cheeky CHEKCD 017* ○	3		11
21 Dec 96	**SALVA MEA (SAVE ME) (REMIX)** *Cheeky CHEKXCD 018*	9		5
26 Apr 97	**REVERENCE** *Cheeky CHEKCD 019*	10		2
15 Nov 97	**DON'T LEAVE** *Cheeky CHEKXCD 024*	21		1
5 Sep 98	**GOD IS A DJ** *Cheeky CHEKCD 028*	6		6
5 Dec 98	**TAKE THE LONG WAY HOME** *Cheeky CHEKCD 031*	15		2
1 May 99	**BRING MY FAMILY BACK** *Cheeky CHEKCD 035*	14		3
16 Jun 01	**WE COME 1** *Cheeky 74321858352*	3		6
29 Sep 01	**MUHAMMAD ALI** *Cheeky 74321886452*	29		1
29 Dec 01	**TARANTULA** *Cheeky 74321903592*	29		2
20 Apr 02	**ONE STEP TOO FAR** *Cheeky 74321926412* FAITHLESS FEATURING DIDO	6		2
4 May 02	**ONE STEP TOO FAR** *Cheeky 74321936742* FAITHLESS FEATURING DIDO	68		
12 Jun 04	**MASS DESTRUCTION** *Cheeky 82876614922*	7		4
4 Sep 04	**I WANT MORE** *BMG 82876641902*	22		1
30 Apr 05	**INSOMNIA** *Cheeky 82876690301*	48		
11 Jun 05	**WHY GO?** *Cheeky 82876699292* FAITHLESS FEATURING ESTELLE	49		
13 Aug 05	**GOD IS A DJ** *Cheeky 82876719861*	66		
13 Aug 05	**WE COME 1** *Cheeky 82876719871*	73		
17 Sep 05	**INSOMNIA 2005 (REMIX)** *Cheeky 82876724692*	17		3
2 Dec 06	**BOMBS** *Columbia 88697027602* FAITHLESS FEATURING HARRY COLLIER	26		2
7 Apr 07	**MUSIC MATTERS** *Download* FAITHLESS FEATURING CASS FOX	38		1

FALCO Austrian singer

Date	Title	Peak Position	Weeks at No.1	Weeks in Top 40
22 Mar 86	**ROCK ME AMADEUS** *A&M AM 278* ● ★	1	1	11
31 May 86	**VIENNA CALLING** *A&M AM 318*	10		6
2 Aug 86	**JEANNY** *A&M AM 333*	68		
27 Sep 86	**THE SOUND OF MUSIK** *WEA U 8591*	61		

CHRISTIAN FALK Swedish producer

Date	Title	Peak Position	Weeks at No.1	Weeks in Top 40
26 Aug 00	**MAKE IT RIGHT** *London LONCD 452* CHRISTIAN FALK FEATURING DEMETREUS	22		2

THOMAS FALKE German producer

Date	Title	Peak Position	Weeks at No.1	Weeks in Top 40
13 Aug 05	**HIGH AGAIN (HIGH ON EMOTION)** *Manifesto 9871558*	55		

FALL UK group

Date	Title	Peak Position	Weeks at No.1	Weeks in Top 40
13 Sep 86	**MR PHARMACIST** *Beggars Banquet BEG 168*	75		
20 Dec 86	**HEY! LUCIANI** *Beggars Banquet BEG 176*	59		
9 May 87	**THERE'S A GHOST IN MY HOUSE** *Beggars Banquet BEG 187*	30		2
31 Oct 87	**HIT THE NORTH** *Beggars Banquet BEG 200*	57		
30 Jan 88	**VICTORIA** *Beggars Banquet BEG 206*	35		2
26 Nov 88	**BIG NEW PRINZ/JERUSALEM** *Beggars Banquet FALL 2/3*	59		
27 Jan 90	**TELEPHONE THING** *Cog Sinister SIN 4*	58		
8 Sep 90	**WHITE LIGHTNING** *Cog Sinister SIN 6*	56		
14 Mar 92	**FREE RANGE** *Cog Sinister SINS 8*	40		1
17 Apr 93	**WHY ARE PEOPLE GRUDGEFUL** *Permanent CDSPERM 9*	43		
25 Dec 93	**BEHIND THE COUNTER** *Permanent CDSPERM 13*	75		
30 Apr 94	**15 WAYS** *Permanent CDSPERM 14*	65		
17 Feb 96	**THE CHISELERS** *Jet JETSCD 500*	60		
21 Feb 98	**MASQUERADE** *Artful CDARTFUYL 1*	69		
14 Dec 02	**THE FALL VS 2003** *Action TAKE 020CD*	64		
10 Jul 04	**THEME FROM SPARTA FC** *Action TAKE23CD*	66		

FALL OUT BOY US group

Date	Title	Peak Position	Weeks at No.1	Weeks in Top 40
21 Jan 06	**SUGAR WE'RE GOIN' DOWN** *Mercury 9884652*	24		2
18 Feb 06	**SUGAR WE'RE GOIN' DOWN** *Mercury 9850371*	8		8
22 Apr 06	**DANCE DANCE** *Mercury 9878031*	8		7
15 Jul 06	**A LITTLE LESS 16 CANDLES, A LITTLE MORE "TOUCH ME"** *Mercury 1701063*	38		1
3 Feb 07	**THIS AIN'T A SCENE IT'S AN ARMS RACE** *Mercury 1718545*	2		10
14 Apr 07	**THNKS FR TH MMRS** *Mercury 1732074*	12		7
14 Jul 07	**THE TAKE OVER THE BREAKS OVER** *Mercury 1739377*	48		

FALLACY UK production duo

Date	Title	Peak Position	Weeks at No.1	Weeks in Top 40
22 Jun 02	**THE GROUNDBREAKER** *Wordplay WORCD 036* FALLACY & FUSION	47		
24 May 03	**BIG N BASHY** *Virgin VSCDT 1847* FALLACY FEATURING TUBBY T	45		

FALLOUT TRUST UK group

Date	Title	Peak Position	Weeks at No.1	Weeks in Top 40
25 Jun 05	**WHEN WE ARE GONE** *At Large FUGCD007*	73		
25 Feb 06	**WASHOUT** *At Large FUGCD014*	75		

Silver-selling ● Gold-selling ● Platinum-selling ● US No.1 ★ | Peak Position | Weeks at No.1 | Weeks in Top 40

HAROLD FALTERMEYER German producer

Date	Title / Label	Peak Position	Weeks at No.1	Weeks in Top 40
23 Mar 85	**AXEL F** *MCA 949* (Silver)	2		13
24 Aug 85	**FLETCH THEME** *MCA 991*	74		

AGNETHA FÄLTSKOG Swedish singer

Date	Title / Label	Peak Position	Weeks at No.1	Weeks in Top 40
28 May 83	**THE HEAT IS ON** *Epic A 3436*	35		3
13 Aug 83	**WRAP YOUR ARMS AROUND ME** *Epic A 3622*	44		
22 Oct 83	**CAN'T SHAKE LOOSE** *Epic A 3812*	63		
24 Apr 04	**IF I THOUGHT YOU'D EVER CHANGE YOUR MIND** *WEA 375CD*	11		3
26 Jun 04	**WHEN YOU WALK IN THE ROOM** *WEA 378CD*	34		1

GEORGIE FAME UK singer/pianist

Date	Title / Label	Peak Position	Weeks at No.1	Weeks in Top 40
17 Dec 64	**YEH YEH** *Columbia DB 7428* GEORGIE FAME & THE BLUE FLAMES	1	2	12
4 Mar 65	**IN THE MEANTIME** *Columbia DB 7494* GEORGIE FAME & THE BLUE FLAMES	22		6
29 Jul 65	**LIKE WE USED TO BE** *Columbia DB 7633* GEORGIE FAME & THE BLUE FLAMES	33		3
28 Oct 65	**SOMETHING** *Columbia DB 7727* GEORGIE FAME & THE BLUE FLAMES	23		5
23 Jun 66	**GET AWAY** *Columbia DB 7946* GEORGIE FAME & THE BLUE FLAMES	1	1	10
22 Sep 66	**SUNNY** *Columbia DB 8015*	13		7
22 Dec 66	**SITTING IN THE PARK** *Columbia DB 8096* GEORGIE FAME & THE BLUE FLAMES	12		8
23 Mar 67	**BECAUSE I LOVE YOU** *CBS 202587*	15		8
13 Sep 67	**TRY MY WORLD** *CBS 2945*	37		2
13 Dec 67	**BALLAD OF BONNIE AND CLYDE** *CBS 3124*	1	1	13
9 Jul 69	**PEACEFUL** *CBS 4295*	16		7
13 Dec 69	**SEVENTH SON** *CBS 4659*	25		5
10 Apr 71	**ROSETTA** *CBS 7108* FAME AND PRICE TOGETHER	11		7

FAMILY UK group

Date	Title / Label	Peak Position	Weeks at No.1	Weeks in Top 40
1 Nov 69	**NO MULE'S FOOL** *Reprise RS 27001*	29		6
22 Aug 70	**STRANGE BAND** *Reprise RS 27009*	11		12
17 Jul 71	**IN MY OWN TIME** *Reprise K 14090*	4		12
23 Sep 72	**BURLESQUE** *Reprise K 14196*	13		10

FAMILY CAT UK group

Date	Title / Label	Peak Position	Weeks at No.1	Weeks in Top 40
28 Aug 93	**AIRPLANE GARDENS/ATMOSPHERIC ROAD** *Dedicated FCUK 00CD*	69		
21 May 94	**WONDERFUL EXCUSE** *Dedicated 74321208432*	48		
30 Jul 94	**GOLDENBOOK** *Dedicated 74321220072*	42		

FAMILY DOGG UK group

Date	Title / Label	Peak Position	Weeks at No.1	Weeks in Top 40
28 May 69	**A WAY OF LIFE** *Bell 1055*	6		12

FAMILY FOUNDATION UK group

Date	Title / Label	Peak Position	Weeks at No.1	Weeks in Top 40
13 Jun 92	**XPRESS YOURSELF** *380 PEW 1*	42		

FAMILY STAND US group

Date	Title / Label	Peak Position	Weeks at No.1	Weeks in Top 40
31 Mar 90	**GHETTO HEAVEN** *East West A 7997*	10		10
17 Jan 98	**GHETTO HEAVEN (REMIX)** *Perfecto PERD 156CD1*	30		1

FANTASTIC FOUR US group

Date	Title / Label	Peak Position	Weeks at No.1	Weeks in Top 40
24 Feb 79	**B.Y.O.F. (BRING YOUR OWN FUNK)** *Atlantic LV 14*	62		

FANTASTICS US group

Date	Title / Label	Peak Position	Weeks at No.1	Weeks in Top 40
27 Mar 71	**SOMETHING OLD, SOMETHING NEW** *Bell 1141*	9		10

FANTASY UFO UK instrumental group

Date	Title / Label	Peak Position	Weeks at No.1	Weeks in Top 40
29 Sep 90	**FANTASY** *XL Recordings XLT 15*	56		
10 Aug 91	**MIND BODY SOUL** *Strictly Underground YZ 591* FANTASY UFO FEATURING JAY GROOVE	50		

FAR CORPORATION Multinational group

Date	Title / Label	Peak Position	Weeks at No.1	Weeks in Top 40
26 Oct 85	**STAIRWAY TO HEAVEN** *Arista ARIST 639*	8		6

DON FARDON UK singer

Date	Title / Label	Peak Position	Weeks at No.1	Weeks in Top 40
18 Apr 70	**BELFAST BOY** *Young Blood YB 1010*	32		2
10 Oct 70	**INDIAN RESERVATION** *Young Blood YB 1015*	3		14

FARGETTA Italian DJ

Date	Title / Label	Peak Position	Weeks at No.1	Weeks in Top 40
23 Jan 93	**MUSIC** *Synthetic CDR 6334* FARGETTA & ANNE-MARIE SMITH	34		1
10 Aug 96	**THE MUSIC IS MOVING** *Arista 74321381572*	74		

CHRIS FARLOWE UK singer

Date	Title / Label	Peak Position	Weeks at No.1	Weeks in Top 40
27 Jan 66	**THINK** *Immediate IM 023*	37		1
23 Jun 66	**OUT OF TIME** *Immediate IM 035*	1	1	12
27 Oct 66	**RIDE ON BABY** *Immediate IM 038*	31		7
16 Feb 67	**MY WAY OF GIVING IN** *Immediate IM 041*	48		
29 Jun 67	**MOANIN'** *Immediate IM 056*	46		
13 Dec 67	**HANDBAGS AND GLADRAGS** *Immediate IM 065*	33		2
27 Sep 75	**OUT OF TIME** *Immediate IMS 101*	44		

FARM UK group

Date	Title / Label	Peak Position	Weeks at No.1	Weeks in Top 40
5 May 90	**STEPPING STONE/FAMILY OF MAN** *Produce MILK 101*	58		
1 Sep 90	**GROOVY TRAIN** *Produce MILK 102*	6		9
8 Dec 90	**ALL TOGETHER NOW** *Produce MILK 103* (Silver)	4		10
13 Apr 91	**SINFUL! (SCARY JIGGIN' WITH DOCTOR LOVE)** *Siren SRN 138* PETE WYLIE WITH THE FARM	28		3
4 May 91	**DON'T LET ME DOWN** *Produce MILK 104*	36		2
24 Aug 91	**MIND** *Produce MILK 105*	31		3
14 Dec 91	**LOVE SEE NO COLOUR** *Produce MILK 106*	58		
4 Jul 92	**RISING SUN** *End Product 6581737*	48		
17 Oct 92	**DON'T YOU WANT ME** *End Product 6584687*	18		4
2 Jan 93	**LOVE SEE NO COLOUR (REMIX)** *End Product 6588682*	35		3
12 Jun 04	**ALL TOGETHER NOW 2004** *DMG ENGLCD2004* FARM FEATURING SFX BOYS CHOIR	5		4

FARMER'S BOYS UK group

Date	Title / Label	Peak Position	Weeks at No.1	Weeks in Top 40
9 Apr 83	**MUCK IT OUT** *EMI 5380*	48		
30 Jul 83	**FOR YOU** *EMI 5401*	66		
4 Aug 84	**IN THE COUNTRY** *EMI FAB 2*	44		
3 Nov 84	**PHEW WOW** *EMI FAB 3*	59		

JOHN FARNHAM Australian singer

Date	Title / Label	Peak Position	Weeks at No.1	Weeks in Top 40
25 Apr 87	**YOU'RE THE VOICE** *Wheatley PB 41093*	6		12

JOANNE FARRELL UK singer

Date	Title / Label	Peak Position	Weeks at No.1	Weeks in Top 40
24 Jun 95	**ALL I WANNA DO** *Big Beat A 8194CD*	40		1

JOE FARRELL US saxophonist

Date	Title / Label	Peak Position	Weeks at No.1	Weeks in Top 40
16 Dec 78	**NIGHT DANCING** *Warner Brothers LV 2*	57		

DIONNE FARRIS US singer

Date	Title / Label	Peak Position	Weeks at No.1	Weeks in Top 40
18 Mar 95	**I KNOW** *Columbia 6613542*	47		
27 May 95	**I KNOW** *Columbia 6613542*	41		
7 Jun 97	**HOPELESS** *Columbia 6645165*	42		

GENE FARRIS US DJ/producer

Date	Title / Label	Peak Position	Weeks at No.1	Weeks in Top 40
20 Dec 03	**WELCOME TO CHICAGO EP** *Defected DFTD081R*	74		

GENE FARROW & G.F. BAND UK production group

Date	Title / Label	Peak Position	Weeks at No.1	Weeks in Top 40
1 Apr 78	**MOVE YOUR BODY** *Magnet MAG 109*	33		1
5 Aug 78	**DON'T STOP NOW** *Magnet MAG 125*	71		

Silver-selling · Gold-selling · Platinum-selling · US No.1 · Peak Position · Weeks at No.1 · Weeks in Top 40

FASCINATIONS US group

Date	Title / Label	Peak Position	Weeks at No.1	Weeks in Top 40
3 Jul 71	**GIRLS ARE OUT TO GET YOU** *Mojo 2092 004*	32		3

FASHION UK group

Date	Title / Label	Peak Position	Weeks at No.1	Weeks in Top 40
3 Apr 82	**STREETPLAYER (MECHANIK)** *Arista ARIST 456*	46		
21 Aug 82	**LOVE SHADOW** *Arista ARIST 483*	51		
18 Feb 84	**EYE TALK** *De Stijl A 4106*	69		

SUSAN FASSBENDER UK singer

Date	Title / Label	Peak Position	Weeks at No.1	Weeks in Top 40
17 Jan 81	**TWILIGHT CAFE** *CBS 9468*	21		6

FAST FOOD ROCKERS UK group

Date	Title / Label	Peak Position	Weeks at No.1	Weeks in Top 40
28 Jun 03	**FAST FOOD SONG** *Better The Devil BTD1CD*	2		11
18 Oct 03	**SAY CHEESE (SMILE PLEASE)** *Better The Devil BTD5CD*	10		2
27 Dec 03	**I LOVE CHRISTMAS** *Better The Devil BTD6CDX*	25		1

FASTBALL US group

Date	Title / Label	Peak Position	Weeks at No.1	Weeks in Top 40
3 Oct 98	**THE WAY** *Polydor 5689472*	21		3

FASTWAY UK group

Date	Title / Label	Peak Position	Weeks at No.1	Weeks in Top 40
2 Apr 83	**EASY LIVIN'** *CBS A 3196*	74		

FAT BOYS US group

Date	Title / Label	Peak Position	Weeks at No.1	Weeks in Top 40
4 May 85	**JAIL HOUSE RAP** *Sutra U 9123*	63		
22 Aug 87	**WIPEOUT** *Urban URB 5* FAT BOYS & THE BEACH BOYS	2		8
18 Jun 88	**THE TWIST (YO, TWIST)** *Urban URB 20* FAT BOYS & CHUBBY CHECKER	2		9
5 Nov 88	**LOUIE LOUIE** *Urban URB 26*	46		

FAT JOE US rapper

Date	Title / Label	Peak Position	Weeks at No.1	Weeks in Top 40
1 Apr 00	**FEELIN' SO GOOD** *Columbia 6691972* JENNIFER LOPEZ FEATURING BIG PUN & FAT JOE	15		3
30 Mar 02	**WE THUGGIN'** *Atlantic AT 0124CD*	48		
25 May 02	**WHAT'S LUV** *Atlantic AT 0128CD* FAT JOE FEATURING ASHANTI	4		5
14 Dec 02	**CRUSH TONIGHT** *Atlantic AT 0142CD* FAT JOE FEATURING GINUWINE	42		
16 Oct 04	**LEAN BACK** *Universal MCSTD 40385* TERROR SQUAD FEATURING FAT JOE & REMY	24		2
28 May 05	**HOLD YOU DOWN** *Epic 6759342* JENNIFER LOPEZ FEATURING FAT JOE	6		5
16 Jul 05	**GET IT POPPIN'** *Atlantic AT0210CD* FAT JOE FEATURING NELLY	34		1

FAT LADY SINGS Irish group

Date	Title / Label	Peak Position	Weeks at No.1	Weeks in Top 40
17 Jul 93	**DRUNKARD LOGIC** *East West YZ 756CD*	56		

FAT LARRY'S BAND US group

Date	Title / Label	Peak Position	Weeks at No.1	Weeks in Top 40
2 Jul 77	**CENTRE CITY** *Atlantic K 10951*	31		3
10 Mar 79	**BOOGIE TOWN** *Fantasy FTC 168* FLB	46		
18 Aug 79	**LOOKING FOR LOVE TONIGHT** *Fantasy FTC 179*	46		
18 Sep 82	**ZOOM** *Virgin VS 546*	2		9

FAT LES UK comedy duo

Date	Title / Label	Peak Position	Weeks at No.1	Weeks in Top 40
20 Jun 98	**VINDALOO** *Telstar CDSTAS 2982*	2		8
19 Dec 98	**NAUGHTY CHRISTMAS (GOBLIN IN THE OFFICE)** *Turtleneck NECKCD 001*	21		4
17 Jun 00	**JERUSALEM** *Parlophone CDRS 6540* FAT LES 2000	10		3

FATBACK BAND US group

Date	Title / Label	Peak Position	Weeks at No.1	Weeks in Top 40
6 Sep 75	**YUM YUM (GIMME SOME)** *Polydor 2066 590*	40		1
6 Dec 75	**(ARE YOU READY) DO THE BUS STOP** *Polydor 2066 637*	18		9
21 Feb 76	**(DO THE) SPANISH HUSTLE** *Polydor 2066 656*	10		7
29 May 76	**PARTY TIME** *Polydor 2066 682*	41		
14 Aug 76	**NIGHT FEVER** *Spring 2066 706*	38		2
12 Mar 77	**DOUBLE DUTCH** *Spring 2066 777*	31		3
9 Aug 80	**BACKSTROKIN'** *Spring POSP 149*	41		
23 Jun 84	**I FOUND LOVIN'** *Master Mix CHE 8401*	49		
4 May 85	**GIRLS ON MY MIND** *Atlantic/Cotillion FBACK 1*	69		
6 Sep 86	**I FOUND LOVIN' (REMIX)** *Important TAN 10*	55		
5 Sep 87	**I FOUND LOVIN'** *Master Mix CHE 8401*	7		7

FATBOY SLIM UK DJ/producer

Date	Title / Label	Peak Position	Weeks at No.1	Weeks in Top 40
3 May 97	**GOING OUT OF MY HEAD** *Skint 19CD*	57		
1 Nov 97	**EVERYBODY NEEDS A 303** *Skint 31CD*	34		1
20 Jun 98	**THE ROCKAFELLER SKANK** *Skint 35CD*	6		7
17 Oct 98	**GANGSTER TRIPPIN** *Skint 39CD*	3		6
16 Jan 99	**PRAISE YOU** *Skint 42CD*	1	1	8
1 May 99	**BADDER BADDER SCHWING** *Eye-Q EYEUK 040CD* FREDDY FRESH FEATURING FATBOY SLIM	34		1
1 May 99	**RIGHT HERE RIGHT NOW** *Skint 46CD*	2		6
28 Oct 00	**SUNSET (BIRD OF PREY)** *Skint 58CD*	9		3
20 Jan 01	**DEMONS** *Skint 60CD* FATBOY SLIM FEATURING MACY GRAY	16		2
5 May 01	**STAR 69** *Skint 64XCD*	10		4
15 Sep 01	**A SONG FOR SHELTER/YA MAMA** *Skint 71CD*	30		1
26 Jan 02	**RETOX** *Skint FAT 18*	73		
2 Oct 04	**SLASH DOT DASH** *Skint SKINT100CDX*	12		2
11 Dec 04	**WONDERFUL NIGHT** *Skint SKINT104CD*	51		
12 Mar 05	**THE JOKER** *Skint SKINT106CD*	32		1
8 Jul 06	**THAT OLD PAIR OF JEANS** *Skint SKINT123CD*	39		1

FATHER ABRAPHART UK singer

Date	Title / Label	Peak Position	Weeks at No.1	Weeks in Top 40
16 Dec 78	**LICK A SMURP FOR CHRISTMAS (ALL FALL DOWN)** *Petrol GAS 1/Magnet MAG 139* FATHER ABRAPHART & THE SMURPS	58		

FATIMA MANSIONS Irish group

Date	Title / Label	Peak Position	Weeks at No.1	Weeks in Top 40
23 May 92	**EVIL MAN** *Radioactive SKX 56*	59		
1 Aug 92	**10** *Radioactive SKX 59*	61		
19 Sep 92	**(EVERYTHING I DO) I DO IT FOR YOU** *Columbia 6583827*	7		5
6 Aug 94	**THE LOYALISER** *Kitchenware SKCD 67*	58		

FATMAN SCOOP US rapper

Date	Title / Label	Peak Position	Weeks at No.1	Weeks in Top 40
1 Nov 03	**BE FAITHFUL** *Def Jam 9812716* FATMAN SCOOP FEATURING THE CROOKLYN CLAN	1	2	12
21 Feb 04	**IT TAKES SCOOP** *Def Jam 9816983* FATMAN SCOOP FEATURING THE CROOKLYN CLAN	9		4

NEWTON FAULKNER UK singer

Date	Title / Label	Peak Position	Weeks at No.1	Weeks in Top 40
4 Aug 07	**DREAM CATCH ME** *Ugly Truth 88697117762*	7		12
11 Aug 07	**TEARDROP** *Ugly Truth GBHKB0600089*	57		
3 Nov 07	**ALL I GOT** *Ugly Truth 88697189852*	59		

FC KAHUNA UK group

Date	Title / Label	Peak Position	Weeks at No.1	Weeks in Top 40
6 Apr 02	**GLITTERBALL** *City Rockers ROCKERS 11CD*	64		
20 Jul 02	**MACHINE SAYS YES** *City Rockers ROCKERS 18CD*	58		
22 Mar 03	**HAYLING** *Skint 84CD*	49		

FEAR FACTORY US group

Date	Title / Label	Peak Position	Weeks at No.1	Weeks in Top 40
9 Oct 99	**CARS** *Roadrunner RR 21893*	57		

PHIL FEARON UK singer

Date	Title / Label	Peak Position	Weeks at No.1	Weeks in Top 40
23 Apr 83	**DANCING TIGHT** *Ensign ENY 501* GALAXY FEATURING PHIL FEARON	4		9
30 Jul 83	**WAIT UNTIL TONIGHT (MY LOVE)** *Ensign ENY 503* GALAXY FEATURING PHIL FEARON	20		6
22 Oct 83	**FANTASY REAL** *Ensign ENY 507* GALAXY FEATURING PHIL FEARON	41		
10 Mar 84	**WHAT DO I DO** *Ensign ENY 510* PHIL FEARON & GALAXY	5		8
14 Jul 84	**EVERYBODY'S LAUGHING** *Ensign ENY 514* PHIL FEARON & GALAXY	10		9
15 Jun 85	**YOU DON'T NEED A REASON** *Ensign ENY 517* PHIL FEARON & GALAXY	42		

Silver-selling ● Gold-selling ● Platinum-selling ✪ US No.1 ★ Peak Position Weeks at No.1 Weeks in Top 40

Date	Title / Label	Peak Position	Weeks at No.1	Weeks in Top 40
27 Jul 85	**THIS KIND OF LOVE** *Ensign ENY521* PHIL FEARON & GALAXY	70		
2 Aug 86	**I CAN PROVE IT** *Ensign PF 1*	8		6
15 Nov 86	**AIN'T NOTHING BUT A HOUSEPARTY** *Ensign PF 2*	60		

FEEDER UK group

Date	Title / Label	Peak Position	Weeks at No.1	Weeks in Top 40
8 Mar 97	**TANGERINE** *Echo ECSCD 32*	60		
10 May 97	**CEMENT** *Echo ECSCX 36*	53		
23 Aug 97	**CRASH** *Echo ECSCD 42*	48		
18 Oct 97	**HIGH** *Echo ECSCD 44*	24		1
28 Feb 98	**SUFFOCATE** *Echo ECSCX 52*	37		1
3 Apr 99	**DAY IN DAY OUT** *Echo ECSCD 75*	31		1
12 Jun 99	**INSOMNIA** *Echo ECSCD 77*	22		1
21 Aug 99	**YESTERDAY WENT TOO SOON** *Echo ECSCD 79*	20		2
20 Nov 99	**PAPERFACES** *Echo ECSCD 85*	41		
20 Jan 01	**BUCK ROGERS** *Echo ECSCX 106*	5		4
14 Apr 01	**SEVEN DAYS IN THE SUN** *Echo ECSCD 107*	14		3
14 Jul 01	**TURN** *Echo ECSCD 116*	27		1
22 Dec 01	**JUST A DAY EP** *Echo ECSCX 121*	12		6
12 Oct 02	**COME BACK AROUND** *Echo ECSCX 130*	14		2
25 Jan 03	**JUST THE WAY I'M FEELING** *Echo ECSCX 133*	10		4
17 May 03	**FORGET ABOUT TOMORROW** *Echo ECSCX 135*	12		3
4 Oct 03	**FIND THE COLOUR** *Echo ECSCD 145*	24		1
29 Jan 05	**TUMBLE AND FALL** *Echo ECSCX157*	5		3
16 Apr 05	**FEELING A MOMENT** *Echo ECSCX163*	13		3
9 Jul 05	**PUSHING THE SENSES** *Echo ECSCX173*	30		1
22 Oct 05	**SHATTER/TENDER** *Echo ECSCX180*	11		2
13 May 06	**LOST & FOUND** *Echo ECSCX184*	12		2
5 Aug 06	**SAVE US** *EMI ECSCD186*	34		1

FEELING UK group

Date	Title / Label	Peak Position	Weeks at No.1	Weeks in Top 40
11 Mar 06	**SEWN** *Island CID920*	7		8
27 May 06	**FILL MY LITTLE WORLD** *Island MCSTD40464*	10		13
2 Sep 06	**NEVER BE LONELY** *Island/Uni-Island 1705007*	9		10
25 Nov 06	**LOVE IT WHEN YOU CALL** *Island 1713050*	18		6
17 Feb 07	**ROSE** *Island/Uni-Island 1723753*	38		1
16 Feb 08	**I THOUGHT IT WAS OVER** *Island 1761837*	9		6

FEIST Canadian singer

Date	Title / Label	Peak Position	Weeks at No.1	Weeks in Top 40
29 Sep 07	**1234** *Polydor 5300680*	8		6

WILTON FELDER US saxophonist/bass player

Date	Title / Label	Peak Position	Weeks at No.1	Weeks in Top 40
1 Nov 80	**INHERIT THE WIND** *MCA 646*	39		1
16 Feb 85	**(NO MATTER HOW HIGH I GET) I'LL STILL BE LOOKIN' UP TO YOU** *MCA 919* WILTON FELDER FEATURING BOBBY WOMACK & INTRODUCING ALLTRINA GRAYSON	63		

JOSE FELICIANO US singer

Date	Title / Label	Peak Position	Weeks at No.1	Weeks in Top 40
18 Sep 68	**LIGHT MY FIRE** *RCA 1715*	6		12
18 Oct 69	**AND THE SUN WILL SHINE** *RCA 1871*	25		5

FELIX UK producer

Date	Title / Label	Peak Position	Weeks at No.1	Weeks in Top 40
8 Aug 92	**DON'T YOU WANT ME** *Deconstruction 74321110507*	6		9
24 Oct 92	**IT WILL MAKE ME CRAZY** *Deconstruction 74321118137*	11		4
22 May 93	**STARS** *Deconstruction 74321147102*	29		2
12 Aug 95	**DON'T YOU WANT ME (REMIX)** *Deconstruction 74321293972*	10		3
19 Oct 96	**DON'T YOU WANT ME (2ND REMIX)** *Deconstruction 74321418142*	17		2

FELIX DA HOUSECAT US producer

Date	Title / Label	Peak Position	Weeks at No.1	Weeks in Top 40
6 Sep 97	**DIRTY MOTHA** *Manifesto FESCD 29* QWILO & FELIX DA HOUSECAT	66		
14 Jul 01	**SILVER SCREEN SHOWER SCENE** *City Rockers ROCKERS 1CD*	55		
2 Mar 02	**WHAT DOES IT FEEL LIKE?** *City Rockers ROCKERS 8CD*	66		
5 Oct 02	**SILVER SCREEN SHOWER SCENE** *City Rockers ROCKERS 19CD*	39		1
14 Aug 04	**ROCKET RIDE** *Rykodisc ENR522*	55		
27 Nov 04	**WATCHING CARS GO BY** *Emperor Norton ENR532*	49		
26 Feb 05	**READY2WEAR** *Emperor Norton ENR562*	62		

JULIE FELIX US singer

Date	Title / Label	Peak Position	Weeks at No.1	Weeks in Top 40
18 Apr 70	**IF I COULD (EL CONDOR PASA)** *RAK 101*	19		10
17 Oct 70	**HEAVEN IS HERE** *RAK 105*	22		7

FELON UK singer

Date	Title / Label	Peak Position	Weeks at No.1	Weeks in Top 40
23 Mar 02	**GET OUT** *Serious SERR 32CD*	31		1

FE-M@IL UK group

Date	Title / Label	Peak Position	Weeks at No.1	Weeks in Top 40
5 Aug 00	**FLEE FLY FLO** *Jive 9250592*	46		

FEMME FATALE US group

Date	Title / Label	Peak Position	Weeks at No.1	Weeks in Top 40
11 Feb 89	**FALLING IN AND OUT OF LOVE** *MCA 1309*	69		

FENDERMEN US duo

Date	Title / Label	Peak Position	Weeks at No.1	Weeks in Top 40
18 Aug 60	**MULE SKINNER BLUES** *Top Rank JAR 395*	32		5

FENIX TX US group

Date	Title / Label	Peak Position	Weeks at No.1	Weeks in Top 40
11 May 02	**THREESOME** *MCA MCSTD 40279*	66		

GEORGE FENTON & JONAS GWANGWA UK/South African duo

Date	Title / Label	Peak Position	Weeks at No.1	Weeks in Top 40
2 Jan 88	**CRY FREEDOM** *MCA 1228*	75		

PETER FENTON UK singer

Date	Title / Label	Peak Position	Weeks at No.1	Weeks in Top 40
10 Nov 66	**MARBLE BREAKS IRON BENDS** *Fontana TF 748*	46		

SHANE FENTON & THE FENTONES UK singer

Date	Title / Label	Peak Position	Weeks at No.1	Weeks in Top 40
26 Oct 61	**I'M A MOODY GUY** *Parlophone R 4827*	22		8
1 Feb 62	**WALK AWAY** *Parlophone R 4866*	38		3
5 Apr 62	**IT'S ALL OVER NOW** *Parlophone R 4883*	29		4
12 Jul 62	**CINDY'S BIRTHDAY** *Parlophone R 4921*	19		6

FENTONES UK group

Date	Title / Label	Peak Position	Weeks at No.1	Weeks in Top 40
19 Apr 62	**THE MEXICAN** *Parlophone R 4899*	41		
27 Sep 62	**THE BREEZE AND I** *Parlophone R 4937*	48		

FERGIE UK DJ/producer

Date	Title / Label	Peak Position	Weeks at No.1	Weeks in Top 40
9 Sep 00	**DECEPTION** *Duty Free DF 020CD*	47		
25 Nov 00	**HOOVERS & HORNS** *Nukleuz NUKC 0185* FERGIE & BK	57		
10 Aug 02	**THE BASS EP** *Duty Free DFTELCDX 004*	47		

FERGIE US singer

Date	Title / Label	Peak Position	Weeks at No.1	Weeks in Top 40
16 Sep 06	**LONDON BRIDGE** *A&M/Polydor 1707129* ★	3		7
24 Feb 07	**GLAMOROUS** *A&M 1730081* FERGIE FEATURING LUDACRIS ★	6		17
23 Jun 07	**BIG GIRLS DON'T CRY (PERSONAL)** *Interscope 1741332* ★	2		23
17 Nov 07	**CLUMSY** *Download*	62		

SHEILA FERGUSON US singer

Date	Title / Label	Peak Position	Weeks at No.1	Weeks in Top 40
5 Feb 94	**WHEN WILL I SEE YOU AGAIN** *XSrhythm CDSTAS 2711*	60		

FERKO STRING BAND US string band

Date	Title / Label	Peak Position	Weeks at No.1	Weeks in Top 40
12 Aug 55	**ALABAMA JUBILEE** *London HL 8140*	20		2

LUISA FERNANDEZ Spanish singer

Date	Title / Label	Peak Position	Weeks at No.1	Weeks in Top 40
11 Nov 78	**LAY LOVE ON YOU** *Warner Brothers K 17061*	31		3

PAMELA FERNANDEZ US singer

Date	Title / Label	Peak Position	Weeks at No.1	Weeks in Top 40
17 Sep 94	**KICKIN' IN THE BEAT** *Ore AG 5CD*	43		
3 Jun 95	**LET'S START OVER/KICKIN' IN THE BEAT (REMIX)** *Ore AG 9CD*	59		

FERRANTE & TEICHER US pianist duo

Date	Title / Label	Peak Position	Weeks at No.1	Weeks in Top 40
18 Aug 60	**THEME FROM *THE APARTMENT*** *London HLT 9164*	44		
9 Mar 61	**THEME FROM *EXODUS*** *London HLT 9298/HMV POP 881*	6		16

JOSE FERRER US singer

Date	Title / Label	Peak Position	Weeks at No.1	Weeks in Top 40
19 Feb 54	**WOMAN (UH-HUH)** *Philips PB 220*	7		5

TONY FERRINO Played by UK comedian Steve Coogan

Date	Title / Label	Peak Position	Weeks at No.1	Weeks in Top 40
23 Nov 96	**HELP YOURSELF/BIGAMY AT CHRISTMAS** *RCA 74321430302*	42		

FERRY AID Multinational charity ensemble

Date	Title / Label	Peak Position	Weeks at No.1	Weeks in Top 40
4 Apr 87	**LET IT BE** *The Sun AID 1* ●	1	3	6

BRYAN FERRY UK singer

Date	Title / Label	Peak Position	Weeks at No.1	Weeks in Top 40
29 Sep 73	**A HARD RAIN'S GONNA FALL** *Island WIP 6170*	10		7
25 May 74	**THE IN CROWD** *Island WIP 6196*	13		5
31 Aug 74	**SMOKE GETS IN YOUR EYES** *Island WIP 6205*	17		6
5 Jul 75	**YOU GO TO MY HEAD** *Island WIP 6234*	33		2
12 Jun 76	**LET'S STICK TOGETHER** *Island WIP 6307* ○	4		10
7 Aug 76	**EXTENDED PLAY EP** *Island IEP 1*	7		9
5 Feb 77	**THIS IS TOMORROW** *Polydor 2001 704*	9		8
14 May 77	**TOKYO JOE** *Polydor 2001 711*	15		6
13 May 78	**WHAT GOES ON** *Polydor POSP 3*	67		
5 Aug 78	**SIGN OF THE TIMES** *Polydor 2001 798*	37		3
11 May 85	**SLAVE TO LOVE** *EG FERRY 1*	10		7
31 Aug 85	**DON'T STOP THE DANCE** *EG FERRY 2*	21		5
7 Dec 85	**WINDSWEPT** *EG FERRY 3*	46		
29 Mar 86	**IS YOUR LOVE STRONG ENOUGH** *EG FERRY 4*	22		4
10 Oct 87	**THE RIGHT STUFF** *Virgin VS 940*	37		1
13 Feb 88	**KISS AND TELL** *Virgin VS 1034*	41		
29 Oct 88	**LET'S STICK TOGETHER (REMIX)** *EG EGO 44*	12		5
11 Feb 89	**THE PRICE OF LOVE (REMIX)** *EG EGO 46*	49		
22 Apr 89	**HE'LL HAVE TO GO** *EG EGO 48*	63		
6 Mar 93	**I PUT A SPELL ON YOU** *Virgin VSCDG 1400*	18		3
29 May 93	**WILL YOU LOVE ME TOMORROW** *Virgin VSCDG 1455*	23		3
4 Sep 93	**GIRL OF MY BEST FRIEND** *Virgin VSCDG 1468*	57		
29 Oct 94	**YOUR PAINTED SMILE** *Virgin VSCDG 1508*	52		
11 Feb 95	**MAMOUNA** *Virgin VSCDG 1528*	57		

FEVER UK production group

Date	Title / Label	Peak Position	Weeks at No.1	Weeks in Top 40
8 Jul 95	**STAYING ALIVE 95** *Telstar CDSTAS 2776* FEATURING TIPPA IRIE	48		

LENA FIAGBE UK singer

Date	Title / Label	Peak Position	Weeks at No.1	Weeks in Top 40
24 Jul 93	**YOU COME FROM EARTH** *Mother MUMCD 42*	69		
23 Oct 93	**GOTTA GET IT RIGHT** *Mother MUMCD 44*	20		3
16 Apr 94	**WHAT'S IT LIKE TO BE BEAUTIFUL** *Mother MUMCD 49*	52		
25 Jun 94	**VISIONS** *Mother MUMCD 53*	48		
10 Feb 96	**AFRICAN DREAM** *Mercury MERCD 453* WASIS DIOP FEATURING LENA FIAGBE	44		

KAREL FIALKA UK singer

Date	Title / Label	Peak Position	Weeks at No.1	Weeks in Top 40
17 May 80	**THE EYES HAVE IT** *Blueprint BLU 2005*	52		
5 Sep 87	**HEY MATTHEW** *IRS IRM 140*	9		6

LUPE FIASCO US rapper

Date	Title / Label	Peak Position	Weeks at No.1	Weeks in Top 40
18 Mar 06	**TOUCH THE SKY** *Roc-A-Fella 9852115* KANYE WEST FEATURING LUPE FIASCO	6		7
1 Jul 06	**KICK PUSH** *Atlantic AT0243CDX*	27		3
16 Sep 06	**DAYDREAMIN'** *Atlantic AT0252CD* LUPE FIASCO FEATURING JILL SCOTT	25		2
19 Jan 08	**SUPERSTAR** *Atlantic ATO298CD2* LUPE FIASCO FEATURING MATTHEW SANTOS	4		10

FIAT LUX UK group

Date	Title / Label	Peak Position	Weeks at No.1	Weeks in Top 40
28 Jan 84	**SECRETS** *Polydor FIAT 2*	65		
17 Mar 84	**BLUE EMOTION** *Polydor FIAT 3*	59		

FICTION FACTORY UK group

Date	Title / Label	Peak Position	Weeks at No.1	Weeks in Top 40
14 Jan 84	**(FEELS LIKE) HEAVEN** *CBS A 3996*	6		7
17 Mar 84	**GHOST OF LOVE** *CBS A 3819*	64		

FIDDLER'S DRAM UK group

Date	Title / Label	Peak Position	Weeks at No.1	Weeks in Top 40
15 Dec 79	**DAY TRIP TO BANGOR (DIDN'T WE HAVE A LOVELY TIME?)** *Dingles SID 211*	3		7

FIDELFATTI Italian producer

Date	Title / Label	Peak Position	Weeks at No.1	Weeks in Top 40
27 Jan 90	**JUST WANNA TOUCH ME** *Urban URB 46* FIDELFATTI FEATURING RONETTE	65		

FIELD MOB US rap duo

Date	Title / Label	Peak Position	Weeks at No.1	Weeks in Top 40
26 Aug 06	**SO WHAT** *Geffen 1705382* FIELD MOBB FEATURING CIARA	56		

BILLY FIELD Australian singer

Date	Title / Label	Peak Position	Weeks at No.1	Weeks in Top 40
12 Jun 82	**YOU WEREN'T IN LOVE WITH ME** *CBS A 2344*	67		

ERNIE FIELDS US bandleader

Date	Title / Label	Peak Position	Weeks at No.1	Weeks in Top 40
25 Dec 59	**IN THE MOOD** *London HL 8985*	13		8

GRACIE FIELDS UK singer

Date	Title / Label	Peak Position	Weeks at No.1	Weeks in Top 40
31 May 57	**AROUND THE WORLD** *Columbia DB 3953*	8		9
6 Nov 59	**LITTLE DONKEY** *Columbia DB 4360*	21		7

RICHARD 'DIMPLES' FIELDS US singer

Date	Title / Label	Peak Position	Weeks at No.1	Weeks in Top 40
20 Feb 82	**I'VE GOT TO LEARN TO SAY NO** *Epic EPC A 1918*	56		

FIELDS OF THE NEPHILIM UK group

Date	Title / Label	Peak Position	Weeks at No.1	Weeks in Top 40
24 Oct 87	**BLUE WATER** *Situation Two SIT 48*	75		
4 Jun 88	**MOONCHILD** *Situation Two SIT 52*	28		2
27 May 89	**PSYCHONAUT** *Situation Two ST 57*	35		2
4 Aug 90	**FOR HER LIGHT** *Beggars Banquet BEG 244T*	54		
24 Nov 90	**SUMERLAND (DREAMED)** *Beggars Banquet BEG 250*	37		1
28 Sep 02	**FROM THE FIRE** *Jungle JUNG 65CD*	62		

FIERCE UK group

Date	Title / Label	Peak Position	Weeks at No.1	Weeks in Top 40
9 Jan 99	**RIGHT HERE RIGHT NOW** *Wildstar CXWILD 13*	25		3
15 May 99	**DAYZ LIKE THAT** *Wildstar CDWILD 19*	11		3
14 Aug 99	**SO LONG** *Wildstar CDWILD 27*	15		3
12 Feb 00	**SWEET LOVE 2K** *Wildstar CDWILD 34*	3		4

FIERCE GIRL UK production duo

Date	Title / Label	Peak Position	Weeks at No.1	Weeks in Top 40
11 Sep 04	**DOUBLE DROP** *Red Flag RF012CDS*	74		
19 Feb 05	**WHAT MAKES A GIRL FIERCE** *Red Flag RF013CDS*	52		

FIERY FURNACES US duo

Date	Title / Label	Peak Position	Weeks at No.1	Weeks in Top 40
6 Mar 04	**TROPICAL ICE-LAND** *Rough Trade RTRADESCD152*	52		
17 Jul 04	**SINGLE AGAIN** *Rough Trade RTRADSCD 190*	49		

FIFTH DIMENSION US group

Date	Title / Label	Peak Position	Weeks at No.1	Weeks in Top 40
16 Apr 69	**AQUARIUS/LET THE SUNSHINE IN (MEDLEY)** *Liberty LBF 15193* ★	11		10
17 Jan 70	**WEDDING BELL BLUES** *Liberty LBF 15288* ★	16		8

50 CENT US rapper

Date	Title / Label	Peak Position	Weeks at No.1	Weeks in Top 40
22 Mar 03	**IN DA CLUB** *Interscope 4978742* ○ ★	3		21
12 Jul 03	**21 QUESTIONS** *Interscope 9807195* 50 CENT FEATURING NATE DOGG	6		7
18 Oct 03	**PIMP (IMPORT)** *Interscope 9811812CD*	74		
25 Oct 03	**PIMP** *Interscope 9812333*	5		5
6 Mar 04	**IF I CAN'T/THEM THANGS** *Interscope 9815279* 50 CENT/G-UNIT	10		5

Silver-selling · Gold-selling · Platinum-selling · US No.1 ★ | Peak Position | Weeks at No.1 | Weeks in Top 40

Date	Title / Label	Peak Position	Weeks at No.1	Weeks in Top 40
26 Feb 05	**HOW WE DO** *Interscope 9880361* GAME FEATURING 50 CENT	5		6
2 Apr 05	**CANDY SHOP** *Interscope 9881293* ★	4		12
21 May 05	**HATE IT OR LOVE IT** *Interscope 9882205* GAME FEATURING 50 CENT	4		8
2 Jul 05	**JUST A LIL BIT** *Interscope 9882950*	10		7
24 Sep 05	**OUTTA CONTROL** *Interscope 9885436* 50 CENT FEATURING MOBB DEEP	7		7
24 Sep 05	**SO SEDUCTIVE** *Interscope 9884360* TONY YAYO FEATURING 50 CENT	28		2
3 Dec 05	**WINDOW SHOPPER** *Interscope 9888358*	11		6
11 Feb 06	**HUSTLER'S AMBITION** *Interscope 9879772*	13		4
21 Oct 06	**HANDS UP** *Atlantic AT0253CD* LLOYD BANKS FEATURING 50 CENT	43		
13 Jan 07	**YOU DON'T KNOW** *Download*	32		1
25 Aug 07	**AYO TECHNOLOGY** *Interscope 1746158* 50 CENT FEATURING JUSTIN TIMBERLAKE & TIMBALAND	2		19

5050 UK production duo

Date	Title / Label	Peak Position	Weeks at No.1	Weeks in Top 40
13 Oct 01	**WHO'S COMING ROUND** *Obsessive FIFTYCD 01*	54		
23 Mar 02	**BAD BOYS HOLLER BOO** *Logic 74321910202*	73		

50 GRIND UK group

Date	Title / Label	Peak Position	Weeks at No.1	Weeks in Top 40
22 Dec 01	**GOTTA CATCH 'EM ALL** *Recognition CDREC 21* 50 GRIND FEATURING POKEMON ALLSTARS	57		

52ND STREET UK group

Date	Title / Label	Peak Position	Weeks at No.1	Weeks in Top 40
2 Nov 85	**TELL ME (HOW IT FEELS)** *10 TEN 74*	54		
11 Jan 86	**YOU'RE MY LAST CHANCE** *10 TEN 89*	49		
8 Mar 86	**I CAN'T LET YOU GO** *10 TEN 114*	57		

56K German group

Date	Title / Label	Peak Position	Weeks at No.1	Weeks in Top 40
19 Apr 03	**SAVE A PRAYER** *Kontor 0146495 KON* 56K FEATURING BEJAY	46		

53RD & A 3RD UK singer

Date	Title / Label	Peak Position	Weeks at No.1	Weeks in Top 40
20 Sep 75	**CHICK-A-BOOM (DON'T YA JES LOVE IT)** *UK 2012 002* 53RD & A 3RD FEATURING THE SOUND OF SHAG	36		3

FIGHT CLUB French producer

Date	Title / Label	Peak Position	Weeks at No.1	Weeks in Top 40
7 Feb 04	**SPREAD LOVE** *Nebula NEBCD054* FIGHT CLUB FEATURING LAURENT KONRAD	70		

FIGHTSTAR UK group

Date	Title / Label	Peak Position	Weeks at No.1	Weeks in Top 40
25 Jun 05	**PAINT YOUR TARGET** *Island CID897*	9		2
12 Nov 05	**GRAND UNIFICATION (PART 1)** *Island CID916*	20		1
18 Mar 06	**WASTE A MOMENT** *Island CID921*	29		1
17 Jun 06	**HAZY EYES** *Island/Uni-Island CIDX929*	47		
29 Sep 07	**WE APOLOGISE FOR NOTHING** *Institute CDINSREC06*	63		

FILO US group

Date	Title / Label	Peak Position	Weeks at No.1	Weeks in Top 40
22 Dec 07	**ANTHEM** *Positiva CDTIVS264* FILO & PERI FEATURING ERIC LUMIERE	39		1

FILTER US group

Date	Title / Label	Peak Position	Weeks at No.1	Weeks in Top 40
11 Oct 97	**(CAN'T YOU) TRIP LIKE I DO** *Epic 6650862* FILTER & THE CRYSTAL METHOD	39		1
18 Mar 00	**TAKE A PICTURE** *Reprise W 515CD*	25		1

FILTERFUNK Dutch producer

Date	Title / Label	Peak Position	Weeks at No.1	Weeks in Top 40
22 Apr 06	**SOS (MESSAGE IN A BOTTLE)** *Gusto CDGUS28*	60		

PERCY FILTH UK production duo

Date	Title / Label	Peak Position	Weeks at No.1	Weeks in Top 40
9 Aug 03	**SHOW ME YOUR MONKEY** *Southern Fried ECB 53CDS*	72		

FINCH US group

Date	Title / Label	Peak Position	Weeks at No.1	Weeks in Top 40
5 Apr 03	**LETTERS TO YOU** *MCA MCSXD 40310*	39		1

FINE YOUNG CANNIBALS UK group

Date	Title / Label	Peak Position	Weeks at No.1	Weeks in Top 40
8 Jun 85	**JOHNNY COME HOME** *London LON 68*	8		10
9 Nov 85	**BLUE** *London LON 79*	41		
11 Jan 86	**SUSPICIOUS MINDS** *London LON 82*	8		7
12 Apr 86	**FUNNY HOW LOVE IS** *London LON 88*	58		
21 Mar 87	**EVER FALLEN IN LOVE** *London LON 121*	9		8
7 Jan 89	**SHE DRIVES ME CRAZY** *London LON 199* ★	5		9
15 Apr 89	**GOOD THING** *London LON 218* ★	7		6
19 Aug 89	**DON'T LOOK BACK** *London LON 220*	34		2
18 Nov 89	**I'M NOT THE MAN I USED TO BE** *London LON 244*	20		5
24 Feb 90	**I'M NOT SATISFIED** *London LON 252*	46		
16 Nov 96	**THE FLAME** *ffrr LONCD 389*	17		1
11 Jan 97	**SHE DRIVES ME CRAZY** *ffrr LONCD 391*	36		1

FINITRIBE UK production group

Date	Title / Label	Peak Position	Weeks at No.1	Weeks in Top 40
11 Jul 92	**FOREVERGREEN** *One Little Indian 74 TP12F*	51		
19 Nov 94	**BRAND NEW** *ffrr FCD 247*	69		

FINK BROTHERS UK duo

Date	Title / Label	Peak Position	Weeks at No.1	Weeks in Top 40
9 Feb 85	**MUTANTS IN MEGA CITY ONE** *Zarjazz JAZZ 2*	50		

NEIL FINN New Zealand guitarist/singer

Date	Title / Label	Peak Position	Weeks at No.1	Weeks in Top 40
13 Jun 98	**SHE WILL HAVE HER WAY** *Parlophone CDR 6495*	26		1
17 Oct 98	**SINNER** *Parlophone CDR 6505*	39		1
7 Apr 01	**WHEREVER YOU ARE** *Parlophone CDRS 6557*	32		1
22 Sep 01	**HOLE IN THE ICE** *Parlophone CDRS 6563*	43		

TIM FINN New Zealand singer

Date	Title / Label	Peak Position	Weeks at No.1	Weeks in Top 40
26 Jun 93	**PERSUASION** *Capitol CDCLS 692*	43		
18 Sep 93	**HIT THE GROUND RUNNING** *Capitol CDCLS 694*	50		

FINN BROTHERS New Zealand duo

Date	Title / Label	Peak Position	Weeks at No.1	Weeks in Top 40
14 Oct 95	**SUFFER NEVER** *Parlophone CDRS 6417* FINN	29		1
9 Dec 95	**ANGEL'S HEAP** *Parlophone CDRS 6421* FINN	41		
21 Aug 04	**WON'T GIVE IN** *Parlophone CDRS 6644*	26		1
20 Nov 04	**NOTHING WRONG WITH YOU** *Parlophone CDRS 6655*	31		1
2 Apr 05	**EDIBLE FLOWERS** *Parlophone CDRS6660*	32		1

ELISA FIORILLO US singer

Date	Title / Label	Peak Position	Weeks at No.1	Weeks in Top 40
28 Nov 87	**WHO FOUND WHO** *Chrysalis CHS JEL 1* JELLYBEAN FEATURING ELISA FIORILLO	10		9
13 Feb 88	**HOW CAN I FORGET YOU** *Chrysalis ELISA 1*	50		

FIRE ISLAND UK production group

Date	Title / Label	Peak Position	Weeks at No.1	Weeks in Top 40
8 Aug 92	**FIRE ISLAND/IN YOUR BONES** *Boy's Own BOIX 11*	66		
12 Mar 94	**THERE BUT FOR THE GRACE OF GOD** *Junior Boy's Own JBO 1BCD* FIRE ISLAND FEATURING LOVE NELSON	32		1
4 Mar 95	**IF YOU SHOULD NEED A FRIEND** *Junior Boy's Own JBO 26CDS* FIRE ISLAND FEATURING MARK ANTHONI	51		
11 Apr 98	**SHOUT TO THE TOP** *JBO JNR 5001573* FIRE ISLAND FEATURING LOLEATTA HOLLOWAY	23		1

FIREBALLS US group

Date	Title / Label	Peak Position	Weeks at No.1	Weeks in Top 40
27 Jul 61	**QUITE A PARTY** *Pye International 7N 25092*	29		6
14 Nov 63	**SUGAR SHACK** *London HLD 9789* JIMMY GILMER & THE FIREBALLS ★	45		

FIREHOUSE US group

Date	Title / Label	Peak Position	Weeks at No.1	Weeks in Top 40
13 Jul 91	**DON'T TREAT ME BAD** *Epic 6567807*	71		
19 Dec 92	**WHEN I LOOK INTO YOUR EYES** *Epic 6588347*	65		

FIRM UK comedy group

Date	Title / Label	Peak Position	Weeks at No.1	Weeks in Top 40
17 Jul 82	**ARTHUR DALEY ('E'S ALRIGHT)** *Bark HID 1*	14		7
6 Jun 87	**STAR TREKKIN'** *Bark TREK 1*	1	2	9
29 Nov 97	**FIRM BIZZ** *Columbia 6651612* FIRM FEATURING DAWN ROBINSON	18		1

FIRST CHOICE US group

Date	Title / Label	Peak Position	Weeks at No.1	Weeks in Top 40
19 May 73	**ARMED AND EXTREMELY DANGEROUS** *Bell 1297*	16		8
4 Aug 73	**SMARTY PANTS** *Bell 1324*	9		9

FIRST CLASS UK group

Date	Title / Label	Peak Position	Weeks at No.1	Weeks in Top 40
15 Jun 74	**BEACH BABY** *UK 66*	13		8

FIRST LIGHT UK duo

Date	Title / Label	Peak Position	Weeks at No.1	Weeks in Top 40
21 May 83	**EXPLAIN THE REASONS** *London LON 26*	65		
28 Jan 84	**WISH YOU WERE HERE** *London LON 43*	71		

FIRSTBORN Irish producer

Date	Title / Label	Peak Position	Weeks at No.1	Weeks in Top 40
19 Jun 99	**THE MOOD CLUB** *Independiente ISOM 28MS*	69		

FISCHER-Z UK group

Date	Title / Label	Peak Position	Weeks at No.1	Weeks in Top 40
26 May 79	**THE WORKER** *United Artists UP 36509*	53		
3 May 80	**SO LONG** *United Artists BP 342*	72		

FISCHERSPOONER US production duo

Date	Title / Label	Peak Position	Weeks at No.1	Weeks in Top 40
20 Jul 02	**EMERGE** *Ministry Of Sound FSMOS 1CDS*	25		1
27 Aug 05	**NEVER WIN** *EMI FSCD3*	55		

FISH UK singer

Date	Title / Label	Peak Position	Weeks at No.1	Weeks in Top 40
18 Oct 86	**SHORT CUT TO SOMEWHERE** *Charisma CB 426* FISH & TONY BANKS	75		
28 Oct 89	**STATE OF MIND** *EMI EM 109*	32		2
6 Jan 90	**BIG WEDGE** *EMI EM 125*	25		3
17 Mar 90	**A GENTLEMAN'S EXCUSE ME** *EMI EM 135*	30		2
28 Sep 91	**INTERNAL EXILE** *Polydor FISHY 1*	37		1
11 Jan 92	**CREDO** *Polydor FISHY 2*	38		1
4 Jul 92	**SOMETHING IN THE AIR** *Polydor FISHY 3*	51		
16 Apr 94	**LADY LET IT LIE** *Dick Bros. DDICK 3CD1*	46		
1 Oct 94	**FORTUNES OF WAR** *Dick Bros. DDICK 008CD1*	67		
26 Aug 95	**JUST GOOD FRIENDS** *Dick Bros. DDICK 014CD1* FISH FEATURING SAM BROWN	63		

FISH GO DEEP Irish production duo

Date	Title / Label	Peak Position	Weeks at No.1	Weeks in Top 40
2 Dec 06	**THE CURE & THE CAUSE** *Defected DFTD145CDS* FISH GO DEEP FEATURING TRACEY K	23		2

FISHBONE US group

Date	Title / Label	Peak Position	Weeks at No.1	Weeks in Top 40
1 Aug 92	**EVERYDAY SUNSHINE/FIGHT THE YOUTH** *Columbia 6581937*	60		
28 Aug 93	**SWIM** *Columbia 6596252*	54		

CEVIN FISHER US producer

Date	Title / Label	Peak Position	Weeks at No.1	Weeks in Top 40
3 Oct 98	**THE FREAKS COME OUT** *Sound Of Ministry MOSCDS 127* CEVIN FISHER'S BIG BREAK	34		1
20 Feb 99	**(YOU GOT ME) BURNING UP** *Wonderboy BOYD 013* CEVIN FISHER FEATURING LOLEATTA HOLLOWAY	14		2
7 Aug 99	**MUSIC SAVED MY LIFE** *Sm:)e Communications SM 90982*	67		
20 Jan 01	**IT'S A GOOD LIFE** *Wonderboy BOYD 022* CEVIN FISHER FEATURING RAMONA KELLY	54		
24 Feb 01	**LOVE YOU SOME MORE** *Subversive SUB 68D* CEVIN FISHER FEATURING SHEILA SMITH	60		

EDDIE FISHER US singer

Date	Title / Label	Peak Position	Weeks at No.1	Weeks in Top 40
2 Jan 53	**OUTSIDE OF HEAVEN** *HMV B 10362*	1	1	17
23 Jan 53	**EVERYTHING I HAVE IS YOURS** *HMV B 10398*	8		5
1 May 53	**DOWNHEARTED** *HMV B 10450*	3		15
22 May 53	**I'M WALKING BEHIND YOU** *HMV B 10489* EDDIE FISHER WITH SALLY SWEETLAND (SOPRANO) ★	1	1	18
6 Nov 53	**WISH YOU WERE HERE** *HMV B 10564* ★	8		9
22 Jan 54	**OH MY PAPA** *HMV B 10614* ★	9		4
29 Oct 54	**I NEED YOU NOW** *HMV B 10755* ★	13		10
18 Mar 55	**WEDDING BELLS** *HMV B 10839*	5		11
23 Nov 56	**CINDY OH CINDY** *HMV POP 273*	5		16

MARK FISHER UK keyboard player

Date	Title / Label	Peak Position	Weeks at No.1	Weeks in Top 40
29 Jun 85	**LOVE SITUATION** *Total Control TOCO 3* MARK FISHER FEATURING DOTTY GREEN	59		

TONI FISHER US singer

Date	Title / Label	Peak Position	Weeks at No.1	Weeks in Top 40
12 Feb 60	**THE BIG HURT** *Top Rank JAR 261*	30		1

FITS OF GLOOM UK/Italian production duo

Date	Title / Label	Peak Position	Weeks at No.1	Weeks in Top 40
4 Jun 94	**HEAVEN** *Media MCSTD 1981*	47		
5 Nov 94	**THE POWER OF LOVE** *Media MCSTD 2016* FITS OF GLOOM FEATURING LIZZY MACK	49		

ELLA FITZGERALD US singer

Date	Title / Label	Peak Position	Weeks at No.1	Weeks in Top 40
23 May 58	**SWINGIN' SHEPHERD BLUES** *HMV POP 486*	15		5
16 Oct 59	**BUT NOT FOR ME** *HMV POP 657*	25		3
21 Apr 60	**MACK THE KNIFE** *HMV POP 736*	19		7
6 Oct 60	**HOW HIGH THE MOON** *HMV POP 782*	46		
22 Nov 62	**DESAFINADO** *Verve VS 502*	38		2
30 Apr 64	**CAN'T BUY ME LOVE** *Verve VS 519*	34		3

SCOTT FITZGERALD UK singer

Date	Title / Label	Peak Position	Weeks at No.1	Weeks in Top 40
14 Jan 78	**IF I HAD WORDS** *Pepper UP 36333* SCOTT FITZGERALD & YVONNE KEELEY & THE ST THOMAS MORE SCHOOL CHOIR	3		10
7 May 88	**GO** *PRT PYS 10*	52		

FIVE UK group

Date	Title / Label	Peak Position	Weeks at No.1	Weeks in Top 40
13 Dec 97	**SLAM DUNK (DA FUNK)** *RCA 74321537352*	10		7
14 Mar 98	**WHEN THE LIGHTS GO OUT** *RCA 74321562312*	4		7
20 Jun 98	**GOT THE FEELIN'** *RCA 74321584892*	3		11
12 Sep 98	**EVERYBODY GET UP** *RCA 74321613752*	2		6
28 Nov 98	**UNTIL THE TIME IS THROUGH** *RCA 74321632602*	2		7
31 Jul 99	**IF YA GETTING' DOWN** *RCA 74321689692*	2		8
6 Nov 99	**KEEP ON MOVIN'** *RCA 74321709862*	1	1	13
18 Mar 00	**DON'T WANNA LET YOU GO** *RCA 74321745302*	9		6
29 Jul 00	**WE WILL ROCK YOU** *RCA 74321774022* FIVE & QUEEN	1	1	8
25 Aug 01	**LET'S DANCE** *RCA 74321875962*	1	2	9
3 Nov 01	**CLOSER TO ME** *RCA 74321900742*	4		6

FIVE FOR FIGHTING US guitarist/singer

Date	Title / Label	Peak Position	Weeks at No.1	Weeks in Top 40
1 Jun 02	**SUPERMAN (IT'S NOT EASY)** *Columbia 6727202*	48		

5,6,7,8'S Japanese group

Date	Title / Label	Peak Position	Weeks at No.1	Weeks in Top 40
17 Jul 04	**WOO HOO** *Sweet Nothing CSSN028*	28		1
18 Sep 04	**I'M BLUE** *Sweet Nothing CSSN029*	71		

FIVE SMITH BROTHERS UK group

Date	Title / Label	Peak Position	Weeks at No.1	Weeks in Top 40
22 Jul 55	**I'M IN FAVOUR OF FRIENDSHIP** *Decca F 10527*	20		1

FIVE STAR UK group

Date	Title / Label	Peak Position	Weeks at No.1	Weeks in Top 40
4 May 85	**ALL FALL DOWN** *Tent PB 40039*	15		10
20 Jul 85	**LET ME BE THE ONE** *Tent PB 40193*	18		8
14 Sep 85	**LOVE TAKE OVER** *Tent PB 40353*	25		6
16 Nov 85	**RSVP** *Tent PB 40445*	45		
11 Jan 86	**SYSTEM ADDICT** *Tent PB 40515*	3		9
12 Apr 86	**CAN'T WAIT ANOTHER MINUTE** *Tent PB 40697*	7		9
26 Jul 86	**FIND THE TIME** *Tent PB 40799*	7		7
13 Sep 86	**RAIN OR SHINE** *Tent PB 40901*	2		10
22 Nov 86	**IF I SAY YES** *Tent PB 40981*	15		8
7 Feb 87	**STAY OUT OF MY LIFE** *Tent PB 41131*	9		7

Silver-selling · Gold-selling · Platinum-selling · US No.1 ★ · Peak Position · Weeks at No.1 · Weeks in Top 40

Date	Title / Label	Peak Position	Weeks at No.1	Weeks in Top 40
18 Apr 87	**THE SLIGHTEST TOUCH** *Tent PB 41265*	4		8
22 Aug 87	**WHENEVER YOU'RE READY** *Tent PB 41477*	11		5
10 Oct 87	**STRONG AS STEEL** *Tent PB 41565*	16		5
5 Dec 87	**SOMEWHERE SOMEBODY** *Tent PB 41661*	23		4
4 Jun 88	**ANOTHER WEEKEND** *Tent PB 42081*	18		3
6 Aug 88	**ROCK MY WORLD** *Tent PB 42145*	28		3
17 Sep 88	**THERE'S A BRAND NEW WORLD** *Tent PB 42235*	61		
19 Nov 88	**LET ME BE YOURS** *Tent PB 42343*	51		
8 Apr 89	**WITH EVERY HEARTBEAT** *Tent PB 42693*	49		
10 Mar 90	**TREAT ME LIKE A LADY** *Tent FIVE 1*	54		
7 Jul 90	**HOT LOVE** *Tent FIVE 2*	68		

FIVE THIRTY UK group

Date	Title / Label	Peak Position	Weeks at No.1	Weeks in Top 40
4 Aug 90	**ABSTAIN** *East West YZ 530*	75		
25 May 91	**13TH DISCIPLE** *East West YZ 577*	67		
3 Aug 91	**SUPERNOVA** *East West YZ 594*	75		
2 Nov 91	**YOU (EP)** *East West YZ 624*	72		

5000 VOLTS UK group

Date	Title / Label	Peak Position	Weeks at No.1	Weeks in Top 40
6 Sep 75	**I'M ON FIRE** *Philips 6006 464*	4		9
24 Jul 76	**DR KISS KISS** *Philips 6006 533*	8		8

FIXATE UK group

Date	Title / Label	Peak Position	Weeks at No.1	Weeks in Top 40
14 Jul 01	**37461** *Epark EPKFIX CD1*	42		

FIXX UK group

Date	Title / Label	Peak Position	Weeks at No.1	Weeks in Top 40
24 Apr 82	**STAND OR FALL** *MCA FIXX 2*	54		
17 Jul 82	**RED SKIES** *MCA FIXX 3*	57		

F.K.W. UK group

Date	Title / Label	Peak Position	Weeks at No.1	Weeks in Top 40
2 Oct 93	**NEVER GONNA (GIVE YOU UP)** *PWL International PWCD 273*	48		
11 Dec 93	**SEIZE THE DAY** *PWL International PWCD 279*	45		
5 Mar 94	**JINGO** *PWL International PWCD 283*	30		1
4 Jun 94	**THIS IS THE WAY** *PWL International PWCD 307*	63		

ROBERTA FLACK US singer

Date	Title / Label	Peak Position	Weeks at No.1	Weeks in Top 40
27 May 72	**THE FIRST TIME EVER I SAW YOUR FACE** *Atlantic K 10161* ★	14		13
5 Aug 72	**WHERE IS THE LOVE** *Atlantic K 10202* ROBERTA FLACK & DONNY HATHAWAY	29		5
17 Feb 73	**KILLING ME SOFTLY WITH HIS SONG** *Atlantic K 10282* ★	6		11
24 Aug 74	**FEEL LIKE MAKING LOVE** *Atlantic K 10467* ★	34		2
6 May 78	**THE CLOSER I GET TO YOU** *Atlantic K 11099* ROBERTA FLACK & DONNY HATHAWAY	42		
17 May 80	**BACK TOGETHER AGAIN** *Atlantic K 11481* ROBERTA FLACK & DONNY HATHAWAY	3		9
30 Aug 80	**DON'T MAKE ME WAIT TOO LONG** *Atlantic K 11555*	44		
20 Aug 83	**TONIGHT I CELEBRATE MY LOVE** *Capitol CL 302* PEABO BRYSON & ROBERTA FLACK	2		10
29 Jul 89	**UH-UH OOH OOH LOOK OUT (HERE IT COMES)** *Atlantic A 8491*	72		

FLAMING LIPS US group

Date	Title / Label	Peak Position	Weeks at No.1	Weeks in Top 40
9 Mar 96	**THIS HERE GIRAFFE** *Warner Brothers W 0335CD*	72		
26 Jun 99	**RACE FOR THE PRIZE** *Warner Brothers W 494CD*	39		1
20 Nov 99	**WAITIN' FOR A SUPERMAN** *Warner Brothers W 505CD*	73		
31 Aug 02	**DO YOU REALISE** *Warner Brothers W 586CD*	32		1
25 Jan 03	**YOSHIMI BATTLES THE PINK ROBOTS PART 1** *Warner Brothers W 595CD*	18		2
5 Jul 03	**FIGHT TEST** *Warner Brothers W 611CD*	28		1
27 Sep 03	**THE GOLDEN PATH** *Virgin CHEMSD 18* CHEMICAL BROTHERS FEATURING THE FLAMING LIPS	17		2
22 Apr 06	**THE YEAH YEAH YEAH SONG** *Warner Brothers W711CD1*	16		2
29 Jul 06	**THE WAND** *Warner Brothers W706CD1*	41		

FLAMINGOS US group

Date	Title / Label	Peak Position	Weeks at No.1	Weeks in Top 40
4 Jun 69	**BOOGALOO PARTY** *Philips BF 1786*	26		1

MICHAEL FLANDERS UK singer

Date	Title / Label	Peak Position	Weeks at No.1	Weeks in Top 40
27 Feb 59	**LITTLE DRUMMER BOY** *Parlophone R 4528* MICHAEL FLANDERS WITH THE MICHAEL SAMMES SINGERS	20		3

FLASH & THE PAN Australian group

Date	Title / Label	Peak Position	Weeks at No.1	Weeks in Top 40
23 Sep 78	**AND THE BAND PLAYED ON (DOWN AMONG THE DEAD MEN)** *Ensign ENY 15*	54		
21 May 83	**WAITING FOR A TRAIN** *Easybeat EASY 1*	7		9

FLASH BROTHERS Israeli trio

Date	Title / Label	Peak Position	Weeks at No.1	Weeks in Top 40
6 Nov 04	**AMEN (DON'T BE AFRAID)** *Direction 6754362*	75		

LESTER FLATT & EARL SCRUGGS US banjo duo

Date	Title / Label	Peak Position	Weeks at No.1	Weeks in Top 40
15 Nov 67	**FOGGY MOUNTAIN BREAKDOWN** *CBS 3038/Mercury MF 1007*	39		2

FOGWELL FLAX & THE ANKLEBITERS FROM FREHOLD JUNIOR SCHOOL UK comedian

Date	Title / Label	Peak Position	Weeks at No.1	Weeks in Top 40
26 Dec 81	**ONE NINE FOR SANTA** *EMI 5255*	68		

FLEE-REKKERS UK instrumental group

Date	Title / Label	Peak Position	Weeks at No.1	Weeks in Top 40
19 May 60	**GREEN JEANS** *Triumph RGM 1008*	23		13

FLEET UK group

Date	Title / Label	Peak Position	Weeks at No.1	Weeks in Top 40
15 Oct 05	**GET DOWN** *Cosmos FLEET01CD*	71		

FLEETWOOD MAC UK/US group

Date	Title / Label	Peak Position	Weeks at No.1	Weeks in Top 40
10 Apr 68	**BLACK MAGIC WOMAN** *Blue Horizon 57 3138*	37		1
17 Jul 68	**NEED YOUR LOVE SO BAD** *Blue Horizon 57 3139*	31		7
4 Dec 68	**ALBATROSS** *Blue Horizon 57 3145*	1	1	18
16 Apr 69	**MAN OF THE WORLD** *Immediate IM 080*	2		12
23 Jul 69	**NEED YOUR LOVE SO BAD** *Blue Horizon 57 3157*	32		4
4 Oct 69	**OH WELL** *Reprise RS 27000*	2		14
23 May 70	**THE GREEN MANALISHI (WITH THE TWO-PRONG CROWN)** *Reprise RS 27007*	10		11
12 May 73	**ALBATROSS** *CBS 8306*	2		13
13 Nov 76	**SAY YOU LOVE ME** *Reprise K 14447*	40		1
19 Feb 77	**GO YOUR OWN WAY** *Warner Brothers K 16872*	38		2
30 Apr 77	**DON'T STOP** *Warner Brothers K 16930*	32		4
9 Jul 77	**DREAMS** *Warner Brothers K 16969* ★	24		8
22 Oct 77	**YOU MAKE LOVING FUN** *Warner Brothers K 17013*	45		
11 Mar 78	**RHIANNON** *Warner Brothers K 14430*	46		
6 Oct 79	**TUSK** *Warner Brothers K 17468*	6		7
22 Dec 79	**SARA** *Warner Brothers K 17533*	37		2
25 Sep 82	**GYPSY** *Warner Brothers K 17997*	46		
18 Dec 82	**OH DIANE** *Warner Brothers FLEET 1*	9		9
4 Apr 87	**BIG LOVE** *Warner Brothers W 8398*	9		9
11 Jul 87	**SEVEN WONDERS** *Warner Brothers W 8317*	56		
26 Sep 87	**LITTLE LIES** *Warner Brothers W 8291*	5		9
26 Dec 87	**FAMILY MAN** *Warner Brothers W 8114*	54		
2 Apr 88	**EVERYWHERE** *Warner Brothers W 8143*	4		8
18 Jun 88	**ISN'T IT MIDNIGHT** *Warner Brothers W 7860*	60		
17 Dec 88	**AS LONG AS YOU FOLLOW** *Warner Brothers W 7644*	66		
5 May 90	**SAVE ME** *Warner Brothers W 9866*	53		
25 Aug 90	**IN THE BACK OF MY MIND** *Warner Brothers W 9739*	58		

FLEETWOODS US group

Date	Title / Label	Peak Position	Weeks at No.1	Weeks in Top 40
24 Apr 59	**COME SOFTLY TO ME** *London HLU 8841* ★	6		8

JOHN 'OO' FLEMING UK DJ/producer

Date	Title / Label	Peak Position	Weeks at No.1	Weeks in Top 40
25 Dec 99	**LOST IN EMOTION** *React CDREACT 170*	74		
12 Aug 00	**FREE** *React CDREACT 186*	61		
2 Feb 02	**BELFAST TRANCE** *Nebula BELFCD 001* JOHN 'OO' FLEMING VS SIMPLE MINDS	74		

FLESH & BONES Belgian production duo

Date	Title / Label	Peak Position	Weeks at No.1	Weeks in Top 40
10 Aug 02	**I LOVE YOU** *Multiply CDMULTY 86*	70		

FLICKMAN Italian production group

Date	Title / Label	Peak Position	Weeks at No.1	Weeks in Top 40
4 Mar 00	**THE SOUND OF BAMBOO** *Inferno CDFERN 25*	11		3
28 Apr 01	**HEY! PARADISE** *Inferno CDFERN 37*	69		

K.C. FLIGHTT US rapper

Date	Title / Label	Peak	Wks No.1	Wks Top 40
1 Apr 89	**PLANET E** *RCA PT 49404*	48		
12 May 01	**VOICES** *Hooj Choons HOOJ 106CD* K.C. FLIGHTT VS FUNKY JUNCTION	59		

BERNIE FLINT UK singer

Date	Title / Label	Peak	Wks No.1	Wks Top 40
19 Mar 77	**I DON'T WANT TO PUT A HOLD ON YOU** *EMI 2599* ○	3		10
23 Jul 77	**SOUTHERN COMFORT** *EMI 2621*	48		

FLINTLOCK UK group

Date	Title / Label	Peak	Wks No.1	Wks Top 40
29 May 76	**DAWN** *Pinnacle P 8419*	30		3

FLIP & FILL UK production duo

Date	Title / Label	Peak	Wks No.1	Wks Top 40
24 Mar 01	**TRUE LOVE NEVER DIES** *All Around The World CDGLOBE 240* FLIP & FILL FEATURING KELLY LLORENNA	34		1
2 Feb 02	**TRUE LOVE NEVER DIES (REMIX)** *All Around The World CDGLOBE 248* FLIP & FILL FEATURING KELLY LLORENNA	7		6
27 Jul 02	**SHOOTING STAR** *All Around The World CDGLOBE 258*	3		5
18 Jan 03	**I WANNA DANCE WITH SOMEBODY** *All Around The World CDGLOBE 275*	13		3
22 Mar 03	**SHAKE YA SHIMMY** *All Around The World CXGLOBE 213* PORN KINGS VERSUS FLIP & FILL FEATURING 740 BOYZ	28		1
28 Jun 03	**FIELD OF DREAMS** *All Around The World CDGLOBE 273* FLIP & FILL FEATURING JO JAMES	28		1
17 Jan 04	**IRISH BLUE** *All Around The World CXGLOBE 309* FLIP & FILL FEATURING JUNIOR	20		2
24 Jul 04	**DISCOLAND** *All Around The World CDGLOBE 346* FLIP & FILL FEATURING KAREN PARRY	11		4

FLIPMODE SQUAD US rap group

Date	Title / Label	Peak	Wks No.1	Wks Top 40
31 Oct 98	**CHA CHA CHA** *Elektra E 3810CD*	54		

FLO-RIDA US rapper

Date	Title / Label	Peak	Wks No.1	Wks Top 40
16 Feb 08	**LOW** *Atlantic AT0302CD* FLO-RIDA FEATURING T-PAIN ★	6		6

FLOATERS US group

Date	Title / Label	Peak	Wks No.1	Wks Top 40
23 Jul 77	**FLOAT ON** *ABC 4187* ○	1	1	11

A FLOCK OF SEAGULLS UK group

Date	Title / Label	Peak	Wks No.1	Wks Top 40
27 Mar 82	**I RAN** *Jive 14*	43		
12 Jun 82	**SPACE AGE LOVE SONG** *Jive 17*	34		2
6 Nov 82	**WISHING (IF I HAD A PHOTOGRAPH OF YOU)** *Jive 25* ○	10		9
23 Apr 83	**NIGHTMARES** *Jive 33*	53		
25 Jun 83	**TRANSFER AFFECTION** *Jive 41*	38		1
14 Jul 84	**THE MORE YOU LIVE, THE MORE YOU LOVE** *Jive 62*	26		6
19 Oct 85	**WHO'S THAT GIRL? (SHE'S GOT IT)** *Jive 106*	66		

FLOETRY UK duo

Date	Title / Label	Peak	Wks No.1	Wks Top 40
26 Apr 03	**FLOETIC** *DreamWorks 4507752*	73		

FLOORPLAY UK production duo

Date	Title / Label	Peak	Wks No.1	Wks Top 40
27 Jan 96	**AUTOMATIC** *Perfecto PERF 115CD*	50		

FLOWERED UP UK group

Date	Title / Label	Peak	Wks No.1	Wks Top 40
28 Jul 90	**IT'S ON** *Heavenly HVN 3*	54		
24 Nov 90	**PHOBIA** *Heavenly HVN 7*	75		
11 May 91	**TAKE IT** *London FUP 1*	34		2
17 Aug 91	**IT'S ON/EGG RUSH** *London FUP 2*	38		1
2 May 92	**WEEKENDER** *Heavenly HVN 16*	20		3

FLOWERPOT MEN UK group

Date	Title / Label	Peak	Wks No.1	Wks Top 40
23 Aug 67	**LET'S GO TO SAN FRANCISCO** *Deram DM 142*	4		11

MIKE FLOWERS POPS UK group

Date	Title / Label	Peak	Wks No.1	Wks Top 40
30 Dec 95	**WONDERWALL** *London LONCD 378* ○	2		5
8 Jun 96	**LIGHT MY FIRE/PLEASE RELEASE ME** *London LONCD 384*	39		1
28 Dec 96	**DON'T CRY FOR ME ARGENTINA** *Love This LUVTHISCD 16*	30		2

EDDIE FLOYD US singer

Date	Title / Label	Peak	Wks No.1	Wks Top 40
2 Feb 67	**KNOCK ON WOOD** *Atlantic 584 041*	19		12
16 Mar 67	**RAISE YOUR HAND** *Stax 601 001*	42		
9 Aug 67	**THINGS GET BETTER** *Stax 601 016*	31		3

FLUFFY UK group

Date	Title / Label	Peak	Wks No.1	Wks Top 40
17 Feb 96	**HUSBAND** *Parkway PARK 006CD*	58		
5 Oct 96	**NOTHING** *Virgin VSCDT 1614*	52		

FLUKE UK production group

Date	Title / Label	Peak	Wks No.1	Wks Top 40
20 Mar 93	**SLID** *Circa YRCD 103*	59		
19 Jun 93	**ELECTRIC GUITAR** *Circa YRCD 104*	58		
11 Sep 93	**GROOVY FEELING** *Circa YRCD 106*	45		
23 Apr 94	**BUBBLE** *Circa YRCD 110*	37		1
29 Jul 95	**BULLET** *Circa YRCD 121*	23		1
16 Dec 95	**TOSH** *Circa YRCD 122*	32		1
16 Nov 96	**ATOM BOMB** *Virgin YRCD 125*	20		1
31 May 97	**ABSURD** *Virgin YRCD 126*	25		1
27 Sep 97	**SQUIRT** *Circa YRCD 127*	46		

FLYING LIZARDS UK group

Date	Title / Label	Peak	Wks No.1	Wks Top 40
4 Aug 79	**MONEY** *Virgin VS 276* ○	5		7
9 Feb 80	**TV** *Virgin VS 325*	43		

FLYING PICKETS UK group

Date	Title / Label	Peak	Wks No.1	Wks Top 40
26 Nov 83	**ONLY YOU** *10 TEN 14* ●	1	5	8
21 Apr 84	**WHEN YOU'RE YOUNG AND IN LOVE** *10 TEN 20*	7		7
8 Dec 84	**WHO'S THAT GIRL** *10 GIRL 1*	71		

FM UK group

Date	Title / Label	Peak	Wks No.1	Wks Top 40
31 Jan 87	**FROZEN HEART** *Portrait DIDGE 1*	64		
20 Jun 87	**LET LOVE BE THE LEADER** *Portrait MERV 1*	71		
5 Aug 89	**BAD LUCK** *Epic 6550317*	54		
7 Oct 89	**SOMEDAY (YOU'LL COME RUNNING)** *CBS DINK 1*	64		
10 Feb 90	**EVERYTIME I THINK OF YOU** *Epic DINK 2*	73		

FOALS UK group

Date	Title / Label	Peak	Wks No.1	Wks Top 40
22 Dec 07	**BALLOONS** *Transgressive TRANS065CD*	39		1
1 Mar 08	**CASSIUS** *Download*	26		2

FOCUS Dutch group

Date	Title / Label	Peak	Wks No.1	Wks Top 40
20 Jan 73	**HOCUS POCUS** *Polydor 2001 211*	20		9
27 Jan 73	**SYLVIA** *Polydor 2001 422*	4		10

FOG US DJ/producer

Date	Title / Label	Peak	Wks No.1	Wks Top 40
19 Feb 94	**BEEN A LONG TIME** *Columbia 6601212*	44		
6 Jun 98	**BEEN A LONG TIME (REMIX)** *Pukka CDPUKKA 16*	27		1

DAN FOGELBERG US guitarist/songwriter

Date	Title / Label	Peak	Wks No.1	Wks Top 40
15 Mar 80	**LONGER** *Epic EPC 8230*	59		

BEN FOLDS FIVE US group

Date	Title / Label	Peak	Wks No.1	Wks Top 40
14 Sep 96	**UNDERGROUND** *Caroline CDCAR 008*	37		1
1 Mar 97	**BATTLE OF WHO COULD CARE LESS** *Epic 6642302*	26		2
7 Jun 97	**KATE** *Epic 6645365*	39		1
18 Apr 98	**BRICK** *Epic 6656612*	26		2
24 Apr 99	**ARMY** *Epic 6672182*	28		1
29 Sep 01	**ROCKIN' THE SUBURBS** *Epic 6718492* BEN FOLDS	53		

FOLK IMPLOSION US duo

Date	Title / Label	Peak Position	Weeks at No.1	Weeks in Top 40
15 Jun 96	**NATURAL ONE** *London LONCD 382*	45		

FONTANA US duo

Date	Title / Label	Peak Position	Weeks at No.1	Weeks in Top 40
4 Mar 00	**CHOCOLATE SENSATION** *ffrr FCD 375* LENNY FONTANA & DJ SHORTY	39		1
24 Mar 01	**POW WOW WOW** *Strictly Rhythm SRUKCD 01* FONTANA FEATURING DARRYL D'BONNEAU	62		

WAYNE FONTANA UK singer

Date	Title / Label	Peak Position	Weeks at No.1	Weeks in Top 40
11 Jul 63	**HELLO JOSEPHINE** *Fontana TF 404* WAYNE FONTANA & THE MINDBENDERS	46		
28 May 64	**STOP LOOK AND LISTEN** *Fontana TF 451* WAYNE FONTANA & THE MINDBENDERS	37		2
8 Oct 64	**UM UM UM UM UM UM** *Fontana TF 497* WAYNE FONTANA & THE MINDBENDERS	5		14
4 Feb 65	**GAME OF LOVE** *Fontana TF 535* WAYNE FONTANA & THE MINDBENDERS ★	2		9
17 Jun 65	**JUST A LITTLE BIT TOO LATE** *Fontana TF 579* WAYNE FONTANA & THE MINDBENDERS	20		5
30 Sep 65	**SHE NEEDS LOVE** *Fontana TF 611* WAYNE FONTANA & THE MINDBENDERS	32		4
9 Dec 65	**IT WAS EASIER TO HURT HER** *Fontana TF 642*	36		3
21 Apr 66	**COME ON HOME** *Fontana TF 684*	16		11
25 Aug 66	**GOODBYE BLUEBIRD** *Fontana TF 737*	49		
8 Dec 66	**PAMELA PAMELA** *Fontana TF 770*	11		10

FOO FIGHTERS US group

Date	Title / Label	Peak Position	Weeks at No.1	Weeks in Top 40
1 Jul 95	**THIS IS A CALL** *Roswell CDCL 753*	5		2
16 Sep 95	**I'LL STICK AROUND** *Roswell CDCL 757*	18		1
2 Dec 95	**FOR ALL THE COWS** *Roswell CDCL 762*	28		1
6 Apr 96	**BIG ME** *Roswell CDCL 768*	19		2
10 May 97	**MONKEY WRENCH** *Roswell CDCLS 788*	12		2
30 Aug 97	**EVERLONG** *Roswell CDCL 792*	18		2
31 Jan 98	**MY HERO** *Roswell CDCL 796*	21		1
29 Aug 98	**WALKING AFTER YOU** *Elektra E 4100CD*	20		1
30 Oct 99	**LEARN TO FLY** *RCA 74321706622*	21		2
30 Sep 00	**BREAKOUT** *RCA 74321790112*	29		1
16 Dec 00	**NEXT YEAR** *RCA 74321809262*	42		
19 Oct 02	**ALL MY LIFE** *RCA 74321973152*	5		4
18 Jan 03	**TIMES LIKE THESE** *RCA 74321989562*	12		2
5 Jul 03	**LOW** *RCA 82876522572*	21		1
4 Oct 03	**HAVE IT ALL** *RCA 82876563702*	37		1
11 Jun 05	**BEST OF YOU** *RCA 82876701212*	4		10
17 Sep 05	**DOA** *RCA 82876735392*	25		1
3 Dec 05	**RESOLVE** *RCA 82876738912*	32		1
25 Mar 06	**NO WAY BACK/COLD DAY IN THE SUN** *RCA 82876804732*	64		
25 Aug 07	**THE PRETENDER** *RCA 88697160702*	8		15
15 Dec 07	**LONG ROAD TO RUIN** *RCA 88697190382*	35		1

FOOL BOONA UK producer

Date	Title / Label	Peak Position	Weeks at No.1	Weeks in Top 40
10 Apr 99	**POPPED!** *Virgin/VC Recordings/Uber Disko VCRD 46*	52		

FOOL'S GARDEN German group

Date	Title / Label	Peak Position	Weeks at No.1	Weeks in Top 40
25 May 96	**LEMON TREE** *Encore CDCOR 014*	61		
3 Aug 96	**LEMON TREE (REMIX)** *Encore CDCOR 018*	26		2

FOOLPROOF US group

Date	Title / Label	Peak Position	Weeks at No.1	Weeks in Top 40
26 Jun 04	**PAPER HOUSE** *Island CID 863*	53		

FOR REAL US group

Date	Title / Label	Peak Position	Weeks at No.1	Weeks in Top 40
1 Jul 95	**YOU DON'T KNOW NOTHIN'** *A&M 5811232*	54		
12 Jul 97	**LIKE I DO** *Rowdy 74321486582*	45		

BILL FORBES UK singer

Date	Title / Label	Peak Position	Weeks at No.1	Weeks in Top 40
15 Jan 60	**TOO YOUNG** *Columbia DB 4386*	29		1

DAVID FORBES UK producer

Date	Title / Label	Peak Position	Weeks at No.1	Weeks in Top 40
25 Aug 01	**QUESTIONS (MUST BE ASKED)** *Serious SERR 031CD*	57		

FORCE & STYLES UK production duo

Date	Title / Label	Peak Position	Weeks at No.1	Weeks in Top 40
25 Jul 98	**HEART OF GOLD** *Diverse VERSE 2CD* FORCE & STYLES FEATURING KELLY LLORENNA	55		

FORCE MDs US group

Date	Title / Label	Peak Position	Weeks at No.1	Weeks in Top 40
12 Apr 86	**TENDER LOVE** *Tommy Boy IS 269*	23		4

CLINTON FORD UK singer

Date	Title / Label	Peak Position	Weeks at No.1	Weeks in Top 40
23 Oct 59	**OLD SHEP** *Oriole CB 1500*	27		1
17 Aug 61	**TOO MANY BEAUTIFUL GIRLS** *Oriole CB 1623*	48		
8 Mar 62	**FANLIGHT FANNY** *Oriole CB 1706*	22		8
5 Jan 67	**RUN TO THE DOOR** *Piccadilly 7N 35361*	25		7

EMILE FORD UK singer

Date	Title / Label	Peak Position	Weeks at No.1	Weeks in Top 40
30 Oct 59	**WHAT DO YOU WANT TO MAKE THOSE EYES AT ME FOR?** *Pye 7N 15225* EMILE FORD & THE CHECKMATES	1	6	23
5 Feb 60	**ON A SLOW BOAT TO CHINA** *Pye 7N 15245* EMILE FORD & THE CHECKMATES	3		14
26 May 60	**YOU'LL NEVER KNOW WHAT YOU'RE MISSING ('TIL YOU TRY)** *Pye 7N 15268* EMILE FORD & THE CHECKMATES	12		9
1 Sep 60	**THEM THERE EYES** *Pye 7N 15282*	18		12
8 Dec 60	**COUNTING TEARDROPS** *Pye 7N 15314* EMILE FORD & THE CHECKMATES	4		12
2 Mar 61	**WHAT AM I GONNA DO?** *Pye 7N 15331* EMILE FORD & THE CHECKMATES	33		2
18 May 61	**HALF OF MY HEART** *Piccadilly 7N 35003*	42		
8 Mar 62	**I WONDER WHO'S KISSING HER NOW** *Piccadilly 7N 35033*	43		

LITA FORD UK singer/guitarist

Date	Title / Label	Peak Position	Weeks at No.1	Weeks in Top 40
17 Dec 88	**KISS ME DEADLY** *RCA PB 49575*	75		
20 May 89	**CLOSE MY EYES FOREVER** *Dreamland PB 49409* LITA FORD DUET WITH OZZY OSBOURNE	47		
11 Jan 92	**SHOT OF POISON** *RCA PB 49145*	63		

MARTYN FORD ORCHESTRA UK orchestra

Date	Title / Label	Peak Position	Weeks at No.1	Weeks in Top 40
14 May 77	**LET YOUR BODY GO DOWNTOWN** *Mountain TOP 26*	38		2

PENNY FORD US singer

Date	Title / Label	Peak Position	Weeks at No.1	Weeks in Top 40
4 May 85	**DANGEROUS** *Experience FB 49975*	43		
29 May 93	**DAYDREAMING** *Columbia 6590592*	43		

TENNESSEE ERNIE FORD US singer

Date	Title / Label	Peak Position	Weeks at No.1	Weeks in Top 40
21 Jan 55	**GIVE ME YOUR WORD** *Capitol CL 14005*	1	7	24
6 Jan 56	**SIXTEEN TONS** *Capitol CL 14500* ★	1	4	11
13 Jan 56	**THE BALLAD OF DAVY CROCKETT** *Capitol CL 14506*	3		7

JULIA FORDHAM UK singer

Date	Title / Label	Peak Position	Weeks at No.1	Weeks in Top 40
2 Jul 88	**HAPPY EVER AFTER** *Circa YR 15*	27		4
25 Feb 89	**WHERE DOES TIME GO** *Circa YR 23*	41		
31 Aug 91	**I THOUGHT IT WAS YOU** *Circa YR 69*	64		
18 Jan 92	**LOVE MOVES IN MYSTERIOUS WAYS** *Circa YR 73*	19		6
30 May 92	**I THOUGHT IT WAS YOU (REMIX)** *Circa YR 90*	45		
30 Apr 94	**DIFFERENT TIME DIFFERENT PLACE** *Circa YRCD 111*	41		
23 Jul 94	**I CAN'T HELP MYSELF** *Circa YRCD 116*	62		

FOREIGNER UK/US group

Date	Title / Label	Peak Position	Weeks at No.1	Weeks in Top 40
6 May 78	**FEELS LIKE THE FIRST TIME** *Atlantic K 11086*	39		2
15 Jul 78	**COLD AS ICE** *Atlantic K 10986*	24		4
28 Oct 78	**HOT BLOODED** *Atlantic K 11167*	42		
24 Feb 79	**BLUE MORNING BLUE DAY** *Atlantic K 11236*	45		
29 Aug 81	**URGENT** *Atlantic K 11664*	54		
10 Oct 81	**JUKE BOX HERO** *Atlantic K 11678*	48		
12 Dec 81	**WAITING FOR A GIRL LIKE YOU** *Atlantic K 11696*	8		10

Key: ◯ Silver-selling · ● Gold-selling · ⊛ Platinum-selling · ★ US No.1 · Peak Position · Weeks at No.1 · Weeks in Top 40

Date	Title / Label	Peak Position	Weeks at No.1	Weeks in Top 40
8 May 82	**URGENT** *Atlantic K 11728*	45		
8 Dec 84	**I WANT TO KNOW WHAT LOVE IS** *Atlantic A 9596* ● ★	1	3	12
6 Apr 85	**THAT WAS YESTERDAY** *Atlantic A 9571*	28		4
22 Jun 85	**COLD AS ICE (REMIX)** *Atlantic A 9539*	64		
19 Dec 87	**SAY YOU WILL** *Atlantic A 9169*	71		
22 Oct 94	**WHITE LIE** *Arista 74321232862*	58		

FORMATIONS US group

Date	Title / Label	Peak Position	Weeks at No.1	Weeks in Top 40
31 Jul 71	**AT THE TOP OF THE STAIRS** *Mojo 2027 001*	28		7

GEORGE FORMBY UK singer/ukulele player

Date	Title / Label	Peak Position	Weeks at No.1	Weeks in Top 40
21 Jul 60	**HAPPY GO LUCKY ME/BANJO BOY** *Pye 7N 15269*	40		1

FORREST US singer

Date	Title / Label	Peak Position	Weeks at No.1	Weeks in Top 40
26 Feb 83	**ROCK THE BOAT** *CBS A 3163* ◯	4		8
14 May 83	**FEEL THE NEED IN ME** *CBS A 3411*	17		5
17 Sep 83	**ONE LOVER (DON'T STOP THE SHOW)** *CBS A 3734*	67		

SHARON FORRESTER US singer

Date	Title / Label	Peak Position	Weeks at No.1	Weeks in Top 40
11 Feb 95	**LOVE INSIDE** *ffrr FCD 253*	50		

LANCE FORTUNE UK singer

Date	Title / Label	Peak Position	Weeks at No.1	Weeks in Top 40
19 Feb 60	**BE MINE** *Pye 7N 15240*	4		11
5 May 60	**THIS LOVE I HAVE FOR YOU** *Pye 7N 15260*	26		5

FORTUNES UK group

Date	Title / Label	Peak Position	Weeks at No.1	Weeks in Top 40
8 Jul 65	**YOU'VE GOT YOUR TROUBLES** *Decca F 12173*	2		12
7 Oct 65	**HERE IT COMES AGAIN** *Decca F 12243*	4		12
3 Feb 66	**THIS GOLDEN RING** *Decca F 12321*	15		7
11 Sep 71	**FREEDOM COME FREEDOM GO** *Capitol CL 15693*	6		12
29 Jan 72	**STORM IN A TEACUP** *Capitol CL 15707*	7		10

45 KING UK DJ/producer

Date	Title / Label	Peak Position	Weeks at No.1	Weeks in Top 40
28 Oct 89	**THE KING IS HERE/THE 900 NUMBER** *Dance Trax DRX 9*	60		
11 Aug 90	**THE KING IS HERE/THE 900 NUMBER** *Dance Trax DRX 9*	73		

49ERS Italian group

Date	Title / Label	Peak Position	Weeks at No.1	Weeks in Top 40
16 Dec 89	**TOUCH ME** *Fourth & Broadway BRW 157*	3		11
17 Mar 90	**DON'T YOU LOVE ME** *Fourth & Broadway BRW 167*	12		5
9 Jun 90	**GIRL TO GIRL** *Fourth & Broadway BRW 174*	31		2
6 Jun 92	**GOT TO BE FREE** *Fourth & Broadway BRW 255*	46		
29 Aug 92	**THE MESSAGE** *Fourth & Broadway BRW 257*	68		
18 Mar 95	**ROCKIN' MY BODY** *Media MCSTD 2021*			
	49ERS FEATURING ANN-MARIE SMITH	31		2

FORWARD, RUSSIA! UK group

Date	Title / Label	Peak Position	Weeks at No.1	Weeks in Top 40
27 Aug 05	**THIRTEEN/FOURTEEN** *Drowned In Sound OPE002CDS*	74		
28 Jan 06	**TWELVE** *Dance To The Radio DTTR006CD*	36		1
13 May 06	**NINE** *Dance To The Radio DTTR011CD*	40		1
5 Aug 06	**EIGHTEEN** *Dance To The Radio DTTR016CD*	44		
25 Nov 06	**NINETEEN** *Dance To The Radio DTTR021CD*	67		

FOSTER & ALLEN Irish duo

Date	Title / Label	Peak Position	Weeks at No.1	Weeks in Top 40
27 Feb 82	**A BUNCH OF THYME** *Ritz 5*	18		8
30 Oct 82	**OLD FLAMES** *Ritz 028*	51		
19 Feb 83	**MAGGIE** *Ritz 025*	27		5
29 Oct 83	**I WILL LOVE YOU ALL MY LIFE** *Ritz 056*	49		
30 Jun 84	**JUST FOR OLD TIME'S SAKE** *Ritz 066*	47		
29 Mar 86	**AFTER ALL THESE YEARS** *Ritz 106*	43		

FOUNDATION US duo

Date	Title / Label	Peak Position	Weeks at No.1	Weeks in Top 40
12 Jul 03	**ALL OUT OF LOVE** *Arista 82876513292*			
	FOUNDATION FEATURING NATALIE ROSSI	40		1

FOUNDATIONS UK group

Date	Title / Label	Peak Position	Weeks at No.1	Weeks in Top 40
27 Sep 67	**BABY NOW THAT I'VE FOUND YOU** *Pye 7N 17366*	1	2	14
24 Jan 68	**BACK ON MY FEET AGAIN** *Pye 7N 17417*	18		9
1 May 68	**ANY OLD TIME (YOU'RE LONELY AND SAD)** *Pye 7N 17503*	48		
20 Nov 68	**BUILD ME UP BUTTERCUP** *Pye 7N 17636*	2		12
12 Mar 69	**IN THE BAD BAD OLD DAYS** *Pye 7N 17702*	8		9
13 Sep 69	**BORN TO LIVE AND BORN TO DIE** *Pye 7N 17809*	46		
12 Dec 98	**BUILD ME UP BUTTERCUP** *Castle NEEX 1001*	71		

FOUNTAINS OF WAYNE US group

Date	Title / Label	Peak Position	Weeks at No.1	Weeks in Top 40
22 Mar 97	**RADIATION VIBE** *Atlantic 7567956262*	32		1
10 May 97	**SINK TO THE BOTTOM** *Atlantic A 5612CD*	42		
26 Jul 97	**SURVIVAL CAR** *Atlantic AT 0004CD*	53		
27 Dec 97	**I WANT AN ALIEN FOR CHRISTMAS** *Atlantic AT 0020CD*	36		1
20 Mar 99	**DENISE** *Atlantic AT 0053CD*	57		
20 Mar 04	**STACY'S MUM** *Virgin VSCDX 1860*	11		4
18 Sep 04	**HEY JULIE** *Virgin VSCDX 1881*	57		

FOUR ACES US group

Date	Title / Label	Peak Position	Weeks at No.1	Weeks in Top 40
30 Jul 54	**THREE COINS IN THE FOUNTAIN** *Brunswick 05308*			
	FOUR ACES FEATURING AL ALBERTS ★	5		6
7 Jan 55	**MR SANDMAN** *Brunswick 05355*			
	FOUR ACES FEATURING AL ALBERTS	9		5
20 May 55	**STRANGER IN PARADISE** *Brunswick 05418*	6		6
18 Nov 55	**LOVE IS A MANY SPLENDOURED THING** *Brunswick 05480*			
	FOUR ACES FEATURING AL ALBERTS ★	2		13
19 Oct 56	**WOMAN IN LOVE** *Brunswick 05589*			
	FOUR ACES FEATURING AL ALBERTS	19		3
4 Jan 57	**FRIENDLY PERSUASION** *Brunswick 05623*			
	FOUR ACES FEATURING AL ALBERTS	29		1
23 Jan 59	**THE WORLD OUTSIDE** *Brunswick 05773*	18		6

FOUR BUCKETEERS UK group

Date	Title / Label	Peak Position	Weeks at No.1	Weeks in Top 40
3 May 80	**THE BUCKET OF WATER SONG** *CBS 8393*	26		3

4 CLUBBERS German production group

Date	Title / Label	Peak Position	Weeks at No.1	Weeks in Top 40
14 Sep 02	**CHILDREN** *Code Blue BLU 026CD*	45		

FOUR ESQUIRES US group

Date	Title / Label	Peak Position	Weeks at No.1	Weeks in Top 40
31 Jan 58	**LOVE ME FOREVER** *London HLO 8533*	23		6

FOUR FOUR TWO UK group

Date	Title / Label	Peak Position	Weeks at No.1	Weeks in Top 40
19 Jun 04	**COME ON ENGLAND** *Gut CDGUT58*	2		4

4 HERO UK group

Date	Title / Label	Peak Position	Weeks at No.1	Weeks in Top 40
24 Nov 90	**MR KIRK'S NIGHTMARE** *Reinforced RIVET 1203*	73		
9 May 92	**COOKIN' UP YAH BRAIN** *Reinforced RIVET 1216*	59		
15 Aug 98	**STAR CHASERS** *Talkin Loud TLCD 36*	41		
3 Nov 01	**LES FLEUR** *Talkin Loud TLCD 66*	53		

400 BLOWS UK group

Date	Title / Label	Peak Position	Weeks at No.1	Weeks in Top 40
29 Jun 85	**MOVIN'** *Illuminated ILL 61*	54		

FOUR KNIGHTS US group

Date	Title / Label	Peak Position	Weeks at No.1	Weeks in Top 40
4 Jun 54	**(OH BABY MINE) I GET SO LONELY** *Capitol CL 14076*	5		11

FOUR LADS Canadian group

Date	Title / Label	Peak Position	Weeks at No.1	Weeks in Top 40
19 Dec 52	**FAITH CAN MOVE MOUNTAINS** *Columbia DB 3154*			
	JOHNNIE RAY & THE FOUR LADS	7		3
22 Oct 54	**RAIN RAIN RAIN** *Philips PB 311*			
	FRANKIE LAINE & THE FOUR LADS	8		16
28 Apr 60	**STANDING ON THE CORNER** *Philips PB 1000*	34		3

4 NON BLONDES US group

Date	Title / Label	Peak Position	Weeks at No.1	Weeks in Top 40
19 Jun 93	**WHAT'S UP** *Interscope A 8412CD* ◯	2		12
16 Oct 93	**SPACEMAN** *Interscope A 8349CD*	53		

Silver-selling ● Gold-selling ● Platinum-selling ● US No.1 ★ · Peak Position · Weeks at No.1 · Weeks in Top 40

4 OF US Irish group

Date	Title / Label	Peak Position	Weeks at No.1	Weeks in Top 40
27 Feb 93	**SHE HITS ME** *Columbia 6589192*	35		1
1 May 93	**I MISS YOU** *Columbia 6591722*	62		

411 UK group

Date	Title / Label	Peak Position	Weeks at No.1	Weeks in Top 40
29 May 04	**ON MY KNEES** *Sony Music 6749382* 411 FEATURING GHOSTFACE KILLAH	4		6
4 Sep 04	**DUMB** *Sony/Streetside 6752622*	3		7
27 Nov 04	**TEARDROPS** *Sony/Streetside 6754812*	23		1

FOUR PENNIES UK group

Date	Title / Label	Peak Position	Weeks at No.1	Weeks in Top 40
16 Jan 64	**DO YOU WANT ME TO** *Philips BF 1296*	47		
2 Apr 64	**JULIET** *Philips BF 1322*	1	1	15
16 Jul 64	**I FOUND OUT THE HARD WAY** *Philips BF 1349*	14		9
29 Oct 64	**BLACK GIRL** *Philips BF 1366*	20		8
7 Oct 65	**UNTIL IT'S TIME FOR YOU TO GO** *Philips BF 1435*	19		8
17 Feb 66	**TROUBLE IS MY MIDDLE NAME** *Philips BF 1469*	32		3

FOUR PREPS US group

Date	Title / Label	Peak Position	Weeks at No.1	Weeks in Top 40
13 Jun 58	**BIG MAN** *Capitol CL 14873*	2		14
26 May 60	**GOT A GIRL** *Capitol CL 15128*	28		5
9 Nov 61	**MORE MONEY FOR YOU AND ME (MEDLEY)** *Capitol CL 15217*	39		1

FOUR SEASONS US group

Date	Title / Label	Peak Position	Weeks at No.1	Weeks in Top 40
4 Oct 62	**SHERRY** *Stateside SS 122* ★	8		14
17 Jan 63	**BIG GIRLS DON'T CRY** *Stateside SS 145* ★	13		8
28 Mar 63	**WALK LIKE A MAN** *Stateside SS 169* ★	12		11
27 Jun 63	**AIN'T THAT A SHAME** *Stateside SS 194*	38		1
27 Aug 64	**RAG DOLL** *Philips BF 1347* FOUR SEASONS WITH THE SOUND OF FRANKIE VALLI	2		12
18 Nov 65	**LET'S HANG ON** *Philips BF 1439* FOUR SEASONS WITH THE SOUND OF FRANKIE VALLI	4		15
31 Mar 66	**WORKING MY WAY BACK TO YOU** *Philips BF 1474* FOUR SEASONS WITH FRANKIE VALLI	50		
2 Jun 66	**OPUS 17 (DON'T YOU WORRY 'BOUT ME)** *Philips BF 1493* FOUR SEASONS WITH FRANKIE VALLI	20		6
29 Sep 66	**I'VE GOT YOU UNDER MY SKIN** *Philips BF 1511* FOUR SEASONS WITH FRANKIE VALLI	12		9
12 Jan 67	**TELL IT TO THE RAIN** *Philips BF 1538* FOUR SEASONS WITH FRANKIE VALLI	37		3
19 Apr 75	**THE NIGHT** *Mowest MW 3024* FRANKIE VALLI & THE FOUR SEASONS	7		8
20 Sep 75	**WHO LOVES YOU?** *Warner Brothers K 16602*	6		8
31 Jan 76	**DECEMBER '63 (OH WHAT A NIGHT)** *Warner Brothers K 16688* ● ★	1	2	10
24 Apr 76	**SILVER STAR** *Warner Brothers K 16742*	3		9
27 Nov 76	**WE CAN WORK IT OUT** *Warner Brothers K 16845*	34		2
18 Jun 77	**RHAPSODY** *Warner Brothers K 16932*	37		1
20 Aug 77	**DOWN THE HALL** *Warner Brothers K 16982*	34		3
29 Oct 88	**DECEMBER '63 (OH WHAT A NIGHT) (REMIX)** *BR 45277* FRANKIE VALLI & THE FOUR SEASONS	49		
14 Jul 07	**BEGGIN'** *679 679L146CD* FRANKIE VALLI & THE FOUR SEASONS	32		1

4 STRINGS Dutch producer

Date	Title / Label	Peak Position	Weeks at No.1	Weeks in Top 40
23 Dec 00	**DAY TIME** *A&M CDAMPM 139*	48		
11 May 02	**TAKE ME AWAY INTO THE NIGHT** *Nebula VCRD 107*	15		3
14 Sep 02	**DIVING** *Nebula VCRD 108*	38		1
13 Sep 03	**LET IT RAIN** *Nebula NEBTCD 049*	49		
31 Jul 04	**TURN IT AROUND** *Nebula NEBCD059*	50		

4 THE CAUSE US group

Date	Title / Label	Peak Position	Weeks at No.1	Weeks in Top 40
10 Oct 98	**STAND BY ME** *RCA 74321622442*	12		5

FOUR TOPS US group

Date	Title / Label	Peak Position	Weeks at No.1	Weeks in Top 40
1 Jul 65	**I CAN'T HELP MYSELF** *Tamla Motown TMG 515*	23		6
2 Sep 65	**IT'S THE SAME OLD SONG** *Tamla Motown TMG 528*	34		3
21 Jul 66	**LOVING YOU IS SWEETER THAN EVER** *Tamla Motown TMG 568*	21		7
13 Oct 66	**REACH OUT I'LL BE THERE** *Tamla Motown TMG 579* ★	1	3	15
12 Jan 67	**STANDING IN THE SHADOWS OF LOVE** *Tamla Motown TMG 589*	6		7
30 Mar 67	**BERNADETTE** *Tamla Motown TMG 601*	8		10
15 Jun 67	**SEVEN ROOMS OF GLOOM** *Tamla Motown TMG 612*	12		9
11 Oct 67	**YOU KEEP RUNNING AWAY** *Tamla Motown TMG 623*	26		6
13 Dec 67	**WALK AWAY RENEE** *Tamla Motown TMG 634*	3		11
13 Mar 68	**IF I WERE A CARPENTER** *Tamla Motown TMG 647*	7		9
21 Aug 68	**YESTERDAY'S DREAMS** *Tamla Motown TMG 665*	23		10
13 Nov 68	**I'M IN A DIFFERENT WORLD** *Tamla Motown TMG 675*	27		8
28 May 69	**WHAT IS A MAN** *Tamla Motown TMG 698*	16		8
27 Sep 69	**DO WHAT YOU GOTTA DO** *Tamla Motown TMG 710*	11		8
21 Mar 70	**I CAN'T HELP MYSELF** *Tamla Motown TMG 732* ★	10		8
30 May 70	**IT'S ALL IN THE GAME** *Tamla Motown TMG 736*	5		14
3 Oct 70	**STILL WATER (LOVE)** *Tamla Motown TMG 752*	10		7
1 May 71	**JUST SEVEN NUMBERS (CAN STRAIGHTEN OUT MY LIFE)** *Tamla Motown TMG 770*	36		3
26 Jun 71	**RIVER DEEP MOUNTAIN HIGH** *Tamla Motown TMG 777* SUPREMES & THE FOUR TOPS	11		10
25 Sep 71	**SIMPLE GAME** *Tamla Motown TMG 785*	3		10
20 Nov 71	**YOU GOTTA HAVE LOVE IN YOUR HEART** *Tamla Motown TMG 793* SUPREMES & THE FOUR TOPS	25		8
11 Mar 72	**BERNADETTE** *Tamla Motown TMG 803*	23		5
5 Aug 72	**WALK WITH ME TALK WITH ME DARLING** *Tamla Motown TMG 823*	32		3
18 Nov 72	**KEEPER OF THE CASTLE** *Probe PRO 575*	18		8
10 Nov 73	**SWEET UNDERSTANDING LOVE** *Probe PRO 604*	29		9
17 Oct 81	**WHEN SHE WAS MY GIRL** *Casablanca CAN 1005* ●	3		7
19 Dec 81	**DON'T WALK AWAY** *Casablanca CAN 1006*	16		9
6 Mar 82	**TONIGHT I'M GONNA LOVE YOU ALL OVER** *Casablanca CAN 1008*	43		
26 Jun 82	**BACK TO SCHOOL AGAIN** *RSO 89*	62		
23 Jul 88	**REACH OUT I'LL BE THERE (REMIX)** *Motown ZB 41943*	11		7
17 Sep 88	**INDESTRUCTIBLE** *Arista 111717* FOUR TOPS FEATURING SMOKEY ROBINSON	55		
3 Dec 88	**LOCO IN ACAPULCO** *Arista 111850*	7		9
25 Feb 89	**INDESTRUCTIBLE** *Arista 112074* FOUR TOPS FEATURING SMOKEY ROBINSON	30		2

4 TUNE 500 UK/Israeli production duo

Date	Title / Label	Peak Position	Weeks at No.1	Weeks in Top 40
16 Aug 03	**DANCING IN THE DARK** *Black Gold BLGD04CSC 01*	75		

4 VINI UK group

Date	Title / Label	Peak Position	Weeks at No.1	Weeks in Top 40
18 May 02	**FOREVER YOUNG** *Botchit & Scarper BOS2CD 033* 4 VINI FEATURING ELIZABETH TROY	75		

4MANDU UK group

Date	Title / Label	Peak Position	Weeks at No.1	Weeks in Top 40
29 Jul 95	**THIS IS IT** *Final Vinyl 74321291222*	45		
17 Feb 96	**DO IT FOR LOVE** *Final Vinyl 74321343902*	45		
15 Jun 96	**BABY DON'T GO** *Final Vinyl 74321375912*	47		

FOURMOST UK group

Date	Title / Label	Peak Position	Weeks at No.1	Weeks in Top 40
12 Sep 63	**HELLO LITTLE GIRL** *Parlophone R 5056*	9		11
26 Dec 63	**I'M IN LOVE** *Parlophone R 5078*	17		10
23 Apr 64	**A LITTLE LOVING** *Parlophone R 5128*	6		11
13 Aug 64	**HOW CAN I TELL HER** *Parlophone R 5157*	33		3
26 Nov 64	**BABY I NEED YOUR LOVIN'** *Parlophone R 5194*	24		8
9 Dec 65	**GIRLS GIRLS GIRLS** *Parlophone R 5379*	33		2

14-18 UK singer/producer

Date	Title / Label	Peak Position	Weeks at No.1	Weeks in Top 40
1 Nov 75	**GOODBYE-EE** *Magnet MAG 48*	33		1

FOX UK group

Date	Title / Label	Peak Position	Weeks at No.1	Weeks in Top 40
15 Feb 75	**ONLY YOU CAN** *GTO GT 8* ●	3		9
10 May 75	**IMAGINE ME IMAGINE YOU** *GTO GT 21*	15		7
10 Apr 76	**S-S-S-SINGLE BED** *GTO GT 57*	4		9

CASS FOX UK singer

Date	Title / Label	Peak Position	Weeks at No.1	Weeks in Top 40
4 Nov 06	**TOUCH ME** *Universal 1712211*	52		
7 Apr 07	**MUSIC MATTERS** *Download* FAITHLESS FEATURING CASS FOX	38		1

GEMMA FOX UK singer

Date	Title / Label	Peak Position	Weeks at No.1	Weeks in Top 40
8 May 04	**GIRLFRIEND'S STORY** *Polydor 9866362* GEMMA FOX FEATURING MC LYTE	38		1

JAMES FOX UK singer

Date	Title / Label	Peak Position	Weeks at No.1	Weeks in Top 40
1 May 04	**HOLD ON TO OUR LOVE** *Sony Music 6748732*	13		5

Silver-selling ○ · Gold-selling ● · Platinum-selling ⊛ · US No.1 ★ · Peak Position · Weeks at No.1 · Weeks in Top 40

NOOSHA FOX UK singer

Date	Title / Label	Peak Position	Weeks at No.1	Weeks in Top 40
12 Nov 77	**GEORGINA BAILEY** *GTO GT 106*	31		4

SAMANTHA FOX UK singer/model

Date	Title / Label	Peak Position	Weeks at No.1	Weeks in Top 40
22 Mar 86	**TOUCH ME (I WANT YOUR BODY)** *Jive FOXY 1* ○	3		9
28 Jun 86	**DO YA DO YA (WANNA PLEASE ME)** *Jive FOXY 2*	10		5
6 Sep 86	**HOLD ON TIGHT** *Jive FOXY 3*	26		4
13 Dec 86	**I'M ALL YOU NEED** *Jive FOXY 4*	41		
30 May 87	**NOTHING'S GONNA STOP ME NOW** *Jive FOXY 5*	8		8
25 Jul 87	**I SURRENDER (TO THE SPIRIT OF THE NIGHT)** *Jive FOXY 6*	25		5
17 Oct 87	**I PROMISE YOU (GET READY)** *Jive FOXY 7*	58		
19 Dec 87	**TRUE DEVOTION** *Jive FOXY 8*	62		
21 May 88	**NAUGHTY GIRLS** *Jive FOXY 9* SAMANTHA FOX FEATURING FULL FORCE	31		2
19 Nov 88	**LOVE HOUSE** *Jive FOXY 10*	32		3
28 Jan 89	**I ONLY WANNA BE WITH YOU** *Jive FOXY 11*	16		6
17 Jun 89	**I WANNA HAVE SOME FUN** *Jive FOXY 12*	63		
28 Mar 98	**SANTA MARIA** *All Around The World CDGLOBE 163* DJ MILANO FEATURING SAMANTHA FOX	31		1

BRUCE FOXTON UK singer/bass player

Date	Title / Label	Peak Position	Weeks at No.1	Weeks in Top 40
30 Jul 83	**FREAK** *Arista BFOX 1*	23		5
29 Oct 83	**THIS IS THE WAY** *Arista BFOX 2*	56		
21 Apr 84	**IT MAKES ME WONDER** *Arista BFOX 3*	74		

INEZ FOXX US singer

Date	Title / Label	Peak Position	Weeks at No.1	Weeks in Top 40
23 Jul 64	**HURT BY LOVE** *Sue WI 323*	40		1
19 Feb 69	**MOCKINGBIRD** *United Artists UP 2269* INEZ & CHARLIE FOXX	33		2

JAMIE FOXX US singer

Date	Title / Label	Peak Position	Weeks at No.1	Weeks in Top 40
1 Oct 05	**GOLD DIGGER** *Roc-A-Fella 9885699* KANYE WEST FEATURING JAMIE FOXX ★	2		19
22 Apr 06	**UNPREDICTABLE** *J Records 82876804772* JAMIE FOXX FEATURING LUDACRIS	16		4
1 Jul 06	**EXTRAVAGANZA** *J Records 82876869422*	43		

JOHN FOXX UK singer

Date	Title / Label	Peak Position	Weeks at No.1	Weeks in Top 40
26 Jan 80	**UNDERPASS** *Virgin VS 318*	31		4
29 Mar 80	**NO-ONE DRIVING (DOUBLE SINGLE)** *Virgin VS 338*	32		3
19 Jul 80	**BURNING CAR** *Virgin VS 360*	35		3
8 Nov 80	**MILES AWAY** *Virgin VS 382*	51		
29 Aug 81	**EUROPE (AFTER THE RAIN)** *Virgin VS 393*	40		1
2 Jul 83	**ENDLESSLY** *Virgin VS 543*	66		
17 Sep 83	**YOUR DRESS** *Virgin VS 615*	61		

FPI PROJECT Italian production group

Date	Title / Label	Peak Position	Weeks at No.1	Weeks in Top 40
9 Dec 89	**GOING BACK TO MY ROOTS/RICH IN PARADISE** *Rumour RUMAT 9*	9		10
9 Mar 91	**EVERYBODY (ALL OVER THE WORLD)** *Rumour RUMA 29*	65		
7 Aug 93	**COME ON (AND DO IT)** *Synthetic SYNTH 006CD*	59		
13 Mar 99	**EVERYBODY (ALL OVER)** *99 North CDNTH 14*	67		

FRAGGLES UK/US group

Date	Title / Label	Peak Position	Weeks at No.1	Weeks in Top 40
18 Feb 84	***FRAGGLE ROCK* THEME** *RCA 389*	33		3

FRAGMA German production group

Date	Title / Label	Peak Position	Weeks at No.1	Weeks in Top 40
25 Sep 99	**TOCA ME** *Positiva CDTIV 120*	11		3
22 Apr 00	**TOCA'S MIRACLE** *Positiva CDTIV 128* ●	1	2	12
13 Jan 01	**EVERYTIME YOU NEED ME** *Positiva CDTIVS 147* FRAGMA FEATURING MARIA RUBIA ○	3		9
19 May 01	**YOU ARE ALIVE** *Positiva CDTIVS 153*	4		6
8 Dec 01	**SAY THAT YOU'RE HERE** *Illustrious CD1LL*	25		1

RODDY FRAME UK singer/guitarist

Date	Title / Label	Peak Position	Weeks at No.1	Weeks in Top 40
19 Sep 98	**REASON FOR LIVING** *Independiente ISOM 18MS*	45		

PETER FRAMPTON UK singer/guitarist

Date	Title / Label	Peak Position	Weeks at No.1	Weeks in Top 40
1 May 76	**SHOW ME THE WAY** *A&M AMS 7218*	10		10
11 Sep 76	**BABY I LOVE YOUR WAY** *A&M AMS 7246*	43		
6 Nov 76	**DO YOU FEEL LIKE WE DO** *A&M AMS 7260*	39		1
23 Jul 77	**I'M IN YOU** *A&M AMS 7298*	41		

CONNIE FRANCIS US singer

Date	Title / Label	Peak Position	Weeks at No.1	Weeks in Top 40
4 Apr 58	**WHO'S SORRY NOW?** *MGM 975*	1	6	25
27 Jun 58	**I'M SORRY I MADE YOU CRY** *MGM 982*	11		10
22 Aug 58	**CAROLINA MOON/STUPID CUPID** *MGM 985*	1	6	19
31 Oct 58	**I'LL GET BY** *MGM 993*	19		6
21 Nov 58	**FALLIN'** *MGM 993*	20		5
26 Dec 58	**YOU ALWAYS HURT THE ONE YOU LOVE** *MGM 998*	13		7
13 Feb 59	**MY HAPPINESS** *MGM 1001*	4		15
3 Jul 59	**LIPSTICK ON YOUR COLLAR** *MGM 1018*	3		16
11 Sep 59	**PLENTY GOOD LOVIN'** *MGM 1036*	18		6
4 Dec 59	**AMONG MY SOUVENIRS** *MGM 1046*	11		10
17 Mar 60	**VALENTINO** *MGM 1060*	27		6
19 May 60	**MAMA/ROBOT MAN** *MGM 1076*	2		19
18 Aug 60	**EVERYBODY'S SOMEBODY'S FOOL** *MGM 1086* ★	5		13
3 Nov 60	**MY HEART HAS A MIND OF ITS OWN** *MGM 1100* ★	3		13
12 Jan 61	**MANY TEARS AGO** *MGM 1111*	12		9
16 Mar 61	**WHERE THE BOYS ARE/BABY ROO** *MGM 1121*	5		13
15 Jun 61	**BREAKIN' IN A BRAND NEW BROKEN HEART** *MGM 1136*	12		11
14 Sep 61	**TOGETHER** *MGM 1138*	6		10
14 Dec 61	**BABY'S FIRST CHRISTMAS** *MGM 1145*	30		1
26 Apr 62	**DON'T BREAK THE HEART THAT LOVES YOU** *MGM 1157* ★	39		2
2 Aug 62	**VACATION** *MGM 1165*	10		8
20 Dec 62	**I'M GONNA BE WARM THIS WINTER** *MGM 1185*	48		
10 Jun 65	**MY CHILD** *MGM 1271*	26		5
20 Jan 66	**JEALOUS HEART** *MGM 1293*	44		

JILL FRANCIS UK singer

Date	Title / Label	Peak Position	Weeks at No.1	Weeks in Top 40
3 Jul 93	**MAKE LOVE TO ME** *Glady Wax GW 003CD*	70		

CLAUDE FRANCOIS French singer

Date	Title / Label	Peak Position	Weeks at No.1	Weeks in Top 40
10 Jan 76	**TEARS ON THE TELEPHONE** *Bradley's BRAD 7528*	35		2

FRANK UK group

Date	Title / Label	Peak Position	Weeks at No.1	Weeks in Top 40
12 Aug 06	**I'M NOT SHY** *Polydor FIMS170*	40		1

FRANK & WALTERS Irish group

Date	Title / Label	Peak Position	Weeks at No.1	Weeks in Top 40
21 Mar 92	**HAPPY BUSMAN** *Setanta HOO 2*	49		
12 Sep 92	**THIS IS NOT A SONG** *Setanta HOO 3*	46		
9 Jan 93	**AFTER ALL** *Setanta HOOCD 4*	11		4
17 Apr 93	**FASHION CRISIS HITS NEW YORK** *Setanta HOOCD 5*	42		

FRANKE UK singer

Date	Title / Label	Peak Position	Weeks at No.1	Weeks in Top 40
7 Nov 92	**UNDERSTAND THIS GROOVE** *China WOK 2028*	60		
21 May 94	**LOVE COME HOME** *Triangle BLUESCD 001* OUR TRIBE WITH FRANKE PHAROAH & KRISTINE W	73		

FRANKEE US singer

Date	Title / Label	Peak Position	Weeks at No.1	Weeks in Top 40
1 May 04	**F.U.R.B. – F U RIGHT BACK (IMPORT)** *All Around The World 5603242CD*	43		
22 May 04	**F.U.R.B. (F U RIGHT BACK)** *All Around The World CDGLOBE 355*	1	3	12

FRANKIE GOES TO HOLLYWOOD UK group

Date	Title / Label	Peak Position	Weeks at No.1	Weeks in Top 40
26 Nov 83	**RELAX** *ZTT ZTAS 1* ⊛	1	5	37
16 Jun 84	**TWO TRIBES** *ZTT ZTAS 3* ⊛	1	9	16
1 Dec 84	**THE POWER OF LOVE** *ZTT ZTAS 5* ●	1	1	9
30 Mar 85	**WELCOME TO THE PLEASURE DOME** *ZTT ZTAS 7* ○	2		7
6 Sep 86	**RAGE HARD** *ZTT ZTAS 22* ○	4		5
22 Nov 86	**WARRIORS (OF THE WASTELAND)** *ZTT ZTAS 25*	19		4
7 Mar 87	**WATCHING THE WILDLIFE** *ZTT ZTAS 26*	28		4
2 Oct 93	**RELAX** *ZTT FGTH 1CD*	5		5
20 Nov 93	**WELCOME TO THE PLEASURE DOME (REMIX)** *ZTT FGTH 2CD*	18		2
18 Dec 93	**THE POWER OF LOVE** *ZTT FGTH 3CD*	10		5
26 Feb 94	**TWO TRIBES (REMIX)** *ZTT FGTH 4CD*	16		2
1 Jul 00	**THE POWER OF LOVE (REMIX)** *ZTT ZTT150CD*	6		4

Silver-selling ● Gold-selling ● Platinum-selling ⊛ US No.1 ★ | Peak Position | Weeks at No.1 | Weeks in Top 40

Date	Title / Label	Peak Position	Weeks at No.1	Weeks in Top 40
9 Sep 00	**TWO TRIBES (REMIX)** *ZTT 154CD*	17		2
18 Nov 00	**WELCOME TO THE PLEASURE DOME (2ND REMIX)** *ZTT 166CD*	45		

ARETHA FRANKLIN US singer

Date	Title / Label	Peak Position	Weeks at No.1	Weeks in Top 40
8 Jun 67	**RESPECT** *Atlantic 584 115* ★	10		11
23 Aug 67	**BABY I LOVE YOU** *Atlantic 584 127*	39		1
20 Dec 67	**CHAIN OF FOOLS/SATISFACTION** *Atlantic 584 157*	43		
10 Jan 68	**SATISFACTION** *Atlantic 584 157*	37		1
13 Mar 68	**SINCE YOU'VE BEEN GONE** *Atlantic 584 172*	47		
22 May 68	**THINK** *Atlantic 584 186*	26		7
7 Aug 68	**I SAY A LITTLE PRAYER FOR YOU** *Atlantic 584 206*	4		13
22 Aug 70	**DON'T PLAY THAT SONG** *Atlantic 2091 027*	13		9
2 Oct 71	**SPANISH HARLEM** *Atlantic 2091 138*	14		9
8 Sep 73	**ANGEL** *Atlantic K 10346*	37		2
16 Feb 74	**UNTIL YOU COME BACK TO ME (THAT'S WHAT I'M GONNA DO)** *Atlantic K 10399*	26		6
6 Dec 80	**WHAT A FOOL BELIEVES** *Arista ARIST 377*	46		
19 Sep 81	**LOVE ALL THE HURT AWAY** *Arista ARIST 428* ARETHA FRANKLIN & GEORGE BENSON	49		
4 Sep 82	**JUMP TO IT** *Arista ARIST 479*	42		
23 Jul 83	**GET IT RIGHT** *Arista ARIST 537*	74		
13 Jul 85	**FREEWAY OF LOVE** *Arista ARIST 624*	68		
2 Nov 85	**SISTERS ARE DOING IT FOR THEMSELVES** *RCA PB 40339* EURYTHMICS & ARETHA FRANKLIN	9		8
23 Nov 85	**WHO'S ZOOMIN' WHO** *Arista ARIST 633*	11		7
22 Feb 86	**ANOTHER NIGHT** *Arista ARIST 657*	54		
10 May 86	**FREEWAY OF LOVE** *Arista ARIST 624*	51		
25 Oct 86	**JUMPIN' JACK FLASH** *Arista ARIST 678*	58		
31 Jan 87	**I KNEW YOU WERE WAITIN' FOR ME** *Epic DUET 2* ARETHA FRANKLIN & GEORGE MICHAEL ● ★	1	2	8
14 Mar 87	**JIMMY LEE** *Arista RIS 6*	46		
6 May 89	**THROUGH THE STORM** *Arista 112185* ARETHA FRANKLIN & ELTON JOHN	41		
9 Sep 89	**IT ISN'T, IT WASN'T, IT AIN'T NEVER GONNA BE** *Arista 112545* ARETHA FRANKLIN & WHITNEY HOUSTON	29		3
7 Apr 90	**THINK** *East West A 7951*	31		1
27 Jul 91	**EVERYDAY PEOPLE** *Arista 114420*	69		
12 Feb 94	**A DEEPER LOVE** *Arista 74321187022*	5		4
25 Jun 94	**WILLING TO FORGIVE** *Arista 74321213342*	17		6
9 May 98	**A ROSE IS STILL A ROSE** *Arista 74321569742*	22		2
26 Sep 98	**HERE WE GO AGAIN** *Arista 74321612742*	68		

ERMA FRANKLIN US singer

Date	Title / Label	Peak Position	Weeks at No.1	Weeks in Top 40
10 Oct 92	**(TAKE A LITTLE) PIECE OF MY HEART** *Epic 6583847*	9		9

RODNEY FRANKLIN US pianist

Date	Title / Label	Peak Position	Weeks at No.1	Weeks in Top 40
19 Apr 80	**THE GROOVE** *CBS 8529*	7		5

CHEVELLE FRANKLYN/BEENIE MAN Jamaican duo

Date	Title / Label	Peak Position	Weeks at No.1	Weeks in Top 40
20 Sep 97	**DANCEHALL QUEEN** *Island Jamaica IJCD 2018*	70		

FRANTIQUE US group

Date	Title / Label	Peak Position	Weeks at No.1	Weeks in Top 40
11 Aug 79	**STRUT YOUR FUNKY STUFF** *Philadelphia International PIR 7728*	10		9

FRANZ FERDINAND UK group

Date	Title / Label	Peak Position	Weeks at No.1	Weeks in Top 40
20 Sep 03	**DARTS OF PLEASURE** *Domino RUG 164CD*	44		
24 Jan 04	**TAKE ME OUT** *Domino RUG 172CD*	3		7
1 May 04	**MATINEE** *Domino RUG 176CD*	8		4
28 Aug 04	**MICHAEL** *Domino RUG184CD1*	17		2
1 Oct 05	**DO YOU WANT TO** *Domino RUG211CDX*	4		6
17 Dec 05	**WALK AWAY** *Domino RUG215CD*	13		2
15 Apr 06	**THE FALLEN/L WELLS** *Domino RUG219CD*	14		1
29 Jul 06	**ELEANOR PUT YOUR BOOTS ON** *Domino RUG234CD*	30		1

ELIZABETH FRASER UK singer

Date	Title / Label	Peak Position	Weeks at No.1	Weeks in Top 40
12 May 90	**CANDLELAND (THE SECOND COMING)** *East West YZ 452* IAN McCULLOCH FEATURING ELIZABETH FRASER	75		
13 Aug 94	**LIFEFORMS** *Virgin VSCD 1484* F.S.O.L. VOCALS BY ELIZABETH FRASER	14		2

FRASH UK group

Date	Title / Label	Peak Position	Weeks at No.1	Weeks in Top 40
18 Feb 95	**HERE I GO AGAIN** *PWL International FLIPCD 1*	69		

FRATELLIS UK group

Date	Title / Label	Peak Position	Weeks at No.1	Weeks in Top 40
17 Jun 06	**HENRIETTA** *Island/Uni-Island CID938*	19		3
2 Sep 06	**CHELSEA DAGGER** *Fallout FALLOUTCD12*	5		11
2 Dec 06	**WHISTLE FOR THE CHOIR** *Fallout 1709876*	9		4
17 Mar 07	**FLATHEAD** *Download*	67		
24 Mar 07	**BABY FRATELLI** *Fallout 1723831*	24		2

FRAY US group

Date	Title / Label	Peak Position	Weeks at No.1	Weeks in Top 40
27 Jan 07	**HOW TO SAVE A LIFE** *Epic 88697072302*	4		28
28 Apr 07	**OVER MY HEAD (CABLE CAR)** *Epic 88697012832*	19		4

FRAZIER CHORUS UK group

Date	Title / Label	Peak Position	Weeks at No.1	Weeks in Top 40
4 Feb 89	**DREAM KITCHEN** *Virgin VS 1145*	57		
15 Apr 89	**TYPICAL!** *Virgin VS 1174*	53		
15 Jul 89	**SLOPPY HEART** *Virgin VS 1192*	73		
9 Jun 90	**CLOUD 8** *Virgin VS 1252*	52		
25 Aug 90	**NOTHING** *Virgin VS 1284*	51		
16 Feb 91	**WALKING ON AIR** *Virgin VS 1330*	60		

FREAKPOWER UK group

Date	Title / Label	Peak Position	Weeks at No.1	Weeks in Top 40
16 Oct 93	**TURN ON, TUNE IN, COP OUT** *Fourth & Broadway BRCD 284*	29		3
26 Feb 94	**RUSH** *Fourth & Broadway BRCD 291*	62		
18 Mar 95	**TURN ON, TUNE IN, COP OUT** *Fourth & Broadway BRCD 317* ●	3		7
8 Jun 96	**NEW DIRECTION** *Fourth & Broadway BRCD 331*	60		
9 May 98	**NO WAY** *Deconstruction 74321578572*	29		1

FREAKS UK duo

Date	Title / Label	Peak Position	Weeks at No.1	Weeks in Top 40
28 May 07	**THE CREEPS (YOU'RE GIVING ME)** *Azuli AZNY237*	9		5

FREAKY REALISTIC UK/Japanese group

Date	Title / Label	Peak Position	Weeks at No.1	Weeks in Top 40
3 Apr 93	**KOOCHIE RYDER** *Frealism FRESCD 2*	52		
3 Jul 93	**LEONARD NIMOY** *Frealism FRESCD 3*	71		

FREAKYMAN Dutch producer

Date	Title / Label	Peak Position	Weeks at No.1	Weeks in Top 40
27 Sep 97	**DISCOBUG '97** *Xtravaganza 0091285 EXT*	68		

STAN FREEBERG US singer

Date	Title / Label	Peak Position	Weeks at No.1	Weeks in Top 40
19 Nov 54	**SH-BOOM** *Capitol CL 14187* STAN FREBERG WITH THE TOADS	15		2
27 Jul 56	**ROCK ISLAND LINE/HEARTBREAK HOTEL** *Capitol CL 14608* STAN FREBERG & HIS SKIFFLE GROUP	24		2
12 May 60	**THE OLD PAYOLA ROLL BLUES** *Capitol CL 15122* STAN FREBERG WITH JESSIE WHITE	40		1

FRED & ROXY UK duo

Date	Title / Label	Peak Position	Weeks at No.1	Weeks in Top 40
5 Feb 00	**SOMETHING FOR THE WEEKEND** *Echo ECSCD 81*	36		1

JOHN FRED & THE PLAYBOY BAND US group

Date	Title / Label	Peak Position	Weeks at No.1	Weeks in Top 40
3 Jan 68	**JUDY IN DISGUISE (WITH GLASSES)** *Pye International 7N 25442* ★	3		11

FREDDIE & THE DREAMERS UK group

Date	Title / Label	Peak Position	Weeks at No.1	Weeks in Top 40
9 May 63	**IF YOU GOTTA MAKE A FOOL OF SOMEBODY** *Columbia DB 7032*	3		14
8 Aug 63	**I'M TELLING YOU NOW** *Columbia DB 7086* ★	2		10
7 Nov 63	**YOU WERE MADE FOR ME** *Columbia DB 7147*	3		14
20 Feb 64	**OVER YOU** *Columbia DB 7214*	13		9
14 May 64	**I LOVE YOU BABY** *Columbia DB 7286*	16		6
16 Jul 64	**JUST FOR YOU** *Columbia DB 7322*	41		
5 Nov 64	**I UNDERSTAND** *Columbia DB 7381*	5		13
22 Apr 65	**A LITTLE YOU** *Columbia DB 7526*	26		5
4 Nov 65	**THOU SHALT NOT STEAL** *Columbia DB 7720*	44		

DEE FREDRIX UK singer

Date	Title / Label	Peak Position	Weeks at No.1	Weeks in Top 40
27 Feb 93	**AND SO I WILL WAIT FOR YOU** *East West YZ 725CD*	56		
3 Jul 93	**DIRTY MONEY** *East West YZ 750CD*	74		

FREE UK group

Date	Title / Label	Peak Position	Weeks at No.1	Weeks in Top 40
6 Jun 70	**ALL RIGHT NOW** *Island WIP 6082*	2		16
1 May 71	**MY BROTHER JAKE** *Island WIP 6100*	4		10
27 May 72	**LITTLE BIT OF LOVE** *Island WIP 6129*	13		9
13 Jan 73	**WISHING WELL** *Island WIP 6146*	7		8
21 Jul 73	**ALL RIGHT NOW** *Island WIP 6082*	15		8
18 Feb 78	**FREE EP** *Island IEP 6*	11		7
23 Oct 82	**FREE EP** *Island IEP 6*	57		
9 Feb 91	**ALL RIGHT NOW** *Island IS 486*	8		7

FREE US group

Date	Title / Label	Peak Position	Weeks at No.1	Weeks in Top 40
12 Apr 97	**MR BIG STUFF** *Motown 5736572* QUEEN LATIFAH, SHADES & FREE	31		1
14 Nov 98	**ANOTHER ONE BITES THE DUST** *DreamWorks DRMCD 22364* QUEEN WITH WYCLEF JEAN FEATURING PRAS MICHEL/FREE	5		4

FREE ASSOCIATION UK group

Date	Title / Label	Peak Position	Weeks at No.1	Weeks in Top 40
12 Apr 03	**EVERYBODY KNOWS** *Ramp 001CDS*	74		
13 Sep 03	**SUGARMAN** *13Amp 9809471*	53		

FREE SPIRIT UK duo

Date	Title / Label	Peak Position	Weeks at No.1	Weeks in Top 40
13 May 95	**NO MORE RAINY DAYS** *Columbia 6612822*	68		

FREEEZ UK group

Date	Title / Label	Peak Position	Weeks at No.1	Weeks in Top 40
7 Jun 80	**KEEP IN TOUCH** *Calibre CAB 103*	49		
7 Feb 81	**SOUTHERN FREEEZ** *Beggars Banquet BEG 51* FREEEZ FEATURING INGRID MANSFIELD ALLMAN	8		8
18 Apr 81	**FLYING HIGH** *Beggars Banquet BEG 55*	35		1
18 Jun 83	**I.O.U.** *Beggars Banquet BEG 96*	2		12
1 Oct 83	**POP GOES MY LOVE** *Beggars Banquet BEG 98*	26		4
17 Jan 87	**I.O.U. (REMIX)** *Citybeat CBE 709* FREEEZ FEATURING JOHN ROCCA	23		5
30 May 87	**SOUTHERN FREEEZ (REMIX)** *Total Control TOCO 14* FREEEZ FEATURING INGRID MANSFIELD ALLMAN	63		

FREEFALL UK/Australian production duo

Date	Title / Label	Peak Position	Weeks at No.1	Weeks in Top 40
28 Nov 98	**SKYDIVE** *Stress CDSTR 89* FREEFALL FEATURING JAN JOHNSTON	75		
22 Jul 00	**SKYDIVE (REMIX)** *Renaissance Recordings RENCDS 002* FREEFALL FEATURING JAN JOHNSTON	43		
8 Sep 01	**SKYDIVE (I FEEL WONDERFUL)** *Incentive CENT 22CDS* FREEFALL FEATURING JAN JOHNSTON	35		1
27 Jul 91	**FEEL SURREAL** *ffrr FX 160* FREEFALL FEATURING PSYCHOTROPIC	63		

FREEFALLER UK group

Date	Title / Label	Peak Position	Weeks at No.1	Weeks in Top 40
5 Feb 05	**DO THIS! DO THAT!** *Velocity VELOCD2*	8		4
14 May 05	**GOOD ENOUGH FOR YOU** *Emap VELOCD3*	21		1
3 Dec 05	**SHE'S MY EVERYTHING/BASKET CASE** *Velocity VELOCDX05*	36		1

FREELAND UK producer

Date	Title / Label	Peak Position	Weeks at No.1	Weeks in Top 40
13 Sep 03	**WE WANT YOUR SOUL** *Maximise Profit FREECDS01*	35		1
7 Feb 04	**SUPERNATURAL THING** *Marine Parade MAPACDS024*	65		

CLAIRE FREELAND UK singer

Date	Title / Label	Peak Position	Weeks at No.1	Weeks in Top 40
21 Jul 01	**FREE** *Statuesque CDSTATU 1*	44		

FREELOADERS UK production group

Date	Title / Label	Peak Position	Weeks at No.1	Weeks in Top 40
23 Apr 05	**SO MUCH LOVE TO GIVE** *All Around The World CDGLOBE412* FREELOADERS FEATURING THE REAL THING	9		4

FREEMASONS UK production duo

Date	Title / Label	Peak Position	Weeks at No.1	Weeks in Top 40
3 Sep 05	**LOVE ON MY MIND** *Loaded LOAD108CD* FREEMASONS FEATURING AMANDA WILSON	11		4
11 Mar 06	**WATCHIN'** *Loaded LOAD111CD* FREEMASONS FEATURING AMANDA WILSON	19		2
13 Jan 07	**RAIN DOWN LOVE** *Loaded LOAD116CD* FREEMASONS FEATURING SIEDAH GARRETT	12		4
20 Oct 07	**UNINVITED** *Loaded LOAD118CD* FREEMASONS FEATURING BAILEY TZUKE	8		10

FREESTYLERS UK group

Date	Title / Label	Peak Position	Weeks at No.1	Weeks in Top 40
7 Feb 98	**B-BOY STANCE** *Freskanova FND 7* FREESTYLERS FEATURING TENOR FLY	23		2
14 Nov 98	**WARNING** *Freskanova FND 14* FREESTYLERS FEATURING NAVIGATOR	68		
24 Jul 99	**HERE WE GO** *Freskanova FND 19*	45		
20 Mar 04	**GET A LIFE** *Against The Grain ATG008*	66		
26 Jun 04	**PUSH UP** *Against The Grain ATG009CD*	22		2
12 Feb 05	**BOOM BLAST** *Against The Grain ATG010R* FREESTYLERS FEATURING MILLION DAN	75		

FREIHEIT German group

Date	Title / Label	Peak Position	Weeks at No.1	Weeks in Top 40
17 Dec 88	**KEEPING THE DREAM ALIVE** *CBS 6529897*	14		7

FRENCH AFFAIR French production duo

Date	Title / Label	Peak Position	Weeks at No.1	Weeks in Top 40
16 Sep 00	**MY HEART GOES BOOM** *Arista 74321780562*	44		

NICKI FRENCH UK singer

Date	Title / Label	Peak Position	Weeks at No.1	Weeks in Top 40
15 Oct 94	**TOTAL ECLIPSE OF THE HEART** *Bags Of Fun BAGSCD 1*	54		
14 Jan 95	**TOTAL ECLIPSE OF THE HEART** *Bags Of Fun BAGSCD 1*	5		11
22 Apr 95	**FOR ALL WE KNOW** *Bags Of Fun BAGSCD 4*	42		
15 Jul 95	**DID YOU EVER REALLY LOVE ME** *Love This LUVTHISCD 2*	55		
27 May 00	**DON'T PLAY THAT SONG AGAIN** *RCA 74321764572*	34		1

FRESH BC UK producer

Date	Title / Label	Peak Position	Weeks at No.1	Weeks in Top 40
25 Oct 03	**SIGNAL/BIG LOVE** *Ram RAMM 46* FRESH	58		
18 Sep 04	**COLOSSUS/HOODED** *Ram RAMM 51*	74		
25 Dec 04	**CAPTURE THE FLAG** *Ram RAMM 53*	70		

DOUG E. FRESH & THE GET FRESH CREW US group

Date	Title / Label	Peak Position	Weeks at No.1	Weeks in Top 40
9 Nov 85	**THE SHOW** *Cooltempo COOL 116*	7		10

FRESH 4 UK group

Date	Title / Label	Peak Position	Weeks at No.1	Weeks in Top 40
7 Oct 89	**WISHING ON A STAR** *10 TEN 287* FRESH 4 FEATURING LIZZ E	10		6

FREDDY FRESH US producer

Date	Title / Label	Peak Position	Weeks at No.1	Weeks in Top 40
1 May 99	**BADDER BADDER SCHWING** *Eye-Q EYEUK 040CD* FREDDY FRESH FEATURING FATBOY SLIM	34		1
31 Jul 99	**WHAT IT IS** *Eye-Q EYEUK 043CD*	63		

FRESHIES UK group

Date	Title / Label	Peak Position	Weeks at No.1	Weeks in Top 40
14 Feb 81	**I'M IN LOVE WITH THE GIRL ON A CERTAIN MANCHESTER VIRGIN MEGASTORE CHECKOUT DESK** *MCA 670*	54		

MATT FRETTON UK singer

Date	Title / Label	Peak Position	Weeks at No.1	Weeks in Top 40
11 Jun 83	**IT'S SO HIGH** *Chrysalis MATT 1*	50		

STEPHEN FRETWELL UK singer

Date	Title / Label	Peak Position	Weeks at No.1	Weeks in Top 40
30 Jul 05	**EMILY** *Fiction 9871977*	42		

Silver-selling ○ · Gold-selling ● · Platinum-selling ⊛ · US No.1 ★ · Peak Position · Weeks at No.1 · Weeks in Top 40

FREUR UK group

Date	Title / Label	Peak Position	Weeks at No.1	Weeks in Top 40
23 Apr 83	**DOOT DOOT** *CBS A 3141*	59		

GLENN FREY US singer

Date	Title / Label	Peak Position	Weeks at No.1	Weeks in Top 40
2 Mar 85	**THE HEAT IS ON** *MCA 941*	12		7
22 Jun 85	**SMUGGLER'S BLUES** *BBC RESL 170*	22		5

FRIDA Norwegian singer

Date	Title / Label	Peak Position	Weeks at No.1	Weeks in Top 40
21 Aug 82	**I KNOW THERE'S SOMETHING GOING ON** *Epic EPC A 2603*	43		
17 Dec 83	**TIME** *Epic A 3983* FRIDA & BA ROBERTSON	45		

FRIDAY HILL UK group

Date	Title / Label	Peak Position	Weeks at No.1	Weeks in Top 40
22 Oct 05	**BABY GOODBYE** *Longside LONG1CDX*	5		6
25 Feb 06	**ONE MORE NIGHT ALONE** *Longside LONG2CDX*	13		2

RALPH FRIDGE German producer

Date	Title / Label	Peak Position	Weeks at No.1	Weeks in Top 40
24 Apr 99	**PARADISE** *Addictive 12AD 036*	68		
8 Apr 00	**ANGEL** *Incentive CENT 6CDS*	20		2

DEAN FRIEDMAN US singer/pianist

Date	Title / Label	Peak Position	Weeks at No.1	Weeks in Top 40
3 Jun 78	**WOMAN OF MINE** *Lifesong LS 401*	52		
23 Sep 78	**LUCKY STARS** *Lifesong LS 402* ○	3		10
18 Nov 78	**LYDIA** *Lifesong LS 403*	31		3

FRIENDS AGAIN UK group

Date	Title / Label	Peak Position	Weeks at No.1	Weeks in Top 40
4 Aug 84	**THE FRIENDS AGAIN EP** *Mercury FA 1*	59		

FRIENDS OF MATTHEW UK group

Date	Title / Label	Peak Position	Weeks at No.1	Weeks in Top 40
10 Jul 99	**OUT THERE** *Serious SERR 007CD*	61		

FRIJID VINEGAR UK production duo

Date	Title / Label	Peak Position	Weeks at No.1	Weeks in Top 40
21 Aug 99	**DOGMONAUT 2000 (IS THERE ANYONE OUT THERE)** *Gut CDGUT 27*	53		

FRIJID PINK US group

Date	Title / Label	Peak Position	Weeks at No.1	Weeks in Top 40
28 Mar 70	**HOUSE OF THE RISING SUN** *Deram DM 288*	4		15

JANE FROMAN US singer

Date	Title / Label	Peak Position	Weeks at No.1	Weeks in Top 40
17 Jun 55	**I WONDER** *Capitol CL 14254*	14		4

FRONT 242 Belgian duo

Date	Title / Label	Peak Position	Weeks at No.1	Weeks in Top 40
1 May 93	**RELIGION** *RRE 106CD*	46		

LIAM FROST & SLOWDOWN FAMILY UK group

Date	Title / Label	Peak Position	Weeks at No.1	Weeks in Top 40
9 Sep 06	**THE CITY IS AT STANDSTILL** *Lavolta LAVOLTA006*	74		

FROU FROU UK duo

Date	Title / Label	Peak Position	Weeks at No.1	Weeks in Top 40
6 Jul 02	**BREATHE IN** *Island CID 799*	44		

CHRISTIAN FRY UK singer

Date	Title / Label	Peak Position	Weeks at No.1	Weeks in Top 40
14 Nov 98	**YOU GOT ME** *Mushroom MUSH 33CDS*	45		
3 Apr 99	**WON'T YOU SAY** *Mushroom MUSH 46CDS*	48		

FUGAZI US group

Date	Title / Label	Peak Position	Weeks at No.1	Weeks in Top 40
20 Oct 01	**FURNITURE** *Dischord DIS 129CD*	61		

FUGEES US group

Date	Title / Label	Peak Position	Weeks at No.1	Weeks in Top 40
6 Apr 96	**FU-GEE-LA** *Columbia 6630662*	21		3
8 Jun 96	**KILLING ME SOFTLY** *Columbia 6633435* ⊛	1	5	15
14 Sep 96	**READY OR NOT** *Columbia 6637215* ●	1	2	9
30 Nov 96	**NO WOMAN NO CRY** *Columbia 6639925*	2		7
15 Mar 97	**RUMBLE IN THE JUNGLE** *Mercury 5740692*	3		6
28 Jun 97	**WE TRYING TO STAY ALIVE** *Columbia 6646815* WYCLEF JEAN & THE REFUGEE ALLSTARS	13		3
6 Sep 97	**THE SWEETEST THING** *Columbia 6649785* REFUGEE ALLSTARS FEATURING LAURYN HILL	18		2
27 Sep 97	**GUANTANAMERA** *Columbia 6650852* WYCLEF JEAN & THE REFUGEE ALLSTARS	25		1
27 Oct 01	**LOVING YOU (OLE OLE OLE)** *Blacklist 0133045 ERE* BRIAN HARVEY & THE REFUGEE CREW	20		2

FULL CIRCLE US group

Date	Title / Label	Peak Position	Weeks at No.1	Weeks in Top 40
7 Mar 87	**WORKIN' UP A SWEAT** *EMI America EA 229*	41		

FULL FORCE US group

Date	Title / Label	Peak Position	Weeks at No.1	Weeks in Top 40
4 May 85	**I WONDER IF I TAKE YOU HOME** *CBS A 6057* LISA LISA & CULT JAM WITH FULL FORCE	12		9
21 Dec 85	**ALICE I WANT YOU JUST FOR ME** *CBS A 6640*	9		8
21 May 88	**NAUGHTY GIRLS** *Jive FOXY 9* SAMANTHA FOX FEATURING FULL FORCE	31		2
4 Jun 88	**I'M REAL** *Scotti Brothers JSB 1* JAMES BROWN FEATURING FULL FORCE	31		3

FULL INTENTION UK group

Date	Title / Label	Peak Position	Weeks at No.1	Weeks in Top 40
6 Apr 96	**AMERICA (I LOVE AMERICA)** *Stress CDSTR 56*	32		1
10 Aug 96	**UPTOWN DOWNTOWN** *Stress CDSTR 67*	61		
26 Jul 97	**SHAKE YOUR BODY (DOWN TO THE GROUND)** *Sugar Daddy CDSTR 82*	34		1
22 Nov 97	**AMERICA (I LOVE AMERICA) (REMIX)** *Sugar Daddy CDSTR 56*	56		
6 Jun 98	**YOU ARE SOMEBODY** *Sugar Daddy CDSD 001*	75		
1 Sep 01	**I'LL BE WAITING** *Rulin 17CDS* FULL INTENTION PRESENTS SHENA	44		

FULL MONTY ALLSTARS UK group

Date	Title / Label	Peak Position	Weeks at No.1	Weeks in Top 40
27 Jul 96	**BRILLIANT FEELING** *Arista 74321380902* FULL MONTY ALLSTARS FEATURING TJ DAVIS	72		

BOBBY FULLER FOUR US singer

Date	Title / Label	Peak Position	Weeks at No.1	Weeks in Top 40
14 Apr 66	**I FOUGHT THE LAW** *London HL 10030*	33		2

FUN BOY THREE UK group

Date	Title / Label	Peak Position	Weeks at No.1	Weeks in Top 40
7 Nov 81	**THE LUNATICS (HAVE TAKEN OVER THE ASYLUM)** *Chrysalis CHS 2563*	20		9
13 Feb 82	**IT AIN'T WHAT YOU DO IT'S THE WAY THAT YOU DO IT** *Chrysalis CHS 2570* FUN BOY THREE & BANANARAMA ○	4		7
10 Apr 82	**REALLY SAYING SOMETHING** *Deram NANA 1* BANANARAMA WITH FUN BOY THREE ○	5		9
8 May 82	**THE TELEPHONE ALWAYS RINGS** *Chrysalis CHS 2609*	17		8
31 Jul 82	**SUMMERTIME** *Chrysalis CHS 2629*	18		6
15 Jan 83	**THE MORE I SEE (THE LESS I BELIEVE)** *Chrysalis CHS 2664*	68		
5 Feb 83	**TUNNEL OF LOVE** *Chrysalis CHS 2678*	10		7
30 Apr 83	**OUR LIPS ARE SEALED** *Chrysalis FUNB 1*	7		8

FUN DMENTAL 03 UK group

Date	Title / Label	Peak Position	Weeks at No.1	Weeks in Top 40
25 Mar 06	**JUMP/PLAYGROUND** *Da Works FUND002X*	44		

FUN LOVIN' CRIMINALS US group

Date	Title / Label	Peak Position	Weeks at No.1	Weeks in Top 40
8 Jun 96	**THE GRAVE AND THE CONSTANT** *Chrysalis CDCHS 5031*	72		
17 Aug 96	**SCOOBY SNACKS** *Chrysalis CDCHSS 5034*	22		2
16 Nov 96	**THE FUN LOVIN' CRIMINAL** *Chrysalis CDCHS 5040*	26		1
29 Mar 97	**KING OF NEW YORK** *Chrysalis CDCHS 5049*	28		1
5 Jul 97	**I'M NOT IN LOVE/SCOOBY SNACKS** *Chrysalis CDCHS 5060*	12		3
15 Aug 98	**LOVE UNLIMITED** *Chrysalis CDCHS 5096*	18		1
17 Oct 98	**BIG NIGHT OUT** *Chrysalis CDCHSS 5101*	29		1
8 May 99	**KOREAN BODEGA** *Chrysalis CDCHSS 5108*	15		2
17 Feb 01	**LOCO** *Chrysalis CDCHSS 5121*	5		3

Date	Title / Label	Peak Position	Weeks at No.1	Weeks in Top 40
1 Sep 01	**BUMP/RUN DADDY RUN** *Chrysalis CDHSS 5128*	50		
13 Sep 03	**TOO HOT** *Sanctuary SANXD 205X*	61		

FUNERAL FOR A FRIEND UK group

Date	Title / Label	Peak Position	Weeks at No.1	Weeks in Top 40
9 Aug 03	**JUNEAU** *Infectious EW 269CD1*	19		2
18 Oct 03	**SHE DROVE ME TO DAYTIME TELEVISION** *Infectious EW 274CD2*	20		1
14 Feb 04	**ESCAPE ARTISTS NEVER DIE** *Infectious EW 283CD*	19		1
11 Jun 05	**STREETCAR** *Atlantic ATUK009CDX*	15		2
10 Sep 05	**MONSTERS** *IHT/Atlantic ATUK012CD*	36		1
26 Nov 05	**HISTORY** *Atlantic ATUK017CD*	21		1
4 Mar 06	**ROSES FOR THE DEAD** *Atlantic ATUK022*	39		1
12 May 07	**INTO OBLIVION (REUNION)** *Atlantic ATUK058CD*	16		3
4 Aug 07	**WALK AWAY** *Atlantic ATUK068CD*	40		1

FARLEY 'JACKMASTER' FUNK US singer

Date	Title / Label	Peak Position	Weeks at No.1	Weeks in Top 40
23 Aug 86	**LOVE CAN'T TURN AROUND** *DJInternational LON 105*	10		10
11 Feb 89	**AS ALWAYS** *Champion CHAMP 90* FARLEY 'JACKMASTER' FUNK FEATURING RICKY DILLARD	49		
14 Dec 96	**LOVE CAN'T TURN AROUND (REMIX)** *4 Liberty LIBTCD 27R* FARLEY 'JACKMASTER' FUNK FEATURING DARRYL PANDY	40		1

FUNK D'VOID Swedish producer

Date	Title / Label	Peak Position	Weeks at No.1	Weeks in Top 40
20 Oct 01	**DIABLA** *Soma 112*	70		
31 Jan 04	**EMOTIONAL CONTENT** *Soma 139R*	74		

FUNK JUNKEEZ US producer

Date	Title / Label	Peak Position	Weeks at No.1	Weeks in Top 40
21 Feb 98	**GOT FUNK** *Evocative EVOKE 1CDS*	57		

FUNK MASTERS UK group

Date	Title / Label	Peak Position	Weeks at No.1	Weeks in Top 40
18 Jun 83	**IT'S OVER** *Master Funk Records 7MP 004*	8		9

FUNKADELIC US group

Date	Title / Label	Peak Position	Weeks at No.1	Weeks in Top 40
9 Dec 78	**ONE NATION UNDER A GROOVE (PART 1)** *Warner Brothers K 17246*	9		9
21 Aug 99	**MOTHERSHIP RECONNECTION** *Virgin DINSD 185* SCOTT GROOVES FEATURING PARLIAMENT/FUNKADELIC	55		

FUNKAPOLITAN UK group

Date	Title / Label	Peak Position	Weeks at No.1	Weeks in Top 40
22 Aug 81	**AS THE TIME GOES BY** *London LON 001*	41		

FUNKDOOBIEST US group

Date	Title / Label	Peak Position	Weeks at No.1	Weeks in Top 40
11 Dec 93	**WOPBABALUBOP** *Immortal 6597112*	37		1
5 Mar 94	**BOW WOW WOW** *Immortal 6594052*	34		1

FUNKSTAR DE LUXE Danish producer

Date	Title / Label	Peak Position	Weeks at No.1	Weeks in Top 40
25 Sep 99	**SUN IS SHINING** *Club Tools 0066895 CLU* BOB MARLEY VERSUS FUNKSTAR DE LUXE ●	3		7
22 Jan 00	**RAINBOW COUNTRY** *Club Tools 0067225 CLU* BOB MARLEY VERSUS FUNKSTAR DE LUXE	11		3
13 May 00	**WALKING IN THE NAME** *Club Tools 0067375 CLU*	42		
25 Nov 00	**PULL UP TO THE BUMPER** *Club Tools 0120375 CLU*	60		

FUNKY CHOAD Australian/Italian production duo

Date	Title / Label	Peak Position	Weeks at No.1	Weeks in Top 40
29 Aug 98	**THE ULTIMATE** *ffrr FCD 341* FUNKY CHOAD FEATURING NICK SKITZ	51		

FUNKY GREEN DOGS US group

Date	Title / Label	Peak Position	Weeks at No.1	Weeks in Top 40
12 Apr 97	**FIRED UP!** *Twisted UK TWCD 10016*	17		2
28 Jun 97	**THE WAY** *Twisted UK TWCD 10026*	43		
20 Jun 98	**UNTIL THE DAY** *Twisted UK TWCD 10034*	75		
27 Feb 99	**BODY** *Twisted UK TWCD 110041*	46		

FUNKY POETS US rap group

Date	Title / Label	Peak Position	Weeks at No.1	Weeks in Top 40
7 May 94	**BORN IN THE GHETTO** *Epic 6603522*	72		

FUNKY WORM UK group

Date	Title / Label	Peak Position	Weeks at No.1	Weeks in Top 40
30 Jul 88	**HUSTLE! (TO THE MUSIC...)** *Fon 15*	13		6
26 Nov 88	**THE SPELL!** *Fon 16*	61		
20 May 89	**U + ME = LOVE** *Fon 19*	46		

FUREYS Irish group

Date	Title / Label	Peak Position	Weeks at No.1	Weeks in Top 40
10 Oct 81	**WHEN YOU WERE SWEET SIXTEEN** *Ritz 003* FUREYS WITH DAVEY ARTHUR	14		8
3 Apr 82	**I WILL LOVE YOU (EV'RY TIME WHEN WE ARE GONE)** *Ritz 012*	54		

FURNITURE UK group

Date	Title / Label	Peak Position	Weeks at No.1	Weeks in Top 40
14 Jun 86	**BRILLIANT MIND** *Stiff BUY 251*	21		7

NELLY FURTADO Canadian singer

Date	Title / Label	Peak Position	Weeks at No.1	Weeks in Top 40
10 Mar 01	**I'M LIKE A BIRD** *DreamWorks 4509192* ●	5		13
1 Sep 01	**TURN OFF THE LIGHT** *DreamWorks DRMDM 50891*	4		7
19 Jan 02	**...ON THE RADIO (REMEMBER THE DAYS)** *DreamWorks DRMDM 50856*	18		2
20 Dec 03	**POWERLESS (SAY WHAT YOU WANT)** *DreamWorks 4504645*	13		7
27 Mar 04	**TRY** *DreamWorks 4505113*	15		3
24 Jul 04	**FORCA** *DreamWorks 9862823*	40		1
10 Jun 06	**MANEATER** *DreamWorks 9859585*	1	3	10
9 Sep 06	**PROMISCUOUS** *Geffen 1706030* NELLY FURTADO FEATURING TIMBALAND ★	3		11
2 Dec 06	**ALL GOOD THINGS (COME TO AN END)** *Geffen 1714378*	4		12
10 Feb 07	**SAY IT RIGHT** *Download*	10		24
14 Apr 07	**GIVE IT TO ME** *Interscope 1732199* TIMBALAND FEATURING NELLY FURTADO & JUSTIN TIMBERLAKE ★	1	1	20
1 Dec 07	**DO IT** *Download*	75		

BILLY FURY UK singer

Date	Title / Label	Peak Position	Weeks at No.1	Weeks in Top 40
27 Feb 59	**MAYBE TOMORROW** *Decca F 11102*	18		9
26 Jun 59	**MARGO** *Decca F 11128*	28		1
10 Mar 60	**COLETTE** *Decca F 11200*	9		6
26 May 60	**THAT'S LOVE** *Decca F 11237* BILLY FURY WITH THE FOUR JAYS	19		10
22 Sep 60	**WONDROUS PLACE** *Decca F 11267*	25		6
19 Jan 61	**A THOUSAND STARS** *Decca F 11311*	14		9
27 Apr 61	**DON'T WORRY** *Decca F 11334* BILLY FURY WITH THE FOUR KESTRELS	40		1
11 May 61	**HALFWAY TO PARADISE** *Decca F 11349*	3		21
7 Sep 61	**JEALOUSY** *Decca F 11384*	2		11
14 Dec 61	**I'D NEVER FIND ANOTHER YOU** *Decca F 11409*	5		14
15 Mar 62	**LETTER FULL OF TEARS** *Decca F 11437*	32		4
3 May 62	**LAST NIGHT WAS MADE FOR LOVE** *Decca F 11458*	4		15
19 Jul 62	**ONCE UPON A DREAM** *Decca F 11485*	7		11
25 Oct 62	**BECAUSE OF LOVE** *Decca F 11508*	18		10
14 Feb 63	**LIKE I'VE NEVER BEEN GONE** *Decca F 11582*	3		15
16 May 63	**WHEN WILL YOU SAY I LOVE YOU?** *Decca F 11655*	3		12
25 Jul 63	**IN SUMMER** *Decca F 11701*	5		10
3 Oct 63	**SOMEBODY ELSE'S GIRL** *Decca F 11744*	18		6
2 Jan 64	**DO YOU REALLY LOVE ME TOO?** *Decca F 11792*	13		10
30 Apr 64	**I WILL** *Decca F 11888*	14		10
23 Jul 64	**IT'S ONLY MAKE BELIEVE** *Decca F 11939*	10		9
14 Jan 65	**I'M LOST WITHOUT YOU** *Decca F 12048*	16		9
22 Jul 65	**IN THOUGHTS OF YOU** *Decca F 12178*	9		9
16 Sep 65	**RUN TO MY LOVIN' ARMS** *Decca F 12230*	25		6
10 Feb 66	**I'LL NEVER QUITE GET OVER YOU** *Decca F 12325*	35		1
4 Aug 66	**GIVE ME YOUR WORD** *Decca F 12459*	27		5
4 Sep 82	**LOVE OR MONEY** *Polydor POSP 488*	57		
13 Nov 82	**DEVIL OR ANGEL** *Polydor POSP 528*	58		
4 Jun 83	**FORGET HIM** *Polydor POSP 558*	59		

FUSED Swedish production duo

Date	Title / Label	Peak Position	Weeks at No.1	Weeks in Top 40
20 Mar 99	**THIS PARTY SUCKS!** *Columbia 6669302*	64		

FUTURE BREEZE German production duo

Date	Title / Label	Peak Position	Weeks at No.1	Weeks in Top 40
6 Sep 97	**WHY DON'T YOU DANCE WITH ME?** *AM:PM 5823312*	50		
20 Jan 01	**SMILE** *Nebula NEBCD 014*	67		
13 Apr 02	**TEMPLE OF DREAMS** *Data 31CDS*	21		3
28 Dec 02	**OCEAN OF ETERNITY** *Data 44CD*	46		

Silver-selling ○ Gold-selling ● Platinum-selling ⊛ US No.1 ★ Peak Position Weeks at No.1 Weeks in Top 40

FUTURE FORCE UK/US duo

Date	Title / Label	Peak Position	Weeks at No.1	Weeks in Top 40
17 Aug 96	**WHAT YOU WANT** *AM:PM 5816592*	47		

FUTURE SOUND OF LONDON UK production duo

Date	Title / Label	Peak Position	Weeks at No.1	Weeks in Top 40
23 May 92	**PAPUA NEW GUINEA** *Jumpin' & Pumpin' TOT 17*	22		4
6 Nov 93	**CASCADE** *Virgin VSCDT 1478*	27		1
30 Jul 94	**EXPANDER** *Jumpin' & Pumpin' CDSTOR 37*	72		
13 Aug 94	**LIFEFORMS** *Virgin VSCD 1484* F.S.O.L. VOCALS BY ELIZABETH FRASER	14		2
27 May 95	**FAR-OUT SON OF LUNG & THE RAMBLINGS OF A MADMAN** *Virgin VSCDT 1540*	22		1
26 Oct 96	**MY KINGDOM** *Virgin VSCDT 1605*	13		2
12 Apr 97	**WE HAVE EXPLOSIVE** *Virgin VSCDX 1616*	12		2
29 Sep 01	**PAPUA NEW GUINEA 2001** *Jumpin' & Pumpin' CDSTOT 44*	28		1

FUTUREHEADS UK group

Date	Title / Label	Peak Position	Weeks at No.1	Weeks in Top 40
9 Aug 03	**FIRST DAY** *Fantastic Plastic FPS 036*	58		
7 Aug 04	**DECENT DAYS AND NIGHTS** *679 679L080CD*	26		1
30 Oct 04	**MEANTIME** *679 Recordings 679L088CD*	49		
5 Mar 05	**HOUNDS OF LOVE** *679 679L099CD2*	8		3
21 May 05	**DECENT DAYS AND NIGHTS** *679 Recordings 679L104CD2*	26		1
10 Dec 05	**AREA** *679 Recordings 679L117CD1*	18		1
3 Jun 06	**SKIP TO THE END** *679 679L128CD*	24		1
26 Aug 06	**WORRY ABOUT IT LATER** *679 679L137CD*	52		
15 Mar 08	**THE BEGINNING OF THE TWIST** *Nul NUL101CD*	20		3

FUTURESHOCK UK production duo

Date	Title / Label	Peak Position	Weeks at No.1	Weeks in Top 40
15 Mar 03	**ON MY MIND** *Junior/Parlophone CDR 6595* FUTURESHOCK FEATURING BEN ONONO	51		
16 Aug 03	**PRIDE'S PARANOIA** *Parlophone CDR 6616*	60		
1 Nov 03	**LATE AT NIGHT** *Parlophone CDR 6617*	73		

FYA UK group

Date	Title / Label	Peak Position	Weeks at No.1	Weeks in Top 40
13 Mar 04	**MUST BE LOVE** *Def Jam UK 9817508* FYA FEATURING SMUJJI	13		4
24 Jul 04	**TOO HOT** *Def Jam 9867145*	49		

G

ALI G UK comedian

Date	Title / Label	Peak Position	Weeks at No.1	Weeks in Top 40
23 Mar 02	**ME JULIE** *Island CID 793* ALI G & SHAGGY ○	2		9

ANDY G UK producer

Date	Title / Label	Peak Position	Weeks at No.1	Weeks in Top 40
3 Oct 98	***STARSKY & HUTCH* – THE THEME** *Virgin VSCDT 1708* ANDY G'S STARSKY & HUTCH ALL STARS	51		

BOBBY G UK singer

Date	Title / Label	Peak Position	Weeks at No.1	Weeks in Top 40
1 Dec 84	**BIG DEAL** *BBC RESL 151*	65		
19 Oct 85	**BIG DEAL** *BBC RESL 151*	46		

GINA G Australian singer

Date	Title / Label	Peak Position	Weeks at No.1	Weeks in Top 40
6 Apr 96	**OOH AAH...JUST A LITTLE BIT** *Eternal 041CD* ⊛	1	1	15
9 Nov 96	**I BELONG TO YOU** *Eternal 081CD*	6		5
22 Mar 97	**FRESH!** *Eternal 095CD*	6		5
7 Jun 97	**TI AMO** *Eternal 107CD1*	11		3
6 Sep 97	**GIMME SOME LOVE** *Eternal 101CD1*	25		1
15 Nov 97	**EVERY TIME I FALL** *Eternal 134CD*	52		
14 Oct 06	**TONIGHT'S THE NIGHT** *Stuntgirl Music CDSTNT1*	57		

KENNY G US saxophonist

Date	Title / Label	Peak Position	Weeks at No.1	Weeks in Top 40
21 Apr 84	**HI! HOW YA DOIN'?** *Arista ARIST 561*	70		
30 Aug 86	**WHAT DOES IT TAKE (TO WIN YOUR LOVE)** *Arista ARIST 672*	64		
4 Jul 87	**SONGBIRD** *Arista RIS 18*	22		5
9 May 92	**MISSING YOU NOW** *Columbia 6579917* MICHAEL BOLTON FEATURING KENNY G	28		2
24 Apr 93	**FOREVER IN LOVE** *Arista 74321145552*	47		
17 Jul 93	**BY THE TIME THIS NIGHT IS OVER** *Arista 74321157142* KENNY G WITH PEABO BRYSON	56		
8 Nov 97	**HOW COULD AN ANGEL BREAK MY HEART** *LaFace 74321531982* TONI BRAXTON WITH KENNY G	22		3

G-CLEFS US group

Date	Title / Label	Peak Position	Weeks at No.1	Weeks in Top 40
30 Nov 61	**I UNDERSTAND** *London HLU 9433*	17		12

WARREN G US rapper

Date	Title / Label	Peak Position	Weeks at No.1	Weeks in Top 40
23 Jul 94	**REGULATE** *Death Row A 8290CD* WARREN G & NATE DOGG ○	5		12
12 Nov 94	**THIS DJ** *RAL RALCD 1*	12		3
25 Mar 95	**DO YOU SEE** *RAL RALCD 3*	29		1
23 Nov 96	**WHAT'S LOVE GOT TO DO WITH IT** *Interscope IND 97008* WARREN G FEATURING ADINA HOWARD	2		10
22 Feb 97	**I SHOT THE SHERIFF** *Def Jam DEFCD 31*	2		4
31 May 97	**SMOKIN' ME OUT** *Def Jam 5744432* WARREN G FEATURING RONALD ISLEY	14		3
10 Jan 98	**PRINCE IGOR** *Def Jam 5749652* RHAPSODY FEATURING WARREN G & SISSEL	15		5
24 Jan. 98	**ALL NIGHT ALL RIGHT** *Mushroom MUSH 21CD* PETER ANDRE FEATURING WARREN G	16		3
16 Mar 02	**LOOKIN' AT YOU** *Universal MCSTD 40275* WARREN G FEATURING TOI	60		

G NATION UK production duo

Date	Title / Label	Peak Position	Weeks at No.1	Weeks in Top 40
9 Aug 97	**FEEL THE NEED** *Cooltempo CDCOOL 327* G NATION FEATURING ROSIE	58		

G UNIT US group

Date	Title / Label	Peak Position	Weeks at No.1	Weeks in Top 40
27 Dec 03	**STUNT 101** *Interscope 9815335*	25		4
6 Mar 04	**IF I CAN'T/THEM THANGS** *Interscope 9815279* 50 CENT/G-UNIT	10		5
17 Apr 04	**WANNA GET TO KNOW YA** *Interscope 9862268*	27		1
24 Apr 04	**RIDE WIT U/MORE & MORE** *Jive 82876609392* JOE FEATURING G UNIT	12		5

G.O.S.H. UK charity group

Date	Title / Label	Peak Position	Weeks at No.1	Weeks in Top 40
28 Nov 87	**THE WISHING WELL** *MBS GOSH 1*	22		5

GA GAS UK group

Date	Title / Label	Peak Position	Weeks at No.1	Weeks in Top 40
12 Feb 05	**SEX** *Sanctuary SANXS328*	71		

ERIC GABLE US singer

Date	Title / Label	Peak Position	Weeks at No.1	Weeks in Top 40
19 Mar 94	**PROCESS OF ELMINATION** *Epic 6602282*	63		

PETER GABRIEL UK singer

Date	Title / Label	Peak Position	Weeks at No.1	Weeks in Top 40
9 Apr 77	**SOLSBURY HILL** *Charisma CB 301*	13		8
9 Feb 80	**GAMES WITHOUT FRONTIERS** *Charisma CB 354* ○	4		9
10 May 80	**NO SELF CONTROL** *Charisma CB 360*	33		1
23 Aug 80	**BIKO** *Charisma CB 370*	38		2
25 Sep 82	**SHOCK THE MONKEY** *Charisma SHOCK 1*	58		
9 Jul 83	**I DON'T REMEMBER** *Charisma GAB 1*	62		
2 Jun 84	**WALK THROUGH THE FIRE** *Virgin VS 689*	69		
26 Apr 86	**SLEDGEHAMMER** *Virgin PGS 1* ○ ★	4		12
1 Nov 86	**DON'T GIVE UP** *Virgin PGS 2* PETER GABRIEL & KATE BUSH	9		7
28 Mar 87	**BIG TIME** *Virgin PGS 3*	13		4
11 Jul 87	**RED RAIN** *Virgin PGS 4*	46		
21 Nov 87	**BIKO (LIVE)** *Virgin PGS 6*	49		
3 Jun 89	**SHAKING THE TREE** *Virgin VS 1167* YOUSSOU N'DOUR & PETER GABRIEL	61		
22 Dec 90	**SOLSBURY HILL/SHAKING THE TREE** *Virgin VS 1322*	57		
19 Sep 92	**DIGGING THE DIRT** *Realworld PGS 7*	24		2

Legend: Silver-selling ○ · Gold-selling ● · Platinum-selling · US No.1 ★ · Peak Position · Weeks at No.1 · Weeks in Top 40

Date	Title / Label	Peak Position	Weeks at No.1	Weeks in Top 40
16 Jan 93	**STEAM** *Realworld PGSDG 8*	10		4
3 Apr 93	**BLOOD OF EDEN** *Realworld PGSDG 9*	43		
25 Sep 93	**KISS THAT FROG** *Realworld PGSDG 10*	46		
25 Jun 94	**LOVETOWN** *Epic 6604802*	49		
3 Sep 94	**SW LIVE EP** *Realworld PGSCD 11*	39		1
11 Jan 03	**MORE THAN THIS** *Realworld PGSCD 14*	47		

GABRIELLA & TROY US duo

Date	Title / Label	Peak Position	Weeks at No.1	Weeks in Top 40
6 Oct 07	**GOTTA GO MY OWN WAY** *Download*	40		1

GABRIELLE UK singer

Date	Title / Label	Peak Position	Weeks at No.1	Weeks in Top 40
19 Jun 93	**DREAMS** *Go! Beat GODCD 99* ●	1	3	13
2 Oct 93	**GOING NOWHERE** *Go! Beat GODCD 106*	9		6
11 Dec 93	**I WISH** *Go! Beat GODCD 108*	26		2
26 Feb 94	**BECAUSE OF YOU** *Go! Beat GOLCD 109*	24		3
24 Feb 96	**GIVE ME A LITTLE MORE TIME** *Go! Beat GODCD 139* ○	5		14
22 Jun 96	**FORGET ABOUT THE WORLD** *Go! Beat GOLCD 146*	23		3
5 Oct 96	**IF YOU REALLY CARED** *Go! Beat GODCD 153*	15		3
2 Nov 96	**IF YOU EVER** *London LONCD 388* EAST 17 FEATURING GABRIELLE ●	2		11
1 Feb 97	**WALK ON BY** *Go! Beat GODCD 159*	7		4
9 Oct 99	**SUNSHINE** *Go! Beat GOBCD 23*	9		6
5 Feb 00	**RISE** *Go! Beat GOLCD 25* ●	1	2	10
17 Jun 00	**WHEN A WOMAN** *Go! Beat GOLCD 27*	6		5
4 Nov 00	**SHOULD I STAY** *Go! Beat GOLCD 32*	13		4
21 Apr 01	**OUT OF REACH** *Go! Beat GOLCD 39* ○	4		13
3 Nov 01	**DON'T NEED THE SUN TO SHINE (TO MAKE ME SMILE)** *Go! Beat GOLCD 47*	9		5
15 May 04	**STAY THE SAME** *Go! Beat 9866529*	20		2
14 Aug 04	**TEN YEARS TIME** *Go! Beat 9867550*	43		
6 Oct 07	**WHY** *Polydor 1747463*	42		

GADJO German production duo

Date	Title / Label	Peak Position	Weeks at No.1	Weeks in Top 40
28 May 05	**SO MANY TIMES** *Manifesto/Subliminal/AATW 9871480* GADJO FEATURING ALEXANDRA PRINCE	22		2

YVONNE GAGE US singer

Date	Title / Label	Peak Position	Weeks at No.1	Weeks in Top 40
16 Jun 84	**DOIN' IT IN A HAUNTED HOUSE** *Epic A 4519*	45		

DANNI'ELLE GAHA Australian singer

Date	Title / Label	Peak Position	Weeks at No.1	Weeks in Top 40
1 Aug 92	**STUCK IN THE MIDDLE** *Epic 6581247*	68		
27 Feb 93	**DO IT FOR LOVE** *Epic 6584612*	52		
12 Jun 93	**SECRET LOVE** *Epic 6592212*	41		

DAVE GAHAN UK singer

Date	Title / Label	Peak Position	Weeks at No.1	Weeks in Top 40
7 Jun 03	**DIRTY STICKY FLOORS** *Mute LCDMUTE 294*	18		1
30 Aug 03	**I NEED YOU** *Mute LCDMUTE 301*	27		1
8 Nov 03	**BOTTLE LIVING** *Mute LCDMUTE 310*	36		1
20 Oct 07	**KINGDOM** *Mute LCDMUTE393*	44		

BILLY & SARAH GAINES US duo

Date	Title / Label	Peak Position	Weeks at No.1	Weeks in Top 40
14 Jun 97	**I FOUND SOMEONE** *Expansion CDEXP 27*	48		

ROSIE GAINES US singer

Date	Title / Label	Peak Position	Weeks at No.1	Weeks in Top 40
11 Nov 95	**I WANT U** *Motown 8604852*	70		
31 May 97	**CLOSER THAN CLOSE** *Big Bang CDBBANG 1* ○	4		10
29 Nov 97	**I SURRENDER** *Big Bang CDBBANG 2*	39		1

GALA Italian singer

Date	Title / Label	Peak Position	Weeks at No.1	Weeks in Top 40
19 Jul 97	**FREED FROM DESIRE** *Big Life BLRD 135* ●	2		12
6 Dec 97	**LET A BOY CRY** *Big Life BLRD 140*	11		6
22 Aug 98	**COME INTO MY LIFE** *Big Life BLRD 147*	38		1

EVE GALLAGHER UK singer

Date	Title / Label	Peak Position	Weeks at No.1	Weeks in Top 40
1 Dec 90	**LOVE COME DOWN** *More Protein PROT 6*	61		
15 Apr 95	**YOU CAN HAVE IT ALL** *Cleveland City CLECD 13023*	43		
28 Oct 95	**LOVE COME DOWN** *Cleveland City CLECD 13028*	57		
6 Jul 96	**HEARTBREAK** *React CDREACT 78* MRS WOOD FEATURING EVE GALLAGHER	44		

LIAM GALLAGHER UK singer

Date	Title / Label	Peak Position	Weeks at No.1	Weeks in Top 40
23 Oct 99	**CARNATION** *Ignition IGNSCD 16* LIAM GALLAGHER & STEVE CRADDOCK	6		3
28 Dec 02	**SCORPIO RISING** *Concrete HARD 54CD* DEATH IN VEGAS FEATURING LIAM GALLAGHER	14		4

GALLAGHER & LYLE UK duo

Date	Title / Label	Peak Position	Weeks at No.1	Weeks in Top 40
28 Feb 76	**I WANNA STAY WITH YOU** *A&M AMS 7211*	6		8
22 May 76	**HEART ON MY SLEEVE** *A&M AMS 7227*	6		9
11 Sep 76	**BREAKAWAY** *A&M AMS 7245*	35		1
29 Jan 77	**EVERY LITTLE TEARDROP** *A&M AMS 7274*	32		3

PATSY GALLANT Canadian singer

Date	Title / Label	Peak Position	Weeks at No.1	Weeks in Top 40
10 Sep 77	**FROM NEW YORK TO L.A.** *EMI 2620*	6		8

GALLEON French group

Date	Title / Label	Peak Position	Weeks at No.1	Weeks in Top 40
20 Apr 02	**SO I BEGIN** *Epic 6724102*	36		1

LUKE GALLIANA UK singer

Date	Title / Label	Peak Position	Weeks at No.1	Weeks in Top 40
12 May 01	**TO DIE FOR** *Jive 9201272*	42		

GALLIANO UK group

Date	Title / Label	Peak Position	Weeks at No.1	Weeks in Top 40
30 May 92	**SKUNK FUNK** *Talkin Loud TLK 23*	41		
1 Aug 92	**PRINCE OF PEACE** *Talkin Loud TLK 24*	47		
10 Oct 92	**JUS' REACH (RECYCLED)** *Talkin Loud TLK 29*	66		
28 May 94	**LONG TIME GONE** *Talkin Loud TLKCD 48*	15		2
30 Jul 94	**TWYFORD DOWN** *Talkin Loud TLKDD 49*	37		1
27 Jul 96	**EASE YOUR MIND** *Talkin Loud TLKDD 10*	45		

GALLOWS UK group

Date	Title / Label	Peak Position	Weeks at No.1	Weeks in Top 40
29 Sep 07	**IN THE BELLY OF A SHARK** *Warner Brothers WEA425CD*	56		
1 Dec 07	**STARING AT THE RUDE BOIS** *Warner Brothers WEA435CD*	31		1

JAMES GALWAY UK flautist

Date	Title / Label	Peak Position	Weeks at No.1	Weeks in Top 40
27 May 78	**ANNIE'S SONG** *RCA Red Seal RB 5085*	3		11

GAMBAFREAKS Italian production duo

Date	Title / Label	Peak Position	Weeks at No.1	Weeks in Top 40
12 Sep 98	**INSTANT REPLAY** *Evocative EVOKE 7CDS* GAMBAFREAKS FEATURING PACO RIVAZ	57		
13 May 00	**DOWN DOWN DOWN** *Azuli AZNYCDX 116*	57		

GAME US rapper

Date	Title / Label	Peak Position	Weeks at No.1	Weeks in Top 40
26 Feb 05	**HOW WE DO** *Interscope 9880361* GAME FEATURING 50 CENT	5		6
21 May 05	**HATE IT OR LOVE IT** *Interscope 9882205* GAME FEATURING 50 CENT	4		8
13 Aug 05	**DREAMS** *Interscope 9883713*	8		5
10 Sep 05	**PLAYA'S ONLY** *Jive 82876725552* R KELLY FEATURING GAME	33		1
19 Nov 05	**PUT YOU ON THE GAME** *Interscope 9887827*	46		
4 Nov 06	**IT'S OKAY** *Geffen 1713921* GAME FEATURING JUNIOR REID	26		3
20 Jan 07	**LET'S RIDE** *Geffen 1718917*	42		

GANG OF FOUR UK group

Date	Title / Label	Peak Position	Weeks at No.1	Weeks in Top 40
16 Jun 79	**AT HOME HE'S A TOURIST** *EMI 2956*	58		
22 May 82	**I LOVE A MAN IN UNIFORM** *EMI 5299*	65		

GANG STARR US duo

Date	Title / Label	Peak Position	Weeks at No.1	Weeks in Top 40
13 Oct 90	**JAZZ THING** *CBS 6563777*	66		
23 Feb 91	**TAKE A REST** *Cooltempo COOL 230*	63		
25 May 91	**LOVESICK** *Cooltempo COOL 234*	50		
13 Jun 92	**2 DEEP** *Cooltempo COOL 256*	67		

Silver-selling ○ Gold-selling ● Platinum-selling ⊛ US No.1 ★ | Peak Position | Weeks at No.1 | Weeks in Top 40

GANT UK production duo

Date	Title / Label	Peak Position	Weeks at No.1	Weeks in Top 40
27 Dec 97	**SOUND BWOY BURIAL/ALL NIGHT LONG** *Positiva CDTIV 85*	67		

GAP BAND US group

Date	Title / Label	Peak Position	Weeks at No.1	Weeks in Top 40
12 Jul 80	**OOPS UPSIDE YOUR HEAD** *Mercury MER 22* ○	6		11
27 Sep 80	**PARTY LIGHTS** *Mercury MER 37*	30		5
27 Dec 80	**BURN RUBBER ON ME (WHY YOU WANNA HURT ME)** *Mercury MER 52*	22		7
11 Apr 81	**HUMPIN'** *Mercury MER 63*	36		2
27 Jun 81	**YEARNING FOR YOUR LOVE** *Mercury MER 73*	47		
5 Jun 82	**EARLY IN THE MORNING** *Mercury MER 97*	55		
19 Feb 83	**OUTSTANDING** *Total Experience TE 001*	68		
31 Mar 84	**SOMEDAY** *Total Experience TE 5*	17		5
23 Jun 84	**JAMMIN' IN AMERICA** *Total Experience TE 6*	64		
13 Dec 86	**BIG FUN** *Total Experience FB 49779*	4		11
14 Mar 87	**HOW MUSIC CAME ABOUT (BOP B DA B DA DA)** *Total Experience FB 49755*	61		
11 Jul 87	**OOPS UPSIDE YOUR HEAD (REMIX)** *Club JAB 54*	20		5
18 Feb 89	**I'M GONNA GET YOU SUCKA** *Arista 112016*	63		
16 Oct 04	**OOPS UPSIDE YOUR HEAD** *All Around The World CDGLOBE376* DJ CASPER FEATURING THE GAP BAND	16		3

GARBAGE US/UK group

Date	Title / Label	Peak Position	Weeks at No.1	Weeks in Top 40
19 Aug 95	**SUBHUMAN** *Mushroom D 1138*	50		
30 Sep 95	**ONLY HAPPY WHEN IT RAINS** *Mushroom D 1199*	29		1
2 Dec 95	**QUEER** *Mushroom D 1237*	13		2
23 Mar 96	**STUPID GIRL** *Mushroom D 1271*	4		5
23 Nov 96	**MILK** *Mushroom D 1494* GARBAGE FEATURING TRICKY	10		3
9 May 98	**PUSH IT** *Mushroom MUSH 28CDS*	9		3
18 Jul 98	**I THINK I'M PARANOID** *Mushroom MUSH 35CDS*	9		3
17 Oct 98	**SPECIAL** *Mushroom MUSH 39CDS*	15		3
6 Feb 99	**WHEN I GROW UP** *Mushroom MUSH 43CDS*	9		3
5 Jun 99	**YOU LOOK SO FINE** *Mushroom MUSH 49CDS*	19		1
27 Nov 99	**THE WORLD IS NOT ENOUGH** *Radioactive RAXTD 40*	11		3
6 Oct 01	**ANDROGYNY** *Mushroom MUSH 94CDSX*	24		1
2 Feb 02	**CHERRY LIPS** *Mushroom MUSH 98CDS*	22		3
20 Apr 02	**BREAKING UP THE GIRL** *Mushroom MUSH 101CDS*	27		1
5 Oct 02	**SHUT YOUR MOUTH** *Mushroom MUSH 106CDSXX*	20		1
16 Apr 05	**WHY DO YOU LOVE ME** *Warner Brothers WEA385CD*	7		4
25 Jun 05	**SEX IS NOT THE ENEMY** *Mushroom WEA391CD*	24		1
28 Jul 07	**TELL ME WHERE IT HURTS** *Warner Brothers WEA424CD*	50		

ADAM GARCIA Australian singer

Date	Title / Label	Peak Position	Weeks at No.1	Weeks in Top 40
16 May 98	**NIGHT FEVER** *Polydor 5697972*	15		3

SCOTT GARCIA UK producer

Date	Title / Label	Peak Position	Weeks at No.1	Weeks in Top 40
1 Nov 97	**A LONDON THING** *Connected CDCONNECT 1* SCOTT GARCIA FEATURING MC STYLES	29		1

BORIS GARDINER Jamaican singer

Date	Title / Label	Peak Position	Weeks at No.1	Weeks in Top 40
17 Jan 70	**ELIZABETHAN REGGAE** *Duke DU 39*	14		12
26 Jul 86	**I WANT TO WAKE UP WITH YOU** *Revue REV 733* ●	1	3	12
4 Oct 86	**YOU'RE EVERYTHING TO ME** *Revue REV 735*	11		6
27 Dec 86	**THE MEANING OF CHRISTMAS** *Revue REV 740*	69		

PAUL GARDINER UK bass player

Date	Title / Label	Peak Position	Weeks at No.1	Weeks in Top 40
25 Jul 81	**STORMTROOPER IN DRAG** *Beggars Banquet BEG 61*	49		

ART GARFUNKEL US singer

Date	Title / Label	Peak Position	Weeks at No.1	Weeks in Top 40
13 Sep 75	**I ONLY HAVE EYES FOR YOU** *CBS 3575* ○	1	2	10
3 Mar 79	**BRIGHT EYES** *CBS 6947* ⊛	1	6	14
7 Jul 79	**SINCE I DON'T HAVE YOU** *CBS 7371*	38		1

JUDY GARLAND US singer/actress

Date	Title / Label	Peak Position	Weeks at No.1	Weeks in Top 40
10 Jun 55	**THE MAN THAT GOT AWAY** *Philips PB 366*	18		2

JESSICA GARLICK UK singer

Date	Title / Label	Peak Position	Weeks at No.1	Weeks in Top 40
25 May 02	**COME BACK** *Columbia 6725662*	13		4

LAURENT GARNIER French DJ/producer

Date	Title / Label	Peak Position	Weeks at No.1	Weeks in Top 40
15 Feb 97	**CRISPY BACON** *F Communications F 055CD*	60		
22 Apr 00	**MAN WITH THE RED FACE** *F Communications F 119CD*	65		
11 Nov 00	**GREED/THE MAN WITH THE RED FACE** *F Communications F127 CDUK*	36		1

LEE GARRETT US singer

Date	Title / Label	Peak Position	Weeks at No.1	Weeks in Top 40
29 May 76	**YOU'RE MY EVERYTHING** *Chrysalis CHS 2087*	15		6

LEIF GARRETT US singer

Date	Title / Label	Peak Position	Weeks at No.1	Weeks in Top 40
20 Jan 79	**I WAS MADE FOR DANCIN'** *Scotti Brothers K 11202* ○	4		8
21 Apr 79	**FEEL THE NEED** *Scotti Brothers K 11274*	38		2

LESLEY GARRETT & AMANDA THOMPSON UK duo

Date	Title / Label	Peak Position	Weeks at No.1	Weeks in Top 40
6 Nov 93	**AVE MARIA** *Internal Affairs KGBD 012*	16		8

SIEDAH GARRETT US singer

Date	Title / Label	Peak Position	Weeks at No.1	Weeks in Top 40
24 Mar 84	**DON'T LOOK ANY FURTHER** *Gordy TMG 1334* DENNIS EDWARDS FEATURING SIEDAH GARRETT	45		
20 Jun 87	**DON'T LOOK ANY FURTHER** *Gordy TMG 1334* DENNIS EDWARDS FEATURING SIEDAH GARRETT	55		
13 Jan 07	**RAIN DOWN LOVE** *Loaded LOAD116CD* FREEMASONS FEATURING SIEDAH GARRETT	12		4

DAVID GARRICK UK singer

Date	Title / Label	Peak Position	Weeks at No.1	Weeks in Top 40
9 Jun 66	**LADY JANE** *Piccadilly 7N 35317*	28		5
22 Sep 66	**DEAR MRS APPLEBEE** *Piccadilly 7N 35335*	22		6

GARY'S GANG US group

Date	Title / Label	Peak Position	Weeks at No.1	Weeks in Top 40
24 Feb 79	**KEEP ON DANCIN'** *CBS 7109*	8		7
2 Jun 79	**LET'S LOVE DANCE TONIGHT** *CBS 7328*	49		
6 Nov 82	**KNOCK ME OUT** *Arista ARIST 499*	45		

GAT DECOR UK production group

Date	Title / Label	Peak Position	Weeks at No.1	Weeks in Top 40
16 May 92	**PASSION** *Effective EFFS 1*	29		3
9 Mar 96	**PASSION (REMIX)** *Way Of Life WAYDA 1*	6		5

STEPHEN GATELY Irish singer

Date	Title / Label	Peak Position	Weeks at No.1	Weeks in Top 40
10 Jun 00	**NEW BEGINNING/BRIGHT EYES** *A&M 5618202* ○	3		4
14 Oct 00	**I BELIEVE** *Polydor 5877482*	11		2
12 May 01	**STAY** *A&M 5870672*	13		2

DAVID GATES US singer

Date	Title / Label	Peak Position	Weeks at No.1	Weeks in Top 40
22 Jul 78	**TOOK THE LAST TRAIN** *Elektra K 12307*	50		

GARETH GATES UK singer

Date	Title / Label	Peak Position	Weeks at No.1	Weeks in Top 40
30 Mar 02	**UNCHAINED MELODY** *S 74321930882* ⊛	1	4	13
20 Jul 02	**ANYONE OF US (STUPID MISTAKE)** *S 74321950602* ●	1	3	11
5 Oct 02	**THE LONG AND WINDING ROAD/SUSPICIOUS MINDS** *S 74321965972* WILL YOUNG & GARETH GATES/GARETH GATES ●	1	2	8
21 Dec 02	**WHAT MY HEART WANTS TO SAY** *S 74321985602*	5		7
22 Mar 03	**SPIRIT IN THE SKY** *S 82876511202* GARETH GATES FEATURING THE KUMARS ⊛	1	2	9
20 Sep 03	**SUNSHINE** *S 82876560042*	3		5
13 Dec 03	**SAY IT ISN'T SO** *S 82876583422*	4		6
21 Apr 07	**CHANGES** *19 1721080*	14		1
30 Jun 07	**ANGEL ON MY SHOULDER** *19 1736009*	22		1

ALEX GAUDINO Italian producer

Date	Title / Label	Peak Position	Weeks at No.1	Weeks in Top 40
24 Mar 07	**DESTINATION CALABRIA** *Data DATA153CDS* ALEX GAUDINO FEATURING CRYSTAL WATERS	4		11

Silver-selling ◦ Gold-selling ● Platinum-selling ✪ US No.1 ★ — Peak Position / Weeks at No.1 / Weeks in Top 40

GAY DAD UK group

Date	Title	Peak Position	Weeks at No.1	Weeks in Top 40
30 Jan 99	**TO EARTH WITH LOVE** *London LONCD 413*	10		3
5 Jun 99	**JOY!** *London LONCD 428*	22		1
14 Aug 99	**OH JIM** *London LONCD 437*	47		
31 Mar 01	**NOW ALWAYS AND FOREVER** *B Unique BUN 004CD*	41		
22 Sep 01	**TRANSMISSION** *B Unique BUN 009CDX*	58		

GAY GORDON & THE MINCE PIES UK group

Date	Title	Peak Position	Weeks at No.1	Weeks in Top 40
6 Dec 86	**THE ESSENTIAL WALLY PARTY MEDLEY** *Lifestyle XY 2*	60		

MARVIN GAYE US singer

Date	Title	Peak Position	Weeks at No.1	Weeks in Top 40
30 Jul 64	**ONCE UPON A TIME** *Stateside SS 316* MARVIN GAYE & MARY WELLS	50		
10 Dec 64	**HOW SWEET IT IS** *Stateside SS 360*	49		
29 Sep 66	**LITTLE DARLIN'** *Tamla Motown TMG 574*	50		
26 Jan 67	**IT TAKES TWO** *Tamla Motown TMG 590* MARVIN GAYE & KIM WESTON	16		9
17 Jan 68	**IF I COULD BUILD MY WHOLE WORLD AROUND YOU** *Tamla Motown TMG 635* MARVIN GAYE & TAMMI TERRELL	41		
12 Jun 68	**AIN'T NOTHING LIKE THE REAL THING** *Tamla Motown TMG 655* MARVIN GAYE & TAMMI TERRELL	34		4
2 Oct 68	**YOU'RE ALL I NEED TO GET BY** *Tamla Motown TMG 668* MARVIN GAYE & TAMMI TERRELL	19		14
22 Jan 69	**YOU AIN'T LIVIN' TILL YOU'RE LOVIN'** *Tamla Motown TMG 681* MARVIN GAYE & TAMMI TERRELL	21		7
12 Feb 69	**I HEARD IT THROUGH THE GRAPEVINE** *Tamla Motown TMG 686* ★	1	3	14
4 Jun 69	**GOOD LOVIN' AIN'T EASY TO COME BY** *Tamla Motown TMG 697* MARVIN GAYE & TAMMI TERRELL	26		5
23 Jul 69	**TOO BUSY THINKING ABOUT MY BABY** *Tamla Motown TMG 705*	5		15
15 Nov 69	**ONION SONG** *Tamla Motown TMG 715* MARVIN GAYE & TAMMI TERRELL	9		10
9 May 70	**ABRAHAM MARTIN AND JOHN** *Tamla Motown TMG 734*	9		13
11 Dec 71	**SAVE THE CHILDREN** *Tamla Motown TMG 796*	41		
22 Sep 73	**LET'S GET IT ON** *Tamla Motown TMG 868* ★	31		5
23 Mar 74	**YOU ARE EVERYTHING** *Tamla Motown TMG 890* DIANA ROSS & MARVIN GAYE ◦	5		10
20 Jul 74	**STOP LOOK LISTEN (TO YOUR HEART)** *Tamla Motown TMG 906* DIANA ROSS & MARVIN GAYE	25		5
7 May 77	**GOT TO GIVE IT UP** *Motown TMG 1069* ★	7		10
24 Feb 79	**POPS WE LOVE YOU** *Motown TMG 1136* DIANA ROSS, MARVIN GAYE, SMOKEY ROBINSON & STEVIE WONDER	66		
30 Oct 82	**(SEXUAL) HEALING** *CBS A 2855* ◦	4		11
8 Jan 83	**MY LOVE IS WAITING** *CBS A 3048*	34		2
18 May 85	**SANCTIFIED LADY** *CBS A 4894*	51		
26 Apr 86	**I HEARD IT THROUGH THE GRAPEVINE** *Tamla Motown ZB 40701*	8		6
14 May 94	**LUCKY LUCKY ME** *Motown TMGCD 1426*	67		
6 Oct 01	**MUSIC** *Polydor 4976222* ERICK SERMON FEATURING MARVIN GAYE	36		1

GAYE BYKERS ON ACID UK group

Date	Title	Peak Position	Weeks at No.1	Weeks in Top 40
31 Oct 87	**GIT DOWN (SHAKE YOUR THANG)** *Purple Fluid VS 1008*	54		

CRYSTAL GAYLE US singer

Date	Title	Peak Position	Weeks at No.1	Weeks in Top 40
12 Nov 77	**DON'T IT MAKE MY BROWN EYES BLUE** *United Artists UP 36307* ◦	5		14
26 Aug 78	**TALKING IN YOUR SLEEP** *United Artists UP 36422* ◦	11		10

MICHELLE GAYLE UK singer

Date	Title	Peak Position	Weeks at No.1	Weeks in Top 40
7 Aug 93	**LOOKING UP** *RCA 74321154532*	11		5
24 Sep 94	**SWEETNESS** *RCA 74321230192* ◦	4		13
17 Dec 94	**I'LL FIND YOU** *RCA 74321247762*	26		5
27 May 95	**FREEDOM** *RCA 74321284692*	16		4
26 Aug 95	**HAPPY JUST TO BE WITH YOU** *RCA 74321302692*	11		5
8 Feb 97	**DO YOU KNOW** *RCA 74321419282*	6		4
26 Apr 97	**SENSATIONAL** *RCA 74321419302*	14		3

GAYLE & GILLIAN Australian duo

Date	Title	Peak Position	Weeks at No.1	Weeks in Top 40
3 Jul 93	**MAD IF YA DON'T** *Mushroom CDMUSH 1*	75		
19 Mar 94	**WANNA BE YOUR LOVER** *Mushroom D 11598*	62		

GLORIA GAYNOR US singer

Date	Title	Peak Position	Weeks at No.1	Weeks in Top 40
7 Dec 74	**NEVER CAN SAY GOODBYE** *MGM 2006 463* ◦	2		11
8 Mar 75	**REACH OUT I'LL BE THERE** *MGM 2006 499*	14		7
9 Aug 75	**ALL I NEED IS YOUR SWEET LOVIN'** *MGM 2006 531*	44		
17 Jan 76	**HOW HIGH THE MOON** *MGM 2006 558*	33		2
3 Feb 79	**I WILL SURVIVE** *Polydor 2095 017* ● ★	1	4	12
6 Oct 79	**LET ME KNOW (I HAVE THE RIGHT)** *Polydor STEP 5*	32		3
24 Dec 83	**I AM WHAT I AM (FROM 'LA CAGE AUX FOLLES')** *Chrysalis CHS 2765*	13		7
26 Jun 93	**I WILL SURVIVE (REMIX)** *Polydor PZCD 270*	5		8
3 Jun 00	**LAST NIGHT** *Logic 74321738082*	67		

GAZ US group

Date	Title	Peak Position	Weeks at No.1	Weeks in Top 40
24 Feb 79	**SING SING** *Salsoul SSOL 116*	60		

GAZZA UK footballer

Date	Title	Peak Position	Weeks at No.1	Weeks in Top 40
10 Nov 90	**FOG ON THE TYNE (REVISITED)** *Best ZB 44083* GAZZA & LINDISFARNE	2		6
22 Dec 90	**GEORDIE BOYS (GAZZA RAP)** *Best ZB 44229*	31		3

GBH UK group

Date	Title	Peak Position	Weeks at No.1	Weeks in Top 40
6 Feb 82	**NO SURVIVORS** *Clay 8*	63		
20 Nov 82	**GIVE ME FIRE** *Clay 16*	69		

NIGEL GEE UK producer

Date	Title	Peak Position	Weeks at No.1	Weeks in Top 40
27 Jan 01	**HOOTIN'** *Neo NEOCD 040*	57		

J GEILS BAND US group

Date	Title	Peak Position	Weeks at No.1	Weeks in Top 40
9 Jun 79	**ONE LAST KISS** *EMI America AM 507*	74		
13 Feb 82	**CENTERFOLD** *EMI America EA 135* ◦ ★	3		8
10 Apr 82	**FREEZE-FRAME** *EMI America EA 134*	27		5
26 Jun 82	**ANGEL IN BLUE** *EMI America EA 138*	55		

PETER GELDERBLOM Dutch producer

Date	Title	Peak Position	Weeks at No.1	Weeks in Top 40
8 Dec 07	**WAITING 4** *Data DATA171CDS*	29		1

BOB GELDOF Irish singer

Date	Title	Peak Position	Weeks at No.1	Weeks in Top 40
1 Nov 86	**THIS IS THE WORLD CALLING** *Mercury BOB 101*	25		4
21 Feb 87	**LOVE LIKE A ROCKET** *Mercury BOB 102*	61		
23 Jun 90	**THE GREAT SONG OF INDIFFERENCE** *Mercury BOB 104*	15		4
7 May 94	**CRAZY** *Vertigo VERCX 85*	65		

GEMINI UK duo

Date	Title	Peak Position	Weeks at No.1	Weeks in Top 40
30 Sep 95	**EVEN THOUGH YOU BROKE MY HEART** *EMI CDEMS 391*	40		1
10 Feb 96	**STEAL YOUR LOVE AWAY** *EMI CDEMS 407*	37		1
29 Jun 96	**COULD IT BE FOREVER** *EMI CDEM 426*	38		1

GEMS FOR JEM UK production duo

Date	Title	Peak Position	Weeks at No.1	Weeks in Top 40
6 May 95	**LIFTING ME HIGHER** *Box 21 CDSBOK 3*	28		1

GENE UK group

Date	Title	Peak Position	Weeks at No.1	Weeks in Top 40
13 Aug 94	**BE MY LIGHT BE MY GUIDE** *Costermonger COST 002CD*	54		
12 Nov 94	**SLEEP WELL TONIGHT** *Costermonger COST 003CD*	36		1
4 Mar 95	**HAUNTED BY YOU** *Costermonger COST 004CD*	32		1
22 Jul 95	**OLYMPIAN** *Costermonger COST 005CD*	18		1
13 Jan 96	**FOR THE DEAD** *Costermonger COST 006CD*	14		2
2 Nov 96	**FIGHTING FIT** *Polydor COST 9CD*	22		1
1 Feb 97	**WE COULD BE KINGS** *Polydor COSCD 10*	17		1
10 May 97	**WHERE ARE THEY NOW?** *Polydor COSCD 11*	22		1
9 Aug 97	**SPEAK TO ME SOMEONE** *Polydor COSCD 12*	30		1
27 Feb 99	**AS GOOD AS IT GETS** *Polydor COSCD 14*	23		1
24 Apr 99	**FILL HER UP** *Polydor COSCD 15*	36		1
25 Dec 04	**LET ME MOVE ON** *Costermonger COST10CD1*	69		

GENE AND JIM ARE INTO SHAKES UK duo

Date	Title	Peak Position	Weeks at No.1	Weeks in Top 40
19 Mar 88	**SHAKE! (HOW ABOUT A SAMPLING GENE)** *Rough Trade RT 216*	68		

GENE LOVES JEZEBEL UK group

Date	Title	Peak Position	Weeks at No.1	Weeks in Top 40
29 Mar 86	**SWEETEST THING** *Beggars Banquet BEG 156*	75		
14 Jun 86	**HEARTACHE** *Beggars Banquet BEG 161*	71		
5 Sep 87	**THE MOTION OF LOVE** *Beggars Banquet BEG 192*	56		
5 Dec 87	**GORGEOUS** *Beggars Banquet BEG 202*	68		

GENERAL LEVY UK rapper

Date	Title	Peak Position	Weeks at No.1	Weeks in Top 40
4 Sep 93	**MONKEY MAN** *ffrr FCD 214*	75		
18 Jun 94	**INCREDIBLE** *Renk 42CD* M-BEAT FEATURING GENERAL LEVY	39		2
10 Sep 94	**INCREDIBLE (REMIX)** *Renk CDRENK 44* M-BEAT FEATURING GENERAL LEVY	8		7
13 Mar 04	**SHAKE (WHAT YA MAMA GAVE YA)** *East West EW281CD* GENERAL LEVY VS ZEUS	51		

GENERAL PUBLIC UK group

Date	Title	Peak Position	Weeks at No.1	Weeks in Top 40
10 Mar 84	**GENERAL PUBLIC** *Virgin VS 659*	60		
2 Jul 94	**I'LL TAKE YOU THERE** *Epic 6605532*	73		

GENERAL SAINT UK singer

Date	Title	Peak Position	Weeks at No.1	Weeks in Top 40
29 Sep 84	**LAST PLANE (ONE WAY TICKET)** *MCA 910* CLINT EASTWOOD & GENERAL SAINT	51		
2 Apr 94	**OH CAROL!** *Copasetic COPCD 0009* CLINT EASTWOOD & GENERAL SAINT	54		
6 Aug 94	**SAVE THE LAST DANCE FOR ME** *Copasetic COPCD 12* GENERAL SAINT FEATURING DON CAMPBELL	75		

GENERATION X UK group

Date	Title	Peak Position	Weeks at No.1	Weeks in Top 40
17 Sep 77	**YOUR GENERATION** *Chrysalis CHS 2165*	36		3
11 Mar 78	**READY STEADY GO** *Chrysalis CHS 2207*	47		
20 Jan 79	**KING ROCKER** *Chrysalis CHS 2261*	11		6
7 Apr 79	**VALLEY OF THE DOLLS** *Chrysalis CHS 2310*	23		6
30 Jun 79	**FRIDAY'S ANGELS** *Chrysalis CHS 2330*	62		
18 Oct 80	**DANCING WITH MYSELF** *Chrysalis CHS 2444*	62		
24 Jan 81	**DANCING WITH MYSELF (EP)** *Chrysalis CHS 2488*	60		

GENERATOR Dutch producer

Date	Title	Peak Position	Weeks at No.1	Weeks in Top 40
23 Oct 99	**WHERE ARE YOU NOW?** *Tidy Trax TIDY 130CD*	60		

GENESIS UK group

Date	Title	Peak Position	Weeks at No.1	Weeks in Top 40
6 Apr 74	**I KNOW WHAT I LIKE (IN YOUR WARDROBE)** *Charisma CB 224*	21		5
26 Feb 77	**YOUR OWN SPECIAL WAY** *Charisma CB 300*	43		
28 May 77	**SPOT THE PIGEON EP** *Charisma GEN 001*	14		5
11 Mar 78	**FOLLOW YOU FOLLOW ME** *Charisma CB 309* ●	7		10
8 Jul 78	**MANY TOO MANY** *Charisma CB 315*	43		
15 Mar 80	**TURN IT ON AGAIN** *Charisma CB 356*	8		7
17 May 80	**DUCHESS** *Charisma CB 363*	46		
13 Sep 80	**MISUNDERSTANDING** *Charisma CB 369*	42		
22 Aug 81	**ABACAB** *Charisma CB 388*	9		6
31 Oct 81	**KEEP IT DARK** *Charisma CB 391*	33		2
13 Mar 82	**MAN ON THE CORNER** *Charisma CB 393*	41		
22 May 82	**3 X 3 EP** *Charisma GEN 1*	10		7
3 Sep 83	**MAMA** *Virgin/Charisma MAMA 1* ●	4		9
12 Nov 83	**THAT'S ALL** *Charisma/Virgin TATA 1*	16		9
11 Feb 84	**ILLEGAL ALIEN** *Charisma/Virgin AL 1*	46		
31 May 86	**INVISIBLE TOUCH** *Virgin GENS 1* ★	15		6
30 Aug 86	**IN TOO DEEP** *Virgin GENS 2*	19		8
22 Nov 86	**LAND OF CONFUSION** *Virgin GENS 3*	14		10
14 Mar 87	**TONIGHT TONIGHT TONIGHT** *Virgin GENS 4*	18		5
20 Jun 87	**THROWING IT ALL AWAY** *Virgin GENS 5*	22		5
2 Nov 91	**NO SON OF MINE** *Virgin GENS 6*	6		4
11 Jan 92	**I CAN'T DANCE** *Virgin GENS 7*	7		6
18 Apr 92	**HOLD ON MY HEART** *Virgin GENS 8*	16		4
25 Jul 92	**JESUS HE KNOWS ME** *Virgin GENS 9*	20		5
21 Nov 92	**INVISIBLE TOUCH (LIVE)** *Virgin GENS 10*	7		3
20 Feb 93	**TELL ME WHY** *Virgin GENDG 11*	40		1
27 Sep 97	**CONGO** *Virgin GENSD 12*	29		1
13 Dec 97	**SHIPWRECKED** *Virgin GENDX 14*	54		
7 Mar 98	**NOT ABOUT US** *Virgin GENSD 15*	66		

GENEVA UK group

Date	Title	Peak Position	Weeks at No.1	Weeks in Top 40
26 Oct 96	**NO ONE SPEAKS** *Nude NUD 22CD*	32		1
8 Feb 97	**INTO THE BLUE** *Nude NUD 25CD*	26		1
31 May 97	**TRANQUILLIZER** *Nude NUD 28CD1*	24		1
16 Aug 97	**BEST REGRETS** *Nude NUD 31CD1*	38		1
27 Nov 99	**DOLLARS IN THE HEAVENS** *Nude NUD 46CD1*	59		
11 Mar 00	**IF YOU HAVE TO GO** *Nude NUD 49CD1*	69		

GENEVIEVE UK singer

Date	Title	Peak Position	Weeks at No.1	Weeks in Top 40
5 May 66	**ONCE** *CBS 202061*	43		

GENIUS US rapper

Date	Title	Peak Position	Weeks at No.1	Weeks in Top 40
2 Mar 96	**COLD WORLD** *Geffen GFSTD 22114* GENIUS/GZA FEATURING D'ANGELO	40		1

GENIUS CRU UK group

Date	Title	Peak Position	Weeks at No.1	Weeks in Top 40
3 Feb 01	**BOOM SELECTION** *Incentive CENT 17CDS*	12		3
27 Oct 01	**COURSE BRUV** *Incentive CENT 28CDS*	39		1

BOBBIE GENTRY US singer

Date	Title	Peak Position	Weeks at No.1	Weeks in Top 40
13 Sep 67	**ODE TO BILLY JOE** *Capitol CL 15511* ★	13		10
30 Aug 69	**I'LL NEVER FALL IN LOVE AGAIN** *Capitol CL 15606*	1	1	18
6 Dec 69	**ALL I HAVE TO DO IS DREAM** *Capitol CL 15619* BOBBIE GENTRY & GLEN CAMPBELL	3		13
21 Feb 70	**RAINDROPS KEEP FALLIN' ON MY HEAD** *Capitol CL 15626*	40		1

GEORDIE UK group

Date	Title	Peak Position	Weeks at No.1	Weeks in Top 40
2 Dec 72	**DON'T DO THAT** *Regal Zonophone RZ 3067*	32		4
17 Mar 73	**ALL BECAUSE OF YOU** *EMI 2008*	6		11
16 Jun 73	**CAN YOU DO IT** *EMI 2031*	13		7
25 Aug 73	**ELECTRIC LADY** *EMI 2048*	32		4

ROBIN GEORGE UK guitarist

Date	Title	Peak Position	Weeks at No.1	Weeks in Top 40
27 Apr 85	**HEARTLINE** *Bronze BRO 191*	68		

SOPHIA GEORGE Jamaican singer

Date	Title	Peak Position	Weeks at No.1	Weeks in Top 40
7 Dec 85	**GIRLIE GIRLIE** *Winner WIN 01*	7		8

GEORGIA SATELLITES US group

Date	Title	Peak Position	Weeks at No.1	Weeks in Top 40
7 Feb 87	**KEEP YOUR HANDS TO YOURSELF** *Elektra EKR 50*	69		
16 May 87	**BATTLESHIP CHAINS** *Elektra EKR 58*	44		
21 Jan 89	**HIPPY HIPPY SHAKE** *Elektra EKR 86*	63		

GEORGIE PORGIE US producer

Date	Title	Peak Position	Weeks at No.1	Weeks in Top 40
12 Aug 95	**EVERYBODY MUST PARTY** *Vibe MCSTD 2068*	61		
4 May 96	**TAKE ME HIGHER** *Music Plant MCSTD 40031*	61		
26 Aug 00	**LIFE GOES ON** *Neo NEOCD 039*	54		

GEORGIO US singer

Date	Title	Peak Position	Weeks at No.1	Weeks in Top 40
20 Feb 88	**LOVER'S LANE** *Motown ZB 41611*	54		

DANYEL GERARD French singer

Date	Title	Peak Position	Weeks at No.1	Weeks in Top 40
18 Sep 71	**BUTTERFLY** *CBS 7454*	11		10

GERIDEAU US singer

Date	Title	Peak Position	Weeks at No.1	Weeks in Top 40
27 Aug 94	**BRING IT BACK 2 LUV** *Fruittree FTREE 10CD* PROJECT FEATURING GERIDEAU	65		
4 Jul 98	**MASQUERADE** *Inferno CDFERN 7*	63		

GERRY & THE PACEMAKERS UK group

Date	Title	Peak Position	Weeks at No.1	Weeks in Top 40
14 Mar 63	**HOW DO YOU DO IT?** *Columbia DB 4987*	1	3	17
30 May 63	**I LIKE IT** *Columbia DB 7041*	1	4	15
10 Oct 63	**YOU'LL NEVER WALK ALONE** *Columbia DB 7126*	1	4	19

Date	Title / Label	Peak Position	Weeks at No.1	Weeks in Top 40
16 Jan 64	**I'M THE ONE** *Columbia DB 7189*	2		13
16 Apr 64	**DON'T LET THE SUN CATCH YOU CRYING** *Columbia DB 7268*	6		9
3 Sep 64	**IT'S GONNA BE ALL RIGHT** *Columbia DB 7353*	24		7
17 Dec 64	**FERRY ACROSS THE MERSEY** *Columbia DB 7437*	8		12
25 Mar 65	**I'LL BE THERE** *Columbia DB 7504*	15		8
18 Nov 65	**WALK HAND IN HAND** *Columbia DB 7738*	29		4

GET CAPE WEAR CAPE FLY US singer

Date	Title / Label	Peak Position	Weeks at No.1	Weeks in Top 40
23 Sep 06	**THE CHRONICLES OF A BOHEMIAN TEENAGER** *Atlantic ATUK042CD*	38		1
9 Dec 06	**WAR OF THE WORLDS** *Atlantic ATUK049CD*	39		1
17 Mar 07	**I SPY** *Atlantic ATUK056CDH*	37		1
15 Mar 08	**FIND THE TIME** *Atlantic ATUK073CD*	33		1

GET READY UK group

Date	Title / Label	Peak Position	Weeks at No.1	Weeks in Top 40
3 Jun 95	**WILD WILD WEST** *Mega GACXCD 2698*	65		

GETO BOYS US group

Date	Title / Label	Peak Position	Weeks at No.1	Weeks in Top 40
11 May 96	**THE WORLD IS A GHETTO** *Virgin America VUSCD 104* GETO BOYS FEATURING FLAJ	49		

STAN GETZ US saxophonist

Date	Title / Label	Peak Position	Weeks at No.1	Weeks in Top 40
8 Nov 62	**DESAFINADO** *HMV POP 1061* STAN GETZ & CHARLIE BYRD	11		12
23 Jul 64	**THE GIRL FROM IPANEMA (GAROTA DE IPANEMA)** *Verve VS 520*	29		7
25Aug 84	**THE GIRL FROM IPANEMA** *Verve IPA 1* STAN GETZ & ASTRUD GILBERTO	55		

G4 Irish group

Date	Title / Label	Peak Position	Weeks at No.1	Weeks in Top 40
26 Mar 05	**BOHEMIAN RHAPSODY** *Sony Music 6758062*	9		3

AMANDA GHOST UK singer

Date	Title / Label	Peak Position	Weeks at No.1	Weeks in Top 40
8 Apr 00	**IDOL** *Warner Brothers W 518CD*	63		
1 May 04	**BREAK MY WORLD** *Island CID 853* DARK GLOBE FEATURING AMANDA GHOST	52		

GHOST DANCE UK group

Date	Title / Label	Peak Position	Weeks at No.1	Weeks in Top 40
17 Jun 89	**DOWN TO THE WIRE** *Chrysalis CHS 3376*	66		

GHOSTFACE KILLAH US rapper

Date	Title / Label	Peak Position	Weeks at No.1	Weeks in Top 40
12 Jul 97	**ALL THAT I GOT IS YOU** *Epic 6646842*	11		3
23 Jan 99	**I WANT YOU FOR MYSELF** *Northwestside 74321643632* ANOTHER LEVEL/GHOSTFACE KILLAH	2		6
4 Nov 00	**MISS FAT BOOTY – PART II** *Rawkus RWK 282CD* MOS DEF FEATURING GHOSTFACE KILLAH	64		
29 May 04	**ON MY KNEES** *Sony Music 6749382* 411 FEATURING GHOSTFACE KILLAH	4		6
17 Jul 04	**PUSH** *Def Jam 9862837* GHOSTFACE FEATURING MISSY ELLIOTT	34		1
16 Oct 04	**LOVE THEM** *Jive 82876639212* EAMON FEATURING GHOSTFACE	27		2
26 Aug 06	**BACK LIKE THAT** *Def Jam 1705586* GHOSTFACE KILLAH FEATURING NE-YO	46		

GHOSTS UK group

Date	Title / Label	Peak Position	Weeks at No.1	Weeks in Top 40
10 Mar 07	**STAY THE NIGHT** *Atlantic ATUK055CD*	25		3
16 Jun 07	**THE WORLD IS OUTSIDE** *Atlantic ATUK064CD*	35		1

ANDY GIBB UK singer

Date	Title / Label	Peak Position	Weeks at No.1	Weeks in Top 40
25 Jun 77	**I JUST WANNA BE YOUR EVERYTHING** *RSO 2090 237* ★	26		5
13 May 78	**SHADOW DANCING** *RSO 001* ★	42		
12 Aug 78	**AN EVERLASTING LOVE** *RSO 015*	10		8
27 Jan 79	**(OUR LOVE) DON'T THROW IT ALL AWAY** *RSO 26*	32		4

ROBIN GIBB UK singer

Date	Title / Label	Peak Position	Weeks at No.1	Weeks in Top 40
9 Jul 69	**SAVED BY THE BELL** *Polydor 56 337*	2		16
7 Feb 70	**AUGUST OCTOBER** *Polydor 56 371*	45		

Date	Title / Label	Peak Position	Weeks at No.1	Weeks in Top 40
11 Feb 84	**ANOTHER LONELY NIGHT IN NEW YORK** *Polydor POSP 668*	71		
1 Feb 03	**PLEASE** *SPV Recordings 05571463*	23		3

BETH GIBBONS AND RUSTIN MAN UK duo

Date	Title / Label	Peak Position	Weeks at No.1	Weeks in Top 40
15 Mar 03	**TOM THE MODEL** *Go! Beat GOBCD 55*	70		

STEVE GIBBONS BAND UK group

Date	Title / Label	Peak Position	Weeks at No.1	Weeks in Top 40
6 Aug 77	**TULANE** *Polydor 2058 889*	12		8
13 May 78	**EDDY VORTEX** *Polydor 2059 017*	56		

GEORGIA GIBBS US singer

Date	Title / Label	Peak Position	Weeks at No.1	Weeks in Top 40
22 Apr 55	**TWEEDLE DEE** *Mercury MB 3196*	20		1
13 Jul 56	**KISS ME ANOTHER** *Mercury MT 110*	24		1

DEBBIE GIBSON US singer

Date	Title / Label	Peak Position	Weeks at No.1	Weeks in Top 40
26 Sep 87	**ONLY IN MY DREAMS** *Atlantic A 9322*	54		
23 Jan 88	**SHAKE YOUR LOVE** *Atlantic A 9187*	7		7
19 Mar 88	**ONLY IN MY DREAMS** *Atlantic A 9322*	11		6
7 May 88	**OUT OF THE BLUE** *Atlantic A 9091*	19		5
9 Jul 88	**FOOLISH BEAT** *Atlantic A 9059* ★	9		8
15 Oct 88	**STAYING TOGETHER** *Atlantic A 9020*	53		
28 Jan 89	**LOST IN YOUR EYES** *Atlantic A 8970* ★	34		4
29 Apr 89	**ELECTRIC YOUTH** *Atlantic A 8919*	14		6
19 Aug 89	**WE COULD BE TOGETHER** *Atlantic A 8896*	22		6
9 Mar 91	**ANYTHING IS POSSIBLE** *Atlantic A 7735*	51		
3 Apr 93	**SHOCK YOUR MAMA** *Atlantic A 7386CD*	74		
24 Jul 93	**YOU'RE THE ONE THAT I WANT** *Epic 6595222* CRAIG McLACHLAN & DEBBIE GIBSON	13		4

DON GIBSON US singer

Date	Title / Label	Peak Position	Weeks at No.1	Weeks in Top 40
31 Aug 61	**SEA OF HEARTBREAK** *RCA 1243*	14		13
1 Feb 62	**LONESOME NUMBER ONE** *RCA 1272*	47		

WAYNE GIBSON UK singer

Date	Title / Label	Peak Position	Weeks at No.1	Weeks in Top 40
3 Sep 64	**KELLY** *Pye 7N 15680*	48		
23 Nov 74	**UNDER MY THUMB** *Pye Disco Demand DDS 2001*	17		10

GIBSON BROTHERS Martinique group

Date	Title / Label	Peak Position	Weeks at No.1	Weeks in Top 40
10 Mar 79	**CUBA** *Island WIP 6483*	41		
21 Jul 79	**OOH! WHAT A LIFE** *Island WIP 6503*	10		9
17 Nov 79	**QUE SERA MI VIDA (IF YOU SHOULD GO)** *Island WIP 6525* ●	5		10
23 Feb 80	**CUBA/BETTER DO IT SALSA** *Island WIP 6561*	12		7
12 Jul 80	**MARIANA** *Island WIP 6617*	11		8
9 Jul 83	**MY HEART'S BEATING WILD (TIC TAC TIC TAC)** *Stiff BUY 184*	56		

GIDEA PARK UK producer

Date	Title / Label	Peak Position	Weeks at No.1	Weeks in Top 40
4 Jul 81	**BEACHBOY GOLD** *Stone SON 2162*	11		9
12 Sep 81	**SEASONS OF GOLD** *Polo 14*	28		4

JOHN GIELEN Belgian producer

Date	Title / Label	Peak Position	Weeks at No.1	Weeks in Top 40
18 Aug 01	**VELVET MOODS** *Data 17T* JOHAN GIELEN PRESENTS ABNEA	74		
22 Sep 01	**THE BEAUTY OF SILENCE** *Xtrahard/Xtravaganza X2H 5CDS* SVENSON & GIELEN	41		

GIFTED UK instrumentalist

Date	Title / Label	Peak Position	Weeks at No.1	Weeks in Top 40
23 Aug 97	**DO I** *Perfecto PERF 140CD*	60		

GIGOLO AUNTS US group

Date	Title / Label	Peak Position	Weeks at No.1	Weeks in Top 40
23 Apr 94	**MRS WASHINGTON** *Fire BLAZE 68CD*	74		
13 May 95	**WHERE I FIND MY HEAVEN** *Fire BLAZE 87CD*	29		1

DONNA GILES US singer

Date	Title / Label	Peak Position	Weeks at No.1	Weeks in Top 40
13 Aug 94	**AND I'M TELLING YOU I'M NOT GOING** *Ore AG 4CD*	43		
10 Feb 96	**AND I'M TELLING YOU I'M NOT GOING (REMIX)** *Ore/XL Recordings AGR 4CD*	27		1

Silver-selling ○ Gold-selling ● Platinum-selling ⊛ US No.1 ★ Peak Position · Weeks at No.1 · Weeks in Top 40

JOHNNY GILL US singer

Date	Title / Label	Peak Position	Weeks at No.1	Weeks in Top 40
23 Feb 91	**WRAP MY BODY TIGHT** *Motown ZB 44271*	57		
28 Nov 92	**SLOW AND SEXY** *Epic 6587727* SHABBA RANKS FEATURING JOHNNY GILL	17		3
17 Jul 93	**THE FLOOR** *Motown TMGCD 1416*	53		
29 Jan 94	**A CUTE SWEET LOVE ADDICTION** *Motown TMGCD 1420*	46		

VINCE GILL US singer

Date	Title / Label	Peak Position	Weeks at No.1	Weeks in Top 40
14 Oct 95	**HOUSE OF LOVE** *A&M 5812332* AMY GRANT WITH VINCE GILL	46		
30 Oct 99	**IF YOU EVER LEAVE ME** *Columbia 6681242* BARBRA STREISAND/VINCE GILL	26		1

GILLAN UK group

Date	Title / Label	Peak Position	Weeks at No.1	Weeks in Top 40
14 Jun 80	**SLEEPIN' ON THE JOB** *Virgin VS 355*	55		
4 Oct 80	**TROUBLE** *Virgin VS 377*	14		5
14 Feb 81	**MUTUALLY ASSURED DESTRUCTION** *Virgin VS 103*	32		3
21 Mar 81	**NEW ORLEANS** *Virgin VS 406*	17		8
20 Jun 81	**NO LAUGHING IN HEAVEN** *Virgin VS 425*	31		4
10 Oct 81	**NIGHTMARE** *Virgin VS 441*	36		4
23 Jan 82	**RESTLESS** *Virgin VS 465*	25		3
4 Sep 82	**LIVING FOR THE CITY** *Virgin VS 519*	50		

STUART GILLIES UK singer

Date	Title / Label	Peak Position	Weeks at No.1	Weeks in Top 40
31 Mar 73	**AMANDA** *Philips 6006 293*	13		8

THEA GILMORE UK singer

Date	Title / Label	Peak Position	Weeks at No.1	Weeks in Top 40
16 Aug 03	**JULIET (KEEP THAT IN MIND)** *Hungry Dog YRGNUHS 2*	35		1
8 Nov 03	**MAINSTREAM** *Hungry Dog YRGNUHS 4*	50		

DAVID GILMOUR UK singer/guitarist

Date	Title / Label	Peak Position	Weeks at No.1	Weeks in Top 40
17 Jun 06	**SMILE** *EMI CDEM696*	72		
6 Jan 07	**ARNOLD LAYNE** *EMI CDEM717*	19		1

JAMES GILREATH US singer

Date	Title / Label	Peak Position	Weeks at No.1	Weeks in Top 40
2 May 63	**LITTLE BAND OF GOLD** *Pye International 7N 25190*	29		7

JIM GILSTRAP US singer

Date	Title / Label	Peak Position	Weeks at No.1	Weeks in Top 40
15 Mar 75	**SWING YOUR DADDY** *Chelsea 2005 021*	4		9

GORDON GILTRAP UK guitarist

Date	Title / Label	Peak Position	Weeks at No.1	Weeks in Top 40
14 Jan 78	**HEARTSONG** *Electric WOT 19*	21		6
28 Apr 79	**FEAR OF THE DARK** *Electric WOT 29* GORDON GILTRAP BAND	58		

GIN BLOSSOMS US group

Date	Title / Label	Peak Position	Weeks at No.1	Weeks in Top 40
5 Feb 94	**HEY JEALOUSY** *Fontana GINCD 3*	24		3
16 Apr 94	**FOUND OUT ABOUT YOU** *Fontana GINCD 4*	40		1
10 Feb 96	**TIL I HEAR IT FROM YOU** *A&M 5812272*	39		1
27 Apr 96	**FOLLOW YOU DOWN** *A&M 5815512*	30		1

GINUWINE US singer

Date	Title / Label	Peak Position	Weeks at No.1	Weeks in Top 40
25 Jan 97	**PONY** *Epic 6641282*	16		4
24 May 97	**TELL ME DO U WANNA** *Epic 6645272*	16		2
6 Sep 97	**WHEN DOVES CRY** *Epic 6649245*	10		3
14 Mar 98	**HOLLER** *Epic 6653372*	13		2
13 Mar 99	**WHAT'S SO DIFFERENT?** *Epic 6670522*	10		2
14 Dec 02	**CRUSH TONIGHT** *Atlantic AT 0142CD* FAT JOE FEATURING GINUWINE	42		
7 Jun 03	**HELL YEAH** *Epic 6739245*	27		1

GIPSY KINGS French group

Date	Title / Label	Peak Position	Weeks at No.1	Weeks in Top 40
3 Sep 94	**HITS MEDLEY** *Columbia 6606022*	53		

MARTINE GIRAULT UK singer

Date	Title / Label	Peak Position	Weeks at No.1	Weeks in Top 40
29 Aug 92	**REVIVAL** *ffrr FX 195*	53		
30 Jan 93	**REVIVAL** *ffrr FCD 205*	37		1
28 Oct 95	**BEEN THINKING ABOUT YOU** *RCA 74321316142*	63		
1 Feb 97	**REVIVAL** *RCA 74321432162*	61		

GIRESSE UK production duo

Date	Title / Label	Peak Position	Weeks at No.1	Weeks in Top 40
14 Apr 01	**MON AMI** *Inferno CDFERN 36*	61		

GIRL UK group

Date	Title / Label	Peak Position	Weeks at No.1	Weeks in Top 40
12 Apr 80	**HOLLYWOOD TEASE** *Jet 176*	50		
1 Jul 00	**LAST ONE STANDING** *RCA 74321762422* GIRL THING	8		6
18 Nov 00	**GIRLS ON TOP** *RCA 74321801172*	25		1

GIRLFRIEND Australian group

Date	Title / Label	Peak Position	Weeks at No.1	Weeks in Top 40
30 Jan 93	**TAKE IT FROM ME** *Arista 74321142252*	47		
15 May 93	**GIRL'S LIFE** *Arista 74321138452*	68		

GIRLS ALOUD UK group

Date	Title / Label	Peak Position	Weeks at No.1	Weeks in Top 40
28 Dec 02	**SOUND OF THE UNDERGROUND** *Polydor 0658272* ⊛	1	4	13
24 May 03	**NO GOOD ADVICE** *Polydor 9800051*	2		6
30 Aug 03	**LIFE GOT COLD** *Polydor 9810656*	3		5
29 Nov 03	**JUMP** *Polydor 9814104*	2		11
10 Jul 04	**THE SHOW** *Polydor 9867041*	2		6
25 Sep 04	**LOVE MACHINE** *Polydor 9867984*	2		7
27 Nov 04	**I'LL STAND BY YOU** *Polydor 9869130*	1	2	9
5 Mar 05	**WAKE ME UP** *Polydor 9870426*	4		5
3 Sep 05	**LONG HOT SUMMER** *Polydor 9873589*	7		4
26 Nov 05	**BIOLOGY** *Polydor 9875297*	4		8
31 Dec 05	**SEE THE DAY** *Polydor 9875965*	9		4
25 Mar 06	**WHOLE LOTTA HISTORY** *Polydor 9877402*	6		4
28 Oct 06	**SOMETHING KINDA OOOOH** *Fascination FASC4*	3		12
23 Dec 06	**I THINK WE'RE ALONE NOW** *Fascination 1714586*	4		5
24 Mar 07	**WALK THIS WAY** *Fascination/island 1724331* SUGABABES VS GIRLS ALOUD	1	1	4
8 Sep 07	**SEXY! NO NO NO** *Fascination 1744981*	5		5
1 Dec 07	**CALL THE SHOTS** *Fascination 1753047*	3		15
12 Jan 08	**THEME TO *ST TRINIAN'S*** *Download*	51		
1 Mar 08	**CAN'T SPEAK FRENCH** *Fascination 1764167*	9		4

GIRLS @ PLAY UK group

Date	Title / Label	Peak Position	Weeks at No.1	Weeks in Top 40
24 Feb 01	**AIRHEAD** *GSM GSMCDR 1*	18		3
13 Oct 01	**RESPECTABLE** *Redbus Music RBMCD 101*	29		1

GIRLS OF FHM UK group

Date	Title / Label	Peak Position	Weeks at No.1	Weeks in Top 40
3 Jul 04	**DA YA THINK I'M SEXY?** *2PSL 2PSLCD5*	10		3
17 Feb 07	**I TOUCH MYSELF** *All Around The World CDGLOBE654* FHM HIGHSTREET HONEYS	34		1

GIRLSCHOOL UK group

Date	Title / Label	Peak Position	Weeks at No.1	Weeks in Top 40
2 Aug 80	**RACE WITH THE DEVIL** *Bronze BRO 100*	49		
21 Feb 81	**ST VALENTINE'S DAY MASSACRE EP** *Bronze BRO 116* MOTORHEAD & GIRLSCHOOL ○	5		6
11 Apr 81	**HIT AND RUN** *Bronze BRO 118*	32		3
11 Jul 81	**C'MON LET'S GO** *Bronze BRO 126*	42		
3 Apr 82	**WILDLIFE (EP)** *Bronze BRO 144*	58		

GITTA Danish/Italian group

Date	Title / Label	Peak Position	Weeks at No.1	Weeks in Top 40
19 Aug 00	**NO MORE TURNING BACK** *Pepper 9230302*	54		

GLADIATOR UK production duo

Date	Title / Label	Peak Position	Weeks at No.1	Weeks in Top 40
29 May 04	**NOW WE ARE FREE** *Universal TV 9866813* GLADIATOR FEATURING IZZY	19		2

GLADIATORS UK group

Date	Title / Label	Peak Position	Weeks at No.1	Weeks in Top 40
30 Nov 96	**THE BOYS ARE BACK IN TOWN** *RCA 74321417002*	70		

GLAM Italian production group

Date	Title / Label	Peak Position	Weeks at No.1	Weeks in Top 40
1 May 93	**HELL'S PARTY** *Six6 SIXCD 001*	42		

GLAM METAL DETECTIVES UK group

Date	Title / Label	Peak Position	Weeks at No.1	Weeks in Top 40
11 Mar 95	**EVERYBODY UP!** *ZTT ZANG 62CD*	29		1

GLAMMA KID UK rapper

Date	Title / Label	Peak Position	Weeks at No.1	Weeks in Top 40
21 Nov 98	**FASHION '98** *WEA 179CD*	49		
17 Apr 99	**TABOO** *WEA 203CD* GLAMMA KID FEATURING SHOLA AMA	10		5
27 Nov 99	**WHY** *WEA 229CD1*	10		3
2 Sep 00	**BILLS 2 PAY** *WEA 268CD1*	17		2

GLASS TIGER Canadian group

Date	Title / Label	Peak Position	Weeks at No.1	Weeks in Top 40
18 Oct 86	**DON'T FORGET ME (WHEN I'M GONE)** *Manhattan MT 13*	29		5
31 Jan 87	**SOMEDAY** *Manhattan MT 17*	66		
26 Oct 91	**MY TOWN** *EMI EM 212*	33		3

GLENN & CHRIS UK footballers

Date	Title / Label	Peak Position	Weeks at No.1	Weeks in Top 40
18 Apr 87	**DIAMOND LIGHTS** *Record Shack Records KICK 1*	12		6

GLITTER BAND UK group

Date	Title / Label	Peak Position	Weeks at No.1	Weeks in Top 40
23 Mar 74	**ANGEL FACE** *Bell 1348* ○	4		9
3 Aug 74	**JUST FOR YOU** *Bell 1368*	10		6
19 Oct 74	**LET'S GET TOGETHER AGAIN** *Bell 1383*	8		6
18 Jan 75	**GOODBYE MY LOVE** *Bell 1395*	2		7
12 Apr 75	**THE TEARS I CRIED** *Bell 1416*	8		7
9 Aug 75	**LOVE IN THE SUN** *Bell 1437*	15		7
28 Feb 76	**PEOPLE LIKE YOU PEOPLE LIKE ME** *Bell 1471*	5		9

GARY GLITTER UK singer

Date	Title / Label	Peak Position	Weeks at No.1	Weeks in Top 40
10 Jun 72	**ROCK AND ROLL (PARTS 1 & 2)** *Bell 1216*	2		14
23 Sep 72	**I DIDN'T KNOW I LOVED YOU (TILL I SAW YOU ROCK 'N' ROLL)** *Bell 1259*	4		10
20 Jan 73	**DO YOU WANNA TOUCH ME (OH YEAH!)** *Bell 1280*	2		11
7 Apr 73	**HELLO! HELLO! I'M BACK AGAIN** *Bell 1299* ○	2		13
21 Jul 73	**I'M THE LEADER OF THE GANG (I AM)** *Bell 1321* ●	1	4	11
17 Nov 73	**I LOVE YOU LOVE ME LOVE** *Bell 1337* ⊛	1	4	14
30 Mar 74	**REMEMBER ME THIS WAY** *Bell 1349* ○	3		6
15 Jun 74	**ALWAYS YOURS** *Bell 1359* ○	1	1	8
23 Nov 74	**OH YES! YOU'RE BEAUTIFUL** *Bell 1391* ○	2		9
3 May 75	**LOVE LIKE YOU AND ME** *Bell 1423*	10		6
21 Jun 75	**DOING ALRIGHT WITH THE BOYS** *Bell 1429*	6		7
8 Nov 75	**PAPA OOM MOW MOW** *Bell 1451*	38		2
13 Mar 76	**YOU BELONG TO ME** *Bell 1473*	40		2
22 Jan 77	**IT TAKES ALL NIGHT LONG** *Arista 85*	25		5
16 Jul 77	**A LITTLE BOOGIE WOOGIE IN THE BACK OF MY MIND** *Arista 112*	31		4
20 Sep 80	**GARY GLITTER (EP)** *GTO GT 282*	57		
10 Oct 81	**AND THEN SHE KISSED ME** *Bell 1497*	39		2
5 Dec 81	**ALL THAT GLITTERS** *Bell 1498*	48		
23 Jun 84	**DANCE ME UP** *Arista ARIST 570*	25		3
1 Dec 84	**ANOTHER ROCK AND ROLL CHRISTMAS** *Arista ARIST 592* ○	7		5
10 Oct 92	**AND THE LEADER ROCKS ON** *EMI EM 252*	58		
21 Nov 92	**THROUGH THE YEARS** *EMI EM 256*	49		
16 Dec 95	**HELLO! HELLO! I'M BACK AGAIN (AGAIN)** *Carlton Sounds 3036000192*	50		

GLITTERATI UK group

Date	Title / Label	Peak Position	Weeks at No.1	Weeks in Top 40
26 Mar 05	**YOU GOT NOTHING ON ME** *Atlantic ATUK005CD*	36		1
4 Jun 05	**HEARTBREAKER** *Atlantic ATUK008CD*	45		
5 Nov 05	**BACK IN POWER** *Atlantic ATUK015CD*	62		

GLOBAL COMMUNICATION UK production duo

Date	Title / Label	Peak Position	Weeks at No.1	Weeks in Top 40
11 Jan 97	**THE WAY/THE DEEP** *Dedicated GLOBA 002CD*	51		

GLOVE UK group

Date	Title / Label	Peak Position	Weeks at No.1	Weeks in Top 40
20 Aug 83	**LIKE AN ANIMAL** *Wonderland SHE 3*	52		

DANA GLOVER US singer

Date	Title / Label	Peak Position	Weeks at No.1	Weeks in Top 40
10 May 03	**THINKING OVER** *DreamWorks 4507762*	38		1

GLOWORM UK/US group

Date	Title / Label	Peak Position	Weeks at No.1	Weeks in Top 40
6 Feb 93	**I LIFT MY CUP** *Pulse 8 CDLOSE 37*	20		2
14 May 94	**CARRY ME HOME** *Go! Beat GODCD 112*	9		8
6 Aug 94	**I LIFT MY CUP** *Pulse 8 CDLOSE 67*	46		

GNARLS BARKLEY US duo

Date	Title / Label	Peak Position	Weeks at No.1	Weeks in Top 40
8 Apr 06	**CRAZY** *Warner Brothers WEA401CD* ⊛	1	9	12
22 Jul 06	**SMILEY FACES** *Warner Brothers WEA410CD1*	10		8
18 Nov 06	**WHO CARES** *Warner Brothers WEA413CD1*	60		
23 Feb 08	**RUN** *Download*	32		1

GO GO LORENZO & THE DAVIS PINCKNEY PROJECT US group

Date	Title / Label	Peak Position	Weeks at No.1	Weeks in Top 40
6 Dec 86	**YOU CAN DANCE (IF YOU WANT TO)** *Boiling Point POSP 836*	46		

GO-GOS US group

Date	Title / Label	Peak Position	Weeks at No.1	Weeks in Top 40
15 May 82	**OUR LIPS ARE SEALED** *IRS GDN 102*	47		
26 Jan 91	**COOL JERK** *IRS AM 712*	60		
18 Feb 95	**THE WHOLE WORLD LOST ITS HEAD** *IRS CDEIRS 190*	29		2

GO! TEAM UK group

Date	Title / Label	Peak Position	Weeks at No.1	Weeks in Top 40
4 Dec 04	**LADYFLASH** *Memphis Industries MI041CDS*	68		
8 Oct 05	**BOTTLE ROCKET** *Memphis Industries MI048CDS*	64		
11 Feb 06	**LADYFLASH** *Memphis Industries MI054CDS*	26		1
14 Jul 07	**GRIP LIKE A VICE** *Memphis Industries MI092CDS*	57		
15 Sep 07	**DOING IT RIGHT** *Memphis Industries MI098CDS*	55		

GO WEST UK duo

Date	Title / Label	Peak Position	Weeks at No.1	Weeks in Top 40
23 Feb 85	**WE CLOSE OUR EYES** *Chrysalis CHS 2850* ○	5		10
11 May 85	**CALL ME** *Chrysalis GOW 1*	12		8
3 Aug 85	**GOODBYE GIRL** *Chrysalis GOW 2*	25		6
23 Nov 85	**DON'T LOOK DOWN – THE SEQUEL** *Chrysalis GOW 3*	13		8
29 Nov 86	**TRUE COLOURS** *Chrysalis GOW 4*	48		
9 May 87	**I WANT TO HEAR IT FROM YOU** *Chrysalis GOW 5*	43		
12 Sep 87	**THE KING IS DEAD** *Chrysalis GOW 6*	67		
28 Jul 90	**THE KING OF WISHFUL THINKING** *Chrysalis GOW 8*	18		6
17 Oct 92	**FAITHFUL** *Chrysalis GOW 9*	13		4
16 Jan 93	**WHAT YOU WON'T DO FOR LOVE** *Chrysalis CDGOWS 10*	15		4
27 Mar 93	**STILL IN LOVE** *Chrysalis CDGOWS 11*	43		
2 Oct 93	**TRACKS OF MY TEARS** *Chrysalis CDGOWS 12*	16		3
4 Dec 93	**WE CLOSE OUR EYES (REMIX)** *Chrysalis CDGOWS 13*	40		1

GOATS US group

Date	Title / Label	Peak Position	Weeks at No.1	Weeks in Top 40
29 May 93	**AAAH D YAAA/TYPICAL AMERICAN** *Ruffhouse 6593032*	53		

GOD MACHINE US group

Date	Title / Label	Peak Position	Weeks at No.1	Weeks in Top 40
30 Jan 93	**HOME** *Fiction FICCD 47*	65		

GODIEGO Japanese/US group

Date	Title / Label	Peak Position	Weeks at No.1	Weeks in Top 40
15 Oct 77	**THE WATER MARGIN** *BBC RESL 50*	37		1
16 Feb 80	**GHANDARA** *BBC RESL 66*	56		

GODLEY & CREME UK duo

Date	Title / Label	Peak Position	Weeks at No.1	Weeks in Top 40
12 Sep 81	**UNDER YOUR THUMB** *Polydor POSP 322* ○	3		9
21 Nov 81	**WEDDING BELLS** *Polydor POSP 369* ○	7		9
30 Mar 85	**CRY** *Polydor POSP 732*	19		6

GOD'S PROPERTY US group

Date	Title / Label	Peak Position	Weeks at No.1	Weeks in Top 40
22 Nov 97	**STOMP** *B-rite Music IND 95559*	60		

Silver-selling ○ Gold-selling ● Platinum-selling ⊛ US No.1 ★ | Peak Position | Weeks at No.1 | Weeks in Top 40

ALEX GOLD UK producer

Date	Title / Label	Peak Position	Weeks at No.1	Weeks in Top 40
26 Apr 03	**LA TODAY** *Xtravaganza XTRAV 37CDS* ALEX GOLD FEATURING PHILIP OAKLEY	68		

ANDREW GOLD US singer/pianist

Date	Title / Label	Peak Position	Weeks at No.1	Weeks in Top 40
2 Apr 77	**LONELY BOY** *Asylum K 13076*	11		8
25 Mar 78	**NEVER LET HER SLIP AWAY** *Asylum K 13112* ○	5		12
24 Jun 78	**HOW CAN THIS BE LOVE** *Asylum K 13126*	19		7
14 Oct 78	**THANK YOU FOR BEING A FRIEND** *Asylum K 13135*	42		

BRIAN & TONY GOLD Jamaican duo

Date	Title / Label	Peak Position	Weeks at No.1	Weeks in Top 40
30 Jul 94	**COMPLIMENTS ON YOUR KISS** *Mango CIDM 820* RED DRAGON WITH BRIAN & TONY GOLD ○	2		11
9 Nov 02	**HEY SEXY LADY** *MCA MCSTD 40304* SHAGGY FEATURING BRIAN AND TONY GOLD	10		4

GOLD BLADE UK group

Date	Title / Label	Peak Position	Weeks at No.1	Weeks in Top 40
22 Mar 97	**STRICTLY HARDCORE** *Ultimate TOPP 056CD*	64		

GOLDBUG UK group

Date	Title / Label	Peak Position	Weeks at No.1	Weeks in Top 40
27 Jan 96	**WHOLE LOTTA LOVE** *Make Dust JAZID 125CD*	3		4

GOLDEN BOY WITH MISS KITTIN Swiss producer with singer

Date	Title / Label	Peak Position	Weeks at No.1	Weeks in Top 40
7 Sep 02	**RIPPIN KITTIN** *Illustrious CDILL 007*	67		

GOLDEN EARRING Dutch group

Date	Title / Label	Peak Position	Weeks at No.1	Weeks in Top 40
8 Dec 73	**RADAR LOVE** *Track 2094 116* ○	7		11
8 Oct 77	**RADAR LOVE** *Polydor 2121 335*	44		

GOLDEN GIRLS UK producer

Date	Title / Label	Peak Position	Weeks at No.1	Weeks in Top 40
3 Oct 98	**KINETIC** *Distinctive DISNCD 46*	38		1
4 Dec 99	**KINETIC '99 (REMIX)** *Distinctive DISNCD 59*	56		

GOLDENSCAN UK production duo

Date	Title / Label	Peak Position	Weeks at No.1	Weeks in Top 40
11 Nov 00	**SUNRISE** *VC Recordings VCRD 79*	52		

GOLDFINGER UK group

Date	Title / Label	Peak Position	Weeks at No.1	Weeks in Top 40
22 Jun 02	**OPEN YOUR EYES** *Jive 9270052*	75		

GOLDFRAPP UK duo

Date	Title / Label	Peak Position	Weeks at No.1	Weeks in Top 40
23 Jun 01	**UTOPIA** *Mute CDMUTE 264*	62		
17 Nov 01	**PILOTS** *Mute LCDMUTE 267*	68		
26 Apr 03	**TRAIN** *Mute LCDMUTE 291*	23		1
2 Aug 03	**STRICT MACHINE** *Mute LCDMUTE 295*	25		1
15 Nov 03	**TWIST** *Mute LCDMUTE 311*	31		1
13 Mar 04	**BLACK CHERRY** *Mute LCDMUTE 320*	28		1
22 May 04	**STRICT MACHINE** *Mute LCDMUTE 335*	20		1
20 Aug 05	**OOH LA LA** *Mute LCDMUTE342*	4		7
12 Nov 05	**NUMBER 1** *Mute LCDMUTE351*	9		3
25 Feb 06	**RIDE A WHITE HORSE** *Mute LCDMUTE356*	15		2
13 May 06	**FLY ME AWAY** *Mute LCDMUTE361*	26		1
16 Feb 08	**A&E** *Mute LCDMUTE389*	10		6

GOLDIE UK group

Date	Title / Label	Peak Position	Weeks at No.1	Weeks in Top 40
27 May 78	**MAKING UP AGAIN** *Bronze BRO 50*	7		8

GOLDIE UK production group

Date	Title / Label	Peak Position	Weeks at No.1	Weeks in Top 40
3 Dec 94	**INNER CITY LIFE** *ffrr FCD 251* GOLDIE PRESENTS METALHEADS	49		
9 Sep 95	**ANGEL** *ffrr FCD 266*	41		
11 Nov 95	**INNER CITY LIFE (REMIX)** *ffrr FCD 267* GOLDIE PRESENTS METALHEADS	39		1
1 Nov 97	**DIGITAL** *ffrr FCD 316* GOLDIE FEATURING KRS ONE	13		2
24 Jan 98	**TEMPERTEMPER** *ffrr FCD 325*	13		2
18 Apr 98	**BELIEVE** *ffrr FCD 332*	36		1

GOLDIE & THE GINGERBREADS US group

Date	Title / Label	Peak Position	Weeks at No.1	Weeks in Top 40
25 Feb 65	**CAN'T YOU HEAR MY HEART BEAT?** *Decca F 12070*	25		4

GOLDIE LOOKIN CHAIN UK group

Date	Title / Label	Peak Position	Weeks at No.1	Weeks in Top 40
1 May 04	**HALF MAN HALF MACHINE/SELF SUICIDE** *Must Destroy DUSTY 019CD*	32		1
28 Aug 04	**GUNS DON'T KILL PEOPLE RAPPERS DO** *Atlantic GLC01CD*	3		7
6 Nov 04	**YOUR MOTHER'S GOT A PENIS** *East West GLC02CD*	14		2
25 Dec 04	**YOU KNOWS I LOVES YOU** *Atlantic GLC03CD*	22		3
17 Sep 05	**YOUR MISSUS IS A NUTTER** *Atlantic ATUK014CDX*	14		3
3 Dec 05	**R 'N' B** *Atlantic ATUK021CD*	26		1

GOLDRUSH UK group

Date	Title / Label	Peak Position	Weeks at No.1	Weeks in Top 40
22 Jun 02	**SAME PICTURE** *Virgin VSCDT 1833*	64		
7 Sep 02	**WIDE OPEN SKY** *Virgin VSCDT 1834*	70		

BOBBY GOLDSBORO US singer

Date	Title / Label	Peak Position	Weeks at No.1	Weeks in Top 40
17 Apr 68	**HONEY** *United Artists UP 2215* ★	2		14
4 Aug 73	**SUMMER (THE FIRST TIME)** *United Artists UP 35558*	9		10
3 Aug 74	**HELLO SUMMERTIME** *United Artists UP 35705*	14		8
29 Mar 75	**HONEY** *United Artists UP 35633*	2		9

GLEN GOLDSMITH UK singer

Date	Title / Label	Peak Position	Weeks at No.1	Weeks in Top 40
7 Nov 87	**I WON'T CRY** *Reproduction PB 41493*	34		3
12 Mar 88	**DREAMING** *Reproduction PB 41711*	12		7
11 Jun 88	**WHAT YOU SEE IS WHAT YOU GET** *Reproduction PB 42075*	33		3
3 Sep 88	**SAVE A LITTLE BIT** *Reproduction PB 42147*	73		

GOLDTRIX UK production duo

Date	Title / Label	Peak Position	Weeks at No.1	Weeks in Top 40
19 Jan 02	**IT'S LOVE (TRIPPIN')** *AM:PM/Serious/Evolve CDAMPM 152* GOLDTRIX PRESENTS ANDREA BROWN	6		7

GOMEZ UK group

Date	Title / Label	Peak Position	Weeks at No.1	Weeks in Top 40
11 Apr 98	**78 STONE WOBBLE** *Hut HUTCD 95*	44		
13 Jun 98	**GET MYSELF ARRESTED** *Hut HUTCD 97*	45		
12 Sep 98	**WHIPPIN' PICCADILLY** *Hut HUTCD 105*	35		1
10 Jul 99	**BRING IT ON** *Hut HUTCD 112*	21		2
11 Sep 99	**RHYTHM & BLUES ALIBI** *Hut HUTCD 114*	18		2
27 Nov 99	**WE HAVEN'T TURNED AROUND** *Hut HUTCD 117*	38		1
16 Mar 02	**SHOT SHOT** *Hut HUTCDX 149*	28		1
15 Jun 02	**SOUND OF SOUNDS/PING ONE DOWN** *Hut HUTDX 154*	48		
20 Mar 04	**CATCH ME UP** *Hut HUTDX 175*	36		1
22 May 04	**SILENCE** *Hut HUTDX 178*	41		
10 Jun 06	**GIRLSHAPEDLOVEDRUG** *Independiente ISOM105SMS*	66		

GOMPIE Dutch group

Date	Title / Label	Peak Position	Weeks at No.1	Weeks in Top 40
20 May 95	**ALICE (WHO THE X IS ALICE?) (LIVING NEXT DOOR TO ALICE)** *Habana HABSCD 5*	34		3
2 Sep 95	**ALICE (WHO THE X IS ALICE?) (LIVING NEXT DOOR TO ALICE)** *Habana HABSCD 5*	17		6

GONZALEZ UK group

Date	Title / Label	Peak Position	Weeks at No.1	Weeks in Top 40
31 Mar 79	**HAVEN'T STOPPED DANCING YET** *Sidewalk SID 102*	15		7

JOSE GONZALEZ Swedish guitarist/singer

Date	Title / Label	Peak Position	Weeks at No.1	Weeks in Top 40
21 Jan 06	**HEARTBEATS** *Peacefrog PFG076CD*	9		9
15 Jul 06	**HAND ON YOUR HEART** *Peacefrog PFG083CD*	29		1

GOO GOO DOLLS US group

Date	Title / Label	Peak Position	Weeks at No.1	Weeks in Top 40
1 Aug 98	**IRIS** *Reprise W0449CD*	50		
27 Mar 99	**SLIDE** *Edel/Hollywood/Third Rail 0102035 HWR*	43		
17 Jul 99	**IRIS** *Hollywood 0102485 HWR*	26		1
21 Oct 06	**IRIS/STAY WITH YOU** *Warner Brothers W736CD1*	39		1

Silver-selling ○ Gold-selling ● Platinum-selling ✪ US No.1 ★

Peak Position · Weeks at No.1 · Weeks in Top 40

GOOD CHARLOTTE US group

Date	Title / Label	Peak Position	Weeks at No.1	Weeks in Top 40
15 Feb 03	**LIFESTYLES OF THE RICH AND FAMOUS** *Epic 6735562*	8		8
17 May 03	**GIRLS AND BOYS** *Epic 6738775*	6		7
30 Aug 03	**THE ANTHEM** *Epic 6742552*	10		3
20 Dec 03	**THE YOUNG AND THE HOPELESS/HOLD ON** *Epic 6745435*	34		1
16 Oct 04	**PREDICTABLE** *Epic 6753882*	12		4
12 Feb 05	**I JUST WANNA LIVE** *Epic 6756492*	9		3
18 Jun 05	**THE CHRONICLES OF LIFE AND DEATH** *Epic 6759432*	30		1
10 Mar 07	**KEEP YOUR HANDS OFF MY GIRL** *Epic 88697063432*	23		4

GOOD GIRLS US group

Date	Title / Label	Peak Position	Weeks at No.1	Weeks in Top 40
24 Jul 93	**JUST CALL ME** *Motown TMGCD 1417*	75		

GOOD SHOES UK group

Date	Title / Label	Peak Position	Weeks at No.1	Weeks in Top 40
6 Jan 07	**THE PHOTOS ON MY WALL** *Brille BRILS15CD*	48		
24 Mar 07	**NEVER MEANT TO HURT YOU** *Brille BRILS20CD*	34		1

GOOD THE BAD & THE QUEEN UK group

Date	Title / Label	Peak Position	Weeks at No.1	Weeks in Top 40
11 Nov 06	**HERCULEAN** *Honest Jons CDR6722*	22		1
27 Jan 07	**KINGDOM OF DOOM** *Honest Jons CDR6732*	20		1
14 Apr 07	**GREEN FIELDS** *Honest Jons CDRS6738*	51		

GOODBOOKS UK group

Date	Title / Label	Peak Position	Weeks at No.1	Weeks in Top 40
28 Jul 07	**PASSCHENDAELE** *Columbia LIBRARY006*	73		

GOODBYE MR MACKENZIE UK group

Date	Title / Label	Peak Position	Weeks at No.1	Weeks in Top 40
20 Aug 88	**GOODBYE MR MACKENZIE** *Capitol CL 501*	62		
11 Mar 89	**THE RATTLER** *Capitol CL 522*	37		2
29 Jul 89	**GOODWILL CITY/I'M SICK OF YOU** *Capitol CL 538*	49		
21 Apr 90	**LOVE CHILD** *Parlophone R 6247*	52		
23 Jun 90	**BLACKER THAN BLACK** *Parlophone R 6257*	61		

ROGER GOODE South African producer

Date	Title / Label	Peak Position	Weeks at No.1	Weeks in Top 40
13 Apr 02	**IN THE BEGINNING** *ffrr DFCDP 004* ROGER GOODE FEATURING TASHA BAXTER	33		1

GOODFELLAS Italian production duo

Date	Title / Label	Peak Position	Weeks at No.1	Weeks in Top 40
21 Jul 01	**SOUL HEAVEN** *Direction 6713852* GOODFELLAS FEATURING LISA MALLETT	27		1

GOODFELLAZ US group

Date	Title / Label	Peak Position	Weeks at No.1	Weeks in Top 40
10 May 97	**SUGAR HONEY ICE TEA** *Wild Card 5736132*	25		1

GOODIES UK comedy group

Date	Title / Label	Peak Position	Weeks at No.1	Weeks in Top 40
7 Dec 74	**THE IN BETWEENIES/FATHER CHRISTMAS DO NOT TOUCH ME** *Bradley's BRAD 7421* ○	7		8
15 Mar 75	**FUNKY GIBBON/SICK MAN BLUES** *Bradley's BRAD 7504*	4		9
21 Jun 75	**BLACK PUDDING BERTHA (THE QUEEN OF NORTHERN SOUL)** *Bradley's BRAD 7517*	19		6
27 Sep 75	**NAPPY LOVE/WILD THING** *Bradley's BRAD 7524*	21		6
13 Dec 75	**MAKE A DAFT NOISE FOR CHRISTMAS** *Bradley's BRAD 7533*	20		5

CUBA GOODING US singer

Date	Title / Label	Peak Position	Weeks at No.1	Weeks in Top 40
19 Nov 83	**HAPPINESS IS JUST AROUND THE BEND** *London LON 41*	72		

GOODMEN Dutch production duo

Date	Title / Label	Peak Position	Weeks at No.1	Weeks in Top 40
7 Aug 93	**GIVE IT UP** *Fresh Fruit TABCD 118* ○	5		4

DELTA GOODREM Australian singer

Date	Title / Label	Peak Position	Weeks at No.1	Weeks in Top 40
22 Mar 03	**BORN TO TRY** *Epic 6736342*	3		11
28 Jun 03	**LOST WITHOUT YOU** *Epic 6739555*	4		9
4 Oct 03	**INNOCENT EYES** *Epic 6743155*	9		6
13 Dec 03	**NOT ME NOT I** *Epic 6745372*	18		2
20 Nov 04	**OUT OF THE BLUE** *Epic 6754732*	9		2
12 Feb 05	**ALMOST HERE** *Sony Music 6757352* BRIAN McFADDEN & DELTA GOODREM	3		6

RON GOODWIN UK orchestra leader

Date	Title / Label	Peak Position	Weeks at No.1	Weeks in Top 40
15 May 53	**TERRY'S THEME FROM LIMELIGHT** *Parlophone R 3686*	3		23
28 Oct 55	**BLUE STAR (THE MEDIC THEME)** *Parlophone R 4074*	20		1

GOODY GOODY US group

Date	Title / Label	Peak Position	Weeks at No.1	Weeks in Top 40
2 Dec 78	**NUMBER ONE DEE JAY** *Atlantic LV 3*	55		

GOOMBAY DANCE BAND Multinational group

Date	Title / Label	Peak Position	Weeks at No.1	Weeks in Top 40
27 Feb 82	**SEVEN TEARS** *Epic EPC A 1242* ●	1	3	9
15 May 82	**SUN OF JAMAICA** *Epic EPC A 2345*	50		

GOONS UK comedy group

Date	Title / Label	Peak Position	Weeks at No.1	Weeks in Top 40
29 Jun 56	**I'M WALKING BACKWARDS FOR CHRISTMAS/ BLUEBOTTLE BLUES** *Decca F 10756*	4		10
14 Sep 56	**BLOODNOK'S ROCK 'N' ROLL CALL/YING TONG SONG** *Decca E 10780*	3		10
21 Jul 73	**YING TONG SONG** *Decca F 13414*	9		8

LONNIE GORDON US singer

Date	Title / Label	Peak Position	Weeks at No.1	Weeks in Top 40
24 Jun 89	**(I'VE GOT YOUR) PLEASURE CONTROL** *ffrr F 106* SIMON HARRIS FEATURING LONNIE GORDON	60		
27 Jan 90	**HAPPENIN' ALL OVER AGAIN** *Supreme SUPE 159*	4		8
11 Aug 90	**BEYOND YOUR WILDEST DREAMS** *Supreme SUPE 167*	48		
17 Nov 90	**IF I HAVE TO STAND ALONE** *Supreme SUPE 181*	68		
4 May 91	**GONNA CATCH YOU** *Supreme SUPE 185*	32		3
7 Oct 95	**LOVE EVICTION** *X:Plode BANG 2CD* QUARTZ LOCK FEATURING LONNIE GORDON	32		1

LESLEY GORE US singer

Date	Title / Label	Peak Position	Weeks at No.1	Weeks in Top 40
20 Jun 63	**IT'S MY PARTY** *Mercury AMT 1205* ★	9		11
24 Sep 64	**MAYBE I KNOW** *Mercury MF 829*	20		7

MARTIN L GORE UK multi-instrumentalist/producer

Date	Title / Label	Peak Position	Weeks at No.1	Weeks in Top 40
26 Apr 03	**STARDUST** *Mute CDMUTE 296*	44		

GORILLAZ UK group

Date	Title / Label	Peak Position	Weeks at No.1	Weeks in Top 40
17 Mar 01	**CLINT EASTWOOD** *Parlophone CDR 6552* ●	4		14
7 Jul 01	**19/2000** *Parlophone CDR 6559*	6		8
3 Nov 01	**ROCK THE HOUSE** *Parlophone CDRS 6565*	18		2
9 Mar 02	**TOMORROW COMES TODAY** *Parlophone CDR 6573*	33		1
3 Aug 02	**LIL' DUB CHEFIN'** *Parlophone CDR 6584* SPACE MONKEY VS GORILLAZ	73		
23 Apr 05	**FEEL GOOD INC** *Parlophone CDR6663*	2		20
10 Sep 05	**DARE** *Parlophone CDRS6668*	1	1	14
3 Dec 05	**DIRTY HARRY** *Parlophone CDRS6676*	6		8
22 Apr 06	**KIDS WITH GUNS/EL MANANA** *Parlophone CDR6685*	27		1

GORKY'S ZYGOTIC MYNCI UK group

Date	Title / Label	Peak Position	Weeks at No.1	Weeks in Top 40
9 Nov 96	**PATIO SONG** *Fontana GZMCD 1*	41		
29 Mar 97	**DIAMOND DEW** *Fontana GZMCD 2*	42		
21 Jun 97	**YOUNG GIRLS & HAPPY ENDINGS/DARK NIGHT** *Fontana GZMCD 3*	49		
6 Jun 98	**SWEET JOHNNY** *Fontana GZMCD 4*	60		
29 Aug 98	**LET'S GET TOGETHER (IN OUR MINDS)** *Fontana GZMCD 5*	43		
2 Oct 99	**SPANISH DANCE TROUPE** *Mantra/Beggars Banquet MNT 47CD*	47		
4 Mar 00	**POODLE ROCKIN'** *Mantra/Beggars Banquet MNT 52CD*	52		
15 Sep 01	**STOOD ON GOLD** *Mantra MNT 64CD*	65		

EYDIE GORME US singer

Date	Title / Label	Peak Position	Weeks at No.1	Weeks in Top 40
24 Jan 58	**LOVE ME FOREVER** *HMV POP 432*	21		5
21 Jun 62	**YES MY DARLING DAUGHTER** *CBS AAG 105*	10		9
31 Jan 63	**BLAME IT ON THE BOSSA NOVA** *CBS AAG 131*	32		4
22 Aug 63	**I WANT TO STAY HERE** *CBS AAG 163* STEVE (Lawrence) & EYDIE (Gorme)	3		11

Silver-selling · Gold-selling · Platinum-selling · US No.1 ★ · Peak Position · Weeks at No.1 · Weeks in Top 40

LUKE GOSS & THE BAND OF THIEVES
UK group

Date	Title / Label	Peak Position	Weeks at No.1	Weeks in Top 40
12 Jun 93	**SWEETER THAN THE MIDNIGHT RAIN** *Sabre CDSAB 1*	52		
21 Aug 93	**GIVE ME ONE MORE CHANCE** *Sabre CDSAB 2*	68		

MATT GOSS UK singer

Date	Title / Label	Peak Position	Weeks at No.1	Weeks in Top 40
26 Aug 95	**THE KEY** *Atlas 5811532*	40		1
27 Apr 96	**IF YOU WERE HERE TONIGHT** *Atlas 5762932*	23		2
15 Nov 03	**I'M COMING WITH YA** *Concept CDCON 49*	22		1
31 Jul 04	**FLY** *Concept CDCON57*	31		1
2 Oct 04	**I NEED THE KEY** *Inferno CDFERN63* MINIMAL CHIC FEATURING MATT GOSS	54		

GOSSIP US group

Date	Title / Label	Peak Position	Weeks at No.1	Weeks in Top 40
11 Nov 06	**STANDING IN THE WAY OF CONTROL** *Back Yard Recordings BACK19CSC1*	7		12
23 Jun 07	**LISTEN UP** *Back Yard Recordings BACK18CSC2*	39		1

IRV GOTTI US producer

Date	Title / Label	Peak Position	Weeks at No.1	Weeks in Top 40
12 Oct 02	**DOWN 4 U** *Murder Inc 0639002* IRV GOTTI PRESENTS JA RULE, ASHANTI, CHARLI BALTIMORE & VITA	4		5

GRAHAM GOULDMAN UK singer/bass player

Date	Title / Label	Peak Position	Weeks at No.1	Weeks in Top 40
23 Jun 79	**SUNBURN** *Mercury SUNNY 1*	52		

GOURYELLA Dutch group

Date	Title / Label	Peak Position	Weeks at No.1	Weeks in Top 40
10 Jul 99	**GOURYELLA** *Code Blue BLU 001CD*	15		5
4 Dec 99	**WALHALLA** *Code Blue BLU 006CD*	27		1
23 Dec 00	**TENSHI** *Code Blue BLU 017CD*	45		

GQ US group

Date	Title / Label	Peak Position	Weeks at No.1	Weeks in Top 40
10 Mar 79	**DISCO NIGHTS (ROCK FREAK)** *Arista ARIST 245*	42		

GRACE UK singer

Date	Title / Label	Peak Position	Weeks at No.1	Weeks in Top 40
8 Apr 95	**NOT OVER YET** *Perfecto PERF 104CD*	6		6
23 Sep 95	**I WANT TO LIVE** *Perfecto PERF 109CD*	30		1
24 Feb 96	**SKIN ON SKIN** *Perfecto PERF 116CD*	21		1
1 Jun 96	**DOWN TO EARTH (REMIX)** *Perfecto PERF 120CD*	20		1
28 Sep 96	**IF I COULD FLY** *Perfecto PERF 127CD*	29		1
3 May 97	**HAND IN HAND** *Perfecto PERF 129CD*	38		1
26 Jul 97	**DOWN TO EARTH** *Perfecto PERF 142CD1*	29		1
14 Aug 99	**NOT OVER YET 99** *Code Blue BLU OO4CD* PLANET PERFECTO FEATURING GRACE	16		2

GRACE BROTHERS UK duo

Date	Title / Label	Peak Position	Weeks at No.1	Weeks in Top 40
20 Apr 96	**ARE YOU BEING SERVED?** *EMI Premier PRESCD 1*	51		

CHARLIE GRACIE US singer

Date	Title / Label	Peak Position	Weeks at No.1	Weeks in Top 40
19 Apr 57	**BUTTERFLY** *Parlophone R 4290* ★	12		8
14 Jun 57	**FABULOUS** *Parlophone R 4313*	8		16
23 Aug 57	**I LOVE YOU SO MUCH IT HURTS** *London HLU 8467*	14		4
23 Aug 57	**WANDERIN' EYES** *London HLU 8467*	6		14
10 Jan 58	**COOL BABY** *London HLU 8521*	26		1

GRAFITI UK DJ

Date	Title / Label	Peak Position	Weeks at No.1	Weeks in Top 40
30 Aug 03	**WHAT IS THE PROBLEM?** *679 Recordings 679L 021CD*	37		1

JAKI GRAHAM UK singer

Date	Title / Label	Peak Position	Weeks at No.1	Weeks in Top 40
23 Mar 85	**COULD IT BE I'M FALLING IN LOVE** *Chrysalis GRAN 6* DAVID GRANT & JAKI GRAHAM	5		9
29 Jun 85	**ROUND AND ROUND** *EMI JAKI 4*	9		9
31 Aug 85	**HEAVEN KNOWS** *EMI JAKI 5*	59		
16 Nov 85	**MATED** *EMI JAKI 6* DAVID GRANT & JAKI GRAHAM	20		6
3 May 86	**SET ME FREE** *EMI JAKI 7*	7		8
9 Aug 86	**BREAKING AWAY** *EMI JAKI 8*	16		6
15 Nov 86	**STEP RIGHT UP** *EMI JAKI 9*	15		8
9 Jul 88	**NO MORE TEARS** *EMI JAKI 12*	60		
24 Jun 89	**FROM NOW ON** *EMI JAKI 15*	73		
16 Jul 94	**AIN'T NOBODY** *Pulse 8 CDLOSE 64*	44		
4 Feb 95	**YOU CAN COUNT ON ME** *Avex UK AVEXCD 1*	62		
8 Jul 95	**ABSOLUTE E-SENSUAL** *Avex UK AVEXCD 5*	69		

LARRY GRAHAM US singer/bass player

Date	Title / Label	Peak Position	Weeks at No.1	Weeks in Top 40
3 Jul 82	**SOONER OR LATER** *Warner Brothers K 17925*	54		

MAX GRAHAM Canadian producer

Date	Title / Label	Peak Position	Weeks at No.1	Weeks in Top 40
28 May 05	**OWNER OF A LONELY HEART** *Data DATA92CDS* MAX GRAHAM VS YES	9		6

MIKEY GRAHAM Irish singer

Date	Title / Label	Peak Position	Weeks at No.1	Weeks in Top 40
10 Jun 00	**YOU'RE MY ANGEL** *Public PR 001CDS*	13		2
14 Apr 01	**YOU COULD BE MY EVERYTHING** *Public PR 003CDS*	62		

RON GRAINER ORCHESTRA UK orchestra

Date	Title / Label	Peak Position	Weeks at No.1	Weeks in Top 40
9 Dec 78	**A TOUCH OF VELVET A STING OF BRASS** *Casino Classics CC 5*	60		

GRAM'MA FUNK US singer

Date	Title / Label	Peak Position	Weeks at No.1	Weeks in Top 40
27 Nov 99	**I SEE YOU BABY** *Pepper 9230002* GROOVE ARMADA FEATURING GRAM'MA FUNK	17		2
2 Sep 00	**CHEEKY ARMADA** *Yola YOLACDX 01* ILLICIT FEATURING GRAM'MA FUNK	72		

GRAND FUNK RAILROAD US group

Date	Title / Label	Peak Position	Weeks at No.1	Weeks in Top 40
6 Feb 71	**INSIDE LOOKING OUT** *Capitol CL 15668*	40		1

GRAND PLAZ UK production group

Date	Title / Label	Peak Position	Weeks at No.1	Weeks in Top 40
8 Sep 90	**WOW WOW – NA NA** *Urban URB 60*	41		

GRAND PRIX UK group

Date	Title / Label	Peak Position	Weeks at No.1	Weeks in Top 40
27 Feb 82	**KEEP ON BELIEVING** *RCA 162*	75		

GRAND PUBA US rapper

Date	Title / Label	Peak Position	Weeks at No.1	Weeks in Top 40
13 Jan 96	**WHY YOU TREAT ME SO BAD** *Virgin VSCDT 1566* SHAGGY FEATURING GRAND PUBA	11		3
30 Mar 96	**WILL YOU BE MY BABY** *GHQ 74321339092* INFINITI FEATURING GRAND PUBA	53		

GRAND THEFT AUDIO UK group

Date	Title / Label	Peak Position	Weeks at No.1	Weeks in Top 40
24 Mar 01	**WE LUV U** *Sci-Fi SCIFI 1CD*	70		

GRANDAD ROBERTS & HIS SON ELVIS
UK duo

Date	Title / Label	Peak Position	Weeks at No.1	Weeks in Top 40
20 Jun 98	**MEAT PIE SAUSAGE ROLL** *WEA 160CD*	67		

GRANDADDY US group

Date	Title / Label	Peak Position	Weeks at No.1	Weeks in Top 40
2 Sep 00	**HEWLETT'S DAUGHTER** *V2 VVR 5014333*	71		
10 Feb 01	**THE CRYSTAL LAKE** *V2 VVR 5015158*	38		1
14 Jun 03	**NOW IT'S ON** *V2 VVR 5022248*	23		1
6 Sep 03	**EL CAMINOS IN THE WEST** *V2 VVR 5023663*	48		

GRANDMASTER FLASH US group

Date	Title / Label	Peak Position	Weeks at No.1	Weeks in Top 40
28 Aug 82	**THE MESSAGE** *Sugarhill SHL 117* GRANDMASTER FLASH & THE FURIOUS FIVE	8		7
22 Jan 83	**MESSAGE II (SURVIVAL)** *Sugarhill SHL 119* MELLE MEL & DUKE BOOTEE	74		
19 Nov 83	**WHITE LINES (DON'T DON'T DO IT)** *Sugarhill SHL 130* GRANDMASTER FLASH & MELLE MEL (Silver-selling)	7		17
30 Jun 84	**BEAT STREET BREAKDOWN** *Atlantic A 9659* GRANDMASTER MELLE MEL & THE FURIOUS FIVE	42		

Date	Title	Peak Position	Weeks at No.1	Weeks in Top 40
22 Sep 84	**WE DON'T WORK FOR FREE** *Sugarhill SH 136* GRANDMASTER MELLE MEL & THE FURIOUS FIVE	45		
15 Dec 84	**STEP OFF (PART 1)** *Sugarhill SHL 139* GRANDMASTER MELLE MEL & THE FURIOUS FIVE	8		8
16 Feb 85	**SIGN OF THE TIMES** *Elektra E 9677*	72		
16 Mar 85	**PUMP ME UP** *Sugarhill SH 141* GRANDMASTER MELLE MEL & THE FURIOUS FIVE	45		
8 Jan 94	**WHITE LINES (DON'T DON'T DO IT) (REMIX)** *WGAF WGAFCD 103* GRANDMASTER FLASH & MELLE MEL	59		
14 Jan 96	**STOMP – THE REMIXES** *QWE07 W0372 CD* QUINCY JONES FEATURING MELLE MEL, COOLIO YO-YO, SHAQUILLE O'NEAL & THE LUNIZ	28		1
17 Jun 95	**WHITE LINES (DON'T DON'T DO IT)** *Parlophone CDDD 19* DURAN DURAN FEATURING MELLE MEL & GRANDMASTER FLASH & THE FURIOUS FIVE	59		

GRANDMIXER DST US producer

Date	Title	Peak Position	Weeks at No.1	Weeks in Top 40
24 Dec 83	**CRAZY CUTS** *Island IS 146*	71		

GRANGE HILL CAST
UK cast of BBC TV children's series *Grange Hill*

Date	Title	Peak Position	Weeks at No.1	Weeks in Top 40
19 Apr 86	**JUST SAY NO** *BBC RESL 183*	5		5

GERRI GRANGER US singer

Date	Title	Peak Position	Weeks at No.1	Weeks in Top 40
30 Sep 78	**I GO TO PIECES (EVERYTIME)** *Casino Classics CC 3*	50		

AMY GRANT US singer

Date	Title	Peak Position	Weeks at No.1	Weeks in Top 40
11 May 91	**BABY BABY** *A&M AM 727* ○ ★	2		11
3 Aug 91	**EVERY HEARTBEAT** *A&M AM 783*	25		5
2 Nov 91	**THAT'S WHAT LOVE IS FOR** *A&M AM 666*	60		
15 Feb 92	**GOOD FOR ME** *A&M AM 810*	60		
13 Aug 94	**LUCKY ONE** *A&M 5807322*	60		
22 Oct 94	**SAY YOU'LL BE MINE** *A&M 5808292*	41		
24 Jun 95	**BIG YELLOW TAXI** *A&M 5809972*	20		8
14 Oct 95	**HOUSE OF LOVE** *A&M 5812332* AMY GRANT WITH VINCE GILL	46		

ANDREA GRANT UK singer

Date	Title	Peak Position	Weeks at No.1	Weeks in Top 40
14 Nov 98	**REPUTATIONS (JUST BE GOOD TO ME)** *WEA 192CD*	75		

DAVID GRANT UK singer

Date	Title	Peak Position	Weeks at No.1	Weeks in Top 40
30 Apr 83	**STOP AND GO** *Chrysalis GRAN 1*	19		6
16 Jul 83	**WATCHING YOU WATCHING ME** *Chrysalis GRAN 2*	10		8
8 Oct 83	**LOVE WILL FIND A WAY** *Chrysalis GRAN 3*	24		5
26 Nov 83	**ROCK THE MIDNIGHT** *Chrysalis GRAN 4*	46		
23 Mar 85	**COULD IT BE I'M FALLING IN LOVE** *Chrysalis GRAN 6* DAVID GRANT & JAKI GRAHAM	5		9
16 Nov 85	**MATED** *EMI JAKI 6* DAVID GRANT & JAKI GRAHAM	20		6
1 Aug 87	**CHANGE** *Polydor POSP 871*	55		
12 May 90	**KEEP IT TOGETHER** *Fourth & Broadway BRW 169*	56		

EDDY GRANT Guyanese singer/multi-instrumentalist

Date	Title	Peak Position	Weeks at No.1	Weeks in Top 40
2 Jun 79	**LIVING ON THE FRONT LINE** *Ensign ENY 26*	11		7
15 Nov 80	**DO YOU FEEL MY LOVE** *Ensign ENY 45* ○	8		9
4 Apr 81	**CAN'T GET ENOUGH OF YOU** *Ensign ENY 207*	13		7
25 Jul 81	**I LOVE YOU, YES I LOVE YOU** *Ensign ENY 216*	37		2
16 Oct 82	**I DON'T WANNA DANCE** *Ice 56* ●	1	3	12
15 Jan 83	**ELECTRIC AVENUE** *Ice 57* ○	2		8
19 Mar 83	**LIVING ON THE FRONT LINE/DO YOU FEEL MY LOVE** *Mercury MER 135*	47		
23 Apr 83	**WAR PARTY** *Ice 58*	42		
29 Oct 83	**TILL I CAN'T TAKE LOVE NO MORE** *Ice 60*	42		
19 May 84	**ROMANCING THE STONE** *Ice 61*	52		
23 Jan 88	**GIMME HOPE JO'ANNA** *Ice 78701*	7		8
27 May 89	**WALKING ON SUNSHINE** *Blue Wave R 6217*	63		
9 Jun 01	**ELECTRIC AVENUE (REMIX)** *Ice EW 232CD* ○	5		7
24 Nov 01	**WALKING ON SUNSHINE (REMIX)** *Ice EW 242CD*	57		

GOGI GRANT US singer

Date	Title	Peak Position	Weeks at No.1	Weeks in Top 40
29 Jun 56	**WAYWARD WIND** *London HLB 8282* ★	9		11

JULIE GRANT UK singer

Date	Title	Peak Position	Weeks at No.1	Weeks in Top 40
3 Jan 63	**UP ON THE ROOF** *Pye 7N 15483*	33		2
28 Mar 63	**COUNT ON ME** *Pye 7N 15508*	24		7
24 Sep 64	**COME TO ME** *Pye 7N 15684*	31		4

RUDY GRANT Guyanese singer

Date	Title	Peak Position	Weeks at No.1	Weeks in Top 40
14 Feb 81	**LATELY** *Ensign ENY 202*	58		

GRAPEFRUIT UK group

Date	Title	Peak Position	Weeks at No.1	Weeks in Top 40
14 Feb 68	**DEAR DELILAH** *RCA 1656*	21		6
14 Aug 68	**C'MON MARIANNE** *RCA 1716*	31		5

GRASS-SHOW Swedish group

Date	Title	Peak Position	Weeks at No.1	Weeks in Top 40
22 Mar 97	**1962** *Food CDFOOD 90*	53		
23 Aug 97	**OUT OF THE VOID** *Food CDFOOD 103*	75		

GRAVEDIGGAZ US group

Date	Title	Peak Position	Weeks at No.1	Weeks in Top 40
11 Mar 95	**SIX FEET DEEP (EP)** *Gee Street GESCD 62*	64		
5 Aug 95	**THE HELL EP** *Fourth & Broadway BRCD 326* TRICKY VS THE GRAVEDIGGAZ	12		2
24 Jan 98	**THE NIGHT THE EARTH CRIED** *Gee Street GEE 5001013*	44		
25 Apr 98	**UNEXPLAINED** *Gee Street GEE 5001623*	48		

DAVID GRAY UK singer

Date	Title	Peak Position	Weeks at No.1	Weeks in Top 40
4 Dec 99	**PLEASE FORGIVE ME** *IHT IHTCDS 003*	72		
1 Jul 00	**BABYLON** *IHT/East West EW 215CD1*	5		9
28 Oct 00	**PLEASE FORGIVE ME** *IHT/East West EW 219CD*	18		3
17 Mar 01	**THIS YEAR'S LOVE** *IHT/East West EW 228CD1*	20		3
28 Jul 01	**SAIL AWAY** *IHT/East West EW 234CD*	26		2
29 Dec 01	**SAY HELLO WAVE GOODBYE** *IHT/East West EW 243CD*	26		3
21 Dec 02	**THE OTHER SIDE** *IHT/East West EW 259CD*	35		1
19 Apr 03	**BE MINE** *IHT/East West EW 264CD*	23		1
10 Sep 05	**THE ONE I LOVE** *IHT/Atlantic ATUK013CD*	8		6
10 Dec 05	**HOSPITAL FOOD** *Atlantic ATUK018CD*	34		1
8 Apr 06	**ALIBI** *Atlantic ATUK027CDX*	71		
17 Nov 07	**YOU'RE THE WORLD TO ME** *Atlantic ATUK071CD2*	53		

DOBIE GRAY US singer

Date	Title	Peak Position	Weeks at No.1	Weeks in Top 40
25 Feb 65	**THE IN CROWD** *London HL 9953*	25		5
27 Sep 75	**OUT ON THE FLOOR** *Black Magic BM 107*	42		

DORIAN GRAY UK singer

Date	Title	Peak Position	Weeks at No.1	Weeks in Top 40
27 Mar 68	**I'VE GOT YOU ON MY MIND** *Parlophone R 5667*	36		3

LES GRAY UK singer

Date	Title	Peak Position	Weeks at No.1	Weeks in Top 40
26 Feb 77	**A GROOVY KIND OF LOVE** *Warner Brothers K 16883*	32		4

MACY GRAY US singer

Date	Title	Peak Position	Weeks at No.1	Weeks in Top 40
3 Jul 99	**DO SOMETHING** *Epic 6675932*	51		
9 Oct 99	**I TRY** *Epic 6681832* ●	6		18
25 Mar 00	**STILL** *Epic 6689622*	18		3
5 Aug 00	**WHY DIDN'T YOU CALL ME** *Epic 6696682*	38		1
20 Jan 01	**DEMONS** *Skint 60CD* FATBOY SLIM FEATURING MACY GRAY	16		2
28 Apr 01	**GETO HEAVEN** *MCA MCSTD 40246* COMMON FEATURING MACY GRAY	48		
12 May 01	**REQUEST & LINE** *Interscope 4975032* BLACK EYED PEAS FEATURING MACY GRAY	31		1
15 Sep 01	**SWEET BABY** *Epic 6718822* MACY GRAY FEATURING ERYKAH BADU	23		2
8 Dec 01	**SEXUAL REVOLUTION** *Epic 6721462*	45		
3 May 03	**WHEN I SEE YOU** *Epic 6738405*	26		2

MICHAEL GRAY UK producer

Date	Title	Peak Position	Weeks at No.1	Weeks in Top 40
13 Nov 04	**THE WEEKEND** *Eye Industries/UMTV 9868865*	7		10
12 Aug 06	**BORDERLINE** *Eye Industries/UMTV 1703606* MICHAEL GRAY FEATURING SHELLEY POOLE	12		3

Silver-selling ○ Gold-selling ● Platinum-selling ⊛ US No.1 ★ | Peak Position | Weeks at No.1 | Weeks in Top 40

BARRY GRAY ORCHESTRA UK orchestra

Date	Title	Peak Position	Weeks at No.1	Weeks in Top 40
11 Jul 81	*THUNDERBIRDS* *PRT 7P 216*	61		
14 Jun 86	*JOE 90* (THEME)/*CAPTAIN SCARLET* THEME *PRT 7PX 354* BARRY GRAY ORCHESTRA WITH PETER BECKETT – KEYBOARDS	53		

GREAT WHITE US group

Date	Title	Peak Position	Weeks at No.1	Weeks in Top 40
24 Feb 90	HOUSE OF BROKEN LOVE *Capitol CL 562*	44		
16 Feb 91	CONGO SQUARE *Capitol CL 605*	62		
7 Sep 91	CALL IT ROCK 'N' ROLL *Capitol CL 625*	67		

MARTIN GRECH UK guitarist/singer

Date	Title	Peak Position	Weeks at No.1	Weeks in Top 40
12 Oct 02	OPEN HEART ZOO *Island CID 811*	68		

BUDDY GRECO US singer/pianist

Date	Title	Peak Position	Weeks at No.1	Weeks in Top 40
7 Jul 60	LADY IS A TRAMP *Fontana H 225*	26		4

GREED UK duo

Date	Title	Peak Position	Weeks at No.1	Weeks in Top 40
18 Mar 95	PUMP UP THE VOLUME *Stress CDSTR 49* GREED FEATURING RICARDO DA FORCE	51		

GREEDIES UK/US/Irish group

Date	Title	Peak Position	Weeks at No.1	Weeks in Top 40
15 Dec 79	A MERRY JINGLE *Vertigo GREED 1*	28		1

ADAM GREEN US singer

Date	Title	Peak Position	Weeks at No.1	Weeks in Top 40
3 Apr 04	JESSICA/KOKOMO *Rough Trade RTRADESCD112*	63		
19 Feb 05	EMILY *Rough Trade RTRADSCD213*	53		

AL GREEN US singer

Date	Title	Peak Position	Weeks at No.1	Weeks in Top 40
9 Oct 71	TIRED OF BEING ALONE *London HL 10337*	4		13
8 Jan 72	LET'S STAY TOGETHER *London HL 10348* ★	7		10
20 May 72	LOOK WHAT YOU DONE FOR ME *London HL 10369*	44		
19 Aug 72	I'M STILL IN LOVE WITH YOU *London HL 10382*	35		3
16 Nov 74	SHA-LA-LA (MAKES ME HAPPY) *London HL 10470*	20		9
15 Mar 75	L.O.V.E. *London HL 10482*	24		6
3 Dec 88	PUT A LITTLE LOVE IN YOUR HEART *A&M AM 484* ANNIE LENNOX & AL GREEN	28		4
21 Oct 89	THE MESSAGE IS LOVE *Breakout USA 668* ARTHUR BAKER & THE BACKSTREET DISCIPLES FEATURING AL GREEN	38		2
2 Oct 93	LOVE IS A BEAUTIFUL THING *Arista 74321162692*	56		

JESSE GREEN Jamaican singer

Date	Title	Peak Position	Weeks at No.1	Weeks in Top 40
7 Aug 76	NICE AND SLOW *EMI 2492*	17		10
18 Dec 76	FLIP *EMI 2564*	26		4
11 Jun 77	COME WITH ME *EMI 2615*	29		5

ROBSON GREEN & JEROME FLYNN
UK actors/singers

Date	Title	Peak Position	Weeks at No.1	Weeks in Top 40
20 May 95	UNCHAINED MELODY/(THERE'LL BE BLUEBIRDS OVER) WHITE CLIFFS OF DOVER *RCA 74321284362* ⊛	1	7	14
11 Nov 95	I BELIEVE/UP ON THE ROOF *RCA 74321326882* ⊛	1	4	11
9 Nov 96	WHAT BECOMES OF THE BROKENHEARTED/SATURDAY NIGHT AT THE MOVIES/YOU'LL NEVER WALK ALONE *RCA 74321424732* ●	1	2	10

GREEN DAY US group

Date	Title	Peak Position	Weeks at No.1	Weeks in Top 40
20 Aug 94	BASKET CASE *Reprise W0257CD*	55		
29 Oct 94	WELCOME TO PARADISE *Reprise W0269CDX*	20		2
28 Jan 95	BASKET CASE *Reprise W0279CDX*	7		4
18 Mar 95	LONGVIEW *Reprise W0287CDX*	30		1
20 May 95	WHEN I COME AROUND *Reprise W0294CD*	27		1
7 Oct 95	GEEK STINK BREATH *Reprise W0320CD*	16		2
6 Jan 96	STUCK WITH ME *Reprise W0327CD1*	24		1
6 Jul 96	BRAIN STEW/JADED *Reprise W0339CD*	28		1
11 Oct 97	HITCHIN' A RIDE *Reprise W0424CD*	25		1
31 Jan 98	TIME OF YOUR LIFE (GOOD RIDDANCE) *Reprise W0430CD1*	11		3
9 May 98	REDUNDANT *Reprise W0438CD1*	27		1
30 Sep 00	MINORITY *Reprise W532CD*	18		2
23 Dec 00	WARNING *Reprise W548CD1*	27		3
10 Nov 01	WAITING *Reprise W570CD*	34		1
25 Sep 04	AMERICAN IDIOT *Reprise W652CD*	3		5
11 Dec 04	BOULEVARD OF BROKEN DREAMS *Reprise W659CD1*	5		13
26 Mar 05	HOLIDAY *Reprise W664CD1*	11		4
25 Jun 05	WAKE ME UP WHEN SEPTEMBER ENDS *Reprise W674CD2*	8		11
26 Nov 05	JESUS OF SUBURBIA *Reprise W691CD*	17		2
4 Aug 07	*THE SIMPSONS* THEME *Download*	19		2
11 Nov 06	THE SAINTS ARE COMING *Mercury 1713137* U2 & GREEN DAY	2		4
24 Mar 07	TIME OF YOUR LIFE (GOOD RIDDANCE) *Reprise W0430CD1*	67		

GREEN JELLY US comedy act

Date	Title	Peak Position	Weeks at No.1	Weeks in Top 40
5 Jun 93	THREE LITTLE PIGS *Zoo 74321151422*	5		7
14 Aug 93	ANARCHY IN THE UK *Zoo 74321174892*	27		2
25 Dec 93	I'M THE LEADER OF THE GANG *Arista 74321174892* HULK HOGAN WITH GREEN JELLY	25		3

GREEN VELVET US producer

Date	Title	Peak Position	Weeks at No.1	Weeks in Top 40
25 May 02	LA LA LAND *Credence CDCRED 025*	29		1

NORMAN GREENBAUM US singer

Date	Title	Peak Position	Weeks at No.1	Weeks in Top 40
21 Mar 70	SPIRIT IN THE SKY *Reprise RS 20885*	1	2	17

LORNE GREENE Canadian singer

Date	Title	Peak Position	Weeks at No.1	Weeks in Top 40
17 Dec 64	RINGO *RCA 1428* ★	22		7

LEE GREENWOOD US singer

Date	Title	Peak Position	Weeks at No.1	Weeks in Top 40
19 May 84	THE WIND BENEATH MY WINGS *MCA 877*	49		

IAIN GREGORY UK singer

Date	Title	Peak Position	Weeks at No.1	Weeks in Top 40
4 Jan 62	CAN'T YOU HEAR THE BEAT OF A BROKEN HEART *Pye 7N 15397*	39		1

RICHARD GREY French producer

Date	Title	Peak Position	Weeks at No.1	Weeks in Top 40
23 Jun 07	TAINTED LOVE *Apollo Recordings APOLLO112CDX*	52		

GREYHOUND Jamaican group

Date	Title	Peak Position	Weeks at No.1	Weeks in Top 40
26 Jun 71	BLACK AND WHITE *Trojan TR 7820*	6		11
8 Jan 72	MOON RIVER *Trojan TR 7848*	12		9
25 Mar 72	I AM WHAT I AM *Trojan TR 7853*	20		7

GRID UK duo

Date	Title	Peak Position	Weeks at No.1	Weeks in Top 40
7 Jul 90	FLOATATION *East West YZ 475*	60		
29 Sep 90	A BEAT CALLED LOVE *East West YZ 498*	64		
25 Jul 92	FIGURE OF 8 *Virgin VSCDT 1421*	50		
3 Oct 92	HEARTBEAT *Virgin VSCDT 1427*	72		
13 Mar 93	CRYSTAL CLEAR *Virgin VSCDT 1442*	27		3
30 Oct 93	TEXAS COWBOYS *Deconstruction 74321167762*	21		2
4 Jun 94	SWAMP THING *Deconstruction 74321205842* ○	3		15
17 Sep 94	ROLLERCOASTER *Deconstruction 74321230772*	19		2
3 Dec 94	TEXAS COWBOYS *Deconstruction 74321244032*	17		4
23 Sep 95	DIABLO *Deconstruction 74321308402*	32		1

ZAINE GRIFF New Zealand singer

Date	Title	Peak Position	Weeks at No.1	Weeks in Top 40
16 Feb 80	TONIGHT *Automatic K 17547*	54		
31 May 80	ASHES AND DIAMONDS *Automatic K 17619*	68		

ALISTAIR GRIFFIN UK singer

Date	Title	Peak Position	Weeks at No.1	Weeks in Top 40
10 Jan 04	BRING IT ON/MY LOVER'S PRAYER *Pro TV9814926*	5		4
27 Mar 04	YOU AND ME (TONIGHT) *Universal TV9817777*	18		1

BILLY GRIFFIN US singer

Date	Title	Peak Position	Weeks at No.1	Weeks in Top 40
8 Jan 83	HOLD ME TIGHTER IN THE RAIN *CBS A 2935*	17		6
14 Jan 84	SERIOUS *CBS A 4053*	64		

GREEN DAY

When, on 27 October 1994, three young American men wearing thrift-store clothes and sporting crudely dyed haircuts appeared on *Top Of The Pops*, it felt like a significant moment. On their first ever UK TV appearance, Green Day were promoting their new single 'Welcome To Paradise', a punked-up confessional about frontman Billie-Joe Armstrong's days as a teenager in the streets and squats of Berkeley, California.

To many, they were the latest young band to come kicking and screaming out of America in the wake of the death of alt-rock icon Kurt Cobain, who had committed suicide six months earlier. Yet for all the vim and vigour of a single and performance that sounded and looked like a band debuting – and all the attention that surrounded the band's attendant album *Dookie* – they were far from an overnight sensation.

Though all three members – Armstrong, bassist Mike Dirnt and drummer Tre Cool – were only in their early twenties, Green Day had already been in existence for seven years, touring in a converted mobile-library van and releasing two decent-selling albums on independent punk label Lookout! Records.

United by a love of heavy metal, 1960s British bands and 1970s punk, in 1987 childhood friends Armstrong and Dirnt formed their first band Sweet Children in their home town of Rodeo, California with drummer Al Sobrante. Sweet Children swiftly evolved into Green Day and for the next three years the teenagers established themselves via a mixture of the melodies of The Kinks and The Who and the energy of punk bands such as The Ramones, Buzzcocks and local ska-punk heroes Operation Ivy. It was quite a concoction.

Drummer Tre Cool (real name Frank Edwin Wright III) replaced Sobrante in 1990 in time for the first of many European tours. These low/no-budget slogs paid dividends, however, when Green Day's second album *Kerplunk* sold 50,000 copies. Recognising the inherent pop appeal of their music, Warner Records signed the band in 1993.

Few could have truly predicted the influence that Green Day would have over the coming decade – especially those who criticised the band for turning their backs on the punk scene. Yet there was an audience for a more colourful and irreverent take on life than the grunge bands were offering when the band's 1994 major label debut single 'Longview' crept into the UK charts at Number 30. That – and the unexpected *Top Of The Pops* appearance – might explain 'Welcome To Paradise's strong chart-placing, which was capitalised on further when charged follow-up, the enduring 'Basket Case' plunged them into the UK Top 10 while their *Dookie* album sold in the millions.

This first flush of success would be hard to match, yet Green Day returned with the more jaded but nevertheless effervescent follow-up album *Insomniac*, which spawned four singles throughout 1995–96: 'Geek Stink Breath', 'Stuck With Me', the double A-side 'Brain Stew / Jaded' and 'Hitchin' A Ride'.

Some critics dismissed the band as having already peaked, yet it was the plaintive 1997 single 'Good Riddance (Time Of Your Life)' that earned their highest chart position in three years and hinted towards Green Day's incredible future. It also featured on the final episode of *Seinfeld*, one of the most watched shows in television's history.

By the time Green Day released their stripped-down, acoustic-leaning 2000 album *Warning*, they had built a strong enough following to ensure that two of its three singles – 'Minority' and 'Warning' – charted in the Top 30, yet the pop-punk sound they had pioneered had been taken on by a new generation of young bands. Maybe their time was up after all?

Not so.

History will judge Green's Day's 2004 album, the conceptual *American Idiot*, and its lead single of the same name, as one of the biggest rock comebacks of all time. It heralded a return to the highly charged sound of their early days, the trio leaner than the slightly flabbier husbands and fathers they had become in the late 1990s. An explosion of power chords and anti-Republican sloganeering released during the US invasion of Iraq, 'American Idiot' charted at Number 3, capturing a wave of public unrest at the increasingly fragile and problematic international climate. *American Idiot* sent their global record sales past the staggering 50 million mark.

Firmly re-established as one of the biggest-selling bands on the planet, against all the odds Green Day have now entered their most successful period yet, with a string of poignant and anthemic radio-friendly singles to match: 'Boulevard Of Broken Dreams' (Number 5), 'Holiday' (Number 11), 'Wake Me Up When September Ends' (Number 8) and 'Jesus of Suburbia' (Number 17).

Silencing the critics, Green Day had evolved into a more socially aware band whose transition into an arena-filling punk band occurred with ease and left their credibility intact. When, in 2006, they collaborated with U2 on The Skids' 'The Saints Are Coming' for victims of Hurricane Katrina, few were surprised by the meeting of these much-loved and ever-playful punks and the world's biggest stadium rockers.

Green Day had come a long way.

Silver-selling · Gold-selling · Platinum-selling · US No.1 ★ · Peak Position · Weeks at No.1 · Weeks in Top 40

CLIVE GRIFFIN UK singer

Date	Title	Peak Position	Weeks at No.1	Weeks in Top 40
24 Jun 89	**HEAD ABOVE WATER** *Mercury STEP 4*	60		
11 May 91	**I'LL BE WAITING** *Mercury STEP 6*	56		

RONI GRIFFITH US singer

Date	Title	Peak Position	Weeks at No.1	Weeks in Top 40
30 Jun 84	**(THE BEST PART OF) BREAKING UP** *Making Waves SURF 101*	63		

GRIFTERS UK production duo

Date	Title	Peak Position	Weeks at No.1	Weeks in Top 40
20 Feb 99	**FLASH** *Duty Free DF 004CD*	63		

GRIM NORTHERN SOCIAL UK group

Date	Title	Peak Position	Weeks at No.1	Weeks in Top 40
6 Sep 03	**URBAN PRESSURE** *One Little Indian 353 TP7CD*	60		

GRINDERMAN Australian group

Date	Title	Peak Position	Weeks at No.1	Weeks in Top 40
3 Mar 07	**NO PUSSY BLUES** *Mute ICDMUTE373*	64		

JOSH GROBAN US singer

Date	Title	Peak Position	Weeks at No.1	Weeks in Top 40
9 Jun 07	**YOU RAISE ME UP** *Download*	74		

GROOVE ARMADA UK production duo

Date	Title	Peak Position	Weeks at No.1	Weeks in Top 40
8 May 99	**IF EVERYBODY LOOKED THE SAME** *Pepper 0530292*	25		1
7 Aug 99	**AT THE RIVER** *Pepper 0530062*	19		4
27 Nov 99	**I SEE YOU BABY** *Pepper 9230002* GROOVE ARMADA FEATURING GRAM'MA FUNK	17		2
25 Aug 01	**SUPERSTYLIN'** *Pepper 9230472*	12		3
17 Nov 01	**MY FRIEND** *Pepper 9230532*	36		1
2 Nov 02	**PURPLE HAZE** *Pepper 9230652*	36		1
17 May 03	**EASY** *Pepper 9230712*	31		1
6 Sep 03	**BUT I FEEL GOOD** *Pepper 82876556812*	50		
2 Oct 04	**I SEE YOU BABY** *Jive 82876649982*	11		3
5 May 07	**GET DOWN** *Columbia 88697074402* GROOVE ARMADA FEATURING STUSH	9		4
14 Jul 07	**SONG 4 MUTYA (OUT OF CONTROL)** *Columbia 88697114322*	8		7

GROOVE CONNEKTION 2 UK producer

Date	Title	Peak Position	Weeks at No.1	Weeks in Top 40
11 Apr 98	**CLUB LONELY** *XL Recordings XLT 94CD*	54		

GROOVE CORPORATION UK group

Date	Title	Peak Position	Weeks at No.1	Weeks in Top 40
16 Apr 94	**RAIN** *Six6 SIXCD 109*	71		

GROOVE COVERAGE German duo

Date	Title	Peak Position	Weeks at No.1	Weeks in Top 40
11 Jun 05	**POISON** *All Around The World CDGLOBE361*	32		1

GROOVE CUTTERS UK production duo

Date	Title	Peak Position	Weeks at No.1	Weeks in Top 40
5 Mar 05	**WE CLOSE OUR EYES** *Nebula NEBCD066*	33		1

GROOVE GENERATION UK production group

Date	Title	Peak Position	Weeks at No.1	Weeks in Top 40
8 Aug 98	**YOU MAKE ME FEEL LIKE DANCING** *Brothers Organisation CDBRUV 8* GROOVE GENERATION FEATURING LEO SAYER	32		1

GROOVE THEORY US duo

Date	Title	Peak Position	Weeks at No.1	Weeks in Top 40
18 Nov 95	**TELL ME** *Epic 6623882*	31		1

GROOVERIDER UK producer

Date	Title	Peak Position	Weeks at No.1	Weeks in Top 40
26 Sep 98	**RAINBOWS OF COLOUR** *Higher Ground HIGHS 13CD*	40		1
19 Jun 99	**WHERE'S JACK THE RIPPER** *Higher Ground HIGHS 20CD*	61		
29 Apr 06	**AIN'T GOT NO – I GOT LIFE** *Sony BMG TV 82876708212* NINA SIMONE VERSUS GROOVEFINDER	30		3

SCOTT GROOVES US producer

Date	Title	Peak Position	Weeks at No.1	Weeks in Top 40
16 May 98	**EXPANSIONS** *Soma Recordings SOMA 65CDS* SCOTT GROOVES FEATURING ROY AYERS	68		
28 Nov 98	**MOTHERSHIP RECONNECTION** *Soma Recordings SOMA 71CDS*	55		
21 Aug 99	**MOTHERSHIP RECONNECTION (REMIX)** *Virgin DINSD 185* SCOTT GROOVES FEATURING PARLIAMENT/FUNKADELIC	55		

HENRY GROSS US singer

Date	Title	Peak Position	Weeks at No.1	Weeks in Top 40
28 Aug 76	**SHANNON** *Life Song ELS 45002*	32		3

GROUND LEVEL Australian production group

Date	Title	Peak Position	Weeks at No.1	Weeks in Top 40
30 Jan 93	**DREAMS OF HEAVEN** *Faze 2 CDFAZE 14*	54		

GROUNDED UK group

Date	Title	Peak Position	Weeks at No.1	Weeks in Top 40
26 Feb 05	**I NEED A GIRL** *Platinum PLATGROUND1A*	43		

GROUP THERAPY US group

Date	Title	Peak Position	Weeks at No.1	Weeks in Top 40
30 Nov 96	**EAST COAST/WEST COAST KILLAS** *Interscope IND 95516*	51		

GSP UK production duo

Date	Title	Peak Position	Weeks at No.1	Weeks in Top 40
3 Oct 92	**THE BANANA SONG** *Yoyo 1*	38		2

GTO UK duo

Date	Title	Peak Position	Weeks at No.1	Weeks in Top 40
4 Aug 90	**PURE** *Cooltempo COOL 218*	57		
7 Sep 91	**LISTEN TO THE RHYTHM FLOW/BULLFROG** *React 7001*	72		
2 May 92	**ELEVATION** *React 4*	59		

GUESS WHO Canadian group

Date	Title	Peak Position	Weeks at No.1	Weeks in Top 40
16 Feb 67	**HIS GIRL** *King KG 1044*	45		
9 May 70	**AMERICAN WOMAN** *RCA 1943* ★	19		11

DAVID GUETTA French producer

Date	Title	Peak Position	Weeks at No.1	Weeks in Top 40
31 Aug 02	**LOVE DON'T LET ME GO** *Virgin DINSD 243* DAVID GUETTA FEATURING CHRIS WILLIS	46		
12 Jul 03	**JUST FOR ONE DAY (HEROES)** *Virgin DINST 263* DAVID GUETTA VS DAVID BOWIE	73		
25 Oct 03	**JUST A LITTLE MORE LOVE** *Virgin DINSD 250* DAVID GUETTA FEATURING CHRIS WILLIS	19		2
5 Mar 05	**THE WORLD IS MINE** *Virgin DINSDX271* DAVID GUETTA FEATURING JD DAVIS	49		
15 Jul 06	**WALKING AWAY** *Gusto CDGUS37* THE EGG VERSUS DAVID GUETTA	56		
19 Aug 06	**LOVE DON'T LET ME GO (WALKING AWAY)** *Gusto CDGUS42* DAVID GUETTA VS THE EGG	3		12
28 Jul 07	**LOVE IS GONE** *Angel ANGECD49*	9		8
8 Dec 07	**BABY WHEN THE LIGHT** *Charisma CASDX13* DAVID GUETTA FEATURING COZI	50		

GUILLEMOTS UK group

Date	Title	Peak Position	Weeks at No.1	Weeks in Top 40
8 Jul 06	**MADE-UP LOVE SONG #43** *Polydor 1700946*	23		1
23 Sep 06	**TRAINS TO BRAZIL** *Polydor 1705998*	36		1
27 Jan 07	**ANNIE LET'S NOT WAIT** *Polydor 1717323*	27		2
29 Mar 08	**GET OVER IT** *Polydor 1760834*	20		1

GUN UK group

Date	Title	Peak Position	Weeks at No.1	Weeks in Top 40
20 Nov 68	**RACE WITH THE DEVIL** *CBS 3734*	8		10

GUN UK group

Date	Title	Peak Position	Weeks at No.1	Weeks in Top 40
1 Jul 89	**BETTER DAYS** *A&M AM 505*	33		3
16 Sep 89	**MONEY (EVERYBODY LOVES HER)** *A&M AM 520*	73		
11 Nov 89	**INSIDE OUT** *A&M AM 531*	57		
10 Feb 90	**TAKING ON THE WORLD** *A&M AM 541*	50		
14 Jul 90	**SHAME ON YOU** *A&M AM 573*	33		2
14 Mar 92	**STEAL YOUR FIRE** *A&M AM 851*	24		3
2 May 92	**HIGHER GROUND** *A&M AM 869*	48		
4 Jul 92	**WELCOME TO THE REAL WORLD** *A&M AM 885*	43		

Date	Title / Label	Peak Position	Weeks at No.1	Weeks in Top 40
9 Jul 94	**WORD UP** *A&M 5806672*	8		6
24 Sep 94	**DON'T SAY IT'S OVER** *A&M 5807572*	19		2
25 Feb 95	**THE ONLY ONE** *A&M 5809552*	29		1
15 Apr 95	**SOMETHING WORTHWHILE** *A&M 5810452*	39		1
26 Apr 97	**CRAZY YOU** *A&M 5821932* G.U.N.	21		1
12 Jul 97	**MY SWEET JANE** *A&M 5822792* G.U.N.	51		

GUNS N' ROSES US group

Date	Title / Label	Peak Position	Weeks at No.1	Weeks in Top 40
3 Oct 87	**WELCOME TO THE JUNGLE** *Geffen GEF 30*	67		
20 Aug 88	**SWEET CHILD O' MINE** *Geffen GEF 43* ★	24		6
29 Oct 88	**WELCOME TO THE JUNGLE/NIGHTRAIN** *Geffen GEF 47*	24		4
18 Mar 89	**PARADISE CITY** *Geffen GEF 50*	6		8
3 Jun 89	**SWEET CHILD O' MINE** *Geffen GEF 55*	6		8
1 Jul 89	**PATIENCE** *Geffen GEF 56*	10		5
2 Sep 89	**NIGHTRAIN** *Geffen GEF 60*	17		3
13 Jul 91	**YOU COULD BE MINE** *Geffen GFS 6*	3		9
21 Sep 91	**DON'T CRY** *Geffen GFS 9*	8		3
21 Dec 91	**LIVE AND LET DIE** *Geffen GFS 17*	5		5
7 Mar 92	**NOVEMBER RAIN** *Geffen GFS 18*	4		4
23 May 92	**KNOCKIN' ON HEAVEN'S DOOR** *Geffen GFS 21*	2		7
21 Nov 92	**YESTERDAYS/NOVEMBER RAIN** *Geffen GFS 27*	8		7
29 May 93	**THE CIVIL WAR EP** *Geffen GEFSTD 43*	11		2
20 Nov 93	**AIN'T IT FUN** *Geffen GFSTD 62*	9		2
4 Jun 94	**SINCE I DON'T HAVE YOU** *Geffen GFSTD 70*	10		4
14 Jan 95	**SYMPATHY FOR THE DEVIL** *Geffen GFSTD 86*	9		5

GUNTHER & THE SUNSHINE GIRLS Swedish singer

Date	Title / Label	Peak Position	Weeks at No.1	Weeks in Top 40
15 May 04	**DING DONG SONG** *WEA 376CD*	14		3

GURU US duo

Date	Title / Label	Peak Position	Weeks at No.1	Weeks in Top 40
11 Sep 93	**TRUST ME** *Cooltempo CDCOOL 278* GURU FEATURING N'DEA DAVENPORT	34		1
13 Nov 93	**NO TIME TO PLAY** *Cooltempo CDCOOL 282* GURU FEATURING DEE C LEE	25		2
19 Aug 95	**WATCH WHAT YOU SAY** *Cooltempo CDCOOL 308* GURU FEATURING CHAKA KHAN	28		1
18 Nov 95	**FEEL THE MUSIC** *Cooltempo CDCOOLS 313*	34		1
13 Jul 96	**LIVIN' IN THIS WORLD/LIFESAVER** *Cooltempo CDCOOL 320*	61		
16 Dec 00	**KEEP YOUR WORRIES** *Virgin VUSCD 177* GURU'S JAZZAMATAZZ FEATURING ANGIE STONE	57		

GURU JOSH UK producer

Date	Title / Label	Peak Position	Weeks at No.1	Weeks in Top 40
24 Feb 90	**INFINITY** *Deconstruction PB 43475*	5		9
16 Jun 90	**WHOSE LAW (IS IT ANYWAY)** *Deconstruction PB 43647*	26		3

ADRIAN GURVITZ UK singer

Date	Title / Label	Peak Position	Weeks at No.1	Weeks in Top 40
30 Jan 82	**CLASSIC** *RAK 339* ○	8		7
12 Jun 82	**YOUR DREAM** *RAK 343*	61		

GUS GUS Icelandic group

Date	Title / Label	Peak Position	Weeks at No.1	Weeks in Top 40
21 Feb 98	**POLYESTERDAY** *4AD BAD 8002CD*	55		
13 Mar 99	**LADYSHAVE** *4AD BAD 9001CD*	64		
24 Apr 99	**STARLOVERS** *4AD BADD 9004CD*	62		
8 Feb 03	**DAVID** *Underwater H2O 022CD*	52		
28 Jun 03	**CALL OF THE WILD** *Underwater H2O 032CD*	75		
10 Apr 04	**DAVID (REMIX)** *Underwater H2O 042P*	72		

GUSTO UK producer

Date	Title / Label	Peak Position	Weeks at No.1	Weeks in Top 40
2 Mar 96	**DISCO'S REVENGE** *Manifesto FESCD 6*	9		4
7 Sep 96	**LET'S ALL CHANT** *Manifesto FESCD 13*	21		1

GWEN GUTHRIE US singer

Date	Title / Label	Peak Position	Weeks at No.1	Weeks in Top 40
19 Jul 86	**AIN'T NOTHING GOIN' ON BUT THE RENT** *Boiling Point POSP 807* ○	5		11
11 Oct 86	**(THEY LONG TO BE) CLOSE TO YOU** *Boiling Point POSP 822*	25		5
14 Feb 87	**GOOD TO GO LOVER/OUTSIDE IN THE RAIN** *Boiling Point POSP 841*	37		2
4 Sep 93	**AIN'T NOTHING GOIN' ON BUT THE RENT (REMIX)** *Polydor PZCD 276*	42		

GUY US group

Date	Title / Label	Peak Position	Weeks at No.1	Weeks in Top 40
4 May 91	**HER** *MCA MCS 1575*	58		

A GUY CALLED GERALD UK producer

Date	Title / Label	Peak Position	Weeks at No.1	Weeks in Top 40
8 Apr 89	**VOODOO RAY** *Rham! RS 804*	12		7
16 Dec 89	**FX/EYES OF SORROW** *Subscape AGCG 1*	52		

GUYS & DOLLS UK group

Date	Title / Label	Peak Position	Weeks at No.1	Weeks in Top 40
1 Mar 75	**THERE'S A WHOLE LOT OF LOVING** *Magnet MAG 20* ○	2		9
17 May 75	**HERE I GO AGAIN** *Magnet MAG 30*	33		2
21 Feb 76	**YOU DON'T HAVE TO SAY YOU LOVE ME** *Magnet MAG 50*	5		7
6 Nov 76	**STONEY GROUND** *Magnet MAG 76*	38		1
13 May 78	**ONLY LOVING DOES IT** *Magnet MAG 115*	42		

GUYVER UK producer

Date	Title / Label	Peak Position	Weeks at No.1	Weeks in Top 40
29 Mar 03	**TRAPPED/DIFFERENCES** *Tidy Two 118*	72		

GYM CLASS HEROES US group

Date	Title / Label	Peak Position	Weeks at No.1	Weeks in Top 40
21 Apr 07	**CUPID'S CHOKEHOLD/BREAKFAST IN AMERICA** *Atlantic AT0271CD*	3		16
25 Aug 07	**CLOTHES OFF** *Atlantic AT0282CDX*	5		8

GYPSYMEN US producer

Date	Title / Label	Peak Position	Weeks at No.1	Weeks in Top 40
11 Aug 01	**BABARABATIN** *Sound Design SDES 09CDS*	32		1

GYRES UK group

Date	Title / Label	Peak Position	Weeks at No.1	Weeks in Top 40
13 Apr 96	**POP COP** *Sugar SUGA 9CD*	71		
6 Jul 96	**ARE YOU READY** *Sugar SUGA 11CD*	71		

H

H & CLAIRE UK duo

Date	Title / Label	Peak Position	Weeks at No.1	Weeks in Top 40
18 May 02	**DJ** *WEA 347CD*	3		4
24 Aug 02	**HALF A HEART** *WEA 359CDX*	8		2
16 Nov 02	**ALL OUT OF LOVE** *WEA 360CDX*	10		3

HABIT UK group

Date	Title / Label	Peak Position	Weeks at No.1	Weeks in Top 40
30 Apr 88	**LUCY** *Virgin VS 1063*	56		

STEVE HACKETT UK singer/guitarist

Date	Title / Label	Peak Position	Weeks at No.1	Weeks in Top 40
2 Apr 83	**CELL 151** *Charisma CELL 1*	66		

HADDAWAY Trinidadian singer

Date	Title / Label	Peak Position	Weeks at No.1	Weeks in Top 40
5 Jun 93	**WHAT IS LOVE** *Logic 74321148502* ●	2		13
25 Sep 93	**LIFE** *Logic 74321164212*	6		7
18 Dec 93	**I MISS YOU** *Logic 74321181522*	9		12
2 Apr 94	**ROCK MY HEART** *Logic 74321194122*	9		7
24 Jun 95	**FLY AWAY** *Logic 74321286942*	20		2
23 Sep 95	**CATCH A FIRE** *Logic 74321306652*	39		1

TONY HADLEY UK singer

Date	Title / Label	Peak Position	Weeks at No.1	Weeks in Top 40
7 Mar 92	**LOST IN YOUR LOVE** *EMI EM 222*	42		
29 Aug 92	**FOR YOUR BLUE EYES ONLY** *EMI EM 234*	67		
16 Jan 93	**GAME OF LOVE** *EMI CDEM 254*	72		
10 May 97	**DANCE WITH ME** *VC Recordings VCRD 17* TIN TIN OUT FEATURING TONY HADLEY	35		1

HADOUKEN UK group

Date	Title / Label	Peak Position	Weeks at No.1	Weeks in Top 40
7 Jul 07	**LIQUID LIVES** *Surface Noise ATUK066CD*	36		1

Silver-selling ○ Gold-selling ● Platinum-selling ⊛ US No.1 ★ | Peak Position · Weeks at No.1 · Weeks in Top 40

SAMMY HAGAR US singer/guitarist

Date	Title / Label	Peak Position	Weeks at No.1	Weeks in Top 40
15 Dec 79	THIS PLANET'S ON FIRE/SPACE STATION NO. 5 *Capitol CL 16114*	52		
16 Feb 80	I'VE DONE EVERYTHING FOR YOU *Capitol CL 16120*	36		2
24 May 80	HEARTBEAT/LOVE OR MONEY *Capitol RED 1*	67		
16 Jan 82	PIECE OF MY HEART *Geffen GEF A 1884*	67		

PAUL HAIG UK singer

Date	Title / Label	Peak Position	Weeks at No.1	Weeks in Top 40
28 May 83	HEAVEN SENT *Island IS 111*	74		

HAIRCUT 100 UK group

Date	Title / Label	Peak Position	Weeks at No.1	Weeks in Top 40
24 Oct 81	FAVOURITE SHIRTS (BOY MEETS GIRL) *Arista CLIP 1* ○	4		8
30 Jan 82	LOVE PLUS ONE *Arista CLIP 2* ●	3		11
10 Apr 82	FANTASTIC DAY *Arista CLIP 3*	9		7
21 Aug 82	NOBODY'S FOOL *Arista CLIP 4*	9		6
6 Aug 83	PRIME TIME *Polydor HC 1*	46		

CURTIS HAIRSTON US singer

Date	Title / Label	Peak Position	Weeks at No.1	Weeks in Top 40
15 Oct 83	I WANT YOU (ALL TONIGHT) *RCA 368*	44		
27 Apr 85	I WANT YOUR LOVIN' (JUST A LITTLE BIT) *London LON 66*	13		6
6 Dec 86	CHILLIN' OUT *Atlantic A 9335*	57		

SEAMUS HAJI UK producer

Date	Title / Label	Peak Position	Weeks at No.1	Weeks in Top 40
18 Dec 04	LAST NIGHT A DJ SAVED MY LIFE (BIG LOVE) *Big Love BL013*	69		
4 Feb 06	TAKE ME AWAY *Big Love BL024CD* HAJI & EMANUEL	73		
31 Mar 07	LAST NIGHT A DJ SAVED MY LIFE *Apollo Recordings APOLLO110CDS*	13		4

HAL Irish group

Date	Title / Label	Peak Position	Weeks at No.1	Weeks in Top 40
8 May 04	WORRY ABOUT THE WIND *Rough Trade RTRADESCD172*	53		
5 Feb 05	WHAT A LOVELY DANCE *Rough Trade RTRADSCD212*	36		1
23 Apr 05	PLAY THE HITS *Rough Trade RTRADSCD226*	38		1
24 May 97	EXTREMIS *Virgin VSCDT 1636* HAL FEATURING GILLIAN ANDERSON	23		1

HALE & PACE & THE STONKERS UK comedy duo

Date	Title / Label	Peak Position	Weeks at No.1	Weeks in Top 40
9 Mar 91	THE STONK *London LON 296*	1	1	6

BILL HALEY & HIS COMETS US group

Date	Title / Label	Peak Position	Weeks at No.1	Weeks in Top 40
17 Dec 54	SHAKE RATTLE AND ROLL *Brunswick 05338*	4		14
7 Jan 55	ROCK AROUND THE CLOCK *Brunswick 05317* ★	17		2
15 Apr 55	MAMBO ROCK *Brunswick 05405*	14		2
14 Oct 55	ROCK AROUND THE CLOCK *Brunswick 05317*	1	5	17
30 Dec 55	ROCK-A-BEATIN' BOOGIE *Brunswick 05509*	4		9
9 Mar 56	SEE YOU LATER ALLIGATOR *Brunswick 05530*	7		13
25 May 56	THE SAINTS ROCK 'N' ROLL *Brunswick 05565*	5		24
17 Aug 56	ROCKIN' THROUGH THE RYE *Brunswick 05582*	3		23
14 Sep 56	RAZZLE DAZZLE *Brunswick 05453*	13		8
21 Sep 56	ROCK AROUND THE CLOCK *Brunswick 05317*	5		17
21 Sep 56	SEE YOU LATER ALLIGATOR *Brunswick 05530*	12		8
9 Nov 56	RIP IT UP *Brunswick 05615*	4		18
9 Nov 56	ROCK 'N' ROLL STAGE SHOW (LP) *Brunswick LAT 8139*	30		1
23 Nov 56	RUDY'S ROCK *Brunswick 05616*	26		5
1 Feb 57	ROCK THE JOINT *London HLF 8371*	20		4
8 Feb 57	DON'T KNOCK THE ROCK *Brunswick 05640*	7		8
3 Apr 68	ROCK AROUND THE CLOCK *MCA MU 1013*	20		8
16 Mar 74	ROCK AROUND THE CLOCK *MCA 128*	12		10
25 Apr 81	HALEY'S GOLDEN MEDLEY *MCA 694*	50		

AARON HALL US singer

Date	Title / Label	Peak Position	Weeks at No.1	Weeks in Top 40
13 Jun 92	DON'T BE AFRAID *MCA MCS 1632*	56		
23 Oct 93	GET A LITTLE FREAKY WITH ME *MCA MCSTD 1936*	66		

AUDREY HALL Jamaican singer

Date	Title / Label	Peak Position	Weeks at No.1	Weeks in Top 40
25 Jan 86	ONE DANCE WON'T DO *Germain DG7-1985*	20		6
5 Jul 86	SMILE *Germain DG 15*	14		7

DARYL HALL US singer

Date	Title / Label	Peak Position	Weeks at No.1	Weeks in Top 40
2 Aug 86	DREAMTIME *RCA HALL 1*	28		5
25 Sep 93	I'M IN A PHILLY MOOD *Epic 6595555*	59		
8 Jan 94	STOP LOVING ME LOVING YOU *Epic 6599982*	30		3
26 Mar 94	I'M IN A PHILLY MOOD *Epic 6595555*	52		
14 May 94	HELP ME FIND A WAY TO YOUR HEART *Epic 6604102*	70		
2 Jul 94	GLORYLAND *Mercury MERCD 404* DARYL HALL & THE SOUNDS OF BLACKNESS	36		2
10 Jun 95	WHEREVER WOULD I BE *Columbia 6620592* DUSTY SPRINGFIELD & DARYL HALL	44		

DARYL HALL & JOHN OATES US duo

Date	Title / Label	Peak Position	Weeks at No.1	Weeks in Top 40
16 Oct 76	SHE'S GONE *Atlantic K 10828*	42		
14 Jun 80	RUNNING FROM PARADISE *RCA RUN 1*	41		
20 Sep 80	YOU'VE LOST THAT LOVIN' FEELIN' *RCA 1*	55		
15 Nov 80	KISS ON MY LIST *RCA 15* ★	33		3
23 Jan 82	I CAN'T GO FOR THAT (NO CAN DO) *RCA 172* ○ ★	8		7
10 Apr 82	PRIVATE EYES *RCA 134* ★	32		3
30 Oct 82	MANEATER *RCA 290* ★	6		7
22 Jan 83	ONE ON ONE *RCA 305*	63		
30 Apr 83	FAMILY MAN *RCA 323*	15		5
12 Nov 83	SAY IT ISN'T SO *RCA 375*	69		
10 Mar 84	ADULT EDUCATION *RCA 396*	63		
20 Oct 84	OUT OF TOUCH *RCA 449* ★	48		
9 Feb 85	METHOD OF MODERN LOVE *RCA 472*	21		4
22 Jun 85	OUT OF TOUCH *RCA PB 49967*	62		
21 Sep 85	A NIGHT AT THE APOLLO LIVE! *RCA PB 49935* DARYL HALL & JOHN OATES FEATURING DAVID RUFFIN & EDDIE KENDRICK	58		
29 Sep 90	SO CLOSE *Arista 113600*	69		
26 Jan 91	EVERYWHERE I LOOK *Arista 113980*	74		

LYNDEN DAVID HALL UK singer

Date	Title / Label	Peak Position	Weeks at No.1	Weeks in Top 40
25 Oct 97	SEXY CINDERELLA *Cooltempo CDCOOL 328*	45		
14 Mar 98	DO I QUALIFY? *Cooltempo CDCOOLS 331*	26		1
4 Jul 98	CRESCENT MOON *Cooltempo CDCOOL 333*	45		
31 Oct 98	SEXY CINDERELLA *Cooltempo CDCOOLS 340*	17		1
11 Mar 00	FORGIVE ME *Cooltempo CDCOOLS 346*	30		1
27 May 00	SLEEPING WITH VICTOR *Cooltempo CDCOOL 348*	49		
23 Sep 00	LET'S DO IT AGAIN *Cooltempo CDCOOL 351*	69		

PAM HALL Jamaican singer

Date	Title / Label	Peak Position	Weeks at No.1	Weeks in Top 40
16 Aug 86	DEAR BOOPSIE *Bluemountain BM 027*	54		

TERRY HALL UK singer

Date	Title / Label	Peak Position	Weeks at No.1	Weeks in Top 40
11 Nov 89	MISSING *Chrysalis CHS 3381*	75		
27 Aug 94	FOREVER J *AnXious ANX 1024CDX*	67		
12 Nov 94	SENSE *AnXious ANX 1027CD*	54		
28 Oct 95	RAINBOWS (EP) *AnXious ANX 1033CD1*	62		
14 Jun 97	BALLAD OF A LANDLORD *Southsea Bubble CDBUBBLE 1*	50		
18 Oct 03	PROBLEM IS *Distinctive DISNCD 107* DUB PISTOLS FEATURING TERRY HALL	66		

GERI HALLIWELL UK singer

Date	Title / Label	Peak Position	Weeks at No.1	Weeks in Top 40
22 May 99	LOOK AT ME *EMI CDEM 542* ●	2		7
28 Aug 99	MI CHICO LATINO *EMI CDEMS 548* ○	1	1	8
13 Nov 99	LIFT ME UP *EMI CDEM 554* ○	1	1	9
25 Mar 00	BAG IT UP *EMI CDEMS 560* ○	1	1	8
12 May 01	IT'S RAINING MEN *EMI CDEMS 584* ●	1	2	11
11 Aug 01	SCREAM IF YOU WANNA GO FASTER *EMI CDEM 595*	8		4
8 Dec 01	CALLING *EMI CDEMS 606*	7		5
4 Dec 04	RIDE IT *Innocent SINDX69*	4		7
11 Jun 05	DESIRE *Innocent SINDX75*	22		1

HALO UK group

Date	Title / Label	Peak Position	Weeks at No.1	Weeks in Top 40
16 Feb 02	COLD LIGHT OF DAY *Sony S2 6723072*	49		
1 Jun 02	SANCTIMONIOUS *Sony S2 6725965*	44		
7 Sep 02	NEVER ENDING *Sony S2 6730125*	56		

HALO JAMES UK group

Date	Title / Label	Peak Position	Weeks at No.1	Weeks in Top 40
7 Oct 89	WANTED *Epic HALO 1*	45		
23 Dec 89	COULD HAVE TOLD YOU SO *Epic HALO 2*	6		7

Date	Title	Peak Position	Weeks at No.1	Weeks in Top 40
17 Mar 90	**BABY** *Epic HALO 3*	43		
19 May 90	**MAGIC HOUR** *Epic HALO 4*	59		

HAMFATTER UK group

Date	Title	Peak Position	Weeks at No.1	Weeks in Top 40
21 Jul 07	**SZIGET (WE GET WRECKED)** *Pink Hedgehog SMILE24*	54		

ASHLEY HAMILTON US singer

Date	Title	Peak Position	Weeks at No.1	Weeks in Top 40
14 Jun 03	**WIMMIN'** *Columbia 6739305*	27		2

GEORGE HAMILTON IV US singer

Date	Title	Peak Position	Weeks at No.1	Weeks in Top 40
7 Mar 58	**WHY DON'T THEY UNDERSTAND?** *HMV POP 429*	22		9
18 Jul 58	**I KNOW WHERE I'M GOING** *HMV POP 505*	23		4

LYNNE HAMILTON UK singer

Date	Title	Peak Position	Weeks at No.1	Weeks in Top 40
29 Apr 89	**ON THE INSIDE (THEME FROM *PRISONER CELL BLOCK H*)** *A1 311*	3		6

RUSS HAMILTON UK singer

Date	Title	Peak Position	Weeks at No.1	Weeks in Top 40
24 May 57	**WE WILL MAKE LOVE** *Oriole CB 1359*	2		20
27 Sep 57	**WEDDING RING** *Oriole CB 1388* RUSS HAMILTON WITH JOHNNY GREGORY & HIS ORCHESTRA WITH THE TONETTES	20		6

HAMILTON, JOE FRANK & REYNOLDS US group

Date	Title	Peak Position	Weeks at No.1	Weeks in Top 40
13 Sep 75	**FALLIN' IN LOVE** *Pye International 7N 25690* ★	33		4

MARVIN HAMLISCH US pianist

Date	Title	Peak Position	Weeks at No.1	Weeks in Top 40
30 Mar 74	**THE ENTERTAINER** *MCA 121*	25		9

MC HAMMER US rapper

Date	Title	Peak Position	Weeks at No.1	Weeks in Top 40
9 Jun 90	**U CAN'T TOUCH THIS** *Capitol CL 578* ○	3		13
6 Oct 90	**HAVE YOU SEEN HER** *Capitol CL 590*	8		5
8 Dec 90	**PRAY** *Capitol CL 599*	8		9
23 Feb 91	**HERE COMES THE HAMMER** *Capitol CL 610*	15		4
1 Jun 91	**YO! SWEETNESS** *Capitol CL 616*	16		4
20 Jul 91	**(HAMMER HAMMER) THEY PUT ME IN THE MIX** *Capitol CL 607*	20		3
26 Oct 91	**2 LEGIT 2 QUIT** *Capitol CL 636* HAMMER	60		
21 Dec 91	**ADDAMS GROOVE** *Capitol CL 642* HAMMER	4		8
21 Mar 92	**DO NOT PASS ME BY** *Capitol CL 650* HAMMER	14		5
12 Mar 94	**IT'S ALL GOOD** *RCA 74321188612* HAMMER	52		
13 Aug 94	**DON'T STOP** *RCA 74321220012* HAMMER	72		
3 Jun 95	**STRAIGHT TO MY FEET** *Priority PTYCD 102* HAMMER FEATURING DEION SAUNDERS	57		

JAN HAMMER Czech instrumentalist

Date	Title	Peak Position	Weeks at No.1	Weeks in Top 40
12 Oct 85	***MIAMI VICE* THEME** *MCA 1000* ○ ★	5		7
19 Sep 87	**CROCKETT'S THEME** *MCA 1193* ○	2		11
1 Jun 91	**CROCKETT'S THEME/CHANCER** *MCA MCS 1541*	47		

ALBERT HAMMOND UK singer

Date	Title	Peak Position	Weeks at No.1	Weeks in Top 40
30 Jun 73	**FREE ELECTRIC BAND** *Mums 1494*	19		9

HAMPENBERG Danish producer

Date	Title	Peak Position	Weeks at No.1	Weeks in Top 40
21 Sep 02	**DUCK TOY** *Serious SERR 49CD*	30		1

HERBIE HANCOCK US keyboard player

Date	Title	Peak Position	Weeks at No.1	Weeks in Top 40
26 Aug 78	**I THOUGHT IT WAS YOU** *CBS 6530*	15		7
3 Feb 79	**YOU BET YOUR LOVE** *CBS 7010*	18		8
30 Jul 83	**ROCKIT** *CBS A 3577*	8		8
8 Oct 83	**AUTO DRIVE** *CBS A 3802*	33		1
21 Jan 84	**FUTURE SHOCK** *CBS A 4075*	54		
4 Aug 84	**HARDROCK** *CBS A 4616*	65		

HANDBAGGERS UK group

Date	Title	Peak Position	Weeks at No.1	Weeks in Top 40
15 Jun 96	**U FOUND OUT** *Tidy Trax TIDY 104CD*	55		

HANDLEY FAMILY UK group

Date	Title	Peak Position	Weeks at No.1	Weeks in Top 40
7 Apr 73	**WAM BAM** *GL 100*	30		4

HANI US producer

Date	Title	Peak Position	Weeks at No.1	Weeks in Top 40
11 Mar 00	**BABY WANTS TO RIDE** *Neo CD025*	70		

JAYN HANNA UK singer

Date	Title	Peak Position	Weeks at No.1	Weeks in Top 40
13 Apr 96	**LOVELIGHT (RIDE ON A LOVE TRAIN)** *VC Recordings VCRD 10*	42		
1 Feb 97	**LOST WITHOUT YOU** *VC Recordings VCRD 16*	44		

HANNAH UK singer

Date	Title	Peak Position	Weeks at No.1	Weeks in Top 40
21 Oct 00	**OUR KIND OF LOVE** *Telstar CDSTAS 3149*	41		

HANOI ROCKS Finnish group

Date	Title	Peak Position	Weeks at No.1	Weeks in Top 40
7 Jul 84	**UP AROUND THE BEND** *CBS A 4513*	61		

HANSON US group

Date	Title	Peak Position	Weeks at No.1	Weeks in Top 40
7 Jun 97	**MMMBOP** *Mercury 5745012* ⊛ ★	1	3	11
13 Sep 97	**WHERE'S THE LOVE** *Mercury 5749032* ○	4		6
22 Nov 97	**I WILL COME TO YOU** *Mercury 5680072*	5		4
28 Mar 98	**WEIRD** *Mercury 5685412*	19		2
4 Jul 98	**THINKING OF YOU** *Mercury 5688132*	23		1
29 Apr 00	**IF ONLY** *Mercury 5627502*	15		2
5 Feb 05	**PENNY AND ME** *Cooking Vinyl FRYCD220X*	10		4
9 Apr 05	**LOST WITHOUT EACH OTHER** *Cooking Vinyl FRYCD224X*	39		1
28 Apr 07	**GO** *Cooking Vinyl FRYCD291X*	44		

HAPPENINGS US group

Date	Title	Peak Position	Weeks at No.1	Weeks in Top 40
18 May 67	**I GOT RHYTHM** *Stateside SS 2013*	28		6
16 Aug 67	**MY MAMMY** *Pye International 25501/BT Puppy BTS 45530*	34		4

HAPPY CLAPPERS UK group

Date	Title	Peak Position	Weeks at No.1	Weeks in Top 40
3 Jun 95	**I BELIEVE** *Shindig SHIN 4CD*	21		2
26 Aug 95	**HOLD ON** *Shindig SHIN 7CD*	27		1
18 Nov 95	**I BELIEVE** *Shindig SHIN 9CD*	7		4
15 Jun 96	**CAN'T HELP IT** *Coliseum TOGA 004CD*	18		2
21 Dec 96	**NEVER AGAIN** *Coliseum TOGA 012CD*	49		
22 Nov 97	**I BELIEVE (REMIX)** *Coliseum COLA 027CD*	28		1

HAPPY MONDAYS UK group

Date	Title	Peak Position	Weeks at No.1	Weeks in Top 40
30 Sep 89	**WFL** *Factory FAC 2327*	68		
25 Nov 89	**MADCHESTER RAVE ON EP** *Factory FAC 2427*	19		7
7 Apr 90	**STEP ON** *Factory FAC 2727*	5		8
9 Jun 90	**LAZYITIS – ONE ARMED BOXER** *Factory FAC 2227* HAPPY MONDAYS & KARL DENVER	46		
20 Oct 90	**KINKY AFRO** *Factory FAC 3027*	5		6
9 Mar 91	**LOOSE FIT** *Factory FAC 3127*	17		4
30 Nov 91	**JUDGE FUDGE** *Factory FAC 3327*	24		2
19 Sep 92	**STINKIN THINKIN** *Factory FAC 3627*	31		2
21 Nov 92	**SUNSHINE AND LOVE** *Factory FAC 3727*	62		
22 May 99	**THE BOYS ARE BACK IN TOWN** *London LONCD 432*	24		1
29 Oct 05	**PLAYGROUND SUPERSTAR** *Big Brother RKIDSCD34*	51		

HAPPYLIFE UK group

Date	Title	Peak Position	Weeks at No.1	Weeks in Top 40
9 Oct 04	**SILENCE WHEN YOU'RE BURNING** *Albert Productions JASCDUK012*	73		

HAR MAR SUPERSTAR US singer

Date	Title	Peak Position	Weeks at No.1	Weeks in Top 40
5 Jul 03	**EZ PASS** *B Unique BUN 054CDS*	59		
4 Sep 04	**DUI** *Record Collection W651CD*	46		

Silver-selling · Gold-selling · Platinum-selling · US No.1 ★ · Peak Position · Weeks at No.1 · Weeks in Top 40

ED HARCOURT UK singer

Date	Title	Label	Peak Position	Weeks at No.1	Weeks in Top 40
2 Feb 02	APPLE OF MY EYE	*Heavenly HVN 107CDS*	61		
15 Feb 03	ALL OF YOUR DAYS WILL BE BLESSED	*Heavenly HVN 127CDS*	35		1
11 Sep 04	THIS ONE'S FOR YOU	*Heavenly HVN 140CD*	41		
13 Nov 04	BORN IN THE 70'S	*Heavenly HVN 146CD*	61		
26 Feb 05	LONELINESS	*Heavenly HVN149CD*	59		

HARD-FI UK group

Date	Title	Label	Peak Position	Weeks at No.1	Weeks in Top 40
30 Apr 05	TIED UP TOO TIGHT	*Necessary HARDFI02CD*	15		2
2 Jul 05	HARD TO BEAT	*Necessary HARD03CD*	9		5
1 Oct 05	LIVING FOR THE WEEKEND	*Necessary HARD04CD*	15		2
7 Jan 06	CASH MACHINE	*Necessary HARD05CDX*	14		8
22 Apr 06	BETTER DO BETTER	*Necessary/Atlantic HARD06CD*	14		2
25 Aug 07	SUBURBAN KNIGHTS	*Necessary/Atlantic HARD07CD*	7		6
24 Nov 07	CAN'T GET ALONG (WITHOUT YOU)	*Necessary/Atlantic HARD08CD*	45		
22 Mar 08	I SHALL OVERCOME	*Necessary/Atlantic HARD09CD*	36		1

PAUL HARDCASTLE UK producer

Date	Title	Label	Peak Position	Weeks at No.1	Weeks in Top 40
7 Apr 84	YOU'RE THE ONE FOR ME – DAYBREAK – AM	*Total Control TOCO 1*	41		
28 Jul 84	GUILTY	*Total Control TOCO 2*	55		
22 Sep 84	RAIN FOREST	*Bluebird BR 8*	41		
17 Nov 84	EAT YOUR HEART OUT	*Cooltempo COOL 102*	59		
4 May 85	19	*Chrysalis CHS 2860*	1	5	12
15 Jun 85	RAIN FOREST	*Bluebird/10 BR 15*	53		
9 Nov 85	JUST FOR MONEY	*Chrysalis CASH 1*	19		4
1 Feb 86	DON'T WASTE MY TIME — PAUL HARDCASTLE FEATURING CAROL KENYON	*Chrysalis PAUL 1*	8		8
21 Jun 86	FOOLIN' YOURSELF	*Chrysalis PAUL 2*	51		
11 Oct 86	THE WIZARD	*Chrysalis PAUL 3*	15		6
9 Apr 88	WALK IN THE NIGHT	*Chrysalis PAUL 4*	54		
4 Jun 88	40 YEARS	*Chrysalis PAUL 5*	53		

HARDCORE RHYTHM TEAM UK production group

Date	Title	Label	Peak Position	Weeks at No.1	Weeks in Top 40
14 Mar 92	HARDCORE – THE FINAL CONFLICT	*Furious FRUT 001*	69		

DUANE HARDEN US singer

Date	Title	Label	Peak Position	Weeks at No.1	Weeks in Top 40
6 Feb 99	YOU DON'T KNOW ME — ARMAND VAN HELDEN FEATURING DUANE HARDEN	*ffrr FCD 357*	1	1	9
22 May 99	WHAT YOU NEED — POWERHOUSE FEATURING DUANE HARDEN	*Defected DEFECT 3CDS*	13		3

HARDFLOOR German group

Date	Title	Label	Peak Position	Weeks at No.1	Weeks in Top 40
26 Dec 92	HARDTRANCE ACPERIENCE	*Harthouse UK HARTUK 1*	56		
10 Apr 93	TRANCESCRIPT	*Harthouse UK HARTUK 5CD*	72		
25 Oct 97	ACPERIENCE	*Eye-Q EYEUK 018CD1*	60		

TIM HARDIN US singer

Date	Title	Label	Peak Position	Weeks at No.1	Weeks in Top 40
5 Jan 67	HANG ON TO A DREAM	*Verve VS 1504*	50		

MIKE HARDING UK comedian

Date	Title	Label	Peak Position	Weeks at No.1	Weeks in Top 40
2 Aug 75	ROCHDALE COWBOY	*Rubber ADUB 3*	22		6

HARDSOUL Dutch production duo

Date	Title	Label	Peak Position	Weeks at No.1	Weeks in Top 40
12 Jun 04	BACK TOGETHER — HARDSOUL FEATURING RON CARROLL	*In The House ITH02CDS*	60		

FRANCOISE HARDY French singer

Date	Title	Label	Peak Position	Weeks at No.1	Weeks in Top 40
25 Jun 64	TOUS LES GARCONS ET LES FILLES	*Pye 7N 15653*	36		3
7 Jan 65	HOWEVER MUCH (ET MEME)	*Pye 7N 15740*	31		1
25 Mar 65	ALL OVER THE WORLD	*Pye 7N 15802*	16		13

MORTEN HARKET Norwegian singer

Date	Title	Label	Peak Position	Weeks at No.1	Weeks in Top 40
19 Aug 95	A KIND OF CHRISTMAS CARD	*Warner Brothers 0304CD*	53		

HARLEQUIN 4S/BUNKER KRU US/UK group

Date	Title	Label	Peak Position	Weeks at No.1	Weeks in Top 40
19 Mar 88	SET IT OFF	*Champion CHAMP 64*	55		

STEVE HARLEY & COCKNEY REBEL UK group

Date	Title	Label	Peak Position	Weeks at No.1	Weeks in Top 40
11 May 74	JUDY TEEN — COCKNEY REBEL	*EMI 2128*	5		9
10 Aug 74	MR SOFT — COCKNEY REBEL	*EMI 2191*	8		8
8 Feb 75	MAKE ME SMILE (COME UP AND SEE ME)	*EMI 2263*	1	2	9
7 Jun 75	MR RAFFLES (MAN IT WAS MEAN)	*EMI 2299*	13		6
31 Jul 76	HERE COMES THE SUN — STEVE HARLEY	*EMI 2505*	10		6
6 Nov 76	LOVE'S A PRIMA DONNA — STEVE HARLEY	*EMI 2539*	41		
20 Oct 79	FREEDOM'S PRISONER — STEVE HARLEY	*EMI 2994*	58		
13 Aug 83	BALLERINA (PRIMA DONNA) — STEVE HARLEY	*Stiletto STL 14*	51		
11 Jan 86	THE PHANTOM OF THE OPERA — SARAH BRIGHTMAN & STEVE HARLEY	*Polydor POSP 800*	7		7
25 Apr 92	MAKE ME SMILE (COME UP AND SEE ME) — STEVE HARLEY	*EMI EMCT 5*	46		
30 Dec 95	MAKE ME SMILE (COME UP AND SEE ME)	*EMI CDHARLEY 1*	33		1
2 Jul 05	MAKE ME SMILE (COME UP AND SEE ME)	*Gott Discs GOTTCD030*	55		

HARLEY QUINNE UK group

Date	Title	Label	Peak Position	Weeks at No.1	Weeks in Top 40
14 Oct 72	NEW ORLEANS	*Bell 1255*	19		8

HARMONIX UK producer

Date	Title	Label	Peak Position	Weeks at No.1	Weeks in Top 40
30 Mar 96	LANDSLIDE	*Deconstruction 74321330762*	28		1

HARMONY GRASS UK group

Date	Title	Label	Peak Position	Weeks at No.1	Weeks in Top 40
29 Jan 69	MOVE IN A LITTLE CLOSER	*RCA 1772*	24		5

BEN HARPER US singer

Date	Title	Label	Peak Position	Weeks at No.1	Weeks in Top 40
4 Apr 98	FADED	*Virgin VUSCD 134*	54		

CHARLIE HARPER UK singer

Date	Title	Label	Peak Position	Weeks at No.1	Weeks in Top 40
19 Jul 80	BARMY LONDON ARMY	*Gem GEMS 35*	68		

HARPERS BIZARRE US group

Date	Title	Label	Peak Position	Weeks at No.1	Weeks in Top 40
30 Mar 67	59TH STREET BRIDGE SONG (FEELING GROOVY)	*Warner Brothers WB 5890*	34		5
4 Oct 67	ANYTHING GOES	*Warner Brothers WB 7063*	33		5

HARPO Swedish singer

Date	Title	Label	Peak Position	Weeks at No.1	Weeks in Top 40
17 Apr 76	MOVIE STAR	*DJM DJS 400*	24		5

ANITA HARRIS UK singer/actress

Date	Title	Label	Peak Position	Weeks at No.1	Weeks in Top 40
29 Jun 67	JUST LOVING YOU	*CBS 2724*	6		26
11 Oct 67	PLAYGROUND	*CBS 2991*	46		
24 Jan 68	ANNIVERSARY WALTZ	*CBS 3211*	21		7
14 Aug 68	DREAM A LITTLE DREAM OF ME	*CBS 3637*	33		4

CALVIN HARRIS UK producer

Date	Title	Label	Peak Position	Weeks at No.1	Weeks in Top 40
10 Mar 07	ACCEPTABLE IN THE 80S	*Columbia 88697063932*	10		11
9 Jun 07	THE GIRLS	*Sony BMG 88697072212*	3		11
25 Aug 07	MERRYMAKING AT MY PLACE	*Columbia FLYEYE011*	43		

EMMYLOU HARRIS US singer

Date	Title	Label	Peak Position	Weeks at No.1	Weeks in Top 40
6 Mar 76	HERE THERE AND EVERYWHERE	*Reprise K 14415*	30		2

JET HARRIS UK bass guitarist

Date	Title	Label	Peak Position	Weeks at No.1	Weeks in Top 40
24 May 62	BESAME MUCHO	*Decca F 11466*	22		7
16 Aug 62	MAIN TITLE THEME FROM *MAN WITH THE GOLDEN ARM*	*Decca F 11488*	12		10

JET HARRIS & TONY MEEHAN UK instrumental duo

Date	Title	Peak Position	Weeks at No.1	Weeks in Top 40
10 Jan 63	**DIAMONDS** *Decca F 11563*	1	3	12
25 Apr 63	**SCARLETT O'HARA** *Decca F 11644*	2		13
5 Sep 63	**APPLEJACK** *Decca F 11710*	4		11

KEITH HARRIS & ORVILLE UK ventriloquist

Date	Title	Peak Position	Weeks at No.1	Weeks in Top 40
18 Dec 82	**ORVILLE'S SONG** *BBC RESL 124* ○	4		8
24 Dec 83	**COME TO MY PARTY** *BBC RESL 138*			
	KEITH HARRIS & ORVILLE WITH DIPPY	44		
14 Dec 85	**WHITE CHRISTMAS** *Columbia DB 9121*	40		1

MAJOR HARRIS US singer

Date	Title	Peak Position	Weeks at No.1	Weeks in Top 40
9 Aug 75	**LOVE WON'T LET ME WAIT** *Atlantic K 10585*	37		2
5 Nov 83	**ALL MY LIFE** *London LON 37*	61		

MAX HARRIS UK orchestra leader

Date	Title	Peak Position	Weeks at No.1	Weeks in Top 40
1 Dec 60	**GURNEY SLADE** *Fontana H 282*	11		9

RAHNI HARRIS US keyboard player

Date	Title	Peak Position	Weeks at No.1	Weeks in Top 40
16 Dec 78	**SIX MILLION STEPS (WEST RUNS SOUTH)** *Mercury 6007 198*			
	RAHNI HARRIS & F.L.O.	43		

RICHARD HARRIS Irish actor

Date	Title	Peak Position	Weeks at No.1	Weeks in Top 40
26 Jun 68	**MACARTHUR PARK** *RCA 1699*	4		11
8 Jul 72	**MACARTHUR PARK** *Probe GFF 101*	38		2

ROLF HARRIS Australian singer/TV personality

Date	Title	Peak Position	Weeks at No.1	Weeks in Top 40
21 Jul 60	**TIE ME KANGAROO DOWN SPORT** *Columbia DB 4483*			
	ROLF HARRIS WITH HIS WOBBLE BOARD AND THE RHYTHM SPINNERS	9		12
25 Oct 62	**SUN ARISE** *Columbia DB 4888*	3		15
28 Feb 63	**JOHNNY DAY** *Columbia DB 8553*	44		
16 Apr 69	**BLUER THAN BLUE** *Columbia DB 8553*	30		5
22 Nov 69	**TWO LITTLE BOYS** *Columbia DB 8630*	1	6	23
13 Feb 93	**STAIRWAY TO HEAVEN** *Vertigo VERCD 73*	7		4
1 Jun 96	**BOHEMIAN RHAPSODY** *Living Beat LBECD 41*	50		
25 Oct 97	**SUN ARISE** *EMI CDROO 001*	26		1
14 Oct 00	**FINE DAY** *Tommy Boy TBCD 2155*	24		2

RONNIE HARRIS UK singer

Date	Title	Peak Position	Weeks at No.1	Weeks in Top 40
24 Sep 54	**STORY OF TINA** *Columbia DB 3499*	12		3

SAM HARRIS US singer

Date	Title	Peak Position	Weeks at No.1	Weeks in Top 40
9 Feb 85	**HEARTS ON FIRE/OVER THE RAINBOW** *Motown TMG 1370*	67		

SIMON HARRIS UK producer

Date	Title	Peak Position	Weeks at No.1	Weeks in Top 40
19 Mar 88	**BASS (HOW LOW CAN YOU GO)** *ffrr FFR 4*	12		5
29 Oct 88	**HERE COMES THAT SOUND** *ffrr FFR 12*	38		2
24 Jun 89	**(I'VE GOT YOUR) PLEASURE CONTROL** *ffrr F 106*			
	SIMON HARRIS FEATURING LONNIE GORDON	60		
18 Nov 89	**ANOTHER MONSTERJAM** *ffrr F 116*			
	SIMON HARRIS FEATURING EINSTEIN	65		
10 Mar 90	**RAGGA HOUSE (ALL NIGHT LONG)** *Living Beat 7SMASH 9*			
	SIMON HARRIS FEATURING DADDY FREDDY	56		

GEORGE HARRISON UK singer/guitarist

Date	Title	Peak Position	Weeks at No.1	Weeks in Top 40
23 Jan 71	**MY SWEET LORD** *Apple R 5884* ★	1	5	15
14 Aug 71	**BANGLA DESH** *Apple R 5912*	10		7
2 Jun 73	**GIVE ME LOVE (GIVE ME PEACE ON EARTH)** *Apple R 5988* ★	8		9
21 Dec 74	**DING DONG** *Apple R 6002*	38		2
11 Oct 75	**YOU** *Apple R 6007*	38		3
10 Mar 79	**BLOW AWAY** *Dark Horse K 17327*	51		
23 May 81	**ALL THOSE YEARS AGO** *Dark Horse K 17807*	13		5
24 Oct 87	**GOT MY MIND SET ON YOU** *Dark Horse W 8178* ○ ★	2		11
6 Feb 88	**WHEN WE WAS FAB** *Dark Horse W 8131*	25		3
25 Jun 88	**THIS IS LOVE** *Dark Horse W 7913*	55		
26 Jan 02	**MY SWEET LORD** *Parlophone CDR 6571*	1	1	5
24 May 03	**ANY ROAD** *Parlophone CDRS 6601*	37		1

NOEL HARRISON UK singer

Date	Title	Peak Position	Weeks at No.1	Weeks in Top 40
26 Feb 69	**WINDMILLS OF YOUR MIND** *Reprise RS 20758*	8		14

HARRISONS UK group

Date	Title	Peak Position	Weeks at No.1	Weeks in Top 40
25 Feb 06	**BLUE NOTE** *Melodic MELO036CD*	69		

HARRY UK group

Date	Title	Peak Position	Weeks at No.1	Weeks in Top 40
2 Nov 02	**SO REAL** *Dirty World DWRCD 003*	53		
19 Apr 03	**UNDER THE COVERS EP** *Dirty World DWRCD 005*	43		

DEBBIE HARRY US singer

Date	Title	Peak Position	Weeks at No.1	Weeks in Top 40
1 Aug 81	**BACKFIRED** *Chrysalis CHS 2526*	32		3
15 Nov 86	**FRENCH KISSIN' IN THE USA** *Chrysalis CHS 3066*	8		9
28 Feb 87	**FREE TO FALL** *Chrysalis CHS 3093*	46		
9 May 87	**IN LOVE WITH LOVE** *Chrysalis CHS 3128*	45		
7 Oct 89	**I WANT THAT MAN** *Chrysalis CHS 3369*			
	DEBORAH HARRY	13		8
2 Dec 89	**BRITE SIDE** *Chrysalis CHS 3452*			
	DEBORAH HARRY	59		
31 Mar 90	**SWEET AND LOW** *Chrysalis CHS 3491*			
	DEBORAH HARRY	57		
5 Jan 91	**WELL DID YOU EVAH!** *Chrysalis CHS 3646*			
	DEBORAH HARRY & IGGY POP	42		
3 Jul 93	**I CAN SEE CLEARLY NOW** *Chrysalis CDCHSS 4900*			
	DEBORAH HARRY	23		2
18 Sep 93	**STRIKE ME PINK** *Chrysalis CDCHSS 5000*			
	DEBORAH HARRY	46		
11 Nov 06	**NEW YORK NEW YORK** *Mute CDMUTE371*			
	MOBY FEATURING DEBBIE HARRY	43		

RICHARD HARTLEY/MICHAEL REED ORCHESTRA UK synthesiser player orchestra

Date	Title	Peak Position	Weeks at No.1	Weeks in Top 40
25 Feb 84	**THE MUSIC OF TORVILL AND DEAN EP** *Safari SKATE 1* ○	9		8

DAN HARTMAN US singer

Date	Title	Peak Position	Weeks at No.1	Weeks in Top 40
21 Oct 78	**INSTANT REPLAY** *Blue Sky 6706* ○	8		12
13 Jan 79	**THIS IS IT** *Blue Sky 6999*	17		6
18 May 85	**SECOND NATURE** *MCA 957*	66		
24 Aug 85	**I CAN DREAM ABOUT YOU** *MCA 988*	12		6
1 Apr 95	**KEEP THE FIRE BURNIN'** *Columbia 6611552*			
	DAN HARTMAN STARRING LOLEATTA HOLLOWAY	49		

HARVEY UK rapper

Date	Title	Peak Position	Weeks at No.1	Weeks in Top 40
7 Sep 02	**GET UP AND MOVE** *Go! Beat GOBCD 52*	24		1

SENSATIONAL ALEX HARVEY BAND UK group

Date	Title	Peak Position	Weeks at No.1	Weeks in Top 40
26 Jul 75	**DELILAH** *Vertigo ALEX 001*	7		7
22 Nov 75	**GAMBLIN' BAR ROOM BLUES** *Vertigo ALEX 002*	38		1
19 Jun 76	**THE BOSTON TEA PARTY** *Mountain TOP 12*	13		9

BRIAN HARVEY UK singer

Date	Title	Peak Position	Weeks at No.1	Weeks in Top 40
2 Dec 00	**TRUE STEP TONIGHT** *NuLife 74321811312*			
	TRUE STEPPERS FEATURING BRIAN HARVEY & DONELL JONES	25		1
28 Apr 01	**STRAIGHT UP NO BENDS** *Edel 0126605ERE*	26		1
27 Oct 01	**LOVING YOU (OLE OLE OLE)** *Blacklist 0133045 ERE*			
	BRIAN HARVEY & THE REFUGEE CREW	20		2

PJ HARVEY UK group

Date	Title	Peak Position	Weeks at No.1	Weeks in Top 40
29 Feb 92	**SHEELA-NA-GIG** *Too Pure PURE 008*	69		
1 May 93	**50FT QUEENIE** *Island CID 538*	27		1
17 Jul 93	**MAN-SIZE** *Island CID 569*	42		
18 Feb 95	**DOWN BY THE WATER** *Island CID 607*	38		1
22 Jul 95	**C'MON BILLY** *Island CIDX 614*	29		1
28 Oct 95	**SEND HIS LOVE TO ME** *Island CID 610*	34		1
9 Mar 96	**HENRY LEE** *Mute CDMUTE 189*			
	NICK CAVE & THE BAD SEEDS & PJ HARVEY	36		1
23 Nov 96	**THAT WAS MY VEIL** *Island CID 648*			
	JOHN PARISH & POLLY JEAN HARVEY	75		
26 Sep 98	**A PERFECT DAY ELISE** *Island CID 718*	25		1

Silver-selling ○ · Gold-selling ● · Platinum-selling · US No.1 ★ · Peak Position · Weeks at No.1 · Weeks in Top 40

Date	Title	Peak Position	Weeks at No.1	Weeks in Top 40
23 Jan 99	**THE WIND** *Island CID 730*	29		1
25 Nov 00	**GOOD FORTUNE** *Island CID 769*	41		
10 Mar 01	**A PLACE CALLED HOME** *Island CID 771*	43		
20 Oct 01	**THIS IS LOVE** *Island CID 785*	41		
29 May 04	**THE LETTER** *Island CIDX 861*	28		1
31 Jul 04	**YOU COME THROUGH** *Island CIDX 869*	41		
2 Oct 04	**SHAME** *Island CID 873*	45		

STEVE HARVEY UK singer

Date	Title	Peak Position	Weeks at No.1	Weeks in Top 40
28 May 83	**SOMETHING SPECIAL** *London LON 25*	46		
29 Oct 83	**TONIGHT** *London LON 36*	63		

HARVEY DANGER US group

Date	Title	Peak Position	Weeks at No.1	Weeks in Top 40
1 Aug 98	**FLAGPOLE SITTA** *Slash LASCD 64*	57		

GORDON HASKELL UK singer/guitarist

Date	Title	Peak Position	Weeks at No.1	Weeks in Top 40
29 Dec 01	**HOW WONDERFUL YOU ARE** *Flying Sparks TDBCDS 04* ○	2		4

LEE HASLAM UK producer

Date	Title	Peak Position	Weeks at No.1	Weeks in Top 40
14 Aug 04	**LIBERATE/HERE COMES THE PAIN** *Tidy Trax TIDYTWO135*	71		

DAVID HASSELHOFF US actor/singer

Date	Title	Peak Position	Weeks at No.1	Weeks in Top 40
13 Nov 93	**IF I COULD ONLY SAY GOODBYE** *Arista 74321172262*	35		1
14 Oct 06	**JUMP IN MY CAR** *Skintight CDHOFF1*	3		3

TONY HATCH UK orchestra leader

Date	Title	Peak Position	Weeks at No.1	Weeks in Top 40
4 Oct 62	**OUT OF THIS WORLD** *Pye 7N 15460*	50		

JULIANA HATFIELD US singer/guitarist

Date	Title	Peak Position	Weeks at No.1	Weeks in Top 40
11 Sep 93	**MY SISTER** *Mammoth YZ 767CD* JULIANA HATFIELD THREE	71		
18 Mar 95	**UNIVERSAL HEART-BEAT** *East West YZ 916CD*	65		

LALAH HATHAWAY US singer

Date	Title	Peak Position	Weeks at No.1	Weeks in Top 40
1 Sep 90	**HEAVEN KNOWS** *Virgin America VUS 28*	66		
2 Feb 91	**BABY DON'T CRY** *Virgin America VUS 35*	54		
27 Jul 91	**FAMILY AFFAIR** *10 TEN 369* B.E.F. FEATURING LALAH HATHAWAY	37		1

CHARLOTTE HATHERLEY UK singer

Date	Title	Peak Position	Weeks at No.1	Weeks in Top 40
21 Aug 04	**SUMMER** *Double Dragon DD2014CD*	31		1
5 Mar 05	**BASTARDO** *Double Dragon DD2019CD*	31		1

HATIRAS Canadian producer

Date	Title	Peak Position	Weeks at No.1	Weeks in Top 40
27 Jan 01	**SPACED INVADER** *Defected DFECT 25CDS* HATIRAS FEATURING SLARTA JOHN	14		2

HAVANA UK production group

Date	Title	Peak Position	Weeks at No.1	Weeks in Top 40
6 Mar 93	**ETHNIC PRAYER** *Limbo 007CD*	71		

HAVEN UK group

Date	Title	Peak Position	Weeks at No.1	Weeks in Top 40
22 Sep 01	**LET IT LIVE** *Radiate RDT 3*	72		
2 Feb 02	**SAY SOMETHING** *Radiate RDTX 4*	24		2
4 May 02	**TIL THE END** *Radiate RDTX 6*	28		1
27 Mar 04	**WOULDN'T CHANGE A THING** *Radiate RDTCD14*	57		

NIC HAVERSON UK singer

Date	Title	Peak Position	Weeks at No.1	Weeks in Top 40
30 Jan 93	**HEAD OVER HEELS** *Telstar CDHOH 1*	48		

CHESNEY HAWKES UK singer

Date	Title	Peak Position	Weeks at No.1	Weeks in Top 40
23 Feb 91	**THE ONE AND ONLY** *Chrysalis CHS 3627* ●	1	5	12
22 Jun 91	**I'M A MAN NOT A BOY** *Chrysalis CHS 3708*	27		3
28 Sep 91	**SECRETS OF THE HEART** *Chrysalis CHS 3681*	57		
29 May 93	**WHAT'S WRONG WITH THIS PICTURE** *Chrysalis CDCHS 3969*	63		
12 Jan 02	**STAY AWAY BABY JANE** *ARC DSART 13*	74		
4 Jun 05	**ANOTHER FINE MESS** *Right Track CHESCD001*	48		

SCREAMIN' JAY HAWKINS US singer

Date	Title	Peak Position	Weeks at No.1	Weeks in Top 40
3 Apr 93	**HEART ATTACK AND VINE** *Columbia 6591092*	42		

SOPHIE B. HAWKINS US singer

Date	Title	Peak Position	Weeks at No.1	Weeks in Top 40
4 Jul 92	**DAMN I WISH I WAS YOUR LOVER** *Columbia 6581077*	14		8
12 Sep 92	**CALIFORNIA HERE I COME** *Columbia 6583177*	53		
6 Feb 93	**I WANT YOU** *Columbia 6587772*	49		
13 Aug 94	**RIGHT BESIDE YOU** *Columbia 6606915*	13		10
26 Nov 94	**DON'T DON'T TELL ME NO** *Columbia 6610152*	36		2
11 Mar 95	**AS I LAY ME DOWN** *Columbia 6612125*	24		4

EDWIN HAWKINS SINGERS US group

Date	Title	Peak Position	Weeks at No.1	Weeks in Top 40
21 May 69	**OH HAPPY DAY** *Buddah 201 048* EDWIN HAWKINS SINGERS FEATURING DOROTHY COMBS MORRISON	2		11

KIRSTY HAWKSHAW UK singer

Date	Title	Peak Position	Weeks at No.1	Weeks in Top 40
24 Jun 00	**DREAMING** *Headspace HEDSCD 002* BT FEATURING KIRSTY HAWKSHAW	38		1
29 Sep 01	**URBAN TRAIN** *VC Recordings/Nebula VCRD 95* DJ TIESTO FEATURING KIRSTY HAWKSHAW	22		2
21 Sep 02	**STEALTH** *Distinctive Breaks DISNCD 90* WAY OUT WEST FEATURING KIRSTY HAWKSHAW	67		
23 Nov 02	**FINE DAY** *Mainline CDMAIN002*	62		
23 Oct 04	**JUST BE** *Nebula NEBCD062* TIESTO FEATURING KIRSTY HAWKSHAW	43		

HAWKWIND UK group

Date	Title	Peak Position	Weeks at No.1	Weeks in Top 40
1 Jul 72	**SILVER MACHINE** *United Artists UP 35381*	3		12
11 Aug 73	**URBAN GUERRILLA** *United Artists UP 35566*	39		1
21 Oct 78	**SILVER MACHINE** *United Artists UP 35381*	34		2
19 Jul 80	**SHOT DOWN IN THE NIGHT** *Bronze BRO 98*	59		
15 Jan 83	**SILVER MACHINE** *United Artists UP 35381*	67		

RICHARD HAWLEY UK singer/guitarist

Date	Title	Peak Position	Weeks at No.1	Weeks in Top 40
16 Sep 06	**HOTEL ROOM** *Mute CDMUTE379*	64		
18 Aug 07	**TONIGHT THE STREETS ARE OURS** *Mute CDMUTE382*	40		1

BILL HAYES US singer

Date	Title	Peak Position	Weeks at No.1	Weeks in Top 40
6 Jan 56	**BALLAD OF DAVY CROCKETT** *London HLA 8220* BILL HAYES WITH ARCHIE BLEYER'S ORCHESTRA ★	2		9

DARREN HAYES Australian singer

Date	Title	Peak Position	Weeks at No.1	Weeks in Top 40
30 Mar 02	**INSATIABLE** *Columbia 6723992*	8		11
20 Jul 02	**STRANGE RELATIONSHIP** *Columbia 6728685*	15		3
16 Nov 02	**I MISS YOU** *Columbia 6733315*	20		2
1 Feb 03	**CRUSH** *Columbia 6734905*	19		1
11 Sep 04	**POP!ULAR** *Columbia 6751112*	12		2
12 Nov 05	**SO BEAUTIFUL** *Columbia 82876739402*	15		2
18 Aug 07	**ON THE VERGE OF SOMETHING WONDERFUL** *Powdered Sugar CXPOWSUG2*	20		1
24 Nov 07	**ME MYSELF AND I** *Powdered Sugar CXPOWSUG3*	59		

GEMMA HAYES Irish singer

Date	Title	Peak Position	Weeks at No.1	Weeks in Top 40
25 May 02	**HANGING AROUND** *Source SOURCD 046*	62		
10 Aug 02	**LET A GOOD THING GO** *Source SOURCDX 051*	54		
18 Mar 06	**UNDERCOVER** *Source SOURDX119*	63		

PJ HARVEY

The daughter of bohemian parents who had a fondness for esoteric music – blues, jazz and 1960s pioneers such as Captain Beefheart and Jimi Hendrix – and raised on a sheep farm in rural Dorset, Polly Jean Harvey was perhaps destined to be an unusual performer and, as such, a unique and exhilarating contributor to the UK singles charts. Such early exposure to the sounds of the counter-culture led to a voracious passion for music from a young age. After playing in a series of short-lived bands during her teens, she formed her eponymous three-piece band in 1991 to showcase her burgeoning songwriting skills. Legend has it that at their debut show in a West Country skittle alley, the promoter begged the band to finish their performance early, as their dark-hearted music was driving paying customers away. Not quite the cold, silent stares of *American Werewolf In London* perhaps, but an auspicious start at least.

Just ten months later PJ Harvey – now a student at London's creatively fertile St Martin's art college – released her debut single 'Dress' on indie label Too Pure, which swiftly found favour with Radio 1 DJ John Peel. Combining blues, grunge and garage rock with a strong sense of introspection, it was the melodic second single and indie dance floor filler 'Sheela Na Gig' that introduced Harvey to a wider audience (despite only hauling itself to Number 69) and pushed her critically adored debut album *Dry* to Number 11 in the charts. A series of enigmatic press interviews and *Rolling Stone*'s claim that she was the world's best new female singer confirmed what her fans already knew: PJ Harvey was a welcome new and unique voice in the alternative rock scene. Island Records agreed and snapped her up after a frenzied bidding war.

Rid Of Me, 1993's Top 5 sophomore album, spawned two singles that further enhanced PJ Harvey's reputation: the raucous punk of '50 ft Queenie' (Number 27) and 'Man-Size' (Number 42) further set her apart from her contemporaries as an acutely focused and elemental writer (and added to her mystique when Steve Albini claimed she ate nothing but potatoes during the album's inception). Harvey remained the antithesis of the flash-in-the-pan singles artist, her live shows swelling her fan base considerably and her albums drawing the type of reviews that most bands could only dream of.

It is Harvey's uncompromising stance to her art and desire to never make the same record twice that has continued to win her respect – and why she is featured here, even though her track record in the singles charts is hardly littered with Top Five radio hits (in fact, she has never been inside the Top Twenty. Released in 1995, *To Bring You My Love* was a dark, impassioned and heady blues record that saw her make serious in-roads to the US market for the first time. It sold a million copies, with the singles 'C'mon Billy', 'Send His Love To Me' and stand-out track (and, given its dark nature, unlikely hit) 'Down By The Water' all registering favourably.

In the mid-1990s, Polly Harvey begin experimenting with her presentation, her appearance moving away from the black-clad young woman of old and growing more outlandish and theatrical. In 1996, a relationship with Nick Cave proved to be a creative match made in heaven when the pair duetted on Cave's murderous ballad 'Henry Lee'. By the release of her 1998 album, *Is This Desire?*, Harvey was one of the most successful artists of her era, a reputation that sustained her through the album's mixed reception, though the single 'A Perfect Day Elise' (Number 25) marked her highest chart placing to date. Harvey herself considered the album among her strongest work.

Written in Paris, New York and Dorset, 2000's *Stories From The City, Stories From The Sea* was another huge commercial success, with Radiohead's Thom Yorke featured on the track 'This Mess We're In'. A slow-burner, the album stayed in the charts for the next twelve months and won PJ Harvey the coveted Mercury Music Prize the following year – on the dark day of 11 September 2001, in fact, when she was staying in a hotel overlooking the Pentagon (for the record, she has also earned seven Brit nominations, five Grammy nods and two Mercury nominations).

Her self-produced and lo-fi seventh album *Uh Huh Her* didn't quite match the success of its predecessor – yet regardless of chart favour, Harvey toured extensively, including in this case a number of shows with Morrissey. She had also begun appearing in low-budget short films and garnered a reputation as a sculptor of some craft. Working with long-term collaborators Flood and John Parish once again, 2007's *White Chalk* heralded Harvey's most radical departure with a set of songs that were almost exclusively piano ballads. The singles were particularly evocative and occasionally harrowing: 'When Under Ether' was released as a download and seven-inch only, while 'The Piano' and 'The Devil' both followed.

It might seem odd to feature a performer widely recognised as 'an album artist' in a book about hit singles; however, it is the inclusion of singers such as PJ Harvey that make the list such an eclectic mix, such an essential staple of British culture. For every reality-show winner or supremely polished boy band, the charts need a raucous, unsettling artist like PJ Harvey. Both have their place.

As she approaches two decades of releasing music, PJ Harvey remains in the rare position of being an artist whose sales figures match the justified critical acclaim. Such success is a direct result of the artistic integrity and creative originality of this genuinely one-off artist.

Silver-selling ○ Gold-selling ● Platinum-selling ⊛ US No.1 ★

Peak Position / Weeks at No.1 / Weeks in Top 40

ISAAC HAYES US singer

Date	Title / Label	Peak Position	Weeks at No.1	Weeks in Top 40
4 Dec 71	**THEME FROM *SHAFT*** *Stax 2025 069* ★	4		12
3 Apr 76	**DISCO CONNECTION** *ABC 4100* ISAAC HAYES MOVEMENT	10		9
26 Dec 98	**CHOCOLATE SALTY BALLS (PS I LOVE YOU)** *Columbia 6667985* CHEF ⊛	1	1	11
30 Sep 00	**THEME FROM *SHAFT*** *LaFace 74321792582*	53		

HAYSI FANTAYZEE UK duo

Date	Title / Label	Peak Position	Weeks at No.1	Weeks in Top 40
24 Jul 82	**JOHN WAYNE IS BIG LEGGY** *Regard RG 100*	11		7
13 Nov 82	**HOLY JOE** *Regard RG 104*	51		
22 Jan 83	**SHINY SHINY** *Regard RG 106*	16		6
25 Jun 83	**SISTER FRICTION** *Regard RG 108*	62		

JUSTIN HAYWARD UK singer/guitarist

Date	Title / Label	Peak Position	Weeks at No.1	Weeks in Top 40
25 Oct 75	**BLUE GUITAR** *Threshold TH 21* JUSTIN HAYWARD & JOHN LODGE	8		7
8 Jul 78	**FOREVER AUTUMN** *CBS 6368* ○	5		11

LEON HAYWOOD US singer

Date	Title / Label	Peak Position	Weeks at No.1	Weeks in Top 40
15 Mar 80	**DON'T PUSH IT, DON'T FORCE IT** *20th Century TC 2443*	12		9

HAYWOODE UK singer

Date	Title / Label	Peak Position	Weeks at No.1	Weeks in Top 40
17 Sep 83	**A TIME LIKE THIS** *CBS A 3651*	48		
29 Sep 84	**I CAN'T LET YOU GO** *CBS A 4664*	63		
13 Apr 85	**ROSES** *CBS A 6069*	65		
5 Oct 85	**GETTING CLOSER** *CBS A 6582*	67		
21 Jun 86	**ROSES** *CBS A 7224*	11		8
13 Sep 86	**I CAN'T LET YOU GO** *CBS 6500767*	50		

OFRA HAZA Israeli singer

Date	Title / Label	Peak Position	Weeks at No.1	Weeks in Top 40
30 Apr 88	**IM NIN'ALU** *WEA YZ 190*	15		5
17 Jun 95	**MY LOVE IS FOR REAL** *Virgin VUSCD 91* PAULA ABDUL FEATURING OFRA HAZA	28		2
3 Apr 99	**BABYLON** *warner.esp WESP 006 CD1* BLACK DOG FEATURING OFRA HAZA	65		

HAZE US producer

Date	Title / Label	Peak Position	Weeks at No.1	Weeks in Top 40
18 Jan 03	**CHANGES** *Defected DFTD 059R* SANDY RIVERA FEATURING HAZE	48		
31 Jul 04	**DREAMS** *Defected DFTD 090CDS* KINGS OF TOMORROW FEATURING HAZE	69		
26 Feb 05	**THRU** *Defected DFTD099CDS* KINGS OF TOMORROW FEATURING HAZE	55		

HAZIZA Swedish production duo

Date	Title / Label	Peak Position	Weeks at No.1	Weeks in Top 40
28 Apr 01	**ONE MORE** *Tidy Trax TIDY 152T*	75		

LEE HAZLEWOOD US singer/producer

Date	Title / Label	Peak Position	Weeks at No.1	Weeks in Top 40
5 Jul 67	**YOU ONLY LIVE TWICE/JACKSON** *Reprise RS 20595* NANCY SINATRA/NANCY SINATRA & LEE HAZLEWOOD	11		14
8 Nov 67	**LADYBIRD** *Reprise RS 20629*	47		
21 Aug 71	**DID YOU EVER** *Reprise K 14093*	2		17

HAZZARDS US ukele duo

Date	Title / Label	Peak Position	Weeks at No.1	Weeks in Top 40
22 Nov 03	**GAY BOYFRIEND** *Better The Devil BTD3CD*	67		

MURRAY HEAD UK singer/actor

Date	Title / Label	Peak Position	Weeks at No.1	Weeks in Top 40
29 Jan 72	**SUPERSTAR** *MCA MMKS 5077*	47		
10 Nov 84	**ONE NIGHT IN BANGKOK** *RCA CHESS 1*	12		10

ROY HEAD US singer

Date	Title / Label	Peak Position	Weeks at No.1	Weeks in Top 40
4 Nov 65	**TREAT HER RIGHT** *Vocalion V-P 928*	30		4

HEAD AUTOMATICA UK production duo

Date	Title / Label	Peak Position	Weeks at No.1	Weeks in Top 40
12 Feb 05	**BEATING HEART BABY** *WEA W663CD*	44		

HEADBANGERS UK group

Date	Title / Label	Peak Position	Weeks at No.1	Weeks in Top 40
10 Oct 81	**STATUS ROCK** *Magnet MAG 206*	60		

HEADBOYS UK group

Date	Title / Label	Peak Position	Weeks at No.1	Weeks in Top 40
22 Sep 79	**THE SHAPE OF THINGS TO COME** *RSO 40*	45		

HEADS UK group

Date	Title / Label	Peak Position	Weeks at No.1	Weeks in Top 40
21 Jun 86	**AZTEC LIGHTNING (THEME FROM 'BBC WORLD CUP GRANDSTAND')** *BBC RESL 184*	45		

HEADS US/UK group

Date	Title / Label	Peak Position	Weeks at No.1	Weeks in Top 40
9 Nov 96	**DON'T TAKE MY KINDNESS FOR WEAKNESS** *Radioactive MCSTD 48024* HEADS WITH SHAUN RYDER	60		

HEADSWIM UK group

Date	Title / Label	Peak Position	Weeks at No.1	Weeks in Top 40
25 Feb 95	**CRAWL** *Epic 6612252*	64		
14 Feb 98	**TOURNIQUET** *Epic 6656442*	30		1
16 May 98	**BETTER MADE** *Epic 6658402*	42		

JEREMY HEALY & AMOS UK DJ and singer

Date	Title / Label	Peak Position	Weeks at No.1	Weeks in Top 40
12 Oct 96	**STAMP!** *Positiva CDTIV 65*	11		3
31 May 97	**ARGENTINA** *Positiva CDTIV 74*	30		1

IMOGEN HEAP UK singer

Date	Title / Label	Peak Position	Weeks at No.1	Weeks in Top 40
6 Mar 99	**BLANKET** *Talkin Loud TLDD 39* URBAN SPECIES FEATURING IMOGEN HEAP	56		
20 May 06	**GOODNIGHT AND GO** *Megaphonic/White 82876822842*	56		
28 Oct 06	**HEADLOCK** *Megaphonic MEGACD004*	74		

HEAR 'N AID Multinational charity ensemble

Date	Title / Label	Peak Position	Weeks at No.1	Weeks in Top 40
19 Apr 86	**STARS** *Vertigo HEAR 1*	26		4

HEAR'SAY UK group

Date	Title / Label	Peak Position	Weeks at No.1	Weeks in Top 40
24 Mar 01	**PURE AND SIMPLE** *Polydor 5870069* ⊛	1	3	14
7 Jul 01	**THE WAY TO YOUR LOVE** *Polydor 5871492*	1	1	7
8 Dec 01	**EVERYBODY** *Polydor 5705122*	4		6
24 Aug 02	**LOVIN' IS EASY** *Polydor 5708552*	6		3

HEART US group

Date	Title / Label	Peak Position	Weeks at No.1	Weeks in Top 40
29 Mar 86	**THESE DREAMS** *Capitol CL 394*	62		
13 Jun 87	**ALONE** *Capitol CL 448* ○ ★	3		10
19 Sep 87	**WHO WILL YOU RUN TO** *Capitol CL 457*	30		4
12 Dec 87	**THERE'S THE GIRL** *Capitol CL 473*	34		3
5 Mar 88	**NEVER/THESE DREAMS** *Capitol CL 482*	8		7
14 May 88	**WHAT ABOUT LOVE** *Capitol CL 487*	14		5
22 Oct 88	**NOTHIN' AT ALL** *Capitol CL 507*	38		1
24 Mar 90	**ALL I WANNA DO IS MAKE LOVE TO YOU** *Capitol CL 569*	8		12
28 Jul 90	**I DIDN'T WANT TO NEED YOU** *Capitol CL 580*	47		
17 Nov 90	**STRANDED** *Capitol CL 595*	60		
14 Sep 91	**YOU'RE THE VOICE** *Capitol CL 624*	56		
20 Nov 93	**WILL YOU BE THERE (IN THE MORNING)** *Capitol CDCLS 700*	19		3

HEARTBEAT UK group

Date	Title / Label	Peak Position	Weeks at No.1	Weeks in Top 40
24 Oct 87	**TEARS FROM HEAVEN** *Priority P 17*	32		2
23 Apr 88	**THE WINNER** *Priority P 19*	70		

HEARTBEAT COUNTRY UK singer

Date	Title / Label	Peak Position	Weeks at No.1	Weeks in Top 40
31 Dec 94	**HEARTBEAT** *MMM 01CD*	75		

HEARTISTS Italian production group

Date	Title / Label	Peak Position	Weeks at No.1	Weeks in Top 40
9 Aug 97	**BELO HORIZONTI** *VC Recordings VCRD 23*	42		
31 Jan 98	**BELO HORIZONTI (REMIX)** *VC Recordings VCRD 28*	40		1

HEARTLESS CREW UK group

Date	Title / Label	Peak Position	Weeks at No.1	Weeks in Top 40
25 May 02	**THE HEARTLESS CREW THEME** *East West HEART 02CD*	21		1
28 Jun 03	**WHY (LOOKING BACK)** *East West HEART 03CD*	50		

TED HEATH UK orchestra leader/trombonist

Date	Title / Label	Peak Position	Weeks at No.1	Weeks in Top 40
16 Jan 53	**VANESSA** *Decca F 9983*	11		1
3 Jul 53	**HOT TODDY** *Decca F 10093*	6		11
23 Oct 53	**DRAGNET** *Decca F 10176*	9		5
12 Feb 54	**SKIN DEEP** *Decca F 10246*	9		3
6 Jul 56	**THE FAITHFUL HUSSAR** *Decca F 10746*	18		9
14 Mar 58	**SWINGIN' SHEPHERD BLUES** *Decca F 11000*	3		14
11 Apr 58	**TEQUILA** *Decca F 11003*	21		6
4 Jul 58	**TOM HARK** *Decca F 11025*	24		2
5 Oct 61	**SUCU SUCU** *Decca F 11392*	36		2

HEATWAVE US/UK group

Date	Title / Label	Peak Position	Weeks at No.1	Weeks in Top 40
22 Jan 77	**BOOGIE NIGHTS** *GTO GT 77*	2		13
7 May 77	**TOO HOT TO HANDLE/SLIP YOUR DISC TO THIS** *GTO GT 91*	15		10
14 Jan 78	**THE GROOVE LINE** *GTO GT 115*	12		8
3 Jun 78	**MIND BLOWING DECISIONS** *GTO GT 226*	12		9
4 Nov 78	**ALWAYS AND FOREVER/MIND BLOWING DECISIONS (REMIX)** *GTO GT 236*	9		12
26 May 79	**RAZZLE DAZZLE** *GTO GT 248*	43		
17 Jan 81	**GANGSTER OF THE GROOVE** *GTO GT 285*	19		6
21 Mar 81	**JITTERBUGGIN'** *GTO GT 290*	34		3
1 Sep 90	**MIND BLOWING DECISIONS** *Brothers Organisation HW 1*	65		

HEAVEN 17 UK group

Date	Title / Label	Peak Position	Weeks at No.1	Weeks in Top 40
21 Mar 81	**(WE DON'T NEED THIS) FASCIST GROOVE THANG** *Virgin VS 400*	45		
5 Sep 81	**PLAY TO WIN** *Virgin VS 433*	46		
14 Nov 81	**PENTHOUSE AND PAVEMENT** *Virgin VS 455*	57		
30 Oct 82	**LET ME GO** *Virgin VS 532*	41		
16 Apr 83	**TEMPTATION** *Virgin VS 570*	2		10
25 Jun 83	**COME LIVE WITH ME** *Virgin VS 607*	5		10
10 Sep 83	**CRUSHED BY THE WHEELS OF INDUSTRY** *Virgin VS 628*	17		6
1 Sep 84	**SUNSET NOW** *Virgin VS 708*	24		4
27 Oct 84	**THIS IS MINE** *Virgin VS 722*	23		4
19 Jan 85	**...(AND THAT'S NO LIE)** *Virgin VS 740*	52		
17 Jan 87	**TROUBLE** *Virgin VS 920*	51		
21 Nov 92	**TEMPTATION (REMIX)** *Virgin VS 1446*	4		6
27 Feb 93	**(WE DON'T NEED THIS) FASCIST GROOVE THANG** *Virgin VSCDT 1451*	40		1
10 Apr 93	**PENTHOUSE AND PAVEMENT (REMIX)** *Virgin VSCDT 1457*	54		

HEAVENS CRY Dutch production duo

Date	Title / Label	Peak Position	Weeks at No.1	Weeks in Top 40
6 Oct 01	**TILL TEARS DO US PART** *Tidy Trax TIDY 158CD*	68		
19 Jan 02	**TILL TEARS DO US PART** *Tidy Trax TIDY 158CD*	71		

HEAVY D. & THE BOYZ US group

Date	Title / Label	Peak Position	Weeks at No.1	Weeks in Top 40
6 Dec 86	**MR BIG STUFF** *MCA 1106*	61		
15 Jul 89	**WE GOT OUR OWN THANG** *MCA 23942*	69		
6 Jul 91	**NOW THAT WE FOUND LOVE** *MCA 1550*	2		11
28 Sep 91	**IS IT GOOD TO YOU** *MCA MCS 1564*	46		
8 Oct 94	**THIS IS YOUR NIGHT** *MCA MCSTD 2010*	30		1

HEAVY PETTIN' UK group

Date	Title / Label	Peak Position	Weeks at No.1	Weeks in Top 40
17 Mar 84	**LOVE TIMES LOVE** *Polydor HEP 3*	69		

HEAVY STEREO UK group

Date	Title / Label	Peak Position	Weeks at No.1	Weeks in Top 40
22 Jul 95	**SLEEP FREAK** *Creation CRESCD 203*	46		
28 Oct 95	**SMILER** *Creation CRESCD 213*	46		
10 Feb 96	**CHINESE BURN** *Creation CRESCD 218*	45		
24 Aug 96	**MOUSE IN A HOLE** *Creation CRESCD 230*	53		

HEAVY WEATHER US singer

Date	Title / Label	Peak Position	Weeks at No.1	Weeks in Top 40
29 Jun 96	**LOVE CAN'T TURN AROUND** *Pukka CDPUKKA 6*	56		

BOBBY HEBB US singer

Date	Title / Label	Peak Position	Weeks at No.1	Weeks in Top 40
8 Sep 66	**SUNNY** *Philips BF 1503*	12		7
19 Aug 72	**LOVE LOVE LOVE** *Philips 6051 023*	32		2

SHARLENE HECTOR UK singer

Date	Title / Label	Peak Position	Weeks at No.1	Weeks in Top 40
17 Apr 04	**I WISH I KNEW HOW IT WOULD FEEL** *Radar RAD0006CD*	28		2

HED BOYS UK production duo

Date	Title / Label	Peak Position	Weeks at No.1	Weeks in Top 40
6 Aug 94	**GIRLS & BOYS** *Deconstruction 74321223322*	21		2
4 Nov 95	**GIRLS & BOYS (REMIX)** *Deconstruction 74321322032*	36		1

HEDGEHOPPERS ANONYMOUS UK group

Date	Title / Label	Peak Position	Weeks at No.1	Weeks in Top 40
30 Sep 65	**IT'S GOOD NEWS WEEK** *Decca F 12241*	5		9

HEFNER UK group

Date	Title / Label	Peak Position	Weeks at No.1	Weeks in Top 40
26 Aug 00	**GOOD FRUIT** *Too Pure PURE 108CDS*	50		
14 Oct 00	**THE GREEDY UGLY PEOPLE** *Too Pure PURE 111CDS*	64		
8 Sep 01	**ALAN BEAN** *Too Pure PURE 118CDS*	58		

NEAL HEFTI US orchestra leader

Date	Title / Label	Peak Position	Weeks at No.1	Weeks in Top 40
9 Apr 88	***BATMAN* THEME** *RCA PB 49571*	55		

DEN HEGARTY UK singer

Date	Title / Label	Peak Position	Weeks at No.1	Weeks in Top 40
31 Mar 79	**VOODOO VOODOO** *Magnet MAG 143*	73		

HEINZ German singer/bass player

Date	Title / Label	Peak Position	Weeks at No.1	Weeks in Top 40
8 Aug 63	**JUST LIKE EDDIE** *Decca F 11693*	5		15
28 Nov 63	**COUNTRY BOY** *Decca F 11768*	26		7
27 Feb 64	**YOU WERE THERE** *Decca F 11831*	26		6
15 Oct 64	**QUESTIONS I CAN'T ANSWER** *Columbia DB 7374*	39		1
18 Mar 65	**DIGGIN' MY POTATOES** *Columbia DB 7482* HEINZ & THE WILD BOYS	49		

HELICOPTER UK production duo

Date	Title / Label	Peak Position	Weeks at No.1	Weeks in Top 40
27 Aug 94	**ON YA WAY** *Helicopter TIG 007CD*	32		1
22 Jun 96	**ON YA WAY (REMIX)** *Systematic SYSCD 27*	37		1

HELIOCENTRIC WORLD UK group

Date	Title / Label	Peak Position	Weeks at No.1	Weeks in Top 40
14 Jan 95	**WHERE'S YOUR LOVE BEEN** *Talkin Loud TLKCD 51*	71		

HELIOTROPIC UK group

Date	Title / Label	Peak Position	Weeks at No.1	Weeks in Top 40
16 Oct 99	**ALIVE** *Multiply CDMULTY 52* HELIOTROPIC FEATURING VERNA V	33		1

HELL IS FOR HEROES UK group

Date	Title / Label	Peak Position	Weeks at No.1	Weeks in Top 40
9 Feb 02	**YOU DROVE ME TO IT** *Wishakismo CDWISH 003*	63		
17 Aug 02	**I CAN CLIMB MOUNTAINS** *Chrysalis CDCHS 5143*	41		
2 Nov 02	**NIGHT VISION** *Chrysalis CDCHSS 5147*	38		1
1 Feb 03	**YOU DROVE ME TO IT** *EMI CDCHSS 5149*	28		1
17 May 03	**RETREAT** *EMI CDEMS 619*	39		1
28 Aug 04	**ONE OF US** *Captains Of Industry CAPT008*	71		
27 Nov 04	**KAMICHI** *Factotum TUM001CD*	72		
12 Mar 05	**MODELS FOR THE PROGRAMME** *Factotum TUM002CD2*	56		

HELLER & FARLEY PROJECT UK duo

Date	Title / Label	Peak Position	Weeks at No.1	Weeks in Top 40
24 Feb 96	**ULTRA FLAVA** *AM:PM 5814372*	22		1
28 Dec 96	**ULTRA FLAVA (REMIX)** *AM:PM 5820551*	32		1
15 May 99	**BIG LOVE** *Essential Recordings ESCD 4* PETE HELLER'S BIG LOVE	12		4

Silver-selling · Gold-selling · Platinum-selling · US No.1 ★ · Peak Position · Weeks at No.1 · Weeks in Top 40

HELLO UK group

Date	Title / Label	Peak Position	Weeks at No.1	Weeks in Top 40
9 Nov 74	**TELL HIM** *Bell 1377* (Silver)	6		10
18 Oct 75	**NEW YORK GROOVE** *Bell 1438*	9		8
12 May 07	**HERE (IN YOUR ARMS)** *Drive Thru 88697098462*	4		14

HELLOWEEN German group

Date	Title / Label	Peak Position	Weeks at No.1	Weeks in Top 40
27 Aug 88	**DR STEIN** *Noise International 7HELLO 1*	57		
12 Nov 88	**I WANT OUT** *Noise International 7HELLO 2*	69		
2 Mar 91	**KIDS OF THE CENTURY** *EMI EM 178*	56		

BOBBY HELMS US singer

Date	Title / Label	Peak Position	Weeks at No.1	Weeks in Top 40
29 Nov 57	**MY SPECIAL ANGEL** *Brunswick 05271* BOBBY HELMS WITH THE ANITA KERR SINGERS	22		3
21 Feb 58	**NO OTHER BABY** *Brunswick 05730*	30		1
1 Aug 58	**JACQUELINE** *Brunswick 05748* BOBBY HELMS WITH THE ANITA KERR SINGERS	20		3

JIMMY HELMS US singer

Date	Title / Label	Peak Position	Weeks at No.1	Weeks in Top 40
24 Feb 73	**GONNA MAKE YOU AN OFFER YOU CAN'T REFUSE** *Cube BUG 27*	8		8

HELTAH SKELTAH US group

Date	Title / Label	Peak Position	Weeks at No.1	Weeks in Top 40
1 Jun 96	**BLAH** *Priority PTYCD 117* HELTAH SKELTAH & ORIGINOO GUNN CLAPPAZ AS THE FABULOUS FIVE	60		

AINSLIE HENDERSON UK singer

Date	Title / Label	Peak Position	Weeks at No.1	Weeks in Top 40
8 Mar 03	**KEEP ME A SECRET** *Mercury 0779812*	5		3

EDDIE HENDERSON US trumpet player

Date	Title / Label	Peak Position	Weeks at No.1	Weeks in Top 40
28 Oct 78	**PRANCE ON** *Capitol CL 16015*	44		

JOE 'MR PIANO' HENDERSON UK pianist

Date	Title / Label	Peak Position	Weeks at No.1	Weeks in Top 40
3 Jun 55	**SING IT WITH JOE** *Polygon P 1167*	14		4
2 Sep 55	**SING IT AGAIN WITH JOE** *Polygon P 1184*	18		3
25 Jul 58	**TRUDIE** *Pye Nixa N 15147*	14		14
23 Oct 59	**TREBLE CHANCE** *Pye 7N 15224*	28		1
24 Mar 60	**OOH! LA! LA!** *Pye 7N 15257*	44		

BILLY HENDRIX German producer

Date	Title / Label	Peak Position	Weeks at No.1	Weeks in Top 40
12 Sep 98	**THE BODY SHINE (EP)** *Hooj Choons HOOJ 65CD*	55		

JIMI HENDRIX US singer/guitarist

Date	Title / Label	Peak Position	Weeks at No.1	Weeks in Top 40
29 Dec 66	**HEY JOE** *Polydor 56 139*	6		8
23 Mar 67	**PURPLE HAZE** *Track 604 001* JIMI HENDRIX EXPERIENCE	3		12
11 May 67	**THE WIND CRIES MARY** *Track 604 004* JIMI HENDRIX EXPERIENCE	6		9
30 Aug 67	**BURNING OF THE MIDNIGHT LAMP** *Track 604 007* JIMI HENDRIX EXPERIENCE	18		7
23 Oct 68	**ALL ALONG THE WATCHTOWER** *Track 604 025* JIMI HENDRIX EXPERIENCE	5		9
16 Apr 69	**CROSSTOWN TRAFFIC** *Track 604 029* JIMI HENDRIX EXPERIENCE	37		2
7 Nov 70	**VOODOO CHILE** *Track 2095 001* JIMI HENDRIX EXPERIENCE	1	1	11
30 Oct 71	**GYPSY EYES/REMEMBER** *Track 2094 010* JIMI HENDRIX EXPERIENCE	35		2
12 Feb 72	**JOHNNY B. GOODE** *Track 2001 277*	35		2
21 Apr 90	**CROSSTOWN TRAFFIC** *Polydor PO 71*	61		
20 Oct 90	**ALL ALONG THE WATCHTOWER (EP)** *Polydor PO 100*	52		

NONA HENDRYX US singer

Date	Title / Label	Peak Position	Weeks at No.1	Weeks in Top 40
16 May 87	**WHY SHOULD I CRY?** *EMI America EA 234*	60		

DON HENLEY US singer

Date	Title / Label	Peak Position	Weeks at No.1	Weeks in Top 40
12 Feb 83	**DIRTY LAUNDRY** *Asylum E 9894*	59		
9 Feb 85	**THE BOYS OF SUMMER** *Geffen A 4945*	12		7
27 Jul 89	**THE END OF THE INNOCENCE** *Geffen GEF 57*	48		
3 Oct 92	**SOMETIMES LOVE JUST AIN'T ENOUGH** *MCA MCS 1692* PATTY SMYTH WITH DON HENLEY	22		5
18 Jul 98	**THE BOYS OF SUMMER** *Geffen GFSTD 22350*	12		3

CASSIUS HENRY UK singer

Date	Title / Label	Peak Position	Weeks at No.1	Weeks in Top 40
30 Mar 02	**BROKE** *Blacklist 0130265 ERE*	31		1
3 Jul 04	**THE ONE** *Universal MCSTD 40334* CASSIUS HENRY FEATURING FREEWAY	56		

CLARENCE 'FROGMAN' HENRY US singer

Date	Title / Label	Peak Position	Weeks at No.1	Weeks in Top 40
4 May 61	**(I DON'T KNOW WHY) BUT I DO** *Pye International 7N 25078*	3		19
13 Jul 61	**YOU ALWAYS HURT THE ONE YOU LOVE** *Pye International 7N 25089*	6		11
21 Sep 61	**LONELY STREET/WHY CAN'T YOU** *Pye International 7N 25108*	42		
17 Jul 93	**(I DON'T KNOW WHY) BUT I DO** *MCA MCSTD 1797*	65		

PAUL HENRY UK actor

Date	Title / Label	Peak Position	Weeks at No.1	Weeks in Top 40
14 Jan 78	**BENNY'S THEME** *Pye 7N 46027* PAUL HENRY & MAYSON GLEN ORCHESTRA	39		1

PAULINE HENRY UK singer

Date	Title / Label	Peak Position	Weeks at No.1	Weeks in Top 40
18 Sep 93	**TOO MANY PEOPLE** *Sony S2 6595942*	38		1
6 Nov 93	**FEEL LIKE MAKING LOVE** *Sony S2 6597972*	12		6
29 Jan 94	**CAN'T TAKE YOUR LOVE** *Sony S2 6599902*	30		2
21 May 94	**WATCH THE MIRACLE START** *Sony S2 6602772*	54		
30 Sep 95	**SUGAR FREE** *Sony S2 6624362*	57		
23 Dec 95	**LOVE HANGOVER** *Sony S2 6626132*	37		1
24 Feb 96	**NEVER KNEW LOVE LIKE THIS** *Sony S2 6629382* PAULINE HENRY FEATURING WAYNE MARSHALL	40		1
1 Jun 96	**HAPPY** *Sony S2 6630692*	46		

PIERRE HENRY French instrumentalist

Date	Title / Label	Peak Position	Weeks at No.1	Weeks in Top 40
4 Oct 97	**PSYCHE ROCK** *Hi-Life 4620312*	58		

HEPBURN UK group

Date	Title / Label	Peak Position	Weeks at No.1	Weeks in Top 40
29 May 99	**I QUIT** *Columbia 6674012*	8		5
28 Aug 99	**BUGS** *Columbia 6677385*	14		2
19 Feb 00	**DEEP DEEP DOWN** *Columbia 6683382*	16		2

HERCULES & LOVE AFFAIR US group

Date	Title / Label	Peak Position	Weeks at No.1	Weeks in Top 40
15 Mar 08	**BLIND** *DFA/EMI DFAEMI2192CD*	40		1

HERD UK production duo

Date	Title / Label	Peak Position	Weeks at No.1	Weeks in Top 40
13 Sep 67	**FROM THE UNDERWORLD** *Fontana TF 856*	6		12
20 Dec 67	**PARADISE LOST** *Fontana TF 887*	15		7
10 Apr 68	**I DON'T WANT OUR LOVING TO DIE** *Fontana TF 925*	5		12
17 Dec 05	**I JUST CAN'T GET ENOUGH** *All Around The World CDGLOBE473* HERD & FITZ FEATURING ABIGAIL BAILEY	11		6

HERMAN'S HERMITS UK group

Date	Title / Label	Peak Position	Weeks at No.1	Weeks in Top 40
20 Aug 64	**I'M INTO SOMETHING GOOD** *Columbia DB 7338*	1	2	14
19 Nov 64	**SHOW ME GIRL** *Columbia DB 7408*	19		8
18 Feb 65	**SILHOUETTES** *Columbia DB 7475*	3		10
29 Apr 65	**WONDERFUL WORLD** *Columbia DB 7546*	7		8
2 Sep 65	**JUST A LITTLE BIT BETTER** *Columbia DB 7670*	15		9
23 Dec 65	**A MUST TO AVOID** *Columbia DB 7791*	6		10
24 Mar 66	**YOU WON'T BE LEAVING** *Columbia DB 7861*	20		7
23 Jun 66	**THIS DOOR SWINGS BOTH WAYS** *Columbia DB 7947*	18		6
6 Oct 66	**NO MILK TODAY** *Columbia DB 8012*	7		10
1 Dec 66	**EAST WEST** *Columbia DB 8076*	33		3
9 Feb 67	**THERE'S A KIND OF HUSH** *Columbia DB 8123*	7		10
17 Jan 68	**I CAN TAKE OR LEAVE YOUR LOVING** *Columbia DB 8327*	11		9
1 May 68	**SLEEPY JOE** *Columbia DB 8404*	12		9
17 Jul 68	**SUNSHINE GIRL** *Columbia DB 8446*	8		12
18 Dec 68	**SOMETHING'S HAPPENING** *Columbia DB 8504*	6		13
23 Apr 69	**MY SENTIMENTAL FRIEND** *Columbia DB 8563*	2		11

Date	Title / Label	Peak Position	Weeks at No.1	Weeks in Top 40
8 Nov 69	**HERE COMES THE STAR** *Columbia DB 8626*	33		4
7 Feb 70	**YEARS MAY COME, YEARS MAY GO** *Columbia DB 8556*	7		11
23 May 70	**BET YER LIFE I DO** *RAK 102*	22		10
14 Nov 70	**LADY BARBARA** *RAK 106* PETER NOONE & HERMAN'S HERMITS	13		9

HERMES HOUSE BAND Dutch group

Date	Title / Label	Peak Position	Weeks at No.1	Weeks in Top 40
15 Dec 01	**COUNTRY ROADS** *Liberty CDHHB 001*	7		10
13 Apr 02	**QUE SERA SERA** *EMI CDHHB 002*	53		
28 Dec 02	**LIVE IS LIFE** *Liberty CDLIVE001* HERMES HOUSE BAND & DJ OTZI	50		

HERNANDEZ UK singer

Date	Title / Label	Peak Position	Weeks at No.1	Weeks in Top 40
15 Apr 89	**ALL MY LOVE** *Epic HER 1*	58		

MARCOS HERNANDEZ US singer

Date	Title / Label	Peak Position	Weeks at No.1	Weeks in Top 40
25 Feb 06	**IF YOU WERE MINE** *TVT TVTUKCD0019*	41		

PATRICK HERNANDEZ French singer

Date	Title / Label	Peak Position	Weeks at No.1	Weeks in Top 40
16 Jun 79	**BORN TO BE ALIVE** *Gem 4* ○	10		9

HERREYS Swedish group

Date	Title / Label	Peak Position	Weeks at No.1	Weeks in Top 40
26 May 84	**DIGGI LOO-DIGGI LEY** *Panther PAN 5*	46		

KRISTIN HERSH US singer/guitarist

Date	Title / Label	Peak Position	Weeks at No.1	Weeks in Top 40
22 Jan 94	**YOUR GHOST** *4AD BAD 4001CD*	45		
16 Apr 94	**STRINGS** *4AD BAD 4006CD*	60		

NICK HEYWARD UK singer

Date	Title / Label	Peak Position	Weeks at No.1	Weeks in Top 40
19 Mar 83	**WHISTLE DOWN THE WIND** *Arista HEY 1*	13		6
4 Jun 83	**TAKE THAT SITUATION** *Arista HEY 2*	11		6
24 Sep 83	**BLUE HAT FOR A BLUE DAY** *Arista HEY 3*	14		6
3 Dec 83	**ON A SUNDAY** *Arista HEY 4*	52		
2 Jun 84	**LOVE ALL DAY** *Arista HEY 5*	31		4
3 Nov 84	**WARNING SIGN** *Arista HEY 6*	25		3
8 Jun 85	**LAURA** *Arista HEY 8*	45		
10 May 86	**OVER THE WEEKEND** *Arista HEY 9*	43		
10 Sep 88	**YOU'RE MY WORLD** *Warner Brothers W 7758*	67		
21 Aug 93	**KITE** *Epic 6594882*	44		
16 Oct 93	**HE DOESN'T LOVE YOU LIKE I DO** *Epic 6597282*	58		
30 Sep 95	**THE WORLD** *Epic 6623845*	47		
13 Jan 96	**ROLLERBLADE** *Epic 6627915*	37		1

HHC UK production duo

Date	Title / Label	Peak Position	Weeks at No.1	Weeks in Top 40
19 Apr 97	**WE'RE NOT ALONE** *Perfecto PERF 138CD*	44		

HI-FIVE US group

Date	Title / Label	Peak Position	Weeks at No.1	Weeks in Top 40
1 Jun 91	**I LIKE THE WAY (THE KISSING GAME)** *Jive 271* ★	43		
24 Oct 92	**SHE'S PLAYING HARD TO GET** *Jive 316*	55		

HI-GATE UK group

Date	Title / Label	Peak Position	Weeks at No.1	Weeks in Top 40
29 Jan 00	**PITCHIN' (IN EVERY DIRECTION)** *Incentive CENT 3CD*	6		4
26 Aug 00	**I CAN HEAR VOICES/CANED AND UNABLE** *Incentive CENT 9CDS*	12		3
7 Apr 01	**GONNA WORK IT OUT** *Incentive CENT 20CDS*	25		1

HI GLOSS US group

Date	Title / Label	Peak Position	Weeks at No.1	Weeks in Top 40
8 Aug 81	**YOU'LL NEVER KNOW** *Epic EPC A 1387*	12		9

HI-LUX UK production duo

Date	Title / Label	Peak Position	Weeks at No.1	Weeks in Top 40
18 Feb 95	**FEEL IT** *Cheeky CHEKCD 006*	41		
2 Sep 95	**NEVER FELT THIS WAY/FEEL IT** *Champion CHAMPCD 319*	58		

HI POWER German group

Date	Title / Label	Peak Position	Weeks at No.1	Weeks in Top 40
1 Sep 90	**CULT OF SNAP/SIMBA GROOVE** *Rumour RUMAT 34*	73		

HI-TACK Dutch production duo

Date	Title / Label	Peak Position	Weeks at No.1	Weeks in Top 40
28 Jan 06	**SAY SAY SAY (WAITING 4 U)** *Gusto CDGUS26*	4		9
22 Sep 07	**LET'S DANCE** *Gusto CDGUS34*	38		1

HI-TEK US producer

Date	Title / Label	Peak Position	Weeks at No.1	Weeks in Top 40
20 Oct 01	**ROUND & ROUND** *Rawkus RWK 3432* HI-TEK FEATURING JONELL	73		

HI-TEK 3 Belgian group

Date	Title / Label	Peak Position	Weeks at No.1	Weeks in Top 40
3 Feb 90	**SPIN THAT WHEEL** *Brothers Organisation BORG 1* HI-TEK 3 FEATURING YA KID K	69		
29 Sep 90	**SPIN THAT WHEEL (TURTLES GET REAL)** *Brothers Organisation BORG 16* HI-TEK 3 FEATURING YA KID K	15		6

HI TENSION UK group

Date	Title / Label	Peak Position	Weeks at No.1	Weeks in Top 40
6 May 78	**HI TENSION** *Island WIP 6422*	13		8
12 Aug 78	**BRITISH HUSTLE/PEACE ON EARTH** *Island WIP 6446*	8		8

AL HIBBLER US singer

Date	Title / Label	Peak Position	Weeks at No.1	Weeks in Top 40
13 May 55	**UNCHAINED MELODY** *Brunswick 05420*	2		17

HINDA HICKS UK singer

Date	Title / Label	Peak Position	Weeks at No.1	Weeks in Top 40
7 Mar 98	**IF YOU WANT ME** *Island CID 689*	25		1
16 May 98	**YOU THINK YOU OWN ME** *Island CID 700*	19		3
15 Aug 98	**I WANNA BE YOUR LADY** *Island CID 709*	14		3
24 Oct 98	**TRULY** *Island CID 721*	31		1
14 Oct 00	**MY REMEDY** *Island CID 765*	61		

HIDDEN CAMERAS Canadian group

Date	Title / Label	Peak Position	Weeks at No.1	Weeks in Top 40
14 Jun 03	**A MIRACLE** *Rough Trade RTRADESCD 105*	70		

BERTIE HIGGINS US singer

Date	Title / Label	Peak Position	Weeks at No.1	Weeks in Top 40
5 Jun 82	**KEY LARGO** *Epic EPC A 2168*	60		

HIGH UK group

Date	Title / Label	Peak Position	Weeks at No.1	Weeks in Top 40
25 Aug 90	**UP AND DOWN** *London LON 272*	53		
27 Oct 90	**TAKE YOUR TIME** *London LON 280*	56		
12 Jan 91	**BOX SET GO** *London LONG 286*	28		2
6 Apr 91	**MORE...** *London LON 297*	67		

HIGH CONTRAST UK producer

Date	Title / Label	Peak Position	Weeks at No.1	Weeks in Top 40
1 Jun 02	**GLOBAL LOVE** *Hospital NHS 44CD*	68		
9 Aug 03	**BASEMENT TRACK** *Hospital NHS 60*	65		
26 Jun 04	**TWILIGHTS LAST GLEAMING/MADE IT LAST** *Hospital NHS 73*	74		
18 Sep 04	**RACING GREEN** *Hospital NHS 76*	73		

HIGH FIDELITY UK group

Date	Title / Label	Peak Position	Weeks at No.1	Weeks in Top 40
25 Jul 98	**LUV DUP** *Plastique FAKE 03CDS*	70		

HIGH NUMBERS UK group

Date	Title / Label	Peak Position	Weeks at No.1	Weeks in Top 40
5 Apr 80	**I'M THE FACE** *Back Door DOOR 4*	49		

HIGH SOCIETY UK group

Date	Title / Label	Peak Position	Weeks at No.1	Weeks in Top 40
15 Nov 80	**I NEVER GO OUT IN THE RAIN** *Eagle ERS 002*	53		

HIGHLY LIKELY UK group

Date	Title / Label	Peak Position	Weeks at No.1	Weeks in Top 40
21 Apr 73	**WHATEVER HAPPENED TO YOU (*LIKELY LADS* THEME)** *BBC RESL 10*	35		2

Silver-selling ● Gold-selling ● Platinum-selling ⊛ US No.1 ★ | Peak Position | Weeks at No.1 | Weeks in Top 40

HIGHWAYMEN US group

Date	Title / Label	Peak Position	Weeks at No.1	Weeks in Top 40
7 Sep 61	**MICHAEL** *HMV POP 910* ★	1	1	12
7 Dec 61	**GYPSY ROVER** *HMV POP 948*	41		

HIJACK UK rap group

Date	Title / Label	Peak Position	Weeks at No.1	Weeks in Top 40
6 Jan 90	**THE BADMAN IS ROBBIN'** *Rhyme Syndicate 6555177*	56		

BENNY HILL UK comedian

Date	Title / Label	Peak Position	Weeks at No.1	Weeks in Top 40
16 Feb 61	**GATHER IN THE MUSHROOMS** *Pye 7N 15327*	12		7
1 Jun 61	**TRANSISTOR RADIO** *Pye 7N 15359*	24		5
16 May 63	**HARVEST OF LOVE** *Pye 7N 15520*	20		6
13 Nov 71	**ERNIE (THE FASTEST MILKMAN IN THE WEST)** *Columbia DB 8833*	1	4	15
30 May 92	**ERNIE (THE FASTEST MILKMAN IN THE WEST)** *EMI ERN 1*	29		2

CHRIS HILL UK DJ

Date	Title / Label	Peak Position	Weeks at No.1	Weeks in Top 40
6 Dec 75	**RENTA SANTA** *Philips 6006 491*	10		7
4 Dec 76	**BIONIC SANTA** *Philips 6006 551*	10		6

DAN HILL Canadian singer

Date	Title / Label	Peak Position	Weeks at No.1	Weeks in Top 40
18 Feb 78	**SOMETIMES WHEN WE TOUCH** *20th Century BTC 2355*	13		10

FAITH HILL US singer

Date	Title / Label	Peak Position	Weeks at No.1	Weeks in Top 40
14 Nov 98	**THIS KISS** *Warner Brothers W 463CD*	13		6
17 Apr 99	**LET ME LET GO** *Warner Brothers W 473CD*	72		
20 May 00	**BREATHE** *WEA W 520CDX*	33		1
21 Apr 01	**THE WAY YOU LOVE ME** *WEA W 541CD1*	15		4
30 Jun 01	**THERE YOU'LL BE** *Warner Brothers W 563CD*	3		10
13 Oct 01	**BREATHE (REMIX)** *Warner Brothers W 572CD*	36		1
26 Oct 02	**CRY** *Warner Brothers W 593CD*	25		1

LAURYN HILL US singer

Date	Title / Label	Peak Position	Weeks at No.1	Weeks in Top 40
6 Sep 97	**THE SWEETEST THING** *Columbia 6649785* REFUGEE ALLSTARS FEATURING LAURYN HILL	18		2
27 Dec 97	**ALL MY TIME** *One World Entertainment OWECD 2* PAID + LIVE FEATURING LAURYN HILL	57		
3 Oct 98	**DOO WOP (THAT THING)** *Ruffhouse 6665152* ● ★	3		5
27 Feb 99	**EX-FACTOR** *Columbia/Ruffhouse 6669452*	4		4
10 Jul 99	**EVERYTHING IS EVERYTHING** *Columbia/Ruffhouse 6675745*	19		3
11 Dec 99	**TURN YOUR LIGHTS DOWN LOW** *Columbia 6684362* BOB MARLEY FEATURING LAURYN HILL	15		5

LONNIE HILL US singer

Date	Title / Label	Peak Position	Weeks at No.1	Weeks in Top 40
22 Mar 86	**GALVESTON BAY** *10 TEN 111*	51		

RONI HILL US singer

Date	Title / Label	Peak Position	Weeks at No.1	Weeks in Top 40
7 May 77	**YOU KEEP ME HANGIN' ON – STOP IN THE NAME OF LOVE (MEDLEY)** *Creole CR 138*	36		1

VINCE HILL UK singer

Date	Title / Label	Peak Position	Weeks at No.1	Weeks in Top 40
7 Jun 62	**THE RIVER'S RUN DRY** *Piccadilly 7N 35043*	41		
6 Jan 66	**TAKE ME TO YOUR HEART AGAIN** *Columbia DB 7781*	13		7
17 Mar 66	**HEARTACHES** *Columbia DB 7852*	28		4
2 Jun 66	**MERCI CHERI** *Columbia DB 7924*	36		1
9 Feb 67	**EDELWEISS** *Columbia DB 8127*	2		15
11 May 67	**ROSES OF PICARDY** *Columbia DB 8185*	13		9
27 Sep 67	**LOVE LETTERS IN THE SAND** *Columbia DB 8268*	23		6
26 Jun 68	**IMPORTANCE OF YOUR LOVE** *Columbia DB 8414*	32		5
12 Feb 69	**DOESN'T ANYBODY KNOW MY NAME?** *Columbia DB 8515*	50		
25 Oct 69	**LITTLE BLUE BIRD** *Columbia DB 8616*	42		
25 Sep 71	**LOOK AROUND (AND YOU'LL FIND ME THERE)** *Columbia DB 8804*	12		13

HILLMAN MINX UK/French group

Date	Title / Label	Peak Position	Weeks at No.1	Weeks in Top 40
5 Sep 98	**I'VE HAD ENOUGH** *Mercury MERCD 509*	72		

HILLTOPPERS US group

Date	Title / Label	Peak Position	Weeks at No.1	Weeks in Top 40
27 Jan 56	**ONLY YOU** *London HLD 8221*	3		23
14 Sep 56	**TRYIN'** *London HLD 8298*	30		1
5 Apr 57	**MARIANNE** *London HLD 8381*	20		6

KERI HILSON US singer

Date	Title / Label	Peak Position	Weeks at No.1	Weeks in Top 40
7 Jul 07	**THE WAY I ARE** *Interscope 1742316* TIMBALAND FEATURING DOE & KERI HILSON	1	2	28
16 Feb 08	**SCREAM** *Interscope 1764136* TIMBALAND FEATURING KERI HILSON & NICOLE SCHERZINGER	12		7

PARIS HILTON US singer

Date	Title / Label	Peak Position	Weeks at No.1	Weeks in Top 40
5 Aug 06	**STARS ARE BLIND** *Warner Brothers W723CD1*	5		7
18 Nov 06	**NOTHING IN THIS WORLD** *Warner Brothers W746CD1*	55		

RONNIE HILTON UK singer

Date	Title / Label	Peak Position	Weeks at No.1	Weeks in Top 40
26 Nov 54	**I STILL BELIEVE** *HMV B 10785*	3		14
10 Dec 54	**VENI VIDI VICI** *HMV B 10785*	12		8
11 Mar 55	**A BLOSSOM FELL** *HMV B 10808*	10		5
26 Aug 55	**STARS SHINE IN YOUR EYES** *HMV B 10901*	13		7
11 Nov 55	**YELLOW ROSE OF TEXAS** *HMV B 10924*	15		2
10 Feb 56	**YOUNG AND FOOLISH** *HMV POP 154*	17		3
20 Apr 56	**NO OTHER LOVE** *HMV POP 198*	1	6	14
29 Jun 56	**WHO ARE WE** *HMV POP 221*	6		12
21 Sep 56	**WOMAN IN LOVE** *HMV POP 248*	30		1
9 Nov 56	**TWO DIFFERENT WORLDS** *HMV POP 274*	13		13
24 May 57	**AROUND THE WORLD** *HMV POP 338*	4		18
2 Aug 57	**WONDERFUL WONDERFUL** *HMV POP 364*	27		2
21 Feb 58	**MAGIC MOMENTS** *HMV POP 446*	22		2
18 Apr 58	**I MAY NEVER PASS THIS WAY AGAIN** *HMV POP 468* RONNIE HILTON WITH THE MICHAEL SAMMES SINGERS	27		3
9 Jan 59	**THE WORLD OUTSIDE** *HMV POP 559* RONNIE HILTON WITH THE MICHAEL SAMMES SINGERS	18		6
21 Aug 59	**THE WONDER OF YOU** *HMV POP 638*	22		3
21 May 64	**DON'T LET THE RAIN COME DOWN** *HMV POP 1291*	21		8
11 Feb 65	**A WINDMILL IN OLD AMSTERDAM** *HMV POP 1378*	23		12

H.I.M. Finnish group

Date	Title / Label	Peak Position	Weeks at No.1	Weeks in Top 40
17 May 03	**BURIED ALIVE BY LOVE** *RCA 82876523182*	30		1
20 Sep 03	**THE SACREMENT** *RCA 82876558892*	23		1
24 Jan 04	**THE FUNERAL OF HEARTS** *RCA 82876585792*	15		3
8 May 04	**SOLITARY MAN** *RCA 82876610652*	9		2
24 Sep 05	**WINGS OF A BUTTERFLY** *Sire W686CD1*	10		2
6 May 06	**KILLING LONELINESS** *Sire W699CD2*	26		1
22 Sep 07	**THE KISS OF DAWN** *Sire W779CD*	59		

HINDSIGHT UK group

Date	Title / Label	Peak Position	Weeks at No.1	Weeks in Top 40
5 Sep 87	**LOWDOWN** *Circa YR 5*	62		

DENI HINES Australian singer

Date	Title / Label	Peak Position	Weeks at No.1	Weeks in Top 40
14 Jun 97	**IT'S ALRIGHT** *Mushroom D 1593*	35		1
20 Sep 97	**I LIKE THE WAY** *Mushroom MUSH 7CDX*	37		1
28 Feb 98	**DELICIOUS** *Mushroom MUSH 20CD* DENI HINES FEATURING DON-E	52		
23 May 98	**JOY** *Mushroom MUSH 30CDS*	47		

HIPSWAY UK group

Date	Title / Label	Peak Position	Weeks at No.1	Weeks in Top 40
13 Jul 85	**THE BROKEN YEARS** *Mercury MER 193*	72		
14 Sep 85	**ASK THE LORD** *Mercury MER 195*	72		
22 Feb 86	**THE HONEYTHIEF** *Mercury MER 212*	17		5
10 May 86	**ASK THE LORD** *Mercury LORD 1*	50		
20 Sep 86	**LONG WHITE CAR** *Mercury MER 230*	55		
1 Apr 89	**YOUR LOVE** *Mercury MER 279*	66		

HISS US group

Date	Title / Label	Peak Position	Weeks at No.1	Weeks in Top 40
1 Mar 03	**TRIUMPH** *Polydor 0657782*	53		
9 Aug 03	**CLEVER KICKS** *Polydor 9809462*	49		
15 Nov 03	**BACK ON THE RADIO** *Polydor 9813415*	65		

HISTORY UK production duo

Date	Title / Label	Peak Position	Weeks at No.1	Weeks in Top 40
21 Apr 90	**AFRIKA** *SBK 7008* HISTORY FEATURING Q-TEE	42		

CAROL HITCHCOCK Australian singer

Date	Title / Label	Peak Position	Weeks at No.1	Weeks in Top 40
30 May 87	**GET READY** *A&M AM 391*	56		

HITHOUSE Dutch producer

Date	Title / Label	Peak Position	Weeks at No.1	Weeks in Top 40
5 Nov 88	**JACK TO THE SOUND OF THE UNDERGROUND** *Supreme SUPE 137*	14		8
19 Aug 89	**MOVE YOUR FEET TO THE RHYTHM OF THE BEAT** *Supreme SUPE 149*	69		

HIVES Swedish group

Date	Title / Label	Peak Position	Weeks at No.1	Weeks in Top 40
23 Feb 02	**HATE TO SAY I TOLD YOU SO** *Burning Heart BHR 1059*	23		2
18 May 02	**MAIN OFFENDER** *Poptones MC 5076SCD*	24		1
17 Jul 04	**WALK IDIOT WALK** *Polydor 9867038*	13		5
30 Oct 04	**TWO TIMING TOUCH AND BROKEN BONES** *Polydor 9868351*	44		
13 Oct 07	**TICK TICK BOOM** *Polydor 1748909*	41		

EDMUND HOCKRIDGE Canadian singer

Date	Title / Label	Peak Position	Weeks at No.1	Weeks in Top 40
17 Feb 56	**YOUNG AND FOOLISH** *Nixa N 15039*	10		9
11 May 56	**NO OTHER LOVE** *Nixa N 15048*	24		4
31 Aug 56	**BY THE FOUNTAINS OF ROME** *Pye Nixa N 15063*	17		5

EDDIE HODGES US singer

Date	Title / Label	Peak Position	Weeks at No.1	Weeks in Top 40
28 Sep 61	**I'M GONNA KNOCK ON YOUR DOOR** *London HLA 9369*	37		4
9 Aug 62	**MADE TO LOVE (GIRLS GIRLS GIRLS)** *London HLA 9576*	37		2

SUSANNA HOFFS US singer

Date	Title / Label	Peak Position	Weeks at No.1	Weeks in Top 40
2 Mar 91	**MY SIDE OF THE BED** *Columbia 6565547*	44		
11 May 91	**UNCONDITIONAL LOVE** *Columbia 6567827*	65		
19 Oct 96	**ALL I WANT** *London LONCD 387*	32		1

HULK HOGAN US wrestler

Date	Title / Label	Peak Position	Weeks at No.1	Weeks in Top 40
25 Dec 93	**I'M THE LEADER OF THE GANG** *Arista 74321174892* HULK HOGAN WITH GREEN JELLY	25		3

HOGGBOY UK group

Date	Title / Label	Peak Position	Weeks at No.1	Weeks in Top 40
27 Apr 02	**SHOULDN'T LET THE SIDE DOWN** *Sobriety SOB 4CDA*	74		

DEMI HOLBORN UK singer

Date	Title / Label	Peak Position	Weeks at No.1	Weeks in Top 40
27 Jul 02	**I'D LIKE TO TEACH THE WORLD TO SING** *Universal Classics & Jazz 0190982*	27		1

HOLDEN & THOMPSON UK duo

Date	Title / Label	Peak Position	Weeks at No.1	Weeks in Top 40
17 May 03	**NOTHING** *Loaded LOAD 98CD*	51		

HOLE US group

Date	Title / Label	Peak Position	Weeks at No.1	Weeks in Top 40
17 Apr 93	**BEAUTIFUL SON** *City Slang EFA 0491603*	54		
9 Apr 94	**MISS WORLD** *City Slang EFA 049362*	64		
15 Apr 95	**DOLL PARTS** *Geffen GFSXD 91*	16		2
29 Jul 95	**VIOLET** *Geffen GFSTD 94*	17		1
12 Sep 98	**CELEBRITY SKIN** *Geffen GFSTD 22345*	19		3
30 Jan 99	**MALIBU** *Geffen GFSTD 22369*	22		1
10 Jul 99	**AWFUL** *Geffen INTDE 97098*	42		

HOLE IN ONE Dutch producer

Date	Title / Label	Peak Position	Weeks at No.1	Weeks in Top 40
15 Feb 97	**LIFE'S TOO SHORT** *Manifesto FESCD 21*	36		1

J. HOLIDAY US singer

Date	Title / Label	Peak Position	Weeks at No.1	Weeks in Top 40
17 Nov 07	**BED** *Charisma CASDX16*	32		1

HOLIDAY PLAN UK group

Date	Title / Label	Peak Position	Weeks at No.1	Weeks in Top 40
26 Jun 04	**STORIES/SUNSHINE** *Island CID 858*	58		

JOOLS HOLLAND UK singer/pianist

Date	Title / Label	Peak Position	Weeks at No.1	Weeks in Top 40
24 Feb 01	**I'M IN THE MOOD FOR LOVE** *warner.esp WSMS 001CD* JOOLS HOLLAND & JAMIROQUAI	29		1

HOLLAND-DOZIER US production duo

Date	Title / Label	Peak Position	Weeks at No.1	Weeks in Top 40
28 Oct 72	**WHY CAN'T WE BE LOVERS** *Invictus INV 525* HOLLAND-DOZIER FEATURING LAMONT DOZIER	29		5

JENNIFER HOLLIDAY US singer

Date	Title / Label	Peak Position	Weeks at No.1	Weeks in Top 40
4 Sep 82	**AND I'M TELLING YOU I'M NOT GOING** *Geffen GEF A 2644*	32		3

MICHAEL HOLLIDAY UK singer

Date	Title / Label	Peak Position	Weeks at No.1	Weeks in Top 40
30 Mar 56	**NOTHIN' TO DO** *Columbia DB 3746*	20		3
15 Jun 56	**GAL WITH THE YALLER SHOES** *Columbia DB 3783*	13		6
22 Jun 56	**HOT DIGGITY (DOG ZIGGITY BOOM)** *Columbia DB 3783*	14		8
5 Oct 56	**TEN THOUSAND MILES** *Columbia DB 3813*	24		3
17 Jan 58	**THE STORY OF MY LIFE** *Columbia DB 4058*	1	2	15
14 Mar 58	**IN LOVE** *Columbia DB 4087*	26		3
16 May 58	**STAIRWAY OF LOVE** *Columbia DB 4121*	3		13
11 Jul 58	**I'LL ALWAYS BE IN LOVE WITH YOU** *Columbia DB 4155*	27		1
1 Jan 60	**STARRY EYED** *Columbia DB 4378* MICHAEL HOLLIDAY WITH THE MICHAEL SAMMES SINGERS	1	1	11
14 Apr 60	**SKYLARK** *Columbia DB 4437*	39		2
1 Sep 60	**LITTLE BOY LOST** *Columbia DB 4475*	50		

HOLLIES UK group

Date	Title / Label	Peak Position	Weeks at No.1	Weeks in Top 40
30 May 63	**(AIN'T THAT) JUST LIKE ME** *Parlophone R 5030*	25		8
29 Aug 63	**SEARCHIN'** *Parlophone R 5052*	12		12
21 Nov 63	**STAY** *Parlophone R 5077*	8		15
27 Feb 64	**JUST ONE LOOK** *Parlophone R 5104*	2		12
21 May 64	**HERE I GO AGAIN** *Parlophone R 5137*	4		8
17 Sep 64	**WE'RE THROUGH** *Parlophone R 5178*	7		9
28 Jan 65	**YES I WILL** *Parlophone R 5232*	9		12
27 May 65	**I'M ALIVE** *Parlophone R 5287*	1	3	13
2 Sep 65	**LOOK THROUGH ANY WINDOW** *Parlophone R 5322*	4		10
9 Dec 65	**IF I NEEDED SOMEONE** *Parlophone R 5392*	20		7
24 Feb 66	**I CAN'T LET GO** *Parlophone R 5409*	2		8
23 Jun 66	**BUS STOP** *Parlophone R 5469*	5		9
13 Oct 66	**STOP STOP STOP** *Parlophone R 5508*	2		10
16 Feb 67	**ON A CAROUSEL** *Parlophone R 5562*	4		10
1 Jun 67	**CARRIE-ANNE** *Parlophone R 5602*	3		10
27 Sep 67	**KING MIDAS IN REVERSE** *Parlophone R 5637*	18		6
27 Mar 68	**JENNIFER ECCLES** *Parlophone R 5680*	7		10
2 Oct 68	**LISTEN TO ME** *Parlophone R 5733*	11		10
5 Mar 69	**SORRY SUZANNE** *Parlophone R 5765*	3		11
4 Oct 69	**HE AIN'T HEAVY, HE'S MY BROTHER** *Parlophone R 5806*	3		12
18 Apr 70	**I CAN'T TELL THE BOTTOM FROM THE TOP** *Parlophone R 5837*	7		8
3 Oct 70	**GASOLINE ALLEY BRED** *Parlophone R 5862*	14		7
22 May 71	**HEY WILLY** *Parlophone R 5905*	22		6
26 Feb 72	**THE BABY** *Polydor 2058 199*	26		5
2 Sep 72	**LONG COOL WOMAN IN A BLACK DRESS** *Parlophone R 5939*	32		4
13 Oct 73	**THE DAY THAT CURLY BILLY SHOT DOWN CRAZY SAM MCGHEE** *Polydor 2058 403*	24		5
9 Feb 74	**THE AIR THAT I BREATHE** *Polydor 2058 435*	2		12
14 Jun 80	**SOLDIER'S SONG** *Polydor 2059 246*	58		
29 Aug 81	**HOLLIEDAZE (MEDLEY)** *EMI 5229*	28		4
3 Sep 88	**HE AIN'T HEAVY, HE'S MY BROTHER** *EMI EM 74*	1	2	10
3 Dec 88	**THE AIR THAT I BREATHE** *EMI EM 80*	60		
20 Mar 93	**THE WOMAN I LOVE** *EMI CDEM 264*	42		

LOLEATTA HOLLOWAY US singer

Date	Title / Label	Peak Position	Weeks at No.1	Weeks in Top 40
31 Aug 91	**GOOD VIBRATIONS** *Interscope A 8764* MARKY MARK & THE FUNKY BUNCH FEATURING LOLEATTA HOLLOWAY ★	14		5
18 Jan 92	**TAKE ME AWAY** *PWL Continental PWL 210* CAPPELLA FEATURING LOLEATTA HOLLOWAY	25		3
26 Mar 94	**STAND UP** *Six6 SIXCD 111*	68		
1 Apr 95	**KEEP THE FIRE BURNIN'** *Columbia 6611552* DAN HARTMAN STARRING LOLEATTA HOLLOWAY	49		
11 Apr 98	**SHOUT TO THE TOP** *JBO JNR 5001573* FIRE ISLAND FEATURING LOLEATTA HOLLOWAY	23		1

Silver-selling ○ · Gold-selling ● · Platinum-selling ⊛ · US No.1 ★ · Peak Position · Weeks at No.1 · Weeks in Top 40

Date	Title	Label	Peak Position	Weeks at No.1	Weeks in Top 40
20 Feb 99	(YOU GOT ME) BURNING UP CEVIN FISHER FEATURING LOLEATTA HOLLOWAY	Wonderboy BOYD 013	14		2
25 Nov 00	DREAMIN'	Defected DFECT 22CDS	59		
10 Jun 06	LOVE SENSATION '06	Gusto CDGUS40	37		1

HOLLOWAY & CO UK producer

Date	Title	Label	Peak Position	Weeks at No.1	Weeks in Top 40
21 Aug 99	I'LL DO ANYTHING – TO MAKE YOU MINE	INCredible INCS 2CD	58		

HOLLOWAYS UK group

Date	Title	Label	Peak Position	Weeks at No.1	Weeks in Top 40
12 Aug 06	TWO LEFT FEET	TVT HOLLOCD1	33		1
28 Oct 06	GENERATOR	TVT HOLLOCD2	30		2
7 Apr 07	DANCEFLOOR	TVT HOLLOCD3	41		
23 Jun 07	GENERATOR	TVT TV61362	14		2
6 Oct 07	TWO LEFT FEET	TVT TV61392	74		

BUDDY HOLLY US singer

Date	Title	Label	Peak Position	Weeks at No.1	Weeks in Top 40
6 Dec 57	PEGGY SUE	Coral Q 72293	6		17
14 Mar 58	LISTEN TO ME	Coral Q 72288	16		2
20 Jun 58	RAVE ON	Coral Q 72325	5		14
29 Aug 58	EARLY IN THE MORNING	Coral Q 72333	17		4
16 Jan 59	HEARTBEAT	Coral Q 72346	30		1
27 Feb 59	IT DOESN'T MATTER ANYMORE	Coral Q 72360	1	3	21
31 Jul 59	MIDNIGHT SHIFT	Brunswick 05800	26		3
11 Sep 59	PEGGY SUE GOT MARRIED	Coral Q 72376	13		10
28 Apr 60	HEARTBEAT	Coral Q 72392	30		1
26 May 60	TRUE LOVE WAYS	Coral Q 72397	25		8
20 Oct 60	LEARNIN' THE GAME	Coral Q 72411	36		2
9 Feb 61	WHAT TO DO	Coral Q 72419	34		6
6 Jul 61	BABY I DON'T CARE/VALLEY OF TEARS	Coral Q 72432	12		12
15 Mar 62	LISTEN TO ME	Coral Q 72449	48		
13 Sep 62	REMINISCING	Coral Q 72455	17		10
14 Mar 63	BROWN-EYED HANDSOME MAN	Coral Q 72459	3		15
6 Jun 63	BO DIDDLEY	Coral Q 72463	4		11
5 Sep 63	WISHING	Coral Q 72466	10		10
19 Dec 63	WHAT TO DO	Coral Q 72469	27		6
14 May 64	YOU'VE GOT LOVE BUDDY HOLLY & THE CRICKETS	Coral Q 72472	40		1
10 Sep 64	LOVE'S MADE A FOOL OF YOU	Coral Q 72475	39		1
3 Apr 68	PEGGY SUE/RAVE ON	MCA MU 1012	32		6
10 Dec 88	TRUE LOVE WAYS	MCA 1302	65		

HOLLY & THE IVYS UK group

Date	Title	Label	Peak Position	Weeks at No.1	Weeks in Top 40
19 Dec 81	CHRISTMAS ON 45	Decca SANTA 1	40		3

HOLLYWOOD ARGYLES US singer

Date	Title	Label	Peak Position	Weeks at No.1	Weeks in Top 40
21 Jul 60	ALLEY OOP	London HLU 9146 ★	24		8

HOLLYWOOD BEYOND UK group

Date	Title	Label	Peak Position	Weeks at No.1	Weeks in Top 40
12 Jul 86	WHAT'S THE COLOUR OF MONEY?	WEA YZ 76	7		7
20 Sep 86	NO MORE TEARS	WEA YZ 81	47		

EDDIE HOLMAN US singer

Date	Title	Label	Peak Position	Weeks at No.1	Weeks in Top 40
19 Oct 74	(HEY THERE) LONELY GIRL	ABC 4012 ○	4		11

DAVE HOLMES UK producer

Date	Title	Label	Peak Position	Weeks at No.1	Weeks in Top 40
26 May 01	DEVOTION	Tidy Trax TIDY 154CD	66		

DAVID HOLMES UK singer

Date	Title	Label	Peak Position	Weeks at No.1	Weeks in Top 40
6 Apr 96	GONE	Go! Discs GODCD 140	75		
23 Aug 97	GRITTY SHAKER	Go! Beat GOBCD 2	53		
10 Jan 98	DON'T DIE JUST YET	Go! Beat GOLCD 6	33		1
4 Apr 98	MY MATE PAUL	Go! Beat GOBCD 8	39		1
19 Aug 00	69 POLICE	Go! Beat GOBCD 30	53		

RUPERT HOLMES US singer

Date	Title	Label	Peak Position	Weeks at No.1	Weeks in Top 40
12 Jan 80	ESCAPE (THE PINA COLADA SONG)	Infinity INF 120 ★	23		6
22 Mar 80	HIM	MCA 565	31		4

JOHN HOLT Jamaican singer

Date	Title	Label	Peak Position	Weeks at No.1	Weeks in Top 40
14 Dec 74	HELP ME MAKE IT THROUGH THE NIGHT	Trojan TR 7909	6		11

NICHOLA HOLT UK singer

Date	Title	Label	Peak Position	Weeks at No.1	Weeks in Top 40
21 Oct 00	THE GAME	RCA 74321798992	72		

PAUL HOLT UK singer

Date	Title	Label	Peak Position	Weeks at No.1	Weeks in Top 40
18 Dec 04	FIFTY GRAND FOR CHRISTMAS	Sanctuary SANXS348	35		1

A HOMEBOY, A HIPPIE & A FUNKI DREDD UK group

Date	Title	Label	Peak Position	Weeks at No.1	Weeks in Top 40
13 Oct 90	TOTAL CONFUSION	Tam Tam 7TTT 031	56		
29 Dec 90	FREEDOM	Tam Tam 7TTT 039	68		
8 Jan 94	HERE WE GO AGAIN	Polydor PZCD 302	57		

HONDY Italian group

Date	Title	Label	Peak Position	Weeks at No.1	Weeks in Top 40
12 Apr 97	HONDY (NO ACCESS)	Manifesto FESCD 20	26		1

HONEYBUS UK group

Date	Title	Label	Peak Position	Weeks at No.1	Weeks in Top 40
20 Mar 68	I CAN'T LET MAGGIE GO	Deram DM 182	8		8

HONEYCOMBS UK group

Date	Title	Label	Peak Position	Weeks at No.1	Weeks in Top 40
23 Jul 64	HAVE I THE RIGHT	Pye 7N 15664	1	2	13
22 Oct 64	IS IT BECAUSE	Pye 7N 15705	38		2
29 Apr 65	SOMETHING BETTER BEGINNING	Pye 7N 15827	39		1
5 Aug 65	THAT'S THE WAY	Pye 7N 15890	12		12

HONEYCRACK UK group

Date	Title	Label	Peak Position	Weeks at No.1	Weeks in Top 40
4 Nov 95	SITTING AT HOME	Epic 6625382	42		
24 Feb 96	GO AWAY	Epic 6628642	41		
11 May 96	KING OF MISERY	Epic 6631475	32		1
20 Jul 96	SITTING AT HOME	Epic 6635032	32		1
16 Nov 96	ANYWAY	EG EGO 52A	67		

HONEYDRIPPERS UK/US group

Date	Title	Label	Peak Position	Weeks at No.1	Weeks in Top 40
2 Feb 85	SEA OF LOVE	Es Paranza YZ 33	56		

HONEYMOON MACHINE UK group

Date	Title	Label	Peak Position	Weeks at No.1	Weeks in Top 40
21 May 05	INTO YOUR HEAD	Easy Street EASYST009CD	66		
22 Oct 05	FAITH IN PEOPLE	Easy Street EASYST011CD	64		

HONEYROOT UK duo

Date	Title	Label	Peak Position	Weeks at No.1	Weeks in Top 40
7 May 05	LOVE WILL TEAR US APART	Just Music TAOS003	70		

HONEYZ UK group

Date	Title	Label	Peak Position	Weeks at No.1	Weeks in Top 40
5 Sep 98	FINALLY FOUND	1st Avenue HNZCD 1 ○	4		10
19 Dec 98	END OF THE LINE	1st Avenue HNZCD 2 ○	5		11
24 Apr 99	LOVE OF A LIFETIME	1st Avenue HNZCD 3	9		5
23 Oct 99	NEVER LET YOU DOWN	1st Avenue HNZCD 4	7		3
11 Mar 00	WON'T TAKE IT LYING DOWN	1st Avenue HNZCD 5	7		4
28 Oct 00	NOT EVEN GONNA TRIP	1st Avenue HNZDD 7	24		1
18 Aug 01	I DON'T KNOW	1st Avenue HNZDD 8	28		1

HONKY UK group

Date	Title	Label	Peak Position	Weeks at No.1	Weeks in Top 40
28 May 77	JOIN THE PARTY	Creole CR 137	28		4
30 Oct 93	THE HONKY DOODLE DAY EP	ZTT ZANG 45CD	61		
19 Feb 94	THE WHISTLER	ZTT ZANG 48CD	41		
20 Apr 96	HIP HOP DON'T YA DROP	Higher Ground HIGHS 1CD	70		
10 Aug 96	WHAT'S GOIN' DOWN	Higher Ground HIGHS 2CD	49		

HOOBASTANK US group

Date	Title	Label	Peak Position	Weeks at No.1	Weeks in Top 40
13 Apr 02	CRAWLING IN THE DARK	Mercury 5828622	47		
12 Jun 04	THE REASON	Mercury 9862567	12		4

Silver-selling · Gold-selling · Platinum-selling · US No.1 ★ · Peak Position · Weeks at No.1 · Weeks in Top 40

FRANK HOOKER & POSITIVE PEOPLE US group

Date	Title / Label	Peak Position	Weeks at No.1	Weeks in Top 40
5 Jul 80	**THIS FEELIN'** *DJM DJS 10947*	48		

JOHN LEE HOOKER US singer/guitarist

Date	Title / Label	Peak Position	Weeks at No.1	Weeks in Top 40
11 Jun 64	**DIMPLES** *Stateside SS 297*	23		8
24 Oct 92	**BOOM BOOM** *Pointblank POB 3*	16		2
16 Jan 93	**BOOGIE AT RUSSIAN HILL** *Pointblank POBDX 4*	53		
15 May 93	**GLORIA** *Exile VANCD 11* VAN MORRISON & JOHN LEE HOOKER	31		2
11 Feb 95	**CHILL OUT (THINGS GONNA CHANGE)** *Pointblank POBD 10*	45		
20 Apr 96	**BABY LEE** *Silvertone ORECD 81* JOHN LEE HOOKER WITH ROBERT CRAY	65		

HOOSIERS UK group

Date	Title / Label	Peak Position	Weeks at No.1	Weeks in Top 40
30 Jun 07	**WORRIED ABOUT RAY** *RCA 88697116512*	5		23
20 Oct 07	**GOODBYE MR A** *RCA 88697156892*	4		17

HOOTERS UK group

Date	Title / Label	Peak Position	Weeks at No.1	Weeks in Top 40
21 Nov 87	**SATELLITE** *CBS 6511687*	22		7

HOOTIE & THE BLOWFISH US group

Date	Title / Label	Peak Position	Weeks at No.1	Weeks in Top 40
25 Feb 95	**HOLD MY HAND** *Atlantic A 7230CD*	50		
27 May 95	**LET HER CRY** *Atlantic A 7188CD*	75		
4 May 96	**OLD MAN AND ME (WHEN I GET TO HEAVEN)** *Atlantic A 5513CD*	57		
7 Nov 98	**I WILL WAIT** *Atlantic AT 0048CD*	57		

HOPE A.D. UK producer

Date	Title / Label	Peak Position	Weeks at No.1	Weeks in Top 40
4 Jun 94	**TREE FROG** *Sun-Up SUN 003CD*	73		

HOPE OF THE STATES UK group

Date	Title / Label	Peak Position	Weeks at No.1	Weeks in Top 40
11 Oct 03	**ENEMIES FRIENDS** *Sony Music 6742572*	25		1
5 Jun 04	**THE RED, THE WHITE, THE BLUE** *Sony Music 6749922*	15		1
28 Aug 04	**NEHEMIAH** *Sony Music 6752472*	30		1
17 Jun 06	**SING IT OUT** *Columbia LEFTCD003*	39		1
2 Sep 06	**LEFT** *Columbia LEFTCD06*	63		

MARY HOPKIN UK singer

Date	Title / Label	Peak Position	Weeks at No.1	Weeks in Top 40
4 Sep 68	**THOSE WERE THE DAYS** *Apple 2*	1	6	18
2 Apr 69	**GOODBYE** *Apple 10*	2		14
31 Jan 70	**TEMMA HARBOUR** *Apple 22*	6		10
28 Mar 70	**KNOCK KNOCK WHO'S THERE** *Apple 26*	2		12
31 Oct 70	**THINK ABOUT YOUR CHILDREN** *Apple 30*	19		6
31 Jul 71	**LET MY NAME BE SORROW** *Apple 34*	46		
20 Mar 76	**IF YOU LOVE ME** *Good Earth GD 2*	32		3

ANTHONY HOPKINS UK actor

Date	Title / Label	Peak Position	Weeks at No.1	Weeks in Top 40
27 Dec 86	**DISTANT STAR** *Juice AA 5*	75		

BRUCE HORNSBY & THE RANGE US group

Date	Title / Label	Peak Position	Weeks at No.1	Weeks in Top 40
2 Aug 86	**THE WAY IT IS** *RCA PB 49805* ★	15		8
25 Apr 87	**MANDOLIN RAIN** *RCA PB 49769*	70		
28 May 88	**THE VALLEY ROAD** *RCA PB 49561*	44		

HORRORS UK group

Date	Title / Label	Peak Position	Weeks at No.1	Weeks in Top 40
10 Mar 07	**GLOVES** *Loog 1725532*	34		1

HORSE UK group

Date	Title / Label	Peak Position	Weeks at No.1	Weeks in Top 40
24 Nov 90	**CAREFUL** *Capitol CL 587*	52		
21 Aug 93	**SHAKE THIS MOUNTAIN** *Oxygen GASPD 7*	52		
23 Oct 93	**GOD'S HOME MOVIE** *Oxygen GASXD 10*	56		
15 Jan 94	**CELEBRATE** *Oxygen GASPD 11*	49		
5 Apr 97	**CAREFUL (STRESS)** *Stress CDSTRX 79*	44		

JOHNNY HORTON US singer

Date	Title / Label	Peak Position	Weeks at No.1	Weeks in Top 40
26 Jun 59	**THE BATTLE OF NEW ORLEANS** *Philips PB 932* ★	16		4
19 Jan 61	**NORTH TO ALASKA** *Philips PB 1062*	23		7

HOT ACTION COP US group

Date	Title / Label	Peak Position	Weeks at No.1	Weeks in Top 40
14 Jun 03	**FEVER FOR THE FLAVA** *Lava AT 0152CD*	41		

HOT BLOOD French instrumental group

Date	Title / Label	Peak Position	Weeks at No.1	Weeks in Top 40
9 Oct 76	**SOUL DRACULA** *Creole CR 132*	32		4

HOT BUTTER US instrumentalist

Date	Title / Label	Peak Position	Weeks at No.1	Weeks in Top 40
22 Jul 72	**POPCORN** *Pye International 7N 25583*	5		13

HOT CHIP UK group

Date	Title / Label	Peak Position	Weeks at No.1	Weeks in Top 40
11 Mar 06	**OVER AND OVER** *EMI CDEM682*	32		1
20 May 06	**BOY FROM SCHOOL** *EMI CDEM690*	40		1
14 Oct 06	**OVER AND OVER** *EMI CDEMS707*	27		1
9 Feb 08	**READY FOR THE FLOOR** *EMI CDEM738*	6		5

HOT CHOCOLATE UK group

Date	Title / Label	Peak Position	Weeks at No.1	Weeks in Top 40
15 Aug 70	**LOVE IS LIFE** *RAK 103*	6		10
6 Mar 71	**YOU COULD HAVE BEEN A LADY** *RAK 110*	22		8
28 Aug 71	**I BELIEVE (IN LOVE)** *RAK 118*	8		9
28 Oct 72	**YOU'LL ALWAYS BE A FRIEND** *RAK 139*	23		7
14 Apr 73	**BROTHER LOUIE** *RAK 149*	7		9
18 Aug 73	**RUMOURS** *RAK 157*	44		
16 Mar 74	**EMMA** *RAK 168*	3		8
30 Nov 74	**CHERI BABE** *RAK 188*	31		7
24 May 75	**DISCO QUEEN** *RAK 202*	11		7
9 Aug 75	**A CHILD'S PRAYER** *RAK 212*	7		8
8 Nov 75	**YOU SEXY THING** *RAK 221*	2		12
20 Mar 76	**DON'T STOP IT NOW** *RAK 230*	11		7
26 Jun 76	**MAN TO MAN** *RAK 238*	14		7
21 Aug 76	**HEAVEN IS IN THE BACK SEAT OF MY CADILLAC** *RAK 240*	25		7
18 Jun 77	**SO YOU WIN AGAIN** *RAK 259*	1	3	11
26 Nov 77	**PUT YOUR LOVE IN ME** *RAK 266*	10		8
4 Mar 78	**EVERY 1'S A WINNER** *RAK 270*	12		9
2 Dec 78	**I'LL PUT YOU TOGETHER AGAIN** *RAK 286*	13		10
19 May 79	**MINDLESS BOOGIE** *RAK 292*	46		
28 Jul 79	**GOING THROUGH THE MOTIONS** *RAK 296*	53		
3 May 80	**NO DOUBT ABOUT IT** *RAK 310*	2		10
19 Jul 80	**ARE YOU GETTING ENOUGH OF WHAT MAKES YOU HAPPY** *RAK 318*	17		6
13 Dec 80	**LOVE ME TO SLEEP** *RAK 324*	50		
30 May 81	**YOU'LL NEVER BE SO WRONG** *RAK 331*	52		
17 Apr 82	**GIRL CRAZY** *RAK 341*	7		9
10 Jul 82	**IT STARTED WITH A KISS** *RAK 344*	5		10
25 Sep 82	**CHANCES** *RAK 350*	32		2
7 May 83	**WHAT KINDA BOY YOU LOOKING FOR (GIRL)** *RAK 357*	10		7
17 Sep 83	**TEARS ON THE TELEPHONE** *RAK 363*	37		2
4 Feb 84	**I GAVE YOU MY HEART (DIDN'T I)** *RAK 369*	13		7
17 Jan 87	**YOU SEXY THING (REMIX)** *EMI 5592*	10		7
4 Apr 87	**EVERY 1'S A WINNER (REMIX)** *EMI 5607*	69		
6 Mar 93	**IT STARTED WITH A KISS** *EMI CDEMCTS 7*	31		3
22 Nov 97	**YOU SEXY THING** *EMI CDHOT 100*	6		7
14 Feb 98	**IT STARTED WITH A KISS** *EMI CDHOT 101* HOT CHOCOLATE FEATURING ERROL BROWN	18		2

HOT HOT HEAT Canadian group

Date	Title / Label	Peak Position	Weeks at No.1	Weeks in Top 40
5 Apr 03	**BANDAGES** *B Unique BUN 045CDS*	25		1
9 Aug 03	**NO, NOT NOW** *Sub Pop W 615CD*	38		1
28 May 05	**GOODNIGHT GOODNIGHT** *Sire W670CD1*	36		1
30 Jul 05	**MIDDLE OF NOWHERE** *Sire W677CD1*	47		

HOT HOUSE UK group

Date	Title / Label	Peak Position	Weeks at No.1	Weeks in Top 40
14 Feb 87	**DON'T COME TO STAY** *Deconstruction CHEZ 1*	74		
24 Sep 88	**DON'T COME TO STAY** *Deconstruction PB 42233*	70		

HOT PANTZ UK duo

Date	Title / Label	Peak Position	Weeks at No.1	Weeks in Top 40
25 Dec 04	**GIVE U ONE 4 CHRISTMAS** *Tug CDSNOG13*	64		

HOT STREAK US group

Date	Title / Label	Peak Position	Weeks at No.1	Weeks in Top 40
10 Sep 83	**BODY WORK** *Polydor POSP 642*	19		6

HOTHOUSE FLOWERS Irish group

Date	Title / Label	Peak Position	Weeks at No.1	Weeks in Top 40
14 May 88	**DON'T GO** *London LON 174*	11		5
23 Jul 88	**I'M SORRY** *London LON 187*	53		
12 May 90	**GIVE IT UP** *London LON 258*	30		3
28 Jul 90	**I CAN SEE CLEARLY NOW** *London LON 269*	23		4
20 Oct 90	**MOVIES** *London LON 276*	68		
13 Feb 93	**EMOTIONAL TIME** *London LONCD 335*	38		2
8 May 93	**ONE TONGUE** *London LOCDP 340*	45		
19 Jun 93	**ISN'T IT AMAZING** *London LOCDP 343*	46		
27 Nov 93	**THIS IS IT (YOUR SOUL)** *London LONCD 346*	67		
16 May 98	**YOU CAN LEAVE ME NOW** *London LONCD 410*	65		

HOTLEGS UK group

Date	Title / Label	Peak Position	Weeks at No.1	Weeks in Top 40
4 Jul 70	**NEANDERTHAL MAN** *Fontana 6007 019*	2		13

HOTSHOTS UK group

Date	Title / Label	Peak Position	Weeks at No.1	Weeks in Top 40
2 Jun 73	**SNOOPY VS. THE RED BARON** *Mooncrest MOON 5*	4		12

STEVEN HOUGHTON UK actor/singer

Date	Title / Label	Peak Position	Weeks at No.1	Weeks in Top 40
29 Nov 97	**WIND BENEATH MY WINGS** *RCA 74321529272*	3		10
7 Mar 98	**TRULY** *RCA 74321558552*	23		1

HOUND DOGS UK/US production group

Date	Title / Label	Peak Position	Weeks at No.1	Weeks in Top 40
31 Dec 05	**I LIKE GIRLS** *Direction 82876777032*	26		5

A HOUSE Irish group

Date	Title / Label	Peak Position	Weeks at No.1	Weeks in Top 40
13 Jun 92	**ENDLESS ART** *Setanta AHOU 1*	46		
8 Aug 92	**TAKE IT EASY ON ME** *Setanta AHOU 2*	55		
25 Jun 94	**WHY ME** *Setanta CDAHOU 4*	52		
1 Oct 94	**HERE COME THE GOOD TIMES** *Setanta CDAHOUS 5*	37		1

HOUSE ENGINEERS UK group

Date	Title / Label	Peak Position	Weeks at No.1	Weeks in Top 40
5 Dec 87	**GHOST HOUSE** *Syncopate SY 8*	69		

HOUSE OF GLASS Italian production duo

Date	Title / Label	Peak Position	Weeks at No.1	Weeks in Top 40
14 Apr 01	**DISCO DOWN** *Azuli AZNY 138*	72		

HOUSE OF LOVE UK group

Date	Title / Label	Peak Position	Weeks at No.1	Weeks in Top 40
22 Apr 89	**NEVER** *Fontana HOL 1*	41		
18 Nov 89	**I DON'T KNOW WHY** *Fontana HOL 2*	41		
3 Feb 90	**SHINE ON** *Fontana HOL 3*	20		3
7 Apr 90	**BEATLES AND THE STONES** *Fontana HOL 4*	36		2
26 Oct 91	**THE GIRL WITH THE LONELIEST EYES** *Fontana HOL 5*	58		
2 May 92	**FEEL** *Fontana HOL 6*	45		
27 Jun 92	**YOU DON'T UNDERSTAND** *Fontana HOL 7*	46		
5 Dec 92	**CRUSH ME** *Fontana HOL 810*	67		
26 Feb 05	**LOVE YOU TOO MUCH** *Art And Industry 2ARTCD*	73		

HOUSE OF PAIN US group

Date	Title / Label	Peak Position	Weeks at No.1	Weeks in Top 40
10 Oct 92	**JUMP AROUND** *Ruffness XLS 32*	32		3
22 May 93	**JUMP AROUND/TOP O' THE MORNING TO YA** *Ruffness XLS 43CD*	8		6
23 Oct 93	**SHAMROCKS AND SHENIGANS/WHO'S THE MAN** *Ruffness XLS 46CD*	23		2
16 Jul 94	**ON POINT** *Ruffness XLS 52CD*	19		2
12 Nov 94	**IT AIN'T A CRIME** *Ruffness XLS 55CD1*	37		1
1 Jul 95	**OVER THERE (I DON'T CARE)** *Ruffness XLS 61CD2*	20		2
5 Oct 96	**FED UP** *Tommy Boy TBCD 7744*	68		
20 Nov 04	**JUMP AROUND (REMIX)** *Tommy Boy 5046760110*	44		
22 Mar 08	**JUMP AROUND (REMIX)** *Tommy Boy 5046760110*	67		

HOUSE OF VIRGINISM Swedish singer/dancer

Date	Title / Label	Peak Position	Weeks at No.1	Weeks in Top 40
20 Nov 93	**I'LL BE THERE FOR YOU (DOYA DODODO DOYA)** *ffrr FCD 221*	29		2
30 Jul 94	**REACHIN** *ffrr FCD 238*	35		1
17 Feb 96	**EXCLUSIVE** *Logic 74321324102* APOLLO PRESENTS HOUSE OF VIRGINISM	67		

HOUSE TRAFFIC Italian/UK production group

Date	Title / Label	Peak Position	Weeks at No.1	Weeks in Top 40
4 Oct 97	**EVERYDAY OF MY LIFE** *Logic 74321249442*	24		2

HOUSEMARTINS UK group

Date	Title / Label	Peak Position	Weeks at No.1	Weeks in Top 40
8 Mar 86	**SHEEP** *Go! Discs GOD 9*	56		
7 Jun 86	**HAPPY HOUR** *Go! Discs GOD 11* ○	3		10
4 Oct 86	**THINK FOR A MINUTE** *Go! Discs GOD 13*	18		6
6 Dec 86	**CARAVAN OF LOVE** *Go! Discs GOD 16* ●	1	1	9
23 May 87	**FIVE GET OVER EXCITED** *Go! Discs GOD 18*	11		5
5 Sep 87	**ME AND THE FARMER** *Go! Discs GOD 19*	15		4
21 Nov 87	**BUILD** *Go! Discs GOD 21*	15		5
23 Apr 88	**THERE IS ALWAYS SOMETHING THERE TO REMIND ME** *Go! Discs GOD 22*	35		2
10 May 03	**CHANGE THE WORLD** *Free 2 Air 0146685 F2A* DINO LENNY VS THE HOUSEMARTINS	51		

HOUSEMASTER BOYZ & THE RUDE BOY OF HOUSE US singer

Date	Title / Label	Peak Position	Weeks at No.1	Weeks in Top 40
9 May 87	**HOUSE NATION** *Magnetic Dance MAGD 1*	48		
12 Sep 87	**HOUSE NATION** *Magnetic Dance MAGD 1*	8		7

HOUSTON US singer

Date	Title / Label	Peak Position	Weeks at No.1	Weeks in Top 40
18 Sep 04	**I LIKE THAT** *Capitol CDCL 861*	11		5
5 Feb 05	**AIN'T NOTHING WRONG** *Capitol CDCL866*	33		1

MARQUES HOUSTON US singer

Date	Title / Label	Peak Position	Weeks at No.1	Weeks in Top 40
20 Mar 04	**CLUBBIN'** *Elektra E 7544CD*	15		3
31 Jul 04	**POP THAT BOOTY** *East West E7609CD* MARQUES HOUSTON FEATURING JERMAINE	23		3
27 Nov 04	**BECAUSE OF YOU** *Atlantic AT0188CD*	51		

THELMA HOUSTON US singer

Date	Title / Label	Peak Position	Weeks at No.1	Weeks in Top 40
5 Feb 77	**DON'T LEAVE ME THIS WAY** *Motown TMG 1060* ★	13		8
27 Jun 81	**IF YOU FEEL IT** *RCA 77*	48		
1 Dec 84	**YOU USED TO HOLD ME SO TIGHT** *MCA 932*	49		
21 Jan 95	**DON'T LEAVE ME THIS WAY** *Dynamo DYND 001*	35		1

WHITNEY HOUSTON US singer

Date	Title / Label	Peak Position	Weeks at No.1	Weeks in Top 40
16 Nov 85	**SAVING ALL MY LOVE FOR YOU** *Arista ARIST 640* ● ★	1	2	11
25 Jan 86	**HOLD ME** *Asylum EKR 32* TEDDY PENDERGRASS & WHITNEY HOUSTON	44		
25 Jan 86	**HOW WILL I KNOW** *Arista ARIST 656* ○ ★	5		11
12 Apr 86	**GREATEST LOVE OF ALL** *Arista ARIST 658* ★	8		7
23 May 87	**I WANNA DANCE WITH SOMEBODY (WHO LOVES ME)** *Arista RIS 1* ● ★	1	2	12
22 Aug 87	**DIDN'T WE ALMOST HAVE IT ALL** *Arista RIS 31* ★	14		6
14 Nov 87	**SO EMOTIONAL** *Arista RIS 43* ★	5		9
12 Mar 88	**WHERE DO BROKEN HEARTS GO** *Arista 109793* ★	14		6
28 May 88	**LOVE WILL SAVE THE DAY** *Arista 111516*	10		4
24 Sep 88	**ONE MOMENT IN TIME** *Arista 111613* ○	1	2	10
9 Sep 89	**IT ISN'T, IT WASN'T, IT AIN'T NEVER GONNA BE** *Arista 112545* ARETHA FRANKLIN & WHITNEY HOUSTON	29		3
20 Oct 90	**I'M YOUR BABY TONIGHT** *Arista 113594* ★	5		7
22 Dec 90	**ALL THE MAN THAT I NEED** *Arista 114000* ★	13		8
6 Jul 91	**MY NAME IS NOT SUSAN** *Arista 114510*	29		3
28 Sep 91	**I BELONG TO YOU** *Arista 114727*	54		
14 Nov 92	**I WILL ALWAYS LOVE YOU** *Arista 74321120657* ⊛ ★	1	10	20
20 Feb 93	**I'M EVERY WOMAN** *Arista 74321131502*	4		9
24 Apr 93	**I HAVE NOTHING** *Arista 74321146142*	3		8
31 Jul 93	**RUN TO YOU** *Arista 74321153332*	15		4
6 Nov 93	**QUEEN OF THE NIGHT** *Arista 74321169302*	14		3
25 Dec 93	**I WILL ALWAYS LOVE YOU** *Arista 74321120657*	25		3
22 Jan 94	**SOMETHING IN COMMON** *MCA MCSTD 1957* BOBBY BROWN & WHITNEY HOUSTON	16		3
18 Nov 95	**EXHALE (SHOOP SHOOP)** *Arista 74321332472* ★	11		5

Key: ○ Silver-selling · ● Gold-selling · ⊛ Platinum-selling · ★ US No.1 · Peak Position · Weeks at No.1 · Weeks in Top 40

Date	Title	Peak Position	Weeks at No.1	Weeks in Top 40
24 Feb 96	**COUNT ON ME** *Arista 74321345842* WHITNEY HOUSTON & CECE WINANS	12		4
21 Dec 96	**STEP BY STEP** *Arista 74321449332*	13		11
29 Mar 97	**I BELIEVE IN YOU AND ME** *Arista 74321468602*	16		2
19 Dec 98	**WHEN YOU BELIEVE (FROM THE PRINCE OF EGYPT)** *Columbia 6667522* MARIAH CAREY & WHITNEY HOUSTON	4		7
6 Mar 99	**IT'S NOT RIGHT BUT IT'S OKAY** *Arista 74321652412* ●	3		12
3 Jul 99	**MY LOVE IS YOUR LOVE** *Arista 74321672872*	2		10
11 Dec 99	**I LEARNED FROM THE BEST** *Arista 74321723992*	19		8
17 Jun 00	**IF I TOLD YOU THAT** *Arista 74321766282* WHITNEY HOUSTON & GEORGE MICHAEL	9		4
14 Oct 00	**COULD I HAVE THIS KISS FOREVER** *Arista 74321795992* WHITNEY HOUSTON & ENRIQUE IGLESIAS	7		6
30 Dec 00	**HEARTBREAK HOTEL** *Arista 74321820572* WHITNEY HOUSTON FEATURING FAITH EVANS & KELLY PRICE	25		3
9 Nov 02	**WHATCHULOOKINAT** *Arista 74321975732*	13		2
29 Dec 07	**WHEN YOU BELIEVE (FROM THE PRINCE OF EGYPT)** *Columbia 6667522* MARIAH CAREY & WHITNEY HOUSTON	65		

ADINA HOWARD US singer

Date	Title	Peak Position	Weeks at No.1	Weeks in Top 40
4 Mar 95	**FREAK LIKE ME** *East West A 4473CD*	33		1
23 Nov 96	**WHAT'S LOVE GOT TO DO WITH IT** *Interscope IND 97008* WARREN G FEATURING ADINA HOWARD	2		10

BILLY HOWARD UK comedian

Date	Title	Peak Position	Weeks at No.1	Weeks in Top 40
13 Dec 75	**KING OF THE COPS** *Penny Farthing PEN 892*	6		11

MIKI HOWARD US singer

Date	Title	Peak Position	Weeks at No.1	Weeks in Top 40
26 May 90	**UNTIL YOU COME BACK (THAT'S WHAT I'M GONNA DO)** *East West 7935*	67		

NICK HOWARD Australian singer

Date	Title	Peak Position	Weeks at No.1	Weeks in Top 40
21 Jan 95	**EVERYBODY NEEDS SOMEBODY** *Bell 74321220942*	64		

DANNY HOWELLS & DICK TREVOR UK production duo

Date	Title	Peak Position	Weeks at No.1	Weeks in Top 40
9 Oct 04	**DUSK TIL DAWN** *C2 CDC2004*	37		1

HOWLIN' WOLF US singer/guitarist

Date	Title	Peak Position	Weeks at No.1	Weeks in Top 40
4 Jun 64	**SMOKESTACK LIGHTNIN'** *Pye International 7N 25244*	42		

H2O UK group

Date	Title	Peak Position	Weeks at No.1	Weeks in Top 40
21 May 83	**DREAM TO SLEEP** *RCA 330*	17		7
13 Aug 83	**JUST OUTSIDE OF HEAVEN** *RCA 349*	38		2

H2O US/Swiss production duo

Date	Title	Peak Position	Weeks at No.1	Weeks in Top 40
14 Sep 96	**NOBODY'S BUSINESS** *AM:PM 5818832* H2O FEATURING BILLIE	19		2
30 Aug 97	**SATISFIED (TAKE ME HIGHER)** *AM:PM 5853252*	66		

H TWO O UK duo

Date	Title	Peak Position	Weeks at No.1	Weeks in Top 40
23 Feb 08	**WHAT'S IT GONNA BE** *Hard2Beat H2B02CDS* H TWO O FEATURING PLATINUM	2		6

AL HUDSON US singer

Date	Title	Peak Position	Weeks at No.1	Weeks in Top 40
9 Sep 78	**DANCE, GET DOWN (FEEL THE GROOVE)/HOW DO YOU DO** *ABC 4229*	57		
15 Sep 79	**YOU CAN DO IT** *MCA 511* AL HUDSON & THE PARTNERS	15		8
8 Dec 79	**MUSIC** *MCA 542* ONE WAY FEATURING AL HUDSON	56		

LAVINE HUDSON UK singer

Date	Title	Peak Position	Weeks at No.1	Weeks in Top 40
21 May 88	**INTERVENTION** *Virgin VS 1067*	57		

HUDSON-FORD UK duo

Date	Title	Peak Position	Weeks at No.1	Weeks in Top 40
18 Aug 73	**PICK UP THE PIECES** *A&M AMS 7078*	8		7
16 Feb 74	**BURN BABY BURN** *A&M AMS 7096*	15		7
29 Jun 74	**FLOATING IN THE WIND** *A&M AMS 7116*	35		2

HUE & CRY UK duo

Date	Title	Peak Position	Weeks at No.1	Weeks in Top 40
13 Jun 87	**LABOUR OF LOVE** *Circa YR 4*	6		9
19 Sep 87	**STRENGTH TO STRENGTH** *Circa YR 6*	46		
30 Jan 88	**I REFUSE** *Circa YR 8*	47		
22 Oct 88	**ORDINARY ANGEL** *Circa YR 18*	42		
28 Jan 89	**LOOKING FOR LINDA** *Circa YR 24*	15		7
6 May 89	**VIOLENTLY (EP)** *Circa YR 29*	21		3
30 Sep 89	**SWEET INVISIBILITY** *Circa YR 37*	55		
25 May 91	**MY SALT HEART** *Circa YR 64*	47		
3 Aug 91	**LONG TERM LOVERS OF PAIN (EP)** *Circa YR 71*	48		
11 Jul 92	**PROFOUNDLY YOURS** *Fidelity FIDEL 1*	74		
13 Mar 93	**LABOUR OF LOVE (REMIX)** *Circa HUESCD 1*	25		3

HUES CORPORATION US group

Date	Title	Peak Position	Weeks at No.1	Weeks in Top 40
27 Jul 74	**ROCK THE BOAT** *RCA APBO 0232* ○ ★	6		9
19 Oct 74	**ROCKIN' SOUL** *RCA PB 10066*	24		4

HUFF & HERB UK production duo

Date	Title	Peak Position	Weeks at No.1	Weeks in Top 40
2 Nov 96	**HELP ME MAKE IT** *Skyway SKYWCD 4* HUFF & PUFF	31		1
21 Jun 97	**HELP ME MAKE IT (REMIX)** *Skyway SKYWCD 8* HUFF & PUFF	37		1
6 Dec 97	**FEELING GOOD** *Planet 3 GXY 2018CD*	31		1
7 Nov 98	**FEELING GOOD '98 (REMIX)** *Planet 3 GXY 2020CD*	69		

DAVID HUGHES UK singer

Date	Title	Peak Position	Weeks at No.1	Weeks in Top 40
21 Sep 56	**BY THE FOUNTAINS OF ROME** *Philips PB 606*	27		1

HUGO & LUIGI US production duo

Date	Title	Peak Position	Weeks at No.1	Weeks in Top 40
24 Jul 59	**LA PLUME DE MA TANTE** *RCA 1127*	29		2

HUMAN LEAGUE UK group

Date	Title	Peak Position	Weeks at No.1	Weeks in Top 40
3 May 80	**HOLIDAY 80 (DOUBLE SINGLE)** *Virgin SV 105*	56		
21 Jun 80	**EMPIRE STATE HUMAN** *Virgin VS 351*	62		
28 Feb 81	**BOYS AND GIRLS** *Virgin VS 395*	48		
2 May 81	**THE SOUND OF THE CROWD** *Virgin VS 416*	12		7
8 Aug 81	**LOVE ACTION (I BELIEVE IN LOVE)** *Virgin VS 435* ○	3		11
10 Oct 81	**OPEN YOUR HEART** *Virgin VS 453* ○	6		8
5 Dec 81	**DON'T YOU WANT ME** *Virgin VS 466* ⊛ ★	1	5	11
9 Jan 82	**BEING BOILED** *EMI FAST 4*	6		7
6 Feb 82	**HOLIDAY 80 (DOUBLE SINGLE)** *Virgin SV 105*	46		
20 Nov 82	**MIRROR MAN** *Virgin VS 522* ○	2		9
23 Apr 83	**(KEEP FEELING) FASCINATION** *Virgin VS 569* ○	2		7
5 May 84	**THE LEBANON** *Virgin VS 672*	11		5
30 Jun 84	**LIFE ON YOUR OWN** *Virgin VS 688*	16		5
17 Nov 84	**LOUISE** *Virgin VS 723*	13		8
23 Aug 86	**HUMAN** *Virgin VS 880* ★	8		6
22 Nov 86	**I NEED YOUR LOVING** *Virgin VS 900*	72		
15 Oct 88	**LOVE IS ALL THAT MATTERS** *Virgin VS 1025*	41		
18 Aug 90	**HEART LIKE A WHEEL** *Virgin VS 1262*	29		3
7 Jan 95	**TELL ME WHEN** *East West YZ 882CD1*	6		7
18 Mar 95	**ONE MAN IN MY HEART** *East West YZ 904CD1*	13		7
17 Jun 95	**FILLING UP WITH HEAVEN** *East West YZ 944CD*	36		1
28 Oct 95	**DON'T YOU WANT ME (REMIX)** *Virgin VSCDT 1557*	16		2
20 Jan 96	**STAY WITH ME TONIGHT** *East West EW 020CD*	40		1
11 Aug 01	**ALL I EVER WANTED** *Papillon BTFLYS 0012*	47		

HUMAN MOVEMENT UK production duo

Date	Title	Peak Position	Weeks at No.1	Weeks in Top 40
3 Feb 01	**LOVE HAS COME AGAIN** *Renaissance Recordings RENCDS 005* HUMAN MOVEMENT FEATURING SOPHIE MOLET	53		

HUMAN NATURE Australian group

Date	Title	Peak Position	Weeks at No.1	Weeks in Top 40
10 May 97	**WISHES** *Epic 6644485*	44		
30 Aug 97	**WHISPER YOUR NAME** *Epic 6649465*	53		
10 Mar 01	**HE DON'T LOVE YOU** *Epic 6708922*	18		2
30 Jun 01	**WHEN WE WERE YOUNG** *Epic 6713792*	43		

Silver-selling · Gold-selling · Platinum-selling · US No.1 ★ — Peak Position · Weeks at No.1 · Weeks in Top 40

HUMAN RESOURCE
Dutch production group

Date	Title	Peak Position	Weeks at No.1	Weeks in Top 40
14 Sep 91	**DOMINATOR** *R&S RSUK 4*	36		2
21 Dec 91	**THE COMPLETE DOMINATOR (REMIX)** *R&S RSUK 4X*	18		5

HUMANOID UK producer

Date	Title	Peak Position	Weeks at No.1	Weeks in Top 40
26 Nov 88	**STAKKER HUMANOID** *Westside WSR 12*	17		7
22 Apr 89	**SLAM** *Westside WSR 14*	54		
8 Aug 92	**STAKKER HUMANOID** *Jumpin' & Pumpin' TOT 27*	40		1
3 Mar 01	**STAKKER HUMANOID (REMIX)** *Jumpin' & Pumpin' CDSTOT 43*	65		

HUMATE German group

Date	Title	Peak Position	Weeks at No.1	Weeks in Top 40
30 Jan 99	**LOVE STIMULATION** *Deviant DVNT 22CDS*	18		2

HUMBLE PIE UK group

Date	Title	Peak Position	Weeks at No.1	Weeks in Top 40
23 Aug 69	**NATURAL BORN BUGIE** *Immediate IM 082*	4		10

ENGELBERT HUMPERDINCK UK singer

Date	Title	Peak Position	Weeks at No.1	Weeks in Top 40
26 Jan 67	**RELEASE ME** *Decca F 12541*	1	6	47
25 May 67	**THERE GOES MY EVERYTHING** *Decca F 12610*	2		26
23 Aug 67	**THE LAST WALTZ** *Decca F 12655*	1	5	26
10 Jan 68	**AM I THAT EASY TO FORGET** *Decca F 12722*	3		13
24 Apr 68	**A MAN WITHOUT LOVE** *Decca F 12770*	2		13
25 Sep 68	**LES BICYCLETTES DE BELSIZE** *Decca F 12834*	5		13
5 Feb 69	**THE WAY IT USED TO BE** *Decca F 12879*	3		12
9 Aug 69	**I'M A BETTER MAN (FOR HAVING LOVED YOU)** *Decca F 12957*	15		10
15 Nov 69	**WINTER WORLD OF LOVE** *Decca F 12980*	7		11
30 May 70	**MY MARIE** *Decca F 13032*	31		4
12 Sep 70	**SWEETHEART** *Decca F 13068*	22		5
11 Sep 71	**ANOTHER TIME ANOTHER PLACE** *Decca F 13212*	13		11
4 Mar 72	**TOO BEAUTIFUL TO LAST** *Decca F 13281*	14		8
20 Oct 73	**LOVE IS ALL** *Decca F 13443*	44		
30 Jan 99	**QUANDO QUANDO QUANDO** *The Hit Label HLC 15*	40		1
6 May 00	**HOW TO WIN YOUR LOVE** *Universal TV 8822682*	59		
12 Jun 04	**RELEASE ME** *Universal TV 9819567*	51		

HUNDRED REASONS UK group

Date	Title	Peak Position	Weeks at No.1	Weeks in Top 40
18 Aug 01	**EP TWO** *Columbia 6713922*	47		
15 Dec 01	**EP THREE** *Columbia 6720782*	37		1
16 Mar 02	**IF I COULD** *Columbia 6724402*	19		2
18 May 02	**SILVER** *Columbia 6726642*	15		1
28 Sep 02	**FALTER** *Columbia 6731455*	38		1
15 Nov 03	**THE GREAT TEST** *Columbia 6743762*	29		1
28 Feb 04	**WHAT YOU GET** *Columbia 6745495*	30		1
16 Oct 04	**HOW SOON IS NOW** *Sore Point SORE029CDS*	47		
18 Mar 06	**KILL YOUR OWN** *V2 VVR5036428*	48		

GERALDINE HUNT US singer

Date	Title	Peak Position	Weeks at No.1	Weeks in Top 40
25 Oct 80	**CAN'T FAKE THE FEELING** *Champagne FIZZ 501*	44		

MARSHA HUNT US singer

Date	Title	Peak Position	Weeks at No.1	Weeks in Top 40
21 May 69	**WALK ON GILDED SPLINTERS** *Track 604 030*	46		
2 May 70	**KEEP THE CUSTOMER SATISFIED** *Track 604 037*	41		

TOMMY HUNT US singer

Date	Title	Peak Position	Weeks at No.1	Weeks in Top 40
11 Oct 75	**CRACKIN' UP** *Spark SRL 1132*	39		1
21 Aug 76	**LOVING ON THE LOSING SIDE** *Spark SRL 1146*	28		9
4 Dec 76	**ONE FINE MORNING** *Spark SRL 1148*	44		

ALFONZO HUNTER US saxophonist

Date	Title	Peak Position	Weeks at No.1	Weeks in Top 40
22 Feb 97	**JUST THE WAY** *Cooltempo CDCOOL 326*	38		1

HUNTER UK gladiator

Date	Title	Peak Position	Weeks at No.1	Weeks in Top 40
9 Dec 95	**SHAKABOOM!** *Telstar HUNTCD 1* HUNTER FEATURING RUBY TURNER	64		

IAN HUNTER UK singer

Date	Title	Peak Position	Weeks at No.1	Weeks in Top 40
3 May 75	**ONCE BITTEN TWICE SHY** *CBS 3194*	14		8

TAB HUNTER US singer

Date	Title	Peak Position	Weeks at No.1	Weeks in Top 40
8 Feb 57	**YOUNG LOVE** *London HLD 8380* ★	1	7	18
12 Apr 57	**99 WAYS** *London HLD 8410*	5		12

TERRY HUNTER US producer

Date	Title	Peak Position	Weeks at No.1	Weeks in Top 40
26 Jul 97	**HARVEST FOR THE WORLD** *Delirious DELICD 4*	48		

HURLEY & TODD UK production duo

Date	Title	Peak Position	Weeks at No.1	Weeks in Top 40
29 Apr 00	**SUNSTORM** *Multiply CDMULTY 58*	38		1

STEVE 'SILK' HURLEY US singer

Date	Title	Peak Position	Weeks at No.1	Weeks in Top 40
10 Jan 87	**JACK YOUR BODY** *DJInternational LON 117*	1	2	8

HURRICANE #1 UK group

Date	Title	Peak Position	Weeks at No.1	Weeks in Top 40
10 May 97	**STEP INTO MY WORLD** *Creation CRESCD 253*	29		1
5 Jul 97	**JUST ANOTHER ILLUSION** *Creation CRESCD 264*	35		1
6 Sep 97	**CHAIN REACTION** *Creation CRESCD 271*	30		1
1 Nov 97	**STEP INTO MY WORLD** *Creation CRESCD 276*	19		1
21 Feb 98	**ONLY THE STRONGEST WILL SURVIVE** *Creation CRESCD 285*	19		1
24 Oct 98	**RISING SIGN** *Creation CRESCD 303*	47		
3 Apr 99	**THE GREATEST HIGH** *Creation CRESCD 309*	43		

PHIL HURTT US singer

Date	Title	Peak Position	Weeks at No.1	Weeks in Top 40
11 Nov 78	**GIVING IT BACK** *Fantasy FTC 161*	36		1

HUSTLERS CONVENTION UK group

Date	Title	Peak Position	Weeks at No.1	Weeks in Top 40
20 May 95	**DANCE TO THE MUSIC** *Stress CDSTR 53* HUSTLERS CONVENTION FEATURING DAVE LAUDAT & ONDRERA DUVERNY	71		

WILLIE HUTCH US singer

Date	Title	Peak Position	Weeks at No.1	Weeks in Top 40
4 Dec 82	**IN AND OUT** *Motown TMG 1285*	51		
6 Jul 85	**KEEP ON JAMMIN'** *Motown ZB 40173*	73		

JUNE HUTTON US singer

Date	Title	Peak Position	Weeks at No.1	Weeks in Top 40
7 Aug 53	**SAY YOU'RE MINE AGAIN** *Capitol CL 13918* JUNE HUTTON & AXEL STORDAHL & THE BOYS NEXT DOOR	6		7

HWA UK producer

Date	Title	Peak Position	Weeks at No.1	Weeks in Top 40
5 Dec 92	**SUPERSONIC** *Internal Affairs KGB 008* HWA FEATURING SONIC THE HEDGEHOG	33		5

HYBRID UK group

Date	Title	Peak Position	Weeks at No.1	Weeks in Top 40
10 Jul 99	**FINISHED SYMPHONY** *Distinctive DISNCD 52*	58		
11 Sep 99	**IF I SURVIVE** *Distinctive DISNCD 55* HYBRID FEATURING JULEE CRUISE	52		
3 Jun 00	**KID 2000** *Virgin VTS CD2* HYBRID FEATURING CHRISSIE HYNDE	32		1
20 Sep 03	**TRUE TO FORM** *Distinctive DISNCD 111* HYBRID FEATURING PETER HOOK	59		

BRIAN HYLAND US singer

Date	Title	Peak Position	Weeks at No.1	Weeks in Top 40
7 Jul 60	**ITSY BITSY TEENY WEENY YELLOW POLKA DOT BIKINI** *London HLR 9161* ★	8		11
20 Oct 60	**FOUR LITTLE HEELS** *London HLR 9203*	29		5
10 May 62	**GINNY COME LATELY** *HMV POP 1013*	5		15
2 Aug 62	**SEALED WITH A KISS** *HMV POP 1051*	3		13
8 Nov 62	**WARMED OVER KISSES** *HMV POP 1079*	28		4
27 Mar 71	**GYPSY WOMAN** *Uni UN 530*	42		
28 Jun 75	**SEALED WITH A KISS** *ABC 4059*	7		10

SHEILA HYLTON Jamaican singer

Date	Title	Peak Position	Weeks at No.1	Weeks in Top 40
15 Sep 79	**BREAKFAST IN BED** *United Artists BP 304*	57		
17 Jan 81	**THE BED'S TOO BIG WITHOUT YOU** *Island WIP 6671*	35		2

PHYLLIS HYMAN US singer

Date	Title	Peak Position	Weeks at No.1	Weeks in Top 40
16 Feb 80	**YOU KNOW HOW TO LOVE ME** *Arista ARIST 323*	47		
12 Sep 81	**YOU SURE LOOK GOOD TO ME** *Arista ARIST 424*	56		

DICK HYMAN TRIO US instrumental group

Date	Title	Peak Position	Weeks at No.1	Weeks in Top 40
16 Mar 56	**THEME FROM *THE THREEPENNY OPERA*** *MGM 890*	9		10

CHRISSIE HYNDE US singer

Date	Title	Peak Position	Weeks at No.1	Weeks in Top 40
3 Aug 85	**I GOT YOU BABE** *DEP International DEP 20* UB40 FEATURING CHRISSIE HYNDE ●	1	1	11
18 Jun 88	**BREAKFAST IN BED** *DEP International DEP 29* UB40 FEATURING CHRISSIE HYNDE	6		9
12 Oct 91	**SPIRITUAL HIGH (STATE OF INDEPENDENCE)** *Arista 114528* MOODSWINGS FEATURING CHRISSIE HYNDE	66		
23 Jan 93	**SPIRITUAL HIGH (STATE OF INDEPENDENCE) (REMIX)** *Arista 74321127712* MOODSWINGS FEATURING CHRISSIE HYNDE	47		
18 Mar 95	**LOVE CAN BUILD A BRIDGE** *London COCD 1* CHER, CHRISSIE HYNDE & NENEH CHERRY WITH ERIC CLAPTON ○	1	1	6
3 Jun 00	**KID 2000** *Virgin VTS CD2* HYBRID FEATURING CHRISSIE HYNDE	32		1
7 Feb 04	**STRAIGHT AHEAD** *Direction 6746222* TUBE & BERGER FEATURING CHRISSIE HYNDE	29		1

HYPER GO GO UK production duo

Date	Title	Peak Position	Weeks at No.1	Weeks in Top 40
22 Aug 92	**HIGH** *Deconstruction 74321110497*	30		3
31 Jul 93	**NEVER LET GO** *Positiva CDTIV 3*	45		
5 Feb 94	**RAISE** *Positiva CDTIV 9*	36		1
26 Nov 94	**IT'S ALRIGHT** *Positiva CDTIV 20*	49		
6 Apr 96	**DO WATCHA DO** *Avex UK AVEXCD 24* HYPER GO GO & ADEVA	54		
12 Oct 96	**HIGH (REMIX)** *Distinctive DISNCD 24*	32		1
12 Apr 97	**DO WATCHA DO (REMIX)** *Distinctive DISNCD 28* HYPER GO GO & ADEVA	60		

HYPERLOGIC UK production duo

Date	Title	Peak Position	Weeks at No.1	Weeks in Top 40
29 Jul 95	**ONLY ME** *Systematic SYSCD 15*	35		1
9 May 98	**ONLY ME (REMIX)** *Tidy Trax TIDY 113CD1*	48		

HYPERSTATE UK production duo

Date	Title	Peak Position	Weeks at No.1	Weeks in Top 40
6 Feb 93	**TIME AFTER TIME** *M&G MAGCD 34*	71		

HYPNOTIST UK producer

Date	Title	Peak Position	Weeks at No.1	Weeks in Top 40
28 Sep 91	**THE HOUSE IS MINE** *Rising High RSN 4*	65		
21 Dec 91	**THE HARDCORE EP** *Rising High RSN 13*	68		

HYPO PSYCHO UK group

Date	Title	Peak Position	Weeks at No.1	Weeks in Top 40
24 Jul 04	**PUBLIC ENEMY NO 1** *Believe Music SMASCD059*	53		

HYSTERIC EGO UK producer

Date	Title	Peak Position	Weeks at No.1	Weeks in Top 40
31 Aug 96	**WANT LOVE** *WEA 070CD*	28		2
21 Jun 97	**MINISTRY OF LOVE** *WEA 094CD*	39		1
28 Feb 98	**WANT LOVE (REMIX)** *WEA 150CD*	46		
13 Feb 99	**TIME TO GET BACK** *WEA 198CD*	50		

HYSTERICS UK group

Date	Title	Peak Position	Weeks at No.1	Weeks in Top 40
12 Dec 81	**JINGLE BELLS LAUGHING ALL THE WAY** *Record Delivery KA 5*	44		

HYSTERIX UK group

Date	Title	Peak Position	Weeks at No.1	Weeks in Top 40
7 May 94	**MUST BE THE MUSIC** *Deconstruction 74321207362*	40		1
18 Feb 95	**EVERYTHING** *Deconstruction 74321236882*	65		

Blur Versus Oasis

How The West Was Won

When Auntie Beeb starts talking about 'the hit parade' on the *Six O'Clock News*, you know something has gone mainstream. This is exactly what happened in August 1995 when Blur and Oasis released their new singles in the same week and the singles charts witnessed one of its biggest ever face-offs. Mockney Essex boys Blur, fronted by the handsome charm of drama student Damon Albarn, were competing against the lairy Mancunian brothers Gallagher, whose own band Oasis had rocketed to fame with a volley of classic singles and profanity-hurling, two-fingered salutes to the media.

Legend has it that after an initially warm relationship, the two bands squared up to each other over a pint in the Camden music-biz watering hole, The Good Mixer. Liam Gallagher's berating of Damon was said to be so relentless that the 'friendship' evaporated and eventually – via a high-profile war of words in the press – the two bands decided to confront each other across the chart listings.

Dubbed 'The Battle of Britain', the furore commenced on 14 August 1995 when shops started selling the respective singles. Some excitable but misinformed sections of the media hailed this as the best chart battle since the days of The Beatles and The Rolling Stones – however, these two legends had in fact staggered their releases for mutual benefit – despite the huge volume of singles both bands put out, they did not clash in this way. The Clash and The Sex Pistols, Spandau Ballet and Duran Duran, and The Stone Roses and The Happy Mondays were always plagued by rumours of rivalry, but nothing from those periods matched this.

The underdogs were the Mancunians. Oasis had enjoyed a previous Number 1 hit ('Some Might Say' in May of that year) whereas Blur had not (their best effort was 'Girls And Boys' at Number 5 in March 1994). However, the southerners had since raised Britain's pop crown aloft with the whimsical yet darkly observant *Parklife* album, a multi-platinum, multi-award-winning critics' favourite. Oasis, meanwhile, had unleashed a string of hit singles and possessed a belligerent but brilliant frontman in the shape of Liam Gallagher, coupled with the songwriting prowess of his witty older brother Noel, and become the favourite of the working man.

The backdrop for the Battle of Britain was Britpop. A backlash against the slacker-driven culture of grunge, the likes of (initially) Suede, Pulp and Blur had focused on Anglo-centric themes, quirky English social traits and highly stylised, romantic dramas. This generally more upbeat pop created a loosely gelled cluster of bands quickly dubbed Britpop. In reality, the extremes of Pulp's Jarvis Cocker's brilliance could not be any further away from the pop sensibility of Elastica, but the music biz loves its pigeon-holes and alongside these three lynchpins were dumped other artists such as the soon-to-be global Radiohead, The Auteurs, Supergrass, Shed Seven, The Bluetones, Marion and Dodgy.

Blur's pivotal second album, *Modern Life Is Rubbish*, openly paraded their Anglo-centric interests. The untimely death of Kurt Cobain and the arrival of Blur's third album *Parklife* sparked the deluge. A revival in the fortunes of Britpop 'forefathers' such as Paul Weller, New Order and Ray Davies added to the mix, as did a sartorial fashion for Fred Perry shirts, trainers, Harrington jackets and Oxfam chic that replaced grunge thrift-store style. With the fading recession and the sense of gloom that had made grunge seem so appropriate in the UK, the kids began to look for something more uplifting. Enter Blur vs Oasis.

The confrontation across the chart listings soon escalated to ludicrous heights: what had begun as handbags at dawn over a pint in north London was soon being portrayed as North vs South, middle-class vs working-class, rock vs pop, intelligence vs brawn, EMI vs Parlophone, Food Records vs Creation Records and so on.

Blur were the bookies' favourite – and with Oasis on tour in Japan for much of the week, Damon was left to take a sword to their chances with some of pop's wittiest put-downs. Fake estate agents' boards pronouncing 'For Sale: Country House. Enquire Within' were erected outside London record shops; when Damon appeared on Chris Evans' Radio 1 morning show, he sang Status Quo's 'Rockin' All Over The World' over the lead line of Oasis's track, and christened them Oasis Quo. Even in his own single's lyrics, Damon made a sly reference to Oasis's forthcoming album title *(What's The Story) Morning Glory?* Better formatting helped Blur sales, as did a cheaper price and a cheekier video – dubbed 'Benny-Hill-on-acid' by some observers – ensured more MTV coverage than Oasis's drab band footage (although Blur later distanced themselves from the Damien Hirst-directed video as the moment they went 'mainstream'). Oasis were decidedly less subtle – Noel said to one paper, 'Blur are a bunch of middle-class wankers trying to play hardball with a bunch of working-class heroes.'

In that same week, Mike Tyson was released from prison after serving a sentence for rape, it was the anniversary of VJ Day and Eastern European atrocities plagued continental politics. But, most importantly of all, the *Daily Sport* were able to use the headline 'It's a Blur Job'.

On the Sunday night, it was Blur who topped the charts – selling 270,000 copies of 'Country House', compared to (a still mighty) 220,000 copies of 'Roll With It'. All sorts of factors were blamed for the Mancs' loss, including bar-code problems, but the reality was that their single was their weakest song to date. 'Country House' – albeit a dark piece about Prozac, the rat race and panic attacks – was simply a better pop song.

What was certain was that British music was enjoying a golden era. Noel Gallagher quaffing drinks at No. 10, Jarvis waving his bottom at Michael Jackson and Robbie Williams getting bladdered with Oasis at Glastonbury were all obvious but fun highlights. 'Cool Britannia' had arrived, London became the über-cool capital of the world, and grinning politicians clamped on to pop stars like some electoral golden ticket.

The Battle of Britain was much more than just two bands going head to head in the charts. It was the moment that Britpop went unconditionally mainstream; liken it to the catwalk model wearing the £3,000 'grunge' denim if you will. Harsh perhaps, but it was certainly the moment when the movement lost its remaining vestiges of alternative cool and became part of the establishment. By the time Blur and Oasis were engaging in this feted battle for the Number 1 slot, there were already dissenters who bemoaned the mainstream prostitution of the scene, just like glam, punk, grunge and many other 'scenes' before it. Internationally, Britpop was impotent, with only Oasis enjoying any real success in a bemused Stateside market. By mid-1996, just a year after 'Country House', the movement was effectively dead. Still, good times ...

There was a Mancunian sting in the tail, however. If Blur had won the battle, Oasis would win the war. Within a year, they were playing to 125,000 at Knebworth and their second album *(What's The Story) Morning Glory?* was racing towards record-breaking sales of 4 million copies, while Blur took a musical diversion into American hardcore and then lost their mercurial guitarist Graham Coxon (he had called the chart battle 'a circle of freaks' and even left the band's own celebration party early).

Besides, the real winner was the singles charts – in the week of the battle, record sales had hit their highest peak for ten years, and of the 1.8 million singles sold, nearly 500,000 were from these two bands. It had been a year dominated by the likes of Robson & Jerome, so even the most churlish of critics welcomed such a rivalry, however much it was fuelled by the media. As a courtesy to the winner of the Battle of Britain, the last word must go to Blur's Damon Albarn: 'Pop people are defects. Pop people are funny in the head and the more pop they get, the funnier their heads become. Pop begins in bedrooms and ends up in supermarkets.'

KEY TO ARTIST ENTRIES

Artist/Group Name — Artist/Group Nationality and Category — Silver-selling — Gold-selling — Platinum-selling — US No.1 — Peak Position — Weeks at No.1 — Weeks in Top 40

DEXY'S MIDNIGHT RUNNERS UK group

Date	Title / Label	Peak Position	Weeks at No.1	Weeks in Top 40
19 Jan 80	**DANCE STANCE** *Oddball Productions R 6028*	40		1
22 Mar 80	**GENO** *Late Night Feelings R 6033* (silver)	1	2	12
12 Jul 80	**THERE THERE MY DEAR** *Late Night Feelings R 6038*	7		6
21 Mar 81	**PLAN B** *Parlophone R 6046*	58		
11 Jul 81	**SHOW ME** *Mercury DEXYS 6*	16		7
20 Mar 82	**THE CELTIC SOUL BROTHERS** *Mercury DEXYS 8* DEXY'S MIDNIGHT RUNNERS WITH THE EMERALD EXPRESS	45		
3 Jul 82	**COME ON EILEEN** *Mercury DEXYS 9* DEXY'S MIDNIGHT RUNNERS WITH THE EMERALD EXPRESS (platinum) ★	1	4	13
2 Oct 82	**JACKIE WILSON SAID (I'M IN HEAVEN WHEN YOU SMILE)** *Mercury DEXYS 10* KEVIN ROWLAND & DEXY'S MIDNIGHT RUNNERS	5		6
4 Dec 82	**LET'S GET THIS STRAIGHT (FROM THE START)/OLD** *Mercury DEXYS 11* KEVIN ROWLAND & DEXY'S MIDNIGHT RUNNERS	17		8
2 Apr 83	**THE CELTIC SOUL BROTHERS** *Mercury DEXYS 12* KEVIN ROWLAND & DEXY'S MIDNIGHT RUNNERS	20		5
22 Nov 86	**BECAUSE OF YOU** *Mercury BRUSH 1*	13		6

Date of entry into Top 75

Artist collaboration or where artist's name has changed

Song Title

Label and Catalogue Number

I AM KLOOT UK group

Date	Title / Label	Peak Position	Weeks at No.1	Weeks in Top 40
21 Jun 03	**LIFE IN A DAY** *Echo ECSCX 140*	43		
20 Sep 03	**3 FEET TALL** *Echo ECSCX 143*	46		
2 Apr 05	**OVER MY SHOULDER** *Echo ECSCD160*	38		1

I DREAM UK duo

Date	Title / Label	Peak Position	Weeks at No.1	Weeks in Top 40
27 Nov 04	**DREAMING** *19/UMTV 9868872* I DREAM FEATURING FRANKIE & CALVIN	19		2

I KAMANCHI UK duo

Date	Title / Label	Peak Position	Weeks at No.1	Weeks in Top 40
14 Jun 03	**NEVER CAN TELL/SOUL BEAT CALLING** *Full Cycle FCY052*	69		

I-LEVEL UK group

Date	Title / Label	Peak Position	Weeks at No.1	Weeks in Top 40
16 Apr 83	**MINEFIELD** *Virgin VS 563*	52		
18 Jun 83	**TEACHER** *Virgin VS 595*	56		

I MONSTER UK production duo

Date	Title / Label	Peak Position	Weeks at No.1	Weeks in Top 40
16 Jun 01	**DAYDREAM IN BLUE** *Instant Karma KARMA 7CD*	20		4

JANIS IAN US singer

Date	Title / Label	Peak Position	Weeks at No.1	Weeks in Top 40
17 Nov 79	**FLY TOO HIGH** *CBS 7936*	44		
28 Jun 80	**THE OTHER SIDE OF THE SUN** *CBS 8611*	44		

IAN VAN DAHL Belgian producer

Date	Title / Label	Peak Position	Weeks at No.1	Weeks in Top 40
21 Jul 01	**CASTLES IN THE SKY** *NuLife 74321867142*	3		13
22 Dec 01	**WILL I?** *NuLife 74321903402*	5		9
1 Jun 02	**REASON** *NuLife 74321938722*	8		5
12 Oct 02	**TRY** *NuLife 74321967942*	15		3
1 Nov 03	**I CAN'T LET YOU GO** *NuLife 82876570712*	20		2
17 Jul 04	**BELIEVE** *NuLife 82876626542*	27		1

ICE CUBE US rapper

Date	Title / Label	Peak Position	Weeks at No.1	Weeks in Top 40
27 Mar 93	**IT WAS A GOOD DAY** *Fourth & Broadway BRCD 270*	27		2
7 Aug 93	**CHECK YO SELF** *Fourth & Broadway BRCD 283* ICE CUBE FEATURING DAS EFX	36		3
11 Sep 93	**WICKED** *Fourth & Broadway BRCD 282*	62		
18 Dec 93	**REALLY DOE** *Fourth & Broadway BRCD 302*	66		
26 Mar 94	**YOU KNOW HOW WE DO IT** *Fourth & Broadway BRCD 303*	41		
27 Aug 94	**BOP GUN (ONE NATION)** *Fourth & Broadway BRCD 308* ICE CUBE FEATURING GEORGE CLINTON	22		2
24 Dec 94	**YOU KNOW HOW WE DO IT** *Fourth & Broadway BRCD 303*	46		
11 Mar 95	**HAND OF THE DEAD BODY** *Virgin America VUSCD 88* SCARFACE FEATURING ICE CUBE	41		
15 Apr 95	**NATURAL BORN KILLAZ** *Death Row A 8197CD* DR DRE & ICE CUBE	45		
22 Mar 97	**THE WORLD IS MINE** *Jive JIVECD 419*	60		
11 Dec 04	**YOU CAN DO IT** *All Around The World CDGLOBE396* ICE CUBE FEATURING MACK 10 & MS TOI	2		10

ICE MC UK rapper

Date	Title / Label	Peak Position	Weeks at No.1	Weeks in Top 40
6 Aug 94	**THINK ABOUT THE WAY (BOM DIGI DIGI BOM...)** *WEA YZ 829CD*	42		
8 Apr 95	**IT'S A RAINY DAY** *Eternal YZ 902CD*	73		
14 Sep 96	**BOM DIGI BOM (THINK ABOUT THE WAY)** *Eternal 073CD*	38		1

ICE-T US rapper

Date	Title / Label	Peak Position	Weeks at No.1	Weeks in Top 40
18 Mar 89	**HIGH ROLLERS** *Sire W 7574*	63		
17 Feb 90	**YOU PLAYED YOURSELF** *Sire W 9994*	64		
29 Sep 90	**SUPERFLY 1990** *Capitol CL 586* CURTIS MAYFIELD & ICE-T	48		
8 May 93	**I AIN'T NEW TA THIS** *Rhyme Syndicate SYNDD 1*	62		
18 Dec 93	**THAT'S HOW I'M LIVIN'** *Rhyme Syndicate SYNDD 2*	21		4
9 Apr 94	**GOTTA LOTTA LOVE** *Rhyme Syndicate SYNDD 3*	24		3
10 Dec 94	**BORN TO RAISE HELL** *Fox 74321230152* MOTORHEAD/ICE-T/WHITFIELD CRANE	47		
1 Jun 96	**I MUST STAND** *Rhyme Syndicate SYNDD 5*	23		1
7 Dec 96	**THE LANE** *Virgin SYNDD 6*	18		2

ICEBERG SLIMM UK rapper

Date	Title / Label	Peak Position	Weeks at No.1	Weeks in Top 40
7 Oct 00	**NURSERY RHYMES** *Polydor 5877632*	37		1
6 Nov 04	**STARSHIP** *V2 ARV5029063* ICEBERG SLIMM FEATURING COREE	73		

ICEHOUSE Australian group

Date	Title / Label	Peak Position	Weeks at No.1	Weeks in Top 40
5 Feb 83	**HEY LITTLE GIRL** *Chrysalis CHS 2670*	17		7
23 Apr 83	**STREET CAFÉ** *Chrysalis COOL 1*	62		
3 May 86	**NO PROMISES** *Chrysalis CHS 2978*	72		
29 Aug 87	**CRAZY** *Chrysalis CHS 3156*	74		
13 Feb 88	**CRAZY** *Chrysalis CHS 3156*	38		1
14 May 88	**ELECTRIC BLUE** *Chrysalis CHS 3239*	53		

ICICLE WORKS UK group

Date	Title / Label	Peak Position	Weeks at No.1	Weeks in Top 40
24 Dec 83	**LOVE IS A WONDERFUL COLOUR** *Beggars Banquet BEG 99*	15		4
10 Mar 84	**BIRDS FLY (WHISPER TO A SCREAM)/IN THE CAULDRON OF LOVE** *Beggars Banquet BEG 108*	53		
26 Jul 86	**UNDERSTANDING JANE** *Beggars Banquet BEG 160*	52		
4 Oct 86	**WHO DO YOU WANT FOR YOUR LOVE** *Beggars Banquet BEG 172*	54		
14 Feb 87	**EVANGELINE** *Beggars Banquet BEG 181*	53		
30 Apr 88	**LITTLE GIRL LOST** *Beggars Banquet BEG 215*	59		
17 Mar 90	**MOTORCYCLE RIDER** *Epic WORKS 100*	73		

ICON UK vocal/instrumental duo

Date	Title / Label	Peak Position	Weeks at No.1	Weeks in Top 40
15 Jun 96	**TAINTED LOVE** *Eternal WEA 057CD*	51		

IDEAL UK producer

Date	Title / Label	Peak Position	Weeks at No.1	Weeks in Top 40
6 Aug 94	**HOT** *Cleveland City CLECD 13019*	49		

IDEAL US US Group

Date	Title / Label	Peak Position	Weeks at No.1	Weeks in Top 40
23 Sep 00	**WHATEVER** *Virgin VUSCD 172* IDEAL US FEATURING LIL' MO	31		1

IDES OF MARCH US group

Date	Title / Label	Peak Position	Weeks at No.1	Weeks in Top 40
6 Jun 70	**VEHICLE** *Warner Brothers WB 7378*	31		5

ERIC IDLE UK comedian

Date	Title / Label	Peak Position	Weeks at No.1	Weeks in Top 40
17 Dec 94	**ONE FOOT IN THE GRAVE** *Victa CDVICTA 1* ERIC IDLE FEATURING RICHARD WILSON	50		

IDLEWILD UK group

Date	Title / Label	Peak Position	Weeks at No.1	Weeks in Top 40
9 May 98	**A FILM FOR THE FUTURE** *Food CDFOOD 111*	53		
25 Jul 98	**EVERYONE SAYS YOU'RE SO FRAGILE** *Food CDFOOD 113*	47		
24 Oct 98	**I'M A MESSAGE** *Food CDFOOD 114*	41		
13 Feb 99	**WHEN I ARGUE I SEE SHAPES** *Food CDFOODS 116*	19		1
2 Oct 99	**LITTLE DISCOURAGE** *Food CDFOODS 124*	24		1
8 Apr 00	**ACTUALLY IT'S DARKNESS** *Food CDFOODS 127*	23		1
24 Jun 00	**THESE WOODEN IDEAS** *Food CDFOODS 132*	32		1
28 Oct 00	**ROSEABILITY** *Food CDFOODS 134*	38		1
4 May 02	**YOU HELD THE WORLD IN YOUR ARMS** *Parlophone CDRS 6575*	9		2
13 Jul 02	**AMERICAN ENGLISH** *Parlophone CDRS 6582*	15		2
2 Nov 02	**LIVE IN A HIDING PLACE** *Parlophone CDRS 6587*	26		1
22 Feb 03	**A MODERN WAY OF LETTING GO** *Parlophone CDR 6598*	28		1
5 Mar 05	**LOVE STEALS US FROM LONELINESS** *Parlophone CDRS6658*	16		1
14 May 05	**I UNDERSTAND IT** *Parlophone CDRS6662*	32		1
23 Jul 05	**EL CAPITAN** *Parlophone CDRS6667*	39		1
10 Mar 07	**NO EMOTION** *Sequel SEQXD008*	36		1

BILLY IDOL UK singer

Date	Title / Label	Peak Position	Weeks at No.1	Weeks in Top 40
11 Sep 82	**HOT IN THE CITY** *Chrysalis CHS 2625*	58		
24 Mar 84	**REBEL YELL** *Chrysalis IDOL 2*	62		
30 Jun 84	**EYES WITHOUT A FACE** *Chrysalis IDOL 3*	18		6
29 Sep 84	**FLESH FOR FANTASY** *Chrysalis IDOL 4*	54		
13 Jul 85	**WHITE WEDDING** *Chrysalis IDOL 5*	6		11
14 Sep 85	**REBEL YELL** *Chrysalis IDOL 6*	6		10
4 Oct 86	**TO BE A LOVER** *Chrysalis IDOL 8*	22		6
7 Mar 87	**DON'T NEED A GUN** *Chrysalis IDOL 9*	26		3
13 Jun 87	**SWEET SIXTEEN** *Chrysalis IDOL 10*	17		6
3 Oct 87	**MONY MONY** *Chrysalis IDOL 11* ★	7		8

Silver-selling · Gold-selling · Platinum-selling · US No.1 ★ · Peak Position · Weeks at No.1 · Weeks in Top 40

Date	Title	Label	Peak Position	Weeks at No.1	Weeks in Top 40
16 Jan 88	HOT IN THE CITY (REMIX)	Chrysalis IDOL 12	13		6
13 Aug 88	CATCH MY FALL	Chrysalis IDOL 13	63		
28 Apr 90	CRADLE OF LOVE	Chrysalis IDOL 14	34		2
11 Aug 90	L.A. WOMAN	Chrysalis IDOL 15	70		
22 Dec 90	PRODIGAL BLUES	Chrysalis IDOL 16	47		
26 Jun 93	SHOCK TO THE SYSTEM	Chrysalis CDCHS 3994	30		2
10 Sep 94	SPEED	Fox 74321223472	47		

IDOLS UK group

Date	Title	Label	Peak Position	Weeks at No.1	Weeks in Top 40
27 Dec 03	HAPPY XMAS (WAR IS OVER)	S 82876583822	5		3

FRANK IFIELD UK singer

Date	Title	Label	Peak Position	Weeks at No.1	Weeks in Top 40
19 Feb 60	LUCKY DEVIL	Columbia DB 4399	22		5
29 Sep 60	GOTTA GET A DATE	Columbia DB 4496	49		
5 Jul 62	I REMEMBER YOU	Columbia DB 4856	1	7	27
25 Oct 62	LOVESICK BLUES	Columbia DB 4913	1	5	16
24 Jan 63	THE WAYWARD WIND	Columbia DB 4960	1	3	13
11 Apr 63	NOBODY'S DARLIN' BUT MINE	Columbia DB 7007	4		14
27 Jun 63	CONFESSIN'	Columbia DB 7062	1	2	16
17 Oct 63	MULE TRAIN	Columbia DB 7131	22		5
9 Jan 64	DON'T BLAME ME	Columbia DB 7184	8		11
23 Apr 64	ANGRY AT THE BIG OAK TREE	Columbia DB 7263	25		6
23 Jul 64	I SHOULD CARE	Columbia DB 7319	33		3
1 Oct 64	SUMMER IS OVER	Columbia DB 7355	25		6
19 Aug 65	PARADISE	Columbia DB 7655	26		7
23 Jun 66	NO ONE WILL EVER KNOW	Columbia DB 7940	25		4
8 Dec 66	CALL HER YOUR SWEETHEART	Columbia DB 8078	24		6
7 Dec 91	THE YODELLING SONG FRANK IFIELD FEATURING THE BACKROOM BOYS	EMI 7YODEL 1	40		1

ENRIQUE IGLESIAS Spanish singer

Date	Title	Label	Peak Position	Weeks at No.1	Weeks in Top 40
11 Sep 99	BAILAMOS	Interscope IND 97131 ★	4		7
18 Dec 99	RHYTHM DIVINE	Interscope 4972242	45		
14 Oct 00	COULD I HAVE THIS KISS FOREVER WHITNEY HOUSTON & ENRIQUE IGLESIAS	Arista 74321795992	7		6
2 Feb 02	HERO	Interscope IND 97671	1	4	17
27 Apr 02	ESCAPE (IMPORT)	Interscope 4976922	71		
25 May 02	ESCAPE	Interscope 4977232	3		11
7 Sep 02	LOVE TO SEE YOU CRY	Interscope IND 97760	12		4
7 Dec 02	MAYBE	Interscope 4978232	12		5
26 Apr 03	TO LOVE A WOMAN LIONEL RICHIE FEATURING ENRIQUE IGLESIAS	Mercury 0779082	19		3
29 Nov 03	ADDICTED	Interscope 9814328	11		3
20 Mar 04	NOT IN LOVE ENRIQUE FEATURING KELIS	Interscope 9862023	5		7
9 Jun 07	DO YOU KNOW (THE PING PONG SONG)	Interscope 1735807	3		17
29 Sep 07	TIRED OF BEING SORRY	Interscope 1747082	20		4

JULIO IGLESIAS Spanish singer

Date	Title	Label	Peak Position	Weeks at No.1	Weeks in Top 40
24 Oct 81	BEGIN THE BEGUINE (VOLVER A EMPEZAR)	CBS A 1612	1	1	12
6 Mar 82	QUIEREME MUCHO (YOURS)	CBS A 1939	3		7
9 Oct 82	AMOR	CBS A 2801	32		2
9 Apr 83	HEY!	CBS JULIO 1	31		5
7 Apr 84	TO ALL THE GIRLS I'VE LOVED BEFORE JULIO IGLESIAS & WILLIE NELSON	CBS A 4252	17		6
7 Jul 84	ALL OF YOU JULIO IGLESIAS & DIANA ROSS	CBS A 4522	43		
6 Aug 88	MY LOVE JULIO IGLESIAS FEATURING STEVIE WONDER	CBS JULIO 2	5		8
4 Jun 94	CRAZY	Columbia 6603695	43		
26 Nov 94	FRAGILE	Columbia 6610192	53		

IGNORANTS UK vocal duo

Date	Title	Label	Peak Position	Weeks at No.1	Weeks in Top 40
25 Dec 93	PHAT GIRLS	Spaghetti CIOCD 8	59		

IL PADRINOS UK production group

Date	Title	Label	Peak Position	Weeks at No.1	Weeks in Top 40
7 Sep 02	THAT'S HOW GOOD YOUR LOVE IS IL PADRINOS FEATURING JOCELYN BROWN	Defected DFTD 057CDS	54		

ILLEGAL MOTION UK duo

Date	Title	Label	Peak Position	Weeks at No.1	Weeks in Top 40
9 Oct 93	SATURDAY LOVE ILLEGAL MOTION FEATURING SIMONE CHAPMAN	Arista 74321163032	67		

ILLICIT UK producer

Date	Title	Label	Peak Position	Weeks at No.1	Weeks in Top 40
2 Sep 00	CHEEKY ARMADA ILLICIT FEATURING GRAM'MA FUNK	Yola YOLACDX 01	72		

IIO US producer

Date	Title	Label	Peak Position	Weeks at No.1	Weeks in Top 40
10 Nov 01	RAPTURE	Made/Data/MoS 27CDS	2		10
14 Jun 03	AT THE END	Free 2 Air 0148065 F2A	20		2

IKARA COLT UK group

Date	Title	Label	Peak Position	Weeks at No.1	Weeks in Top 40
2 Mar 02	RUDD	Fantastic Plastic FPS 029	72		
28 Feb 04	WANNA BE THAT WAY	Fantastic Plastic FPS 038X	49		
5 Jun 04	WAKE IN THE CITY	Fantastic Plastic FPS 040X	55		
23 Oct 04	MODERN FEELING	Fantastic Plastic FPS 042	61		

ILS UK producer

Date	Title	Label	Peak Position	Weeks at No.1	Weeks in Top 40
23 Feb 02	NEXT LEVEL	Marine Parade MAPA 012	75		

IMAANI UK singer

Date	Title	Label	Peak Position	Weeks at No.1	Weeks in Top 40
9 May 98	WHERE ARE YOU	EMI CDEM 510	15		4

IMAGINATION UK group

Date	Title	Label	Peak Position	Weeks at No.1	Weeks in Top 40
16 May 81	BODY TALK	R&B RBS 201	4		11
5 Sep 81	IN AND OUT OF LOVE	R&B RBS 202	16		7
14 Nov 81	FLASHBACK	R&B RBS 206	16		10
6 Mar 82	JUST AN ILLUSION	R&B RBS 208	2		9
26 Jun 82	MUSIC AND LIGHTS	R&B RBS 210	5		7
25 Sep 82	IN THE HEAT OF THE NIGHT	R&B RBS 211	22		7
11 Dec 82	CHANGES	R&B RBS 213	31		3
4 Jun 83	LOOKING AT MIDNIGHT	R&B RBS 214	29		4
5 Nov 83	NEW DIMENSIONS	R&B RBS 216	56		
26 May 84	STATE OF LOVE	R&B RBS 218	67		
24 Nov 84	THANK YOU MY LOVE	R&B RBS 219	22		7
16 Jan 88	INSTINCTUAL	RCA PB 41697	62		

IMAJIN US group

Date	Title	Label	Peak Position	Weeks at No.1	Weeks in Top 40
27 Jun 98	SHORTY (YOU KEEP PLAYIN' WITH MY MIND) IMAJIN FEATURING KEITH MURRAY	Jive 0521212	22		1
20 Feb 99	NO DOUBT	Jive 0521772	42		
24 Apr 99	BOUNCE, ROCK, SKATE, ROLL BABY DC FEATURING IMAJIN	Jive 0522142	45		
12 Feb 00	FLAVA	Jive 9250012	64		

NATALIE IMBRUGLIA Australian singer

Date	Title	Label	Peak Position	Weeks at No.1	Weeks in Top 40
8 Nov 97	TORN	RCA 74321527982	2		16
14 Mar 98	BIG MISTAKE	RCA 74321566782	2		7
6 Jun 98	WISHING I WAS HERE	RCA 74321585062	19		3
17 Oct 98	SMOKE	RCA 74321621942	5		3
10 Nov 01	THAT DAY	RCA 74321896792	11		2
23 Mar 02	WRONG IMPRESSION	RCA 74321928352	10		3
3 Aug 02	BEAUTY ON THE FIRE	RCA 74321950362	26		1
2 Apr 05	SHIVER	Brightside 82876686882	8		8
6 Aug 05	COUNTING DOWN THE DAYS	Brightside 82876715592	23		3
8 Sep 07	GLORIOUS	Brightside 88697137112	23		2
29 Sep 07	TORN	Brightside 74321527982	70		

IMMACULATE FOOLS UK group

Date	Title	Label	Peak Position	Weeks at No.1	Weeks in Top 40
26 Jan 85	IMMACULATE FOOLS	A&M AM 227	51		

IMMATURE US singer

Date	Title	Label	Peak Position	Weeks at No.1	Weeks in Top 40
16 Mar 96	WE GOT IT IMMATURE FEATURING SMOOTH	MCA MCSTD 48009	26		1

IMPALAS US group

Date	Title	Label	Peak Position	Weeks at No.1	Weeks in Top 40
21 Aug 59	SORRY (I RAN ALL THE WAY HOME)	MGM 1015	28		1

IMPEDANCE UK producer

Date	Title / Label	Peak Position	Weeks at No.1	Weeks in Top 40
11 Nov 89	**TAINTED LOVE** *Jumpin' & Pumpin' TOT 4*	54		

IMPERIAL DRAG UK group

Date	Title / Label	Peak Position	Weeks at No.1	Weeks in Top 40
12 Oct 96	**BOY OR A GIRL** *Columbia 6632992*	54		

IMPERIAL TEEN US group

Date	Title / Label	Peak Position	Weeks at No.1	Weeks in Top 40
7 Sep 96	**YOU'RE ONE** *Slash LASCD 57*	69		

IMPERIALS US group

Date	Title / Label	Peak Position	Weeks at No.1	Weeks in Top 40
24 Dec 77	**WHO'S GONNA LOVE ME** *Power Exchange PX 266*	17		6

IMPRESSIONS US group

Date	Title / Label	Peak Position	Weeks at No.1	Weeks in Top 40
22 Nov 75	**FIRST IMPRESSIONS** *Curtom K 16638*	16		9

IN CROWD UK group

Date	Title / Label	Peak Position	Weeks at No.1	Weeks in Top 40
20 May 65	**THAT'S HOW STRONG MY LOVE IS** *Parlophone R 5276*	48		

IN TUA NUA Irish group

Date	Title / Label	Peak Position	Weeks at No.1	Weeks in Top 40
14 May 88	**ALL I WANTED** *Virgin VS 1072*	69		

INAURA UK group

Date	Title / Label	Peak Position	Weeks at No.1	Weeks in Top 40
18 May 96	**COMA AROMA** *EMI CDEM 421*	57		

INCANTATION UK group

Date	Title / Label	Peak Position	Weeks at No.1	Weeks in Top 40
4 Dec 82	**CACHARPAYA (ANDES PUMPSA DAESI)** *Beggars Banquet BEG 84*	12		8

INCOGNITO UK group

Date	Title / Label	Peak Position	Weeks at No.1	Weeks in Top 40
15 Nov 80	**PARISIENNE GIRL** *Ensign ENY 44*	73		
29 Jun 91	**ALWAYS THERE** *Talkin Loud TLK 10* INCOGNITO FEATURING JOCELYN BROWN	6		7
14 Sep 91	**CRAZY FOR YOU** *Talkin Loud TLK 14* INCOGNITO FEATURING CHYNA	59		
6 Jun 92	**DON'T YOU WORRY 'BOUT A THING** *Talkin Loud TLK 21*	19		4
15 Aug 92	**CHANGE** *Talkin Loud TLK 26*	52		
21 Aug 93	**STILL A FRIEND OF MINE** *Talkin Loud TLKCD 42*	47		
20 Nov 93	**GIVIN' IT UP** *Talkin Loud TLKCD 44*	43		
12 Mar 94	**PIECES OF A DREAM** *Talkin Loud TLKCD 46*	35		1
27 May 95	**EVERYDAY** *Talkin Loud TLKCD 55*	23		2
5 Aug 95	**I HEAR YOUR NAME** *Talkin Loud TLKCD 56*	42		
11 May 96	**JUMP TO MY LOVE/ALWAYS THERE** *Talkin Loud TLCD 7* INCOGNITO/INCOGNITO FEATURING JOCELYN BROWN	29		1
26 Oct 96	**OUT OF THE STORM** *Talkin Loud TLCD 14*	57		
10 Apr 99	**NIGHTS OVER EGYPT** *Talkin Loud TLCD 40*	56		

INCUBUS US group

Date	Title / Label	Peak Position	Weeks at No.1	Weeks in Top 40
20 May 00	**PARDON ME** *Epic 6693462*	61		
23 Jun 01	**DRIVE** *Epic 6713782*	40		1
2 Feb 02	**WISH YOU WERE HERE** *Epic 6722552*	27		1
14 Sep 02	**ARE YOU IN** *Epic 6728485*	34		1
7 Feb 04	**MEGLOMANIAC** *Epic 6746465*	23		1
19 Jun 04	**TALK SHOWS ON MUTE** *Epic 6749022*	43		

INDEEP US group

Date	Title / Label	Peak Position	Weeks at No.1	Weeks in Top 40
22 Jan 83	**LAST NIGHT A DJ SAVED MY LIFE** *Sound Of New York SNY 1*	13		7
14 May 83	**WHEN BOYS TALK** *Sound of New York SNY 3*	67		

INDIA US vocalist

Date	Title / Label	Peak Position	Weeks at No.1	Weeks in Top 40
26 Feb 94	**LOVE AND HAPPINESS (YEMAYA Y OCHUN)** *Cooltempo CDCOOL 287* RIVER OCEAN FEATURING INDIA	50		
5 Aug 95	**I CAN'T GET NO SLEEP** *A&M 5811412* MASTERS AT WORK PRESENT INDIA	44		
16 Mar 96	**OYE COMO VA** *Media MCSTD 40013* TITO PUENTE Jr & THE LATIN RHYTHM FEATURING TITO PUENTE, INDIA & CALI ALEMAN	36		1
8 Feb 97	**RUNAWAY** *Talkin Loud TLCD 20* NUYORICAN SOUL FEATURING INDIA	24		2
19 Jul 97	**OYE COMO VA (REMIX)** *Nukleuz MCSTD 40120* TITO PUENTE Jr & THE LATIN RHYTHM FEATURING TITO PUENTE, INDIA & CALI ALEMAN	56		
31 Jul 99	**TO BE IN LOVE** *Defected DEFECT 5CD* MAW PRESENTS INDIA	23		2
6 Jul 02	**BACKFIRED** *Susu CDSUSU 4* MASTERS AT WORK FEATURING INDIA	62		

INDIAN VIBES UK group

Date	Title / Label	Peak Position	Weeks at No.1	Weeks in Top 40
24 Sep 94	**MATHAR** *Virgin International DINSD 136*	68		
2 May 98	**MATHAR (REMIX)** *VC Recordings VCRD 32*	52		

INDIEN UK duo

Date	Title / Label	Peak Position	Weeks at No.1	Weeks in Top 40
9 Aug 03	**SHOW ME LOVE** *Concept CDCON 40*	69		

INDO US rapper

Date	Title / Label	Peak Position	Weeks at No.1	Weeks in Top 40
18 Apr 98	**R U SLEEPING** *Satellite 74321568212*	31		1

INDUSTRY STANDARD UK production duo

Date	Title / Label	Peak Position	Weeks at No.1	Weeks in Top 40
10 Jan 98	**VOLUME 1 (WHAT YOU WANT WHAT YOU NEED)** *Satellite 74321543742*	34		1

INFADELS UK group

Date	Title / Label	Peak Position	Weeks at No.1	Weeks in Top 40
4 Feb 06	**CAN'T GET ENOUGH** *Wall Of Sound WALLD110*	43		

INFARED VS GIL FELIX US production group

Date	Title / Label	Peak Position	Weeks at No.1	Weeks in Top 40
4 Oct 03	**CAPOEIRA** *Infrared INFRA 24CD*	67		

INFERNAL Danish group

Date	Title / Label	Peak Position	Weeks at No.1	Weeks in Top 40
22 Apr 06	**FROM PARIS TO BERLIN** *Apollo APOLLO102CD*	2		18
11 Nov 06	**SELF CONTROL** *Europa EUROPA101CDS*	18		3

INGRAM US group

Date	Title / Label	Peak Position	Weeks at No.1	Weeks in Top 40
11 Jun 83	**SMOOTHIN' GROOVIN'** *Streetwave WAVE 3*	56		

JAMES INGRAM US singer

Date	Title / Label	Peak Position	Weeks at No.1	Weeks in Top 40
12 Feb 83	**BABY COME TO ME** *Qwest K 15005* PATTI AUSTIN & JAMES INGRAM ★	11		9
18 Feb 84	**YAH MO B THERE** *Qwest W 9394* JAMES INGRAM WITH MICHAEL McDONALD	44		
12 Jan 85	**YAH MO B THERE** *Qwest W 9394* JAMES INGRAM WITH MICHAEL McDONALD	12		6
11 Jul 87	**SOMEWHERE OUT THERE** *MCA 1132* LINDA RONSTADT & JAMES INGRAM	8		9
31 Mar 90	**SECRET GARDEN** *Qwest W 9992* QUINCY JONES FEATURING AL B SURE!, JAMES INGRAM, EL DeBARGE & BARRY WHITE	67		
16 Apr 94	**THE DAY I FALL IN LOVE** *Columbia 6600282* DOLLY PARTON & JAMES INGRAM	64		

INK SPOTS US group

Date	Title / Label	Peak Position	Weeks at No.1	Weeks in Top 40
29 Apr 55	**MELODY OF LOVE** *Parlophone R 3977*	10		4

JOHN INMAN UK actor

Date	Title / Label	Peak Position	Weeks at No.1	Weeks in Top 40
25 Oct 75	**ARE YOU BEING SERVED SIR** *DJM DJS 602*	39		3

INMATES UK group

Date	Title / Label	Peak Position	Weeks at No.1	Weeks in Top 40
8 Dec 79	**THE WALK** *Radar ADA 47*	36		2

Silver-selling · Gold-selling · Platinum-selling · US No.1 ★ · Peak Position · Weeks at No.1 · Weeks in Top 40

INME UK group

Date	Title / Label	Peak Position	Weeks at No.1	Weeks in Top 40
27 Jul 02	**UNDERDOSE** *Music For Nations CDKUT 195*	66		
28 Sep 02	**FIREFLY** *Music For Nations CDKUT 197*	43		
18 Jan 03	**CRUSHED LIKE FRUIT** *Music For Nations CDKUT 200*	25		1
26 Apr 03	**NEPTUNE** *Music For Nations CDXKUT 201*	46		
5 Jun 04	**FASTER THE CHASE** *Music For Nations CDXKUT 210*	31		1
30 Jul 05	**7 WEEKS** *Pandora's Box PB002NMECD*	36		1
22 Oct 05	**SO YOU KNOW** *Pandora's Box PB003NMECD*	33		1

INNER CIRCLE Jamaican group

Date	Title / Label	Peak Position	Weeks at No.1	Weeks in Top 40
24 Feb 79	**EVERYTHING IS GREAT** *Island WIP 6472*	37		1
12 May 79	**STOP BREAKING MY HEART** *Island WIP 6488*	50		
31 Oct 92	**SWEAT (A LA LA LA LA LONG)** *Magnet 9031776802*	43		
1 May 93	**SWEAT (A LA LA LA LA LONG)** *Magnet 9031776802*	3		13
31 Jul 93	**BAD BOYS** *Magnet MAG 1017CD*	52		
10 Sep 94	**GAMES PEOPLE PLAY** *Magnet MAG 1026CD*	67		

INNER CITY US duo

Date	Title / Label	Peak Position	Weeks at No.1	Weeks in Top 40
3 Sep 88	**BIG FUN** *10 TEN 240* INNER CITY FEATURING KEVIN SAUNDERSON	8		11
10 Dec 88	**GOOD LIFE** *10 TEN 249*	4		11
22 Apr 89	**AIN'T NOBODY BETTER** *10 TEN 252*	10		5
29 Jul 89	**DO YOU LOVE WHAT YOU FEEL** *10 TEN 237*	16		5
18 Nov 89	**WATCHA GONNA DO WITH MY LOVIN'** *10 TEN 290*	12		6
13 Oct 90	**THAT MAN (HE'S ALL MINE)** *10 TEN 334*	42		
23 Feb 91	**TILL WE MEET AGAIN** *10 TEN 337*	47		
7 Dec 91	**LET IT REIGN** *10 TEN 392*	51		
4 Apr 92	**HALLELUJAH '92** *10 TEN 398*	22		3
13 Jun 92	**PENNIES FROM HEAVEN** *10 TEN 405*	24		3
12 Sep 92	**PRAISE** *10 TENX 408*	59		
27 Feb 93	**TILL WE MEET AGAIN (REMIX)** *10 TENCD 414*	55		
14 Aug 93	**BACK TOGETHER AGAIN** *Six6 SIXCD 104*	49		
5 Feb 94	**DO YA** *Six6 SIXCD 107*	44		
9 Jul 94	**SHARE MY LIFE** *Six6 SIXCD 114*	62		
10 Feb 96	**YOUR LOVE** *Six6 SIXCD 127*	28		1
5 Oct 96	**DO ME RIGHT** *Six6 SIXXCD 2*	47		
6 Feb 99	**GOOD LIFE (BUENA VIDA)** *Pias Recordings PIASX 002CD*	10		3

INNER SANCTUM Canadian producer

Date	Title / Label	Peak Position	Weeks at No.1	Weeks in Top 40
23 May 98	**HOW SOON IS NOW** *Malarky MLKD 6*	75		

INNERZONE ORCHESTRA US producer

Date	Title / Label	Peak Position	Weeks at No.1	Weeks in Top 40
28 Sep 96	**BUG IN THE BASSBIN** *Mo Wax MW 049CD*	68		

INNOCENCE UK group

Date	Title / Label	Peak Position	Weeks at No.1	Weeks in Top 40
3 Mar 90	**NATURAL THING** *Cooltempo COOL 201*	16		5
21 Jul 90	**SILENT VOICE** *Cooltempo COOL 212*	37		1
13 Oct 90	**LET'S PUSH IT** *Cooltempo COOL 220*	25		5
8 Dec 90	**A MATTER OF FACT** *Cooltempo COOL 223*	37		3
30 Mar 91	**REMEMBER THE DAY** *Cooltempo COOL 226*	56		
20 Jun 92	**I'LL BE THERE** *Cooltempo COOL 255*	26		2
3 Oct 92	**ONE LOVE IN MY LIFETIME** *Cooltempo COOL 263*	40		1
21 Nov 92	**BUILD** *Cooltempo COOL 267*	72		

INSANE CLOWN POSSE US duo

Date	Title / Label	Peak Position	Weeks at No.1	Weeks in Top 40
17 Jan 98	**HALLS OF ILLUSION** *Island CID 685*	56		
6 Jun 98	**HOKUS POKUS** *Island CIDX 705*	53		

INSPIRAL CARPETS UK group

Date	Title / Label	Peak Position	Weeks at No.1	Weeks in Top 40
18 Nov 89	**MOVE** *Cow DUNG 6*	49		
17 Mar 90	**THIS IS HOW IT FEELS** *Cow DUNG 7*	14		6
30 Jun 90	**SHE COMES IN THE FALL** *Cow DUNG 10*	27		4
17 Nov 90	**ISLAND HEAD (EP)** *Cow DUNG 11*	21		3
30 Mar 91	**CARAVAN** *Cow DUNG 13*	30		3
22 Jun 91	**PLEASE BE CRUEL** *Cow DUNG 15*	50		
29 Feb 92	**DRAGGING ME DOWN** *Cow DUNG 16*	12		4
30 May 92	**TWO WORLDS COLLIDE** *Cow DUNG 17*	32		1
19 Sep 92	**GENERATIONS** *Cow DUNG 18T*	28		2
14 Nov 92	**BITCHES BREW** *Cow DUNG 20T*	36		1
5 Jun 93	**HOW IT SHOULD BE** *Cow DUNG 22CD*	49		
22 Jan 94	**SATURN 5** *Cow DUNG 23CD*	20		3
5 Mar 94	**I WANT YOU** *Cow DUNG 24CD* INSPIRAL CARPETS FEATURING MARK E SMITH	18		2
7 May 94	**UNIFORM** *Cow DUNG 26CD*	51		
16 Sep 95	**JOE** *Cow DUNG 27CD*	37		1
26 Jul 03	**COME BACK TOMORROW** *Mute DUNG 31CD*	43		

INSPIRATIONAL CHOIR US gospel choir

Date	Title / Label	Peak Position	Weeks at No.1	Weeks in Top 40
22 Dec 84	**ABIDE WITH ME** *Epic A 4997*	44		
14 Dec 85	**ABIDE WITH ME** *Portrait A 4997*	36		1

INSTANT FUNK US group

Date	Title / Label	Peak Position	Weeks at No.1	Weeks in Top 40
20 Jan 79	**GOT MY MIND MADE UP** *Salsoul SSOL 114*	46		

INTASTELLA UK group

Date	Title / Label	Peak Position	Weeks at No.1	Weeks in Top 40
25 May 91	**DREAM SOME PARADISE** *MCA MCS 1520*	69		
24 Aug 91	**PEOPLE** *MCA MCS 1559*	74		
16 Nov 91	**CENTURY** *MCA MCS 1585*	70		
23 Sep 95	**THE NIGHT** *Planet 3 GXY 2005CD*	60		

INTELLIGENT HOODLUM US rapper

Date	Title / Label	Peak Position	Weeks at No.1	Weeks in Top 40
6 Oct 90	**BACK TO REALITY** *A&M AM 598*	55		

INTENSO PROJECT UK duo

Date	Title / Label	Peak Position	Weeks at No.1	Weeks in Top 40
17 Aug 02	**LUV DA SUNSHINE** *Inferno CDFERN 47*	22		1
26 Jul 03	**YOUR MUSIC** *Concept CDCON 43* INTENSO PROJECT FEATURING LAURA JAYE	32		1
4 Dec 04	**GET IT ON** *Inspired INSPMOS1CDS* INTENSO PROJECT FEATURING LISA SCOTT-LEE	23		1

INTERACTIVE German group

Date	Title / Label	Peak Position	Weeks at No.1	Weeks in Top 40
13 Apr 96	**FOREVER YOUNG** *ffrreedom TABCD 235*	28		1
8 Mar 03	**FOREVER YOUNG** *All Around The World CDGLOBE 253*	37		1

INTERPOL US group

Date	Title / Label	Peak Position	Weeks at No.1	Weeks in Top 40
23 Nov 02	**OBSTACLE 1** *Matador OLE 5702*	72		
26 Apr 03	**SAY HELLO TO THE ANGELS/NYC** *Matador OLE 5822*	65		
27 Sep 03	**OBSTACLE 1** *Matador OLE 5942*	41		
25 Sep 04	**SLOW HANDS** *Matador OLE 6362*	36		1
15 Jan 05	**EVIL** *Matador OLE 6376*	18		2
23 Apr 05	**C'MERE** *Matador OLE6642*	19		1
9 Jul 05	**SLOW HANDS** *Matador OLE6692*	44		
14 Jul 07	**THE HEINRICH MANEUVER** *Parlophone CLCD894*	31		1
15 Sep 07	**MAMMOTH** *Parlophone CDCLS896*	44		

INTRUDERS US group

Date	Title / Label	Peak Position	Weeks at No.1	Weeks in Top 40
13 Apr 74	**I'LL ALWAYS LOVE MY MAMA** *Philadelphia International PIR 2149*	32		4
6 Jul 74	**(WIN PLACE OR SHOW) SHE'S A WINNER** *Philadelphia International PIR 2212*	14		7
22 Dec 84	**WHO DO YOU LOVE?** *Streetwave KHAN 34*	65		

INVISIBLE MAN UK producer

Date	Title / Label	Peak Position	Weeks at No.1	Weeks in Top 40
17 Apr 99	**GIVE A LITTLE LOVE** *Serious SERR 006CD*	48		

INXS Australian group

Date	Title / Label	Peak Position	Weeks at No.1	Weeks in Top 40
19 Apr 86	**WHAT YOU NEED** *Mercury INXS 5*	51		
28 Jun 86	**LISTEN LIKE THIEVES** *Mercury INXS 6*	46		
30 Aug 86	**KISS THE DIRT (FALLING DOWN THE MOUNTAIN)** *Mercury INXS 7*	54		
24 Oct 87	**NEED YOU TONIGHT** *Mercury INXS* ★	58		
9 Jan 88	**NEW SENSATION** *Mercury INXS 9*	25		4
12 Mar 88	**DEVIL INSIDE** *Mercury INXS 10*	47		
25 Jun 88	**NEVER TEAR US APART** *Mercury INXS 11*	24		6
12 Nov 88	**NEED YOU TONIGHT** *Mercury INXS 12*	2		10
8 Apr 89	**MYSTIFY** *Mercury INXS 13*	14		5
15 Sep 90	**SUICIDE BLONDE** *Mercury INXS 14*	11		4
8 Dec 90	**DISAPPEAR** *Mercury INXS 15*	21		6
26 Jan 91	**GOOD TIMES** *Atlantic A 7751* JIMMY BARNES & INXS	18		5
30 Mar 91	**BY MY SIDE** *Mercury INXS 16*	42		
13 Jul 91	**BITTER TEARS** *Mercury INXS 17*	30		2
2 Nov 91	**SHINING STAR (EP)** *Mercury INXS 18*	27		2

Date	Title	Label	Peak Position	Weeks at No.1	Weeks in Top 40
18 Jul 92	**HEAVEN SENT**	*Mercury INXS 19*	31		2
5 Sep 92	**BABY DON'T CRY**	*Mercury INXS 20*	20		4
14 Nov 92	**TASTE IT**	*Mercury INXS 23*	21		3
13 Feb 93	**BEAUTIFUL GIRL**	*Mercury INXCD 24*	23		3
23 Oct 93	**THE GIFT**	*Mercury INXCD 25*	11		2
11 Dec 93	**PLEASE (YOU GOT THAT...)**	*Mercury INXCD 26*	50		
22 Oct 94	**THE STRANGEST PARTY (THESE ARE THE TIMES)**	*Mercury INXCD 27*	15		3
22 Mar 97	**ELEGANTLY WASTED**	*Mercury INXCD 28*	20		1
7 Jun 97	**EVERYTHING**	*Mercury INXDD 29*	71		
18 Aug 01	**PRECIOUS HEART** TALL PAUL VS INXS	*Duty Freee/Decode DFTELCD 001*	14		3
3 Nov 01	**I'M SO CRAZY** PAR-T-ONE VS INXS	*Credence CDCRED 016*	19		2

SWEETIE IRIE Jamaican singer

Date	Title	Label	Peak Position	Weeks at No.1	Weeks in Top 40
17 Nov 90	**SMILE** ASWAD FEATURING SWEETIE IRIE	*Mango MNG 767*	53		
3 Aug 91	**TAKE ME IN YOUR ARMS AND LOVE ME** SCRITTI POLITTI & SWEETIE IRIE	*Virgin VS 1346*	47		
15 Sep 01	**WHO?** ED CASE & SWEETIE IRIE	*Columbia 6718302*	29		1

TIPPA IRIE UK singer

Date	Title	Label	Peak Position	Weeks at No.1	Weeks in Top 40
22 Mar 86	**HELLO DARLING**	*UK Bubblers TIPPA 4*	22		5
19 Jul 86	**HEARTBEAT**	*UK Bubblers TIPPA 5*	59		
15 May 93	**SHOUTING FOR THE GUNNERS** ARSENAL FA CUP SQUAD FEATURING TIPPA IRIE & PETER HUNNIGALE	*London LONCD 342*	34		2
8 Jul 95	**STAYING ALIVE 95** FEVER FEATURING TIPPA IRIE	*Telstar CDSTAS 2776*	48		

IRON MAIDEN UK group

Date	Title	Label	Peak Position	Weeks at No.1	Weeks in Top 40
23 Feb 80	**RUNNING FREE**	*EMI 5032*	34		2
7 Jun 80	**SANCTUARY**	*EMI 5065*	29		3
8 Nov 80	**WOMEN IN UNIFORM**	*EMI 5105*	35		2
14 Mar 81	**TWILIGHT ZONE/WRATH CHILD**	*EMI 5145*	31		2
27 Jun 81	**PURGATORY**	*EMI 5184*	52		
26 Sep 81	**MAIDEN JAPAN**	*EMI 5219*	43		
20 Feb 82	**RUN TO THE HILLS**	*EMI 5263*	7		8
15 May 82	**THE NUMBER OF THE BEAST**	*EMI 5287*	18		6
23 Apr 83	**FLIGHT OF ICARUS**	*EMI 5378*	11		5
2 Jul 83	**THE TROOPER**	*EMI 5397*	12		6
18 Aug 84	**2 MINUTES TO MIDNIGHT**	*EMI 5849*	11		5
3 Nov 84	**ACES HIGH**	*EMI 5502*	20		3
5 Oct 85	**RUNNING FREE (LIVE)**	*EMI 5532*	19		3
14 Dec 85	**RUN TO THE HILLS (LIVE)**	*EMI 5542*	26		4
6 Sep 86	**WASTED YEARS**	*EMI 5583*	18		3
22 Nov 86	**STRANGER IN A STRANGE LAND**	*EMI 5589*	22		3
26 Mar 88	**CAN I PLAY WITH MADNESS**	*EMI EM 49*	3		5
13 Aug 88	**THE EVIL THAT MEN DO**	*EMI EM 64*	5		4
19 Nov 88	**THE CLAIRVOYANT**	*EMI EM 79*	6		4
18 Nov 89	**INFINITE DREAMS (LIVE)**	*EMI EM 117*	6		3
22 Sep 90	**HOLY SMOKE**	*EMI EM 153*	3		3
5 Jan 91	**BRING YOUR DAUGHTER...TO THE SLAUGHTER**	*EMI EMPD 171*	1	2	4
25 Apr 92	**BE QUICK OR BE DEAD**	*EMI EM 229*	2		3
11 Jul 92	**FROM HERE TO ETERNITY**	*EMI EMS 240*	21		2
13 Mar 93	**FEAR OF THE DARK (LIVE)**	*EMI CDEMS 263*	8		2
16 Oct 93	**HALLOWED BE THY NAME (LIVE)**	*EMI CDEM 288*	9		2
7 Oct 95	**MAN ON THE EDGE**	*EMI CDEMS 398*	10		2
21 Sep 96	**VIRUS**	*EMI CDEM 443*	16		1
21 Mar 98	**THE ANGEL AND THE GAMBLER**	*EMI CDEM 507*	18		1
20 May 00	**THE WICKER MAN**	*EMI CDEMS 568*	9		3
4 Nov 00	**OUT OF THE SILENT PLANET**	*EMI CDEM 576*	20		1
23 Mar 02	**RUN TO THE HILLS**	*EMI CDEMS 612*	9		3
13 Sep 03	**WILDEST DREAMS**	*EMI CDEM 627*	6		2
6 Dec 03	**RAINMAKER**	*EMI CDEM 633*	13		2
15 Jan 05	**THE NUMBER OF THE BEAST**	*EMI CDEMS 666*	3		4
27 Aug 05	**THE TROOPER**	*EMI CDEM662*	5		2
6 Jan 07	**DIFFERENT WORLD**	*EMI CDEM714*	3		2

IRONHORSE Canadian band

Date	Title	Label	Peak Position	Weeks at No.1	Weeks in Top 40
5 May 79	**SWEET LUI-LOUISE**	*Scotti Brothers K 11271*	64		

IRRITANT UK group

Date	Title	Label	Peak Position	Weeks at No.1	Weeks in Top 40
7 Jul 07	**VOICE OF THE SIREN**	*Download*	70		

BIG DEE IRWIN US singer

Date	Title	Label	Peak Position	Weeks at No.1	Weeks in Top 40
21 Nov 63	**SWINGING ON A STAR**	*Colpix PX 11010*	7		13

CHRIS ISAAK US singer

Date	Title	Label	Peak Position	Weeks at No.1	Weeks in Top 40
24 Nov 90	**WICKED GAME**	*London LON 279*	10		8
2 Feb 91	**BLUE HOTEL**	*Reprise W 0005*	17		4
3 Apr 93	**CAN'T DO A THING (TO STOP ME)**	*Reprise W 0161CD*	36		2
10 Jul 93	**SAN FRANCISCO DAYS**	*Reprise W 0182CD*	62		
2 Oct 99	**BABY DID A BAD BAD THING**	*Reprise W 503CD*	44		

ISHA-D UK duo

Date	Title	Label	Peak Position	Weeks at No.1	Weeks in Top 40
22 Jul 95	**STAY (TONIGHT)**	*Cleveland City Blues CCBCD 15005*	28		1
5 Jul 97	**STAY (REMIX)**	*Satellite 74321498212*	58		

ISLEY BROTHERS US group

Date	Title	Label	Peak Position	Weeks at No.1	Weeks in Top 40
25 Jul 63	**TWIST AND SHOUT**	*Stateside SS 112*	42		
28 Apr 66	**THIS OLD HEART OF MINE**	*Tamla Motown TMG 555*	47		
1 Sep 66	**I GUESS I'LL ALWAYS LOVE YOU**	*Tamla Motown TMG 572*	45		
23 Oct 68	**THIS OLD HEART OF MINE**	*Tamla Motown TMG 555*	3		15
15 Jan 69	**I GUESS I'LL ALWAYS LOVE YOU**	*Tamla Motown TMG 683*	11		7
16 Apr 69	**BEHIND A PAINTED SMILE**	*Tamla Motown TMG 693*	5		10
25 Jun 69	**IT'S YOUR THING**	*Major Minor MM 621*	30		4
30 Aug 69	**PUT YOURSELF IN MY PLACE**	*Tamla Motown TMG 708*	13		10
22 Sep 73	**THAT LADY**	*Epic EPC 1704*	14		7
19 Jan 74	**HIGHWAYS OF MY LIFE**	*Epic EPC 1980*	25		6
25 May 74	**SUMMER BREEZE**	*Epic EPC 2244*	16		6
10 Jul 76	**HARVEST FOR THE WORLD**	*Epic EPC 4369*	10		8
13 May 78	**TAKE ME TO THE NEXT PHASE**	*Epic EPC 6292*	50		
3 Nov 79	**IT'S A DISCO NIGHT (ROCK DON'T STOP)**	*Epic EPC 7911*	14		6
16 Jul 83	**BETWEEN THE SHEETS**	*Epic A 3513*	52		

ISLEY JASPER ISLEY US group

Date	Title	Label	Peak Position	Weeks at No.1	Weeks in Top 40
23 Nov 85	**CARAVAN OF LOVE**	*Epic A 6612*	52		

ISOTONIK UK producer

Date	Title	Label	Peak Position	Weeks at No.1	Weeks in Top 40
11 Jan 92	**DIFFERENT STROKES**	*ffrreedom TAB 101*	12		3
2 May 92	**EVERYWHERE I GO/LET'S GET DOWN**	*ffrreedom TAB 108*	25		3

IT BITES UK group

Date	Title	Label	Peak Position	Weeks at No.1	Weeks in Top 40
12 Jul 86	**CALLING ALL THE HEROES**	*Virgin VS 872*	6		7
18 Oct 86	**WHOLE NEW WORLD**	*Virgin VS 896*	54		
23 May 87	**THE OLD MAN AND THE ANGEL**	*Virgin VS 941*	72		
13 May 89	**STILL TOO YOUNG TO REMEMBER**	*Virgin VS 1184*	66		
24 Feb 90	**STILL TOO YOUNG TO REMEMBER (REMIX)**	*Virgin VS 1238*	60		

IT'S IMMATERIAL UK duo

Date	Title	Label	Peak Position	Weeks at No.1	Weeks in Top 40
12 Apr 86	**DRIVING AWAY FROM HOME (JIM'S TUNE)**	*Siren 15*	18		5
2 Aug 86	**ED'S FUNKY DINER (FRIDAY NIGHT, SATURDAY MORNING)**	*Siren 24*	65		

ITTY BITTY BOOZY WOOZY Dutch production group

Date	Title	Label	Peak Position	Weeks at No.1	Weeks in Top 40
25 Nov 95	**TEMPO FIESTA (PARTY TIME)**	*Systematic SYSCD 23*	34		1

BURL IVES US singer

Date	Title	Label	Peak Position	Weeks at No.1	Weeks in Top 40
25 Jan 62	**A LITTLE BITTY TEAR**	*Brunswick 05863*	9		13
17 May 62	**FUNNY WAY OF LAUGHIN'**	*Brunswick 05868*	29		6

IVY LEAGUE UK group

Date	Title	Label	Peak Position	Weeks at No.1	Weeks in Top 40
4 Feb 65	**FUNNY HOW LOVE CAN BE**	*Piccadilly 7N 35222*	8		8
6 May 65	**THAT'S WHY I'M CRYING**	*Piccadilly 7N 35228*	22		6
24 Jun 65	**TOSSING AND TURNING**	*Piccadilly 7N 35251*	3		11
14 Jul 66	**WILLOW TREE**	*Piccadilly 7N 35326*	50		

IWASACUBSCOUT UK duo

Date	Title	Label	Peak Position	Weeks at No.1	Weeks in Top 40
16 Feb 08	**PINK SQUARES**	*Abeano AX1330A*	71		

Silver-selling · Gold-selling · Platinum-selling · US No.1 ★ · Peak Position · Weeks at No.1 · Weeks in Top 40

IZIT UK group

Date	Title / Label	Peak Position	Weeks at No.1	Weeks in Top 40
2 Dec 89	**STORIES** *ffrr F 122*	52		

J

FRANKIE J Mexican singer

Date	Title / Label	Peak Position	Weeks at No.1	Weeks in Top 40
20 Aug 05	**OBSESSION (NO ES AMOR)** *Columbia 6760212* FRANKIE J FEATURING BABY BASH	38		1

HARRY J. ALL STARS Jamaican group

Date	Title / Label	Peak Position	Weeks at No.1	Weeks in Top 40
25 Oct 69	**THE LIQUIDATOR** *Trojan TR 675*	9		17
29 Mar 80	**THE LIQUIDATOR** *Trojan TRO 9063*	42		

RAY J US singer

Date	Title / Label	Peak Position	Weeks at No.1	Weeks in Top 40
17 Oct 98	**THAT'S WHY I LIE** *Atlantic AT 0049CD*	71		
16 Jun 01	**ANOTHER DAY IN PARADISE** *WEA 327CD1* BRANDY & RAY J	5		8
11 Aug 01	**WAIT A MINUTE** *Atlantic AT 0106CD* RAY J FEATURING LIL' KIM	54		
12 Nov 05	**ONE WISH** *Sanctuary Urban SANXD397*	26		1
25 Mar 06	**ONE WISH** *Sanctuary SANXS424*	13		5

J-KWON US rapper

Date	Title / Label	Peak Position	Weeks at No.1	Weeks in Top 40
24 Jul 04	**TIPSY** *LaFace 82876634162*	4		8

J PAC UK duo

Date	Title / Label	Peak Position	Weeks at No.1	Weeks in Top 40
22 Jul 95	**ROCK 'N' ROLL (DOLE)** *East West YZ 953CD*	51		

JA RULE US rapper

Date	Title / Label	Peak Position	Weeks at No.1	Weeks in Top 40
13 Mar 99	**CAN I GET A...** *Def Jam 5668472* JAY-Z FEATURING AMIL & JA RULE	24		2
3 Mar 01	**BETWEEN YOU AND ME** *Def Jam 5727402* JA RULE FEATURING CHRISTINA MILIAN	26		1
18 Aug 01	**AIN'T IT FUNNY** *Epic 6717592* JENNIFER LOPEZ FEATURING JA RULE & CADILLAC TAH	3		6
10 Nov 01	**I'M REAL** *Epic 6720322* JENNIFER LOPEZ FEATURING JA RULE ★	4		12
10 Nov 01	**LIVIN' IT UP** *Def Jam 5888142* JA RULE FEATURING CASE	27		2
2 Feb 02	**ALWAYS ON TIME** *Def Jam 5889462* JA RULE FEATURING ASHANTI ★	6		10
3 Aug 02	**LIVIN' IT UP** *Def Jam 0639782* JA RULE FEATURING CASE	5		6
24 Aug 02	**RAINY DAYZ** *MCA MCSXD 40288* MARY J BLIGE FEATURING JA RULE	17		3
12 Oct 02	**DOWN 4 U** *Murder Inc 0639002* IRV GOTTI PRESENTS JA RULE, ASHANTI, CHARLI BALTIMORE & VITA	4		5
21 Dec 02	**THUG LOVIN'** *Def Jam 0637872* JA RULE FEATURING BOBBY BROWN	15		6
29 Mar 03	**MESMERIZE** *Murder Inc 0779582* JA RULE FEATURING ASHANTI	12		6
6 Dec 03	**CLAP BACK/REIGNS** *Def Jam 9861552*	9		7
6 Nov 04	**WONDERFUL** *Def Jam 9864606* JA RULE FEATURING R KELLY & ASHANTI	1	1	5
30 Apr 05	**CAUGHT UP** *The Inc 9881232* JA RULE FEATURING LLOYD	20		2

JACK 'N' CHILL UK group

Date	Title / Label	Peak Position	Weeks at No.1	Weeks in Top 40
6 Jun 87	**THE JACK THAT HOUSE BUILT** *Oval TEN 174*	48		
9 Jan 88	**THE JACK THAT HOUSE BUILT** *Oval TEN 174*	6		7
9 Jul 88	**BEATIN' THE HEAT** *10 TEN 234*	42		

TERRY JACKS Canadian singer

Date	Title / Label	Peak Position	Weeks at No.1	Weeks in Top 40
23 Mar 74	**SEASONS IN THE SUN** *Bell 1344* ★	1	4	11
29 Jun 74	**IF YOU GO AWAY** *Bell 1362*	8		7

CHAD JACKSON UK producer

Date	Title / Label	Peak Position	Weeks at No.1	Weeks in Top 40
2 Jun 90	**HEAR THE DRUMMER (GET WICKED)** *Big Wave BWR 36*	3		8

DEE D. JACKSON UK singer

Date	Title / Label	Peak Position	Weeks at No.1	Weeks in Top 40
22 Apr 78	**AUTOMATIC LOVER** *Mercury 6007 171*	4		7
2 Sep 78	**METEOR MAN** *Mercury 6007 182*	48		

FREDDIE JACKSON US singer

Date	Title / Label	Peak Position	Weeks at No.1	Weeks in Top 40
23 Nov 85	**YOU ARE MY LADY** *Capitol CL 379*	49		
22 Feb 86	**ROCK ME TONIGHT (FOR OLD TIME'S SAKE)** *Capitol CL 358*	18		6
11 Oct 86	**TASTY LOVE** *Capitol CL 428*	73		
7 Feb 87	**HAVE YOU EVER LOVED SOMEBODY** *Capitol CL 437*	33		2
9 Jul 88	**NICE 'N' SLOW** *Capitol CL 502*	56		
15 Oct 88	**CRAZY (FOR ME)** *Capitol CL 510*	41		
5 Sep 92	**ME AND MRS JONES** *Capitol CL 668*	32		4
15 Jan 94	**MAKE LOVE EASY** *RCA 74321179162*	70		

GISELE JACKSON US singer

Date	Title / Label	Peak Position	Weeks at No.1	Weeks in Top 40
30 Aug 97	**LOVE COMMANDMENTS** *Manifesto FESCD 28*	54		

JANET JACKSON US singer

Date	Title / Label	Peak Position	Weeks at No.1	Weeks in Top 40
22 Mar 86	**WHAT HAVE YOU DONE FOR ME LATELY?** *A&M AM 308*	3		9
31 May 86	**NASTY** *A&M AM 316*	19		6
9 Aug 86	**WHEN I THINK OF YOU** *A&M AM 337* ★	10		7
1 Nov 86	**CONTROL** *A&M AM 359*	42		
21 Mar 87	**LET'S WAIT AWHILE** *Breakout USA 601*	3		9
13 Jun 87	**PLEASURE PRINCIPLE** *Breakout USA 604*	24		4
14 Nov 87	**FUNNY HOW TIME FLIES (WHEN YOU'RE HAVING FUN)** *Breakout USA 613*	59		
2 Sep 89	**MISS YOU MUCH** *Breakout USA 663* ★	22		6
4 Nov 89	**RHYTHM NATION** *Breakout USA 673*	23		3
27 Jan 90	**COME BACK TO ME** *Breakout USA 681*	20		4
31 Mar 90	**ESCAPADE** *Breakout USA 684* ★	17		6
7 Jul 90	**ALRIGHT** *A&M USA 693*	20		3
8 Sep 90	**BLACK CAT** *A&M EM 587* ★	15		5
27 Oct 90	**LOVE WILL NEVER DO (WITHOUT YOU)** *A&M EM 700* ★	34		2
15 Aug 92	**THE BEST THINGS IN LIFE ARE FREE** *Perspective PERSS 7400* LUTHER VANDROSS & JANET JACKSON WITH SPECIAL GUESTS BBD & RALPH TRESVANT	2		11
8 May 93	**THAT'S THE WAY LOVE GOES** *Virgin VSCDG 1460* ★	2		8
31 Jul 93	**IF** *Virgin VSCDT 1474*	14		4
20 Nov 93	**AGAIN** *Virgin VSCDG 1481* ★	6		9
12 Mar 94	**BECAUSE OF LOVE** *Virgin VSCDG 1488*	19		2
18 Jun 94	**ANY TIME ANY PLACE** *Virgin VSCDT 1501*	13		3
26 Nov 94	**YOU WANT THIS** *Virgin VSCDT 1519*	14		2
18 Mar 95	**WHOOPS NOW/WHAT'LL I DO** *Virgin VSCDT 1533*	9		6
10 Jun 95	**SCREAM** *Epic 6620222* MICHAEL JACKSON & JANET JACKSON	3		7
24 Jun 95	**SCREAM (REMIX)** *Epic 6621277* MICHAEL JACKSON & JANET JACKSON	43		
23 Sep 95	**RUNAWAY** *A&M 5811972*	6		5
16 Dec 95	**THE BEST THINGS IN LIFE ARE FREE (REMIX)** *A&M 5813092* LUTHER VANDROSS & JANET JACKSON WITH SPECIAL GUESTS BBD & RALPH TRESVANT	7		5
6 Apr 96	**TWENTY FOREPLAY** *A&M 5815112*	22		2
4 Oct 97	**GOT 'TIL IT'S GONE** *Virgin VSCDG 1666* JANET FEATURING Q-TIP & JONI	6		7
13 Dec 97	**TOGETHER AGAIN** *Virgin VSCDG 1670* ★	4		16
4 Apr 98	**I GET LONELY** *Virgin VSCDT 1683*	5		5
27 Jun 98	**GO DEEP** *Virgin VSCDT 1680*	13		2
19 Dec 98	**EVERY TIME** *Virgin VSCDT 1720*	46		
17 Apr 99	**GIRLFRIEND/BOYFRIEND** *Interscope IND 95640* BLACKstreet FEATURING JANET	11		4
1 May 99	**WHAT'S IT GONNA BE?!** *Elektra E 3762CD1* BUSTA RHYMES FEATURING JANET	6		5
19 Aug 00	**DOESN'T REALLY MATTER** *Def Soul 5629152* ★	5		6
21 Apr 01	**ALL FOR YOU** *Virgin VSCDT 1801* ★	3		7
11 Aug 01	**SOMEONE TO CALL MY LOVER** *Virgin VSCDT 1813*	11		3
22 Dec 01	**SON OF A GUN (BETCHA THINK THIS SONG IS ABOUT YOU)** *Virgin VUSCDX 232* JANET JACKSON WITH CARLY SIMON FEATURING MISSY ELLIOTT	13		5
28 Sep 02	**FEEL IT BOY** *Virgin VUSCD 258* BEENIE MAN FEATURING JANET JACKSON	9		3
24 Apr 04	**JUST A LITTLE WHILE** *Virgin VUSDX 285*	15		3
19 Jun 04	**ALL NITE (DON'T STOP)/I WANT YOU** *Virgin VUSDX 292*	19		2
30 Sep 06	**CALL ON ME** *Virgin VUSCD330* JANET & NELLY	18		3

Key: ○ Silver-selling · ● Gold-selling · ⊛ Platinum-selling · ★ US No.1 · Peak Position · Weeks at No.1 · Weeks in Top 40

JERMAINE JACKSON US singer

Date	Title / Label	Peak Position	Weeks at No.1	Weeks in Top 40
10 May 80	**LET'S GET SERIOUS** *Motown TMG 1183*	8		9
26 Jul 80	**BURNIN' HOT** *Motown TMG 1194*	32		2
30 May 81	**YOU LIKE ME DON'T YOU?** *Motown TMG 1222*	41		
12 May 84	**SWEETEST SWEETEST** *Arista JJK 1*	52		
27 Oct 84	**WHEN THE RAIN BEGINS TO FALL** *Arista ARIST 584* JERMAINE JACKSON & PIA ZADORA	68		
16 Feb 85	**DO WHAT YOU DO** *Arista ARIST 609* ○	6		9
21 Oct 89	**DON'T TAKE IT PERSONAL** *Arista 112634*	69		

JOE JACKSON UK singer

Date	Title / Label	Peak Position	Weeks at No.1	Weeks in Top 40
4 Aug 79	**IS SHE REALLY GOING OUT WITH HIM?** *A&M AMS 7459*	13		7
12 Jan 80	**IT'S DIFFERENT FOR GIRLS** *A&M AMS 7493* ○	5		6
4 Jul 81	**JUMPIN' JIVE** *A&M AMS 8145* JOE JACKSON'S JUMPIN' JIVE	43		
8 Jan 83	**STEPPIN' OUT** *A&M AMS 8262*	6		6
12 Mar 83	**BREAKING US IN TWO** *A&M AM 101*	59		
28 Apr 84	**HAPPY ENDING** *A&M AM 186*	58		
7 Jul 84	**BE MY NUMBER TWO** *A&M AM 200*	70		
7 Jun 86	**LEFT OF CENTER** *A&M AM 320* SUZANNE VEGA FEATURING JOE JACKSON	32		3

LEON JACKSON US singer

Date	Title / Label	Peak Position	Weeks at No.1	Weeks in Top 40
29 Dec 07	**WHEN YOU BELIEVE** *Syco Music 88697220162*	1	3	6

MICHAEL JACKSON US singer

Date	Title / Label	Peak Position	Weeks at No.1	Weeks in Top 40
12 Feb 72	**GOT TO BE THERE** *Tamla Motown TMG 797*	5		11
20 May 72	**ROCKIN' ROBIN** *Tamla Motown TMG 816*	3		12
19 Aug 72	**AIN'T NO SUNSHINE** *Tamla Motown TMG 826*	8		10
25 Nov 72	**BEN** *Tamla Motown TMG 834* ★	7		13
18 Nov 78	**EASE ON DOWN THE ROAD** *MCA 396* DIANA ROSS & MICHAEL JACKSON	45		
15 Sep 79	**DON'T STOP 'TIL YOU GET ENOUGH** *Epic EPC 7763* ○ ★	3		9
24 Nov 79	**OFF THE WALL** *Epic EPC 8045*	7		8
9 Feb 80	**ROCK WITH YOU** *Epic EPC 8206* ★	7		7
3 May 80	**SHE'S OUT OF MY LIFE** *Epic EPC 8384*	3		7
26 Jul 80	**GIRLFRIEND** *Epic EPC 8782*	41		
23 May 81	**ONE DAY IN YOUR LIFE** *Motown TMG 976* ●	1	2	11
1 Aug 81	**WE'RE ALMOST THERE** *Motown TMG 977*	46		
6 Nov 82	**THE GIRL IS MINE** *Epic A 2729* MICHAEL JACKSON & PAUL McCARTNEY	8		6
29 Jan 83	**BILLIE JEAN** *Epic EPC A 3084* ● ★	1	1	12
9 Apr 83	**BEAT IT** *Epic EPC A 3258* ○ ★	3		9
11 Jun 83	**WANNA BE STARTIN' SOMETHING** *Epic A 3427*	8		6
23 Jul 83	**HAPPY (LOVE THEME FROM LADY SINGS THE BLUES)** *Tamla Motown TMG 986*	52		
15 Oct 83	**SAY SAY SAY** *Parlophone R 6062* PAUL McCARTNEY & MICHAEL JACKSON ○ ★	2		14
19 Nov 83	**THRILLER** *Epic A 3643* ○	10		12
31 Mar 84	**P.Y.T. (PRETTY YOUNG THING)** *Epic A 4136*	11		6
2 Jun 84	**FAREWELL MY SUMMER LOVE** *Motown TMG 1342*	7		9
7 Jul 84	**STATE OF SHOCK** *Epic A 4431* JACKSONS, LEAD VOCALS MICK JAGGER & MICHAEL JACKSON	14		6
11 Aug 84	**GIRL YOU'RE SO TOGETHER** *Motown TMG 1355*	33		3
8 Aug 87	**I JUST CAN'T STOP LOVING YOU** *Epic 6502027* ★	1	2	8
26 Sep 87	**BAD** *Epic 6511557* ★	3		7
5 Dec 87	**THE WAY YOU MAKE ME FEEL** *Epic 6512757* ★	3		8
20 Feb 88	**MAN IN THE MIRROR** *Epic 6513887* ★	21		4
16 Apr 88	**I WANT YOU BACK** *Motown ZB 41913* MICHAEL JACKSON & THE JACKSON 5	8		7
28 May 88	**GET IT** *Motown ZB 41883* STEVIE WONDER & MICHAEL JACKSON	37		2
16 Jul 88	**DIRTY DIANA** *Epic 6515467* ★	4		6
10 Sep 88	**ANOTHER PART OF ME** *Epic 6528447*	15		5
26 Nov 88	**SMOOTH CRIMINAL** *Epic 6530267*	8		9
25 Feb 89	**LEAVE ME ALONE** *Epic 6546727*	2		7
15 Jul 89	**LIBERIAN GIRL** *Epic 6549470*	13		4
23 Nov 91	**BLACK OR WHITE** *Epic 6575987* ○ ★	1	2	8
18 Jan 92	**BLACK OR WHITE (REMIX)** *Epic 6577316*	14		2
15 Feb 92	**REMEMBER THE TIME/COME TOGETHER** *Epic 6577747*	3		5
2 May 92	**IN THE CLOSET** *Epic 6580187*	8		4
25 Jul 92	**WHO IS IT** *Epic 6581797*	10		5
12 Sep 92	**JAM** *Epic 6583607*	13		3
5 Dec 92	**HEAL THE WORLD** *Epic 6584887* ●	2		10
27 Feb 93	**GIVE IN TO ME** *Epic 6590692*	2		8
10 Jul 93	**WILL YOU BE THERE** *Epic 6592222*	9		6
18 Dec 93	**GONE TOO SOON** *Epic 6599762*	33		3
10 Jun 95	**SCREAM** *Epic 6620222* MICHAEL JACKSON & JANET JACKSON	3		7
24 Jun 95	**SCREAM (REMIX)** *Epic 6621277* MICHAEL JACKSON & JANET JACKSON	43		
2 Sep 95	**YOU ARE NOT ALONE** *Epic 6623102* ● ★	1	2	13
9 Dec 95	**EARTH SONG** *Epic 6626955* ⊛	1	6	16
20 Apr 96	**THEY DON'T CARE ABOUT US** *Epic 6629502* ○	4		8
24 Aug 96	**WHY** *Epic 6636482* 3T FEATURING MICHAEL JACKSON	2		5
16 Nov 96	**STRANGER IN MOSCOW** *Epic 6637872*	4		5
3 May 97	**BLOOD ON THE DANCE FLOOR** *Epic 6644625*	1	1	4
19 Jul 97	**HISTORY/GHOSTS** *Epic 6647962*	5		5
20 Oct 01	**YOU ROCK MY WORLD** *Epic 6720292*	2		7
22 Dec 01	**CRY** *Epic 6721822*	25		1
6 Dec 03	**ONE MORE CHANCE** *Epic 6744805*	5		3
4 Mar 06	**DON'T STOP 'TIL YOU GET ENOUGH** *Epic 82876725112*	17		1
11 Mar 06	**ROCK WITH YOU** *Epic 82876725132*	15		1
18 Mar 06	**BILLIE JEAN** *Epic 82876725172*	11		1
25 Mar 06	**BEAT IT** *Epic 82876725182*	15		1
1 Apr 06	**BAD** *Epic 82876725242*	16		1
8 Apr 06	**THE WAY YOU MAKE ME FEEL** *Epic 82876725252*	17		1
15 Apr 06	**DIRTY DIANA** *Epic 82876725272*	17		1
22 Apr 06	**SMOOTH CRIMINAL** *Epic 82876725292*	19		1
29 Apr 06	**LEAVE ME ALONE** *Epic 82876725302*	15		1
6 May 06	**BLACK OR WHITE** *Epic 82876773302*	18		1
13 May 06	**REMEMBER THE TIME** *Epic 82876773322*	22		1
20 May 06	**IN THE CLOSET** *Epic 82876773342*	20		1
27 May 06	**JAM** *Epic 82876773362*	22		1
3 Jun 06	**HEAL THE WORLD** *Epic 82876773382*	27		1
10 Jun 06	**YOU ARE NOT ALONE** *Epic 82876773402*	30		1
17 Jun 06	**EARTH SONG** *Epic 82876773422*	34		1
24 Jun 06	**THEY DON'T CARE ABOUT US** *Epic 82876773442*	26		1
1 Jul 06	**STRANGER IN MOSCOW** *Epic 82876773462*	22		1
8 Jul 06	**BLOOD ON THE DANCE FLOOR** *Epic 82876773482*	19		1
10 Nov 07	**THRILLER** *Download*	57		
2 Feb 08	**THE GIRL IS MINE** *Epic 88697226202* MICHAEL JACKSON FEATURING WILL.I.AM	32		1
1 Mar 08	**WANNA BE STARTIN' SOMETHING 2008** *Download* MICHAEL JACKSON WITH AKON	69		

MICK JACKSON UK singer

Date	Title / Label	Peak Position	Weeks at No.1	Weeks in Top 40
30 Sep 78	**BLAME IT ON THE BOOGIE** *Atlantic K 11102*	15		8
3 Feb 79	**WEEKEND** *Atlantic K 11224*	38		1

MILLIE JACKSON US singer

Date	Title / Label	Peak Position	Weeks at No.1	Weeks in Top 40
18 Nov 72	**MY MAN A SWEET MAN** *Mojo 2093 022*	50		
10 Mar 84	**I FEEL LIKE WALKIN' IN THE RAIN** *Sire W 9348*	55		
15 Jun 85	**ACT OF WAR** *Rocket EJS 8* ELTON JOHN & MILLIE JACKSON	32		3

PAUL JACKSON & STEVE SMITH UK duo

Date	Title / Label	Peak Position	Weeks at No.1	Weeks in Top 40
24 Jan 04	**THE PUSH (FAR FROM HERE)** *Underwater H2O041CD*	51		

JACKSON SISTERS US group

Date	Title / Label	Peak Position	Weeks at No.1	Weeks in Top 40
20 Jun 87	**I BELIEVE IN MIRACLES** *Urban URB 4*	72		

STONEWALL JACKSON US singer

Date	Title / Label	Peak Position	Weeks at No.1	Weeks in Top 40
17 Jul 59	**WATERLOO** *Philips PB 941*	24		2

TONY JACKSON & THE VIBRATIONS UK group

Date	Title / Label	Peak Position	Weeks at No.1	Weeks in Top 40
8 Oct 64	**BYE BYE BABY** *Pye 7N 15685*	38		1

WANDA JACKSON US singer

Date	Title / Label	Peak Position	Weeks at No.1	Weeks in Top 40
1 Sep 60	**LET'S HAVE A PARTY** *Capitol CL 15147*	32		7
26 Jan 61	**MEAN MEAN MAN** *Capitol CL 15176*	40		1

JACKSON 5/JACKSONS US group

Date	Title / Label	Peak Position	Weeks at No.1	Weeks in Top 40
31 Jan 70	**I WANT YOU BACK** *Tamla Motown TMG 724* JACKSON 5 ★	2		12
16 May 70	**ABC** *Tamla Motown TMG 738* JACKSON 5 ★	8		7
1 Aug 70	**THE LOVE YOU SAVE** *Tamla Motown TMG 746* JACKSON 5 ★	7		8

Date	Title / Label / Artist	Peak Position	Weeks at No.1	Weeks in Top 40
21 Nov 70	**I'LL BE THERE** *Tamla Motown TMG 758* JACKSON 5 ★	4		15
10 Apr 71	**MAMA'S PEARL** *Tamla Motown TMG 769* JACKSON 5	25		6
17 Jul 71	**NEVER CAN SAY GOODBYE** *Tamla Motown TMG 778* JACKSON 5	33		4
11 Nov 72	**LOOKIN' THROUGH THE WINDOWS** *Tamla Motown TMG 833* JACKSON 5	9		10
23 Dec 72	**SANTA CLAUS IS COMING TO TOWN** *Tamla Motown TMG 837* JACKSON 5	43		
17 Feb 73	**DOCTOR MY EYES** *Tamla Motown TMG 842* JACKSON 5	9		8
9 Jun 73	**HALLELUJAH DAY** *Tamla Motown TMG 856* JACKSON 5	20		7
8 Sep 73	**SKYWRITER** *Tamla Motown TMG 865* JACKSON 5	25		7
9 Apr 77	**ENJOY YOURSELF** *Epic EPC 5063* JACKSONS	42		
4 Jun 77	**SHOW YOU THE WAY TO GO** *Epic EPC 5266* JACKSONS	1	1	10
13 Aug 77	**DREAMER** *Epic EPC 5458* JACKSONS	22		8
5 Nov 77	**GOIN' PLACES** *Epic EPC 5732* JACKSONS	26		5
11 Feb 78	**EVEN THOUGH YOU'VE GONE** *Epic EPC 5919* JACKSONS	31		2
23 Sep 78	**BLAME IT ON THE BOOGIE** *Epic EPC 6683* JACKSONS	8		10
3 Feb 79	**DESTINY** *Epic EPC 6983* JACKSONS	39		1
24 Mar 79	**SHAKE YOUR BODY (DOWN TO THE GROUND)** *Epic EPC 7181* JACKSONS	4		9
25 Oct 80	**LOVELY ONE** *Epic EPC 9302* JACKSONS	29		3
13 Dec 80	**HEARTBREAK HOTEL** *Epic EPC 9391* JACKSONS	44		
28 Feb 81	**CAN YOU FEEL IT** *Epic EPC 9554* JACKSONS	6		13
4 Jul 81	**WALK RIGHT NOW** *Epic EPC A 1294* JACKSONS	7		7
7 Jul 84	**STATE OF SHOCK** *Epic A 4431* JACKSONS, LEAD VOCALS MICK JAGGER & MICHAEL JACKSON	14		6
8 Sep 84	**TORTURE** *Epic A 4675* JACKSONS	26		4
16 Apr 88	**I WANT YOU BACK** *Motown ZB 41913* MICHAEL JACKSON & THE JACKSON 5	8		7
13 May 89	**NOTHIN' (THAT COMPARES 2 U)** *Epic 6548087* JACKSONS	33		3
27 Jan 07	**I WANT YOU BACK** *Download* JACKSON FIVE GROUP	53		

JACKY Irish singer

Date	Title / Label / Artist	Peak Position	Weeks at No.1	Weeks in Top 40
10 Apr 68	**WHITE HORSES** *Philips BF 1674*	10		12
2 Jan 71	**RUPERT** *Pye 7N 45003* JACKIE LEE	14		13

JADE US group

Date	Title / Label / Artist	Peak Position	Weeks at No.1	Weeks in Top 40
20 Mar 93	**DON'T WALK AWAY** *Giant W 0160CD*	7		7
3 Jul 93	**I WANNA LOVE YOU** *Giant 74321151662*	13		4
18 Sep 93	**ONE WOMAN** *Giant 74321165122*	22		3
5 Feb 94	**ALL THRU THE NITE** *Giant 74321187552* P.O.V. FEATURING JADE	32		1
11 Feb 95	**EVERY DAY OF THE WEEK** *Giant 74321260242*	19		4

JAGGED EDGE UK group

Date	Title / Label / Artist	Peak Position	Weeks at No.1	Weeks in Top 40
15 Sep 90	**YOU DON'T LOVE ME** *Polydor PO 97*	66		
27 Oct 01	**WHERE'S THE PARTY AT** *Columbia 6719012* JAGGED EDGE FEATURING NELLY	25		1
21 Feb 04	**WALKED OUTTA HEAVEN** *Columbia 6745452*	21		3
28 Jan 06	**NASTY GIRL** *Bad Boy AT0229CDX* NOTORIOUS B.I.G. FEATURING DIDDY, NELLY, JAGGED EDGE AND AVERY STORM	1	2	16

MICK JAGGER UK singer

Date	Title / Label / Artist	Peak Position	Weeks at No.1	Weeks in Top 40
14 Nov 70	**MEMO FROM TURNER** *Decca F 13067*	32		2
7 Jul 84	**STATE OF SHOCK** *Epic A 4431* JACKSONS, LEAD VOCALS MICK JAGGER & MICHAEL JACKSON	14		6
16 Feb 85	**JUST ANOTHER NIGHT** *CBS A 4722*	32		4
7 Sep 85	**DANCING IN THE STREET** *EMI America EA 204* DAVID BOWIE & MICK JAGGER	1	4	9
12 Sep 87	**LET'S WORK** *CBS 6510287*	31		2
6 Feb 93	**SWEET THING** *Atlantic A 7410CD*	24		2
23 Mar 02	**VISIONS OF PARADISE** *Virgin VUSCD 240*	43		
6 Nov 04	**OLD HABITS DIE HARD** *Virgin VSCDX1887* MICK JAGGER & DAVE STEWART	45		

JAGS UK group

Date	Title / Label / Artist	Peak Position	Weeks at No.1	Weeks in Top 40
8 Sep 79	**BACK OF MY HAND** *Island WIP 6501*	17		7
2 Feb 80	**WOMAN'S WORLD** *Island WIP 6531*	75		

JAHEIM US rapper

Date	Title / Label / Artist	Peak Position	Weeks at No.1	Weeks in Top 40
24 Mar 01	**COULD IT BE?** *Warner Brothers W 551CDX*	33		1
11 Aug 01	**JUST IN CASE** *Warner Brothers W 564CDX*	34		1
29 Jun 02	**JUST IN CASE (REMIX)** *Warner Brothers W 581CD*	38		1
8 Mar 03	**FABULOUS** *Warner Brothers W 598CD* JAHEIM FEATURING THA RAYNE	41		

JAIMESON UK keyboard player

Date	Title / Label / Artist	Peak Position	Weeks at No.1	Weeks in Top 40
25 Jan 03	**TRUE** *V2/J-Did JAD 5021363* JAIMESON FEATURING ANGEL BLU	4		6
23 Aug 03	**COMPLETE** *V2/J-Did JAD 5021713*	4		6
7 Feb 04	**TAKE CONTROL** *V2/J-Did JAD 5021738* JAIMESON FEATURING ANGEL BLU & CK	16		3

JAKATTA UK producer

Date	Title / Label / Artist	Peak Position	Weeks at No.1	Weeks in Top 40
24 Feb 01	**AMERICAN DREAM** *Rulin 15CDS*	3		8
11 Aug 01	**AMERICAN DREAM (REMIX)** *Rulin 20CDS*	63		
16 Feb 02	**SO LONELY** *Rulin 25CDS*	8		3
12 Oct 02	**MY VISION** *Rulin 26CDS* JAKATTA FEATURING SEAL	6		6
1 Mar 03	**ONE FINE DAY** *Rulin 29CDX*	39		1

J.A.L.N. BAND UK group

Date	Title / Label / Artist	Peak Position	Weeks at No.1	Weeks in Top 40
11 Sep 76	**DISCO MUSIC (I LIKE IT)** *Magnet MAG 73*	21		6
27 Aug 77	**I GOT TO SING** *Magnet MAG 97*	40		1
1 Jul 78	**GET UP** *Magnet MAG 118*	53		

JAM UK group

Date	Title / Label / Artist	Peak Position	Weeks at No.1	Weeks in Top 40
7 May 77	**IN THE CITY** *Polydor 2058 866*	40		1
23 Jul 77	**ALL AROUND THE WORLD** *Polydor 2058 903*	13		8
5 Nov 77	**THE MODERN WORLD** *Polydor 2058 945*	36		2
11 Mar 78	**NEWS OF THE WORLD** *Polydor 2058 995*	27		5
26 Aug 78	**DAVID WATTS/'A' BOMB IN WARDOUR STREET** *Polydor 2059 054*	25		8
21 Oct 78	**DOWN IN THE TUBE STATION AT MIDNIGHT** *Polydor POSP 8*	15		6
17 Mar 79	**STRANGE TOWN** *Polydor POSP 34*	15		7
25 Aug 79	**WHEN YOU'RE YOUNG** *Polydor POSP 69*	17		6
3 Nov 79	**THE ETON RIFLES** *Polydor POSP 83*	3		6
22 Mar 80	**GOING UNDERGROUND/DREAMS OF CHILDREN** *Polydor POSP 113*	1	3	7
26 Apr 80	**ALL AROUND THE WORLD** *Polydor 2058 903*	43		
26 Apr 80	**DAVID WATTS/'A' BOMB IN WARDOUR STREET** *Polydor 2059 054*	54		
26 Apr 80	**IN THE CITY** *Polydor 2058 866*	40		1
26 Apr 80	**NEWS OF THE WORLD** *Polydor 2058 995*	53		
26 Apr 80	**STRANGE TOWN** *Polydor POSP 34*	44		
26 Apr 80	**THE MODERN WORLD** *Polydor 2058 945*	52		
23 Aug 80	**START** *Polydor 2059 266*	1	1	7
7 Feb 81	**THAT'S ENTERTAINMENT** *Metronome 0030 364*	21		6
6 Jun 81	**FUNERAL PYRE** *Polydor POSP 257*	4		5
24 Oct 81	**ABSOLUTE BEGINNERS** *Polydor POSP 350*	4		5
13 Feb 82	**A TOWN CALLED MALICE/PRECIOUS** *Polydor POSP 400*	1	3	7
3 Jul 82	**JUST WHO IS THE FIVE O'CLOCK HERO** *Polydor 2059 504*	8		5
18 Sep 82	**THE BITTEREST PILL (I EVER HAD TO SWALLOW)** *Polydor POSP 505*	2		6
4 Dec 82	**BEAT SURRENDER** *Polydor POSP 540*	1	2	7
22 Jan 83	**ALL AROUND THE WORLD** *Polydor 2058 903*	38		1
22 Jan 83	**DAVID WATTS/'A' BOMB IN WARDOUR STREET** *Polydor 2059 054*	50		
22 Jan 83	**DOWN IN THE TUBE STATION AT MIDNIGHT** *Polydor POSP 8*	30		3
22 Jan 83	**GOING UNDERGROUND/DREAMS OF CHILDREN** *Polydor POSP 113*	21		4
22 Jan 83	**IN THE CITY** *Polydor 2058 866*	47		
22 Jan 83	**STRANGE TOWN** *Polydor POSP 34*	42		
22 Jan 83	**NEWS OF THE WORLD** *Polydor 2058 995*	39		1
22 Jan 83	**THE MODERN WORLD** *Polydor 2058 945*	51		

Date	Title / Label	Peak Position	Weeks at No.1	Weeks in Top 40
22 Jan 83	WHEN YOU'RE YOUNG *Polydor POSP 69*	53		
29 Jan 83	THAT'S ENTERTAINMENT *Polydor POSP 482*	60		
5 Feb 83	START *Polydor 2059 266*	62		
5 Feb 83	THE ETON RIFLES *Polydor POSP 83*	54		
5 Feb 83	A TOWN CALLED MALICE/PRECIOUS *Polydor POSP 400*	73		
29 Jun 91	THAT'S ENTERTAINMENT *Polydor PO 155*	57		
11 Oct 97	THE BITTEREST PILL (I EVER HAD TO SWALLOW) *Polydor 5715992*	30		1
11 May 02	IN THE CITY *Polydor 5876117*	36		1

JAM & SPOON German production duo

Date	Title / Label	Peak Position	Weeks at No.1	Weeks in Top 40
2 May 92	TALES FROM A DANCEOGRAPHIC OCEAN (EP) *R&S RSUK 14*	49		
6 Jun 92	THE COMPLETE STELLA (REMIX) *R&S RSUK 14X*	66		
26 Feb 94	RIGHT IN THE NIGHT (FALL IN LOVE WITH MUSIC) *Epic 6600822* JAM & SPOON FEATURING PLAVKA	31		2
24 Sep 94	FIND ME (ODYSSEY TO ANYOONA) *Epic 6608082* JAM & SPOON FEATURING PLAVKA	37		1
10 Jun 95	RIGHT IN THE NIGHT (FALL IN LOVE WITH MUSIC) *Epic 6620182* JAM & SPOON FEATURING PLAVKA	10		6
16 Sep 95	FIND ME (ODYSSEY TO ANYOONA) *Epic 6623242* JAM & SPOON FEATURING PLAVKA	22		1
25 Nov 95	ANGEL (LADADI O-HEYO) *Epic 6626382* JAM & SPOON FEATURING PLAVKA	26		1
30 Aug 97	KALEIDOSCOPE SKIES *Epic 6647612* JAM & SPOON FEATURING PLAVKA	48		
2 Mar 02	BE ANGLED *NuLife 74321878992* JAM & SPOON FEATURING REA	31		1

JAM MACHINE Italian group

Date	Title / Label	Peak Position	Weeks at No.1	Weeks in Top 40
23 Dec 89	EVERYDAY *Deconstruction PB 43299*	68		

JAM ON THE MUTHA UK group

Date	Title / Label	Peak Position	Weeks at No.1	Weeks in Top 40
11 Aug 90	HOTEL CALIFORNIA *M&G MAGS 3*	62		

JAM TRONIK German group

Date	Title / Label	Peak Position	Weeks at No.1	Weeks in Top 40
24 Mar 90	ANOTHER DAY IN PARADISE *Debut DEBT 3093*	19		6

JAMAICA UNITED Jamaican group

Date	Title / Label	Peak Position	Weeks at No.1	Weeks in Top 40
4 Jul 98	RISE UP *Columbia 6660522*	54		

JAMELIA UK singer

Date	Title / Label	Peak Position	Weeks at No.1	Weeks in Top 40
31 Jul 99	I DO *Parlophone Rhythm CDRHYTHM 21*	36		1
4 Mar 00	MONEY *Parlophone Rhythm CDRHYTHM 27* JAMELIA FEATURING BEENIE MAN	5		5
24 Jun 00	CALL ME *Parlophone Rhythm CDRHYTHS 28*	11		3
21 Oct 00	BOY NEXT DOOR *Parlophone Rhythm CDRHYTHS 29*	42		
21 Jun 03	BOUT *Parlophone CDRS 6597* JAMELIA FEATURING RAH DIGGA	37		1
27 Sep 03	SUPERSTAR *Parlophone CDRS 6615* ○	3		13
6 Mar 04	THANK YOU *Parlophone CDRS 6621*	2		11
24 Jul 04	SEE IT IN A BOY'S EYES *Parlophone CDRS 6635*	5		7
13 Nov 04	DJ/STOP *Parlophone CDR 6646*	9		10
16 Sep 06	SOMETHING ABOUT YOU *Parlophone CDR6713*	9		7
9 Dec 06	BEWARE OF THE DOG *Parlophone CDR6727*	10		6
31 Mar 07	NO MORE *Parlophone CDR6736*	43		

JAMES UK group

Date	Title / Label	Peak Position	Weeks at No.1	Weeks in Top 40
12 May 90	HOW WAS IT FOR YOU *Fontana JIM 5*	32		2
7 Jul 90	COME HOME *Fontana JIM 6*	32		2
8 Dec 90	LOSE CONTROL *Fontana JIM 7*	38		1
30 Mar 91	SIT DOWN *Fontana JIM 8* ○	2		9
30 Nov 91	SOUND *Fontana JIM 9*	9		6
1 Feb 92	BORN OF FRUSTRATION *Fontana JIM 10*	13		4
4 Apr 92	RING THE BELLS *Fontana JIM 11*	37		1
18 Jul 92	SEVEN (EP) *Fontana JIM 12*	46		
11 Sep 93	SOMETIMES *Fontana JIMCD 13*	18		3
13 Nov 93	LAID *Fontana JIMCD 14*	25		3
2 Apr 94	JAM J/SAY SOMETHING *Fontana JIMCD 152*	24		2
22 Feb 97	SHE'S A STAR *Fontana JIMCD 16*	9		3
3 May 97	TOMORROW *Fontana JIMCD 17*	12		2
5 Jul 97	WALTZING ALONG *Fontana JIMCD 18*	23		2
21 Mar 98	DESTINY CALLING *Fontana JIMCD 19*	17		2
6 Jun 98	RUNAGROUND *Fontana JIMCD 20*	29		1
21 Nov 98	SIT DOWN (REMIX) *Fontana JIMCD 21*	7		4
31 Jul 99	I KNOW WHAT I'M HERE FOR *Fontana JIMDD 22*	22		2
16 Oct 99	JUST LIKE FRED ASTAIRE *Mercury JIMCD 23*	17		2
25 Dec 99	WE'RE GOING TO MISS YOU *Mercury JIMCD 24*	48		
7 Jul 01	GETTING AWAY WITH IT (ALL MESSED UP) *Mercury JIMDD 25*	22		1

DAVID JAMES UK producer

Date	Title / Label	Peak Position	Weeks at No.1	Weeks in Top 40
11 Aug 01	ALWAYS A PERMANENT STATE *Hooj Choons HOOJ 108CD*	60		

DICK JAMES UK singer

Date	Title / Label	Peak Position	Weeks at No.1	Weeks in Top 40
20 Jan 56	ROBIN HOOD *Parlophone R 4117*	14		8
18 May 56	ROBIN HOOD/BALLAD OF DAVY CROCKETT *Parlophone R 4117*	29		1
11 Jan 57	GARDEN OF EDEN *Parlophone R 4255*	18		4

DUNCAN JAMES UK duo

Date	Title / Label	Peak Position	Weeks at No.1	Weeks in Top 40
23 Oct 04	I BELIEVE MY HEART *Innocent 8677122* DUNCAN JAMES & KEEDIE	2		5
17 Jun 06	SOONER OR LATER *Innocent SINCD78*	35		1
2 Sep 06	CAN'T STOP A RIVER *Innocent ANGEDX17*	59		

ETTA JAMES US singer

Date	Title / Label	Peak Position	Weeks at No.1	Weeks in Top 40
10 Feb 96	I JUST WANT TO MAKE LOVE TO YOU *Chess MCSTD 48003*	5		5

FREDDIE JAMES US singer

Date	Title / Label	Peak Position	Weeks at No.1	Weeks in Top 40
24 Nov 79	GET UP AND BOOGIE *Warner Brothers K 17478*	54		

JONI JAMES US singer

Date	Title / Label	Peak Position	Weeks at No.1	Weeks in Top 40
6 Mar 53	WHY DON'T YOU BELIEVE ME *MGM 582* ★	11		1
30 Jan 59	THERE MUST BE A WAY *MGM 1002*	24		1

NATE JAMES UK singer

Date	Title / Label	Peak Position	Weeks at No.1	Weeks in Top 40
19 Mar 05	SET THE TONE *4/Onetwo ONETCDS001*	69		
25 Jun 05	LOVIN' YOU *Positiva CDTIVS218* POKER PETS FEATURING NATE JAMES	43		
30 May 05	UNIVERSAL *4/Onetwo ONETCDX002*	72		

RICK JAMES US singer

Date	Title / Label	Peak Position	Weeks at No.1	Weeks in Top 40
8 Jul 78	YOU AND I *Motown TMG 1110*	46		
7 Jul 79	I'M A SUCKER FOR YOUR LOVE *Motown TMG 1146* TEENA MARIE, CO-LEAD VOCALS RICK JAMES	43		
6 Sep 80	BIG TIME *Motown TMG 1198*	41		
4 Jul 81	GIVE IT TO ME BABY *Motown TMG 1229*	47		
12 Jun 82	STANDING ON THE TOP (PART 1) *Motown TMG 1263* TEMPTATIONS FEATURING RICK JAMES	53		
3 Jul 82	DANCE WIT ME *Motown TMG 1266*	53		

SONNY JAMES US singer

Date	Title / Label	Peak Position	Weeks at No.1	Weeks in Top 40
30 Nov 56	THE CAT CAME BACK *Capitol CL 14635*	30		1
8 Feb 57	YOUNG LOVE *Capitol CL 14683* ★	11		7

TYLER JAMES UK singer

Date	Title / Label	Peak Position	Weeks at No.1	Weeks in Top 40
13 Nov 04	WHY DO I DO? *Island/Uni-Island CID872*	25		2
19 Mar 05	FOOLISH *Island CID884*	16		2
3 Sep 05	YOUR WOMAN *Island CIDX900*	60		

WENDY JAMES UK singer

Date	Title / Label	Peak Position	Weeks at No.1	Weeks in Top 40
20 Feb 93	THE NAMELESS ONE *MCA MCSTD 1732*	34		2
17 Apr 93	LONDON'S BRILLIANT *MCA MCSTD 1763*	62		

JAMES BOYS UK duo

Date	Title / Label	Peak Position	Weeks at No.1	Weeks in Top 40
19 May 73	OVER AND OVER *Penny Farthing PEN 806*	39		2

JIMMY JAMES & THE VAGABONDS UK singer

Date	Title / Label	Peak Position	Weeks at No.1	Weeks in Top 40
11 Sep 68	RED RED WINE *Pye 7N 17579*	36		2
24 Apr 76	I'LL GO WHERE YOUR MUSIC TAKES ME *Pye 7N 45585*	23		7

Key: Silver-selling ○ · Gold-selling ● · Platinum-selling ⊛ · US No.1 ★ · Peak Position · Weeks at No.1 · Weeks in Top 40

Date	Title / Label	Peak Position	Weeks at No.1	Weeks in Top 40
17 Jul 76	**NOW IS THE TIME** *Pye 7N 45606*	5		8

TOMMY JAMES & THE SHONDELLS US singer

Date	Title / Label	Peak Position	Weeks at No.1	Weeks in Top 40
21 Jul 66	**HANKY PANKY** *Roulette RK 7000* ★	38		5
5 Jun 68	**MONY MONY** *Major Minor MM 567*	1	1	16

JAMESON & VIPER UK duo

Date	Title / Label	Peak Position	Weeks at No.1	Weeks in Top 40
14 Sep 02	**SELECTA (URBAN HEROES)** *Soundproof SPR 1CD*	51		

JAMESTOWN US producer with singer

Date	Title / Label	Peak Position	Weeks at No.1	Weeks in Top 40
14 Sep 91	**SHE'S GOT SOUL** *A&M AM 819* JAMESTOWN FEATURING JOCELYN BROWN	57		
27 Mar 99	**I BELIEVE** *Playola 0091705 PLA* JAMESTOWN FEATURING JOCELYN BROWN	62		

JAMIROQUAI UK group

Date	Title / Label	Peak Position	Weeks at No.1	Weeks in Top 40
31 Oct 92	**WHEN YOU GONNA LEARN** *Acid Jazz JAZID 46*	52		
20 Feb 93	**WHEN YOU GONNA LEARN** *Acid Jazz JAZID 46*	69		
13 Mar 93	**TOO YOUNG TO DIE** *Sony S2 6590112*	10		5
5 Jun 93	**BLOW YOUR MIND** *Sony S2 6592972*	12		5
14 Aug 93	**EMERGENCY ON PLANET EARTH** *Sony S2 6595782*	32		2
25 Sep 93	**WHEN YOU GONNA LEARN** *Sony S2 6596952*	28		1
8 Oct 94	**SPACE COWBOY** *Sony S2 6608512*	17		3
19 Nov 94	**HALF THE MAN** *Sony S2 6610032*	15		4
1 Jul 95	**STILLNESS IN TIME** *Sony S2 6620255*	9		3
1 Jun 96	**DO U KNOW WHERE YOU'RE COMING FROM** *Renk CDRENK 63* M-BEAT FEATURING JAMIROQUAI	12		3
31 Aug 96	**VIRTUAL INSANITY** *Sony S2 6636132*	3		9
7 Dec 96	**COSMIC GIRL** *Sony S2 6638292*	6		8
10 May 97	**ALRIGHT** *Sony S2 6642352*	6		3
13 Dec 97	**HIGH TIMES** *Sony S2 6653702*	20		2
25 Jul 98	**DEEPER UNDERGROUND** *Sony S2 6662182*	1	1	8
5 Jun 99	**CANNED HEAT** *Sony S2 6673022*	4		5
25 Sep 99	**SUPERSONIC** *Sony S2 6678392*	22		2
11 Dec 99	**KING FOR A DAY** *Sony S2 6679732*	20		1
24 Feb 01	**I'M IN THE MOOD FOR LOVE** *warner.esp WSMS 001CD* JOOLS HOLLAND & JAMIROQUAI	29		1
25 Aug 01	**LITTLE L** *Sony S2 6717182*	5		6
1 Dec 01	**YOU GIVE ME SOMETHING** *Sony S2 6720072*	16		2
9 Mar 02	**LOVE FOOLOSOPHY** *Sony S2 6723255*	14		3
20 Jul 02	**CORNER OF THE EARTH** *Sony S2 6727885*	31		1
18 Jun 05	**FEELS JUST LIKE IT SHOULD** *Sony Music 6759682*	8		4
27 Aug 05	**SEVEN DAYS IN SUNNY JUNE** *Sony Music 6760642*	14		2
19 Nov 05	**(DON'T) GIVE HATE A CHANCE** *Sony Music 82876750652*	27		2
10 Jun 06	**SPACE COWBOY (REMIX)** *Sony Music 82876846001*	71		
4 Nov 06	**RUNAWAY** *Columbia 88697016002*	18		2

JAMMERS US group

Date	Title / Label	Peak Position	Weeks at No.1	Weeks in Top 40
29 Jan 83	**BE MINE TONIGHT** *Salsoul SAL 101*	65		

JAMX & DELEON German production duo

Date	Title / Label	Peak Position	Weeks at No.1	Weeks in Top 40
7 Sep 02	**CAN U DIG IT** *Serious SERR 052CD*	40		1

JAN & DEAN US duo

Date	Title / Label	Peak Position	Weeks at No.1	Weeks in Top 40
24 Aug 61	**HEART AND SOUL** *London HLH 9395*	24		5
15 Aug 63	**SURF CITY** *London LIB 55580* ★	26		8

JAN & KJELD Danish duo

Date	Title / Label	Peak Position	Weeks at No.1	Weeks in Top 40
21 Jul 60	**BANJO BOY** *Ember S 101*	36		2

JANE'S ADDICTION US group

Date	Title / Label	Peak Position	Weeks at No.1	Weeks in Top 40
23 Mar 91	**BEEN CAUGHT STEALING** *Warner Brothers W 0011*	34		2
1 Jun 91	**CLASSIC GIRL** *Warner Brothers W 0031*	60		
26 Jul 03	**JUST BECAUSE** *Capitol CDCL 847*	14		2
8 Nov 03	**TRUE NATURE** *Parlophone CDCLS 850*	41		

HORST JANKOWSKI German pianist

Date	Title / Label	Peak Position	Weeks at No.1	Weeks in Top 40
29 Jul 65	**A WALK IN THE BLACK FOREST** *Mercury MF 861*	3		16

SAMANTHA JANUS UK singer

Date	Title / Label	Peak Position	Weeks at No.1	Weeks in Top 40
11 May 91	**A MESSAGE TO YOUR HEART** *Hollywood HWD 104*	30		2

PHILIP JAP UK singer

Date	Title / Label	Peak Position	Weeks at No.1	Weeks in Top 40
31 Jul 82	**SAVE US** *A&M AMS 8217*	53		
25 Sep 82	**TOTAL ERASURE** *A&M JAP 1*	41		

JAPAN UK group

Date	Title / Label	Peak Position	Weeks at No.1	Weeks in Top 40
18 Oct 80	**GENTLEMEN TAKE POLAROIDS** *Virgin VS 379*	60		
9 May 81	**THE ART OF PARTIES** *Virgin VS 409*	48		
19 Sep 81	**QUIET LIFE** *Hansa 6*	19		7
7 Nov 81	**VISIONS OF CHINA** *Virgin VS 436*	32		3
23 Jan 82	**EUROPEAN SON** *Hansa 10*	31		3
20 Mar 82	**GHOSTS** *Virgin VS 472*	5		6
22 May 82	**CANTONESE BOY** *Virgin VS 502*	24		4
3 Jul 82	**I SECOND THAT EMOTION** *Hansa 12*	9		8
9 Oct 82	**LIFE IN TOKYO** *Hansa 17*	28		3
20 Nov 82	**NIGHT PORTER** *Virgin VS 554*	29		6
12 Mar 83	**ALL TOMORROW'S PARTIES** *Hansa 18*	38		1
21 May 83	**CANTON (LIVE)** *Virgin VS 581*	42		

JARK PRONGO Dutch production duo

Date	Title / Label	Peak Position	Weeks at No.1	Weeks in Top 40
3 Apr 99	**MOVIN' THRU YOUR SYSTEM** *Hooj Choons HOOJ 72CD*	58		

JEAN-MICHEL JARRE French synthesiser player

Date	Title / Label	Peak Position	Weeks at No.1	Weeks in Top 40
27 Aug 77	**OXYGENE PART IV** *Polydor 2001 721* ○	4		9
20 Jan 79	**EQUINOXE PART 5** *Polydor POSP 20*	45		
23 Aug 86	**FOURTH RENDEZ-VOUS** *Polydor POSP 788*	65		
5 Nov 88	**REVOLUTIONS** *Polydor PO 25*	52		
7 Jan 89	**LONDON KID** *Polydor 32* JEAN-MICHEL JARRE FEATURING HANK MARVIN	52		
7 Oct 89	**OXYGENE PART IV (REMIX)** *Polydor PO 55*	65		
26 Jun 93	**CHRONOLOGIE PART 4** *Polydor PZCD 274*	55		
30 Oct 93	**CHRONOLOGIE PART 4 (REMIX)** *Polydor PZ 274*	56		
22 Mar 97	**OXYGENE 8** *Epic 6643232*	17		2
5 Jul 97	**OXYGENE 10** *Epic 6647152*	21		1
11 Jul 98	**RENDEZ-VOUS 98** *Epic 6661102* JEAN-MICHEL JARRE & APOLLO 440	12		4
26 Feb 00	**C'EST LA VIE** *Epic 6689302* JEAN-MICHEL JARRE FEATURING NATACHA ATLAS	40		1

AL JARREAU US singer

Date	Title / Label	Peak Position	Weeks at No.1	Weeks in Top 40
26 Sep 81	**WE'RE IN THIS LOVE TOGETHER** *Warner Brothers K 17849*	55		
14 May 83	**MORNIN'** *WEA U9929*	28		4
16 Jul 83	**TROUBLE IN PARADISE** *WEA International U9871*	36		2
24 Sep 83	**BOOGIE DOWN** *WEA U9814*	63		
16 Nov 85	**DAY BY DAY** *Polydor POSP 770* SHAKATAK FEATURING AL JARREAU	53		
5 Apr 86	**THE MUSIC OF GOODBYE (LOVE THEME FROM *OUT OF AFRICA*)** *MCA 1038*	75		
7 Mar 87	***MOONLIGHTING* THEME** *WEA U8407*	8		6

KENNY 'JAMMIN' JASON & DJ 'FAST' EDDIE SMITH US production duo

Date	Title / Label	Peak Position	Weeks at No.1	Weeks in Top 40
11 Apr 87	**CAN U DANCE** *Champion CHAMP 41*	71		
14 Nov 87	**CAN U DANCE** *Champion CHAMP 41*	67		

JAVELLS UK group

Date	Title / Label	Peak Position	Weeks at No.1	Weeks in Top 40
9 Nov 74	**GOODBYE NOTHING TO SAY** *Pye Disco Demand DDS 2003* JAVELLS FEATURING NOSMO KING	26		5

JAVINE UK singer

Date	Title / Label	Peak Position	Weeks at No.1	Weeks in Top 40
19 Jul 03	**REAL THINGS** *Innocent SINCD 46*	4		7
22 Nov 03	**SURRENDER (YOUR LOVE)** *Innocent SINDX 52*	15		2
26 Jun 04	**BEST OF MY LOVE** *Innocent SINDX 63*	18		1
21 Aug 04	**DON'T WALK AWAY** *Innocent SINDX 65*	16		3
28 May 05	**TOUCH MY FIRE** *Shalit Productions 9871694*	18		2
14 Oct 06	**DON'T LET THE MORNING COME** *Positiva CDTIVS244* SOUL AVENGERZ FEATURING JAVINE	49		

CANDEE JAY Dutch singer

Date	Title / Label	Peak Position	Weeks at No.1	Weeks in Top 40
19 Jun 04	**IF I WERE YOU** *Incentive CENT 58CDX*	14		4
13 Nov 04	**BACK FOR ME** *Incentive CENT 67CDS*	23		1

ORIS JAY Dutch producer

Date	Title / Label	Peak Position	Weeks at No.1	Weeks in Top 40
23 Mar 02	**TRIPPIN'** *Gusto CDGUS 3* ORIS JAY PRESENTS DELSENA	42		

PETER JAY & THE JAYWALKERS UK instrumental group

Date	Title / Label	Peak Position	Weeks at No.1	Weeks in Top 40
8 Nov 62	**CAN CAN 62** *Decca F 11531*	31		7

JAYDEE Dutch producer

Date	Title / Label	Peak Position	Weeks at No.1	Weeks in Top 40
20 Sep 97	**PLASTIC DREAMS** *R&S RS 97117CD*	18		2
10 Jan 04	**PLASTIC DREAMS (REMIX)** *Positiva CDTIVS 198*	35		1

JAYHAWKS US group

Date	Title / Label	Peak Position	Weeks at No.1	Weeks in Top 40
15 Jul 95	**BAD TIME** *American Recordings 74321291632*	70		

JAY-Z US rapper

Date	Title / Label	Peak Position	Weeks at No.1	Weeks in Top 40
1 Mar 97	**CAN'T KNOCK THE HUSTLE** *Northwestside 74321447192* JAY-Z FEATURING MARY J BLIGE	30		1
10 May 97	**AIN'T NO PLAYA** *Northwestside 74321474842* JAY-Z FEATURING FOXY BROWN	31		1
21 Jun 97	**I'LL BE** *Def Jam 5710432* FOXY BROWN FEATURING JAY-Z	9		2
23 Aug 97	**WHO YOU WIT** *Qwest W0411CD*	65		
25 Oct 97	**SUNSHINE** *Northwestside 74321528702* JAY-Z FEATURING BABYFACE & FOXY BROWN	25		1
14 Feb 98	**WISHING ON A STAR** *Northwestside 74321554632* JAY-Z FEATURING GWEN DICKEY	13		3
28 Feb 98	**BE ALONE NO MORE** *Northwestside 74321551982* ANOTHER LEVEL FEATURING JAY-Z	6		6
27 Jun 98	**THE CITY IS MINE** *Northwestside 74321588012* JAY-Z FEATURING BLACKstreet	38		1
12 Dec 98	**HARD KNOCK LIFE (GHETTO ANTHEM)** *Northwestside 74321635332* ●	2		9
13 Mar 99	**CAN I GET A...** *Def Jam 5668472* JAY-Z FEATURING AMIL & JA RULE	24		2
10 Apr 99	**BE ALONE NO MORE** *Northwestside 74321658482* ANOTHER LEVEL FEATURING JAY-Z	11		5
19 Jun 99	**LOBSTER & SCRIMP** *Virgin DINSD 186* TIMBALAND FEATURING JAY-Z	48		
6 Nov 99	**HEARTBREAKER** *Columbia 6683012* MARIAH CAREY FEATURING JAY-Z ★	5		6
4 Dec 99	**WHAT YOU THINK OF THAT** *Def Jam 8708292* MEMPHIS BLEEK FEATURING JAY-Z	58		
26 Feb 00	**ANYTHING** *Def Jam 5626502*	18		2
24 Jun 00	**BIG PIMPIN'** *Def Jam 5627742*	29		2
16 Dec 00	**I JUST WANNA LOVE U (GIVE IT TO ME)** *Def Jam 5727462*	17		6
23 Jun 01	**FIESTA** *Jive 9252142* R KELLY FEATURING JAY-Z	23		2
27 Oct 01	**IZZO (H.O.V.A.)** *Roc-A-Fella 5888152*	21		2
19 Jan 02	**GIRLS GIRLS GIRLS** *Roc-A-Fella/Def Jam 5889062*	11		4
25 May 02	**HONEY** *Jive 9253662* R KELLY & JAY-Z	35		1
1 Feb 03	**03 BONNIE AND CLYDE** *Roc-A-Fella 0770102* JAY-Z FEATURING BEYONCÉ KNOWLES	2		8
26 Apr 03	**EXCUSE ME MISS** *Roc-A-Fella 0779122*	17		3
5 Jul 03	**JOGI/BEWARE OF THE BOYS** *Showbiz/Dharma DHARMA 1CDS* PANJABI MC FEATURING JAY-Z	25		2
16 Aug 03	**FRONTIN'** *Arista 82876553332* PHARRELL WILLIAMS FEATURING JAY-Z	6		7
20 Dec 03	**CHANGE CLOTHES** *Roc-A-Fella 9815226*	32		1
22 May 04	**99 PROBLEMS/DIRT OFF YOUR SHOULDER** *Roc-A-Fella 9862392*	12		4
4 Dec 04	**NUMB/ENCORE** *WEA W660CD* JAY-Z VS LINKIN PARK	14		18
26 Aug 06	**DÉJÀ VU** *Columbia 82876884352* BEYONCE FEATURING JAY-Z	1	1	9
9 Dec 06	**SHOW ME WHAT YOU GOT** *Mercury 1717945*	38		2
26 May 07	**UMBRELLA** *Def Jam 1735491* RIHANNA FEATURING JAY-Z ● ★	1	10	35

MAXI JAZZ UK singer

Date	Title / Label	Peak Position	Weeks at No.1	Weeks in Top 40
20 Apr 02	**MY CULTURE** *Palm Pictures PPCD 70732* 1 GIANT LEAP FEATURING MAXI JAZZ & ROBBIE WILLIAMS	9		4
11 Nov 06	**DANCE4LIFE** *Nebula NEBCD100* TIESTO FEATURING MAXI JAZZ	67		

JAZZ & THE BROTHERS GRIMM UK group

Date	Title / Label	Peak Position	Weeks at No.1	Weeks in Top 40
9 Jul 88	**(LET'S ALL GO BACK) DISCO NIGHTS** *Ensign ENY 616*	57		

JAZZY JEFF & THE FRESH PRINCE US duo

Date	Title / Label	Peak Position	Weeks at No.1	Weeks in Top 40
4 Oct 86	**GIRLS AIN'T NOTHING BUT TROUBLE** *Champion CHAMP 18*	21		4
3 Aug 91	**SUMMERTIME** *Jive 279*	8		7
9 Nov 91	**RING MY BELL** *Jive JIVECD 288*	53		
11 Sep 93	**BOOM! SHAKE THE ROOM** *Jive JIVECD 335* ●	1	2	11
20 Nov 93	**I'M LOOKING FOR THE ONE (TO BE WITH ME)** *Jive JIVECD 345*	24		3
19 Feb 94	**CAN'T WAIT TO BE WITH YOU** *Jive JIVECD 348*	29		2
4 Jun 94	**TWINKLE TWINKLE (I'M NOT A STAR)** *Jive JIVECD 354*	62		
6 Aug 94	**SUMMERTIME** *Jive JIVECD 279*	29		3
	DJ JAZZY JEFF & THE FRESH PRINCE			
2 Dec 95	**BOOM! SHAKE THE ROOM (REMIX)** *Jive JIVECD 387*	40		1
11 Jul 98	**LOVELY DAZE** *Jive 0518902*	37		1

JAZZY M UK producer

Date	Title / Label	Peak Position	Weeks at No.1	Weeks in Top 40
21 Oct 00	**JAZZIN' THE WAY YOU KNOW** *Perfecto PERF 08CDS*	47		

JB'S ALL STARS UK group

Date	Title / Label	Peak Position	Weeks at No.1	Weeks in Top 40
11 Feb 84	**BACKFIELD IN MOTION** *RCA Victor 384*	48		

JC UK producer

Date	Title / Label	Peak Position	Weeks at No.1	Weeks in Top 40
7 Feb 98	**SO HOT** *East West EW 146CD*	74		

JC 001 UK rapper

Date	Title / Label	Peak Position	Weeks at No.1	Weeks in Top 40
24 Apr 93	**NEVER AGAIN** *AnXious ANX 1012CD*	67		
26 Jun 93	**CUPID** *AnXious ANX 1014CD*	56		

JD AKA DREADY UK rapper

Date	Title / Label	Peak Position	Weeks at No.1	Weeks in Top 40
2 Aug 03	**SIGNAL** *Independiente SSB2MS*	64		

JDS UK production duo

Date	Title / Label	Peak Position	Weeks at No.1	Weeks in Top 40
27 Sep 97	**NINE WAYS** *ffrr FCD 310*	61		
23 May 98	**LONDON TOWN** *Jive 0530042*	49		
3 Mar 01	**NINE WAYS (REMIX)** *ffrr FCD 391*	47		

JEALOUSY French group

Date	Title / Label	Peak Position	Weeks at No.1	Weeks in Top 40
16 Sep 06	**LUCY** *Purple City CDPCTY105*	30		2

WYCLEF JEAN US rapper

Date	Title / Label	Peak Position	Weeks at No.1	Weeks in Top 40
28 Jun 97	**WE TRYING TO STAY ALIVE** *Columbia 6646815* WYCLEF JEAN & THE REFUGEE ALLSTARS	13		3
27 Sep 97	**GUANTANAMERA** *Columbia 6650852* WYCLEF JEAN & THE REFUGEE ALLSTARS	25		1
28 Mar 98	**NO NO NO** *Columbia 6656592* DESTINY'S CHILD FEATURING WYCLEF JEAN	5		6
16 May 98	**GONE TILL NOVEMBER** *Columbia 6658712* ●	3		7
14 Nov 98	**ANOTHER ONE BITES THE DUST** *DreamWorks DRMCD 22364* QUEEN WITH WYCLEF JEAN FEATURING PRAS MICHEL/FREE	5		4
23 Oct 99	**NEW DAY** *Columbia 6682122* WYCLEF JEAN FEATURING BONO	23		1
16 Sep 00	**IT DOESN'T MATTER** *Columbia 6697782* WYCLEF JEAN FEATURING THE ROCK & MELKY SEDECK	3		5
16 Dec 00	**911** *Columbia 6706122* WYCLEF FEATURING MARY J BLIGE	9		7
21 Jul 01	**PERFECT GENTLEMAN** *Columbia 6710522* ●	4		12
8 Dec 01	**WISH YOU WERE HERE** *Columbia 6721562*	28		1
6 Jul 02	**TWO WRONGS (DON'T MAKE A RIGHT)** *Columbia 6728902* WYCLEF JEAN FEATURING CLAUDETTE ORTIZ	14		4
17 Jun 06	**HIPS DON'T LIE** *Epic 82876842702* SHAKIRA FEATURING WYCLEF JEAN ★	1	2	28

Silver-selling · Gold-selling · Platinum-selling · US No.1 · Peak Position · Weeks at No.1 · Weeks in Top 40

Date	Title / Label	Peak Position	Weeks at No.1	Weeks in Top 40
1 Dec 07	**SWEETEST GIRL (DOLLAR BILL)** *Download* WYCLEF JEAN FEATURING AKON, LIL WAYNE & NIIA	66		

JEEVAS UK group

Date	Title / Label	Peak Position	Weeks at No.1	Weeks in Top 40
22 Mar 03	**ONCE UPON A TIME IN AMERICA** *Cowboy Music COWCDB 005*	61		
28 Feb 04	**HAVE YOU EVER SEEN THE RAIN?** *Cowboy Music COWCDB 008*	70		

JEFFERSON UK singer

Date	Title / Label	Peak Position	Weeks at No.1	Weeks in Top 40
9 Apr 69	**COLOUR OF MY LOVE** *Pye 7N 17706*	22		7

GARLAND JEFFREYS US singer

Date	Title / Label	Peak Position	Weeks at No.1	Weeks in Top 40
8 Feb 92	**HAIL HAIL ROCK 'N' ROLL** *RCA PB 49171*	72		

JELLYBEAN US producer

Date	Title / Label	Peak Position	Weeks at No.1	Weeks in Top 40
1 Feb 86	**SIDEWALK TALK** *EMI America EA 210* JELLYBEAN FEATURING CATHERINE BUCHANAN	47		
26 Sep 87	**THE REAL THING** *Chrysalis CHS 3167* JELLYBEAN FEATURING STEVEN DANTE	13		8
28 Nov 87	**WHO FOUND WHO** *Chrysalis CHS JEL 1* JELLYBEAN FEATURING ELISA FIORILLO	10		9
12 Dec 87	**JINGO** *Chrysalis JEL 2*	12		8
12 Mar 88	**JUST A MIRAGE** *Chrysalis JEL 3* JELLYBEAN FEATURING ADELE BERTEI	13		7
20 Aug 88	**COMING BACK FOR MORE** *Chrysalis JEL 4* JELLYBEAN FEATURING RICHARD DARBYSHIRE	41		

JELLYFISH US group

Date	Title / Label	Peak Position	Weeks at No.1	Weeks in Top 40
26 Jan 91	**THE KING IS HALF UNDRESSED** *Charisma CUSS 1*	39		1
27 Apr 91	**BABY'S COMING BACK** *Charisma CUSS 2*	51		
3 Aug 91	**THE SCARY-GO-ROUND EP** *Charisma CUSS 3*	49		
26 Oct 91	**I WANNA STAY HOME** *Charisma CUSS 4*	59		
1 May 93	**THE GHOST AT NUMBER ONE** *Charisma CUSDG 10*	43		
17 Jul 93	**NEW MISTAKE** *Charisma CUSDG 11*	55		

JEM UK singer

Date	Title / Label	Peak Position	Weeks at No.1	Weeks in Top 40
26 Mar 05	**THEY** *Ato 82876685182*	6		10
25 Jun 05	**JUST A RIDE** *Ato 82876705862*	16		4
24 Sep 05	**WISH I** *Ato 82876727732*	24		2

JEMINI UK duo

Date	Title / Label	Peak Position	Weeks at No.1	Weeks in Top 40
7 Jun 03	**CRY BABY** *Integral INTEG 001CD*	15		2

KATHERINE JENKINS UK singer

Date	Title / Label	Peak Position	Weeks at No.1	Weeks in Top 40
2 Dec 06	**GREEN GREEN GRASS OF HOME** *UCJ 1717438*	62		

JENTINA UK singer

Date	Title / Label	Peak Position	Weeks at No.1	Weeks in Top 40
3 Jul 04	**BAD ASS STRIPPA** *Virgin VSCDX 1873*	22		2
9 Oct 04	**FRENCH KISSES** *Virgin VSCDX 1877*	20		1

JERU THE DAMAJA US rapper

Date	Title / Label	Peak Position	Weeks at No.1	Weeks in Top 40
7 Dec 96	**YA PLAYIN YASELF** *ffrr FCD 289*	67		

JESSICA Swedish singer

Date	Title / Label	Peak Position	Weeks at No.1	Weeks in Top 40
20 Mar 99	**HOW WILL I KNOW (WHO YOU ARE)** *Jive 0522412*	47		

JESSY Belgian singer

Date	Title / Label	Peak Position	Weeks at No.1	Weeks in Top 40
12 Apr 03	**LOOK AT ME NOW** *Data 46CDS*	29		1
19 Aug 06	**DANCING IN THE DARK** *All Around The World CDGLOBE510* MICKEY MODELLE V JESSY	10		5
30 Dec 06	**OVER YOU** *All Around The World CDGLOBE609* MICKEY MODELLE V JESSY	35		1

JESUS & MARY CHAIN UK group

Date	Title / Label	Peak Position	Weeks at No.1	Weeks in Top 40
2 Mar 85	**NEVER UNDERSTAND** *Blanco Y Negro NEG 8*	47		
8 Jun 85	**YOU TRIP ME UP** *Blanco Y Negro NEG 13*	55		
12 Oct 85	**JUST LIKE HONEY** *Blanco Y Negro NEG 17*	45		
26 Jul 86	**SOME CANDY TALKING** *Blanco Y Negro NEG 19*	13		4
2 May 87	**APRIL SKIES** *Blanco Y Negro NEG 24*	8		5
15 Aug 87	**HAPPY WHEN IT RAINS** *Blanco Y Negro NEG 25*	25		4
7 Nov 87	**DARKLANDS** *Blanco Y Negro NEG 29*	33		3
9 Apr 88	**SIDEWALKING** *Blanco Y Negro NEG 32*	30		2
23 Sep 89	**BLUES FROM A GUN** *Blanco Y Negro NEG 41*	32		1
18 Nov 89	**HEAD ON** *Blanco Y Negro NEG 42*	57		
8 Sep 90	**ROLLERCOASTER (EP)** *Blanco Y Negro NEG 45*	46		
15 Feb 92	**REVERENCE** *Blanco Y Negro NEG 55*	10		2
14 Mar 92	**FAR GONE AND OUT** *Blanco Y Negro NEG 56*	23		2
4 Jul 92	**ALMOST GOLD** *Blanco Y Negro NEG 57*	41		
10 Jul 93	**SOUND OF SPEED (EP)** *Blanco Y Negro NEG 66CD*	30		1
30 Jul 94	**SOMETIMES ALWAYS** *Blanco Y Negro NEG 70CD*	22		2
22 Oct 94	**COME ON** *Blanco Y Negro NEG 73CD1*	52		
17 Jun 95	**I HATE ROCK 'N' ROLL** *Blanco Y Negro NEG 81CD*	61		
18 Apr 98	**CRACKING UP** *Creation CRESCD 292*	35		1
30 May 98	**ILOVEROCKNROLL** *Creation CRESCD 296*	38		1

JESUS JONES UK group

Date	Title / Label	Peak Position	Weeks at No.1	Weeks in Top 40
25 Feb 89	**INFO-FREAKO** *Food 18*	42		
8 Jul 89	**NEVER ENOUGH** *Food 21*	42		
23 Sep 89	**BRING IT ON DOWN** *Food 22*	46		
7 Apr 90	**REAL REAL REAL** *Food 24*	19		7
6 Oct 90	**RIGHT HERE RIGHT NOW** *Food 25*	31		3
12 Jan 91	**INTERNATIONAL BRIGHT YOUNG THING** *Food 27*	7		4
2 Mar 91	**WHO WHERE WHY** *Food 28*	21		6
20 Jul 91	**RIGHT HERE RIGHT NOW** *Food 30*	31		3
9 Jan 93	**THE DEVIL YOU KNOW** *Food CDPERV 1*	10		3
10 Apr 93	**THE RIGHT DECISION** *Food CDPERV 2*	36		1
10 Jul 93	**ZEROES AND ONES** *Food CDFOODS 44*	30		1
14 Jun 97	**THE NEXT BIG THING** *Food CDFOOD 95*	49		
16 Aug 97	**CHEMICAL #1** *Food CDFOOD 102*	71		

JESUS LIZARD US group

Date	Title / Label	Peak Position	Weeks at No.1	Weeks in Top 40
6 Mar 93	**PUSS** *Touch And Go TG 83CD*	12		1

JESUS LOVES YOU UK singer

Date	Title / Label	Peak Position	Weeks at No.1	Weeks in Top 40
11 Nov 89	**AFTER THE LOVE** *More Protein PROT 2*	68		
23 Feb 91	**BOW DOWN MISTER** *More Protein PROT 8*	27		4
8 Jun 91	**GENERATIONS OF LOVE** *More Protein PROT 10*	35		3
12 Dec 92	**SWEET TOXIC LOVE** *Virgin VS 1449*	65		

JET Australian group

Date	Title / Label	Peak Position	Weeks at No.1	Weeks in Top 40
6 Sep 03	**ARE YOU GONNA BE MY GIRL?** *Elektra E 7456CD1*	23		1
15 Nov 03	**ROLLOVER DJ** *Elektra E 7486CD1*	34		1
20 Mar 04	**LOOK WHAT YOU'VE DONE** *Elektra E 7527CD*	28		1
5 Jun 04	**ARE YOU GONNA BE MY GIRL?** *Elektra E 7599CD*	16		3
18 Sep 04	**COLD HARD BITCH** *Elektra E7607CD*	34		1
8 Jan 05	**GET ME OUTTA HERE** *679 679L094CD*	37		1
30 Sep 06	**PUT YOUR MONEY WHERE YOUR MOUTH IS** *Elektra AT0258CD*	23		1
2 Dec 06	**BRING IT ON BACK** *Atlantic AT0263CD*	51		

JETHRO TULL UK group

Date	Title / Label	Peak Position	Weeks at No.1	Weeks in Top 40
1 Jan 69	**LOVE STORY** *Island WIP 6048*	29		5
14 May 69	**LIVING IN THE PAST** *Island WIP 6056*	3		11
1 Nov 69	**SWEET DREAM** *Chrysalis WIP 6070*	7		10
24 Jan 70	**THE WITCH'S PROMISE/TEACHER** *Chrysalis WIP 6077*	4		9
18 Sep 71	**LIFE IS A LONG SONG/UP THE POOL** *Chrysalis WIP 6106*	11		8
11 Dec 76	**RING OUT SOLSTICE BELLS (EP)** *Chrysalis CXP 2*	28		2
15 Sep 84	**LAP OF LUXURY** *Chrysalis TULL 1*	70		
16 Jan 88	**SAID SHE WAS A DANCER** *Chrysalis TULL 4*	55		
21 Mar 92	**ROCKS ON THE ROAD** *Chrysalis TULLX 7*	47		
22 May 93	**LIVING IN THE (SLIGHTLY MORE RECENT) PAST** *Chrysalis CDCHSS 3970*	32		1

JETS UK group

Date	Title / Label	Peak Position	Weeks at No.1	Weeks in Top 40
22 Aug 81	**SUGAR DOLL** *EMI 5211*	55		
31 Oct 81	**YES TONIGHT JOSEPHINE** *EMI 5247*	25		6
6 Feb 82	**LOVE MAKES THE WORLD GO ROUND** *EMI 5262*	21		5
24 Apr 82	**THE HONEYDRIPPER** *EMI 5289*	58		

Silver-selling ● Gold-selling ● Platinum-selling ✪ US No.1 ★ | Peak Position | Weeks at No.1 | Weeks in Top 40

Date	Title	Label	Peak Position	Weeks at No.1	Weeks in Top 40
9 Oct 82	SOMEBODY TO LOVE	EMI 5342	56		
6 Aug 83	BLUE SKIES	EMI 5405	53		
17 Dec 83	ROCKIN' AROUND THE CHRISTMAS TREE	PRT 7P 297	62		
13 Oct 84	PARTY DOLL	PRT JETS 2	72		
31 Jan 87	CRUSH ON YOU	MCA 1048	5		9
25 Apr 87	CURIOSITY	MCA 1119	41		
28 May 88	ROCKET 2 U	MCA 1226	69		

JOAN JETT US singer

Date	Title	Label	Peak Position	Weeks at No.1	Weeks in Top 40
24 Apr 82	I LOVE ROCK 'N' ROLL JOAN JETT & THE BLACKHEARTS (Silver) ★	Epic EPC A 2152	4		8
10 Jul 82	CRIMSON AND CLOVER JOAN JETT & THE BLACKHEARTS	Epic EPC A 2485	60		
20 Aug 88	I HATE MYSELF FOR LOVING YOU JOAN JETT & THE BLACKHEARTS	London LON 195	46		
31 Mar 90	DIRTY DEEDS	Chrysalis CHS 3518	69		
19 Feb 94	I LOVE ROCK 'N' ROLL JOAN JETT & THE BLACKHEARTS	Reprise W 0232CD	75		

JEWEL US singer/guitarist

Date	Title	Label	Peak Position	Weeks at No.1	Weeks in Top 40
14 Jun 97	WHO WILL SAVE YOUR SOUL	Atlantic A 8514CD	52		
9 Aug 97	YOU WERE MEANT FOR ME	Atlantic A 5463CD	53		
22 Nov 97	YOU WERE MEANT FOR ME	Atlantic A 5463CD	32		1
21 Nov 98	HANDS	Atlantic AT 0055CD	41		
26 Jun 99	DOWN SO LONG	Atlantic AT 0069CD	38		1
30 Aug 03	INTUITION	Atlantic W 619CD	52		

JEZ & CHOOPIE UK/Israeli production duo

Date	Title	Label	Peak Position	Weeks at No.1	Weeks in Top 40
21 Mar 98	YIM	Multiply CDMULTY 31	36		1

JFK UK producer

Date	Title	Label	Peak Position	Weeks at No.1	Weeks in Top 40
15 Sep 01	GOOD GOD	Y2K 025CD	71		
26 Jan 02	WHIPLASH	Y2K 027CD	47		
4 May 02	THE SOUND OF BLUE	Y2K 030CD	55		

JHELISA US singer

Date	Title	Label	Peak Position	Weeks at No.1	Weeks in Top 40
1 Jul 95	FRIENDLY PRESSURE	Dorado DOR 040CD	75		

JIBBS US rapper

Date	Title	Label	Peak Position	Weeks at No.1	Weeks in Top 40
3 Feb 07	CHAIN HANG LOW	Geffen 1709267	63		

JIGSAW UK group

Date	Title	Label	Peak Position	Weeks at No.1	Weeks in Top 40
1 Nov 75	SKY HIGH	Splash CPI 1	9		10
6 Aug 77	IF I HAVE TO GO AWAY	Splash CP 11	36		4

JILTED JOHN UK singer

Date	Title	Label	Peak Position	Weeks at No.1	Weeks in Top 40
12 Aug 78	JILTED JOHN (Silver)	EMI International INT 567	4		11

JIMMY EAT WORLD US group

Date	Title	Label	Peak Position	Weeks at No.1	Weeks in Top 40
17 Nov 01	SALT SWEAT SUGAR	DreamWorks 4508782	60		
9 Feb 02	THE MIDDLE	DreamWorks 4508482	26		2
15 Jun 02	SWEETNESS	DreamWorks 4508342	38		1
16 Oct 04	PAIN	Interscope 9864179	38		1
9 Apr 05	WORK	Interscope 9880673	49		
15 Mar 08	ALWAYS BE	Interscope 1763635	37		1

JIMMY THE HOOVER UK group

Date	Title	Label	Peak Position	Weeks at No.1	Weeks in Top 40
25 Jun 83	TANTALISE (WO WO EE YEH YEH)	Innervision A 3406	18		6

JIN US rapper

Date	Title	Label	Peak Position	Weeks at No.1	Weeks in Top 40
19 Mar 05	LEARN CHINESE	Virgin VUSDX300	59		

JINGLE BELLES UK group

Date	Title	Label	Peak Position	Weeks at No.1	Weeks in Top 40
17 Dec 83	CHRISTMAS SPECTRE	Passion PASH 14	37		3

JINNY Italian singer

Date	Title	Label	Peak Position	Weeks at No.1	Weeks in Top 40
29 Jun 91	KEEP WARM	Virgin VS 1356	68		
22 May 93	FEEL THE RHYTHM	Logic 1633001022	74		
15 Jul 95	KEEP WARM (REMIX)	Multiply CDMULTY 5	11		6
16 Dec 95	WANNA BE WITH YOU	Multiply CDMULTY 8	30		1

JIVE BUNNY & THE MASTERMIXERS UK production/mixing group

Date	Title	Label	Peak Position	Weeks at No.1	Weeks in Top 40
15 Jul 89	SWING THE MOOD (Platinum)	Music Factory Dance MFD 001	1	5	17
14 Oct 89	THAT'S WHAT I LIKE (Gold)	Music Factory Dance MFD 002	1	3	10
2 Dec 89	IT TAKES TWO BABY LIZ KERSHAW, BRUNO BROOKES, JIVE BUNNY & LONDONBEAT	Spartan CIN 101	53		
16 Dec 89	LET'S PARTY (Gold)	Music Factory Dance MFD 003	1	1	5
17 Mar 90	THAT SOUNDS GOOD TO ME	Music Factory Dance MFD 004	4		4
25 Aug 90	CAN CAN YOU PARTY	Music Factory Dance MFD 007	8		5
17 Nov 90	LET'S SWING AGAIN	Music Factory Dance MFD 009	19		3
22 Dec 90	THE CRAZY PARTY MIXES	Music Factory Dance MFD 010	13		4
23 Mar 91	OVER TO YOU JOHN (HERE WE GO AGAIN)	Music Factory Dance MFD 012	28		4
20 Jul 91	HOT SUMMER SALSA	Music Factory Dance MFD 013	43		
23 Nov 91	ROCK 'N' ROLL DANCE PARTY	Music Factory Dance MFD 015	48		

JJ UK duo

Date	Title	Label	Peak Position	Weeks at No.1	Weeks in Top 40
9 Feb 91	IF THIS IS LOVE	Columbia 6566097	55		

JJ72 UK duo

Date	Title	Label	Peak Position	Weeks at No.1	Weeks in Top 40
3 Jun 00	LONG WAY SOUTH	Lakota LAK 0015CD	68		
26 Aug 00	OXYGEN	Lakota LAK 0016CD	23		1
4 Nov 00	OCTOBER SWIMMER	Lakota LAK 0018CD	29		1
10 Feb 01	SNOW	Lakota LAK 0019CD	21		1
12 Oct 02	FORMULAE	Columbia 6731595	28		1
22 Feb 03	ALWAYS AND FOREVER	Columbia 6734325	43		
10 Sep 05	COMING HOME	Lakota LAK0035	52		

JKD BAND UK group

Date	Title	Label	Peak Position	Weeks at No.1	Weeks in Top 40
1 Jul 78	DRAGON POWER	Satril SAT 132	58		

JM SILK US duo

Date	Title	Label	Peak Position	Weeks at No.1	Weeks in Top 40
25 Oct 86	I CAN'T TURN AROUND	RCA PB 49793	62		
7 Mar 87	LET THE MUSIC TAKE CONTROL	RCA PB 49767	47		

JO BOXERS UK group

Date	Title	Label	Peak Position	Weeks at No.1	Weeks in Top 40
19 Feb 83	BOXER BEAT	RCA BOXX 1	3		9
21 May 83	JUST GOT LUCKY	RCA BOXX 2	7		7
13 Aug 83	JOHNNY FRIENDLY	RCA BOXX 3	31		3
12 Nov 83	JEALOUS LOVE	RCA BOXX 4	72		

JO JINGLES UK group

Date	Title	Label	Peak Position	Weeks at No.1	Weeks in Top 40
13 Nov 04	WIND THE BOBBIN UP	Jo Jingles JJ21CD	21		2
12 Nov 05	DISCO	Jo Jingles JJ27	44		

JO JO GUNNE US group

Date	Title	Label	Peak Position	Weeks at No.1	Weeks in Top 40
25 Mar 72	RUN RUN RUN	Asylum AYM 501	6		11

JOAN COLLINS FAN CLUB UK comedian

Date	Title	Label	Peak Position	Weeks at No.1	Weeks in Top 40
18 Jun 88	LEADER OF THE PACK	10 TEN 227	60		

JOHN PAUL JOANS UK singer/comedian

Date	Title	Label	Peak Position	Weeks at No.1	Weeks in Top 40
19 Dec 70	MAN FROM NAZARETH	RAK 107	25		4

JOCASTA UK group

Date	Title	Label	Peak Position	Weeks at No.1	Weeks in Top 40
15 Feb 97	GO	Epic 6641415	50		
3 May 97	CHANGE ME	Epic 6643902	60		

Silver-selling ○ Gold-selling ● Platinum-selling ⊛ US No.1 ★ — Peak Position · Weeks at No.1 · Weeks in Top 40

JOCKO US rapper

Date	Title / Label	Peak Position	Weeks at No.1	Weeks in Top 40
23 Feb 80	**RHYTHM TALK** *Philadelphia International PIR 8222*	56		

JODE UK duo

Date	Title / Label	Peak Position	Weeks at No.1	Weeks in Top 40
19 Dec 98	**WALK...(THE DOG) LIKE AN EGYPTIAN** *Logic 74321640332* JODE FEATURING YO-HANS	48		

JODECI US group

Date	Title / Label	Peak Position	Weeks at No.1	Weeks in Top 40
16 Jan 93	**CHERISH** *Uptown MCSTD 1726*	56		
11 Dec 93	**CRY FOR YOU** *Uptown MCSTD 1951*	56		
16 Jul 94	**FEENIN'** *MCA MCSTD 1984*	18		2
28 Jan 95	**CRY FOR YOU** *Uptown MCSTD 2039*	20		2
24 Jun 95	**FREEK 'N YOU** *Uptown MCSTD 2072*	17		2
9 Dec 95	**LOVE U 4 LIFE** *Uptown MCSTD 2105*	23		1
25 May 96	**GET ON UP** *MCA MCSTD 48010*	20		1

JODIE Australian singer

Date	Title / Label	Peak Position	Weeks at No.1	Weeks in Top 40
25 Feb 95	**ANYTHING YOU WANT** *Mercury MERCD 423*	47		

JOE US singer

Date	Title / Label	Peak Position	Weeks at No.1	Weeks in Top 40
22 Jan 94	**I'M IN LUV** *Mercury JOECD 1*	22		3
25 Jun 94	**THE ONE FOR ME** *Mercury JOECD 2*	34		1
22 Oct 94	**ALL OR NOTHING** *Mercury JOECD 3*	56		
27 Apr 96	**ALL THE THINGS (YOUR MAN WON'T DO)** *Island CID 634*	34		1
14 Jun 97	**DON'T WANNA BE A PLAYER** *Jive JIVECD 410*	16		1
27 Sep 97	**THE LOVE SCENE** *Jive JIVECD 430*	22		1
10 Jan 98	**GOOD GIRLS** *Jive JIVECD 442*	29		1
22 Aug 98	**NO ONE ELSE COMES CLOSE** *Jive 0521682*	41		
31 Oct 98	**ALL THAT I AM** *Jive 0518532*	52		
11 Mar 00	**THANK GOD I FOUND YOU** *Columbia 6690582* MARIAH CAREY FEATURING JOE & 98°	10		4
15 Jul 00	**TREAT HER LIKE A LADY** *Jive 9250772*	60		
17 Feb 01	**STUTTER** *Jive 9251632* JOE FEATURING MYSTIKAL ★	7		6
5 May 01	**I WANNA KNOW** *Jive 9252102*	37		1
16 Feb 02	**LET'S STAY HOME TONIGHT** *Jive 9253222*	29		1
14 Sep 02	**WHAT IF A WOMAN** *Jive 9253962*	53		
24 Apr 04	**RIDE WIT U/MORE & MORE** *Jive 82876609392* JOE FEATURING G UNIT	12		5

JOE PUBLIC US group

Date	Title / Label	Peak Position	Weeks at No.1	Weeks in Top 40
11 Jul 92	**LIVE AND LEARN** *Columbia 6575267*	43		
28 Nov 92	**I'VE BEEN WATCHIN'** *Columbia 6587657*	75		

BILLY JOEL US singer/pianist

Date	Title / Label	Peak Position	Weeks at No.1	Weeks in Top 40
11 Feb 78	**JUST THE WAY YOU ARE** *CBS 5872*	19		9
24 Jun 78	**MOVIN' OUT (ANTHONY'S SONG)** *CBS 6412*	35		3
2 Dec 78	**MY LIFE** *CBS 6821* ○	12		12
28 Apr 79	**UNTIL THE NIGHT** *CBS 7242*	50		
12 Apr 80	**ALL FOR LEYNA** *CBS 8325*	40		1
9 Aug 80	**IT'S STILL ROCK AND ROLL TO ME** *CBS 8753* ★	14		9
15 Oct 83	**UPTOWN GIRL** *CBS A 3775* ●	1	5	14
10 Dec 83	**TELL HER ABOUT IT** *CBS A 3655* ○ ★	4		9
18 Feb 84	**AN INNOCENT MAN** *CBS A 4142* ○	8		9
28 Apr 84	**THE LONGEST TIME** *CBS A 4280*	25		4
23 Jun 84	**LEAVE A TENDER MOMENT ALONE/GOODNIGHT SAIGON** *CBS A 4521*	29		4
22 Feb 86	**SHE'S ALWAYS A WOMAN/JUST THE WAY YOU ARE** *CBS A 6862*	53		
20 Sep 86	**A MATTER OF TRUST** *CBS 6500577*	52		
30 Sep 89	**WE DIDN'T START THE FIRE** *CBS JOEL 1* ★	7		9
16 Dec 89	**LENINGRAD** *CBS JOEL 3*	53		
10 Mar 90	**I GO TO EXTREMES** *CBS JOEL 2*	70		
29 Aug 92	**ALL SHOOK UP** *Columbia 6583437*	27		3
31 Jul 93	**THE RIVER OF DREAMS** *Columbia 6595432*	3		12
23 Oct 93	**ALL ABOUT SOUL** *Columbia 6597362*	32		2
26 Feb 94	**NO MAN'S LAND** *Columbia 6599202*	50		

JOHANN German producer

Date	Title / Label	Peak Position	Weeks at No.1	Weeks in Top 40
16 Mar 96	**NEW KICKS** *Perfecto PERF 118CD*	54		

ELTON JOHN UK singer/pianist

Date	Title / Label	Peak Position	Weeks at No.1	Weeks in Top 40
23 Jan 71	**YOUR SONG** *DJM DJS 233*	7		10
22 Apr 72	**ROCKET MAN** *DJM DJX 501*	2		10
9 Sep 72	**HONKY CAT** *DJM DJS 269*	31		5
4 Nov 72	**CROCODILE ROCK** *DJM DJS 271* ★	5		11
20 Jan 73	**DANIEL** *DJM DJS 275*	4		9
7 Jul 73	**SATURDAY NIGHT'S ALRIGHT FOR FIGHTING** *DJM DJX 502*	7		8
29 Sep 73	**GOODBYE YELLOW BRICK ROAD** *DJM DJS 285*	6		10
8 Dec 73	**STEP INTO CHRISTMAS** *DJM DJS 290*	24		5
2 Mar 74	**CANDLE IN THE WIND** *DJM DJS 297*	11		8
1 Jun 74	**DON'T LET THE SUN GO DOWN ON ME** *DJM DJS 302*	16		8
14 Sep 74	**THE BITCH IS BACK** *DJM DJS 322*	15		6
23 Nov 74	**LUCY IN THE SKY WITH DIAMONDS** *DJM DJS 340* ★	10		10
8 Mar 75	**PHILADELPHIA FREEDOM** *DJM DJS 354* ELTON JOHN BAND ★	12		9
28 Jun 75	**SOMEONE SAVED MY LIFE TONIGHT** *DJM DJS 385*	22		4
4 Oct 75	**ISLAND GIRL** *DJM DJS 610* ★	14		7
20 Mar 76	**PINBALL WIZARD** *DJM DJS 652*	7		7
3 Jul 76	**DON'T GO BREAKING MY HEART** *Rocket ROKN 512* ELTON JOHN & KIKI DEE ● ★	1	6	13
25 Sep 76	**BENNIE AND THE JETS** *DJM DJS 10705* ★	37		1
13 Nov 76	**SORRY SEEMS TO BE THE HARDEST WORD** *Rocket ROKN 517*	11		9
26 Feb 77	**CRAZY WATER** *Rocket ROKN 521*	27		5
11 Jun 77	**BITE YOUR LIP (GET UP AND DANCE)** *Rocket ROKN 526*	28		3
15 Apr 78	**EGO** *Rocket ROKN 538*	34		3
21 Oct 78	**PART TIME LOVE** *Rocket XPRES 1* ○	15		8
16 Dec 78	**SONG FOR GUY** *Rocket XPRES 5* ○	4		8
12 May 79	**ARE YOU READY FOR LOVE** *Rocket XPRES 13*	42		
24 May 80	**LITTLE JEANNIE** *Rocket XPRES 32*	33		3
23 Aug 80	**SARTORIAL ELOQUENCE** *Rocket XPRES 41*	44		
21 Mar 81	**I SAW HER STANDING THERE** *DJM DJS 10965* ELTON JOHN BAND FEATURING JOHN LENNON & THE MUSCLE SHOALS HORNS	40		1
23 May 81	**NOBODY WINS** *Rocket XPRES 54*	42		
27 Mar 82	**BLUE EYES** *Rocket XPRES 71*	8		8
12 Jun 82	**EMPTY GARDEN** *Rocket XPRES 77*	51		
30 Apr 83	**I GUESS THAT'S WHY THEY CALL IT THE BLUES** *Rocket XPRES 91*	5		9
30 Jul 83	**I'M STILL STANDING** *Rocket EJS 1* ○	4		9
15 Oct 83	**KISS THE BRIDE** *Rocket EJS 2*	20		6
10 Dec 83	**COLD AS CHRISTMAS** *Rocket EJS 3*	33		3
26 May 84	**SAD SONGS (SAY SO MUCH)** *Rocket PH 7*	7		9
11 Aug 84	**PASSENGERS** *Rocket EJS 5* ○	5		9
20 Oct 84	**WHO WEARS THESE SHOES** *Rocket EJS 6*	50		
2 Mar 85	**BREAKING HEARTS (AIN'T WHAT IT USED TO BE)** *Rocket EJS 7*	59		
15 Jun 85	**ACT OF WAR** *Rocket EJS 8* ELTON JOHN & MILLIE JACKSON	32		3
12 Oct 85	**NIKITA** *Rocket EJS 9* ○	3		10
9 Nov 85	**THAT'S WHAT FRIENDS ARE FOR** *Arista ARIST 638* DIONNE WARWICK & FRIENDS FEATURING ELTON JOHN, STEVIE WONDER & GLADYS KNIGHT ★	16		7
7 Dec 85	**WRAP HER UP** *Rocket EJS 10*	12		7
1 Mar 86	**CRY TO HEAVEN** *Rocket EJS 11*	47		
4 Oct 86	**HEARTACHE ALL OVER THE WORLD** *Rocket EJS 12*	45		
29 Nov 86	**SLOW RIVERS** *Rocket EJS 13* ELTON JOHN & CLIFF RICHARD	44		
20 Jun 87	**FLAMES OF PARADISE** *Columbia 6508657* JENNIFER RUSH & ELTON JOHN	59		
16 Jan 88	**CANDLE IN THE WIND (LIVE)** *Rocket EJS 15*	5		8
4 Jun 88	**I DON'T WANNA GO ON WITH YOU LIKE THAT** *Rocket EJS 16*	30		3
3 Sep 88	**TOWN OF PLENTY** *Rocket EJS 17*	74		
6 May 89	**THROUGH THE STORM** *Arista 112185* ARETHA FRANKLIN & ELTON JOHN	41		
26 Aug 89	**HEALING HANDS** *Rocket EJS 19*	45		
4 Nov 89	**SACRIFICE** *Rocket EJS 20*	55		
9 Jun 90	**SACRIFICE/HEALING HANDS** *Rocket EJS 22* ⊛	1	5	13
18 Aug 90	**CLUB AT THE END OF THE STREET/WHISPERS** *Rocket EJS 23*	47		
20 Oct 90	**YOU GOTTA LOVE SOMEONE** *Rocket EJS 24*	33		2
15 Dec 90	**EASIER TO WALK AWAY** *Rocket EJS 25*	63		
7 Dec 91	**DON'T LET THE SUN GO DOWN ON ME** *Epic 6576467* GEORGE MICHAEL & ELTON JOHN ○ ★	1	2	7
6 Jun 92	**THE ONE** *Rocket EJS 28*	10		6
1 Aug 92	**RUNAWAY TRAIN** *Rocket EJS 29* ELTON JOHN & ERIC CLAPTON	31		2
7 Nov 92	**THE LAST SONG** *Rocket EJS 30*	21		3
22 May 93	**SIMPLE LIFE** *Rocket EJSCD 31*	44		
20 Nov 93	**TRUE LOVE** *Rocket EJSCX 32* ELTON JOHN & KIKI DEE ○	2		8
26 Feb 94	**DON'T GO BREAKING MY HEART** *Rocket EJCD 33* ELTON JOHN WITH RuPAUL	7		5
14 May 94	**AIN'T NOTHING LIKE THE REAL THING** *London LONCD 350* MARCELLA DETROIT & ELTON JOHN	24		3
9 Jul 94	**CAN YOU FEEL THE LOVE TONIGHT** *Mercury EJCD 34*	14		7
8 Oct 94	**CIRCLE OF LIFE** *Rocket EJSCD 35*	11		10

Date	Title / Label	Peak Position	Weeks at No.1	Weeks in Top 40
4 Mar 95	**BELIEVE** *Rocket EJSDD 36*	15		4
20 May 95	**MADE IN ENGLAND** *Rocket EJSDD 37*	18		3
3 Feb 96	**PLEASE** *Rocket EJSCD 40*	33		1
14 Dec 96	**LIVE LIKE HORSES** *Rocket LLHDD 1* ELTON JOHN & LUCIANO PAVAROTTI	9		4
20 Sep 97	**CANDLE IN THE WIND 1997/SOMETHING ABOUT THE WAY YOU LOOK TONIGHT** *Rocket PTCD 1* ⊛ ★	1	5	20
14 Feb 98	**RECOVER YOUR SOUL** *Rocket EJSCD 42*	16		2
13 Jun 98	**IF THE RIVER CAN BEND** *Rocket EJSDD 43*	32		1
6 Mar 99	**WRITTEN IN THE STARS** *Mercury EJSDD 45* ELTON JOHN & LeANN RIMES	10		3
6 Oct 01	**I WANT LOVE** *Rocket 5887072*	9		5
26 Jan 02	**THIS TRAIN DON'T STOP THERE ANYMORE** *Rocket 5888972*	24		1
13 Apr 02	**ORIGINAL SIN** *Rocket 5889992*	39		1
27 Jul 02	**YOUR SONG** *Mercury 639972* ELTON JOHN & ALESSANDRO SAFINA	4		3
21 Dec 02	**SORRY SEEMS TO BE THE HARDEST WORD** *Innocent SINCD 43* BLUE FEATURING ELTON JOHN ○	1	1	12
19 Jul 03	**ARE YOU READY FOR LOVE** *Southern Fried ECB 50LOVE*	66		
6 Sep 03	**ARE YOU READY FOR LOVE** *Southern Fried ECB 50CDS*	1	1	9
13 Nov 04	**ALL THAT I'M ALLOWED (I'M THANKFUL)** *Rocket/Mercury 9868258*	20		2
16 Apr 05	**TURN THE LIGHTS OUT WHEN YOU LEAVE** *Rocket 9870664*	32		1
2 Jul 05	**GHETTO GOSPEL** *Interscope 9883248* 2PAC FEATURING ELTON JOHN	1	3	14
23 Jul 05	**ELECTRICITY** *Rocket 9872184*	4		2
7 Apr 07	**ROCKET MAN** *Download*	62		
22 Dec 07	**STEP INTO CHRISTMAS** *Download*	53		

ROBERT JOHN US singer

Date	Title / Label	Peak Position	Weeks at No.1	Weeks in Top 40
17 Jul 68	**IF YOU DON'T WANT MY LOVE** *CBS 3436*	42		
20 Oct 79	**SAD EYES** *EMI American EA 101* ★	31		5

JOHNNA US singer

Date	Title / Label	Peak Position	Weeks at No.1	Weeks in Top 40
10 Feb 96	**DO WHAT YOU FEEL** *PWL International PWL 323CD*	43		
11 May 96	**IN MY DREAMS** *PWL International PWL 325CD*	66		

JOHNNY & CHARLEY Spanish duo

Date	Title / Label	Peak Position	Weeks at No.1	Weeks in Top 40
14 Oct 65	**LA YENKA** *Pye International 7N 25326*	49		

JOHNNY & THE HURRICANES US group

Date	Title / Label	Peak Position	Weeks at No.1	Weeks in Top 40
9 Oct 59	**RED RIVER ROCK** *London HL 8948*	3		16
25 Dec 59	**REVEILLE ROCK** *London HL 9017*	14		5
17 Mar 60	**BEATNIK FLY** *London HLI 9072*	8		15
16 Jun 60	**DOWN YONDER** *London HLX 9134*	8		10
29 Sep 60	**ROCKING GOOSE** *London HLX 9190*	3		18
2 Mar 61	**JA-DA** *London HLX 9289*	14		9
6 Jul 61	**OLD SMOKEY/HIGH VOLTAGE** *London HLX 9378*	24		5

JOHNNY BOY UK duo

Date	Title / Label	Peak Position	Weeks at No.1	Weeks in Top 40
14 Aug 04	**YOU ARE THE GENERATION THAT BOUGHT MORE SHOES AND YOU GET WHAT YOU DESERVE** *Mercury 9866935*	50		

JOHNNY CORPORATE US duo

Date	Title / Label	Peak Position	Weeks at No.1	Weeks in Top 40
28 Oct 00	**SUNDAY SHOUTIN'** *Defected DFECT 21CDS*	45		

JOHNNY HATES JAZZ UK group

Date	Title / Label	Peak Position	Weeks at No.1	Weeks in Top 40
11 Apr 87	**SHATTERED DREAMS** *Virgin VS 948*	5		9
29 Aug 87	**I DON'T WANT TO BE A HERO** *Virgin VS 1000*	11		8
21 Nov 87	**TURN BACK THE CLOCK** *Virgin VS 1017*	12		9
27 Feb 88	**HEART OF GOLD** *Virgin VS 1045*	19		4
9 Jul 88	**DON'T SAY IT'S LOVE** *Virgin VS 1081*	48		

JOHNSON UK duo

Date	Title / Label	Peak Position	Weeks at No.1	Weeks in Top 40
27 Mar 99	**SAY YOU LOVE ME** *Higher Ground HIGHS 18CD*	56		

ANDREAS JOHNSON Swedish singer

Date	Title / Label	Peak Position	Weeks at No.1	Weeks in Top 40
5 Feb 00	**GLORIOUS** *WEA 254CD*	4		6
27 May 00	**THE GAMES WE PLAY** *WEA 264CD*	41		

BRYAN JOHNSON UK singer

Date	Title / Label	Peak Position	Weeks at No.1	Weeks in Top 40
10 Mar 60	**LOOKING HIGH HIGH HIGH** *Decca F 11213*	20		11

CAREY JOHNSON Australian singer

Date	Title / Label	Peak Position	Weeks at No.1	Weeks in Top 40
25 Apr 87	**REAL FASHION REGGAE STYLE** *Oval TEN 170*	19		5

DENISE JOHNSON UK singer

Date	Title / Label	Peak Position	Weeks at No.1	Weeks in Top 40
24 Aug 91	**DON'T FIGHT IT FEEL IT** *Creation CRE 110* PRIMAL SCREAM FEATURING DENISE JOHNSON	41		
14 May 94	**RAYS OF THE RISING SUN** *Magnet MAG 1022CD*	45		

DON JOHNSON US actor

Date	Title / Label	Peak Position	Weeks at No.1	Weeks in Top 40
18 Oct 86	**HEARTBEAT** *Epic 6500647*	46		
5 Nov 88	**TILL I LOVED YOU (LOVE THEME FROM *GOYA*)** *CBS BARB 2* BARBRA STREISAND & DON JOHNSON	16		4

HOLLY JOHNSON UK singer

Date	Title / Label	Peak Position	Weeks at No.1	Weeks in Top 40
14 Jan 89	**LOVE TRAIN** *MCA 1306* ○	4		9
1 Apr 89	**AMERICANOS** *MCA 1323* ○	4		10
20 May 89	**FERRY 'CROSS THE MERSEY** *PWL 41* CHRISTIANS, HOLLY JOHNSON, PAUL McCARTNEY, GERRY MARSDEN & STOCK AITKEN WATERMAN	1	3	6
24 Jun 89	**ATOMIC CITY** *MCA 1342*	18		3
30 Sep 89	**HEAVEN'S HERE** *MCA 1342*	62		
1 Dec 90	**WHERE HAS LOVE GONE** *MCA 1460*	73		
25 Dec 99	**THE POWER OF LOVE** *Pleasure Dome PLDCD 2005*	56		

HOWARD JOHNSON US singer

Date	Title / Label	Peak Position	Weeks at No.1	Weeks in Top 40
4 Sep 82	**KEEPIN' LOVE NEW/SO FINE** *A&M USA 1221*	45		

JACK JOHNSON US singer

Date	Title / Label	Peak Position	Weeks at No.1	Weeks in Top 40
25 Jun 05	**GOOD PEOPLE** *Island MCSTD40417*	50		
17 Sep 05	**BREAKDOWN** *Island MCSTD40430*	73		
4 Mar 06	**SITTING, WAITING, WISHING** *Brushfire/Island MCSXD40407*	65		
11 Mar 06	**BETTER TOGETHER** *Brushfire/Island 9879916*	24		5
27 May 06	**UPSIDE DOWN** *Brushfire/Island 9853873*	30		2
26 Jan 08	**IF I HAD EYES** *Brushfire/Island 1760759*	60		

JOHNNY JOHNSON & THE BANDWAGON US group

Date	Title / Label	Peak Position	Weeks at No.1	Weeks in Top 40
16 Oct 68	**BREAKIN' DOWN THE WALLS OF HEARTACHE** *Direction 58 3670* BANDWAGON	4		14
5 Feb 69	**YOU** *Direction 58 3923* BANDWAGON	34		1
28 May 69	**LET'S HANG ON** *Direction 58 4180* BANDWAGON	36		1
25 Jul 70	**SWEET INSPIRATION** *Bell 1111*	10		11
28 Nov 70	**(BLAME IT) ON THE PONY EXPRESS** *Bell 1128*	7		10

KEVIN JOHNSON Australian singer

Date	Title / Label	Peak Position	Weeks at No.1	Weeks in Top 40
11 Jan 75	**ROCK 'N ROLL (I GAVE YOU THE BEST YEARS OF MY LIFE)** *UK UKR 84*	23		5

LAURIE JOHNSON UK orchestra leader

Date	Title / Label	Peak Position	Weeks at No.1	Weeks in Top 40
28 Sep 61	**SUCU SUCU** *Pye 7N 15383* LAURIE JOHNSON ORCHESTRA	9		11
17 May 97	**THEME FROM *THE PROFESSIONALS*** *Virgin VSCDT 1643* LAURIE JOHNSON'S LONDON BIG BAND	36		1

L.J. JOHNSON US singer

Date	Title / Label	Peak Position	Weeks at No.1	Weeks in Top 40
7 Feb 76	**YOUR MAGIC PUT A SPELL ON ME** *Philips 6006 492*	27		6

LOU JOHNSON US singer

Date	Title / Label	Peak Position	Weeks at No.1	Weeks in Top 40
26 Nov 64	**MESSAGE TO MARTHA** *London HL 9929*	36		2

Silver-selling ● Gold-selling ● Platinum-selling ⊛ US No.1 ★ Peak Position Weeks at No.1 Weeks in Top 40

MARV JOHNSON US singer

Date	Title / Label	Peak Position	Weeks at No.1	Weeks in Top 40
12 Feb 60	YOU GOT WHAT IT TAKES *London HLT 9013*	7		15
5 May 60	I LOVE THE WAY YOU LOVE *London HLT 9109*	35		2
11 Aug 60	AIN'T GONNA BE THAT WAY *London HLT 9165*	50		
22 Jan 69	I'LL PICK A ROSE FOR MY ROSE *Tamla Motown TMG 680*	10		10
25 Oct 69	I MISS YOU BABY *Tamla Motown TMG 713*	25		6

PAUL JOHNSON UK singer

Date	Title / Label	Peak Position	Weeks at No.1	Weeks in Top 40
21 Feb 87	WHEN LOVE COMES CALLING *CBS PJOHN 1*	52		
25 Feb 89	NO MORE TOMORROWS *CBS PJOHN 7*	67		
25 Sep 99	GET GET DOWN *Defected DEFECT 7CDS*	5		5
27 Aug 05	SHE GOT ME ON *Data DATA86CDS*	70		

PUFF JOHNSON US singer

Date	Title / Label	Peak Position	Weeks at No.1	Weeks in Top 40
18 Jan 97	OVER AND OVER *Columbia 6640345*	20		2
12 Apr 97	FOREVER MORE *Work 6644075*	29		1

ROMINA JOHNSON UK singer

Date	Title / Label	Peak Position	Weeks at No.1	Weeks in Top 40
4 Mar 00	MOVIN TOO FAST *Locked On/XL Recordings LUX 117CD* ● ARTFUL DODGER & ROMINA JOHNSON	2		8
17 Jun 00	MY FORBIDDEN LOVER *51 Lexington CDLEX 1* ROMINA JOHNSON FEATURING LUCI MARTIN & NORMA JEAN	59		

SYLEENA JOHNSON US singer

Date	Title / Label	Peak Position	Weeks at No.1	Weeks in Top 40
26 Oct 02	TONIGHT I'M GONNA LET GO *Jive 9254252*	38		1
19 Jun 04	ALL FALLS DOWN *Roc-A-Fella 9862670* KANYE WEST FEATURING SYLEENA JOHNSON	10		5

ANA JOHNSSON Swedish singer

Date	Title / Label	Peak Position	Weeks at No.1	Weeks in Top 40
14 Aug 04	WE ARE *Epic 6751622*	8		4

JOHNSTON BROTHERS UK group

Date	Title / Label	Peak Position	Weeks at No.1	Weeks in Top 40
3 Apr 53	OH HAPPY DAY *Decca F 10071*	4		8
5 Nov 54	WAIT FOR ME DARLING *Decca F 10362* JOAN REGAN & THE JOHNSTON BROTHERS	18		1
21 Jan 55	HAPPY DAYS AND LONELY NIGHTS *Decca F 10389* SUZI MILLER & THE JOHNSTON BROTHERS	14		2
7 Oct 55	HERNANDO'S HIDEAWAY *Decca F 10608*	1	2	13
30 Dec 55	JOIN IN AND SING AGAIN *Decca F 10636* JOHNSTON BROTHERS & THE GEORGE CHISHOLM SOUR-NOTE SIX	9		1
13 Apr 56	NO OTHER LOVE *Decca F 10721*	22		1
30 Nov 56	IN THE MIDDLE OF THE HOUSE *Decca F 10781*	27		1
7 Dec 56	JOIN IN AND SING (NO. 3) *Decca F 10814*	24		2
8 Feb 57	GIVE HER MY LOVE *Decca F 10828*	27		1
19 Apr 57	HEART *Decca F 10860*	23		3

BRUCE JOHNSTON US keyboard player

Date	Title / Label	Peak Position	Weeks at No.1	Weeks in Top 40
27 Aug 77	PIPELINE *CBS 5514*	33		3

JAN JOHNSTON UK singer

Date	Title / Label	Peak Position	Weeks at No.1	Weeks in Top 40
8 Feb 97	TAKE ME BY THE HAND *AM:PM 5821012* SUBMERGE FEATURING JAN JOHNSTON	28		1
28 Nov 98	SKYDIVE *Stress CDSTR 89* FREEFALL FEATURING JAN JOHNSTON	75		
22 Jul 00	SKYDIVE *Renaissance Recordings RENCDS 002* FREEFALL FEATURING JAN JOHNSTON	43		
21 Apr 01	FLESH *Perfecto PERF 05CDS*	36		1
28 Jul 01	SILENT WORDS *Perfecto PERF 16CDS*	57		
8 Sep 01	SKYDIVE (I FEEL WONDERFUL) *Incentive CENT 22CDS* FREEFALL FEATURING JAN JOHNSTON	35		1

SABRINA JOHNSTON US singer

Date	Title / Label	Peak Position	Weeks at No.1	Weeks in Top 40
7 Sep 91	PEACE *East West YZ 616*	8		8
7 Dec 91	FRIENDSHIP *East West YZ 637*	58		
11 Jul 92	I WANNA SING *East West YZ 661*	46		
3 Oct 92	PEACE (REMIX) *Epic 6584377*	35		1
13 Aug 94	SATISFY MY LOVE *Champion CHAMPCD 311*	62		

JIMMY JOHNSTONE, JIM KERR, SIMPLE MINDS & LAURA MCGHEE UK group

Date	Title / Label	Peak Position	Weeks at No.1	Weeks in Top 40
8 Apr 06	TRIBUTE TO JINKY *Lord Of The Wing LWSP7*	28		3

JOJO US singer

Date	Title / Label	Peak Position	Weeks at No.1	Weeks in Top 40
11 Sep 04	LEAVE (GET OUT) *Mercury 9867841*	2		6
27 Nov 04	BABY IT'S YOU *Mercury 9869056* JOJO FEATURING BOW WOW	8		7
13 Jan 07	TOO LITTLE TOO LATE *Mercury 1716751*	4		11
12 May 07	ANYTHING *Mercury 1734750*	21		3

JOLLY BROTHERS Jamaican group

Date	Title / Label	Peak Position	Weeks at No.1	Weeks in Top 40
28 Jul 79	CONSCIOUS MAN *United Artists UP 36415*	46		

JOLLY ROGER UK singer

Date	Title / Label	Peak Position	Weeks at No.1	Weeks in Top 40
10 Sep 88	ACID MAN *10 TEN 236*	23		5

JOMANDA US group

Date	Title / Label	Peak Position	Weeks at No.1	Weeks in Top 40
22 Apr 89	MAKE MY BODY ROCK *RCA PB 42749*	44		
29 Jun 91	GOT A LOVE FOR YOU *Giant W 0040*	43		
11 Sep 93	I LIKE IT *Big Beat A 8377CD*	67		
13 Nov 93	NEVER *Big Beat A 8347CD*	40		1

JON & VANGELIS UK/Greek duo

Date	Title / Label	Peak Position	Weeks at No.1	Weeks in Top 40
5 Jan 80	I HEAR YOU NOW *Polydor POSP 96*	8		8
12 Dec 81	I'LL FIND MY WAY HOME *Polydor JV 1* ●	6		10
30 Jul 83	HE IS SAILING *Polydor JV 4*	61		
18 Aug 84	STATE OF INDEPENDENCE *Polydor JV 5*	67		

JON OF THE PLEASED WIMMIN UK transvestite DJ

Date	Title / Label	Peak Position	Weeks at No.1	Weeks in Top 40
18 Feb 95	PASSION *Perfecto YZ 884CD*	27		1
6 Apr 96	GIVE ME STRENGTH *Perfecto PERF 119CD*	30		1

JON THE DENTIST VS OLLIE JAYE UK production duo

Date	Title / Label	Peak Position	Weeks at No.1	Weeks in Top 40
24 Jul 99	IMAGINATION *Tidy Trax TIDY 126CD*	72		
10 Jun 00	FEEL SO GOOD *Tidy Trax TIDY 135CD*	72		

JONAH Dutch group

Date	Title / Label	Peak Position	Weeks at No.1	Weeks in Top 40
22 Jul 00	SSSST (LISTEN) *VC Recordings VCRD 69*	25		2

ALED JONES UK boy soprano

Date	Title / Label	Peak Position	Weeks at No.1	Weeks in Top 40
20 Jul 85	MEMORY: THEME FROM THE MUSICAL 'CATS' *BBC RESL 175*	42		
30 Nov 85	WALKING IN THE AIR *HMV ALED 1* ●	5		7
14 Dec 85	PICTURES IN THE DARK *Virgin VS 836* MIKE OLDFIELD FEATURING ALED JONES, ANITA HEGERLAND & BARRY PALMER	50		
20 Dec 86	A WINTER STORY *HMV ALED 2*	51		
29 Dec 07	WALKING IN THE AIR *Download*	72		

BARBARA JONES Jamaican singer

Date	Title / Label	Peak Position	Weeks at No.1	Weeks in Top 40
31 Jan 81	JUST WHEN I NEEDED YOU MOST *Sonet SON 2221*	31		3

CATHERINE ZETA JONES UK actress

Date	Title / Label	Peak Position	Weeks at No.1	Weeks in Top 40
19 Sep 92	FOR ALL TIME *Columbia 6583547*	36		1
26 Nov 94	TRUE LOVE WAYS *Polygram TV TLWCD 2* DAVID ESSEX & CATHERINE ZETA JONES	38		1
1 Apr 95	IN THE ARMS OF LOVE *Wow! WOWCD 7101*	72		

DONELL JONES US singer

Date	Title / Label	Peak Position	Weeks at No.1	Weeks in Top 40
15 Feb 97	KNOCKS ME OFF MY FEET *LaFace 74321458502*	58		
22 Jan 00	U KNOW WHAT'S UP *LaFace 74321722762* ●	2		8
20 May 00	SHORTY (GOT HER EYES ON ME) *LaFace 74321748902*	19		2

Silver-selling · Gold-selling · Platinum-selling · US No.1 ★ · Peak Position · Weeks at No.1 · Weeks in Top 40

Date	Title / Label	Peak Position	Weeks at No.1	Weeks in Top 40
2 Dec 00	**TRUE STEP TONIGHT** *NuLife 74321811312* TRUE STEPPERS FEATURING BRIAN HARVEY & DONELL JONES	25		1
24 Aug 02	**YOU KNOW THAT I LOVE YOU** *Arista 74321956962*	41		

GRACE JONES US singer

Date	Title / Label	Peak Position	Weeks at No.1	Weeks in Top 40
26 Jul 80	**PRIVATE LIFE** *Island WIP 6629*	17		6
20 Jun 81	**PULL UP TO THE BUMPER** *Island WIP 6696*	53		
30 Oct 82	**THE APPLE STRETCHING/NIPPLE TO THE BOTTLE** *Island WIP 6779*	50		
9 Apr 83	**MY JAMAICAN GUY** *Island IS 103*	56		
12 Oct 85	**SLAVE TO THE RHYTHM** *ZTT IS 206*	12		7
18 Jan 86	**PULL UP TO THE BUMPER/LA VIE EN ROSE** *Island IS 240*	12		7
1 Mar 86	**LOVE IS THE DRUG** *Island IS 266*	35		2
15 Nov 86	**I'M NOT PERFECT (BUT I'M PERFECT FOR YOU)** *Manhattan MT 15*	56		
7 May 94	**SLAVE TO THE RHYTHM** *Zance ZANG 50CD1*	28		1
25 Nov 00	**PULL UP TO THE BUMPER (REMIX)** *Club Tools 0120375 CLU* GRACE JONES VS FUNKSTAR DE LUXE	60		

HANNAH JONES US singer

Date	Title / Label	Peak Position	Weeks at No.1	Weeks in Top 40
14 Sep 91	**BRIDGE OVER TROUBLED WATER** *Dance Pool 6565467* PJB FEATURING HANNAH & HER SISTERS	21		6
30 Jan 93	**KEEP IT ON** *TMRC CDTMRC 7*	67		

HOWARD JONES UK singer

Date	Title / Label	Peak Position	Weeks at No.1	Weeks in Top 40
17 Sep 83	**NEW SONG** *WEA HOW 1*	3		9
26 Nov 83	**WHAT IS LOVE** *WEA HOW 2*	2		11
18 Feb 84	**HIDE AND SEEK** *WEA HOW 3*	12		7
26 May 84	**PEARL IN THE SHELL** *WEA HOW 4*	7		7
11 Aug 84	**LIKE TO GET TO KNOW YOU WELL** *WEA HOW 5*	4		10
9 Feb 85	**THINGS CAN ONLY GET BETTER** *WEA HOW 6*	6		7
20 Apr 85	**LOOK MAMA** *WEA HOW 7*	10		5
29 Jun 85	**LIFE IN ONE DAY** *WEA HOW 8*	14		5
15 Mar 86	**NO ONE IS TO BLAME** *WEA HOW 9*	16		5
4 Oct 86	**ALL I WANT** *WEA HOW 10*	35		2
29 Nov 86	**YOU KNOW I LOVE YOU...DON'T YOU** *WEA HOW 11*	43		
21 Mar 87	**A LITTLE BIT OF SNOW** *WEA HOW 12*	70		
4 Mar 89	**EVERLASTING LOVE** *WEA HOW 13*	62		
11 Apr 92	**LIFT ME UP** *WEA HOW 15*	52		

JANIE JONES UK singer

Date	Title / Label	Peak Position	Weeks at No.1	Weeks in Top 40
27 Jan 66	**WITCHES' BREW** *HMV POP 1495*	46		

JIMMY JONES US singer

Date	Title / Label	Peak Position	Weeks at No.1	Weeks in Top 40
17 Mar 60	**HANDY MAN** *MGM 1051*	3		23
16 Jun 60	**GOOD TIMIN'** *MGM 1078*	1	3	15
8 Sep 60	**I JUST GO FOR YOU** *MGM 1091*	35		2
17 Nov 60	**READY FOR LOVE** *MGM 1103*	46		
6 Apr 61	**I TOLD YOU SO** *MGM 1123*	33		1

JUGGY JONES US multi-instrumentalist

Date	Title / Label	Peak Position	Weeks at No.1	Weeks in Top 40
7 Feb 76	**INSIDE AMERICA** *Contempo CS 2080*	39		1

LAVINIA JONES South African singer

Date	Title / Label	Peak Position	Weeks at No.1	Weeks in Top 40
18 Feb 95	**SING IT TO YOU (DEE-DOOB-DEE-DOO)** *Virgin International DINDG 142*	45		

NORAH JONES US singer/pianist

Date	Title / Label	Peak Position	Weeks at No.1	Weeks in Top 40
25 May 02	**DON'T KNOW WHY** *Parlophone CDCL 836*	59		
17 Aug 02	**FEELIN' THE SAME WAY** *Parlophone CDCL 838*	72		
13 Sep 03	**DON'T KNOW WHY/I'LL BE YOUR BABY TONIGHT** *Parlophone CDCL 848*	67		
10 Apr 04	**SUNRISE** *Blue Note CDCL 853*	30		1

ORAN 'JUICE' JONES US singer

Date	Title / Label	Peak Position	Weeks at No.1	Weeks in Top 40
15 Nov 86	**THE RAIN** *Def Jam A 7303*	4		10

PAUL JONES UK singer

Date	Title / Label	Peak Position	Weeks at No.1	Weeks in Top 40
6 Oct 66	**HIGH TIME** *HMV POP 1554*	4		13
19 Jan 67	**I'VE BEEN A BAD BAD BOY** *HMV POP 1576*	5		8
23 Aug 67	**THINKIN' AIN'T FOR ME** *HMV POP 1602*	32		3
5 Feb 69	**AQUARIUS** *Columbia DB 8514*	45		

QUINCY JONES US producer/keyboard player

Date	Title / Label	Peak Position	Weeks at No.1	Weeks in Top 40
29 Jul 78	**STUFF LIKE THAT** *A&M AMS 7367*	34		3
11 Apr 81	**AI NO CORRIDA (I-NO-KO-REE-DA)** *A&M AMS 8109* QUINCY JONES FEATURING DUNE	14		8
20 Jun 81	**RAZZAMATAZZ** *A&M 8140* QUINCY JONES FEATURING PATTI AUSTIN	11		6
5 Sep 81	**BETCHA' WOULDN'T HURT ME** *A&M AMS 8157*	52		
13 Jan 90	**I'LL BE GOOD TO YOU** *Qwest W 2697* QUINCY JONES FEATURING RAY CHARLES & CHAKA KHAN	21		5
31 Mar 90	**SECRET GARDEN** *Qwest W 9992* QUINCY JONES FEATURING AL B SURE!, JAMES INGRAM, EL DeBARGE & BARRY WHITE	67		
14 Sep 96	**STOMP – THE REMIXES** *Qwest W 0372CD* QUINCY JONES FEATURING MELLE MEL, COOLIO, YO-YO, SHAQUILLE O'NEAL & THE LUNIZ	28		1
1 Aug 98	**SOUL BOSSA NOVA** *Manifesto FESCD 48* COOL, THE FAB & THE GROOVY PRESENT QUINCY JONES	47		

RICKIE LEE JONES US singer

Date	Title / Label	Peak Position	Weeks at No.1	Weeks in Top 40
23 Jun 79	**CHUCK E.'S IN LOVE** *Warner Brothers K 17390*	18		6

SONNY JONES German singer

Date	Title / Label	Peak Position	Weeks at No.1	Weeks in Top 40
7 Oct 00	**FOLLOW YOU FOLLOW ME** *Logic 74321772892* SONNY JONES FEATURING TARA CHASE	42		

TAMMY JONES UK singer

Date	Title / Label	Peak Position	Weeks at No.1	Weeks in Top 40
26 Apr 75	**LET ME TRY AGAIN** *Epic EPC 3211*	5		9

TOM JONES UK singer

Date	Title / Label	Peak Position	Weeks at No.1	Weeks in Top 40
11 Feb 65	**IT'S NOT UNUSUAL** *Decca F 12062*	1	1	14
6 May 65	**ONCE UPON A TIME** *Decca F 12121*	32		3
8 Jul 65	**WITH THESE HANDS** *Decca F 12191*	13		9
12 Aug 65	**WHAT'S NEW PUSSYCAT** *Decca F 12203*	11		9
13 Jan 66	**THUNDERBALL** *Decca F 12292*	35		2
19 May 66	**ONCE THERE WAS A TIME/NOT RESPONSIBLE** *Decca F 12390*	18		8
18 Aug 66	**THIS AND THAT** *Decca F 12461*	44		
10 Nov 66	**GREEN GREEN GRASS OF HOME** *Decca F 22511*	1	7	21
16 Feb 67	**DETROIT CITY** *Decca F 22555*	8		9
13 Apr 67	**FUNNY FAMILIAR FORGOTTEN FEELINGS** *Decca F 12599*	7		13
26 Jul 67	**I'LL NEVER FALL IN LOVE AGAIN** *Decca F 12639*	2		18
22 Nov 67	**I'M COMING HOME** *Decca F 12693*	2		14
28 Feb 68	**DELILAH** *Decca F 12747*	2		17
17 Jul 68	**HELP YOURSELF** *Decca F 12812*	5		21
27 Nov 68	**A MINUTE OF YOUR TIME** *Decca F 12854*	14		13
14 May 69	**LOVE ME TONIGHT** *Decca F 12924*	9		10
13 Dec 69	**WITHOUT LOVE (THERE IS NOTHING)** *Decca F 12990*	10		9
18 Apr 70	**DAUGHTER OF DARKNESS** *Decca F 13013*	5		13
15 Aug 70	**I (WHO HAVE NOTHING)** *Decca F 13061*	16		8
16 Jan 71	**SHE'S A LADY** *Decca F 13113*	13		8
5 Jun 71	**PUPPET MAN** *Decca F 13183*	49		
23 Oct 71	**TILL** *Decca F 13236*	2		13
1 Apr 72	**THE YOUNG NEW MEXICAN PUPPETEER** *Decca F 13298*	6		10
14 Apr 73	**LETTER TO LUCILLE** *Decca F 13393*	31		5
7 Sep 74	**SOMETHING 'BOUT YOU BABY I LIKE** *Decca F 13550*	36		3
16 Apr 77	**SAY YOU'LL STAY UNTIL TOMORROW** *EMI 2583*	40		1
18 Apr 87	**A BOY FROM NOWHERE** *Epic OLE 1*	2		10
30 May 87	**IT'S NOT UNUSUAL** *Decca F 103*	17		6
2 Jan 88	**I WAS BORN TO BE ME** *Epic OLE 4*	61		
29 Oct 88	**KISS** *China 11* ART OF NOISE FEATURING TOM JONES	5		5
29 Apr 89	**MOVE CLOSER** *Jive 203*	49		
26 Jan 91	**COULDN'T SAY GOODBYE** *Dover ROJ 10*	51		
16 Mar 91	**CARRYING A TORCH** *Dover ROJ 12*	57		
4 Jul 92	**DELILAH** *The Hit Label TOM 10*	68		
6 Feb 93	**ALL YOU NEED IS LOVE** *Childline CHILDCD 93*	19		2
5 Nov 94	**IF I ONLY KNEW** *ZTT ZANG 59CD*	11		5
25 Sep 99	**BURNING DOWN THE HOUSE** *Gut CDGUT 26* TOM JONES & THE CARDIGANS	7		5
18 Dec 99	**BABY, IT'S COLD OUTSIDE** *Gut CDGUT 29* TOM JONES & CERYS OF CATATONIA	17		3

QUINCY JONES

A handful of artists, songwriters and producers enjoy such phenomenal success that their fame, status and wealth propels them into some kind of super-celebrity ether where mere songs and chart hits seem but entertaining minutiae compared to the more pressing concerns of humanity. Thus Bono/Third World Debt and Geldof/famine are two obvious and essentially inter-linked examples. Quincy Jones is another.

Jones was a musician with his own recording contract, having had eight UK hit singles. However, it will always be for his production and arrangement work that he is best known. He has produced some of the world's biggest records – including *the* biggest record of them all, Michael Jackson's *Thriller*.

Born in Chicago in 1933, Jones was the son of a bank executive and a semi-pro basketball player. Bizarrely, his family tree actually links him distantly to both George Washington and Senator John McCain. As a child he was a keen trumpeter, and this led to his first work on the road with Lionel Hampton; a talent for musical arrangement saw him sprinkle his magic across releases by the likes of such luminaries as Count Basie and Duke Ellington, while also touring with Dizzy Gillespie as trumpeter and musical director.

The 1950s were a financially lean time for Jones following a series of ill-planned and loss-making tours with various jazz orchestras (his extensive tour schedule meant that he never learned to drive), but brighter horizons were ahead when he rose to become vice-president of Mercury Records in 1964 – an important indication that the white domination of the music industry was coming to a timely end. His first real chart hit single was 'It's My Party' for the singer Lesley Gore, which reached Number 9 in the UK singles charts after its March 1963 release. After that, Jones's star was firmly in the ascendant, working as an arranger with, among others, Frank Sinatra, Ella Fitzgerald and Peggy Lee for some of these legendary names' most fertile career periods. In terms of his own musical output, sadly, after suffering a cerebral aneurysm in 1974, for which he underwent major surgery, doctors advised Jones never to play the trumpet again.

Not content with limiting his enormous talent and enviable energy to the LP, he turned his attention to the screen, becoming the music arranger for movies like *Walk, Don't Run*, *The Italian Job* (featuring 'On Days Like These' as sung by Matt Monro) and, in the 80s, the award-winning *The Color Purple* (which he also produced) have benefited from his prolific pen. Television was not immune to his talent either, with *Ironside*, *Roots* and *The Bill Cosby Show* turning Jones's contributions into a badge of honour for their shows. Several years later, Quincy Jones's own hit television show *The Fresh Prince Of Bel Air* launched Will Smith, a chart star and major box-office draw in his own right.

Jones would be famous just for these achievements alone, but his name will always be linked with the world's biggest-selling album of all time, the massively influential *Thriller*, which he produced. In 1978 Jones oversaw the music arrangements for the movie *The Wiz*, an adaptation of the funkified 1975 Broadway musical based on *The Wizard Of Oz*. The film's stellar cast included Richard Prior, Diana Ross and, crucially, a young man named Michael Jackson, who had been in show business from a small boy as part of his famous family's successful singing act, the Jackson 5. Jackson was keen to strike out alone and, impressed by Jones's work on the movie, asked him to produce his debut album, *Off The Wall*. The album spawned several singles, beginning with 'Don't Stop Til You Get Enough', which reached Number 3 in July 1979, followed by 'Rock With You' (Number 7), with the title track and 'She's Out Of My Life' making history as the first time an artist had snagged four Top 10 singles from one album. However, five was too much of a stretch, with the Paul McCartney-penned 'Girlfriend' limping in at Number 51.

Then came *Thriller*. Legend has it that the duo had a shortlist of 300 songs to choose from; they culled them to a rather more manageable nine. 'Billie Jean', a track that Jones thought was weak, topped the UK charts in 1983, the highest placing of no less than seven singles to come from the album. Further chart success from Jackson's *Bad* album came with nine singles hitting the Top 20 and 'I Just Can't Stop Lovin' You' hitting the top slot in March 1987.

However, Quincy's contribution goes way beyond any chart. His 79 Grammy nominations, 27 Grammy wins and even his own Grammy dedicated night tell a deeper story than the lavish ceremonies and glittering trophy cabinets. He has carved a path for Afro-American creatives during a period when institutionalised discrimination was commonplace. At the Oscars, he and his songwriting partner, Bob Russell, became the first African-Americans to be nominated for an Oscar for Best Original Song; he was also the first African-American to be nominated twice in the same year; Jones remains the only African-American to be nominated as Best Producer in the Best Picture category; and so on and so on. The list is impressively long and is not just another catalogue of achievement – these are important landmarks in the social fabric of music history.

Jones's social activism also keeps him busy. He was instrumental in setting up the Institute for Black American Music in the 1960s, and the new millennium has seen his Listen Up foundation build life-changing homes in South Africa; in 2004 he helped launch the 'We Are the Future' humanitarian project for children from poor and deprived areas. Speaking in 2007, he said he had, at the age of 74, over 900 projects to oversee. Jones has received numerous awards outside of the music industry, including the prestigious Légion D'Honneur: no small dice for a musician who left school to go on the road playing his trumpet all those years ago.

Silver-selling ● Gold-selling ● Platinum-selling ✪ US No.1 ★ Peak Position Weeks at No.1 Weeks in Top 40

Date	Title / Label	Peak Position	Weeks at No.1	Weeks in Top 40
18 Mar 00	**MAMA TOLD ME NOT TO COME** *Gut CXGUT 031* TOM JONES & STEREOPHONICS	4		4
20 May 00	**SEX BOMB** *Gut CXGUT 33* TOM JONES & MOUSSE T	3		7
18 Nov 00	**YOU NEED LOVE LIKE I DO** *Gut CXGUT 36* TOM JONES & HEATHER SMALL	24		1
9 Nov 02	**TOM JONES INTERNATIONAL** *V2 VVR 5021083*	31		1
8 Mar 03	**BLACK BETTY/I WHO HAVE NOTHING** *V2 VVR 5021763*	50		
29 Apr 06	**STONED IN LOVE** *Universal TV 9878360* CHICANE FEATURING TOM JONES	7		6

JONESTOWN US duo

Date	Title / Label	Peak Position	Weeks at No.1	Weeks in Top 40
13 Jun 98	**SWEET THANG** *Universal UMD 70376*	49		

ALISON JORDAN UK singer

Date	Title / Label	Peak Position	Weeks at No.1	Weeks in Top 40
9 May 92	**BOY FROM NEW YORK CITY** *Arista 74321100427*	23		3

DAVID JORDAN UK singer

Date	Title / Label	Peak Position	Weeks at No.1	Weeks in Top 40
26 Jan 08	**SUN GOES DOWN** *Mercury 1761142*	4		9

DICK JORDAN UK singer

Date	Title / Label	Peak Position	Weeks at No.1	Weeks in Top 40
17 Mar 60	**HALLELUJAH I LOVE HER SO** *Oriole CB 1534*	47		
9 Jun 60	**LITTLE CHRISTINE** *Oriole CB 1548*	39		1

MONTELL JORDAN US singer

Date	Title / Label	Peak Position	Weeks at No.1	Weeks in Top 40
13 May 95	**THIS IS HOW WE DO IT** *Def Jam DEFCD 07* ★	11		7
2 Sep 95	**SOMETHIN' 4 DA HONEYZ** *Def Jam DEFCD 10*	15		2
19 Oct 96	**I LIKE** *Def Jam DEFCD 19* MONTELL JORDAN FEATURING SLICK RICK	24		1
23 May 98	**LET'S RIDE** *Def Jam 5686912* MONTELL JORDAN FEATURING MASTER P & SILKK THE SHOCKER	25		1
8 Apr 00	**GET IT ON TONITE** *Def Soul 5627222*	15		2

RONNY JORDAN UK guitarist

Date	Title / Label	Peak Position	Weeks at No.1	Weeks in Top 40
1 Feb 92	**SO WHAT!** *Antilles ANN 14*	32		2
25 Sep 93	**UNDER YOUR SPELL** *Island CID 565*	72		
15 Jan 94	**TINSEL TOWN** *Island CID 566*	64		
28 May 94	**COME WITH ME** *Island CID 584* RONNY JORDAN (GUEST VOCALIST FAY SIMPSON)	63		

JORIO US producer

Date	Title / Label	Peak Position	Weeks at No.1	Weeks in Top 40
24 Feb 01	**REMEMBER ME** *Wonderboy WBOYD 021*	54		

DAVID JOSEPH UK singer

Date	Title / Label	Peak Position	Weeks at No.1	Weeks in Top 40
26 Feb 83	**YOU CAN'T HIDE (YOUR LOVE FROM ME)** *Island IS 101*	13		7
28 May 83	**LET'S LIVE IT UP (NITE PEOPLE)** *Island IS 116*	26		3
18 Feb 84	**JOYS OF LIFE** *Island IS 153*	61		
31 May 86	**EXPANSIONS '86 (EXPAND YOUR MIND)** *Fourth & Broadway BRW 48* CHRIS PAUL FEATURING DAVID JOSEPH	58		

MARK JOSEPH UK singer

Date	Title / Label	Peak Position	Weeks at No.1	Weeks in Top 40
1 Mar 03	**GET THROUGH** *Mark Joseph MJR 003*	38		1
30 Aug 03	**FLY** *14th Floor MJM01CD*	28		1
27 Mar 04	**BRINGING BACK THOSE MEMORIES** *14th Floor MJM02CD2*	34		1
26 Feb 05	**LADY LADY** *14th Floor MJM05CD2*	36		1

MARTYN JOSEPH UK singer

Date	Title / Label	Peak Position	Weeks at No.1	Weeks in Top 40
20 Jun 92	**DOLPHINS MAKE ME CRY** *Epic 6581347*	34		2
12 Sep 92	**WORKING MOTHER** *Epic 6582937*	65		
9 Jan 93	**PLEASE SIRE** *Epic 6588552*	45		
3 Jun 95	**TALK ABOUT IT IN THE MORNING** *Epic 6613342*	43		

JOURNEY US group

Date	Title / Label	Peak Position	Weeks at No.1	Weeks in Top 40
27 Feb 82	**DON'T STOP BELIEVIN'** *CBS A 1728*	62		
11 Sep 82	**WHO'S CRYING NOW** *CBS A 2725*	46		

RUTH JOY UK singer

Date	Title / Label	Peak Position	Weeks at No.1	Weeks in Top 40
26 Aug 89	**DON'T PUSH IT** *MCA RJOY 1*	66		
22 Feb 92	**FEEL** *MCA MCS 1574*	67		

JOY DIVISION UK group

Date	Title / Label	Peak Position	Weeks at No.1	Weeks in Top 40
28 Jun 80	**LOVE WILL TEAR US APART** *Factory FAC 23*	13		6
29 Oct 83	**LOVE WILL TEAR US APART** *Factory FAC 23*	19		4
18 Jun 88	**ATMOSPHERE** *Factory FAC 2137*	34		2
17 Jun 95	**LOVE WILL TEAR US APART (REMIX)** *London YOJCD 1*	19		2
6 Oct 07	**LOVE WILL TEAR US APART** *London FAC23CD*	46		

JOY STRINGS UK group

Date	Title / Label	Peak Position	Weeks at No.1	Weeks in Top 40
27 Feb 64	**IT'S AN OPEN SECRET** *Regal Zonophone RZ 501*	32		6
17 Dec 64	**A STARRY NIGHT** *Regal Zonophone RZ 504*	35		3

JOY ZIPPER US duo

Date	Title / Label	Peak Position	Weeks at No.1	Weeks in Top 40
24 Apr 04	**BABY YOU SHOULD KNOW** *13 Amp/Vertigo 9866235*	59		
20 Aug 05	**I** *Vertigo 9872947*	73		

JOYRIDER UK group

Date	Title / Label	Peak Position	Weeks at No.1	Weeks in Top 40
27 Jul 96	**RUSH HOUR** *Paradox PDOXD 012*	22		1
28 Sep 96	**ALL GONE AWAY** *A&M 5819552*	54		

JT & THE BIG FAMILY Italian group

Date	Title / Label	Peak Position	Weeks at No.1	Weeks in Top 40
3 Mar 90	**MOMENTS IN SOUL** *Champion CHAMP 237*	7		6

JT PLAYAZ UK production group

Date	Title / Label	Peak Position	Weeks at No.1	Weeks in Top 40
5 Apr 97	**JUST PLAYIN'** *Pukka CDJTP 1*	30		1
2 May 98	**LET'S GET DOWN** *MCA MCSTD 40161*	64		

JTQ UK group

Date	Title / Label	Peak Position	Weeks at No.1	Weeks in Top 40
3 Apr 93	**LOVE THE LIFE** *Big Life BLRD 93* JTQ WITH NOEL McKOY	34		1
3 Jul 93	**SEE A BRIGHTER DAY** *Big Life BLRDA 97*	49		
25 Feb 95	**LOVE WILL KEEP US TOGETHER** *Acid Jazz JAZID 112CD* JTQ FEATURING ALISON LIMERICK	63		

JUANES Colombian singer

Date	Title / Label	Peak Position	Weeks at No.1	Weeks in Top 40
29 Apr 06	**LA CAMISA NEGRA** *Interscope 9877816*	32		1

JUDAS PRIEST UK group

Date	Title / Label	Peak Position	Weeks at No.1	Weeks in Top 40
20 Jan 79	**TAKE ON THE WORLD** *CBS 6915*	14		6
12 May 79	**EVENING STARS** *CBS 7312*	53		
29 Mar 80	**LIVING AFTER MIDNIGHT** *CBS 8379*	12		5
7 Jun 80	**BREAKING THE LAW** *CBS 8644*	12		5
23 Aug 80	**UNITED** *CBS 8897*	26		4
21 Feb 81	**DON'T GO** *CBS 9520*	51		
25 Apr 81	**HOT ROCKIN'** *CBS A 1153*	60		
21 Aug 82	**YOU'VE GOT ANOTHER THINK COMIN'** *CBS A 2611*	66		
21 Jan 84	**FREEWHEEL BURNIN'** *CBS A 4054*	42		
23 Apr 88	**JOHNNY B. GOODE** *Atlantic A 9114*	64		
15 Sep 90	**PAINKILLER** *CBS 6562737*	74		
23 Mar 91	**A TOUCH OF EVIL** *Columbia 6565897*	58		
24 Apr 93	**NIGHT CRAWLER** *Columbia 6590972*	63		

JUDGE DREAD UK singer/comedian

Date	Title / Label	Peak Position	Weeks at No.1	Weeks in Top 40
26 Aug 72	**BIG SIX** *Big Shot BI 608*	11		19
9 Dec 72	**BIG SEVEN** *Big Shot BI 613*	8		14
21 Apr 73	**BIG EIGHT** *Big Shot BI 619*	14		8
5 Jul 75	**JE T'AIME (MOI NON PLUS)** *Cactus CT 65*	9		9
27 Sep 75	**BIG TEN** *Cactus CT 77*	14		6
6 Dec 75	**CHRISTMAS IN DREADLAND/COME OUTSIDE** *Cactus CT 80*	14		6
8 May 76	**THE WINKLE MAN** *Cactus CT 90*	35		4
28 Aug 76	**Y VIVA SUSPENDERS/CONFESSIONS OF A BOUNCER** *Cactus CT 99*	27		4
2 Apr 77	**5TH ANNIVERSARY EP** *Cactus CT 98*	31		2
14 Jan 78	**UP WITH THE COCK/BIG PUNK** *Cactus CT 110*	49		
16 Dec 78	**HOKEY COKEY/JINGLE BELLS** *EMI 2881*	64		

Silver-selling ○ Gold-selling ● Platinum-selling ⊛ US No.1 ★

JUICE Danish group

Date	Title / Label	Peak Position	Weeks at No.1	Weeks in Top 40
18 Apr 98	**BEST DAYS** *Chrysalis CDCHS 5081*	28		1
22 Aug 98	**I'LL COME RUNNIN'** *Chrysalis CDCHS 5090*	48		

JUICY US duo

Date	Title / Label	Peak Position	Weeks at No.1	Weeks in Top 40
22 Feb 86	**SUGAR FREE** *Epic A 6917*	45		

JUICY LUCY UK group

Date	Title / Label	Peak Position	Weeks at No.1	Weeks in Top 40
7 Mar 70	**WHO DO YOU LOVE** *Vertigo V 1*	14		9
10 Oct 70	**PRETTY WOMAN** *Vertigo 6059 015*	44		

THOMAS JULES-STOCK UK singer

Date	Title / Label	Peak Position	Weeks at No.1	Weeks in Top 40
15 Aug 98	**DIDN'T I TELL YOU TRUE** *Mercury MERCD 501*	59		

JULIA & COMPANY US group

Date	Title / Label	Peak Position	Weeks at No.1	Weeks in Top 40
3 Mar 84	**BREAKIN' DOWN (SUGAR SAMBA)** *London LON 46*	15		6
23 Feb 85	**I'M SO HAPPY** *Next Plateau LON 61*	56		

JULIET US singer

Date	Title / Label	Peak Position	Weeks at No.1	Weeks in Top 40
23 Apr 05	**AVALON** *Virgin VUSDX299*	24		2

JULIETTE & THE LICKS UK group

Date	Title / Label	Peak Position	Weeks at No.1	Weeks in Top 40
21 May 05	**YOU'RE SPEAKING MY LANGUAGE** *Hassle HOFF003CDS*	35		1
1 Oct 05	**GOT LOVE TO KILL** *Hassle HOFF005CDS*	56		
7 Oct 06	**HOT KISS** *Hassle HOFF020CDS*	50		

JULUKA UK/South African group

Date	Title / Label	Peak Position	Weeks at No.1	Weeks in Top 40
12 Feb 83	**SCATTERLINGS OF AFRICA** *Safari ZULU 1*	44		

JUMP UK instrumental group

Date	Title / Label	Peak Position	Weeks at No.1	Weeks in Top 40
1 Mar 97	**FUNKATARIUM** *Heat Recordings HEATCD 005*	56		

WALLY JUMP JR & THE CRIMINAL ELEMENT ORCHESTRA US groups

Date	Title / Label	Peak Position	Weeks at No.1	Weeks in Top 40
28 Feb 87	**TURN ME LOOSE** *London LON 126*	60		
5 Sep 87	**PUT THE NEEDLE TO THE RECORD** *Cooltempo COOL 150* CRIMINAL ELEMENT ORCHESTRA	63		
12 Dec 87	**TIGHTEN UP – I JUST CAN'T STOP DANCING** *Breakout USA 621*	24		5
19 Mar 88	**PRIVATE PARTY** *Breakout USA 624*	57		
6 Oct 90	**EVERYBODY (RAP)** *Deconstruction PB 44701* CRIMINAL ELEMENT ORCHESTRA & WENDELL WILLIAMS	30		2

ROSEMARY JUNE US singer

Date	Title / Label	Peak Position	Weeks at No.1	Weeks in Top 40
23 Jan 59	**I'LL BE WITH YOU IN APPLE BLOSSOM TIME** *Pye International 7N 25005*	14		9

JUNGLE BOOK US group

Date	Title / Label	Peak Position	Weeks at No.1	Weeks in Top 40
8 May 93	**THE JUNGLE BOOK GROOVE** *Hollywood HWCD 128*	14		7

JUNGLE BOYS UK group

Date	Title / Label	Peak Position	Weeks at No.1	Weeks in Top 40
20 Mar 04	**JUNGLE ROCK** *Bushtucker JUNGLE001CD*	30		1
31 Jul 04	**IN THE SUMMERTIME** *MCS JUNGLE002CD*	72		

JUNGLE BROTHERS US group

Date	Title / Label	Peak Position	Weeks at No.1	Weeks in Top 40
22 Oct 88	**I'LL HOUSE YOU** *Gee Street GEE 003* RICHIE RICH MEETS THE JUNGLE BROTHERS	22		3
18 Mar 89	**BLACK IS BLACK/STRAIGHT OUT OF THE JUNGLE** *Gee Street GEE 15*	72		
31 Mar 90	**WHAT 'U' WAITIN' '4'** *Eternal W 9865*	35		3
21 Jul 90	**DOIN' OUR OWN DANG** *Eternal W 9754*	33		4
19 Jul 97	**BRAIN** *Gee Street GEE 5000388*	52		
29 Nov 97	**JUNGLE BROTHER** *Gee Street GEE 5000493*	56		
9 May 98	**JUNGLE BROTHER** *Gee Street GEE 5000493*	18		4
11 Jul 98	**I'LL HOUSE YOU '98 (REMIX)** *Gee Street FCD 338* RICHIE RICH MEETS THE JUNGLE BROTHERS	26		2
28 Nov 98	**BECAUSE I GOT IT LIKE THAT** *Gee Street GEE 5003593*	32		1
10 Jul 99	**VIP** *Gee Street GEE 5007958*	33		1
6 Nov 99	**GET DOWN** *Gee Street GEE 5010153*	52		
25 Mar 00	**FREAKIN' YOU** *Gee Street GEE 5008808*	70		
7 Feb 04	**BREATHE DON'T STOP** *Positiva/Incentive CDTIVS 201* MR ON VS THE JUNGLE BROTHERS	21		3

JUNGLE HIGH German/UK production duo

Date	Title / Label	Peak Position	Weeks at No.1	Weeks in Top 40
27 Nov 93	**FIRE OF LOVE** *Logic 74321170292* JUNGLE HIGH WITH BLUE PEARL	71		

JUNIOR UK singer

Date	Title / Label	Peak Position	Weeks at No.1	Weeks in Top 40
24 Apr 82	**MAMA USED TO SAY** *Mercury MER 98* ○	7		9
10 Jul 82	**TOO LATE** *Mercury MER 112*	20		7
25 Sep 82	**LET ME KNOW/I CAN'T HELP IT** *Mercury MER 116*	53		
23 Apr 83	**COMMUNICATION BREAKDOWN** *Mercury MER 134*	57		
8 Sep 84	**SOMEBODY** *London LON 50*	64		
9 Feb 85	**DO YOU REALLY (WANT MY LOVE)** *London LON 60*	47		
30 Nov 85	**OH LOUISE** *London LON 75*	74		
4 Apr 87	**ANOTHER STEP CLOSER TO YOU** *MCA KIM 5* KIM WILDE & JUNIOR	6		9
25 Aug 90	**STEP OFF** *MCA 1432* JUNIOR GISCOMBE	63		
15 Aug 92	**THEN CAME YOU** *MCA MCS 1676* JUNIOR GISCOMBE	32		2
31 Oct 92	**ALL OVER THE WORLD** *MCA MCS 1691* JUNIOR GISCOMBE	74		

JUNIOR JACK Italian producer

Date	Title / Label	Peak Position	Weeks at No.1	Weeks in Top 40
16 Dec 00	**MY FEELING** *Defected DFECT 24CDS*	31		1
2 Mar 02	**THRILL ME** *VC Recordings VCRD 102*	29		1
27 Sep 03	**E SAMBA** *Defected DFTD 076CDS*	34		1
14 Feb 04	**DA HYPE** *Defected DFTD 083CDS* JUNIOR JACK FEATURING ROBERT SMITH	25		1
3 Jul 04	**STUPIDISCO** *Defected DFTD 089CDS*	26		2
24 Feb 07	**DARE ME (STUPIDISCO)** *Defected DFTD150CDS* JUNIOR JACK FEATURING SHENA	20		2

JUNIOR M.A.F.I.A. US group

Date	Title / Label	Peak Position	Weeks at No.1	Weeks in Top 40
3 Feb 96	**I NEED YOU TONIGHT** *Big Beat A 8130CD* JUNIOR M.A.F.I.A. FEATURING AALIYAH	66		
19 Oct 96	**GETTING' MONEY** *Big Beat A 5674CD*	63		

JUNIOR SENIOR Danish duo

Date	Title / Label	Peak Position	Weeks at No.1	Weeks in Top 40
8 Mar 03	**MOVE YOUR FEET** *Mercury 0198192*	3		15
9 Aug 03	**RHYTHM BANDITS** *Mercury 9810210*	22		2

JUNKIE XL Dutch producer

Date	Title / Label	Peak Position	Weeks at No.1	Weeks in Top 40
22 Jul 00	**ZEROTONINE** *Manifesto FESCD 71*	63		
22 Jun 02	**A LITTLE LESS CONVERSATION** *RCA 74321943572* ELVIS VS JXL ⊛	1	4	10
30 Nov 02	**OBSESSION** *Nebula NEBCD 029* TIESTO & JUNKIE XL	56		
7 Jun 03	**CATCH UP TO MY STEP** *Roadrunner RR 20209* JUNKIE XL FEATURING SOLOMON BURKE	63		
7 May 05	**A LITTLE LESS CONVERSATION** *RCA 82876666832* ELVIS VS JXL	3		2

JUNO REACTOR UK/German production duo

Date	Title / Label	Peak Position	Weeks at No.1	Weeks in Top 40
8 Feb 97	**JUNGLE HIGH** *Perfecto PERF 133CD*	45		

JUPITER ACE UK producer with singer

Date	Title / Label	Peak Position	Weeks at No.1	Weeks in Top 40
23 Jul 05	**1000 YEARS (JUST LEAVE ME NOW)** *Manifesto 9871706* JUPITER ACE FEATURING SHEENA	51		

JURASSIC 5 US group

Date	Title / Label	Peak Position	Weeks at No.1	Weeks in Top 40
25 Jul 98	**JAYOU** *Pan 018CD*	56		
24 Oct 98	**CONCRETE SCHOOLYARD** *Pan 020CD*	35		1

Key: Silver-selling ● Gold-selling ● Platinum-selling ✪ US No.1 ★ — Peak Position / Weeks at No.1 / Weeks in Top 40

CHRISTOPHER JUST Austrian producer

Date	Title / Label	Peak Position	Weeks at No.1	Weeks in Top 40
13 Dec 97	**I'M A DISCO DANCER** *Slut Trax SLUT 001CD*	72		
6 Feb 99	**I'M A DISCO DANCER (REMIX)** *XL Recordings XLS 105CD*	69		

JUST 4 JOKES UK group

Date	Title / Label	Peak Position	Weeks at No.1	Weeks in Top 40
28 Sep 02	**JUMP UP** *Serious SERR 050CD* JUST 4 JOKES FEATURING MC RB	67		

JUST JACK UK singer

Date	Title / Label	Peak Position	Weeks at No.1	Weeks in Top 40
20 Jan 07	**STARZ IN THEIR EYES** *Mercury 1714375*	2		13
14 Apr 07	**GLORY DAYS** *Mercury 1724905*	32		1
30 Jun 07	**WRITER'S BLOCK** *Mercury 1735872*	74		

JUST LUIS Spanish singer

Date	Title / Label	Peak Position	Weeks at No.1	Weeks in Top 40
14 Oct 95	**AMERICAN PIE** *Pro-Activ CDPTV 1*	31		1
17 Feb 96	**AMERICAN PIE (REMIX)** *Pro-Activ CDPTV 1*	70		

JUSTICE French production duo

Date	Title / Label	Peak Position	Weeks at No.1	Weeks in Top 40
15 Jul 06	**WE ARE YOUR FRIENDS** *Ten TENCDX505* JUSTICE VERSUS SIMIAN	20		4
23 Jun 07	**BECAUSE** *Because/Ed Banger BEC5772072*	48		

JIMMY JUSTICE UK singer

Date	Title / Label	Peak Position	Weeks at No.1	Weeks in Top 40
29 Mar 62	**WHEN MY LITTLE GIRL IS SMILING** *Pye 7N 15421*	9		12
14 Jun 62	**AIN'T THAT FUNNY** *Pye 7N 15443*	8		11
23 Aug 62	**SPANISH HARLEM** *Pye 7N 15457*	20		10

JUSTIFIED ANCIENTS OF MU MU UK duo

Date	Title / Label	Peak Position	Weeks at No.1	Weeks in Top 40
9 Nov 91	**IT'S GRIM UP NORTH** *KLF Communications JAMS 028*	10		3

JUSTIN UK singer

Date	Title / Label	Peak Position	Weeks at No.1	Weeks in Top 40
22 Aug 98	**THIS BOY** *Virgin STCDT 1*	34		1
16 Jan 99	**OVER YOU** *Virgin STCDT 2*	11		3
17 Jul 99	**IT'S ALL ABOUT YOU** *Virgin STCDT 3*	34		1
22 Jan 00	**LET IT BE ME** *Innocent STCDTX 4*	15		2

BILL JUSTIS US saxophonist

Date	Title / Label	Peak Position	Weeks at No.1	Weeks in Top 40
10 Jan 58	**RAUNCHY** *London HLS 8517*	11		8

PATRICK JUVET French singer

Date	Title / Label	Peak Position	Weeks at No.1	Weeks in Top 40
2 Sep 78	**GOT A FEELING** *Casablanca CAN 127*	34		4
4 Nov 78	**I LOVE AMERICA** *Casablanca CAN 132*	12		8

JX UK producer

Date	Title / Label	Peak Position	Weeks at No.1	Weeks in Top 40
2 Apr 94	**SON OF A GUN** *Internal Dance IDC 5*	13		5
1 Apr 95	**YOU BELONG TO ME** *ffrreedom TABCD 227*	17		3
19 Aug 95	**SON OF A GUN (REMIX)** *ffrreedom TABCD 233*	6		4
18 May 96	**THERE'S NOTHING I WON'T DO** *ffrreedom TABCD 241* ●	4		10
8 Mar 97	**CLOSE TO YOUR HEART** *ffrreedom TABCD 245*	18		2
6 Mar 04	**RESTLESS** *Tidy Two TIDYTWOJX1C*	22		2

K

FRANK K Italian/US duo

Date	Title / Label	Peak Position	Weeks at No.1	Weeks in Top 40
26 Jan 91	**EVERYBODY LETS SOMEBODY LOVE** *Urban URB 66* FRANK K FEATURING WISTON OFFICE	61		

LEILA K Swedish rapper

Date	Title / Label	Peak Position	Weeks at No.1	Weeks in Top 40
25 Nov 89	**GOT TO GET** *Arista 112696* ROB 'N' RAZ FEATURING LEILA K	8		11
17 Mar 90	**ROK THE NATION** *Arista 112971* ROB 'N' RAZ FEATURING LEILA K	41		
23 Jan 93	**OPEN SESAME** *Polydor PQCD 1*	23		3
3 Jul 93	**CA PLANE POUR MOI** *Polydor PQCD 3*	69		

K-CI & JOJO US duo

Date	Title / Label	Peak Position	Weeks at No.1	Weeks in Top 40
27 Jul 96	**HOW DO YOU WANT IT?** *Death Row 228546532* 2PAC FEATURING K-CI & JOJO ★	17		2
30 Nov 96	**I AIN'T MAD AT CHA** *Death Row DRWCD 5* 2PAC FEATURING K-CI & JOJO	13		7
23 Aug 97	**YOU BRING ME UP** *MCA MCSTD 48057*	21		1
18 Apr 98	**ALL MY LIFE** *MCA MCSTD 48076* ★	8		10
19 Sep 98	**DON'T RUSH (TAKE LOVE SLOWLY)** *MCA MCSD 48090*	16		2
2 Oct 99	**TELL ME IT'S REAL** *MCA MCSXD 40211*	40		1
23 Sep 00	**TELL ME IT'S REAL (REMIX)** *AM:PM CDAMPM 135*	16		3
12 May 01	**CRAZY** *MCA MCSTD 40253*	35		1

K CREATIVE UK group

Date	Title / Label	Peak Position	Weeks at No.1	Weeks in Top 40
7 Mar 92	**THREE TIMES A MAYBE** *Talkin Loud TLK 17*	58		

ERNIE K-DOE US singer

Date	Title / Label	Peak Position	Weeks at No.1	Weeks in Top 40
11 May 61	**MOTHER-IN-LAW** *London HLU 9330* ★	29		6
8 Dec 07	**HERE COME THE GIRLS** *Soul Jazz SJR176CDS*	43		

K-GEE UK producer

Date	Title / Label	Peak Position	Weeks at No.1	Weeks in Top 40
4 Nov 00	**I DON'T REALLY CARE** *Instant Karma 3CD*	22		2

K-KLASS UK group

Date	Title / Label	Peak Position	Weeks at No.1	Weeks in Top 40
4 May 91	**RHYTHM IS A MYSTERY** *Deconstruction CREED 1*	61		
9 Nov 91	**RHYTHM IS A MYSTERY** *Deconstruction R 6302*	3		6
25 Apr 92	**SO RIGHT** *Deconstruction R 6309*	20		3
7 Nov 92	**DON'T STOP** *Deconstruction R 6325*	32		2
27 Nov 93	**LET ME SHOW YOU** *Deconstruction CDR 6367*	13		4
28 May 94	**WHAT YOU'RE MISSING** *Deconstruction CDRS 6380*	24		2
1 Aug 98	**BURNIN'** *Parlophone CDK 2001*	45		

K7 US rapper

Date	Title / Label	Peak Position	Weeks at No.1	Weeks in Top 40
11 Dec 93	**COME BABY COME** *Big Life BLRD 105*	3		13
2 Apr 94	**HI DE HO** *Big Life BLRD 108* K7 & THE SWING KIDS	17		3
25 Jun 94	**ZUNGA ZENG** *Big Life BLRD 111* K7 & THE SWING KIDS	63		

K3M Italian duo

Date	Title / Label	Peak Position	Weeks at No.1	Weeks in Top 40
21 Mar 92	**LISTEN TO THE RHYTHM** *PWL Continental PWL 214*	71		

K2 FAMILY UK production group

Date	Title / Label	Peak Position	Weeks at No.1	Weeks in Top 40
27 Oct 01	**BOUNCING FLOW** *Relentless RELENT 22CD*	27		1

K WARREN UK producer

Date	Title / Label	Peak Position	Weeks at No.1	Weeks in Top 40
5 May 01	**COMING HOME** *Go! Beat GOBCD 41* K WARREN FEATURING LEE O	32		1

KACI US singer

Date	Title / Label	Peak Position	Weeks at No.1	Weeks in Top 40
10 Mar 01	**PARADISE** *Curb CUBC 61*	11		7
28 Jul 01	**TU AMOR** *Curb CUBX 71*	24		1
2 Feb 02	**I THINK I LOVE YOU** *Curb CUBC 076*	10		6
9 Aug 03	**I'M NOT ANYBODY'S GIRL** *Curb CUBC 091*	55		

JOSHUA KADISON US singer

Date	Title / Label	Peak Position	Weeks at No.1	Weeks in Top 40
26 Feb 94	**JESSIE** *SBK CDSBK 43*	69		
1 Oct 94	**JESSIE** *SBK CDSBK 43*	48		
12 Nov 94	**BEAUTIFUL IN MY EYES** *SBK CDSBK 50*	65		
29 Apr 95	**JESSIE (REMIX)** *SBK CDSBK 53*	15		8
12 Aug 95	**BEAUTIFUL IN MY EYES** *SBK CDSBKS 55*	37		2

Silver-selling ○ Gold-selling ● Platinum-selling ✱ US No.1 ★ — Peak Position · Weeks at No.1 · Weeks in Top 40

KADOC UK/Spanish group

Date	Title / Label	Peak Position	Weeks at No.1	Weeks in Top 40
6 Apr 96	**THE NIGHTTRAIN** *Positiva CDTIV 26*	14		6
17 Aug 96	**YOU GOT TO BE THERE** *Positiva CDTIV 58*	45		
23 Aug 97	**ROCK THE BELLS** *Manifesto FESCD 30*	34		1

BERT KAEMPFERT German orchestra leader/producer

Date	Title / Label	Peak Position	Weeks at No.1	Weeks in Top 40
23 Dec 65	**BYE BYE BLUES** *Polydor BM 56 504*	24		8

KAISER CHIEFS UK group

Date	Title / Label	Peak Position	Weeks at No.1	Weeks in Top 40
29 May 04	**OH MY GOD** *Drowned In Sound DIS03*	66		
13 Nov 04	**I PREDICT A RIOT** *B Unique BUN088CD*	22		2
5 Mar 05	**OH MY GOD** *B Unique BUN092CDX*	6		4
28 May 05	**EVERYDAY I LOVE YOU LESS AND LESS** *B Unique/Polydor BUN094CDX*	10		10
6 Aug 05	**I PREDICT A RIOT** *B Unique BUN088CD*	31		2
3 Sep 05	**I PREDICT A RIOT/SINK A SHIP** *B Unique/Polydor BUN96CD*	9		15
19 Nov 05	**MODERN WAY** *B Unique/Polydor BUN100CDX*	11		3
17 Feb 07	**RUBY** *B Unique/Polydor BUN119CD*	1	1	22
26 May 07	**EVERYTHING IS AVERAGE NOWADAYS** *B Unique/Polydor BUN125CD*	19		2
1 Sep 07	**THE ANGRY MOB** *B Unique/Polydor BUN132CD*	20		2

KAJAGOOGOO UK group

Date	Title / Label	Peak Position	Weeks at No.1	Weeks in Top 40
22 Jan 83	**TOO SHY** *EMI 5359* ●	1	2	10
2 Apr 83	**OOH TO BE AH** *EMI 5383*	7		7
4 Jun 83	**HANG ON NOW** *EMI 5394*	13		6
17 Sep 83	**BIG APPLE** *EMI 5423*	8		6
3 Mar 84	**THE LION'S MOUTH** *EMI 5449*	25		4
5 May 84	**TURN YOUR BACK ON ME** *EMI 5646*	47		
21 Sep 85	**SHOULDN'T DO THAT** *Parlophone R 6106* KAJA	63		

KALEEF UK group

Date	Title / Label	Peak Position	Weeks at No.1	Weeks in Top 40
30 Mar 96	**WALK LIKE A CHAMPION** *Payday KACD 5* KALIPHZ FEATURING PRINCE NASEEM	23		1
7 Dec 96	**GOLDEN BROWN** *Unity 010CD*	22		2
14 Jun 97	**TRIALS OF LIFE** *Unity 012CD*	75		
11 Oct 97	**I LIKE THE WAY (THE KISSING GAME)** *Unity 015CD*	58		
24 Jan 98	**SANDS OF TIME** *Unity 016CD*	26		2

PREEYA KALIDAS UK singer

Date	Title / Label	Peak Position	Weeks at No.1	Weeks in Top 40
13 Jul 02	**SHAKALAKA BABY** *Sony Classical 6726322*	38		1

KALIN TWINS US duo

Date	Title / Label	Peak Position	Weeks at No.1	Weeks in Top 40
18 Jul 58	**WHEN** *Brunswick 05751*	1	5	18

KITTY KALLEN US singer

Date	Title / Label	Peak Position	Weeks at No.1	Weeks in Top 40
2 Jul 54	**LITTLE THINGS MEAN A LOT** *Brunswick 05287* ★	1	1	23

GUNTER KALLMAN CHOIR German choir

Date	Title / Label	Peak Position	Weeks at No.1	Weeks in Top 40
24 Dec 64	**ELISABETH SERENADE** *Polydor NH 24678*	39		1

ISRAEL KAMAKAWIWO'OLE US singer

Date	Title / Label	Peak Position	Weeks at No.1	Weeks in Top 40
21 Apr 07	**SOMEWHERE OVER THE RAINBOW** *Download*	68		

KAMASUTRA Italian production duo

Date	Title / Label	Peak Position	Weeks at No.1	Weeks in Top 40
22 Nov 97	**HAPPINESS** *Sony S2 KAMCD 2* KAMASUTRA FEATURING JOCELYN BROWN	45		

NICK KAMEN UK singer

Date	Title / Label	Peak Position	Weeks at No.1	Weeks in Top 40
8 Nov 86	**EACH TIME YOU BREAK MY HEART** *WEA YZ 90* ○	5		9
28 Feb 87	**LOVING YOU IS SWEETER THAN EVER** *WEA YZ 106*	16		7
16 May 87	**NOBODY ELSE** *WEA YZ 122*	47		
28 May 88	**TELL ME** *WEA YZ 184*	40		2
28 Apr 90	**I PROMISED MYSELF** *WEA YZ 454*	50		

INI KAMOZE Jamaican singer

Date	Title / Label	Peak Position	Weeks at No.1	Weeks in Top 40
7 Jan 95	**HERE COMES THE HOTSTEPPER** *Columbia 6610472* ● ★	4		13

KANDI US singer

Date	Title / Label	Peak Position	Weeks at No.1	Weeks in Top 40
11 Nov 00	**DON'T THINK I'M NOT** *Columbia 6705102*	9		9

KANDIDATE UK group

Date	Title / Label	Peak Position	Weeks at No.1	Weeks in Top 40
19 Aug 78	**DON'T WANNA SAY GOODNIGHT** *RAK 280*	47		
17 Mar 79	**I DON'T WANNA LOSE YOU** *RAK 289*	11		8
4 Aug 79	**GIRLS GIRLS GIRLS** *RAK 295*	34		2
22 Mar 80	**LET ME ROCK YOU** *RAK 306*	58		

KANE Dutch duo

Date	Title / Label	Peak Position	Weeks at No.1	Weeks in Top 40
4 Sep 04	**RAIN DOWN ON ME** *BMG 82876634262*	38		1

EDEN KANE UK singer

Date	Title / Label	Peak Position	Weeks at No.1	Weeks in Top 40
1 Jun 61	**WELL I ASK YOU** *Decca F 11353*	1	1	19
14 Sep 61	**GET LOST** *Decca F 11381*	10		9
18 Jan 62	**FORGET ME NOT** *Decca F 11418*	3		13
10 May 62	**I DON'T KNOW WHY** *Decca F 11460*	7		11
30 Jan 64	**BOYS CRY** *Fontana TF 438*	8		12

KANE GANG UK group

Date	Title / Label	Peak Position	Weeks at No.1	Weeks in Top 40
19 May 84	**SMALLTOWN CREED** *Kitchenware SK 11*	60		
7 Jul 84	**CLOSEST THING TO HEAVEN** *Kitchenware SK 15*	12		8
10 Nov 84	**RESPECT YOURSELF** *Kitchenware SK 16*	21		7
9 Mar 85	**GUN LAW** *Kitchenware SK 20*	53		
27 Jun 87	**MOTORTOWN** *Kitchenware SK 30*	45		
16 Apr 88	**DON'T LOOK ANY FURTHER** *Kitchenware SK 33*	52		

KANO UK rapper

Date	Title / Label	Peak Position	Weeks at No.1	Weeks in Top 40
12 Mar 05	**TYPICAL ME** *679 679L096CD2*	22		2
19 Mar 05	**ROUTINE CHECK** *WEA BEATS8* MITCHELL BROTHERS/KANO/THE STREETS	42		
25 Jun 05	**REMEMBER ME** *679 679L101CD1*	71		
24 Sep 05	**NITE NITE** *679 679L108CD2* KANO FEATURING MIKE SKINNER & LEO THE LION	25		2
1 Sep 07	**THIS IS THE GIRL** *679 679L148CD* KANO FEATURING CRAIG DAVID	18		6

KANSAS US group

Date	Title / Label	Peak Position	Weeks at No.1	Weeks in Top 40
1 Jul 78	**CARRY ON WAYWARD SON** *Kirshner KIR 4932*	51		

MORY KANTÉ Guinean singer

Date	Title / Label	Peak Position	Weeks at No.1	Weeks in Top 40
23 Jul 88	**YEKE YEKE** *London LON 171*	29		3
11 Mar 95	**YEKE YEKE (REMIX)** *ffreedom TABCD 226*	25		2
30 Nov 96	**YEKE YEKE (2ND REMIX)** *ffrr FCD 288*	28		1

KAOMA French group

Date	Title / Label	Peak Position	Weeks at No.1	Weeks in Top 40
21 Oct 89	**LAMBADA** *CBS 6550117* ●	4		13
27 Jan 90	**DANCANDO LAMBADA** *CBS 6552357*	62		

KAOTIC CHEMISTRY UK production group

Date	Title / Label	Peak Position	Weeks at No.1	Weeks in Top 40
31 Oct 92	**LSD (EP)** *Moving Shadow SHADOW 20*	68		

KARAJA German singer

Date	Title / Label	Peak Position	Weeks at No.1	Weeks in Top 40
19 Oct 02	**SHE MOVES (LALALA)** *Substance SUBS 14CDS*	42		

KARIYA US singer

Date	Title / Label	Peak Position	Weeks at No.1	Weeks in Top 40
8 Jul 89	**LET ME LOVE YOU FOR TONIGHT** *Sleeping Bag SBUK 4*	44		
21 Oct 89	**LET ME LOVE YOU FOR TONIGHT** *Sleeping Bag SBUK 4*	57		

MICK KARN UK singer/bass player

Date	Title / Label	Peak Position	Weeks at No.1	Weeks in Top 40
9 Jul 83	**AFTER A FASHION** *Musicfest FEST 1* MIDGE URE & MICK KARN	39		2
17 Jan 87	**BUOY** *Virgin VS 910* MICK KARN FEATURING DAVID SYLVIAN	63		

KARTOON KREW US group

Date	Title / Label	Peak Position	Weeks at No.1	Weeks in Top 40
7 Dec 85	**INSPECTOR GADGET** *Champion CHAMP 6*	58		

KASABIAN UK group

Date	Title / Label	Peak Position	Weeks at No.1	Weeks in Top 40
22 May 04	**CLUB FOOT** *BMG PARADISE08*	19		1
21 Aug 04	**LSF** *RCA PARADISE14*	10		3
23 Oct 04	**PROCESSED BEATS** *RCA PARADISE21*	17		1
15 Jan 05	**CUTT OFF** *RCA PARADISE26*	8		3
2 Apr 05	**CLUB FOOT (REMIX)** *RCA PARADISE30*	22		1
5 Aug 06	**EMPIRE** *Columbia PARADISE36*	9		9
11 Nov 06	**SHOOT THE RUNNER** *Columbia PARADISE43*	17		2
10 Feb 07	**ME PLUS ONE** *Columbia PARADISE48*	22		1

KASENETZ-KATZ SINGING ORCHESTRAL CIRCUS US producers

Date	Title / Label	Peak Position	Weeks at No.1	Weeks in Top 40
20 Nov 68	**QUICK JOEY SMALL (RUN JOEY RUN)** *Buddah 201 022*	19		12

KATCHA UK producer

Date	Title / Label	Peak Position	Weeks at No.1	Weeks in Top 40
21 Aug 99	**TOUCHED BY GOD** *Hooj Choons HOOJ 77CD*	57		

KATOI Thai producer

Date	Title / Label	Peak Position	Weeks at No.1	Weeks in Top 40
29 Mar 03	**TOUCH YOU** *Arista Dance 74321964492*	70		

KATRINA & THE WAVES UK/US group

Date	Title / Label	Peak Position	Weeks at No.1	Weeks in Top 40
4 May 85	**WALKING ON SUNSHINE** *Capitol CL 354*	8		8
5 Jul 86	**SUN STREET** *Capitol CL 407*	22		5
8 Jun 96	**WALKING ON SUNSHINE** *EMI Premier PRESCD 2*	53		
10 May 97	**LOVE SHINE A LIGHT** *Eternal WEA 106CD1*	3		7

KAVANA UK singer

Date	Title / Label	Peak Position	Weeks at No.1	Weeks in Top 40
11 May 96	**CRAZY CHANCE** *Nemesis NMSDG 1*	35		2
24 Aug 96	**WHERE ARE YOU** *Nemesis NMSD 2*	26		1
11 Jan 97	**I CAN MAKE YOU FEEL GOOD** *Nemesis NMSDX 3*	8		4
19 Apr 97	**MFEO** *Nemesis NMSD 4*	8		3
13 Sep 97	**CRAZY CHANCE** *Nemesis NMSD 5*	16		1
29 Aug 98	**SPECIAL KIND OF SOMETHING** *Virgin VSCDT 1704*	13		2
12 Dec 98	**FUNKY LOVE** *Virgin VSCDT 1711*	32		1
20 Mar 99	**WILL YOU WAIT FOR ME** *Virgin VSCDT 1726*	29		1

NIAMH KAVANAGH Irish singer

Date	Title / Label	Peak Position	Weeks at No.1	Weeks in Top 40
12 Jun 93	**IN YOUR EYES** *Arista 74321154152*	24		3

KAWALA UK group

Date	Title / Label	Peak Position	Weeks at No.1	Weeks in Top 40
26 Feb 00	**HUMANISTIC** *Pepper 9230022*	68		

JANET KAY UK singer

Date	Title / Label	Peak Position	Weeks at No.1	Weeks in Top 40
9 Jun 79	**SILLY GAMES** *Scope SC 2* ○	2		9
11 Aug 90	**SILLY GAMES** *Arista 113452* LINDY LAYTON FEATURING JANET KAY	22		5
11 Aug 90	**SILLY GAMES (REMIX)** *Music Factory Dance MFD 006*	62		

PETER KAY UK comedian

Date	Title / Label	Peak Position	Weeks at No.1	Weeks in Top 40
26 Mar 05	**(IS THIS THE WAY TO) AMARILLO?** *Universal TV 9828606* TONY CHRISTIE FEATURING PETER KAY ⊛	1	7	21
31 Dec 05	**(IS THIS THE WAY TO) AMARILLO?** *Universal TV 9828606* TONY CHRISTIE FEATURING PETER KAY	58		

DANNY KAYE US actor

Date	Title / Label	Peak Position	Weeks at No.1	Weeks in Top 40
27 Feb 53	**WONDERFUL COPENHAGEN** *Brunswick 05023*	5		10

KAYE SISTERS UK group

Date	Title / Label	Peak Position	Weeks at No.1	Weeks in Top 40
25 May 56	**IVORY TOWER** *HMV POP 209* THREE KAYS	20		5
1 Nov 57	**GOTTA HAVE SOMETHING IN THE BANK FRANK** *Philips PB 751* FRANKIE VAUGHAN & THE KAYE SISTERS	8		11
3 Jan 58	**SHAKE ME I RATTLE/ALONE** *Philips PB 752*	27		1
1 May 59	**COME SOFTLY TO ME** *Philips PB 913* FRANKIE VAUGHAN & THE KAYE SISTERS	9		9
7 Jul 60	**PAPER ROSES** *Philips PB 1024*	7		16

KAYESTONE UK production duo

Date	Title / Label	Peak Position	Weeks at No.1	Weeks in Top 40
29 Jul 00	**ATMOSPHERE** *Distinctive DISNCD 62*	55		

KC & THE SUNSHINE BAND US group

Date	Title / Label	Peak Position	Weeks at No.1	Weeks in Top 40
17 Aug 74	**QUEEN OF CLUBS** *Jayboy BOY 88*	7		10
23 Nov 74	**SOUND YOUR FUNKY HORN** *Jayboy BOY 83*	17		8
29 Mar 75	**GET DOWN TONIGHT** *Jayboy BOY 93* ★	21		6
2 Aug 75	**THAT'S THE WAY (I LIKE IT)** *Jayboy BOY 99* ★	4		9
22 Nov 75	**I'M SO CRAZY ('BOUT YOU)** *Jayboy BOY 101*	34		1
17 Jul 76	**(SHAKE SHAKE SHAKE) SHAKE YOUR BOOTY** *Jayboy BOY 110* ★	22		7
11 Dec 76	**KEEP IT COMIN' LOVE** *Jayboy BOY 112*	31		7
30 Apr 77	**I'M YOUR BOOGIE MAN** *TK XB 2167* ★	41		
6 May 78	**BOOGIE SHOES** *TK TKR 6025*	34		2
22 Jul 78	**IT'S THE SAME OLD SONG** *TK TKR 6037*	47		
8 Dec 79	**PLEASE DON'T GO** *TK TKR 7558* ○ ★	3		10
16 Jul 83	**GIVE IT UP** *Epic EPC 3017* ●	1	3	11
24 Sep 83	**(YOU SAID) YOU'D GIMME SOME MORE** *Epic A 2760*	41		
11 May 91	**THAT'S THE WAY (I LIKE IT) (REMIX)** *Music Factory Dance M7FAC 2*	59		

KE US singer

Date	Title / Label	Peak Position	Weeks at No.1	Weeks in Top 40
13 Apr 96	**STRANGE WORLD** *Venture 74321349412*	73		

KEANE UK group

Date	Title / Label	Peak Position	Weeks at No.1	Weeks in Top 40
28 Feb 04	**SOMEWHERE ONLY WE KNOW** *Island CID 849*	3		7
15 May 04	**EVERYBODY'S CHANGING** *Island CID 855*	4		6
28 Aug 04	**BEDSHAPED** *Island CID 870*	10		5
4 Dec 04	**THIS IS THE LAST TIME** *Island CID880*	18		2
3 Jun 06	**IS IT ANY WONDER** *Island CID934*	3		8
26 Aug 06	**CRYSTAL BALL** *Island/Uni-Island 1704803*	20		3
11 Nov 06	**NOTHING IN MY WAY** *Island 1712175*	19		1
27 Jan 07	**A BAD DREAM** *Island/Uni-Island 1723057*	23		1

JOHNNY KEATING UK orchestra leader

Date	Title / Label	Peak Position	Weeks at No.1	Weeks in Top 40
1 Mar 62	**THEME FROM *Z-CARS*** *Piccadilly 7N 35032*	8		14

RONAN KEATING Irish singer

Date	Title / Label	Peak Position	Weeks at No.1	Weeks in Top 40
7 Aug 99	**WHEN YOU SAY NOTHING AT ALL** *Polydor 5612902* ●	1	2	11
22 Jul 00	**LIFE IS A ROLLERCOASTER** *Polydor 5619362* ●	1	1	11
2 Dec 00	**THE WAY YOU MAKE ME FEEL** *Polydor 5878862*	6		7
28 Apr 01	**LOVIN' EACH DAY** *Polydor 5876912* ○	2		7
18 May 02	**IF TOMORROW NEVER COMES** *Polydor 5707192* ●	1	1	13
21 Sep 02	**I LOVE IT WHEN WE DO** *Polydor 5709042*	5		3
7 Dec 02	**WE'VE GOT TONIGHT** *Polydor 0658612* RONAN KEATING FEATURING LULU	4		9
10 May 03	**THE LONG GOODBYE** *Polydor 0657382*	3		4
22 Nov 03	**LOST FOR WORDS** *Polydor 9813305*	9		2
21 Feb 04	**SHE BELIEVES (IN ME)** *Polydor 9816653*	2		4
15 May 04	**LAST THING ON MY MIND** *Polydor/Curb 9866595* RONAN KEATING & LeANN RIMES	5		5
9 Oct 04	**I HOPE YOU DANCE** *Polydor 9868261*	2		4
25 Dec 04	**FATHER AND SON** *Polydor 9869667* RONAN KEATING & YUSUF ISLAM	2		6
10 Jun 06	**ALL OVER AGAIN** *Polydor 9857872* RONAN KEATING & KATE RUSBY	6		3
26 Aug 06	**IRIS** *Polydor 1705359*	15		3

Silver-selling ○ · Gold-selling ● · Platinum-selling ⊛ · US No.1 ★ · Peak Position · Weeks at No.1 · Weeks in Top 40

KEEDIE *UK singer*

Date	Title	Peak Position	Weeks at No.1	Weeks in Top 40
23 Oct 04	**I BELIEVE MY HEART** *Innocent 8677122* DUNCAN JAMES & KEEDIE	2		5
24 Dec 05	**JERUSALEM** *Hyperactive CXSTUMP1* KEEDIE & THE ENGLAND CRICKET TEAM	19		2

KEVIN KEEGAN *UK footballer*

Date	Title	Peak Position	Weeks at No.1	Weeks in Top 40
9 Jun 79	**HEAD OVER HEELS IN LOVE** *EMI 2965*	31		4

NELSON KEENE *UK singer*

Date	Title	Peak Position	Weeks at No.1	Weeks in Top 40
25 Aug 60	**IMAGE OF A GIRL** *HMV POP 771*	37		3

KEITH *US singer*

Date	Title	Peak Position	Weeks at No.1	Weeks in Top 40
26 Jan 67	**98.6** *Mercury MF 955*	24		6
16 Mar 67	**TELL IT TO MY FACE** *Mercury MF 968*	50		

KEITH 'N' SHANE *Irish duo*

Date	Title	Peak Position	Weeks at No.1	Weeks in Top 40
23 Dec 00	**GIRL YOU KNOW IT'S TRUE** *Polydor 5879462*	36		1

KELIS *US singer*

Date	Title	Peak Position	Weeks at No.1	Weeks in Top 40
26 Feb 00	**CAUGHT OUT THERE (IMPORT)** *Virgin 8965102CD*	52		
4 Mar 00	**CAUGHT OUT THERE** *Virgin VUSCD 158*	4		6
17 Jun 00	**GOOD STUFF** *Virgin VUSDX 164*	19		3
8 Jul 00	**GOT YOUR MONEY** *Elektra E 7077CD* OL' DIRTY BASTARD FEATURING KELIS	11		5
21 Oct 00	**GET ALONG WITH YOU** *Virgin VUSCD 174*	51		
3 Nov 01	**YOUNG FRESH N' NEW** *Virgin VUSCD 212*	32		1
5 Oct 02	**HELP ME** *Perfecto PERF 42CDS* TIMO MAAS FEATURING KELIS	65		
23 Aug 03	**FINEST DREAMS** *Virgin RXCD 2* RICHARD X FEATURING KELIS	8		3
23 Aug 03	**LET'S GET ILL** *Bad Boy/Island MCSTD 40331* P DIDDY FEATURING KELIS	25		1
17 Jan 04	**MILKSHAKE** *Virgin VSCDX 1863* ○	2		12
20 Mar 04	**NOT IN LOVE** *Interscope 9862023* ENRIQUE FEATURING KELIS	5		7
5 Jun 04	**TRICK ME** *Virgin VSCDX 1872*	2		12
30 Oct 04	**MILLIONAIRE** *Virgin VSCDX 1885* KELIS FEATURING ANDRE 3000	3		8
16 Apr 05	**IN PUBLIC** *Virgin VSCDT1893* KELIS FEATURING NAS	17		3
9 Sep 06	**BOSSY** *Virgin VSCDT1914* KELIS FEATURING TOO SHORT	22		2
3 Feb 07	**LIL STAR** *Virgin VSCDT1922* KELIS FEATURING CEE LO	3		12

JERRY KELLER *US singer*

Date	Title	Peak Position	Weeks at No.1	Weeks in Top 40
28 Aug 59	**HERE COMES SUMMER** *London HLR 8890*	1	1	14

FRANK KELLY *Irish actor*

Date	Title	Peak Position	Weeks at No.1	Weeks in Top 40
24 Dec 83	**CHRISTMAS COUNTDOWN** *Ritz 062*	26		3
29 Dec 84	**CHRISTMAS COUNTDOWN** *Ritz 062*	54		

FRANKIE KELLY *US singer*

Date	Title	Peak Position	Weeks at No.1	Weeks in Top 40
2 Nov 85	**AIN'T THAT THE TRUTH** *10 TEN 87*	65		

KEITH KELLY *UK singer*

Date	Title	Peak Position	Weeks at No.1	Weeks in Top 40
5 May 60	**TEASE ME** *Parlophone R 4640*	27		3
18 Aug 60	**LISTEN LITTLE GIRL** *Parlophone R 4676*	47		

R KELLY *US singer*

Date	Title	Peak Position	Weeks at No.1	Weeks in Top 40
9 May 92	**SHE'S GOT THAT VIBE** *Jive JIVET 292* R KELLY & PUBLIC ANNOUNCEMENT	57		
20 Nov 93	**SEX ME** *Jive JIVECD 346* R KELLY & PUBLIC ANNOUNCEMENT	75		
14 May 94	**YOUR BODY'S CALLIN'** *Jive JIVECD 353*	19		2
3 Sep 94	**SUMMER BUNNIES** *Jive JIVECD 358*	23		1
22 Oct 94	**SHE'S GOT THAT VIBE** *Jive JIVECD 364*	3		10
21 Jan 95	**BUMP N' GRIND** *Jive JIVECD 368* ★	8		7
6 May 95	**THE 4 PLAYS EPS** *Jive JIVECD 376*	23		1
11 Nov 95	**YOU REMIND ME OF SOMETHING** *Jive JIVECD 388*	24		1
2 Mar 96	**DOWN LOW (NOBODY HAS TO KNOW)** *Jive JIVERCD 392* R KELLY FEATURING RONALD ISLEY	23		1
22 Jun 96	**THANK GOD IT'S FRIDAY** *Jive JIVERCD 395*	14		3
29 Mar 97	**I BELIEVE I CAN FLY** *Jive JIVECD 415* ⊛	1	3	14
19 Jul 97	**GOTHAM CITY** *Jive JIVECD 428*	9		6
18 Jul 98	**BE CAREFUL** *Jive 0521452* SPARKLE FEATURING R KELLY	7		4
26 Sep 98	**HALF ON A BABY** *Jive 0521802*	16		2
14 Nov 98	**HOME ALONE** *Jive 0522392* R KELLY FEATURING KEITH MURRAY	17		3
28 Nov 98	**I'M YOUR ANGEL** *Epic 6666282* CELINE DION & R KELLY ○ ★	3		9
31 Jul 99	**DID YOU EVER THINK** *Jive 0523612*	20		3
16 Oct 99	**IF I COULD TURN BACK THE HANDS OF TIME (IMPORT)** *Jive 0523182*	57		
30 Oct 99	**IF I COULD TURN BACK THE HANDS OF TIME** *Jive 0523182* ⊛	2		17
19 Feb 00	**SATISFY YOU (IMPORT)** *Bad Boy/Arista 792832* PUFF DADDY FEATURING R KELLY	73		
11 Mar 00	**SATISFY YOU** *Puff Daddy 74321745592* PUFF DADDY FEATURING R KELLY	8		6
22 Apr 00	**ONLY THE LOOT CAN MAKE ME HAPPY/WHEN A WOMAN'S FED UP/I CAN'T SLEEP BABY (IF I)** *Jive 9250282*	24		1
21 Oct 00	**I WISH** *Jive 9251292*	12		5
31 Mar 01	**THE STORM IS OVER** *Jive 9251852*	18		3
23 Jun 01	**FIESTA** *Jive 9252142* R KELLY FEATURING JAY-Z	23		2
2 Mar 02	**THE WORLD'S GREATEST** *Jive 9253242*	4		10
25 May 02	**HONEY** *Jive 9253662* R KELLY & JAY-Z	35		1
17 May 03	**IGNITION** *Jive 9254982* ●	1	4	16
23 Aug 03	**SNAKE** *Jive 82876547232* R KELLY FEATURING BIG TIGGER	10		3
15 Nov 03	**STEP IN THE NAME OF LOVE/THOIA THONG** *Jive 82876573912*	14		2
29 May 04	**HOTEL** *J 82876618612* CASSIDY FEATURING R KELLY	3		12
30 Oct 04	**HAPPY PEOPLE/U SAVED ME** *Jive 82876656182*	6		5
6 Nov 04	**WONDERFUL** *Def Jam 9864606* JA RULE FEATURING R KELLY & ASHANTI	1	1	5
20 Nov 04	**SO SEXY** *Atlantic AT 0187CD* TWISTA FEATURING R KELLY	28		1
10 Sep 05	**PLAYA'S ONLY** *Jive 82876725552* R KELLY FEATURING GAME	33		1
16 Dec 06	**THAT'S THAT S****** *Geffen 1717453* SNOOP DOGG FEATURING R KELLY	38		1
19 May 07	**I'M A FLIRT** *Jive 88697090232* R KELLY FEATURING TI & T-PAIN	18		2
28 Jul 07	**SAME GIRL** *Nonsuch 88697126432* R KELLY & USHER	26		6

ROBERTA KELLY *US singer*

Date	Title	Peak Position	Weeks at No.1	Weeks in Top 40
21 Jan 78	**ZODIACS** *Oasis/Hansa 3*	44		

KELLY FAMILY *Irish group*

Date	Title	Peak Position	Weeks at No.1	Weeks in Top 40
21 Oct 95	**AN ANGEL** *EMI CDEM 390*	69		

JOHNNY KEMP *Bahamian singer*

Date	Title	Peak Position	Weeks at No.1	Weeks in Top 40
27 Aug 88	**JUST GOT PAID** *CBS 6514707*	68		

TARA KEMP *US singer*

Date	Title	Peak Position	Weeks at No.1	Weeks in Top 40
20 Apr 91	**HOLD YOU TIGHT** *Giant W 0020*	69		

GRAHAM KENDRICK *UK singer*

Date	Title	Peak Position	Weeks at No.1	Weeks in Top 40
9 Sep 89	**LET THE FLAME BURN BRIGHTER** *Power P 30*	55		

EDDIE KENDRICKS *US singer*

Date	Title	Peak Position	Weeks at No.1	Weeks in Top 40
3 Nov 73	**KEEP ON TRUCKIN'** *Tamla Motown TMG 873* ★	18		12
16 Mar 74	**BOOGIE DOWN** *Tamla Motown TMG 888*	39		1
21 Sep 85	**A NIGHT AT THE APOLLO LIVE!** *RCA PB 49935* DARYL HALL & JOHN OATES FEATURING DAVID RUFFIN & EDDIE KENDRICK	58		

KENICKIE UK group

Date	Title	Peak Position	Weeks at No.1	Weeks in Top 40
14 Sep 96	**PUNKA** *Emidisc CDDISC 001*	43		
16 Nov 96	**MILLIONAIRE SWEEPER** *Emidisc CDDISC 002*	60		
11 Jan 97	**IN YOUR CAR** *Emidisc CDDISCX 005*	24		2
3 May 97	**NIGHTLIFE** *Emidisc CDDISCX 006*	27		1
5 Jul 97	**PUNKA** *Emidisc CDDISCS 007*	38		1
6 Jun 98	**I WOULD FIX YOU** *EMI CDEM 513*	36		1
22 Aug 98	**STAY IN THE SUN** *EMI CDEMS 520*	43		

JANE KENNAWAY & STRANGE BEHAVIOUR UK group

Date	Title	Peak Position	Weeks at No.1	Weeks in Top 40
24 Jan 81	**I.O.U.** *Deram DM 436*	65		

BRIAN KENNEDY Irish singer

Date	Title	Peak Position	Weeks at No.1	Weeks in Top 40
22 Jun 96	**A BETTER MAN** *RCA 74321382642*	28		1
21 Sep 96	**LIFE, LOVE AND HAPPINESS** *RCA 74321409912*	27		1
5 Apr 97	**PUT THE MESSAGE IN THE BOX** *RCA 74321462272*	37		1
31 Dec 05	**GEORGE BEST - A TRIBUTE** *Curb CUBC116* BRIAN KENNEDY & PETER CORRY	4		9

KEVIN KENNEDY UK singer

Date	Title	Peak Position	Weeks at No.1	Weeks in Top 40
24 Jun 00	**BULLDOG NATION** *D2m 74321759742*	70		

KENNY Irish singer

Date	Title	Peak Position	Weeks at No.1	Weeks in Top 40
3 Mar 73	**HEART OF STONE** *RAK 144*	11		10
30 Jun 73	**GIVE IT TO ME NOW** *RAK 153*	38		1
7 Dec 74	**THE BUMP** *RAK 186*	3		14
8 Mar 75	**FANCY PANTS** *RAK 196*	4		9
7 Jun 75	**BABY I LOVE YOU OK** *RAK 207*	12		6
16 Aug 75	**JULIE ANN** *RAK 214*	10		7

GERARD KENNY US singer

Date	Title	Peak Position	Weeks at No.1	Weeks in Top 40
9 Dec 78	**NEW YORK, NEW YORK** *RCA PB 5117*	43		
21 Jun 80	**FANTASY** *RCA PB 5256*	34		3
18 Feb 84	**THE OTHER WOMAN, THE OTHER MAN** *Impression IMS 3*	69		
4 May 85	**NO MAN'S LAND** *WEA YZ 38*	56		

KENT Swedish group

Date	Title	Peak Position	Weeks at No.1	Weeks in Top 40
13 Mar 99	**747** *RCA 74321645912*	61		

KLARK KENT US singer/drummer

Date	Title	Peak Position	Weeks at No.1	Weeks in Top 40
26 Aug 78	**DON'T CARE** *A&M AMS 7376*	48		

KERBDOG Irish group

Date	Title	Peak Position	Weeks at No.1	Weeks in Top 40
12 Mar 94	**DRY RISER** *Vertigo VERCC 83*	60		
6 Aug 94	**DUMMY CRUSHER** *Vertigo VERCD 86*	37		1
12 Oct 96	**SALLY** *Fontana KERCD 2*	69		
29 Mar 97	**MEXICAN WAVE** *Fontana KERCD 3*	49		

KERRI & MICK Australian duo

Date	Title	Peak Position	Weeks at No.1	Weeks in Top 40
28 Apr 84	**SONS AND DAUGHTERS' THEME** *A1 286*	68		

KERRI-ANN Irish singer

Date	Title	Peak Position	Weeks at No.1	Weeks in Top 40
8 Aug 98	**DO YOU LOVE ME BOY?** *Ragtan Road 5671012*	58		

LIZ KERSHAW & BRUNO BROOKES UK radio DJs

Date	Title	Peak Position	Weeks at No.1	Weeks in Top 40
2 Dec 89	**IT TAKES TWO BABY** *Spartan CIN 101* LIZ KERSHAW, BRUNO BROOKES, JIVE BUNNY & LONDONBEAT	53		
1 Dec 90	**LET'S DANCE** *Jive BRUNO 1* BRUNO & LIZ & THE RADIO 1 POSSE	54		

NIK KERSHAW UK singer

Date	Title	Peak Position	Weeks at No.1	Weeks in Top 40
19 Nov 83	**I WON'T LET THE SUN GO DOWN ON ME** *MCA 816*	47		
28 Jan 84	**WOULDN'T IT BE GOOD** *MCA NIK 2*	4		11
14 Apr 84	**DANCING GIRLS** *MCA NIK 3*	13		8
16 Jun 84	**I WON'T LET THE SUN GO DOWN ON ME** *MCA NIK 4*	2		11
15 Sep 84	**HUMAN RACING** *MCA NIK 5*	19		5
17 Nov 84	**THE RIDDLE** *MCA NIK 6*	3		10
16 Mar 85	**WIDE BOY** *MCA NIK 7*	9		7
3 Aug 85	**DON QUIXOTE** *MCA NIK 8*	10		6
30 Nov 85	**WHEN A HEART BEATS** *MCA NIK 9*	27		4
11 Oct 86	**NOBODY KNOWS** *MCA NIK 10*	44		
13 Dec 86	**RADIO MUSICOLA** *MCA NIK 11*	43		
4 Feb 89	**ONE STEP AHEAD** *MCA NIK 12*	55		
27 Feb 99	**SOMEBODY LOVES YOU** *Eagle EAGXA 023*	70		
7 Aug 99	**SOMETIMES** *Wall Of Sound WALLD 054* LES RYTHMES DIGITALES FEATURING NIK KERSHAW	56		

KEVIN THE GERBIL UK novelty act

Date	Title	Peak Position	Weeks at No.1	Weeks in Top 40
4 Aug 84	**SUMMER HOLIDAY** *Magnet RAT 3*	50		

KEY WEST UK producer

Date	Title	Peak Position	Weeks at No.1	Weeks in Top 40
10 Apr 93	**LOOKS LIKE I'M IN LOVE AGAIN** *PWL Sanctuary PWCD 252* KEY WEST FEATURING ERIK	46		

ALICIA KEYS US singer

Date	Title	Peak Position	Weeks at No.1	Weeks in Top 40
10 Nov 01	**FALLIN'** *J Records 74321903692* ★	3		7
9 Mar 02	**BROTHA PART II** *J Records 74321922142* ANGIE STONE FEATURING ALICIA KEYS & EVE	37		1
30 Mar 02	**A WOMAN'S WORTH** *J Records 74321928692*	18		3
20 Jul 02	**HOW COME YOU DON'T CALL ME** *J Records 74321943122*	26		1
5 Oct 02	**GANGSTA LOVIN'** *Interscope 4978042* EVE FEATURING ALICIA KEYS	6		6
7 Dec 02	**GIRLFRIEND** *J Records 74321974972*	24		2
20 Dec 03	**YOU DON'T KNOW MY NAME** *J Records 82876588652*	19		5
10 Apr 04	**IF I AIN'T GOT YOU** *J Records 82876608172*	18		1
10 Nov 07	**NO ONE** *J Records 88697182452* ★	6		19
8 Mar 08	**LIKE YOU'LL NEVER SEE ME AGAIN** *J Records 88697233992*	53		

CHAKA KHAN US singer

Date	Title	Peak Position	Weeks at No.1	Weeks in Top 40
2 Dec 78	**I'M EVERY WOMAN** *Warner Brothers K 17269*	11		10
31 Mar 84	**AIN'T NOBODY** *Warner Brothers RCK 1* RUFUS & CHAKA KHAN	8		9
20 Oct 84	**I FEEL FOR YOU** *Warner Brothers W 9209*	1	3	13
19 Jan 85	**THIS IS MY NIGHT** *Warner Brothers W 9097*	14		5
20 Apr 85	**EYE TO EYE** *Warner Brothers W 9009*	16		5
12 Jul 86	**LOVE OF A LIFETIME** *Warner Brothers W 8671*	52		
21 Jan 89	**IT'S MY PARTY** *Warner Brothers W 7678*	71		
6 May 89	**I'M EVERY WOMAN (REMIX)** *Warner Brothers W 2963*	8		6
8 Jul 89	**AIN'T NOBODY (REMIX)** *Warner Brothers W 2880* RUFUS & CHAKA KHAN	6		8
7 Oct 89	**I FEEL FOR YOU (REMIX)** *Warner Brothers W 2764*	45		
13 Jan 90	**I'LL BE GOOD TO YOU** *Qwest W 2697* QUINCY JONES FEATURING RAY CHARLES & CHAKA KHAN	21		5
28 Mar 92	**LOVE YOU ALL MY LIFETIME** *Warner Brothers W 0087*	49		
17 Jul 93	**DON'T LOOK AT ME THAT WAY** *Warner Brothers W 0192CD*	73		
19 Aug 95	**WATCH WHAT YOU SAY** *Cooltempo CDCOOL 308* GURU FEATURING CHAKA KHAN	28		1
1 Mar 97	**NEVER MISS THE WATER** *Reprise W 1393CD* CHAKA KHAN FEATURING ME'SHELL NDEGEOCELLO	59		
11 Nov 00	**ALL GOOD** *Tommy Boy TBCD 2154B* DE LA SOUL FEATURING CHAKA KHAN	33		1

PRAGA KHAN Belgian producer

Date	Title	Peak Position	Weeks at No.1	Weeks in Top 40
4 Apr 92	**FREE YOUR BODY/INJECTED WITH A POISON** *Profile PROFT 347* PRAGA KHAN FEATURING JADE 4 U	16		4
11 Jul 92	**RAVE ALERT** *Profile PROF 369*	39		1
24 Nov 01	**INJECTED WITH POISON (REMIX)** *Nukleuz NUKC 0238*	52		

KHIA US singer

Date	Title	Peak Position	Weeks at No.1	Weeks in Top 40
16 Oct 04	**MY NECK MY BACK (LICK IT)** *Direction 6753802*	4		10

Silver-selling ○ · Gold-selling ● · Platinum-selling ✪ · US No.1 ★ · Peak Position · Weeks at No.1 · Weeks in Top 40

MARY KIANI UK singer

Date	Title	Label	Peak Position	Weeks at No.1	Weeks in Top 40
12 Aug 95	WHEN I CALL YOUR NAME	Mercury MERCD 440	18		2
23 Dec 95	I GIVE IT ALL TO YOU/I IMAGINE	Mercury MERCD 449	35		2
27 Apr 96	LET THE MUSIC PLAY	Mercury MERCD 456	19		2
18 Jan 97	100%	Mercury MERCD 469	23		2
21 Jun 97	WITH OR WITHOUT YOU	Mercury MERCD 487	46		

KICK SQUAD UK/German group

Date	Title	Label	Peak Position	Weeks at No.1	Weeks in Top 40
10 Nov 90	SOUND CLASH (CHAMPION SOUND)	Kickin KICK 2	59		

KICKING BACK WITH TAXMAN UK group

Date	Title	Label	Peak Position	Weeks at No.1	Weeks in Top 40
17 Mar 90	DEVOTION	10 TEN 297	47		
7 Jul 90	EVERYTHING	10 TEN 307	54		

KICKS LIKE A MULE UK production duo

Date	Title	Label	Peak Position	Weeks at No.1	Weeks in Top 40
1 Feb 92	THE BOUNCER	Tribal Bass TRIBE 35	7		5

K.I.D. Antilles group

Date	Title	Label	Peak Position	Weeks at No.1	Weeks in Top 40
28 Feb 81	DON'T STOP	EMI 5143	49		

KID CRÈME Belgian producer

Date	Title	Label	Peak Position	Weeks at No.1	Weeks in Top 40
22 Mar 03	DOWN AND UNDER (TOGETHER) KID CRÈME FEATURING MC SHURAKANO	Ink NIBNE 13CD	55		
10 May 03	HYPNOTISING KID CRÈME FEATURING CHARLISE	Positiva CDTIV 189	31		1

KID 'N' PLAY US duo

Date	Title	Label	Peak Position	Weeks at No.1	Weeks in Top 40
18 Jul 87	LAST NIGHT	Cooltempo COOL 148	71		
26 Mar 88	DO THIS MY WAY	Cooltempo COOL 164	48		
17 Sep 88	GITTIN' FUNKY	Cooltempo COOL 168	55		

KID ROCK US rapper

Date	Title	Label	Peak Position	Weeks at No.1	Weeks in Top 40
23 Oct 99	COWBOY	Atlantic AT 0076CD	36		1
9 Sep 00	AMERICAN BAD ASS	Atlantic AT 0085CD	25		2
12 May 01	BAWITDABA	Atlantic AT 0098CD	41		

KID UNKNOWN UK producer Paul Fitzpatrick

Date	Title	Label	Peak Position	Weeks at No.1	Weeks in Top 40
2 May 92	NIGHTMARE	Warp WAP 20CD	64		

CAROL KIDD UK singer

Date	Title	Label	Peak Position	Weeks at No.1	Weeks in Top 40
17 Oct 92	WHEN I DREAM CAROL KIDD FEATURING TERRY WAITE	The Hit Label HLS 1	58		

JOHNNY KIDD & THE PIRATES UK group

Date	Title	Label	Peak Position	Weeks at No.1	Weeks in Top 40
12 Jun 59	PLEASE DON'T TOUCH JOHNNY KIDD	HMV POP 615	25		5
12 Feb 60	YOU GOT WHAT IT TAKES	HMV POP 698	25		3
16 Jun 60	SHAKIN' ALL OVER	HMV POP 753	1	1	18
6 Oct 60	RESTLESS	HMV POP 790	22		5
13 Apr 61	LINDA LU	HMV POP 853	47		
10 Jan 63	SHOT OF RHYTHM AND BLUES	HMV POP 1088	48		
25 Jul 63	I'LL NEVER GET OVER YOU	HMV POP 1173	4		14
28 Nov 63	HUNGRY FOR LOVE	HMV POP 1228	20		6
30 Apr 64	ALWAYS AND EVER	HMV POP 1269	46		

NICOLE KIDMAN Australian actor

Date	Title	Label	Peak Position	Weeks at No.1	Weeks in Top 40
6 Oct 01	COME WHAT MAY NICOLE KIDMAN & EWAN McGREGOR	Interscope 4976302	27		3
22 Dec 01	SOMETHIN' STUPID ROBBIE WILLIAMS & NICOLE KIDMAN ○	Chrysalis CDCHS 5132	1	3	10

KIDS FROM FAME US group

Date	Title	Label	Peak Position	Weeks at No.1	Weeks in Top 40
14 Aug 82	HI-FIDELITY KIDS FROM FAME FEATURING VALERIE LANDSBERG ○	RCA 254	5		7
2 Oct 82	STARMAKER	RCA 280 ●	3		9
11 Dec 82	MANNEQUIN KIDS FROM FAME FEATURING GENE ANTHONY RAY	RCA 299	50		
9 Apr 83	FRIDAY NIGHT (LIVE VERSION)	RCA 320	13		7

GREG KIHN BAND US group

Date	Title	Label	Peak Position	Weeks at No.1	Weeks in Top 40
23 Apr 83	JEOPARDY	Beserkley E 9847	63		

KILLAH PRIEST US rapper

Date	Title	Label	Peak Position	Weeks at No.1	Weeks in Top 40
7 Feb 98	ONE STEP	Geffen GFSTD 22318	45		

KILLCITY UK group

Date	Title	Label	Peak Position	Weeks at No.1	Weeks in Top 40
14 Aug 04	JUST LIKE BRUCE LEE	Poptones MC5091SCD	63		

KILLER MIKE US rapper

Date	Title	Label	Peak Position	Weeks at No.1	Weeks in Top 40
6 Apr 02	THE WHOLE WORLD OUTKAST FEATURING KILLER MIKE	LaFace 74321917592	19		3
27 Jul 02	LAND OF A MILLION DRUMS OUTKAST FEATURING KILLER MIKE & S BROWN	Atlantic AT 0134CD	46		
10 May 03	A.D.I.D.A.S. KILLER MIKE FEATURING BIG BOI	Columbia 6738652	22		1

KILLERS US group

Date	Title	Label	Peak Position	Weeks at No.1	Weeks in Top 40
27 Mar 04	SOMEBODY TOLD ME	Lizard King LIZARD009	28		1
5 Jun 04	MR BRIGHTSIDE	Lizard King LIZARD 010CD2	10		3
11 Sep 04	ALL THESE THINGS THAT I'VE DONE	Lizard King LIZARD012	18		2
22 Jan 05	SOMEBODY TOLD ME	Lizard King LIZARD014CD2	3		4
14 May 05	SMILE LIKE YOU MEAN IT	Lizard King LIZARD015	11		3
23 Sep 06	WHEN YOU WERE YOUNG	Mercury 1707658	2		8
2 Dec 06	BONES	Vertigo 1717078	15		2
24 Feb 07	READ MY MIND	Vertigo 1724567	15		6
7 Jul 07	FOR REASONS UNKNOWN	Vertigo 1736030	53		
20 Oct 07	TRANQUILIZE	Download	13		1
15 Dec 07	DON'T SHOOT ME SANTA	Vertigo 1750323	34		1

KILLING JOKE UK group

Date	Title	Label	Peak Position	Weeks at No.1	Weeks in Top 40
23 May 81	FOLLOW THE LEADERS	Malicious Damage EGMDS 101	55		
20 Mar 82	EMPIRE SONG	Malicious Damage EGO 4	43		
30 Oct 82	BIRDS OF A FEATHER	EG EGO 10	64		
25 Jun 83	LET'S ALL (GO TO THE FIRE DANCES)	EG EGO 11	51		
15 Oct 83	ME OR YOU?	EG EGO 14	57		
7 Apr 84	EIGHTIES	EG EGO 16	60		
21 Jul 84	A NEW DAY	EG EGO 17	56		
2 Feb 85	LOVE LIKE BLOOD	EG EGO 20	16		6
30 Mar 85	KINGS AND QUEENS	EG EGO 21	58		
16 Aug 86	ADORATIONS	EG EGO 27	42		
18 Oct 86	SANITY	EG EGO 30	70		
7 May 94	MILLENNIUM	Butterfly BFLD 12	34		1
16 Jul 94	THE PANDEMONIUM SINGLE	Butterfly BFLDA 17	28		1
4 Feb 95	JANA	Butterfly BFLDA 21	54		
23 Mar 96	DEMOCRACY	Butterfly BFLDB 33	39		1
26 Jul 03	LOOSE CANNON	Zuma Recordings ZUMAD004	25		1
1 Apr 06	HOSANNAS FROM THE BASEMENTS OF HELL	Cooking Vinyl FRYCD251	72		

KILLS UK duo

Date	Title	Label	Peak Position	Weeks at No.1	Weeks in Top 40
26 Apr 03	FRIED MY LITTLE BRAINS	Domino Recordings RUG 154CD	55		
19 Feb 05	THE GOOD ONES	Domino RUG190CD	23		1
11 Jun 05	LOVE IS A DESERTER	Domino RUG198CD	44		
12 Nov 05	NO WOW	Domino RUG207CD	53		

ANDY KIM Canadian singer

Date	Title	Label	Peak Position	Weeks at No.1	Weeks in Top 40
24 Aug 74	ROCK ME GENTLY	Capitol CL 15787 ○ ★	2		11

KINANE Irish singer

Date	Title	Label	Peak Position	Weeks at No.1	Weeks in Top 40
18 May 96	ALL THE LOVER I NEED	Coliseum TOGA 003CD	59		
21 Sep 96	THE WOMAN IN ME	Coliseum TOGA 007CD	73		
16 May 98	HEAVEN	Coalition COLA 047CD	49		
22 Aug 98	SO FINE	Coalition COLA 055CD1	63		

Key: ○ Silver-selling · ● Gold-selling · ✪ Platinum-selling · ★ US No.1 · Peak Position · Weeks at No.1 · Weeks in Top 40

KINESIS UK group

Date	Title / Label	Peak Position	Weeks at No.1	Weeks in Top 40
22 Mar 03	**AND THEY OBEY** *Independiente ISOM 68MS*	63		
28 Jun 03	**FOREVER REELING** *Independiente ISOM 74MS*	65		
27 Sep 03	**ONE WAY MIRROR** *Independiente ISOM 77MS*	71		

KING UK group

Date	Title / Label	Peak Position	Weeks at No.1	Weeks in Top 40
12 Jan 85	**LOVE AND PRIDE** *CBS A 4988* ●	2		10
23 Mar 85	**WON'T YOU HOLD MY HAND NOW** *CBS A 6094*	24		6
17 Aug 85	**ALONE WITHOUT YOU** *CBS A 6308*	8		8
19 Oct 85	**THE TASTE OF YOUR TEARS** *CBS A 6618*	11		7
11 Jan 86	**TORTURE** *CBS A 6761*	23		3

KING ADORA UK group

Date	Title / Label	Peak Position	Weeks at No.1	Weeks in Top 40
4 Nov 00	**SMOULDER** *Superior Quality RQSD 010CD*	62		
3 Mar 01	**SUFFOCATE** *Superior Quality RQS 11DD*	39		1
26 May 01	**BIONIC** *Superior Quality RQS 012DD*	30		1
31 May 03	**BORN TO LOSE/KAMIKAZE** *MHR MHRCD 001*	68		

BB KING US singer/guitarist

Date	Title / Label	Peak Position	Weeks at No.1	Weeks in Top 40
15 Apr 89	**WHEN LOVE COMES TO TOWN** *Island IS 411* U2 FEATURING BB KING	6		5
18 Jul 92	**SINCE I MET YOU BABY** *Virgin VS 1423* GARY MOORE & BB KING	59		

BEN E. KING US singer

Date	Title / Label	Peak Position	Weeks at No.1	Weeks in Top 40
2 Feb 61	**FIRST TASTE OF LOVE** *London HLK 9258*	27		10
22 Jun 61	**STAND BY ME** *London HLK 9358*	27		4
5 Oct 61	**AMOR AMOR** *London HLK 9416*	38		2
14 Feb 87	**STAND BY ME** *Atlantic A 9361* ●	1	3	9
4 Jul 87	**SAVE THE LAST DANCE FOR ME** *Manhattan MT 25*	69		

CAROLE KING US singer

Date	Title / Label	Peak Position	Weeks at No.1	Weeks in Top 40
20 Sep 62	**IT MIGHT AS WELL RAIN UNTIL SEPTEMBER** *London HLU 9591*	3		11
7 Aug 71	**IT'S TOO LATE** *A&M AMS 849* ★	6		10
28 Oct 72	**IT MIGHT AS WELL RAIN UNTIL SEPTEMBER** *London HL 10391*	43		

DAVE KING UK singer

Date	Title / Label	Peak Position	Weeks at No.1	Weeks in Top 40
17 Feb 56	**MEMORIES ARE MADE OF THIS** *Decca F 10684* DAVE KING FEATURING THE KEYNOTES	5		15
13 Apr 56	**YOU CAN'T BE TRUE TO TWO** *Decca F 10720* DAVE KING FEATURING THE KEYNOTES	11		9
21 Dec 56	**CHRISTMAS AND YOU** *Decca F 10791*	23		2
24 Jan 58	**THE STORY OF MY LIFE** *Decca F 10973*	20		3

DIANA KING Jamaican singer

Date	Title / Label	Peak Position	Weeks at No.1	Weeks in Top 40
8 Jul 95	**SHY GUY** *Columbia 6621682* ○	2		11
28 Oct 95	**AIN'T NOBODY** *Work 6625495*	13		3
1 Nov 97	**I SAY A LITTLE PRAYER** *Columbia 6651472*	17		3

EVELYN KING US singer

Date	Title / Label	Peak Position	Weeks at No.1	Weeks in Top 40
13 May 78	**SHAME** *RCA PC 1122* ○ EVELYN 'CHAMPAGNE' KING	39		1
3 Feb 79	**I DON'T KNOW IF IT'S RIGHT** *RCA PB 1386* EVELYN 'CHAMPAGNE' KING	67		
27 Jun 81	**I'M IN LOVE** *RCA 95*	27		6
26 Sep 81	**IF YOU WANT MY LOVIN'** *RCA 131*	43		
28 Aug 82	**LOVE COME DOWN** *RCA 249* ○	7		10
20 Nov 82	**BACK TO LOVE** *RCA 287*	40		1
19 Feb 83	**GET LOOSE** *RCA 315*	45		
9 Nov 85	**YOUR PERSONAL TOUCH** *RCA PB 49915*	37		2
29 Mar 86	**HIGH HORSE** *RCA PB 49891*	55		
23 Jul 88	**HOLD ON TO WHAT YOU'VE GOT** *Manhattan MT 49*	47		
10 Oct 92	**SHAME** *Network NWKTEN 56* ALTERN 8 VS EVELYN KING	74		

JONATHAN KING UK singer

Date	Title / Label	Peak Position	Weeks at No.1	Weeks in Top 40
29 Jul 65	**EVERYONE'S GONE TO THE MOON** *Decca F 12187*	4		10
10 Jan 70	**LET IT ALL HANG OUT** *Decca F 12988*	26		7
29 May 71	**LAZY BONES** *Decca F 13177*	23		6
20 Nov 71	**HOOKED ON A FEELING** *Decca F 13241*	23		8
5 Feb 72	**FLIRT** *Decca F 13276*	22		7
6 Sep 75	**UNA PALOMA BLANCA** *UK 105*	5		10
7 Oct 78	**ONE FOR YOU ONE FOR ME** *GTO GT 237*	29		4
16 Jun 79	**YOU'RE THE GREATEST LOVER** *UK International INT 586*	67		
3 Nov 79	**GLORIA** *Ariola ARO 198*	65		

PAUL KING UK singer

Date	Title / Label	Peak Position	Weeks at No.1	Weeks in Top 40
2 May 87	**I KNOW** *CBS PKING 1*	59		

SOLOMON KING US singer

Date	Title / Label	Peak Position	Weeks at No.1	Weeks in Top 40
3 Jan 68	**SHE WEARS MY RING** *Columbia DB 8325*	3		16
1 May 68	**WHEN WE WERE YOUNG** *Columbia DB 8402*	21		9

KING BEE Dutch rapper

Date	Title / Label	Peak Position	Weeks at No.1	Weeks in Top 40
26 Jan 91	**MUST BEE THE MUSIC** *Columbia 6565827* KING BEE FEATURING MICHELE	44		
23 Mar 91	**BACK BY DOPE DEMAND** *First Bass 7RUFF 6X*	61		

KING BISCUIT TIME UK singer

Date	Title / Label	Peak Position	Weeks at No.1	Weeks in Top 40
8 Oct 05	**C I AM 15** *No Style MC5103SCD*	67		

KING BROTHERS UK group

Date	Title / Label	Peak Position	Weeks at No.1	Weeks in Top 40
31 May 57	**A WHITE SPORT COAT (AND A PINK CARNATION)** *Parlophone R 4310*	6		14
9 Aug 57	**IN THE MIDDLE OF AN ISLAND** *Parlophone R 4338*	19		13
6 Dec 57	**WAKE UP LITTLE SUSIE** *Parlophone R 4367*	22		3
31 Jan 58	**PUT A LIGHT IN THE WINDOW** *Parlophone R 4389*	25		4
14 Apr 60	**STANDING ON THE CORNER** *Parlophone R 4639*	4		11
28 Jul 60	**MAIS OUI** *Parlophone R 4672*	16		9
12 Jan 61	**DOLL HOUSE** *Parlophone R 4715*	21		8
2 Mar 61	**76 TROMBONES** *Parlophone R 4737*	19		10

KING KURT UK group

Date	Title / Label	Peak Position	Weeks at No.1	Weeks in Top 40
15 Oct 83	**DESTINATION ZULULAND** *Stiff BUY 189*	36		3
28 Apr 84	**MACK THE KNIFE** *Stiff BUY 199*	55		
4 Aug 84	**BANANA BANANA** *Stiff BUY 206*	54		
15 Nov 86	**AMERICA** *Polydor KURT 1*	73		
2 May 87	**THE LAND OF RING DANG DO** *Polydor KURT 2*	67		

KING SUN-D'MOET US rapper

Date	Title / Label	Peak Position	Weeks at No.1	Weeks in Top 40
11 Jul 87	**HEY LOVE** *Flame MELT 5*	66		

KING TRIGGER UK group

Date	Title / Label	Peak Position	Weeks at No.1	Weeks in Top 40
14 Aug 82	**THE RIVER** *Chrysalis CHS 2623*	57		

KINGDOM COME German/US group

Date	Title / Label	Peak Position	Weeks at No.1	Weeks in Top 40
16 Apr 88	**GET IT ON** *Polydor KCS 1*	75		
6 May 89	**DO YOU LIKE IT** *Polydor KCS 3*	73		

KINGMAKER UK group

Date	Title / Label	Peak Position	Weeks at No.1	Weeks in Top 40
18 Jan 92	**IDIOTS AT THE WHEEL EP.** *Scorch 3*	30		2
23 May 92	**EAT YOURSELF WHOLE** *Scorch SCORCHG 5*	15		2
31 Oct 92	**ARMCHAIR ANARCHIST** *Scorch SCORCHG 6*	47		
8 May 93	**10 YEARS ASLEEP** *Scorch CDSCORCHS 8*	15		3
19 Jun 93	**QUEEN JANE** *Scorch CDSCORS 9*	29		2
30 Oct 93	**SATURDAY'S NOT WHAT IT USED TO BE** *Scorch CDSCORCH 10*	63		
15 Apr 95	**YOU AND I WILL NEVER SEE THINGS EYE TO EYE** *Chrysalis CDSORCHS 11*	33		1
3 Jun 95	**IN THE BEST POSSIBLE TASTE (PART 2)** *Scorch CDSCORCHS 12*	41		

KINGS OF CONVENIENCE Norwegian duo

Date	Title / Label	Peak Position	Weeks at No.1	Weeks in Top 40
21 Apr 01	**TOXIC GIRL** *Source SOURCDSE 1025*	44		
14 Jul 01	**FAILURE** *Source SOURCD 036*	63		
4 Sep 04	**I'D RATHER DANCE WITH YOU** *Source SOURCDX 102*	60		

Silver-selling ● Gold-selling ● Platinum-selling ● US No.1 ★ | Peak Position | Weeks at No.1 | Weeks in Top 40

KINGS OF LEON US group

Date	Title	Label	Peak Position	Weeks at No.1	Weeks in Top 40
8 Mar 03	HOLY ROLLER NOVACAINE	Hand Me Down HMD21	53		
14 Jun 03	WHAT I SAW	Hand Me Down HMD23	22		1
23 Aug 03	MOLLY'S CHAMBERS	Hand Me Down HMD30	23		1
1 Nov 03	WASTED TIME	Hand Me Down HMD32	51		
28 Feb 04	CALIFORNIA WAITING	Hand Me Down HMD37	61		
6 Nov 04	THE BUCKET	Hand Me Down HMD41	16		1
22 Jan 05	FOUR KICKS	Hand Me Down HMD45	24		1
23 Apr 05	KING OF THE RODEO	Hand Me Down HMD49	41		
24 Mar 07	ON CALL	Hand Me Down 88697073602	18		3
14 Jul 07	FANS	Columbia 88697114112	13		4

KINGS OF SWING ORCHESTRA Australian orchestra

Date	Title	Label	Peak Position	Weeks at No.1	Weeks in Top 40
1 May 82	SWITCHED ON SWING	Philips Swing 1	48		

KINGS OF TOMORROW US production duo

Date	Title	Label	Peak Position	Weeks at No.1	Weeks in Top 40
14 Apr 01	FINALLY KINGS OF TOMORROW FEATURING JULIE McKNIGHT	Distance DI 2029	54		
29 Sep 01	FINALLY (REMIX) KINGS OF TOMORROW FEATURING JULIE McKNIGHT	Defected DEFECT 37CDX	24		1
13 Apr 02	YOUNG HEARTS	Defected DFECT 46CDS	45		
25 Oct 03	DREAMS/THROUGH	Defected DFTD 079	74		
31 Jul 04	DREAMS (REMIX) KINGS OF TOMORROW FEATURING HAZE	Defected DFTD 090CDS	69		
26 Feb 05	THRU KINGS OF TOMORROW FEATURING HAZE	Defected DFTD099CDS	55		

KINGSMEN US group

Date	Title	Label	Peak Position	Weeks at No.1	Weeks in Top 40
30 Jan 64	LOUIE LOUIE	Pye International 7N 25231	26		7

SEAN KINGSTON US singer

Date	Title	Label	Peak Position	Weeks at No.1	Weeks in Top 40
1 Sep 07	BEAUTIFUL GIRLS	RCA 88697168302 ★	1	4	13
3 Nov 07	ME LOVE	RCA 88697204762	32		1
1 Mar 08	TAKE YOU THERE	Download	47		
29 Mar 08	LOVE LIKE THIS NATASHA BEDINGFIELD FEATURING SEAN KINGSTON	Phonogenic 88697287252	27		1

KINGSTON TRIO US group

Date	Title	Label	Peak Position	Weeks at No.1	Weeks in Top 40
21 Nov 58	TOM DOOLEY	Capitol CL 14951 ★	5		14
4 Dec 59	SAN MIGUEL	Capitol CL 15073	29		1

KINKS UK group

Date	Title	Label	Peak Position	Weeks at No.1	Weeks in Top 40
13 Aug 64	YOU REALLY GOT ME	Pye 7N 15673	1	2	11
29 Oct 64	ALL DAY AND ALL OF THE NIGHT	Pye 7N 15714	2		12
21 Jan 65	TIRED OF WAITING FOR YOU	Pye 7N 15759	1	1	10
25 Mar 65	EVERYBODY'S GONNA BE HAPPY	Pye 7N 15813	17		6
27 May 65	SET ME FREE	Pye 7N 15854	9		9
5 Aug 65	SEE MY FRIEND	Pye 7N 15919	10		8
2 Dec 65	TILL THE END OF THE DAY	Pye 7N 15981	8		12
3 Mar 66	DEDICATED FOLLOWER OF FASHION	Pye 7N 17064	4		10
9 Jun 66	SUNNY AFTERNOON	Pye 7N 17125	1	2	13
24 Nov 66	DEAD END STREET	Pye 7N 17222	5		11
11 May 67	WATERLOO SUNSET	Pye 7N 17321	2		10
18 Oct 67	AUTUMN ALMANAC	Pye 7N 17400	3		10
17 Apr 68	WONDERBOY	Pye 7N 17468	36		5
17 Jul 68	DAYS	Pye 7N 17573	12		9
16 Apr 69	PLASTIC MAN	Pye 7N 17724	31		3
10 Jan 70	VICTORIA	Pye 7N 17865	33		3
4 Jul 70	LOLA	Pye 7N 17961	2		13
12 Dec 70	APEMAN	Pye 7N 45016	5		13
27 May 72	SUPERSONIC ROCKET SHIP	RCA 2211	16		7
27 Jun 81	BETTER THINGS	Arista ARIST 415	46		
6 Aug 83	COME DANCING	Arista ARIST 502	12		6
15 Oct 83	DON'T FORGET TO DANCE	Arista ARIST 524	58		
15 Oct 83	YOU REALLY GOT ME	PRT KD1	47		
18 Jan 97	THE DAYS EP	When! WENX 1016	35		1
18 Sep 04	YOU REALLY GOT ME	Sanctuary SANXD317	42		

KINKY UK rapper

Date	Title	Label	Peak Position	Weeks at No.1	Weeks in Top 40
24 Aug 96	EVERYBODY	Feverpitch CDFVR 1009	71		

KINKY MACHINE UK group

Date	Title	Label	Peak Position	Weeks at No.1	Weeks in Top 40
6 Mar 93	SUPERNATURAL GIVER	Lemon 006CD	70		
29 May 93	SHOCKAHOLIC	Oxygen GASPD 5	70		
14 Aug 93	GOING OUT WITH GOD	Oxygen GASPD 9	74		
2 Jul 94	10 SECOND BIONIC MAN	Oxygen GASPD 14	66		

FERN KINNEY US singer

Date	Title	Label	Peak Position	Weeks at No.1	Weeks in Top 40
16 Feb 80	TOGETHER WE ARE BEAUTIFUL	WEA K 79111 ●	1	1	9

KIOKI Japanese singer

Date	Title	Label	Peak Position	Weeks at No.1	Weeks in Top 40
17 Aug 02	DO AND DON'T FOR LOVE	V2 VVR 5020803	66		

KIRA Belgian singer

Date	Title	Label	Peak Position	Weeks at No.1	Weeks in Top 40
1 Mar 03	I'LL BE YOUR ANGEL	NuLife 74321970362	9		3

KATHY KIRBY UK singer

Date	Title	Label	Peak Position	Weeks at No.1	Weeks in Top 40
15 Aug 63	DANCE ON	Decca F 11682	11		12
7 Nov 63	SECRET LOVE	Decca F 11759	4		15
20 Feb 64	LET ME GO LOVER	Decca F 11832	10		11
7 May 64	YOU'RE THE ONE	Decca F 11892	17		8
4 Mar 65	I BELONG	Decca F 12087	36		2

BO KIRKLAND & RUTH DAVIS US duo

Date	Title	Label	Peak Position	Weeks at No.1	Weeks in Top 40
4 Jun 77	YOU'RE GONNA GET NEXT TO ME	EMI International INT 532	12		8

KISS US group

Date	Title	Label	Peak Position	Weeks at No.1	Weeks in Top 40
30 Jun 79	I WAS MADE FOR LOVIN' YOU	Casablanca CAN 152	50		
20 Feb 82	A WORLD WITHOUT HEROES	Casablanca KISS 002	55		
30 Apr 83	CREATURES OF THE NIGHT	Casablanca KISS 4	34		2
29 Oct 83	LICK IT UP	Vertigo KISS 5	31		2
8 Sep 84	HEAVEN'S ON FIRE	Vertigo VER 12	43		
9 Nov 85	TEARS ARE FALLING	Vertigo KISS 6	57		
3 Oct 87	CRAZY CRAZY NIGHTS	Vertigo KISS 7	4		8
5 Dec 87	REASON TO LIVE	Vertigo KISS 8	33		4
10 Sep 88	TURN ON THE NIGHT	Vertigo KISS 9	41		
18 Nov 89	HIDE YOUR HEART	Vertigo KISS 10	59		
31 Mar 90	FOREVER	Vertigo KISS 11	65		
11 Jan 92	GOD GAVE ROCK AND ROLL TO YOU II	Interscope A 8696	4		7
9 May 92	UNHOLY	Vertigo KISS 12	26		1

KISS AMC UK rapper

Date	Title	Label	Peak Position	Weeks at No.1	Weeks in Top 40
1 Jul 89	A BIT OF...	Syncopate SY 29	58		
19 Aug 89	A BIT OF U2	Syncopate SY 29	58		
3 Feb 90	MY DOCS	Syncopate XAMC 1	66		

KISSING THE PINK UK group

Date	Title	Label	Peak Position	Weeks at No.1	Weeks in Top 40
5 Mar 83	LAST FILM	Magnet KTP 3	19		8

MAC & KATIE KISSOON UK duo

Date	Title	Label	Peak Position	Weeks at No.1	Weeks in Top 40
19 Jun 71	CHIRPY CHIRPY CHEEP CHEEP	Young Blood YB 1026	41		
18 Jan 75	SUGAR CANDY KISSES	Polydor 2058 531 ●	3		8
3 May 75	DON'T DO IT BABY	State STAT 4	9		7
30 Aug 75	LIKE A BUTTERFLY	State STAT 9	18		8
15 May 76	THE TWO OF US	State STAT 21	46		

KEVIN KITCHEN UK singer

Date	Title	Label	Peak Position	Weeks at No.1	Weeks in Top 40
20 Apr 85	PUT MY ARMS AROUND YOU	China WOK 1	64		

JOY KITIKONTI Italian producer

Date	Title	Label	Peak Position	Weeks at No.1	Weeks in Top 40
17 Nov 01	JOYENERGIZER	BXR BXRC 0347	57		

EARTHA KITT US singer

Date	Title	Label	Peak Position	Weeks at No.1	Weeks in Top 40
1 Apr 55	UNDER THE BRIDGES OF PARIS	HMV B 10647	7		10
3 Dec 83	WHERE IS MY MAN	Record Shack SOHO 11	36		4
7 Jul 84	I LOVE MEN	Record Shack SOHO 21	50		

Silver-selling · Gold-selling · Platinum-selling · US No.1 ★ · Peak Position · Weeks at No.1 · Weeks in Top 40

Date	Title / Label	Peak Position	Weeks at No.1	Weeks in Top 40
12 Apr 86	**THIS IS MY LIFE** *Record Shack SOHO 61*	73		
1 Jul 89	**CHA CHA HEELS** *Arista 112331* EARTHA KITT & BRONSKI BEAT	32		3
5 Mar 94	**IF I LOVE YA THEN I NEED YA IF I NEED YA THEN I WANT YOU AROUND** *RCA 74321190342*	43		

KITTIE Canadian group

Date	Title / Label	Peak Position	Weeks at No.1	Weeks in Top 40
25 Mar 00	**BRACKISH** *Epic 6691292*	46		
22 Jul 00	**CHARLOTTE** *Epic 6696222*	60		

KLAXONS Belgian group

Date	Title / Label	Peak Position	Weeks at No.1	Weeks in Top 40
10 Dec 83	**THE CLAP CLAP SOUND** *PRT 7P 290*	45		
11 Nov 06	**MAGICK** *Polydor RINSE1CD*	29		1
20 Jan 07	**GOLDEN SKANS** *Polydor RINSE002CD*	7		8
21 Apr 07	**GRAVITY'S RAINBOW** *Rinse RINSE003CD*	35		1
16 Jun 07	**IT'S NOT OVER YET** *Rinse RINSE004CD*	13		8

KLEA Dutch group

Date	Title / Label	Peak Position	Weeks at No.1	Weeks in Top 40
7 Sep 02	**TIC TOC** *Incentive CENT 41CDS*	61		

KLEEER US group

Date	Title / Label	Peak Position	Weeks at No.1	Weeks in Top 40
17 Mar 79	**KEEEP YOUR BODY WORKING** *Atlantic LV 21*	51		
14 Mar 81	**GET TOUGH** *Atlantic 11560*	49		

KLESHAY UK group

Date	Title / Label	Peak Position	Weeks at No.1	Weeks in Top 40
19 Sep 98	**REASONS** *Epic KLE 1CD*	33		1
20 Feb 99	**RUSH** *Epic KLE 2CD*	19		2

KLF UK duo

Date	Title / Label	Peak Position	Weeks at No.1	Weeks in Top 40
11 Aug 90	**WHAT TIME IS LOVE (LIVE AT TRANCENTRAL)** *KLF Communications KLF 004* KLF FEATURING THE CHILDREN OF THE REVOLUTION	5		10
19 Jan 91	**3AM ETERNAL** *KLF Communications KLF 005* KLF FEATURING THE CHILDREN OF THE REVOLUTION	1	2	10
4 May 91	**LAST TRAIN TO TRANCENTRAL** *KLF Communications KLF 008* KLF FEATURING THE CHILDREN OF THE REVOLUTION	2		8
7 Dec 91	**JUSTIFIED AND ANCIENT** *KLF Communications KLF099* KLF, GUEST VOCALS TAMMY WYNETTE	2		10
7 Mar 92	**AMERICA: WHAT TIME IS LOVE** *KLF Communications KLFUSA 004*	4		5

KLUBHEADS Dutch production group

Date	Title / Label	Peak Position	Weeks at No.1	Weeks in Top 40
11 May 96	**KLUBHOPPING** *AM:PM 5815572*	10		5
16 Aug 97	**DISCOHOPPING** *AM:PM 5823032*	35		1
15 Aug 98	**KICKIN' HARD** *Wonderboy WBOYD 011*	36		1

KLUSTER French production duo

Date	Title / Label	Peak Position	Weeks at No.1	Weeks in Top 40
28 Apr 01	**MY LOVE** *Scorpio Music 1928112* KLUSTER FEATURING RON CARROL	73		

KMC Italian production group

Date	Title / Label	Peak Position	Weeks at No.1	Weeks in Top 40
25 May 02	**I FEEL SO FINE** *Incentive CENT 39CDS* KMC FEATURING DAHNY	33		1

KNACK US group

Date	Title / Label	Peak Position	Weeks at No.1	Weeks in Top 40
30 Jun 79	**MY SHARONA** *Capitol CL 16087* ★	6		6
13 Oct 79	**GOOD GIRLS DON'T** *Capitol CL 16097*	66		

BEVERLEY KNIGHT UK singer

Date	Title / Label	Peak Position	Weeks at No.1	Weeks in Top 40
8 Apr 95	**FLAVOUR OF THE OLD SCHOOL** *Dome CDDOME 101*	50		
2 Sep 95	**DOWN FOR THE ONE** *Dome CDDOME 102*	55		
21 Oct 95	**FLAVOUR OF THE OLD SCHOOL** *Dome CDDOME 105*	33		1
23 Mar 96	**MOVING ON UP (ON THE RIGHT SIDE)** *Dome CDDOME 107*	42		
30 May 98	**MADE IT BACK** *Parlophone Rhythm CDRHYTHM 11* BEVERLEY KNIGHT FEATURING REDMAN	21		1
22 Aug 98	**REWIND (FIND A WAY)** *Parlophone Rhythm CDRHYTHS 13*	40		1
10 Apr 99	**MADE IT BACK 99 (REMIX)** *Parlophone Rhythm CDRHYTHS 18* BEVERLEY KNIGHT FEATURING REDMAN	19		3
17 Jul 99	**GREATEST DAY** *Parlophone Rhythm CDRHYTHS 22*	14		3
4 Dec 99	**SISTA SISTA** *Parlophone Rhythm CDRHYTHS 26*	31		1
17 Nov 01	**GET UP** *Parlophone CDRS 6564*	17		2
9 Mar 02	**SHOULDA WOULDA COULDA** *Parlophone CDRS 6570*	10		5
6 Jul 02	**GOLD** *Parlophone CDRS 6580*	27		2
3 Jul 04	**COME AS YOU ARE** *Parlophone CDRS 6636*	9		7
9 Oct 04	**NOT TOO LATE FOR LOVE** *Parlophone CDRS 6645*	31		1
22 Jan 05	**NO MORE** *VVRECSUK003CD* RONI SIZE FEATURING BEVERLEY KNIGHT	26		2
26 Mar 05	**KEEP THIS FIRE BURNING** *Parlophone CDRS6657*	16		4
25 Mar 06	**PIECE OF MY HEART** *Parlophone CDR6684*	16		5
12 May 07	**NO MAN'S LAND** *Parlophone CDR6737*	43		

FREDERICK KNIGHT US singer

Date	Title / Label	Peak Position	Weeks at No.1	Weeks in Top 40
10 Jun 72	**I'VE BEEN LONELY FOR SO LONG** *Stax 2025 098*	22		8

GLADYS KNIGHT & THE PIPS US group

Date	Title / Label	Peak Position	Weeks at No.1	Weeks in Top 40
8 Jun 67	**TAKE ME IN YOUR ARMS AND LOVE ME** *Tamla Motown TMG 604*	13		11
27 Dec 67	**I HEARD IT THROUGH THE GRAPEVINE** *Tamla Motown TMG 629*	47		
17 Jun 72	**JUST WALK IN MY SHOES** *Tamla Motown TMG 813*	35		3
25 Nov 72	**HELP ME MAKE IT THROUGH THE NIGHT** *Tamla Motown TMG 830*	11		15
3 Mar 73	**LOOK OF LOVE** *Tamla Motown TMG 844*	21		7
26 May 73	**NEITHER ONE OF US** *Tamla Motown TMG 855*	31		5
5 Apr 75	**THE WAY WE WERE – TRY TO REMEMBER** *Buddah BDS 428*	4		14
2 Aug 75	**BEST THING THAT EVER HAPPENED TO ME** *Buddah BDS 432*	7		9
15 Nov 75	**PART TIME LOVE** *Buddah BDS 438*	30		4
8 May 76	**MIDNIGHT TRAIN TO GEORGIA** *Buddah BDS 444* ★	10		8
21 Aug 76	**MAKE YOURS A HAPPY HOME** *Buddah BDS 447*	35		2
6 Nov 76	**SO SAD THE SONG** *Buddah BDS 448*	20		8
15 Jan 77	**NOBODY BUT YOU** *Buddah BDS 451*	34		1
28 May 77	**BABY DON'T CHANGE YOUR MIND** *Buddah BDS 458*	4		12
24 Sep 77	**HOME IS WHERE THE HEART IS** *Buddah BDS 460*	35		2
8 Apr 78	**THE ONE AND ONLY** *Buddah BDS 470*	32		2
24 Jun 78	**COME BACK AND FINISH WHAT YOU STARTED** *Buddah BDS 473*	15		9
30 Sep 78	**IT'S A BETTER THAN GOOD TIME** *Buddah BDS 478*	59		
30 Aug 80	**TASTE OF BITTER LOVE** *CBS 8890*	35		2
8 Nov 80	**BOURGIE BOURGIE** *CBS 9081*	32		3
26 Dec 81	**WHEN A CHILD IS BORN** *CBS S 1758* JOHNNY MATHIS & GLADYS KNIGHT	74		
9 Nov 85	**THAT'S WHAT FRIENDS ARE FOR** *Arista ARIST 638* DIONNE WARWICK & FRIENDS FEATURING ELTON JOHN, STEVIE WONDER & GLADYS KNIGHT ★	16		7
16 Jan 88	**LOVE OVERBOARD** *MCA 1223*	42		
10 Jun 89	**LICENCE TO KILL** *MCA 1339* GLADYS KNIGHT	6		9

JORDAN KNIGHT US singer

Date	Title / Label	Peak Position	Weeks at No.1	Weeks in Top 40
16 Oct 99	**GIVE IT TO YOU** *Interscope 4971672*	5		5

ROBERT KNIGHT US singer

Date	Title / Label	Peak Position	Weeks at No.1	Weeks in Top 40
17 Jan 68	**EVERLASTING LOVE** *Monument MON 1008*	40		1
24 Nov 73	**LOVE ON A MOUNTAIN TOP** *Monument MNT 1875*	10		13
9 Mar 74	**EVERLASTING LOVE** *Monument MNT 2106*	19		6

MARK KNOPFLER UK singer/guitarist

Date	Title / Label	Peak Position	Weeks at No.1	Weeks in Top 40
12 Mar 83	**GOING HOME (THEME OF 'LOCAL HERO')** *Vertigo DSTR 4*	56		
16 Mar 96	**DARLING PRETTY** *Vertigo VERCD 88*	33		1
25 May 96	**CANNIBALS** *Vertigo VERCD 89*	42		
2 Oct 04	**BOOM LIKE THAT** *Mercury 9867839*	34		1

KNOWLEDGE Italian production duo

Date	Title / Label	Peak Position	Weeks at No.1	Weeks in Top 40
8 Nov 97	**AS (UNTIL THE DAY)** *ffrr FCD 312*	70		

BEYONCÉ KNOWLES US singer

Date	Title / Label	Peak Position	Weeks at No.1	Weeks in Top 40
27 Jul 02	**WORK IT OUT** *Columbia 6729822*	7		6
1 Feb 03	**03 BONNIE AND CLYDE** *Roc-A-Fella 0770102* JAY-Z FEATURING BEYONCÉ KNOWLES	2		8
12 Jul 03	**CRAZY IN LOVE** *Columbia 6740675* ★	1	3	13
18 Oct 03	**BABY BOY** *Columbia 6744082* BEYONCÉ FEATURING SEAN PAUL ★	2		6
24 Jan 04	**ME, MYSELF & I** *Columbia 6745445*	11		5
17 Apr 04	**NAUGHTY GIRL** *Columbia 6748282*	10		6

Silver-selling ○ · Gold-selling ● · Platinum-selling · US No.1 ★ · Peak Position · Weeks at No.1 · Weeks in Top 40

Date	Title	Peak Position	Weeks at No.1	Weeks in Top 40
28 Jan 06	**CHECK ON IT** *Columbia 82876772532* BEYONCÉ FEATURING SLIM THUG ★	3		8
26 Aug 06	**DÉJÀ VU** *Columbia 82876884352* BEYONCE FEATURING JAY-Z	1	1	9
28 Oct 06	**IRREPLACEABLE** *Columbia 88697024472* ★	4		17
3 Feb 07	**LISTEN** *Columbia 88697059602*	16		4
14 Apr 07	**BEAUTIFUL LIAR** *Columbia 88697091242* BEYONCÉ & SHAKIRA ○	1	3	19
11 Aug 07	**GREEN LIGHT FREEMASONS EP** *Download*	12		4

BUDDY KNOX US singer

Date	Title	Peak Position	Weeks at No.1	Weeks in Top 40
10 May 57	**PARTY DOLL** *Columbia DB 3914* ★	29		3
16 Aug 62	**SHE'S GONE** *Liberty LIB 55473*	45		

FRANKIE KNUCKLES US singer

Date	Title	Peak Position	Weeks at No.1	Weeks in Top 40
17 Jun 89	**TEARS** *ffrr F 108* FRANKIE KNUCKLES PRESENTS SATOSHI TOMIIE	50		
21 Oct 89	**YOUR LOVE** *Trax TRAXT 3*	59		
27 Jul 91	**THE WHISTLE SONG** *Virgin America VUS 47*	17		3
23 Nov 91	**IT'S HARD SOMETIMES** *Virgin America VUS 52*	67		
6 Jun 92	**RAIN FALLS** *Virgin America VUST 60* FRANKIE KNUCKLES FEATURING LISA MICHAELIS	48		
27 May 95	**TOO MANY FISH** *Virgin VUSCD 89* FRANKIE KNUCKLES FEATURING ADEVA	34		1
18 Nov 95	**WHADDA U WANT (FROM ME)** *Virgin VUSCD 98* FRANKIE KNUCKLES FEATURING ADEVA	36		1

MOE KOFFMAN QUARTETTE Canadian flautist

Date	Title	Peak Position	Weeks at No.1	Weeks in Top 40
28 Mar 58	**SWINGIN' SHEPHERD BLUES** *London HLJ 8549*	23		2

MIKE KOGLIN German producer

Date	Title	Peak Position	Weeks at No.1	Weeks in Top 40
28 Nov 98	**THE SILENCE** *Multiply CDMULTY 44*	20		1
29 May 99	**ON MY WAY** *Multiply CDMULTY 51* MIKE KOGLIN FEATURING BEATRICE	28		1

KOKOMO US pianist

Date	Title	Peak Position	Weeks at No.1	Weeks in Top 40
13 Apr 61	**ASIA MINOR** *London HLU 9305*	35		3
29 May 82	**A LITTLE BIT FURTHER AWAY** *CBS A 2064*	45		

KON KAN Canadian duo

Date	Title	Peak Position	Weeks at No.1	Weeks in Top 40
4 Mar 89	**I BEG YOUR PARDON** *Atlantic A 8969* ○	5		10

JOHN KONGOS South African singer/multi-instrumentalist

Date	Title	Peak Position	Weeks at No.1	Weeks in Top 40
22 May 71	**HE'S GONNA STEP ON YOU AGAIN** *Fly BUG 8*	4		11
20 Nov 71	**TOKOLOSHE MAN** *Fly BUG 14*	4		10

KONKRETE UK production duo

Date	Title	Peak Position	Weeks at No.1	Weeks in Top 40
22 Sep 01	**LAW UNTO MYSELF** *Perfecto PERF 23CDS*	60		

KONTAKT UK production duo

Date	Title	Peak Position	Weeks at No.1	Weeks in Top 40
20 Sep 03	**SHOW ME A SIGN** *NuLife 82876557432*	19		2

KOOKS UK group

Date	Title	Peak Position	Weeks at No.1	Weeks in Top 40
23 Jul 05	**EDDIE'S GUN** *Virgin VSCDT2000*	35		1
29 Oct 05	**SOFA SONG** *Virgin VSCDT1904*	28		1
21 Jan 06	**YOU DON'T LOVE ME** *Virgin VSCDX1910*	12		3
1 Apr 06	**NAÏVE** *Virgin VSCDT1911*	5		20
1 Jul 06	**SHE MOVES IN HER OWN WAY** *Virgin VSCDT1913*	7		18
28 Oct 06	**OOH LA** *Virgin VSCDT1918*	20		2

KOOL & THE GANG US group

Date	Title	Peak Position	Weeks at No.1	Weeks in Top 40
27 Oct 79	**LADIES NIGHT** *Mercury KOOL 7*	9		7
19 Jan 80	**TOO HOT** *Mercury KOOL 8*	23		6
12 Jul 80	**HANGIN' OUT** *Mercury KOOL 9*	52		
1 Nov 80	**CELEBRATION** *De-Lite KOOL 10* ○ ★	7		10
21 Feb 81	**JONES VS JONES/SUMMER MADNESS** *De-Lite KOOL 11*	17		8
30 May 81	**TAKE IT TO THE TOP** *De-Lite DE 2*	15		7
31 Oct 81	**STEPPIN' OUT** *De-Lite DE 4*	12		7
19 Dec 81	**GET DOWN ON IT** *De-Lite DE 5* ○	3		10
6 Mar 82	**TAKE MY HEART (YOU CAN HAVE IT IF YOU WANT IT)** *De-Lite DE 6*	29		4
7 Aug 82	**BIG FUN** *De-Lite DE 7*	14		6
16 Oct 82	**OOH LA LA LA (LET'S GO DANCIN')** *De-Lite DE 9*	6		7
4 Dec 82	**HI DE HI, HI DE HO** *De-Lite DE 14*	29		5
10 Dec 83	**STRAIGHT AHEAD** *De-Lite DE 15*	15		8
11 Feb 84	**JOANNA/TONIGHT** *De-Lite DE 16* ○	2		9
14 Apr 84	**(WHEN YOU SAY YOU LOVE SOMEBODY) IN THE HEART** *De-Lite DE 17*	7		7
24 Nov 84	**FRESH** *De-Lite DE 18* ○	11		10
9 Feb 85	**MISLED** *De-Lite DE 19*	28		3
11 May 85	**CHERISH** *De-Lite DE 20* ○	4		16
2 Nov 85	**EMERGENCY** *De-Lite DE 21*	50		
22 Nov 86	**VICTORY** *Club JAB 44*	30		4
21 Mar 87	**STONE LOVE** *Club JAB 47*	45		
31 Dec 88	**CELEBRATION (REMIX)** *Club JAB 78*	56		
6 Jul 91	**GET DOWN ON IT (REMIX)** *Mercury MER 346*	69		
27 Dec 03	**LADIES NIGHT** *Innocent SINDX53* ATOMIC KITTEN FEATURING KOOL & THE GANG	8		8

KOOPA UK group

Date	Title	Peak Position	Weeks at No.1	Weeks in Top 40
3 Dec 05	**NO TREND** *Mad Cow MCR741*	71		
20 Jan 07	**BLAG STEAL & BORROW** *Download*	31		1
23 Jun 07	**THE ONE-OFF SONG FOR THE SUMMER** *Download*	21		1
10 Nov 07	**THE CRASH** *Juxtaposition JXCD904*	16		1

KORGIS UK duo

Date	Title	Peak Position	Weeks at No.1	Weeks in Top 40
23 Jun 79	**IF I HAD YOU** *Rialto TREB 103*	13		7
24 May 80	**EVERYBODY'S GOT TO LEARN SOMETIME** *Rialto TREB 115* ○	5		9
30 Aug 80	**IF IT'S ALRIGHT WITH YOU BABY** *Rialto TREB 118*	56		

KORN US group

Date	Title	Peak Position	Weeks at No.1	Weeks in Top 40
19 Oct 96	**NO PLACE TO HIDE** *Epic 6638452*	26		1
15 Feb 97	**A.D.I.D.A.S.** *Epic 6642042*	22		1
7 Jun 97	**GOOD GOD** *Epic 6646585*	25		1
22 Aug 98	**GOT THE LIFE** *Epic 6663912*	23		1
8 May 99	**FREAK ON A LEASH** *Epic 6672525*	24		1
12 Feb 00	**FALLING AWAY FROM ME** *Epic 6688692*	24		1
3 Jun 00	**MAKE ME BAD** *Epic 6694332*	25		1
1 Jun 02	**HERE TO STAY** *Epic 6727422*	12		3
21 Sep 02	**THOUGHTLESS** *Epic 6731572*	37		1
23 Aug 03	**DID MY TIME** *Epic 6741422*	15		2
3 Dec 05	**TWISTED TRANSISTOR** *Virgin VUSCD316*	27		1
24 Jun 06	**COMING UNDONE** *Virgin VUSCD323*	63		

KOSHEEN UK production duo

Date	Title	Peak Position	Weeks at No.1	Weeks in Top 40
17 Jun 00	**EMPTY SKIES/HIDE U** *Moksha Recordings MOKSHA 05CD*	73		
14 Apr 01	**(SLIP & SLIDE) SUICIDE** *Moksha Recordings MOKSHA 07CD*	50		
1 Sep 01	**HIDE U (REMIX)** *Moksha/Arista 74321879412*	6		1
22 Dec 01	**CATCH** *Moksha/Arista 74321913732*	15		6
4 May 02	**HUNGRY** *Moksha/Arista 74321934392*	13		3
31 Aug 02	**HARDER** *Moksha/Arista 74321954462*	53		
9 Aug 03	**ALL IN MY HEAD** *Moksha/Arista 82876527252*	7		3
1 Nov 03	**WASTING MY TIME** *Moksha/Arista 82876570032*	49		

KP & ENVYI US vocal/rap duo

Date	Title	Peak Position	Weeks at No.1	Weeks in Top 40
13 Jun 98	**SWING MY WAY** *East West E 3849CD*	14		2

KRAFTWERK German group

Date	Title	Peak Position	Weeks at No.1	Weeks in Top 40
10 May 75	**AUTOBAHN** *Vertigo 6147 012*	11		9
28 Oct 78	**NEON LIGHTS** *Capitol CL 15998*	53		
9 May 81	**POCKET CALCULATOR** *EMI 5175*	39		1
11 Jul 81	**THE MODEL/COMPUTER LOVE** *EMI 5207*	36		2
26 Dec 81	**THE MODEL/COMPUTER LOVE** *EMI 5207* ●	1	1	9
20 Feb 82	**SHOWROOM DUMMIES** *EMI 5272*	25		4
6 Aug 83	**TOUR DE FRANCE** *EMI 5413*	22		6
25 Aug 84	**TOUR DE FRANCE (REMIX)** *EMI 5413*	24		5
1 Jun 91	**THE ROBOTS** *EMI EM 192*	20		3
2 Nov 91	**RADIOACTIVITY** *EMI EM 201*	43		
23 Oct 99	**TOUR DE FRANCE** *EMI 8874210*	61		
18 Mar 00	**EXPO 2000** *EMI CDEM 562*	27		1
19 Jul 03	**TOUR DE FRANCE 2003** *EMI CDEM 626*	20		2
27 Mar 04	**AERODYNAMIK** *EMI CDEM 637*	33		1

BILLY J. KRAMER & THE DAKOTAS UK group

Date	Title / Label	Peak Position	Weeks at No.1	Weeks in Top 40
2 May 63	**DO YOU WANT TO KNOW A SECRET?** *Parlophone R 5023*	2		13
1 Aug 63	**BAD TO ME** *Parlophone R 5049*	1	3	12
7 Nov 63	**I'LL KEEP YOU SATISFIED** *Parlophone R 5073*	4		12
27 Feb 64	**LITTLE CHILDREN** *Parlophone R 5105*	1	2	13
23 Jul 64	**FROM A WINDOW** *Parlophone R 5156*	10		8
20 May 65	**TRAINS AND BOATS AND PLANES** *Parlophone R 5285*	12		7

KRANKIES UK comedy duo

Date	Title / Label	Peak Position	Weeks at No.1	Weeks in Top 40
7 Feb 81	**FAN'DABI'DOZI** *Monarch MON 21*	46		

LENNY KRAVITZ US singer/multi-instrumentalist

Date	Title / Label	Peak Position	Weeks at No.1	Weeks in Top 40
2 Jun 90	**MR CABDRIVER** *Virgin America VUS 20*	58		
4 Aug 90	**LET LOVE RULE** *Virgin America VUS 26*	39		2
30 Mar 91	**ALWAYS ON THE RUN** *Virgin America VUS 34*	41		
15 Jun 91	**IT AIN'T OVER TIL IT'S OVER** *Virgin America VUS 43*	11		7
14 Sep 91	**STAND BY MY WOMAN** *Virgin America VUS 45*	55		
20 Feb 93	**ARE YOU GONNA GO MY WAY** *Virgin America VUSDG 65* ● (silver)	4		9
22 May 93	**BELIEVE** *Virgin America VUSCD 72*	30		4
28 Aug 93	**HEAVEN HELP** *Virgin America VUSDG 73*	20		5
4 Dec 93	**BUDDHA OF SUBURBIA** *Arista 74321177052* DAVID BOWIE FEATURING LENNY KRAVITZ	35		2
4 Dec 93	**IS THERE ANY LOVE IN YOUR HEART** *Virgin America VUSDG 76*	52		
9 Sep 95	**ROCK AND ROLL IS DEAD** *Virgin America VUSCD 93*	22		2
23 Dec 95	**CIRCUS** *Virgin America VUSCD 96*	54		
2 Mar 96	**CAN'T GET YOU OFF MY MIND** *Virgin America VUSCD 100*	54		
16 May 98	**IF YOU CAN'T SAY NO** *Virgin VUSCD 130*	48		
10 Oct 98	**I BELONG TO YOU** *Virgin VUSCD 138*	75		
20 Feb 99	**FLY AWAY** *Virgin VUSCD 141* ● (silver)	1	1	8
6 Apr 02	**STILLNESS OF HEART** *Virgin VUSCD 236*	44		
7 Feb 04	**SHOW ME YOUR SOUL** *Puff Daddy MCSTD 40350* P DIDDY, LENNY KRAVITZ, PHARRELL WILLIAMS & LOON	35		1
24 Jul 04	**CALIFORNIA** *Virgin VUSCD 294*	62		

KRAY TWINZ UK production duo

Date	Title / Label	Peak Position	Weeks at No.1	Weeks in Top 40
12 Nov 05	**WHAT WE DO** *Gana/W10 GANA01CDS* KRAY TWINZ FEATURING TWISTA & LETHAL B	23		1

KRAZE US group

Date	Title / Label	Peak Position	Weeks at No.1	Weeks in Top 40
22 Oct 88	**THE PARTY** *MCA 1288*	29		3
17 Jun 89	**LET'S PLAY HOUSE** *MCA 1337*	71		

KREUZ UK group

Date	Title / Label	Peak Position	Weeks at No.1	Weeks in Top 40
8 Jul 95	**PARTY ALL NIGHT** *Diesel DES 004C*	75		

CHANTAL KREVIAZUK Canadian singer/pianist

Date	Title / Label	Peak Position	Weeks at No.1	Weeks in Top 40
6 Mar 99	**LEAVING ON A JET PLANE** *Epic 6666272*	59		

KREW-KATS UK group

Date	Title / Label	Peak Position	Weeks at No.1	Weeks in Top 40
9 Mar 61	**TRAMBONE** *HMV POP 840*	33		5

CHAD KROEGER Canadian singer

Date	Title / Label	Peak Position	Weeks at No.1	Weeks in Top 40
22 Jun 02	**HERO** *Roadrunner RR 20463* CHAD KROEGER FEATURING JOSEY SCOTT ● (silver)	4		11

KRIS KROSS US duo

Date	Title / Label	Peak Position	Weeks at No.1	Weeks in Top 40
30 May 92	**JUMP** *Ruffhouse 6578547* ★	2		7
25 Jul 92	**WARM IT UP** *Ruffhouse 6582187*	16		4
17 Oct 92	**I MISSED THE BUS** *Ruffhouse 6583927*	57		
19 Dec 92	**IT'S A SHAME** *Ruffhouse 6588587*	31		3
11 Sep 93	**ALRIGHT** *Ruffhouse 6595652*	47		

KROKUS Swiss group

Date	Title / Label	Peak Position	Weeks at No.1	Weeks in Top 40
16 May 81	**INDUSTRIAL STRENGTH (EP)** *Ariola ARO 258*	62		

KRS ONE US rapper

Date	Title / Label	Peak Position	Weeks at No.1	Weeks in Top 40
18 May 96	**RAPPAZ R N DAINJA** *Jive JIVECD 396*	47		
8 Feb 97	**WORD PERFECT** *Jive JIVECD 418*	70		
26 Apr 97	**STEP INTO A WORLD (RAPTURE'S DELIGHT)** *Jive JIVECD 411*	24		1
20 Sep 97	**HEARTBEAT/A FRIEND** *Jive JIVECD 431*	66		
1 Nov 97	**DIGITAL** *ffrr FCD 316* GOLDIE FEATURING KRS ONE	13		2

KRUSH UK trio

Date	Title / Label	Peak Position	Weeks at No.1	Weeks in Top 40
5 Dec 87	**HOUSE ARREST** *Club JAB 63* ● (silver)	3		10
14 Nov 92	**WALKING ON SUNSHINE** *Network NWK 55*	71		
16 Jan 93	**LET'S GET TOGETHER (SO GROOVY NOW)** *Perspective PERD 7416* KRUSH PERSPECTIVE	61		

KRUST UK group

Date	Title / Label	Peak Position	Weeks at No.1	Weeks in Top 40
23 Oct 99	**CODED LANGUAGE** *Talkin Loud TLCD 51* KRUST FEATURING SAUL WILLIAMS	66		
26 Jan 02	**SNAPPED IT** *Full Cycle FCY 034*	58		

KUBB UK group

Date	Title / Label	Peak Position	Weeks at No.1	Weeks in Top 40
3 Sep 05	**REMAIN** *Mercury 9873116*	45		
19 Nov 05	**WICKED SOUL** *Mercury 9874772*	25		2
18 Feb 06	**GROW** *Mercury 9876852*	18		2

KUJAY DADA UK production group

Date	Title / Label	Peak Position	Weeks at No.1	Weeks in Top 40
17 Jan 04	**YOUNG HEARTS** *Nebula NEBCD 057*	41		

KULA SHAKER UK group

Date	Title / Label	Peak Position	Weeks at No.1	Weeks in Top 40
4 May 96	**GRATEFUL WHEN YOU'RE DEAD – JERRY WAS THERE** *Columbia KULACD 2*	35		1
6 Jul 96	**TATTVA** *Columbia KULACD 3K*	4		5
7 Sep 96	**HEY DUDE** *Columbia KULACD 4*	2		4
23 Nov 96	**GOVINDA** *Columbia KULACD 5*	7		4
8 Mar 97	**HUSH** *Columbia KULACD 6* ● (silver)	2		6
2 May 98	**SOUND OF DRUMS** *Columbia KULA 21CD*	3		3
6 Mar 99	**MYSTICAL MACHINE GUN** *Columbia KULA 22CD*	14		2
15 May 99	**SHOWER YOUR LOVE** *Columbia KULA 23CD*	14		2

KULAY Filipino group

Date	Title / Label	Peak Position	Weeks at No.1	Weeks in Top 40
12 Sep 98	**DELICIOUS** *INCredible INCRL 4CD*	73		

KUMARA Dutch production duo

Date	Title / Label	Peak Position	Weeks at No.1	Weeks in Top 40
7 Oct 00	**SNAP YOUR FINGAZ** *Y2K 018CD*	70		

CHARLIE KUNZ US pianist

Date	Title / Label	Peak Position	Weeks at No.1	Weeks in Top 40
17 Dec 54	**PIANO MEDLEY NO. 114** *Decca F 10419*	16		4

KURSAAL FLYERS UK group

Date	Title / Label	Peak Position	Weeks at No.1	Weeks in Top 40
20 Nov 76	**LITTLE DOES SHE KNOW** *CBS 4689*	14		9

KURUPT US rapper

Date	Title / Label	Peak Position	Weeks at No.1	Weeks in Top 40
25 Aug 01	**WHERE I WANNA BE** *London LONCD 461* SHADE SHEIST FEATURING NATE DOGG & KURUPT	14		3
13 Oct 01	**IT'S OVER** *PIAS Recordings PIASB 024CDX*	21		2

KUT KLOSE US group

Date	Title / Label	Peak Position	Weeks at No.1	Weeks in Top 40
29 Apr 95	**I LIKE** *Elektra EKR 200CD*	72		

LI KWAN UK producer

Date	Title / Label	Peak Position	Weeks at No.1	Weeks in Top 40
17 Dec 94	**I NEED A MAN** *Deconstruction 74321252192*	51		

TALIB KWELI US singer

Date	Title	Peak Position	Weeks at No.1	Weeks in Top 40
18 Dec 04	**I TRY** *Island MCSTD40390* TALIB KWELI FEATURING MARY J BLIGE	59		

KWS UK production duo

Date	Title	Peak Position	Weeks at No.1	Weeks in Top 40
25 Apr 92	**PLEASE DON'T GO/GAME BOY** *Network NWK 46* ●	1	5	15
22 Aug 92	**ROCK YOUR BABY** *Network NWK 54*	8		5
12 Dec 92	**HOLD BACK THE NIGHT** *Network NWK 65* KWS FEATURES GUEST VOCAL FROM THE TRAMMPS	30		3
5 Jun 93	**CAN'T GET ENOUGH OF YOUR LOVE** *Network NWKCD 72*	71		
9 Apr 94	**IT SEEMS TO HANG ON** *X-clusive SCLU 006CD*	58		
2 Jul 94	**AIN'T NOBODY (LOVES ME BETTER)** *X-clusive XCLU 010CD* KWS & GWEN DICKEY	21		3
19 Nov 94	**THE MORE I GET THE MORE I WANT** *X-clusive XCLU 011CD* KWS FEATURING TEDDY PENDERGRASS	35		1

L

JONNY L UK singer

Date	Title	Peak Position	Weeks at No.1	Weeks in Top 40
28 Aug 93	**OOH I LIKE IT** *XL Recordings XLS 44CD*	73		
31 Oct 98	**20 DEGREES** *XL Recordings XLS 103CD*	66		

LA BELLE EPOQUE French group

Date	Title	Peak Position	Weeks at No.1	Weeks in Top 40
27 Aug 77	**BLACK IS BLACK** *Harvest HAR 5133* ●	2		13

LA BIONDA Italian group

Date	Title	Peak Position	Weeks at No.1	Weeks in Top 40
7 Oct 78	**ONE FOR YOU ONE FOR ME** *Philips 6198 227*	54		

LA BOUCHE US duo

Date	Title	Peak Position	Weeks at No.1	Weeks in Top 40
24 Sep 94	**SWEET DREAMS** *Bell 74321223912*	63		
15 Jul 95	**BE MY LOVER** *Arista 74321265402*	27		3
30 Sep 95	**FALLING IN LOVE** *Arista 74321305102*	43		
2 Mar 96	**BE MY LOVER** *Arista 74321339822*	25		2
7 Sep 96	**SWEET DREAMS** *Arista 74321398542*	44		

LA FLEUR Belgian group

Date	Title	Peak Position	Weeks at No.1	Weeks in Top 40
30 Jul 83	**BOOGIE NIGHTS** *Proto ENA 111*	51		

LA GANZ US group

Date	Title	Peak Position	Weeks at No.1	Weeks in Top 40
9 Nov 96	**LIKE A PLAYA** *Jive JIVECD 405*	75		

L.A. GUNS US group

Date	Title	Peak Position	Weeks at No.1	Weeks in Top 40
30 Nov 91	**SOME LIE 4 LOVE** *Mercury MER 358*	61		
21 Dec 91	**THE BALLAD OF JAYNE** *Mercury MER 361*	53		

L.A. MIX UK group

Date	Title	Peak Position	Weeks at No.1	Weeks in Top 40
10 Oct 87	**DON'T STOP (JAMMIN')** *Breakout USA 615*	47		
21 May 88	**CHECK THIS OUT** *Breakout USA 629*	6		6
8 Jul 89	**GET LOOSE** *Breakout USA 659* L.A. MIX PERFORMED BY JAZZI P	25		4
16 Sep 89	**LOVE TOGETHER** *Breakout USA 662* L.A. MIX FEATURING KEVIN HENRY	66		
15 Sep 90	**COMING BACK FOR MORE** *A&M AM 579*	50		
19 Jan 91	**MYSTERIES OF LOVE** *A&M AM 707*	46		
23 Mar 91	**WE SHOULDN'T HOLD HANDS IN THE DARK** *A&M AM 755*	69		

SAM LA MORE Australian producer

Date	Title	Peak Position	Weeks at No.1	Weeks in Top 40
5 Apr 03	**TAKIN' HOLD** *Underwater H20 023X*	70		

DANNY LA RUE Irish singer

Date	Title	Peak Position	Weeks at No.1	Weeks in Top 40
18 Dec 68	**ON MOTHER KELLY'S DOORSTEP** *Page One POF 108*	33		4

DENISE LA SALLE US singer

Date	Title	Peak Position	Weeks at No.1	Weeks in Top 40
15 Jun 85	**MY TOOT TOOT** *Epic A 6334*	6		9

LABELLE US group

Date	Title	Peak Position	Weeks at No.1	Weeks in Top 40
22 Mar 75	**LADY MARMALADE (VOULEZ-VOUS COUCHER AVEC MOI CE SOIR)** *Epic EPC 2852* ★	17		8

PATTI LABELLE US singer

Date	Title	Peak Position	Weeks at No.1	Weeks in Top 40
3 May 86	**ON MY OWN** *MCA 1045* PATTI LABELLE & MICHAEL McDONALD ● ★	2		11
2 Aug 86	**OH, PEOPLE** *MCA 1075*	26		4
3 Sep 94	**THE RIGHT KINDA LOVER** *MCA MCSTD 1995*	50		

NICK LACHEY US singer

Date	Title	Peak Position	Weeks at No.1	Weeks in Top 40
10 Feb 07	**WHAT'S LEFT OF ME** *Jive 82876848622*	47		

LACUNA COIL Italian group

Date	Title	Peak Position	Weeks at No.1	Weeks in Top 40
1 Apr 06	**OUR TRUTH** *Century Media 776598*	40		1
8 Jul 06	**ENJOY THE SILENCE** *Century Media 776618*	41		

LADIES CHOICE UK group

Date	Title	Peak Position	Weeks at No.1	Weeks in Top 40
25 Jan 86	**FUNKY SENSATION** *Sure Delight SD 01*	41		

LADIES FIRST UK trio

Date	Title	Peak Position	Weeks at No.1	Weeks in Top 40
24 Nov 01	**MESSIN'** *Polydor 5873422*	30		1
13 Apr 02	**I CAN'T WAIT** *Polydor 5706912*	19		3

LADY OF RAGE US rapper

Date	Title	Peak Position	Weeks at No.1	Weeks in Top 40
8 Oct 94	**AFRO PUFFS** *Interscope A 8288CD*	72		

LADY SAW Jamaican singer

Date	Title	Peak Position	Weeks at No.1	Weeks in Top 40
16 Dec 00	**BUMP N GRIND (I AM FEELING HOT TONIGHT)** *Telstar CDSTAS 3129* M DUBS FEATURING LADY SAW	59		
20 Oct 01	**SINCE I MET YOU LADY/SPARKLE OF MY EYES** *DEP International DEPD 55* UB40 FEATURING LADY SAW	40		1
12 Oct 02	**UNDERNEATH IT ALL** *Interscope 4977792* NO DOUBT FEATURING LADY SAW	18		3

LADY SOVEREIGN UK rapper

Date	Title	Peak Position	Weeks at No.1	Weeks in Top 40
26 Mar 05	**RANDOM** *Casual CDLOUPE15*	73		
20 Aug 05	**9 TO 5** *Island CIDX898*	33		1
3 Dec 05	**HOODIE** *Island/Uni-Island CIDX914*	44		
27 May 06	**NINE 2FIVE** *Polydor BUN105CD* ORDINARY BOYS FEATURING LADY SOVEREIGN	6		5
27 Jan 07	**LOVE ME OR HATE ME** *Island/Uni-Island 1722848*	26		2

LADYFUZZ UK/Australian group

Date	Title	Peak Position	Weeks at No.1	Weeks in Top 40
1 Apr 06	**BOUNCY BALL** *Transgressive TRANS024CD*	52		

LADYSMITH BLACK MAMBAZO South African group

Date	Title	Peak Position	Weeks at No.1	Weeks in Top 40
3 Jun 95	**SWING LOW SWEET CHARIOT** *Polygram TV SWLDW 2* LADYSMITH BLACK MAMBAZO FEATURING CHINA BLACK	15		5
3 Jun 95	**WORLD IN UNION '95** *Polygram TV RUGBY 2* LADYSMITH BLACK MAMBAZO FEATURING PJ POWERS	47		
15 Nov 97	**INKANYEZI NEZAZI (THE STAR AND THE WISEMAN)** *A&M 5823892*	33		1
11 Jul 98	**THE STAR AND THE WISEMAN** *AM:PM 5825692*	63		
16 Oct 99	**AIN'T NO SUNSHINE** *Universal Music TV 1564332* LADYSMITH BLACK MAMBAZO FEATURING DES'REE	42		
18 Dec 99	**I SHALL BE THERE** *Glow Worm 6683332* B*WITCHED FEATURING LADYSMITH BLACK MAMBAZO	13		5

LADYTRON UK group

Date	Title	Peak Position	Weeks at No.1	Weeks in Top 40
7 Dec 02	**SEVENTEEN** *Invicta Hi-Fi/Telstar CDSTAS 3284*	68		
22 Mar 03	**BLUE JEANS** *Invicta Hi-Fi/Telstar CDSTAS 3311*	43		
12 Jul 03	**EVIL** *Invicta Hi-Fi/Telstar CXSTAS 3331*	44		
2 Jul 05	**SUGAR** *Island CID896*	45		
1 Oct 05	**DESTROY EVERYTHING YOU TOUCH** *Island CIDX905*	42		

LAGUNA Spanish production duo

Date	Title	Peak Position	Weeks at No.1	Weeks in Top 40
1 Nov 97	**SPILLER FROM RIO (DO IT EASY)** *Positiva CDTIV 83*	40		1

LAHAYNA UK group

Date	Title	Peak Position	Weeks at No.1	Weeks in Top 40
24 Nov 07	**IN THE CITY** *Download*	33		1

LAID BACK Danish duo

Date	Title	Peak Position	Weeks at No.1	Weeks in Top 40
5 May 90	**BAKERMAN** *Arista 112356*	44		

CLEO LAINE UK singer

Date	Title	Peak Position	Weeks at No.1	Weeks in Top 40
29 Dec 60	**LET'S SLIP AWAY** *Fontana H 269*	42		
14 Sep 61	**YOU'LL ANSWER TO ME** *Fontana H 326*	5		13

FRANKIE LAINE US singer

Date	Title	Peak Position	Weeks at No.1	Weeks in Top 40
14 Nov 52	**HIGH NOON (DO NOT FORSAKE ME)** *Columbia DB 3113*	7		7
14 Nov 52	**SUGARBUSH** *Columbia DB 3123* DORIS DAY & FRANKIE LAINE	8		8
20 Mar 53	**GIRL IN THE WOOD** *Columbia DB 2907*	11		1
3 Apr 53	**I BELIEVE** *Philips PB 117*	1	18	36
4 Sep 53	**WHERE THE WINDS BLOW** *Philips PB 167*	2		12
8 May 53	**TELL ME A STORY** *Philips PB 126* FRANKIE LAINE & JIMMY BOYD	5		16
16 Oct 53	**HEY JOE** *Philips PB 172*	1	2	8
30 Oct 53	**ANSWER ME** *Philips PB 196*	1	8	17
8 Jan 54	**BLOWING WILD** *Philips PB 207*	2		12
26 Mar 54	**GRANADA** *Philips PB 242*	9		2
16 Apr 54	**THE KID'S LAST FIGHT** *Philips PB 258*	3		10
13 Aug 54	**MY FRIEND** *Philips PB 316*	3		15
8 Oct 54	**THERE MUST BE A REASON** *Philips PB 306*	9		9
22 Oct 54	**RAIN RAIN RAIN** *Philips PB 311* FRANKIE LAINE & THE FOUR LADS	8		16
11 Mar 55	**IN THE BEGINNING** *Philips PB 404*	20		1
24 Jun 55	**COOL WATER** *Philips PB 465* FRANKIE LAINE WITH THE MELLOMEN	2		22
15 Jul 55	**STRANGE LADY IN TOWN** *Philips PB 478*	6		13
11 Nov 55	**HUMMING BIRD** *Philips PB 498*	16		1
25 Nov 55	**HAWKEYE** *Philips PB 519*	7		8
20 Jan 56	**SIXTEEN TONS** *Philips PB 539* FRANKIE LAINE WITH THE MELLOMEN	10		3
4 May 56	**HELL HATH NO FURY** *Philips PB 585*	28		1
7 Sep 56	**A WOMAN IN LOVE** *Philips PB 617*	1	4	21
28 Dec 56	**MOONLIGHT GAMBLER** *Philips PB 638*	13		13
26 Apr 57	**LOVE IS A GOLDEN RING** *Philips PB 676*	19		5
4 Oct 57	**GOOD EVENING FRIENDS/UP ABOVE MY HEAD I HEAR MUSIC IN THE AIR** *Philips PB 708* FRANKIE LAINE & JOHNNIE RAY	25		4
13 Nov 59	**RAWHIDE** *Philips PB 965*	6		17
11 May 61	**GUNSLINGER** *Philips PB 1135*	50		

CHRIS LAKE UK producer

Date	Title	Peak Position	Weeks at No.1	Weeks in Top 40
30 Sep 06	**CHANGES** *Apollo APOLLO107CDX* CHRIS LAKE FEATURING LAURA V	27		3

GREG LAKE UK singer

Date	Title	Peak Position	Weeks at No.1	Weeks in Top 40
6 Dec 75	**I BELIEVE IN FATHER CHRISTMAS** *Manticore K 13511*	2		7
25 Dec 82	**I BELIEVE IN FATHER CHRISTMAS** *Manticore K 13511*	72		
24 Dec 83	**I BELIEVE IN FATHER CHRISTMAS** *Manticore K 13511*	65		

SETH LAKEMAN UK singer

Date	Title	Peak Position	Weeks at No.1	Weeks in Top 40
19 Aug 06	**LADY OF THE SEA (HEAR HER CALLING)** *Relentless RELCD28*	52		
4 Nov 06	**THE WHITE HARE** *Relentless RELCD29*	47		

LAMB UK duo

Date	Title	Peak Position	Weeks at No.1	Weeks in Top 40
29 Mar 97	**GORECKI** *Fontana LAMCD 4*	30		1
3 Apr 99	**B LINE** *Fontana LAMCD 5*	52		
22 May 99	**ALL IN YOUR HANDS** *Fontana LAMCD 6*	71		
27 Aug 83	**RIDERS ON THE STORM** *A&M AM 131* ANNABEL LAMB	27		4

LAMBCHOP US group

Date	Title	Peak Position	Weeks at No.1	Weeks in Top 40
20 May 00	**UP WITH THE PEOPLE** *City Slang 201592*	66		

LAMBRETTAS UK group

Date	Title	Peak Position	Weeks at No.1	Weeks in Top 40
1 Mar 80	**POISON IVY** *Rocket XPRESS 25*	7		8
24 May 80	**D-A-A-ANCE** *Rocket XPRESS 33*	12		6
23 Aug 80	**ANOTHER DAY (ANOTHER GIRL)** *Rocket XPRESS 36*	49		

RAY LAMONTAGNE US singer

Date	Title	Peak Position	Weeks at No.1	Weeks in Top 40
29 Jul 06	**TROUBLE** *14th Floor 14FLR15CD*	25		4

LAMPIES US group

Date	Title	Peak Position	Weeks at No.1	Weeks in Top 40
22 Dec 01	**LIGHT UP THE WORLD FOR CHRISTMAS** *Bluecrest LAMPCD 001*	48		

LANCASTRIANS UK group

Date	Title	Peak Position	Weeks at No.1	Weeks in Top 40
24 Dec 64	**WE'LL SING IN THE SUNSHINE** *Pye 7N 15732*	44		

MAJOR LANCE US singer

Date	Title	Peak Position	Weeks at No.1	Weeks in Top 40
13 Feb 64	**UM UM UM UM UM UM** *Columbia DB 7205*	40		1

LANDSCAPE UK group

Date	Title	Peak Position	Weeks at No.1	Weeks in Top 40
28 Feb 81	**EINSTEIN A GO-GO** *RCA 22*	5		10
23 May 81	**NORMAN BATES** *RCA 60*	40		1

RONNIE LANE & SLIM CHANCE UK group

Date	Title	Peak Position	Weeks at No.1	Weeks in Top 40
12 Jan 74	**HOW COME?** *GM GMS 011*	11		7
15 Jun 74	**THE POACHER** *GM GMS 024*	36		3

DON LANG UK singer

Date	Title	Peak Position	Weeks at No.1	Weeks in Top 40
4 Nov 55	**CLOUDBURST** *HMV POP 115* DON LANG & THE MAIRANTS-LANGHORN BIG SIX	16		4
5 Jul 57	**SCHOOL DAY (RING! RING! GOES THE BELL)** *HMV POP 350* DON LANG & HIS FRANTIC FIVE	26		2
23 May 58	**WITCH DOCTOR** *HMV POP 488* DON LANG & HIS FRANTIC FIVE	5		11
10 Mar 60	**SINK THE BISMARK** *HMV POP 714*	43		

k.d. lang Canadian singer

Date	Title	Peak Position	Weeks at No.1	Weeks in Top 40
16 May 92	**CONSTANT CRAVING** *Sire W0100*	52		
22 Aug 92	**CRYING** *Virgin America VUS 63* ROY ORBISON (DUET WITH k d lang)	13		4
27 Feb 93	**CONSTANT CRAVING** *Sire W0157CD*	15		5
1 May 93	**THE MIND OF LOVE** *Sire W0170CD1*	72		
26 Jun 93	**MISS CHATELAINE** *Sire W0181CDX*	68		
11 Dec 93	**JUST KEEP ME MOVING** *Sire W0227CD*	59		
30 Sep 95	**IF I WERE YOU** *Sire W0319CD*	53		
18 May 96	**YOU'RE OK** *Warner Brothers W0332CD*	44		

THOMAS LANG UK singer

Date	Title	Peak Position	Weeks at No.1	Weeks in Top 40
30 Jan 88	**THE HAPPY MAN** *Epic VOW 4*	67		

LANGE UK producer

Date	Title	Peak Position	Weeks at No.1	Weeks in Top 40
19 Jun 99	**I BELIEVE** *Addictive 12 ADD039* LANGE FEATURING SARAH DWYER	68		
19 Jan 02	**DRIFTING AWAY** *VC Recordings VCRD 101* LANGE FEATURING SKYE	9		4
22 Feb 03	**DON'T THINK IT (FEEL IT)** *Nebula NEBCD 037* LANGE FEATURING LEAH	59		

Silver-selling · Gold-selling · Platinum-selling · US No.1 ★ · Peak Position · Weeks at No.1 · Weeks in Top 40

LANTERNS UK trio

Date	Title	Label	Peak	Wks No.1	Wks Top 40
6 Feb 99	HIGHRISE TOWN	Columbia 6665712	50		

MARIO LANZA US tenor

Date	Title	Label	Peak	Wks No.1	Wks Top 40
14 Nov 52	BECAUSE YOU'RE MINE	HMV DA 2017	3		24
4 Feb 55	DRINKING SONG	HMV DA 2065	13		1
18 Feb 55	I'LL WALK WITH GOD	HMV DA 2062	18		2
22 Apr 55	SERENADE	HMV DA 2065	15		3
14 Sep 56	SERENADE	HMV DA 2085	25		2

LAPTOP US singer

Date	Title	Label	Peak	Wks No.1	Wks Top 40
12 Jun 99	NOTHING TO DECLARE	Island CID 744	74		

YVES LAROCK Swiss producer

Date	Title	Label	Peak	Wks No.1	Wks Top 40
4 Aug 07	RISE UP	Data DATA159CDS	13		6

JULIUS LAROSA US singer

Date	Title	Label	Peak	Wks No.1	Wks Top 40
4 Jul 58	TORERO	RCA 1063	15		9

LARRIKIN LOVE UK group

Date	Title	Label	Peak	Wks No.1	Wks Top 40
15 Apr 06	EDWOULD	Infectious WEA403CD	49		
8 Jul 06	DOWNING STREET KINDLING	Infectious WEA409CD	35		1
23 Sep 06	HAPPY AS ANNIE	Infectious WEA412CD	32		1
3 Feb 07	A DAY IN THE LIFE	Infectious WEA415CD	31		1

LA'S UK group

Date	Title	Label	Peak	Wks No.1	Wks Top 40
14 Jan 89	THERE SHE GOES	Go! Discs GOLAS 2	59		
15 Sep 90	TIMELESS MELODY	Go! Discs GOLAS 4	57		
3 Nov 90	THERE SHE GOES	Go! Discs GOLAS 5	13		6
16 Feb 91	FEELIN'	Go! Discs GOLAS 6	43		
10 May 97	FEVER PITCH THE EP — PRETENDERS, LA'S, ORLANDO, NICK HORNBY	Blanco Y Negro NEG 104CD	65		
2 Oct 99	THERE SHE GOES	Polydor 5614032	65		

LAS KETCHUP Spanish group

Date	Title	Label	Peak	Wks No.1	Wks Top 40
21 Sep 02	KETCHUP SONG (ASEREJE) (IMPORT)	Columbia 9729602CD	49		
19 Oct 02	THE KETCHUP SONG (ASEREJE)	Columbia 6731932	1	1	18

LASGO Belgian production group

Date	Title	Label	Peak	Wks No.1	Wks Top 40
9 Mar 02	SOMETHING	Positiva CDTIV 169	4		12
24 Aug 02	ALONE	Positiva CDTIV 176	7		4
30 Nov 02	PRAY	Positiva CDTIVS 182	17		3
1 May 04	SURRENDER	Positiva CDTIVS 205	24		2

LISA LASHES UK producer

Date	Title	Label	Peak	Wks No.1	Wks Top 40
8 Jul 00	UNBELIEVABLE	Tidy Trax TIDY 138CD	63		
25 Oct 03	WHAT CAN YOU DO 4 ME?	Tidy Trax TIDY 194C	52		

JAMES LAST BAND German orchestra leader

Date	Title	Label	Peak	Wks No.1	Wks Top 40
3 May 80	THE SEDUCTION (LOVE THEME)	Polydor PD 2071	48		

LAST RHYTHM Italian production group

Date	Title	Label	Peak	Wks No.1	Wks Top 40
14 Sep 96	LAST RHYTHM	Stress CDSTR 76	62		

LATE SHOW UK group

Date	Title	Label	Peak	Wks No.1	Wks Top 40
3 Mar 79	BRISTOL STOMP	Decca F 13822	40		1

LATIN QUARTER UK group

Date	Title	Label	Peak	Wks No.1	Wks Top 40
18 Jan 86	RADIO AFRICA	Rockin' Horse RH 102	19		5
18 Apr 87	NOMZAMO (ONE PEOPLE ONE CAUSE)	Rockin' Horse RH 113	73		

LATIN THING Canadian/Spanish group

Date	Title	Label	Peak	Wks No.1	Wks Top 40
13 Jul 96	LATIN THING	Faze 2 CDFAZE 33	41		

GINO LATINO Italian producer

Date	Title	Label	Peak	Wks No.1	Wks Top 40
20 Jan 90	WELCOME	ffrr F 126	17		6

LaTOUR US singer/producer

Date	Title	Label	Peak	Wks No.1	Wks Top 40
8 Jun 91	PEOPLE ARE STILL HAVING SEX	Polydor PO 147	15		5

STACY LATTISHAW US singer

Date	Title	Label	Peak	Wks No.1	Wks Top 40
14 Jun 80	JUMP TO THE BEAT	Cotillion K 11496	3		9
30 Aug 80	DYNAMITE	Atlantic K 11554	51		

CYNDI LAUPER US singer

Date	Title	Label	Peak	Wks No.1	Wks Top 40
14 Jan 84	GIRLS JUST WANT TO HAVE FUN	Portrait A 3943	2		9
24 Mar 84	TIME AFTER TIME	Portrait A 4290 ★	54		
16 Jun 84	TIME AFTER TIME	Portrait A 4290	3		10
1 Sep 84	SHE BOP	Portrait A 4620	46		
17 Nov 84	ALL THROUGH THE NIGHT	Portrait A 4849	64		
20 Sep 86	TRUE COLORS	Portrait 65000267 ★	12		9
27 Dec 86	CHANGE OF HEART	Portrait CYNDI 1	67		
28 Mar 87	WHAT'S GOING ON	Portrait CYN 1	57		
20 May 89	I DROVE ALL NIGHT	Epic CYN 4	7		9
5 Aug 89	MY FIRST NIGHT WITHOUT YOU	Epic CYN 5	53		
30 Dec 89	HEADING WEST	Epic CYN 6	68		
6 Jun 92	THE WORLD IS STONE	Epic 6579707	15		5
13 Nov 93	THAT'S WHAT I THINK	Epic 6598782	31		2
8 Jan 94	WHO LET IN THE RAIN	Epic 6590392	32		2
17 Sep 94	HEY NOW (GIRLS JUST WANT TO HAVE FUN)	Epic 6608072	4		11
11 Feb 95	I'M GONNA BE STRONG	Epic 6611962	37		1
26 Aug 95	COME ON HOME	Epic 6614255	39		1
1 Feb 97	YOU DON'T KNOW	Epic 6641845	27		1

LAURA Swedish group

Date	Title	Label	Peak	Wks No.1	Wks Top 40
5 May 07	RELEASE ME	Download	47		

LAUREL & HARDY UK/US comedians

Date	Title	Label	Peak	Wks No.1	Wks Top 40
22 Nov 75	THE TRAIL OF THE LONESOME PINE — LAUREL & HARDY WITH THE AVALON BOYS FEATURING CHILL WILLS	United Artists UP 36026	2		9

LAUREL & HARDY UK duo

Date	Title	Label	Peak	Wks No.1	Wks Top 40
2 Apr 83	CLUNK CLICK	CBS A 3213	65		

LAURNEA US singer

Date	Title	Label	Peak	Wks No.1	Wks Top 40
12 Jul 97	DAYS OF YOUTH	Epic 6646932	36		1

AVRIL LAVIGNE Canadian singer

Date	Title	Label	Peak	Wks No.1	Wks Top 40
7 Sep 02	COMPLICATED (IMPORT)	RCA 74321955782	64		
5 Oct 02	COMPLICATED	RCA 74321965962	3		8
28 Dec 02	SK8ER BOI	RCA 74321979782	8		8
12 Apr 03	I'M WITH YOU	Arista 82876506712	7		7
19 Jul 03	LOSING GRIP	Arista 82876534542	22		1
22 May 04	DON'T TELL ME	Arista 82876617322	5		5
14 Aug 04	MY HAPPY ENDING	Arista 82876636492	5		6
27 Nov 04	NOBODY'S HOME	Arista 82876663652	24		2
9 Apr 05	HE WASN'T	Arista 82876683052	23		1
10 Mar 07	GIRLFRIEND	Arista 88697073522 ★	2		13
23 Jun 07	WHEN YOU'RE GONE	RCA 88697119262	3		12
27 Oct 07	HOT	RCA 88697170362	30		2

JOANNA LAW UK singer

Date	Title	Label	Peak	Wks No.1	Wks Top 40
7 Jul 90	FIRST TIME EVER	Citybeat CBE 752	67		
14 Sep 96	THE GIFT — WAY OUT WEST/MISS JOANNA LAW	Deconstruction 74321401912	15		3

STEVE LAWLER UK producer

Date	Title / Label	Peak Position	Weeks at No.1	Weeks in Top 40
11 Nov 00	**RISE 'IN** *Bedrock BEDRCDS 008*	50		

LAWRENCE BELLE UK singer

Date	Title / Label	Peak Position	Weeks at No.1	Weeks in Top 40
30 Mar 02	**EVERGREEN** *Euphoric CDUPH 024*	73		

JOEY LAWRENCE US singer

Date	Title / Label	Peak Position	Weeks at No.1	Weeks in Top 40
26 Jun 93	**NOTHIN' MY LOVE CAN'T FIX** *EMI CDEM 271*	13		5
28 Aug 93	**I CAN'T HELP MYSELF** *EMI CDEM 277*	27		3
30 Oct 93	**STAY FOREVER** *EMI CDEM 289*	41		
19 Sep 98	**NEVER GONNA CHANGE MY MIND** *Curb CUBC 34*	49		

LEE LAWRENCE UK singer

Date	Title / Label	Peak Position	Weeks at No.1	Weeks in Top 40
20 Nov 53	**CRYING IN THE CHAPEL** *Decca F 10177*			
	LEE LAWRENCE WITH RAY MARTIN & HIS ORCHESTRA	7		6
2 Dec 55	**SUDDENLY THERE'S A VALLEY** *Columbia DB 3681*			
	LEE LAWRENCE WITH RAY MARTIN & HIS ORCHESTRA	14		4

SOPHIE LAWRENCE UK singer/actress

Date	Title / Label	Peak Position	Weeks at No.1	Weeks in Top 40
3 Aug 91	**LOVE'S UNKIND** *IQ ZB 44821*	21		4

STEVE LAWRENCE US singer

Date	Title / Label	Peak Position	Weeks at No.1	Weeks in Top 40
21 Apr 60	**FOOTSTEPS** *HMV POP 726*	4		13
18 Aug 60	**GIRLS GIRLS GIRLS** *London HLT 9166*	49		
22 Aug 63	**I WANT TO STAY HERE** *CBS AAG 163*			
	STEVE (Lawrence) & EYDIE (Gorme)	3		11

MARIA LAWSON UK singer

Date	Title / Label	Peak Position	Weeks at No.1	Weeks in Top 40
26 Aug 06	**SLEEPWALKING** *Phonogenic 82876885032*	20		2

LAYO & BUSHWACKA UK group

Date	Title / Label	Peak Position	Weeks at No.1	Weeks in Top 40
22 Jun 02	**LOVE STORY** *XL Recordings XLS 144CD*	30		1
25 Jan 03	**LOVE STORY (VS FINALLY)** *XL Recordings XLS 154CD*	8		5
16 Aug 03	**IT'S UP TO YOU (SHINING THROUGH)** *XL Recordings XLS 163CD*	25		1

LINDY LAYTON UK singer

Date	Title / Label	Peak Position	Weeks at No.1	Weeks in Top 40
10 Feb 90	**DUB BE GOOD TO ME** *Go! Beat GOD 39*			
	BEATS INTERNATIONAL FEATURING LINDY LAYTON ●	1	4	12
11 Aug 90	**SILLY GAMES** *Arista 113452*			
	LINDY LAYTON FEATURING JANET KAY	22		5
26 Jan 91	**ECHO MY HEART** *Arista 113845*	42		
31 Aug 91	**WITHOUT YOU (ONE AND ONE)** *Arista 114636*	71		
24 Apr 93	**WE GOT THE LOVE** *PWL International PWCD 250*	38		2
30 Oct 93	**SHOW ME** *PWL International PWCD 275*	47		

PETER LAZONBY UK producer

Date	Title / Label	Peak Position	Weeks at No.1	Weeks in Top 40
10 Jun 00	**SACRED CYCLES** *Hooj Choons HOOJ 93CD*	49		

DOUG LAZY US rapper/producer

Date	Title / Label	Peak Position	Weeks at No.1	Weeks in Top 40
15 Jul 89	**LET IT ROLL** *Atlantic A 8866*			
	RAZE PRESENTS DOUG LAZY	27		2
4 Nov 89	**LET THE RHYTHM PUMP** *Atlantic A 8784*	45		
26 May 90	**LET THE RHYTHM PUMP (REMIX)** *East West A 7919*	63		

LAZY-B Danish singer

Date	Title / Label	Peak Position	Weeks at No.1	Weeks in Top 40
26 Aug 06	**UNDERWEAR GOES INSIDE THE PANTS** *Universal TV 9878961*	30		2

LAZY TOWN Icelandic group

Date	Title / Label	Peak Position	Weeks at No.1	Weeks in Top 40
16 Dec 06	**BING BANG (TIME TO DANCE)** *GTV CDGTV01*	4		4

LCD UK production group

Date	Title / Label	Peak Position	Weeks at No.1	Weeks in Top 40
27 Jun 98	**ZORBA'S DANCE** *Virgin VSCDT 1693*	20		4
9 Oct 99	**ZORBA'S DANCE** *Virgin VSCDT 1757*	22		3

LCD SOUNDSYSTEM US production duo

Date	Title / Label	Peak Position	Weeks at No.1	Weeks in Top 40
20 Nov 04	**MOVEMENT** *EMI DFAEMI2141CD*	52		
12 Mar 05	**DAFT PUNK IS PLAYING AT MY HOUSE** *DFA/EMI DFAEMI2143CD*	29		1
18 Jun 05	**DISCO INFILTRATOR** *DFA/EMI DFAEMI2145CD*	49		
8 Oct 05	**TRIBULATIONS** *DFA/EMI DFAEMI2151CD*	59		
17 Mar 07	**NORTH AMERICAN SCUM** *DFA/EMI DFAEMI2165CD*	40		1
9 Jun 07	**ALL MY FRIENDS** *DFA/EMI DFAEMI2169CD*	41		

LE CLICK US group

Date	Title / Label	Peak Position	Weeks at No.1	Weeks in Top 40
30 Aug 97	**CALL ME** *Logic 74321509672*	38		1

FEDDE LE GRANDE Dutch producer

Date	Title / Label	Peak Position	Weeks at No.1	Weeks in Top 40
9 Sep 06	**PUT YOUR HANDS UP FOR DETROIT** *Data DATA140CDX*	53		
4 Nov 06	**PUT YOUR HANDS UP FOR DETROIT** *Data DATA140CDS*	1	1	16
10 Mar 07	**THE CREEPS** *Data DATA155CDS*			
	CAMILLE JONES & FEDDE LE GRANDE	7		9
29 Sep 07	**LET ME THINK ABOUT IT** *Data DATA170CDS*			
	IDA CORR & FEDDE LE GRANDE	2		10

KELE LE ROC UK singer

Date	Title / Label	Peak Position	Weeks at No.1	Weeks in Top 40
31 Oct 98	**LITTLE BIT OF LOVIN'** *1st Avenue 5672812*	8		5
27 Mar 99	**MY LOVE** *1st Avenue 5636112*	8		4
30 Sep 00	**THINKING OF YOU** *Telstar CDSTAS 3136*			
	CURTIS LYNCH JR FEATURING KELE LE ROCK & RED RAT	70		
7 Jun 03	**FEELIN' U** *London FCD 409*			
	SHY FX & T-POWER FEATURING KELE LE ROC	34		1

DAN LE SAC VS SCROOBIUS PIP UK duo

Date	Title / Label	Peak Position	Weeks at No.1	Weeks in Top 40
14 Apr 07	**THOU SHALT ALWAYS KILL** *Download*	34		1

LE TIGRE US group

Date	Title / Label	Peak Position	Weeks at No.1	Weeks in Top 40
15 Jan 05	**TKO** *Universal MCSTD40398*	50		
7 May 05	**AFTER DARK** *Universal MCSTD40411*	63		

JOE LEAN & THE JING JANG JONG UK group

Date	Title / Label	Peak Position	Weeks at No.1	Weeks in Top 40
22 Mar 08	**LONELY BUOY** *Vertigo 1758362*	43		

VICKY LEANDROS Greek singer

Date	Title / Label	Peak Position	Weeks at No.1	Weeks in Top 40
8 Apr 72	**COME WHAT MAY** *Philips 6000 049*	2		15
23 Dec 72	**THE LOVE IN YOUR EYES** *Philips 6000 081*	40		1
7 Jul 73	**WHEN BOUZOUKIS PLAYED** *Philips 6000 111*	44		

DENIS LEARY US comedian

Date	Title / Label	Peak Position	Weeks at No.1	Weeks in Top 40
13 Jan 96	**ASSHOLE** *A&M 5813352*	58		

LEAVES Icelandic group

Date	Title / Label	Peak Position	Weeks at No.1	Weeks in Top 40
18 May 02	**RACE** *B Unique BUN 020CDS*	66		

LED ZEPPELIN UK group

Date	Title / Label	Peak Position	Weeks at No.1	Weeks in Top 40
13 Sep 97	**WHOLE LOTTA LOVE** *Atlantic AT 0013CD*	21		1
24 Nov 07	**STAIRWAY TO HEAVEN** *Download*	37		2
24 Nov 07	**WHOLE LOTTA LOVE** *Download*	64		

ANGEL LEE UK singer

Date	Title / Label	Peak Position	Weeks at No.1	Weeks in Top 40
3 Jun 00	**WHAT'S YOUR NAME?** *WEA 258CD1*	39		1

ANN LEE UK singer

Date	Title / Label	Peak Position	Weeks at No.1	Weeks in Top 40
11 Sep 99	**2 TIMES (IMPORT)** *ZYX 90188*	57		
16 Oct 99	**2 TIMES** *Systematic SYSX 31* ●	2		9
4 Mar 00	**VOICES** *Systematic SYSCD 32*	27		1

Silver-selling ● Gold-selling ● Platinum-selling ● US No.1 ★ — Peak Position · Weeks at No.1 · Weeks in Top 40

BRENDA LEE US singer

Date	Title / Label	Peak Position	Weeks at No.1	Weeks in Top 40
17 Mar 60	**SWEET NOTHIN'S** *Brunswick 05819*	4		18
30 Jun 60	**I'M SORRY** *Brunswick 05833* ★	12		14
20 Oct 60	**I WANT TO BE WANTED** *Brunswick 05839* ★	31		2
19 Jan 61	**LET'S JUMP THE BROOMSTICK** *Brunswick 05823*	12		12
6 Apr 61	**EMOTIONS** *Brunswick 05847*	45		
20 Jul 61	**DUM DUM** *Brunswick 05854*	22		7
16 Nov 61	**FOOL NUMBER ONE** *Brunswick 05860*	38		1
8 Feb 62	**BREAK IT TO ME GENTLY** *Brunswick 05864*	46		
5 Apr 62	**SPEAK TO ME PRETTY** *Brunswick 05867*	3		11
21 Jun 62	**HERE COMES THAT FEELING** *Brunswick 05871*	5		11
13 Sep 62	**IT STARTED ALL OVER AGAIN** *Brunswick 05876*	15		8
29 Nov 62	**ROCKIN' AROUND THE CHRISTMAS TREE** *Brunswick 05880*	6		7
17 Jan 63	**ALL ALONE AM I** *Brunswick 05882*	7		14
28 Mar 63	**LOSING YOU** *Brunswick 05886*	10		13
18 Jul 63	**I WONDER** *Brunswick 05891*	14		8
31 Oct 63	**SWEET IMPOSSIBLE YOU** *Brunswick 05896*	28		5
9 Jan 64	**AS USUAL** *Brunswick 05899*	5		14
9 Apr 64	**THINK** *Brunswick 05903*	26		5
10 Sep 64	**IS IT TRUE** *Brunswick 05915*	17		8
10 Dec 64	**CHRISTMAS WILL BE JUST ANOTHER LONELY DAY** *Brunswick 05921*	25		3
4 Feb 65	**THANKS A LOT** *Brunswick 05927*	41		
29 Jul 65	**TOO MANY RIVERS** *Brunswick 05936*	22		9

CURTIS LEE US singer

Date	Title / Label	Peak Position	Weeks at No.1	Weeks in Top 40
31 Aug 61	**PRETTY LITTLE ANGEL EYES** *London HLX 9397*	47		

DEE C. LEE UK singer

Date	Title / Label	Peak Position	Weeks at No.1	Weeks in Top 40
9 Nov 85	**SEE THE DAY** *CBS A 6570* ●	3		10
8 Mar 86	**COME HELL OR WATERS HIGH** *CBS A 6869*	46		
13 Nov 93	**NO TIME TO PLAY** *Cooltempo CDCOOL 282* GURU FEATURING DEE C LEE	25		2

GARRY LEE & SHOWDOWN Canadian group

Date	Title / Label	Peak Position	Weeks at No.1	Weeks in Top 40
31 Jul 93	**THE RODEO SONG** *Party Dish VCD 101*	44		

LEAPY LEE UK singer

Date	Title / Label	Peak Position	Weeks at No.1	Weeks in Top 40
21 Aug 68	**LITTLE ARROWS** *MCA MU 1028*	2		17
20 Dec 69	**GOOD MORNING** *MCA MK 5021*	29		4

PEGGY LEE US singer

Date	Title / Label	Peak Position	Weeks at No.1	Weeks in Top 40
24 May 57	**MR WONDERFUL** *Brunswick 05671*	5		13
15 Aug 58	**FEVER** *Capitol CL 14902*	5		11
23 Mar 61	**TILL THERE WAS YOU** *Capitol CL 15184*	30		3
22 Aug 92	**FEVER** *Capitol PEG 1*	75		

TONEY LEE US singer

Date	Title / Label	Peak Position	Weeks at No.1	Weeks in Top 40
29 Jan 83	**REACH UP** *TMT 2*	64		

TRACEY LEE US rapper

Date	Title / Label	Peak Position	Weeks at No.1	Weeks in Top 40
19 Jul 97	**THE THEME** *Universal UND 56133*	51		

LEE-CABRERA US duo

Date	Title / Label	Peak Position	Weeks at No.1	Weeks in Top 40
12 Apr 03	**SHAKE IT (NO TE MUEVAS TANTO)** *Credence 12CRED 035*	58		
6 Sep 03	**SHAKE IT (MOVE A LITTLE CLOSER)** *Credence CDCRED 039* LEE CABRERA FEATURING ALEX CARTANA	16		3
15 Nov 03	**SPECIAL 2003** *Credence CDCRED 040*	45		
10 Jul 04	**VOODOO LOVE** *C2 CDC2001*	58		

LEEDS UNITED F.C. UK football club

Date	Title / Label	Peak Position	Weeks at No.1	Weeks in Top 40
29 Apr 72	**LEEDS UNITED** *Chapter One SCH 168*	10		8
25 Apr 92	**LEEDS LEEDS LEEDS** *Q Music LUFC 2*	54		

RAYMOND LEFEVRE French orchestra leader

Date	Title / Label	Peak Position	Weeks at No.1	Weeks in Top 40
15 May 68	**SOUL COAXING** *Major Minor MM 559*	46		

LEFTFIELD UK production duo

Date	Title / Label	Peak Position	Weeks at No.1	Weeks in Top 40
12 Dec 92	**SONG OF LIFE** *Hard Hands HAND 002T*	59		
13 Nov 93	**OPEN UP** *Hard Hands HAND 009CD* LEFTFIELD LYDON	13		3
25 Mar 95	**ORIGINAL** *Hard Hands HAND 18CD* LEFTFIELD FEATURING TONI HALLIDAY	18		2
5 Aug 95	**THE AFRO-LEFT EP** *Hard Hands HAND 23CD* LEFTFIELD FEATURING DJUM DJUM	22		1
20 Jan 96	**RELEASE THE PRESSURE** *Hard Hands HAND 29CD*	13		2
18 Sep 99	**AFRIKA SHOX** *Hard Hands HAND 057CD1* LEFTFIELD/BAMBAATAA	7		3
11 Dec 99	**DUSTED** *Hard Hands HAND 058CD1* LEFTFIELD/ROOTS MANUVA	28		1

JOHN LEGEND US singer/pianist

Date	Title / Label	Peak Position	Weeks at No.1	Weeks in Top 40
26 Mar 05	**USED TO LOVE U** *Columbia 6758022*	29		1
18 Jun 05	**ORDINARY PEOPLE** *Columbia 6759642*	27		5
3 Sep 05	**NUMBER ONE** *Columbia 82876724532*	62		

LEGEND B German production duo

Date	Title / Label	Peak Position	Weeks at No.1	Weeks in Top 40
22 Feb 97	**LOST IN LOVE** *Perfecto PERF 132CD*	45		

JODY LEI South African singer

Date	Title / Label	Peak Position	Weeks at No.1	Weeks in Top 40
22 Feb 03	**SHOWDOWN** *Independiente ISOM 66SMS*	34		1

LEILANI UK singer

Date	Title / Label	Peak Position	Weeks at No.1	Weeks in Top 40
6 Feb 99	**MADNESS THING** *ZTT 124CD*	19		3
12 Jun 99	**DO YOU WANT ME?** *ZTT 134CD*	40		1
3 Jun 00	**FLYING ELVIS** *ZTT 145CD*	73		

PAUL LEKAKIS US singer

Date	Title / Label	Peak Position	Weeks at No.1	Weeks in Top 40
30 May 87	**BOOM BOOM (LET'S GO BACK TO MY ROOM)** *Champion CHAMP 43*	60		

LEMAR UK singer

Date	Title / Label	Peak Position	Weeks at No.1	Weeks in Top 40
30 Aug 03	**DANCE (WITH U)** *Sony Music 6741322*	2		8
29 Nov 03	**50:50/LULLABY** *Sony Music 6744185*	5		6
6 Mar 04	**ANOTHER DAY** *Sony Music 6746595*	9		4
27 Nov 04	**IF THERE'S ANY JUSTICE** *Sony Music 6756072*	3		13
9 Apr 05	**TIME TO GROW** *Sony Music 6758122*	9		7
13 Aug 05	**DON'T GIVE IT UP** *Sony Music 6760452*	21		2
9 Sep 06	**IT'S NOT THAT EASY** *White Rabbit 82876894632*	7		7
25 Nov 06	**SOMEONE SHOULD TELL YOU** *White Rabbit 88697008982*	21		2
31 Mar 07	**TICK TOCK** *White Rabbit 88697076622*	45		

LEMON JELLY UK production duo

Date	Title / Label	Peak Position	Weeks at No.1	Weeks in Top 40
19 Oct 02	**SPACE WALK** *Impotent Fury/XL Recordings IFXLS 150CD*	36		1
1 Feb 03	**NICE WEATHER FOR DUCKS** *Impotent Fury/XL Recordings IFXL 156CD*	16		2
4 Dec 04	**STAY WITH YOU** *XL Recordings IFXLS201CD*	31		1
5 Feb 05	**THE SHOUTY TRACK** *XL Recordings IFXLS205CD1*	21		1
23 Jul 05	**MAKE THINGS RIGHT** *XL Recordings IFXLS211CD*	33		1

LEMON PIPERS US group

Date	Title / Label	Peak Position	Weeks at No.1	Weeks in Top 40
7 Feb 68	**GREEN TAMBOURINE** *Pye International 7N 25444* ★	7		10
1 May 68	**RICE IS NICE** *Pye International 7N 25454*	41		

LEMON TREES UK group

Date	Title / Label	Peak Position	Weeks at No.1	Weeks in Top 40
26 Sep 92	**LOVE IS IN YOUR EYES** *Oxygen GASP 1*	75		
7 Nov 92	**THE WAY I FEEL** *Oxygen GASP 2*	62		
13 Feb 93	**LET IT LOOSE** *Oxygen GASPD 3*	55		
17 Apr 93	**CHILD OF LOVE** *Oxygen GASPD 4*	55		
3 Jul 93	**I CAN'T FACE THE WORLD** *Oxygen GASPD 6*	52		

LEMONESCENT UK group

Date	Title / Label	Peak Position	Weeks at No.1	Weeks in Top 40
29 Jun 02	**BEAUTIFUL** *Supertone SUPTCD 1*	70		
9 Nov 02	**SWING MY HIPS (SEX DANCE)** *Supertone SUPTCD 2*	48		
5 Apr 03	**HELP ME MAMA** *Supertone SUPTCD 4*	36		1

Silver-selling ○ Gold-selling ● Platinum-selling ✪ US No.1 ★ — Peak Position · Weeks at No.1 · Weeks in Top 40

Date	Title	Peak Position	Weeks at No.1	Weeks in Top 40
21 Jun 03	**CINDERELLA** *Supertone SUPTCD 8*	31		1
3 Jul 04	**ALL RIGHT NOW** *Supertone SUPTCD 12*	37		1

LEMONHEADS US group

Date	Title	Peak Position	Weeks at No.1	Weeks in Top 40
17 Oct 92	**IT'S A SHAME ABOUT RAY** *Atlantic A 7423*	70		
5 Dec 92	**MRS ROBINSON/BEIN' AROUND** *Atlantic A 7401*	19		7
6 Feb 93	**CONFETTI/MY DRUG BUDDY** *Atlantic A 7430CD*	44		
10 Apr 93	**IT'S A SHAME ABOUT RAY** *Atlantic A 5764CD*	31		2
16 Oct 93	**INTO YOUR ARMS** *Atlantic A 7302CD*	14		2
27 Nov 93	**IT'S ABOUT TIME** *Atlantic A 7296CD*	57		
14 May 94	**BIG GAY HEART** *Atlantic A 7259CD*	55		
28 Sep 96	**IF I COULD TALK I'D TELL YOU** *Atlantic A 5661CD1*	39		1
14 Dec 96	**IT'S ALL TRUE** *Atlantic A 5635CD*	61		

LEN Canadian group

Date	Title	Peak Position	Weeks at No.1	Weeks in Top 40
18 Dec 99	**STEAL MY SUNSHINE** *Columbia 6685062*	8		11
10 Jun 00	**CRYPTIK SOULS CREW** *Columbia 6693832*	28		1

JOHN LENNON UK singer/guitarist

Date	Title	Peak Position	Weeks at No.1	Weeks in Top 40
9 Jul 69	**GIVE PEACE A CHANCE** *Apple 13* PLASTIC ONO BAND	2		10
1 Nov 69	**COLD TURKEY** *Apple APPLES 1001* PLASTIC ONO BAND	14		8
21 Feb 70	**INSTANT KARMA** *Apple APPLES 1003* LENNON, ONO & THE PLASTIC ONO BAND	5		8
20 Mar 71	**POWER TO THE PEOPLE** *Apple R 5892* JOHN LENNON & THE PLASTIC ONO BAND	7		8
9 Dec 72	**HAPPY XMAS (WAR IS OVER)** *Apple R 5970* JOHN & YOKO & THE PLASTIC ONO BAND WITH THE HARLEM COMMUNITY CHOIR	4		7
24 Nov 73	**MIND GAMES** *Apple R 5994*	26		8
19 Oct 74	**WHATEVER GETS YOU THRU' THE NIGHT** *Apple R 5998* JOHN LENNON WITH THE PLASTIC ONO NUCLEAR BAND ★	36		1
4 Jan 75	**HAPPY XMAS (WAR IS OVER)** *Apple R 5970* JOHN & YOKO & THE PLASTIC ONO BAND WITH THE HARLEM COMMUNITY CHOIR	48		
8 Feb 75	**#9 DREAM** *Apple R 6003*	23		6
3 May 75	**STAND BY ME** *Apple R 6005*	30		5
1 Nov 75	**IMAGINE** *Apple R 6009* ○	6		10
8 Nov 80	**(JUST LIKE) STARTING OVER** *Geffen K 79186* ● ★	1	1	13
20 Dec 80	**HAPPY XMAS (WAR IS OVER)** *Apple R 5970* JOHN & YOKO & THE PLASTIC ONO BAND WITH THE HARLEM COMMUNITY CHOIR	2		6
27 Dec 80	**IMAGINE** *Apple R 6009* ○	1	4	11
24 Jan 81	**WOMAN** *Geffen K 79195* ○	1	2	9
24 Jan 81	**GIVE PEACE A CHANCE** *Apple 13* PLASTIC ONO BAND	33		2
21 Mar 81	**I SAW HER STANDING THERE** *DJM DJS 10965* ELTON JOHN BAND FEATURING JOHN LENNON & THE MUSCLE SHOALS HORNS	40		1
4 Apr 81	**WATCHING THE WHEELS** *Geffen K 79207*	30		3
19 Dec 81	**HAPPY XMAS (WAR IS OVER)** *Apple R 5970* JOHN & YOKO & THE PLASTIC ONO BAND WITH THE HARLEM COMMUNITY CHOIR	28		3
20 Nov 82	**LOVE** *Parlophone R 6059*	41		
25 Dec 82	**HAPPY XMAS (WAR IS OVER)** *Apple R 5970* JOHN & YOKO & THE PLASTIC ONO BAND WITH THE HARLEM COMMUNITY CHOIR	56		
21 Jan 84	**NOBODY TOLD ME** *Ono Music/Polydor POSP 700*	6		4
17 Mar 84	**BORROWED TIME** *Polydor POSP 701*	32		3
30 Nov 85	**JEALOUS GUY** *Parlophone R 6117*	65		
10 Dec 88	**IMAGINE/JEALOUS GUY/HAPPY XMAS (WAR IS OVER)** *Parlophone R 6199*	45		
25 Dec 99	**IMAGINE** *Parlophone CDR 6534* ●	3		6
20 Dec 03	**HAPPY XMAS (WAR IS OVER)** *Parlophone CDR 6627* JOHN & YOKO & THE PLASTIC ONO BAND	33		1
15 Dec 07	**HAPPY XMAS (WAR IS OVER)** *Download* JOHN & YOKO & THE PLASTIC ONO BAND	40		1

JULIAN LENNON UK singer

Date	Title	Peak Position	Weeks at No.1	Weeks in Top 40
6 Oct 84	**TOO LATE FOR GOODBYES** *Charisma JL 1*	6		7
15 Dec 84	**VALOTTE** *Charisma JL 2*	55		
9 Mar 85	**SAY YOU'RE WRONG** *Charisma JL 3*	75		
7 Dec 85	**BECAUSE** *EMI 5538*	40		1
11 Mar 89	**NOW YOU'RE IN HEAVEN** *Virgin VS 1154*	59		
24 Aug 91	**SALTWATER** *Virgin VS 1361*	6		9
30 Nov 91	**HELP YOURSELF** *Virgin VS 1379*	53		
25 Apr 92	**GET A LIFE** *Virgin VS 1398*	56		

Date	Title	Peak Position	Weeks at No.1	Weeks in Top 40
23 May 98	**DAY AFTER DAY** *Music From Another JULIAN 4CD*	66		

ANNIE LENNOX UK singer

Date	Title	Peak Position	Weeks at No.1	Weeks in Top 40
3 Dec 88	**PUT A LITTLE LOVE IN YOUR HEART** *A&M AM 484* ANNIE LENNOX & AL GREEN	28		4
28 Mar 92	**WHY** *RCA PB 45317*	5		6
6 Jun 92	**PRECIOUS** *RCA 74321100257*	23		3
22 Aug 92	**WALKING ON BROKEN GLASS** *RCA 74321107227*	8		7
31 Oct 92	**COLD** *RCA 74321116902*	26		2
13 Feb 93	**LITTLE BIRD/LOVE SONG FOR A VAMPIRE** *RCA 74321133832* ○	3		10
18 Feb 95	**NO MORE 'I LOVE YOUS'** *RCA 74321257162* ○	2		7
10 Jun 95	**A WHITER SHADE OF PALE** *RCA 74321284822*	16		4
30 Sep 95	**WAITING IN VAIN** *RCA 74321316132*	31		1
9 Dec 95	**SOMETHING SO RIGHT** *RCA 74321332392* ANNIE LENNOX FEATURING PAUL SIMON	44		
6 Oct 07	**DARK ROAD** *RCA 88697157432*	58		

DINO LENNY Italian producer

Date	Title	Peak Position	Weeks at No.1	Weeks in Top 40
4 May 02	**I FEEL STEREO** *Incentive CENT 40CDS*	60		
10 May 03	**CHANGE THE WORLD** *Free 2 Air 0146685 F2A* DINO LENNY VS THE HOUSEMARTINS	51		
21 Apr 07	**FEELS LIKE HOME** *Free 2 Air F2A27CD* MECK FEATURING DINO	31		1

PHILLIP LEO UK singer

Date	Title	Peak Position	Weeks at No.1	Weeks in Top 40
23 Jul 94	**SECOND CHANCE** *EMI CDEM 327*	57		
25 Mar 95	**THINKING ABOUT YOUR LOVE** *EMI CDEM 358*	64		

KRISTIAN LEONTIOU UK singer

Date	Title	Peak Position	Weeks at No.1	Weeks in Top 40
5 Jun 04	**THE STORY OF MY LIFE** *Polydor 9866632*	9		4
28 Aug 04	**SHINING** *Polydor 9867640*	13		4
4 Dec 04	**SOME SAY** *Polydor 9868904*	54		

LES RYTHMES DIGITALES UK multi-instrumentalist

Date	Title	Peak Position	Weeks at No.1	Weeks in Top 40
25 Apr 98	**MUSIC MAKES YOU LOSE CONTROL** *Wall Of Sound WALLD 037*	69		
7 Aug 99	**SOMETIMES** *Wall Of Sound WALLD 054* LES RYTHMES DIGITALES FEATURING NIK KERHSAW	56		
30 Oct 99	**JACQUES YOUR BODY (MAKE ME SWEAT)** *Wall Of Sound WALLD 060*	60		
10 Sep 05	**JACQUES YOUR BODY (MAKE ME SWEAT)** *Data DATA93CDS*	9		4

LESS THAN JAKE US group

Date	Title	Peak Position	Weeks at No.1	Weeks in Top 40
5 Aug 00	**ALL MY BEST FRIENDS ARE METALHEADS** *Golf CDSHOLE 027*	51		
8 Sep 01	**GAINESVILLE ROCK CITY** *Golf CDSHOLE 48*	57		
24 May 03	**SHE'S GONNA BREAK SOON** *Sire W 606CD*	39		1
27 May 06	**OVERRATED (EVERYTHING IS)/A STILL LIFE** *Sire W713CD2*	61		

KETTY LESTER US singer

Date	Title	Peak Position	Weeks at No.1	Weeks in Top 40
19 Apr 62	**LOVE LETTERS** *London HLN 9527*	4		12
19 Jul 62	**BUT NOT FOR ME** *London HLN 9574*	45		

LET LOOSE UK group

Date	Title	Peak Position	Weeks at No.1	Weeks in Top 40
24 Apr 93	**CRAZY FOR YOU** *Vertigo VERCD 74*	44		
9 Apr 94	**SEVENTEEN** *Mercury MERCD 400*	44		
25 Jun 94	**CRAZY FOR YOU** *Mercury MERCD 402* ●	2		16
22 Oct 94	**SEVENTEEN (REMIX)** *Mercury MERCD 406*	11		4
28 Jan 95	**ONE NIGHT STAND** *Mercury MERCD 419*	12		4
29 Apr 95	**BEST IN ME** *Mercury MERDD 428*	8		3
4 Nov 95	**EVERYBODY SAY EVERYBODY DO** *Mercury MERDD 446*	29		1
22 Jun 96	**MAKE IT WITH YOU** *Mercury MERDD 464*	7		4
7 Sep 96	**TAKE IT EASY** *Mercury MERCD 472*	25		1
16 Nov 96	**DARLING BE HOME SOON** *Mercury MERCD 475*	65		

LETHAL BIZZLE UK group

Date	Title	Peak Position	Weeks at No.1	Weeks in Top 40
1 Jan 05	**POW (FORWARD)** *Relentless RELDX15*	11		4
6 Aug 05	**UH OH (I'M BACK)** *V2/J-Did JAD5033613*	47		
29 Oct 05	**FIRE** *V2/J-Did JAD5035653*	34		1
12 Nov 05	**WHAT WE DO** *Gana/W10 GANA01CDS* KRAY TWINZ FEATURING TWISTA & LETHAL B	23		1
13 Oct 07	**POLICE ON MY BACK** *V2 VVR5044933*	37		1

LeTOYA US singer

Date	Title / Label	Peak Position	Weeks at No.1	Weeks in Top 40
7 Oct 06	**TORN** *EMI CDEM705*	35		1

LETTERMEN US group

Date	Title / Label	Peak Position	Weeks at No.1	Weeks in Top 40
23 Nov 61	**THE WAY YOU LOOK TONIGHT** *Capitol CL 15222*	36		1

LEVEL 42 UK group

Date	Title / Label	Peak Position	Weeks at No.1	Weeks in Top 40
30 Aug 80	**LOVE MEETING LOVE** *Polydor POSP 170*	61		
18 Apr 81	**LOVE GAMES** *Polydor POSP 234*	38		2
8 Aug 81	**TURN IT ON** *Polydor POSP 286*	57		
14 Nov 81	**STARCHILD** *Polydor POSP 343*	47		
8 May 82	**ARE YOU HEARING (WHAT I HEAR)?** *Polydor POSP 396*	49		
2 Oct 82	**WEAVE YOUR SPELL** *Polydor POSP 500*	43		
15 Jan 83	**THE CHINESE WAY** *Polydor POSP 538*	24		6
16 Apr 83	**OUT OF SIGHT, OUT OF MIND** *Polydor POSP 570*	41		
30 Jul 83	**THE SUN GOES DOWN (LIVING IT UP)** *Polydor POSP 622*	10		10
22 Oct 83	**MICRO KID** *Polydor POSP 643*	37		1
1 Sep 84	**HOT WATER** *Polydor POSP 697*	18		7
3 Nov 84	**THE CHANT HAS BEGUN** *Polydor POSP 710*	41		
21 Sep 85	**SOMETHING ABOUT YOU** *Polydor POSP 759* ○	6		11
7 Dec 85	**LEAVING ME NOW** *Polydor POSP 776*	15		9
26 Apr 86	**LESSONS IN LOVE** *Polydor POSP 790* ○	3		10
14 Feb 87	**RUNNING IN THE FAMILY** *Polydor POSP 842*	6		8
25 Apr 87	**TO BE WITH YOU AGAIN** *Polydor POSP 855*	10		6
12 Sep 87	**IT'S OVER** *Polydor POSP 900*	10		7
12 Dec 87	**CHILDREN SAY** *Polydor POSP 911*	22		5
3 Sep 88	**HEAVEN IN MY HANDS** *Polydor PO 14*	12		4
29 Oct 88	**TAKE A LOOK** *Polydor PO 24*	32		3
21 Jan 89	**TRACIE** *Polydor PO 34*	25		4
28 Oct 89	**TAKE CARE OF YOURSELF** *Polydor PO 58*	39		2
17 Aug 91	**GUARANTEED** *RCA PB 44745*	17		2
19 Oct 91	**OVERTIME** *RCA PB 44997*	62		
18 Apr 92	**MY FATHER'S SHOES** *RCA PB 45271*	55		
26 Feb 94	**FOREVER NOW** *RCA 74321190272*	19		2
30 Apr 94	**ALL OVER YOU** *RCA 74321205662*	26		1
6 Aug 94	**LOVE IN A PEACEFUL WORLD** *RCA 74321220332*	31		1

LEVELLERS UK group

Date	Title / Label	Peak Position	Weeks at No.1	Weeks in Top 40
21 Sep 91	**ONE WAY** *China WOK 2008*	51		
7 Dec 91	**FAR FROM HOME** *China WOK 2010*	71		
23 May 92	**15 YEARS (EP)** *China WOKX 2020*	11		3
10 Jul 93	**BELARUSE** *China WOKCD 2034*	12		3
30 Oct 93	**THIS GARDEN** *China WOKCD 2039*	12		3
14 May 94	**JULIE (EP)** *China WOKCD 2042*	17		2
12 Aug 95	**HOPE ST** *China WOKCD 2059*	12		3
14 Oct 95	**FANTASY** *China WOKCD 2067*	16		1
23 Dec 95	**JUST THE ONE** *China WOKCD 2076* LEVELLERS, SPECIAL GUEST JOE STRUMMER	12		6
20 Jul 96	**EXODUS – LIVE** *China WOKCD 2082*	24		1
9 Aug 97	**WHAT A BEAUTIFUL DAY** *China WOKCD 2088*	13		4
18 Oct 97	**CELEBRATE** *China WOKCD 2089*	28		1
20 Dec 97	**DOG TRAIN** *China WOKCD 2090*	24		3
14 Mar 98	**TOO REAL** *China WOKCD 2091*	46		
24 Oct 98	**BOZOS** *China WOKCD 2096*	44		
6 Feb 99	**ONE WAY** *China WOKCD 2102*	33		1
9 Sep 00	**HAPPY BIRTHDAY REVOLUTION** *China EW 218CD*	57		
21 Sep 02	**COME ON** *Eagle EHAGXS 001*	44		
18 Jan 03	**WILD AS ANGELS EP** *Eagle EHAGXS 003*	34		1
30 Apr 05	**MAKE YOU HAPPY** *Eagle EOTFXS303*	38		1

LEVERT US group

Date	Title / Label	Peak Position	Weeks at No.1	Weeks in Top 40
22 Aug 87	**CASANOVA** *Atlantic A 9217*	9		8

LEVERT SWEAT GILL US group

Date	Title / Label	Peak Position	Weeks at No.1	Weeks in Top 40
14 Mar 98	**MY BODY** *East West E 3857CD*	21		1
6 Jun 98	**CURIOUS** *East West E 3842CD*	23		1
12 Sep 98	**DOOR #1** *East West E 3817CD*	45		

HANK LEVINE US orchestra leader

Date	Title / Label	Peak Position	Weeks at No.1	Weeks in Top 40
21 Dec 61	**IMAGE** *HMV POP 947*	45		

LEVITICUS UK producer

Date	Title / Label	Peak Position	Weeks at No.1	Weeks in Top 40
25 Mar 95	**BURIAL** *ffrr FCD 255*	66		

BARRINGTON LEVY Jamaican singer

Date	Title / Label	Peak Position	Weeks at No.1	Weeks in Top 40
2 Feb 85	**HERE I COME** *London LON 62*	41		
15 Jun 91	**TRIBAL BASE** *Desire WANT 44* REBEL MC FEATURING TENOR FLY & BARRINGTON LEVY	20		4
24 Sep 94	**WORK** *MCA MCSTD 2003*	65		
13 Oct 01	**HERE I COME (SING DJ)** *NuLife 74321895622* TALISMAN P MEETS BARRINGTON LEVY	37		1

JONA LEWIE UK singer

Date	Title / Label	Peak Position	Weeks at No.1	Weeks in Top 40
10 May 80	**YOU'LL ALWAYS FIND ME IN THE KITCHEN AT PARTIES** *Stiff BUY 73*	16		7
29 Nov 80	**STOP THE CAVALRY** *Stiff BUY 104* ●	3		9
22 Dec 07	**STOP THE CAVALRY** *Download*	48		

ANDY LEWIS & PAUL WELLER UK duo

Date	Title / Label	Peak Position	Weeks at No.1	Weeks in Top 40
22 Sep 07	**ARE YOU TRYING TO BE LONELY** *Acid Jazz AJX193CD*	31		1

C.J. LEWIS UK singer

Date	Title / Label	Peak Position	Weeks at No.1	Weeks in Top 40
23 Apr 94	**SWEETS FOR MY SWEET** *Black Market BMITD 017*	3		9
23 Jul 94	**EVERYTHING IS ALRIGHT (UPTIGHT)** *Black Market BMITD 019*	10		5
8 Oct 94	**BEST OF MY LOVE** *Black Market BMITD 021*	13		4
17 Dec 94	**DOLLARS** *Black Market BMITD 023*	34		2
9 Sep 95	**R TO THE A** *Black Market BMITD 030*	34		1

DANNY J. LEWIS UK producer

Date	Title / Label	Peak Position	Weeks at No.1	Weeks in Top 40
20 Jun 98	**SPEND THE NIGHT** *Locked On LOX 98CD*	29		1

DEE LEWIS US singer

Date	Title / Label	Peak Position	Weeks at No.1	Weeks in Top 40
18 Jun 88	**BEST OF MY LOVE** *Mercury DEE 3*	47		

DONNA LEWIS UK singer

Date	Title / Label	Peak Position	Weeks at No.1	Weeks in Top 40
7 Sep 96	**I LOVE YOU ALWAYS FOREVER** *Atlantic A 5495CD* ○	5		11
8 Feb 97	**WITHOUT LOVE** *Atlantic A 5468CD*	39		1

GARY LEWIS & THE PLAYBOYS US singer

Date	Title / Label	Peak Position	Weeks at No.1	Weeks in Top 40
8 Feb 75	**MY HEART'S SYMPHONY** *United Artists UP 35780*	36		5

HUEY LEWIS & THE NEWS US group

Date	Title / Label	Peak Position	Weeks at No.1	Weeks in Top 40
27 Oct 84	**IF THIS IS IT** *Chrysalis CHS 2803*	39		2
31 Aug 85	**THE POWER OF LOVE** *Chrysalis HUEY 1* ★	11		8
23 Nov 85	**HEART AND SOUL (EP)** *Chrysalis HUEY 2*	61		
8 Feb 86	**THE POWER OF LOVE/DO YOU BELIEVE IN LOVE** *Chrysalis HUEY 3* ○	9		9
10 May 86	**THE HEART OF ROCK AND ROLL** *Chrysalis HUEY 4*	49		
23 Aug 86	**STUCK WITH YOU** *Chrysalis HUEY 5* ★	12		10
6 Dec 86	**HIP TO BE SQUARE** *Chrysalis HUEY 6*	41		
21 Mar 87	**SIMPLE AS THAT** *Chrysalis HUEY 7*	47		
16 Jul 88	**PERFECT WORLD** *Chrysalis HUEY 10*	48		

JERRY LEWIS US actor/comedian

Date	Title / Label	Peak Position	Weeks at No.1	Weeks in Top 40
8 Feb 57	**ROCK-A-BYE YOUR BABY (WITH A DIXIE MELODY)** *Brunswick 05636*	12		8

JERRY LEE LEWIS US singer

Date	Title / Label	Peak Position	Weeks at No.1	Weeks in Top 40
27 Sep 57	**WHOLE LOTTA SHAKIN' GOIN' ON** *London HLS 8457*	8		11
20 Dec 57	**GREAT BALLS OF FIRE** *London HLS 8529*	1	2	12
11 Apr 58	**BREATHLESS** *London HLS 8592*	8		7
23 Jan 59	**HIGH SCHOOL CONFIDENTIAL** *London HLS 8780*	12		6
1 May 59	**LOVIN' UP A STORM** *London HLS 8840*	28		1
9 Jun 60	**BABY BABY BYE BYE** *London HLS 9131*	47		
4 May 61	**WHAT'D I SAY** *London HLS 9335*	10		12
6 Sep 62	**SWEET LITTLE SIXTEEN** *London HLS 9584*	38		2
14 Mar 63	**GOOD GOLLY MISS MOLLY** *London HLS 9688*	31		4
6 May 72	**CHANTILLY LACE** *Mercury 6052 141*	33		4

LINDA LEWIS UK singer

Date	Title	Peak Position	Weeks at No.1	Weeks in Top 40
2 Jun 73	**ROCK-A-DOODLE-DOO** *Raft RA 18502*	15		9
12 Jul 75	**IT'S IN HIS KISS** *Arista 17*	6		7
17 Apr 76	**BABY I'M YOURS** *Arista 43*	33		3
2 Jun 79	**I'D BE SURPRISINGLY GOOD FOR YOU** *Ariola ARO 166*	40		1
19 Aug 00	**REACH OUT** *Skint 54CD* MIDFIELD GENERAL FEATURING LINDA LEWIS	61		

LEONA LEWIS UK singer

Date	Title	Peak Position	Weeks at No.1	Weeks in Top 40
30 Dec 06	**A MOMENT LIKE THIS** *Syco Music 88697050872* ⊛	1	3	9
3 Nov 07	**BLEEDING LOVE** *Syco Music 88697175622* ⊛ ★	1	7	20
3 Nov 07	**FORGIVENESS** *Download*	46		
24 Nov 07	**WHATEVER IT TAKES** *Download*	61		
24 Nov 07	**FOOTPRINTS IN THE SAND** *Download*	25		2
24 Nov 07	**THE FIRST TIME EVER I SAW YOUR FACE** *Download*	73		
1 Mar 08	**BETTER IN TIME/FOOTPRINTS IN THE SAND** *Syco Music 88697272002*	2		2
8 Mar 08	**BETTER IN TIME** *Download*	23		2

RAMSEY LEWIS US pianist

Date	Title	Peak Position	Weeks at No.1	Weeks in Top 40
15 Apr 72	**WADE IN THE WATER** *Chess 6145 004*	31		4

SHAZNAY LEWIS UK singer

Date	Title	Peak Position	Weeks at No.1	Weeks in Top 40
17 Jul 04	**NEVER FELT LIKE THIS BEFORE** *London LONCD484*	8		7
30 Oct 04	**YOU** *London LONCD486*	56		

JOHN LEYTON UK singer

Date	Title	Peak Position	Weeks at No.1	Weeks in Top 40
3 Aug 61	**JOHNNY REMEMBER ME** *Top Rank JAR 577*	1	3	15
5 Oct 61	**WILD WIND** *Top Rank JAR 585*	2		10
28 Dec 61	**SON THIS IS SHE** *HMV POP 956*	15		9
15 Mar 62	**LONE RIDER** *HMV POP 992*	40		1
3 May 62	**LONELY CITY** *HMV POP 1014*	14		9
23 Aug 62	**DOWN THE RIVER NILE** *HMV POP 1054*	42		
21 Feb 63	**CUPBOARD LOVE** *HMV POP 1122*	22		10
18 Jul 63	**I'LL CUT YOUR TAIL OFF** *HMV POP 1175*	36		1
20 Feb 64	**MAKE LOVE TO ME** *HMV POP 1264* JOHN LEYTON & THE LeROYS	49		

LEYTON BUZZARDS UK group

Date	Title	Peak Position	Weeks at No.1	Weeks in Top 40
3 Mar 79	**SATURDAY NIGHT (BENEATH THE PLASTIC PALM TREES)** *Chrysalis CHS 2288*	53		

LFO UK instrumental group

Date	Title	Peak Position	Weeks at No.1	Weeks in Top 40
14 Jul 90	**LFO** *Warp WAP 5*	12		7
6 Jul 91	**WE ARE BACK/NURTURE** *Warp 7WAP 14*	47		
1 Feb 92	**WHAT IS HOUSE (EP)** *Warp WAP 17*	62		

LIARS US group

Date	Title	Peak Position	Weeks at No.1	Weeks in Top 40
21 Feb 04	**THERE'S ALWAYS ROOM ON THE BROOM** *Mute CDMUTE 317*	74		

LIBERACE US pianist

Date	Title	Peak Position	Weeks at No.1	Weeks in Top 40
17 Jun 55	**UNCHAINED MELODY** *Philips PB 430*	20		1
19 Oct 56	**I DON'T CARE (AS LONG AS YOU CARE FOR ME)** *Columbia DB 3834*	28		1

LIBERATION UK production duo

Date	Title	Peak Position	Weeks at No.1	Weeks in Top 40
24 Oct 92	**LIBERATION** *ZYX 68657*	28		1

LIBERTINES UK group

Date	Title	Peak Position	Weeks at No.1	Weeks in Top 40
15 Jun 02	**WHAT A WASTER** *Rough Trade RTRADESCD 054*	37		1
12 Oct 02	**UP THE BRACKET** *Rough Trade RTRADESCD 064*	29		1
25 Jan 03	**TIME FOR HEROES** *Rough Trade RTRADESCD 074*	20		1
30 Aug 03	**DON'T LOOK BACK INTO THE SUN** *Rough Trade RTRADESCD 120*	11		2
21 Aug 04	**CAN'T STAND ME NOW** *Rough Trade RTRADSCDX 163*	2		3
6 Nov 04	**WHAT BECAME OF THE LIKELY LADS** *Rough Trade RTRADSCD 215*	9		2

LIBERTY X UK group

Date	Title	Peak Position	Weeks at No.1	Weeks in Top 40
6 Oct 01	**THINKING IT OVER** *V2 VVR 5017773* LIBERTY	5		6
15 Dec 01	**DOIN' IT** *V2 VVR 5017798* LIBERTY	14		5
25 May 02	**JUST A LITTLE** *V2 VVR 5018968* ●	1	1	14
21 Sep 02	**GOT TO HAVE YOUR LOVE** *V2 VVR 5020508*	2		8
14 Dec 02	**HOLDING ON FOR YOU** *V2 VVR 5020768*	5		7
29 Mar 03	**BEING NOBODY** *Virgin RXCD1* RICHARD X VS LIBERTY X	3		6
1 Nov 03	**JUMPIN'** *V2 VVR 5023549*	6		4
24 Jan 04	**EVERYBODY CRIES** *V2 VVR5023558*	13		3
8 Oct 05	**SONG 4 LOVERS** *Virgin/EMI VTSCDX8*	5		7
26 Nov 05	**A NIGHT TO REMEMBER** *EMI Virgin/Unique VTSCDX9*	6		4
1 Jul 06	**X** *EMI Virgin/Unique VTSCD10*	47		

LIBIDO Norwegian group

Date	Title	Peak Position	Weeks at No.1	Weeks in Top 40
31 Jan 98	**OVERTHROWN** *Fire BLAZE 119CD*	53		

LIBRA PRESENTS TAYLOR US production duo

Date	Title	Peak Position	Weeks at No.1	Weeks in Top 40
26 Oct 96	**ANOMALY – CALLING YOUR NAME** *Platipus PLATCD 24*	71		
18 Mar 00	**ANOMALY – CALLING YOUR NAME (REMIX)** *Platipus PLATCD 56*	43		

LICK THE TINS UK group

Date	Title	Peak Position	Weeks at No.1	Weeks in Top 40
29 Mar 86	**CAN'T HELP FALLING IN LOVE** *Sedition EDIT 3308*	42		

OLIVER LIEB German producer

Date	Title	Peak Position	Weeks at No.1	Weeks in Top 40
30 Sep 00	**METROPOLIS** *Duty Free DF 019CD*	72		

BEN LIEBRAND Dutch producer

Date	Title	Peak Position	Weeks at No.1	Weeks in Top 40
9 Jun 90	**PULS(T)AR** *Epic LIEB 1*	68		

LIEUTENANT PIGEON UK group

Date	Title	Peak Position	Weeks at No.1	Weeks in Top 40
16 Sep 72	**MOULDY OLD DOUGH** *Decca F 13278*	1	4	16
16 Dec 72	**DESPERATE DAN** *Decca F 13365*	17		9

LIFEHOUSE US group

Date	Title	Peak Position	Weeks at No.1	Weeks in Top 40
8 Sep 01	**HANGING BY A MOMENT** *DreamWorks 4508942*	25		2

LIGHT OF THE WORLD UK group

Date	Title	Peak Position	Weeks at No.1	Weeks in Top 40
14 Apr 79	**SWINGIN'** *Ensign ENY 22*	45		
14 Jul 79	**MIDNIGHT GROOVIN'** *Ensign ENY 29*	72		
18 Oct 80	**LONDON TOWN** *Ensign ENY 43*	41		
17 Jan 81	**I SHOT THE SHERIFF** *Ensign ENY 46*	40		1
28 Mar 81	**I'M SO HAPPY/TIME** *Ensign ENY 64*	35		2
21 Nov 81	**RIDE THE LOVE TRAIN** *EMI 5242*	49		

LIGHTER SHADE OF BROWN US rappers

Date	Title	Peak Position	Weeks at No.1	Weeks in Top 40
9 Jul 94	**HEY DJ** *Mercury MERCD 401*	33		2

GORDON LIGHTFOOT Canadian singer

Date	Title	Peak Position	Weeks at No.1	Weeks in Top 40
19 Jun 71	**IF YOU COULD READ MY MIND** *Reprise K 20974*	30		6
3 Aug 74	**SUNDOWN** *Reprise K 14327* ★	33		4
15 Jan 77	**THE WRECK OF THE EDMUND FITZGERALD** *Reprise K 14451*	40		1
16 Sep 78	**DAYLIGHT KATY** *Warner Brothers K 17214*	41		

TERRY LIGHTFOOT & HIS NEW ORLEANS JAZZMEN UK singer/clarinettist and group

Date	Title	Peak Position	Weeks at No.1	Weeks in Top 40
7 Sep 61	**TRUE LOVE** *Columbia DB 4696*	33		2
23 Nov 61	**KING KONG** *Columbia SCD 2165*	29		3
3 May 62	**TAVERN IN THE TOWN** *Columbia DB 4822*	49		

LIGHTFORCE German production duo

Date	Title	Peak Position	Weeks at No.1	Weeks in Top 40
28 Oct 00	**JOIN ME** *Slinky Music SLINKY004CD*	53		

Silver-selling ○ Gold-selling ● Platinum-selling ⊛ US No.1 ★ | Peak Position | Weeks at No.1 | Weeks in Top 40

LIGHTHOUSE FAMILY UK group

Date	Title	Peak Position	Weeks at No.1	Weeks in Top 40
27 May 95	**LIFTED** *Wild Card CARDW 17*	61		
14 Oct 95	**OCEAN DRIVE** *Wild Card 5797072*	34		1
10 Feb 96	**LIFTED** *Wild Card 5779432* ○	4		7
1 Jun 96	**OCEAN DRIVE** *Wild Card 5766192*	11		6
21 Sep 96	**GOODBYE HEARTBREAK** *Wild Card 5753492*	14		3
21 Dec 96	**LOVING EVERY MINUTE** *Wild Card 5731012*	20		5
11 Oct 97	**RAINCLOUD** *Wild Card 5717932*	6		4
10 Jan 98	**HIGH** *Wild Card 5691492* ○	4		12
27 Jun 98	**LOST IN SPACE** *Polydor 5670592*	6		6
10 Oct 98	**QUESTION OF FAITH** *Wild Card 5673932*	21		2
9 Jan 99	**POSTCARD FROM HEAVEN** *Wild Card 5633952*	24		2
24 Nov 01	**(I WISH I KNEW HOW IT WOULD FEEL TO BE) FREE/ONE** *Wild Card 5873812*	6		4
9 Mar 02	**RUN** *Wild Card 5705702*	30		1
6 Jul 02	**HAPPY** *Wild Card 5707912*	51		

LIGHTNING SEEDS UK group

Date	Title	Peak Position	Weeks at No.1	Weeks in Top 40
22 Jul 89	**PURE** *Ghetto GTG 4*	16		5
14 Mar 92	**THE LIFE OF RILEY** *Virgin VS 1402*	28		3
30 May 92	**SENSE** *Virgin VS 1414*	31		2
20 Aug 94	**LUCKY YOU** *Epic 6606282*	43		
14 Jan 95	**CHANGE** *Epic 6609865*	13		5
15 Apr 95	**MARVELLOUS** *Epic 6614265*	24		3
22 Jul 95	**PERFECT** *Epic 6621792*	18		4
21 Oct 95	**LUCKY YOU** *Epic 6625182*	15		4
9 Mar 96	**READY OR NOT** *Epic 6629672*	20		2
1 Jun 96	**THREE LIONS (THE OFFICIAL SONG OF THE ENGLAND FOOTBALL TEAM)** *Epic 6632732* BADDIEL & SKINNER & LIGHTNING SEEDS ⊛	1	2	13
2 Nov 96	**WHAT IF...** *Epic 6638635*	14		2
18 Jan 97	**SUGAR COATED ICEBERG** *Epic 6640435*	12		3
26 Apr 97	**YOU SHOWED ME** *Epic 6643282*	8		3
13 Dec 97	**WHAT YOU SAY** *Epic 6653572*	41		
20 Jun 98	**THREE LIONS (THE OFFICIAL SONG OF THE ENGLAND FOOTBALL TEAM)** *Epic 6660982* BADDIEL & SKINNER & LIGHTNING SEEDS ⊛	1	3	13
27 Nov 99	**LIFE'S TOO SHORT** *Epic 6681502*	27		1
18 Mar 00	**SWEET SOUL SENSATIONS** *Epic 6689422*	67		
15 Jun 02	**THREE LIONS** *Epic 6728152* BADDIEL & SKINNER & LIGHTNING SEEDS	16		3
10 Jun 06	**THREE LIONS** *Epic 82876856672* BADDIEL & SKINNER & LIGHTNING SEEDS	9		4

LIGHTSPEED CHAMPION US vocalist/guitarist

Date	Title	Peak Position	Weeks at No.1	Weeks in Top 40
26 Jan 08	**TELL ME WHAT IT'S WORTH** *Domino RUG273CD*	72		

LIL BOW WOW US rapper

Date	Title	Peak Position	Weeks at No.1	Weeks in Top 40
14 Apr 01	**BOW WOW (THAT'S MY NAME)** *So So Def 6709832*	6		4
27 Nov 04	**BABY IT'S YOU** *Mercury 9869056* JOJO FEATURING BOW WOW	8		7
8 Oct 05	**LET ME HOLD YOU (IMPORT)** *Sony BMG 6760602* BOW WOW FEATURING OMARION	64		
22 Oct 05	**LET ME HOLD YOU** *Columbia 6760605* BOW WOW FEATURING OMARION	27		3
18 Mar 06	**LIKE YOU** *Columbia 82876779522* BOW WOW FEATURING CIARA	17		3

LIL' CHRIS UK singer

Date	Title	Peak Position	Weeks at No.1	Weeks in Top 40
30 Sep 06	**CHECKIN' IT OUT** *RCA 88697002812*	3		8
16 Dec 06	**GETTING' ENOUGH** *RCA 88697035232*	17		5
10 Mar 07	**FIGURE IT OUT** *RCA 88697061382*	57		
29 Sep 07	**WE DON'T HAVE TO TAKE OUR CLOTHES OFF** *Download*	63		

LIL' DEVIOUS UK production duo

Date	Title	Peak Position	Weeks at No.1	Weeks in Top 40
15 Sep 01	**COME HOME** *Rulin 16CDS*	55		

LIL' FLIP US rapper

Date	Title	Peak Position	Weeks at No.1	Weeks in Top 40
11 Sep 04	**NEVER REALLY WAS** *Bad Boy MCSTD40372* MARIO WINANS FEATURING LIL' FLIP	44		
30 Oct 04	**SUNSHINE** *Columbia 6751842*	14		2

LIL' JON US rapper

Date	Title	Peak Position	Weeks at No.1	Weeks in Top 40
27 Mar 04	**YEAH** *Arista 82876606012* USHER FEATURING LIL' JON & LUDACRIS ★	1	2	12
12 Feb 05	**ROLL CALL/WHAT U GON' DO** *TVT TVTUKCDX2* LIL JON & THE EAST SIDE BOYZ	38		1
26 Feb 05	**LET'S GO** *Atlantic AT0193CD* TRICK DADDY FEATURING TWISTA & LIL' JON	26		1
14 May 05	**GET LOW/LOVERS & FRIENDS** *TVT TVTUKCD9* LIL JON & THE EAST SIDE BOYZ	10		4
16 Jul 05	**GIRLFIGHT** *Virgin VUSDX301* BROOKE VALENTINE FEATURING BIG BOI & LIL' JON	35		1

LIL' KIM US rapper

Date	Title	Peak Position	Weeks at No.1	Weeks in Top 40
26 Apr 97	**NO TIME** *Atlantic A 5594CD* LIL' KIM FEATURING PUFF DADDY	45		
5 Jul 97	**CRUSH ON YOU** *Atlantic AT 0002CD*	36		1
16 Aug 97	**NOT TONIGHT** *Atlantic AT 0007CD*	11		3
25 Oct 97	**CRUSH ON YOU** *Atlantic AT 0002CD*	23		1
22 Aug 98	**HIT 'EM WIT DA HEE** *East West E 3824CD1* MISSY 'MISDEMEANOR' ELLIOTT FEATURING LIL' KIM	25		1
5 Feb 00	**NOTORIOUS B.I.G.** *Puff Daddy 74321737312* NOTORIOUS B.I.G. FEATURING PUFF DADDY AND LIL' KIM	16		3
2 Sep 00	**NO MATTER WHAT THEY SAY** *Atlantic 7567846972*	35		1
30 Jun 01	**LADY MARMALADE** *Interscope 4975612* CHRISTINA AGUILERA/LIL' KIM/MYA/PINK ● ★	1	1	13
11 Aug 01	**WAIT A MINUTE** *Atlantic AT 0106CD* RAY J FEATURING LIL' KIM	54		
22 Sep 01	**IN THE AIR TONITE** *WEA 331CD* LIL' KIM FEATURING PHIL COLLINS	26		1
10 May 03	**THE JUMP OFF** *Atlantic AT 0151CD* LIL' KIM FEATURING MR CHEEKS	16		2
20 Sep 03	**CAN'T HOLD US DOWN** *RCA 82876556332* CHRISTINA AGUILERA FEATURING LIL' KIM	6		6
19 Nov 05	**LIGHTERS UP** *Atlantic AT0226CD*	12		4
27 May 06	**WHOA** *Atlantic AT0241CDX*	43		

LIL' LOUIS US producer

Date	Title	Peak Position	Weeks at No.1	Weeks in Top 40
29 Jul 89	**FRENCH KISS** *ffrr FX 115* ○	2		9
13 Jan 90	**I CALLED U** *ffrr F 123*	16		5
26 Sep 92	**SAVED MY LIFE** *ffrr FX 197* LIL' LOUIS & THE WORLD	74		
12 Aug 00	**HOW'S YOUR EVENING SO FAR** *ffrr FCD 384* JOSH WINK & LIL' LOUIS	23		1

LIL' LOVE Italian duo

Date	Title	Peak Position	Weeks at No.1	Weeks in Top 40
27 Aug 05	**LITTLE LOVE** *Positiva CDTIVS222*	34		1

LIL' MO US rapper

Date	Title	Peak Position	Weeks at No.1	Weeks in Top 40
21 Nov 98	**5 MINUTES** *Elektra E 3803CD* LIL' MO FEATURING MISSY 'MISDEMEANOR' ELLIOTT	72		
23 Sep 00	**WHATEVER** *Virgin VUSCD 172* IDEAL US FEATURING LIL' MO	31		1
6 Apr 02	**WHERE'S MY** *EMI CDEMS 598* ADAM F FEATURING LIL' MO	37		1
15 Feb 03	**IF I COULD GO** *Elektra E 7331CD* ANGIE MARTINEZ FEATURING LIL MO	61		
16 Aug 03	**CAN'T LET YOU GO** *Elektra E 7408CD* FABOLOUS FEATURING MIKE SHOREY & LIL' MO	14		3
9 Mar 96	**REACH** *Multiply CDMULTY 9* LIL MO' YIN YANG	28		1

LIL' ROMEO US rapper

Date	Title	Peak Position	Weeks at No.1	Weeks in Top 40
22 Sep 01	**MY BABY** *Priority PTYCD 136*	67		

LIL' WAYNE US rapper

Date	Title	Peak Position	Weeks at No.1	Weeks in Top 40
19 Feb 05	**SOLDIER** *Columbia 6757622* DESTINY'S CHILD FEATURING TI & LIL' WAYNE	4		5
22 Jul 06	**GIMME THAT REMIX** *Jive 82876880762* CHRIS BROWN FEATURING LIL' WAYNE	23		3
1 Dec 07	**SWEETEST GIRL (DOLLAR BILL)** *Download* WYCLEF JEAN FEATURING AKON, LIL WAYNE & NIIA	66		

LILYS US group

Date	Title	Peak Position	Weeks at No.1	Weeks in Top 40
21 Feb 98	**A NANNY IN MANHATTAN** *Che 77CD*	16		2

LIMAHL UK singer

Date	Title	Peak Position	Weeks at No.1	Weeks in Top 40
5 Nov 83	**ONLY FOR LOVE** *EMI LML 1*	16		5
2 Jun 84	**TOO MUCH TROUBLE** *EMI LML 2*	64		
13 Oct 84	**NEVER ENDING STORY** *EMI LML 3*	4		10

ALISON LIMERICK UK singer

Date	Title	Peak Position	Weeks at No.1	Weeks in Top 40
30 Mar 91	**WHERE LOVE LIVES** *Arista 114208*	27		5
12 Oct 91	**COME BACK (FOR REAL LOVE)** *Arista 114530*	53		
21 Dec 91	**MAGIC'S BACK (THEME FROM 'THE GHOSTS OF OXFORD STREET')** *RCA PB 45223* MALCOLM McLAREN FEATURING ALISON LIMERICK	42		
29 Feb 92	**MAKE IT ON MY OWN** *Arista 114996*	16		4
18 Jul 92	**GETTING' IT RIGHT** *Arista 74321102867*	57		
28 Nov 92	**HEAR MY CALL** *Arista 115337*	73		
8 Jan 94	**TIME OF OUR LIVES** *Arista 74321180332*	36		2
19 Mar 94	**LOVE COME DOWN** *Arista 74321191952*	36		1
25 Feb 95	**LOVE WILL KEEP US TOGETHER** *Acid Jazz JAZID 112CD* JTQ FEATURING ALISON LIMERICK	63		
6 Jul 96	**WHERE LOVE LIVES (REMIX)** *Arista 74321381592*	9		5
14 Sep 96	**MAKE IT ON MY OWN (REMIX)** *Arista 74321407812*	30		1
23 Aug 97	**PUT YOUR FAITH IN ME** *MBA XES 9001*	42		
15 Mar 03	**WHERE LOVE LIVES (2ND REMIX)** *Arista Dance 74321981442*	44		

LIMIT Dutch duo

Date	Title	Peak Position	Weeks at No.1	Weeks in Top 40
5 Jan 85	**SAY YEAH** *Portrait A 4808*	17		6

LIMMIE & THE FAMILY COOKIN' US singer

Date	Title	Peak Position	Weeks at No.1	Weeks in Top 40
21 Jul 73	**YOU CAN DO MAGIC** *Avco 6105 019*	3		11
20 Oct 73	**DREAMBOAT** *Avco 6105 025*	31		4
6 Apr 74	**A WALKIN' MIRACLE** *Avco 6105 027*	6		9

LIMP BIZKIT US group

Date	Title	Peak Position	Weeks at No.1	Weeks in Top 40
15 Jul 00	**TAKE A LOOK AROUND** *Interscope 4973692*	3		11
11 Nov 00	**MY GENERATION** *Interscope IND 97448*	15		2
27 Jan 01	**ROLLIN'** *Interscope IND 97474*	1	2	10
23 Jun 01	**MY WAY** *Interscope 4975732*	6		5
10 Nov 01	**BOILER** *Interscope 4976362*	18		3
27 Sep 03	**EAT YOU ALIVE** *Interscope 9811757*	10		2
6 Dec 03	**BEHIND BLUE EYES** *Interscope 9814744*	18		2

LINA US singer

Date	Title	Peak Position	Weeks at No.1	Weeks in Top 40
3 Mar 01	**PLAYA NO MO'** *Atlantic AT 0094CD*	46		

BOB LIND US singer

Date	Title	Peak Position	Weeks at No.1	Weeks in Top 40
10 Mar 66	**ELUSIVE BUTTERFLY** *Fontana TF 670*	5		8
26 May 66	**REMEMBER THE RAIN** *Fontana TF 702*	46		

LINDISFARNE UK group

Date	Title	Peak Position	Weeks at No.1	Weeks in Top 40
26 Feb 72	**MEET ME ON THE CORNER** *Charisma CB 173*	5		11
13 May 72	**LADY ELEANOR** *Charisma CB 153*	3		9
23 Sep 72	**ALL FALL DOWN** *Charisma CB 191*	34		4
3 Jun 78	**RUN FOR HOME** *Mercury 6007 177*	10		10
7 Oct 78	**JUKE BOX GYPSY** *Mercury 6007 187*	56		
10 Nov 90	**FOG ON THE TYNE (REVISITED)** *Best ZB 44083* GAZZA & LINDISFARNE	2		6

LINDSAY UK singer

Date	Title	Peak Position	Weeks at No.1	Weeks in Top 40
12 May 01	**NO DREAM IMPOSSIBLE** *Universal TV 1589562*	32		2

LINER UK group

Date	Title	Peak Position	Weeks at No.1	Weeks in Top 40
10 Mar 79	**KEEP REACHING OUT FOR LOVE** *Atlantic K 11235*	49		
26 May 79	**YOU AND ME** *Atlantic K 11285*	44		

ANDY LING UK producer

Date	Title	Peak Position	Weeks at No.1	Weeks in Top 40
13 May 00	**FIXATION** *Hooj Choons HOOJ 094CD*	55		

LAURIE LINGO & THE DIPSTICKS UK Radio 1 DJs

Date	Title	Peak Position	Weeks at No.1	Weeks in Top 40
17 Apr 76	**CONVOY G.B.** *State STAT 23*	4		6

LINK US rapper

Date	Title	Peak Position	Weeks at No.1	Weeks in Top 40
7 Nov 98	**WHATCHA GONE DO?** *Relativity 6666055*	48		

LINKIN PARK US group

Date	Title	Peak Position	Weeks at No.1	Weeks in Top 40
27 Jan 01	**ONE STEP CLOSER** *Warner Brothers W 550CD*	24		1
21 Apr 01	**CRAWLING** *Warner Brothers W 556CD*	16		5
30 Jun 01	**PAPERCUT** *Warner Brothers W 562CD*	14		3
20 Oct 01	**IN THE END** *Warner Brothers W 569CD*	8		6
3 Aug 02	**HIGH VOLTAGE/POINTS OF AUTHORITY** *Warner Brothers W 588CD*	9		3
29 Mar 03	**SOMEWHERE I BELONG** *Warner Brothers W 602CD*	10		5
21 Jun 03	**FAINT** *Warner Brothers W 610CD*	15		5
20 Sep 03	**NUMB** *Warner Brothers W 622CD*	14		3
19 Jun 04	**BREAKING THE HABIT** *Warner Brothers W 645CD*	39		1
4 Dec 04	**NUMB/ENCORE** *WEA W660CD* JAY-Z VS LINKIN PARK	14		18
14 Apr 07	**WHAT I'VE DONE** *Warner Brothers W762CD1*	6		11
25 Aug 07	**BLEED IT** *Warner Brothers W772CD*	29		3
24 Nov 07	**SHADOW OF THE DAY** *Warner Brothers W790CD*	46		

LINOLEUM UK group

Date	Title	Peak Position	Weeks at No.1	Weeks in Top 40
12 Jul 97	**MARQUIS** *Lino Vinyl LINO 004CD1*	73		

LINX UK duo

Date	Title	Peak Position	Weeks at No.1	Weeks in Top 40
20 Sep 80	**YOU'RE LYING** *Chrysalis CHS 2461*	15		6
7 Mar 81	**INTUITION** *Chrysalis CHS 2500*	7		8
13 Jun 81	**THROW AWAY THE KEY** *Chrysalis CHS 2519*	21		7
5 Sep 81	**SO THIS IS ROMANCE** *Chrysalis CHS 2546*	15		7
21 Nov 81	**CAN'T HELP MYSELF** *Chrysalis CHS 2565*	55		
10 Jul 82	**PLAYTHING** *Chrysalis CHS 2621*	48		

LIONROCK UK producer

Date	Title	Peak Position	Weeks at No.1	Weeks in Top 40
5 Dec 92	**LIONROCK** *Deconstruction 74321124381*	63		
8 May 93	**PACKET OF PEACE** *Deconstruction 74321144372*	32		1
23 Oct 93	**CARNIVAL** *Deconstruction 74321164862*	34		1
27 Aug 94	**TRIPWIRE** *Deconstruction 74321204702*	44		
6 Apr 96	**STRAIGHT AT YER HEAD** *Deconstruction 74321342972*	33		1
27 Jul 96	**FIRE UP THE SHOESAW** *Deconstruction 74321382652*	43		
14 Mar 98	**RUDE BOY ROCK** *Concrete HARD 31CD*	20		2
30 May 98	**SCATTER & SWING** *Concrete HARD 35CD*	54		

LIPPS INC US group

Date	Title	Peak Position	Weeks at No.1	Weeks in Top 40
17 May 80	**FUNKY TOWN** *Casablanca CAN 194* ★	2		11

LIQUID UK production duo

Date	Title	Peak Position	Weeks at No.1	Weeks in Top 40
21 Mar 92	**SWEET HARMONY** *XL Recordings XLS 28*	15		4
5 Sep 92	**THE FUTURE MUSIC (EP)** *XL Recordings XLT 33*	59		
20 Mar 93	**TIME TO GET UP** *XL Recordings XLS 40CD*	46		
8 Jul 95	**SWEET HARMONY (REMIX)/ONE LOVE FAMILY** *XL Recordings XLS 65CD*	14		4
21 Oct 95	**CLOSER** *XL Recordings XLS 66CD*	47		
25 Jul 98	**STRONG** *Higher Ground HIGHS 7CD*	59		
21 Oct 00	**ORLANDO DAWN** *Xtravaganza XTRAV 16CDS*	53		

LIQUID CHILD German production duo

Date	Title	Peak Position	Weeks at No.1	Weeks in Top 40
23 Oct 99	**DIVING FACES** *Essential Recordings ESCD 9*	25		1

LIQUID GOLD UK group

Date	Title	Peak Position	Weeks at No.1	Weeks in Top 40
2 Dec 78	**ANYWAY YOU DO IT** *Creole CR 159*	41		
23 Feb 80	**DANCE YOURSELF DIZZY** *Polo 1*	2		10
31 May 80	**SUBSTITUTE** *Polo 4*	8		7

Silver-selling ● Gold-selling ● Platinum-selling ⊛ US No.1 ★ | Peak Position | Weeks at No.1 | Weeks in Top 40

Date	Title	Label	Peak Position	Weeks at No.1	Weeks in Top 40
1 Nov 80	THE NIGHT THE WINE THE ROSES	*Polo 6*	32		4
28 Mar 81	DON'T PANIC	*Polo 8*	42		
21 Aug 82	WHERE DID WE GO WRONG	*Polo 23*	56		

LIQUID OXYGEN US producer

Date	Title	Label	Peak Position	Weeks at No.1	Weeks in Top 40
28 Apr 90	THE PLANET DANCE (MOVE YA BODY)	*Champion CHAMP 242*	56		

LIQUID PEOPLE UK production duo

Date	Title	Label	Peak Position	Weeks at No.1	Weeks in Top 40
20 Jul 02	MONSTER LIQUID PEOPLE VS SIMPLE MINDS	*Defected DFECT 49R*	67		
21 Jun 03	IT'S MY LIFE LIQUID PEOPLE VS TALK TALK	*Nebula NEBCD 045*	64		

LIQUID STATE UK production group

Date	Title	Label	Peak Position	Weeks at No.1	Weeks in Top 40
30 Mar 02	FALLING LIQUID STATE FEATURING MARCELLA WOODS	*Perfecto PERF 29CDS*	60		

LISA LISA & CULT JAM US group

Date	Title	Label	Peak Position	Weeks at No.1	Weeks in Top 40
4 May 85	I WONDER IF I TAKE YOU HOME LISA LISA & CULT JAM WITH FULL FORCE	*CBS A 6057*	12		9
31 Oct 87	LOST IN EMOTION	*CBS 6510367* ★	58		
13 Jul 91	LET THE BEAT HIT 'EM	*Columbia 6572867*	17		5
24 Aug 91	LET THE BEAT HIT 'EM PART 2	*Columbia 6573747*	49		
26 Mar 94	SKIP TO MY LU LISA LISA	*Chrysalis CDCHS 5006*	34		1

LISA MARIE EXPERIENCE UK production duo

Date	Title	Label	Peak Position	Weeks at No.1	Weeks in Top 40
27 Apr 96	KEEP ON JUMPIN'	*ffrr FCD 271*	7		6
10 Aug 96	DO THAT TO ME	*Positiva CDTIV 57*	33		1
16 Jun 07	KEEP ON JUMPIN' CORENELL & LISA MARIE EXPERIENCE	*Gusto CDGUS46*	37		1

LISBON LIONS UK group

Date	Title	Label	Peak Position	Weeks at No.1	Weeks in Top 40
11 May 02	THE BEST DAYS OF OUR LIVES LISBON LIONS FEATURING MARTIN O'NEILL	*Concept CDCON 32*	17		2

LIT US group

Date	Title	Label	Peak Position	Weeks at No.1	Weeks in Top 40
26 Jun 99	MY OWN WORST ENEMY	*RCA 74321669992*	16		2
25 Sep 99	ZIP - LOCK	*RCA 74321701852*	60		
19 Aug 00	OVER MY HEAD	*Capitol 8889532*	37		1

LITHIUM & SONYA MADAN US/UK duo

Date	Title	Label	Peak Position	Weeks at No.1	Weeks in Top 40
1 Mar 97	RIDE A ROCKET	*ffrr FCD 293*	40		1

LITTLE'ANS UK group

Date	Title	Label	Peak Position	Weeks at No.1	Weeks in Top 40
29 Oct 05	THEIR WAY LITTL'ANS FEATURING PETER DOHERTY	*Rough Trade RTRADSCD267*	22		1

DE ETTA LITTLE & NELSON PIGFORD US duo

Date	Title	Label	Peak Position	Weeks at No.1	Weeks in Top 40
13 Aug 77	YOU TAKE MY HEART AWAY	*United Artists UP 36257*	35		3

LITTLE ANGELS UK group

Date	Title	Label	Peak Position	Weeks at No.1	Weeks in Top 40
4 Mar 89	BIG BAD EP	*Polydor LTLEP 2*	74		
24 Feb 90	KICKING UP DUST	*Polydor LTL 5*	46		
12 May 90	RADICAL YOUR LOVER LITTLE ANGELS FEATURING THE BIG BAD HORNS	*Polydor LTL 6*	34		2
4 Aug 90	SHE'S A LITTLE ANGEL	*Polydor LTL 7*	21		2
2 Feb 91	BONEYARD	*Polydor LTL 8*	33		2
30 Mar 91	PRODUCT OF THE WORKING CLASS	*Polydor LTL 9*	40		1
1 Jun 91	YOUNG GODS	*Polydor LTL 10*	34		1
20 Jul 91	I AIN'T GONNA CRY	*Polydor LTL 11*	26		2
7 Nov 92	TOO MUCH TOO YOUNG	*Polydor LTL 12*	22		2
9 Jan 93	WOMANKIND	*Polydor LTLCD 13*	12		4
24 Apr 93	SOAPBOX	*Polydor LTLCD 14*	33		2
25 Sep 93	SAIL AWAY	*Polydor LTLCD 15*	45		
9 Apr 94	TEN MILES HIGH	*Polydor LTLCD 16*	18		2

LITTLE ANTHONY & THE IMPERIALS US group

Date	Title	Label	Peak Position	Weeks at No.1	Weeks in Top 40
31 Jul 76	BETTER USE YOUR HEAD	*United Artists UP 36141*	42		

LITTLE BARRIE UK group

Date	Title	Label	Peak Position	Weeks at No.1	Weeks in Top 40
5 Feb 05	FREE SALUTE	*Genuine GEN032CD*	73		

LITTLE BENNY & THE MASTERS US group

Date	Title	Label	Peak Position	Weeks at No.1	Weeks in Top 40
2 Feb 85	WHO COMES TO BOOGIE	*Bluebird/10 BR 13*	33		2

LITTLE CAESAR UK singer

Date	Title	Label	Peak Position	Weeks at No.1	Weeks in Top 40
9 Jun 90	THE WHOLE OF THE MOON	*A1 EAU 1*	68		

LITTLE EVA US singer

Date	Title	Label	Peak Position	Weeks at No.1	Weeks in Top 40
6 Sep 62	THE LOCO-MOTION	*London HL 9581* ★	2		15
3 Jan 63	KEEP YOUR HANDS OFF MY BABY	*London HLU 9633*	30		3
7 Mar 63	LET'S TURKEY TROT	*London HLU 9687*	13		11
29 Jul 72	THE LOCO-MOTION	*London HL 9581*	11		9

LITTLE MAN TATE UK group

Date	Title	Label	Peak Position	Weeks at No.1	Weeks in Top 40
3 Jun 06	WHAT? WHAT YOU GOT?	*V2 VVR5040553*	40		1
9 Sep 06	HOUSE PARTY AT BOOTHY'S	*V2 VVR5041733*	29		1
25 Nov 06	MAN I HATE YOUR BAND	*V2 VVR5042293*	26		1
3 Feb 07	SEXY IN LATIN	*V2 VVR5042913*	20		1
14 Apr 07	THIS MUST BE LOVE	*V2 VVR5044713*	33		1

LITTLE RICHARD US singer/pianist

Date	Title	Label	Peak Position	Weeks at No.1	Weeks in Top 40
14 Dec 56	RIP IT UP	*London HLO 8336*	30		1
8 Feb 57	LONG TALL SALLY	*London HLO 8366*	3		16
22 Feb 57	TUTTI FRUTTI	*London HLO 8366*	29		1
8 Mar 57	SHE'S GOT IT	*London HLO 8382*	15		9
15 Mar 57	THE GIRL CAN'T HELP IT	*London HLO 8382*	9		11
28 Jun 57	LUCILLE	*London HLO 8446*	10		9
13 Sep 57	JENNY JENNY	*London HLO 8470*	11		5
29 Nov 57	KEEP A KNOCKIN'	*London HLO 8509*	21		7
28 Feb 58	GOOD GOLLY MISS MOLLY	*London HLU 8560*	8		9
11 Jul 58	OOH MY SOUL	*London HLO 8647*	22		4
2 Jan 59	BABY FACE	*London HLU 8770*	2		15
3 Apr 59	BY THE LIGHT OF THE SILVERY MOON	*London HLU 8831*	17		5
5 Jun 59	KANSAS CITY	*London HLU 8868*	26		5
11 Oct 62	HE GOT WHAT HE WANTED (BUT HE LOST WHAT HE HAD)	*Mercury AMT 1189*	38		1
4 Jun 64	BAMA LAMA BAMA LOO	*London HL 9896*	20		6
2 Jul 77	GOOD GOLLY MISS MOLLY/RIP IT UP	*Creole CR 140*	37		2
14 Jun 86	GREAT GOSH A'MIGHTY (IT'S A MATTER OF TIME)	*MCA 1049*	62		
25 Oct 86	OPERATOR	*WEA YZ 89*	67		

LITTLE STEVEN US singer/guitarist

Date	Title	Label	Peak Position	Weeks at No.1	Weeks in Top 40
23 May 87	BITTER FRUIT	*Manhattan MT 21*	66		

LITTLE TONY Italian singer

Date	Title	Label	Peak Position	Weeks at No.1	Weeks in Top 40
15 Jan 60	TOO GOOD	*Decca F 11190*	19		3

LITTLE TREES Danish group

Date	Title	Label	Peak Position	Weeks at No.1	Weeks in Top 40
1 Sep 01	HELP! I'M A FISH	*RCA 74321874652*	11		5

LIVE US group

Date	Title	Label	Peak Position	Weeks at No.1	Weeks in Top 40
18 Feb 95	I ALONE	*Radioactive RAXTD 13*	48		
1 Jul 95	SELLING THE DRAMA	*Radioactive RAXXD 17*	30		1
7 Oct 95	ALL OVER YOU	*Radioactive RAXTD 20*	48		
13 Jan 96	LIGHTNING CRASHES	*Radioactive RAXXD 23*	33		1
15 Mar 97	LAKINI'S JUICE	*Radioactive RAD 49023*	29		1
12 Jul 97	FREAKS	*Radioactive RAXTD 29*	60		
5 Feb 00	THE DOLPHINS CRY	*Radioactive RAXTD 39*	62		

LIVE ELEMENT US duo

Date	Title	Label	Peak Position	Weeks at No.1	Weeks in Top 40
26 Jan 02	BE FREE	*Strictly Rhythm SRUKCD 11*	26		1

Silver-selling ○ Gold-selling ● Platinum-selling US No.1 ★ Peak Position Weeks at No.1 Weeks in Top 40

LIVE REPORT UK group

Date	Title / Label	Peak Position	Weeks at No.1	Weeks in Top 40
20 May 89	**WHY DO I ALWAYS GET IT WRONG?** *Brouhaha CUE 7*	73		

LIVERPOOL EXPRESS UK group

Date	Title / Label	Peak Position	Weeks at No.1	Weeks in Top 40
26 Jun 76	**YOU ARE MY LOVE** *Warner Brothers K 16743*	11		8
16 Oct 76	**HOLD TIGHT** *Warner Brothers K 16799*	46		
18 Dec 76	**EVERY MAN MUST HAVE A DREAM** *Warner Brothers K 16854*	17		10
4 Jun 77	**DREAMIN'** *Warner Brothers K 16933*	40		1

LIVERPOOL F.C. UK football club

Date	Title / Label	Peak Position	Weeks at No.1	Weeks in Top 40
28 May 77	**WE CAN DO IT (EP)** *State STAT 50*	15		4
23 Apr 83	**LIVERPOOL (WE'RE NEVER GONNA...)/LIVERPOOL (ANTHEM)** *Mean 102*	54		
17 May 86	**SITTING ON TOP OF THE WORLD** *Columbia DB 9116*	50		
14 May 88	**ANFIELD RAP (RED MACHINE IN FULL EFFECT)** *Virgin LFC 1*	3		5
18 May 96	**PASS & MOVE (IT'S THE LIVERPOOL GROOVE)** *Telstar LFCCD 96* LIVERPOOL FC & THE BOOT ROOM BOYS	4		4

LIVIN' JOY Italian group

Date	Title / Label	Peak Position	Weeks at No.1	Weeks in Top 40
3 Sep 94	**DREAMER** *Undiscovered MCSTD 1993*	18		4
13 May 95	**DREAMER** *Undiscovered MCSTD 2056*	1	1	7
15 Jun 96	**DON'T STOP MOVIN'** *Undiscovered MCSTD 40041* ○	5		12
2 Nov 96	**FOLLOW THE RULES** *Undiscovered MCSTD 40081*	9		3
5 Apr 97	**WHERE CAN I FIND LOVE** *Undiscovered MCSTD 40108*	12		3
23 Aug 97	**DEEP IN YOU** *Undiscovered MCSTD 40136*	17		3

LIVING COLOUR US group

Date	Title / Label	Peak Position	Weeks at No.1	Weeks in Top 40
27 Oct 90	**TYPE** *Epic LCL 7*	75		
2 Feb 91	**LOVE REARS ITS UGLY HEAD** *Epic 6565937*	12		8
1 Jun 91	**SOLACE OF YOU** *Epic 6569087*	33		2
26 Oct 91	**CULT OF PERSONALITY** *Epic 6575357*	67		
20 Feb 93	**LEAVE IT ALONE** *Epic 6589762*	34		1
17 Apr 93	**AUSLANDER** *Epic 6591732*	53		

LIVING IN A BOX UK group

Date	Title / Label	Peak Position	Weeks at No.1	Weeks in Top 40
4 Apr 87	**LIVING IN A BOX** *Chrysalis LIB 1*	5		10
13 Jun 87	**SCALES OF JUSTICE** *Chrysalis LIB 2*	30		4
26 Sep 87	**SO THE STORY GOES** *Chrysalis LIB 3* LIVING IN A BOX FEATURING BOBBY WOMACK	34		2
30 Jan 88	**LOVE IS THE ART** *Chrysalis LIB 4*	45		
18 Feb 89	**BLOW THE HOUSE DOWN** *Chrysalis LIB 5*	10		7
10 Jun 89	**GATECRASHING** *Chrysalis LIB 6*	36		3
23 Sep 89	**ROOM IN YOUR HEART** *Chrysalis LIB 7* ○	5		10
30 Dec 89	**DIFFERENT AIR** *Chrysalis LIB 8*	57		

DANDY LIVINGSTONE Jamaican singer

Date	Title / Label	Peak Position	Weeks at No.1	Weeks in Top 40
2 Sep 72	**SUZANNE BEWARE OF THE DEVIL** *Horse HOSS 16*	14		9
13 Jan 73	**BIG CITY/THINK ABOUT THAT** *Horse HOSS 26*	26		7

LL COOL J US rapper

Date	Title / Label	Peak Position	Weeks at No.1	Weeks in Top 40
4 Jul 87	**I'M BAD** *Def Jam 6508567*	71		
12 Sep 87	**I NEED LOVE** *Def Jam 6511017*	8		7
21 Nov 87	**GO CUT CREATOR GO** *Def Jam LLCJ 1*	66		
13 Feb 88	**GOING BACK TO CALI/JACK THE RIPPER** *Def Jam LLCJ 2*	37		2
10 Jun 89	**I'M THAT TYPE OF GUY** *Def Jam LLCJ 3*	43		
1 Dec 90	**AROUND THE WAY GIRL/MAMA SAID KNOCK YOU OUT** *Def Jam 6564470*	41		
9 Mar 91	**AROUND THE WAY GIRL (REMIX)** *Columbia 6564470*	36		3
10 Apr 93	**HOW I'M COMIN'** *Def Jam 6591692*	37		1
20 Jan 96	**HEY LOVER** *Def Jam DEFCD 14* LL COOL J FEATURING BOYZ II MEN	17		2
1 Jun 96	**DOIN' IT** *Def Jam DEFCD 15*	15		2
5 Oct 96	**LOUNGIN** *Def Jam DEFCD 30*	7		6
8 Feb 97	**AIN'T NOBODY** *Geffen GFSTD 22195*	1	1	5
5 Apr 97	**HIT 'EM HIGH (THE MONSTARS' ANTHEM)** *Atlantic A 5449CD* B REAL/BUSTA RHYMES/COOLIO/LL COOL J/METHOD MAN	8		4
1 Nov 97	**PHENOMENON** *Def Jam 5681172*	9		3
28 Mar 98	**FATHER** *Def Jam 5685292*	10		3
11 Jul 98	**ZOOM** *Interscope IND 95594* DR DRE & LL COOL J	15		2
5 Dec 98	**INCREDIBLE** *Jive 0522102* KEITH MURRAY FEATURING LL COOL J	52		
26 Oct 02	**LUV U BETTER** *Def Jam 0638722*	7		4
22 Feb 03	**PARADISE** *Def Jam 0637242* LL COOL J FEATURING AMERIE	18		3
22 Mar 03	**ALL I HAVE** *Epic 6736782* JENNIFER LOPEZ FEATURING LL COOL J ★	2		11
28 Aug 04	**HEADSPRUNG** *Def Jam 9863759*	25		2
26 Feb 05	**HUSH** *Def Jam 2103774* LL COOL J FEATURING 7 AURELIUS	3		6
13 May 06	**CONTROL MYSELF** *Def Jam 9856569* LL COOL J FEATURING JENNIFER LOPEZ	2		10

LLAMA FARMERS UK group

Date	Title / Label	Peak Position	Weeks at No.1	Weeks in Top 40
6 Feb 99	**BIG WHEELS** *Beggars Banquet BBQ 333CD*	67		
15 May 99	**GET THE KEYS AND GO** *Beggars Banquet BBQ 335CD*	74		

KELLY LLORENNA UK singer

Date	Title / Label	Peak Position	Weeks at No.1	Weeks in Top 40
7 May 94	**SET YOU FREE** *All Around The World CDGLOBE 124* N-TRANCE FEATURING KELLY LLORENNA	39		1
24 Feb 96	**BRIGHTER DAY** *Pukka CDPUKKA 5*	43		
14 Jan 95	**SET YOU FREE** *All Around The World CXGLOBE 126* N-TRANCE FEATURING KELLY LLORENNA ●	2		11
25 Jul 98	**HEART OF GOLD** *Diverse VERSE 2CD* FORCE & STYLES FEATURING KELLY LLORENNA	55		
24 Mar 01	**TRUE LOVE NEVER DIES** *All Around The World CDGLOBE 240* FLIP & FILL FEATURING KELLY LLORENNA	34		1
2 Feb 02	**TRUE LOVE NEVER DIES (REMIX)** *All Around The World CDGLOBE 248* FLIP & FILL FEATURING KELLY LLORENNA	7		6
6 Jul 02	**TELL IT TO MY HEART** *All Around The World CDGLOBE 256*	9		6
30 Nov 02	**HEART OF GOLD** *All Around The World CXGLOBE 271*	19		2
6 Mar 04	**THIS TIME I KNOW IT'S FOR REAL** *All Around The World CXGLOBE 295*	14		2

LLOYD US rapper

Date	Title / Label	Peak Position	Weeks at No.1	Weeks in Top 40
30 Apr 05	**CAUGHT UP** *The Inc 9881232* JA RULE FEATURING LLOYD	20		2
2 Jun 07	**YOU** *The Inc 1734409* LLOYD FEATURING LIL WAYNE	45		
18 Aug 07	**GET IT SHAWTY** *Universal 1743495*	72		

LMC UK duo

Date	Title / Label	Peak Position	Weeks at No.1	Weeks in Top 40
7 Feb 04	**TAKE ME TO THE CLOUDS ABOVE** *All Around The World CXGLOBE 313* LMC VS U2	1	2	10
4 Feb 06	**YOU GET WHAT YOU GIVE** *All Around The World CDGLOBE423* LMC FEATURING RACHEL McFARLANE	30		1

LNM PROJEKT UK group

Date	Title / Label	Peak Position	Weeks at No.1	Weeks in Top 40
19 Mar 05	**EVERYWHERE** *Hed Kandi HEDKCDS012* LNM PROJECT FEATURING BONNIE BAILEY	38		1

LNR US vocal/instrumental house duo

Date	Title / Label	Peak Position	Weeks at No.1	Weeks in Top 40
3 Jun 89	**WORK IT TO THE BONE** *Kool Kat KOOL 501*	64		

LO FIDELITY ALLSTARS UK group

Date	Title / Label	Peak Position	Weeks at No.1	Weeks in Top 40
11 Oct 97	**DISCO MACHINE GUN** *Skint 30CD*	50		
2 May 98	**VISION INCISION** *Skint 33CD*	30		1
28 Nov 98	**BATTLEFLAG** *Skint 38CD* LO FIDELITY ALLSTARS FEATURING PIGEONHED	36		1

LO-RIDER UK production duo

Date	Title / Label	Peak Position	Weeks at No.1	Weeks in Top 40
2 Dec 06	**SKINNY** *Absolution CDABSOL8* LO-RIDER FEATURING CUMBERBATCH	44		

LOBO US singer

Date	Title / Label	Peak Position	Weeks at No.1	Weeks in Top 40
19 Jun 71	**ME AND YOU AND A DOG NAMED BOO** *Philips 6073 801*	4		12
8 Jun 74	**I'D LOVE YOU TO WANT ME** *UK 68*	5		10
25 Jul 81	**THE CARIBBEAN DISCO SHOW** *Polydor POSP 302*	8		9

LOC UK production group

Date	Title / Label	Peak Position	Weeks at No.1	Weeks in Top 40
9 Jul 05	**RING DING DING** *Street Tuff STRCDS3539*	58		

Silver-selling ○ Gold-selling ● Platinum-selling ✪ US No.1 ★ — Peak Position, Weeks at No.1, Weeks in Top 40

TONE LOC US rapper

Date	Title / Label	Peak Position	Weeks at No.1	Weeks in Top 40
11 Feb 89	**WILD THING/LOC'ED AFTER DARK** *Fourth & Broadway BRW 121*	21		5
20 May 89	**FUNKY COLD MEDINA/ON FIRE** *Fourth & Broadway BRW 129*	13		6
5 Aug 89	**I GOT IT GOIN' ON** *Fourth & Broadway BRW 140*	55		

LOCK 'N' LOAD Dutch production group

Date	Title / Label	Peak Position	Weeks at No.1	Weeks in Top 40
15 Apr 00	**BLOW YA MIND** *Pepper 9230162* ○	6		8
3 Mar 01	**HOUSE SOME MORE** *Pepper 9230422*	45		

KIMBERLEY LOCKE US singer

Date	Title / Label	Peak Position	Weeks at No.1	Weeks in Top 40
31 Jul 04	**8TH WORLD WONDER** *Curb CUBC097*	49		

HANK LOCKLIN US singer

Date	Title / Label	Peak Position	Weeks at No.1	Weeks in Top 40
11 Aug 60	**PLEASE HELP ME I'M FALLING** *RCA 1188*	9		17
15 Feb 62	**FROM HERE TO THERE TO YOU** *RCA 1273*	44		
15 Nov 62	**WE'RE GONNA GO FISHIN'** *RCA 1305*	18		9
5 May 66	**I FEEL A CRY COMING ON** *RCA 1510*	29		5

LOCKSMITH US group

Date	Title / Label	Peak Position	Weeks at No.1	Weeks in Top 40
23 Aug 80	**UNLOCK THE FUNK** *Arista ARIST 364*	42		

LOCOMOTIVE UK group

Date	Title / Label	Peak Position	Weeks at No.1	Weeks in Top 40
16 Oct 68	**RUDI'S IN LOVE** *Parlophone R 5718*	25		7

LODGER UK group

Date	Title / Label	Peak Position	Weeks at No.1	Weeks in Top 40
2 May 98	**I'M LEAVING** *Island CID 693*	40		1

LISA LOEB & NINE STORIES US group

Date	Title / Label	Peak Position	Weeks at No.1	Weeks in Top 40
3 Sep 94	**STAY (I MISSED YOU)** *RCA 74321212522* ★	6		13
16 Sep 95	**DO YOU SLEEP?** *Geffen GFSTD 96*	45		

NILS LOFGREN US singer/guitarist

Date	Title / Label	Peak Position	Weeks at No.1	Weeks in Top 40
8 Jun 85	**SECRETS IN THE STREET** *Towerbell TOW 68*	53		

JOHNNY LOGAN Irish singer

Date	Title / Label	Peak Position	Weeks at No.1	Weeks in Top 40
3 May 80	**WHAT'S ANOTHER YEAR** *Epic EPC 8572* ○	1	2	7
23 May 87	**HOLD ME NOW** *Epic LOG 1* ○	2		9
22 Aug 87	**I'M NOT IN LOVE** *Epic LOG 2*	51		

KENNY LOGGINS US singer

Date	Title / Label	Peak Position	Weeks at No.1	Weeks in Top 40
28 Apr 84	**FOOTLOOSE** *CBS A 4101* ★	6		7
1 Nov 86	**DANGER ZONE** *CBS A 7188*	45		

LOGO UK production duo

Date	Title / Label	Peak Position	Weeks at No.1	Weeks in Top 40
8 Dec 01	**DON'T PANIC** *Manifesto FESCD 89* LOGO FEATURING DAWN JOSEPH	42		

LINDSAY LOHAN US singer/actress

Date	Title / Label	Peak Position	Weeks at No.1	Weeks in Top 40
7 May 05	**OVER** *Universal MCSTD40412*	27		1

LOLA US singer

Date	Title / Label	Peak Position	Weeks at No.1	Weeks in Top 40
28 Mar 87	**WAX THE VAN** *Syncopate SY 1*	65		

LOLLY UK singer

Date	Title / Label	Peak Position	Weeks at No.1	Weeks in Top 40
10 Jul 99	**VIVA LA RADIO** *Polydor 5639512*	6		6
18 Sep 99	**MICKEY** *Polydor 5613692* ○	4		7
4 Dec 99	**BIG BOYS DON'T CRY/ROCKIN' ROBIN** *Polydor 5615552*	10		7
6 May 00	**PER SEMPRE AMORE (FOREVER IN LOVE)** *Polydor 5617882*	11		3
9 Sep 00	**GIRLS JUST WANNA HAVE FUN** *Polydor 5619762*	14		3

LONDON BOYS UK duo

Date	Title / Label	Peak Position	Weeks at No.1	Weeks in Top 40
10 Dec 88	**REQUIEM** *WEA YZ 345*	59		
1 Apr 89	**REQUIEM** *WEA YZ 345* ○	4		11
1 Jul 89	**LONDON NIGHTS** *WEA YZ 393* ○	2		8
16 Sep 89	**HARLEM DESIRE** *WEA YZ 415*	17		6
2 Dec 89	**MY LOVE** *WEA YZ 433*	46		
16 Jun 90	**CHAPEL OF LOVE** *East West YZ 458*	75		
19 Jan 91	**FREEDOM** *East West YZ 554*	54		

JULIE LONDON US singer

Date	Title / Label	Peak Position	Weeks at No.1	Weeks in Top 40
5 Apr 57	**CRY ME A RIVER** *London HLU 8240*	22		3

LAURIE LONDON UK singer

Date	Title / Label	Peak Position	Weeks at No.1	Weeks in Top 40
8 Nov 57	**HE'S GOT THE WHOLE WORLD IN HIS HANDS** *Parlophone R 4359* ★	12		12

LONDON STRING CHORALE
UK orchestra and choir

Date	Title / Label	Peak Position	Weeks at No.1	Weeks in Top 40
15 Dec 73	**GALLOPING HOME** *Polydor 2058 280*	31		5

LONDON SYMPHONY ORCHESTRA
UK orchestra

Date	Title / Label	Peak Position	Weeks at No.1	Weeks in Top 40
6 Jan 79	**THEME FROM *SUPERMAN* (MAIN TITLE)** *Warner Brothers K 17292*	32		4

LONDONBEAT UK/US/Trinidadian group

Date	Title / Label	Peak Position	Weeks at No.1	Weeks in Top 40
26 Nov 88	**9 A.M. (THE COMFORT ZONE)** *AnXious ANX 008*	19		6
18 Feb 89	**FALLING IN LOVE AGAIN** *AnXious ANX 007*	60		
2 Dec 89	**IT TAKES TWO BABY** *Spartan CIN 101* LIZ KERSHAW, BRUNO BROOKES, JIVE BUNNY & LONDONBEAT	53		
1 Sep 90	**I'VE BEEN THINKING ABOUT YOU** *AnXious ANX 14* ○ ★	2		10
24 Nov 90	**A BETTER LOVE** *AnXious ANX 21*	52		
2 Mar 91	**NO WOMAN NO CRY** *AnXious ANX 25*	64		
20 Jul 91	**A BETTER LOVE** *AnXious ANX 32*	23		4
27 Jun 92	**YOU BRING ON THE SUN** *AnXious ANX 37*	32		2
24 Oct 92	**THAT'S HOW I FEEL ABOUT YOU** *AnXious ANX 40*	69		
8 Apr 95	**I'M JUST YOUR PUPPET ON A ... (STRING)** *AnXious 74321270982*	55		
20 May 95	**COME BACK** *AnXious 74321226682*	69		

LONE JUSTICE US group

Date	Title / Label	Peak Position	Weeks at No.1	Weeks in Top 40
7 Mar 87	**I FOUND LOVE** *Geffen GEF 18*	45		

LONESTAR US group

Date	Title / Label	Peak Position	Weeks at No.1	Weeks in Top 40
15 Apr 00	**AMAZED** *Grapevine 74321742582* ★	21		17
7 Oct 00	**SMILE** *Grapevine 74321786132*	55		

SHORTY LONG US singer

Date	Title / Label	Peak Position	Weeks at No.1	Weeks in Top 40
17 Jul 68	**HERE COMES THE JUDGE** *Tamla Motown TMG 663*	30		6

LONG & THE SHORT UK group

Date	Title / Label	Peak Position	Weeks at No.1	Weeks in Top 40
10 Sep 64	**THE LETTER** *Decca F 11964*	35		4
24 Dec 64	**CHOC ICE** *Decca F 12043*	40		1

LONG BLONDES UK group

Date	Title / Label	Peak Position	Weeks at No.1	Weeks in Top 40
8 Jul 06	**WEEKEND WITHOUT MAKEUP** *Rough Trade RTRADSCD351*	28		1
4 Nov 06	**ONCE AND NEVER AGAIN** *Rough Trade RTRADSCD373*	30		1
17 Feb 07	**GIDDY STRATOSPHERES** *Rough Trade RTRADSCD387*	37		1

LONG RYDERS US group

Date	Title / Label	Peak Position	Weeks at No.1	Weeks in Top 40
5 Oct 85	**LOOKING FOR LEWIS AND CLARK** *Island IS 237*	59		

LONGPIGS UK group

Date	Title / Label	Peak Position	Weeks at No.1	Weeks in Top 40
22 Jul 95	**SHE SAID** *Mother MUMCD 66*	67		
28 Oct 95	**JESUS CHRIST** *Mother MUMCD 68*	61		
17 Feb 96	**FAR** *Mother MUMCD 71*	37		1

Silver-selling · Gold-selling · Platinum-selling · US No.1 ★ — Peak Position · Weeks at No.1 · Weeks in Top 40

Date	Title / Label	Peak Position	Weeks at No.1	Weeks in Top 40
13 Apr 96	**ON AND ON** *Mother MUMCD 74*	16		1
22 Jun 96	**SHE SAID** *Mother MUMXD 77*	16		3
5 Oct 96	**LOST MYSELF** *Mother MUMCD 82*	22		2
9 Oct 99	**BLUE SKIES** *Mother MUMCD 113*	21		1
18 Dec 99	**THE FRANK SONATA** *Mother MUMCD 114*	57		

JOE LONGTHORNE UK singer

Date	Title / Label	Peak Position	Weeks at No.1	Weeks in Top 40
30 Apr 94	**YOUNG GIRL** *EMI CDEM 310*	61		
10 Dec 94	**PASSING STRANGERS** *EMI CDEM 362* JOE LONGTHORNE & LIZ DAWN	34		1

LONGVIEW UK group

Date	Title / Label	Peak Position	Weeks at No.1	Weeks in Top 40
26 Oct 02	**WHEN YOU SLEEP** *4.45 Recordings LVIEW 02CD*	74		
8 Feb 03	**NOWHERE** *4.45 Recordings LVIEW 03CD*	72		
19 Jul 03	**FURTHER** *14th Floor 14FLR 01CD*	27		1
11 Oct 03	**CAN'T EXPLAIN** *14th Floor 14FLR 02CD*	51		
10 Jul 04	**IN A DREAM** *14th Floor 14FLR 06CD*	38		1
22 Jan 05	**COMING DOWN/WHEN YOU SLEEP** *14th Floor 14FLR09CD*	32		1
20 Aug 05	**FURTHER** *14th Floor 14FLR12CD*	24		2

LONYO UK singer

Date	Title / Label	Peak Position	Weeks at No.1	Weeks in Top 40
8 Jul 00	**SUMMER OF LOVE** *Riverhorse RIVH CD3X* LONYO - COMME CI COMME CA	8		4
7 Apr 01	**GARAGE GIRLS** *Riverhorse RIVHCD 12* LONYO FEATURING MC ONYX STONE	39		1

LOOK UK group

Date	Title / Label	Peak Position	Weeks at No.1	Weeks in Top 40
20 Dec 80	**I AM THE BEAT** *MCA 647*	6		7
29 Aug 81	**FEEDING TIME** *MCA 736*	50		

LOON US rapper

Date	Title / Label	Peak Position	Weeks at No.1	Weeks in Top 40
10 Aug 02	**I NEED A GIRL (PART ONE)** *Puff Daddy 74321947242* P DIDDY FEATURING USHER & LOON	4		8
8 Mar 03	**HIT THE FREEWAY** *Arista 82876506372* TONI BRAXTON FEATURING LOON	29		1
7 Feb 04	**SHOW ME YOUR SOUL** *Puff Daddy MCSTD 40350* P DIDDY, LENNY KRAVITZ, PHARRELL WILLIAMS & LOON	35		1

LOOP DA LOOP UK producer

Date	Title / Label	Peak Position	Weeks at No.1	Weeks in Top 40
7 Jun 97	**GO WITH THE FLOW** *Manifesto FESCD 24*	47		
20 Feb 99	**HAZEL** *Manifesto FESCD 53*	20		2

LOOSE ENDS UK group

Date	Title / Label	Peak Position	Weeks at No.1	Weeks in Top 40
23 Feb 84	**TELL ME WHAT YOU WANT** *Virgin VS 658*	74		
28 Apr 84	**EMERGENCY (DIAL 999)** *Virgin VS 677*	41		
21 Jul 84	**CHOOSE ME (RESCUE ME)** *Virgin VS 697*	59		
23 Feb 85	**HANGIN' ON A STRING (CONTEMPLATING)** *Virgin VS 748*	13		8
11 May 85	**MAGIC TOUCH** *Virgin VS 761*	16		6
27 Jul 85	**GOLDEN TOUCH** *Virgin VS 795*	59		
14 Jun 86	**STAY A LITTLE WHILE, CHILD** *Virgin VS 819*	52		
20 Sep 86	**SLOW DOWN** *Virgin VS 884*	27		5
29 Nov 86	**NIGHTS OF PLEASURE** *Virgin VS 919*	42		
4 Jun 88	**MR BACHELOR** *Virgin VS 1080*	50		
25 Aug 90	**DON'T BE A FOOL** *10 TEN 312*	13		5
17 Nov 90	**LOVE'S GOT ME** *10 TEN 330*	40		1
20 Jun 92	**HANGIN' ON A STRING (CONTEMPLATING) (REMIX)** *10 TEN 406*	25		3
5 Sep 92	**MAGIC TOUCH (REMIX)** *10 TEN 409*	75		

LISA LEFT EYE LOPES US singer

Date	Title / Label	Peak Position	Weeks at No.1	Weeks in Top 40
1 Apr 00	**NEVER BE THE SAME AGAIN** *Virgin VSCDT 1786* MELANIE C & LISA LEFT EYE LOPES	1	1	10
27 Oct 01	**THE BLOCK PARTY** *LaFace 74321895912*	16		2

JENNIFER LOPEZ US singer

Date	Title / Label	Peak Position	Weeks at No.1	Weeks in Top 40
3 Jul 99	**IF YOU HAD MY LOVE** *Columbia 6675772* ★	4		10
13 Nov 99	**WAITING FOR TONIGHT** *Columbia 6683072*	5		5
1 Apr 00	**FEELIN' SO GOOD** *Columbia 6691972* JENNIFER LOPEZ FEATURING BIG PUN & FAT JOE	15		3
20 Jan 01	**LOVE DON'T COST A THING** *Epic 6707282*	1	1	7
12 May 01	**PLAY** *Epic 6712272*	3		6
18 Aug 01	**AIN'T IT FUNNY** *Epic 6717592* JENNIFER LOPEZ FEATURING JA RULE & CADILLAC TAH	3		6
10 Nov 01	**I'M REAL** *Epic 6720322* JENNIFER LOPEZ FEATURING JA RULE ★	4		12
23 Mar 02	**AIN'T IT FUNNY** *Epic 6724922* ★	4		10
13 Jul 02	**I'M GONNA BE ALRIGHT** *Epic 6728442* JENNIFER LOPEZ FEATURING NAS	3		8
30 Nov 02	**JENNY FROM THE BLOCK** *Epic 6733572*	3		8
22 Mar 03	**ALL I HAVE** *Epic 6736782* JENNIFER LOPEZ FEATURING LL COOL J ★	2		11
21 Jun 03	**I'M GLAD** *Epic 6740152*	11		5
20 Mar 04	**BABY I LOVE U** *Epic 6747902*	3		6
26 Feb 05	**GET RIGHT** *Epic 6757562*	1		10
28 May 05	**HOLD YOU DOWN** *Epic 6759342* JENNIFER LOPEZ FEATURING FAT JOE	6		5
13 May 06	**CONTROL MYSELF** *Def Jam 9856569* LL COOL J FEATURING JENNIFER LOPEZ	2		10
6 Oct 07	**DO IT WELL** *RCA 88697176452*	11		5
2 Feb 08	**HOLD IT, DON'T DROP IT** *Download*	72		

TRINI LOPEZ US singer

Date	Title / Label	Peak Position	Weeks at No.1	Weeks in Top 40
12 Sep 63	**IF I HAD A HAMMER** *Reprise R 20198*	4		14
12 Dec 63	**KANSAS CITY** *Reprise R 20236*	35		1
12 May 66	**I'M COMING HOME CINDY** *Reprise R 20455*	28		3
6 Apr 67	**GONNA GET ALONG WITHOUT YA NOW** *Reprise R 20547*	41		
19 Dec 81	**TRINI TRAX** *RCA 154*	59		

LORD ROCKINGHAM'S XI UK group

Date	Title / Label	Peak Position	Weeks at No.1	Weeks in Top 40
24 Oct 58	**HOOTS MON** *Decca F 11059*	1	3	17
6 Feb 59	**WEE TOM** *Decca F 11104*	16		3
25 Sep 93	**HOOTS MON** *Decca 8820982*	60		

LORD TANAMO Jamaican singer

Date	Title / Label	Peak Position	Weeks at No.1	Weeks in Top 40
1 Dec 90	**I'M IN THE MOOD FOR LOVE** *Mooncrest MOON 1009*	58		

LORD TARIQ & PETER GUNZ US duo

Date	Title / Label	Peak Position	Weeks at No.1	Weeks in Top 40
2 May 98	**DEJA VU (UPTOWN BABY)** *Columbia 6658722*	21		1

JERRY LORDAN UK singer

Date	Title / Label	Peak Position	Weeks at No.1	Weeks in Top 40
8 Jan 60	**I'LL STAY SINGLE** *Parlophone R 4588*	26		2
26 Feb 60	**WHO COULD BE BLUER** *Parlophone R 4627*	16		9
2 Jun 60	**SING LIKE AN ANGEL** *Parlophone R 4653*	36		1

LORDI Finnish group

Date	Title / Label	Peak Position	Weeks at No.1	Weeks in Top 40
10 Jun 06	**HARD ROCK HALLELUJAH** *Sony BMG 82876806762*	25		2

TRACI LORDS US singer/actress

Date	Title / Label	Peak Position	Weeks at No.1	Weeks in Top 40
7 Oct 95	**FALLEN ANGEL** *Radioactive RAXTD 18*	72		

LORENZ Italian singer

Date	Title / Label	Peak Position	Weeks at No.1	Weeks in Top 40
16 Sep 06	**SET ME FREE** *Superstar Music LORENZ17CD*	35		1

TREY LORENZ US singer

Date	Title / Label	Peak Position	Weeks at No.1	Weeks in Top 40
21 Nov 92	**SOMEONE TO HOLD** *Epic 6587857*	65		
30 Jan 93	**PHOTOGRAPH OF MARY** *Epic 6589542*	38		1

LORI & THE CHAMELEONS UK group

Date	Title / Label	Peak Position	Weeks at No.1	Weeks in Top 40
8 Dec 79	**TOUCH** *Sire SIR 4025*	70		

LORRAINE Norwegian group

Date	Title / Label	Peak Position	Weeks at No.1	Weeks in Top 40
22 Apr 06	**I FEEL IT** *Waterfall/Columbia 82876822702*	29		1

LOS BRAVOS Spanish/German group

Date	Title / Label	Peak Position	Weeks at No.1	Weeks in Top 40
30 Jun 66	**BLACK IS BLACK** *Decca F 22419*	2		12
8 Sep 66	**I DON'T CARE** *Decca F 22484*	16		9

Silver-selling ◌ Gold-selling ● Platinum-selling ✱ US No.1 ★ | Peak Position | Weeks at No.1 | Weeks in Top 40

LOS DEL MAR Canadian group

Date	Title / Label	Peak Position	Weeks at No.1	Weeks in Top 40
8 Jun 96	MACARENA *Pulse 8 CDLOSE 101* LOS DEL MAR FEATURING WILL VELOZ	43		

LOS DEL RIO Spanish duo

Date	Title / Label	Peak Position	Weeks at No.1	Weeks in Top 40
1 Jun 96	MACARENA *RCA 74321345372* ● ★	2		15

LOS INDIOS TABAJARAS Brazilian Indian guitarists

Date	Title / Label	Peak Position	Weeks at No.1	Weeks in Top 40
31 Oct 63	MARIA ELENA *RCA 1365*	5		16

LOS LOBOS US group

Date	Title / Label	Peak Position	Weeks at No.1	Weeks in Top 40
6 Apr 85	DON'T WORRY BABY/WILL THE WOLF SURVIVE *London LASH 4*	57		
18 Jul 87	LA BAMBA *Slash LASH 13* ★	1	2	9
26 Sep 87	COME ON LET'S GO *Slash LASH 14*	18		6

LOS POP TOPS Spanish group

Date	Title / Label	Peak Position	Weeks at No.1	Weeks in Top 40
9 Oct 71	MAMY BLUE *A&M AMS 859*	35		2

LOS UMERELLOS Multinational group

Date	Title / Label	Peak Position	Weeks at No.1	Weeks in Top 40
3 Oct 98	NO TENGO DINERO *Virgin VUSCD 139*	33		1

JOE LOSS ORCHESTRA UK bandleader and orchestra

Date	Title / Label	Peak Position	Weeks at No.1	Weeks in Top 40
29 Jun 61	WHEELS CHA CHA *HMV POP 880*	21		19
19 Oct 61	SUCU SUCU *HMV POP 937*	48		
29 Mar 62	THE MAIGRET THEME *HMV POP 995*	20		7
1 Nov 62	MUST BE MADISON *HMV POP 1075*	20		12
5 Nov 64	MARCH OF THE MODS *HMV POP 1351*	31		3

LOST UK production duo

Date	Title / Label	Peak Position	Weeks at No.1	Weeks in Top 40
22 Jun 91	TECHNO FUNK *Perfecto PT 44560*	75		

LOST BOYZ US group

Date	Title / Label	Peak Position	Weeks at No.1	Weeks in Top 40
2 Nov 96	MUSIC MAKES ME HIGH *Universal MCSTD 48015*	42		
12 Jul 97	LOVE, PEACE & HAPPINESS *Universal UND 56131*	57		

LOST BROTHERS UK group

Date	Title / Label	Peak Position	Weeks at No.1	Weeks in Top 40
20 Dec 03	CRY LITTLE SISTER (I NEED U NOW) *Incentive CENT 60CDS* LOST BROTHERS FEATURING G TOM MAC	21		6

LOST IT.COM UK production duo

Date	Title / Label	Peak Position	Weeks at No.1	Weeks in Top 40
7 Apr 01	ANIMAL *Perfecto PERF 13CDS*	70		

LOST TRIBE UK group

Date	Title / Label	Peak Position	Weeks at No.1	Weeks in Top 40
11 Sep 99	GAMEMASTER *Hooj Choons HOOJ 81CD*	24		1
6 Dec 03	GAMEMASTER (REMIX) *Liquid Asset ASSETCD 12015*	61		

LOST WITNESS UK group

Date	Title / Label	Peak Position	Weeks at No.1	Weeks in Top 40
29 May 99	HAPPINESS HAPPENING *Ministry Of Sound MOSCDS 129*	18		2
18 Sep 99	RED SUN RISING *Sound Of Ministry MOSCDS 133*	22		2
16 Dec 00	7 COLOURS *Data 15CDS*	28		1
18 May 02	DID I DREAM (SONG TO THE SIREN) *Data 28CDS*	28		1

LOSTPROPHETS UK group

Date	Title / Label	Peak Position	Weeks at No.1	Weeks in Top 40
8 Dec 01	SHINOBI VS DRAGON NINJA *Visible Noise TORMENT 17*	41		
23 Mar 02	THE FAKE SOUND OF PROGRESS *Visible Noise TORMENT 20*	21		2
15 Nov 03	BURN BURN *Visible Noise TORMENT 30CD*	17		2
7 Feb 04	LAST TRAIN HOME *Visible Noise TORMENT 37CD*	8		5
15 May 04	WAKE UP *Visible Noise TORMENT 40CD*	18		2
4 Sep 04	LAST SUMMER *Visible Noise TORMENT 43CD*	13		3
4 Dec 04	GOODBYE TONIGHT *Visible Noise TORMENT47CD*	42		
24 Jun 06	ROOFTOPS (A LIBERATION BROADCAST) *Visible Noise TORMENT73CD*	8		7
16 Sep 06	A TOWN CALLED HYPOCRISY *Visible Noise TORMENT86CD*	23		2
9 Dec 06	CAN'T CATCH TOMORROW *Visible Noise TORMENT96CD*	35		1
5 May 07	4 AM FOREVER *Visible Noise TORMENT105*	34		1

LOTUS EATERS UK duo

Date	Title / Label	Peak Position	Weeks at No.1	Weeks in Top 40
2 Jul 83	THE FIRST PICTURE OF YOU *Sylvan SYL 1*	15		9
8 Oct 83	YOU DON'T NEED SOMEONE NEW *Sylvan SYL 2*	53		

BONNIE LOU US singer

Date	Title / Label	Peak Position	Weeks at No.1	Weeks in Top 40
5 Feb 54	TENNESSEE WIG WALK *Parlophone R 3730*	4		10

LIPPY LOU UK rapper

Date	Title / Label	Peak Position	Weeks at No.1	Weeks in Top 40
22 Apr 95	LIBERATION *More Protein PROCD 105*	57		

LOUCHIE LOU & MICHIE ONE UK duo

Date	Title / Label	Peak Position	Weeks at No.1	Weeks in Top 40
29 May 93	SHOUT (IT OUT) *ffrr FCD 211*	7		6
14 Aug 93	SOMEBODY ELSE'S GUY *ffrr FCD 216*	54		
26 Aug 95	GET DOWN ON IT *China WOKCD 2054*	58		
13 Apr 96	CECILIA *WEA 042CD1* SUGGS FEATURING LOUCHIE LOU & MICHIE ONE ◌	4		11
15 Jun 96	GOOD SWEET LOVIN' *Indochina ID 050CD*	34		1
21 Sep 96	NO MORE ALCOHOL *WEA 065CD1* SUGGS FEATURING LOUCHIE LOU & MICHIE ONE	24		2

LOUD UK group

Date	Title / Label	Peak Position	Weeks at No.1	Weeks in Top 40
28 Mar 92	EASY *China WOK 2016*	67		

JOHN D. LOUDERMILK US singer

Date	Title / Label	Peak Position	Weeks at No.1	Weeks in Top 40
4 Jan 62	THE LANGUAGE OF LOVE *RCA 1269*	13		8

LOUIE LOUIE US singer

Date	Title / Label	Peak Position	Weeks at No.1	Weeks in Top 40
19 Dec 92	THE THOUGHT OF IT *Hardback YZ 724*	34		2

LOUIS XIV US group

Date	Title / Label	Peak Position	Weeks at No.1	Weeks in Top 40
30 Jul 05	GOD KILLED THE QUEEN *Atlantic AT0211CD*	68		
22 Oct 05	FINDING OUT TRUE LOVE IS BLIND *Atlantic AT0214CD*	57		

LOUISE UK singer

Date	Title / Label	Peak Position	Weeks at No.1	Weeks in Top 40
7 Oct 95	LIGHT OF MY LIFE *EMI CDEMS 397*	8		5
16 Mar 96	IN WALKED LOVE *EMI CDEMS 413*	17		5
8 Jun 96	NAKED *EMI CDEM 431*	5		6
31 Aug 96	UNDIVIDED LOVE *EMI CDEM 441*	5		4
30 Nov 96	ONE KISS FROM HEAVEN *EMI CDEM 454*	9		3
4 Oct 97	ARMS AROUND THE WORLD *EMI CDEM 490*	4		5
29 Nov 97	LET'S GO ROUND AGAIN *EMI CDEM 500*	10		7
4 Apr 98	ALL THAT MATTERS *1st Avenue CDEM 506*	11		4
29 Jul 00	2 FACED *1st Avenue CDEMS 570*	3		6
11 Nov 00	BEAUTIFUL INSIDE *1st Avenue CDEMS 575*	13		2
8 Sep 01	STUCK IN THE MIDDLE WITH YOU *1st Avenue CDEM 600*	4		7
27 Sep 03	PANDORA'S KISS *Positive POSCDS002*	5		3

ALI LOVE UK singer

Date	Title / Label	Peak Position	Weeks at No.1	Weeks in Top 40
28 Jul 07	SECRET SUNDAY LOVER *Columbia ALCD003*	45		

COURTNEY LOVE US singer/guitarist

Date	Title / Label	Peak Position	Weeks at No.1	Weeks in Top 40
27 Mar 04	MONO *Virgin VUSDX 283*	41		

DARLENE LOVE US singer

Date	Title / Label	Peak Position	Weeks at No.1	Weeks in Top 40
19 Dec 92	ALL ALONE ON CHRISTMAS *Arista 74321124767*	31		2
1 Jan 94	ALL ALONE ON CHRISTMAS *Arista 74321124767*	72		

HELEN LOVE UK group

Date	Title / Label	Peak Position	Weeks at No.1	Weeks in Top 40
20 Sep 97	DOES YOUR HEART GO BOOM *Che 72CD*	71		
19 Sep 98	LONG LIVE THE UK MUSIC SCENE *Che 82CD*	65		

Silver-selling · Gold-selling · Platinum-selling · US No.1 ★ · Peak Position · Weeks at No.1 · Weeks in Top 40

MONIE LOVE *UK singer*

Date	Title	Peak Position	Weeks at No.1	Weeks in Top 40
4 Feb 89	**I CAN DO THIS** *Cooltempo COOL 177*	37		2
24 Jun 89	**GRANDPA'S PARTY** *Cooltempo COOL 184*	16		6
14 Jul 90	**MONIE IN THE MIDDLE** *Cooltempo COOL 210*	46		
22 Sep 90	**IT'S A SHAME (MY SISTER)** *Cooltempo COOL 219* MONIE LOVE FEATURING TRUE IMAGE	12		7
1 Dec 90	**DOWN TO EARTH** *Cooltempo COOL 222*	31		2
6 Apr 91	**RING MY BELL** *Cooltempo COOL 224* MONIE LOVE Vs ADEVA	20		4
25 Jul 92	**FULL TERM LOVE** *Cooltempo COOL 258*	34		2
13 Mar 93	**BORN 2 B.R.E.E.D.** *Cooltempo CDCOOL 269*	18		4
12 Jun 93	**IN A WORD OR 2/THE POWER** *Cooltempo CDCOOL 273*	33		2
21 Aug 93	**NEVER GIVE UP** *Cooltempo CDCOOL 276*	41		
22 Apr 00	**SLICE OF DA PIE** *Relentless RELENT 2CDS*	29		1

LOVE AFFAIR *UK group*

Date	Title	Peak Position	Weeks at No.1	Weeks in Top 40
3 Jan 68	**EVERLASTING LOVE** *CBS 3125*	1	2	12
17 Apr 68	**RAINBOW VALLEY** *CBS 3366*	5		11
11 Sep 68	**A DAY WITHOUT LOVE** *CBS 3674*	6		11
19 Feb 69	**ONE ROAD** *CBS 3994*	16		8
16 Jul 69	**BRINGING ON BACK THE GOOD TIMES** *CBS 4300*	9		8

LOVE & MONEY *UK group*

Date	Title	Peak Position	Weeks at No.1	Weeks in Top 40
24 May 86	**CANDYBAR EXPRESS** *Mercury MONEY 1*	56		
25 Apr 87	**LOVE AND MONEY** *Mercury MONEY 4*	68		
17 Sep 88	**HALLELUIAH MAN** *Mercury MONEY 5*	63		
14 Jan 89	**STRANGE KIND OF LOVE** *Mercury MONEY 6*	45		
25 Mar 89	**JOCELYN SQUARE** *Mercury MONEY 7*	51		
16 Nov 91	**WINTER** *Mercury MONEY 9*	52		

LOVE BITE *Italian production group*

Date	Title	Peak Position	Weeks at No.1	Weeks in Top 40
7 Oct 00	**TAKE YOUR TIME** *AM:PM CDAMPM 134*	56		

LOVE CITY GROOVE *UK group*

Date	Title	Peak Position	Weeks at No.1	Weeks in Top 40
8 Apr 95	**LOVE CITY GROOVE** *Planet 3 GXY 2003CD*	7		8

LOVE CONNECTION *Italian/German production group*

Date	Title	Peak Position	Weeks at No.1	Weeks in Top 40
2 Dec 00	**THE BOMB** *Multiply CDMULTY 63*	53		

LOVE DECADE *UK group*

Date	Title	Peak Position	Weeks at No.1	Weeks in Top 40
6 Jul 91	**DREAM ON (IS THIS A DREAM)** *All Around The World GLOBE 100*	52		
23 Nov 91	**SO REAL** *All Around The World GLOBE 106*	14		3
11 Apr 92	**I FEEL YOU** *All Around The World GLOBE 107*	34		2
6 Feb 93	**WHEN THE MORNING COMES** *All Around The World CDGLOBE 114*	69		
17 Feb 96	**IS THIS A DREAM?** *All Around The World CDGLOBE 132*	39		1

LOVE DECREE *UK group*

Date	Title	Peak Position	Weeks at No.1	Weeks in Top 40
16 Sep 89	**SOMETHING SO REAL (CHINHEADS THEME)** *Ariola 112642*	61		

LOVE/HATE *US group*

Date	Title	Peak Position	Weeks at No.1	Weeks in Top 40
30 Nov 91	**EVIL TWIN** *Columbia 6575967*	59		
4 Apr 92	**WASTED IN AMERICA** *Columbia 6578897*	38		2

LOVE INC *Jamaican/Canadian production duo*

Date	Title	Peak Position	Weeks at No.1	Weeks in Top 40
28 Dec 02	**YOU'RE A SUPERSTAR** *NuLife 74321978042*	7		11
31 May 03	**BROKEN BONES** *NuLife 8286523172*	8		5
6 Mar 04	**INTO THE NIGHT** *NuLife 82876585782*	39		1

LOVE INCORPORATED *UK production duo*

Date	Title	Peak Position	Weeks at No.1	Weeks in Top 40
9 Feb 91	**LOVE IS THE MESSAGE** *Love EVOL 1* LOVE INCORPORATED FEATURING MC NOISE	59		

LOVE SCULPTURE *UK group*

Date	Title	Peak Position	Weeks at No.1	Weeks in Top 40
27 Nov 68	**SABRE DANCE** *Parlophone R 5744*	5		11

A LOVE SUPREME *UK group*

Date	Title	Peak Position	Weeks at No.1	Weeks in Top 40
17 Apr 99	**NIALL QUINN'S DISCO PANTS** *A Love Supreme/Cherry Red CDVINNIE 3*	59		

(LOVE) TATTOO *Australian producer*

Date	Title	Peak Position	Weeks at No.1	Weeks in Top 40
6 Oct 01	**DROP SOME DRUMS** *Positiva CDTIV 162*	58		

LOVE TO INFINITY *UK group*

Date	Title	Peak Position	Weeks at No.1	Weeks in Top 40
24 Jun 95	**KEEP LOVE TOGETHER** *Mushroom D 00467*	38		1
18 Nov 95	**SOMEDAY** *Mushroom D 1143*	75		
3 Aug 96	**PRAY FOR LOVE** *Mushroom D 1213*	69		

LOVE TRIBE *US group*

Date	Title	Peak Position	Weeks at No.1	Weeks in Top 40
29 Jun 96	**STAND UP** *AM:PM 5816272*	23		2

LOVE UNLIMITED *US group*

Date	Title	Peak Position	Weeks at No.1	Weeks in Top 40
17 Jun 72	**WALKIN' IN THE RAIN WITH THE ONE I LOVE** *Uni UN 539*	14		8
25 Jan 75	**IT MAY BE WINTER OUTSIDE (BUT IN MY HEART IT'S SPRING)** *20th Century BTC 2149*	11		8

LOVE UNLIMITED ORCHESTRA *US orchestra*

Date	Title	Peak Position	Weeks at No.1	Weeks in Top 40
2 Feb 74	**LOVE'S THEME** *Pye International 7N 25635* ★	10		9

LOVE BITES *UK group*

Date	Title	Peak Position	Weeks at No.1	Weeks in Top 40
29 Oct 05	**YOU BROKE MY HEART** *Island MCSXD40427*	13		2
11 Mar 06	**HE'S FIT** *Island MCSXD40446*	48		

LOVEBUG *UK group*

Date	Title	Peak Position	Weeks at No.1	Weeks in Top 40
18 Oct 03	**WHO'S THE DADDY** *Sony Music 6742705*	35		1

LOVEBUG STARSKI *US rapper*

Date	Title	Peak Position	Weeks at No.1	Weeks in Top 40
31 May 86	**AMITYVILLE (THE HOUSE ON THE HILL)** *Epic A 7182*	12		7

LOVEFREEKZ *UK producer*

Date	Title	Peak Position	Weeks at No.1	Weeks in Top 40
5 Feb 05	**SHINE** *Positiva CDTIVS214*	6		4

LOVEHAPPY *US/UK group*

Date	Title	Peak Position	Weeks at No.1	Weeks in Top 40
18 Feb 95	**MESSAGE OF LOVE** *MCA MCSTD 2040*	37		1
20 Jul 96	**MESSAGE OF LOVE (REMIX)** *MCA MCSTD 40052*	70		

BILL LOVELADY *UK singer*

Date	Title	Peak Position	Weeks at No.1	Weeks in Top 40
18 Aug 79	**REGGAE FOR IT NOW** *Charisma CB 337*	12		8

LOVELAND *UK group*

FEATURING RACHEL McFARLANE VS DARLENE LEWIS

Date	Title	Peak Position	Weeks at No.1	Weeks in Top 40
16 Apr 94	**LET THE MUSIC (LIFT YOU UP)** *KMS/Eastern Bloc KMSCD 10*	16		3
5 Nov 94	**(KEEP ON) SHINING/HOPE (NEVER GIVE UP)** *Eastern Bloc BLOCCD 016*	37		1
14 Jan 95	**I NEED SOMEBODY** *Eastern Bloc BLOCCDX 019*	21		2
10 Jun 95	**DON'T MAKE ME WAIT** *Eastern Bloc BLOC 20CD*	22		2
2 Sep 95	**THE WONDER OF LOVE** *Eastern Bloc BLOC 22CD*	53		
11 Nov 95	**I NEED SOMEBODY** *Eastern Bloc BLOC 23CD*	38		2

LOVER SPEAKS *UK duo*

Date	Title	Peak Position	Weeks at No.1	Weeks in Top 40
16 Aug 86	**NO MORE 'I LOVE YOU'S** *A&M AM 326*	58		

LINUS LOVES *US producer*

Date	Title	Peak Position	Weeks at No.1	Weeks in Top 40
22 Nov 03	**STAND BACK** *Data 62CDS* LINUS LOVES FEATURING SAM OBERNIK	31		1

Silver-selling ● Gold-selling ● Platinum-selling ● US No.1 ★ | Peak Position | Weeks at No.1 | Weeks in Top 40

MICHAEL LOVESMITH US singer

Date	Title / Label	Peak Position	Weeks at No.1	Weeks in Top 40
5 Oct 85	**AIN'T NOTHIN' LIKE IT** *Motown ZB 40369*	75		

LOVESTATION UK group

Date	Title / Label	Peak Position	Weeks at No.1	Weeks in Top 40
13 Mar 93	**SHINE ON ME** *RCA 74321137912* LOVESTATION FEATURING LISA HUNT	71		
13 Nov 93	**BEST OF MY LOVE** *Fresh FRSHD 1*	73		
18 Mar 95	**LOVE COME RESCUE ME** *Fresh FRSHD 22*	42		
1 Aug 98	**TEARDROPS** *Fresh FRSHD 65*	14		5
5 Dec 98	**SENSUALITY** *Fresh FRSHD 71*	16		2
5 Feb 00	**TEARDROPS (FOOTSTEPS ON THE DANCEFLOOR) (REMIX)** *Fresh FRSHD 79*	24		2

LENE LOVICH US singer

Date	Title / Label	Peak Position	Weeks at No.1	Weeks in Top 40
17 Feb 79	**LUCKY NUMBER** *Stiff BUY 42* ●	3		9
12 May 79	**SAY WHEN** *Stiff BUY 46*	19		9
20 Oct 79	**BIRD SONG** *Stiff BUY 53*	39		2
29 Mar 80	**WHAT WILL I DO WITHOUT YOU** *Stiff BUY 69*	58		
14 Mar 81	**NEW TOY** *Stiff BUY 97*	53		
27 Nov 82	**IT'S ONLY YOU (MEIN SCHMERZ** *Stiff BUY 164*	68		

LOVIN' SPOONFUL US group

Date	Title / Label	Peak Position	Weeks at No.1	Weeks in Top 40
14 Apr 66	**DAYDREAM** *Pye International 7N 25361*	2		12
14 Jul 66	**SUMMER IN THE CITY** *Kama Sutra KAS 200* ★	8		10
5 Jan 67	**NASHVILLE CATS** *Kama Sutra KAS 204*	26		5
9 Mar 67	**DARLING BE HOME SOON** *Kama Sutra KAS 207*	44		

LOVINDEER Jamaican singer

Date	Title / Label	Peak Position	Weeks at No.1	Weeks in Top 40
27 Sep 86	**MAN SHORTAGE** *TSOJ TS 1*	69		

LOW US group

Date	Title / Label	Peak Position	Weeks at No.1	Weeks in Top 40
5 Mar 05	**CALIFORNIA** *Rough Trade RTRADSCD221*	57		

GARY LOW Italian singer

Date	Title / Label	Peak Position	Weeks at No.1	Weeks in Top 40
8 Oct 83	**I WANT YOU** *Savoir Faire FAIS 004*	52		

JIM LOWE & THE HIGH FIVES
US singer and backing group

Date	Title / Label	Peak Position	Weeks at No.1	Weeks in Top 40
26 Oct 56	**THE GREEN DOOR** *London HLD 8317* ★	8		9

NICK LOWE UK singer

Date	Title / Label	Peak Position	Weeks at No.1	Weeks in Top 40
11 Mar 78	**I LOVE THE SOUND OF BREAKING GLASS** *Radar ADA 1*	7		8
9 Jun 79	**CRACKIN' UP** *Radar ADA 34*	34		2
25 Aug 79	**CRUEL TO BE KIND** *Radar ADA 43*	12		8
26 May 84	**HALF A BOY HALF A MAN** *F. Beat XX 34*	53		

LOWGOLD UK group

Date	Title / Label	Peak Position	Weeks at No.1	Weeks in Top 40
30 Sep 00	**BEAUTY DIES YOUNG** *Nude NUD 52CD*	67		
10 Feb 01	**MERCURY** *Nude NUD 53CD*	48		
12 May 01	**COUNTERFEIT** *Nude NUD 55CD*	52		
8 Sep 01	**BEAUTY DIES YOUNG** *Nude NUD 59CD1*	40		1

LOWRELL US singer

Date	Title / Label	Peak Position	Weeks at No.1	Weeks in Top 40
24 Nov 79	**MELLOW MELLOW RIGHT ON** *AVI AVIS 108*	37		1

L7 US group

Date	Title / Label	Peak Position	Weeks at No.1	Weeks in Top 40
4 Apr 92	**PRETEND WE'RE DEAD** *Slash LASH 34*	21		4
30 May 92	**EVERGLADE** *Slash LASH 36*	27		2
12 Sep 92	**MONSTER** *Slash LASH 38*	33		1
28 Nov 92	**PRETEND WE'RE DEAD** *Slash LASH 42*	50		
9 Jul 94	**ANDRES** *Slash LASCD 48*	34		1

LSG German producer

Date	Title / Label	Peak Position	Weeks at No.1	Weeks in Top 40
10 May 97	**NETHERWORLD** *Hooj Choons HOOJCD 52*	63		

LTD US group

Date	Title / Label	Peak Position	Weeks at No.1	Weeks in Top 40
9 Sep 78	**HOLDING ON (WHEN LOVE IS GONE)** *A&M AMS 7378*	70		

LUCAS US rapper

Date	Title / Label	Peak Position	Weeks at No.1	Weeks in Top 40
6 Aug 94	**LUCAS WITH THE LID OFF** *WEA YZ 832CD*	37		2

CARRIE LUCAS US singer

Date	Title / Label	Peak Position	Weeks at No.1	Weeks in Top 40
16 Jun 79	**DANCE WITH YOU** *Solar FB 1482*	40		1

LUCIANA UK singer

Date	Title / Label	Peak Position	Weeks at No.1	Weeks in Top 40
23 Apr 94	**GET IT UP FOR LOVE** *Chrysalis CDCHS 5008*	55		
6 Aug 94	**IF YOU WANT** *Chrysalis CDCHS 5009*	47		
5 Nov 94	**WHAT GOES AROUND/ONE MORE RIVER** *Chrysalis CDCHS 5015*	67		
4 Nov 06	**YEAH YEAH** *Eye Industries/UMTV 1712693* BODYROX FEATURING LUCIANA	2		14
21 Jul 07	**BIGGER THAN BIG** *Eye Industries/UMTV 1740243* SUPER MAL FEATURING LUCIANA	19		2

LUCID UK group

Date	Title / Label	Peak Position	Weeks at No.1	Weeks in Top 40
8 Aug 98	**I CAN'T HELP MYSELF** *ffrr FCD 339*	7		5
27 Feb 99	**CRAZY** *ffrr FCDP 355*	14		3
16 Oct 99	**STAY WITH ME TILL DAWN** *ffrr FCD 368*	25		1

LUCKY MONKEYS UK production group

Date	Title / Label	Peak Position	Weeks at No.1	Weeks in Top 40
9 Nov 96	**BJANGO** *Hi-Life 5757132*	50		

LUCY PEARL US group

Date	Title / Label	Peak Position	Weeks at No.1	Weeks in Top 40
29 Jul 00	**DANCE TONIGHT** *Virgin VSCDT 1775*	36		1
25 Nov 00	**DON'T MESS WITH MY MAN** *Virgin VSCDT 1778*	20		2
28 Jul 01	**WITHOUT YOU** *Virgin VSCDT 1805*	51		

LUDACRIS US rapper

Date	Title / Label	Peak Position	Weeks at No.1	Weeks in Top 40
9 Jun 01	**WHAT'S YOUR FANTASY** *Def Jam 5729842*	19		3
18 Aug 01	**ONE MINUTE MAN** *The Gold Mind/Elektra E 7245CD* MISSY ELLIOTT FEATURING LUDACRIS	10		4
29 Sep 01	**AREA CODES** *Def Jam 5887722* LUDACRIS FEATURING NATE DOGG	25		2
22 Jun 02	**ROLLOUT (MY BUSINESS)** *Def Jam 5829632*	20		3
5 Oct 02	**SATURDAY (OOOH OOOH)** *Def Jam 639142*	31		1
9 Nov 02	**WHY DON'T WE FALL IN LOVE** *Columbia 6732212* AMERIE FEATURING LUDACRIS	40		1
22 Mar 03	**GOSSIP FOLKS** *Elektra E 7380CD* MISSY ELLIOTT FEATURING LUDACRIS	9		7
22 Nov 03	**STAND UP** *Def Jam South 9814001* ★	14		3
27 Mar 04	**YEAH** *Arista 82876606012* USHER FEATURING LIL' JON & LUDACRIS ★	1	2	12
21 May 05	**NUMBER ONE SPOT** *Def Jam 9881720*	30		1
13 Aug 05	**OH** *LaFace 82876711372* CIARA FEATURING LUDACRIS	4		7
22 Apr 06	**UNPREDICTABLE** *J 82876804772* JAMIE FOXX FEATURING LUDACRIS	16		4
27 Jan 07	**RUNAWAY LOVE** *Def Jam 1723705* LUDACRIS FEATURING MARY J. BLIGE	52		
24 Feb 07	**GLAMOROUS** *A&M 1730081* FERGIE FEATURING LUDACRIS ★	6		17

LUDES UK group

Date	Title / Label	Peak Position	Weeks at No.1	Weeks in Top 40
18 Dec 04	**RADIO** *Double Dragon DD2018CD*	68		

BAZ LUHRMANN Australian film director

Date	Title / Label	Peak Position	Weeks at No.1	Weeks in Top 40
12 Jun 99	**EVERYBODY'S FREE (TO WEAR SUNSCREEN)** *EMI CDBAZ 001* ●	1	1	7

ROBIN LUKE US singer

Date	Title / Label	Peak Position	Weeks at No.1	Weeks in Top 40
17 Oct 58	**SUSIE DARLIN'** *London HLD 8676*	23		6

LUKK US group

Date	Title / Label	Peak Position	Weeks at No.1	Weeks in Top 40
28 Sep 85	**ON THE ONE** *Important TAN 6* LUKK FEATURING FELICIA COLLINS	72		

LULU UK singer

Date	Title / Label	Peak Position	Weeks at No.1	Weeks in Top 40
14 May 64	**SHOUT** *Decca F 11884* LULU & THE LUVVERS	7		10
12 Nov 64	**HERE COMES THE NIGHT** *Decca F 12017*	50		
17 Jun 65	**LEAVE A LITTLE LOVE** *Decca F 12169*	8		9
2 Sep 65	**TRY TO UNDERSTAND** *Decca F 12214*	25		5
13 Apr 67	**THE BOAT THAT I ROW** *Columbia DB 8169*	6		9
29 Jun 67	**LET'S PRETEND** *Columbia DB 8221*	11		9
8 Nov 67	**LOVE LOVES TO LOVE LOVE** *Columbia DB 8295*	32		5
28 Feb 68	**ME THE PEACEFUL HEART** *Columbia DB 8358*	9		9
5 Jun 68	**BOY** *Columbia DB 8425*	15		7
6 Nov 68	**I'M A TIGER** *Columbia DB 8500*	9		12
12 Mar 69	**BOOM BANG-A-BANG** *Columbia DB 8550*	2		12
22 Nov 69	**OH ME OH MY (I'M A FOOL FOR YOU BABY)** *Atco 226 008*	47		
26 Jan 74	**THE MAN WHO SOLD THE WORLD** *Polydor 2001 490* ○	3		8
19 Apr 75	**TAKE YOUR MAMA FOR A RIDE** *Chelsea 2005 022*	37		1
12 Dec 81	**I COULD NEVER MISS YOU (MORE THAN I DO)** *Alfa 1700*	62		
19 Jul 86	**SHOUT** *Jive LULU 1/Decca SHOUT 1* LULU & THE LUVVERS	8		6
30 Jan 93	**INDEPENDENCE** *Dome CDDOME 1001*	11		4
3 Apr 93	**I'M BACK FOR MORE** *Dome CDDOME 1002* LULU & BOBBY WOMACK	27		3
4 Sep 93	**LET ME WAKE UP IN YOUR ARMS** *Dome CDDOME 1005*	51		
9 Oct 93	**RELIGHT MY FIRE** *RCA 74321167722* TAKE THAT FEATURING LULU ○	1	2	6
27 Nov 93	**HOW 'BOUT US** *Dome CDDOME 1007*	46		
27 Aug 94	**GOODBYE BABY AND AMEN** *Dome CDDOME 1011*	40		1
26 Nov 94	**EVERY WOMAN KNOWS** *Dome CDDOME 1013*	44		
29 May 99	**HURT ME SO BAD** *Rocket/Mercury 5726132*	42		
8 Jan 00	**BETTER GET READY** *Mercury 5625852*	59		
18 Mar 00	**WHERE THE POOR BOYS DANCE** *Mercury 1568452*	24		3
7 Dec 02	**WE'VE GOT TONIGHT** *Polydor 0658612* RONAN KEATING FEATURING LULU	4		9

BOB LUMAN US singer

Date	Title / Label	Peak Position	Weeks at No.1	Weeks in Top 40
8 Sep 60	**LET'S THINK ABOUT LIVING** *Warner Brothers WB 18*	6		16
15 Dec 60	**WHY WHY BYE BYE** *Warner Brothers WB 28*	46		
4 May 61	**THE GREAT SNOWMAN** *Warner Brothers WB 37*	49		

LUMIDEE US rapper

Date	Title / Label	Peak Position	Weeks at No.1	Weeks in Top 40
9 Aug 03	**NEVER LEAVE YOU (UH OOOH UH OOOH)** *Universal MCSTD 40328*	2		10
29 Nov 03	**CRASHIN' A PARTY** *Universal MCSTD 40341* LUMIDEE FEATURING NORE	55		
11 Aug 07	**CRAZY** *TVT TVTUKCD24*	74		

LUNIZ US duo

Date	Title / Label	Peak Position	Weeks at No.1	Weeks in Top 40
17 Feb 96	**I GOT 5 ON IT** *Noo Trybe VUSCD 101* ○	3		11
11 May 96	**PLAYA HATA** *Virgin VUSCDX 103*	20		1
14 Sep 96	**STOMP – THE REMIXES** *Q West 0372 CD* QUINCY JONES FEATURING MELLE MEL, COOLIO, YO-YO, SHAQVILLE O'NEAL & THE LUNIZ	28		1
31 Oct 98	**I GOT 5 ON IT (REMIX)** *Virgin VCRD 41*	28		1

LUPINE HOWL UK group

Date	Title / Label	Peak Position	Weeks at No.1	Weeks in Top 40
22 Jan 00	**VAPORIZER** *Vinyl Hiss VHISSCD 001*	68		

LURKERS UK group

Date	Title / Label	Peak Position	Weeks at No.1	Weeks in Top 40
3 Jun 78	**AIN'T GOT A CLUE** *Beggars Banquet BEG 6*	45		
5 Aug 78	**I DON'T NEED TO TELL HER** *Beggars Banquet BEG 9*	49		
3 Feb 79	**JUST THIRTEEN** *Beggars Banquet BEG 14*	66		
9 Jun 79	**OUT IN THE DARK/CYANIDE** *Beggars Banquet BEG 19*	72		
17 Nov 79	**NEW GUITAR IN TOWN** *Beggars Banquet BEG 28*	72		

LUSCIOUS JACKSON US group

Date	Title / Label	Peak Position	Weeks at No.1	Weeks in Top 40
18 Mar 95	**DEEP SHAG/CITYSONG** *Capitol CDCL 739*	69		
21 Oct 95	**HERE** *Capitol CDCL 758*	59		
12 Apr 97	**NAKED EYE** *Capitol CDCL 786*	25		1
3 Jul 99	**LADYFINGERS** *Grand Royal CDCL 813*	43		

LUSH UK group

Date	Title / Label	Peak Position	Weeks at No.1	Weeks in Top 40
10 Mar 90	**MAD LOVE (EP)** *4AD BAD 003*	55		
27 Oct 90	**SWEETNESS AND LIGHT** *4AD BAD 0013*	47		
19 Oct 91	**NOTHING NATURAL** *4AD AD 1016*	43		
11 Jan 92	**FOR LOVE (EP)** *4AD BAD 2001*	35		1
11 Jun 94	**DESIRE LINES** *4AD BAD 4010CD*	60		
11 Jun 94	**HYPOCRITE** *4AD BAD 4008CD*	52		
20 Jan 96	**SINGLE GIRL** *4AD BAD 6001CD*	21		2
9 Mar 96	**LADYKILLERS** *4AD BAD 6002CD*	22		2
27 Jul 96	**500 (SHAKE BABY SHAKE)** *4AD BADD 6009CD*	21		1

LUSTRAL UK production duo

Date	Title / Label	Peak Position	Weeks at No.1	Weeks in Top 40
18 Oct 97	**EVERYTIME** *Hooj Choons HOOJCD 55*	60		
4 Dec 99	**EVERYTIME (REMIX)** *Hooj Choons HOOJ 83CD*	30		1

LUZON US producer

Date	Title / Label	Peak Position	Weeks at No.1	Weeks in Top 40
14 Jul 01	**THE BAGUIO TRACK** *Renaissance RENCDS 006*	67		

LV US rapper

Date	Title / Label	Peak Position	Weeks at No.1	Weeks in Top 40
28 Oct 95	**GANGSTA'S PARADISE** *Tommy Boy MCSTD 2104* COOLIO FEATURING LV ⊛ ★	1	2	18
23 Dec 95	**THROW YOUR HANDS UP/GANGSTA'S PARADISE** *Tommy Boy TBCD 699*	24		3
4 May 96	**I AM LV** *Tommy Boy TBCD 7724*	64		

ANNABELLA LWIN Burmese singer

Date	Title / Label	Peak Position	Weeks at No.1	Weeks in Top 40
28 Jan 95	**DO WHAT YOU DO** *Sony S2 6611235*	61		

LWS Italian group

Date	Title / Label	Peak Position	Weeks at No.1	Weeks in Top 40
29 Oct 94	**GOSP** *Transworld TRANNY 4CD*	65		

JOHN LYDON UK singer

Date	Title / Label	Peak Position	Weeks at No.1	Weeks in Top 40
13 Nov 93	**OPEN UP** *Hard Hands HAND 009CD* LEFTFIELD LYDON	13		3
2 Aug 97	**SUN** *Virgin VUSCD 122*	42		

FRANKIE LYMON US singer

Date	Title / Label	Peak Position	Weeks at No.1	Weeks in Top 40
29 Jun 56	**WHY DO FOOLS FALL IN LOVE** *Columbia DB 3772* TEENAGERS FEATURING FRANKIE LYMON	1	3	16
29 Mar 57	**I'M NOT A TEENAGE DELINQUENT** *Columbia DB 3878* FRANKIE LYMON & THE TEENAGERS	12		7
12 Apr 57	**BABY BABY** *Columbia DB 3878* FRANKIE LYMON & THE TEENAGERS	4		12
20 Sep 57	**GOODY GOODY** *Columbia DB 3983* FRANKIE LYMON & THE TEENAGERS	24		3

DES LYNAM UK sports presenter

Date	Title / Label	Peak Position	Weeks at No.1	Weeks in Top 40
12 Dec 98	**IF – READ TO FAURE'S 'PAVANE'** *BBC Worldwide WMSS 60062* DES LYNAM FEATURING WIMBLEDON CHORAL SOCIETY	45		

CURTIS LYNCH JR UK producer

Date	Title / Label	Peak Position	Weeks at No.1	Weeks in Top 40
30 Sep 00	**THINKING OF YOU** *Telstar CDSTAS 3136* CURTIS LYNCH JR FEATURING KELE LE ROC & RED RAT	70		

KENNY LYNCH UK singer

Date	Title / Label	Peak Position	Weeks at No.1	Weeks in Top 40
30 Jun 60	**MOUNTAIN OF LOVE** *HMV POP 751*	33		1
13 Sep 62	**PUFF** *HMV POP 1057*	33		4
6 Dec 62	**UP ON THE ROOF** *HMV POP 1090*	10		11
20 Jun 63	**YOU CAN NEVER STOP ME LOVING YOU** *HMV POP 1165*	10		12
16 Apr 64	**STAND BY ME** *HMV POP 1280*	39		2
27 Aug 64	**WHAT AM I TO YOU** *HMV POP 1321*	37		1
17 Jun 65	**I'LL STAY BY YOU** *HMV POP 1430*	29		5
20 Aug 83	**HALF THE DAY'S GONE AND WE HAVEN'T EARNT A PENNY** *Satril SAT 510*	50		

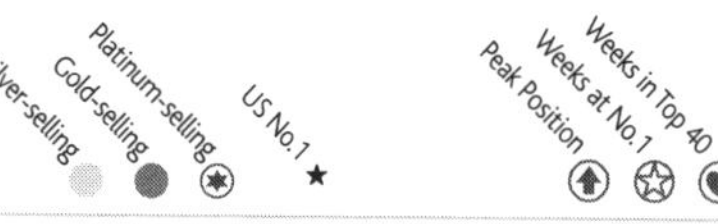

LIAM LYNCH US singer

Date	Title	Peak Position	Weeks at No.1	Weeks in Top 40
7 Dec 02	**UNITED STATES OF WHATEVER** *Global Warming WARMCD 17*	10		7

CHERYL LYNN US singer

Date	Title	Peak Position	Weeks at No.1	Weeks in Top 40
8 Sep 84	**ENCORE** *Streetwave KHAN 23*	68		

PATTI LYNN UK singer

Date	Title	Peak Position	Weeks at No.1	Weeks in Top 40
10 May 62	**JOHNNY ANGEL** *Fontana H 391*	37		4

TAMI LYNN US singer

Date	Title	Peak Position	Weeks at No.1	Weeks in Top 40
22 May 71	**I'M GONNA RUN AWAY FROM YOU** *Mojo 2092 001*	4		12
3 May 75	**I'M GONNA RUN AWAY FROM YOU** *Contempo Raries CS 9026*	36		3

VERA LYNN UK singer

Date	Title	Peak Position	Weeks at No.1	Weeks in Top 40
14 Nov 52	**AUF WIEDERSEHEN SWEETHEART** *Decca F 9927* ★	10		1
14 Nov 52	**FORGET-ME-NOT** *Decca F 9985*	5		6
14 Nov 52	**HOMING WALTZ** *Decca F 9959*	9		3
5 Jun 53	**THE WINDSOR WALTZ** *Decca F 10092*	11		1
15 Oct 54	**MY SON MY SON** *Decca F 10372* VERA LYNN WITH FRANK WEIR, HIS SAXOPHONE, HIS ORCHESTRA & CHORUS	1	2	14
8 Jun 56	**WHO ARE WE** *Decca F 10715*	30		1
26 Oct 56	**A HOUSE WITH LOVE IN IT** *Decca F 10799*	17		13
15 Mar 57	**THE FAITHFUL HUSSAR (DON'T CRY MY LOVE)** *Decca F 10846*	29		2
21 Jun 57	**TRAVELLIN' HOME** *Decca F 10903*	20		5

JEFF LYNNE UK singer/guitarist

Date	Title	Peak Position	Weeks at No.1	Weeks in Top 40
30 Jun 90	**EVERY LITTLE THING** *Reprise W 9799*	59		

SHELBY LYNNE US singer

Date	Title	Peak Position	Weeks at No.1	Weeks in Top 40
29 Apr 00	**LEAVIN'** *Mercury 5627372*	73		

PHIL LYNOTT Irish singer/guitarist

Date	Title	Peak Position	Weeks at No.1	Weeks in Top 40
5 Apr 80	**DEAR MISS LONELY HEARTS** *Vertigo SOLO 1* PHILIP LYNOTT	32		3
21 Jun 80	**KING'S CALL** *Vertigo SOLO 2*	35		1
21 Mar 81	**YELLOW PEARL** *Vertigo SOLO 3*	56		
26 Dec 81	**YELLOW PEARL** *Vertigo SOLO 3*	14		6
18 May 85	**OUT IN THE FIELDS** *10 TEN 49* GARY MOORE & PHIL LYNOTT	5		8
24 Jan 87	**KING'S CALL (REMIX)** *Vertigo LYN 1* GARY MOORE & PHIL LYNOTT	68		

LYNYRD SKYNYRD US group

Date	Title	Peak Position	Weeks at No.1	Weeks in Top 40
11 Sep 76	**FREE BIRD EP** *MCA 251*	31		3
22 Dec 79	**FREE BIRD EP** *MCA 251*	43		
19 Jun 82	**FREE BIRD EP** *MCA 251*	21		5
20 Jan 07	**SWEET HOME ALABAMA** *Download*	61		

BARBARA LYON US singer

Date	Title	Peak Position	Weeks at No.1	Weeks in Top 40
24 Jun 55	**STOWAWAY** *Columbia DB 3619*	12		8
21 Dec 56	**LETTER TO A SOLDIER** *Columbia DB 3865*	27		4

LYTE FUNKIE ONES US group

Date	Title	Peak Position	Weeks at No.1	Weeks in Top 40
22 May 99	**CAN'T HAVE YOU** *Logic 74321649152*	54		
18 Sep 99	**SUMMER GIRLS** *Logic 74321701162*	16		3
5 Feb 00	**GIRL ON TV** *Logic 74321717582*	6		5
27 Apr 02	**EVERY OTHER TIME** *Logic 74321925502*	24		2

HUMPHREY LYTTELTON BAND
UK bandleader and orchestra

Date	Title	Peak Position	Weeks at No.1	Weeks in Top 40
13 Jul 56	**BAD PENNY BLUES** *Parlophone R 4184*	19		6

KEVIN LYTTLE St Vincent singer

Date	Title	Peak Position	Weeks at No.1	Weeks in Top 40
25 Oct 03	**TURN ME ON** *Atlantic AT 0167CD*	2		16
29 May 04	**LAST DROP** *Atlantic AT 0176CD*	22		2

Sex Pistols 'Don't' Get to Number 1

One of the greatest myths in chart history remains the failure of the Sex Pistols' single, 'God Save The Queen' to get to Number 1, despite – according to numerous sources – selling more copies that week than any other single. Or did it?

In 2008, debate over whether a single did or did not sell enough copies to reach the top spot is an impossibility – the OCC extracts sales data from over 6,000 shops with clinical precision and therefore no such argument can arise. However, what The Sex Pistols' record represents is not so much a 'did they/didn't they?' statistical query, but rather more a moment in time when the charts crystallised with spectacular clarity a deep social division in Britain. While up and down this Sceptred Isle the royalist – or at least mainstream – nation was eating sausage rolls at street parties festooned with Union Jacks, there was a grimy undercurrent of disaffected youth, turned off by the festivities, alienated by the lack of opportunity, fractious at their devalued social status and bored of the self-important and seeming never-ending self-indulgence of the so-called prog-rock acts.

The Sex Pistols had already been beaten to the punch by The Damned's 'New Rose' as punk's first-ever single; with a stumbling lack of live shows and a deliriously incompetent new bass player in the form of Sid Vicious, as well as record company rejections and controversy by the bucket load, some observers might have suggested The Pistols' chances of a chart-topping single were, at best, slim. The Damned was not the only punk band making progress – The Clash, The Stranglers and others were all moving forward either on the live scene or with records of their own. Did the Pistols really have no future?

When they signed to Richard Branson's hippy Virgin Records, it seemed the two new partners were impossible bedfellows, but it was a masterstroke by both sides. 'You thought you'd got rid of us but you haven't. The Sex Pistols are back', a leering Rotten snarled at the press pack. As was often the case, he wasn't wrong.

Rarely has a single attracted so much hatred as 'God Save The Queen'. Initially there were problems even finding a pressing plant to manufacture the record, after several refused. Then, when the song was pressed, several major chainstores – including Woolworths and WHSmiths – would not stock it. TV and radio were almost universal in their blanket refusal to play it and critics up and down the land cried foul over its content, vilifying it as an example of all that was wrong with youth and punk. Christians met in Trafalgar Square – fronted by Cliff Richard – to protest, and even the supposedly modernistic publication *Sounds* altered the advert for the single so that Jamie Reid's ground-breaking original record sleeve was no longer 'defacing' the Queen.

In the week of release, The Sex Pistols' song eventually stalled at Number 2 – or did it? Well, the history books tell us it did, but champions of the conspiracy theory have suggested that Gallup – the governing body of the charts at the time – changed the rules concerning chart singles that week in order to snatch a supposedly humbling defeat from the jaws of victory.

The print media at the time produced numerous varied listings that only added to the mire (the definitive listing of 2008 was not yet existent). Some charts, such as that in the *NME*, listed 'God Save The Queen' as Number 1, and some radio stations even announced it as the top-selling song, then refused actually to air it. Someone should have phoned Mulder and Scully ...

Drunken boat trips down the Thames, arrests, knife, machete and razor attacks on Johnny Rotten and his cohorts, plus countless cancelled live shows fuelled the Pistols' myth yet more, before the band imploded with the death of Vicious and the splintering of a musical team that had momentarily seemed to threaten the very lifeblood of the establishment.

The history of punk has been written, rewritten, invented, re-invented and argued over many times and it is not the place of this book to enter into that argument further. However, the importance of The Pistols in the charts cannot be underestimated. Their flame burned brightly but staggeringly briefly – their initial chart career spanned less than three years and included seven Top 10 hits. Can any other band lay claim to have exploded on youth, fashion, art and popular culture so hugely and in such a short space of time?

You won't find The Sex Pistols in any Top 100 chart lists or any 'longest stays in the charts'. Of course, thankfully, they did come back again to irritate and entertain with several shows from the mid-1990s onwards; for the record, the frequently ridiculed reunion dates have actually been of surprisingly high quality, particularly the first at Finsbury Park in 1996 – don't be fooled by cultural snobbery now, any more than people were in 1976. Yet that first Pistols' chart career was wonderful in its brevity, and 'God Save The Queen' was an absolute watershed moment in UK singles chart history. It's hard to imagine a song inciting such national outrage in today's climate but that's exactly what happened and, for that, the single will always hold a unique place in the chart's history.

M–P

KEY TO ARTIST ENTRIES

Artist/Group Name — Artist/Group Nationality and Category — Silver-selling ● Gold-selling ● Platinum-selling ⊛ US No.1 ★ Peak Position Weeks at No.1 Weeks in Top 40

DEXY'S MIDNIGHT RUNNERS UK group

Date of entry into Top 75	Song Title / Label and Catalogue Number	Peak Position	Weeks at No.1	Weeks in Top 40
19 Jan 80	**DANCE STANCE** *Oddball Productions R 6028*	40		1
22 Mar 80	**GENO** *Late Night Feelings R 6033* ●	1	2	12
12 Jul 80	**THERE THERE MY DEAR** *Late Night Feelings R 6038*	7		6
21 Mar 81	**PLAN B** *Parlophone R 6046*	58		
11 Jul 81	**SHOW ME** *Mercury DEXYS 6*	16		7
20 Mar 82	**THE CELTIC SOUL BROTHERS** *Mercury DEXYS 8* DEXY'S MIDNIGHT RUNNERS WITH THE EMERALD EXPRESS	45		
3 Jul 82	**COME ON EILEEN** *Mercury DEXYS 9* DEXY'S MIDNIGHT RUNNERS WITH THE EMERALD EXPRESS ⊛ ★	1	4	13
2 Oct 82	**JACKIE WILSON SAID (I'M IN HEAVEN WHEN YOU SMILE)** *Mercury DEXYS 10* KEVIN ROWLAND & DEXY'S MIDNIGHT RUNNERS	5		6
4 Dec 82	**LET'S GET THIS STRAIGHT (FROM THE START)/OLD** *Mercury DEXYS 11* KEVIN ROWLAND & DEXY'S MIDNIGHT RUNNERS	17		8
2 Apr 83	**THE CELTIC SOUL BROTHERS** *Mercury DEXYS 12* KEVIN ROWLAND & DEXY'S MIDNIGHT RUNNERS	20		5
22 Nov 86	**BECAUSE OF YOU** *Mercury BRUSH 1*	13		6

Artist collaboration or where artist's name has changed

Song Title — Label and Catalogue Number

Silver-selling ● Gold-selling ● Platinum-selling ✪ US No.1 ★ — Peak Position, Weeks at No.1, Weeks in Top 40

M UK singer/multi-instrumentalist

Date	Title	Label	Peak Position	Weeks at No.1	Weeks in Top 40
7 Apr 79	**POP MUZIK**	*MCA 413* ● ★	2		11
8 Dec 79	**MOONLIGHT AND MUZAK**	*MCA 541*	33		5
15 Mar 80	**THAT'S THE WAY THE MONEY GOES**	*MCA 570*	45		
22 Nov 80	**OFFICIAL SECRETS**	*MCA 650*	64		
10 Jun 89	**POP MUZIK**	*Freestyle FRS 1*	15		5

BOBBY M US singer

Date	Title	Label	Peak Position	Weeks at No.1	Weeks in Top 40
29 Jan 83	**LET'S STAY TOGETHER** BOBBY M FEATURING JEAN CARN	*Gordy TMG 1288*	53		

M & O BAND UK group

Date	Title	Label	Peak Position	Weeks at No.1	Weeks in Top 40
28 Feb 76	**LET'S DO THE LATIN HUSTLE**	*Creole CR 120*	16		5

M&S UK group

Date	Title	Label	Peak Position	Weeks at No.1	Weeks in Top 40
7 Apr 01	**SALSOUL NUGGET (IF U WANNA)** M&S PRESENTS GIRL NEXT DOOR	*ffrr FCD 398*	6		6

M-BEAT UK producer

Date	Title	Label	Peak Position	Weeks at No.1	Weeks in Top 40
18 Jun 94	**INCREDIBLE** M-BEAT FEATURING GENERAL LEVY	*Renk 42CD*	39		2
10 Sep 94	**INCREDIBLE (REMIX)** M-BEAT FEATURING GENERAL LEVY	*Renk CDRENK 44*	8		7
17 Dec 94	**SWEET LOVE** M-BEAT FEATURING NAZLYN	*Renk CDRENK 49*	18		5
1 Jun 96	**DO U KNOW WHERE YOU'RE COMING FROM** M-BEAT FEATURING JAMIROQUAI	*Renk CDRENK 63*	12		3

M DUBS UK producer

Date	Title	Label	Peak Position	Weeks at No.1	Weeks in Top 40
16 Dec 00	**BUMP N GRIND (I AM FEELING HOT TONIGHT)** M DUBS FEATURING LADY SAW	*Telstar CDSTAS 3129*	59		

M FACTOR UK production duo

Date	Title	Label	Peak Position	Weeks at No.1	Weeks in Top 40
6 Jul 02	**MOTHER**	*Serious SERR 042CD*	18		2
26 Jul 03	**COME TOGETHER**	*Credence CDCRED 037*	46		

M1 UK producer

Date	Title	Label	Peak Position	Weeks at No.1	Weeks in Top 40
22 Feb 03	**HEAVEN SENT**	*Inferno CDFERN 51*	72		

M PEOPLE UK group

Date	Title	Label	Peak Position	Weeks at No.1	Weeks in Top 40
26 Oct 91	**HOW CAN I LOVE YOU MORE**	*Deconstruction PB 44855*	29		4
7 Mar 92	**COLOUR MY LIFE**	*Deconstruction PB 45241*	35		2
18 Apr 92	**SOMEDAY** M PEOPLE WITH HEATHER SMALL	*Deconstruction PB 45369*	38		2
10 Oct 92	**EXCITED**	*Deconstruction 74321116337*	29		3
6 Feb 93	**HOW CAN I LOVE YOU MORE (REMIX)**	*Deconstruction 74321130232*	8		6
26 Jun 93	**ONE NIGHT IN HEAVEN**	*Deconstruction 74321151852*	6		10
25 Sep 93	**MOVING ON UP**	*Deconstruction 74321166162*	2		9
4 Dec 93	**DON'T LOOK ANY FURTHER**	*Deconstruction 74321177112*	9		7
12 Mar 94	**RENAISSANCE**	*Deconstruction 74321194132*	5		5
17 Sep 94	**ELEGANTLY AMERICAN: ONE NIGHT IN HEAVEN/ MOVING ON UP**	*Deconstruction 74321231882*	31		1
19 Nov 94	**SIGHT FOR SORE EYES**	*Deconstruction 74321245472*	6		7
4 Feb 95	**OPEN YOUR HEART**	*Deconstruction 74321261532*	9		5
24 Jun 95	**SEARCH FOR THE HERO**	*Deconstruction 74321287962*	9		6
14 Oct 95	**LOVE RENDEZVOUS**	*Deconstruction 74321319282*	32		2
25 Nov 95	**ITCHYCOO PARK**	*Deconstruction 74321330732*	11		6
4 Oct 97	**JUST FOR YOU**	*M People 74321523002*	8		5
6 Dec 97	**FANTASY ISLAND**	*M People 74321542932*	33		1
28 Mar 98	**ANGEL STREET**	*M People 74321564182*	8		4
7 Nov 98	**TESTIFY**	*M People 74321621742*	12		3
13 Feb 99	**DREAMING**	*M People 74321645362*	13		2

M + M Canadian duo

Date	Title	Label	Peak Position	Weeks at No.1	Weeks in Top 40
28 Jul 84	**BLACK STATIONS WHITE STATIONS**	*RCA 426*	46		

M3 UK group

Date	Title	Label	Peak Position	Weeks at No.1	Weeks in Top 40
30 Oct 99	**BAILAMOS**	*Inferno CDFERN 21*	40		1

M2M Norwegian duo

Date	Title	Label	Peak Position	Weeks at No.1	Weeks in Top 40
1 Apr 00	**DON'T SAY YOU LOVE ME**	*Atlantic AT 0081CD1*	16		4

TIMO MAAS German producer

Date	Title	Label	Peak Position	Weeks at No.1	Weeks in Top 40
1 Apr 00	**DER SCHIEBER**	*48k/Perfecto SPECT 07CDS*	50		
30 Sep 00	**UBIK** TIMO MAAS FEATURING MARTIN BETTINGHAUS	*Perfecto PERF 10CDS2*	33		1
23 Feb 02	**TO GET DOWN (ROCK THING)**	*Perfecto PERF 30CDS*	14		3
11 May 02	**SHIFTER** TIMO MAAS FEATURING MC CHICKABOO	*Perfecto PERF 31CDS*	38		1
5 Oct 02	**HELP ME** TIMO MAAS FEATURING KELIS	*Perfecto PERF 42CDS*	65		

PETE MAC JR US singer

Date	Title	Label	Peak Position	Weeks at No.1	Weeks in Top 40
15 Oct 77	**THE WATER MARGIN**	*BBC RESL 50*	37		1

STEVE MAC/STEVE SMITH UK production duo

Date	Title	Label	Peak Position	Weeks at No.1	Weeks in Top 40
22 Oct 05	**LOVIN' YOU MORE**	*Ministry Of Sound C2MOS1CDS*	73		

MAC BAND US group

Date	Title	Label	Peak Position	Weeks at No.1	Weeks in Top 40
18 Jun 88	**ROSES ARE RED** MAC BAND FEATURING THE McCAMPBELL BROTHERS	*MCA 1264*	8		9
10 Sep 88	**STALEMATE** MAC BAND FEATURING THE McCAMPBELL BROTHERS	*MCA 1271*	40		1

KEITH MAC PROJECT UK group

Date	Title	Label	Peak Position	Weeks at No.1	Weeks in Top 40
25 Jun 94	**DE DAH DAH (SPICE OF LIFE)**	*Public Demand PPDCD 3*	66		

DAVID McALMONT UK singer

Date	Title	Label	Peak Position	Weeks at No.1	Weeks in Top 40
27 May 95	**YES** McALMONT & BUTLER	*Hut HUTCD 53*	8		6
4 Nov 95	**YOU DO** McALMONT & BUTLER	*Hut HUTDG 57*	17		2
27 Apr 96	**HYMN** ULTRAMARINE FEATURING DAVID McALMONT	*Blanco Y Negro NEG 87CD*	65		
9 Aug 97	**LOOK AT YOURSELF**	*Hut HUTCD 87*	40		1
22 Nov 97	**DIAMONDS ARE FOREVER** DAVID McALMONT & DAVID ARNOLD	*East West EW 141CD*	39		1
10 Aug 02	**FALLING**	*Chrysalis CDCHS 5141*	23		2
9 Nov 02	**BRING IT BACK**	*Chrysalis CDCHSS 5145*	36		1

NEIL MacARTHUR UK singer

Date	Title	Label	Peak Position	Weeks at No.1	Weeks in Top 40
5 Feb 69	**SHE'S NOT THERE**	*Deram DM 225*	34		2

DAVID MacBETH UK singer

Date	Title	Label	Peak Position	Weeks at No.1	Weeks in Top 40
30 Oct 59	**MR BLUE**	*Pye 7N 15231*	18		4

NICKO McBRAIN UK singer/drummer

Date	Title	Label	Peak Position	Weeks at No.1	Weeks in Top 40
13 Jul 91	**RHYTHM OF THE BEAST**	*EMI NICK 1*	72		

FRANKIE McBRIDE Irish singer

Date	Title	Label	Peak Position	Weeks at No.1	Weeks in Top 40
9 Aug 67	**FIVE LITTLE FINGERS**	*Emerald MD 1081*	19		11

MACCABEES UK group

Date	Title	Label	Peak Position	Weeks at No.1	Weeks in Top 40
25 Nov 06	**FIRST LOVE**	*Fiction 1707085*	40		1
10 Mar 07	**ABOUT YOUR DRESS**	*Fiction/Polydor 1724475*	33		1
19 May 07	**PRECIOUS TIME**	*Fiction/Polydor 1732766*	49		
19 Jan 08	**TOOTHPASTE KISSES**	*Fiction/Polydor 1746533*	70		

DAN McCAFFERTY UK singer

Date	Title / Label	Peak Position	Weeks at No.1	Weeks in Top 40
13 Sep 75	**OUT OF TIME** *Mountain TOP 1*	41		

CW McCALL US singer

Date	Title / Label	Peak Position	Weeks at No.1	Weeks in Top 40
14 Feb 76	**CONVOY** *MGM 2006 560* ★	2		9

DAVID McCALLUM UK singer/actor

Date	Title / Label	Peak Position	Weeks at No.1	Weeks in Top 40
14 Apr 66	**COMMUNICATION** *Capitol CL 15439*	32		2

JESSE McCARTNEY US singer

Date	Title / Label	Peak Position	Weeks at No.1	Weeks in Top 40
11 Feb 06	**BEAUTIFUL SOUL** *Angel ANGEDX7*	16		4
7 Oct 06	**RIGHT WHERE YOU WANT ME** *Angel ANGECD20*	54		

LINDA McCARTNEY US singer

Date	Title / Label	Peak Position	Weeks at No.1	Weeks in Top 40
21 Nov 98	**WIDE PRAIRIE** *Parlophone CDR 6510* LINDA McCARTNEY	74		
6 Feb 99	**THE LIGHT COMES FROM WITHIN** *Parlophone CDR 6513* LINDA McCARTNEY	56		

PAUL McCARTNEY UK singer

Date	Title / Label	Peak Position	Weeks at No.1	Weeks in Top 40
28 Aug 71	**BACK SEAT OF MY CAR** *Apple R 5914* PAUL & LINDA McCARTNEY	39		1
27 Feb 71	**ANOTHER DAY** *Apple R 5889*	2		10
28 Aug 71	**BACK SEAT OF MY CAR** *Apple R 5914* PAUL & LINDA McCARTNEY	39		1
26 Feb 72	**GIVE IRELAND BACK TO THE IRISH** *Apple R 5936* WINGS	16		5
27 May 72	**MARY HAD A LITTLE LAMB** *Apple R 5949* WINGS	9		11
9 Dec 72	**HI HI HI/C MOON** *Apple R 5973* WINGS	5		12
7 Apr 73	**MY LOVE** *Apple R 5985* PAUL McCARTNEY & WINGS ★	9		9
9 Jun 73	**LIVE AND LET DIE** *Apple R 5987* WINGS	9		11
3 Nov 73	**HELEN WHEELS** *Apple R 5993* PAUL McCARTNEY & WINGS	12		11
2 Mar 74	**JET** *Apple R 5996* PAUL McCARTNEY & WINGS	7		9
6 Jul 74	**BAND ON THE RUN** *Apple R 5997* PAUL McCARTNEY & WINGS ★	3		10
9 Nov 74	**JUNIOR'S FARM** *Apple R 5999* PAUL McCARTNEY & WINGS	16		6
31 May 75	**LISTEN TO WHAT THE MAN SAID** *Capitol R 6006* WINGS ★	6		8
18 Oct 75	**LETTING GO** *Capitol R 6008* WINGS	41		
15 May 76	**SILLY LOVE SONGS** *Parlophone R 6014* WINGS ★	2		11
7 Aug 76	**LET 'EM IN** *Parlophone R 6015* WINGS	2		10
19 Feb 77	**MAYBE I'M AMAZED** *Parlophone R 6017* WINGS	28		4
19 Nov 77	**MULL OF KINTYRE/GIRLS' SCHOOL** *Parlophone R 6018* WINGS	1	9	15
8 Apr 78	**WITH A LITTLE LUCK** *Parlophone R 6019* WINGS ★	5		7
1 Jul 78	**I'VE HAD ENOUGH** *Parlophone R 6020* WINGS	42		
9 Sep 78	**LONDON TOWN** *Parlophone R 6021* WINGS	60		
7 Apr 79	**GOODNIGHT TONIGHT** *Parlophone R 6023* WINGS	5		8
16 Jun 79	**OLD SIAM SIR** *MPL R 6026* WINGS	35		3
1 Sep 79	**GETTING CLOSER/BABY'S REQUEST** *R 6027* WINGS	60		
1 Dec 79	**WONDERFUL CHRISTMASTIME** *Parlophone R 6029*	6		6
19 Apr 80	**COMING UP** *Parlophone R 6035* ★	2		6
21 Jun 80	**WATERFALLS** *Parlophone R 6037*	9		6
10 Apr 82	**EBONY AND IVORY** *Parlophone R 6054* PAUL McCARTNEY & STEVIE WONDER ★	1	3	9
3 Jul 82	**TAKE IT AWAY** *Parlophone R 6056*	15		8
9 Oct 82	**TUG OF WAR** *Parlophone R 6057*	53		
6 Nov 82	**THE GIRL IS MINE** *Epic A 2729* MICHAEL JACKSON & PAUL McCARTNEY	8		6
15 Oct 83	**SAY SAY SAY** *Parlophone R 6062* PAUL McCARTNEY & MICHAEL JACKSON ★	2		14
17 Dec 83	**PIPES OF PEACE** *Parlophone R 6064*	1	2	8
6 Oct 84	**NO MORE LONELY NIGHTS (BALLAD)** *Parlophone R 6080*	2		11
24 Nov 84	**WE ALL STAND TOGETHER** *Parlophone R 6086* PAUL McCARTNEY & THE FROG CHORUS	3		10
30 Nov 85	**SPIES LIKE US** *Parlophone R 6118*	13		8
21 Dec 85	**WE ALL STAND TOGETHER** *Parlophone R 6086* PAUL McCARTNEY & THE FROG CHORUS	32		2
26 Jul 86	**PRESS** *Parlophone R 6133*	25		5
13 Dec 86	**ONLY LOVE REMAINS** *Parlophone R 6148*	34		4
28 Nov 87	**ONCE UPON A LONG AGO** *Parlophone R 6170*	10		7
20 May 89	**FERRY 'CROSS THE MERSEY** *PWL 41* CHRISTIANS, HOLLY JOHNSON, PAUL McCARTNEY, GERRY MARSDEN & STOCK AITKEN WATERMAN	1	3	6
20 May 89	**MY BRAVE FACE** *Parlophone R 6213*	18		3
29 Jul 89	**THIS ONE** *Parlophone R 6223*	18		4
25 Nov 89	**FIGURE OF EIGHT** *Parlophone R 6235*	42		
17 Feb 90	**PUT IT THERE** *Parlophone R 6246*	32		1
20 Oct 90	**BIRTHDAY** *Parlophone R 6271*	29		2
8 Dec 90	**ALL MY TRIALS** *Parlophone R 6278*	35		2
9 Jan 93	**HOPE OF DELIVERANCE** *Parlophone CDR 6330*	18		5
6 Mar 93	**C'MON PEOPLE** *Parlophone CDRS 6338*	41		
10 May 97	**YOUNG BOY** *Parlophone CDRS 6462*	19		1
19 Jul 97	**THE WORLD TONIGHT** *Parlophone CDR 6472*	23		1
27 Dec 97	**BEAUTIFUL NIGHT** *Parlophone CDR 6489*	25		2
6 Nov 99	**NO OTHER BABY/BROWN EYED HANDSOME MAN** *Parlophone CDR 6527*	42		
10 Nov 01	**FROM A LOVER TO A FRIEND** *Parlophone CDR 6567*	45		
2 Oct 04	**TROPIC ISLAND HUM/WE ALL STAND TOGETHER** *Parlophone CDR 6649*	21		2
10 Sep 05	**FINE LINE** *Parlophone CDR6673*	20		1
3 Dec 05	**JENNY WREN** *Parlophone CDRS6678*	22		1
30 Jun 07	**DANCE TONIGHT** *Download*	26		2
22 Dec 07	**WONDERFUL CHRISTMASTIME** *Download*	44		

LIZ McCLARNON UK singer

Date	Title / Label	Peak Position	Weeks at No.1	Weeks in Top 40
25 Feb 06	**WOMAN IN LOVE/I GET THE SWEETEST FEELING** *All Around The World CXGLOBE476*	5		3

KIRSTY MacCOLL UK singer

Date	Title / Label	Peak Position	Weeks at No.1	Weeks in Top 40
13 Jun 81	**THERE'S A GUY WORKS DOWN THE CHIPSHOP SWEARS HE'S ELVIS** *Polydor POSP 250*	14		6
19 Jan 85	**A NEW ENGLAND** *Stiff BUY 216*	7		8
15 Nov 86	**GREETINGS TO THE NEW BRUNETTE** *Go! Discs GOD 15* BILLY BRAGG WITH JOHNNY MARR & KIRSTY MacCOLL	58		
5 Dec 87	**FAIRYTALE OF NEW YORK** *Pogue Mahone NY 7* POGUES FEATURING KIRSTY MacCOLL	2		8
8 Apr 89	**FREE WORLD** *Virgin KMA 1*	43		
1 Jul 89	**DAYS** *Virgin KMA 2*	12		7
25 May 91	**WALKING DOWN MADISON** *Virgin VS 1348*	23		5
17 Aug 91	**MY AFFAIR** *Virgin VS 1354*	56		
14 Dec 91	**FAIRYTALE OF NEW YORK** *PM YZ 628* POGUES FEATURING KIRSTY MacCOLL	36		2
4 Mar 95	**CAROLINE** *Virgin VSCDX 1517*	58		
24 Jun 95	**PERFECT DAY** *Virgin VSCDT 1552* KIRSTY MacCOLL & EVAN DANDO	75		
29 Jul 95	**DAYS** *Virgin VSCDT 1558*	42		
31 Dec 05	**FAIRYTALE OF NEW YORK** *Warner Brothers WEA400CD* POGUES FEATURING KIRSTY MacCOLL	3		3
9 Dec 06	**FAIRYTALE OF NEW YORK** *Warner Brothers WEA400CD* POGUES FEATURING KIRSTY MacCOLL	6		4
8 Dec 07	**FAIRYTALE OF NEW YORK** *Warner Brothers WEA400CD* POGUES FEATURING KIRSTY MacCOLL	4		5

MARILYN McCOO & BILLY DAVIS JR US duo

Date	Title / Label	Peak Position	Weeks at No.1	Weeks in Top 40
19 Mar 77	**YOU DON'T HAVE TO BE A STAR (TO BE IN MY SHOW)** *ABC 4147* ★	7		8

VAN McCOY US producer/orchestra leader

Date	Title / Label	Peak Position	Weeks at No.1	Weeks in Top 40
31 May 75	**THE HUSTLE** *Avco 6105 038* VAN McCOY WITH THE SOUL CITY SYMPHONY	3		12
1 Nov 75	**CHANGE WITH THE TIMES** *H&L 6105 042*	36		2
12 Feb 77	**SOUL CHA CHA** *H&L 6105 065*	34		3
9 Apr 77	**THE SHUFFLE** *H&L 6105 076* ★	4		12

Silver-selling ○ Gold-selling ● Platinum-selling ⊛ US No.1 ★

McCOYS US group

Date	Title / Label	Peak Position	Weeks at No.1	Weeks in Top 40
2 Sep 65	**HANG ON SLOOPY** *Immediate IM 001* ★	5		12
16 Dec 65	**FEVER** *Immediate IM 021*	44		

GEORGE McCRAE US singer

Date	Title / Label	Peak Position	Weeks at No.1	Weeks in Top 40
29 Jun 74	**ROCK YOUR BABY** *Jayboy BOY 85* ● ★	1	3	12
5 Oct 74	**I CAN'T LEAVE YOU ALONE** *Jayboy BOY 90*	9		8
14 Dec 74	**YOU CAN HAVE IT ALL** *Jayboy BOY 92*	23		5
22 Mar 75	**SING A HAPPY SONG** *Jayboy BOY 95*	38		1
19 Jul 75	**IT'S BEEN SO LONG** *Jayboy BOY 100* ○	4		10
18 Oct 75	**I AIN'T LYIN'** *Jayboy BOY 105*	12		6
24 Jan 76	**HONEY I** *Jayboy BOY 107*	33		3
25 Feb 84	**ONE STEP CLOSER (TO LOVE)** *President PT 522*	57		

GWEN McCRAE US singer

Date	Title / Label	Peak Position	Weeks at No.1	Weeks in Top 40
30 Apr 88	**ALL THIS LOVE I'M GIVING** *Flame MELT 7*	63		
13 Feb 93	**ALL THIS LOVE I'M GIVING** *KTDA CDKTDA 2* MUSIC & MYSTERY FEATURING GWEN McCRAE	36		1

McCRARYS US group

Date	Title / Label	Peak Position	Weeks at No.1	Weeks in Top 40
31 Jul 82	**LOVE ON A SUMMER NIGHT** *Capitol CL 251*	52		

MINDY McCREADY US singer

Date	Title / Label	Peak Position	Weeks at No.1	Weeks in Top 40
1 Aug 98	**OH ROMEO** *BNA 74321597242*	41		

DAVE McCULLEN Dutch producer

Date	Title / Label	Peak Position	Weeks at No.1	Weeks in Top 40
24 Dec 05	**B*TCH** *Nebula NEBCD078*	54		

IAN McCULLOCH UK singer

Date	Title / Label	Peak Position	Weeks at No.1	Weeks in Top 40
15 Dec 84	**SEPTEMBER SONG** *Korova KOW 40*	51		
2 Sep 89	**PROUD TO FALL** *WEA YZ 417*	51		
12 May 90	**CANDLELAND (THE SECOND COMING)** *East West YZ 452* IAN McCULLOCH FEATURING ELIZABETH FRASER	75		
22 Feb 92	**LOVER LOVER LOVER** *East West YZ 643*	47		
26 Apr 03	**SLIDLING** *Cooking Vinyl FRYCD 146X*	61		

MARTINE McCUTCHEON UK singer

Date	Title / Label	Peak Position	Weeks at No.1	Weeks in Top 40
18 Nov 95	**ARE YOU MAN ENOUGH** *Avex UK AVEXCD 14* UNO CLIO FEATURING MARTINE McCUTCHEON	62		
17 Apr 99	**PERFECT MOMENT** *Innocent SINCD 7* ⊛	1	2	10
11 Sep 99	**I'VE GOT YOU** *Innocent SINCD 12*	6		6
4 Dec 99	**TALKING IN YOUR SLEEP/LOVE ME** *Innocent SINCD 14* ○	6		8
4 Nov 00	**I'M OVER YOU** *Innocent SINCD 20*	2		6
3 Feb 01	**ON THE RADIO** *Innocent SINCD 21*	7		4

GENE McDANIELS US singer

Date	Title / Label	Peak Position	Weeks at No.1	Weeks in Top 40
16 Nov 61	**TOWER OF STRENGTH** *London HLG 9448*	49		

JULIE McDERMOT UK singer

Date	Title / Label	Peak Position	Weeks at No.1	Weeks in Top 40
12 Oct 96	**DON'T GO** *Soundprooof MCSTD 40082* THIRD DIMENSION FEATURING JULIE McDERMOTT	34		1
26 Oct 96	**DON'T GO (2ND REMIX)** *XL Recordings XLS 78CD* AWESOME 3 FEATURING JULIE McDERMOTT	27		1

CHARLES McDEVITT SKIFFLE GROUP UK group

Date	Title / Label	Peak Position	Weeks at No.1	Weeks in Top 40
12 Apr 57	**FREIGHT TRAIN** *Oriole CB 1352* FEATURING NANCY WHISKEY	5		18
14 Jun 57	**GREENBACK DOLLAR** *Oriole CB 1371* FEATURING NANCY WHISKEY	28		2

AMY MacDONALD UK singer/guitarist

Date	Title / Label	Peak Position	Weeks at No.1	Weeks in Top 40
28 Jul 07	**MR ROCK & ROLL** *Vertigo 1736026*	12		7
27 Oct 07	**LA** *Vertigo 1749279*	48		
8 Dec 07	**THIS IS THE LIFE** *Vertigo 1755264*	28		8
15 Mar 08	**RUN** *Vertigo 1762441*	75		

JANE McDONALD UK singer

Date	Title / Label	Peak Position	Weeks at No.1	Weeks in Top 40
26 Dec 98	**CRUISE INTO CHRISTMAS MEDLEY** *Focus Music Int CDFM 2*	10		3

MICHAEL McDONALD US singer

Date	Title / Label	Peak Position	Weeks at No.1	Weeks in Top 40
18 Feb 84	**YAH MO B THERE** *Qwest W 9394* JAMES INGRAM WITH MICHAEL McDONALD	44		
12 Jan 85	**YAH MO B THERE** *Qwest W 9394* JAMES INGRAM WITH MICHAEL McDONALD	12		6
3 May 86	**ON MY OWN** *MCA 1045* PATTI LABELLE & MICHAEL McDONALD ○ ★	2		11
26 Jul 86	**I KEEP FORGETTIN'** *Warner Brothers K 17992*	43		
6 Sep 86	**SWEET FREEDOM** *MCA 1073*	12		6
24 Jan 87	**WHAT A FOOL BELIEVES** *Warner Brothers W 8451* DOOBIE BROTHERS FEATURING MICHAEL McDONALD	57		
5 Oct 02	**SWEET FREEDOM** *Serious SERR 55CD* SAFRI DUO FEATURING MICHAEL McDONALD	54		

CARRIE McDOWELL US singer

Date	Title / Label	Peak Position	Weeks at No.1	Weeks in Top 40
26 Sep 87	**UH UH NO NO CASUAL SEX** *Motown ZV 41501*	68		

JOHN McENROE & PAT CASH US/Australian tennis players

Date	Title / Label	Peak Position	Weeks at No.1	Weeks in Top 40
13 Jul 91	**ROCK 'N' ROLL** *Music For Nations KUT 141* JOHN McENROE & PAT CASH WITH THE FULL METAL RACKETS	66		

REBA McENTIRE US singer

Date	Title / Label	Peak Position	Weeks at No.1	Weeks in Top 40
19 Jun 99	**DOES HE LOVE YOU** *MCA Nashville MCSTD 55569*	62		

MACEO & THE MACKS US saxophonist

Date	Title / Label	Peak Position	Weeks at No.1	Weeks in Top 40
16 May 87	**CROSS THE TRACK (WE BETTER GO BACK)** *Urban IRBX 1*	54		

BRIAN McFADDEN Irish singer

Date	Title / Label	Peak Position	Weeks at No.1	Weeks in Top 40
18 Sep 04	**REAL TO ME** *Modest/Sony Music 6753032*	1	1	6
4 Dec 04	**IRISH SON** *Modest/Sony Music 6754872*	6		7
12 Feb 05	**ALMOST HERE** *Sony Music 6757352* BRIAN McFADDEN & DELTA GOODREM	3		6
4 Jun 05	**DEMONS** *Modest/Sony Music 6759102*	28		1
7 Oct 06	**EVERYBODY'S SOMEONE** *Curb/London CUBC128* LeANN RIMES & BRIAN McFADDEN	48		

McFADDEN & WHITEHEAD US duo

Date	Title / Label	Peak Position	Weeks at No.1	Weeks in Top 40
19 May 79	**AIN'T NO STOPPIN' US NOW** *Philadelphia International PIR 7365* ○	5		8

RACHEL McFARLANE UK singer

Date	Title / Label	Peak Position	Weeks at No.1	Weeks in Top 40
1 Aug 98	**LOVER** *Multiply CDMULTY 37*	38		1
29 Jan 05	**LOVER (REMIX)** *All Around The World CDGLOBE250*	36		1
4 Feb 06	**YOU GET WHAT YOU GIVE** *All Around The World CDGLOBE423* LMC FEATURING RACHEL McFARLANE	30		1

BOBBY McFERRIN US singer

Date	Title / Label	Peak Position	Weeks at No.1	Weeks in Top 40
24 Sep 88	**DON'T WORRY BE HAPPY** *Manhattan MT 56* ★	2		8
17 Dec 88	**THINKIN' ABOUT YOUR BODY** *Manhattan BLUE 6*	46		

McFLY UK group

Date	Title / Label	Peak Position	Weeks at No.1	Weeks in Top 40
10 Apr 04	**FIVE COLOURS IN HER HAIR** *Universal MCSXD 40357*	1	2	8
3 Jul 04	**OBVIOUSLY** *Universal MCSXD 40364*	1		9
18 Sep 04	**THAT GIRL** *Universal MCSXD 40378*	3		5
27 Nov 04	**ROOM ON THE 3RD FLOOR** *Island MCSXD40389*	5		7
19 Mar 05	**ALL ABOUT YOU/YOU'VE GOT A FRIEND** *Island MCSTD40409* ○	1	1	10
27 Aug 05	**I'LL BE OK** *Island MCSXD40428*	1	1	4
29 Oct 05	**I WANNA HOLD YOU** *Island MCSXD40436*	3		3
24 Dec 05	**ULTRAVIOLET/THE BALLAD OF PAUL K** *Island MCSXD40442*	9		2
29 Jul 06	**DON'T STOP ME NOW/PLEASE, PLEASE** *Universal 1703585*	1	1	5
4 Nov 06	**STAR GIRL** *Island 1709444*	1	1	4
30 Dec 06	**SORRY'S NOT GOOD ENOUGH/FRIDAY NIGHT** *Island 1718992*	3		3
19 May 07	**BABY'S COMING BACK/TRANSYLVANIA** *Island/Uni-Island 1733933*	1	1	3
3 Nov 07	**THE HEART NEVER LIES** *Island 1749617*	3		4

Silver-selling ● · Gold-selling ● · Platinum-selling ✪ · US No.1 ★ · Peak Position · Weeks at No.1 · Weeks in Top 40

McGANNS UK group

Date	Title / Label	Peak Position	Weeks at No.1	Weeks in Top 40
14 Nov 98	**JUST MY IMAGINATION** *Coalition COLA 062CD*	59		
6 Feb 99	**A HEARTBEAT AWAY** *Coalition COLA 069CD*	42		

MIKE McGEAR UK singer

Date	Title / Label	Peak Position	Weeks at No.1	Weeks in Top 40
5 Oct 74	**LEAVE IT** *Warner Brothers K 16446*	36		2

MAUREEN McGOVERN US singer

Date	Title / Label	Peak Position	Weeks at No.1	Weeks in Top 40
5 Jun 76	**THE CONTINENTAL** *20th Century BTC 2222*	16		6

SHANE McGOWAN UK singer

Date	Title / Label	Peak Position	Weeks at No.1	Weeks in Top 40
12 Dec 92	**WHAT A WONDERFUL WORLD** *Mute 151* NICK CAVE & SHANE McGOWAN	72		
3 Sep 94	**THE CHURCH OF THE HOLY SPOOK** *ZTT ZANG 57CD* SHANE MacGOWAN & THE POPES	74		
15 Oct 94	**THAT WOMAN'S GOT ME DRINKING** *ZTT ZANG 57CD* SHANE MacGOWAN & THE POPES	34		1
29 Apr 95	**HAUNTED** *ZTT BANG 65CD* SHANE MacGOWAN & SINEAD O'CONNOR	30		1
20 Apr 96	**MY WAY** *ZTT ZANG 79CD*	29		1

EWAN McGREGOR UK actor

Date	Title / Label	Peak Position	Weeks at No.1	Weeks in Top 40
15 Nov 97	**CHOOSE LIFE** *Positiva CDTIV 84* PF PROJECT FEATURING EWAN McGREGOR	6		9
6 Oct 01	**COME WHAT MAY** *Interscope 4976302* NICOLE KIDMAN & EWAN McGREGOR	27		3

FREDDIE McGREGOR Jamaican singer

Date	Title / Label	Peak Position	Weeks at No.1	Weeks in Top 40
27 Jun 87	**JUST DON'T WANT TO BE LONELY** *Germain DG 24*	9		7
19 Sep 87	**THAT GIRL (GROOVY SITUATION)** *Polydor POSP 884*	47		

MARY MacGREGOR US singer

Date	Title / Label	Peak Position	Weeks at No.1	Weeks in Top 40
19 Feb 77	**TORN BETWEEN TWO LOVERS** *Ariola America AA 111* ● ★	4		10

McGUINNESS FLINT US singer

Date	Title / Label	Peak Position	Weeks at No.1	Weeks in Top 40
21 Nov 70	**WHEN I'M DEAD AND GONE** *Capitol CL 15662*	2		12
1 May 71	**MALT AND BARLEY BLUES** *Capitol CL 15682*	5		9

BARRY McGUIRE US singer

Date	Title / Label	Peak Position	Weeks at No.1	Weeks in Top 40
9 Sep 65	**EVE OF DESTRUCTION** *RCA 1469* ★	3		13

McGUIRE SISTERS US trio

Date	Title / Label	Peak Position	Weeks at No.1	Weeks in Top 40
1 Apr 55	**NO MORE** *Vogue Coral Q 72050*	20		4
15 Jul 55	**SINCERELY** *Vogue Coral Q 72050* ★	14		1
1 Jun 56	**DELILAH JONES** *Vogue Coral Q 72161*	24		2
14 Feb 58	**SUGARTIME** *Coral Q 72305* ★	14		6
1 May 59	**MAY YOU ALWAYS** *Coral Q 72356*	15		11

MACHEL Trinidadian singer

Date	Title / Label	Peak Position	Weeks at No.1	Weeks in Top 40
14 Sep 96	**COME DIG IT** *London LONCD 386*	56		

MACHINE HEAD US group

Date	Title / Label	Peak Position	Weeks at No.1	Weeks in Top 40
27 May 95	**OLD** *Roadrunner RR 23403*	43		
6 Dec 97	**TAKE MY SCARS** *Roadrunner RR 22573*	73		
18 Dec 99	**FROM THIS DAY** *Roadrunner RR 21383*	74		

STEPHANIE McINTOSH Australian singer

Date	Title / Label	Peak Position	Weeks at No.1	Weeks in Top 40
7 Jul 07	**MISTAKE** *Universal TV 1739005*	47		

BILLY MACK UK singer

Date	Title / Label	Peak Position	Weeks at No.1	Weeks in Top 40
27 Dec 03	**CHRISTMAS IS ALL AROUND** *Island CID 841*	26		1

CRAIG MACK US rapper

Date	Title / Label	Peak Position	Weeks at No.1	Weeks in Top 40
12 Nov 94	**FLAVA IN YOUR EAR** *Bad Boy 74321242582*	57		
1 Apr 95	**GET DOWN** *Puff Daddy 74321263402*	54		
7 Jun 97	**SPIRIT** *Perspective 5822312* SOUNDS OF BLACKNESS FEATURING CRAIG MACK	35		1

LIZZY MACK UK singer

Date	Title / Label	Peak Position	Weeks at No.1	Weeks in Top 40
5 Nov 94	**THE POWER OF LOVE** *Media MCSTD 2016* FITS OF GLOOM FEATURING LIZZY MACK	49		
4 Nov 95	**DON'T GO** *Power Station MCSTD 40004*	52		

LONNIE MACK US guitarist

Date	Title / Label	Peak Position	Weeks at No.1	Weeks in Top 40
14 Apr 79	**MEMPHIS** *Lightning LIG 9011*	47		

MACK VIBE US duo

Date	Title / Label	Peak Position	Weeks at No.1	Weeks in Top 40
4 Feb 95	**I CAN'T LET YOU GO** *MCA MCSTD 2020* MACK VIBE FEATURING JAQUELINE	53		

McKAY US singer

Date	Title / Label	Peak Position	Weeks at No.1	Weeks in Top 40
23 Aug 03	**TAKE ME OVER** *Go! Beat GOBCD 57*	65		

MARIA McKEE US singer

Date	Title / Label	Peak Position	Weeks at No.1	Weeks in Top 40
15 Sep 90	**SHOW ME HEAVEN** *Epic 6563037*	1	4	12
26 Jan 91	**BREATHE** *Geffen GFS 1*	59		
1 Aug 92	**SWEETEST CHILD** *Geffen GFS 23*	45		
22 May 93	**I'M GONNA SOOTHE YOU** *Geffen GFSTD 39*	35		1
18 Sep 93	**I CAN'T MAKE IT ALONE** *Geffen GFSTD 53*	74		

KENNETH McKELLAR UK singer

Date	Title / Label	Peak Position	Weeks at No.1	Weeks in Top 40
10 Mar 66	**A MAN WITHOUT LOVE** *Decca F 12341*	30		2

GISELE MacKENZIE Canadian singer

Date	Title / Label	Peak Position	Weeks at No.1	Weeks in Top 40
17 Jul 53	**SEVEN LONELY DAYS** *Capitol CL 13920*	6		6

SCOTT McKENZIE US singer

Date	Title / Label	Peak Position	Weeks at No.1	Weeks in Top 40
12 Jul 67	**SAN FRANCISCO (BE SURE TO WEAR SOME FLOWERS IN YOUR HAIR)** *CBS 2816*	1	4	16
1 Nov 67	**LIKE AN OLD TIME MOVIE** *CBS 3009* VOICE OF SCOTT McKENZIE	50		

KEN MACKINTOSH UK orchestra leader

Date	Title / Label	Peak Position	Weeks at No.1	Weeks in Top 40
15 Jan 54	**THE CREEP** *HMV BD 1295*	10		2
7 Feb 58	**RAUNCHY** *HMV POP 426*	19		6
10 Mar 60	**NO HIDING PLACE** *HMV POP 713*	45		

BEN MACKLIN UK producer

Date	Title / Label	Peak Position	Weeks at No.1	Weeks in Top 40
20 Jan 07	**FEEL TOGETHER** *Free2Air F2A25CDX* BEN MACKLIN FEATURING TIGER LILY	71		

BRIAN McKNIGHT US singer

Date	Title / Label	Peak Position	Weeks at No.1	Weeks in Top 40
6 Jun 98	**ANYTIME** *Motown 8607752*	48		
3 Oct 98	**YOU SHOULD BE MINE** *Motown 8608412* BRIAN McKNIGHT FEATURING MASE	36		1

JULIE McKNIGHT US singer

Date	Title / Label	Peak Position	Weeks at No.1	Weeks in Top 40
14 Apr 01	**FINALLY** *Distance DI 2029* KINGS OF TOMORROW FEATURING JULIE McKNIGHT	54		
29 Sep 01	**FINALLY (REMIX)** *Defected DEFECT 37CDX* KINGS OF TOMORROW FEATURING JULIE McKNIGHT	24		1
15 Jun 02	**HOME** *Defected DFECT 51CDS*	61		
23 Nov 02	**DIAMOND LIFE** *Distance D12409* LOUIE VEGA & JAY 'SINISTER' SEALEE STARRING JULIE McKNIGHT	52		

VIVIENNE McKONE UK singer

Date	Title / Label	Peak Position	Weeks at No.1	Weeks in Top 40
25 Jul 92	**SING (OOH-EE-OOH)** *ffrr F 183*	47		
31 Oct 92	**BEWARE** *ffrr F 202*	69		

McKOY UK group

Date	Title / Label	Peak Position	Weeks at No.1	Weeks in Top 40
6 Mar 93	**FIGHT** *Rightrack CDTUM 1*	54		

CRAIG McLACHLAN Australian actor/singer

Date	Title / Label	Peak Position	Weeks at No.1	Weeks in Top 40
16 Jun 90	**MONA** *Epic 6557847* CRAIG McLACHLAN & CHECK 1-2	2		9
4 Aug 90	**AMANDA** *Epic 6561707* CRAIG McLACHLAN & CHECK 1-2	19		5
10 Nov 90	**I ALMOST FELT LIKE CRYING** *Epic 6563107* CRAIG McLACHLAN & CHECK 1-2	50		
23 May 92	**ONE REASON WHY** *Epic 6580677*	29		4
14 Nov 92	**ON MY OWN** *Epic 6584677*	59		
24 Jul 93	**YOU'RE THE ONE THAT I WANT** *Epic 6595222* CRAIG McLACHLAN & DEBBIE GIBSON	13		4
25 Dec 93	**GREASE** *Epic 6600242*	44		
8 Jul 95	**EVERYDAY** *MDMC DEVCS 6* CRAIG McLACHLAN & THE CULPRITS	65		

SARAH McLACHLAN Canadian singer

Date	Title / Label	Peak Position	Weeks at No.1	Weeks in Top 40
3 Oct 98	**ADIA** *Arista 74321613902*	18		3
14 Oct 00	**SILENCE** *Nettwerk 331082* DELERIUM FEATURING SARAH McLACHLAN	3		10
2 Feb 02	**ANGEL** *Nettwerk 331492*	36		1
20 Mar 04	**FALLEN** *Arista 82876599282*	50		
26 Jun 04	**WORLD ON FIRE** *Arista 82876628632*	72		
27 Nov 04	**SILENCE 2004 (REMIX)** *Nettwerk 332422* DELERIUM FEATURING SARAH McLACHLAN	38		1

TOMMY McLAIN US singer

Date	Title / Label	Peak Position	Weeks at No.1	Weeks in Top 40
8 Sep 66	**SWEET DREAMS** *London HL 10065*	49		

MALCOLM McLAREN UK producer

Date	Title / Label	Peak Position	Weeks at No.1	Weeks in Top 40
4 Dec 82	**BUFFALO GALS** *Charisma MALC 1* MALCOLM McLAREN & THE WORLD'S FAMOUS SUPREME TEAM	9		11
26 Feb 83	**SOWETO** *Charisma MALC 2* MALCOLM McLAREN & THE McLARENETTES	32		3
2 Jul 83	**DOUBLE DUTCH** *Charisma MALC 3*	3		10
17 Dec 83	**DUCK FOR THE OYSTER** *Charisma MALC 4*	54		
1 Sep 84	**MADAM BUTTERFLY (UN BEL DI VEDREMO)** *Charisma MALC 5*	13		7
27 May 89	**WALTZ DARLING** *Epic WALTZ 2* MALCOLM McLAREN & THE BOOTZILLA ORCHESTRA	31		3
19 Aug 89	**SOMETHING'S JUMPIN' IN YOUR SHIRT** *Epic WALTZ 3* MALCOLM McLAREN & THE BOOTZILLA ORCHESTRA FEATURING LISA MARIE	29		4
25 Nov 89	**HOUSE OF THE BLUE DANUBE** *Epic WALTZ 4*	73		
8 Dec 90	**OPERA HOUSE** *Virgin VS1273CD* MALCOLM McLAREN PRESENTS THE WORLD'S FAMOUS SUPREME TEAM SHOW	75		
21 Dec 91	**MAGIC'S BACK (THEME FROM 'THE GHOSTS OF OXFORD STREET')** *RCA PB 45223* MALCOLM McLAREN FEATURING ALISON LIMERICK	42		
3 Oct 98	**BUFFALO GALS STAMPEDE** *Virgin VSCDT 1717* MALCOLM McLAREN & THE WORLD'S FAMOUS SUPREME TEAM PLUS RAKIM & ROGER SANCHEZ	65		

BITTY McLEAN UK singer

Date	Title / Label	Peak Position	Weeks at No.1	Weeks in Top 40
31 Jul 93	**IT KEEP'S RAININ' (TEARS FROM MY EYES)** *Brilliant CDBRIL 1*	2		12
30 Oct 93	**PASS IT ON** *Brilliant CDBRIL 2*	35		2
15 Jan 94	**HERE I STAND** *Brilliant CDBRIL 3*	10		5
9 Apr 94	**DEDICATED TO THE ONE I LOVE** *Brilliant CDBRIL 4*	6		7
6 Aug 94	**WHAT GOES AROUND** *Brilliant CDBRIL 5*	36		1
8 Apr 95	**OVER THE RIVER** *Brilliant CDBRIL 9*	27		3
17 Jun 95	**WE'VE ONLY JUST BEGUN** *Brilliant CDBRIL 10*	23		3
30 Sep 95	**NOTHING CAN CHANGE THIS LOVE** *Brilliant CDBRIL 11*	55		
27 Jan 96	**NATURAL HIGH** *Brilliant CDBRIL 12*	63		
5 Oct 96	**SHE'S ALRIGHT** *Kuff KUFFD 9*	53		

DON McLEAN US singer

Date	Title / Label	Peak Position	Weeks at No.1	Weeks in Top 40
22 Jan 72	**AMERICAN PIE** *United Artists UP 35325* ★	2		15
13 May 72	**VINCENT** *United Artists UP 35359*	1	2	14
14 Apr 73	**EVERYDAY** *United Artists UP 35519*	38		1
10 May 80	**CRYING** *EMI 5051*	1	3	11
17 Apr 82	**CASTLES IN THE AIR** *EMI 5258*	47		
5 Oct 91	**AMERICAN PIE** *Liberty EMCT 3*	12		7

JACKIE McLEAN US saxophonist

Date	Title / Label	Peak Position	Weeks at No.1	Weeks in Top 40
7 Jul 79	**DR JACKYLL AND MISTER FUNK** *RCA PB 1575*	53		

PHIL McLEAN US singer/radio DJ

Date	Title / Label	Peak Position	Weeks at No.1	Weeks in Top 40
18 Jan 62	**SMALL SAD SAM** *Top Rank JAR 597*	34		3

McLUSKY UK group

Date	Title / Label	Peak Position	Weeks at No.1	Weeks in Top 40
8 May 04	**THAT MAN WILL NOT HANG** *Too Pure PURE153CDS*	71		

IAN McNABB UK singer

Date	Title / Label	Peak Position	Weeks at No.1	Weeks in Top 40
23 Jan 93	**IF LOVE WAS LIKE GUITARS** *This Way Up WAY 233*	67		
2 Jul 94	**YOU MUST BE PREPARED TO DREAM** *This Way Up WAY 3199*	54		
17 Sep 94	**GO INTO THE LIGHT** *This Way Up WAY 3699*	66		
27 Apr 96	**DON'T PUT YOUR SPELL ON ME** *This Way Up WAY 5033*	72		
6 Jul 96	**MERSEYBEAT** *This Way Up WAY 5266*	74		
28 May 05	**LET THE YOUNG GIRL DO WHAT SHE WANTS TO** *Fairfield FAIRCD5*	38		1

LUTRICIA McNEAL US singer

Date	Title / Label	Peak Position	Weeks at No.1	Weeks in Top 40
29 Nov 97	**AIN'T THAT JUST THE WAY** *Wildstar CDSTAS 2907*	6		15
23 May 98	**STRANDED** *Wildstar CXSTAS 2973*	3		10
26 Sep 98	**SOMEONE LOVES YOU HONEY** *Wildstar CDWILD 9*	9		6
19 Dec 98	**THE GREATEST LOVE YOU'LL NEVER KNOW** *Wildstar CDWILD 11*	17		3

PATRICK MacNEE & HONOR BLACKMAN UK actors

Date	Title / Label	Peak Position	Weeks at No.1	Weeks in Top 40
1 Dec 90	**KINKY BOOTS** *Deram KINKY 1*	5		6

RITA MacNEIL Canadian singer

Date	Title / Label	Peak Position	Weeks at No.1	Weeks in Top 40
6 Oct 90	**WORKING MAN** *Polydor PO 98*	11		7

CLYDE McPHATTER US singer

Date	Title / Label	Peak Position	Weeks at No.1	Weeks in Top 40
24 Aug 56	**TREASURE OF LOVE** *London HLE 8293*	27		1

TOM McRAE UK singer

Date	Title / Label	Peak Position	Weeks at No.1	Weeks in Top 40
24 May 03	**KARAOKE SOUL** *DB DB016CDE7JC2*	48		

RALPH McTELL UK singer

Date	Title / Label	Peak Position	Weeks at No.1	Weeks in Top 40
7 Dec 74	**STREETS OF LONDON** *Reprise K 14380*	2		11
20 Dec 75	**DREAMS OF YOU** *Warner Brothers K 16648*	36		1

MAD COBRA Jamaican rapper

Date	Title / Label	Peak Position	Weeks at No.1	Weeks in Top 40
15 May 93	**LEGACY** *Columbia 6592852* MAD COBRA FEATURING RICHIE STEPHENS	64		

MAD DONNA US group

Date	Title / Label	Peak Position	Weeks at No.1	Weeks in Top 40
4 May 02	**THE WHEELS ON THE BUS** *Star Harbour/All Around The World DISCO 0202CR*	17		3

MAD JOCKS UK group

Date	Title / Label	Peak Position	Weeks at No.1	Weeks in Top 40
19 Dec 87	**JOCK MIX 1** *Debut DEBT 3037* MAD JOCKS FEATURING JOCKMASTER B.A.	46		
18 Dec 93	**PARTY FOUR (EP)** *SMP CDSSKM 24* MAD JOCKS FEATURING JOCKMASTER B.A.	57		

Silver-selling ○ Gold-selling ● Platinum-selling ⊛ US No.1 ★

Peak Position · Weeks at No.1 · Weeks in Top 40

MAD MOSES US producer

Date	Title / Label	Peak Position	Weeks at No.1	Weeks in Top 40
16 Aug 97	**PANTHER PARTY** *Hi-Life 5744932*	50		

MADASUN UK group

Date	Title / Label	Peak Position	Weeks at No.1	Weeks in Top 40
11 Mar 00	**DON'T YOU WORRY** *V2 VVR 5011523*	14		3
27 May 00	**WALKING ON WATER** *V2 VVR 5012418*	14		2
2 Sep 00	**FEEL GOOD** *V2 VVR 5012983*	29		1

DANNY MADDEN US singer

Date	Title / Label	Peak Position	Weeks at No.1	Weeks in Top 40
14 Jul 90	**THE FACTS OF LIFE** *Eternal YZ 473*	72		

MADDER ROSE US group

Date	Title / Label	Peak Position	Weeks at No.1	Weeks in Top 40
26 Mar 94	**PANIC ON** *Atlantic A 8301CD*	65		
16 Jul 94	**CAR SONG** *Seed A 7256CD*	68		

MADE IN LONDON UK/Norwegian group

Date	Title / Label	Peak Position	Weeks at No.1	Weeks in Top 40
13 May 00	**DIRTY WATER** *RCA 74321746192*	15		3
9 Sep 00	**SHUT YOUR MOUTH** *RCA 74321772602*	74		

MADELYNE Dutch producer

Date	Title / Label	Peak Position	Weeks at No.1	Weeks in Top 40
7 Sep 02	**BEAUTIFUL CHILD (A DEEPER LOVE)** *Xtravaganza XTRAV 36CDS*	63		

MADEMOISELLE French production duo

Date	Title / Label	Peak Position	Weeks at No.1	Weeks in Top 40
8 Sep 01	**DO YOU LOVE ME** *RCA 74321878952*	56		

MADHOUSE French production group

Date	Title / Label	Peak Position	Weeks at No.1	Weeks in Top 40
17 Aug 02	**LIKE A PRAYER** *Serious SERR 046CD*	3		8
9 Nov 02	**HOLIDAY** *Serious SER 058CD*	24		1

MADISON AVENUE Australian duo

Date	Title / Label	Peak Position	Weeks at No.1	Weeks in Top 40
13 Nov 99	**DON'T CALL ME BABY** *VC Recordings VCRD 56*	30		1
20 May 00	**DON'T CALL ME BABY** *VC Recordings VCRD 64* ○	1	1	8
21 Oct 00	**WHO THE HELL ARE YOU** *VC Recordings VCRD 70*	10		3
27 Jan 01	**EVERYTHING YOU NEED** *VC Recordings VCRD 82*	33		1

MADNESS UK group

Date	Title / Label	Peak Position	Weeks at No.1	Weeks in Top 40
1 Sep 79	**THE PRINCE** *2 Tone TT 3*	16		7
10 Nov 79	**ONE STEP BEYOND** *Stiff BUY 56* ○	7		10
5 Jan 80	**MY GIRL** *Stiff BUY 62* ○	3		7
5 Apr 80	**WORK REST AND PLAY (EP)** *Stiff BUY 71*	6		6
13 Sep 80	**BAGGY TROUSERS** *Stiff BUY 84* ●	3		11
22 Nov 80	**EMBARRASSMENT** *Stiff BUY 102* ●	4		11
24 Jan 81	**RETURN OF THE LOS PALMAS SEVEN** *Stiff BUY 108* ○	7		9
25 Apr 81	**GREY DAY** *Stiff BUY 112* ○	4		7
26 Sep 81	**SHUT UP** *Stiff BUY 126* ○	7		7
5 Dec 81	**IT MUST BE LOVE** *Stiff BUY 134* ●	4		10
20 Feb 82	**CARDIAC ARREST** *Stiff BUY 140*	14		7
22 May 82	**HOUSE OF FUN** *Stiff BUY 146* ○	1	2	7
24 Jul 82	**DRIVING IN MY CAR** *Stiff BUY 153* ○	4		6
27 Nov 82	**OUR HOUSE** *Stiff BUY 163* ●	5		11
19 Feb 83	**TOMORROW'S (JUST ANOTHER DAY)/MADNESS (IS ALL IN THE MIND)** *Stiff BUY 169*	8		6
20 Aug 83	**WINGS OF A DOVE** *Stiff BUY 181* ○	2		8
5 Nov 83	**THE SUN AND THE RAIN** *Stiff BUY 192*	5		7
11 Feb 84	**MICHAEL CAINE** *Stiff BUY 196*	11		6
2 Jun 84	**ONE BETTER DAY** *Stiff BUY 201*	17		5
31 Aug 85	**YESTERDAY'S MEN** *Zarjazz JAZZ 5*	18		5
26 Oct 85	**UNCLE SAM** *Zarjazz JAZZ 7*	21		6
1 Feb 86	**SWEETEST GIRL** *Zarjazz JAZZ 8*	35		2
8 Nov 86	**(WAITING FOR) THE GHOST TRAIN** *Zarjazz JAZZ 9*	18		5
19 Mar 88	**I PRONOUNCE YOU** *Virgin VS 1054*	44		
15 Feb 92	**IT MUST BE LOVE** *Virgin VS 1405*	6		7
25 Apr 92	**HOUSE OF FUN** *Virgin VS 1413*	40		1
8 Aug 92	**MY GIRL** *Virgin VS 1425*	27		2
28 Nov 92	**THE HARDER THEY COME** *Go! Discs GOD 93*	44		
27 Feb 93	**NIGHT BOAT TO CAIRO** *Virgin VSCDT 1447*	56		
31 Jul 99	**LOVESTRUCK** *Virgin VSCDT 1737*	10		4
6 Nov 99	**JOHNNY THE HORSE** *Virgin VSCDT 1740*	44		
11 Mar 00	**DRIP FED FRED** *Virgin VSCDT 1768* MADNESS FEATURING IAN DURY	55		
6 Aug 05	**SHAME & SCANDAL** *V2 VVR5033243*	38		1
17 Mar 07	**SORRY** *Lucky Seven Records LUCKY701CDS*	23		1
26 Jan 08	**NW5** *Lucky Seven Records LUCKY70021CDS*	24		1

MADONNA US singer

Date	Title / Label	Peak Position	Weeks at No.1	Weeks in Top 40
14 Jan 84	**HOLIDAY** *Sire W 9405* ●	6		9
17 Mar 84	**LUCKY STAR** *Sire W 9522*	14		7
2 Jun 84	**BORDERLINE** *Sire W 9260*	56		
17 Nov 84	**LIKE A VIRGIN** *Sire W 9210* ● ★	3		15
2 Mar 85	**MATERIAL GIRL** *Sire W 9083* ●	3		8
8 Jun 85	**CRAZY FOR YOU** *Geffen A 6323* ● ★	2		13
27 Jul 85	**INTO THE GROOVE** *Sire W 8934*	1	4	12
3 Aug 85	**HOLIDAY** *Sire W 9405*	2		8
21 Sep 85	**ANGEL** *Sire W 8881* ○	5		7
12 Oct 85	**GAMBLER** *Geffen A 6585* ○	4		8
7 Dec 85	**DRESS YOU UP** *Sire W 8848* ●	5		8
25 Jan 86	**BORDERLINE** *Sire W 9260* ○	2		7
26 Apr 86	**LIVE TO TELL** *Sire W 8717* ○ ★	2		8
28 Jun 86	**PAPA DON'T PREACH** *Sire W 8636* ● ★	1	3	11
4 Oct 86	**TRUE BLUE** *Sire W 8550* ○	1	1	9
13 Dec 86	**OPEN YOUR HEART** *Sire W 8480* ○ ★	4		8
4 Apr 87	**LA ISLA BONITA** *Sire W 8378* ○	1	2	10
18 Jul 87	**WHO'S THAT GIRL** *Sire W 8341* ○ ★	1	1	9
19 Sep 87	**CAUSING A COMMOTION** *Sire W 8224*	4		7
12 Dec 87	**THE LOOK OF LOVE** *Sire W 8115*	9		6
18 Mar 89	**LIKE A PRAYER** *Sire W 7539* ● ★	1	3	9
3 Jun 89	**EXPRESS YOURSELF** *Sire W 2948* ○	5		8
16 Sep 89	**CHERISH** *Sire W 2883*	3		6
16 Dec 89	**DEAR JESSIE** *Sire W 2668* ○	5		7
7 Apr 90	**VOGUE** *Sire W 9851* ● ★	1	4	12
21 Jul 90	**HANKY PANKY** *Sire W 9789* ○	2		8
8 Dec 90	**JUSTIFY MY LOVE** *Sire W 9000* ○ ★	2		8
2 Mar 91	**CRAZY FOR YOU (REMIX)** *Sire W 0008* ○	2		6
13 Apr 91	**RESCUE ME** *Sire W 0024*	3		6
8 Jun 91	**HOLIDAY** *Sire W 0037*	5		4
25 Jul 92	**THIS USED TO BE MY PLAYGROUND** *Sire W 0122* ○ ★	3		7
17 Oct 92	**EROTICA** *Maverick W 0138*	3		5
12 Dec 92	**DEEPER AND DEEPER** *Maverick W 0146*	6		7
6 Mar 93	**BAD GIRL** *Maverick W 0145CD*	10		4
3 Apr 93	**FEVER** *Maverick W 0168CD*	6		4
31 Jul 93	**RAIN** *Maverick W 0190CD*	7		5
2 Apr 94	**I'LL REMEMBER (THEME FROM WITH HONORS)** *Maverick W 0240CD*	7		5
8 Oct 94	**SECRET** *Maverick W 0268CD*	5		7
17 Dec 94	**TAKE A BOW** *Maverick W 0278CD* ★	16		6
25 Feb 95	**BEDTIME STORY** *Maverick W 0285CD*	4		3
26 Aug 95	**HUMAN NATURE** *Maverick W 0300CD*	8		3
4 Nov 95	**YOU'LL SEE** *Maverick W 0324CDX*	5		11
6 Jan 96	**OH FATHER** *Maverick W 0326CDX*	16		3
23 Mar 96	**ONE MORE CHANCE** *Maverick W 0337CD*	11		2
2 Nov 96	**YOU MUST LOVE ME** *Warner Brothers W 0378CD*	10		3
28 Dec 96	**DON'T CRY FOR ME ARGENTINA** *Warner Brothers W 0384CD* ○	3		9
29 Mar 97	**ANOTHER SUITCASE IN ANOTHER HALL** *Warner Brothers W 0388CD*	7		2
7 Mar 98	**FROZEN** *Maverick W 0433CD* ●	1	1	9
9 May 98	**RAY OF LIGHT** *Maverick W 0444CD* ○	2		7
5 Sep 98	**DROWNED WORLD (SUBSTITUTE FOR LOVE)** *Maverick W 0453CD1*	10		3
5 Dec 98	**THE POWER OF GOODBYE/LITTLE STAR** *Maverick W 459CD*	6		6
13 Mar 99	**NOTHING REALLY MATTERS** *Maverick W 471CD1* ○	7		4
19 Jun 99	**BEAUTIFUL STRANGER** *Maverick W 495CD* ●	2		13
11 Mar 00	**AMERICAN PIE** *Maverick W 519CD* ●	1	1	8
2 Sep 00	**MUSIC** *Maverick W 537CD1* ● ★	1	1	15
9 Dec 00	**DON'T TELL ME** *Maverick W 547CD1*	4		8
28 Apr 01	**WHAT IT FEELS LIKE FOR A GIRL** *Maverick W 533CD1*	7		5
9 Nov 02	**DIE ANOTHER DAY** *Warner Brothers W 595CD*	3		10
19 Apr 03	**AMERICAN LIFE (IMPORT)** *Maverick 166582*	57		
26 Apr 03	**AMERICAN LIFE** *Maverick W 603CD*	2		5
19 Jul 03	**HOLLYWOOD** *Maverick W 614CD*	2		4
22 Nov 03	**ME AGAINST THE MUSIC** *Jive 82876576432* BRITNEY SPEARS FEATURING MADONNA	2		6
20 Dec 03	**NOTHING FAILS/LOVE PROFUSION** *Maverick W 634CD1*	11		2
19 Nov 05	**HUNG UP** *Warner Brothers W695CD2*	1	3	18
4 Mar 06	**SORRY** *Warner Brothers W703CD1*	1		11
29 Jul 06	**GET TOGETHER** *Warner Brothers W725CD*	7		3
11 Nov 06	**JUMP** *Warner Brothers W744CD1*	9		3
29 Mar 08	**4 MINUTES** *Download* MADONNA FEATURING JUSTIN TIMBERLAKE	7		1

LISA MAFFIA UK rapper

Date	Title / Label	Peak Position	Weeks at No.1	Weeks in Top 40
30 Dec 00	**NO GOOD 4 ME** *East West OXIDE 02CD* OXIDE & NEUTRINO FEATURING MEGAMAN, ROMEO & LISA MAFFIA	6		6
3 May 03	**ALL OVER** *Independiente ISOM 69SMS*	2		6
9 Aug 03	**IN LOVE** *Independiente ISOM 75SMS*	13		3
8 Sep 07	**BAD GIRL (AT NIGHT)** *Toolroom/Apollo APOLLO114CDX* DAVE SPOON FEATURING LISA MAFFIA	36		1

MAGAZINE UK group

Date	Title / Label	Peak Position	Weeks at No.1	Weeks in Top 40
11 Feb 78	**SHOT BY BOTH SIDES** *Virgin VS 200*	41		
26 Jul 80	**SWEET HEART CONTRACT** *Virgin VS 368*	54		

MAGIC AFFAIR US/German group

Date	Title / Label	Peak Position	Weeks at No.1	Weeks in Top 40
4 Jun 94	**OMEN III** *EMI CDEM 317*	17		3
27 Aug 94	**GIVE ME ALL YOUR LOVE** *EMI CDEM 340*	30		1
5 Nov 94	**IN THE MIDDLE OF THE NIGHT** *EMI CDEM 349*	38		1

MAGIC LADY US group

Date	Title / Label	Peak Position	Weeks at No.1	Weeks in Top 40
14 May 88	**BETCHA CAN'T LOSE (WITH MY LOVE)** *Motown ZB 42003*	58		

MAGIC LANTERNS UK group

Date	Title / Label	Peak Position	Weeks at No.1	Weeks in Top 40
7 Jul 66	**EXCUSE ME BABY** *CBS 202094*	44		

MAGIC NUMBERS US group

Date	Title / Label	Peak Position	Weeks at No.1	Weeks in Top 40
4 Jun 05	**FOREVER LOST** *Heavenly HVN151CD*	15		2
20 Aug 05	**LOVE ME LIKE YOU** *Heavenly HVN153CDS*	12		3
5 Nov 05	**LOVE'S A GAME** *Heavenly HVN154CD*	24		1
25 Feb 06	**I SEE YOU YOU SEE ME** *Heavenly HVN156CD*	20		1
28 Oct 06	**TAKE A CHANCE** *Heavenly HVN163CD*	16		2
3 Mar 07	**THIS IS A SONG** *Heavenly HVN165CD*	36		1

MAGNOLIA Italian producer

Date	Title / Label	Peak Position	Weeks at No.1	Weeks in Top 40
24 Jul 04	**IT'S ALL VAIN** *Data 69CDS*	55		

MAGNUM Uk group

Date	Title / Label	Peak Position	Weeks at No.1	Weeks in Top 40
22 Mar 80	**MAGNUM (DOUBLE SINGLE)** *Jet 175*	47		
12 Jul 86	**LONELY NIGHT** *Polydor POSP 798*	70		
19 Mar 88	**DAYS OF NO TRUST** *Polydor POSP 910*	32		2
7 May 88	**START TALKING LOVE** *Polydor POSP 920*	22		3
2 Jul 88	**IT MUST HAVE BEEN LOVE** *Polydor POSP 930*	33		2
23 Jun 90	**ROCKIN' CHAIR** *Polydor PO 88*	27		3
25 Aug 90	**HEARTBROKE AND BUSTED** *Polydor PO 94*	49		

MAGOO US rapper

Date	Title / Label	Peak Position	Weeks at No.1	Weeks in Top 40
13 Mar 99	**HERE WE COME** *Virgin DINSD 179* TIMBALAND/MISSY ELLIOTT & MAGOO	43		
13 Mar 04	**COP THAT SHIT** *Unique Corp TIMBACD001* TIMBALAND/MAGOO/MISSY ELLIOTT	22		2
4 Apr 98	**BLACK SABBATH/SWEET LEAF** *Fierce Panda NING 47CD* MAGOO : MOGWAI	60		

SEAN MAGUIRE UK actor/singer

Date	Title / Label	Peak Position	Weeks at No.1	Weeks in Top 40
20 Aug 94	**SOMEONE TO LOVE** *Parlophone CDRS 6390*	14		5
5 Nov 94	**TAKE THIS TIME** *Parlophone CDRS 6395*	27		2
25 Mar 95	**SUDDENLY** *Parlophone CDRS 6403*	18		3
24 Jun 95	**NOW I'VE FOUND YOU** *Parlophone CDLEEPYS 1*	22		2
18 Nov 95	**YOU TO ME ARE EVERYTHING** *Parlophone CDR 6420*	16		2
25 May 96	**GOOD DAY** *Parlophone CDR 6432*	12		3
3 Aug 96	**DON'T PULL YOUR LOVE** *Parlophone CDRS 6440*	14		2
29 Mar 97	**TODAY'S THE DAY** *Parlophone CDR 6459*	27		1

MAI TAI Dutch group

Date	Title / Label	Peak Position	Weeks at No.1	Weeks in Top 40
25 May 85	**HISTORY** *Virgin VS 773*	8		9
3 Aug 85	**BODY AND SOUL** *Virgin VS 801*	9		8
15 Feb 86	**FEMALE INTUITION** *Virgin VS 844*	54		

MAIN INGREDIENT US group

Date	Title / Label	Peak Position	Weeks at No.1	Weeks in Top 40
29 Jun 74	**JUST DON'T WANT TO BE LONELY** *RCA APBO 0205*	27		4

MAISONETTES UK group

Date	Title / Label	Peak Position	Weeks at No.1	Weeks in Top 40
11 Dec 82	**HEARTACHE AVENUE** *Ready Steady Go! RSG 1*	7		8

J MALIK US producer

Date	Title / Label	Peak Position	Weeks at No.1	Weeks in Top 40
5 May 01	**LOVE IS NOT A GAME** *Defected DFECT 31CDS* J MAJIK FEATURING KATHY BROWN	34		1
27 Apr 02	**METROSOUND** *Kaos 001P* ADAM F & J MAJIK	54		
22 May 04	**SCOOBY DOO/SPYCATCHER** *Infared INFRA28* J MAJIK & WICKAMAN	67		

MAKADOPOULOS & HIS GREEK SERENADERS Greek group

Date	Title / Label	Peak Position	Weeks at No.1	Weeks in Top 40
20 Oct 60	**NEVER ON SUNDAY** *Palette PG 9005*	36		7

MAKAVELI US rapper

Date	Title / Label	Peak Position	Weeks at No.1	Weeks in Top 40
12 Apr 97	**TO LIVE AND DIE IN LA** *Interscope IND 95529*	10		2
9 Aug 97	**TOSS IT UP** *Interscope IND 95521*	15		2
14 Feb 98	**HAIL MARY** *Interscope IND 95575*	43		

JACK E MAKOSSA US multi-instrumentalist

Date	Title / Label	Peak Position	Weeks at No.1	Weeks in Top 40
12 Sep 87	**THE OPERA HOUSE** *Champion CHAMP 50*	48		

MALAIKA US singer

Date	Title / Label	Peak Position	Weeks at No.1	Weeks in Top 40
31 Jul 93	**GOTTA KNOW (YOUR NAME)** *A&M 5802732*	68		

CARL MALCOLM Jamaican singer

Date	Title / Label	Peak Position	Weeks at No.1	Weeks in Top 40
13 Sep 75	**FATTIE BUM BUM** *UK 108*	8		8

STEPHEN MALKMUS US singer/guitarist

Date	Title / Label	Peak Position	Weeks at No.1	Weeks in Top 40
28 Apr 01	**DISCRETION GROVE** *Domino RUG 123CD*	60		

RAUL MALO US guitarist/singer

Date	Title / Label	Peak Position	Weeks at No.1	Weeks in Top 40
18 May 02	**I SAID I LOVE YOU** *Gravity 74321923082*	57		

MAMA CASS US singer

Date	Title / Label	Peak Position	Weeks at No.1	Weeks in Top 40
14 Aug 68	**DREAM A LITTLE DREAM OF ME** *RCA 1726*	11		10
16 Aug 69	**IT'S GETTING BETTER** *Stateside SS 8021*	8		12

MAMAS & THE PAPAS US group

Date	Title / Label	Peak Position	Weeks at No.1	Weeks in Top 40
28 Apr 66	**CALIFORNIA DREAMIN'** *RCA 1503*	23		7
12 May 66	**MONDAY MONDAY** *RCA 1516* ★	3		13
28 Jul 66	**I SAW HER AGAIN** *RCA 1533*	11		9
9 Feb 67	**WORDS OF LOVE** *RCA 1564*	47		
6 Apr 67	**DEDICATED TO THE ONE I LOVE** *RCA 1576*	2		16
26 Jul 67	**CREEQUE ALLEY** *RCA 1613*	9		10
2 Aug 97	**CALIFORNIA DREAMIN'** *MCA MCSTD 48058*	9		5

A MAN CALLED ADAM UK group

Date	Title / Label	Peak Position	Weeks at No.1	Weeks in Top 40
29 Sep 90	**BAREFOOT IN THE HEAD** *Big Life BLR 28*	60		

MAN TO MAN US group

Date	Title / Label	Peak Position	Weeks at No.1	Weeks in Top 40
13 Sep 86	**MALE STRIPPER** *Bolts 4* MAN TO MAN MEET MAN PARRISH	64		
3 Jan 87	**MALE STRIPPER** *Bolts 4* MAN TO MAN MEET MAN PARRISH	4		
4 Jul 87	**I NEED A MAN/ENERGY IS EUROBEAT** *Bolts 5*	43		

Silver-selling ○ Gold-selling ● Platinum-selling ✪ US No.1 ★ — Peak Position / Weeks at No.1 / Weeks in Top 40

MAN WITH NO NAME UK producer

Date	Title	Peak Position	Weeks at No.1	Weeks in Top 40
30 Sep 95	**FLOOR-ESSENCE** *Perfecto PERF 108CD*	68		
20 Jan 96	**PAINT A PICTURE** *Perfecto PERF 114CD* MAN WITH NO NAME FEATURING HANNAH	42		
12 Oct 96	**TELEPORT/SUGAR RUSH** *Perfecto PERF 126CD*	55		
2 May 98	**VAVOOM!** *Perfecto PERF 159CD1*	43		
18 Jul 98	**THE FIRST DAY (HORIZON)** *Perfecto PERF 164CD*	72		

MANCHESTER UNITED FOOTBALL CLUB
UK football club

Date	Title	Peak Position	Weeks at No.1	Weeks in Top 40
8 May 76	**MANCHESTER UNITED** *Decca F 13633*	50		
21 May 83	**GLORY GLORY MAN. UNITED** *EMI 5390*	13		4
18 May 85	**WE ALL FOLLOW MAN. UNITED** *Columbia DB 9107*	10		4
19 Jun 93	**UNITED (WE LOVE YOU)** *Living Beat LBECD 026* MANCHESTER UNITED & THE CHAMPIONS	37		1
30 Apr 94	**COME ON YOU REDS** *Polygram TV MANU 2* ○	1	2	12
13 May 95	**WE'RE GONNA DO IT AGAIN** *Polygram TV MANU 952* MANCHESTER UNITED FEATURING STRYKER	6		5
4 May 96	**MOVE MOVE MOVE (THE RED TRIBE)** *Music Collection MANUCD 1* ○	6		7
29 May 99	**LIFT IT HIGH (ALL ABOUT BELIEF)** *Music Collection MANUCD 4* 1999 MANCHESTER UNITED SQUAD	11		3

MANCHILD UK production duo

Date	Title	Peak Position	Weeks at No.1	Weeks in Top 40
16 Sep 00	**THE CLICHES ARE TRUE** *One Little Indian 176TP7CD* MANCHILD FEATURING KELLY JONES	60		
25 Aug 01	**NOTHING WITHOUT ME** *One Little Indian 183TP7CD*	40		1

HENRY MANCINI US orchestra leader

Date	Title	Peak Position	Weeks at No.1	Weeks in Top 40
7 Dec 61	**MOON RIVER** *RCA 1256*	44		
24 Sep 64	**HOW SOON** *RCA 1414*	10		10
25 Mar 72	**THEME FROM *CADE'S COUNTY*** *RCA 2182*	42		
11 Feb 84	**MAIN THEME FROM *THE THORNBIRDS*** *Warner Brothers 9677*	23		5

MANDO DIAO Swedish group

Date	Title	Peak Position	Weeks at No.1	Weeks in Top 40
5 Mar 05	**YOU CAN'T STEAL MY LOVE** *Majesty 8708962*	73		
18 Jun 05	**GOD KNOWS** *Majesty 8726022*	64		

MANFRED MANN UK group

Date	Title	Peak Position	Weeks at No.1	Weeks in Top 40
23 Jan 64	**5-4-3-2-1** *HMV POP 1252*	5		11
16 Apr 64	**HUBBLE BUBBLE TOIL AND TROUBLE** *HMV POP 1282*	11		7
16 Jul 64	**DO WAH DIDDY DIDDY** *HMV POP 1320* ★	1	2	14
15 Oct 64	**SHA LA LA** *HMV POP 1346*	3		11
14 Jan 65	**COME TOMORROW** *HMV POP 1381*	4		9
15 Apr 65	**OH NO NOT MY BABY** *HMV POP 1413*	11		9
16 Sep 65	**IF YOU GOTTA GO GO NOW** *HMV POP 1466*	2		11
21 Apr 66	**PRETTY FLAMINGO** *HMV POP 1523*	1	3	12
7 Jul 66	**YOU GAVE ME SOMEBODY TO LOVE** *HMV POP 1541*	36		3
4 Aug 66	**JUST LIKE A WOMAN** *Fontana TF 730*	10		10
27 Oct 66	**SEMI-DETACHED SUBURBAN MR. JAMES** *Fontana TF 757*	2		11
30 Mar 67	**HA HA SAID THE CLOWN** *Fontana TF 812*	4		9
25 May 67	**SWEET PEA** *Fontana TF 828*	36		2
24 Jan 68	**MIGHTY QUINN** *Fontana TF 897*	1	2	10
12 Jun 68	**MY NAME IS JACK** *Fontana TF 943*	8		10
18 Dec 68	**FOX ON THE RUN** *Fontana TF 985*	5		9
30 Apr 69	**RAGAMUFFIN MAN** *Fontana TF 1013*	8		10
8 Sep 73	**JOYBRINGER** *Vertigo 6059 083* MANFRED MANNS EARTH BAND	9		9
28 Aug 76	**BLINDED BY THE LIGHT** *Bronze BRO 29* MANFRED MANNS EARTH BAND ★	6		9
20 May 78	**DAVY'S ON THE ROAD AGAIN** *Bronze BRO 52* MANFRED MANNS EARTH BAND ○	6		10
17 Mar 79	**YOU ANGEL YOU** *Bronze BRO 68* MANFRED MANNS EARTH BAND	54		
7 Jul 79	**DON'T KILL IT CAROL** *Bronze BRO 77* MANFRED MANNS EARTH BAND	45		

MANHATTAN TRANSFER US group

Date	Title	Peak Position	Weeks at No.1	Weeks in Top 40
7 Feb 76	**TUXEDO JUNCTION** *Atlantic K 10670*	24		5
5 Feb 77	**CHANSON D'AMOUR** *Atlantic K 10886* ●	1	3	13
28 May 77	**DON'T LET GO** *Atlantic K 10930*	32		5
18 Feb 78	**WALK IN LOVE** *Atlantic K 11075*	12		9
20 May 78	**ON A LITTLE STREET IN SINGAPORE** *Atlantic K 11136*	20		7
16 Sep 78	**WHERE DID OUR LOVE GO/JE VOULAIS TE DIRE (QUE JE T'ATTENDS)** *Atlantic K 11182*	40		1
23 Dec 78	**WHO WHAT WHEN WHERE WHY** *Atlantic K 11233*	49		
17 May 80	**TWILIGHT ZONE - TWILIGHT TONE (MEDLEY)** *Atlantic K 11476*	25		5
21 Jan 84	**SPICE OF LIFE** *Atlantic A 9728*	19		6

MANHATTANS US group

Date	Title	Peak Position	Weeks at No.1	Weeks in Top 40
19 Jun 76	**KISS AND SAY GOODBYE** *CBS 4317* ○ ★	4		10
2 Oct 76	**HURT** *CBS 4562* ○	4		11
23 Apr 77	**IT'S YOU** *CBS 5093*	43		
26 Jul 80	**SHINING STAR** *CBS 8624*	45		
6 Aug 83	**CRAZY** *CBS A 3578*	63		

MANIA UK duo

Date	Title	Peak Position	Weeks at No.1	Weeks in Top 40
7 Aug 04	**LOOKING FOR A PLACE** *RCA 82876617862*	29		1

M.A.N.I.C. UK production duo

Date	Title	Peak Position	Weeks at No.1	Weeks in Top 40
18 Apr 92	**I'M COMIN' HARDCORE** *Union City UCRT 2*	60		

MANIC MC's UK production duo

Date	Title	Peak Position	Weeks at No.1	Weeks in Top 40
12 Aug 89	**MENTAL** *RCA PB 43037* MANIC MC's FEATURING SARAH CARLSON	30		3

MANIC STREET PREACHERS UK group

Date	Title	Peak Position	Weeks at No.1	Weeks in Top 40
25 May 91	**YOU LOVE US** *Heavenly HVN 10*	62		
10 Aug 91	**STAY BEAUTIFUL** *Columbia 6573377*	40		1
9 Nov 91	**LOVE'S SWEET EXILE/REPEAT** *Columbia 6575827*	26		2
1 Feb 92	**YOU LOVE US** *Columbia 6577247*	16		3
28 Mar 92	**SLASH 'N' BURN** *Columbia 6578737*	20		3
13 Jun 92	**MOTORCYCLE EMPTINESS** *Columbia 6580837*	17		4
19 Sep 92	**THEME FROM *MASH* (SUICIDE IS PAINLESS)** *Columbia 6583827*	7		5
21 Nov 92	**LITTLE BABY NOTHING** *Columbia 6587967*	29		1
12 Jun 93	**FROM DESPAIR TO WHERE** *Columbia 6593372*	25		3
31 Jul 93	**LA TRISTESSE DURERA (SCREAM TO A SIGH)** *Columbia 6594772*	22		3
2 Oct 93	**ROSES IN THE HOSPITAL** *Columbia 6597272*	15		2
12 Feb 94	**LIFE BECOMING A LANDSLIDE** *Columbia 6600702*	36		1
11 Jun 94	**FASTER/PCP** *Epic 6604472*	16		2
13 Aug 94	**REVOL** *Epic 6606862*	22		2
15 Oct 94	**SHE IS SUFFERING** *Epic 6608952*	25		2
27 Apr 96	**A DESIGN FOR LIFE** *Epic 6630705* ○	2		7
3 Aug 96	**EVERYTHING MUST GO** *Epic 6634685*	5		3
12 Oct 96	**KEVIN CARTER** *Epic 6637752*	9		3
14 Dec 96	**AUSTRALIA** *Epic 6640445*	7		4
13 Sep 97	**STAY BEAUTIFUL** *Epic MANIC 1CD*	52		
13 Sep 97	**LOVE'S SWEET EXILE** *Epic MANIC 2CD*	55		
13 Sep 97	**YOU LOVE US** *Epic MANIC 3CD*	49		
13 Sep 97	**SLASH 'N' BURN** *Epic MANIC 4CD*	54		
13 Sep 97	**MOTORCYCLE EMPTINESS** *Epic MANIC 5CD*	41		
13 Sep 97	**LITTLE BABY NOTHING** *Epic MANIC 6CD*	50		
5 Sep 98	**IF YOU TOLERATE THIS YOUR CHILDREN WILL BE NEXT** *Epic 6663452* ○	1	1	6
12 Dec 98	**THE EVERLASTING** *Epic 6666862*	11		6
20 Mar 99	**YOU STOLE THE SUN FROM MY HEART** *Epic 6669532*	5		4
17 Jul 99	**TSUNAMI** *Epic 6674112*	11		2
22 Jan 00	**THE MASSES AGAINST THE CLASSES** *Epic 6685302*	1	1	4
10 Mar 01	**SO WHY SO SAD** *Epic 6708322*	8		3
10 Mar 01	**FOUND THAT SOUL** *Epic 6708332*	9		2
16 Jun 01	**OCEAN SPRAY** *Epic 6712532*	15		1
22 Sep 01	**LET ROBESON SING** *Epic 6717732*	19		1
26 Oct 02	**THERE BY THE GRACE OF GOD** *Epic 6731662*	6		2
30 Oct 04	**THE LOVE OF RICHARD NIXON** *Sony Music 6753422*	2		2
22 Jan 05	**EMPTY SOULS** *Columbia 6756102*	2		2
5 May 07	**YOUR LOVE ALONE IS NOT ENOUGH** *Columbia 88697075602*	2		7
4 Aug 07	**AUTUMNSONG** *Columbia 88697118302*	10		1
13 Oct 07	**INDIAN SUMMER** *Columbia 88697159322*	22		1
22 Mar 08	**UMBRELLA** *Download*	47		

MANIJAMA Danish group

Date	Title	Peak Position	Weeks at No.1	Weeks in Top 40
8 Feb 03	**NO NO NO** *Defected DFTD 058CDS* MANIJAMA FEATURING MUKUPA & LIL' T	66		

BARRY MANILOW US singer

Date	Title	Peak Position	Weeks at No.1	Weeks in Top 40
22 Feb 75	**MANDY** *Arista 1* ★	11		7
6 May 78	**CAN'T SMILE WITHOUT YOU** *Arista 176*	43		

Legend: Silver-selling · Gold-selling · Platinum-selling · US No.1 ★ · Peak Position · Weeks at No.1 · Weeks in Top 40

Date	Title / Label	Peak Position	Weeks at No.1	Weeks in Top 40
29 Jul 78	**SOMEWHERE IN THE NIGHT/COPACABANA (AT THE COPA)** *Arista 196*	42		
23 Dec 78	**COULD IT BE MAGIC** *Arista ARIST 229*	25		7
8 Nov 80	**LONELY TOGETHER** *Arista ARIST 373*	21		11
7 Feb 81	**I MADE IT THROUGH THE RAIN** *Arista ARIST 384*	37		2
11 Apr 81	**BERMUDA TRIANGLE** *Arista ARIST 406*	15		6
26 Sep 81	**LET'S HANG ON** *Arista ARIST 429*	12		9
12 Dec 81	**THE OLD SONGS** *Arista ARIST 443*	48		
20 Feb 82	**IF I SHOULD LOVE AGAIN** *Arista ARIST 453*	66		
17 Apr 82	**STAY** *Arista ARIST 464* BARRY MANILOW FEATURING KEVIN DISIMONE & JAMES JOLIS	23		4
16 Oct 82	**I WANNA DO IT WITH YOU** *Arista ARIST 495* ★	8		7
4 Dec 82	**I'M GONNA SIT RIGHT DOWN AND WRITE MYSELF A LETTER** *Arista ARIST 503*	36		3
25 Jun 83	**SOME KIND OF FRIEND** *Arista ARIST 516*	48		
27 Aug 83	**YOU'RE LOOKING HOT TONIGHT** *Arista ARIST 542*	47		
10 Dec 83	**READ 'EM AND WEEP** *Arista ARIST 551*	17		6
8 Apr 89	**PLEASE DON'T BE SCARED** *Arista 112186*	35		3
10 Apr 93	**COPACABANA (AT THE COPA) (REMIX)** *Arista 74321136912*	22		2
20 Nov 93	**COULD IT BE MAGIC** *Arista 74321174882*	36		2
6 Aug 94	**LET ME BE YOUR WINGS** *EMI CDEM 336* BARRY MANILOW & DEBRA BYRD	73		

MANIX UK production group

Date	Title / Label	Peak Position	Weeks at No.1	Weeks in Top 40
23 Nov 91	**MANIC MINDS** *Reinforced RIVET 1209*	63		
7 Mar 92	**OBLIVION (HEAD IN THE CLOUDS) (EP)** *Reinforced RIVET 1212*	43		
8 Aug 92	**RAINBOW PEOPLE** *Reinforced RIVET 1221*	57		

MANKEY UK producer

Date	Title / Label	Peak Position	Weeks at No.1	Weeks in Top 40
16 Nov 96	**BELIEVE IN ME** *Frisky DISKY 3*	74		

MANKIND UK group

Date	Title / Label	Peak Position	Weeks at No.1	Weeks in Top 40
25 Nov 78	**DR WHO** *Pinnacle PIN 71*	25		8

AIMEE MANN US singer

Date	Title / Label	Peak Position	Weeks at No.1	Weeks in Top 40
31 Oct 87	**TIME STAND STILL** *Vertigo RUSH 13* RUSH WITH AIMEE MANN	42		
28 Aug 93	**I SHOULD'VE KNOWN** *Imago 72787250437*	55		
20 Nov 93	**STUPID THING** *Imago 74321174227*	47		
5 Mar 94	**I SHOULD'VE KNOWN** *Imago 72787250602*	45		

JOHNNY MANN SINGERS US choir

Date	Title / Label	Peak Position	Weeks at No.1	Weeks in Top 40
12 Jul 67	**UP, UP AND AWAY** *Liberty LIB 55972*	6		10

MANSUN UK group

Date	Title / Label	Peak Position	Weeks at No.1	Weeks in Top 40
6 Apr 96	**ONE EP** *Parlophone CDR 6430*	37		1
15 Jun 96	**TWO EP** *Parlophone CDR 6437*	32		1
21 Sep 96	**THREE EP** *Parlophone CDR 6447*	19		2
7 Dec 96	**WIDE OPEN SPACE** *Parlophone CDR 6453*	15		2
15 Feb 97	**SHE MAKES MY NOSE BLEED** *Parlophone CDR 6458*	9		2
10 May 97	**TAXLOSS** *Parlophone CDRS 6465*	15		1
18 Oct 97	**CLOSED FOR BUSINESS** *Parlophone CDR 6482*	10		2
11 Jul 98	**LEGACY EP** *Parlophone CDR 6497*	7		2
5 Sep 98	**BEING A GIRL (PART ONE) EP** *Parlophone CDR 6503*	13		1
7 Nov 98	**NEGATIVE** *Parlophone CDR 6508*	27		1
13 Feb 99	**SIX** *Parlophone CDRS 6511*	16		1
12 Aug 00	**I CAN ONLY DISAPPOINT U** *Parlophone CDRS 6544*	8		3
18 Nov 00	**ELECTRIC MAN** *Parlophone CDRS 6550*	23		1
10 Feb 01	**FOOL** *Parlophone CDRS 6553*	28		1
2 Oct 04	**SLIPPING AWAY** *Parlophone R6650*	55		

MANTOVANI UK orchestra leader

Date	Title / Label	Peak Position	Weeks at No.1	Weeks in Top 40
19 Dec 52	**WHITE CHRISTMAS** *Decca F 10017*	6		3
29 May 53	**THE SONG FROM MOULIN ROUGE** *Decca F 10094*	1	1	23
23 Oct 53	**SWEDISH RHAPSODY** *Decca F 10168*	2		18
18 Jun 54	**CARA MIA** *Decca F 10327* DAVID WHITFIELD, WITH CHORUS AND MANTOVANI AND HIS ORCHESTRA	1	10	25
11 Feb 55	**LONELY BALLERINA** *Decca F 10395*	16		4
25 Nov 55	**WHEN YOU LOSE THE ONE YOU LOVE** *Decca F 10627* DAVID WHITFIELD WITH CHORUS & MANTOVANI & HIS ORCHESTRA	7		11
31 May 57	**AROUND THE WORLD** *Decca F 10888*	20		4
14 Feb 58	**CRY MY HEART** *Decca F 10978* DAVID WHITFIELD WITH CHORUS & MANTOVANI & HIS ORCHESTRA	22		3

MANTRONIX US/Jamaican duo

Date	Title / Label	Peak Position	Weeks at No.1	Weeks in Top 40
15 Aug 98	**STRICTLY BUSINESS** *Parlophone CDR 6502* MANTRONIK VS EPMD	43		
22 Feb 86	**LADIES** *10 TEN 116*	55		
17 May 86	**BASSLINE** *10 TEN 118*	34		3
7 Feb 87	**WHO IS IT** *10 TEN 137*	40		1
4 Jul 87	**SCREAM (PRIMAL SCREAM)** *10 TEN 169*	46		
30 Jan 88	**SING A SONG (BREAK IT DOWN)** *10 TEN 206*	61		
12 Mar 88	**SIMPLE SIMON (YOU GOTTA REGARD)** *10 TEN 217*	72		
6 Jan 90	**GOT TO HAVE YOUR LOVE** *Capitol CL 559* MANTRONIX FEATURING WONDRESS	4		10
12 May 90	**TAKE YOUR TIME** *Capitol CL 573* MANTRONIX FEATURING WONDRESS	10		5
2 Mar 91	**DON'T GO MESSIN' WITH MY HEART** *Capitol CL 608*	22		4
22 Jun 91	**STEP TO ME (DO ME)** *Capitol CL 613*	59		
15 Aug 98	**STRICTLY BUSINESS** *Parlophone CDR 6502*	43		
9 Nov 02	**77 STRINGS** *Southern Fried ECB 35* KURTIS MANTRONIK PRESENTS CHAMONIX	71		
28 Jun 03	**HOW DID YOU KNOW** *Southern Fried ECB 43CDS* KURTIS MANTRONIK PRESENTS CHAMONIX	16		2

MANUEL & HIS MUSIC OF THE MOUNTAINS UK orchestra leader

Date	Title / Label	Peak Position	Weeks at No.1	Weeks in Top 40
28 Aug 59	**THE HONEYMOON SONG** *Columbia DB 4323*	22		9
13 Oct 60	**NEVER ON SUNDAY** *Columbia DB 4515*	29		7
13 Oct 66	**SOMEWHERE MY LOVE** *Columbia DB 7969*	42		
31 Jan 76	**RODRIGO'S GUITAR CONCERTO DE ARANJUEZ (THEME FROM 2ND MOVEMENT)** *EMI 2383*	3		9

ROOTS MANUVA UK rapper

Date	Title / Label	Peak Position	Weeks at No.1	Weeks in Top 40
11 Dec 99	**DUSTED** *Hard Hands HAND 058CD1* LEFTFIELD/ROOTS MANUVA	28		1
4 Aug 01	**WITNESS (1 HOPE)** *Big Dada BDCDS 022*	45		
20 Oct 01	**DREAMY DAYS** *Big Dada BDCDS 033*	53		
8 May 04	**OH YOU WANT MORE** *Big Dada BDCDS 066* TY FEATURING ROOTS MANUVA	65		
29 Jan 05	**COLOSSAL INSIGHT** *Big Dada BDCDS073*	33		1
2 Apr 05	**TOO COLD** *Big Dada BDCDS078*	39		1
29 Apr 06	**TRUE SKOOL** *Ninja Tune ZENCDS178* COLDCUT FEATURING ROOTS MANUVA	61		

MARATHON German/UK group

Date	Title / Label	Peak Position	Weeks at No.1	Weeks in Top 40
25 Jan 92	**MOVIN'** *10 TEN 395*	36		2

MARAUDERS UK group

Date	Title / Label	Peak Position	Weeks at No.1	Weeks in Top 40
8 Aug 63	**THAT'S WHAT I WANT** *Decca F 11695*	43		

MARBLES UK duo

Date	Title / Label	Peak Position	Weeks at No.1	Weeks in Top 40
25 Sep 68	**ONLY ONE WOMAN** *Polydor 56 272*	5		11
26 Mar 69	**THE WALLS FELL DOWN** *Polydor 56 310*	28		5

MARC ET CLAUDE German production group

Date	Title / Label	Peak Position	Weeks at No.1	Weeks in Top 40
21 Nov 98	**LA** *Positiva CDTIV 104*	28		1
22 Jul 00	**I NEED YOUR LOVIN' (LIKE THE SUNSHINE)** *Positiva CDTIV 136*	12		4
6 Apr 02	**TREMBLE** *Positiva CDTIV 170*	29		1
19 Apr 03	**LOVING YOU '03** *Positiva CDTIV 190*	37		1

MARCELS US group

Date	Title / Label	Peak Position	Weeks at No.1	Weeks in Top 40
13 Apr 61	**BLUE MOON** *Pye International 7N 25073* ★	1	2	11
8 Jun 61	**SUMMERTIME** *Pye International 7N 25083*	46		

LITTLE PEGGY MARCH US singer

Date	Title / Label	Peak Position	Weeks at No.1	Weeks in Top 40
12 Sep 63	**HELLO HEARTACHE GOODBYE LOVE** *RCA 1362*	29		5

MARCO POLO Italian production duo

Date	Title / Label	Peak Position	Weeks at No.1	Weeks in Top 40
8 Apr 95	**A PRAYER TO THE MUSIC** *Hi-Life HICD 7*	65		

Silver-selling ○ Gold-selling ● Platinum-selling ⊛ US No.1 ★ | Peak Position | Weeks at No.1 | Weeks in Top 40

MARCY PLAYGROUND US group

Date	Title / Label	Peak Position	Weeks at No.1	Weeks in Top 40
18 Apr 98	**SEX AND CANDY** *EMI CDEM 508*	29		1

MARDI GRAS UK group

Date	Title / Label	Peak Position	Weeks at No.1	Weeks in Top 40
5 Aug 72	**TOO BUSY THINKING 'BOUT MY BABY** *Bell 1226*	19		7

MARDOUS UK group

Date	Title / Label	Peak Position	Weeks at No.1	Weeks in Top 40
20 Aug 05	**REVOLUTION OVER THE PHONE** *Poptones MC5102SCD*	74		

KELLY MARIE UK singer

Date	Title / Label	Peak Position	Weeks at No.1	Weeks in Top 40
2 Aug 80	**FEELS LIKE I'M IN LOVE** *Calibre Plus 1* ●	1	2	12
18 Oct 80	**LOVING JUST FOR FUN** *Calibre Plus 4*	21		6
7 Feb 81	**HOT LOVE** *Calibre Plus 5*	22		7
30 May 81	**LOVE TRIAL** *Calibre Plus 7*	51		

ROSE MARIE Irish singer

Date	Title / Label	Peak Position	Weeks at No.1	Weeks in Top 40
19 Nov 83	**WHEN I LEAVE THE WORLD BEHIND** *A1 284*	63		

TEENA MARIE US singer

Date	Title / Label	Peak Position	Weeks at No.1	Weeks in Top 40
7 Jul 79	**I'M A SUCKER FOR YOUR LOVE** *Motown TMG 1146* TEENA MARIE, CO-LEAD VOCALS RICK JAMES	43		
31 May 80	**BEHIND THE GROOVE** *Motown TMG 1185*	6		7
11 Oct 80	**I NEED YOUR LOVIN'** *Motown TMG 1203*	28		4
26 Mar 88	**OOO LA LA LA** *Epic 6514237*	74		
10 Nov 90	**SINCE DAY ONE** *Epic 6564297*	69		

MARILLION UK group

Date	Title / Label	Peak Position	Weeks at No.1	Weeks in Top 40
20 Nov 82	**MARKET SQUARE HEROES** *EMI 5351*	60		
12 Feb 83	**HE KNOWS YOU KNOW** *EMI 5362*	35		2
16 Apr 83	**MARKET SQUARE HEROES** *EMI 5351*	53		
18 Jun 83	**GARDEN PARTY** *EMI 5393*	16		4
11 Feb 84	**PUNCH AND JUDY** *EMI MARIL 1*	29		3
12 May 84	**ASSASSING** *EMI MARIL 2*	22		3
18 May 85	**KAYLEIGH** *EMI MARIL 3* ○	2		11
7 Sep 85	**LAVENDER** *EMI MARIL 4*	5		7
30 Nov 85	**HEART OF LOTHIAN** *EMI MARIL 5*	29		2
23 May 87	**INCOMMUNICADO** *EMI MARIL 6*	6		4
25 Jul 87	**SUGAR MICE** *EMI MARIL 7*	22		4
7 Nov 87	**WARM WET CIRCLES** *EMI MARIL 8*	22		3
26 Nov 88	**FREAKS (LIVE)** *EMI MARIL 9*	24		2
9 Sep 89	**HOOKS IN YOU** *Capitol MARIL 10*	30		2
9 Dec 89	**UNINVITED GUEST** *EMI MARIL 11*	53		
14 Apr 90	**EASTER** *EMI MARIL 12*	34		2
8 Jun 91	**COVER MY EYES (PAIN AND HEAVEN)** *EMI MARIL 13*	34		2
3 Aug 91	**NO ONE CAN** *EMI MARIL 14*	33		3
5 Oct 91	**DRY LAND** *EMI MARIL 15*	34		1
23 May 92	**SYMPATHY** *EMI MARIL 16*	17		2
1 Aug 92	**NO ONE CAN** *EMI MARIL 17*	26		2
26 Mar 94	**THE HOLLOW MAN** *EMI CDEMS 307*	30		1
7 May 94	**ALONE AGAIN IN THE LAP OF LUXURY** *EMI CDEMS 318*	53		
10 Jun 95	**BEAUTIFUL** *EMI CDMARILS 18*	29		1
1 May 04	**YOU'RE GONE** *Intact CXINTACT1*	7		2
24 Jul 04	**DON'T HURT YOURSELF** *Intact CXINTACT2*	16		1
7 Apr 07	**SEE IT LIKE A BABY** *Download*	45		
23 Jun 07	**THANKYOU WHOEVER YOU ARE** *Intact CXINTACT4*	15		1

MARILYN UK singer

Date	Title / Label	Peak Position	Weeks at No.1	Weeks in Top 40
5 Nov 83	**CALLING YOUR NAME** *Mercury MAZ 1* ○	4		10
11 Feb 84	**CRY AND BE FREE** *Mercury MAZ 2*	31		3
21 Apr 84	**YOU DON'T LOVE ME** *Mercury MAZ 3*	40		2
13 Apr 85	**BABY U LEFT ME (IN THE COLD)** *Mercury MAZ 4*	70		

MARILYN MANSON US group

Date	Title / Label	Peak Position	Weeks at No.1	Weeks in Top 40
7 Jun 97	**THE BEAUTIFUL PEOPLE** *Interscope IND 95541*	18		2
20 Sep 97	**TOURNIQUET** *Interscope IND 95552*	28		1
21 Nov 98	**THE DOPE SHOW** *Interscope IND 95610*	12		1
26 Jun 99	**ROCK IS DEAD** *Maverick W 486CD*	23		2
18 Nov 00	**DISPOSABLE TEENS** *Nothing 4974372*	12		2
3 Mar 01	**THE FIGHT SONG** *Interscope 4974912*	24		1
15 Sep 01	**THE NOBODIES** *Interscope IND 97604*	34		1
30 Mar 02	**TAINTED LOVE** *Maverick W 579CD1*	5		8
14 Jun 03	**MOBSCENE** *Interscope 9807726*	13		3
13 Sep 03	**THIS IS THE NEW SHIT** *Interscope 9810793*	29		1
16 Oct 04	**PERSONAL JESUS** *Interscope 9864166*	13		3
9 Jun 07	**HEART-SHAPED GLASSES** *Interscope 1736138*	19		1

MARINO MARINI & HIS QUARTET
Italian singer/pianist

Date	Title / Label	Peak Position	Weeks at No.1	Weeks in Top 40
3 Oct 58	**VOLARE** *Durium DC 16632*	13		7
10 Oct 58	**COME PRIMA** *Durium DC 16632*	2		14
20 Mar 59	**CIAO CIAO BAMBINA** *Durium DC 16636*	24		2

MARIO US singer

Date	Title / Label	Peak Position	Weeks at No.1	Weeks in Top 40
12 Apr 03	**JUST A FRIEND** *J Records 82876508082*	18		3
12 Jul 03	**C'MON** *J Records 82876528282*	28		1
19 Mar 05	**LET ME LOVE YOU (IMPORT)** *J Records 82876679752* ★	53		
2 Apr 05	**LET ME LOVE YOU** *J Records 82876682562* ★	2		11
9 Jul 05	**HERE I GO AGAIN** *J Records 82876705592*	11		5
18 Aug 07	**HOW DO I BREATHE** *J Records 88697121652*	21		4

MARION UK group

Date	Title / Label	Peak Position	Weeks at No.1	Weeks in Top 40
25 Feb 95	**SLEEP** *London LONCD 360*	53		
13 May 95	**TOYS FOR BOYS** *London LONCD 366*	57		
21 Oct 95	**LET'S ALL GO TOGETHER** *London LONCD 371*	37		1
3 Feb 96	**TIME** *London LONCD 377*	29		1
30 Mar 96	**SLEEP (REMIX)** *London LONCD 381*	17		1
7 Mar 98	**MIYAKO HIEAWAY** *London LONCD 403*	45		

MARK' OH German producer

Date	Title / Label	Peak Position	Weeks at No.1	Weeks in Top 40
6 May 95	**TEARS DON'T LIE** *Systematic SYSCD 9*	24		2

PIGMEAT MARKHAM US singer

Date	Title / Label	Peak Position	Weeks at No.1	Weeks in Top 40
17 Jul 68	**HERE COMES THE JUDGE** *Chess CRS 8077*	19		8

BIZ MARKIE US rapper

Date	Title / Label	Peak Position	Weeks at No.1	Weeks in Top 40
26 May 90	**JUST A FRIEND** *Cold Chillin' W 9823*	55		

YANNIS MARKOPOULOS
Greek orchestra leader

Date	Title / Label	Peak Position	Weeks at No.1	Weeks in Top 40
17 Dec 77	**WHO PAYS THE FERRYMAN** *BBC RESL 51*	11		8

GUY MARKS US singer/comedian

Date	Title / Label	Peak Position	Weeks at No.1	Weeks in Top 40
13 May 78	**LOVING YOU HAS MADE ME BANANAS** *ABC 4211*	25		5

MARKY MARK & THE FUNKY BUNCH
US singer

Date	Title / Label	Peak Position	Weeks at No.1	Weeks in Top 40
31 Aug 91	**GOOD VIBRATIONS** *Interscope A 8764* MARKY MARK & THE FUNKY BUNCH FEATURING LOLEATTA HOLLOWAY ★	14		5
2 Nov 91	**WILDSIDE** *Interscope A 8674*	42		
12 Dec 92	**YOU GOTTA BELIEVE** *Interscope A 8680*	54		

DAMIAN 'JR GONG' MARLEY Jamaican singer

Date	Title / Label	Peak Position	Weeks at No.1	Weeks in Top 40
1 Oct 05	**WELCOME TO JAMROCK** *Island MCSD40432*	13		3
24 Dec 05	**THE MASTER HAS COME BACK** *Island MCSTD40443*	74		
29 Apr 06	**BEAUTIFUL** *Tuff Gong MCSTD40452*	39		1

ZIGGY MARLEY & THE MELODY MAKERS
Jamaican group

Date	Title / Label	Peak Position	Weeks at No.1	Weeks in Top 40
11 Jun 88	**TOMORROW PEOPLE** *Virgin VS 1049*	22		5
23 Sep 89	**LOOK WHO'S DANCING** *Virgin America VUS 5*	65		

BOB MARLEY & THE WAILERS
Jamaican singer and backing group

Date	Title / Label	Peak Position	Weeks at No.1	Weeks in Top 40
27 Sep 75	**NO WOMAN NO CRY** *Island WIP 6244*	22		7
25 Jun 77	**EXODUS** *Island WIP 6390*	14		8

Silver-selling ● Gold-selling ● Platinum-selling ⊛ US No.1 ★ | Peak Position | Weeks at No.1 | Weeks in Top 40

Date	Title / Label	Peak Position	Weeks at No.1	Weeks in Top 40
10 Sep 77	**WAITING IN VAIN** *Island WIP 6402*	27		5
10 Dec 77	**JAMMING/PUNKY REGGAE PARTY** *Island WIP 6410* ●	9		11
25 Feb 78	**IS THIS LOVE** *Island WIP 6420*	9		9
10 Jun 78	**SATISFY MY SOUL** *Island WIP 6440*	21		7
20 Oct 79	**SO MUCH TROUBLE IN THE WORLD** *Island WIP 6510*	56		
21 Jun 80	**COULD YOU BE LOVED** *Island WIP 6610*	5		10
13 Sep 80	**THREE LITTLE BIRDS** *Island WIP 6641*	17		7
13 Jun 81	**NO WOMAN NO CRY** *Island WIP 6244* ●	8		8
7 May 83	**BUFFALO SOLDIER** *Island/Tuff Gong IS 180*	4		9
21 Apr 84	**ONE LOVE – PEOPLE GET READY** *Island IS 169*	5		9
23 Jun 84	**WAITING IN VAIN** *Island IS 180*	31		4
8 Dec 84	**COULD YOU BE LOVED** *Island IS 210*	71		
18 May 91	**ONE LOVE – PEOPLE GET READY** *Tuff Gong TGX 1*	42		
19 Sep 92	**IRON LION ZION** *Tuff Gong TGX 2*	5		6
28 Nov 92	**WHY SHOULD I/EXODUS** *Tuff Gong TFX 3*	42		
20 May 95	**KEEP ON MOVING** *Tuff Gong TGXCD 4*	17		3
8 Jun 96	**WHAT GOES AROUND COMES AROUND** *Anansi ANACS 002*	42		
25 Sep 99	**SUN IS SHINING** *Club Tools 0066895 CLU* BOB MARLEY VERSUS FUNKSTAR DE LUXE ●	3		7
11 Dec 99	**TURN YOUR LIGHTS DOWN LOW** *Columbia 6684362* BOB MARLEY FEATURING LAURYN HILL	15		5
22 Jan 00	**RAINBOW COUNTRY** *Club Tools 0067225 CLU* BOB MARLEY VERSUS FUNKSTAR DELUXE	11		3
24 Jun 00	**JAMMIN'** *Tuff Gong TFXCD 9* BOB MARLEY FEATURING MC LYTE	42		
12 Nov 05	**NO WOMAN NO CRY** *Tuff Gong TGXCD13*	58		
19 Nov 05	**I SHOT THE SHERIFF** *Tuff Gong TGXCD14*	67		
26 Nov 05	**SUN IS SHINING** *Tuff Gong TGXCD15*	54		
3 Dec 05	**SLOGANS** *Tuff Gong TGXCDS11*	45		
10 Dec 05	**AFRICA UNITE** *Tuff Gong TGXCD16*	49		
17 Dec 05	**STAND UP JAMROCK** *Tuff Gong TGXCD17*	56		

LENE MARLIN Norwegian singer

Date	Title / Label	Peak Position	Weeks at No.1	Weeks in Top 40
11 Mar 00	**SITTING DOWN HERE** *Virgin DINSD 183* ●	5		8
16 Sep 00	**UNFORGIVABLE SINNER** *Virgin DINSCX 202*	13		3
13 Jan 01	**WHERE I'M HEADED** *Virgin DINSD 196*	31		1
4 Oct 03	**YOU WEREN'T THERE** *Virgin DINSD 262*	59		

MARLO UK group

Date	Title / Label	Peak Position	Weeks at No.1	Weeks in Top 40
24 Jul 99	**HOW DO I KNOW?** *Polydor 5611362*	56		

MARLY Danish singer

Date	Title / Label	Peak Position	Weeks at No.1	Weeks in Top 40
28 Aug 04	**YOU NEVER KNOW** *All Around The World CDGLOBE 363*	23		1

MARMALADE UK group

Date	Title / Label	Peak Position	Weeks at No.1	Weeks in Top 40
22 May 68	**LOVIN' THINGS** *CBS 3412*	6		10
23 Oct 68	**WAIT FOR ME MARIANNE** *CBS 3708*	30		5
4 Dec 68	**OB-LA-DI OB-LA-DA** *CBS 3892*	1	3	17
11 Jun 69	**BABY MAKE IT SOON** *CBS 4287*	9		12
20 Dec 69	**REFLECTIONS OF MY LIFE** *Decca F 12982*	3		11
18 Jul 70	**RAINBOW** *Decca F 13035*	3		12
27 Mar 71	**MY LITTLE ONE** *Decca F 13135*	15		9
4 Sep 71	**COUSIN NORMAN** *Decca F 13214*	6		10
27 Nov 71	**BACK ON THE ROAD** *Decca F 13251*	35		4
1 Apr 72	**RADANCER** *Decca F 13297*	6		10
21 Feb 76	**FALLING APART AT THE SEAMS** *Target TGT 105*	9		9

MARMIO Spanish/Dutch production duo

Date	Title / Label	Peak Position	Weeks at No.1	Weeks in Top 40
18 May 96	**SCHONEBERG** *Hooj Choons HOOJCD 43*	53		
14 Feb 98	**SCHONEBERG (REMIX)** *ffrr FCD 324*	56		

MAROON 5 US group

Date	Title / Label	Peak Position	Weeks at No.1	Weeks in Top 40
31 Jan 04	**HARDER TO BREATHE** *J Records 82876566922*	13		5
1 May 04	**THIS LOVE** *J Records 82876608452*	3		12
4 Sep 04	**SHE WILL BE LOVED** *J Records 82876643632*	4		8
18 Dec 04	**SUNDAY MORNING** *J Records 82876668042*	27		4
23 Apr 05	**MUST GET OUT** *J Records 82876689062*	39		1
19 May 07	**MAKES ME WONDER** *A&M/Polydor 1734956*	2		12
25 Aug 07	**WAKE UP CALL** *A&M 1744501*	33		2
24 Nov 07	**WON'T GO HOME WITHOUT YOU** *Download*	44		

MARRADONA UK group

Date	Title / Label	Peak Position	Weeks at No.1	Weeks in Top 40
26 Feb 94	**OUT OF MY HEAD** *Peach PWCD 282*	38		1
26 Jul 97	**OUT OF MY HEAD (REMIX)** *Soopa SPCD 1*	39		1

M/A/R/R/S UK group

Date	Title / Label	Peak Position	Weeks at No.1	Weeks in Top 40
5 Sep 87	**PUMP UP THE VOLUME/ANITINA (THE FIRST TIME I SEE SHE DANCE)** *4AD AD 70* ●	1	2	12

MARS VOLTA US group

Date	Title / Label	Peak Position	Weeks at No.1	Weeks in Top 40
11 Oct 03	**INERTIATIC ESP** *Universal MCSTD 40332*	42		
13 Mar 04	**TELEVATORS** *Universal MCSTD 40352*	41		
26 Mar 05	**THE WIDOW** *Universal MCSTD40408*	20		1
23 Jul 05	**L'VIA L'VIAQUEZ** *Universal MCSTD40420*	53		

MATTHEW MARSDEN UK singer

Date	Title / Label	Peak Position	Weeks at No.1	Weeks in Top 40
11 Jul 98	**THE HEART'S LONE DESIRE** *Columbia 6661152*	13		6
7 Nov 98	**SHE'S GONE** *Columbia 6664915* MATTHEW MARSDEN FEATURING DESTINY'S CHILD	24		1

KYM MARSH UK singer

Date	Title / Label	Peak Position	Weeks at No.1	Weeks in Top 40
19 Apr 03	**CRY** *Island MCSXD 40314*	2		7
19 Jul 03	**COME ON OVER** *Universal MCSXD 40323*	10		3
8 Nov 03	**SENTIMENTAL** *Universal MCSTD 40340*	35		1

STEVIE MARSH UK singer

Date	Title / Label	Peak Position	Weeks at No.1	Weeks in Top 40
4 Dec 59	**IF YOU WERE THE ONLY BOY IN THE WORLD** *Decca F 11181*	24		4

JOY MARSHALL UK singer

Date	Title / Label	Peak Position	Weeks at No.1	Weeks in Top 40
23 Jun 66	**THE MORE I SEE YOU** *Decca F 12422*	34		1

KEITH MARSHALL UK singer

Date	Title / Label	Peak Position	Weeks at No.1	Weeks in Top 40
4 Apr 81	**ONLY CRYING** *Arrival PIK 2*	12		9

WAYNE MARSHALL UK singer

Date	Title / Label	Peak Position	Weeks at No.1	Weeks in Top 40
1 Oct 94	**OOH AAH (G-SPOT)** *Soultown SOULCDS 322*	29		2
3 Jun 95	**SPIRIT** *Soultown SOULCDS 00352*	58		
24 Feb 96	**NEVER KNEW LOVE LIKE THIS** *Sony S2 6629382* PAULINE HENRY FEATURING WAYNE MARSHALL	40		1
7 Dec 96	**G SPOT (REMIX)** *MBA INTER 9006*	50		

MARSHALL HAIN UK duo

Date	Title / Label	Peak Position	Weeks at No.1	Weeks in Top 40
3 Jun 78	**DANCING IN THE CITY** *Harvest HAR 5157* ●	3		12
14 Oct 78	**COMING HOME** *Harvest HAR 5168*	39		1

MARTAY UK rapper

Date	Title / Label	Peak Position	Weeks at No.1	Weeks in Top 40
16 Oct 99	**GIMME ALL YOUR LOVIN' 2000** *Riverhorse RIVHCD 2* MARTAY FEATURING ZZ TOP	28		1

LENA MARTELL UK singer

Date	Title / Label	Peak Position	Weeks at No.1	Weeks in Top 40
29 Sep 79	**ONE DAY AT A TIME** *Pye 7N 46021* ●	1	3	14

MARTHA & THE MUFFINS Canadian group

Date	Title / Label	Peak Position	Weeks at No.1	Weeks in Top 40
1 Mar 80	**ECHO BEACH** *Dindisc DIN 9*	10		7

MARTIKA US singer

Date	Title / Label	Peak Position	Weeks at No.1	Weeks in Top 40
29 Jul 89	**TOY SOLDIERS** *CBS 6550497* ● ★	5		8
14 Oct 89	**I FEEL THE EARTH MOVE** *CBS 6552947*	7		9
13 Jan 90	**MORE THAN YOU KNOW** *CBS 6555267*	15		6
17 Mar 90	**WATER** *CBS 6557317*	59		
17 Aug 91	**LOVE...THY WILL BE DONE** *Columbia 6573137*	9		8
30 Nov 91	**MARTIKA'S KITCHEN** *Columbia 6575687*	17		8
22 Feb 92	**COLOURED KISSES** *Columbia 6577097*	41		

Silver-selling ● Gold-selling ● Platinum-selling ⊛ US No.1 ★ | Peak Position | Weeks at No.1 | Weeks in Top 40

BILLIE RAY MARTIN German singer

Date	Title / Label	Peak Position	Weeks at No.1	Weeks in Top 40
19 Nov 94	**YOUR LOVING ARMS** *Magnet MAG 1028CD*	38		1
20 May 95	**YOUR LOVING ARMS** *Magnet MAG 1031CD*	6		8
2 Sep 95	**RUNNING AROUND TOWN** *Magnet MAG 1035CD*	29		1
6 Jan 96	**IMITATION OF LIFE** *Magnet MAG 1040CD*	29		1
6 Apr 96	**SPACE OASIS** *Magnet MAG 1042CD*	66		
21 Aug 99	**HONEY** *React CDREACT 129*	54		

DEAN MARTIN US singer/actor

Date	Title / Label	Peak Position	Weeks at No.1	Weeks in Top 40
18 Sep 53	**KISS** *Capitol CL 13893*	5		8
22 Jan 54	**THAT'S AMORE** *Capitol CL 14008*	2		11
1 Oct 54	**SWAY** *Capitol CL 14138*	6		7
22 Oct 54	**HOW DO YOU SPEAK TO AN ANGEL** *Capitol CL 14150*	15		6
28 Jan 55	**NAUGHTY LADY OF SHADY LANE** *Capitol CL 14226*	5		9
4 Feb 55	**MAMBO ITALIANO** *Capitol CL 14227*	14		2
25 Feb 55	**LET ME GO LOVER** *Capitol CL 14226*	3		10
1 Apr 55	**UNDER THE BRIDGES OF PARIS** *Capitol CL 14255*	6		8
10 Feb 56	**MEMORIES ARE MADE OF THIS** *Capitol CL 14523* ★	1	4	16
2 Mar 56	**YOUNG AND FOOLISH** *Capitol CL 14519*	20		1
27 Apr 56	**INNAMORATA** *Capitol CL 14507*	21		3
22 Mar 57	**THE MAN WHO PLAYS THE MANDOLINO** *Capitol CL 14690*	21		2
13 Jun 58	**RETURN TO ME** *Capitol CL 14844*	2		22
29 Aug 58	**VOLARE** *Capitol CL 14910*	2		14
27 Aug 64	**EVERYBODY LOVES SOMEBODY** *Reprise R 20281* ★	11		11
12 Nov 64	**THE DOOR IS STILL OPEN TO MY HEART** *Reprise R 20307*	42		
5 Feb 69	**GENTLE ON MY MIND** *Reprise R 23343*	2		20
22 Jun 96	**THAT'S AMORE** *EMI Premier PRESCD 3*	43		
21 Aug 99	**SWAY** *Capitol CDSWAY 001*	66		

JUAN MARTIN Spanish classical guitarist

Date	Title / Label	Peak Position	Weeks at No.1	Weeks in Top 40
28 Jan 84	**LOVE THEME FROM THE THORN BIRDS** *WEA X 9518*	10		5

LINDA MARTIN Irish singer

Date	Title / Label	Peak Position	Weeks at No.1	Weeks in Top 40
30 May 92	**WHY ME** *Columbia 6581317*	59		

RAY MARTIN UK orchestra leader

Date	Title / Label	Peak Position	Weeks at No.1	Weeks in Top 40
14 Nov 52	**BLUE TANGO** *Columbia DB 3051*	8		4
4 Dec 53	**SWEDISH RHAPSODY** *Columbia DB 3346*	4		4
15 Jun 56	**CAROUSEL WALTZ** *Columbia DB 3771*	24		3

RICKY MARTIN Puerto Rican singer

Date	Title / Label	Peak Position	Weeks at No.1	Weeks in Top 40
20 Sep 97	**(UN, DOS, TRES) MARIA** *Columbia 6649595*	6		4
11 Jul 98	**THE CUP OF LIFE** *Columbia 6661502*	29		2
17 Jul 99	**LIVIN' LA VIDA LOCA** *Columbia 6676405* ⊛ ★	1	3	12
20 Nov 99	**SHAKE YOUR BON-BON** *Columbia 6683412*	12		3
29 Apr 00	**PRIVATE EMOTION** *Columbia 6692692* RICKY MARTIN FEATURING MEJA	9		7
4 Nov 00	**SHE BANGS** *Columbia 6705422* ●	3		11
10 Mar 01	**NOBODY WANTS TO BE LONELY** *Columbia 6709462* RICKY MARTIN WITH CHRISTINA AGUILERA	4		6
28 Jul 01	**LOADED** *Columbia 6714642*	19		2
15 Oct 05	**DON'T CARE** *Sony BMG 6760667*	11		4

TONY MARTIN US singer

Date	Title / Label	Peak Position	Weeks at No.1	Weeks in Top 40
22 Apr 55	**STRANGER IN PARADISE** *HMV B 10849*	6		13
13 Jul 56	**WALK HAND IN HAND** *HMV POP 222*	2		15

WINK MARTINDALE US singer

Date	Title / Label	Peak Position	Weeks at No.1	Weeks in Top 40
4 Dec 59	**DECK OF CARDS** *London HLD 8962*	18		7
18 Apr 63	**DECK OF CARDS** *London HLD 8962*	5		19
20 Oct 73	**DECK OF CARDS** *Dot 109*	22		7

ALICE MARTINEAU UK singer

Date	Title / Label	Peak Position	Weeks at No.1	Weeks in Top 40
23 Nov 02	**IF I FALL** *Epic 6732332*	45		

ANGIE MARTINEZ FEATURING LIL' MO
US duo

Date	Title / Label	Peak Position	Weeks at No.1	Weeks in Top 40
15 Feb 03	**IF I COULD GO** *Elektra E 7331CD*	61		

AL MARTINO US singer

Date	Title / Label	Peak Position	Weeks at No.1	Weeks in Top 40
14 Nov 52	**HERE IN MY HEART** *Capitol CL 13779* ★	1	9	18
21 Nov 52	**TAKE MY HEART** *Capitol CL 13769*	9		1
30 Jan 53	**NOW** *Capitol CL 13835*	3		12
10 Jul 53	**RACHEL** *Capitol CL 13879*	10		5
4 Jun 54	**WANTED** *Capitol CL 14128*	4		16
1 Oct 54	**THE STORY OF TINA** *Capitol CL 14163*	10		8
23 Sep 55	**THE MAN FROM LARAMIE** *Capitol CL 14343*	19		3
31 Mar 60	**SUMMERTIME** *Top Rank JAR 312*	49		
29 Aug 63	**I LOVE YOU BECAUSE** *Capitol CL 15300*	48		
22 Aug 70	**SPANISH EYES** *Capitol CL 15430*	49		
14 Jul 73	**SPANISH EYES** *Capitol CL 15430*	5		17

MARVELETTES US group

Date	Title / Label	Peak Position	Weeks at No.1	Weeks in Top 40
15 Jun 67	**WHEN YOU'RE YOUNG AND IN LOVE** *Tamla Motown TMG 609*	13		6

MARVIN & TAMARA UK duo

Date	Title / Label	Peak Position	Weeks at No.1	Weeks in Top 40
7 Aug 99	**GROOVE MACHINE** *Epic 6675582*	11		3
25 Dec 99	**NORTH, SOUTH, EAST, WEST** *Epic 6684902*	38		1

HANK MARVIN UK guitarist/singer

Date	Title / Label	Peak Position	Weeks at No.1	Weeks in Top 40
13 Sep 69	**THROW DOWN A LINE** *Columbia DB 8615* CLIFF RICHARD & HANK MARVIN	7		8
21 Feb 70	**JOY OF LIVING** *Columbia DB 8657* CLIFF (Richard) & HANK (Marvin)	25		7
6 Mar 82	**DON'T TALK** *Polydor POSP 420*	49		
22 Mar 86	**LIVING DOLL** *WEA YZ 65* CLIFF RICHARD & THE YOUNG ONES FEATURING HANK B MARVIN ●	1	3	9
7 Jan 89	**LONDON KID** *Polydor 32* JEAN-MICHEL JARRE FEATURING HANK MARVIN	52		
17 Oct 92	**WE ARE THE CHAMPIONS** *PolyGram TV PO 229* HANK MARVIN FEATURING BRIAN MAY	66		

LEE MARVIN US actor

Date	Title / Label	Peak Position	Weeks at No.1	Weeks in Top 40
7 Feb 70	**WAND'RIN' STAR** *Paramount PARA 3004*	1	3	17

MARVIN THE PARANOID ANDROID
UK robot TV character

Date	Title / Label	Peak Position	Weeks at No.1	Weeks in Top 40
16 May 81	**MARVIN** *Polydor POSP 261*	53		

RICHARD MARX US singer

Date	Title / Label	Peak Position	Weeks at No.1	Weeks in Top 40
27 Feb 88	**SHOULD'VE KNOWN BETTER** *Manhattan MT 32*	50		
14 May 88	**ENDLESS SUMMER NIGHTS** *Manhattan MT 39*	50		
17 Jun 89	**SATISFIED** *EMI-USA MT 64* ★	52		
2 Sep 89	**RIGHT HERE WAITING** *EMI-USA MT 72* ● ★	2		9
11 Nov 89	**ANGELIA** *EMI-USA MT 74*	45		
24 Mar 90	**TOO LATE TO SAY GOODBYE** *EMI-USA MT 80*	38		2
7 Jul 90	**CHILDREN OF THE NIGHT** *EMI-USA MT 84*	54		
1 Sep 90	**ENDLESS SUMMER NIGHTS/HOLD ON TO THE NIGHTS** *EMI-USA MT 89*	60		
19 Oct 91	**KEEP COMING BACK** *Capitol CL 634*	55		
9 May 92	**HAZARD** *Capitol CL 654* ●	3		13
29 Aug 92	**TAKE THIS HEART** *Capitol CL 667*	13		4
28 Nov 92	**CHAINS AROUND MY HEART** *Capitol CL 676*	29		2
29 Jan 94	**NOW AND FOREVER** *Capitol CDCLS 703*	13		5
30 Apr 94	**SILENT SCREAM** *Capitol CDCLS 714*	32		1
13 Aug 94	**THE WAY SHE LOVES ME** *Capitol CDCL 721*	38		1

MARXMAN UK group

Date	Title / Label	Peak Position	Weeks at No.1	Weeks in Top 40
6 Mar 93	**ALL ABOUT EVE** *Talkin Loud TLKCD 35*	28		2
1 May 93	**SHIP AHOY** *Talkin Loud TLKCD 39*	64		

MARY JANE GIRLS US group

Date	Title / Label	Peak Position	Weeks at No.1	Weeks in Top 40
21 May 83	**CANDY MAN** *Motown TMG 1301*	60		
25 Jun 83	**ALL NIGHT LONG** *Gordy TMG 1309*	13		6
8 Oct 83	**BOYS** *Gordy TMG 1315*	74		
18 Feb 95	**ALL NIGHT LONG (REMIX)** *Motown TMGCD 1436*	51		

MARY MARY US duo

Date	Title	Peak Position	Weeks at No.1	Weeks in Top 40
10 Jun 00	**SHACKLES (PRAISE YOU)** *Columbia 6694202*	5		11
18 Nov 00	**I SINGS** *Columbia 6699742*	32		1

CAROLYNE MAS US singer

Date	Title	Peak Position	Weeks at No.1	Weeks in Top 40
2 Feb 80	**QUOTE GOODBYE QUOTE** *Mercury 6167 873*	71		

MASAI UK duo

Date	Title	Peak Position	Weeks at No.1	Weeks in Top 40
1 Mar 03	**DO THAT THANG** *Concept CDCON 36X*	42		

MASE US rapper

Date	Title	Peak Position	Weeks at No.1	Weeks in Top 40
29 Mar 97	**CAN'T NOBODY HOLD ME DOWN** *Puff Daddy 74321464552* PUFF DADDY FEATURING MASE ★	19		2
9 Aug 97	**MO MONEY MO PROBLEMS** *Puff Daddy 74321492492* NOTORIOUS B.I.G. FEATURING PUFF DADDY & MASE ★	6		8
27 Dec 97	**FEEL SO GOOD** *Puff Daddy 74321526442*	10		6
18 Apr 98	**WHAT YOU WANT** *Puff Daddy 74321578772* MASE FEATURING TOTAL	15		3
19 Sep 98	**HORSE AND CARRIAGE** *Epic 6662612* CAM'RON FEATURING MASE	12		3
3 Oct 98	**YOU SHOULD BE MINE** *Motown 8608412* BRIAN McKNIGHT FEATURING MASE	36		1
10 Oct 98	**TOP OF THE WORLD** *Atlantic AT 0046CD* BRANDY FEATURING MASE	2		5
12 Dec 98	**TAKE ME THERE** *Interscope IND 95620* BLACKstreet & MYA FEATURING MASE & BLINKY BLINK	7		7
10 Jul 99	**GET READY** *Puff Daddy 74321682612* MASE FEATURING BLACKstreet	32		2
20 Nov 04	**WELCOME BACK/BREATHE STRETCH SHAKE** *Bad Boy MCSTD40392*	29		1

MASH US group

Date	Title	Peak Position	Weeks at No.1	Weeks in Top 40
10 May 80	**THEME FROM *MASH* (SUICIDE IS PAINLESS)** *CBS 8536*	1	3	9

MASH! UK/US group

Date	Title	Peak Position	Weeks at No.1	Weeks in Top 40
21 May 94	**U DON'T HAVE TO SAY U LOVE ME** *React CDREACT 37*	37		1
4 Feb 95	**LET'S SPEND THE NIGHT TOGETHER** *Playa CDXPLAYA 2*	66		

MASON VS PRINCESS SUPERSTAR
Dutch producer with US rapper

Date	Title	Peak Position	Weeks at No.1	Weeks in Top 40
27 Jan 07	**EXCEEDER** *Boss DATA150CDS*	3		11

BARBARA MASON US singer

Date	Title	Peak Position	Weeks at No.1	Weeks in Top 40
21 Jan 84	**ANOTHER MAN** *Streetwave KHAN 3*	45		

GLEN MASON UK singer

Date	Title	Peak Position	Weeks at No.1	Weeks in Top 40
28 Sep 56	**GLENDORA** *Parlophone R 4203*	28		2
16 Nov 56	**GREEN DOOR** *Parlophone R 4244*	24		5

MARY MASON UK singer

Date	Title	Peak Position	Weeks at No.1	Weeks in Top 40
8 Oct 77	**ANGEL OF THE MORNING - ANY WAY THAT YOU WANT ME (MEDLEY)** *Epic EPC 5552*	27		5

WILLY MASON US singer

Date	Title	Peak Position	Weeks at No.1	Weeks in Top 40
26 Feb 05	**OXYGEN** *Virgin VSCDX1892*	23		1
14 May 05	**SO LONG** *Virgin VSCDX1898*	45		
3 Mar 07	**SAVE MYSELF** *Virgin VSCDT1928*	42		
26 May 07	**WE CAN BE STRONG** *Radiate VSCDT1939*	52		

MASQUERADE UK group

Date	Title	Peak Position	Weeks at No.1	Weeks in Top 40
11 Jan 86	**ONE NATION** *Streetwave KHAN 59*	54		
5 Jul 86	**(SOLUTION TO) THE PROBLEM** *Streetwave KHAN 67*	64		

MASS ORDER US duo

Date	Title	Peak Position	Weeks at No.1	Weeks in Top 40
14 Mar 92	**LIFT EVERY VOICE (TAKE ME AWAY)** *Columbia 6577487*	35		2
23 May 92	**LET'S GET HAPPY** *Columbia 6580737*	45		

MASS PRODUCTION US group

Date	Title	Peak Position	Weeks at No.1	Weeks in Top 40
12 Mar 77	**WELCOME TO OUR WORLD (OF MERRY MUSIC)** *Atlantic K 10898*	44		
17 May 80	**SHANTE** *Atlantic K 11475*	59		

MASS SYNDICATE US producer

Date	Title	Peak Position	Weeks at No.1	Weeks in Top 40
24 Oct 98	**YOU DON'T KNOW** *ffrr FCD 347* MASS SYNDICATE FEATURING SU SU BOBIEN	71		

ZEITIA MASSIAH UK singer

Date	Title	Peak Position	Weeks at No.1	Weeks in Top 40
12 Mar 94	**I SPECIALIZE IN LOVE** *Union City UCRCD 27* ARIZONA FEATURING ZEITIA	74		
24 Sep 94	**THIS IS THE PLACE** *Virgin VSCDT 1511*	62		

MASSIEL Spanish singer

Date	Title	Peak Position	Weeks at No.1	Weeks in Top 40
24 Apr 68	**LA LA LA** *Philips BF 1667*	35		3

MASSIVE ATTACK UK group

Date	Title	Peak Position	Weeks at No.1	Weeks in Top 40
23 Feb 91	**UNFINISHED SYMPATHY** *Wild Bunch WBRS 2* MASSIVE	13		6
8 Jun 91	**SAFE FROM HARM** *Wild Bunch WBRS 3*	25		3
22 Feb 92	**MASSIVE ATTACK EP** *Wild Bunch WBRS 4*	27		3
29 Oct 94	**SLY** *Wild Bunch WBRDX 5*	24		2
21 Jan 95	**PROTECTION** *Virgin WBRX 6* MASSIVE ATTACK FEATURING TRACEY THORN	14		3
1 Apr 95	**KARMACOMA** *Virgin WBRX 7*	28		2
19 Jul 97	**RISINGSON** *Circa WBRX 8*	11		2
9 May 98	**TEARDROP** *Virgin WBRX 9*	10		4
25 Jul 98	**ANGEL** *Virgin WBRX 10*	30		1
8 Mar 03	**SPECIAL CASES** *Virgin VSCDT 1839*	15		1
25 Mar 06	**LIVE WITH ME** *Virgin VSCDX1912*	17		3

MASSIVO UK production group

Date	Title	Peak Position	Weeks at No.1	Weeks in Top 40
26 May 90	**LOVING YOU** *Debut DEBT 3097* MASSIVO FEATURING TRACY	25		5

MASTER BLASTER Dutch production group

Date	Title	Peak Position	Weeks at No.1	Weeks in Top 40
7 Aug 04	**HYPNOTIC TANGO** *Mondo Pop 9867100*	64		

MASTER SINGERS UK group

Date	Title	Peak Position	Weeks at No.1	Weeks in Top 40
14 Apr 66	**HIGHWAY CODE** *Parlophone R 5428*	25		6
17 Nov 66	**WEATHER FORECAST** *Parlophone R 5523*	45		

MASTERS AT WORK US group

Date	Title	Peak Position	Weeks at No.1	Weeks in Top 40
5 Aug 95	**I CAN'T GET NO SLEEP** *A&M 5811412* MASTERS AT WORK PRESENT INDIA	44		
31 Jul 99	**TO BE IN LOVE** *Defected DEFECT 5CD* MAW PRESENTS INDIA	23		2
6 Jul 02	**BACKFIRED** *Susu CDSUSU 4* MASTERS AT WORK FEATURING INDIA	62		

SAMMY MASTERS US singer

Date	Title	Peak Position	Weeks at No.1	Weeks in Top 40
9 Jun 60	**ROCKIN' RED WING** *Warner Brothers WB 10*	36		5

PAUL MASTERSON UK producer

Date	Title	Peak Position	Weeks at No.1	Weeks in Top 40
2 Nov 02	**THE EARTHSHAKER** *NuLife 74321970372* PAUL MASTERSON PRESENTS SUSHI	35		2

MATCH UK group

Date	Title	Peak Position	Weeks at No.1	Weeks in Top 40
16 Jun 79	**BOOGIE MAN** *Flamingo FM 2*	48		

MATCHBOX UK group

Date	Title	Peak Position	Weeks at No.1	Weeks in Top 40
3 Nov 79	**ROCKABILLY REBEL** *Magnet MAG 155*	18		9
19 Jan 80	**BUZZ BUZZ A DIDDLE IT** *Magnet MAG 157*	22		6
10 May 80	**MIDNITE DYNAMOS** *Magnet MAG 169*	14		7
27 Sep 80	**WHEN YOU ASK ABOUT LOVE** *Magnet MAG 191*	4		9

Date	Title / Label	Peak Position	Weeks at No.1	Weeks in Top 40
29 Nov 80	OVER THE RAINBOW - YOU BELONG TO ME (MEDLEY) *Magnet MAG 192*	15		9
4 Apr 81	BABES IN THE WOOD *Magnet MAG 193*	46		
1 Aug 81	LOVE'S MADE A FOOL OF YOU *Magnet MAG 194*	63		
29 May 82	ONE MORE SATURDAY NIGHT *Magnet MAG 223*	63		

MATCHBOX 20 US group

Date	Title / Label	Peak Position	Weeks at No.1	Weeks in Top 40
11 Apr 98	PUSH *Atlantic AT 0021CD*	38		1
4 Jul 98	3AM *Atlantic AT 0034CD*	64		
17 Feb 01	IF YOU'RE GONE *Atlantic AT 0090CD*	50		
22 Feb 03	DISEASE *Atlantic AT 0145CD*	50		

MIREILLE MATHIEU French singer

Date	Title / Label	Peak Position	Weeks at No.1	Weeks in Top 40
13 Dec 67	LA DERNIERE VALSE *Columbia DB 8323*	26		5

JOHNNY MATHIS US singer

Date	Title / Label	Peak Position	Weeks at No.1	Weeks in Top 40
23 May 58	TEACHER TEACHER *Fontana H 130*	27		5
26 Sep 58	A CERTAIN SMILE *Fontana H 142*	4		16
19 Dec 58	WINTER WONDERLAND *Fontana H 165*	17		3
7 Aug 59	SOMEONE *Fontana H 199*	6		15
27 Nov 59	THE BEST OF EVERYTHING *Fontana H 218*	30		1
29 Jan 60	MISTY *Fontana H 219*	12		9
24 Mar 60	YOU ARE BEAUTIFUL *Fontana H 234*	38		3
28 Jul 60	STARBRIGHT *Fontana H 254*	47		
6 Oct 60	MY LOVE FOR YOU *Fontana H 267*	9		18
4 Apr 63	WHAT WILL MARY SAY *CBS AAG 135*	49		
25 Jan 75	I'M STONE IN LOVE WITH YOU *CBS 2653*	10		10
13 Nov 76	WHEN A CHILD IS BORN (SOLEADO) *CBS 4599* ●	1	3	10
25 Mar 78	TOO MUCH TOO LITTLE TOO LATE *CBS 6164* JOHNNY MATHIS & DENIECE WILLIAMS ★	3		12
29 Jul 78	YOU'RE ALL I NEED TO GET BY *CBS 6483* JOHNNY MATHIS & DENIECE WILLIAMS	45		
11 Aug 79	GONE GONE GONE *CBS 7730*	15		8
26 Dec 81	WHEN A CHILD IS BORN *CBS S 1758* JOHNNY MATHIS & GLADYS KNIGHT	74		

IVAN MATAIS US singer

Date	Title / Label	Peak Position	Weeks at No.1	Weeks in Top 40
6 Apr 96	SO GOOD (TO COME HOME TO)/I'VE HAD ENOUGH *Arista 74321345072*	69		

MATT BIANCO UK group

Date	Title / Label	Peak Position	Weeks at No.1	Weeks in Top 40
11 Feb 84	GET OUT YOUR LAZY BED *WEA BIANCO 1*	15		6
14 Apr 84	SNEAKING OUT THE BACK DOOR/MATT'S MOOD *WEA YZ 3*	44		
10 Nov 84	HALF A MINUTE *WEA YZ 26*	23		4
2 Mar 85	MORE THAN I CAN BEAR *WEA YZ 34*	50		
5 Oct 85	YEH YEH *WEA YZ 46*	13		7
1 Mar 86	JUST CAN'T STAND IT *WEA YZ 62*	66		
14 Jun 86	DANCING IN THE STREET *WEA YZ 72*	64		
4 Jun 88	DON'T BLAME IT ON THAT GIRL/WAP-BAM-BOOGIE *WEA YZ 188*	11		11
27 Aug 88	GOOD TIMES *WEA YZ 302*	55		
4 Feb 89	NERVOUS/WAP-BAM-BOOGIE (REMIX) *WEA YZ 328*	59		

MATTAFIX UK duo

Date	Title / Label	Peak Position	Weeks at No.1	Weeks in Top 40
20 Aug 05	BIG CITY LIFE *Buddhist Punk ANGEDX1*	15		5

AL MATTHEWS US singer

Date	Title / Label	Peak Position	Weeks at No.1	Weeks in Top 40
23 Aug 75	FOOL *CBS 3429*	16		7

CERYS MATTHEWS UK singer

Date	Title / Label	Peak Position	Weeks at No.1	Weeks in Top 40
7 Mar 98	THE BALLAD OF TOM JONES *Gut CDGUT 18* SPACE WITH CERYS OF CATATONIA ○	4		6
18 Dec 99	BABY, IT'S COLD OUTSIDE *Gut CDGUT 29* TOM JONES & CERYS OF CATATONIA	17		3
2 Aug 03	CAUGHT IN THE MIDDLE *Blanco Y Negro NEG 147CD*	47		
19 Aug 06	OPEN ROADS *Rough Trade RTRADSCD357*	53		

DAVE MATTHEWS BAND South African/US group

Date	Title / Label	Peak Position	Weeks at No.1	Weeks in Top 40
1 Dec 01	THE SPACE BETWEEN *RCA 74321883192*	35		1

SCOTT MATTHEWS UK singer

Date	Title / Label	Peak Position	Weeks at No.1	Weeks in Top 40
30 Sep 06	ELUSIVE *Island REMOCDS001*	56		

SUMMER MATTHEWS UK singer

Date	Title / Label	Peak Position	Weeks at No.1	Weeks in Top 40
28 Feb 04	LITTLE MISS PERFECT *Sony Music 6744732*	32		1

MATTHEWS SOUTHERN COMFORT UK singer/guitarist

Date	Title / Label	Peak Position	Weeks at No.1	Weeks in Top 40
26 Sep 70	WOODSTOCK *Uni UNS 526*	1	3	15

MATUMBI UK group

Date	Title / Label	Peak Position	Weeks at No.1	Weeks in Top 40
29 Sep 79	POINT OF VIEW *Matumbi RIC 101*	35		1

SUSAN MAUGHAN UK singer

Date	Title / Label	Peak Position	Weeks at No.1	Weeks in Top 40
11 Oct 62	BOBBY'S GIRL *Philips 326544 BF*	3		17
14 Feb 63	HAND A HANDKERCHIEF TO HELEN *Philips 326562 BF*	41		
9 May 63	SHE'S NEW TO YOU *Philips 326586 BF*	45		

MAUREEN UK singer

Date	Title / Label	Peak Position	Weeks at No.1	Weeks in Top 40
26 Nov 88	SAY A LITTLE PRAYER *Rhythm King DOOD 3* BOMB THE BASS FEATURING MAUREEN	10		8
16 Jun 90	THINKING OF YOU *Urban URB 55*	11		7
12 Jan 91	WHERE HAS ALL THE LOVE GONE *Urban URB 65*	51		

PAUL MAURIAT French orchestra leader

Date	Title / Label	Peak Position	Weeks at No.1	Weeks in Top 40
21 Feb 68	LOVE IS BLUE (L'AMOUR EST BLEU) *Philips BF 1637* ★	12		12

MAVERICKS US group

Date	Title / Label	Peak Position	Weeks at No.1	Weeks in Top 40
2 May 98	DANCE THE NIGHT AWAY *MCA Nashville MCSTD 48081* ●	4		16
26 Sep 98	I'VE GOT THIS FEELING *MCA Nashville MCSTD 48095*	27		1
5 Jun 99	SOMEONE SHOULD TELL HER *MCA Nashville MCSTD 55567*	45		

MAX LINEN UK production duo

Date	Title / Label	Peak Position	Weeks at No.1	Weeks in Top 40
17 Nov 01	THE SOULSHAKER *Global Cuts GC 73CD*	55		

MAX Q Australian duo

Date	Title / Label	Peak Position	Weeks at No.1	Weeks in Top 40
17 Feb 90	SOMETIMES *Mercury MXQ 2*	53		

MAX WEBSTER Canadian group

Date	Title / Label	Peak Position	Weeks at No.1	Weeks in Top 40
19 May 79	PARADISE SKIES *Capitol CL 16079*	43		

MAXEE US singer

Date	Title / Label	Peak Position	Weeks at No.1	Weeks in Top 40
17 Mar 01	WHEN I LOOK INTO YOUR EYES *Mercury 5628702*	55		

MAXIM UK singer

Date	Title / Label	Peak Position	Weeks at No.1	Weeks in Top 40
10 Jun 00	CARMEN QUEASY *XL Recordings XLS 119CD*	33		1
23 Sep 00	SCHEMING *XL Recordings XLS 121CD*	53		

MAXIMA UK/Spanish singer

Date	Title / Label	Peak Position	Weeks at No.1	Weeks in Top 40
14 Aug 93	IBIZA *Yo! Yo! CDLILY 1* MAXIMA FEATURING LILY	55		

MAXIMO PARK UK group

Date	Title / Label	Peak Position	Weeks at No.1	Weeks in Top 40
5 Mar 05	APPLY SOME PRESSURE *Warp WAP185CD*	20		1
14 May 05	GRAFFITI *Warp WAP187CDR*	15		2
30 Jul 05	GOING MISSING *Warp WAP190CDR*	20		1
5 Nov 05	APPLY SOME PRESSURE *Warp WAP198CD*	17		2
4 Mar 06	I WANT YOU TO STAY *Warp WAP201CD*	21		1
24 Mar 07	OUR VELOCITY *Warp WAP220CD*	9		7
23 Jun 07	BOOKS FROM BOXES *Warp WAP223CD*	16		1
1 Sep 07	GIRLS WHO PLAY GUITARS *Warp WAP227CD*	31		1

Silver-selling · Gold-selling · Platinum-selling · US No.1 ★ · Peak Position · Weeks at No.1 · Weeks in Top 40

MAXTREME Dutch production group

Date	Title	Peak	Wks No.1	Wks Top 40
9 Mar 02	**MY HOUSE IS YOUR HOUSE** *Y2K 028CD*	66		

MAXWELL US singer

Date	Title	Peak	Wks No.1	Wks Top 40
11 May 96	**...TIL THE COPS COME KNOCKIN'** *Columbia 6631792*	63		
24 Aug 96	**ASCENSION NO ONE'S GONNA LOVE YOU, SO DON'T EVER WONDER** *Columbia 6636265*	39		1
1 Mar 97	**SUMTHIN' SUMTHIN' THE MANTRA** *Columbia 6638642*	27		1
24 May 97	**ASCENSION NO ONE'S GONNA LOVE YOU, SO DON'T EVER WONDER** *Columbia 6645952*	28		2

MAXX UK/Swedish/German group

Date	Title	Peak	Wks No.1	Wks Top 40
21 May 94	**GET-A-WAY** *Pulse 8 CDLOSE 59*	4		10
6 Aug 94	**NO MORE (I CAN'T STAND IT)** *Pulse 8 CDLOSE 66*	8		6
29 Oct 94	**YOU CAN GET IT** *Pulse 8 CDLOSE 75*	21		2
22 Jul 95	**I CAN MAKE YOU FEEL LIKE** *Pulse 8 CDLOSE 88*	56		

BILLY MAY US bandleader

Date	Title	Peak	Wks No.1	Wks Top 40
27 Apr 56	**MAIN TITLE THEME FROM *MAN WITH THE GOLDEN ARM*** *Capitol 14551*	9		10

BRIAN MAY UK singer/guitarist

Date	Title	Peak	Wks No.1	Wks Top 40
5 Nov 83	**STAR FLEET** *EMI 5436* BRIAN MAY & FRIENDS	65		
7 Dec 91	**DRIVEN BY YOU** *Parlophone R 6304*	6		7
5 Sep 92	**TOO MUCH LOVE WILL KILL YOU** *Parlophone R 6320*	5		7
17 Oct 92	**WE ARE THE CHAMPIONS** *PolyGram TV PO 229* HANK MARVIN FEATURING BRIAN MAY	66		
21 Nov 92	**BACK TO THE LIGHT** *Parlophone R 6329*	19		1
19 Jun 93	**RESURRECTION** *Parlophone CDRS 6351* BRIAN MAY WITH COZY POWELL	23		2
18 Dec 93	**LAST HORIZON** *Parlophone CDR 6371*	51		
6 Jun 98	**THE BUSINESS** *Parlophone CDR 6498*	51		
12 Sep 98	**WHY DON'T WE TRY AGAIN** *Parlophone CDR 6504*	44		

LISA MAY UK singer

Date	Title	Peak	Wks No.1	Wks Top 40
15 Jul 95	**WISHING ON A STAR** *Urban Gorilla UG 3CD* 88.3 FEATURING LISA MAY	61		
14 Sep 96	**THE CURSE OF VOODOO RAY** *Fontana VOOCD 1*	64		

MARY MAY UK singer

Date	Title	Peak	Wks No.1	Wks Top 40
27 Feb 64	**ANYONE WHO HAD A HEART** *Fontana TF 440*	49		

SHERNETTE MAY UK singer

Date	Title	Peak	Wks No.1	Wks Top 40
6 Jun 98	**ALL THE MAN THAT I NEED** *Virgin VSCDT 1691*	50		

SIMON MAY UK orchestra leader

Date	Title	Peak	Wks No.1	Wks Top 40
9 Oct 76	**SUMMER OF MY LIFE** *Pye 7N 45627*	7		8
21 May 77	**WE'LL GATHER LILACES – ALL MY LOVING (MEDLEY)** *Pye 7N 45688*	49		
26 Oct 85	**HOWARD'S WAY** *BBC RESL 174* SIMON MAY ORCHESTRA	21		6
9 Aug 86	**ANYONE CAN FALL IN LOVE** *BBC RESL 191* ANITA DOBSON FEATURING THE SIMON MAY ORCHESTRA	4		7
20 Sep 86	**ALWAYS THERE** *BBC RESL 190* MARTI WEBB & THE SIMON MAY ORCHESTRA	13		9

JOHN MAYER US singer

Date	Title	Peak	Wks No.1	Wks Top 40
23 Aug 03	**NO SUCH THING** *Columbia 6732322*	42		
28 Feb 04	**BIGGER THAN MY BODY** *Columbia 6744392*	72		

CURTIS MAYFIELD US singer

Date	Title	Peak	Wks No.1	Wks Top 40
31 Jul 71	**MOVE ON UP** *Buddah 2011 080*	12		8
2 Dec 78	**NO GOODBYES** *Atlantic LV 1*	65		
30 May 87	**(CELEBRATE) THE DAY AFTER YOU** *RCA MONK 6* BLOW MONKEYS WITH CURTIS MAYFIELD	52		
29 Sep 90	**SUPERFLY 1990** *Capitol CL 586* CURTIS MAYFIELD & ICE-T	48		
16 Jun 01	**ASTOUNDED** *Virgin VUSCD 194* BRAN VAN 3000 FEATURING CURTIS MAYFIELD	40		1

MAYTALS Jamaican group

Date	Title	Peak	Wks No.1	Wks Top 40
25 Apr 70	**MONKEY MAN** *Trojan TR 7711*	47		

MAYTE US singer

Date	Title	Peak	Wks No.1	Wks Top 40
18 Nov 95	**IF EYE LOVE U 2 NIGHT** *NPG 0061635*	67		

MAZE US group

Date	Title	Peak	Wks No.1	Wks Top 40
20 Jul 85	**TOO MANY GAMES** *Capitol CL 363* MAZE FEATURING FRANKIE BEVERLY	36		3
23 Aug 86	**I WANNA BE WITH YOU** *Capitol CL 421* MAZE FEATURING FRANKIE BEVERLY	55		
27 May 89	**JOY AND PAIN** *Capitol CL 531*	57		

KYM MAZELLE US singer

Date	Title	Peak	Wks No.1	Wks Top 40
12 Nov 88	**USELESS (I DON'T NEED YOU NOW)** *Syncopate SY 18*	53		
14 Jan 89	**WAIT** *RCA PB 42595* ROBERT HOWARD & KYM MAZELLE	7		8
25 Mar 89	**GOT TO GET YOU BACK** *Syncopate SY 25*	29		3
7 Oct 89	**LOVE STRAIN** *Syncopate SY 30*	52		
20 Jan 90	**WAS THAT ALL IT WAS** *Syncopate SY 32*	33		3
26 May 90	**USELESS (I DON'T NEED YOU NOW) (REMIX)** *Syncopate SY 36*	48		
24 Nov 90	**MISSING YOU** *10 TEN 345* SOUL II SOUL FEATURING KYM MAZELLE	22		3
25 May 91	**NO ONE CAN LOVE YOU MORE THAN ME** *Parlophone R 6287*	62		
26 Dec 92	**LOVE ME THE RIGHT WAY** *Logic 74321128097* RAPINATION & KYM MAZELLE	22		5
11 Jun 94	**NO MORE TEARS (ENOUGH IS ENOUGH)** *Ding Dong 74321209032* KYM MAZELLE & JOCELYN BROWN	13		4
8 Oct 94	**GIMME ALL YOUR LOVIN'** *Ding Dong 74321231322* KYM MAZELLE & JOCELYN BROWN	22		2
23 Dec 95	**SEARCHING FOR THE GOLDEN EYE** *Eternal 027CD* MOTIV 8 & KYM MAZELLE	40		1
28 Sep 96	**LOVE ME THE RIGHT WAY (REMIX)** *Logic 74321404442* RAPINATION & KYM MAZELLE	55		
16 Aug 97	**YOUNG HEARTS RUN FREE** *EMI CDEM 488*	20		2
19 Feb 00	**TRULY** *Island Blue PFACD 4* PESHAY FEATURING KYM MAZELLE	55		

MAZZY STAR US duo

Date	Title	Peak	Wks No.1	Wks Top 40
27 Aug 94	**FADE INTO YOU** *Capitol CDCL 720*	48		
2 Nov 96	**FLOWERS IN DECEMBER** *Capitol CDCL 781*	40		1

MC DUKE UK rapper

Date	Title	Peak	Wks No.1	Wks Top 40
11 Mar 89	**I'M RIFFIN (ENGLISH RASTA)** *Music Of Life 7NOTE 25*	75		

MC JIG German rapper

Date	Title	Peak	Wks No.1	Wks Top 40
21 Feb 04	**CHA CHA SLIDE (IMPORT)** *ZYX 95838*	37		1
13 Mar 04	**CHA CHA SLIDE** *NM Music SLIDE001*	33		1

MC LETHAL UK producer

Date	Title	Peak	Wks No.1	Wks Top 40
14 Nov 92	**THE RAVE DIGGER** *Network NWKT 60*	66		

MC LYTE US rapper

Date	Title	Peak	Wks No.1	Wks Top 40
15 Jan 94	**RUFFNECK** *Atlantic A 8336CD*	67		
29 Jun 96	**KEEP ON, KEEPIN' ON** *East West A 4287CD* MC LYTE FEATURING XSCAPE	39		1
18 Jan 97	**COLD ROCK A PARTY** *East West A 3975CD*	15		3
19 Apr 97	**KEEP ON, KEEPIN' ON** *East West A 3950CD1* MC LYTE FEATURING XSCAPE	27		1
5 Sep 98	**I CAN'T MAKE A MISTAKE** *Elektra E 3813CD*	46		
19 Dec 98	**IT'S ALL YOURS** *East West E 3789CD* MC LYTE FEATURING GINA THOMPSON	36		1
24 Jun 00	**JAMMIN'** *Tuff Gong TGXCD 9* BOB MARLEY FEATURING MC LYTE	42		
8 May 04	**GIRLFRIEND'S STORY** *Polydor 9866362* GEMMA FOX FEATURING MC LYTE	38		1

Silver-selling ● Gold-selling ● Platinum-selling ⊛ US No.1 ★ | Peak Position | Weeks at No.1 | Weeks in Top 40

MC MIKER 'G' & DEEJAY SVEN Dutch duo

Date	Title / Label	Peak Position	Weeks at No.1	Weeks in Top 40
6 Sep 86	**HOLIDAY RAP** *Debut DEBT 3008*	6		5

MC RB UK rapper

Date	Title / Label	Peak Position	Weeks at No.1	Weeks in Top 40
1 Apr 00	**CHEQUE ONE-TWO** *Filter FILT 044* SUNSHIP FEATURING M.C.R.B.	75		
28 Sep 02	**JUMP UP** *Serious SERR 050CD* JUST 4 JOKES FEATURING MC RB	67		

MC ONYX STONE UK rapper

Date	Title / Label	Peak Position	Weeks at No.1	Weeks in Top 40
7 Apr 01	**GARAGE GIRLS** *Riverhorse RIVHCD 12* LONYO FEATURING MC ONYX STONE	39		1
16 Mar 02	**WHADDA WE LIKE?** *Cooltempo CDCOOL 358* ROUND SOUND PRESENTS ONYX STONE & MC MALIBU	69		

MC SKAT CAT US cartoon cat

Date	Title / Label	Peak Position	Weeks at No.1	Weeks in Top 40
9 Nov 91	**SKAT STRUT** *Virgin America VUS 51* MC SKAT KAT & THE STRAY MOB	64		

MC SOLAAR French rapper

Date	Title / Label	Peak Position	Weeks at No.1	Weeks in Top 40
20 Aug 94	**LISTEN** *Talkin Loud TLKCD 50* URBAN SPECIES FEATURING MC SOLAAR	47		
25 Sep 99	**ALL N MY GRILL** *Elektra E 3742CD* MISSY 'MISDEMEANOR' ELLIOTT FEATURING MC SOLAAR	20		2

MC SPY-D + FRIENDS UK group

Date	Title / Label	Peak Position	Weeks at No.1	Weeks in Top 40
11 Mar 95	**THE AMAZING SPIDER MAN** *Parlophone CDR 6404*	37		1

MC TUNES UK rapper

Date	Title / Label	Peak Position	Weeks at No.1	Weeks in Top 40
2 Jun 90	**THE ONLY RHYME THAT BITES** *ZTT ZANG 3* MC TUNES VERSUS 808 STATE	10		8
15 Sep 90	**TUNES SPLITS THE ATOM** *ZTT ZANG 6* MC TUNES VERSUS 808 STATE	18		5
1 Dec 90	**PRIMARY RHYMING** *ZTT ZANG 10*	67		
6 Mar 99	**THE ONLY RHYME THAT BITES 99** *ZTT 125CD* MC TUNES VERSUS 808 STATE	53		

MC WILDSKI UK rapper

Date	Title / Label	Peak Position	Weeks at No.1	Weeks in Top 40
8 Jul 89	**WON'T TALK ABOUT IT/BLAME IT ON THE BASSLINE** *Go! Beat GOD 33* NORMAN COOK FEATURING BILLY BRAGG/NORMAN COOK FEATURING MC WILDSKI	29		4
3 Mar 90	**WARRIOR** *Arista 112956*	49		

M-D-EMM UK producer

Date	Title / Label	Peak Position	Weeks at No.1	Weeks in Top 40
22 Feb 92	**GET DOWN** *Strictly Underground 7STUR 13*	55		
30 May 92	**MOVE YOUR FEET** *Strictly Underground 7STUR 15*	67		

MDM UK producer

Date	Title / Label	Peak Position	Weeks at No.1	Weeks in Top 40
27 Oct 01	**MASH IT UP** *NuLife 74321870472*	66		

ME & YOU UK group

Date	Title / Label	Peak Position	Weeks at No.1	Weeks in Top 40
28 Jul 79	**YOU NEVER KNOW WHAT YOU'VE GOT** *Laser LAS 8* ME & YOU FEATURING WE THE PEOPLE BAND	31		4

ME ME ME UK group

Date	Title / Label	Peak Position	Weeks at No.1	Weeks in Top 40
17 Aug 96	**HANGING AROUND** *Indolent DUFF 005CD*	19		2

ABIGAIL MEAD & NIGEL GOULDING UK/US duo

Date	Title / Label	Peak Position	Weeks at No.1	Weeks in Top 40
26 Sep 87	**FULL METAL JACKET (I WANNA BE YOUR DRILL INSTRUCTOR)** *Warner Brothers W 8187* ●	2		9

LEE MEAD UK singer

Date	Title / Label	Peak Position	Weeks at No.1	Weeks in Top 40
23 Jun 07	**ANY DREAM WILL DO** *Polydor 1739785*	2		6

MEAT BEAT MANIFESTO UK production group

Date	Title / Label	Peak Position	Weeks at No.1	Weeks in Top 40
20 Feb 93	**MINDSTREAM** *Play It Again Sam BIAS 232CD*	55		

MEAT LOAF US singer

Date	Title / Label	Peak Position	Weeks at No.1	Weeks in Top 40
20 May 78	**YOU TOOK THE WORDS RIGHT OUT OF MY MOUTH** *Epic EPC 5980*	33		3
19 Aug 78	**TWO OUT OF THREE AIN'T BAD** *Epic EPC 6281*	32		4
10 Feb 79	**BAT OUT OF HELL** *Epic EPC 7018*	15		5
26 Sep 81	**I'M GONNA LOVE HER FOR BOTH OF US** *Epic EPC A 1580*	62		
28 Nov 81	**DEAD RINGER FOR LOVE** *Epic EPC A 1697* ●	5		14
28 May 83	**IF YOU REALLY WANT TO** *Epic A 3357*	59		
24 Sep 83	**MIDNIGHT AT THE LOST AND FOUND** *Epic A 3748*	17		6
14 Jan 84	**RAZOR'S EDGE** *Epic A 4080*	41		
6 Oct 84	**MODERN GIRL** *Arista ARIST 585*	17		7
22 Dec 84	**NOWHERE FAST** *Arista ARIST 600*	67		
23 Mar 85	**PIECE OF THE ACTION** *Arista ARIST 603*	47		
30 Aug 86	**ROCK 'N' ROLL MERCENARIES** *Arista ARIST 666* MEAT LOAF FEATURING JOHN PARR	31		4
22 Jun 91	**DEAD RINGER FOR LOVE** *Epic 6569827*	53		
27 Jun 92	**TWO OUT OF THREE AIN'T BAD** *Epic 6574917*	69		
9 Oct 93	**I'D DO ANYTHING FOR LOVE (BUT I WON'T DO THAT)** *Virgin VSCDT 1443* ⊛ ★	1	7	16
18 Dec 93	**BAT OUT OF HELL** *Epic 6600062*	8		6
19 Feb 94	**ROCK AND ROLL DREAMS COME THROUGH** *Virgin VSCDT 1479*	11		3
7 May 94	**OBJECTS IN THE REAR VIEW MIRROR MAY APPEAR CLOSER THAN THEY ARE** *Virgin VSCDT 1492*	26		2
28 Oct 95	**I'D LIE FOR YOU (AND THAT'S THE TRUTH)** *Virgin VSCDT 1563* ●	2		7
27 Jan 96	**NOT A DRY EYE IN THE HOUSE** *Virgin VSCDT 1567*	7		4
27 Apr 96	**RUNNIN' FOR THE RED LIGHT (I GOTTA LIFE)** *Virgin VSCDX 1582*	21		2
17 Apr 99	**IS NOTHING SACRED** *Virgin VSCDT 1734* MEAT LOAF FEATURING PATTI RUSSO	15		3
26 Apr 03	**COULDN'T HAVE SAID IT BETTER** *Mercury 0656842*	31		1
6 Dec 03	**MAN OF STEEL** *Mercury 9815114*	21		2
21 Oct 06	**IT'S ALL COMING BACK TO ME NOW** *Mercury 1707714* MEAT LOAF FEATURING MARION RAVEN	6		5
19 May 07	**CRY OVER ME** *Mercury 1733477*	47		

MECK UK producer

Date	Title / Label	Peak Position	Weeks at No.1	Weeks in Top 40
18 Feb 06	**THUNDER IN MY HEART AGAIN** *Apollo/Free 2 Air APOLLO101CDX* MECK FEATURING LEO SAYER	1	2	13
21 Apr 07	**FEELS LIKE HOME** *Free2Air F2A27CDS* MECK FEATURING DINO	39		1

MECO US orchestra leader

Date	Title / Label	Peak Position	Weeks at No.1	Weeks in Top 40
1 Oct 77	***STAR WARS* THEME - CANTINA BAND** *RCA XB 102* ★	7		8

GLENN MEDEIROS US singer

Date	Title / Label	Peak Position	Weeks at No.1	Weeks in Top 40
18 Jun 88	**NOTHING'S GONNA CHANGE MY LOVE FOR YOU** *London LON 184* ●	1	4	10
3 Sep 88	**LONG AND LASTING LOVE (ONCE IN A LIFETIME)** *London LON 202*	42		
30 Jun 90	**SHE AIN'T WORTH IT** *London LON 265* GLENN MEDEIROS FEATURING BOBBY BROWN ★	12		7

MEDICINE HEAD UK duo

Date	Title / Label	Peak Position	Weeks at No.1	Weeks in Top 40
26 Jun 71	**(AND THE) PICTURES IN THE SKY** *Dandelion DAN 7003*	22		5
5 May 73	**ONE AND ONE IS ONE** *Polydor 2001 432*	3		11
4 Aug 73	**RISING SUN** *Polydor 2058 389*	11		9
9 Feb 74	**SLIP AND SLIDE** *Polydor 2058 436*	22		5

BILL MEDLEY US singer

Date	Title / Label	Peak Position	Weeks at No.1	Weeks in Top 40
31 Oct 87	**(I'VE HAD) THE TIME OF MY LIFE** *RCA PB 49625* BILL MEDLEY & JENNIFER WARNES ★	6		9
27 Aug 88	**HE AIN'T HEAVY, HE'S MY BROTHER** *Scotti Brothers PO 10*	25		4
15 Dec 90	**(I'VE HAD) THE TIME OF MY LIFE** *RCA PB 49625* BILL MEDLEY & JENNIFER WARNES ●	8		6

Silver-selling ○ Gold-selling ● Platinum-selling ⊛ US No.1 ★ — Peak Position — Weeks at No.1 — Weeks in Top 40

MEDWAY US producer

Date	Title	Peak Position	Weeks at No.1	Weeks in Top 40
29 Apr 00	**FAT BASTARD (EP)** *Hooj Choons HOOJ 92CD*	69		
10 Mar 01	**RELEASE** *Hooj Choons HOOJ 105CD*	67		

MICHAEL MEDWIN, BERNARD BRESSLAW, ALFIE BASS & LESLIE FYSON UK actors

Date	Title	Peak Position	Weeks at No.1	Weeks in Top 40
30 May 58	**THE SIGNATURE TUNE OF THE ARMY GAME** *HMV POP 490*	5		9

MEECHIE US singer

Date	Title	Peak Position	Weeks at No.1	Weeks in Top 40
2 Sep 95	**YOU BRING ME JOY** *Vibe MCSTD 2069*	74		

TONY MEEHAN COMBO US singer

Date	Title	Peak Position	Weeks at No.1	Weeks in Top 40
16 Jan 64	**SONG OF MEXICO** *Decca F 11801*	39		1

MEEKER UK production duo

Date	Title	Peak Position	Weeks at No.1	Weeks in Top 40
26 Feb 00	**SAVE ME** *Underwater H2O 009 CD*	60		

MEGA CITY FOUR UK group

Date	Title	Peak Position	Weeks at No.1	Weeks in Top 40
19 Oct 91	**WORDS THAT SAY** *Big Life MEGA 2*	66		
8 Feb 92	**STOP (EP)** *Big Life MEGA 3*	36		1
16 May 92	**SHIVERING SAND** *Big Life MEGA 4*	35		1
1 May 93	**IRON** *Big Life MEGAD 5*	48		
17 Jul 93	**WALLFLOWER** *Big Life MEGAD 6*	69		

MEGADETH US group

Date	Title	Peak Position	Weeks at No.1	Weeks in Top 40
19 Dec 87	**WAKE UP DEAD** *Capitol CL 476*	65		
27 Feb 88	**ANARCHY IN THE UK** *Capitol CL 480*	45		
21 May 88	**MARY JANE** *Capitol CL 489*	46		
13 Jan 90	**NO MORE MR. NICE GUY** *SBK 4*	13		5
29 Sep 90	**HOLY WARS...THE PUNISHMENT DUE** *Capitol CLP 588*	24		2
16 Mar 91	**HANGAR 18** *Capitol CLS 604*	26		3
27 Jun 92	**SYMPHONY OF DESTRUCTION** *Capitol CLS 662*	15		2
24 Oct 92	**SKIN O' MY TEETH** *Capitol CLP 669*	13		1
29 May 93	**SWEATING BULLETS** *Capitol CDCL 682*	26		2
7 Jan 95	**TRAIN OF CONSEQUENCES** *Capitol CDCL 730*	22		2

MEJA Swedish singer

Date	Title	Peak Position	Weeks at No.1	Weeks in Top 40
24 Oct 98	**ALL 'BOUT THE MONEY** *Columbia 6665662*	12		4
29 Apr 00	**PRIVATE EMOTION** *Columbia 6692692* RICKY MARTIN FEATURING MEJA	9		7

MEKKA UK producer

Date	Title	Peak Position	Weeks at No.1	Weeks in Top 40
24 Mar 01	**DIAMOND BACK** *Perfecto PERF 12CDS*	67		

MEKON UK producer

Date	Title	Peak Position	Weeks at No.1	Weeks in Top 40
23 Sep 00	**WHAT'S GOING ON** *Wall Of Sound WALD 064* MEKON FEATURING ROXANNE SHANTE	43		
13 Mar 04	**D-FUNKTIONAL** *Wall Of Sound WALLD092* MEKON FEATURING AFRIKA BAMBAATAA	72		

MEL & KIM UK duo

Date	Title	Peak Position	Weeks at No.1	Weeks in Top 40
20 Sep 86	**SHOWING OUT (GET FRESH AT THE WEEKEND)** *Supreme SUPE 107* ○	3		12
7 Mar 87	**RESPECTABLE** *Supreme SUPE 111* ●	1	1	13
11 Jul 87	**F.L.M.** *Supreme SUPE 113*	7		7
27 Feb 88	**THAT'S THE WAY IT IS** *Supreme SUPE 117*	10		5

GEORGE MELACHRINO ORCHESTRA UK orchestra

Date	Title	Peak Position	Weeks at No.1	Weeks in Top 40
12 Oct 56	**AUTUMN CONCERTO** *HMV B 10958*	18		9

MELANIE US singer

Date	Title	Peak Position	Weeks at No.1	Weeks in Top 40
26 Sep 70	**RUBY TUESDAY** *Buddah 2011 038*	9		13
16 Jan 71	**WHAT HAVE THEY DONE TO MY SONG MA** *Buddah 2011 038*	39		1
1 Jan 72	**BRAND NEW KEY** *Buddah 2011 105* ★	4		11
16 Feb 74	**WILL YOU LOVE ME TOMORROW** *Neighbourhood NBH 9*	37		2
24 Sep 83	**EVERY BREATH OF THE WAY** *Neighbourhood HOOD NB1*	70		

MELKY SEDECK US duo

Date	Title	Peak Position	Weeks at No.1	Weeks in Top 40
8 May 99	**RAW** *MCA MCSTD 48107*	50		
16 Sep 00	**IT DOESN'T MATTER** *Columbia 6697782* WYCLEF JEAN FEATURING THE ROCK & MELKY SEDECK	3		5

JOHN COUGAR MELLENCAMP US singer

Date	Title	Peak Position	Weeks at No.1	Weeks in Top 40
23 Oct 82	**JACK AND DIANE** *Riva 37* JOHN COUGAR ★	25		5
1 Feb 86	**SMALL TOWN** *Riva JCM 5*	53		
10 May 86	**R.O.C.K. IN THE USA** *Riva JCM 6*	67		
3 Sep 94	**WILD NIGHT** *Mercury MERCD 409* JOHN MELLENCAMP FEATURING ME'SHELL NDEGEOCELLO	34		1

THE MELLOMAN US group

Date	Title	Peak Position	Weeks at No.1	Weeks in Top 40
1 Oct 54	**IF I GIVE MY HEART TO YOU** *Philips PB 325* DORIS DAY WITH THE MELLOMAN	4		11
17 Dec 54	**MAMBO ITALIANO** *Philips PB 382* ROSEMARY CLOONEY WITH THE MELLOMEN	1	3	16
20 May 55	**WHERE WILL THE BABY'S DIMPLE BE** *Philips PB 428* ROSEMARY CLOONEY WITH THE MELLOMEN	6		13
24 Jun 55	**COOL WATER** *Philips PB 465* FRANKIE LAINE WITH THE MELLOMEN	2		22
20 Jan 56	**SIXTEEN TONS** *Philips PB 539* FRANKIE LAINE WITH THE MELLOMEN	10		3
28 Feb 63	**ONE BROKEN HEART FOR SALE** *RCA 1337* ELVIS PRESLEY WITH THE MELLOMEN	12		7

WILL MELLOR UK singer/actor

Date	Title	Peak Position	Weeks at No.1	Weeks in Top 40
28 Feb 98	**WHEN I NEED YOU** *Unity 017RCD*	5		3
27 Jun 98	**NO MATTER WHAT I DO** *Jive 0540012*	23		1

MELLOW TRAX German producer

Date	Title	Peak Position	Weeks at No.1	Weeks in Top 40
14 Oct 00	**OUTTA SPACE** *Substance SUBS 3CDS*	41		

MELODIANS Jamaican group

Date	Title	Peak Position	Weeks at No.1	Weeks in Top 40
10 Jan 70	**SWEET SENSATION** *Trojan TR 695*	41		

MELT UK producer

Date	Title	Peak Position	Weeks at No.1	Weeks in Top 40
8 Apr 00	**HARD HOUSE MUSIC** *WEA 257CD* MELT FEATURING LITTLE MS MARCIE	59		

MELTDOWN UK/US production duo

Date	Title	Peak Position	Weeks at No.1	Weeks in Top 40
27 Apr 96	**MY LIFE IS IN YOUR HANDS** *Sony S3 DANU 7CD*	44		

KATIE MELUA Georgian singer

Date	Title	Peak Position	Weeks at No.1	Weeks in Top 40
13 Dec 03	**THE CLOSEST THING TO CRAZY** *Dramatico DRAMCDS 0003*	10		18
27 Mar 04	**CALL OFF THE SEARCH** *Dramatico DRAMCDS0005*	19		1
31 Jul 04	**CRAWLING UP A HILL** *Dramatico DRAMCDS0007*	46		
1 Oct 05	**NINE MILLION BICYCLES** *Dramatico DRAMCDS0012*	5		9
17 Dec 05	**I CRIED FOR YOU/JUST LIKE HEAVEN** *Dramatico DRAMCDS0013*	35		1
29 Apr 06	**SPIDER'S WEB** *Dramatico DRAMCDS0017*	52		
23 Sep 06	**IT'S ONLY PAIN** *Dramatico DRAMCDS0020*	41		
6 Oct 07	**IF YOU WERE A SAILBOAT** *Dramatico DRAMCDS0029*	23		2
22 Dec 07	**WHAT A WONDERFUL WORLD** *Dramatico TD001* EVA CASSIDY & KATIE MELUA	1	1	3

HAROLD MELVIN & THE BLUENOTES US group

Date	Title	Peak Position	Weeks at No.1	Weeks in Top 40
13 Jan 73	**IF YOU DON'T KNOW ME BY NOW** *CBS 8496*	9		8
12 Jan 74	**THE LOVE I LOST** *Philadelphia International PIR 1879*	21		6
13 Apr 74	**SATISFACTION GUARANTEED (OR TAKE YOUR LOVE BACK)** *Philadelphia International PIR 2187*	32		4
31 May 75	**GET OUT (AND LET ME CRY)** *Route RT 06*	35		2
28 Feb 76	**WAKE UP EVERYBODY** *Philadelphia International PIR 3866*	23		5

Silver-selling ○ · Gold-selling ● · Platinum-selling · US No.1 ★ · Peak Position · Weeks at No.1 · Weeks in Top 40

Date	Title	Peak Position	Weeks at No.1	Weeks in Top 40
22 Jan 77	**DON'T LEAVE ME THIS WAY** *Philadelphia International PIR 4909* HAROLD MELVIN & THE BLUENOTES FEATURING THEODORE PENDERGRASS ○	5		10
2 Apr 77	**REACHING FOR THE WORLD** *ABC 4161*	48		
28 Apr 84	**DON'T GIVE ME UP** *London LON 47*	59		
4 Aug 84	**TODAY'S YOUR LUCKY DAY** *London LON 52* HAROLD MELVIN & THE BLUENOTES FEATURING NIKKO	66		

MEMBERS UK group

Date	Title	Peak Position	Weeks at No.1	Weeks in Top 40
3 Feb 79	**THE SOUND OF THE SUBURBS** *Virgin VS 242*	12		8
7 Apr 79	**OFFSHORE BANKING BUSINESS** *Virgin VS 248*	31		3

MEMBERS OF MAYDAY German production duo

Date	Title	Peak Position	Weeks at No.1	Weeks in Top 40
23 Jun 01	**10 IN 01** *Deviant DVNT 42CDS*	31		1
13 Apr 02	**SONIC EMPIRE** *Deviant DVNT 49CDS*	59		

MEMPHIS BLEEK US rapper

Date	Title	Peak Position	Weeks at No.1	Weeks in Top 40
4 Dec 99	**WHAT YOU THINK OF THAT** *Def Jam 8708292* MEMPHIS BLEEK FEATURING JAY-Z	58		

MEN AT WORK Australian group

Date	Title	Peak Position	Weeks at No.1	Weeks in Top 40
30 Oct 82	**WHO CAN IT BE NOW?** *Epic A 2392* ★	45		
8 Jan 83	**DOWN UNDER** *Epic EPC A 1980* ● ★	1	3	10
9 Apr 83	**OVERKILL** *Epic EPC A 3220*	21		7
2 Jul 83	**IT'S A MISTAKE** *Epic EPC A 3475*	33		2
10 Sep 83	**DR HECKYLL AND MR. JIVE** *Epic EPC A 3668*	31		3

MEN OF VIZION US group

Date	Title	Peak Position	Weeks at No.1	Weeks in Top 40
27 Mar 99	**DO YOU FEEL ME? (...FREAK YOU)** *MJJ 6670912*	36		1

MEN THEY COULDN'T HANG UK group

Date	Title	Peak Position	Weeks at No.1	Weeks in Top 40
2 Apr 88	**THE COLOURS** *Magnet SELL 6*	61		

MEN WITHOUT HATS Canadian group

Date	Title	Peak Position	Weeks at No.1	Weeks in Top 40
8 Oct 83	**THE SAFETY DANCE** *Statik TAK 1* ○	6		8

SERGIO MENDES Brazilian pianist

Date	Title	Peak Position	Weeks at No.1	Weeks in Top 40
9 Jul 83	**NEVER GONNA LET YOU GO** *A&M AM 118*	45		
24 Jun 06	**MAS QUE NADA** *Concord/UCJ 9859631* SERGIO MENDES & THE BLACK EYED PEAS	6		8

ANDREA MENDEZ UK singer

Date	Title	Peak Position	Weeks at No.1	Weeks in Top 40
3 Aug 96	**BRING ME LOVE** *AM:PM 5817872*	44		

MENSWEAR UK group

Date	Title	Peak Position	Weeks at No.1	Weeks in Top 40
15 Apr 95	**I'LL MANAGE SOMEHOW** *Laurel LAUCD 4*	49		
1 Jul 95	**DAYDREAMER** *Laurel LAUCD 5*	14		3
30 Sep 95	**STARDUST** *Laurel LAUCD 6*	16		2
16 Dec 95	**SLEEPING IN** *Laurel LAUCD 7*	24		1
23 Mar 96	**BEING BRAVE** *Laurel LAUCD 8*	10		2
7 Sep 96	**WE LOVE YOU** *Laurel LAUCD 11*	22		1

MENTAL AS ANYTHING
Australian/New Zealand group

Date	Title	Peak Position	Weeks at No.1	Weeks in Top 40
7 Feb 87	**LIVE IT UP** *Epic ANY 1* ○	3		10

FREDDIE MERCURY UK singer

Date	Title	Peak Position	Weeks at No.1	Weeks in Top 40
22 Sep 84	**LOVE KILLS** *CBS A 4735*	10		6
20 Apr 85	**I WAS BORN TO LOVE YOU** *CBS A 6019*	11		8
13 Jul 85	**MADE IN HEAVEN** *CBS A 6413*	57		
21 Sep 85	**LIVING ON MY OWN** *CBS A 6555*	50		
24 May 86	**TIME** *EMI 5559*	32		4
7 Mar 87	**THE GREAT PRETENDER** *Parlophone R 6151*	4		8
7 Nov 87	**BARCELONA** *Polydor POSP 887* FREDDIE MERCURY & MONTSERRAT CABALLE	8		5
8 Aug 92	**BARCELONA** *Polydor PO 221* FREDDIE MERCURY & MONTSERRAT CABALLE	2		6
12 Dec 92	**IN MY DEFENCE** *Parlophone R 6331*	8		5
6 Feb 93	**THE GREAT PRETENDER** *Parlophone CDR 6336*	29		2
31 Jul 93	**LIVING ON MY OWN (REMIX)** *Parlophone CDR 6355* ●	1	2	11

MERCURY REV US group

Date	Title	Peak Position	Weeks at No.1	Weeks in Top 40
14 Nov 98	**GODDESS ON A HIWAY** *V2 VVR 5003323*	51		
6 Feb 99	**DELTA SUN BOTTLENECK STOMP** *V2 VVR 5005413*	26		1
22 May 99	**OPUS 40** *V2 VVR 5006963*	31		1
28 Aug 99	**GODDESS ON A HIWAY** *V2 VVR 5008498*	26		1
6 Oct 01	**NITE AND FOG** *V2 VVR 5017728*	47		
26 Jan 02	**THE DARK IS RISING** *V2 VVR 5018713*	16		2
27 Jul 02	**LITTLE RHYMES** *V2 VVR 5019788*	51		
29 Jan 05	**IN A FUNNY WAY** *V2 VVR 5029223*	28		1
2 Apr 05	**ACROSS YER OCEAN** *V2 VVR5031033*	54		

MERCY MERCY UK group

Date	Title	Peak Position	Weeks at No.1	Weeks in Top 40
21 Sep 85	**WHAT ARE WE GONNA DO ABOUT IT?** *Ensign ENY 522*	59		

MERLIN UK rapper

Date	Title	Peak Position	Weeks at No.1	Weeks in Top 40
27 Aug 88	**MEGABLAST/DON'T MAKE ME WAIT** *Mister-ron DOOD 2* BOMB THE BASS FEATURING MERLIN & ANTONIA/BOMB THE BASS FEATURING LORRAINE	6		8
22 Apr 89	**WHO'S IN THE HOUSE** *Rhythm King LEFT 31* BEATMASTERS FEATURING MERLIN	8		7

MERO UK duo

Date	Title	Peak Position	Weeks at No.1	Weeks in Top 40
25 Mar 00	**IT MUST BE LOVE** *RCA 74321664772*	33		1

TONY MERRICK UK singer

Date	Title	Peak Position	Weeks at No.1	Weeks in Top 40
2 Jun 66	**LADY JANE** *Columbia DB 7913*	49		

AVID MERRION/DAVINA McCALL/ PATSY KENSIT UK comedian/TV presenter/actress

Date	Title	Peak Position	Weeks at No.1	Weeks in Top 40
25 Dec 04	**I GOT YOU BABE/SODA POP** *BMG 82876669872*	5		4

MERSEYBEATS UK group

Date	Title	Peak Position	Weeks at No.1	Weeks in Top 40
12 Sep 63	**IT'S LOVE THAT REALLY COUNTS** *Fontana TF 412*	24		10
16 Jan 64	**I THINK OF YOU** *Fontana TF 431*	5		14
16 Apr 64	**DON'T TURN AROUND** *Fontana TF 459*	13		8
9 Jul 64	**WISHIN' AND HOPIN'** *Fontana TF 482*	13		9
5 Nov 64	**LAST NIGHT** *Fontana TF 504*	40		1
14 Oct 65	**I LOVE YOU, YES I DO** *Fontana TF 607*	22		5
20 Jan 66	**I STAND ACCUSED** *Fontana TF 645*	38		1

MERSEYS UK duo

Date	Title	Peak Position	Weeks at No.1	Weeks in Top 40
28 Apr 66	**SORROW** *Fontana TF 694*	4		11

MERTON PARKAS UK group

Date	Title	Peak Position	Weeks at No.1	Weeks in Top 40
4 Aug 79	**YOU NEED WHEELS** *Beggars Banquet BEG 22*	40		1

MERZ UK singer

Date	Title	Peak Position	Weeks at No.1	Weeks in Top 40
17 Jul 99	**MANY WEATHERS APART** *Epic 6674972*	48		
16 Oct 99	**LOVELY DAUGHTER** *Epic 6679132*	60		

MESH 29 UK group

Date	Title	Peak Position	Weeks at No.1	Weeks in Top 40
14 Jul 07	**OVER THE BARRICADE** *Download*	35		1

MADY MESPLE & DANIELLE MILLET
French duo

Date	Title	Peak Position	Weeks at No.1	Weeks in Top 40
6 Apr 85	**FLOWER DUET (FROM LAKME)** *EMI 5481* MADY MESPLE & DANIELLE MILLET WITH THE PARIS OPERACOMIQUE ORCHESTRA CONDUCTED BY ALAIN LOMBARD	47		

Silver-selling ○ · Gold-selling ● · Platinum-selling ⊛ · US No.1 ★ · Peak Position · Weeks at No.1 · Weeks in Top 40

MESSIAH UK duo

Date	Title	Peak Position	Weeks at No.1	Weeks in Top 40
20 Jun 92	**TEMPLE OF DREAMS** *Kickin KICK 125*	20		4
26 Sep 92	**I FEEL LOVE** *Kickin KICK 225* MESSIAH FEATURING PRECIOUS WILSON	19		3
27 Nov 93	**THUNDERDOME** *WEA YZ 790CD1*	29		2

METAL GURUS UK group

Date	Title	Peak Position	Weeks at No.1	Weeks in Top 40
8 Dec 90	**MERRY XMAS EVERYBODY** *Mercury GURU 1*	55		

METALLICA US group

Date	Title	Peak Position	Weeks at No.1	Weeks in Top 40
22 Aug 87	**THE $5.98 EP - GARAGE DAYS REVISITED** *Vertigo METAL 112*	27		3
3 Sep 88	**HARVESTER OF SORROW** *Vertigo METAL 212*	20		2
22 Apr 89	**ONE** *Vertigo METAL 5*	13		5
10 Aug 91	**ENTER SANDMAN** *Vertigo METAL 7*	5		3
9 Nov 91	**THE UNFORGIVEN** *Vertigo METAL 8*	15		3
2 May 92	**NOTHING ELSE MATTERS** *Vertigo METAL 10*	6		5
31 Oct 92	**WHEREVER I MAY ROAM** *Vertigo METAL 9*	25		3
20 Feb 93	**SAD BUT TRUE** *Vertigo METCD 11*	20		2
1 Jun 96	**UNTIL IT SLEEPS** *Vertigo UKMETCX 12*	5		3
28 Sep 96	**HERO OF THE DAY** *Vertigo METCD 13*	17		2
7 Dec 96	**MAMA SAID** *Vertigo METCD 14*	19		1
22 Nov 97	**THE MEMORY REMAINS** *Vertigo METCD 15*	13		2
7 Mar 98	**THE UNFORGIVEN II** *Vertigo METDD 17*	15		2
4 Jul 98	**FUEL** *Vertigo METCD 16*	31		1
27 Feb 99	**WHISKEY IN THE JAR** *Vertigo METCD 19*	29		1
12 Aug 00	**I DISAPPEAR** *Hollywood 0113875 HWR*	35		1
5 Jul 03	**ST ANGER** *Vertigo 9865413*	9		3
4 Oct 03	**FRANTIC** *Vertigo 9811514*	16		2
24 Jan 04	**THE UNNAMED FEELING** *Vertigo 9815881*	42		

METEOR SEVEN German producer

Date	Title	Peak Position	Weeks at No.1	Weeks in Top 40
18 May 02	**UNIVERSAL MUSIC** *Bulletproof PROOF 16CD*	71		

METEORS UK group

Date	Title	Peak Position	Weeks at No.1	Weeks in Top 40
26 Feb 83	**JOHNNY REMEMBER ME** *ID EYE 1*	66		

METHOD MAN US rapper

Date	Title	Peak Position	Weeks at No.1	Weeks in Top 40
29 Apr 95	**RELEASE YO' SELF** *Def Jam DEFCD 6*	46		
29 Jul 95	**I'LL BE THERE FOR YOU – YOU'RE ALL I NEED TO GET BY** *Def Jam DEFDX11* METHOD MAN FEATURING MARY J BLIGE	10		3
5 Apr 97	**HIT 'EM HIGH (THE MONSTARS' ANTHEM)** *Atlantic A 5449CD* B REAL/BUSTA RHYMES/COOLIO/LL COOL J/METHOD MAN	8		4
22 May 99	**BREAK UPS 2 MAKE UPS** *Def Jam 8709272* METHOD MAN FEATURING D'ANGELO	33		1
27 Sep 03	**LOVE @ 1ST SIGHT** *MCA MCSTD 40338* MARY J BLIGE FEATURING METHOD MAN	18		3
22 May 04	**WHAT'S HAPPENIN'** *Def Jam 9862518* METHOD MAN FEATURING BUSTA RHYMES	17		3

METRIC Canadian group

Date	Title	Peak Position	Weeks at No.1	Weeks in Top 40
19 Aug 06	**MONSTER HOSPITAL** *Drowned In Sound DISO021CD*	55		

MEW Danish group

Date	Title	Peak Position	Weeks at No.1	Weeks in Top 40
5 Apr 03	**COMFORTING SOUNDS** *Epic 6736432*	48		
28 Jun 03	**AM I WRY NO** *Epic 6739395*	47		
27 Dec 03	**SHE CAME HOME FOR CHRISTMAS** *Epic 6744942*	55		
30 Jul 05	**APOCALYPSO** *Evil Office EVIL02*	75		
1 Oct 05	**SPECIAL** *Evil Office 6760621*	46		
18 Feb 06	**WHY ARE YOU LOOKING GRAVE?** *Evil Office 82876755712*	53		

MEZZOFORTE Icelandic group

Date	Title	Peak Position	Weeks at No.1	Weeks in Top 40
5 Mar 83	**GARDEN PARTY** *Steinar STE 705*	17		6
11 Jun 83	**ROCKALL** *Steinar STE 710*	75		

MFSB US group

Date	Title	Peak Position	Weeks at No.1	Weeks in Top 40
27 Apr 74	**TSOP (THE SOUND OF PHILADELPHIA)** *Philadelphia International PIR 2289* MFSB FEATURING THE THREE DEGREES ★	22		6
26 Jul 75	**SEXY** *Philadelphia International PIR 3381*	37		3
31 Jan 81	**MYSTERIES OF THE WORLD** *Sound Of Philadelphia PIR 9501*	41		

MGMT US group

Date	Title	Peak Position	Weeks at No.1	Weeks in Top 40
15 Mar 08	**TIME TO PRETEND** *Columbia 88697235412*	49		

MIA UK singer

Date	Title	Peak Position	Weeks at No.1	Weeks in Top 40
13 Oct 07	**JIMMY** *XL Recordings XLS287CD*	66		

MIAMI SOUND MACHINE US group

Date	Title	Peak Position	Weeks at No.1	Weeks in Top 40
11 Aug 84	**DR BEAT** *Epic A 4614* ○	6		10
17 May 86	**BAD BOY** *Epic A 6537*	16		8
16 Jul 88	**ANYTHING FOR YOU** *Epic 6516737* GLORIA ESTEFAN & MIAMI SOUND MACHINE ★	10		10
22 Oct 88	**1-2-3-** *Epic 6529587* GLORIA ESTEFAN & MIAMI SOUND MACHINE	9		6
17 Dec 88	**RHYTHM IS GONNA GET YOU** *Epic 6545147* GLORIA ESTEFAN & MIAMI SOUND MACHINE	16		6
11 Feb 89	**CAN'T STAY AWAY FROM YOU** *Epic 6514447* GLORIA ESTEFAN & MIAMI SOUND MACHINE	7		9
17 Sep 05	**DOCTOR PRESSURE** *Breastfed BFD017CD2* MYLO VS MIAMI SOUND MACHINE	3		13

GEORGE MICHAEL UK singer

Date	Title	Peak Position	Weeks at No.1	Weeks in Top 40
4 Aug 84	**CARELESS WHISPER** *Epic A 4603* ⊛ ★	1	3	15
5 Apr 86	**A DIFFERENT CORNER** *Epic A 7033* ●	1	3	9
31 Jan 87	**I KNEW YOU WERE WAITIN' FOR ME** *Epic DUET 2* ARETHA FRANKLIN & GEORGE MICHAEL ● ★	1	2	8
13 Jun 87	**I WANT YOUR SEX** *Epic LUST 1*	3		7
24 Oct 87	**FAITH** *Epic EMU 3* ★	2		7
9 Jan 88	**FATHER FIGURE** *Epic EMU 4* ★	11		4
23 Apr 88	**ONE MORE TRY** *Epic EMU 5* ★	8		5
16 Jul 88	**MONKEY** *Epic EMU 6* ★	13		5
3 Dec 88	**KISSING A FOOL** *Epic EMU 7*	18		4
25 Aug 90	**PRAYING FOR TIME** *Epic GEO 1* ★	6		5
27 Oct 90	**WAITING FOR THAT DAY** *Epic GEO 2*	23		4
15 Dec 90	**FREEDOM 90** *Epic GEO 3*	28		4
16 Feb 91	**HEAL THE PAIN** *Epic 6566477*	31		3
30 Mar 91	**COWBOYS AND ANGELS** *Epic 6567747*	45		
7 Dec 91	**DON'T LET THE SUN GO DOWN ON ME** *Epic 6576467* GEORGE MICHAEL & ELTON JOHN ○ ★	1	2	7
13 Jun 92	**TOOFUNKY** *Epic 6580587*	4		7
1 May 93	**FIVE LIVE EP** *Parlophone CDRS 6340* GEORGE MICHAEL & QUEEN WITH LISA STANSFIELD ●	1	3	9
20 Jan 96	**JESUS TO A CHILD** *Virgin VSCDG 1571* ○	1	1	6
4 May 96	**FASTLOVE** *Virgin VSCDG 1579* ●	1	3	10
31 Aug 96	**SPINNING THE WHEEL** *Virgin VSCDG 1595* ○	2		9
1 Feb 97	**OLDER/I CAN'T MAKE YOU LOVE ME** *Virgin VSCDG 1626*	3		4
10 May 97	**STAR PEOPLE '97** *Virgin VSCDG 1641*	2		4
7 Jun 97	**WALTZ AWAY DREAMING** *Aegean AECD 01* TOBY BOURKE/GEORGE MICHAEL	10		3
20 Sep 97	**YOU HAVE BEEN LOVED/THE STRANGEST THING '97** *Virgin VSCD 1663*	2		4
31 Oct 98	**OUTSIDE** *Epic 6665625* ○	2		8
13 Mar 99	**AS** *Epic 6670122* GEORGE MICHAEL & MARY J BLIGE ○	4		7
17 Jun 00	**IF I TOLD YOU THAT** *Arista 74321766282* WHITNEY HOUSTON & GEORGE MICHAEL	9		4
30 Mar 02	**FREEEK!** *Polydor 5706822*	7		3
10 Aug 02	**SHOOT THE DOG** *Polydor 5709242*	12		2
13 Mar 04	**AMAZING** *Aegean 6747265*	4		5
10 Jul 04	**FLAWLESS (GO TO THE CITY)** *Aegean 6750682*	8		6
13 Nov 04	**ROUND HERE** *Aegean/Sony 6754702*	32		1
8 Jul 06	**AN EASIER AFFAIR** *Epic 82876869462*	13		3
18 Nov 06	**THIS IS NOT REAL LOVE** *Aegean/Sony 88697019792* GEORGE MICHAEL & MUTYA	15		3

MICHAELA UK singer

Date	Title	Peak Position	Weeks at No.1	Weeks in Top 40
2 Sep 89	**H-A-P-P-Y RADIO** *London H 1*	62		
28 Apr 90	**TAKE GOOD CARE OF MY HEART** *London WAC 90*	66		

PRAS MICHEL US rapper

Date	Title	Peak Position	Weeks at No.1	Weeks in Top 40
27 Jun 98	**GHETTO SUPERSTAR (THAT IS WHAT YOU ARE)** *Interscope IND 95593* PRAS MICHEL FEATURING OL' DIRTY BASTARD INTRODUCING MYA ⊛	2		14

Silver-selling ○ Gold-selling ● Platinum-selling US No.1 ★ — Peak Position / Weeks at No.1 / Weeks in Top 40

Date	Title / Label	Peak Position	Weeks at No.1	Weeks in Top 40
7 Nov 98	**BLUE ANGELS** *Ruffhouse 6666215*	6		5
14 Nov 98	**ANOTHER ONE BITES THE DUST** *DreamWorks DRMCD 22364* QUEEN WITH WYCLEF JEAN FEATURING PRAS MICHEL/FREE	5		4
1 Sep 01	**MISS CALIFORNIA** *Elektra E 7192CD* DANTE THOMAS FEATURING PRAS	25		1

KEITH MICHELL Australian actor

Date	Title / Label	Peak Position	Weeks at No.1	Weeks in Top 40
27 Mar 71	**I'LL GIVE YOU THE EARTH (TOUS LES BATEAUX, TOUS LES OISEAUX)** *Spark SRL 1046*	30		5
26 Jan 80	**CAPTAIN BEAKY/WILFRED THE WEASEL** *Polydor POSP 106* ○	5		7
29 Mar 80	**THE TRIAL OF HISSING SID** *Polydor HISS 1* KEITH MICHELL, CAPTAIN BEAKY & HIS BAND	53		

MICHELLE Trinidadian singer

Date	Title / Label	Peak Position	Weeks at No.1	Weeks in Top 40
8 Jun 96	**STANDING HERE ALL ALONE** *Positiva CDTIV 54*	69		
17 Jan 04	**ALL THIS TIME** *S 82876590652*	1	3	9
17 Apr 04	**THE MEANING OF LOVE** *S 82876604032*	16		2

YVETTE MICHELLE US singer

Date	Title / Label	Peak Position	Weeks at No.1	Weeks in Top 40
5 Apr 97	**I'M NOT FEELING YOU** *Loud 74321465222*	36		1

MICROBE UK singer

Date	Title / Label	Peak Position	Weeks at No.1	Weeks in Top 40
14 May 69	**GROOVY BABY** *CBS 4158*	29		6

MICRODISNEY Irish group

Date	Title / Label	Peak Position	Weeks at No.1	Weeks in Top 40
21 Feb 87	**TOWN TO TOWN** *Virgin VS 927*	55		

MIDAS UK group

Date	Title / Label	Peak Position	Weeks at No.1	Weeks in Top 40
31 Mar 07	**DON'T DANCE** *Midas MID001*	59		

MIDDLE OF THE ROAD UK group

Date	Title / Label	Peak Position	Weeks at No.1	Weeks in Top 40
5 Jun 71	**CHIRPY CHIRPY CHEEP CHEEP** *RCA 2047*	1	5	23
4 Sep 71	**TWEEDLE DEE TWEEDLE DUM** *RCA 2110*	2		14
11 Dec 71	**SOLEY SOLEY** *RCA 2151*	5		11
25 Mar 72	**SACRAMENTO (A WONDERFUL TOWN)** *RCA 2184*	23		5
29 Jul 72	**SAMSON AND DELILAH** *RCA 2237*	26		4

MIDDLESBROUGH F.C. UK football club

Date	Title / Label	Peak Position	Weeks at No.1	Weeks in Top 40
24 May 97	**LET'S DANCE** *Magnet EW 112CD* MIDDLESBROUGH FC FEATURING BOB MORTIMER & CHRIS REA	44		

MALCOLM MIDDLETON UK singer/guitarist

Date	Title / Label	Peak Position	Weeks at No.1	Weeks in Top 40
29 Dec 07	**WE'RE ALL GOING TO DIE** *Full Time Hobby FTH045S*	31		1

MIDFIELD GENERAL UK producer with singer

Date	Title / Label	Peak Position	Weeks at No.1	Weeks in Top 40
19 Aug 00	**REACH OUT** *Skint 54CD* MIDFIELD GENERAL FEATURING LINDA LEWIS	61		

MIDGET UK group

Date	Title / Label	Peak Position	Weeks at No.1	Weeks in Top 40
31 Jan 98	**ALL FALL DOWN** *Radarscope TINYCDS 6X*	57		
18 Apr 98	**INVISIBLE BALLOON** *Radarscope TINYCDS 7*	66		

MIDI XPRESS UK duo

Date	Title / Label	Peak Position	Weeks at No.1	Weeks in Top 40
11 May 96	**CHASE** *Labello Dance LAD 26CD*	73		

BETTE MIDLER US singer/actress

Date	Title / Label	Peak Position	Weeks at No.1	Weeks in Top 40
17 Jun 89	**WIND BENEATH MY WINGS** *Atlantic A 8972* ★	5		8
13 Oct 90	**FROM A DISTANCE** *Atlantic A 7820*	45		
15 Jun 91	**FROM A DISTANCE** *Atlantic A 7820*	6		7
5 Dec 98	**MY ONE TRUE FRIEND** *Warner Brothers W 460CD*	58		

MIDNIGHT COWBOY SOUNDTRACK US orchestra

Date	Title / Label	Peak Position	Weeks at No.1	Weeks in Top 40
8 Nov 80	**MIDNIGHT COWBOY** *United Artists UP 634*	47		

MIDNIGHT OIL Australian group

Date	Title / Label	Peak Position	Weeks at No.1	Weeks in Top 40
23 Apr 88	**BEDS ARE BURNING** *Sprint OIL 1*	48		
2 Jul 88	**THE DEAD HEART** *Sprint OIL 2*	68		
25 Mar 89	**BEDS ARE BURNING** *Sprint OIL 3*	6		8
1 Jul 89	**THE DEAD HEART** *Sprint OIL 4*	62		
10 Feb 90	**BLUE SKY MINE** *CBS OIL 5*	66		
17 Apr 93	**TRUGANINI** *Columbia 6590492*	29		1
3 Jul 93	**MY COUNTRY** *Columbia 6593702*	66		
6 Nov 93	**IN THE VALLEY** *Columbia 6598492*	60		

MIDNIGHT STAR US group

Date	Title / Label	Peak Position	Weeks at No.1	Weeks in Top 40
23 Feb 85	**OPERATOR** *Solar MCA 942*	66		
28 Jun 86	**HEADLINES** *Solar MCA 1065*	16		6
4 Oct 86	**MIDAS TOUCH** *Solar MCA 1096*	8		8
7 Feb 87	**ENGINE NO 9** *Solar MCA 1117*	64		
2 May 87	**WET MY WHISTLE** *Solar MCA 1127*	60		

MIGHTY AVENGERS UK group

Date	Title / Label	Peak Position	Weeks at No.1	Weeks in Top 40
26 Nov 64	**SO MUCH IN LOVE** *Decca F 11962*	46		

MIGHTY DUB KATZ UK singer

Date	Title / Label	Peak Position	Weeks at No.1	Weeks in Top 40
7 Dec 96	**JUST ANOTHER GROOVE** *ffrr FCD 287*	43		
2 Aug 97	**MAGIC CARPET RIDE** *ffrr FCD 306*	24		2
7 Dec 02	**LET THE DRUMS SPEAK** *Southern Fried ECB 31X*	73		

MIGHTY LEMON DROPS UK group

Date	Title / Label	Peak Position	Weeks at No.1	Weeks in Top 40
13 Sep 86	**THE OTHER SIDE OF YOU** *Blue Guitar AZUR 1*	67		
18 Apr 87	**OUT OF HAND** *Blue Guitar AZUR 4*	66		
23 Jan 88	**INSIDE OUT** *Blue Guitar AZUR 6*	74		

MIGHTY MIGHTY BOSSTONES US group

Date	Title / Label	Peak Position	Weeks at No.1	Weeks in Top 40
25 Apr 98	**THE IMPRESSION THAT I GET** *Mercury 5748432*	12		3
27 Jun 98	**THE RASCAL KING** *Mercury 5661092*	63		

MIGHTY MORPH'N POWER RANGERS US TV characters

Date	Title / Label	Peak Position	Weeks at No.1	Weeks in Top 40
17 Dec 94	**POWER RANGERS** *RCA 74321253022* ○	3		6

MIGIL FIVE UK group

Date	Title / Label	Peak Position	Weeks at No.1	Weeks in Top 40
19 Mar 64	**MOCKIN' BIRD HILL** *Pye 7N 15597*	10		10
4 Jun 64	**NEAR YOU** *Pye 7N 15645*	31		4

MIG29 Italian production group

Date	Title / Label	Peak Position	Weeks at No.1	Weeks in Top 40
22 Feb 92	**MIG29** *Champion CHAMP 292*	62		

MIKA Lebanese singer

Date	Title / Label	Peak Position	Weeks at No.1	Weeks in Top 40
20 Jan 07	**GRACE KELLY** *Island 1721083* ○	1	4	23
17 Feb 07	**LOLLIPOP** *Download*	59		
7 Apr 07	**LOVE TODAY** *Casablanca/Island 1732069*	6		11
14 Jul 07	**BIG GIRL (YOU ARE BEAUTIFUL)** *Casablanca/Island 1741590*	9		10
13 Oct 07	**HAPPY ENDING** *Casablanca/Island 1749143*	7		13
29 Dec 07	**RELAX TAKE IT EASY** *Casablanca/Island 1706314*	18		10

MIKE UK producer

Date	Title / Label	Peak Position	Weeks at No.1	Weeks in Top 40
19 Nov 94	**TWANGLING THREE FINGERS IN A BOX** *Pukka CDMIKE 100*	40		1

MIKE + THE MECHANICS UK group

Date	Title / Label	Peak Position	Weeks at No.1	Weeks in Top 40
15 Feb 86	**SILENT RUNNING (ON DANGEROUS GROUND)** *WEA U 8908*	21		5
31 May 86	**ALL I NEED IS A MIRACLE** *WEA U 8765*	53		
14 Jan 89	**THE LIVING YEARS** *WEA U 7717* ● ★	2		9

Date	Title / Label	Peak Position	Weeks at No.1	Weeks in Top 40
16 Mar 91	**WORD OF MOUTH** *Virgin VS 1345*	13		6
15 Jun 91	**A TIME AND PLACE** *Virgin VS 1351*	58		
8 Feb 92	**EVERYBODY GETS A SECOND CHANCE** *Virgin VS 1396*	56		
25 Feb 95	**OVER MY SHOULDER** *Virgin VSCDX 1526*	12		6
17 Jun 95	**A BEGGAR ON A BEACH OF GOLD** *Virgin VSCD 1535*	33		2
2 Sep 95	**ANOTHER CUP OF COFFEE** *Virgin VSCDT 1554*	51		
17 Feb 96	**ALL I NEED IS A MIRACLE '96** *Virgin VSCDG 1576*	27		2
1 Jun 96	**SILENT RUNNING** *Virgin VSCDT 1585*	61		
5 Jun 99	**NOW THAT YOU'VE GONE** *Virgin VSCD 1732*	35		1
28 Aug 99	**WHENEVER I STOP** *Virgin VSCDT 1743*	73		

MIKI & GRIFF UK duo

Date	Title / Label	Peak Position	Weeks at No.1	Weeks in Top 40
2 Oct 59	**HOLD BACK TOMORROW** *Pye 7N 15213*	26		2
13 Oct 60	**ROCKIN' ALONE** *Pye 7N 15296*	44		
1 Feb 62	**LITTLE BITTY TEAR** *Pye 7N 15412*	16		10
22 Aug 63	**I WANNA STAY HERE** *Pye 7N 15555*	23		5

MILBURN UK group

Date	Title / Label	Peak Position	Weeks at No.1	Weeks in Top 40
8 Apr 06	**SEND IN THE BOYS** *Mercury 9853112*	22		1
22 Jul 06	**CHESHIRE CAT SMILE** *Mercury 9858662*	32		1
11 Nov 06	**WHAT YOU COULD'VE WON** *Mercury 1708383*	66		
29 Sep 07	**WHAT WILL YOU DO (WHEN THE MONEY GOES)** *Mercury 1744520*	44		

JOHN MILES UK singer/multi-instrumentalist

Date	Title / Label	Peak Position	Weeks at No.1	Weeks in Top 40
18 Oct 75	**HIGH FLY** *Decca F 13595*	17		5
20 Mar 76	**MUSIC** *Decca F 13627* ○	3		8
16 Oct 76	**REMEMBER YESTERDAY** *Decca F 13667*	32		3
18 Jun 77	**SLOW DOWN** *Decca F 13709*	10		9

ROBERT MILES Italian producer

Date	Title / Label	Peak Position	Weeks at No.1	Weeks in Top 40
24 Feb 96	**CHILDREN** *Deconstruction 74321348322* ⊛	2		16
8 Jun 96	**FABLE** *Deconstruction 74321382622*	7		5
16 Nov 96	**ONE & ONE** *Deconstruction 74321427692* ROBERT MILES FEATURING MARIA NAYLER ●	3		13
29 Nov 97	**FREEDOM** *Deconstruction 74321536952* ROBERT MILES FEATURING KATHY SLEDGE	15		2
28 Jul 01	**PATHS** *Salt 002CDX* ROBERT MILES FEATURING NINA MIRANDA	74		

CHRISTINA MILIAN US singer

Date	Title / Label	Peak Position	Weeks at No.1	Weeks in Top 40
3 Mar 01	**BETWEEN YOU AND ME** *Def Jam 5727402* JA RULE FEATURING CHRISTINA MILIAN	26		1
26 Jan 02	**AM TO PM** *Def Soul 5889332*	3		7
29 Jun 02	**WHEN YOU LOOK AT ME** *Def Soul 5829802*	3		8
9 Nov 02	**IT'S ALL GRAVY** *Relentless RELENT 32CD* ROMEO FEATURING CHRISTINA MILIAN	9		4
15 May 04	**DIP IT LOW** *Def Jam UK 9862395*	2		9
16 Oct 04	**WHATEVER U WANT** *Def Jam 9864266* CHRISTINA MILIAN FEATURING JOE BUDDEN	9		4
20 May 06	**SAY I** *Def Jam 9857779* CHRISTINA MILIAN FEATURING YOUNG JEEZY	4		6

MILK & HONEY Israeli group

Date	Title / Label	Peak Position	Weeks at No.1	Weeks in Top 40
14 Apr 79	**HALLELUJAH** *Polydor 2001 870* MILK & HONEY FEATURING GALI ATARI ○	5		6

MILK & SUGAR German production duo

Date	Title / Label	Peak Position	Weeks at No.1	Weeks in Top 40
12 Jan 02	**LOVE IS IN THE AIR** *Positiva CDTIV 166* MILK & SUGAR/JOHN PAUL YOUNG	25		2
11 Oct 03	**LET THE SUNSHINE IN** *Data 64CDS* MILK & SUGAR FEATURING LIZZY PATTINSON	18		2

MILK INCORPORATED Belgian production group

Date	Title / Label	Peak Position	Weeks at No.1	Weeks in Top 40
28 Feb 98	**GOOD ENOUGH (LA VACHE)** *Malarky MLKD 5*	23		1
25 May 02	**IN MY EYES** *All Around The World CDGLOBE 252*	9		5
21 Sep 02	**WALK ON WATER** *Positiva CDTIV 179*	10		4
11 Jan 03	**LAND OF THE LIVING** *Positiva CDTIV 184*	18		2

MILKY German singer

Date	Title / Label	Peak Position	Weeks at No.1	Weeks in Top 40
31 Aug 02	**JUST THE WAY YOU ARE** *Multiply CDMULTY 87*	8		4
7 Dec 02	**IN MY MIND** *Multiply CDMULTY 92*	48		

MILLA US singer

Date	Title / Label	Peak Position	Weeks at No.1	Weeks in Top 40
18 Jun 94	**GENTLEMAN WHO FELL** *SBK CDSBK 49*	65		

FRANKIE MILLER UK singer

Date	Title / Label	Peak Position	Weeks at No.1	Weeks in Top 40
4 Jun 77	**BE GOOD TO YOURSELF** *Chrysalis CHS 2147*	27		5
14 Oct 78	**DARLIN'** *Chrysalis CHS 2255* ○	6		10
20 Jan 79	**WHEN I'M AWAY FROM YOU** *Chrysalis CHS 2276*	42		
21 Mar 92	**CALEDONIA** *MCS 2001*	45		

GARY MILLER UK singer

Date	Title / Label	Peak Position	Weeks at No.1	Weeks in Top 40
21 Oct 55	**YELLOW ROSE OF TEXAS** *Pye Nixa N 15004*	13		5
13 Jan 56	**ROBIN HOOD** *Pye Nixa N 15020*	10		6
11 Jan 57	**GARDEN OF EDEN** *Pye Nixa N 15070*	14		7
19 Jul 57	**WONDERFUL WONDERFUL** *Pye Nixa N 15094*	29		1
17 Jan 58	**STORY OF MY LIFE** *Pye Nixa N 15120*	14		6
21 Dec 61	**THERE GOES THAT SONG AGAIN/THE NIGHT IS YOUNG** *Pye Nixa N 15404*	29		8

GLENN MILLER US orchestra leader/trombonist

Date	Title / Label	Peak Position	Weeks at No.1	Weeks in Top 40
12 Mar 54	**MOONLIGHT SERENADE** *HMV BD 5942*	12		1
24 Jan 76	**MOONLIGHT SERENADE/LITTLE BROWN JUG/IN THE MOOD** *RCA 2644*	13		7

JODY MILLER US singer

Date	Title / Label	Peak Position	Weeks at No.1	Weeks in Top 40
21 Oct 65	**HOME OF THE BRAVE** *Capitol CL 15415*	49		

MITCH MILLER US orchestra leader

Date	Title / Label	Peak Position	Weeks at No.1	Weeks in Top 40
7 Oct 55	**YELLOW ROSE OF TEXAS** *Philips PB 505* ★	2		13

NED MILLER US singer

Date	Title / Label	Peak Position	Weeks at No.1	Weeks in Top 40
14 Feb 63	**FROM A JACK TO A KING** *London HL 9658*	2		19
18 Feb 65	**DO WHAT YOU DO WELL** *London HL 9937*	48		

ROGER MILLER US singer

Date	Title / Label	Peak Position	Weeks at No.1	Weeks in Top 40
18 Mar 65	**KING OF THE ROAD** *Philips BF 1397*	1	1	15
3 Jun 65	**ENGINE ENGINE NO. 9** *Philips BF 1416*	33		3
21 Oct 65	**KANSAS CITY STAR** *Philips BF 1437*	48		
16 Dec 65	**ENGLAND SWINGS** *Philips BF 1456*	13		7
27 Mar 68	**LITTLE GREEN APPLES** *Mercury MF 1021*	19		9
2 Apr 69	**LITTLE GREEN APPLES** *Mercury MF 1021*	39		1

STEVE MILLER BAND US group

Date	Title / Label	Peak Position	Weeks at No.1	Weeks in Top 40
23 Oct 76	**ROCK 'N ME** *Mercury 6078 804*	11		7
19 Jun 82	**ABRACADABRA** *Mercury STEVE 3* ○ ★	2		9
4 Sep 82	**KEEPS IN ME IN WONDERLAND** *Mercury STEVE 4*	52		
11 Aug 90	**THE JOKER** *Capitol CL 583* ○ ★	1	2	10

SUZI MILLER & THE JOHNSTON BROTHERS UK singer and backing group

Date	Title / Label	Peak Position	Weeks at No.1	Weeks in Top 40
21 Jan 55	**HAPPY DAYS AND LONELY NIGHTS** *Decca F 10389*	14		2

LISA MILLETT UK singer

Date	Title / Label	Peak Position	Weeks at No.1	Weeks in Top 40
3 Sep 94	**WALKIN' ON** *Go! Beat GODCD 115* SHEER BRONZE FEATURING LISA MILLETT	63		
16 Sep 00	**BAD HABIT** *Defected DEFECT 8CDS* A.T.F.C. PRESENTS ONEPHATDEEVA FEATURING LISA MILLETT	17		2
21 Jul 01	**SOUL HEAVEN** *Direction 6713852* GOODFELLAS FEATURING LISA MILLETT	27		1
9 Feb 02	**SLEEP TALK** *Defected DFECT 43CDS* A.T.F.C. FEATURING LISA MILLETT	33		1

Silver-selling ● Gold-selling ● Platinum-selling ⊛ US No.1 ★ Peak Position Weeks at No.1 Weeks in Top 40

MILLI VANILLI French/German duo

Date	Title / Label	Peak Position	Weeks at No.1	Weeks in Top 40
1 Oct 88	**GIRL YOU KNOW IT'S TRUE** *Cooltempo COOL 170* ●	3		9
17 Dec 88	**BABY DON'T FORGET MY NUMBER** *Cooltempo COOL 178* ★	16		6
22 Jul 89	**BLAME IT ON THE RAIN** *Cooltempo COOL 180* ★	53		
30 Sep 89	**GIRL I'M GONNA MISS YOU** *Cooltempo COOL 191* ● ★	2		10
2 Dec 89	**BLAME IT ON THE RAIN** *Cooltempo COOL 180*	52		
10 Mar 90	**ALL OR NOTHING** *Cooltempo COOL 199*	74		

MILLICAN & NESBITT UK duo

Date	Title / Label	Peak Position	Weeks at No.1	Weeks in Top 40
1 Dec 73	**VAYA CON DOS** *Pye 7N 45310*	20		9
18 May 74	**FOR OLD TIME'S SAKE** *Pye 7N 45357*	38		1

MILLIE Jamaican singer

Date	Title / Label	Peak Position	Weeks at No.1	Weeks in Top 40
12 Mar 64	**MY BOY LOLLIPOP** *Fontana TF 449*	2		15
25 Jun 64	**SWEET WILLIAM** *Fontana TF 479*	30		6
11 Nov 65	**BLOODSHOT EYES** *Fontana TF 617*	48		
25 Jul 87	**MY BOY LOLLIPOP** *Island WIP 6574*	46		

MILLION DAN UK producer

Date	Title / Label	Peak Position	Weeks at No.1	Weeks in Top 40
27 Sep 03	**DOGZ N SLEDGEZ** *Gut CDGUT 52*	66		
12 Feb 05	**BOOM BLAST** *Against The Grain ATG010R* FREESTYLERS FEATURING MILLION DAN	75		

MILLION DEAD UK group

Date	Title / Label	Peak Position	Weeks at No.1	Weeks in Top 40
29 May 04	**I GAVE MY EYES TO STEVIE WONDER** *Xtra Mile XMR101*	72		
2 Apr 05	**LIVING THE DREAM** *Xtra Mile XMR105*	60		

MILLIONAIRE HIPPIES UK producer

Date	Title / Label	Peak Position	Weeks at No.1	Weeks in Top 40
18 Dec 93	**I AM THE MUSIC HEAR ME!** *Deconstruction 74321175432*	52		
10 Sep 94	**C'MON** *Deconstruction 74321229372*	59		

GARRY MILLS UK singer

Date	Title / Label	Peak Position	Weeks at No.1	Weeks in Top 40
7 Jul 60	**LOOK FOR A STAR** *Top Rank JAR 336*	7		11
20 Oct 60	**TOP TEEN BABY** *Top Rank JAR 500*	24		10
22 Jun 61	**I'LL STEP DOWN** *Decca F 11358*	39		1

HAYLEY MILLS UK actress

Date	Title / Label	Peak Position	Weeks at No.1	Weeks in Top 40
19 Oct 61	**LET'S GET TOGETHER** *Decca F 21396*	17		10

STEPHANIE MILLS US singer

Date	Title / Label	Peak Position	Weeks at No.1	Weeks in Top 40
18 Oct 80	**NEVER KNEW LOVE LIKE THIS BEFORE** *20th Century TC 2460* ●	4		11
23 May 81	**TWO HEARTS** *20th Century TC 2492* STEPHANIE MILLS FEATURING TEDDY PENDERGRASS	49		
15 Sep 84	**THE MEDICINE SONG** *Club JAB 8*	29		6
5 Sep 87	**(YOU'RE PUTTIN') A RUSH ON ME** *MCA 1187*	62		
1 May 93	**NEVER DO YOU WRONG** *MCA MCSTD 1767*	57		
10 Jul 93	**ALL DAY ALL NIGHT** *MCA MCSTD 1778*	68		

WARREN MILLS Zambian singer

Date	Title / Label	Peak Position	Weeks at No.1	Weeks in Top 40
28 Sep 85	**SUNSHINE** *Jive 99*	74		

MILLS BROTHERS US group

Date	Title / Label	Peak Position	Weeks at No.1	Weeks in Top 40
30 Jan 53	**GLOW WORM** *Brunswick 05007* ★	10		1

MILLTOWN BROTHERS UK group

Date	Title / Label	Peak Position	Weeks at No.1	Weeks in Top 40
2 Feb 91	**WHICH WAY SHOULD I JUMP** *A&M AM 711*	38		2
13 Apr 91	**HERE I STAND** *A&M AM 758*	41		
6 Jul 91	**APPLE GREEN** *A&M AM 787*	43		
22 May 93	**TURN OFF** *A&M 5802692*	55		
17 Jul 93	**IT'S ALL OVER NOW BABY BLUE** *A&M 5803332*	48		

MILLWALL F.C. UK football club

Date	Title / Label	Peak Position	Weeks at No.1	Weeks in Top 40
29 May 04	**OH MILLWALL** *Absolute CDAME4*	41		

C.B. MILTON Dutch singer

Date	Title / Label	Peak Position	Weeks at No.1	Weeks in Top 40
21 May 94	**IT'S A LOVING THING** *Logic 74321208062*	49		
25 Mar 95	**IT'S A LOVING THING (REMIX)** *Logic 74321267212*	34		1
19 Aug 95	**HOLD ON** *Logic 74321292112*	62		

GARNET MIMMS & TRUCKIN' CO US singer

Date	Title / Label	Peak Position	Weeks at No.1	Weeks in Top 40
25 Jun 77	**WHAT IT IS** *Arista 109*	44		

MIMS US rapper

Date	Title / Label	Peak Position	Weeks at No.1	Weeks in Top 40
12 May 07	**THIS IS WHY I'M HOT** *Capitol ANGECD43* ★	18		3

MIND OF KANE UK producer

Date	Title / Label	Peak Position	Weeks at No.1	Weeks in Top 40
27 Jul 91	**STABBED IN THE BACK** *Déjà Vu DJV 007*	64		

MINDBENDERS UK group

Date	Title / Label	Peak Position	Weeks at No.1	Weeks in Top 40
11 Jul 63	**HELLO JOSEPHINE** *Fontana TF 404* WAYNE FONTANA & THE MIND BENDERS	46		
28 May 64	**STOP LOOK AND LISTEN** *Fontana TF 451* WAYNE FONTANA & THE MIND BENDERS	37		2
8 Oct 64	**UM UM UM UM UM UM** *Fontana TF 497* WAYNE FONTANA & THE MIND BENDERS	5		14
4 Feb 65	**GAME OF LOVE** *Fontana TF 535* ★	2		9
17 Jun 65	**JUST A LITTLE BIT TOO LATE** *Fontana TF 579* WAYNE FONTANA & THE MIND BENDERS	20		5
30 Sep 65	**SHE NEEDS LOVE** *Fontana TF 611* WAYNE FONTANA & THE MIND BENDERS	32		4
13 Jan 66	**A GROOVY KIND OF LOVE** *Fontana TF 644*	2		14
5 May 66	**CAN'T LIVE WITH YOU (CAN'T LIVE WITHOUT YOU)** *Fontana TF 697*	28		6
25 Aug 66	**ASHES TO ASHES** *Fontana TF 731*	14		6
20 Sep 67	**THE LETTER** *Fontana TF 869*	42		

MINDS OF MEN UK group

Date	Title / Label	Peak Position	Weeks at No.1	Weeks in Top 40
22 Jun 96	**BRAND NEW DAY** *Perfecto PERF 121CD*	41		

SAL MINEO US actor

Date	Title / Label	Peak Position	Weeks at No.1	Weeks in Top 40
12 Jul 57	**START MOVIN' (IN MY DIRECTION)** *Philips PB 707*	16		11

MARCELLO MINERBI Italian orchestra leader

Date	Title / Label	Peak Position	Weeks at No.1	Weeks in Top 40
22 Jul 65	**ZORBA'S DANCE** *Durium DRS 54001*	6		14

MINI POPS UK group

Date	Title / Label	Peak Position	Weeks at No.1	Weeks in Top 40
26 Dec 87	**SONGS FOR CHRISTMAS '87 EP** *Bright BULB 9*	39		1

MINIMAL CHIC Italian production duo

Date	Title / Label	Peak Position	Weeks at No.1	Weeks in Top 40
2 Oct 04	**I NEED THE KEY** *Inferno CDFERN63* MINIMAL CHIC FEATURING MATT GOSS	54		

MINIMAL FUNK 2 Italian production duo

Date	Title / Label	Peak Position	Weeks at No.1	Weeks in Top 40
18 Jul 98	**THE GROOVY THANG** *Cleveland City CLECD 13046*	65		
18 May 02	**DEFINITION OF HOUSE** *Junior BRG 033*	63		

MINIMALISTIX Belgian production group

Date	Title / Label	Peak Position	Weeks at No.1	Weeks in Top 40
16 Mar 02	**CLOSE COVER** *Data 32CDS*	12		3
19 Jul 03	**MAGIC FLY** *Data 48CDS*	36		1

MINISTERS DE LA FUNK US production group

Date	Title / Label	Peak Position	Weeks at No.1	Weeks in Top 40
11 Mar 00	**BELIEVE** *Defected DFECT 14CDS* MINISTERS DE LA FUNK FEATURING JOCELYN BROWN	45		
27 Jan 01	**BELIEVE (REMIX)** *Defected DFECT 26CDS* MINISTERS DE LA FUNK FEATURING JOCELYN BROWN	42		

Key: ○ Silver-selling · ● Gold-selling · ⊛ Platinum-selling · ★ US No.1

MINISTRY US group

Date	Title / Label	Peak Position	Weeks at No.1	Weeks in Top 40
8 Aug 92	**NOW** *Sire W0125TE*	49		
6 Jan 96	**THE FALL** *Warner Brothers W0328CD*	53		

MINK DE VILLE UK group

Date	Title / Label	Peak Position	Weeks at No.1	Weeks in Top 40
6 Aug 77	**SPANISH STROLL** *Capitol CLX 103*	20		8

MINKY UK producer

Date	Title / Label	Peak Position	Weeks at No.1	Weeks in Top 40
30 Oct 99	**THE WEEKEND HAS LANDED** *Offbeat OFFCD 1001*	70		

LIZA MINNELLI US singer/actress

Date	Title / Label	Peak Position	Weeks at No.1	Weeks in Top 40
12 Aug 89	**LOSING MY MIND** *Epic ZEE 1*	6		5
7 Oct 89	**DON'T DROP BOMBS** *Epic ZEE 2*	46		
25 Nov 89	**SO SORRY I SAID** *Epic ZEE 3*	62		
3 Mar 90	**LOVE PAINS** *Epic ZEE 4*	41		

DANNII MINOGUE Australian singer

Date	Title / Label	Peak Position	Weeks at No.1	Weeks in Top 40
30 Mar 91	**LOVE AND KISSES** *MCA MCS 1529*	8		7
18 May 91	**SUCCESS** *MCA MCS 1538*	11		5
27 Jul 91	**JUMP TO THE BEAT** *MCA MCS 1556*	8		4
19 Oct 91	**BABY LOVE** *MCA MCS 1580*	14		4
14 Dec 91	**I DON'T WANNA TAKE THIS PAIN** *MCA MCS 1600*	40		1
1 Aug 92	**SHOW YOU THE WAY TO GO** *MCA MCS 1671*	30		2
12 Dec 92	**LOVE'S ON EVERY CORNER** *MCA MCSR 1723*	44		
17 Jul 93	**THIS IS IT** *MCA MCSTD 1790*	10		7
2 Oct 93	**THIS IS THE WAY** *MCA MCSTD 1935*	27		2
11 Jun 94	**GET INTO YOU** *Mushroom D 11751*	36		1
23 Aug 97	**ALL I WANNA DO** *Eternal WEA 119CD*	4		6
1 Nov 97	**EVERYTHING I WANTED** *Eternal WEA 137CD*	15		3
28 Mar 98	**DISREMEMBRANCE** *Eternal WEA 153CD*	21		1
1 Dec 01	**WHO DO YOU LOVE NOW (STRINGER)** *ffrr DFCD 002* RIVA FEATURING DANNII MINOGUE	3		9
16 Nov 02	**PUT THE NEEDLE ON IT** *London LONCD 470*	7		3
15 Mar 03	**I BEGIN TO WONDER** *London LONCD 473*	2		6
21 Jun 03	**DON'T WANNA LOSE THIS FEELING** *London LONCD 478*	5		3
6 Nov 04	**YOU WON'T FORGET ABOUT ME** *All Around The World CXGLOBE379* DANNII MINOGUE VS FLOWER POWER	7		3
29 Oct 05	**PERFECTION** *All Around The World CDGLOBE483* DANNII MINOGUE & SOUL SEEKERZ	11		1
24 Jun 06	**SO UNDER PRESSURE** *All Around The World CXGLOBE541*	20		1
15 Dec 07	**TOUCH ME LIKE THAT** *All Around The World CDGLOBE795* DANNII MINOGUE VS JASON NEVINS	48		

KYLIE MINOGUE Australian singer

Date	Title / Label	Peak Position	Weeks at No.1	Weeks in Top 40
23 Jan 88	**I SHOULD BE SO LUCKY** *PWL 8* ●	1	5	13
14 May 88	**GOT TO BE CERTAIN** *PWL 12* ○	2		10
6 Aug 88	**THE LOCO-MOTION** *PWL 14*	2		9
22 Oct 88	**JE NE SAIS PAS POURQUOI** *PWL 21* ○	2		9
10 Dec 88	**ESPECIALLY FOR YOU** *PWL 24* KYLIE MINOGUE & JASON DONOVAN ●	1	3	12
6 May 89	**HAND ON YOUR HEART** *PWL 35* ●	1	1	9
5 Aug 89	**WOULDN'T CHANGE A THING** *PWL 42*	2		8
4 Nov 89	**NEVER TOO LATE** *PWL 45* ○	4		8
20 Jan 90	**TEARS ON MY PILLOW** *PWL 47* ○	1	1	7
12 May 90	**BETTER THE DEVIL YOU KNOW** *PWL 56* ○	2		9
3 Nov 90	**STEP BACK IN TIME** *PWL 64*	4		6
2 Feb 91	**WHAT DO I HAVE TO DO** *PWL 72*	6		6
1 Jun 91	**SHOCKED** *PWL 81*	6		6
7 Sep 91	**WORD IS OUT** *PWL 204*	16		3
2 Nov 91	**IF YOU WERE WITH ME NOW** *PWL 208* KYLIE MINOGUE & KEITH WASHINGTON	4		6
30 Nov 91	**KEEP ON PUMPIN' IT** *PWL 207* VISIONMASTERS WITH TONY KING & KYLIE MINOGUE	49		
25 Jan 92	**GIVE ME JUST A LITTLE MORE TIME** *PWL 212*	2		6
25 Apr 92	**FINER FEELINGS** *PWL International PWL 227*	11		4
22 Aug 92	**WHAT KIND OF FOOL (HEARD IT ALL BEFORE)** *PWL International PWL 241*	14		3
28 Nov 92	**CELEBRATION** *PWL International PWL 257*	20		4
10 Sep 94	**CONFIDE IN ME** *Deconstruction 74321227482* ○	2		6
26 Nov 94	**PUT YOURSELF IN MY PLACE** *Deconstruction 74321246572*	11		7
22 Jul 95	**WHERE IS THE FEELING?** *Deconstruction 74321293612*	16		2
14 Oct 95	**WHERE THE WILD ROSES GROW** *Mute CDMUTE 185* NICK CAVE + KYLIE MINOGUE	11		3
20 Sep 97	**SOME KIND OF BLISS** *Deconstruction 74321517252*	22		1
6 Dec 97	**DID IT AGAIN** *Deconstruction 74321535702*	14		2
21 Mar 98	**BREATHE** *Deconstruction 74321570132*	14		2
31 Oct 98	**GBI** *Athrob ART 021CD* TOWA TEI FEATURING KYLIE MINOGUE	63		
1 Jul 00	**SPINNING AROUND** *Parlophone CDRS 6542* ○	1	1	6
23 Sep 00	**ON A NIGHT LIKE THIS** *Parlophone CDRS 6546*	2		5
21 Oct 00	**KIDS** *Chrysalis CDCHSS 5119* ROBBIE WILLIAMS & KYLIE MINOGUE ○	2		10
23 Dec 00	**PLEASE STAY** *Parlophone CDRS 6551*	10		5
29 Sep 01	**CAN'T GET YOU OUT OF MY HEAD** *Parlophone CDRS 6562* ⊛	1	4	20
2 Mar 02	**IN YOUR EYES** *Parlophone CDRS 6569* ○	3		7
22 Jun 02	**LOVE AT FIRST SIGHT** *Parlophone CDRS 6577*	2		6
23 Nov 02	**COME INTO MY WORLD** *Parlophone CDR 6590*	8		4
15 Nov 03	**SLOW** *Parlophone CDRS 6625*	1	1	5
13 Mar 04	**RED BLOODED WOMAN** *Parlophone CDRS 6633*	5		5
10 Jul 04	**CHOCOLATE** *Parlophone CDRS 6639*	6		5
18 Dec 04	**I BELIEVE IN YOU** *Parlophone CDRS 6656*	2		8
9 Apr 05	**GIVING YOU UP** *Parlophone CDRS6661*	6		5
17 Nov 07	**2 HEARTS** *Parlophone CDRS6751*	4		10
29 Dec 07	**WOW** *Parlophone CDRS6754*	5		13

MORRIS MINOR & THE MAJORS UK group

Date	Title / Label	Peak Position	Weeks at No.1	Weeks in Top 40
19 Dec 87	**STUTTER RAP (NO SLEEP 'TIL BEDTIME)** *10 TEN 203*	4		8

SUGAR MINOTT Jamaican singer

Date	Title / Label	Peak Position	Weeks at No.1	Weeks in Top 40
28 Mar 81	**GOOD THING GOING (WE'VE GOT A GOOD THING GOING)** *RCA 58* ○	4		9
17 Oct 81	**NEVER MY LOVE** *RCA 138*	52		

MINT CONDITION US group

Date	Title / Label	Peak Position	Weeks at No.1	Weeks in Top 40
21 Jun 97	**WHAT KIND OF MAN WOULD I BE** *Wild Card 5710492*	38		1
4 Oct 97	**LET ME BE THE ONE** *Wild Card 5717132*	63		

MINT JULEPS UK group

Date	Title / Label	Peak Position	Weeks at No.1	Weeks in Top 40
22 Mar 86	**ONLY LOVE CAN BREAK YOUR HEART** *Stiff BUY 241*	62		
30 May 87	**EVERY KINDA PEOPLE** *Stiff BUY 257*	58		

MINT ROYALE UK production duo

Date	Title / Label	Peak Position	Weeks at No.1	Weeks in Top 40
5 Feb 00	**DON'T FALTER** *Faith & Hope FHCD 014* MINT ROYALE FEATURING LAUREN LAVERNE	15		3
6 May 00	**TAKE IT EASY** *Faith & Hope FHCD 016* MINT ROYALE FEATURING LAUREN LAVERNE	66		
7 Sep 02	**SEXIEST MAN IN JAMAICA** *Faith & Hope FHCD 025*	20		2
8 Feb 03	**BLUE SONG** *Illustrious/Epic FHCD 030*	35		1
3 Sep 05	**SINGIN' IN THE RAIN** *Direction 82876720492*	20		3

MINTY Australian singer

Date	Title / Label	Peak Position	Weeks at No.1	Weeks in Top 40
23 Jan 99	**I WANNA BE FREE** *Virgin VSCDT 1728*	67		

MINUTEMAN Swiss group

Date	Title / Label	Peak Position	Weeks at No.1	Weeks in Top 40
20 Jul 02	**BIGBOY** *Ignition IGNSCD 225*	69		
21 Sep 02	**5000 MINUTES OF PAIN** *Ignition IGNSCD 27*	75		
15 Feb 03	**BIGBOY/MOTHER FIXATION** *Ignition IGNSCD 28X*	45		

MIRACLES US group

Date	Title / Label	Peak Position	Weeks at No.1	Weeks in Top 40
24 Feb 66	**GOING TO A GO-GO** *Tamla Motown TMG 547*	44		
22 Dec 66	**(COME 'ROUND HERE) I'M THE ONE YOU NEED** *Tamla Motown TMG 584*	37		
27 Dec 67	**I SECOND THAT EMOTION** *Tamla Motown TMG 631* SMOKEY ROBINSON & THE MIRACLES	27		8
3 Apr 68	**IF YOU CAN WANT** *Tamla Motown TMG 648* SMOKEY ROBINSON & THE MIRACLES	50		
7 May 69	**TRACKS OF MY TEARS** *Tamla Motown TMG 696* SMOKEY ROBINSON & THE MIRACLES	9		11
1 Aug 70	**TEARS OF A CLOWN** *Tamla Motown TMG 745* SMOKEY ROBINSON & THE MIRACLES ★	1	1	14
30 Jan 71	**(COME 'ROUND HERE) I'M THE ONE YOU NEED** *Tamla Motown TMG 761* SMOKEY ROBINSON & THE MIRACLES	13		8
5 Jun 71	**I DON'T BLAME YOU AT ALL** *Tamla Motown TMG 774* SMOKEY ROBINSON & THE MIRACLES	11		9

Silver-selling ● Gold-selling ● Platinum-selling ⊛ US No.1 ★ | Peak Position | Weeks at No.1 | Weeks in Top 40

Date	Title / Label	Peak Position	Weeks at No.1	Weeks in Top 40
10 Jan 76	**LOVE MACHINE (PART 1)** *Tamla Motown TMG 1015* ● ★	3		9
2 Oct 76	**TEARS OF A CLOWN** *Tamla Motown TMG 1048* SMOKEY ROBINSON & THE MIRACLES	34		3

MIRAGE UK group

Date	Title / Label	Peak Position	Weeks at No.1	Weeks in Top 40
14 Jan 84	**GIVE ME THE NIGHT** *Passion PASH 15* MIRAGE FEATURING ROY GAYLE	49		
9 May 87	**JACK MIX II/JACK MIX III** *Debut DEBT 3022*	4		9
25 Jul 87	**SERIOUS MIX** *Debut DEBT 3028*	42		
7 Nov 87	**JACK MIX IV** *Debut DEBT 3035*	8		6
27 Feb 88	**JACK MIX VII** *Debut DEBT 3042*	50		
2 Jul 88	**PUSH THE BEAT** *Debut DEBT 3050*	67		
11 Nov 89	**LATINO HOUSE** *Debut DEBT 3085*	70		

DANNY MIRROR Dutch singer

Date	Title / Label	Peak Position	Weeks at No.1	Weeks in Top 40
17 Sep 77	**I REMEMBER ELVIS PRESLEY (THE KING IS DEAD)** *Sonet SON 2121* ●	4		8

MIRRORBALL UK production duo

Date	Title / Label	Peak Position	Weeks at No.1	Weeks in Top 40
13 Feb 99	**GIVEN UP** *Multiply CDMULTY 46*	12		2
24 Jun 00	**BURNIN'** *Multiply CDMULTY 56*	47		

MIRWAIS French producer

Date	Title / Label	Peak Position	Weeks at No.1	Weeks in Top 40
20 May 00	**DISCO SCIENCE** *Epic 6693102*	68		
23 Dec 00	**NAÏVE SONG** *Epic 6706922*	50		

MIS-TEEQ UK group

Date	Title / Label	Peak Position	Weeks at No.1	Weeks in Top 40
20 Jan 01	**WHY** *Inferno CDFERN 35*	8		5
23 Jun 01	**ALL I WANT** *Telstar CDSTAS 3184*	2		10
27 Oct 01	**ONE NIGHT STAND** *Inferno/Telstar CDTAS 3208*	5		7
2 Mar 02	**B WITH ME** *Inferno/Telstar CDSTAS 3243*	5		6
29 Jun 02	**ROLL ON/THIS IS HOW WE DO IT** *Inferno/Telstar CDSTAS 3255*	7		5
29 Mar 03	**SCANDALOUS** *Telstar CDSTAS 3319*	2		8
12 Jul 03	**CAN'T GET IT BACK** *Telstar CXSTAS 3337*	8		6
29 Nov 03	**STYLE** *Telstar CDSTAS 3369*	13		3

MISH MASH UK group

Date	Title / Label	Peak Position	Weeks at No.1	Weeks in Top 40
15 Apr 06	**SPEECHLESS** *Data DATA100CDS*	16		2

MISHKA Bermudan singer

Date	Title / Label	Peak Position	Weeks at No.1	Weeks in Top 40
15 May 99	**GIVE YOU ALL THE LOVE** *Creation CRESCD 311*	34		1

MISS BEHAVIN' UK DJ

Date	Title / Label	Peak Position	Weeks at No.1	Weeks in Top 40
18 Jan 03	**SUCH A GOOD FEELIN'** *Tidy Two 115C*	62		

MISS JANE UK singer

Date	Title / Label	Peak Position	Weeks at No.1	Weeks in Top 40
30 Oct 99	**IT'S A FINE DAY** *G1 Recordings G 1001CD*	62		

MISS SHIVA German singer

Date	Title / Label	Peak Position	Weeks at No.1	Weeks in Top 40
10 Nov 01	**DREAMS** *VC Recordings VCRCD 99*	30		1

MISS X UK singer

Date	Title / Label	Peak Position	Weeks at No.1	Weeks in Top 40
1 Aug 63	**CHRISTINE** *Ember S 175*	37		2

MISSION UK group

Date	Title / Label	Peak Position	Weeks at No.1	Weeks in Top 40
14 Jun 86	**SERPENTS KISS** *Chapter 22 CHAP 6*	70		
26 Jul 86	**GARDEN OF DELIGHT/LIKE A HURRICANE** *Chapter 22 CHAP 7*	49		
18 Oct 86	**STAY WITH ME** *Mercury MYTH 1*	30		3
17 Jan 87	**WASTELAND** *Mercury MYTH 2*	11		5
14 Mar 87	**SEVERINA** *Mercury MYTH 3*	25		4
13 Feb 88	**TOWER OF STRENGTH** *Mercury MYTH 4*	12		5
23 Apr 88	**BEYOND THE PALE** *Mercury MYTH 6*	32		3
13 Jan 90	**BUTTERFLY ON A WHEEL** *Mercury MYTH 8*	12		3
10 Mar 90	**DELIVERANCE** *Mercury MYTH 9*	27		3
2 Jun 90	**INTO THE BLUE** *Mercury MYTH 10*	32		2
17 Nov 90	**HANDS ACROSS THE OCEAN** *Mercury MYTH 11*	28		1
25 Apr 92	**NEVER AGAIN** *Mercury MYTH 12*	34		1
20 Jun 92	**LIKE A CHILD AGAIN** *Mercury MYTH 13*	30		1
17 Oct 92	**SHADES OF GREEN** *Vertigo MYTH 14*	49		
8 Jan 94	**TOWER OF STRENGTH (REMIX)** *Vertigo MYTCD 15*	33		2
26 Mar 94	**AFTERGLOW** *Vertigo MYTCD 16*	53		
4 Feb 95	**SWOON** *Neverland HOOKCD 002*	73		

MISSJONES US singer

Date	Title / Label	Peak Position	Weeks at No.1	Weeks in Top 40
10 Oct 98	**2 WAY STREET** *Motown 8608572*	49		

MRS MILLS UK pianist

Date	Title / Label	Peak Position	Weeks at No.1	Weeks in Top 40
14 Dec 61	**MRS MILLS MEDLEY** *Parlophone R 4856*	18		4
31 Dec 64	**MRS MILLS PARTY MEDLEY** *Parlophone R 5214*	50		

MRS WOOD UK singer/pianist

Date	Title / Label	Peak Position	Weeks at No.1	Weeks in Top 40
16 Sep 95	**JOANNA** *React CDREACT 066*	40		1
6 Jul 96	**HEARTBREAK** *React CDREACT 78* MRS WOOD FEATURING EVE GALLAGHER	44		
4 Oct 97	**JOANNA (REMIX)** *React CDXREACT 107*	34		1
15 Aug 98	**1234** *React CDREACT 121*	54		

MISTA E UK producer

Date	Title / Label	Peak Position	Weeks at No.1	Weeks in Top 40
10 Dec 88	**DON'T BELIEVE THE HYPE** *Urban URB 28*	41		

MR & MRS SMITH UK production group

Date	Title / Label	Peak Position	Weeks at No.1	Weeks in Top 40
12 Oct 96	**GOTTA GET LOOSE** *Hooj Choons HOOJCD 46*	70		

MR BEAN UK comedian/actor

Date	Title / Label	Peak Position	Weeks at No.1	Weeks in Top 40
4 Apr 92	**(I WANT TO BE) ELECTED** *London LON 319* MR BEAN & SMEAR CAMPAIGN FEATURING BRUCE DICKINSON	9		4

MR BIG UK group

Date	Title / Label	Peak Position	Weeks at No.1	Weeks in Top 40
12 Feb 77	**ROMEO** *EMI 2567* ●	4		10
21 May 77	**FEEL LIKE CALLING HOME** *EMI 2610*	35		1
7 Mar 92	**TO BE WITH YOU** *Atlantic A 7514* ★	3		9
23 May 92	**JUST TAKE MY HEART** *Atlantic A 7490*	26		3
8 Aug 92	**GREEN TINTED SIXTIES MIND** *Atlantic A 7468*	72		
20 Nov 93	**WILD WORLD** *Atlantic A 7310CD*	59		

MR BLOBBY UK TV character

Date	Title / Label	Peak Position	Weeks at No.1	Weeks in Top 40
4 Dec 93	**MR BLOBBY** *Destiny Music CDDMUS 104* ⊛	1	3	9
16 Dec 95	**CHRISTMAS IN BLOBBYLAND** *Destiny DMUSCD 108*	36		3

MR BLOE UK group

Date	Title / Label	Peak Position	Weeks at No.1	Weeks in Top 40
9 May 70	**GROOVIN' WITH MR. BLOE** *DJM DJS 216*	2		17

MR FINGERS US producer

Date	Title / Label	Peak Position	Weeks at No.1	Weeks in Top 40
17 Mar 90	**WHAT ABOUT THIS LOVE** *ffrr F 131*	74		
7 Mar 92	**CLOSER** *MCA MCS 1601*	50		
23 May 92	**ON MY WAY** *MCA MCS 1630*	71		

MR FOOD UK singer

Date	Title / Label	Peak Position	Weeks at No.1	Weeks in Top 40
9 Jun 90	**...AND THAT'S BEFORE ME TEA!** *Tangible TGB 005*	62		

MR HANKEY US cartoon character

Date	Title / Label	Peak Position	Weeks at No.1	Weeks in Top 40
25 Dec 99	**MR HANKEY THE CHRISTMAS POO** *Columbia 6685582*	4		5

MR HUDSON & THE LIBRARY UK group

Date	Title / Label	Peak Position	Weeks at No.1	Weeks in Top 40
3 Mar 07	**TOO LATE TOO LATE** *Mercury 1721391*	53		

MR JACK Italian producer

Date	Title / Label	Peak Position	Weeks at No.1	Weeks in Top 40
25 Jan 97	**WIGGLY WORLD** *Xtravaganza 0090965*	32		1

Silver-selling ○ Gold-selling ● Platinum-selling ⊛ US No.1 ★ Peak Position · Weeks at No.1 · Weeks in Top 40

MR LEE US producer

Date	Title	Peak Position	Weeks at No.1	Weeks in Top 40
6 Aug 88	**PUMP UP LONDON** *Breakout USA 639*	64		
11 Nov 89	**GET BUSY** *Jive 231*	71		
24 Feb 90	**GET BUSY** *Jive 231*	41		

MR MISTER US group

Date	Title	Peak Position	Weeks at No.1	Weeks in Top 40
21 Dec 85	**BROKEN WINGS** *RCA PB 49945* ★	4		8
1 Mar 86	**KYRIE** *RCA PB 49927* ★	11		7

MR OIZO French producer

Date	Title	Peak Position	Weeks at No.1	Weeks in Top 40
3 Apr 99	**FLAT BEAT** *F Communications/PIAS Recordings F 104CDUK* ⊛	1	2	7

MR ON UK producer

Date	Title	Peak Position	Weeks at No.1	Weeks in Top 40
7 Feb 04	**BREATHE DON'T STOP** *Positiva/Incentive CDTIVS 201* MR ON VS THE JUNGLE BROTHERS	21		1

MR PINK US producer

Date	Title	Peak Position	Weeks at No.1	Weeks in Top 40
19 Jan 02	**LOVE AND AFFECTION** *Manifesto FESCD 90* MR PINK PRESENTS THE PROGRAM	22		2

MR PRESIDENT German group

Date	Title	Peak Position	Weeks at No.1	Weeks in Top 40
14 Jun 97	**COCO JAMBOO** *WEA 110CD* ○	8		9
20 Sep 97	**I GIVE YOU MY HEART** *WEA 126CD*	52		
25 Apr 98	**JOJO ACTION** *WEA 156CD*	73		

MR REDZ VS DJ SKRIBBLE UK/US duo

Date	Title	Peak Position	Weeks at No.1	Weeks in Top 40
24 May 03	**EVERYBODY COME ON (CAN U FEEL IT)** *ffrr FCD 410*	13		4

MR ROY UK production group

Date	Title	Peak Position	Weeks at No.1	Weeks in Top 40
7 May 94	**SOMETHING ABOUT YOU** *Fresh FRSHD 11*	74		
21 Jan 95	**SAVED** *Fresh FRSHD 21*	24		2
16 Dec 95	**SOMETHING ABOUT YOU (CAN'T BE BEAT) (REMIX)** *Fresh FRSHD 33*	49		

MR SCRUFF UK producer

Date	Title	Peak Position	Weeks at No.1	Weeks in Top 40
14 Dec 02	**SWEETSMOKE** *Ninja Tune ZEN 12124*	75		

MR SMASH & FRIENDS UK producer

Date	Title	Peak Position	Weeks at No.1	Weeks in Top 40
8 Jun 02	**WE'RE COMING OVER** *RGR RGRCD 2*	67		

MR V UK producer

Date	Title	Peak Position	Weeks at No.1	Weeks in Top 40
6 Aug 94	**GIVE ME LIFE** *Cheeky CHEKCD 005*	40		1

MR VEGAS Jamaican singer

Date	Title	Peak Position	Weeks at No.1	Weeks in Top 40
22 Aug 98	**HEADS HIGH** *Greensleeves GRECD 650*	71		
13 Nov 99	**HEADS HIGH** *Greensleeves GRECD 785*	16		4

MISTURA US group

Date	Title	Peak Position	Weeks at No.1	Weeks in Top 40
15 May 76	**THE FLASHER** *Route RT 30* MISTURA FEATURING LLOYD MICHELS	23		8

MITCHELL BROTHERS UK duo

Date	Title	Peak Position	Weeks at No.1	Weeks in Top 40
19 Mar 05	**ROUTINE CHECK** *WEA BEATS8* THE MITCHELL BROTHERS/KANO/THE STREETS	42		
4 Jun 05	**HARVEY NICKS** *WEA BEATS15* MITCHELL BROTHERS FEATURING SWAY	62		
20 Aug 05	**EXCUSE MY BROTHER** *The Beats BEATS19*	58		
17 Nov 07	**MICHAEL JACKSON** *Beat Recordings BEATS58*	65		

DES MITCHELL UK/Belgian production group

Date	Title	Peak Position	Weeks at No.1	Weeks in Top 40
29 Jan 00	**(WELCOME) TO THE DANCE** *Code Blue BLU 008CD1*	5		4

GUY MITCHELL US singer

Date	Title	Peak Position	Weeks at No.1	Weeks in Top 40
14 Nov 52	**FEET UP** *Columbia DB 3151*	2		10
13 Feb 53	**SHE WEARS RED FEATHERS** *Columbia DB 3238*	1	4	16
24 Apr 53	**PRETTY LITTLE BLACK EYED SUSIE** *Columbia DB 3255*	2		11
28 Aug 53	**LOOK AT THAT GIRL** *Philips PB 162*	1	6	14
6 Nov 53	**CHICKA BOOM** *Philips PB 178*	4		15
18 Dec 53	**CLOUD LUCKY SEVEN** *Philips PB 210*	2		16
19 Feb 54	**CUFF OF MY SHIRT** *Philips PB 225*	9		3
26 Feb 54	**SIPPIN' SODA** *Philips PB 210*	11		1
30 Apr 54	**DIME AND A DOLLAR** *Philips PB 248*	8		5
7 Dec 56	**SINGING THE BLUES** *Philips PB 650* ★	1	3	22
15 Feb 57	**KNEE DEEP IN THE BLUES** *Philips PB 669*	3		12
26 Apr 57	**ROCK-A-BILLY** *Philips PB 685*	1	1	14
26 Jul 57	**IN THE MIDDLE OF A DARK DARK NIGHT/SWEET STUFF** *Philips PB 712*	25		4
11 Oct 57	**CALL ROSIE ON THE PHONE** *Philips PB 743*	17		6
27 Nov 59	**HEARTACHES BY THE NUMBER** *Philips PB 964* ★	5		15

JONI MITCHELL Canadian singer

Date	Title	Peak Position	Weeks at No.1	Weeks in Top 40
13 Jun 70	**BIG YELLOW TAXI** *Reprise RS 20906*	11		11
4 Oct 97	**GOT 'TIL IT'S GONE** *Virgin VSCDG 1666* JANET FEATURING Q-TIP & JONI ○	6		7

WILLIE MITCHELL US singer/trumpeter

Date	Title	Peak Position	Weeks at No.1	Weeks in Top 40
24 Apr 68	**SOUL SERENADE** *London HLU 10186*	43		
11 Dec 76	**THE CHAMPION** *London HL 10545*	47		

MIX FACTORY UK group

Date	Title	Peak Position	Weeks at No.1	Weeks in Top 40
30 Jan 93	**TAKE ME AWAY (PARADISE)** *All Around The World CDGLOBE 120*	51		

MIXMASTER Italian producer

Date	Title	Peak Position	Weeks at No.1	Weeks in Top 40
4 Nov 89	**GRAND PIANO** *BCM 344*	9		6

MIXTURES Australian group

Date	Title	Peak Position	Weeks at No.1	Weeks in Top 40
16 Jan 71	**THE PUSHBIKE SONG** *Polydor 2058 083*	2		17

HANK MIZELL US singer

Date	Title	Peak Position	Weeks at No.1	Weeks in Top 40
20 Mar 76	**JUNGLE ROCK** *Charly CS 1005* ○	3		13

MK US producer

Date	Title	Peak Position	Weeks at No.1	Weeks in Top 40
4 Feb 95	**ALWAYS** *Activ CDTV 3* MK FEATURING ALANA	69		
27 May 95	**BURNING** *Activ CDTVR 6*	44		

MN8 UK group

Date	Title	Peak Position	Weeks at No.1	Weeks in Top 40
4 Feb 95	**I'VE GOT A LITTLE SOMETHING FOR YOU** *Columbia 6608802* ○	2		9
29 Apr 95	**IF YOU ONLY LET ME IN** *Columbia 6613252*	6		4
15 Jul 95	**HAPPY** *Columbia 6622192*	8		4
4 Nov 95	**BABY IT'S YOU** *Columbia 6624522*	22		1
24 Feb 96	**PATHWAY TO THE MOON** *Columbia 6629212*	25		1
31 Aug 96	**TUFF ACT TO FOLLOW** *Columbia 6635345*	15		2
26 Oct 96	**DREAMING** *Columbia 6638302*	21		1

MNO Belgian group

Date	Title	Peak Position	Weeks at No.1	Weeks in Top 40
28 Sep 91	**GOD OF ABRAHAM** *A&M AM 820*	66		

MOBB DEEP US duo

Date	Title	Peak Position	Weeks at No.1	Weeks in Top 40
24 Sep 05	**OUTTA CONTROL** *Interscope 9885436* 50 CENT FEATURING MOBB DEEP	7		7
15 Jul 06	**PUT EM' IN THEIR PLACE** *Interscope 9877787*	75		

MOBILES UK group

Date	Title	Peak Position	Weeks at No.1	Weeks in Top 40
9 Jan 82	**DROWNING IN BERLIN** *Rialto RIA 3*	9		8
27 Mar 82	**AMOUR AMOUR** *Rialto RIA 5*	45		

Silver-selling ● Gold-selling ● Platinum-selling ● US No.1 ★ · Peak Position · Weeks at No.1 · Weeks in Top 40

MOBO ALLSTARS UK/US group

Date	Title / Label	Peak Position	Weeks at No.1	Weeks in Top 40
26 Dec 98	**AIN'T NO STOPPING US NOW** *PolyGram TV 5632302*	47		

MOBY US singer

Date	Title / Label	Peak Position	Weeks at No.1	Weeks in Top 40
27 Jul 91	**GO** *Outer Rhythm FOOT 15*	46		
19 Oct 91	**GO** *Outer Rhythm FOOT 15*	10		5
3 Jul 93	**I FEEL IT** *Equator AXISCD 001*	38		1
11 Sep 93	**MOVE** *Mute CDMUTE 158*	21		3
28 May 94	**HYMN** *Mute CDMUTE 161*	31		1
29 Oct 94	**FEELING SO REAL** *Mute CDMUTE 173*	30		1
25 Feb 95	**EVERY TIME YOU TOUCH ME** *Mute CDMUTE 176*	28		2
1 Jul 95	**INTO THE BLUE** *Mute CDMUTE 179A*	34		1
7 Sep 96	**THAT'S WHEN I REACH FOR MY REVOLVER** *Mute CDMUTE 184*	50		
15 Nov 97	**JAMES BOND THEME** *Mute CDMUTE 210*	8		3
5 Sep 98	**HONEY** *Mute CDMUTE 218*	33		1
8 May 99	**RUN ON** *Mute LCDMUTE 221*	33		1
24 Jul 99	**BODYROCK** *Mute LCDMUTE 225*	38		1
23 Oct 99	**WHY DOES MY HEART FEEL SO BAD/HONEY** *Mute CDMUTE 230* MOBY/MOBY (FEATURING KELIS)	16		2
18 Mar 00	**NATURAL BLUES** *Mute CDMUTE 251*	11		4
24 Jun 00	**PORCELAIN** *Mute LCDMUTE 252*	5		4
28 Oct 00	**WHY DOES MY HEART FEEL SO BAD** *Mute LCDMUTE 255*	17		2
11 May 02	**WE ARE ALL MADE OF STARS** *Mute LCDMUTE 268*	11		2
31 Aug 02	**EXTREME WAYS** *Mute LCDMUTE 270*	39		1
16 Nov 02	**IN THIS WORLD** *Mute LCDMUTE 276*	35		1
12 Mar 05	**LIFT ME UP** *Mute LCDMUTE340*	18		2
11 Jun 05	**SPIDERS** *Mute LCDMUTE350*	50		
4 Feb 06	**SLIPPING AWAY** *Mute LCDMUTE365*	53		
11 Nov 06	**NEW YORK NEW YORK** *Mute CDMUTE371* MOBY FEATURING DEBBIE HARRY	43		
1 Sep 07	**EXTREME WAYS** *Mute CDMUTE270*	45		

MOCK TURTLES UK group

Date	Title / Label	Peak Position	Weeks at No.1	Weeks in Top 40
9 Mar 91	**CAN YOU DIG IT** *Siren SRN 136*	18		8
29 Jun 91	**AND THEN SHE SMILES** *Siren SRN 139*	44		
15 Mar 03	**CAN YOU DIG IT** *Virgin CDMOCK 001*	19		2

MICKEY MODELLE V JESSY UK/Dutch duo

Date	Title / Label	Peak Position	Weeks at No.1	Weeks in Top 40
19 Aug 06	**DANCING IN THE DARK** *All Around The World CDGLOBE510*	10		5
30 Dec 06	**OVER YOU** *All Around The World CDGLOBE609*	35		1

MODERN UK group

Date	Title / Label	Peak Position	Weeks at No.1	Weeks in Top 40
26 Nov 05	**JANE FALLS DOWN** *Mercury 9874798*	35		1

MODERN ROMANCE UK group

Date	Title / Label	Peak Position	Weeks at No.1	Weeks in Top 40
15 Aug 81	**EVERYBODY SALSA** *WEA K 18815*	12		7
7 Nov 81	**AY AY AY AY MOOSEY** *WEA K 18883*	10		9
30 Jan 82	**QUEEN OF THE RAPPING SCENE (NOTHING EVER GOES THE WAY YOU PLAN)** *WEA K 18928*	37		1
14 Aug 82	**CHERRY PINK AND APPLE BLOSSOM WHITE** *WEA K 19245* MODERN ROMANCE FEATURING JOHN DU PREZ	15		6
13 Nov 82	**BEST YEARS OF OUR LIVES** *WEA ROM 1* ●	4		11
26 Feb 83	**HIGH LIFE** *WEA ROM 2*	8		6
7 May 83	**DON'T STOP THAT CRAZY RHYTHM** *WEA ROM 3*	14		4
6 Aug 83	**WALKING IN THE RAIN** *WEA X 9733* ●	7		10

MODERN TALKING German duo

Date	Title / Label	Peak Position	Weeks at No.1	Weeks in Top 40
15 Jun 85	**YOU'RE MY HEART, YOU'RE MY SOUL** *Magnet MAG 277*	56		
12 Oct 85	**YOU CAN WIN IF YOU WANT** *Magnet MAG 282*	70		
16 Aug 86	**BROTHER LOUIE** *RCA PB 40875* ●	4		8
4 Oct 86	**ATLANTIS IS CALLING (S.O.S. FOR LOVE)** *RCA PB 40969*	55		

MODEST MOUSE US group

Date	Title / Label	Peak Position	Weeks at No.1	Weeks in Top 40
24 Jul 04	**FLOAT ON** *Epic 6750692*	46		

MODETTES UK/US group

Date	Title / Label	Peak Position	Weeks at No.1	Weeks in Top 40
12 Jul 80	**PAINT IT BLACK** *Deram DET-R 1*	42		
18 Jul 81	**TONIGHT** *Deram DET 3*	68		

MODJO French group

Date	Title / Label	Peak Position	Weeks at No.1	Weeks in Top 40
16 Sep 00	**LADY (HEAR ME TONIGHT)** *Sound Of Barclay 5877582* ●	1	2	11
14 Apr 01	**CHILLIN'** *Polydor 5870092*	12		2
6 Oct 01	**WHAT I MEAN** *Polydor 5873462*	59		

DOMENICO MODUGNO Italian singer

Date	Title / Label	Peak Position	Weeks at No.1	Weeks in Top 40
5 Sep 58	**VOLARE** *Oriole ICB 5000* ★	10		12
27 Mar 59	**CIAO CIAO BAMBINA (PIOVE)** *Oriole ICB 1489*	29		1

MODEY LEMON US duo

Date	Title / Label	Peak Position	Weeks at No.1	Weeks in Top 40
22 May 04	**CROWS** *Mute CDMUTE 328*	75		
28 May 05	**SLEEPWALKERS** *Mute CDMUTE331*	71		

MOFFATTS Canadian group

Date	Title / Label	Peak Position	Weeks at No.1	Weeks in Top 40
20 Feb 99	**CRAZY** *Chrysalis CDEM 533*	16		2
26 Jun 99	**UNTIL YOU LOVED ME** *Chrysalis CDEMS 541*	36		1
23 Oct 99	**MISERY** *EMI CDEM 551*	47		

MOGUAI German producer

Date	Title / Label	Peak Position	Weeks at No.1	Weeks in Top 40
8 Feb 03	**U KNOW Y** *Hope Recordings HOPECDS 038*	62		

MOGWAI UK group

Date	Title / Label	Peak Position	Weeks at No.1	Weeks in Top 40
4 Apr 98	**SWEET LEAF/BLACK SABBATH** *Fierce Panda NING 47CD* MAGOO : MOGWAI	60		
11 Apr 98	**FEAR SATAN** *Eye-Q EYEUK 032CD*	57		
11 Jul 98	**NO EDUCATION NO FUTURE (F**K THE CURFEW)** *Chemikal Underground CHEM 026CD*	68		
11 Feb 06	**FRIEND OF THE NIGHT** *PIAS PIASX064CD*	38		1

MOHAIR UK group

Date	Title / Label	Peak Position	Weeks at No.1	Weeks in Top 40
17 Dec 05	**END OF THE LINE** *Pebble Beach ECYCD025*	52		

MOHAWKS UK keyboard player

Date	Title / Label	Peak Position	Weeks at No.1	Weeks in Top 40
24 Jan 87	**THE CHAMP** *Pama PM 1*	58		

FRANK'O MOIRAGHI Italian producer

Date	Title / Label	Peak Position	Weeks at No.1	Weeks in Top 40
1 Jun 96	**FEEL MY BODY** *Multiply CDMULTY 10* FRANK'O MOIRAGHI FEATURING AMNESIA	39		1
26 Oct 96	**FEEL MY BODY (REMIX)** *Multiply CDMULTY 15* FRANK'O MOIRAGHI FEATURING AMNESIA	40		1

MOIST Canadian group

Date	Title / Label	Peak Position	Weeks at No.1	Weeks in Top 40
12 Nov 94	**PUSH** *Chrysalis CDCHS 5016*	35		1
25 Feb 95	**SILVER** *Chrysalis CDCHS 5019*	50		
29 Apr 95	**FREAKY BE BEAUTIFUL** *Chrysalis CDCHS 5022*	47		
19 Aug 95	**PUSH** *Chrysalis CDCHS 5024*	20		2

MOJO UK group

Date	Title / Label	Peak Position	Weeks at No.1	Weeks in Top 40
22 Aug 81	**DANCE ON** *Creole CR 17*	70		

MOJOLATORS US production group

Date	Title / Label	Peak Position	Weeks at No.1	Weeks in Top 40
6 Oct 01	**DRIFTING** *Multiply CDMULTY81* MOJOLATERS FEATURING CAMILLA	52		

MOJOS UK group

Date	Title / Label	Peak Position	Weeks at No.1	Weeks in Top 40
26 Mar 64	**EVERYTHING'S ALRIGHT** *Decca F 11853*	9		10
11 Jun 64	**WHY NOT TONIGHT** *Decca F 11918*	25		7
10 Sep 64	**SEVEN DAFFODILS** *Decca F 11959*	30		4

MOKENSTEF US group

Date	Title / Label	Peak Position	Weeks at No.1	Weeks in Top 40
23 Sep 95	**HE'S MINE** *Def Jam DEFCD 13*	70		

Silver-selling ○ · Gold-selling ● · Platinum-selling · US No.1 ★ · Peak Position · Weeks at No.1 · Weeks in Top 40

MOLELLA Italian singer

Date	Title / Label	Peak Position	Weeks at No.1	Weeks in Top 40
16 Dec 95	IF YOU WANNA PARTY *Stip 030CD* MOLELLA FEATURING THE OUTHERE BROTHERS	9		8

MOLLY HALF HEAD UK group

Date	Title / Label	Peak Position	Weeks at No.1	Weeks in Top 40
3 Jun 95	SHINE *Columbia 6620732*	73		

MOLOKO UK/Irish duo

Date	Title / Label	Peak Position	Weeks at No.1	Weeks in Top 40
24 Feb 96	DOMINOID *Echo ECSCD 016*	65		
25 May 96	FUN FOR ME *Echo ECSCD 20*	36		1
20 Jun 98	THE FLIPSIDE *Echo ECSCD 54*	53		
27 Mar 99	SING IT BACK *Echo ECSCD 71*	45		
4 Sep 99	SING IT BACK (REMIX) *Echo ECSCD 82* ○	4		6
1 Apr 00	THE TIME IS NOW *Echo ECSCD 88* ○	2		7
5 Aug 00	PURE PLEASURE SEEKER *Echo ECSCD 99*	21		2
25 Nov 00	INDIGO *Echo ECSCD 104*	51		
1 Mar 03	FAMILIAR FEELING *Echo ECSCD 131*	10		2
5 Jul 03	FOREVER MORE *Echo ECSCD 136*	17		2

MOMBASSA UK production duo

Date	Title / Label	Peak Position	Weeks at No.1	Weeks in Top 40
8 Mar 97	CRY FREEDOM *Soundproof SPCD 021*	63		

MOMENTS US group

Date	Title / Label	Peak Position	Weeks at No.1	Weeks in Top 40
8 Mar 75	GIRLS *All Platinum 6146 302* MOMENTS & WHATNAUTS ○	3		9
19 Jul 75	DOLLY MY LOVE *All Platinum 6146 306*	10		8
25 Oct 75	LOOK AT ME (I'M IN LOVE) *All Platinum 6146 309*	42		
22 Jan 77	JACK IN THE BOX *All Platinum 6146 318* ○	7		8

TONY MOMRELLE UK singer

Date	Title / Label	Peak Position	Weeks at No.1	Weeks in Top 40
15 Aug 98	LET ME SHOW YOU *Art & Soul ART 1CDS*	67		

MONACO UK duo

Date	Title / Label	Peak Position	Weeks at No.1	Weeks in Top 40
15 Mar 97	WHAT DO YOU WANT FROM ME? *Polydor 5731912*	11		4
31 May 97	SWEET LIPS *Polydor 5710552*	18		2
20 Sep 97	SHINE (SOMEONE WHO NEEDS ME) *Polydor 5714182*	55		

PHAROAHE MONCH US rapper

Date	Title / Label	Peak Position	Weeks at No.1	Weeks in Top 40
19 Feb 00	SIMON SAYS *Rawkus RWK 205CD*	24		1
19 Aug 00	LIGHT *Rawkus RWK 259CD*	72		
3 Feb 01	OH NO *Rawkus RWK 302* MOS DEF & NATE DOGG FEATURING PHAROAHE MONCH	24		3
1 Dec 01	GOT YOU *Priority PTYCD 145*	27		1
14 Sep 02	THE LIFE *MCA MCSTD 40292* STYLES & PHAROAHE MONCH	50		

JAY MONDI & THE LIVING BASS UK group

Date	Title / Label	Peak Position	Weeks at No.1	Weeks in Top 40
24 Mar 90	ALL NIGHT LONG *10 TEN 304*	63		

MONDO KANE UK group

Date	Title / Label	Peak Position	Weeks at No.1	Weeks in Top 40
16 Aug 86	NEW YORK AFTERNOON *Lisson DOLE 2*	70		

MONÉ US singer

Date	Title / Label	Peak Position	Weeks at No.1	Weeks in Top 40
12 Aug 95	WE CAN MAKE IT *A&M 5811592*	64		
16 Mar 96	MOVIN' *AM:PM 5814392*	48		

ZOOT MONEY & THE BIG ROLL BAND UK group

Date	Title / Label	Peak Position	Weeks at No.1	Weeks in Top 40
18 Aug 66	BIG TIME OPERATOR *Columbia DB 7975*	25		6

MONEY MARK US rapper

Date	Title / Label	Peak Position	Weeks at No.1	Weeks in Top 40
28 Feb 98	HAND IN YOUR HEAD *Mo Wax MW 066CD*	40		1
6 Jun 98	MAYBE I'M DEAD *Mo Wax MW 089CD1*	45		

MONICA US singer

Date	Title / Label	Peak Position	Weeks at No.1	Weeks in Top 40
29 Jul 95	DON'T TAKE IT PERSONAL (JUST ONE OF DEM DAYS) *Arista 74321301452*	32		1
17 Feb 96	LIKE THIS AND LIKE THAT *Rowdy 74321344222*	33		1
8 Jun 96	BEFORE YOU WALK OUT OF MY LIFE *Rowdy 74321374042*	22		2
24 May 97	FOR YOU I WILL *Atlantic A 5437CD*	27		1
6 Jun 98	THE BOY IS MINE *Atlantic AT 0036CD* BRANDY & MONICA ○ ★	2		18
17 Oct 98	THE FIRST NIGHT *Rowdy 74321619342* ★	6		4
4 Sep 99	ANGEL OF MINE *Arista 74321692892* ★	55		

MONIFAH US singer

Date	Title / Label	Peak Position	Weeks at No.1	Weeks in Top 40
30 Jan 99	TOUCH IT *Universal UMD 56218*	29		1

TS MONK US group

Date	Title / Label	Peak Position	Weeks at No.1	Weeks in Top 40
7 Mar 81	BON BON VIE *Mirage K 11653*	63		
25 Apr 81	CANDIDATE FOR LOVE *Mirage K 11648*	58		

MONKEES UK/US group

Date	Title / Label	Peak Position	Weeks at No.1	Weeks in Top 40
5 Jan 67	I'M A BELIEVER *RCA 1560* ★	1	4	15
26 Jan 67	LAST TRAIN TO CLARKSVILLE *RCA 1547* ★	23		6
6 Apr 67	A LITTLE BIT ME A LITTLE BIT YOU *RCA 1580*	3		10
22 Jun 67	ALTERNATE TITLE *RCA 1604*	2		12
16 Aug 67	PLEASANT VALLEY SUNDAY *RCA 1620*	11		7
15 Nov 67	DAYDREAM BELIEVER *RCA 1645* ★	5		16
27 Mar 68	VALLERI *RCA 1673*	12		7
26 Jun 68	D. W. WASHBURN *RCA 1706*	17		6
26 Mar 69	TEARDROP CITY *RCA 1802*	44		
25 Jun 69	SOMEDAY MAN *RCA 1824*	47		
15 Mar 80	THE MONKEES EP *Arista ARIST 326*	33		5
18 Oct 86	THAT WAS THEN, THIS IS NOW *Arista ARIST 673*	68		
1 Apr 89	THE MONKEES EP *Arista 112157*	62		

MONKEY BARS US production duo

Date	Title / Label	Peak Position	Weeks at No.1	Weeks in Top 40
8 May 04	SHUGGIE LOVE *Subliminal SUB117CD* MONKEY BARS/GABRIELLE WIDMAN	61		

MONKEY HANGERZ UK group

Date	Title / Label	Peak Position	Weeks at No.1	Weeks in Top 40
19 Nov 05	2 LITTLE BOYS/NEVER SAY DIE 2005 *Poolie Pride 1908*	24		1

MONKEY MAFIA UK production duo

Date	Title / Label	Peak Position	Weeks at No.1	Weeks in Top 40
10 Aug 96	WORK MI BODY *Heavenly HVN 53CD* MONKEY MAFIA FEATURING PATRA	75		
7 Jun 97	15 STEPS (EP) *Heavenly HVN 67CD*	67		
2 May 98	LONG AS I CAN SEE THE LIGHT *Heavenly HVN 84CD*	51		

MONKS UK duo

Date	Title / Label	Peak Position	Weeks at No.1	Weeks in Top 40
21 Apr 79	NICE LEGS SHAME ABOUT HER FACE *Carrere CAR 104*	19		6

MONO UK duo

Date	Title / Label	Peak Position	Weeks at No.1	Weeks in Top 40
2 May 98	LIFE IN MONO *Echo ECSCD 64*	60		

MONOBOY Irish producer

Date	Title / Label	Peak Position	Weeks at No.1	Weeks in Top 40
7 Jul 01	THE MUSIC IN YOU – THEME FROM AROUND THE WORLD IN 80 RAVES *Perfecto PERF 18CDS* MONOBOY FEATURING DELORES	50		

MATT MONRO UK singer

Date	Title / Label	Peak Position	Weeks at No.1	Weeks in Top 40
15 Dec 60	PORTRAIT OF MY LOVE *Parlophone R 4714*	3		13
9 Mar 61	MY KIND OF GIRL *Parlophone R 4755*	5		11
18 May 61	WHY NOT NOW/CAN THIS BE LOVE *Parlophone R 4775*	24		7
28 Sep 61	GONNA BUILD A MOUNTAIN *Parlophone R 4819*	44		
8 Feb 62	SOFTLY AS I LEAVE YOU *Parlophone R 4868*	10		14
14 Jun 62	WHEN LOVE COMES ALONG *Parlophone R 4911*	46		
8 Nov 62	MY LOVE AND DEVOTION *Parlophone R 4954*	29		3
14 Nov 63	FROM RUSSIA WITH LOVE *Parlophone R 5068*	20		10
17 Sep 64	WALK AWAY *Parlophone R 5171*	4		19
24 Dec 64	FOR MAMA *Parlophone R 5215*	23		3

Silver-selling · Gold-selling · Platinum-selling · US No.1 ★ · Peak Position · Weeks at No.1 · Weeks in Top 40

Date	Title / Label	Peak Position	Weeks at No.1	Weeks in Top 40
25 Mar 65	**WITHOUT YOU** *Parlophone R 5251*	37		2
21 Oct 65	**YESTERDAY** *Parlophone R 5348*	8		12
24 Nov 73	**AND YOU SMILED** *EMI 2091*	28		6

MONROE UK group

Date	Title / Label	Peak Position	Weeks at No.1	Weeks in Top 40
31 Jul 04	**SMILE** *Zu ZUDB001*	60		

GERRY MONROE UK singer

Date	Title / Label	Peak Position	Weeks at No.1	Weeks in Top 40
23 May 70	**SALLY** *Chapter One CH 122*	4		16
19 Sep 70	**CRY** *Chapter One CH 128*	38		1
14 Nov 70	**MY PRAYER** *Chapter One CH 132*	9		10
17 Apr 71	**IT'S A SIN TO TELL A LIE** *Chapter One CH 144*	13		11
21 Aug 71	**LITTLE DROPS OF SILVER** *Chapter One CH 152*	37		6
12 Feb 72	**GIRL OF MY DREAMS** *Chapter One CH 159*	43		

HOLLIS P MONROE Canadian producer

Date	Title / Label	Peak Position	Weeks at No.1	Weeks in Top 40
24 Apr 99	**I'M LONELY** *City Beat CBE 778CD*	51		

MONSOON UK group

Date	Title / Label	Peak Position	Weeks at No.1	Weeks in Top 40
3 Apr 82	**EVER SO LONELY** *Mobile Suit Corporation CORP 2*	12		8
5 Jun 82	**SHAKTI (THE MEANING OF WITHIN)** *Mobile Suit Corporation CORP 4*	41		

MONSTA BOY UK production duo

Date	Title / Label	Peak Position	Weeks at No.1	Weeks in Top 40
7 Oct 00	**SORRY (I DIDN'T KNOW)** *Locked On LOX 125C* MONSTA BOY FEATURING DENZIE	25		1

MONSTER MAGNET US group

Date	Title / Label	Peak Position	Weeks at No.1	Weeks in Top 40
29 May 93	**TWIN EARTH** *A&M 5802812*	67		
18 Mar 95	**NEGASONIC TEENAGE WARHEAD** *A&M 5809812*	49		
6 May 95	**DOPES TO INFINITY** *A&M 5810332*	58		
23 Jan 99	**POWERTRIP** *A&M 5828232*	39		1
6 Mar 99	**SPACE LORD** *A&M 5632752*	45		

MONTAGE UK group

Date	Title / Label	Peak Position	Weeks at No.1	Weeks in Top 40
15 Feb 97	**THERE AIN'T NOTHIN' LIKE THE LOVE** *Wild Card 5733172*	64		

MONTANA SEXTET US group

Date	Title / Label	Peak Position	Weeks at No.1	Weeks in Top 40
15 Jan 83	**HEAVY VIBES** *Virgin VS 560*	59		

MONTANO VS THE TRUMPET MAN UK production duo

Date	Title / Label	Peak Position	Weeks at No.1	Weeks in Top 40
18 Sep 99	**ITZA TRUMPET THING** *Serious SERR 010CD*	46		

HUGO MONTENEGRO US orchestra leader

Date	Title / Label	Peak Position	Weeks at No.1	Weeks in Top 40
11 Sep 68	**THE GOOD THE BAD THE UGLY** *RCA 1727* HUGO MONTENEGRO & HIS ORCHESTRA & CHORUS	1	4	21
8 Jan 69	**HANG 'EM HIGH** *RCA 1771*	50		

CHRIS MONTEZ US singer

Date	Title / Label	Peak Position	Weeks at No.1	Weeks in Top 40
4 Oct 62	**LET'S DANCE** *London HLU 9596*	2		16
17 Jan 63	**SOME KINDA FUN** *London HLU 9650*	10		7
30 Jun 66	**THE MORE I SEE YOU** *Pye International 7N 25369*	3		13
22 Sep 66	**THERE WILL NEVER BE ANOTHER YOU** *Pye International 7N 25381*	37		1
14 Oct 72	**LET'S DANCE** *London HL 10205*	9		11
14 Apr 79	**LET'S DANCE** *Lightning LIG 9011*	47		

MONTROSE US group

Date	Title / Label	Peak Position	Weeks at No.1	Weeks in Top 40
28 Jun 80	**SPACE STATION NO. 5/GOOD ROCKIN' TONIGHT** *WB HM 9*	71		

MONTROSE AVENUE UK group

Date	Title / Label	Peak Position	Weeks at No.1	Weeks in Top 40
28 Mar 98	**WHERE DO I STAND?** *Columbia 6656072*	38		1
20 Jun 98	**SHINE** *Columbia 6660012*	58		
17 Oct 98	**START AGAIN** *Columbia 6664255*	59		

MONTY PYTHON UK comedy group

Date	Title / Label	Peak Position	Weeks at No.1	Weeks in Top 40
5 Oct 91	**ALWAYS LOOK ON THE BRIGHT SIDE OF LIFE** *Virgin PYTH 1*	3		7

MONYAKA US group

Date	Title / Label	Peak Position	Weeks at No.1	Weeks in Top 40
10 Sep 83	**GO DEH YAKA (GO TO THE TOP)** *Polydor POSP 641*	14		6

MOOD UK group

Date	Title / Label	Peak Position	Weeks at No.1	Weeks in Top 40
6 Feb 82	**DON'T STOP** *RCA 171*	59		
22 May 82	**PARIS IS ONE DAY AWAY** *RCA 211*	42		
30 Oct 82	**PASSION IN DARK ROOMS** *RCA 276*	74		

MOOD II SWING US production duo

Date	Title / Label	Peak Position	Weeks at No.1	Weeks in Top 40
31 Jan 04	**CAN'T GET AWAY** *Defected DFTD 078CDS*	45		

MOODSWINGS UK group

Date	Title / Label	Peak Position	Weeks at No.1	Weeks in Top 40
12 Oct 91	**SPIRITUAL HIGH (STATE OF INDEPENDENCE)** *Arista 114528* MOODSWINGS FEATURING CHRISSIE HYNDE	66		
23 Jan 93	**SPIRITUAL HIGH (STATE OF INDEPENDENCE) (REMIX)** *Arista 74321127712* MOODSWINGS FEATURING CHRISSIE HYNDE	47		

MOODY BLUES UK group

Date	Title / Label	Peak Position	Weeks at No.1	Weeks in Top 40
10 Dec 64	**GO NOW** *Decca F 12022*	1	1	13
4 Mar 65	**I DON'T WANT TO GO ON WITHOUT YOU** *Decca F 12095*	33		5
10 Jun 65	**FROM THE BOTTOM OF MY HEART** *Decca F 12166*	22		7
18 Nov 65	**EVERYDAY** *Decca F 12266*	44		
27 Dec 67	**NIGHTS IN WHITE SATIN** *Deram DM 161*	19		9
7 Aug 68	**VOICES IN THE SKY** *Deram DM 196*	27		8
4 Dec 68	**RIDE MY SEE-SAW** *Deram DM 213*	42		
2 May 70	**QUESTION** *Threshold TH 4*	2		12
6 May 72	**ISN'T LIFE STRANGE** *Threshold TH 9*	13		9
2 Dec 72	**NIGHTS IN WHITE SATIN** *Deram DM 161*	9		10
10 Feb 73	**I'M JUST A SINGER (IN A ROCK 'N' ROLL BAND)** *Threshold TH 13*	36		2
10 Nov 79	**NIGHTS IN WHITE SATIN** *Deram DM 161*	14		8
20 Aug 83	**BLUE WORLD** *Threshold TH 30*	35		2
25 Jun 88	**I KNOW YOU'RE OUT THERE SOMEWHERE** *Polydor POSP 921*	52		

MICHAEL MOOG US producer

Date	Title / Label	Peak Position	Weeks at No.1	Weeks in Top 40
11 Dec 99	**THAT SOUND** *ffrr FCD 374*	32		1
25 Aug 01	**YOU BELONG TO ME** *Strictly Rhythm SRUKECD 04*	62		

MOOGWAI Swiss/Dutch production duo

Date	Title / Label	Peak Position	Weeks at No.1	Weeks in Top 40
6 May 00	**VIOLA** *Platipus PLATCD 71*	55		
26 May 01	**THE LABYRINTH** *Platipus PLATCD 83*	68		

MOONEY SUZUKI US group

Date	Title / Label	Peak Position	Weeks at No.1	Weeks in Top 40
29 Jan 05	**ALIVE AND AMPLIFIED** *Columbia SAMMY006*	38		1

MOONMAN Dutch singer

Date	Title / Label	Peak Position	Weeks at No.1	Weeks in Top 40
9 Aug 97	**DON'T BE AFRAID** *Heat Recordings HEATCD 009*	60		
27 Nov 99	**DON'T BE AFRAID '99 (REMIX)** *Heat Recordings HEATCD 022*	41		
7 Oct 00	**GALAXIA** *Heat Recordings HEATCD 025* MOONMAN FEATURING CHANTAL	50		

MOONTREKKERS UK group

Date	Title / Label	Peak Position	Weeks at No.1	Weeks in Top 40
2 Nov 61	**NIGHT OF THE VAMPIRE** *Parlophone R 4814*	50		

MOONY Italian singer

Date	Title / Label	Peak Position	Weeks at No.1	Weeks in Top 40
15 Jun 02	**DOVE (I'LL BE LOVING YOU)** *Positiva/Cream CDMNY1*	9		3
1 Mar 03	**ACROBATS (LOOKING FOR BALANCE)** *WEA 363CD*	64		

CHANTE MOORE US singer

Date	Title / Label	Peak Position	Weeks at No.1	Weeks in Top 40
20 Mar 93	**LOVE'S TAKEN OVER** *MCA MCSTD 1744*	54		
4 Mar 95	**FREE/SAIL ON** *MCA MCSTD 2042*	69		
7 Apr 01	**STRAIGHT UP** *MCA MCSTD 40250*	11		4

DOROTHY MOORE US singer

Date	Title / Label	Peak Position	Weeks at No.1	Weeks in Top 40
19 Jun 76	**MISTY BLUE** *Contempo CS 2087*	5		11
16 Oct 76	**FUNNY HOW TIME SLIPS AWAY** *Contempo CS 2092*	38		1
15 Oct 77	**I BELIEVE YOU** *Epic EPC 5573*	20		8

GARY MOORE UK singer/guitarist

Date	Title / Label	Peak Position	Weeks at No.1	Weeks in Top 40
21 Apr 79	**PARISIENNE WALKWAYS** *MCA 419*	8		9
21 Jan 84	**HOLD ON TO LOVE** *10 TEN 13*	65		
11 Aug 84	**EMPTY ROOMS** *10 TEN 25*	51		
18 May 85	**OUT IN THE FIELDS** *10 TEN 49* GARY MOORE & PHIL LYNOTT	5		8
27 Jul 85	**EMPTY ROOMS** *10 TEN 58*	23		6
20 Dec 86	**OVER THE HILLS AND FAR AWAY** *10 TEN 134*	20		6
28 Feb 87	**WILD FRONTIER** *10 TEN 159*	35		3
9 May 87	**FRIDAY ON MY MIND** *10 TEN 164*	26		3
29 Aug 87	**THE LONER** *10 TEN 178*	53		
5 Dec 87	**TAKE A LITTLE TIME (DOUBLE SINGLE)** *10 TEN 190*	75		
14 Jan 89	**AFTER THE WAR** *Virgin GMS 1*	37		2
18 Mar 89	**READY FOR LOVE** *Virgin GMS 2*	56		
24 Mar 90	**OH PRETTY WOMAN** *Virgin VS 1233* GARY MOORE FEATURING ALBERT KING	48		
12 May 90	**STILL GOT THE BLUES (FOR YOU)** *Virgin VS 1267*	31		4
18 Aug 90	**WALKING BY MYSELF** *Virgin VS 1281*	48		
15 Dec 90	**TOO TIRED** *Virgin VS 1306*	71		
22 Feb 92	**COLD DAY IN HELL** *Virgin VS 1393*	24		2
9 May 92	**STORY OF THE BLUES** *Virgin VS 1412*	40		1
18 Jul 92	**SINCE I MET YOU BABY** *Virgin VS 1423* GARY MOORE & BB KING	59		
24 Oct 92	**SEPARATE WAYS** *Virgin VS 1437*	59		
8 May 93	**PARISIENNE WALKWAYS (LIVE)** *Virgin VSCDX 1456*	32		2
17 Jun 95	**NEED YOUR LOVE SO BAD** *Virgin VSCDG 1546*	48		

JACKIE MOORE US singer

Date	Title / Label	Peak Position	Weeks at No.1	Weeks in Top 40
15 Sep 79	**THIS TIME BABY** *CBS 7722*	49		

MANDY MOORE US singer

Date	Title / Label	Peak Position	Weeks at No.1	Weeks in Top 40
6 May 00	**CANDY** *Epic 6693452*	6		4
19 Aug 00	**I WANNA BE WITH YOU** *Epic 6695922*	21		2

MELBA MOORE US singer

Date	Title / Label	Peak Position	Weeks at No.1	Weeks in Top 40
15 May 76	**THIS IS IT** *Buddah BDS 443*	9		7
26 May 79	**PICK ME UP I'LL DANCE** *Epic EPC 7234*	48		
9 Oct 82	**LOVE'S COMIN' AT YA** *EMI America EA 146*	15		7
15 Jan 83	**MIND UP TONIGHT** *Capitol CL 272*	22		5
5 Mar 83	**UNDERLOVE** *Capitol CL 281*	60		

RAY MOORE UK radio DJ/singer

Date	Title / Label	Peak Position	Weeks at No.1	Weeks in Top 40
29 Nov 86	**O' MY FATHER HAD A RABBIT** *Play 213*	24		4
5 Dec 87	**BOG EYED JOG** *Play 224*	61		

SAM MOORE & LOU REED US duo

Date	Title / Label	Peak Position	Weeks at No.1	Weeks in Top 40
17 Jan 87	**SOUL MAN** *A&M AM 364*	30		4

TINA MOORE US singer

Date	Title / Label	Peak Position	Weeks at No.1	Weeks in Top 40
30 Aug 97	**NEVER GONNA LET YOU GO** *Delirious 74321511052*	7		13
25 Apr 98	**NOBODY BETTER** *Delirious 74321571612*	20		1

LISA MOORISH UK singer

Date	Title / Label	Peak Position	Weeks at No.1	Weeks in Top 40
7 Jan 95	**JUST THE WAY IT IS** *Go! Beat GODCD 123*	42		
19 Aug 95	**I'M YOUR MAN** *Go! Beat GODCD 128*	24		1
3 Feb 96	**MR FRIDAY NIGHT** *Go! Beat GODCD 137*	24		2
18 May 96	**LOVE FOR LIFE** *Go! Beat GODCD 145*	37		1

M.O.P. US duo

Date	Title / Label	Peak Position	Weeks at No.1	Weeks in Top 40
12 May 01	**COLD AS ICE** *Epic 6711762*	4		8
18 Aug 01	**ANTE UP** *Epic 6717882* M.O.P. FEATURING BUSTA RHYMES	7		4
1 Dec 01	**STAND CLEAR** *Chrysalis CDEM 597* ADAM F FEATURING M.O.P.	43		
8 Jun 02	**STAND CLEAR** *Kaos KAOSCD 002* ADAM F FEATURING M.O.P.	50		

ANGEL MORAES US producer

Date	Title / Label	Peak Position	Weeks at No.1	Weeks in Top 40
16 Nov 96	**HEAVEN KNOWS - DEEP DEEP DOWN** *ffrr FCD 282*	72		
17 May 97	**I LIKE IT** *AM:PM 5871792*	70		

DAVID MORALES US producer

Date	Title / Label	Peak Position	Weeks at No.1	Weeks in Top 40
10 Jul 93	**GIMME LUV (EENIE MEENIE MINY MO)** *Mercury MERCD 390* DAVID MORALES & THE BAD YARD CLUB FEATURING PAPA SAN	37		2
20 Nov 93	**THE PROGRAM** *Mercury MERCD 396* DAVID MORALES & THE BAD YARD CLUB	66		
24 Aug 96	**IN DE GHETTO** *Manifesto FESCD 12* DAVID MORALES & THE BAD YARD CLUB FEATURING CRYSTAL WATERS & DELTA	35		1
15 Aug 98	**NEEDIN' YOU** *Manifesto FESCD 46* DAVID MORALES PRESENTS THE FACE	8		5
24 Jun 00	**HIGHER** *Azuli AZNYCDX 120* DAVID MORALES & ALBERT CABRERA PRESENT MOCA FEATURING DEANNA	41		
20 Jan 01	**NEEDIN' U II (REMIX)** *Manifesto FESCD 78* DAVID MORALES PRESENTS THE FACE FEATURING JULIET ROBERTS	11		3
2 Oct 04	**HOW WOULD U FEEL** *DMI DM102* DAVID MORALES FEATURING LEA LORIEN	71		

MORCHEEBA UK group

Date	Title / Label	Peak Position	Weeks at No.1	Weeks in Top 40
13 Jul 96	**TAPE LOOP** *Indochina ID 045CD*	42		
5 Oct 96	**TRIGGER HIPPIE** *Indochina ID 052CDR*	40		1
15 Feb 97	**THE MUSIC THAT WE HEAR (MOOG ISLAND)** *Indochina ID 054CD*	47		
11 Oct 97	**SHOULDER HOLSTER** *Indochina ID 064CD*	53		
11 Apr 98	**BLINDFOLD** *Indochina ID 070CD*	56		
20 Jun 98	**LET ME SEE** *Indochina ID 076CD*	46		
29 Aug 98	**PART OF THE PROCESS** *China WOKCD 2097*	38		1
5 Aug 00	**ROME WASN'T BUILT IN A DAY** *East West EW 214CD*	34		1
31 Mar 01	**WORLD LOOKING IN** *East West EW 225CD*	48		
6 Jul 02	**OTHERWISE** *East West EW 247CD*	64		

MORE UK group

Date	Title / Label	Peak Position	Weeks at No.1	Weeks in Top 40
14 Mar 81	**WE ARE THE BAND** *Atlantic K 11561*	59		

MORE FIRE CREW UK group

Date	Title / Label	Peak Position	Weeks at No.1	Weeks in Top 40
16 Mar 02	**OI** *Go! Beat GOBCD 48* PLATINUM 45 FEATURING MORE FIRE CREW	8		5
25 Jan 03	**BACK THEN** *Go! Beat GOBCD 54*	45		

MOREL US singer

Date	Title / Label	Peak Position	Weeks at No.1	Weeks in Top 40
12 Aug 00	**TRUE (THE FAGGOT IS YOU)** *Hooj Choons HOOJ 097CD*	64		

GEORGE MOREL US singer

Date	Title / Label	Peak Position	Weeks at No.1	Weeks in Top 40
26 Oct 96	**LET'S GROOVE** *Positiva CDTIV 62* GEORGE MOREL FEATURING HEATHER WILDMAN	42		

MORGAN UK vocal/instrumental duo

Date	Title / Label	Peak Position	Weeks at No.1	Weeks in Top 40
27 Nov 99	**MISS PARKER** *Source CDSOUR 002*	74		

DEBELAH MORGAN US singer

Date	Title / Label	Peak Position	Weeks at No.1	Weeks in Top 40
24 Feb 01	**DANCE WITH ME** *Atlantic AT 0087CD*	10		5

DERRICK MORGAN Jamaican singer

Date	Title / Label	Peak Position	Weeks at No.1	Weeks in Top 40
17 Jan 70	**MOON HOP** *Crab 32*	49		

JAMIE J. MORGAN US singer

Date	Title / Label	Peak Position	Weeks at No.1	Weeks in Top 40
10 Feb 90	**WALK ON THE WILD SIDE** *Tabu 6555967*	27		3

Silver-selling ○ Gold-selling ● Platinum-selling ⊛ US No.1 ★ — Peak Position / Weeks at No.1 / Weeks in Top 40

JANE MORGAN US singer

Date	Title	Peak Position	Weeks at No.1	Weeks in Top 40
5 Dec 58	**THE DAY THE RAINS CAME** *London HLR 8751*	1	1	16
22 May 59	**IF ONLY I COULD LIVE MY LIFE AGAIN** *London HLR 8810*	27		1
21 Jul 60	**ROMANTICA** *London HLR 9120*	39		1

MELI'SA MORGAN US singer

Date	Title	Peak Position	Weeks at No.1	Weeks in Top 40
9 Aug 86	**FOOL'S PARADISE** *Capitol CL 415*	41		
25 Jun 88	**GOOD LOVE** *Capitol CL 483*	59		

RAY MORGAN UK singer

Date	Title	Peak Position	Weeks at No.1	Weeks in Top 40
25 Jul 70	**THE LONG AND WINDING ROAD** *B&C CB 128*	32		4

ERICK 'MORE' MORILLO US producer

Date	Title	Peak Position	Weeks at No.1	Weeks in Top 40
4 Feb 95	**HIGHER (FEEL IT)** *A&M 5809412* ERICK 'MORE' MORILLO PRESENTS RAW	74		
26 Jun 04	**BREAK DOWN THE DOORS** *Subliminal SUB124CD* MORILLO FEATURING THE AUDIOBULLYS	44		
12 Feb 05	**WHAT DO YOU WANT?** *Subliminal SUB138CD* MORILLO FEATURING TERRA DEVA	61		

ALANIS MORISSETTE Canadian singer

Date	Title	Peak Position	Weeks at No.1	Weeks in Top 40
5 Aug 95	**YOU OUGHTA KNOW** *Maverick W03070CD*	22		5
28 Oct 95	**HAND IN MY POCKET** *Maverick W0312CD1*	26		2
24 Feb 96	**YOU LEARN** *Maverick W0334CD*	24		2
20 Apr 96	**IRONIC** *Maverick W0343CD*	11		7
3 Aug 96	**HEAD OVER FEET** *Maverick W0355CD*	7		5
7 Dec 96	**ALL I REALLY WANT** *Maverick W0382CD*	59		
31 Oct 98	**THANK U** *Maverick W0458CD*	5		6
13 Mar 99	**JOINING YOU** *Maverick W 472CD*	28		1
31 Jul 99	**SO PURE** *Maverick W 492CD1*	38		1
2 Mar 02	**HANDS CLEAN** *Maverick W 574CD*	12		3
17 Aug 02	**PRECIOUS ILLUSIONS** *Maverick W 582CD*	53		
22 May 04	**EVERYTHING** *Maverick W 641CD*	22		1
31 Jul 04	**OUT IS THROUGH** *Maverick W 647CD*	56		
12 Nov 05	**CRAZY** *Maverick W694CD1*	65		

MORJAC Danish production duo

Date	Title	Peak Position	Weeks at No.1	Weeks in Top 40
11 Oct 03	**STARS** *Credence CDCRED 036* MORJAC FEATURING RAZ CONWAY	38		1

MORNING RUNNER UK group

Date	Title	Peak Position	Weeks at No.1	Weeks in Top 40
4 Jun 05	**DRAWING SHAPES EP** *Parlophone CDR6666*	70		
13 Aug 05	**GONE UP IN FLAMES** *Parlophone CDRS6669*	39		1
5 Nov 05	**BE ALL YOU WANT ME TO BE** *Parlophone CDR6674*	44		
4 Mar 06	**BURNING BENCHES** *Parlophone CDRS6683*	19		1
27 May 06	**THE GREAT ESCAPE** *Parlophone CDRS6696*	56		

GIORGIO MORODER Italian producer/keyboard player

Date	Title	Peak Position	Weeks at No.1	Weeks in Top 40
24 Sep 77	**FROM HERE TO ETERNITY** *Oasis 1*	16		9
17 Mar 79	**CHASE** *Casablanca CAN 144*	48		
22 Sep 84	**TOGETHER IN ELECTRIC DREAMS** *Virgin VS 713* GIORGIO MORODER & PHIL OAKEY ○	3		10
29 Jun 85	**GOODBYE BAD TIMES** *Virgin VS 772* GIORGIO MORODER & PHIL OAKEY	44		
11 Jul 98	**CARRY ON** *Almighty CDALMY 120* DONNA SUMMER & GIORGIO MORODER	65		
12 Feb 00	**THE CHASE** *Logic 74321732112* DJ EMPIRE PRESENTS GIORGIO MORODER	46		

ENNIO MORRICONE Italian orchestra leader

Date	Title	Peak Position	Weeks at No.1	Weeks in Top 40
11 Apr 81	**CHI MAI (THEME FROM THE TV SERIES *THE LIFE AND TIMES OF DAVID LLOYD GEORGE*)** *BBC RESL 92* ●	2		10

JAMES MORRISON UK singer

Date	Title	Peak Position	Weeks at No.1	Weeks in Top 40
22 Jul 06	**YOU GIVE ME SOMETHING** *Polydor 9858670*	5		10
21 Oct 06	**WONDERFUL WORLD** *Polydor 1709432*	8		9
23 Dec 06	**THE PIECES DON'T FIT ANYMORE** *Polydor 1717533*	30		2
24 Mar 07	**UNDISCOVERED** *Download*	63		

MARK MORRISON UK singer

Date	Title	Peak Position	Weeks at No.1	Weeks in Top 40
22 Apr 95	**CRAZY** *WEA YZ 907CD*	19		3
16 Sep 95	**LET'S GET DOWN** *WEA 001CD*	39		1
16 Mar 96	**RETURN OF THE MACK** *WEA 040CD* ⊛	1	2	17
27 Jul 96	**CRAZY (REMIX)** *WEA 054CD1*	6		4
19 Oct 96	**TRIPPIN'** *WEA 079CD1*	8		4
21 Dec 96	**HORNY** *WEA 090CD1*	5		8
15 Mar 97	**MOAN AND GROAN** *WEA 096CD1*	7		3
20 Sep 97	**WHO'S THE MACK** *WEA 128CD1*	13		3
4 Sep 99	**BEST FRIEND** *WEA 221CD1* MARK MORRISON & CONNOR REEVES	23		1
14 Aug 04	**JUST A MAN/BACKSTABBERS** *2 Wikid WKDCD007*	48		
22 Apr 06	**INNOCENT MAN** *Mona MONASP5CDS* MARK MORRISON FEATURING DMX	46		

VAN MORRISON UK singer

Date	Title	Peak Position	Weeks at No.1	Weeks in Top 40
20 Oct 79	**BRIGHT SIDE OF THE ROAD** *Mercury 6001 121*	63		
1 Jul 89	**HAVE I TOLD YOU LATELY** *Polydor VANS 1*	74		
9 Dec 89	**WHENEVER GOD SHINES HIS LIGHT** *Polydor VANS 2* VAN MORRISON WITH CLIFF RICHARD	20		5
15 May 93	**GLORIA** *Exile VANCD 11* VAN MORRISON & JOHN LEE HOOKER	31		2
18 Mar 95	**HAVE I TOLD YOU LATELY THAT I LOVE YOU** *RCA 74321271702* CHIEFTAINS WITH VAN MORRISON	71		
10 Jun 95	**DAYS LIKE THIS** *Exile VANCD 12*	65		
2 Dec 95	**NO RELIGION** *Exile 5775792*	54		
1 Mar 97	**THE HEALING GAME** *Exile 5733912*	46		
6 Mar 99	**PRECIOUS TIME** *Pointblank POBDX 14*	36		1
22 May 99	**BACK ON TOP** *Exile/Pointblank/Virgin POBD 15*	69		
18 May 02	**HEY MR DJ** *Exile 5705962*	58		

MORRISSEY UK singer

Date	Title	Peak Position	Weeks at No.1	Weeks in Top 40
27 Feb 88	**SUEDEHEAD** *HMV POP 1618*	5		4
11 Jun 88	**EVERYDAY IS LIKE SUNDAY** *HMV POP 1619*	9		5
11 Feb 89	**LAST OF THE FAMOUS INTERNATIONAL PLAYBOYS** *HMV POP 1620*	6		3
29 Apr 89	**INTERESTING DRUG** *HMV POP 1621*	9		3
25 Nov 89	**OUIJA BOARD OUIJA BOARD** *HMV POP 1622*	18		2
5 May 90	**NOVEMBER SPAWNED A MONSTER** *HMV POP 1623*	12		2
20 Oct 90	**PICCADILLY PALARE** *HMV POP 1624*	18		2
23 Feb 91	**OUR FRANK** *HMV POP 1625*	26		2
13 Apr 91	**SING YOUR LIFE** *HMV POP 1626*	33		1
27 Jul 91	**PREGNANT FOR THE LAST TIME** *HMV POP 1627*	25		3
12 Oct 91	**MY LOVE LIFE** *HMV POP 1628*	29		1
9 May 92	**WE HATE IT WHEN OUR FRIENDS BECOME SUCCESSFUL** *HMV POP 1629*	17		2
18 Jul 92	**YOU'RE THE ONE FOR ME, FATTY** *HMV POP 1630*	19		2
19 Dec 92	**CERTAIN PEOPLE I KNOW** *HMV POP 1631*	35		1
12 Mar 94	**THE MORE YOU IGNORE ME THE CLOSER I GET** *Parlophone CDR 6372*	8		2
11 Jun 94	**HOLD ON TO YOUR FRIENDS** *Parlophone CDR 6383*	47		
20 Aug 94	**INTERLUDE** *Parlophone CDR 6365* MORRISSEY & SIOUXSIE	25		1
28 Jan 95	**BOXERS** *Parlophone CDR 6400*	23		1
2 Sep 95	**DAGENHAM DAVE** *RCA Victor 74321299802*	26		1
9 Dec 95	**THE BOY RACER** *RCA Victor 74321332952*	36		1
23 Dec 95	**SUNNY** *Parlophone CDR 6243*	42		
2 Aug 97	**ALMA MATTERS** *Island CID 667*	16		1
18 Oct 97	**ROY'S KEEN** *Island CID 671*	42		
10 Jan 98	**SATAN REJECTED MY SOUL** *Island CID 686*	39		1
22 May 04	**IRISH BLOOD ENGLISH HEART** *Attack ATKXS002*	3		3
24 Jul 04	**FIRST OF THE GANG TO DIE** *Attack ATKXS003*	6		5
23 Oct 04	**LET ME KISS YOU** *Attack ATKXS008*	8		2
25 Dec 04	**I HAVE FORGIVEN JESUS** *Attack ATKXS011*	10		3
9 Apr 05	**REDONDO BEACH/THERE IS A LIGHT THAT NEVER GOES OUT** *Attack ATKXD015*	11		2
8 Apr 06	**YOU HAVE KILLED ME** *Attack ATKXS017*	3		2
17 Jun 06	**THE YOUNGEST WAS THE MOST LOVED** *Attack ATKXS018*	14		1
2 Sep 06	**IN THE FUTURE WHEN ALL'S WELL** *Attack ATKXS021*	17		1
16 Dec 06	**I JUST WANT TO SEE THE BOY HAPPY** *Attack ATKXD023*	16		1
16 Feb 08	**THAT'S HOW PEOPLE GROW UP** *Decca 4780362*	14		2

BUDDY MORROW US orchestra leader

Date	Title	Peak Position	Weeks at No.1	Weeks in Top 40
20 Mar 53	**NIGHT TRAIN** *HMV B 10347*	12		1

BOB MORTIMER UK comedian

Date	Title	Peak Position	Weeks at No.1	Weeks in Top 40
8 Jul 95	**I'M A BELIEVER** *Parlophone CDR 6412* EMF/REEVES & MORTIMER	3		5
24 May 97	**LET'S DANCE** *Magnet EW 112CD* MIDDLESBROUGH FC FEATURING BOB MORTIMER & CHRIS REA	44		

MORTIIS Norwegian singer/bass player

Date	Title	Peak Position	Weeks at No.1	Weeks in Top 40
28 Aug 04	**THE GRUDGE** *Earache MOSH284CD*	51		
7 May 05	**DECADENT & DESPERATE** *Earache MOSH306CD*	49		

MOS DEF US rapper

Date	Title	Peak Position	Weeks at No.1	Weeks in Top 40
24 Jun 00	**UMI SAYS** *Rawkus RWK 232CD*	60		
4 Nov 00	**MISS FAT BOOTY - PART II** *Rawkus RWK 282CD* MOS DEF FEATURING GHOSTFACE KILLAH	64		
3 Feb 01	**OH NO** *Rawkus RWK 302* MOS DEF & NATE DOGG FEATURING PHAROAHE MONCH	24		3

MICKIE MOST UK singer

Date	Title	Peak Position	Weeks at No.1	Weeks in Top 40
25 Jul 63	**MISTER PORTER** *Decca F 11664*	45		

MOTELS US group

Date	Title	Peak Position	Weeks at No.1	Weeks in Top 40
11 Oct 80	**WHOSE PROBLEM?** *Capitol CL 16162*	42		
10 Jan 81	**DAYS ARE O.K.** *Capitol CL 16149*	41		

WENDY MOTEN US singer

Date	Title	Peak Position	Weeks at No.1	Weeks in Top 40
5 Feb 94	**COME IN OUT OF THE RAIN** *EMI-USA CDMT 105*	8		7
14 May 94	**SO CLOSE TO LOVE** *EMI-USA CDMTS 106*	35		2

MOTHER UK production duo

Date	Title	Peak Position	Weeks at No.1	Weeks in Top 40
12 Jun 93	**ALL FUNKED UP** *Bosting BYSNCD 101*	34		1
1 Oct 94	**GET BACK** *Six6 SIXT 119*	73		
31 Aug 96	**ALL FUNKED UP (REMIX)** *Six6 SIXXCD 1*	66		

MOTHER'S PRIDE UK production duo

Date	Title	Peak Position	Weeks at No.1	Weeks in Top 40
21 Mar 98	**FLORIBUNDA** *Heat Recordings HEATCD 013*	42		
6 Nov 99	**LEARNING TO FLY** *Devolution DEVR 001CDS*	54		

MOTIV 8 UK producer

Date	Title	Peak Position	Weeks at No.1	Weeks in Top 40
17 Jul 93	**ROCKIN' FOR MYSELF** *Nuff Respect NUFF 002CD* MOTIV 8 FEATURING ANGIE BROWN	67		
7 May 94	**ROCKIN' FOR MYSELF (REMIX)** *WEA YZ 814CD*	18		3
21 Oct 95	**BREAK THE CHAIN** *Eternal 010CD*	31		1
23 Dec 95	**SEARCHING FOR THE GOLDEN EYE** *Eternal 027CD* MOTIV 8 & KYM MAZELLE	40		1
19 Feb 05	**RIDING ON THE WINGS** *Concept CDCON52X*	44		

MOTIVATION Dutch producer

Date	Title	Peak Position	Weeks at No.1	Weeks in Top 40
17 Nov 01	**PARA MI** *Definitive CDDEF 1*	71		

MOTLEY CRUE US group

Date	Title	Peak Position	Weeks at No.1	Weeks in Top 40
24 Aug 85	**SMOKIN' IN THE BOYS ROOM** *Elektra EKR 16*	71		
8 Feb 86	**HOME SWEET HOME/SMOKIN' IN THE BOYS ROOM** *Elektra EKR 33*	51		
1 Aug 87	**GIRLS GIRLS GIRLS** *Elektra EKR 59*	26		5
16 Jan 88	**YOU'RE ALL I NEED/WILD SIDE** *Elektra EKR 65*	23		3
4 Nov 89	**DR FEELGOOD** *Elektra EKR 97*	50		
12 May 90	**WITHOUT YOU** *Elektra EKR 109*	39		2
7 Sep 91	**PRIMAL SCREAM** *Elektra EKR 133*	32		1
11 Jan 92	**HOME SWEET HOME** *Elektra EKR 136*	37		1
5 Mar 94	**HOOLIGAN'S HOLIDAY** *Elektra EKR 180CDX*	36		1
19 Jul 97	**AFRAID** *Elektra E 3936 CD1*	58		
4 Jun 05	**IF I DIE TOMORROW** *Mercury 9871754*	63		

MOTORCYCLE US group

Date	Title	Peak Position	Weeks at No.1	Weeks in Top 40
17 Jan 04	**AS THE RUSH COMES** *Positiva CDTIVS 203*	11		6

MOTORHEAD UK group

Date	Title	Peak Position	Weeks at No.1	Weeks in Top 40
16 Sep 78	**LOUIE LOUIE** *Bronze BRO 60*	68		
10 Mar 79	**OVERKILL** *Bronze BRO 67*	39		1
30 Jun 79	**NO CLASS** *Bronze BRO 78*	61		
1 Dec 79	**BOMBER** *Bronze BRO 85*	34		1
3 May 80	**THE GOLDEN YEARS EP** *Bronze BRO 92*	8		5
1 Nov 80	**ACE OF SPADES** *Bronze BRO 106*	15		5
22 Nov 80	**BEER DRINKERS AND HELL RAISERS** *Big Beat SWT 61*	43		
21 Feb 81	**ST VALENTINE'S DAY MASSACRE EP** *Bronze BRO 116* MOTORHEAD & GIRLSCHOOL ●	5		6
11 Jul 81	**MOTORHEAD LIVE** *Bronze BRO 124*	6		5
3 Apr 82	**IRON FIST** *Bronze BRO 146*	29		4
21 May 83	**I GOT MINE** *Bronze BRO 165*	46		
30 Jul 83	**SHINE** *Bronze BRO 167*	59		
1 Sep 84	**KILLED BY DEATH** *Bronze BRO 185*	51		
5 Jul 86	**DEAF FOREVER** *GWR 2*	67		
5 Jan 91	**THE ONE TO SING THE BLUES** *Epic 6565787*	45		
14 Nov 92	**92 TOUR (EP)** *Epic 6588096*	63		
11 Sep 93	**ACE OF SPADES** *WGAF CDWGAF 101*	23		3
10 Dec 94	**BORN TO RAISE HELL** *Fox 74321230152* MOTORHEAD/ICE-T/WHITFIELD CRANE	47		

MOTORS UK group

Date	Title	Peak Position	Weeks at No.1	Weeks in Top 40
24 Sep 77	**DANCING THE NIGHT AWAY** *Virgin VS 186*	42		
10 Jun 78	**AIRPORT** *Virgin VS 219* ●	4		9
19 Aug 78	**FORGET ABOUT YOU** *Virgin VS 222*	13		7
12 Apr 80	**LOVE AND LONELINESS** *Virgin VS 263*	58		

MOTT THE HOOPLE UK group

Date	Title	Peak Position	Weeks at No.1	Weeks in Top 40
12 Aug 72	**ALL THE YOUNG DUDES** *CBS 8271*	3		9
16 Jun 73	**HONALOOCHIE BOOGIE** *CBS 1530*	12		8
8 Sep 73	**ALL THE WAY FROM MEMPHIS** *CBS 1764*	10		7
24 Nov 73	**ROLL AWAY THE STONE** *CBS 1895*	8		12
30 Mar 74	**GOLDEN AGE OF ROCK AND ROLL** *CBS 2177*	16		7
22 Jun 74	**FOXY FOXY** *CBS 2439*	33		4
2 Nov 74	**SATURDAY GIGS** *CBS 2754*	41		

MOUNT RUSHMORE UK production duo

Date	Title	Peak Position	Weeks at No.1	Weeks in Top 40
3 Apr 99	**YOU BETTER** *Universal MCSTD 40192* MOUNT RUSHMORE PRESENTS THE KNACK	53		

NANA MOUSKOURI Greek singer

Date	Title	Peak Position	Weeks at No.1	Weeks in Top 40
11 Jan 86	**ONLY LOVE** *Philips PH 38*	2		9

MOUSSE T German remixer

Date	Title	Peak Position	Weeks at No.1	Weeks in Top 40
6 Jun 98	**HORNY** *AM:PM 5826712* MOUSSE T VERSUS HOT 'N' JUICY ●	2		13
20 May 00	**SEX BOMB** *Gut CXGUT 33* TOM JONES & MOUSSE T	3		7
10 Aug 02	**FIRE** *Serious SERR 44CDX* MOUSSE T FEATURING EMMA LANFORD	58		
4 Sep 04	**IS IT COS I'M COOL?** *Free 2 Air F2A1CDX* MOUSSE T FEATURING EMMA LANFORD	9		7
18 Dec 04	**RIGHT ABOUT NOW** *Free2Air F2A2CDX* MOUSSE T FEATURING EMMA LANFORD	28		1
12 Aug 06	**HORNY AS A DANDY** *Feverpitch/Free2air CDFEV14* MOUSSE T VS DANDY WARHOLS	17		2

MOUTH & MACNEAL Dutch duo

Date	Title	Peak Position	Weeks at No.1	Weeks in Top 40
4 May 74	**I SEE A STAR** *Decca F 13504*	8		7

MOVE UK group

Date	Title	Peak Position	Weeks at No.1	Weeks in Top 40
5 Jan 67	**NIGHT OF FEAR** *Deram DM 109*	2		9
6 Apr 67	**I CAN HEAR THE GRASS GROW** *Deram DM 117*	5		9
6 Sep 67	**FLOWERS IN THE RAIN** *Regal Zonophone RZ 3001*	2		12
7 Feb 68	**FIRE BRIGADE** *Regal Zonophone RZ 3005*	3		11
25 Dec 68	**BLACKBERRY WAY** *Regal Zonophone RZ 3015*	1	1	9
23 Jul 69	**CURLY** *Regal Zonophone RZ 3021*	12		10
25 Apr 70	**BRONTOSAURUS** *Regal Zonophone RZ 3026*	7		10
3 Jul 71	**TONIGHT** *Harvest HAR 5038*	11		8
23 Oct 71	**CHINATOWN** *Harvest HAR 5043*	23		8
13 May 72	**CALIFORNIA MAN** *Harvest HAR 5050*	7		12

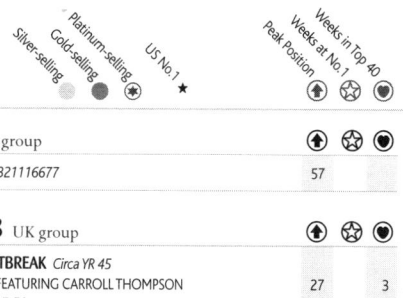

Silver-selling · Gold-selling · Platinum-selling · US No.1 · Peak Position · Weeks at No.1 · Weeks in Top 40

MOVEMENT US group

Date	Title / Label	Peak Position	Weeks at No.1	Weeks in Top 40
24 Oct 92	**JUMP!** *Arista 74321116677*	57		

MOVEMENT 98 UK group

Date	Title / Label	Peak Position	Weeks at No.1	Weeks in Top 40
19 May 90	**JOY AND HEARTBREAK** *Circa YR 45* MOVEMENT 98 FEATURING CARROLL THOMPSON	27		3
15 Sep 90	**SUNRISE** *Circa YR 51* MOVEMENT 98 FEATURING CARROLL THOMPSON	58		

MOVIN' MELODIES Dutch producer

Date	Title / Label	Peak Position	Weeks at No.1	Weeks in Top 40
22 Oct 94	**LA LUNA** *Effective EFFS 017CD* MOVIN' MELODIES PRODUCTION	64		
29 Jun 96	**INDICA** *Hooj Choons HOOJCD 44*	62		
26 Jul 97	**ROLLERBLADE** *Movin' Melodies 5822352*	71		

ALISON MOYET UK singer

Date	Title / Label	Peak Position	Weeks at No.1	Weeks in Top 40
23 Jun 84	**LOVE RESURRECTION** *CBS A 4497*	10		8
13 Oct 84	**ALL CRIED OUT** *CBS A 4757*	8		9
1 Dec 84	**INVISIBLE** *CBS A 4930*	21		9
16 Mar 85	**THAT OLE DEVIL CALLED LOVE** *CBS A 6044*	2		8
29 Nov 86	**IS THIS LOVE?** *CBS MOYET 1*	3		12
7 Mar 87	**WEAK IN THE PRESENCE OF BEAUTY** *CBS MOYET 2*	6		8
30 May 87	**ORDINARY GIRL** *CBS MOYET 3*	43		
28 Nov 87	**LOVE LETTERS** *CBS MOYET 5*	4		8
6 Apr 91	**IT WON'T BE LONG** *Columbia 6567577*	50		
1 Jun 91	**WISHING YOU WERE HERE** *Columbia 6569397*	72		
12 Oct 91	**THIS HOUSE** *Columbia 6575157*	40		1
16 Oct 93	**FALLING** *Columbia 6595962*	42		
12 Mar 94	**WHISPERING YOUR NAME** *Columbia 6601622*	18		5
28 May 94	**GETTING INTO SOMETHING** *Columbia 6603565*	51		
22 Oct 94	**ODE TO BOY** *Columbia 6607952*	59		
26 Aug 95	**SOLID WOOD** *Columbia 6623265*	44		

MOZAIC UK group

Date	Title / Label	Peak Position	Weeks at No.1	Weeks in Top 40
5 Aug 95	**SING IT (THE HALLELUJAH SONG)** *Perfecto PERF 106CD*	14		2
10 Aug 96	**RAYS OF THE RISING SUN** *Perfecto PERF 123CD*	32		1
30 Nov 96	**MOVING UP MOVING ON** *Perfecto PERF 131CD*	62		

MS DYNAMITE UK singer

Date	Title / Label	Peak Position	Weeks at No.1	Weeks in Top 40
23 Jun 01	**BOOO!** *ffrr FCD 399* STICKY FEATURING MS DYNAMITE	12		4
1 Jun 02	**IT TAKES MORE** *Polydor 5707982*	7		6
7 Sep 02	**DY-NA-MI-TEE** *Polydor 5709782*	5		7
14 Dec 02	**PUT HIM OUT** *Polydor 0658942*	19		4
8 Oct 05	**JUDGEMENT DAY** *Polydor 9873970*	25		2

MTUME US group

Date	Title / Label	Peak Position	Weeks at No.1	Weeks in Top 40
14 May 83	**JUICY FRUIT** *Epic A 3424*	34		5
22 Sep 84	**PRIME TIME** *Epic A 4720*	57		

MUD UK group

Date	Title / Label	Peak Position	Weeks at No.1	Weeks in Top 40
10 Mar 73	**CRAZY** *RAK 146*	12		10
23 Jun 73	**HYPNOSIS** *RAK 152*	16		10
27 Oct 73	**DYNA-MITE** *RAK 159*	4		12
19 Jan 74	**TIGER FEET** *RAK 166*	1	4	10
13 Apr 74	**THE CAT CREPT IN** *RAK 170*	2		7
27 Jul 74	**ROCKET** *RAK 178*	6		8
30 Nov 74	**LONELY THIS CHRISTMAS** *RAK 187*	1	4	9
15 Feb 75	**THE SECRETS THAT YOU KEEP** *RAK 194*	3		8
26 Apr 75	**OH BOY** *RAK 201*	1	2	8
21 Jun 75	**MOONSHINE SALLY** *RAK 208*	10		7
2 Aug 75	**ONE NIGHT** *RAK 213*	32		3
4 Oct 75	**L-L-LUCY** *Private Stock PVT 41*	10		6
29 Nov 75	**SHOW ME YOU'RE A WOMAN** *Private Stock PVT 45*	8		8
15 May 76	**SHAKE IT DOWN** *Private Stock PVT 65*	12		8
27 Nov 76	**LEAN ON ME** *Private Stock PVT 85*	7		9
21 Dec 85	**LONELY THIS CHRISTMAS** *RAK 187*	61		

MUDHONEY US group

Date	Title / Label	Peak Position	Weeks at No.1	Weeks in Top 40
17 Aug 91	**LET IT SLIDE** *Subpop SP 15154*	60		
24 Oct 92	**SUCK YOU DRY** *Reprise W0137*	65		

MUDLARKS UK group

Date	Title / Label	Peak Position	Weeks at No.1	Weeks in Top 40
2 May 58	**LOLLIPOP** *Columbia DB 4099*	2		9
6 Jun 58	**BOOK OF LOVE** *Columbia DB 4133*	8		9
27 Feb 59	**THE LOVE GAME** *Columbia DB 4250*	30		1

IDRIS MUHAMMAD US drummer

Date	Title / Label	Peak Position	Weeks at No.1	Weeks in Top 40
17 Sep 77	**COULD HEAVEN EVER BE LIKE THIS** *Kudu 935*	42		

MUKKAA UK production duo

Date	Title / Label	Peak Position	Weeks at No.1	Weeks in Top 40
27 Feb 93	**BURUCHACCA** *Limbo 008*	74		

MARIA MULDAUR US singer

Date	Title / Label	Peak Position	Weeks at No.1	Weeks in Top 40
29 Jun 74	**MIDNIGHT AT THE OASIS** *Reprise K 14331*	21		6

MULL HISTORICAL SOCIETY UK group

Date	Title / Label	Peak Position	Weeks at No.1	Weeks in Top 40
21 Jul 01	**ANIMAL CANNABUS** *Rough Trade RTRADESCD 021*	53		
9 Feb 02	**WATCHING XANADU** *Blanco Y Negro NEG 138CD*	36		1
1 Mar 03	**THE FINAL ARREARS** *Blanco Y Negro NEG 144CD*	32		1
14 Jun 03	**AM I WRONG?** *Blanco Y Negro NEG 146CD*	51		
24 Jul 04	**HOW 'BOUT I LOVE YOU MORE?** *B Unique BUN080CDS*	37		1

SHAWN MULLINS US singer

Date	Title / Label	Peak Position	Weeks at No.1	Weeks in Top 40
6 Mar 99	**LULLABY** *Columbia 6669595*	9		6
2 Oct 99	**WHAT IS LIFE** *Columbia 6678212*	62		

MULU UK duo

Date	Title / Label	Peak Position	Weeks at No.1	Weeks in Top 40
2 Aug 97	**PUSSYCAT** *Dedicated MULU 003CD1*	50		

OMERO MUMBA Irish singer

Date	Title / Label	Peak Position	Weeks at No.1	Weeks in Top 40
20 Jul 02	**LIL' BIG MAN** *Polydor 5708862*	42		

SAMANTHA MUMBA Irish singer

Date	Title / Label	Peak Position	Weeks at No.1	Weeks in Top 40
8 Jul 00	**GOTTA TELL YOU** *Wild Card 5618832*	2		10
28 Oct 00	**BODY II BODY** *Wild Card 5877752*	5		5
3 Mar 01	**ALWAYS COME BACK TO YOUR LOVE** *Wild Card 5879252*	3		9
22 Sep 01	**BABY COME ON OVER** *Wild Card 5872352*	5		5
22 Dec 01	**LATELY** *Wild Card 5705232*	6		9
26 Oct 02	**I'M RIGHT HERE** *Wild Card 0659372*	5		4

MUMM RA UK group

Date	Title / Label	Peak Position	Weeks at No.1	Weeks in Top 40
4 Nov 06	**OUT OF THE QUESTION** *Columbia BEXHILL06*	45		
3 Mar 07	**WHAT WOULD STEVE DO** *Columbia BEXHILL10*	40		1
26 May 07	**SHE'S GOT YOU HIGH** *Columbia BEXHILL14*	41		

MUNDY Irish singer

Date	Title / Label	Peak Position	Weeks at No.1	Weeks in Top 40
3 Aug 96	**TO YOU I BESTOW** *Epic MUNDY 1CD*	60		
5 Oct 96	**LIFE'S A CINCH** *Epic MUNDY 2CD*	75		

MUNGO JERRY UK group

Date	Title / Label	Peak Position	Weeks at No.1	Weeks in Top 40
6 Jun 70	**IN THE SUMMERTIME** *Dawn DNX 2502*	1	7	16
6 Feb 71	**BABY JUMP** *Dawn DNX 2505*	1	2	12
29 May 71	**LADY ROSE** *Dawn DNX 2510*	5		10
18 Sep 71	**YOU DON'T HAVE TO BE IN THE ARMY TO FIGHT IN THE WAR** *Dawn DNX 2513*	13		6
22 Apr 72	**OPEN UP** *Dawn DNX 2514*	21		6
7 Jul 73	**ALRIGHT ALRIGHT ALRIGHT** *Dawn DNS 1037*	3		10
10 Nov 73	**WILD LOVE** *Dawn DNS 1051*	32		4
6 Apr 74	**LONG LEGGED WOMAN DRESSED IN BLACK** *Dawn DNS 1061*	13		8
29 May 99	**SUPPORT THE TOON - IT'S YOUR DUTY (EP)** *Saraja TOONCD 001* MUNGO JERRY & TOON TRAVELLERS	57		

MUNICH MACHINE German group

Date	Title / Label	Peak Position	Weeks at No.1	Weeks in Top 40
10 Dec 77	**GET ON THE FUNK TRAIN** *Oasis 2*	41		
4 Nov 78	**A WHITER SHADE OF PALE** *Oasis 5* MUNICH MACHINE INTRODUCING CHRIS BENNETT	42		

Silver-selling ○ Gold-selling ● Platinum-selling ✪ US No.1 ★ — Peak Position / Weeks at No.1 / Weeks in Top 40

MUPPETS US TV puppet characters

Date	Title / Label	Peak Position	Weeks at No.1	Weeks in Top 40
28 May 77	**HALFWAY DOWN THE STAIRS** *Pye 7N 45698*	7		8
17 Dec 77	**THE MUPPET SHOW MUSIC HALL EP** *Pye 7NX 8004*	19		5

MURDERDOLLS US group

Date	Title / Label	Peak Position	Weeks at No.1	Weeks in Top 40
16 Nov 02	**DEAD IN HOLLYWOOD** *Roadrunner RR 20223*	54		
26 Jul 03	**WHITE WEDDING** *Roadrunner RR 20155*	24		1

LYDIA MURDOCK US singer

Date	Title / Label	Peak Position	Weeks at No.1	Weeks in Top 40
24 Sep 83	**SUPERSTAR** *Korova KOW 30*	14		6

SHIRLEY MURDOCK US singer

Date	Title / Label	Peak Position	Weeks at No.1	Weeks in Top 40
12 Apr 86	**TRUTH OR DARE** *Elektra EKR 36*	60		

NOEL MURPHY Irish singer

Date	Title / Label	Peak Position	Weeks at No.1	Weeks in Top 40
27 Jun 87	**MURPHY AND THE BRICKS** *Murphy's STACK 1*	57		

ROISIN MURPHY UK singer

Date	Title / Label	Peak Position	Weeks at No.1	Weeks in Top 40
16 Jun 01	**NEVER ENOUGH** *Positiva CDTIV 156* BORIS DLUGOSCH FEATURING ROISIN MURPHY	16		3
19 Jan 02	**WONDERLAND** *Echo ECSCD 120* PSYCHEDELIC WALTONS FEATURING ROISIN MURPHY	37		1
20 Oct 07	**LET ME KNOW** *EMI CDEMS728*	28		1

WALTER MURPHY US orchestra leader

Date	Title / Label	Peak Position	Weeks at No.1	Weeks in Top 40
10 Jul 76	**A FIFTH OF BEETHOVEN** *Private Stock PVT 59* WALTER MURPHY & THE BIG APPLE BAND ★	28		7

ANNE MURRAY Canadian singer

Date	Title / Label	Peak Position	Weeks at No.1	Weeks in Top 40
24 Oct 70	**SNOWBIRD** *Capitol CL 15654*	23		15
21 Oct 72	**DESTINY** *Capitol CL 15734*	41		
9 Dec 78	**YOU NEEDED ME** *Capitol CL 16011* ★	22		6
21 Apr 79	**I JUST FALL IN LOVE AGAIN** *Capitol CL 16069*	58		
19 Apr 80	**DAYDREAM BELIEVER** *Capitol CL 16123*	61		

KEITH MURRAY US singer

Date	Title / Label	Peak Position	Weeks at No.1	Weeks in Top 40
2 Nov 96	**THE RHYME** *Jive JIVECD 407*	59		
27 Jun 98	**SHORTY (YOU KEEP PLAYIN' WITH MY MIND)** *Jive 0521212* IMAJIN FEATURING KEITH MURRAY	22		1
14 Nov 98	**HOME ALONE** *Jive 0522392* R KELLY FEATURING KEITH MURRAY	17		3
5 Dec 98	**INCREDIBLE** *Jive 0522102* KEITH MURRAY FEATURING LL COOL J	52		

PAULINE MURRAY UK singer

Date	Title / Label	Peak Position	Weeks at No.1	Weeks in Top 40
2 Aug 80	**DREAM SEQUENCE (ONE)** *Illusive IVE 1* PAULINE MURRAY & THE INVISIBLE GIRLS	67		

RUBY MURRAY UK singer

Date	Title / Label	Peak Position	Weeks at No.1	Weeks in Top 40
3 Dec 54	**HEARTBEAT** *Columbia DB 3542*	3		16
28 Jan 55	**SOFTLY SOFTLY** *Columbia DB 3558*	1	3	23
4 Feb 55	**HAPPY DAYS AND LONELY NIGHTS** *Columbia DB 3577*	6		8
4 Mar 55	**LET ME GO LOVER** *Columbia DB 3577*	5		7
18 Mar 55	**IF ANYONE FINDS THIS I LOVE YOU** *Columbia DB 3580* RUBY MURRAY WITH ANNE WARREN	4		11
1 Jul 55	**EVERMORE** *Columbia DB 3617*	3		17
14 Oct 55	**I'LL COME WHEN YOU CALL** *Columbia DB 3643*	6		7
31 Aug 56	**YOU ARE MY FIRST LOVE** *Columbia DB 3770*	16		5
12 Dec 58	**REAL LOVE** *Columbia DB 4192*	18		6
5 Jun 59	**GOODBYE JIMMY GOODBYE** *Columbia DB 4305*	10		14

JUNIOR MURVIN Jamaican singer

Date	Title / Label	Peak Position	Weeks at No.1	Weeks in Top 40
3 May 80	**POLICE AND THIEVES** *Island WIP 6539*	23		8

MUSE UK group

Date	Title / Label	Peak Position	Weeks at No.1	Weeks in Top 40
26 Jun 99	**UNO** *Mushroom MUSH 50CDS*	73		
18 Sep 99	**CAVE** *Mushroom MUSH 58CDS*	52		
4 Dec 99	**MUSCLE MUSEUM** *Mushroom MUSH 66CDS*	43		
4 Mar 00	**SUNBURN** *Mushroom MUSH 68CDS*	22		1
17 Jun 00	**UNINTENDED** *Mushroom MUSH 72CDSX*	20		2
21 Oct 00	**MUSCLE MUSEUM** *Mushroom MUSH 84CDSX*	25		1
24 Mar 01	**PLUG IN BABY** *Mushroom MUSH 89CDSX*	11		2
16 Jun 01	**NEW BORN** *Mushroom MUSH 92CDSX*	12		2
1 Sep 01	**BLISS** *Mushroom MUSH 96CDSX*	22		1
1 Dec 01	**HYPER MUSIC/FEELING GOOD** *Mushroom MUSH 97CDS*	24		1
29 Jun 02	**DEAD STAR/IN YOUR WORLD** *Mushroom MUSH 104CDS*	13		2
20 Sep 03	**TIME IS RUNNING OUT** *East West EW 272CD*	8		4
13 Dec 03	**HYSTERIA** *Taste Media/EastWest EW 278CD*	17		1
29 May 04	**SING FOR ABSOLUTION** *Taste Media/East West EW 285CD*	16		2
2 Oct 04	**BUTTERFLIES AND HURRICANES** *Atlantic ATUK003CD*	14		2
24 Jun 06	**SUPER MASSIVE BLACK HOLE** *Warner Brothers HEL3001CD*	4		7
9 Sep 06	**STARLIGHT** *Helium 3/Warner Bros HEL3003CD*	13		7
9 Dec 06	**KNIGHTS OF CYDONIA** *Helium 3/Warner Bros HEL3004CD*	10		2
21 Apr 07	**INVINCIBLE** *Helium 3/Warner Bros HEL3005CD*	21		1
30 Jun 07	**MAP OF THE PROBLEMATIQUE** *Download*	18		1

MUSIC UK group

Date	Title / Label	Peak Position	Weeks at No.1	Weeks in Top 40
31 Aug 02	**TAKE THE LONG ROAD AND WALK IT** *Hut HUTDX 158*	14		2
30 Nov 02	**GETAWAY** *Hut HUTCD 162*	26		1
1 Mar 03	**THE TRUTH IS NO WORDS** *Hut HUTCD 164*	18		1
18 Sep 04	**FREEDOM FIGHTERS** *Virgin VSCDX 1883*	15		2
22 Jan 05	**BREAKIN'** *Virgin VSCDX1894*	20		1

MUSIC & MYSTERY UK production duo

Date	Title / Label	Peak Position	Weeks at No.1	Weeks in Top 40
13 Feb 93	**ALL THIS LOVE I'M GIVING** *KTDA CDKTDA 2* MUSIC & MYSTERY FEATURING GWEN McCRAE	36		1

MUSIC RELIEF '94 UK group

Date	Title / Label	Peak Position	Weeks at No.1	Weeks in Top 40
5 Nov 94	**WHAT'S GOING ON** *Jive RWANDACD 1*	70		

MUSICAL YOUTH UK group

Date	Title / Label	Peak Position	Weeks at No.1	Weeks in Top 40
25 Sep 82	**PASS THE DUTCHIE** *MCA YOU 1* ●	1	3	8
20 Nov 82	**YOUTH OF TODAY** *MCA YOU 2*	13		8
12 Feb 83	**NEVER GONNA GIVE YOU UP** *MCA YOU 3*	6		7
16 Apr 83	**HEARTBREAKER** *MCA YOU 4*	44		
9 Jul 83	**TELL ME WHY** *MCA YOU 5*	33		3
22 Oct 83	**007** *MCA YOU 6*	26		3
14 Jan 84	**SIXTEEN** *MCA YOU 7*	23		5

MUSIQUE US group

Date	Title / Label	Peak Position	Weeks at No.1	Weeks in Top 40
18 Nov 78	**IN THE BUSH** *CBS 6791*	16		10

MUSIQUE VS U2 UK production duo

Date	Title / Label	Peak Position	Weeks at No.1	Weeks in Top 40
2 Jun 01	**NEW YEARS DUB** *Serious SERRO 030CD*	15		2

MUTINY UK UK production duo

Date	Title / Label	Peak Position	Weeks at No.1	Weeks in Top 40
19 May 01	**SECRETS** *Sunflower VCRD 86*	47		
25 Aug 01	**VIRUS** *VC Recordings VCRD 91*	42		

MVP US group

Date	Title / Label	Peak Position	Weeks at No.1	Weeks in Top 40
2 Jul 05	**ROC YA BODY (MIC CHECK 1 2)** *Positiva CDTIVS219*	5		11
1 Apr 06	**BOUNCE SHAKE MOVE STOP** *Positiva CDTIVS227*	22		2

MXM Italian group

Date	Title / Label	Peak Position	Weeks at No.1	Weeks in Top 40
2 Jun 90	**NOTHING COMPARES 2 U** *London LON 267*	68		

MY BLOODY VALENTINE UK group

Date	Title / Label	Peak Position	Weeks at No.1	Weeks in Top 40
5 May 90	**SOON** *Creation CRE 073*	41		
16 Feb 91	**TO HERE KNOWS WHEN** *Creation CRE 085*	29		1

Silver-selling ○ Gold-selling ● Platinum-selling ⊛ US No.1 ★

MY CHEMICAL ROMANCE US group

Date	Title	Peak Position	Weeks at No.1	Weeks in Top 40
25 Dec 04	**THANK YOU FOR THE VENOM** *Reprise W661*	71		
19 Mar 05	**I'M NOT OKAY (I PROMISE)** *Reprise W666CD1*	19		1
4 Jun 05	**HELENA** *Reprise W671CD*	20		2
10 Sep 05	**THE GHOST OF YOU** *Reprise W683CD1*	27		1
19 Nov 05	**I'M NOT OKAY (I PROMISE)** *Reprise W666CD1*	28		2
14 Oct 06	**WELCOME TO THE BLACK PARADE** *Reprise W740CD*	1	2	15
20 Jan 07	**FAMOUS LAST WORDS** *Reprise W754CD*	8		4
31 Mar 07	**I DON'T LOVE YOU** *Reprise W758CD*	13		4
23 Jun 07	**TEENAGERS** *Reprise W771CD*	9		10

MY LIFE STORY UK group

Date	Title	Peak Position	Weeks at No.1	Weeks in Top 40
17 Aug 96	**12 REASONS WHY I LOVE HER** *Parlophone CDR 6442*	32		1
9 Nov 96	**SPARKLE** *Parlophone CDR 6450*	34		1
1 Mar 97	**THE KING OF KISSINGDOM** *Parlophone CDRS 6457*	35		1
17 May 97	**STRUMPET** *Parlophone CDR 6464*	27		1
23 Aug 97	**DUCHESS** *Parlophone CDR 6474*	39		1
19 Jun 99	**IT'S A GIRL THING** *IT ITR 001*	37		1
30 Oct 99	**EMPIRE LINE** *IT ITR 003*	58		
19 Feb 00	**WALK/DON'T WALK** *IT ITR 007*	48		

MY RED CELL UK group

Date	Title	Peak Position	Weeks at No.1	Weeks in Top 40
12 Jun 04	**IN A CAGE (ON PROZAC)** *V2 VVR 5027133*	61		

MY VITRIOL UK group

Date	Title	Peak Position	Weeks at No.1	Weeks in Top 40
22 Jul 00	**CEMENTED SHOES** *Infectious INFECT 89CDS*	65		
11 Nov 00	**PIECES** *Infectious INFECT 94CDS*	56		
24 Feb 01	**ALWAYS YOUR WAY** *Infectious INFECT 95CDSX*	31		1
19 May 01	**GROUNDED** *Infectious INFECT 97CD*	29		1
27 Jul 02	**MOODSWINGS/THE GENTLE ART OF CHOKING** *Infectious INFEC 107CDSX*	39		1

PRAS MICHEL US singer

Date	Title	Peak Position	Weeks at No.1	Weeks in Top 40
27 Jun 98	**GHETTO SUPERSTAR (THAT IS WHAT YOU ARE)** *Interscope IND 95593* PRAS MICHEL FEATURING OL' DIRTY BASTARD INTRODUCING MYA ⊛	2		14

MYA US singer

Date	Title	Peak Position	Weeks at No.1	Weeks in Top 40
12 Dec 98	**TAKE ME THERE** *Interscope IND 95620* BLACKstreet & MYA FEATURING MASE & BLINKY BLINK	7		7
10 Feb 01	**CASE OF THE EX (WHATCHA GONNA DO)** *Interscope 4974772*	3		6
24 Mar 01	**GIRLS DEM SUGAR** *Virgin VUSCD 173* BEENIE MAN FEATURING MYA	13		4
9 Jun 01	**FREE** *Interscope 4975002*	11		3
30 Jun 01	**LADY MARMALADE** *Interscope 4975612* CHRISTINA AGUILERA/LIL' KIM/MYA/PINK ● ★	1	1	13
20 Sep 03	**MY LOVE IS LIKE...WO!** *Interscope 9810302*	33		1

ALICIA MYERS US singer

Date	Title	Peak Position	Weeks at No.1	Weeks in Top 40
1 Sep 84	**YOU GET THE BEST FROM ME (SAY SAY SAY)** *MCA 914*	58		

BILLIE MYERS UK singer

Date	Title	Peak Position	Weeks at No.1	Weeks in Top 40
11 Apr 98	**KISS THE RAIN** *Universal UND 56182*	4		7
25 Jul 98	**TELL ME** *Universal UND 56201*	28		1

RICHARD MYHILL UK singer

Date	Title	Peak Position	Weeks at No.1	Weeks in Top 40
1 Apr 78	**IT TAKES TWO TO TANGO** *Mercury 6007 167*	17		6

ALANNAH MYLES Canadian singer

Date	Title	Peak Position	Weeks at No.1	Weeks in Top 40
17 Mar 90	**BLACK VELVET** *East West A 8742* ○ ★	2		11
16 Jun 90	**LOVE IS** *East West A 8918*	61		

MYLO UK producer

Date	Title	Peak Position	Weeks at No.1	Weeks in Top 40
30 Oct 04	**DROP THE PRESSURE** *Breastfed BFD009CD*	19		2
5 Feb 05	**DESTROY ROCK AND ROLL** *Breastfed BFD014CD*	15		2
28 May 05	**IN MY ARMS** *Breastfed BFD016CD*	13		4
17 Sep 05	**DOCTOR PRESSURE** *Breastfed BFD017CD2* MYLO VS MIAMI SOUND MACHINE	3		13
21 Jan 06	**MUSCLE CAR** *Breastfed BFD019CD* MYLO FEATURING FREEFORM FIVE	38		1

MYNC PROJECT UK production duo

Date	Title	Peak Position	Weeks at No.1	Weeks in Top 40
22 Jul 06	**SOMETHING ON YOUR MIND** *Island APOLLO103CD* MYNC PROJECT FEATURING ABIGAIL BAILEY	71		

MARIE MYRIAM French singer

Date	Title	Peak Position	Weeks at No.1	Weeks in Top 40
28 May 77	**L'OISEAU ET L'ENFANT** *Polydor 2056 634*	42		

MYRON US singer

Date	Title	Peak Position	Weeks at No.1	Weeks in Top 40
22 Nov 97	**WE CAN GET DOWN** *Island Black Music CID 677*	74		

MYSTERY Dutch production duo

Date	Title	Peak Position	Weeks at No.1	Weeks in Top 40
6 Oct 01	**MYSTERY** *Inferno CDFERN 42*	56		
10 Aug 02	**ALL I EVER WANTED (DEVOTION)** *Xtravaganza XTRAV 33CDS*	57		

MYSTERY JETS UK group

Date	Title	Peak Position	Weeks at No.1	Weeks in Top 40
24 Sep 05	**YOU CAN'T FOOL ME DENNIS** *679 679L109CD*	44		
17 Dec 05	**ALAS AGNES** *679 679L115CD*	34		1
11 Mar 06	**THE BOY WHO RAN AWAY** *679 679L122CD*	23		1
3 Jun 06	**YOU CAN'T FOOL ME DENNIS** *679 679L129CD*	41		
16 Sep 06	**DIAMONDS IN THE DARK EP** *679 679L138CD*	47		
15 Mar 08	**YOUNG LOVE** *679 679L152CD*	34		1

MYSTIC MERLIN US group

Date	Title	Peak Position	Weeks at No.1	Weeks in Top 40
26 Apr 80	**JUST CAN'T GIVE YOU UP** *Capitol CL 16133*	20		7

MYSTIC 3 UK/Italian production group

Date	Title	Peak Position	Weeks at No.1	Weeks in Top 40
24 Jun 00	**SOMETHING'S GOIN' ON** *Rulin 2CDS*	63		

MYSTICA Israeli production group

Date	Title	Peak Position	Weeks at No.1	Weeks in Top 40
24 Jan 98	**EVER REST** *Perfecto PERF 152CD*	62		
9 May 98	**AFRICAN HORIZON** *Perfecto PERF 161CD*	59		

MYSTIKAL US rapper

Date	Title	Peak Position	Weeks at No.1	Weeks in Top 40
9 Dec 00	**SHAKE YA ASS** *Jive 9251552*	30		1
17 Feb 01	**STUTTER** *Jive 9251632* JOE FEATURING MYSTIKAL ★	7		6
3 Mar 01	**DANGER (BEEN SO LONG)** *Jive 9251722* MYSTIKAL FEATURING NIVEA	28		1
29 Dec 01	**DON'T STOP (FUNKIN' 4 JAMAICA)** *Virgin VUSCD 228* MARIAH CAREY FEATURING MYSTIKAL	32		2
23 Feb 02	**BOUNCIN' BACK** *Jive 9253272*	45		

MYTOWN Irish group

Date	Title	Peak Position	Weeks at No.1	Weeks in Top 40
13 Mar 99	**PARTY ALL NIGHT** *Universal UND 56231*	22		1

N

N-DUBZ UK group

Date	Title	Peak Position	Weeks at No.1	Weeks in Top 40
26 May 07	**FEVA LAS VEGAS** *LRC LRC0010*	57		
3 Nov 07	**YOU BETTER NOT WASTE MY TIME** *LRC 1744153*	26		1

N-JOI UK production duo

Date	Title	Peak Position	Weeks at No.1	Weeks in Top 40
27 Oct 90	**ANTHEM** *Deconstruction PB 44041*	45		
2 Mar 91	**ADRENALIN (EP)** *Deconstruction PT 44344*	23		3
6 Apr 91	**ANTHEM** *Deconstruction PB 44445*	8		6
22 Feb 92	**LIVE IN MANCHESTER (PARTS 1 + 2)** *Deconstruction PT 45252*	12		3
24 Jul 93	**THE DRUMSTRUCK (EP)** *Deconstruction 74321154832*	33		2

Silver-selling · Gold-selling · Platinum-selling · US No.1 ★ · Peak Position · Weeks at No.1 · Weeks in Top 40

Date	Title / Label	Peak Position	Weeks at No.1	Weeks in Top 40
17 Dec 94	**PAPILLON** *Deconstruction 74321252132*	70		
8 Jul 95	**BAD THINGS** *Deconstruction 74321277292*	57		

N + G UK production duo

Date	Title / Label	Peak Position	Weeks at No.1	Weeks in Top 40
1 Apr 00	**RIGHT BEFORE MY EYES** *Urban Heat UHTCD003* N + G FEATURING KALLAGHAN & MC NEAT	12		4

N SYNC US group

Date	Title / Label	Peak Position	Weeks at No.1	Weeks in Top 40
13 Sep 97	**TEARIN' UP MY HEART** *Arista 74321505152*	40		1
22 Nov 97	**I WANT YOU BACK** *Arista 74321541122*	62		
27 Feb 99	**I WANT YOU BACK** *Transcontinental 74321646982*	5		4
26 Jun 99	**TEARIN' UP MY HEART** *Northwestside 74321675832*	9		5
8 Jan 00	**MUSIC OF MY HEART** *Epic 6678052* N SYNC & GLORIA ESTEFAN	34		2
11 Mar 00	**BYE BYE BYE** *Jive 9250202*	3		5
22 Jul 00	**I'LL NEVER STOP** *Jive 9250762*	13		3
16 Sep 00	**IT'S GONNA BE ME** *Jive 9251082* ★	9		3
2 Dec 00	**THIS I PROMISE YOU** *Jive 9251302*	21		2
21 Jul 01	**POP** *Jive 9252422*	9		4
8 Dec 01	**GONE** *Jive 9252772*	24		1
27 Apr 02	**GIRLFRIEND** *Jive 9253312* N SYNC FEATURING NELLY	2		8

N-TRANCE UK group

Date	Title / Label	Peak Position	Weeks at No.1	Weeks in Top 40
7 May 94	**SET YOU FREE** *All Around The World CDGLOBE 124* N-TRANCE FEATURING KELLY LLORENNA	39		1
22 Oct 94	**TURN UP THE POWER** *All Around The World CDGLOBE 125*	23		2
14 Jan 95	**SET YOU FREE (REMIX)** *All Around The World CXGLOBE 126* N-TRANCE FEATURING KELLY LLORENNA	2		11
16 Sep 95	**STAYIN' ALIVE** *All Around The World CDGLOBE 131* N-TRANCE FEATURING RICARDO DA FORCE	2		8
24 Feb 96	**ELECTRONIC PLEASURE** *All Around The World CDGLOBE 135*	11		2
5 Apr 97	**D.I.S.C.O.** *All Around The World CDGLOBE 153*	11		4
23 Aug 97	**THE MIND OF THE MACHINE** *All Around The World CDGLOBE 159*	15		3
1 Nov 97	**DA YA THINK I'M SEXY?** *All Around The World CDGLOBE 150* N-TRANCE FEATURING ROD STEWART	7		6
12 Sep 98	**PARADISE CITY** *All Around The World CDGLOBE 140*	28		1
19 Dec 98	**TEARS IN THE RAIN** *All Around The World CDGLOBE 185*	53		
20 May 00	**SHAKE YA BODY** *All Around The World CDGLOBE 204*	37		1
22 Sep 01	**SET YOU FREE (2ND REMIX)** *All Around The World CXGLOBE 242*	4		7
14 Sep 02	**FOREVER** *All Around The World CXGLOBE 257*	6		4
19 Jul 03	**DESTINY** *All Around The World CDGLOBE 282*	37		1
4 Dec 04	**I'M IN HEAVEN** *All Around The World CDGLOBE343*	46		
8 Jan 05	**SET YOU FREE (2ND REMIX)** *All Around The World CXGLOBE 242*	64		

N-TYCE UK group

Date	Title / Label	Peak Position	Weeks at No.1	Weeks in Top 40
5 Jul 97	**HEY DJ! (PLAY THAT SONG)** *Telstar CDSTAS 2885*	20		1
13 Sep 97	**WE COME TO PARTY** *Telstar CDSTAS 2915*	12		3
28 Feb 98	**TELEFUNKIN'** *Telstar CXSTAS 2944*	16		3
6 Jun 98	**BOOM BOOM** *Telstar CDSTAS 2971*	18		3

NADA SURF US group

Date	Title / Label	Peak Position	Weeks at No.1	Weeks in Top 40
24 May 03	**INSIDE OF LOVE** *Heavenly HVN 133CD*	73		

NADIA Portuguese singer

Date	Title / Label	Peak Position	Weeks at No.1	Weeks in Top 40
11 Dec 04	**A LITTLE BIT OF ACTION** *Virgin/EMI VTSCDX6*	27		1

JIMMY NAIL UK actor/singer

Date	Title / Label	Peak Position	Weeks at No.1	Weeks in Top 40
27 Apr 85	**LOVE DON'T LIVE HERE ANYMORE** *Virgin VS 764*	3		8
11 Jul 92	**AIN'T NO DOUBT** *East West YZ 686*	1	3	11
3 Oct 92	**LAURA** *East West YZ 702*	58		
26 Nov 94	**CROCODILE SHOES** *East West YZ 867CD*	4		9
11 Feb 95	**COWBOY DREAMS** *East West YZ 878CD*	13		4
6 May 95	**CALLING OUT YOUR NAME** *East West YZ 935CD*	65		
28 Oct 95	**BIG RIVER** *East West EW008CD*	18		2
23 Dec 95	**LOVE** *East West EW018CD1*	33		2
3 Feb 96	**BIG RIVER (REMIX)** *East West EW024CD*	72		
16 Nov 96	**COUNTRY BOY** *East West EW070CD*	25		4
21 Nov 98	**THE FLAME STILL BURNS** *London LONCD 420* JIMMY NAIL WITH STRANGE FRUIT	47		

YAEL NAIM French singer

Date	Title / Label	Peak Position	Weeks at No.1	Weeks in Top 40
16 Feb 08	**NEW SOUL** *Tôt Ou Tard FR79W0700370*	36		1

NAKATOMI Dutch production group

Date	Title / Label	Peak Position	Weeks at No.1	Weeks in Top 40
7 Feb 98	**CHILDREN OF THE NIGHT** *Peach PCHCD 006*	47		
26 Oct 02	**CHILDREN OF THE NIGHT (REMIX)** *Jive 9254212*	31		1

NAKED EYES UK duo

Date	Title / Label	Peak Position	Weeks at No.1	Weeks in Top 40
23 Jul 83	**ALWAYS SOMETHING THERE TO REMIND ME** *EMI 5334*	59		

NALIN I.N.C. German production duo

Date	Title / Label	Peak Position	Weeks at No.1	Weeks in Top 40
28 Mar 98	**PLANET VIOLET** *Logic 74321565702*	51		

NALIN & KANE German production duo

Date	Title / Label	Peak Position	Weeks at No.1	Weeks in Top 40
1 Nov 97	**BEACHBALL** *ffrr FCD 318*	48		
3 Oct 98	**BEACHBALL (REMIX)** *London FCD 349*	17		3

NAPOLEON XIV US producer

Date	Title / Label	Peak Position	Weeks at No.1	Weeks in Top 40
4 Aug 66	**THEY'RE COMING TO TAKE ME AWAY HA-HAAA!** *Warner Brothers WB 5831*	4		9

NARCOTIC THRUST UK group

Date	Title / Label	Peak Position	Weeks at No.1	Weeks in Top 40
10 Aug 02	**SAFE FROM HARM** *ffrr FCD 406*	24		2
17 Apr 04	**I LIKE IT** *Free 2 Air 0153656F2A*	9		5
22 Jan 05	**WHEN THE DAWN BREAKS** *Free2Air F2A3CDX*	28		1

NAS US singer

Date	Title / Label	Peak Position	Weeks at No.1	Weeks in Top 40
28 May 94	**IT AIN'T HARD TO TELL** *Columbia 6604702*	64		
17 Aug 96	**IF I RULED THE WORLD** *Columbia 6634022*	12		6
25 Jan 97	**STREET DREAMS** *Columbia 6641302*	12		2
14 Jun 97	**HEAD OVER HEELS** *Epic 6645942* ALLURE FEATURING NAS	18		1
29 May 99	**HATE ME NOW** *Columbia 6672565* NAS FEATURING PUFF DADDY	14		3
15 Jan 00	**NASTRADAMUS** *Columbia 6685572*	24		2
22 Jan 00	**HOT BOYZ** *Elektra E 7002CD* MISSY MISDEMEANOR ELLIOTT FEATURING NAS, EVE & Q-TIP	18		2
21 Apr 01	**OOCHIE WALLY** *Columbia 6710852* QB FINEST FEATURING NAS & BRAVEHEARTS	30		1
2 Feb 02	**GOT UR SELF A** *Columbia 6723022*	30		1
13 Jul 02	**I'M GONNA BE ALRIGHT** *Epic 6728442* JENNIFER LOPEZ FEATURING NAS	3		8
25 Jan 03	**MADE YOU LOOK** *Columbia 6734792*	27		1
5 Apr 03	**I CAN** *Columbia 6737385*	19		3
20 Nov 04	**BRIDGING THE GAP** *Columbia 6754682*	18		2
16 Apr 05	**IN PUBLIC** *Virgin VSCDT1893* KELIS FEATURING NAS	17		3
3 Feb 07	**HIP HOP IS DEAD** *Def Jam 1721323* NAS FEATURING WILL I AM	35		1

JOHNNY NASH US singer

Date	Title / Label	Peak Position	Weeks at No.1	Weeks in Top 40
7 Aug 68	**HOLD ME TIGHT** *Regal Zonophone RZ 3010*	5		14
8 Jan 69	**YOU GOT SOUL** *Major Minor MM 586*	6		11
2 Apr 69	**CUPID** *Major Minor MM 603*	6		10
1 Apr 72	**STIR IT UP** *CBS 7800*	13		9
24 Jun 72	**I CAN SEE CLEARLY NOW** *CBS 8113* ★	5		13
7 Oct 72	**THERE ARE MORE QUESTIONS THAN ANSWERS** *CBS 8351*	9		9
14 Jun 75	**TEARS ON MY PILLOW** *CBS 3220*	1	1	11
11 Oct 75	**LET'S BE FRIENDS** *CBS 3597*	42		
12 Jun 76	**(WHAT A) WONDERFUL WORLD** *Epic EPC 4294*	25		6
9 Nov 85	**ROCK ME BABY** *2000 AD FED 19*	47		
15 Apr 89	**I CAN SEE CLEARLY NOW (REMIX)** *Epic JN 1*	54		

KATE NASH UK singer

Date	Title / Label	Peak Position	Weeks at No.1	Weeks in Top 40
7 Jul 07	**FOUNDATIONS** *Fiction/Polydor 1735509*	2		18
22 Sep 07	**MOUTHWASH** *Fiction/Polydor 1744949*	23		2
15 Dec 07	**PUMPKIN SOUP** *Fiction/Polydor 1754566*	23		6

Silver-selling ● Gold-selling ● Platinum-selling ⊛ US No.1 ★ — Peak Position · Weeks at No.1 · Weeks in Top 40

NASHVILLE TEENS UK group

Date	Title / Label	Peak Position	Weeks at No.1	Weeks in Top 40
9 Jul 64	**TOBACCO ROAD** *Decca F 11930*	6		10
22 Oct 64	**GOOGLE EYE** *Decca F 12000*	10		9
4 Mar 65	**FIND MY WAY BACK HOME** *Decca F 12089*	34		1
20 May 65	**THIS LITTLE BIRD** *Decca F 12143*	38		2
3 Feb 66	**THE HARD WAY** *Decca F 12316*	45		

NATASHA UK singer

Date	Title / Label	Peak Position	Weeks at No.1	Weeks in Top 40
5 Jun 82	**IKO IKO** *Towerbell TOW 22*	10		9
4 Sep 82	**THE BOOM BOOM ROOM** *Towerbell TOW 25*	44		

ULTRA NATÉ US singer

Date	Title / Label	Peak Position	Weeks at No.1	Weeks in Top 40
9 Dec 89	**IT'S OVER NOW** *Eternal YZ 440*	62		
23 Feb 91	**IS IT LOVE** *Eternal YZ 509* BASEMENT BOYS PRESENT ULTRA NATE	71		
29 Jan 94	**SHOW ME** *Warner Brothers W 0219CD*	62		
14 Jun 97	**FREE** *AM:PM 5822432* ●	4		14
24 Jan 98	**FREE (REMIX)** *AM:PM 5825012*	33		1
18 Apr 98	**FOUND A CURE** *AM:PM 5826452*	6		5
25 Jul 98	**NEW KIND OF MEDICINE** *AM:PM 5827492*	14		3
22 Jul 00	**DESIRE** *AM:PM CDAMPM 133*	40		1
9 Jun 01	**GET IT UP (THE FEELING)** *AM:PM CDAMPM 140*	51		
28 May 05	**FREAK ON** *Hed Kandi HEDKCDX010* STONEBRIDGE VS ULTRA NATE	37		1

NATHAN UK singer

Date	Title / Label	Peak Position	Weeks at No.1	Weeks in Top 40
12 Mar 05	**COME INTO MY ROOM** *V2 JAD5029593*	37		1
24 Mar 07	**DO WITHOUT MY LOVE** *Mona MONA7NATCDS*	44		

NATIVE UK production duo

Date	Title / Label	Peak Position	Weeks at No.1	Weeks in Top 40
10 Feb 01	**FEEL THE DRUMS** *Slinky Music SLINKY 009CD*	46		

NATURAL US group

Date	Title / Label	Peak Position	Weeks at No.1	Weeks in Top 40
10 Aug 02	**PUT YOUR ARMS AROUND ME** *Ariola 74321947892*	32		1

NATURAL BORN CHILLERS UK production duo

Date	Title / Label	Peak Position	Weeks at No.1	Weeks in Top 40
1 Nov 97	**ROCK THE FUNKY BEAT** *East West EW 138CD1* NATURAL BORN CHILLERS	30		1

NATURAL BORN GROOVES Belgian production group

Date	Title / Label	Peak Position	Weeks at No.1	Weeks in Top 40
2 Nov 96	**FORERUNNER** *XL Recordings XLS 76CD*	64		
19 Apr 97	**GROOVEBIRD** *Positiva CDTIV 75*	21		1

NATURAL LIFE UK group

Date	Title / Label	Peak Position	Weeks at No.1	Weeks in Top 40
7 Mar 92	**NATURAL LIFE** *Tribe NLIFE 3*	47		

NATURAL SELECTION US duo

Date	Title / Label	Peak Position	Weeks at No.1	Weeks in Top 40
9 Nov 91	**DO ANYTHING** *East West A 8724*	69		

NATURALS UK group

Date	Title / Label	Peak Position	Weeks at No.1	Weeks in Top 40
20 Aug 64	**I SHOULD HAVE KNOWN BETTER** *Parlophone R 5165*	24		8

DAVID NAUGHTON US singer

Date	Title / Label	Peak Position	Weeks at No.1	Weeks in Top 40
25 Aug 79	**MAKIN' IT** *RSO 32*	44		

NAUGHTY BOY UK production duo

Date	Title / Label	Peak Position	Weeks at No.1	Weeks in Top 40
14 Jan 06	**PHAT BEACH (I'LL BE READY)** *Ministry Of Sound PHAT01CDS*	36		1

NAUGHTY BY NATURE US group

Date	Title / Label	Peak Position	Weeks at No.1	Weeks in Top 40
9 Nov 91	**O.P.P.** *Big Life BLR 62*	73		
20 Jun 92	**O.P.P.** *Big Life BLR 74*	35		2
30 Jan 93	**HIP HOP HOORAY** *Big Life BLRD 89*	22		2
19 Jun 93	**IT'S ON** *Big Life BLRD 99*	48		
27 Nov 93	**HIP HOP HOORAY (REMIX)** *Big Life BLRDA 104*	20		2
29 Apr 95	**FEEL ME FLOW** *Big Life BLRD 115*	23		1
11 Sep 99	**JAMBOREE** *Arista 74321692882* NAUGHTY BY NATURE FEATURING ZHANE	51		
19 Oct 02	**FEELS GOOD (DON'T WORRY BOUT A THING)** *Island CID 806* NAUGHTY BY NATURE FEATURING 3LW	44		
8 Jan 05	**O.P.P.** *Tommy Boy 5046759840*	71		

MARIA NAYLER UK singer

Date	Title / Label	Peak Position	Weeks at No.1	Weeks in Top 40
9 Mar 96	**BE AS ONE** *7pm 74321342962* SASHA & MARIA	17		3
16 Nov 96	**ONE & ONE** *Deconstruction 74321427692* ROBERT MILES FEATURING MARIA NAYLER ●	3		13
7 Mar 98	**NAKED AND SACRED** *Deconstruction 74321534242*	32		1
5 Sep 98	**WILL YOU BE WITH ME/LOVE IS THE GOD** *Deconstruction 74321591772*	65		
27 May 00	**ANGRY SKIES** *Deconstruction 74321759492*	42		

NAZARETH UK group

Date	Title / Label	Peak Position	Weeks at No.1	Weeks in Top 40
5 May 73	**BROKEN DOWN ANGEL** *Mooncrest MOON 1*	9		9
21 Jul 73	**BAD BAD BOY** *Mooncrest MOON 9*	10		8
13 Oct 73	**THIS FLIGHT TONIGHT** *Mooncrest MOON 14*	11		8
23 Mar 74	**SHANGHAI'D IN SHANGHAI** *Mooncrest MOON 22*	41		
14 Jun 75	**MY WHITE BICYCLE** *Mooncrest MOON 47*	14		8
15 Nov 75	**HOLY ROLLER** *Mountain TOP 3*	36		2
24 Sep 77	**HOT TRACKS EP** *Mountain NAZ 1*	15		10
18 Feb 78	**GONE DEAD TRAIN** *Mountain NAZ 002*	49		
13 May 78	**PLACE IN YOUR HEART** *Mountain TOP 37*	70		
27 Jan 79	**MAY THE SUN SHINE** *Mountain NAZ 003*	22		6
28 Jul 79	**STAR** *Mountain TOP 45*	54		

ME'SHELL NDEGEOCELLO US singer/bass player

Date	Title / Label	Peak Position	Weeks at No.1	Weeks in Top 40
12 Feb 94	**IF THAT'S YOUR BOYFIEND (HE WASN'T LAST NIGHT)** *Maverick W 0223CD1*	74		
3 Sep 94	**WILD NIGHT** *Mercury MERCD 409* JOHN MELLENCAMP FEATURING ME'SHELL NDEGEOCELLO	34		1
1 Mar 97	**NEVER MISS THE WATER** *Reprise W 1393CD* CHAKA KHAN FEATURING ME'SHELL NDEGEOCELLO	59		

YOUSSOU N'DOUR Senegalese singer

Date	Title / Label	Peak Position	Weeks at No.1	Weeks in Top 40
3 Jun 89	**SHAKING THE TREE** *Virgin VS 1167* YOUSSOU N'DOUR & PETER GABRIEL	61		
22 Dec 90	**SHAKING THE TREE** *Virgin VS 1322* YOUSSOU N'DOUR & PETER GABRIEL	57		
25 Jun 94	**7 SECONDS** *Columbia 6605082* YOUSSOU N'DOUR (FEATURING NENEH CHERRY) ●	3		18
14 Jan 95	**UNDECIDED** *Columbia 6609712*	53		
10 Oct 98	**HOW COME** *Interscope IND 95598* YOUSSOU N'DOUR & CANIBUS	52		

NE-YO US singer

Date	Title / Label	Peak Position	Weeks at No.1	Weeks in Top 40
25 Mar 06	**SO SICK** *Def Jam 9854185* ★	1	1	11
1 Jul 06	**SEXY LOVE** *Def Jam 1701192*	5		9
26 Aug 06	**BACK LIKE THAT** *Def Jam 1705586* GHOSTFACE KILLAH FEATURING NE-YO	46		
14 Apr 07	**BECAUSE OF YOU** *Def Jam 1732579*	4		11
13 Oct 07	**CAN WE CHILL** *Def Jam 1747442*	62		
20 Oct 07	**HATE THAT I LOVE YOU** *Def Jam 1751369* RIHANNA FEATURING NE-YO	15		15

NEARLY GOD UK rapper

Date	Title / Label	Peak Position	Weeks at No.1	Weeks in Top 40
20 Apr 96	**POEMS** *Durban Poison DPCD 3*	28		1

TERRY NEASON UK singer/comedian

Date	Title / Label	Peak Position	Weeks at No.1	Weeks in Top 40
25 Jun 94	**LIFEBOAT** *WEA YZ 830*	72		

NEBULA II UK group

Date	Title / Label	Peak Position	Weeks at No.1	Weeks in Top 40
1 Feb 92	**SÉANCE/ATHEAMA** *Reinforced RIVET 1211*	55		
16 May 92	**FLATLINERS** *J4M 12NEBULA 2*	54		

Silver-selling ○ Gold-selling ● Platinum-selling ⊛ US No.1 ★ | Peak Position | Weeks at No.1 | Weeks in Top 40

NED'S ATOMIC DUSTBIN UK group

Date	Title / Label	Peak Position	Weeks at No.1	Weeks in Top 40
14 Jul 90	**KILL YOUR TELEVISION** *Chapter 22 CHAP 48*	53		
27 Oct 90	**UNTIL YOU FIND OUT** *Chapter 22 CHAP 52*	51		
9 Mar 91	**HAPPY** *Columbia 6566807*	16		2
21 Sep 91	**TRUST** *Furtive 6574627*	21		2
10 Oct 92	**NOT SLEEPING AROUND** *Furtive 6583866*	19		2
5 Dec 92	**INTACT** *Furtive 6588166*	36		2
25 Mar 95	**ALL I ASK OF MYSELF IS THAT I HOLD TOGETHER** *Furtive 6613565*	33		1
15 Jul 95	**STUCK** *Furtive 6620562*	64		

RAJA NEE US singer

Date	Title / Label	Peak Position	Weeks at No.1	Weeks in Top 40
4 Mar 95	**TURN IT UP** *Perspective 5874872*	42		

JOEY NEGRO UK producer

Date	Title / Label	Peak Position	Weeks at No.1	Weeks in Top 40
16 Nov 91	**DO WHAT YOU FEEL** *10 TEN 391*	36		2
21 Dec 91	**REACHIN'** *Republic LIC 160* JOEY NEGRO PRESENTS PHASE II	70		
18 Jul 92	**ENTER YOUR FANTASY EP** *10 TEN 397*	35		1
25 Sep 93	**WHAT HAPPENED TO THE MUSIC** *Virgin VSCD 1466*	51		
19 Feb 00	**MUST BE THE MUSIC** *Incentive CENT 4CDS* JOEY NEGRO FEATURING TAKA BOOM	8		3
16 Sep 00	**SATURDAY** *Yola CDX03* JOEY NEGRO FEATURING TAKA BOOM	41		
18 Mar 06	**MAKE A MOVE ON ME** *Data DATA82CDS*	11		6

NEIL UK actor

Date	Title / Label	Peak Position	Weeks at No.1	Weeks in Top 40
14 Jul 84	**HOLE IN MY SHOE** *WEA YZ 10* ○	2		8

VINCE NEIL US singer

Date	Title / Label	Peak Position	Weeks at No.1	Weeks in Top 40
3 Oct 92	**YOU'RE INVITED (BUT YOUR FRIEND CAN'T COME)** *Hollywood HWD 123*	63		

NEIL'S CHILDREN UK group

Date	Title / Label	Peak Position	Weeks at No.1	Weeks in Top 40
18 Jun 05	**ALWAYS THE SAME** *Poptones MC5100SCD*	56		

NEJA Italian singer

Date	Title / Label	Peak Position	Weeks at No.1	Weeks in Top 40
26 Sep 98	**RESTLESS (I KNOW YOU KNOW)** *Panorama CDPAN 1*	47		

NEK Italian singer

Date	Title / Label	Peak Position	Weeks at No.1	Weeks in Top 40
29 Aug 98	**LAURA** *Coalition COLA 054CD*	59		

NELLY US rapper

Date	Title / Label	Peak Position	Weeks at No.1	Weeks in Top 40
11 Nov 00	**(HOT S**T) COUNTRY GRAMMAR** *Universal MCSTD 40242*	7		5
24 Feb 01	**EI** *Universal MCSTD 40249*	11		3
19 May 01	**RIDE WIT ME** *Universal MCSTD 40252* NELLY FEATURING CITY SPUD ○	3		9
15 Sep 01	**BATTER UP** *Universal MCSTD 40261* NELLY & ST LUNATICS	28		1
27 Oct 01	**WHERE'S THE PARTY AT** *Columbia 6719012* JAGGED EDGE FEATURING NELLY	25		1
27 Apr 02	**GIRLFRIEND** *Jive 9253312* N SYNC FEATURING NELLY	2		8
29 Jun 02	**HOT IN HERRE** *Universal MCSTD 40289* ○ ★	4		13
26 Oct 02	**DILEMMA** *Universal MCSTD 40299* NELLY FEATURING KELLY ROWLAND ⊛ ★	1	2	17
15 Mar 03	**WORK IT** *Universal MCSXD 40312* NELLY FEATURING JUSTIN TIMBERLAKE	7		5
20 Sep 03	**SHAKE YA TAILFEATHER** *Bad Boy MCSTD 40337* NELLY, P DIDDY & MURPHY LEE ★	10		5
13 Dec 03	**IZ U** *Universal MCSTD 40346*	36		1
11 Sep 04	**MY PLACE/FLAP YOUR WINGS** *Universal MCSTD 40379*	1	1	8
4 Dec 04	**TILT YA HEAD BACK** *Universal MCSTD40396* NELLY & CHRISTINA AGUILERA	5		9
5 Mar 05	**OVER AND OVER** *Curb/Derrty/Island MCSTD40402* NELLY FEATURING TIM McGRAW	1	1	9
25 Jun 05	**N DEY SAY** *Universal MCSXD40414*	6		4
16 Jul 05	**GET IT POPPIN'** *Atlantic AT0210CD* FAT JOE FEATURING NELLY	34		1
28 Jan 06	**NASTY GIRL** *Bad Boy AT0229CDX* NOTORIOUS B.I.G. FEATURING DIDDY, NELLY, JAGGED EDGE AND AVERY STORM	1	2	16
25 Mar 06	**GRILLZ** *Universal MCSTD40453* NELLY FEATURING PAUL WALL, ALI & GIPP	24		4
30 Sep 06	**CALL ON ME** *Virgin VUSCD330* JANET & NELLY	18		3

NELSON US duo

Date	Title / Label	Peak Position	Weeks at No.1	Weeks in Top 40
27 Oct 90	**(CAN'T LIVE WITHOUT YOUR) LOVE AND AFFECTION** *DGC GEF 82* ★	54		

BILL NELSON UK singer/multi-instrumentalist

Date	Title / Label	Peak Position	Weeks at No.1	Weeks in Top 40
24 Feb 79	**FURNITURE MUSIC** *Harvest HAR 5176* BILL NELSON'S RED NOISE	59		
5 May 79	**REVOLT IN STYLE** *Harvest HAR 5183* BILL NELSON'S RED NOISE	69		
5 Jul 80	**DO YOU DREAM IN COLOUR?** *Cocteau COQ 1*	52		
13 Jun 81	**YOUTH OF NATION ON FIRE** *Mercury WILL 2*	73		

PHYLLIS NELSON US singer

Date	Title / Label	Peak Position	Weeks at No.1	Weeks in Top 40
23 Feb 85	**MOVE CLOSER** *Carrere CAR 337* ●	1	1	15
21 May 94	**MOVE CLOSER** *EMI CDEMCT 9*	34		1

RICKY NELSON US singer

Date	Title / Label	Peak Position	Weeks at No.1	Weeks in Top 40
21 Feb 58	**STOOD UP** *London HLP 8542*	27		2
22 Aug 58	**POOR LITTLE FOOL** *London HLP 8670* ★	4		14
7 Nov 58	**SOMEDAY** *London HLP 8732*	9		13
21 Nov 58	**I GOT A FEELING** *London HLP 8732*	27		1
17 Apr 59	**IT'S LATE** *London HLP 8817*	3		20
15 May 59	**NEVER BE ANYONE ELSE BUT YOU** *London HLP 8817*	14		10
4 Sep 59	**SWEETER THAN YOU** *London HLP 8927*	19		3
11 Sep 59	**JUST A LITTLE TOO MUCH** *London HLP 8927*	11		8
15 Jan 60	**I WANNA BE LOVED** *London HLP 9021*	30		1
7 Jul 60	**YOUNG EMOTIONS** *London HLP 9121*	48		
1 Jun 61	**HELLO MARY LOU/TRAVELLIN' MAN** *London HLP 9347* ★	2		18
16 Nov 61	**EVERLOVIN'** *London HLP 9440*	23		5
29 Mar 62	**YOUNG WORLD** *London HLP 9524*	19		12
30 Aug 62	**TEENAGE IDOL** *London HLP 9583*	39		2
17 Jan 63	**IT'S UP TO YOU** *London HLP 9648*	22		8
17 Oct 63	**FOOLS RUSH IN** *Brunswick 05895*	12		9
30 Jan 64	**FOR YOU** *Brunswick 05900*	14		10
21 Oct 72	**GARDEN PARTY** *MCA MU 1165*	41		
24 Aug 91	**HELLO MARY LOU (GOODBYE HEART)** *Liberty EMCT 2*	45		

SANDY NELSON US drummer

Date	Title / Label	Peak Position	Weeks at No.1	Weeks in Top 40
6 Nov 59	**TEEN BEAT** *Top Rank JAR 197*	9		12
14 Dec 61	**LET THERE BE DRUMS** *London HLP 9466*	3		13
22 Mar 62	**DRUMS ARE MY BEAT** *London HLP 9521*	30		4
7 Jun 62	**DRUMMIN' UP A STORM** *London HLP 9558*	39		1

SHARA NELSON UK singer

Date	Title / Label	Peak Position	Weeks at No.1	Weeks in Top 40
24 Jul 93	**DOWN THAT ROAD** *Cooltempo CDCOOL 275*	19		4
18 Sep 93	**ONE GOODBYE IN TEN** *Cooltempo CDCOOL 279*	21		4
12 Feb 94	**UPTIGHT** *Cooltempo CDCOOL 286*	19		3
4 Jun 94	**NOBODY** *Cooltempo CDCOOL 290*	49		
10 Sep 94	**INSIDE OUT/DOWN THAT ROAD (REMIX)** *Cooltempo CDCOOLX 295*	34		2
16 Sep 95	**ROUGH WITH THE SMOOTH** *Cooltempo CDCOOL 311*	30		1
5 Dec 98	**SENSE OF DANGER** *Pagan 024CDS* PRESENCE FEATURING SHARA NELSON	61		

WILLIE NELSON US singer

Date	Title / Label	Peak Position	Weeks at No.1	Weeks in Top 40
31 Jul 82	**ALWAYS ON MY MIND** *CBS A 2511*	49		
7 Apr 84	**TO ALL THE GIRLS I'VE LOVED BEFORE** *CBS A 4252* JULIO IGLESIAS & WILLIE NELSON	17		6

NENA German group

Date	Title / Label	Peak Position	Weeks at No.1	Weeks in Top 40
4 Feb 84	**99 RED BALLOONS** *Epic A 4074* ●	1	3	10
5 May 84	**JUST A DREAM** *Epic A 3249*	70		

NEO CORTEX Danish production group

Date	Title / Label	Peak Position	Weeks at No.1	Weeks in Top 40
23 Oct 04	**ELEMENTS** *All Around The World CDGLOBE332*	67		

Silver-selling ○ Gold-selling ● Platinum-selling ⊛ US No.1 ★ Peak Position / Weeks at No.1 / Weeks in Top 40

N*E*R*D *US group*

Date	Title / Label / Artist	Peak Position	Weeks at No.1	Weeks in Top 40
9 Jun 01	**LAPDANCE** *Virgin VUSCD 196* N*E*R*D FEATURING LEE HARVEY & VITA	33		1
26 Jan 02	**DIDDY** *Puff Daddy 74321911652* P DIDDY FEATURING THE NEPTUNES	19		1
8 Jun 02	**PASS THE COURVOISIER - PART II** *J Records 74321937902* BUSTA RHYMES, P DIDDY & PHARRELL	16		3
10 Aug 02	**BOYS** *Jive 9253912* BRITNEY SPEARS FEATURING PHARRELL WILLIAMS	7		4
10 Aug 02	**ROCK STAR** *Virgin VUSCD 253*	15		2
29 Mar 03	**PROVIDER/LAPDANCE** *Virgin VUSCD 262*	20		2
5 Apr 03	**BEAUTIFUL** *Capitol CDCL 842* SNOOP DOGG FEATURING PHARRELL	23		4
16 Aug 03	**FRONTIN'** *Arista 82876553332* PHARRELL WILLIAMS FEATURING JAY-Z	6		7
29 Nov 03	**LIGHT YOUR ASS ON FIRE** *Arista 82876572512* BUSTA RHYMES FEATURING PHARRELL	62		
7 Feb 04	**SHOW ME YOUR SOUL** *Puff Daddy MCSTD 40350* P DIDDY, LENNY KRAVITZ, PHARRELL WILLIAMS & LOON	35		1
27 Mar 04	**SHE WANTS TO MOVE** *Virgin VUSDX 284*	5		9
15 May 04	**PASS THE COURVOISIER - PART II** *J Records 74321937902* BUSTA RHYMES, P DIDDY & PHARRELL	71		
26 Jun 04	**MAYBE** *Virgin VUSDX 291*	25		1
11 Dec 04	**DROP IT LIKE IT'S HOT** *Geffen 2103461* SNOOP DOGG FEATURING PHARRELL ★	10		8
5 Mar 05	**LET'S GET BLOWN** *Geffen 9880425* SNOOP DOGG FEATURING PHARRELL	13		3
12 Nov 05	**CAN I HAVE IT LIKE THAT** *Virgin VUSCD315* PHARRELL FEATURING GWEN STEFANI	3		7
4 Feb 06	**ANGEL** *Virgin VUSCD317*	15		3
26 Aug 06	**NUMBER ONE** *Virgin VUSDX333* PHARRELL FEATURING KANYE WEST	31		1

FRANCES NERO *US singer*

Date	Title / Label / Artist	Peak Position	Weeks at No.1	Weeks in Top 40
13 Apr 91	**FOOTSTEPS FOLLOWING ME** *Debut DEBT 3109*	17		7

NERO & THE GLADIATORS *UK group*

Date	Title / Label / Artist	Peak Position	Weeks at No.1	Weeks in Top 40
23 Mar 61	**ENTRY OF THE GLADIATORS** *Decca F 11329*	37		2
27 Jul 61	**IN THE HALL OF THE MOUNTAIN KING** *Decca F 11367*	48		

ANN NESBY *US singer*

Date	Title / Label / Artist	Peak Position	Weeks at No.1	Weeks in Top 40
21 Dec 96	**WITNESS (EP)** *AM:PM 5875612*	42		
17 May 97	**HOLD ON (EP)** *AM:PM 5822332*	75		

MICHAEL NESMITH *US singer*

Date	Title / Label / Artist	Peak Position	Weeks at No.1	Weeks in Top 40
26 Mar 77	**RIO** *Island WIP 6373*	28		5

NETWORK *UK group*

Date	Title / Label / Artist	Peak Position	Weeks at No.1	Weeks in Top 40
12 Dec 92	**BROKEN WINGS** *Chrysalis CHS 3923*	46		

NEVADA *UK group*

Date	Title / Label / Artist	Peak Position	Weeks at No.1	Weeks in Top 40
8 Jan 83	**IN THE BLEAK MID WINTER** *Polydor POSP 203*	71		

ROBBIE NEVIL *US singer*

Date	Title / Label / Artist	Peak Position	Weeks at No.1	Weeks in Top 40
20 Dec 86	**C'EST LA VIE** *Manhattan MT 14*	3		7
2 May 87	**DOMINOES** *Manhattan MT 19*	26		4
11 Jul 87	**WOT'S IT TO YA** *Manhattan MT 24*	43		

TOM NEVILLE *UK producer*

Date	Title / Label / Artist	Peak Position	Weeks at No.1	Weeks in Top 40
6 Mar 04	**JUST FUCK** *Nukleuz 0555PNUK*	60		

NEVILLE BROTHERS *US group*

Date	Title / Label / Artist	Peak Position	Weeks at No.1	Weeks in Top 40
25 Nov 89	**WITH GOD ON OUR SIDE** *A&M AM 545*	47		
7 Jul 90	**BIRD ON A WIRE** *A&M AM 568*	72		

JASON NEVINS *US producer*

Date	Title / Label / Artist	Peak Position	Weeks at No.1	Weeks in Top 40
21 Feb 98	**IT'S LIKE THAT (GERMAN IMPORT)** *Columbia 6652932* RUN DMC VERSUS JASON NEVINS	63		
14 Mar 98	**IT'S LIKE THAT (AMERICAN IMPORT)** *Columbia 6652932* RUN DMC VERSUS JASON NEVINS	65		
21 Mar 98	**IT'S LIKE THAT** *Sm:)e Communications SM 90652* RUN DMC VERSUS JASON NEVINS ⊛	1	6	14
18 Apr 98	**IT'S TRICKY (IMPORT)** *Epidrome EPD 6656982* RUN DMC VERSUS JASON NEVINS	74		
26 Jun 99	**INSANE IN THE BRAIN** *INCredible INCRL 17CD* JASON NEVINS VERSUS CYPRESS HILL	19		2
16 Aug 03	**I'M IN HEAVEN** *Free 2 Air/Incentive 0148665 F2A* JASON NEVINS PRESENTS UKNY FEATURING HOLLY JAMES	9		3
15 Dec 07	**TOUCH ME LIKE THAT** *All Around The World CDGLOBE795* DANNII MINOGUE VS JASON NEVINS	48		

NEW ATLANTIC *UK duo*

Date	Title / Label / Artist	Peak Position	Weeks at No.1	Weeks in Top 40
29 Feb 92	**I KNOW** *3 Beat 3BT 1*	12		5
3 Oct 92	**INTO THE FUTURE** *3 Beat 3BT 2* NEW ATLANTIC FEATURING LINDA WRIGHT	70		
13 Feb 93	**TAKE OFF SOME TIME** *3 Beat 3BTCD 14*	64		
26 Nov 94	**THE SUNSHINE AFTER THE RAIN** *3 Beat TABCD 223* NEW ATLANTIC/U4EA FEATURING BERRI	26		4

NEW EDITION *US group*

Date	Title / Label / Artist	Peak Position	Weeks at No.1	Weeks in Top 40
16 Apr 83	**CANDY GIRL** *London LON 21* ○	1	1	9
13 Aug 83	**POPCORN LOVE** *London LON 31*	43		
23 Feb 85	**MR TELEPHONE MAN** *MCA 938*	19		5
15 Apr 89	**CRUCIAL** *MCA 23934*	70		
10 Aug 96	**HIT ME OFF** *MCA MCSTD 48014*	20		2
7 Jun 97	**SOMETHING ABOUT YOU** *MCA MCSTD 48032*	16		3

NEW FOUND GLORY *US group*

Date	Title / Label / Artist	Peak Position	Weeks at No.1	Weeks in Top 40
16 Jun 01	**HIT OR MISS (WAITED TOO LONG)** *MCA 1558232*	58		
3 Aug 02	**MY FRIENDS OVER YOU** *MCA MCSXD 40286*	30		1
19 Oct 02	**HEAD ON COLLISION** *MCA MCSXD 40298*	64		
12 Jun 04	**ALL DOWNHILL FROM HERE** *Geffen 9862523*	58		
11 Sep 04	**FAILURE'S NOT FLATTERING** *Geffen MCSTD40380*	67		
26 Feb 05	**I DON'T WANNA KNOW** *Geffen 2103972*	48		

A NEW GENERATION *UK group*

Date	Title / Label / Artist	Peak Position	Weeks at No.1	Weeks in Top 40
26 Jun 68	**SMOKEY BLUES AWAY** *Spark SRL 1007*	38		1

NEW KIDS ON THE BLOCK *US group*

Date	Title / Label / Artist	Peak Position	Weeks at No.1	Weeks in Top 40
16 Sep 89	**HANGIN' TOUGH** *CBS BLOCK 1*	52		
11 Nov 89	**YOU GOT IT (THE RIGHT STUFF)** *CBS BLOCK 2* ●	1	3	11
6 Jan 90	**HANGIN' TOUGH** *CBS BLOCK 3* ★	1	2	8
17 Mar 90	**I'LL BE LOVING YOU (FOREVER)** *CBS BLOCK 4* ★	5		7
12 May 90	**COVER GIRL** *CBS BLOCK 5*	4		6
16 Jun 90	**STEP BY STEP** *CBS BLOCK 6* ○ ★	2		5
4 Aug 90	**TONIGHT** *CBS BLOCK 7*	3		9
13 Oct 90	**LET'S TRY AGAIN/DIDN'T I BLOW YOUR MIND** *CBS BLOCK 8*	8		4
8 Dec 90	**THIS ONE'S FOR THE CHILDREN** *CBS BLOCK 9*	9		6
9 Feb 91	**GAMES** *CBS 6566267*	14		4
18 May 91	**CALL IT WHAT YOU WANT** *Columbia 6567857*	12		4
14 Dec 91	**IF YOU GO AWAY** *Columbia 6576667*	9		4
19 Feb 94	**DIRTY DAWG** *Columbia 6600362* NKOTB	27		2
26 Mar 94	**NEVER LET YOU GO** *Columbia 6602072* NKOTB	42		

NEW MODEL ARMY *UK group*

Date	Title / Label / Artist	Peak Position	Weeks at No.1	Weeks in Top 40
27 Apr 85	**NO REST** *EMI NMA 1*	28		3
3 Aug 85	**THE ACOUSTICS (EP)** *EMI NMA 2*	49		
30 Nov 85	**BRAVE NEW WORLD** *EMI NMA 3*	57		
8 Nov 86	**51ST STATE** *EMI NMA 4*	71		
28 Feb 87	**POISON STREET** *EMI NMA 5*	64		
26 Sep 87	**WHITE COATS (EP)** *EMI NMA 6*	50		
21 Jan 89	**STUPID QUESTION** *EMI NMA 7*	31		2
11 Mar 89	**VAGABONDS** *EMI NMA 8*	37		2
10 Jun 89	**GREEN AND GREY** *EMI NMA 9*	37		2
8 Sep 90	**GET ME OUT** *EMI NMA 10*	34		2
3 Nov 90	**PURITY** *EMI NMA 11*	61		
8 Jun 91	**SPACE** *EMI NMA 12*	39		1

Date	Title / Label	Peak Position	Weeks at No.1	Weeks in Top 40
20 Feb 93	HERE COMES THE WAR *Epic 6589352*	25		1
24 Jul 93	LIVING IN THE ROSE (THE BALLADS EP) *Epic 6592492*	51		

NEW MUSIK UK group

Date	Title / Label	Peak Position	Weeks at No.1	Weeks in Top 40
6 Oct 79	STRAIGHT LINES *GTO GT 255*	53		
19 Jan 80	LIVING BY NUMBERS *GTO GT 261*	13		6
26 Apr 80	THIS WORLD OF WATER *GTO GT 268*	31		5
12 Jul 80	SANCTUARY *GTO GT 275*	31		4

NEW ORDER UK group

Date	Title / Label	Peak Position	Weeks at No.1	Weeks in Top 40
14 Mar 81	CEREMONY *Factory FAC 33*	34		3
3 Oct 81	PROCESSION/EVERYTHING'S GONE GREEN *Factory FAC 53*	38		2
22 May 82	TEMPTATION *Factory FAC 63*	29		5
19 Mar 83	BLUE MONDAY *Factory FAC 73*	12		11
13 Aug 83	BLUE MONDAY *Factory FAC 73*	9		10
3 Sep 83	CONFUSION *Factory FAC 93*	12		5
28 Apr 84	THIEVES LIKE US *Factory FAC 103*	18		4
25 May 85	THE PERFECT KISS *Factory FAC 123*	46		
9 Nov 85	SUB-CULTURE *Factory FAC 133*	63		
29 Mar 86	SHELLSHOCK *Factory FAC 143*	28		3
27 Sep 86	STATE OF THE NATION *Factory FAC 153*	30		2
27 Sep 86	THE PEEL SESSIONS (1ST JUNE 1982) *Strange Fruit SFPS 001*	54		
15 Nov 86	BIZARRE LOVE TRIANGLE *Factory FAC 163*	56		
1 Aug 87	TRUE FAITH *Factory FAC 183/7*	4		8
19 Dec 87	TOUCHED BY THE HAND OF GOD *Factory FAC 1937*	20		5
7 May 88	BLUE MONDAY (REMIX) *Factory FAC 737*	3		7
10 Dec 88	FINE TIME *Factory FAC 2237*	11		6
11 Mar 89	ROUND AND ROUND *Factory FAC 2637*	21		5
9 Sep 89	RUN 2 *Factory FAC 273*	49		
2 Jun 90	WORLD IN MOTION *Factory/MCA FAC 2937* ENGLANDNEWORDER ●	1	2	10
17 Apr 93	REGRET *Centredate Co NUOCD 1*	4		5
3 Jul 93	RUINED IN A DAY *Centredate Co NUOCD 2*	22		2
4 Sep 93	WORLD (THE PRICE OF LOVE) *Centredate Co NUOCD 3*	13		3
18 Dec 93	SPOOKY *Centredate Co NUOCD 4*	22		1
19 Nov 94	TRUE FAITH (REMIX) *Centredate Co NUOCD 5*	9		4
21 Jan 95	NINETEEN63 *London NUOCD 6*	21		3
5 Aug 95	BLUE MONDAY (2ND REMIX) *London NUOCD 7*	17		3
25 Aug 01	CRYSTAL *London NUOCD 8*	8		2
1 Dec 01	60 MILES AN HOUR *London NOUCD 9*	29		1
27 Apr 02	HERE TO STAY *London NUOCD 11*	15		1
15 Jun 02	WORLD IN MOTION *London NUOCD 12* ENGLANDNEWORDER	43		
30 Nov 02	CONFUSION (REMIX) *Whacked WACKT 002CD* ARTHUR BAKER VS NEW ORDER	64		
19 Mar 05	KRAFTY *London NUOCD13*	8		2
28 May 05	JETSTREAM *London NUOCD14* NEW ORDER FEATURING ANA MANTRONIC	20		1
8 Oct 05	WAITING FOR THE SIRENS' CALL *London NUOCD15*	21		1
11 Mar 06	BLUE MONDAY (REMIX) *New State NSER017*	73		

NEW POWER GENERATION US group

Date	Title / Label	Peak Position	Weeks at No.1	Weeks in Top 40
31 Aug 91	GETT OFF *Paisley Park W 0056* PRINCE & THE NEW POWER GENERATION	4		7
21 Sep 91	CREAM *Paisley Park W 0061* PRINCE & THE NEW POWER GENERATION ★	15		4
7 Dec 91	DIAMONDS AND PEARLS *Paisley Park W 0075* PRINCE & THE NEW POWER GENERATION	25		5
28 Mar 92	MONEY DON'T MATTER 2 NIGHT *Paisley Park W 0091* PRINCE & THE NEW POWER GENERATION	19		3
27 Jun 92	THUNDER *Paisley Park W 01132P* PRINCE & THE NEW POWER GENERATION	28		2
18 Jul 92	SEXY MF/STROLLIN' *Paisley Park W 0123* PRINCE & THE NEW POWER GENERATION	4		5
10 Oct 92	MY NAME IS PRINCE *Paisley Park W 0132* PRINCE & THE NEW POWER GENERATION	7		4
14 Nov 92	MY NAME IS PRINCE (REMIX) *Paisley Park W 0142T* PRINCE & THE NEW POWER GENERATION	51		
5 Dec 92	7 *Paisley Park W 0147* PRINCE & THE NEW POWER GENERATION	27		2
13 Mar 93	THE MORNING PAPERS *Paisley Park W 0162CD* PRINCE & THE NEW POWER GENERATION	52		
1 Apr 95	GET WILD *NPG 0061045*	19		2
19 Aug 95	THE GOOD LIFE *NPG 0061515*	29		1
5 Jul 97	THE GOOD LIFE *NPG 0061515*	15		2
21 Nov 98	COME ON *RCA 74321634722*	65		

NEW RADICALS US group

Date	Title / Label	Peak Position	Weeks at No.1	Weeks in Top 40
3 Apr 99	YOU GET WHAT YOU GIVE *MCA MCSTD 48111* ○	5		13
25 Sep 99	SOMEDAY WE'LL KNOW *MCA MCSTD 40217*	48		

NEW RHODES UK group

Date	Title / Label	Peak Position	Weeks at No.1	Weeks in Top 40
7 Aug 04	I WISH I WAS YOU *Moshi Moshi MOSHI11CD*	63		
26 Feb 05	YOU'VE GIVEN ME SOMETHING THAT I CAN'T GIVE BACK *Moshi Moshi MOSHI15CD*	38		1
27 Aug 05	FROM THE BEGINNING *Moshi Moshi MOSHI24CD*	64		

NEW SEEKERS UK/Australian group

Date	Title / Label	Peak Position	Weeks at No.1	Weeks in Top 40
17 Oct 70	WHAT HAVE THEY DONE TO MY SONG MA *Philips 6006 027*	44		
10 Jul 71	NEVER ENDING SONG OF LOVE *Philips 6006 125*	2		15
18 Dec 71	I'D LIKE TO TEACH THE WORLD TO SING (IN PERFECT HARMONY) *Polydor 2058 184*	1	4	19
4 Mar 72	BEG, STEAL OR BORROW *Polydor 2058 201*	2		12
10 Jun 72	CIRCLES *Polydor 2058 242*	4		14
2 Dec 72	COME SOFTLY TO ME *Polydor 2058 315* NEW SEEKERS FEATURING MARTY KRISTIAN	20		8
24 Feb 73	PINBALL WIZARD – SEE ME FEEL ME (MEDLEY) *Polydor 2058 338*	16		7
7 Apr 73	NEVERTHELESS *Polydor 2058 340* EVE GRAHAM & THE NEW SEEKERS	34		1
16 Jun 73	GOODBYE IS JUST ANOTHER WORD *Polydor 2058 368*	36		2
24 Nov 73	YOU WON'T FIND ANOTHER FOOL LIKE ME *Polydor 2058 421* ●	1	1	16
9 Mar 74	I GET A LITTLE SENTIMENTAL OVER YOU *Polydor 2058 439* ○	5		8
14 Aug 76	IT'S SO NICE (TO HAVE YOU HOME) *CBS 4391*	44		
29 Jan 77	I WANNA GO BACK *CBS 4786*	25		2
15 Jul 78	ANTHEM (ONE DAY IN EVERY WEEK) *CBS 6413*	21		5

NEW VAUDEVILLE BAND UK group

Date	Title / Label	Peak Position	Weeks at No.1	Weeks in Top 40
8 Sep 66	WINCHESTER CATHEDRAL *Fontana TF 741* ★	4		17
26 Jan 67	PEEK-A-BOO *Fontana TF 784* NEW VAUDEVILLE BAND FEATURING TRISTRAM	7		10
11 May 67	FINCHLEY CENTRAL *Fontana TF 824*	11		8
2 Aug 67	GREEN STREET GREEN *Fontana TF 853*	37		1

NEW VISION US duo

Date	Title / Label	Peak Position	Weeks at No.1	Weeks in Top 40
29 Jan 00	(JUST) ME AND YOU *AM:PM CDAMPM 128*	23		1

NEW WORLD Australian group

Date	Title / Label	Peak Position	Weeks at No.1	Weeks in Top 40
27 Feb 71	ROSE GARDEN *RAK 111*	15		9
3 Jul 71	TOM-TOM TURNAROUND *RAK 117*	6		14
4 Dec 71	KARA KARA *RAK 123*	17		11
13 May 72	SISTER JANE *RAK 130*	9		12
12 May 73	ROOF TOP SINGING *RAK 148*	50		

NEW YORK CITY US group

Date	Title / Label	Peak Position	Weeks at No.1	Weeks in Top 40
21 Jul 73	I'M DOING FINE NOW *RCA 2351*	20		9

NEW YORK SKYY US group

Date	Title / Label	Peak Position	Weeks at No.1	Weeks in Top 40
16 Jan 82	LET'S CELEBRATE *Epic EPC A 1898*	67		

NEW YOUNG PONY CLUB UK group

Date	Title / Label	Peak Position	Weeks at No.1	Weeks in Top 40
31 Mar 07	THE BOMB *Island/Modular NYPCCD002*	47		
14 Jul 07	ICE CREAM *Island/Modular MODCDS40*	40		1

NEWBEATS US trio

Date	Title / Label	Peak Position	Weeks at No.1	Weeks in Top 40
10 Sep 64	BREAD AND BUTTER *Hickory 1269*	15		8
23 Oct 71	RUN BABY RUN *London HL 10341*	10		11

BOOKER NEWBURY III US singer

Date	Title / Label	Peak Position	Weeks at No.1	Weeks in Top 40
28 May 83	LOVE TOWN *Polydor POSP 613*	6		7
8 Oct 83	TEDDY BEAR *Polydor POSP 637*	44		

MICKEY NEWBURY US singer

Date	Title / Label	Peak Position	Weeks at No.1	Weeks in Top 40
1 Jul 72	AMERICAN TRILOGY *Elektra K 12047*	42		

Silver-selling ○ Gold-selling ● Platinum-selling ⊛ US No.1 ★ — Peak Position / Weeks at No.1 / Weeks in Top 40

NEWCLEUS US group

Date	Title	Label	Peak Position	Weeks at No.1	Weeks in Top 40
3 Sep 83	JAM ON REVENGE (THE WIKKI WIKKI SONG)	*Beckett BKS 8*	44		

ANTHONY NEWLEY UK singer/actor

Date	Title	Label	Peak Position	Weeks at No.1	Weeks in Top 40
1 May 59	I'VE WAITED SO LONG	*Decca F 11127*	3		15
8 May 59	IDLE ON PARADE EP	*Decca DFE 6566*	13		4
12 Jun 59	PERSONALITY	*Decca F 11142*	6		12
15 Jan 60	WHY	*Decca F 11194*	1	4	17
24 Mar 60	DO YOU MIND	*Decca F 11220*	1	1	15
14 Jul 60	IF SHE SHOULD COME TO YOU	*Decca F 11254*	4		14
24 Nov 60	STRAWBERRY FAIR	*Decca F 11295*	3		9
16 Mar 61	AND THE HEAVENS CRIED	*Decca F 11331*	6		11
15 Jun 61	POP GOES THE WEASEL/BEE BOM	*Decca F 11362*	12		8
3 Aug 61	WHAT KIND OF FOOL AM I?	*Decca F 11376*	36		6
25 Jan 62	D-DARLING	*Decca F 11419*	25		5
26 Jul 62	THAT NOISE	*Decca F 11486*	34		4

BRAD NEWMAN UK singer

Date	Title	Label	Peak Position	Weeks at No.1	Weeks in Top 40
22 Feb 62	SOMEBODY TO LOVE	*Fontana H 357*	47		

DAVE NEWMAN UK singer

Date	Title	Label	Peak Position	Weeks at No.1	Weeks in Top 40
15 Apr 72	THE LION SLEEPS TONIGHT	*Pye 7N 45134*	34		1

NEWS UK group

Date	Title	Label	Peak Position	Weeks at No.1	Weeks in Top 40
29 Aug 81	AUDIO VIDEO	*George 1*	52		

NEWTON UK singer

Date	Title	Label	Peak Position	Weeks at No.1	Weeks in Top 40
15 Jul 95	SKY HIGH	*Bags Of Fun BAGSCD 6*	56		
15 Feb 97	SOMETIMES WHEN WE TOUCH	*Dominion CDDMIN 202*	32		2
16 Aug 97	DON'T WORRY	*Dominion CDDMIN 206*	61		

JUICE NEWTON US singer

Date	Title	Label	Peak Position	Weeks at No.1	Weeks in Top 40
2 May 81	ANGEL OF THE MORNING	*Capitol CL 16189*	43		

OLIVIA NEWTON-JOHN UK singer

Date	Title	Label	Peak Position	Weeks at No.1	Weeks in Top 40
20 Mar 71	IF NOT FOR YOU	*Pye International 7N 25543*	7		11
23 Oct 71	BANKS OF THE OHIO	*Pye International 7N 25568*	6		15
11 Mar 72	WHAT IS LIFE	*Pye International 7N 25575*	16		6
13 Jan 73	TAKE ME HOME COUNTRY ROADS	*Pye International 7N 25599*	15		12
16 Mar 74	LONG LIVE LOVE	*Pye International 7N 25638*	11		7
12 Oct 74	I HONESTLY LOVE YOU	*EMI 2216* ★	22		6
11 Jun 77	SAM	*EMI 2616*	6		11
20 May 78	YOU'RE THE ONE THAT I WANT JOHN TRAVOLTA & OLIVIA NEWTON-JOHN ⊛ ★	*RSO 006*	1	9	20
16 Sep 78	SUMMER NIGHTS JOHN TRAVOLTA & OLIVIA NEWTON-JOHN ⊛	*RSO 18*	1	7	12
4 Nov 78	HOPELESSLY DEVOTED TO YOU	*RSO 17* ●	2		7
16 Dec 78	A LITTLE MORE LOVE	*EMI 2879* ○	4		9
30 Jun 79	DEEPER THAN THE NIGHT	*EMI 2954*	64		
21 Jun 80	XANADU OLIVIA NEWTON-JOHN & ELECTRIC LIGHT ORCHESTRA ○	*Jet 185*	1	2	10
23 Aug 80	MAGIC	*Jet 196* ★	32		3
25 Oct 80	SUDDENLY OLIVIA NEWTON-JOHN & CLIFF RICHARD	*Jet 7002*	15		5
10 Oct 81	PHYSICAL	*EMI 5234* ○ ★	7		12
16 Jan 82	LANDSLIDE	*EMI 5257*	18		6
17 Apr 82	MAKE A MOVE ON ME	*EMI 5291*	43		
23 Oct 82	HEART ATTACK	*EMI 5347*	46		
15 Jan 83	I HONESTLY LOVE YOU	*EMI 5360*	52		
12 Nov 83	TWIST OF FATE	*EMI 5438*	57		
22 Dec 90	GREASE MEGAMIX JOHN TRAVOLTA & OLIVIA NEWTON-JOHN	*Polydor PO 114*	3		8
23 Mar 91	GREASE - THE DREAM MIX FRANKIE VALLI, JOHN TRAVOLTA & OLIVIA NEWTON-JOHN	*PWL/Polydor PO 136*	47		
4 Jul 92	I NEED LOVE	*Mercury MER 370*	75		
9 Dec 95	HAD TO BE CLIFF RICHARD & OLIVIA NEWTON-JOHN	*EMI CDEMS 410*	22		1
25 Jul 98	YOU'RE THE ONE THAT I WANT JOHN TRAVOLTA & OLIVIA NEWTON-JOHN	*Polydor 0441332*	4		4

NEXT US group

Date	Title	Label	Peak Position	Weeks at No.1	Weeks in Top 40
6 Jun 98	TOO CLOSE	*Arista 74321580672* ★	24		2
16 Sep 00	WIFEY	*Arista 74321790912*	19		3

NEXT OF KIN UK group

Date	Title	Label	Peak Position	Weeks at No.1	Weeks in Top 40
20 Feb 99	24 HOURS FROM YOU	*Universal MCSTD 40201*	13		3
19 Jun 99	MORE LOVE	*Universal MCSTD 40207*	33		1

NIAGRA UK production duo

Date	Title	Label	Peak Position	Weeks at No.1	Weeks in Top 40
27 Sep 97	CLOUDBURST	*Freeflow FLOW CD2*	65		

NICE UK group

Date	Title	Label	Peak Position	Weeks at No.1	Weeks in Top 40
10 Jul 68	AMERICA	*Immediate IM 068*	21		15

PAUL NICHOLAS UK singer/actor

Date	Title	Label	Peak Position	Weeks at No.1	Weeks in Top 40
17 Apr 76	REGGAE LIKE IT USED TO BE	*RSO 2090 185*	17		7
9 Oct 76	DANCING WITH THE CAPTAIN	*RSO 2090 206*	8		8
4 Dec 76	GRANDMA'S PARTY	*RSO 2090 216* ○	9		10
9 Jul 77	HEAVEN ON THE 7TH FLOOR	*RSO 2090 249*	40		1

SUE NICHOLLS UK actress

Date	Title	Label	Peak Position	Weeks at No.1	Weeks in Top 40
3 Jul 68	WHERE WILL YOU BE	*Pye 7N 17565*	17		7

NICKELBACK Canadian group

Date	Title	Label	Peak Position	Weeks at No.1	Weeks in Top 40
23 Feb 02	HOW YOU REMIND ME (IMPORT)	*Roadrunner 23203323CD*	65		
9 Mar 02	HOW YOU REMIND ME	*Roadrunner 23203325* ● ★	4		16
7 Sep 02	TOO BAD	*Roadrunner RR 20375*	9		4
7 Dec 02	NEVER AGAIN	*Roadrunner RR 20255*	30		1
27 Sep 03	SOMEDAY	*Roadrunner RR 20088*	6		7
27 Mar 04	FEELIN' WAY TOO DAMN GOOD	*Roadrunner RR39983*	39		1
8 Oct 05	PHOTOGRAPH	*Roadrunner RR39553*	29		1
25 Feb 06	FAR AWAY	*Roadrunner RR39483*	40		1
27 Oct 07	ROCKSTAR	*Roadrunner RR39323* ○	2		20
2 Feb 08	HOW YOU REMIND ME	*Download*	55		

STEVIE NICKS US singer

Date	Title	Label	Peak Position	Weeks at No.1	Weeks in Top 40
15 Aug 81	STOP DRAGGIN' MY HEART AROUND STEVIE NICKS WITH TOM PETTY & THE HEARTBREAKERS	*WEA K 79231*	50		
25 Jan 86	I CAN'T WAIT	*Parlophone R 6110*	54		
29 Mar 86	TALK TO ME	*Parlophone R 6124*	68		
6 May 89	ROOMS ON FIRE	*EMI EM 90*	16		5
12 Aug 89	LONG WAY TO GO	*EMI EM 97*	60		
11 Nov 89	WHOLE LOTTA TROUBLE	*EMI EM 114*	62		
24 Aug 91	SOMETIMES IT'S A BITCH	*EMI EM 203*	40		1
9 Nov 91	I CAN'T WAIT	*EMI EM 214*	47		
2 Jul 94	MAYBE LOVE	*EMI CDEMS 328*	42		
29 Apr 06	DREAMS DEEP DISH FEATURING STEVIE NICKS	*Positiva CDTIV232*	14		3

NICOLE German singer

Date	Title	Label	Peak Position	Weeks at No.1	Weeks in Top 40
8 May 82	A LITTLE PEACE	*CBS A 2365* ○	1	2	6
21 Aug 82	GIVE ME MORE TIME	*CBS A 2467*	75		

NICOLE US singer

Date	Title	Label	Peak Position	Weeks at No.1	Weeks in Top 40
28 Dec 85	NEW YORK EYES NICOLE WITH TIMMY THOMAS	*Portrait A 6805*	41		
26 Dec 92	ROCK THE HOUSE SOURCE FEATURING NICOLE	*React 12REACT 12*	63		
6 Jul 96	RUNNIN' AWAY	*Ore AG 18CD*	69		

REMI NICOLE UK singer

Date	Title	Label	Peak Position	Weeks at No.1	Weeks in Top 40
1 Sep 07	GO MR SUNSHINE	*Island 1744537*	57		

NICOLETTE UK singer

Date	Title	Label	Peak Position	Weeks at No.1	Weeks in Top 40
23 Dec 95	NO GOVERNMENT	*Talkin Loud TLCD 1*	67		

NIGEL & MARVIN Trinidadian duo

Date	Title	Peak Position	Weeks at No.1	Weeks in Top 40
18 May 02	**FOLLOW DA LEADER** *Relentless RELENT 19CD*	5		6

NIGHTBREED UK producer

Date	Title	Peak Position	Weeks at No.1	Weeks in Top 40
9 Oct 04	**PACK OF WOLVES** *Ram RAMM52CD*	45		

NIGHTCRAWLERS UK production duo

Date	Title	Peak Position	Weeks at No.1	Weeks in Top 40
15 Oct 94	**PUSH THE FEELING ON** *ffrr FCD 245*	22		2
4 Mar 95	**PUSH THE FEELING ON (REMIX)** *ffrr FCD 257*	3		9
27 May 95	**SURRENDER YOUR LOVE** *Final Vinyl 74321283982* NIGHTCRAWLERS FEATURING JOHN REID	7		6
9 Sep 95	**DON'T LET THE FEELING GO** *Final Vinyl 74321298822* NIGHTCRAWLERS FEATURING JOHN REID	13		2
20 Jan 96	**LET'S PUSH IT** *Final Vinyl 74321328142* NIGHTCRAWLERS FEATURING JOHN REID	23		3
20 Apr 96	**SHOULD I EVER (FALL IN LOVE)** *Arista 74321358072* NIGHTCRAWLERS FEATURING JOHN REID	34		1
27 Jul 96	**KEEP ON PUSHING OUR LOVE** *Arista 74321390422* NIGHTCRAWLERS FEATURING JOHN REID & ALYSHA WARREN	30		1
3 Jul 99	**NEVER KNEW LOVE** *Riverhorse RIVHCD 1*	59		

MAXINE NIGHTINGALE UK singer

Date	Title	Peak Position	Weeks at No.1	Weeks in Top 40
1 Nov 75	**RIGHT BACK WHERE WE STARTED FROM** *United Artists UP 36015*	8		7
12 Mar 77	**LOVE HIT ME** *United Artists UP 36215*	11		7

NIGHTMARES ON WAX UK duo

Date	Title	Peak Position	Weeks at No.1	Weeks in Top 40
27 Oct 90	**AFTERMATH/I'M FOR REAL** *Warp WAP 6*	38		1
26 Jun 99	**FINER** *Warp WAP 123CD*	63		

NIGHTWISH Finnish group

Date	Title	Peak Position	Weeks at No.1	Weeks in Top 40
9 Oct 04	**WISH I HAD AN ANGEL** *Nuclear Blast NB1336CD*	60		

NIGHTWRITERS US duo

Date	Title	Peak Position	Weeks at No.1	Weeks in Top 40
23 May 92	**LET THE MUSIC USE YOU** *ffrreedom TABX 112*	51		

NIKKE? NICOLE! US rapper

Date	Title	Peak Position	Weeks at No.1	Weeks in Top 40
1 Jun 91	**NIKKE DOES IT BETTER** *Love EVOL 5*	73		

MARKUS NIKOLAI German producer

Date	Title	Peak Position	Weeks at No.1	Weeks in Top 40
6 Oct 01	**BUSHES** *Southern Fried ECB 24CD*	74		

KURT NILSEN Norwegian singer

Date	Title	Peak Position	Weeks at No.1	Weeks in Top 40
29 May 04	**SHE'S SO HIGH** *RCA 82876610882*	25		1

NILSSON US singer

Date	Title	Peak Position	Weeks at No.1	Weeks in Top 40
27 Sep 69	**EVERYBODY'S TALKIN'** *RCA 1876*	23		7
5 Feb 72	**WITHOUT YOU** *RCA 2165* ★	1	5	17
3 Jun 72	**COCONUT** *RCA 2214*	42		
16 Oct 76	**WITHOUT YOU** *RCA 2733*	22		7
20 Aug 77	**ALL I THINK ABOUT IS YOU** *RCA PB 9104*	43		
19 Feb 94	**WITHOUT YOU** *RCA 74321193092*	47		

CHARLOTTE NILSSON Swedish singer

Date	Title	Peak Position	Weeks at No.1	Weeks in Top 40
3 Jul 99	**TAKE ME TO YOUR HEAVEN** *Arista 74321686952*	20		2

NINA & FREDERICK Danish duo

Date	Title	Peak Position	Weeks at No.1	Weeks in Top 40
18 Dec 59	**MARY'S BOY CHILD** *Columbia DB 4375*	26		1
10 Mar 60	**LISTEN TO THE OCEAN** *Columbia DB 4332*	46		
17 Nov 60	**LITTLE DONKEY** *Columbia DB 4536*	3		9
28 Sep 61	**LONGTIME BOY** *Columbia DB 4703*	43		
5 Oct 61	**SUCU SUCU** *Columbia DB 4632*	23		10

NINA SKY US duo

Date	Title	Peak Position	Weeks at No.1	Weeks in Top 40
17 Jul 04	**MOVE YA BODY** *Universal MCSTD40373*	6		8

NINE BLACK ALPS UK group

Date	Title	Peak Position	Weeks at No.1	Weeks in Top 40
19 Mar 05	**SHOT DOWN** *Island CID885*	25		1
4 Jun 05	**NOT EVERYONE** *Island CID892*	31		1
20 Aug 05	**UNSATISFIED** *Island CID899*	30		1
12 Nov 05	**JUST FRIENDS** *Island CID915*	52		
4 Aug 07	**BURN FASTER** *Island/Uni-Island 1741825*	42		

NINE INCH NAILS US group

Date	Title	Peak Position	Weeks at No.1	Weeks in Top 40
14 Sep 91	**HEAD LIKE A HOLE** *TVT IS 484*	45		
16 Nov 91	**SIN** *TVT IS 508*	35		1
9 Apr 94	**MARCH OF THE PIGS** *TVT CID 592*	45		
18 Jun 94	**CLOSER** *TVT CID 596*	25		1
13 Sep 97	**THE PERFECT DRUG** *Interscope IND 95542*	43		
18 Dec 99	**WE'RE IN THIS TOGETHER** *Island 4971832*	39		1
30 Apr 05	**THE HAND THAT FEEDS** *Island CID888*	7		2
6 Aug 05	**ONLY** *Island CID903*	20		1
21 Apr 07	**SURVIVALISM** *Interscope 1730194*	29		1

999 UK group

Date	Title	Peak Position	Weeks at No.1	Weeks in Top 40
25 Nov 78	**HOMICIDE** *United Artists UP 36467*	40		1
27 Oct 79	**FOUND OUT TOO LATE** *Radar ADA 46*	69		
16 May 81	**OBSESSED** *Albion ION 1011*	71		
18 Jul 81	**LIL RED RIDING HOOD** *Albion ION 1017*	59		
14 Nov 81	**INDIAN RESERVATION** *Albion ION 1023*	51		

911 UK group

Date	Title	Peak Position	Weeks at No.1	Weeks in Top 40
11 May 96	**NIGHT TO REMEMBER** *Ginga CDGINGA 1*	38		1
10 Aug 96	**LOVE SENSATION** *Ginga CDGINGA 2*	21		2
9 Nov 96	**DON'T MAKE ME WAIT** *Ginga VSCDT 1618*	10		3
22 Feb 97	**THE DAY WE FIND LOVE** *Virgin VSCDG 1619*	4		4
3 May 97	**BODYSHAKIN'** *Virgin VSCDT 1634*	3		6
12 Jul 97	**THE JOURNEY** *Virgin VSCDT 1645*	3		4
1 Nov 97	**PARTY PEOPLE...FRIDAY NIGHT** *Ginga VSCDT 1658*	5		4
4 Apr 98	**ALL I WANT IS YOU** *Virgin VSCDT 1681*	4		4
4 Jul 98	**HOW DO YOU WANT ME TO LOVE YOU?** *Ginga VSCDT 1686*	10		2
24 Oct 98	**MORE THAN A WOMAN** *Virgin VSCDT 1707*	2		4
23 Jan 99	**A LITTLE BIT MORE** *Virgin VSCDT 1719* ●	1	1	5
15 May 99	**PRIVATE NUMBER** *Virgin VSCDT 1730*	3		4
23 Oct 99	**WONDERLAND** *Virgin VSCDT 1755*	13		2

9.9 US group

Date	Title	Peak Position	Weeks at No.1	Weeks in Top 40
6 Jul 85	**ALL OF ME FOR ALL OF YOU** *RCA PB 49951*	53		

NINE YARDS UK group

Date	Title	Peak Position	Weeks at No.1	Weeks in Top 40
21 Nov 98	**LONELINESS IS GONE** *Virgin VSCDT 1696*	70		
10 Apr 99	**MATTER OF TIME** *Virgin VSCDT 1723*	59		
28 Aug 99	**ALWAYS FIND A WAY** *Virgin VSCDT 1746*	50		

1910 FRUITGUM CO. US group

Date	Title	Peak Position	Weeks at No.1	Weeks in Top 40
20 Mar 68	**SIMON SAYS** *Pye International 7N 25447*	2		14

1927 Australian group

Date	Title	Peak Position	Weeks at No.1	Weeks in Top 40
22 Apr 89	**THAT'S WHEN I THINK OF YOU** *WEA YZ 351*	46		

98° US group

Date	Title	Peak Position	Weeks at No.1	Weeks in Top 40
29 Nov 97	**INVISIBLE MAN** *Motown 8607092*	66		
31 Oct 98	**TRUE TO YOUR HEART** *Motown 8608832* 98° FEATURING STEVIE WONDER	51		
13 Mar 99	**BECAUSE OF YOU** *Motown 8609012*	36		1
11 Mar 00	**THANK GOD I FOUND YOU** *Columbia 6690582* MARIAH CAREY FEATURING JOE & 98°	10		4
11 Mar 00	**THE HARDEST THING** *Universal MCSTD 40228*	29		1
2 Dec 00	**GIVE ME JUST ONE MORE NIGHT (UNA NOCHE)** *Universal MCSTD 40243*	61		

Silver-selling ○ · Gold-selling ● · Platinum-selling · US No.1 ★ · Peak Position · Weeks at No.1 · Weeks in Top 40

99TH FLOOR ELEVATORS UK group

Date	Title	Peak Position	Weeks at No.1	Weeks in Top 40
12 Aug 95	**HOOKED** *Labello Dance LAD 18CD* 99TH FLOOR ELEVATORS FEATURING TONY DE VIT	28		1
30 Mar 96	**I'LL BE THERE** *Labello Dance LAD 25CD2* 99TH FLOOR ELEVATORS FEATURING TONY DE VIT	37		1
8 Apr 00	**HOOKED (REMIX)** *Tripoli Trax TTRAX 061CD*	66		

NIO Irish singer

Date	Title	Peak Position	Weeks at No.1	Weeks in Top 40
23 Aug 03	**DO YOU THINK YOU'RE SPECIAL?** *Echo ECSCX 132*	52		

NIRVANA UK/Irish group

Date	Title	Peak Position	Weeks at No.1	Weeks in Top 40
15 May 68	**RAINBOW CHASER** *Island WIP 6029*	34		4

NIRVANA US group

Date	Title	Peak Position	Weeks at No.1	Weeks in Top 40
30 Nov 91	**SMELLS LIKE TEEN SPIRIT** *DGC DGCS 5*	7		6
14 Mar 92	**COME AS YOU ARE** *DGC DGCS 7*	9		3
25 Jul 92	**LITHIUM** *DGC DGCS 9*	11		4
12 Dec 92	**IN BLOOM** *Geffen GFS 34*	28		5
6 Mar 93	**OH THE GUILT** *Touch And Go TG 83CD*	12		1
11 Sep 93	**HEART-SHAPED BOX** *Geffen GFSTD 54*	5		3
18 Dec 93	**ALL APOLOGIES/RAPE ME** *Geffen GFSTD 66*	32		3

NITRO DELUXE US producer

Date	Title	Peak Position	Weeks at No.1	Weeks in Top 40
14 Feb 87	**THIS BRUTAL HOUSE** *Cooltempo COOL 142*	47		
13 Jun 87	**THIS BRUTAL HOUSE (REMIX)** *Cooltempo COOL 142*	62		
6 Feb 88	**LET'S GET BRUTAL** *Cooltempo COOL 142*	24		4

NITZER EBB UK group

Date	Title	Peak Position	Weeks at No.1	Weeks in Top 40
11 Jan 92	**GODHEAD** *Mute 1MUTE 135T*	56		
11 Apr 92	**ASCEND** *Mute CDMUTE 145*	52		
4 Mar 95	**KICK IT** *Mute LCDMUTE 155*	75		

NIVEA US singer

Date	Title	Peak Position	Weeks at No.1	Weeks in Top 40
3 Mar 01	**DANGER (BEEN SO LONG)** *Jive 9251722* MYSTIKAL FEATURING NIVEA	28		1
4 May 02	**RUN AWAY (I WANNA BE WITH U)/DON'T MESS WITH THE RADIO** *Jive 9253362*	48		
21 Sep 02	**DON'T MESS WITH MY MAN** *Jive 9254082* NIVEA FEATURING BRIAN & BRANDON CASEY	41		
10 May 03	**LAUNDROMAT/DON'T MESS WITH MY MAN** *Jive 9254822*	33		1

NIZLOPI UK duo

Date	Title	Peak Position	Weeks at No.1	Weeks in Top 40
24 Dec 05	**JCB SONG** *FDM FDMNIZ004* ●	1		13

NO AUTHORITY US group

Date	Title	Peak Position	Weeks at No.1	Weeks in Top 40
14 Mar 98	**DON'T STOP** *Epic 6655592*	54		

NO DICE UK group

Date	Title	Peak Position	Weeks at No.1	Weeks in Top 40
5 May 79	**COME DANCING** *EMI 2927*	65		

NO DOUBT US group

Date	Title	Peak Position	Weeks at No.1	Weeks in Top 40
26 Oct 96	**JUST A GIRL** *Interscope IND 80034*	38		1
22 Feb 97	**DON'T SPEAK** *Interscope IND 95515* ●	1	3	14
5 Jul 97	**JUST A GIRL** *Interscope IND 95539*	3		5
4 Oct 97	**SPIDERWEBS** *Interscope IND 95551*	16		2
20 Dec 97	**SUNDAY MORNING** *Interscope IND 95566*	50		
12 Jun 99	**NEW** *Higher Ground HIGHS 22CD*	30		1
25 Mar 00	**EX-GIRLFRIEND** *Interscope 4972992*	23		1
7 Oct 00	**SIMPLE KIND OF LIFE** *Interscope 4974162*	69		
16 Feb 02	**HEY BABY** *Interscope 4976682* NO DOUBT FEATURING BOUNTY KILLER	2		4
15 Jun 02	**HELLA GOOD** *Interscope 4977362*	12		4
12 Oct 02	**UNDERNEATH IT ALL** *Interscope 4977792* NO DOUBT FEATURING LADYSAW	18		3
6 Dec 03	**IT'S MY LIFE** *Interscope 9813724*	20		2
13 Mar 04	**IT'S MY LIFE/BATHWATER** *Interscope 9861993*	17		4

NO MERCY US group

Date	Title	Peak Position	Weeks at No.1	Weeks in Top 40
18 Jan 97	**WHERE DO YOU GO** *Arista 74321401502* ●	2		14
24 May 97	**PLEASE DON'T GO** *Arista 74321481372*	4		4
6 Sep 97	**KISS YOU ALL OVER** *Arista 74321514452*	16		2

NO REASON UK group

Date	Title	Peak Position	Weeks at No.1	Weeks in Top 40
11 Sep 04	**MAN LIKE ME** *Mad As Toast TOAST001*	53		

NO SWEAT Irish group

Date	Title	Peak Position	Weeks at No.1	Weeks in Top 40
13 Oct 90	**HEART AND SOUL** *London LON 274*	64		
2 Feb 91	**TEAR DOWN THE WALLS** *London LON 257*	61		

NO WAY JOSE US group

Date	Title	Peak Position	Weeks at No.1	Weeks in Top 40
3 Aug 85	**TEQUILA** *Fourth & Broadway BRW 28*	47		

NO WAY SIS US group

Date	Title	Peak Position	Weeks at No.1	Weeks in Top 40
21 Dec 96	**I'D LIKE TO TEACH THE WORLD TO SING** *EMI CDEM 461*	27		3

NODDY UK cartoon character

Date	Title	Peak Position	Weeks at No.1	Weeks in Top 40
20 Dec 03	**MAKE WAY FOR NODDY** *BMG 82876582142*	29		2

NODESHA US singer

Date	Title	Peak Position	Weeks at No.1	Weeks in Top 40
6 Sep 03	**MISS PERFECT** *BMG 82876556742* ABS FEATURING NODESHA	5		5
1 Nov 03	**GET IT WHILE IT'S HOT** *Arista 82876559592*	55		

JIM NOIR UK singer

Date	Title	Peak Position	Weeks at No.1	Weeks in Top 40
13 May 06	**MY PATCH** *My Dad Recordings MY013CD*	65		
22 Jul 06	**EANIE MEANY** *My Dad Recordings MY011CDX*	67		

NOISE NEXT DOOR UK group

Date	Title	Peak Position	Weeks at No.1	Weeks in Top 40
6 Nov 04	**LOCK UP YA DAUGHTERS/MINISTRY OF MAYHEM** *Us & Them USTHEMS10*	12		3
19 Feb 05	**CALENDAR GIRL** *Us & Them USTHEMS12*	11		2
11 Jun 05	**SHE MIGHT** *Us & Them WEA386CD1*	27		1

NOISETTES UK group

Date	Title	Peak Position	Weeks at No.1	Weeks in Top 40
2 Dec 06	**DON'T GIVE UP** *Vertigo 9844295*	73		
10 Feb 07	**SISTER ROSETTA (CAPTURE THE SPIRIT)** *Vertigo 1723267*	63		

BERNIE NOLAN Irish singer

Date	Title	Peak Position	Weeks at No.1	Weeks in Top 40
6 Mar 04	**MACUSHLA** *Laurel Bank 4KATECD1*	38		2

NOLANS Irish group

Date	Title	Peak Position	Weeks at No.1	Weeks in Top 40
6 Oct 79	**SPIRIT BODY AND SOUL** *Epic EPC 7796* NOLAN SISTERS	34		4
22 Dec 79	**I'M IN THE MOOD FOR DANCING** *Epic EPC 8068* ●	3		10
12 Apr 80	**DON'T MAKE WAVES** *Epic EPC 8349*	12		8
13 Sep 80	**GOTTA PULL MYSELF TOGETHER** *Epic EPC 8878* ○	9		9
6 Dec 80	**WHO'S GONNA ROCK YOU** *Epic EPC 9325*	12		8
14 Mar 81	**ATTENTION TO ME** *Epic EPC 9571* ○	9		10
15 Aug 81	**CHEMISTRY** *Epic EPC A 1485*	15		6
20 Feb 82	**DON'T LOVE ME TOO HARD** *Epic EPC A 1927*	14		8
1 Apr 95	**I'M IN THE MOOD FOR DANCING** *Living Beat LBECD 31*	51		

NOMAD UK duo

Date	Title	Peak Position	Weeks at No.1	Weeks in Top 40
2 Feb 91	**(I WANNA GIVE YOU) DEVOTION** *Rumour RUMA 25* NOMAD FEATURING MC MIKEE FREEDOM ○	2		9
4 May 91	**JUST A GROOVE** *Rumour RUMA 33*	16		5
28 Sep 91	**SOMETHING SPECIAL** *Rumour RUMA 35*	73		
25 Apr 92	**YOUR LOVE IS LIFTING ME** *Rumour RUMA 48*	60		
7 Nov 92	**24 HOURS A DAY** *Rumour RUMA 60*	61		
25 Nov 95	**(I WANNA GIVE YOU) DEVOTION (REMIX)** *Rumour RUMACD 75*	42		

NONCHALANT US singer

Date	Title / Label	Peak Position	Weeks at No.1	Weeks in Top 40
29 Jun 96	**5 O'CLOCK** *MCA MCSTD 48011*	44		

PETER NOONE UK singer

Date	Title / Label	Peak Position	Weeks at No.1	Weeks in Top 40
22 May 71	**OH YOU PRETTY THING** *RAK 114*	12		9

NOOTROPIC UK production duo

Date	Title / Label	Peak Position	Weeks at No.1	Weeks in Top 40
16 Mar 96	**I SEE ONLY YOU** *Hi-Life 5779832*	42		

NORE US rapper

Date	Title / Label	Peak Position	Weeks at No.1	Weeks in Top 40
21 Sep 02	**NOTHIN'** *Def Jam 639262*	11		3
29 Nov 03	**CRASHIN' A PARTY** *Universal MCSTD 40341* LUMIDEE FEATURING NORE	55		
22 May 04	**NOTHIN'** *Def Jam 639262*	72		

NORTH & SOUTH UK group

Date	Title / Label	Peak Position	Weeks at No.1	Weeks in Top 40
17 May 97	**I'M A MAN NOT A BOY** *RCA 74321461142*	7		4
9 Aug 97	**TARANTINO'S NEW STAR** *RCA 74321501242*	18		3
8 Nov 97	**BREATHING** *RCA 74321528422*	27		1
4 Apr 98	**NO SWEAT '98** *RCA 74321562212*	29		1

NORTHERN HEIGHTZ UK production group

Date	Title / Label	Peak Position	Weeks at No.1	Weeks in Top 40
20 Mar 04	**LOOK AT US** *Iconic CDXICO02*	29		1

NORTHERN LINE UK group

Date	Title / Label	Peak Position	Weeks at No.1	Weeks in Top 40
9 Oct 99	**RUN FOR YOUR LIFE** *Global Talent GTR 002CDS1*	18		2
11 Mar 00	**LOVE ON THE NORTHERN LINE** *Global Talent GTR 003CDS1*	15		3
17 Jun 00	**ALL AROUND THE WORLD** *Global Talent GTR 004CDS1*	27		1

NORTHERN UPROAR UK group

Date	Title / Label	Peak Position	Weeks at No.1	Weeks in Top 40
21 Oct 95	**ROLLERCOASTER/ROUGH BOYS** *Heavenly HVN 047CD*	41		
3 Feb 96	**FROM A WINDOW/THIS MORNING** *Heavenly HVN 051CD*	17		1
20 Apr 96	**LIVIN' IT UP** *Heavenly HVN 52CD*	24		1
22 Jun 96	**TOWN** *Heavenly HVN 54CD*	48		
7 Jun 97	**ANY WAY YOU LOOK** *Heavenly HVN 70CD*	36		1
23 Aug 97	**A GIRL I ONCE KNEW** *Heavenly HVN 73CD*	63		

NORTHSIDE UK group

Date	Title / Label	Peak Position	Weeks at No.1	Weeks in Top 40
9 Jun 90	**SHALL WE TAKE A TRIP/MOODY PLACES** *Factory FAC 268*	50		
3 Nov 90	**MY RISING STAR** *Factory FAC 2987*	32		2
1 Jun 91	**TAKE 5** *Factory FAC 3087*	40		1

FREDDIE NOTE & THE RUDIES Jamaican group

Date	Title / Label	Peak Position	Weeks at No.1	Weeks in Top 40
10 Oct 70	**MONTEGO BAY** *Trojan TR 7791*	45		

NOTORIOUS B.I.G. US rapper

Date	Title / Label	Peak Position	Weeks at No.1	Weeks in Top 40
29 Oct 94	**JUICY** *Bad Boy 74321240102*	72		
1 Apr 95	**BIG POPPA** *Puff Daddy 74321263412*	63		
15 Jul 95	**CAN'T YOU SEE** *Tommy Boy TBCD 700* TOTAL FEATURING THE NOTORIOUS B.I.G.	43		
19 Aug 95	**ONE MORE CHANCE/STAY WITH ME** *Puff Daddy 74321300782*	34		1
3 May 97	**HYPNOTIZE** *Puff Daddy 74321466412* ★	10		2
9 Aug 97	**MO MONEY MO PROBLEMS** *Puff Daddy 74321492492* NOTORIOUS B.I.G. FEATURING PUFF DADDY & MASE ★	6		8
14 Feb 98	**SKY'S THE LIMIT** *Puff Daddy 74321587992* NOTORIOUS B.I.G. FEATURING 112	35		1
18 Jul 98	**RUNNIN'** *Black Jam BJAM 9005* 2PAC & THE NOTORIOUS B.I.G.	15		1
5 Feb 00	**NOTORIOUS B.I.G.** *Puff Daddy 74321737312* NOTORIOUS B.I.G. FEATURING PUFF DADDY AND LIL' KIM	16		3
31 Jan 04	**RUNNIN' (DYIN' TO LIVE)** *Interscope 9815329* 2PAC & THE NOTORIOUS B.I.G.	17		3
28 Jan 06	**NASTY GIRL** *Bad Boy AT0229CDX* NOTORIOUS B.I.G. FEATURING DIDDY, NELLY, JAGGED EDGE AND AVERY STORM	1	2	16
6 May 06	**SPIT YOUR GAME** *Bad Boy AT0240CDX*	64		

NOTTINGHAM FOREST F.C. UK football club

Date	Title / Label	Peak Position	Weeks at No.1	Weeks in Top 40
4 Mar 78	**WE'VE GOT THE WHOLE WORLD IN OUR HANDS** *Warner Brothers K 17110* NOTTINGHAM FOREST FC & PAPER LACE	24		5

HEATHER NOVA US singer

Date	Title / Label	Peak Position	Weeks at No.1	Weeks in Top 40
25 Feb 95	**WALK THIS WORLD** *Butterfly BFLD 19*	69		

NANCY NOVA UK singer

Date	Title / Label	Peak Position	Weeks at No.1	Weeks in Top 40
4 Sep 82	**NO NO NO** *EMI 5328*	63		

NOVACANE German production team

Date	Title / Label	Peak Position	Weeks at No.1	Weeks in Top 40
15 Jun 02	**LOVE BE MY LOVER (PLAYA SOL)** *Direction 6727792* NOVACANE VS NO ONE DRIVING	69		

NOVASPACE German producer

Date	Title / Label	Peak Position	Weeks at No.1	Weeks in Top 40
22 Feb 03	**TIME AFTER TIME** *Substance SUBS 15CDS*	29		1

TOM NOVY German producer

Date	Title / Label	Peak Position	Weeks at No.1	Weeks in Top 40
2 May 98	**SUPERSTAR** *D:disco 74321569352* NOVY VS ENIAC	32		1
3 Jun 00	**PUMPIN'** *Positiva CDTIVS 132* NOVY VS ENIAC	19		1
2 Sep 00	**I ROCK** *Rulin 3CDS*	55		
4 Aug 01	**NOW OR NEVER** *Rulin 14CDS* TOM NOVY FEATURING LIMA	64		
3 Dec 05	**YOUR BODY** *Data DATA102CDS* TOM NOVY FEATURING MICHAEL MARSHALL	10		11
12 Aug 06	**TAKE IT (CLOSING TIME)** *Data DATA132CDS* TOM NOVY & LIMA	31		1

NRG UK DJ/production duo

Date	Title / Label	Peak Position	Weeks at No.1	Weeks in Top 40
29 Mar 97	**NEVER LOST HIS HARDCORE** *Top Banana TOPCD 04*	71		
12 Dec 98	**NEVER LOST HIS HARDCORE (REMIX)** *Top Banana TOPCD 010*	61		
20 Mar 04	**NEVER LOST HIS HARDCORE (2ND REMIX)** *Tidy Trax TIDY200T2*	59		

NT GANG German group

Date	Title / Label	Peak Position	Weeks at No.1	Weeks in Top 40
2 Apr 88	**WAM BAM** *Cooltempo COOL 163*	71		

NU-BIRTH UK production duo

Date	Title / Label	Peak Position	Weeks at No.1	Weeks in Top 40
6 Sep 97	**ANYTIME** *XL Recordings XLS 85CD*	48		
6 Jun 98	**ANYTIME** *Locked On LOX 97CD*	41		

NU CIRCLES UK duo

Date	Title / Label	Peak Position	Weeks at No.1	Weeks in Top 40
8 Feb 03	**WHAT YOU NEED (TONIGHT)** *East West EW 258CD* NU CIRCLES FEATURING EMMA B	46		

NU COLOURS UK group

Date	Title / Label	Peak Position	Weeks at No.1	Weeks in Top 40
6 Jun 92	**TEARS** *Wild Card CARD 1*	55		
10 Oct 92	**POWER** *Wild Card CARD 3*	64		
5 Jun 93	**WHAT IN THE WORLD** *Wild Card CARDD 4*	57		
27 Nov 93	**POWER (REMIX)** *Wild Card CARDD 5*	40		1
25 May 96	**DESIRE** *Wild Card 5763652*	31		1
24 Aug 96	**SPECIAL KIND OF LOVER** *Wild Card 5752012*	38		1

NU GENERATION UK producer

Date	Title / Label	Peak Position	Weeks at No.1	Weeks in Top 40
29 Jan 00	**IN YOUR ARMS (RESCUE ME)** *Concept CDCON 7*	8		6
21 Oct 00	**NOWHERE TO RUN 2000** *Concept CDCON 16*	66		

NU MATIC UK duo

Date	Title / Label	Peak Position	Weeks at No.1	Weeks in Top 40
8 Aug 92	**SPRING IN MY STEP** *XL Recordings XLS 31*	58		

Key: Silver-selling ○ · Gold-selling ● · Platinum-selling · US No.1 ★ · Peak Position · Weeks at No.1 · Weeks in Top 40

NU SHOOZ US duo

Date	Title / Label	Peak Position	Weeks at No.1	Weeks in Top 40
24 May 86	**I CAN'T WAIT** *Atlantic A 9446* ○	2		11
26 Jul 86	**POINT OF NO RETURN** *Atlantic A 9392*	48		

NU SOUL US duo

Date	Title / Label	Peak Position	Weeks at No.1	Weeks in Top 40
13 Jan 96	**HIDE-A-WAY** *ffrr FCD 269* NU SOUL FEATURING KELLI RICH	27		1

NUANCE US group

Date	Title / Label	Peak Position	Weeks at No.1	Weeks in Top 40
19 Jan 85	**LOVERIDE** *Fourth & Broadway BRW 20* NUANCE FEATURING VIKKI LOVE	59		

NUKLEUZ DJs UK group

Date	Title / Label	Peak Position	Weeks at No.1	Weeks in Top 40
24 Aug 02	**DJ NATION** *Nukleuz NUKFB 0440*	40		1
8 Feb 03	**DJ NATION (BOOTLEG EDITION)** *Nukleuz 0468 FNUK*	33		1
9 Aug 03	**SUMMER EDITION** *Nukleuz 0542 FNUK* DJNATION	59		
15 Nov 03	**DJ NATION - HARDER EDITION** *Nukleuz 0572 FBNUK*	48		
17 Jan 04	**DJ NATION (BOOTLEG EDITION)** *Nukleuz 0468 FNUK*	63		
27 Mar 04	**X-RATED** *Amato 0501FBNUK* DJNATION	52		

GARY NUMAN UK singer

Date	Title / Label	Peak Position	Weeks at No.1	Weeks in Top 40
19 May 79	**ARE 'FRIENDS' ELECTRIC?** *Beggars Banquet BEG 18* TUBEWAY ARMY ●	1	4	12
1 Sep 79	**CARS** *Beggars Banquet BEG 23* ●	1	1	9
24 Nov 79	**COMPLEX** *Beggars Banquet BEG 29* ○	6		6
24 May 80	**WE ARE GLASS** *Beggars Banquet BEG 35*	5		6
30 Aug 80	**I DIE: YOU DIE** *Beggars Banquet BEG 46*	6		5
20 Dec 80	**THIS WRECKAGE** *Beggars Banquet BEG 50*	20		6
29 Aug 81	**SHE'S GOT CLAWS** *Beggars Banquet BEG 62*	6		6
5 Dec 81	**LOVE NEEDS NO DISGUISE** *Beggars Banquet BEG 33* GARY NUMAN & DRAMATIS	33		2
6 Mar 82	**MUSIC FOR CHAMELEONS** *Beggars Banquet BEG 70*	19		6
19 Jun 82	**WE TAKE MYSTERY (TO BED)** *Beggars Banquet BEG 77*	9		4
28 Aug 82	**WHITE BOYS AND HEROES** *Beggars Banquet BEG 81*	20		3
3 Sep 83	**WARRIORS** *Beggars Banquet BEG 95*	20		4
22 Oct 83	**SISTER SURPRISE** *Beggars Banquet BEG 101*	32		2
3 Nov 84	**BERSERKER** *Numa NU 4*	32		3
22 Dec 84	**MY DYING MACHINE** *Numa NU 6*	66		
9 Feb 85	**CHANGE YOUR MIND** *Polydor POSP 722* SHARPE & NUMAN	17		5
25 May 85	**THE LIVE EP** *Numa NUM 7*	27		4
10 Aug 85	**YOUR FASCINATION** *Numa NU 9*	46		
21 Sep 85	**CALL OUT THE DOGS** *Numa NU 11*	49		
16 Nov 85	**MIRACLES** *Numa NU 13*	49		
19 Apr 86	**THIS IS LOVE** *Numa NU 16*	28		2
28 Jun 86	**I CAN'T STOP** *Numa NU 17*	27		3
4 Oct 86	**NEW THING FROM LONDON TOWN** *Numa NU 19* SHARPE & NUMAN	52		
6 Dec 86	**I STILL REMEMBER** *Numa NU 21*	74		
28 Mar 87	**RADIO HEART** *GFM 109* RADIO HEART FEATURING GARY NUMAN	35		2
13 Jun 87	**LONDON TIMES** *GFM 112* RADIO HEART FEATURING GARY NUMAN	48		
19 Sep 87	**CARS (E REG MODEL) (REMIX)/ ARE 'FRIENDS' ELECTRIC? (REMIX)** *Beggars Banquet BEG 199*	16		6
30 Jan 88	**NO MORE LIES** *Polydor POSP 894* SHARPE & NUMAN	34		3
1 Oct 88	**NEW ANGER** *Illegal ILS 1003*	46		
3 Dec 88	**AMERICA** *Illegal ILS 1004*	49		
3 Jun 89	**I'M ON AUTOMATIC** *Polydor PO 43* SHARPE & NUMAN	44		
16 Mar 91	**HEART** *IRS NUMAN 1*	43		
21 Mar 92	**THE SKIN GAME** *Numa NU 23*	68		
1 Aug 92	**MACHINE + SOUL** *Numa NUM 124*	72		
4 Sep 93	**CARS (2ND REMIX)** *Beggars Banquet BEG 264CD*	53		
16 Mar 96	**CARS (REMIX)** *Polygram TV PRMCD 1*	17		3
13 Jul 02	**RIP** *Jagged Halo JHCD5*	29		1
5 Jul 03	**CRAZIER** *Jagged Halo JHCDX6* GARY NUMAN VS RICO	13		1
29 Jul 06	**IN A DARK PLACE** *Cooking Vinyl MORTALCDS001*	63		
11 Aug 07	**THE LEATHER SEA** *Submission Ltd SUB03CD2* GARY NUMAN VS ADE FENTON	72		

NUMBER ONE CUP US group

Date	Title / Label	Peak Position	Weeks at No.1	Weeks in Top 40
2 Mar 96	**DIVEBOMB** *Blue Rose BRRC 10032*	61		

JOSE NUNEZ US producer

Date	Title / Label	Peak Position	Weeks at No.1	Weeks in Top 40
5 Sep 98	**IN MY LIFE** *Ministry Of Sound MOSCDS 126* JOSE NUNEZ FEATURING OCTAHVIA	56		
5 Jun 99	**HOLD ON** *Ministry Of Sound MOSCDS 130* JOSE NUNEZ FEATURING OCTAHVIA	44		

BOBBY NUNN US singer

Date	Title / Label	Peak Position	Weeks at No.1	Weeks in Top 40
4 Feb 84	**DON'T KNOCK IT (UNTIL YOU TRY IT)** *Motown TMG 1323*	65		

NUSH UK production duo

Date	Title / Label	Peak Position	Weeks at No.1	Weeks in Top 40
23 Jul 94	**U GIRLS** *Blunted Vinyl BLNCDX 006*	58		
22 Apr 95	**MOVE THAT BODY** *Blunted Vinyl BLNCD 012*	46		
16 Sep 95	**U GIRLS (LOOK SO SEXY) (REMIX)** *Blunted Vinyl BLNCD 13*	15		2

NUT UK singer

Date	Title / Label	Peak Position	Weeks at No.1	Weeks in Top 40
8 Jun 96	**BRAINS** *Epic NUTCD 2*	64		
21 Sep 96	**CRAZY** *Epic NUTCD 5*	56		
11 Jan 97	**SCREAM** *Epic NUTCD 6*	43		

PAOLO NUTINI UK singer

Date	Title / Label	Peak Position	Weeks at No.1	Weeks in Top 40
8 Jul 06	**LAST REQUEST** *Atlantic ATUK034CD*	5		11
30 Sep 06	**JENNY DON'T BE HASTY** *Atlantic ATUK043CD*	20		5
9 Dec 06	**REWIND** *Atlantic ATUK050CD*	27		1
10 Mar 07	**NEW SHOES** *Atlantic ATUK057CD*	21		9

NUTTIN' NYCE US group

Date	Title / Label	Peak Position	Weeks at No.1	Weeks in Top 40
10 Jun 95	**DOWN 4 WHATEVA** *Jive JIVECD 365*	62		
12 Aug 95	**FROGGY STYLE** *Jive JIVECD 381*	68		

NUYORICAN SOUL US group

Date	Title / Label	Peak Position	Weeks at No.1	Weeks in Top 40
8 Feb 97	**RUNAWAY** *Talkin Loud TLCD 20* NUYORICAN SOUL FEATURING INDIA	24		2
10 May 97	**IT'S ALRIGHT, I FEEL IT!** *Talkin Loud TLCD 22* NUYORICAN SOUL FEATURING JOCELYN BROWN	26		1
25 Oct 97	**I AM THE BLACK GOLD OF THE SUN** *Talkin Loud TLCD 26* NUYORICAN SOUL FEATURING JOCELYN BROWN	31		1

NWA US group

Date	Title / Label	Peak Position	Weeks at No.1	Weeks in Top 40
9 Sep 89	**EXPRESS YOURSELF** *Fourth & Broadway BRW 144*	50		
26 May 90	**EXPRESS YOURSELF** *Fourth & Broadway BRW 144*	26		3
1 Sep 90	**GANGSTA, GANGSTA** *Fourth & Broadway BRW 191*	70		
10 Nov 90	**100 MILES AND RUNNIN'** *Fourth & Broadway BRW 200*	38		2
23 Nov 91	**ALWAYZ INTO SOMETHIN'** *Fourth & Broadway BRW 238*	60		

NYCC German group

Date	Title / Label	Peak Position	Weeks at No.1	Weeks in Top 40
30 May 98	**FIGHT FOR YOUR RIGHT (TO PARTY)** *Control 0042645 CON*	14		3
19 Sep 98	**CAN YOU FEEL IT (ROCK DA HOUSE)** *Control 0042785 CON*	68		

NYLON Norwegian group

Date	Title / Label	Peak Position	Weeks at No.1	Weeks in Top 40
22 Jul 06	**LOSING A FRIEND** *Believer Music BELIEVECDS1*	29		1
4 Nov 06	**CLOSER** *Believer Music BELIEVECDS2*	64		

NYLON MOON Italian duo

Date	Title / Label	Peak Position	Weeks at No.1	Weeks in Top 40
13 Apr 96	**SKY PLUS** *Positiva CDTIV 50*	43		

MICHAEL NYMAN UK composer/pianist

Date	Title / Label	Peak Position	Weeks at No.1	Weeks in Top 40
19 Mar 94	**THE HEART ASKS PLEASURE FIRST/THE PROMISE** *Virgin VEND 3*	60		

O

O-TOWN US group

Date	Title / Label	Peak Position	Weeks at No.1	Weeks in Top 40
28 Apr 01	**LIQUID DREAMS** *J Records 74321853212*	3		7
4 Aug 01	**ALL OR NOTHING** *J Records 74321877952*	4		6
3 Nov 01	**WE FIT TOGETHER** *J Records 74321893692*	20		1
23 Feb 02	**LOVE SHOULD BE A CRIME** *J Records 74321920232*	38		1
15 Feb 03	**THESE ARE THE DAYS** *J Records 82876503052*	36		1

O-ZONE Moldovan group

Date	Title / Label	Peak Position	Weeks at No.1	Weeks in Top 40
19 Jun 04	**DRAGOSTEA DIN TEI** *Jive 82876618412*	3		14

PAUL OAKENFOLD UK producer

Date	Title / Label	Peak Position	Weeks at No.1	Weeks in Top 40
25 Aug 01	**PLANET ROCK** *Tommy Boy TBCD 2266* PAUL OAKENFOLD PRESENTS AFRIKA BAMBAATAA	47		
22 Jun 02	**SOUTHERN SUN/READY STEADY GO** *Perfecto PERF 17CDS*	16		3
31 Aug 02	**STARRY EYED SURPRISE** *Perfecto PERF 27CDS*	6		6
22 Feb 03	**THE HARDER THEY COME** *Perfecto PERF 49CDSX*	38		1
27 Sep 03	**HYPNOTISED** *Perfecto EW 271CD*	57		
3 Jun 06	**FASTER KILL PUSSYCAT** *Perfecto CDPER008* PAUL OAKENFOLD FEATURING BRITTANY MURPHY	7		8

PHILIP OAKLEY UK singer

Date	Title / Label	Peak Position	Weeks at No.1	Weeks in Top 40
22 Sep 84	**TOGETHER IN ELECTRIC DREAMS** *Virgin VS 713* GIORGIO MORODER & PHIL OAKEY ○	3		10
29 Jun 85	**GOODYBYE BAD TIMES** *Virgin VS 772* GIORGIO MORODER & PHIL OAKEY	44		
26 Apr 03	**LA TODAY** *Xtravaganza XTRAV 37CDS* ALEX GOLD FEATURING PHILIP OAKEY	68		

OASIS UK group

Date	Title / Label	Peak Position	Weeks at No.1	Weeks in Top 40
23 Apr 94	**SUPERSONIC** *Creation CRESCD 176*	31		1
2 Jul 94	**SHAKERMAKER** *Creation CRESCD 182*	11		3
20 Aug 94	**LIVE FOREVER** *Creation CRESCD 185* ○	10		4
22 Oct 94	**CIGARETTES AND ALCOHOL** *Creation CRESCD 190* ○	7		3
31 Dec 94	**WHATEVER** *Creation CRESCD 195* ●	3		7
6 May 95	**SOME MIGHT SAY** *Creation CRESCD 204* ●	1	1	6
13 May 95	**SOME MIGHT SAY** *Creation CRE 204T*	71		
26 Aug 95	**ROLL WITH IT** *Creation CRESCD 212* ●	2		6
11 Nov 95	**WONDERWALL** *Creation CRESCD 215* ⊛	2		17
25 Nov 95	**WIBBLING RIVALRY (INTERVIEWS WITH NOEL AND LIAM GALLAGHER)** *Fierce Panda NING 12CD*	52		
2 Mar 96	**DON'T LOOK BACK IN ANGER** *Creation CRESCD 221* ⊛	1	1	11
19 Jul 97	**D'YOU KNOW WHAT I MEAN?** *Creation CRESCD 256* ⊛	1	1	8
4 Oct 97	**STAND BY ME** *Creation CRESCD 273* ●	2		7
24 Jan 98	**ALL AROUND THE WORLD** *Creation CRESCD 282*	1	1	5
19 Feb 00	**GO LET IT OUT** *Big Brother RKIDSCD 001* ○	1	1	4
29 Apr 00	**WHO FEELS LOVE?** *Big Brother RKIDSCD 003*	4		3
15 Jul 00	**SUNDAY MORNING CALL** *Big Brother RKIDSCD 004*	4		4
27 Apr 02	**THE HINDU TIMES** *Big Brother RKIDSCD 23* ○	1	1	5
29 Jun 02	**STOP CRYING YOUR HEART OUT** *Big Brother RKIDSCD 24* ○	2		6
5 Oct 02	**LITTLE BY LITTLE/SHE IS LOVE** *Big Brother RKIDSCD 26*	2		6
15 Feb 03	**SONGBIRD** *Big Brother RKIDSCD 27*	3		5
28 May 05	**LYLA** *Big Brother RKIDSCD29*	1	1	5
3 Sep 05	**THE IMPORTANCE OF BEING IDLE** *Big Brother RKIDSCD31*	1		8
10 Dec 05	**LET THERE BE LOVE** *Big Brother RKIDSCD32*	2		4
3 Nov 07	**LORD DON'T SLOW ME DOWN** *Download*	10		2

SAM OBERNIK Irish singer

Date	Title / Label	Peak Position	Weeks at No.1	Weeks in Top 40
20 Jul 02	**IT JUST WON'T DO** *Underwater H2O 016CD* TIM DELUXE FEATURING SAM OBERNIK	14		4
22 Nov 03	**STAND BACK** *Data 62CDS* LINUS LOVES FEATURING SAM OBERNIK	31		1

OBERNKIRCHEN CHILDREN'S CHOIR German school choir

Date	Title / Label	Peak Position	Weeks at No.1	Weeks in Top 40
22 Jan 54	**HAPPY WANDERER** *Parlophone R 3799*	2		26

OBI PROJECT UK rap group

Date	Title / Label	Peak Position	Weeks at No.1	Weeks in Top 40
4 Aug 01	**BABY, CAN I GET YOUR NUMBER** *East West EW 235CD* OBI PROJECT FEATURING HARRY, ASHER D & DJ WHAT?	75		

DERMOT O'BRIEN Irish singer/accordionist

Date	Title / Label	Peak Position	Weeks at No.1	Weeks in Top 40
20 Oct 66	**THE MERRY PLOUGHBOY** *Envoy ENV 016*	46		

BILLY OCEAN UK singer

Date	Title / Label	Peak Position	Weeks at No.1	Weeks in Top 40
21 Feb 76	**LOVE REALLY HURTS WITHOUT YOU** *GTO GT 52* ○	2		10
10 Jul 76	**L.O.D. (LOVE ON DELIVERY)** *GTO GT 62*	19		7
13 Nov 76	**STOP ME (IF YOU'VE HEARD IT ALL BEFORE)** *GTO GT 72*	12		10
19 Mar 77	**RED LIGHT SPELLS DANGER** *GTO GT 85* ○	2		9
1 Sep 79	**AMERICAN HEARTS** *GTO GT 244*	54		
19 Jan 80	**ARE YOU READY** *GTO GT 259*	42		
13 Oct 84	**CARIBBEAN QUEEN (NO MORE LOVE ON THE RUN)** *Jive 77* ○ ★	6		9
19 Jan 85	**LOVERBOY** *Jive 80*	15		9
11 May 85	**SUDDENLY** *Jive 90* ○	4		10
17 Aug 85	**MYSTERY LADY** *Jive 98*	49		
25 Jan 86	**WHEN THE GOING GETS TOUGH, THE TOUGH GET GOING** *Jive 114* ●	1	4	12
12 Apr 86	**THERE'LL BE SAD SONGS (TO MAKE YOU CRY)** *Jive 117* ★	12		9
9 Aug 86	**LOVE ZONE** *Jive 124*	49		
11 Oct 86	**BITTERSWEET** *Jive 133*	44		
10 Jan 87	**LOVE IS FOREVER** *Jive 134*	34		4
6 Feb 88	**GET OUTTA MY DREAMS GET INTO MY CAR** *Jive BOS 1* ○ ★	3		10
7 May 88	**CALYPSO CRAZY** *Jive BOS 2*	35		2
6 Aug 88	**THE COLOUR OF LOVE** *Jive BOS 3*	65		
6 Feb 93	**PRESSURE** *Jive BOSCD 6*	55		

OCEAN COLOUR SCENE UK group

Date	Title / Label	Peak Position	Weeks at No.1	Weeks in Top 40
23 Mar 91	**YESTERDAY TODAY** *!Phfft FIT 2*	49		
17 Feb 96	**THE RIVERBOAT SONG** *MCA MCSTD 40021*	15		3
6 Apr 96	**YOU'VE GOT IT BAD** *MCA MCSTD 40036*	7		2
15 Jun 96	**THE DAY WE CAUGHT THE TRAIN** *MCA MCSTD 40046*	4		9
28 Sep 96	**THE CIRCLE** *MCA MCSTD 40077*	6		3
28 Jun 97	**HUNDRED MILE HIGH CITY** *MCA MCSTD 40133*	4		5
6 Sep 97	**TRAVELLERS TUNE** *MCA MCSTD 40144*	5		3
22 Nov 97	**BETTER DAY** *MCA MCSTD 40151*	9		3
28 Feb 98	**IT'S A BEAUTIFUL THING** *MCA MCSTD 40157*	12		2
4 Sep 99	**PROFIT IN PEACE** *Island CID 757*	13		4
27 Nov 99	**SO LOW** *Island CID 759*	34		1
8 Jul 00	**JULY/I AM THE NEWS** *Island CID 763*	31		1
7 Apr 01	**UP ON THE DOWN SIDE** *Island CID 774*	19		2
14 Jul 01	**MECHANICAL WONDER** *Island CID 779*	49		
22 Dec 01	**CRAZY LOWDOWN WAYS** *Island CID 787*	64		
12 Jul 03	**I JUST NEED MYSELF** *Sanctuary SANXD 159X*	13		2
6 Sep 03	**MAKE THE DEAL** *Sanctuary SANXD 219*	35		1
10 Jan 04	**GOLDEN GATE BRIDGE** *Sanctuary SANXD 244*	40		1
19 Mar 05	**FREE MY NAME** *Sanctuary SANXS344*	23		1
2 Jul 05	**THIS DAY SHOULD LAST FOREVER** *Sanctuary SANXS380*	53		
28 Apr 07	**I TOLD YOU SO** *Moseley Shoals CXOCS1*	34		1

OCEANIC UK group

Date	Title / Label	Peak Position	Weeks at No.1	Weeks in Top 40
24 Aug 91	**INSANITY** *Dead Dead Good GOOD 4* ○	3		13
30 Nov 91	**WICKED LOVE** *Dead Dead Good GOOD 5*	25		2
13 Jun 92	**CONTROLLING ME** *Dead Dead Good GOOD 14*	14		4
14 Nov 92	**IGNORANCE** *Dead Dead Good GOOD 22* OCEANIC FEATURING SIOBHAN MAHER	72		

OCEANLAB UK/Dutch production group

Date	Title / Label	Peak Position	Weeks at No.1	Weeks in Top 40
27 Apr 02	**CLEAR BLUE WATER** *Code Blue BLU 024CD1* OCEANLAB FEATURING JUSTINE SUISSA	48		
1 May 04	**SATELLITE** *NuLife 82876614002*	19		3

OCEANSIZE UK group

Date	Title / Label	Peak Position	Weeks at No.1	Weeks in Top 40
14 Feb 04	**CATALYST** *Beggars Banquet BBQ 375CD*	73		

DES O'CONNOR UK singer

Date	Title / Label	Peak Position	Weeks at No.1	Weeks in Top 40
1 Nov 67	**CARELESS HANDS** *Columbia DB 8275* DES O'CONNOR WITH THE MICHAEL SAMMES SINGERS	6		13
8 May 68	**I PRETEND** *Columbia DB 8397*	1	1	23
20 Nov 68	**1-2-3 O'LEARY** *Columbia DB 8492*	4		11

Silver-selling ○ · Gold-selling ● · Platinum-selling ⊛ · US No.1 ★ · Peak Position · Weeks at No.1 · Weeks in Top 40

Date	Title / Label	Peak Position	Weeks at No.1	Weeks in Top 40
7 May 69	**DICK-A-DUM-DUM (KING'S ROAD)** *Columbia DB 8566*	14		7
29 Nov 69	**LONELINESS** *Columbia DB 8632*	18		8
14 Mar 70	**I'LL GO ON HOPING** *Columbia DB 8661*	30		3
26 Sep 70	**THE TIPS OF MY FINGERS** *Columbia DB 8713*	15		13
8 Nov 86	**THE SKYE BOAT SONG** *Tembo TML 119* ROGER WHITTAKER & DES O'CONNOR	10		7

HAZEL O'CONNOR UK singer

Date	Title / Label	Peak Position	Weeks at No.1	Weeks in Top 40
16 Aug 80	**EIGHTH DAY** *A&M AMS 7553* ○	5		9
25 Oct 80	**GIVE ME AN INCH** *A&M AMS 7569*	41		
21 Mar 81	**D-DAYS** *Albion ION 1009* ○	10		7
23 May 81	**WILL YOU** *A&M AMS 8131* ○	8		7
1 Aug 81	**(COVER PLUS) WE'RE ALL GROWN UP** *Albion ION 1018*	41		
3 Oct 81	**HANGING AROUND** *Albion ION 1022*	45		
23 Jan 82	**CALLS THE TUNE** *A&M AMS 8203*	60		

SINEAD O'CONNOR Irish singer

Date	Title / Label	Peak Position	Weeks at No.1	Weeks in Top 40
16 Jan 88	**MANDINKA** *Ensign ENY 611*	17		6
20 Jan 90	**NOTHING COMPARES 2 U** *Ensign ENY 630* ⊛ ★	1	4	12
21 Jul 90	**THE EMPEROR'S NEW CLOTHES** *Ensign ENY 633*	31		2
20 Oct 90	**THREE BABIES** *Ensign ENY 635*	42		
8 Jun 91	**MY SPECIAL CHILD** *Ensign ENY 646*	42		
14 Dec 91	**SILENT NIGHT** *Ensign ENY 652*	60		
12 Sep 92	**SUCCESS HAS MADE A FAILURE OF OUR HOME** *Ensign ENY 656*	18		3
12 Dec 92	**DON'T CRY FOR ME ARGENTINA** *Ensign ENY 657*	53		
19 Feb 94	**YOU MADE ME THE THIEF OF YOUR HEART** *Island CID 588*	42		
26 Nov 94	**THANK YOU FOR HEARING ME** *Ensign CDENYS 662*	13		5
29 Apr 95	**HAUNTED** *ZTT BANG 65CD* SHANE MacGOWAN & SINEAD O'CONNOR	30		1
26 Aug 95	**FAMINE** *Ensign CDENY 663*	51		
17 May 97	**GOSPEL OAK EP** *Chrysalis CDCHS 5051*	28		1
6 Dec 97	**THIS IS A REBEL SONG** *Columbia 6652992*	60		
24 Aug 02	**TROY (THE PHOENIX FROM THE FLAME)** *Devolution DEVR 003CDS*	48		
29 Sep 07	**ILLEGAL ATTACKS** *Fiction 1724668* IAN BROWN FEATURING SINEAD O'CONNOR	16		1

OCTOPUS UK group

Date	Title / Label	Peak Position	Weeks at No.1	Weeks in Top 40
22 Jun 96	**YOUR SMILE** *Food CDFOODS 78*	42		
14 Sep 96	**SAVED** *Food CDFOODS 84*	40		1
23 Nov 96	**JEALOUSY** *Food CDFOODS 87*	59		

OCTAVE ONE US group

Date	Title / Label	Peak Position	Weeks at No.1	Weeks in Top 40
16 Feb 02	**BLACKWATER** *Concept/430 West CDCON 26* FEATURING ANN SAUNDERSON	47		
28 Sep 02	**BLACKWATER (REMIX)** *Concept/430 West CDCON 34* FEATURING ANN SAUNDERSON	69		

ALAN O'DAY US pianist/singer

Date	Title / Label	Peak Position	Weeks at No.1	Weeks in Top 40
2 Jul 77	**UNDERCOVER ANGEL** *Atlantic K 10926* ★	43		

DANIEL O'DONNELL Irish singer

Date	Title / Label	Peak Position	Weeks at No.1	Weeks in Top 40
12 Sep 92	**I JUST WANT TO DANCE WITH YOU** *Ritz 250P*	20		5
2 Jan 93	**THE THREE BELLS** *Ritz RITZCD 239*	71		
8 May 93	**THE LOVE IN YOUR EYES** *Ritz RITZCD 257*	47		
7 Aug 93	**WHAT EVER HAPPENED TO OLD FASHIONED LOVE** *Ritz RITZCD 262*	21		3
16 Apr 94	**SINGING THE BLUES** *Ritz RITZCD 270*	23		2
26 Nov 94	**THE GIFT** *Ritz RITZCD 275*	46		
10 Jun 95	**SECRET LOVE** *Ritz RITZCD 285* DANIEL O'DONNELL & MARY DUFF	28		1
9 Mar 96	**TIMELESS** *Ritz RITZCD 293* DANIEL O'DONNELL & MARY DUFF	32		1
28 Sep 96	**FOOTSTEPS** *Ritz RITZCD 300*	25		3
7 Jun 97	**THE LOVE SONGS EP** *Ritz RITZCD 306*	27		2
11 Apr 98	**GIVE A LITTLE LOVE** *Ritz RITZCD 315*	7		3
17 Oct 98	**THE MAGIC IS THERE** *Ritz RZCD 320*	16		2
20 Mar 99	**THE WAY DREAMS ARE** *Ritz RZCD 325*	18		2
24 Jul 99	**UNO MAS** *Ritz RZCD 326*	25		1
18 Dec 99	**A CHRISTMAS KISS** *Ritz RZCD 330*	20		3
15 Apr 00	**LIGHT A CANDLE** *Ritz RZCD 335*	23		2
16 Dec 00	**MORNING HAS BROKEN** *Ritz RZCD 341*	32		1
13 Dec 03	**YOU RAISE ME UP** *Rosette ROSCD 310*	22		2
23 Sep 06	**CRUSH ON YOU** *Rosette ROSCD325*	21		2

ODYSSEY US group

Date	Title / Label	Peak Position	Weeks at No.1	Weeks in Top 40
24 Dec 77	**NATIVE NEW YORKER** *RCA PC 1129* ○	5		9
21 Jun 80	**USE IT UP AND WEAR IT OUT** *RCA PB 1962* ○	1	2	10
13 Sep 80	**IF YOU'RE LOOKING FOR A WAY OUT** *RCA 5* ○	6		12
17 Jan 81	**HANG TOGETHER** *RCA 23*	36		3
30 May 81	**GOING BACK TO MY ROOTS** *RCA 85* ○	4		9
19 Sep 81	**IT WILL BE ALRIGHT** *RCA 128*	43		
12 Jun 82	**INSIDE OUT** *RCA 226* ○	3		9
11 Sep 82	**MAGIC TOUCH** *RCA 275*	41		
17 Aug 85	**(JOY) I KNOW IT** *Mirror BUTCH 12*	51		

ESTHER & ABI OFARIM Israeli duo

Date	Title / Label	Peak Position	Weeks at No.1	Weeks in Top 40
14 Feb 68	**CINDERELLA ROCKEFELLA** *Philips BF 1640*	1	3	13
19 Jun 68	**ONE MORE DANCE** *Philips BF 1678*	13		8

OFF-SHORE German production duo

Date	Title / Label	Peak Position	Weeks at No.1	Weeks in Top 40
22 Dec 90	**I CAN'T TAKE THE POWER** *CBS 6565707*	7		6
17 Aug 91	**I GOT A LITTLE SONG** *Dance Pool 6568257*	64		

OFFSPRING US group

Date	Title / Label	Peak Position	Weeks at No.1	Weeks in Top 40
25 Feb 95	**SELF ESTEEM** *Epitaph CDSHOLE 001*	37		2
19 Aug 95	**GOTTA GET AWAY** *Out Of Step WOOS 2CDS*	43		
1 Feb 97	**ALL I WANT** *Epitaph 64912*	31		1
26 Apr 97	**GONE AWAY** *Epitaph 64982*	42		
30 Jan 99	**PRETTY FLY (FOR A WHITE GUY)** *Columbia 6668802* ●	1	1	7
8 May 99	**WHY DON'T YOU GET A JOB** *Columbia 6673545*	2		5
11 Sep 99	**THE KIDS AREN'T ALRIGHT** *Columbia 6677632*	11		3
4 Dec 99	**SHE'S GOT ISSUES** *Columbia 6683772*	41		
18 Nov 00	**ORIGINAL PRANKSTER** *Columbia 6699972*	6		4
31 Mar 01	**WANT YOU BAD** *Columbia 6709292*	15		5
7 Jul 01	**MILLION MILES AWAY** *Columbia 6714082*	21		2
31 Jan 04	**HIT THAT** *Columbia 6745475*	11		4
5 Jun 04	**(CAN'T GET MY) HEAD AROUND YOU** *Columbia 6748262*	48		

OH WELL German producer

Date	Title / Label	Peak Position	Weeks at No.1	Weeks in Top 40
14 Oct 89	**OH WELL** *Parlophone R 6236*	28		4
3 Mar 90	**RADAR LOVE** *Parlophone R 6244*	65		

OHIO EXPRESS US group

Date	Title / Label	Peak Position	Weeks at No.1	Weeks in Top 40
5 Jun 68	**YUMMY YUMMY YUMMY** *Pye International 7N 25459*	5		12

OHIO PLAYERS US group

Date	Title / Label	Peak Position	Weeks at No.1	Weeks in Top 40
10 Jul 76	**WHO'D SHE COO** *Mercury PLAY 001*	43		

O'JAYS US group

Date	Title / Label	Peak Position	Weeks at No.1	Weeks in Top 40
23 Sep 72	**BACK STABBERS** *CBS 8270*	14		7
3 Mar 73	**LOVE TRAIN** *CBS 1181* ★	9		11
31 Jan 76	**I LOVE MUSIC** *Philadelphia International PIR 3879*	13		8
12 Feb 77	**DARLIN' DARLIN' BABY (SWEET, TENDER, LOVE)** *Philadelphia International PIR 4834*	24		6
8 Apr 78	**I LOVE MUSIC** *Philadelphia International PIR 6093*	36		1
17 Jun 78	**USED TA BE MY GIRL** *Philadelphia International PIR 6332*	12		9
30 Sep 78	**BRANDY** *Philadelphia International PIR 6658*	21		6
29 Sep 79	**SING A HAPPY SONG** *Philadelphia International PIR 7825*	39		2
30 Jul 83	**PUT OUR HEADS TOGETHER** *Philadelphia International A 3642*	45		

OK GO US group

Date	Title / Label	Peak Position	Weeks at No.1	Weeks in Top 40
22 Mar 03	**GET OVER IT** *Capitol CDR 6603*	21		2
25 Feb 06	**A MILLION WAYS** *Angel ANGECD9*	43		
30 Sep 06	**HERE IT GOES AGAIN** *Angel ANGECD22*	36		1

JOHN O'KANE UK singer

Date	Title / Label	Peak Position	Weeks at No.1	Weeks in Top 40
9 May 92	**STAY WITH ME** *Circa YR 88*	41		

OL' DIRTY BASTARD US rapper

Date	Title / Label	Peak Position	Weeks at No.1	Weeks in Top 40
2 Aug 97	**SAY NOTHIN'** *RCA 74321 502862* OMAR FEATURING OL' DIRTY BASTARD OF WU – TANG CLAN	29		1

Date	Title / Label	Peak Position	Weeks at No.1	Weeks in Top 40
27 Jun 98	**GHETTO SUPERSTAR (THAT IS WHAT YOU ARE)** *Interscope IND 95593* PRAS MICHEL FEATURING OL' DIRTY BASTARD INTRODUCING MYA	2		14
8 Jul 00	**GOT YOUR MONEY** *Elektra E 7077CD* OL' DIRTY BASTARD FEATURING KELIS	11		5

OLD SKOOL ORCHESTRA UK production duo

Date	Title / Label	Peak Position	Weeks at No.1	Weeks in Top 40
23 Jan 99	**B-BOY HUMP** *East West EW 186CD1*	55		

MIKE OLDFIELD UK singer/multi-instrumentalist

Date	Title / Label	Peak Position	Weeks at No.1	Weeks in Top 40
13 Jul 74	**MIKE OLDFIELD'S SINGLE (THEME FROM TUBULAR BELLS)** *Virgin VS 101*	31		3
20 Dec 75	**IN DULCE JUBILO/ON HORSEBACK** *Virgin VS 131*	4		9
27 Nov 76	**PORTSMOUTH** *Virgin VS 163*	3		11
23 Dec 78	**TAKE 4 (EP)** *Virgin VS 238*	72		
21 Apr 79	**GUILTY** *Virgin VS 245*	22		7
8 Dec 79	**BLUE PETER** *Virgin VS 317*	19		7
20 Mar 82	**FIVE MILES OUT** *Virgin VS 464* MIKE OLDFIELD FEATURING MAGGIE REILLY	43		
12 Jun 82	**FAMILY MAN** *Virgin VS 489* MIKE OLDFIELD FEATURING MAGGIE REILLY	45		
28 May 83	**MOONLIGHT SHADOW** *Virgin VS 586* MIKE OLDFIELD WITH VOCALS BY MAGGIE REILLY	4		13
14 Jan 84	**CRIME OF PASSION** *Virgin VS 648* MIKE OLDFIELD FEATURING MAGGIE REILLY	61		
30 Jun 84	**TO FRANCE** *Virgin VS 686* MIKE OLDFIELD FEATURING MAGGIE REILLY	48		
14 Dec 85	**PICTURES IN THE DARK** *Virgin VS 836* MIKE OLDFIELD FEATURING ALED JONES, ANITA HEGERLAND & BARRY PALMER	50		
3 Oct 92	**SENTINEL** *WEA YZ 698*	10		4
19 Dec 92	**TATTOO** *WEA YZ 708*	33		3
17 Apr 93	**THE BELL** *WEA YZ 737CD*	50		
9 Oct 93	**MOONLIGHT SHADOW** *Virgin VSCDT 1477*	52		
17 Dec 94	**HIBERNACULUM** *WEA YZ 871CD*	47		
2 Sep 95	**LET THERE BE LIGHT** *WEA YZ 880CD*	51		
22 Nov 97	**WOMEN OF IRELAND** *WEA YZ 093CD*	70		
24 Apr 99	**FAR ABOVE THE CLOUDS** *WEA 206CD1*	53		

SALLY OLDFIELD UK singer

Date	Title / Label	Peak Position	Weeks at No.1	Weeks in Top 40
9 Dec 78	**MIRRORS** *Bronze BRO 66*	19		9

MISTY OLDLAND UK singer

Date	Title / Label	Peak Position	Weeks at No.1	Weeks in Top 40
16 Oct 93	**GOT ME A FEELING** *Columbia 6597872*	59		
12 Mar 94	**A FAIR AFFAIR (JE T'AIME)** *Columbia 6601612*	49		
9 Jul 94	**I WROTE YOU A SONG** *Columbia 6603732*	73		

OLGA Italian singer

Date	Title / Label	Peak Position	Weeks at No.1	Weeks in Top 40
1 Oct 94	**I'M A BITCH** *UMM 144UKCD*	68		

OLIVE UK group

Date	Title / Label	Peak Position	Weeks at No.1	Weeks in Top 40
7 Sep 96	**YOU'RE NOT ALONE** *RCA 74321406272*	42		
15 Mar 97	**MIRACLE** *RCA 74321461242*	41		
17 May 97	**YOU'RE NOT ALONE** *RCA 74321473232*	1	2	8
16 Aug 97	**OUTLAW** *RCA 74321508372*	14		3
8 Nov 97	**MIRACLE (REMIX)** *RCA 74321530842*	41		

OLIVER US singer

Date	Title / Label	Peak Position	Weeks at No.1	Weeks in Top 40
9 Aug 69	**GOOD MORNING STARSHINE** *CBS 4435*	6		15

FRANKIE OLIVER UK singer

Date	Title / Label	Peak Position	Weeks at No.1	Weeks in Top 40
7 Jun 97	**GIVE HER WHAT SHE WANTS** *Island Jamaica IJCD 2011*	58		

OLLIE & JERRY US duo

Date	Title / Label	Peak Position	Weeks at No.1	Weeks in Top 40
23 Jun 84	**BREAKIN'...THERE'S NO STOPPING US** *Polydor POSP 690*	5		8
9 Mar 85	**ELECTRIC BOOGALOO** *Polydor POSP 730*	57		

OLYMPIC ORCHESTRA UK orchestra

Date	Title / Label	Peak Position	Weeks at No.1	Weeks in Top 40
1 Oct 83	**REILLY** *Red Bus RBUS 82*	26		8

OLYMPIC RUNNERS UK group

Date	Title / Label	Peak Position	Weeks at No.1	Weeks in Top 40
13 May 78	**WHATEVER IT TAKES** *RCA PC 5078*	61		
14 Oct 78	**GET IT WHILE YOU CAN** *Polydor RUN 7*	35		3
20 Jan 79	**SIR DANCEALOT** *Polydor POSP 17*	35		1
28 Jul 79	**THE BITCH** *Polydor POSP 63*	37		2

OLYMPICS US group

Date	Title / Label	Peak Position	Weeks at No.1	Weeks in Top 40
3 Oct 58	**WESTERN MOVIES** *HMV POP 528*	12		8
19 Jan 61	**I WISH I COULD SHIMMY LIKE MY SISTER KATE** *Vogue V 9174*	40		1

OMAR UK singer

Date	Title / Label	Peak Position	Weeks at No.1	Weeks in Top 40
22 Jun 91	**THERE'S NOTHING LIKE THIS** *Talkin Loud TLK 9*	14		6
23 May 92	**YOUR LOSS MY GAIN** *Talkin Loud TLK 22*	47		
26 Sep 92	**MUSIC** *Talkin Loud TLK 28*	53		
23 Jul 94	**OUTSIDE/SATURDAY** *RCA 74321213982*	43		
15 Oct 94	**KEEP STEPPIN'** *RCA 74321233682*	57		
2 Aug 97	**SAY NOTHIN'** *RCA 74321502872* OMAR FEATURING OL' DIRTY BASTARD OF WU – TANG CLAN	29		1
18 Oct 97	**GOLDEN BROWN** *RCA 74321525122*	37		1

OMARION US singer

Date	Title / Label	Peak Position	Weeks at No.1	Weeks in Top 40
23 Jul 05	**O** *Epic 6759862*	47		
8 Oct 05	**LET ME HOLD YOU (IMPORT)** *Sony BMG 6760602* BOW WOW FEATURING OMARION	64		
22 Oct 05	**LET ME HOLD YOU** *Columbia 6760605* BOW WOW FEATURING OMARION	27		3
17 Feb 07	**ICE BOX** *Epic 88697079682*	14		8
9 Jun 07	**ENTOURAGE** *Columbia/Sony Urban 88697098442*	58		

OMC New Zealand singer

Date	Title / Label	Peak Position	Weeks at No.1	Weeks in Top 40
20 Jul 96	**HOW BIZARRE** *Polydor 5776202*	5		14
18 Jan 97	**ON THE RUN** *Polydor 5732452*	56		

JO O'MEARA UK singer

Date	Title / Label	Peak Position	Weeks at No.1	Weeks in Top 40
8 Oct 05	**WHAT HURTS THE MOST** *Sanctuary SANXS403*	13		3

OMNI TRIO UK producer

Date	Title / Label	Peak Position	Weeks at No.1	Weeks in Top 40
7 Jul 01	**THE ANGELS & SHADOWS PROJECT** *Moving Shadow SHADOW 150CD*	44		
26 Jul 03	**RENEGADE SNARES** *Moving Shadow SHADOW 166*	61		

ONE UK group

Date	Title / Label	Peak Position	Weeks at No.1	Weeks in Top 40
11 Jan 97	**ONE MORE CHANCE** *Mercury MERDD 478*	31		1

MICHIE ONE UK singer

Date	Title / Label	Peak Position	Weeks at No.1	Weeks in Top 40
29 Oct 05	**WATERMAN** *Positiva CDTIVS224* OLAV BASOSKI FEATURING MICHIE ONE	45		

PHOEBE ONE UK singer

Date	Title / Label	Peak Position	Weeks at No.1	Weeks in Top 40
12 Dec 98	**DOIN' OUR THING/ONE MAN'S BITCH** *Mecca Recordings MECX 1020*	59		
15 May 99	**GET ON IT** *Mecca Recordings MECX 1026*	38		1

ONE DOVE UK group

Date	Title / Label	Peak Position	Weeks at No.1	Weeks in Top 40
7 Aug 93	**WHITE LOVE** *Boy's Own BOICD 14*	43		
16 Oct 93	**BREAKDOWN** *Boy's Own BOICD 15*	24		1
15 Jan 94	**WHY DON'T YOU TAKE ME** *Boy's Own BOICD 16*	30		1

187 LOCKDOWN UK production duo

Date	Title / Label	Peak Position	Weeks at No.1	Weeks in Top 40
15 Nov 97	**GUNMAN** *East West EW 140CD*	16		2
25 Apr 98	**KUNG-FU** *East West EW 155CD*	9		3
25 Jul 98	**GUNMAN** *East West EW 176CD*	17		2
3 Oct 98	**THE DON** *East West EW 180CD*	29		1
13 Feb 99	**ALL 'N' ALL** *East West EW 194CD* 187 LOCKDOWN (FEATURING D'EMPRESS)	43		

Silver-selling ○ · Gold-selling ● · Platinum-selling ⊛ · US No.1 ★ · Peak Position · Weeks at No.1 · Weeks in Top 40

1 GIANT LEAP *UK production group*

Date	Title / Label	Peak Position	Weeks at No.1	Weeks in Top 40
20 Apr 02	**MY CULTURE** *Palm Pictures PPCD 70732* 1 GIANT LEAP FEATURING MAXI JAZZ & ROBBIE WILLIAMS	9		4

100% *UK production duo*

Date	Title / Label	Peak Position	Weeks at No.1	Weeks in Top 40
25 Dec 04	**JUST CAN'T WAIT (SATURDAY)** *CR2 CDC2X005* 100% FEATURING JENNIFER JOHN	28		4

ONE HUNDRED TON & A FEATHER *UK singer*

Date	Title / Label	Peak Position	Weeks at No.1	Weeks in Top 40
26 Jun 76	**IT ONLY TAKES A MINUTE** *UK 135* ONE HUNDRED TON & A FEATHER	9		8

ONE MINUTE SILENCE *UK group*

Date	Title / Label	Peak Position	Weeks at No.1	Weeks in Top 40
20 Jan 01	**FISH OUT OF WATER** *V2 VVR 5013213*	56		
5 Jul 03	**I WEAR MY SKIN** *Taste Media TMCDSX 5005*	44		

ONE NIGHT ONLY *UK group*

Date	Title / Label	Peak Position	Weeks at No.1	Weeks in Top 40
10 Nov 07	**YOU AND ME** *Vertigo 1747365*	46		
2 Feb 08	**JUST FOR TONIGHT** *Vertigo 1753471*	9		8

112 *US group*

Date	Title / Label	Peak Position	Weeks at No.1	Weeks in Top 40
28 Jun 97	**I'LL BE MISSING YOU** *Puff Daddy 74321499102* PUFF DADDY & FAITH EVANS FEATURING 112 ⊛ ★	1	6	18
10 Jan 98	**ALL CRIED OUT** *Epic 6652715* ALLURE FEATURING 112	12		4
14 Feb 98	**SKY'S THE LIMIT** *Puff Daddy 74321587992* NOTORIOUS B.I.G. FEATURING 112	35		1
30 Jun 01	**IT'S OVER NOW** *Puff Daddy 74321849912*	22		2
8 Sep 01	**PEACHES AND CREAM** *Arista 74321882632*	32		1

ONE REPUBLIC *US group*

Date	Title / Label	Peak Position	Weeks at No.1	Weeks in Top 40
13 Oct 07	**APOLOGIZE** *Interscope 1750152* TIMBALAND PRESENTS ONE REPUBLIC	3		24
23 Feb 08	**STOP AND STARE** *Interscope 1763784*	4		6

ONE THE JUGGLER *UK group*

Date	Title / Label	Peak Position	Weeks at No.1	Weeks in Top 40
19 Feb 83	**PASSION KILLER** *Regard RG 107*	71		

1000 CLOWNS *US group*

Date	Title / Label	Peak Position	Weeks at No.1	Weeks in Top 40
22 May 99	**(NOT THE) GREATEST RAPPER** *Elektra E 3759CD*	23		3

ONE TRUE VOICE *UK group*

Date	Title / Label	Peak Position	Weeks at No.1	Weeks in Top 40
28 Dec 02	**SACRED TRUST/AFTER YOU'RE GONE** *Ebul/Jive 9201532* ●	2		7
14 Jun 03	**SHAKESPEARE'S WAY WITH WORDS** *Ebul/Jive 9201582*	10		2

ONE 2 MANY *Norwegian group*

Date	Title / Label	Peak Position	Weeks at No.1	Weeks in Top 40
12 Nov 88	**DOWNTOWN** *A&M AM 476*	65		
3 Jun 89	**DOWNTOWN** *A&M AM 456*	43		

ONE WAY *US group*

Date	Title / Label	Peak Position	Weeks at No.1	Weeks in Top 40
8 Dec 79	**MUSIC** *MCA 542* ONE WAY FEATURING AL HUDSON	56		
29 Jun 85	**LET'S TALK ABOUT SHHH** *MCA 972*	64		

ONE WORLD PROJECT *Multinational charity group*

Date	Title / Label	Peak Position	Weeks at No.1	Weeks in Top 40
5 Feb 05	**GRIEF NEVER GROWS OLD** *One World OWR1*	4		3

ALEXANDER O'NEAL *US singer*

Date	Title / Label	Peak Position	Weeks at No.1	Weeks in Top 40
28 Dec 85	**SATURDAY LOVE** *Tabu A 6829* CHERRELLE WITH ALEXANDER O'NEAL	6		9
15 Feb 86	**IF YOU WERE HERE TONIGHT** *Tabu A 6391*	13		7
5 Apr 86	**A BROKEN HEART CAN MEND** *Tabu A 6244*	53		
6 Jun 87	**FAKE** *Tabu 6508917*	33		2
31 Oct 87	**CRITICIZE** *Tabu 6512117*	4		10
6 Feb 88	**NEVER KNEW LOVE LIKE THIS** *Tabu 6513827* ALEXANDER O'NEAL FEATURING CHERRELLE	26		5
28 May 88	**THE LOVERS** *Tabu 6515957*	28		3
23 Jul 88	**(WHAT CAN I SAY) TO MAKE YOU LOVE ME** *Tabu 6528527*	27		4
24 Sep 88	**FAKE '88 (REMIX)** *Tabu 6529497*	16		5
10 Dec 88	**CHRISTMAS SONG (CHESTNUTS ROASTING ON AN OPEN FIRE)/THANK YOU FOR A GOOD YEAR** *Tabu 6531827*	30		4
25 Feb 89	**HEARSAY '89** *Tabu 6544667*	56		
2 Sep 89	**SUNSHINE** *Tabu 6551917*	72		
9 Dec 89	**HITMIX (OFFICIAL BOOTLEG MEGA-MIX)** *Tabu 6555047*	19		5
24 Mar 90	**SATURDAY LOVE (REMIX)** *Tabu 6558007* CHERRELLE WITH ALEXANDER O'NEAL	55		
12 Jan 91	**ALL TRUE MAN** *Tabu 6565717*	18		4
23 Mar 91	**WHAT IS THIS THING CALLED LOVE** *Tabu 6567317*	53		
11 May 91	**SHAME ON ME** *Tabu 6568737*	71		
9 May 92	**SENTIMENTAL** *Tabu 6580147*	53		
30 Jan 93	**LOVE MAKES NO SENSE** *Tabu AMCD 7708*	26		2
3 Jul 93	**IN THE MIDDLE** *Tabu 5877152*	32		2
25 Sep 93	**ALL THAT MATTERS TO ME** *Tabu 6577232*	67		
2 Nov 96	**LET'S GET TOGETHER** *EMI Premier PRESCD 11*	38		1
2 Aug 97	**BABY COME TO ME** *One World Entertainment OWECD 1* ALEXANDER O'NEAL FEATURING CHERRELLE	56		
12 Dec 98	**CRITICIZE '98 MIX** *One World Entertainment OWECD 3*	51		

SHAQUILLE O'NEAL *US singer/basketball player*

Date	Title / Label	Peak Position	Weeks at No.1	Weeks in Top 40
26 Mar 94	**I'M OUTSTANDING** *Jive JIVECD 349*	70		
14 Sep 96	**STOMP - THE REMIXES** *Qwest W0372CD* QUINCY JONES FEATURING MELLE MEL, COOLIO, YO-YO, SHAQUILLE O'NEAL & THE LUNIZ	28		1
1 Feb 97	**YOU CAN'T STOP THE REIGN** *Interscope IND 95522*	40		1
17 Oct 98	**THE WAY IT'S GOIN' DOWN (T.W.I.S.M. FOR LIFE)** *A&M 5827932*	62		

ONES *US group*

Date	Title / Label	Peak Position	Weeks at No.1	Weeks in Top 40
20 Oct 01	**FLAWLESS** *Positiva CDTIV 164*	7		6
1 Mar 03	**SUPERSTAR** *Positiva CDTIVS 186*	45		

ONLY ONES *UK group*

Date	Title / Label	Peak Position	Weeks at No.1	Weeks in Top 40
1 Feb 92	**ANOTHER GIRL - ANOTHER PLANET** *Columbia 6577507*	57		

YOKO ONO *Japanese singer*

Date	Title / Label	Peak Position	Weeks at No.1	Weeks in Top 40
28 Feb 81	**WALKING ON THIN ICE** *Geffen K 79202*	35		3
14 Jun 03	**WALKING ON THIN ICE (REMIX)** *Parlophone CDMINDS 002*	35		1

BEN ONONO *UK singer*

Date	Title / Label	Peak Position	Weeks at No.1	Weeks in Top 40
15 Mar 03	**ON MY MIND** *Junior/Parlophone CDR 6595* FUTURESHOCK FEATURING BEN ONONO	51		
17 May 03	**MY LOVE IS ALWAYS** *Illustrious CDILL 016* SAFFRON HILL FEATURING BEN ONONO	28		1

ONSLAUGHT *UK group*

Date	Title / Label	Peak Position	Weeks at No.1	Weeks in Top 40
6 May 89	**LET THERE BE ROCK** *London LON 224*	50		

ONYX *US group*

Date	Title / Label	Peak Position	Weeks at No.1	Weeks in Top 40
28 Aug 93	**SLAM** *Columbia 6596302*	31		2
27 Nov 93	**THROW YA GUNZ** *Columbia 6598312*	34		1
20 Feb 99	**ROC-IN-IT** *Independiente ISOM 21MS* DEEJAY PUNK-ROC VS ONYX	59		
11 Dec 04	**EVERY LITTLE TIME** *Data DATA78CDS* ONYX FEATURING GEMMA J	66		

OO LA LA *UK group*

Date	Title / Label	Peak Position	Weeks at No.1	Weeks in Top 40
5 Sep 92	**OO...AH...CANTONA** *North Speed OOAH 1*	64		

OOBERMAN *UK group*

Date	Title / Label	Peak Position	Weeks at No.1	Weeks in Top 40
8 May 99	**BLOSSOMS FALLING** *Independiente ISOM 26MS*	39		1
17 Jul 99	**MILLION SUNS** *Independiente ISOM 30MS*	43		
23 Oct 99	**TEARS FROM A WILLOW** *Independiente ISOM 37MS*	63		
8 Apr 00	**SHORLEY WALL** *Independiente ISOM 41MS*	47		

Legend: Silver-selling ● Gold-selling ● Platinum-selling ✪ US No.1 ★ | Peak Position | Weeks at No.1 | Weeks in Top 40

OPEN UK group

Date	Title	Label	Peak Position	Weeks at No.1	Weeks in Top 40
13 Mar 04	CLOSE MY EYES	*Polydor 9817294*	46		
3 Jul 04	JUST WANT TO LIVE	*Loog 9866489*	52		
11 Sep 04	ELEVATION	*Loog 9867495*	54		
13 Nov 04	NEVER ENOUGH	*Loog 9868779*	53		

OPEN ARMS UK production duo

Date	Title	Label	Peak Position	Weeks at No.1	Weeks in Top 40
15 Jun 96	HEY MR DJ OPEN ARMS FEATURING ROWETTA	*All Around The World CDGLOBE 136*	62		

OPERABABES UK duo

Date	Title	Label	Peak Position	Weeks at No.1	Weeks in Top 40
6 Jul 02	ONE FINE DAY	*Sony Classical 6727062*	54		

OPM US group

Date	Title	Label	Peak Position	Weeks at No.1	Weeks in Top 40
14 Jul 01	HEAVEN IS A HALFPIPE	*Atlantic AT 0107CD* ●	4		11
12 Jan 02	EL CAPITAN	*East West AT 0118CD*	20		2

OPTIMYSTIC UK group

Date	Title	Label	Peak Position	Weeks at No.1	Weeks in Top 40
17 Sep 94	CAUGHT UP IN MY HEART	*WEA YZ 841CD*	49		
10 Dec 94	NOTHING BUT LOVE	*WEA YZ 864CD1*	37		1
13 May 95	BEST THING IN THE WORLD	*WEA YZ 920CD*	70		

OPUS Austrian group

Date	Title	Label	Peak Position	Weeks at No.1	Weeks in Top 40
15 Jun 85	LIVE IS LIFE	*Polydor POSP 743* ●	6		11

OPUS III UK production group

Date	Title	Label	Peak Position	Weeks at No.1	Weeks in Top 40
22 Feb 92	IT'S A FINE DAY	*PWL International PWL 215*	5		6
27 Jun 92	I TALK TO THE WIND	*PWL International PWL 235*	52		
11 Jun 94	WHEN YOU MADE THE MOUNTAIN	*PWL International PWL 302*	71		

ORANGE UK group

Date	Title	Label	Peak Position	Weeks at No.1	Weeks in Top 40
8 Oct 94	JUDY OVER THE RAINBOW	*Chrysalis CDCHS 5012*	73		

ORANGE JUICE UK group

Date	Title	Label	Peak Position	Weeks at No.1	Weeks in Top 40
7 Nov 81	L.O.V.E...LOVE	*Polydor POSP 357*	65		
30 Jan 82	FELICITY	*Polydor POSP 386*	63		
21 Aug 82	TWO HEARTS TOGETHER/HOKOYO	*Polydor POSP 470*	60		
23 Oct 82	I CAN'T HELP MYSELF	*Polydor POSP 522*	42		
19 Feb 83	RIP IT UP	*Polydor POSP 547*	8		8
4 Jun 83	FLESH OF MY FLESH	*Polydor OJ 4*	41		
25 Feb 84	BRIDGE	*Polydor OJ 5*	67		
12 May 84	WHAT PRESENCE?	*Polydor OJ 6*	47		
27 Oct 84	LEAN PERIOD	*Polydor OJ 7*	74		

ORB UK group

Date	Title	Label	Peak Position	Weeks at No.1	Weeks in Top 40
15 Jun 91	PERPETUAL DAWN	*Big Life BLRD 46*	61		
20 Jun 92	BLUE ROOM	*Big Life BLRT 75*	8		4
17 Oct 92	ASSASSIN	*Big Life BLRT 81*	12		3
13 Nov 93	LITTLE FLUFFY CLOUDS	*Big Life BLRD 98*	10		3
5 Feb 94	PERPETUAL DAWN	*Big Life BLRD 46*	18		3
27 May 95	OXBOW LAKES	*Island CID 609*	38		1
8 Feb 97	TOXYGENE	*Island CID 652*	4		3
24 May 97	ASYLUM	*Island CID 657*	20		1
24 Feb 01	ONCE MORE	*Island CIDX 767*	38		1

ROY ORBISON US singer

Date	Title	Label	Peak Position	Weeks at No.1	Weeks in Top 40
28 Jul 60	ONLY THE LONELY	*London HLU 9149*	1	2	23
27 Oct 60	BLUE ANGEL	*London HLU 9207*	11		14
25 May 61	RUNNING SCARED	*London HLU 9342* ★	9		15
28 Sep 61	CRYIN'	*London HLU 9405*	25		8
8 Mar 62	DREAM BABY	*London HLU 9511*	2		13
28 Jun 62	THE CROWD	*London HLU 9561*	40		1
8 Nov 62	WORKIN' FOR THE MAN	*London HLU 9607*	50		
28 Feb 63	IN DREAMS	*London HLU 9676*	6		22
30 May 63	FALLING	*London HLU 9727*	9		11
19 Sep 63	BLUE BAYOU/MEAN WOMAN BLUES	*London HLU 9777*	3		17
20 Feb 64	BORNE ON THE WIND	*London HLU 9845*	15		9
30 Apr 64	IT'S OVER	*London HLU 9882*	1	2	18
10 Sep 64	OH PRETTY WOMAN	*London HLU 9919* ★	1	3	15
19 Nov 64	PRETTY PAPER	*London HLU 9930*	6		10
11 Feb 65	GOODNIGHT	*London HLU 9951*	14		8
22 Jul 65	(SAY) YOU'RE MY GIRL	*London HLU 9978*	23		6
9 Sep 65	RIDE AWAY	*London HLU 9986*	34		4
4 Nov 65	CRAWLIN' BACK	*London HLU 10000*	19		6
27 Jan 66	BREAKIN' UP IS BREAKIN' MY HEART	*London HLU 10015*	22		5
7 Apr 66	TWINKLE TOES	*London HLU 10034*	29		5
16 Jun 66	LANA	*London HLU 10051*	15		8
18 Aug 66	TOO SOON TO KNOW	*London HLU 10067*	3		16
1 Dec 66	THERE WON'T BE MANY COMING HOME	*London HLU 10096*	12		8
23 Feb 67	SO GOOD	*London HLU 10113*	32		4
24 Jul 68	WALK ON	*London HLU 10206*	39		2
25 Sep 68	HEARTACHE	*London HLU 10222*	44		
30 Apr 69	MY FRIEND	*London HLU 10261*	35		3
13 Sep 69	PENNY ARCADE	*London HLU 10285*	27		8
14 Jan 89	YOU GOT IT	*Virgin VS 1166* ●	3		9
1 Apr 89	SHE'S A MYSTERY TO ME	*Virgin VS 1173*	27		3
4 Jul 92	I DROVE ALL NIGHT	*MCA MCS 1652*	7		9
22 Aug 92	CRYING ROY ORBISON (DUET WITH k d lang)	*Virgin America VUS 63*	13		4
7 Nov 92	HEARTBREAK RADIO	*Virgin America VUS 68*	36		2
13 Nov 93	I DROVE ALL NIGHT	*Virgin America VUSCD 79*	47		

WILLIAM ORBIT UK producer

Date	Title	Label	Peak Position	Weeks at No.1	Weeks in Top 40
26 Jun 93	WATER FROM A VINE LEAF	*Guerilla VSCDT 1465*	59		
18 Dec 99	BARBER'S ADAGIO FOR STRINGS	*WEA 247CD* ●	4		10
6 May 00	RAVEL'S PAVANE POUR UNE INFANTE DEFUNTE	*WEA 269CD*	31		1
19 Jul 03	FEEL GOOD TIME PINK FEATURING WILLIAM ORBIT	*Columbia 6741062*	3		7

ORBITAL UK duo

Date	Title	Label	Peak Position	Weeks at No.1	Weeks in Top 40
24 Mar 90	CHIME	*ffrr F 85*	17		4
22 Sep 90	OMEN	*ffrr 145*	46		
19 Jan 91	SATAN	*ffrr FX 149*	31		2
15 Feb 92	MUTATIONS EP	*ffrr FX 181*	24		2
26 Sep 92	RADICCIO EP	*Internal LIARX 1*	37		1
21 Aug 93	LUSH	*Internal LIECD 7*	43		
24 Sep 94	ARE WE HERE	*Internal LIECD 15*	33		1
27 May 95	BELFAST	*Volume VOLCD 1*	53		
27 Apr 96	THE BOX	*Internal LIECD 30*	11		2
11 Jan 97	SATAN	*Internal LIECD 37*	3		4
19 Apr 97	THE SAINT	*ffrr FCD 296*	3		3
20 Mar 99	STYLE	*ffrr FCD 358*	13		2
17 Jul 99	NOTHING LEFT	*ffrr FCDP 365*	32		1
11 Mar 00	BEACHED ORBITAL & ANGELO BADALAMENTI	*ffrr FCD 377*	36		1
28 Apr 01	FUNNY BREAK (ONE IS ENOUGH)	*ffrr FCDP 395*	21		2
8 Jun 02	REST AND PLAY EP	*ffrr FCD 407*	33		1
17 Jul 04	ONE PERFECT SUNRISE	*Orbital Music ORBITALCD03X*	29		1

ORCHESTRA ON THE HALF SHELL US group

Date	Title	Label	Peak Position	Weeks at No.1	Weeks in Top 40
15 Dec 90	TURTLE RHAPSODY	*SBK 17*	36		3

ORCHESTRAL MANOEUVRES IN THE DARK UK group

Date	Title	Label	Peak Position	Weeks at No.1	Weeks in Top 40
9 Feb 80	RED FRAME WHITE LIGHT	*Dindisc DIN 6*	67		
10 May 80	MESSAGES	*Dindisc DIN 15*	13		8
4 Oct 80	ENOLA GAY	*Dindisc DIN 22* ●	8		10
29 Aug 81	SOUVENIR	*Dindisc DIN 24* ●	3		9
24 Oct 81	JOAN OF ARC	*Dindisc DIN 36* ●	5		8
23 Jan 82	MAID OF ORLEANS (THE WALTZ JOAN OF ARC)	*Dindisc DIN 40* ●	4		9
19 Feb 83	GENETIC ENGINEERING	*Virgin VS 527*	20		6
9 Apr 83	TELEGRAPH	*Virgin VS 580*	42		
14 Apr 84	LOCOMOTION	*Virgin VS 660*	5		9
16 Jun 84	TALKING LOUD AND CLEAR	*Virgin VS 685*	11		8
8 Sep 84	TESLA GIRLS	*Virgin VS 705*	21		5
10 Nov 84	NEVER TURN AWAY	*Virgin VS 727*	70		
25 May 85	SO IN LOVE	*Virgin VS 766*	27		5
20 Jul 85	SECRET	*Virgin VS 796*	34		4
26 Oct 85	LA FEMME ACCIDENT	*Virgin VS 811*	42		
3 May 86	IF YOU LEAVE	*Virgin VS 843*	48		
6 Sep 86	(FOREVER) LIVE AND DIE	*Virgin VS 888*	11		7
15 Nov 86	WE LOVE YOU	*Virgin VS 911*	54		
2 May 87	SHAME	*Virgin VS 938*	52		
6 Feb 88	DREAMING	*Virgin VS 987*	50		
2 Jul 88	DREAMING	*Virgin VS 987*	60		
30 Mar 91	SAILING ON THE SEVEN SEAS	*Virgin VS 1310*	3		10

Silver-selling ● Gold-selling ● Platinum-selling ● US No.1 ★ | Peak Position | Weeks at No.1 | Weeks in Top 40

Date	Title	Label	Peak Position	Weeks at No.1	Weeks in Top 40
6 Jul 91	PANDORA'S BOX	*Virgin VS 1331*	7		7
14 Sep 91	THEN YOU TURN AWAY	*Virgin VS 1368*	50		
7 Dec 91	CALL MY NAME	*Virgin VS 1380*	50		
15 May 93	STAND ABOVE ME	*Virgin VSCDG 1444*	21		3
17 Jul 93	DREAM OF ME (BASED ON LOVE'S THEME)	*Virgin VSCDT 1461*	24		3
18 Sep 93	EVERYDAY	*Virgin VSCDT 1471*	59		
17 Aug 96	WALKING ON THE MILKY WAY	*Virgin VSCDT 1599*	17		3
2 Nov 96	UNIVERSAL	*Virgin VSCDT 1606*	55		
26 Sep 98	THE OMD REMIXES EP	*Virgin VSCDT 1694*	35		1

ORDINARY BOYS UK group

Date	Title	Label	Peak Position	Weeks at No.1	Weeks in Top 40
17 Apr 04	WEEK IN WEEK OUT	*B Unique WEA372CD*	36		1
10 Jul 04	TALK TALK TALK	*B Unique WEA377CD*	17		1
2 Oct 04	SEASIDE	*B Unique WEA379CD*	27		1
18 Jun 05	BOYS WILL BE BOYS	*B Unique WEA389CD2*	16		1
10 Sep 05	LIFE WILL BE THE DEATH OF ME	*B Unique WEA394CD1*	50		
21 Jan 06	BOYS WILL BE BOYS	*B Unique WEA389CD2*	3		9
27 May 06	NINE 2FIVE	*Polydor BUN105CD*			
	ORDINARY BOYS FEATURING LADY SOVEREIGN		6		5
21 Oct 06	LONELY AT THE TOP	*B Unique/Polydor BUN112CD*	10		3
13 Jan 07	I LUV U	*B Unique/Polydor BUN118CD*	7		6

RAUL ORELLANA Spanish producer

Date	Title	Label	Peak Position	Weeks at No.1	Weeks in Top 40
30 Sep 89	THE REAL WILD HOUSE	*RCA BCM 322*	29		4

O.R.G.A.N. Spanish producer

Date	Title	Label	Peak Position	Weeks at No.1	Weeks in Top 40
16 May 98	TO THE WORLD	*Multiply CDMULTY 34*	33		1

ORIGIN UK production duo

Date	Title	Label	Peak Position	Weeks at No.1	Weeks in Top 40
12 Aug 00	WIDE EYED ANGEL	*Lost Language LOST 001CD*	73		

ORIGIN UNKNOWN UK production duo

Date	Title	Label	Peak Position	Weeks at No.1	Weeks in Top 40
13 Jul 96	VALLEY OF THE SHADOWS	*Ram RAMM 16CD*	60		
11 May 02	TRULY ONE	*Ram RAMM 38CD*	53		
20 Sep 03	HOTNESS	*Ram RAMM 45*			
	DYNAMITE MC & ORIGIN UNKNOWN		66		

ORIGINAL US duo

Date	Title	Label	Peak Position	Weeks at No.1	Weeks in Top 40
14 Jan 95	I LUV U BABY	*Ore AG 8CD*	31		1
19 Aug 95	I LUV U BABY (REMIX)	*Ore/XL Recordings AGR 8CD* ●	2		7
11 Nov 95	B 2 GETHER	*Ore/XL Recordings AG 12CD*	29		1

ORION UK group

Date	Title	Label	Peak Position	Weeks at No.1	Weeks in Top 40
7 Oct 00	ETERNITY	*Incentive CENT 11CDS*	38		1

ORION TOO Belgian group

Date	Title	Label	Peak Position	Weeks at No.1	Weeks in Top 40
9 Nov 02	HOPE AND WAIT	*Data 4CDS*	46		

TONY ORLANDO US singer

Date	Title	Label	Peak Position	Weeks at No.1	Weeks in Top 40
5 Oct 61	BLESS YOU	*Fontana H 330*	5		10

ORLONS US group

Date	Title	Label	Peak Position	Weeks at No.1	Weeks in Top 40
27 Dec 62	DON'T HANG UP	*Cameo Parkway C 231*	39		1

ORN UK producer

Date	Title	Label	Peak Position	Weeks at No.1	Weeks in Top 40
1 Mar 97	SNOW	*Deconstruction 74321447612*	61		

STACIE ORRICO US singer

Date	Title	Label	Peak Position	Weeks at No.1	Weeks in Top 40
23 Aug 03	STUCK	*Virgin VUSCD 269*	9		5
1 Nov 03	THERE'S GOTTA BE MORE TO LIFE	*Virgin VUSCD 275*	12		5
24 Jan 04	I PROMISE	*Virgin VUSDX 280*	22		2
12 Jun 04	I COULD BE THE ONE	*Virgin VUSDX 289*	34		1
2 Sep 06	I'M NOT MISSING YOU	*Virgin VUSCD329*	22		2

ORSON UK group

Date	Title	Label	Peak Position	Weeks at No.1	Weeks in Top 40
11 Mar 06	NO TOMORROW	*Mercury 9876828*	1		15
20 May 06	BRIGHT IDEA	*Mercury 9856127*	11		7
12 Aug 06	HAPPINESS	*Mercury 1703849*	27		2
20 Oct 07	AIN'T NO PARTY	*Mercury 1746453*	21		2

BETH ORTON UK singer

Date	Title	Label	Peak Position	Weeks at No.1	Weeks in Top 40
1 Feb 97	TOUCH ME WITH YOUR LOVE	*Heavenly HVN 64CD*	60		
5 Apr 97	SOMEONE'S DAUGHTER	*Heavenly HVN 65CD*	49		
14 Jun 97	SHE CRIES YOUR NAME	*Heavenly HVN 68CD*	40		1
13 Dec 97	BEST BIT EP	*Heavenly HVN 72CD*			
	BETH ORTON FEATURING TERRY CALLIER		36		1
13 Mar 99	STOLEN CAR	*Heavenly HVN 89CD*	34		1
25 Sep 99	CENTRAL RESERVATION	*Heavenly HVN 92CD1*	37		1
16 Nov 02	ANYWHERE	*Heavenly HVN 125CDS*	55		
12 Apr 03	THINKING ABOUT TOMORROW	*Heavenly HVN 129CD*	57		
11 Feb 06	CONCEIVED	*EMI CDEM681*	44		

JEFFREY OSBORNE US singer

Date	Title	Label	Peak Position	Weeks at No.1	Weeks in Top 40
17 Sep 83	DON'T YOU GET SO MAD	*A&M AM 140*	54		
14 Apr 84	STAY WITH ME TONIGHT	*A&M AM 188*	18		6
23 Jun 84	ON THE WINGS OF LOVE	*A&M AM 198*	11		9
20 Oct 84	DON'T STOP	*A&M AM 222*	61		
26 Jul 86	SOWETO	*A&M AM 334*	44		
15 Aug 87	LOVE POWER	*Arista RIS 27*			
	DIONNE WARWICK & JEFFREY OSBORNE		63		

JOAN OSBORNE US singer

Date	Title	Label	Peak Position	Weeks at No.1	Weeks in Top 40
10 Feb 96	ONE OF US	*Blue Gorilla JOACD 1*	6		8
8 Jun 96	ST TERESA	*Blue Gorilla JOACD 3*	33		1

TONY OSBORNE SOUND UK orchestra

Date	Title	Label	Peak Position	Weeks at No.1	Weeks in Top 40
23 Feb 61	MAN FROM MADRID	*HMV POP 827*			
	TONY OSBORNE SOUND FEATURING JOANNE BROWN		50		
3 Feb 73	THE SHEPHERD'S SONG	*Philips 6006 266*	46		

KELLY OSBOURNE UK singer

Date	Title	Label	Peak Position	Weeks at No.1	Weeks in Top 40
24 Aug 02	PAPA DON'T PREACH (IMPORT)	*Epic 6729152CD*	65		
21 Sep 02	PAPA DON'T PREACH	*Epic 6731602*	3		5
8 Feb 03	SHUT UP	*Epic 6735552*	12		4
20 Dec 03	CHANGES	*Sanctuary SANXD 34*			
	OZZY & KELLY OSBOURNE ●		1	1	13
21 May 05	ONE WORD	*Sanctuary SANXS349*	9		4

OZZY OSBOURNE UK singer

Date	Title	Label	Peak Position	Weeks at No.1	Weeks in Top 40
13 Sep 80	CRAZY TRAIN	*Jet 197*			
	OZZY OSBOURNE'S BLIZZARD OF OZ		49		
15 Nov 80	MR CROWLEY	*Jet 7003*			
	OZZY OSBOURNE'S BLIZZARD OF OZ		46		
26 Nov 83	BARK AT THE MOON	*Epic A 3915*	21		6
2 Jun 84	SO TIRED	*Epic A 4452*	20		7
1 Feb 86	SHOT IN THE DARK	*Epic A 6859*	20		5
9 Aug 86	THE ULTIMATE SIN/LIGHTNING STRIKES	*Epic A 7311*	72		
20 May 89	CLOSE MY EYES FOREVER	*Dreamland PB 49409*			
	LITA FORD DUET WITH OZZY OSBOURNE		47		
28 Sep 91	NO MORE TEARS	*Epic 6574407*	32		2
30 Nov 91	MAMA I'M COMING HOME	*Epic 6576177*	46		
25 Nov 95	PERRY MASON	*Epic 6626395*	23		1
31 Aug 96	I JUST WANT YOU	*Epic 6635702*	43		
8 Jun 02	DREAMER/GETS ME THROUGH	*Epic 6724122*	18		4
20 Dec 03	CHANGES	*Sanctuary SANXD 34*			
	OZZY & KELLY OSBOURNE ●		1	1	13
24 Dec 05	IN MY LIFE	*Epic 82876743122*	63		

OSIBISA Ghanaian/Nigerian group

Date	Title	Label	Peak Position	Weeks at No.1	Weeks in Top 40
17 Jan 76	SUNSHINE DAY	*Bronze BRO 20*	17		4
5 Jun 76	DANCE THE BODY MUSIC	*Bronze BRO 26*	31		4

DONNY OSMOND US singer

Date	Title	Label	Peak Position	Weeks at No.1	Weeks in Top 40
17 Jun 72	PUPPY LOVE	*MGM 2006 104*	1	5	17
16 Sep 72	TOO YOUNG	*MGM 2006 113*	5		11

Platinum-selling · Gold-selling · Silver-selling · US No.1 ★ · Peak Position · Weeks at No.1 · Weeks in Top 40

Date	Title	Label	Peak Position	Weeks at No.1	Weeks in Top 40
11 Nov 72	WHY	MGM 2006 119	3		15
10 Mar 73	THE TWELFTH OF NEVER	MGM 2006 199	1	1	12
18 Aug 73	YOUNG LOVE	MGM 2006 300	1	4	9
10 Nov 73	WHEN I FALL IN LOVE	MGM 2006 365	4		11
9 Nov 74	WHERE DID ALL THE GOOD TIMES GO	MGM 2006 468	18		5
26 Sep 87	I'M IN IT FOR LOVE	Virgin VS 994	70		
6 Aug 88	SOLDIER OF LOVE	Virgin VS 1094	29		3
12 Nov 88	IF IT'S LOVE THAT YOU WANT	Virgin VS 1140	70		
9 Feb 91	MY LOVE IS A FIRE	Capitol CL 600	64		
2 Oct 04	BREEZE ON BY	Decca 9863140	8		2

DONNY & MARIE OSMOND
US duo

Date	Title	Label	Peak Position	Weeks at No.1	Weeks in Top 40
3 Aug 74	I'M LEAVING IT (ALL) UP TO YOU	MGM 2006 446	2		11
14 Dec 74	MORNING SIDE OF THE MOUNTAIN	MGM 2006 274	5		9
21 Jun 75	MAKE THE WORLD GO AWAY	MGM 2006 523	18		6
17 Jan 76	DEEP PURPLE	MGM 2006 561	25		7

LITTLE JIMMY OSMOND US singer

Date	Title	Label	Peak Position	Weeks at No.1	Weeks in Top 40
25 Nov 72	LONG HAIRED LOVER FROM LIVERPOOL	MGM 2006 109	1	5	22
31 Mar 73	TWEEDLE DEE	MGM 2006 175	4		10
23 Mar 74	I'M GONNA KNOCK ON YOUR DOOR	MGM 2006 389	11		8

MARIE OSMOND US singer

Date	Title	Label	Peak Position	Weeks at No.1	Weeks in Top 40
17 Nov 73	PAPER ROSES	MGM 2006 315	2		14

OSMOND BOYS US group

Date	Title	Label	Peak Position	Weeks at No.1	Weeks in Top 40
9 Nov 91	BOYS WILL BE BOYS	Curb 6573847	65		
11 Jan 92	SHOW ME THE WAY	Curb 6577227	60		

OSMONDS US group

Date	Title	Label	Peak Position	Weeks at No.1	Weeks in Top 40
25 Mar 72	DOWN BY THE LAZY RIVER	MGM 2006 096	40		2
11 Nov 72	CRAZY HORSES	MGM 2006 142	2		16
14 Jul 73	GOING HOME	MGM 2006 288	4		9
27 Oct 73	LET ME IN	MGM 2006 321	2		13
20 Apr 74	I CAN'T STOP	MCA 129	12		8
24 Aug 74	LOVE ME FOR A REASON	MGM 2006 458	1	3	8
1 Mar 75	HAVING A PARTY	MGM 2006 492	28		5
24 May 75	THE PROUD ONE	MGM 2006 520	5		8
15 Nov 75	I'M STILL GONNA NEED YOU	MGM 2006 551	32		2
30 Oct 76	I CAN'T LIVE A DREAM	Polydor 2066 726	37		1
23 Sep 95	CRAZY HORSES (REMIX)	Polydor 5793212	50		
12 Jun 99	CRAZY HORSES	Polydor 5611372	34		1

GILBERT O'SULLIVAN Irish singer/pianist

Date	Title	Label	Peak Position	Weeks at No.1	Weeks in Top 40
28 Nov 70	NOTHING RHYMED	MAM 3	8		9
3 Apr 71	UNDERNEATH THE BLANKET GO	MAM 13	40		1
24 Jul 71	WE WILL	MAM 30	16		9
27 Nov 71	NO MATTER HOW I TRY	MAM 53	5		13
4 Mar 72	ALONE AGAIN (NATURALLY)	MAM 66 ★	3		11
17 Jun 72	OOH-WAKKA-DOO-WAKKA-DAY	MAM 78	8		10
21 Oct 72	CLAIR	MAM 84	1	2	13
17 Mar 73	GET DOWN	MAM 96	1	2	12
15 Sep 73	OOH BABY	MAM 107	18		6
10 Nov 73	WHY OH WHY OH WHY	MAM 111	6		12
9 Feb 74	HAPPINESS IS ME AND YOU	MAM 114	19		5
24 Aug 74	A WOMAN'S PLACE	MAM 122	42		
14 Dec 74	CHRISTMAS SONG	MAM 124	12		5
14 Jun 75	I DON'T LOVE YOU BUT I THINK I LIKE YOU	MAM 130	14		5
27 Sep 80	WHAT'S IN A KISS?	CBS 8929	19		7
24 Feb 90	SO WHAT	Dover ROJ 3	70		

OTHER TWO UK duo

Date	Title	Label	Peak Position	Weeks at No.1	Weeks in Top 40
9 Nov 91	TASTY FISH	Factory FAC 3297	41		
6 Nov 93	SELFISH	London TWOCD 1	46		

OTHERS UK group

Date	Title	Label	Peak Position	Weeks at No.1	Weeks in Top 40
29 May 04	THIS IS FOR THE POOR	Poptones MC5090SCD	42		
6 Nov 04	STAN BOWLES	Vertigo 9868521	36		1
29 Jan 05	LACKEY	Vertigo 9869350	21		1
16 Apr 05	WILLIAM	Poptones 9870861	29		1

JOHNNY OTIS US singer

Date	Title	Label	Peak Position	Weeks at No.1	Weeks in Top 40
22 Nov 57	MA HE'S MAKING EYES AT ME JOHNNY OTIS & HIS ORCHESTRA WITH MARIE ADAMS & THE THREE TONS OF JOY	Capitol CL 14794	2		15
10 Jan 58	BYE BYE BABY JOHNNY OTIS SHOW, VOCALS BY MARIE ADAMS & JOHNNY OTIS	Capitol CL 14817	20		7

OTT Irish group

Date	Title	Label	Peak Position	Weeks at No.1	Weeks in Top 40
15 Feb 97	LET ME IN	Epic 6642052	12		4
17 May 97	FOREVER GIRL	Epic 6645082	24		1
23 Aug 97	ALL OUT OF LOVE	Epic 6649152	11		3
24 Jan 98	THE STORY OF LOVE	Epic OTT 1CD	11		4

OTTOWAN Martiniquan duo

Date	Title	Label	Peak Position	Weeks at No.1	Weeks in Top 40
13 Sep 80	D.I.S.C.O.	Carrere CAR 161	2		11
13 Dec 80	YOU'RE OK	Carrere CAR 168	56		
29 Aug 81	HANDS UP (GIVE ME YOUR HEART)	Carrere CAR 183	3		11
5 Dec 81	HELP, GET ME SOME HELP!	Carrere CAR 215	49		

JOHN OTWAY & WILD WILLY BARRETT
UK duo

Date	Title	Label	Peak Position	Weeks at No.1	Weeks in Top 40
3 Dec 77	REALLY FREE	Polydor 2058 951	27		6
5 Jul 80	DK 50-80 OTWAY AND BARRET	Polydor 2059 250	45		
12 Oct 02	BUNSEN BURNER JOHN OTWAY	U-vibe OTWAY 02Z	9		2

OUI 3 US group

Date	Title	Label	Peak Position	Weeks at No.1	Weeks in Top 40
20 Feb 93	FOR WHAT IT'S WORTH	MCA MCSTD 1736	28		4
24 Apr 93	ARMS OF SOLITUDE	MCA MCSTD 1759	54		
17 Jul 93	BREAK FROM THE OLD ROUTINE	MCA MCSTD 1793	17		4
23 Oct 93	FOR WHAT IT'S WORTH (REMIX)	MCA MCSTD 1941	26		2
29 Jan 94	FACT OF LIFE	MCA MCSTD 1939	38		1
27 May 95	JOY OF LIVING	MCA MCSTD 2057	55		

OUR DAUGHTER'S WEDDING US group

Date	Title	Label	Peak Position	Weeks at No.1	Weeks in Top 40
1 Aug 81	LAWNCHAIRS	EMI America EA 124	49		

OUR HOUSE Australian production duo

Date	Title	Label	Peak Position	Weeks at No.1	Weeks in Top 40
31 Aug 96	FLOOR SPACE	Perfecto PERF 125CD	52		

OUR KID UK group

Date	Title	Label	Peak Position	Weeks at No.1	Weeks in Top 40
29 May 76	YOU JUST MIGHT SEE ME CRY	Polydor 2058 729	2		10

OUR LADY PEACE Canadian group

Date	Title	Label	Peak Position	Weeks at No.1	Weeks in Top 40
15 Jan 00	ONE MAN ARMY	Epic 6688662	70		

OUR TRIBE/ONE TRIBE UK/US duo

Date	Title	Label	Peak Position	Weeks at No.1	Weeks in Top 40
20 Jun 92	WHAT HAVE YOU DONE (IS THIS ALL) ONE TRIBE FEATURING GEM	Inner Rhythm HEART 03	52		
27 Mar 93	I BELIEVE IN YOU OUR TRIBE	ffrreedom TABCD 117	42		
30 Apr 94	HOLD THAT SUCKER DOWN OT QUARTET	Cheeky CHEKCD 004	24		2
21 May 94	LOVE COME HOME OUR TRIBE WITH FRANKE PHAROAH & KRISTINE W	Triangle BLUESCD 001	73		
13 May 95	HIGH AS A KITE ONE TRIBE FEATURING ROGER	ffrr FCD 259	55		
30 Sep 95	HOLD THAT SUCKER DOWN (REMIX) OT QUARTET	Cheeky CHEKCD 009	26		2
9 Dec 00	HOLD THAT SUCKER DOWN OT QUARTET	Champion CHAMPCD 786	45		

OUT OF MY HAIR UK group

Date	Title	Label	Peak Position	Weeks at No.1	Weeks in Top 40
1 Jul 95	MISTER JONES	RCA 74321267812	73		

Silver-selling ○ Gold-selling ● Platinum-selling ✪ US No.1 ★ — Peak Position / Weeks at No.1 / Weeks in Top 40

OUT OF OFFICE UK group

Date	Title	Label	Peak Position	Weeks at No.1	Weeks in Top 40
22 Sep 07	HANDS UP	*Frenetic FRE1CDX*	52		
23 Feb 08	BREAK OF DAWN 2008	*Frenetic FRE7CDX*	41		

OUTHERE BROTHERS US group

Date	Title	Label	Peak Position	Weeks at No.1	Weeks in Top 40
18 Mar 95	DON'T STOP (WIGGLE WIGGLE)	*Stip YZ 917CD* ●	1	1	13
17 Jun 95	BOOM BOOM BOOM	*Stip YZ 938CD* ●	1	4	13
23 Sep 95	LA LA LA HEY HEY	*Stip YZ 974CD*	7		5
16 Dec 95	IF YOU WANNA PARTY MOLELLA FEATURING THE OUTHERE BROTHERS	*Stip 030CD*	9		8
25 Jan 97	LET ME HEAR YOU SAY 'OLE OLE'	*Stip 089CD*	18		2

OUTKAST US duo

Date	Title	Label	Peak Position	Weeks at No.1	Weeks in Top 40
23 Dec 00	B.O.B. (BOMBS OVER BAGHDAD)	*LaFace 74321822942*	61		
3 Feb 01	MS JACKSON (IMPORT)	*LaFace 73008245252*	48		
3 Mar 01	MS JACKSON	*LaFace 74321836822* ○ ★	2		8
9 Jun 01	SO FRESH SO CLEAN	*LaFace 74321863402*	16		2
6 Apr 02	THE WHOLE WORLD OUTKAST FEATURING KILLER MIKE	*LaFace 74321917592*	19		3
27 Jul 02	LAND OF A MILLION DRUMS OUTKAST FEATURING KILLER MIKE & SLEEPY BROWN	*Atlantic AT 0134CD*	46		
4 Oct 03	GHETTO MUSICK	*Arista 82876567232*	55		
22 Nov 03	HEY YA!	*Arista 82876580102* ★	3		19
3 Apr 04	THE WAY YOU MOVE OUTKAST FEATURING SLEEPY BROWN ★	*Arista 82876605672*	7		7
3 Jul 04	ROSES	*Arista 82876624392*	4		4
9 Sep 06	MORRIS BROWN	*LaFace 82876808422*	43		

OUTLANDER Belgian producer

Date	Title	Label	Peak Position	Weeks at No.1	Weeks in Top 40
31 Aug 91	VAMP	*R&S RSUK 1*	51		
7 Feb 98	THE VAMP (REVISITED)	*R&S RS 97113CDX*	62		

OUTLANDISH Danish/Honduran group

Date	Title	Label	Peak Position	Weeks at No.1	Weeks in Top 40
31 May 03	GUANTANAMO	*RCA 82876517702*	31		1

OUTLAWS UK group

Date	Title	Label	Peak Position	Weeks at No.1	Weeks in Top 40
13 Apr 61	SWINGIN' LOW	*HMV POP 844*	46		
8 Jun 61	AMBUSH	*HMV POP 877*	43		

OUTRAGE US singer

Date	Title	Label	Peak Position	Weeks at No.1	Weeks in Top 40
11 Mar 95	TALL 'N' HANDSOME	*Effective ECFL 001CD*	57		
23 Nov 96	TALL 'N' HANDSOME (REMIX)	*Positiva CDTIV 64*	51		

OUTSIDAZ US group

Date	Title	Label	Peak Position	Weeks at No.1	Weeks in Top 40
2 Mar 02	I'M LEAVIN' OUTSIDAZ FEATURING RAH DIGGA & MELANIE BLATT	*Rufflife RLCDM 03*	41		

OUTWORK Italian producer

Date	Title	Label	Peak Position	Weeks at No.1	Weeks in Top 40
16 Dec 06	ELEKTRO OUTWORK FEATURING MR GEE	*Defected DFTD137CDS*	49		

OVERCAST UK group

Date	Title	Label	Peak Position	Weeks at No.1	Weeks in Top 40
10 Mar 07	NO BIG DEAL OVERCAST & BECKY MEASURES	*Logik BECKY1*	67		

OVERLANDERS UK group

Date	Title	Label	Peak Position	Weeks at No.1	Weeks in Top 40
13 Jan 66	MICHELLE	*Pye 7N 17034*	1	3	9

OVERWEIGHT POOCH US rapper

Date	Title	Label	Peak Position	Weeks at No.1	Weeks in Top 40
18 Jan 92	I LIKE IT OVERWEIGHT POOCH FEATURING CE CE PENISTON	*A&M AM 847*	58		

MARK OWEN UK singer

Date	Title	Label	Peak Position	Weeks at No.1	Weeks in Top 40
30 Nov 96	CHILD	*RCA 74321424422* ○	3		6
15 Feb 97	CLEMENTINE	*RCA 74321454992*	3		4
23 Aug 97	I AM WHAT I AM	*RCA 74321501222*	29		1
16 Aug 03	FOUR MINUTE WARNING	*Universal MCSTD 40329*	4		6
8 Nov 03	ALONE WITHOUT YOU	*Universal MCSXD 40342*	26		1
19 Jun 04	MAKIN' OUT	*Sedna CXSEDNA1*	30		1
3 Sep 05	BELIEVE IN THE BOOGIE	*Sedna SEDNACS1*	57		

REG OWEN UK orchestra leader

Date	Title	Label	Peak Position	Weeks at No.1	Weeks in Top 40
27 Feb 59	MANHATTAN SPIRITUAL	*Pye International 7N 25009*	20		8
27 Oct 60	OBSESSION	*Palette PG 9004*	43		

SID OWEN UK singer

Date	Title	Label	Peak Position	Weeks at No.1	Weeks in Top 40
16 Dec 95	BETTER BELIEVE IT (CHILDREN IN NEED) SID OWEN & PATSY PALMER	*Trinity TDM 001CD*	60		
8 Jul 00	GOOD THING GOING	*Mushroom MUSH 74CDS*	14		3

ROBERT OWENS US singer

Date	Title	Label	Peak Position	Weeks at No.1	Weeks in Top 40
7 Dec 91	I'LL BE YOUR FRIEND	*Perfecto PB 45161*	75		
26 Apr 97	I'LL BE YOUR FRIEND (REMIX)	*Perfecto PERF 137CD1*	25		1
24 Feb 01	MINE TO GIVE PHOTEK FEATURING ROBERT OWENS	*Science QEDCD 10*	44		
15 Feb 03	LAST NIGHT A DJ BLEW MY MIND FAB FOR FEATURING ROBERT OWENS	*Illustrious CDILL 013*	34		1

OXIDE & NEUTRINO UK duo

Date	Title	Label	Peak Position	Weeks at No.1	Weeks in Top 40
6 May 00	BOUND 4 DA RELOAD (CASUALTY)	*East West OXIDE01CD1* ○	1	1	7
30 Dec 00	NO GOOD 4 ME OXIDE & NEUTRINO FEATURING MEGAMAN, ROMEO & LISA MAFFIA	*East West OXIDE02CD*	6		6
26 May 01	UP MIDDLE FINGER	*East West OXIDE 03CD*	7		3
28 Jul 01	DEVIL'S NIGHTMARE	*East West OXIDE 07CD1*	16		3
8 Dec 01	RAP DIS/ONLY WANNA KNOW U COS URE FAMOUS	*East West OXIDE 08CD*	12		6
28 Sep 02	DEM GIRLZ (I DON'T KNOW WHY) OXIDE & NEUTRINO FEATURING KOWDEAN	*East West OXIDE 09CD*	10		3

OXYGEN UK production duo

Date	Title	Label	Peak Position	Weeks at No.1	Weeks in Top 40
11 Jan 03	AM I ON YOUR MIND OXYGEN FEATURING ANDREA BRITTON	*Innocent SINCD 40*	30		1

OYSTAR UK group

Date	Title	Label	Peak Position	Weeks at No.1	Weeks in Top 40
19 Jan 08	I FOUGHT THE LLOYDS	*Download*	25		1

OZOMATLI US group

Date	Title	Label	Peak Position	Weeks at No.1	Weeks in Top 40
20 Mar 99	CUT CHEMIST SUITE	*Almo Sounds CDALM 62*	58		
22 May 99	SUPER BOWL SUNDAE	*Almo Sounds CDALM 63*	68		

P

JAMESY P St Vincent singer

Date	Title	Label	Peak Position	Weeks at No.1	Weeks in Top 40
24 Sep 05	NOOKIE	*Smoove SMOOVE04CDS*	14		3

JAZZI P UK rapper

Date	Title	Label	Peak Position	Weeks at No.1	Weeks in Top 40
8 Jul 89	GET LOOSE L.A. MIX PERFORMED BY JAZZI P	*Breakout USA 659*	25		4
9 Jun 90	FEEL THE RHYTHM	*A&M USA 691*	51		
3 Aug 91	REBEL WOMAN DNA FEATURING JAZZI P	*DNA 7DNA 001*	42		

TALISMAN P UK producer

Date	Title	Peak Position	Weeks at No.1	Weeks in Top 40
13 Oct 01	**HERE I COME (SING DJ)** *NuLife 74321895622* TALISMAN P MEETS BARRINGTON LEVY	37		1

PETEY PABLO US rapper

Date	Title	Peak Position	Weeks at No.1	Weeks in Top 40
9 Feb 02	**I** *Jive 9253092*	51		
15 Jan 05	**GOODIES (IMPORT)** *Jive 82876648252* CIARA FEATURING PETEY PABLO	68		
29 Jan 05	**GOODIES** *LaFace 82876673132* CIARA FEATURING PETEY PABLO ★	1	1	6

THOM PACE US singer

Date	Title	Peak Position	Weeks at No.1	Weeks in Top 40
19 May 79	**MAYBE** *RSO 34*	14		9

PACIFICA UK production duo

Date	Title	Peak Position	Weeks at No.1	Weeks in Top 40
31 Jul 99	**LOST IN THE TRANSLATION** *Wildstar CDWILD 25*	54		

PACK UK group

Date	Title	Peak Position	Weeks at No.1	Weeks in Top 40
8 Dec 90	**STAND AND FIGHT** *IQ ZB 44237* PACK FEATURING NIGEL BENN	61		

PACKABEATS UK group

Date	Title	Peak Position	Weeks at No.1	Weeks in Top 40
23 Feb 61	**GYPSY BEAT** *Parlophone R 4729*	49		

PADDINGTONS UK group

Date	Title	Peak Position	Weeks at No.1	Weeks in Top 40
23 Oct 04	**21/SOME OLD GIRL** *Poptones MC5093SCD*	47		
7 May 05	**PANIC ATTACK** *Poptones 9870603*	25		1
23 Jul 05	**50 TO A POUND** *Poptones 9872739*	32		1
29 Oct 05	**SORRY** *Poptones 9873961*	41		

JOSE PADILLA Spanish producer

Date	Title	Peak Position	Weeks at No.1	Weeks in Top 40
8 Aug 98	**WHO DO YOU LOVE** *Manifesto FESCD 45* JOSE PADILLA FEATURING ANGELA JOHN	59		

PAFFENDORF German group

Date	Title	Peak Position	Weeks at No.1	Weeks in Top 40
15 Jun 02	**BE COOL** *Data 29CDS*	7		5
26 Apr 03	**CRAZY SEXY MARVELLOUS** *Data 51CDS*	52		

PAGANINI TRAXX Italian producer

Date	Title	Peak Position	Weeks at No.1	Weeks in Top 40
1 Feb 97	**ZOE** *Sony S3 DANCUCD 18X*	47		

JIMMY PAGE UK guitarist

Date	Title	Peak Position	Weeks at No.1	Weeks in Top 40
17 Dec 94	**GALLOWS POLE** *Fontana PPCD 2* JIMMY PAGE & ROBERT PLANT	35		1
11 Apr 98	**MOST HIGH** *Mercury 5687512* JIMMY PAGE & ROBERT PLANT	26		1
1 Aug 98	**COME WITH ME (IMPORT)** *Epic 34K78954* PUFF DADDY FEATURING JIMMY PAGE	75		
8 Aug 98	**COME WITH ME** *Epic 6662842* PUFF DADDY FEATURING JIMMY PAGE	2		7

PATTI PAGE US singer

Date	Title	Peak Position	Weeks at No.1	Weeks in Top 40
27 Mar 53	**(HOW MUCH IS) THAT DOGGIE IN THE WINDOW** *Oriole CB 1156* ★	9		5

TOMMY PAGE US singer

Date	Title	Peak Position	Weeks at No.1	Weeks in Top 40
26 May 90	**I'LL BE YOUR EVERYTHING** *Sire W 9959* ★	53		

PAGLIARO Canadian singer

Date	Title	Peak Position	Weeks at No.1	Weeks in Top 40
19 Feb 72	**LOVING YOU AIN'T EASY** *Pye 7N 45111*	31		4

PAID + LIVE US production duo

Date	Title	Peak Position	Weeks at No.1	Weeks in Top 40
27 Dec 97	**ALL MY TIME** *World Entertainment OWECD 2* PAID + LIVE FEATURING LAURYN HILL	57		

ELAINE PAIGE UK singer

Date	Title	Peak Position	Weeks at No.1	Weeks in Top 40
21 Oct 78	**DON'T WALK AWAY TILL I TOUCH YOU** *EMI 2862*	46		
6 Jun 81	**MEMORY** *Polydor POSP 279* ●	6		9
30 Jan 82	**MEMORY** *Polydor POSP 279*	67		
14 Apr 84	**SOMETIMES (THEME FROM CHAMPIONS)** *Island IS 174*	72		
5 Jan 85	**I KNOW HIM SO WELL** *RCA CHESS 3* ELAINE PAIGE & BARBARA DICKSON ●	1	4	13
21 Nov 87	**THE SECOND TIME (THEME FROM BILITIS)** *WEA YZ 163*	69		
21 Jan 95	**HYMNE A L'AMOUR (IF YOU LOVE ME)** *WEA YZ 899CD*	68		
24 Oct 98	**MEMORY** *WEA 197CD*	36		1

HAL PAIGE & THE WHALERS US group

Date	Title	Peak Position	Weeks at No.1	Weeks in Top 40
25 Aug 60	**GOING BACK TO MY HOME TOWN** *Melodisc MEL 1553*	50		

JENNIFER PAIGE US singer

Date	Title	Peak Position	Weeks at No.1	Weeks in Top 40
12 Sep 98	**CRUSH** *EAR 0039425 ERE* ○	4		10
20 Mar 99	**SOBER** *EAR 0044185 ERE*	68		

ORCHESTRE DE CHAMBRE JEAN-FRANÇOIS PAILLARD French orchestra

Date	Title	Peak Position	Weeks at No.1	Weeks in Top 40
20 Aug 88	**THEME FROM 'VIETNAM' (CANON IN D)** *Debut DEBT 3053*	61		

PALE Irish group

Date	Title	Peak Position	Weeks at No.1	Weeks in Top 40
13 Jun 92	**DOGS WITH NO TAILS** *A&M AM 866*	51		

PALE FOUNTAINS UK group

Date	Title	Peak Position	Weeks at No.1	Weeks in Top 40
27 Nov 82	**THANK YOU** *Virgin VS 557*	48		

PALE SAINTS UK group

Date	Title	Peak Position	Weeks at No.1	Weeks in Top 40
6 Jul 91	**KINKY LOVE** *4AD AD 1009*	72		

PALE X Dutch producer

Date	Title	Peak Position	Weeks at No.1	Weeks in Top 40
3 Feb 01	**NITRO** *Nukleuz NUKP 0280*	74		

PALLADIUM UK group

Date	Title	Peak Position	Weeks at No.1	Weeks in Top 40
17 Nov 07	**HIGH 5** *Virgin VSCDT1957*	44		

NERINA PALLOT UK singer

Date	Title	Peak Position	Weeks at No.1	Weeks in Top 40
18 Aug 01	**PATIENCE** *Polydor 5872122*	61		
27 May 06	**EVERYBODY'S GONE TO WAR** *14th Floor 14FLR13CD*	14		5
14 Oct 06	**SOPHIA** *14th Floor 14FLR16CD*	32		1
20 Jan 07	**LEARNING TO BREATHE** *14th Floor 14FLR18CD*	70		

JHAY PALMER Jamaican singer

Date	Title	Peak Position	Weeks at No.1	Weeks in Top 40
27 Apr 02	**HELLO** *Bagatrix CDBTX 002* JHAY PALMER FEATURING MC IMAGE	69		

ROBERT PALMER UK singer

Date	Title	Peak Position	Weeks at No.1	Weeks in Top 40
20 May 78	**EVERY KINDA PEOPLE** *Island WIP 6425*	53		
7 Jul 79	**BAD CASE OF LOVIN' YOU (DOCTOR DOCTOR)** *Island WIP 6481*	61		
6 Sep 80	**JOHNNY AND MARY** *Island WIP 6638*	44		
22 Nov 80	**LOOKING FOR CLUES** *Island WIP 6651*	33		6
13 Feb 82	**SOME GUYS HAVE ALL THE LUCK** *Island WIP 6754*	16		6
2 Apr 83	**YOU ARE IN MY SYSTEM** *Island IS 104*	53		
18 Jun 83	**YOU CAN HAVE IT (TAKE MY HEART)** *Island IS 121*	66		
10 May 86	**ADDICTED TO LOVE** *Island IS 270* ○ ★	5		12
19 Jul 86	**I DIDN'T MEAN TO TURN YOU ON** *Island IS 283*	9		7
1 Nov 86	**DISCIPLINE OF LOVE** *Island IS 242*	68		
26 Mar 88	**SWEET LIES** *Island IS 352*	58		
11 Jun 88	**SIMPLY IRRESISTIBLE** *EMI EM 61*	44		

Silver-selling ◌ Gold-selling ● Platinum-selling ⊛ US No.1 ★ | Peak Position | Weeks at No.1 | Weeks in Top 40

Date	Title / Label	Peak Position	Weeks at No.1	Weeks in Top 40
15 Oct 88	**SHE MAKES MY DAY** *EMI EM 65*	6		8
13 May 89	**CHANGE HIS WAYS** *EMI EM 85*	28		4
26 Aug 89	**IT COULD HAPPEN TO YOU** *EMI EM 99*	71		
3 Nov 90	**I'LL BE YOUR BABY TONIGHT** *EMI EM 167* ROBERT PALMER & UB40	6		8
5 Jan 91	**MERCY MERCY ME - I WANT YOU** *EMI EM 173*	9		7
15 Jun 91	**DREAMS TO REMEMBER** *EMI 193*	68		
7 Mar 92	**EVERY KINDA PEOPLE (REMIX)** *Island IS 498*	43		
17 Oct 92	**WITCHCRAFT** *EMI EM 251*	50		
9 Jul 94	**GIRL U WANT** *EMI CDEMS 331*	57		
3 Sep 94	**KNOW BY NOW** *EMI CDEMS 343*	25		4
24 Dec 94	**YOU BLOW ME AWAY** *EMI CDEMS 350*	38		2
14 Oct 95	**RESPECT YOURSELF** *EMI CDEMS 399*	45		
18 Jan 03	**ADDICTED TO LOVE** *Serious SER 606CD* SHAKE B4 USE VS ROBERT PALMER	42		

SUZANNE PALMER UK singer

Date	Title / Label	Peak Position	Weeks at No.1	Weeks in Top 40
18 Jan 97	**I BELIEVE** *AM:PM 5820752* ABSOLUTE FEATURING SUZANNE PALMER	38		1
14 Nov 98	**ALRIGHT** *Twisted UK TWCD 10039* CLUB 69 FEATURING SUZANNE PALMER	70		
29 Jun 02	**643 (LOVE'S ON FIRE)** *Nebula VCRD 106* DJ TIESTO FEATURING SUZANNE PALMER	36		1

PAN POSITION Italian/Venezuelan group

Date	Title / Label	Peak Position	Weeks at No.1	Weeks in Top 40
18 Jun 94	**ELEPHANT PAW (GET DOWN TO THE FUNK)** *Positiva CDTIV 13*	55		

PANDORA'S BOX US group

Date	Title / Label	Peak Position	Weeks at No.1	Weeks in Top 40
21 Oct 89	**IT'S ALL COMING BACK TO ME NOW** *Virgin VS 1216*	51		

DARRYL PANDY US singer

Date	Title / Label	Peak Position	Weeks at No.1	Weeks in Top 40
14 Dec 96	**LOVE CAN'T TURN AROUND** *4 Liberty LIBTCD 27R* FARLEY 'JACKMASTER' FUNK FEATURING DARRYL PANDY	40		1
20 Feb 99	**RAISE YOUR HANDS** *VC Recordings VCRD 44* BIG ROOM GIRL FEATURING DARRYL PANDY	40		1
2 Oct 99	**SUNSHINE & HAPPINESS** *Azuli AZNYCD 103* DARRYL PANDY/NERIO'S DUBWORK	68		

JOHNNY PANIC UK group

Date	Title / Label	Peak Position	Weeks at No.1	Weeks in Top 40
18 Sep 04	**BURN YOUR YOUTH** *Concept CDCON59*	69		
14 May 05	**MINORITY OF ONE** *Concept CDCON63*	60		

JOHNNY PANIC & THE BIBLE OF DREAMS UK duo

Date	Title / Label	Peak Position	Weeks at No.1	Weeks in Top 40
2 Feb 91	**JOHNNY PANIC AND THE BIBLE OF DREAMS** *Fontana PANIC 1* JOHNNY PANIC & THE BIBLE OF DREAMS	70		

PANIC! AT THE DISCO US group

Date	Title / Label	Peak Position	Weeks at No.1	Weeks in Top 40
13 May 06	**BUT IT'S BETTER IF YOU DO** *Decaydance/Fueled By Ramen AT0242CD*	23		2
19 Aug 06	**LYING IS THE MOST FUN A GIRL CAN HAVE** *Decaydance/Fueled By Ramen AT0247CD*	39		1
4 Nov 06	**I WRITE SINS NOT TRAGEDIES** *Decaydance/Fueled By Ramen AT0259CD*	25		3
22 Mar 08	**NINE IN THE AFTERNOON** *Decaydance/Fueled By Ramen AT0303CD*	13		2

PANJABI MC UK singer

Date	Title / Label	Peak Position	Weeks at No.1	Weeks in Top 40
4 Jan 03	**MUNDIAN TO BACH KE (IMPORT)** *Big Star Big CDM 076CD*	59		
25 Jan 03	**MUNDIAN TO BACH KE** *Showbiz/Instant Karma KARMA 28CD*	5		7
5 Jul 03	**JOGI/BEWARE OF THE BOYS** *Showbiz/Dharma DHARMA 1CDS* PANJABI MC FEATURING JAY-Z	25		2

PANTERA US group

Date	Title / Label	Peak Position	Weeks at No.1	Weeks in Top 40
10 Oct 92	**MOUTH FOR WAR** *Atco A 5845T*	73		
27 Feb 93	**WALK** *Atco B 6076CD*	35		1
19 Mar 94	**I'M BROKEN** *Atco B 5832CD1*	19		1
22 Oct 94	**PLANET CARAVAN** *East West A 5836CD1*	26		1

PAPA ROACH US group

Date	Title / Label	Peak Position	Weeks at No.1	Weeks in Top 40
17 Feb 01	**LAST RESORT** *DreamWorks 4509212*	3		6
5 May 01	**BETWEEN ANGELS AND INSECTS** *DreamWorks 4509092*	17		3
22 Jun 02	**SHE LOVES ME NOT** *DreamWorks 4508182*	14		3
2 Nov 02	**TIME AND TIME AGAIN** *DreamWorks 4508052*	54		
18 Sep 04	**GETTING AWAY WITH MURDER** *Geffen 9863647*	45		

PAPER DOLLS UK group

Date	Title / Label	Peak Position	Weeks at No.1	Weeks in Top 40
13 Mar 68	**SOMETHING HERE IN MY HEART (KEEPS A-TELLIN' ME NO)** *Pye 7N 17456*	11		10

PAPER LACE UK group

Date	Title / Label	Peak Position	Weeks at No.1	Weeks in Top 40
23 Feb 74	**BILLY, DON'T BE A HERO** *Bus Stop BUS 1014* ●	1	3	12
4 May 74	**THE NIGHT CHICAGO DIED** *Bus Stop BUS 1016* ◌ ★	3		10
24 Aug 74	**THE BLACK EYED BOYS** *Bus Stop BUS 1019*	11		8
4 Mar 78	**WE'VE GOT THE WHOLE WORLD IN OUR HANDS** *Warner Brothers K 17110* NOTTINGHAM FOREST FC & PAPER LACE	24		5

PAPERDOLLS UK group

Date	Title / Label	Peak Position	Weeks at No.1	Weeks in Top 40
12 Sep 98	**GONNA MAKE YOU BLUSH** *MCA MCSTD 40175*	65		

PAPPA BEAR German rapper

Date	Title / Label	Peak Position	Weeks at No.1	Weeks in Top 40
16 May 98	**CHERISH** *Universal UMD 70316* PAPPA BEAR FEATURING VAN DER TOORN	47		

PAR-T-ONE Italian producer

Date	Title / Label	Peak Position	Weeks at No.1	Weeks in Top 40
3 Nov 01	**I'M SO CRAZY** *Credence CDCRED 016* PAR-T-ONE VS INXS	19		2

PARA BEATS UK production duo

Date	Title / Label	Peak Position	Weeks at No.1	Weeks in Top 40
27 Aug 05	**U GOT ME** *Onetwo ONETCDS003* PARA BEATS FEATURING CARMEN REECE	59		

VANESSA PARADIS French singer

Date	Title / Label	Peak Position	Weeks at No.1	Weeks in Top 40
13 Feb 88	**JOE LE TAXI** *FA Productions POSP 902*	3		8
10 Oct 92	**BE MY BABY** *Remark PO 235*	6		8
27 Feb 93	**SUNDAY MORNINGS** *Remark PZCD 251*	49		
24 Jul 93	**JUST AS LONG AS YOU ARE THERE** *Remark PZCD 272*	57		

PARADISE UK group

Date	Title / Label	Peak Position	Weeks at No.1	Weeks in Top 40
10 Sep 83	**ONE MIND, TWO HEARTS** *Priority P 1*	42		
9 Jul 05	**SEE THE LIGHT** *Turbulence CDTURB1*	73		

PARADISE LOST UK group

Date	Title / Label	Peak Position	Weeks at No.1	Weeks in Top 40
20 May 95	**THE LAST TIME** *Music For Nations CDKUT 165*	60		
7 Oct 95	**FOREVER FAILURE** *Music For Nations CDKUT 169*	66		
28 Jun 97	**SAY JUST WORDS** *Music For Nations CDKUT 174*	53		

PARADISE ORGANISATION UK group

Date	Title / Label	Peak Position	Weeks at No.1	Weeks in Top 40
23 Jan 93	**PRAYER TOWER** *Cowboy RODEO 13*	70		

PARADOX UK producer

Date	Title / Label	Peak Position	Weeks at No.1	Weeks in Top 40
24 Feb 90	**JAILBREAK** *Ronin 7R2*	66		

NORRIE PARAMOR UK producer/orchestra leader

Date	Title / Label	Peak Position	Weeks at No.1	Weeks in Top 40
17 Mar 60	**THEME FROM *A SUMMER PLACE*** *Columbia DB 4419*	36		1
22 Mar 62	**THEME FROM *Z CARS*** *Columbia DB 4789*	33		2

PARAMORE US group

Date	Title / Label	Peak Position	Weeks at No.1	Weeks in Top 40
30 Jun 07	**MISERY BUSINESS (AUSTRALIA RELEASE)** *Atlantic AT0279CD*	17		2
8 Dec 07	**CRUSH CRUSH CRUSH** *Fueled By Ramen AT0295CD*	61		

Key: Silver-selling ● (light) · Gold-selling ● (dark) · Platinum-selling ⊛ · US No.1 ★ · Peak Position · Weeks at No.1 · Weeks in Top 40

PARAMOUNTS UK group

Date	Title / Label	Peak Position	Weeks at No.1	Weeks in Top 40
16 Jan 64	**POISON IVY** *Parlophone R 5093*	35		3

PARCHMENT UK group

Date	Title / Label	Peak Position	Weeks at No.1	Weeks in Top 40
16 Sep 72	**LIGHT UP THE FIRE** *Pye 7N 45178*	31		2

PARIS UK group

Date	Title / Label	Peak Position	Weeks at No.1	Weeks in Top 40
19 Jun 82	**NO GETTING OVER YOU** *RCA 222*	49		

PARIS US singer

Date	Title / Label	Peak Position	Weeks at No.1	Weeks in Top 40
21 Jan 95	**GUERRILLA FUNK** *Virgin PTYCD 100*	38		1

PARIS & SHARP UK production duo

Date	Title / Label	Peak Position	Weeks at No.1	Weeks in Top 40
1 Dec 01	**APHRODITE** *Cream 16CD*	61		

PARIS ANGELS Irish group

Date	Title / Label	Peak Position	Weeks at No.1	Weeks in Top 40
3 Nov 90	**SCOPE** *Sheer Joy SHEER 0047*	75		
20 Jul 91	**PERFUME** *Virgin VS 1360*	55		
21 Sep 91	**FADE** *Virgin VS 1365*	70		

MICA PARIS UK singer

Date	Title / Label	Peak Position	Weeks at No.1	Weeks in Top 40
7 May 88	**MY ONE TEMPTATION** *Fourth & Broadway BRW 85*	7		7
30 Jul 88	**LIKE DREAMERS DO** *Fourth & Broadway BRW 108* MICA PARIS FEATURING COURTNEY PINE	26		4
22 Oct 88	**BREATHE LIFE INTO ME** *Fourth & Broadway BRW 115*	26		5
21 Jan 89	**WHERE IS THE LOVE** *Fourth & Broadway BRW 122* MICA PARIS & WILL DOWNING	19		4
6 Oct 90	**CONTRIBUTION** *Fourth & Broadway BRW 188* MICA PARIS FEATURING RAKIM	33		2
1 Dec 90	**SOUTH OF THE RIVER** *Fourth & Broadway BRW 199*	50		
23 Feb 91	**IF I LOVE U 2 NITE** *Fourth & Broadway BRW 207*	43		
31 Aug 91	**YOUNG SOUL REBELS** *Big Life BLR 57*	61		
3 Apr 93	**I NEVER FELT LIKE THIS BEFORE** *Fourth & Broadway BRCD 263*	15		4
5 Jun 93	**I WANNA HOLD ON TO YOU** *Fourth & Broadway BRCD 275*	27		2
7 Aug 93	**TWO IN A MILLION** *Fourth & Broadway BRCD 285*	51		
4 Dec 93	**WHISPER A PRAYER** *Fourth & Broadway BRCD 287*	65		
8 Apr 95	**ONE** *Cooltempo CDCOOL 304*	29		2
16 May 98	**STAY** *Cooltempo CDCOOL 334*	40		1
14 Nov 98	**BLACK ANGEL** *Cooltempo CDCOOL 341*	72		

PARIS RED US/German duo

Date	Title / Label	Peak Position	Weeks at No.1	Weeks in Top 40
29 Feb 92	**GOOD FRIEND** *Columbia 6569417*	61		
15 May 93	**PROMISES** *Columbia 6592342*	59		

RYAN PARIS Italian singer

Date	Title / Label	Peak Position	Weeks at No.1	Weeks in Top 40
3 Sep 83	**DOLCE VITA** *Carrere CAR 289*	5		7

JOHN PARISH & POLLY JEAN HARVEY UK guitarist and singer

Date	Title / Label	Peak Position	Weeks at No.1	Weeks in Top 40
23 Nov 96	**THAT WAS MY VEIL** *Island CID 648*	75		

SIMON PARK ORCHESTRA UK orchestra leader

Date	Title / Label	Peak Position	Weeks at No.1	Weeks in Top 40
25 Nov 72	**EYE LEVEL** *Columbia DB 8946*	41		
15 Sep 73	**EYE LEVEL** *Columbia DB 8946* ⊛	1	4	18

GRAHAM PARKER UK singer

Date	Title / Label	Peak Position	Weeks at No.1	Weeks in Top 40
19 Mar 77	**THE PINK PARKER EP** *Vertigo PARK 001*	24		5
22 Apr 78	**HEY LORD DON'T ASK ME QUESTIONS** *Vertigo PARK 002* GRAHAM PARKER & THE RUMOUR	32		1
20 Mar 82	**TEMPORARY BEAUTY** *RCA PARK 100* GRAHAM PARKER & THE RUMOUR	50		

RAY PARKER JR US singer/guitarist

Date	Title / Label	Peak Position	Weeks at No.1	Weeks in Top 40
25 Aug 84	**GHOSTBUSTERS** *Arista ARIST 580* ● ★	2		24
18 Jan 86	**GIRLS ARE MORE FUN** *Arista ARIST 641*	46		
3 Oct 87	**I DON'T THINK THAT MAN SHOULD SLEEP ALONE** *Geffen GEF 27*	13		6
30 Jan 88	**OVER YOU** *Geffen GEF 33*	65		
10 Nov 07	**GHOSTBUSTERS** *Download*	70		

ROBERT PARKER US singer

Date	Title / Label	Peak Position	Weeks at No.1	Weeks in Top 40
4 Aug 66	**BAREFOOTIN'** *Island WI 286*	24		6

SARA PARKER US singer

Date	Title / Label	Peak Position	Weeks at No.1	Weeks in Top 40
12 Apr 97	**MY LOVE IS DEEP** *Manifesto FESCD 22*	22		1

JIMMY PARKINSON Australian singer

Date	Title / Label	Peak Position	Weeks at No.1	Weeks in Top 40
2 Mar 56	**THE GREAT PRETENDER** *Columbia DB 3729*	9		13
17 Aug 56	**WALK HAND IN HAND** *Columbia DB 3775*	26		2
9 Nov 56	**IN THE MIDDLE OF THE HOUSE** *Columbia DB 3833*	26		4

ALEX PARKS UK singer

Date	Title / Label	Peak Position	Weeks at No.1	Weeks in Top 40
29 Nov 03	**MAYBE THAT'S WHAT IT TAKES** *Polydor 9814581*	3		4
28 Feb 04	**CRY** *Polydor 9816986*	13		2
4 Feb 06	**HONESTY** *Polydor 9876837*	56		

PARKS & WILSON UK production duo

Date	Title / Label	Peak Position	Weeks at No.1	Weeks in Top 40
9 Sep 00	**FEEL THE DRUM (EP)** *Hooj Choons HOOJ 099CD*	71		

JOHN PARR UK singer

Date	Title / Label	Peak Position	Weeks at No.1	Weeks in Top 40
14 Sep 85	**ST ELMO'S FIRE (MAN IN MOTION)** *London LON 73* ● ★	6		9
18 Jan 86	**NAUGHTY NAUGHTY** *London 80*	58		
30 Aug 86	**ROCK 'N' ROLL MERCENARIES** *Arista ARIST 666* MEAT LOAF FEATURING JOHN PARR	31		4
24 Jun 06	**NEW HORIZON** *Gusto CDGUS35* JOHN PARR VERSUS TOMMYKNOCKERS	43		

DEAN PARRISH US singer

Date	Title / Label	Peak Position	Weeks at No.1	Weeks in Top 40
8 Feb 75	**I'M ON MY WAY** *UK USA 2*	38		1

MAN PARISH US producer

Date	Title / Label	Peak Position	Weeks at No.1	Weeks in Top 40
26 Mar 83	**HIP HOP, BE BOP (DON'T STOP)** *Polydor POSP 575*	41		
23 Mar 85	**BOOGIE DOWN (BRONX)** *Boiling Point POSP 731*	56		
13 Sep 86	**MALE STRIPPER** *Bolts 4* MAN 2 MAN MEET MAN PARRISH	64		
3 Jan 87	**MALE STRIPPER** *Bolts 4* MAN 2 MAN MEET MAN PARRISH ●	4		10

KAREN PARRY UK singer

Date	Title / Label	Peak Position	Weeks at No.1	Weeks in Top 40
28 Dec 02	**I THINK WE'RE ALONE NOW** *All Around The World CDGLOBE267* PASCAL FEATURING KAREN PARRY	23		3
24 Jul 04	**DISCOLAND** *All Around The World CDGLOBE 346* FLIP & FILL FEATURING KAREN PARRY	11		4

BILL PARSONS US singer

Date	Title / Label	Peak Position	Weeks at No.1	Weeks in Top 40
10 Apr 59	**ALL AMERICAN BOY** *London HL 8798*	22		2

ALAN PARSONS PROJECT UK group

Date	Title / Label	Peak Position	Weeks at No.1	Weeks in Top 40
15 Jan 83	**OLD AND WISE** *Arista ARIST 494*	74		
10 Mar 84	**DON'T ANSWER ME** *Arista ARIST 553*	58		

PARTIZAN UK group

Date	Title / Label	Peak Position	Weeks at No.1	Weeks in Top 40
8 Feb 97	**DRIVE ME CRAZY** *Multiply CDMULTY 17*	36		1
6 Dec 97	**KEEP YOUR LOVE** *Multiply CDMULTY 29* PARTIZAN FEATURING NATALIE ROBB	53		

Silver-selling ● Gold-selling ● Platinum-selling ● US No.1 ★ | Peak Position | Weeks at No.1 | Weeks in Top 40

PARTNERS IN KRYME US group

Date	Title	Peak Position	Weeks at No.1	Weeks in Top 40
21 Jul 90	**TURTLE POWER** *SBK TURTLE 1*	1	4	9

DAVID PARTON UK singer

Date	Title	Peak Position	Weeks at No.1	Weeks in Top 40
15 Jan 77	**ISN'T SHE LOVELY** *Pye 7N 45663*	4		9

DOLLY PARTON US singer

Date	Title	Peak Position	Weeks at No.1	Weeks in Top 40
15 May 76	**JOLENE** *RCA 2675*	7		9
21 Feb 81	**9 TO 5** *RCA 325* ★	47		
12 Nov 83	**ISLANDS IN THE STREAM** *RCA 378* KENNY ROGERS & DOLLY PARTON ★	7		11
7 Apr 84	**HERE YOU COME AGAIN** *RCA 395*	75		
16 Apr 94	**THE DAY I FALL IN LOVE** *Columbia 6600282* DOLLY PARTON & JAMES INGRAM	64		
19 Oct 02	**IF** *Sanctuary SANX 139X*	73		

STELLA PARTON US singer

Date	Title	Peak Position	Weeks at No.1	Weeks in Top 40
22 Oct 77	**THE DANGER OF A STRANGER** *Elektra K 12272*	35		1

DON PARTRIDGE UK singer

Date	Title	Peak Position	Weeks at No.1	Weeks in Top 40
7 Feb 68	**ROSIE** *Columbia DB 8330*	4		12
29 May 68	**BLUE EYES** *Columbia DB 8416*	3		11
19 Feb 69	**BREAKFAST ON PLUTO** *Columbia DB 8538*	26		5

PARTRIDGE FAMILY US group

Date	Title	Peak Position	Weeks at No.1	Weeks in Top 40
13 Feb 71	**I THINK I LOVE YOU** *Bell 1130* PARTRIDGE FAMILY STARRING SHIRLEY JONES FEATURING DAVID CASSIDY ★	18		8
26 Feb 72	**IT'S ONE OF THOSE NIGHTS (YES LOVE)** *Bell 1203* PARTRIDGE FAMILY STARRING SHIRLEY JONES FEATURING DAVID CASSIDY	11		10
8 Jul 72	**BREAKING UP IS HARD TO DO** *Bell MABEL 1* PARTRIDGE FAMILY STARRING SHIRLEY JONES FEATURING DAVID CASSIDY	3		13
3 Feb 73	**LOOKING THROUGH THE EYES OF LOVE** *Bell 1278* PARTRIDGE FAMILY STARRING DAVID CASSIDY	9		8
19 May 73	**WALKING IN THE RAIN** *Bell 1293* PARTRIDGE FAMILY STARRING DAVID CASSIDY	10		9

PARTY ANIMALS Dutch production duo

Date	Title	Peak Position	Weeks at No.1	Weeks in Top 40
1 Jun 96	**HAVE YOU EVER BEEN MELLOW** *Mokum DB 17553*	56		
19 Oct 96	**HAVE YOU EVER BEEN MELLOW (EP)** *Mokum DB 17413*	43		

PARTY BOYS UK group

Date	Title	Peak Position	Weeks at No.1	Weeks in Top 40
10 Jan 04	**BUILD ME UP BUTTERCUP 2003** *Liberty CDUP 001*	44		

PARTY FAITHFUL UK group

Date	Title	Peak Position	Weeks at No.1	Weeks in Top 40
22 Jul 95	**BRASS, LET THERE BE HOUSE** *Ore AG 10CD*	54		

PASADENAS UK group

Date	Title	Peak Position	Weeks at No.1	Weeks in Top 40
28 May 88	**TRIBUTE (RIGHT ON)** *CBS PASA 1*	5		9
17 Sep 88	**RIDING ON A TRAIN** *CBS PASA 2*	13		8
26 Nov 88	**ENCHANTED LADY** *CBS PASA 3*	31		3
12 May 90	**LOVE THING** *CBS PASA 4*	22		3
14 Jul 90	**REELING** *CBS PASA 5*	75		
1 Feb 92	**I'M DOING FINE NOW** *Columbia 6577187*	4		8
4 Apr 92	**MAKE IT WITH YOU** *Columbia 6579257*	20		3
6 Jun 92	**I BELIEVE IN MIRACLES** *Columbia 6580567*	34		2
29 Aug 92	**MOVING IN THE RIGHT DIRECTION** *Columbia 6583417*	49		
21 Nov 92	**LET'S STAY TOGETHER** *Columbia 6587747*	22		2

PASCAL UK production group

Date	Title	Peak Position	Weeks at No.1	Weeks in Top 40
28 Dec 02	**I THINK WE'RE ALONE NOW** *All Around The World CDGLOBE267* PASCAL FEATURING KAREN PARRY	23		3

PASSENGERS UK/Irish/Italian group

Date	Title	Peak Position	Weeks at No.1	Weeks in Top 40
2 Dec 95	**MISS SARAJEVO** *Island CID 625*	6		6

PASSION UK group

Date	Title	Peak Position	Weeks at No.1	Weeks in Top 40
25 Jan 97	**SHARE YOUR LOVE (NO DIGGITY)** *Charm CRTCDS 269*	62		

PASSIONS UK group

Date	Title	Peak Position	Weeks at No.1	Weeks in Top 40
31 Jan 81	**I'M IN LOVE WITH A GERMAN FILM STAR** *Polydor POSP 222*	25		6

PAT & MICK UK radio DJs

Date	Title	Peak Position	Weeks at No.1	Weeks in Top 40
9 Apr 88	**LET'S ALL CHANT/ON THE NIGHT** *PWL 10*	11		7
25 Mar 89	**I HAVEN'T STOPPED DANCING YET** *PWL 33*	9		7
14 Apr 90	**USE IT UP AND WEAR IT OUT** *PWL 55*	22		4
23 Mar 91	**GIMME SOME** *PWL 75*	53		
15 May 93	**HOT HOT HOT** *PWL International PARKCD 1*	47		

PATIENCE & PRUDENCE US duo

Date	Title	Peak Position	Weeks at No.1	Weeks in Top 40
2 Nov 56	**TONIGHT YOU BELONG TO ME** *London HLU 8321*	28		3
1 Mar 57	**GONNA GET ALONG WITHOUT YA NOW** *London HLU 8369*	22		5

PATRA Jamaican singer

Date	Title	Peak Position	Weeks at No.1	Weeks in Top 40
25 Dec 93	**FAMILY AFFAIR** *Polydor PZCD 304* SHABBA RANKS FEATURING PATRA & TERRY & MONICA	18		6
30 Sep 95	**PULL UP TO THE BUMPER** *Epic 6623942*	50		
10 Aug 96	**WORK MI BODY** *Heavenly HVN 53CD* MONKEY MAFIA FEATURING PATRA	75		

PATRIC UK singer

Date	Title	Peak Position	Weeks at No.1	Weeks in Top 40
9 Jul 94	**LOVE ME** *Bell 74321215352*	54		

DEE PATTEN UK producer

Date	Title	Peak Position	Weeks at No.1	Weeks in Top 40
30 Jan 99	**WHO'S THE BAD MAN** *Higher Ground HIGHS 15CD*	42		

KELLEE PATTERSON US singer

Date	Title	Peak Position	Weeks at No.1	Weeks in Top 40
18 Feb 78	**IF IT DON'T FIT DON'T FORCE IT** *EMI International INT 544*	44		

RAHSAAN PATTERSON US singer

Date	Title	Peak Position	Weeks at No.1	Weeks in Top 40
26 Jul 97	**STOP BY** *MCA MCSTD 48055*	50		
21 Mar 98	**WHERE YOU ARE** *MCA MCSTD 48073*	55		

BILLY PAUL US singer

Date	Title	Peak Position	Weeks at No.1	Weeks in Top 40
13 Jan 73	**ME AND MRS JONES** *Epic EPC 1055* ★	12		7
12 Jan 74	**THANKS FOR SAVING MY LIFE** *Philadelphia International PIR 1928*	33		4
22 May 76	**LET'S MAKE A BABY** *Philadelphia International PIR 4144*	30		4
30 Apr 77	**LET 'EM IN** *Philadelphia International PIR 5143*	26		4
16 Jul 77	**YOUR SONG** *Philadelphia International PIR 5391*	37		2
19 Nov 77	**ONLY THE STRONG SURVIVE** *Philadelphia International PIR 5699*	33		4
14 Jul 79	**BRING THE FAMILY BACK** *Philadelphia International PIR 7456*	51		
12 Oct 02	**SEX** *352 Recordings 352 CD001* ROBBIE RIVERA FEATURING BILLY PAUL W	55		

CHRIS PAUL UK producer/guitarist

Date	Title	Peak Position	Weeks at No.1	Weeks in Top 40
31 May 86	**EXPANSIONS '86 (EXPAND YOUR MIND)** *Fourth & Broadway BRW 48* CHRIS PAUL FEATURING DAVID JOSEPH	58		
21 Nov 87	**BACK IN MY ARMS** *Syncopate SY 5*	74		
13 Aug 88	**TURN THE MUSIC UP** *Syncopate SY 13*	73		

LES PAUL & MARY FORD US duo

Date	Title	Peak Position	Weeks at No.1	Weeks in Top 40
20 Nov 53	**VAYA CON DIOS** *Capitol CL 13943* ★	7		4

LYN PAUL UK singer

Date	Title	Peak Position	Weeks at No.1	Weeks in Top 40
28 Jun 75	**IT OUGHTA SELL A MILLION** *Polydor 2058 602*	37		1

OWEN PAUL UK singer

Date	Title	Peak Position	Weeks at No.1	Weeks in Top 40
31 May 86	**MY FAVOURITE WASTE OF TIME** *Epic A 7125* ○	3		10

SEAN PAUL Jamaican singer

Date	Title	Peak Position	Weeks at No.1	Weeks in Top 40
21 Sep 02	**GIMME THE LIGHT** *VP VPCD 6400*	32		1
15 Feb 03	**GIMME THE LIGHT** *VP/Atlantic AT 0146CD*	5		6
24 May 03	**GET BUSY** *VP/Atlantic AT 0155CD* ★	4		6
19 Jul 03	**BREATHE (IMPORT)** *Arista 82876534002* BLU CANTRELL FEATURING SEAN PAUL	59		
9 Aug 03	**BREATHE** *Arista 82876545722* BLU CANTRELL FEATURING SEAN PAUL ○	1	4	15
6 Sep 03	**LIKE GLUE** *VP/Atlantic AT 0162CD*	3		7
18 Oct 03	**BABY BOY** *Columbia 6744082* BEYONCÉ FEATURING SEAN PAUL ★	2		6
17 Jan 04	**I'M STILL IN LOVE WITH YOU** *VP/Atlantic AT 0170CDX* SEAN PAUL FEATURING SASHA	6		9
24 Sep 05	**WE BE BURNIN'** *VP/Atlantic AT0218CDX*	2		12
10 Dec 05	**EVER BLAZIN'** *VP/Atlantic AT0227CD*	12		6
25 Mar 06	**TEMPERATURE** *VP/Atlantic AT0235CD* ★	11		8
20 May 06	**CRY BABY CRY** *Arista 82876804672* SANTANA FEATURING SEAN PAUL & JOSS STONE	71		
22 Jul 06	**NEVER GONNA BE THE SAME** *VP/Atlantic AT0248CD*	22		3
23 Sep 06	**DO IT TO IT** *Capitol CDCL878* CHERISH FEATURING SEAN PAUL	30		2
4 Nov 06	**(WHEN YOU GONNA) GIVE IT UP TO ME** *VP/Atlantic AT0265CD* SEAN PAUL FEATURING KEYSHIA COLE	31		1

PAUL & PAULA US duo

Date	Title	Peak Position	Weeks at No.1	Weeks in Top 40
14 Feb 63	**HEY PAULA** *Philips 304012 BF* ★	8		13
18 Apr 63	**YOUNG LOVERS** *Philips 304016 BF*	9		12

LUCIANO PAVAROTTI Italian tenor

Date	Title	Peak Position	Weeks at No.1	Weeks in Top 40
16 Jun 90	**NESSUN DORMA** *Decca PAV 03* ●	2		8
24 Oct 92	**MISERERE** *London LON 329* ZUCCHERO WITH LUCIANO PAVAROTTI	15		4
30 Jul 94	**LIBIAMO/LA DONNA E MOBILE** *Teldec YZ 843CD* JOSE CARRERAS, PLACIDO DOMINGO & LUCIANO PAVAROTTI	21		2
14 Dec 96	**LIVE LIKE HORSES** *Rocket LLHDD 1* ELTON JOHN & LUCIANO PAVAROTTI	9		4
25 Jul 98	**YOU'LL NEVER WALK ALONE** *Decca 4607982* CARRERAS/DOMINGO/PAVAROTTI WITH MEHTA	35		1
15 Sep 07	**NESSUN DORMA** *Decca PAVOX3*	24		3

PAVEMENT US group

Date	Title	Peak Position	Weeks at No.1	Weeks in Top 40
28 Nov 92	**WATERY, DOMESTIC (EP)** *Big Cat ABB 38T*	58		
12 Feb 94	**CUT YOUR HAIR** *Big Cat ABB 55SCD*	52		
8 Feb 97	**STEREO** *Domino RUG 51CD*	48		
3 May 97	**SHADY LANE** *Domino RUG 53CD*	40		1
22 May 99	**CARROT ROPE** *Domino RUG 90CD1*	27		1

RITA PAVONE Italian singer

Date	Title	Peak Position	Weeks at No.1	Weeks in Top 40
1 Dec 66	**HEART** *RCA 1553*	27		6
19 Jan 67	**YOU ONLY YOU** *RCA 1561*	21		5

PAY AS U GO UK group

Date	Title	Peak Position	Weeks at No.1	Weeks in Top 40
27 Apr 02	**CHAMPAGNE DANCE** *So Urban 6721362*	13		2

FREDA PAYNE US singer

Date	Title	Peak Position	Weeks at No.1	Weeks in Top 40
5 Sep 70	**BAND OF GOLD** *Invictus INV 502*	1	6	18
21 Nov 70	**DEEPER AND DEEPER** *Invictus INV 505*	33		5
27 Mar 71	**CHERISH WHAT IS DEAR TO YOU** *Invictus INV 509*	46		

TAMMY PAYNE UK singer

Date	Title	Peak Position	Weeks at No.1	Weeks in Top 40
20 Jul 91	**TAKE ME NOW** *Talkin Loud TLK 12*	55		

HEATHER PEACE UK singer

Date	Title	Peak Position	Weeks at No.1	Weeks in Top 40
13 May 00	**THE ROSE** *RCA 74321742892*	56		

PEACE BY PIECE UK group

Date	Title	Peak Position	Weeks at No.1	Weeks in Top 40
21 Sep 96	**SWEET SISTER** *Blanco Y Negro 94CD*	46		
25 Apr 98	**NOBODY'S BUSINESS** *Blanco Y Negro 110CD1*	50		

PEACH UK/Belgian production group

Date	Title	Peak Position	Weeks at No.1	Weeks in Top 40
17 Jan 98	**ON MY OWN** *Mute CDMUTE 215*	69		

PEACHES Canadian singer

Date	Title	Peak Position	Weeks at No.1	Weeks in Top 40
15 Jun 02	**SET IT OFF** *Epic 6726862*	36		1
17 Jan 04	**KICK IT** *XL Recordings XLS176CD* PEACHES FEATURING IGGY POP	39		1
15 Jul 06	**DOWNTOWN** *XL Recordings XLS235CD*	50		

PEACHES & HERB US duo

Date	Title	Peak Position	Weeks at No.1	Weeks in Top 40
20 Jan 79	**SHAKE YOUR GROOVE THING** *Polydor 2066 992*	26		6
21 Apr 79	**REUNITED** *Polydor POSP 43* ○ ★	4		10

PEARL JAM US group

Date	Title	Peak Position	Weeks at No.1	Weeks in Top 40
15 Feb 92	**ALIVE** *Epic 6575727*	16		4
18 Apr 92	**EVEN FLOW** *Epic 6578577*	27		2
26 Sep 92	**JEREMY** *Epic 6582587*	15		2
1 Jan 94	**DAUGHTER** *Epic 6600202*	18		3
28 May 94	**DISSIDENT** *Epic 6604415*	14		3
26 Nov 94	**SPIN THE BLACK CIRCLE** *Epic 6610362*	10		2
25 Feb 95	**NOT FOR YOU** *Epic 6612032*	34		1
16 Dec 95	**MERKINBALL EP** *Epic 6627162*	25		1
17 Aug 96	**WHO YOU ARE** *Epic 6635392*	18		1
31 Jan 98	**GIVEN TO FLY** *Epic 6653942*	12		2
23 May 98	**WISHLIST** *Epic 6657902*	30		1
14 Aug 99	**LAST KISS** *Epic 6674792*	42		
13 May 00	**NOTHING AS IT SEEMS** *Epic 6693742*	22		1
22 Jul 00	**LIGHT YEARS** *Epic 6696282*	52		
9 Nov 02	**I AM MINE** *Epic 6733082*	26		1

PEARLS UK duo

Date	Title	Peak Position	Weeks at No.1	Weeks in Top 40
27 May 72	**THIRD FINGER, LEFT HAND** *Bell 1217*	31		3
23 Sep 72	**YOU CAME YOU SAW YOU CONQUERED** *Bell 1254*	32		3
24 Mar 73	**YOU ARE EVERYTHING** *Bell 1284*	41		
1 Jun 74	**GUILTY** *Bell 1352*	10		7

JOHNNY PEARSON UK orchestra leader

Date	Title	Peak Position	Weeks at No.1	Weeks in Top 40
18 Dec 71	**SLEEPY SHORES** *Penny Farthing PEN 778*	8		15

PEBBLES US singer

Date	Title	Peak Position	Weeks at No.1	Weeks in Top 40
19 Mar 88	**GIRLFRIEND** *MCA 1233*	8		7
28 May 88	**MERCEDES BOY** *MCA 1248*	42		
27 Oct 90	**GIVING YOU THE BENEFIT** *MCA 1448*	73		

PEDDLERS UK group

Date	Title	Peak Position	Weeks at No.1	Weeks in Top 40
7 Jan 65	**LET THE SUNSHINE IN** *Philips BF 1375*	50		
23 Aug 69	**BIRTH** *CBS 4449*	17		6
31 Jan 70	**GIRLIE** *CBS 4720*	34		4

PEE BEE SQUAD UK singer

Date	Title	Peak Position	Weeks at No.1	Weeks in Top 40
5 Oct 85	**RUGGED AND MEAN, BUTCH AND ON SCREEN** *Project PRO 3*	52		

ANN PEEBLES US singer

Date	Title	Peak Position	Weeks at No.1	Weeks in Top 40
20 Apr 74	**I CAN'T STAND THE RAIN** *London HL 10428*	41		

PEECH BOYS US group

Date	Title	Peak Position	Weeks at No.1	Weeks in Top 40
30 Oct 82	**DON'T MAKE ME WAIT** *TMT 7001*	49		

Silver-selling · Gold-selling · Platinum-selling · US No.1 · Peak Position · Weeks at No.1 · Weeks in Top 40

DONALD PEERS UK singer

Date	Title / Label	Peak Position	Weeks at No.1	Weeks in Top 40
29 Dec 66	GAMES THAT LOVERS PLAY *Columbia DB 8079*	46		
18 Dec 68	PLEASE DON'T GO *Columbia DB 8502*	3		18
24 Jun 72	GIVE ME ONE MORE CHANCE *Decca F 13302*	36		1

PELE UK group

Date	Title / Label	Peak Position	Weeks at No.1	Weeks in Top 40
15 Feb 92	MEGALOMANIA *M&G MAGS 20*	73		
13 Jun 92	FAIR BLOWS THE WIND FOR FRANCE *M&G MAGS 24*	62		
31 Jul 93	FAT BLACK HEART *M&G MAGCD 43*	75		

MARTI PELLOW UK singer

Date	Title / Label	Peak Position	Weeks at No.1	Weeks in Top 40
16 Jun 01	CLOSE TO YOU *Mercury MERDD 532*	9		4
1 Dec 01	I'VE BEEN AROUND THE WORLD *Mercury 5887772*	28		1
22 Nov 03	A LOT OF LOVE *Universal TV 9813763*	59		

JACK PENATE UK singer

Date	Title / Label	Peak Position	Weeks at No.1	Weeks in Top 40
30 Jun 07	TORN ON THE PLATFORM *XL Recordings XLS276CD*	7		7
29 Sep 07	SECOND, MINUTE OR HOUR *XL Recordings XLS290CD*	17		3
22 Dec 07	HAVE I BEEN A FOOL *XL Recordings XLS391CD*	73		

DEBBIE PENDER US singer

Date	Title / Label	Peak Position	Weeks at No.1	Weeks in Top 40
30 May 98	MOVIN' ON *AM:PM 5826492*	41		

TEDDY PENDERGRASS US singer

Date	Title / Label	Peak Position	Weeks at No.1	Weeks in Top 40
21 May 77	THE WHOLE TOWN'S LAUGHING AT ME *Philadelphia International PIR 5116*	44		
28 Oct 78	ONLY YOU/CLOSE THE DOOR *Philadelphia International PIR 6713*	41		
23 May 81	TWO HEARTS *20th Century TC 2492* STEPHANIE MILLS FEATURING TEDDY PENDERGRASS	49		
25 Jan 86	HOLD ME *Asylum EKR 32* TEDDY PENDERGRASS & WHITNEY HOUSTON	44		
28 May 88	JOY *Elektra EKR 75*	58		
19 Nov 94	THE MORE I GET THE MORE I WANT *X-clusive XCLU 011CD* KWS FEATURING TEDDY PENDERGRASS	35		1

PENDULUM UK production group

Date	Title / Label	Peak Position	Weeks at No.1	Weeks in Top 40
6 Mar 04	ANOTHER PLANET/VOYAGER *Breakbeat Kaos BBK003*	46		
30 Apr 05	GUNS AT DAWN *Breakbeat Kaos BBK008* DJ BARON FEATURING PENDULUM	71		
9 Jul 05	TARANTULA/FASTEN YOUR SEATBELT *Breakbeat Kaos BBK009SCD* PENDULUM & FRESH FEATURING SPYDA	60		
1 Oct 05	SLAM/OUT HERE *Breakbeat Kaos BBK011SCD*	34		1
9 Jun 07	BLOOD SUGAR/AXLE GRINDER *Download*	62		
17 Nov 07	GRANITE *Warner Brothers WEA436CD*	29		2

CE CE PENISTON US singer

Date	Title / Label	Peak Position	Weeks at No.1	Weeks in Top 40
12 Oct 91	FINALLY *A&M AM 822*	29		5
11 Jan 92	WE GOT A LOVE THANG *A&M AM 846*	6		6
18 Jan 92	I LIKE IT *A&M AM 847* OVERWEIGHT POOCH FEATURING CE CE PENISTON	58		
21 Mar 92	FINALLY *A&M AM 858*	2		7
23 May 92	KEEP ON WALKIN' *A&M AM 878*	10		4
5 Sep 92	CRAZY LOVE *A&M AM 0060*	44		
12 Dec 92	INSIDE THAT I CRIED *A&M AM 0121*	42		
15 Jan 94	I'M IN THE MOOD *A&M 5804552*	16		3
2 Apr 94	KEEP GIVIN' ME YOUR LOVE *A&M 5805492*	36		1
6 Aug 94	HIT BY LOVE *A&M 5806932*	33		1
13 Sep 97	FINALLY (REMIX) *AM:PM 5823432*	26		1
7 Feb 98	SOMEBODY ELSE'S GUY *AM:PM 5825112*	13		2

DAWN PENN Jamaican singer

Date	Title / Label	Peak Position	Weeks at No.1	Weeks in Top 40
11 Jun 94	YOU DON'T LOVE ME (NO NO NO) *Big Beat A 8295CD*	3		9

BARBARA PENNINGTON US singer

Date	Title / Label	Peak Position	Weeks at No.1	Weeks in Top 40
27 Apr 85	FAN THE FLAME *Record Shack SOHO 37*	62		
27 Jul 85	ON A CROWDED STREET *Record Shack SOHO 49*	57		

TRICIA PENROSE UK singer

Date	Title / Label	Peak Position	Weeks at No.1	Weeks in Top 40
7 Dec 96	WHERE DID OUR LOVE GO *RCA 74321428152*	71		
4 Mar 00	DON'T WANNA BE ALONE *Doop DP 2001CD*	44		

PENTANGLE UK group

Date	Title / Label	Peak Position	Weeks at No.1	Weeks in Top 40
28 May 69	ONCE I HAD A SWEETHEART *Big T BIG 124*	46		
14 Feb 70	LIGHT FLIGHT *Big T BIG 128*	43		

PENTHOUSE 4 UK duo

Date	Title / Label	Peak Position	Weeks at No.1	Weeks in Top 40
23 Apr 88	BUST THIS HOUSE DOWN *Syncopate SY 10*	56		

PEOPLE'S CHOICE US group

Date	Title / Label	Peak Position	Weeks at No.1	Weeks in Top 40
20 Sep 75	DO IT ANY WAY YOU WANNA *Philadelphia International PIR 3500*	36		3
21 Jan 78	JAM JAM JAM *Philadelphia International PIR 5891*	40		1

PEPE DELUXE Finnish production group

Date	Title / Label	Peak Position	Weeks at No.1	Weeks in Top 40
26 May 01	BEFORE YOU LEAVE *Catskills 6712392*	20		2

DANNY PEPPERMINT & THE JUMPING JACKS US group

Date	Title / Label	Peak Position	Weeks at No.1	Weeks in Top 40
18 Jan 62	PEPPERMINT TWIST *London HLL 9478*	26		4

PEPPERS French duo

Date	Title / Label	Peak Position	Weeks at No.1	Weeks in Top 40
26 Oct 74	PEPPER BOX *Spark SRL 1100*	6		9

PEPSI & SHIRLIE UK duo

Date	Title / Label	Peak Position	Weeks at No.1	Weeks in Top 40
17 Jan 87	HEARTACHE *Polydor POSP 837*	2		9
30 May 87	GOODBYE STRANGER *Polydor POSP 865*	9		6
26 Sep 87	CAN'T GIVE ME NOW *Polydor POSP 885*	58		
12 Dec 87	ALL RIGHT NOW *Polydor POSP 896*	50		

PERAN Dutch producer

Date	Title / Label	Peak Position	Weeks at No.1	Weeks in Top 40
23 Mar 02	GOOD TIME *Incentive CENT 37CDS*	37		1

PERCEPTION UK group

Date	Title / Label	Peak Position	Weeks at No.1	Weeks in Top 40
7 Mar 92	FEED THE FEELING *Talkin Loud TLK 17*	58		

LANCE PERCIVAL UK actor

Date	Title / Label	Peak Position	Weeks at No.1	Weeks in Top 40
28 Oct 65	SHAME AND SCANDAL IN THE FAMILY *Parlophone R 5335*	37		1

A PERFECT CIRCLE US group

Date	Title / Label	Peak Position	Weeks at No.1	Weeks in Top 40
18 Nov 00	THE HOLLOW *Virgin VUSCD 181*	72		
13 Jan 01	3 LIBRAS *Virgin VUSCD 184*	49		

PERFECT DAY UK group

Date	Title / Label	Peak Position	Weeks at No.1	Weeks in Top 40
21 Jan 89	LIBERTY TOWN *London LON 214*	58		
1 Apr 89	JANE *London LON 188*	68		

PERFECT PHASE Dutch production duo

Date	Title / Label	Peak Position	Weeks at No.1	Weeks in Top 40
25 Dec 99	HORNY HORNS *Positiva CDTIV 123*	21		5
12 Jun 04	BLOW YOUR HORNY HORNS *Feverpitch 12FEV3*	75		

PERFECTLY ORDINARY PEOPLE UK group

Date	Title / Label	Peak Position	Weeks at No.1	Weeks in Top 40
22 Oct 88	THEME FROM P.O.P. *Urban URB 25*	61		

PERFECTO ALLSTARZ UK group

Date	Title / Label	Peak Position	Weeks at No.1	Weeks in Top 40
4 Feb 95	REACH UP (PAPA'S GOT A BRAND NEW PIG BAG) *Perfecto YZ 892CD*	6		8

Silver-selling ○ Gold-selling ● Platinum-selling ✪ US No.1 ★ | Peak Position | Weeks at No.1 | Weeks in Top 40

PERFUME UK group

Date	Title / Label	Peak Position	Weeks at No.1	Weeks in Top 40
10 Feb 96	**HAVEN'T SEEN YOU** *Aromasound AROMA 005CDS*	71		

EMILIO PERICOLI Italian singer/actor

Date	Title / Label	Peak Position	Weeks at No.1	Weeks in Top 40
28 Jun 62	**AL DI LA** *Warner Brothers WB 69*	30		11

CARL PERKINS US singer

Date	Title / Label	Peak Position	Weeks at No.1	Weeks in Top 40
18 May 56	**BLUE SUEDE SHOES** *London HLU 8271*	10		8

PERPETUAL MOTION UK production duo

Date	Title / Label	Peak Position	Weeks at No.1	Weeks in Top 40
2 May 98	**KEEP ON DANCIN' (LET'S GO)** *Positiva CDTIV 90*	12		3

STEVE PERRY UK singer

Date	Title / Label	Peak Position	Weeks at No.1	Weeks in Top 40
4 Aug 60	**STEP BY STEP** *HMV POP 745*	41		

NINA PERSSON & DAVID ARNOLD Swedish/UK duo

Date	Title / Label	Peak Position	Weeks at No.1	Weeks in Top 40
29 Apr 00	**THEME FROM *RANDALL & HOPKIRK (DECEASED)*** *Island CID 762*	49		

JON PERTWEE UK actor

Date	Title / Label	Peak Position	Weeks at No.1	Weeks in Top 40
1 Mar 80	**WORZEL SONG** *Decca F 13885*	33		3

PESHAY UK producer

Date	Title / Label	Peak Position	Weeks at No.1	Weeks in Top 40
9 May 98	**MILES FROM HOME** *Mo Wax MW 092*	75		
17 Jul 99	**SWITCH** *Island Blue PFACD 1*	59		
19 Feb 00	**TRULY** *Island Blue PFACD 4* PESHAY FEATURING KYM MAZELLE	55		
4 May 02	**YOU GOT ME BURNING/FUZION** *Cubik Music CUBIKSAMPCD 001* PESHAY FEATURING CO-ORDINATE	41		
24 Aug 02	**SATISFY MY LOVE** *Cubik Music CUBIK 002CD* PESHAY VERSUS FLYTRONIX	67		

PET SHOP BOYS UK duo

Date	Title / Label	Peak Position	Weeks at No.1	Weeks in Top 40
23 Nov 85	**WEST END GIRLS** *Parlophone R 6115* ● ★	1	2	12
8 Mar 86	**LOVE COMES QUICKLY** *Parlophone R 6116*	19		6
31 May 86	**OPPORTUNITIES (LET'S MAKE LOTS OF MONEY)** *Parlophone R 6129*	11		6
4 Oct 86	**SUBURBIA** *Parlophone R 6140*	8		7
27 Jun 87	**IT'S A SIN** *Parlophone R 6158* ○	1	3	9
22 Aug 87	**WHAT HAVE I DONE TO DESERVE THIS** *Parlophone R 6163* PET SHOP BOYS & DUSTY SPRINGFIELD ○	2		7
24 Oct 87	**RENT** *Parlophone R 6168*	8		5
12 Dec 87	**ALWAYS ON MY MIND** *Parlophone R 6171* ●	1	4	9
2 Apr 88	**HEART** *Parlophone R 6177* ○	1	2	8
24 Sep 88	**DOMINO DANCING** *Parlophone R 6190*	7		6
26 Nov 88	**LEFT TO MY OWN DEVICES** *Parlophone R 6198*	4		7
8 Jul 89	**IT'S ALRIGHT** *Parlophone R 6220*	5		6
6 Oct 90	**SO HARD** *Parlophone R 6269*	4		5
24 Nov 90	**BEING BORING** *Parlophone R 6275*	20		3
23 Mar 91	**WHERE THE STREETS HAVE NO NAME - CAN'T TAKE MY EYES OFF YOU/HOW CAN YOU EXPECT ME TO BE TAKEN SERIOUSLY** *Parlophone R 6285*	4		5
8 Jun 91	**JEALOUSY** *Parlophone R 6283*	12		3
26 Oct 91	**DJ CULTURE** *Parlophone R 6301*	13		2
23 Nov 91	**DJ CULTURE (REMIX)** *Parlophone 12RX 6301*	40		1
21 Dec 91	**WAS IT WORTH IT** *Parlophone R 6306*	24		3
12 Jun 93	**CAN YOU FORGIVE HER** *Parlophone CDR 6348*	7		5
18 Sep 93	**GO WEST** *Parlophone CDR 6356*	2		7
11 Dec 93	**I WOULDN'T NORMALLY DO THIS KIND OF THING** *Parlophone CDR 6370*	13		5
16 Apr 94	**LIBERATION** *Parlophone CDR 6377*	14		3
11 Jun 94	**ABSOLUTELY FABULOUS** *Spaghetti CDR 6382* ABSOLUTELY FABULOUS	6		4
10 Sep 94	**YESTERDAY WHEN I WAS MAD** *Parlophone CDRS 6386*	13		2
5 Aug 95	**PANINARO '95** *Parlophone CDRS 6414*	15		3
4 May 96	**BEFORE** *Parlophone CDRS 6431*	7		2
24 Aug 96	**SE A VIDA E (THAT'S THE WAY LIFE IS)** *Parlophone CDR 6443*	8		5
23 Nov 96	**SINGLE** *Parlophone CDRS 6452*	14		2
29 Mar 97	**RED LETTER DAY** *Parlophone CDR 6460*	9		1
5 Jul 97	**SOMEWHERE** *Parlophone CDR 6470*	9		3
31 Jul 99	**I DON'T KNOW WHAT YOU WANT BUT I CAN'T GIVE IT TO YOU** *Parlophone CDR 6523*	15		2
9 Oct 99	**NEW YORK CITY BOY** *Parlophone CDR 6525*	14		2
15 Jan 00	**YOU ONLY TELL ME YOU LOVE ME WHEN YOU'RE DRUNK** *Parlophone CDR 6533*	8		3
30 Mar 02	**HOME AND DRY** *Parlophone CDRS 6572*	14		2
27 Jul 02	**I GET ALONG** *Parlophone CDRS 6581*	18		1
29 Nov 03	**MIRACLES** *Parlophone CDRS 6620*	10		2
10 Apr 04	**FLAMBOYANT** *Parlophone CDRS 6629*	12		1
20 May 06	**I'M WITH STUPID** *Parlophone CDR6690*	8		2
5 Aug 06	**MINIMAL** *Parlophone CDR6708*	19		1
28 Oct 06	**NUMB** *Parlophone CDR6723*	23		1
17 Mar 07	**SHE'S MADONNA** *Chrysalis CDCHS5163* ROBBIE WILLIAMS & PET SHOP BOYS	16		2

PETER & GORDON UK duo

Date	Title / Label	Peak Position	Weeks at No.1	Weeks in Top 40
12 Mar 64	**A WORLD WITHOUT LOVE** *Columbia DB 7225* ★	1	2	14
4 Jun 64	**NOBODY I KNOW** *Columbia DB 7292*	10		10
8 Apr 65	**TRUE LOVE WAYS** *Columbia DB 7524*	2		13
24 Jun 65	**TO KNOW YOU IS TO LOVE YOU** *Columbia DB 7617*	5		8
21 Oct 65	**BABY I'M YOURS** *Columbia DB 7729*	19		7
24 Feb 66	**WOMAN** *Columbia DB 7834*	28		3
22 Sep 66	**LADY GODIVA** *Columbia DB 8003*	16		9

PETER BJORN & JOHN Swedish group

Date	Title / Label	Peak Position	Weeks at No.1	Weeks in Top 40
19 Aug 06	**YOUNG FOLKS** *Wichita WEBB107SCD* PETER BJORN & JOHN FEATURING BERGSMAN	35		1
8 Sep 07	**YOUNG FOLKS** *Wichita WEBB107SCD* PETER BJORN & JOHN FEATURING BERGSMAN	13		7

PETER, PAUL & MARY US group

Date	Title / Label	Peak Position	Weeks at No.1	Weeks in Top 40
10 Oct 63	**BLOWING IN THE WIND** *Warner Brothers WB 104*	13		13
16 Apr 64	**TELL IT ON THE MOUNTAIN** *Warner Brothers WB 127*	33		2
15 Oct 64	**THE TIMES THEY ARE A-CHANGIN'** *Warner Brothers WB 142*	44		
17 Jan 70	**LEAVIN' ON A JET PLANE** *Warner Brothers WB 7340* ★	2		13

PETERS & LEE UK duo

Date	Title / Label	Peak Position	Weeks at No.1	Weeks in Top 40
26 May 73	**WELCOME HOME** *Philips 6006 307*	1	1	21
3 Nov 73	**BY YOUR SIDE** *Philips 6006 339*	39		1
20 Apr 74	**DON'T STAY AWAY TOO LONG** *Philips 6006 388* ○	3		12
17 Aug 74	**RAINBOW** *Philips 6006 406*	17		7
6 Mar 76	**HEY MR. MUSIC MAN** *Philips 6006 502*	16		6

JONATHAN PETERS US producer

Date	Title / Label	Peak Position	Weeks at No.1	Weeks in Top 40
24 Jul 99	**FLOWER DUET** *Pelican PELID 001* JONATHAN PETERS PRESENTS LUMINAIRE	75		

RAY PETERSON US singer

Date	Title / Label	Peak Position	Weeks at No.1	Weeks in Top 40
4 Sep 59	**THE WONDER OF YOU** *RCA 1131*	23		1
24 Mar 60	**ANSWER ME** *RCA 1175*	47		
19 Jan 61	**CORRINE, CORRINA** *London HLX 9246*	41		

TOM PETTY US singer

Date	Title / Label	Peak Position	Weeks at No.1	Weeks in Top 40
25 Jun 77	**ANYTHING THAT'S ROCK 'N' ROLL** *Shelter WIP 6396* TOM PETTY & THE HEARTBREAKERS	36		1
13 Aug 77	**AMERICAN GIRL** *Shelter WIP 6403* TOM PETTY & THE HEARTBREAKERS	40		1
15 Aug 81	**STOP DRAGGIN' MY HEART AROUND** *WEA K 79231* STEVIE NICKS WITH TOM PETTY & THE HEARTBREAKERS	50		
13 Apr 85	**DON'T COME AROUND HERE NO MORE** *MCA 926* TOM PETTY & THE HEARTBREAKERS	50		
13 May 89	**I WON'T BACK DOWN** *MCA 1334*	28		5
12 Aug 89	**RUNNIN' DOWN A DREAM** *MCA 1359*	55		
25 Nov 89	**FREE FALLIN'** *MCA 1381*	64		
29 Jun 91	**LEARNING TO FLY** *MCA MCS 1555* TOM PETTY & THE HEARTBREAKERS	46		
4 Apr 92	**TOO GOOD TO BE TRUE** *MCA MCS 1616* TOM PETTY & THE HEARTBREAKERS	34		2
30 Oct 93	**SOMETHING IN THE AIR** *MCA MCSTD 1945*	53		
12 Mar 94	**MARY JANE'S LAST DANCE** *MCA MCSTD 1966*	52		

Key: Silver-selling ● | Gold-selling ● | Platinum-selling | US No.1 ★ | Peak Position | Weeks at No.1 | Weeks in Top 40

PEYTON US duo

Date	Title / Label	Peak Position	Weeks at No.1	Weeks in Top 40
22 May 04	**A HIGHER PLACE** *Hed Kandi HEDK12006*	68		

PF PROJECT
UK group featuring songwriters and producers with actor

Date	Title / Label	Peak Position	Weeks at No.1	Weeks in Top 40
15 Nov 97	**CHOOSE LIFE** *Positiva CDTIV 84* PF PROJECT FEATURING EWAN MCGREGOR	6		9

PHANTOM PLANET US group

Date	Title / Label	Peak Position	Weeks at No.1	Weeks in Top 40
19 Mar 05	**CALIFORNIA** *Epic 6726672*	9		10

PHARAO German group

Date	Title / Label	Peak Position	Weeks at No.1	Weeks in Top 40
4 Mar 95	**THERE IS A STAR** *Epic 6611832*	43		

PHARCYDE US group

Date	Title / Label	Peak Position	Weeks at No.1	Weeks in Top 40
31 Jul 93	**PASSIN' ME BY** *Atlantic A 8360CD*	55		
6 Apr 96	**RUNNIN'** *Go! Beat GODCD 142*	36		1
10 Aug 96	**SHE SAID** *Go! Beat GODCD 144*	51		

PHASE II UK producer

Date	Title / Label	Peak Position	Weeks at No.1	Weeks in Top 40
18 Mar 89	**REACHIN'** *Republic LICT 006*	70		
21 Dec 91	**REACHIN' (REMIX)** *Republic LICT 160* JOEY NEGRO PRESENTS PHASE II	70		

PHAT 'N' PHUNKY UK production duo

Date	Title / Label	Peak Position	Weeks at No.1	Weeks in Top 40
14 Jun 97	**LET'S GROOVE** *Chase CDCHASE 8*	61		

PHATS & SMALL UK production duo

Date	Title / Label	Peak Position	Weeks at No.1	Weeks in Top 40
10 Apr 99	**TURN AROUND** *Multiply CDMULTY 49* (gold)	2		12
14 Aug 99	**FEEL GOOD** *Multiply CDMULTY 54*	7		4
4 Dec 99	**TONITE** *Multiply CDMULTY 57*	11		2
30 Jun 01	**THIS TIME AROUND** *Multiply CDMULTY 75*	15		3
24 Nov 01	**CHANGE** *Multiply CDMULTY 80*	45		

PHATT B Dutch producer

Date	Title / Label	Peak Position	Weeks at No.1	Weeks in Top 40
11 Nov 00	**AND DA DRUM MACHINE** *NuLife 74321801902*	58		

PhD UK duo

Date	Title / Label	Peak Position	Weeks at No.1	Weeks in Top 40
3 Apr 82	**I WON'T LET YOU DOWN** *WEA K 79209* (silver)	3		9

BARRINGTON PHELOUNG
Australian conductor/arranger

Date	Title / Label	Peak Position	Weeks at No.1	Weeks in Top 40
13 Mar 93	***INSPECTOR MORSE* THEME** *Virgin VSCDT 1458*	61		

PHILADELPHIA INTERNATIONAL ALL-STARS
US charity ensemble

Date	Title / Label	Peak Position	Weeks at No.1	Weeks in Top 40
13 Aug 77	**LET'S CLEAN UP THE GHETTO** *Philadelphia International PIR 5451*	34		5

PHILHARMONIA ORCHESTRA, CONDUCTOR LORIN MAAZEL UK orchestra with US conductor

Date	Title / Label	Peak Position	Weeks at No.1	Weeks in Top 40
30 Jul 69	**THUS SPAKE ZARATHUSTRA** *Columbia DB 8607*	33		3

CHYNNA PHILLIPS US singer

Date	Title / Label	Peak Position	Weeks at No.1	Weeks in Top 40
3 Feb 96	**NAKED AND SACRED** *EMI CDEM 409*	62		

ESTHER PHILLIPS US singer

Date	Title / Label	Peak Position	Weeks at No.1	Weeks in Top 40
4 Oct 75	**WHAT A DIFFERENCE A DAY MAKES** *Kudu 925*	6		7

PHIXX UK group

Date	Title / Label	Peak Position	Weeks at No.1	Weeks in Top 40
8 Nov 03	**HOLD ON ME** *Concept CDCON 51X*	10		3
20 Mar 04	**LOVE REVOLUTION** *Concept CDCON 55X*	13		3
3 Jul 04	**WILD BOYS** *Concept CON 56X*	12		2
5 Feb 05	**STRANGE LOVE** *Concept CDCON60X*	19		1

PHOENIX French group

Date	Title / Label	Peak Position	Weeks at No.1	Weeks in Top 40
3 Feb 01	**IF I EVER FEEL BETTER** *Source DINSD 210*	65		
1 May 04	**RUN RUN RUN** *Source SOURCD094*	66		
24 Jul 04	**EVERYTHING IS EVERYTHING** *Source SOURCDX097*	74		

PAUL PHOENIX UK singer

Date	Title / Label	Peak Position	Weeks at No.1	Weeks in Top 40
3 Nov 79	**NUNC DIMITTIS** *Different HAVE 20*	56		

PHOTEK UK producer

Date	Title / Label	Peak Position	Weeks at No.1	Weeks in Top 40
22 Mar 97	**NI-TEN-ICHI-RYU (TWO SWORDS TECHNIQUE)** *Science QEDCD 2*	37		1
28 Feb 98	**MODUS OPERANDI** *Virgin QEDCD 6*	66		
24 Feb 01	**MINE TO GIVE** *Science QEDCD 10* PHOTEK FEATURING ROBERT OWENS	44		

PHOTOS UK group

Date	Title / Label	Peak Position	Weeks at No.1	Weeks in Top 40
17 May 80	**IRENE** *Epic EPC 8517*	56		

PHUNKY PHANTOM UK producer

Date	Title / Label	Peak Position	Weeks at No.1	Weeks in Top 40
16 May 98	**GET UP STAND UP** *Club For Life DISNCD 44*	27		1

PHUTURE ASSASSINS
UK production group

Date	Title / Label	Peak Position	Weeks at No.1	Weeks in Top 40
6 Jun 92	**FUTURE SOUND (EP)** *Suburban Base SUBBASE 010*	64		

EDITH PIAF French singer

Date	Title / Label	Peak Position	Weeks at No.1	Weeks in Top 40
12 May 60	**MILORD** *Columbia DC 754*	41		
3 Nov 60	**MILORD** *Columbia DC 754*	24		10

PIANOHEADZ US production duo

Date	Title / Label	Peak Position	Weeks at No.1	Weeks in Top 40
11 Jul 98	**IT'S OVER (DISTORTION)** *Incredible Music INCRL 3CD*	39		1

PIANOMAN UK producer

Date	Title / Label	Peak Position	Weeks at No.1	Weeks in Top 40
15 Jun 96	**BLURRED** *ffrreedom TABCD 243*	6		5
26 Apr 97	**PARTY PEOPLE (LIVE YOUR LIFE BE FREE)** *3 Beat 3 BTDCD 1*	43		

MARK PICCHIOTTI US producer

Date	Title / Label	Peak Position	Weeks at No.1	Weeks in Top 40
19 Jan 02	**RUNNIN'** *Black & Blue NEOCD 073* MARK PICCHIOTTI PRESENTS BASSTOY FEATURING DANA	13		2

BOBBY 'BORIS' PICKETT & THE CRYPT-KICKERS US group

Date	Title / Label	Peak Position	Weeks at No.1	Weeks in Top 40
1 Sep 73	**MONSTER MASH** *London HL 10320* (silver) ★	3		10

WILSON PICKETT US singer

Date	Title / Label	Peak Position	Weeks at No.1	Weeks in Top 40
23 Sep 65	**IN THE MIDNIGHT HOUR** *Atlantic AT 4036*	12		9
25 Nov 65	**DON'T FIGHT IT** *Atlantic AT 4052*	29		5
10 Mar 66	**634-5789** *Atlantic AT 4072*	36		1
1 Sep 66	**LAND OF 1000 DANCES** *Atlantic 584-039*	22		8
15 Dec 66	**MUSTANG SALLY** *Atlantic 584-066*	28		6
27 Sep 67	**FUNKY BROADWAY** *Atlantic 584 130*	43		
11 Sep 68	**I'M A MIDNIGHT MOVER** *Atlantic 584 203*	38		2
8 Jan 69	**HEY JUDE** *Atlantic 584 236*	16		7
21 Nov 87	**IN THE MIDNIGHT HOUR** *Motown ZB 41583*	62		

Key: ○ Silver-selling · ● Gold-selling · ⊛ Platinum-selling · ★ US No.1 · Peak Position · Weeks at No.1 · Weeks in Top 40

PICKETTYWITCH UK group

Date	Title	Label	Peak Position	Weeks at No.1	Weeks in Top 40
28 Feb 70	THAT SAME OLD FEELING	Pye 7N 17887	5		12
4 Jul 70	(IT'S LIKE A) SAD OLD KINDA MOVIE	Pye 7N 17951	16		9
7 Nov 70	BABY I WON'T LET YOU DOWN	Pye 7N 45002	27		7

MAURO PICOTTO Italian producer

Date	Title	Label	Peak Position	Weeks at No.1	Weeks in Top 40
12 Jun 99	LIZARD (GONNA GET YOU)	VC Recordings VCRD 50	27		2
20 Nov 99	LIZARD (GONNA GET YOU) (REMIX)	VC Recordings VCRD 57	33		1
15 Jul 00	IGUANA	VC Recordings VCRD 68	33		1
13 Jan 01	KOMODO (SAVE A SOUL)	VC Recordings VCRDX 85	13		3
11 Aug 01	LIKE THIS LIKE THAT	VC Recordings VCRD 92	21		2
25 Aug 01	VERDI	BXR BXRP 0318	74		
16 Mar 02	PULSAR 2002	BXR/Nukleuz BXRCA 0162	35		1
3 Aug 02	BACK TO CALI	BXR BXRC 0433	42		

PIGBAG UK group

Date	Title	Label	Peak Position	Weeks at No.1	Weeks in Top 40
7 Nov 81	SUNNY DAY	Y Records Y 12	53		
27 Feb 82	GETTING UP	Y Records Y 16	61		
3 Apr 82	PAPA'S GOT A BRAND NEW PIGBAG	Y Records Y 10	3		8
10 Jul 82	THE BIG BEAN	Y Records Y 24	40		1

PIGLETS UK group

Date	Title	Label	Peak Position	Weeks at No.1	Weeks in Top 40
6 Nov 71	JOHNNY REGGAE	Bell 1180	3		11

PIGEON DETECTIVES UK group

Date	Title	Label	Peak Position	Weeks at No.1	Weeks in Top 40
18 Nov 06	I FOUND OUT	Dance To The Radio DTTR018CD	39		1
10 Mar 07	ROMANTIC TYPE	Dance To The Radio DTTR026CD	19		1
26 May 07	I'M NOT SORRY	Dance To The Radio DTTR029CD	12		3
18 Aug 07	TAKE HER BACK	Dance To The Radio DTTR034CD	20		4
24 Nov 07	I FOUND OUT	Dance To The Radio DTTR040CD	42		

PILOT UK group

Date	Title	Label	Peak Position	Weeks at No.1	Weeks in Top 40
2 Nov 74	MAGIC	EMI 2217	11		11
18 Jan 75	JANUARY	EMI 2255 ○	1	3	9
19 Apr 75	CALL ME ROUND	EMI 2287	34		2
27 Sep 75	JUST A SMILE	EMI 2338	31		3

PILTDOWN MEN US group

Date	Title	Label	Peak Position	Weeks at No.1	Weeks in Top 40
8 Sep 60	MACDONALD'S CAVE	Capitol CL 15149	14		15
12 Jan 61	PILTDOWN RIDES AGAIN	Capitol CL 15175	14		9
9 Mar 61	GOODNIGHT MRS. FLINTSTONE	Capitol CL 15186	18		6

COURTNEY PINE UK saxophonist

Date	Title	Label	Peak Position	Weeks at No.1	Weeks in Top 40
30 Jul 88	LIKE DREAMERS DO MICA PARIS FEATURING COURTNEY PINE	Fourth & Broadway BRW 108	26		4
7 Jul 90	I'M STILL WAITING COURTNEY PINE FEATURING CARROLL THOMPSON	Mango MNG 749	66		

PING PING & AL VERLANE Belgian duo

Date	Title	Label	Peak Position	Weeks at No.1	Weeks in Top 40
28 Sep 61	SUCU SUCU	Oriole CB 1589	41		

P!NK US singer

Date	Title	Label	Peak Position	Weeks at No.1	Weeks in Top 40
10 Jun 00	THERE YOU GO	LaFace 74321757602	6		6
30 Sep 00	MOST GIRLS	LaFace 74321792012	5		7
27 Jan 01	YOU MAKE ME SICK	LaFace 74321828702	9		4
30 Jun 01	LADY MARMALADE CHRISTINA AGUILERA/LIL' KIM/MYA/P!NK ● ★	Interscope 4975612	1	1	13
26 Jan 02	GET THE PARTY STARTED	Arista 74321913382 ○	2		12
25 May 02	DON'T LET ME GET ME	Arista 74321939212	6		8
28 Sep 02	JUST LIKE A PILL	Arista 74321959652	1	1	9
14 Dec 02	FAMILY PORTRAIT (IMPORT)	Arista 74321982102	66		
21 Dec 02	FAMILY PORTRAIT	Arista 74321982052	11		7
19 Jul 03	FEEL GOOD TIME P!NK FEATURING WILLIAM ORBIT	Columbia 6741062	3		7
8 Nov 03	TROUBLE	Arista 82876572172	7		6
7 Feb 04	GOD IS A DJ	Arista 82876589472	11		4
1 May 04	LAST TO KNOW	Arista 82876611732	21		2
25 Mar 06	STUPID GIRLS	RCA 82876811902	4		9
3 Jun 06	WHO KNEW	LaFace 82876847012	5		14
2 Sep 06	U & UR HAND	LaFace 82876880802	10		10
2 Dec 06	NOBODY KNOWS	LaFace 88697032862	27		2
10 Mar 07	LEAVE ME ALONE (I'M LONELY)	Download	34		2

PINK FLOYD UK group

Date	Title	Label	Peak Position	Weeks at No.1	Weeks in Top 40
30 Mar 67	ARNOLD LAYNE	Columbia DB 8156	20		6
22 Jun 67	SEE EMILY PLAY	Columbia DB 8214	6		10
1 Dec 79	ANOTHER BRICK IN THE WALL (PART 2)	Harvest HAR 5194 ⊛ ★	1	5	10
7 Aug 82	WHEN THE TIGERS BROKE FREE	Harvest HAR 5222	39		1
7 May 83	NOT NOW JOHN	Harvest HAR 5224	30		3
19 Dec 87	ON THE TURNING AWAY	EMI EM 34	55		
25 Jun 88	ONE SLIP	EMI EM 52	50		
4 Jun 94	TAKE IT BACK	EMI CDEMS 309	23		2
29 Oct 94	HIGH HOPES/KEEP TALKING	EMI CDEMS 342	26		2

PINK GREASE UK group

Date	Title	Label	Peak Position	Weeks at No.1	Weeks in Top 40
26 Jun 04	THE PINK GREASE	Mute CDMUTE316	75		
22 Jan 05	STRIP	Mute CDMUTE325	36		1
9 Apr 05	PEACHES	Mute CDMUTE343	44		

PINKEES UK group

Date	Title	Label	Peak Position	Weeks at No.1	Weeks in Top 40
18 Sep 82	DANGER GAMES	Creole CR 39	8		6

PINKERTON'S ASSORTED COLOURS UK group

Date	Title	Label	Peak Position	Weeks at No.1	Weeks in Top 40
13 Jan 66	MIRROR MIRROR	Decca F 12307	9		9
21 Apr 66	DON'T STOP LOVIN' ME BABY	Decca F 12377	50		

PINKY & PERKY UK puppet duo

Date	Title	Label	Peak Position	Weeks at No.1	Weeks in Top 40
29 May 93	REET PETITE	Telstar CDPIGGY 1	47		

LISA PIN-UP UK producer

Date	Title	Label	Peak Position	Weeks at No.1	Weeks in Top 40
25 May 02	TURN UP THE SOUND	Nukleuz NUKC 0406	60		
21 Dec 02	BLOW YOUR MIND (I AM THE WOMAN)	Nukleuz 0450 FNUK	60		

PIONEERS Jamaican group

Date	Title	Label	Peak Position	Weeks at No.1	Weeks in Top 40
18 Oct 69	LONG SHOT KICK DE BUCKET	Trojan TR 672	21		8
31 Jul 71	LET YOUR YEAH BE YEAH	Trojan TR 7825	5		9
15 Jan 72	GIVE AND TAKE	Trojan TR 7846	35		3
29 Mar 80	LONG SHOT KICK DE BUCKET	Trojan TRO 9063	42		

BILLIE PIPER UK singer

Date	Title	Label	Peak Position	Weeks at No.1	Weeks in Top 40
11 Jul 98	BECAUSE WE WANT TO BILLIE ○	Innocent SINCD 2	1	1	8
17 Oct 98	GIRLFRIEND BILLIE ○	Innocent SINCD 3	1	1	8
19 Dec 98	SHE WANTS YOU BILLIE ○	Innocent SINDXX 6	3		5
3 Apr 99	HONEY TO THE BEE BILLIE ○	Innocent SINCD 8	3		5
19 Apr 99	THANK ABBA FOR THE MUSIC STEPS/TINA COUSINS/CLEOPATRA/B*WITCHED/BILLIE	EPIC ABCA1	4		11
27 May 00	DAY & NIGHT	Innocent SINDX 11 ○	1	1	7
30 Sep 00	SOMETHING DEEP INSIDE	Innocent SINDX 19	4		3
23 Dec 00	WALK OF LIFE	Innocent SINDX 23	25		3
27 Jan 07	HONEY TO THE BEE	Innocent SINCD 8	17		1

PIPETTES UK group

Date	Title	Label	Peak Position	Weeks at No.1	Weeks in Top 40
26 Nov 05	DIRTY MIND	Memphis Industries MI053CDS	63		
8 Apr 06	YOUR KISSES ARE WASTED ON ME	Memphis Industries MI062CDS	35		1
15 Jul 06	PULL SHAPES	Memphis Industries MI071CDS	26		1
7 Oct 06	JUDY	Memphis Industries MI077CDS	46		

PIPKINS UK duo

Date	Title	Label	Peak Position	Weeks at No.1	Weeks in Top 40
28 Mar 70	GIMME DAT DING	Columbia DB 8662	6		9

Key: Silver-selling ● · Gold-selling ● · Platinum-selling ⊛ · US No.1 ★ · Peak Position · Weeks at No.1 · Weeks in Top 40

PIRANHAS UK group

Date	Title / Label	Peak Position	Weeks at No.1	Weeks in Top 40
2 Aug 80	**TOM HARK** *Sire SIR 4044* ●	6		9
16 Oct 82	**ZAMBESI** *Dakota DAK 6* PIRANHAS FEATURING BORING BOB GROVER	17		7

PIRATES UK group

Date	Title / Label	Peak Position	Weeks at No.1	Weeks in Top 40
11 Sep 04	**YOU SHOULD READILY KNOW** *Relentless RELDX6* PIRATES FEATURING ENYA, SHOLA AMA, NAILA BOSS & ISHANI	8		6

PITCHSHIFTER UK group

Date	Title / Label	Peak Position	Weeks at No.1	Weeks in Top 40
28 Feb 98	**GENIUS** *Geffen GFSTD 22324*	71		
26 Sep 98	**MICROWAVED** *Geffen GFSTD 22348*	54		
21 Oct 00	**DEAD BATTERY** *MCA MCSTD 40241*	71		
29 Jun 02	**SHUTDOWN** *Mayan MYNX 008X*	66		

GENE PITNEY US singer

Date	Title / Label	Peak Position	Weeks at No.1	Weeks in Top 40
23 Mar 61	**(I WANNA) LOVE MY LIFE AWAY** *London HL 9270*	26		8
8 Mar 62	**TOWN WITHOUT PITY** *HMV POP 952*	32		4
5 Dec 63	**TWENTY FOUR HOURS FROM TULSA** *United Artists UP 1035*	5		17
5 Mar 64	**THAT GIRL BELONGS TO YESTERDAY** *United Artists UP 1045*	7		10
15 Oct 64	**IT HURTS TO BE IN LOVE** *United Artists UP 1063*	36		1
12 Nov 64	**I'M GONNA BE STRONG** *Stateside SS 358*	2		13
18 Feb 65	**I MUST BE SEEING THINGS** *Stateside SS 390*	6		9
10 Jun 65	**LOOKING THROUGH THE EYES OF LOVE** *Stateside SS 420*	3		11
4 Nov 65	**PRINCESS IN RAGS** *Stateside SS 471*	9		10
17 Feb 66	**BACKSTAGE** *Stateside SS 490*	4		8
9 Jun 66	**NOBODY NEEDS YOUR LOVE** *Stateside SS 518*	2		12
10 Nov 66	**JUST ONE SMILE** *Stateside SS 558*	8		10
23 Feb 67	**(IN THE) COLD LIGHT OF DAY** *Stateside SS 597*	38		5
15 Nov 67	**SOMETHING'S GOTTEN HOLD OF MY HEART** *Stateside SS 2060*	5		12
3 Apr 68	**SOMEWHERE IN THE COUNTRY** *Stateside SS 2103*	19		9
27 Nov 68	**YOURS UNTIL TOMORROW** *Stateside SS 2131*	34		4
5 Mar 69	**MARIA ELENA** *Stateside SS 2142*	25		5
14 Mar 70	**A STREET CALLED HOPE** *Stateside SS 2164*	37		2
3 Oct 70	**SHADY LADY** *Stateside SS 2177*	29		6
28 Apr 73	**24 SYCAMORE** *Pye International 7N 25606*	34		2
2 Nov 74	**BLUE ANGEL** *Bronze BRO 11*	39		1
14 Jan 89	**SOMETHING'S GOTTEN HOLD OF MY HEART** *Parlophone R 6201* MARC ALMOND FEATURING SPECIAL GUEST STAR GENE PITNEY ●	1	4	10

MARIO PIU Italian producer

Date	Title / Label	Peak Position	Weeks at No.1	Weeks in Top 40
11 Dec 99	**COMMUNICATION (SOMEBODY ANSWER THE PHONE)** *Incentive CENT 2CDS*	5		7
10 Mar 01	**THE VISION** *BXR BXRC 0253* MARIO PIU PRESENTS DJ ARABESQUE	16		2

PIXIES US group

Date	Title / Label	Peak Position	Weeks at No.1	Weeks in Top 40
1 Apr 89	**MONKEY GONE TO HEAVEN** *4AD AD 904*	60		
1 Jul 89	**HERE COMES YOUR MAN** *4AD AD 909*	54		
28 Jul 90	**VELOURIA** *4AD AD 0009*	28		1
10 Nov 90	**DIG FOR FIRE** *4AD AD 0014*	62		
8 Jun 91	**PLANET OF SOUND** *4AD AD 1008*	27		2
4 Oct 97	**DEBASER** *4AD BADO 7010CD*	23		1

PIZZAMAN UK production group

Date	Title / Label	Peak Position	Weeks at No.1	Weeks in Top 40
27 Aug 94	**TRIPPIN' ON SUNSHINE** *Loaded CDLOAD 16*	33		1
10 Jun 95	**SEX ON THE STREETS** *Cowboy CDLOAD 24*	24		2
18 Nov 95	**HAPPINESS** *Cowboy CDLOAD 29*	19		2
6 Jan 96	**SEX ON THE STREETS** *Cowboy CDLOAD 24*	23		2
1 Jun 96	**TRIPPIN' ON SUNSHINE** *Cowboy CDLOAD 32*	18		2
14 Sep 96	**HELLO HONKY TONKS (ROCK YOUR BODY)** *Cowboy CDLOAD 39*	41		

PIZZICATO FIVE Japanese group

Date	Title / Label	Peak Position	Weeks at No.1	Weeks in Top 40
1 Nov 97	**MON AMOUR TOKYO** *Matador OLE 2902*	72		

PJ Canadian producer

Date	Title / Label	Peak Position	Weeks at No.1	Weeks in Top 40
20 Sep 97	**HAPPY DAYS** *Deconstruction 74321511822*	72		
4 Sep 99	**HAPPY DAYS (REMIX)** *Defected DFECT 6CDS*	57		

PJB US group

Date	Title / Label	Peak Position	Weeks at No.1	Weeks in Top 40
14 Sep 91	**BRIDGE OVER TROUBLED WATER** *Dance Pool 6565467* PJB FEATURING HANNAH & HER SISTERS	21		6

PKA UK producer

Date	Title / Label	Peak Position	Weeks at No.1	Weeks in Top 40
20 Apr 91	**TEMPERATURE RISING** *Stress SS 4*	68		
7 Mar 92	**POWERSIGN (ONLY YOUR LOVE)** *Stress PKA 1*	70		

PLACEBO US/Swedish group

Date	Title / Label	Peak Position	Weeks at No.1	Weeks in Top 40
28 Sep 96	**TEENAGE ANGST** *Elevator Music FLOORCD 3*	30		1
1 Feb 97	**NANCY BOY** *Elevator Music FLOORCD 4*	4		4
24 May 97	**BRUISE PRISTINE** *Elevator Music FLOORCD 5*	14		1
15 Aug 98	**PURE MORNING** *Hut FLOORCD 6*	4		4
10 Oct 98	**YOU DON'T CARE ABOUT US** *Hut FLOORCD 7*	5		3
6 Feb 99	**EVERY YOU EVERY ME** *Hut FLOORDX 9*	11		2
29 Jul 00	**TASTE IN MEN** *Hut FLOORD 11*	16		2
7 Oct 00	**SLAVE TO THE WAGE** *Hut FLOORDX 12*	19		2
22 Mar 03	**BITTER END** *Hut FLOORDX 16*	12		3
28 Jun 03	**THIS PICTURE** *Hut FLOORCD 18*	23		1
27 Sep 03	**SPECIAL NEEDS** *Hut FLOORCD 19*	27		1
6 Mar 04	**ENGLISH SUMMER RAIN** *Hut FLOORDX 21*	23		1
30 Oct 04	**TWENTY YEARS** *Virgin FLOORDX24*	18		1
18 Mar 06	**BECAUSE I WANT YOU** *Virgin FLOORCD25*	13		2
1 Jul 06	**INFRA-RED** *Virgin FLOORCD29*	42		
21 Oct 06	**MEDS** *Virgin FLOORCD30* PLACEBO FEATURING ALISON MOSSHART	35		1
3 Feb 07	**RUNNING UP THAT HILL** *Download*	66		

PLAIN WHITE T'S US group

Date	Title / Label	Peak Position	Weeks at No.1	Weeks in Top 40
28 Jul 07	**HEY THERE DELILAH** *Hollywood/Angel ANGECDX52* ★	2		25
19 Jan 08	**HATE (I REALLY DON'T LIKE YOU)** *Hollywood/Angel CASD9*	53		

PLAN B UK rapper

Date	Title / Label	Peak Position	Weeks at No.1	Weeks in Top 40
22 Jul 06	**MAMA (LOVES A CRACKHEAD)** *679 679L135CD*	41		

PLANET FUNK Italian group

Date	Title / Label	Peak Position	Weeks at No.1	Weeks in Top 40
10 Feb 01	**CHASE THE SUN** *Virgin VSCDT 1749*	5		4
26 Apr 03	**WHO SAID (STUCK IN THE UK)** *Illustrious/Bustin L CDILL 015*	36		1
16 Aug 03	**THE SWITCH** *Illustrious/Epic CDILL 017*	52		
19 Mar 05	**THE SWITCH** *Direction 6757882*	66		

PLANET PATROL US group

Date	Title / Label	Peak Position	Weeks at No.1	Weeks in Top 40
17 Sep 83	**CHEAP THRILLS** *Polydor POSP 639*	64		

PLANET PERFECTO UK producer

Date	Title / Label	Peak Position	Weeks at No.1	Weeks in Top 40
14 Aug 99	**NOT OVER YET 99** *Code Blue BLU 004CD* PLANET PERFECTO FEATURING GRACE	16		2
13 Nov 99	**BULLET IN THE GUN** *Perfecto PERF 3CDS*	15		2
16 Sep 00	**BULLET IN THE GUN 2000 (REMIX)** *Perfecto PERF 03CDSX*	7		4
29 Sep 01	**BITES DA DUST** *Perfecto PERF 19CDS*	52		

PLANETS UK group

Date	Title / Label	Peak Position	Weeks at No.1	Weeks in Top 40
18 Aug 79	**LINES** *Rialto TREB 104*	36		2
25 Oct 80	**DON'T LOOK DOWN** *Rialto TREB 116*	66		

PLANK 15 UK group

Date	Title / Label	Peak Position	Weeks at No.1	Weeks in Top 40
2 Feb 02	**STRINGS OF LIFE** *Multiply CDMULTY 82*	60		

ROBERT PLANT UK singer

Date	Title / Label	Peak Position	Weeks at No.1	Weeks in Top 40
9 Oct 82	**BURNING DOWN ONE SIDE** *Swansong SSK 19429*	73		
16 Jul 83	**BIG LOG** *WEA B 9848*	11		7
30 Jan 88	**HEAVEN KNOWS** *Es Paranza A 9373*	33		2
28 Apr 90	**HURTING KIND (I'VE GOT MY EYES ON YOU)** *Es Paranza A 8985*	45		
8 May 93	**29 PALMS** *Fontana FATEX 1*	21		3
3 Jul 93	**I BELIEVE** *Fontana FATEX 2*	64		
25 Dec 93	**IF I WERE A CARPENTER** *Fontana FATEX 4*	63		
17 Dec 94	**GALLOWS POLE** *Fontana PPCD 2* JIMMY PAGE & ROBERT PLANT	35		1

Date	Title / Label	Peak Position	Weeks at No.1	Weeks in Top 40
11 Apr 98	**MOST HIGH** *Mercury 5687512* JIMMY PAGE & ROBERT PLANT	26		1
7 May 05	**SHINE IT ALL AROUND** *Universal MCSTD40412* ROBERT PLANT & THE STRANGE SENSATION	32		1

PLASMATICS US group

Date	Title / Label	Peak Position	Weeks at No.1	Weeks in Top 40
26 Jul 80	**BUTCHER BABY** *Stiff BUY 76*	55		

PLASTIC BERTRAND Belgian singer

Date	Title / Label	Peak Position	Weeks at No.1	Weeks in Top 40
13 May 78	**CA PLANE POUR MOI** *Sire 6078 616*	8		9
5 Aug 78	**SHA LA LA LA LEE** *Vertigo 6059 209*	39		1

PLASTIC BOY Belgian producer

Date	Title / Label	Peak Position	Weeks at No.1	Weeks in Top 40
22 Nov 03	**LIVE ANOTHER LIFE** *Inferno CDFERN 59* PLASTIC BOY FEATURING ROZALLA	55		

PLASTIC PENNY UK group

Date	Title / Label	Peak Position	Weeks at No.1	Weeks in Top 40
3 Jan 68	**EVERYTHING I AM** *Page One POF 051*	6		10

PLATINUM 45 UK producer

Date	Title / Label	Peak Position	Weeks at No.1	Weeks in Top 40
16 Mar 02	**OI** *Go! Beat GOBCD 48* PLATINUM 45 FEATURING MORE FIRE CREW	8		5

PLATINUM HOOK US R&B group

Date	Title / Label	Peak Position	Weeks at No.1	Weeks in Top 40
2 Sep 78	**STANDING ON THE VERGE (OF GETTING IT ON)** *Motown TMG 1115*	72		

PLATTERS US group

Date	Title / Label	Peak Position	Weeks at No.1	Weeks in Top 40
7 Sep 56	**THE GREAT PRETENDER/ONLY YOU** *Mercury MT 117* ★	5		16
2 Nov 56	**MY PRAYER** *Mercury MT 120* ★	4		13
25 Jan 57	**YOU'LL NEVER NEVER KNOW/IT ISN'T RIGHT** *Mercury MT 130*	23		3
17 May 57	**I'M SORRY** *Mercury MT 145*	18		8
16 May 58	**TWILIGHT TIME** *Mercury MT 214* ★	3		18
16 Jan 59	**SMOKE GETS IN YOUR EYES** *Mercury AMT 1016* ★	1	1	20
28 Aug 59	**REMEMBER WHEN** *Mercury AMT 1053*	25		2
29 Jan 60	**HARBOUR LIGHTS** *Mercury AMT 1081*	11		11

PLAYER US group

Date	Title / Label	Peak Position	Weeks at No.1	Weeks in Top 40
25 Feb 78	**BABY COME BACK** *RSO 2090 254* ★	32		6

PLAYERS ASSOCIATION US group

Date	Title / Label	Peak Position	Weeks at No.1	Weeks in Top 40
10 Mar 79	**TURN THE MUSIC UP** *Vanguard VS 5011*	8		7
5 May 79	**RIDE THE GROOVE** *Vanguard VS 5012*	42		
9 Feb 80	**WE GOT THE GROOVE** *Vanguard VS 5016*	61		

PLAYGROUP UK producer

Date	Title / Label	Peak Position	Weeks at No.1	Weeks in Top 40
24 Nov 01	**NUMBER ONE** *Source SOURCD 026*	66		

PLAYTHING Italian production duo

Date	Title / Label	Peak Position	Weeks at No.1	Weeks in Top 40
5 May 01	**INTO SPACE** *Manifesto FESCD 81*	48		
24 Aug 02	**DO YOU SEE THE LIGHT** *Data 33CDS* SNAP VS PLAYTHING	14		3

PLUMB US singer

Date	Title / Label	Peak Position	Weeks at No.1	Weeks in Top 40
14 Feb 04	**REAL** *Curb CUBC 095*	41		

PLUMMET US duo

Date	Title / Label	Peak Position	Weeks at No.1	Weeks in Top 40
26 Apr 03	**DAMAGED** *Serious SER 68CD*	12		7
8 May 04	**CHERISH THE DAY** *Manifesto 9866389*	35		1

PLUS 44 US group

Date	Title / Label	Peak Position	Weeks at No.1	Weeks in Top 40
24 Feb 07	**WHEN YOUR HEART STOPS BEATING** *Interscope 1724085*	47		

PLUS ONE UK group

Date	Title / Label	Peak Position	Weeks at No.1	Weeks in Top 40
19 May 90	**IT'S HAPPENIN'** *MCA 1405* PLUS ONE FEATURING SIRRON	40		1

PLUX US group

Date	Title / Label	Peak Position	Weeks at No.1	Weeks in Top 40
4 May 96	**OVER & OVER** *ffrr FCD 277* PLUX FEATURING GEORGIA JONES	33		1

PM DAWN US duo

Date	Title / Label	Peak Position	Weeks at No.1	Weeks in Top 40
8 Jun 91	**A WATCHER'S POINT OF VIEW (DON'T CHA THINK)** *Gee Street GEE 32*	36		2
17 Aug 91	**SET ADRIFT ON A MEMORY BLISS** *Gee Street GEE 33* ★	3		7
19 Oct 91	**PAPER DOLL** *Gee Street GEE 35*	49		
22 Feb 92	**REALITY USED TO BE A GOOD FRIEND OF MINE** *Gee Street GEE 37*	29		2
7 Nov 92	**I'D DIE WITHOUT YOU** *Gee Street GEE 39*	30		3
13 Mar 93	**LOOKING THROUGH PATIENT EYES** *Gee Street GESCD 47*	11		5
12 Jun 93	**MORE THAN LIKELY** *Gee Street GESCD 49* PM DAWN FEATURING BOY GEORGE	40		1
30 Sep 95	**DOWNTOWN VENUS** *Gee Street GESCD 63*	58		
6 Apr 96	**SOMETIMES I MISS YOU SO MUCH** *Gee Street GESCD 65*	58		
31 Oct 98	**GOTTA…MOVIN' ON UP** *Gee Street GEE 5003933* PM DAWN FEATURING KY-MANI	68		

POB UK producer

Date	Title / Label	Peak Position	Weeks at No.1	Weeks in Top 40
11 Dec 99	**BLUEBOTTLE/FLY** *Platipus PLAT 63CD* POB FEATURING DJ PATRICK REID	74		

P.O.D. US group

Date	Title / Label	Peak Position	Weeks at No.1	Weeks in Top 40
2 Feb 02	**ALIVE** *Atlantic AT 0119CD*	19		4
18 May 02	**YOUTH OF THE NATION** *East West AT 0127CD*	36		1
7 Jun 03	**SLEEPING AWAKE** *Maverick W 608CD*	42		
24 Jan 04	**WILL YOU** *Atlantic AT 0169CD*	68		

POETS UK group

Date	Title / Label	Peak Position	Weeks at No.1	Weeks in Top 40
29 Oct 64	**NOW WE'RE THRU** *Decca F 11995*	31		5

POGUES UK group

Date	Title / Label	Peak Position	Weeks at No.1	Weeks in Top 40
6 Apr 85	**A PAIR OF BROWN EYES** *Stiff BUY 220*	72		
22 Jun 85	**SALLY MACLENNANE** *Stiff BUY 224*	51		
14 Sep 85	**DIRTY OLD TOWN** *Stiff BUY 229*	62		
8 Mar 86	**POGUETRY IN MOTION EP** *Stiff BUY 243*	29		4
30 Aug 86	**HAUNTED** *MCA 1084*	42		
28 Mar 87	**THE IRISH ROVER** *Stiff BUY 258* POGUES & THE DUBLINERS	8		6
5 Dec 87	**FAIRYTALE OF NEW YORK** *Pogue Mahone NY 7* POGUES FEATURING KIRSTY MacCOLL ●	2		8
5 Mar 88	**IF I SHOULD FALL FROM GRACE WITH GOD** *Pogue Mahone PG 1*	58		
16 Jul 88	**FIESTA** *Pogue Mahone PG 2*	24		3
17 Dec 88	**YEAH YEAH YEAH YEAH YEAH** *Pogue Mahone YZ 355*	43		
8 Jul 89	**MISTY MORNING, ALBERT BRIDGE** *PM YZ 407*	41		
16 Jun 90	**JACK'S HEROES/WHISKEY IN THE JAR** *Pogue Mahone YZ 500* POGUES & THE DUBLINERS	63		
15 Sep 90	**SUMMER IN SIAM** *PM YZ 519*	64		
21 Sep 91	**A RAINY NIGHT IN SOHO** *PM YZ 603*	67		
14 Dec 91	**FAIRYTALE OF NEW YORK** *PM YZ 628* POGUES FEATURING KIRSTY MacCOLL	36		2
30 May 92	**HONKY TONK WOMEN** *PM YZ 673*	56		
21 Aug 93	**TUESDAY MORNING** *PM YZ 758CD*	18		3
22 Jan 94	**ONCE UPON A TIME** *PM YZ 771CD*	66		
31 Dec 05	**FAIRYTALE OF NEW YORK** *Warner Brothers WEA400CD* POGUES FEATURING KIRSTY MacCOLL	3		3
9 Dec 06	**FAIRYTALE OF NEW YORK** *Warner Brothers WEA400CD* POGUES FEATURING KIRSTY MacCOLL	6		4
8 Dec 07	**FAIRYTALE OF NEW YORK** *Warner Brothers WEA400CD* POGUES FEATURING KIRSTY MacCOLL	4		5

POINT BREAK UK group

Date	Title / Label	Peak Position	Weeks at No.1	Weeks in Top 40
9 Oct 99	**DO WE ROCK** *Eternal WEA 216CD1*	29		1
22 Jan 00	**STAND TOUGH** *Eternal WEA 248CD2*	7		3
22 Apr 00	**FREAKYTIME** *Eternal WEA 265CD1*	13		3

Silver-selling ○ Gold-selling ● Platinum-selling US No.1 ★ Peak Position Weeks at No.1 Weeks in Top 40

Date	Title / Label	Peak Position	Weeks at No.1	Weeks in Top 40
5 Aug 00	**YOU** *Eternal WEA 290CD1*	14		3
2 Dec 00	**WHAT ABOUT US** *Eternal WEA 314CD1*	24		1

POINTER SISTERS US group

Date	Title / Label	Peak Position	Weeks at No.1	Weeks in Top 40
3 Feb 79	**EVERYBODY IS A STAR** *Planet K 12324*	61		
17 Mar 79	**FIRE** *Planet K 12339*	34		4
22 Aug 81	**SLOWHAND** *Planet K 12530*	10		9
5 Dec 81	**SHOULD I DO IT?** *Reprise K 12578*	50		
14 Apr 84	**AUTOMATIC** *Planet RPS 105* ○	2		10
23 Jun 84	**JUMP (FOR MY LOVE)** *Planet RPS 106*	6		9
11 Aug 84	**I NEED YOU** *Planet RPS 107*	25		5
27 Oct 84	**I'M SO EXCITED** *Planet RPS 108*	11		7
12 Jan 85	**NEUTRON DANCE** *Planet RPS 109*	31		3
20 Jul 85	**DARE ME** *RCA PB 49957*	17		6

POISON US group

Date	Title / Label	Peak Position	Weeks at No.1	Weeks in Top 40
23 May 87	**TALK DIRTY TO ME** *Music For Nations KUT 125*	67		
7 May 88	**NOTHIN' BUT A GOOD TIME** *Capitol CL 486*	35		1
5 Nov 88	**FALLEN ANGEL** *Capitol CL 500*	59		
11 Feb 89	**EVERY ROSE HAS ITS THORN** *Capitol CL 520* ★	13		8
29 Apr 89	**YOUR MAMA DON'T DANCE** *Capitol CL 523*	13		5
23 Sep 89	**NOTHIN' BUT A GOOD TIME** *Capitol CL 539*	48		
30 Jun 90	**UNSKINNY BOP** *Capitol CL 582*	15		6
27 Oct 90	**SOMETHING TO BELIEVE IN** *Enigma CL 594*	35		3
23 Nov 91	**SO TELL ME WHY** *Capitol CL 640*	25		2
13 Feb 93	**STAND** *Capitol CDCL 679*	25		1
24 Apr 93	**UNTIL YOU SUFFER SOME (FIRE AND ICE)** *Capitol CDCL 685*	32		2

POKER PETS UK production duo

Date	Title / Label	Peak Position	Weeks at No.1	Weeks in Top 40
25 Jun 05	**LOVIN' YOU** *Positiva CDTIVS218* POKER PETS FEATURING NATE JAMES	43		

POLECATS UK group

Date	Title / Label	Peak Position	Weeks at No.1	Weeks in Top 40
7 Mar 81	**JOHN I'M ONLY DANCING/BIG GREEN CAR** *Mercury POLE 1*	35		4
16 May 81	**ROCKABILLY GUY** *Mercury POLE 2*	35		3
22 Aug 81	**JEEPSTER/MARIE CELESTE** *Mercury POLE 3*	53		

POLICE UK/US group

Date	Title / Label	Peak Position	Weeks at No.1	Weeks in Top 40
7 Oct 78	**CAN'T STAND LOSING YOU** *A&M AMS 7381*	42		
28 Apr 79	**ROXANNE** *A&M AMS 7348*	12		7
7 Jul 79	**CAN'T STAND LOSING YOU** *A&M AMS 7381* ○	2		8
22 Sep 79	**MESSAGE IN A BOTTLE** *A&M AMS 7474* ●	1	3	8
17 Nov 79	**FALL OUT** *Illegal IL 001*	47		
1 Dec 79	**WALKING ON THE MOON** *A&M AMS 7494* ●	1	1	8
16 Feb 80	**SO LONELY** *A&M AMS 7402* ○	6		7
14 Jun 80	**SIX PACK** *A&M AMPP 6001*	17		3
27 Sep 80	**DON'T STAND SO CLOSE TO ME** *A&M AMS 7564* ●	1	4	8
13 Dec 80	**DE DO DO DO, DE DA DA DA** *A&M AMS 7578* ●	5		7
26 Sep 81	**INVISIBLE SUN** *A&M AMS 8164* ○	2		6
24 Oct 81	**EVERY LITTLE THING SHE DOES IS MAGIC** *A&M AMS 8174* ○	1	1	8
12 Dec 81	**SPIRITS IN THE MATERIAL WORLD** *A&M AMS 8194* ○	12		7
28 May 83	**EVERY BREATH YOU TAKE** *A&M AM 117* ○ ★	1	4	10
23 Jul 83	**WRAPPED AROUND YOUR FINGER** *A&M AM 127*	7		6
5 Nov 83	**SYNCHRONICITY II** *A&M AM 153*	17		3
14 Jan 84	**KING OF PAIN** *A&M AM 176*	17		3
11 Oct 86	**DON'T STAND SO CLOSE TO ME (REMIX)** *A&M AM 354*	24		3
13 May 95	**CAN'T STAND LOSING YOU (LIVE)** *A&M 5810372*	27		1
20 Dec 97	**ROXANNE '97 (REMIX)** *A&M 5824552* STING & THE POLICE	17		3
5 Aug 00	**WHEN THE WORLD IS RUNNING DOWN** *Pagan 039CDS* DIFFERENT GEAR VERSUS THE POLICE	28		1

SU POLLARD UK actress

Date	Title / Label	Peak Position	Weeks at No.1	Weeks in Top 40
5 Oct 85	**COME TO ME (I AM WOMAN)** *Rainbow RBR 1*	71		
1 Feb 86	**STARTING TOGETHER** *Rainbow RBR 4* ○	2		7

JIM POLO US singer

Date	Title / Label	Peak Position	Weeks at No.1	Weeks in Top 40
9 Nov 91	**NEVER GOIN' DOWN/BORN TO BE ALIVE** *MCA MCS 1578* ADAMSKI FEATURING JIMI POLO/ADAMSKI FEATURING SOHO	51		
1 Aug 92	**EXPRESS YOURSELF** *Perfecto 74321101827*	59		
9 Aug 97	**EXPRESS YOURSELF (REMIX)** *Perfecto PERF 146CD1*	62		

POLOROID UK singer

Date	Title / Label	Peak Position	Weeks at No.1	Weeks in Top 40
11 Oct 03	**SO DAMN BEAUTIFUL** *Decode/Telstar CXSTAS 3351*	28		1

POLTERGEIST UK producer

Date	Title / Label	Peak Position	Weeks at No.1	Weeks in Top 40
6 Jul 96	**VICIOUS CIRCLES** *Manifesto FESCD 8*	32		1

PETER POLYCARPOU UK singer/actor

Date	Title / Label	Peak Position	Weeks at No.1	Weeks in Top 40
20 Feb 93	**LOVE HURTS** *Soundtrack Music CDEM 259*	26		2

POLYGON WINDOW UK producer

Date	Title / Label	Peak Position	Weeks at No.1	Weeks in Top 40
3 Apr 93	**QUOTH** *Warp WAP 33CD*	49		

POLYPHONIC SPREE US group

Date	Title / Label	Peak Position	Weeks at No.1	Weeks in Top 40
2 Nov 02	**HANGING AROUND** *679 Recordings 679L 012CD*	39		1
22 Feb 03	**LIGHT AND DAY** *679 Recordings 679L 015CD*	40		1
26 Jul 03	**SOLDIER GIRL** *679 Recordings 679L 014CD*	26		1
7 Aug 04	**HOLD ME NOW** *Good CDPOLY1*	72		

PONDLIFE UK group

Date	Title / Label	Peak Position	Weeks at No.1	Weeks in Top 40
18 Jun 05	**RING DING DING** *Gut CDSNOG14*	11		5

PONI-TAILS US group

Date	Title / Label	Peak Position	Weeks at No.1	Weeks in Top 40
19 Sep 58	**BORN TOO LATE** *HMV POP 516*	5		11
10 Apr 59	**EARLY TO BED** *HMV POP 596*	26		3

BRIAN POOLE & THE TREMELOES UK group

Date	Title / Label	Peak Position	Weeks at No.1	Weeks in Top 40
4 Jul 63	**TWIST AND SHOUT** *Decca F 11694*	4		13
12 Sep 63	**DO YOU LOVE ME** *Decca F 11739*	1	3	14
28 Nov 63	**I CAN DANCE** *Decca F 11771*	31		6
30 Jan 64	**CANDY MAN** *Decca F 11823*	6		11
7 May 64	**SOMEONE SOMEONE** *Decca F 11893*	2		15
20 Aug 64	**TWELVE STEPS TO LOVE** *Decca F 11951*	32		6
31 Dec 64	**THREE BELLS** *Decca F 12037*	17		8
22 Jul 65	**I WANT CANDY** *Decca F 12197*	25		6

GLYN POOLE UK singer

Date	Title / Label	Peak Position	Weeks at No.1	Weeks in Top 40
20 Oct 73	**MILLY MOLLY MANDY** *York SYK 565*	35		4

IAN POOLEY German producer

Date	Title / Label	Peak Position	Weeks at No.1	Weeks in Top 40
10 Mar 01	**900 DEGREES** *V2 VVR 5015143*	57		
11 Aug 01	**BALMES** *V2 VVR 5016613* IAN POOLEY FEATURING ESTHERO	65		
23 Nov 02	**PIHA** *Honchos Music HONM019CD* IAN POOLEY & MAGIK J	53		

POP! UK group

Date	Title / Label	Peak Position	Weeks at No.1	Weeks in Top 40
12 Jun 04	**HEAVEN AND EARTH** *Jive 82876619582*	14		1
11 Sep 04	**CAN'T SAY GOODBYE** *Jive 82876639492*	26		1
22 Jan 05	**SERIOUS** *Ebul/Jive 82876668682*	16		2

IGGY POP US singer

Date	Title / Label	Peak Position	Weeks at No.1	Weeks in Top 40
13 Dec 86	**REAL WILD CHILD (WILD ONE)** *A&M AM 368*	10		5
10 Feb 90	**LIVIN' ON THE EDGE OF THE NIGHT** *Virgin America VUS 18*	51		
13 Oct 90	**CANDY** *Virgin America VUS 29*	67		
5 Jan 91	**WELL DID YOU EVAH!** *Chrysalis CHS 3646* DEBORAH HARRY & IGGY POP	42		
4 Sep 93	**THE WILD AMERICA (EP)** *Virgin America VUSCD 74*	63		
21 May 94	**BESIDE YOU** *Virgin America VUSCD 77*	47		
23 Nov 96	**LUST FOR LIFE** *Virgin VUSCDT 116*	26		1
7 Mar 98	**THE PASSENGER** *Virgin VSCDT 1689*	22		2
17 Jan 04	**KICK IT** *XL Recordings XLS 176CD* PEACHES FEATURING IGGY POP	39		1

POP WILL EAT ITSELF UK group

Date	Title / Label	Peak Position	Weeks at No.1	Weeks in Top 40
30 Jan 88	**THERE IS NO LOVE BETWEEN US ANYMORE** *Chapter 22 CHAP 20*	66		
23 Jul 88	**DEF CON ONE** *Chapter 22 PWEI 001*	63		
11 Feb 89	**CAN U DIG IT** *RCA PB 42621*	38		2
22 Apr 89	**WISE UP! SUCKER** *RCA PB 42761*	41		
2 Sep 89	**VERY METAL NOISE POLLUTION (EP)** *RCA PB 42883*	45		
9 Jun 90	**TOUCHED BY THE HAND OF CICCIOLINA** *RCA PB 43735*	28		3
13 Oct 90	**DANCE OF THE MAD** *RCA PB 44023*	32		2
12 Jan 91	**X Y & ZEE** *RCA PB 44243*	15		3
1 Jun 91	**92 DEGREES** *RCA PB 44555*	23		2
6 Jun 92	**KARMADROME/EAT ME DRINK ME LOVE ME** *RCA PB 45467*	17		2
29 Aug 92	**BULLETPROOF!** *RCA 74321110137*	24		1
16 Jan 93	**GET THE GIRL! KILL THE BADDIES!** *RCA 74321128802*	9		2
16 Oct 93	**RSVP/FAMILIUS HORRIBILUS** *Infectious INFECT 1CD*	27		1
12 Mar 94	**ICH BIN EIN AUSLANDER** *Infectious INFECT 4CD*	28		1
10 Sep 94	**EVERYTHING'S COOL** *Infectious INFECT 9CD*	23		1

POPPERS PRESENTS AURA UK production group

Date	Title / Label	Peak Position	Weeks at No.1	Weeks in Top 40
25 Oct 97	**EVERY LITTLE TIME** *VC Recordings VCRD 26*	44		

POPPY FAMILY Canadian group

Date	Title / Label	Peak Position	Weeks at No.1	Weeks in Top 40
15 Aug 70	**WHICH WAY YOU GOIN' BILLY** *Decca F 22976*	7		11

POPPYFIELDS UK group

Date	Title / Label	Peak Position	Weeks at No.1	Weeks in Top 40
21 Feb 04	**45 RPM** *Snapper Music SMASCD055*	28		1

PORN KINGS UK production group

Date	Title / Label	Peak Position	Weeks at No.1	Weeks in Top 40
28 Sep 96	**UP TO NO GOOD** *All Around The World CDGLOBE 145*	28		1
21 Jun 97	**AMOUR (C'MON)** *All Around The World CDGLOBE 152*	17		2
16 Jan 99	**UP TO THE WILDSTYLE** *All Around The World CDGLOBE 170* PORN KINGS VERSUS DJ SUPREME	10		3
10 Feb 01	**SLEDGER** *All Around The World CDGLOBE 229*	71		
22 Mar 03	**SHAKE YA SHIMMY** *All Around The World CXGLOBE 213* PORN KINGS VERSUS FLIP & FILL FEATURING 740 BOYZ	28		1

PORNO Italian production group

Date	Title / Label	Peak Position	Weeks at No.1	Weeks in Top 40
4 Feb 06	**MUSIC POWER** *Data DATA96CDS*	72		

PORNO FOR PYROS US group

Date	Title / Label	Peak Position	Weeks at No.1	Weeks in Top 40
5 Jun 93	**PETS** *Warner Brothers W 0177CD*	53		

PORTISHEAD UK group

Date	Title / Label	Peak Position	Weeks at No.1	Weeks in Top 40
13 Aug 94	**SOUR TIMES** *Go! Beat GOLCD 116*	57		
14 Jan 95	**GLORY BOX** *Go! Beat GODCD 120*	13		5
22 Apr 95	**SOUR TIMES** *Go! Beat GOLCD 116*	13		3
20 Sep 97	**ALL MINE** *Go! Beat 5715972*	8		2
22 Nov 97	**OVER** *Go! Beat 5710932*	25		1
14 Mar 98	**ONLY YOU** *Go! Beat 5694752*	35		1

GARY PORTNOY US singer

Date	Title / Label	Peak Position	Weeks at No.1	Weeks in Top 40
25 Feb 84	**THEME FROM *CHEERS*** *Starblend CHEER 1*	58		

PORTOBELLA UK group

Date	Title / Label	Peak Position	Weeks at No.1	Weeks in Top 40
26 Jun 04	**COVERED IN PUNK** *Island CID 862*	54		

PORTRAIT US group

Date	Title / Label	Peak Position	Weeks at No.1	Weeks in Top 40
27 Mar 93	**HERE WE GO AGAIN** *Capitol CDCL 683*	37		1
8 Apr 95	**I CAN CALL YOU** *Capitol CDCL 740*	61		
8 Jul 95	**HOW DEEP IS YOUR LOVE** *Capitol CDCL 751*	41		

PORTSMOUTH SINFONIA UK orchestra

Date	Title / Label	Peak Position	Weeks at No.1	Weeks in Top 40
12 Sep 81	**CLASSICAL MUDDLEY** *Island WIP 6736*	38		1

SANDY POSEY US singer

Date	Title / Label	Peak Position	Weeks at No.1	Weeks in Top 40
15 Sep 66	**BORN A WOMAN** *MGM 1321*	24		9
5 Jan 67	**SINGLE GIRL** *MGM 1330*	15		12
13 Apr 67	**WHAT A WOMAN IN LOVE WON'T DO** *MGM 1335*	48		
6 Sep 75	**SINGLE GIRL** *MGM 2006 533*	35		4

POSIES US group

Date	Title / Label	Peak Position	Weeks at No.1	Weeks in Top 40
19 Mar 94	**DEFINITE DOOR** *Geffen GFSTD 68*	67		

POSITIVE FORCE US group

Date	Title / Label	Peak Position	Weeks at No.1	Weeks in Top 40
22 Dec 79	**WE GOT THE FUNK** *Sugarhill SHL 102*	18		5

POSITIVE GANG UK group

Date	Title / Label	Peak Position	Weeks at No.1	Weeks in Top 40
17 Apr 93	**SWEET FREEDOM** *PWL Continental PWCD 261*	34		3
31 Jul 93	**SWEET FREEDOM PART 2** *PWL Continental PWCD 264*	67		

POSITIVE K US rapper

Date	Title / Label	Peak Position	Weeks at No.1	Weeks in Top 40
15 May 93	**I GOT A MAN** *Fourth & Broadway BRCD 280*	43		

MIKE POST US orchestra leader

Date	Title / Label	Peak Position	Weeks at No.1	Weeks in Top 40
9 Aug 75	**AFTERNOON OF THE RHINO** *Warner Brothers K 16588* MIKE POST COALITION	47		
16 Jan 82	**THEME FROM *HILL STREET BLUES*** *Elektron K 12576* MIKE POST FEATURING LARRY CARLTON	25		8
29 Sep 84	**THE A TEAM** *RCA 443*	45		

ROBERT POST Norwegian singer

Date	Title / Label	Peak Position	Weeks at No.1	Weeks in Top 40
3 Sep 05	**GOT NONE** *Mercury 9872370*	42		

POTTERS UK group

Date	Title / Label	Peak Position	Weeks at No.1	Weeks in Top 40
1 Apr 72	**WE'LL BE WITH YOU** *Pye JT 100*	34		2

P.O.V. US group

Date	Title / Label	Peak Position	Weeks at No.1	Weeks in Top 40
5 Feb 94	**ALL THRU THE NITE** *Giant 74321187552* P.O.V. FEATURING JADE	32		1

POWDER UK group

Date	Title / Label	Peak Position	Weeks at No.1	Weeks in Top 40
24 Jun 95	**AFRODISIAC** *Parkway PARK 002CD*	72		

BRYAN POWELL UK singer

Date	Title / Label	Peak Position	Weeks at No.1	Weeks in Top 40
13 Mar 93	**IT'S ALRIGHT** *Talkin Loud TLKCD 34*	73		
15 May 93	**I THINK OF YOU** *Talkin Loud TLKCD 38*	61		
7 Aug 93	**NATURAL** *Talkin Loud TLKCD 41*	73		

COZY POWELL UK drummer

Date	Title / Label	Peak Position	Weeks at No.1	Weeks in Top 40
8 Dec 73	**DANCE WITH THE DEVIL** *RAK 164*	3		13
25 May 74	**THE MAN IN BLACK** *RAK 173*	18		7
10 Aug 74	**NA NA NA** *RAK 180*	10		9
10 Nov 79	**THEME ONE** *Ariola ARO 189*	62		
19 Jun 93	**RESURRECTION** *Parlophone CDRS 6351* BRIAN MAY WITH COZY POWELL	23		2

POWER OF DREAMS Irish group

Date	Title / Label	Peak Position	Weeks at No.1	Weeks in Top 40
19 Jan 91	**AMERICAN DREAM** *Polydor PO 117*	74		
11 Apr 92	**THERE I GO AGAIN** *Polydor PO 200*	65		

POWER STATION UK/US group

Date	Title / Label	Peak Position	Weeks at No.1	Weeks in Top 40
16 Mar 85	**SOME LIKE IT HOT** *Parlophone R 6091*	14		6
11 May 85	**GET IT ON** *Parlophone R 6096*	22		5
9 Nov 85	**COMMUNICATION** *Parlophone R 6114*	75		
12 Oct 96	**SHE CAN ROCK IT** *Chrysalis CDCHS 5039*	63		

Silver-selling ○ Gold-selling ● Platinum-selling ⊛ US No.1 ★ — Peak Position / Weeks at No.1 / Weeks in Top 40

POWERCUT US group

Date	Title	Peak Position	Weeks at No.1	Weeks in Top 40
22 Jun 91	**GIRLS** *Eternal YZ 570*			
	POWERCUT FEATURING NUBIAN PRINZ	50		

POWERHOUSE UK production duo

Date	Title	Peak Position	Weeks at No.1	Weeks in Top 40
20 Dec 97	**RHYTHM OF THE NIGHT** *Satellite 74321522592*	38		1
22 May 99	**WHAT YOU NEED** *Defected DEFECT 3CDS*			
	POWERHOUSE FEATURING DUANE HARDEN	13		3

POWERPILL UK producer

Date	Title	Peak Position	Weeks at No.1	Weeks in Top 40
6 Jun 92	**PAC-MAN** *ffrreedom TABX 110*	43		

WILL POWERS US singer

Date	Title	Peak Position	Weeks at No.1	Weeks in Top 40
1 Oct 83	**KISSING WITH CONFIDENCE** *Island IS 134*	17		6

POWERS THAT BE UK producer

Date	Title	Peak Position	Weeks at No.1	Weeks in Top 40
26 Jul 03	**PLANET ROCK/FUNKY PLANET** *Defected DFTD 074*	63		

DANIEL POWTER Canadian singer/pianist

Date	Title	Peak Position	Weeks at No.1	Weeks in Top 40
6 Aug 05	**BAD DAY** *Warner Brothers W682CD1* ★	2		25

PPK Russian group

Date	Title	Peak Position	Weeks at No.1	Weeks in Top 40
8 Dec 01	**RESURRECTION** *Perfecto PERF 32CDS*	3		11
26 Oct 02	**RELOAD** *Perfecto PERF 41CDS*	39		1

PQM US producer

Date	Title	Peak Position	Weeks at No.1	Weeks in Top 40
9 Dec 00	**THE FLYING SONG** *Renaissance/Yoshitoshi RENCD 004*			
	PQM FEATURING CICA	68		

PEREZ 'PREZ' PRADO Cuban orchestra leader

Date	Title	Peak Position	Weeks at No.1	Weeks in Top 40
25 Mar 55	**CHERRY PINK AND APPLE BLOSSOM WHITE** *HMV B 10833*			
	PEREZ 'PREZ' PRADO & HIS ORCHESTRA, THE KING OF THE MAMBO ★	1	2	17
25 Jul 58	**PATRICIA** *RCA 1067*	8		16
10 Dec 94	**GUAGLIONE** *RCA 74321250192*			
	PEREZ 'PREZ' PRADO & HIS ORCHESTRA	41		
8 Apr 95	**GUAGLIONE** *RCA 74321250192*			
	PEREZ 'PREZ' PRADO & HIS ORCHESTRA ●	2		10

PRAISE UK group

Date	Title	Peak Position	Weeks at No.1	Weeks in Top 40
2 Feb 91	**ONLY YOU** *Epic 6566117*	4		6

PRAISE CATS US producer

Date	Title	Peak Position	Weeks at No.1	Weeks in Top 40
26 Oct 02	**SHINED ON ME** *PIAS Recordings PIASX 028CD*			
	PRAISE CATS FEATURING ANDREA LOVE	56		
21 May 05	**SHINED ON ME** *All Around The World CDGLOBE380*			
	PRAISE CATS FEATURING ANDREA LOVE	24		2

PRATT & MCCLAIN US duo

Date	Title	Peak Position	Weeks at No.1	Weeks in Top 40
1 Oct 77	**HAPPY DAYS** *Reprise K 14435*			
	PRATT & McCLAIN WITH BROTHERLOVE	31		5

PRAXIS US duo producer

Date	Title	Peak Position	Weeks at No.1	Weeks in Top 40
25 Nov 95	**TURN ME OUT (TURN TO SUGAR)** *Stress CDSTR 40*			
	PRAXIS FEATURING KATHY BROWN	44		
20 Sep 97	**TURN ME OUT (TURN TO SUGAR) (REMIX)** *ffrr FCD 314*			
	PRAXIS FEATURING KATHY BROWN	35		1

PRAYING MANTIS UK group

Date	Title	Peak Position	Weeks at No.1	Weeks in Top 40
31 Jan 81	**CHEATED** *Arista ARIST 378*	69		

PRECIOUS UK group

Date	Title	Peak Position	Weeks at No.1	Weeks in Top 40
29 May 99	**SAY IT AGAIN** *EMI CDEM 544* ○	6		5
1 Apr 00	**REWIND** *EMI CDEM 557*	11		3
15 Jul 00	**IT'S GONNA BE MY WAY** *EMI CDEMS 569*	27		1
25 Nov 00	**NEW BEGINNING** *EMI CDEM 573*	50		

PRECOCIOUS BRATS UK production duo

Date	Title	Peak Position	Weeks at No.1	Weeks in Top 40
6 May 00	**BIG GIRL** *Virgin VTSCD 1*			
	PRECOCIOUS BRATS FEATURING KEVIN & PERRY	16		3

PREFAB SPROUT UK group

Date	Title	Peak Position	Weeks at No.1	Weeks in Top 40
28 Jan 84	**DON'T SING** *Kitchenware SK 9*	62		
20 Jul 85	**FARON YOUNG** *Kitchenware SK 22*	74		
9 Nov 85	**WHEN LOVE BREAKS DOWN** *Kitchenware SK 21*	25		4
8 Feb 86	**JOHNNY JOHNNY** *Kitchenware SK 24*	64		
13 Feb 88	**CARS AND GIRLS** *Kitchenware SK 35*	44		
30 Apr 88	**THE KING OF ROCK 'N' ROLL** *Kitchenware SK 37*	7		7
23 Jul 88	**HEY MANHATTAN** *Kitchenware SK 38*	72		
18 Aug 90	**LOOKING FOR ATLANTIS** *Kitchenware SK 47*	51		
20 Oct 90	**WE LET THE STARS GO** *Kitchenware SK 48*	50		
5 Jan 91	**JORDAN: THE EP** *Kitchenware SK 49*	35		2
13 Jun 92	**THE SOUND OF CRYING** *Kitchenware SK 58*	23		3
8 Aug 92	**IF YOU DON'T LOVE ME** *Kitchenware SK 60*	33		3
3 Oct 92	**ALL THE WORLD LOVES LOVERS** *Kitchenware SK 62*	61		
9 Jan 93	**LIFE OF SURPRISES** *Kitchenware SKCD 63*	24		3
10 May 97	**A PRISONER OF THE PAST** *Columbia SKZD 70*	30		1
2 Aug 97	**ELECTRIC GUITARS** *Columbia SKZD 71*	53		

PRELUDE UK group

Date	Title	Peak Position	Weeks at No.1	Weeks in Top 40
26 Jan 74	**AFTER THE GOLDRUSH** *Dawn DNS 1052*	21		8
26 Apr 80	**PLATINUM BLONDE** *EMI 5046*	45		
22 May 82	**AFTER THE GOLDRUSH** *After Hours AFT 02*	28		5
31 Jul 82	**ONLY THE LONELY** *After Hours AFT 06*	55		

PRESENCE UK production group

Date	Title	Peak Position	Weeks at No.1	Weeks in Top 40
5 Dec 98	**SENSE OF DANGER** *Pagan 024CDS*			
	PRESENCE FEATURING SHARA NELSON	61		
19 Jun 99	**FUTURE LOVE** *Pagan 028CDS*	66		

PRESIDENTS OF THE UNITED STATES OF AMERICA US group

Date	Title	Peak Position	Weeks at No.1	Weeks in Top 40
6 Jan 96	**LUMP** *Columbia 6624962*	15		5
20 Apr 96	**PEACHES** *Columbia 6631072*	8		6
20 Jul 96	**DUNE BUGGY** *Columbia 6634892*	15		2
2 Nov 96	**MACH 5** *Columbia 6638812*	29		1
1 Aug 98	**VIDEO KILLED THE RADIO STAR** *Maverick W 0450CD*	52		

ELVIS PRESLEY US singer

Date	Title	Peak Position	Weeks at No.1	Weeks in Top 40
11 May 56	**HEARTBREAK HOTEL** *HMV POP 182* ★	2		22
25 May 56	**BLUE SUEDE SHOES** *HMV POP 213*	9		10
3 Aug 56	**I WANT YOU I NEED YOU I LOVE YOU** *HMV POP 235* ★	14		11
21 Sep 56	**HOUND DOG** *HMV POP 249* ★	2		23
16 Nov 56	**BLUE MOON** *HMV POP 272*	9		11
23 Nov 56	**I DON'T CARE IF THE SUN DON'T SHINE** *HMV POP 272*	23		4
7 Dec 56	**LOVE ME TENDER** *HMV POP 253* ★	11		9
15 Feb 57	**MYSTERY TRAIN** *HMV POP 295*	25		5
8 Mar 57	**RIP IT UP** *HMV POP 305*	27		1
10 May 57	**TOO MUCH** *HMV POP 330*			
	ELVIS PRESLEY WITH THE JORDANAIRES ★	6		9
14 Jun 57	**ALL SHOOK UP** *HMV POP 359*			
	ELVIS PRESLEY WITH THE JORDANAIRES ★	1	7	21
12 Jul 57	**(LET ME BE YOUR) TEDDY BEAR** *RCA 1013*			
	ELVIS PRESLEY WITH THE JORDANAIRES ★	3		19
30 Aug 57	**PARALYSED** *HMV POP 378*	8		10
4 Oct 57	**PARTY** *RCA 1020*			
	ELVIS PRESLEY WITH THE JORDANAIRES	2		15
18 Oct 57	**GOT A LOT O' LIVIN' TO DO** *RCA 1020*			
	ELVIS PRESLEY WITH THE JORDANAIRES	17		4
1 Nov 57	**TRYING TO GET TO YOU** *HMV POP 408*	16		4
1 Nov 57	**LOVING YOU** *RCA 1013*			
	ELVIS PRESLEY WITH THE JORDANAIRES	24		2
8 Nov 57	**LAWDY MISS CLAWDY** *HMV POP 408*	15		5
15 Nov 57	**SANTA BRING MY BABY BACK TO ME** *RCA 1025*	7		8

Silver-selling ○ Gold-selling ● Platinum-selling ⊛ US No.1 ★

Date	Title	Peak Position	Weeks at No.1	Weeks in Top 40
17 Jan 58	**I'M LEFT YOU'RE RIGHT SHE'S GONE** *HMV POP 428*	21		3
24 Jan 58	**JAILHOUSE ROCK** *RCA 1028* ★	1	3	14
31 Jan 58	**JAILHOUSE ROCK EP** *RCA RCX 106* ELVIS PRESLEY WITH THE JORDANAIRES	18		5
28 Feb 58	**DON'T** *RCA 1043* ELVIS PRESLEY WITH THE JORDANAIRES ★	2		11
2 May 58	**WEAR MY RING AROUND YOUR NECK** *RCA 1058* ELVIS PRESLEY WITH THE JORDANAIRES	3		10
25 Jul 58	**HARD HEADED WOMAN** *RCA 1070* ELVIS PRESLEY WITH THE JORDANAIRES ★	2		11
3 Oct 58	**KING CREOLE** *RCA 1081* ELVIS PRESLEY WITH THE JORDANAIRES	2		15
23 Jan 59	**ONE NIGHT/I GOT STUNG** *RCA 1100*	1	3	12
24 Apr 59	**A FOOL SUCH AS I/I NEED YOUR LOVE TONIGHT** *RCA 1113* ELVIS PRESLEY WITH THE JORDANAIRES	1	5	15
24 Jul 59	**A BIG HUNK O' LOVE** *RCA 1136* ELVIS PRESLEY WITH THE JORDANAIRES ★	4		9
12 Feb 60	**STRICTLY ELVIS EP** *RCA RCX 175*	26		1
7 Apr 60	**STUCK ON YOU** *RCA 1187* ELVIS PRESLEY WITH THE JORDANAIRES ★	3		13
28 Jul 60	**A MESS OF BLUES** *RCA 1194* ELVIS PRESLEY WITH THE JORDANAIRES	2		17
3 Nov 60	**IT'S NOW OR NEVER** *RCA 1207* ELVIS PRESLEY WITH THE JORDANAIRES ★	1	8	18
19 Jan 61	**ARE YOU LONESOME TONIGHT** *RCA 1216* ELVIS PRESLEY WITH THE JORDANAIRES ★	1	4	14
9 Mar 61	**WOODEN HEART** *RCA 1226*	1	6	22
25 May 61	**SURRENDER** *RCA 1227* ELVIS PRESLEY WITH THE JORDANAIRES ★	1	4	15
7 Sep 61	**WILD IN THE COUNTRY/I FEEL SO BAD** *RCA 1244* ELVIS PRESLEY WITH THE JORDANAIRES	4		11
2 Nov 61	**(MARIE'S THE NAME) HIS LATEST FLAME/LITTLE SISTER** *RCA 1258*	1	4	13
1 Feb 62	**ROCK A HULA BABY/CAN'T HELP FALLING IN LOVE** *RCA 1270* ELVIS PRESLEY WITH THE JORDANAIRES	1	4	19
10 May 62	**GOOD LUCK CHARM** *RCA 1280* ELVIS PRESLEY WITH THE JORDANAIRES ★	1	5	16
21 Jun 62	**FOLLOW THAT DREAM EP** *RCA RCX 211*	34		2
30 Aug 62	**SHE'S NOT YOU** *RCA 1303* ELVIS PRESLEY WITH THE JORDANAIRES	1	3	13
29 Nov 62	**RETURN TO SENDER** *RCA 1320* ELVIS PRESLEY WITH THE JORDANAIRES	1	3	13
28 Feb 63	**ONE BROKEN HEART FOR SALE** *RCA 1337* ELVIS PRESLEY WITH THE MELLOMEN	12		7
4 Jul 63	**(YOU'RE THE) DEVIL IN DISGUISE** *RCA 1355* ELVIS PRESLEY WITH THE JORDANAIRES	1	1	11
24 Oct 63	**BOSSA NOVA BABY** *RCA 1374* ELVIS PRESLEY WITH THE JORDANAIRES	13		6
19 Dec 63	**KISS ME QUICK** *RCA 1375* ELVIS PRESLEY WITH THE JORDANAIRES	14		10
12 Mar 64	**VIVA LAS VEGAS** *RCA 1390* ELVIS PRESLEY WITH THE JORDANAIRES	17		8
25 Jun 64	**KISSIN' COUSINS** *RCA 1404* ELVIS PRESLEY WITH THE JORDANAIRES	10		9
20 Aug 64	**SUCH A NIGHT** *RCA 1411* ELVIS PRESLEY WITH THE JORDANAIRES	13		9
29 Oct 64	**AIN'T THAT LOVIN' YOU BABY** *RCA 1422*	15		7
3 Dec 64	**BLUE CHRISTMAS** *RCA 1430* ELVIS PRESLEY WITH THE JORDANAIRES	11		6
11 Mar 65	**DO THE CLAM** *RCA 1443* ELVIS PRESLEY WITH THE JORDANAIRES JUBILEE FOUR AND CAROL LOMBARD TRIO	19		7
27 May 65	**CRYING IN THE CHAPEL** *RCA 1455* ELVIS PRESLEY WITH THE JORDANAIRES	1	2	14
11 Nov 65	**TELL ME WHY** *RCA 1489* ELVIS PRESLEY WITH THE JORDANAIRES	15		8
24 Feb 66	**BLUE RIVER** *RCA 1504*	22		6
7 Apr 66	**FRANKIE AND JOHNNY** *RCA 1509*	21		8
7 Jul 66	**LOVE LETTERS** *RCA 1526*	6		10
13 Oct 66	**ALL THAT I AM** *RCA 1545* ELVIS PRESLEY WITH THE JORDANAIRES	18		8
1 Dec 66	**IF EVERY DAY WAS LIKE CHRISTMAS** *RCA 1557* ELVIS PRESLEY WITH THE JORDANAIRES AND IMPERIALS QUARTET	9		6
9 Feb 67	**INDESCRIBABLY BLUE** *RCA 1565* ELVIS PRESLEY WITH THE JORDANAIRES AND IMPERIALS QUARTET	21		5
11 May 67	**YOU GOTTA STOP/LOVE MACHINE** *RCA 1593*	38		3
16 Aug 67	**LONG LEGGED GIRL (WITH THE SHORT DRESS ON)** *RCA 1616* ELVIS PRESLEY WITH THE JORDANAIRES	49		
21 Feb 68	**GUITAR MAN** *RCA 1663*	19		7
15 May 68	**U.S. MALE** *RCA 1688* ELVIS PRESLEY WITH THE JORDANAIRES	15		7
17 Jul 68	**YOUR TIME HASN'T COME YET BABY** *RCA 1714* ELVIS PRESLEY WITH THE JORDANAIRES	22		7
16 Oct 68	**YOU'LL NEVER WALK ALONE** *RCA 1747* ELVIS PRESLEY WITH THE JORDANAIRES	44		
26 Feb 69	**IF I CAN DREAM** *RCA 1795*	11		10
11 Jun 69	**IN THE GHETTO** *RCA 1831*	2		14
6 Sep 69	**CLEAN UP YOUR OWN BACK YARD** *RCA 1869*	21		5
29 Nov 69	**SUSPICIOUS MINDS** *RCA 1900* ★	2		12
28 Feb 70	**DON'T CRY DADDY** *RCA 1916*	8		10
16 May 70	**KENTUCKY RAIN** *RCA 1949*	21		10
11 Jul 70	**THE WONDER OF YOU** *RCA 1974*	1	6	18
14 Nov 70	**I'VE LOST YOU** *RCA 1999*	9		9
9 Jan 71	**YOU DON'T HAVE TO SAY YOU LOVE ME** *RCA 2046*	9		10
20 Mar 71	**THERE GOES MY EVERYTHING** *RCA 2060* ELVIS PRESLEY, VOCAL ACCOMPANIMENT: THE IMPERIALS QUARTET	6		10
15 May 71	**RAGS TO RICHES** *RCA 2084*	9		9
17 Jul 71	**HEARTBREAK HOTEL/HOUND DOG** *RCA Maximillion 2104*	10		10
2 Oct 71	**I'M LEAVIN'** *RCA 2125* ELVIS PRESLEY, VOCAL ACCOMPANIMENT: THE IMPERIALS QUARTET	23		8
4 Dec 71	**I JUST CAN'T HELP BELIEVING** *RCA 2158* ELVIS PRESLEY, VOCAL ACCOMPANIMENT: THE IMPERIALS QUARTET AND THE SWEET INSPIRATIONS	6		13
11 Dec 71	**JAILHOUSE ROCK** *RCA Maximillion 2153*	42		
1 Apr 72	**UNTIL IT'S TIME FOR YOU TO GO** *RCA 2188* ELVIS PRESLEY, VOCAL ACCOMPANIMENT: THE IMPERIALS QUARTET	5		8
17 Jun 72	**AMERICAN TRILOGY** *RCA 2229*	8		10
30 Sep 72	**BURNING LOVE** *RCA 2267*	7		9
16 Dec 72	**ALWAYS ON MY MIND** *RCA 2304* ELVIS PRESLEY, VOCAL ACCOMPANIMENT: JD SUMNER AND THE STAMPS	9		12
26 May 73	**POLK SALAD ANNIE** *RCA 2359*	23		6
11 Aug 73	**FOOL** *RCA 2393*	15		10
24 Nov 73	**RAISED ON ROCK** *RCA 2435*	36		2
16 Mar 74	**I'VE GOT A THING ABOUT YOU BABY** *RCA APBO 0196* ELVIS PRESLEY, VOCAL ACCOMPANIMENT: JD SUMNER AND THE STAMPS	33		4
13 Jul 74	**IF YOU TALK IN YOUR SLEEP** *RCA APBO 0280*	40		1
16 Nov 74	**MY BOY** *RCA 2458* ○	5		12
18 Jan 75	**PROMISED LAND** *RCA PB 10074*	9		7
24 May 75	**T.R.O.U.B.L.E.** *RCA 2562*	31		3
29 Nov 75	**GREEN GREEN GRASS OF HOME** *RCA 2635*	29		5
1 May 76	**HURT** *RCA 2674*	37		1
4 Sep 76	**GIRL OF MY BEST FRIEND** *RCA 2729*	9		11
25 Dec 76	**SUSPICION** *RCA 2768*	9		9
5 Mar 77	**MOODY BLUE** *RCA PB 0857* ELVIS PRESLEY, VOCAL ACCOMPANIMENT JD SUMNER AND THE STAMPS QUARTET, KATHY WESTMORELAND, MYRNA SMITH	6		9
13 Aug 77	**WAY DOWN** *RCA PB 0998* ELVIS PRESLEY, VOCAL ACCOMPANIMENT JD SUMNER AND THE STAMPS QUARTET, K WESTMORELAND, S NEILSON AND M SMITH ●	1	5	11
3 Sep 77	**ALL SHOOK UP** *RCA PB 2694* ELVIS PRESLEY WITH THE JORDANAIRES	41		
3 Sep 77	**ARE YOU LONESOME TONIGHT** *RCA PB 2699* ELVIS PRESLEY WITH THE JORDANAIRES	46		
3 Sep 77	**CRYING IN THE CHAPEL** *RCA PB 2708* ELVIS PRESLEY WITH THE JORDANAIRES	43		
3 Sep 77	**IT'S NOW OR NEVER** *RCA PB 2698* ELVIS PRESLEY WITH THE JORDANAIRES	39		1
3 Sep 77	**JAILHOUSE ROCK** *RCA PB 2695* ELVIS PRESLEY WITH THE JORDANAIRES	44		
3 Sep 77	**RETURN TO SENDER** *RCA PB 2706* ELVIS PRESLEY WITH THE JORDANAIRES	42		
3 Sep 77	**THE WONDER OF YOU** *RCA PB 2709*	48		
3 Sep 77	**WOODEN HEART** *RCA PB 2700*	49		
10 Dec 77	**MY WAY** *RCA PB 1165* ELVIS PRESLEY, VOCAL ACCOMPANIMENT JD SUMNER AND THE STAMPS, THE SWEET INSPIRATIONS AND KATHY WESTMORELAND	9		8
24 Jun 78	**DON'T BE CRUEL** *RCA PB 9265* ★	24		6
15 Dec 79	**IT WON'T SEEM LIKE CHRISTMAS (WITHOUT YOU)** *RCA PB 9464*	13		4
30 Aug 80	**IT'S ONLY LOVE/BEYOND THE REEF** *RCA 4* ○	3		8
6 Dec 80	**SANTA CLAUS IS BACK IN TOWN** *RCA 16*	41		
14 Feb 81	**GUITAR MAN** *RCA 43*	43		
18 Apr 81	**LOVING ARMS** *RCA 48*	47		
13 Mar 82	**ARE YOU LONESOME TONIGHT** *RCA 196* ELVIS PRESLEY, VOCAL ACCOMPANIMENT JD SUMNER AND THE STAMPS, THE SWEET INSPIRATIONS AND KATHY WESTMORELAND	25		6
26 Jun 82	**THE SOUND OF YOUR CRY** *RCA 232*	59		
5 Feb 83	**JAILHOUSE ROCK** *RCA 1028*	27		3
7 May 83	**BABY I DON'T CARE** *RCA 332*	61		
3 Dec 83	**I CAN HELP** *RCA 369*	30		5
10 Nov 84	**THE LAST FAREWELL** *RCA 459*	48		
19 Jan 85	**THE ELVIS MEDLEY** *RCA 476* ELVIS PRESLEY WITH THE JORDANAIRES	51		
10 Aug 85	**ALWAYS ON MY MIND** *RCA PB 49944*	59		
11 Apr 87	**AIN'T THAT LOVIN' YOU BABY/BOSSA NOVA BABY** *RCA ARON 1*	47		
22 Aug 87	**LOVE ME TENDER/IF I CAN DREAM** *RCA ARON 2*	56		

Silver-selling ● Gold-selling ● Platinum-selling ⊛ US No.1 ★ — Peak Position · Weeks at No.1 · Weeks in Top 40

Date	Title / Label	Peak Position	Weeks at No.1	Weeks in Top 40
16 Jan 88	**STUCK ON YOU** *RCA PB 49595* ELVIS PRESLEY WITH THE JORDANAIRES	58		
17 Aug 91	**ARE YOU LONESOME TONIGHT (LIVE)** *RCA PB 49177*	68		
29 Aug 92	**DON'T BE CRUEL** *RCA 74321110777* ELVIS PRESLEY WITH THE JORDANAIRES	42		
11 Nov 95	**THE TWELFTH OF NEVER** *RCA 74321320122* ELVIS PRESLEY, VOCAL ACCOMPANIMENT THE VOICE	21		2
18 May 96	**HEARTBREAK HOTEL/I WAS THE ONE** *RCA 74321336862*	45		
24 May 97	**ALWAYS ON MY MIND** *RCA 74321485412*	13		3
14 Apr 01	**SUSPICIOUS MINDS** *RCA 74321855822*	15		3
10 Nov 01	**AMERICA THE BEAUTIFUL** *RCA 74321904022*	69		
22 Jun 02	**A LITTLE LESS CONVERSATION** *RCA 74321943572* ELVIS VS JXL ⊛	1	4	10
4 Oct 03	**RUBBERNECKIN'** *RCA 82876543412*	5		4
17 Jul 04	**THAT'S ALL RIGHT** *RCA 82876619212*	3		2
15 Jan 05	**JAILHOUSE ROCK** *RCA 82876667152*	1	1	4
22 Jan 05	**ONE NIGHT/I GOT STUNG** *RCA 82876666682*	1	1	5
29 Jan 05	**A FOOL SUCH AS I/I NEED YOUR LOVE TONIGHT** *RCA 82876666582*	2		4
5 Feb 05	**IT'S NOW OR NEVER** *RCA 82876666592*	1	1	3
12 Feb 05	**ARE YOU LONESOME TONIGHT?** *RCA 82876666602*	2		3
19 Feb 05	**WOODEN HEART** *RCA 82876666612*	2		2
26 Feb 05	**SURRENDER** *RCA 82876666692*	2		3
5 Mar 05	**(MARIE'S THE NAME) HIS LATEST FLAME** *RCA 82876666702*	3		2
12 Mar 05	**ROCK-A-HULA BABY** *RCA 82876666732*	3		2
19 Mar 05	**GOOD LUCK CHARM** *RCA 82876666752*	2		2
26 Mar 05	**SHE'S NOT YOU** *RCA 82876666762*	3		2
2 Apr 05	**RETURN TO SENDER** *RCA 82876666772*	5		2
9 Apr 05	**(YOU'RE THE) DEVIL IN DISGUISE** *RCA 82876666782*	2		2
16 Apr 05	**CRYING IN THE CHAPEL** *RCA 82876666802*	2		2
23 Apr 05	**THE WONDER OF YOU** *RCA 82876666812*	4		2
30 Apr 05	**WAY DOWN** *RCA 82876666822*	2		2
7 May 05	**A LITTLE LESS CONVERSATION** *RCA 82876666832* ELVIS VS JXL	3		2
25 Aug 07	**SUSPICIOUS MINDS** *RCA Victor 88697147212*	11		2
1 Sep 07	**BLUE SUEDE SHOES** *RCA Victor 88697122382*	11		1
1 Sep 07	**MY BABY LEFT ME** *Memphis Recording Service MHC400451001*	18		1
8 Sep 07	**HOUND DOG** *RCA 88697122402*	14		1
15 Sep 07	**(LET ME BE YOUR) TEDDY BEAR** *RCA 88697124782*	14		1
22 Sep 07	**PARTY** *RCA 88697125142*	14		1
29 Sep 07	**DON'T** *RCA 88697125152*	14		1
6 Oct 07	**HARD HEADED WOMAN** *RCA 88697125162*	15		1
13 Oct 07	**KING CREOLE** *RCA 88697125172*	15		1
20 Oct 07	**A BIG HUNK O' LOVE** *RCA 88697125182*	12		1
27 Oct 07	**WEAR MY RING AROUND YOUR NECK** *RCA 88697125192*	16		1
3 Nov 07	**IF I CAN DREAM** *RCA 88697125202*	17		1
10 Nov 07	**VIVA LAS VEGAS** *RCA 88697125212*	15		1
17 Nov 07	**IN THE GHETTO** *RCA 88697125222*	13		1
24 Nov 07	**YOU DON'T HAVE TO SAY YOU LOVE ME** *RCA 88697125232*	16		1
1 Dec 07	**ALWAYS ON MY MIND** *RCA 88697125242*	17		1
8 Dec 07	**AN AMERICAN TRILOGY** *RCA 88697125252*	12		1
15 Dec 07	**BURNING LOVE** *RCA 88697125262*	13		1

LISA MARIE PRESLEY US singer

Date	Title / Label	Peak Position	Weeks at No.1	Weeks in Top 40
12 Jul 03	**LIGHTS OUT** *Capitol CDCL 844*	16		2

PRESSURE DROP UK group

Date	Title / Label	Peak Position	Weeks at No.1	Weeks in Top 40
21 Mar 98	**SILENTLY BAD MINDED** *Higher Ground HIGHS 6CD*	53		
17 Mar 01	**WARRIOR SOUND** *Higher Ground 6697192*	72		

BILLY PRESTON US singer and pianist

Date	Title / Label	Peak Position	Weeks at No.1	Weeks in Top 40
23 Apr 69	**GET BACK** *Apple R 5777* BEATLES WITH BILLY PRESTON ★	1	6	15
2 Jul 69	**THAT'S THE WAY GOD PLANNED IT** *Apple 12*	11		7
16 Sep 72	**OUTA SPACE** *A&M AMS 7007*	44		
3 Apr 76	**GET BACK** *Apple R 5777* BEATLES WITH BILLY PRESTON	28		4
15 Dec 79	**WITH YOU I'M BORN AGAIN** *Motown TMG 1159* BILLY PRESTON & SYREETA ●	2		7
8 Mar 80	**IT WILL COME IN TIME** *Motown TMG 1175* BILLY PRESTON & SYREETA	47		
22 Apr 89	**GET BACK** *Apple R 5777* BEATLES WITH BILLY PRESTON	74		

JOHNNY PRESTON US singer

Date	Title / Label	Peak Position	Weeks at No.1	Weeks in Top 40
12 Feb 60	**RUNNING BEAR** *Mercury AMT 1079* ★	1	2	14
21 Apr 60	**CRADLE OF LOVE** *Mercury AMT 1092*	2		14
28 Jul 60	**I'M STARTING TO GO STEADY** *Mercury AMT 1104*	49		
11 Aug 60	**FEEL SO FINE** *Mercury AMT 1104*	18		9
8 Dec 60	**CHARMING BILLY** *Mercury AMT 1114*	34		1

MIKE PRESTON UK singer

Date	Title / Label	Peak Position	Weeks at No.1	Weeks in Top 40
30 Oct 59	**MR BLUE** *Decca F 11167*	12		8
25 Aug 60	**I'D DO ANYTHING** *Decca F 11255*	23		6
22 Dec 60	**TOGETHERNESS** *Decca F 11287*	41		
9 Mar 61	**MARRY ME** *Decca F 11335*	14		9

PRETENDERS UK/US group

Date	Title / Label	Peak Position	Weeks at No.1	Weeks in Top 40
10 Feb 79	**STOP YOUR SOBBING** *Real ARE 6*	34		3
14 Jul 79	**KID** *Real ARE 9*	33		4
17 Nov 79	**BRASS IN POCKET** *Real ARE 11* ●	1	2	11
5 Apr 80	**TALK OF THE TOWN** *Real ARE 12*	8		7
14 Feb 81	**MESSAGE OF LOVE** *Real ARE 15*	11		5
12 Sep 81	**DAY AFTER DAY** *Real ARE 17*	45		
14 Nov 81	**I GO TO SLEEP** *Real ARE 18*	7		8
2 Oct 82	**BACK ON THE CHAIN GANG** *Real ARE 19*	17		8
26 Nov 83	**2000 MILES** *Real ARE 20*	15		6
9 Jun 84	**THIN LINE BETWEEN LOVE AND HATE** *Real ARE 22*	49		
11 Oct 86	**DON'T GET ME WRONG** *Real YZ 85*	10		7
13 Dec 86	**HYMN TO HER** *Real YZ 93*	8		9
15 Aug 87	**IF THERE WAS A MAN** *Real YZ 149* PRETENDERS FOR 007	49		
23 Apr 94	**I'LL STAND BY YOU** *Real YZ 815CD*	10		8
2 Jul 94	**NIGHT IN MY VEINS** *Real YZ 825CD*	25		3
15 Oct 94	**977** *WEA YZ 848CD1*	66		
14 Oct 95	**KID** *WEA 014CD*	73		
10 May 97	**FEVER PITCH THE EP** *Blanco Y Negro NEG 104CD* PRETENDERS, LA'S, ORLANDO, NICK HORNBY	65		
15 May 99	**HUMAN** *WEA 207CD*	33		1

PRETTY BOY FLOYD US group

Date	Title / Label	Peak Position	Weeks at No.1	Weeks in Top 40
10 Mar 90	**ROCK AND ROLL (IS GONNA SET THE NIGHT ON FIRE)** *MCA 1393*	75		

PRETTY RICKY US group

Date	Title / Label	Peak Position	Weeks at No.1	Weeks in Top 40
24 Sep 05	**GRIND WITH ME** *Atlantic AT0212CDX*	26		2
25 Feb 06	**YOUR BODY** *Atlantic AT0231CD1*	37		1

PRETTY THINGS UK group

Date	Title / Label	Peak Position	Weeks at No.1	Weeks in Top 40
18 Jun 64	**ROSALYN** *Fontana TF 469*	41		
22 Oct 64	**DON'T BRING ME DOWN** *Fontana TF 503*	10		10
25 Feb 65	**HONEY I NEED** *Fontana TF 537*	13		8
15 Jul 65	**CRY TO ME** *Fontana TF 585*	28		6
20 Jan 66	**MIDNIGHT TO SIX MAN** *Fontana TF 647*	46		
5 May 66	**COME SEE ME** *Fontana TF 688*	43		
21 Jul 66	**A HOUSE IN THE COUNTRY** *Fontana TF 722*	50		

ALAN PRICE UK singer/keyboard player

Date	Title / Label	Peak Position	Weeks at No.1	Weeks in Top 40
31 Mar 66	**I PUT A SPELL ON YOU** *Decca F 12367* ALAN PRICE SET	9		9
14 Jul 66	**HI LILI HI LO** *Decca F 12442* ALAN PRICE SET	11		10
2 Mar 67	**SIMON SMITH AND HIS AMAZING DANCING BEAR** *Decca F 12570* ALAN PRICE SET	4		10
2 Aug 67	**THE HOUSE THAT JACK BUILT** *Decca F 12641* *ALAN PRICE SET*	*4*		*10*
15 Nov 67	**SHAME** *Decca F 12691* ALAN PRICE SET	45		
31 Jan 68	**DON'T STOP THE CARNIVAL** *Decca F 12731* ALAN PRICE SET	13		8
10 Apr 71	**ROSETTA** *CBS 7108* FAME & PRICE TOGETHER	11		7
25 May 74	**JARROW SONG** *Warner Brothers K 16372*	6		7
29 Apr 78	**JUST FOR YOU** *Jet UP 36358*	43		
17 Feb 79	**BABY OF MINE/JUST FOR YOU** *Jet 135*	32		2
30 Apr 88	**CHANGES** *Ariola 109911*	54		

KELLY PRICE US singer

Date	Title / Label	Peak Position	Weeks at No.1	Weeks in Top 40
7 Nov 98	**FRIEND OF MINE** *Island Black Music CID 723*	25		1
8 May 99	**SECRET LOVE** *Island Black Music CID 739*	26		1
30 Dec 00	**HEARTBREAK HOTEL** *Arista 74321820572* WHITNEY HOUSTON FEATURING FAITH EVANS & KELLY PRICE	25		3

Weeks in Top 40 / Weeks at No.1 / Peak Position

LLOYD PRICE US singer

Date	Title / Label	Peak Position	Weeks at No.1	Weeks in Top 40
13 Feb 59	**STAGGER LEE** *HMV POP 580* ★	7		14
15 May 59	**WHERE WERE YOU (ON OUR WEDDING DAY)?** *HMV POP 598*	15		6
12 Jun 59	**PERSONALITY** *HMV POP 626*	9		10
11 Sep 59	**I'M GONNA GET MARRIED** *HMV POP 650*	23		5
21 Apr 60	**LADY LUCK** *HMV POP 712*	45		

PRICKLY HEAT UK producer

Date	Title / Label	Peak Position	Weeks at No.1	Weeks in Top 40
26 Dec 98	**OOOIE, OOOIE, OOOIE** *Virgin VSCDT 1727*	57		

DICKIE PRIDE UK singer

Date	Title / Label	Peak Position	Weeks at No.1	Weeks in Top 40
30 Oct 59	**PRIMROSE LANE** *Columbia DB 4340*	28		1

MAXI PRIEST UK singer

Date	Title / Label	Peak Position	Weeks at No.1	Weeks in Top 40
29 Mar 86	**STROLLIN' ON** *10 TEN 84*	32		4
12 Jul 86	**IN THE SPRINGTIME** *10 TEN 127*	54		
8 Nov 86	**CRAZY LOVE** *10 TEN 135*	67		
4 Apr 87	**LET ME KNOW** *10 TEN 156*	49		
24 Oct 87	**SOME GUYS HAVE ALL THE LUCK** *10 TEN 198*	12		8
20 Feb 88	**HOW CAN WE EASE THE PAIN** *10 TEN 207* MAXI PRIEST FEATURING BERES HAMMOND	41		
4 Jun 88	**WILD WORLD** *10 TEN 221*	5		8
27 Aug 88	**GOODBYE TO LOVE AGAIN** *10 TEN 238*	57		
9 Jun 90	**CLOSE TO YOU** *10 TEN 294* ★	7		8
1 Sep 90	**PEACE THROUGHOUT THE WORLD** *10 TEN 317* MAXI PRIEST FEATURING JAZZIE B	41		
1 Dec 90	**HUMAN WORK OF ART** *10 TEN 328*	71		
24 Aug 91	**HOUSECALL** *Epic 6573477* SHABBA RANKS FEATURING MAXI PRIEST	31		4
5 Oct 91	**THE MAXI PRIEST EP** *10 TEN 343*	62		
26 Sep 92	**GROOVIN' IN THE MIDNIGHT** *10 TEN 412*	50		
28 Nov 92	**JUST WANNA KNOW/FE' REAL** *10 TEN 416* MAXI PRIEST/MAXI PRIEST FEATURING APACHE INDIAN	33		2
20 Mar 93	**ONE MORE CHANCE** *10 TENCD 420*	40		1
8 May 93	**HOUSECALL (REMIX)** *Epic 6592842* SHABBA RANKS FEATURING MAXI PRIEST	8		6
31 Jul 93	**WAITING IN VAIN** *GRP MCSTD 1921* LEE RITENOUR & MAXI PRIEST	65		
22 Jun 96	**THAT GIRL** *Virgin VUSDX 106* MAXI PRIEST FEATURING SHAGGY	15		5
21 Sep 96	**WATCHING THE WORLD GO BY** *Virgin VUSD 108*	36		1

PRIMA DONNA UK group

Date	Title / Label	Peak Position	Weeks at No.1	Weeks in Top 40
26 Apr 80	**LOVE ENOUGH FOR TWO** *Ariola ARO 221*	48		

LOUIS PRIMA US singer/trumpeter

Date	Title / Label	Peak Position	Weeks at No.1	Weeks in Top 40
21 Feb 58	**BUONA SERA** *Capitol CL 14841*	25		1

PRIMAL SCREAM UK group

Date	Title / Label	Peak Position	Weeks at No.1	Weeks in Top 40
3 Mar 90	**LOADED** *Creation CRE 070*	16		5
18 Aug 90	**COME TOGETHER** *Creation CRE 078*	26		4
22 Jun 91	**HIGHER THAN THE SUN** *Creation CRE 096*	40		1
24 Aug 91	**DON'T FIGHT IT FEEL IT** *Creation CRE 110* PRIMAL SCREAM FEATURING DENISE JOHNSON	41		
8 Feb 92	**DIXIE-NARCO EP** *Creation CRE 117*	11		3
12 Mar 94	**ROCKS/FUNKY JAM** *Creation CRESCD 129*	7		3
18 Jun 94	**JAILBIRD** *Creation CRESCD 145*	29		1
10 Dec 94	**(I'M GONNA) CRY MYSELF BLIND** *Creation CRESCD 183*	49		
15 Jun 96	**THE BIG MAN AND THE SCREAM TEAM MEET THE BARMY ARMY UPTOWN** *Creation CRESCD 194* PRIMAL SCREAM, IRVINE WELSH & ON U-SOUND	17		1
17 May 97	**KOWALSKI** *Creation CRESCD 245*	8		2
28 Jun 97	**STAR** *Creation CRESCD 263*	16		1
25 Oct 97	**BURNING WHEEL** *Creation CRESCD 272*	17		1
20 Nov 99	**SWASTIKA EYES** *Creation CRESCD 326*	22		1
1 Apr 00	**KILL ALL HIPPIES** *Creation CRESCD 332*	24		1
23 Sep 00	**ACCELERATOR** *Creation CRESCD 333*	34		1
3 Aug 02	**MISS LUCIFER** *Columbia 6728252*	25		1
9 Nov 02	**AUTOBAHN 66** *Columbia 6733122*	44		
29 Nov 03	**SOME VELVET MORING** *Columbia 6744022*	44		
27 May 06	**COUNTRY GIRL** *Columbia 82876834272*	5		8
19 Aug 06	**DOLLS** *Columbia 82876871632*	40		1

PRIME MOVERS US group

Date	Title / Label	Peak Position	Weeks at No.1	Weeks in Top 40
8 Feb 86	**ON THE TRAIL** *Island IS 263*	74		

PRIMITIVE RADIO GODS US singer

Date	Title / Label	Peak Position	Weeks at No.1	Weeks in Top 40
30 Mar 96	**STANDING OUTSIDE A BROKEN PHONE BOOTH WITH MONEY IN MY HAND** *Columbia 6627692*	74		

PRIMITIVES UK group

Date	Title / Label	Peak Position	Weeks at No.1	Weeks in Top 40
27 Feb 88	**CRASH** *Lazy PB 41761*	5		8
30 Apr 88	**OUT OF REACH** *Lazy PB 42011*	25		3
3 Sep 88	**WAY BEHIND ME** *Lazy PB 42209*	36		2
29 Jul 89	**SICK OF IT** *Lazy PB 42947*	24		3
30 Sep 89	**SECRETS** *Lazy PB 43173*	49		
3 Aug 91	**YOU ARE THE WAY** *RCA PB 44481*	58		

PRINCE US singer/guitarist/producer

Date	Title / Label	Peak Position	Weeks at No.1	Weeks in Top 40
19 Jan 80	**I WANNA BE YOUR LOVER** *Warner Brothers K 17537*	41		
29 Jan 83	**1999** *Warner Brothers W 9896*	25		5
30 Apr 83	**LITTLE RED CORVETTE** *Warner Brothers W 9688*	54		
26 Nov 83	**LITTLE RED CORVETTE** *Warner Brothers W 9436*	66		
30 Jun 84	**WHEN DOVES CRY** *Warner Brothers W 9286* ● ★	4		11
22 Sep 84	**PURPLE RAIN** *Warner Brothers W 9174* PRINCE & THE REVOLUTION	8		7
8 Dec 84	**I WOULD DIE 4 U** *Warner Brothers W 9121* PRINCE & THE REVOLUTION	58		
19 Jan 85	**1999/LITTLE RED CORVETTE** *Warner Brothers W 1999* PRINCE & THE REVOLUTION ●	2		9
23 Feb 85	**LET'S GO CRAZY/TAKE ME WITH YOU** *Warner Brothers W 2000* PRINCE & THE REVOLUTION ★	7		6
25 May 85	**PAISLEY PARK** *WEA W 9052* PRINCE & THE REVOLUTION	18		6
27 Jul 85	**RASPBERRY BERET** *WEA W 8929* PRINCE & THE REVOLUTION	25		5
26 Oct 85	**POP LIFE** *Paisley Park W 8858* PRINCE & THE REVOLUTION	60		
8 Mar 86	**KISS** *Paisley Park W 8751* PRINCE & THE REVOLUTION ★	6		7
14 Jun 86	**MOUNTAINS** *Paisley Park W 8711* PRINCE & THE REVOLUTION	45		
16 Aug 86	**GIRLS AND BOYS** *Paisley Park W 8586* PRINCE & THE REVOLUTION	11		6
1 Nov 86	**ANOTHERLOVERHOLENYOHEAD** *Paisley Park W 8521* PRINCE & THE REVOLUTION	36		2
14 Mar 87	**SIGN O' THE TIMES** *Paisley Park W 8399*	10		7
20 Jun 87	**IF I WAS YOUR GIRLFRIEND** *Paisley Park W 8334*	20		5
15 Aug 87	**U GOT THE LOOK** *Paisley Park W 8289*	11		7
28 Nov 87	**I COULD NEVER TAKE THE PLACE OF YOUR MAN** *Paisley Park W 8288*	29		3
7 May 88	**ALPHABET STREET** *Paisley Park W 7900*	9		4
23 Jul 88	**GLAM SLAM** *Paisley Park W 7806*	29		2
5 Nov 88	**I WISH U HEAVEN** *Paisley Park W 7745*	24		4
24 Jun 89	**BATDANCE** *Warner Brothers W 2924* ● ★	2		10
9 Sep 89	**PARTYMAN** *Warner Brothers W 2814*	14		4
18 Nov 89	**THE ARMS OF ORION** *Warner Brothers W 2757* PRINCE WITH SHEENA EASTON	27		4
4 Aug 90	**THIEVES IN THE TEMPLE** *Paisley Park W 9751*	7		4
10 Nov 90	**NEW POWER GENERATION** *Paisley Park W 9525*	26		3
31 Aug 91	**GETT OFF** *Paisley Park W 0056* PRINCE & THE NEW POWER GENERATION	4		7
21 Sep 91	**CREAM** *Paisley Park W 0061* PRINCE & THE NEW POWER GENERATION	15		4
7 Dec 91	**DIAMONDS AND PEARLS** *Paisley Park W 0075* PRINCE & THE NEW POWER GENERATION	25		5
28 Mar 92	**MONEY DON'T MATTER 2 NIGHT** *Paisley Park W 0091* PRINCE & THE NEW POWER GENERATION	19		3
27 Jun 92	**THUNDER** *Paisley Park W 01132P* PRINCE & THE NEW POWER GENERATION	28		2
18 Jul 92	**SEXY MF/STROLLIN'** *Paisley Park W 0123* PRINCE & THE NEW POWER GENERATION	4		5
10 Oct 92	**MY NAME IS PRINCE** *Paisley Park W 0132* PRINCE & THE NEW POWER GENERATION	7		4
14 Nov 92	**MY NAME IS PRINCE (REMIX)** *Paisley Park W 0142T* PRINCE & THE NEW POWER GENERATION	51		
5 Dec 92	**7** *Paisley Park W 0147* PRINCE & THE NEW POWER GENERATION	27		2
13 Mar 93	**THE MORNING PAPERS** *Paisley Park W 0162CD* PRINCE & THE NEW POWER GENERATION	52		
16 Oct 93	**PEACH** *Paisley Park W 0210CD*	14		3

Silver-selling · Gold-selling · Platinum-selling · US No.1 ★ · Peak Position · Weeks at No.1 · Weeks in Top 40

Date	Title / Label	Peak Position	Weeks at No.1	Weeks in Top 40
11 Dec 93	**CONTROVERSY** *Paisley Park W0215CD15*	5		2
9 Apr 94	**THE MOST BEAUTIFUL GIRL IN THE WORLD** *NPG 60155* SYMBOL	1	3	10
4 Jun 94	**THE BEAUTIFUL EXPERIENCE** *NPG 60212* SYMBOL	18		2
10 Sep 94	**LETITGO** *Warner Brothers W0260CD*	30		2
18 Mar 95	**PURPLE MEDLEY** *Warner Brothers W0289CD*	33		1
23 Sep 95	**EYE HATE U** *Warner Brothers W0315CD* ARTIST FORMERLY KNOWN AS PRINCE (AFKAP)	20		1
9 Dec 95	**GOLD** *Warner Brothers W0325CDX* ARTIST FORMERLY KNOWN AS PRINCE (AFKAP)	10		8
3 Aug 96	**DINNER WITH DELORES** *Warner Brothers 9362437422* ARTIST FORMERLY KNOWN AS PRINCE (AFKAP)	36		1
14 Dec 96	**BETCHA BY GOLLY WOW!** *NPG CDEMS 463* ARTIST	11		4
8 Mar 97	**THE HOLY RIVER** *EMI CDEM 467* ARTIST	19		2
9 Jan 99	**1999** *Warner Brothers W467CD*	10		3
18 Dec 99	**1999** *Warner Brothers W467CD*	40		1
26 Feb 00	**THE GREATEST ROMANCE EVER SOLD** *NPG 74321745002* ARTIST	65		
20 Nov 04	**CINNAMON GIRL** *Columbia 6751422*	43		
8 Apr 06	**BLACK SWEAT** *Universal MCSTD40457*	43		
10 Jun 06	**FURY** *Universal MCSTD40462*	60		

PRINCE BUSTER Jamaican singer

Date	Title / Label	Peak Position	Weeks at No.1	Weeks in Top 40
23 Feb 67	**AL CAPONE** *Blue Beat BB 324*	18		9
4 Apr 98	**WHINE AND GRINE** *Island CID 691*	21		2

PRINCE CHARLES & THE CITY BEAT BAND US group

Date	Title / Label	Peak Position	Weeks at No.1	Weeks in Top 40
22 Feb 86	**WE CAN MAKE IT HAPPEN** *PRT 7P 348*	56		

PRINCESS UK singer

Date	Title / Label	Peak Position	Weeks at No.1	Weeks in Top 40
3 Aug 85	**SAY I'M YOUR NO. 1** *Supreme SUPE 101*	7		9
9 Nov 85	**AFTER THE LOVE HAS GONE** *Supreme SUPE 103*	28		8
19 Apr 86	**I'LL KEEP ON LOVING YOU** *Supreme SUPE 105*	16		7
5 Jul 86	**TELL ME TOMORROW** *Supreme SUPE 106*	34		2
25 Oct 86	**IN THE HEAT OF A PASSIONATE MOMENT** *Supreme SUPE 109*	74		
13 Jun 87	**RED HOT** *Polydor POSP 868*	58		

PRINCESS IVORI US rapper

Date	Title / Label	Peak Position	Weeks at No.1	Weeks in Top 40
17 Mar 90	**WANTED** *Supreme SUPE 163*	69		

PRINCESS SUPERSTAR US rapper

Date	Title / Label	Peak Position	Weeks at No.1	Weeks in Top 40
2 Mar 02	**BAD BABYSITTER** *Rapster/!K7 RR 007CDM*	11		5
27 Jan 07	**EXCEEDER** *Boss DATA150CDS* MASON VS PRINCESS SUPERSTAR	3		11

PRIVATE LIVES UK group

Date	Title / Label	Peak Position	Weeks at No.1	Weeks in Top 40
11 Feb 84	**LIVING IN A WORLD (TURNED UPSIDE DOWN)** *EMI PRIV 2*	53		

PRIZNA UK group

Date	Title / Label	Peak Position	Weeks at No.1	Weeks in Top 40
29 Apr 95	**FIRE** *Labello Blanco NLBCDX 18* PRIZNA FEATURING DEMOLITION MAN	33		1

P.J. PROBY US singer

Date	Title / Label	Peak Position	Weeks at No.1	Weeks in Top 40
28 May 64	**HOLD ME** *Decca F 11904*	3		14
3 Sep 64	**TOGETHER** *Decca F 11967*	8		10
10 Dec 64	**SOMEWHERE** *Liberty LIB 10182*	6		11
25 Feb 65	**I APOLOGISE** *Liberty LIB 10188*	11		7
8 Jul 65	**LET THE WATER RUN DOWN** *Liberty LIB 10206*	19		8
30 Sep 65	**THAT MEANS A LOT** *Liberty LIB 10215*	30		6
25 Nov 65	**MARIA** *Liberty LIB 10218*	8		9
10 Feb 66	**YOU'VE COME BACK** *Liberty LIB 10223*	25		6
16 Jun 66	**TO MAKE A BIG MAN CRY** *Liberty LIB 10236*	34		1
27 Oct 66	**I CAN'T MAKE IT ALONE** *Liberty LIB 10250*	37		1
6 Mar 68	**IT'S YOUR DAY TODAY** *Liberty LIB 15046*	32		2
28 Dec 96	**YESTERDAY HAS GONE** *EMI Premier CDPRESX 13* PJ PROBY & MARC ALMOND FEATURING THE MY LIFE STORY ORCHESTRA	58		

PROCLAIMERS UK duo

Date	Title / Label	Peak Position	Weeks at No.1	Weeks in Top 40
14 Nov 87	**LETTER FROM AMERICA** *Chrysalis CHS 3178*	3		8
5 Mar 88	**MAKE MY HEART FLY** *Chrysalis CLAIM 1*	63		
27 Aug 88	**I'M GONNA BE (500 MILES)** *Chrysalis CLAIM 2*	11		8
12 Nov 88	**SUNSHINE ON LEITH** *Chrysalis CLAIM 3*	41		
11 Feb 89	**I'M ON MY WAY** *Chrysalis CLAIM 4*	43		
24 Nov 90	**KING OF THE ROAD (EP)** *Chrysalis CLAIM 5*	9		7
19 Feb 94	**LET'S GET MARRIED** *Chrysalis CDCLAIMS 6*	21		3
16 Apr 94	**WHAT MAKES YOU CRY** *Chrysalis CDCLAIMS 7*	38		1
22 Oct 94	**THESE ARMS OF MINE** *Chrysalis CDCLAIM 8*	51		
24 Mar 07	**I'M GONNA BE (500 MILES)** *EMI COMICCD01* PROCLAIMERS FEATURING BRIAN POTTER & ANDY PIPKIN	1	3	8
24 Mar 07	**I'M GONNA BE (500 MILES)** *Download*	26		2
8 Sep 07	**LIFE WITH YOU** *W14 1742097*	58		

PROCOL HARUM UK group

Date	Title / Label	Peak Position	Weeks at No.1	Weeks in Top 40
25 May 67	**A WHITER SHADE OF PALE** *Deram DM 126*	1	6	15
4 Oct 67	**HOMBURG** *Regal Zonophone RZ 3003*	6		10
24 Apr 68	**QUITE RIGHTLY SO** *Regal Zonophone RZ 3007*	50		
18 Jun 69	**SALTY DOG** *Regal Zonophone RZ 3109*	44		
22 Apr 72	**A WHITER SHADE OF PALE** *Magnifly ECHO 10*	13		10
5 Aug 72	**CONQUISTADOR** *Chrysalis CHS 2003*	22		6
23 Aug 75	**PANDORA'S BOX** *Chrysalis CHS 2073*	16		6

PRODIGY UK group

Date	Title / Label	Peak Position	Weeks at No.1	Weeks in Top 40
24 Aug 91	**CHARLY** *XL Recordings XLS 21*	3		8
4 Jan 92	**EVERYBODY IN THE PLACE (EP)** *XL Recordings XLS 26*	2		6
26 Sep 92	**FIRE/JERICHO** *XL Recordings XLS 30*	11		3
21 Nov 92	**OUT OF SPACE/RUFF IN THE JUNGLE BIZNESS** *XL Recordings XLS 35*	5		11
17 Apr 93	**WIND IT UP (REWOUND)** *XL Recordings XLS 39CD*	11		5
16 Oct 93	**ONE LOVE** *XL Recordings XLS 47CD*	8		4
28 May 94	**NO GOOD (START THE DANCE)** *XL Recordings XLS 51CD*	4		10
24 Sep 94	**VOODOO PEOPLE** *XL Recordings XLS 54CD*	13		3
18 Mar 95	**POISON** *XL Recordings XLS 58CD*	15		3
30 Mar 96	**FIRESTARTER** *XL Recordings XLS 70CD*	1	3	9
20 Apr 96	**CHARLY** *XL Recordings XLS 21*	66		
20 Apr 96	**FIRE/JERICHO** *XL Recordings XLS 30*	63		
20 Apr 96	**NO GOOD (START THE DANCE)** *XL Recordings XLS 51CD*	57		
20 Apr 96	**OUT OF SPACE/RUFF IN THE JUNGLE BIZNESS** *XL Recordings XLS 35*	52		
20 Apr 96	**POISON** *XL Recordings XLS 58CD*	62		
20 Apr 96	**VOODOO PEOPLE** *XL Recordings XLS 54CD*	75		
20 Apr 96	**WIND IT UP (REWOUND)** *XL Recordings XLS 39CD*	71		
27 Apr 96	**EVERYBODY IN THE PLACE (EP)** *XL Recordings XLS 26*	69		
23 Nov 96	**BREATHE** *XL Recordings XLS 80CD*	1	2	12
14 Dec 96	**FIRESTARTER** *XL Recordings XLS 70CD*	53		
29 Nov 97	**SMACK MY BITCH UP** *XL Recordings XLS 90CD*	8		4
13 Jul 02	**BABY'S GOT A TEMPER** *XL Recordings XLS 145CD*	5		2
11 Sep 04	**GIRLS** *XL Recordings XLS 195CD*	19		2
4 Dec 04	**CHARLY** *XL Recordings XLXV1506*	73		
15 Oct 05	**VOODOO PEOPLE (REMIX)/OUT OF SPACE (REMIX)** *XL Recordings XLS219CD*	20		2

PROFESSIONALS UK group

Date	Title / Label	Peak Position	Weeks at No.1	Weeks in Top 40
11 Oct 80	**1-2-3-** *Virgin VS 376*	43		

PROGRESS FUNK Italian production group

Date	Title / Label	Peak Position	Weeks at No.1	Weeks in Top 40
11 Oct 97	**AROUND MY BRAIN** *Deconstruction 74321518182*	73		

PROGRESS UK producer

Date	Title / Label	Peak Position	Weeks at No.1	Weeks in Top 40
18 Dec 99	**EVERYBODY** *Manifesto FESCD 65* PROGRESS PRESENTS THE BOY WUNDA	7		8

PROJECT US duo

Date	Title / Label	Peak Position	Weeks at No.1	Weeks in Top 40
27 Aug 94	**BRING IT BACK 2 LUV** *Fruittree FTREE 10CD* PROJECT FEATURING GERIDEAU	65		

PROJECT 1 UK producer

Date	Title / Label	Peak Position	Weeks at No.1	Weeks in Top 40
16 May 92	**ROUGHNECK (EP)** *Rising High RSN 22*	49		
29 Aug 92	**DON GARGON COMIN'** *Rising High RSN 35*	64		

LIAM HOWLETT of THE PRODIGY

Few bands have had as controversial an impact on the singles charts as Essex's The Prodigy. Initially the brainchild of raver and teen DJ Liam Howlett, the band have sold around 20 million albums worldwide and have helped to redefine genre and industry preconceptions of the demographic and commercial potential of dance music.

Although the band is perhaps best known for the 1996 smash single, 'Firestarter', their incendiary attack on the charts and the moral majority actually began many years before. Crawling out from within the rave culture and the morass of illegal parties in and around the M25 at the turn of the 1990s, Howlett hailed from a small satellite village near Braintree. Initially listening obsessively to hip-hop, Howlett quickly immersed himself in the thunderous beats-per-minute of early rave and began using his rudimentary Roland W30 and Akai 950 keyboards to compose pioneering hard-dance tunes. Given that rave culture was anti-establishment, drug-riddled and relatively faceless, the chances of a new act breaking into the commercial mainstream were almost zero. However, Howlett then hooked up with Keith Flint and Leeroy Thornhill, two ravers who were widely known as exceptional dancers and colourful characters, not least because of their penchant for dancing together, despite the 6' 7" Thornhill towering over Flint.

Once the MC talents of Peterborough-based vocal tornado Maxim Reality had been secured (plus a split with departing member, Sharky), the line-up of The Prodigy was sealed. As mentioned in the Introduction, a nineteen-year-old Howlett then presented XL Records with a completed demo tape so expertly crafted and programmed that the label could effectively press the records and ship them to the shops. Not satisfied with pioneering home studio songwriting, Howlett proceeded to crash into the charts at Number 3 with his debut single, 'Charly', which cleverly morphed a voice-over from a Public Service Announcement about kids avoiding strangers and married this to a brutal succession of beats and hooks. The Prodigy had arrived.

Despite dissenters within the rave scene criticising The Prodigy for betraying their roots, the band were on a course that left no room for genre loyalties. Follow-up single 'Everybody In The Place' went one better at Number 2 and the debut album, *Experience*, also fared well, but it was with Howlett's seminal second album, *Music For The Jilted Generation* that dance-music history began to be rewritten. Using inspired sampling ('Teen Spirit' for example on 'Voodoo People'), concept pieces ('The Narcotic Suite') and ingenious beats, Howlett captured the zeitgeist effortlessly, mobilising a generation fighting against the Criminal Justice Bill. As they began to morph a sea of musical genres together – most notably with the inclusion of a live drummer and guitarist for their live show – The Prodigy began to break out of the dance circuit and appear on the main stages of UK rock festivals.

However, it was the release in March 1996 of the historic single 'Firestarter' that jettisoned The Prodigy into global infamy. Sung by the maniacal alter-ego of Flint, the song was a juggernaut sonic assault and came complete with a watershed black-and-white video showing Flint and cohorts running amok deep below London in a disused Underground tunnel. When the song hit Number 1 in the UK, the BBC aired the video on *Top Of The Pops* (the band refused ever to appear on the show in person) and saw their switchboard inundated with complaints, including some suggesting that Flint needed urgent medical help.

The accompanying album, *The Fat Of The Land*, was a colossal global smash, selling over 12 million copies. At a time when Oasis were being heralded for charting at Number 1 in a dozen countries, The Prodigy's opus – seen now as one of the greatest albums of all time – smashed in at number 1 in twenty-four territories. In the process, the band forced the media and the music industry to rethink exactly what constituted a 'dance' and/or 'rock' band. Headline slots at Reading Festival and major rock and dance venues around the globe since have proved that The Prodigy are one of those rare acts that can successfully straddle various genres with equal popularity.

Even the controversy over 'Firestarter' was overshadowed by the furore following the release of the November 1997 single, 'Smack My Bitch Up'. Based around the lead line – in fact a sampling of the Ultramagnetic MCs – the song was criticised by womens' groups and even the former tabloid-baiting misbehavers the Beastie Boys (without a hint of irony). It mattered little, with the song still piercing the Top 10.

An unfortunate seven-year hiatus followed while Howlett worked on the follow-up to *The Fat Of The Land*, before 2004's *Always Outnumbered, Never Outgunned* was released. The critics were less impressed and the singles charted lower, but time has crystallised opinion that although this was a flawed album in many ways, there are some flashes of Howlett's genius, such as the breathtaking 'Spitfire'. With the band touring relentlessly, playing massive festivals and gigs such as Moscow's Red Square, it is hard to deny them their status as arguably the most successful hard-dance band of all time.

Silver-selling ● Gold-selling ● Platinum-selling ● US No.1 ★ Peak Position · Weeks at No.1 · Weeks in Top 40

PRONG US group

Date	Title / Label	Peak Position	Weeks at No.1	Weeks in Top 40
25 Apr 92	**WHOSE FIST IS THIS ANYWAY EP** *Epic 6580026*	58		

PROPAGANDA German group

Date	Title / Label	Peak Position	Weeks at No.1	Weeks in Top 40
17 Mar 84	**DR MABUSE** *ZTT ZTAS 2*	27		3
4 May 85	**DUEL** *ZTT ZTAS 8*	21		6
10 Aug 85	**P MACHINERY** *ZTT ZTAS 12*	50		
28 Apr 90	**HEAVEN GIVE ME WORDS** *Virgin VS 1245*	36		2
8 Sep 90	**ONLY ONE WORD** *Virgin VS 1271*	71		

PROPELLERHEADS UK duo

Date	Title / Label	Peak Position	Weeks at No.1	Weeks in Top 40
7 Dec 96	**TAKE CALIFORNIA** *Wall Of Sound WALLD 024*	69		
17 May 97	**SPYBREAK!** *Wall Of Sound WALLD 029X*	40		1
18 Oct 97	**ON HER MAJESTY'S SECRET SERVICE** *East West EW 136CD* PROPELLERHEADS & DAVID ARNOLD	7		3
20 Dec 97	**HISTORY REPEATING** *Wall Of Sound WALLD 036* PROPELLERHEADS & SHIRLEY BASSEY	19		4
27 Jun 98	**BANG ON!** *Wall Of Sound WALLD 039*	53		

PROPHETS OF SOUND UK production duo

Date	Title / Label	Peak Position	Weeks at No.1	Weeks in Top 40
14 Nov 98	**HIGH** *Distinctive DISNCD 47*	73		
23 Feb 02	**NEW DAWN** *Ink NIBNE 10CD*	51		

PROSPECT PARK/CAROLYN HARDING UK duo

Date	Title / Label	Peak Position	Weeks at No.1	Weeks in Top 40
8 Aug 98	**MOVIN' ON** *AM:PM 5827312*	55		

BRIAN PROTHEROE UK singer

Date	Title / Label	Peak Position	Weeks at No.1	Weeks in Top 40
7 Sep 74	**PINBALL** *Chrysalis CHS 2043*	22		6

PROTOCOL UK group

Date	Title / Label	Peak Position	Weeks at No.1	Weeks in Top 40
22 Oct 05	**SHE WAITS FOR ME** *Polydor 9871400*	65		
4 Feb 06	**WHERE'S THE PLEASURE** *Polydor 9876559*	27		1

PROUD MARY UK group

Date	Title / Label	Peak Position	Weeks at No.1	Weeks in Top 40
25 Aug 01	**VERY BEST FRIEND** *Sour Mash JDNCSCD 004*	75		

DOROTHY PROVINE US singer

Date	Title / Label	Peak Position	Weeks at No.1	Weeks in Top 40
7 Dec 61	**DON'T BRING LULU** *Warner Brothers WB 53*	17		9
28 Jun 62	**CRAZY WORDS CRAZY TUNE** *Warner Brothers WB 70*	45		

ERIC PRYDZ Swedish producer

Date	Title / Label	Peak Position	Weeks at No.1	Weeks in Top 40
21 Aug 04	**WOZ NOT WOZ** *C2 CDC2002* ERIC PRYDZ & STEVE ANGELLO	55		
25 Sep 04	**CALL ON ME** *Data 68CDS*	1	5	19
13 Jan 07	**PROPER EDUCATION** *Data/Positiva DATA144CDS* ERIC PRYDZ VS FLOYD	2		8

PSEUDO ECHO Australian group

Date	Title / Label	Peak Position	Weeks at No.1	Weeks in Top 40
18 Jul 87	**FUNKY TOWN** *RCA PB 49705*	8		8

PSYCHEDELIC FURS UK group

Date	Title / Label	Peak Position	Weeks at No.1	Weeks in Top 40
2 May 81	**DUMB WAITERS** *CBS A 1166*	59		
27 Jun 81	**PRETTY IN PINK** *CBS A 1327*	43		
31 Jul 82	**LOVE MY WAY** *CBS A 2549*	42		
31 Mar 84	**HEAVEN** *CBS A 4300*	29		3
16 Jun 84	**GHOST IN YOU** *CBS A 4470*	68		
23 Aug 86	**PRETTY IN PINK** *CBS A 7242*	18		6
9 Jul 88	**ALL THAT MONEY WANTS** *CBS FURS 4*	75		

PSYCHEDELIC WALTONS UK production duo

Date	Title / Label	Peak Position	Weeks at No.1	Weeks in Top 40
19 Jan 02	**WONDERLAND** *Echo ECSCD 120* PSYCHEDELIC WALTONS FEATURING ROISIN MURPHY	37		1

PSYCHIC TV UK group

Date	Title / Label	Peak Position	Weeks at No.1	Weeks in Top 40
26 Apr 86	**GODSTAR** *Temple TOPY 009*	67		
20 Sep 86	**GOOD VIBRATIONS/ROMAN P** *Temple TOPY 23*	65		

PUBLIC ANNOUNCEMENT US group

Date	Title / Label	Peak Position	Weeks at No.1	Weeks in Top 40
9 May 92	**SHE'S GOT THAT VIBE** *Jive JIVET 292* R KELLY & PUBLIC ANNOUNCEMENT	57		
20 Nov 93	**SEX ME** *Jive JIVECD 346* R KELLY & PUBLIC ANNOUNCEMENT	75		
4 Jul 98	**BODY BUMPIN' (YIPPIE-YI-YO)** *A&M 5826972*	38		1

PUBLIC DEMAND UK group

Date	Title / Label	Peak Position	Weeks at No.1	Weeks in Top 40
15 Feb 97	**INVISIBLE** *ZTT ZANG 85CD*	41		

PUBLIC DOMAIN UK group

Date	Title / Label	Peak Position	Weeks at No.1	Weeks in Top 40
2 Dec 00	**OPERATION BLADE (BASS IN THE PLACE)** *Xtravaganza X2H1 CDS* PUBLIC DOMAIN FEATURING CHUCK D ●	5		10
23 Jun 01	**ROCK DA FUNKY BEATS** *Xtrahard X2H3 CDS* PUBLIC DOMAIN FEATURING CHUCK D	19		2
12 Jan 02	**TOO MANY MC'S/LET ME CLEAR MY THROAT** *Xtrahard X2H 8CDS*	34		1

PUBLIC ENEMY US group

Date	Title / Label	Peak Position	Weeks at No.1	Weeks in Top 40
21 Nov 87	**REBEL WITHOUT A PAUSE** *Def Jam 6512457*	37		2
9 Jan 88	**BRING THE NOISE** *Def Jam 6513357*	32		2
2 Jul 88	**DON'T BELIEVE THE HYPE** *Def Jam 6528337*	18		3
15 Oct 88	**NIGHT OF THE LIVING BASEHEADS** *Def Jam 6530460*	63		
24 Jun 89	**FIGHT THE POWER** *Motown ZB 42877*	29		4
20 Jan 90	**WELCOME TO THE TERRORDOME** *Def Jam 6554760*	18		3
7 Apr 90	**911 IS A JOKE** *Def Jam 6558377*	41		
23 Jun 90	**BROTHERS GONNA WORK IT OUT** *Def Jam 6560181*	46		
3 Nov 90	**CAN'T DO NUTTIN' FOR YA MAN** *Def Jam 6563857*	53		
12 Oct 91	**CAN'T TRUSS IT** *Def Jam 6575307*	22		2
25 Jan 92	**SHUT 'EM DOWN** *Def Jam 6577617*	21		2
11 Apr 92	**NIGHTTRAIN** *Def Jam 6578647*	55		
13 Aug 94	**GIVE IT UP** *Def Jam DEFCD1*	18		2
29 Jul 95	**SO WATCHA GONNA DO NOW** *Def Jam DEFCD5*	50		
6 Jun 98	**HE GOT GAME** *Def Jam 5689852* PUBLIC ENEMY FEATURING STEPHEN STILLS	16		2
25 Sep 99	**DO YOU WANNA GO OUR WAY???** *PIAS Recordings PIASX 005CDX*	66		

PUBLIC IMAGE LTD UK group

Date	Title / Label	Peak Position	Weeks at No.1	Weeks in Top 40
21 Oct 78	**PUBLIC IMAGE** *Virgin VS 228*	9		6
7 Jul 79	**DEATH DISCO (PARTS 1 & 2)** *Virgin VS 274*	20		5
20 Oct 79	**MEMORIES** *Virgin VS 299*	60		
4 Apr 81	**FLOWERS OF ROMANCE** *Virgin VS 397*	24		6
17 Sep 83	**THIS IS NOT A LOVE SONG** *Virgin VS 529*	5		8
19 May 84	**BAD LIFE** *Virgin VS 675*	71		
1 Feb 86	**RISE** *Virgin VS 841*	11		7
3 May 86	**HOME** *Virgin VS 855*	75		
22 Aug 87	**SEATTLE** *Virgin VS 988*	47		
6 May 89	**DISAPPOINTED** *Virgin VS 1181*	38		2
20 Oct 90	**DON'T ASK ME** *Virgin VS 1231*	22		4
22 Feb 92	**CRUEL** *Virgin VS 1390*	49		

PUDDLE OF MUDD US group

Date	Title / Label	Peak Position	Weeks at No.1	Weeks in Top 40
23 Feb 02	**CONTROL** *Geffen 4976822*	15		3
15 Jun 02	**BLURRY** *Geffen 4977352*	8		5
28 Sep 02	**SHE HATES ME** *Geffen 4978052*	14		5
13 Dec 03	**AWAY FROM ME** *Geffen 9814810*	55		

TITO PUENTE US multi-instrumentalist

Date	Title / Label	Peak Position	Weeks at No.1	Weeks in Top 40
16 Mar 96	**OYE COMO VA** *Media MCSTD 40013* TITO PUENTE Jr & THE LATIN RHYTHM FEATURING TITO PUENTE, INDIA & CALI ALEMAN	36		1
19 Jul 97	**OYE COMO VA (REMIX)** *Nukleuz MCSTD 40120* TITO PUENTE Jr & THE LATIN RHYTHM FEATURING TITO PUENTE, INDIA & CALI ALEMAN	56		

Key: ○ Silver-selling · ● Gold-selling · ⊛ Platinum-selling · ★ US No.1 · Peak Position · Weeks at No.1 · Weeks in Top 40

PUFF DADDY US rapper/producer

		Peak Position	Weeks at No.1	Weeks in Top 40
29 Mar 97	**CAN'T NOBODY HOLD ME DOWN** *Puff Daddy 74321464552* PUFF DADDY FEATURING MASE ★	19		2
26 Apr 97	**NO TIME** *Atlantic A 5594CD* LIL' KIM FEATURING PUFF DADDY	45		
28 Jun 97	**I'LL BE MISSING YOU** *Puff Daddy 74321499102* PUFF DADDY & FAITH EVANS FEATURING 112 ⊛ ★	1	6	18
9 Aug 97	**MO MONEY MO PROBLEMS** *Puff Daddy 74321492492* NOTORIOUS B.I.G. FEATURING PUFF DADDY & MASE ★	6		8
13 Sep 97	**SOMEONE** *RCA 74321513942* SWV FEATURING PUFF DADDY	34		1
1 Nov 97	**BEEN AROUND THE WORLD** *Puff Daddy 74321539442* PUFF DADDY & THE FAMILY	20		2
7 Feb 98	**IT'S ALL ABOUT THE BENJAMINS** *Puff Daddy 74321561972* PUFF DADDY & THE FAMILY	18		1
1 Aug 98	**COME WITH ME (IMPORT)** *Epic 34K78954* PUFF DADDY FEATURING JIMMY PAGE	75		
8 Aug 98	**COME WITH ME** *Epic 6662842* PUFF DADDY FEATURING JIMMY PAGE	2		7
1 May 99	**ALL NIGHT LONG** *Puff Daddy 74321625592* FAITH EVANS FEATURING PUFF DADDY	23		2
29 May 99	**HATE ME NOW** *Columbia 6672565* NAS FEATURING PUFF DADDY	14		3
21 Aug 99	**PE 2000** *Puff Daddy 74321694982* PUFF DADDY FEATURING HURRICANE G	13		2
20 Nov 99	**BEST FRIEND** *Puff Daddy 74321712312* PUFF DADDY FEATURING MARIO WINANS	24		3
5 Feb 00	**NOTORIOUS B.I.G.** *Puff Daddy 74321737312* NOTORIOUS B.I.G. FEATURING PUFF DADDY AND LIL' KIM	16		3
19 Feb 00	**SATISFY YOU (IMPORT)** *Bad Boy/Arista 792832* PUFF DADDY FEATURING R KELLY	73		
11 Mar 00	**SATISFY YOU** *Puff Daddy 74321745592* PUFF DADDY FEATURING R KELLY	8		6
6 Oct 01	**BAD BOY FOR LIFE** *Arista 74321889982* P DIDDY FEATURING BLACK ROB & MARK CURRY	13		5
26 Jan 02	**DIDDY** *Puff Daddy 74321911652* P DIDDY FEATURING THE NEPTUNES	19		1
8 Jun 02	**PASS THE COURVOISIER - PART II** *J Records 74321937902* BUSTA RHYMES, P DIDDY & PHARRELL	16		3
10 Aug 02	**I NEED A GIRL (PART ONE)** *Puff Daddy 74321947242* P DIDDY FEATURING USHER & LOON	4		8
29 Mar 03	**BUMP BUMP BUMP** *Epic 6736452* B2K FEATURING P DIDDY	11		6
23 Aug 03	**LET'S GET ILL** *Bad Boy MCSTD 40331* P DIDDY FEATURING KELIS	25		1
20 Sep 03	**SHAKE YA TAILFEATHER** *Bad Boy MCSTD 40337* NELLY, P DIDDY & MURPHY LEE ★	10		5
7 Feb 04	**SHOW ME YOUR SOUL** *Puff Daddy MCSTD 40350* P DIDDY, LENNY KRAVITZ, PHARRELL WILLIAMS & LOON	35		1
15 May 04	**PASS THE COURVOISIER - PART II** *J Records 74321937902* BUSTA RHYMES, P DIDDY & PHARRELL	71		
5 Jun 04	**I DON'T WANNA KNOW (IMPORT)** *Universal 9862372PMI* MARIO WINANS FEATURING ENYA & P DIDDY	71		
12 Jun 04	**I DON'T WANNA KNOW** *Bad Boy MCSTD40369* MARIO WINANS FEATURING ENYA & P DIDDY ○	1	1	12
28 Jan 06	**NASTY GIRL** *Bad Boy AT0229CDX* NOTORIOUS B.I.G. FEATURING DIDDY, NELLY, JAGGED EDGE AND AVERY STORM	1	2	16
7 Oct 06	**COME TO ME** *Atlantic AT0260CD* P DIDDY FEATURING NICOLE SCHERZINGER	4		9
16 Dec 06	**TELL ME** *Atlantic AT0268CD* P DIDDY FEATURING CHRISTINA AGUILERA	8		13
3 Mar 07	**LAST NIGHT** *Atlantic AT0273CD* P DIDDY FEATURING KEYSHIA COLE	14		10
14 Jul 07	**I'LL BE MISSING YOU** *Download* PUFF DADDY FEATURING FAITH EVANS	32		1
8 Sep 07	**THROUGH THE PAIN (SHE TOLD ME)** *Bad Boy AT0283CD* P DIDDY FEATURING MARIO WINANS	50		

PULP UK group

Date	Title / Label	Peak Position	Weeks at No.1	Weeks in Top 40
27 Nov 93	**LIP GLOSS** *Island CID 567*	50		
2 Apr 94	**DO YOU REMEMBER THE FIRST TIME** *Island CID 574*	33		1
4 Jun 94	**THE SISTERS EP** *Island CID 595*	19		2
3 Jun 95	**COMMON PEOPLE** *Island CID 613* ○	2		10
7 Oct 95	**MIS-SHAPES/SORTED FOR ES & WIZZ** *Island CIDX 620* ○	2		5
9 Dec 95	**DISCO 2000** *Island CID 623* ○	7		8
6 Apr 96	**SOMETHING CHANGED** *Island CID 632*	10		3
7 Sep 96	**DO YOU REMEMBER THE FIRST TIME** *Island CID 574*	73		
22 Nov 97	**HELP THE AGED** *Island CID 679*	8		2
28 Mar 98	**THIS IS HARDCORE** *Island CID 695*	12		2
20 Jun 98	**A LITTLE SOUL** *Island CID 708*	22		1
19 Sep 98	**PARTY HARD** *Island CID 719*	29		1
20 Oct 01	**THE TREES/SUNRISE** *Island CID 786*	23		1
27 Apr 02	**BAD COVER VERSION** *Island CIDX 794*	27		1

PULSE US duo

		Peak Position	Weeks at No.1	Weeks in Top 40
25 May 96	**THE LOVER THAT YOU ARE** *ffrr FCD 278* PULSE FEATURING ANTOINETTE ROBERTSON	22		1

PUNK CHIC Swedish producer

Date	Title / Label	Peak Position	Weeks at No.1	Weeks in Top 40
6 Oct 01	**DJ SPINNIN'** *WEA 333CD*	69		

PUNX German producer

Date	Title / Label	Peak Position	Weeks at No.1	Weeks in Top 40
16 Nov 02	**THE ROCK** *Data 38CDS*	59		

PURE REASON REVOLUTION UK group

Date	Title / Label	Peak Position	Weeks at No.1	Weeks in Top 40
1 May 04	**APPRENTICE OF THE UNIVERSE** *Poptones MC5089SCD*	74		
23 Apr 05	**THE BRIGHT AMBASSADORS OF MORNING** *Sony Music 6758072*	68		

PURE SUGAR US group

Date	Title / Label	Peak Position	Weeks at No.1	Weeks in Top 40
24 Oct 98	**DELICIOUS** *Geffen GFSTD 22355*	70		

PURESSENCE UK group

Date	Title / Label	Peak Position	Weeks at No.1	Weeks in Top 40
23 May 98	**THIS FEELING** *Island CID 688*	33		1
8 Aug 98	**IT DOESN'T MATTER ANYMORE** *Island CID 703*	47		
21 Nov 98	**ALL I WANT** *Island CID 722*	39		1
5 Oct 02	**WALKING DEAD** *Island CIDX 803*	40		1
22 Sep 07	**DROP DOWN TO EARTH** *Reaction REACTRR002*	56		

PURETONE Australian producer

Date	Title / Label	Peak Position	Weeks at No.1	Weeks in Top 40
12 Jan 02	**ADDICTED TO BASS** *Gut GDGUS 6*	2		11
10 May 03	**STUCK IN A GROOVE** *Illustrious CDILL 014*	26		1

JAMES & BOBBY PURIFY US duo

Date	Title / Label	Peak Position	Weeks at No.1	Weeks in Top 40
24 Apr 76	**I'M YOUR PUPPET** *Mercury 6167 324*	12		9
7 Aug 76	**MORNING GLORY** *Mercury 6167 380*	27		5

PURPLE HEARTS UK group

Date	Title / Label	Peak Position	Weeks at No.1	Weeks in Top 40
22 Sep 79	**MILLIONS LIKE US** *Fiction FICS 003*	57		
8 Mar 80	**JIMMY** *Fiction FICS 9*	60		

PURPLE KINGS UK duo

Date	Title / Label	Peak Position	Weeks at No.1	Weeks in Top 40
15 Oct 94	**THAT'S THE WAY YOU DO IT** *Positiva CDTIV 21*	26		2

PUSH Belgian producer

		Peak Position	Weeks at No.1	Weeks in Top 40
15 May 99	**UNIVERSAL NATION** *Inferno CDFERN 16*	36		1
9 Oct 99	**UNIVERSAL NATION (REMIX)** *Inferno CDFERN 20*	35		1
23 Sep 00	**TILL WE MEET AGAIN** *Inferno CDFERN 29*	46		
12 May 01	**STRANGE WORLD** *Inferno CDFERN 38*	21		2
20 Oct 01	**PLEASE SAVE ME** *Five AM/Inferno FAMFERN 1CD* SUNSCREEM VS PUSH	36		1
3 Nov 01	**THE LEGACY** *Inferno CDFERN 43*	22		2
4 May 02	**TRANZY STATE OF MIND** *Inferno CDFERN 45*	31		1
5 Oct 02	**STRANGE WORLD/THE LEGACY** *Inferno CDFERN 49*	55		
15 Mar 03	**UNIVERSAL NATION** *Inferno CDFERN 53*	54		

PUSSY 2000 UK production duo

Date	Title / Label	Peak Position	Weeks at No.1	Weeks in Top 40
3 Nov 01	**IT'S GONNA BE ALRIGHT** *Ink NIBNE 9CD*	70		

PUSSYCAT Dutch group

Date	Title / Label	Peak Position	Weeks at No.1	Weeks in Top 40
28 Aug 76	**MISSISSIPPI** *Sonet SON 2077* ●	1	4	19
25 Dec 76	**SMILE** *Sonet SON 2096*	24		5

PUSSYCAT DOLLS US group

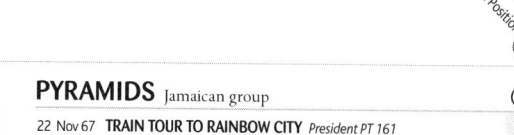

Date	Title	Peak Position	Weeks at No.1	Weeks in Top 40
10 Sep 05	**DON'T CHA (IMPORT)** *Polydor AMB000468322* PUSSYCAT DOLLS FEATURING BUSTA RHYMES	44		
17 Sep 05	**DON'T CHA** *A&M/Polydor 9885052* PUSSYCAT DOLLS FEATURING BUSTA RHYMES ○	1	3	23
10 Dec 05	**STICKWITU** *A&M 9888583* ★	1		12
11 Mar 06	**BEEP** *A&M 9852860* PUSSYCAT DOLLS FEATURING WLL.I.AM	2		11
1 Jul 06	**BUTTONS** *A&M 1700854* PUSSYCAT DOLLS FEATURING SNOOP DOGG	3		9
30 Sep 06	**I DON'T NEED A MAN** *A&M/Polydor 1709094*	7		6

PYRAMIDS Jamaican group

Date	Title	Peak Position	Weeks at No.1	Weeks in Top 40
22 Nov 67	**TRAIN TOUR TO RAINBOW CITY** *President PT 161*	35		3

PYTHON LEE JACKSON Australian group

Date	Title	Peak Position	Weeks at No.1	Weeks in Top 40
30 Sep 72	**IN A BROKEN DREAM** *Young Blood YB 1002*	3		10

Nirvana

Grunge is What Happens When the Children of Divorce Get Their Hands on Guitars

One of the UK charts' most seismic moments actually centred round a single that peaked at just Number 7 in November 1991: Nirvana's 'Smells Like Teen Spirit'. For the purposes of this book's UK slant, let's start the tale at the end: Reading Festival, 1992. Nirvana were the headliners amidst a swirl of controversy, drug rumour and speculation about the ill health of their heroin-using lead singer, Kurt Cobain.

There was a palpable sense of anticipation – both among industry people behind the scenes and in the mass of festival goers out front – about Cobain's state of mind. As the day dragged on and there was no sign of him, the anticipation turned first to apprehension and then to genuine concern. For three days, Reading Festival had been immersed in another episode of the rapidly escalating Nirvana saga – would they appear, were they still together as a band, had Cobain overdosed, were he and his wife Courtney Love still together? These and many other questions raced through the minds of all the people who stood ankle deep in that cold muddy Berkshire field, waiting for the headline performance by arguably the most important band of the decade.

Then, suddenly, Kurt Cobain, wearing a blond wig and white gown, was pushed onstage in a battered wheelchair in front of 40,000 bewildered music fans. The sense of melodrama cranked up yet another notch. After singing one line of the opening song, Cobain collapsed onto the floor, motionless, only to then jump up and launch into his band's last ever UK gig. It was a truly blistering performance and even as the field emptied itself of the tired revellers, kicking their way home through the streams of plastic water bottles and flyers, there was a feeling that we had all just witnessed music history.

Less than two years later, shortly after a drug-and alcohol-induced coma, Cobain, who had been depressed and feeling increasingly isolated, was dead, killed by a single gunshot wound to the head in his family home.

Most music fans remember the moment they first heard 'Smells Like Teen Spirit'. It sliced through the haze of standard radio programming like a missile and almost instantly made a generation of music seem outmoded. It was that shocking – a statement that sounds outdated, exaggerated even, when you look at the breadth of radio programming and music TV today, but back in 1991 this song – that was named after a deodorant marketed at teenagers – really was that different.

Raucous music was not new to the charts, of course – see elsewhere for the impact of punk on the charts and society; take your pick from a multitude of edgier bands, my own favourites might include MC5, The Stooges, Black Sabbath, Napalm Death, The Wedding Present, up through The Prodigy and on to Gallows, the list is endless. But with Nirvana, there was something very deep-rooted about their impact.

That famous riff spawned a monster, albeit unwittingly. It wasn't just Nirvana, there were hordes of other brilliant bands around that time that were lumped in with the newly christened 'grunge' scene – Tad, Mudhoney, the enormo-rockers Pearl Jam, Skinny Puppy, The Screaming Trees, U-Men, to name just a few. This loosely affiliated cluster of bands had originally been an underground scene from the cold and wet north-western coast town of Seattle, which boasted

Jimi Hendrix, Queensryche, Robert Cray and Kenny G as some of its forefathers. Then Nirvana broke, the media called it grunge and, when it pierced the charts in late 1991, it changed the UK's music scene for ever.

To the youth of the period, it sounded revolutionary; older detractors derided grunge's fusion of hardcore and metal as merely re-hashing seventies rock, but this mattered little to those who were experiencing such music for the first time. It felt like they were living through something *important*.

The media feeding frenzy was startling. Britain and indeed the world was gripped by 'Nirvana-mania' as every mainstream tabloid and glossy magazine now wanted a piece of a band who only six months previously they had not even heard of. When grunge hit the mainstream with this seminal single, it was but a precursor to the avalanche that was Nirvana's second album, *Nevermind*. This 20-million-selling record single-handedly changed the face of modern music programming, live shows, record store buying policies and just about every facet of the music and entertainment industries. Prior to Nirvana, the mainstream music industry was still an ultra-conservative place. Even though MTV had launched over ten years previously, it remained largely the domain of the big hitters, the anodyne pop stars and the innocuous novelty hit. Likewise UK radio programming, which only boasted a few bastions of alternative thinking such as the likes of John Peel and Steve Lamacq. The norm had been to be normal. However, over the next two years, grunge changed the world; it altered the very DNA of the music business.

The chart success was reflected directly on the streets as followers of grunge – the crassly termed 'loser kids' – swamped a thousand glistening shopping malls with their scruffy thrift-store chic. Boys were bedecked in flannel shirts, oversized shorts cut off just below the knee, a pair of Dr Martens and long, lank hair; girls often wore flowery dresses with thick leggings, or trousers with oversized band T-shirts.

Unfortunately, as with so many subcultures, once grunge entered the mainstream it was effectively rendered culturally impotent by its own success. Nirvana's debut album was produced for just $606.17 – now, cheque-book waving A&R men were jetting into Seattle and throwing six-figure sums at almost any band. Some of these gambles paid off with multi-million-selling albums, but many bands never achieved what they promised, unprepared as they were for the intense heat of the worldwide spotlight.

Million-dollar marketing campaigns targeted all the latest 'grungers', while cheesy TV shows ran features on what to say to your 'loser' teenager. Elevator music albums were released with muzak versions of grunge classics and, perhaps worst of all, haute couture designers started to copy the style. Milan and Paris catwalks exhibited horrendous copies of the grunge look, with obscenely priced and hideously shaped versions of the thrift-store style. Record stores reported fashion journalists, dripping in designer garments, running in and asking for albums by grunge bands. Some even tried to rename the designer wear 'frunge'. Lumberjack shirts with designer labels were selling for over $500 and a corduroy jacket, similar to the thousands of second-hand coats worn by grunge fans, was offered for sale for $3,000. 'Smells Like Teen Spirit' was even used to advertise antique cars in America.

Once 'Smells Like Teen Spirit' had charted, this anti-establishment band – reluctant heroes to 'losers' the world over – was suddenly a core part of the mainstream. The trio had become a 'radio friendly unit shifter', as a perplexed and increasingly troubled Cobain termed it. Nirvana became so bored of their breakthrough single that it was even briefly dropped from their live set.

And then, of course, it all stopped.

The shot that was heard across the world, when Kurt Cobain committed suicide in early 1994, effectively put an end to grunge, although for many it had already become listless amidst the corporate hijack, the growing drug problems and the increasingly feeble music. In the vacuum left by Cobain's death, the grunge movement splintered and stumbled. Nirvana's drummer Dave Grohl started the all-conquering Foo Fighters, while the bassist, Krist Noveselic, went on to campaign for electoral reform. Then Britpop arrived in the UK to brutally sweep away the last vestiges of grunge's impact . . . but that's another story (morning glory).

Q–T

KEY TO ARTIST ENTRIES

Artist/Group Name — Artist/Group Nationality and Category — Silver-selling — Gold-selling — Platinum-selling — US No.1 ★ — Peak Position — Weeks at No.1 — Weeks in Top 40

DEXY'S MIDNIGHT RUNNERS UK group

Date	Title / Label	Peak Position	Weeks at No.1	Weeks in Top 40
19 Jan 80	**DANCE STANCE** *Oddball Productions R 6028*	40		1
22 Mar 80	**GENO** *Late Night Feelings R 6033* ●	1	2	12
12 Jul 80	**THERE THERE MY DEAR** *Late Night Feelings R 6038*	7		6
21 Mar 81	**PLAN B** *Parlophone R 6046*	58		
11 Jul 81	**SHOW ME** *Mercury DEXYS 6*	16		7
20 Mar 82	**THE CELTIC SOUL BROTHERS** *Mercury DEXYS 8* DEXY'S MIDNIGHT RUNNERS WITH THE EMERALD EXPRESS	45		
3 Jul 82	**COME ON EILEEN** *Mercury DEXYS 9* DEXY'S MIDNIGHT RUNNERS WITH THE EMERALD EXPRESS ⊛ ★	1	4	13
2 Oct 82	**JACKIE WILSON SAID (I'M IN HEAVEN WHEN YOU SMILE)** *Mercury DEXYS 10* KEVIN ROWLAND & DEXY'S MIDNIGHT RUNNERS	5		6
4 Dec 82	**LET'S GET THIS STRAIGHT (FROM THE START)/OLD** *Mercury DEXYS 11* KEVIN ROWLAND & DEXY'S MIDNIGHT RUNNERS	17		8
2 Apr 83	**THE CELTIC SOUL BROTHERS** *Mercury DEXYS 12* KEVIN ROWLAND & DEXY'S MIDNIGHT RUNNERS	20		5
22 Nov 86	**BECAUSE OF YOU** *Mercury BRUSH 1*	13		6

Date of entry into Top 75

Artist collaboration or where artist's name has changed

Song Title

Label and Catalogue Number

Silver-selling · Gold-selling · Platinum-selling · US No.1 ★ · Peak Position · Weeks at No.1 · Weeks in Top 40

Q UK production duo

Date	Title / Label	Peak Position	Weeks at No.1	Weeks in Top 40
5 Jun 93	**GET HERE** *Arista 74321145972* Q FEATURING TRACY ACKERMAN	37		2
12 Mar 94	**(EVERYTHING I DO) I DO IT FOR YOU** *Bell 74321193062* Q FEATURING TONY JACKSON	47		

QATTARA UK production duo

Date	Title / Label	Peak Position	Weeks at No.1	Weeks in Top 40
15 Mar 97	**COME WITH ME** *Positiva CDTIV 71*	31		1

QB FINEST US group

Date	Title / Label	Peak Position	Weeks at No.1	Weeks in Top 40
21 Apr 01	**OOCHIE WALLY** *Columbia 6710852* QB FINEST FEATURING NAS & BRAVEHEARTS	30		1

Q-BASS UK production duo

Date	Title / Label	Peak Position	Weeks at No.1	Weeks in Top 40
8 Feb 92	**HARDCORE WILL NEVER DIE** *Suburban Base SUBBASE 007*	64		

Q-CLUB Italian group

Date	Title / Label	Peak Position	Weeks at No.1	Weeks in Top 40
6 Jan 96	**TELL IT TO MY HEART** *Manifesto FESCD 5*	28		2

QFX UK producer

Date	Title / Label	Peak Position	Weeks at No.1	Weeks in Top 40
6 May 95	**FREEDOM (EP)** *Epidemic EPICD 004*	41		
3 Feb 96	**EVERYTIME YOU TOUCH ME** *Epidemic EPICD 006*	22		3
3 Aug 96	**YOU GOT THE POWER** *Epidemic EPICD 007*	33		1
18 Jan 97	**FREEDOM 2** *Epidemic EPICD 008*	21		2
20 Mar 99	**SAY YOU'LL BE MINE** *Quality Recordings QUAL 005CD*	34		1
23 Aug 03	**FREEDOM** *Data 57CDS*	36		1

Q-TEE UK rapper

Date	Title / Label	Peak Position	Weeks at No.1	Weeks in Top 40
21 Apr 90	**AFRIKA** *SBK 7008* HISTORY FEATURING Q-TEE	42		
10 Feb 96	**GIMME THAT BODY** *Heavenly HVN 48CD*	40		1

Q-TEX UK group

Date	Title / Label	Peak Position	Weeks at No.1	Weeks in Top 40
9 Apr 94	**THE POWER OF LOVE** *Stoatin' VSCDG 1666*	65		
26 Nov 94	**BELIEVE** *23rd Precinct THIRD 2CD*	41		
15 Jun 96	**LET THE LOVE** *23rd Precinct THIRD 4CD*	30		1
30 Nov 96	**DO YOU WANT ME** *23rd Precinct THIRD 5CD*	48		
28 Jun 97	**POWER OF LOVE '97 (REMIX)** *23rd Precinct THIRD 7CD*	49		

Q-TIP US rapper

Date	Title / Label	Peak Position	Weeks at No.1	Weeks in Top 40
4 Oct 97	**GOT 'TIL IT'S GONE** *Virgin VSCDG 1666* JANET FEATURING Q-TIP & JONI	6		7
19 Jun 99	**GET INVOLVED** *Hollywood 0101185 HWR*	36		1
22 Jan 00	**HOT BOYZ** *Elektra E 7002CD* MISSY MISDEMEANOR ELLIOTT FEATURING NAS, EVE & Q-TIP	18		2
12 Feb 00	**BREATHE AND STOP** *Arista 74321727062*	12		4
6 May 00	**VIVRANT THING** *Arista 74321751302*	39		1

QUAD CITY DJS US group

Date	Title / Label	Peak Position	Weeks at No.1	Weeks in Top 40
15 Nov 97	**SPACE JAM** *Atlantic EW 773*	57		

QUADROPHONIA Belgian production group

Date	Title / Label	Peak Position	Weeks at No.1	Weeks in Top 40
13 Apr 91	**QUADROPHONIA** *ARS 6567687*	14		6
6 Jul 91	**THE WAVE OF THE FUTURE** *ARS 6569937*	40		1
21 Dec 91	**FIND THE TIME (PART ONE)** *ARS 6576260*	41		

QUADS UK group

Date	Title / Label	Peak Position	Weeks at No.1	Weeks in Top 40
22 Sep 79	**THERE MUST BE THOUSANDS** *Big Bear BB 23*	66		

QUAKE UK producer

Date	Title / Label	Peak Position	Weeks at No.1	Weeks in Top 40
29 Aug 98	**THE DAY WILL COME** *ffrr FCD 344* QUAKE FEATURING MARCIA RAE	53		

QUANTUM JUMP UK group

Date	Title / Label	Peak Position	Weeks at No.1	Weeks in Top 40
2 Jun 79	**THE LONE RANGER** *Electric WOT 33*	5		8

QUARTERFLASH US group

Date	Title / Label	Peak Position	Weeks at No.1	Weeks in Top 40
27 Feb 82	**HARDEN MY HEART** *Geffen GEF A 1838*	49		

QUARTZ UK instrumental group

Date	Title / Label	Peak Position	Weeks at No.1	Weeks in Top 40
17 Mar 90	**WE'RE COMIN' AT YA** *Mercury ITMR 2* QUARTZ FEATURING STEPZ	65		
2 Feb 91	**IT'S TOO LATE** *Mercury ITM 3* QUARTZ INTRODUCING DINA CARROLL	8		9
15 Jun 91	**NAKED LOVE (JUST SAY YOU WANT ME)** *Mercury ITM 4* QUARTZ & DINA CARROLL	39		1

JAKIE QUARTZ French singer

Date	Title / Label	Peak Position	Weeks at No.1	Weeks in Top 40
11 Mar 89	**A LA VIE, A L'AMOUR** *PWL 30*	55		

QUARTZ LOCK UK production duo

Date	Title / Label	Peak Position	Weeks at No.1	Weeks in Top 40
7 Oct 95	**LOVE EVICTION** *X-Plode BANG 2CD* QUARTZ LOCK FEATURING LONNIE GORDON	32		1

SUZI QUATRO US singer/bass player

Date	Title / Label	Peak Position	Weeks at No.1	Weeks in Top 40
19 May 73	**CAN THE CAN** *RAK 150*	1	1	11
28 Jul 73	**48 CRASH** *RAK 158*	3		8
27 Oct 73	**DAYTONA DEMON** *RAK 161*	14		6
9 Feb 74	**DEVIL GATE DRIVE** *RAK 167*	1	2	9
29 Jun 74	**TOO BIG** *RAK 175*	14		5
9 Nov 74	**THE WILD ONE** *RAK 185*	7		6
8 Feb 75	**YOUR MAMA WON'T LIKE ME** *RAK 191*	31		4
5 Mar 77	**TEAR ME APART** *RAK 248*	27		4
18 Mar 78	**IF YOU CAN'T GIVE ME LOVE** *RAK 271*	4		10
22 Jul 78	**THE RACE IS ON** *RAK 278*	43		
11 Nov 78	**STUMBLIN' IN** *RAK 285* SUZI QUATRO & CHRIS NORMAN	41		
20 Oct 79	**SHE'S IN LOVE WITH YOU** *RAK 299*	11		7
19 Jan 80	**MAMA'S BOY** *RAK 303*	34		2
5 Apr 80	**I'VE NEVER BEEN IN LOVE** *RAK 307*	56		
25 Oct 80	**ROCK HARD** *Dreamland DLSP 6*	68		
13 Nov 82	**HEART OF STONE** *Polydor POSP 477*	60		

FINLEY QUAYE UK singer

Date	Title / Label	Peak Position	Weeks at No.1	Weeks in Top 40
21 Jun 97	**SUNDAY SHINING** *Epic 6644552*	16		4
13 Sep 97	**EVEN AFTER ALL** *Epic 6649712*	10		3
29 Nov 97	**IT'S GREAT WHEN WE'RE TOGETHER** *Epic 6653382*	29		1
7 Mar 98	**YOUR LOVE GETS SWEETER** *Epic 6656065*	16		3
15 Aug 98	**ULTRA STIMULATION** *Epic 6660792*	51		
23 Sep 00	**SPIRITUALIZED** *Epic 6698032*	26		1

QUEEN UK group

Date	Title / Label	Peak Position	Weeks at No.1	Weeks in Top 40
9 Mar 74	**SEVEN SEAS OF RHYE** *EMI 2121*	10		8
26 Oct 74	**KILLER QUEEN** *EMI 2229*	2		12
25 Jan 75	**NOW I'M HERE** *EMI 2256*	11		7
8 Nov 75	**BOHEMIAN RHAPSODY** *EMI 2375*	1	9	16
3 Jul 76	**YOU'RE MY BEST FRIEND** *EMI 2494*	7		8
27 Nov 76	**SOMEBODY TO LOVE** *EMI 2565*	2		9
19 Mar 77	**TIE YOUR MOTHER DOWN** *EMI 2593*	31		2
4 Jun 77	**QUEEN'S FIRST EP** *EMI 2623*	17		10
22 Oct 77	**WE ARE THE CHAMPIONS** *EMI 2708*	2		11
25 Feb 78	**SPREAD YOUR WINGS** *EMI 2757*	34		4
28 Oct 78	**BICYCLE RACE/FAT BOTTOMED GIRLS** *EMI 2870*	11		8
10 Feb 79	**DON'T STOP ME NOW** *EMI 2910*	9		10
14 Jul 79	**LOVE OF MY LIFE** *EMI 2959*	63		
20 Oct 79	**CRAZY LITTLE THING CALLED LOVE** *EMI 5001* ★	2		12
2 Feb 80	**SAVE ME** *EMI 5022*	11		5
14 Jun 80	**PLAY THE GAME** *EMI 5076*	14		7
6 Sep 80	**ANOTHER ONE BITES THE DUST** *EMI 5102* ★	7		7
6 Dec 80	**FLASH** *EMI 5126*	10		10
14 Nov 81	**UNDER PRESSURE** *EMI 5250* QUEEN & DAVID BOWIE	1	2	9
1 May 82	**BODY LANGUAGE** *EMI 5293*	25		3
12 Jun 82	**LAS PALABRAS DE AMOR** *EMI 5316*	17		7
21 Aug 82	**BACKCHAT** *EMI 5325*	40		1

Date	Title / Label	Peak Position	Weeks at No.1	Weeks in Top 40
4 Feb 84	**RADIO GA GA** *EMI QUEEN 1* ○	2		8
14 Apr 84	**I WANT TO BREAK FREE** *EMI QUEEN 2* ○	3		11
28 Jul 84	**IT'S A HARD LIFE** *EMI QUEEN 3*	6		7
22 Sep 84	**HAMMER TO FALL** *EMI QUEEN 4*	13		5
8 Dec 84	**THANK GOD IT'S CHRISTMAS** *EMI QUEEN 5*	21		4
16 Nov 85	**ONE VISION** *EMI QUEEN 6*	7		6
29 Mar 86	**A KIND OF MAGIC** *EMI QUEEN 7*	3		9
21 Jun 86	**FRIENDS WILL BE FRIENDS** *EMI QUEEN 8*	14		6
27 Sep 86	**WHO WANTS TO LIVE FOREVER** *EMI QUEEN 9*	24		4
13 May 89	**I WANT IT ALL** *Parlophone QUEEN 10* ○	3		5
1 Jul 89	**BREAKTHRU'** *Parlophone QUEEN 11*	7		4
19 Aug 89	**THE INVISIBLE MAN** *Parlophone QUEEN 12*	12		4
21 Oct 89	**SCANDAL** *Parlophone QUEEN 14*	25		3
9 Dec 89	**THE MIRACLE** *Parlophone QUEEN 15*	21		2
26 Jan 91	**INNUENDO** *Parlophone QUEEN 16* ○	1	1	4
16 Mar 91	**I'M GOING SLIGHTLY MAD** *Parlophone QUEEN 17*	22		3
25 May 91	**HEADLONG** *Parlophone QUEEN 18*	14		3
26 Oct 91	**THE SHOW MUST GO ON** *Parlophone QUEEN 19*	16		3
21 Dec 91	**BOHEMIAN RHAPSODY/THESE ARE THE DAYS OF OUR LIVES** *Parlophone QUEEN 20* ⊛	1	5	12
1 May 93	**FIVE LIVE EP** *Parlophone CDRS 6340* GEORGE MICHAEL & QUEEN WITH LISA STANSFIELD ●	1	3	9
4 Nov 95	**HEAVEN FOR EVERYONE** *Parlophone CDQUEEN 21* ○	2		10
23 Dec 95	**A WINTER'S TALE** *Parlophone CDQUEENS 22*	6		3
9 Mar 96	**TOO MUCH LOVE WILL KILL YOU** *Parlophone CDQUEEN 23*	15		3
29 Jun 96	**LET ME LIVE** *Parlophone CDQUEENS 24*	9		2
30 Nov 96	**YOU DON'T FOOL ME – THE REMIXES** *Parlophone CDQUEEN 25*	17		2
17 Jan 98	**NO-ONE BUT YOU/TIE YOUR MOTHER DOWN** *Parlophone CDQUEEN 27*	13		2
14 Nov 98	**ANOTHER ONE BITES THE DUST** *DreamWorks DRMCD 22364* QUEEN WITH WYCLEF JEAN FEATURING PRAS MICHEL/FREE	5		4
18 Dec 99	**UNDER PRESSURE (REMIX)** *Parlophone CDQUEEN 28* QUEEN & DAVID BOWIE	14		3
29 Jul 00	**WE WILL ROCK YOU** *RCA 74321774022* FIVE & QUEEN	1	1	8
29 Mar 03	**FLASH** *Nebula NEBCD 041* QUEEN & VANGUARD	15		3
23 Dec 06	**ANOTHER ONE BITES THE DUST** *Positiva CDTIVS250* QUEEN VS THE MIAMI PROJECT	31		2

QUEEN LATIFAH US rapper

Date	Title / Label	Peak Position	Weeks at No.1	Weeks in Top 40
24 Mar 90	**MAMA GAVE BIRTH TO THE SOUL CHILDREN** *Gee Street GEE 26* QUEEN LATIFAH + DE LA SOUL	14		6
26 May 90	**FIND A WAY** *Ahead Of Our Time CCUT 8* COLDCUT FEATURING QUEEN LATIFAH	52		
31 Aug 91	**FLY GIRL** *Gee Street GEE 34*	67		
26 Jun 93	**WHAT'CHA GONNA DO** *Epic 6593072* SHABBA RANKS FEATURING QUEEN LATIFAH	21		2
26 Mar 94	**U.N.I.T.Y.** *Motown TMGCD 1422*	74		
12 Apr 97	**MR BIG STUFF** *Motown 5736572* QUEEN LATIFAH, SHADES & FREE	31		1

QUEEN PEN US rapper

Date	Title / Label	Peak Position	Weeks at No.1	Weeks in Top 40
7 Mar 98	**MAN BEHIND THE MUSIC** *Interscope IND 95562*	38		1
9 May 98	**ALL MY LOVE** *Interscope IND 95584* QUEEN PEN FEATURING ERIC WILLIAMS	11		4
5 Sep 98	**IT'S TRUE** *Interscope IND 95597*	24		1

QUEENS OF THE STONE AGE US group

Date	Title / Label	Peak Position	Weeks at No.1	Weeks in Top 40
26 Aug 00	**THE LOST ART OF KEEPING A SECRET** *Interscope 4973922*	31		1
16 Nov 02	**NO ONE KNOWS** *Interscope 4978122*	15		3
19 Apr 03	**GO WITH THE FLOW** *Interscope 4978702*	21		1
30 Aug 03	**FIRST IT GIVETH** *Interscope 9810505*	33		1
26 Mar 05	**LITTLE SISTER** *Interscope 9880670*	18		2
23 Jul 05	**IN MY HEAD** *Interscope 9883541*	44		
16 Jun 07	**3'S & 7'S** *Interscope 1735379*	19		1

QUEENSRYCHE US group

Date	Title / Label	Peak Position	Weeks at No.1	Weeks in Top 40
13 May 89	**EYES OF A STRANGER** *EMI USA MT 65*	59		
10 Nov 90	**EMPIRE** *EMI USA MT 90*	61		
20 Apr 91	**SILENT LUCIDITY** *EMI USA MT 94*	34		2
6 Jul 91	**BEST I CAN** *EMI USA MT 97*	36		1
7 Sep 91	**JET CITY WOMAN** *EMI USA MT 98*	39		1
8 Aug 92	**SILENT LUCIDITY** *EMI USA MT 104*	18		3
28 Jan 95	**I AM I** *EMI CDMT 109*	40		1
25 Mar 95	**BRIDGE** *EMI CDMTS 111*	40		1

QUENCH Australian production duo

Date	Title / Label	Peak Position	Weeks at No.1	Weeks in Top 40
17 Feb 96	**DREAMS** *Infectious INFECT 3CD*	75		

QUENTIN & ASH UK duo

Date	Title / Label	Peak Position	Weeks at No.1	Weeks in Top 40
6 Jul 96	**TELL HIM** *East West EW 049CD*	25		2

? (QUESTION MARK) & THE MYSTERIANS US group

Date	Title / Label	Peak Position	Weeks at No.1	Weeks in Top 40
17 Nov 66	**96 TEARS** *Cameo Parkway C 428* ★	37		3

QUESTIONS UK group

Date	Title / Label	Peak Position	Weeks at No.1	Weeks in Top 40
23 Apr 83	**PRICE YOU PAY** *Respond KOB 702*	56		
17 Sep 83	**TEAR SOUP** *Respond KOB 705*	66		
10 Mar 84	**TUESDAY SUNSHINE** *Respond KOB 707*	46		

QUICK UK duo

Date	Title / Label	Peak Position	Weeks at No.1	Weeks in Top 40
15 May 82	**RHYTHM OF THE JUNGLE** *Epic EPC A 2013*	41		

TOMMY QUICKLY & THE REMO FOUR UK group

Date	Title / Label	Peak Position	Weeks at No.1	Weeks in Top 40
22 Oct 64	**WILD SIDE OF LIFE** *Pye 7N 15708*	33		5

QUIET FIVE UK group

Date	Title / Label	Peak Position	Weeks at No.1	Weeks in Top 40
13 May 65	**WHEN THE MORNING SUN DRIES THE DEW** *Parlophone R 5273*	45		
21 Apr 66	**HOMWARD BOUND** *Parlophone R 5421*	44		

QUIET RIOT US group

Date	Title / Label	Peak Position	Weeks at No.1	Weeks in Top 40
3 Dec 83	**METAL HEALTH/CUM ON FEEL THE NOIZE** *Epic A 3968*	45		

EIMEAR QUINN Irish singer

Date	Title / Label	Peak Position	Weeks at No.1	Weeks in Top 40
15 Jun 96	**THE VOICE** *Polydor 5768842*	40		1

PAUL QUINN & EDWYN COLLINS UK duo

Date	Title / Label	Peak Position	Weeks at No.1	Weeks in Top 40
11 Aug 84	**PALE BLUE EYES** *Swamplands SWP 1*	72		

SINEAD QUINN Irish singer

Date	Title / Label	Peak Position	Weeks at No.1	Weeks in Top 40
22 Feb 03	**I CAN'T BREAK DOWN** *Mercury 0637282*	2		6
12 Jul 03	**WHAT YOU NEED IS** *Fontana 9808972*	19		1

QUIREBOYS UK group

Date	Title / Label	Peak Position	Weeks at No.1	Weeks in Top 40
4 Nov 89	**7 O'CLOCK** *Parlophone R 6230*	36		1
6 Jan 90	**HEY YOU** *Parlophone R 6241*	14		6
7 Apr 90	**I DON'T LOVE YOU ANYMORE** *Parlophone R 6248*	24		5
8 Sep 90	**THERE SHE GOES AGAIN/MISLED** *Parlophone R 6267*	37		2
10 Oct 92	**TRAMPS AND THIEVES** *Parlophone R 6323*	41		
20 Feb 93	**BROTHER LOUIE** *Parlophone CDR 6335*	32		2

QUIVVER UK production duo

Date	Title / Label	Peak Position	Weeks at No.1	Weeks in Top 40
5 Mar 94	**SAXY LADY** *A&M 5805152*	56		
18 Nov 95	**BELIEVE IN ME** *Perfecto PERF 111CD*	56		

QUO VADIS UK production group

Date	Title / Label	Peak Position	Weeks at No.1	Weeks in Top 40
16 Dec 00	**SONIC BOOM (LIFE'S TOO SHORT)** *Serious SERR 028CD*	49		

QWILO & FELIX DA HOUSECAT US duo

Date	Title / Label	Peak Position	Weeks at No.1	Weeks in Top 40
6 Sep 97	**DIRTY MOTHA** *Manifesto FESCD 29*	66		

R

EDDIE RABBITT US singer/guitarist

Date	Title	Label	Peak Position	Weeks at No.1	Weeks in Top 40
27 Jan 79	EVERY WHICH WAY BUT LOOSE	Elektra K 12331	41		
28 Feb 81	I LOVE A RAINY NIGHT	Elektra K 12498 ★	53		

STEVE RACE UK pianist

Date	Title	Label	Peak Position	Weeks at No.1	Weeks in Top 40
28 Feb 63	PIED PIPER (THE BEEJE)	Parlophone R 4981	29		5

RACEY UK group

Date	Title	Label	Peak Position	Weeks at No.1	Weeks in Top 40
25 Nov 78	LAY YOUR LOVE ON ME	RAK 284 ●	3		12
31 Mar 79	SOME GIRLS	RAK 291 ●	2		9
18 Aug 79	BOY OH BOY	RAK 297	22		6
20 Dec 80	RUNAROUND SUE	RAK 325	13		7

RACING CARS UK group

Date	Title	Label	Peak Position	Weeks at No.1	Weeks in Top 40
12 Feb 77	THEY SHOOT HORSES DON'T THEY	Chrysalis CHS 2129	14		6

RACONTEURS US group

Date	Title	Label	Peak Position	Weeks at No.1	Weeks in Top 40
6 May 06	STEADY AS SHE GOES	XL Recordings XLS229CD	4		6
12 Aug 06	HANDS	XL Recordings XLS236CD	29		1
4 Nov 06	BROKEN BOY SOLDIER	XL Recordings XLS248CD	22		1

JIMMY RADCLIFFE US singer

Date	Title	Label	Peak Position	Weeks at No.1	Weeks in Top 40
4 Feb 65	LONG AFTER TONIGHT IS ALL OVER	Stateside SS 374	40		1

RADHA KRISHNA TEMPLE Multinational group

Date	Title	Label	Peak Position	Weeks at No.1	Weeks in Top 40
13 Sep 69	HARE KRISHNA MANTRA	Apple 15	12		7
28 Mar 70	GOVINDA	Apple 25	23		7

RADICAL ROB UK producer

Date	Title	Label	Peak Position	Weeks at No.1	Weeks in Top 40
11 Jan 92	MONKEY WAH	R&S RSUK 8	67		

RADIO 4 US group

Date	Title	Label	Peak Position	Weeks at No.1	Weeks in Top 40
24 Jul 04	PARTY CRASHERS	City Slang 5494920	75		
18 Sep 04	ABSOLUTE AFFIRMATION	Labels 5498032	61		

RADIO HEART UK group

Date	Title	Label	Peak Position	Weeks at No.1	Weeks in Top 40
28 Mar 87	RADIO HEART (RADIO HEART FEATURING GARY NUMAN)	GFM 109	35		2
13 Jun 87	LONDON TIMES (RADIO HEART FEATURING GARY NUMAN)	GFM 112	48		

RADIO STARS UK group

Date	Title	Label	Peak Position	Weeks at No.1	Weeks in Top 40
4 Feb 78	NERVOUS WRECK	Chiswick NS 23	39		2

RADIOHEAD UK group

Date	Title	Label	Peak Position	Weeks at No.1	Weeks in Top 40
13 Feb 93	ANYONE CAN PLAY GUITAR	Parlophone CDR 6333	32		1
22 May 93	POP IS DEAD	Parlophone CDR 6345	42		
18 Sep 93	CREEP	Parlophone CDR 6359	7		5
8 Oct 94	MY IRON LUNG	Parlophone CDR 6394	24		1
11 Mar 95	HIGH AND DRY/PLANET TELEX	Parlophone CDRS 6405	17		2
27 May 95	FAKE PLASTIC TREES	Parlophone CDR 6411	20		3
2 Sep 95	JUST	Parlophone CDR 6415	19		1
3 Feb 96	STREET SPIRIT (FADE OUT)	Parlophone CDRS 6419	5		2
7 Jun 97	PARANOID ANDROID	Parlophone CDODATA 01	3		3
6 Sep 97	KARMA POLICE	Parlophone CDODATAS 03	8		2
24 Jan 98	NO SURPRISES	Parlophone CDODATAS 04	4		3
2 Jun 01	PYRAMID SONG	Parlophone CDSFHEIT 45102	5		2
18 Aug 01	KNIVES OUT	Parlophone CDFEIT 45103	13		2
7 Jun 03	THERE THERE	Parlophone CDR 6608	4		2
30 Aug 03	GO TO SLEEP	Parlophone CDRS 6613	12		2
29 Nov 03	2 + 2 = 5	Parlophone CDRS 6623	15		1
26 Jan 08	JIGSAW FALLING INTO PLACE	XL Recordings XLS326CD	30		1

RADISH US group

Date	Title	Label	Peak Position	Weeks at No.1	Weeks in Top 40
30 Aug 97	LITTLE PINK STARS	Mercury MERCD 494	32		1
15 Nov 97	SIMPLE SINCERITY	Mercury MERCD 498	50		

CORINNE BAILEY RAE UK singer

Date	Title	Label	Peak Position	Weeks at No.1	Weeks in Top 40
19 Nov 05	LIKE A STAR	EMI CDEM678	34		1
4 Mar 06	PUT YOUR RECORDS ON	Good Groove/EMI CDEM683	2		13
10 Jun 06	TROUBLE SLEEPING	Good Groove/EMI CDEM692	40		1
14 Oct 06	LIKE A STAR	EMI CDEM710	32		1

FONDA RAE US singer

Date	Title	Label	Peak Position	Weeks at No.1	Weeks in Top 40
6 Oct 84	TUCH ME	Streetwave KHAN 28	49		

JESSE RAE UK singer

Date	Title	Label	Peak Position	Weeks at No.1	Weeks in Top 40
11 May 85	OVER THE SEA	Scotland Video YZ 36	65		

RAE UK production duo

Date	Title	Label	Peak Position	Weeks at No.1	Weeks in Top 40
6 Mar 99	ALL I ASK (RAE & CHRISTIAN FEATURING VEBA)	Grand Central GCD 120	67		

RAF Italian producer

Date	Title	Label	Peak Position	Weeks at No.1	Weeks in Top 40
14 Mar 92	WE'VE GOT TO LIVE TOGETHER	PWL Continental PWL 218	34		2
5 Mar 94	TAKE ME HIGHER	Media MRLCD 0012	71		
23 Mar 96	TAKE ME HIGHER (REMIX)	Media MCSTD 40026	59		
27 Jul 96	ANGEL'S SYMPHONY	Media MCSTD 40051	73		

GERRY RAFFERTY UK singer/guitarist

Date	Title	Label	Peak Position	Weeks at No.1	Weeks in Top 40
18 Feb 78	BAKER STREET	United Artists UP 36346 ●	3		12
26 May 79	NIGHT OWL	United Artists UP 36512 ○	5		10
18 Aug 79	GET IT RIGHT NEXT TIME	United Artists BP 301	30		6
22 Mar 80	BRING IT ALL HOME	United Artists BP 340	54		
21 Jun 80	ROYAL MILE	United Artists BP 354	67		
10 Mar 90	BAKER STREET (REMIX)	EMI EM 132	53		

RAGE UK production group

Date	Title	Label	Peak Position	Weeks at No.1	Weeks in Top 40
31 Oct 92	RUN TO YOU	Pulse 8 LOSE 33	3		7
27 Feb 93	WHY DON'T YOU	Pulse 8 CDLOSE 39	44		
15 May 93	HOUSE OF THE RISING SUN	Pulse 8 CDLOSE 43	41		

RAGE AGAINST THE MACHINE US group

Date	Title	Label	Peak Position	Weeks at No.1	Weeks in Top 40
27 Feb 93	KILLING IN THE NAME	Epic 6584922	25		3
8 May 93	BULLET IN THE HEAD	Epic 6592582	16		2
4 Sep 93	BOMBTRACK	Epic 6594712	37		1
13 Apr 96	BULLS ON PARADE	Epic 6631522	8		2
7 Sep 96	PEOPLE OF THE SUN	Epic 6636282	26		1
6 Nov 99	GUERRILLA RADIO	Epic 6683142	32		1
15 Apr 00	SLEEP NOW IN THE FIRE	Epic 6691362	43		

RAGGA TWINS UK duo

Date	Title	Label	Peak Position	Weeks at No.1	Weeks in Top 40
10 Nov 90	ILLEGAL GUNSHOT/SPLIFFHEAD	Shut Up And Dance SUAD 7	51		
6 Apr 91	WIPE THE NEEDLE/JUGGLING	Shut Up And Dance SUAD 12S	71		
6 Jul 91	HOOLIGAN 69	Shut Up And Dance SUAD 16S	56		
7 Mar 92	MIXED TRUTH/BRING UP THE MIC SOME MORE	Shut Up And Dance SUAD 27S	65		
11 Jul 92	SHINE EYE (RAGGA TWINS FEATURING JUNIOR REID)	Shut Up And Dance SUAD 32S	63		

RAGHAV Canadian singer

Date	Title	Label	Peak Position	Weeks at No.1	Weeks in Top 40
24 Jan 04	SO CONFUSED (2PLAY FEATURING RAGHAV & JUCXI)	2PSL 2PSLCD02	6		9
22 May 04	IT CAN'T BE RIGHT (2PLAY FEATURING RAGHAV & NAILA BOSS)	2PSL/Inferno 2PSLCD04	8		4
28 Feb 04	CAN'T GET ENOUGH	A&R ANR1CDS	10		3

Date	Title / Label	Peak Position	Weeks at No.1	Weeks in Top 40
4 Sep 04	**LET'S WORK IT OUT** *V2 ARV5028628* RAGHAV FEATURING JAHAZIEL	15		2
19 Feb 05	**ANGEL EYES** *A&R/V2 ARV5028638*	7		4

RAGING SPEEDHORN UK group

Date	Title / Label	Peak Position	Weeks at No.1	Weeks in Top 40
16 Jun 01	**THE GUSH** *ZTT GIR004CD*	47		
6 Jul 02	**THE HATE SONG** *ZTT RSH001CD*	69		

RAGTIMERS UK group

Date	Title / Label	Peak Position	Weeks at No.1	Weeks in Top 40
16 Mar 74	**THE STING** *Pye 7N 45323*	31		5

RAH BAND UK multi-instrumentalist

Date	Title / Label	Peak Position	Weeks at No.1	Weeks in Top 40
9 Jul 77	**THE CRUNCH** *Good Earth GD 7*	6		11
1 Nov 80	**FALCON** *DJM DJS 10954*	35		3
7 Feb 81	**SLIDE** *DJM DJS 10964*	50		
1 May 82	**PERFUMED GARDEN** *KR 5*	45		
9 Jul 83	**MESSAGES FROM THE STARS** *TMT 5*	42		
19 Jan 85	**ARE YOU SATISFIED? (FUNKA NOVA)** *RCA 470*	70		
30 Mar 85	**CLOUDS ACROSS THE MOON** *RCA PB 40025*	6		7

RAILWAY CHILDREN UK group

Date	Title / Label	Peak Position	Weeks at No.1	Weeks in Top 40
24 Mar 90	**EVERY BEAT OF THE HEART** *Virgin VS 1237*	68		
2 Jun 90	**MUSIC STOP** *Virgin VS 1255*	66		
20 Oct 90	**SO RIGHT** *Virgin VS 1289*	68		
2 Feb 91	**EVERY BEAT OF THE HEART** *Virgin VS 1237*	24		4
20 Apr 91	**SOMETHING SO GOOD** *Virgin VS 1318*	57		

RAIN BAND UK group

Date	Title / Label	Peak Position	Weeks at No.1	Weeks in Top 40
1 Mar 03	**EASY RIDER** *Temptation TEMPTCD 003*	63		
19 Jul 03	**KNEE DEEP AND DOWN** *Temptation TEMPTCD 007*	56		

RAIN TREE CROW UK group

Date	Title / Label	Peak Position	Weeks at No.1	Weeks in Top 40
30 Mar 91	**BLACKWATER** *Virgin VS 1340*	62		

RAINBOW UK group

Date	Title / Label	Peak Position	Weeks at No.1	Weeks in Top 40
17 Sep 77	**KILL THE KING** *Polydor 2066 845*	44		
8 Apr 78	**LONG LIVE ROCK 'N' ROLL** *Polydor 2066 913*	33		3
30 Sep 78	**L.A. CONNECTION** *Polydor 2066 968*	40		1
15 Sep 79	**SINCE YOU'VE BEEN GONE** *Polydor POSP 70*	6		9
16 Feb 80	**ALL NIGHT LONG** *Polydor POSP 104*	5		10
31 Jan 81	**I SURRENDER** *Polydor POSP 221*	3		9
20 Jun 81	**CAN'T HAPPEN HERE** *Polydor POSP 251*	20		6
11 Jul 81	**KILL THE KING** *Polydor POSP 274*	41		
3 Apr 82	**STONE COLD** *Polydor POSP 421*	34		2
27 Aug 83	**STREET OF DREAMS** *Polydor POSP 631*	52		
5 Nov 83	**CAN'T LET YOU GO** *Polydor POSP 654*	43		

RAINBOW COTTAGE UK group

Date	Title / Label	Peak Position	Weeks at No.1	Weeks in Top 40
6 Mar 76	**SEAGULL** *Penny Farthing PEN 906*	33		2

RAINBOW (GEORGE & ZIPPY)

UK singer with TV puppet characters

Date	Title / Label	Peak Position	Weeks at No.1	Weeks in Top 40
14 Dec 02	**IT'S A RAINBOW** *BBC Music ZIPPCD1X*	15		5

RAINMAKERS US group

Date	Title / Label	Peak Position	Weeks at No.1	Weeks in Top 40
7 Mar 87	**LET MY PEOPLE GO-GO** *Mercury MER 238*	18		6

MARVIN RAINWATER US singer

Date	Title / Label	Peak Position	Weeks at No.1	Weeks in Top 40
7 Mar 58	**WHOLE LOTTA WOMAN** *MGM 974*	1	3	15
6 Jun 58	**I DIG YOU BABY** *MGM 980*	19		7

RAISSA UK singer

Date	Title / Label	Peak Position	Weeks at No.1	Weeks in Top 40
12 Feb 00	**HOW LONG DO I GET** *Polydor 5616282*	47		

BONNIE RAITT US singer

Date	Title / Label	Peak Position	Weeks at No.1	Weeks in Top 40
14 Dec 91	**I CAN'T MAKE YOU LOVE ME** *Capitol CL 639*	50		
9 Apr 94	**LOVE SNEAKIN' UP ON YOU** *Capitol CDCL 713*	69		
18 Jun 94	**YOU** *Capitol CDCLS 718*	31		1
11 Nov 95	**ROCK STEADY** *Capitol CDCL 763* BONNIE RAITT & BRYAN ADAMS	50		

DIONNE RAKEEM UK singer

Date	Title / Label	Peak Position	Weeks at No.1	Weeks in Top 40
4 Aug 01	**SWEETER THAN WINE** *Virgin VSCDT 1809*	46		

RAKES UK group

Date	Title / Label	Peak Position	Weeks at No.1	Weeks in Top 40
9 Oct 04	**STRASBOURG** *City Rockers ROCKERS28CD*	57		
30 Apr 05	**RETREAT** *Moshi Moshi MOSHI18CD*	24		1
13 Aug 05	**WORK WORK WORK (PUB CLUB SLEEP)** *V2 VVR5032778*	28		1
12 Nov 05	**22 GRAND JOB** *V2 VVR5034618*	39		1
11 Mar 06	**ALL TOO HUMAN** *V2 VVR5036208*	22		1
24 Mar 07	**WE DANCED TOGETHER** *V2 VVR5042753*	38		1

RAKIM US rapper

Date	Title / Label	Peak Position	Weeks at No.1	Weeks in Top 40
6 Oct 90	**CONTRIBUTION** *4th & Broadway BRW188* MICA PARIS FEATURING RAKIM	33		2
27 Dec 97	**GUESS WHO'S BACK** *Universal UND 56151*	32		1
22 Aug 98	**STAY A WHILE** *Universal UND 56203*	53		
3 Oct 98	**BUFFALO GALS STAMPEDE** *Virgin VSCDT 1717* MALCOLM McLAREN & THE WORLD'S FAMOUS SUPREME TEAM PLUS RAKIM & ROGER SANCHEZ	65		
31 Aug 02	**ADDICTIVE** *Interscope 4977782* TRUTH HURTS FEATURING RAKIM	3		9

TONY RALLO & THE MIDNIGHT BAND

French group

Date	Title / Label	Peak Position	Weeks at No.1	Weeks in Top 40
23 Feb 80	**HOLDIN' ON** *Calibre CAB 150*	34		1

SHERYL LEE RALPH US singer/actress

Date	Title / Label	Peak Position	Weeks at No.1	Weeks in Top 40
26 Jan 85	**IN THE EVENING** *Arista ARIST 595*	64		

RAM JAM US group

Date	Title / Label	Peak Position	Weeks at No.1	Weeks in Top 40
10 Sep 77	**BLACK BETTY** *Epic EPC 5492*	7		12
17 Feb 90	**BLACK BETTY (REMIX)** *Epic 6554307*	13		5

RAM TRILOGY UK group

Date	Title / Label	Peak Position	Weeks at No.1	Weeks in Top 40
6 Jul 02	**CHAPTER FOUR** *Ram RAMM 39*	71		
20 Jul 02	**CHAPTER FIVE** *Ram RAMM 40*	62		
3 Aug 02	**CHAPTER SIX** *Ram RAMM 41*	60		

RAMBLERS (FROM THE ABBEY HEY JUNIOR SCHOOL) UK group

Date	Title / Label	Peak Position	Weeks at No.1	Weeks in Top 40
13 Oct 79	**THE SPARROW** *Decca F 13860*	11		11

KAREN RAMIREZ UK singer

Date	Title / Label	Peak Position	Weeks at No.1	Weeks in Top 40
28 Mar 98	**TROUBLED GIRL** *Manifesto FESCD 31*	50		
27 Jun 98	**LOOKING FOR LOVE** *Manifesto FESCD 44*	8		8
21 Nov 98	**IF WE TRY** *Manifesto FESCD 50*	23		1

RAMMSTEIN German group

Date	Title / Label	Peak Position	Weeks at No.1	Weeks in Top 40
25 May 02	**ICH WILL** *Universal MCSXD 40280*	30		1
23 Nov 02	**FEUER FREI** *Universal MCSXD 40302*	35		1
14 Aug 04	**MEIN TEIL (IMPORT)** *Universal 9866978*	61		
30 Oct 04	**AMERIKA** *Universal MCSTD 40394*	38		1
12 Mar 05	**KEINE LUST** *Universal MCSTD40405*	35		1
29 Oct 05	**BENZIN** *Universal 9874302*	58		
1 Apr 06	**MANN GEGEN MANN** *Universal MCSXD40451*	59		

Silver-selling · Gold-selling · Platinum-selling · US No.1 ★ · Peak Position · Weeks at No.1 · Weeks in Top 40

RAMONES US group

Date	Title / Label	Peak Position	Weeks at No.1	Weeks in Top 40
21 May 77	**SHEENA IS A PUNK ROCKER** *Sire RAM 001*	22		6
6 Aug 77	**SWALLOW MY PRIDE** *Sire 6078 607*	36		1
30 Sep 78	**DON'T COME CLOSE** *Sire SRE 1031*	39		1
8 Sep 79	**ROCK 'N' ROLL HIGH SCHOOL** *Sire SRE 4021*	67		
26 Jan 80	**BABY I LOVE YOU** *Sire SIR 4031*	8		7
19 Apr 80	**DO YOU REMEMBER ROCK 'N' ROLL RADIO** *Sire SIR 4037*	54		
10 May 86	**SOMEBODY PUT SOMETHING IN MY DRINK/SOMETHING TO BELIEVE IN** *Beggars Banquet BEG 157*	69		
19 Dec 92	**POISON HEART** *Chrysalis CHS 3917*	69		

RAMP US group

Date	Title / Label	Peak Position	Weeks at No.1	Weeks in Top 40
8 Jun 96	**ROCK THE DISCOTEK** *Loaded LOADCD 30*	49		

RAMPAGE UK production duo

Date	Title / Label	Peak Position	Weeks at No.1	Weeks in Top 40
25 Nov 95	**THE MONKEES** *Almo Sounds CDALMOS 017*	51		

RAMPAGE US rapper

Date	Title / Label	Peak Position	Weeks at No.1	Weeks in Top 40
18 Oct 97	**TAKE IT TO THE STREETS** *Elektra E 3914CD*			
	RAMPAGE FEATURING BILLY LAWRENCE	58		

RAMRODS US instrumental group

Date	Title / Label	Peak Position	Weeks at No.1	Weeks in Top 40
23 Feb 61	**RIDERS IN THE SKY** *London HLU 9282*	8		12

RAMSEY & FEN UK production duo with singer

Date	Title / Label	Peak Position	Weeks at No.1	Weeks in Top 40
10 Jun 00	**LOVE BUG** *Nebula VCNEBD 4*			
	RAMSEY & FEN FEATURING LYNSEY MOORE	75		

RANCID US group

Date	Title / Label	Peak Position	Weeks at No.1	Weeks in Top 40
7 Oct 95	**TIME BOMB** *Out Of Step WOOS 8CDS*	56		
27 Sep 03	**FALL BACK DOWN** *Hellcat W 618CD*	42		

RANGERS F.C. UK football club

Date	Title / Label	Peak Position	Weeks at No.1	Weeks in Top 40
4 Oct 97	**GLASGOW RANGERS (NINE IN A ROW)** *Gers GERSCD 1*	54		

RANK 1 Dutch production duo

Date	Title / Label	Peak Position	Weeks at No.1	Weeks in Top 40
15 Apr 00	**AIRWAVE** *Manifesto FESCD 69*	10		3

SHABBA RANKS Jamaican singer

Date	Title / Label	Peak Position	Weeks at No.1	Weeks in Top 40
16 Mar 91	**SHE'S A WOMAN** *Virgin VS 1333*			
	SCRITTI POLITTI FEATURING SHABBA RANKS	20		3
18 May 91	**TRAILER LOAD A GIRLS** *Epic 6568747*	63		
24 Aug 91	**HOUSECALL** *Epic 6573477*			
	SHABBA RANKS FEATURING MAXI PRIEST	31		4
8 Aug 92	**MR LOVERMAN** *Epic 6582517*	23		4
28 Nov 92	**SLOW AND SEXY** *Epic 6587727*			
	SHABBA RANKS FEATURING JOHNNY GILL	17		3
6 Mar 93	**I WAS A KING** *Motown TMGCD 1414*			
	EDDIE MURPHY FEATURING SHABBA RANKS	64		
13 Mar 93	**MR LOVERMAN** *Epic 6590782*	3		9
8 May 93	**HOUSECALL (REMIX)** *Epic 6592842*			
	SHABBA RANKS FEATURING MAXI PRIEST	8		6
26 Jun 93	**WHAT'CHA GONNA DO** *Epic 6593072*			
	SHABBA RANKS FEATURING QUEEN LATIFAH	21		2
25 Dec 93	**FAMILY AFFAIR** *Polydor PZCD 304*			
	SHABBA RANKS FEATURING PATRA & TERRY & MONICA	18		6
29 Apr 95	**LET'S GET IT ON** *Epic 6614122*	22		2
5 Aug 95	**SHINE EYE GAL** *Epic 6622332*			
	SHABBA RANKS (FEATURING MYKAL ROSE)	46		

RAPINATION Italian production duo

Date	Title / Label	Peak Position	Weeks at No.1	Weeks in Top 40
26 Dec 92	**LOVE ME THE RIGHT WAY** *Logic 74321128097*			
	RAPINATION & KYM MAZELLE	22		5
10 Jul 93	**HERE'S MY A** *Logic 74321153092*			
	RAPINATION FEATURING CAROL KENYON	69		
28 Sep 96	**LOVE ME THE RIGHT WAY (REMIX)** *Logic 74321404442*			
	RAPINATION & KYM MAZELLE	55		

RAPPIN' 4-TAY US rapper

Date	Title / Label	Peak Position	Weeks at No.1	Weeks in Top 40
24 Jun 95	**I'LL BE AROUND** *Cooltempo CDCOOL 306*			
	RAPPIN' 4-TAY FEATURING THE SPINNERS	30		2
30 Sep 95	**PLAYAZ CLUB** *Cooltempo CDCOOL 310*	63		

RAPTURE US group

Date	Title / Label	Peak Position	Weeks at No.1	Weeks in Top 40
6 Sep 03	**HOUSE OF JEALOUS LOVERS** *XL Recordings XLS 167CD*	27		1
13 Dec 03	**SISTER SAVIOUR** *DFA/Output/Vertigo 9814181*	51		
21 Feb 04	**LOVE IS ALL** *DFA/Output/Vertigo 9816876*	38		1
16 Sep 06	**GET MYSELF INTO IT** *Vertigo 1705165*	36		1
16 Dec 06	**WAYUH (PEOPLE DON'T DANCE NO MORE)** *Vertigo 1713573*	65		

RARE UK group

Date	Title / Label	Peak Position	Weeks at No.1	Weeks in Top 40
17 Feb 96	**SOMETHING WILD** *Equator AXISCD 011*	57		

RARE BIRD UK group

Date	Title / Label	Peak Position	Weeks at No.1	Weeks in Top 40
14 Feb 70	**SYMPATHY** *Charisma CB 120*	27		5

DIZZEE RASCAL UK rapper

Date	Title / Label	Peak Position	Weeks at No.1	Weeks in Top 40
7 Jun 03	**I LUV U** *XL Recordings XLS 165CD*	29		1
30 Aug 03	**FIX UP LOOK SHARP** *XL Recordings XLS 167CD*	17		3
22 Nov 03	**LUCKY STAR** *XL Recordings XLS 172CD*			
	BASEMENT JAXX FEATURING DIZZEE RASCAL	23		1
6 Dec 03	**JUS' A RASCAL** *XL Recordings XLS 175CD*	30		1
4 Sep 04	**STAND UP TALL** *XL Recordings XLS 198CD*	10		3
20 Nov 04	**DREAM** *XL Recordings XLS 204CD1*	14		4
2 Apr 05	**OFF 2 WORK** *XL Recordings XLS208CD1*	44		
2 Jun 07	**SIRENS** *XL Recordings XLS272CD*	20		2
11 Aug 07	**PUSSYOLE (OLD SKOOL)** *XL Recordings XLS285CD*	22		3
17 Nov 07	**FLEX** *XL Recordings XLS312CD*	23		2

RASMUS Finnish group

Date	Title / Label	Peak Position	Weeks at No.1	Weeks in Top 40
17 Apr 04	**IN THE SHADOWS** *Universal MCSXD 40351*	3		13
21 Aug 04	**GUILTY** *Universal MCSTD 40376*	15		4
13 Nov 04	**FIRST DAY OF MY LIFE** *Universal MCSTD 40391*	50		
17 Sep 05	**NO FEAR** *Universal MCSXD40429*	43		

ROLAND RAT SUPERSTAR UK TV puppet character

Date	Title / Label	Peak Position	Weeks at No.1	Weeks in Top 40
19 Nov 83	**RAT RAPPING** *Rodent RAT 1*	14		10
28 Apr 84	**LOVE ME TENDER** *Rodent RAT 2*	32		3
2 Mar 85	**NO. 1 RAT FAN** *Rodent RAT 4*	72		

RATPACK UK production duo

Date	Title / Label	Peak Position	Weeks at No.1	Weeks in Top 40
6 Jun 92	**SEARCHIN' FOR MY RIZLA** *Big Giant BIGT 02*	58		

RATTLES German group

Date	Title / Label	Peak Position	Weeks at No.1	Weeks in Top 40
3 Oct 70	**THE WITCH** *Decca F 23058*	8		9

RATTY German/UK production group

Date	Title / Label	Peak Position	Weeks at No.1	Weeks in Top 40
24 Mar 01	**SUNRISE (HERE I AM)** *Neo NEOCD 051*	51		

RAVEN MAIZE UK producer

Date	Title / Label	Peak Position	Weeks at No.1	Weeks in Top 40
5 Aug 89	**FOREVER TOGETHER** *Republic LIC 014*	67		
18 Aug 01	**THE REAL LIFE** *Rulin 18CDS*	12		3
17 Aug 02	**FASCINATED** *Rulin 27CDS*	37		1

RAVEONETTES Danish duo

Date	Title / Label	Peak Position	Weeks at No.1	Weeks in Top 40
21 Dec 02	**ATTACK OF THE GHOSTRIDERS** *Columbia 6733892*	73		
30 Aug 03	**THAT GREAT LOVE SOUND** *Columbia RAVEON005*	34		1
20 Dec 03	**HEARTBREAK STROLL** *Columbia RAVEON008*	49		
22 May 04	**THAT GREAT LOVE SOUND (REMIX)** *Columbia RAVEON010*	52		
23 Jul 05	**LOVE IN A TRASHCAN** *Columbia RAVEON017*	26		1

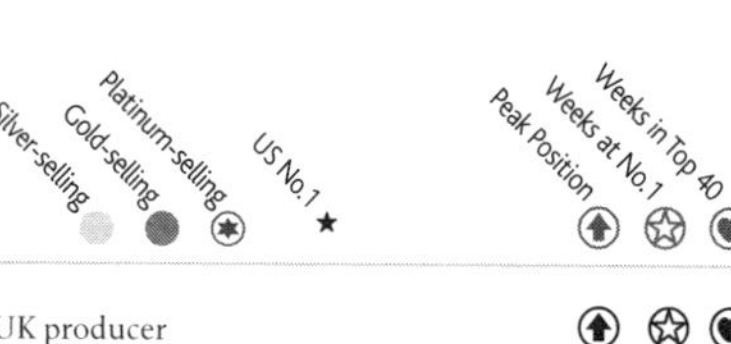

RAVESIGNAL III UK producer

Date	Title	Peak Position	Weeks at No.1	Weeks in Top 40
14 Dec 91	**HORSEPOWER** *R&S RSUK 6*	61		

RAW SILK US group

Date	Title	Peak Position	Weeks at No.1	Weeks in Top 40
16 Oct 82	**DO IT TO THE MUSIC** *KR 14*	18		8
10 Sep 83	**JUST IN TIME** *West End WEND 2*	49		

RAW STYLUS UK duo

Date	Title	Peak Position	Weeks at No.1	Weeks in Top 40
26 Oct 96	**BELIEVE IN ME** *Wired 234*	66		

LOU RAWLS US singer

Date	Title	Peak Position	Weeks at No.1	Weeks in Top 40
31 Jul 76	**YOU'LL NEVER FIND ANOTHER LOVE LIKE MINE** *Philadelphia International PIR 4372*	10		9

JIMMY RAY UK singer

Date	Title	Peak Position	Weeks at No.1	Weeks in Top 40
25 Oct 97	**ARE YOU JIMMY RAY?** *Sony S2 6650125*	13		3
14 Feb 98	**GOIN' TO VEGAS** *Sony S2 6654652*	49		

JOHNNIE RAY US singer

Date	Title	Peak Position	Weeks at No.1	Weeks in Top 40
14 Nov 52	**WALKING MY BABY BACK HOME** *Columbia DB 3060*	12		1
19 Dec 52	**FAITH CAN MOVE MOUNTAINS** *Columbia DB 3154* JOHNNIE RAY & THE FOUR LADS	7		3
3 Apr 53	**MA SAYS PA SAYS** *Columbia DB 3242* DORIS DAY & JOHNNIE RAY	12		1
10 Apr 53	**SOMEBODY STOLE MY GAL** *Philips PB 123*	6		7
17 Apr 53	**FULL TIME JOB** *Columbia DB 3242* DORIS DAY & JOHNNIE RAY	11		1
24 Jul 53	**LET'S WALK THATA-WAY** *Philips PB 157* DORIS DAY & JOHNNIE RAY	4		14
9 Apr 54	**SUCH A NIGHT** *Philips PB 244*	1	1	18
8 Apr 55	**IF YOU BELIEVE** *Philips PB 379*	7		11
20 May 55	**PATHS OF PARADISE** *Philips PB 441*	20		1
7 Oct 55	**HERNANDO'S HIDEAWAY** *Philips PB 495*	11		5
14 Oct 55	**HEY THERE** *Philips PB 495*	5		9
28 Oct 55	**SONG OF THE DREAMER** *Philips PB 516*	10		5
17 Feb 56	**WHO'S SORRY NOW** *Philips PB 546*	17		2
20 Apr 56	**AIN'T MISBEHAVIN'** *Philips PB 580*	17		7
12 Oct 56	**JUST WALKIN' IN THE RAIN** *Philips PB 624*	1	7	19
18 Jan 57	**YOU DON'T OWE ME A THING** *Philips PB 655*	12		15
8 Feb 57	**LOOK HOMEWARD ANGEL** *Philips PB 655*	7		16
10 May 57	**YES TONIGHT JOSEPHINE** *Philips PB 686*	1	3	16
6 Sep 57	**BUILD YOUR LOVE (ON A STRONG FOUNDATION)** *Philips PB 721*	17		7
4 Oct 57	**GOOD EVENING FRIENDS/UP ABOVE MY HEAD I HEAR MUSIC IN THE AIR** *Philips PB 708* FRANKIE LAINE & JOHNNIE RAY	25		4
4 Dec 59	**I'LL NEVER FALL IN LOVE AGAIN** *Philips PB 952*	26		6

NICOLE RAY US rapper

Date	Title	Peak Position	Weeks at No.1	Weeks in Top 40
22 Aug 98	**MAKE IT HOT** *East West E 3821CD* NICOLE FEATURING MISSY 'MISDEMEANOR' ELLIOTT	22		2
5 Dec 98	**I CAN'T SEE** *East West E 3801CD*	55		

RAYDIO US group

Date	Title	Peak Position	Weeks at No.1	Weeks in Top 40
8 Apr 78	**JACK AND JILL** *Arista 161*	11		9
8 Jul 78	**IS THIS A LOVE THING** *Arista 193*	27		4

DANA RAYNE US singer

Date	Title	Peak Position	Weeks at No.1	Weeks in Top 40
15 Jan 05	**OBJECT OF MY DESIRE** *Incentive CENTMOS1CDS*	7		6

RAYVON Barbadian singer

Date	Title	Peak Position	Weeks at No.1	Weeks in Top 40
8 Jul 95	**IN THE SUMMERTIME** *Virgin VSCDT 1542* SHAGGY FEATURING RAYVON	5		8
9 Jun 01	**ANGEL** *MCA MCSTD 40257* SHAGGY FEATURING RAYVON ● ★	1	3	13
3 Aug 02	**2-WAY** *MCA MCSTD 40287*	67		

RAZE US group

Date	Title	Peak Position	Weeks at No.1	Weeks in Top 40
1 Nov 86	**JACK THE GROOVE** *Champion CHAMP 23*	20		5
28 Feb 87	**LET THE MUSIC MOVE U** *Champion CHAMP 27*	57		
31 Dec 88	**BREAK 4 LOVE** *Champion CHAMP 67*	28		5
15 Jul 89	**LET IT ROLL** *Atlantic A 8866* RAZE PRESENTS DOUG LAZY	27		2
2 Sep 89	**BREAK 4 LOVE** *Champion CHAMP 67*	59		
27 Jan 90	**ALL 4 LOVE (BREAK 4 LOVE 1990)** *Champion CHAMP 228* RAZE FEATURING LADY J & SECRETARY OF ENTERTAINMENT	30		3
10 Feb 90	**CAN YOU FEEL IT/CAN YOU FEEL IT** *Champion CHAMP 227* RAZE/CHAMPIONSHIP LEGEND	62		
24 Sep 94	**BREAK 4 LOVE (REMIX)** *Champion CHAMPCD 314*	44		
29 Mar 03	**BREAK 4 LOVE (REMIX)** *Champion CHAMPCD 784*	64		

RAZORLIGHT UK group

Date	Title	Peak Position	Weeks at No.1	Weeks in Top 40
30 Aug 03	**ROCK 'N' ROLL LIES** *Vertigo 9800413*	56		
22 Nov 03	**RIP IT UP** *Vertigo 9814046*	42		
7 Feb 04	**STUMBLE AND FALL** *Vertigo 9816397*	27		1
26 Jun 04	**GOLDEN TOUCH** *Vertigo 9866836*	9		3
25 Sep 04	**VICE** *Vertigo 9867759*	18		2
11 Dec 04	**RIP IT UP** *Vertigo 9869077*	20		1
23 Apr 05	**SOMEWHERE ELSE** *Vertigo 9869893*	2		8
8 Jul 06	**IN THE MORNING** *Vertigo 1701088*	3		13
7 Oct 06	**AMERICA** *Vertigo 1705368*	1	1	20
23 Dec 06	**BEFORE I FALL TO PIECES** *Vertigo 1714372*	17		6
31 Mar 07	**I CAN'T STOP THIS FEELING I'VE GOT** *Vertigo 1724345*	44		

RE-FLEX UK group

Date	Title	Peak Position	Weeks at No.1	Weeks in Top 40
28 Jan 84	**THE POLITICS OF DANCING** *EMI FLEX 2*	28		4

CHRIS REA UK singer/guitarist

Date	Title	Peak Position	Weeks at No.1	Weeks in Top 40
7 Oct 78	**FOOL (IF YOU THINK IT'S OVER)** *Magnet MAG 111*	30		2
21 Apr 79	**DIAMONDS** *Magnet MAG 144*	44		
27 Mar 82	**LOVING YOU** *Magnet MAG 215*	65		
1 Oct 83	**I CAN HEAR YOUR HEARTBEAT** *Magnet MAG 244*	60		
17 Mar 84	**I DON'T KNOW WHAT IT IS BUT I LOVE IT** *Magnet MAG 255*	65		
30 Mar 85	**STAINSBY GIRLS** *Magnet MAG 276*	26		5
29 Jun 85	**JOSEPHINE** *Magnet MAG 280*	67		
29 Mar 86	**IT'S ALL GONE** *Magnet MAG 283*	69		
31 May 86	**ON THE BEACH** *Magnet MAG 294*	57		
6 Jun 87	**LET'S DANCE** *Magnet MAG 299*	12		8
29 Aug 87	**LOVING YOU AGAIN** *Magnet MAG 300*	47		
5 Dec 87	**JOYS OF CHRISTMAS** *Magnet MAG 314*	67		
13 Feb 88	**QUE SERA** *Magnet MAG 318*	73		
13 Aug 88	**ON THE BEACH SUMMER '88** *WEA YZ 195*	12		5
22 Oct 88	**I CAN HEAR YOUR HEARTBEAT** *WEA YZ 320*	74		
17 Dec 88	**DRIVING HOME FOR CHRISTMAS (EP)** *WEA YZ 325*	53		
18 Feb 89	**WORKING ON IT** *WEA YZ 350*	53		
14 Oct 89	**THE ROAD TO HELL (PART 2)** *WEA YZ 431*	10		8
10 Feb 90	**TELL ME THERE'S A HEAVEN** *East West YZ 455*	24		4
5 May 90	**TEXAS** *East West YZ 468*	69		
16 Feb 91	**AUBERGE** *East West YZ 555*	16		4
6 Apr 91	**HEAVEN** *East West YZ 566*	57		
29 Jun 91	**LOOKING FOR THE SUMMER** *East West YZ 584*	49		
9 Nov 91	**WINTER SONG** *East West YZ 629*	27		2
24 Oct 92	**NOTHING TO FEAR** *East West YZ 699*	16		3
28 Nov 92	**GOD'S GREAT BANANA SKIN** *East West YZ 706*	31		1
30 Jan 93	**SOFT TOP HARD SHOULDER** *East West YZ 710CD*	53		
23 Oct 93	**JULIA** *East West YZ 722CD*	18		4
12 Nov 94	**YOU CAN GO YOUR OWN WAY** *East West YZ 835CD*	28		2
24 Dec 94	**TELL ME THERE'S A HEAVEN** *East West YZ 885CD*	70		
16 Nov 96	**DISCO' LA PASSIONE** *East West EW 072CD* CHRIS REA & SHIRLEY BASSEY	41		
24 May 97	**LET'S DANCE** *Magnet EW 112CD* MIDDLESBROUGH FC FEATURING BOB MORTIMER & CHRIS REA	44		
15 Dec 07	**DRIVING HOME FOR CHRISTMAS** *Download*	33		2

REACT 2 RHYTHM UK production duo

Date	Title	Peak Position	Weeks at No.1	Weeks in Top 40
28 Jun 97	**INTOXICATION** *Jackpot WIN 014CD*	73		

REACTOR UK group

Date	Title	Peak Position	Weeks at No.1	Weeks in Top 40
10 Apr 04	**FEELING THE LOVE** *Liberty CDREACT001*	56		

EDDI READER UK singer

Date	Title	Peak Position	Weeks at No.1	Weeks in Top 40
4 Jun 94	**PATIENCE OF ANGELS** *Blanco Y Negro NEG 68CD*	33		3
13 Aug 94	**JOKE (I'M LAUGHING)** *Blanco Y Negro NEG 72CD*	42		
5 Nov 94	**DEAR JOHN** *Blanco Y Negro NEG 75CD1*	48		
22 Jun 96	**TOWN WITHOUT PITY** *Blanco Y Negro NEG 90CDX*	26		1
21 Aug 99	**FRAGILE THING** *Track 0004A* BIG COUNTRY FEATURING EDDI READER	69		

READY FOR THE WORLD US group

Date	Title	Peak Position	Weeks at No.1	Weeks in Top 40
26 Oct 85	**OH SHEILA** *MCA 1005* ★	50		
14 Mar 87	**LOVE YOU DOWN** *MCA 1110*	60		

REAL & RICHARDSON UK production duo

Date	Title	Peak Position	Weeks at No.1	Weeks in Top 40
10 May 03	**SUNSHINE ON A RAINY DAY** *Nukleuz 0489 CNUK* REAL & RICHARDSON FEATURING JOBABE	69		

REAL EMOTION UK group

Date	Title	Peak Position	Weeks at No.1	Weeks in Top 40
1 Jul 95	**BACK FOR GOOD** *Living Beat LBECD 34*	67		

REAL McCOY German/US group

Date	Title	Peak Position	Weeks at No.1	Weeks in Top 40
6 Nov 93	**ANOTHER NIGHT** *Logic 74321173732* (MC SAR &) THE REAL McCOY	61		
5 Nov 94	**ANOTHER NIGHT (REMIX)** *Logic 74321236992* (MC SAR &) THE REAL McCOY	2		11
28 Jan 95	**RUN AWAY** *Logic 74321258822* (MC SAR &) THE REAL McCOY	6		8
22 Apr 95	**LOVE AND DEVOTION** *Logic 74321272702* (MC SAR &) THE REAL McCOY	11		6
26 Aug 95	**COME AND GET YOUR LOVE** *Logic 74321301272*	19		3
11 Nov 95	**AUTOMATIC LOVER (CALL FOR LOVE)** *Logic 74321325042*	58		

REAL PEOPLE UK group

Date	Title	Peak Position	Weeks at No.1	Weeks in Top 40
16 Feb 91	**OPEN YOUR MIND (LET ME IN)** *CBS 6566127*	70		
20 Apr 91	**THE TRUTH** *Columbia 6567877*	73		
6 Jul 91	**WINDOW PANE (EP)** *Columbia 6569327*	60		
11 Jan 92	**THE TRUTH** *Columbia 6576987*	41		
23 May 92	**BELIEVER** *Columbia 6580067*	38		1

REAL ROXANNE US rapper

Date	Title	Peak Position	Weeks at No.1	Weeks in Top 40
28 Jun 86	**BANG ZOOM (LET'S GO GO)** *Cooltempo COOL 124* REAL ROXANNE WITH HITMAN HOWIE TEE	11		7
12 Nov 88	**RESPECT** *Cooltempo COOL 176*	71		

REAL THING UK group

Date	Title	Peak Position	Weeks at No.1	Weeks in Top 40
5 Jun 76	**YOU TO ME ARE EVERYTHING** *Pye International 7N 25709*	1	3	11
4 Sep 76	**CAN'T GET BY WITHOUT YOU** *Pye 7N 45618*	2		10
12 Feb 77	**YOU'LL NEVER KNOW WHAT YOU'RE MISSING** *Pye 7N 45662*	16		8
30 Jul 77	**LOVE'S SUCH A WONDERFUL THING** *Pye 7N 45701*	33		2
4 Mar 78	**WHENEVER YOU WANT MY LOVE** *Pye 7N 46045*	18		8
3 Jun 78	**LET'S GO DISCO** *Pye 7N 46078*	39		1
12 Aug 78	**RAININ' THROUGH MY SUNSHINE** *Pye 7N 46113*	40		1
17 Feb 79	**CAN YOU FEEL THE FORCE** *Pye 7N 46147*	5		9
21 Jul 79	**BOOGIE DOWN (GET FUNKY NOW)** *Pye 7P 109*	33		3
22 Nov 80	**SHE'S A GROOVY FREAK** *Calibre CAB 105*	52		
8 Mar 86	**YOU TO ME ARE EVERYTHING (THE DECADE REMIX 78-86)** *PRT 7P 349*	5		9
24 May 86	**CAN'T GET BY WITHOUT YOU (THE SECOND DECADE REMIX)** *PRT 7P 352*	6		10
2 Aug 86	**CAN YOU FEEL THE FORCE ('86 REMIX)** *PRT 7P 358*	24		4
25 Oct 86	**STRAIGHT TO THE HEART** *Jive 129*	71		
23 Apr 05	**SO MUCH LOVE TO GIVE** *All Around The World CDGLOBE412* FREELOADERS FEATURING THE REAL THING	9		4

REAL TO REEL US group

Date	Title	Peak Position	Weeks at No.1	Weeks in Top 40
21 Apr 84	**LOVE ME LIKE THIS** *Arista ARIST 565*	68		

REBEL MC UK rapper

Date	Title	Peak Position	Weeks at No.1	Weeks in Top 40
27 May 89	**JUST KEEP ROCKIN'** *Desire WANT 9* DOUBLE TROUBLE & THE REBEL MC	11		10
7 Oct 89	**STREET TUFF** *Desire WANT 18* DOUBLE TROUBLE & THE REBEL MC	3		10
31 Mar 90	**BETTER WORLD** *Desire WANT 25*	20		5
2 Jun 90	**REBEL MUSIC** *Desire WANT 31*	53		
6 Apr 91	**WICKEDEST SOUND** *Desire WANT 40* REBEL MC FEATURING TENOR FLY	43		
15 Jun 91	**TRIBAL BASE** *Desire WANT 44* REBEL MC FEATURING TENOR FLY & BARRINGTON LEVY	20		4
31 Aug 91	**BLACK MEANING GOOD** *Desire WANT 47*	73		
21 Mar 92	**RICH AH GETTING RICHER** *Big Life BLR 70* REBEL MC INTRODUCING LITTLE T	48		
8 Aug 92	**HUMANITY** *Big Life BLR 78* REBEL MC FEATURING PRINCE/LINCOLN THOMPSON	62		

EZZ RECO & THE LAUNCHERS WITH BOSIE GRANT Jamaican trombonist with singer

Date	Title	Peak Position	Weeks at No.1	Weeks in Top 40
5 Mar 64	**KING OF KINGS** *Columbia DB 7217*	44		

RECOIL UK group

Date	Title	Peak Position	Weeks at No.1	Weeks in Top 40
21 Mar 92	**FAITH HEALER** *Mute 110*	60		

RED UK production duo

Date	Title	Peak Position	Weeks at No.1	Weeks in Top 40
20 Jan 01	**HEAVEN & EARTH** *Slinky Music SLINKY 008CD*	41		

RED BOX UK group

Date	Title	Peak Position	Weeks at No.1	Weeks in Top 40
24 Aug 85	**LEAN ON ME (AH-LI-AYO)** *Sire W 8926*	3		10
25 Oct 86	**FOR AMERICA** *Sire YZ 84*	10		11
31 Jan 87	**HEART OF THE SUN** *Sire YZ 100*	71		

RED CAR AND THE BLUE CAR UK group

Date	Title	Peak Position	Weeks at No.1	Weeks in Top 40
14 Dec 91	**HOME FOR CHRISTMAS DAY** *Virgin VS 1394*	44		

RED CARPET Belgian production duo

Date	Title	Peak Position	Weeks at No.1	Weeks in Top 40
11 Dec 04	**ALRIGHT** *Positiva CDTIVS212*	58		
14 Jan 06	**ALRIGHT** *Positiva CDTIVS231*	74		

RED DRAGON Jamaican singer

Date	Title	Peak Position	Weeks at No.1	Weeks in Top 40
30 Jul 94	**COMPLIMENTS ON YOUR KISS** *Mango CIDM 820* RED DRAGON WITH BRIAN & TONY GOLD	2		11

RED EYE UK production duo

Date	Title	Peak Position	Weeks at No.1	Weeks in Top 40
3 Dec 94	**KUT IT** *Champion CHAMPCD 315*	62		

RED 5 German producer

Date	Title	Peak Position	Weeks at No.1	Weeks in Top 40
10 May 97	**I LOVE YOU...STOP!** *Multiply CDMULTY 20*	11		3
20 Dec 97	**LIFT ME UP** *Multiply CDMULTY 30*	26		1

RED HILL CHILDREN UK group

Date	Title	Peak Position	Weeks at No.1	Weeks in Top 40
30 Nov 96	**WHEN CHILDREN RULE THE WORLD** *Really Useful 5797262*	40		1

RED HOT CHILI PEPPERS US group

Date	Title	Peak Position	Weeks at No.1	Weeks in Top 40
10 Feb 90	**HIGHER GROUND** *EMI-USA MT 75*	55		
23 Jun 90	**TASTE THE PAIN** *EMI-USA MT 85*	29		2
8 Sep 90	**HIGHER GROUND** *EMI-USA MT 88*	54		
14 Mar 92	**UNDER THE BRIDGE** *Warner Brothers W 0084*	26		2
15 Aug 92	**BREAKING THE GIRL** *Warner Brothers W 0126*	41		
5 Feb 94	**GIVE IT AWAY** *Warner Brothers W 0225CD1*	9		3
30 Apr 94	**UNDER THE BRIDGE** *Warner Brothers W 0237CDX*	13		5
2 Sep 95	**WARPED** *Warner Brothers W 0316CD*	31		1
21 Oct 95	**MY FRIENDS** *Warner Brothers W 0317CD*	29		1
17 Feb 96	**AEROPLANE** *Warner Brothers W 0331CD*	11		2

Silver-selling ○ Gold-selling ● Platinum-selling ⊛ US No.1 ★ — Peak Position · Weeks at No.1 · Weeks in Top 40

Date	Title	Label	Peak Position	Weeks at No.1	Weeks in Top 40
14 Jun 97	LOVE ROLLERCOASTER	Geffen GFSTD 22188	7		6
12 Jun 99	SCAR TISSUE	Warner Brothers W 490CD	15		4
4 Sep 99	AROUND THE WORLD	Warner Brothers W 500CD1	35		1
12 Feb 00	OTHERSIDE	Warner Brothers W 510CD1	33		1
19 Aug 00	CALIFORNICATION	Warner Brothers W 534CD1	16		2
13 Jan 01	ROAD TRIPPIN'	Warner Brothers W 546CD1	30		1
13 Jul 02	BY THE WAY	Warner Brothers W 580CD1	2		7
2 Nov 02	THE ZEPHYR SONG	Warner Brothers W 592CD	11		4
22 Feb 03	CAN'T STOP	Warner Brothers W 599CD	22		3
28 Jun 03	UNIVERSALLY SPEAKING	Warner Brothers W 609CD	27		1
22 Nov 03	FORTUNE FADED	Warner Brothers W 630CD	11		3
6 May 06	DANI CALIFORNIA	Warner Brothers W715CD1	2		12
22 Jul 06	TELL ME BABY	Warner Brothers W726CD1	16		4
25 Nov 06	SNOW (HEY HO)	Warner Brothers W751CD1	16		4
24 Feb 07	DESECRATION SMILE	Warner Brothers W756CD2	27		1
12 May 07	HUMP DE BUMP	Warner Brothers W763CDX	41		

RED 'N' WHITE MACHINES UK group

Date	Title	Label	Peak Position	Weeks at No.1	Weeks in Top 40
24 May 03	SOUTHAMPTON BOYS	Centric CEN 008	16		1

RED RAW UK duo

Date	Title	Label	Peak Position	Weeks at No.1	Weeks in Top 40
28 Oct 95	OOH LA LA LA RED RAW FEATURING 007	Media MCSTD 2065	59		

RED SNAPPER UK group

Date	Title	Label	Peak Position	Weeks at No.1	Weeks in Top 40
21 Nov 98	IMAGE OF YOU	Warp WAP 111CD	60		

REDBONE US/Indian group

Date	Title	Label	Peak Position	Weeks at No.1	Weeks in Top 40
25 Sep 71	THE WITCH QUEEN OF NEW ORLEANS	Epic EPC 7351	2		11

REDD KROSS US group

Date	Title	Label	Peak Position	Weeks at No.1	Weeks in Top 40
5 Feb 94	VISIONARY	This Way Up WAY 2733	75		
10 Sep 94	YESTERDAY ONCE MORE	A&M 5807932	45		
1 Feb 97	GET OUT OF MYSELF	This Way Up WAY 5466	63		

REDD SQUARE UK duo

Date	Title	Label	Peak Position	Weeks at No.1	Weeks in Top 40
26 Oct 02	IN YOUR HANDS REDD SQUARE FEATURING TIFF LACEY	Inferno CDFERN 50	64		

SHARON REDD US singer

Date	Title	Label	Peak Position	Weeks at No.1	Weeks in Top 40
28 Feb 81	CAN YOU HANDLE IT	Epic EPC 9572	31		4
2 Oct 82	NEVER GIVE YOU UP	Prelude PRL A 2755	20		8
15 Jan 83	IN THE NAME OF LOVE	Prelude PRL A 2905	31		3
22 Oct 83	LOVE HOW YOU FEEL	Prelude A 3868	39		2
1 Feb 92	CAN YOU HANDLE IT DNA FEATURING SHARON REDD	EMI EM 219	17		3

OTIS REDDING US singer

Date	Title	Label	Peak Position	Weeks at No.1	Weeks in Top 40
25 Nov 65	MY GIRL	Atlantic AT 4050	11		13
7 Apr 66	SATISFACTION	Atlantic AT 4080	33		3
14 Jul 66	MY LOVER'S PRAYER	Atlantic 584 019	37		3
25 Aug 66	I CAN'T TURN YOU LOOSE	Atlantic 584 030	29		6
24 Nov 66	FA FA FA FA FA (SAD SONG)	Atlantic 584 049	23		8
26 Jan 67	TRY A LITTLE TENDERNESS	Atlantic 584 070	46		
23 Mar 67	DAY TRIPPER	Stax 601 005	43		
4 May 67	LET ME COME ON HOME	Stax 601 007	48		
15 Jun 67	SHAKE	Stax 601 011	28		8
19 Jul 67	TRAMP OTIS REDDING & CARLA THOMAS	Stax 601 012	18		9
11 Oct 67	KNOCK ON WOOD OTIS REDDING & CARLA THOMAS	Stax 601 021	35		2
14 Feb 68	MY GIRL	Atlantic 584 092	36		6
21 Feb 68	(SITTIN' ON) THE DOCK OF THE BAY	Stax 601 031 ★	3		14
29 May 68	THE HAPPY SONG (DUM-DUM)	Stax 601 040	24		4
31 Jul 68	HARD TO HANDLE	Atlantic 584 199	15		11
9 Jul 69	LOVE MAN	Atco 226 001	43		

HELEN REDDY Australian singer

Date	Title	Label	Peak Position	Weeks at No.1	Weeks in Top 40
18 Jan 75	ANGIE BABY	Capitol CL 15799 ★	5		8
28 Nov 81	I CAN'T SAY GOODBYE TO YOU	MCA 744	43		

REDHEAD KINGPIN & THE FBI US group

Date	Title	Label	Peak Position	Weeks at No.1	Weeks in Top 40
22 Jul 89	DO THE RIGHT THING	10 TEN 271	13		7
2 Dec 89	SUPERBAD SUPERSLICK	10 TEN 286	68		

REDMAN US rapper

Date	Title	Label	Peak Position	Weeks at No.1	Weeks in Top 40
25 Apr 98	RAP SCHOLAR DAS EFX FEATURING REDMAN	East West E 3853CD	42		
30 May 98	MADE IT BACK BEVERLEY KNIGHT FEATURING REDMAN	Parlophone Rhythm CDRHYTHM 11	21		1
24 Oct 98	HOW DEEP IS YOUR LOVE DRU HILL FEATURING REDMAN	Island Black Music CID 725	9		4
10 Apr 99	MADE IT BACK 99 (REMIX) BEVERLEY KNIGHT FEATURING REDMAN	Parlophone Rhythm CDRHYTHS 18	19		3
12 Jun 99	DA GOODNESS	Def Jam 8709232	52		
22 Jul 00	OOOH DE LA SOUL FEATURING REDMAN	Tommy Boy TBCD 2102B	29		1
15 Sep 01	SMASH SUMTHIN' REDMAN FEATURING ADAM F	Def Jam 5886932	11		3
31 Aug 02	SMASH SUMTHIN'(REMIX) ADAM F FEATURING REDMAN	Kaos KOASCD 003	47		
23 Nov 02	DIRRTY CHRISTINA AGUILERA FEATURING REDMAN ⊛	RCA 74321962722	1	2	7
11 Jan 03	REACT ERICK SERMON FEATURING REDMAN	J Records 74321988492	14		3

REDNEX Swedish group

Date	Title	Label	Peak Position	Weeks at No.1	Weeks in Top 40
17 Dec 94	COTTON EYE JOE	Internal Affairs KGBCD 016 ⊛	1	2	14
25 Mar 95	OLD POP IN AN OAK	Internal Affairs KGBCD 019	12		3
21 Oct 95	WILD 'N FREE	Internal Affairs KGBCD 024	55		

REDS UNITED UK group

Date	Title	Label	Peak Position	Weeks at No.1	Weeks in Top 40
6 Dec 97	SING UP FOR THE CHAMPIONS	Music Collection MANUCD 2 ○	12		6
9 May 98	UNITED CALYPSO '98	Music Collection MANUCD 3	33		1

REDSKINS UK group

Date	Title	Label	Peak Position	Weeks at No.1	Weeks in Top 40
10 Nov 84	KEEP ON KEEPIN' ON	Decca F 1	43		
22 Jun 85	BRING IT DOWN (THIS INSANE THING)	Decca F 2	33		3
22 Feb 86	THE POWER IS YOURS	Decca F 3	59		

ALEX REECE UK producer

Date	Title	Label	Peak Position	Weeks at No.1	Weeks in Top 40
16 Dec 95	FEEL THE SUNSHINE	Blunted Vinyl BLNCD 016	69		
11 May 96	FEEL THE SUNSHINE (REMIX)	Fourth & Broadway BRCD 332	26		1
27 Jul 96	CANDLES	Fourth & Broadway BRCD 333	33		1
16 Nov 96	ACID LAB	Fourth & Broadway BRCD 344	64		

JIMMY REED US singer/guitarist

Date	Title	Label	Peak Position	Weeks at No.1	Weeks in Top 40
10 Sep 64	SHAME SHAME SHAME	Stateside SS 330	45		

LOU REED US singer

Date	Title	Label	Peak Position	Weeks at No.1	Weeks in Top 40
12 May 73	WALK ON THE WILD SIDE	RCA 2303	10		8
17 Jan 87	SOUL MAN SAM MOORE & LOU REED	A&M AM 364	30		4
31 Jul 04	SATELLITE OF LOVE 04	NuLife 82876636472	10		4

DAN REED NETWORK US group

Date	Title	Label	Peak Position	Weeks at No.1	Weeks in Top 40
20 Jan 90	COME BACK BABY	Mercury DRN 2	51		
17 Mar 90	RAINBOW CHILD	Mercury DRN 3	60		
21 Jul 90	STARDATE 1990/RAINBOW CHILD	Mercury DRN 4	39		1
8 Sep 90	LOVER/MONEY	Mercury DRN 5	45		
13 Jul 91	MIX IT UP	Mercury MER 345	49		
21 Sep 91	BABY NOW I	Mercury MER 352	65		

REEF UK group

Date	Title / Label	Peak Position	Weeks at No.1	Weeks in Top 40
15 Apr 95	**GOOD FEELING** *Sony S2 6613602*	24		2
3 Jun 95	**NAKED** *Sony S2 6620622*	11		3
5 Aug 95	**WEIRD** *Sony S2 6622772*	19		1
2 Nov 96	**PLACE YOUR HANDS** *Sony S2 6635712*	6		5
25 Jan 97	**COME BACK BRIGHTER** *Sony S2 6640972*	8		3
5 Apr 97	**CONSIDERATION** *Sony S2 6643125*	13		2
2 Aug 97	**YER OLD** *Sony S2 6647032*	21		1
10 Apr 99	**I'VE GOT SOMETHING TO SAY** *Sony S2 6669545*	15		3
5 Jun 99	**SWEETY** *Sony S2 6673732*	46		
11 Sep 99	**NEW BIRD** *Sony S2 6678512*	73		
12 Aug 00	**SET THE RECORD STRAIGHT** *Sony S2 6695952*	19		1
16 Dec 00	**SUPERHERO** *Sony S2 6699382*	55		
19 May 01	**ALL I WANT** *Sony S2 6708222*	51		
25 Jan 03	**GIVE ME YOUR LOVE** *Sony S2 6731645*	44		
28 Jun 03	**WASTER** *Reef Recordings SMASCD 051X*	56		

REEL Irish group

Date	Title / Label	Peak Position	Weeks at No.1	Weeks in Top 40
24 Nov 01	**LIFT ME UP** *Universal TV 0154632*	39		1
8 Jun 02	**YOU TAKE ME AWAY** *Universal TV 0190182*	31		1

REEL BIG FISH US group

Date	Title / Label	Peak Position	Weeks at No.1	Weeks in Top 40
6 Apr 02	**SOLD OUT EP** *Jive 9270002*	62		

REEL 2 REAL US duo

Date	Title / Label	Peak Position	Weeks at No.1	Weeks in Top 40
12 Feb 94	**I LIKE TO MOVE IT** *Positiva CDTIV 10* REEL 2 REAL FEATURING THE MAD STUNTMAN	5		17
2 Jul 94	**GO ON MOVE** *Positiva CDTIV 15* REEL 2 REAL FEATURING THE MAD STUNTMAN	7		6
1 Oct 94	**CAN YOU FEEL IT** *Positiva CDTIV 22* REEL 2 REAL FEATURING THE MAD STUNTMAN	13		3
3 Dec 94	**RAISE YOUR HANDS** *Positiva CDTIV 27* REEL 2 REAL FEATURING THE MAD STUNTMAN	14		3
6 Jul 96	**JAZZ IT UP** *Positiva CDTIV 59*	7		5
1 Apr 95	**CONWAY** *Positiva CDTIVS 30* REEL 2 REAL FEATURING THE MAD STUNTMAN	27		2
5 Oct 96	**ARE YOU READY FOR SOME MORE?** *Positiva CDTIV 56*	24		1

REELISTS UK production duo

Date	Title / Label	Peak Position	Weeks at No.1	Weeks in Top 40
25 May 02	**FREAK MODE** *Go! Beat GOBCD 45*	16		2

MAUREEN REES UK singer/TV personality

Date	Title / Label	Peak Position	Weeks at No.1	Weeks in Top 40
20 Dec 97	**DRIVING IN MY CAR** *Eagle EAGXS 014*	49		

TONY REES & THE COTTAGERS UK group

Date	Title / Label	Peak Position	Weeks at No.1	Weeks in Top 40
10 May 75	**VIVA EL FULHAM** *Sonet SON 2059*	46		

REESE PROJECT US producer

Date	Title / Label	Peak Position	Weeks at No.1	Weeks in Top 40
8 Aug 92	**THE COLOUR OF LOVE** *Network NWK 1*	52		
12 Dec 92	**I BELIEVE** *Network NWKT 63*	74		
13 Mar 93	**SO DEEP** *Network NWKCD 68*	54		
24 Sep 94	**THE COLOUR OF LOVE (REMIX)** *Network NWKCD 81*	55		
6 May 95	**DIRECT-ME** *Network NWKCD 87*	44		

CONNOR REEVES UK singer

Date	Title / Label	Peak Position	Weeks at No.1	Weeks in Top 40
30 Aug 97	**MY FATHER'S SON** *Wildstar CDWILD 1*	12		3
22 Nov 97	**EARTHBOUND** *Wildstar CDWILD 2*	14		2
11 Apr 98	**READ MY MIND** *Wildstar CXWILD 4*	19		3
3 Oct 98	**SEARCHING FOR A SOUL** *Wildstar CDWILD 6*	28		1
4 Sep 99	**BEST FRIEND** *WEA 221CD1* MARK MORRISON & CONNOR REEVES	23		1

JIM REEVES US singer

Date	Title / Label	Peak Position	Weeks at No.1	Weeks in Top 40
24 Mar 60	**HE'LL HAVE TO GO** *RCA 1168*	12		30
16 Mar 61	**WHISPERING HOPE** *RCA 1223*	50		
23 Nov 61	**YOU'RE THE ONLY GOOD THING (THAT HAPPENED TO ME)** *RCA 1261*	17		17
28 Jun 62	**ADIOS AMIGO** *RCA 1293*	23		16
22 Nov 62	**I'M GONNA CHANGE EVERYTHING** *RCA 1317*	42		
13 Jun 63	**WELCOME TO MY WORLD** *RCA 1342*	6		13
17 Oct 63	**GUILTY** *RCA 1364*	29		3
20 Feb 64	**I LOVE YOU BECAUSE** *RCA 1385*	5		37
18 Jun 64	**I WON'T FORGET YOU** *RCA 1400*	3		25
5 Nov 64	**THERE'S A HEARTACHE FOLLOWING ME** *RCA 1423*	6		13
4 Feb 65	**IT HURTS SO MUCH (TO SEE YOU)** *RCA 1437*	8		7
15 Apr 65	**NOT UNTIL NEXT TIME** *RCA 1446*	13		10
6 May 65	**HOW LONG HAS IT BEEN** *RCA 1445*	45		
15 Jul 65	**THIS WORLD IS NOT MY HOME** *RCA 1412*	22		7
11 Nov 65	**IS IT REALLY OVER** *RCA 1488*	17		8
18 Aug 66	**DISTANT DRUMS** *RCA 1537*	1	5	25
2 Feb 67	**I WON'T COME IN WHILE HE'S THERE** *RCA 1563*	12		10
26 Jul 67	**TRYING TO FORGET** *RCA 1611*	33		4
22 Nov 67	**I HEARD A HEART BREAK LAST NIGHT** *RCA 1643*	38		1
27 Mar 68	**PRETTY BROWN EYES** *RCA 1672*	33		1
25 Jun 69	**WHEN TWO WORLDS COLLIDE** *RCA 1830*	17		13
6 Dec 69	**BUT YOU LOVE ME, DADDY** *RCA 1899*	15		10
21 Mar 70	**NOBODY'S FOOL** *RCA 1915*	32		4
12 Sep 70	**ANGELS DON'T LIE** *RCA 1997*	32		2
26 Jun 71	**I LOVE YOU BECAUSE/HE'LL HAVE TO GO/MOONLIGHT & ROSES** *RCA Maximillion 2092*	34		5
19 Feb 72	**YOU'RE FREE TO GO** *RCA 2174*	48		

MARTHA REEVES & THE VANDELLAS US group

Date	Title / Label	Peak Position	Weeks at No.1	Weeks in Top 40
29 Oct 64	**DANCING IN THE STREET** *Stateside SS 345*	28		6
1 Apr 65	**NOWHERE TO RUN** *Tamla Motown TMG 502*	26		8
1 Dec 66	**I'M READY FOR LOVE** *Tamla Motown TMG 582*	22		7
30 Mar 67	**JIMMY MACK** *Tamla Motown TMG 599*	21		6
17 Jan 68	**HONEY CHILE** *Tamla Motown TMG 636*	30		5
15 Jan 69	**DANCING IN THE STREET** *Tamla Motown TMG 684*	4		10
16 Apr 69	**NOWHERE TO RUN** *Tamla Motown TMG 694*	42		
29 Aug 70	**JIMMY MACK** *Tamla Motown TMG 599*	21		10
13 Feb 71	**FORGET ME NOT** *Tamla Motown TMG 762*	11		7
8 Jan 72	**BLESS YOU** *Tamla Motown TMG 794*	33		3
23 Jul 88	**NOWHERE TO RUN** *A&M AM 444*	52		

VIC REEVES UK comedian

Date	Title / Label	Peak Position	Weeks at No.1	Weeks in Top 40
27 Apr 91	**BORN FREE** *Sense SIGH 710* VIC REEVES & THE ROMAN NUMERALS	6		5
26 Oct 91	**DIZZY** *Sense SIGH 712* VIC REEVES & THE WONDER STUFF	1	2	11
14 Dec 91	**ABIDE WITH ME** *Sense SIGH 713*	47		
8 Jul 95	**I'M A BELIEVER** *Parlophone CDR 6412* EMF/REEVES & MORTIMER	3		5

REFLEKT UK production duo

Date	Title / Label	Peak Position	Weeks at No.1	Weeks in Top 40
5 Mar 05	**NEED TO FEEL LOVED** *Positiva CDTIVS213* REFLEKT FEATURING DELLINE BASS	14		3

REFLEX UK production duo

Date	Title / Label	Peak Position	Weeks at No.1	Weeks in Top 40
19 May 01	**PUT YOUR HANDS UP** *Gusto CDGUS 2* REFLEX FEATURING MC VIPER	72		

REFUGEE ALLSTARS US group

Date	Title / Label	Peak Position	Weeks at No.1	Weeks in Top 40
28 Jun 97	**WE TRYING TO STAY ALIVE** *Columbia 6646815* WYCLEF JEAN & THE REFUGEE ALLSTARS	13		3
6 Sep 97	**THE SWEETEST THING** *Columbia 6649785* REFUGEE ALLSTARS FEATURING LAURYN HILL	18		2
27 Sep 97	**GUANTANAMERA** *Columbia 6650852* WYCLEF JEAN & THE REFUGEE ALLSTARS	25		1
27 Oct 01	**LOVING YOU (OLE OLE OLE)** *Blacklist 0133045 ERE* BRIAN HARVEY & THE REFUGEE CREW	20		2

JOAN REGAN UK singer

Date	Title / Label	Peak Position	Weeks at No.1	Weeks in Top 40
11 Dec 53	**RICOCHET** *Decca F 10193* JOAN REGAN & THE SQUADRONAIRES	8		5
14 May 54	**SOMEONE ELSE'S ROSES** *Decca F 10257*	5		8
1 Oct 54	**IF I GIVE MY HEART TO YOU** *Decca F 10373*	3		11
5 Nov 54	**WAIT FOR ME DARLING** *Decca F 10362* JOAN REGAN & THE JOHNSTON BROTHERS	18		1
25 Mar 55	**PRIZE OF GOLD** *Decca F 10432*	6		8
6 May 55	**OPEN UP YOUR HEART** *Decca F 10474* JOAN & RUSTY REGAN	19		1
1 May 59	**MAY YOU ALWAYS** *HMV POP 593*	9		16

Silver-selling · Gold-selling · Platinum-selling · US No.1 ★ · Peak Position · Weeks at No.1 · Weeks in Top 40

Date	Title	Peak Position	Weeks at No.1	Weeks in Top 40
5 Feb 60	**HAPPY ANNIVERSARY** *Pye 7N 15238*	29		2
28 Jul 60	**PAPA LOVES MAMA** *Pye 7N 15278*	29		3
24 Nov 60	**ONE OF THE LUCKY ONES** *Pye 7N 15310*	47		
5 Jan 61	**IT MUST BE SANTA** *Pye 7N 15303*	42		

REGENTS UK group

Date	Title	Peak Position	Weeks at No.1	Weeks in Top 40
22 Dec 79	**7TEEN** *Rialto TREB 111*	11		7
7 Jun 80	**SEE YOU LATER** *Arista ARIST 350*	55		

REGGAE BOYZ Jamaican group

Date	Title	Peak Position	Weeks at No.1	Weeks in Top 40
27 Jun 98	**KICK IT** *Universal MCSTD 40167*	59		

REGGAE PHILHARMONIC ORCHESTRA UK group

Date	Title	Peak Position	Weeks at No.1	Weeks in Top 40
19 Nov 88	**MINNIE THE MOOCHER** *Mango IS 378*	35		3
28 Jul 90	**LOVELY THING** *Mango MNG 742*	71		

REGINA US singer

Date	Title	Peak Position	Weeks at No.1	Weeks in Top 40
1 Feb 86	**BABY LOVE** *Funkin' Marvellous MARV 01*	50		

REID UK group

Date	Title	Peak Position	Weeks at No.1	Weeks in Top 40
8 Oct 88	**ONE WAY OUT** *Syncopate SY 16*	66		
11 Feb 89	**REAL EMOTION** *Syncopate SY 24*	65		
15 Apr 89	**GOOD TIMES** *Syncopate SY 27*	55		
21 Oct 89	**LOVIN' ON THE SIDE** *Syncopate REID 1*	71		

JUNIOR REID Jamaican singer

Date	Title	Peak Position	Weeks at No.1	Weeks in Top 40
10 Sep 88	**STOP THIS CRAZY THING** *Ahead Of Our Time CCUT 4* COLDCUT FEATURING JUNIOR REID & THE AHEAD OF OUR TIME ORCHESTRA	21		5
14 Jul 90	**I'M FREE** *Raw TV RTV 9* SOUP DRAGONS FEATURING JUNIOR REID	5		11
11 Jul 92	**SHINE EYE** *Shut Up And Dance SUAD 32S* RAGGA TWINS FEATURING JUNIOR REID	63		
4 Nov 06	**IT'S OKAY** *Geffen 1713921* GAME FEATURING JUNIOR REID	26		3

MIKE REID UK actor/comedian

Date	Title	Peak Position	Weeks at No.1	Weeks in Top 40
22 Mar 75	**UGLY DUCKLING** *Pye 7N 45434*	10		7
24 Apr 99	**THE MORE I SEE YOU** *Telstar TV CDSTAS 3049* BARBARA WINDSOR & MIKE REID	46		

NEIL REID UK singer

Date	Title	Peak Position	Weeks at No.1	Weeks in Top 40
1 Jan 72	**MOTHER OF MINE** *Decca F 13264*	2		15
8 Apr 72	**THAT'S WHAT I WANT TO BE** *Decca F 13300*	45		

KEITH RELF UK singer

Date	Title	Peak Position	Weeks at No.1	Weeks in Top 40
26 May 66	**MR ZERO** *Columbia DB 7920*	50		

R.E.M. US group

Date	Title	Peak Position	Weeks at No.1	Weeks in Top 40
28 Nov 87	**THE ONE I LOVE** *IRS IRM 46*	51		
30 Apr 88	**FINEST WORKSONG** *IRS IRM 161*	50		
4 Feb 89	**STAND** *Warner Brothers W 7577*	51		
3 Jun 89	**ORANGE CRUSH** *Warner Brothers W 2960*	28		3
12 Aug 89	**STAND** *Warner Brothers W 2833*	48		
9 Mar 91	**LOSING MY RELIGION** *Warner Brothers W 0015*	19		7
18 May 91	**SHINY HAPPY PEOPLE** *Warner Brothers W 0027*	6		9
17 Aug 91	**NEAR WILD HEAVEN** *Warner Brothers W 0055*	27		2
21 Sep 91	**THE ONE I LOVE** *IRS IRM 178*	16		5
16 Nov 91	**RADIO SONG** *Warner Brothers W 0072*	28		1
14 Dec 91	**IT'S THE END OF THE WORLD AS WE KNOW IT** *IRS IRM 180*	39		1
3 Oct 92	**DRIVE** *Warner Brothers W 0136*	11		3
28 Nov 92	**MAN ON THE MOON** *Warner Brothers W 0143*	18		3
20 Feb 93	**THE SIDEWINDER SLEEPS TONITE** *Warner Brothers W 0152CD1*	17		3
17 Apr 93	**EVERYBODY HURTS** *Warner Brothers W 0169CD1*	7		11
24 Jul 93	**NIGHTSWIMMING** *Warner Brothers W 0184CD*	27		2
11 Dec 93	**FIND THE RIVER** *Warner Brothers W 0211CD*	54		
17 Sep 94	**WHAT'S THE FREQUENCY, KENNETH** *Warner Brothers W 0265CD*	9		4
12 Nov 94	**BANG AND BLAME** *Warner Brothers W 0275CD*	15		2
4 Feb 95	**CRUSH WITH EYELINER** *Warner Brothers W 0281CD*	23		2
15 Apr 95	**STRANGE CURRENCIES** *Warner Brothers W 0290CD*	9		3
29 Jul 95	**TONGUE** *Warner Brothers W 0308CD*	13		3
31 Aug 96	**E – BOW THE LETTER** *Warner Brothers W 0369CD*	4		3
2 Nov 96	**BITTERSWEET ME** *Warner Brothers W 0377CDX*	19		1
14 Dec 96	**ELECTROLITE** *Warner Brothers W 0383CDX*	29		1
24 Oct 98	**DAYSLEEPER** *Warner Brothers W 0455CD*	6		3
19 Dec 98	**LOTUS** *Warner Brothers W 466CD*	26		1
20 Mar 99	**AT MY MOST BEAUTIFUL** *Warner Brothers W 477CD*	10		2
5 Feb 00	**THE GREAT BEYOND** *Warner Brothers W 516CD*	3		7
12 May 01	**IMITATION OF LIFE** *Warner Brothers W 559CD*	6		4
4 Aug 01	**ALL THE WAY TO RENO** *Warner Brothers W 568CDX*	24		1
1 Dec 01	**I'LL TAKE THE RAIN** *Warner Brothers W 573CD*	44		
25 Oct 03	**BAD DAY** *Warner Brothers W 624CD1*	8		3
17 Jan 04	**ANIMAL** *Warner Brothers W 633CD*	33		1
9 Oct 04	**LEAVING NEW YORK** *Warner Brothers W 654CD1*	5		3
11 Dec 04	**AFTERMATH** *Warner Brothers W658CD2*	41		
12 Mar 05	**ELECTRON BLUE** *Warner Brothers W665CD2*	26		1
23 Jul 05	**WANDERLUST** *Warner Brothers W676CD2*	27		1
23 Feb 08	**SUPERNATURAL SUPERSERIOUS** *Download*	54		

REMBRANDTS US duo

Date	Title	Peak Position	Weeks at No.1	Weeks in Top 40
2 Sep 95	**I'LL BE THERE FOR YOU (THEME FROM *FRIENDS*)** *Elektra A 4390CD*	3		10
20 Jan 96	**THIS HOUSE IS NOT A HOME** *East West A 4336CD*	58		
24 May 97	**I'LL BE THERE FOR YOU (THEME FROM *FRIENDS*)** *East West A 4390CD*	5		13

REMY ZERO US group

Date	Title	Peak Position	Weeks at No.1	Weeks in Top 40
27 Apr 02	**SAVE ME** *Elektra E 7297CD*	55		

RENAISSANCE UK group

Date	Title	Peak Position	Weeks at No.1	Weeks in Top 40
15 Jul 78	**NORTHERN LIGHTS** *Warner Brothers K 17177*	10		8

RENE & ANGELA US duo

Date	Title	Peak Position	Weeks at No.1	Weeks in Top 40
15 Jun 85	**SAVE YOUR LOVE (FOR NUMBER 1)** *Club JAB 14* RENE & ANGELA FEATURING KURTIS BLOW	66		
7 Sep 85	**I'LL BE GOOD** *Club JAB 18*	22		7
2 Nov 85	**SECRET RENDEZVOUS** *Champion CHAMP 5*	54		

RENE & YVETTE UK actors

Date	Title	Peak Position	Weeks at No.1	Weeks in Top 40
22 Nov 86	**JE T'AIME (ALLO ALLO)/RENE DMC (DEVASTATING MACHO CHARISMA)** *Sedition EDIT 3319*	57		

NICOLA RENEE US singer

Date	Title	Peak Position	Weeks at No.1	Weeks in Top 40
12 Dec 98	**STRAWBERRY** *Atlantic AT 0050CD*	55		

RENEE & RENATO UK/Italian duo

Date	Title	Peak Position	Weeks at No.1	Weeks in Top 40
30 Oct 82	**SAVE YOUR LOVE** *Hollywood HWD 003*	1	4	13
12 Feb 83	**JUST ONE MORE KISS** *Hollywood HWD 006*	48		

RENEGADE SOUNDWAVE UK group

Date	Title	Peak Position	Weeks at No.1	Weeks in Top 40
3 Feb 90	**PROBABLY A ROBBERY** *Mute 102*	38		1
5 Feb 94	**RENEGADE SOUNDWAVE** *Mute CDMUTE 146*	64		

REO SPEEDWAGON US group

Date	Title	Peak Position	Weeks at No.1	Weeks in Top 40
11 Apr 81	**KEEP ON LOVING YOU** *Epic EPC 9544* ★	7		9
27 Jun 81	**TAKE IT ON THE RUN** *Epic EPC A 1207*	19		10
16 Mar 85	**CAN'T FIGHT THIS FEELING** *Epic A 4880* ★	16		6

REPARATA & THE DELRONS US group

Date	Title	Peak Position	Weeks at No.1	Weeks in Top 40
20 Mar 68	**CAPTAIN OF YOUR SHIP** *Bell 1002*	13		10
18 Oct 75	**SHOES** *Dart 2066 562* REPARATA	43		

REPUBLICA UK group

Date	Title / Label	Peak	Wks No.1	Wks Top 40
27 Apr 96	**READY TO GO** *Deconstruction 74321326132*	43		
1 Mar 97	**READY TO GO (REMIX)** *Deconstruction 74321421332*	13		5
3 May 97	**DROP DEAD GORGEOUS** *Deconstruction 74321408442*	7		5
3 Oct 98	**FROM RUSH HOUR WITH LOVE** *Deconstruction 74321610472*	20		1

RESEARCH UK group

Date	Title / Label	Peak	Wks No.1	Wks Top 40
27 Nov 04	**SHE'S NOT LEAVING** *At Large FUGCD005*	73		
3 Sep 05	**C'MON CHAMELEON/I LOVE YOU BUT** *At Large FUGCD008*	63		
29 Oct 05	**THE WAY YOU USED TO SMILE** *At Large FUGCD010*	66		
25 Feb 06	**LONELY HEARTS STILL BEAT THE SAME** *At Large FUGCD013*	50		
17 Jun 06	**THE HARD TIMES** *At Large FUGCD015*	73		

RESONANCE US producer

Date	Title / Label	Peak	Wks No.1	Wks Top 40
26 May 01	**DJ** *Strictly Rhythm SRUKCD 02* RESONANCE FEATURING THE BURRELLS	67		

RESOURCE German production group

Date	Title / Label	Peak	Wks No.1	Wks Top 40
31 May 03	**I JUST DIED IN YOUR ARMS** *Substance SUBS17CDS*	42		

REST ASSURED UK production group

Date	Title / Label	Peak	Wks No.1	Wks Top 40
28 Feb 98	**TREAT INFAMY** *ffrr FCD 333*	14		4

REUBEN UK group

Date	Title / Label	Peak	Wks No.1	Wks Top 40
19 Jun 04	**FREDDY KREUGER** *Xtra Mile XMR102*	53		
28 Aug 04	**MOVING TO BLACKWATER** *Xtra Mile XMR104*	59		
25 Jun 05	**A KICK I N THE MOUTH** *Xtra Mile XMR108*	58		
17 Sep 05	**KEEP IT TO YOURSELF** *Xtra Mile XMR109*	62		

REUNION US group

Date	Title / Label	Peak	Wks No.1	Wks Top 40
21 Sep 74	**LIFE IS A ROCK (BUT THE RADIO ROLLED ME)** *RCA PB 10056*	33		3

REVELATION UK production group

Date	Title / Label	Peak	Wks No.1	Wks Top 40
10 May 03	**JUST BE DUB TO ME** *Multiply CDMULTY99*	36		1

REVEREND & THE MAKERS UK group

Date	Title / Label	Peak	Wks No.1	Wks Top 40
19 May 07	**HEAVYWEIGHT CHAMPION OF THE WORLD** *Wall Of Sound WOS009CD*	8		10
8 Sep 07	**HE SAID HE LOVED ME** *Wall Of Sound WOS014CD*	16		4
1 Dec 07	**OPEN YOUR WINDOW** *Wall Of Sound WOS020CD*	65		

REVIVAL 3000 UK production group

Date	Title / Label	Peak	Wks No.1	Wks Top 40
1 Nov 97	**THE MIGHTY HIGH** *Hi-Life 5718092*	47		

REVOLTING COCKS US group

Date	Title / Label	Peak	Wks No.1	Wks Top 40
18 Sep 93	**DA YA THINK I'M SEXY** *Devotion CDDVN 111*	61		

DEBBIE REYNOLDS US singer

Date	Title / Label	Peak	Wks No.1	Wks Top 40
30 Aug 57	**TAMMY** *Coral Q 72274* ★	2		17

JODY REYNOLDS US singer

Date	Title / Label	Peak	Wks No.1	Wks Top 40
14 Apr 79	**ENDLESS SLEEP** *Lightning LIG 9015*	66		

LJ REYNOLDS US singer

Date	Title / Label	Peak	Wks No.1	Wks Top 40
30 Jun 84	**DON'T LET NOBODY HOLD YOU DOWN** *Club JAB 5*	53		

REYNOLDS GIRLS UK duo

Date	Title / Label	Peak	Wks No.1	Wks Top 40
25 Feb 89	**I'D RATHER JACK** *PWL 25*	8		8

REZILLOS UK group

Date	Title / Label	Peak	Wks No.1	Wks Top 40
12 Aug 78	**TOP OF THE POPS** *Sire SIR 4001*	17		7
25 Nov 78	**DESTINATION VENUS** *Sire SIR 4008*	43		
18 Aug 79	**I WANNA BE YOUR MAN/I CAN'T STAND MY BABY** *Sensible SAB 1*	71		
26 Jan 80	**MOTORBIKE BEAT** *Dindisc DIN 5* REVILLOS	45		

REZONANCE Q UK production duo

Date	Title / Label	Peak	Wks No.1	Wks Top 40
1 Mar 03	**SOMEDAY** *All Around The World CXGLOBE 266*	29		1

RHAPSODY US group

Date	Title / Label	Peak	Wks No.1	Wks Top 40
10 Jan 98	**PRINCE IGOR** *Def Jam 5749652* RHAPSODY FEATURING WARREN G & SISSEL	15		5

RHC Belgian duo

Date	Title / Label	Peak	Wks No.1	Wks Top 40
11 Jan 92	**FEVER CALLED LOVE** *R&S RSUK 9*	65		

RHIANNA UK singer

Date	Title / Label	Peak	Wks No.1	Wks Top 40
1 Jun 02	**OH BABY** *Sony S2 6726232*	18		3
14 Sep 02	**WORD LOVE** *Sony S2 6730115*	41		

RHODA WITH THE SPECIAL A.K.A. UK singer with group

Date	Title / Label	Peak	Wks No.1	Wks Top 40
23 Jan 82	**THE BOILER** *2 Tone CHSTT 18*	35		2

RHYMEFEST US rapper

Date	Title / Label	Peak	Wks No.1	Wks Top 40
25 Feb 06	**BRAND NEW** *J Records 82876778842* RHYMEFEST FEATURING KANYE WEST	32		1

BUSTA RHYMES US rapper

Date	Title / Label	Peak	Wks No.1	Wks Top 40
11 May 96	**WOO-HAH!! GOT YOU ALL IN CHECK** *Elektra EKR 220CD*	8		4
21 Sep 96	**IT'S A PARTY** *Elektra EKR 226CD* BUSTA RHYMES FEATURING ZHANE	23		1
5 Apr 97	**HIT 'EM HIGH (THE MONSTARS' ANTHEM)** *Atlantic A 5449CD* B REAL/BUSTA RHYMES/COOLIO/LL COOL J/METHOD MAN	8		4
3 May 97	**DO MY THING** *Elektra EKR 235CD*	39		1
18 Oct 97	**PUT YOUR HANDS WHERE MY EYES COULD SEE** *Elektra E 3900CD*	16		2
20 Dec 97	**DANGEROUS** *Elektra E 3877CD*	32		1
18 Apr 98	**TURN IT UP/FIRE IT UP** *Elektra E 3847CD* ○	2		7
11 Jul 98	**ONE** *Elektra E 3833CD1* BUSTA RHYMES FEATURING ERYKAH BADU	23		1
30 Jan 99	**GIMME SOME MORE** *Elektra E 3782CD*	5		3
1 May 99	**WHAT'S IT GONNA BE?!** *Elektra E 3762CD1* BUSTA RHYMES FEATURING JANET	6		5
22 Jul 00	**GET OUT** *Elektra E 7075CD*	57		
16 Dec 00	**FIRE** *East West E 7136CD*	60		
18 Aug 01	**ANTE UP** *Epic 6717882* M.O.P. FEATURING BUSTA RHYMES	7		4
16 Mar 02	**BREAK YA NECK** *J Records 74321922332*	11		4
8 Jun 02	**PASS THE COURVOISIER – PART II** *J Records 74321937902* BUSTA RHYMES, P DIDDY & PHARRELL	16		3
8 Feb 03	**MAKE IT CLAP** *J Records 82876502062* BUSTA RHYMES FEATURING SPLIFF STAR	16		2
7 Jun 03	**I KNOW WHAT YOU WANT** *J Records 82876528292*	3		11
29 Nov 03	**LIGHT YOUR ASS ON FIRE** *Arista 82876572512* BUSTA RHYMES FEATURING PHARRELL	62		
15 May 04	**PASS THE COURVOISIER – PART II** *J Records 74321937902* BUSTA RHYMES, P DIDDY & PHARRELL	71		
22 May 04	**WHAT'S HAPPENIN'** *Def Jam 9862518* METHOD MAN FEATURING BUSTA RHYMES	17		3
10 Sep 05	**DON'T CHA (IMPORT)** *Polydor AMB000468322* PUSSYCAT DOLLS FEATURING BUSTA RHYMES	44		
17 Sep 05	**DON'T CHA** *A&M/Polydor 9885052* PUSSYCAT DOLLS FEATURING BUSTA RHYMES ○	1	3	23
20 May 06	**TOUCH IT** *Interscope 9855966*	6		7
15 Jul 06	**I LOVE MY CHICK** *Interscope 1702859*	8		7

DYLAN RHYMES UK producer

Date	Title / Label	Peak	Wks No.1	Wks Top 40
29 Jan 05	**SALTY** *Kingsize KS093D1* DYLAN RHYMES FEATURING KATHERINE ELLIS	70		

RHYTHIM IS RHYTHIM US producer

Date	Title	Peak Position	Weeks at No.1	Weeks in Top 40
11 Nov 89	**STRINGS OF LIFE** *Kool Kat KOOL 509*	74		

RHYTHM ETERNITY UK group

Date	Title	Peak Position	Weeks at No.1	Weeks in Top 40
23 May 92	**PINK CHAMPAGNE** *Dead Dead Good GOOD 15T*	72		

RHYTHM FACTOR UK group

Date	Title	Peak Position	Weeks at No.1	Weeks in Top 40
29 Apr 95	**YOU BRING ME JOY** *Multiply CDMULTY 4*	53		

RHYTHM MASTERS UK/Maltese production duo

Date	Title	Peak Position	Weeks at No.1	Weeks in Top 40
16 Aug 97	**COME ON YALL** *Faze 2 CDFAZE 37*	49		
6 Dec 97	**ENTER THE SCENE** *Distinctive DISNCD 40* DJ SUPREME VS THE RHYTHM MASTERS	49		
18 Aug 01	**UNDERGROUND** *Black & Blue NEOCD 056*	50		
30 Mar 02	**GHETTO** *Black & Blue NEOCD 074* RHYTHM MASTERS FEATURING JOE WATSON	71		

RHYTHM-N-BASS UK group

Date	Title	Peak Position	Weeks at No.1	Weeks in Top 40
19 Sep 92	**ROSES** *Epic 6582907*	56		
3 Jul 93	**CAN'T STOP THIS FEELING** *Epic 6592002*	59		

RHYTHM OF LIFE UK producer

Date	Title	Peak Position	Weeks at No.1	Weeks in Top 40
13 May 00	**YOU PUT ME IN HEAVEN WITH YOUR TOUCH** *Xtravaganza XTRAV 4CDS*	24		1

RHYTHM ON THE LOOSE UK producer

Date	Title	Peak Position	Weeks at No.1	Weeks in Top 40
19 Aug 95	**BREAK OF DAWN** *Six6 SIXCD 126*	36		1

RHYTHM QUEST UK producer

Date	Title	Peak Position	Weeks at No.1	Weeks in Top 40
20 Jun 92	**CLOSER TO ALL YOUR DREAMS** *Network NWK 40*	45		

RHYTHM SECTION UK group

Date	Title	Peak Position	Weeks at No.1	Weeks in Top 40
18 Jul 92	**MIDSUMMER MADNESS (EP)** *Rhythm Section RSEC 006*	66		

RHYTHM SOURCE UK group

Date	Title	Peak Position	Weeks at No.1	Weeks in Top 40
17 Jun 95	**LOVE SHINE** *A&M 5810672*	74		

RHYTHMATIC UK duo

Date	Title	Peak Position	Weeks at No.1	Weeks in Top 40
12 May 90	**TAKE ME BACK** *Network NWK 8*	71		
3 Nov 90	**FREQUENCY** *Network NWK 13*	62		

RHYTHMATIC JUNKIES UK production group

Date	Title	Peak Position	Weeks at No.1	Weeks in Top 40
15 May 99	**THE FEELIN (CLAP YOUR HANDS)** *Sound Of Ministry RIDE 2CDS*	67		

RHYTHMKILLAZ Dutch production duo

Date	Title	Peak Position	Weeks at No.1	Weeks in Top 40
31 Mar 01	**WACK ASS MF** *Incentive CENT 18CDS*	32		1

RIALTO UK group

Date	Title	Peak Position	Weeks at No.1	Weeks in Top 40
8 Nov 97	**MONDAY MORNING 5:19** *East West EW 116CD*	37		1
17 Jan 98	**UNTOUCHABLE** *East West EW 107CD1*	20		2
28 Mar 98	**DREAM ANOTHER DREAM** *East West EW 156CD1*	39		1
17 Oct 98	**SUMMER'S OVER** *China WOKCDR 2099*	60		

ROSIE RIBBONS UK singer

Date	Title	Peak Position	Weeks at No.1	Weeks in Top 40
2 Nov 02	**BLINK** *T2 CDSTAS 3288*	12		2
25 Jan 03	**A LITTLE BIT** *T2 CDSTAS 3312*	19		2

DAMIEN RICE Irish singer/guitarist

Date	Title	Peak Position	Weeks at No.1	Weeks in Top 40
1 Nov 03	**CANNONBALL** *DRM/14th Floor DR03CD1*	32		1
17 Jul 04	**CANNONBALL** *DRM/14th Floor DR03CD1*	19		5
25 Dec 04	**THE BLOWER'S DAUGHTER** *14th Floor DR06CD1*	27		2
2 Apr 05	**VOLCANO** *DRM/14th Floor DR07CD1*	29		1
2 Jul 05	**UNPLAYED PIANO** *DRM/14th Floor DR08CD* DAMIEN RICE & LISA HANNIGAN	24		1
2 Dec 06	**9 CRIMES** *DRM/14th Floor DR09CD*	29		1
17 Feb 07	**ROOTLESS TREE** *Heffa/14th Floor DR10CD*	50		

REVA RICE & GREG ELLIS UK duo

Date	Title	Peak Position	Weeks at No.1	Weeks in Top 40
27 Mar 93	**NEXT TIME YOU FALL IN LOVE** *Really Useful RURCD 12*	59		

CHARLIE RICH US singer

Date	Title	Peak Position	Weeks at No.1	Weeks in Top 40
16 Feb 74	**THE MOST BEAUTIFUL GIRL** *CBS 1897* ★	2		12
13 Apr 74	**BEHIND CLOSED DOORS** *Epic EPC 1539*	16		8
1 Feb 75	**WE LOVE EACH OTHER** *Epic EPC 2868*	37		1

RICHIE RICH UK singer

Date	Title	Peak Position	Weeks at No.1	Weeks in Top 40
16 Jul 88	**TURN IT UP** *Club JAR 68*	48		
22 Oct 88	**I'LL HOUSE YOU** *Gee Street GEE 003* RICHIE RICH MEETS THE JUNGLE BROTHERS	22		3
10 Dec 88	**MY DJ (PUMP IT UP SOME)** *Gee Street GEE 7*	74		
2 Sep 89	**SALSA HOUSE** *ffrr F 113*	50		
9 Mar 91	**YOU USED TO SALSA** *ffrr F 156* RICHIE RICH FEATURING RALPHI ROSARIO	52		
29 Mar 97	**STAY WITH ME** *Castle CATX 1001* RICHIE RICH & ESERA TUAOLO	58		

RISHI RICH PROJECT UK producer

Date	Title	Peak Position	Weeks at No.1	Weeks in Top 40
20 Sep 03	**DANCE WITH YOU (NACHNA TERE NAAL)** *Relentless RELCD1* RISHI RICH PROJECT FEATURING JAY SEAN	12		3
3 Jul 04	**EYES ON YOU** *Relentless RELDX5* JAY SEAN FEATURING RISHI RICH PROJECT	6		8

TONY RICH PROJECT US singer

Date	Title	Peak Position	Weeks at No.1	Weeks in Top 40
4 May 96	**NOBODY KNOWS** *LaFace 74321356422*	4		15
31 Aug 96	**LIKE A WOMAN** *LaFace 74321401612*	27		2
14 Dec 96	**LEAVIN'** *LaFace 74321438382*	52		

RICH KIDS UK group

Date	Title	Peak Position	Weeks at No.1	Weeks in Top 40
28 Jan 78	**RICH KIDS** *EMI 2738*	24		5

CLIFF RICHARD UK singer

Date	Title	Peak Position	Weeks at No.1	Weeks in Top 40
12 Sep 58	**MOVE IT** *Columbia DB 4178* CLIFF RICHARD & THE DRIFTERS	2		17
21 Nov 58	**HIGH CLASS BABY** *Columbia DB 4203* CLIFF RICHARD & THE DRIFTERS	7		10
30 Jan 59	**LIVIN' LOVIN' DOLL** *Columbia DB 4249* CLIFF RICHARD & THE DRIFTERS	20		6
8 May 59	**MEAN STREAK** *Columbia DB 4290* CLIFF RICHARD & THE DRIFTERS	10		9
15 May 59	**NEVER MIND** *Columbia DB 4290* CLIFF RICHARD & THE DRIFTERS	21		2
10 Jul 59	**LIVING DOLL** *Columbia DB 4306* CLIFF RICHARD & THE SHADOWS	1	6	23
9 Oct 59	**TRAVELLIN' LIGHT** *Columbia DB 4351* CLIFF RICHARD & THE SHADOWS	1	5	17
9 Oct 59	**DYNAMITE** *Columbia DB 4351* CLIFF RICHARD & THE SHADOWS	16		4
15 Jan 60	**EXPRESSO BONGO EP** *Columbia SEG 7971* CLIFF RICHARD & THE SHADOWS	14		7
22 Jan 60	**A VOICE IN THE WILDERNESS** *Columbia DB 4398* CLIFF RICHARD & THE SHADOWS	2		13
24 Mar 60	**FALL IN LOVE WITH YOU** *Columbia DB 4431* CLIFF RICHARD & THE SHADOWS	2		15
30 Jun 60	**PLEASE DON'T TEASE** *Columbia DB 4479* CLIFF RICHARD & THE SHADOWS	1	4	18
22 Sep 60	**NINE TIMES OUT OF TEN** *Columbia DB 4506* CLIFF RICHARD & THE SHADOWS	3		12
1 Dec 60	**I LOVE YOU** *Columbia DB 4547* CLIFF RICHARD & THE SHADOWS	1	2	15

		Peak Position	Weeks at No.1	Weeks in Top 40
2 Mar 61	**THEME FOR A DREAM** *Columbia DB 4593* CLIFF RICHARD & THE SHADOWS	3		13
30 Mar 61	**GEE WHIZ IT'S YOU** *Columbia DC 756* CLIFF RICHARD & THE SHADOWS	4		13
22 Jun 61	**A GIRL LIKE YOU** *Columbia DB 4667* CLIFF RICHARD & THE SHADOWS	3		14
19 Oct 61	**WHEN THE GIRL IN YOUR ARMS IS THE GIRL IN YOUR HEART** *Columbia DB 4716*	3		13
11 Jan 62	**THE YOUNG ONES** *Columbia DB 4761* CLIFF RICHARD & THE SHADOWS	1	6	19
10 May 62	**I'M LOOKING OUT THE WINDOW/DO YOU WANNA DANCE** *Columbia DB 4828* CLIFF RICHARD & THE SHADOWS	2		15
6 Sep 62	**IT'LL BE ME** *Columbia DB 4886* CLIFF RICHARD & THE SHADOWS	2		11
6 Dec 62	**THE NEXT TIME/BACHELOR BOY** *Columbia DB 4950* CLIFF RICHARD & THE SHADOWS	1	3	16
21 Feb 63	**SUMMER HOLIDAY** *Columbia DB 4977* CLIFF RICHARD & THE SHADOWS	1	3	17
9 May 63	**LUCKY LIPS** *Columbia DB 7034* CLIFF RICHARD & THE SHADOWS	4		14
22 Aug 63	**IT'S ALL IN THE GAME** *Columbia DB 7089*	2		12
7 Nov 63	**DON'T TALK TO HIM** *Columbia DB 7150* CLIFF RICHARD & THE SHADOWS	2		13
6 Feb 64	**I'M THE LONELY ONE** *Columbia DB 7203* CLIFF RICHARD & THE SHADOWS	8		9
30 Apr 64	**CONSTANTLY** *Columbia DB 7272*	4		12
2 Jul 64	**ON THE BEACH** *Columbia DB 7305* CLIFF RICHARD & THE SHADOWS	7		12
8 Oct 64	**THE TWELFTH OF NEVER** *Columbia DB 7372*	8		9
10 Dec 64	**I COULD EASILY FALL (IN LOVE WITH YOU)** *Columbia DB 7420* CLIFF RICHARD & THE SHADOWS	6		10
11 Mar 65	**THE MINUTE YOU'RE GONE** *Columbia DB 7496*	1	1	13
10 Jun 65	**ON MY WORD** *Columbia DB 7596*	12		9
19 Aug 65	**THE TIME IN BETWEEN** *Columbia DB 7660* CLIFF RICHARD & THE SHADOWS	22		6
4 Nov 65	**WIND ME UP (LET ME GO)** *Columbia DB 7745*	2		15
24 Mar 66	**BLUE TURNS TO GREY** *Columbia DB 7866* CLIFF RICHARD & THE SHADOWS	15		8
21 Jul 66	**VISIONS** *Columbia DB 7968*	7		11
13 Oct 66	**TIME DRAGS BY** *Columbia DB 8017* CLIFF RICHARD & THE SHADOWS	10		10
15 Dec 66	**IN THE COUNTRY** *Columbia DB 8094* CLIFF RICHARD & THE SHADOWS	6		9
16 Mar 67	**IT'S ALL OVER** *Columbia DB 8150*	9		9
8 Jun 67	**I'LL COME RUNNING** *Columbia DB 8210*	26		6
16 Aug 67	**THE DAY I MET MARIE** *Columbia DB 8245*	10		13
15 Nov 67	**ALL MY LOVE** *Columbia DB 8293*	6		11
20 Mar 68	**CONGRATULATIONS** *Columbia DB 8376*	1	2	13
26 Jun 68	**I'LL LOVE YOU FOREVER TODAY** *Columbia DB 8437*	27		6
25 Sep 68	**MARIANNE** *Columbia DB 8476*	22		6
27 Nov 68	**DON'T FORGET TO CATCH ME** *Columbia DB 8503* CLIFF RICHARD & THE SHADOWS	21		7
26 Feb 69	**GOOD TIMES (BETTER TIMES)** *Columbia DB 8548*	12		11
28 May 69	**BIG SHIP** *Columbia DB 8581*	8		10
13 Sep 69	**THROW DOWN A LINE** *Columbia DB 8615* CLIFF RICHARD & HANK MARVIN	7		8
6 Dec 69	**WITH THE EYES OF A CHILD** *Columbia DB 8641*	20		4
21 Feb 70	**JOY OF LIVING** *Columbia DB 8657* CLIFF (Richard) & HANK (Marvin)	25		7
6 Jun 70	**GOODBYE SAM HELLO SAMANTHA** *Columbia DB 8685*	6		14
5 Sep 70	**I AIN'T GOT TIME ANYMORE** *Columbia DB 8708*	21		7
23 Jan 71	**SUNNY HONEY GIRL** *Columbia DB 8747*	19		8
10 Apr 71	**SILVERY RAIN** *Columbia DB 8774*	27		6
17 Jul 71	**FLYING MACHINE** *Columbia DB 8797*	37		1
13 Nov 71	**SING A SONG OF FREEDOM** *Columbia DB 8836*	13		10
11 Mar 72	**JESUS** *Columbia DB 8864*	35		3
26 Aug 72	**LIVING IN HARMONY** *Columbia DB 8917*	12		8
17 Mar 73	**POWER TO ALL OUR FRIENDS** *EMI 2012*	4		10
12 May 73	**HELP IT ALONG/TOMORROW RISING** *EMI 2022*	29		4
1 Dec 73	**TAKE ME HIGH** *EMI 2088*	27		10
18 May 74	**(YOU KEEP ME) HANGIN' ON** *EMI 2150*	13		7
7 Feb 76	**MISS YOU NIGHTS** *EMI 2376*	15		8
8 May 76	**DEVIL WOMAN** *EMI 2458*	9		7
21 Aug 76	**I CAN'T ASK FOR ANY MORE THAN YOU** *EMI 2499*	17		7
4 Dec 76	**HEY MR. DREAM MAKER** *EMI 2559*	31		3
5 Mar 77	**MY KINDA LIFE** *EMI 2584*	15		7
16 Jul 77	**WHEN TWO WORLDS DRIFT APART** *EMI 2633*	46		
31 Mar 79	**GREEN LIGHT** *EMI 2920*	57		
21 Jul 79	**WE DON'T TALK ANY MORE** *EMI 2975* ●	1	4	13
3 Nov 79	**HOT SHOT** *EMI 5003*	46		
2 Feb 80	**CARRIE** *EMI 5006* ○	4		7
16 Aug 80	**DREAMIN'** *EMI 5095* ○	8		8
25 Oct 80	**SUDDENLY** *Jet 7002* OLIVIA NEWTON-JOHN & CLIFF RICHARD	15		5
24 Jan 81	**A LITTLE IN LOVE** *EMI 5123*	15		7
29 Aug 81	**WIRED FOR SOUND** *EMI 5221* ○	4		8
21 Nov 81	**DADDY'S HOME** *EMI 5251* ●	2		11
17 Jul 82	**THE ONLY WAY OUT** *EMI 5318*	10		7
25 Sep 82	**WHERE DO WE GO FROM HERE** *EMI 5341*	60		
4 Dec 82	**LITTLE TOWN** *EMI 5348*	11		5
19 Feb 83	**SHE MEANS NOTHING TO ME** *Capitol CL 276* PHIL EVERLY & CLIFF RICHARD	9		7
16 Apr 83	**TRUE LOVE WAYS** *EMI 5385* CLIFF RICHARD WITH THE LONDON PHILHARMONIC ORCHESTRA	8		7
4 Jun 83	**DRIFTING** *DJM SHEILA 1* SHEILA WALSH & CLIFF RICHARD	64		
3 Sep 83	**NEVER SAY DIE (GIVE A LITTLE BIT MORE)** *EMI 5415*	15		6
26 Nov 83	**PLEASE DON'T FALL IN LOVE** *EMI 5437* ○	7		8
31 Mar 84	**BABY YOU'RE DYNAMITE/OCEAN DEEP** *EMI 5457*	27		3
3 Nov 84	**SHOOTING FROM THE HEART** *EMI RICH 1*	51		
9 Feb 85	**HEART USER** *EMI RICH 2*	46		
14 Sep 85	**SHE'S SO BEAUTIFUL** *EMI 5531*	17		8
7 Dec 85	**IT'S IN EVERY ONE OF US** *EMI 5537*	45		
22 Mar 86	**LIVING DOLL** *WEA YZ 65* CLIFF RICHARD & THE YOUNG ONES FEATURING HANK B MARVIN ●	1	3	9
4 Oct 86	**ALL I ASK OF YOU** *Polydor POSP 802* CLIFF RICHARD & SARAH BRIGHTMAN ○	3		14
29 Nov 86	**SLOW RIVERS** *Rocket EJS 13* ELTON JOHN & CLIFF RICHARD	44		
20 Jun 87	**MY PRETTY ONE** *EMI EM 4*	6		7
29 Aug 87	**SOME PEOPLE** *EMI EM 18* ○	3		9
31 Oct 87	**REMEMBER ME** *EMI EM 31*	35		3
13 Feb 88	**TWO HEARTS** *EMI EM 42*	34		1
3 Dec 88	**MISTLETOE AND WINE** *EMI EM 78* ●	1	4	7
10 Jun 89	**THE BEST OF ME** *EMI EM 78* ○	2		5
26 Aug 89	**I JUST DON'T HAVE THE HEART** *EMI EM 101* ○	3		6
14 Oct 89	**LEAN ON YOU** *EMI EM 105*	17		5
9 Dec 89	**WHENEVER GOD SHINES HIS LIGHT** *Polydor VANS 2* VAN MORRISON WITH CLIFF RICHARD	20		5
24 Feb 90	**STRONGER THAN THAT** *EMI EM 129*	14		3
25 Aug 90	**SILHOUETTES** *EMI EM 152*	10		5
13 Oct 90	**FROM A DISTANCE** *EMI EM 155*	11		4
8 Dec 90	**SAVIOUR'S DAY** *EMI XMAS 90* ○	1	1	6
14 Sep 91	**MORE TO LIFE** *EMI EM 205*	23		3
7 Dec 91	**WE SHOULD BE TOGETHER** *EMI XMAS 91*	10		5
11 Jan 92	**THIS NEW YEAR** *EMI EMS 216*	30		1
5 Dec 92	**I STILL BELIEVE IN YOU** *EMI EM 255*	7		5
27 Mar 93	**PEACE IN OUR TIME** *EMI CDEMS 265*	8		3
12 Jun 93	**HUMAN WORK OF ART** *EMI CDEMS 267*	24		2
2 Oct 93	**NEVER LET GO** *EMI CDEM 281*	32		1
18 Dec 93	**HEALING LOVE** *EMI CDEM 294*	19		3
10 Dec 94	**ALL I HAVE TO DO IS DREAM/MISS YOU NIGHTS** *EMI CDEMS 359* PHIL EVERLY & CLIFF RICHARD/CLIFF RICHARD	14		4
21 Oct 95	**MISUNDERSTOOD MAN** *EMI CDEM 394*	19		2
9 Dec 95	**HAD TO BE** *EMI CDEMS 410* CLIFF RICHARD & OLIVIA NEWTON-JOHN	22		1
30 Mar 96	**THE WEDDING** *EMI CDEM 422* CLIFF RICHARD FEATURING HELEN HOBSON	40		1
25 Jan 97	**BE WITH ME ALWAYS** *EMI CDEM 453*	52		
24 Oct 98	**CAN'T KEEP THIS FEELING IN** *EMI CDEM 526*	10		2
7 Aug 99	**THE MIRACLE** *Blacknight CDEM 546*	23		1
27 Nov 99	**THE MILLENNIUM PRAYER** *Papillon PROMISECD 01* ⊛	1	3	9
15 Dec 01	**SOMEWHERE OVER THE RAINBOW/WHAT A WONDERFUL WORLD** *Papillon CLIFFCX 1*	11		4
13 Apr 02	**LET ME BE THE ONE** *Papillon CLIFFCD 2*	29		2
20 Dec 03	**SANTA'S LIST** *EMI SANTA 02*	5		2
23 Oct 04	**SOMETHIN' IS GOIN' ON** *Decca/UCJ 4756419*	9		2
25 Dec 04	**I CANNOT GIVE YOU MY LOVE** *Decca/UCJ 4756611*	13		2
21 May 05	**WHAT CAR** *Decca/UCJ 4756943*	12		2
23 Dec 06	**21ST CENTURY CHRISTMAS/MOVE IT** *EMI 3799312*	2		2
10 Nov 07	**WHEN I NEED YOU** *EMI 5114522*	38		1
29 Dec 07	**MISTLETOE AND WINE** *Download*	68		

CALVIN RICHARDSON US singer

		Peak Position	Weeks at No.1	Weeks in Top 40
27 Mar 04	**I'VE GOT TO MOVE** *Hollywood HOL004CD*	74		

LIONEL RICHIE US singer

		Peak Position	Weeks at No.1	Weeks in Top 40
12 Sep 81	**ENDLESS LOVE** *Motown TMG 1240* DIANA ROSS & LIONEL RICHIE ★	7		9
20 Nov 82	**TRULY** *Motown TMG 1284* ○ ★	6		10
29 Jan 83	**YOU ARE** *Motown TMG 1290*	43		
7 May 83	**MY LOVE** *Motown TMG 1300*	70		
1 Oct 83	**ALL NIGHT LONG (ALL NIGHT)** *Motown TMG 1319* ★	2		12

Silver-selling ○ Gold-selling ● Platinum-selling ⊛ US No.1 ★ — Peak Position / Weeks at No.1 / Weeks in Top 40

Date	Title / Label	Peak Position	Weeks at No.1	Weeks in Top 40
3 Dec 83	**RUNNING WITH THE NIGHT** *Motown TMG 1324*	9		6
10 Mar 84	**HELLO** *Motown TMG 1330* ● ★	1	6	13
23 Jun 84	**STUCK ON YOU** *Motown TMG 1341*	12		10
20 Oct 84	**PENNY LOVER** *Motown TMG 1356*	18		6
16 Nov 85	**SAY YOU, SAY ME** *Motown ZB 40421* ★	8		10
26 Jul 86	**DANCING ON THE CEILING** *Motown LIO 1*	7		9
11 Oct 86	**LOVE WILL CONQUER ALL** *Motown LIO 2*	45		
20 Dec 86	**BALLERINA GIRL/DEEP RIVER WOMAN** *Motown LIO 3*	17		6
28 Mar 87	**SELA** *Motown LIO 4*	43		
9 May 92	**DO IT TO ME** *Motown TMG 1407*	33		3
22 Aug 92	**MY DESTINY** *Motown TMG 1408*	7		12
28 Nov 92	**LOVE OH LOVE** *Motown TMG 1413*	52		
6 Apr 96	**DON'T WANNA LOSE YOU** *Mercury MERDD 461*	17		2
23 Nov 96	**STILL IN LOVE** *Mercury MERDD 477*	66		
27 Jun 98	**CLOSEST THING TO HEAVEN** *Mercury 5661312*	26		1
21 Oct 00	**ANGEL** *Mercury 5726702*	18		3
23 Dec 00	**DON'T STOP THE MUSIC** *Mercury 5688992*	34		1
17 Mar 01	**TENDER HEART** *Mercury 5728462*	29		1
23 Jun 01	**I FORGOT** *Mercury 5729922*	34		1
26 Apr 03	**TO LOVE A WOMAN** *Mercury 0779082* LIONEL RICHIE FEATURING ENRIQUE IGLESIAS	19		3
20 Mar 04	**JUST FOR YOU** *Mercury 9862072*	20		2
30 Sep 06	**I CALL IT LOVE** *Def Jam 1707683*	45		

SHANE RICHIE UK singer

Date	Title / Label	Peak Position	Weeks at No.1	Weeks in Top 40
6 Dec 03	**I'M YOUR MAN** *BMG 82876576932* ●	2		9

JONATHAN RICHMAN & THE MODERN LOVERS US group

Date	Title / Label	Peak Position	Weeks at No.1	Weeks in Top 40
16 Jul 77	**ROADRUNNER** *Beserkley BZZ 1*	11		9
29 Oct 77	**EGYPTIAN REGGAE** *Beserkley BZZ 2* ○	5		11
21 Jan 78	**MORNING OF OUR LIVES** *Beserkley BZZ 7* MODERN LOVERS	29		4

ADAM RICKITT UK singer/actor

Date	Title / Label	Peak Position	Weeks at No.1	Weeks in Top 40
26 Jun 99	**I BREATHE AGAIN** *Polydor 5611862* ○	5		6
16 Oct 99	**EVERYTHING MY HEART DESIRES** *Polydor 5614492*	15		3
5 Feb 00	**BEST THING** *Polydor 5616142*	25		1

RICKY UK group

Date	Title / Label	Peak Position	Weeks at No.1	Weeks in Top 40
18 Sep 04	**THAT EXTRA MILE** *Garcia GARCIA005CD*	50		
5 Feb 05	**THE JOURNEY/STOP KNOCKING THE WALLS DOWN** *Beat Crazy BEAT001CD* AMSTERDAM/RICKY	32		1
1 Jul 06	**WE ARE ENGLAND** *Beat Crazy BEAT007CD*	54		

RIDE UK group

Date	Title / Label	Peak Position	Weeks at No.1	Weeks in Top 40
27 Jan 90	**RIDE (EP)** *Creation CRE 072T*	71		
14 Apr 90	**PLAY EP** *Creation CRE 077T2*	32		1
29 Sep 90	**FALL EP** *Creation CRE 075T*	34		2
16 Mar 91	**TODAY FOREVER** *Creation CRE 100T*	14		2
15 Feb 92	**LEAVE THEM ALL BEHIND** *Creation CRE 123T*	9		2
25 Apr 92	**TWISTERELLA** *Creation CRE 150T*	36		1
30 Apr 94	**BIRDMAN** *Creation CRESCD 155*	38		1
25 Jun 94	**HOW DOES IT FEEL TO FEEL** *Creation CRESCD 184*	58		
8 Oct 94	**I DON'T KNOW WHERE IT COMES FROM** *Creation CRESCD 189R*	46		
24 Feb 96	**BLACK NITE CRASH** *Creation CRESCD 199*	67		

RIDER & TERRY VENABLES
UK group with former footballer

Date	Title / Label	Peak Position	Weeks at No.1	Weeks in Top 40
1 Jun 02	**ENGLAND CRAZY** *East West EW 248CD*	46		

ANDREW RIDGELEY UK singer

Date	Title / Label	Peak Position	Weeks at No.1	Weeks in Top 40
31 Mar 90	**SHAKE** *Epic AJR 1*	58		

STAN RIDGWAY US singer

Date	Title / Label	Peak Position	Weeks at No.1	Weeks in Top 40
5 Jul 86	**CAMOUFLAGE** *IRS IRM 114*	4		9

RIFLES UK group

Date	Title / Label	Peak Position	Weeks at No.1	Weeks in Top 40
11 Jun 05	**WHEN I'M ALONE** *Xtra Mile XMR007CD*	64		
5 Nov 05	**LOCAL BOY** *Right Hook RHK001CD*	36		1
18 Mar 06	**REPEATED OFFENDER** *Red Ink 82876786922*	26		1
15 Jul 06	**SHE'S GOT STANDARDS** *Red Ink 82876856172*	32		1
28 Oct 06	**PEACE & QUIET** *Red Ink 82876897652*	48		

RIGHEIRA Italian group

Date	Title / Label	Peak Position	Weeks at No.1	Weeks in Top 40
24 Sep 83	**VAMOS A LA PLAYA** *A&M AM 137*	53		

RIGHT SAID FRED UK group

Date	Title / Label	Peak Position	Weeks at No.1	Weeks in Top 40
27 Jul 91	**I'M TOO SEXY** *Tug SNOG 1* ● ★	2		15
7 Dec 91	**DON'T TALK JUST KISS** *Tug SNOG 2* RIGHT SAID FRED, GUEST VOCALS: JOCELYN BROWN	3		9
21 Mar 92	**DEEPLY DIPPY** *Tug SNOG 3* ○	1	3	12
1 Aug 92	**THOSE SIMPLE THINGS/ WHAT A DAY FOR A DAYDREAM** *Tug SNOG 4*	29		3
27 Feb 93	**STICK IT OUT** *Tug CDCOMIC 1* RIGHT SAID FRED & FRIENDS	4		6
23 Oct 93	**BUMPED** *Tug CDSNOG 7*	32		3
18 Dec 93	**HANDS UP (4 LOVERS)** *Tug CDSNOG 8*	60		
19 Mar 94	**WONDERMAN** *Tug CDSNOG 9*	55		
13 Oct 01	**YOU'RE MY MATE** *Kingsize 74321895632*	18		4
12 May 07	**I'M TOO SEXY 2007** *Gut CDSNOG20*	56		

RIGHTEOUS BROTHERS US duo

Date	Title / Label	Peak Position	Weeks at No.1	Weeks in Top 40
14 Jan 65	**YOU'VE LOST THAT LOVIN' FEELIN'** *London HLU 9943* ★	1	2	10
12 Aug 65	**UNCHAINED MELODY** *London HL 9975*	14		11
13 Jan 66	**EBB TIDE** *London HL 10011*	48		
14 Apr 66	**(YOU'RE MY) SOUL AND INSPIRATION** *Verve VS 535* ★	15		9
10 Nov 66	**WHITE CLIFFS OF DOVER** *London HL 10086*	21		6
22 Dec 66	**ISLAND IN THE SUN** *Verve VS 547*	24		4
12 Feb 69	**YOU'VE LOST THAT LOVIN' FEELIN'** *London HL 10241*	10		11
19 Nov 77	**YOU'VE LOST THAT LOVIN' FEELIN'** *Phil Spector International 2010 022*	42		
27 Oct 90	**UNCHAINED MELODY** *Verve/Polydor PO 101* ⊛	1	4	12
15 Dec 90	**YOU'VE LOST THAT LOVIN' FEELIN'/EBB TIDE** *Verve/Polydor PO 116*	3		7

RIHANNA Barbadian singer

Date	Title / Label	Peak Position	Weeks at No.1	Weeks in Top 40
3 Sep 05	**PON DE REPLAY** *Def Jam 9884878*	2		8
10 Dec 05	**IF IT'S LOVIN' THAT YOU WANT** *Def Jam 9888412*	11		5
22 Apr 06	**SOS** *Def Jam 9877821* ★	2		13
22 Jul 06	**UNFAITHFUL** *Def Jam 1702249*	2		12
28 Oct 06	**WE RIDE** *Def Jam 1709084*	17		2
26 May 07	**UMBRELLA** *Def Jam 1735491* RIHANNA FEATURING JAY-Z ○ ★	1	10	35
28 Jul 07	**SHUT UP AND DRIVE** *Def Jam 1746118*	5		14
20 Oct 07	**HATE THAT I LOVE YOU** *Def Jam 1751369* RIHANNA FEATURING NE-YO	15		15
15 Dec 07	**DON'T STOP THE MUSIC** *Def Jam 1762161* ○	4		15

RIKKI & DAZ UK production duo

Date	Title / Label	Peak Position	Weeks at No.1	Weeks in Top 40
30 Nov 02	**RHINESTONE COWBOY (GIDDY UP GIDDY UP)** *Serious SER 059CD* RIKKI & DAZ FEATURING GLEN CAMPBELL	12		3

CHERYL PEPSII RILEY US singer

Date	Title / Label	Peak Position	Weeks at No.1	Weeks in Top 40
28 Jan 89	**THANKS FOR MY CHILD** *CBS 6531537*	75		

JEANNIE C. RILEY US singer

Date	Title / Label	Peak Position	Weeks at No.1	Weeks in Top 40
16 Oct 68	**HARPER VALLEY P.T.A.** *Polydor 56 748* ★	12		14

TEDDY RILEY US singer/producer

Date	Title / Label	Peak Position	Weeks at No.1	Weeks in Top 40
21 Mar 92	**IS IT GOOD TO YOU** *MCA MCS 1611* TEDDY RILEY FEATURING TAMMY LUCAS	53		
19 Jun 93	**BABY BE MINE** *MCA MCSTD 1772* BLACKstreet FEATURING TEDDY RILEY	37		1

RIHANNA

Robyn Rihanna Fenty was born 18 February 1988, in St Michael's Parish on the West Indies island of Barbados. The child of an accountant mother and warehouse supervisor father, her famed good looks come from her parents' mixed Barbadian and Guyanese heritage. A young woman of startling beauty with piercing green eyes, she had already won the local school beauty pageant by the age of sixteen, yet has described herself as something of a tomboy, most happy fooling around with her two younger brothers and thirteen male cousins. The liberal clubbing laws of Barbados allowed her to immerse herself in the club scene as early as fourteen and her youthful vocals were honed on a diet of R&B divas like Mariah Carey, and reggae music, as well the more obvious dancehall influences of her home town.

Urban legend has it that Rihanna was discovered by hip-hop master Jay-Z, some laughable anecdotes even suggesting he was on holiday in Barbados when he heard her singing on a beach. This would make great reading, but the truth is rather more prosaic. Producers Evan Rogers and Carl Sturken – who previously had brought us *N Sync's slush-fest 'God Must Have Spent A Little More Time On You' as well as working on tracks by Jessica Simpson and Christina Aguilera – were her route to fame. Rogers was on holiday in Barbados with his wife, who had been born there, and a friend of Rihanna's introduced them. By then, Rihanna had formed a girl group with two classmates and they auditioned for Rogers, where he immediately saw her talent and potential. He arranged for her to travel to New York where she recorded a four-song demo and then set about playing that tape to various record business executives. Meanwhile, he put her up in his family house and kept a watchful eye over the West Indian teenager a long way from home.

Jay-Z was handed her demo in the normal course of business and liked what he heard – a lot. He summoned her to his office for a meeting and there she sang a few songs unaccompanied. She later admitted to physically shaking while waiting to go into the room; he later admitted he knew she was a mega-star within two minutes of meeting her. He was clearly blown away by her a cappella performance as he insisted she didn't leave his office until the ink had dried on a recording contract, which it did twelve hours later. She was only sixteen.

Her debut single (a Number 2 single in the UK) was the addictive 'Pon De Replay', at that stage a pretty straight dancehall-flavoured piece that Rihanna herself did not not initially like; both that and the later hit single 'SOS' were penned by her champions, Rogers and Sturken. The debut album *Music Of The Sun* was more patchy, which may explain why the follow-up long player, *A Girl Like Me*, was released only eight months after her first record had hit the streets. This time, however, her growing confidence and a live show that was accomplished beyond her years, combined with songs such as 'Unfaithful' met with more critical acclaim (although still a little mixed) and healthy chart performances.

Her third album, *Good Girl Gone Bad*, was a stark, more obviously commercial departure from her first two albums and saw her profile click up another notch, with appearances on that record from Justin Timberlake, Ne-Yo and Timbaland. Gone was the innocent girl from Barbados, replaced by a sophisticated young woman with a powerful and textured vocal range (and, after being awarded the 'Celebrity Legs of a Goddess' accolade she insured them for $1 million). However, it was the hit Number 1 single, 'Umbrella' that cemented her place on the modern pop pantheon. It was perhaps the summer single of 2007, hitting the top of the charts in the UK for ten weeks as well as many other countries, going on to sell over 558,000 copies in the UK alone. Then, in February 2008, she scooped her first Grammy for 'Best Rap/Sung Collaboration' for her work with Jay-Z on the single. Later single releases were also very strong – the Number 1 'Take A Bow' and 'Hate That I Love You' being obvious cases – although it may well be that 'Umbrella' becomes her signature career tune. Her US success is startling – to date eleven Number 1s – but her UK triumphs are equally impressive. With a highly lucrative cosmetics contract in place and rumours of her own fashion range to follow, Rihanna's impact on the charts is surely only just beginning.

Silver-selling ○ Gold-selling ● Platinum-selling ⊛ US No.1 ★ | Peak Position | Weeks at No.1 | Weeks in Top 40

RIMES UK rapper

Date	Title	Peak Position	Weeks at No.1	Weeks in Top 40
22 May 99	**IT'S OVER** *Universal MCSTD 40199* RIMES FEATURING SHAILA PROSPERE	51		

LeANN RIMES US singer

Date	Title	Peak Position	Weeks at No.1	Weeks in Top 40
7 Mar 98	**HOW DO I LIVE** *Curb CUBCX 30* ⊛	7		30
12 Sep 98	**LOOKING THROUGH YOUR EYES/COMMITMENT** *Curb CUBC 32*	38		1
12 Dec 98	**BLUE** *Curb CUBC 39*	23		4
6 Mar 99	**WRITTEN IN THE STARS** *Mercury EJSDD 45* ELTON JOHN & LeANN RIMES	10		3
18 Dec 99	**CRAZY** *Curb CUBC 52*	36		1
25 Nov 00	**CAN'T FIGHT THE MOONLIGHT** *Curb CUBCX 58* ●	1	1	13
31 Mar 01	**I NEED YOU** *Curb CUBCX 60*	13		4
23 Feb 02	**BUT I DO LOVE YOU** *Curb CUBC 075*	20		2
12 Oct 02	**LIFE GOES ON** *Curb CUBCX 085*	11		5
8 Mar 03	**SUDDENLY** *Curb CUBC 088*	47		
23 Aug 03	**WE CAN** *Curb CUBC 092*	27		1
14 Feb 04	**THIS LOVE** *Curb CUNC 096*	54		
15 May 04	**LAST THING ON MY MIND** *Polydor/Curb 9866595* RONAN KEATING & LeANN RIMES	5		5
10 Jun 06	**AND IT FEELS LIKE** *Curb/London CUBC122*	22		1
7 Oct 06	**EVERYBODY'S SOMEONE** *Curb/London CUBC128* LeANN RIMES & BRIAN McFADDEN	48		
6 Oct 07	**NOTHIN' BETTER TO DO** *Curb CUBC145*	48		

RIMSHOTS US group

Date	Title	Peak Position	Weeks at No.1	Weeks in Top 40
19 Jul 75	**7-6-5-4-3-2-1 (BLOW YOUR WHISTLE)** *All Platinum 6146 304*	26		4

RIO & MARS French/UK duo

Date	Title	Peak Position	Weeks at No.1	Weeks in Top 40
28 Jan 95	**BOY I GOTTA HAVE YOU** *Dome CDDOME 1014*	43		
13 Apr 96	**BOY I GOTTA HAVE YOU** *Feverpitch CDFVR 1007*	46		

MIGUEL RIOS Spanish singer

Date	Title	Peak Position	Weeks at No.1	Weeks in Top 40
11 Jul 70	**SONG OF JOY** *A&M AMS 790*	16		9

RIOT ACT US group

Date	Title	Peak Position	Weeks at No.1	Weeks in Top 40
4 Jun 05	**CALIFORNIA SOUL** *Nebula NEBCD070*	59		

RIP PRODUCTIONS UK production group

Date	Title	Peak Position	Weeks at No.1	Weeks in Top 40
29 Nov 97	**THE CHANT (WE R)/RIP PRODUCTIONS** *Satellite 74321534022*	50		

MINNIE RIPERTON US singer

Date	Title	Peak Position	Weeks at No.1	Weeks in Top 40
12 Apr 75	**LOVING YOU** *Epic EPC 3121* ○ ★	2		9

RISE UK production duo

Date	Title	Peak Position	Weeks at No.1	Weeks in Top 40
3 Sep 94	**THE SINGLE** *East West YZ 839CD*	70		

RITCHIE FAMILY US group

Date	Title	Peak Position	Weeks at No.1	Weeks in Top 40
23 Aug 75	**BRAZIL** *Polydor 2058 625*	41		
18 Sep 76	**THE BEST DISCO IN TOWN** *Polydor 2058 777*	10		9
17 Feb 79	**AMERICAN GENERATION** *Mercury 6007 199*	49		

LEE RITENOUR & MAXI PRIEST

US guitarist & UK singer

Date	Title	Peak Position	Weeks at No.1	Weeks in Top 40
31 Jul 93	**WAITING IN VAIN** *GRP MCSTD 1921*	65		

RITMO-DYNAMIC French producer

Date	Title	Peak Position	Weeks at No.1	Weeks in Top 40
15 Nov 03	**CALINDA** *Xtravaganza XTRAV42CDS*	68		

TEX RITTER US singer

Date	Title	Peak Position	Weeks at No.1	Weeks in Top 40
22 Jun 56	**WAYWARD WIND** *Capitol CL 14581*	8		14

RIVAL SCHOOLS US group

Date	Title	Peak Position	Weeks at No.1	Weeks in Top 40
30 Mar 02	**USED FOR GLUE** *Mercury 5889652*	42		
20 Jul 02	**GOOD THINGS** *Mercury 5829662*	74		

RIVER CITY PEOPLE UK group

Date	Title	Peak Position	Weeks at No.1	Weeks in Top 40
12 Aug 89	**(WHAT'S WRONG WITH) DREAMING** *EMI EM 95*	70		
3 Mar 90	**WALKING ON ICE** *EMI EM 130*	62		
30 Jun 90	**CARRY THE BLAME/CALIFORNIA DREAMIN'** *EMI EM 145*	13		8
22 Sep 90	**(WHAT'S WRONG WITH) DREAMING** *EMI EM 156*	40		1
2 Mar 91	**WHEN I WAS YOUNG** *EMI EM 176*	62		
28 Sep 91	**SPECIAL WAY** *EMI EM 207*	44		
22 Feb 92	**STANDING IN THE NEED OF LOVE** *EMI EM 216*	36		1

RIVER DETECTIVES UK duo

Date	Title	Peak Position	Weeks at No.1	Weeks in Top 40
29 Jul 89	**CHAINS** *WEA YZ 383*	51		

RIVER OCEAN US producer

Date	Title	Peak Position	Weeks at No.1	Weeks in Top 40
26 Feb 94	**LOVE AND HAPPINESS (YEMAYA Y OCHUN)** *Cooltempo CDCOOL 287* RIVER OCEAN FEATURING INDIA	50		

ROBBIE RIVERA Italian DJ

Date	Title	Peak Position	Weeks at No.1	Weeks in Top 40
2 Sep 00	**BANG** *Multiply CDMULTY 64* ROBBIE RIVERA PRESENTS RHYTHM BANGERS	13		2
12 Oct 02	**SEX** *352 Recordings 352 CD001* ROBBIE RIVERA FEATURING BILLY PAUL W	55		

SANDY RIVERA US producer

Date	Title	Peak Position	Weeks at No.1	Weeks in Top 40
18 Jan 03	**CHANGES** *Defected DFTD 059R* SANDY RIVERA FEATURING HAZE	48		
5 Apr 03	**I CAN'T STOP** *Defected DFTD 063R*	58		
5 May 07	**LOLLIPOP** *Data DATA158CDS* DADA FEATURING SANDY RIVERA & TRIX	18		2

DANNY RIVERS UK singer

Date	Title	Peak Position	Weeks at No.1	Weeks in Top 40
12 Jan 61	**CAN'T YOU HEAR MY HEART** *Decca F 11294*	36		1

RM PROJECT UK/Maltese production duo

Date	Title	Peak Position	Weeks at No.1	Weeks in Top 40
3 Jul 99	**GET IT UP** *Inferno CDFERN 15*	49		

RMXCRW Dutch production duo

Date	Title	Peak Position	Weeks at No.1	Weeks in Top 40
17 Jan 04	**TURN ME ON** *Digi Dance 871486697203* RMXCRW FEATURING EBON-E PLUS AMBUSH	52		

ROACH MOTEL UK duo

Date	Title	Peak Position	Weeks at No.1	Weeks in Top 40
21 Aug 93	**AFRO SLEEZE/TRANSATLANTIC** *Junior Boy's Own JBO 1412*	73		
10 Dec 94	**HAPPY BIZZNESS/WILD LUV** *Junior Boy's Own JBO 24*	75		

ROACHFORD UK group

Date	Title	Peak Position	Weeks at No.1	Weeks in Top 40
18 Jun 88	**CUDDLY TOY** *CBS ROA 2*	61		
14 Jan 89	**CUDDLY TOY** *CBS ROA 4*	4		8
18 Mar 89	**FAMILY MAN** *CBS ROA 5*	25		3
1 Jul 89	**KATHLEEN** *CBS ROA 6*	43		
13 Apr 91	**GET READY!** *Columbia 6567057*	22		5
19 Mar 94	**ONLY TO BE WITH YOU** *Columbia 6601562*	21		5
18 Jun 94	**LAY YOUR LOVE ON ME** *Columbia 6603722*	36		1
20 Aug 94	**THIS GENERATION** *Columbia 6607452*	38		1
3 Dec 94	**CRY FOR ME** *Columbia 6610742*	46		
1 Apr 95	**I KNOW YOU DON'T LOVE ME** *Columbia 6612525*	42		
11 Oct 97	**THE WAY I FEEL** *Columbia 6650142*	20		3
14 Feb 98	**HOW COULD I? (INSECURITY)** *Columbia 6653462*	34		1
11 Jul 98	**NAKED WITHOUT YOU** *Columbia 6659362*	53		

ROB 'N' RAZ Swedish production duo

Date	Title	Peak Position	Weeks at No.1	Weeks in Top 40
25 Nov 89	**GOT TO GET** *Arista 112696* ROB 'N' RAZ FEATURING LEILA K	8		11
17 Mar 90	**ROK THE NATION** *Arista 112971* ROB 'N' RAZ FEATURING LEILA K	41		

KATE ROBBINS & BEYOND UK singer/actress

Date	Title	Peak Position	Weeks at No.1	Weeks in Top 40
30 May 81	**MORE THAN IN LOVE** *RCA 69* ●	2		9

MARTY ROBBINS US singer

Date	Title	Peak Position	Weeks at No.1	Weeks in Top 40
29 Jan 60	**EL PASO** *Fontana H 233* ★	19		7
26 May 60	**BIG IRON** *Fontana H 229*	48		
27 Sep 62	**DEVIL WOMAN** *CBS AAG 114*	5		16
17 Jan 63	**RUBY ANN** *CBS AAG 128*	24		4

AUSTIN ROBERTS US singer

Date	Title	Peak Position	Weeks at No.1	Weeks in Top 40
25 Oct 75	**ROCKY** *Private Stock PVT 33*	22		5

JOE ROBERTS UK singer

Date	Title	Peak Position	Weeks at No.1	Weeks in Top 40
28 Aug 93	**BACK IN MY LIFE** *ffrr FCD 215*	59		
29 Jan 94	**LOVER** *ffrr FCD 220*	22		4
14 May 94	**BACK IN MY LIFE** *ffrr FCD 230*	39		2
6 Aug 94	**ADORE** *ffrr FCD 240*	45		
18 Feb 95	**YOU ARE EVERYTHING** *Columbia 6611755* MELANIE WILLIAMS & JOE ROBERTS	28		2
24 Feb 96	**HAPPY DAYS** *Grass Green GRASS 10CD* SWEET MERCY FEATURING JOE ROBERTS	63		

JULIET ROBERTS UK singer

Date	Title	Peak Position	Weeks at No.1	Weeks in Top 40
31 Jul 93	**CAUGHT IN THE MIDDLE** *Cooltempo CDCOOL 272*	24		5
6 Nov 93	**FREE LOVE** *Cooltempo CDCOOL 281*	25		1
19 Mar 94	**AGAIN/I WANT YOU** *Cooltempo CDCOOL 285*	33		2
2 Jul 94	**CAUGHT IN THE MIDDLE (REMIX)** *Cooltempo CDCOOL 291*	14		3
15 Oct 94	**I WANT YOU** *Cooltempo CDCOOL 297*	28		1
31 Jan 98	**SO GOOD/FREE LOVE 98 (REMIX)** *Delirious 74321554002*	15		2
23 Jan 99	**BAD GIRLS/I LIKE** *Delirious DELICD 11*	17		3
20 Jan 01	**NEEDIN' U II (REMIX)** *Manifesto FESCD 78* DAVID MORALES PRESENTS THE FACE FEATURING JULIET ROBERTS	11		3

MALCOLM ROBERTS UK singer

Date	Title	Peak Position	Weeks at No.1	Weeks in Top 40
11 May 67	**TIME ALONE WILL TELL** *RCA 1578*	45		
30 Oct 68	**MAY I HAVE THE NEXT DREAM WITH YOU** *Major Minor MM 581*	8		13
22 Nov 69	**LOVE IS ALL** *Major Minor MM 637*	12		9

B.A. ROBERTSON UK singer

Date	Title	Peak Position	Weeks at No.1	Weeks in Top 40
28 Jul 79	**BANG BANG** *Asylum K 13152* ○	2		9
27 Oct 79	**KNOCKED IT OFF** *Asylum K 12396* ○	8		5
1 Mar 80	**KOOL IN THE KAFTAN** *Asylum K 12427*	17		7
31 May 80	**TO BE OR NOT TO BE** *Asylum K 12449*	9		8
17 Oct 81	**HOLD ME** *Swansong BAM 1* B.A. ROBERTSON & MAGGIE BELL	11		7
17 Dec 83	**TIME** *Epic A 3983* FRIDA & B.A. ROBERTSON	45		

DON ROBERTSON US pianist/whistler

Date	Title	Peak Position	Weeks at No.1	Weeks in Top 40
11 May 56	**THE HAPPY WHISTLER** *Capitol CL 14575*	8		9

ROBBIE ROBERTSON Canadian singer

Date	Title	Peak Position	Weeks at No.1	Weeks in Top 40
23 Jul 88	**SOMEWHERE DOWN THE CRAZY RIVER** *Geffen GEF 40*	15		6
11 Apr 98	**TAKE YOUR PARTNER BY THE HAND** *Polydor 5693272* HOWIE B FEATURING ROBBIE ROBERTSON	74		

IVO ROBIC Croatian singer

Date	Title	Peak Position	Weeks at No.1	Weeks in Top 40
6 Nov 59	**MORGEN** *Polydor 23923*	23		1

FLOYD ROBINSON US singer

Date	Title	Peak Position	Weeks at No.1	Weeks in Top 40
16 Oct 59	**MAKIN' LOVE** *RCA 1146*	9		9

SMOKEY ROBINSON US singer

Date	Title	Peak Position	Weeks at No.1	Weeks in Top 40
27 Dec 67	**I SECOND THAT EMOTION** *Tamla Motown TMG 631* SMOKEY ROBINSON & THE MIRACLES	27		8
3 Apr 68	**IF YOU CAN WANT** *Tamla Motown TMG 648* SMOKEY ROBINSON & THE MIRACLES	50		
7 May 69	**TRACKS OF MY TEARS** *Tamla Motown TMG 696* SMOKEY ROBINSON & THE MIRACLES	9		11
1 Aug 70	**TEARS OF A CLOWN** *Tamla Motown TMG 745* SMOKEY ROBINSON & THE MIRACLES ★	1	1	14
30 Jan 71	**(COME 'ROUND HERE) I'M THE ONE YOU NEED** *Tamla Motown TMG 761* SMOKEY ROBINSON & THE MIRACLES	13		8
5 Jun 71	**I DON'T BLAME YOU AT ALL** *Tamla Motown TMG 774* SMOKEY ROBINSON & THE MIRACLES	11		9
23 Feb 74	**JUST MY SOUL RESPONDING** *Tamla Motown TMG 883*	35		3
2 Oct 76	**TEARS OF A CLOWN** *Tamla Motown TMG 1048* SMOKEY ROBINSON & THE MIRACLES	34		3
24 Feb 79	**POPS WE LOVE YOU** *Motown TMG 1136* DIANA ROSS, MARVIN GAYE, SMOKEY ROBINSON & STEVIE WONDER	66		
9 May 81	**BEING WITH YOU** *Motown TMG 1223* ●	1	2	11
13 Mar 82	**TELL ME TOMORROW** *Motown TMG 1255*	51		
28 Mar 87	**JUST TO SEE HER** *Motown ZB 41147*	52		
17 Sep 88	**INDESTRUCTIBLE** *Arista 111717* FOUR TOPS FEATURING SMOKEY ROBINSON	55		
25 Feb 89	**INDESTRUCTIBLE** *Arista 112074* FOUR TOPS FEATURING SMOKEY ROBINSON	30		2

TOM ROBINSON UK singer

Date	Title	Peak Position	Weeks at No.1	Weeks in Top 40
22 Oct 77	**2-4-6-8 MOTORWAY** *EMI 2715* TOM ROBINSON BAND ○	5		9
18 Feb 78	**DON'T TAKE NO FOR AN ANSWER** *EMI 2749* TOM ROBINSON BAND	18		5
13 May 78	**UP AGAINST THE WALL** *EMI 2787* TOM ROBINSON BAND	33		4
17 Mar 79	**BULLY FOR YOU** *EMI 2916* TOM ROBINSON BAND	68		
25 Jun 83	**WAR BABY** *Panic NIC 2*	6		8
12 Nov 83	**LISTEN TO THE RADIO: ATMOSPHERICS** *Panic NIC 3*	39		2
15 Sep 84	**RIKKI DON'T LOSE THAT NUMBER** *Castaway TR 2*	58		

VICKI SUE ROBINSON US singer

Date	Title	Peak Position	Weeks at No.1	Weeks in Top 40
27 Sep 97	**HOUSE OF JOY** *Logic 74321511492*	48		

ROBYN Swedish singer

Date	Title	Peak Position	Weeks at No.1	Weeks in Top 40
20 Jul 96	**YOU'VE GOT THAT SOMETHIN'** *RCA 74321393462*	54		
16 Aug 97	**DO YOU KNOW (WHAT IT TAKES)** *RCA 74321509932*	26		1
7 Mar 98	**SHOW ME LOVE** *RCA 74321555032*	8		5
30 May 98	**DO YOU REALLY WANT ME** *RCA 74321582982*	20		2
11 Aug 07	**WITH EVERY HEARTBEAT** *Konichiwa KORMCD008* ROBYN WITH KLEERUP	1	1	15
3 Nov 07	**HANDLE ME** *Konichiwa 1751222*	17		4
12 Jan 08	**BE MINE** *Konichiwa 1759899*	10		8

ROC PROJECT US producer

Date	Title	Peak Position	Weeks at No.1	Weeks in Top 40
12 Apr 03	**NEVER (PAST TENSE)** *Illustrious CDILL 010* ROC PROJECT FEATURING TINA ARENA	42		

ERIN ROCHA UK singer

Date	Title	Peak Position	Weeks at No.1	Weeks in Top 40
27 Dec 03	**CAN'T DO RIGHT FOR DOING WRONG** *Flying Sparks TDBCDS76*	36		1

ROCHELLE US singer

Date	Title	Peak Position	Weeks at No.1	Weeks in Top 40
1 Feb 86	**MY MAGIC MAN** *Warner Brothers W 8838*	27		5

CHUBB ROCK US rapper

Date	Title	Peak Position	Weeks at No.1	Weeks in Top 40
19 Jan 91	**TREAT 'EM RIGHT** *Champion CHAMP 272*	67		

Key: ○ Silver-selling · ● Gold-selling · ⊛ Platinum-selling · ★ US No.1 · Peak Position · Weeks at No.1 · Weeks in Top 40

ROCK AID ARMENIA UK charity ensemble

Date	Title / Label	Peak Position	Weeks at No.1	Weeks in Top 40
16 Dec 89	**SMOKE ON THE WATER** *Life Aid Armenia ARMEN 001*	39		1

ROCK CANDY UK group

Date	Title / Label	Peak Position	Weeks at No.1	Weeks in Top 40
11 Sep 71	**REMEMBER** *MCA MK 5069*	32		3

ROCK GODDESS UK group

Date	Title / Label	Peak Position	Weeks at No.1	Weeks in Top 40
5 Mar 83	**MY ANGEL** *A&M AMS 8311*	64		
24 Mar 84	**I DIDN'T KNOW I LOVED YOU (TILL I SAW YOU ROCK 'N' ROLL)** *A&M AMS 185*	57		

ROCKER'S REVENGE US group

Date	Title / Label	Peak Position	Weeks at No.1	Weeks in Top 40
14 Aug 82	**WALKING ON SUNSHINE** *London LON 11* ROCKER'S REVENGE FEATURING DONNIE CALVIN ○	4		10
29 Jan 83	**THE HARDER THEY COME** *London LON 18*	30		4

ROCKET FROM THE CRYPT US group

Date	Title / Label	Peak Position	Weeks at No.1	Weeks in Top 40
27 Jan 96	**BORN IN 69** *Elemental ELM 32CD*	68		
13 Apr 96	**YOUNG LIVERS** *Elemental ELM 33CDS*	67		
14 Sep 96	**ON A ROPE** *Elemental ELM 38CDS1*	12		3
29 Aug 98	**LIPSTICK** *Elemental ELM 48CDS1*	64		

ROCKFORD FILES UK duo

Date	Title / Label	Peak Position	Weeks at No.1	Weeks in Top 40
11 Mar 95	**YOU SEXY DANCER** *Escapade/Rumour CDJAPE 7*	34		1
6 Apr 96	**YOU SEXY DANCER** *Escapade CDJAPE 14*	59		

ROCKIN' BERRIES UK group

Date	Title / Label	Peak Position	Weeks at No.1	Weeks in Top 40
1 Oct 64	**I DIDN'T MEAN TO HURT YOU** *Piccadilly 7N 35197*	43		
15 Oct 64	**HE'S IN TOWN** *Piccadilly 7N 35203*	3		12
21 Jan 65	**WHAT IN THE WORLD'S COME OVER YOU** *Piccadilly 7N 35217*	23		5
13 May 65	**POOR MAN'S SON** *Piccadilly 7N 35236*	5		10
26 Aug 65	**YOU'RE MY GIRL** *Piccadilly 7N 35254*	40		1
6 Jan 66	**THE WATER IS OVER MY HEAD** *Piccadilly 7N 35270*	43		

ROCKSTEADY CREW US group

Date	Title / Label	Peak Position	Weeks at No.1	Weeks in Top 40
1 Oct 83	**(HEY YOU) THE ROCKSTEADY CREW** *Charisma/Virgin RSC 1* ○	6		8
5 May 84	**UPROCK** *Charisma/Virgin RSC 2*	64		

ROCKWELL US singer

Date	Title / Label	Peak Position	Weeks at No.1	Weeks in Top 40
4 Feb 84	**SOMEBODY'S WATCHING ME** *Motown TMG 1331*	6		9

ROCOCO UK/Italian group

Date	Title / Label	Peak Position	Weeks at No.1	Weeks in Top 40
16 Dec 89	**ITALO HOUSE MIX** *Mercury MER 314*	54		

RODEO JONES UK/Grenadine group

Date	Title / Label	Peak Position	Weeks at No.1	Weeks in Top 40
30 Jan 93	**NATURAL WORLD** *A&M AMCD 0165*	75		
3 Apr 93	**SHADES OF SUMMER** *A&M AMCD 212*	59		

CLODAGH RODGERS UK singer

Date	Title / Label	Peak Position	Weeks at No.1	Weeks in Top 40
26 Mar 69	**COME BACK AND SHAKE ME** *RCA 1792*	3		12
9 Jul 69	**GOODNIGHT MIDNIGHT** *RCA 1852*	4		10
8 Nov 69	**BILJO** *RCA 1891*	22		8
4 Apr 70	**EVERYBODY GO HOME THE PARTY'S OVER** *RCA 1930*	47		
20 Mar 71	**JACK IN THE BOX** *RCA 2066*	4		9
9 Oct 71	**LADY LOVE BUG** *RCA 2117*	28		8

JIMMIE RODGERS US singer

Date	Title / Label	Peak Position	Weeks at No.1	Weeks in Top 40
1 Nov 57	**HONEYCOMB** *Columbia DB 3986* ★	30		1
20 Dec 57	**KISSES SWEETER THAN WINE** *Columbia DB 4052*	7		11
28 Mar 58	**OH OH, I'M FALLING IN LOVE AGAIN** *Columbia DB 4078*	18		6
19 Dec 58	**WOMAN FROM LIBERIA** *Columbia DB 4206*	18		6
14 Jun 62	**ENGLISH COUNTRY GARDEN** *Columbia DB 4847*	5		13

PAUL RODGERS UK singer

Date	Title / Label	Peak Position	Weeks at No.1	Weeks in Top 40
12 Feb 94	**MUDDY WATER BLUES** *Victory ROGCD 1*	45		

TOMMY ROE US singer

Date	Title / Label	Peak Position	Weeks at No.1	Weeks in Top 40
6 Sep 62	**SHEILA** *HMV POP 1060* ★	3		13
6 Dec 62	**SUSIE DARLIN'** *HMV POP 1092*	37		2
21 Mar 63	**THE FOLK SINGER** *HMV POP 1138*	4		12
26 Sep 63	**EVERYBODY** *HMV POP 1207*	9		10
16 Apr 69	**DIZZY** *Stateside SS 2143* ★	1	1	16
23 Jul 69	**HEATHER HONEY** *Stateside SS 2152*	24		8

ROFO UK production duo

Date	Title / Label	Peak Position	Weeks at No.1	Weeks in Top 40
1 Aug 92	**ROFO'S THEME** *PWL Continental PWLT 236*	44		

ROGER US singer

Date	Title / Label	Peak Position	Weeks at No.1	Weeks in Top 40
17 Oct 87	**I WANT TO BE YOUR MAN** *Reprise W 8229*	61		
12 Nov 88	**BOOM! THERE SHE WAS** *Virgin VS 1143* SCRITTI POLITTI FEATURING ROGER	55		
13 May 95	**HIGH AS A KITE** *ffrr FCD 259* ONE TRIBE FEATURING ROGER	55		

JULIE ROGERS UK singer

Date	Title / Label	Peak Position	Weeks at No.1	Weeks in Top 40
13 Aug 64	**THE WEDDING** *Mercury MF 820* JULIE ROGERS WITH JOHNNY ARTHEY & HIS ORCHESTRA & CHORUS	3		21
10 Dec 64	**LIKE A CHILD** *Mercury MF 838*	20		6
25 Mar 65	**HAWAIIAN WEDDING SONG** *Mercury MF 849*	31		3

KENNY ROGERS US singer

Date	Title / Label	Peak Position	Weeks at No.1	Weeks in Top 40
18 Oct 69	**RUBY DON'T TAKE YOUR LOVE TO TOWN** *Reprise RS 20829* KENNY ROGERS & THE FIRST EDITION	2		18
7 Feb 70	**SOMETHING'S BURNING** *Reprise RS 20888* KENNY ROGERS & THE FIRST EDITION	8		13
30 Apr 77	**LUCILLE** *United Artists UP 36242* ○	1	1	13
17 Sep 77	**DAYTIME FRIENDS** *United Artists UP 36289*	39		3
2 Jun 79	**SHE BELIEVES IN ME** *United Artists UP 36533*	42		
26 Jan 80	**COWARD OF THE COUNTY** *United Artists UP 614* ●	1	2	10
15 Nov 80	**LADY** *United Artists UP 635* ★	12		9
12 Feb 83	**WE'VE GOT TONIGHT** *Liberty UP 658* KENNY ROGERS & SHEENA EASTON	28		3
22 Oct 83	**EYES THAT SEE IN THE DARK** *RCA 358*	61		
12 Nov 83	**ISLANDS IN THE STREAM** *RCA 378* KENNY ROGERS & DOLLY PARTON ○ ★	7		11
20 Oct 07	**THE GAMBLER** *Download*	22		1

ROGUE TRADERS Australian group

Date	Title / Label	Peak Position	Weeks at No.1	Weeks in Top 40
15 Jul 06	**VOODOO CHILD** *RCA 82876866312*	3		13
28 Oct 06	**WATCHING YOU** *Sony BMG 88697019672*	33		1

ROKOTTO UK group

Date	Title / Label	Peak Position	Weeks at No.1	Weeks in Top 40
22 Oct 77	**BOOGIE ON UP** *State STAT 62*	40		1
10 Jun 78	**FUNK THEORY** *State STAT 80*	49		

ROLL DEEP UK group

Date	Title / Label	Peak Position	Weeks at No.1	Weeks in Top 40
30 Jul 05	**THE AVENUE** *Relentless RELDX19*	11		5
22 Oct 05	**SHAKE A LEG** *Relentless RELDX22*	24		2

ROLLERGIRL German singer

Date	Title / Label	Peak Position	Weeks at No.1	Weeks in Top 40
16 Sep 00	**DEAR JESSIE** *Neo NEOCD038*	22		2

ROLLING STONES UK group

Date	Title / Label	Peak Position	Weeks at No.1	Weeks in Top 40
25 Jul 63	**COME ON** *Decca F 11675*	21		12
14 Nov 63	**I WANNA BE YOUR MAN** *Decca F 11764*	12		15
27 Feb 64	**NOT FADE AWAY** *Decca F 11845*	3		13
2 Jul 64	**IT'S ALL OVER NOW** *Decca F 11934*	1	1	15
19 Nov 64	**LITTLE RED ROOSTER** *Decca F 12014*	1	1	11
4 Mar 65	**THE LAST TIME** *Decca F 12104*	1	3	12
26 Aug 65	**(I CAN'T GET NO) SATISFACTION** *Decca F 12220* ★	1	2	11
28 Oct 65	**GET OFF OF MY CLOUD** *Decca F 12263* ★	1	3	12

Silver-selling ○ Gold-selling ● Platinum-selling ⊛ US No.1 ★ | Peak Position | Weeks at No.1 | Weeks in Top 40

Date	Title / Label	Peak Position	Weeks at No.1	Weeks in Top 40
10 Feb 66	**NINETEENTH NERVOUS BREAKDOWN** *Decca F 12331*	2		8
19 May 66	**PAINT IT, BLACK** *Decca F 12395* ★	1	1	9
29 Sep 66	**HAVE YOU SEEN YOUR MOTHER BABY STANDING IN THE SHADOW** *Decca F 12497*	5		8
19 Jan 67	**LET'S SPEND THE NIGHT TOGETHER/RUBY TUESDAY** *Decca F 12546*	3		10
23 Aug 67	**WE LOVE YOU/DANDELION** *Decca F 12654*	8		8
29 May 68	**JUMPING JACK FLASH** *Decca F 12782*	1	2	11
9 Jul 69	**HONKY TONK WOMEN** *Decca F 12952* ★	1	5	16
24 Apr 71	**BROWN SUGAR/BITCH/LET IT ROCK** *Rolling Stones RS 19100* ★	2		12
3 Jul 71	**STREET FIGHTING MAN** *Decca F 13195*	21		6
29 Apr 72	**TUMBLING DICE** *Rolling Stones RS 19103*	5		8
1 Sep 73	**ANGIE** *Rolling Stones RS 19105* ○ ★	5		9
3 Aug 74	**IT'S ONLY ROCK AND ROLL** *Rolling Stones RS 19114*	10		7
20 Sep 75	**OUT OF TIME** *Decca F 13597*	45		
1 May 76	**FOOL TO CRY** *Rolling Stones RS 19121*	6		9
3 Jun 78	**MISS YOU/FAR AWAY EYES** *Rolling Stones EMI 2802* ○ ★	3		10
30 Sep 78	**RESPECTABLE** *Rolling Stones EMI 2861*	23		8
5 Jul 80	**EMOTIONAL RESCUE** *Rolling Stones RSR 105*	9		5
4 Oct 80	**SHE'S SO COLD** *Rolling Stones RSR 106*	33		2
29 Aug 81	**START ME UP** *Rolling Stones RSR 108*	7		7
12 Dec 81	**WAITING ON A FRIEND** *Rolling Stones RSR 109*	50		
12 Jun 82	**GOING TO A GO GO** *Rolling Stones RSR 110*	26		4
2 Oct 82	**TIME IS ON MY SIDE** *Rolling Stones RSR 111*	62		
12 Nov 83	**UNDERCOVER OF THE NIGHT** *Rolling Stones RSR 113*	11		5
11 Feb 84	**SHE WAS HOT** *Rolling Stones RSR 114*	42		
21 Jul 84	**BROWN SUGAR** *Rolling Stones SUGAR 1*	58		
15 Mar 86	**HARLEM SHUFFLE** *Rolling Stones A 6864*	13		5
2 Sep 89	**MIXED EMOTIONS** *Rolling Stones 6551937*	36		3
2 Dec 89	**ROCK AND A HARD PLACE** *Rolling Stones 6554227*	63		
23 Jun 90	**PAINT IT, BLACK** *London LON 264*	61		
30 Jun 90	**ALMOST HEAR YOU SIGH** *Rolling Stones 6560657*	31		3
30 Mar 91	**HIGHWIRE** *Rolling Stones 6567567*	29		2
1 Jun 91	**RUBY TUESDAY (LIVE)** *Rolling Stones 6568927*	59		
16 Jul 94	**LOVE IS STRONG** *Virgin VSCDT 1503*	14		2
8 Oct 94	**YOU GOT ME ROCKING** *Virgin VSCDG 1518*	23		2
10 Dec 94	**OUT OF TEARS** *Virgin VSCDT 1524*	36		2
15 Jul 95	**I GO WILD** *Virgin VSCDX 1539*	29		1
11 Nov 95	**LIKE A ROLLING STONE** *Virgin VSCDT 1562*	12		3
4 Oct 97	**ANYBODY SEEN MY BABY?** *Virgin VSCDT 1653*	22		1
7 Feb 98	**SAINT OF ME** *Virgin VSCDT 1667*	26		1
22 Aug 98	**OUT OF CONTROL** *Virgin VSCDT 1700*	51		
28 Dec 02	**DON'T STOP** *Virgin VSCDT 1838*	36		1
13 Sep 03	**SYMPATHY FOR THE DEVIL** *Mercury 9810612*	14		3
3 Sep 05	**STREETS OF LOVE/ROUGH JUSTICE** *Virgin VSCDT1905*	15		2
17 Dec 05	**RAIN FALL DOWN** *Virgin VSCDX1907*	33		1
2 Sep 06	**BIGGEST MISTAKE** *Virgin VSCDX1916*	51		
2 Jun 07	**PAINT IT, BLACK** *Download*	70		

ROLLINS BAND US group

Date	Title / Label	Peak Position	Weeks at No.1	Weeks in Top 40
12 Sep 92	**TEARING** *Imago 72787250187*	54		
10 Sep 94	**LIAR/DISCONNECTED** *Imago 74321213052*	27		1

ROLLO UK producer

Date	Title / Label	Peak Position	Weeks at No.1	Weeks in Top 40
29 Jan 94	**GET OFF YOUR HIGH HORSE** *Cheeky CHEKCD 003* ROLLO GOES CAMPING	43		
1 Oct 94	**GET OFF YOUR HIGH HORSE** *Cheeky CHEKCD 003* ROLLO GOES CAMPING	47		
10 Jun 95	**LOVE, LOVE, LOVE – HERE I COME** *Cheeky CHEKCD 007* ROLLO GOES MYSTIC	32		1
8 Jun 96	**LET THIS BE A PRAYER** *Cheeky CHEKCD 013* ROLLO GETS SPIRITUAL WITH PAULINE TAYLOR	26		1

ROMAN HOLIDAY UK group

Date	Title / Label	Peak Position	Weeks at No.1	Weeks in Top 40
2 Apr 83	**STAND BY** *Jive 31*	61		
2 Jul 83	**DON'T TRY TO STOP IT** *Jive 39*	14		8
24 Sep 83	**MOTORMANIA** *Jive 49*	40		1

ROMEO UK rapper

Date	Title / Label	Peak Position	Weeks at No.1	Weeks in Top 40
30 Dec 00	**NO GOOD 4 ME** *East West OXIDE 02CD* OXIDE & NEUTRINO FEATURING MEGAMAN, ROMEO & LISA MAFFIA	6		6
24 Aug 02	**ROMEO DUNN** *Relentless RELENT 29CD*	3		6
9 Nov 02	**IT'S ALL GRAVY** *Relentless RELENT 32CD* ROMEO FEATURING CHRISTINA MILIAN	9		4
6 Dec 03	**I SEE GIRLS (CRAZY)** *Multiply CDMULTY 109* STUDIO B/ROMEO & HARRY BROOKS	52		

MAX ROMEO Jamaican singer

Date	Title / Label	Peak Position	Weeks at No.1	Weeks in Top 40
28 May 69	**WET DREAM** *Unity UN 503*	10		20

HARRY 'CHOO CHOO' ROMERO US producer

Date	Title / Label	Peak Position	Weeks at No.1	Weeks in Top 40
22 May 99	**JUST CAN'T GET ENOUGH** *AM:PM CDAMPM 121* HARRY 'CHOO CHOO' ROMERO PRESENTS INAYA DAY	39		1
1 Sep 01	**I WANT OUT (I CAN'T BELIEVE)** *Perfecto PERF 22CDS*	51		

RONALDO'S REVENGE UK group

Date	Title / Label	Peak Position	Weeks at No.1	Weeks in Top 40
1 Aug 98	**MAS QUE MANCADA** *AM:PM 5827532*	37		1

RONDO VENEZIANO Italian group

Date	Title / Label	Peak Position	Weeks at No.1	Weeks in Top 40
22 Oct 83	**LA SERENISSIMA (THEME FROM 'VENICE IN PERIL')** *Ferroway 7 RON 1*	58		

RONETTES US group

Date	Title / Label	Peak Position	Weeks at No.1	Weeks in Top 40
17 Oct 63	**BE MY BABY** *London HLU 9793*	4		11
9 Jan 64	**BABY I LOVE YOU** *London HLU 9826*	11		12
27 Aug 64	**(THE BEST PART OF) BREAKING UP** *London HLU 9905*	43		
8 Oct 64	**DO I LOVE YOU** *London HLU 9922*	35		1

MARK RONSON US producer

Date	Title / Label	Peak Position	Weeks at No.1	Weeks in Top 40
1 Nov 03	**OOH WEE** *Elektra E 7490CD*	15		3
25 Mar 06	**JUST** *Columbia 88697272032* MARK RONSON FEATURING ALEX GREENWALD	48		
14 Apr 07	**STOP ME** *Columbia 88697078762* MARK RONSON FEATURING DANIEL MERRIWEATHER	2		9
21 Apr 07	**GOD PUT A SMILE ON YOUR FACE** *Download* RONSON FEATURING DAPTONE HORNS	63		
21 Apr 07	**NO ONE KNOWS** *Download*	66		
7 Jul 07	**OH MY GOD** *Columbia 88697113172* MARK RONSON FEATURING LILY ALLEN	8		8
29 Sep 07	**VALERIE** *Columbia 88697186332* MARK RONSON FEATURING AMY WINEHOUSE	2		26
8 Mar 08	**JUST** *Columbia 88697272032* MARK RONSON FEATURING PHANTOM PLANET	36		1

MICK RONSON UK guitarist

Date	Title / Label	Peak Position	Weeks at No.1	Weeks in Top 40
7 May 94	**DON'T LOOK DOWN** *Epic 6603582* MICK RONSON WITH JOE ELLIOTT	55		

LINDA RONSTADT US singer

Date	Title / Label	Peak Position	Weeks at No.1	Weeks in Top 40
8 May 76	**TRACKS OF MY TEARS** *Asylum K 13034*	42		
28 Jan 78	**BLUE BAYOU** *Asylum K 13106*	35		3
26 May 79	**ALISON** *Asylum K 13149*	66		
11 Jul 87	**SOMEWHERE OUT THERE** *MCA 1132* LINDA RONSTADT & JAMES INGRAM	8		9
11 Nov 89	**DON'T KNOW MUCH** *Elektra EKR 101* LINDA RONSTADT & AARON NEVILLE ○	2		10

ROOFTOP SINGERS US group

Date	Title / Label	Peak Position	Weeks at No.1	Weeks in Top 40
31 Jan 63	**WALK RIGHT IN** *Fontana TF 271700* ★	10		10

ROOM 5 Italian producer

Date	Title / Label	Peak Position	Weeks at No.1	Weeks in Top 40
5 Apr 03	**MAKE LUV** *Positiva CDTIV 187* ROOM 5 FEATURING OLIVER CHEATHAM ○	1	4	10
6 Dec 03	**MUSIC AND YOU** *Positiva CDTIVS 197* ROOM 5 FEATURING OLIVER CHEATHAM	38		1

ROONEY US group

Date	Title / Label	Peak Position	Weeks at No.1	Weeks in Top 40
26 Jun 04	**I'M SHAKIN'** *Geffen 9862557*	73		
15 Sep 07	**WHEN DID YOUR HEART GO MISSING?** *Geffen 1745789*	45		

ROOSTER UK group

Date	Title / Label	Peak Position	Weeks at No.1	Weeks in Top 40
23 Oct 04	**COME GET SOME** *Brightside 82876652382*	7		5
22 Jan 05	**STARING AT THE SUN** *Brightside 82876670952*	5		6

MARK RONSON

It's not uncommon for children to dream of international superstardom. What young fantasist, discovering music for the first time, hasn't imagined themself inspiring the reverence of a sea of sweaty devotees? For most, this aspiration will remain forever unrealised. But even the quickest inquiry into Mark Ronson's upbringing reveals his success as less of an ambition fulfilled than a foregone conclusion.

Born on 4 September 1975 in London, Mark was immediately inducted into the London elite by virtue of his socialite heritage – the son of writer Ann Dexter-Jones and band manager Laurence Ronson (he is also the nephew of property tycoon Gerald Ronson). The Ronson household played host to a galaxy of pop culture luminaries: Keith Moon was teaching him drums at age two; Andy Warhol was assessing his doodles; Mick Jagger and Keith Richards were regular dinner guests; the McCartneys lived but a few doors away; John Lennon's son Sean was one of his close childhood friends. Fortunately for Mark some of the talent rubbed off on him; as young as four he began composing music. When Mark was six, his parents split, and two years later he moved with his mother and sisters to New York.

As he moved into his late teens, something strange happened. His eccentric, rapacious tastes led him away from British guitar music to hip-hop, first making beats on an old drum machine of his stepfather's. In his last year of high school he began DJing and immersed himself in the downtown New York scene, where he soon became one of the most sought after bookings in the city – despite initially charging only $50 per set. The tag of 'DJ to the stars' was one hard earned – he played at the launches of various fashion shows, as well as a couple of P Diddy parties – but it also proved hard to shake off. Rumour has it that Diddy once gave him a $100 bill with his phone number on it when Ronson's DJ selection had completely rammed a dance floor. He was soon signed to Elektra Records and started recording his debut album.

The subsequent release, 2003's *Here Comes The Fuzz*, was only a modest seller despite critical acclaim. However, it spawned the successful single 'Ooh Wee' featuring the talents of US rappers Nate Dogg, Ghostface Killah and Trife Da God; it skips along on a nimble Latin-tinged beat, a sample of Boney M's 'Sunny' shimmering in the production. It reached Number 15 in the UK, and Number 10 in the US Hot 100.

After the release of *Here Comes The Fuzz*, Elektra Records dissolved and Ronson decided to focus on producing, as well as setting up his own label, Allido Records. In between working on two of the biggest albums of 2006, Lily Allen's *Alright, Still* and Amy Winehouse's *Back To Black*, he found the time to contribute a cover of 'Just' for a Radiohead tribute album. It featured Alex Greenwald of Phantom Planet on vocals. Although the track only reached Number 48 in the UK, it was effectively the genesis of Ronson's second album *Version*, which would be comprised entirely of covers.

The first single from the album was 'Stop Me', a reworking of The Smiths' 1987 single 'Stop Me If You Think That You've Heard This One Before' with childhood friend Daniel Merriweather on vocals. It infuses a distinctly soulful vibe into Morrissey and Marr's classic with a rich orchestral arrangement, even working in lyrics from The Supremes' 'You Keep Me Hanging On'. Released on 2 April 2007 on Columbia Records, it was a massive hit, debuting at Number 2 in the UK singles chart and Number 1 in the UK download chart.

The next official single was Lily Allen singing 'Oh My God', originally by Leeds-based Kaiser Chiefs. When Mark first met Allen she was still unknown, inspiring his ire by pinning a badge to an expensive leather jacket. But the quality of her demos helped him forgive this misdemeanour, and since she had previously covered 'Oh My God' for an early mix tape, she was an obvious choice for *Version*. It peaked at Number 8 in the UK and Ronson was able to celebrate his second Top 10 hit. The big hitter was still to come – the third single from the album would be Amy Winehouse's 'Valerie' (see separate Amy Winehouse feature, p. 456). By now, he was an established artist in his own right and was able to scoop three Grammys and a Brit for 'Best Male Artist' (several of his previous singles received hefty download sales boosts in the week after the award ceremony).

But what do the artists think of Ronson's reworkings outshining their originals? The famously humble and mildly spoken Ronson maintains that most are happy to see their songs achieve renewed success. The Kaiser Chiefs certainly don't mind – singer Ricky Wilson has performed 'Oh My God' with Ronson on a variety of occasions, and the band have reportedly enlisted his services for their third album. And with his singles repeatedly hitting the Top 10, any artists who are embarrassed by his version outselling their original, will – to paraphrase Ronson – be able to get over it as they drive their gold Rolls Royce around.

Silver-selling ○ Gold-selling ● Platinum-selling ⊛ US No.1 ★ Peak Position Weeks at No.1 Weeks in Top 40

Date	Title / Label	Peak Position	Weeks at No.1	Weeks in Top 40
7 May 05	**YOU'RE SO RIGHT FOR ME** *Wichita WEBB078SCD*	14		3
23 Jul 05	**DEEP AND MEANINGLESS** *Brightside 82876708392*	29		1
22 Jul 06	**HOME** *Brightside 82876862852*	33		1

ROOTJOOSE UK group

Date	Title / Label	Peak Position	Weeks at No.1	Weeks in Top 40
17 May 97	**CAN'T KEEP LIVING THIS WAY** *Rage RAGECD 2*	73		
2 Aug 97	**MR FIXIT** *Rage RAGECDX 3*	54		
4 Oct 97	**LONG WAY** *Rage RAGECD 5*	68		

ROOTS US group

Date	Title / Label	Peak Position	Weeks at No.1	Weeks in Top 40
3 May 97	**WHAT THEY DO** *Geffen GFSTD 22240*	49		
6 Mar 99	**YOU GOT ME** *MCA MCSTD 48110* ROOTS FEATURING ERYKAH BADU	31		1
12 Apr 03	**THE SEED (2.0)** *MCA MCSTD 40316* ROOTS FEATURING CODY CHESTNUTT	33		1
16 Aug 03	**BREAKS YOU OFF** *MCA MCSTD 40330* ROOTS FEATURING MUSIQ	59		

ROSE OF ROMANCE ORCHESTRA UK orchestra

Date	Title / Label	Peak Position	Weeks at No.1	Weeks in Top 40
9 Jan 82	**TARA'S THEME FROM *GONE WITH THE WIND*** *BBC RESL 108*	71		

ROSE ROYCE US group

Date	Title / Label	Peak Position	Weeks at No.1	Weeks in Top 40
25 Dec 76	**CAR WASH** *MCA 267* ★	9		10
22 Jan 77	**PUT YOUR MONEY WHERE YOUR MOUTH IS** *MCA 259*	44		
2 Apr 77	**I WANNA GET NEXT TO YOU** *MCA 278*	14		7
24 Sep 77	**DO YOUR DANCE** *Whitfield K 17006*	30		5
14 Jan 78	**WISHING ON A STAR** *Whitfield K 17060* ○	3		13
6 May 78	**IT MAKES YOU FEEL LIKE DANCIN'** *Whitfield K 17148*	16		6
16 Sep 78	**LOVE DON'T LIVE HERE ANYMORE** *Whitfield K 17236* ●	2		8
3 Feb 79	**I'M IN LOVE (AND I LOVE THE FEELING)** *Whitfield K 17291*	51		
17 Nov 79	**IS IT LOVE YOU'RE AFTER** *Whitfield K 17456*	13		11
8 Mar 80	**OOH BOY** *Whitfield K 17575*	46		
21 Nov 81	**R.R. EXPRESS** *Warner Brothers K 17875*	52		
1 Sep 84	**MAGIC TOUCH** *Streetwave KHAN 21*	43		
6 Apr 85	**LOVE ME RIGHT NOW** *Streetwave KHAN 39*	60		
11 Jun 88	**CAR WASH/IS IT LOVE YOU'RE AFTER** *MCA 1253*	20		5
31 Oct 98	**CAR WASH** *MCA MCSTD 48096* ROSE ROYCE FEATURING GWEN DICKEY	18		1

ROSE TATTOO Australian group

Date	Title / Label	Peak Position	Weeks at No.1	Weeks in Top 40
11 Jul 81	**ROCK 'N' ROLL OUTLAW** *Carrere CAR 200*	60		

JIMMY ROSELLI US singer

Date	Title / Label	Peak Position	Weeks at No.1	Weeks in Top 40
5 Mar 83	**WHEN YOUR OLD WEDDING RING WAS NEW** *A1 282*	51		
20 Jun 87	**WHEN YOUR OLD WEDDING RING WAS NEW** *First Night SCORE 9*	52		

MARIO ROSENSTOCK Irish comedian

Date	Title / Label	Peak Position	Weeks at No.1	Weeks in Top 40
4 Mar 06	**JOSE AND HIS AMAZING TECHNICOLOR OVERCOAT** *Angel ANGECD11*	45		

ROSETTA LIFE UK duo

Date	Title / Label	Peak Position	Weeks at No.1	Weeks in Top 40
12 Nov 05	**WE LAUGHED** *Cooking Vinyl FRYCD252* ROSETTA LIFE FEATURING BILLY BRAGG	11		3

DIANA ROSS US singer

Date	Title / Label	Peak Position	Weeks at No.1	Weeks in Top 40
30 Aug 67	**REFLECTIONS** *Tamla Motown TMG 616* DIANA ROSS & THE SUPREMES	5		12
29 Nov 67	**IN AND OUT OF LOVE** *Tamla Motown TMG 632* DIANA ROSS & THE SUPREMES	13		12
10 Apr 68	**FOREVER CAME TODAY** *Tamla Motown TMG 650* DIANA ROSS & THE SUPREMES	28		7
3 Jul 68	**SOME THINGS YOU NEVER GET USED TO** *Tamla Motown TMG 662* DIANA ROSS & THE SUPREMES	34		4
20 Nov 68	**LOVE CHILD** *Tamla Motown TMG 677* DIANA ROSS & THE SUPREMES ★	15		5
29 Jan 69	**I'M GONNA MAKE YOU LOVE ME** *Tamla Motown TMG 685* DIANA ROSS & THE SUPREMES & THE TEMPTATIONS	3		11
23 Apr 69	**I'M LIVING IN SHAME** *Tamla Motown TMG 695* DIANA ROSS & THE SUPREMES	14		8
16 Jul 69	**NO MATTER WHAT SIGN YOU ARE** *Tamla Motown TMG 704* DIANA ROSS & THE SUPREMES	37		5
20 Sep 69	**I SECOND THAT EMOTION** *Tamla Motown TMG 709* DIANA ROSS & THE SUPREMES & THE TEMPTATIONS	18		8
13 Dec 69	**SOMEDAY WE'LL BE TOGETHER** *Tamla Motown TMG 721* DIANA ROSS & THE SUPREMES ★	13		10
21 Mar 70	**WHY (MUST WE FALL IN LOVE)** *Tamla Motown TMG 730* DIANA ROSS & THE SUPREMES & THE TEMPTATIONS	31		4
18 Jul 70	**REACH OUT AND TOUCH** *Tamla Motown TMG 743*	33		3
12 Sep 70	**AIN'T NO MOUNTAIN HIGH ENOUGH** *Tamla Motown TMG 751* ★	6		11
3 Apr 71	**REMEMBER ME** *Tamla Motown TMG 768*	7		11
31 Jul 71	**I'M STILL WAITING** *Tamla Motown TMG 781*	1	4	13
30 Oct 71	**SURRENDER** *Tamla Motown TMG 792*	10		10
13 May 72	**DOOBEDOOD'NDOOBE DOOBEDOOD'NDOOBE** *Tamla Motown TMG 812*	12		7
14 Jul 73	**TOUCH ME IN THE MORNING** *Tamla Motown TMG 861* ★	9		10
5 Jan 74	**ALL OF MY LIFE** *Tamla Motown TMG 880*	9		10
23 Mar 74	**YOU ARE EVERYTHING** *Tamla Motown TMG 890* DIANA ROSS & MARVIN GAYE ○	5		10
4 May 74	**LAST TIME I SAW HIM** *Tamla Motown TMG 893*	35		3
20 Jul 74	**STOP LOOK LISTEN (TO YOUR HEART)** *Tamla Motown TMG 906* DIANA ROSS & MARVIN GAYE	25		5
24 Aug 74	**BABY LOVE** *Tamla Motown TMG 915* DIANA ROSS & THE SUPREMES	12		7
28 Sep 74	**LOVE ME** *Tamla Motown TMG 917*	38		1
29 Mar 75	**SORRY DOESN'T ALWAYS MAKE IT RIGHT** *Tamla Motown TMG 941*	23		6
3 Apr 76	**THEME FROM MAHOGANY (DO YOU KNOW WHERE YOU'RE GOING TO)** *Tamla Motown TMG 1010* ★	5		8
24 Apr 76	**LOVE HANGOVER** *Tamla Motown TMG 1024* ★	10		9
10 Jul 76	**I THOUGHT IT TOOK A LITTLE TIME** *Tamla Motown TMG 1032*	32		4
16 Oct 76	**I'M STILL WAITING** *Tamla Motown TMG 1041*	41		
19 Nov 77	**GETTIN' READY FOR LOVE** *Motown TMG 1090*	23		6
22 Jul 78	**LOVIN' LIVIN' AND GIVIN'** *Motown TMG 1112*	54		
18 Nov 78	**EASE ON DOWN THE ROAD** *MCA 396* DIANA ROSS & MICHAEL JACKSON	45		
24 Feb 79	**POPS WE LOVE YOU** *Motown TMG 1136* DIANA ROSS, MARVIN GAYE, SMOKEY ROBINSON & STEVIE WONDER	66		
21 Jul 79	**THE BOSS** *Motown TMG 1150*	40		1
6 Oct 79	**NO ONE GETS THE PRIZE** *Motown TMG 1160*	59		
24 Nov 79	**IT'S MY HOUSE** *Motown TMG 1169*	32		6
19 Jul 80	**UPSIDE DOWN** *Motown TMG 1195* ○ ★	2		10
20 Sep 80	**MY OLD PIANO** *Motown TMG 1202* ○	5		7
15 Nov 80	**I'M COMING OUT** *Motown TMG 1210*	13		8
17 Jan 81	**IT'S MY TURN** *Motown TMG 1217*	16		5
28 Mar 81	**ONE MORE CHANCE** *Motown TMG 1227*	49		
13 Jun 81	**CRYIN' MY HEART OUT FOR YOU** *Motown TMG 1233*	58		
12 Sep 81	**ENDLESS LOVE** *Motown TMG 1240* DIANA ROSS & LIONEL RICHIE ★	7		9
7 Nov 81	**WHY DO FOOLS FALL IN LOVE** *Capitol CL 226* ○	4		11
23 Jan 82	**TENDERNESS** *Motown TMG 1248*	73		
30 Jan 82	**MIRROR MIRROR** *Capitol CL 234*	36		2
29 May 82	**WORK THAT BODY** *Capitol CL 241*	7		8
7 Aug 82	**IT'S NEVER TOO LATE** *Capitol CL 256*	41		
23 Oct 82	**MUSCLES** *Capitol CL 268*	15		7
15 Jan 83	**SO CLOSE** *Capitol CL 277*	43		
23 Jul 83	**PIECES OF ICE** *Capitol CL 298*	46		
7 Jul 84	**ALL OF YOU** *CBS A 4522* JULIO IGLESIAS & DIANA ROSS	43		
15 Sep 84	**TOUCH BY TOUCH** *Capitol CL 337*	47		
28 Sep 85	**EATEN ALIVE** *Capitol CL 372*	71		
25 Jan 86	**CHAIN REACTION** *Capitol CL 386* ●	1	3	12
3 May 86	**EXPERIENCE** *Capitol CL 400*	47		
13 Jun 87	**DIRTY LOOKS** *EMI EM 2*	49		
8 Oct 88	**MR LEE** *EMI EM 73*	58		
26 Nov 88	**LOVE HANGOVER (REMIX)** *Motown ZB 42307*	75		
18 Feb 89	**STOP! IN THE NAME OF LOVE** *Motown ZB 41963* DIANA ROSS & THE SUPREMES	62		
6 May 89	**WORKIN' OVERTIME** *EMI EM 91*	32		2
29 Jul 89	**PARADISE** *EMI EM 94*	61		
7 Jul 90	**I'M STILL WAITING (REMIX)** *Motown ZB 43781*	21		5
30 Nov 91	**WHEN YOU TELL ME THAT YOU LOVE ME** *EMI EM 217* ○	2		10
15 Feb 92	**THE FORCE BEHIND THE POWER** *EMI EM 221*	27		2
20 Jun 92	**ONE SHINING MOMENT** *EMI EM 239*	10		7
28 Nov 92	**IF WE HOLD ON TOGETHER** *EMI EM 257*	11		8
13 Mar 93	**HEART (DON'T CHANGE MY MIND)** *EMI CDEM 261*	31		2
9 Oct 93	**CHAIN REACTION** *EMI CDEM 290*	20		4
11 Dec 93	**YOUR LOVE** *EMI CDEM 299*	14		4
2 Apr 94	**THE BEST YEARS OF MY LIFE** *EMI CDEM 305*	28		2
9 Jul 94	**WHY DO FOOLS FALL IN LOVE/I'M COMING OUT (REMIX)** *EMI CDEM 332*	36		1
2 Sep 95	**TAKE ME HIGHER** *EMI CDEM 388*	32		3
25 Nov 95	**I'M GONE** *EMI CDEMS 402*	36		1
17 Feb 96	**I WILL SURVIVE** *EMI CDEM 415*	14		2
21 Dec 96	**IN THE ONES YOU LOVE** *EMI CDEM 457*	34		1

Silver-selling ○ · Gold-selling ● · Platinum-selling ⊛ · US No.1 ★ · Peak Position · Weeks at No.1 · Weeks in Top 40

Date	Title / Label	Peak Position	Weeks at No.1	Weeks in Top 40
6 Nov 99	**NOT OVER YOU YET** *EMI CDEM 553*	9		3
24 Dec 05	**WHEN YOU TELL ME THAT YOU LOVE ME** *S 82876767382* WESTLIFE FEATURING DIANA ROSS	2		5

RICKY ROSS UK singer

Date	Title / Label	Peak Position	Weeks at No.1	Weeks in Top 40
18 May 96	**RADIO ON** *Epic 6631352*	35		1
10 Aug 96	**GOOD EVENING PHILADELPHIA** *Epic 6635335*	58		

FRANCIS ROSSI UK singer/guitarist

Date	Title / Label	Peak Position	Weeks at No.1	Weeks in Top 40
11 May 85	**MODERN ROMANCE (I WANT TO FALL IN LOVE AGAIN)** *Vertigo FROS 1* FRANCIS ROSSI & BERNARD FROST	54		
3 Aug 96	**GIVE MYSELF TO LOVE** *Virgin VSCDT 1594*	42		

NINI ROSSO Italian singer

Date	Title / Label	Peak Position	Weeks at No.1	Weeks in Top 40
26 Aug 65	**IL SILENZIO** *Durium DRS 54000*	8		13

DAVID LEE ROTH US singer

Date	Title / Label	Peak Position	Weeks at No.1	Weeks in Top 40
23 Feb 85	**CALIFORNIA GIRLS** *Warner Brothers W 9102*	68		
5 Mar 88	**JUST LIKE PARADISE** *Warner Brothers W 8119*	27		4
3 Sep 88	**DAMN GOOD/STAND UP** *Warner Brothers W 7753*	72		
12 Jan 91	**A LIL' AIN'T ENOUGH** *Warner Brothers W 0002*	32		2
19 Feb 94	**SHE'S MY MACHINE** *Reprise W 0229CD*	64		
28 May 94	**NIGHT LIFE** *Reprise W 0249CD*	72		

ROTTERDAM TERMINATION SOURCE
Dutch production duo

Date	Title / Label	Peak Position	Weeks at No.1	Weeks in Top 40
7 Nov 92	**POING** *SEP EDGE 74*	27		3
25 Dec 93	**MERRY X-MESS** *React CDREACT 33*	73		

ROUND SOUND UK group

Date	Title / Label	Peak Position	Weeks at No.1	Weeks in Top 40
16 Mar 02	**WHADDA WE LIKE?** *Cooltempo CDCOOL 358* ROUND SOUND PRESENTS ONYX STONE & MC MALIBU	69		

DEMIS ROUSSOS Greek singer

Date	Title / Label	Peak Position	Weeks at No.1	Weeks in Top 40
22 Nov 75	**HAPPY TO BE ON AN ISLAND IN THE SUN** *Philips 6042 033* ○	5		9
28 Feb 76	**CAN'T SAY HOW MUCH I LOVE YOU** *Philips 6042 114*	35		1
26 Jun 76	**THE ROUSSOS PHENOMENON EP** *Philips DEMIS 001* ○	1	1	12
2 Oct 76	**WHEN FOREVER HAS GONE** *Philips 6042 186* ○	2		10
19 Mar 77	**BECAUSE** *Philips 6042 245*	39		1
18 Jun 77	**KYRILA (EP)** *Philips DEMIS 002*	33		2

ROUTE ONE UK production group

Date	Title / Label	Peak Position	Weeks at No.1	Weeks in Top 40
22 Oct 05	**CRASH LANDING** *All Around The World CDGLOBE446* ROUTE ONE FEATURING JENNY FROST	47		

ROUTERS US group

Date	Title / Label	Peak Position	Weeks at No.1	Weeks in Top 40
27 Dec 62	**LET'S GO** *Warner Brothers WB 77*	32		3

MARIA ROWE UK singer

Date	Title / Label	Peak Position	Weeks at No.1	Weeks in Top 40
20 May 95	**SEXUAL** *ffrr FCD 248*	67		

KELLY ROWLAND US singer

Date	Title / Label	Peak Position	Weeks at No.1	Weeks in Top 40
26 Oct 02	**DILEMMA** *Universal MCSTD 40299* NELLY FEATURING KELLY ROWLAND ⊛ ★	1	2	17
28 Dec 02	**STOLE (IMPORT)** *Columbia 6732122*	57		
8 Feb 03	**STOLE** *Columbia 6735182*	2		8
10 May 03	**CAN'T NOBODY** *Columbia 6738142*	5		5
16 Aug 03	**TRAIN ON A TRACK** *Columbia 6742155*	20		2
15 Apr 06	**HERE WE GO** *Atlantic AT0238CD* TRINA FEATURING KELLY ROWLAND	15		4
16 Jun 07	**LIKE THIS** *Columbia 88697110322* KELLY ROWLAND FEATURING EVE	4		10
19 Jan 08	**WORK** *RCA 88697268382*	4		10

JOHN ROWLES New Zealand singer

Date	Title / Label	Peak Position	Weeks at No.1	Weeks in Top 40
13 Mar 68	**IF I ONLY HAD TIME** *MCA MU 1000*	3		17
19 Jun 68	**HUSH NOT A WORD TO MARY** *MCA MU 1023*	12		9

LISA ROXANNE UK singer

Date	Title / Label	Peak Position	Weeks at No.1	Weeks in Top 40
9 Jun 01	**NO FLOW** *Palm Pictures PPCD 70542*	18		1

ROXETTE Swedish duo

Date	Title / Label	Peak Position	Weeks at No.1	Weeks in Top 40
22 Apr 89	**THE LOOK** *EMI EM 87* ★	7		8
15 Jul 89	**DRESSED FOR SUCCESS** *EMI EM 96*	48		
28 Oct 89	**LISTEN TO YOUR HEART** *EMI EM 108* ★	62		
2 Jun 90	**IT MUST HAVE BEEN LOVE** *EMI EM 141* ○ ★	3		12
11 Aug 90	**LISTEN TO YOUR HEART/DANGEROUS** *EMI EM 149*	6		7
27 Oct 90	**DRESSED FOR SUCCESS** *EMI EM 162*	18		6
9 Mar 91	**JOYRIDE** *EMI EM 177* ★	4		9
11 May 91	**FADING LIKE A FLOWER (EVERY TIME YOU LEAVE)** *EMI EM 190*	12		5
7 Sep 91	**THE BIG L** *EMI EM 204*	21		4
23 Nov 91	**SPENDING MY TIME** *EMI EM 215*	22		2
28 Mar 92	**CHURCH OF YOUR HEART** *EMI EM 227*	21		3
1 Aug 92	**HOW DO YOU DO!** *EMI EM 241*	13		5
7 Nov 92	**QUEEN OF RAIN** *EMI EM 253*	28		3
24 Jul 93	**ALMOST UNREAL** *EMI CDEM 268*	7		7
18 Sep 93	**IT MUST HAVE BEEN LOVE** *EMI CDEM 285*	10		6
26 Mar 94	**SLEEPING IN MY CAR** *EMI CDEM 314*	14		4
4 Jun 94	**CRASH! BOOM! BANG!** *EMI CDEM 324*	26		3
17 Sep 94	**FIREWORKS** *EMI CDEM 345*	30		2
3 Dec 94	**RUN TO YOU** *EMI CDEMS 360*	27		2
8 Apr 95	**VULNERABLE** *EMI CDEM 369*	44		
25 Nov 95	**THE LOOK (REMIX)** *EMI CDEMS 406*	28		1
30 Mar 96	**YOU DON'T UNDERSTAND ME** *EMI CDEM 418*	42		
20 Jul 96	**JUNE AFTERNOON** *EMI CDEM 437*	52		
20 Mar 99	**WISH I COULD FLY** *EMI CDEM 537*	11		3
9 Oct 99	**STARS** *EMI CDEM 550*	56		
6 Aug 05	**FADING LIKE A FLOWER (REMIX)** *All Around The World CDGLOBE426* DANCING DJS VS ROXETTE	18		4

ROXY MUSIC UK group

Date	Title / Label	Peak Position	Weeks at No.1	Weeks in Top 40
19 Aug 72	**VIRGINIA PLAIN** *Island WIP 6144*	4		10
10 Mar 73	**PYJAMARAMA** *Island WIP 6159*	10		9
17 Nov 73	**STREET LIFE** *Island WIP 6173*	9		10
12 Oct 74	**ALL I WANT IS YOU** *Island WIP 6208*	12		6
11 Oct 75	**LOVE IS THE DRUG** *Island WIP 6248* ○	2		10
27 Dec 75	**BOTH ENDS BURNING** *Island WIP 6262*	25		7
22 Oct 77	**VIRGINIA PLAIN** *Polydor 2001 739*	11		6
3 Mar 79	**TRASH** *Polydor POSP 32*	40		1
28 Apr 79	**DANCE AWAY** *Polydor POSP 44* ●	2		11
11 Aug 79	**ANGEL EYES** *Polydor POSP 67* ○	4		9
17 May 80	**OVER YOU** *Polydor POSP 93* ○	5		8
2 Aug 80	**OH YEAH (ON THE RADIO)** *Polydor 2001 972*	5		7
8 Nov 80	**THE SAME OLD SCENE** *Polydor ROXY 1*	12		6
21 Feb 81	**JEALOUS GUY** *EG ROXY 2* ●	1	2	9
3 Apr 82	**MORE THAN THIS** *EG ROXY 3* ○	6		6
19 Jun 82	**AVALON** *EG ROXY 4*	13		5
25 Sep 82	**TAKE A CHANCE WITH ME** *EG ROXY 5*	26		4
27 Apr 96	**LOVE IS THE DRUG (REMIX)** *EG VSCDT 1580*	33		1

BILLY JOE ROYAL US singer

Date	Title / Label	Peak Position	Weeks at No.1	Weeks in Top 40
7 Oct 65	**DOWN IN THE BOONDOCKS** *CBS 201802*	38		3

CENTRAL BAND OF THE ROYAL AIR FORCE UK military band

Date	Title / Label	Peak Position	Weeks at No.1	Weeks in Top 40
21 Oct 55	**THE DAMBUSTERS MARCH** *HMV B 10877* CENTRAL BAND OF THE ROYAL AIRFORCE CONDUCTOR W/CDR A.E. SIMS O.B.E	18		1

ROYAL BALLET SINFONIA & GAVIN SUTHERLAND UK orchestra with conductor

Date	Title / Label	Peak Position	Weeks at No.1	Weeks in Top 40
8 Apr 06	**RADIO 4 UK THEME** *Sweetspot SSUKCDS001*	29		2

ROYAL GIGOLOS UK production duo

Date	Title / Label	Peak Position	Weeks at No.1	Weeks in Top 40
31 Jul 04	**CALIFORNIA DREAMIN'** *Manifesto 9866931*	44		

Key: ○ Silver-selling · ● Gold-selling · Platinum-selling · ★ US No.1 · Peak Position · Weeks at No.1 · Weeks in Top 40

ROYAL GUARDSMEN US group

Date	Title / Label	Peak Position	Weeks at No.1	Weeks in Top 40
19 Jan 67	**SNOOPY VS. THE RED BARON** *Stateside SS 574*	8		11
6 Apr 67	**RETURN OF THE RED BARON** *Stateside SS 2010*	37		2

ROYAL HOUSE US group

Date	Title / Label	Peak Position	Weeks at No.1	Weeks in Top 40
10 Sep 88	**CAN YOU PARTY** *Champion CHAMP 79*	14		6
7 Jan 89	**YEAH! BUDDY** *Champion CHAMP 91*	35		2

ROYAL PHILHARMONIC ORCHESTRA
UK orchestra

Date	Title / Label	Peak Position	Weeks at No.1	Weeks in Top 40
25 Jul 81	**HOOKED ON CLASSICS** *RCA 109* ROYAL PHILHARMONIC ORCHESTRA ARRANGED & CONDUCTED BY LOUIS CLARK ○	2		9
24 Oct 81	**HOOKED ON CAN-CAN** *RCA 151* ROYAL PHILHARMONIC ORCHESTRA ARRANGED & CONDUCTED BY LOUIS CLARK	47		
10 Jul 82	**BBC WORLD CUP GRANDSTAND** *BBC RESL 116*	61		
7 Aug 82	**IF YOU KNEW SOUSA (AND FRIENDS)** *RCA 256* ROYAL PHILHARMONIC ORCHESTRA ARRANGED & CONDUCTED BY LOUIS CLARK	71		

PIPES & DRUMS & MILITARY BAND OF THE ROYAL SCOTS DRAGOON GUARDS
UK military band

Date	Title / Label	Peak Position	Weeks at No.1	Weeks in Top 40
1 Apr 72	**AMAZING GRACE** *RCA 2191*	1	5	21
19 Aug 72	**HEYKENS SERENADE/THE DAY IS ENDED** *RCA 2251*	30		6
2 Dec 72	**LITTLE DRUMMER BOY** *RCA 2301*	13		8

ROYALLE DELITE US group

Date	Title / Label	Peak Position	Weeks at No.1	Weeks in Top 40
14 Sep 85	**(I'LL BE A) FREAK FOR YOU** *Streetwave KHAN 51*	45		

ROYKSOPP Norwegian production duo

Date	Title / Label	Peak Position	Weeks at No.1	Weeks in Top 40
15 Dec 01	**POOR LENO** *Wall Of Sound WALLD 073*	59		
17 Aug 02	**REMIND ME/SO EASY** *Wall Of Sound WALLD 074X*	21		2
30 Nov 02	**POOR LENO** *Wall Of Sound WALLD 079V*	38		1
8 Mar 03	**EPLE** *Wall Of Sound WALLD 080V*	16		2
28 Jun 03	**SPARKS** *Wall Of Sound WALLD 084V*	41		
9 Jul 05	**ONLY THIS MOMENT** *Wall Of Sound WALLD104*	33		1
8 Oct 05	**49 PERCENT** *Wall Of Sound WALLD107X*	55		
17 Dec 05	**WHAT ELSE IS THERE?** *Wall Of Sound WALLD111*	32		2

LITA ROZA UK singer

Date	Title / Label	Peak Position	Weeks at No.1	Weeks in Top 40
13 Mar 53	**(HOW MUCH IS) THAT DOGGIE IN THE WINDOW** *Decca F 10070*	1	1	11
7 Oct 55	**HEY THERE** *Decca F 10611*	17		2
23 Mar 56	**JIMMY UNKNOWN** *Decca F 10679*	15		5

ROZALLA Zambian singer

Date	Title / Label	Peak Position	Weeks at No.1	Weeks in Top 40
27 Apr 91	**FAITH (IN THE POWER OF LOVE)** *Pulse 8 LOSE 7*	65		
7 Sep 91	**EVERYBODY'S FREE (TO FEEL GOOD)** *Pulse 8 LOSE 13* ○	6		10
16 Nov 91	**FAITH (IN THE POWER OF LOVE)** *Pulse 8 LOSE 15*	11		3
22 Feb 92	**ARE YOU READY TO FLY** *Pulse 8 LOSE 21*	14		5
9 May 92	**LOVE BREAKDOWN** *Pulse 8 LOSE 25*	65		
15 Aug 92	**IN 4 CHOONS LATER** *Pulse 8 LOSE 29*	50		
30 Oct 93	**DON'T PLAY WITH ME** *Pulse 8 CDLOSE 52*	50		
5 Feb 94	**I LOVE MUSIC** *Epic 6598932*	18		3
6 Aug 94	**THIS TIME I FOUND LOVE** *Epic 6603742*	33		2
29 Oct 94	**YOU NEVER LOVE THE SAME WAY TWICE** *Epic 6609052*	16		4
4 Mar 95	**BABY** *Epic 6611955*	26		2
31 Aug 96	**EVERYBODY'S FREE (TO FEEL GOOD) (REMIX)** *Pulse 8 CDLOSE 110*	30		1
22 Nov 03	**LIVE ANOTHER LIFE** *Inferno CDFERN 59* PLASTIC BOY FEATURING ROZALLA	55		

RUBBADUBB UK group

Date	Title / Label	Peak Position	Weeks at No.1	Weeks in Top 40
18 Jul 98	**TRIBUTE TO OUR ANCESTORS** *Perfecto PERF 165CD*	56		

RUBETTES UK group

Date	Title / Label	Peak Position	Weeks at No.1	Weeks in Top 40
4 May 74	**SUGAR BABY LOVE** *Polydor 2058 442* ●	1	4	10
13 Jul 74	**TONIGHT** *Polydor 2058 499*	12		8
16 Nov 74	**JUKE BOX JIVE** *Polydor 2058 529* ○	3		12
8 Mar 75	**I CAN DO IT** *State STAT 1*	7		8
21 Jun 75	**FOE-DEE-O-DEE** *State STAT 7*	15		5
22 Nov 75	**LITTLE DARLING** *State STAT 13*	30		4
1 May 76	**YOU'RE THE REASON WHY** *State STAT 20*	28		4
25 Sep 76	**UNDER ONE ROOF** *State STAT 27*	40		1
12 Feb 77	**BABY I KNOW** *State STAT 37*	10		8

MARIA RUBIA UK singer

Date	Title / Label	Peak Position	Weeks at No.1	Weeks in Top 40
13 Jan 01	**EVERYTIME YOU NEED ME** *Positiva CDTIVS 147* FRAGMA FEATURING MARIA RUBIA ○	3		9
19 May 01	**SAY IT** *Neo NEOCD 055*	40		1

PAULINA RUBIO Mexican singer

Date	Title / Label	Peak Position	Weeks at No.1	Weeks in Top 40
28 Sep 02	**DON'T SAY GOODBYE** *Universal MCSXD 40291*	68		

RUBY & THE ROMANTICS US group

Date	Title / Label	Peak Position	Weeks at No.1	Weeks in Top 40
28 Mar 63	**OUR DAY WILL COME** *London HLR 9679* ★	38		4

RUFF DRIVERZ UK production group

Date	Title / Label	Peak Position	Weeks at No.1	Weeks in Top 40
7 Feb 98	**DON'T STOP** *Inferno CDFERN 003*	30		1
23 May 98	**DEEPER LOVE** *Inferno CDFERN 006*	19		2
24 Oct 98	**SHAME** *Inferno CXFERN 9*	51		
28 Nov 98	**DREAMING** *Inferno CXFERN 11* RUFF DRIVERZ PRESENTS ARROLA	10		3
24 Apr 99	**LA MUSICA** *Inferno CDFERN 14* RUFF DRIVERZ PRESENTS ARROLA	14		3
2 Oct 99	**WAITING FOR THE SUN** *Inferno CDFERN 19*	37		1

RUFF ENDZ US group

Date	Title / Label	Peak Position	Weeks at No.1	Weeks in Top 40
19 Aug 00	**NO MORE** *Epic 6696202*	11		4

FRANCES RUFFELLE UK singer

Date	Title / Label	Peak Position	Weeks at No.1	Weeks in Top 40
16 Apr 94	**LONELY SYMPHONY** *Virgin VSCDT 1499*	25		5

BRUCE RUFFIN Jamaican singer

Date	Title / Label	Peak Position	Weeks at No.1	Weeks in Top 40
1 May 71	**RAIN** *Trojan TR 7814*	19		7
24 Jun 72	**MAD ABOUT YOU** *Rhino RNO 101*	9		10

DAVID RUFFIN US singer

Date	Title / Label	Peak Position	Weeks at No.1	Weeks in Top 40
17 Jan 76	**WALK AWAY FROM LOVE** *Tamla Motown TMG 1017*	10		7
21 Sep 85	**A NIGHT AT THE APOLLO LIVE!** *RCA PB 49935* DARYL HALL & JOHN OATES FEATURING DAVID RUFFIN & EDDIE KENDRICK	58		

JIMMY RUFFIN US singer

Date	Title / Label	Peak Position	Weeks at No.1	Weeks in Top 40
27 Oct 66	**WHAT BECOMES OF THE BROKENHEARTED** *Tamla Motown TMG 577*	10		11
9 Feb 67	**I'VE PASSED THIS WAY BEFORE** *Tamla Motown TMG 593*	29		6
20 Apr 67	**GONNA GIVE HER ALL THE LOVE I'VE GOT** *Tamla Motown TMG 603*	26		4
9 Aug 69	**I'VE PASSED THIS WAY BEFORE** *Tamla Motown TMG 703*	33		2
28 Feb 70	**FAREWELL IS A LONELY SOUND** *Tamla Motown TMG 726*	8		13
4 Jul 70	**I'LL SAY FOREVER MY LOVE** *Tamla Motown TMG 740*	7		11
17 Oct 70	**IT'S WONDERFUL (TO BE LOVED BY YOU)** *Tamla Motown TMG 753*	6		12
27 Jul 74	**WHAT BECOMES OF THE BROKENHEARTED** *Tamla Motown TMG 911* ○	4		11
2 Nov 74	**FAREWELL IS A LONELY SOUND** *Tamla Motown TMG 922*	30		5
16 Nov 74	**TELL ME WHAT YOU WANT** *Polydor 2058 433*	39		1
3 May 80	**HOLD ON TO MY LOVE** *RSO 57*	7		7
26 Jan 85	**THERE WILL NEVER BE ANOTHER YOU** *EMI 5541*	68		

RUFFNECK US group

Date	Title / Label	Peak Position	Weeks at No.1	Weeks in Top 40
11 Nov 95	**EVERYBODY BE SOMEBODY** *Positiva CDTIV 46* RUFFNECK FEATURING YAVAHN	13		3
7 Sep 96	**MOVE YOUR BODY** *Positiva CDTIV 61* RUFFNECK FEATURING YAVAHN	60		
1 Dec 01	**EVERYBODY BE SOMEBODY (REMIX)** *Strictly Rhythm SRUKCD 08* RUFFNECK FEATURING YAVAHN	66		

Silver-selling ● Gold-selling ● Platinum-selling ⊛ US No.1 ★ | Peak Position | Weeks at No.1 | Weeks in Top 40

RUFUS & CHAKA KHAN US group

Date	Title / Label	Peak	No.1	Top 40
31 Mar 84	**AIN'T NOBODY** *Warner Brothers RCK 1* ●	8		9
8 Jul 89	**AIN'T NOBODY (REMIX)** *Warner Brothers W 2880*	6		8

RUMBLE STRIPS US group

Date	Title / Label	Peak	No.1	Top 40
31 Mar 07	**ALARM CLOCK** *Fallout 1723936*	41		
23 Jun 07	**MOTORCYCLE** *Fallout 1727123*	46		
15 Sep 07	**GIRLS AND BOYS IN LOVE** *Fallout 1745159*	64		

RUMPLE-STILTS-SKIN US group

Date	Title / Label	Peak	No.1	Top 40
24 Sep 83	**I THINK I WANT TO DANCE WITH YOU** *Polydor POSP 649*	51		

RUN TINGS UK production duo

Date	Title / Label	Peak	No.1	Top 40
16 May 92	**FIRES BURNING** *Suburban Base SUBBASE 009*	58		

TODD RUNDGREN US singer/multi instrumentalist

Date	Title / Label	Peak	No.1	Top 40
30 Jun 73	**I SAW THE LIGHT** *Bearsville K 15506*	36		4
14 Dec 85	**LOVING YOU'S A DIRTY JOB BUT SOMEBODY'S GOTTA DO IT** *CBS A 6662* BONNIE TYLER, GUEST VOCALS TODD RUNDGREN	73		

RUN D.M.C. US group

Date	Title / Label	Peak	No.1	Top 40
19 Jul 86	**MY ADIDAS/PETER PIPER** *London LON 101*	62		
6 Sep 86	**WALK THIS WAY** *London LON 104*	8		8
7 Feb 87	**YOU BE ILLIN'** *Profile LON 118*	42		
30 May 87	**IT'S TRICKY** *Profile LON 130*	16		5
12 Dec 87	**CHRISTMAS IN HOLLIS** *Profile LON 163*	56		
21 May 88	**RUN'S HOUSE** *London LON 177*	37		1
2 Sep 89	**GHOSTBUSTERS** *MCA 1360*	65		
1 Dec 90	**WHAT'S IT ALL ABOUT** *Profile PROF 315*	48		
27 Mar 93	**DOWN WITH THE KING** *Profile PROFCD 39*	69		
21 Feb 98	**IT'S LIKE THAT (GERMAN IMPORT)** *Columbia 6652932* RUN DMC VERSUS JASON NEVINS	63		
14 Mar 98	**IT'S LIKE THAT (AMERICAN IMPORT)** *Columbia 6652932* RUN DMC VERSUS JASON NEVINS	65		
21 Mar 98	**IT'S LIKE THAT** *Sm:)e Communications SM 90652* RUN DMC VERSUS JASON NEVINS ⊛	1	6	14
18 Apr 98	**IT'S TRICKY (IMPORT)** *Epidrome EPD 6656982* RUN DMC VERSUS JASON NEVINS	74		
19 Apr 03	**IT'S TRICKY 2003** *Arista 82876513712* RUN DMC FEATURING JACKNIFE LEE	20		2

RUNRIG UK group

Date	Title / Label	Peak	No.1	Top 40
29 Sep 90	**CAPTURE THE HEART (EP)** *Chrysalis CHS 3594*	49		
7 Sep 91	**HEARTHAMMER (EP)** *Chrysalis CHS 3754*	25		2
9 Nov 91	**FLOWER OF THE WEST** *Chrysalis CHS 3805*	43		
6 Mar 93	**WONDERFUL** *Chrysalis CDCHS 3952*	29		1
15 May 93	**THE GREATEST FLAME** *Chrysalis CDCHS 3975*	36		2
7 Jan 95	**THIS TIME OF YEAR** *Chrysalis CDCHS 5018*	38		1
6 May 95	**AN UBHAL AS AIRDE (THE HIGHEST APPLE)** *Chrysalis CDCHS 5021*	18		3
4 Nov 95	**THINGS THAT ARE** *Chrysalis CDCHS 5029*	40		1
12 Oct 96	**RHYTHM OF MY HEART** *Chrysalis CDCHS 5035*	24		1
11 Jan 97	**THE GREATEST FLAME (REMIX)** *Chrysalis CDCHSS 5045*	30		1
24 Nov 07	**LOCH LOMOND** *Ridge RRS48* RUNRIG & THE TARTAN ARMY	9		3

RuPAUL US singer

Date	Title / Label	Peak	No.1	Top 40
26 Jun 93	**SUPERMODEL (YOU BETTER WORK)** *Union City UCRD 21*	39		1
18 Sep 93	**HOUSE OF LOVE/BACK TO MY ROOTS** *Union City UCRD 23*	40		1
22 Jan 94	**SUPERMODEL/LITTLE DRUMMER BOY** *Union City UCRD 25*	61		
26 Feb 94	**DON'T GO BREAKING MY HEART** *Rocket EJCD 33* ELTON JOHN WITH RuPAUL	7		5
25 May 94	**HOUSE OF LOVE (REMIX)** *Union City UCRDG 29*	68		
28 Feb 98	**IT'S RAINING MEN...THE SEQUEL** *Logic 74321555412* MARTHA WASH FEATURING RuPAUL	21		2

RUPEE Barbadian singer

Date	Title / Label	Peak	No.1	Top 40
23 Oct 04	**TEMPTED TO TOUCH** *Atlantic AT0185CD*	44		

RUSH Canadian group

Date	Title / Label	Peak	No.1	Top 40
11 Feb 78	**CLOSER TO THE HEART** *Mercury RUSH 7*	36		1
15 Mar 80	**SPIRIT OF RADIO** *Mercury RADIO 7*	13		6
28 Mar 81	**VITAL SIGNS/A PASSAGE TO BANGKOK** *Mercury VITAL 7*	41		
28 Mar 81	**A PASSAGE TO BANGKOK** *Mercury VITAL 7*	41		
31 Oct 81	**TOM SAWYER** *Mercury Exit 7*	25		5
4 Sep 82	**NEW WORLD MAN** *Mercury RUSH 8*	42		
30 Oct 82	**SUBDIVISIONS** *Mercury RUSH 9*	53		
7 May 83	**COUNTDOWN/NEW WORLD MAN (LIVE)** *Mercury RUSH 10*	36		2
26 May 84	**THE BODY ELECTRIC** *Mercury RUSH 11*	56		
12 Oct 85	**THE BIG MONEY** *Vertigo RUSH 12*	46		
31 Oct 87	**TIME STAND STILL** *Vertigo RUSH 13* RUSH WITH AIMEE MANN	42		
23 Apr 88	**PRIME MOVER** *Vertigo RUSH 14*	43		
7 Mar 92	**ROLL THE BONES** *Atlantic A 7524*	49		

DONELL RUSH US singer

Date	Title / Label	Peak	No.1	Top 40
5 Dec 92	**SYMPHONY** *ID 6587977*	66		

ED RUSH & OPTICAL US production duo

Date	Title / Label	Peak	No.1	Top 40
1 Jun 02	**PACMAN/VESSEL** *Virus VRS 010* ED RUSH & OPTICAL/UNIVERSAL PROJECT	61		
20 Nov 04	**REMIXES – VOLUME 2** *Virus VRS014B*	69		

JENNIFER RUSH US singer

Date	Title / Label	Peak	No.1	Top 40
29 Jun 85	**THE POWER OF LOVE** *CBS A 5003* ⊛	1	5	18
14 Dec 85	**RING OF ICE** *CBS A 4745*	14		7
20 Jun 87	**FLAMES OF PARADISE** *Columbia 6508657* JENNIFER RUSH & ELTON JOHN	59		
27 May 89	**TILL I LOVED YOU** *CBS 6548437* PLACIDO DOMINGO & JENNIFER RUSH	24		4

PATRICE RUSHEN US singer

Date	Title / Label	Peak	No.1	Top 40
1 Mar 80	**HAVEN'T YOU HEARD** *Elektra K 12414*	62		
24 Jan 81	**NEVER GONNA GIVE YOU UP (WON'T LET YOU BE)** *Elektra K 12494*	66		
24 Apr 82	**FORGET ME NOTS** *Elektra K 13173*	8		8
10 Jul 82	**I WAS TIRED OF BEING ALONE** *Elektra K 13184*	39		2
9 Jun 84	**FEELS SO REAL (WON'T LET GO)** *Elektra E 9742*	51		

RUSLANA Ukrainian singer

Date	Title / Label	Peak	No.1	Top 40
19 Jun 04	**WILD DANCES** *Liberty 5490542*	47		

RUSSELL US singer

Date	Title / Label	Peak	No.1	Top 40
27 May 00	**FOOL FOR LOVE** *Rulin ICDS*	52		

BRENDA RUSSELL US singer

Date	Title / Label	Peak	No.1	Top 40
19 Apr 80	**SO GOOD SO RIGHT/IN THE THICK OF IT** *A&M AM 7515*	51		
12 Mar 88	**PIANO IN THE DARK** *Breakout USA 623*	23		7

RUTH UK group

Date	Title / Label	Peak	No.1	Top 40
12 Apr 97	**I DON'T KNOW** *Arc 5737812*	66		

PAUL RUTHERFORD UK singer

Date	Title / Label	Peak	No.1	Top 40
8 Oct 88	**GET REAL** *Fourth & Broadway BRW 113*	47		
19 Aug 89	**OH WORLD** *Fourth & Broadway BRW 136*	61		

RUTHLESS RAP ASSASSINS UK group

Date	Title / Label	Peak	No.1	Top 40
9 Jun 90	**JUST MELLOW** *Syncopate SY 35*	75		
1 Sep 90	**AND IT WASN'T A DREAM** *Syncopate SY 38*	75		

RUTLES UK group

Date	Title / Label	Peak	No.1	Top 40
15 Apr 78	**I MUST BE IN LOVE** *Warner Brothers K 17125*	39		1
16 Nov 96	**SHANGRI-LA** *Virgin America VUSCD 117*	68		

RUTS UK group

Date	Title / Label	Peak Position	Weeks at No.1	Weeks in Top 40
16 Jun 79	**BABYLON'S BURNING** *Virgin VS 271*	7		7
8 Sep 79	**SOMETHING THAT I SAID** *Virgin VS 285*	29		2
19 Apr 80	**STARING AT THE RUDE BOYS** *Virgin VS 327*	22		5
30 Aug 80	**WEST ONE (SHINE ON ME)** *Virgin VS 370*	43		

BARRY RYAN UK singer

Date	Title / Label	Peak Position	Weeks at No.1	Weeks in Top 40
23 Oct 68	**ELOISE** *MGM 1442*	2		11
19 Feb 69	**LOVE IS LOVE** *MGM 1464*	25		4
4 Oct 69	**HUNT** *Polydor 56 348*	34		3
21 Feb 70	**MAGICAL SPIEL** *Polydor 56 370*	49		
16 May 70	**KITSCH** *Polydor 2001 035*	37		1
15 Jan 72	**CAN'T LET YOU GO** *Polydor 2001 256*	32		4

JOSHUA RYAN US singer

Date	Title / Label	Peak Position	Weeks at No.1	Weeks in Top 40
27 Jan 01	**PISTOL WHIP** *NuLife 74321825482*	29		1

LEE RYAN UK singer

Date	Title / Label	Peak Position	Weeks at No.1	Weeks in Top 40
30 Jul 05	**ARMY OF LOVERS** *Brightside 82876713182*	3		6
22 Oct 05	**TURN YOUR CAR AROUND** *Brightside 82876743372*	12		3
11 Feb 06	**WHEN I THINK OF YOU** *Brightside 82876782892*	15		3

MARION RYAN UK singer

Date	Title / Label	Peak Position	Weeks at No.1	Weeks in Top 40
24 Jan 58	**LOVE ME FOREVER** *Pye Nixa N 15121*	5		11

PAUL & BARRY RYAN UK duo

Date	Title / Label	Peak Position	Weeks at No.1	Weeks in Top 40
11 Nov 65	**DON'T BRING ME YOUR HEARTACHES** *Decca F 12260*	13		9
3 Feb 66	**HAVE PITY ON THE BOY** *Decca F 12319*	18		5
12 May 66	**I LOVE HER** *Decca F 12391*	17		6
14 Jul 66	**I LOVE HOW YOU LOVE ME** *Decca F 12445*	21		5
29 Sep 66	**HAVE YOU EVER LOVED SOMEBODY** *Decca F 12494*	49		
8 Dec 66	**MISSY MISSY** *Decca F 12520*	43		
2 Mar 67	**KEEP IT OUT OF SIGHT** *Decca F 12567*	30		5
29 Jun 67	**CLAIRE** *Decca F 12633*	47		

REBEKAH RYAN UK singer

Date	Title / Label	Peak Position	Weeks at No.1	Weeks in Top 40
18 May 96	**YOU LIFT ME UP** *MCA MCSTD 40022*	26		1
7 Sep 96	**JUST A LITTLE BIT OF LOVE** *MCA MCSTD 40063*	51		
17 May 97	**WOMAN IN LOVE** *MCA MCSTD 40109*	64		

RYANDAN Canadian duo

Date	Title / Label	Peak Position	Weeks at No.1	Weeks in Top 40
29 Sep 07	**LIKE THE SUN** *UCJ 1747339*	69		

BOBBY RYDELL US singer

Date	Title / Label	Peak Position	Weeks at No.1	Weeks in Top 40
10 Mar 60	**WILD ONE** *Columbia DB 4429*	7		12
1 Sep 60	**VOLARE** *Columbia DB 4495*	22		5
30 Jun 60	**SWINGING SCHOOL** *Columbia DB 4471*	44		
15 Dec 60	**SWAY** *Columbia DB 4545*	12		12
23 Mar 61	**GOOD TIME BABY** *Columbia DB 4600*	42		
19 Apr 62	**TEACH ME TO TWIST** *Columbia DB 4802* CHUBBY CHECKER & BOBBY RYDELL	45		
20 Dec 62	**JINGLE BELL ROCK** *Cameo Parkway C 205* CHUBBY CHECKER & BOBBY RYDELL	40		1
23 May 63	**FORGET HIM** *Cameo Parkway C 108*	13		12

MARK RYDER UK producer

Date	Title / Label	Peak Position	Weeks at No.1	Weeks in Top 40
31 Mar 01	**JOY** *Relentless/Public Demand RELENT9CDS*	34		1

MITCH RYDER & THE DETROIT WHEELS US group

Date	Title / Label	Peak Position	Weeks at No.1	Weeks in Top 40
10 Feb 66	**JENNY TAKE A RIDE** *Stateside SS 481*	33		3

SHAUN RYDER UK singer

Date	Title / Label	Peak Position	Weeks at No.1	Weeks in Top 40
9 Nov 96	**DON'T TAKE MY KINDNESS FOR WEAKNESS** *Radioactive MCSTD 48024* HEADS WITH SHAUN RYDER	60		
22 Jul 00	**BARCELONA (FRIENDS UNTIL THE END)** *Decca 46672772* RUSSELL WATSON & SHAUN RYDER	68		

RYTHM SYNDICATE US group

Date	Title / Label	Peak Position	Weeks at No.1	Weeks in Top 40
27 Jul 91	**P.A.S.S.I.O.N.** *Impact American EM 197*	58		

RYZE UK group

Date	Title / Label	Peak Position	Weeks at No.1	Weeks in Top 40
2 Nov 02	**IN MY LIFE** *Inferno Cool CDFERN 48*	46		

S

ROBIN S US singer

Date	Title / Label	Peak Position	Weeks at No.1	Weeks in Top 40
16 Jan 93	**SHOW ME LOVE** *Champion CHAMPCD 300*	59		
13 Mar 93	**SHOW ME LOVE** *Champion CHAMPCD 300*	6		10
31 Jul 93	**LUV 4 LUV** *Champion CHAMPCD 301*	11		6
4 Dec 93	**WHAT I DO BEST** *Champion CHAMPCD 307*	43		
19 Mar 94	**I WANT TO THANK YOU** *Champion CHAMPCD 310*	48		
5 Nov 94	**BACK IT UP** *Champion CHAMPCD 312*	43		
8 Mar 97	**SHOW ME LOVE (REMIX)** *Champion CHAMPCD 326*	9		3
12 Jul 97	**IT MUST BE LOVE** *Atlantic A 5596CD*	37		1
4 Oct 97	**YOU GOT THE LOVE** *Champion CHAMPCD 330* T2 FEATURING ROBIN S	62		
7 Dec 02	**SHOW ME LOVE (2ND REMIX)** *Champion CHAMPCD 796*	61		

S CLUB JUNIORS UK group

Date	Title / Label	Peak Position	Weeks at No.1	Weeks in Top 40
4 May 02	**ONE STEP CLOSER** *Polydor 5707332*	2		11
3 Aug 02	**AUTOMATIC HIGH** *Polydor 5708922*	2		8
19 Oct 02	**NEW DIRECTION** *Polydor 0659702*	2		6
21 Dec 02	**PUPPY LOVE/SLEIGH RIDE** *Polydor 0658442*	6		5
12 Jul 03	**FOOL NO MORE** *Polydor 9808754* S CLUB 8	4		5
11 Oct 03	**SUNDOWN** *19/Universal 9811790* S CLUB 8	4		5
10 Jan 04	**DON'T TELL ME YOU'RE SORRY** *Polydor 9815342* S CLUB 8	11		3

S CLUB 7 UK group

Date	Title / Label	Peak Position	Weeks at No.1	Weeks in Top 40
19 Jun 99	**BRING IT ALL BACK** *Polydor 5610852*	1	1	11
2 Oct 99	**S CLUB PARTY** *Polydor 5614172*	2		9
25 Dec 99	**TWO IN A MILLION/YOU'RE MY NUMBER ONE** *Polydor 5615962*	2		9
3 Jun 00	**REACH** *Polydor 5618302*	2		15
23 Sep 00	**NATURAL** *Polydor 5677602*	3		7
9 Dec 00	**NEVER HAD A DREAM COME TRUE** *Polydor 5879032*	1	1	11
5 May 01	**DON'T STOP MOVIN'** *Polydor 5870842*	1	2	16
1 Dec 01	**HAVE YOU EVER** *Polydor 5705002*	1	1	10
23 Feb 02	**YOU** *Polydor 5705822*	2		8
30 Nov 02	**ALIVE** *Polydor 0658912* S CLUB	5		7
7 Jun 03	**SAY GOODBYE/LOVE AIN'T GONNA WAIT FOR YOU** *Polydor 9807140* S CLUB	2		7

S-EXPRESS UK group

Date	Title / Label	Peak Position	Weeks at No.1	Weeks in Top 40
16 Apr 88	**THEME FROM S-EXPRESS** *Rhythm King LEFT 21*	1	2	10
23 Jul 88	**SUPERFLY GUY** *Rhythm King LEFT 28*	5		8
18 Feb 89	**HEY MUSIC LOVER** *Rhythm King LEFT 30*	6		8
16 Sep 89	**MANTRA FOR A STATE MIND** *Rhythm King LEFT 35*	21		6
15 Sep 90	**NOTHING TO LOSE** *Rhythm King SEXY 01*	32		3
30 May 92	**FIND 'EM, FOOL 'EM, FORGET 'EM** *Rhythm King 6580137*	43		
11 May 96	**THEME FROM S-EXPRESS (REMIX)** *Rhythm King SEXY 9CD*	14		2

S-J UK singer

Date	Title / Label	Peak Position	Weeks at No.1	Weeks in Top 40
11 Jan 97	**FEVER** *React CDREACT 93*	46		
24 Jan 98	**I FEEL DIVINE** *React CDREACT 113*	30		1
7 Nov 98	**SHIVER** *React CDREACT 138*	59		

Silver-selling ○ Gold-selling ● Platinum-selling ⊛ US No.1 ★ — Peak Position / Weeks at No.1 / Weeks in Top 40

RAPHAEL SAADIQ US singer

Date	Title / Label	Peak Position	Weeks at No.1	Weeks in Top 40
23 Nov 96	**STRESSED OUT** *Jive JIVECD 404* A TRIBE CALLED QUEST FEATURING FAITH EVANS & RAPHAEL SAADIQ	33		1
19 Jun 99	**GET INVOLVED** *Hollywood 0101185 HWR* RAPHAEL SAADIQ & Q-TIP	36		1

SABRE Jamaican duo

Date	Title / Label	Peak Position	Weeks at No.1	Weeks in Top 40
19 Aug 95	**WRONG OR RIGHT** *Greensleeves GRECD 485* SABRE FEATURING PREZIDENT BROWN	71		

SABRES OF PARADISE UK group

Date	Title / Label	Peak Position	Weeks at No.1	Weeks in Top 40
2 Oct 93	**SMOKEBELCH II** *Sabres Of Paradise PT 009CD*	55		
9 Apr 94	**THEME** *Sabres Of Paradise PT 014CD*	56		
17 Sep 94	**WILMOT** *Warp WAP 50CD*	36		1

SABRINA Italian singer

Date	Title / Label	Peak Position	Weeks at No.1	Weeks in Top 40
6 Feb 88	**BOYS (SUMMERTIME LOVE)** *Ibiza IBIZ 1*	60		
11 Jun 88	**BOYS (SUMMERTIME LOVE)** *Ibiza IBIZ 1* ○	3		9
1 Oct 88	**ALL OF ME** *PWL 19*	25		5
1 Jul 89	**LIKE A YO-YO** *Videogram DCUP 1*	72		

SACRED SPIRIT German multi-instrumentalist

Date	Title / Label	Peak Position	Weeks at No.1	Weeks in Top 40
15 Apr 95	**YEHA-NOHA (WISHES OF HAPPINESS AND PROSPERITY)** *Virgin VSCDT 1514*	71		
18 Nov 95	**YEHA-NOHA (WISHES OF HAPPINESS AND PROSPERITY)** *Virgin VSCDT 1514*	37		1
16 Mar 96	**WINTER CEREMONY (TOR-CHENEY-NAHANA)** *Virgin VSCDT 1574*	45		

SAD CAFÉ UK group

Date	Title / Label	Peak Position	Weeks at No.1	Weeks in Top 40
22 Sep 79	**EVERY DAY HURTS** *RCA PB 5180* ○	3		10
19 Jan 80	**STRANGE LITTLE GIRL** *RCA PB 5202*	32		3
15 Mar 80	**MY OH MY** *RCA SAD 3*	14		7
21 Jun 80	**NOTHING LEFT TOULOUSE** *RCA SAD 4*	62		
27 Sep 80	**LA-DI-DA** *RCA SAD 5*	41		
20 Dec 80	**I'M IN LOVE AGAIN** *RCA SAD 6*	40		1

SADE UK group

Date	Title / Label	Peak Position	Weeks at No.1	Weeks in Top 40
25 Feb 84	**YOUR LOVE IS KING** *Epic A 4137*	6		7
26 May 84	**WHEN AM I GONNA MAKE A LIVING** *Epic A 4437*	36		3
15 Sep 84	**SMOOTH OPERATOR** *Epic A 4655*	19		8
12 Oct 85	**THE SWEETEST TABOO** *Epic A 6609*	31		3
11 Jan 86	**IS IT A CRIME** *Epic A 6742*	49		
2 Apr 88	**LOVE IS STRONGER THAN PRIDE** *Epic SADE 1*	44		
4 Jun 88	**PARADISE** *Epic SADE 2*	29		4
10 Oct 92	**NO ORDINARY LOVE** *Epic 6583567*	26		2
28 Nov 92	**FEEL NO PAIN** *Epic 6588297*	56		
8 May 93	**KISS OF LIFE** *Epic 6591162*	44		
5 Jun 93	**NO ORDINARY LOVE** *Epic 6583562*	14		6
31 Jul 93	**CHERISH THE DAY** *Epic 6594812*	53		
18 Nov 00	**BY YOUR SIDE** *Epic 6699992*	17		3
24 Mar 01	**KING OF SORROW** *Epic 6708672*	59		

STAFF SERGEANT BARRY SADLER US singer

Date	Title / Label	Peak Position	Weeks at No.1	Weeks in Top 40
24 Mar 66	**BALLAD OF THE GREEN BERETS** *RCA 1506* ★	24		6

SAFFRON UK singer

Date	Title / Label	Peak Position	Weeks at No.1	Weeks in Top 40
16 Jan 93	**CIRCLES** *WEA SAFF 9CD*	60		

SAFFRON HILL UK producer

Date	Title / Label	Peak Position	Weeks at No.1	Weeks in Top 40
17 May 03	**MY LOVE IS ALWAYS** *Illustrious CDILL 016* SAFFRON HILL FEATURING BEN ONONO	28		1

SAFRI DUO Danish group

Date	Title / Label	Peak Position	Weeks at No.1	Weeks in Top 40
3 Feb 01	**PLAYED A LIVE (THE BONGO SONG)** *AM:PM CDAMPM 141*	6		6
5 Oct 02	**SWEET FREEDOM** *Serious SERR 55CD* SAFRI DUO FEATURING MICHAEL McDONALD	54		

MIKE SAGAR & THE CRESTERS UK group

Date	Title / Label	Peak Position	Weeks at No.1	Weeks in Top 40
8 Dec 60	**DEEP FEELING** *HMV POP 819*	44		

SAGAT US rapper

Date	Title / Label	Peak Position	Weeks at No.1	Weeks in Top 40
4 Dec 93	**FUNK DAT** *ffrr FCD 224*	25		2
3 Dec 94	**LUVSTUFF** *ffrr FCD 250*	71		

CAROLE BAYER SAGER US singer

Date	Title / Label	Peak Position	Weeks at No.1	Weeks in Top 40
28 May 77	**YOU'RE MOVING OUT TODAY** *Elektra K 12257*	6		8

BALLY SAGOO Indian singer

Date	Title / Label	Peak Position	Weeks at No.1	Weeks in Top 40
3 Sep 94	**CHURA LIYA** *Columbia 6607092*	64		
22 Apr 95	**CHOLI KE PEECHE** *Columbia 6613352*	45		
19 Oct 96	**DIL CHEEZ (MY HEART...)** *Higher Ground 6634882*	12		2
1 Feb 97	**TUM BIN JIYA** *Higher Ground 6641372*	21		1

SAILOR UK group

Date	Title / Label	Peak Position	Weeks at No.1	Weeks in Top 40
6 Dec 75	**A GLASS OF CHAMPAGNE** *Epic EPC 3770* ○	2		11
27 Mar 76	**GIRLS GIRLS GIRLS** *Epic EPC 3858*	7		7
19 Feb 77	**ONE DRINK TOO MANY** *Epic EPC 4804*	35		2

SAINT UK group

Date	Title / Label	Peak Position	Weeks at No.1	Weeks in Top 40
12 Apr 03	**SHOW ME HEAVEN** *Inferno CXFERN 52* SAINT FEATURING SUZANNA DEE	36		1

ST ANDREWS CHORALE UK church choir

Date	Title / Label	Peak Position	Weeks at No.1	Weeks in Top 40
14 Feb 76	**CLOUD 99** *Decca F 13617*	31		4

ST CECILIA UK singer

Date	Title / Label	Peak Position	Weeks at No.1	Weeks in Top 40
19 Jun 71	**LEAP UP AND DOWN (WAVE YOUR KNICKERS IN THE AIR)** *Polydor 2058 104*	12		15

SAINT ETIENNE UK group

Date	Title / Label	Peak Position	Weeks at No.1	Weeks in Top 40
18 May 91	**NOTHING CAN STOP US/SPEEDWELL** *Heavenly HVN 009*	54		
7 Sep 91	**ONLY LOVE CAN BREAK YOUR HEART/FILTHY** *Heavenly HVN 12*	39		1
16 May 92	**JOIN OUR CLUB/PEOPLE GET REAL** *Heavenly HVN 15*	21		2
17 Oct 92	**AVENUE** *Heavenly HVN 2312*	40		1
13 Feb 93	**YOU'RE IN A BAD WAY** *Heavenly HVN 25CD*	12		3
22 May 93	**HOBART PAVING/WHO DO YOU THINK YOU ARE** *Heavenly HVN 29CD*	23		3
18 Dec 93	**I WAS BORN ON CHRISTMAS DAY** *Heavenly HVN 36CD* SAINT ETIENNE CO STARRING TIM BURGESS	37		2
19 Feb 94	**PALE MOVIE** *Heavenly HVN 37CD*	28		2
28 May 94	**LIKE A MOTORWAY** *Heavenly HVN 40CD*	47		
1 Oct 94	**HUG MY SOUL** *Heavenly HVN 42CD*	32		1
11 Nov 95	**HE'S ON THE PHONE** *Heavenly HVN 50CDR* SAINT ETIENNE FEATURING ETIENNE DAHO	11		4
7 Feb 98	**SYLVIE** *Creation CRESCD 279X*	12		2
2 May 98	**THE BAD PHOTOGRAPHER** *Creation CRESCD 290*	27		1
20 May 00	**TELL ME WHY (THE RIDDLE)** *Deviant DVNT 36CDS* PAUL VAN DYK FEATURING SAINT ETIENNE	7		4
24 Jun 00	**HEART FAILED (IN THE BACK OF A TAXI)** *Mantra MNT 54CD*	50		
20 Jan 01	**BOY IS CRYING** *Mantra MNT 60CD1*	34		1
7 Sep 02	**ACTION** *Mantra MNT 73CD*	41		
29 Mar 03	**SOFT LIKE ME** *Mantra MNT 78CD*	40		1
18 Jun 05	**SIDE STREETS** *Sanctuary SANXS378*	36		1
12 Nov 05	**A GOOD THING** *Sanctuary SANXS412*	70		

ST GERMAIN French group

Date	Title / Label	Peak Position	Weeks at No.1	Weeks in Top 40
31 Aug 96	**ALABAMA BLUES (REVISITED)** *F Communications F 050CD*	50		
10 Mar 01	**ROSE ROUGE** *Blue Note CDROSE 001*	54		

BARRY ST JOHN UK singer

Date	Title / Label	Peak Position	Weeks at No.1	Weeks in Top 40
9 Dec 65	**COME AWAY MELINDA** *Columbia DB 7783*	47		

ST JOHN'S COLLEGE SCHOOL CHOIR & THE BAND OF THE GRENADIER GUARDS
UK school choir and military band

Date	Title / Label	Peak Position	Weeks at No.1	Weeks in Top 40
3 May 86	**THE QUEEN'S BIRTHDAY SONG** *Columbia Q1*	40		1

ST LOUIS UNION UK group

Date	Title / Label	Peak Position	Weeks at No.1	Weeks in Top 40
13 Jan 66	**GIRL** *Decca F 12318*	11		9

CRISPIAN ST PETERS UK singer/guitarist

Date	Title / Label	Peak Position	Weeks at No.1	Weeks in Top 40
6 Jan 66	**YOU WERE ON MY MIND** *Decca F 12287*	2		12
31 Mar 66	**PIED PIPER** *Decca F 12359*	5		11
15 Sep 66	**CHANGES** *Decca F 12480*	47		

ST PHILIPS CHOIR UK choir

Date	Title / Label	Peak Position	Weeks at No.1	Weeks in Top 40
12 Dec 87	**SING FOR EVER** *BBC RESL 222*	49		

ST WINIFRED'S SCHOOL CHOIR
UK school choir

Date	Title / Label	Peak Position	Weeks at No.1	Weeks in Top 40
22 Nov 80	**THERE'S NO ONE QUITE LIKE GRANDMA** *MFP FP 900* ●	1	2	8

BUFFY SAINTE-MARIE Canadian singer

Date	Title / Label	Peak Position	Weeks at No.1	Weeks in Top 40
17 Jul 71	**SOLDIER BLUE** *RCA 2081*	7		14
18 Mar 72	**I'M GONNA BE A COUNTRY GIRL AGAIN** *Vanguard VRS 35143*	34		2
8 Feb 92	**THE BIG ONES GET AWAY** *Ensign ENY 650*	39		2
4 Jul 92	**FALLEN ANGELS** *Ensign ENY 655*	57		

SAINTS Australian group

Date	Title / Label	Peak Position	Weeks at No.1	Weeks in Top 40
16 Jul 77	**THIS PERFECT DAY** *Harvest HAR 5130*	34		2

KYU SAKAMOTO Japanese singer

Date	Title / Label	Peak Position	Weeks at No.1	Weeks in Top 40
27 Jun 63	**SUKIYAKI** *HMV POP 1171* ★	6		12

RYUICHI SAKAMOTO Japanese synthesiser player

Date	Title / Label	Peak Position	Weeks at No.1	Weeks in Top 40
7 Aug 82	**BAMBOO HOUSES/BAMBOO MUSIC** *Virgin VS 510* SYLVIAN SAKAMOTO	30		3
2 Jul 83	**FORBIDDEN COLOURS** *Virgin VS 601* DAVID SYLVIAN & RYUICHI SAKAMOTO	16		7
13 Jun 92	**HEARTBEAT (TAINAI KAIKI II) RETURNING TO THE WOMB** *Virgin America VUS 57* DAVID SYLVIAN/RYUICHI SAKAMOTO FEATURING INGRID CHAVEZ	58		

SAKKARIN UK singer

Date	Title / Label	Peak Position	Weeks at No.1	Weeks in Top 40
3 Apr 71	**SUGAR SUGAR** *RCA 2064*	12		11

SALAD UK/Dutch group

Date	Title / Label	Peak Position	Weeks at No.1	Weeks in Top 40
11 Mar 95	**DRINK THE ELIXIR** *Island Red CIRD 104*	66		
13 May 95	**MOTORBIKE TO HEAVEN** *Island Red CIRD 106*	42		
16 Sep 95	**GRANITE STATUE** *Island Red CIRD 108*	50		
26 Oct 96	**I WANT YOU** *Island CID 646*	60		
17 May 97	**CARDBOY KING** *Island CID 654*	65		

SALFORD JETS UK group

Date	Title / Label	Peak Position	Weeks at No.1	Weeks in Top 40
31 May 80	**WHO YOU LOOKING AT** *RCA PB 5239*	72		

SALIVA US group

Date	Title / Label	Peak Position	Weeks at No.1	Weeks in Top 40
15 Mar 03	**ALWAYS** *Mercury 0637082*	47		

SALT TANK UK production duo

Date	Title / Label	Peak Position	Weeks at No.1	Weeks in Top 40
11 May 96	**EUGINA** *Internal LIECD 29*	40		1
3 Jul 99	**DIMENSION** *Hooj Choons HOOJ 74CD*	52		
9 Dec 00	**EUGINA (REMIX)** *Lost Language LOST 004CD*	58		

SALT-N-PEPA US duo

Date	Title / Label	Peak Position	Weeks at No.1	Weeks in Top 40
26 Mar 88	**PUSH IT/I AM DOWN** *ffrr FFR 2*	41		
25 Jun 88	**PUSH IT/TRAMP** *Champion CHAMP 51/ffrr FFR 2* ○	2		10
3 Sep 88	**SHAKE YOUR THANG (IT'S YOUR THING)** *ffrr FFR 11* SALT-N-PEPA FEATURING E.U.	22		6
12 Nov 88	**TWIST AND SHOUT** *ffrr FFR 16*	4		6
14 Apr 90	**EXPRESSION** *ffrr F 127*	40		1
25 May 91	**DO YOU WANT ME** *ffrr F 151*	5		9
31 Aug 91	**LET'S TALK ABOUT SEX** *ffrr F 162* SALT-N-PEPA FEATURING PSYCHOTROPIC ○	2		11
30 Nov 91	**YOU SHOWED ME** *ffrr F 174*	15		7
28 Mar 92	**EXPRESSION (REMIX)** *ffrr F 182*	23		4
3 Oct 92	**START ME UP** *ffrr F 196*	39		2
9 Oct 93	**SHOOP** *ffrr FCD 219*	29		2
19 Mar 94	**WHATTA MAN** *ffrr FCD 222* SALT-N-PEPA WITH EN VOGUE	7		8
28 May 94	**SHOOP (REMIX)** *ffrr FCD 234*	13		5
12 Nov 94	**NONE OF YOUR BUSINESS** *ffrr FCD 244*	19		2
21 Dec 96	**CHAMPAGNE** *MCA MCSTD 48025*	23		4
29 Nov 97	**R U READY** *ffrr FCDP 322*	24		1
11 Dec 99	**THE BRICK TRACK VERSUS GITTY UP** *ffrr FCD 373*	22		1

SAM & DAVE US duo

Date	Title / Label	Peak Position	Weeks at No.1	Weeks in Top 40
16 Mar 67	**SOOTHE ME** *Stax 601 004*	35		3
1 Nov 67	**SOUL MAN** *Stax 601 023*	24		12
13 Mar 68	**I THANK YOU** *Stax 601 030*	34		3
29 Jan 69	**SOUL SISTER BROWN SUGAR** *Atlantic 584 237*	15		7

SAM & MARK UK duo

Date	Title / Label	Peak Position	Weeks at No.1	Weeks in Top 40
21 Feb 04	**WITH A LITTLE HELP FROM MY FRIENDS/MEASURE OF A MAN** *19 19RECS9*	1	1	4
5 Jun 04	**THE SUN HAS COME YOUR WAY** *19/UMTV 9866906*	19		2

SAM THE SHAM & THE PHARAOHS US group

Date	Title / Label	Peak Position	Weeks at No.1	Weeks in Top 40
24 Jun 65	**WOOLY BULLY** *MGM 1269*	11		11
4 Aug 66	**LIL' RED RIDING HOOD** *MGM 1315*	46		

SAMANDA UK duo

Date	Title / Label	Peak Position	Weeks at No.1	Weeks in Top 40
20 Oct 07	**BARBIE GIRL** *BMG 88697186502*	26		2

RICHIE SAMBORA US singer/guitarist

Date	Title / Label	Peak Position	Weeks at No.1	Weeks in Top 40
7 Sep 91	**BALLAD OF YOUTH** *Mercury MER 350*	59		
7 Mar 98	**HARD TIMES COME EASY** *Mercury 5686972*	37		1
1 Aug 98	**IN IT FOR LOVE** *Mercury 5660632*	58		

SAMIM German producer

Date	Title / Label	Peak Position	Weeks at No.1	Weeks in Top 40
3 Nov 07	**HEATER** *Data DATA176CDS*	12		5

MICHAEL SAMMES SINGERS UK group

Date	Title / Label	Peak Position	Weeks at No.1	Weeks in Top 40
3 May 57	**ROUND AND ROUND** *Decca F 10875* JIMMY YOUNG WITH THE MICHAEL SAMMES SINGERS	30		1
21 Mar 58	**TO BE LOVED** *HMV POP 459* MALCOLM VAUGHAN WITH THE MICHAEL SAMMES SINGERS	14		12
18 Apr 58	**I MAY NEVER PASS THIS WAY AGAIN** *HMV POP 468* RONNIE HILTON WITH THE MICHAEL SAMMES SINGERS	27		3
17 Oct 58	**MORE THAN EVER (COME PRIMA)** *HMV POP 538* MALCOLM VAUGHAN WITH THE MICHAEL SAMMES SINGERS	5		14
9 Jan 59	**THE WORLD OUTSIDE** *HMV POP 559* RONNIE HILTON WITH THE MICHAEL SAMMES SINGERS	18		6
27 Feb 59	**LITTLE DRUMMER BOY** *Parlophone R 4528* MICHAEL FLANDERS WITH THE MICHAEL SAMMES SINGERS	20		3
1 Jan 60	**STARRY EYED** *Columbia DB 4378* MICHAEL HOLLIDAY WITH THE MICHAEL SAMMES SINGERS	1	1	11
15 Dec 60	**DONALD WHERE'S YOUR TROOSERS** *Top Rank JAR 427* ANDY STEWART WITH THE MICHAEL SAMMES SINGERS	37		1
12 Jan 61	**A SCOTTISH SOLDIER** *Top Rank JAR 512* ANDY STEWART WITH THE MICHAEL SAMMES SINGERS	19		36
1 Jun 61	**THE BATTLE'S O'ER** *Top Rank JAR 565* ANDY STEWART WITH THE MICHAEL SAMMES SINGERS	28		8
26 Mar 64	**UNCHAINED MELODY** *Columbia DB 7234* JIMMY YOUNG WITH THE MICHAEL SAMMES SINGERS	43		
15 Sep 66	**SOMEWHERE MY LOVE** *HMV POP 1546*	22		15

Silver-selling · Gold-selling · Platinum-selling · US No.1 ★ · Peak Position · Weeks at No.1 · Weeks in Top 40

Date	Title	Peak Position	Weeks at No.1	Weeks in Top 40
12 Jul 67	**SOMEWHERE MY LOVE** *HMV POP 1546*	14		11
1 Nov 67	**CARELESS HANDS** *Columbia DB 8275* DES O'CONNOR WITH THE MICHAEL SAMMES SINGERS	6		13

DAZ SAMPSON UK singer

Date	Title	Peak Position	Weeks at No.1	Weeks in Top 40
20 May 06	**TEENAGE LIFE** *Ebul/Jive 82876834222*	8		4

DAVE SAMPSON UK singer

Date	Title	Peak Position	Weeks at No.1	Weeks in Top 40
19 May 60	**SWEET DREAMS** *Columbia DB 4449*	29		4

SAMSON UK group

Date	Title	Peak Position	Weeks at No.1	Weeks in Top 40
4 Jul 81	**RIDING WITH THE ANGELS** *RCA 67*	55		
24 Jul 82	**LOSING MY GRIP** *Polydor POSP 471*	63		
5 Mar 83	**RED SKIES** *Polydor POSP 554*	65		

SAN JOSÉ UK instrumental group

Date	Title	Peak Position	Weeks at No.1	Weeks in Top 40
17 Jun 78	**ARGENTINE MELODY (CANCION DE ARGENTINA)** *MCA 369* SAN JOSE FEATURING RODRIGUEZ ARGENTINA	14		5

SAN REMO STRINGS US violinists

Date	Title	Peak Position	Weeks at No.1	Weeks in Top 40
18 Dec 71	**FESTIVAL TIME** *Tamla Motown TMG 795*	39		3

JUNIOR SANCHEZ US producer

Date	Title	Peak Position	Weeks at No.1	Weeks in Top 40
16 Oct 99	**B WITH U** *Manifesto FESCD 62* JUNIOR SANCHEZ FEATURING DAJAE	31		1

ROGER SANCHEZ US producer

Date	Title	Peak Position	Weeks at No.1	Weeks in Top 40
3 Oct 98	**BUFFALO GALS STAMPEDE** *Virgin VSCDT 1717* MALCOLM McLAREN & THE WORLD'S FAMOUS SUPREME TEAM PLUS RAKIM & ROGER SANCHEZ	65		
20 Feb 99	**I WANT YOUR LOVE** *Perpetual PERPCDS 001* ROGER SANCHEZ PRESENTS TWILIGHT	31		1
29 Jan 00	**I NEVER KNEW** *INCredible INCS 4CD*	24		1
14 Jul 01	**ANOTHER CHANCE** *Defected DFECT 35CD*	1	1	8
15 Dec 01	**YOU CAN'T CHANGE ME** *Defected DFECT 41CDS* ROGER SANCHEZ FEATURING ARMAND VAN HELDEN AND N'DEA DAVENPORT	25		1

HAYLEY SANDERSON UK singer

Date	Title	Peak Position	Weeks at No.1	Weeks in Top 40
19 Aug 06	**SOMETHING IN THE AIR** *Transistor Project CDTRANSP2*	61		

CHRIS SANDFORD UK singer/actor

Date	Title	Peak Position	Weeks at No.1	Weeks in Top 40
12 Dec 63	**NOT TOO LITTLE NOT TOO MUCH** *Decca F 11778*	17		8

SANDPIPERS US group

Date	Title	Peak Position	Weeks at No.1	Weeks in Top 40
15 Sep 66	**GUANTANAMERA** *Pye International 7N 25380*	7		15
5 Jun 68	**QUANDO M'INNAMORO (A MAN WITHOUT LOVE)** *A&M AMS 723*	33		4
26 Mar 69	**KUMBAYA** *A&M AMS 744*	38		1
27 Nov 76	**HANG ON SLOOPY** *Satril SAT 114*	32		2

SANDRA German singer

Date	Title	Peak Position	Weeks at No.1	Weeks in Top 40
17 Dec 88	**EVERLASTING LOVE** *Siren SRN 85*	45		

JODIE SANDS US singer

Date	Title	Peak Position	Weeks at No.1	Weeks in Top 40
17 Oct 58	**SOMEDAY (YOU'LL WANT ME TO WANT YOU)** *HMV POP 533*	14		10

TOMMY SANDS US singer

Date	Title	Peak Position	Weeks at No.1	Weeks in Top 40
4 Aug 60	**OLD OAKEN BUCKET** *Capitol CL 15143*	25		4

SANDSTORM US producer

Date	Title	Peak Position	Weeks at No.1	Weeks in Top 40
13 May 00	**THE RETURN OF NOTHING** *Renaissance Recordings RENCDS 001*	54		

SAMANTHA SANG Australian singer

Date	Title	Peak Position	Weeks at No.1	Weeks in Top 40
4 Feb 78	**EMOTION** *Private Stock PVT 128*	11		12

SANTA UK group

Date	Title	Peak Position	Weeks at No.1	Weeks in Top 40
31 Dec 05	**IS THIS THE WAY TO AMARILLO (SANTA'S GROTTO)** *Sony 82876767312*	30		1

SANTA CLAUS & THE CHRISTMAS TREES UK group

Date	Title	Peak Position	Weeks at No.1	Weeks in Top 40
11 Dec 82	**SINGALONG-A-SANTA** *Polydor IVY 1*	19		4
10 Dec 83	**SINGALONG-A-SANTA AGAIN** *Polydor IVY 2*	39		2

SANTA ESMERELDA & LEROY GOMEZ US group

Date	Title	Peak Position	Weeks at No.1	Weeks in Top 40
12 Nov 77	**DON'T LET ME BE MISUNDERSTOOD** *Philips 6042 325*	41		

SANTANA US group

Date	Title	Peak Position	Weeks at No.1	Weeks in Top 40
28 Sep 74	**SAMBA PA TI** *CBS 2561*	27		5
15 Oct 77	**SHE'S NOT THERE** *CBS 5671*	11		10
25 Nov 78	**WELL ALL RIGHT** *CBS 6755*	53		
22 Mar 80	**ALL I EVER WANTED** *CBS 8160*	57		
23 Oct 99	**SMOOTH** *Arista 74321709492* SANTANA FEATURING ROB THOMAS ★	75		
1 Apr 00	**SMOOTH** *Arista 74321748762* SANTANA FEATURING ROB THOMAS	3		8
5 Aug 00	**MARIA MARIA** *Arista 74321769372* SANTANA FEATURING THE PRODUCT G&B ★	6		7
23 Nov 02	**THE GAME OF LOVE** *Arista 74321959442* SANTANA FEATURING MICHELLE BRANCH	16		3
20 May 06	**CRY BABY CRY** *Arista 82876804672* SANTANA FEATURING SEAN PAUL & JOSS STONE	71		
23 Dec 06	**ILLEGAL** *Epic 88697009202* SHAKIRA FEATURING CARLOS SANTANA	34		1

JUELZ SANTANA US singer

Date	Title	Peak Position	Weeks at No.1	Weeks in Top 40
17 Aug 02	**OH BOY** *Roc-A-Fella 0639642* CAM'RON FEATURING JUELZ SANTANA	13		5
8 Feb 03	**HEY MA** *Roc-A-Fella 0637242* CAM'RON FEATURING JUELZ SANTANA	8		8
11 Feb 06	**RUN IT!** *Jive 82876780532* CHRIS BROWN FEATURING JUELZ SANTANA ★	2		9
25 Mar 06	**THERE IT GO (THE WHISTLE SONG)** *Def Jam 9853444*	47		

SANTO & JOHNNY US guitarists

Date	Title	Peak Position	Weeks at No.1	Weeks in Top 40
16 Oct 59	**SLEEP WALK** *Pye International 7N 25037* ★	22		4
31 Mar 60	**TEARDROP** *Parlophone R 4619*	50		

SANTOS Italian producer

Date	Title	Peak Position	Weeks at No.1	Weeks in Top 40
20 Jan 01	**CAMELS** *Incentive CENT 15CDS*	9		3

MIKE SARNE UK singer

Date	Title	Peak Position	Weeks at No.1	Weeks in Top 40
10 May 62	**COME OUTSIDE** *Parlophone R 4902* MIKE SARNE WITH WENDY RICHARD	1	2	17
30 Aug 62	**WILL I WHAT** *Parlophone R 4932* MIKE SARNE WITH BILLIE DAVIS	18		10
10 Jan 63	**JUST FOR KICKS** *Parlophone R 4974*	22		6
28 Mar 63	**CODE OF LOVE** *Parlophone R 5010*	29		6

JOY SARNEY UK singer

Date	Title	Peak Position	Weeks at No.1	Weeks in Top 40
7 May 77	**NAUGHTY NAUGHTY NAUGHTY** *Alaska ALA 2005*	26		5

SARR BAND Italian/UK/French group

Date	Title	Peak Position	Weeks at No.1	Weeks in Top 40
16 Sep 78	**MAGIC MANDRAKE** *Calendar Day 111*	68		

PETER SARSTEDT UK singer

Date	Title	Peak Position	Weeks at No.1	Weeks in Top 40
5 Feb 69	**WHERE DO YOU GO TO MY LOVELY** *United Artists UP 2262*	1	4	13
4 Jun 69	**FROZEN ORANGE JUICE** *United Artists UP 35021*	10		8

ROBIN SARSTEDT UK singer

Date	Title / Label	Peak	Wks No.1	Wks Top 40
8 May 76	**MY RESISTANCE IS LOW** *Decca F 13624*	3		8

SARTORELLO Italian Duo

Date	Title / Label	Peak	Wks No.1	Wks Top 40
10 Aug 96	**MOVE BABY MOVE** *Multiply CDMULTY 12*	56		

SASH! German producer

Date	Title / Label	Peak	Wks No.1	Wks Top 40
1 Mar 97	**ENCORE UNE FOIS** *Multiply CDMULTY 18* ●	2		12
5 Jul 97	**ECUADOR** *Multiply CDMULTY 23* SASH! FEATURING RODRIGUEZ ●	2		10
18 Oct 97	**STAY** *Multiply CDMULTY 26* SASH! FEATURING LA TREC ●	2		9
4 Apr 98	**LA PRIMAVERA** *Multiply CXMULTY 32* ○	3		7
15 Aug 98	**MYSTERIOUS TIMES** *Multiply CDMULTY 40* SASH! FEATURING TINA COUSINS ○	2		8
28 Nov 98	**MOVE MANIA** *Multiply CDMULTY 45* SASH! FEATURING SHANNON	8		8
3 Apr 99	**COLOUR THE WORLD** *Multiply CDMULTY 48*	15		3
12 Feb 00	**ADELANTE** *Multiply CDMULTY 60*	2		6
22 Apr 00	**JUST AROUND THE HILL** *Multiply CDMULTY 62*	8		6
23 Sep 00	**WITH MY OWN EYES** *Multiply CDMULTY 67*	10		3

SASHA UK producer

Date	Title / Label	Peak	Wks No.1	Wks Top 40
31 Jul 93	**TOGETHER** *ffrr FCD 212* DANNY CAMPBELL & SASHA	57		
19 Feb 94	**HIGHER GROUND** *Deconstruction 74321189002* SASHA WITH SAM MOLLISON	19		2
27 Aug 94	**MAGIC** *Deconstruction 74321221862* SASHA WITH SAM MOLLISON	32		2
9 Mar 96	**BE AS ONE** *7pm 74321342962* SASHA & MARIA	17		3
23 Sep 00	**SCORCHIO** *Arista 74321788222* SASHA/EMERSON	23		2
31 Aug 02	**WAVY GRAVY** *Arista 74321960602*	64		

JOE SATRIANI US guitarist

Date	Title / Label	Peak	Wks No.1	Wks Top 40
13 Feb 93	**THE SATCH EP** *Relativity 6589532*	53		

SATURATED SOUL US production duo

Date	Title / Label	Peak	Wks No.1	Wks Top 40
14 Aug 04	**GOT TO RELEASE** *Defected DFTD093* SATURATED SOUL FEATURING MISS BUNTY	56		

SATURDAY NIGHT BAND US group

Date	Title / Label	Peak	Wks No.1	Wks Top 40
1 Jul 78	**COME ON DANCE DANCE** *CBS 6367*	16		6

ANNE SAVAGE UK producer

Date	Title / Label	Peak	Wks No.1	Wks Top 40
19 Apr 03	**HELLRAISER** *Tidy Trax TIDY 186T*	74		

CHANTAY SAVAGE US singer

Date	Title / Label	Peak	Wks No.1	Wks Top 40
4 May 96	**I WILL SURVIVE** *RCA 74321377682*	12		6
8 Nov 97	**REMINDING ME (OF SEF)** *Relativity 6560762* COMMON FEATURING CHANTAY SAVAGE	59		

EDNA SAVAGE UK singer

Date	Title / Label	Peak	Wks No.1	Wks Top 40
13 Jan 56	**ARRIVEDERCI DARLING** *Parlophone R 4097*	19		1

SAVAGE GARDEN Australian duo

Date	Title / Label	Peak	Wks No.1	Wks Top 40
21 Jun 97	**I WANT YOU** *Columbia 6645452*	11		4
27 Sep 97	**TO THE MOON AND BACK** *Columbia 6648932*	55		
28 Feb 98	**TRULY MADLY DEEPLY** *Columbia 6656022* ⊛ ★	4		19
22 Aug 98	**TO THE MOON AND BACK** *Columbia 6662882* ●	3		12
12 Dec 98	**I WANT YOU '98 (REMIX)** *Columbia 6667332*	12		7
10 Jul 99	**THE ANIMAL SONG** *Columbia 6675882*	16		4
13 Nov 99	**I KNEW I LOVED YOU** *Columbia 6683102* ★	10		4
1 Apr 00	**CRASH AND BURN** *Columbia 6690442*	14		4
29 Jul 00	**AFFIRMATION** *Columbia 6696882*	8		7
25 Nov 00	**HOLD ME** *Columbia 6706032*	16		2
31 Mar 01	**THE BEST THING** *Columbia 6709852*	35		1

TELLY SAVALAS US actor

Date	Title / Label	Peak	Wks No.1	Wks Top 40
22 Feb 75	**IF** *MCA 174* ○	1	2	9
31 May 75	**YOU'VE LOST THAT LOVIN' FEELIN'** *MCA 189*	47		

SAVANA Jamaican singer

Date	Title / Label	Peak	Wks No.1	Wks Top 40
24 Jul 04	**PRETTY LADY** *Jetstar JECDS1805*	48		

SAVANNA UK group

Date	Title / Label	Peak	Wks No.1	Wks Top 40
10 Oct 81	**I CAN'T TURN AWAY** *R&B RBS 203*	61		

SAW DOCTORS Irish group

Date	Title / Label	Peak	Wks No.1	Wks Top 40
12 Nov 94	**SMALL BIT OF LOVE** *Shamtown SAW001CD*	24		1
27 Jan 96	**WORLD OF GOOD** *Shamtown SAW002CD*	15		2
13 Jul 96	**TO WIN JUST ONCE** *Shamtown SAW004CD*	14		1
6 Dec 97	**SIMPLE THINGS** *Shamtown SAW006CD*	56		
1 Jun 02	**THIS IS ME** *Shamtown SAW012CD*	31		1
15 Oct 05	**STARS OVER CLOUGHANOVER** *Shamtown SAW014CD*	69		

NITIN SAWHNEY UK multi-instrumentalist

Date	Title / Label	Peak	Wks No.1	Wks Top 40
28 Jul 01	**SUNSET** *V2 VVR 5016768* NITIN SAWHNEY FEATURING ESKA	65		

SAXON UK group

Date	Title / Label	Peak	Wks No.1	Wks Top 40
22 Mar 80	**WHEELS OF STEEL** *Carrere CAR 143*	20		6
21 Jun 80	**747 (STRANGERS IN THE NIGHT)** *Carrere CAR 151*	13		7
28 Jun 80	**BACKS TO THE WALL** *Carrere HM 6*	64		
28 Jun 80	**BIG TEASER/RAINBOW THEME** *Carrere HM 5*	66		
29 Nov 80	**STRONG ARM OF THE LAW** *Carrere CAR 170*	63		
11 Apr 81	**AND THE BANDS PLAYED ON** *Carrere CAR 180*	12		6
18 Jul 81	**NEVER SURRENDER** *Carrere CAR 204*	18		5
31 Oct 81	**PRINCESS OF THE NIGHT** *Carrere CAR 208*	57		
23 Apr 83	**POWER AND THE GLORY** *Carrere SAXON 1*	32		2
30 Jul 83	**NIGHTMARE** *Carrere CAR 284*	50		
31 Aug 85	**BACK ON THE STREETS** *Parlophone R 6103*	75		
29 Mar 86	**ROCK 'N' ROLL GYPSY** *Parlophone R 6112*	72		
30 Aug 86	**WAITING FOR THE NIGHT** *EMI 5575*	66		
5 Mar 88	**RIDE LIKE THE WIND** *EMI EM 43*	52		
30 Apr 88	**I CAN'T WAIT ANYMORE** *EMI EM 54*	71		

AL SAXON UK singer

Date	Title / Label	Peak	Wks No.1	Wks Top 40
16 Jan 59	**YOU'RE THE TOP CHA** *Fontana H 164*	17		4
28 Aug 59	**ONLY SIXTEEN** *Fontana H 205*	24		3
22 Dec 60	**BLUE-EYED BOY** *Fontana H 278*	39		1
7 Sep 61	**THERE I'VE SAID IT AGAIN** *Piccadilly 7N 35011*	48		

LEO SAYER UK singer

Date	Title / Label	Peak	Wks No.1	Wks Top 40
15 Dec 73	**THE SHOW MUST GO ON** *Chrysalis CHS 2023* ●	2		11
15 Jun 74	**ONE MAN BAND** *Chrysalis CHS 2045*	6		8
14 Sep 74	**LONG TALL GLASSES** *Chrysalis CHS 2052*	4		7
30 Aug 75	**MOONLIGHTING** *Chrysalis CHS 2076* ○	2		8
30 Oct 76	**YOU MAKE ME FEEL LIKE DANCING** *Chrysalis CHS 2119* ○ ★	2		11
29 Jan 77	**WHEN I NEED YOU** *Chrysalis CHS 2127* ● ★	1	3	12
9 Apr 77	**HOW MUCH LOVE** *Chrysalis CHS 2140*	10		7
10 Sep 77	**THUNDER IN MY HEART** *Chrysalis CHS 2163*	22		8
16 Sep 78	**I CAN'T STOP LOVIN' YOU (THOUGH I TRY)** *Chrysalis CHS 2240* ○	6		8
25 Nov 78	**RAINING IN MY HEART** *Chrysalis CHS 2277*	21		8
5 Jul 80	**MORE THAN I CAN SAY** *Chrysalis CHS 2442* ○	2		9
13 Mar 82	**HAVE YOU EVER BEEN IN LOVE** *Chrysalis CHS 2596*	10		6
19 Jun 82	**HEART (STOP BEATING IN TIME)** *Chrysalis CHS 2616*	22		6
12 Mar 83	**ORCHARD ROAD** *Chrysalis CHS 2677*	16		6
15 Oct 83	**TILL YOU COME BACK TO ME** *Chrysalis LEO 01*	51		
8 Feb 86	**UNCHAINED MELODY** *Chrysalis LEO 3*	54		
13 Feb 93	**WHEN I NEED YOU** *Chrysalis CDCHS 3926*	65		
8 Aug 98	**YOU MAKE ME FEEL LIKE DANCING** *Brothers Organisation CDBRUV 8* GROOVE GENERATION FEATURING LEO SAYER	32		1
18 Feb 06	**THUNDER IN MY HEART AGAIN** *Apollo/Free 2 Air APOLLO101CDX* MECK FEATURING LEO SAYER	1	2	13

ALEXEI SAYLE UK comedian

Date	Title / Label	Peak	Wks No.1	Wks Top 40
25 Feb 84	**'ULLO JOHN GOT A NEW MOTOR?** *Island IS 162*	15		6

Silver-selling ● Gold-selling ● Platinum-selling ● US No.1 ★ | Peak Position · Weeks at No.1 · Weeks in Top 40

SCAFFOLD UK group

Date	Title / Label	Peak Position	Weeks at No.1	Weeks in Top 40
22 Nov 67	**THANK U VERY MUCH** *Parlophone R 5643*	4		12
27 Mar 68	**DO YOU REMEMBER** *Parlophone R 5679*	34		3
6 Nov 68	**LILY THE PINK** *Parlophone R 5734*	1	4	22
1 Nov 69	**GIN GAN GOOLIE** *Parlophone R 5812*	38		3
1 Jun 74	**LIVERPOOL LOU** *Warner Brothers K 16400*	7		8

BOZ SCAGGS US singer

Date	Title / Label	Peak Position	Weeks at No.1	Weeks in Top 40
30 Oct 76	**LOWDOWN** *CBS 4563*	28		3
22 Jan 77	**WHAT CAN I SAY** *CBS 4869*	10		9
14 May 77	**LIDO SHUFFLE** *CBS 5136*	13		8
10 Dec 77	**HOLLYWOOD** *CBS 5836*	33		4

SCANTY SANDWICH UK producer

Date	Title / Label	Peak Position	Weeks at No.1	Weeks in Top 40
29 Jan 00	**BECAUSE OF YOU** *Southern Fried ECB 18CDS*	3		5

SCARFACE US rapper

Date	Title / Label	Peak Position	Weeks at No.1	Weeks in Top 40
11 Mar 95	**HAND OF THE DEAD BODY** *Virgin America VUSCD 88* SCARFACE FEATURING ICE CUBE	41		
5 Aug 95	**I SEEN A MAN DIE** *Virgin America VUSCD 94*	55		
5 Jul 97	**GAME OVER** *Virgin VUSCD 121*	34		1

SCARFO UK group

Date	Title / Label	Peak Position	Weeks at No.1	Weeks in Top 40
19 Jul 97	**ALKALINE** *Deceptive BLUFF 044CD*	61		
18 Oct 97	**COSMONAUT NO. 7** *Deceptive BLUFF 053CD*	67		

SCARLET UK duo

Date	Title / Label	Peak Position	Weeks at No.1	Weeks in Top 40
21 Jan 95	**INDEPENDENT LOVE SONG** *WEA YZ 820CD*	12		10
29 Apr 95	**I WANNA BE FREE (TO BE WITH HIM)** *WEA YZ 913CD*	21		2
5 Aug 95	**LOVE HANGOVER** *WEA YZ 969CD*	54		
6 Jul 96	**BAD GIRL** *WEA 046CD*	54		

SCARLET FANTASTIC UK duo

Date	Title / Label	Peak Position	Weeks at No.1	Weeks in Top 40
3 Oct 87	**NO MEMORY** *Arista RIS 36*	24		6
23 Jan 88	**PLUG ME IN (TO THE CENTRAL LOVE LINE)** *Arista 109693*	67		

SCARLET PARTY UK group

Date	Title / Label	Peak Position	Weeks at No.1	Weeks in Top 40
16 Oct 82	**101 DAM-NATIONS** *Parlophone R 6058*	44		

SCATMAN JOHN US singer

Date	Title / Label	Peak Position	Weeks at No.1	Weeks in Top 40
13 May 95	**SCATMAN (SKI-BA-BOP-BA-DOP-BOP)** *RCA 74321281712* ●	3		10
2 Sep 95	**SCATMAN'S WORLD** *RCA 74321289952*	10		5

MICHAEL SCHENKER GROUP German/UK group

Date	Title / Label	Peak Position	Weeks at No.1	Weeks in Top 40
13 Sep 80	**ARMED AND READY** *Chrysalis CHS 2455*	53		
8 Nov 80	**CRY FOR THE NATIONS** *Chrysalis CHS 2471*	56		
11 Sep 82	**DANCER** *Chrysalis CHS 2636*	52		

NICOLE SCHERZINGER US singer

Date	Title / Label	Peak Position	Weeks at No.1	Weeks in Top 40
7 Oct 06	**COME TO ME** *Atlantic AT0260CD* P DIDDY FEATURING NICOLE SCHERZINGER	4		9
20 Oct 07	**BABY LOVE** *Polydor 1753014* NICOLE SCHERZINGER FEATURING WILL.I.AM	14		7
16 Feb 08	**SCREAM** *Interscope 1764136* TIMBALAND FEATURING KERI HILSON & NICOLE SCHERZINGER	12		7

SCHNAPPI German cartoon crocodile

Date	Title / Label	Peak Position	Weeks at No.1	Weeks in Top 40
15 Oct 05	**SCHNAPPI** *Universal TV 9873701*	32		1

SCENT Italian/UK production group

Date	Title / Label	Peak Position	Weeks at No.1	Weeks in Top 40
21 Aug 04	**UP AND DOWN** *Positiva CDTIVS209*	23		2

LALO SCHIFRIN Argentinian orchestra leader

Date	Title / Label	Peak Position	Weeks at No.1	Weeks in Top 40
9 Oct 76	**JAWS** *CTI CTSP 005*	14		8
25 Oct 97	**BULLITT** *warner.esp WESP 002CD*	36		1

SCHILLER German production duo

Date	Title / Label	Peak Position	Weeks at No.1	Weeks in Top 40
28 Apr 01	**DAS GLOCKENSPIEL** *Data 22CDS*	17		2

PETER SCHILLING German singer

Date	Title / Label	Peak Position	Weeks at No.1	Weeks in Top 40
5 May 84	**MAJOR TOM (COMING HOME)** *PSP/WEA X 9438*	42		

PHILIP SCHOFIELD UK singer/TV presenter

Date	Title / Label	Peak Position	Weeks at No.1	Weeks in Top 40
5 Dec 92	**CLOSE EVERY DOOR** *Really Useful RUR 11*	27		2

SCHOOL OF ROCK US group

Date	Title / Label	Peak Position	Weeks at No.1	Weeks in Top 40
21 Feb 04	**SCHOOL OF ROCK** *Atlantic AT 0172CD*	51		

SCIENCE DEPT UK production duo

Date	Title / Label	Peak Position	Weeks at No.1	Weeks in Top 40
10 Nov 01	**BREATHE** *Renaissance RENCDS 010* SCIENCE DEPT FEATURING ERIRE	64		

SCIENTIST UK producer

Date	Title / Label	Peak Position	Weeks at No.1	Weeks in Top 40
6 Oct 90	**THE EXORCIST** *Kickin KICK 1*	62		
1 Dec 90	**THE EXORCIST (REMIX)** *Kickin KICK 1TR*	46		
15 Dec 90	**THE BEE** *Kickin KICK 35*	47		
11 May 91	**SPIRAL SYMPHONY** *Kickin KICK 5*	74		

SCISSOR SISTERS US group

Date	Title / Label	Peak Position	Weeks at No.1	Weeks in Top 40
8 Nov 03	**LAURA** *Polydor 9812788*	54		
31 Jan 04	**COMFORTABLY NUMB** *Polydor 9815883*	10		4
10 Apr 04	**TAKE YOUR MAMA** *Polydor 9866277*	17		3
19 Jun 04	**LAURA** *Polydor 9866833*	12		6
23 Oct 04	**MARY** *Polydor 9868282*	14		4
8 Jan 05	**COMFORTABLY NUMB** *Polydor 9815883*	74		
15 Jan 05	**FILTHY/GORGEOUS** *Polydor 9869799*	5		7
9 Sep 06	**I DON'T FEEL LIKE DANCIN'** *Polydor 1705491*	1	4	26
9 Dec 06	**LAND OF A THOUSAND WORDS** *Polydor 1712488*	19		1
17 Mar 07	**SHE'S MY MAN** *Polydor 1721313*	29		1
9 Jun 07	**KISS YOU OFF** *Polydor 1726298*	43		
14 Jul 07	**I CAN'T DECIDE** *Download*	64		

SCOOBIE UK group

Date	Title / Label	Peak Position	Weeks at No.1	Weeks in Top 40
22 Dec 01	**THE MAGNIFICENT 7** *Big Tongue BTR 001CDS*	58		
1 Jun 02	**THE MAGNIFICENT 7 (REMIX)** *Big Tongue BTR 001CDSX*	71		

SCOOCH UK group

Date	Title / Label	Peak Position	Weeks at No.1	Weeks in Top 40
6 Nov 99	**WHEN MY BABY** *Accolade CDACS 002*	29		1
22 Jan 00	**MORE THAN I NEEDED TO KNOW** *Accolade CDACS 003*	5		3
6 May 00	**THE BEST IS YET TO COME** *Accolade CDAC 004*	12		2
5 Aug 00	**FOR SURE** *Accolade CDACS 005*	15		3
31 Mar 07	**FLYING THE FLAG (FOR YOU)** *Warner Brothers WEA421CD*	5		3

SCOOTER UK/German group

Date	Title / Label	Peak Position	Weeks at No.1	Weeks in Top 40
21 Oct 95	**MOVE YOUR ASS** *Club Tools 0061675 CLU*	23		3
17 Feb 96	**BACK IN THE UK** *Club Tools 0061955 CLU*	18		2
25 May 96	**REBEL YELL** *Club Tools 0062575 CLU*	30		1
19 Oct 96	**I'M RAVING** *Club Tools 0063015 CLU*	33		1
17 May 97	**FIRE** *Club Tools 0060005 CLU*	45		
22 Jun 02	**THE LOGICAL SONG** *Sheffield Tunes 0139295 STU* ●	2		13
21 Sep 02	**NESSAJA** *Sheffield Tunes 0142165 STU*	4		7
7 Dec 02	**POSSE (I NEED YOU ON THE FLOOR)** *Sheffield Tunes 0143775 STU*	15		4
5 Apr 03	**WEEKEND** *Sheffield Tunes 0147315 STU*	12		5
5 Jul 03	**THE NIGHT** *Sheffield Tunes 0149005 STU*	16		2
18 Oct 03	**MARIA (I LIKE IT LOUD)** *Sheffield Tunes 0151135 STU* SCOOTER VS MARC ACARDIPANE & DICK RULES	16		2
10 Jul 04	**JIGGA JIGGA** *All Around The World CXGLOBE 348*	48		

SCORPIONS German group

Date	Title / Label	Peak Position	Weeks at No.1	Weeks in Top 40
26 May 79	**IS THERE ANYBODY THERE/ANOTHER PIECE OF MEAT** *Harvest HAR 5185*	39		1
25 Aug 79	**LOVEDRIVE** *Harvest HAR 5188*	69		
31 May 80	**MAKE IT REAL** *Harvest HAR 5206*	72		
20 Sep 80	**THE ZOO** *Harvest HAR 5212*	75		
3 Apr 82	**NO ONE LIKE YOU** *Harvest HAR 5219*	64		
17 Jul 82	**CAN'T LIVE WITHOUT YOU** *Harvest HAR 5221*	63		
4 Jun 88	**RHYTHM OF LOVE** *Harvest HAR 5240*	59		
18 Feb 89	**PASSION RULES THE GAME** *Harvest HAR 5242*	74		
1 Jun 91	**WIND OF CHANGE** *Vertigo VER 54*	53		
28 Sep 91	**WIND OF CHANGE** *Vertigo VER 58* ●	2		8
30 Nov 91	**SEND ME AN ANGEL** *Vertigo VER 60*	27		1

SCOTLAND WORLD CUP SQUAD Scottish football team

Date	Title / Label	Peak Position	Weeks at No.1	Weeks in Top 40
22 Jun 74	**EASY EASY** *Polydor 2058 452*	20		3
27 May 78	**OLE OLA (MULHER BRASILEIRA)** *Riva 15* ROD STEWART FEATURING THE SCOTTISH WORLD CUP FOOTBALL SQUAD	4		5
1 May 82	**WE HAVE A DREAM** *WEA K 19145*	5		7
9 Jun 90	**SAY IT WITH PRIDE** *RCA PB 43791*	45		
15 Jun 96	**PURPLE HEATHER** *Warner Brothers W 0354CD* ROD STEWART WITH THE SCOTTISH EURO '96 SQUAD	16		3

JACK SCOTT Canadian singer

Date	Title / Label	Peak Position	Weeks at No.1	Weeks in Top 40
10 Oct 58	**MY TRUE LOVE** *London HLU 8626*	9		10
25 Sep 59	**THE WAY I WALK** *London HLL 8912*	30		1
10 Mar 60	**WHAT IN THE WORLD'S COME OVER YOU** *Top Rank JAR 280*	11		14
2 Jun 60	**BURNING BRIDGES** *Top Rank JAR 375*	32		2

JAMIE SCOTT UK singer

Date	Title / Label	Peak Position	Weeks at No.1	Weeks in Top 40
4 Sep 04	**JUST** *Sony Music 6752282*	29		1
22 Jan 05	**SEARCHING** *Sony Music 6757332*	33		1
8 Sep 07	**WHEN WILL I SEE YOUR FACE AGAIN** *Polydor 1742251* JAMIE SCOTT & THE TOWN	41		

JILL SCOTT US singer

Date	Title / Label	Peak Position	Weeks at No.1	Weeks in Top 40
4 Nov 00	**GETTIN' IN THE WAY** *Epic 6705272*	30		1
7 Apr 01	**A LONG WALK** *Epic 6710382*	54		
6 Nov 04	**GOLDEN** *Epic 6751772*	59		
16 Sep 06	**DAYDREAMIN'** *Atlantic AT0252CD* LUPE FIASCO FEATURING JILL SCOTT	25		2

LINDA SCOTT US singer

Date	Title / Label	Peak Position	Weeks at No.1	Weeks in Top 40
18 May 61	**I'VE TOLD EVERY LITTLE STAR** *Columbia DB 4638*	7		11
14 Sep 61	**DON'T BET MONEY HONEY** *Columbia DB 4692*	50		

MIKE SCOTT UK singer/multi-instrumentalist

Date	Title / Label	Peak Position	Weeks at No.1	Weeks in Top 40
16 Sep 95	**BRING 'EM ALL IN** *Chrysalis CDCHS 5025*	56		
11 Nov 95	**BUILDING THE CITY OF LIGHT** *Chrysalis CDCHS 5026*	60		
27 Sep 97	**LOVE ANYWAY** *Chrysalis CDCHS 5064*	50		
14 Feb 98	**RARE, PRECIOUS AND GONE** *Chrysalis CDCHS 5073*	74		

MILLIE SCOTT US singer

Date	Title / Label	Peak Position	Weeks at No.1	Weeks in Top 40
12 Apr 86	**PRISONER OF LOVE** *Fourth & Broadway BRW 45*	52		
23 Aug 86	**AUTOMATIC** *Fourth & Broadway BRW 51*	56		
21 Feb 87	**EV'RY LITTLE BIT** *Fourth & Broadway BRW 58*	63		

SIMON SCOTT UK singer

Date	Title / Label	Peak Position	Weeks at No.1	Weeks in Top 40
13 Aug 64	**MOVE IT BABY** *Parlophone R 5164*	37		2

TONY SCOTT Dutch rapper

Date	Title / Label	Peak Position	Weeks at No.1	Weeks in Top 40
15 Apr 89	**THAT'S HOW I'M LIVING/THE CHIEF** *Champion CHAMP 97*	48		
10 Feb 90	**GET INTO IT/THAT'S HOW I'M LIVING** *Champion CHAMP 232*	63		

SCOTT & LEON UK production duo

Date	Title / Label	Peak Position	Weeks at No.1	Weeks in Top 40
30 Sep 00	**YOU USED TO HOLD ME** *AM:PM CDAMPM 137*	19		2
19 May 01	**SHINE ON** *AM:PM CDAMPM 143*	34		1

LISA SCOTT-LEE UK singer

Date	Title / Label	Peak Position	Weeks at No.1	Weeks in Top 40
24 May 03	**LATELY** *Fontana 9800295*	6		5
20 Sep 03	**TOO FAR GONE** *Fontana 9811643*	11		2
4 Dec 04	**GET IT ON** *Inspired INSPMOS1CDS* INTENSO PROJECT FEATURING LISA SCOTT-LEE	23		1
22 Oct 05	**ELECTRIC** *Concept CDCON68X*	13		1

SCOTTISH RUGBY TEAM Scottish rugby team

Date	Title / Label	Peak Position	Weeks at No.1	Weeks in Top 40
2 Jun 90	**FLOWER OF SCOTLAND** *Greentrax STRAX 1001* SCOTTISH RUGBY TEAM WITH RONNIE BROWNE	73		

SCOUTING FOR GIRLS UK group

Date	Title / Label	Peak Position	Weeks at No.1	Weeks in Top 40
30 Jun 07	**IT'S NOT ABOUT YOU** *Epic 88697102422*	31		1
8 Sep 07	**SHE'S SO LOVELY** *Epic 88697147742*	7		22
15 Dec 07	**ELVIS AIN'T DEAD** *Epic 88697191162*	8		14
29 Mar 08	**HEARTBEAT** *Epic 88697271242*	64		

SCREAMING BLUE MESSIAHS UK group

Date	Title / Label	Peak Position	Weeks at No.1	Weeks in Top 40
16 Jan 88	**I WANNA BE A FLINTSTONE** *WEA YZ 166*	28		3

SCREAMING TREES US group

Date	Title / Label	Peak Position	Weeks at No.1	Weeks in Top 40
6 Mar 93	**NEARLY LOST YOU EP** *Epic 6582372*	50		
1 May 93	**DOLLAR BILL** *Epic 6591792*	52		

SCRITTI POLITTI UK group

Date	Title / Label	Peak Position	Weeks at No.1	Weeks in Top 40
21 Nov 81	**THE SWEETEST GIRL** *Rough Trade RT 091*	64		
22 May 82	**FAITHLESS** *Rough Trade RT 101*	56		
7 Aug 82	**ASYLUMS IN JERUSALEM/JACQUES DERRIDA** *Rough Trade RT 111*	43		
10 Mar 84	**WOOD BEEZ (PRAY LIKE ARETHA FRANKLIN)** *Virgin VS 657*	10		7
9 Jun 84	**ABSOLUTE** *Virgin VS 680*	17		7
17 Nov 84	**HYPNOTIZE** *Virgin VS 725*	68		
11 May 85	**THE WORD GIRL** *Virgin VS 747* SCRITTI POLITTI FEATURING RANKING ANN	6		9
7 Sep 85	**PERFECT WAY** *Virgin VS 780*	48		
7 May 88	**OH PATTI (DON'T FEEL SORRY FOR LOVERBOY)** *Virgin VS 1006*	13		6
27 Aug 88	**FIRST BOY IN THIS TOWN (LOVE SICK)** *Virgin VS 1082*	63		
12 Nov 88	**BOOM! THERE SHE WAS** *Virgin VS 1143* SCRITTI POLITTI FEATURING ROGER	55		
16 Mar 91	**SHE'S A WOMAN** *Virgin VS 1333* SCRITTI POLITTI FEATURING SHABBA RANKS	20		3
3 Aug 91	**TAKE ME IN YOUR ARMS AND LOVE ME** *Virgin VS 1346* SCRITTI POLITTI & SWEETIE IRIE	47		
31 Jul 99	**TINSELTOWN TO THE BOOGIEDOWN** *Virgin VSCDT 1731*	46		

SCUMFROG Dutch producer

Date	Title / Label	Peak Position	Weeks at No.1	Weeks in Top 40
11 May 02	**LOVING THE ALIEN** *Positiva CDTIV 172* SCUMFROG VS BOWIE	41		
31 May 03	**MUSIC REVOLUTION** *Positiva CDTIV 191*	46		

SE:SA German/UK duo

Date	Title / Label	Peak Position	Weeks at No.1	Weeks in Top 40
1 Dec 07	**LIKE THIS LIKE THAT** *Positiva CDTIVS263* SE:SA FEATURING SHARON PHILIPS	63		

SEA FRUIT UK group

Date	Title / Label	Peak Position	Weeks at No.1	Weeks in Top 40
24 Jul 99	**HELLO WORLD** *Electric Canyon ECCD 3055*	59		

SEA LEVEL US group

Date	Title / Label	Peak Position	Weeks at No.1	Weeks in Top 40
17 Feb 79	**FIFTY-FOUR** *Capricorn POSP 28*	63		

SEAFOOD UK group

Date	Title / Label	Peak Position	Weeks at No.1	Weeks in Top 40
28 Jul 01	**CLOAKING** *Infectious INFEC 103CDS*	71		
1 May 04	**GOOD REASON** *Cooking Vinyl FRYCD189*	65		

Silver-selling ○ · Gold-selling ● · Platinum-selling · US No.1 ★ · Peak Position · Weeks at No.1 · Weeks in Top 40

SEAGULLS SKA UK group

Date	Title	Peak Position	Weeks at No.1	Weeks in Top 40
15 Jan 05	**TOM HARK (WE WANT FALMER)** *Falmer For All FALMER001*	17		1

SEAHORSES UK group

Date	Title	Peak Position	Weeks at No.1	Weeks in Top 40
10 May 97	**LOVE IS THE LAW** *Geffen GFSTD 22243*	3		5
26 Jul 97	**BLINDED BY THE SUN** *Geffen GFSTD 22266*	7		4
11 Oct 97	**LOVE ME AND LEAVE ME** *Geffen GFSTD 22292*	16		2
13 Dec 97	**YOU CAN TALK TO ME** *Geffen GFSTD 22297*	15		6

SEAL UK singer

Date	Title	Peak Position	Weeks at No.1	Weeks in Top 40
8 Dec 90	**CRAZY** *ZTT ZANG 8* ○	2		12
4 May 91	**FUTURE LOVE EP** *ZTT ZANG 11*	12		5
20 Jul 91	**THE BEGINNING** *ZTT ZANG 21*	24		4
16 Nov 91	**KILLER (EP)** *ZTT ZANG 23*	8		4
29 Feb 92	**VIOLET** *ZTT ZANG 27*	39		1
21 May 94	**PRAYER FOR THE DYING** *ZTT ZANG 51CD*	14		3
30 Jul 94	**KISS FROM A ROSE** *ZTT ZANG 52CD1*	20		3
5 Nov 94	**NEWBORN FRIEND** *ZTT ZANG 58CD*	45		
15 Jul 95	**KISS FROM A ROSE/I'M ALIVE** *ZTT ZANG 70CD* ○ ★	4		11
9 Dec 95	**DON'T CRY/PRAYER FOR THE DYING** *ZTT ZANG 75CD*	51		
29 Mar 97	**FLY LIKE AN EAGLE** *ZTT ZEAL 1CD*	13		2
14 Nov 98	**HUMAN BEINGS** *Warner Brothers W 464CD*	50		
12 Oct 02	**MY VISION** *Rulin 26CDS* JAKATTA FEATURING SEAL	6		6
20 Sep 03	**GET IT TOGETHER** *Warner Brothers W 620CD*	25		1
22 Nov 03	**LOVE'S DIVINE** *Warner Brothers W 629CD*	68		
17 Nov 07	**AMAZING** *Warner Brothers W788CD*	74		

JAY SEAN UK singer

Date	Title	Peak Position	Weeks at No.1	Weeks in Top 40
20 Sep 03	**DANCE WITH YOU (NACHNA TERE NAAL)** *Relentless RELCD1* RISHI RICH PROJECT FEATURING JAY SEAN & JUGGY D	12		3
3 Jul 04	**EYES ON YOU** *Relentless RELDX5* JAY SEAN FEATURING RISHI RICH PROJECT	6		8
6 Nov 04	**STOLEN** *Relentless RELDX11*	4		4
2 Feb 08	**RIDE IT** *2Point9 CXJAY2P91*	11		8

SEARCHERS UK group

Date	Title	Peak Position	Weeks at No.1	Weeks in Top 40
27 Jun 63	**SWEETS FOR MY SWEET** *Pye 7N 15533*	1	2	14
10 Oct 63	**SWEET NOTHINS** *Phillips BF 1274*	48		
24 Oct 63	**SUGAR AND SPICE** *Pye 7N 15566*	2		12
16 Jan 64	**NEEDLES AND PINS** *Pye 7N 15594*	1	3	14
16 Apr 64	**DON'T THROW YOUR LOVE AWAY** *Pye 7N 15630*	1	2	11
16 Jul 64	**SOMEDAY WE'RE GONNA LOVE AGAIN** *Pye 7N 15670*	11		7
17 Sep 64	**WHEN YOU WALK IN THE ROOM** *Pye 7N 15694*	3		11
3 Dec 64	**WHAT HAVE THEY DONE TO THE RAIN** *Pye 7N 15739*	13		9
4 Mar 65	**GOODBYE MY LOVE** *Pye 7N 15794*	4		8
8 Jul 65	**HE'S GOT NO LOVE** *Pye 7N 15878*	12		8
14 Oct 65	**WHEN I GET HOME** *Pye 7N 15950*	35		2
16 Dec 65	**TAKE ME FOR WHAT I'M WORTH** *Pye 7N 15992*	20		7
21 Apr 66	**TAKE IT OR LEAVE IT** *Pye 7N 17094*	31		4
13 Oct 66	**HAVE YOU EVER LOVED SOMEBODY** *Pye 7N 17170*	48		

SEASHELLS UK group

Date	Title	Peak Position	Weeks at No.1	Weeks in Top 40
9 Sep 72	**MAYBE I KNOW** *CBS 8218*	32		2

SEB UK keyboard player

Date	Title	Peak Position	Weeks at No.1	Weeks in Top 40
18 Feb 95	**SUGAR SHACK** *React CDREACT 50*	61		

SEBADOH US group

Date	Title	Peak Position	Weeks at No.1	Weeks in Top 40
27 Jul 96	**BEAUTY OF THE RIDE** *Domino RUG 47CD*	74		
30 Jan 99	**FLAME** *Domino RUG 80CD1*	30		1

JON SECADA US singer

Date	Title	Peak Position	Weeks at No.1	Weeks in Top 40
18 Jul 92	**JUST ANOTHER DAY** *SBK 35* ○	5		12
31 Oct 92	**DO YOU BELIEVE IN US** *SBK 37*	30		3
6 Feb 93	**ANGEL** *SBK CDSBK 39*	23		3
17 Jul 93	**DO YOU REALLY WANT ME** *SBK CDSBK 41*	30		2
16 Oct 93	**I'M FREE** *SBK CDSBK 44*	50		
14 May 94	**IF YOU GO** *SBK CDSBK 51*	39		2
4 Feb 95	**MENTAL PICTURE** *SBK CDSBK 54*	44		
16 Dec 95	**IF I NEVER KNEW YOU (LOVE THEME FROM *POCAHONTAS*)** *Walt Disney WD 7023C* JON SECADA & SHANICE	51		
14 Jun 97	**TOO LATE, TOO SOON** *SBK CDSBK 57*	43		

SECCHI Italian producer

Date	Title	Peak Position	Weeks at No.1	Weeks in Top 40
4 May 91	**I SAY YEAH** *Epic 6568467* SECCHI FEATURING ORLANDO JOHNSON	46		

HARRY SECOMBE UK singer/comedian

Date	Title	Peak Position	Weeks at No.1	Weeks in Top 40
9 Dec 55	**ON WITH THE MOTLEY** *Philips PB 523*	16		3
3 Oct 63	**IF I RULED THE WORLD** *Philips BF 1261*	18		14
23 Feb 67	**THIS IS MY SONG** *Philips BF 1539*	2		13

SECOND CITY SOUND UK group

Date	Title	Peak Position	Weeks at No.1	Weeks in Top 40
20 Jan 66	**TCHAIKOVSKY ONE** *Decca F 12310*	22		5
2 Apr 69	**DREAM OF OLWEN** *Major Minor MM 600*	43		

SECOND IMAGE UK group

Date	Title	Peak Position	Weeks at No.1	Weeks in Top 40
24 Jul 82	**STAR** *Polydor POSP 457*	60		
2 Apr 83	**BETTER TAKE TIME** *Polydor POSP 565*	67		
26 Nov 83	**DON'T YOU** *MCA 848*	68		
11 Aug 84	**SING AND SHOUT** *MCA 882*	53		
2 Feb 85	**STARTING AGAIN** *MCA 936*	65		

SECOND PHASE US production duo

Date	Title	Peak Position	Weeks at No.1	Weeks in Top 40
21 Sep 91	**MENTASM** *R&S RSUK 2*	48		

SECOND PROTOCOL UK production duo

Date	Title	Peak Position	Weeks at No.1	Weeks in Top 40
23 Sep 00	**BASSLICK** *East West 216CD*	58		

SECRET AFFAIR UK group

Date	Title	Peak Position	Weeks at No.1	Weeks in Top 40
1 Sep 79	**TIME FOR ACTION** *I-Spy SEE 1*	13		7
10 Nov 79	**LET YOUR HEART DANCE** *I-Spy SEE 3*	32		3
8 Mar 80	**MY WORLD** *I-Spy SEE 5*	16		7
23 Aug 80	**SOUND OF CONFUSION** *I-Spy SEE 8*	45		
17 Oct 81	**DO YOU KNOW?** *I-Spy SEE 10*	57		

SECRET KNOWLEDGE UK/US duo

Date	Title	Peak Position	Weeks at No.1	Weeks in Top 40
27 Apr 96	**LOVE ME NOW** *Deconstruction 74321342432*	66		
24 Aug 96	**SUGAR DADDY** *Deconstruction 74321400242*	75		

SECRET LIFE UK group

Date	Title	Peak Position	Weeks at No.1	Weeks in Top 40
12 Dec 92	**AS ALWAYS** *Cowboy 7RODEO 9*	45		
7 Aug 93	**LOVE SO STRONG** *Cowboy RODEO 18CD*	38		1
7 May 94	**SHE HOLDS THE KEY** *Pulse 8 CDLOSE 58*	63		
29 Oct 94	**I WANT YOU** *Pulse 8 CDLOSE 71*	70		
28 Jan 95	**LOVE SO STRONG (REMIX)** *Pulse 8 CDLOSE 79*	37		1

SECRET MACHINES US group

Date	Title	Peak Position	Weeks at No.1	Weeks in Top 40
7 Aug 04	**NOWHERE AGAIN** *Reprise W648CD*	49		
8 Jan 05	**SAD AND LONELY** *East West E 7625*	38		1
23 Apr 05	**THE ROAD LEADS WHERE IT'S LED** *679 Recordings W669CD2*	56		
8 Apr 06	**LIGHTNING BLUE EYES** *Warner Brothers W707CD1*	57		

SECTION-X French duo

Date	Title	Peak Position	Weeks at No.1	Weeks in Top 40
8 Mar 97	**ATLANTIS** *Perfecto PERF 136CD*	42		

NEIL SEDAKA US singer

Date	Title	Peak Position	Weeks at No.1	Weeks in Top 40
24 Apr 59	**I GO APE** *RCA 1115*	9		13
13 Nov 59	**OH CAROL** *RCA 1152*	3		17
14 Apr 60	**STAIRWAY TO HEAVEN** *RCA 1178*	8		15
1 Sep 60	**YOU MEAN EVERYTHING TO ME** *RCA 1198*	45		
2 Feb 61	**CALENDAR GIRL** *RCA 1220*	8		11
18 May 61	**LITTLE DEVIL** *RCA 1236*	9		11

Date	Title	Peak Position	Weeks at No.1	Weeks in Top 40
21 Dec 61	**HAPPY BIRTHDAY SWEET SIXTEEN** *RCA 1266*	3		15
19 Apr 62	**KING OF CLOWNS** *RCA 1282*	23		9
19 Jul 62	**BREAKING UP IS HARD TO DO** *RCA 1298* ★	7		15
22 Nov 62	**NEXT DOOR TO AN ANGEL** *RCA 1319*	29		3
30 May 63	**LET'S GO STEADY AGAIN** *RCA 1343*	42		
7 Oct 72	**OH CAROL/BREAKING UP IS HARD TO DO/LITTLE DEVIL** *RCA Maximillion 2259*	19		12
4 Nov 72	**BEAUTIFUL YOU** *RCA 2269*	43		
24 Feb 73	**THAT'S WHEN THE MUSIC TAKES ME** *RCA 2310*	18		8
2 Jun 73	**STANDING ON THE INSIDE** *MGM 2006 267*	26		6
25 Aug 73	**OUR LAST SONG TOGETHER** *MGM 2006 307*	31		4
9 Feb 74	**A LITTLE LOVIN'** *Polydor 2058 434*	34		3
22 Jun 74	**LAUGHTER IN THE RAIN** *Polydor 2058 494* ★	15		7
22 Mar 75	**THE QUEEN OF 1964** *Polydor 2058 546*	35		3

MAX SEDGLEY UK producer/drummer

Date	Title	Peak Position	Weeks at No.1	Weeks in Top 40
17 Jul 04	**HAPPY** *Sunday Best SBESTC14*	30		1

SEDUCTION US group

Date	Title	Peak Position	Weeks at No.1	Weeks in Top 40
21 Apr 90	**HEARTBEAT** *Breakout USA 685*	75		

SEEKERS Australian group

Date	Title	Peak Position	Weeks at No.1	Weeks in Top 40
7 Jan 65	**I'LL NEVER FIND ANOTHER YOU** *Columbia DB 7431*	1	2	15
15 Apr 65	**A WORLD OF OUR OWN** *Columbia DB 7532*	3		15
28 Oct 65	**THE CARNIVAL IS OVER** *Columbia DB 7711*	1	3	15
24 Mar 66	**SOMEDAY ONE DAY** *Columbia DB 7867*	11		10
8 Sep 66	**WALK WITH ME** *Columbia DB 8000*	10		11
24 Nov 66	**MORNINGTOWN RIDE** *Columbia DB 8060*	2		14
23 Feb 67	**GEORGY GIRL** *Columbia DB 8134*	3		11
20 Sep 67	**WHEN WILL THE GOOD APPLES FALL** *Columbia DB 8273*	11		10
13 Dec 67	**EMERALD CITY** *Columbia DB 8313*	50		

SEELENLUFT Swiss producer

Date	Title	Peak Position	Weeks at No.1	Weeks in Top 40
4 Oct 03	**MANILA** *Back Yard BACK 10CSC1* SEELENLUFT FEATURING MICHAEL SMITH	70		

BOB SEGER & THE SILVER BULLET BAND US group

Date	Title	Peak Position	Weeks at No.1	Weeks in Top 40
30 Sep 78	**HOLLYWOOD NIGHTS** *Capitol CL 16004* ROB SEGER	42		
3 Feb 79	**WE'VE GOT TONITE** *Capitol CL 16028* ROB SEGER	41		
24 Oct 81	**HOLLYWOOD NIGHTS** *Capitol CL 223*	49		
6 Feb 82	**WE'VE GOT TONITE** *Capitol CL 235*	60		
9 Apr 83	**EVEN NOW** *Capitol CL 284*	73		
28 Jan 95	**WE'VE GOT TONIGHT** *Capitol CDCLS 734*	22		4
29 Apr 95	**NIGHT MOVES** *Capitol CDCL 741*	45		
29 Jul 95	**HOLLYWOOD NIGHTS** *Capitol CDCL 749*	52		
10 Feb 96	**LOCK AND LOAD** *Capitol CDCL 765*	57		

SHEA SEGER US singer

Date	Title	Peak Position	Weeks at No.1	Weeks in Top 40
5 May 01	**CLUTCH** *RCA 74321828142*	47		

SEIKO & DONNIE WAHLBERG Japanese/US duo

Date	Title	Peak Position	Weeks at No.1	Weeks in Top 40
18 Aug 90	**THE RIGHT COMBINATION** *Epic 6562037*	44		

SELECTER UK group

Date	Title	Peak Position	Weeks at No.1	Weeks in Top 40
13 Oct 79	**ON MY RADIO** *2 Tone CHSTT 4*	8		6
2 Feb 80	**THREE MINUTE HERO** *2 Tone CHSTT 8*	16		6
29 Mar 80	**MISSING WORDS** *2 Tone CHSTT 10*	23		6
23 Aug 80	**THE WHISPER** *Chrysalis CHS 1*	36		1

SELENA VS X MEN UK singer and production duo

Date	Title	Peak Position	Weeks at No.1	Weeks in Top 40
14 Jul 01	**GIVE IT UP** *Go! Beat GOBCD 40*	61		

SELFISH CUNT UK duo

Date	Title	Peak Position	Weeks at No.1	Weeks in Top 40
17 Jul 04	**AUTHORITY CONFRONTATION** *Horseglue UHU008*	66		

PETER SELLERS UK comedian and actor

Date	Title	Peak Position	Weeks at No.1	Weeks in Top 40
2 Aug 57	**ANY OLD IRON** *Parlophone R 4337*	17		11
10 Nov 60	**GOODNESS GRACIOUS ME** *Parlophone R 4702* PETER SELLERS & SOPHIA LOREN	4		14
12 Jan 61	**BANGERS AND MASH** *Parlophone R 4724* PETER SELLERS & SOPHIA LOREN	22		5
23 Dec 65	**A HARD DAY'S NIGHT** *Parlophone R 5393*	14		7
27 Nov 93	**A HARD DAY'S NIGHT (EP)** *EMI CDEMS 293*	52		

MICHAEL SEMBELLO US singer/guitarist

Date	Title	Peak Position	Weeks at No.1	Weeks in Top 40
20 Aug 83	**MANIAC** *Casablanca CAN 1017* ★	43		

SEMISONIC US group

Date	Title	Peak Position	Weeks at No.1	Weeks in Top 40
10 Jul 99	**SECRET SMILE** *MCA MCSTD 40210*	13		8
6 Nov 99	**CLOSING TIME** *MCA MCDXD 40221*	25		2
1 Apr 00	**SINGING IN MY SLEEP** *MCA MCSTD 40227*	39		1
3 Mar 01	**CHEMISTRY** *MCA MCSTD 40248*	35		1

SEMPRINI UK pianist

Date	Title	Peak Position	Weeks at No.1	Weeks in Top 40
16 Mar 61	**THEME FROM *EXODUS*** *HMV POP 842*	25		7

SENSELESS THINGS UK group

Date	Title	Peak Position	Weeks at No.1	Weeks in Top 40
22 Jun 91	**EVERYBODY'S GONE** *Epic 6569807*	73		
28 Sep 91	**GOT IT AT THE DELMAR** *Epic 6574497*	50		
11 Jan 92	**EASY TO SMILE** *Epic 6576957*	18		3
11 Apr 92	**HOLD IT DOWN** *Epic 6579267*	19		2
5 Dec 92	**HOMOPHOBIC ASSHOLE** *Epic 6588337*	52		
13 Feb 93	**PRIMARY INSTINCT** *Epic 6589402*	41		
12 Jun 93	**TOO MUCH KISSING** *Epic 6592502*	69		
5 Nov 94	**CHRISTINE KEELER** *Epic 6609572*	56		
28 Jan 95	**SOMETHING TO MISS** *Epic 6611162*	57		

SENSER UK group

Date	Title	Peak Position	Weeks at No.1	Weeks in Top 40
25 Sep 93	**THE KEY** *Ultimate TOPP 019CD*	47		
19 Mar 94	**SWITCH** *Ultimate TOPP 022CD*	39		1
23 Jul 94	**AGE OF PANIC** *Ultimate TOPP 027CD*	52		
17 Aug 96	**CHARMING DEMONS** *Ultimate TOPP 045CD*	42		

SEPULTURA Brazilian group

Date	Title	Peak Position	Weeks at No.1	Weeks in Top 40
2 Oct 93	**TERRITORY** *Roadrunner RR 23823*	66		
26 Feb 94	**REFUSE-RESIST** *Roadrunner RR 23773*	51		
4 Jun 94	**SLAVE NEW WORLD** *Roadrunner RR 23745*	46		
24 Feb 96	**ROOTS BLOODY ROOTS** *Roadrunner RR 23205*	19		1
17 Aug 96	**RATAMAHATTA** *Roadrunner RR 23145*	23		1
14 Dec 96	**ATTITUDE** *Roadrunner RR 22995*	46		

SERAFIN UK group

Date	Title	Peak Position	Weeks at No.1	Weeks in Top 40
17 May 03	**THINGS FALL APART** *Taste Media TMCDSX 5003*	49		
16 Aug 03	**DAY BY DAY** *Taste Media TMCDSX 5006*	49		

SERAPHIM SUITE UK production group

Date	Title	Peak Position	Weeks at No.1	Weeks in Top 40
27 Mar 04	**HEART** *Inferno CDFERN61*	45		

SERIAL DIVA UK production group

Date	Title	Peak Position	Weeks at No.1	Weeks in Top 40
18 Jan 97	**KEEP HOPE ALIVE** *Sound Of Ministry SOMCD 26*	57		
15 May 99	**PEARL RIVER** *Low Sense SENSECD 24* THREE 'N' ONE PRESENTS JOHNNY SHAKER FEATURING SERIAL DIVA	32		1

SERIOUS DANGER UK producer

Date	Title	Peak Position	Weeks at No.1	Weeks in Top 40
20 Dec 97	**DEEPER** *Fresh FRSHD 68*	40		1
2 May 98	**HIGH NOON** *Fresh FRSHD 69*	54		

SERIOUS INTENTION UK group

Date	Title	Peak Position	Weeks at No.1	Weeks in Top 40
16 Nov 85	**YOU DON'T KNOW (OH-OH-OH)** *Important TAN 8*	75		
5 Apr 86	**SERIOUS** *Pow Wow LON 93*	51		

Silver-selling ● Gold-selling ● Platinum-selling ● US No.1 ★ Peak Position · Weeks at No.1 · Weeks in Top 40

SERIOUS ROPE UK group

Date	Title	Peak Position	Weeks at No.1	Weeks in Top 40
22 May 93	HAPPINESS *Rumour RUMACD 64* SERIOUS ROPE PRESENTS SHARON DEE CLARK	54		
1 Oct 94	HAPPINESS – YOU MAKE ME HAPPY (REMIX) *Mercury MERCD 407*	70		

ERICK SERMON US rapper

Date	Title	Peak Position	Weeks at No.1	Weeks in Top 40
6 Oct 01	MUSIC *Polydor 4976222* ERICK SERMON FEATURING MARVIN GAYE	36		1
11 Jan 03	REACT *J Records 74321988492* ERICK SERMON FEATURING REDMAN	14		3
19 Apr 03	LOVE IZ *J Records 82876510971*	72		

SERTAB Turkish singer

Date	Title	Peak Position	Weeks at No.1	Weeks in Top 40
21 Jun 03	EVERY WAY THAT I CAN *Columbia 6739621*	72		

SET THE TONE UK group

Date	Title	Peak Position	Weeks at No.1	Weeks in Top 40
22 Jan 83	DANCE SUCKER *Island WIP 6836*	62		
26 Mar 83	RAP YOUR LOVE *Island IS 110*	67		

SETTLERS UK group

Date	Title	Peak Position	Weeks at No.1	Weeks in Top 40
16 Oct 71	THE LIGHTNING TREE *York SYK 505*	36		3

BRIAN SETZER ORCHESTRA US singer and guitarist

Date	Title	Peak Position	Weeks at No.1	Weeks in Top 40
3 Apr 99	JUMP JIVE AN' WAIL *Interscope IND 95601*	34		1

TAJA SEVELLE US singer

Date	Title	Peak Position	Weeks at No.1	Weeks in Top 40
20 Feb 88	LOVE IS CONTAGIOUS *Paisley Park W 8257*	7		6
14 May 88	WOULDN'T YOU LOVE TO LOVE ME *Paisley Park W 8127*	59		

702 US group

Date	Title	Peak Position	Weeks at No.1	Weeks in Top 40
14 Dec 96	STEELO *Motown 8606072*	41		
29 Nov 97	NO DOUBT *Motown 8607052*	59		
7 Aug 99	WHERE MY GIRLS AT? *Motown TMGCD 1500*	22		2
27 Nov 99	YOU DON'T KNOW *Motown TMGCD 1502*	36		1

740 BOYZ US duo

Date	Title	Peak Position	Weeks at No.1	Weeks in Top 40
4 Nov 95	SHIMMY SHAKE *MCA MCSTD 40002*	54		
22 Mar 03	SHAKE YA SHIMMY *All Around The World CXGLOBE 213* PORN KINGS VERSUS FLIP & FILL FEATURING 740 BOYZ	28		1

SEVEN GRAND HOUSING AUTHORITY UK producer

Date	Title	Peak Position	Weeks at No.1	Weeks in Top 40
23 Oct 93	THE QUESTION *Olympic ELYCD 010*	70		

7669 US group

Date	Title	Peak Position	Weeks at No.1	Weeks in Top 40
18 Jun 94	JOY *Motown TMGCD 1429*	60		

7TH HEAVEN UK group

Date	Title	Peak Position	Weeks at No.1	Weeks in Top 40
14 Sep 85	HOT FUN *Mercury MER 199*	47		

SEVERINE French singer

Date	Title	Peak Position	Weeks at No.1	Weeks in Top 40
24 Apr 71	UN BANC, UN ABRE, UNE RUE *Philips 6009 135*	9		9

DAVID SEVILLE US singer

Date	Title	Peak Position	Weeks at No.1	Weeks in Top 40
23 May 58	WITCH DOCTOR *London HLU 8619* ★	11		6

SEX CLUB US duo

Date	Title	Peak Position	Weeks at No.1	Weeks in Top 40
28 Jan 95	BIG DICK MAN *Club Tools CLU 60775* SEX CLUB FEATURING BROWN SUGAR	67		

SEX-O-SONIQUE UK group

Date	Title	Peak Position	Weeks at No.1	Weeks in Top 40
6 Dec 97	I THOUGHT IT WAS YOU *ffrr FCD 321*	32		1

SEX PISTOLS UK group

Date	Title	Peak Position	Weeks at No.1	Weeks in Top 40
18 Dec 76	ANARCHY IN THE U.K. *EMI 2566*	38		3
4 Jun 77	GOD SAVE THE QUEEN *Virgin VS 181* ●	2		9
9 Jul 77	PRETTY VACANT *Virgin VS 184* ●	6		7
22 Oct 77	HOLIDAYS IN THE SUN *Virgin VS 191*	8		6
8 Jul 78	NO ONE IS INNOCENT/MY WAY *Virgin VS 220* SEX PISTOLS, PUNK PRAYER BY RONALD BIGGS	7		7
3 Mar 79	SOMETHING ELSE/FRIGGIN' IN THE RIGGIN' *Virgin VS 240* ●	3		10
7 Apr 79	SILLY THING *Virgin VS 256* ●	6		6
30 Jun 79	C'MON EVERYBODY *Virgin VS 272* ●	3		7
13 Oct 79	THE GREAT ROCK 'N' ROLL SWINDLE *Virgin VS 290*	21		6
14 Jun 80	(I'M NOT YOUR) STEPPING STONE *Virgin VS 339*	21		6
3 Oct 92	ANARCHY IN THE U.K. *Virgin VS 1431*	33		2
5 Dec 92	PRETTY VACANT *Virgin VS 1448*	56		
27 Jul 96	PRETTY VACANT (LIVE) *Virgin VUSCD 113*	18		2
8 Jun 02	GOD SAVE THE QUEEN *Virgin VSCDT 1832*	15		2
13 Oct 07	ANARCHY IN THE U.K. *Virgin EMI2566*	70		
20 Oct 07	GOD SAVE THE QUEEN *Virgin VS181*	42		
27 Oct 07	PRETTY VACANT *Virgin VS 184*	65		
3 Nov 07	HOLIDAYS IN THE SUN *Virgin VS 191*	74		

DENNY SEYTON & THE SABRES UK group

Date	Title	Peak Position	Weeks at No.1	Weeks in Top 40
17 Sep 64	THE WAY YOU LOOK TONIGHT *Mercury MF 824*	48		

SFX UK production group

Date	Title	Peak Position	Weeks at No.1	Weeks in Top 40
15 May 93	LEMMINGS *Parlophone CDR 6343*	51		

SHABOOM UK production group

Date	Title	Peak Position	Weeks at No.1	Weeks in Top 40
31 Jul 99	SWEET SENSATION *WEA 218CD1*	64		

SHACK UK group

Date	Title	Peak Position	Weeks at No.1	Weeks in Top 40
26 Jun 99	COMEDY *London LONCD 427*	44		
14 Aug 99	NATALIE'S PARTY *London LONCD 436*	63		
11 Mar 00	OSCAR *London LONCD 445*	67		
4 Oct 03	BYRDS TURN TO STONE *North Country NCCDB 002*	63		

SHADES US group

Date	Title	Peak Position	Weeks at No.1	Weeks in Top 40
12 Apr 97	MR BIG STUFF *Motown 5736572* QUEEN LATIFAH, SHADES & FREE	31		1
20 Sep 97	SERENADE *Motown 8606892*	75		

SHADES OF LOVE US production duo

Date	Title	Peak Position	Weeks at No.1	Weeks in Top 40
22 Apr 95	KEEP IN TOUCH (BODY TO BODY) *Vicious Muzik MUZCD 102*	64		

SHADES OF RHYTHM UK production group

Date	Title	Peak Position	Weeks at No.1	Weeks in Top 40
2 Feb 91	HOMICIDE/EXORCIST *ZTT ZANG 13*	53		
13 Apr 91	SWEET SENSATION *ZTT ZANG 18*	54		
20 Jul 91	THE SOUND OF EDEN *ZTT ZANG 22*	35		2
30 Nov 91	EXTACY *ZTT ZANG 24*	16		3
20 Feb 93	SWEET REVIVAL (KEEP IT COMIN') *ZTT ZANG 40CD*	61		
11 Sep 93	THE SOUND OF EDEN *ZTT ZANG 44CD*	37		1
5 Nov 94	THE WANDERING DRAGON *Public Demand PPDCD 5*	55		
21 Jun 97	PSYCHO BASE *Coalition CRUM 002CD*	57		

SHADOWS UK group

Date	Title	Peak Position	Weeks at No.1	Weeks in Top 40
12 Sep 58	MOVE IT *Columbia DB 4178* CLIFF RICHARD & THE DRIFTERS	2		17
21 Nov 58	HIGH CLASS BABY *Columbia DB 4203* CLIFF RICHARD & THE DRIFTERS	7		10
30 Jan 59	LIVIN' LOVIN' DOLL *Columbia DB 4249* CLIFF RICHARD & THE DRIFTERS	20		6
8 May 59	MEAN STREAK *Columbia DB 4290* CLIFF RICHARD & THE DRIFTERS	10		9
15 May 59	NEVER MIND *Columbia DB 4290* CLIFF RICHARD & THE DRIFTERS	21		2

Silver-selling ○ · Gold-selling ● · Platinum-selling ⊛ · US No.1 ★ · Peak Position · Weeks at No.1 · Weeks in Top 40

Date	Title / Label	Peak Position	Weeks at No.1	Weeks in Top 40
10 Jul 59	**LIVING DOLL** *Columbia DB 4306* CLIFF RICHARD & THE SHADOWS	1	6	23
9 Oct 59	**TRAVELLIN' LIGHT** *Columbia DB 4351* CLIFF RICHARD & THE SHADOWS	1	5	17
9 Oct 59	**DYNAMITE** *Columbia DB 4351* CLIFF RICHARD & THE SHADOWS	16		4
15 Jan 60	**EXPRESSO BONGO EP** *Columbia SEG 7971* CLIFF RICHARD & THE SHADOWS	14		7
22 Jan 60	**A VOICE IN THE WILDERNESS** *Columbia DB 4398* CLIFF RICHARD & THE SHADOWS	2		13
24 Mar 60	**FALL IN LOVE WITH YOU** *Columbia DB 4431* CLIFF RICHARD & THE SHADOWS	2		15
30 Jun 60	**PLEASE DON'T TEASE** *Columbia DB 4479* CLIFF RICHARD & THE SHADOWS	1	4	18
21 Jul 60	**APACHE** *Columbia DB 4484*	1	5	20
22 Sep 60	**NINE TIMES OUT OF TEN** *Columbia DB 4506* CLIFF RICHARD & THE SHADOWS	3		12
10 Nov 60	**MAN OF MYSTERY/THE STRANGER** *Columbia DB 4530*	5		13
1 Dec 60	**I LOVE YOU** *Columbia DB 4547* CLIFF RICHARD & THE SHADOWS	1	2	15
9 Feb 61	**F.B.I.** *Columbia DB 4580*	6		18
2 Mar 61	**THEME FOR A DREAM** *Columbia DB 4593* CLIFF RICHARD & THE SHADOWS	3		13
30 Mar 61	**GEE WHIZ IT'S YOU** *Columbia DC 756* CLIFF RICHARD & THE SHADOWS	4		13
11 May 61	**FRIGHTENED CITY** *Columbia DB 4637*	3		18
22 Jun 61	**A GIRL LIKE YOU** *Columbia DB 4667* CLIFF RICHARD & THE SHADOWS	3		14
7 Sep 61	**KON-TIKI** *Columbia DB 4698*	1	1	12
16 Nov 61	**THE SAVAGE** *Columbia DB 4726*	10		8
11 Jan 62	**THE YOUNG ONES** *Columbia DB 4761* CLIFF RICHARD & THE SHADOWS	1	6	19
1 Mar 62	**WONDERFUL LAND** *Columbia DB 4790*	1	8	18
10 May 62	**I'M LOOKING OUT THE WINDOW/DO YOU WANNA DANCE** *Columbia DB 4828* CLIFF RICHARD & THE SHADOWS	2		15
2 Aug 62	**GUITAR TANGO** *Columbia DB 4870*	4		14
6 Sep 62	**IT'LL BE ME** *Columbia DB 4886* CLIFF RICHARD & THE SHADOWS	2		11
6 Dec 62	**THE NEXT TIME/BACHELOR BOY** *Columbia DB 4950* CLIFF RICHARD & THE SHADOWS	1	3	16
13 Dec 62	**DANCE ON!** *Columbia DB 4948*	1	1	13
21 Feb 63	**SUMMER HOLIDAY** *Columbia DB 4977* CLIFF RICHARD & THE SHADOWS	1	3	17
7 Mar 63	**FOOT TAPPER** *Columbia DB 4984*	1	1	15
9 May 63	**LUCKY LIPS** *Columbia DB 7034* CLIFF RICHARD & THE SHADOWS	4		14
6 Jun 63	**ATLANTIS** *Columbia DB 7047*	2		15
19 Sep 63	**SHINDIG** *Columbia DB 7106*	6		11
7 Nov 63	**DON'T TALK TO HIM** *Columbia DB 7150* CLIFF RICHARD & THE SHADOWS	2		13
5 Dec 63	**GERONIMO** *Columbia DB 7163*	11		11
6 Feb 64	**I'M THE LONELY ONE** *Columbia DB 7203* CLIFF RICHARD & THE SHADOWS	8		9
5 Mar 64	**THEME FOR YOUNG LOVERS** *Columbia DB 7231*	12		10
7 May 64	**THE RISE AND FALL OF FLINGEL BUNT** *Columbia DB 7261*	5		12
2 Jul 64	**ON THE BEACH** *Columbia DB 7305* CLIFF RICHARD & THE SHADOWS	7		12
3 Sep 64	**RHYTHM AND GREENS** *Columbia DB 7342*	22		7
3 Dec 64	**GENIE WITH THE LIGHT BROWN LAMP** *Columbia DB 7416*	17		10
10 Dec 64	**I COULD EASILY FALL (IN LOVE WITH YOU)** *Columbia DB 7420* CLIFF RICHARD & THE SHADOWS	6		10
11 Feb 65	**MARY ANNE** *Columbia DB 7476*	17		7
10 Jun 65	**STINGRAY** *Columbia DB 7588*	19		6
5 Aug 65	**DON'T MAKE MY BABY BLUE** *Columbia DB 7650*	10		9
19 Aug 65	**THE TIME IN BETWEEN** *Columbia DB 7660* CLIFF RICHARD & THE SHADOWS	22		6
4 Nov 65	**WIND ME UP (LET ME GO)** *Columbia DB 7745* CLIFF RICHARD & THE SHADOWS	21		5
25 Nov 65	**WAR LORD** *Columbia DB 7769*	18		8
17 Mar 66	**I MET A GIRL** *Columbia DB 7853*	22		4
24 Mar 66	**BLUE TURNS TO GREY** *Columbia DB 7866* CLIFF RICHARD & THE SHADOWS	15		8
7 Jul 66	**A PLACE IN THE SUN** *Columbia DB 7952*	24		5
13 Oct 66	**TIME DRAGS BY** *Columbia DB 8017* CLIFF RICHARD & THE SHADOWS	10		10
3 Nov 66	**THE DREAMS I DREAM** *Columbia DB 8034*	42		
15 Dec 66	**IN THE COUNTRY** *Columbia DB 8094* CLIFF RICHARD & THE SHADOWS	6		9
13 Apr 67	**MAROC 7** *Columbia DB 8170*	24		6
27 Nov 68	**DON'T FORGET TO CATCH ME** *Columbia DB 8503* CLIFF RICHARD & THE SHADOWS	21		7
8 Mar 75	**LET ME BE THE ONE** *EMI 2269*	12		7
16 Dec 78	**DON'T CRY FOR ME ARGENTINA** *EMI 2890* ○	5		9
28 Apr 79	**THEME FROM *THE DEER HUNTER* (CAVATINA)** *EMI 2939* ○	9		9
26 Jan 80	**RIDERS IN THE SKY** *EMI 5027*	12		7
23 Aug 80	**EQUINOXE (PART V)** *Polydor POSP 148*	50		
2 May 81	**THE THIRD MAN** *Polydor POSP 255*	44		

SHAFT UK producer

Date	Title / Label	Peak Position	Weeks at No.1	Weeks in Top 40
21 Dec 91	**ROOBARB AND CUSTARD** *ffrreedom TAB 100*	7		6
25 Jul 92	**MONKEY** *ffrreedom TAB 114*	61		
4 Sep 99	**(MUCHO MAMBO) SWAY** *Wonderboy WBYD 015* ○	2		9
20 May 00	**MAMBO ITALIANO** *Wonderboy WBDD 017*	12		4
21 Jul 01	**KIKI RIRI BOOM** *Wonderboy WBOYD 026*	62		

SHAG UK singer

Date	Title / Label	Peak Position	Weeks at No.1	Weeks in Top 40
14 Oct 72	**LOOP DI LOVE** *UK 7*	4		11
20 Sep 75	**CHICK-A-BOOM (DON'T YA JES LOVE IT)** *UK 2012 002* 53RD & A 3RD FEATURING THE SOUND OF SHAG	36		3

SHAGGY Jamaican singer

Date	Title / Label	Peak Position	Weeks at No.1	Weeks in Top 40
6 Feb 93	**OH CAROLINA** *Greensleeves GRECD 361* ●	1	2	15
10 Jul 93	**SOON BE DONE** *Greensleeves GRECD 380*	46		
8 Jul 95	**IN THE SUMMERTIME** *Virgin VSCDT 1542* SHAGGY FEATURING RAYVON	5		8
23 Sep 95	**BOOMBASTIC** *Virgin VSCDT 1536* ●	1	1	10
13 Jan 96	**WHY YOU TREAT ME SO BAD** *Virgin VSCDT 1566* SHAGGY FEATURING GRAND PUBA	11		3
23 Mar 96	**SOMETHING DIFFERENT/THE TRAIN IS COMING** *Virgin VSCDX 1581* SHAGGY FEATURING WAYNE WONDER	21		4
22 Jun 96	**THAT GIRL** *Virgin VUSDX 106* MAXI PRIEST FEATURING SHAGGY	15		5
19 Jul 97	**PIECE OF MY HEART** *Virgin VSCDT 1647* SHAGGY FEATURING MARSHA	7		5
17 Feb 01	**IT WASN'T ME (IMPORT)** *MCA 1558032* SHAGGY FEATURING RICARDO 'RIKROK' DU CENT	31		3
10 Mar 01	**IT WASN'T ME** *MCA 1558022* SHAGGY FEATURING RICARDO 'RIKROK' DU CENT ⊛ ★	1	1	16
9 Jun 01	**ANGEL** *MCA MCSTD 40257* SHAGGY FEATURING RAYVON ● ★	1	3	13
29 Sep 01	**LUV ME LUV ME** *MCA MCSTD 40263*	5		6
1 Dec 01	**DANCE AND SHOUT/HOPE** *MCA MCSTD 40272* SHAGGY/SHAGGY FEATURING PRINCE MYDAS	19		2
23 Mar 02	**ME JULIE** *Island CID 793* ALI G & SHAGGY ○	2		9
9 Nov 02	**HEY SEXY LADY** *MCA MCSTD 40304* SHAGGY FEATURING BRIAN AND TONY GOLD	10		4
3 Jul 04	**YOUR EYES** *VP VPCD6415* RIK ROK FEATURING SHAGGY	57		
17 Sep 05	**WILD 2NITE** *Geffen MCSXD40431* SHAGGY FEATURING OLIVIA	61		

SHAH UK singer

Date	Title / Label	Peak Position	Weeks at No.1	Weeks in Top 40
6 Jun 98	**SECRET LOVE** *Evocative EVOKE 5CDS*	69		

SHAI US group

Date	Title / Label	Peak Position	Weeks at No.1	Weeks in Top 40
19 Dec 92	**IF I EVER FALL IN LOVE** *MCA MCS 1727*	36		1

SHAKATAK UK group

Date	Title / Label	Peak Position	Weeks at No.1	Weeks in Top 40
8 Nov 80	**FEELS LIKE THE RIGHT TIME** *Polydor POSP 188*	41		
7 Mar 81	**LIVING IN THE UK** *Polydor POSP 230*	52		
25 Jul 81	**BRAZILIAN DAWN** *Polydor POSP 282*	48		
21 Nov 81	**EASIER SAID THAN DONE** *Polydor POSP 375*	12		8
3 Apr 82	**NIGHT BIRDS** *Polydor POSP 407*	9		7
19 Jun 82	**STREETWALKIN'** *Polydor POSP 452*	38		3
4 Sep 82	**INVITATIONS** *Polydor POSP 502*	24		3
6 Nov 82	**STRANGER** *Polydor POSP 530*	43		
4 Jun 83	**DARK IS THE NIGHT** *Polydor POSP 595*	15		6
27 Aug 83	**IF YOU COULD SEE ME NOW** *Polydor POSP 635*	49		
7 Jul 84	**DOWN ON THE STREET** *Polydor POSP 688*	9		8
15 Sep 84	**DON'T BLAME IT ON LOVE** *Polydor POSP 699*	55		
16 Nov 85	**DAY BY DAY** *Polydor POSP 770* SHAKATAK FEATURING AL JARREAU	53		
24 Oct 87	**MR MANIC AND SISTER COOL** *Polydor MANIC 1*	56		

Silver-selling ○ · Gold-selling ● · Platinum-selling ⊛ · US No.1 ★ · Peak Position · Weeks at No.1 · Weeks in Top 40

SHAKE B4 USE UK production group

Date	Title / Label	Peak Position	Weeks at No.1	Weeks in Top 40
18 Jan 03	**ADDICTED TO LOVE** *Serious SER 606CD* SHAKE B4 USE VS ROBERT PALMER	42		

SHAKEDOWN Swiss group

Date	Title / Label	Peak Position	Weeks at No.1	Weeks in Top 40
11 May 02	**AT NIGHT** *Defected DFECT 50CDS*	6		5
28 Jun 03	**DROWSY WITH HOPE** *Defected DFTD 071CDS*	46		

SHAKESPEARS SISTER UK/US duo

Date	Title / Label	Peak Position	Weeks at No.1	Weeks in Top 40
29 Jul 89	**YOU'RE HISTORY** *ffrr F 112*	7		7
14 Oct 89	**RUN SILENT** *ffrr F 119*	54		
10 Mar 90	**DIRTY MIND** *ffrr F 128*	71		
12 Oct 91	**GOODBYE CRUEL WORLD** *London LON 309*	59		
25 Jan 92	**STAY** *London LON 314* ●	1	8	15
16 May 92	**I DON'T CARE** *London LON 318*	7		6
18 Jul 92	**GOODBYE CRUEL WORLD** *London LON 322*	32		2
7 Nov 92	**HELLO (TURN YOUR RADIO ON)** *London LON 330*	14		4
27 Feb 93	**MY 16TH APOLOGY (EP)** *London LONCD 337*	61		
22 Jun 96	**I CAN DRIVE** *London LONCD 383*	30		1

SHAKIRA Colombian singer

Date	Title / Label	Peak Position	Weeks at No.1	Weeks in Top 40
9 Mar 02	**WHENEVER WHEREVER** *Epic 6724262* ●	2		16
3 Aug 02	**UNDERNEATH YOUR CLOTHES** *Epic 6729532*	3		13
23 Nov 02	**OBJECTION (TANGO)** *Epic 6733402*	17		3
11 Mar 06	**DON'T BOTHER** *Epic 82876792812*	9		3
17 Jun 06	**HIPS DON'T LIE** *Epic 82876842702* SHAKIRA FEATURING WYCLEF JEAN ★	1	2	28
23 Dec 06	**ILLEGAL** *Epic 88697009202* SHAKIRA FEATURING CARLOS SANTANA	34		1
14 Apr 07	**BEAUTIFUL LIAR** *Columbia 88697091242* BEYONCÉ & SHAKIRA ○	1	3	19

SHALAMAR US group

Date	Title / Label	Peak Position	Weeks at No.1	Weeks in Top 40
14 May 77	**UPTOWN FESTIVAL** *Soul Train FB 0885*	30		4
9 Dec 78	**TAKE THAT TO THE BANK** *RCA FB 1379*	20		6
24 Nov 79	**THE SECOND TIME AROUND** *Solar FB 1709*	45		
9 Feb 80	**RIGHT IN THE SOCKET** *Solar SO 2*	44		
30 Aug 80	**I OWE YOU ONE** *Solar SO 11*	13		8
28 Mar 81	**MAKE THAT MOVE** *Solar SO 17*	30		5
27 Mar 82	**I CAN MAKE YOU FEEL GOOD** *Solar K 12599*	7		8
12 Jun 82	**A NIGHT TO REMEMBER** *Solar K 13162*	5		9
4 Sep 82	**THERE IT IS** *Solar K 13194* ○	5		8
27 Nov 82	**FRIENDS** *Solar CHUM 1*	12		8
11 Jun 83	**DEAD GIVEAWAY** *Solar E 9819*	8		8
13 Aug 83	**DISAPPEARING ACT** *Solar E 9807*	18		6
15 Oct 83	**OVER AND OVER** *Solar E 9792*	23		4
24 Mar 84	**DANCING IN THE SHEETS** *CBS A 4171*	41		
31 Mar 84	**DEADLINE USA** *MCA 866*	52		
24 Nov 84	**AMNESIA** *Solar/MCA SHAL 1*	61		
2 Feb 85	**MY GIRL LOVES ME** *MCA SHAL 2*	45		
26 Apr 86	**A NIGHT TO REMEMBER (REMIX)** *MCA SHAL 3*	52		

SHAM ROCK Irish group

Date	Title / Label	Peak Position	Weeks at No.1	Weeks in Top 40
7 Nov 98	**TELL ME MA** *Jive 0522352*	13		5

SHAM 69 UK group

Date	Title / Label	Peak Position	Weeks at No.1	Weeks in Top 40
13 May 78	**ANGELS WITH DIRTY FACES** *Polydor 2059 023*	19		6
29 Jul 78	**IF THE KIDS ARE UNITED** *Polydor 2059 050*	9		8
14 Oct 78	**HURRY UP HARRY** *Polydor POSP 7*	10		7
24 Mar 79	**QUESTIONS AND ANSWERS** *Polydor POSP 27*	18		6
4 Aug 79	**HERSHAM BOYS** *Polydor PSOP 64*	6		7
27 Oct 79	**YOU'RE A BETTER MAN THAN I** *Polydor POSP 82*	49		
12 Apr 80	**TELL THE CHILDREN** *Polydor POSP 136*	45		
24 Jun 06	**HURRY UP ENGLAND – THE PEOPLE'S ANTHEM** *Parlophone CDR6704* SHAM 69 & THE SPECIAL ASSEMBLY	10		2

SHAMEN UK group

Date	Title / Label	Peak Position	Weeks at No.1	Weeks in Top 40
7 Apr 90	**PRO-GEN** *One Little Indian 36 TP7*	55		
22 Sep 90	**MAKE IT MINE** *One Little Indian 46 TP7*	42		
6 Apr 91	**HYPERREAL** *One Little Indian 48 TP7*	29		4
27 Jul 91	**MOVE ANY MOUNTAIN (REMIX)/PRO-GEN '91** *One Little Indian 52 TP7*	4		8
18 Jul 92	**LSI** *One Little Indian 68 TP7*	6		7
5 Sep 92	**EBENEEZER GOODE** *One Little Indian 78 TP7* ○	1	4	9
7 Nov 92	**BOSS DRUM** *One Little Indian 88 TP7*	4		6
7 Nov 92	**BOSS DRUM (REMIX)** *One Little Indian 88 TP12*	58		
19 Dec 92	**PHOREVER PEOPLE** *One Little Indian 98 TP7* ○	5		8
6 Mar 93	**RE:EVOLUTION** *One Little Indian 118 TP7CD* SHAMEN WITH TERENCE McKENNA	18		1
6 Nov 93	**THE SOS EP** *One Little Indian 108 TP7CD*	14		3
19 Aug 95	**DESTINATION ESCHATON** *One Little Indian 128 TP7CDL*	15		2
21 Oct 95	**TRANSAMAZONIA** *One Little Indian 138 TP7CD*	28		1
10 Feb 96	**HEAL (THE SEPARATION)** *One Little Indian 158 TP7CDL*	31		1
21 Dec 96	**MOVE ANY MOUNTAIN (2ND REMIX)** *One Little Indian 169 TP7CD*	35		1

SHAMPOO UK duo

Date	Title / Label	Peak Position	Weeks at No.1	Weeks in Top 40
30 Jul 94	**TROUBLE** *Food CDFOOD 51*	11		10
15 Oct 94	**VIVA LA MEGABABES** *Food CDFOOD 54*	27		3
18 Feb 95	**DELICIOUS** *Food CDFOOD 58*	21		3
5 Aug 95	**TROUBLE** *Food CDFOODS 66*	36		1
13 Jul 96	**GIRL POWER** *Food CDFOOD 76*	25		2
21 Sep 96	**I KNOW WHAT BOYS LIKE** *Food CDFOOD 83*	42		

JIMMY SHAND UK accordionist

Date	Title / Label	Peak Position	Weeks at No.1	Weeks in Top 40
23 Dec 55	**BLUEBELL POLKA** *Parlophone R 3436*	20		2

PAUL SHANE & THE YELLOWCOATS UK actor and backing group

Date	Title / Label	Peak Position	Weeks at No.1	Weeks in Top 40
16 May 81	**HI DE HI (HOLIDAY ROCK)** *EMI 5180*	36		2

SHANGRI-LAS US group

Date	Title / Label	Peak Position	Weeks at No.1	Weeks in Top 40
8 Oct 64	**REMEMBER (WALKIN' IN THE SAND)** *Red Bird RB 10008*	14		9
14 Jan 65	**LEADER OF THE PACK** *Red Bird RB 10014* ★	11		8
14 Oct 72	**LEADER OF THE PACK** *Kama Sutra 2013 024*	3		12
5 Jun 76	**LEADER OF THE PACK** *Charly CS 1009/Contempo CS 7032*	7		9
12 Jun 76	**LEADER OF THE PACK** *Contempo CS 9032*	7		8

SHANICE US singer

Date	Title / Label	Peak Position	Weeks at No.1	Weeks in Top 40
23 Nov 91	**I LOVE YOUR SMILE** *Motown ZB 44907*	55		
22 Feb 92	**I LOVE YOUR SMILE (REMIX)** *Motown TMG 1401*	2		9
14 Nov 92	**LOVIN' YOU** *Motown TMG 1409*	54		
16 Jan 93	**SAVING FOREVER FOR YOU** *Giant W 0148CD*	42		
13 Aug 94	**I LIKE** *Motown TMGCD 1427*	49		
16 Dec 95	**IF I NEVER KNEW YOU (LOVE THEME FROM *POCAHONTAS*)** *Walt Disney WD 7023C* JON SECADA & SHANICE	51		

SHANKS & BIGFOOT UK production duo

Date	Title / Label	Peak Position	Weeks at No.1	Weeks in Top 40
29 May 99	**SWEET LIKE CHOCOLATE** *Chocolate Boy 0530352* ⊛	1	2	12
29 Jul 00	**SING-A-LONG** *Pepper 9230232*	12		4

SHANNON US singer

Date	Title / Label	Peak Position	Weeks at No.1	Weeks in Top 40
19 Nov 83	**LET THE MUSIC PLAY** *Club LET 1*	14		9
7 Apr 84	**GIVE ME TONIGHT** *Club JAB 1*	24		4
30 Jun 84	**SWEET SOMEBODY** *Club JAB 3*	25		5
20 Jul 85	**STRONGER TOGETHER** *Club JAB 15*	46		
6 Dec 97	**IT'S OVER LOVE** *Manifesto FESCD 37* TODD TERRY PRESENTS SHANNON	16		2
28 Nov 98	**MOVE MANIA** *Multiply CDMULTY 45* SASH! FEATURING SHANNON	8		8

DEL SHANNON US singer

Date	Title / Label	Peak Position	Weeks at No.1	Weeks in Top 40
27 Apr 61	**RUNAWAY** *London HLX 9317* ★	1	3	19
14 Sep 61	**HATS OFF TO LARRY** *London HLX 9402*	6		11
7 Dec 61	**SO LONG BABY** *London HLX 9462*	10		10
15 Mar 62	**HEY LITTLE GIRL** *London HLX 9515*	2		13
6 Sep 62	**CRY MYSELF TO SLEEP** *London HLX 9587*	29		5
11 Oct 62	**SWISS MAID** *London HLX 0609*	2		15
17 Jan 63	**LITTLE TOWN FLIRT** *London HLX 9653*	4		9
25 Apr 63	**TWO KINDS OF TEARDROPS** *London HLX 9710*	5		12
22 Aug 63	**TWO SILHOUETTES** *London HLX 9761*	23		6
24 Oct 63	**SUE'S GOTTA BE MINE** *London HLU 9800*	21		6

Silver-selling ○ Gold-selling ● Platinum-selling ⊛ US No.1 ★ | Peak Position | Weeks at No.1 | Weeks in Top 40

Date	Title / Label	Peak Position	Weeks at No.1	Weeks in Top 40
12 Mar 64	**MARY JANE** *Stateside SS 269*	35		2
30 Jul 64	**HANDY MAN** *Stateside SS 317*	36		1
14 Jan 65	**KEEP SEARCHIN' (WE'LL FOLLOW THE SUN)** *Stateside SS 368*	3		10
18 Mar 65	**STRANGER IN TOWN** *Stateside SS 395*	40		1

ROXANNE SHANTE US singer

Date	Title / Label	Peak Position	Weeks at No.1	Weeks in Top 40
1 Aug 87	**HAVE A NICE DAY** *Breakout USA 612*	58		
4 Jun 88	**GO ON GIRL** *Breakout USA 633*	55		
29 Oct 88	**SHARP AS A KNIFE** *Club JAB 73* BRANDON COOKE FEATURING ROXANNE SHANTE	45		
14 Apr 90	**GO ON GIRL (REMIX)** *Breakout USA 689*	74		
23 Sep 00	**WHAT'S GOING ON** *Wall Of Sound WALLD 064* MEKON FEATURING ROXANNE SHANTE	43		

SHAPESHIFTERS UK/Swedish duo

Date	Title / Label	Peak Position	Weeks at No.1	Weeks in Top 40
24 Jul 04	**LOLA'S THEME** *Positiva CDTIVS 207* ○	1	1	12
26 Mar 05	**BACK TO BASICS** *Positiva CDTIVS216*	10		4
18 Mar 06	**INCREDIBLE** *Positiva CDTIVS233*	12		3
5 Aug 06	**SENSITIVITY** *Positiva CDTIV238* SHAPESHIFTERS & CHIC	40		1
14 Jul 07	**PUSHER** *Positiva CDTIVS258*	56		
27 Oct 07	**NEW DAY** *Positiva CDTIVS262*	72		

HELEN SHAPIRO UK singer

Date	Title / Label	Peak Position	Weeks at No.1	Weeks in Top 40
23 Mar 61	**DON'T TREAT ME LIKE A CHILD** *Columbia DB 4589*	3		18
29 Jun 61	**YOU DON'T KNOW** *Columbia DB 4670*	1	3	20
28 Sep 61	**WALKIN' BACK TO HAPPINESS** *Columbia DB 4715*	1	3	18
15 Feb 62	**TELL ME WHAT HE SAID** *Columbia DB 4782*	2		14
3 May 62	**LET'S TALK ABOUT LOVE** *Columbia DB 4824*	23		6
12 Jul 62	**LITTLE MISS LONELY** *Columbia DB 4869*	8		10
18 Oct 62	**KEEP AWAY FROM OTHER GIRLS** *Columbia DB 4908*	40		3
7 Feb 63	**QUEEN FOR TONIGHT** *Columbia DB 4966*	33		3
25 Apr 63	**WOE IS ME** *Columbia DB 7026*	35		3
24 Oct 63	**LOOK WHO IT IS** *Columbia DB 7130*	47		
23 Jan 64	**FEVER** *Columbia DB 7190*	38		2

SHARADA HOUSE GANG Italian group

Date	Title / Label	Peak Position	Weeks at No.1	Weeks in Top 40
12 Aug 95	**KEEP IT UP** *Media MCSTD 2071*	36		1
11 May 96	**LET THE RHYTHM MOVE YOU** *Media MCSTD 40035*	50		
18 Oct 97	**GYPSY BOY, GYPSY GIRL** *Gut CXGUT 12*	52		

SHARAM US producer

Date	Title / Label	Peak Position	Weeks at No.1	Weeks in Top 40
30 Dec 06	**PATT (PARTY ALL THE TIME)** *Data DATA138CDS*	8		9

SHARKEY UK DJ and producer

Date	Title / Label	Peak Position	Weeks at No.1	Weeks in Top 40
8 Mar 97	**REVOLUTIONS (EP)** *React CDREACT 95*	53		

FEARGAL SHARKEY UK singer

Date	Title / Label	Peak Position	Weeks at No.1	Weeks in Top 40
13 Oct 84	**LISTEN TO YOUR FATHER** *Zarjazz JAZZ 1*	23		5
29 Jun 85	**LOVING YOU** *Virgin VS 770*	26		6
12 Oct 85	**A GOOD HEART** *Virgin VS 808* ●	1	2	13
4 Jan 86	**YOU LITTLE THIEF** *Virgin VS 840*	5		7
5 Apr 86	**SOMEONE TO SOMEBODY** *Virgin VS 828*	64		
16 Jan 88	**MORE LOVE** *Virgin VS 992*	44		
16 Mar 91	**I'VE GOT NEWS FOR YOU** *Virgin VS 1294*	12		7

SHARONETTES UK group

Date	Title / Label	Peak Position	Weeks at No.1	Weeks in Top 40
26 Apr 75	**PAPA OOM MOW MOW** *Black Magic BM 102*	26		4
12 Jul 75	**GOING TO A GO-GO** *Black Magic BM 104*	46		

DEE DEE SHARP US singer

Date	Title / Label	Peak Position	Weeks at No.1	Weeks in Top 40
25 Apr 63	**DO THE BIRD** *Cameo Parkway C 244*	46		

SHARPAY US singer

Date	Title / Label	Peak Position	Weeks at No.1	Weeks in Top 40
6 Oct 07	**FABULOUS** *Download*	64		

SHARPE & NUMAN UK duo

Date	Title / Label	Peak Position	Weeks at No.1	Weeks in Top 40
9 Feb 85	**CHANGE YOUR MIND** *Polydor POSP 722*	17		5
4 Oct 86	**NEW THING FROM LONDON TOWN** *Numa NU 19*	52		
30 Jan 88	**NO MORE LIES** *Polydor POSP 894*	34		3
3 Jun 89	**I'M ON AUTOMATIC** *Polydor PO 43*	44		

ROCKY SHARPE & THE REPLAYS UK group

Date	Title / Label	Peak Position	Weeks at No.1	Weeks in Top 40
16 Dec 78	**RAMA LAMA DING DONG** *Chiswick CHIS 104*	17		5
24 Mar 79	**IMAGINATION** *Chiswick CHIS 110*	39		1
25 Aug 79	**LOVE WILL MAKE YOU FAIL IN SCHOOL** *Chiswick CHIS 114* ROCKY SHARPE & THE REPLAYS FEATURING THE TOP LINERS	60		
9 Feb 80	**MARTIAN HOP** *Chiswick CHIS 121*	55		
17 Apr 82	**SHOUT SHOUT (KNOCK YOURSELF OUT)** *Chiswick DICE 3*	19		6
7 Aug 82	**CLAP YOUR HANDS** *RAK 345*	54		
26 Feb 83	**IF YOU WANNA BE HAPPY** *Polydor POSP 560*	46		

SHAUN THE SHEEP UK animated TV character

Date	Title / Label	Peak Position	Weeks at No.1	Weeks in Top 40
22 Dec 07	**LIFE'S A TREAT** *Tug CDSNOG24*	20		2

BEN SHAW UK producer

Date	Title / Label	Peak Position	Weeks at No.1	Weeks in Top 40
14 Jul 01	**SO STRONG** *Fire Recordings ERIF 009CDS* BEN SHAW FEATURING ADELE HOLNESS	72		

MARK SHAW UK singer

Date	Title / Label	Peak Position	Weeks at No.1	Weeks in Top 40
17 Nov 90	**LOVE SO BRIGHT** *EMI EM 161*	54		

SANDIE SHAW UK singer

Date	Title / Label	Peak Position	Weeks at No.1	Weeks in Top 40
8 Oct 64	**(THERE'S) ALWAYS SOMETHING THERE TO REMIND ME** *Pye 7N 15704*	1	3	9
10 Dec 64	**GIRL DON'T COME** *Pye 7N 15743*	3		12
18 Feb 65	**I'LL STOP AT NOTHING** *Pye 7N 15783*	4		9
13 May 65	**LONG LIVE LOVE** *Pye 7N 15841*	1	3	12
23 Sep 65	**MESSAGE UNDERSTOOD** *Pye 7N 15940*	6		8
18 Nov 65	**HOW CAN YOU TELL** *Pye 7N 15987*	21		8
27 Jan 66	**TOMORROW** *Pye 7N 17036*	9		7
19 May 66	**NOTHING COMES EASY** *Pye 7N 17086*	14		7
8 Sep 66	**RUN** *Pye 7N 17163*	32		3
24 Nov 66	**THINK SOMETIMES ABOUT ME** *Pye 7N 17212*	32		3
19 Jan 67	**I DON'T NEED ANYTHING** *Pye 7N 17239*	50		
16 Mar 67	**PUPPET ON A STRING** *Pye 7N 17272*	1	3	15
12 Jul 67	**TONIGHT IN TOKYO** *Pye 7N 17346*	21		5
4 Oct 67	**YOU'VE NOT CHANGED** *Pye 7N 17378*	18		9
7 Feb 68	**TODAY** *Pye 7N 17441*	27		5
12 Feb 69	**MONSIEUR DUPONT** *Pye 7N 17675*	6		13
14 May 69	**THINK IT ALL OVER** *Pye 7N 17726*	42		
21 Apr 84	**HAND IN GLOVE** *Rough Trade RT 130*	27		3
14 Jun 86	**ARE YOU READY TO BE HEARTBROKEN** *Polydor POSP 793*	68		
12 Nov 94	**NOTHING LESS THAN BRILLIANT** *Virgin VSCDT 1521*	66		

TRACY SHAW UK singer

Date	Title / Label	Peak Position	Weeks at No.1	Weeks in Top 40
4 Jul 98	**HAPPENIN' ALL OVER AGAIN** *Recognition CDREC 2*	46		

WINIFRED SHAW US singer

Date	Title / Label	Peak Position	Weeks at No.1	Weeks in Top 40
14 Aug 76	**LULLABY OF BROADWAY** *United Artists UP 36131*	42		

SHE ROCKERS UK group

Date	Title / Label	Peak Position	Weeks at No.1	Weeks in Top 40
13 Jan 90	**JAM IT JAM** *Jive 233*	58		

GEORGE SHEARING UK pianist

Date	Title / Label	Peak Position	Weeks at No.1	Weeks in Top 40
19 Jul 62	**LET THERE BE LOVE** *Capitol CL 15257* NAT 'KING' COLE WITH GEORGE SHEARING	11		12
4 Oct 62	**BAUBLES, BANGLES AND BEADS** *Capitol CL 15269*	49		

GARY SHEARSTON Australian singer

Date	Title / Label	Peak Position	Weeks at No.1	Weeks in Top 40
5 Oct 74	**I GET A KICK OUT OF YOU** *Charisma CB 234*	7		8

Silver-selling | Gold-selling | Platinum-selling | US No.1 ★ | Peak Position | Weeks at No.1 | Weeks in Top 40

SHED SEVEN UK group

Date	Title / Label	Peak Position	Weeks at No.1	Weeks in Top 40
25 Jun 94	**DOLPHIN** *Polydor YORCD 2*	28		2
27 Aug 94	**SPEAKEASY** *Polydor YORCD 3*	24		2
12 Nov 94	**OCEAN PIE** *Polydor YORCD 4*	33		1
13 May 95	**WHERE HAVE YOU BEEN TONIGHT?** *Polydor YORCD 5*	23		1
27 Jan 96	**GETTING BETTER** *Polydor 5778912*	14		2
23 Mar 96	**GOING FOR GOLD** *Polydor 5762152*	8		4
18 May 96	**BULLY BOY** *Polydor 5765972*	22		1
31 Aug 96	**ON STANDBY** *Polydor 5752732*	12		3
23 Nov 96	**CHASING RAINBOWS** *Polydor 5759292*	17		3
14 Mar 98	**SHE LEFT ME ON FRIDAY** *Polydor 5695412*	11		2
23 May 98	**THE HEROES** *Polydor 5699172*	18		2
22 Aug 98	**DEVIL IN YOUR SHOES (WALKING ALL OVER)** *Polydor 5672072*	37		1
5 Jun 99	**DISCO DOWN** *Polydor 5638752*	13		3
5 May 01	**CRY FOR HELP** *Artful CDX 35ARTFUL*	30		1
24 May 03	**WHY CAN'T I BE YOU?** *Taste Media TMCDSX 5004*	23		1

SHEEP ON DRUGS UK duo

Date	Title / Label	Peak Position	Weeks at No.1	Weeks in Top 40
27 Mar 93	**15 MINUTES OF FAME** *Transglobal CID 564*	44		
30 Oct 93	**FROM A TO H AND BACK AGAIN** *Transglobal CID 575*	40		1
14 May 94	**LET THE GOOD TIMES ROLL** *Transglobal CID 576*	56		

SHEER BRONZE UK duo

Date	Title / Label	Peak Position	Weeks at No.1	Weeks in Top 40
3 Sep 94	**WALKIN' ON** *Go! Beat GODCD 115* SHEER BRONZE FEATURING LISA MILLETT	63		

SHEER ELEGANCE UK group

Date	Title / Label	Peak Position	Weeks at No.1	Weeks in Top 40
20 Dec 75	**MILKY WAY** *Pye International 7N 25697*	18		7
3 Apr 76	**LIFE IS TOO SHORT GIRL** *Pye International 7N 25703*	9		8
24 Jul 76	**IT'S TEMPTATION** *Pye International 7N 25717*	41		

SHADE SHEIST US group

Date	Title / Label	Peak Position	Weeks at No.1	Weeks in Top 40
25 Aug 01	**WHERE I WANNA BE** *London LONCD 461* SHADE SHEIST FEATURING NATE DOGG & KURUPT	14		3

DOUG SHELDON UK singer

Date	Title / Label	Peak Position	Weeks at No.1	Weeks in Top 40
9 Nov 61	**RUNAROUND SUE** *Decca F 11398*	36		2
4 Jan 62	**YOUR MA SAID YOU CRIED IN YOUR SLEEP LAST NIGHT** *Decca F 11416*	29		5
7 Feb 63	**I SAW LINDA YESTERDAY** *Decca F 11564*	36		3

PETE SHELLEY UK singer

Date	Title / Label	Peak Position	Weeks at No.1	Weeks in Top 40
12 Mar 83	**TELEPHONE OPERATOR** *Genetic XX1*	66		

PETER SHELLEY UK singer

Date	Title / Label	Peak Position	Weeks at No.1	Weeks in Top 40
14 Sep 74	**GEE BABY** *Magnet MAG 12*	4		9
22 Mar 75	**LOVE ME LOVE MY DOG** *Magnet MAG 22*	3		10

ANNE SHELTON UK singer

Date	Title / Label	Peak Position	Weeks at No.1	Weeks in Top 40
16 Dec 55	**ARRIVEDERCI DARLING** *HMV POP 146*	17		4
13 Apr 56	**SEVEN DAYS** *Philips PB 567*	20		4
24 Aug 56	**LAY DOWN YOUR ARMS** *Philips PB 616*	1	4	14
20 Nov 59	**VILLAGE OF ST. BERNADETTE** *Philips PB 969*	27		1
26 Jan 61	**SAILOR** *Philips PB 1096*	10		7

SHENA UK singer

Date	Title / Label	Peak Position	Weeks at No.1	Weeks in Top 40
2 Aug 97	**LET THE BEAT HIT 'EM** *VC Recordings VCRD 24*	28		1
1 Sep 01	**I'LL BE WAITING** *Rulin 17CDS* FULL INTENTION PRESENTS SHENA	44		
4 Oct 03	**WILDERNESS** *Direction 6742692* JURGEN VRIES FEATURING SHENA	20		2
24 Feb 07	**DARE ME (STUPIDISCO)** *Defected DFTD150CDS* JUNIOR JACK FEATURING SHENA	20		2
14 Apr 07	**GUILTY** *Hed Kandi HK32CDS* DE SOUZA FEATURING SHENA	46		

VONDA SHEPARD US singer

Date	Title / Label	Peak Position	Weeks at No.1	Weeks in Top 40
5 Dec 98	**SEARCHIN' MY SOUL** *Epic 6666332*	10		3

SHEPHERD SISTERS US group

Date	Title / Label	Peak Position	Weeks at No.1	Weeks in Top 40
15 Nov 57	**ALONE** *HMV POP 411*	14		6

SHERBET Australian group

Date	Title / Label	Peak Position	Weeks at No.1	Weeks in Top 40
25 Sep 76	**HOWZAT** *Epic EPC 4574*	4		9

TONY SHERIDAN & THE BEATLES UK singer and group

Date	Title / Label	Peak Position	Weeks at No.1	Weeks in Top 40
6 Jun 63	**MY BONNIE** *Polydor NH 66833*	48		

ALLAN SHERMAN US singer/comedian

Date	Title / Label	Peak Position	Weeks at No.1	Weeks in Top 40
12 Sep 63	**HELLO MUDDAH HELLO FADDAH** *Warner Brothers WB 106*	14		9

BOBBY SHERMAN US singer/actor

Date	Title / Label	Peak Position	Weeks at No.1	Weeks in Top 40
31 Oct 70	**JULIE DO YA LOVE ME** *CBS 5144*	28		2

SHERRICK US singer

Date	Title / Label	Peak Position	Weeks at No.1	Weeks in Top 40
1 Aug 87	**JUST CALL** *Warner Brothers W 8380*	23		6
21 Nov 87	**LET'S BE LOVERS TONIGHT** *Warner Brothers W 8146*	63		

PLUTO SHERVINGTON Jamaican singer

Date	Title / Label	Peak Position	Weeks at No.1	Weeks in Top 40
7 Feb 76	**DAT** *Opal Pal 5*	6		7
10 Apr 76	**RAM GOAT LIVER** *Trojan TR 7978*	43		
6 Mar 82	**YOUR HONOUR** *KR 4*	19		6

HOLLY SHERWOOD US singer

Date	Title / Label	Peak Position	Weeks at No.1	Weeks in Top 40
5 Feb 72	**DAY BY DAY** *Bell 1182*	29		6

TONY SHEVETON UK singer

Date	Title / Label	Peak Position	Weeks at No.1	Weeks in Top 40
13 Feb 64	**MILLION DRUMS** *Oriole CB 1895*	49		

SHIFTY US singer

Date	Title / Label	Peak Position	Weeks at No.1	Weeks in Top 40
11 Sep 04	**SLIDE ALONG SIDE** *Maverick W649CD*	29		1

SHIMMON & WOOLFSON UK production duo

Date	Title / Label	Peak Position	Weeks at No.1	Weeks in Top 40
10 Jan 98	**WELCOME TO THE FUTURE** *React CDREACT 119*	69		

SHIMON & ANDY C UK duo

Date	Title / Label	Peak Position	Weeks at No.1	Weeks in Top 40
15 Sep 01	**BODY ROCK** *Ram RAMM 34CD*	58		
12 Jan 02	**BODY ROCK** *Ram RAMM 34CD*	28		3

SHINEHEAD Jamaican singer

Date	Title / Label	Peak Position	Weeks at No.1	Weeks in Top 40
3 Apr 93	**JAMAICAN IN NEW YORK** *Elektra EKR 161CD*	30		4
26 Jun 93	**LET 'EM IN** *Elektra EKR 168CD*	70		

SHINING UK group

Date	Title / Label	Peak Position	Weeks at No.1	Weeks in Top 40
6 Jul 02	**I WONDER HOW** *Zuma ZUMAD 002*	58		
14 Sep 02	**YOUNG AGAIN** *Zuma ZUMASCD 03B*	52		

SHINS US group

Date	Title / Label	Peak Position	Weeks at No.1	Weeks in Top 40
13 Mar 04	**SO SAYS I** *Sub Pop SPCD621*	73		
3 Feb 07	**PHANTOM LIMB** *Transgressive TRANS046CD*	42		
21 Apr 07	**AUSTRALIA** *Transgressive TRANS051CD*	62		

SHIRELLES US group

Date	Title / Label	Peak Position	Weeks at No.1	Weeks in Top 40
9 Feb 61	**WILL YOU LOVE ME TOMORROW** *Top Rank JAR 540* ★	4		14
31 May 62	**SOLDIER BOY** *HMV POP 1019* ★	23		7
23 May 63	**FOOLISH LITTLE GIRL** *Stateside SS 181*	38		2

Silver-selling · Gold-selling · Platinum-selling · US No.1 ★ · Peak Position · Weeks at No.1 · Weeks in Top 40

SHIRLEY & COMPANY US group

Date	Title / Label	Peak Position	Weeks at No.1	Weeks in Top 40
8 Feb 75	**SHAME SHAME SHAME** *All Platinum 6146 301*	6		8

SHITDISCO UK group

Date	Title / Label	Peak Position	Weeks at No.1	Weeks in Top 40
4 Nov 06	**REACTOR PARTY** *Fierce Panda NING191CD*	73		

SHIVA UK group

Date	Title / Label	Peak Position	Weeks at No.1	Weeks in Top 40
13 May 95	**WORK IT OUT** *ffrr FCD 261*	36		1
19 Aug 95	**FREEDOM** *ffrr FCD 263*	18		2

SHIVAREE US group

Date	Title / Label	Peak Position	Weeks at No.1	Weeks in Top 40
17 Feb 01	**GOODNIGHT MOON** *Capitol CDCL 825*	63		

SHO NUFF US group

Date	Title / Label	Peak Position	Weeks at No.1	Weeks in Top 40
24 May 80	**IT'S ALRIGHT** *Ensign ENY 37*	53		

MICHELLE SHOCKED US singer/songwriter/guitarist

Date	Title / Label	Peak Position	Weeks at No.1	Weeks in Top 40
8 Oct 88	**ANCHORAGE** *Cooking Vinyl LON 193*	60		
14 Jan 89	**IF LOVE WAS A TRAIN** *Cooking Vinyl LON 212*	63		
11 Mar 89	**WHEN I GROW UP** *Cooking Vinyl LON 219*	67		

SHOCKING BLUE Dutch group

Date	Title / Label	Peak Position	Weeks at No.1	Weeks in Top 40
17 Jan 70	**VENUS** *Penny Farthing PEN 702* ★	8		10
25 Apr 70	**MIGHTY JOE** *Penny Farthing PEN 713*	43		

SHOLAN UK/German duo

Date	Title / Label	Peak Position	Weeks at No.1	Weeks in Top 40
5 Apr 03	**CAN YOU FEEL (WHAT I'M GOING THROUGH)** *Data 39CDS*	47		

TROY SHONDELL US singer

Date	Title / Label	Peak Position	Weeks at No.1	Weeks in Top 40
2 Nov 61	**THIS TIME** *London HLG 9432*	22		8

SHOOTING PARTY UK duo

Date	Title / Label	Peak Position	Weeks at No.1	Weeks in Top 40
31 Mar 90	**LET'S HANG ON** *Lisson DOLE 15*	66		

SHORTIE Italian production duo

Date	Title / Label	Peak Position	Weeks at No.1	Weeks in Top 40
4 Aug 01	**SOMEBODY** *WEA 328CDX* SHORTIE VS BLACK LEGEND	37		1

SHOUT OUT LOUDS Swedish group

Date	Title / Label	Peak Position	Weeks at No.1	Weeks in Top 40
24 Sep 05	**THE COMEBACK** *EMI CDEM668*	63		
4 Mar 06	**PLEASE PLEASE PLEASE** *EMI CDEM684*	53		

SHOWADDYWADDY UK group

Date	Title / Label	Peak Position	Weeks at No.1	Weeks in Top 40
18 May 74	**HEY ROCK AND ROLL** *Bell 1357*	2		11
17 Aug 74	**ROCK 'N' ROLL LADY** *Bell 1374*	15		8
30 Nov 74	**HEY MR. CHRISTMAS** *Bell 1387*	13		5
22 Feb 75	**SWEET MUSIC** *Bell 1403*	14		7
17 May 75	**THREE STEPS TO HEAVEN** *Bell 1426*	2		10
6 Sep 75	**HEARTBEAT** *Bell 1450*	7		7
15 Nov 75	**HEAVENLY** *Bell 1460*	34		3
29 May 76	**TROCADERO** *Bell 1476*	32		2
6 Nov 76	**UNDER THE MOON OF LOVE** *Bell 1495*	1	3	15
5 Mar 77	**WHEN** *Arista 91*	3		10
23 Jul 77	**YOU GOT WHAT IT TAKES** *Arista 126*	2		9
5 Nov 77	**DANCIN' PARTY** *Arista 149*	4		10
25 Mar 78	**I WONDER WHY** *Arista 174*	2		9
24 Jun 78	**A LITTLE BIT OF SOAP** *Arista 191*	5		8
4 Nov 78	**PRETTY LITTLE ANGEL EYES** *Arista ARIST 222*	5		10
31 Mar 79	**REMEMBER THEN** *Arista 247*	17		6
28 Jul 79	**SWEET LITTLE ROCK 'N' ROLLER** *Arista 278*	15		7
10 Nov 79	**A NIGHT AT DADDY GEE'S** *Arista 314*	39		1
27 Sep 80	**WHY DO LOVERS BREAK EACH OTHER'S HEARTS** *Arista ARIST 359*	22		6
29 Nov 80	**BLUE MOON** *Arista ARIST 379*	32		6
13 Jun 81	**MULTIPLICATION** *Arista ARIST 416*	39		1
28 Nov 81	**FOOTSTEPS** *Bell 1499*	31		6
28 Aug 82	**WHO PUT THE BOMP (IN THE BOMP-A-BOMP-A-BOMP)** *RCA 236*	37		2

SHOWDOWN US group

Date	Title / Label	Peak Position	Weeks at No.1	Weeks in Top 40
17 Dec 77	**KEEP DOIN' IT** *State STAT 63*	41		

SHOWSTOPPERS US group

Date	Title / Label	Peak Position	Weeks at No.1	Weeks in Top 40
13 Mar 68	**AIN'T NOTHING BUT A HOUSEPARTY** *Beacon 3-100*	11		14
13 Nov 68	**EENY MEENY** *MGM 1436*	33		4
30 Jan 71	**AIN'T NOTHING BUT A HOUSEPARTY** *Beacon BEA 100*	33		2

SHRIEKBACK UK group

Date	Title / Label	Peak Position	Weeks at No.1	Weeks in Top 40
28 Jul 84	**HAND ON MY HEART** *Arista SHRK 1*	52		

SHRINK Dutch production group

Date	Title / Label	Peak Position	Weeks at No.1	Weeks in Top 40
10 Oct 98	**NERVOUS BREAKDOWN** *VC Recordings VCRD 42*	42		
19 Aug 00	**ARE YOU READY TO PARTY** *NuLife 74321783772*	39		1

SHUT UP & DANCE UK duo

Date	Title / Label	Peak Position	Weeks at No.1	Weeks in Top 40
21 Apr 90	**£20 TO GET IN** *Shut Up And Dance SUAD 3*	56		
28 Jul 90	**LAMBORGHINI** *Shut Up And Dance SUAD 4*	55		
8 Feb 92	**AUTOBIOGRAPHY OF A CRACKHEAD/THE GREEN MAN** *Shut Up And Dance SUAD 21*	43		
30 May 92	**RAVING I'M RAVING** *Shut Up And Dance SUAD 30S* SHUT UP & DANCE FEATURING PETER BOUNCER	2		2
15 Aug 92	**THE ART OF MOVING BUTTS** *Shut Up And Dance SUAD 34S* SHUT UP & DANCE FEATURING ERIN	69		
1 Apr 95	**SAVE IT 'TIL THE MOURNING AFTER** *Pulse 8 PULS 84CD*	25		2
8 Jul 95	**I LUV U** *Pulse 8 PULS 90CD* SHUT UP & DANCE FEATURING RICHIE DAVIS & PROFESSOR T	68		

SHY UK group

Date	Title / Label	Peak Position	Weeks at No.1	Weeks in Top 40
19 Apr 80	**GIRL (IT'S ALL I HAVE)** *Gallery GA 1*	60		

SHY FX UK producer

Date	Title / Label	Peak Position	Weeks at No.1	Weeks in Top 40
1 Oct 94	**ORIGINAL NUTTAH** *Sound Of Underground SOUR 008CD* U.K. APACHI WITH SHY FX	39		1
20 Mar 99	**BAMBAATA 2012** *Ebony EBR 020CD*	60		
6 Apr 02	**SHAKE UR BODY** *Positiva CDTIV 171* SHY FX & T-POWER FEATURING DI	7		7
23 Nov 02	**DON'T WANNA KNOW** *ffrr FCD 408* SHY FX/T POWER/DI & SKIBADEE	19		2
28 Dec 02	**WOLF** *Ebony Dubs EBD001*	60		
7 Jun 03	**FEELIN' U** *London FCD 409* SHY FX & T-POWER FEATURING KELE LE ROC	34		1
21 Jan 06	**EVERYDAY** *Soundboy SBOY002* SHY FX & TPOWER FEATURING TOP CAT	75		

SHYEIM US rapper

Date	Title / Label	Peak Position	Weeks at No.1	Weeks in Top 40
8 Jun 96	**THIS IZ REAL** *Noo Trybe VUSCD 105*	61		

SHYSTIE UK rapper

Date	Title / Label	Peak Position	Weeks at No.1	Weeks in Top 40
17 Jul 04	**ONE WISH** *Polydor 9866875*	40		1
2 Oct 04	**MAKE IT EASY** *Polydor 9867988*	59		

SIA Australian singer

Date	Title / Label	Peak Position	Weeks at No.1	Weeks in Top 40
3 Jun 00	**TAKEN FOR GRANTED** *Long Lost Brother S002CD1*	10		3
18 Aug 01	**DESTINY** *Ultimate Dilemma UDRCDS 043* ZERO 7 FEATURING SIA & SOPHIE	30		1
1 May 04	**BREATHE ME** *Go! Beat 9866392*	71		
29 May 04	**SOMERSAULT** *Ultimate Dilemma EW290CD* ZERO 7 FEATURING SIA	56		

LABI SIFFRE UK singer

Date	Title / Label	Peak Position	Weeks at No.1	Weeks in Top 40
27 Nov 71	**IT MUST BE LOVE** *Pye International 7N 25572*	14		11
25 Mar 72	**CRYING LAUGHING LOVING LYING** *Pye International 7N 25576*	11		7

Silver-selling ● Gold-selling ● Platinum-selling ✪ US No.1 ★ Peak Position Weeks at No.1 Weeks in Top 40

Date	Title / Label	Peak Position	Weeks at No.1	Weeks in Top 40
29 Jul 72	**WATCH ME** *Pye International 7N 25586*	29		4
4 Apr 87	**(SOMETHING INSIDE) SO STRONG** *China WOK 12*	4		9
21 Nov 87	**NOTHIN'S GONNA CHANGE** *China WOK 16*	52		

SIGNAL 1 & SIGNAL 2 UK group

Date	Title / Label	Peak Position	Weeks at No.1	Weeks in Top 40
3 Jun 06	**STANDING TOGETHER – WORLD CUP 2006** *Signal 1 SIGNAL1CDS*	67		

SIGNUM Dutch production duo

Date	Title / Label	Peak Position	Weeks at No.1	Weeks in Top 40
28 Nov 98	**WHAT YA GOT 4 ME** *Tidy Trax TIDY 118CD*	70		
31 Jul 99	**COMING ON STRONG** *Tidy Trax TIDY 128T* SIGNUM FEATURING SCOTT MAC	66		
9 Feb 02	**WHAT YA GOT 4 ME** *Tidy Trax TIDY 163CD*	35		1
29 Jun 02	**COMING ON STRONG** *Tidy Two TIDYTWO 104CD*	50		

SIGUE SIGUE SPUTNIK UK group

Date	Title / Label	Peak Position	Weeks at No.1	Weeks in Top 40
1 Mar 86	**LOVE MISSILE F1-11** *Parlophone SSS 1* ●	3		6
7 Jun 86	**TWENTY-FIRST CENTURY BOY** *Parlophone SSS 2*	20		3
19 Nov 88	**SUCCESS** *Parlophone SSS 3*	31		1
1 Apr 89	**DANCERAMA** *Parlophone SSS 5*	50		
20 May 89	**ALBINONI VS STAR WARS** *Parlophone SSS 4*	75		

SIGUR ROS Icelandic group

Date	Title / Label	Peak Position	Weeks at No.1	Weeks in Top 40
24 May 03	**( )** *Pias Recordings CD10FAT02*	72		
10 Dec 05	**HOPPIPOLLA** *EMI CDEM673*	24		4

SIL Dutch production duo

Date	Title / Label	Peak Position	Weeks at No.1	Weeks in Top 40
11 Apr 98	**WINDOWS '98** *Hooj Choons HOOJCD 60*	58		
25 Jun 88	**PAINTED MOON** *RCA HUSH 1*	57		
27 May 89	**SCOTTISH RAIN** *RCA PB 42701*	71		
15 May 93	**I CAN FEEL IT** *RCA 74321147112*	62		

SILENT UNDERDOG UK producer

Date	Title / Label	Peak Position	Weeks at No.1	Weeks in Top 40
16 Feb 85	**PAPA'S GOT A BRAND NEW PIGBAG** *Kaz 50*	73		

SILICONE SOUL UK production duo

Date	Title / Label	Peak Position	Weeks at No.1	Weeks in Top 40
6 Oct 01	**RIGHT ON!** *Soma/VC Recordings VCRD 96* SILICONE SOUL FEATURING LOUISE CLARE MARSHALL	15		3

SILJE Norwegian singer

Date	Title / Label	Peak Position	Weeks at No.1	Weeks in Top 40
15 Dec 90	**TELL ME WHERE YOU'RE GOING** *EMI EM 159*	55		

SILK US group

Date	Title / Label	Peak Position	Weeks at No.1	Weeks in Top 40
24 Apr 93	**FREAK ME** *Elektra EKR 165CD* ★	46		
5 Jun 93	**GIRL U FOR ME** *Elektra EKR 167CD*	67		
9 Oct 93	**BABY IT'S YOU** *Elektra EKR 173CD*	44		
26 Feb 94	**FREAK ME** *Elektra EKR 165CD*	72		
23 Sep 65	**YOU'VE GOT TO HIDE YOUR LOVE AWAY** *Fontana TF 603*	28		5

SILSOE UK keyboard player

Date	Title / Label	Peak Position	Weeks at No.1	Weeks in Top 40
21 Jun 86	**AZTEC GOLD** *CBS A 7231*	48		

LUCIE SILVAS UK singer

Date	Title / Label	Peak Position	Weeks at No.1	Weeks in Top 40
17 Jun 00	**IT'S TOO LATE** *EMI CDEM 565*	62		
16 Oct 04	**WHAT YOU'RE MADE OF** *Mercury 9867463*	7		5
29 Jan 05	**BREATHE IN** *Mercury 2103631*	6		5
14 May 05	**THE GAME IS WON** *Mercury 9870820*	38		1
6 Aug 05	**DON'T LOOK BACK** *Mercury 9872943*	34		1

JOHN SILVER German producer

Date	Title / Label	Peak Position	Weeks at No.1	Weeks in Top 40
25 Jan 03	**COME ON OVER** *Cream 20CD*	35		1

SILVER BULLET UK rapper

Date	Title / Label	Peak Position	Weeks at No.1	Weeks in Top 40
2 Sep 89	**BRING FORTH THE GUILLOTINE** *Tam Tam TTT 013*	70		
9 Dec 89	**20 SECONDS TO COMPLY** *Tam Tam 7TTT 019*	11		7
3 Mar 90	**BRING FORTH THE GUILLOTINE** *Tam Tam TTT 013*	45		
13 Apr 91	**UNDERCOVER ANARCHIST** *Parlophone R 6284*	33		2

SILVER CITY UK duo

Date	Title / Label	Peak Position	Weeks at No.1	Weeks in Top 40
30 Oct 93	**LOVE INFINITY** *Silver City GFJMCD 1*	62		

SILVER CONVENTION German/US group

Date	Title / Label	Peak Position	Weeks at No.1	Weeks in Top 40
5 Apr 75	**SAVE ME** *Magnet MAG 26*	30		4
15 Nov 75	**FLY ROBIN FLY** *Magnet MAG 43* ★	28		5
3 Apr 76	**GET UP AND BOOGIE** *Magnet MAG 55*	7		10
19 Jun 76	**TIGER BABY/NO NO JOE** *Magnet MAG 69*	41		
29 Jan 77	**EVERYBODY'S TALKIN' 'BOUT LOVE** *Magnet MAG 81*	25		4

SILVER SUN UK group

Date	Title / Label	Peak Position	Weeks at No.1	Weeks in Top 40
2 Nov 96	**LAVA** *Polydor 5756872*	54		
22 Feb 97	**LAST DAY** *Polydor 5732432*	48		
3 May 97	**GOLDEN SKIN** *Polydor 5738272*	32		1
5 Jul 97	**JULIA** *Polydor 5711752*	51		
18 Oct 97	**LAVA** *Polydor 5714242*	35		1
20 Jun 98	**TOO MUCH, TOO LITTLE, TOO LATE** *Polydor 5699152*	20		2
26 Sep 98	**I'LL SEE YOU AROUND** *Polydor 5674532*	26		1

SILVERCHAIR Australian group

Date	Title / Label	Peak Position	Weeks at No.1	Weeks in Top 40
29 Jul 95	**PURE MASSACRE** *Murmur 6622642*	71		
9 Sep 95	**TOMORROW** *Murmur 6623952*	59		
5 Apr 97	**FREAK** *Murmur 6640765*	34		1
19 Jul 97	**ABUSE ME** *Murmur 6647905*	40		1
15 May 99	**ANA'S SONG** *Columbia 6673452*	45		

DOOLEY SILVERSPOON US singer

Date	Title / Label	Peak Position	Weeks at No.1	Weeks in Top 40
31 Jan 76	**LET ME BE THE NUMBER 1 (LOVE OF YOUR LIFE)** *Seville SEV 1020*	44		

HARRY SIMEONE CHORALE US choir

Date	Title / Label	Peak Position	Weeks at No.1	Weeks in Top 40
13 Feb 59	**LITTLE DRUMMER BOY** *Top Rank JAR 101*	13		7
22 Dec 60	**ONWARD CHRISTIAN SOLDIERS** *Ember EMBS 118*	35		2
21 Dec 61	**ONWARD CHRISTIAN SOLDIERS** *Ember EMBS 118*	36		1
20 Dec 62	**ONWARD CHRISTIAN SOLDIERS** *Ember EMBS 144*	38		1

SIMIAN UK group

Date	Title / Label	Peak Position	Weeks at No.1	Weeks in Top 40
14 Jun 03	**LA BREEZE** *Source SOURCD 069*	55		
15 Jul 06	**WE ARE YOUR FRIENDS** *Ten TENCDX505* JUSTICE VERSUS SIMIAN	20		4

SIMILOU Swedish duo

Date	Title / Label	Peak Position	Weeks at No.1	Weeks in Top 40
5 Aug 06	**ALL THIS LOVE** *Direction 82876883502*	20		3

GENE SIMMONS US singer/bass player

Date	Title / Label	Peak Position	Weeks at No.1	Weeks in Top 40
27 Jan 79	**RADIOACTIVE** *Casablanca CAN 134*	41		

SIMON UK producer

Date	Title / Label	Peak Position	Weeks at No.1	Weeks in Top 40
31 Mar 01	**FREE AT LAST** *Positiva CDTIV 152*	36		1

CARLY SIMON US singer

Date	Title / Label	Peak Position	Weeks at No.1	Weeks in Top 40
16 Dec 72	**YOU'RE SO VAIN** *Elektra K 12077* ★	3		13
31 Mar 73	**THE RIGHT THING TO DO** *Elektra K 12095*	17		8
16 Mar 74	**MOCKINGBIRD** *Elektra K 12134* CARLY SIMON & JAMES TAYLOR	34		3
6 Aug 77	**NOBODY DOES IT BETTER** *Elektra K 12261* ●	7		11
21 Aug 82	**WHY** *WEA K 79300*	10		9
24 Jan 87	**COMING AROUND AGAIN** *Arista ARIST 687*	10		8
10 Jun 89	**WHY** *WEA U 7501*	56		
20 Apr 91	**YOU'RE SO VAIN** *Elektra EKR 123*	41		
22 Dec 01	**SON OF A GUN (BETCHA THINK THIS SONG IS ABOUT YOU)** *Virgin VUSCDX 232* JANET JACKSON WITH CARLY SIMON FEATURING MISSY ELLIOTT	13		5

Silver-selling ○ Gold-selling ● Platinum-selling ⊛ US No.1 ★ Peak Position Weeks at No.1 Weeks in Top 40

JOE SIMON US singer

Date	Title	Peak Position	Weeks at No.1	Weeks in Top 40
16 Jun 73	**STEP BY STEP** *Mojo 2093 030*	14		9

PAUL SIMON US singer

Date	Title	Peak Position	Weeks at No.1	Weeks in Top 40
19 Feb 72	**MOTHER AND CHILD REUNION** *CBS 7793*	5		10
29 Apr 72	**ME AND JULIO DOWN BY THE SCHOOLYARD** *CBS 7964*	15		8
16 Jun 73	**TAKE ME TO THE MARDI GRAS** *CBS 1578*	7		10
22 Sep 73	**LOVES ME LIKE A ROCK** *CBS 1700*	39		1
10 Jan 76	**50 WAYS TO LEAVE YOUR LOVER** *CBS 3887* ★	23		5
3 Dec 77	**SLIP SLIDIN' AWAY** *CBS 5770*	36		1
6 Sep 80	**LATE IN THE EVENING** *Warner Brothers K 17666*	58		
13 Sep 86	**YOU CAN CALL ME AL** *Warner Brothers W 8667* ○	4		9
13 Dec 86	**THE BOY IN THE BUBBLE** *Warner Brothers W 8509*	26		6
6 Oct 90	**THE OBVIOUS CHILD** *Warner Brothers W 9549*	15		7
9 Dec 95	**SOMETHING SO RIGHT** *RCA 74321332392* ANNIE LENNOX FEATURING PAUL SIMON	44		
3 Jun 06	**FATHER AND DAUGHTER** *Warner Brothers W719CD*	31		1

RONNI SIMON UK singer

Date	Title	Peak Position	Weeks at No.1	Weeks in Top 40
13 Aug 94	**B GOOD 2 ME** *Network NWKCD 80*	73		
10 Jun 95	**TAKE YOU THERE** *Network NWKCD 85*	58		

TITO SIMON Jamaican singer

Date	Title	Peak Position	Weeks at No.1	Weeks in Top 40
8 Feb 75	**THIS MONDAY MORNING FEELING** *Horse HOSS 57*	45		

SIMON & GARFUNKEL US folk-rock duo

Date	Title	Peak Position	Weeks at No.1	Weeks in Top 40
24 Mar 66	**HOMEWARD BOUND** *CBS 202045*	9		11
16 Jun 66	**I AM A ROCK** *CBS 202303*	17		9
10 Jul 68	**MRS. ROBINSON** *CBS 3443* ★	4		9
8 Jan 69	**MRS. ROBINSON (EP)** *CBS EP 6400*	9		5
30 Apr 69	**THE BOXER** *CBS 4162*	6		10
21 Feb 70	**BRIDGE OVER TROUBLED WATER** *CBS 4790* ★	1	3	17
7 Oct 72	**AMERICA** *CBS 8336*	25		6
7 Dec 91	**A HAZY SHADE OF WINTER/SILENT NIGHT/SEVEN O'CLOCK NEWS** *Columbia 6576537*	30		4
15 Feb 92	**THE BOXER** *Columbia 6578067*	75		

SIMONE US group

Date	Title	Peak Position	Weeks at No.1	Weeks in Top 40
23 Nov 91	**MY FAMILY DEPENDS ON ME** *Strictly Rhythm A 8678*	75		

NINA SIMONE US singer

Date	Title	Peak Position	Weeks at No.1	Weeks in Top 40
5 Aug 65	**I PUT A SPELL ON YOU** *Philips BF 1415*	49		
16 Oct 68	**AIN'T GOT NO-I GOT LIFE/DO WHAT YOU GOTTA DO** *RCA 1743*	2		15
15 Jan 69	**TO LOVE SOMEBODY** *RCA 1779*	5		7
15 Jan 69	**I PUT A SPELL ON YOU** *Philips BF 1736*	28		3
31 Oct 87	**MY BABY JUST CARES FOR ME** *Charly CYZ 7112* ○	5		9
9 Jul 94	**FEELING GOOD** *Mercury MERCD 403*	40		1
29 Apr 06	**AIN'T GOT NO-I GOT LIFE (REMIX)** *Sony BMG TV 82876708212* NINA SIMONE VERSUS GROOVEFINDER	30		3

VICTOR SIMONELLI US producer

Date	Title	Peak Position	Weeks at No.1	Weeks in Top 40
2 Nov 96	**FEELS SO RIGHT** *Soundproof MCSTD 40068* VICTOR SIMONELLI PRESENTS SOLUTION	63		

SIMPLE KID Irish singer

Date	Title	Peak Position	Weeks at No.1	Weeks in Top 40
13 Sep 03	**THE AVERAGE MAN** *2M 2M005CD*	72		
14 Feb 04	**TRUCK ON** *2M 2M007CD*	38		1

SIMPLE MINDS UK group

Date	Title	Peak Position	Weeks at No.1	Weeks in Top 40
12 May 79	**LIFE IN A DAY** *Zoom ZUM 10*	62		
23 May 81	**THE AMERICAN** *Virgin VS 410*	59		
15 Aug 81	**LOVE SONG** *Virgin VS 434*	47		
7 Nov 81	**SWEAT IN A BULLET** *Virgin VS 451*	52		
10 Apr 82	**PROMISED YOU A MIRACLE** *Virgin VS 488*	13		9
28 Aug 82	**GLITTERING PRIZE** *Virgin VS 511*	16		8
13 Nov 82	**SOMEONE SOMEWHERE (IN SUMMERTIME)** *Virgin VS 538*	36		1
26 Nov 83	**WATERFRONT** *Virgin VS 636*	13		7
28 Jan 84	**SPEED YOUR LOVE TO ME** *Virgin VS 649*	20		3
24 Mar 84	**UP ON THE CATWALK** *Virgin VS 661*	27		4
20 Apr 85	**DON'T YOU FORGET ABOUT ME** *Virgin VS 749* ○ ★	7		9
12 Oct 85	**ALIVE AND KICKING** *Virgin VS 817*	7		7
1 Feb 86	**SANCTIFY YOURSELF** *Virgin SM 1*	10		5
12 Apr 86	**ALL THE THINGS SHE SAID** *Virgin VS 860*	9		6
15 Nov 86	**GHOSTDANCING** *Virgin VS 907*	13		4
20 Jun 87	**PROMISED YOU A MIRACLE** *Virgin SM 2*	19		5
18 Feb 89	**BELFAST CHILD** *Virgin SMX 3* ○	1	2	7
22 Apr 89	**THIS IS YOUR LAND** *Virgin SMX 4*	13		3
29 Jul 89	**KICK IT IN** *Virgin SM 5*	15		4
9 Dec 89	**THE AMSTERDAM EP** *Virgin SMX 6*	18		4
23 Mar 91	**LET THERE BE LOVE** *Virgin VS 1332*	6		5
25 May 91	**SEE THE LIGHTS** *Virgin VS 1343*	20		3
31 Aug 91	**STAND BY LOVE** *Virgin VS 1358*	13		2
26 Oct 91	**REAL LIFE** *Virgin VS 1382*	34		2
10 Oct 92	**LOVE SONG (REMIX)/ALIVE AND KICKING** *Virgin VS 1440*	6		5
28 Jan 95	**SHE'S A RIVER** *Virgin VSCDX 1509*	9		3
8 Apr 95	**HYPNOTISED** *Virgin VSCDX 1534*	18		3
14 Mar 98	**GLITTERBALL** *Chrysalis CDCHSS 5078*	18		1
30 May 98	**WAR BABIES** *Chrysalis CDCHSS 5088*	43		
2 Feb 02	**BELFAST TRANCE** *Nebula BELFCD 001* JOHN 'OO' FLEMING VS SIMPLE MINDS	74		
30 Mar 02	**CRY** *Eagle EAGXS 218*	47		
20 Jul 02	**MONSTER** *Defected DFECT 49R* LIQUID PEOPLE VS SIMPLE MINDS	67		
17 Sep 05	**HOME** *Sanctuary SANXS388*	41		
8 Apr 06	**TRIBUTE TO JINKY** *Lord Of The Wing LWSP7* JIMMY JOHNSTONE, JIM KERR, SIMPLE MINDS & LAURA McGHEE	28		3

SIMPLE PLAN Canadian group

Date	Title	Peak Position	Weeks at No.1	Weeks in Top 40
5 Jul 03	**ADDICTED** *Lava/Atlantic AT 0158CD*	63		
5 Mar 05	**SHUT UP** *Lava AT0195CD*	44		
2 Jul 05	**WELCOME TO MY LIFE** *Lava AT0206CD1*	49		
23 Feb 08	**WHEN I'M GONE** *Atlantic AT0297CDX*	26		2

SIMPLICIOUS US group

Date	Title	Peak Position	Weeks at No.1	Weeks in Top 40
29 Sep 84	**LET HER FEEL IT** *Fourth & Broadway BRW 13*	65		
2 Feb 85	**LET HER FEEL IT** *Fourth & Broadway BRW 18*	34		3

SIMPLY RED UK group

Date	Title	Peak Position	Weeks at No.1	Weeks in Top 40
15 Jun 85	**MONEY'S TOO TIGHT TO MENTION** *Elektra EKR 9*	13		7
21 Sep 85	**COME TO MY AID** *Elektra EKR 19*	66		
16 Nov 85	**HOLDING BACK THE YEARS** *Elektra EKR 29* ★	51		
8 Mar 86	**JERICHO** *WEA YZ 63*	53		
17 May 86	**HOLDING BACK THE YEARS** *WEA YZ 70* ○	2		10
9 Aug 86	**OPEN UP THE RED BOX** *WEA YZ 75*	61		
14 Feb 87	**THE RIGHT THING** *WEA YZ 103*	11		7
23 May 87	**INFIDELITY** *Elektra YZ 114*	31		3
28 Nov 87	**EV'RY TIME WE SAY GOODBYE** *Elektra YZ 161*	11		6
12 Mar 88	**I WON'T FEEL BAD** *Elektra YZ 172*	68		
28 Jan 89	**IT'S ONLY LOVE** *Elektra YZ 349*	13		6
8 Apr 89	**IF YOU DON'T KNOW ME BY NOW** *Elektra YZ 377* ○ ★	2		8
8 Jul 89	**A NEW FLAME** *WEA YZ 404*	17		6
28 Oct 89	**YOU'VE GOT IT** *WEA YZ 424*	46		
21 Sep 91	**SOMETHING GOT ME STARTED** *East West YZ 614*	11		7
30 Nov 91	**STARS** *East West YZ 626*	8		8
8 Feb 92	**FOR YOUR BABIES** *East West YZ 642*	9		6
2 May 92	**THRILL ME** *East West YZ 671*	33		2
25 Jul 92	**YOUR MIRROR** *East West YZ 689*	17		3
21 Nov 92	**MONTREUX EP** *East West YZ 716*	11		9
30 Sep 95	**FAIRGROUND** *East West EW 001CD2* ⊛	1	4	11
16 Dec 95	**REMEMBERING THE FIRST TIME** *East West EW 015CD1*	22		4
24 Feb 96	**NEVER NEVER LOVE** *East West EW 029CD1*	18		2
22 Jun 96	**WE'RE IN THIS TOGETHER** *East West EW 046CDX*	11		4
9 Nov 96	**ANGEL** *East West EW 074CD1* ○	4		4
20 Sep 97	**NIGHT NURSE** *East West EW 129CD1* SLY & ROBBIE FEATURING SIMPLY RED	14		6
16 May 98	**SAY YOU LOVE ME** *East West EW 164CD*	7		4
22 Aug 98	**THE AIR I BREATHE** *East West EW 181CD1*	6		4
12 Dec 98	**GHETTO GIRL** *East West EW 191CD1*	34		1
30 Oct 99	**AIN'T THAT A LOT OF LOVE** *East West EW 208CD1*	14		3
19 Feb 00	**YOUR EYES** *East West EW 212CD1*	26		1
29 Mar 03	**SUNRISE** *Simplyred.com SRS 001CD*	7		7
19 Jul 03	**FAKE** *Simplyred.com SRS 002CD*	21		3
13 Dec 03	**YOU MAKE ME FEEL BRAND NEW** *Simplyred.com SRS 003CD*	7		7
10 Apr 04	**HOME** *Simplyred.com SRS 004CD*	40		1
22 Oct 05	**PERFECT LOVE** *Simplyred.com SRS005CD2*	30		2
7 Oct 06	**OH! WHAT A GIRL!** *Simplyred.com SRS007CD1*	57		
17 Mar 07	**SO NOT OVER YOU** *Simplyred.com SRS009CD2*	34		1
9 Jun 07	**STAY** *Simplyred.com SRS010CD*	36		1

Silver-selling ○ Gold-selling ● Platinum-selling ✪ US No.1 ★ | Peak Position | Weeks at No.1 | Weeks in Top 40

SIMPLY RED & WHITE UK group

Date	Title / Label	Peak Position	Weeks at No.1	Weeks in Top 40
6 Apr 96	DAYDREAM BELIEVER (CHEER UP PETER REID) *Ropery SHAYISGOD 1D*	41		

SIMPLY SMOOTH US group

Date	Title / Label	Peak Position	Weeks at No.1	Weeks in Top 40
17 Oct 98	LADY (YOU BRING ME UP) *Big Bang CDBANG 07*	70		

ASHLEE SIMPSON US singer

Date	Title / Label	Peak Position	Weeks at No.1	Weeks in Top 40
9 Oct 04	PIECES OF ME *Geffen 9863812*	4		7
5 Feb 05	LALA *Geffen 2103876*	11		4
11 Feb 06	BOYFRIEND *Geffen 9850111*	12		4

JESSICA SIMPSON US singer

Date	Title / Label	Peak Position	Weeks at No.1	Weeks in Top 40
22 Apr 00	I WANNA LOVE YOU FOREVER *Columbia 6691272*	7		5
15 Jul 00	I THINK I'M IN LOVE WITH YOU *Columbia 6695942*	15		3
14 Jul 01	IRRESISTIBLE *Columbia 6714102*	11		3
26 Jun 04	WITH YOU *Columbia 6748302*	7		4
10 Sep 05	THESE BOOTS ARE MADE FOR WALKIN' *Columbia 6760652*	4		6
10 Feb 07	A PUBLIC AFFAIR *Columbia 88697060712*	20		2

PAUL SIMPSON US producer

Date	Title / Label	Peak Position	Weeks at No.1	Weeks in Top 40
25 Mar 89	MUSICAL FREEDOM (MOVING ON UP) *Cooltempo COOL 182* PAUL SIMPSON FEATURING ADEVA	22		6

VIDA SIMPSON US singer

Date	Title / Label	Peak Position	Weeks at No.1	Weeks in Top 40
18 Feb 95	OOHHH BABY *Hi-Life HICD 6*	70		

SIMPSONS US cartoon characters

Date	Title / Label	Peak Position	Weeks at No.1	Weeks in Top 40
26 Jan 91	DO THE BARTMAN *Geffen GEF 87* ●	1	3	11
6 Apr 91	DEEP DEEP TROUBLE *Geffen GEF 88* SIMPSONS FEATURING BART & HOMER	7		6
11 Aug 07	SPIDER PIG *Download*	23		3

JOYCE SIMS US singer

Date	Title / Label	Peak Position	Weeks at No.1	Weeks in Top 40
19 Apr 86	ALL AND ALL *London LON 94*	16		7
13 Jun 87	LIFETIME LOVE *London LON 137*	34		4
9 Jan 88	COME INTO MY LIFE *London LON 161*	7		7
23 Apr 88	WALK AWAY *London LON 176*	24		4
17 Jun 89	LOOKING FOR A LOVE *ffrr F 109*	39		2
27 May 95	COME INTO MY LIFE (REMIX) *Club Tools 0060435 CLU*	72		

KYM SIMS US singer

Date	Title / Label	Peak Position	Weeks at No.1	Weeks in Top 40
7 Dec 91	TOO BLIND TO SEE IT *Atco B 8667* ○	5		10
28 Mar 92	TAKE MY ADVICE *Atco B 8591*	13		5
27 Jun 92	A LITTLE BIT MORE *Atco B 8528*	30		2
8 Jun 96	WE GOTTA LOVE *Pulse 8 CDLOSE 104*	58		

SIN WITH SEBASTIAN German singer

Date	Title / Label	Peak Position	Weeks at No.1	Weeks in Top 40
16 Sep 95	SHUT UP (AND SLEEP WITH ME) *Sing Sing 74321253592*	44		
27 Jan 96	SHUT UP (AND SLEEP WITH ME) (REMIX) *Sing Sing 74321337972*	46		

FRANK SINATRA US singer

Date	Title / Label	Peak Position	Weeks at No.1	Weeks in Top 40
9 Jul 54	YOUNG AT HEART *Capitol CL 14064*	12		1
16 Jul 54	THREE COINS IN THE FOUNTAIN *Capitol CL 14120*	1	3	19
10 Jun 55	YOU MY LOVE *Capitol CL 14240*	13		5
5 Aug 55	LEARNIN' THE BLUES *Capitol CL 14296* ★	2		13
2 Sep 55	NOT AS A STRANGER *Capitol CL 14326*	18		1
13 Jan 56	LOVE AND MARRIAGE *Capitol CL 14503*	3		8
20 Jan 56	(LOVE IS) THE TENDER TRAP *Capitol CL 14511*	2		9
15 Jun 56	SONGS FOR SWINGING LOVERS (LP) *Capitol LCT 6106*	12		8
22 Nov 57	ALL THE WAY *Capitol CL 14800*	3		19
29 Nov 57	CHICAGO *Capitol CL 14800*	21		2
7 Feb 58	WITCHCRAFT *Capitol CL 14819*	12		8
14 Nov 58	MR SUCCESS *Capitol CL 14956*	25		4
10 Apr 59	FRENCH FOREIGN LEGION *Capitol CL 14997*	18		5
15 May 59	COME DANCE WITH ME (LP) *Capitol LCT 6179*	30		1
28 Aug 59	HIGH HOPES *Capitol CL 15052*	6		13
7 Apr 60	IT'S NICE TO GO TRAV'LING *Capitol CL 15116*	48		
16 Jun 60	RIVER STAY 'WAY FROM MY DOOR *Capitol CL 15135*	18		9
8 Sep 60	NICE 'N' EASY *Capitol CL 15150*	15		12
24 Nov 60	OL' MACDONALD *Capitol CL 15168*	11		8
20 Apr 61	MY BLUE HEAVEN *Capitol CL 15193*	33		5
28 Sep 61	GRANADA *Reprise R 20010*	15		7
23 Nov 61	THE COFFEE SONG *Reprise R 20035*	39		1
5 Apr 62	EVERYBODY'S TWISTING *Reprise R 20063*	22		10
13 Dec 62	ME AND MY SHADOW *Reprise R 20128* FRANK SINATRA & SAMMY DAVIS JR	20		5
7 Mar 63	MY KIND OF GIRL *Reprise R 20148* FRANK SINATRA WITH COUNT BASIE	35		3
24 Sep 64	HELLO DOLLY *Reprise R 20351* FRANK SINATRA WITH COUNT BASIE	47		
12 May 66	STRANGERS IN THE NIGHT *Reprise R 23052* ★	1	3	19
29 Sep 66	SUMMER WIND *Reprise R 20509*	36		4
15 Dec 66	THAT'S LIFE *Reprise RS 20531*	44		
23 Mar 67	SOMETHIN' STUPID *Reprise RS 23166* NANCY SINATRA & FRANK SINATRA ★	1	2	15
23 Aug 67	THE WORLD WE KNEW *Reprise R 20610*	33		6
2 Apr 69	MY WAY *Reprise RS 20817*	5		73
4 Oct 69	LOVE'S BEEN GOOD TO ME *Reprise R 20852*	8		14
6 Mar 71	I WILL DRINK THE WINE *Reprise R 23487*	16		10
20 Dec 75	I BELIEVE I'M GONNA LOVE YOU *Reprise K 14400*	34		3
9 Aug 80	THEME FROM NEW YORK, NEW YORK *Reprise K 14502*	59		
22 Feb 86	THEME FROM NEW YORK, NEW YORK *Reprise K 14502* ○	4		7
4 Dec 93	I'VE GOT YOU UNDER MY SKIN *Island CID 578* FRANK SINATRA WITH BONO	4		6
16 Apr 94	MY WAY *Reprise W 0163CD*	45		
30 Jan 99	THEY ALL LAUGHED *Reprise W 469CD*	41		

NANCY SINATRA US singer

Date	Title / Label	Peak Position	Weeks at No.1	Weeks in Top 40
27 Jan 66	THESE BOOTS ARE MADE FOR WALKIN' *Reprise R 20432* ★	1	4	14
28 Apr 66	HOW DOES THAT GRAB YOU DARLIN' *Reprise R 20461*	19		6
19 Jan 67	SUGAR TOWN *Reprise RS 20527*	8		9
23 Mar 67	SOMETHIN' STUPID *Reprise RS 23166* NANCY SINATRA & FRANK SINATRA ★	1	2	15
5 Jul 67	YOU ONLY LIVE TWICE/JACKSON *Reprise RS 20595* NANCY SINATRA/NANCY SINATRA & LEE HAZLEWOOD	11		14
8 Nov 67	LADYBIRD *Reprise RS 20629* NANCY SINATRA & LEE HAZLEWOOD	47		
29 Nov 69	THE HIGHWAY SONG *Reprise RS 20869*	21		8
21 Aug 71	DID YOU EVER *Reprise K 14093* NANCY SINATRA & LEE HAZLEWOOD	2		17
23 Oct 04	LET ME KISS YOU *Attack ATKXS005*	46		
4 Jun 05	SHOT YOU DOWN *Source SOURCDX111* AUDIO BULLYS FEATURING NANCY SINATRA	3		14

SINCLAIR UK singer

Date	Title / Label	Peak Position	Weeks at No.1	Weeks in Top 40
21 Aug 93	AIN'T NO CASANOVA *Dome CDDOME 1004*	28		3
26 Feb 94	(I WANNA KNOW) WHY *Dome CDDOME 1009*	58		
6 Aug 94	DON'T LIE *Dome CDDOME 1010*	70		

BOB SINCLAR French producer

Date	Title / Label	Peak Position	Weeks at No.1	Weeks in Top 40
20 Mar 99	MY ONLY LOVE *East West EW 196CD* BOB SINCLAR FEATURING LEE A GENESIS	56		
19 Aug 00	I FEEL FOR YOU *Defected DFECT 18CDS*	9		3
7 Apr 01	DARLIN' *Defected DFECT 30CDS* BOB SINCLAR FEATURING JAMES WILLIAMS	46		
25 Jan 03	THE BEAT GOES ON *Defected DFTD 062CDS*	33		1
2 Aug 03	KISS MY EYES *Defected DFTD 070CDX*	67		
22 Oct 05	LOVE GENERATION *Defected DFTD111CDX* BOB SINCLAR FEATURING GARY NESTA PINE	12		9
15 Jul 06	WORLD, HOLD ON (CHILDREN OF THE SKY) *Defected DFTD132CDX* BOB SINCLAR FEATURING STEVE EDWARDS	9		9
7 Oct 06	ROCK THIS PARTY (EVERYBODY DANCE NOW) *Defected DFTD142CDX* BOB SINCLAR & CUTEE B	3		10
9 Jun 07	SOUND OF FREEDOM *Defected DFTD157CDS* BOB SINCLAR, CUTEE B & DOLLARMAN	14		2

SINDY UK doll character

Date	Title / Label	Peak Position	Weeks at No.1	Weeks in Top 40
5 Oct 96	SATURDAY NIGHT *Love This LUVTHISCD 13*	70		

SINE US group

Date	Title / Label	Peak Position	Weeks at No.1	Weeks in Top 40
10 Jun 78	JUST LET ME DO MY THING *CBS 6351*	33		4

SINGING CORNER UK duo

Date	Title	Peak Position	Weeks at No.1	Weeks in Top 40
1 Dec 90	**JENNIFER JUNIPER** *Fontana SYP 1* SINGING CORNER MEETS DONOVAN	68		

SINGING DOGS Danish recording of dogs

Date	Title	Peak Position	Weeks at No.1	Weeks in Top 40
25 Nov 55	**THE SINGING DOGS (MEDLEY)/OH SUSANNA** *Nixa N 15009* DON CHARLES PRESENTS THE SINGING DOGS	13		4

SINGING NUN Belgian singer

Date	Title	Peak Position	Weeks at No.1	Weeks in Top 40
5 Dec 63	**DOMINIQUE** *Philips BF 1293* ★	7		12

SINGING SHEEP UK computerised sheep vocals

Date	Title	Peak Position	Weeks at No.1	Weeks in Top 40
18 Dec 82	**BAA BAA BLACK SHEEP** *Sheep BAA 1*	42		

MAXINE SINGLETON US singer

Date	Title	Peak Position	Weeks at No.1	Weeks in Top 40
2 Apr 83	**YOU CAN'T RUN FROM LOVE** *Creole CR 50*	57		

SINITTA US singer

Date	Title	Peak Position	Weeks at No.1	Weeks in Top 40
8 Mar 86	**SO MACHO/CRUISING** *Fanfare FAN 7*	2		13
11 Oct 86	**FEELS LIKE THE FIRST TIME** *Fanfare FAN 8*	45		
25 Jul 87	**TOY BOY** *Fanfare FAN 12*	4		11
12 Dec 87	**G.T.O.** *Fanfare FAN 14*	15		7
19 Mar 88	**CROSS MY BROKEN HEART** *Fanfare FAN 15*	6		7
24 Sep 88	**I DON'T BELIEVE IN MIRACLES** *Fanfare FAN 16*	22		6
3 Jun 89	**RIGHT BACK WHERE WE STARTED FROM** *Fanfare FAN 18*	4		8
7 Oct 89	**LOVE ON A MOUNTAIN TOP** *Fanfare FAN 21*	20		5
21 Apr 90	**HITCHIN' A RIDE** *Fanfare FAN 24*	24		4
22 Sep 90	**LOVE AND AFFECTION** *Fanfare FAN 31*	62		
4 Jul 92	**SHAME SHAME SHAME** *Arista 74321100327*	28		3
17 Apr 93	**THE SUPREME EP** *Arista 74321139592*	49		

SINNAMON US group

Date	Title	Peak Position	Weeks at No.1	Weeks in Top 40
28 Sep 96	**I NEED YOU NOW** *Worx WORXCD 003*	70		

SIOUXSIE & THE BANSHEES UK group

Date	Title	Peak Position	Weeks at No.1	Weeks in Top 40
26 Aug 78	**HONG KONG GARDEN** *Polydor 2059 052*	7		7
31 Mar 79	**THE STAIRCASE (MYSTERY)** *Polydor POSP 9*	24		8
7 Jul 79	**PLAYGROUND TWIST** *Polydor POSP 59*	28		2
29 Sep 79	**MITTAGEISEN (METAL POSTCARD)** *Polydor 2059 151*	47		
15 Mar 80	**HAPPY HOUSE** *Polydor POSP 117*	17		7
7 Jun 80	**CHRISTINE** *Polydor 2059 249*	22		7
6 Dec 80	**ISRAEL** *Polydor POSP 205*	41		
30 May 81	**SPELLBOUND** *Polydor POSP 273*	22		7
1 Aug 81	**ARABIAN KNIGHTS** *Polydor PSOP 309*	32		5
29 May 82	**FIRE WORKS** *Polydor POSPG 450*	22		5
9 Oct 82	**SLOWDIVE** *Polydor POSP 510*	41		
4 Dec 82	**MELT/IL EST NE LE DIVIN ENFANT** *Polydor POSP 539*	49		
1 Oct 83	**DEAR PRUDENCE** *Wonderland SHE 4*	3		7
24 Mar 84	**SWIMMING HORSES** *Wonderland SHE 6*	28		3
2 Jun 84	**DAZZLE** *Wonderland SHE 7*	33		2
27 Oct 84	**THE THORN EP** *Wonderland SHE 8*	47		
26 Oct 85	**CITIES IN DUST** *Wonderland SHE 9*	21		5
8 Mar 86	**CANDYMAN** *Wonderland SHE 10*	34		3
17 Jan 87	**THIS WHEEL'S ON FIRE** *Wonderland SHE 11*	14		5
28 Mar 87	**THE PASSENGER** *Wonderland SHE 12*	41		
25 Jul 87	**SONG FROM THE EDGE OF THE WORLD** *Wonderland SHE 13*	59		
30 Jul 88	**PEEK-A-BOO** *Wonderland SHE 14*	16		4
8 Oct 88	**THE KILLING JAR** *Wonderland SHE 15*	41		
3 Dec 88	**THE LAST BEAT OF MY HEART** *Wonderland SHE 16*	44		
25 May 91	**KISS THEM FOR ME** *Wonderland SHE 19*	32		3
13 Jul 91	**SHADOWTIME** *Wonderland SHE 20*	57		
25 Jul 92	**FACE TO FACE** *Wonderland SHE 21*	21		3
20 Aug 94	**INTERLUDE** *Parlophone CDR 6365* MORRISSEY & SIOUXSIE	25		1
7 Jan 95	**O BABY** *Wonderland SHECD 22*	34		1
18 Feb 95	**STARGAZER** *Wonderland SHECD 23*	64		
15 Sep 07	**INTO A SWAN** *W14 1742056* SIOUXSIE	59		

SIR DOUGLAS QUINTET US group

Date	Title	Peak Position	Weeks at No.1	Weeks in Top 40
17 Jun 65	**SHE'S ABOUT A MOVER** *London HLU 9964*	15		9

SIR KILLALOT VS ROBO BABE UK rapper/singer

Date	Title	Peak Position	Weeks at No.1	Weeks in Top 40
30 Dec 00	**ROBOT WARS (ANDROID LOVE)** *Polydor 5879362*	51		

SIR MIX-A-LOT US rapper

Date	Title	Peak Position	Weeks at No.1	Weeks in Top 40
8 Aug 92	**BABY GOT BACK** *Def American DEFA 20* ★	56		

SIRENS UK group

Date	Title	Peak Position	Weeks at No.1	Weeks in Top 40
28 Aug 04	**BABY (OFF THE WALL)** *Kitchenware SKCD742*	49		

SISQO US singer

Date	Title	Peak Position	Weeks at No.1	Weeks in Top 40
12 Feb 00	**GOT TO GET IT** *Def Soul 5626442*	14		3
22 Apr 00	**THONG SONG** *Def Soul 5688902*	3		11
30 Sep 00	**UNLEASH THE DRAGON** *Def Soul 5726432*	6		5
16 Dec 00	**INCOMPLETE** *Def Soul 5727542* ★	13		6
28 Jul 01	**DANCE FOR ME** *Def Soul 5887002*	6		6

SISTER BLISS UK producer

Date	Title	Peak Position	Weeks at No.1	Weeks in Top 40
15 Oct 94	**CANTGETAMAN CANTGETAJOB (LIFE'S A BITCH)** *Go! Beat GODCD 124* SISTER BLISS WITH COLETTE	31		2
15 Jul 95	**OH! WHAT A WORLD** *Go! Beat GODCD 126* SISTER BLISS WITH COLETTE	40		1
29 Jun 96	**BADMAN** *Junk Dog JDOGCD 1*	51		
7 Oct 00	**SISTER SISTER** *Multiply CDMULTY 68*	34		1
24 Mar 01	**DELIVER ME** *Multiply CXMULTY 72* SISTER BLISS FEATURING JOHN MARTYN	31		1

SISTER SLEDGE US group

Date	Title	Peak Position	Weeks at No.1	Weeks in Top 40
21 Jun 75	**MAMA NEVER TOLD ME** *Atlantic K 10619*	20		5
17 Mar 79	**HE'S THE GREATEST DANCER** *Cotillion K 11257*	6		8
26 May 79	**WE ARE FAMILY** *Cotillion K 11293*	8		7
11 Aug 79	**LOST IN MUSIC** *Cotillion K 11337*	17		8
19 Jan 80	**GOT TO LOVE SOMEBODY** *Cotillion K 11404*	34		2
28 Feb 81	**ALL AMERICAN GIRLS** *Atlantic K 11656*	41		
26 May 84	**THINKING OF YOU** *Cotillion B 9744*	11		10
8 Sep 84	**LOST IN MUSIC (REMIX)** *Cotillion B 9718*	4		10
17 Nov 84	**WE ARE FAMILY (REMIX)** *Cotillion B 9692*	33		2
1 Jun 85	**FRANKIE** *Atlantic A 9547*	1	4	13
31 Aug 85	**DANCING ON THE JAGGED EDGE** *Atlantic A 9520*	50		
23 Jan 93	**WE ARE FAMILY (2ND REMIX)** *Atlantic A 4508CD*	5		5
13 Mar 93	**LOST IN MUSIC (2ND REMIX)** *Atlantic A 4509CD*	14		3
12 Jun 93	**THINKING OF YOU (REMIX)** *Atlantic A 4515CD*	17		3

SISTER 2 SISTER Australian duo

Date	Title	Peak Position	Weeks at No.1	Weeks in Top 40
22 Apr 00	**SISTER** *Mushroom MUSH 70CDS*	18		2
28 Oct 00	**WHAT'S A GIRL TO DO** *Mushroom MUSH 76CDS*	61		

SISTERS OF MERCY UK group

Date	Title	Peak Position	Weeks at No.1	Weeks in Top 40
16 Jun 84	**BODY AND SOUL/TRAIN** *Merciful Release MR 029*	46		
20 Oct 84	**WALK AWAY** *Merciful Release MR 033*	45		
9 Mar 85	**NO TIME TO CRY** *Merciful Release MR 035*	63		
3 Oct 87	**THIS CORROSION** *Merciful Release MR 39*	7		4
27 Feb 88	**DOMINION** *Merciful Release MR 43*	13		4
18 Jun 88	**LUCRETIA MY REFLECTION** *Merciful Release MR 45*	20		2
13 Oct 90	**MORE** *Merciful Release MR 47*	14		3
22 Dec 90	**DOCTOR JEEP** *Merciful Release MR 51*	37		2
2 May 92	**TEMPLE OF LOVE** *Merciful Release MR 53*	3		4
28 Aug 93	**UNDER THE GUN** *Merciful Release MR 59CDX*	19		2

SIVUCA Brazilian accordionist

Date	Title	Peak Position	Weeks at No.1	Weeks in Top 40
28 Jul 84	**AIN'T NO SUNSHINE** *London LON 51*	56		

SIX BY SEVEN UK group

Date	Title	Peak Position	Weeks at No.1	Weeks in Top 40
9 May 98	**CANDLELIGHT** *Mantra MNT 34CD*	70		
2 Mar 02	**IOU LOVE** *Mantra MNT 68CD1*	48		

6 BY SIX UK production duo

Date	Title	Peak Position	Weeks at No.1	Weeks in Top 40
4 May 96	**INTO YOUR HEART** *Six6 SIXCD 130*	51		

Silver-selling ● Gold-selling ● Platinum-selling ⊛ US No.1 ★ | Peak Position | Weeks at No.1 | Weeks in Top 40

SIX CHIX UK group

Date	Title / Label	Peak Position	Weeks at No.1	Weeks in Top 40
26 Feb 00	**ONLY THE WOMEN KNOW** *EMI CDCHIX 001*	72		

666 German group

Date	Title / Label	Peak Position	Weeks at No.1	Weeks in Top 40
3 Oct 98	**ALARMA** *Danceteria CDDAN 001*	58		
25 Nov 00	**DEVIL** *Echo ECSCD 102*	18		3

SIXPENCE NONE THE RICHER US group

Date	Title / Label	Peak Position	Weeks at No.1	Weeks in Top 40
29 May 99	**KISS ME** *Elektra E 3750CD* ●	4		10
18 Sep 99	**THERE SHE GOES** *Elektra E 3728CD*	14		3

60FT DOLLS UK group

Date	Title / Label	Peak Position	Weeks at No.1	Weeks in Top 40
3 Feb 96	**STAY** *Indolent DOLLS 002CD*	48		
11 May 96	**TALK TO ME** *Indolent DOLLS 003CD*	37		1
20 Jul 96	**HAPPY SHOPPER** *Indolent DOLLS 005CD*	38		1
9 May 98	**ALISON'S ROOM** *Indolent DOLLS 007CD1*	61		

SIZE 9 US singer

Date	Title / Label	Peak Position	Weeks at No.1	Weeks in Top 40
17 Jun 95	**I'M READY** *Virgin America VUSCD 92*	52		
11 Nov 95	**I'M READY** *VC Recordings VCRD 2* JOSH WINK'S SIZE 9	30		1

RONI SIZE UK producer

Date	Title / Label	Peak Position	Weeks at No.1	Weeks in Top 40
14 Jun 97	**SHARE THE FALL** *Talkin Loud TLCD 21* RONI SIZE REPRAZENT	37		1
13 Sep 97	**HEROES** *Talkin Loud TLCD 25* RONI SIZE REPRAZENT	31		1
15 Nov 97	**BROWN PAPER BAG** *Talkin Loud TLCD 28* RONI SIZE REPRAZENT	20		1
14 Mar 98	**WATCHING WINDOWS** *Talkin Loud TLCD 31* RONI SIZE REPRAZENT	28		1
7 Oct 00	**WHO TOLD YOU** *Talkin Loud TLCD 61* RONI SIZE REPRAZENT	17		2
24 Mar 01	**DIRTY BEATS** *Talkin Loud TLCDD 63* RONI SIZE REPRAZENT	32		1
23 Jun 01	**LUCKY PRESSURE** *Talkin Loud TLCD 64* RONI SIZE REPRAZENT	58		
19 Oct 02	**SOUND ADVICE** *Full Cycle FCY 044*	69		
9 Nov 02	**PLAYTIME** *Full Cycle FCY 045*	53		
7 Dec 02	**SCRAMBLED EGGS/SWINGS & ROUNDABOUTS** *Full Cycle FCY 046*	57		
18 Jan 03	**FEEL THE HEAT** *Full Cycle FCY 048*	55		
22 Feb 03	**SNAPSHOT 3/SORRY FOR YOU** *Full Cycle FCY 033*	61		
12 Jul 03	**SIREN SOUNDS/AT THE MOVIES** *Full Cycle FCY 054*	67		
6 Sep 03	**SOUND ADVICE/FORGET ME KNOTS** *Full Cycle FCY 056*	61		
17 Apr 04	**STRICTLY SOCIAL/AUTUMN** *Liquid V LQD001*	70		
24 Apr 04	**BAMBAKITA/FASSY HOLE** *V Recordings V045*	60		
9 Oct 04	**OUT OF BREATH** *V VRECUK002X* RONI SIZE FEATURING RAHZEL	44		
22 Jan 05	**NO MORE** *V VRECSUK003CD* RONI SIZE FEATURING BEVERLEY KNIGHT	26		2

SIZZLA Jamaican rapper

Date	Title / Label	Peak Position	Weeks at No.1	Weeks in Top 40
17 Apr 99	**RAIN SHOWERS** *Xterminator EXTCDS 76*	51		

SKANDAL UK group

Date	Title / Label	Peak Position	Weeks at No.1	Weeks in Top 40
14 Oct 00	**CHAMPAGNE HIGHWAY** *Prestige Management CDGING 1*	53		

SKANDI GIRLS Finnish/Norwegian/Swedish group

Date	Title / Label	Peak Position	Weeks at No.1	Weeks in Top 40
25 Dec 04	**DO THE CAN CAN** *Intelligent IR001CDX*	38		1

SKATALITES Jamaican group formed

Date	Title / Label	Peak Position	Weeks at No.1	Weeks in Top 40
20 Apr 67	**GUNS OF NAVARONE** *Island WI 168*	36		3

SKEE-LO US rapper

Date	Title / Label	Peak Position	Weeks at No.1	Weeks in Top 40
9 Dec 95	**I WISH** *Wild Card 5777752*	15		6
27 Apr 96	**TOP OF THE STAIRS** *Wild Card 5763352*	38		1

PETER SKELLERN UK pianist/singer

Date	Title / Label	Peak Position	Weeks at No.1	Weeks in Top 40
23 Sep 72	**YOU'RE A LADY** *Decca F 13333*	3		8
29 Mar 75	**HOLD ON TO LOVE** *Decca F 13568*	14		7
28 Oct 78	**LOVE IS THE SWEETEST THING** *Mercury 6008 603* PETER SKELLERN FEATURING GRIMETHORPE COLLIERY BAND	60		

SKID ROW US group

Date	Title / Label	Peak Position	Weeks at No.1	Weeks in Top 40
18 Nov 89	**YOUTH GONE WILD** *Atlantic A 8935*	42		
3 Feb 90	**18 AND LIFE** *Atlantic A 8883*	12		5
31 Mar 90	**I REMEMBER YOU** *East West A 8836*	36		2
15 Jun 91	**MONKEY BUSINESS** *Atlantic A 7673*	19		2
14 Sep 91	**SLAVE TO THE GRIND** *Atlantic A 7603*	43		
23 Nov 91	**WASTED TIME** *Atlantic A 7570*	20		2
29 Aug 92	**YOUTH GONE WILD/DELIVERING THE GOODS** *Atlantic A 7444*	22		3
18 Nov 95	**BREAKIN' DOWN** *Atlantic A 7135CD1*	48		

SKIDS UK group

Date	Title / Label	Peak Position	Weeks at No.1	Weeks in Top 40
23 Sep 78	**SWEET SUBURBIA** *Virgin VS 227*	70		
4 Nov 78	**THE SAINTS ARE COMING** *Virgin VS 232*	48		
17 Feb 79	**INTO THE VALLEY** *Virgin VS 241*	10		8
26 May 79	**MASQUERADE** *Virgin VS 262*	14		7
29 Sep 79	**CHARADE** *Virgin VS 288*	31		2
24 Nov 79	**WORKING FOR THE YANKEE DOLLAR** *Virgin VS 306*	20		10
1 Mar 80	**ANIMATION** *Virgin VS 323*	56		
16 Aug 80	**CIRCUS GAMES** *Virgin VS 359*	32		5
18 Oct 80	**GOODBYE CIVILIAN** *Virgin VS 373*	52		
6 Dec 80	**WOMAN IN WINTER** *Virgin VSK 101*	49		

SKIN German/UK group

Date	Title / Label	Peak Position	Weeks at No.1	Weeks in Top 40
25 Dec 93	**THE SKIN UP (EP)** *Parlophone CDR 6363*	67		
12 Mar 94	**HOUSE OF LOVE** *Parlophone CDR 6374*	45		
30 Apr 94	**MONEY/UNBELIEVABLE** *Parlophone CDRS 6381*	18		2
23 Jul 94	**TOWER OF STRENGTH** *Parlophone CDRS 6387*	19		2
15 Oct 94	**LOOK BUT DON'T TOUCH (EP)** *Parlophone CDRS 6391*	33		2
20 May 95	**TAKE ME DOWN TO THE RIVER** *Parlophone CDRS 6409*	26		1
23 Mar 96	**HOW LUCKY YOU ARE** *Parlophone CDR 6425*	32		1
18 May 96	**PERFECT DAY** *Parlophone CDR 6433*	33		1

SKIN UK singer

Date	Title / Label	Peak Position	Weeks at No.1	Weeks in Top 40
20 Jul 02	**GOOD TIMES** *Columbia 6727672* ED CASE & SKIN	49		
7 Jun 03	**TRASHED** *EMI CDEM 622*	30		1
20 Sep 03	**FAITHFULNESS** *EMI CDEM 624*	64		

SKIN UP UK producer

Date	Title / Label	Peak Position	Weeks at No.1	Weeks in Top 40
7 Sep 91	**IVORY** *Love EVOL 4*	48		
14 Mar 92	**A JUICY RED APPLE** *Love EVOL 11*	32		3
18 Jul 92	**ACCELERATE** *Love EVOL 17*	45		

SKINNY UK producer

Date	Title / Label	Peak Position	Weeks at No.1	Weeks in Top 40
11 Apr 98	**FAILURE** *Cheeky CHEKCD 023*	31		1

SKIP RAIDERS US producer

Date	Title / Label	Peak Position	Weeks at No.1	Weeks in Top 40
15 Jul 00	**ANOTHER DAY** *Perfecto PERF 4CDS* SKIP RAIDERS FEATURING JADA	46		

SKIPWORTH & TURNER US duo

Date	Title / Label	Peak Position	Weeks at No.1	Weeks in Top 40
27 Apr 85	**THINKING ABOUT YOUR LOVE** *Fourth & Broadway BRW 23*	24		5
21 Jan 89	**MAKE IT LAST** *Fourth & Broadway BRW 118*	60		

SKUNK ANANSIE UK group

Date	Title / Label	Peak Position	Weeks at No.1	Weeks in Top 40
25 Mar 95	**SELLING JESUS** *One Little Indian 101 TP7CD*	46		
17 Jun 95	**I CAN DREAM** *One Little Indian 121 TP7CD*	41		
2 Sep 95	**CHARITY** *One Little Indian 131 TP7CD*	40		1
27 Jan 96	**WEAK** *One Little Indian 141 TP7CD*	20		4
27 Apr 96	**CHARITY** *One Little Indian 151 TP7CD*	20		2
28 Sep 96	**ALL I WANT** *One Little Indian 161 TP7CD*	14		2
30 Nov 96	**TWISTED (EVERYDAY HURTS)** *One Little Indian 171 TP7CDL*	26		2

Date	Title / Label	Peak Position	Weeks at No.1	Weeks in Top 40
1 Feb 97	**HEDONISM (JUST BECAUSE YOU FEEL GOOD)** *One Little Indian 181 TP7CD*	13		4
14 Jun 97	**BRAZEN 'WEEP'** *One Little Indian 191 TP7CD1*	11		3
13 Mar 99	**CHARLIE BIG POTATO** *Virgin VSCDT 1725*	17		2
22 May 99	**SECRETLY** *Virgin VSCDT 1733*	16		2
7 Aug 99	**LATELY** *Virgin VSCDT 1738*	33		1

SKY UK group

Date	Title / Label	Peak Position	Weeks at No.1	Weeks in Top 40
5 Apr 80	**TOCCATA** *Ariola ARO 300*	5		6

SKYHOOKS Australian group

Date	Title / Label	Peak Position	Weeks at No.1	Weeks in Top 40
9 Jun 79	**WOMEN IN UNIFORM** *United Artists UP 36508*	73		

SKYLARK UK producer

Date	Title / Label	Peak Position	Weeks at No.1	Weeks in Top 40
27 Mar 04	**THAT'S MORE LIKE IT** *Credence CDCRED042*	62		

SLACKER UK group

Date	Title / Label	Peak Position	Weeks at No.1	Weeks in Top 40
26 Apr 97	**SCARED** *XL Recordings XLS 84CD*	36		1
30 Aug 97	**YOUR FACE** *XL Recordings XLS 87CD*	33		1

SLADE UK group

Date	Title / Label	Peak Position	Weeks at No.1	Weeks in Top 40
19 Jun 71	**GET DOWN AND GET WITH IT** *Polydor 2058 112*	16		11
30 Oct 71	**COZ I LUV YOU** *Polydor 2058 155*	1	4	13
5 Feb 72	**LOOK WOT YOU DUN** *Polydor 2058 195*	4		10
3 Jun 72	**TAKE ME BAK 'OME** *Polydor 2058 231*	1	1	11
2 Sep 72	**MAMA WEER ALL CRAZEE NOW** *Polydor 2058 274*	1	3	10
25 Nov 72	**GUDBUY T' JANE** *Polydor 2058 312*	2		11
3 Mar 73	**CUM ON FEEL THE NOIZE** *Polydor 2058 339*	1	4	10
30 Jun 73	**SKWEEZE ME PLEEZE ME** *Polydor 2058 377* ○	1	3	9
6 Oct 73	**MY FREND STAN** *Polydor 2058 407* ○	2		8
15 Dec 73	**MERRY XMAS EVERYBODY** *Polydor 2058 422* ⊛	1	5	9
6 Apr 74	**EVERYDAY** *Polydor 2058 453* ○	3		6
6 Jul 74	**THE BANGIN' MAN** *Polydor 2058 492*	3		7
19 Oct 74	**FAR FAR AWAY** *Polydor 2058 522* ○	2		6
15 Feb 75	**HOW DOES IT FEEL** *Polydor 2058 547*	15		7
17 May 75	**THANKS FOR THE MEMORY (WHAM BAM THANK YOU MAM)** *Polydor 2058 585*	7		7
22 Nov 75	**IN FOR A PENNY** *Polydor 2058 663*	11		7
7 Feb 76	**LET'S CALL IT QUITS** *Polydor 2058 690*	11		6
5 Feb 77	**GYPSY ROAD HOG** *Barn 2014 105*	48		
29 Oct 77	**MY BABY LEFT ME – THAT'S ALL RIGHT (MEDLEY)** *Barn 2014 114*	32		2
18 Oct 80	**SLADE LIVE AT READING '80 (EP)** *Cheapskate CHEAP 5*	44		
27 Dec 80	**MERRY XMAS EVERYBODY** *Cheapskate CHEAP 11* SLADE & THE READING CHOIR	70		
31 Jan 81	**WE'LL BRING THE HOUSE DOWN** *Cheapskate CHEAPO 16*	10		6
4 Apr 81	**WHEELS AIN'T COMING DOWN** *Cheapskate CHEAPO 21*	60		
19 Sep 81	**LOCK UP YOUR DAUGHTERS** *RCA 124*	29		5
19 Dec 81	**MERRY XMAS EVERYBODY** *Polydor 2058 422*	32		2
27 Mar 82	**RUBY RED** *RCA 191*	51		
27 Nov 82	**(AND NOW – THE WALTZ) C'EST LA VIE** *RCA 291*	50		
25 Dec 82	**MERRY XMAS EVERYBODY** *Polydor 2058 422*	67		
19 Nov 83	**MY OH MY** *RCA 373* ●	2		9
10 Dec 83	**MERRY XMAS EVERYBODY** *Polydor 2058 422*	20		4
4 Feb 84	**RUN RUN AWAY** *RCA 385*	7		8
17 Nov 84	**ALL JOIN HANDS** *RCA 455*	15		8
15 Dec 84	**MERRY XMAS EVERYBODY** *Polydor 2058 422*	47		
26 Jan 85	**7 YEAR BITCH** *RCA 475*	60		
23 Mar 85	**MYZSTERIOUS MIZSTER JONES** *RCA PB 40027*	50		
30 Nov 85	**DO YOU BELIEVE IN MIRACLES** *RCA PB 40449*	54		
21 Dec 85	**MERRY XMAS EVERYBODY** *Polydor POSP 780*	48		
27 Dec 86	**MERRY XMAS EVERYBODY** *Polydor POSP 780*	71		
21 Feb 87	**STILL THE SAME** *RCA PB 41137*	73		
19 Oct 91	**RADIO WALL OF SOUND** *Polydor PO 180*	21		4
26 Dec 98	**MERRY XMAS EVERYBODY '98 REMIX** *Polydor 5633532* SLADE VERSUS FLUSH	30		2
9 Dec 06	**MERRY XMAS EVERYBODY** *Universal TV 1713754*	21		4
15 Dec 07	**MERRY XMAS EVERYBODY** *Universal TV 1713754*	20		3

SLAM UK production duo

Date	Title / Label	Peak Position	Weeks at No.1	Weeks in Top 40
17 Feb 01	**POSITIVE EDUCATION** *VC Recordings VCRD 84*	44		
17 Mar 01	**NARCO TOURISTS** *Soma 100CD* SLAM VS UNKLE	66		
7 Jul 01	**LIFETIMES** *Soma 107CDS* SLAM FEATURING TYRONE PALMER	61		

SLAMM UK group

Date	Title / Label	Peak Position	Weeks at No.1	Weeks in Top 40
17 Jul 93	**ENERGIZE** *PWL International PWCD 266*	57		
23 Oct 93	**VIRGINIA PLAIN** *PWL International PWCD 274*	60		
22 Oct 94	**THAT'S WHERE MY MIND GOES** *PWL International PWCD 310*	68		
4 Feb 95	**CAN'T GET BY** *PWL International PWCD 316*	47		

LUKE SLATER UK producer

Date	Title / Label	Peak Position	Weeks at No.1	Weeks in Top 40
16 Sep 00	**ALL EXHALE** *Novamute CDNOMU 79*	74		
6 Apr 02	**NOTHING AT ALL** *Mute CDMUTE 261*	70		

SLAUGHTER US group

Date	Title / Label	Peak Position	Weeks at No.1	Weeks in Top 40
29 Sep 90	**UP ALL NIGHT** *Chrysalis CHS 3556*	62		
2 Feb 91	**FLY TO THE ANGELS** *Chrysalis CHS 3634*	55		

SLAVE US group

Date	Title / Label	Peak Position	Weeks at No.1	Weeks in Top 40
8 Mar 80	**JUST A TOUCH OF LOVE** *Atlantic/Cotillion K 11442*	64		

SLAYER US group

Date	Title / Label	Peak Position	Weeks at No.1	Weeks in Top 40
13 Jun 87	**CRIMINALLY INSANE** *Def Jam LON 133*	64		
26 Oct 91	**SEASONS IN THE ABYSS** *Def American DEFA 9*	51		
9 Sep 95	**SERENITY IN MURDER** *American Recordings 74321312482*	50		

SLEAZE SISTERS UK producer

Date	Title / Label	Peak Position	Weeks at No.1	Weeks in Top 40
29 Jul 95	**SEX** *Pulse 8 CDLOSE 92* SLEAZESISTERS WITH VIKKI SHEPARD	53		
30 Mar 96	**LET'S WHIP IT UP (YOU GO GIRL)** *Pulse 8 CDLOSE 102* SLEAZESISTERS WITH VIKKI SHEPARD	46		
26 Sep 98	**WORK IT UP** *Logic 74321616622*	74		

KATHY SLEDGE US singer

Date	Title / Label	Peak Position	Weeks at No.1	Weeks in Top 40
16 May 92	**TAKE ME BACK TO LOVE AGAIN** *Epic 6579837*	62		
18 Feb 95	**ANOTHER STAR** *NRC DEACD*	54		
29 Nov 97	**FREEDOM** *Deconstruction 74321536952* ROBERT MILES FEATURING KATHY SLEDGE	15		2

PERCY SLEDGE US singer

Date	Title / Label	Peak Position	Weeks at No.1	Weeks in Top 40
12 May 66	**WHEN A MAN LOVES A WOMAN** *Atlantic 584 001* ★	4		14
4 Aug 66	**WARM AND TENDER LOVE** *Atlantic 584 034*	34		4
14 Feb 87	**WHEN A MAN LOVES A WOMAN** *Atlantic YZ 96* ○	2		9

SLEEPER UK group

Date	Title / Label	Peak Position	Weeks at No.1	Weeks in Top 40
21 May 94	**DELICIOUS** *Indolent SLEEP 003CD*	75		
21 Jan 95	**INBETWEENER** *Indolent SLEEP 006CD*	16		3
8 Apr 95	**VEGAS** *Indolent SLEEP 008CD*	33		1
7 Oct 95	**WHAT DO I DO NOW?** *Indolent SLEEP 009CD*	14		3
4 May 96	**SALE OF THE CENTURY** *Indolent SLEEP 011CD*	10		4
13 Jul 96	**NICE GUY EDDIE** *Indolent SLEEP 013CD*	10		3
5 Oct 96	**STATUESQUE** *Indolent SLEEP 014CD1*	17		1
4 Oct 97	**SHE'S A GOOD GIRL** *Indolent SLEEP 015CD*	28		1
6 Dec 97	**ROMEO ME** *Indolent SLEEP 17CD1*	39		1

SLEEPY JACKSON Australian group

Date	Title / Label	Peak Position	Weeks at No.1	Weeks in Top 40
19 Jul 03	**VAMPIRE RACECOURSE** *Virgin DINSD 261*	50		
25 Oct 03	**GOOD DANCERS** *Virgin DINSD 265*	71		
29 Jul 06	**GOD LEAD YOUR SOUL** *Virgin DINSDX278*	69		

SLICK US group

Date	Title / Label	Peak Position	Weeks at No.1	Weeks in Top 40
16 Jun 79	**SPACE BASS** *Fantasy FTC 176*	16		6
15 Sep 79	**SEXY CREAM** *Fantasy FTC 182*	47		

GRACE SLICK US singer

Date	Title / Label	Peak Position	Weeks at No.1	Weeks in Top 40
24 May 80	**DREAMS** *RCA PB 9534*	50		

Platinum-selling · Gold-selling · Silver-selling · US No.1 ★ · Peak Position · Weeks at No.1 · Weeks in Top 40

SLICK RICK US rapper

Date	Title / Label	Peak Position	Weeks at No.1	Weeks in Top 40
10 Jun 89	**IF I'M NOT YOUR LOVER** *Uptown W 2908* AL B SURE! FEATURING SLICK RICK	54		
19 Oct 96	**I LIKE** *Def Jam DEFCD 19* MONTELL JORDAN FEATURING SLICK RICK	24		1
6 Oct 07	**HIP HOP POLICE** *Universal 1751125* CHAMILLIONAIRE FEATURING SLICK RICK	50		

SLIK UK group

Date	Title / Label	Peak Position	Weeks at No.1	Weeks in Top 40
17 Jan 76	**FOREVER AND EVER** *Bell 1464* (Gold)	1	1	9
8 May 76	**REQUIEM** *Bell 1478*	24		7

SLIPKNOT US group

Date	Title / Label	Peak Position	Weeks at No.1	Weeks in Top 40
11 Mar 00	**WAIT AND BLEED** *Roadrunner RR21125*	27		2
16 Sep 00	**SPIT IT OUT** *Roadrunner RR20903*	28		1
10 Nov 01	**LEFT BEHIND** *Roadrunner 23203352*	24		2
20 Jul 02	**MY PLAGUE** *Roadrunner RR 20453*	43		
26 Jun 04	**DUALITY** *Roadrunner RR 39880*	15		2
30 Oct 04	**VERMILION** *Roadrunner RR 39770*	31		1
25 Jun 05	**BEFORE I FORGET** *Roadrunner RR39688*	35		1

SLIPMATT UK producer

Date	Title / Label	Peak Position	Weeks at No.1	Weeks in Top 40
19 Apr 03	**SPACE** *Concept CDCON 37*	41		

SLIPSTREEM UK group

Date	Title / Label	Peak Position	Weeks at No.1	Weeks in Top 40
19 Dec 92	**WE ARE RAVING – THE ANTHEM** *Boogie Food 7BF 1*	18		5

SLITS UK group

Date	Title / Label	Peak Position	Weeks at No.1	Weeks in Top 40
13 Oct 79	**TYPICAL GIRLS/I HEARD IT THROUGH THE GRAPEVINE** *Island WIP 6505*	60		

SLK UK group

Date	Title / Label	Peak Position	Weeks at No.1	Weeks in Top 40
19 Mar 05	**HYPE! HYPE!** *Smoove SMOOVE01CDS*	22		1

P.F. SLOAN US singer

Date	Title / Label	Peak Position	Weeks at No.1	Weeks in Top 40
4 Nov 65	**SINS OF THE FAMILY** *RCA 1482*	38		1

SLO-MOSHUN UK production duo

Date	Title / Label	Peak Position	Weeks at No.1	Weeks in Top 40
5 Feb 94	**BELLS OF NY** *Six6 SIXCD 108*	29		2
30 Jul 94	**HELP MY FRIEND** *Six6 SIXCD 117*	52		

SLOWDIVE UK group

Date	Title / Label	Peak Position	Weeks at No.1	Weeks in Top 40
15 Jun 91	**CATCH THE BREEZE/SHINE** *Creation CRE 112*	52		
29 May 93	**OUTSIDE YOUR ROOM (EP)** *Creation CRESCD 119*	69		

SL2 UK production duo

Date	Title / Label	Peak Position	Weeks at No.1	Weeks in Top 40
2 Nov 91	**DJS TAKE CONTROL/WAY IN MY BRAIN** *XL Recordings XLS 24*	11		4
18 Apr 92	**ON A RAGGA TIP** *XL Recordings XLS 29* (Silver)	2		10
19 Dec 92	**WAY IN MY BRAIN (REMIX)/DRUMBEATS** *XL Recordings XLS 36*	26		4
15 Feb 97	**ON A RAGGA TIP '97 (REMIX)** *XL Recordings XLSR 29CD*	31		1

SLUSNIK LUNA Finnish production duo

Date	Title / Label	Peak Position	Weeks at No.1	Weeks in Top 40
1 Sep 01	**SUN** *Incentive CENT 29CDS*	40		1

SLY & THE FAMILY STONE US group

Date	Title / Label	Peak Position	Weeks at No.1	Weeks in Top 40
10 Jul 68	**DANCE TO THE MUSIC** *Direction 58 3568*	7		13
2 Oct 68	**M'LADY** *Direction 58 3707*	32		4
19 Mar 69	**EVERYDAY PEOPLE** *Direction 58 3938* ★	36		2
8 Jan 72	**FAMILY AFFAIR** *Epic EPC 7632* ★	15		8
15 Apr 72	**RUNNIN' AWAY** *Epic EPC 7810*	17		7

SLY FOX US duo

Date	Title / Label	Peak Position	Weeks at No.1	Weeks in Top 40
31 May 86	**LET'S GO ALL THE WAY** *Capitol CL 403*	3		11

SLY & ROBBIE Jamaican duo

Date	Title / Label	Peak Position	Weeks at No.1	Weeks in Top 40
4 Apr 87	**BOOPS (HERE TO GO)** *Fourth & Broadway BRW 61*	12		8
25 Jul 87	**FIRE** *Fourth & Broadway BRW 71*	60		
20 Sep 97	**NIGHT NURSE** *East West EW 129CD1* SLY & ROBBIE FEATURING SIMPLY RED	14		6

SMALL ADS UK group

Date	Title / Label	Peak Position	Weeks at No.1	Weeks in Top 40
18 Apr 81	**SMALL ADS** *Bronze BRO 115*	63		

SMALL FACES UK group

Date	Title / Label	Peak Position	Weeks at No.1	Weeks in Top 40
2 Sep 65	**WHATCHA GONNA DO ABOUT IT** *Decca F 12208*	14		10
10 Feb 66	**SHA LA LA LA LEE** *Decca F 12317*	3		11
12 May 66	**HEY GIRL** *Decca F 12393*	10		9
11 Aug 66	**ALL OR NOTHING** *Decca F 12470*	1	1	11
17 Nov 66	**MY MIND'S EYE** *Decca F 12500*	4		10
9 Mar 67	**I CAN'T MAKE IT** *Decca F 12565*	26		5
8 Jun 67	**HERE COME THE NICE** *Immediate IM 050*	12		10
9 Aug 67	**ITCHYCOO PARK** *Immediate IM 057*	3		13
6 Dec 67	**TIN SOLDIER** *Immediate IM 062*	9		11
17 Apr 68	**LAZY SUNDAY** *Immediate IM 064*	2		10
10 Jul 68	**UNIVERSAL** *Immediate IM 069*	16		10
19 Mar 69	**AFTERGLOW OF YOUR LOVE** *Immediate IM 077*	36		1
13 Dec 75	**ITCHYCOO PARK** *Immediate IMS 102*	9		10
20 Mar 76	**LAZY SUNDAY** *Immediate IMS 106*	39		1

HEATHER SMALL UK singer

Date	Title / Label	Peak Position	Weeks at No.1	Weeks in Top 40
18 Apr 92	**SOMEDAY** *Deconstruction PB45369* M PEOPLE WITH HEATHER SMALL	38		2
20 May 00	**PROUD** *Arista 74321757112*	16		3
19 Aug 00	**HOLDING ON** *Arista 74321781332*	58		
30 Jul 05	**PROUD** *Arista 82876669182*	33		1
18 Nov 00	**YOU NEED LOVE LIKE I DO** *Gut CXGUT 36* TOM JONES & HEATHER SMALL	24		1

SMALLER UK group

Date	Title / Label	Peak Position	Weeks at No.1	Weeks in Top 40
28 Sep 96	**WASTED** *Better BETSCD 006*	72		
29 Mar 97	**IS** *Better BETSCD 008*	55		

SMART E'S UK production group

Date	Title / Label	Peak Position	Weeks at No.1	Weeks in Top 40
11 Jul 92	**SESAME'S TREET** *Suburban Base SUBBASE 125*	2		7

S*M*A*S*H UK group

Date	Title / Label	Peak Position	Weeks at No.1	Weeks in Top 40
6 Aug 94	**(I WANT TO) KILL SOMEBODY** *Hi-Rise FLATSCD 5*	26		1

SMASH MOUTH US group

Date	Title / Label	Peak Position	Weeks at No.1	Weeks in Top 40
25 Oct 97	**WALKIN' ON THE SUN** *Interscope IND 95555*	19		3
31 Jul 99	**ALL STAR** *Interscope IND 4971182*	24		2

SMASHING PUMPKINS US group

Date	Title / Label	Peak Position	Weeks at No.1	Weeks in Top 40
5 Sep 92	**I AM ONE** *Hut HUTT 18*	73		
3 Jul 93	**CHERUB ROCK** *Hut HUTCD 31*	31		1
25 Sep 93	**TODAY** *Hut HUTCD 37*	44		
5 Mar 94	**DISARM** *Hut HUTCD 43*	11		2
28 Oct 95	**BULLET WITH BUTTERFLY WINGS** *Virgin HUTCD 63*	20		2
10 Feb 96	**1979** *Virgin HUTCD 67*	16		2
18 May 96	**TONIGHT TONIGHT** *Virgin HUTDX 69*	7		4
23 Nov 96	**THIRTY THREE** *Virgin HUTCD 78*	21		1
14 Jun 97	**THE END IS THE BEGINNING IS THE END** *Warner Brothers W 0404CD*	10		2
23 Aug 97	**THE END IS THE BEGINNING IS THE END (REMIX)** *Warner Brothers W 0410CD*	72		
30 May 98	**AVA ADORE** *Hut HUTCD 101*	11		2
19 Sep 98	**PERFECT** *Hut HUTCD 106*	24		1
4 Mar 00	**STAND INSIDE YOUR LOVE** *Hut HUTCD 127*	23		1
23 Sep 00	**TRY TRY TRY** *Hut HUTCD 140*	73		
14 Jul 07	**TARANTULA** *Warner Brothers W769CD*	59		

SMELLS LIKE HEAVEN Italian producer

Date	Title / Label	Peak Position	Weeks at No.1	Weeks in Top 40
10 Jul 93	**LONDRES STRUTT** *Deconstruction 74321154312*	57		

Key: ○ Silver-selling · ● Gold-selling · ⊛ Platinum-selling · ★ US No.1 · Peak Position · Weeks at No.1 · Weeks in Top 40

AARON SMITH US producer

Date	Title / Label	Peak Position	Weeks at No.1	Weeks in Top 40
14 Jan 06	**DANCIN'** *Boss BOSSMOS02CDS* AARON SMITH FEATURING LUVLI	20		3

ANNE-MARIE SMITH UK singer

Date	Title / Label	Peak Position	Weeks at No.1	Weeks in Top 40
23 Jan 93	**MUSIC** *Synthetic CDR 6334* FARGETTA & ANNE-MARIE SMITH	34		1
18 Mar 95	**ROCKIN' MY BODY** *Media MCSTD 2021* 49ERS FEATURING ANN-MARIE SMITH	31		2
15 Jul 95	**(YOU'RE MY ONE AND ONLY) TRUE LOVE** *Media MCSTD 2060*	46		

ELLIOTT SMITH US singer

Date	Title / Label	Peak Position	Weeks at No.1	Weeks in Top 40
19 Dec 98	**WALTZ #2 (XO)** *DreamWorks DRMCD 22347*	52		
1 May 99	**BABY BRITAIN** *DreamWorks DRMDM 50950*	55		
8 Jul 00	**SON OF SAM** *DreamWorks DRMCD 4509492*	55		

HURRICANE SMITH UK singer/trumpeter

Date	Title / Label	Peak Position	Weeks at No.1	Weeks in Top 40
12 Jun 71	**DON'T LET IT DIE** *Columbia DB 8785*	2		10
29 Apr 72	**OH BABE WHAT WOULD YOU SAY?** *Columbia DB 8878*	4		14
2 Sep 72	**WHO WAS IT** *Columbia DB 8916*	23		5

JIMMY SMITH US organist

Date	Title / Label	Peak Position	Weeks at No.1	Weeks in Top 40
28 Apr 66	**GOT MY MOJO WORKING** *Verve VS 536*	48		

KEELY SMITH US singer

Date	Title / Label	Peak Position	Weeks at No.1	Weeks in Top 40
18 Mar 65	**YOU'RE BREAKIN' MY HEART** *Reprise R 20346*	14		10

MANDY SMITH UK singer

Date	Title / Label	Peak Position	Weeks at No.1	Weeks in Top 40
20 May 89	**DON'T YOU WANT ME BABY** *PWL 37*	59		

MEL SMITH UK singer and comedian

Date	Title / Label	Peak Position	Weeks at No.1	Weeks in Top 40
5 Dec 87	**ROCKIN' AROUND THE CHRISTMAS TREE** *10 TEN 2* MEL & KIM ○	3		7
21 Dec 91	**ANOTHER BLOOMING CHRISTMAS** *Epic 6576877*	59		

MURIEL SMITH US singer

Date	Title / Label	Peak Position	Weeks at No.1	Weeks in Top 40
15 May 53	**HOLD ME THRILL ME KISS ME** *Philips PB 122*	3		17

O.C. SMITH US singer

Date	Title / Label	Peak Position	Weeks at No.1	Weeks in Top 40
29 May 68	**SON OF HICKORY HOLLER'S TRAMP** *CBS 3343*	2		14
26 Mar 77	**TOGETHER** *Caribou CRB 4910*	25		6

PATTI SMITH GROUP US singer

Date	Title / Label	Peak Position	Weeks at No.1	Weeks in Top 40
29 Apr 78	**BECAUSE THE NIGHT** *Arista 181* ○	5		9
19 Aug 78	**PRIVILEGE (SET ME FREE)** *Arista 197*	72		
2 Jun 79	**FREDERICK** *Arista 264*	63		

REX SMITH & RACHEL SWEET US duo

Date	Title / Label	Peak Position	Weeks at No.1	Weeks in Top 40
22 Aug 81	**EVERLASTING LOVE** *CBS A 1405*	35		4

RICHARD JON SMITH South African singer

Date	Title / Label	Peak Position	Weeks at No.1	Weeks in Top 40
16 Jul 83	**SHE'S THE MASTER OF THE GAME** *Jive 38*	63		

WHISTLING JACK SMITH UK whistler

Date	Title / Label	Peak Position	Weeks at No.1	Weeks in Top 40
2 Mar 67	**I WAS KAISER BILL'S BATMAN** *Deram DM 112*	5		10

WILL SMITH US actor/singer

Date	Title / Label	Peak Position	Weeks at No.1	Weeks in Top 40
16 Aug 97	**MEN IN BLACK** *Columbia 6648682* ⊛	1	4	13
13 Dec 97	**JUST CRUISIN'** *Columbia 6653482*	23		4
7 Feb 98	**GETTIN' JIGGY WIT IT** *Columbia 6655605* ○ ★	3		9
1 Aug 98	**JUST THE TWO OF US** *Columbia 6662092*	2		7
5 Dec 98	**MIAMI** *Columbia 6666782*	3		11
13 Feb 99	**BOY YOU KNOCK ME OUT** *MJJ 6674742* TATYANA ALI FEATURING WILL SMITH ○	3		5
10 Jul 99	**WILD WILD WEST** *Columbia 6675962* WILL SMITH FEATURING DRU HILL ● ★	2		12
20 Nov 99	**WILL 2K** *Columbia 6684452*	2		10
25 Mar 00	**FREAKIN' IT** *Columbia 6691052*	15		3
10 Aug 02	**BLACK SUITS COMIN' (NOD YA HEAD)** *Columbia 6730135* WILL SMITH FEATURING TRA-KNOX	3		7
2 Apr 05	**SWITCH** *Interscope 9881083*	4		19
5 Nov 05	**PARTY STARTER** *Interscope 9886574*	19		2

SMITHS UK group

Date	Title / Label	Peak Position	Weeks at No.1	Weeks in Top 40
12 Nov 83	**THIS CHARMING MAN** *Rough Trade RT 136*	25		5
28 Jan 84	**WHAT DIFFERENCE DOES IT MAKE** *Rough Trade RT 146*	12		8
2 Jun 84	**HEAVEN KNOWS I'M MISERABLE NOW** *Rough Trade RT 156*	10		6
1 Sep 84	**WILLIAM, IT WAS REALLY NOTHING** *Rough Trade RT 166*	17		4
9 Feb 85	**HOW SOON IS NOW** *Rough Trade RT 176*	24		4
30 Mar 85	**SHAKESPEARE'S SISTER** *Rough Trade RT 181*	26		3
13 Jul 85	**THE JOKE ISN'T FUNNY ANYMORE** *Rough Trade RT 186*	49		
5 Oct 85	**THE BOY WITH THE THORN IN HIS SIDE** *Rough Trade RT 191*	23		4
31 May 86	**BIG MOUTH STRIKES AGAIN** *Rough Trade RT 192*	26		3
2 Aug 86	**PANIC** *Rough Trade RT 193*	11		6
1 Nov 86	**ASK** *Rough Trade RT 194*	14		4
7 Feb 87	**SHOPLIFTERS OF THE WORLD UNITE** *Rough Trade RT 195*	12		3
25 Apr 87	**SHEILA TAKE A BOW** *Rough Trade RT 196*	10		4
22 Aug 87	**GIRLFRIEND IN A COMA** *Rough Trade RT 197*	13		4
14 Nov 87	**I STARTED SOMETHING I COULDN'T FINISH** *Rough Trade RT 198*	23		3
19 Dec 87	**LAST NIGHT I DREAMT THAT SOMEBODY LOVED ME** *Rough Trade RT 200*	30		2
15 Aug 92	**THIS CHARMING MAN** *WEA YZ 0001*	8		3
12 Sep 92	**HOW SOON IS NOW** *WEA YX 0002*	16		3
24 Oct 92	**THERE IS A LIGHT THAT NEVER GOES OUT** *WEA YZ 0003*	25		2
18 Feb 95	**ASK** *WEA YZ 0004CDX*	62		

SMOKE UK group

Date	Title / Label	Peak Position	Weeks at No.1	Weeks in Top 40
9 Mar 67	**MY FRIEND JACK** *Columbia DB 8115*	45		

SMOKE CITY UK group

Date	Title / Label	Peak Position	Weeks at No.1	Weeks in Top 40
12 Apr 97	**UNDERWATER LOVE** *Jive JIVECD 422*	4		4

SMOKE 2 SEVEN UK group

Date	Title / Label	Peak Position	Weeks at No.1	Weeks in Top 40
16 Mar 02	**BEEN THERE DONE THAT** *Curb CUBCX 077*	26		1

SMOKIE UK group

Date	Title / Label	Peak Position	Weeks at No.1	Weeks in Top 40
19 Jul 75	**IF YOU THINK YOU KNOW HOW TO LOVE ME** *RAK 206* SMOKEY	3		9
4 Oct 75	**DON'T PLAY YOUR ROCK 'N' ROLL TO ME** *RAK 217* SMOKEY	8		6
31 Jan 76	**SOMETHING'S BEEN MAKING ME BLUE** *RAK 227*	17		7
25 Sep 76	**I'LL MEET YOU AT MIDNIGHT** *RAK 241*	11		8
4 Dec 76	**LIVING NEXT DOOR TO ALICE** *RAK 244* ○	5		11
19 Mar 77	**LAY BACK IN THE ARMS OF SOMEONE** *RAK 251*	12		8
16 Jul 77	**IT'S YOUR LIFE** *RAK 260*	5		8
15 Oct 77	**NEEDLES AND PINS** *RAK 263* ○	10		8
28 Jan 78	**FOR A FEW DOLLARS MORE** *RAK 267*	17		6
20 May 78	**OH CAROL** *RAK 276* ○	5		9
23 Sep 78	**MEXICAN GIRL** *RAK 283*	19		6
19 Apr 80	**TAKE GOOD CARE OF MY BABY** *RAK 309*	34		2
13 May 95	**LIVING NEXT DOOR TO ALICE (WHO THE F**K IS ALICE)** *NOW CDWAG 245* SMOKIE FEATURING ROY CHUBBY BROWN	64		
26 Aug 95	**LIVING NEXT DOOR TO ALICE (WHO THE F**K IS ALICE)** *NOW CDWAG 245* SMOKIE FEATURING ROY CHUBBY BROWN ○	3		14

SMOKIN' BEATS UK production group

Date	Title / Label	Peak Position	Weeks at No.1	Weeks in Top 40
17 Jan 98	**DREAMS** *AM:PM 5624711* SMOKIN' BEATS FEATURING LYN EDEN	23		1

SMOKIN' MOJO FILTERS UK/US charity ensemble

Date	Title / Label	Peak Position	Weeks at No.1	Weeks in Top 40
23 Dec 95	**COME TOGETHER (WAR CHILD)** *Go! Discs GODCD 136*	19		3

Silver-selling ○ Gold-selling ● Platinum-selling US No.1 ★ | Peak Position | Weeks at No.1 | Weeks in Top 40

SMOOTH US rapper

Date	Title	Peak	Wks No.1	Wks Top 40
22 Jul 95	**MIND BLOWIN'** *Jive JIVECD 379*	36		1
7 Oct 95	**IT'S SUMMERTIME (LET IT GET INTO YOU)** *Jive JIVECD 383*	46		
16 Mar 96	**LOVE GROOVE (GROOVE WITH YOU)** *Jive JIVECD 390*	46		
16 Mar 96	**WE GOT IT** *MCA MCSTD 48009* IMMATURE FEATURING SMOOTH	26		1
6 Jul 96	**UNDERCOVER LOVER** *Jive JIVECD 397*	41		

JOE SMOOTH US producer

Date	Title	Peak	Wks No.1	Wks Top 40
4 Feb 89	**PROMISED LAND** *DJinternational DJIN 6*	56		

SMOOTH TOUCH US production duo

Date	Title	Peak	Wks No.1	Wks Top 40
2 Apr 94	**HOUSE OF LOVE (IN MY HOUSE)** *Six6 SIXCD 112*	58		

JEAN JACQUES SMOOTHIE UK producer

Date	Title	Peak	Wks No.1	Wks Top 40
13 Oct 01	**2 PEOPLE** *Echo ECSCD 112*	12		4

SMUJJI Jamaican singer

Date	Title	Peak	Wks No.1	Wks Top 40
13 Mar 04	**MUST BE LOVE** *Def Jam UK 9817508* FYA FEATURING SMUJJI	13		4
31 Jul 04	**KO** *Def Jam 9867077*	43		

SMURFS Dutch cartoon characters

Date	Title	Peak	Wks No.1	Wks Top 40
3 Jun 78	**THE SMURF SONG** *Decca F 13759* FATHER ABRAHAM & THE SMURFS ●	2		14
30 Sep 78	**DIPPETY DAY** *Decca F 13798* FATHER ABRAHAM & THE SMURFS ○	13		8
2 Dec 78	**CHRISTMAS IN SMURFLAND** *Decca F 13819* FATHER ABRAHAM & THE SMURFS	19		6
7 Sep 96	**I'VE GOT A LITTLE PUPPY** *EMI TV CDSMURF 100*	4		7
21 Dec 96	**YOUR CHRISTMAS WISH** *EMI TV CDSMURF 102*	8		4

PATTY SMYTH US singer

Date	Title	Peak	Wks No.1	Wks Top 40
3 Oct 92	**SOMETIMES LOVE JUST AIN'T ENOUGH** *MCA MCS 1692* PATTY SMYTH WITH DON HENLEY	22		5

SNAKEBITE Italian group

Date	Title	Peak	Wks No.1	Wks Top 40
9 Aug 97	**THE BIT GOES ON** *Multiply CDMULTY 22*	25		1

SNAP US/German group

Date	Title	Peak	Wks No.1	Wks Top 40
24 Mar 90	**THE POWER** *Arista 113133* ○	1	2	12
16 Jun 90	**OOOPS UP** *Arista 113296* ○	5		10
22 Sep 90	**CULT OF SNAP** *Arista 113596*	8		5
8 Dec 90	**MARY HAD A LITTLE BOY** *Arista 113831*	8		8
30 Mar 91	**SNAP MEGAMIX** *Arista 114169*	10		4
21 Dec 91	**THE COLOUR OF LOVE** *Arista 114678*	54		
4 Jul 92	**RHYTHM IS A DANCER** *Arista 115309* ●	1	6	17
9 Jan 93	**EXTERMINATE!** *Arista 74321106962* SNAP FEATURING NIKI HARIS	2		9
12 Jun 93	**DO YOU SEE THE LIGHT (LOOKING FOR)** *Arista 74321147622* SNAP FEATURING NIKI HARIS	10		6
17 Sep 94	**WELCOME TO TOMORROW** *Arista 74321223852* SNAP FEATURING SUMMER ○	6		11
1 Apr 95	**THE FIRST THE LAST THE ETERNITY (TIL THE END)** *Arista 74321254672* SNAP FEATURING SUMMER	15		6
28 Oct 95	**THE WORLD IN MY HANDS** *Arista 74321314792* SNAP FEATURING SUMMER	44		
13 Apr 96	**RAME** *Arista 74321368902* SNAP FEATURING RUKMANI	50		
24 Aug 96	**THE POWER 96** *Arista 74321398672* SNAP FEATURING EINSTEIN	42		
24 Aug 02	**DO YOU SEE THE LIGHT (REMIX)** *Data 33CDS* SNAP VS PLAYTHING	14		3
17 May 03	**RHYTHM IS A DANCER (REMIX)** *Data 47CDS*	17		3
6 Sep 03	**THE POWER (OF BHANGRA)** *Data 60CDS* SNAP VS MOTIVO	34		1

SNEAKER PIMPS UK group

Date	Title	Peak	Wks No.1	Wks Top 40
19 Oct 96	**6 UNDERGROUND** *Clean Up CUP 023CDD*	15		3
15 Mar 97	**SPIN SPIN SUGAR** *Clean Up CUP 033CDS*	21		2
7 Jun 97	**6 UNDERGROUND** *Clean Up CUP 036CDS*	9		3
30 Aug 97	**POST MODERN SLEAZE** *Clean Up CUP 038CDM*	22		1
7 Feb 98	**SPIN SPIN SUGAR (REMIX)** *Clean Up CUP 037X*	46		
21 Aug 99	**LOW FIVE** *Clean Up CUP 052CDS*	39		1
30 Oct 99	**TEN TO TWENTY** *Clean Up CUP 054CDS*	56		

DAVID SNEDDON UK singer

Date	Title	Peak	Wks No.1	Wks Top 40
25 Jan 03	**STOP LIVING THE LIE** *Mercury 0637292*	1	2	10
3 May 03	**DON'T LET GO** *Mercury 9800069*	3		4
23 Aug 03	**BEST OF ORDER** *Fontana 9810277*	19		1
8 Nov 03	**BABY GET HIGHER** *Fontana 9813422*	38		1

SNIFF 'N' THE TEARS UK group

Date	Title	Peak	Wks No.1	Wks Top 40
23 Jun 79	**DRIVER'S SEAT** *Chiswick CHIS 105*	42		

SNOOP DOGGY DOGG US rapper

Date	Title	Peak	Wks No.1	Wks Top 40
4 Dec 93	**WHAT'S MY NAME?** *Death Row A 8337CD*	20		5
12 Feb 94	**GIN AND JUICE** *Death Row A 8316CD*	39		1
20 Aug 94	**DOGGY DOGG WORLD** *Death Row A 8289CD*	32		1
14 Dec 96	**SNOOP'S UPSIDE YA HEAD** *Interscope IND 95520* SNOOP DOGGY DOGG FEATURING CHARLIE WILSON	12		5
26 Apr 97	**WANTED DEAD OR ALIVE** *Def Jam 5744052* 2PAC & SNOOP DOGGY DOGG	16		2
3 May 97	**VAPORS** *Interscope IND 95530*	18		1
20 Sep 97	**WE JUST WANNA PARTY WITH YOU** *Columbia 6649902* SNOOP DOGGY DOGG FEATURING JD	21		1
24 Jan 98	**THA DOGGFATHER** *Interscope IND 95550*	36		1
12 Dec 98	**COME AND GET WITH ME** *Elektra E 3787CD* KEITH SWEAT FEATURING SNOOP DOGG	58		
25 Mar 00	**STILL DRE** *Interscope 4972862* DR DRE FEATURING SNOOP DOGGY DOGG	6		6
3 Feb 01	**THE NEXT EPISODE** *Interscope 4974762* DR DRE FEATURING SNOOP DOGGY DOGG	3		7
17 Mar 01	**X** *Epic 6709072* XZIBIT FEATURING SNOOP DOOG	14		4
28 Apr 01	**SNOOP DOGG** *Priority PTYCD 134*	13		3
30 Nov 02	**FROM THA CHUUUCH TO DA PALACE** *Priority 5516102*	27		2
1 Mar 03	**THE STREETS** *Def Jam 0779852* WC FEATURING SNOOP DOGG & NATE DOGG	48		
5 Apr 03	**BEAUTIFUL** *Capitol CDCL 842* SNOOP DOGG FEATURING PHARRELL	23		4
14 Feb 04	**THE NEXT EPISODE** *Interscope 4974762* DR DRE FEATURING SNOOP DOGGY DOGG	58		
14 Aug 04	**I WANNA THANK YOU** *J Records 82876624782* ANGIE STONE FEATURING SNOOP DOGG	31		1
11 Dec 04	**DROP IT LIKE IT'S HOT** *Geffen 2103461* SNOOP DOGG FEATURING PHARRELL ★	10		8
5 Mar 05	**LET'S GET BLOWN** *Geffen 9880425* SNOOP DOGG FEATURING PHARRELL	13		3
7 May 05	**SIGNS** *Geffen 9881782* SNOOP DOGG FEATURING CHARLIE WILSON & JUSTIN TIMBERLAKE	2		10
27 Aug 05	**UPS AND DOWN** *Geffen 9883732*	36		1
1 Jul 06	**BUTTONS** *A&M 1700854* PUSSYCAT DOLLS FEATURING SNOOP DOGG	3		9
28 Oct 06	**GANGSTA WALK** *All Around The World CDGLOBE565* COOLIO FEATURING SNOOP DOGG	67		
16 Dec 06	**THAT'S THAT S****** *Geffen 1717453* SNOOP DOGG FEATURING R KELLY	38		1
13 Jan 07	**I WANNA LOVE YOU** *Universal 1722994* AKON FEATURING SNOOP DOGGY DOGG	3		14

SNOW Canadian rapper

Date	Title	Peak	Wks No.1	Wks Top 40
13 Mar 93	**INFORMER** *East West America A 8436CD* ○ ★	2		14
5 Jun 93	**GIRL I'VE BEEN HURT** *East West America A 8417CD*	48		
4 Sep 93	**UHH IN YOU** *Atlantic A 8378CD*	67		

MARK SNOW US composer/pianist

Date	Title	Peak	Wks No.1	Wks Top 40
30 Mar 96	**THE X FILES** *Warner Brothers W 0341CD* ○	2		11

PHOEBE SNOW US singer

Date	Title	Peak	Wks No.1	Wks Top 40
6 Jan 79	**EVERY NIGHT** *CBS 6842*	37		3

SNOW PATROL UK group

Date	Title / Label	Peak Position	Weeks at No.1	Weeks in Top 40
27 Sep 03	**SPITTING GAMES** *Polydor 9809350*	54		
7 Feb 04	**RUN** *Fiction/Polydor 9816353*	5		6
24 Apr 04	**CHOCOLATE** *Fiction/Polydor 9866355*	24		2
24 Jul 04	**SPITTING GAMES** *Fiction/Polydor 9867126*	23		2
6 Nov 04	**HOW TO BE DEAD** *Polydor 9868777*	39		1
29 Apr 06	**YOU'RE ALL I HAVE** *Fiction 9853867*	7		7
29 Jul 06	**CHASING CARS** *Fiction 1704397*	6		17
18 Nov 06	**SET THE FIRE TO THE THIRD BAR** *Fiction 1714673* SNOW PATROL FEATURING MARTHA WAINWRIGHT	18		6
13 Jan 07	**CHASING CARS** *Fiction 1704397*	9		13
10 Feb 07	**OPEN YOUR EYES** *Fiction/Polydor 1723992*	26		2
12 May 07	**SIGNAL FIRE** *Fiction/Polydor 1734375*	4		6

SNOWMEN UK group

Date	Title / Label	Peak Position	Weeks at No.1	Weeks in Top 40
12 Dec 81	**HOKEY COKEY** *Stiff ODB 1*	18		6
18 Dec 82	**XMAS PARTY** *Solid STOP 006*	44		

SNUG UK group

Date	Title / Label	Peak Position	Weeks at No.1	Weeks in Top 40
18 Apr 98	**BEATNIK GIRL** *WEA 151CDX*	55		

SO UK group

Date	Title / Label	Peak Position	Weeks at No.1	Weeks in Top 40
13 Feb 88	**ARE YOU SURE?** *Parlophone R 6173*	62		

SO SOLID CREW UK group

Date	Title / Label	Peak Position	Weeks at No.1	Weeks in Top 40
18 Aug 01	**21 SECONDS** *Relentless RELENT 16CD*	1	1	11
17 Nov 01	**THEY DON'T KNOW** *Relentless RELENT 26CD*	3		4
19 Jan 02	**HATERS** *Relentless/Independiente RELENT 23CD* SO SOLID CREW PRESENTS MR SHABZ	8		5
20 Apr 02	**RIDE WID US** *Relentless ISOM 55SMS*	19		2
27 Sep 03	**BROKEN SILENCE** *Independiente ISOM 71MS*	9		3
3 Apr 04	**SO GRIMEY** *Independiente ISOM 82MS*	62		

S.O.A.P. Danish production duo

Date	Title / Label	Peak Position	Weeks at No.1	Weeks in Top 40
25 Jul 98	**THIS IS HOW WE PARTY** *Columbia 6661295*	36		1

SOAPY UK instrumental and production duo

Date	Title / Label	Peak Position	Weeks at No.1	Weeks in Top 40
14 Sep 96	**HORNY AS FUNK** *WEA 074CD*	35		1

GINO SOCCIO Canadian singer and keyboard player

Date	Title / Label	Peak Position	Weeks at No.1	Weeks in Top 40
28 Apr 79	**DANCER** *Warner Brothers K 17357*	46		

SODA CLUB UK production duo

Date	Title / Label	Peak Position	Weeks at No.1	Weeks in Top 40
9 Nov 02	**TAKE MY BREATH AWAY** *Concept CDCON 33* SODA CLUB FEATURING HANNAH ALETHA	16		2
8 Mar 03	**HEAVEN IS A PLACE ON EARTH** *Concept CDCON 39* SODA CLUB FEATURING HANNAH ALETHA	13		3
23 Aug 03	**KEEP LOVE TOGETHER** *Concept CDCON 44X* SODA CLUB FEATURING ANDREA ANATOLA	31		1
28 Aug 04	**AIN'T NO LOVE (AIN'T NO USE)** *Concept CDCON58X* SODA CLUB FEATURING ASHLEY JADE	40		1

SOFT CELL UK duo

Date	Title / Label	Peak Position	Weeks at No.1	Weeks in Top 40
1 Aug 81	**TAINTED LOVE** *Some Bizzare BZS 2*	1	2	13
14 Nov 81	**BED SITTER** *Some Bizzare BZS 6*	4		11
6 Feb 82	**SAY HELLO WAVE GOODBYE** *Some Bizzare BZS 7*	3		8
29 May 82	**TORCH** *Some Bizzare BZS 9*	2		7
21 Aug 82	**WHAT** *Some Bizzare BZS 11*	3		7
4 Dec 82	**WHERE THE HEART IS** *Some Bizzare BZS 16*	21		6
5 Mar 83	**NUMBERS/BARRIERS** *Some Bizzare BZS 17*	25		3
24 Sep 83	**SOUL INSIDE** *Some Bizzare BZS 20*	16		4
25 Feb 84	**DOWN IN THE SUBWAY** *Some Bizzare BZS 22*	24		4
9 Feb 85	**TAINTED LOVE** *Some Bizzare BZS 2*	43		
23 Mar 91	**SAY HELLO WAVE GOODBYE '91** *Mercury SOFT 1* SOFT CELL/MARC ALMOND	38		2
18 May 91	**TAINTED LOVE** *Mercury SOFT 2* SOFT CELL/MARC ALMOND	5		7
28 Sep 02	**MONOCULTURE** *Cooking Vinyl FRYCD 132X*	52		
8 Feb 03	**THE NIGHT** *Cooking Vinyl FRYCD 135X*	39		1

SOHO UK group

Date	Title / Label	Peak Position	Weeks at No.1	Weeks in Top 40
5 May 90	**HIPPY CHICK** *Savage 7SAV 106*	67		
19 Jan 91	**HIPPY CHICK** *Savage 7SAV 106*	8		7
9 Nov 91	**BORN TO BE ALIVE** *MCA MCS 1578* ADAMSKI & SOHO	51		

SOHO DOLLS UK group

Date	Title / Label	Peak Position	Weeks at No.1	Weeks in Top 40
27 Nov 04	**PRINCE HARRY** *Poptones MC5096SCD*	57		

SOIL US group

Date	Title / Label	Peak Position	Weeks at No.1	Weeks in Top 40
9 Nov 02	**HALO** *J Records 74321970132*	74		
5 Jun 04	**REDEFINE** *J Records 82876618512*	68		

SOLAR STONE UK production duo

Date	Title / Label	Peak Position	Weeks at No.1	Weeks in Top 40
21 Feb 98	**THE IMPRESSIONS EP** *Hooj Choons HOOJCD 57*	75		
6 Nov 99	**SEVEN CITIES** *Hooj Choons HOOJ 85CD*	39		1
28 Sep 02	**SEVEN CITIES (REMIX)** *Lost Language LOST 018CD*	44		

SOLID GOLD CHARTBUSTERS UK production group

Date	Title / Label	Peak Position	Weeks at No.1	Weeks in Top 40
25 Dec 99	**I WANNA 1-2-1 WITH YOU** *Virgin VSCDT 1765*	62		

SOLID HARMONIE UK/US group

Date	Title / Label	Peak Position	Weeks at No.1	Weeks in Top 40
31 Jan 98	**I'LL BE THERE FOR YOU** *Jive JIVECD 437*	18		2
18 Apr 98	**I WANT YOU TO WANT ME** *Jive JIVECD 452*	16		2
15 Aug 98	**I WANNA LOVE YOU** *Jive 0521742*	20		1
21 Nov 98	**TO LOVE ONCE AGAIN** *Jive 0522472*	55		

SOLID SESSIONS Dutch production duo

Date	Title / Label	Peak Position	Weeks at No.1	Weeks in Top 40
14 Sep 02	**JANEIRO** *Positiva CDTIV 175*	47		

SOLITAIRE UK production duo

Date	Title / Label	Peak Position	Weeks at No.1	Weeks in Top 40
29 Nov 03	**I LIKE LOVE (I LOVE LOVE)** *Susu CDSUSU21*	57		
26 Mar 05	**YOU GOT THE LOVE** *Susu CDSUSU30*	63		

SOLO UK producer

Date	Title / Label	Peak Position	Weeks at No.1	Weeks in Top 40
20 Jul 91	**RAINBOW (SAMPLE FREE)** *Reverb RVBT 003*	59		
18 Jan 92	**COME ON!** *Reverb RVBT 008*	75		
11 Sep 93	**COME ON! (REMIX)** *Stoatin' STOAT 003CD*	63		

SOLO (US) US group

Date	Title / Label	Peak Position	Weeks at No.1	Weeks in Top 40
3 Feb 96	**HEAVEN** *Perspective 5875212*	35		1
30 Mar 96	**WHERE DO U WANT ME TO PUT IT** *Perspective 5875312*	45		

SAL SOLO UK singer

Date	Title / Label	Peak Position	Weeks at No.1	Weeks in Top 40
15 Dec 84	**SAN DAMIANO (HEART AND SOUL)** *MCA 930*	15		6
6 Apr 85	**MUSIC AND YOU** *MCA 946* SAL SOLO WITH THE LONDON COMMUNITY GOSPEL CHOIR	52		

SOLU MUSIC US production duo

Date	Title / Label	Peak Position	Weeks at No.1	Weeks in Top 40
17 Jun 06	**FADE** *Ministry Of Sound HK19CDS* SOLU MUSIC FEATURING KIMBLEE	18		3

MARTIN SOLVEIG French producer

Date	Title / Label	Peak Position	Weeks at No.1	Weeks in Top 40
24 Apr 04	**ROCKING MUSIC** *Defected DFTD082CDS*	35		1
26 Jun 04	**I'M A GOOD MAN** *Defected DFTD091CDS*	57		
6 Aug 05	**EVERYBODY** *Defected DFTD107CDS*	22		3
11 Feb 06	**JEALOUSY** *Defected DFTD121CDX*	62		

BELOUIS SOME UK singer

Date	Title / Label	Peak Position	Weeks at No.1	Weeks in Top 40
27 Apr 85	**IMAGINATION** *Parlophone R 6097*	50		
18 Jan 86	**IMAGINATION** *Parlophone R 1986*	17		7
12 Apr 86	**SOME PEOPLE** *Parlophone R 6130*	33		3

Silver-selling ○ Gold-selling ● Platinum-selling ⊛ US No.1 ★ — Peak Position · Weeks at No.1 · Weeks in Top 40

Date	Title	Peak Position	Weeks at No.1	Weeks in Top 40
16 May 87	**LET IT BE WITH YOU** *Parlophone R 6154*	53		

JIMMY SOMERVILLE UK singer

Date	Title	Peak Position	Weeks at No.1	Weeks in Top 40
11 Nov 89	**COMMENT TE DIRE ADIEU** *London LON 241* JIMMY SOMERVILLE FEATURING JUNE MILES-KINGSTON	14		6
13 Jan 90	**YOU MAKE ME FEEL (MIGHTY REAL)** *London LON 249*	5		7
17 Mar 90	**READ MY LIPS (ENOUGH IS ENOUGH)** *London LON 254*	26		4
3 Nov 90	**TO LOVE SOMEBODY** *London LON 281*	8		7
2 Feb 91	**SMALLTOWN BOY (REMIX)** *London LON 287* JIMMY SOMERVILLE WITH BRONSKI BEAT	32		2
10 Aug 91	**RUN FROM LOVE** *London LON 301*	52		
28 Jan 95	**HEARTBEAT** *London LONCD 358*	24		2
27 May 95	**HURT SO GOOD** *London LONCD 364*	15		4
28 Oct 95	**BY YOUR SIDE** *London LONCD 372*	41		
13 Sep 97	**DARK SKY** *Gut CXGUT 11*	66		

SOMETHIN' FOR THE PEOPLE US group

Date	Title	Peak Position	Weeks at No.1	Weeks in Top 40
7 Feb 98	**MY LOVE IS THE SHHH!** *Warner Brothers W 0427CD* SOMETHIN' FOR THE PEOPLE FEATURING TRINA & TAMARA	64		

SOMETHING CORPORATE US group

Date	Title	Peak Position	Weeks at No.1	Weeks in Top 40
29 Mar 03	**PUNK ROCK PRINCESS** *MCA MCSTD 40315*	33		1
12 Jul 03	**IF YOU C JORDAN** *MCA MCSTD 40324*	68		

SOMORE US production group

Date	Title	Peak Position	Weeks at No.1	Weeks in Top 40
24 Jan 98	**I REFUSE (WHAT YOU WANT)** *XL Recordings XLS 93CD* SOMORE FEATURING DAMON TRUEITT	21		1

SON OF DORK UK group

Date	Title	Peak Position	Weeks at No.1	Weeks in Top 40
19 Nov 05	**TICKET OUTTA LOSERVILLE** *Mercury 9875191*	3		4
28 Jan 06	**EDDIE'S SONG** *Mercury 9876652*	10		2

SONGSTRESS US production duo

Date	Title	Peak Position	Weeks at No.1	Weeks in Top 40
27 Feb 99	**SEE LINE WOMAN '99** *Locked On LOX 106CD*	64		

SONIA UK singer

Date	Title	Peak Position	Weeks at No.1	Weeks in Top 40
24 Jun 89	**YOU'LL NEVER STOP ME LOVING YOU** *Chrysalis CHS 3385*	1	2	11
7 Oct 89	**CAN'T FORGET YOU** *Chrysalis CHS 3419*	17		4
9 Dec 89	**LISTEN TO YOUR HEART** *Chrysalis CHS 3465*	10		8
7 Apr 90	**COUNTING EVERY MINUTE** *Chrysalis CHS 3492*	16		5
23 Jun 90	**YOU'VE GOT A FRIEND** *Jive CHILD 90* BIG FUN & SONIA FEATURING GARY BARNACLE	14		5
25 Aug 90	**END OF THE WORLD** *Chrysalis CHS 3557*	18		5
1 Jun 91	**ONLY FOOLS (NEVER FALL IN LOVE)** *IQ ZB 44613*	10		7
31 Aug 91	**BE YOUNG BE FOOLISH BE HAPPY** *IQ ZB 44935*	22		4
16 Nov 91	**YOU TO ME ARE EVERYTHING** *IQ ZB 45121*	13		4
12 Sep 92	**BOOGIE NIGHTS** *Arista 74321113467*	30		2
1 May 93	**BETTER THE DEVIL YOU KNOW** *Arista 74321146872*	15		6
30 Jul 94	**HOPELESSLY DEVOTED TO YOU** *Cockney COCCD 2*	61		

SONIC SOLUTION UK/Belgian production duo

Date	Title	Peak Position	Weeks at No.1	Weeks in Top 40
4 Apr 92	**BEATSTIME** *R&S RSUK 11*	59		

SONIC SURFERS Dutch production duo

Date	Title	Peak Position	Weeks at No.1	Weeks in Top 40
20 Mar 93	**TAKE ME UP** *A&M AMCD 210* SONIC SURFERS FEATURING JOCELYN BROWN	61		
30 Jul 94	**DON'T GIVE IT UP** *Brilliant CDBRIL 6*	54		

SONIC YOUTH US group

Date	Title	Peak Position	Weeks at No.1	Weeks in Top 40
11 Jul 92	**1** *DGC DGCS 11*	28		2
7 Nov 92	**YOUTH AGAINST FASCISM** *Geffen GFS 26*	52		
3 Apr 93	**SUGAR KANE** *Geffen GFSTD 37*	26		2
7 May 94	**BULL IN THE HEATHER** *Geffen GFSTD 72*	24		1
10 Sep 94	**SUPERSTAR** *A&M 5807932*	45		
11 Jul 98	**SUNDAY** *Geffen GFSTD 22332*	72		

SONIQUE UK singer

Date	Title	Peak Position	Weeks at No.1	Weeks in Top 40
13 Jun 98	**I PUT A SPELL ON YOU** *Serious SERR 001CD*	36		1
5 Dec 98	**IT FEELS SO GOOD** *Serious SERR 004CD1*	24		1
3 Jun 00	**IT FEELS SO GOOD (REMIX)** *Universal MCSTD 40233* ⊛	1	3	14
16 Sep 00	**SKY** *Universal MCSTD 40240*	2		8
9 Dec 00	**I PUT A SPELL ON YOU** *Universal MCSTD 40245*	8		7
31 May 03	**CAN'T MAKE MY MIND UP** *Serious 9807217*	17		3
13 Sep 03	**ALIVE** *Serious 9811500*	70		

SONNY US singer

Date	Title	Peak Position	Weeks at No.1	Weeks in Top 40
19 Aug 65	**LAUGH AT ME** *Atlantic AT 4038*	9		9

SONNY & CHER US duo

Date	Title	Peak Position	Weeks at No.1	Weeks in Top 40
12 Aug 65	**I GOT YOU BABE** *Atlantic AT 4035* ★	1	2	12
16 Sep 65	**BABY DON'T GO** *Reprise R 20309*	11		9
21 Oct 65	**BUT YOU'RE MINE** *Atlantic AT 4047*	17		6
17 Feb 66	**WHAT NOW MY LOVE** *Atlantic AT 4069*	13		9
30 Jun 66	**HAVE I STAYED TOO LONG** *Atlantic 584 018*	42		
8 Sep 66	**LITTLE MAN** *Atlantic 584 040*	4		10
17 Nov 66	**LIVING FOR YOU** *Atlantic 584 057*	44		
2 Feb 67	**THE BEAT GOES ON** *Atlantic 584 078*	29		4
15 Jan 72	**ALL I EVER NEED IS YOU** *MCA MU 1145*	8		10
22 May 93	**I GOT YOU BABE** *Epic 6592402*	66		

SONO German production duo

Date	Title	Peak Position	Weeks at No.1	Weeks in Top 40
16 Jun 01	**KEEP CONTROL** *Code Blue BLU 020CD1*	66		

SON'Z OF A LOOP DA LOOP ERA UK producer

Date	Title	Peak Position	Weeks at No.1	Weeks in Top 40
15 Feb 92	**FAR OUT** *Suburban Base SUBBASE 008*	36		1
17 Oct 92	**PEACE + LOVEISM** *Suburban Base SUBBASE 14*	60		

SONS & DAUGHTERS UK group

Date	Title	Peak Position	Weeks at No.1	Weeks in Top 40
16 Oct 04	**JOHNNY CASH** *Domino RUG186CD*	68		
4 Jun 05	**DANCE ME IN** *Domino RUG196CD*	40		1
27 Aug 05	**TASTE THE LAST GIRL** *Domino RUG206CD*	75		

SOOPA HOOPZ UK group

Date	Title	Peak Position	Weeks at No.1	Weeks in Top 40
16 Oct 04	**SOOPA HOOPZ** *Sniper Alley SNIPER001* SOOPA HOOPZ FEATURING QPR MASSIVE	54		

SORROWS UK group

Date	Title	Peak Position	Weeks at No.1	Weeks in Top 40
16 Sep 65	**TAKE A HEART** *Piccadilly 7N 35260*	21		6

S.O.S. BAND US group

Date	Title	Peak Position	Weeks at No.1	Weeks in Top 40
19 Jul 80	**TAKE YOUR TIME (DO IT RIGHT) PART 1** *Tabu TBU 8564*	51		
26 Feb 83	**GROOVIN' (THAT'S WHAT WE'RE DOIN')** *Tabu TBU A 3120*	72		
7 Apr 84	**JUST BE GOOD TO ME** *Tabu A 3626*	13		7
4 Aug 84	**JUST THE WAY YOU LIKE IT** *Tabu A 4621*	32		3
13 Oct 84	**WEEKEND GIRL** *Tabu A 4785*	51		
29 Mar 86	**THE FINEST** *Tabu A 6997*	17		7
5 Jul 86	**BORROWED LOVE** *Tabu A 7241*	50		
2 May 87	**NO LIES** *Tabu 6504447*	64		

AARON SOUL UK singer

Date	Title	Peak Position	Weeks at No.1	Weeks in Top 40
2 Jun 01	**RING RING RING** *Def Soul 5689042*	14		2

DAVID SOUL US singer/actor

Date	Title	Peak Position	Weeks at No.1	Weeks in Top 40
18 Dec 76	**DON'T GIVE UP ON US BABY** *Private Stock PVT 84* ⊛ ★	1	4	16
26 Mar 77	**GOING IN WITH MY EYES OPEN** *Private Stock PVT 99* ○	2		8
27 Aug 77	**SILVER LADY** *Private Stock PVT 115* ●	1	3	14
17 Dec 77	**LET'S HAVE A QUIET NIGHT IN** *Private Stock PVT 130*	8		9
27 May 78	**IT SURE BRINGS OUT THE LOVE IN YOUR EYES** *Private Stock PVT 137*	12		8

JIMMY SOUL US singer

Date	Title / Label	Peak Position	Weeks at No.1	Weeks in Top 40
11 Jul 63	**IF YOU WANNA BE HAPPY** *Stateside SS 178* ★	39		1
15 Jun 91	**IF YOU WANNA BE HAPPY** *Epic 6569647*	68		

SOUL ASYLUM US group

Date	Title / Label	Peak Position	Weeks at No.1	Weeks in Top 40
19 Jun 93	**RUNAWAY TRAIN** *Columbia 6593902*	37		3
4 Sep 93	**SOMEBODY TO SHOVE** *Columbia 6596492*	34		2
13 Nov 93	**RUNAWAY TRAIN** *Columbia 6593902*	7		9
22 Jan 94	**BLACK GOLD** *Columbia 6598442*	26		2
26 Mar 94	**SOMEBODY TO SHOVE** *Columbia 6602245*	32		1
15 Jul 95	**MISERY** *Columbia 6621092*	30		1
2 Dec 95	**JUST LIKE ANYONE** *Columbia 6624785*	52		

SOUL AVENGERZ UK production duo

Date	Title / Label	Peak Position	Weeks at No.1	Weeks in Top 40
14 Oct 06	**DON'T LET THE MORNING COME** *Positiva CDTIVS244* SOUL AVENGERZ FEATURING JAVINE	49		

SOUL BROTHERS UK group

Date	Title / Label	Peak Position	Weeks at No.1	Weeks in Top 40
22 Apr 65	**I KEEP RINGING MY BABY** *Decca F 12116*	43		

SOUL CENTRAL UK production duo

Date	Title / Label	Peak Position	Weeks at No.1	Weeks in Top 40
22 Jan 05	**STRINGS OF LIFE (STRONGER ON MY OWN)** *Defected DFTD094CDS* SOUL CENTRAL FEATURING KATHY BROWN	6		4

SOUL CITY ORCHESTRA UK production group

Date	Title / Label	Peak Position	Weeks at No.1	Weeks in Top 40
11 Dec 93	**IT'S JURASSIC** *London JURCD 1*	70		

SOUL CONTROL German duo

Date	Title / Label	Peak Position	Weeks at No.1	Weeks in Top 40
18 Sep 04	**CHOCOLATE (CHOCO CHOCO)** *Tug CDSNOG12*	25		1

SOUL FAMILY SENSATION UK/US group

Date	Title / Label	Peak Position	Weeks at No.1	Weeks in Top 40
11 May 91	**I DON'T EVEN KNOW IF I SHOULD CALL YOU BABY** *One Little Indian 47 TP7*	49		

SOUL FOR REAL US group

Date	Title / Label	Peak Position	Weeks at No.1	Weeks in Top 40
8 Jul 95	**CANDY RAIN** *Uptown MCSTD 2052*	23		1
23 Mar 96	**EVERY LITTLE THING I DO** *Uptown MCSTD 48005*	31		1

SOUL II SOUL UK group

Date	Title / Label	Peak Position	Weeks at No.1	Weeks in Top 40
21 May 88	**FAIRPLAY** *10 TEN 228* SOUL II SOUL FEATURING ROSE WINDROSS	63		
17 Sep 88	**FEEL FREE** *10 TEN 239* SOUL II SOUL FEATURING DO'REEN	64		
18 Mar 89	**KEEP ON MOVING** *10 TEN 263* SOUL II SOUL FEATURING CARON WHEELER	5		10
10 Jun 89	**BACK TO LIFE (HOWEVER DO YOU WANT ME)** *10 TEN 265* SOUL II SOUL FEATURING CARON WHEELER ●	1	4	11
9 Dec 89	**GET A LIFE** *10 TEN 284* ●	3		10
5 May 90	**A DREAM'S A DREAM** *10 TEN 300*	6		5
24 Nov 90	**MISSING YOU** *10 TEN 345* SOUL II SOUL FEATURING KYM MAZELLE	22		3
4 Apr 92	**JOY** *10 TEN 350*	4		5
13 Jun 92	**MOVE ME NO MOUNTAIN** *10 TEN 400* SOUL II SOUL, LEAD VOCALS KOFI	31		2
26 Sep 92	**JUST RIGHT** *10 TEN 410*	38		1
6 Nov 93	**WISH** *Virgin VSCDG 1480*	24		2
22 Jul 95	**LOVE ENUFF** *Virgin VSCDT 1527*	12		4
21 Oct 95	**I CARE** *Virgin VSCDT 1560*	17		2
19 Oct 96	**KEEP ON MOVING** *Virgin VSCDT 1612* SOUL II SOUL FEATURING CARON WHEELER	31		1
30 Aug 97	**REPRESENT** *Island CID 668*	39		1
8 Nov 97	**PLEASURE DOME** *Island CID 669*	51		

SOUL PROVIDERS UK/US production duo

Date	Title / Label	Peak Position	Weeks at No.1	Weeks in Top 40
14 Jul 01	**RISE** *AM:PM CDAMPM 147* SOUL PROVIDERS FEATURING MICHELLE SHELLERS	59		

S.O.U.L. S.Y.S.T.E.M. US group

Date	Title / Label	Peak Position	Weeks at No.1	Weeks in Top 40
16 Jan 93	**IT'S GONNA BE A LOVELY DAY** *Arista 74321125692* S.O.U.L. S.Y.S.T.E.M. INTRODUCING MICHELLE VISAGE	17		3

SOUL U*NIQUE UK group

Date	Title / Label	Peak Position	Weeks at No.1	Weeks in Top 40
19 Feb 00	**BE MY FRIEND** *M&J MAJCD 2*	53		
29 Jul 00	**3IL (THRILL)** *M&J MAJCD 3*	66		

SOULED OUT Italian/US/UK group

Date	Title / Label	Peak Position	Weeks at No.1	Weeks in Top 40
9 May 92	**IN MY LIFE** *Columbia 6578367*	75		

SOULJA BOY US singer

Date	Title / Label	Peak Position	Weeks at No.1	Weeks in Top 40
24 Nov 07	**CRANK THAT (SOULJA BOY)** *Interscope 1755233* ★	2		18

SOULSEARCHER UK production duo

Date	Title / Label	Peak Position	Weeks at No.1	Weeks in Top 40
13 Feb 99	**CAN'T GET ENOUGH** *Defected DEFECT 1CDS*	8		4
8 Apr 00	**DO IT TO ME AGAIN** *Defected DEFECT 15CDS*	32		1

SOULWAX Belgian group

Date	Title / Label	Peak Position	Weeks at No.1	Weeks in Top 40
25 Mar 00	**CONVERSATION INTERCOM** *Pias Recordings PIASB 018CD*	65		
24 Jun 00	**MUCH AGAINST EVERYONE'S ADVICE** *Pias Recordings PIASB 026CD*	56		
30 Sep 00	**TOO MANY DJ'S** *Pias Recordings PIASB 036CD*	40		1
3 Mar 01	**CONVERSATION INTERCOM (REMIX)** *Pias Recordings PIASB 046CD*	50		
21 Aug 04	**ANY MINUTE NOW** *Pias Recordings PIASB 126CDM*	34		1
29 Jan 05	**E TALKING** *PIAS PIASB136CD*	27		1
9 Jul 05	**EXCUSE** *PIAS PIASB156CD*	35		1

SOUND BLUNTZ Canadian production group

Date	Title / Label	Peak Position	Weeks at No.1	Weeks in Top 40
30 Nov 02	**BILLIE JEAN** *Incentive CENT 51CDS*	32		1

SOUND DE-ZIGN Dutch production duo

Date	Title / Label	Peak Position	Weeks at No.1	Weeks in Top 40
14 Apr 01	**HAPPINESS** *NuLife 74321844002*	19		4

SOUND FACTORY Swedish duo

Date	Title / Label	Peak Position	Weeks at No.1	Weeks in Top 40
5 Jun 93	**2 THE RHYTHM** *Logic 74321149422*	72		

SOUND 5 UK duo

Date	Title / Label	Peak Position	Weeks at No.1	Weeks in Top 40
24 Apr 99	**ALA KABOO** *Gut CDGUT 23*	69		

SOUND 9418 UK singer

Date	Title / Label	Peak Position	Weeks at No.1	Weeks in Top 40
7 Feb 76	**IN THE MOOD** *UK 121*	46		

SOUND OF ONE US duo

Date	Title / Label	Peak Position	Weeks at No.1	Weeks in Top 40
20 Nov 93	**AS I AM** *Cooltempo CDCOOL 280* SOUND OF ONE FEATURING GLADEZZ	65		

SOUNDBWOY ENT UK group

Date	Title / Label	Peak Position	Weeks at No.1	Weeks in Top 40
29 Apr 06	**NEVER WANNA SAY** *Smoove SMOOVE05CDS* SOUNDBWOY ENT FEATURING DOCTOR	18		2

SOUNDGARDEN US group

Date	Title / Label	Peak Position	Weeks at No.1	Weeks in Top 40
11 Apr 92	**JESUS CHRIST POSE** *A&M AM 862*	30		2
20 Jun 92	**RUSTY CAGE** *A&M AM 874*	41		
21 Nov 92	**OUTSHINED** *A&M AM 0102*	50		
26 Feb 94	**SPOONMAN** *A&M 5805392*	20		1
30 Apr 94	**THE DAY I TRIED TO LIVE** *A&M 5805952*	42		
20 Aug 94	**BLACK HOLE SUN** *A&M 5807532*	12		4
28 Jan 95	**FELL ON BLACK DAYS** *A&M 5809472*	24		1
18 May 96	**PRETTY NOOSE** *A&M 5816202*	14		2
28 Sep 96	**BURDEN IN MY HAND** *A&M 5818552*	33		1
28 Dec 96	**BLOW UP THE OUTSIDE WORLD** *A&M 5819862*	40		1

Silver-selling · Gold-selling · Platinum-selling · US No.1 ★ · Peak Position · Weeks at No.1 · Weeks in Top 40

SOUNDMAN UK production group

Date	Title / Label	Peak Position	Weeks at No.1	Weeks in Top 40
25 Feb 95	**GREATER LOVE** *Sound Of Underground SOJURCD 016* SOUNDMAN & DON LLOYDIE WITH ELISABETH TROY	49		

SOUNDS INCORPORATED UK group

Date	Title / Label	Peak Position	Weeks at No.1	Weeks in Top 40
23 Apr 64	**THE SPARTANS** *Columbia DB 7239*	30		5
30 Jul 64	**SPANISH HARLEM** *Columbia DB 7321*	35		2

SOUNDS NICE UK group

Date	Title / Label	Peak Position	Weeks at No.1	Weeks in Top 40
6 Sep 69	**LOVE AT FIRST SIGHT (JE T'AIME...MOI NON PLUS)** *Parlophone R 5797*	18		8

SOUNDS OF BLACKNESS US choir

Date	Title / Label	Peak Position	Weeks at No.1	Weeks in Top 40
22 Jun 91	**OPTIMISTIC** *Perspective PERSS 786*	45		
28 Sep 91	**THE PRESSURE PART 1** *Perspective PERSS 816*	71		
15 Feb 92	**OPTIMISTIC** *Perspective PERSS 849*	28		3
25 Apr 92	**THE PRESSURE PART 1 (REMIX)** *Perspective PERSS 867*	49		
8 May 93	**I'M GOING ALL THE WAY** *Perspective 5874252*	27		2
26 Mar 94	**I BELIEVE** *A&M 5874512*	17		2
2 Jul 94	**GLORYLAND** *Mercury MERCD 404* DARYL HALL & THE SOUNDS OF BLACKNESS	36		2
20 Aug 94	**EVERYTHING IS GONNA BE ALRIGHT** *A&M 5874672*	29		2
14 Jan 95	**I'M GOING ALL THE WAY** *A&M 5874832*	14		2
7 Jun 97	**SPIRIT** *Perspective 5822312* SOUNDS OF BLACKNESS FEATURING CRAIG MACK	35		1
14 Feb 98	**THE PRESSURE (2ND REMIX)** *AM:PM 5824872*	46		

SOUNDS ORCHESTRAL UK orchestra

Date	Title / Label	Peak Position	Weeks at No.1	Weeks in Top 40
3 Dec 64	**CAST YOUR FATE TO THE WIND** *Piccadilly 7N 35206*	5		14
8 Jul 65	**MOONGLOW** *Piccadilly 7N 35248*	43		

SOUNDSATION UK production group

Date	Title / Label	Peak Position	Weeks at No.1	Weeks in Top 40
14 Jan 95	**PEACE AND JOY** *ffrreedom TABCD 224*	48		

SOUNDSCAPE UK production group

Date	Title / Label	Peak Position	Weeks at No.1	Weeks in Top 40
14 Feb 98	**DUBPLATE CULTURE** *Satellite 74321552002*	61		

SOUNDSOURCE UK/Swedish production group

Date	Title / Label	Peak Position	Weeks at No.1	Weeks in Top 40
11 Jan 92	**TAKE ME UP** *ffrr FX 177*	62		

SOUNDTRACK OF OUR LIVES Swedish group

Date	Title / Label	Peak Position	Weeks at No.1	Weeks in Top 40
12 Mar 05	**HEADING FOR A BREAKDOWN** *WEA WEA383CD*	70		

SOUP DRAGONS UK group

Date	Title / Label	Peak Position	Weeks at No.1	Weeks in Top 40
20 Jun 87	**CAN'T TAKE NO FOR AN ANSWER** *Raw TV RTV 3*	65		
5 Sep 87	**SOFT AS YOUR FACE** *Raw TV RTV 4*	66		
14 Jul 90	**I'M FREE** *Raw TV RTV 9* SOUP DRAGONS FEATURING JUNIOR REID	5		11
20 Oct 90	**MOTHER UNIVERSE** *Big Life BLR 30*	26		4
11 Apr 92	**DIVINE THING** *Big Life BLR 68*	53		

SOURCE UK producer

Date	Title / Label	Peak Position	Weeks at No.1	Weeks in Top 40
2 Feb 91	**YOU GOT THE LOVE** *Truelove TLOVE 7001* SOURCE FEATURING CANDI STATON	4		10
26 Dec 92	**ROCK THE HOUSE** *React 12REACT 12* SOURCE FEATURING NICOLE	63		
1 Mar 97	**YOU GOT THE LOVE (REMIX)** *React CDREACT 89* SOURCE FEATURING CANDI STATON	3		5
23 Aug 97	**CLOUDS** *XL Recordings XLS 83CD*	38		1
1 Jan 05	**YOU GOT THE LOVE (REMIX)** *ZYX GDC22218* SOURCE FEATURING CANDI STATON	60		
18 Feb 06	**YOU GOT THE LOVE (2ND REMIX)** *Positiva CDTIVS230* SOURCE FEATURING CANDI STATON	7		9

SOURMASH UK production group

Date	Title / Label	Peak Position	Weeks at No.1	Weeks in Top 40
23 Dec 00	**PILGRIMAGE/MESCALITO** *Hooj Choons HOOJ 102CD*	73		

SOUTH UK group

Date	Title / Label	Peak Position	Weeks at No.1	Weeks in Top 40
17 Mar 01	**PAINT THE SILENCE** *Mo Wax MWR 134CD*	69		
23 Aug 03	**LOOSEN YOUR HOLD** *Double Dragon DD 2010CD*	73		
3 Apr 04	**COLOURS IN WAVES** *Sanctuary SANXD249*	60		
14 Aug 04	**MOTIVELESS CRIME** *Sanctuary SANXD286*	72		

JOE SOUTH US singer

Date	Title / Label	Peak Position	Weeks at No.1	Weeks in Top 40
5 Mar 69	**GAMES PEOPLE PLAY** *Capitol CL 15579*	6		11

SOUTH ST. PLAYER US producer

Date	Title / Label	Peak Position	Weeks at No.1	Weeks in Top 40
2 Sep 00	**WHO KEEPS CHANGING YOUR MIND** *Cream 4CD*	49		

JERI SOUTHERN US singer/pianist

Date	Title / Label	Peak Position	Weeks at No.1	Weeks in Top 40
21 Jun 57	**FIRE DOWN BELOW** *Brunswick 05665*	22		3

SOUTHLANDERS UK group

Date	Title / Label	Peak Position	Weeks at No.1	Weeks in Top 40
22 Nov 57	**ALONE** *Decca F 10946*	17		10

SOUTHSIDE SPINNERS Dutch production duo

Date	Title / Label	Peak Position	Weeks at No.1	Weeks in Top 40
27 May 00	**LUVSTRUCK** *AM:PM CDAMPM 132*	9		4

SOUVERNANCE Dutch production duo

Date	Title / Label	Peak Position	Weeks at No.1	Weeks in Top 40
31 Aug 02	**HAVIN' A GOOD TIME** *Positiva CDTIV 174*	63		

SOUVLAKI UK producer

Date	Title / Label	Peak Position	Weeks at No.1	Weeks in Top 40
15 Feb 97	**INFERNO** *Wonderboy WBOYD 003*	24		1
8 Aug 98	**MY TIME** *Wonderboy WBOYD 009*	63		

SOVEREIGN COLLECTION UK orchestra

Date	Title / Label	Peak Position	Weeks at No.1	Weeks in Top 40
3 Apr 71	**MOZART 40** *Capitol CL 15676*	27		5

RED SOVINE US singer

Date	Title / Label	Peak Position	Weeks at No.1	Weeks in Top 40
13 Jun 81	**TEDDY BEAR** *Starday SD 142*	4		6

SOX UK group

Date	Title / Label	Peak Position	Weeks at No.1	Weeks in Top 40
15 Apr 95	**GO FOR THE HEART** *Living Beat LBECD 33*	47		

BOB B SOXX & THE BLUE JEANS US group

Date	Title / Label	Peak Position	Weeks at No.1	Weeks in Top 40
31 Jan 63	**ZIP-A-DEE-DOO-DAH** *London HLU 9646*	45		

KIM SOZZI US singer

Date	Title / Label	Peak Position	Weeks at No.1	Weeks in Top 40
9 Jun 07	**BREAK UP** *Substance SUBS25CDS*	23		2

SPACE French group

Date	Title / Label	Peak Position	Weeks at No.1	Weeks in Top 40
13 Aug 77	**MAGIC FLY** *Pye International 7N 25746*	2		11

SPACE UK group

Date	Title / Label	Peak Position	Weeks at No.1	Weeks in Top 40
6 Apr 96	**NEIGHBOURHOOD** *Gut CDGUT 1*	56		
8 Jun 96	**FEMALE OF THE SPECIES** *Gut CDGUT 2*	14		9
7 Sep 96	**ME AND YOU VERSUS THE WORLD** *Gut CXGUT 4*	9		4
2 Nov 96	**NEIGHBOURHOOD** *Gut GXGUT 5*	11		4
22 Feb 97	**DARK CLOUDS** *Gut CDGUT 6*	14		2
10 Jan 98	**AVENGING ANGELS** *Gut CDGUT 16*	6		5
7 Mar 98	**THE BALLAD OF TOM JONES** *Gut CDGUT 18* SPACE WITH CERYS OF CATATONIA	4		6
4 Jul 98	**BEGIN AGAIN** *Gut CDGUT 019*	21		2
5 Dec 98	**THE BAD DAYS EP** *Gut CDGUT 22*	20		2
8 Jul 00	**DIARY OF A WIMP** *Gut CDGUT 34*	49		
6 Mar 04	**SUBURBAN ROCK 'N' ROLL** *R&M Entertainment RAMCDS001*	67		

SPACE BABY UK producer

Date	Title	Peak Position	Weeks at No.1	Weeks in Top 40
8 Jul 95	**FREE YOUR MIND** *Hooj Choons HOOJ 34CD*	55		

SPACE BROTHERS UK production duo

Date	Title	Peak Position	Weeks at No.1	Weeks in Top 40
17 May 97	**SHINE** *Manifesto FESCD 23*	23		1
13 Dec 97	**FORGIVEN (I FEEL YOUR LOVE)** *Manifesto FESCD 36*	27		1
10 Jul 99	**LEGACY (SHOW ME LOVE)** *Manifesto FESCD 55*	31		1
9 Oct 99	**HEAVEN WILL COME** *Manifesto FESCD 61*	25		1
5 Feb 00	**SHINE 2000 (REMIX)** *Manifesto FESCD 67*	18		2

SPACE COWBOY UK producer

Date	Title	Peak Position	Weeks at No.1	Weeks in Top 40
6 Jul 02	**I WOULD DIE 4 U** *Southern Fried ECB 29*	55		
2 Aug 03	**JUST PUT YOUR HAND IN MINE** *Southern Fried ECB 37CD*	71		
3 Feb 07	**MY EGYPTIAN LOVER** *Tiger Trax TIGDRE25CD* SPACE COWBOY FEATURING NADIA OH	45		

SPACE FROG German production group

Date	Title	Peak Position	Weeks at No.1	Weeks in Top 40
16 Mar 02	**X RAY FOLLOW ME** *Tripoli Trax TTRAX 082CD*	70		

SPACE KITTENS UK production group

Date	Title	Peak Position	Weeks at No.1	Weeks in Top 40
13 Apr 96	**STORM** *Hooj Choons HOOJCD 41*	58		

SPACE MANOEUVRES UK producer

Date	Title	Peak Position	Weeks at No.1	Weeks in Top 40
29 Jan 00	**STAGE ONE** *Hooj Choons HOOJ 79CD*	25		1

SPACE MONKEY UK producer

Date	Title	Peak Position	Weeks at No.1	Weeks in Top 40
8 Oct 83	**CAN'T STOP RUNNING** *Innervision A 3742*	53		

SPACE MONKEY VS GORILLAZ UK group

Date	Title	Peak Position	Weeks at No.1	Weeks in Top 40
3 Aug 02	**LIL' DUB CHEFIN'** *Parlophone CDR 6584*	73		

SPACE RAIDERS UK production trio

Date	Title	Peak Position	Weeks at No.1	Weeks in Top 40
28 Mar 98	**GLAM RAID** *Skint 32CD*	68		

SPACE 2000 UK production group

Date	Title	Peak Position	Weeks at No.1	Weeks in Top 40
12 Aug 95	**DO U WANNA FUNK** *Wired 218*	50		

SPACECORN Swedish producer

Date	Title	Peak Position	Weeks at No.1	Weeks in Top 40
28 Apr 01	**AXEL F** *69 SN 069CD*	74		

SPACEDUST UK production duo

Date	Title	Peak Position	Weeks at No.1	Weeks in Top 40
24 Oct 98	**GYM AND TONIC** *East West EW 188CD*	1	1	4
27 Mar 99	**LET'S GET DOWN** *East West EW 195CD*	20		1

SPACEHOG UK group

Date	Title	Peak Position	Weeks at No.1	Weeks in Top 40
11 May 96	**IN THE MEANTIME** *Sire 7559643162*	70		
28 Dec 96	**IN THE MEANTIME** *Sire 7559643162*	29		5
7 Feb 98	**CARRY ON** *Sire W 0428CD*	43		

SPACEMAID UK group

Date	Title	Peak Position	Weeks at No.1	Weeks in Top 40
5 Apr 97	**BABY COME ON** *Big Star STARC 105*	70		

SPAGHETTI SURFERS UK production duo

Date	Title	Peak Position	Weeks at No.1	Weeks in Top 40
22 Jul 95	**MISIRLOU (THE THEME TO THE MOTION PICTURE *PULP FICTION*)** *Tempo Toons CDTOON 4*	55		

SPAGNA Italian singer

Date	Title	Peak Position	Weeks at No.1	Weeks in Top 40
25 Jul 87	**CALL ME** *CBS 6502797*	2		9
17 Oct 87	**EASY LADY** *CBS 6511697*	62		
20 Aug 88	**EVERY GIRL AND BOY** *CBS SPAG 1*	23		5

SPAN Norwegian group

Date	Title	Peak Position	Weeks at No.1	Weeks in Top 40
21 Feb 04	**DON'T THINK THE WAY THEY DO** *Island CID 846*	52		

SPANDAU BALLET UK group

Date	Title	Peak Position	Weeks at No.1	Weeks in Top 40
15 Nov 80	**TO CUT A LONG STORY SHORT** *Reformation CHS 2473*	5		9
24 Jan 81	**THE FREEZE** *Reformation CHS 2486*	17		6
4 Apr 81	**MUSCLEBOUND/GLOW** *Reformation CHS 2509*	10		7
18 Jul 81	**CHANT NO. 1 (I DON'T NEED THIS PRESSURE ON)** *Reformation CHS 2528*	3		8
14 Nov 81	**PAINT ME DOWN** *Reformation CHS 2560*	30		3
30 Jan 82	**SHE LOVED LIKE DIAMOND** *Reformation CHS 2585*	49		
17 Apr 82	**INSTINCTION** *Reformation CHS 2602*	10		8
2 Oct 82	**LIFELINE** *Reformation CHS 2642*	7		6
12 Feb 83	**COMMUNICATION** *Reformation CHS 2662*	12		8
23 Apr 83	**TRUE** *Reformation SPAN 1*	1	4	10
13 Aug 83	**GOLD** *Reformation SPAN 2*	2		8
9 Jun 84	**ONLY WHEN YOU LEAVE** *Reformation SPAN 3*	3		6
25 Aug 84	**I'LL FLY FOR YOU** *Reformation SPAN 4*	9		7
20 Oct 84	**HIGHLY STRUNG** *Reformation SPAN 5*	15		4
8 Dec 84	**ROUND AND ROUND** *Reformation SPAN 6*	18		7
26 Jul 86	**FIGHT FOR OURSELVES** *Reformation A 7264*	15		5
8 Nov 86	**THROUGH THE BARRICADES** *Reformation SPANS 1*	6		8
14 Feb 87	**HOW MANY LIES** *Reformation SPANS 2*	34		2
3 Sep 88	**RAW** *CBS SPANS 3*	47		
26 Aug 89	**BE FREE WITH YOUR LOVE** *CBS SPANS 4*	42		

SPANKOX Italian producer

Date	Title	Peak Position	Weeks at No.1	Weeks in Top 40
9 Oct 04	**TO THE CLUB** *Inferno CDFERN62*	69		

SPARKLE US singer

Date	Title	Peak Position	Weeks at No.1	Weeks in Top 40
18 Jul 98	**BE CAREFUL** *Jive 0521452* SPARKLE FEATURING R KELLY	7		4
7 Nov 98	**TIME TO MOVE ON** *Jive 0522032*	40		1
28 Aug 99	**LOVIN' YOU YOU** *Jive 0523452*	65		

SPARKLEHORSE US group

Date	Title	Peak Position	Weeks at No.1	Weeks in Top 40
31 Aug 96	**RAINMAKER** *Capitol CDCL 777*	61		
17 Oct 98	**SICK OF GOODBYES** *Parlophone CDCLS 808*	57		

SPARKS US duo

Date	Title	Peak Position	Weeks at No.1	Weeks in Top 40
4 May 74	**THIS TOWN AIN'T BIG ENOUGH FOR BOTH OF US** *Island WIP 6193*	2		9
20 Jul 74	**AMATEUR HOUR** *Island WIP 6203*	7		7
19 Oct 74	**NEVER TURN YOUR BACK ON MOTHER EARTH** *Island WIP 6211*	13		7
18 Jan 75	**SOMETHING FOR THE GIRL WITH EVERYTHING** *Island WIP 6221*	17		5
19 Jul 75	**GET IN THE SWING** *Island WIP 6236*	27		4
4 Oct 75	**LOOKS LOOKS LOOKS** *Island WIP 6249*	26		3
21 Apr 79	**THE NUMBER ONE SONG IN HEAVEN** *Virgin VS 244*	14		9
21 Jul 79	**BEAT THE CLOCK** *Virgin VS 270*	10		6
27 Oct 79	**TRYOUTS FOR THE HUMAN RACE** *Virgin VS 289*	45		
29 Oct 94	**WHEN DO I GET TO SING 'MY WAY'** *Logic 74321234472*	38		1
11 Mar 95	**WHEN I KISS YOU (I HEAR CHARLIE PARKER PLAYING)** *Logic 74321264272*	36		1
20 May 95	**WHEN DO I GET TO SING 'MY WAY'** *Logic 74321274002*	32		1
9 Mar 96	**NOW THAT I OWN THE BBC** *Logic 74321348672*	60		
25 Oct 97	**THE NUMBER ONE SONG IN HEAVEN** *Roadrunner RR 22692*	70		
13 Dec 97	**THIS TOWN AIN'T BIG ENOUGH FOR BOTH OF US** *Roadrunner RR 22513* SPARKS VERSUS FAITH NO MORE	40		1

SAM SPARRO Australian singer/producer

Date	Title	Peak Position	Weeks at No.1	Weeks in Top 40
29 Mar 08	**BLACK & GOLD** *Download*	23		1

BUBBA SPARXXX US rapper

Date	Title	Peak Position	Weeks at No.1	Weeks in Top 40
24 Nov 01	**UGLY** *Interscope 4976542*	7		4
9 Mar 02	**LOVELY** *Interscope 4976752*	24		1
20 Mar 04	**DELIVERANCE** *Interscope 9862013*	55		

Silver-selling ○ · Gold-selling ● · Platinum-selling ⊛ · US No.1 ★ · Peak Position · Weeks at No.1 · Weeks in Top 40

SPEAR OF DESTINY UK group

Date	Title / Label	Peak Position	Weeks at No.1	Weeks in Top 40
21 May 83	**THE WHEEL** *Epic A 3372*	59		
21 Jan 84	**PRISONER OF LOVER** *Epic A 4068*	59		
14 Apr 84	**LIBERATOR** *Epic A 4310*	67		
15 Jun 85	**ALL MY LOVE (ASK NOTHING)** *Epic A 6333*	61		
10 Aug 85	**COME BACK** *Epic A 6445*	55		
7 Feb 87	**STRANGERS IN OUR TOWN** *10 TEN 148*	49		
4 Apr 87	**NEVER TAKE ME ALIVE** *10 TEN 162*	14		8
25 Jul 87	**WAS THAT YOU** *10 TEN 173*	55		
3 Oct 87	**THE TRAVELLER** *10 TEN 189*	44		
24 Sep 88	**SO IN LOVE WITH YOU** *Virgin VS 1123*	36		2

SPEARHEAD US group

Date	Title / Label	Peak Position	Weeks at No.1	Weeks in Top 40
17 Dec 94	**OF COURSE YOU CAN** *Capitol CDCL 733*	74		
22 Apr 95	**HOLE IN THE BUCKET** *Capitol CDCL 742*	55		
15 Jul 95	**PEOPLE IN THA MIDDLE** *Capitol CDCLS 752*	49		
15 Mar 97	**WHY OH WHY** *Capitol CDCL 785*	45		

BILLIE JO SPEARS US singer

Date	Title / Label	Peak Position	Weeks at No.1	Weeks in Top 40
12 Jul 75	**BLANKET ON THE GROUND** *United Artists UP 35805*	6		12
17 Jul 76	**WHAT I'VE GOT IN MIND** *United Artists UP 36118*	4		11
11 Dec 76	**SING ME AN OLD FASHIONED SONG** *United Artists UP 36179*	34		5
21 Jul 79	**I WILL SURVIVE** *United Artists UP 601*	47		

BRITNEY SPEARS US singer

Date	Title / Label	Peak Position	Weeks at No.1	Weeks in Top 40
27 Feb 99	**BABY ONE MORE TIME** *Jive 0521692* ⊛ ★	1	2	18
26 Jun 99	**SOMETIMES** *Jive 0523202* ●	3		13
2 Oct 99	**(YOU DRIVE ME) CRAZY** *Jive 0550582* ○	5		9
29 Jan 00	**BORN TO MAKE YOU HAPPY** *Jive 9250022* ○	1	1	9
13 May 00	**OOPS!...I DID IT AGAIN** *Jive 9250542* ●	1	1	11
26 Aug 00	**LUCKY** *Jive 9251022* ○	5		8
16 Dec 00	**STRONGER** *Jive 9251502*	7		7
7 Apr 01	**DON'T LET ME BE THE LAST TO KNOW** *Jive 9252032*	12		4
27 Oct 01	**I'M A SLAVE 4 U** *Jive 9252892*	4		6
2 Feb 02	**OVERPROTECTED** *Jive 9253072*	4		7
13 Apr 02	**I'M NOT A GIRL NOT YET A WOMAN** *Jive 9253472*	2		7
10 Aug 02	**BOYS** *Jive 9253912* BRITNEY SPEARS FEATURING PHARRELL WILLIAMS	7		4
16 Nov 02	**I LOVE ROCK 'N' ROLL** *Jive 9254222*	13		4
22 Nov 03	**ME AGAINST THE MUSIC** *Jive 82876576432* BRITNEY SPEARS FEATURING MADONNA	2		6
13 Mar 04	**TOXIC** *Jive 82876602092* ○	1	1	11
26 Jun 04	**EVERYTIME** *Jive 82876626202*	1		11
13 Nov 04	**MY PREROGATIVE** *Jive 82876652582*	3		7
12 Mar 05	**DO SOMETHIN'** *Jive 82876682132*	6		6
27 Oct 07	**GIMME MORE** *Jive 88697186762*	3		11
29 Dec 07	**PIECE OF ME** *Jive 88697221762*	2		12

SPECIAL D German singer

Date	Title / Label	Peak Position	Weeks at No.1	Weeks in Top 40
17 Apr 04	**COME WITH ME** *All Around The World CDGLOBE 340*	6		8

SPECIAL NEEDS UK group

Date	Title / Label	Peak Position	Weeks at No.1	Weeks in Top 40
16 Oct 04	**FRANCESCA – THE MADDENING GLARE/WINTER** *Poptones MC5092SCD*	69		
25 Jun 05	**BLUES SKIES** *Mercury 9872234*	56		

SPECIALS UK group

Date	Title / Label	Peak Position	Weeks at No.1	Weeks in Top 40
28 Jul 79	**GANGSTERS** *2 Tone CHSTT 1* SPECIAL A.K.A. ○	6		8
27 Oct 79	**A MESSAGE TO YOU RUDY/NITE CLUB** *2 Tone CHSTT 5* SPECIALS (FEATURING RICO) ○	10		6
26 Jan 80	**THE SPECIAL A.K.A. LIVE! EP** *2 Tone CHSTT 7* SPECIAL A.K.A. ○	1	2	7
24 May 80	**RAT RACE/RUDE BUOYS OUTA JAIL** *2 Tone CHSTT 11*	5		7
20 Sep 80	**STEREOTYPE/INTERNATIONAL JET SET** *2 Tone CHSTT 13*	6		5
13 Dec 80	**DO NOTHING/MAGGIE'S FARM** *2 Tone CHSTT 16* ○	4		9
20 Jun 81	**GHOST TOWN** *2 Tone CHSTT 17* ●	1	3	11
23 Jan 82	**THE BOILER** *2 Tone CHSTT 18* RHODA WITH THE SPECIAL A.K.A.	35		2
3 Sep 83	**RACIST FRIENDS/BRIGHT LIGHTS** *2 Tone CHSTT 25* SPECIAL A.K.A.	60		
17 Mar 84	**NELSON MANDELA** *2 Tone CHSTT 26* SPECIAL A.K.A.	9		8
8 Sep 84	**WHAT I LIKE MOST ABOUT YOU IS YOUR GIRLFRIEND** *2 Tone CHSTT 27* SPECIAL A.K.A.	51		
10 Feb 96	**HYPROCRITE** *Kuff KUFFD 3*	66		

SPECTRUM UK production group

Date	Title / Label	Peak Position	Weeks at No.1	Weeks in Top 40
26 Sep 92	**TRUE LOVE WILL FIND YOU IN THE END** *Silvertone ORE 44*	70		

CHRIS SPEDDING UK singer/guitarist

Date	Title / Label	Peak Position	Weeks at No.1	Weeks in Top 40
23 Aug 75	**MOTOR BIKING** *RAK 210*	14		6

SPEECH US rapper

Date	Title / Label	Peak Position	Weeks at No.1	Weeks in Top 40
17 Feb 96	**LIKE MARVIN GAYE SAID (WHAT'S GOING ON)** *Cooltempo CDCOOL 314*	35		1

SPEEDWAY UK group

Date	Title / Label	Peak Position	Weeks at No.1	Weeks in Top 40
6 Sep 03	**GENIE IN A BOTTLE/SAVE YOURSELF** *Innocent SINCD 47*	10		2
21 Feb 04	**CAN'T TURN BACK** *Innocent SINDX 55*	12		2
19 Jun 04	**IN AND OUT** *Innocent SINDX 61*	31		1

SPEEDY UK group

Date	Title / Label	Peak Position	Weeks at No.1	Weeks in Top 40
9 Nov 96	**BOY WONDER** *Boiler House! BOIL 2CD*	56		

REGINA SPEKTOR Russian singer

Date	Title / Label	Peak Position	Weeks at No.1	Weeks in Top 40
15 Jul 06	**ON THE RADIO** *Sire W718CD*	60		
3 Mar 07	**FIDELITY** *Sire W737CD1*	45		

SPEKTRUM UK group

Date	Title / Label	Peak Position	Weeks at No.1	Weeks in Top 40
18 Sep 04	**KINDA NEW** *Non Stop SPEKD004*	70		

SPELLBOUND Indian duo

Date	Title / Label	Peak Position	Weeks at No.1	Weeks in Top 40
31 May 97	**HEAVEN ON EARTH** *East West EW 098CD*	73		

JOHNNIE SPENCE UK orchestra leader

Date	Title / Label	Peak Position	Weeks at No.1	Weeks in Top 40
1 Mar 62	**THEME FROM *DR KILDARE*** *Parlophone R 4872*	15		13

DON SPENCER Australian singer

Date	Title / Label	Peak Position	Weeks at No.1	Weeks in Top 40
21 Mar 63	**FIREBALL** *HMV POP 1087*	32		3

TRACIE SPENCER US singer

Date	Title / Label	Peak Position	Weeks at No.1	Weeks in Top 40
4 May 91	**THIS HOUSE** *Capitol CL 612*	65		
6 Nov 99	**IT'S ALL ABOUT YOU (NOT ABOUT ME)** *Parlophone Rhythm Series CDCL 815*	65		

JON SPENCER BLUES EXPLOSION US group

Date	Title / Label	Peak Position	Weeks at No.1	Weeks in Top 40
10 May 97	**WAIL** *Mute CDMUTE 204*	66		
6 Apr 02	**SHE SAID** *Mute LCDMUTE 263*	58		
6 Jul 02	**SWEET N SOUR** *Mute LCDMUTE 271*	66		

SPHINX US group

Date	Title / Label	Peak Position	Weeks at No.1	Weeks in Top 40
25 Mar 95	**WHAT HOPE HAVE I** *Champion CHAMPCD 318*	43		

SPICE GIRLS UK group

Date	Title / Label	Peak Position	Weeks at No.1	Weeks in Top 40
20 Jul 96	**WANNABE** *Virgin VSCDX 1588* ⊛ ★	1	7	18
26 Oct 96	**SAY YOU'LL BE THERE** *Virgin VSCDT 1601* ⊛	1	2	12
28 Dec 96	**2 BECOME 1** *Virgin VSCDT 1607* ⊛	1	3	16
15 Mar 97	**MAMA/WHO DO YOU THINK YOU ARE** *Virgin VSCDT 1623* ⊛	1	3	10
25 Oct 97	**SPICE UP YOUR LIFE** *Virgin VSCDT 1660* ⊛	1	1	12
27 Dec 97	**TOO MUCH** *Virgin VSCDR 1669* ⊛	1	2	7
21 Mar 98	**STOP** *Virgin VSCDT 1679* ○	2		8
1 Aug 98	**VIVA FOREVER** *Virgin VSCDT 1692* ⊛	1	2	9
26 Dec 98	**GOODBYE** *Virgin VSCDT 1721* ⊛	1	1	16

THE SPECIALS

Rarely has a video so perfectly captured not only a song but also a moment in time as when The Specials were pictured driving an old car along a dingy, dimly lit tunnel, threading their way through an urban wasteland soundtracked by the ethereal horns and disturbing vocals of their Number 1 hit single, 'Ghost Town'. The view looking back through the windscreen at the band crammed into the car is one of music's most memorable sights – the song undoubtedly remains one of the OCC's finest chart-toppers.

The Specials were the most critically lauded band to emerge from the so-called Two Tone scene – named after their own independent music label. The backdrop was the grim, grey Midlands city of Coventry, famous for Lady Godiva, bicycles, cars and the ferocious Second World War bombing raids that razed it to the ground. From the post-war rubble sprang up a modern dystopia, intended to revitalise the ravaged city, but which proved to be little more than a series of desolate grey buildings and large, barren housing estates. By 1979 Coventry – and indeed much of inner-city Britain – was spilling over with disaffected youth, unemployment was high and the rebellion of punk was already falling on deaf ears.

The chief architect of The Specials' songs was the mercurial gap-toothed Jerry Dammers. The son of a clergyman, art and film student Dammers was a fan of soul, funk and reggae legends such as Don Drummond, Desmond Dekker and Prince Buster. A litter of early line-ups under the Coventry Automatics banner introduced him to most of the key players in The Specials' story, including punks Terry Hall and Roddy Byers (one story has Dammers catching the train to London to persuade Johnny Rotten to join – he was unsuccessful). The band had to rehearse in Dammers' flat rather than at a studio because his keyboard would not fit through the front door. An incendiary live reputation exploded them on to the national music scene, despite disgruntled punks frequently bottling them onstage.

Re-named The Specials, the band's initially unfashionable mix of punk and reggae nevertheless enjoyed strong live circuit success; after adopting more ska overtones and dropping the overt reggae sounds, the band's career really started to take off. The debut single 'Gangsters' – released on their own titular Two Tone label and distributed by Chrysalis, an industry pioneering deal – hit Number 6 in the summer of 1979.

The band quickly became the epicentre of a movement that swamped discos, youth clubs, gigs and schoolyards the country over (other main players in this latest subculture included The Beat and Selecter) and along with Madness – whom they toured with in the autumn of 1979 – they began to capture the attention of the media and critics alike. With that ensuing press interest and misrepresentation, it is important not to ignore the chart success this most alternative-minded group of musicians enjoyed. Their singles read like a list of classics – 'A Message To You, Rudy', 'The Special Aka Live EP' (their first Number 1), 'Rat Race', and then the watershed 'Ghost Town'.

That song hit the top just as Britain's inner cities ignited in a rash of rioting in Toxteth, Brixton and Handsworth. The song justifiably became the definitive snapshot of the times. It reflected the desperation of inner-city life, the poverty of some people in early-Thatcherite Britain, and the dissatisfaction and frustration of the sections of society that were being ostracised by the Iron Lady. The sartorial badges of pride were just as important, with pork pie hats, loafers, Fred Perry shirts which made up the wardrobe of the Rude Boy (actually a term that originated in the deprived townships of late 1950s Jamaica; ska itself was first imported to the UK via the West Indian immigrant population). The most popular dance was termed the 'skank'. It was a full-on youth subculture that has on-going fashion and musical ramifications to this day.

Problems with right-wing 'fans' disrupting gigs began to stifle the movement, which was ironic given that elements of its musical genesis were deeply rooted in the Jamaican mento, jazz, ya-ya and Calypso. As a retort to this, Dammers and many of the key figures of the scene became involved in movements such as Rock Against Racism, and later the Nelson Mandela Freedom Campaign (including the Number 9 single, 'Nelson Mandela').

Despite its sizeable impact on British youth culture, the movement was relatively short-lived, with The Specials' line-up splintering off into various solo projects; however, whenever that video is played, with that ramshackle troupe of musical pioneers stuffed into that classic old car, cruising around their very own Ghost Town, their unique brilliance is brought powerfully right back into the present.

Silver-selling · Gold-selling · Platinum-selling · US No.1 ★ · Peak Position · Weeks at No.1 · Weeks in Top 40

Date	Title / Label	Peak Position	Weeks at No.1	Weeks in Top 40
4 Nov 00	**HOLLER/LET LOVE LEAD THE WAY** *Virgin VSCDT 1788*	1	1	7
17 Nov 07	**HEADLINES (FRIENDSHIP NEVER ENDS)** *Virgin HEADCD100*	11		4

SPIDER US group

Date	Title / Label	Peak Position	Weeks at No.1	Weeks in Top 40
5 Mar 83	**WHY D'YA LIE TO ME** *RCA 313*	65		
10 Mar 84	**HERE WE GO ROCK 'N' ROLL** *A&M AM 180*	57		

SPILLER UK/Italian group

Date	Title / Label	Peak Position	Weeks at No.1	Weeks in Top 40
26 Aug 00	**GROOVEJET (IF THIS AIN'T LOVE)** *Positiva CDTIV 137*	1	1	12
2 Feb 02	**CRY BABY** *Positiva CDTIVS 167*	40		1

SPIN CITY Irish group

Date	Title / Label	Peak Position	Weeks at No.1	Weeks in Top 40
26 Aug 00	**LANDSLIDE** *Epic 6696132*	30		1

SPIN DOCTORS US group

Date	Title / Label	Peak Position	Weeks at No.1	Weeks in Top 40
15 May 93	**TWO PRINCES** *Epic 6591452*	3		13
14 Aug 93	**LITTLE MISS CAN'T BE WRONG** *Epic 6584892*	23		3
9 Oct 93	**JIMMY OLSEN'S BLUES** *Epic 6597582*	40		1
4 Dec 93	**WHAT TIME IS IT** *Epic 6599552*	56		
25 Jun 94	**CLEOPATRA'S CAT** *Epic 6604192*	29		1
30 Jul 94	**YOU LET YOUR HEART GO TOO FAST** *Epic 6606612*	66		
29 Oct 94	**MARY JANE** *Epic 6609772*	55		
8 Jun 96	**SHE USED TO BE MINE** *Epic 6632682*	55		

SPINAL TAP UK/US group

Date	Title / Label	Peak Position	Weeks at No.1	Weeks in Top 40
28 Mar 92	**BITCH SCHOOL** *MCA 1624*	35		1
2 May 92	**THE MAJESTY OF ROCK** *MCA MCS 1629*	61		

SPINTO BAND US group

Date	Title / Label	Peak Position	Weeks at No.1	Weeks in Top 40
3 Jun 06	**DID I TELL YOU** *Radiate RDTCDX17*	55		
26 Aug 06	**OH MANDY** *Radiate RDTCDX18*	54		

SPIRAL TRIBE UK group

Date	Title / Label	Peak Position	Weeks at No.1	Weeks in Top 40
29 Aug 92	**BREACH THE PEACE (EP)** *Butterfly BLRT 79*	66		
21 Nov 92	**FORWARD THE REVOLUTION** *Butterfly BLRT 85*	70		

SPIRITS UK group

Date	Title / Label	Peak Position	Weeks at No.1	Weeks in Top 40
19 Nov 94	**DON'T BRING ME DOWN** *MCA MCSTD 2018*	31		1
8 Apr 95	**SPIRIT INSIDE** *MCA MCSTD 2045*	39		1

SPIRITUALIZED UK group

Date	Title / Label	Peak Position	Weeks at No.1	Weeks in Top 40
30 Jun 90	**ANYWAY THAT YOU WANT ME/STEP INTO THE BREEZE** *Dedicated ZB 43783*	75		
17 Aug 91	**RUN** *Dedicated SPIRT 002*	59		
25 Jul 92	**MEDICATION** *Dedicated SPIRT 005T*	55		
23 Oct 93	**ELECTRIC MAINLINE** *Dedicated SPIRT 007CD*	49		
4 Feb 95	**LET IT FLOW** *Dedicated SPIRT 009CD* SPIRITUALIZED ELECTRIC MAINLINE	30		1
9 Aug 97	**ELECTRICITY** *Dedicated SPIRIT 012CD1*	32		1
14 Feb 98	**I THINK I'M IN LOVE** *Dedicated SPIRIT 014CD*	27		1
6 Jun 98	**THE ABBEY ROAD EP** *Dedicated SPIRT 015CD*	39		1
15 Sep 01	**STOP YOUR CRYING** *Spaceman OPM 002*	18		2
8 Dec 01	**OUT OF SIGHT** *Spaceman OPM 005*	65		
23 Feb 02	**DO IT ALL OVER AGAIN** *Spaceman OPM 007*	31		1
13 Sep 03	**SHE KISSED ME (IT FELT LIKE A HIT)** *Sanctuary SANXD 222*	38		1

SPIRO & WIX UK duo

Date	Title / Label	Peak Position	Weeks at No.1	Weeks in Top 40
10 Aug 96	**TARA'S THEME** *EMI Premier PRESCD 4*	29		1

SPITTING IMAGE UK TV puppets

Date	Title / Label	Peak Position	Weeks at No.1	Weeks in Top 40
10 May 86	**THE CHICKEN SONG** *Virgin SPIT 1*	1	3	8
6 Dec 86	**SANTA CLAUS IS ON THE DOLE/FIRST ATHEIST TABERNACLE CHOIR** *Virgin VS 921*	22		4

SPLINTER UK duo

Date	Title / Label	Peak Position	Weeks at No.1	Weeks in Top 40
2 Nov 74	**COSTAFINE TOWN** *Dark Horse AMS 7135*	17		6

SPLIT ENZ New Zealand group

Date	Title / Label	Peak Position	Weeks at No.1	Weeks in Top 40
16 Aug 80	**I GOT YOU** *A&M AMS 7546*	12		8
23 May 81	**HISTORY NEVER REPEATS** *A&M AMS 8128*	63		

A SPLIT SECOND Belgian/Italian production group

Date	Title / Label	Peak Position	Weeks at No.1	Weeks in Top 40
14 Dec 91	**FLESH** *ffrr FX 178*	68		

SPLODGENESSABOUNDS UK group

Date	Title / Label	Peak Position	Weeks at No.1	Weeks in Top 40
14 Jun 80	**SIMON TEMPLAR/TWO PINTS OF LAGER AND A PACKET OF CRISPS PLEASE** *Deram BUM 1*	7		6
6 Sep 80	**TWO LITTLE BOYS/HORSE** *Deram ROLF 1*	26		5
13 Jun 81	**COWPUNK MEDLUM** *Deram BUM 3*	69		

SPOILED & ZIGO Israeli group

Date	Title / Label	Peak Position	Weeks at No.1	Weeks in Top 40
12 Aug 00	**MORE & MORE** *Manifesto FESCD 72*	31		1

SPONGE US group

Date	Title / Label	Peak Position	Weeks at No.1	Weeks in Top 40
19 Aug 95	**PLOWED** *Work 6623162*	74		

SPOOKS US group

Date	Title / Label	Peak Position	Weeks at No.1	Weeks in Top 40
27 Jan 01	**THINGS I'VE SEEN** *Artemis ANTCD 6706722*	6		7
5 May 01	**KARMA HOTEL** *Artemis ANTCD 6709012*	15		4
15 Sep 01	**SWEET REVENGE** *Artemis 6718072*	67		

SPOOKY UK duo

Date	Title / Label	Peak Position	Weeks at No.1	Weeks in Top 40
13 Mar 93	**SCHMOO** *Guerilla GRRR 45CD*	72		

DAVE SPOON UK duo

Date	Title / Label	Peak Position	Weeks at No.1	Weeks in Top 40
8 Sep 07	**BAD GIRL (AT NIGHT)** *Toolroom/Apollo APOLLO114CDX* DAVE SPOON FEATURING LISA MAFFIA	36		1

SPORTY THIEVZ US group

Date	Title / Label	Peak Position	Weeks at No.1	Weeks in Top 40
10 Jul 99	**NO PIGEONS** *Columbia 6676022*	21		4

SPOTNICKS Swedish instrumental group

Date	Title / Label	Peak Position	Weeks at No.1	Weeks in Top 40
14 Jun 62	**ORANGE BLOSSOM SPECIAL** *Oriole CB 1724*	29		7
6 Sep 62	**ROCKET MAN** *Oriole CB 1755*	38		6
31 Jan 63	**HAVA NAGILA** *Oriole CB 1790*	13		10
25 Apr 63	**JUST LISTEN TO MY HEART** *Oriole CB 1818*	36		4

DUSTY SPRINGFIELD UK singer

Date	Title / Label	Peak Position	Weeks at No.1	Weeks in Top 40
21 Nov 63	**I ONLY WANT TO BE WITH YOU** *Philips BF 1292*	4		15
20 Feb 64	**STAY AWHILE** *Philips BF 1313*	13		9
2 Jul 64	**I JUST DON'T KNOW WHAT TO DO WITH MYSELF** *Philips BF 1348*	3		11
22 Oct 64	**LOSING YOU** *Philips BF 1369*	9		13
18 Feb 65	**YOUR HURTIN' KIND OF LOVE** *Philips BF 1396*	37		2
1 Jul 65	**IN THE MIDDLE OF NOWHERE** *Philips BF 1418*	8		9
16 Sep 65	**SOME OF YOUR LOVIN'** *Philips BF 1430*	8		10
27 Jan 66	**LITTLE BY LITTLE** *Philips BF 1466*	17		7
31 Mar 66	**YOU DON'T HAVE TO SAY YOU LOVE ME** *Philips BF 1482*	1	1	11
7 Jul 66	**GOING BACK** *Philips BF 1502*	10		9
15 Sep 66	**ALL I SEE IS YOU** *Philips BF 1510*	9		10
23 Feb 67	**I'LL TRY ANYTHING** *Philips BF 1553*	13		7
25 May 67	**GIVE ME TIME** *Philips BF 1577*	24		5
10 Jul 68	**I CLOSE MY EYES AND COUNT TO TEN** *Philips BF 1682*	4		12
4 Dec 68	**SON OF A PREACHER MAN** *Philips BF 1730*	9		8
20 Sep 69	**AM I THE SAME GIRL** *Philips BF 1811*	43		
19 Sep 70	**HOW CAN I BE SURE?** *Philips 6006 045*	36		2
20 Oct 79	**BABY BLUE** *Mercury DUSTY 4*	61		
22 Aug 87	**WHAT HAVE I DONE TO DESERVE THIS** *Parlophone R 6163* PET SHOP BOYS & DUSTY SPRINGFIELD	2		7
25 Feb 89	**NOTHING HAS BEEN PROVED** *Parlophone R 6207*	16		6
2 Dec 89	**IN PRIVATE** *Parlophone R 6234*	14		9
26 May 90	**REPUTATION** *Parlophone R 6253*	38		2
24 Nov 90	**ARRESTED BY YOU** *Parlophone R 6266*	70		
30 Oct 93	**HEART AND SOUL** *Columbia 6598562* CILLA BLACK WITH DUSTY SPRINGFIELD	75		

Silver-selling ○ · Gold-selling ● · Platinum-selling · US No.1 ★ · Peak Position · Weeks at No.1 · Weeks in Top 40

Date	Title / Label	Peak Position	Weeks at No.1	Weeks in Top 40
10 Jun 95	**WHEREVER WOULD I BE?** *Columbia 6620592* DUSTY SPRINGFIELD & DARYL HALL	44		
4 Nov 95	**ROLL AWAY** *Columbia 6623682*	68		

RICK SPRINGFIELD Australian singer

Date	Title / Label	Peak Position	Weeks at No.1	Weeks in Top 40
14 Jan 84	**HUMAN TOUCH/SOULS** *RCA RICK 1*	23		5
24 Mar 84	**JESSIE'S GIRL** *RCA RICK 2* ★	43		

SPRINGFIELDS UK group

Date	Title / Label	Peak Position	Weeks at No.1	Weeks in Top 40
31 Aug 61	**BREAKAWAY** *Philips BF 1168*	31		6
16 Nov 61	**BAMBINO** *Philips BF 1178*	16		10
13 Dec 62	**ISLAND OF DREAMS** *Philips 326557 BF*	5		23
28 Mar 63	**SAY I WON'T BE THERE** *Philips 326577 BF*	5		13
25 Jul 63	**COME ON HOME** *Philips BF 1253*	31		5

BRUCE SPRINGSTEEN US singer/guitarist

Date	Title / Label	Peak Position	Weeks at No.1	Weeks in Top 40
22 Nov 80	**HUNGRY HEART** *CBS 9309*	44		
13 Jun 81	**THE RIVER** *CBS A 1179*	35		2
26 May 84	**DANCING IN THE DARK** *CBS A 4436*	28		5
6 Oct 84	**COVER ME** *CBS A 4662*	38		2
12 Jan 85	**DANCING IN THE DARK** *CBS A 4436* ○	4		13
23 Mar 85	**COVER ME** *CBS A 4662*	16		5
15 Jun 85	**I'M ON FIRE/BORN IN THE USA** *CBS A 6342* ○	5		10
3 Aug 85	**GLORY DAYS** *CBS A 6375*	17		4
14 Dec 85	**SANTA CLAUS IS COMIN' TO TOWN/MY HOMETOWN** *CBS A 6773* ○	9		4
29 Nov 86	**WAR** *CBS 6501937*	18		4
7 Feb 87	**FIRE** *CBS 6503817*	54		
23 May 87	**BORN TO RUN** *CBS BRUCE 2*	16		3
3 Oct 87	**BRILLIANT DISGUISE** *CBS 6511417*	20		3
12 Dec 87	**TUNNEL OF LOVE** *CBS 6512957*	45		
18 Jun 88	**TOUGHER THAN THE REST** *CBS BRUCE 3*	13		7
24 Sep 88	**SPARE PARTS** *CBS BRUCE 4*	32		2
21 Mar 92	**HUMAN TOUCH** *Columbia 6578727*	11		3
23 May 92	**BETTER DAYS** *Columbia 6578907*	34		1
25 Jul 92	**57 CHANNELS (AND NOTHIN' ON)** *Columbia 6581387*	32		2
24 Oct 92	**LEAP OF FAITH** *Columbia 6583697*	46		
10 Apr 93	**LUCKY TOWN (LIVE)** *Columbia 6592282*	48		
19 Mar 94	**STREETS OF PHILADELPHIA** *Columbia 6600652* ○	2		10
22 Apr 95	**SECRET GARDEN** *Columbia 6612955*	44		
11 Nov 95	**HUNGRY HEART** *Columbia 6626252*	28		1
4 May 96	**THE GHOST OF TOM JOAD** *Columbia 6630315*	26		1
19 Apr 97	**SECRET GARDEN** *Columbia 6643245*	17		3
14 Dec 02	**LONESOME DAY** *Columbia 6734082*	39		1
29 Dec 07	**SANTA CLAUS IS COMIN' TO TOWN** *Download*	60		

SPRINGWATER UK instrumentalist

Date	Title / Label	Peak Position	Weeks at No.1	Weeks in Top 40
23 Oct 71	**I WILL RETURN** *Polydor 2058 141*	5		12

SPRINKLER US group

Date	Title / Label	Peak Position	Weeks at No.1	Weeks in Top 40
11 Jul 98	**LEAVE 'EM SOMETHING TO DESIRE** *Island CID 706*	45		

SPUNGE UK group

Date	Title / Label	Peak Position	Weeks at No.1	Weeks in Top 40
15 Jun 02	**JUMP ON DEMAND** *B Unique BUN 022CDX*	39		1
24 Aug 02	**ROOTS** *B Unique BUN 030CDX*	52		

SPYRO GYRA US instrumental group

Date	Title / Label	Peak Position	Weeks at No.1	Weeks in Top 40
21 Jul 79	**MORNING DANCE** *Infinity INF 111*	17		6

SQUEEZE UK group

Date	Title / Label	Peak Position	Weeks at No.1	Weeks in Top 40
8 Apr 78	**TAKE ME I'M YOURS** *A&M AMS 7335*	19		7
10 Jun 78	**BANG BANG** *A&M AMS 7360*	49		
18 Nov 78	**GOODBYE GIRL** *A&M AMS 7398*	63		
24 Mar 79	**COOL FOR CATS** *A&M AMS 7426* ●	2		9
2 Jun 79	**UP THE JUNCTION** *A&M AMS 7444* ○	2		8
8 Sep 79	**SLAP AND TICKLE** *A&M AMS 7466*	24		6
1 Mar 80	**ANOTHER NAIL IN MY HEART** *A&M AMS 7507*	17		7
10 May 80	**PULLING MUSSELS (FROM THE SHELL)** *A&M AMS 7523*	44		
16 May 81	**IS THAT LOVE** *A&M AMS 8129*	35		4
25 Jul 81	**TEMPTED** *A&M AMS 8147*	41		
10 Oct 81	**LABELLED WITH LOVE** *A&M AMS 8166* ○	4		7
24 Apr 82	**BLACK COFFEE IN BED** *A&M AMS 8219*	51		
23 Oct 82	**ANNIE GET YOUR GUN** *A&M AMS 8259*	43		
15 Jun 85	**LAST TIME FOREVER** *A&M AM 255*	45		
8 Aug 87	**HOURGLASS** *A&M AM 4000*	16		5
17 Oct 87	**TRUST ME TO OPEN MY MOUTH** *A&M AM 412*	72		
25 Apr 92	**COOL FOR CATS** *A&M AM 860*	62		
24 Jul 93	**THIRD RAIL** *A&M 5803372*	39		1
11 Sep 93	**SOME FANTASTIC PLACE** *A&M 5803792*	73		
9 Sep 95	**THIS SUMMER** *A&M 5811912*	36		1
18 Nov 95	**ELECTRIC TRAINS** *A&M 5812692*	44		
15 Jun 96	**HEAVEN KNOWS** *A&M 5816052*	27		1
24 Aug 96	**THIS SUMMER (REMIX)** *A&M 5818412*	32		1

BILLY SQUIER US singer

Date	Title / Label	Peak Position	Weeks at No.1	Weeks in Top 40
3 Oct 81	**THE STROKE** *Capitol CL 214*	52		

JOHN SQUIRE UK singer/guitaris

Date	Title / Label	Peak Position	Weeks at No.1	Weeks in Top 40
2 Nov 02	**JOE LOUIS** *North Country NCCDB 001*	43		
14 Feb 04	**ROOM IN BROOKLYN** *North Country NCCDA 003*	44		

DOROTHY SQUIRES UK singer

Date	Title / Label	Peak Position	Weeks at No.1	Weeks in Top 40
5 Jun 53	**I'M WALKING BEHIND YOU** *Polygon P 1068*	12		1
24 Aug 61	**SAY IT WITH FLOWERS** *Columbia DB 4665* DOROTHY SQUIRES & RUSS CONWAY	23		7
20 Sep 69	**FOR ONCE IN MY LIFE** *President PT 267*	24		6
21 Feb 70	**TILL** *President PT 281*	25		6
8 Aug 70	**MY WAY** *President PT 305*	25		9

STABBS Finnish producer

Date	Title / Label	Peak Position	Weeks at No.1	Weeks in Top 40
24 Dec 94	**JOY AND HAPPINESS** *Hi-Life HICD 3*	65		

STACCATO UK/Dutch duo

Date	Title / Label	Peak Position	Weeks at No.1	Weeks in Top 40
20 Jul 96	**I WANNA KNOW** *Multiply CDMULTY 11*	65		

WARREN STACEY UK singer

Date	Title / Label	Peak Position	Weeks at No.1	Weeks in Top 40
23 Mar 02	**MY GIRL MY GIRL** *Def Soul 5889932*	26		1

JIM STAFFORD UK singer

Date	Title / Label	Peak Position	Weeks at No.1	Weeks in Top 40
27 Apr 74	**SPIDERS AND SNAKES** *MGM 2006 374*	14		7
6 Jul 74	**MY GIRL BILL** *MGM 2006 423*	20		7

JO STAFFORD US singer

Date	Title / Label	Peak Position	Weeks at No.1	Weeks in Top 40
14 Nov 52	**YOU BELONG TO ME** *Columbia DB 3152* ★	1	1	19
19 Dec 52	**JAMBALAYA** *Columbia DB 3169*	11		2
7 May 54	**MAKE LOVE TO ME** *Philips PB 233* ★	8		1
9 Dec 55	**SUDDENLY THERE'S A VALLEY** *Philips PB 509*	12		6

TERRY STAFFORD US singer

Date	Title / Label	Peak Position	Weeks at No.1	Weeks in Top 40
7 May 64	**SUSPICION** *London HLU 9871*	31		5

STAGECOACH UK group

Date	Title / Label	Peak Position	Weeks at No.1	Weeks in Top 40
18 Oct 03	**ANGEL LOOKING THROUGH** *Stagecoach Theatre SCR00001* STAGECOACH FEATURING PENNY FOSTER	59		

STAIFFI & HIS MUSTAFAS French group

Date	Title / Label	Peak Position	Weeks at No.1	Weeks in Top 40
28 Jul 60	**MUSTAFA CHA CHA CHA** *Pye International 7N 25057*	43		

STAIND US group

Date	Title / Label	Peak Position	Weeks at No.1	Weeks in Top 40
15 Sep 01	**IT'S BEEN A WHILE** *Elektra E 7252CD1*	15		4
1 Dec 01	**OUTSIDE** *Elektra E 7277CD*	33		1
23 Feb 02	**FOR YOU** *Elektra E 7281CD*	55		
24 May 03	**PRICE TO PAY** *Elektra E 7417CD*	36		1

Silver-selling ○ Gold-selling ● Platinum-selling ⊛ US No.1 ★

Peak Position · Weeks at No.1 · Weeks in Top 40

STAKKA BO Swedish producer

Date	Title / Label	Peak Position	Weeks at No.1	Weeks in Top 40
25 Sep 93	**HERE WE GO** *Polydor PZCD 280*	13		6
18 Dec 93	**DOWN THE DRAIN** *Polydor PZCD 301*	64		

FRANK STALLONE US singer

Date	Title / Label	Peak Position	Weeks at No.1	Weeks in Top 40
22 Oct 83	**FAR FROM OVER** *RSO 95*	68		

STAMFORD AMP UK group

Date	Title / Label	Peak Position	Weeks at No.1	Weeks in Top 40
12 Oct 02	**ANYTHING FOR YOU** *Mercury 638982*	33		1

STAMFORD BRIDGE UK group

Date	Title / Label	Peak Position	Weeks at No.1	Weeks in Top 40
16 May 70	**CHELSEA** *Penny Farthing PEN 715*	47		

STAN UK duo

Date	Title / Label	Peak Position	Weeks at No.1	Weeks in Top 40
31 Jul 93	**SUNTAN** *Hug CDBUM 1*	40		1

STANDS UK group

Date	Title / Label	Peak Position	Weeks at No.1	Weeks in Top 40
16 Aug 03	**WHEN THIS RIVER ROLLS OVER YOU** *Echo ECSCD 142*	32		1
25 Oct 03	**I NEED YOU** *Echo ECSCX 146*	39		1
21 Feb 04	**HERE SHE COMES AGAIN** *Echo ECSCX 148*	25		1
5 Jun 04	**OUTSIDE YOUR DOOR** *Echo ECSCX 151*	49		
21 May 05	**DO IT LIKE YOU LIKE** *Echo ECSCX165*	28		1

LISA STANSFIELD UK singer

Date	Title / Label	Peak Position	Weeks at No.1	Weeks in Top 40
25 Mar 89	**PEOPLE HOLD ON** *Ahead Of Our Time CCUT 5* COLDCUT FEATURING LISA STANSFIELD	11		7
12 Aug 89	**THIS IS THE RIGHT TIME** *Arista 112512*	13		6
28 Oct 89	**ALL AROUND THE WORLD** *Arista 112693* ●	1	2	11
10 Feb 90	**LIVE TOGETHER** *Arista 112914*	10		4
12 May 90	**WHAT DID I DO TO YOU (EP)** *Arista 113168*	25		3
19 Oct 91	**CHANGE** *Arista 114820*	10		5
21 Dec 91	**ALL WOMAN** *Arista 115000*	20		6
14 Mar 92	**TIME TO MAKE YOU MINE** *Arista 115113*	14		7
6 Jun 92	**SET YOUR LOVING FREE** *Arista 74321100587*	28		2
19 Dec 92	**SOMEDAY (I'M COMING BACK)** *Arista 74321123567*	10		7
1 May 93	**FIVE LIVE EP** *Parlophone CDRS 6340* GEORGE MICHAEL & QUEEN WITH LISA STANSFIELD ●	1	3	9
5 Jun 93	**IN ALL THE RIGHT PLACES** *MCA MCSTD 1780*	8		9
23 Oct 93	**SO NATURAL** *Arista 74321169132*	15		3
11 Dec 93	**LITTLE BIT OF HEAVEN** *Arista 74321178202*	32		1
18 Jan 97	**PEOPLE HOLD ON** *Arista 74321452012* LISA STANSFIELD Vs THE DIRTY ROTTEN SCOUNDRELS	4		4
22 Mar 97	**THE REAL THING** *Arista 74321463222*	9		3
21 Jun 97	**NEVER NEVER GONNA GIVE YOU UP** *Arista 74321490392*	25		1
4 Oct 97	**THE LINE** *RCA 74321511372*	64		
23 Jun 01	**LET'S CALL IT LOVE** *Arista 74321863422*	48		

STANTON WARRIORS UK production duo

Date	Title / Label	Peak Position	Weeks at No.1	Weeks in Top 40
22 Sep 01	**DA ANTIDOTE** *Mob MOBCD 006*	69		

STAPLE SINGERS US group

Date	Title / Label	Peak Position	Weeks at No.1	Weeks in Top 40
10 Jun 72	**I'LL TAKE YOU THERE** *Stax 2025 110* ★	30		7
8 Jun 74	**IF YOU'RE READY (COME GO WITH ME)** *Stax 2025 224*	34		3

CYRIL STAPLETON UK orchestra leader

Date	Title / Label	Peak Position	Weeks at No.1	Weeks in Top 40
27 May 55	**ELEPHANT TANGO** *Decca F 10488*	19		4
23 Sep 55	**BLUE STAR (THE MEDIC THEME)** *Decca F 10599* CYRIL STAPLETON ORCHESTRA FEATURING JULIE DAWN	2		12
6 Apr 56	**THE ITALIAN THEME** *Decca F 10703*	18		2
1 Jun 56	**THE HAPPY WHISTLER** *Decca F 10735* CYRIL STAPLETON ORCHESTRA FEATURING DESMOND LANE, PENNY WHISTLE	22		4
19 Jul 57	**FORGOTTEN DREAMS** *Decca F 10912*	27		5

STAR SPANGLES US group

Date	Title / Label	Peak Position	Weeks at No.1	Weeks in Top 40
19 Apr 03	**STAY AWAY FROM ME** *Parlophone CDR 6604*	52		
12 Jul 03	**I LIVE FOR SPEED** *Capitol CDR 6609*	60		

STARCHASER Italian production group

Date	Title / Label	Peak Position	Weeks at No.1	Weeks in Top 40
22 Jun 02	**LOVE WILL SET YOU FREE (JAMBE MYTH)** *Rulin 23CDS*	24		1

STARDUST French group

Date	Title / Label	Peak Position	Weeks at No.1	Weeks in Top 40
8 Oct 77	**ARIANA** *Satril SAT 120*	42		
1 Aug 98	**MUSIC SOUNDS BETTER WITH YOU (IMPORT)** *Roule 305*	55		
22 Aug 98	**MUSIC SOUNDS BETTER WITH YOU** *Virgin DINSD 175* ⊛	2		15

ALVIN STARDUST UK singer

Date	Title / Label	Peak Position	Weeks at No.1	Weeks in Top 40
3 Nov 73	**MY COO-CA-CHOO** *Magnet MAG 1* ●	2		18
16 Feb 74	**JEALOUS MIND** *Magnet MAG 5*	1	1	9
4 May 74	**RED DRESS** *Magnet MAG 8*	7		6
31 Aug 74	**YOU YOU YOU** *Magnet MAG 13* ○	6		9
30 Nov 74	**TELL ME WHY** *Magnet MAG 19*	16		7
1 Feb 75	**GOOD LOVE CAN NEVER DIE** *Magnet MAG 21*	11		7
12 Jul 75	**SWEET CHEATIN' RITA** *Magnet MAG 32*	37		1
5 Sep 81	**PRETEND** *Stiff BUY 124* ○	4		8
21 Nov 81	**A WONDERFUL TIME UP THERE** *Stiff BUY 132*	56		
5 May 84	**I FEEL LIKE BUDDY HOLLY** *Chrysalis CHS 2784*	7		7
27 Oct 84	**I WON'T RUN AWAY** *Chrysalis CHS 2829*	7		9
15 Dec 84	**SO NEAR TO CHRISTMAS** *Chrysalis CHS 2835*	29		3
23 Mar 85	**GOT A LITTLE HEARTACHE** *Chrysalis CHS 2856*	55		

STARFIGHTER Belgian producer

Date	Title / Label	Peak Position	Weeks at No.1	Weeks in Top 40
5 Feb 00	**APACHE** *Sound Of Ministry MOSCDS 136*	31		1

STARGARD US group

Date	Title / Label	Peak Position	Weeks at No.1	Weeks in Top 40
28 Jan 78	**THEME FROM *WHICH WAY IS UP*** *MCA 346*	19		6
15 Apr 78	**LOVE IS SO EASY** *MCA 354*	45		
9 Sep 78	**WHAT YOU WAITING FOR** *MCA 382*	39		1

STARGATE Norwegian production group

Date	Title / Label	Peak Position	Weeks at No.1	Weeks in Top 40
7 Sep 02	**EASIER SAID THAN DONE** *Telstar CDSTAS 3269*	55		

STARGAZERS UK group

Date	Title / Label	Peak Position	Weeks at No.1	Weeks in Top 40
13 Feb 53	**BROKEN WINGS** *Decca F 10047*	1	1	12
19 Feb 54	**I SEE THE MOON** *Decca F 10213*	1	6	15
9 Apr 54	**HAPPY WANDERER** *Decca F 10259*	12		1
17 Dec 54	**FINGER OF SUSPICION** *Decca F 10394* DICKIE VALENTINE WITH THE STARGAZERS	1	3	15
4 Mar 55	**SOMEBODY** *Decca F 10437*	20		1
3 Jun 55	**CRAZY OTTO RAG** *Decca F 10523*	18		3
9 Sep 55	**CLOSE THE DOOR** *Decca F 10594*	6		9
11 Nov 55	**TWENTY TINY FINGERS** *Decca F 10626*	4		11
22 Jun 56	**HOT DIGGITY (DOG ZIGGITY BOOM)** *Decca F 10731*	28		1
6 Feb 82	**GROOVE BABY GROOVE (EP)** *Epic EPC A 1924*	56		

STARJETS UK group

Date	Title / Label	Peak Position	Weeks at No.1	Weeks in Top 40
8 Sep 79	**WAR STORIES** *Epic EPC 7770*	51		

STARLAND VOCAL BAND US group

Date	Title / Label	Peak Position	Weeks at No.1	Weeks in Top 40
7 Aug 76	**AFTERNOON DELIGHT** *RCA 2716* ★	18		7

STARLIGHT Italian studio project

Date	Title / Label	Peak Position	Weeks at No.1	Weeks in Top 40
19 Aug 89	**NUMERO UNO** *Citybeat CBE 742*	9		9

STARPARTY Dutch group

Date	Title / Label	Peak Position	Weeks at No.1	Weeks in Top 40
26 Feb 00	**I'M IN LOVE** *Incentive CENT 5CDS*	26		1

EDWIN STARR US singer

Date	Title / Label	Peak Position	Weeks at No.1	Weeks in Top 40
12 May 66	**STOP HER ON SIGHT (SOS)** *Polydor BM 56 702*	35		4
18 Aug 66	**HEADLINE NEWS** *Polydor 56 717*	39		2
11 Dec 68	**STOP HER ON SIGHT (SOS)/HEADLINE NEWS** *Polydor 56 753*	11		11
13 Sep 69	**25 MILES** *Tamla Motown TMG 672*	36		3
24 Oct 70	**WAR** *Tamla Motown TMG 754* ★	3		11
20 Feb 71	**STOP THE WAR NOW** *Tamla Motown TMG 764*	33		1

Date	Title / Label	Peak Position	Weeks at No.1	Weeks in Top 40
27 Jan 79	**CONTACT** *20th Century BTC 2396* ○	6		9
26 May 79	**H.A.P.P.Y. RADIO** *20th Century TC 2408*	9		9
1 Jun 85	**IT AIN'T FAIR** *Hippodrome HIP 101*	56		
30 Oct 93	**WAR** *Weekend CDWEEK 103* EDWIN STARR & SHADOW	69		
20 May 00	**FUNKY MUSIC SHO NUFF TURNS ME ON** *Echo ECSCX83* UTAH SAINTS SPECIAL GUEST VOCAL EDWIN STARR	23		1

FREDDIE STARR UK comedian

Date	Title / Label	Peak Position	Weeks at No.1	Weeks in Top 40
23 Feb 74	**IT'S YOU** *Tiffany 6121 501*	9		9
20 Dec 75	**WHITE CHRISTMAS** *Thunderbird THE 102*	41		

KAY STARR US singer

Date	Title / Label	Peak Position	Weeks at No.1	Weeks in Top 40
5 Dec 52	**COMES A-LONG A-LOVE** *Capitol CL 13808*	1	1	16
24 Apr 53	**SIDE BY SIDE** *Capitol CL 13871*	7		4
19 Mar 54	**CHANGING PARTNERS** *Capitol CL 14050*	4		14
15 Oct 54	**AM I A TOY OR A TREASURE** *Capitol CL 14151*	17		4
17 Feb 56	**ROCK AND ROLL WALTZ** *HMV POP 168* ★	1	1	20

RINGO STARR UK drummer

Date	Title / Label	Peak Position	Weeks at No.1	Weeks in Top 40
17 Apr 71	**IT DON'T COME EASY** *Apple R 5898*	4		10
1 Apr 72	**BACK OFF BOOGALOO** *Apple R 5944*	2		9
27 Oct 73	**PHOTOGRAPH** *Apple R 5992* ★	8		8
23 Feb 74	**YOU'RE SIXTEEN** *Apple R 5995* ○ ★	4		10
30 Nov 74	**ONLY YOU** *Apple R 6000*	28		10
6 Jun 92	**WEIGHT OF THE WORLD** *Private Music 115392*	74		

STARS ON 54 US group

Date	Title / Label	Peak Position	Weeks at No.1	Weeks in Top 40
28 Nov 98	**IF YOU COULD READ MY MIND** *Tommy Boy TBCD 7497* STARS ON 54, ULTRA NATE, AMBER, JOCELYN ENRIQUEZ	23		1

STARSAILOR UK group

Date	Title / Label	Peak Position	Weeks at No.1	Weeks in Top 40
17 Feb 01	**FEVER** *Chrysalis 555123*	18		1
5 May 01	**GOOD SOULS** *Chrysalis CDCHS 5125*	12		3
29 Sep 01	**ALCOHOLIC** *Chrysalis CDCHSS 5130*	10		3
22 Dec 01	**LULLABY** *Chrysalis CDCHS 5131*	36		1
30 Mar 02	**POOR MISGUIDED FOOL** *Chrysalis CDCHS 5136*	23		1
13 Sep 03	**SILENCE IS EASY** *EMI CDEM 625*	9		3
29 Nov 03	**BORN AGAIN** *EMI CDEMS 632*	40		1
13 Mar 04	**FOUR TO THE FLOOR** *EMI CDEM634*	24		2
15 Oct 05	**THE CROSSFIRE** *EMI CDEM671*	22		1
4 Feb 06	**THIS TIME** *EMI CDEM679*	24		1
20 May 06	**KEEP US TOGETHER** *EMI CDEM691*	47		

STARSHIP US group

Date	Title / Label	Peak Position	Weeks at No.1	Weeks in Top 40
26 Jan 80	**JANE** *Grunt FB 1750* JEFFERSON STARSHIP	21		8
16 Nov 85	**WE BUILT THIS CITY** *RCA PB 49929* ★	12		9
8 Feb 86	**SARA** *RCA PB 49893* ★	66		
11 Apr 87	**NOTHING'S GONNA STOP US NOW** *Grunt FB 49757* ● ★	1	4	15

STARSOUND Dutch producer

Date	Title / Label	Peak Position	Weeks at No.1	Weeks in Top 40
18 Apr 81	**STARS ON 45** *CBS A 1102* ● ★	2		10
4 Jul 81	**STARS ON 45 VOLUME 2** *CBS A 1407* ○	2		8
19 Sep 81	**STARS ON 45 VOLUME 3** *CBS A 1521*	17		5
27 Feb 82	**STARS ON STEVIE** *CBS A 2041*	14		6

STARTRAX UK group

Date	Title / Label	Peak Position	Weeks at No.1	Weeks in Top 40
1 Aug 81	**STARTRAX CLUB DISCO** *Picksy KSY 1001*	18		6

STARTURN ON 45 (PINTS) UK group

Date	Title / Label	Peak Position	Weeks at No.1	Weeks in Top 40
24 Oct 81	**STARTURN ON 45 (PINTS)** *V Tone 003*	45		
30 Apr 88	**PUMP UP THE BITTER** *Pacific DRINK 1*	12		4

STARVATION Multinational charity ensemble

Date	Title / Label	Peak Position	Weeks at No.1	Weeks in Top 40
9 Mar 85	**STARVATION/TAM-TAM POUR L'ETHIOPE** *Zarjazz JAZZ 3*	33		3

STARVING SOULS UK rapper

Date	Title / Label	Peak Position	Weeks at No.1	Weeks in Top 40
21 Oct 95	**I BE THE PROPHET** *Durban Poison DPCD 1*	66		

STATE OF MIND UK group

Date	Title / Label	Peak Position	Weeks at No.1	Weeks in Top 40
18 Apr 98	**THIS IS IT** *Ministry Of Sound MOSCDS 123*	30		1
25 Jul 98	**TAKE CONTROL** *Ministry Of Sound MOSCDS 124*	46		

STATE ONE German producer

Date	Title / Label	Peak Position	Weeks at No.1	Weeks in Top 40
27 Sep 03	**FOREVER AND A DAY** *Incentive CENT 54CDS*	62		

STATIC REVENGER US producer

Date	Title / Label	Peak Position	Weeks at No.1	Weeks in Top 40
7 Jul 01	**HAPPY PEOPLE** *Incentive/Rulin CENRUL 1CDS*	23		1

STATIC-X US group

Date	Title / Label	Peak Position	Weeks at No.1	Weeks in Top 40
6 Oct 01	**BLACK AND WHITE** *Warner Brothers W 560CD*	65		

STATLER BROTHERS US group

Date	Title / Label	Peak Position	Weeks at No.1	Weeks in Top 40
24 Feb 66	**FLOWERS ON THE WALL** *CBS 201976*	38		1

CANDI STATON US singer

Date	Title / Label	Peak Position	Weeks at No.1	Weeks in Top 40
29 May 76	**YOUNG HEARTS RUN FREE** *Warner Brothers K 16730* ○	2		12
18 Sep 76	**DESTINY** *Warner Brothers K 16806*	41		
23 Jul 77	**NIGHTS ON BROADWAY** *Warner Brothers K 16972* ○	6		12
3 Jun 78	**HONEST I DO LOVE YOU** *Warner Brothers K 17164*	48		
24 Apr 82	**SUSPICIOUS MINDS** *Sugarhill SH 112*	31		5
31 May 86	**YOUNG HEARTS RUN FREE** *Warner Brothers W 8680*	47		
2 Feb 91	**YOU GOT THE LOVE** *Truelove TLOVE 7001* SOURCE FEATURING CANDI STATON ○	4		10
1 Mar 97	**YOU GOT THE LOVE (REMIX)** *React CDREACT 89* SOURCE FEATURING CANDI STATON	3		5
17 Apr 99	**LOVE ON LOVE** *React CDREACT 143*	27		1
7 Aug 99	**YOUNG HEARTS RUN FREE** *React CDREACT 158*	29		1
1 Jan 05	**YOU GOT THE LOVE (REMIX)** *ZYX GDC22218* SOURCE FEATURING CANDI STATON	60		
18 Feb 06	**YOU GOT THE LOVE (2ND REMIX)** *Positiva CDTIVS230* SOURCE FEATURING CANDI STATON	7		9

STATUS IV US group

Date	Title / Label	Peak Position	Weeks at No.1	Weeks in Top 40
9 Jul 83	**YOU AIN'T REALLY DOWN** *TMT 4*	56		

STATUS QUO UK group

Date	Title / Label	Peak Position	Weeks at No.1	Weeks in Top 40
24 Jan 68	**PICTURES OF MATCHSTICK MEN** *Pye 7N 17449*	7		11
21 Aug 68	**ICE IN THE SUN** *Pye 7N 17581*	8		11
28 May 69	**ARE YOU GROWING TIRED OF MY LOVE** *Pye 7N 17728*	46		
2 May 70	**DOWN THE DUSTPIPE** *Pye 7N 17907*	12		14
7 Nov 70	**IN MY CHAIR** *Pye 7N 17998*	21		10
13 Jan 73	**PAPER PLANE** *Vertigo 6059 071*	8		9
14 Apr 73	**MEAN GIRL** *Pye 7N 45229*	20		8
8 Sep 73	**CAROLINE** *Vertigo 6059 085* ○	5		11
4 May 74	**BREAK THE RULES** *Vertigo 6059 101*	8		8
7 Dec 74	**DOWN DOWN** *Vertigo 6059 114* ○	1	1	10
17 May 75	**ROLL OVER LAY DOWN** *Vertigo QUO 13*	9		8
14 Feb 76	**RAIN** *Vertigo 6059 133*	7		7
10 Jul 76	**MYSTERY SONG** *Vertigo 6059 146*	11		8
11 Dec 76	**WILD SIDE OF LIFE** *Vertigo 6059 153* ○	9		12
8 Oct 77	**ROCKIN' ALL OVER THE WORLD** *Vertigo 6059 184* ●	3		15
2 Sep 78	**AGAIN AND AGAIN** *Vertigo QUO 1*	13		7
25 Nov 78	**ACCIDENT PRONE** *Vertigo QUO 2*	36		2
22 Sep 79	**WHATEVER YOU WANT** *Vertigo 6059 242* ○	4		8
24 Nov 79	**LIVING ON AN ISLAND** *Vertigo 6059 248*	16		8
11 Oct 80	**WHAT YOU'RE PROPOSING** *Vertigo QUO 3* ○	2		9
6 Dec 80	**LIES/DON'T DRIVE MY CAR** *Vertigo QUO 4* ○	11		9
28 Feb 81	**SOMETHING 'BOUT YOU BABY I LIKE** *Vertigo QUO 5*	9		6
28 Nov 81	**ROCK 'N' ROLL** *Vertigo QUO 6* ○	8		9
27 Mar 82	**DEAR JOHN** *Vertigo QUO 7*	10		7
12 Jun 82	**SHE DON'T FOOL ME** *Vertigo QUO 8*	36		2
30 Oct 82	**CAROLINE (LIVE AT THE NEC)** *Vertigo QUO 10*	13		5
10 Sep 83	**OL' RAG BLUES** *Vertigo QUO 11*	9		6
5 Nov 83	**A MESS OF THE BLUES** *Vertigo QUO 12*	15		4
10 Dec 83	**MARGUERITA TIME** *Vertigo QUO 14* ○	3		9
19 May 84	**GOING DOWN TOWN TONIGHT** *Vertigo QUO 15*	20		5

Date	Title / Label	Peak Position	Weeks at No.1	Weeks in Top 40
27 Oct 84	**THE WANDERER** *Vertigo QUO 16*	7		7
17 May 86	**ROLLIN' HOME** *Vertigo QUO 18*	9		5
26 Jul 86	**RED SKY** *Vertigo QUO 19*	19		6
4 Oct 86	**IN THE ARMY NOW** *Vertigo QUO 20*	2		11
6 Dec 86	**DREAMIN'** *Vertigo QUO 21*	15		6
26 Mar 88	**AIN'T COMPLAINING** *Vertigo QUO 22*	19		4
21 May 88	**WHO GETS THE LOVE** *Vertigo QUO 23*	34		2
20 Aug 88	**RUNNING ALL OVER THE WORLD** *Vertigo QUAID 1*	17		5
3 Dec 88	**BURNING BRIDGES (ON AND OFF AND ON AGAIN)** *Vertigo QUO 25*	5		8
28 Oct 89	**NOT AT ALL** *Vertigo QUO 26*	50		
29 Sep 90	**ANNIVERSARY WALTZ – PART 1** *Vertigo QUO 28*	2		8
15 Dec 90	**ANNIVERSARY WALTZ – PART 2** *Vertigo QUO 29*	16		5
7 Sep 91	**CAN'T GIVE YOU MORE** *Vertigo QUO 30*	37		1
18 Jan 92	**ROCK 'TIL YOU DROP** *Vertigo QUO 32*	38		2
10 Oct 92	**ROADHOUSE MEDLEY (ANNIVERSARY WALTZ PART 25)** *Vertigo QUO 33*	21		2
6 Aug 94	**I DIDN'T MEAN IT** *Vertigo QUOCD 34*	21		3
22 Oct 94	**SHERRI DON'T FAIL ME NOW** *Vertigo QUOCD 35*	38		1
3 Dec 94	**RESTLESS** *Polydor QUOCD 36*	39		1
4 Nov 95	**WHEN YOU WALK IN THE ROOM** *Polygram TV 5775122*	34		1
2 Mar 96	**FUN FUN FUN** *Polygram TV 5762972* STATUS QUO WITH THE BEACH BOYS	24		1
13 Apr 96	**DON'T STOP** *Polygram TV 5766352*	35		1
9 Nov 96	**ALL AROUND MY HAT** *Polygram TV 5759452* STATUS QUO WITH MADDY PRIOR FROM STEELEYE SPAN	47		
20 Mar 99	**THE WAY IT GOES** *Eagle EAGXS 075*	39		1
12 Jun 99	**LITTLE WHITE LIES** *Eagle EAGXS 101*	47		
2 Oct 99	**TWENTY WILD HORSES** *Eagle EAGXS 105*	53		
13 May 00	**MONY MONY** *Universal TV 1580132*	48		
17 Aug 02	**JAM SIDE DOWN** *Universal TV 0192352*	17		2
9 Nov 02	**ALL STAND UP (NEVER SAY NEVER)** *Universal TV 0194872*	51		
25 Sep 04	**YOU'LL COME 'ROUND** *Universal TV 9868038*	14		2
4 Dec 04	**THINKING OF YOU** *Universal TV 9825824*	21		1
24 Sep 05	**THE PARTY AIN'T OVER YET** *Sanctuary SANXS400*	11		2
12 Nov 05	**ALL THAT COUNTS IS LOVE** *Sanctuary SANXS413*	29		1
22 Sep 07	**BEGINNING OF THE END** *Fourth Cord QUOSP002*	48		

STAXX UK production group

Date	Title / Label	Peak Position	Weeks at No.1	Weeks in Top 40
2 Oct 93	**JOY** *Champion CHAMPCD 303*	25		4
20 May 95	**YOU** *Champion CHAMPCD 316* STAXX FEATURING CAROL LEEMING	50		
13 Sep 97	**JOY (REMIX)** *Champion CHAMPCD 328*	14		2

STEALERS WHEEL UK group

Date	Title / Label	Peak Position	Weeks at No.1	Weeks in Top 40
26 May 73	**STUCK IN THE MIDDLE WITH YOU** *A&M AMS 7036*	8		10
1 Sep 73	**EVERYTHING'L TURN OUT FINE** *A&M AMS 7079*	33		4
26 Jan 74	**STAR** *A&M AMS 7094*	25		5

STEAM US group

Date	Title / Label	Peak Position	Weeks at No.1	Weeks in Top 40
31 Jan 70	**NA NA HEY HEY KISS HIM GOODBYE** *Fontana TF 1058* ★	9		12

ANTHONY STEEL & THE RADIO REVELLERS US group

Date	Title / Label	Peak Position	Weeks at No.1	Weeks in Top 40
10 Sep 54	**WEST OF ZANZIBAR** *Polygon P 1114*	11		6

STEEL PULSE UK group

Date	Title / Label	Peak Position	Weeks at No.1	Weeks in Top 40
1 Apr 78	**KU KLUX KHAN** *Island WIP 6428*	41		
8 Jul 78	**PRODIGAL SON** *Island WIP 6449*	35		2
23 Jun 79	**SOUND SYSTEM** *Island WIP 6490*	71		

TOMMY STEELE UK singer

Date	Title / Label	Peak Position	Weeks at No.1	Weeks in Top 40
26 Oct 56	**ROCK WITH THE CAVEMAN** *Decca F 10795* TOMMY STEELE & THE STEELMEN	13		5
14 Dec 56	**SINGING THE BLUES** *Decca F 10819* TOMMY STEELE & THE STEELMEN	1	1	15
15 Feb 57	**KNEE DEEP IN THE BLUES** *Decca F 10849* TOMMY STEELE & THE STEELMEN	15		9
3 May 57	**BUTTERFINGERS** *Decca F 10877* TOMMY STEELE & THE STEELMEN	8		18
16 Aug 57	**WATER WATER/HANDFUL OF SONGS** *Decca F 10923* TOMMY STEELE & THE STEELMEN	5		16
30 Aug 57	**SHIRALEE** *Decca F 10896*	11		4
22 Nov 57	**HEY YOU** *Decca F 10941*	28		1
7 Mar 58	**NAIROBI** *Decca F 10991*	3		11
25 Apr 58	**HAPPY GUITAR** *Decca F 10976*	20		5
18 Jul 58	**THE ONLY MAN ON THE ISLAND** *Decca F 11041*	16		8
14 Nov 58	**COME ON, LET'S GO** *Decca F 11072*	10		13
14 Aug 59	**TALLAHASSEE LASSIE** *Decca F 11152*	16		4
28 Aug 59	**GIVE GIVE GIVE** *Decca F 11152*	28		2
4 Dec 59	**LITTLE WHITE BULL** *Decca F 11177*	6		16
23 Jun 60	**WHAT A MOUTH** *Decca F 11245*	5		10
29 Dec 60	**MUST BE SANTA** *Decca F 11299*	40		1
17 Aug 61	**WRITING ON THE WALL** *Decca F 11372*	30		3

STEELEYE SPAN UK group

Date	Title / Label	Peak Position	Weeks at No.1	Weeks in Top 40
8 Dec 73	**GAUDETE** *Chrysalis CHS 2007*	14		8
15 Nov 75	**ALL AROUND MY HAT** *Chrysalis CHS 2078*	5		8

STEELY DAN US group

Date	Title / Label	Peak Position	Weeks at No.1	Weeks in Top 40
30 Aug 75	**DO IT AGAIN** *ABC 4075*	39		2
11 Dec 76	**HAITIAN DIVORCE** *ABC 4152*	17		8
29 Jul 78	**FM (NO STATIC AT ALL)** *MCA 374*	49		
10 Mar 79	**RIKKI DON'T LOSE THAT NUMBER** *ABC 4241*	58		

GWEN STEFANI US singer

Date	Title / Label	Peak Position	Weeks at No.1	Weeks in Top 40
25 Aug 01	**LET ME BLOW YA MIND** *Interscope 4976052* EVE FEATURING GWEN STEFANI	4		10
27 Nov 04	**WHAT YOU WAITING FOR** *Interscope 9864986*	4		11
26 Mar 05	**RICH GIRL** *Interscope 9880219* GWEN STEFANI FEATURING EVE	4		9
4 Jun 05	**HOLLABACK GIRL** *Interscope 9882326* ★	8		11
10 Sep 05	**COOL** *Interscope 9884356*	11		5
12 Nov 05	**CAN I HAVE IT LIKE THAT** *Virgin VUSCD315* PHARRELL FEATURING GWEN STEFANI	3		7
17 Dec 05	**LUXURIOUS** *Interscope 9888344*	44		
16 Dec 06	**WIND IT UP** *Interscope 1717388*	3		7
3 Feb 07	**THE SWEET ESCAPE** *Interscope 1724450* GWEN STEFANI FEATURING AKON	2		19
16 Jun 07	**4 IN THE MORNING** *Interscope 1735560*	22		3
20 Oct 07	**NOW THAT YOU GOT IT** *Interscope 1747456*	59		

JIM STEINMAN US producer

Date	Title / Label	Peak Position	Weeks at No.1	Weeks in Top 40
4 Jul 81	**ROCK 'N' ROLL DREAMS COME THROUGH** *Epic EPC A 1236* JIM STEINMAN,VOCALS BY RORY DODD	52		
23 Jun 84	**TONIGHT IS WHAT IT MEANS TO BE YOUNG** *MCA 889* JIM STEINMAN AND FIRE INC.	67		

STEINSKI US production group

Date	Title / Label	Peak Position	Weeks at No.1	Weeks in Top 40
31 Jan 87	**WE'LL BE RIGHT BACK** *Fourth & Broadway BRW 59* STEINSKI & MASS MEDIA	63		

STELLA BROWNE UK production duo

Date	Title / Label	Peak Position	Weeks at No.1	Weeks in Top 40
20 May 00	**EVERY WOMAN NEEDS LOVE** *Perfecto PERF 06*	55		
9 Feb 02	**NEVER KNEW LOVE** *Perfecto PERF 26CDS*	42		

STELLASTARR* US group

Date	Title / Label	Peak Position	Weeks at No.1	Weeks in Top 40
31 May 03	**SOMEWHERE ACROSS FOREVER** *Twenty-20 TWENTYCDS001*	73		
27 Sep 03	**JENNY** *Twenty-20 TWENTYCDS002*	61		
20 Mar 04	**MY COCO** *RCA 82876599082*	46		

STELLAR PROJECT Italian production group

Date	Title / Label	Peak Position	Weeks at No.1	Weeks in Top 40
14 Aug 04	**GET UP STAND UP** *Data 74CDS* STELLAR PROJECT FEATURING BRANDI EMMA	14		3

RICHIE STEPHENS Jamaican singer

Date	Title / Label	Peak Position	Weeks at No.1	Weeks in Top 40
15 May 93	**LEGACY** *Columbia 6592852* MAD COBRA FEATURING RICHIE STEPHENS	64		
9 Aug 97	**COME GIVE ME YOUR LOVE** *Delirious 74321450442*	62		

MARTIN STEPHENSON & THE DAINTEES UK group

Date	Title / Label	Peak Position	Weeks at No.1	Weeks in Top 40
8 Nov 86	**BOAT TO BOLIVIA** *Kitchenware SL 27*	70		
17 Jan 87	**TROUBLE TOWN** *Kitchenware SK 13*	58		

Date	Title / Label	Peak Position	Weeks at No.1	Weeks in Top 40
27 Jun 92	**BIG SKY NEW LIGHT** *Kitchenware SK 57*	71		

STEPPENWOLF Canadian group

Date	Title / Label	Peak Position	Weeks at No.1	Weeks in Top 40
11 Jun 69	**BORN TO BE WILD** *Stateside SS 8017*	30		6
27 Feb 99	**BORN TO BE WILD** *MCA MCSTD 48104*	18		2

STEPS UK group

Date	Title / Label	Peak Position	Weeks at No.1	Weeks in Top 40
22 Nov 97	**5, 6, 7, 8** *Jive JIVECD 438*	14		14
2 May 98	**LAST THING ON MY MIND** *Jive 0518492*	6		10
5 Sep 98	**ONE FOR SORROW** *Jive 0519092*	2		9
21 Nov 98	**HEARTBEAT/TRAGEDY** *Ebul/Jive 0519142*	1	1	23
20 Mar 99	**BETTER BEST FORGOTTEN** *Ebul/Jive 0519242*	2		8
24 Jul 99	**LOVE'S GOT A HOLD ON MY HEART** *Ebul/Jive 0519372*	2		7
23 Oct 99	**AFTER THE LOVE HAS GONE** *Ebul/Jive 0519462*	5		5
25 Dec 99	**SAY YOU'LL BE MINE/BETTER THE DEVIL YOU KNOW** *Ebul/Jive 9201008*	4		9
15 Apr 00	**DEEPER SHADE OF BLUE** *Ebul/Jive 9201022*	4		7
15 Jul 00	**WHEN I SAID GOODBYE/SUMMER OF LOVE** *Ebul/Jive 9201162*	5		6
28 Oct 00	**STOMP** *Ebul/Jive 9201212*	1	1	7
6 Jan 01	**IT'S THE WAY YOU MAKE ME FEEL/TOO BUSY THINKING ABOUT MY BABY** *Ebul/Jive 9201232*	2		7
16 Jun 01	**HERE AND NOW/YOU'LL BE SORRY** *Ebul/Jive 9201372*	4		5
6 Oct 01	**CHAIN REACTION/ONE FOR SORROW (REMIX)** *Ebul/Jive 9201442*	2		8
15 Dec 01	**WORDS ARE NOT ENOUGH/I KNOW HIM SO WELL** *Ebul/Jive 9201452*	5		6

STEREO MC'S UK group

Date	Title / Label	Peak Position	Weeks at No.1	Weeks in Top 40
29 Sep 90	**ELEVATE MY MIND** *Fourth & Broadway BRW 186*	74		
9 Mar 91	**LOST IN MUSIC** *Fourth & Broadway BRW 198*	46		
26 Sep 92	**CONNECTED** *Fourth & Broadway BRW 262*	18		5
5 Dec 92	**STEP IT UP** *Fourth & Broadway BRW 266*	12		9
20 Feb 93	**GROUND LEVEL** *Fourth & Broadway BRCD 268*	19		3
29 May 93	**CREATION** *Fourth & Broadway BRCD 276*	19		3
26 May 01	**DEEP DOWN AND DIRTY** *Island CID 777*	17		2
1 Sep 01	**WE BELONG IN THIS WORLD TOGETHER** *Island CID 782*	59		

STEREO NATION UK duo

Date	Title / Label	Peak Position	Weeks at No.1	Weeks in Top 40
17 Aug 96	**I'VE BEEN WAITING** *EMI Premier PRESCD 5*	53		
27 Oct 01	**LAILA** *Wizard WIZ 015* TAZ & STEREO NATION	44		

STEREO STAR UK production duo

Date	Title / Label	Peak Position	Weeks at No.1	Weeks in Top 40
23 Apr 05	**UTOPIA (WHERE I WANT TO BE)** *Free2Air F2A5CDX* STEREO STAR FEATURING MIA J	66		

STEREOLAB UK/French group

Date	Title / Label	Peak Position	Weeks at No.1	Weeks in Top 40
8 Jan 94	**JENNY ONDIOLINE/FRENCH DISCO** *Duophonic UHF DUHFCD 01*	75		
30 Jul 94	**PING PONG** *Duophonic UHF DUHFCD 04*	45		
12 Nov 94	**WOW AND FLUTTER** *Duophonic UHF DUHFCD 07*	70		
2 Mar 96	**CYBELE'S REVERIE** *Duophonic UHF DUHFCD 10*	62		
13 Sep 97	**MISS MODULAR** *Duophonic UHF DUHFCD 16*	60		

STEREOPHONICS UK group

Date	Title / Label	Peak Position	Weeks at No.1	Weeks in Top 40
29 Mar 97	**LOCAL BOY IN THE PHOTOGRAPH** *V2 SPHD 2*	51		
31 May 97	**MORE LIFE IN A TRAMP'S VEST** *V2 SPHD 4*	33		1
23 Aug 97	**A THOUSAND TREES** *V2 VVR 5000443*	22		1
8 Nov 97	**TRAFFIC** *V2 VVR 5000948*	20		1
21 Feb 98	**LOCAL BOY IN THE PHOTOGRAPH** *V2 VVR 5001283*	14		2
21 Nov 98	**THE BARTENDER AND THE THIEF** *V2 VVR 5004653*	3		4
6 Mar 99	**JUST LOOKING** *V2 VVR 5005310*	4		5
15 May 99	**PICK A PART THAT'S NEW** *V2 VVR 5006778*	4		6
4 Sep 99	**I WOULDN'T BELIEVE YOUR RADIO** *V2 VVR 5008823*	11		3
20 Nov 99	**HURRY UP AND WAIT** *V2 VVR 5009323*	11		2
18 Mar 00	**MAMA TOLD ME NOT TO COME** *Gut CXGUT 031* TOM JONES & STEREOPHONICS	4		4
31 Mar 01	**MR WRITER** *V2 VVR 5015938*	5		7
23 Jun 01	**HAVE A NICE DAY** *V2 VVR 5016248*	5		5
6 Oct 01	**STEP ON MY OLD SIZE NINES** *V2 VVR 5016253*	16		2
15 Dec 01	**HANDBAGS AND GLADRAGS** *V2 VVR 5017752*	4		12
13 Apr 02	**VEGAS TWO TIMES** *V2 VVR 5019173*	23		1
31 May 03	**MADAME HELGA** *V2 VVR 5021743*	4		3
2 Aug 03	**MAYBE TOMORROW** *V2 VVR 5021898*	3		7
22 Nov 03	**SINCE I TOLD YOU IT'S OVER** *V2 VVR 5022628*	16		2
21 Feb 04	**MOVIESTAR** *V2 VVR 5024658*	5		3
12 Mar 05	**DAKOTA** *V2 VVR5031048*	1	1	9
2 Jul 05	**SUPERMAN** *V2 VVR5031068*	13		2
1 Oct 05	**DEVIL** *V2 VVR5034058*	11		1
3 Dec 05	**REWIND** *V2 VVR5035048*	17		1
6 Oct 07	**IT MEANS NOTHING** *V2 VVR5048643*	12		4
22 Dec 07	**MY FRIENDS** *V2 1754688*	32		1

STEREOPOL UK group

Date	Title / Label	Peak Position	Weeks at No.1	Weeks in Top 40
29 Mar 03	**DANCIN' TONIGHT** *Rulin 28CDS* STEREOPOL FEATURING NEVADA	36		1

STERIOGRAM New Zealand group

Date	Title / Label	Peak Position	Weeks at No.1	Weeks in Top 40
20 Nov 04	**WALKIE TALKIE MAN** *EMI CDEMS652*	19		2

STETSASONIC US group

Date	Title / Label	Peak Position	Weeks at No.1	Weeks in Top 40
24 Sep 88	**TALKIN' ALL THAT JAZZ** *Breakout USA 640*	73		
7 Nov 98	**TALKIN' ALL THAT JAZZ (REMIX)** *Tommy Boy TBCD 7310A*	54		

CAT STEVENS UK singer

Date	Title / Label	Peak Position	Weeks at No.1	Weeks in Top 40
20 Oct 66	**I LOVE MY DOG** *Deram DM 102*	28		6
12 Jan 67	**MATTHEW AND SON** *Deram DM 110*	2		10
30 Mar 67	**I'M GONNA GET ME A GUN** *Deram DM 118*	6		8
2 Aug 67	**A BAD NIGHT** *Deram DM 140*	20		6
20 Dec 67	**KITTY** *Deram DM 156*	47		
27 Jun 70	**LADY D'ARBANVILLE** *Island WIP 6086*	8		11
28 Aug 71	**MOON SHADOW** *Island WIP 6092*	22		7
1 Jan 72	**MORNING HAS BROKEN** *Island WIP 6121*	9		9
9 Dec 72	**CAN'T KEEP IT IN** *Island WIP 6152*	13		11
24 Aug 74	**ANOTHER SATURDAY NIGHT** *Island WIP 6206*	19		6
2 Jul 77	**(REMEMBER THE DAYS OF THE) OLD SCHOOL YARD** *Island WIP 6387*	44		
25 Dec 04	**FATHER AND SON** *Polydor 9869667* RONAN KEATING & YUSUF ISLAM	2		6
7 Apr 07	**WILD WORLD** *Download*	52		

CONNIE STEVENS US singer

Date	Title / Label	Peak Position	Weeks at No.1	Weeks in Top 40
5 May 60	**KOOKIE KOOKIE (LEND ME YOUR COMB)** *Warner Brothers WB 5* EDWARD BYRNES & CONNIE STEVENS	27		6
5 May 60	**SIXTEEN REASONS** *Warner Brothers WB 3* CONNIE STEVENS WITH THE BIG SOUND OF DON RALKE	9		9

RACHEL STEVENS UK singer

Date	Title / Label	Peak Position	Weeks at No.1	Weeks in Top 40
27 Sep 03	**SWEET DREAMS MY LA EX** *Polydor 9811874*	2		7
20 Dec 03	**FUNKY DORY** *Polydor 9814984*	26		1
24 Jul 04	**SOME GIRLS** *Polydor 9867433*	2		9
16 Oct 04	**MORE MORE MORE** *Polydor 9868325*	3		6
9 Apr 05	**NEGOTIATE WITH LOVE** *Polydor 9870784*	10		4
16 Jul 05	**SO GOOD** *Polydor 9872237*	10		3
15 Oct 05	**I SAID NEVER AGAIN (BUT HERE WE ARE)** *Polydor 9874240*	12		3

RAY STEVENS US singer

Date	Title / Label	Peak Position	Weeks at No.1	Weeks in Top 40
16 May 70	**EVERYTHING IS BEAUTIFUL** *CBS 4953* ★	6		16
13 Mar 71	**BRIDGET THE MIDGET (THE QUEEN OF THE BLUES)** *CBS 7070*	2		13
25 Mar 72	**TURN YOUR RADIO ON** *CBS 7634*	33		3
25 May 74	**THE STREAK** *Janus 6146 201* ★	1	1	10
21 Jun 75	**MISTY** *Janus 6146 204*	2		10
27 Sep 75	**INDIAN LOVE CALL** *Janus 6146 205*	34		3
5 Mar 77	**IN THE MOOD** *Warner Brothers K 16875*	31		3

RICKY STEVENS UK singer

Date	Title / Label	Peak Position	Weeks at No.1	Weeks in Top 40
14 Dec 61	**I CRIED FOR YOU** *Columbia DB 4739*	34		4

SHAKIN' STEVENS UK singer

Date	Title / Label	Peak Position	Weeks at No.1	Weeks in Top 40
16 Feb 80	**HOT DOG** *Epic EPC 8090*	24		6
16 Aug 80	**MARIE MARIE** *Epic EPC 8725*	19		7
28 Feb 81	**THIS OLE HOUSE** *Epic EPC 9555*	1	3	13
2 May 81	**YOU DRIVE ME CRAZY** *Epic A 1165*	2		11
25 Jul 81	**GREEN DOOR** *Epic A 1354*	1	4	9

Silver-selling ○ Gold-selling ● Platinum-selling ⊛ US No.1 ★

Date	Title / Label	Peak Position	Weeks at No.1	Weeks in Top 40
10 Oct 81	**IT'S RAINING** *Epic A 1643* ○	10		7
16 Jan 82	**OH JULIE** *Epic EPCA 1742* ●	1	1	9
24 Apr 82	**SHIRLEY** *Epic EPCA 2087*	6		5
21 Aug 82	**GIVE ME YOUR HEART TONIGHT** *Epic EPCA 2656*	11		7
16 Oct 82	**I'LL BE SATISFIED** *Epic EPCA 2846*	10		6
11 Dec 82	**THE SHAKIN' STEVENS EP** *Epic SHAKY 1* ○	2		6
23 Jul 83	**IT'S LATE** *Epic A 3565*	11		6
5 Nov 83	**CRY JUST A LITTLE BIT** *Epic A 3774* ○	3		11
7 Jan 84	**A ROCKIN' GOOD WAY** *Epic A 4071* SHAKY & BONNIE	5		6
24 Mar 84	**A LOVE WORTH WAITING FOR** *Epic A 4291* ○	2		9
15 Sep 84	**A LETTER TO YOU** *Epic A 4677*	10		7
24 Nov 84	**TEARDROPS** *Epic A 4882* ○	5		8
2 Mar 85	**BREAKING UP MY HEART** *Epic A 6072*	14		5
12 Oct 85	**LIPSTICK POWDER AND PAINT** *Epic A 6610*	11		7
7 Dec 85	**MERRY CHRISTMAS EVERYONE** *Epic A 6769* ●	1	2	7
8 Feb 86	**TURNING AWAY** *Epic A 6819*	15		5
1 Nov 86	**BECAUSE I LOVE YOU** *Epic SHAKY 2*	14		7
20 Dec 86	**MERRY CHRISTMAS EVERYONE** *Epic A 6769*	58		
27 Jun 87	**A LITTLE BOOGIE WOOGIE (IN THE BACK OF MY MIND)** *Epic SHAKY 3*	12		6
19 Sep 87	**COME SEE ABOUT ME** *Epic SHAKY 4*	24		4
28 Nov 87	**WHAT DO YOU WANT TO MAKE THOSE EYES AT ME FOR** *Epic SHAKY 5*	5		7
23 Jul 88	**FEEL THE NEED IN ME** *Epic SHAKY 6*	26		4
15 Oct 88	**HOW MANY TEARS CAN YOU HIDE** *Epic SHAKY 7*	47		
10 Dec 88	**TRUE LOVE** *Epic SHAKY 8*	23		4
18 Feb 89	**JEZEBEL** *Epic SHAKY 9*	58		
13 May 89	**LOVE ATTACK** *Epic SHAKY 10*	28		3
24 Feb 90	**I MIGHT** *Epic SHAKY 11*	18		5
12 May 90	**YES I DO** *Epic SHAKY 12*	60		
18 Aug 90	**PINK CHAMPAGNE** *Epic SHAKY 13*	59		
13 Oct 90	**MY CUTIE CUTIE** *Epic SHAKY 14*	75		
15 Dec 90	**THE BEST CHRISTMAS OF THEM ALL** *Epic SHAKY 15*	19		4
7 Dec 91	**I'LL BE HOME THIS CHRISTMAS** *Epic 6576507*	34		2
10 Oct 92	**RADIO** *Epic 6584367* SHAKY FEATURING ROGER TAYLOR	37		2
25 Jun 05	**TROUBLE/THIS OLE HOUSE** *Virgin/EMI VTSCD7*	20		2
15 Dec 07	**MERRY CHRISTMAS EVERYONE** *Download*	22		3

STEVENSON'S ROCKET UK group

Date	Title / Label	Peak Position	Weeks at No.1	Weeks in Top 40
29 Nov 75	**ALRIGHT BABY** *Magnet MAG 47*	37		1

AL STEWART UK singer

Date	Title / Label	Peak Position	Weeks at No.1	Weeks in Top 40
29 Jan 77	**YEAR OF THE CAT** *RCA 2771*	31		3

AMII STEWART US singer

Date	Title / Label	Peak Position	Weeks at No.1	Weeks in Top 40
7 Apr 79	**KNOCK ON WOOD** *Atlantic/Hansa K 11214* ★	6		10
16 Jun 79	**LIGHT MY FIRE/137 DISCO HEAVEN (MEDLEY)** *Atlantic/Hansa K 11278*	5		8
3 Nov 79	**JEALOUSY** *Atlantic/Hansa K 11386*	58		
19 Jan 80	**THE LETTER/PARADISE BIRD** *Atlantic/Hansa K 11424*	39		1
19 Jul 80	**MY GUY – MY GIRL (MEDLEY)** *Atlantic/Hansa K 11550* AMII STEWART & JOHNNY BRISTOL	39		1
29 Dec 84	**FRIENDS** *RCA 471*	12		7
17 Aug 85	**KNOCK ON WOOD/LIGHT MY FIRE (REMIX)** *Sedition EDIT 3303* ★	7		8
25 Jan 86	**MY GUY – MY GIRL (MEDLEY)** *Sedition EDIT 3310* AMII STEWART & DEON ESTUS	63		

ANDY STEWART UK singer

Date	Title / Label	Peak Position	Weeks at No.1	Weeks in Top 40
15 Dec 60	**DONALD WHERE'S YOUR TROOSERS** *Top Rank JAR 427* ANDY STEWART WITH THE MICHAEL SAMMES SINGERS	37		1
12 Jan 61	**A SCOTTISH SOLDIER** *Top Rank JAR 512* ANDY STEWART WITH THE MICHAEL SAMMES SINGERS	19		36
1 Jun 61	**THE BATTLE'S O'ER** *Top Rank JAR 565* ANDY STEWART WITH THE MICHAEL SAMMES SINGERS	28		8
12 Aug 65	**DR FINLAY** *HMV POP 1454*	43		
9 Dec 89	**DONALD WHERE'S YOUR TROOSERS** *Stone SON 2353* ○	4		6

BILLY STEWART US singer

Date	Title / Label	Peak Position	Weeks at No.1	Weeks in Top 40
8 Sep 66	**SUMMERTIME** *Chess CRS 8040*	39		1

DAVE STEWART UK keyboard player

Date	Title / Label	Peak Position	Weeks at No.1	Weeks in Top 40
14 Mar 81	**WHAT BECOMES OF THE BROKENHEARTED** *Stiff BROKEN 1* DAVE STEWART. GUEST VOCALS: COLIN BLUNSTONE	13		7
19 Sep 81	**IT'S MY PARTY** *Stiff BROKEN 2* DAVE STEWART WITH BARBARA GASKIN ●	1	4	10
13 Aug 83	**BUSY DOING NOTHING** *Broken 5* DAVE STEWART WITH BARBARA GASKIN	49		
14 Jun 86	**THE LOCOMOTION** *Broken 8* DAVE STEWART WITH BARBARA GASKIN	70		

DAVE STEWART UK guitarist

Date	Title / Label	Peak Position	Weeks at No.1	Weeks in Top 40
24 Feb 90	**LILY WAS HERE** *RCA ZB 43045* DAVID A STEWART FEATURING CANDY DULFER	6		10
18 Aug 90	**JACK TALKING** *RCA PB 43907* DAVE STEWART & THE SPIRITUAL COWBOYS	69		
3 Sep 94	**HEART OF STONE** *East West YZ 845CD*	36		1
6 Nov 04	**OLD HABITS DIE HARD** *Virgin VSCDX1887* MICK JAGGER & DAVE STEWART	45		

JERMAINE STEWART US singer

Date	Title / Label	Peak Position	Weeks at No.1	Weeks in Top 40
9 Aug 86	**WE DON'T HAVE TO...** *10 TEN 96* ○	2		11
1 Nov 86	**JODY** *10 TEN 143*	50		
16 Jan 88	**SAY IT AGAIN** *10 TEN 188*	7		9
2 Apr 88	**GET LUCKY** *Siren SRN 82*	13		6
24 Sep 88	**DON'T TALK DIRTY TO ME** *Siren SRN 86*	61		

JOHN STEWART US singer

Date	Title / Label	Peak Position	Weeks at No.1	Weeks in Top 40
30 Jun 79	**GOLD** *RSO 35*	43		

ROD STEWART UK singer

Date	Title / Label	Peak Position	Weeks at No.1	Weeks in Top 40
4 Sep 71	**REASON TO BELIEVE/MAGGIE MAY** *Mercury 6052 097* ★	1	5	19
12 Aug 72	**YOU WEAR IT WELL** *Mercury 6052 171*	1	1	11
18 Nov 72	**ANGEL/WHAT MADE MILWAUKEE FAMOUS (HAS MADE A LOSER OUT OF ME)** *Mercury 6052 198*	4		10
5 May 73	**I'VE BEEN DRINKING** *RAK RR4* JEFF BECK & ROD STEWART	27		5
8 Sep 73	**OH NO NOT MY BABY** *Mercury 6052 371*	6		8
5 Oct 74	**FAREWELL – BRING IT ON HOME TO ME/YOU SEND ME** *Mercury 6167 033*	7		6
7 Dec 74	**YOU CAN MAKE ME DANCE SING OR ANYTHING (EVEN TAKE THE DOG FOR A WALK, MEND A FUSE, FOLD AWAY THE IRONING BOARD, OR ANY OTHER DOMESTIC SHORTCOMINGS)** *Warner Brothers K 16494* ROD STEWART & THE FACES	12		8
16 Aug 75	**SAILING** *Warner Brothers K 16600* ●	1	4	11
15 Nov 75	**THIS OLD HEART OF MINE** *Riva 1*	4		9
5 Jun 76	**TONIGHT'S THE NIGHT** *Riva 3* ★	5		8
21 Aug 76	**THE KILLING OF GEORGIE** *Riva 4*	2		10
4 Sep 76	**SAILING** *Warner Brothers K 16600* ○	3		15
20 Nov 76	**GET BACK** *Riva 6*	11		8
4 Dec 76	**MAGGIE MAY** *Mercury 6160 006*	31		4
23 Apr 77	**I DON'T WANT TO TALK ABOUT IT/FIRST CUT IS THE DEEPEST** *Riva 7* ○	1	4	12
15 Oct 77	**YOU'RE IN MY HEART** *Riva 11* ○	3		9
28 Jan 78	**HOTLEGS/I WAS ONLY JOKING** *Riva 10* ○	5		8
27 May 78	**OLE OLA (MULHER BRASILEIRA)** *Riva 15* ROD STEWART FEATURING THE SCOTTISH WORLD CUP FOOTBALL SQUAD	4		5
18 Nov 78	**DA 'YA THINK I'M SEXY** *Riva 17* ● ★	1	1	11
3 Feb 79	**AIN'T LOVE A BITCH** *Riva 18* ○	11		6
5 May 79	**BLONDES (HAVE MORE FUN)** *Riva 19*	63		
31 May 80	**IF LOVING YOU IS WRONG (I DON'T WANT TO BE RIGHT)** *Riva 23*	23		7
8 Nov 80	**PASSION** *Riva 26*	17		7
20 Dec 80	**MY GIRL** *Riva 28*	32		2
17 Oct 81	**TONIGHT I'M YOURS (DON'T HURT ME)** *Riva 33*	8		8
12 Dec 81	**YOUNG TURKS** *Riva 34*	11		8
27 Feb 82	**HOW LONG** *Riva 35*	41		
4 Jun 83	**BABY JANE** *Warner Brothers W 9608* ○	1	3	12
27 Aug 83	**WHAT AM I GONNA DO** *Warner Brothers W 9564*	3		7
10 Dec 83	**SWEET SURRENDER** *Warner Brothers W 9440*	23		5
26 May 84	**INFATUATION** *Warner Brothers W 9256*	27		4
28 Jul 84	**SOME GUYS HAVE ALL THE LUCK** *Warner Brothers W 9204*	15		7
24 May 86	**LOVE TOUCH** *Warner Brothers W 8668*	27		3
12 Jul 86	**EVERY BEAT OF MY HEART** *Warner Brothers W 8625* ○	2		8
20 Sep 86	**ANOTHER HEARTACHE** *Warner Brothers W 8631*	54		
28 Mar 87	**SAILING** *Warner Brothers K 16600*	41		
28 May 88	**LOST IN YOU** *Warner Brothers W 7927*	21		4
13 Aug 88	**FOREVER YOUNG** *Warner Brothers W 7796*	57		
6 May 89	**MY HEART CAN'T TELL YOU NO** *Warner Brothers W 7729*	49		
11 Nov 89	**THIS OLD HEART OF MINE** *Warner Brothers W 2686*	51		

Silver-selling ◯ · Gold-selling ● · Platinum-selling ⊛ · US No.1 ★ · Peak Position · Weeks at No.1 · Weeks in Top 40

Date	Title / Label	Peak Position	Weeks at No.1	Weeks in Top 40
13 Jan 90	**DOWNTOWN TRAIN** *Warner Brothers W 2647*	10		7
24 Nov 90	**IT TAKES TWO** *Warner Brothers ROD 1* ROD STEWART & TINA TURNER	5		7
16 Mar 91	**RHYTHM OF MY HEART** *Warner Brothers W 0017* ◯	3		9
15 Jun 91	**THE MOTOWN SONG** *Warner Brothers W 0030* ROD STEWART WITH THE TEMPTATIONS	10		6
7 Sep 91	**BROKEN ARROW** *Warner Brothers W 0059*	54		
7 Mar 92	**PEOPLE GET READY** *Epic 6577567* JEFF BECK & ROD STEWART	49		
18 Apr 92	**YOUR SONG/BROKEN ARROW** *Warner Brothers W 0104*	41		
5 Dec 92	**TOM TRAUBERT'S BLUES (WALTZING MATILDA)** *Warner Brothers W 0144* ◯	6		6
20 Feb 93	**RUBY TUESDAY** *Warner Brothers W 0158CD*	11		4
17 Apr 93	**SHOTGUN WEDDING** *Warner Brothers W 0171CD*	21		3
26 Jun 93	**HAVE I TOLD YOU LATELY** *Warner Brothers W 0185CD*	5		7
21 Aug 93	**REASON TO BELIEVE (REMIX)** *Warner Brothers W 0198CD1*	51		
18 Dec 93	**PEOPLE GET READY (REMIX)** *Warner Brothers W 0226CD1*	45		
15 Jan 94	**ALL FOR LOVE** *A&M 5804772* BRYAN ADAMS, ROD STEWART & STING ◯ ★	2		11
20 May 95	**YOU'RE THE STAR** *Warner Brothers W 0296CD*	19		3
19 Aug 95	**LADY LUCK** *Warner Brothers W 0310CD1*	56		
15 Jun 96	**PURPLE HEATHER** *Warner Brothers W 0354CD* ROD STEWART WITH THE SCOTTISH EURO '96 SQUAD	16		3
14 Dec 96	**IF WE FALL IN LOVE TONIGHT** *Warner Brothers W 0380CD*	58		
1 Nov 97	**DA YA THINK I'M SEXY?** *All Around The World CDGLOBE 150* N-TRANCE FEATURING ROD STEWART	7		6
30 May 98	**OOH LA LA** *Warner Brothers W 0446CD*	16		3
5 Sep 98	**ROCKS** *Warner Brothers W 0452CD1*	55		
17 Apr 99	**FAITH OF THE HEART** *Universal UND 56235*	60		
24 Mar 01	**I CAN'T DENY IT** *Atlantic AT 0096CD*	26		1

STEX UK group

Date	Title / Label	Peak Position	Weeks at No.1	Weeks in Top 40
19 Jan 91	**STILL FEEL THE RAIN** *Some Bizzare SBZ 7002*	63		

STICKY UK producer

Date	Title / Label	Peak Position	Weeks at No.1	Weeks in Top 40
23 Jun 01	**BOOO!** *ffrr FCD 399* STICKY FEATURING MS DYNAMITE	12		4

STIFF LITTLE FINGERS Irish group

Date	Title / Label	Peak Position	Weeks at No.1	Weeks in Top 40
29 Sep 79	**STRAW DOGS** *Chrysalis CHS 2368*	44		
16 Feb 80	**AT THE EDGE** *Chrysalis CHS 2406*	15		5
24 May 80	**NOBODY'S HERO/TIN SOLDIERS** *Chrysalis CHS 2424*	36		2
2 Aug 80	**BACK TO FRONT** *Chrysalis CHS 2447*	49		
28 Mar 81	**JUST FADE AWAY** *Chrysalis CHS 2510*	47		
30 May 81	**SILVER LINING** *Chrysalis CHS 2517*	68		
23 Jan 82	**LISTEN EP** *Chrysalis CHS 2580*	33		4
18 Sep 82	**BITS OF KIDS** *Chrysalis CHS 2637*	73		

CURTIS STIGERS US singer

Date	Title / Label	Peak Position	Weeks at No.1	Weeks in Top 40
18 Jan 92	**I WONDER WHY** *Arista 114716*	5		8
28 Mar 92	**YOU'RE ALL THAT MATTERS TO ME** *Arista 115273*	6		10
11 Jul 92	**SLEEPING WITH THE LIGHTS ON** *Arista 74321102307*	53		
17 Oct 92	**NEVER SAW A MIRACLE** *Arista 74321117257*	34		1
3 Jun 95	**THIS TIME** *Arista 74321286962*	28		1
2 Dec 95	**KEEP ME FROM THE COLD** *Arista 74321319162*	57		

STILLS Canadian group

Date	Title / Label	Peak Position	Weeks at No.1	Weeks in Top 40
6 Sep 03	**REMEMBERESE** *679 Recordings 679L 026CD*	75		
28 Feb 04	**LOLA STARS AND STRIPES** *679 Recordings 679L 036CD1*	39		1
8 May 04	**CHANGES ARE NO GOOD** *679 Recordings 679L 072CD2*	51		
28 Aug 04	**STILL IN LOVE SONG** *679 Recordings 679L079CD2*	45		

STEPHEN STILLS US singer

Date	Title / Label	Peak Position	Weeks at No.1	Weeks in Top 40
13 Mar 71	**LOVE THE ONE YOU'RE WITH** *Atlantic 2091 046*	37		3
6 Jun 98	**HE GOT GAME** *Def Jam 5689852* PUBLIC ENEMY FEATURING STEPHEN STILLS	16		2

STILTSKIN UK group

Date	Title / Label	Peak Position	Weeks at No.1	Weeks in Top 40
7 May 94	**INSIDE** *White Water LEV 1CD* ◯	1	1	11
24 Sep 94	**FOOTSTEPS** *White Water WWRD 2*	34		1

STING UK singer/bass player

Date	Title / Label	Peak Position	Weeks at No.1	Weeks in Top 40
14 Aug 82	**SPREAD A LITTLE HAPPINESS** *A&M AMS 8242*	16		6
8 Jun 85	**IF YOU LOVE SOMEBODY SET THEM FREE** *A&M AM 258*	26		4
24 Aug 85	**LOVE IS THE SEVENTH WAVE** *A&M AM 272*	41		
19 Oct 85	**FORTRESS AROUND YOUR HEART** *A&M AM 286*	49		
7 Dec 85	**RUSSIANS** *A&M AM 292*	12		8
15 Feb 86	**MOON OVER BOURBON STREET** *A&M AM 305*	44		
7 Nov 87	**WE'LL BE TOGETHER** *A&M AM 410*	41		
20 Feb 88	**ENGLISHMAN IN NEW YORK** *A&M AM 431*	51		
9 Apr 88	**FRAGILE** *A&M AM 439*	70		
11 Aug 90	**ENGLISHMAN IN NEW YORK (REMIX)** *A&M AM 580*	15		5
12 Jan 91	**ALL THIS TIME** *A&M AM 713*	22		3
9 Mar 91	**MAD ABOUT YOU** *A&M AM 721*	56		
4 May 91	**THE SOUL CAGES** *A&M AM 759*	57		
29 Aug 92	**IT'S PROBABLY ME** *A&M AM 883* STING WITH ERIC CLAPTON	30		4
13 Feb 93	**IF I EVER LOSE MY FAITH IN YOU** *A&M AMCD 0172*	14		3
24 Apr 93	**SEVEN DAYS** *A&M 5802232*	25		2
19 Jun 93	**FIELDS OF GOLD** *A&M 5803012*	16		4
4 Sep 93	**SHAPE OF MY HEART** *A&M 5803532*	57		
20 Nov 93	**DEMOLITION MAN** *A&M 5804512*	21		2
15 Jan 94	**ALL FOR LOVE** *A&M 5804772* BRYAN ADAMS, ROD STEWART & STING ◯ ★	2		11
26 Feb 94	**NOTHING 'BOUT ME** *A&M 5805292*	32		2
29 Oct 94	**WHEN WE DANCE** *A&M 5808612*	9		4
11 Feb 95	**THIS COWBOY SONG** *A&M 5809652* STING FEATURING PATO BANTON	15		4
20 Jan 96	**SPIRITS IN THE MATERIAL WORLD** *MCA MCSTD 2113* PATO BANTON WITH STING	36		1
2 Mar 96	**LET YOUR SOUL BE YOUR PILOT** *A&M 5813312*	15		3
11 May 96	**YOU STILL TOUCH ME** *A&M 5815472*	27		1
22 Jun 96	**LIVE AT TFI FRIDAY EP** *A&M 5817652*	53		
14 Sep 96	**I WAS BROUGHT TO MY SENSES** *A&M 5818912*	31		1
30 Nov 96	**I'M SO HAPPY I CAN'T STOP CRYING** *A&M 5820312*	54		
20 Dec 97	**ROXANNE '97** *A&M 5824552* STING & THE POLICE	17		3
25 Sep 99	**BRAND NEW DAY** *A&M 4971522*	13		3
29 Jan 00	**DESERT SONG** *A&M 4972412* STING FEATURING CHEB MAMI	15		5
22 Apr 00	**AFTER THE RAIN HAS GONE** *A&M 4973262*	31		1
10 May 03	**RISE & FALL** *Wildstar CDWILD 45* CRAIG DAVID FEATURING STING	2		7
27 Sep 03	**SEND YOUR LOVE** *A&M 9810103*	30		1
20 Dec 03	**WHENEVER I SAY YOUR NAME** *A&M 9815304* STING & MARY J BLIGE	60		
29 May 04	**STOLEN CAR (TAKE ME DANCING)** *A&M 9862266*	60		

BYRON STINGILY US singer

Date	Title / Label	Peak Position	Weeks at No.1	Weeks in Top 40
25 Jan 97	**GET UP (EVERYBODY)** *Manifesto FESCD 19*	14		3
1 Nov 97	**SING A SONG** *Manifesto FESCD 35*	38		1
31 Jan 98	**YOU MAKE ME FEEL (MIGHTY REAL)** *Manifesto FESCD 38*	13		2
13 Jun 98	**TESTIFY** *Manifesto FESCD 42*	48		
12 Feb 00	**THAT'S THE WAY LOVE IS** *Manifesto FESCD 66*	32		1

STINX UK duo

Date	Title / Label	Peak Position	Weeks at No.1	Weeks in Top 40
24 Mar 01	**WHY DO YOU KEEP ON RUNNING BOY** *HEBS 1*	49		

STIX 'N' STONED UK production duo

Date	Title / Label	Peak Position	Weeks at No.1	Weeks in Top 40
20 Jul 96	**OUTRAGEOUS** *Positiva CDTIV 52*	39		1

CATHERINE STOCK UK singer

Date	Title / Label	Peak Position	Weeks at No.1	Weeks in Top 40
18 Oct 86	**TO HAVE AND TO HOLD** *Sierra FED 29*	17		4

STOCK AITKEN WATERMAN UK production group

Date	Title / Label	Peak Position	Weeks at No.1	Weeks in Top 40
25 Jul 87	**ROADBLOCK** *Breakout USA 611*	13		7
24 Oct 87	**MR SLEAZE** *London NANA 14* ◯	3		9
12 Dec 87	**PACKJAMMED (WITH THE PARTY POSSE)** *Breakout USA 620*	41		
21 May 88	**ALL THE WAY** *MCA GOAL 1* ENGLAND FOOTBALL TEAM & THE SOUND OF STOCK, AITKEN & WATERMAN	64		
3 Dec 88	**SS PAPARAZZI** *PWL 22*	68		
20 May 89	**FERRY 'CROSS THE MERSEY** *PWL 41* CHRISTIANS, HOLLY JOHNSON, PAUL McCARTNEY, GERRY MARSDEN & STOCK AITKEN WATERMAN	1	3	6

Silver-selling ● Gold-selling ● Platinum-selling ✪ US No.1 ★ | Peak Position · Weeks at No.1 · Weeks in Top 40

RHET STOLLER UK guitarist

Date	Title	Peak	Wks at No.1	Wks in Top 40
12 Jan 61	**CHARIOT** *Decca F 11302*	26		5

MORRIS STOLOFF US orchestra leader

Date	Title	Peak	Wks at No.1	Wks in Top 40
1 Jun 56	**MOONGLOW/THEME FROM PICNIC** *Brunswick 05553* ★	7		11

ANGIE STONE US singer

Date	Title	Peak	Wks at No.1	Wks in Top 40
15 Apr 00	**LIFE STORY** *Arista 74321748492*	22		1
16 Dec 00	**KEEP YOUR WORRIES** *Virgin VUSCD 177* GURU'S JAZZAMATAZZ FEATURING ANGIE STONE	57		
9 Mar 02	**BROTHA PART II** *J Records 74321922142* ANGIE STONE FEATURING ALICIA KEYS & EVE	37		1
27 Jul 02	**WISH I DIDN'T MISS YOU** *J Records 74321939182*	30		1
27 Dec 03	**SIGNED SEALED DELIVERED I'M YOURS** *Innocent SINCD 54* BLUE FEATURING STEVIE WONDER & ANGIE STONE	11		6
14 Aug 04	**I WANNA THANK YOU** *J Records 82876624782* ANGIE STONE FEATURING SNOOP DOGG	31		1

JOSS STONE UK singer

Date	Title	Peak	Wks at No.1	Wks in Top 40
7 Feb 04	**FELL IN LOVE WITH A BOY** *Relentless RELCD3*	18		3
22 May 04	**SUPER DUPER LOVE (ARE YOU DIGGIN ON ME)** *Relentless RELCD4*	18		3
25 Sep 04	**YOU HAD ME** *Relentless RELDX10*	9		5
11 Dec 04	**RIGHT TO BE WRONG** *Relentless RELDX13*	29		3
26 Mar 05	**SPOILED** *Relentless RELCD16*	32		1
16 Jul 05	**DON'T CHA WANNA RIDE** *Relentless RELCD20*	20		2
20 May 06	**CRY BABY CRY** *Arista 82876804672* SANTANA FEATURING SEAN PAUL & JOSS STONE	71		
17 Mar 07	**TELL ME 'BOUT IT** *Relentless/Virgin RELCD35*	28		2

R & J STONE US duo

Date	Title	Peak	Wks at No.1	Wks in Top 40
10 Jan 76	**WE DO IT** *RCA 2616* ●	5		8

STONE ROSES UK group

Date	Title	Peak	Wks at No.1	Wks in Top 40
29 Jul 89	**SHE BANGS THE DRUMS** *Silvertone ORE 6*	36		1
25 Nov 89	**WHAT THE WORLD IS WAITING FOR/FOOL'S GOLD** *Silvertone ORE 13* ●	8		7
6 Jan 90	**SALLY CINNAMON** *Revolver REV 36*	46		
3 Mar 90	**ELEPHANT STONE** *Silvertone ORE 1*	8		4
17 Mar 90	**MADE OF STONE** *Silvertone ORE 2*	20		2
31 Mar 90	**SHE BANGS THE DRUMS** *Silvertone ORE 6*	34		1
14 Jul 90	**ONE LOVE** *Silvertone ORE 17*	4		4
15 Sep 90	**WHAT THE WORLD IS WAITING FOR/FOOL'S GOLD** *Silvertone ORE 13*	22		4
14 Sep 91	**I WANNA BE ADORED** *Silvertone ORE 31*	20		2
11 Jan 92	**WATERFALL** *Silvertone ORE 35*	27		2
11 Apr 92	**I AM THE RESURRECTION** *Silvertone ORE 40*	33		1
30 May 92	**FOOL'S GOLD** *Silvertone ORET 13*	73		
3 Dec 94	**LOVE SPREADS** *Geffen GFSTD 84*	2		5
11 Mar 95	**TEN STOREY LOVE SONG** *Geffen GFSTD 87*	11		2
29 Apr 95	**FOOL'S GOLD** *Silvertone ORECD 71*	25		2
11 Nov 95	**BEGGING YOU** *Geffen GFSTD 22060*	15		1
6 Mar 99	**FOOL'S GOLD (REMIX)** *Jive Electro 0523092*	25		1

STONE SOUR US group

Date	Title	Peak	Wks at No.1	Wks in Top 40
15 Mar 03	**BOTHER** *Roadrunner RR 20243*	28		1
19 Jul 03	**INHALE** *Roadrunner RR 20093*	63		

STONE TEMPLE PILOTS US group

Date	Title	Peak	Wks at No.1	Wks in Top 40
27 Mar 93	**SEX TYPE THING** *Atlantic A 5769CD*	60		
4 Sep 93	**PLUSH** *Atlantic A 7349CD*	23		3
27 Nov 93	**SEX TYPE THING** *Atlantic A 7293CD*	55		
20 Aug 94	**VASOLINE** *Atlantic A 5650CD*	48		
10 Dec 94	**INTERSTATE LOVE SONG** *Atlantic A 7192CD*	53		

STONEBRIDGE Swedish DJ/producer

Date	Title	Peak	Wks at No.1	Wks in Top 40
13 Mar 04	**PUT EM HIGH** *Hed Kandi HEDK12004* STONEBRIDGE FEATURING THERESE	59		
28 Aug 04	**PUT EM HIGH (REMIX)** *Hed Kandi HEDKCDS008* STONEBRIDGE FEATURING THERESE	6		6
29 Jan 05	**TAKE ME AWAY** *Hed Kandi HEDKCDS009* STONEBRIDGE FEATURING THERESE	9		3
28 May 05	**FREAK ON** *Hed Kandi HEDKCDX010* STONEBRIDGE VS ULTRA NATE	37		1

STONEBRIDGE McGUINNESS UK duo

Date	Title	Peak	Wks at No.1	Wks in Top 40
14 Jul 79	**OO-EEH BABY** *RCA PB 5163*	54		

STONEFREE UK singer

Date	Title	Peak	Wks at No.1	Wks in Top 40
23 May 87	**CAN'T SAY 'BYE** *Ensign ENY 607*	73		

STONEPROOF UK producer

Date	Title	Peak	Wks at No.1	Wks in Top 40
15 May 99	**EVERYTHING'S NOT YOU** *VC Recordings VCRD 47*	68		

STOP THE VIOLENCE US group

Date	Title	Peak	Wks at No.1	Wks in Top 40
18 Feb 89	**SELF DESTRUCTION** *Jive BDPST 1*	75		

STORM UK group

Date	Title	Peak	Wks at No.1	Wks in Top 40
17 Nov 79	**IT'S MY HOUSE** *Scope SC 10*	36		3

STORM German prodouction duo

Date	Title	Peak	Wks at No.1	Wks in Top 40
29 Aug 98	**STORM** *Positiva CDTIV 94*	32		1
12 Aug 00	**TIME TO BURN** *Data 16CDS* ●	3		8
23 Dec 00	**STORM ANIMAL** *Data 20CDS*	21		4
26 May 01	**STORM (REMIX)** *Positiva CDTIV 154*	32		1

DANNY STORM UK singer

Date	Title	Peak	Wks at No.1	Wks in Top 40
12 Apr 62	**HONEST I DO** *Piccadilly 7N 35025*	42		

REBECCA STORM UK actress

Date	Title	Peak	Wks at No.1	Wks in Top 40
13 Jul 85	**THE SHOW (THEME FROM *CONNIE*)** *Towerbell TVP 3*	22		5

STORY OF THE YEAR US group

Date	Title	Peak	Wks at No.1	Wks in Top 40
12 Jun 04	**UNTIL THE DAY I DIE** *Maverick W 643CD*	62		

IZZY STRADLIN' US guitarist

Date	Title	Peak	Wks at No.1	Wks in Top 40
26 Sep 92	**PRESSURE DROP** *Geffen GFS 25*	45		

NICK STRAKER BAND UK group

Date	Title	Peak	Wks at No.1	Wks in Top 40
2 Aug 80	**A WALK IN THE PARK** *CBS 8525*	20		9
15 Nov 80	**LEAVING ON THE MIDNIGHT TRAIN** *CBS 9088*	61		

PETER STRAKER & THE HANDS OF DR TELENY UK group

Date	Title	Peak	Wks at No.1	Wks in Top 40
19 Feb 72	**THE SPIRIT IS WILLING** *RCA 2163*	40		1

STRANGELOVE UK group

Date	Title	Peak	Wks at No.1	Wks in Top 40
20 Apr 96	**LIVING WITH THE HUMAN MACHINES** *Food CDFOOD 70*	53		
15 Jun 96	**BEAUTIFUL ALONE** *Food CDFOOD 81*	35		1
19 Oct 96	**SWAY** *Food CDFOOD 82*	47		
26 Jul 97	**THE GREATEST SHOW ON EARTH** *Food CDFOOD 97*	36		1
11 Oct 97	**FREAK** *Food CDFOOD 105*	43		
21 Feb 98	**ANOTHER NIGHT IN** *Food CDFOOD 110*	46		

STRANGLERS UK group

Date	Title	Peak	Wks at No.1	Wks in Top 40
19 Feb 77	**(GET A) GRIP (ON YOURSELF)** *United Artists UP 36211*	44		
21 May 77	**PEACHES/GO BUDDY GO** *United Artists UP 36248* ●	8		14
30 Jul 77	**SOMETHING BETTER CHANGE/STRAIGHTEN OUT** *United Artists UP 36277*	9		8
24 Sep 77	**NO MORE HEROES** *United Artists UP 36300*	8		8
4 Feb 78	**FIVE MINUTES** *United Artists UP 36350*	11		7
6 May 78	**NICE 'N' SLEAZY** *United Artists UP 36379*	18		7

(Column key: Silver-selling ○ · Gold-selling ● · Platinum-selling · US No.1 ★ · Peak Position · Weeks at No.1 · Weeks in Top 40)

Date	Title / Label	Peak Position	Weeks at No.1	Weeks in Top 40
12 Aug 78	**WALK ON BY** *United Artists UP 36429*	21		6
18 Aug 79	**DUCHESS** *United Artists BP 308*	14		6
20 Oct 79	**NUCLEAR DEVICE (THE WIZARD OF AUS)** *United Artists BP 318*	36		3
1 Dec 79	**DON'T BRING HARRY (EP)** *United Artists STR 1*	41		
22 Mar 80	**BEAR CAGE** *United Artists BP 344*	36		1
7 Jun 80	**WHO WANTS THE WORLD?** *United Artists BPX 355*	39		1
31 Jan 81	**THROWN AWAY** *Liberty BP 383*	42		
14 Nov 81	**LET ME INTRODUCE YOU TO THE FAMILY** *Liberty BP 405*	42		
9 Jan 82	**GOLDEN BROWN** *Liberty BP 407* ●	2		10
24 Apr 82	**LA FOLIE** *Liberty BP 410*	47		
24 Jul 82	**STRANGE LITTLE GIRL** *Liberty BP 412*	7		8
8 Jan 83	**EUROPEAN FEMALE** *Epic EPC A 2893*	9		5
26 Feb 83	**MIDNIGHT SUMMER DREAM** *Epic EPC A 3167*	35		2
6 Aug 83	**PARADISE** *Epic A 3387*	48		
6 Oct 84	**SKIN DEEP** *Epic A 4738*	15		6
1 Dec 84	**NO MERCY** *Epic A 4921*	37		2
16 Feb 85	**LET ME DOWN EASY** *Epic A 6045*	48		
23 Aug 86	**NICE IN NICE** *Epic 6500557*	30		4
18 Oct 86	**ALWAYS THE SUN** *Epic SOLAR 1*	30		3
13 Dec 86	**BIG IN AMERICA** *Epic HUGE 1*	48		
7 Mar 87	**SHAKIN' LIKE A LEAF** *Epic SHEIK 1*	58		
9 Jan 88	**ALL DAY AND ALL OF THE NIGHT** *Epic VICE 1*	7		6
28 Jan 89	**GRIP '89 (GET A) GRIP (ON YOURSELF) (REMIX)** *EMI EM 84*	33		2
17 Feb 90	**96 TEARS** *Epic TEARS 1*	17		4
21 Apr 90	**SWEET SMELL OF SUCCESS** *Epic TEARS 2*	65		
5 Jan 91	**ALWAYS THE SUN (REMIX)** *Epic 6564307*	29		2
30 Mar 91	**GOLDEN BROWN (REMIX)** *Epic 6567617*	68		
22 Aug 92	**HEAVEN OR HELL** *Psycho WOK 2025*	46		
14 Feb 04	**BIG THING COMING** *Liberty 5480692*	31		1
24 Apr 04	**LONG BLACK VEIL** *EMI 05489062*	51		
23 Sep 06	**THE SPECTRE OF LOVE** *Liberty 3750342*	57		

STRAW UK group

Date	Title / Label	Peak Position	Weeks at No.1	Weeks in Top 40
6 Feb 99	**THE AEROPLANE SONG** *WEA 196CD*	37		1
24 Apr 99	**MOVING TO CALIFORNIA** *WEA 205CD*	50		
3 Mar 01	**SAILING OFF THE EDGE OF THE WORLD** *Columbia 6708452*	52		

STRAWBERRY SWITCHBLADE UK duo

Date	Title / Label	Peak Position	Weeks at No.1	Weeks in Top 40
17 Nov 84	**SINCE YESTERDAY** *Korova KOW 38*	5		8
23 Mar 85	**LET HER GO** *Korova KOW 39*	59		
21 Sep 85	**JOLENE** *Korova KOW 42*	53		

STRAWBS UK group

Date	Title / Label	Peak Position	Weeks at No.1	Weeks in Top 40
28 Oct 72	**LAY DOWN** *A&M AMS 7035*	12		11
27 Jan 73	**PART OF THE UNION** *A&M AMS 7047*	2		10
6 Oct 73	**SHINE ON SILVER SUN** *A&M AMS 7082*	34		1

STRAY CATS US group

Date	Title / Label	Peak Position	Weeks at No.1	Weeks in Top 40
29 Nov 80	**RUNAWAY BOYS** *Arista SCAT 1* ○	9		8
7 Feb 81	**ROCK THIS TOWN** *Arista SCAT 2*	9		7
25 Apr 81	**STRAY CAT STRUT** *Arista SCAT 3*	11		7
20 Jun 81	**THE RACE IS ON** *Swansong SSK 19425* DAVE EDMUNDS & THE STRAY CATS	34		3
7 Nov 81	**YOU DON'T BELIEVE ME** *Arista SCAT 4*	57		
6 Aug 83	**(SHE'S) SEXY AND 17** *Arista SCAT 6*	29		4
4 Mar 89	**BRING IT BACK AGAIN** *EMI USA MT 62*	64		

STREETBAND UK group

Date	Title / Label	Peak Position	Weeks at No.1	Weeks in Top 40
4 Nov 78	**TOAST/HOLD ON** *Logo GO 325*	18		5

STREETS UK producer

Date	Title / Label	Peak Position	Weeks at No.1	Weeks in Top 40
20 Oct 01	**HAS IT COME TO THIS** *679 Recordings 679L001CD1*	18		2
27 Apr 02	**LET'S PUSH THINGS FORWARD** *Locked On/679 679005CD1*	30		2
3 Aug 02	**WEAK BECOME HEROES** *Locked On/679 Recordings 679007CD*	27		1
2 Nov 02	**DON'T MUG YOURSELF** *Locked On/679 Recordings 008CDX*	21		1
8 May 04	**FIT BUT YOU KNOW IT** *Locked On/679 Recordings 679L071CD2*	4		7
31 Jul 04	**DRY YOUR EYES** *Locked On/679 Recordings 679L077CD1*	1	1	8
9 Oct 04	**BLINDED BY THE LIGHTS** *Locked On/679 Recordings 679L085CD*	10		3
11 Dec 04	**COULD WELL BE IN** *Locked On/679 Recordings 679L092CD*	30		1
19 Mar 05	**ROUTINE CHECK** *WEA BEATS8* MITCHELL BROTHERS/KANO/THE STREETS	42		
24 Sep 05	**NITE NITE** *679 679L108CD2* KANO FEATURING MIKE SKINNER & LEO THE LION	25		2
8 Apr 06	**WHEN YOU WASN'T FAMOUS** *679 679L125CD1*	8		5
10 Jun 06	**NEVER WENT TO CHURCH** *679 679L132CD1*	20		2
30 Sep 06	**PRANGIN' OUT** *Locked On/679 679L141CD1* STREETS FEATURING PETE DOHERTY	25		2

BARBRA STREISAND US singer/actress

Date	Title / Label	Peak Position	Weeks at No.1	Weeks in Top 40
20 Jan 66	**SECOND HAND ROSE** *CBS 202025*	14		10
30 Jan 71	**STONEY END** *CBS 5321*	27		8
30 Mar 74	**THE WAY WE WERE** *CBS 1915* ★	31		5
9 Apr 77	**LOVE THEME FROM *A STAR IS BORN* (EVERGREEN)** *CBS 4855* ○ ★	3		18
25 Nov 78	**YOU DON'T BRING ME FLOWERS** *CBS 6803* BARBRA (Streisand) & NEIL (Diamond) ● ★	5		9
3 Nov 79	**NO MORE TEARS (ENOUGH IS ENOUGH)** *Casablanca CAN 174/CBS 8000* DONNA SUMMER & BARBRA STREISAND ○ ★	3		10
4 Oct 80	**WOMAN IN LOVE** *CBS 8966* ● ★	1	3	10
6 Dec 80	**GUILTY** *CBS 9315* BARBRA STREISAND & BARRY GIBB	34		1
30 Jan 82	**COMIN' IN AND OUT OF YOUR LIFE** *CBS A 1789*	66		
20 Mar 82	**MEMORY** *CBS A 1903*	34		4
5 Nov 88	**TILL I LOVED YOU (LOVE THEME FROM *GOYA*)** *CBS BARB 2* BARBRA STREISAND & DON JOHNSON	16		4
7 Mar 92	**PLACES THAT BELONG TO YOU** *Columbia 6577947*	17		3
5 Jun 93	**WITH ONE LOOK** *Columbia 6593422*	30		1
15 Jan 94	**THE MUSIC OF THE NIGHT** *Columbia 6597382* BARBRA STREISAND (DUET WITH MICHAEL CRAWFORD)	54		
30 Apr 94	**AS IF WE NEVER SAID GOODBYE (FROM *SUNSET BOULEVARD*)** *Columbia 6603572*	20		2
8 Feb 97	**I FINALLY FOUND SOMEONE** *A&M 5820832* BARBRA STREISAND & BRYAN ADAMS	10		5
15 Nov 97	**TELL HIM** *Epic 6653052* BARBRA STREISAND & CELINE DION ●	3		10
30 Oct 99	**IF YOU EVER LEAVE ME** *Columbia 6681242* BARBRA STREISAND/VINCE GILL	26		1

STRESS UK group

Date	Title / Label	Peak Position	Weeks at No.1	Weeks in Top 40
13 Oct 90	**BEAUTIFUL PEOPLE** *Eternal YZ 495*	74		

STRETCH UK group

Date	Title / Label	Peak Position	Weeks at No.1	Weeks in Top 40
8 Nov 75	**WHY DID YOU DO IT?** *Anchor ANC 1021*	16		8

STRETCH 'N' VERN UK production duo

Date	Title / Label	Peak Position	Weeks at No.1	Weeks in Top 40
14 Sep 96	**I'M ALIVE** *ffrr FCD 284* STRETCH 'N' VERN PRESENT MADDOG	6		7
9 Aug 97	**GET UP! GO INSANE!** *ffrr FCD 304* STRETCH 'N' VERN PRESENT MADDOG	17		3

STRICT INSTRUCTOR Russian singer

Date	Title / Label	Peak Position	Weeks at No.1	Weeks in Top 40
24 Oct 98	**STEP-TWO-THREE-FOUR** *All Around The World CDGLOBE 155*	49		

STRIKE UK/Australian group

Date	Title / Label	Peak Position	Weeks at No.1	Weeks in Top 40
24 Dec 94	**U SURE DO** *Fresh FRSHD 19*	31		2
1 Apr 95	**U SURE DO** *Fresh FRSHD 19*	4		7
23 Sep 95	**THE MORNING AFTER (FREE AT LAST)** *Fresh FRSHD 37*	38		1
29 Jun 96	**INSPIRATION** *Fresh FRSHD 45*	27		1
16 Nov 96	**MY LOVE IS FOR REAL** *Fresh FRSHD 46*	35		1
31 May 97	**I HAVE PEACE** *Fresh FRSHD 58*	17		3
25 Sep 99	**U SURE DO (REMIX)** *Fresh FRSHD 78*	53		

STRIKERS US group

Date	Title / Label	Peak Position	Weeks at No.1	Weeks in Top 40
6 Jun 81	**BODY MUSIC** *Epic A 1290*	45		

STRING-A-LONGS US group

Date	Title / Label	Peak Position	Weeks at No.1	Weeks in Top 40
23 Feb 61	**WHEELS** *London HLU 9278*	8		12

STRINGS OF LOVE Italian group

Date	Title / Label	Peak Position	Weeks at No.1	Weeks in Top 40
3 Mar 90	**NOTHING HAS BEEN PROVED** *Breakout USA 688*	59		

Silver-selling ○ Gold-selling ● Platinum-selling ⊛ US No.1 ★ — Peak Position / Weeks at No.1 / Weeks in Top 40

STROKES US group

Date	Title / Label	Peak Position	Weeks at No.1	Weeks in Top 40
7 Jul 01	**HARD TO EXPLAIN/NEW YORK CITY COPS** *Rough Trade RTRADESCD 023*	16		2
7 Jul 01	**MODERN AGE** *Rough Trade RTRADESCD 010*	68		
17 Nov 01	**LAST NIGHT** *Rough Trade RTRADESCD 041*	14		3
5 Oct 02	**SOMEDAY** *Rough Trade RTRADESCD 063*	27		1
18 Oct 03	**12.51** *Rough Trade RTRADESCD 140*	7		2
21 Feb 04	**REPTILLA** *Rough Trade RTRADESCD 155*	17		2
13 Nov 04	**THE END HAS NO END** *Rough Trade RTRADSCD 205*	27		1
17 Dec 05	**JUICEBOX** *Rough Trade RTRADSCDX282*	5		3
1 Apr 06	**HEART IN A CAGE** *Rough Trade RTRADSCDX305*	25		1

JOE STRUMMER UK singer and guitarist

Date	Title / Label	Peak Position	Weeks at No.1	Weeks in Top 40
2 Aug 86	**LOVE KILLS** *CBS A 7244*	69		
23 Dec 95	**JUST THE ONE** *China WOKCD 2076* LEVELLERS, SPECIAL GUEST JOE STRUMMER	12		6
29 Jun 96	**ENGLAND'S IRIE** *Radioactive RAXTD 25* BLACK GRAPE FEATURING JOE STRUMMER & KEITH ALLEN	6		3
18 Oct 03	**COMA GIRL** *Hellcat 11362* JOE STRUMMER & THE MESCALEROS	33		1
27 Dec 03	**REDEMPTION SONG/ARMS ALOFT** *Hellcat 11482* JOE STRUMMER & THE MESCALEROS	46		

STUART Dutch producer

Date	Title / Label	Peak Position	Weeks at No.1	Weeks in Top 40
5 Apr 03	**FREE (LET IT BE)** *Product/Incentive PFT 07CDS*	41		

CHAD STUART & JEREMY CLYDE UK duo

Date	Title / Label	Peak Position	Weeks at No.1	Weeks in Top 40
28 Nov 63	**YESTERDAY'S GONE** *Ember EMBS 180*	37		4

STUDIO B UK production group

Date	Title / Label	Peak Position	Weeks at No.1	Weeks in Top 40
6 Dec 03	**I SEE GIRLS (CRAZY)** *Multiply CDMULTY 109* STUDIO B/ROMEO & HARRY BROOKS	52		
9 Apr 05	**I SEE GIRLS** *Data BOSSMOS1CDS*	12		12
22 Apr 06	**C'MON GET IT ON** *Loaded LOAD110CD*	28		1

STUDIO 45 German production duo

Date	Title / Label	Peak Position	Weeks at No.1	Weeks in Top 40
20 Feb 99	**FREAK IT!** *Azuli AZNYCD 090*	36		1

STUDIO 2 Jamaican singer

Date	Title / Label	Peak Position	Weeks at No.1	Weeks in Top 40
27 Jun 98	**TRAVELLING MAN** *Multiply CDMULTY 35*	40		1

AMY STUDT UK singer

Date	Title / Label	Peak Position	Weeks at No.1	Weeks in Top 40
13 Jul 02	**JUST A LITTLE GIRL** *Polydor 5708802*	14		4
21 Jun 03	**MISFIT** *Polydor 9800107*	6		8
11 Oct 03	**UNDER THE THUMB** *Polydor 9811793*	10		4
24 Jan 04	**ALL I WANNA DO** *19/Polydor 9815012*	21		2

STUMP UK group

Date	Title / Label	Peak Position	Weeks at No.1	Weeks in Top 40
13 Aug 88	**CHARLTON HESTON** *Ensign ENY 614*	72		

STUNT UK production duo

Date	Title / Label	Peak Position	Weeks at No.1	Weeks in Top 40
21 Jan 06	**RAINDROPS** *Data DATA108CDS*	51		
3 Mar 01	**THE LADYBOY IS MINE** *East West EW 226CD*	10		5

STUTZ BEARCATS UK group

Date	Title / Label	Peak Position	Weeks at No.1	Weeks in Top 40
24 Apr 82	**THE SONG THAT I SING (THEME FROM *WE'LL MEET AGAIN*)** *Multi-Media Tapes MMT 6* STUTZ BEARCATS & THE DENIS KING ORCHESTRA	36		2

STYLE COUNCIL UK group

Date	Title / Label	Peak Position	Weeks at No.1	Weeks in Top 40
19 Mar 83	**SPEAK LIKE A CHILD** *Polydor TSC 1* ○	4		7
28 May 83	**MONEY GO ROUND (PART 1)** *Polydor TSC 2*	11		4
13 Aug 83	**LONG HOT SUMMER/PARIS MATCH** *Polydor TSC 3* ○	3		7
19 Nov 83	**SOLID BOND IN YOUR HEART** *Polydor TSC 4*	11		5
18 Feb 84	**MY EVER CHANGING MOODS** *Polydor TSC 5*	5		6
26 May 84	**GROOVIN' (YOU'RE THE BEST THING)/BIG BOSS GROOVE** *Polydor TSC 6*	5		6
13 Oct 84	**SHOUT TO THE TOP** *Polydor TSC 7*	7		6
11 May 85	**WALLS COME TUMBLING DOWN!** *Polydor TSC 8*	6		5
6 Jul 85	**COME TO MILTON KEYNES** *Polydor TSC 9*	23		3
28 Sep 85	**THE LODGERS** *Polydor TSC 10*	13		4
5 Apr 86	**HAVE YOU EVER HAD IT BLUE** *Polydor CINE 1*	14		5
17 Jan 87	**IT DIDN'T MATTER** *Polydor TSC 12*	9		4
14 Mar 87	**WAITING** *Polydor TSC 13*	52		
31 Oct 87	**WANTED** *Polydor TSC 14*	20		3
28 May 88	**LIFE AT A TOP PEOPLE'S HEALTH FARM** *Polydor TSC 15*	28		2
23 Jul 88	**HOW SHE THREW IT ALL AWAY (EP)** *Polydor TSC 16*	41		
18 Feb 89	**PROMISED LAND** *Polydor TSC 17*	27		3
27 May 89	**LONG HOT SUMMER 89 (REMIX)** *Polydor LHS 1*	48		

STYLES P US rapper

Date	Title / Label	Peak Position	Weeks at No.1	Weeks in Top 40
14 Sep 02	**THE LIFE** *MCA MCSTD 40292* STYLES & PHAROAHE MONCH	50		
25 Dec 04	**LOCKED UP** *Universal E9864569* AKON FEATURING STYLES P	61		

DARREN STYLES/MARK BREEZE UK production duo

Date	Title / Label	Peak Position	Weeks at No.1	Weeks in Top 40
5 Apr 03	**LET ME FLY** *Nukleuz 0432 CNUK*	59		
31 Jul 04	**YOU'RE SHINING** *All Around The World CDGLOBE346*	19		3
12 Mar 05	**HEARTBEATZ** *All Around The World CDGLOBE342* STYLES & BREEZE FEATURING KAREN DANZIG	16		2
7 Apr 07	**SAVE ME** *All Around The World CXGLOBE566* DARREN STYLES	70		
8 Sep 07	**SURE FEELS GOOD** *All Around The World CDGLOBE696* ULTRABEAT VERSUS DARREN STYLES	52		

STYLISTICS US group

Date	Title / Label	Peak Position	Weeks at No.1	Weeks in Top 40
24 Jun 72	**BETCHA BY GOLLY WOW** *Avco 6105 011*	13		11
4 Nov 72	**I'M STONE IN LOVE WITH YOU** *Avco 6105 015*	9		9
17 Mar 73	**BREAK UP TO MAKE UP** *Avco 6105 020*	34		3
30 Jun 73	**PEEK-A-BOO** *Avco 6105 023*	35		4
19 Jan 74	**ROCKIN' ROLL BABY** *Avco 6105 026*	6		8
13 Jul 74	**YOU MAKE ME FEEL BRAND NEW** *Avco 6105 028* ○	2		12
19 Oct 74	**LET'S PUT IT ALL TOGETHER** *Avco 6105 032*	9		8
25 Jan 75	**STAR ON A TV SHOW** *Avco 6105 035*	12		7
10 May 75	**SING BABY SING** *Avco 6105 036* ○	3		10
26 Jul 75	**CAN'T GIVE YOU ANYTHING (BUT MY LOVE)** *Avco 6105 039* ●	1	3	11
15 Nov 75	**NA NA IS THE SADDEST WORD** *Avco 6105 041* ○	5		9
14 Feb 76	**FUNKY WEEKEND** *Avco 6105 044*	10		6
24 Apr 76	**CAN'T HELP FALLING IN LOVE** *Avco 6105 050*	4		7
7 Aug 76	**16 BARS** *H&L 6105 059*	7		8
27 Nov 76	**YOU'LL NEVER GET TO HEAVEN EP** *H&L STYL 001*	24		7
26 Mar 77	**7000 DOLLARS AND YOU** *H&L 6105 073*	24		4

STYLUS TROUBLE UK producer

Date	Title / Label	Peak Position	Weeks at No.1	Weeks in Top 40
23 Jun 01	**SPUTNIK** *Junior London BRG 014*	63		

STYX US group

Date	Title / Label	Peak Position	Weeks at No.1	Weeks in Top 40
5 Jan 80	**BABE** *A&M AMS 7489* ○ ★	6		8
24 Jan 81	**THE BEST OF TIMES** *A&M AMS 8102*	42		
18 Jun 83	**DON'T LET IT END** *A&M AM 120*	56		

SUB FOCUS UK producer

Date	Title / Label	Peak Position	Weeks at No.1	Weeks in Top 40
19 Mar 05	**X RAY/SCARECROW** *Ramm Records RAMM 054*	60		

SUB SUB UK group

Date	Title / Label	Peak Position	Weeks at No.1	Weeks in Top 40
10 Apr 93	**AIN'T NO LOVE (AIN'T NO USE)** *Rob's CDROB 9* SUB SUB FEATURING MELANIE WILLIAMS ○	3		9
19 Feb 94	**RESPECT** *Rob's CDROB 19*	49		

SUBCIRCUS UK/Danish group

Date	Title / Label	Peak Position	Weeks at No.1	Weeks in Top 40
26 Apr 97	**YOU LOVE YOU** *Echo ECSCD 34*	61		
12 Jul 97	**86'D** *Echo ECSCX 43*	56		

SUBLIME US group

Date	Title	Label	Peak Position	Weeks at No.1	Weeks in Top 40
5 Jul 97	WHAT I GOT	Gasoline Alley MCSTD 48045	71		

SUBLIMINAL CUTS Dutch producer

Date	Title	Label	Peak Position	Weeks at No.1	Weeks in Top 40
15 Oct 94	LE VOIE LE SOLEIL	XL Recordings XLS 53CD	69		
20 Jul 96	LE VOIE LE SOLEIL (REMIX)	XL Recordings XLSR 53CD	23		1

SUBMERGE US producer

Date	Title	Label	Peak Position	Weeks at No.1	Weeks in Top 40
8 Feb 97	TAKE ME BY THE HAND	AM:PM 5821012			
	SUBMERGE FEATURING JAN JOHNSTON		28		1

SUBSONIC 2 UK duo

Date	Title	Label	Peak Position	Weeks at No.1	Weeks in Top 40
13 Jul 91	THE UNSUNG HEROES OF HIP HOP	Unity 6577947	63		

SUBTERRANIA Swedish duo

Date	Title	Label	Peak Position	Weeks at No.1	Weeks in Top 40
5 Jun 93	DO IT FOR LOVE	Champion CHAMPCD 297			
	SUBTERRANIA FEATURING ANN CONSUELO		68		

SUBWAYS UK group

Date	Title	Label	Peak Position	Weeks at No.1	Weeks in Top 40
2 Apr 05	OH YEAH	WEA WEA384CD1	25		1
2 Jul 05	ROCK & ROLL QUEEN	Infectious WEA390CD1	22		1
24 Sep 05	WITH YOU	Infectious WEA392CD	29		1
24 Dec 05	NO GOODBYES	Infectious WEA398CD	27		1

SUEDE UK group

Date	Title	Label	Peak Position	Weeks at No.1	Weeks in Top 40
23 May 92	THE DROWNERS/TO THE BIRDS	Nude NUD 1CD	49		
26 Sep 92	METAL MICKEY	Nude NUD 3CD	17		2
6 Mar 93	ANIMAL NITRATE	Nude NUD 4CD	7		5
29 May 93	SO YOUNG	Nude NUD 5CD	22		1
26 Feb 94	STAY TOGETHER	Nude NUD 9CD	3		4
24 Sep 94	WE ARE THE PIGS	Nude NUD 10CD	18		2
19 Nov 94	THE WILD ONES	Nude NUD 11CD1	18		1
11 Feb 95	NEW GENERATION	Nude NUD 12CD2	21		2
10 Aug 96	TRASH	Nude NUD 21CD1	3		4
26 Oct 96	BEAUTIFUL ONES	Nude NUD 23CD1	8		3
25 Jan 97	SATURDAY NIGHT	Nude NUD 24CD1	6		3
19 Apr 97	LAZY	Nude NUD 27CD	9		2
23 Aug 97	FILMSTAR	Nude NUD 30CD1	9		2
24 Apr 99	ELECTRICITY	Nude NUD 43CD1	5		3
3 Jul 99	SHE'S IN FASHION	Nude NUD 44CD1	13		3
18 Sep 99	EVERYTHING WILL FLOW	Nude NUD 45CD1	24		1
20 Nov 99	CAN'T GET ENOUGH	Nude NUD 47CD1	23		1
28 Sep 02	POSITIVITY	Epic 6729495	16		1
30 Nov 02	OBSESSIONS	Epic 6732942	29		1
18 Oct 03	ATTITUDE/GOLDEN GUN	Sony Music 6743585	14		1

SUENO LATINO Italian production duo

Date	Title	Label	Peak Position	Weeks at No.1	Weeks in Top 40
23 Sep 89	SUENO LATINO	BCM 323			
	SUENO LATINO FEATURING CAROLINA DAMAS		47		
11 Nov 00	SUENO LATINO (REMIX)	Distinctive DISNCD 64	68		

SUGABABES UK group

Date	Title	Label	Peak Position	Weeks at No.1	Weeks in Top 40
23 Sep 00	OVERLOAD	London LONCD 449	6		7
30 Dec 00	NEW YEAR	London LONCD 455	12		4
21 Apr 01	RUN FOR COVER	London LONCD 459	13		3
28 Jul 01	SOUL SOUND	London LONCD 460	30		1
4 May 02	FREAK LIKE ME	Island CID 798	1	1	8
24 Aug 02	ROUND ROUND	Island CIDX 804	1	1	10
23 Nov 02	STRONGER/ANGELS WITH DIRTY FACES	Island CIDX 813	7		9
22 Mar 03	SHAPE	Island CIDX 817	11		4
25 Oct 03	HOLE IN THE HEAD	Island CIDX 836	1	1	7
27 Dec 03	TOO LOST IN YOU	Island CID 844	10		9
3 Apr 04	IN THE MIDDLE	Island MCSXD 40360	8		4
4 Sep 04	CAUGHT IN A MOMENT	Universal MCSXD 40371	8		5
8 Oct 05	PUSH THE BUTTON	Island CID911	1	3	16
17 Dec 05	UGLY	Island CIDX918	3		11
18 Mar 06	RED DRESS	Island CID922	4		7
17 Jun 06	FOLLOW ME HOME	Island CID936	32		1
11 Nov 06	EASY	Island 1712313	8		4
24 Mar 07	WALK THIS WAY	Fascination/Island 1724331			
	SUGABABES VS GIRLS ALOUD		1	1	4
29 Sep 07	ABOUT YOU NOW	Island 1748657	1	4	20
8 Dec 07	CHANGE	Island 1755606	13		9
8 Mar 08	DENIAL	Download	15		3

SUGACOMA UK group

Date	Title	Label	Peak Position	Weeks at No.1	Weeks in Top 40
13 Apr 02	YOU DRIVE ME CRAZY/WINGDINGS	Music For Nations CDKUT 190	57		

SUGAR US group

Date	Title	Label	Peak Position	Weeks at No.1	Weeks in Top 40
31 Oct 92	A GOOD IDEA	Creation CRE 143	65		
30 Jan 93	IF I CAN'T CHANGE YOUR MIND	Creation CRESCD 149	30		1
21 Aug 93	TILTED	Creation CRECD 156	48		
3 Sep 94	YOUR FAVOURITE THING	Creation CRESCD 186	40		1
29 Oct 94	BELIEVE WHAT YOU'RE SAYING	Creation CRESCD 193	73		

SUGAR CANE US group

Date	Title	Label	Peak Position	Weeks at No.1	Weeks in Top 40
30 Sep 78	MONTEGO BAY	Ariola Hansa AHA 524	54		

SUGAR RAY US group

Date	Title	Label	Peak Position	Weeks at No.1	Weeks in Top 40
31 Jan 98	FLY	Atlantic AT 0008CD	58		
29 May 99	EVERY MORNING	Lava AT 0065CD	10		6
20 Oct 01	WHEN IT'S OVER	Atlantic 020114CD	32		1

SUGARCUBES Icelandic group

Date	Title	Label	Peak Position	Weeks at No.1	Weeks in Top 40
14 Nov 87	BIRTHDAY	One Little Indian 7TP 7	65		
30 Jan 88	COLD SWEAT	One Little Indian 7TP 9	56		
16 Apr 88	DEUS	One Little Indian 7TP 10	51		
3 Sep 88	BIRTHDAY	One Little Indian 7TP 11	65		
16 Sep 89	REGINA	One Little Indian 26 TP7	55		
11 Jan 92	HIT	One Little Indian 62 TP7	17		5
3 Oct 92	BIRTHDAY (REMIX)	One Little Indian 104 TP12	64		

SUGARHILL GANG US group

Date	Title	Label	Peak Position	Weeks at No.1	Weeks in Top 40
1 Dec 79	RAPPER'S DELIGHT	Sugarhill SHL 101	3		10
11 Sep 82	THE LOVER IN YOU	Sugarhill SH 116	54		
25 Nov 89	RAPPER'S DELIGHT (REMIX)	Sugarhill SHRD 0007	58		

SUGGS UK singer

Date	Title	Label	Peak Position	Weeks at No.1	Weeks in Top 40
12 Aug 95	I'M ONLY SLEEPING/OFF ON HOLIDAY	WEA YZ 975CD	7		4
14 Oct 95	CAMDEN TOWN	WEA 019CD	14		4
16 Dec 95	THE TUNE	WEA 031CD	33		1
13 Apr 96	CECILIA	WEA 042CD1			
	SUGGS FEATURING LOUCHIE LOU & MICHIE ONE		4		11
21 Sep 96	NO MORE ALCOHOL	WEA 065CD1			
	SUGGS FEATURING LOUCHIE LOU & MICHIE ONE		24		2
17 May 97	BLUE DAY	WEA 112CD			
	SUGGS & CO FEATURING CHELSEA TEAM		22		3
5 Sep 98	I AM	WEA 174CD	38		1

JUSTINE SUISSA Dutch singer

Date	Title	Label	Peak Position	Weeks at No.1	Weeks in Top 40
27 Apr 02	CLEAR BLUE WATER	Code Blue BLU 024CD1			
	OCEANLAB FEATURING JUSTINE SUISSA		48		
20 Mar 04	BURNED WITH DESIRE	Nebula NEBCDX 055			
	ARMIN VAN BUUREN FEATURING JUSTINE SUISSA		45		

SULTANA Italian production group

Date	Title	Label	Peak Position	Weeks at No.1	Weeks in Top 40
26 Mar 94	TE AMO	Union City UCRD 28	57		

SULTANS OF PING FC Irish group

Date	Title	Label	Peak Position	Weeks at No.1	Weeks in Top 40
8 Feb 92	WHERE'S ME JUMPER?	Divine ATHY 01	67		
9 May 92	STUPID KID	Divine ATHY 02	67		
10 Oct 92	VERONICA	Divine ATHY 03	69		
9 Jan 93	YOU TALK TOO MUCH	Rhythm King 6588872	26		2
11 Sep 93	TEENAGE PUNKS	Epic 6595792	49		
30 Oct 93	MICHIKO	Epic 6598222	43		
19 Feb 94	WAKE UP AND SCRATCH ME	Epic 6601122	50		

Silver-selling ○ Gold-selling ● Platinum-selling US No.1 ★ — Peak Position / Weeks at No.1 / Weeks in Top 40

SUM 41 Canadian group

Date	Title	Label	Peak Position	Weeks at No.1	Weeks in Top 40
13 Oct 01	**FAT LIP**	*Def Jam 5888012*	8		5
15 Dec 01	**IN TOO DEEP**	*Mercury 5888982*	13		7
6 Apr 02	**MOTIVATION**	*Mercury 5889452*	21		2
29 Jun 02	**IT'S WHAT WE'RE ALL ABOUT**	*Columbia 6728642*	32		2
30 Nov 02	**STILL WAITING**	*Mercury 0638342*	16		3
22 Feb 03	**THE HELL SONG**	*Mercury 0637202*	35		1

DONNA SUMMER US singer

Date	Title	Label	Peak Position	Weeks at No.1	Weeks in Top 40
17 Jan 76	**LOVE TO LOVE YOU BABY**	*GTO GT 17*	4		9
29 May 76	**COULD IT BE MAGIC**	*GTO GT 60*	40		1
25 Dec 76	**WINTER MELODY**	*GTO GT 76*	27		3
9 Jul 77	**I FEEL LOVE**	*GTO GT 100* ●	1	4	11
20 Aug 77	**DOWN DEEP INSIDE (THEME FROM *THE DEEP*)**	*Casablanca CAN 111* ○	5		9
24 Sep 77	**I REMEMBER YESTERDAY**	*GTO GT 107*	14		7
3 Dec 77	**LOVE'S UNKIND**	*GTO GT 113* ●	3		13
10 Dec 77	**I LOVE YOU**	*Casablanca CAN 114*	10		9
25 Feb 78	**RUMOUR HAS IT**	*Casablanca CAN 122*	19		8
22 Apr 78	**BACK IN LOVE AGAIN**	*GTO GT 117*	29		5
10 Jun 78	**LAST DANCE**	*Casablanca TGIF 2*	51		
14 Oct 78	**MACARTHUR PARK**	*Casablanca CAN 131* ○ ★	5		8
17 Feb 79	**HEAVEN KNOWS**	*Casablanca CAN 141*	34		4
12 May 79	**HOT STUFF**	*Casablanca CAN 151* ★	11		7
7 Jul 79	**BAD GIRLS**	*Casablanca CAN 155* ○ ★	14		7
1 Sep 79	**DIM ALL THE LIGHTS**	*Casablanca CAN 162*	29		4
3 Nov 79	**NO MORE TEARS (ENOUGH IS ENOUGH)** DONNA SUMMER & BARBRA STREISAND	*Casablanca CAN 174/CBS 8000* ○ ★	3		10
16 Feb 80	**ON THE RADIO**	*Casablanca NB 2236*	32		3
21 Jun 80	**SUNSET PEOPLE**	*Casablanca CAN 198*	46		
27 Sep 80	**THE WANDERER**	*Geffen K 79180*	48		
17 Jan 81	**COLD LOVE**	*Geffen K 79193*	44		
10 Jul 82	**LOVE IS IN CONTROL (FINGER ON THE TRIGGER)**	*Warner Brothers K 79302*	18		9
6 Nov 82	**STATE OF INDEPENDENCE**	*Warner Brothers K 79344*	14		6
4 Dec 82	**I FEEL LOVE (REMIX)**	*Casablanca FEEL 7*	21		8
5 Mar 83	**THE WOMAN IN ME**	*Warner Brothers U 9983*	62		
18 Jun 83	**SHE WORKS HARD FOR THE MONEY**	*Mercury DONNA 1*	25		6
24 Sep 83	**UNCONDITIONAL LOVE**	*Mercury DONNA 2*	14		7
21 Jan 84	**STOP LOOK AND LISTEN**	*Mercury DONNA 3*	57		
24 Oct 87	**DINNER WITH GERSHWIN**	*Warner Brothers U 8237*	13		6
23 Jan 88	**ALL SYSTEMS GO**	*WEA U 8122*	54		
25 Feb 89	**THIS TIME I KNOW IT'S FOR REAL**	*Warner Brothers U 7780* ○	3		11
27 May 89	**I DON'T WANNA GET HURT**	*Warner Brothers U 7567*	7		7
26 Aug 89	**LOVE'S ABOUT TO CHANGE MY HEART**	*Warner Brothers U 7494*	20		5
25 Nov 89	**WHEN LOVE TAKES OVER YOU**	*WEA U 7361*	72		
17 Nov 90	**STATE OF INDEPENDENCE**	*Warner Brothers U 2857*	45		
12 Jan 91	**BREAKAWAY**	*Warner Brothers U 3308*	49		
30 Nov 91	**WORK THAT MAGIC**	*Warner Brothers U 5937*	74		
12 Nov 94	**MELODY OF LOVE (WANNA BE LOVED)**	*Mercury MERCD 418*	21		2
9 Sep 95	**I FEEL LOVE**	*Manifesto FESCD 1*	8		8
6 Apr 96	**STATE OF INDEPENDENCE (REMIX)** DONNA SUMMER FEATURING THE ALL STAR CHOIR	*Manifesto FESCD 7*	13		3
11 Jul 98	**CARRY ON** DONNA SUMMER & GIORGIO MORODER	*Almighty CDALMY 120*	65		
30 Oct 99	**I WILL GO WITH YOU (CON TE PARTIRO)**	*Epic 6682092*	44		

SUMMER DAZE UK production duo

Date	Title	Label	Peak Position	Weeks at No.1	Weeks in Top 40
26 Oct 96	**SAMBA MAGIC**	*VC Recordings VCRD 14*	61		

MARK SUMMERS UK producer

Date	Title	Label	Peak Position	Weeks at No.1	Weeks in Top 40
26 Jan 91	**SUMMER'S MAGIC**	*Fourth & Broadway BRW 205*	27		5

SUNBLOCK Dutch production duo

Date	Title	Label	Peak Position	Weeks at No.1	Weeks in Top 40
21 Jan 06	**I'LL BE READY**	*Manifesto 9876550*	4		9
20 May 06	**FIRST TIME**	*Manifesto 9878335*	9		3
28 Apr 07	**BABY BABY** SUNBLOCK FEATURING SANDY	*Universal TV 1727061*	16		2

SUNBURST UK producer

Date	Title	Label	Peak Position	Weeks at No.1	Weeks in Top 40
8 Jul 00	**EYEBALL (EYEBALL PAUL'S THEME)**	*Virgin/EMI VTSCD 4*	48		

SUNDANCE UK production duo

Date	Title	Label	Peak Position	Weeks at No.1	Weeks in Top 40
8 Nov 97	**SUNDANCE**	*React CDREACT 109*	33		1
3 Oct 98	**SUNDANCE '98 (REMIX)**	*React CDREACTX 136*	37		1
27 Feb 99	**THE LIVING DREAM**	*React CDREACT 134*	56		
5 Feb 00	**WON'T LET THIS FEELING GO**	*Inferno CDFERN 23*	40		1

SUNDAYS UK group

Date	Title	Label	Peak Position	Weeks at No.1	Weeks in Top 40
11 Feb 89	**CAN'T BE SURE**	*Rough Trade RT 218*	45		
3 Oct 92	**GOODBYE**	*Parlophone R 6319*	27		1
20 Sep 97	**SUMMERTIME**	*Parlophone CDRS 6475*	15		3
22 Nov 97	**CRY**	*Parlophone CDR 6487*	43		

SUNDRAGON UK duo

Date	Title	Label	Peak Position	Weeks at No.1	Weeks in Top 40
21 Feb 68	**GREEN TAMBOURINE**	*MGM 1380*	50		

SUNFIRE US group

Date	Title	Label	Peak Position	Weeks at No.1	Weeks in Top 40
12 Mar 83	**YOUNG, FREE AND SINGLE**	*Warner Brothers W 9897*	20		7

SUNFREAKZ Belgian producer

Date	Title	Label	Peak Position	Weeks at No.1	Weeks in Top 40
28 Jul 07	**COUNTING DOWN THE DAYS** SUNFREAKZ FEATURING ANDREA BRITTON	*Positiva CDTIVS245*	37		1

SUNKIDS US production duo

Date	Title	Label	Peak Position	Weeks at No.1	Weeks in Top 40
13 Nov 99	**RESCUE ME** SUNKIDS FEATURING CHANCE	*AM:PM CDAMPM 126*	50		

SUNNY UK singer

Date	Title	Label	Peak Position	Weeks at No.1	Weeks in Top 40
30 Mar 74	**DOCTOR'S ORDERS**	*CBS 2068*	7		8

SUNSCREEM UK group

Date	Title	Label	Peak Position	Weeks at No.1	Weeks in Top 40
29 Feb 92	**PRESSURE**	*Sony S2 6578017*	60		
18 Jul 92	**LOVE U MORE**	*Sony S2 6581727*	23		3
17 Oct 92	**PERFECT MOTION**	*Sony S2 6584057*	18		3
9 Jan 93	**BROKEN ENGLISH**	*Sony S2 6589032*	13		3
27 Mar 93	**PRESSURE US (REMIX)**	*Sony S2 6591102*	19		3
2 Sep 95	**WHEN**	*Sony S2 6623222*	47		
18 Nov 95	**EXODUS**	*Sony S2 6625342*	40		1
20 Jan 96	**WHITE SKIES**	*Sony S2 6627425*	25		1
23 Mar 96	**SECRETS**	*Sony S2 6629342*	36		1
6 Sep 97	**CATCH**	*Pulse 8 CDLOSE 117*	55		
20 Oct 01	**PLEASE SAVE ME** SUNSCREEM VS PUSH	*Five AM/Inferno FAMFERN 1CD*	36		1
16 Nov 02	**PERFECT MOTION (REMIX)**	*Five AM FAM 15CD*	71		

SUNSET STRIPPERS UK production group

Date	Title	Label	Peak Position	Weeks at No.1	Weeks in Top 40
19 Mar 05	**FALLING STARS**	*Direction 6758312*	3		9

SUNSHINE UNDERGROUND UK group

Date	Title	Label	Peak Position	Weeks at No.1	Weeks in Top 40
28 Jan 06	**COMMERCIAL BREAKDOWN**	*City Rockers ROCKERS32CD*	48		
27 May 06	**I AIN'T LOSING ANY SLEEP**	*City Rockers ROCKERS33CD*	47		
26 Aug 06	**PUT YOU IN YOUR PLACE**	*City Rockers ROCKERS35CD*	39		1
11 Nov 06	**COMMERCIAL BREAKDOWN**	*City Rockers ROCKERS37CD*	46		
17 Mar 07	**BORDERS**	*City Rockers ROCKERS38CD*	56		

SUNSHIP UK producer with singer

Date	Title	Label	Peak Position	Weeks at No.1	Weeks in Top 40
1 Apr 00	**CHEQUE ONE-TWO** SUNSHIP FEATURING M.C.R.B.	*Filter FILT 044*	75		

SUPAFLY INC Australian production group

Date	Title	Label	Peak Position	Weeks at No.1	Weeks in Top 40
17 Sep 05	**LET'S GET DOWN** SUPAFLY VS FISHBOWL	*Eye Industries/UMTV 9873464*	22		2
9 Sep 06	**MOVING TOO FAST**	*Data DATA133CDS*	23		2

SUPATONIC UK duo

Date	Title / Label	Peak Position	Weeks at No.1	Weeks in Top 40
6 Nov 04	**I WISH IT WASN'T TRUE** *Fluff Alley FLUFFA0001*	69		

SUPER FURRY ANIMALS UK group

Date	Title / Label	Peak Position	Weeks at No.1	Weeks in Top 40
9 Mar 96	**HOMETOWN UNICORN** *Creation CRESCD 222*	47		
11 May 96	**GOD! SHOW ME MAGIC** *Creation CRESCD 231*	33		1
13 Jul 96	**SOMETHING 4 THE WEEKEND** *Creation CRESCD 235*	18		2
12 Oct 96	**IF YOU DON'T WANT ME TO DESTROY YOU** *Creation CRESCD 243*	18		1
14 Dec 96	**THE MAN DON'T GIVE A FUCK** *Creation CRESCD 247*	22		1
24 May 97	**HERMANN LOVES PAULINE** *Creation CRESCD 252*	26		1
26 Jul 97	**THE INTERNATIONAL LANGUAGE OF SCREAMING** *Creation CRESCD 269*	24		1
4 Oct 97	**PLAY IT COOL** *Creation CRESCD 275*	27		1
6 Dec 97	**DEMONS** *Creation CRESCD 283*	27		1
6 Jun 98	**ICE HOCKEY HAIR** *Creation CRESCD 288*	12		1
22 May 99	**NORTHERN LITES** *Creation CRESCD 314*	11		2
21 Aug 99	**FIRE IN MY HEART** *Creation CRESCD 323*	25		1
29 Jan 00	**DO OR DIE** *Creation CRESCD 329*	20		1
21 Jul 01	**JUXTAPOZED WITH U** *Epic 6712242*	14		2
20 Oct 01	**(DRAWING) RINGS AROUND THE WORLD** *Epic 6719082*	28		1
26 Jan 02	**IT'S NOT THE END OF THE WORLD?** *Epic 6721752*	30		1
26 Jul 03	**GOLDEN RETRIEVER** *Epic 6739062*	13		2
1 Nov 03	**HELLO SUNSHINE** *Epic 6743602*	31		1
9 Oct 04	**THE MAN DON'T GIVE A FUCK** *Epic 6753041*	16		1
27 Aug 05	**LAZER BEAM** *Epic 6760111*	28		1
25 Aug 07	**SHOW YOUR HAND** *Rough Trade RTRADSCD402*	46		

SUPER MAL UK production group

Date	Title / Label	Peak Position	Weeks at No.1	Weeks in Top 40
21 Jul 07	**BIGGER THAN BIG** *Eye Industries/UMTV 1740243* SUPER MAL FEATURING LUCIANA	19		2

SUPERCAR Italian production duo

Date	Title / Label	Peak Position	Weeks at No.1	Weeks in Top 40
13 Feb 99	**TONITE** *Pepper 0530202*	15		3
21 Aug 99	**COMPUTER LOVE** *Pepper 0530392* SUPERCAR FEATURING MIKAELA	67		

SUPERCAT Jamaican singer

Date	Title / Label	Peak Position	Weeks at No.1	Weeks in Top 40
1 Aug 92	**IT FE DONE** *Columbia 6582737*	66		
6 May 95	**MY GIRL JOSEPHINE** *Columbia 6614702* SUPERCAT FEATURING JACK RADICS	22		3

SUPERFUNK French production group

Date	Title / Label	Peak Position	Weeks at No.1	Weeks in Top 40
4 Mar 00	**LUCKY STAR** *Virgin DINSD 198* SUPERFUNK FEATURING RON CARROLL	42		
10 Jun 00	**THE YOUNG MC** *Virgin DINSD 206*	62		

SUPERGRASS UK group

Date	Title / Label	Peak Position	Weeks at No.1	Weeks in Top 40
29 Oct 94	**CAUGHT BY THE FUZZ** *Parlophone CDR 6396*	43		
18 Feb 95	**MANSIZE ROOSTER** *Parlophone CDR 6402*	20		2
25 Mar 95	**LOSE IT** *Sub Pop SP 281*	75		
13 May 95	**LENNY** *Parlophone CDR 6410*	10		2
15 Jul 95	**ALRIGHT/TIME** *Parlophone CDR 6413*	2		8
9 Mar 96	**GOING OUT** *Parlophone CDR 6428*	5		3
12 Apr 97	**RICHARD III** *Parlophone CDR 6461*	2		3
21 Jun 97	**SUN HITS THE SKY** *Parlophone CDR 6469*	10		2
18 Oct 97	**LATE IN THE DAY** *Parlophone CDRS 6484*	18		2
5 Jun 99	**PUMPING ON YOUR STEREO** *Parlophone CDR 6518*	11		4
18 Sep 99	**MOVING** *Parlophone CDR 6524*	9		3
4 Dec 99	**MARY** *Parlophone CDR 6531*	36		1
13 Jul 02	**NEVER DONE NOTHING LIKE THAT BEFORE** *Parlophone R 6583*	75		
28 Sep 02	**GRACE** *Parlophone CDRS 6586*	13		3
8 Feb 03	**SEEN THE LIGHT** *Parlophone CDR 6592*	22		2
5 Jun 04	**KISS OF LIFE** *Parlophone CDR 6638*	23		1
20 Aug 05	**ST PETERSBURG** *Parlophone CDR6670*	22		1
5 Nov 05	**LOW C** *Parlophone CDR6675*	52		
29 Mar 08	**BAD BLOOD** *Parlophone CDR6755*	73		

SUPERMEN LOVERS French group with singer

Date	Title / Label	Peak Position	Weeks at No.1	Weeks in Top 40
15 Sep 01	**STARLIGHT** *Independiente ISOM 53MS* SUPERMEN LOVERS FEATURING MANI HOFFMAN	2		9

SUPERMODE Swedish production duo

Date	Title / Label	Peak Position	Weeks at No.1	Weeks in Top 40
29 Jul 06	**TELL ME WHY** *Data DATA121CDS*	13		7

SUPERNATURALS UK group

Date	Title / Label	Peak Position	Weeks at No.1	Weeks in Top 40
26 Oct 96	**LAZY LOVER** *Food CDFOOD 85*	34		1
8 Feb 97	**THE DAY BEFORE YESTERDAY'S MAN** *Food CDFOODS 88*	25		1
26 Apr 97	**SMILE** *Food CDFOOD 92*	23		1
12 Jul 97	**LOVE HAS PASSED AWAY** *Food CDFOOD 99*	38		1
25 Oct 97	**PREPARE TO LAND** *Food CDFOODS 106*	48		
1 Aug 98	**I WASN'T BUILT TO GET UP** *Food CDFOOD 112*	25		1
24 Oct 98	**SHEFFIELD SONG** *Food CDFOODS 115*	45		
13 Mar 99	**EVEREST** *Food CDFOOD 119*	52		

SUPERNOVA UK producer

Date	Title / Label	Peak Position	Weeks at No.1	Weeks in Top 40
11 May 96	**SOME MIGHT SAY** *Sing Sing 74321369442*	55		

SUPERSISTER UK group

Date	Title / Label	Peak Position	Weeks at No.1	Weeks in Top 40
14 Oct 00	**COFFEE** *Gut CXGUT 35*	16		2
25 Aug 01	**SHOPPING** *Gut CXGUT 37*	36		1
17 Nov 01	**SUMMER GONNA COME AGAIN** *Gut CDGUT 38*	51		

SUPERSTAR UK group

Date	Title / Label	Peak Position	Weeks at No.1	Weeks in Top 40
7 Feb 98	**EVERY DAY I FALL APART** *Camp Fabulous CFAB 003CD*	66		
25 Apr 98	**SUPERSTAR** *Camp Fabulous CFAB 007CD*	49		

SUPERTRAMP UK group

Date	Title / Label	Peak Position	Weeks at No.1	Weeks in Top 40
15 Feb 75	**DREAMER** *A&M AMS 7132*	13		7
25 Jun 77	**GIVE A LITTLE BIT** *A&M AMS 7293*	29		5
31 Mar 79	**THE LOGICAL SONG** *A&M AMS 7427*	7		9
30 Jun 79	**BREAKFAST IN AMERICA** *A&M AMS 7451*	9		8
27 Oct 79	**GOODBYE STRANGER** *A&M AMS 7481*	57		
30 Oct 82	**IT'S RAINING AGAIN** *A&M AMS 8255* SUPERTRAMP FEATURING VOCALS BY ROGER HODGSON	26		9

SUPREMES US group

Date	Title / Label	Peak Position	Weeks at No.1	Weeks in Top 40
3 Sep 64	**WHERE DID OUR LOVE GO** *Stateside SS 327* ★	3		14
22 Oct 64	**BABY LOVE** *Stateside SS 350* ★	1	2	14
21 Jan 65	**COME SEE ABOUT ME** *Stateside SS 376* ★	27		4
25 Mar 65	**STOP IN THE NAME OF LOVE** *Tamla Motown TMG 501* ★	7		9
10 Jun 65	**BACK IN MY ARMS AGAIN** *Tamla Motown TMG 516* ★	40		2
9 Dec 65	**I HEAR A SYMPHONY** *Tamla Motown TMG 543* ★	39		1
8 Sep 66	**YOU CAN'T HURRY LOVE** *Tamla Motown TMG 575* ★	3		11
1 Dec 66	**YOU KEEP ME HANGIN' ON** *Tamla Motown TMG 585* ★	8		10
2 Mar 67	**LOVE IS HERE AND NOW YOU'RE GONE** *Tamla Motown TMG 597* ★	17		8
11 May 67	**THE HAPPENING** *Tamla Motown TMG 607* ★	6		11
30 Aug 67	**REFLECTIONS** *Tamla Motown TMG 616* DIANA ROSS & THE SUPREMES	5		12
29 Nov 67	**IN AND OUT OF LOVE** *Tamla Motown TMG 632* DIANA ROSS & THE SUPREMES	13		12
10 Apr 68	**FOREVER CAME TODAY** *Tamla Motown TMG 650* DIANA ROSS & THE SUPREMES	28		7
3 Jul 68	**SOME THINGS YOU NEVER GET USED TO** *Tamla Motown TMG 662* DIANA ROSS & THE SUPREMES	34		4
20 Nov 68	**LOVE CHILD** *Tamla Motown TMG 677* DIANA ROSS & THE SUPREMES ★	15		5
29 Jan 69	**I'M GONNA MAKE YOU LOVE ME** *Tamla Motown TMG 685* DIANA ROSS & THE SUPREMES & THE TEMPTATIONS	3		11
23 Apr 69	**I'M LIVING IN SHAME** *Tamla Motown TMG 695* DIANA ROSS & THE SUPREMES	14		8
16 Jul 69	**NO MATTER WHAT SIGN YOU ARE** *Tamla Motown TMG 704* DIANA ROSS & THE SUPREMES	37		5
20 Sep 69	**I SECOND THAT EMOTION** *Tamla Motown TMG 709* DIANA ROSS & THE SUPREMES & THE TEMPTATIONS	18		8
13 Dec 69	**SOMEDAY WE'LL BE TOGETHER** *Tamla Motown TMG 721* DIANA ROSS & THE SUPREMES ★	13		10
21 Mar 70	**WHY (MUST WE FALL IN LOVE)** *Tamla Motown TMG 730* DIANA ROSS & THE SUPREMES & THE TEMPTATIONS	31		4
2 May 70	**UP THE LADDER TO THE ROOF** *Tamla Motown TMG 735*	6		12
16 Jan 71	**STONED LOVE** *Tamla Motown TMG 760*	3		12
26 Jun 71	**RIVER DEEP MOUNTAIN HIGH** *Tamla Motown TMG 777* SUPREMES & THE FOUR TOPS	11		10
21 Aug 71	**NATHAN JONES** *Tamla Motown TMG 782*	5		10
20 Nov 71	**YOU GOTTA HAVE LOVE IN YOUR HEART** *Tamla Motown TMG 793* SUPREMES & THE FOUR TOPS	25		8

Silver-selling ○ Gold-selling ● Platinum-selling ⊛ US No.1 ★ — Peak Position / Weeks at No.1 / Weeks in Top 40

Date	Title	Label	Peak Position	Weeks at No.1	Weeks in Top 40
4 Mar 72	**FLOY JOY**	*Tamla Motown TMG 804*	9		7
15 Jul 72	**AUTOMATICALLY SUNSHINE**	*Tamla Motown TMG 821*	10		8
21 Apr 73	**BAD WEATHER**	*Tamla Motown TMG 847*	37		1
24 Aug 74	**BABY LOVE** — DIANA ROSS & THE SUPREMES	*Tamla Motown TMG 915*	12		7
18 Feb 89	**STOP! IN THE NAME OF LOVE** — DIANA ROSS & THE SUPREMES	*Motown ZB 41963*	62		

AL B SURE! US singer

Date	Title	Label	Peak Position	Weeks at No.1	Weeks in Top 40
16 Apr 88	**NITE AND DAY**	*Uptown W 8192*	44		
30 Jul 88	**OFF ON YOUR OWN (GIRL)**	*Uptown W 7870*	70		
10 Jun 89	**IF I'M NOT YOUR LOVER** — AL B SURE! FEATURING SLICK RICK	*Uptown W 2908*	54		
31 Mar 90	**SECRET GARDEN** — QUINCY JONES FEATURING AL B SURE!, JAMES INGRAM, EL DeBARGE & BARRY WHITE	*Qwest W 9992*	67		
12 Jun 93	**BLACK TIE WHITE NOISE** — DAVID BOWIE FEATURING AL B. SURE!	*Arista 74321148682*	36		1

SUREAL US singer

Date	Title	Label	Peak Position	Weeks at No.1	Weeks in Top 40
7 Oct 00	**YOU TAKE MY BREATH AWAY**	*Cream 7CD*	15		2

SURFACE US group

Date	Title	Label	Peak Position	Weeks at No.1	Weeks in Top 40
23 Jul 83	**FALLING IN LOVE**	*Salsoul SAL 104*	67		
23 Jun 84	**WHEN YOUR 'EX' WANTS YOU BACK**	*Salsoul SAL 106*	52		
28 Feb 87	**HAPPY**	*CBS 6503937*	56		
12 Jan 91	**THE FIRST TIME**	*Columbia 6564767* ★	60		

SURFACE NOISE UK producer

Date	Title	Label	Peak Position	Weeks at No.1	Weeks in Top 40
31 May 80	**THE SCRATCH**	*WEA K 18291*	26		5
30 Aug 80	**DANCIN' ON A WIRE**	*Groove Productions GP 102*	59		

SURFARIS US group

Date	Title	Label	Peak Position	Weeks at No.1	Weeks in Top 40
25 Jul 63	**WIPE OUT**	*London HLD 9751*	5		13

SURPRISE SISTERS UK group

Date	Title	Label	Peak Position	Weeks at No.1	Weeks in Top 40
13 Mar 76	**LA BOOGA ROOGA**	*Good Earth GD 1*	38		1

SURVIVOR US group

Date	Title	Label	Peak Position	Weeks at No.1	Weeks in Top 40
31 Jul 82	**EYE OF THE TIGER**	*Scotti Brothers SCT A 2411* ● ★	1	4	12
1 Feb 86	**BURNING HEART**	*Scotti Brothers A 6708*	5		8
27 Jan 07	**EYE OF THE TIGER**	*Download*	47		

SUTHERLAND BROTHERS UK group

Date	Title	Label	Peak Position	Weeks at No.1	Weeks in Top 40
3 Apr 76	**ARMS OF MARY** — SUTHERLAND BROTHERS & QUIVER	*CBS 4001*	5		11
20 Nov 76	**SECRETS** — SUTHERLAND BROTHERS & QUIVER	*CBS 4668*	35		1
2 Jun 79	**EASY COME EASY GO**	*CBS 7121*	50		

PAT SUZUKI US singer

Date	Title	Label	Peak Position	Weeks at No.1	Weeks in Top 40
14 Apr 60	**I ENJOY BEING A GIRL**	*RCA 1171*	49		

SVENSON & GIELEN Belgian duo

Date	Title	Label	Peak Position	Weeks at No.1	Weeks in Top 40
22 Sep 01	**THE BEAUTY OF SILENCE**	*Xtrahard/Xtravaganza X2H 5CDS*	41		

BILLY SWAN US singer

Date	Title	Label	Peak Position	Weeks at No.1	Weeks in Top 40
14 Dec 74	**I CAN HELP**	*Monument MNT 2752* ○ ★	6		9
24 May 75	**DON'T BE CRUEL**	*Monument MNT 3244*	42		

SWAN LAKE US producer

Date	Title	Label	Peak Position	Weeks at No.1	Weeks in Top 40
17 Sep 88	**IN THE NAME OF LOVE**	*Champion CHAMP 86*	53		

SWANS WAY UK group

Date	Title	Label	Peak Position	Weeks at No.1	Weeks in Top 40
4 Feb 84	**SOUL TRAIN**	*Exit EXT 3*	20		4
26 May 84	**ILLUMINATIONS**	*Balgier PH 5*	57		

SWAY UK singer

Date	Title	Label	Peak Position	Weeks at No.1	Weeks in Top 40
28 Jan 06	**LITTLE DEREK**	*All City ACM0017CDS*	38		1

PATRICK SWAYZE US actor

Date	Title	Label	Peak Position	Weeks at No.1	Weeks in Top 40
26 Mar 88	**SHE'S LIKE THE WIND** — PATRICK SWAYZE FEATURING WENDY FRASER	*RCA PB 49565*	17		6

KEITH SWEAT US singer

Date	Title	Label	Peak Position	Weeks at No.1	Weeks in Top 40
20 Feb 88	**I WANT HER**	*Vintertainment EKR 68*	26		6
14 May 88	**SOMETHING JUST AIN'T RIGHT**	*Vintertainment EKR 72*	55		
14 May 94	**HOW DO YOU LIKE IT**	*Elektra EKR 185CD*	71		
22 Jun 96	**TWISTED**	*Elektra EKR 223CD*	39		1
23 Nov 96	**JUST A TOUCH**	*Elektra EKR 227CD*	35		1
3 May 97	**NOBODY** — KEITH SWEAT FEATURING ATHENA CAGE	*Elektra EKR 233CD*	30		1
6 Dec 97	**I WANT HER (REMIX)**	*Elektra E 3887CD*	44		
12 Dec 98	**COME AND GET WITH ME** — KEITH SWEAT FEATURING SNOOP DOGG	*Elektra E 3787CD*	58		
27 Mar 99	**I'M NOT READY**	*Elektra E 3767CD*	53		

MICHELLE SWEENEY Canadian singer/actress

Date	Title	Label	Peak Position	Weeks at No.1	Weeks in Top 40
29 Oct 94	**THIS TIME**	*Big Beat A 8229CD*	57		

SWEET UK group

Date	Title	Label	Peak Position	Weeks at No.1	Weeks in Top 40
13 Mar 71	**FUNNY FUNNY**	*RCA 2051*	13		12
12 Jun 71	**CO-CO**	*RCA 2087*	2		14
16 Oct 71	**ALEXANDER GRAHAM BELL**	*RCA 2121*	33		3
5 Feb 72	**POPPA JOE**	*RCA 2164*	11		10
10 Jun 72	**LITTLE WILLY**	*RCA 2225*	4		11
9 Sep 72	**WIG-WAM BAM**	*RCA 2260*	4		11
13 Jan 73	**BLOCKBUSTER**	*RCA 2305*	1	5	13
5 May 73	**HELL RAISER**	*RCA 2357*	2		9
22 Sep 73	**THE BALLROOM BLITZ**	*RCA 2403* ○	2		8
19 Jan 74	**TEENAGE RAMPAGE**	*RCA LPBO 5004* ○	2		8
13 Jul 74	**THE SIX TEENS**	*RCA LPBO 5037*	9		6
9 Nov 74	**TURN IT DOWN**	*RCA 2480*	41		
15 Mar 75	**FOX ON THE RUN**	*RCA 2524* ○	2		8
12 Jul 75	**ACTION**	*RCA 2578*	15		5
24 Jan 76	**LIES IN YOUR EYES**	*RCA 2641*	35		4
28 Jan 78	**LOVE IS LIKE OXYGEN**	*Polydor POSP 1* ○	9		8
26 Jan 85	**IT'S...IT'S...THE SWEET MIX**	*Anagram ANA 28*	45		

RACHEL SWEET US singer

Date	Title	Label	Peak Position	Weeks at No.1	Weeks in Top 40
9 Dec 78	**B-A-B-Y**	*Stiff BUY 39*	35		4
22 Aug 81	**EVERLASTING LOVE** — REX SMITH & RACHEL SWEET	*CBS A 1405*	35		4

SWEET DREAMS UK duo

Date	Title	Label	Peak Position	Weeks at No.1	Weeks in Top 40
20 Jul 74	**HONEY HONEY**	*Bradley's BRAD 7408*	10		11

SWEET DREAMS UK group

Date	Title	Label	Peak Position	Weeks at No.1	Weeks in Top 40
9 Apr 83	**I'M NEVER GIVING UP**	*Ariola ARO 333*	21		4

SWEET FEMALE ATTITUDE UK group

Date	Title	Label	Peak Position	Weeks at No.1	Weeks in Top 40
15 Apr 00	**FLOWERS**	*Milkk 267CD* ○	2		9
7 Oct 00	**8 DAYS A WEEK**	*WEA 296CD*	43		

SWEET MERCY UK production duo

Date	Title	Label	Peak Position	Weeks at No.1	Weeks in Top 40
24 Feb 96	**HAPPY DAYS** — SWEET MERCY FEATURING JOE ROBERTS	*Grass Green GRASS 10CD*	63		

SWEET PEOPLE French instrumental group

Date	Title / Label	Peak Position	Weeks at No.1	Weeks in Top 40
4 Oct 80	**ET LES OISEAUX CHANTAIENT (AND THE BIRDS WERE SINGING)** *Polydor POSP 179*	4		5
29 Aug 87	**ET LES OISEAUX CHANTAIENT (AND THE BIRDS WERE SINGING)** *Polydor POSP 179*	73		

SWEET SENSATION UK group

Date	Title / Label	Peak Position	Weeks at No.1	Weeks in Top 40
14 Sep 74	**SAD SWEET DREAMER** *Pye 7N 45385* (silver)	1	1	8
18 Jan 75	**PURELY BY COINCIDENCE** *Pye 7N 45421*	11		6

SWEET TEE US rapper

Date	Title / Label	Peak Position	Weeks at No.1	Weeks in Top 40
16 Jan 88	**IT'S LIKE THAT Y'ALL/I GOT DA FEELIN'** *Cooltempo COOL 160*	31		3
13 Aug 94	**THE FEELING** *Deep Distraxion OILYCD 029* TIN TIN OUT FEATURING SWEET TEE	32		1

SWEETBACK UK group

Date	Title / Label	Peak Position	Weeks at No.1	Weeks in Top 40
29 Mar 97	**YOU WILL RISE** *Epic 6643155*	64		

SWEETBOX US rapper

Date	Title / Label	Peak Position	Weeks at No.1	Weeks in Top 40
22 Aug 98	**EVERYTHING'S GONNA BE ALRIGHT** *RCA 74321606842*	5		8

SWERVEDRIVER UK group

Date	Title / Label	Peak Position	Weeks at No.1	Weeks in Top 40
10 Aug 91	**SANDBLASTED (EP)** *Creation CRE 102*	67		
30 May 92	**NEVER LOST THAT FEELING** *Creation CRE 120*	62		
14 Aug 93	**DUEL** *Creation CRESCD 136*	60		

MAMPI SWIFT UK producer

Date	Title / Label	Peak Position	Weeks at No.1	Weeks in Top 40
5 Jun 04	**HI-TEK/DRUNKEN STARS** *Charge Recordings CHRG024*	72		

SWIMMING WITH SHARKS German duo

Date	Title / Label	Peak Position	Weeks at No.1	Weeks in Top 40
7 May 88	**CARELESS LOVE** *WEA YZ 173*	63		

SWING US rapper

Date	Title / Label	Peak Position	Weeks at No.1	Weeks in Top 40
29 Apr 95	**SWEET DREAMS** *Logic 74321251552* SWING FEATURING DR ALBAN	59		

SWING 52 US group

Date	Title / Label	Peak Position	Weeks at No.1	Weeks in Top 40
25 Feb 95	**COLOR OF MY SKIN** *ffrr FCD 256*	60		

SWING OUT SISTER UK group

Date	Title / Label	Peak Position	Weeks at No.1	Weeks in Top 40
25 Oct 86	**BREAKOUT** *Mercury SWING 2* (silver)	4		12
10 Jan 87	**SURRENDER** *Mercury SWING 3*	7		7
18 Apr 87	**TWILIGHT WORLD** *Mercury SWING 4*	32		3
11 Jul 87	**FOOLED BY A SMILE** *Mercury SWING 5*	43		
8 Apr 89	**YOU ON MY MIND** *Fontana SWING 6*	28		5
8 Jul 89	**WHERE IN THE WORLD** *Fontana SWING 7*	47		
11 Apr 92	**AM I THE SAME GIRL** *Fontana SWING 9*	21		4
20 Jun 92	**NOTGONNACHANGE** *Fontana SWING 10*	49		
27 Aug 94	**LA LA (MEANS I LOVE YOU)** *Fontana SWIDD 11*	37		1

SWINGING BLUE JEANS UK group

Date	Title / Label	Peak Position	Weeks at No.1	Weeks in Top 40
20 Jun 63	**IT'S TOO LATE NOW** *HMV POP 1170*	30		2
12 Dec 63	**HIPPY HIPPY SHAKE** *HMV POP 1242*	2		14
19 Mar 64	**GOOD GOLLY MISS MOLLY** *HMV POP 1273*	11		9
4 Jun 64	**YOU'RE NO GOOD** *HMV POP 1304*	3		12
20 Jan 66	**DON'T MAKE ME OVER** *HMV POP 1501*	31		4

SWIRL 360 US duo

Date	Title / Label	Peak Position	Weeks at No.1	Weeks in Top 40
14 Nov 98	**HEY NOW NOW** *Mercury 5665352*	61		

SWITCH US group

Date	Title / Label	Peak Position	Weeks at No.1	Weeks in Top 40
10 Nov 84	**KEEPING SECRETS** *Total Experience RCA XE 502*	61		

SWITCHES UK group

Date	Title / Label	Peak Position	Weeks at No.1	Weeks in Top 40
10 Feb 07	**DRAMA QUEEN** *Atlantic ATUK052CD*	61		
28 Apr 07	**LAY DOWN THE LAW** *Atlantic ATUK059CD*	51		

SWITCHFOOT US group

Date	Title / Label	Peak Position	Weeks at No.1	Weeks in Top 40
14 Aug 04	**MEANT TO LIVE** *Columbia 6750812*	29		1

SWV US group

Date	Title / Label	Peak Position	Weeks at No.1	Weeks in Top 40
1 May 93	**I'M SO INTO YOU** *RCA 74321144972*	17		4
26 Jun 93	**WEAK** *RCA 74321153352* ★	33		2
28 Aug 93	**RIGHT HERE** *RCA 74321160482*	3		10
26 Feb 94	**DOWNTOWN** *RCA 74321189012*	19		3
11 Jun 94	**ANYTHING** *RCA 74321212212*	24		2
25 May 96	**YOU'RE THE ONE** *RCA 74321383312*	13		2
21 Dec 96	**IT'S ALL ABOUT U** *RCA 74321442152*	36		1
12 Apr 97	**CAN WE** *Jive JIVECD 423*	18		3
13 Sep 97	**SOMEONE** *RCA 74321513942* SWV FEATURING PUFF DADDY	34		1

SYBIL US singer

Date	Title / Label	Peak Position	Weeks at No.1	Weeks in Top 40
1 Nov 86	**FALLING IN LOVE** *Champion CHAMP 22*	68		
25 Apr 87	**LET YOURSELF GO** *Champion CHAMP 42*	32		4
29 Aug 87	**MY LOVE IS GUARANTEED** *Champion CHAMPX 55*	42		
22 Jul 89	**DON'T MAKE ME OVER** *Champion CHAMP 213*	59		
14 Oct 89	**DON'T MAKE ME OVER** *Champion CHAMP 213*	19		4
27 Jan 90	**WALK ON BY** *PWL 48*	6		7
21 Apr 90	**CRAZY FOR YOU** *PWL 53*	71		
16 Jan 93	**THE LOVE I LOST** *PWL Sanctuary PWCD 253* WEST END FEATURING SYBIL	3		11
20 Mar 93	**WHEN I'M GOOD AND READY** *PWL International PWCD 260*	5		11
26 Jun 93	**BEYOND YOUR WILDEST DREAMS** *PWL International PWCD 265*	41		
11 Sep 93	**STRONGER TOGETHER** *PWL International PWCD 269*	41		
11 Dec 93	**MY LOVE IS GUARANTEED (REMIX)** *PWL International PWCD 277*	48		
9 Mar 96	**SO TIRED OF BEING ALONE** *PWL International PWL 324CD*	53		
8 Mar 97	**WHEN I'M GOOD AND READY (REMIX)** *Next Plateau NP 14183*	66		
26 Jul 97	**STILL A THRILL** *Coalition COLA 007CD*	55		

SYLK 130 US group

Date	Title / Label	Peak Position	Weeks at No.1	Weeks in Top 40
25 Apr 98	**LAST NIGHT A DJ SAVED MY LIFE** *Sony S2 SYLK 1CD*	33		1

SYLVER Belgian production duo

Date	Title / Label	Peak Position	Weeks at No.1	Weeks in Top 40
1 Jun 02	**TURN THE TIDE** *Pepper 9230562*	56		

SYLVESTER US singer

Date	Title / Label	Peak Position	Weeks at No.1	Weeks in Top 40
19 Aug 78	**YOU MAKE ME FEEL (MIGHTY REAL)** *Fantasy FTC 160* (silver)	8		13
18 Nov 78	**DANCE (DISCO HEAT)** *Fantasy FTC 163*	29		7
31 Mar 79	**I (WHO HAVE NOTHING)** *Fantasy FTC 171*	46		
7 Jul 79	**STARS** *Fantasy FTC 177*	47		
11 Sep 82	**DO YOU WANNA FUNK** *London LON 13* SYLVESTER WITH PATRICK COWLEY	32		3
3 Sep 83	**BAND OF GOLD** *London LON 33*	67		

SYLVIA US singer

Date	Title / Label	Peak Position	Weeks at No.1	Weeks in Top 40
23 Jun 73	**PILLOW TALK** *London HL 10415*	14		8

SYLVIA Swedish singer

Date	Title / Label	Peak Position	Weeks at No.1	Weeks in Top 40
10 Aug 74	**Y VIVA ESPANA** *Sonet SON 2037* (gold)	4		17
26 Apr 75	**HASTA LA VISTA** *Sonet SON 2055*	38		2

DAVID SYLVIAN UK singer

Date	Title / Label	Peak Position	Weeks at No.1	Weeks in Top 40
7 Aug 82	**BAMBOO HOUSES/BAMBOO MUSIC** *Virgin VS 510* SYLVIAN SAKAMOTO	30		3
2 Jul 83	**FORBIDDEN COLOURS** *Virgin VS 601* DAVID SYLVIAN & RYUICHI SAKAMOTO	16		7
2 Jun 84	**RED GUITAR** *Virgin VS 633*	17		4
18 Aug 84	**THE INK IN THE WELL** *Virgin VS 700*	36		2
3 Nov 84	**PULLING PUNCHES** *Virgin VS 717*	56		
14 Dec 85	**WORDS WITH THE SHAMEN** *Virgin VS 835*	72		
9 Aug 86	**TAKING THE VEIL** *Virgin VS 815*	53		

Silver-selling ● Gold-selling ● Platinum-selling ⊛ US No.1 ★ | Peak Position | Weeks at No.1 | Weeks in Top 40

Date	Title / Label	Peak Position	Weeks at No.1	Weeks in Top 40
17 Jan 87	**BUOY** *Virgin VS 910* MICK KARN FEATURING DAVID SYLVIAN	63		
10 Oct 87	**LET THE HAPPINESS IN** *Virgin VS 1001*	66		
13 Jun 92	**HEARTBEAT (TAINAI KAIKI II) RETURNING TO THE WOMB** *Virgin America VUS 57* DAVID SYLVIAN/RYUICHI SAKAMOTO FEATURING INGRID CHAVEZ	58		
28 Aug 93	**JEAN THE BIRDMAN** *Virgin VSCDG 1462* DAVID SYLVIAN & ROBERT FRIPP	68		
27 Mar 99	**I SURRENDER** *Virgin VSCDT 1722*	40		1

SYMARIP UK group

Date	Title / Label	Peak Position	Weeks at No.1	Weeks in Top 40
2 Feb 80	**SKINHEAD MOONSTOMP** *Trojan TRO 9062*	54		

SYMBOLS UK group

Date	Title / Label	Peak Position	Weeks at No.1	Weeks in Top 40
2 Aug 67	**BYE BYE BABY** *President PT 144*	44		
3 Jan 68	**BEST PART OF BREAKING UP** *President PT 173*	25		8

TERRI SYMON UK singer

Date	Title / Label	Peak Position	Weeks at No.1	Weeks in Top 40
10 Jun 95	**I WANT TO KNOW WHAT LOVE IS** *A&M 5810592*	54		

SYMPOSIUM UK group

Date	Title / Label	Peak Position	Weeks at No.1	Weeks in Top 40
22 Mar 97	**FAREWELL TO TWILIGHT** *Infectious INFECT 34CD*	25		1
31 May 97	**THE ANSWER TO WHY I HATE YOU** *Infectious INFECT 37CD*	32		1
30 Aug 97	**FAIRWEATHER FRIEND** *Infectious INFECT 44CD*	25		1
14 Mar 98	**AVERAGE MAN** *Infectious INFECT 52CD*	45		
16 May 98	**BURY YOU** *Infectious INFECT 55CDS*	41		
18 Jul 98	**BLUE** *Infectious INFECT 57CD*	48		

SYNTAX UK producer

Date	Title / Label	Peak Position	Weeks at No.1	Weeks in Top 40
8 Feb 03	**PRAY** *Illustrious/Epic CDILL 012*	28		1
28 Feb 04	**BLISS** *Illustrious/Epic CDILLX 020*	69		

SYREETA US singer

Date	Title / Label	Peak Position	Weeks at No.1	Weeks in Top 40
21 Sep 74	**SPINNIN' AND SPINNIN'** *Tamla Motown TMG 912*	49		
1 Feb 75	**YOUR KISS IS SWEET** *Tamla Motown TMG 933*	12		7
12 Jul 75	**HARMOUR LOVE** *Tamla Motown TMG 954*	32		3
15 Dec 79	**WITH YOU I'M BORN AGAIN** *Motown TMG 1159* BILLY PRESTON & SYREETA ●	2		7
8 Mar 80	**IT WILL COME IN TIME** *Motown TMG 1175* BILLY PRESTON & SYREETA	47		

SYSTEM US duo

Date	Title / Label	Peak Position	Weeks at No.1	Weeks in Top 40
9 Jun 84	**I WANNA MAKE YOU FEEL GOOD** *Polydor POSP 685*	73		

SYSTEM F Dutch producer

Date	Title / Label	Peak Position	Weeks at No.1	Weeks in Top 40
3 Apr 99	**OUT OF THE BLUE** *Essential Recordings 5704052*	14		3
6 May 00	**CRY** *Essential Recordings ESCD 14*	19		3

SYSTEM OF A DOWN US group

Date	Title / Label	Peak Position	Weeks at No.1	Weeks in Top 40
3 Nov 01	**CHOP SUEY** *Columbia 6720342*	17		2
23 Mar 02	**TOXICITY** *Columbia 6725022*	25		1
27 Jul 02	**ARIELS** *Columbia 6728692*	34		1
10 Sep 05	**QUESTION** *American/Columbia 6760562*	41		
26 Nov 05	**HPNOTIZE** *American/Columbia 82876741302*	48		

SYSTEM OF LIFE UK production group

Date	Title / Label	Peak Position	Weeks at No.1	Weeks in Top 40
29 May 04	**LUV IS COOL** *Freedream CDFDREAM1*	63		

SYSTEM UK group

Date	Title / Label	Peak Position	Weeks at No.1	Weeks in Top 40
8 Nov 03	**IF YOU LEAVE ME NOW** *All Around The World CDGLOBE 288* SYSTEM PRESENTS KERRI B	55		

SYSTEM 7 French/UK duo

Date	Title / Label	Peak Position	Weeks at No.1	Weeks in Top 40
13 Feb 93	**7:7 EXPANSION** *Butterfly BFLD 2*	39		1
17 Jul 93	**SINBAD QUEST** *Butterfly BFLD 8*	74		

T

JAMIE T UK singer

Date	Title / Label	Peak Position	Weeks at No.1	Weeks in Top 40
15 Jul 06	**SHEILA** *Virgin VSCDT1917*	15		7
21 Oct 06	**IF YOU GOT THE MONEY** *Virgin VSCDT1921*	13		2
20 Jan 07	**CALM DOWN DEAREST** *Virgin VSCDT1923*	9		4

T-BOZ US singer

Date	Title / Label	Peak Position	Weeks at No.1	Weeks in Top 40
23 Nov 96	**TOUCH MYSELF** *LaFace 74321422882*	48		
14 Apr 01	**MY GETAWAY** *Maverick W 549CD* TIONNE T-BOZ WATKINS	44		

T-CONNECTION US group

Date	Title / Label	Peak Position	Weeks at No.1	Weeks in Top 40
18 Jun 77	**DO WHAT YOU WANNA DO** *TK XC 9109*	11		7
14 Jan 78	**ON FIRE** *TK TKR 6006*	16		5
10 Jun 78	**LET YOURSELF GO** *TK TKR 6024*	52		
24 Feb 79	**AT MIDNIGHT** *TK TKR 7517*	53		
5 May 79	**SATURDAY NIGHT** *TK TKR 7536*	41		

T-EMPO UK producer

Date	Title / Label	Peak Position	Weeks at No.1	Weeks in Top 40
7 May 94	**SATURDAY NIGHT SUNDAY MORNING** *ffrr FCD 232*	19		2
9 Nov 96	**THE LOOK OF LOVE/THE BLUE ROOM** *ffrr FCD 281*	71		

T FACTORY Italian production group

Date	Title / Label	Peak Position	Weeks at No.1	Weeks in Top 40
13 Apr 02	**MESSAGE IN A BOTTLE** *Inferno CDFERN 44*	51		

T-PAIN US rapper

Date	Title / Label	Peak Position	Weeks at No.1	Weeks in Top 40
13 May 06	**I'M SPRUNG** *Jive 82876734862*	30		3
19 May 07	**I'M A FLIRT** *Jive 88697090232* R KELLY FEATURING TI & T-PAIN	18		2
22 Sep 07	**GOOD LIFE** *Def Jam 1752306* KANYE WEST FEATURING T-PAIN	23		8
3 Nov 07	**KISS KISS** *Download* CHRIS BROWN FEATURING T-PAIN ★	38		3
16 Feb 08	**LOW** *Atlantic AT0302CD* FLO-RIDA FEATURING T-PAIN ★	6		6
8 Mar 08	**CHURCH** *Jive 88697280942* T-PAIN FEATURING TEDDY VERSETI	42		

T-POWER UK producer

Date	Title / Label	Peak Position	Weeks at No.1	Weeks in Top 40
13 Apr 96	**POLICE STATE** *Sound Of Underground TPOWCD 001*	63		
6 Apr 02	**SHAKE UR BODY** *Positiva CDTIV 171* SHY FX & T-POWER FEATURING DI	7		7
7 Jun 03	**FEELIN' U** *London FCD 409* SHY FX & T-POWER FEATURING KELE LE ROC	34		1

T.REX UK group

Date	Title / Label	Peak Position	Weeks at No.1	Weeks in Top 40
8 May 68	**DEBORA** *Regal Zonophone RZ 3008* TYRANNOSAURUS REX	34		4
4 Sep 68	**ONE INCH ROCK** *Regal Zonophone RZ 3011* TYRANNOSAURUS REX	28		4
9 Aug 69	**KING OF THE RUMBLING SPIRES** *Regal Zonophone RZ 3022* TYRANNOSAURUS REX	44		
24 Oct 70	**RIDE A WHITE SWAN** *Fly BUG 1*	2		18
27 Feb 71	**HOT LOVE** *Fly BUG 6*	1	6	16
10 Jul 71	**GET IT ON** *Fly BUG 10*	1	4	13
13 Nov 71	**JEEPSTER** *Fly BUG 16*	2		13
29 Jan 72	**TELEGRAM SAM** *T Rex 101*	1	2	9
1 Apr 72	**DEBORA/ONE INCH ROCK** *Magnifly ECHO 102* TYRANNOSAURUS REX	7		8
13 May 72	**METAL GURU** *EMI MARC 1*	1	4	11
16 Sep 72	**CHILDREN OF THE REVOLUTION** *EMI MARC 2*	2		9
9 Dec 72	**SOLID GOLD EASY ACTION** *EMI MARC 3*	2		10
10 Mar 73	**20TH CENTURY BOY** *EMI MARC 4*	3		9
16 Jun 73	**THE GROOVER** *EMI MARC 5*	4		7
24 Nov 73	**TRUCK ON (TYKE)** *EMI MARC 6*	12		10

Silver-selling ○ Gold-selling ● Platinum-selling ⊛ US No.1 ★ Peak Position | Weeks at No.1 | Weeks in Top 40

Date	Title	Peak Position	Weeks at No.1	Weeks in Top 40
9 Feb 74	**TEENAGE DREAM** *EMI MARC 7* MARC BOLAN & T REX	13		5
13 Jul 74	**LIGHT OF LOVE** *EMI MARC 8*	22		4
16 Nov 74	**ZIP GUN BOOGIE** *EMI MARC 9* MARC BOLAN & T REX	41		
12 Jul 75	**NEW YORK CITY** *EMI MARC 10*	15		8
11 Oct 75	**DREAMY LADY** *EMI MARC 11* T REX DISCO PARTY	30		4
6 Mar 76	**LONDON BOYS** *EMI MARC 13*	40		1
19 Jun 76	**I LOVE TO BOOGIE** *EMI MARC 14*	13		8
2 Oct 76	**LASER LOVE** *EMI MARC 15*	41		
2 Apr 77	**THE SOUL OF MY SUIT** *EMI MARC 16*	42		
9 May 81	**RETURN OF THE ELECTRIC WARRIOR (EP)** *Rarn MBSF 001* MARC BOLAN	50		
19 Sep 81	**YOU SCARE ME TO DEATH** *Cherry Red CHERRY 29* MARC BOLAN	51		
27 Mar 82	**TELEGRAM SAM** *T Rex 101*	69		
18 May 85	**MEGAREX** *Marc On Wax TANX 1*	72		
9 May 87	**GET IT ON (REMIX)** *Marc On Wax MARC*	54		
24 Aug 91	**20TH CENTURY BOY** *Marc On Wax MARC 501* MARC BOLAN & T REX	13		7
7 Oct 00	**GET IT ON** *All Around The World CDGLOBE 225* BUS STOP FEATURING T REX	59		
22 Sep 07	**GET IT ON** *Universal TV 1744374*	71		

T-SHIRT UK duo

Date	Title	Peak Position	Weeks at No.1	Weeks in Top 40
13 Sep 97	**YOU SEXY THING** *Eternal WEA 122CD*	63		

T-SPOON Dutch group

Date	Title	Peak Position	Weeks at No.1	Weeks in Top 40
19 Sep 98	**SEX ON THE BEACH** *Control 0042395 CON* ○	2		10
23 Jan 99	**TOM'S PARTY** *Control 0043505 CON*	27		1

T2 US duo

Date	Title	Peak Position	Weeks at No.1	Weeks in Top 40
4 Oct 97	**YOU GOT THE LOVE** *Champion CHAMPCD 330* T2 FEATURING ROBIN S	62		
24 Nov 07	**HEARTBROKEN** *All Around The World CDGLOBE760* T2 & JODIE ○	2		14
22 Mar 08	**GONNA BE MINE** *Gusto/2NV CDGUST59* ADDICTIVE FEATURING T2	47		

TABERNACLE UK group

Date	Title	Peak Position	Weeks at No.1	Weeks in Top 40
4 Mar 95	**I KNOW THE LORD** *Good Groove CDGG 1*	62		
3 Feb 96	**I KNOW THE LORD (REMIX)** *Good Groove CDGGX 1*	55		

TACK HEAD US group

Date	Title	Peak Position	Weeks at No.1	Weeks in Top 40
30 Jun 90	**DANGEROUS SEX** *SBK 7014*	48		

TAFFY UK singer

Date	Title	Peak Position	Weeks at No.1	Weeks in Top 40
10 Jan 87	**I LOVE MY RADIO (MY DEE JAY'S RADIO)** *Transglobal TYPE 1*	6		8
18 Jul 87	**STEP BY STEP** *Transglobal TYPE 5*	59		

TAG TEAM US duo

Date	Title	Peak Position	Weeks at No.1	Weeks in Top 40
8 Jan 94	**WHOOMP! (THERE IT IS)** *Club Tools SHXCD 1*	34		2
29 Jan 94	**ADDAMS FAMILY (WHOOMP!)** *Atlas PZCD 305*	53		
10 Sep 94	**WHOOMP! (THERE IT IS) (REMIX)** *Club Tools SHXR 1*	48		

TAIKO German production duo

Date	Title	Peak Position	Weeks at No.1	Weeks in Top 40
29 Jun 02	**SILENCE** *Nukleuz NUKC 0330*	72		

TAK TIX US group

Date	Title	Peak Position	Weeks at No.1	Weeks in Top 40
20 Jan 96	**FEEL LIKE SINGING** *Dub Dub 5813212*	33		1

TAKE 5 US group

Date	Title	Peak Position	Weeks at No.1	Weeks in Top 40
7 Nov 98	**I GIVE** *Edel 0039635 ERE*	70		
27 Mar 99	**NEVER HAD IT SO GOOD** *Edel 0043975 ERE*	34		1

TAKE THAT UK group

Date	Title	Peak Position	Weeks at No.1	Weeks in Top 40
23 Nov 91	**PROMISES** *RCA PB 45085*	38		2
8 Feb 92	**ONCE YOU'VE TASTED LOVE** *RCA PB 45257*	47		
6 Jun 92	**IT ONLY TAKES A MINUTE** *RCA 74321101007*	7		7
15 Aug 92	**I FOUND HEAVEN** *RCA 74321108137*	15		4
10 Oct 92	**A MILLION LOVE SONGS** *RCA 74321116307*	7		7
12 Dec 92	**COULD IT BE MAGIC** *RCA 74321123137* ○	3		10
20 Feb 93	**WHY CAN'T I WAKE UP WITH YOU** *RCA 74321133102* ○	2		6
17 Jul 93	**PRAY** *RCA 74321154502* ●	1	4	9
9 Oct 93	**RELIGHT MY FIRE** *RCA 74321167722* TAKE THAT FEATURING LULU ○	1	2	6
18 Dec 93	**BABE** *RCA 74321182122* ⊛	1	1	7
9 Apr 94	**EVERYTHING CHANGES** *RCA 74321167732* ○	1	2	6
9 Jul 94	**LOVE AIN'T HERE ANYMORE** *RCA 74321214832* ○	3		7
15 Oct 94	**SURE** *RCA 74321236622* ○	1	2	5
8 Apr 95	**BACK FOR GOOD** *RCA 74321271462* ⊛	1	4	10
5 Aug 95	**NEVER FORGET** *RCA 74321299572* ●	1	3	7
9 Mar 96	**HOW DEEP IS YOUR LOVE** *RCA 74321355592* ⊛	1	3	8
25 Nov 06	**PATIENCE** *Polydor 1714832* ●	1	4	22
10 Feb 07	**SHINE** *Polydor 1724294* ●	1	1	21
30 Jun 07	**I'D WAIT FOR LIFE** *Polydor 1736401*	17		1
27 Oct 07	**RULE THE WORLD** *Polydor 1746285* ●	2		22

TAKING BACK SUNDAY US group

Date	Title	Peak Position	Weeks at No.1	Weeks in Top 40
2 Oct 04	**A DECADE UNDER THE INFLUENCE** *Victory VR236CD*	70		
3 Jun 06	**MAKEDAMN SURE** *Warner Brothers W716CD1*	36		1
2 Sep 06	**TWENTY-TWENTY SURGERY** *Warner Brothers W728CD2*	60		

TALI New Zealand rapper

Date	Title	Peak Position	Weeks at No.1	Weeks in Top 40
10 Aug 02	**LYRIC ON MY LIP** *Full Cycle FCY 042*	75		
7 Feb 04	**BLAZIN'** *Full Cycle FCYCDS 059*	42		
15 May 04	**LYRIC ON MY LIP** *Full Cycle FCYCDS 065*	39		1

TALK TALK UK group

Date	Title	Peak Position	Weeks at No.1	Weeks in Top 40
24 Apr 82	**TALK TALK** *EMI 5284*	52		
24 Jul 82	**TODAY** *EMI 5314*	14		12
13 Nov 82	**TALK TALK (REMIX)** *EMI 5352*	23		7
19 Mar 83	**MY FOOLISH FRIEND** *EMI 5373*	57		
14 Jan 84	**IT'S MY LIFE** *EMI 5443*	46		
7 Apr 84	**SUCH A SHAME** *EMI 5433*	49		
11 Aug 84	**DUM DUM GIRL** *EMI 5480*	74		
18 Jan 86	**LIFE'S WHAT YOU MAKE IT** *EMI 5540*	16		6
15 Mar 86	**LIVING IN ANOTHER WORLD** *EMI 5551*	48		
17 May 86	**GIVE IT UP** *Parlophone R 6131*	59		
19 May 90	**IT'S MY LIFE** *Parlophone R 6254*	13		7
1 Sep 90	**LIFE'S WHAT YOU MAKE IT** *Parlophone R 6264*	23		4
21 Jun 03	**IT'S MY LIFE** *Nebula NEBCD 045* LIQUID PEOPLE VS TALK TALK	64		

TALKING HEADS US group

Date	Title	Peak Position	Weeks at No.1	Weeks in Top 40
7 Feb 81	**ONCE IN A LIFETIME** *Sire SIR 4048*	14		8
9 May 81	**HOUSES IN MOTION** *Sire SIR 4050*	50		
21 Jan 84	**THIS MUST BE THE PLACE** *sire W 9451*	51		
3 Nov 84	**SLIPPERY PEOPLE** *EMI 5504*	68		
12 Oct 85	**ROAD TO NOWHERE** *EMI 5530*	6		11
8 Feb 86	**AND SHE WAS** *EMI 5543*	17		6
6 Sep 86	**WILD WILD LIFE** *EMI 5567*	43		
16 May 87	**RADIO HEAD** *EMI EM 1*	52		
13 Aug 88	**BLIND** *EMI EM 68*	59		
10 Oct 92	**LIFETIME PILING UP** *EMI EM 250*	50		

TALKSPORT ALLSTARS UK group

Date	Title	Peak Position	Weeks at No.1	Weeks in Top 40
17 Jun 06	**WE'RE ENGLAND (TOM HARK)** *Nonsuch 82876857452*	37		1

TALL PAUL UK producer

Date	Title	Peak Position	Weeks at No.1	Weeks in Top 40
29 Mar 97	**ROCK DA HOUSE** *VC Recordings VCRD 18*	12		2
29 May 99	**BE THERE** *Duty Free DF 009CD*	45		
8 Apr 00	**FREEBASE** *Duty Free DF 015CD*	43		
2 Jun 01	**ROCK DA HOUSE (REMIX)** *VC Recordings VCRD 89*	29		1
18 Aug 01	**PRECIOUS HEART** *Duty Freee/Decode DFTELCD 001* TALL PAUL VS INXS	14		3
13 Apr 02	**EVERYBODY'S A ROCK STAR** *Duty Free DFTELCD 003*	60		

Silver-selling · Gold-selling · Platinum-selling · US No.1 ★ · Peak Position · Weeks at No.1 · Weeks in Top 40

TAMBA TRIO Argentinian group

Date	Title / Label	Peak Position	Weeks at No.1	Weeks in Top 40
18 Jul 98	**MAS QUE NADA** *Talkin Loud TLCD 34*	34		1

TAMPERER Italian production duo

Date	Title / Label	Peak Position	Weeks at No.1	Weeks in Top 40
25 Apr 98	**FEEL IT** *Pepper 0530032* TAMPERER FEATURING MAYA	1	1	11
14 Nov 98	**IF YOU BUY THIS RECORD YOUR LIFE WILL BE BETTER** *Pepper 0530082* TAMPERER FEATURING MAYA	3		9
12 Feb 00	**HAMMER TO THE HEART** *Pepper 9230038* TAMPERER FEATURING MAYA	6		4

TAMS US group

Date	Title / Label	Peak Position	Weeks at No.1	Weeks in Top 40
14 Feb 70	**BE YOUNG BE FOOLISH BE HAPPY** *Stateside SS 2123*	32		4
31 Jul 71	**HEY GIRL DON'T BOTHER ME** *Probe PRO 532*	1	3	16
21 Nov 87	**THERE AIN'T NOTHING LIKE SHAGGIN'** *Virgin VS 1029*	21		3

NORMA TANEGA US singer

Date	Title / Label	Peak Position	Weeks at No.1	Weeks in Top 40
7 Apr 66	**WALKING MY CAT NAMED DOG** *Stateside SS 496*	22		7

CHILDREN OF TANSLEY SCHOOL
UK children's school choir

Date	Title / Label	Peak Position	Weeks at No.1	Weeks in Top 40
28 Mar 81	**MY MUM IS ONE IN A MILLION** *EMI 5151*	27		1

JIMMY TARBUCK UK comedian

Date	Title / Label	Peak Position	Weeks at No.1	Weeks in Top 40
16 Nov 85	**AGAIN** *Safari SAFE 68*	68		

BILL TARMEY UK actor

Date	Title / Label	Peak Position	Weeks at No.1	Weeks in Top 40
3 Apr 93	**ONE VOICE** *Arista 74321140852*	16		3
19 Feb 94	**WIND BENEATH MY WINGS** *EMI CDEM 304*	40		1
19 Nov 94	**IOU** *EMI CDEM 361*	55		

TARRIERS US trio

Date	Title / Label	Peak Position	Weeks at No.1	Weeks in Top 40
14 Dec 56	**CINDY OH CINDY** *London HLN 8340* VINCE MARTIN & THE TARRIERS	26		1
1 Mar 57	**BANANA BOAT SONG** *Columbia DB 3891*	15		5

TARTAN ARMY UK group

Date	Title / Label	Peak Position	Weeks at No.1	Weeks in Top 40
6 Jun 98	**SCOTLAND BE GOOD** *Precious Organisation JWLCD 33* TARTAN ARMY FEATURING THE WEEIST PIPE BAND IN THE WORLD	54		
24 Nov 07	**LOCH LOMOND** *Ridge RRS48* RUNRIG WITH THE TARTAN ARMY	9		3

A TASTE OF HONEY US group

Date	Title / Label	Peak Position	Weeks at No.1	Weeks in Top 40
17 Jun 78	**BOOGIE OOGIE OOGIE** *Capitol CL 15988* ★	3		13
18 May 85	**BOOGIE OOGIE OOGIE (REMIX)** *Capitol CL 357*	59		

TASTE XPERIENCE UK production group

Date	Title / Label	Peak Position	Weeks at No.1	Weeks in Top 40
6 Nov 99	**SUMMERSAULT** *Manifesto FESCD 64* TASTE EXPERIENCE FEATURING NATASHA PEARL	66		

TATA BOX INHIBITORS Dutch production duo

Date	Title / Label	Peak Position	Weeks at No.1	Weeks in Top 40
3 Feb 01	**FREET** *Hooj Choons HOOJ 103CD*	67		

TATJANA Croatian singer

Date	Title / Label	Peak Position	Weeks at No.1	Weeks in Top 40
21 Sep 96	**SANTA MARIA** *Love This LUVTHISCDX 4*	40		1

tATu Russian duo

Date	Title / Label	Peak Position	Weeks at No.1	Weeks in Top 40
25 Jan 03	**ALL THE THINGS SHE SAID (IMPORT)** *Interscope 0193332*	44		
8 Feb 03	**ALL THE THINGS SHE SAID** *Interscope 0196972*	1	4	12
31 May 03	**NOT GONNA GET US** *Interscope 9806961*	7		4
8 Oct 05	**ALL ABOUT US** *Interscope 9885764*	8		4
18 Feb 06	**FRIEND OR FOE** *Interscope 9850070*	48		

TAVARES US group

Date	Title / Label	Peak Position	Weeks at No.1	Weeks in Top 40
10 Jul 76	**HEAVEN MUST BE MISSING AN ANGEL** *Capitol CL 15876*	4		11
9 Oct 76	**DON'T TAKE AWAY THE MUSIC** *Capitol CL 15886*	4		10
5 Feb 77	**MIGHTY POWER OF LOVE** *Capitol CL 15905*	25		6
9 Apr 77	**WHODUNNIT** *Capitol CL 15914*	5		10
2 Jul 77	**ONE STEP AWAY** *Capitol CL 15930*	16		7
18 Mar 78	**THE GHOST OF LOVE** *Capitol CL 15968*	29		4
6 May 78	**MORE THAN A WOMAN** *Capitol CL 15977*	7		9
12 Aug 78	**SLOW TRAIN TO PARADISE** *Capitol CL 15996*	62		
22 Feb 86	**HEAVEN MUST BE MISSING AN ANGEL (REMIX)** *Capitol TAV 1*	12		6
3 May 86	**IT ONLY TAKES A MINUTE** *Capitol TAV 2*	46		

ANDY TAYLOR UK singer/guitarist

Date	Title / Label	Peak Position	Weeks at No.1	Weeks in Top 40
20 Oct 90	**LOLA** *A&M AM 596*	60		

BECKY TAYLOR UK singer

Date	Title / Label	Peak Position	Weeks at No.1	Weeks in Top 40
16 Jun 01	**SONG OF DREAMS** *EMI Classics 8794880*	60		

FELICE TAYLOR US singer

Date	Title / Label	Peak Position	Weeks at No.1	Weeks in Top 40
25 Oct 67	**I FEEL LOVE COMIN' ON** *President PT 155*	11		11

JAMES TAYLOR US singer

Date	Title / Label	Peak Position	Weeks at No.1	Weeks in Top 40
21 Nov 70	**FIRE AND RAIN** *Warner Brothers WB 6104*	42		
28 Aug 71	**YOU'VE GOT A FRIEND** *Warner Brothers K 16085* ★	4		14
16 Mar 74	**MOCKINGBIRD** *Elektra K 12134* CARLY SIMON & JAMES TAYLOR	34		3

JOHN TAYLOR UK singer/bass player

Date	Title / Label	Peak Position	Weeks at No.1	Weeks in Top 40
15 Mar 86	**I DO WHAT I DO…THEME FOR 9½ WEEKS** *Parlophone R 6125*	42		

JOHNNIE TAYLOR US singer

Date	Title / Label	Peak Position	Weeks at No.1	Weeks in Top 40
24 Apr 76	**DISCO LADY** *CBS 4044* ★	25		6

J.T. TAYLOR US singer

Date	Title / Label	Peak Position	Weeks at No.1	Weeks in Top 40
24 Aug 91	**LONG HOT SUMMER NIGHT** *MCA MCS 1567*	63		
30 Nov 91	**FEEL THE NEED** *MCA MCS 1592*	57		
18 Apr 92	**FOLLOW ME** *MCA MCS 1617*	59		

PAULINE TAYLOR UK singer

Date	Title / Label	Peak Position	Weeks at No.1	Weeks in Top 40
8 Jun 96	**LET THIS BE A PRAYER** *Cheeky CHEKCD 013* ROLLO GOES SPIRITUAL WITH PAULINE TAYLOR	26		1
9 Nov 96	**CONSTANTLY WAITING** *Cheeky CHEKCD 015*	51		

R. DEAN TAYLOR Canadian singer

Date	Title / Label	Peak Position	Weeks at No.1	Weeks in Top 40
19 Jun 68	**GOTTA SEE JANE** *Tamla Motown TMG 656*	17		10
3 Apr 71	**INDIANA WANTS ME** *Tamla Motown TMG 763*	2		14
11 May 74	**THERE'S A GHOST IN MY HOUSE** *Tamla Motown TMG 896*	3		11
31 Aug 74	**WINDOW SHOPPING** *Polydor 2058 502*	36		3
21 Sep 74	**GOTTA SEE JANE** *Tamla Motown TMG 918*	41		

ROGER TAYLOR UK singer/drummer

Date	Title / Label	Peak Position	Weeks at No.1	Weeks in Top 40
18 Apr 81	**FUTURE MANAGEMENT** *EMI 5157*	49		
16 Jun 84	**MAN ON FIRE** *EMI 5478*	66		
10 Oct 92	**RADIO** *Epic 6584367* SHAKY FEATURING ROGER TAYLOR	37		2
14 May 94	**NAZIS** *Parlophone CDR 6379*	22		1
1 Oct 94	**FOREIGN SAND** *Parlophone CDR 6389* ROGER TAYLOR & YOSHIKI	26		1
26 Nov 94	**HAPPINESS** *Parlophone CDRS 6399*	32		1
10 Oct 98	**PRESSURE ON** *Parlophone CDR 6507*	45		
10 Apr 99	**SURRENDER** *Parlophone CDRS 6517*	38		1

TAZ UK duo

Date	Title / Label	Peak Position	Weeks at No.1	Weeks in Top 40
27 Oct 01	**LAILA** *Wizard WIZ 015* TAZ & STEREO NATION	44		
26 Jun 04	**CAN'T CONTAIN ME** *Def Jam UK/Mercury 9866825*	46		

TC 1991 Italian production duo

Date	Title / Label	Peak Position	Weeks at No.1	Weeks in Top 40
14 Mar 92	**BERRY** *Union City UCRT 13*	73		
21 Nov 92	**FUNKY GUITAR** *Union City UCRT 13* TC 1992	40		1
10 Jul 93	**HARMONY** *Union City UCRD 20* TC 1993	51		

KIRI TE KANAWA New Zealand soprano

Date	Title / Label	Peak Position	Weeks at No.1	Weeks in Top 40
28 Sep 91	**WORLD IN UNION** *Columbia 6574817*	4		8

TEACH-IN Dutch group

Date	Title / Label	Peak Position	Weeks at No.1	Weeks in Top 40
12 Apr 75	**DING-A-DONG** *Polydor 2058 570*	13		6

TEAM UK group

Date	Title / Label	Peak Position	Weeks at No.1	Weeks in Top 40
1 Jun 85	**WICKY WACKY HOUSE PARTY** *EMI 5519*	55		

TEAM DEEP Belgian production duo

Date	Title / Label	Peak Position	Weeks at No.1	Weeks in Top 40
17 May 97	**MORNINGLIGHT** *Multiply CDMULTY 19*	42		

TEARDROP EXPLODES UK group

Date	Title / Label	Peak Position	Weeks at No.1	Weeks in Top 40
27 Sep 80	**WHEN I DREAM** *Mercury TEAR 1*	47		
31 Jan 81	**REWARD** *Vertigo TEAR 2*	6		7
2 May 81	**TREASON (IT'S JUST A STORY)** *Mercury TEAR 3*	18		6
29 Aug 81	**PASSIONATE FRIEND** *Mercury TEAR 5*	25		7
21 Nov 81	**COLOURS FLY AWAY** *Mercury TEAR 6*	54		
19 Jun 82	**TINY CHILDREN** *Mercury TEAR 7*	44		
19 Mar 83	**YOU DISAPPEAR FROM VIEW** *Mercury TEAR 8*	41		

TEARS UK duo

Date	Title / Label	Peak Position	Weeks at No.1	Weeks in Top 40
7 May 05	**REFUGEES** *Independiente ISOM92MS*	9		2
9 Jul 05	**LOVERS** *Independiente ISOM95MS*	24		1

TEARS FOR FEARS UK duo

Date	Title / Label	Peak Position	Weeks at No.1	Weeks in Top 40
2 Oct 82	**MAD WORLD** *Mercury IDEA 3*	3		10
5 Feb 83	**CHANGE** *Mercury IDEA 4*	4		7
30 Apr 83	**PALE SHELTER** *Mercury IDEA 5*	5		6
3 Dec 83	**THE WAY YOU ARE** *Mercury IDEA 6*	24		7
18 Aug 84	**MOTHER'S TALK** *Mercury IDEA 7*	14		7
1 Dec 84	**SHOUT** *Mercury IDEA 8* ★	4		13
30 Mar 85	**EVERYBODY WANTS TO RULE THE WORLD** *Mercury IDEA 9* ★	2		11
22 Jun 85	**HEAD OVER HEELS** *Mercury IDEA 10*	12		7
31 Aug 85	**SUFFER THE CHILDREN** *Mercury IDEA 1*	52		
7 Sep 85	**PALE SHELTER** *Mercury IDEA 2*	73		
12 Oct 85	**I BELIEVE (A SOULFUL RECORDING)** *Mercury IDEA 11*	23		3
22 Feb 86	**EVERYBODY WANTS TO RULE THE WORLD** *Mercury IDEA 9*	73		
31 May 86	**EVERYBODY WANTS TO RUN THE WORLD** *Mercury RACE 1*	5		4
2 Sep 89	**SOWING THE SEEDS OF LOVE** *Fontana IDEA 12*	5		7
18 Nov 89	**WOMAN IN CHAINS** *Fontana IDEA 13*	26		3
3 Mar 90	**ADVICE FOR THE YOUNG AT HEART** *Fontana IDEA 14*	36		3
22 Feb 92	**LAID SO LOW (TEARS ROLL DOWN)** *Fontana IDEA 17*	17		3
25 Apr 92	**WOMAN IN CHAINS** *Fontana IDEA 16* TEARS FOR FEARS FEATURING OLETA ADAMS	57		
29 May 93	**BREAK IT DOWN AGAIN** *Mercury IDECD 18*	20		3
31 Jul 93	**COLD** *Mercury IDECD 19*	72		
7 Oct 95	**RAOUL AND THE KINGS OF SPAIN** *Epic 6624765*	31		1
29 Jun 96	**GOD'S MISTAKE** *Epic 6634185*	61		
5 Mar 05	**CLOSEST THING TO HEAVEN** *Gut CDGUT66*	40		1

TECHNATION UK production duo

Date	Title / Label	Peak Position	Weeks at No.1	Weeks in Top 40
7 Apr 01	**SEA OF BLUE** *Slinky Music SLINK 012CD*	56		

TECHNICIAN 2 UK group

Date	Title / Label	Peak Position	Weeks at No.1	Weeks in Top 40
14 Nov 92	**PLAYING WITH THE BOY** *MCA MCS 1710*	70		

TECHNIQUE UK duo

Date	Title / Label	Peak Position	Weeks at No.1	Weeks in Top 40
10 Apr 99	**SUN IS SHINING** *Creation CRESCD 306*	64		
28 Aug 99	**YOU + ME** *Creation CRESCD 315*	56		

TECHNO TWINS UK duo

Date	Title / Label	Peak Position	Weeks at No.1	Weeks in Top 40
16 Jan 82	**FALLING IN LOVE AGAIN** *PRT 7P 224*	70		

TECHNOCAT UK producer

Date	Title / Label	Peak Position	Weeks at No.1	Weeks in Top 40
2 Dec 95	**TECHNOCAT** *Pukka CDPUKKA 4* TECHNOCAT FEATURING TOM WILSON	33		1

TECHNOHEAD UK duo

Date	Title / Label	Peak Position	Weeks at No.1	Weeks in Top 40
3 Feb 96	**I WANNA BE A HIPPY** *Mokum DB 17703*	6		12
27 Apr 96	**HAPPY BIRTHDAY** *Mokum DB 17593*	18		3
12 Oct 96	**BANANA-NA-NA (DUMB DI DUMB)** *Mokum DB 17473*	64		

TECHNOTRONIC Belgian group

Date	Title / Label	Peak Position	Weeks at No.1	Weeks in Top 40
2 Sep 89	**PUMP UP THE JAM** *Swanyard SYR 4* TECHNOTRONIC FEATURING FELLY	2		13
3 Feb 90	**GET UP (BEFORE THE NIGHT IS OVER)** *Swanyard SYR 8* TECHNOTRONIC FEATURING YA KID K	2		8
7 Apr 90	**THIS BEAT IS TECHNOTRONIC** *Swanyard SYR 9* TECHNOTRONIC FEATURING MC ERIC	14		5
14 Jul 90	**ROCKIN' OVER THE BEAT** *Swanyard SYR 14* TECHNOTRONIC FEATURING YA KID K	9		8
6 Oct 90	**MEGAMIX** *Swanyard SYR 19*	6		7
15 Dec 90	**TURN IT UP** *Swanyard SYD 9* TECHNOTRONIC FEATURING MELISSA & EINSTEIN	42		
25 May 91	**MOVE THAT BODY** *ARS 6568377* TECHNOTRONIC FEATURING REGGIE	12		6
3 Aug 91	**WORK** *ARS 6573317* TECHNOTRONIC FEATURING REGGIE	40		1
14 Dec 96	**PUMP UP THE JAM (REMIX)** *Worx WORXCD 004* TECHNOTRONIC FEATURING FELLY	36		1
5 Nov 05	**PUMP UP THE JAM (2ND REMIX)** *Data DATA94CDS* DONS FEATURING TECHNOTRONIC	22		2

TEDDY BEARS US group

Date	Title / Label	Peak Position	Weeks at No.1	Weeks in Top 40
19 Dec 58	**TO KNOW HIM IS TO LOVE HIM** *London HLN 8733* ★	2		16
14 Apr 79	**TO KNOW HIM IS TO LOVE HIM** *Lightning LIG 9015*	66		

TEEBONE UK producer

Date	Title / Label	Peak Position	Weeks at No.1	Weeks in Top 40
5 Aug 00	**FLY BI** *East West EW 217CD* TEEBONE FEATURING MC KIE & MC SPARKS	43		

TEENAGE FANCLUB UK group

Date	Title / Label	Peak Position	Weeks at No.1	Weeks in Top 40
24 Aug 91	**STAR SIGN** *Creation CRE 105*	44		
2 Nov 91	**THE CONCEPT** *Creation CRE 111*	51		
8 Feb 92	**WHAT YOU DO TO ME (EP)** *Creation CRE 115*	31		1
26 Jun 93	**RADIO** *Creation CRESCD 130*	31		1
2 Oct 93	**NORMAN 3** *Creation CRESCD 142*	50		
2 Apr 94	**FALLIN'** *Epic 6602622* TEENAGE FANCLUB & DE LA SOUL	59		
8 Apr 95	**MELLOW DOUBT** *Creation CRESCD 175*	34		1
27 May 95	**SPARKY'S DREAM** *Creation CRESCD 201*	40		1
2 Sep 95	**NEIL JUNG** *Creation CRESCD 210*	62		
16 Dec 95	**HAVE LOST IT (EP)** *Creation CRESCD 216*	53		
12 Jul 97	**AIN'T THAT ENOUGH** *Creation CRESCD 228*	17		1
30 Aug 97	**I DON'T WANT CONTROL OF YOU** *Creation CRESCD 238*	43		
29 Nov 97	**START AGAIN** *Creation CRESCD 280*	54		
28 Oct 00	**I NEED DIRECTION** *Columbia 6699512*	48		
2 Mar 02	**NEAR TO ME** *Geographic GEOG 013CD* TEENAGE FANCLUB & JAD FAIR	68		
4 Sep 04	**ASSOCIATION** *Geographic GEOG 29CD* INTERNATIONAL AIRPORT/TEENAGE FANCLUB	75		

TOWA TEI Japanese producer

Date	Title / Label	Peak Position	Weeks at No.1	Weeks in Top 40
31 Oct 98	**GBI** *Athrob ART 021CD* TOWA TEI FEATURING KYLIE MINOGUE	63		

TEKNOO TOO UK duo

Date	Title / Label	Peak Position	Weeks at No.1	Weeks in Top 40
13 Jul 91	**JET-STAR** *D-Zone DANCE 012*	56		

Silver-selling ○ | Gold-selling ● | Platinum-selling ⊛ | US No.1 ★ | Peak Position | Weeks at No.1 | Weeks in Top 40

TELEPOPMUSIK French group

Date	Title	Peak	Wks at No.1	Wks in Top 40
2 Mar 02	**BREATHE** *Chrysalis CDCHS 5133*	42		

TELETUBBIES UK children's TV characters

Date	Title	Peak	Wks at No.1	Wks in Top 40
13 Dec 97	**TELETUBBIES SAY EH-OH!** *BBC Worldwide Music WMXS 00092* ⊛	1	2	9

TELEVISION US group

Date	Title	Peak	Wks at No.1	Wks in Top 40
16 Apr 77	**MARQUEE MOON** *Elektra K 12252*	30		3
30 Jul 77	**PROVE IT** *Elektra K 12262*	25		4
22 Apr 78	**FOXHOLE** *Elektra K 12287*	36		1

TELEX Belgian group

Date	Title	Peak	Wks at No.1	Wks in Top 40
21 Jul 79	**ROCK AROUND THE CLOCK** *Sire SIR 4020*	34		3

SEBASTIEN TELLIER French singer/multi-instrumentalist

Date	Title	Peak	Wks at No.1	Wks in Top 40
8 Oct 05	**LA RITOURNELLE** *Lucky Number LUCKY004CD*	66		

TEMPERANCE SEVEN UK group

Date	Title	Peak	Wks at No.1	Wks in Top 40
30 Mar 61	**YOU'RE DRIVING ME CRAZY** *Parlophone R 4757*	1	1	16
15 Jun 61	**PASADENA** *Parlophone R 4781*	4		16
28 Sep 61	**HARD HEARTED HANNAH/CHILI BOM BOM** *Parlophone R 4823*	28		3
7 Dec 61	**CHARLESTON** *Parlophone R 4851*	22		6

TEMPLE OF THE DOG US group

Date	Title	Peak	Wks at No.1	Wks in Top 40
24 Oct 92	**HUNGER STRIKE** *A&M AM 0091*	51		

NINO TEMPO & APRIL STEVENS US duo

Date	Title	Peak	Wks at No.1	Wks in Top 40
7 Nov 63	**DEEP PURPLE** *London HLK 9782* ★	17		9
16 Jan 64	**WHISPERING** *London HLK 9829*	20		7

TEMPTATIONS US group

Date	Title	Peak	Wks at No.1	Wks in Top 40
18 Mar 65	**MY GIRL** *Stateside SS 378* ★	43		
1 Apr 65	**IT'S GROWING** *Tamla Motown TMG 504*	45		
14 Jul 66	**AIN'T TOO PROUD TO BEG** *Tamla Motown TMG 565*	21		8
6 Oct 66	**BEAUTY IS ONLY SKIN DEEP** *Tamla Motown TMG 578*	18		9
15 Dec 66	**(I KNOW) I'M LOSING YOU** *Tamla Motown TMG 587*	19		7
6 Sep 67	**YOU'RE MY EVERYTHING** *Tamla Motown TMG 620*	26		11
6 Mar 68	**I WISH IT WOULD RAIN** *Tamla Motown TMG 641*	45		
12 Jun 68	**I COULD NEVER LOVE ANOTHER** *Tamla Motown TMG 658*	47		
29 Jan 69	**I'M GONNA MAKE YOU LOVE ME** *Tamla Motown TMG 685* DIANA ROSS & THE SUPREMES & THE TEMPTATIONS	3		11
5 Mar 69	**GET READY** *Tamla Motown TMG 688*	10		9
23 Aug 69	**CLOUD NINE** *Tamla Motown TMG 707*	15		9
20 Sep 69	**I SECOND THAT EMOTION** *Tamla Motown TMG 709* DIANA ROSS & THE SUPREMES & THE TEMPTATIONS	18		8
17 Jan 70	**I CAN'T GET NEXT TO YOU** *Tamla Motown TMG 722* ★	13		9
21 Mar 70	**WHY (MUST WE FALL IN LOVE)** *Tamla Motown TMG 730* DIANA ROSS & THE SUPREMES & THE TEMPTATIONS	31		4
13 Jun 70	**PSYCHEDELIC SHACK** *Tamla Motown TMG 741*	33		5
19 Sep 70	**BALL OF CONFUSION (THAT'S WHAT THE WORLD IS TODAY)** *Tamla Motown TMG 749*	7		11
22 May 71	**JUST MY IMAGINATION (RUNNING AWAY WITH ME)** *Tamla Motown TMG 773* ★	8		16
5 Feb 72	**SUPERSTAR (REMEMBER HOW YOU GOT WHERE YOU ARE)** *Tamla Motown TMG 800*	32		3
15 Apr 72	**TAKE A LOOK AROUND** *Tamla Motown TMG 808*	13		9
13 Jan 73	**PAPA WAS A ROLLIN' STONE** *Tamla Motown TMG 839* ★	14		7
29 Sep 73	**LAW OF THE LAND** *Tamla Motown TMG 866*	41		
12 Jun 82	**STANDING ON THE TOP (PART 1)** *Motown TMG 1263* TEMPTATIONS FEATURING RICK JAMES	53		
17 Nov 84	**TREAT HER LIKE A LADY** *Motown TMG 1365*	12		7
15 Aug 87	**PAPA WAS A ROLLIN' STONE (REMIX)** *Motown ZB 41431*	31		3
6 Feb 88	**LOOK WHAT YOU STARTED** *Motown ZB 41733*	63		
21 Oct 89	**ALL I WANT FROM YOU** *Motown ZB 43233*	71		
15 Jun 91	**THE MOTOWN SONG** *Warner Bros W0030* ROD STEWART WITH THE TEMPTATIONS	10		6
15 Feb 92	**MY GIRL** *Epic 6576767*	2		9
22 Feb 92	**THE JONES'** *Motown TMG 1403*	69		

10 C.C. UK group

Date	Title	Peak	Wks at No.1	Wks in Top 40
23 Sep 72	**DONNA** *UK 6*	2		11
19 May 73	**RUBBER BULLETS** *UK 36*	1	1	12
25 Aug 73	**THE DEAN AND I** *UK 48*	10		8
15 Jun 74	**WALL STREET SHUFFLE** *UK 69*	10		9
14 Sep 74	**SILLY LOVE** *UK 77*	24		6
5 Apr 75	**LIFE IS A MINESTRONE** *Mercury 6008 010*	7		6
31 May 75	**I'M NOT IN LOVE** *Mercury 6008 014* ○	1	2	10
29 Nov 75	**ART FOR ART'S SAKE** *Mercury 6008 017*	5		9
20 Mar 76	**I'M MANDY FLY ME** *Mercury 6008 019*	6		9
11 Dec 76	**THINGS WE DO FOR LOVE** *Mercury 6008 022* ●	6		11
16 Apr 77	**GOOD MORNING JUDGE** *Mercury 6008 025* ○	5		11
12 Aug 78	**DREADLOCK HOLIDAY** *Mercury 6008 035* ●	1	1	11
7 Aug 82	**RUN AWAY** *Mercury MER 113*	50		
18 Mar 95	**I'M NOT IN LOVE** *Avex UK AVEXCD 2*	29		1

TEN CITY US group

Date	Title	Peak	Wks at No.1	Wks in Top 40
21 Jan 89	**THAT'S THE WAY LOVE IS** *Atlantic A 8963*	8		8
8 Apr 89	**DEVOTION** *Atlantic A 8916*	29		3
22 Jul 89	**WHERE DO WE GO** *Atlantic A 8864*	60		
27 Oct 90	**WHATEVER MAKES YOU HAPPY** *Atlantic A 7819*	60		
15 Aug 92	**ONLY TIME WILL TELL/MY PEACE OF HEAVEN** *East West America A 8516*	63		
11 Sep 93	**FANTASY** *Columbia 6595042*	45		

10 REVOLUTIONS UK group

Date	Title	Peak	Wks at No.1	Wks in Top 40
30 Aug 03	**TIME FOR THE REVOLUTION** *Incentive CENT 53CDS*	59		

TEN SHARP Dutch duo

Date	Title	Peak	Wks at No.1	Wks in Top 40
21 Mar 92	**YOU** *Columbia 6566647*	10		10
20 Jun 92	**AIN'T MY BEATING HEART** *Columbia 6580947*	63		

10,000 MANIACS US group

Date	Title	Peak	Wks at No.1	Wks in Top 40
12 Sep 92	**THESE ARE DAYS** *Elektra EKR 156*	58		
10 Apr 93	**CANDY EVERYBODY WANTS** *Elektra EKR 160CD1*	47		
23 Oct 93	**BECAUSE THE NIGHT** *Elektra EKR 175CD*	65		

TEN YEARS AFTER UK group

Date	Title	Peak	Wks at No.1	Wks in Top 40
6 Jun 70	**LOVE LIKE A MAN** *Deram DM 299*	10		15

TENACIOUS D US duo

Date	Title	Peak	Wks at No.1	Wks in Top 40
23 Nov 02	**WONDERBOY** *Epic 6733512*	34		1
11 Nov 06	**POD** *Columbia 88697029612*	24		1

DANNY TENAGLIA US producer

Date	Title	Peak	Wks at No.1	Wks in Top 40
5 Sep 98	**MUSIC IS THE ANSWER (DANCING' & PRANCIN')** *Twisted UK TWCD 10038* DANNY TENAGLIA & CELEDA	36		1
10 Apr 99	**TURN ME ON** *Twisted UK TWCD 10045* DANNY TENAGLIA FEATURING LIZ TORRES	53		
23 Oct 99	**MUSIC IS THE ANSWER (REMIX)** *Twisted UK TWCD 10052* DANNY TENAGLIA & CELEDA	50		

TENOR FLY UK singer

Date	Title	Peak	Wks at No.1	Wks in Top 40
6 Apr 91	**WICKEDEST SOUND** *Desire WANT 40* REBEL MC FEATURING TENOR FLY	43		
15 Jun 91	**TRIBAL BASE** *Desire WANT 44* REBEL MC FEATURING TENOR FLY & BARRINGTON LEVY	20		4
7 Jan 95	**BRIGHT SIDE OF LIFE** *Mango CIDM 825*	51		
7 Feb 98	**B-BOY STANCE** *Freskanova FND 7* FREESTYLERS FEATURING TENOR FLY	23		2

TENPOLE TUDOR UK group

Date	Title	Peak	Wks at No.1	Wks in Top 40
7 Apr 79	**WHO KILLED BAMBI** *Virgin VS 256* ○	6		6
13 Oct 79	**ROCK AROUND THE CLOCK** *Virgin VS 290*	21		6
25 Apr 81	**SWORDS OF A THOUSAND MEN** *Stiff BUY 109* ○	6		9
1 Aug 81	**WUNDERBAR** *Stiff BUY 120*	16		7
14 Nov 81	**THROWING MY BABY OUT WITH BATHWATER** *Stiff BUY 129*	49		

TENTH PLANET UK group

Date	Title / Label	Peak Position	Weeks at No.1	Weeks in Top 40
14 Apr 01	**GHOSTS** *Nebula NEBCD 015*	59		

TERRA FIRMA Italian producer

Date	Title / Label	Peak Position	Weeks at No.1	Weeks in Top 40
18 May 96	**FLOATING** *Platipus PLAT 21CD*	64		

TERRIS UK group

Date	Title / Label	Peak Position	Weeks at No.1	Weeks in Top 40
17 Mar 01	**FABRICATED LUNACY** *Blanco Y Negro NEG 130CD*	62		

TERROR SQUAD US group

Date	Title / Label	Peak Position	Weeks at No.1	Weeks in Top 40
16 Oct 04	**LEAN BACK** *Universal MCSTD 40385* TERROR SQUAD FEATURING FAT JOE & REMY	24		2

TERRORIZE UK producer

Date	Title / Label	Peak Position	Weeks at No.1	Weeks in Top 40
2 May 92	**IT'S JUST A FEELING** *Hamster STER 1*	52		
22 Aug 92	**FEEL THE RHYTHM** *Hamster 12STER2*	69		
14 Nov 92	**IT'S JUST A FEELING** *Hamster STER 8*	47		

TERRORVISION UK group

Date	Title / Label	Peak Position	Weeks at No.1	Weeks in Top 40
19 Jun 93	**AMERICAN TV** *Total Vegas CDVEGAS 3*	63		
30 Oct 93	**NEW POLICY ONE** *Total Vegas CDVEGAS 4*	42		
8 Jan 94	**MY HOUSE** *Total Vegas CDVEGAS 5*	29		2
9 Apr 94	**OBLIVION** *Total Vegas CDVEGAS 6*	21		2
25 Jun 94	**MIDDLEMAN** *Total Vegas CDVEGAS 7*	25		2
3 Sep 94	**PRETEND BEST FRIEND** *Total Vegas CDVEGASS 8*	25		2
29 Oct 94	**ALICE WHAT'S THE MATTER** *Total Vegas CDVEGAS 9*	24		3
18 Mar 95	**SOME PEOPLE SAY** *Total Vegas CDVEGAS 10*	22		2
2 Mar 96	**PERSEVERANCE** *Total Vegas CDVEGAS 11*	5		3
4 May 96	**CELEBRITY HIT LIST** *Total Vegas CDVEGAS 12*	20		1
20 Jul 96	**BAD ACTRESS** *Total Vegas CDVEGAS 13*	10		2
11 Jan 97	**EASY** *Total Vegas CDVEGAS 14*	12		2
3 Oct 98	**JOSEPHINE** *Total Vegas CDVEGAS 15*	23		1
30 Jan 99	**TEQUILA** *Total Vegas CDVEGAS 16*	2		6
15 May 99	**III WISHES** *Total Vegas CDVEGAS 17*	42		
27 Jan 01	**D'YA WANNA GO FASTER** *Papillon BTFLYX0007*	28		1

HELEN TERRY UK singer

Date	Title / Label	Peak Position	Weeks at No.1	Weeks in Top 40
12 May 84	**LOVE LIES LOST** *Virgin VS 678*	34		2

TONY TERRY US singer

Date	Title / Label	Peak Position	Weeks at No.1	Weeks in Top 40
27 Feb 88	**LOVEY DOVEY** *Epic TONY 2*	44		

TODD TERRY PROJECT US remixer/producer

Date	Title / Label	Peak Position	Weeks at No.1	Weeks in Top 40
12 Nov 88	**WEEKEND** *Sleeping Bag SBUK 1T*	56		
3 Dec 88	**A DAY IN THE LIFE/WARLOCK** *Champion CHAMP 75* TODD TERRY PRESENTS BLACK RIOT	68		
14 Oct 95	**WEEKEND (REMIX)** *Ore AG 13CD*	28		1
13 Jul 96	**KEEP ON JUMPIN'** *Manifesto FESCD 11* TODD TERRY FEATURING MARTHA WASH & JOCELYN BROWN	8		5
12 Jul 97	**SOMETHING GOIN' ON** *Manifesto FESCD 25* TODD TERRY FEATURING MARTHA WASH & JOCELYN BROWN	5		7
6 Dec 97	**IT'S OVER LOVE** *Manifesto FESCD 37* TODD TERRY PRESENTS SHANNON	16		2
11 Apr 98	**READY FOR A NEW DAY** *Manifesto FESCD 40* TODD TERRY FEATURING MARTHA WASH	20		1
3 Jul 99	**LET IT RIDE** *Innocent RESTCD 1*	58		

TESLA US group

Date	Title / Label	Peak Position	Weeks at No.1	Weeks in Top 40
27 Apr 91	**SIGNS** *Geffen GFS 3*	70		

TEST ICICLES UK/US group

Date	Title / Label	Peak Position	Weeks at No.1	Weeks in Top 40
13 Aug 05	**BOA VS PYTHON** *Domino RUG205CD*	46		
5 Nov 05	**CIRCLE SQUARE TRIANGLE** *Domino RUG210CD*	25		1
28 Jan 06	**WHAT'S YOUR DAMAGE?** *Domino RUG217CD*	31		1

JOE TEX US singer

Date	Title / Label	Peak Position	Weeks at No.1	Weeks in Top 40
23 Apr 77	**AIN'T GONNA BUMP NO MORE (WITH NO BIG FAT WOMAN)** *Epic EPC 5035*	2		11

TEXAS UK group

Date	Title / Label	Peak Position	Weeks at No.1	Weeks in Top 40
4 Feb 89	**I DON'T WANT A LOVER** *Mercury TEX 1*	8		8
6 May 89	**THRILL HAS GONE** *Mercury TEX 2*	60		
5 Aug 89	**EVERYDAY NOW** *Mercury TEX 3*	44		
2 Dec 89	**PRAYER FOR YOU** *Mercury TEX 4*	73		
7 Sep 91	**WHY BELIEVE IN YOU** *Mercury TEX 5*	66		
26 Oct 91	**IN MY HEART** *Mercury TEX 6*	74		
8 Feb 92	**ALONE WITH YOU** *Mercury TEX 7*	32		1
25 Apr 92	**TIRED OF BEING ALONE** *Mercury TEX 8*	19		4
11 Sep 93	**SO CALLED FRIEND** *Mercury TEXCD 9*	30		2
30 Oct 93	**YOU OWE IT ALL TO ME** *Vertigo TEXCD 10*	39		2
12 Feb 94	**SO IN LOVE WITH YOU** *Vertigo TEXCD 11*	28		1
18 Jan 97	**SAY WHAT YOU WANT** *Mercury MERDD 480*	3		9
19 Apr 97	**HALO** *Mercury MERCD 482*	10		4
9 Aug 97	**BLACK EYED BOY** *Mercury MERCD 490*	5		5
15 Nov 97	**PUT YOUR ARMS AROUND ME** *Mercury MERCD 497*	10		3
21 Mar 98	**SAY WHAT YOU WANT/INSANE** *Mercury MERCD 499* TEXAS FEATURING THE WU TANG CLAN	4		5
1 May 99	**IN OUR LIFETIME** *Mercury MERCD 517*	4		5
28 Aug 99	**SUMMER SON** *Mercury MERDD 520*	5		5
27 Nov 99	**WHEN WE ARE TOGETHER** *Mercury MERDD 525*	12		3
14 Oct 00	**IN DEMAND** *Mercury MERDD 528*	6		5
20 Jan 01	**INNER SMILE** *Mercury MERDD 531*	6		4
21 Jul 01	**I DON'T WANT A LOVER (REMIX)** *Mercury MERCD 533*	16		2
18 Oct 03	**CARNIVAL GIRL** *Mercury 9812254* TEXAS FEATURING KARDINAL OFFISHALL	9		3
20 Dec 03	**I'LL SEE IT THROUGH** *Mercury 9815221*	40		1
13 Aug 05	**GETAWAY** *Mercury 9872946*	6		3
12 Nov 05	**CAN'T RESIST** *Mercury 9874784*	13		1
21 Jan 06	**SLEEP** *Mercury 9876292*	6		5

THAT KID CHRIS US producer

Date	Title / Label	Peak Position	Weeks at No.1	Weeks in Top 40
22 Feb 97	**FEEL THA VIBE** *Manifesto FESCD 16*	52		

THAT PETROL EMOTION UK group

Date	Title / Label	Peak Position	Weeks at No.1	Weeks in Top 40
11 Apr 87	**BIG DECISION** *Polydor TPE 1*	43		
11 Jul 87	**DANCE** *Polydor TPE 2*	64		
17 Oct 87	**GENIUS MOVE** *Virgin VS 1002*	65		
31 Mar 90	**ABANDON** *Virgin VS 1242*	73		
1 Sep 90	**HEY VENUS** *Virgin VS 1290*	49		
9 Feb 91	**TINGLE** *Virgin VS 1312*	49		
27 Apr 91	**SENSITIZE** *Virgin VS 1261*	55		

THE THE UK group

Date	Title / Label	Peak Position	Weeks at No.1	Weeks in Top 40
4 Dec 82	**UNCERTAIN SMILE** *Epic EPC A 2787*	68		
17 Sep 83	**THIS IS THE DAY** *Epic A 3710*	71		
9 Aug 86	**HEARTLAND** *Some Bizzare TRUTH 2*	29		5
25 Oct 86	**INFECTED** *Some Bizzare TRUTH 3*	48		
24 Jan 87	**SLOW TRAIN TO DAWN** *Some Bizzare TENSE 1*	64		
23 May 87	**SWEET BIRD OF TRUTH** *Epic TENSE 2*	55		
1 Apr 89	**THE BEAT(EN) GENERATION** *Epic EMU 8*	18		3
22 Jul 89	**GRAVITATE TO ME** *Epic EMU 9*	63		
7 Oct 89	**ARMAGEDDON DAYS ARE HERE (AGAIN)** *Epic EMU 10*	70		
2 Mar 91	**SHADES OF BLUE (EP)** *Epic 6557968*	54		
16 Jan 93	**DOGS OF LUST** *Epic 6584572*	25		3
17 Apr 93	**SLOW EMOTION REPLAY** *Epic 6590772*	35		1
19 Jun 93	**LOVE IS STRONGER THAN DEATH** *Epic 6593712*	39		1
15 Jan 94	**DIS-INFECTED EP** *Epic 6598112*	17		3
4 Feb 95	**I SAW THE LIGHT** *Epic 6610912*	31		1

THEATRE OF HATE UK group

Date	Title / Label	Peak Position	Weeks at No.1	Weeks in Top 40
23 Jan 82	**DO YOU BELIEVE IN THE WESTWORLD** *Burning Rome BRR 2*	40		2
29 May 82	**THE HOP** *Burning Rome BRR 3*	70		

THEAUDIENCE UK group

Date	Title / Label	Peak Position	Weeks at No.1	Weeks in Top 40
7 Mar 98	**IF YOU CAN'T DO IT WHEN YOU'RE YOUNG, WHEN CAN YOU DO IT?** *Mercury AUDCD 2*	48		
23 May 98	**A PESSIMIST IS NEVER DISAPPOINTED** *Mercury AUDCD 3*	27		1
8 Aug 98	**I KNOW ENOUGH (I DON'T GET ENOUGH)** *Elleffe AUCD 4*	25		1

Silver-selling · Gold-selling · Platinum-selling · US No.1 ★ · Peak Position · Weeks at No.1 · Weeks in Top 40

THEE UNSTRUNG UK group

Date	Title / Label	Peak Position	Weeks at No.1	Weeks in Top 40
13 Nov 04	CONTRARY MARY/YOU *Poptones MC5094SCD*	59		
7 May 05	PSYCHO *Vertigo 9870969*	41		

THEM UK group

Date	Title / Label	Peak Position	Weeks at No.1	Weeks in Top 40
7 Jan 65	BABY PLEASE DON'T GO *Decca F 12018*	10		9
25 Mar 65	HERE COMES THE NIGHT *Decca 12094*	2		11
9 Feb 91	BABY PLEASE DON'T GO *London LON 292*	65		

THEN JERICO UK group

Date	Title / Label	Peak Position	Weeks at No.1	Weeks in Top 40
31 Jan 87	LET HER FALL *London LON 97*	65		
25 Jul 87	THE MOTIVE (LIVING WITHOUT YOU) *London LON 145*	18		6
24 Oct 87	MUSCLE DEEP *London LON 156*	48		
28 Jan 89	BIG AREA *London LON 204*	13		5
8 Apr 89	WHAT DOES IT TAKE *London LON 223*	33		3
12 Aug 89	SUGAR BOX *London LON 235*	22		4

THERAPY? UK group

Date	Title / Label	Peak Position	Weeks at No.1	Weeks in Top 40
31 Oct 92	TEETHGRINDER *A&M AM 0097*	30		1
20 Mar 93	SHORTSHARPSHOCK EP *A&M AMCD 208*	9		3
12 Jun 93	FACE THE STRANGE EP *A&M 5803052*	18		2
28 Aug 93	OPAL MANTRA *A&M 5803612*	13		2
29 Jan 94	NOWHERE *A&M 5805052*	18		3
12 Mar 94	TRIGGER INSIDE *A&M 5805352*	22		1
11 Jun 94	DIE LAUGHING *A&M 5805892*	29		1
27 May 95	INNOCENT X *Volume VOLCD 1*	53		
3 Jun 95	STORIES *A&M 5811052*	14		1
29 Jul 95	LOOSE *A&M 5811652*	25		1
18 Nov 95	DIANE *A&M 5812912*	26		1
14 Mar 98	CHURCH OF NOISE *A&M 5825392*	29		1
30 May 98	LONELY, CRYIN', ONLY *A&M 0441212*	32		1

THERESE Swedish singer

Date	Title / Label	Peak Position	Weeks at No.1	Weeks in Top 40
28 Aug 04	PUT EM HIGH *Hed Kandi HEDKCDS008* STONEBRIDGE FEATURING THERESE	6		6
29 Jan 05	TAKE ME AWAY *Hed Kandi HEDKCDS009* STONEBRIDGE FEATURING THERESE	9		3
19 May 07	FEELIN' ME *Positiva CDTIVS255*	61		

THESE ANIMAL MEN UK group

Date	Title / Label	Peak Position	Weeks at No.1	Weeks in Top 40
24 Sep 94	THIS IS THE SOUND OF YOUTH *Hi-Rise FLATSCD 7*	72		
8 Feb 97	LIFE SUPPORTING MACHINE *Hut HUTCD 76*	62		
12 Apr 97	LIGHT EMITTING ELECTRICAL WAVE *Hut HUTCD 81*	72		

THEY MIGHT BE GIANTS US group

Date	Title / Label	Peak Position	Weeks at No.1	Weeks in Top 40
3 Mar 90	BIRDHOUSE IN YOUR SOUL *Elektra EKR 104*	6		8
2 Jun 90	ISTANBUL (NOT CONSTANTINOPLE) *Elektra EKR 110*	61		
28 Jul 01	BOSS OF ME *PIAS PIASREST 001CD*	21		3

THICK D US producer

Date	Title / Label	Peak Position	Weeks at No.1	Weeks in Top 40
12 Oct 02	INSATIABLE *Multiply CDMULTY 88*	35		1

ROBIN THICKE US singer

Date	Title / Label	Peak Position	Weeks at No.1	Weeks in Top 40
30 Jun 07	LOST WITHOUT U *Interscope 1736885*	11		4

THIN LIZZY Irish group

Date	Title / Label	Peak Position	Weeks at No.1	Weeks in Top 40
20 Jan 73	WHISKEY IN THE JAR *Decca F 13355*	6		11
29 May 76	THE BOYS ARE BACK IN TOWN *Vertigo 6059 139*	8		9
14 Aug 76	JAILBREAK *Vertigo 6059 150*	31		3
15 Jan 77	DON'T BELIEVE A WORD *Vertigo LIZZY 001*	12		7
13 Aug 77	DANCIN' IN THE MOONLIGHT (IT'S CAUGHT ME IN THE SPOTLIGHT) *Vertigo 6059 177*	14		8
13 May 78	ROSALIE – COWGIRLS' SONG (MEDLEY) *Vertigo LIZZY 2*	20		8
3 Mar 79	WAITING FOR AN ALIBI *Vertigo LIZZY 003*	9		7
16 Jun 79	DO ANYTHING YOU WANT TO *Vertigo LIZZY 004*	14		7
20 Oct 79	SARAH *Vertigo LIZZY 5*	24		6
24 May 80	CHINATOWN *Vertigo LIZZY 6*	21		8
27 Sep 80	KILLER ON THE LOOSE *Vertigo LIZZY 7*	10		6
2 May 81	KILLERS LIVE EP *Vertigo LIZZY 8*	19		5
8 Aug 81	TROUBLE BOYS *Vertigo LIZZY 9*	53		
6 Mar 82	HOLLYWOOD (DOWN ON YOUR LUCK) *Vertigo LIZZY 10*	53		
12 Feb 83	COLD SWEAT *Vertigo LIZZY 11*	27		3
7 May 83	THUNDER AND LIGHTNING *Vertigo LIZZY 12*	39		1
6 Aug 83	THE SUN GOES DOWN *Vertigo LIZZY 13*	52		
26 Jan 91	DEDICATION *Vertigo LIZZY 14*	35		2
23 Mar 91	THE BOYS ARE BACK IN TOWN *Vertigo LIZZY 15*	63		

3RD BASS US group

Date	Title / Label	Peak Position	Weeks at No.1	Weeks in Top 40
10 Feb 90	THE GAS FACE *Def Jam 6556270*	71		
7 Apr 90	BROOKLYN-QUEENS *Def Jam 6558307*	61		
22 Jun 91	POP GOES THE WEASEL *Def Jam 6569547*	64		

THIRD DIMENSION UK group

Date	Title / Label	Peak Position	Weeks at No.1	Weeks in Top 40
12 Oct 96	DON'T GO *Soundproof MCSTD 40082* THIRD DIMENSION FEATURING JULIE McDERMOTT	34		1

3RD EDGE UK group

Date	Title / Label	Peak Position	Weeks at No.1	Weeks in Top 40
31 Aug 02	IN AND OUT *Q Zone/Parlophone CDR 6568*	15		3
8 Feb 03	KNOW YOU WANNA *Parlophone CDRS 6596*	17		2

THIRD EYE BLIND UK group

Date	Title / Label	Peak Position	Weeks at No.1	Weeks in Top 40
27 Sep 97	SEMI-CHARMED LIFE *Elektra E 3907CD*	33		3
21 Mar 98	HOW'S IT GOING TO BE *Elektra E 3863CD*	51		

3RD STOREE US group

Date	Title / Label	Peak Position	Weeks at No.1	Weeks in Top 40
5 Jun 99	IF EVER *Yab Yum E 3752CD*	53		

3RD WISH US group

Date	Title / Label	Peak Position	Weeks at No.1	Weeks in Top 40
18 Dec 04	OBSESSION (SI ES AMOR) *Three8 CXTHREE8004*	15		5

THIRD WORLD Jamaican group

Date	Title / Label	Peak Position	Weeks at No.1	Weeks in Top 40
23 Sep 78	NOW THAT WE'VE FOUND LOVE *Island WIP 6457*	10		7
6 Jan 79	COOL MEDITATION *Island WIP 6469*	17		7
16 Jun 79	TALK TO ME *Island WIP 6496*	56		
6 Jun 81	DANCING ON THE FLOOR (HOOKED ON LOVE) *CBS A 1214*	10		12
17 Apr 82	TRY JAH LOVE *CBS A 2063*	47		
9 Mar 85	NOW THAT WE'VE FOUND LOVE *Island IS 219*	22		5

THIRST UK group

Date	Title / Label	Peak Position	Weeks at No.1	Weeks in Top 40
6 Jul 91	THE ENEMY WITHIN *10 TEN 379*	61		

THIRTEEN SENSES UK group

Date	Title / Label	Peak Position	Weeks at No.1	Weeks in Top 40
12 Jun 04	DO NO WRONG *Vertigo 9866746*	38		1
25 Sep 04	INTO THE FIRE *Vertigo 9867851*	35		1
22 Jan 05	THRU THE GLASS *Vertigo 9869347*	18		1
9 Apr 05	THE SALT WOUND ROUTINE *Vertigo 9870781*	45		

1300 DRUMS UK duo

Date	Title / Label	Peak Position	Weeks at No.1	Weeks in Top 40
18 May 96	OOH! AAH! CANTONA *Dynamo DYND 5* 1300 DRUMS FEATURING THE UNJUSTIFIED ANCIENTS OF MU	11		3

30 SECONDS TO MARS US group

Date	Title / Label	Peak Position	Weeks at No.1	Weeks in Top 40
12 May 07	THE KILL *Virgin 3933652*	64		
22 Sep 07	THE KILL (REBIRTH) *Virgin 3933652*	28		3
16 Feb 08	FROM YESTERDAY *Virgin VUSCD340*	37		1

THIS ISLAND EARTH UK group

Date	Title / Label	Peak Position	Weeks at No.1	Weeks in Top 40
5 Jan 85	SEE THAT GLOW *Magnet MAG 266*	47		

THIS MORTAL COIL UK group

Date	Title / Label	Peak Position	Weeks at No.1	Weeks in Top 40
22 Oct 83	SONG TO THE SIREN *4AD AD 310*	66		

Legend: Silver-selling ● · Gold-selling ● · Platinum-selling ● · US No.1 ★ · Peak Position · Weeks at No.1 · Weeks in Top 40

THIS WAY UP UK duo

Date	Title / Label	Peak Position	Weeks at No.1	Weeks in Top 40
22 Aug 87	**TELL ME WHY** *Virgin VS 954*	72		

THIS YEAR'S BLONDE UK group

Date	Title / Label	Peak Position	Weeks at No.1	Weeks in Top 40
10 Oct 81	**PLATINUM POP** *Creole CR 19*	46		
14 Nov 87	**WHO'S THAT MIX** *Debut DEBT 3034*	62		

SANDI THOM UK singer

Date	Title / Label	Peak Position	Weeks at No.1	Weeks in Top 40
15 Oct 05	**I WISH I WAS A PUNK ROCKER (WITH FLOWERS IN MY HAIR)** *Viking Legacy VIKINGS04*	55		
27 May 06	**I WISH I WAS A PUNK ROCKER (WITH FLOWERS IN MY HAIR)** *RCA 82876843422*	1		17
2 Sep 06	**WHAT IF I'M RIGHT** *RCA 82876891252*	22		2

B.J. THOMAS US singer

Date	Title / Label	Peak Position	Weeks at No.1	Weeks in Top 40
21 Feb 70	**RAINDROPS KEEP FALLING ON MY HEAD** *Wand WN 1* ★	38		1

DANTE THOMAS US singer

Date	Title / Label	Peak Position	Weeks at No.1	Weeks in Top 40
1 Sep 01	**MISS CALIFORNIA** *Elektra E 7192CD* DANTE THOMAS FEATURING PRAS	25		1

EVELYN THOMAS US singer

Date	Title / Label	Peak Position	Weeks at No.1	Weeks in Top 40
24 Jan 76	**WEAK SPOT** *20th Century BTC 1014*	26		6
17 Apr 76	**DOOMSDAY** *20th Century BTC 1017*	41		
21 Apr 84	**HIGH ENERGY** *Record Shack SOHO 18*	5		11
25 Aug 84	**MASQUERADE** *Record Shack SOHO 25*	60		

JAMO THOMAS US singer

Date	Title / Label	Peak Position	Weeks at No.1	Weeks in Top 40
26 Feb 69	**I SPY FOR THE FBI** *Polydor 56 755*	44		

KENNY THOMAS UK singer

Date	Title / Label	Peak Position	Weeks at No.1	Weeks in Top 40
26 Jan 91	**OUTSTANDING** *Cooltempo COOL 227*	12		8
1 Jun 91	**THINKING ABOUT YOUR LOVE** *Cooltempo COOL 235*	4		12
5 Oct 91	**BEST OF YOU** *Cooltempo COOL 243*	11		5
30 Nov 91	**TENDER LOVE** *Cooltempo COOL 247*	26		5
10 Jul 93	**STAY** *Cooltempo CDCOOL 271*	22		4
4 Sep 93	**TRIPPIN' ON YOUR LOVE** *Cooltempo CDCOOL 277*	17		3
6 Nov 93	**PIECE BY PIECE** *Cooltempo CDCOOL 283*	36		2
14 May 94	**DESTINY** *Cooltempo CDCOOL 289*	59		
2 Sep 95	**WHEN I THINK OF YOU** *Cooltempo CDCOOL 309*	27		2

LILLO THOMAS US singer

Date	Title / Label	Peak Position	Weeks at No.1	Weeks in Top 40
27 Apr 85	**SETTLE DOWN** *Capitol CL 356*	66		
21 Mar 87	**SEXY GIRL** *Capitol CL 445*	23		4
30 May 87	**I'M IN LOVE** *Capitol CL 450*	54		

NATASHA THOMAS Danish singer

Date	Title / Label	Peak Position	Weeks at No.1	Weeks in Top 40
22 Apr 06	**SKIN DEEP** *Simply Vinyl SIMPCD003*	54		

NICKY THOMAS Jamaican singer

Date	Title / Label	Peak Position	Weeks at No.1	Weeks in Top 40
13 Jun 70	**LOVE OF THE COMMON PEOPLE** *Trojan TR 7750*	9		13

ROB THOMAS US singer

Date	Title / Label	Peak Position	Weeks at No.1	Weeks in Top 40
23 Oct 99	**SMOOTH** *Arista 74321709492* SANTANA FEATURING ROB THOMAS	75		
1 Apr 00	**SMOOTH** *Arista 74321748762* SANTANA FEATURING ROB THOMAS ★	3		8
28 May 05	**LONELY NO MORE** *Atlantic AT0203CD*	11		5
1 Oct 05	**THIS IS HOW A HEART BREAKS** *Atlantic AT0219CD*	67		

RUFUS THOMAS US singer

Date	Title / Label	Peak Position	Weeks at No.1	Weeks in Top 40
11 Apr 70	**DO THE FUNKY CHICKEN** *Stax 144*	18		10

TASHA THOMAS US singer

Date	Title / Label	Peak Position	Weeks at No.1	Weeks in Top 40
20 Jan 79	**SHOOT ME (WITH YOUR LOVE)** *Atlantic LV 4*	59		

TIMMY THOMAS US singer

Date	Title / Label	Peak Position	Weeks at No.1	Weeks in Top 40
24 Feb 73	**WHY CAN'T WE LIVE TOGETHER** *Mojo 2027 012*	12		10
28 Dec 85	**NEW YORK EYES** *Portrait A 6805* NICOLE WITH TIMMY THOMAS	41		
14 Jul 90	**WHY CAN'T WE LIVE TOGETHER (REMIX)** *TK TKR 1*	54		

THOMAS & TAYLOR US duo

Date	Title / Label	Peak Position	Weeks at No.1	Weeks in Top 40
17 May 86	**YOU CAN'T BLAME LOVE** *Cooltempo COOL 123*	53		

CARROLL THOMPSON UK singer

Date	Title / Label	Peak Position	Weeks at No.1	Weeks in Top 40
19 May 90	**JOY AND HEARTBREAK** *Circa YR 45* MOVEMENT 98 FEATURING CARROLL THOMPSON	27		3
7 Jul 90	**I'M STILL WAITING** *Mango MNG 749* COURTNEY PINE FEATURING CARROLL THOMPSON	66		
15 Sep 90	**SUNRISE** *Circa YR 51* MOVEMENT 98 FEATURING CARROLL THOMPSON	58		

CHRIS THOMPSON UK singer

Date	Title / Label	Peak Position	Weeks at No.1	Weeks in Top 40
27 Oct 79	**IF YOU REMEMBER ME** *Planet K 12389*	42		

SUE THOMPSON US singer

Date	Title / Label	Peak Position	Weeks at No.1	Weeks in Top 40
2 Nov 61	**SAD MOVIES (MAKE ME CRY)** *Polydor NH 66967*	46		
21 Jan 65	**PAPER TIGER** *Hickory 1284*	30		5

THOMPSON TWINS UK/New Zealand group

Date	Title / Label	Peak Position	Weeks at No.1	Weeks in Top 40
6 Nov 82	**LIES** *Arista ARIST 486*	67		
29 Jan 83	**LOVE ON YOUR SIDE** *Arista ARIST 504*	9		10
16 Apr 83	**WE ARE DETECTIVE** *Arista ARIST 526*	7		7
16 Jul 83	**WATCHING** *Arista TWINS 1*	33		3
19 Nov 83	**HOLD ME NOW** *Arista TWINS 2*	4		13
4 Feb 84	**DOCTOR DOCTOR** *Arista TWINS 3*	3		9
31 Mar 84	**YOU TAKE ME UP** *Arista TWINS 4*	2		8
7 Jul 84	**SISTER OF MERCY** *Arista TWINS 5*	11		6
8 Dec 84	**LAY YOUR HANDS ON ME** *Arista TWINS 6*	13		7
31 Aug 85	**DON'T MESS WITH DOCTOR DREAM** *Arista TWINS 9*	15		5
19 Oct 85	**KING FOR A DAY** *Arista TWINS 7*	22		4
7 Dec 85	**REVOLUTION** *Arista TWINS 10*	56		
21 Mar 87	**GET THAT LOVE** *Arista TWINS 12*	66		
15 Oct 88	**IN THE NAME OF LOVE '88** *Arista 111808*	46		
28 Sep 91	**COME INSIDE** *Warner Brothers W 0058*	56		
25 Jan 92	**THE SAINT** *Warner Brothers W 0080*	53		

EDDIE THONEICK & KURD MAVERICK German production duo

Date	Title / Label	Peak Position	Weeks at No.1	Weeks in Top 40
27 May 06	**LOVE SENSATION 2006** *All Around The World CDGLOBE531*	39		1

TRACEY THORNE UK singer

Date	Title / Label	Peak Position	Weeks at No.1	Weeks in Top 40
21 Jan 95	**PROTECTION** *Virgin WBRX 6* MASSIVE ATTACK FEATURING TRACEY THORN	14		3
10 Mar 07	**IT'S ALL TRUE** *Virgin VSCDX1932*	75		

DAVID THORNE US singer

Date	Title / Label	Peak Position	Weeks at No.1	Weeks in Top 40
24 Jan 63	**ALLEY CAT SONG** *Stateside SS 141*	21		5

KEN THORNE UK pianist

Date	Title / Label	Peak Position	Weeks at No.1	Weeks in Top 40
18 Jul 63	**THEME FROM THE FILM *THE LEGION'S LAST PATROL*** *HMV POP 1176*	4		12

THOSE 2 GIRLS UK duo

Date	Title / Label	Peak Position	Weeks at No.1	Weeks in Top 40
5 Nov 94	**WANNA MAKE YOU GO...UUH!** *Final Vinyl 74321233782*	74		
4 Mar 95	**ALL I WANT** *Final Vinyl 74321254202*	36		1

THOUSAND YARD STARE UK group

Date	Title / Label	Peak Position	Weeks at No.1	Weeks in Top 40
26 Oct 91	**SEASONSTREAM (EP)** *Stifled Aardvark AARD 5T*	65		
8 Feb 92	**COMEUPPANCE** *Stifled Aardvark AARD 007*	37		1
11 Jul 92	**SPINDRIFT (EP)** *Stifled Aardvark AARDT 010*	58		
8 May 93	**VERSION OF ME** *Polydor AARDC 012*	57		

THRASHING DOVES UK group

Date	Title / Label	Peak Position	Weeks at No.1	Weeks in Top 40
24 Jan 87	**BEAUTIFUL IMBALANCE** *A&M TDOVE 1*	50		

THREE AMIGOS UK production group

Date	Title / Label	Peak Position	Weeks at No.1	Weeks in Top 40
3 Jul 99	**LOUIE LOUIE** *Inferno CDFERN 17*	15		3
24 Mar 01	**25 MILES 2001** *Wonderboy WBOYD 25*	30		1

3 COLOURS RED UK group

Date	Title / Label	Peak Position	Weeks at No.1	Weeks in Top 40
18 Jan 97	**NUCLEAR HOLIDAY** *Creation CRESCD 250*	22		1
15 Mar 97	**SIXTY MILE SMILE** *Creation CRESCD 254*	20		1
10 May 97	**PURE** *Creation CRESCD 265*	28		1
12 Jul 97	**COPPER GIRL** *Creation CRESCD 270*	30		1
8 Nov 97	**THIS IS MY HOLLYWOOD** *Creation CRESCD 277*	48		
23 Jan 99	**BEAUTIFUL DAY** *Creation CRESCD 308*	11		4
29 May 99	**THIS IS MY TIME** *Creation CRESCD 313*	36		1

THREE DEGREES US group

Date	Title / Label	Peak Position	Weeks at No.1	Weeks in Top 40
13 Apr 74	**YEAR OF DECISION** *Philadelphia International PIR 2073*	13		9
27 Apr 74	**TSOP (THE SOUND OF PHILADELPHIA)** *Philadelphia International PIR 2289* MFSB FEATURING THE THREE DEGREES ★	22		6
13 Jul 74	**WHEN WILL I SEE YOU AGAIN** *Philadelphia International PIR 2155* ●	1	2	14
2 Nov 74	**GET YOUR LOVE BACK** *Philadelphia International PIR 2737*	34		3
12 Apr 75	**TAKE GOOD CARE OF YOURSELF** *Philadelphia International PIR 3177* ○	9		8
5 Jul 75	**LONG LOST LOVER** *Philadelphia International PIR 3352*	40		1
1 May 76	**TOAST OF LOVE** *Epic EPC 4215*	36		1
7 Oct 78	**GIVIN' UP GIVIN' IN** *Ariola ARO 130*	12		8
13 Jan 79	**WOMAN IN LOVE** *Ariola ARO 141* ●	3		9
24 Mar 79	**THE RUNNER** *Ariola ARO 154* ○	10		8
23 Jun 79	**THE GOLDEN LADY** *Ariola ARO 170*	56		
29 Sep 79	**JUMP THE GUN** *Ariola ARO 183*	48		
24 Nov 79	**MY SIMPLE HEART** *Ariola ARO 202* ○	9		9
5 Oct 85	**THE HEAVEN I NEED** *Supreme SUPE 102*	42		
26 Dec 98	**LAST CHRISTMAS** *Wildstar CDWILD 15* ALIEN VOICES FEATURING THE THREE DEGREES	54		

THREE DOG NIGHT US group

Date	Title / Label	Peak Position	Weeks at No.1	Weeks in Top 40
8 Aug 70	**MAMA TOLD ME NOT TO COME** *Stateside SS 8052* ★	3		11
29 May 71	**JOY TO THE WORLD** *Probe PRO 523* ★	24		7

THREE DRIVES Dutch group

Date	Title / Label	Peak Position	Weeks at No.1	Weeks in Top 40
27 Jun 98	**GREECE 2000** *Hooj Choons HOOJCD 63*	44		
30 Jan 99	**GREECE 2000** *Hooj Choons HOOJ 70CD*	12		3
17 Nov 01	**SUNSET ON IBIZA** *Xtravaganza XTRAV 27CDS* THREE DRIVES ON A VINYL	44		
7 Jun 03	**CARRERA 2** *Nebula NEBCD 043*	57		
14 Aug 04	**AIR TRAFFIC** *Nebula NEBCD 056*	75		

THREE GOOD REASONS UK group

Date	Title / Label	Peak Position	Weeks at No.1	Weeks in Top 40
10 Mar 66	**NOWHERE MAN** *Mercury MF 899*	47		

3 JAYS UK group

Date	Title / Label	Peak Position	Weeks at No.1	Weeks in Top 40
31 Jul 99	**FEELING IT TOO** *Multiply CDMULTY 53*	17		3

3LW US group

Date	Title / Label	Peak Position	Weeks at No.1	Weeks in Top 40
2 Jun 01	**NO MORE (BABY I'MA DO RIGHT)** *Epic 6712722*	6		6
8 Sep 01	**PLAYAS GON' PLAY** *Epic 6717932*	21		2
19 Oct 02	**FEELS GOOD (DON'T WORRY BOUT A THING)** *Island CID 806* NAUGHTY BY NATURE FEATURING 3LW	44		

THREE 'N' ONE German production duo

Date	Title / Label	Peak Position	Weeks at No.1	Weeks in Top 40
7 Jun 97	**REFLECT** *ffrr FCD 301*	66		
15 May 99	**PEARL RIVER** *Low Sense SENSECD 24* THREE 'N' ONE PRESENTS JOHNNY SHAKER FEATURING SERIAL DIVA	32		1

365 UK group

Date	Title / Label	Peak Position	Weeks at No.1	Weeks in Top 40
25 Nov 06	**ONE TOUCH** *Innocent ANGEDX24*	60		

THREE 6 MAFIA US group

Date	Title / Label	Peak Position	Weeks at No.1	Weeks in Top 40
18 Feb 06	**STAY FLY** *Sony Urban 82876783062*	33		1

3SL UK group

Date	Title / Label	Peak Position	Weeks at No.1	Weeks in Top 40
20 Apr 02	**TAKE IT EASY** *Epic 6724042*	11		3
7 Sep 02	**TOUCH ME TEASE ME** *Epic 6727875*	16		2

3 OF A KIND UK group

Date	Title / Label	Peak Position	Weeks at No.1	Weeks in Top 40
21 Aug 04	**BABYCAKES** *Relentless RELDX6* ○	1	1	12

3T US group

Date	Title / Label	Peak Position	Weeks at No.1	Weeks in Top 40
27 Jan 96	**ANYTHING** *MJJ 6627152* ●	2		10
4 May 96	**37461** *MJJ 6631995*	11		4
24 Aug 96	**WHY** *Epic 6636482* 3T FEATURING MICHAEL JACKSON	2		5
7 Dec 96	**I NEED YOU** *Epic 6639912* ○	3		7
5 Apr 97	**GOTTA BE YOU** *Epic 6643645* 3T: RAP BY HERBIE	10		3

THRICE US group

Date	Title / Label	Peak Position	Weeks at No.1	Weeks in Top 40
18 Oct 03	**ALL THAT'S LEFT** *Island US 9811957*	69		

THRILLS Irish group

Date	Title / Label	Peak Position	Weeks at No.1	Weeks in Top 40
22 Mar 03	**ONE HORSE TOWN** *Virgin VSCDT 1845*	18		1
21 Jun 03	**BIG SUR** *Virgin VSCDT 1852*	17		3
6 Sep 03	**SANTA CRUZ (YOU'RE NOT THAT FAR)** *Virgin VSCDT 1862*	33		1
6 Dec 03	**DON'T STEAL OUR SUN** *Virgin VSCD 1864*	45		
11 Sep 04	**WHATEVER HAPPENED TO COREY HAIM?** *Virgin VSCDX 1876*	22		2
27 Nov 04	**NOT FOR ALL THE LOVE IN THE WORLD** *Virgin VSCDX1890*	39		1
2 Apr 05	**THE IRISH KEEP GATE-CRASHING** *Virgin VSCDT1895*	48		
28 Jul 07	**NOTHING CHANGES AROUND HERE** *Virgin VSCDT1947*	40		1

THRILLSEEKERS UK producer

Date	Title / Label	Peak Position	Weeks at No.1	Weeks in Top 40
17 Feb 01	**SYNAESTHESIA (FLY AWAY)** *Neo NEOCD1 050* THRILLSEEKERS FEATURING SHERYL DEANE	28		1
7 Sep 02	**DREAMING OF YOU** *Data 36CDS*	48		

THROWING MUSES US group

Date	Title / Label	Peak Position	Weeks at No.1	Weeks in Top 40
9 Feb 91	**COUNTING BACKWARDS** *4AD AD 1001*	70		
1 Aug 92	**FIREPILE (EP)** *4AD BAD 2012*	46		
24 Dec 94	**BRIGHT YELLOW GUN** *4AD BAD 4018CD*	51		
10 Aug 96	**SHARK** *4AD BAD 6016CD*	53		

THS – THE HORN SECTION US group

Date	Title / Label	Peak Position	Weeks at No.1	Weeks in Top 40
18 Aug 84	**LADY SHINE (SHINE ON)** *Fourth & Broadway BRW 10*	54		

HARRY THUMANN German keyboard player

Date	Title / Label	Peak Position	Weeks at No.1	Weeks in Top 40
21 Feb 81	**UNDERWATER** *Decca F 13901*	41		

THUNDER UK group

Date	Title / Label	Peak Position	Weeks at No.1	Weeks in Top 40
17 Feb 90	**DIRTY LOVE** *EMI EM 126*	32		2
12 May 90	**BACKSTREET SYMPHONY** *EMI EM 137*	25		2
14 Jul 90	**GIMME SOME LOVIN'** *EMI EM 148*	36		2
29 Sep 90	**SHE'S SO FINE** *EMI EM 158*	34		2
23 Feb 91	**LOVE WALKED IN** *EMI EM 175*	21		3
15 Aug 92	**LOW LIFE IN HIGH PLACES** *EMI EM 242*	22		3

Silver-selling ○ · Gold-selling ● · Platinum-selling ✪ · US No.1 ★

Date	Title	Label	Peak Position	Weeks at No.1	Weeks in Top 40
10 Oct 92	**EVERYBODY WANTS HER**	*EMI EM 249*	36		1
13 Feb 93	**A BETTER MAN**	*EMI CDBETTER 1*	18		2
19 Jun 93	**LIKE A SATELLITE (EP)**	*EMI CDEM 272*	28		1
7 Jan 95	**STAND UP**	*EMI CDEM 365*	23		2
25 Feb 95	**RIVER OF PAIN**	*EMI CDEM 367*	31		1
6 May 95	**CASTLES IN THE SAND**	*EMI CDEMS 372*	30		2
23 Sep 95	**IN A BROKEN DREAM**	*EMI CDEMS 384*	26		1
25 Jan 97	**DON'T WAIT UP**	*Raw Power RAWX 1020*	27		1
5 Apr 97	**LOVE WORTH DYING FOR**	*Raw Power RAWX 1043*	60		
7 Feb 98	**THE ONLY ONE**	*Eagle EAGXA 016*	31		1
27 Jun 98	**PLAY THAT FUNKY MUSIC**	*Eagle EAGXS 030*	39		1
20 Mar 99	**YOU WANNA KNOW**	*Eagle EAGXA 037*	49		
31 May 03	**LOSER**	*STC Recordings STC20032*	48		
4 Dec 04	**I LOVE YOU MORE THAN ROCK N ROLL**	*STC STC20044*	27		1
16 Dec 06	**THE DEVIL MADE ME DO IT**	*STC STC20066*	40		1

THUNDERBUGS UK/French/German group

Date	Title	Label	Peak Position	Weeks at No.1	Weeks in Top 40
18 Sep 99	**FRIENDS FOREVER**	*1st Avenue 6676932*	5		5
18 Dec 99	**IT'S ABOUT TIME YOU WERE MINE**	*1st Avenue 6683972*	43		

THUNDERCLAP NEWMAN UK group

Date	Title	Label	Peak Position	Weeks at No.1	Weeks in Top 40
11 Jun 69	**SOMETHING IN THE AIR**	*Track 604 031*	1	3	11
27 Jun 70	**ACCIDENTS**	*Track 2094 001*	46		

THUNDERTHIGHS UK group

Date	Title	Label	Peak Position	Weeks at No.1	Weeks in Top 40
22 Jun 74	**CENTRAL PARK ARREST**	*Philips 6006 386*	30		4

THURSDAY US group

Date	Title	Label	Peak Position	Weeks at No.1	Weeks in Top 40
25 Oct 03	**SIGNALS OVER THE AIR**	*Island US 9812292*	62		

BOBBY THURSTON US singer

Date	Title	Label	Peak Position	Weeks at No.1	Weeks in Top 40
29 Mar 80	**CHECK OUT THE GROOVE**	*Epic EPC 8348*	10		7

TI US rapper

Date	Title	Label	Peak Position	Weeks at No.1	Weeks in Top 40
19 Feb 05	**SOLDIER** DESTINY'S CHILD FEATURING TI & LIL' WAYNE	*Columbia 6757622*	4		5
26 Mar 05	**BRING EM OUT**	*Atlantic AT0196CD*	59		
17 Jun 06	**WHY YOU WANNA**	*Atlantic AT0244CD*	22		3
18 Nov 06	**MY LOVE** JUSTIN TIMBERLAKE FEATURING TI ★	*Jive 88697020502*	2		12
27 Jan 07	**PAC'S LIFE** 2PAC FEATURING TI & ASHANTI	*Interscope 1723503*	21		2
19 May 07	**I'M A FLIRT** R KELLY FEATURING TI & T-PAIN	*Jive 88697090232*	18		2

TIFFANY US singer

Date	Title	Label	Peak Position	Weeks at No.1	Weeks in Top 40
16 Jan 88	**I THINK WE'RE ALONE NOW**	*MCA 1211* ● ★	1	3	10
19 Mar 88	**COULD'VE BEEN**	*MCA TIFF 2* ★	4		7
4 Jun 88	**I SAW HIM STANDING THERE**	*MCA TIFF 3*	8		5
6 Aug 88	**FEELINGS OF FOREVER**	*MCA TIFF 4*	52		
12 Nov 88	**RADIO ROMANCE**	*MCA TIFF 5*	13		9
11 Feb 89	**ALL THIS TIME**	*MCA TIFF 6*	47		

TIGA Canadian duo

Date	Title	Label	Peak Position	Weeks at No.1	Weeks in Top 40
11 May 02	**SUNGLASSES AT NIGHT** TIGA & ZYNTHERIUS	*City Rockers ROCKERS 15CD*	25		1
6 Sep 03	**HOT IN HERRE**	*Skint 90CD*	46		
19 Jun 04	**PLEASURE FROM THE BASS**	*Different DIFB1028CDM*	57		
29 Oct 05	**YOU GONNA WANT ME**	*Different DIFB1043CDM*	64		
6 May 06	**(FAR FROM) HOME**	*Different DIFB1048CDM*	65		

TIGER UK/Irish group

Date	Title	Label	Peak Position	Weeks at No.1	Weeks in Top 40
31 Aug 96	**RACE**	*Trade 2 TRDCD 004*	37		1
16 Nov 96	**MY PUPPET PAL**	*Trade 2 TRDCD 005*	62		
22 Feb 97	**ON THE ROSE**	*Trade 2 TRDCD 008*	57		
22 Aug 98	**FRIENDS**	*Trade 2 TRDCD 013*	72		

TIGERTAILZ US group

Date	Title	Label	Peak Position	Weeks at No.1	Weeks in Top 40
24 Jun 89	**LOVE BOMB BABY**	*Music For Nations KUT 132*	75		
16 Feb 91	**HEAVEN**	*Music For Nations KUT 137*	71		

TIGHT FIT UK group

Date	Title	Label	Peak Position	Weeks at No.1	Weeks in Top 40
18 Jul 81	**BACK TO THE SIXTIES**	*Jive 002*	4		9
26 Sep 81	**BACK TO THE SIXTIES PART 2**	*Jive 005*	33		3
23 Jan 82	**THE LION SLEEPS TONIGHT**	*Jive 9* ●	1	3	11
1 May 82	**FANTASY ISLAND**	*Jive 13* ○	5		10
31 Jul 82	**SECRET HEART**	*Jive 20*	41		

TIK & TOK UK duo

Date	Title	Label	Peak Position	Weeks at No.1	Weeks in Top 40
8 Oct 83	**COOL RUNNING**	*Survival SUR 0116*	69		

TANITA TIKARAM UK singer

Date	Title	Label	Peak Position	Weeks at No.1	Weeks in Top 40
30 Jul 88	**GOOD TRADITION**	*WEA YZ 196*	10		7
22 Oct 88	**TWIST IN MY SOBRIETY**	*WEA YZ 321*	22		7
14 Jan 89	**CATHEDRAL SONG**	*WEA YZ 331*	48		
18 Mar 89	**WORLD OUTSIDE YOUR WINDOW**	*WEA YZ 363*	58		
13 Jan 90	**WE ALMOST GOT IT TOGETHER**	*WEA YZ 443*	52		
9 Feb 91	**ONLY THE ONES WE LOVE**	*East West YZ 558*	69		
4 Feb 95	**I MIGHT BE CRYING**	*East West YZ 879CD*	64		
6 Jun 98	**STOP LISTENING**	*Mother MUMCD 102*	67		
29 Aug 98	**I DON'T WANNA LOSE AT LOVE**	*Mother MUMCD 105*	73		

TILLMAN + REIS German production duo

Date	Title	Label	Peak Position	Weeks at No.1	Weeks in Top 40
16 Sep 00	**BASSFLY**	*Liquid Asset ASSETCD 004*	70		

TILLMANN UHRMACHER German producer

Date	Title	Label	Peak Position	Weeks at No.1	Weeks in Top 40
23 Mar 02	**ON THE RUN**	*Direction 6721352*	16		2

JOHNNY TILLOTSON US singer

Date	Title	Label	Peak Position	Weeks at No.1	Weeks in Top 40
1 Dec 60	**POETRY IN MOTION**	*London HLA 9231*	1	2	15
2 Feb 61	**JIMMY'S GIRL**	*London HLA 9275*	43		
12 Jul 62	**IT KEEPS RIGHT ON A HURTIN'**	*London HLA 9550*	31		7
4 Oct 62	**SEND ME THE PILLOW YOU DREAM ON**	*London HLA 9598*	21		8
27 Dec 62	**I CAN'T HELP IT**	*London HLA 9642*	41		
9 May 63	**OUT OF MY MIND**	*London HLA 9695*	34		2
14 Apr 79	**POETRY IN MOTION/PRINCESS PRINCESS**	*Lightning LIG 9016*	67		

TILT UK production group

Date	Title	Label	Peak Position	Weeks at No.1	Weeks in Top 40
2 Dec 95	**I DREAM**	*Perfecto PERF 112CD*	69		
10 May 97	**MY SPIRIT**	*Perfecto PERF 139CD*	61		
13 Sep 97	**PLACES**	*Perfecto PERF 149CD*	64		
7 Feb 98	**BUTTERFLY** TILT FEATURING ZEE	*Perfecto PERF 154CD1*	41		
27 Mar 99	**CHILDREN**	*Deconstruction 74321648172*	51		
8 May 99	**INVISIBLE**	*Hooj Choons HOOJ 73CD*	20		1
12 Feb 00	**DARK SCIENCE (EP)**	*Hooj Choons HOOJ 87CD*	55		

TIMBALAND US rapper

Date	Title	Label	Peak Position	Weeks at No.1	Weeks in Top 40
23 Jan 99	**GET ON THE BUS** DESTINY'S CHILD FEATURING TIMBALAND	*East West E 3780CD*	15		3
13 Mar 99	**HERE WE COME** TIMBALAND/MISSY ELLIOTT & MAGOO	*Virgin DINSD 179*	43		
19 Jun 99	**LOBSTER & SCRIMP** TIMBALAND FEATURING JAY-Z	*Virgin DINSD 186*	48		
21 Jul 01	**WE NEED A RESOLUTION** AALIYAH FEATURING TIMBALAND	*Blackground VUSCD 206*	20		2
13 Mar 04	**COP THAT SHIT** TIMBALAND/MAGOO/MISSY ELLIOTT	*Unique Corp TIMBACD001*	22		2
9 Sep 06	**PROMISCUOUS** NELLY FURTADO FEATURING TIMBALAND ★	*Geffen 1706030*	3		11
14 Apr 07	**GIVE IT TO ME** TIMBALAND FEATURING NELLY FURTADO & JUSTIN TIMBERLAKE ★	*Interscope 1732199*	1	1	20
30 Jun 07	**ANONYMOUS** BOBBY VALENTINO FEATURING TIMBALAND	*Def Jam 1736310*	25		2
7 Jul 07	**THE WAY I ARE** TIMBALAND FEATURING DOE & KERI HILSON	*Interscope 1742316*	1	2	28
25 Aug 07	**AYO TECHNOLOGY** 50 CENT FEATURING JUSTIN TIMBERLAKE & TIMBALAND	*Interscope 1746158*	2		19

TIMBALAND

TIMBALAND

In an era when the charts are more fluid than ever, when rules are there to be broken and no one can afford to rest on their laurels, a new generation of artists have emerged who are multi-faceted and creatively amorphous. Timbaland is one such super-creator. His impact on the UK singles chart is, on the surface, relatively modest; yet dig a little deeper and his contribution is very much more. Super-producer, remixer, DJ, songwriter, lyricist, performer, record label CEO and artist in his own right ...

His early years were unremarkable – born Timothy Mosley in March 1971 in Norfolk, Virginia, he credits hearing Prince's 1979 song, 'I Wanna Be Your Lover' as the moment he realised he wanted to be in music – at just eight years of age. Despite his phenomenal success, Timbaland maintains that no one can touch Prince and has he spent twenty years trying – unsuccessfully, in his own opinion – to mimic the diminutive one's snare drum sound. His earliest musical experiences were as a DJ, making his own mix tapes and backing tracks on a Casio keyboard. Initially, his sole aim in life was to be a working DJ, and he was known as 'DJ Timmy Tim' or 'DJ Tiny Tim'. Then Rick James's 'Super Freak' turned him on to the idea of being a producer, and so when his school friend Missy Elliott suggested he work with her R&B group Sista on some sounds, he grasped the opportunity to produce music.

After signing to Swing Mob Records in New York, the label owner DeVante Swing renamed Mosley as Timbaland, after the yellow sand boots that were the hip-hop artist's footwear of choice at the time. Also on the label was Ginuwine and it was this artist who gave Timbaland his first commercially massive album production credit, with his 1996 debut *Ginuwine ... the Bachelor*. Shortly after, the singer Aaliyah contracted him to work on her album, *One In A Million*, which went on to sell 11 million copies.

From then on, his rise to fame was meteoric and sustained. From the mid-1990s, his production work reads like a who's who of hip-hop, new jack swing and innovative R&B: Missy Elliott, Jodeci, Aaliyah, Lil' Kim, The Game, Destiny's Child, Ludacris, Snoop Dogg and Jay-Z, to name but a few. His own hip-hop group, Timbaland and Magoo has also enjoyed critical success. The only dip in his prolific creativity came when his close friend Aaliyah was killed in a plane crash in 2001.

His reputation was built as much on his ability to inject innovative sounds as it was for the more conventional producer role of shaping and moulding songs. Obvious examples of this gift for unique sonic twists include his Indian influences, most notably on songs such as the remix of Xscape's 'My Secret'; then, of course, there's his unmistakable murmurs and mumblings in a song's background which somehow become the addictive part that the listener ends up singing endlessly. Urban music historians credit Timbaland as defining much of the 1990s evolution of the genre, splicing new, unusual beats, complex sounds and eclectic effects on to songs by countless artists. Famously, he does not use samples.

Inevitably, his expansive ambitions turned to other ideas and he built a massive, 5,000-square-foot recording complex in Virginia; this inexorably slid into founding his own label, Mosley Music Group in 2006. This is when Timbaland first started to hit the radar of most UK singles buyers – one of the artists on the label was the enigmatic Nelly Furtado and his production of her 2006 album *Loose* and singles such as 'Promiscuous' definitively reinvented this quirky female singer-songwriter into a hip-hop experimenter and alumnus with devastating commercial success. His latter-day work with Justin Timberlake and most recently Madonna's 2008 album *Hard Candy* replicated this stunning track record and he has since enjoyed involvement in several UK Number 1 singles, including 'Apologise' by One Republic.

Arguably boasting a greater Midas touch than any other post-2000 producer, Timbaland is now one of, if not *the*, most sought-after men to collaborate with on big albums. Additionally, he is rightly being compared to genre- and era-defining producers such as Brian Eno and Phil Spector, and this perception has only increased with his growing profile as an artist, such as his second solo album, 2007's *Timbaland Presents Shock Value*. He prides himself on ignoring genre labels and seems at ease working with purist hip-hop as well as such artistically different singers as Celine Dion and Bjork with absolute equanimity – giving him that rare dichotomy of commerciality and credibility. Likewise his influences; surprisingly, he cites industrial-goth legend Trent Reznor as his all-time-favourite producer. As an aside, one of his personal obsessions is body-building and he is reported to adhere to a strict diet and exhausting training regime, despite his intimidating workload.

In keeping with the apparently limitless horizons he sees to his career, in 2008 Timbaland became the first artist to provide material for the exclusive use of mobile phones, when he hooked up with US phone network Verizon Wireless. Speaking at the time of the announcement, Timbaland said, 'Every place don't get a CD but everybody has a mobile phone.'

Silver-selling ○ Gold-selling ● Platinum-selling ⊛ US No.1 ★

Date	Title / Label	Peak Position	Weeks at No.1	Weeks in Top 40
13 Oct 07	**APOLOGIZE** *Interscope 1750152* TIMBALAND PRESENTS ONE REPUBLIC	3		24
16 Feb 08	**SCREAM** *Interscope 1764136* TIMBALAND FEATURING KERI HILSON & NICOLE SCHERZINGER	12		7

JUSTIN TIMBERLAKE US singer

Date	Title / Label	Peak Position	Weeks at No.1	Weeks in Top 40
2 Nov 02	**LIKE I LOVE YOU** *Jive 9254342* ○	2		12
15 Feb 03	**CRY ME A RIVER** *Jive 9254632*	2		10
15 Mar 03	**WORK IT** *Universal MCSXD 40312* NELLY FEATURING JUSTIN TIMBERLAKE	7		5
24 May 03	**ROCK YOUR BODY (IMPORT)** *Jive 9254962*	46		
31 May 03	**ROCK YOUR BODY** *Jive 9254952*	2		10
27 Sep 03	**SENORITA** *Jive 82876563442*	13		4
7 May 05	**SIGNS** *Geffen 9881782* SNOOP DOGG FEATURING CHARLIE WILSON & JUSTIN TIMBERLAKE	2		10
2 Sep 06	**SEXYBACK** *Jive 82876870882*	1	1	17
18 Nov 06	**MY LOVE** *Jive 88697020502* JUSTIN TIMBERLAKE FEATURING TI ★	2		12
3 Feb 07	**WHAT GOES AROUND COMES AROUND** *Jive 88697058012* ★	4		17
14 Apr 07	**GIVE IT TO ME** *Interscope 1732199* TIMBALAND FEATURING NELLY FURTADO & JUSTIN TIMBERLAKE ★	1	1	20
23 Jun 07	**LOVESTONED I THINK SHE KNOWS** *Download*	11		9
25 Aug 07	**AYO TECHNOLOGY** *Interscope 1746158* 50 CENT FEATURING JUSTIN TIMBERLAKE & TIMBALAND	2		19
29 Mar 08	**4 MINUTES** *Download* MADONNA FEATURING JUSTIN TIMBERLAKE	7		1

TIMBUK 3 US duo

Date	Title / Label	Peak Position	Weeks at No.1	Weeks in Top 40
31 Jan 87	**THE FUTURE'S SO BRIGHT I GOTTA WEAR SHADES** *IRS IRM 126*	21		4

TIME FREQUENCY UK group

Date	Title / Label	Peak Position	Weeks at No.1	Weeks in Top 40
6 Jun 92	**REAL LOVE** *Jive JIVET 307*	60		
9 Jan 93	**NEW EMOTION** *Internal Affairs KGBCD 009*	36		4
12 Jun 93	**THE ULTIMATE HIGH/THE POWER ZONE** *Internal Affairs KGBCD 010*	17		7
6 Nov 93	**REAL LOVE (REMIX)** *Internal Affairs KGBCD 011*	8		5
28 May 94	**SUCH A PHANTASY** *Internal Affairs KGBCD 013*	25		2
8 Oct 94	**DREAMSCAPE '94** *Internal Affairs KGBCD 015*	32		1
31 Aug 02	**REAL LOVE 2002 (2ND REMIX)** *Jive 9253782*	43		

TIME OF THE MUMPH UK producer

Date	Title / Label	Peak Position	Weeks at No.1	Weeks in Top 40
11 Feb 95	**CONTROL** *Fresh FRSHD 24*	69		

TIME UK UK group

Date	Title / Label	Peak Position	Weeks at No.1	Weeks in Top 40
8 Oct 83	**THE CABARET** *Red Bus/Aroadia TIM 123*	63		

TIME ZONE UK/US group

Date	Title / Label	Peak Position	Weeks at No.1	Weeks in Top 40
19 Jan 85	**WORLD DESTRUCTION** *Virgin VS 743*	44		

TIMEBOX UK group

Date	Title / Label	Peak Position	Weeks at No.1	Weeks in Top 40
24 Jul 68	**BEGGIN'** *Deram DM 194*	38		1

TIMELORDS UK duo

Date	Title / Label	Peak Position	Weeks at No.1	Weeks in Top 40
4 Jun 88	**DOCTORIN' THE TARDIS** *KLF Communications KLF 003*	1	1	8

TIMEX SOCIAL CLUB US group

Date	Title / Label	Peak Position	Weeks at No.1	Weeks in Top 40
13 Sep 86	**RUMORS** *Cooltempo COOL 133*	13		7

TIN MACHINE UK/US group

Date	Title / Label	Peak Position	Weeks at No.1	Weeks in Top 40
1 Jul 89	**UNDER THE GOD** *EMI-USA MT 68*	51		
9 Sep 89	**TIN MACHINE/MAGGIE'S FARM (LIVE)** *EMI-USA MT 73*	48		
24 Aug 91	**YOU BELONG IN ROCK 'N' ROLL** *London LON 305*	33		2
2 Nov 91	**BABY UNIVERSAL** *London LON 310*	48		

TIN TIN OUT UK duo

Date	Title / Label	Peak Position	Weeks at No.1	Weeks in Top 40
13 Aug 94	**THE FEELING** *Deep Distraxion OILYCD 029* TIN TIN OUT FEATURING SWEET TEE	32		1
25 Mar 95	**ALWAYS SOMETHING THERE TO REMIND ME** *WEA YZ 911CD* TIN TIN OUT FEATURING ESPIRITU	14		3
8 Feb 97	**ALL I WANNA DO** *VC Recordings VCRD 15*	31		1
10 May 97	**DANCE WITH ME** *VC Recordings VCRD 17* TIN TIN OUT FEATURING TONY HADLEY	35		1
20 Sep 97	**STRINGS FOR YASMIN** *VC Recordings VCRD 20*	31		1
28 Mar 98	**HERE'S WHERE THE STORY ENDS** *VC Recordings VCRD 30* TIN TIN OUT FEATURING SHELLEY NELSON	7		7
12 Sep 98	**SOMETIMES** *VC Recordings VCRD 34* TIN TIN OUT FEATURING SHELLEY NELSON	20		2
11 Sep 99	**ELEVEN TO FLY** *VC Recordings VCRDX 52* TIN TIN OUT FEATURING WENDY PAGE	26		1
13 Nov 99	**WHAT I AM** *VC Recordings VCRD 53* TIN TIN OUT FEATURING EMMA BUNTON ○	2		7

TINDERSTICKS UK group

Date	Title / Label	Peak Position	Weeks at No.1	Weeks in Top 40
5 Feb 94	**KATHLEEN (EP)** *This Way Up WAY 2833CD*	61		
18 Mar 95	**NO MORE AFFAIRS** *This Way Up WAY 3833*	58		
12 Aug 95	**TRAVELLING LIGHT** *This Way Up WAY 4533*	51		
7 Jun 97	**BATHTIME** *This Way Up WAY 6166*	38		1
1 Nov 97	**RENTED ROOMS** *This Way Up WAY 6566*	56		
4 Sep 99	**CAN WE START AGAIN?** *Island CID 756*	54		
2 Aug 03	**SOMETIMES IT HURTS** *Beggars Banquet BBQ369CD*	60		

TINGO TANGO UK group

Date	Title / Label	Peak Position	Weeks at No.1	Weeks in Top 40
21 Jul 90	**IT IS JAZZ** *Champion CHAMP 250*	68		

TINMAN UK producer

Date	Title / Label	Peak Position	Weeks at No.1	Weeks in Top 40
20 Aug 94	**EIGHTEEN STRINGS** *ffrr FCD 242*	9		5
3 Jun 95	**GUDVIBE** *ffrr FCD 262*	49		

TINY DANCERS UK group

Date	Title / Label	Peak Position	Weeks at No.1	Weeks in Top 40
31 Mar 07	**I WILL WAIT FOR YOU** *Parlophone CDR6733*	36		1
9 Jun 07	**HANNAH WE KNOW** *Parlophone CDR6740*	33		1

TINY TIM US singer

Date	Title / Label	Peak Position	Weeks at No.1	Weeks in Top 40
5 Feb 69	**GREAT BALLS OF FIRE** *Reprise RS 20802*	45		

ROB TISSERA & VINYLGROOVER UK duo

Date	Title / Label	Peak Position	Weeks at No.1	Weeks in Top 40
10 Jul 04	**STAY** *Tidy Trax TIDYTWO133C*	61		

TITANIC Norwegian/UK group

Date	Title / Label	Peak Position	Weeks at No.1	Weeks in Top 40
25 Sep 71	**SULTANA** *CBS 5365*	5		11

TITIYO Swedish singer

Date	Title / Label	Peak Position	Weeks at No.1	Weeks in Top 40
3 Mar 90	**AFTER THE RAIN** *Arista 112722*	60		
6 Oct 90	**FLOWERS** *Arista 113212*	71		
5 Feb 94	**TELL ME I'M NOT DREAMING** *Arista 74321185622*	45		

TJR UK group

Date	Title / Label	Peak Position	Weeks at No.1	Weeks in Top 40
27 Sep 97	**JUST GETS BETTER** *Multiply CDMULTY 25* TJR FEATURING XAVIER	28		1

TLC US group

Date	Title / Label	Peak Position	Weeks at No.1	Weeks in Top 40
20 Jun 92	**AIN'T 2 PROUD 2 BEG** *Arista 115265*	13		4
22 Aug 92	**BABY-BABY-BABY** *LaFace 74321111297*	55		
24 Oct 92	**WHAT ABOUT YOUR FRIENDS** *LaFace 74321118177*	59		
21 Jan 95	**CREEP** *LaFace 74321254212* ★	22		3
22 Apr 95	**RED LIGHT SPECIAL** *LaFace 74321273662*	18		2
5 Aug 95	**WATERFALLS** *LaFace 74321298812* ○ ★	4		12
4 Nov 95	**DIGGIN' ON YOU** *LaFace 74321319252*	18		3
13 Jan 96	**CREEP** *LaFace 74321340942*	6		5
3 Apr 99	**NO SCRUBS** *LaFace 74321660952* ⊛ ★	3		16
28 Aug 99	**UNPRETTY** *LaFace 74321695842* ★	6		9
18 Dec 99	**DEAR LIE** *LaFace 74321724012*	31		5
14 Dec 02	**GIRL TALK** *Arista 74321983502*	30		1

Silver-selling ● Gold-selling ● Platinum-selling ✪ US No.1 ★ | Peak Position | Weeks at No.1 | Weeks in Top 40

T99 Belgian group

Date	Title / Label	Peak Position	Weeks at No.1	Weeks in Top 40
11 May 91	**ANASTHASIA** *XL Recordings XLS 19*	14		5
19 Oct 91	**NOCTURNE** *Emphasis 6574097*	33		3

ART & DOTTY TODD US duo

Date	Title / Label	Peak Position	Weeks at No.1	Weeks in Top 40
13 Feb 53	**BROKEN WINGS** *HMV B 10399*	6		7

TOGETHER UK group

Date	Title / Label	Peak Position	Weeks at No.1	Weeks in Top 40
4 Aug 90	**HARDCORE UPROAR** *ffrr F 143*	12		6

TOKENS US group

Date	Title / Label	Peak Position	Weeks at No.1	Weeks in Top 40
21 Dec 61	**THE LION SLEEPS TONIGHT (WIMOWEH)** *RCA 1263* ★	11		11

TOKYO DRAGONS UK group

Date	Title / Label	Peak Position	Weeks at No.1	Weeks in Top 40
26 Jun 04	**TEENAGE SCREAMERS** *Island CID 864*	61		
23 Oct 04	**GET 'EM OFF** *Island CID 876*	75		
5 Mar 05	**WHAT THE HELL** *Island/Uni-Island CID883*	59		

TOKYO GHETTO PUSSY German duo

Date	Title / Label	Peak Position	Weeks at No.1	Weeks in Top 40
16 Sep 95	**EVERYBODY ON THE FLOOR (PUMP IT)** *Epic 6611132*	26		1
16 Mar 96	**I KISS YOUR LIPS** *Epic 6623212*	55		

TOL & TOL Dutch duo

Date	Title / Label	Peak Position	Weeks at No.1	Weeks in Top 40
14 Apr 90	**ELENI** *Dover ROJ 5*	73		

TOM TOM CLUB US group

Date	Title / Label	Peak Position	Weeks at No.1	Weeks in Top 40
20 Jun 81	**WORDY RAPPINGHOOD** *Island WIP 6694*	7		8
10 Oct 81	**GENIUS OF LOVER** *Island WIP 6735*	65		
7 Aug 82	**UNDER THE BOARDWALK** *Island WIP 6762*	22		7

TOMBA VIRA Dutch duo

Date	Title / Label	Peak Position	Weeks at No.1	Weeks in Top 40
16 Jun 01	**THE SOUND OF OH YEAH** *VC Recordings VCRD 88*	51		

TOMCAT UK group

Date	Title / Label	Peak Position	Weeks at No.1	Weeks in Top 40
14 Oct 00	**CRAZY** *Virgin VSCSDT 1785*	48		

TOMCRAFT German producer

Date	Title / Label	Peak Position	Weeks at No.1	Weeks in Top 40
10 May 03	**LONELINESS** *Data 52CDS*	1	1	9
25 Oct 03	**BRAINWASHED (CALL YOU)** *Data 63CDS*	43		

RICKY TOMLINSON UK actor/comedian

Date	Title / Label	Peak Position	Weeks at No.1	Weeks in Top 40
10 Nov 01	**ARE YOU LOOKIN' AT ME** *All Around The World CDRICKY 1*	28		2
23 Dec 06	**CHRISTMAS MY A*SE** *Liberty 3837292*	25		2

TOMMI UK producer

Date	Title / Label	Peak Position	Weeks at No.1	Weeks in Top 40
5 Jul 03	**LIKE WHAT** *Sony Music 6739095*	12		2

TOMSKI UK producer

Date	Title / Label	Peak Position	Weeks at No.1	Weeks in Top 40
18 Apr 98	**14 HOURS TO SAVE THE EARTH** *Xtravaganza 0091515 EXT*	42		
12 Feb 00	**LOVE WILL COME** *Xtravaganza XTRAV 6CDS* TOMSKI FEATURING JAN JOHNSTON	31		1

TONEDEF ALLSTARS UK group

Date	Title / Label	Peak Position	Weeks at No.1	Weeks in Top 40
17 Jun 06	**WHO DO YOU THINK YOU ARE KIDDING JURGEN KLINSMANN** *Tone Def CDTONE1*	13		2

TONGUE 'N' CHEEK UK group

Date	Title / Label	Peak Position	Weeks at No.1	Weeks in Top 40
27 Feb 88	**NOBODY (CAN LOVE ME)** *Criminal BUS 6* TONGUE IN CHEEK	59		
25 Nov 89	**ENCORE** *Syncopate SY 33*	41		
14 Apr 90	**TOMORROW** *Syncopate SY 34*	20		5
4 Aug 90	**FORGET ME NOTS** *Syncopate SY 37*	37		2
19 Jan 91	**NOBODY** *Syncopate SY 39*	26		4

TONIGHT UK group

Date	Title / Label	Peak Position	Weeks at No.1	Weeks in Top 40
28 Jan 78	**DRUMMER MAN** *Target TDS 1*	14		8
20 May 78	**MONEY THAT'S YOUR PROBLEM** *Target TDS 2*	66		

TONY! TONI! TONÉ! US group

Date	Title / Label	Peak Position	Weeks at No.1	Weeks in Top 40
30 Jun 90	**OAKLAND STROKE** *Wing 7*	50		
9 Mar 91	**IT NEVER RAINS (IN SOUTHERN CALIFORNIA)** *Wing 10*	69		
4 Sep 93	**IF I HAD NO LOOT** *Polydor PZCD 292*	44		
3 May 97	**LET'S GET DOWN** *Mercury MERCD 485* TONY TONI TONE FEATURING DJ QUIK	33		1

TOP UK group

Date	Title / Label	Peak Position	Weeks at No.1	Weeks in Top 40
20 Jul 91	**NUMBER ONE DOMINATOR** *Island IS 496*	67		

TOPLOADER UK group

Date	Title / Label	Peak Position	Weeks at No.1	Weeks in Top 40
22 May 99	**ACHILLES HEEL** *Sony S2 6671612*	64		
7 Aug 99	**LET THE PEOPLE KNOW** *Sony S2 6677132*	52		
4 Mar 00	**DANCING IN THE MOONLIGHT** *Sony S2 6689412*	19		4
13 May 00	**ACHILLES HEEL** *Sony S2 6691872*	8		5
2 Sep 00	**JUST HOLD ON** *Sony S2 6696242*	20		2
25 Nov 00	**DANCING IN THE MOONLIGHT** *Sony S2 6699852* ●	7		19
21 Apr 01	**ONLY FOR A WHILE** *Sony S2 6708612*	19		1
17 Aug 02	**TIME OF MY LIFE** *Sony S2 6728862*	18		2

TOPOL Israeli actor

Date	Title / Label	Peak Position	Weeks at No.1	Weeks in Top 40
20 Apr 67	**IF I WERE A RICH MAN** *CBS 202651*	9		18

MEL TORMÉ US singer

Date	Title / Label	Peak Position	Weeks at No.1	Weeks in Top 40
27 Apr 56	**MOUNTAIN GREENERY** *Vogue Coral Q 72150*	4		24
3 Jan 63	**COMING HOME BABY** *London HLK 9643*	13		7

TORNADOS UK group

Date	Title / Label	Peak Position	Weeks at No.1	Weeks in Top 40
30 Aug 62	**TELSTAR** *Decca F 11494* ★	1	5	24
10 Jan 63	**GLOBETROTTER** *Decca F 11562*	5		11
21 Mar 63	**ROBOT** *Decca F 11606*	17		11
6 Jun 63	**THE ICE CREAM MAN** *Decca F 11662*	18		9
10 Oct 63	**DRAGONFLY** *Decca F 11745*	41		

MITCHELL TOROK US singer

Date	Title / Label	Peak Position	Weeks at No.1	Weeks in Top 40
28 Sep 56	**WHEN MEXICO GAVE UP THE RHUMBA** *Brunswick 05586*	6		18
11 Jan 57	**RED LIGHT GREEN LIGHT** *Brunswick 05626*	29		1

EMILIANA TORRINI Norwegian singer

Date	Title / Label	Peak Position	Weeks at No.1	Weeks in Top 40
10 Jun 00	**EASY** *One Little Indian 274 TP7CD*	63		
9 Sep 00	**UNEMPLOYED IN SUMMERTIME** *One Little Indian 275 TP7CD*	63		
3 Feb 01	**TO BE FREE** *One Little Indian 276TP 7CDL*	44		

PETE TOSH Jamaican singer

Date	Title / Label	Peak Position	Weeks at No.1	Weeks in Top 40
21 Oct 78	**(YOU GOTTA WALK) DON'T LOOK BACK** *Rolling Stones 2859*	43		
2 Apr 83	**JOHNNY B GOODE** *EMI RIC 115*	48		

TOTAL US group

Date	Title / Label	Peak Position	Weeks at No.1	Weeks in Top 40
15 Jul 95	**CAN'T YOU SEE** *Tommy Boy TBCD 700* TOTAL FEATURING THE NOTORIOUS B.I.G.	43		
14 Sep 96	**KISSIN' YOU** *Arista 74321404172*	29		1
15 Feb 97	**DO YOU THINK ABOUT US** *Puff Daddy 74321458492*	49		
18 Apr 98	**WHAT YOU WANT** *Puff Daddy 74321578772* MASE FEATURING TOTAL	15		3

Date	Title	Peak Position	Weeks at No.1	Weeks in Top 40
30 Sep 00	**I WONDER WHY HE'S THE GREATEST DJ** *Tommy Boy TBCD 2100* TONY TOUCH FEATURING TOTAL	68		

TOTAL CONTRAST UK group

Date	Title	Peak Position	Weeks at No.1	Weeks in Top 40
3 Aug 85	**TAKES A LITTLE TIME** *London LON 71*	17		6
19 Oct 85	**HIT AND RUN** *London LON 76*	41		
1 Mar 86	**THE RIVER** *London LON 83*	44		
10 May 86	**WHAT YOU GONNA DO ABOUT IT** *London LON 95*	63		

TOTO US group

Date	Title	Peak Position	Weeks at No.1	Weeks in Top 40
10 Feb 79	**HOLD THE LINE** *CBS 6784*	14		6
5 Feb 83	**AFRICA** *CBS A 2510* ○ ★	3		9
9 Apr 83	**ROSANNA** *CBS A 2079*	12		6
18 Jun 83	**I WON'T HOLD YOU BACK** *CBS A 3392*	37		2
18 Nov 95	**I WILL REMEMBER** *Columbia 6626552*	64		

TOTO COELO UK group

Date	Title	Peak Position	Weeks at No.1	Weeks in Top 40
7 Aug 82	**I EAT CANNIBALS PART 1** *Radialchoice TIC 10*	8		8
13 Nov 82	**DRACULA'S TANGO/MUCHO MACHO** *Radialchoice TIC 11*	54		

TOTTENHAM HOTSPUR F.A. CUP FINAL SQUAD UK football club

Date	Title	Peak Position	Weeks at No.1	Weeks in Top 40
9 May 81	**OSSIE'S DREAM (SPURS ARE ON THEIR WAY TO WEMBLEY)** *Rockney SHELF 1*	5		5
1 May 82	**TOTTENHAM TOTTENHAM** *Rockney SHELF 2*	19		5
9 May 87	**HOT SHOT TOTTENHAM** *Rainbow RBR 16*	18		3
11 May 91	**WHEN THE YEAR ENDS IN 1** *A1 A 1324*	44		

TONY TOUCH US producer

Date	Title	Peak Position	Weeks at No.1	Weeks in Top 40
30 Sep 00	**I WONDER WHY HE'S THE GREATEST DJ** *Tommy Boy TBCD 2100* TONY TOUCH FEATURING TOTAL	68		

TOUCH & GO UK group

Date	Title	Peak Position	Weeks at No.1	Weeks in Top 40
7 Nov 98	**WOULD YOU...?** *V2 VVR 5003083* ○	3		7

TOUCH OF SOUL UK group

Date	Title	Peak Position	Weeks at No.1	Weeks in Top 40
19 May 90	**WE GOT THE LOVE** *Cooltempo COOL 204*	46		

TOUR DE FORCE UK group

Date	Title	Peak Position	Weeks at No.1	Weeks in Top 40
16 May 98	**CATALAN** *East West EW 161CD*	71		

TOURISTS UK group

Date	Title	Peak Position	Weeks at No.1	Weeks in Top 40
9 Jun 79	**BLIND AMONG THE FLOWERS** *Logo GO 350*	52		
8 Sep 79	**THE LONELIEST MAN IN THE WORLD** *Logo GO 360*	32		3
10 Nov 79	**I ONLY WANT TO BE WITH YOU** *Logo GO 370* ●	4		11
9 Feb 80	**SO GOOD TO BE BACK HOME AGAIN** *Logo TOUR 1*	8		6
18 Oct 80	**DON'T SAY I TOLD YOU SO** *RCA TOUR 2*	40		1

TOUTES LES FILLES UK group

Date	Title	Peak Position	Weeks at No.1	Weeks in Top 40
4 Sep 99	**THAT'S WHAT LOVE CAN DO** *London LONCD 434*	44		

TOWERS OF LONDON UK group

Date	Title	Peak Position	Weeks at No.1	Weeks in Top 40
19 Mar 05	**ON A NOOSE** *TVT TOLCD01*	32		1
9 Jul 05	**FUCK IT UP** *TVT TOLCD2*	46		
26 Nov 05	**HOW RUDE SHE WAS** *TVT TOLCD3*	30		1
27 May 06	**AIR GUITAR** *TVT TOLCD4*	32		1
24 Feb 07	**I'M A RAT** *TVT TOLCD5*	46		

CAROL LYNN TOWNES US singer

Date	Title	Peak Position	Weeks at No.1	Weeks in Top 40
4 Aug 84	**99.5** *Polydor POSP 693*	47		
19 Jan 85	**BELIEVE IN THE BEAT** *Polydor POSP 720*	56		

FUZZ TOWNSHEND UK producer

Date	Title	Peak Position	Weeks at No.1	Weeks in Top 40
6 Sep 97	**HELLO DARLIN'** *Echo ECSCD 46*	51		

PETE TOWNSHEND UK singer/guitarist

Date	Title	Peak Position	Weeks at No.1	Weeks in Top 40
5 Apr 80	**ROUGH BOYS** *Atco K 11460*	39		1
21 Jun 80	**LET MY LOVE OPEN YOUR DOOR** *Atco k 11486*	46		
21 Aug 82	**UNIFORMS (CORPS D'ESPRIT)** *Atco K 11751*	48		

TOXIC TWO US production duo

Date	Title	Peak Position	Weeks at No.1	Weeks in Top 40
7 Mar 92	**RAVE GENERATOR** *PWL International PWL 223*	13		5

TOY – BOX Danish duo

Date	Title	Peak Position	Weeks at No.1	Weeks in Top 40
18 Sep 99	**BEST FRIENDS** *Edel 0058245 ERE*	41		

TOY DOLLS UK group

Date	Title	Peak Position	Weeks at No.1	Weeks in Top 40
1 Dec 84	**NELLIE THE ELEPHANT** *Volume VOL 11*	4		8

TOYAH UK singer

Date	Title	Peak Position	Weeks at No.1	Weeks in Top 40
14 Feb 81	**FOUR FROM TOYAH EP** *Safari TOY 1* ○	4		10
16 May 81	**I WANT TO BE FREE** *Safari SAFE 34* ○	8		9
3 Oct 81	**THUNDER IN THE MOUNTAINS** *Safari SAFE 38* ○	4		8
28 Nov 81	**FOUR MORE FROM TOYAH EP** *Safari TOY 2*	14		8
22 May 82	**BRAVE NEW WORLD** *Safari SAFE 45*	21		7
17 Jul 82	**IEYA** *Safari SAFE 28*	48		
9 Oct 82	**BE LOUD BE PROUD (BE HEARD)** *Safari SAFE 52*	30		4
24 Sep 83	**REBEL RUN** *Safari SAFE 56*	24		3
19 Nov 83	**THE VOW** *Safari SAFE 58*	50		
27 Apr 85	**DON'T FALL IN LOVE (I SAID)** *Portrait A 6160*	22		4
29 Jun 85	**SOUL PASSING THROUGH SOUL** *Portrait A 6359*	57		
25 Apr 87	**ECHO BEACH** *EG EGO 31*	54		

TOYS US group

Date	Title	Peak Position	Weeks at No.1	Weeks in Top 40
4 Nov 65	**A LOVER'S CONCERTO** *Stateside SS 460*	5		12
27 Jan 66	**ATTACK** *Stateside SS 483*	36		2

T'PAU UK group

Date	Title	Peak Position	Weeks at No.1	Weeks in Top 40
8 Aug 87	**HEART AND SOUL** *Siren SRN 41*	4		9
24 Oct 87	**CHINA IN YOUR HAND** *Siren SRN 64* ●	1	5	13
30 Jan 88	**VALENTINE** *Siren SRN 69*	9		7
2 Apr 88	**SEX TALK (LIVE)** *Siren SRN 80*	23		5
25 Jun 88	**I WILL BE WITH YOU** *Siren SRN 87*	14		5
1 Oct 88	**SECRET GARDEN** *Siren SRN 93*	18		6
3 Dec 88	**ROAD TO OUR DREAM** *Siren SRN 100*	42		
25 Mar 89	**ONLY THE LONELY** *Siren SRN 107*	28		5
18 May 91	**WHENEVER YOU NEED ME** *Siren SRN 140*	16		5
27 Jul 91	**WALK ON AIR** *Siren SRN 142*	62		
20 Feb 93	**VALENTINE** *Virgin VALEG 1*	53		

TQ US rapper

Date	Title	Peak Position	Weeks at No.1	Weeks in Top 40
30 Jan 99	**WESTSIDE** *Epic 6668105*	4		7
1 May 99	**BYE BYE BABY** *Epic 6672372*	7		4
21 Aug 99	**BETTER DAYS** *Epic 6677535*	32		1
4 Sep 99	**SUMMERTIME** *Northwestside 74321694672* ANOTHER LEVEL FEATURING TQ	7		4
29 Apr 00	**DAILY** *Epic 6692752*	14		3
13 Oct 01	**LET'S GET BACK TO BED...BOY** *Epic 6718662* SARAH CONNOR FEATURING TQ	16		3

TRACIE UK singer

Date	Title	Peak Position	Weeks at No.1	Weeks in Top 40
26 Mar 83	**THE HOUSE THAT JACK BUILT** *Respond KOB 701*	9		7
16 Jul 83	**GIVE IT SOME EMOTION** *Respond KOB 704*	24		7
14 Apr 84	**SOUL'S ON FIRE** *Respond KOB 708*	73		
9 Jun 84	**(I LOVE YOU) WHEN YOU SLEEP** *Respond KOB 710*	59		
17 Aug 85	**I CAN'T LEAVE YOU ALONE** *Respond SBS 1* TRACIE YOUNG	60		

Legend: ○ Silver-selling · ● Gold-selling · ⊛ Platinum-selling · ★ US No.1 · Peak Position · Weeks at No.1 · Weeks in Top 40

JEANIE TRACY US singer

Date	Title / Label	Peak Position	Weeks at No.1	Weeks in Top 40
11 Jun 94	IF THIS IS LOVE *Pulse 8 CDLOSE 63*	73		
5 Nov 94	DO YOU BELIEVE IN THE WONDER *Pulse 8 CDLOSE 74*	57		
13 May 95	IT'S A MAN'S MAN'S MAN'S WORLD *Pulse 8 CDLOSE 89* JEANIE TRACY & BOBBY WOMACK	73		

TRAFFIC UK group

Date	Title / Label	Peak Position	Weeks at No.1	Weeks in Top 40
1 Jun 67	PAPER SUN *Island WIP 6002*	5		9
6 Sep 67	HOLE IN MY SHOE *Island WIP 6017*	2		12
29 Nov 67	HERE WE GO ROUND THE MULBERRY BUSH *Island WIP 6025*	8		11
6 Mar 68	NO FACE, NO NAME, NO NUMBER *Island WIP 6030*	40		1

TRAIN US group

Date	Title / Label	Peak Position	Weeks at No.1	Weeks in Top 40
11 Aug 01	DROPS OF JUPITER (TELL ME) *Columbia 6714472*	10		7
2 Mar 02	SHE'S ON FIRE *Columbia 6722812*	49		

TRAMAINE US gospel singer

Date	Title / Label	Peak Position	Weeks at No.1	Weeks in Top 40
5 Oct 85	FALL DOWN (SPIRIT OF LOVE) *A&M AM 281*	60		

TRAMMPS US group

Date	Title / Label	Peak Position	Weeks at No.1	Weeks in Top 40
23 Nov 74	ZING WENT THE STRINGS OF MY HEART *Buddah BDS 405*	29		6
1 Feb 75	SIXTY MINUTE MAN *Buddah BDS 415*	40		1
11 Oct 75	HOLD BACK THE NIGHT *Buddah BDS 437*	5		7
13 Mar 76	THAT'S WHERE THE HAPPY PEOPLE GO *Atlantic K 10703*	35		3
24 Jul 76	SOUL SEARCHIN' TIME *Atlantic K 10797*	42		
14 May 77	DISCO INFERNO *Atlantic K 10914*	16		7
24 Jun 78	DISCO INFERNO *Atlantic K 11135*	47		
12 Dec 92	HOLD BACK THE NIGHT *Network NWK 65* KWS FEATURES GUEST VOCAL FROM THE TRAMMPS	30		3

TRANCESETTERS Dutch duo

Date	Title / Label	Peak Position	Weeks at No.1	Weeks in Top 40
4 Mar 00	ROACHES *Hooj Choons HOOJ 89CD*	55		
9 Jun 01	SYNERGY *Hooj Choons HOOJ 107CD*	72		

TRANS-X Canadian group

Date	Title / Label	Peak Position	Weeks at No.1	Weeks in Top 40
13 Jul 85	LIVING ON VIDEO *Boiling Point POSP 650*	9		7

TRANSA UK/production duo

Date	Title / Label	Peak Position	Weeks at No.1	Weeks in Top 40
30 Aug 97	PROPHASE *Perfecto PERF 147CD*	65		
21 Feb 98	ENERVATE *Perfecto PERF 155CD*	42		

TRANSATLANTIC SOUL US producer

Date	Title / Label	Peak Position	Weeks at No.1	Weeks in Top 40
22 Mar 97	RELEASE YO SELF *Deconstruction 74321459102*	43		

TRANSFER UK duo

Date	Title / Label	Peak Position	Weeks at No.1	Weeks in Top 40
3 Nov 01	POSSESSION *Multiply CDMULTY 76*	54		

TRANSFORMER 2 Belgian duo

Date	Title / Label	Peak Position	Weeks at No.1	Weeks in Top 40
24 Feb 96	JUST CAN'T GET ENOUGH *Positiva CDTIV 49*	45		

TRANSISTER UK/US group

Date	Title / Label	Peak Position	Weeks at No.1	Weeks in Top 40
28 Mar 98	LOOK WHO'S PERFECT NOW *Virgin VSCDT 1678*	56		

TRANSPLANTS US group

Date	Title / Label	Peak Position	Weeks at No.1	Weeks in Top 40
19 Apr 03	DIAMONDS AND GUNS *Hellcat 11082*	27		1
19 Jul 03	DJ DJ *Hellcat 11122*	49		
17 Sep 05	GANGSTERS AND THUGS *Atlantic AT0213CD*	35		1

TRANSVISION VAMP UK group

Date	Title / Label	Peak Position	Weeks at No.1	Weeks in Top 40
16 Apr 88	TELL THAT GIRL TO SHUT UP *MCA TVV 2*	45		
25 Jun 88	I WANT YOUR LOVE *MCA TVV 3*	5		8
17 Sep 88	REVOLUTION BABY *MCA TVV 4*	30		4
19 Nov 88	SISTER MOON *MCA TVV 5*	41		
1 Apr 89	BABY I DON'T CARE *MCA TVV 6*	3		9
10 Jun 89	THE ONLY ONE *MCA TVV 7*	15		4
5 Aug 89	LANDSLIDE OF LOVE *MCA TVV 8*	14		4
4 Nov 89	BORN TO BE SOLD *MCA TVV 9*	22		3
13 Apr 91	(I JUST WANNA) B WITH U *MCA TVV 10*	30		2
22 Jun 91	IF LOOKS COULD KILL *MCA TVV 11*	41		

TRASH UK group

Date	Title / Label	Peak Position	Weeks at No.1	Weeks in Top 40
25 Oct 69	GOLDEN SLUMBERS/CARRY THAT WEIGHT *Apple 17*	35		2

TRASH CAN SINATRAS UK group

Date	Title / Label	Peak Position	Weeks at No.1	Weeks in Top 40
24 Apr 93	HAYFEVER *Go! Discs GODCD 98*	61		

TRAVEL French producer

Date	Title / Label	Peak Position	Weeks at No.1	Weeks in Top 40
24 Apr 99	BULGARIAN *Tidy Trax TIDY 121CD*	67		

TRAVELING WILBURYS UK/US group

Date	Title / Label	Peak Position	Weeks at No.1	Weeks in Top 40
29 Oct 88	HANDLE WITH CARE *Wilbury W 7732*	21		7
11 Mar 89	END OF THE LINE *Wilbury W 7637*	52		
30 Jun 90	NOBODY'S CHILD *Wilbury W 9773*	44		

TRAVIS UK group

Date	Title / Label	Peak Position	Weeks at No.1	Weeks in Top 40
12 Apr 97	U16 GIRLS *Independiente ISOM 1MS*	40		1
28 Jun 97	ALL I WANT TO DO IS ROCK *Independiente ISOM 3MS*	39		1
23 Aug 97	TIED TO THE 90'S *Independiente ISOM 5MS*	30		1
25 Oct 97	HAPPY *Independiente ISOM 6SMS*	38		1
11 Apr 98	MORE THAN US EP *Independiente ISOM 11MS*	16		2
20 Mar 99	WRITING TO REACH YOU *Independiente ISOM 22MS*	14		3
29 May 99	DRIFTWOOD *Independiente ISOM 27SMS*	13		3
14 Aug 99	WHY DOES IT ALWAYS RAIN ON ME *Independiente ISOM 33MS*	10		6
20 Nov 99	TURN *Independiente ISOM 39SMS*	8		4
17 Jun 00	COMING AROUND *Independiente ISOM 45SMS*	5		3
9 Jun 01	SING *Independiente ISOM 49SMS*	3		5
29 Sep 01	SIDE *Independiente ISOM 54SMS*	14		2
6 Apr 02	FLOWERS IN THE WINDOW *Independiente ISOM 56SMS*	18		3
11 Oct 03	RE-OFFENDER *Independiente ISOM 78SMS*	7		2
27 Dec 03	THE BEAUTIFUL OCCUPATION *Independiente ISOM 81SMS*	48		
3 Apr 04	LOVE WILL COME THROUGH *Independiente ISOM 84MS*	28		1
30 Oct 04	WALKING IN THE SUN *Independiente ISOM 88SMS*	20		1
28 Apr 07	CLOSER *Independiente ISOM118MS*	10		5
21 Jul 07	SELFISH JEAN *Independiente ISOM123MS*	30		1
29 Sep 07	MY EYES *Independiente ISOM124MS*	60		

RANDY TRAVIS US singer

Date	Title / Label	Peak Position	Weeks at No.1	Weeks in Top 40
21 May 88	FOREVER AND EVER, AMEN *Warner Brothers W 8384*	55		

JOHN TRAVOLTA US singer/actor

Date	Title / Label	Peak Position	Weeks at No.1	Weeks in Top 40
20 May 78	YOU'RE THE ONE THAT I WANT *RSO 006* JOHN TRAVOLTA & OLIVIA NEWTON-JOHN ⊛ ★	1	9	20
16 Sep 78	SUMMER NIGHTS *RSO 18* JOHN TRAVOLTA & OLIVIA NEWTON-JOHN ⊛	1	7	12
7 Oct 78	SANDY *Polydor POSP 6* ●	2		10
2 Dec 78	GREASED LIGHTNIN' *Polydor POSP 14* ○	11		7
22 Dec 90	GREASE MEGAMIX *Polydor PO 114* JOHN TRAVOLTA & OLIVIA NEWTON-JOHN	3		8
23 Mar 91	GREASE – THE DREAM MIX *PWL/Polydor PO 136* FRANKIE VALLI, JOHN TRAVOLTA & OLIVIA NEWTON-JOHN	47		
25 Jul 98	YOU'RE THE ONE THAT I WANT *Polydor 0441332* JOHN TRAVOLTA & OLIVIA NEWTON-JOHN	4		4

TREMELOES UK group

Date	Title / Label	Peak Position	Weeks at No.1	Weeks in Top 40
4 Jul 63	TWIST AND SHOUT *Decca F 11694* BRIAN POOLE & THE TREMELOES	4		13
12 Sep 63	DO YOU LOVE ME *Decca F 11739* BRIAN POOLE & THE TREMELOES	1	3	14
28 Nov 63	I CAN DANCE *Decca F 11771* BRIAN POOLE & THE TREMELOES	31		6
30 Jan 64	CANDY MAN *Decca F 11823* BRIAN POOLE & THE TREMELOES	6		11
7 May 64	SOMEONE SOMEONE *Decca F 11893* BRIAN POOLE & THE TREMELOES	2		15

Date	Title	Peak Position	Weeks at No.1	Weeks in Top 40
20 Aug 64	**TWELVE STEPS TO LOVE** *Decca F 11951* BRIAN POOLE & THE TREMELOES	32		6
31 Dec 64	**THREE BELLS** *Decca F 12037* BRIAN POOLE & THE TREMELOES	17		8
22 Jul 65	**I WANT CANDY** *Decca F 12197* BRIAN POOLE & THE TREMELOES	25		6
2 Feb 67	**HERE COMES MY BABY** *CBS 202519*	4		10
27 Apr 67	**SILENCE IS GOLDEN** *CBS 2723*	1	3	15
2 Aug 67	**EVEN THE BAD TIMES ARE GOOD** *CBS 2930*	4		13
8 Nov 67	**BE MINE** *CBS 3043*	39		1
17 Jan 68	**SUDDENLY YOU LOVE ME** *CBS 3234*	6		10
8 May 68	**HELULE HELULE** *CBS 2889*	14		8
18 Sep 68	**MY LITTLE LADY** *CBS 3680*	6		9
11 Dec 68	**I SHALL BE RELEASED** *CBS 3873*	29		3
19 Mar 69	**HELLO WORLD** *CBS 4065*	14		8
1 Nov 69	**(CALL ME) NUMBER ONE** *CBS 4582*	2		12
21 Mar 70	**BY THE WAY** *CBS 4815*	35		3
12 Sep 70	**ME AND MY LIFE** *CBS 5139*	4		15
10 Jul 71	**HELLO BUDDY** *CBS 7294*	32		2

JACKIE TRENT UK singer

Date	Title	Peak Position	Weeks at No.1	Weeks in Top 40
22 Apr 65	**WHERE ARE YOU NOW (MY LOVE)** *Pye 7N 15776*	1	1	10
1 Jul 65	**WHEN THE SUMMERTIME IS OVER** *Pye 7N 15865*	39		1
2 Apr 69	**I'LL BE THERE** *Pye 7N 17693*	38		1

RALPH TRESVANT US singer

Date	Title	Peak Position	Weeks at No.1	Weeks in Top 40
12 Jan 91	**SENSITIVITY** *MCA MCS 1462*	18		6
15 Aug 92	**THE BEST THINGS IN LIFE ARE FREE** *Perspective PERSS 7400* LUTHER VANDROSS & JANET JACKSON WITH SPECIAL GUESTS BBD & RALPH TRESVANT	2		11
16 Dec 95	**THE BEST THINGS IN LIFE ARE FREE (REMIX)** *A&M 5813092* LUTHER VANDROSS & JANET JACKSON WITH SPECIAL GUESTS BBD & RALPH TRESVANT	7		5

TREVOR & SIMON UK production duo

Date	Title	Peak Position	Weeks at No.1	Weeks in Top 40
10 Jun 00	**HANDS UP** *Substance SUBS 1CDS*	12		3

TRI UK group

Date	Title	Peak Position	Weeks at No.1	Weeks in Top 40
2 Sep 95	**WE GOT THE LOVE** *Epic 6623642*	61		

TRIBAL HOUSE US group

Date	Title	Peak Position	Weeks at No.1	Weeks in Top 40
3 Feb 90	**MOTHERLAND-A-FRI-CA** *Cooltempo COOL 198*	57		

TONY TRIBE Jamaican singer

Date	Title	Peak Position	Weeks at No.1	Weeks in Top 40
16 Jul 69	**RED RED WINE** *Downtown DT 419*	46		

A TRIBE CALLED QUEST US group

Date	Title	Peak Position	Weeks at No.1	Weeks in Top 40
18 Aug 90	**BONITA APPLEBUM** *Jive 256*	47		
19 Jan 91	**CAN I KICK IT** *Jive 265*	15		6
11 Jun 94	**OH MY GOD** *Jive JIVECD 355*	68		
13 Jul 96	**1NCE AGAIN** *Jive JIVECD 399*	34		1
23 Nov 96	**STRESSED OUT** *Jive JIVECD 404* A TRIBE CALLED QUEST FEATURING FAITH EVANS & RAPHAEL SAADIQ	33		1
23 Aug 97	**THE JAM EP** *Jive JIVECD 427*	61		
29 Aug 98	**FIND A WAY** *Jive 0518982*	41		

TRIBE OF TOFFS UK group

Date	Title	Peak Position	Weeks at No.1	Weeks in Top 40
24 Dec 88	**JOHN KETLEY (IS A WEATHERMAN)** *Completely Different DAFT 1*	21		3

OBIE TRICE US rapper

Date	Title	Peak Position	Weeks at No.1	Weeks in Top 40
1 Nov 03	**GOT SOME TEETH** *Interscope 9813061*	8		4
14 Feb 04	**THE SET UP (YOU DON'T KNOW)** *Interscope 9815333* OBIE TRICE FEATURING NATE DOGG	32		1
16 Sep 06	**SNITCH** *Interscope 1705438* OBIE TRICE FEATURING AKON	44		

TRICK DADDY US rapper

Date	Title	Peak Position	Weeks at No.1	Weeks in Top 40
26 Feb 05	**LET'S GO** *Atlantic AT0193CD* TRICK DADDY FEATURING TWISTA & LIL' JON	26		1
28 May 05	**SUGAR (GIMME SOME)** *Atlantic AT0202CDX*	61		

TRICKBABY UK group

Date	Title	Peak Position	Weeks at No.1	Weeks in Top 40
12 Oct 96	**INDIE-YARN** *Logic 74321423152*	47		

TRICKSTER UK producer

Date	Title	Peak Position	Weeks at No.1	Weeks in Top 40
4 Apr 98	**MOVE ON UP** *AM:PM 5825812*	19		2

TRICKY UK rapper

Date	Title	Peak Position	Weeks at No.1	Weeks in Top 40
5 Feb 94	**AFTERMATH** *Fourth & Broadway BRCD 288*	69		
28 Jan 95	**OVERCOME** *Fourth & Broadway BRCD 304*	34		1
15 Apr 95	**BLACK STEEL** *Fourth & Broadway BRCDX 320*	28		1
5 Aug 95	**THE HELL EP** *Fourth & Broadway BRCD 326* TRICKY VS THE GRAVEDIGGAZ	12		2
11 Nov 95	**PUMPKIN** *Fourth & Broadway BRCD 330*	26		1
9 Nov 96	**CHRISTIANSANDS** *Fourth & Broadway BRCD 340*	36		1
23 Nov 96	**MILK** *Mushroom D 1494* GARBAGE FEATURING TRICKY	10		3
11 Jan 97	**TRICKY KID** *Fourth & Broadway BRCD 341*	28		1
3 May 97	**MAKES ME WANNA DIE** *Fourth & Broadway BRCD 348*	29		1
30 May 98	**MONEY GREED/BROKEN HOMES** *Island CID 701*	25		1
21 Aug 99	**FOR REAL** *Island CID 753*	45		

TRICKY DISCO UK producer

Date	Title	Peak Position	Weeks at No.1	Weeks in Top 40
28 Jul 90	**TRICKY DISCO** *Warp WAP 7*	14		6
20 Apr 91	**HOUSE FLY** *Warp 7WAP 11*	55		

TRIFFIDS Australian group

Date	Title	Peak Position	Weeks at No.1	Weeks in Top 40
6 Feb 88	**A TRICK OF THE LIGHT** *Island IS 350*	73		

TRINA & TAMARA US duo

Date	Title	Peak Position	Weeks at No.1	Weeks in Top 40
7 Feb 98	**MY LOVE IS THE SHHH!** *Warner Brothers W 0427CD* SOMETHIN' FOR THE PEOPLE FEATURING TRINA & TAMARA	64		
12 Jun 99	**WHAT'D YOU COME HERE FOR?** *Columbia 6673382*	46		
19 Oct 02	**NO PANTIES** *Atlantic AT 0141CD* TRINA	45		
15 Apr 06	**HERE WE GO** *Atlantic AT0238CD* TRINA FEATURING KELLY ROWLAND	15		4

TRINIDAD & TOBAGO TARTAN ARMY Trinidadian group

Date	Title	Peak Position	Weeks at No.1	Weeks in Top 40
17 Jun 06	**SCOTLAND SCOTLAND JASON SCOTLAND** *1745 Trading QUEST001*	30		2

TRINIDAD OIL COMPANY Trinidadian group

Date	Title	Peak Position	Weeks at No.1	Weeks in Top 40
21 May 77	**THE CALENDAR SONG (JANUARY, FEBRUARY, MARCH, APRIL, MAY)** *Harvest HAR 5122*	34		2

TRINITY-X UK group

Date	Title	Peak Position	Weeks at No.1	Weeks in Top 40
19 Oct 02	**FOREVER** *All Around The World CXGLOBE 255*	19		2

TRIO German group

Date	Title	Peak Position	Weeks at No.1	Weeks in Top 40
3 Jul 82	**DA DA DA** *Mobile Suit Corporation CORP 5*	2		7

TRIPLE EIGHT UK group

Date	Title	Peak Position	Weeks at No.1	Weeks in Top 40
3 May 03	**KNOCK OUT** *Polydor 9800048*	8		3
2 Aug 03	**GIVE ME A REASON** *Polydor 9809137*	9		3
11 Jun 05	**GOOD 2 GO** *Osmosis OSMU88802*	42		

TRIPLE X Italian duo

Date	Title	Peak Position	Weeks at No.1	Weeks in Top 40
30 Oct 99	**FEEL THE SAME** *Ministry Of Sound MOSCDS 135*	32		1

TRIPPING DAISY US group

Date	Title / Label	Peak Position	Weeks at No.1	Weeks in Top 40
30 Mar 96	**PIRANHA** *Island CID 638*	72		

TRISCO UK duo

Date	Title / Label	Peak Position	Weeks at No.1	Weeks in Top 40
30 Jun 01	**MUSAK** *Positiva CDTIV 155*	28		1

TRIUMPH Canadian group

Date	Title / Label	Peak Position	Weeks at No.1	Weeks in Top 40
22 Nov 80	**I LIVE FOR THE WEEKEND** *RCA 13*	59		

TRIVIUM US group

Date	Title / Label	Peak Position	Weeks at No.1	Weeks in Top 40
14 Oct 06	**ANTHEM (WE ARE THE FIRE)** *Roadrunner RR39293*	40		1

TROGGS UK group

Date	Title / Label	Peak Position	Weeks at No.1	Weeks in Top 40
5 May 66	**WILD THING** *Fontana TF 689* ★	2		10
14 Jul 66	**WITH A GIRL LIKE YOU** *Fontana TF 717*	1	2	11
29 Sep 66	**I CAN'T CONTROL MYSELF** *Page One POF 001*	2		11
15 Dec 66	**ANY WAY YOU WANT ME** *Page One POF 010*	8		9
16 Feb 67	**GIVE IT TO ME** *Page One POF 015*	12		8
1 Jun 67	**NIGHT OF THE LONG GRASS** *Page One POF 022*	17		6
26 Jul 67	**HI HI HAZEL** *Page One POF 030*	42		
18 Oct 67	**LOVE IS ALL AROUND** *Page One POF 040*	5		12
28 Feb 68	**LITTLE GIRL** *Page One POF 056*	37		1
30 Oct 93	**WILD THING** *Weekend CDWEEK 103* TROGGS & WOLF	69		

TRONIKHOUSE US producer

Date	Title / Label	Peak Position	Weeks at No.1	Weeks in Top 40
14 Mar 92	**UP TEMPO** *KMS UK KMSUK 1*	68		

TROPHY BOYZ UK group

Date	Title / Label	Peak Position	Weeks at No.1	Weeks in Top 40
6 Aug 05	**DU THE DUDEK** *Diablo DIACD010*	49		

TROUBADOURS DU ROI BAUDOUIN Congolese group

Date	Title / Label	Peak Position	Weeks at No.1	Weeks in Top 40
19 Mar 69	**SANCTUS (MISSA LUBA)** *Philips BF 1732*	28		9

TROUBLE FUNK US group

Date	Title / Label	Peak Position	Weeks at No.1	Weeks in Top 40
27 Jun 87	**WOMAN OF PRINCIPLE** *Fourth & Broadway BRW 70*	65		

TROY US duo

Date	Title / Label	Peak Position	Weeks at No.1	Weeks in Top 40
6 Oct 07	**GOTTA GO MY OWN WAY** *Download* GABRIELLA & TROY	40		1
6 Oct 07	**BET ON IT** *Download*	65		

DORIS TROY US singer

Date	Title / Label	Peak Position	Weeks at No.1	Weeks in Top 40
19 Nov 64	**WHATCHA GONNA DO ABOUT IT** *Atlantic AT 4011*	37		3

TRU FAITH UK group

Date	Title / Label	Peak Position	Weeks at No.1	Weeks in Top 40
9 Sep 00	**FREAK LIKE ME** *Public Demand CDTIV 138* TRU FAITH & DUB CONSPIRACY	12		3

TRUBBLE UK singer

Date	Title / Label	Peak Position	Weeks at No.1	Weeks in Top 40
26 Dec 98	**DANCING BABY (OOGA-CHAKA)** *Island YYCD 1*	21		3

TRUCE UK group

Date	Title / Label	Peak Position	Weeks at No.1	Weeks in Top 40
2 Sep 95	**THE FINEST** *Big Life BLRD 118*	54		
30 Mar 96	**CELEBRATION OF LIFE** *Big Life BLRD 126*	51		
29 Nov 97	**NOTHIN' BUT A PARTY** *Big Life BLRD 138*	71		
5 Sep 98	**EYES DON'T LIE** *Big Life BLRD 146*	20		1

TRUCKS UK/Norwegian group

Date	Title / Label	Peak Position	Weeks at No.1	Weeks in Top 40
5 Oct 02	**IT'S JUST PORN MUM** *Gut CDGUT 43*	35		1

ANDREA TRUE CONNECTION US singer

Date	Title / Label	Peak Position	Weeks at No.1	Weeks in Top 40
17 Apr 76	**MORE MORE MORE** *Buddah BDS 442*	5		9
4 Mar 78	**WHAT'S YOUR NAME WHAT'S YOUR NUMBER** *Buddah BDS 467*	34		1

TRUE FAITH US group

Date	Title / Label	Peak Position	Weeks at No.1	Weeks in Top 40
2 Mar 91	**TAKE ME AWAY** *Network NWK 20* TRUE FAITH & BRIDGETTE GRACE WITH FINAL CUT	51		

TRUE PARTY UK group

Date	Title / Label	Peak Position	Weeks at No.1	Weeks in Top 40
2 Dec 00	**WHAZZUP** *Positiva CDBUD 001*	13		4

TRUE STEPPERS UK producers

Date	Title / Label	Peak Position	Weeks at No.1	Weeks in Top 40
29 Apr 00	**BUGGIN'** *NuLife 74321753342* TRUE STEPPERS FEATURING DANE BOWERS	6		6
26 Aug 00	**OUT OF YOUR MIND** *NuLife 74321782942* TRUE STEPPERS & DANE BOWERS FEATURING VICTORIA BECKHAM ●	2		8
2 Dec 00	**TRUE STEP TONIGHT** *NuLife 74321811312* TRUE STEPPERS FEATURING BRIAN HARVEY & DONELL JONES	25		1

TRUMAN & WOLFF UK duo

Date	Title / Label	Peak Position	Weeks at No.1	Weeks in Top 40
22 Aug 98	**COME AGAIN** *Multiply CDMULTY 38* TRUMAN & WOLFF FEATURING STEEL HORSES	57		

JONNY TRUNK & WISBEY US group

Date	Title / Label	Peak Position	Weeks at No.1	Weeks in Top 40
1 Sep 07	**THE LADIES' BRAS** *Download*	27		2

TRUSSEL US group

Date	Title / Label	Peak Position	Weeks at No.1	Weeks in Top 40
8 Mar 80	**LOVE INJECTION** *Elektra K 12412*	43		

TRUTH UK duo

Date	Title / Label	Peak Position	Weeks at No.1	Weeks in Top 40
3 Feb 66	**GIRL** *Pye 7N 17035*	27		5
11 Jun 83	**CONFUSION (HITS US EVERY TIME)** *Formation TRUTH 1*	22		4
27 Aug 83	**A STEP IN THE RIGHT DIRECTION** *Formation TRUTH 2*	32		3
4 Feb 84	**NO STONE UNTURNED** *Formation TRUTH 3*	66		

TRUTH HURTS US singer

Date	Title / Label	Peak Position	Weeks at No.1	Weeks in Top 40
31 Aug 02	**ADDICTIVE** *Interscope 4977782* TRUTH HURTS FEATURING RAKIM	3		9

TSD UK group

Date	Title / Label	Peak Position	Weeks at No.1	Weeks in Top 40
17 Feb 96	**HEART AND SOUL** *Avex UK AVEXCD 21*	69		
30 Mar 96	**BABY I LOVE YOU** *Avex UK AVEXCD 34*	64		

TUBBY T UK singer

Date	Title / Label	Peak Position	Weeks at No.1	Weeks in Top 40
21 Sep 02	**TALES OF THE HOOD** *Go! Beat GOBCD 51*	47		
24 May 03	**BIG N BASHY** *Virgin VSCDT 1847* FALLACY FEATURING TUBBY T	45		

TUBE & BERGER Belgian duo

Date	Title / Label	Peak Position	Weeks at No.1	Weeks in Top 40
7 Feb 04	**STRAIGHT AHEAD** *Direction 6746222* TUBE & BERGER FEATURING CHRISSIE HYNDE	29		1

TUBES US group

Date	Title / Label	Peak Position	Weeks at No.1	Weeks in Top 40
19 Nov 77	**WHITE PUNKS ON DOPE** *A&M AMS 7323*	28		2
28 Apr 79	**PRIME TIME** *A&M AMS 7423*	34		4
12 Sep 81	**DON'T WANT TO WAIT ANYMORE** *Capitol CL 208*	60		

BARBARA TUCKER US singer

Date	Title / Label	Peak Position	Weeks at No.1	Weeks in Top 40
5 Mar 94	**BEAUTIFUL PEOPLE** *Positiva CDTIV 11*	23		2
26 Nov 94	**I GET LIFTED** *Positiva CDTIV 23*	33		1
23 Sep 95	**STAY TOGETHER** *Positiva CDTIV 39*	46		
8 Aug 98	**EVERYBODY DANCE (THE HORN SONG)** *Positiva CDTIV 96*	28		1

Silver-selling ○ Gold-selling ● Platinum-selling ⊛ US No.1 ★ | Peak Position | Weeks at No.1 | Weeks in Top 40

Date	Title / Label	Peak Position	Weeks at No.1	Weeks in Top 40
18 Mar 00	**STOP PLAYING WITH MY MIND** *Positiva CDTIV 127* BARBARA TUCKER FEATURING DARYL D'BONNEAU	17		3
14 May 05	**MOST PRECIOUS LOVE** *Defected DFTD100CDS* BLAZE PRESENTS UDA FEATURING BARBARA TUCKER	44		
29 Apr 06	**MOST PRECIOUS LOVE** *Defected DFTD125CDX* BLAZE FEATURING BARBARA TUCKER	17		2

JUNIOR TUCKER UK singer

Date	Title / Label	Peak Position	Weeks at No.1	Weeks in Top 40
2 Jun 90	**DON'T TEST** *10 TEN 299*	54		

LOUISE TUCKER UK singer

Date	Title / Label	Peak Position	Weeks at No.1	Weeks in Top 40
9 Apr 83	**MIDNIGHT BLUE** *Ariola ARO 289*	59		

TOMMY TUCKER US singer

Date	Title / Label	Peak Position	Weeks at No.1	Weeks in Top 40
26 Mar 64	**HI-HEEL SNEAKERS** *Pye 7N 25238*	23		7

TUFF JAM UK production duo

Date	Title / Label	Peak Position	Weeks at No.1	Weeks in Top 40
10 Oct 98	**NEED GOOD LOVE** *Locked On LOX 99CD*	44		

TUKAN Danish production duo

Date	Title / Label	Peak Position	Weeks at No.1	Weeks in Top 40
15 Dec 01	**LIGHT A RAINBOW** *Incentive CENT 33CDS*	38		1

KT TUNSTALL UK singer/guitarist

Date	Title / Label	Peak Position	Weeks at No.1	Weeks in Top 40
5 Mar 05	**BLACK HORSE AND THE CHERRY TREE** *Relentless RELCD14*	28		2
21 May 05	**OTHER SIDE OF THE WORLD** *Relentless RELCD18*	13		5
10 Sep 05	**SUDDENLY I SEE** *Relentless RELCD21*	12		10
17 Dec 05	**UNDER THE WEATHER** *Relentless RELCD23*	39		1
25 Mar 06	**ANOTHER PLACE TO FALL** *Relentless RELCD24*	52		
25 Aug 07	**HOLD ON** *Relentless RELCD40*	21		6
1 Dec 07	**SAVING MY FACE** *Relentless RELCD46*	50		
15 Mar 08	**IF ONLY** *Relentless RELCD48*	45		

TURIN BRAKES UK duo

Date	Title / Label	Peak Position	Weeks at No.1	Weeks in Top 40
3 Mar 01	**THE DOOR** *Source SOURCDS 024*	67		
12 May 01	**UNDERDOG (SAVE ME)** *Source SOURCDSE 1015*	39		1
11 Aug 01	**MIND OVER MONEY** *Source SOURCD 038*	31		1
27 Oct 01	**EMERGENCY 72** *Source SOURCD 041*	41		
2 Nov 02	**LONG DISTANCE** *Source SOURCDX 064*	22		1
1 Mar 03	**PAIN KILLER** *Source SOURCD 068*	5		2
7 Jun 03	**AVERAGE MAN** *Source SOURCD 085*	35		1
11 Oct 03	**5 MILE (THESE ARE THE DAYS)** *Source SOURCD 089*	31		1
28 May 05	**FISHING FOR A DREAM** *Source SOURCDX109*	32		1
13 Aug 05	**OVER AND OVER** *Source SOURCDX114*	62		

IKE & TINA TURNER US duo

Date	Title / Label	Peak Position	Weeks at No.1	Weeks in Top 40
9 Jun 66	**RIVER DEEP MOUNTAIN HIGH** *London HL 10046*	3		12
28 Jul 66	**TELL HER I'M NOT HOME** *Warner Brothers WB 5753*	48		
27 Oct 66	**A LOVE LIKE YOURS (DON'T COME KNOCKIN' EVERY DAY)** *London HL 10083*	16		10
12 Feb 69	**RIVER DEEP MOUNTAIN HIGH** *London HLU 10242*	33		2
8 Sep 73	**NUTBUSH CITY LIMITS** *United Artists UP 35582*	4		10

RUBY TURNER UK singer

Date	Title / Label	Peak Position	Weeks at No.1	Weeks in Top 40
25 Jan 86	**IF YOU'RE READY (COME GO WITH ME)** *Jive 109* RUBY TURNER FEATURING JONATHAN BUTLER	30		4
29 Mar 86	**I'M IN LOVE** *Jive 118*	61		
13 Sep 86	**BYE BABY** *Jive 126*	52		
14 Mar 87	**I'D RATHER GO BLIND** *Jive RTS 1*	24		6
16 May 87	**I'M IN LOVE** *Jive RTS 2*	57		
13 Jan 90	**IT'S GONNA BE ALRIGHT** *Jive RTS 7*	57		
5 Feb 94	**STAY WITH ME BABY** *M&G MAGCD 53*	39		1
9 Dec 95	**SHAKABOOM!** *Telstar HUNTCD 1* HUNTER FEATURING RUBY TURNER	64		

SAMMY TURNER US singer

Date	Title / Label	Peak Position	Weeks at No.1	Weeks in Top 40
13 Nov 59	**ALWAYS** *London HLX 8963*	26		2

TINA TURNER US singer

Date	Title / Label	Peak Position	Weeks at No.1	Weeks in Top 40
19 Nov 83	**LET'S STAY TOGETHER** *Capitol CL 316* ○	6		11
25 Feb 84	**HELP** *Capitol CL 325*	40		3
16 Jun 84	**WHAT'S LOVE GOT TO DO WITH IT** *Capitol CL 334* ○ ★	3		13
15 Sep 84	**BETTER BE GOOD TO ME** *Capitol CL 338*	45		
17 Nov 84	**PRIVATE DANCER** *Capitol CL 343*	26		5
2 Mar 85	**I CAN'T STAND THE RAIN** *Capitol CL 352*	57		
20 Jul 85	**WE DON'T NEED ANOTHER HERO (THUNDERDOME)** *Capitol CL 364* ○	3		10
12 Oct 85	**ONE OF THE LIVING** *Capitol CL 376*	55		
2 Nov 85	**IT'S ONLY LOVE** *A&M AM 285* BRYAN ADAMS & TINA TURNER	29		4
23 Aug 86	**TYPICAL MALE** *Capitol CL 419*	33		4
8 Nov 86	**TWO PEOPLE** *Capitol CL 430*	43		
14 Mar 87	**WHAT YOU GET IS WHAT YOU SEE** *Capitol CL 439*	30		4
13 Jun 87	**BREAK EVERY RULE** *Capitol CL 452*	43		
20 Jun 87	**TEARING US APART** *Duck W 8299* ERIC CLAPTON & TINA TURNER	56		
19 Mar 88	**ADDICTED TO LOVE (LIVE)** *Capitol CL 484*	71		
2 Sep 89	**THE BEST** *Capitol CL 543* ○	5		10
18 Nov 89	**I DON'T WANNA LOSE YOU** *Capitol CL 553*	8		7
17 Feb 90	**STEAMY WINDOWS** *Capitol CL 560*	13		4
11 Aug 90	**LOOK ME IN THE HEART** *Capitol CL 584*	31		3
13 Oct 90	**BE TENDER WITH ME BABY** *Capitol CL 593*	28		3
24 Nov 90	**IT TAKES TWO** *Warner Brothers ROD 1* ROD STEWART & TINA TURNER	5		7
21 Sep 91	**NUTBUSH CITY LIMITS** *Capitol CL 630*	23		4
23 Nov 91	**WAY OF THE WORLD** *Capitol CL 637*	13		6
15 Feb 92	**LOVE THING** *Capitol CL 644*	29		2
6 Jun 92	**I WANT YOU NEAR ME** *Capitol CL 659*	22		2
22 May 93	**I DON'T WANNA FIGHT** *Parlophone CDRS 6346*	7		7
28 Aug 93	**DISCO INFERNO** *Parlophone CDR 6357*	12		4
30 Oct 93	**WHY MUST WE WAIT UNTIL TONIGHT** *Parlophone CDR 6366*	16		3
18 Nov 95	**GOLDENEYE** *Parlophone CDR 007 1001*	10		7
23 Mar 96	**WHATEVER YOU WANT** *Parlophone CDRS 6429*	23		2
8 Jun 96	**ON SILENT WINGS** *Parlophone CDR 6434*	13		3
27 Jul 96	**MISSING YOU** *Parlophone CDRS 6441*	12		3
19 Oct 96	**SOMETHING BEAUTIFUL REMAINS** *Parlophone CDR 6448*	27		1
21 Dec 96	**IN YOUR WILDEST DREAMS** *Parlophone CDR 6451* TINA TURNER FEATURING BARRY WHITE	32		2
30 Oct 99	**WHEN THE HEARTACHE IS OVER** *Parlophone CDR 6529*	10		4
12 Feb 00	**WHATEVER YOU NEED** *Parlophone CDRS 6532*	27		1
6 Nov 04	**OPEN ARMS** *Parlophone CDCLS862*	25		2

TURNTABLE ORCHESTRA UK producer

Date	Title / Label	Peak Position	Weeks at No.1	Weeks in Top 40
21 Jan 89	**YOU'RE GONNA MISS ME** *Republic LIC 012*	52		

TURTLES US group

Date	Title / Label	Peak Position	Weeks at No.1	Weeks in Top 40
23 Mar 67	**HAPPY TOGETHER** *London HL 10115* ★	12		10
15 Jun 67	**SHE'D RATHER BE WITH ME** *London HLU 10135*	4		14
30 Oct 68	**ELENORE** *London HL 10223*	7		10

T.W.A. UK group

Date	Title / Label	Peak Position	Weeks at No.1	Weeks in Top 40
16 Sep 95	**NASTY GIRLS** *Mercury MERCD 441*	51		

SHANIA TWAIN Canadian singer

Date	Title / Label	Peak Position	Weeks at No.1	Weeks in Top 40
28 Feb 98	**YOU'RE STILL THE ONE** *Mercury 5684932*	10		7
13 Jun 98	**WHEN** *Mercury 5661192*	18		2
28 Nov 98	**FROM THIS MOMENT ON** *Mercury 5665632*	9		3
22 May 99	**THAT DON'T IMPRESS ME MUCH** *Mercury 8708032* ⊛	3		19
2 Oct 99	**MAN! I FEEL LIKE A WOMAN** *Mercury 5623242* ○	3		11
26 Feb 00	**DON'T BE STUPID (YOU KNOW I LOVE YOU)** *Mercury 1721492*	5		4
16 Nov 02	**I'M GONNA GETCHA GOOD!** *Mercury 1722732*	4		9
22 Mar 03	**KA-CHING** *Mercury 1722872*	8		5
14 Jun 03	**FOREVER AND FOR ALWAYS** *Mercury 9807734*	6		6
6 Sep 03	**THANK YOU BABY! (FOR MAKIN' SOMEDAY COME SO SOON)** *Mercury 9810628*	11		3
29 Nov 03	**WHEN YOU KISS ME/UP!** *Mercury 9814004*	21		1
4 Dec 04	**PARTY FOR TWO** *Mercury 2103240* SHANIA TWAIN & MARK McGRATH	10		3
12 Mar 05	**DON'T** *Mercury 9880435*	30		1

TWANG UK group

Date	Title / Label	Peak	No.1	Weeks
24 Mar 07	**WIDE AWAKE** *B Unique/Polydor BUN121CD*	15		3
2 Jun 07	**EITHER WAY** *B Unique/Polydor BUN126CD*	8		5
8 Sep 07	**TWO LOVERS** *B Unique/Polydor BUN134CDS*	34		1
8 Dec 07	**PUSH THE GHOST** *B Unique/Polydor BUN137CDS*	63		

TWEENIES UK childrens' TV characters

Date	Title / Label	Peak	No.1	Weeks
11 Nov 00	**NUMBER 1** *BBC Music WMSS 60332* ○	5		12
31 Mar 01	**BEST FRIENDS FOREVER** *BBC Music WMSS 60382*	12		6
4 Aug 01	**DO THE LOLLIPOP** *BBC Music WMSS 60452*	17		6
15 Dec 01	**I BELIEVE IN CHRISTMAS** *BBC Music WMSS 60502*	9		5
14 Sep 02	**HAVE FUN GO MAD** *BBC Music WMSS 60572*	20		3

TWEET US singer

Date	Title / Label	Peak	No.1	Weeks
11 May 02	**OOPS (OH MY)** *Elektra E 7306CD*	5		5
7 Sep 02	**CALL ME** *Elektra E 7326CD*	35		1
19 Mar 05	**TURN DA LIGHTS OFF** *Atlantic AT0200CD* TWEET FEATURING MISSY ELLIOTT	29		1

TWEETS UK instrumental group

Date	Title / Label	Peak	No.1	Weeks
12 Sep 81	**THE BIRDIE SONG (BIRDIE DANCE)** *PRT 7P 219* ●	2		20
5 Dec 81	**LET'S ALL SING LIKE THE BIRDIES SING** *PRT 7P 226*	44		
18 Dec 82	**THE BIRDIE SONG (BIRDIE DANCE)** *PRT 7P 219*	46		

20 FINGERS US group

Date	Title / Label	Peak	No.1	Weeks
26 Nov 94	**SHORT DICK MAN** *Multiply CDMULT 12* 20 FINGERS FEATURING GILLETTE	21		3
30 Sep 95	**LICK IT** *ZYX 75908* 20 FINGERS FEATURING ROULA	48		
30 Sep 95	**SHORT SHORT MAN (REMIX)** *Multiply CXMULTY 7* 20 FINGERS FEATURING GILLETTE	11		5

21ST CENTURY GIRLS UK group

Date	Title / Label	Peak	No.1	Weeks
12 Jun 99	**21ST CENTURY GIRLS** *EMI NTNCDS 001*	16		2

24 Dutch producer

Date	Title / Label	Peak	No.1	Weeks
12 Feb 05	**THE LONGEST DAY** *Nebula NEBCD064*	56		

TWENTY 4 SEVEN Irish group

Date	Title / Label	Peak	No.1	Weeks
12 Jun 04	**HIDE** *Diablo Music MND2*	42		

TWENTY 4 SEVEN German production duo

Date	Title / Label	Peak	No.1	Weeks
22 Sep 90	**I CAN'T STAND IT** *BCM BCMR 395* TWENTY 4 SEVEN FEATURING CAPTAIN HOLLYWOOD	7		9
24 Nov 90	**ARE YOU DREAMING** *BCM 07504* TWENTY 4 SEVEN FEATURING CAPTAIN HOLLYWOOD	17		9

29 PALMS UK producer

Date	Title / Label	Peak	No.1	Weeks
25 May 02	**TOUCH THE SKY** *Mushroom PERF 35CDS*	51		

22-20'S UK group

Date	Title / Label	Peak	No.1	Weeks
17 Apr 04	**WHY DON'T YOU DO IT FOR ME** *Heavenly HVN 138CD*	41		
10 Jul 04	**SHOOT YOUR GUN** *Heavenly HVN 141CD*	30		1
25 Sep 04	**22 DAYS** *Heavenly HVN 144CDS*	34		1
12 Feb 05	**SUCH A FOOL** *Heavenly HVN148CDS*	29		1

TWICE AS MUCH UK duo

Date	Title / Label	Peak	No.1	Weeks
16 Jun 66	**SITTIN' ON A FENCE** *Immediate IM 033*	25		8

TWIGGY UK singer/model

Date	Title / Label	Peak	No.1	Weeks
14 Aug 76	**HERE I GO AGAIN** *Mercury 6007 100*	17		9

TWIN HYPE US duo

Date	Title / Label	Peak	No.1	Weeks
15 Jul 89	**DO IT TO THE CROWD** *Profile PROF 255*	65		

TWINKLE UK singer

Date	Title / Label	Peak	No.1	Weeks
26 Nov 64	**TERRY** *Decca F 12013*	4		14
25 Feb 65	**GOLDEN LIGHTS** *Decca F 12076*	21		5

TWISTA US rapper

Date	Title / Label	Peak	No.1	Weeks
10 Apr 04	**SLOW JAMZ** *Atlantic AT 0174CD* ★	3		8
3 Jul 04	**OVERNIGHT CELEBRITY** *Atlantic AT 0180CD*	16		3
14 Aug 04	**SUNSHINE (IMPORT)** *Atlantic 7567932652CD*	60		
11 Sep 04	**SUNSHINE** *Atlantic AT 0181CD*	3		7
20 Nov 04	**SO SEXY** *Atlantic AT 0187CD* TWISTA FEATURING R KELLY	28		1
9 Apr 05	**HOPE** *Capitol 8694660* TWISTA FEATURING FAITH EVANS	25		3
26 Feb 05	**LET'S GO** *Atlantic AT0193CD* TRICK DADDY FEATURING TWISTA & LIL' JON	26		1
12 Nov 05	**WHAT WE DO** *Gana/W10 GANA01CDS* KRAY TWINZ FEATURING TWISTA & LETHAL B	23		1
26 Nov 05	**GIRL TONITE** *Atlantic AT0225CDX* TWISTA FEATURING TREY SONGZ	47		

TWISTED INDIVIDUAL UK drum/bass producer

Date	Title / Label	Peak	No.1	Weeks
9 Aug 03	**BANDWAGON BLUES** *Formation FORM 12102*	51		

TWISTED SISTER US group

Date	Title / Label	Peak	No.1	Weeks
26 Mar 83	**I AM (I'M ME)** *Atlantic A 9854*	18		7
28 May 83	**THE KIDS ARE BACK** *Atlantic A 9827*	32		3
20 Aug 83	**YOU CAN'T STOP ROCK 'N' ROLL** *Atlantic A 9792*	43		
2 Jun 84	**WE'RE NOT GONNA TAKE IT** *Atlantic A 9657*	58		
18 Jan 86	**LEADER OF THE PACK** *Atlantic A 9478*	47		

TWISTED X UK group

Date	Title / Label	Peak	No.1	Weeks
19 Jun 04	**BORN IN ENGLAND** *Universal TV 9867021*	9		2

CONWAY TWITTY US singer

Date	Title / Label	Peak	No.1	Weeks
14 Nov 58	**IT'S ONLY MAKE BELIEVE** *MGM 992* ★	1	5	15
27 Mar 59	**STORY OF MY LOVE** *MGM 1003*	30		1
21 Aug 59	**MONA LISA** *MGM 1029*	5		14
21 Jul 60	**IS A BLUE BIRD BLUE** *MGM 1082*	43		
23 Feb 61	**C'EST SI BON** *MGM 1118*	40		1

2 BAD MICE UK group

Date	Title / Label	Peak	No.1	Weeks
15 Feb 92	**HOLD IT DOWN** *Moving Shadow SHADOW 14*	70		
8 Aug 92	**HOLD IT DOWN** *Moving Shadow SHADOW 14*	48		
7 Sep 96	**BOMBSCARE** *Arista 74321397662*	46		

TWO COWBOYS Italian group

Date	Title / Label	Peak	No.1	Weeks
9 Jul 94	**EVERYBODY GONFI-GON** *3 Beat TABCD 221*	7		8

2 EIVISSA German duo

Date	Title / Label	Peak	No.1	Weeks
4 Oct 97	**OH LA LA LA** *Club Tools 0063475 CLU*	13		4

2 FOR JOY UK duo

Date	Title / Label	Peak	No.1	Weeks
1 Dec 90	**IN A STATE** *Mercury MER 333*	61		
9 Nov 91	**LET THE BASS KICK** *All Around The World GLOBE 102*	67		

2 FUNKY 2 UK group

Date	Title / Label	Peak	No.1	Weeks
6 Nov 93	**BROTHERS AND SISTERS** *Logic 74321170772* 2 FUNKY 2 FEATURING KATHRYN DION	56		
30 Nov 96	**BROTHERS AND SISTERS (REMIX)** *All Around The World CDGLOBE 138* 2 FUNKY 2 FEATURING KATHRYN DION	36		1

Silver-selling ○ | Gold-selling ● | Platinum-selling ⊛ | US No.1 ★ | Peak Position | Weeks at No.1 | Weeks in Top 40

2 HOUSE US duo

Date	Title	Peak Position	Weeks at No.1	Weeks in Top 40
21 Mar 92	**GO TECHNO** *Atlantic A 7519*	65		

2 IN A ROOM US duo

Date	Title	Peak Position	Weeks at No.1	Weeks in Top 40
18 Nov 89	**SOMEBODY IN THE HOUSE SAY YEAH!** *Big Life BLR 12*	66		
26 Jan 91	**WIGGLE IT** *Positiva CDTIV 18* ○	3		7
6 Apr 91	**SHE'S GOT ME GOING CRAZY** *SBK 23*	54		
22 Oct 94	**EL TRAGO (THE DRINK)** *SBK 19*	34		1
8 Apr 95	**AHORA ES (NOW IS THE TIME)** *Positiva CDTIV 32*	43		
17 Aug 96	**GIDDY-UP** *Encore CDCOR 008*	74		

2 IN A TENT UK production duo

Date	Title	Peak Position	Weeks at No.1	Weeks in Top 40
17 Dec 94	**WHEN I'M CLEANING WINDOWS (TURNED OUT NICE AGAIN)** *Love This SPONCD 1*	25		4
13 May 95	**BOOGIE WOOGIE BUGLE BOY (DON'T STOP)** *Bald Cat BALCD 1* 2 IN A TANK	48		
6 Jan 96	**WHEN I'M CLEANING WINDOWS (TURNED OUT NICE AGAIN)** *Love This SPONCD 1*	62		

2 MAD UK duo

Date	Title	Peak Position	Weeks at No.1	Weeks in Top 40
9 Feb 91	**THINKING ABOUT YOUR BODY** *Big Life BLR 37*	43		

TWO MAN SOUND UK production duo

Date	Title	Peak Position	Weeks at No.1	Weeks in Top 40
20 Jan 79	**QUE TAL AMERICA** *Miracle M 1*	46		

TWO MEN, A DRUM MACHINE & A TRUMPET UK production duo

Date	Title	Peak Position	Weeks at No.1	Weeks in Top 40
9 Jan 88	**I'M TIRED OF GETTING PUSHED AROUND** *London LON 141*	18		5
25 Jun 88	**HEAT IT UP** *Jive 174* WEE PAPA GIRL RAPPERS FEATURING TWO MEN & A DRUM MACHINE	21		5

TWO NATIONS UK group

Date	Title	Peak Position	Weeks at No.1	Weeks in Top 40
20 Jun 87	**THAT'S THE WAY IT FEELS** *10 TEN 168*	74		

TWO PEOPLE UK group

Date	Title	Peak Position	Weeks at No.1	Weeks in Top 40
31 Jan 87	**HEAVEN** *Polydor POSP 844*	63		

2WO THIRD3 UK group

Date	Title	Peak Position	Weeks at No.1	Weeks in Top 40
19 Feb 94	**HEAR ME CALLING** *Epic 6600642*	48		
11 Jun 94	**EASE THE PRESSURE** *Epic 6604782*	45		
8 Oct 94	**I WANT THE WORLD** *Epic 6608542*	20		4
17 Dec 94	**I WANT TO BE ALONE** *Epic 6610852*	29		3

2-4 FAMILY UK/US group

Date	Title	Peak Position	Weeks at No.1	Weeks in Top 40
29 May 99	**LEAN ON ME (WITH THE FAMILY)** *Epic 6670132*	69		

2 UNLIMITED Dutch duo

Date	Title	Peak Position	Weeks at No.1	Weeks in Top 40
5 Oct 91	**GET READY FOR THIS** *PWL Continental PWL 206*	2		14
25 Jan 92	**TWILIGHT ZONE** *PWL Continental PWL 211*	2		9
2 May 92	**WORKAHOLIC** *PWL Continental PWL 228*	4		6
15 Aug 92	**THE MAGIC FRIEND** *PWL Continental PWL 240*	11		6
30 Jan 93	**NO LIMIT** *PWL Continental PWCD 256*	1	5	14
8 May 93	**TRIBAL DANCE** *PWL Continental PWCD 262*	4		8
4 Sep 93	**FACES** *PWL Continental PWCD 268*	8		5
20 Nov 93	**MAXIMUM OVERDRIVE** *PWL Continental PWCD 276*	15		4
19 Feb 94	**LET THE BEAT CONTROL YOUR BODY** *PWL Continental PWCD 280*	6		7
21 May 94	**THE REAL THING** *PWL Continental PWCD 306*	6		5
1 Oct 94	**NO ONE** *PWL Continental PWCD 314*	17		3
25 Mar 95	**HERE I GO** *PWL Continental PWCD 317*	22		1
21 Oct 95	**DO WHAT'S GOOD FOR ME** *PWL 322CD*	16		2
11 Jul 98	**WANNA GET UP** *Big Life BLRD 143*	38		1

2K UK duo

Date	Title	Peak Position	Weeks at No.1	Weeks in Top 40
25 Oct 97	*****K THE MILLENNIUM** *Blast First BFFP 146CDK*	28		1

2PAC US rapper

Date	Title	Peak Position	Weeks at No.1	Weeks in Top 40
13 Apr 96	**CALIFORNIA LOVE** *Death Row DRWCD 3* 2PAC FEATURING DR DRE	6		5
27 Jul 96	**HOW DO YOU WANT IT?** *Death Row 228546532* 2PAC FEATURING K-CI & JOJO ★	17		2
30 Nov 96	**I AIN'T MAD AT CHA** *Death Row DRWCD 5* 2PAC FEATURING K-CI & JOJO	13		7
26 Apr 97	**WANTED DEAD OR ALIVE** *Def Jam 5744052* 2PAC & SNOOP DOGGY DOGG	16		2
10 Jan 98	**I WONDER IF HEAVEN GOT A GHETTO** *Jive JIVECD 446*	21		2
13 Jun 98	**DO FOR LOVE** *Jive 0518512* 2PAC FEATURING ERIC WILLIAMS	12		3
18 Jul 98	**RUNNIN'** *Black Jam BJAM 9005* 2PAC & THE NOTORIOUS B.I.G.	15		1
28 Nov 98	**HAPPY HOME** *Eagle EAGXS 058*	17		1
20 Feb 99	**CHANGES** *Jive 0522832* ○	3		10
3 Jul 99	**DEAR MAMA** *Jive 0523702*	27		1
23 Jun 01	**UNTIL THE END OF TIME** *Interscope 4975812*	4		8
10 Nov 01	**LETTER 2 MY UNBORN** *Interscope 4976142*	21		3
22 Feb 03	**THUGZ MANSION** *Interscope 4978542*	24		2
31 Jan 04	**RUNNIN' (DYIN' TO LIVE)** *Interscope 9815329* 2PAC & THE NOTORIOUS B.I.G.	17		3
2 Jul 05	**GHETTO GOSPEL** *Interscope 9883248* 2PAC FEATURING ELTON JOHN	1	3	14
27 Jan 07	**PAC'S LIFE** *Interscope 1723503* 2PAC FEATURING TI & ASHANTI	21		2

2PLAY US rapper

Date	Title	Peak Position	Weeks at No.1	Weeks in Top 40
24 Jan 04	**SO CONFUSED** *2PSL 2PSLCD02* 2PLAY FEATURING RAGHAV & JUCXI	6		9
4 Dec 04	**CARELESS WHISPER** *Inferno 2PSLCD06* 2PLAY FEATURING THOMAS JULES/JUCXI D	29		1

TY UK rapper

Date	Title	Peak Position	Weeks at No.1	Weeks in Top 40
8 May 04	**OH YOU WANT MORE** *Big Dada BDCDS 066* TY FEATURING ROOTS MANUVA	65		

TYGERS OF PAN TANG UK group

Date	Title	Peak Position	Weeks at No.1	Weeks in Top 40
14 Feb 81	**HELLBOUND** *MCA 672*	48		
27 Mar 82	**LOVE POTION NO. 9** *MCA 769*	45		
10 Jul 82	**RENDEZVOUS** *MCA 777*	49		
11 Sep 82	**PARIS BY AIR** *MCA 790*	63		

BONNIE TYLER UK singer

Date	Title	Peak Position	Weeks at No.1	Weeks in Top 40
30 Oct 76	**LOST IN FRANCE** *RCA 2734*	9		9
19 Mar 77	**MORE THAN A LOVER** *RCA PB 5008*	27		4
3 Dec 77	**IT'S A HEARTACHE** *RCA PB 5057* ●	4		12
30 Jun 79	**MARRIED MEN** *RCA PB 5164*	35		4
19 Feb 83	**TOTAL ECLIPSE OF THE HEART** *CBS TYLER 1* ● ★	1	2	10
7 May 83	**FASTER THAN THE SPEED OF NIGHT** *CBS A 3338*	43		
25 Jun 83	**HAVE YOU EVER SEEN THE RAIN** *CBS A 3517*	47		
7 Jan 84	**A ROCKIN' GOOD WAY** *Epic A 4071* SHAKY & BONNIE	5		6
31 Aug 85	**HOLDING OUT FOR A HERO** *CBS A 4251* ○	2		11
14 Dec 85	**LOVING YOU'S A DIRTY JOB BUT SOMEBODY'S GOTTA DO IT** *CBS A 6662* BONNIE TYLER, GUEST VOCALS TODD RUNDGREN	73		
28 Dec 91	**HOLDING OUT FOR A HERO** *Total TYLER 10*	69		
27 Jan 96	**MAKING LOVE (OUT OF NOTHING AT ALL)** *East West EW 010CD*	45		

TYMES US group

Date	Title	Peak Position	Weeks at No.1	Weeks in Top 40
25 Jul 63	**SO MUCH IN LOVE** *Cameo Parkway P 871* ★	21		6
15 Jan 69	**PEOPLE** *Direction 58 3903*	16		9
21 Sep 74	**YOU LITTLE TRUSTMAKER** *RCA 2456*	18		7
21 Dec 74	**MS GRACE** *RCA 2493* ○	1	1	10
17 Jan 76	**GOD'S GONNA PUNISH YOU** *RCA 2626*	41		

TYMES 4 UK group

Date	Title	Peak Position	Weeks at No.1	Weeks in Top 40
25 Aug 01	**BODYROCK** *Edel 0118635 ERE*	23		2
15 Dec 01	**SHE GOT GAME** *Blacklist 0133135 EREP*	40		1

TYPICALLY TROPICAL UK duo

Date	Title	Peak Position	Weeks at No.1	Weeks in Top 40
5 Jul 75	**BARBADOS** *Gull GULS 14* (Silver)	1	1	11

TYREE US producer

Date	Title	Peak Position	Weeks at No.1	Weeks in Top 40
25 Feb 89	**TURN UP THE BASS** *ffrr FFR 24* TYREE FEATURING KOOL ROCK STEADY	12		5
6 May 89	**HARDCORE HIP HOUSE** *DJinternational DJIN 11*	70		
2 Dec 89	**MOVE YOUR BODY** *CBS 6554707* TYREE FEATURING JMD	72		

TYRESE US singer

Date	Title	Peak Position	Weeks at No.1	Weeks in Top 40
31 Jul 99	**NOBODY ELSE** *RCA 74321688282*	59		
25 Sep 99	**SWEET LADY** *RCA 74321700842*	55		
26 Jul 03	**HOW YOU GONNA ACT LIKE THAT** *J Records 82876544892*	30		2
23 Sep 06	**PULLIN' ME BACK** *Capitol CDR6710* CHINGY FEATURING TYRESE	44		

TYRREL CORPORATION UK duo

Date	Title	Peak Position	Weeks at No.1	Weeks in Top 40
14 Mar 92	**THE BOTTLE** *Volante TYR 1*	71		
15 Aug 92	**GOING HOME** *Volante TYR 2*	58		
10 Oct 92	**WAKING WITH A STRANGER/ONE DAY** *Volante TYRS 3*	59		
24 Sep 94	**YOU'RE NOT HERE** *Cooltempo CDCOOL 292*	42		
14 Jan 95	**BETTER DAYS AHEAD** *Cooltempo CDCOOLS 303*	29		1

TZANT UK duo

Date	Title	Peak Position	Weeks at No.1	Weeks in Top 40
7 Sep 96	**HOT AND WET (BELIEVE IT)** *Logic 74321376832*	36		1
25 Apr 98	**SOUNDS OF WICKEDNESS** *Logic 74321568842*	11		4
22 Aug 98	**BOUNCE WITH THE MASSIVE** *Logic 74321602102*	39		1

JUDIE TZUKE UK singer

Date	Title	Peak Position	Weeks at No.1	Weeks in Top 40
14 Jul 79	**STAY WITH ME TILL DAWN** *Rocket XPRES 17*	16		7

'Please Can I See Your 12 inch?'

How Frankie Goes to Hollywood Made the Charts Dangerous Again

Multi-formatting is now an established part of the music business. The charts have very tight and carefully evolved criteria for the qualification of such multi-formatting. It wasn't always so. There are several historical precursors for this phenomenon – in 1984 one specific example of note utterly captivated the nation when the controversial Liverpudlian band Frankie Goes to Hollywood briefly ruled the charts. Initially circulating on the S&M/gay cabaret scene, the band was touted as a self-proclaimed 'post-punk S&M gay cabaret act'. Fronted by Sudanese-born former labourer and pizza chef Holly Johnson, the band appeared on the seminal TV show *The Tube*, and was signed soon after to legendary producer Trevor Horn's ZTT label.

Chart history tells us that Radio 1 DJ Mike Read 'banned' the sexually provocative single 'Relax' – a compulsive dance track centred around a booming repetitive bass thump and overtly sexual/homoerotic lyrics – but actually all he did was object to the lyrics and pull the song off before it had finished. This was despite the song having been previously played on other shows many times. It was his employer, the BBC, who formally banned the song (even though the band had already recorded full Radio 1 sessions for John Peel and Kid Jensen the previous year).

Whoever is to blame, the action made the song the most talked-about single for years. The controversy was stoked by the suggestive graphics and the band's own S&M-styled stage gear. By the time of the eventual single release, anticipation was immense. The lowly initial chart position of 77 was soon a distant memory as the song rocketed to Number 1 where it stayed for five weeks, remaining in the charts for an entire year ('Gay Sex Tops Pops' as one tabloid put it with fantastic political incorrectness).

The black and white sloganeering of the band's merchandise – 'Frankie Says ... ' – made the shirts the most easily and widely bootlegged merchandise in music history. It mattered little – total sales of the single ended up around the 2 million mark. Its year-long chart life was buoyed by the band's second single, the even better 'Two Tribes', a crunching Cold War dance behemoth – complete with wrestling Russian – American heads of state in the video – that hit the top spot in June 1984. In the process, its predecessor climbed back up to Number 2, giving the band a rare one-two, matched only by the likes of legends such as The Beatles, John Lennon, Madonna and, er, John Travolta. Coming in 1984, the Orwellian overtones of the song's voiceover and the multiple mixes and formats ensured that the single captured the very zeitgeist and became a commercial giant. Frankie picked up the baton first clutched by New Order with their seminal 12-inch hit, 'Blue Monday' a year previously. Then, when their third single 'Power Of Love' also hit the top spot, they became only the second act at that point – other than Gerry And The Pacemakers – to enjoy three Number 1s with their first three singles. Frankie Goes To Hollywood will be remembered for a rash of brilliant singles, but in chart terms their contribution to the way a song is marketed, remixed, reshaped and reformatted is perhaps even more considerable.

U–X

KEY TO ARTIST ENTRIES

Artist/Group Name — Artist/Group Nationality and Category — Silver-selling — Gold-selling — Platinum-selling — US No.1 — Peak Position — Weeks at No.1 — Weeks in Top 40

DEXY'S MIDNIGHT RUNNERS UK group

Date	Title / Label	Peak	Wks No.1	Wks Top 40
19 Jan 80	**DANCE STANCE** *Oddball Productions R 6028*	40		1
22 Mar 80	**GENO** *Late Night Feelings R 6033*	1	2	12
12 Jul 80	**THERE THERE MY DEAR** *Late Night Feelings R 6038*	7		6
21 Mar 81	**PLAN B** *Parlophone R 6046*	58		
11 Jul 81	**SHOW ME** *Mercury DEXYS 6*	16		7
20 Mar 82	**THE CELTIC SOUL BROTHERS** *Mercury DEXYS 8* DEXY'S MIDNIGHT RUNNERS WITH THE EMERALD EXPRESS	45		
3 Jul 82	**COME ON EILEEN** *Mercury DEXYS 9* DEXY'S MIDNIGHT RUNNERS WITH THE EMERALD EXPRESS ★	1	4	13
2 Oct 82	**JACKIE WILSON SAID (I'M IN HEAVEN WHEN YOU SMILE)** *Mercury DEXYS 10* KEVIN ROWLAND & DEXY'S MIDNIGHT RUNNERS	5		6
4 Dec 82	**LET'S GET THIS STRAIGHT (FROM THE START)/OLD** *Mercury DEXYS 11* KEVIN ROWLAND & DEXY'S MIDNIGHT RUNNERS	17		8
2 Apr 83	**THE CELTIC SOUL BROTHERS** *Mercury DEXYS 12* KEVIN ROWLAND & DEXY'S MIDNIGHT RUNNERS	20		5
22 Nov 86	**BECAUSE OF YOU** *Mercury BRUSH 1*	13		6

Date of entry into Top 75

Artist collaboration or where artist's name has changed

Song Title

Label and Catalogue Number

UB40 UK group

Date	Title / Label	Peak Position	Weeks at No.1	Weeks in Top 40
8 Mar 80	**KING/FOOD FOR THOUGHT** *Graduate GRAD 6* ○	4		9
14 Jun 80	**MY WAY OF THINKING/I THINK IT'S GOING TO RAIN** *Graduate GRAD 8*	6		8
1 Nov 80	**THE EARTH DIES SCREAMING/DREAM A LIE** *Graduate GRAD 10*	10		10
23 May 81	**DON'T LET IT PASS YOU BY/DON'T SLOW DOWN** *DEP International DEP 1*	16		7
8 Aug 81	**ONE IN TEN** *DEP International DEP 2*	7		8
13 Feb 82	**I WON'T CLOSE MY EYES** *DEP International DEP 3*	32		3
15 May 82	**LOVE IS ALL IS ALRIGHT** *DEP International DEP 4*	29		4
28 Aug 82	**SO HERE I AM** *DEP International DEP 5*	25		8
5 Feb 83	**I'VE GOT MINE** *DEP International DEP 6*	45		
20 Aug 83	**RED RED WINE** *DEP International DEP 7* ● ★	1	3	13
15 Oct 83	**PLEASE DON'T MAKE ME CRY** *DEP International DEP 8*	10		7
10 Dec 83	**MANY RIVERS TO CROSS** *DEP International DEP 9*	16		7
17 Mar 84	**CHERRY OH BABY** *DEP International DEP 10*	12		5
22 Sep 84	**IF IT HAPPENS AGAIN** *DEP International DEP 11*	9		7
1 Dec 84	**RIDDLE ME** *DEP International DEP 15*	59		
3 Aug 85	**I GOT YOU BABE** *DEP International DEP 20* UB40 FEATURING CHRISSIE HYNDE ●	1	1	11
26 Oct 85	**DON'T BREAK MY HEART** *DEP International DEP 22* ○	3		12
12 Jul 86	**SING OUR OWN SONG** *DEP International DEP 23*	5		7
27 Sep 86	**ALL I WANT TO DO** *DEP International DEP 24*	41		
17 Jan 87	**RAT IN MI KITCHEN** *DEP International DEP 25*	12		6
9 May 87	**WATCHDOGS** *DEP International DEP 26*	39		2
10 Oct 87	**MAYBE TOMORROW** *DEP International DEP 27*	14		5
27 Feb 88	**RECKLESS** *EMI EM 41* AFRIKA BAMBAATAA FEATURING UB40 & FAMILY	17		6
18 Jun 88	**BREAKFAST IN BED** *DEP International DEP 29* UB40 FEATURING CHRISSIE HYNDE	6		9
20 Aug 88	**WHERE DID I GO WRONG** *DEP International DEP 30*	26		4
17 Jun 89	**I WOULD DO FOR YOU** *DEP International DEP 32*	45		
18 Nov 89	**HOMELY GIRL** *DEP International DEP 33*	6		8
27 Jan 90	**HERE I AM (COME AND TAKE ME)** *DEP International DEP 34*	46		
31 Mar 90	**KINGSTON TOWN** *DEP International DEP 35* ○	4		10
28 Jul 90	**WEAR YOU TO THE BALL** *DEP International DEP 36*	35		2
3 Nov 90	**I'LL BE YOUR BABY TONIGHT** *EMI EM 167* ROBERT PALMER & UB40	6		8
1 Dec 90	**IMPOSSIBLE LOVE** *DEP International DEP 37*	47		
2 Feb 91	**THE WAY YOU DO THE THINGS YOU DO** *DEP International DEP 38*	49		
12 Dec 92	**ONE IN TEN** *ZTT ZANG 39* 808 STATE Vs UB40	17		7
22 May 93	**(I CAN'T HELP) FALLING IN LOVE WITH YOU** *DEP International DEPDG 40* ⊛ ★	1	2	14
21 Aug 93	**HIGHER GROUND** *DEP International DEPD 41*	8		7
11 Dec 93	**BRING ME YOUR CUP** *DEP International DEPD 42*	24		4
2 Apr 94	**C'EST LA VIE** *DEP International DEPD 43*	37		1
27 Aug 94	**REGGAE MUSIC** *DEP International DEPDG 44*	28		1
4 Nov 95	**UNTIL MY DYING DAY** *DEP International DEPD 45*	15		3
30 Aug 97	**TELL ME IS IT TRUE** *DEP International DEPD 48*	14		2
15 Nov 97	**ALWAYS THERE** *DEP International DEPD 49*	53		
10 Oct 98	**COME BACK DARLING** *DEP International DEPD 50*	10		4
19 Dec 98	**HOLLY HOLY** *DEP International DEPD 51*	31		1
1 May 99	**THE TRAIN IS COMING** *DEP International DEPD 52*	30		1
9 Dec 00	**LIGHT MY FIRE** *DEP International DEPD 53*	63		
20 Oct 01	**SINCE I MET YOU LADY/SPARKLE OF MY EYES** *DEP International DEPD 55* UB40 FEATURING LADY SAW	40		1
2 Mar 02	**COVER UP** *DEP International DEPD 56*	54		
8 Nov 03	**SWING LOW** *DEP International DEPX 58* UB40 FEATURING UNITED COLOURS OF SOUND	15		10
18 Jun 05	**KISS AND SAY GOODBYE** *DEP International DEPDX59*	19		2
10 Sep 05	**REASONS** *DEP International DEPDX60* UB40/HUNTERZ/DHOL BLASTERS	75		

UBM German group

Date	Title / Label	Peak Position	Weeks at No.1	Weeks in Top 40
23 May 98	**LOVIN' YOU** *Logic 74321571692*	46		

UD PROJECT UK/German group

Date	Title / Label	Peak Position	Weeks at No.1	Weeks in Top 40
4 Oct 03	**SUMMER JAM** *Free 2 Air/Kontor 0150795KON*	14		4
21 Feb 04	**SATURDAY NIGHT** *Free 2 Air/Kontor 0152955KON*	19		2

UFO UK/German group

Date	Title / Label	Peak Position	Weeks at No.1	Weeks in Top 40
5 Aug 78	**ONLY YOU CAN ROCK ME** *Chrysalis CHS 2241*	50		
27 Jan 79	**DOCTOR DOCTOR** *Chrysalis CHS 2287*	35		2
31 Mar 79	**SHOOT SHOOT** *Chrysalis CHS 2318*	48		
12 Jan 80	**YOUNG BLOOD** *Chrysalis CHS 2399*	36		2
17 Jan 81	**LONELY HEART** *Chrysalis CHS 2482*	41		
30 Jan 82	**LET IT RAIN** *Chrysalis CHS 2576*	62		
19 Mar 83	**WHEN IT'S TIME TO ROCK** *Chrysalis CHS 2672*	70		

UGLY DUCKLING US group

Date	Title / Label	Peak Position	Weeks at No.1	Weeks in Top 40
13 Oct 01	**A LITTLE SAMBA** *XL Recordings XLS 135CD*	70		

UGLY KID JOE US group

Date	Title / Label	Peak Position	Weeks at No.1	Weeks in Top 40
16 May 92	**EVERYTHING ABOUT YOU** *Mercury MER 367*	3		8
22 Aug 92	**NEIGHBOUR** *Mercury MER 374*	28		3
31 Oct 92	**SO DAMN COOL** *Mercury MER 383*	44		
13 Mar 93	**CAT'S IN THE CRADLE** *Mercury MERCD 385*	7		8
19 Jun 93	**BUSY BEE** *Mercury MERCD 389*	39		1
8 Jul 95	**MILKMAN'S SON** *Mercury MERDD 435*	39		1

UGLY RUMOURS UK group

Date	Title / Label	Peak Position	Weeks at No.1	Weeks in Top 40
10 Mar 07	**WAR** *Download*	21		1

UHF US singer/producer

Date	Title / Label	Peak Position	Weeks at No.1	Weeks in Top 40
14 Dec 91	**UHF/EVERYTHING** *XL Recordings XLS 25*	46		

UK UK group

Date	Title / Label	Peak Position	Weeks at No.1	Weeks in Top 40
30 Jun 79	**NOTHING TO LOSE** *Polydor POSP 55*	67		

UK Canadian/Spanish duo

Date	Title / Label	Peak Position	Weeks at No.1	Weeks in Top 40
3 Aug 96	**SMALL TOWN BOY** *Media MCSTD 40049*	74		

U.K. APACHI UK singer

Date	Title / Label	Peak Position	Weeks at No.1	Weeks in Top 40
1 Oct 94	**ORIGINAL NUTTAH** *Sound Of Underground SOUR 008CD* U.K. APACHI WITH SHY FX	39		1
28 Jul 01	**SIGNS** *Outcaste OUT 38CD1* DJ BADMARSH & SHRI FEATURING UK APACHE	63		

UK MIXMASTERS UK producer

Date	Title / Label	Peak Position	Weeks at No.1	Weeks in Top 40
2 Feb 91	**THE NIGHT FEVER MEGAMIX** *IQ ZB 44339*	23		4
27 Jul 91	**LUCKY 7 MEGAMIX** *IQ ZB 44731*	43		
7 Dec 91	**BARE NECESSITIES MEGAMIX** *Connect ZB 35135*	14		6

UK PLAYERS UK group

Date	Title / Label	Peak Position	Weeks at No.1	Weeks in Top 40
14 May 83	**LOVE'S GONNA GET YOU** *RCA 326*	52		

UK SUBS UK group

Date	Title / Label	Peak Position	Weeks at No.1	Weeks in Top 40
23 Jun 79	**STRANGLEHOLD** *Gem GEMS 5*	26		4
8 Sep 79	**TOMORROW'S GIRLS** *Gem GEMS 10*	28		3
1 Dec 79	**SHE'S NOT THERE/KICKS (EP)** *Gem GEMS 14*	36		2
8 Mar 80	**WARHEAD** *Gem GEMS 23*	30		2
17 May 80	**TEENAGE** *Gem GEMS 30*	32		3
25 Oct 80	**PARTY IN PARIS** *Gem GEMS 42*	37		2
18 Apr 81	**KEEP ON RUNNIN' (TILL YOU BURN)** *Gem GEMS 45*	41		

TRACEY ULLMAN UK singer/comedienne

Date	Title / Label	Peak Position	Weeks at No.1	Weeks in Top 40
19 Mar 83	**BREAKAWAY** *Stiff BUY 168* ○	4		9
24 Sep 83	**THEY DON'T KNOW** *Stiff BUY 180* ○	2		9
3 Dec 83	**MOVE OVER DARLING** *Stiff BUY 195*	8		8
3 Mar 84	**MY GUY** *Stiff BUY 197*	23		4
28 Jul 84	**SUNGLASSES** *Stiff BUY 205*	18		6
27 Oct 84	**HELPLESS** *Stiff BUY 211*	61		

ULTIMATE KAOS UK group

Date	Title / Label	Peak Position	Weeks at No.1	Weeks in Top 40
22 Oct 94	**SOME GIRLS** *Wild Card CARDD 12*	9		6
21 Jan 95	**HOOCHIE BOOTY** *Wild Card CARDW 14*	17		3
1 Apr 95	**SHOW A LITTLE LOVE** *Wild Card CARDW 18*	23		4
1 Jul 95	**RIGHT HERE** *Wild Card 5795832*	18		2
8 Mar 97	**CASANOVA** *Polydor 5759312*	24		2
18 Jul 98	**CASANOVA** *Mercury MERCD 505*	29		1
5 Jun 99	**ANYTHING YOU WANT (I'VE GOT IT)** *Mercury MERCD 510*	52		

Silver-selling · Gold-selling · Platinum-selling · US No.1 · Peak Position · Weeks at No.1 · Weeks in Top 40

ULTRA UK group

Date	Title / Label	Peak Position	Weeks at No.1	Weeks in Top 40
18 Apr 98	**SAY YOU DO** *East West EW 124CD*	11		4
4 Jul 98	**SAY IT ONCE** *East West EW 171CD*	16		4
10 Oct 98	**THE RIGHT TIME** *East West EW 182CD*	28		1
16 Jan 99	**RESCUE ME** *East West EW 193CD1*	8		4

ULTRA HIGH UK singer

Date	Title / Label	Peak Position	Weeks at No.1	Weeks in Top 40
2 Dec 95	**STAY WITH ME** *MCA MCSTD 40007*	36		1
20 Jul 96	**ARE YOU READY FOR LOVE** *MCA MCSTD 40039*	45		

ULTRABEAT UK group

Date	Title / Label	Peak Position	Weeks at No.1	Weeks in Top 40
16 Aug 03	**PRETTY GREEN EYES** *All Around The World CXGLOBE 281*	2		12
27 Dec 03	**FEELIN' FINE** *All Around The World CXGLOBE 320*	12		9
11 Sep 04	**BETTER THAN LIFE** *All Around The World CDGLOBE 360*	23		2
8 Jan 05	**PRETTY GREEN EYES** *All Around The World CXGLOBE 281*	68		
1 Oct 05	**FEEL IT WITH ME** *All Around The World CDGLOBE410*	57		
6 May 06	**ELYSIUM (I GO CRAZY)** *All Around The World CDGLOBE488* ULTRABEAT VERSUS SCOTT BROWN	35		1
8 Sep 07	**SURE FEELS GOOD** *All Around The World CDGLOBE696* ULTRABEAT VERSUS DARREN STYLES	52		

ULTRACYNIC UK group

Date	Title / Label	Peak Position	Weeks at No.1	Weeks in Top 40
29 Aug 92	**NOTHING IS FOREVER** *380 PEW 2*	50		
19 Apr 97	**NOTHING IS FOREVER (REMIX)** *All Around The World CDGLOBE 139*	47		

ULTRAMARINE UK duo

Date	Title / Label	Peak Position	Weeks at No.1	Weeks in Top 40
24 Jul 93	**KINGDOM** *Blanco Y Negro NEG 65CD*	46		
29 Jan 94	**BAREFOOT (EP)** *Blanco Y Negro NEG 67CD*	61		
27 Apr 96	**HYMN** *Blanco Y Negro NEG 87CD* ULTRAMARINE FEATURING DAVID McALMONT	65		

ULTRA-SONIC UK duo

Date	Title / Label	Peak Position	Weeks at No.1	Weeks in Top 40
3 Sep 94	**OBSESSION** *Clubscene DCSRT 027*	75		
21 Sep 96	**DO YOU BELIEVE IN LOVE** *Clubscene DCSRT 070*	47		

ULTRASOUND UK group

Date	Title / Label	Peak Position	Weeks at No.1	Weeks in Top 40
7 Mar 98	**BEST WISHES** *Nude NUD 33CD*	68		
13 Jun 98	**STAY YOUNG** *Nude NUD 35CD1*	30		1
10 Apr 99	**FLOODLIT WORLD** *Nude NUD 41CD1*	39		1

ULTRAVOX UK group

Date	Title / Label	Peak Position	Weeks at No.1	Weeks in Top 40
5 Jul 80	**SLEEPWALK** *Chrysalis CHS 2441*	29		7
18 Oct 80	**PASSING STRANGERS** *Chrysalis CHS 2457*	57		
17 Jan 81	**VIENNA** *Chrysalis CHS 2481* ●	2		11
28 Mar 81	**SLOW MOTION** *Island WIP 6691*	33		3
6 Jun 81	**ALL STOOD STILL** *Chrysalis CHS 2522* ●	8		7
22 Aug 81	**THE THIN WALL** *Chrysalis CHS 2540*	14		7
7 Nov 81	**THE VOICE** *Chrysalis CHS 2559*	16		6
25 Sep 82	**REAP THE WILD WIND** *Chrysalis CHS 2639*	12		7
27 Nov 82	**HYMN** *Chrysalis CHS 2657* ●	11		10
19 Mar 83	**VISIONS IN BLUE** *Chrysalis CHS 2676*	15		4
4 Jun 83	**WE CAME TO DANCE** *Chrysalis VOX 1*	18		5
11 Feb 84	**ONE SMALL DAY** *Chrysalis VOX 2*	27		4
19 May 84	**DANCING WITH TEARS IN MY EYES** *Chrysalis UV 1*	3		8
7 Jul 84	**LAMENT** *Chrysalis UV 2*	22		5
20 Oct 84	**LOVE'S GREAT ADVENTURE** *Chrysalis UV 3*	12		7
27 Sep 86	**SAME OLD STORY** *Chrysalis UV 4*	31		2
22 Nov 86	**ALL FALL DOWN** *Chrysalis UV 5*	30		3
6 Feb 93	**VIENNA** *Chrysalis CDCHSS 3936*	13		3

UMBOZA UK duo

Date	Title / Label	Peak Position	Weeks at No.1	Weeks in Top 40
23 Sep 95	**CRY INDIA** *Positiva CDTIV 43*	19		3
20 Jul 96	**SUNSHINE** *Positiva CDTIV 47*	14		3

PIERO UMILIANI Italian orchestra leader

Date	Title / Label	Peak Position	Weeks at No.1	Weeks in Top 40
30 Apr 77	**MAH NA MAH NA** *EMI International INT 530*	8		8

UN-CUT UK group

Date	Title / Label	Peak Position	Weeks at No.1	Weeks in Top 40
29 Mar 03	**MIDNIGHT** *WEA 364CD2*	26		1
28 Jun 03	**FALLIN'** *WEA 368CD*	63		

UNO MAS UK production duo

Date	Title / Label	Peak Position	Weeks at No.1	Weeks in Top 40
6 Apr 02	**I WILL FOLLOW** *Defected DFECT 47CDS*	55		

UNATION UK group

Date	Title / Label	Peak Position	Weeks at No.1	Weeks in Top 40
5 Jun 93	**HIGHER AND HIGHER** *MCA MCSTD 1773*	42		
7 Aug 93	**DO YOU BELIEVE IN LOVE** *MCA MCSTD 1796*	75		

UNBELIEVABLE TRUTH UK group

Date	Title / Label	Peak Position	Weeks at No.1	Weeks in Top 40
14 Feb 98	**HIGHER THAN REASON** *Virgin VSCDT 1676*	38		1
9 May 98	**SOLVED** *Virgin VSCDT 1684*	39		1
18 Jul 98	**SETTLE DOWN/DUNE SEA** *Virgin VSCDT 1697*	46		

UNCANNY ALLIANCE US duo

Date	Title / Label	Peak Position	Weeks at No.1	Weeks in Top 40
19 Dec 92	**I GOT MY EDUCATION** *A&M AM 0128*	39		1

UNCLE KRACKER US rapper

Date	Title / Label	Peak Position	Weeks at No.1	Weeks in Top 40
8 Sep 01	**FOLLOW ME** *Atlantic AT 0108CD*	3		13

UNCLE SAM US singer

Date	Title / Label	Peak Position	Weeks at No.1	Weeks in Top 40
16 May 98	**I DON'T EVER WANT TO SEE YOU AGAIN** *Epic 6656382*	30		1

UNDERCOVER UK group

Date	Title / Label	Peak Position	Weeks at No.1	Weeks in Top 40
15 Aug 92	**BAKER STREET** *PWL International PWL 239*	2		13
14 Nov 92	**NEVER LET HER SLIP AWAY** *PWL International PWL 255*	5		9
6 Feb 93	**I WANNA STAY WITH YOU** *PWL International PWL 258*	28		2
14 Aug 93	**LOVESICK** *PWL International PWCD 271* UNDERCOVER FEATURING JOHN MATTHEWS	62		
3 Jul 04	**VIVA ENGLAND** *MCS MCSRECS1*	49		

UNDERTAKERS UK group

Date	Title / Label	Peak Position	Weeks at No.1	Weeks in Top 40
9 Apr 64	**JUST A LITTLE BIT** *Pye 7N 15607*	49		

UNDERTONES UK group

Date	Title / Label	Peak Position	Weeks at No.1	Weeks in Top 40
21 Oct 78	**TEENAGE KICKS** *Sire SIR 4007*	31		3
3 Feb 79	**GET OVER YOU** *Sire SIR 4010*	57		
28 Apr 79	**JIMMY JIMMY** *Sire SIR 4015*	16		7
21 Jul 79	**HERE COMES THE SUMMER** *Sire SIR 4022*	34		2
20 Oct 79	**YOU'VE GOT MY NUMBER (WHY DON'T YOU USE IT)** *Sire SIR 4024*	32		3
5 Apr 80	**MY PERFECT COUSIN** *Sire SIR 4038*	9		6
5 Jul 80	**WEDNESDAY WEEK** *Sire SIR 4042*	11		7
2 May 81	**IT'S GOING TO HAPPEN!** *Ardeck ARDS 8*	18		6
25 Jul 81	**JULIE OCEAN** *Ardeck ARDS 9*	41		
9 Jul 83	**TEENAGE KICKS** *Ardeck ARDS 1*	60		

UNDERWORLD UK group

Date	Title / Label	Peak Position	Weeks at No.1	Weeks in Top 40
18 Dec 93	**SPIKEE/DOGMAN GO WOOF** *Junior Boy's Own JBO 17CD*	63		
25 Jun 94	**DARK AND LONG** *Junior Boy's Own JBO 19CDS*	57		
13 May 95	**BORN SLIPPY** *Junior Boy's Own JBO 29CDS*	52		
18 May 96	**PEARL'S GIRL** *Junior Boy's Own JBO 38CDS1*	24		1
13 Jul 96	**BORN SLIPPY (REMIX)** *Junior Boy's Own JBO 44CDS1* ●	2		14
9 Nov 96	**PEARL'S GIRL** *Junior Boy's Own JBO 45CDS1*	22		1
27 Mar 99	**PUSH UPSTAIRS** *Junior Boy's Own JBO 5006173*	12		2
5 Jun 99	**JUMBO** *JBO 5007193*	21		1
28 Aug 99	**KING OF SNAKE** *JBO 5008798*	17		1
2 Sep 00	**COWGIRL** *JBO 5012518*	24		1
14 Sep 02	**TWO MONTHS OFF** *JBO 5020098*	12		2
1 Feb 03	**DINOSAUR ADVENTURE 3D** *JBO 05020528*	34		1
8 Nov 03	**BORN SLIPPY NUXX (2ND REMIX)** *JBO 5024703*	27		1

UNDISPUTED TRUTH US group

Date	Title / Label	Peak Position	Weeks at No.1	Weeks in Top 40
22 Jan 77	**YOU + ME = LOVE** *Warner Brothers K 16804*	43		

U96 German producer

Date	Title	Peak Position	Weeks at No.1	Weeks in Top 40
29 Aug 92	**DAS BOOT** *M&G MAGS 28*	18		4
4 Jun 94	**INSIDE YOUR DREAMS** *Logic 74321209722*	44		
29 Jun 96	**CLUB BIZARRE** *Urban 5750152*	70		

UNION UK/Dutch group

Date	Title	Peak Position	Weeks at No.1	Weeks in Top 40
12 Oct 91	**SWING LOW (RUN WITH THE BALL)** *Columbia 6575317* UNION FEATURING THE WORLD CUP SQUAD	16		4

UNION GAP US group

Date	Title	Peak Position	Weeks at No.1	Weeks in Top 40
17 Apr 68	**YOUNG GIRL** *CBS 3365* UNION GAP FEATURING GARY PUCKETT	1	4	16
7 Aug 68	**LADY WILLPOWER** *CBS 3551* UNION GAP FEATURING GARY PUCKETT	5		15
28 Aug 68	**WOMAN WOMAN** *CBS 3110* GARY PUCKETT AND THE UNION GAP	48		
15 Jun 74	**YOUNG GIRL** *CBS 8202* GARY PUCKETT AND THE UNION GAP (silver)	6		11

UNIQUE US group

Date	Title	Peak Position	Weeks at No.1	Weeks in Top 40
10 Sep 83	**WHAT I GOT IS WHAT YOU NEED** *Prelude A 3707*	27		5

UNIQUE 3 UK group

Date	Title	Peak Position	Weeks at No.1	Weeks in Top 40
4 Nov 89	**THE THEME** *10 TEN 285*	61		
14 Apr 90	**MUSICAL MELODY/WEIGHT FOR THE BASS** *10 TEN 298*	29		3
10 Nov 90	**RHYTHM TAKES CONTROL** *10 TEN 327* UNIQUE 3 FEATURING KARIN	41		
16 Nov 91	**NO MORE** *10 TEN 387*	74		

UNIT FOUR PLUS TWO UK group

Date	Title	Peak Position	Weeks at No.1	Weeks in Top 40
13 Feb 64	**GREEN FIELDS** *Decca F 11821*	48		
25 Feb 65	**CONCRETE AND CLAY** *Decca F 12071*	1	1	13
13 May 65	**YOU'VE NEVER BEEN IN LOVE LIKE THIS BEFORE** *Decca F 12144*	14		10
17 Mar 66	**BABY NEVER SAY GOODBYE** *Decca F 12333*	49		

UNITED CITIZEN UK production group

Date	Title	Peak Position	Weeks at No.1	Weeks in Top 40
14 Feb 98	**STARSHIP TROOPERS** *Coalition COLA 040CD* UNITED CITIZEN FEDERATION FEATURING SARAH BRIGHTMAN	58		

UNITED KINGDOM SYMPHONY ORCHESTRA CONDUCTED BY DONALD GOULD UK orchestra

Date	Title	Peak Position	Weeks at No.1	Weeks in Top 40
27 Jul 85	**SHADES (THEME FROM THE CROWN PAINT TELEVISION COMMERCIAL)** *Food For Thought YUM 108*	68		

UNITING NATIONS UK duo

Date	Title	Peak Position	Weeks at No.1	Weeks in Top 40
4 Dec 04	**OUT OF TOUCH** *Gusto CDGUS13*	7		16
6 Aug 05	**YOU AND ME** *Gusto CDGUS18*	15		5
19 Nov 05	**AI NO CORRIDA** *Gusto CDGUS25* UNITING NATIONS FEATURING LAURA MORE	18		3
8 Dec 07	**DO IT YOURSELF (GO OUT AND GET IT)** *Gusto CDGUS55*	64		

UNITONE UK production duo

Date	Title	Peak Position	Weeks at No.1	Weeks in Top 40
26 Jun 93	**CHILDREN OF THE REVOLUTION** *The Hit Label HLC 4* UNITONE ROCKERS FEATURING STEEL	60		

UNITY UK group

Date	Title	Peak Position	Weeks at No.1	Weeks in Top 40
31 Aug 91	**UNITY** *Cardiac CNY 6*	64		

UNIVERSAL Australian group

Date	Title	Peak Position	Weeks at No.1	Weeks in Top 40
2 Aug 97	**ROCK ME GOOD** *London LONCD 397*	19		3
18 Oct 97	**MAKE IT WITH YOU** *London LONCD 404*	33		1

UNKLE UK production duo

Date	Title	Peak Position	Weeks at No.1	Weeks in Top 40
20 Feb 99	**BE THERE** *Mo Wax MW 108CD1* UNKLE FEATURING IAN BROWN	8		3
17 Mar 01	**NARCO TOURISTS** *Soma 100CD* SLAM VS UNKLE	66		
6 Sep 03	**EYE FOR AN EYE** *Mo Wax/Island CIDX 826*	31		1
15 Nov 03	**IN A STATE** *Mo Wax/Island CID 839*	44		
27 Nov 04	**REIGN** *Mo Wax GUSIN007CDS* UNKLE FEATURING IAN BROWN	40		1

UNKLEJAM UK group

Date	Title	Peak Position	Weeks at No.1	Weeks in Top 40
10 Mar 07	**LOVE YA** *Virgin VSCDX1925*	54		
16 Jun 07	**WHAT AM I FIGHTING FOR** *Virgin VSCDX1937*	16		2

UNO CLIO UK group

Date	Title	Peak Position	Weeks at No.1	Weeks in Top 40
18 Nov 95	**ARE YOU MAN ENOUGH** *Avex UK AVEXCD 14* UNO CLIO FEATURING MARTINE McCUTCHEON	62		

UNTOUCHABLES US group

Date	Title	Peak Position	Weeks at No.1	Weeks in Top 40
6 Apr 85	**FREE YOURSELF** *Stiff BUY 221*	26		6
27 Jul 85	**I SPY FOR THE FBI** *Stiff BUY 227*	59		

UP YER RONSON UK group

Date	Title	Peak Position	Weeks at No.1	Weeks in Top 40
5 Aug 95	**LOST IN LOVE** *Hi-Life 5795572* UP YER RONSON FEATURING MARY PEARCE	27		1
30 Mar 96	**ARE YOU GONNA BE THERE?** *Hi-Life 5763272* UP YER RONSON FEATURING MARY PEARCE	27		1
19 Apr 97	**I WILL BE RELEASED** *Hi-Life 5737352* UP YER RONSON FEATURING MARY PEARCE	32		1

PHIL UPCHURCH COMBO US guitarist

Date	Title	Peak Position	Weeks at No.1	Weeks in Top 40
5 May 66	**YOU CAN'T SIT DOWN** *Sue WI 4005*	39		1

UPPER ROOM UK group

Date	Title	Peak Position	Weeks at No.1	Weeks in Top 40
11 Mar 06	**ALL OVER THIS TOWN** *Columbia 82876728002*	38		1
20 May 06	**BLACK AND WHITE** *Columbia 82876836562*	22		2

UPPER STREET UK/US group

Date	Title	Peak Position	Weeks at No.1	Weeks in Top 40
4 Nov 06	**THE ONE** *Concept CDCON70*	35		1

UPSETTERS Jamaican group

Date	Title	Peak Position	Weeks at No.1	Weeks in Top 40
4 Oct 69	**RETURN OF DJANGO/DOLLAR IN THE TEETH** *Upsetter US 301*	5		12

UPSIDE DOWN UK group

Date	Title	Peak Position	Weeks at No.1	Weeks in Top 40
20 Jan 96	**CHANGE YOUR MIND** *World CDWORLD 1A*	11		5
13 Apr 96	**EVERY TIME I FALL IN LOVE** *World CDWORLD 2A*	18		2
29 Jun 96	**NEVER FOUND A LOVE LIKE THIS BEFORE** *World CDWORLD 3A*	19		1
23 Nov 96	**IF YOU LEAVE ME NOW** *World CDWORLD 4A*	27		1

URBAN ALL STARS UK producer

Date	Title	Peak Position	Weeks at No.1	Weeks in Top 40
27 Aug 88	**IT BEGAN IN AFRICA** *Urban URB 23*	64		

URBAN BLUES US group

Date	Title	Peak Position	Weeks at No.1	Weeks in Top 40
10 Aug 96	**LOVE DON'T LIVE** *AM:PM 5817932* URBAN BLUES PROJECT PRESENTS MICHAEL PROCTER	55		

URBAN COOKIE COLLECTIVE UK group

Date	Title	Peak Position	Weeks at No.1	Weeks in Top 40
10 Jul 93	**THE KEY THE SECRET** *Pulse 8 CDLOSE 48* (silver)	2		13
13 Nov 93	**FEELS LIKE HEAVEN** *Pulse 8 CDLOSE 55*	5		5
19 Feb 94	**SAIL AWAY** *Pulse 8 CDLOSE 56*	18		2
23 Apr 94	**HIGH ON A HAPPY VIBE** *Pulse 8 CDLOSE 60*	31		2
15 Oct 94	**BRING IT ON HOME** *Pulse 8 CDLOSE 73*	56		
27 May 95	**SPEND THE DAY** *Pulse 8 CDLOSE 85*	59		
9 Sep 95	**REST OF MY LOVE** *Pulse 8 CDLOSE 93*	67		
16 Dec 95	**SO BEAUTIFUL** *Pulse 8 CDLOSE 100*	68		

Silver-selling ○ Gold-selling ● Platinum-selling ✪ US No.1 ★ — Peak Position | Weeks at No.1 | Weeks in Top 40

Date	Title	Peak Position	Weeks at No.1	Weeks in Top 40
24 Aug 96	THE KEY THE SECRET (REMIX) *Pulse 8 CDLOSE 109*	52		
15 Jan 05	THE KEY THE SECRET 2005 *Feverpitch CDFEVS4*	31		1

URBAN DISCHARGE US group

Date	Title	Peak Position	Weeks at No.1	Weeks in Top 40
27 Jan 96	WANNA DROP A HOUSE (ON THAT BITCH) *MCA MCSTD 40020* URBAN DISCHARGE FEATURING SHE	51		

URBAN HYPE UK group

Date	Title	Peak Position	Weeks at No.1	Weeks in Top 40
11 Jul 92	A TRIP TO TRUMPTON *Faze 2 FAZE 5*	6		6
17 Oct 92	THE FEELING *Faze 2 FAZE 10*	67		
9 Jan 93	LIVING IN A FANTASY *Faze 2 CDFAZE 13*	57		

URBAN SHAKEDOWN UK/Italian production group

Date	Title	Peak Position	Weeks at No.1	Weeks in Top 40
27 Jun 92	SOME JUSTICE *Urban Shakedown URBST 1*	23		3
12 Sep 92	BASS SHAKE *Urban Shakedown URBST 2* URBAN SHAKEDOWN FEATURING MICKY FINN	59		
10 Jun 95	SOME JUSTICE *Urban Shakedown URBCD 3* URBAN SHAKEDOWN FEATURING DBO	49		

URBAN SOUL UK/US group

Date	Title	Peak Position	Weeks at No.1	Weeks in Top 40
30 Mar 91	ALRIGHT *Cooltempo COOL 231*	60		
21 Sep 91	ALRIGHT (REMIX) *Cooltempo COOL 244*	43		
28 Mar 92	ALWAYS *Cooltempo COOL 251*	41		
13 Jun 98	LOVE IS SO NICE *VC Recordings VCRD 33*	75		

URBAN SPECIES UK group

Date	Title	Peak Position	Weeks at No.1	Weeks in Top 40
12 Feb 94	SPIRITUAL LOVE *Talkin Loud TLKCD 45*	35		2
16 Apr 94	BROTHER *Talkin Loud TLKCD 47*	40		1
20 Aug 94	LISTEN *Talkin Loud TLKCD 50* URBAN SPECIES FEATURING MC SOLAAR	47		
6 Mar 99	BLANKET *Talkin Loud TLDD 39* URBAN SPECIES FEATURING IMOGEN HEAP	56		

URBNRI UK group

Date	Title	Peak Position	Weeks at No.1	Weeks in Top 40
9 Feb 08	YOUNG FREE AND SINGLE *Fortress XPH001*	34		1

MIDGE URE UK singer

Date	Title	Peak Position	Weeks at No.1	Weeks in Top 40
12 Jun 82	NO REGRETS *Chrysalis CHS 2618*	9		7
9 Jul 83	AFTER A FASHION *Musicfest FEST 1* MIDGE URE & MICK KARN	39		2
14 Sep 85	IF I WAS *Chrysalis URE 1* ○	1	1	10
16 Nov 85	THAT CERTAIN SMILE *Chrysalis URE 2*	28		3
8 Feb 86	WASTELANDS *Chrysalis URE 3*	46		
7 Jun 86	CALL OF THE WILD *Chrysalis URE 4*	27		6
20 Aug 88	ANSWERS TO NOTHING *Chrysalis URE 5*	49		
19 Nov 88	DEAR GOD *Chrysalis URE 6*	55		
17 Aug 91	COLD COLD HEART *Arista 114555*	17		5
25 May 96	BREATHE *Arista 74321371172*	70		

URGE OVERKILL US group

Date	Title	Peak Position	Weeks at No.1	Weeks in Top 40
21 Aug 93	SISTER HAVANA *Geffen GFSTD 51*	67		
16 Oct 93	POSITIVE BLEEDING *Geffen GFSTD 57*	61		
19 Nov 94	GIRL, YOU'LL BE A WOMAN SOON *MCA MCSTD 2024*	37		2

URUSEI YATSURA UK group

Date	Title	Peak Position	Weeks at No.1	Weeks in Top 40
22 Feb 97	STRATEGIC HAMLETS *Che 67CD*	64		
28 Jun 97	FAKE FUR *Che 70CD*	58		
21 Feb 98	HELLO TIGER *Che 75CD1*	40		1
6 Jun 98	SLAIN BY ELF *Che 80CD1*	63		

US5 UK duo

Date	Title	Peak Position	Weeks at No.1	Weeks in Top 40
7 Oct 06	MARIA *Triple-M Trans Con 2401001*	38		1

US3 UK duo

Date	Title	Peak Position	Weeks at No.1	Weeks in Top 40
10 Jul 93	RIDDIM *Blue Note CDCL 686* US3 FEATURING TUKKA YOOT	34		4
25 Sep 93	CANTALOOP *Blue Note CDCL 696* US3 FEATURING & RAHSAAN	23		4
28 May 94	I GOT IT GOIN' ON *Blue Note CDCL 708* US3 FEATURING KOBIE POWELL & RAHSAAN	52		
1 Mar 97	COME ON EVERYBODY (GET DOWN) *Blue Note CDCL 784*	38		1

USA FOR AFRICA Multinational charity group

Date	Title	Peak Position	Weeks at No.1	Weeks in Top 40
13 Apr 85	WE ARE THE WORLD *CBS USAID 1* ○ ★	1	2	7

USED US group

Date	Title	Peak Position	Weeks at No.1	Weeks in Top 40
22 Mar 03	THE TASTE OF INK *Reprise W601CD*	52		
5 Feb 05	TAKE IT AWAY *Reprise W662CD2*	44		

USHER US singer

Date	Title	Peak Position	Weeks at No.1	Weeks in Top 40
18 Mar 95	THINK OF YOU *LaFace 74321269252*	70		
31 Jan 98	YOU MAKE ME WANNA... *LaFace 74321560652* ○	1	1	7
2 May 98	NICE AND SLOW *LaFace 74321579102* ★	24		2
3 Feb 01	POP YA COLLAR *LaFace 74321828692*	2		6
7 Jul 01	U REMIND ME *LaFace 74321863382* ★	3		7
20 Oct 01	U GOT IT BAD *LaFace 74321898552* ★	5		6
20 Apr 02	U TURN *LaFace 74321934092*	16		4
10 Aug 02	I NEED A GIRL (PART ONE) *Puff Daddy 74321947242* P DIDDY FEATURING USHER & LOON	4		8
27 Mar 04	YEAH *Arista 82876606012* USHER FEATURING LIL' JON & LUDACRIS ★	1	2	12
10 Jul 04	BURN *LaFace 82876624362* ★	1	2	10
13 Nov 04	CONFESSIONS PART II/MY BOO *LaFace 82876655292* ★	5		11
5 Mar 05	CAUGHT UP *LaFace 82876679142*	9		5
28 Jul 07	SAME GIRL *Nonsuch 88697126432* R KELLY & USHER	26		6

USURA Italian production group

Date	Title	Peak Position	Weeks at No.1	Weeks in Top 40
23 Jan 93	OPEN YOUR MIND *Deconstruction 74321128042*	7		7
10 Jul 93	SWEAT *Deconstruction 74321154602*	29		2
6 Dec 97	OPEN YOUR MIND (REMIX) *Malarky MLKD 4*	21		2

UTAH SAINTS UK production duo

Date	Title	Peak Position	Weeks at No.1	Weeks in Top 40
24 Aug 91	WHAT CAN YOU DO FOR ME *ffrr F 164*	10		9
6 Jun 92	SOMETHING GOOD *ffrr F 187*	4		8
8 May 93	BELIEVE IN ME *ffrr FCD 209*	8		5
17 Jul 93	I WANT YOU *ffrr FCD 213*	25		2
25 Jun 94	I STILL THINK OF YOU *ffrr FCD 225*	32		1
2 Sep 95	OHIO *ffrr FCD 264*	42		
5 Feb 00	LOVE SONG *Echo ECSCD 83*	37		1
20 May 00	FUNKY MUSIC (SHO NUFF TURNS ME ON) *Echo ECSCX 96* UTAH SAINTS SPECIAL GUEST VOCAL EDWIN STARR ★	23		1
23 Feb 08	SOMETHING GOOD 08 *Data DATA183CDS*	8		6

U2 Irish group

Date	Title	Peak Position	Weeks at No.1	Weeks in Top 40
8 Aug 81	FIRE *Island WIP 6679*	35		5
17 Oct 81	GLORIA *Island WIP 6733*	55		
3 Apr 82	A CELEBRATION *Island WIP 6770*	47		
22 Jan 83	NEW YEARS DAY *Island WIP 6848*	10		6
2 Apr 83	TWO HEARTS BEAT AS ONE *Island IS 109*	18		3
15 Sep 84	PRIDE (IN THE NAME OF LOVE) *Island IS 202*	3		9
4 May 85	THE UNFORGETTABLE FIRE *Island IS 220*	6		5
28 Mar 87	WITH OR WITHOUT YOU *Island IS 319* ★	4		8
6 Jun 87	I STILL HAVEN'T FOUND WHAT I'M LOOKING FOR *Island IS 328* ★	6		7
12 Sep 87	WHERE THE STREETS HAVE NO NAME *Island IS 340*	4		4
26 Dec 87	IN GOD'S COUNTRY (IMPORT) *Island 7-99385*	48		
1 Oct 88	DESIRE *Island IS 400* ○	1	1	6
17 Dec 88	ANGEL OF HARLEM *Island IS 402*	9		5
15 Apr 89	WHEN LOVE COMES TO TOWN *Island IS 411* U2 FEATURING BB KING	6		5
24 Jun 89	ALL I WANT IS YOU *Island IS 422*	4		5
2 Nov 91	THE FLY *Island IS 500* ○	1	1	4
14 Dec 91	MYSTERIOUS WAYS *Island IS 509*	13		4
7 Mar 92	ONE *Island IS 515*	7		4
20 Jun 92	EVEN BETTER THAN THE REAL THING *Island IS 525*	12		3
11 Jul 92	EVEN BETTER THAN THE REAL THING (REMIX) *Island REAL U2*	8		4
5 Dec 92	WHO'S GONNA RIDE YOUR WILD HORSES *Island IS 550*	14		5
4 Dec 93	STAY (FARAWAY, SO CLOSE) *Island CID 578* ○	4		6
17 Jun 95	HOLD ME, THRILL ME, KISS ME, KILL ME *Atlantic A 7131CD* ●	2		11
15 Feb 97	DISCOTHEQUE *Island CID 649* ○	1	1	5
26 Apr 97	STARING AT THE SUN *Island CID 658*	3		3

Date	Title / Label	Peak Position	Weeks at No.1	Weeks in Top 40
2 Aug 97	**LAST NIGHT ON EARTH** *Island CID 664*	10		2
4 Oct 97	**PLEASE** *Island CIDX 673*	7		2
20 Dec 97	**IF GOD WILL SEND HIS ANGELS** *Island CID 684*	12		3
31 Oct 98	**SWEETEST THING** *Island CID 727* ○	3		6
21 Oct 00	**BEAUTIFUL DAY** *Island CIDX 766* ○	1	1	5
10 Feb 01	**STUCK IN A MOMENT YOU CAN'T GET OUT OF** *Island CIDX 770*	2		6
2 Jun 01	**NEW YEARS DUB** *Serious SERRO 030CD* MUSIQUE VS U2	15		2
28 Jul 01	**ELEVATION** *Island CIDX 780*	3		4
1 Dec 01	**WALK ON** *Island CIDX 788*	5		2
2 Nov 02	**ELECTRICAL STORM** *Island CIDX 808*	5		4
7 Feb 04	**TAKE ME TO THE CLOUDS ABOVE** *All Around The World CXGLOBE 313* LMC VS U2	1	2	10
20 Nov 04	**VERTIGO** *Island CIDX 878*	1	1	9
19 Feb 05	**SOMETIMES YOU CAN'T MAKE IT ON YOUR OWN** *Island CIDX886*	1	1	6
19 Feb 05	**ALL BECAUSE OF YOU (IMPORT)** *Island 0249870322CD*	51		
18 Jun 05	**CITY OF BLINDING LIGHTS** *Island CIDX890*	2		4
22 Oct 05	**ALL BECAUSE OF YOU** *Island CIDX906*	4		2
8 Apr 06	**ONE** *Geffen MCSTD40458* MARY J BLIGE & U2	2		10
11 Nov 06	**THE SAINTS ARE COMING** *Mercury 1713137* U2 & GREEN DAY	2		4
13 Jan 07	**WINDOW IN THE SKIES** *Mercury 1718124*	4		3

V

V UK group

Date	Title / Label	Peak Position	Weeks at No.1	Weeks in Top 40
5 Jun 04	**BLOOD SWEAT & TEARS** *Universal MCSXD 40362*	6		4
21 Aug 04	**HIP TO HIP/CAN YOU FEEL IT** *Universal MCSXD 40374*	5		4
20 Nov 04	**YOU STOOD UP** *Universal MCSXD 40388*	12		2

HOLLY VALANCE Australian singer

Date	Title / Label	Peak Position	Weeks at No.1	Weeks in Top 40
11 May 02	**KISS KISS** *London LONCD 464* ○	1	1	13
12 Oct 02	**DOWN BOY** *London LONCD 469*	2		5
21 Dec 02	**NAUGHTY GIRL** *London LONCD 472*	16		5
8 Nov 03	**STATE OF MIND** *London LONCD 482*	8		4

RICKY VALANCE UK singer

Date	Title / Label	Peak Position	Weeks at No.1	Weeks in Top 40
25 Aug 60	**TELL LAURA I LOVE HER** *Columbia DB 4493*	1	3	15

RITCHIE VALENS US singer

Date	Title / Label	Peak Position	Weeks at No.1	Weeks in Top 40
6 Mar 59	**DONNA** *London HL 8803*	29		1
1 Aug 87	**LA BAMBA** *RCA PB 41435*	49		

CATERINA VALENTE French singer

Date	Title / Label	Peak Position	Weeks at No.1	Weeks in Top 40
19 Aug 55	**THE BREEZE AND I** *Polydor BM 6002* CATERINA VALENTE WITH WERNER MULLER & THE RIAS DANCE ORCHESTRA	5		14

VALENTINE BROTHERS US duo

Date	Title / Label	Peak Position	Weeks at No.1	Weeks in Top 40
23 Apr 83	**MONEY'S TOO TIGHT TO MENTION** *Energy NRG 1*	73		

BROOKE VALENTINE US singer

Date	Title / Label	Peak Position	Weeks at No.1	Weeks in Top 40
16 Jul 05	**GIRLFIGHT** *Virgin VUSDX301* BROOKE VALENTINE FEATURING BIG BOI & LIL' JON	35		1

DICKIE VALENTINE UK singer

Date	Title / Label	Peak Position	Weeks at No.1	Weeks in Top 40
20 Feb 53	**BROKEN WINGS** *Decca F 9954*	12		1
13 Mar 53	**ALL THE TIME AND EVERYWHERE** *Decca F 10038*	9		3
5 Jun 53	**IN A GOLDEN COACH** *Decca F 10098*	7		1
5 Nov 54	**ENDLESS** *Decca F 10346*	19		1
17 Dec 54	**FINGER OF SUSPICION** *Decca F 10394* DICKIE VALENTINE WITH THE STARGAZERS	1	3	15
17 Dec 54	**MR SANDMAN** *Decca F 10415* DICKIE VALENTINE WITH THE GLEN SOMERS ORCHESTRA	5		12
18 Feb 55	**A BLOSSOM FELL** *Decca F 10430* DICKIE VALENTINE WITH THE GLEN SOMERS ORCHESTRA	9		10
3 Jun 55	**I WONDER** *Decca F 10493* DICKIE VALENTINE WITH THE GLEN SOMERS ORCHESTRA	4		15
25 Nov 55	**CHRISTMAS ALPHABET** *Decca F 10628* DICKIE VALENTINE WITH THE GLEN SOMERS ORCHESTRA	1	3	7
16 Dec 55	**OLD PIANO RAG** *Decca F 10645*	15		5
7 Dec 56	**CHRISTMAS ISLAND** *Decca F 10798* DICKIE VALENTINE WITH THE GLEN SOMERS ORCHESTRA	8		5
27 Dec 57	**SNOWBOUND FOR CHRISTMAS** *Decca F 10950* DICKIE VALENTINE WITH THE GLEN SOMERS ORCHESTRA	28		1
13 Mar 59	**VENUS** *Pye Nixa 7N 15192*	20		8
23 Oct 59	**ONE MORE SUNRISE (MORGEN)** *Pye 7N 15221*	14		8

BOBBY VALENTINO US rapper

Date	Title / Label	Peak Position	Weeks at No.1	Weeks in Top 40
2 Jul 05	**SLOW DOWN** *Def Jam 9883239*	4		7
8 Oct 05	**TELL ME WHY (THE RIDDLE)** *Def Jam 9885686*	38		1
30 Jun 07	**ANONYMOUS** *Def Jam 1736310* BOBBY VALENTINO FEATURING TIMBALAND	25		2

JOE VALINO US singer

Date	Title / Label	Peak Position	Weeks at No.1	Weeks in Top 40
18 Jan 57	**THE GARDEN OF EDEN** *HMV POP 283*	23		2

FRANKIE VALLI US singer

Date	Title / Label	Peak Position	Weeks at No.1	Weeks in Top 40
12 Dec 70	**YOU'RE READY NOW** *Philips 320226*	11		9
1 Feb 75	**MY EYES ADORED YOU** *Private Stock PVT 1* ○ ★	5		11
21 Jun 75	**SWEARIN' TO GOD** *Private Stock PVT 21*	31		4
17 Apr 76	**FALLEN ANGEL** *Private Stock PVT 51*	11		7
26 Aug 78	**GREASE** *RSO 012* ● ★	3		11
23 Mar 91	**GREASE – THE DREAM MIX** *PWL/Polydor PO 136* FRANKIE VALLI, JOHN TRAVOLTA & OLIVIA NEWTON-JOHN	47		

VAMPIRE WEEKEND Dutch producer

Date	Title / Label	Peak Position	Weeks at No.1	Weeks in Top 40
9 Feb 08	**A PUNK** *XL Recordings GBBKS0700527*	55		

MARK VAN DALE Dutch producer

Date	Title / Label	Peak Position	Weeks at No.1	Weeks in Top 40
3 Oct 98	**WATER WAVE** *Club Tools 0065815 CLU* MARK VAN DALE WITH ENRICO	71		

DAVID VAN DAY UK singer

Date	Title / Label	Peak Position	Weeks at No.1	Weeks in Top 40
14 May 83	**YOUNG AMERICANS TALKING** *WEA DAY 1*	43		

RON VAN DEN BEUKEN Dutch producer

Date	Title / Label	Peak Position	Weeks at No.1	Weeks in Top 40
19 Jun 04	**TIMELESS (KEEP ON MOVIN')** *Manifesto 9866717*	65		

GEORGE VAN DUSEN UK singer/yodeler

Date	Title / Label	Peak Position	Weeks at No.1	Weeks in Top 40
17 Dec 88	**IT'S PARTY TIME AGAIN** *Bri-Tone 7BT 001*	43		

PAUL VAN DYK German producer

Date	Title / Label	Peak Position	Weeks at No.1	Weeks in Top 40
17 May 97	**FORBIDDEN FRUIT** *Deviant DVNT 18CDR*	69		
15 Nov 97	**WORDS** *Deviant DVNT 26CDS* PAUL VAN DYK FEATURING TONI HALLIDAY	54		
5 Sep 98	**FOR AN ANGEL** *Deviant DVNT 24CDS*	28		1
20 Nov 99	**ANOTHER WAY/AVENUE** *Deviant DVNT 35CDS*	13		3
20 May 00	**TELL ME WHY (THE RIDDLE)** *Deviant DVNT 36CDS* PAUL VAN DYK FEATURING SAINT ETIENNE	7		4
2 Dec 00	**WE ARE ALIVE** *Deviant DVNT 38CDS*	15		3
12 Jul 03	**NOTHING BUT YOU** *Positiva CDTIVS 192* PAUL VAN DYK FEATURING HEMSTOCK	14		3
18 Oct 03	**TIMES OF OUR LIVES/CONNECTED** *Positiva CDTIVS 196* PAUL VAN DYK FEATURING VEGA 4	28		1
17 Apr 04	**CRUSH** *Positiva CDTIVS 204* PAUL VAN DYK FEATURING SECOND SUN	42		
17 Sep 05	**THE OTHER SIDE** *Positiva CDTIVS221* PAUL VAN DYK FEATURING WAYNE JACKSON	58		

LEROY VAN DYKE US singer

Date	Title / Label	Peak Position	Weeks at No.1	Weeks in Top 40
4 Jan 62	**WALK ON BY** *Mercury AMT 1166*	5		13
26 Apr 62	**BIG MAN IN A BIG HOUSE** *Mercury AMT 1173*	34		2

Key: ○ Silver-selling · ● Gold-selling · Platinum-selling · ★ US No.1

NIELS VAN GOGH German producer

Date	Title	Label	Peak	Wks at No.1	Wks in Top 40
10 Apr 99	PULVERTURM	Logic 74321649192	75		

VAN HALEN US group

Date	Title	Label	Peak	Wks at No.1	Wks in Top 40
28 Jun 80	RUNNIN' WITH THE DEVIL	Warner Brothers HM 10	52		
4 Feb 84	JUMP	Warner Brothers W 9384 ★	7		8
19 May 84	PANAMA	Warner Brothers W 9273	61		
5 Apr 86	WHY CAN'T THIS BE LOVE	Warner Brothers W 8740	8		9
12 Jul 86	DREAMS	Warner Brothers W 8642	62		
6 Aug 88	WHEN IT'S LOVE	Warner Brothers W 7816	28		3
1 Apr 89	FEELS SO GOOD	Warner Brothers W 7565	63		
22 Jun 91	POUNDCAKE	Warner Brothers W 0045	74		
19 Oct 91	TOP OF THE WORLD	Warner Brothers W 0066	63		
27 Mar 93	JUMP (LIVE)	Warner Brothers W 0155CD	26		2
21 Jan 95	DON'T TELL ME	Warner Brothers W 0280CD	27		1
1 Apr 95	CAN'T STOP LOVING YOU	Warner Brothers W 0288CD	33		1

ARMAND VAN HELDEN US producer

Date	Title	Label	Peak	Wks at No.1	Wks in Top 40
8 Mar 97	THE FUNK PHENOMENA	ZYX 8523U8	38		1
8 Nov 97	ULTRAFUNKULA	ffrr FCD 317	46		
6 Feb 99	YOU DON'T KNOW ME ARMAND VAN HELDEN FEATURING DUANE HARDEN	ffrr FCD 357	1	1	9
1 May 99	FLOWERZ ARMAND VAN HELDEN FEATURING ROLAND CLARK	ffrr FCD 361	18		3
20 May 00	KOOCHY	ffrr FCDP 379	4		4
3 Nov 01	WHY CAN'T YOU FREE SOME TIME	ffrr FCD 402	34		1
15 Dec 01	YOU CAN'T CHANGE ME ROGER SANCHEZ FEATURING ARMAND VAN HELDEN AND N'DEA DAVENPORT	Defected DFECT 41CDS	25		1
1 May 04	HEAR MY NAME ARMAND VAN HELDEN FEATURING SPALDING ROCKWELL	Southern Fried ECB64CDS	34		1
11 Sep 04	MY MY MY	Southern Fried ECB67CDS	15		5
2 Jul 05	INTO YOUR EYES	Southern Fried ECB78CDS	48		
1 Oct 05	WHEN THE LIGHTS GO DOWN	Southern Fried ECB85CDS	70		
17 Jun 06	MYMYMY (REMIX) ARMAND VAN HELDEN FEATURING TARA	Southern Fried ECB97CDS	12		9
12 May 07	NYC BEAT	Southern Fried ECB113CDS	22		4
1 Sep 07	I WANT YOUR SOUL	Southern Fried ECD125CDS	19		4

DENISE VAN OUTEN UK TV and radio presenter/singer

Date	Title	Label	Peak	Wks at No.1	Wks in Top 40
26 Dec 98	ESPECIALLY FOR YOU DENISE & JOHNNY	RCA 74321644722	3		12
29 Jun 02	CAN'T TAKE MY EYES OFF YOU ANDY WILLIAMS & DENISE VAN OUTEN	Columbia 6721052	23		2

VAN TWIST Belgian/Congolese group

Date	Title	Label	Peak	Wks at No.1	Wks in Top 40
16 Feb 85	SHAFT	Polydor POSP 729	57		

DESPINA VANDI Greek singer

Date	Title	Label	Peak	Wks at No.1	Wks in Top 40
20 Mar 04	GIA	Positiva CDTIVS 199	63		

LUTHER VANDROSS US singer

Date	Title	Label	Peak	Wks at No.1	Wks in Top 40
19 Feb 83	NEVER TOO MUCH	Epic EPC A 3101	44		
26 Jul 86	GIVE ME THE REASON	Epic A 7288	60		
21 Feb 87	GIVE ME THE REASON	Epic 6502167	71		
28 Mar 87	SEE ME	Epic LUTH 1	60		
11 Jul 87	I REALLY DIDN'T MEAN IT	Epic LUTH 3	16		7
5 Sep 87	STOP TO LOVE	Epic LUTH 2	24		4
7 Nov 87	SO AMAZING	Epic LUTH 4	33		2
23 Jan 88	GIVE ME THE REASON	Epic LUTH 5	26		4
16 Apr 88	I GAVE IT UP (WHEN I FELL IN LOVE)	Epic LUTH 6	28		3
9 Jul 88	THERE'S NOTHING BETTER THAN LOVE LUTHER VANDROSS, DUET WITH GREGORY HINES	Epic LUTH 7	72		
8 Oct 88	ANY LOVE	Epic LUTH 8	31		2
4 Feb 89	SHE WON'T TALK TO ME	Epic LUTH 9	34		2
22 Apr 89	COME BACK	Epic LUTH 10	53		
28 Oct 89	NEVER TOO MUCH (REMIX)	Epic LUTH 12	13		6
6 Jan 90	HERE AND NOW	Epic LUTH 13	43		
27 Apr 91	POWER OF LOVE – LOVE POWER	Epic 6568227	46		
18 Jan 92	THE RUSH	Epic 6577237	53		
15 Aug 92	THE BEST THINGS IN LIFE ARE FREE LUTHER VANDROSS & JANET JACKSON WITH SPECIAL GUESTS BBD & RALPH TRESVANT	Perspective PERSS 7400	2		11
22 May 93	LITTLE MIRACLES (HAPPEN EVERY DAY)	Epic 6590442	28		2
18 Sep 93	HEAVEN KNOWS	Epic 6596522	34		2
4 Dec 93	LOVE IS ON THE WAY	Epic 6599592	38		1
17 Sep 94	ENDLESS LOVE LUTHER VANDROSS & MARIAH CAREY	Epic 6608062	3		7
26 Nov 94	LOVE THE ONE YOU'RE WITH	Epic 6610612	31		3
4 Feb 95	ALWAYS AND FOREVER	Epic 6611942	20		4
15 Apr 95	AIN'T NO STOPPING US NOW	Epic 6614242	22		1
11 Nov 95	POWER OF LOVE – LOVE POWER (REMIX)	Epic 6625902	31		2
16 Dec 95	THE BEST THINGS IN LIFE ARE FREE (REMIX) LUTHER VANDROSS & JANET JACKSON WITH SPECIAL GUESTS BBD & RALPH TRESVANT	A&M 5813092	7		5
23 Dec 95	EVERY YEAR EVERY CHRISTMAS	Epic 6627762	43		
12 Oct 96	YOUR SECRET LOVE	Epic 6638385	14		3
28 Dec 96	I CAN MAKE IT BETTER	Epic 6640632	44		
20 Oct 01	TAKE YOU OUT	J Records 74321899442	59		
28 Feb 04	DANCE WITH MY FATHER	J Records 82876569982	21		3
21 Oct 06	SHINE	J Records 88697025032	50		

VANESSA-MAE UK violinist

Date	Title	Label	Peak	Wks at No.1	Wks in Top 40
28 Jan 95	TOCCATA AND FUGUE	EMI Classics MAE 886812	16		8
20 May 95	RED HOT	EMI CDMAE 2	37		1
18 Nov 95	CLASSICAL GAS	EMI CDEM 404	41		
26 Oct 96	I'M A DOUN FOR LACK O' JOHNNIE (A LITTLE SCOTTISH FANTASY)	EMI CDMAE 3	28		1
25 Oct 97	STORM	EMI CDEM 497	54		
20 Dec 97	I FEEL LOVE	EMI CDEM 503	41		
5 Dec 98	DEVIL'S THRILL/REFLECTION	EMI CDEM 530	53		
28 Jul 01	WHITE BIRD	EMI CDVAN 002	66		

VANGELIS Greek keyboard player

Date	Title	Label	Peak	Wks at No.1	Wks in Top 40
9 May 81	CHARIOTS OF FIRE – TITLES	Polydor POSP 246 ★	12		7
11 Jul 81	HEAVEN AND HELL, THIRD MOVEMENT (THEME FROM THE BBC-TV SERIES *THE COSMOS*)	BBC 1	48		
24 Apr 82	CHARIOTS OF FIRE – TITLES	Polydor POSP 246	41		
31 Oct 92	CONQUEST OF PARADISE	East West YZ 704	60		

VANILLA UK group

Date	Title	Label	Peak	Wks at No.1	Wks in Top 40
22 Nov 97	NO WAY NO WAY	EMI CDEM 487	14		6
23 May 98	TRUE TO US	EMI CDEM 509	36		1

VANILLA FUDGE US group

Date	Title	Label	Peak	Wks at No.1	Wks in Top 40
9 Aug 67	YOU KEEP ME HANGIN' ON	Atlantic 584 123	18		9

VANILLA ICE US rapper

Date	Title	Label	Peak	Wks at No.1	Wks in Top 40
24 Nov 90	ICE ICE BABY	SBK 18 ★	1	4	12
2 Feb 91	PLAY THAT FUNKY MUSIC	SBK 20	10		5
30 Mar 91	I LOVE YOU	SBK 22	45		
29 Jun 91	ROLLIN' IN MY 5.0	SBK 27	27		3
10 Aug 91	SATISFACTION	SBK 29	22		3

VANITY FARE UK group

Date	Title	Label	Peak	Wks at No.1	Wks in Top 40
28 Aug 68	I LIVE FOR THE SUN	Page One POF 075	20		7
23 Jul 69	EARLY IN THE MORNING	Page One POF 142	8		12
27 Dec 69	HITCHIN' A RIDE	Page One POF 158	16		10

JOE T. VANNELLI PROJECT Italian producer

Date	Title	Label	Peak	Wks at No.1	Wks in Top 40
17 Jun 95	SWEETEST DAY OF MAY	Positiva CDTIV 36	45		

RANDY VANWARMER US singer

Date	Title	Label	Peak	Wks at No.1	Wks in Top 40
4 Aug 79	JUST WHEN I NEEDED YOU MOST	Bearsville WIP 6516	8		9

VAPORS UK group

Date	Title	Label	Peak	Wks at No.1	Wks in Top 40
9 Feb 80	TURNING JAPANESE	United Artists BP 334	3		9
5 Jul 80	NEWS AT TEN	United Artists BP 345	44		
11 Jul 81	JIMMIE JONES	Liberty BP 401	44		

VARDIS UK group

Date	Title	Label	Peak	Wks at No.1	Wks in Top 40
27 Sep 80	LET'S GO	Logo VAR 1	59		

Silver-selling ● Gold-selling ● Platinum-selling ● US No.1 ★ Peak Position · Weeks at No.1 · Weeks in Top 40

HALO VARGAS US producer

Date	Title	Peak Position	Weeks at No.1	Weeks in Top 40
9 Dec 00	**FUTURE** *Hooj Choons HOOJ 101CD*	67		

VARIOUS ARTISTS (EPS & LPS)

Date	Title	Peak Position	Weeks at No.1	Weeks in Top 40
15 Jun 56	**'CAROUSEL' – ORIGINAL SOUNDTRACK (LP)** *Capitol LCT 6105*	26		2
29 Jun 56	**ALL STAR HIT PARADE** *Decca F 10752*	2		9
26 Jul 57	**ALL STAR HIT PARADE NO. 2** *Decca 10915*	15		7
9 Dec 89	**THE FOOD CHRISTMAS EP** *Food 23*	63		
20 Jan 90	**THE FURTHER ADVENTURES OF NORTH** *Deconstruction PT 43372*	64		
2 Nov 91	**THE APPLE EP** *Apple APP 1*	60		
11 Jul 92	**FOURPLAY (EP)** *XL Recordings XLFP 1*	45		
7 Nov 92	**THE FRED EP** *Heavenly HVN 19*	26		1
24 Apr 93	**GIMME SHELTER (EP)** *Food CDORDERA 1*	23		2
5 Jun 93	**SUBPLATES VOLUME 1 (EP)** *Suburban Base SUBBASE 24CD*	69		
9 Oct 93	**THE TWO TONE EP** *2 Tone CHSTT 31*	30		2
4 Nov 95	**HELP (EP)** *Go! Discs GODCD 135*	51		
16 Mar 96	**NEW YORK UNDERCOVER 4-TRACK EP** *Uptown MCSTD 48002*	39		1
30 Mar 96	**DANGEROUS MINDS EP** *MCA MCSTD 48007*	35		1
29 Nov 97	**PERFECT DAY** *Chrysalis CDNEED 01* ●	1	3	13
12 Sep 98	**THE FULL MONTY-MONSTER MIX** *RCA Victor 74321602582*	62		
26 Sep 98	**TRADE (EP) (DISC 2)** *Tidy Trax TREP 2*	75		
25 Dec 99	**IT'S ONLY ROCK 'N' ROLL** *Universal TV 1566012*	19		4
17 Jun 00	**PERFECT DAY (RE-RECORDING)** *Chrysalis 8887840*	69		
10 Nov 01	**HARD BEAT EP 19** *Nukleuz NUKPA 0369*	71		
19 Nov 05	**UNITED NATIONS OF HOUSE – VOLUME 1** *CR2 CDC2014*	71		
3 Dec 05	**EVER FALLEN IN LOVE (WITH SOMEONE YOU SHOULDN'T'VE)** *EMI PEELCD1*	28		1

VARIOUS ARTISTS (MONTAGES)

Date	Title	Peak Position	Weeks at No.1	Weeks in Top 40
17 May 80	**CALIBRE CUTS** *Calibre CAB 502*	75		
25 Nov 89	**DEEP HEAT '89** *Deep Heat DEEP 10*	12		9
3 Mar 90	**THE BRITS 1990** *RCA PB 43565*	2		5
28 Apr 90	**THE SIXTH SENSE** *Deep Heat DEEP 12*	49		
10 Nov 90	**TIME TO MAKE THE FLOOR BURN** *Megabass MEGAX 1*	16		6

JUNIOR VASQUEZ US producer

Date	Title	Peak Position	Weeks at No.1	Weeks in Top 40
15 Jul 95	**GET YOUR HANDS OFF MY MAN!** *Tribal UK/Positiva CDTIV 37*	22		1
31 Aug 96	**IF MADONNA CALLS** *Multiply CDMULTY 13*	24		1

VAST Australian group

Date	Title	Peak Position	Weeks at No.1	Weeks in Top 40
16 Sep 00	**FREE** *Mushroom MUSH 79CDS*	55		

SVEN VATH German producer

Date	Title	Peak Position	Weeks at No.1	Weeks in Top 40
24 Jul 93	**L'ESPERANZA** *Eye Q YZ 757*	63		
6 Nov 93	**AN ACCIDENT IN PARADISE** *Eye Q YZ 778CD*	57		
22 Oct 94	**HARLEQUIN – THE BEAUTY AND THE BEAST** *Eye Q YZ 857*	72		

FRANKIE VAUGHAN UK singer

Date	Title	Peak Position	Weeks at No.1	Weeks in Top 40
29 Jan 54	**ISTANBUL (NOT CONSTANTINOPLE)** *HMV B 10599* FRANKIE VAUGHAN WITH THE PETER KNIGHT SINGERS	11		1
28 Jan 55	**HAPPY DAYS AND LONELY NIGHTS** *HMV B 10783*	12		3
22 Apr 55	**TWEEDLE DEE** *Philips PB 423*	17		1
2 Dec 55	**SEVENTEEN** *Philips PB 511*	18		3
3 Feb 56	**MY BOY FLAT TOP** *Philips PB 544*	20		2
9 Nov 56	**GREEN DOOR** *Philips PB 640*	2		15
11 Jan 57	**THE GARDEN OF EDEN** *Philips PB 660*	1	4	13
4 Oct 57	**MAN ON FIRE/WANDERIN' EYES** *Philips PB 729*	6		12
1 Nov 57	**GOTTA HAVE SOMETHING IN THE BANK FRANK** *Philips PB 751* FRANKIE VAUGHAN & THE KAYE SISTERS	8		11
20 Dec 57	**KISSES SWEETER THAN WINE** *Philips PB 775*	8		11
7 Mar 58	**CAN'T GET ALONG WITHOUT YOU/WE ARE NOT ALONE** *Philips PB 793*	11		6
9 May 58	**KEWPIE DOLL** *Philips PB 825*	10		12
1 Aug 58	**WONDERFUL THINGS** *Philips PB 834*	22		6
10 Oct 58	**AM I WASTING MY TIME ON YOU** *Philips PB 865*	25		4
30 Jan 59	**THAT'S MY DOLL** *Philips PB 895*	28		2
1 May 59	**COME SOFTLY TO ME** *Philips PB 913* FRANKIE VAUGHAN & THE KAYE SISTERS	9		9
24 Jul 59	**THE HEART OF A MAN** *Philips PB 930*	5		14
18 Sep 59	**WALKIN' TALL** *Philips PB 931*	28		2
29 Jan 60	**WHAT MORE DO YOU WANT** *Philips PB 985*	25		2
22 Sep 60	**KOOKIE LITTLE PARADISE** *Philips PB 1054*	31		2
27 Oct 60	**MILORD** *Philips PB 1066*	34		5
9 Nov 61	**TOWER OF STRENGTH** *Philips PB 1195*	1	3	12
1 Feb 62	**DON'T STOP TWIST** *Philips PB 1219*	22		7
27 Sep 62	**HERCULES** *Philips 326542 BF*	42		
24 Jan 63	**LOOP-DE-LOOP** *Philips 326566 BF*	5		11
20 Jun 63	**HEY MAMA** *Philips BF 1254*	21		8
4 Jun 64	**HELLO DOLLY** *Philips BF 1339*	18		8
11 Mar 65	**SOMEONE MUST HAVE HURT YOU A LOT** *Philips BF 1394*	46		
23 Aug 67	**THERE MUST BE A WAY** *Columbia DB 8248*	7		21
15 Nov 67	**SO TIRED** *Columbia DB 8298*	21		9
28 Feb 68	**NEVERTHELESS** *Columbia DB 8354*	29		4

MALCOLM VAUGHAN UK singer

Date	Title	Peak Position	Weeks at No.1	Weeks in Top 40
1 Jul 55	**EVERY DAY OF MY LIFE** *HMV B 10874*	5		16
27 Jan 56	**WITH YOUR LOVE** *HMV POP 130* MALCOLM VAUGHAN WITH THE PETER KNIGHT SINGERS	18		3
26 Oct 56	**ST. THERESE OF THE ROSES** *HMV POP 250*	3		20
12 Apr 57	**THE WORLD IS MINE** *HMV POP 303*	29		3
10 May 57	**CHAPEL OF THE ROSES** *HMV POP 325*	13		8
29 Nov 57	**MY SPECIAL ANGEL** *HMV POP 419*	3		14
21 Mar 58	**TO BE LOVED** *HMV POP 459* MALCOLM VAUGHAN WITH THE MICHAEL SAMMES SINGERS	14		12
17 Oct 58	**MORE THAN EVER (COME PRIMA)** *HMV POP 538* MALCOLM VAUGHAN WITH THE MICHAEL SAMMES SINGERS	5		14
27 Feb 59	**WAIT FOR ME/WILLINGLY** *HMV POP 590*	13		15

NORMAN VAUGHAN UK comedian/TV presenter

Date	Title	Peak Position	Weeks at No.1	Weeks in Top 40
17 May 62	**SWINGING IN THE RAIN** *Pye 7N 15438*	34		2

SARAH VAUGHAN US singer

Date	Title	Peak Position	Weeks at No.1	Weeks in Top 40
27 Sep 57	**PASSING STRANGERS** *Mercury MT 164* BILLY ECKSTINE & SARAH VAUGHAN	22		2
11 Sep 59	**BROKEN HEARTED MELODY** *Mercury AMT 1057*	7		13
29 Dec 60	**LET'S/SERENATA** *Columbia DB 4542*	37		1
12 Mar 69	**PASSING STRANGERS** *Mercury MF 1082* BILLY ECKSTINE & SARAH VAUGHAN	20		13

BILLY VAUGHN US singer

Date	Title	Peak Position	Weeks at No.1	Weeks in Top 40
27 Jan 56	**SHIFTING WHISPERING SANDS** *London HLD 8205* BILLY VAUGHN ORCHESTRA & CHORUS, NARRATION BY KEN NORDENE	20		1
23 Mar 56	**THEME FROM THE *THREEPENNY OPERA*** *London HLD 8238*	12		7

VAULTS UK group

Date	Title	Peak Position	Weeks at No.1	Weeks in Top 40
20 Mar 04	**NO SLEEP NO NEED EP** *Red Flag RFO9CDS*	70		

V-BIRDS UK group

Date	Title	Peak Position	Weeks at No.1	Weeks in Top 40
3 May 03	**VIRTUALITY** *Liberty CDVIRT001*	21		2

BOBBY VEE US singer

Date	Title	Peak Position	Weeks at No.1	Weeks in Top 40
19 Jan 61	**RUBBER BALL** *London HLG 9255*	4		10
13 Apr 61	**MORE THAN I CAN SAY/STAYING IN** *London HLG 9316*	4		16
3 Aug 61	**HOW MANY TEARS** *London HLG 9389*	10		12
26 Oct 61	**TAKE GOOD CARE OF MY BABY** *London HLG 9438* ★	3		14
21 Dec 61	**RUN TO HIM** *London HLG 9470*	6		14
8 Mar 62	**PLEASE DON'T ASK ABOUT BARBARA** *Liberty LIB 55419*	29		7
7 Jun 62	**SHARING YOU** *Liberty LIB 55451*	10		11
27 Sep 62	**A FOREVER KIND OF LOVE** *Liberty LIB 10046*	13		15
7 Feb 63	**THE NIGHT HAS A THOUSAND EYES** *Liberty LIB 10069*	3		11
20 Jun 63	**BOBBY TOMORROW** *Liberty LIB 55530*	21		7

LITTLE LOUIE VEGA US producer

Date	Title	Peak Position	Weeks at No.1	Weeks in Top 40
5 Oct 91	**RIDE ON THE RHYTHM** *Atlantic A 7602* LITTLE LOUIE VEGA & MARC ANTHONY	71		
23 May 92	**RIDE ON THE RHYTHM** *Atlantic A 7486* LOUIE VEGA & MARC ANTHONY	70		
31 Jan 98	**RIDE ON THE RHYTHM (REMIX)** *Perfecto PERF 151CD1* LITTLE LOUIE & MARC ANTHONY	36		1
23 Nov 02	**DIAMOND LIFE** *Distance D12409* LOUIE VEGA & JAY 'SINISTER' SEALEE STARRING JULIE McKNIGHT	52		

Silver-selling ○ Gold-selling ● Platinum-selling ⊛ US No.1 ★ — Peak Position / Weeks at No.1 / Weeks in Top 40

SUZANNE VEGA US singer

Date	Title / Label	Peak Position	Weeks at No.1	Weeks in Top 40
18 Jan 86	**SMALL BLUE THING** *A&M AM 294*	65		
22 Mar 86	**MARLENE ON THE WALL** *A&M AM 309*	21		5
7 Jun 86	**LEFT OF CENTER** *A&M AM 320* SUZANNE VEGA FEATURING JOE JACKSON	32		3
23 May 87	**LUKA** *A&M VEGA 1*	23		5
18 Jul 87	**TOM'S DINER** *A&M VEGA 2*	58		
19 May 90	**BOOK OF DREAMS** *A&M AM 559*	66		
28 Jul 90	**TOM'S DINER (REMIX)** *A&M AM 592* DNA FEATURING SUZANNE VEGA ○	2		9
22 Aug 92	**IN LIVERPOOL** *A&M AM 0029*	52		
24 Oct 92	**99.9°F** *A&M AM 0085*	46		
19 Dec 92	**BLOOD MAKES NOISE** *A&M AM 0112*	60		
6 Mar 93	**WHEN HEROES GO DOWN** *A&M AMCD 0158*	58		
22 Feb 97	**NO CHEAP THRILL** *A&M 5818692*	40		1

TATA VEGA US singer

Date	Title / Label	Peak Position	Weeks at No.1	Weeks in Top 40
26 May 79	**GET IT UP FOR LOVE/I JUST KEEP THINKING ABOUT YOU BABY** *Motown TMG 1140*	52		

VEGAS UK vocal/instrumental duo

Date	Title / Label	Peak Position	Weeks at No.1	Weeks in Top 40
19 Sep 92	**POSSESSED** *RCA 74321110437*	32		2
28 Nov 92	**SHE** *RCA 74321124657*	43		
3 Apr 93	**WALK INTO THE WIND** *RCA 74321122462*	65		

VEILS New Zealand group

Date	Title / Label	Peak Position	Weeks at No.1	Weeks in Top 40
7 Feb 04	**THE WILD SON** *Rough Trade RTRADESCD 154*	74		
19 Jun 04	**THE TIDE THAT LEFT AND NEVER CAME BACK** *Rough Trade RTRADSCD 164*	63		

TOM VEK UK multi-instrumentalist

Date	Title / Label	Peak Position	Weeks at No.1	Weeks in Top 40
2 Apr 05	**I AIN'T SAYING MY GOODBYES** *Go Beat/Polydor 9870674*	45		
2 Jul 05	**C-C (YOU SET THE FIRE IN ME)** *Go Beat/Polydor 9871846*	60		
5 Nov 05	**NOTHING BUT GREEN LIGHTS** *Go Beat 9874748*	59		

ROSIE VELA US singer

Date	Title / Label	Peak Position	Weeks at No.1	Weeks in Top 40
17 Jan 87	**MAGIC SMILE** *A&M AM 369*	27		4

VELVELETTES US group

Date	Title / Label	Peak Position	Weeks at No.1	Weeks in Top 40
31 Jul 71	**THESE THINGS WILL KEEP ME LOVING YOU** *Tamla Motown TMG 780*	34		5

VELVET REVOLVER US group

Date	Title / Label	Peak Position	Weeks at No.1	Weeks in Top 40
24 Jul 04	**SLITHER** *RCA 82876633312*	35		1
23 Oct 04	**FALL TO PIECES** *RCA 82876647692*	32		1

VELVET UNDERGROUND US group

Date	Title / Label	Peak Position	Weeks at No.1	Weeks in Top 40
12 Mar 94	**VENUS IN FURS (LIVE)** *Sire W 0224CD*	71		

VELVETS US group

Date	Title / Label	Peak Position	Weeks at No.1	Weeks in Top 40
11 May 61	**THAT LUCKY OLD SUN** *London HLU 9328*	46		
17 Aug 61	**TONIGHT (COULD BE THE NIGHT)** *London HLU 9372*	50		

VENGABOYS Multinational group

Date	Title / Label	Peak Position	Weeks at No.1	Weeks in Top 40
28 Nov 98	**UP AND DOWN** *Positiva CDTIV 105* ●	4		11
13 Mar 99	**WE LIKE TO PARTY (THE VENGABUS)** *Positiva CDTIV 108* ●	3		10
26 Jun 99	**BOOM BOOM BOOM BOOM!!** *Positiva CDTIV 114* ●	1	1	11
11 Sep 99	**WE'RE GOING TO IBIZA! (IMPORT)** *Jive 550422*	69		
18 Sep 99	**WE'RE GOING TO IBIZA!** *Positiva CDTIVS 119* ●	1	1	8
18 Dec 99	**KISS (WHEN THE SUN DON'T SHINE)** *Positiva CDTIV 122* ○	3		11
11 Mar 00	**SHALALA LALA** *Positiva CDTIV 126* ○	5		8
8 Jul 00	**UNCLE JOHN FROM JAMAICA** *Positiva CDTIV 135*	6		5
14 Oct 00	**CHEEKAH BOW WOW (THAT COMPUTER SONG)** *Positiva CDTIV 142* VENGABOYS FEATURING CHEEKAH ○	19		2
24 Feb 01	**FOREVER AS ONE** *Positiva CDTIV 148*	28		1

VENT 414 UK group

Date	Title / Label	Peak Position	Weeks at No.1	Weeks in Top 40
28 Sep 96	**FIXER** *Polydor 5753292*	71		

VENTURES US group

Date	Title / Label	Peak Position	Weeks at No.1	Weeks in Top 40
8 Sep 60	**WALK DON'T RUN** *Top Rank JAR 417*	8		10
1 Dec 60	**PERFIDIA** *London HLG 9232*	4		13
9 Mar 61	**RAM-BUNK-SHUSH** *London HLG 9292*	45		
11 May 61	**LULLABY OF THE LEAVES** *London HLG 9344*	43		

VERACOCHA Dutch group

Date	Title / Label	Peak Position	Weeks at No.1	Weeks in Top 40
15 May 99	**CARTE BLANCHE** *Positiva CDTIV 110*	22		2

VERBALICIOUS UK singer

Date	Title / Label	Peak Position	Weeks at No.1	Weeks in Top 40
5 Mar 05	**DON'T PLAY NICE** *All Around The World/Adventure VERCD1*	11		4

VERKA SERDUCHKA Dutch group

Date	Title / Label	Peak Position	Weeks at No.1	Weeks in Top 40
26 May 07	**DANCING LASHA TUMBAI (UKRAINE)** *Download*	28		1

VERNONS GIRLS UK group

Date	Title / Label	Peak Position	Weeks at No.1	Weeks in Top 40
17 May 62	**LOVER PLEASE** *Decca F 11450*	16		10
23 Aug 62	**LOVER PLEASE/YOU KNOW WHAT I MEAN** *Decca F 11450*	39		10
6 Sep 62	**LOCO-MOTION** *Decca F 11495*	47		
3 Jan 63	**FUNNY ALL OVER** *Decca F 11549*	31		3
18 Apr 63	**DO THE BIRD** *Decca F 11629*	44		

VERNON'S WONDERLAND German producer

Date	Title / Label	Peak Position	Weeks at No.1	Weeks in Top 40
25 May 96	**VERNON'S WONDERLAND** *Eye Q Classics EYECL 004CD*	59		

VERTICAL HORIZONS US group

Date	Title / Label	Peak Position	Weeks at No.1	Weeks in Top 40
26 Aug 00	**EVERYTHING YOU WANT** *RCA 74321748692* ★	42		

VERUCA SALT US group

Date	Title / Label	Peak Position	Weeks at No.1	Weeks in Top 40
2 Jul 94	**SEETHER** *Scared Hitless FRET 003CD*	61		
3 Dec 94	**SEETHER** *Hi-Rise FLATSDG 12*	73		
4 Feb 95	**NUMBER ONE BLIND** *Hi-Rise FLATSDG 16*	68		
22 Feb 97	**VOLCANO GIRLS** *Outpost OPRCD 22197*	56		
30 Aug 97	**BENJAMIN** *Outpost OPRCD 22261*	75		

VERVE UK group

Date	Title / Label	Peak Position	Weeks at No.1	Weeks in Top 40
4 Jul 92	**SHE'S A SUPERSTAR** *Hut 16*	66		
22 May 93	**BLUE** *Hut HUTCD 29*	69		
13 May 95	**THIS IS MUSIC** *Hut HUTCD 54*	35		1
24 Jun 95	**ON YOUR OWN** *Hut HUTCD 55*	28		1
30 Sep 95	**HISTORY** *Hut HUTDX 59*	24		1
28 Jun 97	**BITTER SWEET SYMPHONY** *Hut HUTDG 82* ○	2		9
13 Sep 97	**THE DRUGS DON'T WORK** *Hut HUTDG 88* ○	1	1	10
6 Dec 97	**LUCKY MAN** *Hut HUTDG 92*	7		8
30 May 98	**SONNET (IMPORT)** *Hut 8950752*	74		

A VERY GOOD FRIEND OF MINE Italian group

Date	Title / Label	Peak Position	Weeks at No.1	Weeks in Top 40
3 Jul 99	**JUST ROUND** *Positiva CDTIV 109*	55		

VEX RED UK group

Date	Title / Label	Peak Position	Weeks at No.1	Weeks in Top 40
2 Mar 02	**CAN'T SMILE** *Virgin VUSCD 237*	45		

VHS OR BETA US group

Date	Title / Label	Peak Position	Weeks at No.1	Weeks in Top 40
16 Apr 05	**THE MELTING MOON** *Astralwerks ASW68320*	63		
6 Aug 05	**NIGHT ON FIRE** *Astralwerks ASWCD12624*	69		

VIBRATORS UK group

Date	Title / Label	Peak Position	Weeks at No.1	Weeks in Top 40
18 Mar 78	**AUTOMATIC LOVER** *Epic EPC 6137*	35		2
17 Jun 78	**JUDY SAYS (KNOCK YOU IN THE HEAD)** *Epic EPC 6393*	70		

VICE SQUAD UK group

Date	Title / Label	Peak Position	Weeks at No.1	Weeks in Top 40
13 Feb 82	OUT OF REACH *Zonophone Z 26*	68		

VICIOUS CIRCLES UK producer

Date	Title / Label	Peak Position	Weeks at No.1	Weeks in Top 40
16 Dec 00	VICIOUS CIRCLES *Platipus PLATCD 82*	68		

VICIOUS PINK UK duo

Date	Title / Label	Peak Position	Weeks at No.1	Weeks in Top 40
15 Sep 84	CCCAN'T YOU SEE *Parlophone R 6074*	67		

MARIA VIDAL US singer

Date	Title / Label	Peak Position	Weeks at No.1	Weeks in Top 40
24 Aug 85	BODY ROCK *EMI America EA 189*	11		10

VIDEO KIDS Dutch duo

Date	Title / Label	Peak Position	Weeks at No.1	Weeks in Top 40
5 Oct 85	WOODPECKERS FROM SPACE *Epic A 6504*	72		

VIDEO SYMPHONIC UK orchestra

Date	Title / Label	Peak Position	Weeks at No.1	Weeks in Top 40
24 Oct 81	THE FLAME TREES OF THIKA *EMI 5222*	42		

VIENNA PHILHARMONIC ORCHESTRA Austrian orchestra

Date	Title / Label	Peak Position	Weeks at No.1	Weeks in Top 40
18 Dec 71	THEME FROM *THE ONEDIN LINE* *Decca F 13259*	15		13

VIEW UK group

Date	Title / Label	Peak Position	Weeks at No.1	Weeks in Top 40
12 Aug 06	WASTED LITTLE DJS *1965 OLIVECD007*	15		3
28 Oct 06	SUPERSTAR TRADESMAN *1965 OLIVECD006*	15		1
20 Jan 07	SAME JEANS *1965 OLIVECD015*	3		9
5 May 07	THE DON *1965 OLIVECD021*	33		1
7 Jul 07	FACE FOR THE RADIO *1965 OLIVECD024*	69		

VIEW FROM THE HILL UK group

Date	Title / Label	Peak Position	Weeks at No.1	Weeks in Top 40
19 Jul 86	NO CONVERSATION *EMI 5565*	58		
21 Feb 87	I'M NO REBEL *EMI 5580*	59		

VIKKI UK singer

Date	Title / Label	Peak Position	Weeks at No.1	Weeks in Top 40
4 May 85	LOVE IS... *PRT 7P 326*	49		

VILLAGE PEOPLE US group

Date	Title / Label	Peak Position	Weeks at No.1	Weeks in Top 40
3 Dec 77	SAN FRANCISCO (YOU'VE GOT ME) *DJM DJS 10817*	45		
25 Nov 78	Y.M.C.A. *Mercury 6007 192* ◉	1	3	13
17 Mar 79	IN THE NAVY *Mercury 6007 209* ○	2		7
16 Jun 79	GO WEST *Mercury 6007 221*	15		7
9 Aug 80	CAN'T STOP THE MUSIC *Mercury MER 16*	11		8
9 Feb 85	SEX OVER THE PHONE *Record Shack SOHO 34*	59		
4 Dec 93	Y.M.C.A. (REMIX) *Bell 74321177182*	12		6
28 May 94	IN THE NAVY (REMIX) *Bell 74321198192*	36		1
27 Nov 99	Y.M.C.A. (2ND REMIX) *Wrasse WRASX 002*	35		1

V.I.M. UK group

Date	Title / Label	Peak Position	Weeks at No.1	Weeks in Top 40
26 Jan 91	MAGGIE'S LAST PARTY *F2 BOZ 1*	68		

GENE VINCENT US singer

Date	Title / Label	Peak Position	Weeks at No.1	Weeks in Top 40
13 Jul 56	BE BOP A LULA *Capitol CL 14599*	16		7
12 Oct 56	RACE WITH THE DEVIL *Capitol CL 14628*	28		1
19 Oct 56	BLUE JEAN BOP *Capitol CL 14637*	16		5
8 Jan 60	WILD CAT *Capitol CL 15099*	21		4
10 Mar 60	MY HEART *Capitol CL 15115*	16		5
16 Jun 60	PISTOL PACKIN' MAMA *Capitol CL 15136*	15		8
1 Jun 61	SHE SHE LITTLE SHEILA *Capitol CL 15202*	22		7
31 Aug 61	I'M GOING HOME (TO SEE MY BABY) *Capitol CL 15215*	36		3

VINDALOO SUMMER SPECIAL UK group

Date	Title / Label	Peak Position	Weeks at No.1	Weeks in Top 40
19 Jul 86	ROCKIN' WITH RITA (HEAD TO TOE) *Vindaloo UGH 13*	56		

VINES Australian group

Date	Title / Label	Peak Position	Weeks at No.1	Weeks in Top 40
20 Apr 02	HIGHLY EVOLVED *Heavenly HVN 112CD*	32		1
29 Jun 02	GET FREE *Heavenly HVN 113CD*	24		1
19 Oct 02	OUTTATHAWAY *Heavenly HVN 120CDS*	20		1
20 Mar 04	RIDE *Heavenly HVN 137CD*	25		1
5 Jun 04	WINNING DAYS *Heavenly HVN 139CDS*	42		
17 Jun 06	ANYSOUND *Heavenly HVN160CD*	63		
14 Oct 06	DON'T LISTEN TO THE RADIO *Heavenly HVN162CD*	66		

BOBBY VINTON US singer

Date	Title / Label	Peak Position	Weeks at No.1	Weeks in Top 40
2 Aug 62	ROSES ARE RED (MY LOVE) *Columbia DB 4878*	15		6
19 Dec 63	THERE I'VE SAID IT AGAIN *Columbia DB 7179* ★	34		5
29 Sep 90	BLUE VELVET *Epic 6505240* ★	2		9
17 Nov 90	ROSES ARE RED (MY LOVE) *Epic 6564677* ★	71		

VINYLGROOVER UK production duo

Date	Title / Label	Peak Position	Weeks at No.1	Weeks in Top 40
27 Jan 01	ROK DA HOUSE *Nukleuz NUKP 0285* VINYLGROOVER & THE RED HED	72		
10 Jul 04	STAY *Tidy Trax TIDYTWO133C* ROB TISSERA & VINYLGROOVER	61		

VIOLENT DELIGHT UK group

Date	Title / Label	Peak Position	Weeks at No.1	Weeks in Top 40
1 Mar 03	I WISH I WAS A GIRL *WEA 362CD*	25		1
21 Jun 03	ALL YOU EVER DO *WEA 367CD*	38		1
13 Sep 03	TRANSMISSION *WEA 370CD*	64		

VIOLINSKI UK instrumental group

Date	Title / Label	Peak Position	Weeks at No.1	Weeks in Top 40
17 Feb 79	CLOG DANCE *Jet 136*	17		6

VIPER Belgian production group

Date	Title / Label	Peak Position	Weeks at No.1	Weeks in Top 40
7 Feb 98	THE TWISTER *Hooj Choons HOOJCD 59*	55		

VIPER UK rapper

Date	Title / Label	Peak Position	Weeks at No.1	Weeks in Top 40
19 May 01	PUT YOUR HANDS UP *Gusto CDGUS 2* REFLEX FEATURING MC VIPER	72		
14 Sep 02	SELECTA (URBAN HEROES) *Soundproof SPR 1CD* JAMESON & VIPER	51		

VIPERS SKIFFLE GROUP UK group

Date	Title / Label	Peak Position	Weeks at No.1	Weeks in Top 40
25 Jan 57	DON'T YOU ROCK ME DADDY-O *Parlophone R 4261*	10		9
22 Mar 57	CUMBERLAND GAP *Parlophone R 4289*	10		6
31 May 57	STREAMLINE TRAIN *Parlophone R 4308*	23		3

V.I.P.'S UK group

Date	Title / Label	Peak Position	Weeks at No.1	Weeks in Top 40
6 Sep 80	THE QUARTER MOON *Gem GEMS 39*	55		

VIRUS UK production duo

Date	Title / Label	Peak Position	Weeks at No.1	Weeks in Top 40
26 Aug 95	SUN *Perfecto PERF 107CD*	62		
25 Jan 97	MOON *Perfecto PERF 134CD*	36		1

VISAGE UK group

Date	Title / Label	Peak Position	Weeks at No.1	Weeks in Top 40
20 Dec 80	FADE TO GREY *Polydor POSP 194* ○	8		9
14 Mar 81	MIND OF A TOY *Polydor POSP 236*	13		7
11 Jul 81	VISAGE *Polydor POSP 293*	21		7
13 Mar 82	DAMNED DON'T CRY *Polydor POSP 390*	11		7
26 Jun 82	NIGHT TRAIN *Polydor POSP 441*	12		7
13 Nov 82	PLEASURE BOYS *Polydor POSP 523*	44		
1 Sep 84	LOVE GLOVE *Polydor POSP 691*	54		
28 Aug 93	FADE TO GREY (REMIX) *Polydor PZCD 282*	39		1

VISCOUNTS UK group

Date	Title / Label	Peak Position	Weeks at No.1	Weeks in Top 40
13 Oct 60	SHORT'NIN' BREAD *Pye 7N 15287*	16		6
14 Sep 61	WHO PUT THE BOMP *Pye 7N 15379*	21		7

Silver-selling · Gold-selling · Platinum-selling · US No.1 ★ · Peak Position · Weeks at No.1 · Weeks in Top 40

VISION UK group

Date	Title	Label	Peak Position	Weeks at No.1	Weeks in Top 40
9 Jul 83	LOVE DANCE	MVM 2886	74		

VISIONMASTERS UK production duo

Date	Title	Label	Peak Position	Weeks at No.1	Weeks in Top 40
30 Nov 91	KEEP ON PUMPIN' IT VISIONMASTERS WITH TONY KING & KYLIE MINOGUE	PWL 207	49		

VITA US singer

Date	Title	Label	Peak Position	Weeks at No.1	Weeks in Top 40
9 Jun 01	LAPDANCE N*E*R*D FEATURING LEE HARVEY & VITA	Virgin VUSCD 196	33		1
12 Oct 02	DOWN 4 U IRV GOTTI PRESENTS JA RULE, ASHANTI, CHARLI BALTIMORE & VITA	Murder Inc 0639002	4		5

VITAMIN C US singer

Date	Title	Label	Peak Position	Weeks at No.1	Weeks in Top 40
19 Jul 03	LAST NITE	V2 VVR 5023283	70		

SORAYA VIVIAN UK singer

Date	Title	Label	Peak Position	Weeks at No.1	Weeks in Top 40
16 Mar 02	WHEN YOU'RE GONE	Activ 8 ACT 501	59		

VIXEN US group

Date	Title	Label	Peak Position	Weeks at No.1	Weeks in Top 40
3 Sep 88	EDGE OF A BROKEN HEART	Manhattan MT 48	51		
4 Mar 89	CRYIN'	EMI Manhattan MT 60	27		3
3 Jun 89	LOVE MADE ME	EMI-USA MT 66	36		3
2 Sep 89	EDGE OF A BROKEN HEART	EMI-USA MT 48	59		
28 Jul 90	HOW MUCH LOVE	EMI-USA MT 87	35		1
20 Oct 90	LOVE IS A KILLER	EMI-USA MT 91	41		
16 Mar 91	NOT A MINUTE TOO SOON	EMI America MT 93	37		1

VOGGUE Canadian duo

Date	Title	Label	Peak Position	Weeks at No.1	Weeks in Top 40
18 Jul 81	DANCIN' THE NIGHT AWAY	Mercury MER 76	39		1

VOICE OF THE BEEHIVE UK/US group

Date	Title	Label	Peak Position	Weeks at No.1	Weeks in Top 40
14 Nov 87	I SAY NOTHING	London LON 151	45		
5 Mar 88	I WALK THE EARTH	London LON 169	42		
14 May 88	DON'T CALL ME BABY	London LON 175	15		7
23 Jul 88	I SAY NOTHING	London LON 190	22		4
22 Oct 88	I WALK THE EARTH	London LON 206	46		
13 Jul 91	MONSTERS AND ANGELS	London LON 302	17		8
28 Sep 91	I THINK I LOVE YOU	London LON 308	25		4
11 Jan 92	PERFECT PLACE	London LON 312	37		2

VOICES OF LIFE US duo

Date	Title	Label	Peak Position	Weeks at No.1	Weeks in Top 40
21 Mar 98	THE WORD IS LOVE (SAY THE WORD)	AM:PM 5825272	26		1

STERLING VOID UK instrumentalist and singer

Date	Title	Label	Peak Position	Weeks at No.1	Weeks in Top 40
4 Feb 89	RUNAWAY GIRL/IT'S ALL RIGHT	ffrr FFR 21	53		

VOLATILE AGENTS UK duo

Date	Title	Label	Peak Position	Weeks at No.1	Weeks in Top 40
15 Dec 01	HOOKED ON YOU VOLATILE AGENTS FEATURING SIMONE BENN	Melting Pot MPRCD 10	54		

VOLCANO Norwegian group

Date	Title	Label	Peak Position	Weeks at No.1	Weeks in Top 40
23 Jul 94	MORE TO LOVE	Deconstruction 74321221832	32		2
18 Nov 95	THAT'S THE WAY LOVE IS VOLCANO WITH SAM CARTWRIGHT	EXP EXPCD 002	72		

VON BONDIES US group

Date	Title	Label	Peak Position	Weeks at No.1	Weeks in Top 40
14 Feb 04	C'MON C'MON	Sire W 635CD	21		1
15 May 04	TELL ME WHAT YOU SEE	Sire W 639CD	43		

VOODOO & SERANO German production duo

Date	Title	Label	Peak Position	Weeks at No.1	Weeks in Top 40
3 Feb 01	BLOOD IS PUMPIN'	Xtrahard X2H2 CDS	19		2
16 Aug 03	OVERLOAD	All Around The World CDGLOBE 284	30		1

VOYAGE French/UK group

Date	Title	Label	Peak Position	Weeks at No.1	Weeks in Top 40
17 Jun 78	FROM EAST TO WEST/SCOTS MACHINE	GTO GT 224	13		9
25 Nov 78	SOUVENIRS	GTO GT 241	56		
24 Mar 79	LET'S FLY AWAY	GTO GT 245	38		3
26 May 79	HALFWAY HOTEL	Mountain VOY 001	33		2

JURGEN VRIES UK producer

Date	Title	Label	Peak Position	Weeks at No.1	Weeks in Top 40
14 Sep 02	THE THEME	Direction 6730952	13		2
1 Feb 03	THE OPERA SONG (BRAVE NEW WORLD) JURGEN VRIES FEATURING CMC	Direction 6734642	3		7
4 Oct 03	WILDERNESS JURGEN VRIES FEATURING SHENA	Direction 6742692	20		2
19 Jun 04	TAKE MY HAND JURGEN VRIES FEATURING ANDREA BRITTON	Direction 6749932	23		2

VS UK group

Date	Title	Label	Peak Position	Weeks at No.1	Weeks in Top 40
6 Mar 04	LOVE YOU LIKE MAD	Innocent SINCD 59	7		5
19 Jun 04	CALL U SEXY	Innocent SINDX 62	11		3
23 Oct 04	MAKE IT HOT	Innocent SINDX 66	29		1

VYBE US group

Date	Title	Label	Peak Position	Weeks at No.1	Weeks in Top 40
7 Oct 95	WARM SUMMER DAZE	Fourth & Broadway BRCD 315	60		

W

KRISTINE W US singer

Date	Title	Label	Peak Position	Weeks at No.1	Weeks in Top 40
21 May 94	LOVE COME HOME OUR TRIBE WITH FRANKE PHAROAH & KRISTINE W	Triangle BLUESCD 001	73		
25 Jun 94	FEEL WHAT YOU WANT	Champion CHAMPCD 304	33		1
25 May 96	ONE MORE TRY	Champion CHAMPCD 317	41		
21 Dec 96	LAND OF THE LIVING	Champion CHAMPCD 324	57		
5 Jul 97	FEEL WHAT YOU WANT (REMIX)	Champion CHAMPCD 329	40		1

ADAM WADE US singer

Date	Title	Label	Peak Position	Weeks at No.1	Weeks in Top 40
8 Jun 61	TAKE GOOD CARE OF HER	HMV POP 843	38		3

WAG YA TAIL UK group player

Date	Title	Label	Peak Position	Weeks at No.1	Weeks in Top 40
3 Oct 92	XPAND YA MIND (EXPANSIONS)	PWL International PWL 238	49		

WAH! UK group

Date	Title	Label	Peak Position	Weeks at No.1	Weeks in Top 40
25 Dec 82	THE STORY OF THE BLUES	Eternal JF 1	3		8
19 Mar 83	HOPE (I WISH YOU'D BELIEVE ME)	WEA X 9880	37		2
30 Jun 84	COME BACK MIGHTY WAH	Beggars Banquet BEG 111	20		6

WAIKIKIS Belgian group

Date	Title	Label	Peak Position	Weeks at No.1	Weeks in Top 40
11 Mar 65	HAWAII TATTOO	Pye International 7N 25286	41		

RUFUS WAINWRIGHT Canadian singer

Date	Title	Label	Peak Position	Weeks at No.1	Weeks in Top 40
7 Aug 04	I DON'T KNOW WHAT IT IS	DreamWorks 9863229	74		
19 May 07	GOING TO A TOWN	Download	54		

JOHN WAITE UK singer

Date	Title	Label	Peak Position	Weeks at No.1	Weeks in Top 40
29 Sep 84	MISSING YOU	EMI America EA 182 ★	9		8
13 Feb 93	MISSING YOU	Chrysalis CDCHS 3938	56		

WAITRESSES US group

Date	Title	Label	Peak Position	Weeks at No.1	Weeks in Top 40
18 Dec 82	CHRISTMAS WRAPPING	Ze/Island WIP 6821	45		

JOHNNY WAKELIN UK singer

Date	Title / Label	Peak Position	Weeks at No.1	Weeks in Top 40
18 Jan 75	**BLACK SUPERMAN (MUHAMMAD ALI)** *Pye 7N 45420* JOHNNY WAKELIN & THE KINSHASA BAND	7		8
24 Jul 76	**IN ZAIRE** *Pye 7N 45595*	4		9

NARADA MICHAEL WALDEN US singer/producer

Date	Title / Label	Peak Position	Weeks at No.1	Weeks in Top 40
23 Feb 80	**TONIGHT I'M ALL RIGHT** *Atlantic K 11437*	34		4
26 Apr 80	**I SHOULDA LOVED YA** *Atlantic K 11413*	8		7
23 Apr 88	**DIVINE EMOTIONS** *Reprise W 7967* NARADA	8		7

DOUG WALKER UK singer

Date	Title / Label	Peak Position	Weeks at No.1	Weeks in Top 40
15 Mar 08	**THE MYSTERY** *Download*	36		1

GARY WALKER US singer

Date	Title / Label	Peak Position	Weeks at No.1	Weeks in Top 40
24 Feb 66	**YOU DON'T LOVE ME** *CBS 202036*	26		5
26 May 66	**TWINKIE LEE** *CBS 202081*	26		4

JOHN WALKER US singer

Date	Title / Label	Peak Position	Weeks at No.1	Weeks in Top 40
5 Jul 67	**ANNABELLA** *Philips BF 1593*	24		4

SCOTT WALKER US singer

Date	Title / Label	Peak Position	Weeks at No.1	Weeks in Top 40
6 Dec 67	**JACKIE** *Philips BF 1628*	22		7
1 May 68	**JOANNA** *Philips BF 1662*	7		11
11 Jun 69	**LIGHTS OF CINCINNATI** *Philips BF 1793*	13		8

JUNIOR WALKER & THE ALL-STARS
US singer/saxophonist and backing group

Date	Title / Label	Peak Position	Weeks at No.1	Weeks in Top 40
18 Aug 66	**HOW SWEET IT IS** *Tamla Motown TMG 571*	22		6
2 Apr 69	**(I'M A) ROAD RUNNER** *Tamla Motown TMG 691*	12		10
18 Oct 69	**WHAT DOES IT TAKE (TO WIN YOUR LOVE)** *Tamla Motown TMG 712*	13		9
26 Aug 72	**WALK IN THE NIGHT** *Tamla Motown TMG 824*	16		10
27 Jan 73	**TAKE ME GIRL I'M READY** *Tamla Motown TMG 840*	16		9
30 Jun 73	**WAY BACK HOME** *Tamla Motown TMG 857*	35		2

TERRI WALKER UK singer

Date	Title / Label	Peak Position	Weeks at No.1	Weeks in Top 40
1 Mar 03	**GUESS YOU DIDN'T LOVE ME** *Def Soul 779962*	60		
17 May 03	**CHING CHING (LOVIN' YOU STILL)** *Def Soul 9800075*	38		1
26 Mar 05	**WHOOPSIE DAISY** *Mercury 9870690*	41		

WALKER BROTHERS US group

Date	Title / Label	Peak Position	Weeks at No.1	Weeks in Top 40
29 Apr 65	**LOVE HER** *Philips BF 1409*	20		11
19 Aug 65	**MAKE IT EASY ON YOURSELF** *Philips BF 1428*	1	1	13
2 Dec 65	**MY SHIP IS COMING IN** *Philips BF 1454*	3		12
3 Mar 66	**THE SUN AIN'T GONNA SHINE ANYMORE** *Philips BF 1473*	1	4	11
14 Jul 66	**(BABY) YOU DON'T HAVE TO TELL ME** *Philips BF 1497*	13		7
22 Sep 66	**ANOTHER TEAR FALLS** *Philips BF 1514*	12		7
15 Dec 66	**DEADLIER THAN THE MALE** *Philips BF 1537*	32		5
9 Feb 67	**STAY WITH ME BABY** *Philips BF 1548*	26		5
18 May 67	**WALKING IN THE RAIN** *Philips BF 1576*	26		4
17 Jan 76	**NO REGRETS** *GTO GT 42*	7		9

WALKMEN US group

Date	Title / Label	Peak Position	Weeks at No.1	Weeks in Top 40
1 May 04	**THE RAT** *WEA W640CD*	45		
10 Jul 04	**LITTLE HOUSE OF SAVAGES** *Record Collection W646CD*	72		

WALL OF SOUND US group

Date	Title / Label	Peak Position	Weeks at No.1	Weeks in Top 40
31 Jul 93	**CRITICAL (IF ONLY YOU KNEW)** *Positiva CDTIV 4* WALL OF SOUND FEATURING GERALD LETHAN	73		

WALL OF VOODOO US group

Date	Title / Label	Peak Position	Weeks at No.1	Weeks in Top 40
19 Mar 83	**MEXICAN RADIO** *Illegal ILS 36*	64		

JERRY WALLACE US singer

Date	Title / Label	Peak Position	Weeks at No.1	Weeks in Top 40
23 Jun 60	**YOU'RE SINGING OUR LOVE SONG TO SOMEBODY ELSE** *London HLH 9110*	46		

RIK WALLER UK singer

Date	Title / Label	Peak Position	Weeks at No.1	Weeks in Top 40
16 Mar 02	**I WILL ALWAYS LOVE YOU** *Liberty CDRIK 001*	6		4
6 Jul 02	**SOMETHING INSIDE (SO STRONG)** *Liberty CDRIK 002*	25		2

WALLFLOWERS US group

Date	Title / Label	Peak Position	Weeks at No.1	Weeks in Top 40
12 Jul 97	**ONE HEADLIGHT** *Interscope IND 95532*	54		

BOB WALLIS & HIS STORYVILLE JAZZ BAND
UK singer/trumpeter and backing group

Date	Title / Label	Peak Position	Weeks at No.1	Weeks in Top 40
6 Jul 61	**I'M SHY MARY ELLEN (I'M SHY)** *Pye Jazz 7NJ 2043*	44		
4 Jan 62	**COME ALONG PLEASE** *Pye Jazz 7NJ 2048*	33		4

JOE WALSH US singer

Date	Title / Label	Peak Position	Weeks at No.1	Weeks in Top 40
16 Jul 77	**ROCKY MOUNTAIN EP** *ABC ABE 12002*	39		2
8 Jul 78	**LIFE'S BEEN GOOD** *Asylum K 13129*	14		8

SHEILA WALSH US singer

Date	Title / Label	Peak Position	Weeks at No.1	Weeks in Top 40
4 Jun 83	**DRIFTING** *DJM SHEILA 1* SHEILA WALSH & CLIFF RICHARD	64		

STEVE WALSH UK singer

Date	Title / Label	Peak Position	Weeks at No.1	Weeks in Top 40
18 Jul 87	**I FOUND LOVIN'** *A1 299*	9		6
12 Dec 87	**LET'S GET TOGETHER (TONITE)** *A1 303*	74		
30 Jul 88	**AIN'T NO STOPPING US NOW (PARTY FOR THE WORLD)** *A1 304*	44		

TREVOR WALTERS UK reggae singer

Date	Title / Label	Peak Position	Weeks at No.1	Weeks in Top 40
24 Oct 81	**LOVE ME TONIGHT** *Magnet MAG 198*	27		6
21 Jul 84	**STUCK ON YOU** *Sanity IS 002*	9		7
1 Dec 84	**NEVER LET HER SLIP AWAY** *Polydor POSP 716*	73		

WAMDUE PROJECT US/Argentinian group

Date	Title / Label	Peak Position	Weeks at No.1	Weeks in Top 40
20 Nov 99	**KING OF MY CASTLE (IMPORT)** *Orange ORCDM 53584CD*	61		
27 Nov 99	**KING OF MY CASTLE** *AM:PM CDAMPM 127* ●	1	1	10
15 Apr 00	**YOU'RE THE REASON** *AM:PM CDAMPM 130*	39		1

WANG CHUNG UK group

Date	Title / Label	Peak Position	Weeks at No.1	Weeks in Top 40
28 Jan 84	**DANCE HALL DAYS** *Geffen A 3837*	21		5

WANNADIES Swedish group

Date	Title / Label	Peak Position	Weeks at No.1	Weeks in Top 40
18 Nov 95	**MIGHT BE STARS** *Indolent DIE 003CD1*	51		
24 Feb 96	**HOW DOES IT FEEL** *Indolent DIE 004CD1*	53		
20 Apr 96	**YOU & ME SONG** *Indolent DIE 005CD*	18		2
7 Sep 96	**SOMEONE SOMEWHERE** *Indolent DIE 006CD*	38		1
26 Apr 97	**HIT** *Indolent DIE 009CD1*	20		1
5 Jul 97	**SHORTY** *Indolent DIE 010CD1*	41		
4 Mar 00	**YEAH** *RCA 74321745552*	56		

DEXTER WANSELL US keyboard player

Date	Title / Label	Peak Position	Weeks at No.1	Weeks in Top 40
20 May 78	**ALL NIGHT LONG** *Philadelphia International PIR 6255*	59		

WAR US group

Date	Title / Label	Peak Position	Weeks at No.1	Weeks in Top 40
24 Jan 76	**LOW RIDER** *Island WIP 6267*	12		7
26 Jun 76	**ME AND BABY BROTHER** *Island WIP 6303*	21		6
14 Jan 78	**GALAXY** *MCA 339*	14		7
15 Apr 78	**HEY SENORITA** *MCA 359*	40		1
10 Apr 82	**YOU GOT THE POWER** *RCA 201*	58		
6 Apr 85	**GROOVIN'** *Bluebird BR 16*	43		

Silver-selling ○ Gold-selling ● Platinum-selling ⊛ US No.1 ★ | Peak Position | Weeks at No.1 | Weeks in Top 40

ANITA WARD US singer

Date	Title / Label	Peak Position	Weeks at No.1	Weeks in Top 40
2 Jun 79	**RING MY BELL** *TK TKR 7543* ● ★	1	2	8

BILLY WARD AND THE DOMINOES US group

Date	Title / Label	Peak Position	Weeks at No.1	Weeks in Top 40
13 Sep 57	**STARDUST** *London HLU 8465*	13		12
29 Nov 57	**DEEP PURPLE** *London HLU 8502*	30		1

CHRISSY WARD US singer

Date	Title / Label	Peak Position	Weeks at No.1	Weeks in Top 40
24 Jun 95	**RIGHT AND EXACT** *Ore AG 6CD*	62		
8 Feb 97	**RIGHT AND EXACT (REMIX)** *Ore AG 21CD*	59		

CLIFFORD T. WARD UK singer

Date	Title / Label	Peak Position	Weeks at No.1	Weeks in Top 40
30 Jun 73	**GAYE** *Charisma CB 205*	8		9
26 Jan 74	**SCULLERY** *Charisma CB 221*	37		1

MICHAEL WARD UK singer

Date	Title / Label	Peak Position	Weeks at No.1	Weeks in Top 40
29 Sep 73	**LET THERE BE PEACE ON EARTH (LET IT BEGIN WITH ME)** *Philips 6006 340*	15		10

SHAYNE WARD UK singer

Date	Title / Label	Peak Position	Weeks at No.1	Weeks in Top 40
31 Dec 05	**THAT'S MY GOAL** *Syco Music 82876779272* ⊛	1	4	13
22 Apr 06	**NO PROMISES** *Syco Music 82876825902*	2		9
22 Jul 06	**STAND BY ME** *Syco Music 82876869132*	14		2
6 Oct 07	**NO U HANG UP/IF THAT'S OKAY WITH YOU** *Syco Music 88697131702*	2		10
1 Dec 07	**BREATHLESS** *Syco Music 88697188422*	6		8
8 Dec 07	**IF THAT'S OK WITH YOU** *Download*	72		

WARD BROTHERS UK group

Date	Title / Label	Peak Position	Weeks at No.1	Weeks in Top 40
10 Jan 87	**CROSS THAT BRIDGE** *Siren 37*	32		3

MATHIAS WARE German producer

Date	Title / Label	Peak Position	Weeks at No.1	Weeks in Top 40
9 Mar 02	**HEY LITTLE GIRL** *Manifesto FESCD 91* MATHIAS WARE FEATURING ROB TAYLOR	42		

WARM JETS UK group

Date	Title / Label	Peak Position	Weeks at No.1	Weeks in Top 40
14 Feb 98	**NEVER NEVER** *Island WAY 6766*	37		1
25 Apr 98	**HURRICANE** *Island CID 697*	34		1

WARM SOUNDS UK duo

Date	Title / Label	Peak Position	Weeks at No.1	Weeks in Top 40
4 May 67	**BIRDS AND BEES** *Deram DM 120*	27		5

TONI WARNE UK singer

Date	Title / Label	Peak Position	Weeks at No.1	Weeks in Top 40
25 Apr 87	**BEN** *Mint CHEW 110*	50		

JENNIFER WARNES US singer

Date	Title / Label	Peak Position	Weeks at No.1	Weeks in Top 40
15 Jan 83	**UP WHERE WE BELONG** *Island WIP 6830* JOE COCKER & JENNIFER WARNES ○ ★	7		10
25 Jul 87	**FIRST WE TAKE MANHATTAN** *Cypress PB 49709*	74		
31 Oct 87	**(I'VE HAD) THE TIME OF MY LIFE** *RCA PB 49625* BILL MEDLEY & JENNIFER WARNES ★	6		9
15 Dec 90	**(I'VE HAD) THE TIME OF MY LIFE** *RCA PB 49625* BILL MEDLEY & JENNIFER WARNES ○	8		6

WARP BROTHERS German production group

Date	Title / Label	Peak Position	Weeks at No.1	Weeks in Top 40
11 Nov 00	**PHATT BASS (IMPORT)** *Dos Or Die BMSCDM 40009* WARP BROTHERS VERSUS AQUAGEN	58		
9 Dec 00	**PHATT BASS** *NuLife 74321817102*	9		6
17 Feb 01	**WE WILL SURVIVE** *NuLife 74321832722*	19		2
29 Dec 01	**BLAST THE SPEAKERS** *NuLife 74321899162*	40		1

WARRANT US group

Date	Title / Label	Peak Position	Weeks at No.1	Weeks in Top 40
17 Nov 90	**CHERRY PIE** *CBS 6562587*	59		
9 Mar 91	**CHERRY PIE** *Columbia 6566867*	35		2

ALYSHA WARREN UK singer

Date	Title / Label	Peak Position	Weeks at No.1	Weeks in Top 40
24 Sep 94	**I'M SO IN LOVE** *Wild Card CARDD 10*	61		
25 Mar 95	**I THOUGHT I MEANT THE WORLD TO YOU** *Wild Card CARDD 16*	40		1
27 Jul 96	**KEEP ON PUSHING OUR LOVE** *Arista 74321390422* NIGHTCRAWLERS FEATURING JOHN REID & ALYSHA WARREN	30		1

NIKITA WARREN Italian singer

Date	Title / Label	Peak Position	Weeks at No.1	Weeks in Top 40
13 Jul 96	**I NEED YOU** *VC Recordings VCRD 12*	48		

WARRIOR UK dance duo

Date	Title / Label	Peak Position	Weeks at No.1	Weeks in Top 40
21 Oct 00	**WARRIOR** *Incentive CENT 12CDS*	19		2
30 Jun 01	**VOODOO** *Incentive CENT 26CDS*	37		1
4 Oct 03	**X** *Incentive CENT 56CDS*	64		

DIONNE WARWICK US singer

Date	Title / Label	Peak Position	Weeks at No.1	Weeks in Top 40
13 Feb 64	**ANYONE WHO HAD A HEART** *Pye International 7N 25234*	42		
16 Apr 64	**WALK ON BY** *Pye International 7N 25241*	9		12
30 Jul 64	**YOU'LL NEVER GET TO HEAVEN** *Pye International 7N 25256*	20		6
8 Oct 64	**REACH OUT FOR ME** *Pye International 7N 25265*	23		5
1 Apr 65	**YOU CAN HAVE HIM** *Pye International 7N 25290*	37		1
13 Mar 68	**VALLEY OF THE DOLLS** *Pye International 7N 25445*	28		6
15 May 68	**DO YOU KNOW THE WAY TO SAN JOSÉ** *Pye International 7N 25457*	8		10
19 Oct 74	**THEN CAME YOU** *Atlantic K 10495* DIONNE WARWICK & THE DETROIT SPINNERS ★	29		4
23 Oct 82	**HEARTBREAKER** *Arista ARIST 496* ○	2		8
11 Dec 82	**ALL THE LOVE IN THE WORLD** *Arista ARIST 507* ○	10		8
26 Feb 83	**YOURS** *Arista ARIST 518*	66		
28 May 83	**I'LL NEVER LOVE THIS WAY AGAIN** *Arista ARIST 530*	62		
9 Nov 85	**THAT'S WHAT FRIENDS ARE FOR** *Arista ARIST 638* DIONNE WARWICK & FRIENDS FEATURING ELTON JOHN, STEVIE WONDER & GLADYS KNIGHT ★	16		7
15 Aug 87	**LOVE POWER** *Arista RIS 27* DIONNE WARWICK & JEFFREY OSBORNE	63		

WAS (NOT WAS) US group

Date	Title / Label	Peak Position	Weeks at No.1	Weeks in Top 40
3 Mar 84	**OUT COME THE FREAKS** *Ze/Geffen A 4178*	41		
18 Jul 87	**SPY IN THE HOUSE OF LOVE** *Fontana WAS 2*	51		
3 Oct 87	**WALK THE DINOSAUR** *Fontana WAS 3*	10		8
6 Feb 88	**SPY IN THE HOUSE OF LOVE** *Fontana WAS 2*	21		6
7 May 88	**OUT COME THE FREAKS (AGAIN)** *Fontana WAS 4*	44		
16 Jul 88	**ANYTHING CAN HAPPEN** *Fontana WAS 5*	67		
26 May 90	**PAPA WAS A ROLLING STONE** *Fontana WAS 7*	12		6
11 Aug 90	**HOW THE HEART BEHAVES** *Fontana WAS 8*	53		
23 May 92	**LISTEN LIKE THIEVES** *Fontana WAS 10*	58		
11 Jul 92	**SHAKE YOUR HEAD** *Fontana WAS 11*	4		8
26 Sep 92	**SOMEWHERE IN AMERICA (THERE'S A STREET NAMED AFTER MY DAD)** *Fontana WAS 12*	57		

MARTHA WASH US singer

Date	Title / Label	Peak Position	Weeks at No.1	Weeks in Top 40
28 Nov 92	**CARRY ON** *RCA 74321125457*	74		
6 Mar 93	**GIVE IT TO YOU** *RCA 74321136562*	37		2
10 Jul 93	**RUNAROUND/CARRY ON (REMIX)** *RCA 74321153702*	49		
18 Feb 95	**I FOUND LOVE/TAKE A TOKE** *Columbia 6612112* C & C MUSIC FACTORY/C & C MUSIC FACTORY FEATURING MARTHA WASH	26		1
13 Jul 96	**KEEP ON JUMPIN'** *Manifesto FESCD 11* TODD TERRY FEATURING MARTHA WASH & JOCELYN BROWN	8		5
12 Jul 97	**SOMETHING GOIN' ON** *Manifesto FESCD 25* TODD TERRY FEATURING MARTHA WASH & JOCELYN BROWN	5		7
25 Oct 97	**CARRY ON (2ND REMIX)** *Delirious DELICD 6*	49		
28 Feb 98	**IT'S RAINING MEN...THE SEQUEL** *Logic 74321555412* MARTHA WASH FEATURING RuPAUL	21		2
11 Apr 98	**READY FOR A NEW DAY** *Manifesto FESCD 40* TODD TERRY FEATURING MARTHA WASH	20		1
15 Aug 98	**CATCH THE LIGHT** *Logic 74321587912*	45		
3 Jul 99	**COME** *Logic 74321653942*	64		
5 Feb 00	**IT'S RAINING MEN (REMIX)** *Logic 74321726282*	56		

Silver-selling ● Gold-selling ● Platinum-selling ● US No.1 ★ Peak Position · Weeks at No.1 · Weeks in Top 40

DINAH WASHINGTON US singer

Date	Title	Label	Peak Position	Weeks at No.1	Weeks in Top 40
30 Nov 61	SEPTEMBER IN THE RAIN	*Mercury AMT 1162*	35		1
4 Apr 92	MAD ABOUT THE BOY	*Mercury DINAH 1*	41		

GROVER WASHINGTON JR US saxophonist

Date	Title	Label	Peak Position	Weeks at No.1	Weeks in Top 40
16 May 81	JUST THE TWO OF US	*Elektra K 12514*	34		3

SARAH WASHINGTON UK singer

Date	Title	Label	Peak Position	Weeks at No.1	Weeks in Top 40
14 Aug 93	I WILL ALWAYS LOVE YOU	*Almighty CDALMY 33*	12		5
27 Nov 93	CARELESS WHISPER	*Almighty CDALMY 43*	45		
25 May 96	HEAVEN	*AM:PM 5815332*	28		1
12 Oct 96	EVERYTHING	*AM:PM 5818872*	30		1

GENO WASHINGTON & THE RAM JAM BAND US group

Date	Title	Label	Peak Position	Weeks at No.1	Weeks in Top 40
19 May 66	WATER	*Piccadilly 7N 35312*	39		2
21 Jul 66	HI HI HAZEL	*Piccadilly 7N 35329*	45		
6 Oct 66	QUE SERA SERA	*Piccadilly 7N 35346*	43		
2 Feb 67	MICHAEL	*Piccadilly 7N 35359*	39		2

W.A.S.P. US group

Date	Title	Label	Peak Position	Weeks at No.1	Weeks in Top 40
31 May 86	WILD CHILD	*Capitol CL 388*	71		
11 Oct 86	95 – NASTY	*Capitol CL 432*	70		
29 Aug 87	SCREAM UNTIL YOU LIKE IT	*Capitol CL 458*	32		2
31 Oct 87	I DON'T NEED NO DOCTOR (LIVE)	*Capitol CL 469*	31		2
20 Feb 88	LIVE ANIMAL (F**K LIKE A BEAST)	*Music For Nations KUT 109*	61		
4 Mar 89	MEAN MAN	*Capitol CL 521*	21		3
27 May 89	THE REAL ME	*Capitol CL 534*	23		3
9 Sep 89	FOREVER FREE	*Capitol CL 546*	25		3
4 Apr 92	CHAINSAW CHARLIE (MURDERS IN THE NEW MORGUE)	*Parlophone RS 6308*	17		2
6 Jun 92	THE IDOL	*Parlophone RPD 6314*	41		
31 Oct 92	I AM ONE	*Parlophone 10RG 6324*	56		
23 Oct 93	SUNSET AND BABYLON	*Capitol CDCL 698*	38		1

WATER BABIES UK group

Date	Title	Label	Peak Position	Weeks at No.1	Weeks in Top 40
24 Dec 05	UNDER THE TREE	*Angel ANGECD8*	27		2

WATERBOYS UK group

Date	Title	Label	Peak Position	Weeks at No.1	Weeks in Top 40
2 Nov 85	THE WHOLE OF THE MOON	*Ensign ENY 520*	26		5
14 Jan 89	FISHERMAN'S BLUES	*Ensign ENY 621*	32		2
1 Jul 89	AND A BANG ON THE EAR	*Ensign ENY 624*	51		
6 Apr 91	THE WHOLE OF THE MOON	*Ensign ENY 642*	3		8
8 Jun 91	FISHERMAN'S BLUES	*Ensign ENY 645*	75		
15 May 93	THE RETURN OF PAN	*Geffen GFSTD 42*	24		2
24 Jul 93	GLASTONBURY SONG	*Geffen GFSTD 49*	29		1

WATERFRONT UK duo

Date	Title	Label	Peak Position	Weeks at No.1	Weeks in Top 40
15 Apr 89	BROKEN ARROW	*Polydor WON 3*	63		
27 May 89	CRY	*Polydor WON 1*	17		7
9 Sep 89	NATURE OF LOVE	*Polydor WON 2*	63		

WATERGATE Turkish/Belgian production group

Date	Title	Label	Peak Position	Weeks at No.1	Weeks in Top 40
13 May 00	HEART OF ASIA	*Positiva CDTIV 129*	3		7

DENNIS WATERMAN UK actor

Date	Title	Label	Peak Position	Weeks at No.1	Weeks in Top 40
25 Oct 80	I COULD BE SO GOOD FOR YOU DENNIS WATERMAN & GEORGE COLE ●	*EMI 5009*	3		10
17 Dec 83	WHAT ARE WE GONNA GET 'ER INDOORS DENNIS WATERMAN WITH THE DENNIS WATERMAN BAND	*EMI MIN 101*	21		3

CRYSTAL WATERS US singer

Date	Title	Label	Peak Position	Weeks at No.1	Weeks in Top 40
18 May 91	GYPSY WOMAN (LA DA DEE) ●	*A&M AM 772*	2		7
7 Sep 91	MAKIN' HAPPY	*A&M AM 790*	18		4
11 Jan 92	MEGAMIX	*A&M AM 843*	39		2
3 Oct 92	GYPSY WOMAN (LA DA DEE) (REMIX)	*Epic 6584377*	35		1
23 Apr 94	100% PURE LOVE	*A&M 8586692*	15		6
2 Jul 94	GHETTO DAY	*A&M 8589592*	40		1
25 Nov 95	RELAX	*Manifesto FESCD 4*	37		1
24 Aug 96	IN DE GHETTO DAVID MORALES & THE BAD YARD CLUB FEATURING CRYSTAL WATERS & DELTA	*Manifesto FESCD 12*	35		1
19 Apr 97	SAY...IF YOU FEEL ALRIGHT	*Mercury 5742912*	45		
20 Sep 03	MY TIME DUTCH FEATURING CRYSTAL WATERS	*Illustrious/Epic CDILL 018*	22		1
24 Mar 07	DESTINATION CALABRIA ALEX GAUDINO FEATURING CRYSTAL WATERS	*Data DATA153CDS*	4		11

MUDDY WATERS US singer/guitarist

Date	Title	Label	Peak Position	Weeks at No.1	Weeks in Top 40
16 Jul 88	MANNISH BOY	*Epic MUD 1*	51		

ROGER WATERS UK singer/bass guitarist

Date	Title	Label	Peak Position	Weeks at No.1	Weeks in Top 40
30 May 87	RADIO WAVES	*Harvest EM 6*	74		
26 Dec 87	THE TIDE IS TURNING (AFTER LIVE AID)	*Harvest EM 37*	54		
5 Sep 92	WHAT GOD WANTS PART 1	*Columbia 6581395*	35		1

LAUREN WATERWORTH UK singer

Date	Title	Label	Peak Position	Weeks at No.1	Weeks in Top 40
1 Jun 02	BABY NOW THAT I'VE FOUND YOU	*Jive 9253622*	24		1

MICHAEL WATFORD US singer

Date	Title	Label	Peak Position	Weeks at No.1	Weeks in Top 40
26 Feb 94	SO INTO YOU	*East West A 8309CD*	53		

JODY WATLEY US singer

Date	Title	Label	Peak Position	Weeks at No.1	Weeks in Top 40
9 May 87	LOOKING FOR A NEW LOVE	*MCA 1107*	13		7
17 Oct 87	DON'T YOU WANT ME	*MCA 1198*	55		
8 Apr 89	REAL LOVE	*MCA 1324*	31		5
12 Aug 89	FRIENDS JODY WATLEY WITH ERIC B & RAKIM	*MCA 1352*	21		3
10 Feb 90	EVERYTHING	*MCA 1395*	74		
11 Apr 92	I'M THE ONE YOU NEED	*MCA MCS 1608*	50		
21 May 94	WHEN A MAN LOVES A WOMAN	*MCA MCSTD 1964*	33		1
25 Apr 98	OFF THE HOOK	*Atlantic AT 0024CD1*	51		

JOHNNY 'GUITAR' WATSON US singer/guitarist

Date	Title	Label	Peak Position	Weeks at No.1	Weeks in Top 40
28 Aug 76	I NEED IT	*DJM DJS 10694*	35		2
23 Apr 77	A REAL MOTHER FOR YA	*DJM DJS 10762*	44		

RUSSELL WATSON UK tenor

Date	Title	Label	Peak Position	Weeks at No.1	Weeks in Top 40
30 Oct 99	SWING LOW '99	*Universal TV 4669502*	38		1
22 Jul 00	BARCELONA (FRIENDS UNTIL THE END) RUSSELL WATSON & SHAUN RYDER	*Decca 46672772*	68		
18 May 02	SOMEONE LIKE YOU RUSSELL WATSON & FAYE TOZER	*Decca 4730002*	10		3
21 Dec 02	NOTHING SACRED – A SONG FOR KIRSTY	*Decca 4737402*	17		4
29 Apr 06	CAN'T HELP FALLING IN LOVE	*Decca 4757841*	69		

BEN WATT UK producer

Date	Title	Label	Peak Position	Weeks at No.1	Weeks in Top 40
12 Feb 05	OUTSPOKEN – PART 1 BEN WATT	*Buzzin Fly 010BUZZCD*	74		

BARRATT WAUGH UK singer

Date	Title	Label	Peak Position	Weeks at No.1	Weeks in Top 40
26 Jul 03	SKIP A BEAT	*BNW BNWCD02*	56		

WAVELENGTH UK group

Date	Title	Label	Peak Position	Weeks at No.1	Weeks in Top 40
10 Jul 82	HURRY HOME	*Ariola ARO 281*	17		8

WAX US/UK duo

Date	Title	Label	Peak Position	Weeks at No.1	Weeks in Top 40
12 Apr 86	RIGHT BETWEEN THE EYES	*RCA PB 40509*	60		
1 Aug 87	BRIDGE TO YOUR HEART	*RCA PB 41405*	12		8

ANTHONY WAY UK chorister

Date	Title	Label	Peak Position	Weeks at No.1	Weeks in Top 40
15 Apr 95	PANIS ANGELICUS	*Decca 4481642*	55		

Silver-selling ● Gold-selling ● Platinum-selling ⊛ US No.1 ★ | Peak Position | Weeks at No.1 | Weeks in Top 40

A WAY OF LIFE US group

Date	Title	Label	Peak	Wks No.1	Wks Top 40
21 Apr 90	TRIPPIN' ON YOUR LOVE	Eternal YZ 4664	55		

WAY OF THE WEST UK new group

Date	Title	Label	Peak	Wks No.1	Wks Top 40
25 Apr 81	DON'T SAY THAT'S JUST FOR WHITE BOYS	Mercury MER 66	54		

WAY OUT WEST UK dance duo

Date	Title	Label	Peak	Wks No.1	Wks Top 40
3 Dec 94	AJARE	Deconstruction 74321243802	52		
2 Mar 96	DOMINATION	Deconstruction 74321342822	38		1
14 Sep 96	THE GIFT WAY OUT WEST/MISS JOANNA LAW	Deconstruction 74321401912	15		3
30 Aug 97	BLUE	Deconstruction 74321477512	41		
29 Nov 97	AJARE	Deconstruction 74321521352	36		1
9 Dec 00	THE FALL	Wow 005CD	61		
18 Aug 01	INTENSIFY	Distinctive Breaks DISNCD 74	46		
30 Mar 02	MINDCIRCUS WAY OUT WEST FEATURING TRICIA LEE KELSHALL	Distinctive Breaks DISNCD 80	39		1
21 Sep 02	STEALTH WAY OUT WEST FEATURING KIRSTY HAWKSHAW	Distinctive Breaks DISNCD 90	67		

BRUCE WAYNE German producer

Date	Title	Label	Peak	Wks No.1	Wks Top 40
13 Dec 97	READY	Logic 74321527012	44		
4 Jul 98	NO GOOD FOR ME	Logic 74321587052	70		

JAN WAYNE German producer

Date	Title	Label	Peak	Wks No.1	Wks Top 40
9 Nov 02	BECAUSE THE NIGHT	Product PDT 02CDS	14		3
29 Mar 03	TOTAL ECLIPSE OF THE HEART	Product PDT 10CDS	28		1

JEFF WAYNE US producer

Date	Title	Label	Peak	Wks No.1	Wks Top 40
9 Sep 78	THE EVE OF THE WAR JEFF WAYNE'S WAR OF THE WORLDS	CBS 6496	36		2
10 Jul 82	MATADOR	CBS A 2493	57		
25 Nov 89	THE EVE OF THE WAR (REMIX) JEFF WAYNE'S WAR OF THE WORLDS	CBS 6551267	3		8

WE ARE SCIENTISTS US group

Date	Title	Label	Peak	Wks No.1	Wks Top 40
9 Jul 05	NOBODY MOVE NOBODY GET HURT	Virgin VUSCD303	56		
15 Oct 05	THE GREAT ESCAPE	Virgin VUSDX308	37		1
4 Mar 06	IT'S A HIT	Virgin VUSCD319	29		1
13 May 06	NOBODY MOVE NOBODY GET HURT	Virgin VUSCD325	21		2
15 Mar 08	AFTER HOURS	Virgin VSCDT1970	15		2

WEATHER GIRLS US duo

Date	Title	Label	Peak	Wks No.1	Wks Top 40
27 Aug 83	IT'S RAINING MEN	CBS A 2924	73		
3 Mar 84	IT'S RAINING MEN	CBS A 2924 ●	2		8

WEATHER PROPHETS UK group

Date	Title	Label	Peak	Wks No.1	Wks Top 40
28 Mar 87	SHE COMES FROM THE RAIN	Elevation ACID 1	62		

WEATHERMEN UK singer

Date	Title	Label	Peak	Wks No.1	Wks Top 40
16 Jan 71	IT'S THE SAME OLD SONG	B&C CB 139	19		8

MARTI WEBB UK singer

Date	Title	Label	Peak	Wks No.1	Wks Top 40
9 Feb 80	TAKE THAT LOOK OFF YOUR FACE	Polydor POSP 100 ●	3		9
19 Apr 80	TELL ME ON A SUNDAY	Polydor POSP 111	67		
20 Sep 80	YOUR EARS SHOULD BE BURNING NOW	Polydor POSP 166	61		
8 Jun 85	BEN	Starblend STAR 6	5		8
20 Sep 86	ALWAYS THERE MARTI WEBB & THE SIMON MAY ORCHESTRA	BBC RESL 190	13		9
6 Jun 87	I CAN'T LET GO	Rainbow RBR 12	65		

WEBB BROTHERS US duo

Date	Title	Label	Peak	Wks No.1	Wks Top 40
17 Feb 01	I CAN'T BELIEVE YOU'RE GONE	WEA 320CD	69		

SIMON WEBBE UK singer

Date	Title	Label	Peak	Wks No.1	Wks Top 40
3 Sep 05	LAY YOUR HANDS	Innocent SINCD76	4		7
19 Nov 05	NO WORRIES	Innocent SINDX77	4		12
4 Mar 06	AFTER ALL THIS TIME	Innocent SINDX79	16		2
4 Nov 06	COMING AROUND AGAIN	Angel ANGECD25	12		5
17 Feb 07	MY SOUL PLEADS FOR YOU	Innocent ANGECD28	45		
30 Jun 07	GRACE/RIDE THE STORM	Angel ANGECD46	36		1

JOAN WEBER US singer

Date	Title	Label	Peak	Wks No.1	Wks Top 40
18 Feb 55	LET ME GO LOVER	Philips PB 389 ★	16		1

NIKKI WEBSTER Australian singer

Date	Title	Label	Peak	Wks No.1	Wks Top 40
8 Jun 02	STRAWBERRY KISSES	Gotham 74321943642	64		

WEDDING PRESENT UK group

Date	Title	Label	Peak	Wks No.1	Wks Top 40
5 Mar 88	NOBODY'S TWISTING YOUR ARM	Reception REC 009	46		
1 Oct 88	WHY ARE YOU BEING SO REASONABLE NOW	Reception REC 011	42		
7 Oct 89	KENNEDY	RCA PB 43117	33		2
17 Feb 90	BRASSNECK	RCA PB 43403	24		2
29 Sep 90	3 SONGS EP	RCA PB 44021	25		2
11 May 91	DALLIANCE	RCA PB 44495	29		2
27 Jul 91	LOVENEST	RCA PT 44750	58		
18 Jan 92	BLUE EYES	RCA PB 45185	26		1
15 Feb 92	GO-GO DANCER	RCA PB 45183	20		1
14 Mar 92	THREE	RCA PB 45181	14		1
18 Apr 92	SILVER SHORTS	RCA PB 45311	14		1
16 May 92	COME PLAY WITH ME	RCA PB 45313	10		1
13 Jun 92	CALIFORNIA	RCA PB 43515	16		1
18 Jul 92	FLYING SAUCER	RCA 74321101157	22		1
15 Aug 92	BOING!	RCA 74321101177	19		1
19 Sep 92	LOVE SLAVE	RCA 74321101167	17		1
17 Oct 92	STICKY	RCA 74321116917	17		1
14 Nov 92	THE QUEEN OF OUTER SPACE	RCA 74321116927	23		1
19 Dec 92	NO CHRISTMAS	RCA 74321116937	25		1
10 Sep 94	YEAH YEAH YEAH YEAH YEAH	Island CID 585	51		
26 Nov 94	IT'S A GAS	Island CID 591	71		
31 Aug 96	2, 3, GO	Cooking Vinyl FRYCD 048	67		
25 Jan 97	MONTREAL	Cooking Vinyl FRYCD 053	40		1
27 Nov 04	INTERSTATE 5	Scopitones TONECD018	62		
12 Feb 05	I'M FROM FURTHER NORTH THAN YOU	Scopitones TONECD019	34		1

FRED WEDLOCK UK singer

Date	Title	Label	Peak	Wks No.1	Wks Top 40
31 Jan 81	OLDEST SWINGER IN TOWN	Rocket XPRES 46 ●	6		7

WEE PAPA GIRL RAPPERS UK duo

Date	Title	Label	Peak	Wks No.1	Wks Top 40
12 Mar 88	FAITH	Jive 164	60		
25 Jun 88	HEAT IT UP WEE PAPA GIRL RAPPERS FEATURING TWO MEN & A DRUM MACHINE	Jive 174	21		5
1 Oct 88	WEE RULE	Jive 185	6		8
24 Dec 88	SOULMATE	Jive 193	45		
25 Mar 89	BLOW THE HOUSE DOWN	Jive 197	65		

BERT WEEDON UK guitarist

Date	Title	Label	Peak	Wks No.1	Wks Top 40
15 May 59	GUITAR BOOGIE SHUFFLE	Top Rank JAR 117	10		9
20 Nov 59	NASHVILLE BOOGIE	Top Rank JAR 221	29		2
10 Mar 60	BIG BEAT BOOGIE	Top Rank JAR 300	37		1
9 Jun 60	TWELFTH STREET RAG	Top Rank JAR 360	47		
28 Jul 60	APACHE	Top Rank JAR 415	24		2
27 Oct 60	SORRY ROBBIE	Top Rank JAR 517	28		6
2 Feb 61	GINCHY	Top Rank JAR 537	35		3
4 May 61	MR GUITAR	Top Rank JAR 559	47		

WEEKEND Multinational group

Date	Title	Label	Peak	Wks No.1	Wks Top 40
14 Dec 85	CHRISTMAS MEDLEY/AULD LANG SYNE	Lifestyle XY 1	47		

WEEKEND PLAYERS UK group

Date	Title	Label	Peak	Wks No.1	Wks Top 40
8 Sep 01	21ST CENTURY	Multiply CXMULTY78	22		2
16 Mar 02	INTO THE SUN	Multiply CXMULTY84	42		

MICHELLE WEEKS US singer

Date	Title / Label	Peak Position	Weeks at No.1	Weeks in Top 40
2 Aug 97	**MOMENT OF MY LIFE** *Ministry Of Sound MOSCDS 1* BOBBY D'AMBROSIO FEATURING MICHELLE WEEKS	23		1
8 Nov 97	**DON'T GIVE UP** *Ministry Of Sound MOSCDS 2*	28		1
11 Jul 98	**GIVE ME LOVE** *VC Recordings VCRD 37* DJ DADO VS MICHELLE WEEKS	59		
3 May 03	**THE LIGHT** *Defected DFTD 064X*	69		

WEEN US duo

Date	Title / Label	Peak Position	Weeks at No.1	Weeks in Top 40
29 Aug 98	**BEACON LIGHT** *Elektra E 4100CD*	20		1

WEEZER US group

Date	Title / Label	Peak Position	Weeks at No.1	Weeks in Top 40
11 Feb 95	**UNDONE – THE SWEATER SONG** *Geffen GFSTD 85*	35		1
6 May 95	**BUDDY HOLLY** *Geffen GFSTD 88*	12		5
22 Jul 95	**SAY IT AIN'T SO** *Geffen GFSTD 95*	37		1
5 Oct 96	**EL SCORCHO** *Geffen GFSTD 22167*	50		
14 Jul 01	**HASH PIPE** *Geffen 4975642*	21		2
3 Nov 01	**ISLAND IN THE SUN** *Geffen 4976162*	31		1
14 Sep 02	**KEEP FISHIN'** *Geffen 04977922*	29		1
14 May 05	**BEVERLY HILLS** *Geffen 9881791*	9		3
27 Aug 05	**WE ARE ALL ON DRUGS** *Geffen 9883495*	47		

FRANK WEIR UK saxophonist/orchestra leader

Date	Title / Label	Peak Position	Weeks at No.1	Weeks in Top 40
15 Sep 60	**CARIBBEAN HONEYMOON** *Oriole CB 1559*	42		

WEIRD SCIENCE UK production duo

Date	Title / Label	Peak Position	Weeks at No.1	Weeks in Top 40
1 Jul 00	**FEEL THE NEED** *NuLife 74321751982*	62		

DENISE WELCH UK actress

Date	Title / Label	Peak Position	Weeks at No.1	Weeks in Top 40
4 Nov 95	**YOU DON'T HAVE TO SAY YOU LOVE ME/CRY ME A RIVER** *Virgin VSCDT 1569*	23		2

PAUL WELLER UK singer

Date	Title / Label	Peak Position	Weeks at No.1	Weeks in Top 40
18 May 91	**INTO TOMORROW** *Freedom High FHP 1* PAUL WELLER MOVEMENT	36		2
15 Aug 92	**UH HUH OH YEH** *Go! Discs GOD 86*	18		2
10 Oct 92	**ABOVE THE CLOUDS** *Go! Discs GOD 91*	47		
17 Jul 93	**SUNFLOWER** *Go! Discs GODCD 102*	16		3
4 Sep 93	**WILD WOOD** *Go! Discs GODCD 104*	14		2
13 Nov 93	**THE WEAVER (EP)** *Go! Discs GODCD 107*	18		2
9 Apr 94	**HUNG UP** *Go! Discs GODCD 111*	11		2
5 Nov 94	**OUT OF THE SINKING** *Go! Discs GODCD 121*	20		2
6 May 95	**THE CHANGINGMAN** *Go! Discs GODCD 127*	7		3
22 Jul 95	**YOU DO SOMETHING TO ME** *Go! Discs GODCD 130*	9		5
30 Sep 95	**BROKEN STONES** *Go! Discs GODCD 132*	20		2
9 Mar 96	**OUT OF THE SINKING** *Go! Discs GODCD 143*	16		1
17 Aug 96	**PEACOCK SUIT** *Go! Discs GODCD 149*	5		2
9 Aug 97	**BRUSHED** *Island CID 666*	14		2
11 Oct 97	**FRIDAY STREET** *Island CID 676*	21		1
6 Dec 97	**MERMAIDS** *Island CID 683*	30		1
14 Nov 98	**BRAND NEW START** *Island CID 711*	16		2
9 Jan 99	**WILD WOOD** *Island CID 734*	22		2
2 Sep 00	**SWEET PEA, MY SWEET PEA** *Island CID 764*	44		
14 Sep 02	**IT'S WRITTEN IN THE STARS** *Independiente ISOM 63SMS*	7		2
30 Nov 02	**LEAFY MYSTERIES** *Independiente ISOM 65SMS*	23		1
26 Jun 04	**THE BOTTLE** *V2 VVR 5026913*	13		1
11 Sep 04	**WISHING ON A STAR** *V2 VVR 5026928*	11		3
27 Nov 04	**THINKING OF YOU** *V2 VVR5028463*	18		1
26 Mar 05	**EARLY MORNING RAIN** *V2 VVR5030597*	40		1
30 Jul 05	**FROM THE FLOORBOARDS UP** *V2 VVR5033413*	6		2
8 Oct 05	**COME ON/LET'S GO** *V2 VVR5033223*	15		1
17 Dec 05	**HERE'S THE GOOD NEWS** *V2 VVR5034603*	21		1
18 Nov 06	**WILD BLUE YONDER** *V2 VVR5043983*	22		1
21 Jul 07	**THIS OLD TOWN** *Download* PAUL WELLER & GRAHAM COXON	39		1
22 Sep 07	**ARE YOU TRYING TO BE LONELY** *Acid Jazz AJX193CD* ANDY LEWIS & PAUL WELLER	31		1

BRANDI WELLS US singer

Date	Title / Label	Peak Position	Weeks at No.1	Weeks in Top 40
20 Feb 82	**WATCH OUT** *Virgin VS 479*	74		

HOUSTON WELLS UK singer

Date	Title / Label	Peak Position	Weeks at No.1	Weeks in Top 40
1 Aug 63	**ONLY THE HEARTACHES** *Parlophone R 5031*	22		8

MARY WELLS US singer

Date	Title / Label	Peak Position	Weeks at No.1	Weeks in Top 40
21 May 64	**MY GUY** *Stateside SS 288* ★	5		13
30 Jul 64	**ONCE UPON A TIME** *Stateside SS 316* MARVIN GAYE & MARY WELLS	50		
8 Jul 72	**MY GUY** *Tamla Motown TMG 820*	14		8

TERRI WELLS US singer

Date	Title / Label	Peak Position	Weeks at No.1	Weeks in Top 40
2 Jul 83	**YOU MAKE IT HEAVEN** *Phillyworld PWS 111*	53		
5 May 84	**I'LL BE AROUND** *Phillyworld LON 48*	17		5

ALEX WELSH UK group

Date	Title / Label	Peak Position	Weeks at No.1	Weeks in Top 40
10 Aug 61	**TANSY** *Columbia DB 4686*	45		

WENDY & LISA US soul duo

Date	Title / Label	Peak Position	Weeks at No.1	Weeks in Top 40
5 Sep 87	**WATERFALL** *Virgin VS 999*	66		
16 Jan 88	**SIDE SHOW** *Virgin VS 1012*	49		
18 Feb 89	**ARE YOU MY BABY** *Virgin VS 1156*	70		
29 Apr 89	**LOLLY LOLLY** *Virgin VS 1175*	64		
8 Jul 89	**SATISFACTION** *Virgin VS 1194*	27		4
18 Nov 89	**WATERFALL (REMIX)** *Virgin VS 1223*	69		
30 Jun 90	**STRUNG OUT** *Virgin VS 1272*	44		
10 Nov 90	**RAINBOW LAKE** *Virgin VS 1280*	70		

WES French singer

Date	Title / Label	Peak Position	Weeks at No.1	Weeks in Top 40
14 Feb 98	**ALANE** *Epic 6654682*	11		4
27 Jun 98	**I LOVE FOOTBALL** *Epic 6660772*	75		

DODIE WEST UK singer

Date	Title / Label	Peak Position	Weeks at No.1	Weeks in Top 40
14 Jan 65	**GOING OUT OF MY HEAD** *Decca F 12046*	39		1

KANYE WEST US rapper

Date	Title / Label	Peak Position	Weeks at No.1	Weeks in Top 40
3 Apr 04	**THROUGH THE WIRE** *Roc-A-Fella 9862270*	9		7
19 Jun 04	**ALL FALLS DOWN** *Roc-A-Fella 9862670* KANYE WEST FEATURING SYLEENA JOHNSON	10		5
26 Jun 04	**TALK ABOUT OUR LOVE** *Atlantic AT 0177CD* BRANDY FEATURING KANYE WEST	6		5
11 Sep 04	**JESUS WALKS** *Roc-A-Fella 9863964*	16		4
16 Jul 05	**DIAMONDS FROM SIERRA LEONE** *Roc-A-Fella 9883229*	8		7
1 Oct 05	**GOLD DIGGER** *Roc-A-Fella 9885699* KANYE WEST FEATURING JAMIE FOXX ★	2		19
17 Dec 05	**HEARD 'EM SAY** *Roc-A-Fella 9888416* KANYE WEST FEATURING ADAM LEVINE	22		4
25 Feb 06	**BRAND NEW** *J Records 82876778842* RHYMEFEST FEATURING KANYE WEST	32		1
18 Mar 06	**TOUCH THE SKY** *Roc-A-Fella 9852115* KANYE WEST FEATURING LUPE FIASCO	6		7
26 Aug 06	**NUMBER ONE** *Virgin VUSDX333* PHARRELL FEATURING KANYE WEST	31		1
18 Aug 07	**STRONGER** *Def Jam 1744463* ★	1	2	17
29 Sep 07	**GOOD LIFE** *Def Jam 1752306* KANYE WEST FEATURING T-PAIN	23		8
5 Jan 08	**HOMECOMING** *Def Jam 1761789* KANYE WEST FEATURING CHRIS MARTIN	9		8
15 Mar 08	**AMERICAN BOY** *Atlantic AT0304CD* ESTELLE FEATURING KANYE WEST	1	1	1

KEITH WEST UK singer

Date	Title / Label	Peak Position	Weeks at No.1	Weeks in Top 40
9 Aug 67	**EXCERPT FROM 'A TEENAGE OPERA'** *Parlophone R 5623*	2		15
22 Nov 67	**SAM** *Parlophone R 5651*	38		1

TILL WEST & DJ DELICIOUS German production duo

Date	Title / Label	Peak Position	Weeks at No.1	Weeks in Top 40
15 Jul 06	**SAME MAN** *Data DATA119CDS*	36		1

WEST END UK group

Date	Title / Label	Peak Position	Weeks at No.1	Weeks in Top 40
19 Aug 95	**LOVE RULES** *RCA 74321292702*	44		

Silver-selling ○ Gold-selling ● Platinum-selling ⊛ US No.1 ★ | Peak Position | Weeks at No.1 | Weeks in Top 40

WEST END UK production duo

Date	Title / Label	Peak	No.1	Top 40
16 Jan 93	**THE LOVE I LOST** *PWL Sanctuary PWCD 253* WEST END FEATURING SYBIL	3		11

WEST HAM UNITED CUP SQUAD UK football club

Date	Title / Label	Peak	No.1	Top 40
10 May 75	**I'M FOREVER BLOWING BUBBLES** *Pye 7N 45470*	31		1

WEST STREET MOB US production group

Date	Title / Label	Peak	No.1	Top 40
8 Oct 83	**BREAK DANCIN' – ELECTRIC BOOGIE** *Sugarhill SH 128*	64		

WESTBAM German producer

Date	Title / Label	Peak	No.1	Top 40
9 Jul 94	**CELEBRATION GENERATION** *Low Spirit PQCD 5*	48		
19 Nov 94	**BAM BAM BAM** *Low Spirit PZCD 329*	57		
3 Jun 95	**WIZARDS OF THE SONIC** *Urban PZCD 344*	32		1
23 Mar 96	**ALWAYS MUSIC** *Low Spirit 5779152* WESTBAM/KOON + STEPHENSON	51		
13 Jun 98	**WIZARDS OF THE SONIC (REMIX)** *Wonderboy WBOYD 010* WESTBAM VS RED JERRY	43		
28 Nov 98	**ROOF IS ON FIRE** *Logic 74321633162*	58		

WESTLIFE Irish group

Date	Title / Label	Peak	No.1	Top 40
1 May 99	**SWEAR IT AGAIN** *RCA 74321662062* ●	1	2	8
21 Aug 99	**IF I LET YOU GO** *RCA 74321692352* ○	1	1	9
30 Oct 99	**FLYING WITHOUT WINGS** *RCA 74321709162* ○	1	1	9
25 Dec 99	**I HAVE A DREAM/SEASONS IN THE SUN** *RCA 74321726012* ⊛	1	4	11
8 Apr 00	**FOOL AGAIN** *RCA 74321751562*	1	1	6
30 Sep 00	**AGAINST ALL ODDS (TAKE A LOOK AT ME NOW)** *Columbia 6698872* MARIAH CAREY FEATURING WESTLIFE ○	1	2	8
11 Nov 00	**MY LOVE** *RCA 74321802802*	1	1	9
30 Dec 00	**WHAT MAKES A MAN** *RCA 74321826252* ●	2		11
17 Mar 01	**UPTOWN GIRL** *RCA 74321841692* ○	1	1	11
17 Nov 01	**QUEEN OF MY HEART** *RCA 74321899142* ○	1	1	9
2 Mar 02	**WORLD OF OUR OWN** *RCA 74321919242* ○	1	1	6
1 Jun 02	**BOP BOP BABY** *S 74321940452*	5		4
16 Nov 02	**UNBREAKABLE** *S 74321975222* ○	1	1	9
5 Apr 03	**TONIGHT/MISS YOU NIGHTS** *S 74321986802*	3		7
27 Sep 03	**HEY WHATEVER** *S 82876560862*	4		5
29 Nov 03	**MANDY** *S 82876570742*	1	1	5
6 Mar 04	**OBVIOUS** *S 82876596322*	3		6
5 Nov 05	**YOU RAISE ME UP** *S 82876739522*	1	2	12
24 Dec 05	**WHEN YOU TELL ME THAT YOU LOVE ME** *S 82876767382* WESTLIFE FEATURING DIANA ROSS	2		5
4 Mar 06	**AMAZING** *S 82876806252*	4		3
18 Nov 06	**THE ROSE** *S 88697032652*	1	1	7
10 Nov 07	**HOME** *S 88697189872*	3		10
8 Dec 07	**I'M ALREADY THERE** *Download*	62		
1 Mar 08	**US AGAINST THE WORLD** *S 88697253142*	8		4

WESTWORLD UK/US group

Date	Title / Label	Peak	No.1	Top 40
21 Feb 87	**SONIC BOOM BOY** *RCA BOOM 1*	11		6
2 May 87	**BA-NA-NA-BAM-BOO** *RCA BOOM 2*	37		2
25 Jul 87	**WHERE THE ACTION IS** *RCA BOOM 3*	54		
17 Oct 87	**SILVERMAC** *RCA BOOM 4*	42		
15 Oct 88	**EVERYTHING GOOD IS BAD** *RCA PB 42243*	72		

WET WET WET UK group

Date	Title / Label	Peak	No.1	Top 40
11 Apr 87	**WISHING I WAS LUCKY** *Precious Organisation JEWEL 3*	6		10
25 Jul 87	**SWEET LITTLE MYSTERY** *Precious Organisation JEWEL 4*	5		9
5 Dec 87	**ANGEL EYES (HOME AND AWAY)** *Precious Organisation JEWEL 6*	5		10
19 Mar 88	**TEMPTATION** *Precious Organisation JEWEL 7*	12		6
14 May 88	**WITH A LITTLE HELP FROM MY FRIENDS** *Childline CHILD 1* ○	1	4	10
30 Sep 89	**SWEET SURRENDER** *Precious Organisation JEWEL 9*	6		7
9 Dec 89	**BROKE AWAY** *Precious Organisation JEWEL 10*	19		5
10 Mar 90	**HOLD BACK THE RIVER** *Precious Organisation JEWEL 11*	31		3
11 Aug 90	**STAY WITH ME HEARTACHE/I FEEL FINE** *Precious Organisation JEWEL 13*	30		3
14 Sep 91	**MAKE IT TONIGHT** *Precious Organisation JEWEL 15*	37		2
2 Nov 91	**PUT THE LIGHT ON** *Precious Organisation JEWEL 16*	56		
4 Jan 92	**GOODNIGHT GIRL** *Precious Organisation JEWEL 17*	1	4	10
21 Mar 92	**MORE THAN LOVE** *Precious Organisation JEWEL 18*	19		3
11 Jul 92	**LIP SERVICE (EP)** *Precious Organisation JEWEL 19*	15		4
8 May 93	**BLUE FOR YOU/THIS TIME (LIVE)** *Precious Organisation JWLCD 20*	38		1
6 Nov 93	**SHED A TEAR** *Precious Organisation JWLCD 21*	22		3
8 Jan 94	**COLD COLD HEART** *Precious Organisation JWLCD 22*	20		2
21 May 94	**LOVE IS ALL AROUND** *Precious Organisation JWLCD 23* ⊛	1	15	26
25 Mar 95	**JULIA SAYS** *Precious Organisation JWLDD 24* ○	3		6
17 Jun 95	**DON'T WANT TO FORGIVE ME NOW** *Precious Organisation JWLDD 25*	7		5
30 Sep 95	**SOMEWHERE SOMEHOW** *Precious Organisation JWLDD 26*	7		5
2 Dec 95	**SHE'S ALL ON MY MIND** *Precious Organisation JWLDD 27*	17		5
30 Mar 96	**MORNING** *Precious Organisation JWLDD 28*	16		3
22 Mar 97	**IF I NEVER SEE YOU AGAIN** *Precious Organisation JWLCD 29*	3		5
14 Jun 97	**STRANGE** *Precious Organisation JWLCD 30*	13		3
16 Aug 97	**YESTERDAY** *Precious Organisation JWLCD 31*	4		4
13 Nov 04	**ALL I WANT** *Mercury 9868448*	14		2
17 Nov 07	**TOO MANY PEOPLE** *Dry DRY2SCX*	46		
16 Feb 08	**WEIGHTLESS** *Dry DRY3SCX*	10		1

WE'VE GOT A FUZZBOX & WE'RE GONNA USE IT UK group

Date	Title / Label	Peak	No.1	Top 40
26 Apr 86	**XX SEX/RULES AND REGULATIONS** *Vindaloo UGH 11*	41		
15 Nov 86	**LOVE IS THE SLUG** *Vindaloo UGH 14*	31		2
7 Feb 87	**WHAT'S THE POINT** *Vindaloo YZ 101*	51		
25 Feb 89	**INTERNATIONAL RESCUE** *WEA YZ 347*	11		7
20 May 89	**PINK SUNSHINE** *WEA YZ 401*	14		8
5 Aug 89	**SELF!** *WEA YZ 408*	24		4

WHALE Swedish group

Date	Title / Label	Peak	No.1	Top 40
19 Mar 94	**HOBO HUMPIN' SLOBO BABE** *East West YZ 798CD*	46		
15 Jul 95	**I'LL DO YA** *Hut HUTDG 51*	53		
25 Nov 95	**HOBO HUMPIN' SLOBO BABE** *Hut HUTCD 64*	15		2
4 Jul 98	**FOUR BIG SPEAKERS** *Hut HUTCD 96* WHALE FEATURING BUS 75	69		

WHAM! UK duo

Date	Title / Label	Peak	No.1	Top 40
16 Oct 82	**YOUNG GUNS (GO FOR IT)** *Innervision IVL A 2766* ○	3		11
15 Jan 83	**WHAM RAP** *Innervision IVL A 2442*	8		8
14 May 83	**BAD BOYS** *Innervision A 3143* ○	2		11
30 Jul 83	**CLUB TROPICANA** *Innervision A 3613*	4		9
3 Dec 83	**CLUB FANTASTIC MEGAMIX** *Innervision A 3586*	15		7
26 May 84	**WAKE ME UP BEFORE YOU GO GO** *Epic A 4440* ● ★	1	2	12
13 Oct 84	**FREEDOM** *Epic A 4743* ●	1	3	12
15 Dec 84	**LAST CHRISTMAS/EVERYTHING SHE WANTS** *Epic A 4949* ⊛	2		11
23 Nov 85	**I'M YOUR MAN** *Epic A 6716* ●	1	2	10
14 Dec 85	**LAST CHRISTMAS** *Epic WHAM 1*	6		6
21 Jun 86	**THE EDGE OF HEAVEN/WHERE DID YOUR HEART GO** *Epic FIN 1* ○	1	2	8
20 Dec 86	**LAST CHRISTMAS** *Epic 6502697*	45		
8 Dec 07	**LAST CHRISTMAS** *Download*	14		4

SARAH WHATMORE UK singer

Date	Title / Label	Peak	No.1	Top 40
21 Sep 02	**WHEN I LOST YOU** *RCA 74321965952*	6		7
22 Feb 03	**AUTOMATIC** *RCA 82876504612*	11		4

REBECCA WHEATLEY UK actress

Date	Title / Label	Peak	No.1	Top 40
26 Feb 00	**STAY WITH ME (BABY)** *BBC Music WMSS 60222*	10		3

WHEATUS US group

Date	Title / Label	Peak	No.1	Top 40
17 Feb 01	**TEENAGE DIRTBAG** *Columbia 6707962* ●	2		19
14 Jul 01	**A LITTLE RESPECT** *Columbia 6714282*	3		8
26 Jan 02	**WANNABE GANGSTER/LEROY** *Columbia 6721272*	22		1
6 Sep 03	**AMERICAN IN AMSTERDAM** *Columbia 6741072*	59		

CARON WHEELER UK singer

Date	Title / Label	Peak	No.1	Top 40
18 Mar 89	**KEEP ON MOVING** *10 TEN 263* SOUL II SOUL FEATURING CARON WHEELER	5		10
10 Jun 89	**BACK TO LIFE (HOWEVER DO YOU WANT ME)** *10 TEN 265* SOUL II SOUL FEATURING CARON WHEELER ○	1	4	11
8 Sep 90	**LIVIN' IN THE LIGHT** *RCA PB 43939*	14		4
10 Nov 90	**UK BLAK** *RCA PB 43719*	40		1
9 Feb 91	**DON'T QUIT** *RCA PB 44259*	53		
7 Nov 92	**I ADORE YOU** *Perspective PERSS 7407*	59		
11 Sep 93	**BEACH OF THE WAR GODDESS** *EMI CDEM 282*	75		

WESTLIFE

On 1 June 2008, Westlife played a stadium concert at Dublin's Croke Park, the home ground of Gaelic football. Over 82,000 tickets were available – they'd sold out in less than one day. One month later, the band began a 'year off', the first time in ten years that they had enjoyed an extended period of rest since beginning their careers as fresh-faced Irish teens back in mid-1998. As they walked on to the stage at Croke Park, they stood proud as the most successful boy band of all time in the singles charts, having enjoyed 14 Number 1s, a feat beaten only by The Beatles and Elvis Presley. Nine albums in as many years had grossed 50 million sales and their combined statistics dwarfed those of other high-profile 'boy/man' bands such as Take That and their Irish predecessors, Boyzone.

Westlife had begun their stellar rise when three founder members – Shane Filan, Mark Feehily and Kian Egan – took part in school musicals such as *Grease* in their home town of Sligo on the west coast of Ireland. Local celebrity swiftly followed before a fateful call by Filan's mother to music business legend and Boyzone manager Louis Walsh. Within a few days, Walsh had secured the fledgling band a support slot with American boy band The Backstreet Boys, in front of 6,000 girls at The Point. Prior to Walsh's intervention, some of the band had actually queued overnight to buy tickets to see the show.

Record company showcases followed – including performances in front of an unimpressed Simon Cowell – before Walsh instigated the departure of three members as well as setting up auditions for replacements. The core line-up was finally cemented with the addition of Dubliners Nicky Byrne (a former Leeds United professional) and Brian McFadden. Cowell had been particularly unimpressed with Filan, so Walsh had the singer dye his brown hair blond and re-auditioned for the music mogul with the two new members, telling Cowell that the newly blond Filan was one of 'the new guys'. Cowell didn't recognise Filan and agreed to sign the band after thirty seconds of the first song.

With a support tour alongside Boyzone under their belts, the band went into the studio with revered songwriters such as Stevie Mac and Wayne Hector and launched what is an arguably unprecedented assault on the singles charts. Not only did their debut single, May 1999's 'Swear It Again', go straight in at Number 1, but so did their next six singles. All records were broken as the band took a sword to all their rivals, dominating their genre for the next decade.

Paradoxically, their biggest-selling first week sales were for their first song, not to hit Number 1 – their eighth single, December 2000's 'What Makes A Man'. Worse still, their run of hit singles was curtailed by none other than Bob The Builder, a fact which the band made no secret of being gutted about. A return to form followed with the Comic Relief single, 'Uptown Girl' a Billy Joel cover that shifted in excess of 750,000 in the UK alone. Their dominance of the Number 1 slot was re-ignited with the next three songs, meaning that had Bob The Builder not 'fixed it' for himself, Westlife would have enjoyed a staggering eleven consecutive singles hitting Number 1. They have scored a current total of fourteen chart-topping singles and have never seen a song miss the Top Ten.

Often unfairly and incorrectly criticised for being record company puppets, the band showed their true colours when McFadden left two weeks before a European tour, a departure which saw the remaining four members close ranks and perform a critically lauded, commercially massive and triumphant series of arena shows. Having brilliantly re-invented themselves as a cohesive four-piece, the band's continued singles sales were colossal. Meanwhile, their years of work on the road and in the studio had turned their vocal talents into formidable tools, such that a Rat Pack-style album, *Allow Us To Be Frank*, was delivered with consummate ease. The industry began to proffer them – finally – a deserved nod of respect.

In September 2004, they became the inaugural Number 1 on the Official Chart Company's brand new Download Chart (see also Introduction). Sales of Westlife records are repeatedly vast: few singles dip below a quarter of a million units and if an album falls short of one million copies, it is considered a relative disappointment. For one particular project, a 'crisis' meeting was held after sales stalled at 750,000 copies. Their success – with the perennial exclusion of America – was genuinely global too, with multi-million selling hits in most major territories of the world.

Despite these staggering statistics, and known within the industry for being one of the hardest-working bands for years, Westlife have enjoyed little critical generosity. They may not be the critics' favourite, but are popular to work with and are renowned for their caustic wit and unrivalled ability to 'work a room' with their Irish charm. The single 'Us Against The World', released in March 2008, suggested a promising, more edgy, tone in their song choices and bodes very well for their highly anticipated return to the pop arena in 2010.

Key: ○ Silver-selling · ● Gold-selling · ⊛ Platinum-selling · ★ US No.1 · Peak Position · Weeks at No.1 · Weeks in Top 40

BILL WHELAN Irish composer

Date	Title / Label	Peak Position	Weeks at No.1	Weeks in Top 40
17 Dec 94	**RIVERDANCE** *Son RTEBUACD 1* BILL WHELAN FEATURING ANUNA & THE RTE CONCERT ORCHESTRA ○	9		11

WHEN IN ROME UK group

Date	Title / Label	Peak Position	Weeks at No.1	Weeks in Top 40
28 Jan 89	**THE PROMISE** *10 TEN 244*	58		

WHIGFIELD Danish singer

Date	Title / Label	Peak Position	Weeks at No.1	Weeks in Top 40
17 Sep 94	**SATURDAY NIGHT** *Systematic SYSCD 3* ⊛	1	4	17
10 Dec 94	**ANOTHER DAY** *Systematic SYSCD 6* ○	7		7
10 Jun 95	**THINK OF YOU** *Systematic SYCDP 10*	7		9
9 Sep 95	**CLOSE TO YOU** *Systematic SYCDP 18*	13		4
16 Dec 95	**LAST CHRISTMAS/BIG TIME** *Systematic SYSCD 24*	21		2
10 Oct 98	**SEXY EYES – REMIXES** *ZYX 8085R8*	68		

WHIPPING BOY Irish group

Date	Title / Label	Peak Position	Weeks at No.1	Weeks in Top 40
14 Oct 95	**WE DON'T NEED NOBODY ELSE** *Columbia 6622205*	51		
3 Feb 96	**WHEN WE WERE YOUNG** *Columbia 6628062*	46		
25 May 96	**TWINKLE** *Columbia 6632272*	55		

WHISPERS US group

Date	Title / Label	Peak Position	Weeks at No.1	Weeks in Top 40
2 Feb 80	**AND THE BEAT GOES ON** *Solar SO 1* ○	2		9
10 May 80	**LADY** *Solar SO 4*	55		
12 Jul 80	**MY GIRL** *Solar SO 8*	26		4
14 Mar 81	**IT'S A LOVE THING** *Solar SO 16*	9		9
13 Jun 81	**I CAN MAKE IT BETTER** *Solar SO 19*	44		
19 Jan 85	**CONTAGIOUS** *MCA 937*	56		
28 Mar 87	**AND THE BEAT GOES ON** *Solar MCA 1126*	45		
23 May 87	**ROCK STEADY** *Solar MCA 1152*	38		1
15 Aug 87	**SPECIAL F/X** *Solar MCA 1178*	69		

WHISTLE US group

Date	Title / Label	Peak Position	Weeks at No.1	Weeks in Top 40
1 Mar 86	**(NOTHIN' SERIOUS) JUST BUGGIN'** *Champion CHAMP 12*	7		7

ALEX WHITCOMBE & BIG C UK duo

Date	Title / Label	Peak Position	Weeks at No.1	Weeks in Top 40
23 May 98	**ICE RAIN** *Xtravaganza 0091075 EXT*	44		

BARRY WHITE US singer

Date	Title / Label	Peak Position	Weeks at No.1	Weeks in Top 40
9 Jun 73	**I'M GONNA LOVE YOU JUST A LITTLE BIT MORE BABY** *Pye International 7N 25610*	23		6
26 Jan 74	**NEVER NEVER GONNA GIVE YA UP** *Pye International 7N 25633*	14		9
17 Aug 74	**CAN'T GET ENOUGH OF YOUR LOVE BABE** *Pye International 7N 25661* ★	8		10
2 Nov 74	**YOU'RE THE FIRST THE LAST MY EVERYTHING** *20th Century BTC 2133* ○	1	2	12
8 Mar 75	**WHAT AM I GONNA DO WITH YOU** *20th Century BTC 2177*	5		7
24 May 75	**I'LL DO ANYTHING YOU WANT ME TO** *20th Century BTC 2208*	20		5
27 Dec 75	**LET THE MUSIC PLAY** *20th Century BTC 2265*	9		6
6 Mar 76	**YOU SEE THE TROUBLE WITH ME** *20th Century BTC 2277* ○	2		9
21 Aug 76	**BABY, WE BETTER TRY TO GET IT TOGETHER** *20th Century BTC 2298*	15		7
13 Nov 76	**DON'T MAKE ME WAIT TOO LONG** *20th Century BTC 2309*	17		8
5 Mar 77	**I'M QUALIFIED TO SATISFY** *20th Century BTC 2328*	37		1
15 Oct 77	**IT'S ECSTASY WHEN YOU LAY DOWN NEXT TO ME** *20th Century BTC 2350*	40		1
16 Dec 78	**JUST THE WAY YOU ARE** *20th Century BTC 2380* ○	12		9
24 Mar 79	**SHA LA LA MEANS I LOVE YOU** *20th Century BTC 1041*	55		
7 Nov 87	**SHO' YOU RIGHT** *Breakout USA 614*	14		5
16 Jan 88	**NEVER NEVER GONNA GIVE YA UP (REMIX)** *Club JAB 59*	63		
31 Mar 90	**SECRET GARDEN** *Qwest W 9992* QUINCY JONES FEATURING AL B SURE!, JAMES INGRAM, EL DeBARGE & BARRY WHITE	67		
21 Jan 95	**PRACTICE WHAT YOU PREACH/LOVE IS THE ICON** *A&M 5808992*	20		3
8 Apr 95	**I ONLY WANT TO BE WITH YOU** *A&M 5810252*	36		1
21 Dec 96	**IN YOUR WILDEST DREAMS** *Parlophone CDR 6451* TINA TURNER FEATURING BARRY WHITE	32		2
4 Nov 00	**LET THE MUSIC PLAY (REMIX)** *Wonderboy WBOYD 020*	45		

CHRIS WHITE UK singer/bass player

Date	Title / Label	Peak Position	Weeks at No.1	Weeks in Top 40
20 Mar 76	**SPANISH WINE** *Charisma CB 272*	37		2

KARYN WHITE US singer

Date	Title / Label	Peak Position	Weeks at No.1	Weeks in Top 40
5 Nov 88	**THE WAY YOU LOVE ME** *Warner Brothers W 7773*	42		
18 Feb 89	**SECRET RENDEZVOUS** *Warner Brothers W 7562*	52		
10 Jun 89	**SUPERWOMAN** *Warner Brothers W 2920*	11		10
9 Sep 89	**SECRET RENDEZVOUS** *Warner Brothers W 2855*	22		5
17 Aug 91	**ROMANTIC** *Warner Brothers W 0028* ★	23		3
18 Jan 92	**THE WAY I FEEL ABOUT YOU** *Warner Brothers W 0073*	65		
24 Sep 94	**HUNGAH** *Warner Brothers W 0264CD*	69		

KEISHA WHITE UK singer

Date	Title / Label	Peak Position	Weeks at No.1	Weeks in Top 40
27 Mar 04	**WATCHA GONNA DO** *Radar RAD005CD*	53		
5 Mar 05	**DON'T CARE WHO KNOWS** *Warner Brothers WEA382CD2*	29		1
11 Mar 06	**THE WEAKNESS IN ME** *Korova KOW1001CD1*	17		4
1 Jul 06	**DON'T MISTAKE ME** *Korova KOW1007CD1*	48		
30 Sep 06	**I CHOOSE LIFE** *Korova KOW1012CD1*	63		

SNOWY WHITE UK singer/guitarist

Date	Title / Label	Peak Position	Weeks at No.1	Weeks in Top 40
24 Dec 83	**BIRD OF PARADISE** *Towerbell TOW 42* ○	6		7
28 Dec 85	**FOR YOU** *R4 FOR 3*	65		

TAM WHITE UK singer

Date	Title / Label	Peak Position	Weeks at No.1	Weeks in Top 40
15 Mar 75	**WHAT IN THE WORLD'S COME OVER YOU** *RAK 193*	36		3

TONY JOE WHITE US singer

Date	Title / Label	Peak Position	Weeks at No.1	Weeks in Top 40
6 Jun 70	**GROUPIE GIRL** *Monument MON 1043*	22		9

WHITE & TORCH UK duo

Date	Title / Label	Peak Position	Weeks at No.1	Weeks in Top 40
2 Oct 82	**PARADE** *Chrysalis CHS 2641*	54		

WHITE PLAINS UK group

Date	Title / Label	Peak Position	Weeks at No.1	Weeks in Top 40
7 Feb 70	**MY BABY LOVES LOVIN'** *Deram DM 280*	9		9
18 Apr 70	**I'VE GOT YOU ON MY MIND** *Deram DM 291*	17		10
24 Oct 70	**JULIE DO YA LOVE ME** *Deram DM 315* WHITE PLAINS WITH PETE NELSON	8		12
12 Jun 71	**WHEN YOU ARE A KING** *Deram DM 333*	13		9
17 Feb 73	**STEP INTO A DREAM** *Deram DM 371* WHITE PLAINS WITH GERRY BUTLER STRINGS	21		7

WHITE ROSE MOVEMENT UK group

Date	Title / Label	Peak Position	Weeks at No.1	Weeks in Top 40
12 Nov 05	**ALSATIAN** *Independiente ISOM99MS*	54		

WHITE STRIPES US duo

Date	Title / Label	Peak Position	Weeks at No.1	Weeks in Top 40
24 Nov 01	**HOTEL YORBA** *XL Recordings XLS 139CD*	26		1
9 Mar 02	**FELL IN LOVE WITH A GIRL** *XL Recordings XLS 142CD*	21		1
14 Sep 02	**DEAD LEAVES AND THE DIRTY GROUND** *XL Recordings 148CD*	25		1
3 May 03	**7 NATION ARMY** *XL Recordings XLS 162CD*	7		3
13 Sep 03	**I JUST DON'T KNOW WHAT TO DO WITH MYSELF** *XL Recordings XLS 166CD*	13		3
29 Nov 03	**THE HARDEST BUTTON TO BUTTON** *XL Recordings XLS 173CD*	23		1
27 Nov 04	**JOLENE – LIVE UNDER BLACKPOOL LIGHTS** *XL Recordings XLS207CD*	16		2
11 Jun 05	**BLUE ORCHID** *XL Recordings XLS216CD1*	9		4
3 Sep 05	**MY DOORBELL** *XL Recordings XLS218CD*	10		4
26 Nov 05	**THE DENIAL TWIST** *XL Recordings XLS223CD*	10		3
16 Jun 07	**ICKY THUMP** *XL Recordings XLS277CD*	2		4
22 Sep 07	**YOU DON'T KNOW WHAT LOVE IS** *XL Recordings XLS293CD*	18		1
12 Jan 08	**CONQUEST** *XL Recordings XLS320A*	30		1

WHITE TOWN Indian singer

Date	Title / Label	Peak Position	Weeks at No.1	Weeks in Top 40
25 Jan 97	**YOUR WOMAN** *Chrysalis CDCHS 5052* ○	1	1	7
24 May 97	**UNDRESSED** *Chrysalis CDCHS 5058*	57		

WHITE ZOMBIE US group

Date	Title / Label	Peak Position	Weeks at No.1	Weeks in Top 40
20 May 95	**MORE HUMAN THAN HUMAN** *Geffen GFSTD 92*	51		
18 May 96	**ELECTRIC HEAD PART 2 (THE ECSTASY)** *Geffen GFSXD 22140*	31		1

WHITEHEAD BROTHERS US group

Date	Title / Label	Peak Position	Weeks at No.1	Weeks in Top 40
14 Jan 95	**YOUR LOVE IS A 187** *Motown TMGCD 1434*	32		1
13 May 95	**FORGET I WAS A G** *Motown TMGCD 1441*	40		1

WHITEHOUSE US/UK duo

Date	Title / Label	Peak Position	Weeks at No.1	Weeks in Top 40
15 Aug 98	**AIN'T NO MOUNTAIN HIGH ENOUGH** *Beautiful Noise BNOISE 2CD*	60		

WHITEOUT UK group

Date	Title / Label	Peak Position	Weeks at No.1	Weeks in Top 40
24 Sep 94	**DETROIT** *Silvertone ORECD 66*	73		
18 Feb 95	**JACKIE'S RACING** *Silvertone ORECD 68*	72		

WHITESNAKE UK group

Date	Title / Label	Peak Position	Weeks at No.1	Weeks in Top 40
24 Jun 78	**SNAKE BITE (EP)** *EMI International INEP 751* DAVID COVERDALE'S WHITESNAKE	61		
10 Nov 79	**LONG WAY FROM HOME** *United Artists BP 324*	55		
26 Apr 80	**FOOL FOR YOUR LOVING** *United Artists BP 352*	13		7
12 Jul 80	**READY AN' WILLING (SWEET SATISFACTION)** *United Artists BP 363*	43		
22 Nov 80	**AIN'T NO LOVE IN THE HEART OF THE CITY** *Sunburst/Liberty BP 381*	51		
11 Apr 81	**DON'T BREAK MY HEART AGAIN** *Liberty BP 395*	17		6
6 Jun 81	**WOULD I LIE TO YOU** *Liberty BP 399*	37		2
6 Nov 82	**HERE I GO AGAIN/BLOODY LUXURY** *Liberty BP 416* ★	34		4
13 Aug 83	**GUILTY OF LOVE** *Liberty BP 420*	31		3
14 Jan 84	**GIVE ME MORE TIME** *Liberty BP 422*	29		3
28 Apr 84	**STANDING IN THE SHADOW** *Liberty BP 423*	62		
9 Feb 85	**LOVE AIN'T NO STRANGER** *Liberty BP 424*	44		
28 Mar 87	**STILL OF THE NIGHT** *EMI 5606*	16		6
6 Jun 87	**IS THIS LOVE** *EMI EM 3*	9		9
31 Oct 87	**HERE I GO AGAIN (REMIX)** *EMI EM 35*	9		8
6 Feb 88	**GIVE ME ALL YOUR LOVE** *EMI EM 23*	18		4
2 Dec 89	**FOOL FOR YOUR LOVING** *EMI EM 123*	43		
10 Mar 90	**THE DEEPER THE LOVE** *EMI EM 128*	35		2
25 Aug 90	**NOW YOU'RE GONE** *EMI EM 150*	31		3
6 Aug 94	**IS THIS LOVE/SWEET LADY LUCK** *EMI CDEM 329*	25		2
7 Jun 97	**TOO MANY TEARS** *EMI CDEM 471* DAVID COVERDALE & WHITESNAKE	46		

WHITEY UK producer

Date	Title / Label	Peak Position	Weeks at No.1	Weeks in Top 40
5 Mar 05	**NON STOP/A WALK IN THE DARK** *1234 1234CDS06*	67		

DAVID WHITFIELD UK singer

Date	Title / Label	Peak Position	Weeks at No.1	Weeks in Top 40
2 Oct 53	**BRIDGE OF SIGHS** *Decca F 10129*	9		1
16 Oct 53	**ANSWER ME** *Decca F 10192*	1	2	14
11 Dec 53	**RAGS TO RICHES** *Decca F 10207* DAVID WHITFIELD WITH STANLEY BLACK & HIS ORCHESTRA	3		11
19 Feb 54	**THE BOOK** *Decca F 10242*	5		15
18 Jun 54	**CARA MIA** *Decca F 10327* DAVID WHITFIELD, WITH CHORUS AND MANTOVANI AND HIS ORCHESTRA	1	10	25
12 Nov 54	**SANTO NATALE (MERRY CHRISTMAS)** *Decca F 10399*	2		10
11 Feb 55	**BEYOND THE STARS** *Decca F 10458*	8		9
27 May 55	**MAMA** *Decca F 10515*	12		11
8 Jul 55	**EV'RYWHERE** *Decca F 10515* DAVID WHITFIELD WITH THE ROLAND SHAW ORCHESTRA	3		20
25 Nov 55	**WHEN YOU LOSE THE ONE YOU LOVE** *Decca F 10627* DAVID WHITFIELD WITH CHORUS & MANTOVANI & HIS ORCHESTRA	7		11
2 Mar 56	**MY SEPTEMBER LOVE** *Decca F 10690*	3		23
24 Aug 56	**MY SON JOHN** *Decca F 10769*	22		4
31 Aug 56	**MY UNFINISHED SYMPHONY** *Decca F 10769*	29		1
25 Jan 57	**ADORATION WALTZ** *Decca F 10833* DAVID WHITFIELD WITH THE ROLAND SHAW ORCHESTRA	9		11
5 Apr 57	**I'LL FIND YOU** *Decca F 10864*	27		4
14 Feb 58	**CRY MY HEART** *Decca F 10978* DAVID WHITFIELD WITH CHORUS & MANTOVANI & HIS ORCHESTRA	22		3
16 May 58	**ON THE STREET WHERE YOU LIVE** *Decca F 11018* DAVID WHITFIELD WITH CYRIL STAPLETON & HIS ORCHESTRA	16		14
8 Aug 58	**THE RIGHT TO LOVE** *Decca F 11039*	30		1
24 Nov 60	**I BELIEVE** *Decca F 11289*	49		

SLIM WHITMAN US singer

Date	Title / Label	Peak Position	Weeks at No.1	Weeks in Top 40
15 Jul 55	**ROSE MARIE** *London HL 8061*	1	11	19
29 Jul 55	**INDIAN LOVE CALL** *London L 1149*	7		12
23 Sep 55	**CHINA DOLL** *London L 1149*	15		2
9 Mar 56	**TUMBLING TUMBLEWEEDS** *London HLU 8230*	19		2
13 Apr 56	**I'M A FOOL** *London HLU 8252*	16		4
22 Jun 56	**SERENADE** *London HLU 8287*	8		15
12 Apr 57	**I'LL TAKE YOU HOME AGAIN KATHLEEN** *London HLP 8403*	7		13
5 Oct 74	**HAPPY ANNIVERSARY** *United Artists UP 35728*	14		8

ROGER WHITTAKER Kenyan singer

Date	Title / Label	Peak Position	Weeks at No.1	Weeks in Top 40
8 Nov 69	**DURHAM TOWN (THE LEAVIN')** *Columbia DB 8613*	12		13
11 Apr 70	**I DON'T BELIEVE IN 'IF' ANYMORE** *Columbia DB 8664*	8		16
10 Oct 70	**NEW WORLD IN THE MORNING** *Columbia DB 8718*	17		9
3 Apr 71	**WHY** *Columbia DB 8752*	47		
2 Oct 71	**MAMMY BLUE** *Columbia DB 8822*	31		7
26 Jul 75	**THE LAST FAREWELL** *EMI 2294* ●	2		13
8 Nov 86	**THE SKYE BOAT SONG** *Tembo TML 119* ROGER WHITTAKER & DES O'CONNOR	10		7

WHO UK group

Date	Title / Label	Peak Position	Weeks at No.1	Weeks in Top 40
18 Feb 65	**I CAN'T EXPLAIN** *Brunswick 05926*	8		12
27 May 65	**ANYWAY ANYHOW ANYWHERE** *Brunswick 05935*	10		11
4 Nov 65	**MY GENERATION** *Brunswick 05944*	2		12
10 Mar 66	**SUBSTITUTE** *Reaction 591 001*	5		11
24 Mar 66	**A LEGAL MATTER** *Brunswick 05956*	32		5
1 Sep 66	**I'M A BOY** *Reaction 591 004*	2		12
1 Sep 66	**THE KIDS ARE ALRIGHT** *Brunswick 05965*	41		
15 Dec 66	**HAPPY JACK** *Reaction 591 010*	3		10
27 Apr 67	**PICTURES OF LILY** *Track 604 002*	4		9
26 Jul 67	**THE LAST TIME/UNDER MY THUMB** *Track 604 006*	44		
18 Oct 67	**I CAN SEE FOR MILES** *Track 604 011*	10		9
19 Jun 68	**DOGS** *Track 604 023*	25		4
23 Oct 68	**MAGIC BUS** *Track 604 024*	26		5
19 Mar 69	**PINBALL WIZARD** *Track 604 027*	4		12
4 Apr 70	**THE SEEKER** *Track 604 036*	19		8
8 Aug 70	**SUMMERTIME BLUES** *Track 2094 002*	38		3
10 Jul 71	**WON'T GET FOOLED AGAIN** *Track 2094 009*	9		10
23 Oct 71	**LET'S SEE ACTION** *Track 2094 012*	16		9
24 Jun 72	**JOIN TOGETHER** *Track 2094 102*	9		9
13 Jan 73	**RELAY** *Track 2094 106*	21		5
13 Oct 73	**5.15** *Track 2094 115*	20		6
24 Jan 76	**SQUEEZE BOX** *Polydor 2121 275*	10		8
30 Oct 76	**SUBSTITUTE** *Polydor 2058 803*	7		7
22 Jul 78	**WHO ARE YOU** *Polydor WHO 1*	18		10
28 Apr 79	**LONG LIVE ROCK** *Polydor WHO 2*	48		
7 Mar 81	**YOU BETTER YOU BET** *Polydor WHO 004*	9		6
9 May 81	**DON'T LET GO THE COAT** *Polydor WHO 005*	47		
2 Oct 82	**ATHENA** *Polydor WHO 6*	40		1
26 Nov 83	**READY STEADY WHO (EP)** *Polydor WHO 7*	58		
20 Feb 88	**MY GENERATION** *Polydor POSP 907*	68		
27 Jul 96	**MY GENERATION** *Polydor 8546372*	31		1

WHO DA FUNK US production group

Date	Title / Label	Peak Position	Weeks at No.1	Weeks in Top 40
26 Oct 02	**SHINY DISCO BALLS (IMPORT)** *Subusa 5000007432304* WHO DA FUNK FEATURING JESSICA EVE	69		
2 Nov 02	**SHINY DISCO BALLS** *Cream 22CD* WHO DA FUNK FEATURING JESSICA EVE	15		3
15 Feb 03	**STING ME RED (YOU THINK YOU'RE SO)** *Cream 19CDS* WHO DA FUNK FEATURING TERRA DEVA	32		1

WHODINI US group

Date	Title / Label	Peak Position	Weeks at No.1	Weeks in Top 40
25 Dec 82	**MAGIC'S WAND** *Jive 28*	47		
17 Mar 84	**MAGIC'S WAND (THE WHODINI ELECTRIC EP)** *Jive 61*	63		

WHOOLIGANZ US duo

Date	Title / Label	Peak Position	Weeks at No.1	Weeks in Top 40
13 Aug 94	**PUT YOUR HANDZ UP** *Positiva CDTIV 17*	53		

WHOOSH UK production group

Date	Title / Label	Peak Position	Weeks at No.1	Weeks in Top 40
13 Sep 97	**WHOOSH** *Wonderboy WBOYD 006*	72		

WHYCLIFFE UK singer

Date	Title / Label	Peak Position	Weeks at No.1	Weeks in Top 40
20 Nov 93	**HEAVEN** *MCA MCSTD 1944*	56		
2 Apr 94	**ONE MORE TIME** *MCA MCSTD 1955*	72		

Silver-selling ○ Gold-selling ● Platinum-selling ✪ US No.1 ★ — Peak Position, Weeks at No.1, Weeks in Top 40

WIDEBOYS UK group

Date	Title / Label	Peak Position	Weeks at No.1	Weeks in Top 40
27 Oct 01	SAMBUCA *Locked On/679 Recordings 679L 002CD* WIDEBOYS FEATURING DENNIS G	15		3

JANE WIEDLIN US singer/guitarist

Date	Title / Label	Peak Position	Weeks at No.1	Weeks in Top 40
6 Aug 88	RUSH HOUR *Manhattan MT 36*	12		8
29 Oct 88	INSIDE A DREAM *Manhattan MT 55*	64		

WIFI UK group

Date	Title / Label	Peak Position	Weeks at No.1	Weeks in Top 40
17 Mar 07	BE WITHOUT YOU *All Around The World CDGLOBE625* WIFI FEATURING MELANIE M	42		

WIGAN'S CHOSEN FEW Canadian instrumental group

Date	Title / Label	Peak Position	Weeks at No.1	Weeks in Top 40
18 Jan 75	FOOTSEE *Pye Disco Demand DDS 111*	9		9

WIGAN'S OVATION UK group

Date	Title / Label	Peak Position	Weeks at No.1	Weeks in Top 40
15 Mar 75	SKIING IN THE SNOW *Spark SRL 1122*	12		8
28 Jun 75	PER-SO-NAL-LY *Spark SRL 1129*	38		1
29 Nov 75	SUPER LOVE *Spark SRL 1133*	41		

WIGWAM UK duo

Date	Title / Label	Peak Position	Weeks at No.1	Weeks in Top 40
15 Apr 06	WIGWAM *Instant Karma DHARMA9CD2*	60		

WILCO US group

Date	Title / Label	Peak Position	Weeks at No.1	Weeks in Top 40
17 Apr 99	CAN'T STAND IT *Reprise W 475CD1*	67		

JACK WILD UK actor

Date	Title / Label	Peak Position	Weeks at No.1	Weeks in Top 40
2 May 70	SOME BEAUTIFUL *Capitol CL 15635*	46		

WILD CHERRY US group

Date	Title / Label	Peak Position	Weeks at No.1	Weeks in Top 40
9 Oct 76	PLAY THAT FUNKY MUSIC *Epic EPC 4593* ★	7		11

WILD COLOUR UK group

Date	Title / Label	Peak Position	Weeks at No.1	Weeks in Top 40
14 Oct 95	DREAMS *Perfecto PERF 105CD*	25		1

WILD WEEKEND UK group

Date	Title / Label	Peak Position	Weeks at No.1	Weeks in Top 40
29 Apr 89	BREAKIN' UP *Parlophone R 6204*	74		
5 May 90	WHO'S AFRAID OF THE BIG BAD LOVE *Parlophone R 6249*	70		

WILDCHILD UK producer

Date	Title / Label	Peak Position	Weeks at No.1	Weeks in Top 40
22 Apr 95	LEGENDS OF THE DARK BLACK – PART 2 *Hi-Life HICD 9*	34		1
21 Oct 95	RENEGADE MASTER *Hi-Life 5771312*	11		3
23 Nov 96	JUMP TO MY BEAT *Hi-Life 5757372*	30		1
17 Jan 98	RENEGADE MASTER *Hi-Life 5692792* ○	3		7
25 Apr 98	BAD BOY *Polydor 5716072* WILDCHILD FEATURING JOMALSKI	38		1

EUGENE WILDE US singer

Date	Title / Label	Peak Position	Weeks at No.1	Weeks in Top 40
13 Oct 84	GOTTA GET YOU HOME TONIGHT *Fourth & Broadway BRW 15*	18		7
2 Feb 85	PERSONALITY *Fourth & Broadway BRW 18*	34		3

KIM WILDE UK singer

Date	Title / Label	Peak Position	Weeks at No.1	Weeks in Top 40
21 Feb 81	KIDS IN AMERICA *RAK 327* ●	2		9
9 May 81	CHEQUERED LOVE *RAK 330* ○	4		7
1 Aug 81	WATER ON GLASS/BOYS *RAK 334*	11		7
14 Nov 81	CAMBODIA *RAK 336*	12		9
17 Apr 82	VIEW FROM A BRIDGE *RAK 342*	16		5
16 Oct 82	CHILD COME AWAY *RAK 352*	43		
30 Jul 83	LOVE BLONDE *RAK 360*	23		6
12 Nov 83	DANCING IN THE DARK *RAK 365*	67		
13 Oct 84	THE SECOND TIME *MCA KIM 1*	29		4
8 Dec 84	THE TOUCH *MCA KIM 2*	56		
27 Apr 85	RAGE TO LOVE *MCA KIM 3*	19		5
25 Oct 86	YOU KEEP ME HANGIN' ON *MCA KIM 4* ○ ★	2		12
4 Apr 87	ANOTHER STEP CLOSER TO YOU *MCA KIM 5* KIM WILDE & JUNIOR	6		9
8 Aug 87	SAY YOU REALLY WANT ME *MCA KIM 6*	29		3
5 Dec 87	ROCKIN' AROUND THE CHRISTMAS TREE *10 TEN 2* MEL & KIM ○	3		7
14 May 88	HEY MISTER HEARTACHE *MCA KIM 7*	31		3
16 Jul 88	YOU CAME *MCA KIM 8* ○	3		10
1 Oct 88	NEVER TRUST A STRANGER *MCA KIM 9*	7		7
3 Dec 88	FOUR LETTER WORD *MCA KIM 10*	6		9
4 Mar 89	LOVE IN THE NATURAL WAY *MCA KIM 11*	32		2
14 Apr 90	IT'S HERE *MCA KIM 12*	42		
16 Jun 90	TIME *MCA KIM 13*	71		
15 Dec 90	I CAN'T SAY GOODBYE *MCA KIM 14*	51		
2 May 92	LOVE IS HOLY *MCA KIM 15*	16		5
27 Jun 92	HEART OVER MIND *MCA KIM 16*	34		1
12 Sep 92	WHO DO YOU THINK YOU ARE? *MCA KIM 17*	49		
10 Jul 93	IF I CAN'T HAVE YOU *MCA KIMTD 18*	12		5
13 Nov 93	IN MY LIFE *MCA KIMTD 19*	54		
14 Oct 95	BREAKIN' AWAY *MCA KIMTD 21*	43		
10 Feb 96	THIS I SWEAR *MCA KIMTD 22*	46		

MARTY WILDE UK singer

Date	Title / Label	Peak Position	Weeks at No.1	Weeks in Top 40
11 Jul 58	ENDLESS SLEEP *Philips PB 835*	4		14
6 Mar 59	DONNA *Philips PB 902*	3		18
5 Jun 59	A TEENAGER IN LOVE *Philips PB 926*	2		17
25 Sep 59	SEA OF LOVE *Philips PB 959*	3		12
11 Dec 59	BAD BOY *Philips PB 972*	7		8
10 Mar 60	JOHNNY ROCCO *Philips PB 1002*	30		4
19 May 60	THE FIGHT *Philips PB 1022*	47		
22 Dec 60	LITTLE GIRL *Philips PB 1078*	16		9
26 Jan 61	RUBBER BALL *Philips PB 1101*	9		7
27 Jul 61	HIDE AND SEEK *Philips PB 1240*	47		
9 Nov 61	TOMORROW'S CLOWN *Philips PB 1191*	33		4
24 May 62	JEZEBEL *Philips PB 1240*	19		8
25 Oct 62	EVER SINCE YOU SAID GOODBYE *Philips 326546 BF*	31		3

MATTHEW WILDER US singer

Date	Title / Label	Peak Position	Weeks at No.1	Weeks in Top 40
21 Jan 84	BREAK MY STRIDE *Epic A 3908* ○	4		10

WILDHEARTS UK group

Date	Title / Label	Peak Position	Weeks at No.1	Weeks in Top 40
20 Nov 93	TV TAN *Bronze YZ 784CD*	53		
19 Feb 94	CAFFEINE BOMB *Bronze YZ 794CD*	31		1
9 Jul 94	SUCKERPUNCH *Bronze YZ 828CD*	38		1
28 Jan 95	IF LIFE IS LIKE A LOVE BANK I WANT AN OVERDRAFT/GEORDIE IN WONDERLAND *Bronze YZ 874CD*	31		1
6 May 95	I WANNA GO WHERE THE PEOPLE GO *East West YZ 923CD*	16		2
29 Jul 95	JUST IN LUST *East West YZ 967CD*	28		1
20 Apr 96	SICK OF DRUGS *Round WILD 1CDX*	14		2
29 Jun 96	RED LIGHT GREEN LIGHT EP *Round WILD 2CD*	30		1
16 Aug 97	ANTHEM *Mushroom MUSH 6CD*	21		1
18 Oct 97	URGE *Mushroom MUSH 14CD*	26		1
12 Oct 02	VANILLA RADIO *Round/Snapper SMASCD 048X*	26		1
1 Feb 03	STORMY IN THE NORTH KARMA IN THE SOUTH *Snapper Music SMASCD 049X*	17		1
24 May 03	SO INTO YOU *Gut CXGUT 49*	22		1
15 Nov 03	TOP OF THE WORLD *Gut CXGUT 54*	26		1

WILEY UK rapper

Date	Title / Label	Peak Position	Weeks at No.1	Weeks in Top 40
17 Apr 04	WOT DO U CALL IT? *XL Recordings XLS179CD*	31		1
21 Aug 04	PIES *XL Recordings XLS188CD*	45		

JONATHAN WILKES UK singer

Date	Title / Label	Peak Position	Weeks at No.1	Weeks in Top 40
17 Mar 01	JUST ANOTHER DAY *Innocent SINCD 25*	24		1

SUE WILKINSON UK singer

Date	Title / Label	Peak Position	Weeks at No.1	Weeks in Top 40
2 Aug 80	YOU GOTTA BE A HUSTLER IF YOU WANNA GET ON *Cheapskate CHEAP 2*	25		6

WILL.I.AM US singer

Date	Title	Peak Position	Weeks at No.1	Weeks in Top 40
11 Mar 06	**BEEP** *A&M 9852860* PUSSYCAT DOLLS FEATURING WILL.I.AM	2		11
3 Feb 07	**HIP HOP IS DEAD** *Def Jam 1721323* NAS FEATURING WILL.I.AM	35		1
22 Sep 07	**I GOT IT FROM MY MAMA** *Interscope 1747759*	38		1
20 Oct 07	**BABY LOVE** *Polydor 1753014* NICOLE SCHERZINGER FEATURING WILL.I.AM	14		7
2 Feb 08	**THE GIRL IS MINE** *Epic 88697226202* MICHAEL JACKSON FEATURING WILL.I.AM	32		1
29 Mar 08	**HEARTBREAKER** *Download*	74		

WILL TO POWER US group

Date	Title	Peak Position	Weeks at No.1	Weeks in Top 40
7 Jan 89	**BABY I LOVE YOUR WAY – FREEBIRD** *Epic 6530947* ★	6		8
22 Dec 90	**I'M NOT IN LOVE** *Epic 6565377*	29		3

ALYSON WILLIAMS US singer

Date	Title	Peak Position	Weeks at No.1	Weeks in Top 40
4 Mar 89	**SLEEP TALK** *Def Jam 6546567*	17		6
6 May 89	**MY LOVE IS SO RAW** *Def Jam 6548987* ALYSON WILLIAMS FEATURING NIKKI D	34		2
19 Aug 89	**I NEED YOUR LOVIN'** *Def Jam 6551437*	8		9
18 Nov 89	**I SECOND THAT EMOTION** *Def Jam 6554567* ALYSON WILLIAMS WITH CHUCK STANLEY	44		

ANDY WILLIAMS US singer

Date	Title	Peak Position	Weeks at No.1	Weeks in Top 40
19 Apr 57	**BUTTERFLY** *London HLA 8399* ★	1	2	16
21 Jun 57	**I LIKE YOUR KIND OF LOVE** *London HLA 8437*	16		10
14 Jun 62	**STRANGER ON THE SHORE** *CBS AAG 103*	30		5
21 Mar 63	**CAN'T GET USED TO LOSING YOU** *CBS AAG 138*	2		16
27 Feb 64	**A FOOL NEVER LEARNS** *CBS AAG 182*	40		1
16 Sep 65	**ALMOST THERE** *CBS 201813*	2		16
24 Feb 66	**MAY EACH DAY** *CBS 202042*	19		6
22 Sep 66	**IN THE ARMS OF LOVE** *CBS 202300*	33		6
4 May 67	**MUSIC TO WATCH GIRLS BY** *CBS 2675*	33		5
2 Aug 67	**MORE AND MORE** *CBS 2886*	45		
13 Mar 68	**CAN'T TAKE MY EYES OFF YOU** *CBS 3298*	5		14
7 May 69	**HAPPY HEART** *CBS 4062*	19		9
14 Mar 70	**CAN'T HELP FALLING IN LOVE** *CBS 4818*	3		13
1 Aug 70	**IT'S SO EASY** *CBS 5113*	13		10
21 Nov 70	**HOME LOVIN' MAN** *CBS 5267*	7		10
20 Mar 71	**(WHERE DO I BEGIN) LOVE STORY** *CBS 7020*	4		15
5 Aug 72	**LOVE THEME FROM *THE GODFATHER* (SPEAK SOFTLY LOVE)** *CBS 8166*	42		
8 Dec 73	**SOLITAIRE** *CBS 1824*	4		13
18 May 74	**GETTING OVER YOU** *CBS 2181*	35		2
31 May 75	**YOU LAY SO EASY ON MY MIND** *CBS 3167*	32		3
6 Mar 76	**THE OTHER SIDE OF ME** *CBS 3903*	42		
27 Mar 99	**MUSIC TO WATCH GIRLS BY** *Columbia 6671322*	9		3
29 Jun 02	**CAN'T TAKE MY EYES OFF YOU** *Columbia 6721052* ANDY WILLIAMS & DENISE VAN OUTEN	23		2
8 Dec 07	**IT'S THE MOST WONDERFUL TIME OF THE YEAR** *Sony BMG 88697207452*	21		3

ANDY & DAVID WILLIAMS US duo

Date	Title	Peak Position	Weeks at No.1	Weeks in Top 40
24 Mar 73	**I DON'T KNOW WHY** *MCA MUS 1183*	37		2

BILLY WILLIAMS US singer

Date	Title	Peak Position	Weeks at No.1	Weeks in Top 40
2 Aug 57	**I'M GONNA SIT RIGHT DOWN AND WRITE MYSELF A LETTER** *Vogue Coral Q 72266*	22		9

DANNY WILLIAMS UK singer

Date	Title	Peak Position	Weeks at No.1	Weeks in Top 40
25 May 61	**WE WILL NEVER BE THIS YOUNG AGAIN** *HMV POP 839*	44		
6 Jul 61	**THE MIRACLE OF YOU** *HMV POP 885*	41		
2 Nov 61	**MOON RIVER** *HMV POP 932*	1	2	17
18 Jan 62	**JEANNIE** *HMV POP 968*	14		11
12 Apr 62	**WONDERFUL WORLD OF THE YOUNG** *HMV POP 1002*	8		12
5 Jul 62	**TEARS** *HMV POP 1035*	22		6
28 Feb 63	**MY OWN TRUE LOVE** *HMV POP 1112*	45		
30 Jul 77	**DANCIN' EASY** *Ensign ENY 3*	30		5

DENIECE WILLIAMS US singer

Date	Title	Peak Position	Weeks at No.1	Weeks in Top 40
2 Apr 77	**FREE** *CBS 4978* ●	1	2	10
30 Jul 77	**THAT'S WHAT FRIENDS ARE FOR** *CBS 5432* ●	8		10
12 Nov 77	**BABY BABY MY LOVE'S ALL FOR YOU** *CBS 5779*	32		3
25 Mar 78	**TOO MUCH TOO LITTLE TOO LATE** *CBS 6164* JOHNNY MATHIS & DENIECE WILLIAMS ★	3		12
29 Jul 78	**YOU'RE ALL I NEED TO GET BY** *CBS 6483* JOHNNY MATHIS & DENIECE WILLIAMS	45		
5 May 84	**LET'S HEAR IT FOR THE BOY** *CBS A 4319* ● ★	2		9

DIANA WILLIAMS US singer

Date	Title	Peak Position	Weeks at No.1	Weeks in Top 40
25 Jul 81	**TEDDY BEAR'S LAST RIDE** *Capitol CL 207*	54		

DON WILLIAMS US singer

Date	Title	Peak Position	Weeks at No.1	Weeks in Top 40
19 Jun 76	**I RECALL A GYPSY WOMAN** *ABC 4098*	13		9
23 Oct 76	**YOU'RE MY BEST FRIEND** *ABC 4144*	35		2

ERIC WILLIAMS US singer

Date	Title	Peak Position	Weeks at No.1	Weeks in Top 40
9 May 98	**ALL MY LOVE** *Interscope IND 95584* QUEEN PEN FEATURING ERIC WILLIAMS	11		4
13 Jun 98	**DO FOR LOVE** *Jive 0518512* 2PAC FEATURING ERIC WILLIAMS	12		3

FREEDOM WILLIAMS US rapper

Date	Title	Peak Position	Weeks at No.1	Weeks in Top 40
15 Dec 90	**GONNA MAKE YOU SWEAT (EVERYBODY DANCE NOW)** *CBS 6564540* C & C MUSIC FACTORY (FEATURING FREEDOM WILLIAMS) ★	3		11
30 Mar 91	**HERE WE GO** *Columbia 6567557* C & C MUSIC FACTORY (FEATURING FREEDOM WILLIAMS)	20		5
6 Jul 91	**THINGS THAT MAKE YOU GO HMMM** *Columbia 6566907* C & C MUSIC FACTORY (FEATURING FREEDOM WILLIAMS)	4		10
5 Jun 93	**VOICE OF FREEDOM** *Columbia 6593342*	62		

GEOFFREY WILLIAMS UK R&B singer

Date	Title	Peak Position	Weeks at No.1	Weeks in Top 40
11 Apr 92	**IT'S NOT A LOVE THING** *EMI EM 228*	63		
22 Aug 92	**SUMMER BREEZE** *EMI EM 245*	56		
18 Jan 97	**DRIVE** *Hands On CDHOR 11*	52		
19 Apr 97	**SEX LIFE** *Hands On CDHOR 12*	71		

IRIS WILLIAMS UK singer

Date	Title	Peak Position	Weeks at No.1	Weeks in Top 40
27 Oct 79	**HE WAS BEAUTIFUL (CAVATINA) (THE THEME FROM *THE DEER HUNTER*)** *Columbia DB 9070*	18		5

JOHN WILLIAMS Australian guitarist

Date	Title	Peak Position	Weeks at No.1	Weeks in Top 40
19 May 79	**CAVATINA** *Cube BUG 80*	13		7

JOHN WILLIAMS US orchestra leader

Date	Title	Peak Position	Weeks at No.1	Weeks in Top 40
18 Dec 82	**THEME FROM *E.T. (THE EXTRA-TERRESTRIAL)*** *MCA 800*	17		6
14 Aug 93	**THEME FROM *JURASSIC PARK*** *MCA MCSTD 1927*	45		
4 Jun 05	**BATTLE OF THE HEROES – *STAR WARS*** *Sony Classical 6759562* JOHN WILLIAMS & THE LSO	25		1

KENNY WILLIAMS US singer

Date	Title	Peak Position	Weeks at No.1	Weeks in Top 40
19 Nov 77	**(YOU'RE) FABULOUS BABE** *Decca FR 13731*	35		3

LARRY WILLIAMS US singer

Date	Title	Peak Position	Weeks at No.1	Weeks in Top 40
20 Sep 57	**SHORT FAT FANNY** *London HLN 8472*	21		8
17 Jan 58	**BONY MORONIE** *London HLU 8532*	11		10

LENNY WILLIAMS US singer

Date	Title	Peak Position	Weeks at No.1	Weeks in Top 40
5 Nov 77	**SHOO DOO FU FU OOH** *ABC 4194*	38		2
16 Sep 78	**YOU GOT ME BURNING** *ABC 4228*	67		

MASON WILLIAMS US guitarist

Date	Title	Peak Position	Weeks at No.1	Weeks in Top 40
28 Aug 68	**CLASSICAL GAS** *Warner Brothers WB 7190*	9		12

Key: ○ Silver-selling · ● Gold-selling · ⊛ Platinum-selling · ★ US No.1 · Peak Position · Weeks at No.1 · Weeks in Top 40

MAURICE WILLIAMS & THE ZODIACS US group

Date	Title / Label	Peak Position	Weeks at No.1	Weeks in Top 40
5 Jan 61	**STAY** *Top Rank JAR 526* ★	14		9

MELANIE WILLIAMS UK singer

Date	Title / Label	Peak Position	Weeks at No.1	Weeks in Top 40
10 Apr 93	**AIN'T NO LOVE (AIN'T NO USE)** *Rob's CDROB 9* SUB SUB FEATURING MELANIE WILLIAMS ○	3		9
9 Apr 94	**ALL CRIED OUT** *Columbia 6601872*	60		
11 Jun 94	**EVERYDAY THANG** *Columbia 6604712*	38		1
17 Sep 94	**NOT ENOUGH** *Columbia 6607752*	65		
18 Feb 95	**YOU ARE EVERYTHING** *Columbia 6611755* MELANIE WILLIAMS & JOE ROBERTS	28		2

ROBBIE WILLIAMS UK singer

Date	Title / Label	Peak Position	Weeks at No.1	Weeks in Top 40
10 Aug 96	**FREEDOM** *Chrysalis CDFREE 1* ○	2		4
26 Apr 97	**OLD BEFORE I DIE** *Chrysalis CDCHS 5055*	2		4
26 Jul 97	**LAZY DAYS** *Chrysalis CDCHS 5063*	8		3
27 Sep 97	**SOUTH OF THE BORDER** *Chrysalis CDCHS 5068*	14		2
13 Dec 97	**ANGELS** *Chrysalis CDCHS 5072* ⊛	4		17
28 Mar 98	**LET ME ENTERTAIN YOU** *Chrysalis CDCHSS 5080* ○	3		7
19 Sep 98	**MILLENNIUM** *Chrysalis CDCHS 5099* ●	1	1	9
12 Dec 98	**NO REGRETS** *Chrysalis CDCHS 5100*	4		10
27 Mar 99	**STRONG** *Chrysalis CDCHS 5107*	4		6
20 Nov 99	**SHE'S THE ONE/IT'S ONLY US** *Chrysalis CDCHS 5112* ●	1	1	11
12 Aug 00	**ROCK DJ** *Chrysalis CDCHS 5118* ⊛	1	1	11
21 Oct 00	**KIDS** *Chrysalis CDCHSS 5119* ROBBIE WILLIAMS & KYLIE MINOGUE ○	2		10
23 Dec 00	**SUPREME** *Chrysalis CDCHSS 5120*	4		6
21 Apr 01	**LET LOVE BE YOUR ENERGY** *Chrysalis CDCHS 5124*	10		3
21 Jul 01	**ETERNITY/THE ROAD TO MANDALAY** *Chrysalis CDCHS 5126*	1	2	10
22 Dec 01	**SOMETHIN' STUPID** *Chrysalis CDCHS 5132* ROBBIE WILLIAMS & NICOLE KIDMAN ○	1	3	10
20 Apr 02	**MY CULTURE** *Palm Pictures PPCD 70732* 1 GIANT LEAP FEATURING MAXI JAZZ & ROBBIE WILLIAMS	9		4
14 Dec 02	**FEEL** *Chrysalis CDCHS 5150*	4		11
26 Apr 03	**COME UNDONE** *Chrysalis CDCHS 5151*	4		6
9 Aug 03	**SOMETHING BEAUTIFUL** *Chrysalis CDCHS 5152*	3		6
15 Nov 03	**SEXED UP** *Chrysalis CDCHS 5153*	10		3
16 Oct 04	**RADIO** *Chrysalis CDCHSS 5156*	1	1	6
18 Dec 04	**MISUNDERSTOOD** *Chrysalis CDCHSS 5157*	8		5
15 Oct 05	**TRIPPING** *Chrysalis CDCHSS5158*	2		11
24 Dec 05	**ADVERTISING SPACE** *Chrysalis CDCHSS5159*	8		5
3 Jun 06	**SIN SIN SIN** *Chrysalis CDCHS5160*	22		1
9 Sep 06	**RUDEBOX** *Chrysalis CDCHS5161*	4		6
18 Nov 06	**LOVELIGHT** *Chrysalis CDCHS5162*	8		5
17 Mar 07	**SHE'S MADONNA** *Chrysalis CDCHS5163* ROBBIE WILLIAMS & PET SHOP BOYS	16		2

VANESSA WILLIAMS US singer

Date	Title / Label	Peak Position	Weeks at No.1	Weeks in Top 40
20 Aug 88	**THE RIGHT STUFF** *Wing 3*	71		
25 Mar 89	**DREAMIN'** *Wing 4*	74		
19 Aug 89	**THE RIGHT STUFF (REMIX)** *Wing WINR 3*	62		
21 Mar 92	**SAVE THE BEST FOR LAST** *Polydor PO 192* ★	3		9
8 Apr 95	**THE SWEETEST DAYS** *Mercury MERCD 422*	41		
8 Jul 95	**THE WAY THAT YOU LOVE ME** *Mercury MERCD 439*	52		
16 Sep 95	**COLOURS OF THE WIND** *Walt Disney WD 7677CD*	21		2

VESTA WILLIAMS US singer

Date	Title / Label	Peak Position	Weeks at No.1	Weeks in Top 40
20 Dec 86	**ONCE BITTEN TWICE SHY** *A&M AM 362*	14		7

WENDELL WILLIAMS US singer

Date	Title / Label	Peak Position	Weeks at No.1	Weeks in Top 40
6 Oct 90	**EVERYBODY (RAP)** *Deconstruction PB 44701* CRIMINAL ELEMENT ORCHESTRA & WENDELL WILLIAMS	30		2
18 May 91	**SO GROOVY** *Deconstruction PB 44567*	74		

BRUCE WILLIS US actor

Date	Title / Label	Peak Position	Weeks at No.1	Weeks in Top 40
7 Mar 87	**RESPECT YOURSELF** *Motown ZB 41117*	7		8
30 May 87	**UNDER THE BOARDWALK** *Motown ZB 41349* ○	2		13
12 Sep 87	**SECRET AGENT MAN – JAMES BOND IS BACK** *Motown ZB 41437*	43		
23 Jan 88	**COMIN' RIGHT UP** *Motown ZB 41453*	73		

MATT WILLIS UK singer/bass player

Date	Title / Label	Peak Position	Weeks at No.1	Weeks in Top 40
27 May 06	**UP ALL NIGHT** *Mercury 9858520*	7		2
26 Aug 06	**HEY KID** *Mercury 1705075*	11		2
16 Dec 06	**DON'T LET IT GO TO WASTE** *Mercury 1713567*	19		2
28 Apr 07	**CRASH** *Mercury 1729795*	31		1

VIOLA WILLS US singer

Date	Title / Label	Peak Position	Weeks at No.1	Weeks in Top 40
6 Oct 79	**GONNA GET ALONG WITHOUT YOU NOW** *Ariola/Hansa AHA 546* ○	8		7
15 Mar 86	**BOTH SIDES NOW/DARE TO DREAM** *Streetwave KHAN 66*	35		3

MARIA WILLSON UK singer

Date	Title / Label	Peak Position	Weeks at No.1	Weeks in Top 40
9 Aug 03	**CHOOZA LOOZA** *Telstar CDSTAS 3343*	29		1
1 Nov 03	**MR ALIBI** *Telstar CDSTAS 3355*	43		

AL WILSON US singer/drummer

Date	Title / Label	Peak Position	Weeks at No.1	Weeks in Top 40
23 Aug 75	**THE SNAKE** *Bell 1436*	41		

BRIAN WILSON US singer

Date	Title / Label	Peak Position	Weeks at No.1	Weeks in Top 40
2 Oct 04	**WONDERFUL** *Must Destroy MDA001X*	29		1
18 Dec 04	**GOOD VIBRATIONS** *Nonesuch NS001CD*	30		1
17 Dec 05	**WHAT I REALLY WANT FOR CHRISTMAS** *Arista 82876764802*	66		

CHARLIE WILSON US singer

Date	Title / Label	Peak Position	Weeks at No.1	Weeks in Top 40
14 Dec 96	**SNOOP'S UPSIDE YA HEAD** *Interscope IND 95520* SNOOP DOGGY DOGG FEATURING CHARLIE WILSON	12		5
7 May 05	**SIGNS** *Geffen 9881782* SNOOP DOGG FEATURING CHARLIE WILSON & JUSTIN TIMBERLAKE	2		10

DOOLEY WILSON US singer/actor

Date	Title / Label	Peak Position	Weeks at No.1	Weeks in Top 40
3 Dec 77	**AS TIME GOES BY** *United Artists UP 36331*	15		6

GRETCHEN WILSON US singer

Date	Title / Label	Peak Position	Weeks at No.1	Weeks in Top 40
4 Sep 04	**REDNECK WOMAN** *Epic 6751732*	42		

JACKIE WILSON US singer

Date	Title / Label	Peak Position	Weeks at No.1	Weeks in Top 40
15 Nov 57	**REET PETITE (THE SWEETEST GIRL IN TOWN)** *Coral Q 72290*	6		14
14 Mar 58	**TO BE LOVED** *Coral Q 72306*	23		8
15 Sep 60	**(YOU WERE MADE FOR) ALL MY LOVE** *Coral Q 72407*	33		1
22 Dec 60	**ALONE AT LAST** *Coral Q 72412*	50		
14 May 69	**(YOUR LOVE KEEPS LIFTING ME) HIGHER AND HIGHER** *MCA BAG 2*	11		9
29 Jul 72	**I GET THE SWEETEST FEELING** *MCA MU 1160*	9		11
3 May 75	**I GET THE SWEETEST FEELING/(YOUR LOVE KEEPS LIFTING ME) HIGHER AND HIGHER** *Brunswick BR 18*	25		6
29 Nov 86	**REET PETITE (THE SWEETEST GIRL IN TOWN)** *SMP SKM 3* ●	1	4	13
28 Feb 87	**I GET THE SWEETEST FEELING** *SMP SKM 1* ○	3		9
4 Jul 87	**(YOUR LOVE KEEPS LIFTING ME) HIGHER AND HIGHER** *SMP SKM 10*	15		5

MARI WILSON UK singer

Date	Title / Label	Peak Position	Weeks at No.1	Weeks in Top 40
6 Mar 82	**BEAT THE BEAT** *Compact PINK 2*	59		
8 May 82	**BABY IT'S TRUE** *Compact PINK 3*	42		
11 Sep 82	**JUST WHAT I ALWAYS WANTED** *Compact PINK 4*	8		8
13 Nov 82	**(BEWARE) BOYFRIEND** *Compact PINK 5*	51		
19 Mar 83	**CRY ME A RIVER** *Compact PINK 6*	27		5
11 Jun 83	**WONDERFUL** *Compact PINK 7*	47		

MERI WILSON US singer

Date	Title / Label	Peak Position	Weeks at No.1	Weeks in Top 40
27 Aug 77	**TELEPHONE MAN** *Pye International 7N 25747* ○	6		9

MIKE 'HITMAN' WILSON US producer

Date	Title / Label	Peak Position	Weeks at No.1	Weeks in Top 40
22 Sep 90	**ANOTHER SLEEPLESS NIGHT** *Arista 113506* MIKE 'HITMAN' WILSON FEATURING SHAWN CHRISTOPHER	74		

TONY WILSON

He couldn't – to the best of anyone's knowledge – sing. He didn't know his way around a recording studio. He didn't write songs. He didn't mix and he couldn't dance. Yet during the 1980s and 1990s Tony Wilson was one of the most influential and recognisable figures in the music charts (and industry) and his musical judgements are as apparent in today's charts as they were thirty years ago.

'Mr Manchester', as he became known, was actually born in the neighbouring city of Salford on 20 February 1950. He went to Cambridge before getting his break into television at Independent Television News (ITN) in London. But a return to the north-west of England and a job at Granada Television in Manchester would shape Wilson's future. His day job was as a roving news reporter, but his forte was presenting the provocative music ands arts show *So It Goes*. After seeing The Sex Pistols at Manchester's Lesser Free Trade Hall in 1976, in September Wilson cajoled his bosses into putting the band on television for the first time The Pistols performed 'Anarchy In The UK', trashed the set and entered the public consciousness. 'Anarchy' entered the Top 40 three months later. How many bands have been influenced by The Pistols? How many owe Wilson a debt of thanks for seeing their potential?

When *So It Goes* was taken off air after a profanity-strewn performance by Iggy Pop, Wilson decided to release music himself via his own label, Factory Records. The label had far more misses than hits, even letting acts like Orchestral Manoeuvres In The Dark and James slip through their fingers to enjoy major success elsewhere. However, an early Wilson discovery was Joy Division, four young men from Salford and Macclesfield, whose early punk leanings were soon put aside in favour of a starker, more brooding sheen influenced by various underground pioneers such as Kraftwerk. Initial releases were swamped with critical praise from the weekly music press but failed to cross over to the mainstream and trouble the chart compilers. When lead singer Ian Curtis took his own life in May 1980, the wave of disbelief – along with a beautiful melody – took their single 'Love Will Tear Us Apart' to Number 13 in the charts a month later. Joy Division's influence has since reached global proportions with everyone from Editors to Interpol using their post-punk blueprint to tremendous commercial – and chart – appeal.

The money generated by the single would be ploughed into the next Factory venture, a nightclub housed in a former Manchester yacht showroom. The result was The Haçienda, a playful mix of gig venue and arts centre that would require a great deal more cash to keep its doors open once the initial novelty value wore off. That money was provided by the band that grew from the remains of Joy Division: New Order. With guitarist Bernard Sumner now installed as lead singer, that band started a run of hits in March 1981 with 'Ceremony', which charted at Number 34. But it would be their immersion in dance with 'Blue Monday' that would unite the usually antagonistic worlds of rock and dance. The single, with its loping beat and shuddering synthesiser riff, would prove to be an unstoppable seller, becoming the biggest-selling 12-inch single in UK chart history. It's claimed that the sleeve for 'Blue Monday' – designed by Factory's in-house taste-maker Peter Saville – was so elaborate that the label lost money every time a copy was sold. The ubiquity of this story shows one of two things: either that Factory's insistence on aesthetics over commercial considerations was unshakable, or that Wilson had a winning way with a good tale. Either way, enough money was squeezed out of the song to keep The Haçienda's doors open until the world caught up with its lofty design and ambitions. Dance music, DJ culture and ecstasy would make Wilson's club the centre of the music universe by the late 1980s. Factory's third major success, Happy Mondays, provided the perfect soundtrack. Madchester was in the house, Wilson was at its hedonistic helm and the city and its music became omnipresent. New Order even scored their first Number 1 with the world's 'least worst' football song 'World In Motion'.

Things would never quite be the same after the club's closure in 1997 following problems with drugs and gang culture: New Order finally returned from a lengthy sabbatical before the departure of bass player Peter Hook brought them effectively to an end in 2006; Happy Mondays split and then re-formed, ever the unpredictable mavericks; Ian Curtis's grim story was immortalised in the film *Control* in 2007. Wilson's expansive character has also been the basis of a film: in *24-Hour Party People* comic actor Steve Coogan played Wilson as wide-eyed enthusiast, eager to be part of the next big thing, be it punk or rave.

Tony Wilson died from a heart attack after lengthy cancer treatment in August 2007. He introduced Britain's television viewers to punk rock. He discovered one of the UK's most revered bands. He helped nurture the dance boom of the 1980s. He also gave away most of the proceeds from the biggest-selling 12-inch single of alltime. 'Youth cultural revolutions', Wilson once told the author David Nolan, 'to me they are the most wonderful things.' Tony Wilson was a professional enthusiast. He changed the face of music and the world has been a rather duller place since he left it.

AMY WINEHOUSE

In recent times, few artists have captivated the tabloids and *Heat*-reading celebrity-obsessed generation like Amy Winehouse. Sadly, this is more for her tempestuous life rather than her spectacular talent. But before any (inevitable and necessary) summary of her 'highs' and lows, it is worth dwelling for a moment on the rather postmodern amalgam of influences, looks, sounds and themes that her remarkable talent captures.

Her early years (she is still only twenty-four at the time of writing) were relatively unremarkable, at least compared to her latter-day hell-raising antics. The middle-class Jewish daughter of a pharmacist and a taxi driver, Amy was a handful at school, expelled from the renowned Sylvia Young academy for apathy and piercing her own nose – a little wild perhaps, but hardly tabloid fodder.

Her debut album *Frank* – which she now effectively disowns – was a modest success and even secured a Mercury Award nomination, but was merely a nod towards the maelstrom of material gestating in her increasingly volatile mind. Amy made a name for herself for being outspoken, and her wit and cutting tongue did nothing if not signal the arrival of a sharp personality possessed of a mighty voice.

However, it was with the release of the six-times-platinum album *Back To Black* that Amy Winehouse propelled herself into the stratosphere of British music greats. The lead single, 'Rehab' started the deluge, and the subsequent volley of stunning singles such as 'You Know I'm No Good' and 'Love Is A Losing Game' reignited sales of the album month after month. She was later nominated for six Grammys, winning five, a staggering performance.

The sound of her voice is truly electrifying – at once sending the listener back to the smoky jazz clubs of Ella Fitzgerald, passing through the recording booths of Sarah Vaughan and Dinah Washington, slipping across to the improvisational jams of James Taylor and the rich beauty of Carole King, yet somehow simultaneously placing Amy very much at the forefront of post-millennial musical innovation. When she piles her hair up in that famous black beehive, errant strands tumbling down over her tattooed shoulders, we recall an icon of the past, her voice a classic from another life, yet she sings of subjects that are all too modern. It's a compelling mix. Hers is a stunning contrast of seemingly oppositional traits, yet somehow the sum is mightier even than the not inconsiderable parts. Amy Winehouse is, arguably, the greatest female voice of her generation.

There are several key moments in her singles history of note – perhaps most oddly her highest-profile hit is as guest vocalist on Mark Ronson's 'Valerie', itself a remix of the The Zuton's 2006 number (Ronson had co-produced *Back To Black*). The lush production and technically acrobatic vocal performance from Winehouse saw the song as one of the biggest singles for years, easily outselling the original in reaching Number 2 (its sales to date are near 500,000 while the original Zutons track sold just 150,000). Elsewhere, her totem hit, 'Rehab' remains a brilliantly characterful song, but it seems it will be forever overshadowed by the poignancy of her subsequent abuse issues.

Her singing is the vocal expression of a musically educated brain – maybe this is why it is so frustrating to see her lifestyle spiralling seemingly out of control. In her own words, she explained the disparity between the health/wealth/wisdom of Amy on *Frank* and her second album as being down to the fact 'I started drinking and I fell in love.'

If you look at photos of Amy during the *Frank* era, you will see a beautiful young woman in peak health who is, to be blunt, unrecognisable from the Amy Winehouse of today who famously falls out of pubs/hits by-standers/gets arrested etc. Countless tabloid column inches have already questioned her life expectancy and lifestyle habits, so there's no point repeating them here – not least because that's the point about Amy Winehouse and the media: we've read all about her already. There is no foil, no shield, no bubble. Never before has a celebrity seemed to care so little about what she shows to the world at large.

Of course, Amy is responsible for her own decisions – an undeniable if uncomfortable truth – but while Leona Lewis was conquering the US charts and becoming Britain's first Number 1 female artist in the world's biggest music territory for the best part of two decades, the public seemed more concerned about what was happening in Amy's life. One tabloid ran a single column of only several hundred words about Leona's quite remarkable feat in the US, crammed in the corner of a double-page splash about Amy Winehouse's latest shocking escapades. Ironically, Amy herself has been welcomed by the music literati in America and seems capable of replicating Lewis's phenomenal success, but her drug use may yet scupper her chances in a country where customs legislation is notoriously puritanical.

But despite the chaotic headlines, the court appearances and so on – or perhaps *because* of those factors – when you hear her lyrics, they seem to mirror the harsh glare of her exposed public profile. When she sings about rehab, we know it is not a rock star's posturings. The pain in her voice is not an effect born out of drama school. And all of this is, of course, expressed, played out and documented in the papers. Hers is a life lived through a lens, indeed.

Silver-selling · Gold-selling · Platinum-selling · US No.1 ★ · Peak Position · Weeks at No.1 · Weeks in Top 40

TOM WILSON UK producer

Date	Title	Peak Position	Weeks at No.1	Weeks in Top 40
2 Dec 95	**TECHNOCAT** *Pukka CDPUKKA 4* TECHNOCAT FEATURING TOM WILSON	33		1
16 Mar 96	**LET YOUR BODY GO** *Clubscene DCSRT 050*	60		

VICTORIA WILSON JAMES US singer

Date	Title	Peak Position	Weeks at No.1	Weeks in Top 40
9 Aug 97	**REACH 4 THE MELODY** *Sony S3 VWJCD1*	72		

WILSON PHILLIPS US group

Date	Title	Peak Position	Weeks at No.1	Weeks in Top 40
26 May 90	**HOLD ON** *SBK 6* ★	6		10
18 Aug 90	**RELEASE ME** *SBK 11* ★	36		4
10 Nov 90	**IMPULSIVE** *SBK 16*	42		
11 May 91	**YOU'RE IN LOVE** *SBK 25* ★	29		3
23 May 92	**YOU WON'T SEE ME CRY** *SBK 34*	18		4
22 Aug 92	**GIVE IT UP** *SBK 36*	36		1

WILT Irish group

Date	Title	Peak Position	Weeks at No.1	Weeks in Top 40
8 Apr 00	**RADIO DISCO** *Mushroom MUSH 71CDS*	56		
8 Jul 00	**OPEN ARMS** *Mushroom MUSH 75CDS*	59		
13 Jul 02	**DISTORTION** *Mushroom MUSH 103CDS*	66		

W.I.P. UK production group

Date	Title	Peak Position	Weeks at No.1	Weeks in Top 40
16 Feb 02	**I WON'T LET YOU DOWN** *Decode/Telstar CDSTAS 3210* W.I.P. FEATURING EMMIE	53		

WIMBLEDON CHORAL SOCIETY UK vocal choir

Date	Title	Peak Position	Weeks at No.1	Weeks in Top 40
4 Jul 98	**WORLD CUP '98 – PAVANE** *Telstar CDSTAS 2979*	26		4
12 Dec 98	**IF – READ TO FAURE'S 'PAVANNE'** *BBC Worldwide WMSS 60062* DES LYNAM FEATURING WIMBLEDON CHORAL SOCIETY	45		

WIN UK group

Date	Title	Peak Position	Weeks at No.1	Weeks in Top 40
4 Apr 87	**SUPER POPOID GROOVE** *Swamplands LON 128*	63		

WINANS US group

Date	Title	Peak Position	Weeks at No.1	Weeks in Top 40
30 Nov 85	**LET MY PEOPLE GO (PART 1)** *Qwest W 8874*	71		

MARIO WINANS US singer

Date	Title	Peak Position	Weeks at No.1	Weeks in Top 40
20 Nov 99	**BEST FRIEND** *Puff Daddy 74321712312* PUFF DADDY FEATURING MARIO WINANS	24		3
5 Jun 04	**I DON'T WANNA KNOW (IMPORT)** *Universal 9862372PMI* MARIO WINANS FEATURING ENYA & P DIDDY	71		
12 Jun 04	**I DON'T WANNA KNOW** *Bad Boy MCSTD40369* MARIO WINANS FEATURING ENYA & P DIDDY	1	1	12
11 Sep 04	**NEVER REALLY WAS** *Bad Boy MCSTD40372* MARIO WINANS FEATURING LIL' FLIP	44		
8 Sep 07	**THROUGH THE PAIN (SHE TOLD ME)** *Bad Boy AT0283CD* P DIDDY FEATURING MARIO WINANS	50		

WINDJAMMER US group

Date	Title	Peak Position	Weeks at No.1	Weeks in Top 40
30 Jun 84	**TOSSING AND TURNING** *MCA 897*	18		7

BARBARA WINDSOR & MIKE REID UK actors

Date	Title	Peak Position	Weeks at No.1	Weeks in Top 40
24 Apr 99	**THE MORE I SEE YOU** *Telstar CDSTAS 3049*	46		

AMY WINEHOUSE UK singer

Date	Title	Peak Position	Weeks at No.1	Weeks in Top 40
18 Oct 03	**STRONGER THAN ME** *Island CID 830*	71		
24 Jan 04	**TAKE THE BOX** *Island CID 840*	57		
17 Apr 04	**IN MY BED/YOU SENT ME FLYING** *Island CID 852*	60		
4 Sep 04	**PUMPS/HELP YOURSELF** *Island CID 865*	69		
28 Oct 06	**REHAB** *Island 1709534*	7		20
13 Jan 07	**YOU KNOW I'M NO GOOD** *Island 1720848*	18		5
14 Apr 07	**BACK TO BLACK** *Island/Uni-Island 1732325*	25		6
4 Aug 07	**TEARS DRY ON THEIR OWN** *Island 1744544*	16		10
29 Sep 07	**VALERIE** *Columbia 88697186332* MARK RONSON FEATURING AMY WINEHOUSE	2		26
13 Oct 07	**VALERIE** *Download*	37		1
22 Dec 07	**LOVE IS A LOSING GAME** *Island 1755398*	46		

WING & A PRAYER FIFE & DRUM CORPS US group

Date	Title	Peak Position	Weeks at No.1	Weeks in Top 40
24 Jan 76	**BABY FACE** *Atlantic K 10705*	12		7

WINGER US group

Date	Title	Peak Position	Weeks at No.1	Weeks in Top 40
19 Jan 91	**MILES AWAY** *Atlantic A 7802*	56		

PETE WINGFIELD UK singer

Date	Title	Peak Position	Weeks at No.1	Weeks in Top 40
28 Jun 75	**EIGHTEEN WITH A BULLET** *Island WIP 6231*	7		6

JOSH WINK US producer

Date	Title	Peak Position	Weeks at No.1	Weeks in Top 40
6 May 95	**DON'T LAUGH** *XL Recordings XLS 62CD* WINX	38		1
21 Oct 95	**HIGHER STATE OF CONSCIOUSNESS** *Manifesto FESCD 3*	8		?
2 Mar 96	**HYPNOTIZIN'** *XL Recordings XLS 71CD* WINX	35		1
27 Jul 96	**HIGHER STATE OF CONSCIOUSNESS '96 REMIXES** *Manifesto FESCD 9*	7		8
12 Aug 00	**HOW'S YOUR EVENING SO FAR** *ffrr FCD 384* JOSH WINK & LIL' LOUIS	23		1
11 Aug 07	**HIGHER STATE OF CONSCIOUSNESS** *Strictly Rhythm SR12640CDX*	70		

KATE WINSLET UK actress

Date	Title	Peak Position	Weeks at No.1	Weeks in Top 40
8 Dec 01	**WHAT IF** *EMI/Liberty CDKATE 001*	6		12

EDGAR WINTER GROUP US singer

Date	Title	Peak Position	Weeks at No.1	Weeks in Top 40
26 May 73	**FRANKENSTEIN** *Epic EPC 1440* ★	18		6

RUBY WINTERS US singer

Date	Title	Peak Position	Weeks at No.1	Weeks in Top 40
5 Nov 77	**I WILL** *Creole CR 141*	4		12
29 Apr 78	**COME TO ME** *Creole CR 153*	11		9
26 Aug 78	**I WON'T MENTION IT AGAIN** *Creole CR 160*	45		
16 Jun 79	**BABY LAY DOWN** *Creole CR 171*	43		

STEVE WINWOOD UK singer/multi-instrumentalist

Date	Title	Peak Position	Weeks at No.1	Weeks in Top 40
17 Jan 81	**WHILE YOU SEE A CHANCE** *Island WIP 6655*	45		
9 Oct 82	**VALERIE** *Island WIP 6818*	51		
28 Jun 86	**HIGHER LOVE** *Island IS 288* ★	13		7
13 Sep 86	**FREEDOM OVERSPILL** *Island IS 294*	69		
24 Jan 87	**BACK IN THE HIGH LIFE AGAIN** *Island IS 303*	53		
19 Sep 87	**VALERIE (REMIX)** *Island IS 336*	19		5
11 Jun 88	**ROLL WITH IT** *Virgin VS 1085* ★	53		

WIRE UK group

Date	Title	Peak Position	Weeks at No.1	Weeks in Top 40
27 Jan 79	**OUTDOOR MINER** *Harvest HAR 5172*	51		
13 May 89	**EARDRUM BUZZ** *Mute 87*	68		

NICKY WIRE UK bass player/singer

Date	Title	Peak Position	Weeks at No.1	Weeks in Top 40
30 Sep 06	**BREAK MY HEART SLOWLY** *Red Ink ENOLAD001*	74		

WIRED Dutch/Finnish duo

Date	Title	Peak Position	Weeks at No.1	Weeks in Top 40
20 Feb 99	**TRANSONIC** *Future Groove CDFGR 001*	73		

WIRELESS UK group

Date	Title	Peak Position	Weeks at No.1	Weeks in Top 40
28 Jun 97	**I NEED YOU** *Chrysalis CHCHS 5059*	68		
7 Feb 98	**IN LOVE WITH THE FAMILIAR** *Chrysalis CDCHS 5075*	69		

NORMAN WISDOM UK comedian/actor

Date	Title	Peak Position	Weeks at No.1	Weeks in Top 40
19 Feb 54	**DON'T LAUGH AT ME** *Columbia DB 3133*	3		15
15 Mar 57	**WISDOM OF A FOOL** *Columbia DB 3903*	13		5

Silver-selling ○ Gold-selling ● Platinum-selling ⊛ US No.1 ★ — Peak Position / Weeks at No.1 / Weeks in Top 40

WISDOME Italian group

Date	Title / Label	Peak Position	Weeks at No.1	Weeks in Top 40
11 Mar 00	**OFF THE WALL** *Positiva CDTIV 125*	33		1

WISEGUYS UK producer

Date	Title / Label	Peak Position	Weeks at No.1	Weeks in Top 40
6 Jun 98	**OOH LA LA** *Wall Of Sound WALLD 038*	55		
12 Sep 98	**START THE COMMOTION** *Wall Of Sound WALLD 044*	66		
5 Jun 99	**OOH LA LA** *Wall Of Sound WALLD 038X* ○	2		6
11 Sep 99	**START THE COMMOTION** *Wall Of Sound WALLD 059*	47		

BILL WITHERS US singer

Date	Title / Label	Peak Position	Weeks at No.1	Weeks in Top 40
12 Aug 72	**LEAN ON ME** *A&M AMS 7004* ★	18		8
14 Jan 78	**LOVELY DAY** *CBS 5773*	7		8
25 May 85	**OH YEAH!** *CBS A 6154*	60		
10 Sep 88	**LOVELY DAY (REMIX)** *CBS 6530017*	4		8

WITNESS UK group

Date	Title / Label	Peak Position	Weeks at No.1	Weeks in Top 40
13 Mar 99	**SCARS** *Island CID 740*	71		
19 Jun 99	**AUDITION** *Island CID 749*	71		

WIZZARD UK group

Date	Title / Label	Peak Position	Weeks at No.1	Weeks in Top 40
9 Dec 72	**BALL PARK INCIDENT** *Harvest HAR 5062*	6		10
21 Apr 73	**SEE MY BABY JIVE** *Harvest HAR 5070* ●	1	4	14
1 Sep 73	**ANGEL FINGERS** *Harvest HAR 5076* ○	1	1	9
8 Dec 73	**I WISH IT COULD BE CHRISTMAS EVERY DAY** *Harvest HAR 5079* WIZZARD FEATURING VOCAL BACKING BY THE SUEDETTES PLUS THE STOCKLAND GREEN BILATERAL SCHOOL FIRST YEAR CHOIR WITH ADDITIONAL NOISES BY MISS SNOB AND CLASS 3C ○	4		8
27 Apr 74	**ROCK 'N' ROLL WINTER** *Warner Brothers K 16357*	6		7
10 Aug 74	**THIS IS THE STORY OF MY LIFE (BABY)** *Warner Brothers K 16434*	34		3
21 Dec 74	**ARE YOU READY TO ROCK** *Warner Brothers K 16497*	8		7
19 Dec 81	**I WISH IT COULD BE CHRISTMAS EVERY DAY** *Harvest HAR 5173* WIZZARD FEATURING VOCAL BACKING BY THE SUEDETTES PLUS THE STOCKLAND GREEN BILATERAL SCHOOL FIRST YEAR CHOIR WITH ADDITIONAL NOISES BY MISS SNOB AND CLASS 3C	41		
15 Dec 84	**I WISH IT COULD BE CHRISTMAS EVERY DAY** *Harvest HAR 5173* WIZZARD FEATURING VOCAL BACKING BY THE SUEDETTES PLUS THE STOCKLAND GREEN BILATERAL SCHOOL FIRST YEAR CHOIR WITH ADDITIONAL NOISES BY MISS SNOB AND CLASS 3C	23		3
8 Dec 07	**I WISH IT COULD BE CHRISTMAS EVERY DAY** *Download*	16		3

ANDREW WK US singer

Date	Title / Label	Peak Position	Weeks at No.1	Weeks in Top 40
10 Nov 01	**PARTY HARD** *Mercury 5888132*	19		2
9 Mar 02	**SHE IS BEAUTIFUL** *Mercury 5889522*	55		

JAH WOBBLE'S INVADERS OF THE HEART

UK singer/multi-instrumentalist

Date	Title / Label	Peak Position	Weeks at No.1	Weeks in Top 40
1 Feb 92	**VISIONS OF YOU** *Oval 103*	35		2
30 Apr 94	**BECOMING MORE LIKE GOD** *Island CID 571*	36		1
25 Jun 94	**THE SUN DOES RISE** *Island CIDX 587* JAH WOBBLE'S INVADERS OF THE HEART FEATURING DOLORES FROM THE CRANBERRIES	41		

TERRY WOGAN Irish DJ

Date	Title / Label	Peak Position	Weeks at No.1	Weeks in Top 40
7 Jan 78	**FLORAL DANCE** *Philips 6006 592*	21		5

PATRICK WOLF Irish singer

Date	Title / Label	Peak Position	Weeks at No.1	Weeks in Top 40
12 Feb 05	**THE LIBERTINE** *Tomlab TOM46*	67		
21 Apr 07	**THE MAGIC POSITION** *A&M/Polydor 1726001*	69		

WOLFMAN UK singer

Date	Title / Label	Peak Position	Weeks at No.1	Weeks in Top 40
24 Apr 04	**FOR LOVERS** *Rough Trade RTRADSCD177* WOLFMAN FEATURING PETE DOHERTY	7		4
11 Dec 04	**NAPOLEON** *Beyond Bedlam BEBAD001CDS*	44		
4 Jun 05	**ICE CREAM GUERILLA** *Beyond Bedlam BEBAD002CDS*	60		

WOLFMOTHER Australian group

Date	Title / Label	Peak Position	Weeks at No.1	Weeks in Top 40
29 Apr 06	**DIMENSION** *Modular CID928*	49		
29 Jul 06	**WOMAN** *Modular CID933*	31		1
30 Sep 06	**LOVE TRAIN** *Modular 1707877*	62		
2 Dec 06	**JOKER & THE THIEF** *Island/Modular 1715494*	64		

WOLFSBANE UK group

Date	Title / Label	Peak Position	Weeks at No.1	Weeks in Top 40
5 Oct 91	**EZY** *Def American DEFA 11*	68		

BOBBY WOMACK US singer

Date	Title / Label	Peak Position	Weeks at No.1	Weeks in Top 40
16 Jun 84	**TELL ME WHY** *Motown TMG 1339*	60		
16 Feb 85	**(NO MATTER HOW HIGH I GET) I'LL STILL BE LOOKIN' UP TO YOU** *MCA 919* WILTON FELDER FEATURING BOBBY WOMACK & INTRODUCING ALLTRINA GRAYSON	63		
5 Oct 85	**I WISH HE DIDN'T TRUST ME SO MUCH** *MCA 994*	64		
26 Sep 87	**SO THE STORY GOES** *Chrysalis LIB 3* LIVING IN A BOX FEATURING BOBBY WOMACK	34		2
7 Nov 87	**LIVING IN A BOX** *MCA 1210*	70		
3 Apr 93	**I'M BACK FOR MORE** *Dome CDDOME 1002* LULU & BOBBY WOMACK	27		3
13 May 95	**IT'S A MAN'S MAN'S MAN'S WORLD** *Pulse 8 CDLOSE 89* JEANIE TRACY & BOBBY WOMACK	73		
19 Jun 04	**CALIFORNIA DREAMIN'** *EMI WOMACK001*	59		

LEE ANN WOMACK US singer

Date	Title / Label	Peak Position	Weeks at No.1	Weeks in Top 40
9 Jun 01	**I HOPE YOU DANCE** *MCA Nashville MCSTD 40254*	40		1

WOMACK & WOMACK US duo

Date	Title / Label	Peak Position	Weeks at No.1	Weeks in Top 40
28 Apr 84	**LOVE WARS** *Elektra E 9799*	14		6
30 Jun 84	**BABY I'M SCARED OF YOU** *Elektra E 9733*	72		
6 Dec 86	**SOUL LOVE – SOUL MAN** *Manhattan MT 16*	58		
6 Aug 88	**TEARDROPS** *Fourth & Broadway BRW 101* ○	3		14
12 Nov 88	**LIFE'S JUST A BALLGAME** *Fourth & Broadway BRW 116*	32		3
25 Feb 89	**CELEBRATE THE WORLD** *Fourth & Broadway BRW 125*	19		5
5 Feb 94	**SECRET STAR** *Warner Brothers W 0222CD* HOUSE OF ZEKKARIYAS AKA WOMACK & WOMACK	46		

WOMBATS UK production group

Date	Title / Label	Peak Position	Weeks at No.1	Weeks in Top 40
28 Apr 07	**BACKFIRE AT THE DISCO** *Kids KIDS012CD*	67		
7 Jul 07	**KILL THE DIRECTOR** *14th Floor 14FLR22CD*	35		1
20 Oct 07	**LET'S DANCE TO JOY DIVISION** *14th Floor 14FLR26CD*	15		5
19 Jan 08	**MOVING TO NEW YORK** *14th Floor 14FLR28CD*	13		8

WOMBLES UK TV puppet characters

Date	Title / Label	Peak Position	Weeks at No.1	Weeks in Top 40
26 Jan 74	**THE WOMBLING SONG** *CBS 1794*	4		19
6 Apr 74	**REMEMBER YOU'RE A WOMBLE** *CBS 2241*	3		12
22 Jun 74	**BANANA ROCK** *CBS 2465*	9		8
12 Oct 74	**MINUETTO ALLEGRETTO** *CBS 2710*	16		7
7 Dec 74	**WOMBLING MERRY CHRISTMAS** *CBS 2842* ○	2		6
10 May 75	**WOMBLING WHITE TIE AND TAILS** *CBS 3266*	22		6
9 Aug 75	**SUPER WOMBLE** *CBS 3480*	20		6
13 Dec 75	**LET'S WOMBLE TO THE PARTY TONIGHT** *CBS 3794*	34		3
21 Mar 98	**REMEMBER YOU'RE A WOMBLE** *Columbia 6656202*	13		3
13 Jun 98	**WOMBLING SONG (UNDERGROUND OVERGROUND)** *Columbia 6660412*	27		1
30 Dec 00	**I WISH IT COULD BE A WOMBLING CHRISTMAS** *Dramatico DRAMCDS 0001X* WOMBLES FEATURING ROY WOOD	22		2

STEVIE WONDER US singer

Date	Title / Label	Peak Position	Weeks at No.1	Weeks in Top 40
3 Feb 66	**UPTIGHT** *Tamla Motown TMG 545*	14		8
18 Aug 66	**BLOWIN' IN THE WIND** *Tamla Motown TMG 570*	36		4
5 Jan 67	**A PLACE IN THE SUN** *Tamla Motown TMG 588*	20		3
26 Jul 67	**I WAS MADE TO LOVE HER** *Tamla Motown TMG 613*	5		12
25 Oct 67	**I'M WONDERING** *Tamla Motown TMG 626*	22		6
8 May 68	**SHOO BE DOO BE DOO DA DAY** *Tamla Motown TMG 653*	46		
18 Dec 68	**FOR ONCE IN MY LIFE** *Tamla Motown TMG 679*	3		12
19 Mar 69	**I DON'T KNOW WHY (I LOVE YOU)** *Tamla Motown TMG 690*	14		9
16 Jul 69	**MY CHERIE AMOUR** *Tamla Motown TMG 690*	4		14
15 Nov 69	**YESTER-ME YESTER-YOU YESTERDAY** *Tamla Motown TMG 717*	2		12
28 Mar 70	**NEVER HAD A DREAM COME TRUE** *Tamla Motown TMG 731*	6		9
18 Jul 70	**SIGNED SEALED DELIVERED I'M YOURS** *Tamla Motown TMG 744*	15		9
21 Nov 70	**HEAVEN HELP US ALL** *Tamla Motown TMG 757*	29		6
15 May 71	**WE CAN WORK IT OUT** *Tamla Motown TMG 772*	27		6
22 Jan 72	**IF YOU REALLY LOVE ME** *Tamla Motown TMG 798*	20		6

Silver-selling ○ · Gold-selling ● · Platinum-selling (P) · US No.1 ★ · Peak Position · Weeks at No.1 · Weeks in Top 40

Date	Title / Label / Artist	Peak Position	Weeks at No.1	Weeks in Top 40
3 Feb 73	**SUPERSTITION** *Tamla Motown TMG 841* ★	11		8
19 May 73	**YOU ARE THE SUNSHINE OF MY LIFE** *Tamla Motown TMG 852* ★	7		9
13 Oct 73	**HIGHER GROUND** *Tamla Motown TMG 869*	29		3
12 Jan 74	**LIVING FOR THE CITY** *Tamla Motown TMG 881*	15		8
13 Apr 74	**HE'S MISSTRA KNOW IT ALL** *Tamla Motown TMG 892*	10		9
19 Oct 74	**YOU HAVEN'T DONE NOTHIN'** *Tamla Motown TMG 921* ★	30		4
11 Jan 75	**BOOGIE ON REGGAE WOMAN** *Tamla Motown TMG 928*	12		7
18 Dec 76	**I WISH** *Tamla Motown TMG 1054* ○ ★	5		10
9 Apr 77	**SIR DUKE** *Motown TMG 1068* ○ ★	2		9
10 Sep 77	**ANOTHER STAR** *Motown TMG 1083*	29		5
24 Feb 79	**POPS WE LOVE YOU** *Motown TMG 1136* DIANA ROSS, MARVIN GAYE, SMOKEY ROBINSON & STEVIE WONDER	66		
24 Nov 79	**SEND ONE YOUR LOVE** *Motown TMG 1149*	52		
26 Jan 80	**BLACK ORCHID** *Motown TMG 1173*	63		
29 Mar 80	**OUTSIDE MY WINDOW** *Motown TMG 1179*	52		
13 Sep 80	**MASTERBLASTER (JAMMIN')** *Motown TMG 1204* ○	2		9
27 Dec 80	**I AIN'T GONNA STAND FOR IT** *Motown TMG 1215*	10		6
7 Mar 81	**LATELY** *Motown TMG 1226* ○	3		10
25 Jul 81	**HAPPY BIRTHDAY** *Motown TMG 1235* ○	2		9
23 Jan 82	**THAT GIRL** *Motown TMG 1254*	39		1
10 Apr 82	**EBONY AND IVORY** *Parlophone R 6054* PAUL McCARTNEY & STEVIE WONDER ● ★	1	3	9
5 Jun 82	**DO I DO** *Motown TMG 1269*	10		6
25 Sep 82	**RIBBON IN THE SKY** *Motown TMG 1280*	45		
25 Aug 84	**I JUST CALLED TO SAY I LOVE YOU** *Motown TMG 1349* (P) ★	1	6	18
1 Dec 84	**LOVE LIGHT IN FLIGHT** *Motown TMG 1364*	44		
29 Dec 84	**DON'T DRIVE DRUNK** *Motown TMG 1372*	62		
7 Sep 85	**PART-TIME LOVER** *Motown ZB 40351* ○ ★	3		10
9 Nov 85	**THAT'S WHAT FRIENDS ARE FOR** *Arista ARIST 638* DIONNE WARWICK & FRIENDS FEATURING ELTON JOHN, STEVIE WONDER & GLADYS KNIGHT ★	16		7
23 Nov 85	**GO HOME** *Motown ZB 40501*	67		
8 Mar 86	**OVERJOYED** *Motown ZB 40567*	17		5
17 Jan 87	**STRANGER ON THE SHORE OF LOVE** *Motown WOND 2*	55		
31 Oct 87	**SKELETONS** *Motown ZB 41439*	59		
28 May 88	**GET IT** *Motown ZB 41883* STEVIE WONDER & MICHAEL JACKSON	37		2
6 Aug 88	**MY LOVE** *CBS JULIO 2* JULIO IGLESIAS FEATURING STEVIE WONDER	5		8
20 May 89	**FREE** *Motown ZB 42855*	49		
12 Oct 91	**FUN DAY** *Motown ZB 44957*	63		
25 Feb 95	**FOR YOUR LOVE** *Motown TMGCD 1437*	23		2
22 Jul 95	**TOMORROW ROBINS WILL SING** *Motown 8603732*	71		
19 Jul 97	**HOW COME, HOW LONG** *Epic 6646202* BABYFACE FEATURING STEVIE WONDER	10		3
31 Oct 98	**TRUE TO YOUR HEART** *Motown 8608832* 98o FEATURING STEVIE WONDER	51		
27 Dec 03	**SIGNED SEALED DELIVERED I'M YOURS** *Innocent SINCD 54* BLUE FEATURING STEVIE WONDER & ANGIE STONE	11		6
28 May 05	**SO WHAT THE FUSS** *Motown TMGCDX1510*	19		3
10 Dec 05	**POSITIVITY** *Motown TMGCD1512* STEVIE WONDER FEATURING AISHA MORRIS	54		

WAYNE WONDER Jamaican singer

Date	Title / Label / Artist	Peak Position	Weeks at No.1	Weeks in Top 40
23 Mar 96	**SOMETHING DIFFERENT/THE TRAIN IS COMING** *Virgin VSCDX 1581* SHAGGY FEATURING WAYNE WONDER	21		4
28 Jun 03	**NO LETTING GO** *VP/Atlantic AT 0154CD*	3		7
8 Nov 03	**BOUNCE ALONG** *Atlantic AT 0165CD*	19		3

WONDER DOGS German producer

Date	Title / Label / Artist	Peak Position	Weeks at No.1	Weeks in Top 40
21 Aug 82	**RUFF MIX** *Flip 001*	31		3

WONDER STUFF UK group

Date	Title / Label / Artist	Peak Position	Weeks at No.1	Weeks in Top 40
7 May 88	**GIVE GIVE GIVE ME MORE MORE MORE** *Polydor GONE 3*	72		
16 Jul 88	**A WISH AWAY** *Polydor GONE 4*	43		
24 Sep 88	**IT'S YER MONEY I'M AFTER BABY** *Polydor GONE 5*	40		1
11 Mar 89	**WHO WANTS TO BE THE DISCO KING** *Polydor GONE 6*	28		2
23 Sep 89	**DON'T LET ME DOWN GENTLY** *Polydor GONE 7*	19		3
11 Nov 89	**GOLDEN GREEN/GET TOGETHER** *Polydor GONE 8*	33		2
12 May 90	**CIRCLESQUARE** *Polydor GONE 10*	20		3
13 Apr 91	**THE SIZE OF A COW** *Polydor GONE 11*	5		6
25 May 91	**CAUGHT IN MY SHADOW** *Polydor GONE 12*	18		2
7 Sep 91	**SLEEP ALONE** *Polydor GONE 13*	43		
26 Oct 91	**DIZZY** *Sense SIGH 712* VIC REEVES & THE WONDER STUFF ○	1	2	11
25 Jan 92	**WELCOME TO THE CHEAP SEATS (EP)** *Polydor GONE 14*	8		4
25 Sep 93	**ON THE ROPES (EP)** *Polydor GONCD 15*	10		3
27 Nov 93	**FULL OF LIFE (HAPPY NOW)** *Polydor GONCD 16*	28		2
26 Mar 94	**HOT LOVE NOW** *Polydor GONCD 17*	19		2
10 Sep 94	**UNBEARABLE** *Polydor GONCD 18*	16		2

WONDERS US group

Date	Title / Label / Artist	Peak Position	Weeks at No.1	Weeks in Top 40
22 Feb 97	**THAT THING YOU DO!** *Play-Tone 6640552*	22		2

BRENTON WOOD US singer

Date	Title / Label / Artist	Peak Position	Weeks at No.1	Weeks in Top 40
27 Dec 67	**GIMME LITTLE SIGN** *Liberty LBF 15021*	8		14

ROY WOOD UK singer

Date	Title / Label / Artist	Peak Position	Weeks at No.1	Weeks in Top 40
11 Aug 73	**DEAR ELAINE** *Harvest HAR 5074*	18		6
1 Dec 73	**FOREVER** *Harvest HAR 5078*	8		11
15 Jun 74	**GOING DOWN THE ROAD** *Harvest HAR 5083*	13		7
31 May 75	**OH WHAT A SHAME** *Jet 754*	13		6
22 Nov 86	**WATERLOO** *IRS IRM 125* DOCTOR & THE MEDICS FEATURING ROY WOOD	45		
23 Dec 95	**I WISH IT COULD BE CHRISTMAS EVERYDAY** *Woody 001CD* ROY WOOD BIG BAND	59		
30 Dec 00	**I WISH IT COULD BE A WOMBLING CHRISTMAS** *Dramatico DRAMCDS 0001X* WOMBLES FEATURING ROY WOOD	22		2

WOODENTOPS UK group

Date	Title / Label / Artist	Peak Position	Weeks at No.1	Weeks in Top 40
11 Oct 86	**EVERYDAY LIVING** *Rough Trade RT 178*	72		

MARCELLA WOODS UK singer

Date	Title / Label / Artist	Peak Position	Weeks at No.1	Weeks in Top 40
15 Jul 00	**BEAUTIFUL** *Incentive CENT 7CDS* MATT DAREY'S MASH UP PRESENTS MARCELLA WOODS	21		2
30 Mar 02	**FALLING** *Perfecto PERF 29CDS* LIQUID STATE FEATURING MARCELLA WOODS	60		
20 Apr 02	**BEAUTIFUL** *Incentive CENT 38CDS* MATT DAREY FEATURING MARCELLA WOODS	10		4
14 Dec 02	**U SHINE ON** *Incentive CENT 50CDS* MATT DAREY & MARCELLA WOODS	34		1

MICHAEL WOODS UK producer

Date	Title / Label / Artist	Peak Position	Weeks at No.1	Weeks in Top 40
21 Jun 03	**IF U WANT ME** *Incentive CENT 48CDS* MICHAEL WOODS FEATURING IMOGEN BAILEY	46		
29 Nov 03	**SOLEX (CLOSE TO THE EDGE)** *Free 2 Air 0151865F2A*	52		

EDWARD WOODWARD UK actor

Date	Title / Label / Artist	Peak Position	Weeks at No.1	Weeks in Top 40
16 Jan 71	**THE WAY YOU LOOK TONIGHT** *DJM DJS 232*	42		

WOOKIE UK producer

Date	Title / Label / Artist	Peak Position	Weeks at No.1	Weeks in Top 40
3 Jun 00	**WHAT'S GOING ON** *Soul II Soul S2CD 001*	45		
12 Aug 00	**BATTLE** *Soul II Soul S2SPCD 001* WOOKIE FEATURING LAIN	10		5
12 May 01	**BACK UP (TO ME)** *Soul II Soul S2SPCD 003* WOOKIE FEATURING LAIN	38		1

SHEB WOOLEY US singer/actor

Date	Title / Label / Artist	Peak Position	Weeks at No.1	Weeks in Top 40
20 Jun 58	**PURPLE PEOPLE EATER** *MGM 981* ★	12		8

WOOLPACKERS UK actors

Date	Title / Label / Artist	Peak Position	Weeks at No.1	Weeks in Top 40
16 Nov 96	**HILLBILLY ROCK HILLBILLY ROLL** *RCA 74321425412* ○	5		10
29 Nov 97	**LINE DANCE PARTY** *RCA 74321512262*	25		2

WORKING WEEK UK group

Date	Title / Label / Artist	Peak Position	Weeks at No.1	Weeks in Top 40
9 Jun 84	**VENCEREMOS – WE WILL WIN** *Virgin VS 684*	64		

WORLD OF TWIST UK group

Date	Title / Label / Artist	Peak Position	Weeks at No.1	Weeks in Top 40
24 Nov 90	**THE STORM** *Circa YR 55*	42		
23 Mar 91	**SONS OF THE STAGE** *Circa YR 62*	47		
12 Oct 91	**SWEETS** *Circa YR 72*	58		
22 Feb 92	**SHE'S A RAINBOW** *Circa YR 82*	62		

WORLD PARTY UK singer/multi-instrumentalist

Date	Title / Label	Peak Position	Weeks at No.1	Weeks in Top 40
14 Feb 87	**SHIP OF FOOLS** *Ensign ENY 606*	42		
16 Jun 90	**MESSAGE IN THE BOX** *Ensign ENY 631*	39		1
15 Sep 90	**WAY DOWN NOW** *Ensign ENY 634*	66		
18 May 91	**THANK YOU WORLD** *Ensign ENY 643*	68		
10 Apr 93	**IS IT LIKE TODAY** *Ensign CDENY 658*	19		3
10 Jul 93	**GIVE IT ALL AWAY** *Ensign CDENY 659*	43		
2 Oct 93	**ALL I GAVE** *Ensign CDENY 658*	37		1
7 Jun 97	**BEAUTIFUL DREAM** *Chrysalis CDCHS 5053*	31		1

WORLD PREMIERE US group

Date	Title / Label	Peak Position	Weeks at No.1	Weeks in Top 40
28 Jan 84	**SHARE THE NIGHT** *Epic A 4133*	64		

WORLD WARRIOR UK producer

Date	Title / Label	Peak Position	Weeks at No.1	Weeks in Top 40
16 Apr 94	**STREET FIGHTER II** *Living Beat LBECD 27*	70		

WORLDS APART UK group

Date	Title / Label	Peak Position	Weeks at No.1	Weeks in Top 40
27 Mar 93	**HEAVEN MUST BE MISSING AN ANGEL** *Arista 74321139362*	29		2
3 Jul 93	**WONDERFUL WORLD** *Arista 74321153402*	51		
25 Sep 93	**EVERLASTING LOVE** *Bell 74321164802*	20		3
26 Mar 94	**COULD IT BE I'M FALLING IN LOVE** *Bell 74321189952*	15		4
4 Jun 94	**BEGGIN' TO BE WRITTEN** *Bell 74321211982*	29		1

WORLD'S FAMOUS SUPREME TEAM US group

Date	Title / Label	Peak Position	Weeks at No.1	Weeks in Top 40
4 Dec 82	**BUFFALO GALS** *Charisma MALC 1* MALCOLM McLAREN & THE WORLD'S FAMOUS SUPREME TEAM	9		11
25 Feb 84	**HEY DJ** *Charisma TEAM 1*	52		
8 Dec 90	**OPERAA HOUSE** *Virgin VS 1273* WORLD'S FAMOUS SUPREME TEAM SHOW	75		
3 Oct 98	**BUFFALO GALS STAMPEDE** *Virgin VSCDT 1717* MALCOLM McLAREN & THE WORLD'S FAMOUS SUPREME TEAM PLUS RAKIM & ROGER SANCHEZ	65		

W.O.S.P. UK duo

Date	Title / Label	Peak Position	Weeks at No.1	Weeks in Top 40
17 Nov 01	**GETTING' INTO U** *Data 26CDS*	48		

WRECKX-N-EFFECT US group

Date	Title / Label	Peak Position	Weeks at No.1	Weeks in Top 40
13 Jan 90	**JUICY** *Motown ZB 43295* WRECKS-N-EFFECT	29		4
5 Dec 92	**RUMP SHAKER** *MCA MCS 1725*	24		3
7 May 94	**WRECKX SHOP** *MCA MCSTD 1969* WRECKX-N-EFFECT FEATURING APACHE INDIAN	26		1
13 Aug 94	**RUMP SHAKER** *MCA MCSTD 1989*	40		1

BETTY WRIGHT US singer

Date	Title / Label	Peak Position	Weeks at No.1	Weeks in Top 40
25 Jan 75	**SHOORAH SHOORAH** *RCA 2491*	27		6
19 Apr 75	**WHERE IS THE LOVE** *RCA 2548*	25		6
8 Feb 86	**PAIN** *Cooltempo COOL 117*	42		
9 Sep 89	**KEEP LOVE NEW** *Sure Delight SD 11*	71		

IAN WRIGHT UK footballer

Date	Title / Label	Peak Position	Weeks at No.1	Weeks in Top 40
28 Aug 93	**DO THE RIGHT THING** *M&G MAGCD 45*	43		

RUBY WRIGHT US singer

Date	Title / Label	Peak Position	Weeks at No.1	Weeks in Top 40
16 Apr 54	**BIMBO** *Parlophone R 3816*	7		5
22 May 59	**THREE STARS** *Parlophone R 4556*	19		10

STEVE WRIGHT UK radio DJ

Date	Title / Label	Peak Position	Weeks at No.1	Weeks in Top 40
27 Nov 82	**I'M ALRIGHT** *RCA 296* YOUNG STEVE & THE AFTERNOON BOYS	40		1
15 Oct 83	**GET SOME THERAPY** *RCA 362* STEVE WRIGHT & THE SISTERS OF SOUL	75		
1 Dec 84	**THE GAY CAVALIEROS (THE STORY SO FAR)** *MCA 925*	61		

WUBBLE-U UK production group

Date	Title / Label	Peak Position	Weeks at No.1	Weeks in Top 40
7 Mar 98	**PETAL** *Indolent DGOL 003CD1*	55		

WURZELS UK group

Date	Title / Label	Peak Position	Weeks at No.1	Weeks in Top 40
2 Feb 67	**DRINK UP THY ZIDER** *Columbia DB 8081* ADGE CUTLER & THE WURZELS	45		
15 May 76	**COMBINE HARVESTER (BRAND NEW KEY)** *EMI 2450*	1	2	11
11 Sep 76	**I AM A CIDER DRINKER (PALOMA BLANCA)** *EMI 2520*	3		9
25 Jun 77	**FARMER BILL'S COWMAN (I WAS KAISER BILL'S BATMAN)** *EMI 2637*	32		2
11 Aug 01	**COMBINE HARVESTER 2001 (REMIX)** *EMI Gold CDWURZ 001*	39		1
12 Oct 02	**DON'T LOOK BACK IN ANGER** *EMI Gold 5515082*	59		
5 May 07	**I AM A CIDER DRINKER 2007** *EMI Gold 3926532* WURZELS FEATURING TONY BLACKBURN	57		
6 Oct 07	**ONE FOR THE BRISTOL CITY** *CIA CIA004* BRISTOL CITY & THE WURZELS	66		

WU-TANG CLAN US group

Date	Title / Label	Peak Position	Weeks at No.1	Weeks in Top 40
16 Aug 97	**TRIUMPH** *Loud 74321510212* WU-TANG CLAN FEATURING CAPPADONNA	46		
21 Mar 98	**SAY WHAT YOU WANT/INSANE** *Mercury MERCD 499* TEXAS FEATURING THE WU TANG CLAN	4		5
25 Nov 00	**GRAVEL PIT** *Loud 6705182*	6		11

WWF SUPERSTARS US/UK wrestlers

Date	Title / Label	Peak Position	Weeks at No.1	Weeks in Top 40
12 Dec 92	**SLAM JAM** *Arista 74321124887*	4		6
3 Apr 93	**WRESTLEMANIA** *Arista 74321136832*	14		4
10 Jul 93	**USA** *Arista 74321153092* WWF SUPERSTARS FEATURING HACKSAW JIM DUGGAN	71		

ROBERT WYATT UK singer

Date	Title / Label	Peak Position	Weeks at No.1	Weeks in Top 40
28 Sep 74	**I'M A BELIEVER** *Virgin VS 114*	29		4
7 May 83	**SHIPBUILDING** *Rough Trade RT 115*	35		2

MICHAEL WYCOFF US singer

Date	Title / Label	Peak Position	Weeks at No.1	Weeks in Top 40
23 Jul 83	**(DO YOU REALLY LOVE ME) TELL ME LOVE** *RCA 348*	60		

PETE WYLIE UK singer

Date	Title / Label	Peak Position	Weeks at No.1	Weeks in Top 40
3 May 86	**SINFUL** *Eternal MDM 7*	13		7
13 Sep 86	**DIAMOND GIRL** *Eternal MDM 12*	57		
13 Apr 91	**SINFUL! (SCARY JIGGIN' WITH DOCTOR LOVE)** *Siren SRN 138* PETE WYLIE WITH THE FARM	28		3

BILL WYMAN UK singer/bass player

Date	Title / Label	Peak Position	Weeks at No.1	Weeks in Top 40
25 Jul 81	**(SI SI) JE SUIS UN ROCK STAR** *A&M AMS 8144*	14		7
20 Mar 82	**A NEW FASHION** *A&M AMS 8209*	37		1

TAMMY WYNETTE US singer

Date	Title / Label	Peak Position	Weeks at No.1	Weeks in Top 40
26 Apr 75	**STAND BY YOUR MAN** *Epic EPC 7137*	1	3	11
28 Jun 75	**D.I.V.O.R.C.E.** *Epic EPC 3361*	12		7
12 Jun 76	**I DON'T WANNA PLAY HOUSE** *Epic EPC 4091*	37		2
7 Dec 91	**JUSTIFIED AND ANCIENT** *KLF Communications KLF099* KLF, GUEST VOCALS TAMMY WYNETTE	2		10

MARK WYNTER UK singer

Date	Title / Label	Peak Position	Weeks at No.1	Weeks in Top 40
25 Aug 60	**IMAGE OF A GIRL** *Decca F 11263*	11		10
10 Nov 60	**KICKING UP THE LEAVES** *Decca F 11279*	24		8
9 Mar 61	**DREAM GIRL** *Decca F 11323*	27		3
8 Jun 61	**EXCLUSIVELY YOURS** *Decca F 11354*	32		5
4 Oct 62	**VENUS IN BLUE JEANS** *Pye 7N 15466*	4		12
13 Dec 62	**GO AWAY LITTLE GIRL** *Pye 7N 15492*	6		11
6 Jun 63	**SHY GIRL** *Pye 7N 15525*	28		5
14 Nov 63	**IT'S ALMOST TOMORROW** *Pye 7N 15577*	12		9
9 Apr 64	**ONLY YOU (AND YOU ALONE)** *Pye 7N 15626*	38		2

X

MALCOLM X US political orator

Date	Title	Peak Position	Weeks at No.1	Weeks in Top 40
7 Apr 84	**NO SELL OUT** *Tommy Boy IS 165*	60		

RICHARD X UK producer

Date	Title	Peak Position	Weeks at No.1	Weeks in Top 40
29 Mar 03	**BEING NOBODY** *Virgin RXCD1* RICHARD X VS LIBERTY X	3		6
23 Aug 03	**FINEST DREAMS** *Virgin RXCD 2* RICHARD X FEATURING KELIS	8		3

XAVIER US group

Date	Title	Peak Position	Weeks at No.1	Weeks in Top 40
20 Mar 82	**WORK THAT SUCKER TO DEATH/LOVE IS ON THE ONE** *Liberty UP 651*	53		
27 Sep 97	**JUST GETS BETTER** *Multiply CDMULTY 25* TJR FEATURING XAVIER	28		1
27 Aug 05	**GIVE ME THE NIGHT** *Virgin TENCDX501*	65		

X-ECUTIONERS US group

Date	Title	Peak Position	Weeks at No.1	Weeks in Top 40
13 Apr 02	**IT'S GOIN' DOWN** *Epic 6725642* X-ECUTIONERS FEATURING MIKE SHINODA AND MR HAHN OF LINKIN PARK	7		4

XPANSIONS UK producer

Date	Title	Peak Position	Weeks at No.1	Weeks in Top 40
6 Oct 90	**ELEVATION** *Optimism 113683*	49		
23 Feb 91	**MOVE YOUR BODY** *Arista 113683*	7		8
15 Jun 91	**WHAT YOU WANT** *Arista 114246* XPANSIONS FEATURING DALE JOYNER	55		
26 Aug 95	**MOVE YOUR BODY** *Arista 74321294982* XPANSIONS 95	14		3
30 Nov 02	**ELEVATION (MOVE YOUR BODY) 2002** *RM RMRCD 10*	70		

X-PRESS 2 UK group

Date	Title	Peak Position	Weeks at No.1	Weeks in Top 40
5 Jun 93	**LONDON X-PRESS** *Junior Boy's Own JBO 12*	59		
16 Oct 93	**SAY WHAT!** *Junior Boy's Own JBO 16CD*	32		1
30 Jul 94	**ROCK 2 HOUSE/ HIP HOUSIN'** *Junior Boy's Own JBO 21CD* X-PRESS 2 FEATURING LO-PRO	55		
9 Mar 96	**THE SOUND** *Junior Boy's Own JBO 36CD*	38		1
12 Oct 96	**TRANZ EURO XPRESS** *Junior Boy's Own JBO 42CD*	45		
30 Sep 00	**AC/DC** *Skint 57*	60		
28 Apr 01	**MUZIKIZUM** *Skint 65*	52		
20 Oct 01	**SMOKE MACHINE** *Skint 69*	43		
20 Apr 02	**LAZY** *Skint 74CD* X-PRESS 2 FEATURING DAVID BYRNE	2		9
21 Sep 02	**I WANT YOU BACK** *Skint 81CD* X-PRESS 2 FEATURING DIETER MEIER	50		
8 Oct 05	**GIVE IT** *Skint SKINT111CD* X-PRESS 2 FEATURING KURT WAGNER	33		1
30 Sep 06	**KILL 100** *Skint SKINT124CD*	59		

X-RAY SPEX UK group

Date	Title	Peak Position	Weeks at No.1	Weeks in Top 40
29 Apr 78	**THE DAY THE WORLD TURNED DAY-GLO** *EMI International INT 553*	23		5
22 Jul 78	**IDENTITY** *EMI International INT 563*	24		6
4 Nov 78	**GERM FREE ADOLESCENCE** *EMI International INT 573*	19		6
21 Apr 79	**HIGHLY INFLAMMABLE** *EMI International INT 583*	45		

XSCAPE US group

Date	Title	Peak Position	Weeks at No.1	Weeks in Top 40
20 Nov 93	**JUST KICKIN' IT** *Columbia 6598622*	49		
5 Nov 94	**JUST KICKIN' IT** *Columbia 6608642*	54		
7 Oct 95	**FEELS SO GOOD** *Columbia 6625022*	34		1
27 Jan 96	**WHO CAN I RUN TO** *Columbia 6628112*	31		1
29 Jun 96	**KEEP ON, KEEPIN' ON** *East West A 4287CD* MC LYTE FEATURING XSCAPE	39		1
19 Apr 97	**KEEP ON, KEEPIN' ON** *East West A 3950CD1* MC LYTE FEATURING XSCAPE	27		1
22 Aug 98	**THE ARMS OF THE ONE WHO LOVES YOU** *Columbia 6662522*	46		

XSTASIA UK production duo

Date	Title	Peak Position	Weeks at No.1	Weeks in Top 40
17 Mar 01	**SWEETNESS** *Liquid Asset ASSETCD 005*	65		

X-STATIC Italian group

Date	Title	Peak Position	Weeks at No.1	Weeks in Top 40
4 Feb 95	**I'M STANDING (HIGHER)** *Positiva CDTIV 25*	41		

XTC UK group

Date	Title	Peak Position	Weeks at No.1	Weeks in Top 40
12 May 79	**LIFE BEGINS AT THE HOP** *Virgin VS 259*	54		
22 Sep 79	**MAKING PLANS FOR NIGEL** *Virgin VS 282*	17		7
6 Sep 80	**GENERALS AND MAJORS/DON'T LOSE YOUR TEMPER** *Virgin VS 365*	32		4
18 Oct 80	**TOWERS OF LONDON** *Virgin VS 372*	31		2
24 Jan 81	**SGT ROCK (IS GOING TO HELP ME)** *Virgin VS 384*	16		7
23 Jan 82	**SENSES WORKING OVERTIME** *Virgin VS 462*	10		6
27 Mar 82	**BALL AND CHAIN** *Virgin VS 482*	58		
15 Oct 83	**LOVE ON A FARMBOY'S WAGES** *Virgin VS 613*	50		
29 Sep 84	**ALL YOU PRETTY GIRLS** *Virgin VS 709*	55		
28 Jan 89	**MAYOR OF SIMPLETON** *Virgin VS 1158*	46		
4 Apr 92	**THE DISAPPOINTED** *Virgin VS 1404*	33		1
13 Jun 92	**THE BALLAD OF PETER PUMPKINHEAD** *Virgin VS 1415*	71		

XTM & DJ CHUCKY Spanish production duo

Date	Title	Peak Position	Weeks at No.1	Weeks in Top 40
7 Jun 03	**FLY ON THE WINGS OF LOVE** *Serious SER 62CD* XTM & DJ CHUCKY PRESENTS ANNIA	8		15
2 Apr 05	**GIVE ME YOUR LOVE** *Wonderboy 9870368* XTM & DJ CHUCKY PRESENTS ANNIA	28		1

XZIBIT US rapper

Date	Title	Peak Position	Weeks at No.1	Weeks in Top 40
17 Mar 01	**X** *Epic 6709072* XZIBIT FEATURING SNOOP DOOG	14		4
16 Nov 02	**MULTIPLY** *Epic 6731552*	39		1
5 Feb 05	**HEY NOW (MEAN MUGGIN')** *Columbia 6756482*	9		4

Reality TV Talent Shows

Saviours or Sinners?

The success of reality TV talent shows like *The X Factor* shows no sign of abating. Year in, year out, tens of thousands of pop wannabes queue to 'enjoy' their few minutes in the spotlight. Despite standing in line for hours and hours, the hopefuls will be lucky to get more than a passing, 'Stand on the star, a verse and a chorus.' They don't care, they stand and sing, they take the cutting criticism, the rolling eyes of the judges and the near-inevitable rejection because pop's cattle market is a means to an end, their chance – probably their only chance – to make it.

Pete Waterman once said that shows like this are 'the cheapest and most brutal way to find out that you are no good ... '

... and we, the Great British public, can't get enough of them.

It was not always like this. Talent shows have existed for years and have proved popular TV fayre. *New Faces* is an obvious early example. The first incarnation of the new generation was *Pop Stars*, which brought Hear'say and the deft dance-pop of also-rans Liberty X into the UK market, then came *Pop Stars – The Rivals* with the hugely successful Girls Aloud, and the painfully short-lived and universally berated vocal harmonies of One True Voice. Then, Simon Cowell reinvented the wheel and brought us *X Factor*, which has broken pretty much every phone-in record in the UK TV industry. But, what this new seam of shows has done is take the popularity on to a whole new level. When the auditions for the Spice Girls took place, 400 girls turned up; when Kim Marsh left Hear'say (the very first band formed from this generation of reality talent shows) *3,000* girls queued for the auditions to replace her. That's the difference. The TV talent show has been super-sized.

You might have thought that after a near-decade of such programmes, the impact might be fading.

Not so.

Enter Leona Lewis.

By 2007, it had become almost *de rigeur* for most reality talent show winners to fall off the radar quite swiftly – Will Young and Girls Aloud aside. So when the 2006 *X Factor* series winner Leona Lewis didn't release a second single for almost twelve months, eyebrows were raised. Her debut single had been a predictable smash. Coming off the back of the TV show, 'A Moment Like This', was released in December 2006, breaking a world record after it was downloaded over 50,000 times within thirty minutes. One music chainstore was selling 100 copies a minute.

Then nothing.

What was going on?

It's all part of a plan, we were told, she's in America (aren't they always?) working with songwriters and musicians. Legendary record-biz mogul Clive Davis – whom we have to thank for discovering Whitney Houston among many others – was a big fan, apparently. Simon Cowell was predicting great things.

Just how great would not become apparent until the release of her debut single, 'Bleeding Love' in October 2007. The single was a massive smash, selling nearly 900,000 copies in the UK alone and spending 7 weeks at Number 1. It was easily the year's biggest-selling song. The song topped over thirty national singles charts and – perhaps most impressively of all – hit Number 1 in the US in April 2008 (the first time a female Brit had done so since Kim Wilde in 1987). The song even slipped from the American top spot only to return *twice* ('Le Freak' by Chic being the only other song to achieve this). Matters became even more impressive when her long-awaited debut album was put in shops – *Spirit* debuted at Number 1 in the US *Billboard* 200 chart and made Lewis the first British solo artist to top the chart with a debut album. She is also PETA's Sexiest Vegetarian 2008.

A product of the renowned Sylvia Young Theatre School and later the Italia Conti Academy and the BRIT School, some cynics complained Lewis was not a genuine 'discovery' as she had this pedigree and previous record business experience. Others even cruelly said she had enjoyed preferential treatment because her parents paid for such expensive specialist tuition – uncharitably forgetting to note that they were youth and social workers living in Hackney, the UK's second most deprived borough.

The relevance of the US charts on that of the UK and vice versa has long been the source of many arguments both within the trade and in the general public, but this Stateside success was important because it had been so long since a UK female had made such an impact. This in turn seemed to rubber-stamp her quality and therefore the impression she made on the UK charts and record business. At the time of writing, with a near-$10 million US record deal signed, Leona Lewis is set to become the most high-profile and successful product of the heavily criticised yet enduringly popular reality talent-show genre.

These latest shows have set many precedents, not just in terms of statistics and records sold. What is also new is the extent of the criticism levelled at them. They have ruined the mystery of the music biz, we are told (even though the TV shows are so highly edited they often represent little more than a soap opera with the willing public as extras). The cynicism is perplexing because, at heart, we are only being shown the audition process. Further, these are entirely consenting experiences – people queue willingly, they audition, they might get through to see the panel of judges and they then enter a process that they have already seen many times before on television. Sure enough, the brutality of the comments can seem harsh but, at the same time, the ultimate Svengali, Simon Cowell, is alarmingly accurate and is only dispensing the sort of 'reality checks' that will be a daily occurrence should an aspiring pop wannabe actually sign a record deal.

We all know the judges 'hating' each other and storming off is pantomime, but we are willing voyeurs on a spectacle, just like WWF or *Big Brother*. Let's be honest, we tune in to laugh at the guy who works in a chicken factory, the woman who thinks she is the next Mariah Carey yet can't actually sing a note or the pushy mum who tells the judges they've ruined her little sweetheart's life. It is Jerry Springer for music fans and that is why it is so popular.

For certain, there have been casualties and you have to feel for the likes of Steve Brookstein, certain members of Hear'say and One True Voice. They were, after all, only trying to catch a break.

However, in terms of the shows' impact on the UK singles charts, it is relatively minor. Each series may produce perhaps two, maybe three 'stars' who reach the upper echelons of the charts. The headline-grabbers usually become one of the Top 100 or so selling singles of alltime by virtue of the fact the song is an impulse purchase by the millions of people who follow the show. A few further down the auditions will get small record deals and keep trying, usually to no avail. But each week there are on average 160 songs released. So why do the dozen or so reality songs released each year trouble us so much? Is it because we don't like to see people fast-tracked to success? Do we resent them not 'earning their stripes' in some dingy spit-and-sawdust-style gig circuit?

Cultural commentators might sneer, but the public can't get enough of it. In the UK, *X Factor* is huge; in the States, *American Idol* is exponentially bigger. Each season's winner ends up with, to paraphrase *The League Of Gentlemen*, 'twelvty billion' phone votes. In 2002, more people voted for Will Young and Gareth Gates than for the Conservative Party at the election. That tells you either that Will and Gareth were part of a post-millennial cultural phenomenon or the Tories were in deep trouble.

One fair criticism is that the annual festive release of the *X Factor* winner's single has ruined the yearly battle for the Christmas Number 1. Previously an exciting chart perennial that attracted much publicity and hype, the ritual has now been reduced to an annual dead-cert one-horse race.

It's not just the UK singles chart that has changed shape as a result of reality shows. In China, the winner of the *Super Girl 2005* competition caused genuine political unrest as fears of vulgarity and democratic pretensions unsettled the authorities. Some suggested the democratic measures used to select a winner – a free phone vote – might give people the wrong idea about government. This was despite the final including entirely partisan renditions of folk songs, communist favourites and sterile Western numbers such as 'The Colour Of My Love' by Celine Dion, and Ricky Martin's 'Maria'. Even so, not everyone was happy with the show's methods or its result. The *China Daily* asked: 'How come an imitation of a democratic system ends up selecting the singer who has the least ability to carry a tune?'

Isn't that exactly the point?

Yet all this venom against hugely popular TV shows is set against a backdrop of 'authentic' TV shows turning out to be anything but: wildlife documentaries faking animals' environments, intrepid explorers supposedly out in the wilderness for days, not mentioning that they'd actually just been to the local pub for a slap-up carvery, celebrity chefs taking home fish they'd 'caught' when actually they hadn't. Even the Queen was 'faked' storming out of a photograph session. For that, questions were asked in Parliament; for *The X Factor,* we just get a snobbish dismissal from self-appointed culture curators.

But I, like thousands of others, have seen Shayne Ward sing live, I've been to a Will Young gig and I've heard Leona Lewis's much-vaunted vocals. All I can say from that is regardless of how we found them, we are lucky to have them and the charts are a better place for it. If Shayne Ward was still selling clothes in a Manchester store then there'd be a lot more to worry about in the state of the music business – or rather its inability to find those with genuine talent – than a few hit singles per year from TV talent-show winners.

Y–Z

KEY TO ARTIST ENTRIES

Artist/Group Name — Artist/Group Nationality and Category — Silver-selling — Gold-selling — Platinum-selling — US No.1 ★ — Peak Position — Weeks at No.1 — Weeks in Top 40

DEXY'S MIDNIGHT RUNNERS UK group

Date	Title / Label	Peak Position	Weeks at No.1	Weeks in Top 40
19 Jan 80	**DANCE STANCE** *Oddball Productions R 6028*	40		1
22 Mar 80	**GENO** *Late Night Feelings R 6033* ●	1	2	12
12 Jul 80	**THERE THERE MY DEAR** *Late Night Feelings R 6038*	7		6
21 Mar 81	**PLAN B** *Parlophone R 6046*	58		
11 Jul 81	**SHOW ME** *Mercury DEXYS 6*	16		7
20 Mar 82	**THE CELTIC SOUL BROTHERS** *Mercury DEXYS 8* DEXY'S MIDNIGHT RUNNERS WITH THE EMERALD EXPRESS	45		
3 Jul 82	**COME ON EILEEN** *Mercury DEXYS 9* DEXY'S MIDNIGHT RUNNERS WITH THE EMERALD EXPRESS ⊛ ★	1	4	13
2 Oct 82	**JACKIE WILSON SAID (I'M IN HEAVEN WHEN YOU SMILE)** *Mercury DEXYS 10* KEVIN ROWLAND & DEXY'S MIDNIGHT RUNNERS	5		6
4 Dec 82	**LET'S GET THIS STRAIGHT (FROM THE START)/OLD** *Mercury DEXYS 11* KEVIN ROWLAND & DEXY'S MIDNIGHT RUNNERS	17		8
2 Apr 83	**THE CELTIC SOUL BROTHERS** *Mercury DEXYS 12* KEVIN ROWLAND & DEXY'S MIDNIGHT RUNNERS	20		5
22 Nov 86	**BECAUSE OF YOU** *Mercury BRUSH 1*	13		6

Date of entry into Top 75

Artist collaboration or where artist's name has changed

Song Title — Label and Catalogue Number

Y?N-VEE US group

Date	Title / Label	Peak Position	Weeks at No.1	Weeks in Top 40
17 Dec 94	**CHOCOLATE** *RAL RALCD 2*	65		

Y&T US group

Date	Title / Label	Peak Position	Weeks at No.1	Weeks in Top 40
13 Aug 83	**MEAN STREAK** *A&M AM 135*	41		

Y-TRAXX Belgian producer

Date	Title / Label	Peak Position	Weeks at No.1	Weeks in Top 40
24 May 97	**MYSTERY LAND (EP)** *ffrr FCD 292*	63		
20 Sep 03	**MYSTERY LAND** *Nebula NEBT 047* Y-TRAXX FEATURING NEVE	70		

Y-TRIBE UK production duo

Date	Title / Label	Peak Position	Weeks at No.1	Weeks in Top 40
18 Dec 99	**ENOUGH IS ENOUGH** *Northwest 10 NORTHCD 002* Y-TRIBE FEATURING ELISABETH TROY	49		

WEIRD AL YANKOVIC US singer

Date	Title / Label	Peak Position	Weeks at No.1	Weeks in Top 40
7 Apr 84	**EAT IT** *Scotti Brothers A 4257*	36		2
4 Jul 92	**SMELLS LIKE NIRVANA** *Scotti Brothers PO 219*	58		

YARBOROUGH & PEOPLES US duo

Date	Title / Label	Peak Position	Weeks at No.1	Weeks in Top 40
27 Dec 80	**DON'T STOP THE MUSIC** *Mercury MER 53* (silver)	7		8
5 May 84	**DON'T WASTE YOUR TIME** *Total Experience XE 501*	60		
11 Jan 86	**GUILTY** *Total Experience FB 49905*	53		
5 Jul 86	**I WOULDN'T LIE** *Total Experience FB 49841*	61		

YARDBIRDS UK group

Date	Title / Label	Peak Position	Weeks at No.1	Weeks in Top 40
12 Nov 64	**GOOD MORNING LITTLE SCHOOLGIRL** *Columbia DB 7391*	44		
18 Mar 65	**FOR YOUR LOVE** *Columbia DB 7499*	3		10
17 Jun 65	**HEART FULL OF SOUL** *Columbia DB 7594*	2		12
14 Oct 65	**EVIL HEARTED YOU/STILL I'M SAD** *Columbia DB 7706*	3		10
3 Mar 66	**SHAPES OF THINGS** *Columbia DB 7848*	3		9
2 Jun 66	**OVER UNDER SIDEWAYS DOWN** *Columbia DB 7928*	10		8
27 Oct 66	**HAPPENINGS TEN YEARS TIME AGO** *Columbia DB 8024*	43		

TONY YAYO US rapper

Date	Title / Label	Peak Position	Weeks at No.1	Weeks in Top 40
24 Sep 05	**SO SEDUCTIVE** *Interscope 9884360* TONY YAYO FEATURING 50 CENT	28		2

YAZOO UK duo

Date	Title / Label	Peak Position	Weeks at No.1	Weeks in Top 40
17 Apr 82	**ONLY YOU** *Mute 020* (silver)	2		10
17 Jul 82	**DON'T GO** *Mute YAZ 001* (silver)	3		9
20 Nov 82	**THE OTHER SIDE OF LOVE** *Mute YAZ 002*	13		9
21 May 83	**NOBODY'S DIARY** *Mute YAZ 003* (silver)	3		9
8 Dec 90	**SITUATION** *Mute YAZ 4*	14		7
4 Sep 99	**ONLY YOU (REMIX)** *Mute CDYAZ 5*	38		1

YAZZ UK singer

Date	Title / Label	Peak Position	Weeks at No.1	Weeks in Top 40
20 Feb 88	**DOCTORIN' THE HOUSE** *Ahead Of Our Time CCUT 2* COLDCUT FEATURING YAZZ & THE PLASTIC POPULATION	6		7
23 Jul 88	**THE ONLY WAY IS UP** *Big Life BLR 4* YAZZ & THE PLASTIC POPULATION (gold)	1	5	13
29 Oct 88	**STAND UP FOR YOUR LOVE RIGHTS** *Big Life BLR 5* (silver)	2		9
4 Feb 89	**FINE TIME** *Big Life BLR 6*	9		6
29 Apr 89	**WHERE HAS ALL THE LOVE GONE** *Big Life BLR 8*	16		5
23 Jun 90	**TREAT ME GOOD** *Big Life BLR 24*	20		4
28 Mar 92	**ONE TRUE WOMAN** *Polydor PO 198*	60		
31 Jul 93	**HOW LONG** *Polydor PZCD 252* YAZZ & ASWAD	31		4
2 Apr 94	**HAVE MERCY** *Polydor PZCD 309*	42		
9 Jul 94	**EVERYBODY'S GOT TO LEARN SOMETIME** *Polydor PZCD 316*	56		
28 Sep 96	**GOOD THING GOING** *East West EW 062CD*	53		
22 Mar 97	**NEVER CAN SAY GOODBYE** *East West EW 081CD*	61		

YEAH YEAH YEAHS US group

Date	Title / Label	Peak Position	Weeks at No.1	Weeks in Top 40
16 Nov 02	**MACHINE** *Wichita Recordings WEBB 036SCD*	37		1
26 Apr 03	**DATE WITH THE NIGHT** *Dress Up 0657442*	16		1
5 Jul 03	**PIN** *Dress Up 9808085*	29		1
4 Oct 03	**MAPS** *Dress Up 9811413*	26		1
13 Nov 04	**Y CONTROL** *Dress Up 9868816*	54		
1 Apr 06	**GOLD LION** *Fiction 9877351*	18		2
1 Jul 06	**TURN INTO** *Fiction 1700277*	53		

TRISHA YEARWOOD US singer

Date	Title / Label	Peak Position	Weeks at No.1	Weeks in Top 40
9 Aug 97	**HOW DO I LIVE** *MCA MCSTD 48064*	66		

YELL! UK duo

Date	Title / Label	Peak Position	Weeks at No.1	Weeks in Top 40
20 Jan 90	**INSTANT REPLAY** *Fanfare FAN 22*	10		6

YELLO Swiss duo

Date	Title / Label	Peak Position	Weeks at No.1	Weeks in Top 40
25 Jun 83	**I LOVE YOU** *Stiff BUY 176*	41		
26 Nov 83	**LOST AGAIN** *Stiff BUY 191*	73		
9 Aug 86	**GOLDRUSH** *Mercury MER 218*	54		
22 Aug 87	**THE RHYTHM DIVINE** *Mercury MER 253* YELLO FEATURING SHIRLEY BASSEY	54		
27 Aug 88	**THE RACE** *Mercury YELLO 1*	7		9
17 Dec 88	**TIED UP** *Mercury YELLO 2*	60		
25 Mar 89	**OF COURSE I'M LYING** *Mercury YELLO 3*	23		5
22 Jul 89	**BLAZING SADDLES** *Mercury YELLO 4*	47		
8 Jun 91	**RUBBERBANDMAN** *Mercury YELLO 5*	58		
5 Sep 92	**JUNGLE BILL** *Mercury MER 376*	61		
7 Nov 92	**THE RACE/BOSTICH** *Mercury MER 382*	55		
15 Oct 94	**HOW HOW** *Mercury MERCD 414*	59		

YELLOW DOG UK group

Date	Title / Label	Peak Position	Weeks at No.1	Weeks in Top 40
4 Feb 78	**JUST ONE MORE NIGHT** *Virgin VS 195* (silver)	8		8
22 Jul 78	**WAIT UNTIL MIDNIGHT** *Virgin VS 217*	54		

YELLOW MAGIC ORCHESTRA Japanese group

Date	Title / Label	Peak Position	Weeks at No.1	Weeks in Top 40
14 Jun 80	**COMPUTER GAME (THEME FROM *THE INVADERS*)** *A&M AMS 7502*	17		8

YELLOWCARD US group

Date	Title / Label	Peak Position	Weeks at No.1	Weeks in Top 40
12 Jun 04	**WAY AWAY** *Capitol CDCLS 855*	63		
18 Sep 04	**OCEAN AVENUE** *Capitol CDCLS 860*	65		
18 Mar 06	**LIGHTS AND SOUNDS** *Parlophone CDCLS875*	59		

YEOVIL TOWN F.C. UK football club

Date	Title / Label	Peak Position	Weeks at No.1	Weeks in Top 40
28 Feb 04	**YEOVIL TRUE** *Yeovil Town FC YEOVILTOWN188*	36		1

YES UK group

Date	Title / Label	Peak Position	Weeks at No.1	Weeks in Top 40
17 Sep 77	**WONDEROUS STORIES** *Atlantic K 10999*	7		9
26 Nov 77	**GOING FOR THE ONE** *Atlantic K 11047*	24		3
9 Sep 78	**DON'T KILL THE WHALE** *Atlantic K 11184*	36		1
12 Nov 83	**OWNER OF A LONELY HEART** *Atco B 9817* ★	28		5
31 Mar 84	**LEAVE IT** *Atco B 9787*	56		
3 Oct 87	**LOVE WILL FIND A WAY** *Atco B 9449*	73		
28 May 05	**OWNER OF A LONELY HEART** *Data DATA92CDS* MAX GRAHAM VS YES	9		6

YETI UK group

Date	Title / Label	Peak Position	Weeks at No.1	Weeks in Top 40
9 Apr 05	**NEVER LOSE YOUR SENSE OF WONDER** *Moshi Moshi MOSHI17CD*	36		1
10 Sep 05	**KEEP PUSHIN' ON** *Moshi Moshi MOSHI23CD*	57		

YIN & YAN UK duo

Date	Title / Label	Peak Position	Weeks at No.1	Weeks in Top 40
29 Mar 75	**IF** *EMI 2282*	25		4

YING YANG TWINS US duo

Date	Title / Label	Peak Position	Weeks at No.1	Weeks in Top 40
17 Sep 05	**WAIT (THE WHISPER SONG)** *TVT TVTUKCD16*	47		
18 Feb 06	**SHAKE** *TVT TVTUKCD0020* YING YANG TWINS FEATURING PITBULL	49		

Silver-selling ○ Gold-selling ● Platinum-selling ⊛ US No.1 ★

DWIGHT YOAKAM US singer/guitarist

Date	Title / Label	Peak Position	Weeks at No.1	Weeks in Top 40
10 Jul 99	**CRAZY LITTLE THING CALLED LOVE** *Reprise W 497CD*	43		

YOMANDA UK producer

Date	Title / Label	Peak Position	Weeks at No.1	Weeks in Top 40
24 Jul 99	**SYNTH & STRINGS** *1st Avenue FESCD 59*	8		7
11 Mar 00	**SUNSHINE** *1st Avenue FESCD 68*	16		3
2 Sep 00	**ON THE LEVEL** *Manifesto FESCD 73*	28		1
26 Jul 03	**YOU'RE FREE** *Incentive CENT 55CDS*	22		2

YORK German production duo

Date	Title / Label	Peak Position	Weeks at No.1	Weeks in Top 40
9 Oct 99	**THE AWAKENING** *Manifesto FESCD 60*	11		3
10 Jun 00	**ON THE BEACH** *Manifesto FESCD 70*	4		7
18 Nov 00	**FAREWELL TO THE MOON** *Manifesto FESCD 76*	37		1
27 Jan 01	**THE FIELDS OF LOVE** *Club Tools 0124095 CLU* ATB FEATURING YORK	16		2

THOM YORKE UK singer/guitarist

Date	Title / Label	Peak Position	Weeks at No.1	Weeks in Top 40
2 Sep 06	**HARROWDOWN HILL** *XL Recordings XLS238CD*	23		1

YOSH Dutch producer

Date	Title / Label	Peak Position	Weeks at No.1	Weeks in Top 40
29 Jul 95	**IT'S WHAT'S UPFRONT THAT COUNTS** *Limbo LIMB 46CD* YOSH PRESENTS LOVEDEEJAY AKEMI	69		
2 Dec 95	**IT'S WHAT'S UPFRONT THAT COUNTS (REMIX)** *Limbo LIMB 50CD* YOSH PRESENTS LOVEDEEJAY AKEMI	31		1
20 Apr 96	**THE SCREAMER** *Limbo LIMB 54CD* YOSH PRESENTS LOVEDEEJAY AKEMI	38		1

YOTHU YINDI Australian Aboriginal group

Date	Title / Label	Peak Position	Weeks at No.1	Weeks in Top 40
15 Feb 92	**TREATY** *Hollywood HWD 116*	72		

FARON YOUNG US singer/guitarist

Date	Title / Label	Peak Position	Weeks at No.1	Weeks in Top 40
15 Jul 72	**IT'S FOUR IN THE MORNING** *Mercury 6052 140*	3		19

JIMMY YOUNG UK singer

Date	Title / Label	Peak Position	Weeks at No.1	Weeks in Top 40
9 Jan 53	**FAITH CAN MOVE MOUNTAINS** *Decca F 9986*	11		1
21 Aug 53	**ETERNALLY** *Decca F 10130*	8		9
6 May 55	**UNCHAINED MELODY** *Decca F 10502*	1	3	19
16 Sep 55	**THE MAN FROM LARAMIE** *Decca F 10597*	1	4	12
23 Dec 55	**SOMEONE ON YOUR MIND** *Decca F 10640*	13		5
16 Mar 56	**CHAIN GANG** *Decca F 10694*	9		6
8 Jun 56	**WAYWARD WIND** *Decca F 10736*	27		1
22 Jun 56	**RICH MAN POOR MAN** *Decca F 10736*	25		1
28 Sep 56	**MORE** *Decca F 10774*	4		17
3 May 57	**ROUND AND ROUND** *Decca F 10875* JIMMY YOUNG WITH THE MICHAEL SAMMES SINGERS	30		1
10 Oct 63	**MISS YOU** *Columbia DB 7119*	15		10
26 Mar 64	**UNCHAINED MELODY** *Columbia DB 7234* JIMMY YOUNG WITH THE MICHAEL SAMMES SINGERS	43		

JOHN PAUL YOUNG UK singer

Date	Title / Label	Peak Position	Weeks at No.1	Weeks in Top 40
29 Apr 78	**LOVE IS IN THE AIR** *Ariola ARO 117* ○	5		10
14 Nov 92	**LOVE IS IN THE AIR (REMIX)** *Columbia 6587697*	49		
12 Jan 02	**LOVE IS IN THE AIR** *Positiva CDTIV 166* MILK & SUGAR/JOHN PAUL YOUNG	25		2

KAREN YOUNG UK singer

Date	Title / Label	Peak Position	Weeks at No.1	Weeks in Top 40
6 Sep 69	**NOBODY'S CHILD** *Major Minor MM 625*	6		19

KAREN YOUNG US singer

Date	Title / Label	Peak Position	Weeks at No.1	Weeks in Top 40
19 Aug 78	**HOT SHOT** *Atlantic K 11180*	34		3
24 Feb 79	**HOT SHOT** *Atlantic LV 8*	75		
15 Nov 97	**HOT SHOT '97 (REMIX)** *Distinctive DISNCD 37*	68		

NEIL YOUNG Canadian singer/guitarist

Date	Title / Label	Peak Position	Weeks at No.1	Weeks in Top 40
11 Mar 72	**HEART OF GOLD** *Reprise K 14140* ★	10		9
6 Jan 79	**FOUR STRONG WINDS** *Reprise K 14493*	57		
27 Feb 93	**HARVEST MOON** *Reprise W 0139CD*	36		2
17 Jul 93	**THE NEEDLE AND THE DAMAGE DONE** *Reprise W 0191CD*	75		
30 Oct 93	**LONG MAY YOU RUN (LIVE)** *Reprise W 0207CD*	71		
9 Apr 94	**PHILADELPHIA** *Reprise W 0242CD*	62		

PAUL YOUNG UK singer

Date	Title / Label	Peak Position	Weeks at No.1	Weeks in Top 40
18 Jun 83	**WHEREVER I LAY MY HAT (THAT'S MY HOME)** *CBS A 3371* ●	1	3	12
10 Sep 83	**COME BACK AND STAY** *CBS A 3636* ○	4		8
19 Nov 83	**LOVE OF THE COMMON PEOPLE** *CBS A 3585* ●	2		11
13 Oct 84	**I'M GONNA TEAR YOUR PLAYHOUSE DOWN** *CBS A 4786*	9		6
8 Dec 84	**EVERYTHING MUST CHANGE** *CBS A 4972* ○ ★	9		9
9 Mar 85	**EVERY TIME YOU GO AWAY** *CBS A 6300* ○	4		9
22 Jun 85	**TOMB OF MEMORIES** *CBS A 6321*	16		5
4 Oct 86	**WONDERLAND** *CBS YOUNG 1*	24		4
29 Nov 86	**SOME PEOPLE** *CBS YOUNG 2*	56		
7 Feb 87	**WHY DOES A MAN HAVE TO BE STRONG** *CBS YOUNG 3*	63		
12 May 90	**SOFTLY WHISPERING I LOVE YOU** *CBS YOUNG 4*	21		4
7 Jul 90	**OH GIRL** *CBS YOUNG 5*	25		4
6 Oct 90	**HEAVEN CAN WAIT** *CBS YOUNG 6*	71		
12 Jan 91	**CALLING YOU** *CBS YOUNG 7*	57		
30 Mar 91	**SENZA UNA DONNA (WITHOUT A WOMAN)** *London LON 294* ZUCCHERO & PAUL YOUNG	4		9
10 Aug 91	**BOTH SIDES NOW** *MCA MCS 1546* CLANNAD & PAUL YOUNG	74		
26 Oct 91	**DON'T DREAM IT'S OVER** *Columbia 6574117*	20		3
25 Sep 93	**NOW I KNOW WHAT MADE OTIS BLUE** *Columbia 6596412*	14		5
27 Nov 93	**HOPE IN A HOPELESS WORLD** *Columbia 6598652*	42		
23 Apr 94	**IT WILL BE YOU** *Columbia 6602812*	34		1
17 May 97	**I WISH YOU LOVE** *East West EW 100CD1*	33		1

RETTA YOUNG US singer

Date	Title / Label	Peak Position	Weeks at No.1	Weeks in Top 40
24 May 75	**SENDING OUT AN S.O.S.** *All Platinum 6146 305*	28		5

WILL YOUNG UK singer

Date	Title / Label	Peak Position	Weeks at No.1	Weeks in Top 40
9 Mar 02	**EVERGREEN/ANYTHING IS POSSIBLE** *S 74321926142* ⊛	1	3	12
8 Jun 02	**LIGHT MY FIRE** *S 74321943002* ●	1	2	10
5 Oct 02	**THE LONG AND WINDING ROAD/SUSPICIOUS MINDS** *S 74321965972* WILL YOUNG & GARETH GATES/GARETH GATES ●	1	2	8
30 Nov 02	**DON'T LET ME DOWN/YOU AND I** *S 74321981272* ○	2		7
6 Dec 03	**LEAVE RIGHT NOW** *S 82876578562* ●	1	2	14
27 Mar 04	**YOUR GAME** *S 82876603622*	3		5
17 Jul 04	**FRIDAY'S CHILD** *S 82876634152*	4		5
26 Nov 05	**SWITCH IT ON** *S 82876752292*	5		4
28 Jan 06	**ALL TIME LOVE** *Sony BMG 82876779602*	3		10
29 Apr 06	**WHO AM I** *Sony BMG 82876821792*	11		6

YOUNG & COMPANY US group

Date	Title / Label	Peak Position	Weeks at No.1	Weeks in Top 40
1 Nov 80	**I LIKE (WHAT YOU'RE DOING TO ME)** *Excalibur EXC 501*	20		7

YOUNG & MOODY BAND UK group

Date	Title / Label	Peak Position	Weeks at No.1	Weeks in Top 40
10 Oct 81	**DON'T DO THAT** *Bronze BRO 130*	63		

YOUNG BLACK TEENAGERS US group

Date	Title / Label	Peak Position	Weeks at No.1	Weeks in Top 40
9 Apr 94	**TAP THE BOTTLE** *MCA MCSTD 1967*	39		1

YOUNG BUCK US rapper

Date	Title / Label	Peak Position	Weeks at No.1	Weeks in Top 40
23 Oct 04	**LET ME IN** *Interscope 9864517*	62		

YOUNG DISCIPLES UK group

Date	Title / Label	Peak Position	Weeks at No.1	Weeks in Top 40
13 Oct 90	**GET YOURSELF TOGETHER** *Talkin Loud TLK 2*	68		
23 Feb 91	**APPARENTLY NOTHIN'** *Talkin Loud TLK 5*	46		
3 Aug 91	**APPARENTLY NOTHIN'** *Talkin Loud TLK 5*	13		5
5 Oct 91	**GET YOURSELF TOGETHER** *Talkin Loud TLK 15*	65		
5 Sep 92	**YOUNG DISCIPLES (EP)** *Talkin Loud TLKX 18*	48		

YOUNG HEART ATTACK US group

Date	Title / Label	Peak Position	Weeks at No.1	Weeks in Top 40
10 Apr 04	**TOMMY SHOTS** *XL RecordingsXLS183CD*	54		
17 Jul 04	**STARLITE** *XL Recordings XLS191CD*	69		

YOUNG IDEA UK duo

Date	Title	Peak Position	Weeks at No.1	Weeks in Top 40
29 Jun 67	**WITH A LITTLE HELP FROM MY FRIENDS** *Columbia DB 8205*	10		4

YOUNG JEEZY US rapper

Date	Title	Peak Position	Weeks at No.1	Weeks in Top 40
4 Feb 06	**SOUL SURVIVOR** *Def Jam 9889047* YOUNG JEEZY FEATURING AKON	16		3
20 May 06	**SAY I** *Def Jam 9857779* CHRISTINA MILIAN FEATURING YOUNG JEEZY	4		6

YOUNG KNIVES UK group

Date	Title	Peak Position	Weeks at No.1	Weeks in Top 40
11 Mar 06	**HERE COMES THE RUMOUR MILL** *Transgressive TRANS020CD*	36		1
1 Jul 06	**SHE'S ATTRACTED TO** *Transgressive TRANS031CD*	38		1
26 Aug 06	**WEEKENDS AND BLEAK DAYS (HOT SUMMER)** *Transgressive TRANS035CD*	35		1
11 Nov 06	**THE DECISION** *Transgressive TRANS042CD*	60		
10 Nov 07	**TERRA FIRMA** *Transgressive TRANS056CD*	43		
8 Mar 08	**UP ALL NIGHT** *Download*	45		

YOUNG MC US rapper

Date	Title	Peak Position	Weeks at No.1	Weeks in Top 40
15 Jul 89	**BUST A MOVE** *Delicious Vinyl BRW 137*	73		
17 Feb 90	**PRINCIPAL'S OFFICE** *Delicious Vinyl BRW 161*	54		
17 Aug 91	**THAT'S THE WAY LOVE GOES** *Capitol CL 623*	65		

YOUNG OFFENDERS Irish group

Date	Title	Peak Position	Weeks at No.1	Weeks in Top 40
7 Mar 98	**THAT'S WHY WE LOSE CONTROL** *Columbia 6651942*	60		

YOUNG RASCALS US group

Date	Title	Peak Position	Weeks at No.1	Weeks in Top 40
25 May 67	**GROOVIN'** *Atlantic 584 111* ★	8		11
16 Aug 67	**A GIRL LIKE YOU** *Atlantic 584 128*	37		1

YOUNG STANLEY UK group

Date	Title	Peak Position	Weeks at No.1	Weeks in Top 40
10 Jun 06	**SING IT FOR ENGLAND** *Young Stanley YSCD442*	58		

SYDNEY YOUNGBLOOD US singer

Date	Title	Peak Position	Weeks at No.1	Weeks in Top 40
26 Aug 89	**IF ONLY I COULD** *Circa YR 34* ●	3		11
9 Dec 89	**SIT AND WAIT** *Circa YR 40*	16		7
31 Mar 90	**I'D RATHER GO BLIND** *Circa YR 43*	44		
29 Jun 91	**HOOKED ON YOU** *Circa YR 65*	72		
20 Mar 93	**ANYTHING** *RCA 74321138672*	48		

YOUNGER YOUNGER 28'S UK group

Date	Title	Peak Position	Weeks at No.1	Weeks in Top 40
5 Jun 99	**WE'RE GOING OUT** *V2 VVR 5006943*	61		

YOURCODENAMEIS:MILO UK group

Date	Title	Peak Position	Weeks at No.1	Weeks in Top 40
16 Oct 04	**SCHTEEVE** *Fiction 9868526*	58		
23 Apr 05	**17** *Fiction 9871093*	65		

Z

Z FACTOR UK producer

Date	Title	Peak Position	Weeks at No.1	Weeks in Top 40
21 Feb 98	**GOTTA KEEP PUSHIN'** *ffrr FCD 329*	47		
17 Nov 01	**RIDE THE RHYTHM** *Direction 6718482*	52		

Z2 UK production duo

Date	Title	Peak Position	Weeks at No.1	Weeks in Top 40
26 Feb 00	**I WANT YOU** *Platipus PLATCD 67* Z2 VOCAL BY ALISON RIVERS	61		

HELMUT ZACHARIAS German violinist

Date	Title	Peak Position	Weeks at No.1	Weeks in Top 40
29 Oct 64	**TOKYO MELODY** *Polydor YNH 52341*	9		11

PIA ZADORA US actress

Date	Title	Peak Position	Weeks at No.1	Weeks in Top 40
27 Oct 84	**WHEN THE RAIN BEGINS TO FALL** *Arista ARIST 584* JERMAINE JACKSON & PIA ZADORA	68		
12 Nov 88	**DANCE OUT OF MY HEAD** *Epic 6528867*	65		

ZAGER & EVANS US duo

Date	Title	Peak Position	Weeks at No.1	Weeks in Top 40
9 Aug 69	**IN THE YEAR 2525 (EXORDIUM AND TERMINUS)** *RCA 1860* ★	1	3	13

MICHAEL ZAGER BAND US producer

Date	Title	Peak Position	Weeks at No.1	Weeks in Top 40
1 Apr 78	**LET'S ALL CHANT** *Private Stock PVT 143*	8		8

GHEORGHE ZAMFIR Romanian pan-pipe player

Date	Title	Peak Position	Weeks at No.1	Weeks in Top 40
21 Aug 76	**(LIGHT OF EXPERIENCE) DOINA DE JALE** *Epic EPC 4310*	4		8

TOMMY ZANG US singer

Date	Title	Peak Position	Weeks at No.1	Weeks in Top 40
16 Feb 61	**HEY GOOD LOOKING** *Polydor NH 66957*	45		

ZAPP US group

Date	Title	Peak Position	Weeks at No.1	Weeks in Top 40
25 Jan 86	**IT DOESN'T REALLY MATTER** *Warner Brothers W 8879*	57		
24 May 86	**COMPUTER LOVE (PART 1)** *Warner Brothers W 8805*	64		

FRANCESCO ZAPPALA Italian producer

Date	Title	Peak Position	Weeks at No.1	Weeks in Top 40
10 Aug 91	**WE GOTTA DO IT** *Fourth & Broadway BRW 225* DJ PROFESSOR FEATURING FRANCESCO ZAPPALA	57		
2 May 92	**NO WAY OUT** *PWL Continental PWL 230*	69		

LENA ZAVARONI UK singer

Date	Title	Peak Position	Weeks at No.1	Weeks in Top 40
9 Feb 74	**MA HE'S MAKING EYES AT ME** *Philips 6006 367* ●	10		10
1 Jun 74	**PERSONALITY** *Philips 6006 391*	33		2

ZED BIAS UK group

Date	Title	Peak Position	Weeks at No.1	Weeks in Top 40
15 Jul 00	**NEIGHBOURHOOD** *Locked On LOX 122CD*	25		1

ZEE UK singer

Date	Title	Peak Position	Weeks at No.1	Weeks in Top 40
6 Jul 96	**DREAMTIME** *Perfecto PERF 122CD*	31		1
22 Mar 97	**SAY MY NAME** *Perfecto PERF 135CD*	36		1
7 Feb 98	**BUTTERFLY** *Perfecto PERF 154CD1* TILT FEATURING ZEE	41		

ZENA UK singer

Date	Title	Peak Position	Weeks at No.1	Weeks in Top 40
19 Jul 03	**LET'S GET THIS PARTY STARTED** *Serious SER 69CD*	69		
14 Aug 04	**BEEN AROUND THE WORLD** *Mercury 9867014* ZENA FEATURING VYBZ KARTEL	44		

ZEPHYRS UK group

Date	Title	Peak Position	Weeks at No.1	Weeks in Top 40
18 Mar 65	**SHE'S LOST YOU** *Columbia DB 7481*	48		

ZERO B UK producer

Date	Title	Peak Position	Weeks at No.1	Weeks in Top 40
22 Feb 92	**THE EP** *ffreedom TAB 102*	32		2
24 Jul 93	**RECONNECTION (EP)** *Internal LIECD 6*	54		

ZERO 7 UK production duo

Date	Title	Peak Position	Weeks at No.1	Weeks in Top 40
18 Aug 01	**DESTINY** *Ultimate Dilemma UDRCDS 043* ZERO 7 FEATURING SIA & SOPHIE	30		1
17 Nov 01	**IN THE WAITING LINE** *Ultimate Dilemma UDRCDS 045* ZERO 7 FEATURING SOPHIE BARKER	47		
30 Mar 02	**DISTRACTIONS** *Ultimate Dilemma UDRCDS 046* ZERO 7 FEATURING SIA	45		

Silver-selling · Gold-selling · Platinum-selling · US No.1 ★ · Peak Position · Weeks at No.1 · Weeks in Top 40

Date	Title / Label	Peak Position	Weeks at No.1	Weeks in Top 40
29 May 04	**SOMERSAULT** *Ultimate Dilemma EW290CD*	56		

ZERO VU UK production group

Date	Title / Label	Peak Position	Weeks at No.1	Weeks in Top 40
15 Mar 97	**FEELS SO GOOD** *Avex UK AVEXCD 53* ZERO VU FEATURING LORNA B	69		

ZERO ZERO UK production group

Date	Title / Label	Peak Position	Weeks at No.1	Weeks in Top 40
10 Aug 91	**ZEROXED** *Kickin KICK 9*	71		

ZHANÉ US duo

Date	Title / Label	Peak Position	Weeks at No.1	Weeks in Top 40
11 Sep 93	**HEY MR. DJ** *Epic 6596102*	26		2
19 Mar 94	**GROOVE THANG** *Motown TMGCD 1423*	34		1
20 Aug 94	**VIBE** *Motown TMGCD 1430*	67		
25 Feb 95	**SHAME** *Jive JIVECD 372*	66		
21 Sep 96	**IT'S A PARTY** *Elektra EKR 226CD* BUSTA RHYMES FEATURING ZHANÉ	23		1
8 Mar 97	**4 MORE** *Tommy Boy TBCD 7779A* DE LA SOUL FEATURING ZHANÉ	52		
26 Apr 97	**REQUEST LINE** *Motown 8606452*	22		1
30 Aug 97	**CRUSH** *Motown 5716712*	44		
11 Sep 99	**JAMBOREE** *Arista 74321692882* NAUGHTY BY NATURE FEATURING ZHANÉ	51		

ZIG & ZAG Irish TV puppets

Date	Title / Label	Peak Position	Weeks at No.1	Weeks in Top 40
24 Dec 94	**THEM GIRLS THEM GIRLS** *RCA 74321251042*	5		7
1 Jul 95	**HANDS UP! HANDS UP!** *RCA 74321284392*	21		2

ZIMMERS UK group

Date	Title / Label	Peak Position	Weeks at No.1	Weeks in Top 40
9 Jun 07	**MY GENERATION** *Xphonics XPH006*	26		2

ZION TRAIN UK group

Date	Title / Label	Peak Position	Weeks at No.1	Weeks in Top 40
27 Jul 96	**RISE** *China WOKCD 2085*	61		

ZODIAC MINDWARP & THE LOVE REACTION US group

Date	Title / Label	Peak Position	Weeks at No.1	Weeks in Top 40
9 May 87	**PRIME MOVER** *Mercury ZOD 1*	18		5
14 Nov 87	**BACKSEAT EDUCATION** *Mercury ZOD 2*	49		
2 Apr 88	**PLANET GIRL** *Mercury ZOD 3*	63		

ZOE UK singer

Date	Title / Label	Peak Position	Weeks at No.1	Weeks in Top 40
10 Nov 90	**SUNSHINE ON A RAINY DAY** *M&G MAGS 6*	53		
24 Aug 91	**SUNSHINE ON A RAINY DAY (REMIX)** *M&G MAGS 14*	4		10
2 Nov 91	**LIGHTNING** *M&G MAGS 18*	37		3
29 Feb 92	**HOLY DAYS** *M&G MAGS 21*	72		

ZOMBIE NATION German production duo

Date	Title / Label	Peak Position	Weeks at No.1	Weeks in Top 40
2 Sep 00	**KERNKRAFT 400 (IMPORT)** *TRANSK 002*	61		
30 Sep 00	**KERNKRAFT 400** *Data 11CDS*	2		9

ROB ZOMBIE US singer

Date	Title / Label	Peak Position	Weeks at No.1	Weeks in Top 40
26 Dec 98	**DRAGULA** *Geffen GFSTD 22367*	44		

ZOMBIES UK group

Date	Title / Label	Peak Position	Weeks at No.1	Weeks in Top 40
13 Aug 64	**SHE'S NOT THERE** *Decca F 11940*	12		10
11 Feb 65	**TELL HER NO** *Decca F 12072*	42		

ZOO EXPERIENCE UK group

Date	Title / Label	Peak Position	Weeks at No.1	Weeks in Top 40
22 Aug 92	**LOVE'S GOTTA HOLD ON ME** *Cooltempo COOL 261* ZOO EXPERIENCE FEATURING DESTRY	66		

ZUCCHERO Italian singer/guitarist

Date	Title / Label	Peak Position	Weeks at No.1	Weeks in Top 40
30 Mar 91	**SENZA UNA DONNA (WITHOUT A WOMAN)** *London LON 294* ZUCCHERO & PAUL YOUNG	4		9
18 Jan 92	**DIAMANTE** *London LON 313* ZUCCHERO WITH RANDY CRAWFORD	44		
24 Oct 92	**MISERERE** *London LON 329* ZUCCHERO WITH LUCIANO PAVAROTTI	15		4

ZUTONS UK group

Date	Title / Label	Peak Position	Weeks at No.1	Weeks in Top 40
31 Jan 04	**PRESSURE POINT** *Deltasonic DLTCDV016*	19		1
17 Apr 04	**YOU WILL YOU WON'T** *Must Destroy DARK03CD*	22		1
3 Jul 04	**REMEMBER ME** *Deltasonic DLTCD 2024*	39		1
30 Oct 04	**DON'T EVER THINK (TOO MUCH)** *Deltasonic DLTCD 2026*	15		2
25 Dec 04	**CONFUSION** *Deltasonic DLTCD 030*	37		1
15 Apr 06	**WHY WON'T YOU GIVE ME YOUR LOVE** *Deltasonic DLTCD2046*	9		4
24 Jun 06	**VALERIE** *Deltasonic DLTCD047*	9		9
30 Sep 06	**OH STACEY (LOOK WHAT YOU'VE DONE!)** *Deltasonic DLTCD053*	24		1
9 Dec 06	**IT'S THE LITTLE THINGS WE DO** *Deltasonic DLTCD2058*	47		

ZWAN US group

Date	Title / Label	Peak Position	Weeks at No.1	Weeks in Top 40
8 Mar 03	**HONESTLY** *Reprise W 600CD*	28		1
14 Jun 03	**LYRIC** *Reprise W 607CD*	44		

ZZ TOP US group

Date	Title / Label	Peak Position	Weeks at No.1	Weeks in Top 40
3 Sep 83	**GIMME ALL YOUR LOVIN'** *Warner Brothers W 9693*	61		
26 Nov 83	**SHARP DRESSED MAN** *Warner Brothers W 9576*	53		
31 Mar 84	**TV DINNERS** *Warner Brothers W 9334*	67		
6 Oct 84	**GIMME ALL YOUR LOVIN'** *Warner Brothers W 9693*	10		7
15 Dec 84	**SHARP DRESSED MAN** *Warner Brothers W 9576*	22		4
23 Feb 85	**LEGS** *Warner Brothers W 9272*	16		4
13 Jul 85	**SUMMER HOLIDAY (EP)** *Warner Brothers W 8946*	51		
19 Oct 85	**SLEEPING BAG** *Warner Brothers W 2001*	27		4
15 Feb 86	**STAGES** *Warner Brothers W 2002*	43		
19 Apr 86	**ROUGH BOY** *Warner Brothers W 2003*	23		4
4 Oct 86	**VELCRO FLY** *Warner Brothers W 8650*	54		
21 Jul 90	**DOUBLEBACK** *Warner Brothers W 9812*	29		3
13 Apr 91	**MY HEAD'S IN MISSISSIPPI** *Warner Brothers W 0009*	37		2
11 Apr 92	**VIVA LAS VEGAS** *Warner Brothers W 0098*	10		6
20 Jun 92	**ROUGH BOY** *Warner Brothers W 0111*	49		
29 Jan 94	**PINCUSHION** *RCA 74321184732*	15		2
7 May 94	**BREAKAWAY** *RCA 74321192282*	60		
29 Jun 96	**WHAT'S UP WITH THAT** *RCA 74321394822*	58		
16 Oct 99	**GIMME ALL YOUR LOVIN' 2000** *Riverhorse RIVHCD 2* MARTAY FEATURING ZZ TOP	28		1

Social Networking

Space – The Final Front Ear

There is music in the air, music all around us; the world is full of it, and you simply take as much as you require.

Edward Elgar

In the Introduction to this book, the analysis of the download era briefly touched on the evolution of so-called social network sites and their respective impact on the singles charts and music business in general. In fact, this subject is arguably the biggest sea change in music distribution since the rise of the independent labels in the 1970s. Back then it was the assertion that bands didn't need to be on a major label; in 2008, bands are saying they don't necessarily need to be on a label *at all*. At the forefront of this huge shift is the social network chart topper, with exciting acts at the vanguard including Arctic Monkeys, Enter Shikari, Lily Allen and Kate Nash, all partly developing their careers on websites such as MySpace, Second Life and Bebo.

So how did this come about?

Click on rewind and head back to the mid-1990s. Computing had come a long way since the days of ZX Spectrums and monstrous, room-filling mainframes that filled whole floors of office blocks. Increases in processing power, allied to ever-cheaper hardware, made it economical at last for the PC (or Mac) to be as ubiquitous as the toaster. Crucially, too, the World Wide Web was up and running, enabling unprecedented access to a vast online repository of information. As more and more people came online, message boards and online diaries called weblogs – blogs – became powerful allies to email in delivering information. Suddenly, it seemed, any fan of a band could fire up the PC, log into the dial-up connection and type in that band's web address, where you could chat to other fans of the band or write blog reviews of your favourite tracks for all the world to see. Very quickly, people began emailing songs to each other of bands they liked, setting in motion a new era which directly paralleled the tape swaps of the playground – albeit in digital representation this time around. This would soon have serious repercussions on the charts as we have already seen.

Sticking with the tech-y part a little while longer (sadly we must), the first-generation high-resolution audio took an age to download due to the comparatively low connection speeds. By 1995, however, Mpeg-1 Audio Layer 3 (MP3s) had spread over the internet like wildfire and become the music delivery format of many people's choice. MP3s are compression algorithms that allow perceptually faithful audio reproduction while using far less data; for those readers who only speak English, this means that these tiny-by-comparison files sat nicely on hard drives, CD players and MP3 players alike, allowing for music collections to become completely digitised and save shelf space in homes across the land. In 1997, the Winamp music player enabled the user to create playlists of their favourite tracks, which were being swapped all over the place by now, before music swappers were partying in 1999 with the release of a peer-to-peer file-sharing program called Napster. Peer To Peer (P2P), in contrast to email, allowed users to directly link the contents of the shared folders of their online computers, and Napster's software made swapping entire music collections as easy as logging on had become.

The problem, of course, was that by virtue of having been digitised – or ripped – from CD, the songs had turned into files, an important shift of concept, and one which for many stripped away their entire financial value (see Introduction). Bands and labels alike began to shout foul, with Metallica famously at the forefront of the anti-file-sharing movement after their track 'I Disappear' was widely shared before it was even authorised for any kind of release. If everyone was sharing files for free, after all, who was going to be bothered buying the records ever again? As already mentioned, Napster in this form was shut down in July 2001, before returning as a fully legal subscription site the next year.

If these formative web clashes were the first heavy skirmishes, the real battles began in the early years of the new millennium, when a new breed of websites began to sneak into the online lives of a whole generation. These sites brought together email, profile and contact information, message boards, photos and blogs into one easy-to-search portal. By dint of being based round the users themselves and enabling searchable 'buddying up' with other online friends with shared interests, these web destinations became known as Social Networking Sites.

There are various early examples. The likes of Friends Reunited brought together many long-lost school pals and because the interaction was online, physical location was no longer important. Also chief among the new sites was Friendster, which swept across the web faster than anything ever had before as users rushed to become part of their own, self-selecting network. The UK charts themselves could be said to be the same – buying a record is both a statement of support for the artist as well as a strong indicator that you are part of a group of like-minded people. The Top 10 singles have always been the nexus of a wider base of fans with shared interests.

Critically, however, Friendster's limit (at the time) of 500 'friends' made it vulnerable to other sites, who were eyeing hungrily the multi-million userbase and the potentially enormous ad revenues on offer. Many came and went before one application, MySpace, cornered the market. By 2005, MySpace was king, its music player proving popular with its userbase. Crucially, MySpace also allowed bands themselves to sign up, and because fans of those bands could chat to each other instantly about tracks and gigs, a unique line of communication between artist and consumer was introduced into the chart-creating mix.

One of the first and most famous MySpace success stories was the rapid and inexorable rise of Sheffield band Arctic Monkeys, who seemingly appeared from nowhere to become, quite literally, the voice of a new generation. After signing to indie Domino records, their first single, 'I Bet You Look Good On The Dancefloor', slammed in at the top of the UK Charts on 17 October 2005, while debut album, *Whatever People Say I Am, That's What I'm Not*, soared to Number 1 on 23 January 2006. No wonder: their fans had long been singing the tracks in their packed-out gigs, including several sold-out nights at London's Astoria.

Proof of the power of MySpace?

The popular reading of the tale may suggest so, but in truth Arctic Monkeys had been working very hard and touring steadily for a good two years previous to their 'overnight success', often handing out demo CDs free to their growing fanbase. These delighted fans were encouraged to spread the word and – off their own bat – emailed, copied and put those tracks up on message boards. The fans' shared enthusiasm for what they heard was enough to mobilise the sales potential of the live concerts. MySpace was therefore merely a tool in the whole process rather than any significant tipping point for an 'unknown' band, who had been building momentum by rather more traditional means for some time since their inception in 2002.

One other aspect of MySpace is its blog section, which allows a direct insight into the thoughts of the user who runs the page. For musicians this often takes the form of tour diaries, news of upcoming TV/radio/live appearances and so on, but occasionally it is a much richer experience. In the case of Lily Allen, her penchant for blogging in various states of mind quickly drew empathetic attention. Allen, the daughter of actor Keith, was an aspiring musician whose first forays into music was an unreleased folk album on Warner Brothers in 2002. An avid MySpacer, when her new-sounding demo tracks were placed on there, the positive feedback was instrumental in the major chart success of her (physically released) hit single 'Smile' and her subsequent album *Alright, Still*. The record sales reflected both the punters' love for the music and their love for Lily, whose honesty and occasional vulnerability in her blogging drew in masses of fans.

Unfortunately, so powerful was the attraction and so great was the potential of these new sites to the music lover/music biz that the innocent appeal couldn't last. Social Network sites were very soon jumped on by every part of a corporate music industry eager to show that the digital era was not a threat to the old guard, but an opportunity to utilise technology to inform and spread the word about acts and therefore secure that most elusive of beasts: a hit single.

Sites like MySpace enabled artists to quickly show their music, videos, pictures, gig dates and blogs off to all and sundry, and therefore it was the industry's method of choice throughout 2005 and 2006. It was, in a sense, 'the internet made easy' – a series of already existing online experiences brought together in one digestible package. Suddenly, if a band did not have a MySpace page they were a rarity, old fashioned, out of touch. High-profile radio sessions were booked directly with bands through MySpace, whole albums were previewed on there prior to physical release and because the site also offered fans the chance to email the band *direct* as well as chat among themselves, MySpace became a massive mobilisation point for individuals. The difference between this and the old model was that no gatekeepers were required; as with Arctic Monkeys, bands, fans and movements – and subsequent record sales – meant groups could chart without going anywhere near a record company to 'launch' their career.

This concept was strengthened by the changes in the chart rulings in April 2006, which made records eligible to chart on download sales alone, in the week before any physical release. As previously mentioned, the first single to hit the top without any physical sales whatsoever was Gnarls Barkley, who shot to Number 1 on 2 April with their soul-hop song, 'Crazy'. It happened to be a great track that, due in part to some delays in the original timeline, had been building up momentum and anticipation, thanks to huge pre-release radio play. When it was finally made available to buy, the results were instant and proved that a blend of innovation, a great media, radio and TV campaign and technological savvy could have great rewards.

Along, of course, with a very good song.

There was a small fly in the ointment in social network-land, however, when English folk/punk geezer Billy Bragg noticed that MySpace's 'Terms and Conditions of Use' contained a clause that seemed to indicate that bands signing up to the site were by default also granting MySpace the rights to reproduce and use that content without any remuneration. After much noise in the media and some successful campaigning, the clause was reworded to a simpler one that made it clear that the rights remained with the artist. And with MySpace building in TV previews, sponsoring music concerts and running a record label, they had even begun to get into the content business themselves; then Rupert Murdoch's News Corporation bought the site in 2005 for nearly $600 million and the end of an era, however brief, seemed imminent.

Other developments further diluted the power of the Social Network sites in terms of infecting the charts – within twelve months, record companies went from being really excited and impressed that a band they'd never heard of had a billion-squillion 'friends', to realising that for a matter of pounds you could buy a software 'robot' that could add friends at a faster rate than a lottery winner down the pub. The focus shifted once more. There can never be another band that breaks in the same way as these pioneers, that particular innovative portal has closed. Music in the new millennium is many things, but it is a fast moving target for a fact.

Social Networking websites have nonetheless really proved their worth as part of a contemporary strategy for success, and although they are by no means a fast-track to anywhere, they have in part enabled a new method of approaching a career. MySpace still had much to contribute too. Post-hardcore band Enter Shikari formed in 2003, but despite much record company interest they decided at an early stage to retain control of as much of their careers as was possible and formed their own label, while gigging hard and gathering a fanbase both online and in the physical world.

The technology had finally caught up with the ideal: recording hardware and software was now financially viable for high-quality bedroom recording, and access to a potential fanbase for those tracks was a few clicks away on a broadband computer set-up. This, in theory, removed several obstacles between music and its audience, and since the chart rules had been updated, there was no longer any need for any outlay on physical product. It's difficult to quantify exactly how remarkable this is. For Enter Shikari, it was instrumental in their decision to go it alone and, after clocking up a million plays on their MySpace page, their debut single

'Mothership' was single of the week on the iTunes store in August 2006, followed by a string of chart appearances around the mid-100s on downloads alone. An indicator of their success is that by the end of 2006 they were filling venues as large as London Astoria partly on the buzz created by being able to communicate directly with their fanbase. Many more acts would look at self-releasing their records in the future.

As ever the independent labels (and certain enlightened individuals at the major record companies) were at the forefront of the technology, taking advantage of their small size to move quickly and lead the way. Take Transgressive Records, whose 17 November 2006 four-band road-show was piped into the graphical social network Second Life – a mix of a 3D-world computer game and a social network, where each person controls their own avatar, or representative character. As the bands played that night in the 'real world' gig at Leeds University, their virtual equivalents were bopping away in Second Life's virtual representation of a Dublin club to an audience of logged-in Second Lifers from all over the world. This was powerful in raising further awareness for their acts, some of whom went on, as in the case of Subways, Young Knives and The Foals, to have chart success during the following twelve months. It was a lesson not lost on the industry as a whole. The ante had been upped once more, the target shifted yet again.

The Introduction to this book touches on the big boys' tamperings with the web – Radiohead for example – but 2007 was a historic year for unsigned acts too. In January the chart rules altered to state that no actual physical release would be necessary for chart eligibility. The first act to benefit from this UK chart change was indie-rock outfit Koopa, who since 2000 had been scratching about on the fringes of a largely disinterested music business. In 2005 their single, 'No Trend' had got to Number 71, while 2006 saw follow-up 'Stand Up For England' hit Number 79. Those feats were blown out of the water, however, when on 14 January, Koopa became the first 'unsigned' act to hit the Top 40, 'Blag, Steal And Borrow' whizzing in at Number 34. That astonishing feat, built on the power of word-of-mouth and hard gigging while the fans mobilised through social networks (online and the traditional networking at gigs), was bettered later that year by their 'One Off Song For The Summer' which levelled at Number 17 in the UK Charts and finally 'The Crash' hitting Number 16 on 29 October. On the back of the success, Koopa announced through MySpace that they would sign to Pied Piper Records, having put themselves in a strong position by virtue of their independent chart assault. At the time of writing, they are in a top Californian studio working on their debut album.

The concept of going it alone using the power of social networks was echoed – albeit on a far vaster scale – by Coldplay, who streamed the whole of their long-awaited fourth album, *Viva La Vida Or Death And All His Friends* on MySpace on 6 June 2008, partly in response to leaked tracks circulating on the internet. Given that it was the biggest pre-sale in iTunes history, one can speculate that the MySpace preview plus the leaked tracks were powerful indicators as to the massive anticipation for Coldplay's first album for three years. On 12 June the album's physical release date, it effortlessly soared to Number 1 in the charts, selling a cool 400,000 copies in that first week.

There are now a bewildering array of sites out there, from the featured artist on the front of MySpace itself, Facebook's Fan Pages, Bebo, last.fm with its software that recommends similar tracks and artists you might like and even those virtual concerts in Second Life. The online world is an ever-changing place where no sooner is a boundary identified then it is immediately knocked down. At the crux of it all, though, is the truism that people like to talk to each other online and in doing so they talk about their favourite musicians. Social Networking, then, is hardly a new idea – what is a gig if not a place to hang out with your peers? The groups provide the soundtrack and their own particular musical church within which to gather and, again, *if the songs are good enough* then people will buy sufficient copies to bother the UK chart compilers. It's when the great songs dry up that it's time to really worry.

A–D

KEY TO INDEX ENTRIES

	Song Title / Artist/Group	Peak Position	Year of Entry
	ALL I REALLY WANT ALANIS MORISSETTE	59	1996
	ALL I REALLY WANT TO DO BYRDS	4	1965
	ALL I REALLY WANT TO DO CHER	9	1965
	ALL I SEE IS YOU DUSTY SPRINGFIELD	9	1966
	ALL I THINK ABOUT IS YOU NILSSON	43	1977
Same letter denotes different versions of the same song	ALL I WANNA DO [A] SHERYL CROW	4	1994
	ALL I WANNA DO [A] JOANNE FARRELL	40	1995
	ALL I WANNA DO [A] AMY STUDT	21	2004
Different letters denote different songs with the same name	ALL I WANNA DO [B] TIN TIN OUT	31	1997
	ALL I WANNA DO [C] DANNII	4	1997
	ALL I WANNA DO IS MAKE LOVE TO YOU HEART	37	1993

	Peak Position	Year of Entry
( ) SIGUR ROS	72	2003

A

	Peak Position	Year of Entry
A BA NI BI IZHAR COHEN & ALPHABETA	20	1978
'A' BOMB IN WARDOUR STREET JAM	1	1978
A9 ARIEL	28	2000
THE A TEAM MIKE POST	45	1984
A&E GOLDFRAPP	10	2008
AAAH D YAAA GOATS	53	1993
AARON'S PARTY (COME GET IT) AARON CARTER	51	2000
ABACAB GENESIS	9	1981
ABACUS (WHEN I FALL IN LOVE) AXUS	62	1998
ABANDON [A] DARE	71	1989
ABANDON [B] THAT PETROL EMOTION	73	1990
ABANDON SHIP BLAGGERS I.T.A.	48	1994
ABBA-ESQUE EP ERASURE	1	1992
THE ABBEY ROAD EP SPIRITUALIZED	39	1998
ABC JACKSON 5	8	1970
ABC AND D... BLUE BAMBOO	23	1994
A.B.C. (FALLING IN LOVE'S NOT EASY) DIRECT DRIVE	75	1985
ABIDE WITH ME INSPIRATIONAL CHOIR	36	1984
ABIDE WITH ME VIC REEVES	47	1991
ABOUT LOVE ROY DAVIS JR	70	2004
ABOUT 3AM DARK STAR	50	1999
ABOUT YOU NOW SUGABABES	1	2007
ABOUT YOUR DRESS MACCABEES	33	2007
ABOVE THE CLOUDS PAUL WELLER	47	1992
ABRACADABRA STEVE MILLER BAND	2	1982
ABRAHAM MARTIN AND JOHN MARVIN GAYE	9	1970
ABSENT FRIENDS DIVINE COMEDY	38	2004
ABSOLUT(E) CLAUDIA BRUCKEN	71	1990
ABSOLUTE SCRITTI POLITTI	17	1984
ABSOLUTE AFFIRMATION RADIO 4	61	2004
ABSOLUTE BEGINNERS [A] JAM	4	1981
ABSOLUTE BEGINNERS [B] DAVID BOWIE	2	1986
ABSOLUTE E-SENSUAL JAKI GRAHAM	69	1995
ABSOLUTE REALITY ALARM	35	1985
ABSOLUTELY EVERYBODY VANESSA AMOROSI	7	2000
ABSOLUTELY FABULOUS ABSOLUTELY FABULOUS	6	1994
ABSTAIN FIVE THIRTY	75	1990
ABSURD FLUKE	25	1997
ABUSE ME SILVERCHAIR	40	1997
AC/DC X-PRESS 2	60	2000
ACAPULCO 1922 KENNY BALL & HIS JAZZMEN	27	1963
ACCELERATE SKIN UP	45	1992
ACCELERATOR PRIMAL SCREAM	34	2000
ACCEPTABLE IN THE 80S CALVIN HARRIS	10	2007
ACCESS DJ MISJAH & DJ TIM	16	1996
ACCIDENT OF BIRTH BRUCE DICKINSON	54	1997
ACCIDENT PRONE STATUS QUO	36	1978
ACCIDENT WAITING TO HAPPEN (EP) BILLY BRAGG	33	1992
ACCIDENTLY IN LOVE COUNTING CROWS	28	2004
ACCIDENTS THUNDERCLAP NEWMAN	46	1970
ACCIDENTS WILL HAPPEN ELVIS COSTELLO	28	1979
ACE OF SPADES MOTORHEAD	15	1980
ACES HIGH IRON MAIDEN	20	1984
ACHILLES HEEL TOPLOADER	8	2000
ACHY BREAKY HEART ALVIN & THE CHIPMUNKS FEATURING BILLY RAY CYRUS	53	1992
ACHY BREAKY HEART BILLY RAY CYRUS	3	1992
ACID LAB ALEX REECE	64	1996
ACID MAN JOLLY ROGER	23	1988
ACID TRAK DILLINJA	71	2004
ACKEE 1-2-3 BEAT	54	1983
THE ACOUSTICS (EP) NEW MODEL ARMY	49	1985
ACPERIENCE HARDFLOOR	60	1997
ACROBATS (LOOKING FOR BALANCE) MOONY	64	2003
ACROSS YER OCEAN MERCURY REV	54	2005
ACRYLIC COURTEENERS	44	2007
ACT OF WAR ELTON JOHN & MILLIE JACKSON	32	1985
ACTION [A] SWEET	15	1975
ACTION [A] DEF LEPPARD	14	1994
ACTION [B] SAINT ETIENNE	41	2002
ACTION AND DRAMA BIS	50	1999
ACTIV 8 (COME WITH ME) ALTERN 8	3	1991
ACTIVATED GERALD ALSTON	73	1989
ACTUALLY IT'S DARKNESS IDLEWILD	23	2000
ADAGIO FOR STRINGS TIESTO	37	2005
ADDAMS FAMILY (WHOOMP!) TAG TEAM	53	1994
ADDAMS GROOVE HAMMER	4	1991
ADDICTED [A] SIMPLE PLAN	63	2003
ADDICTED [B] ENRIQUE IGLESIAS	11	2003
ADDICTED TO BASS PURETONE	2	2002
ADDICTED TO LOVE ROBERT PALMER	5	1986
ADDICTED TO LOVE SHAKE B4 USE VS ROBERT PALMER	42	2002
ADDICTED TO LOVE (LIVE) TINA TURNER	71	1988
ADDICTED TO YOU ALEC EMPIRE	64	2002
ADDICTION ALMIGHTY	38	1993
ADDICTIVE TRUTH HURTS	3	2002
ADELANTE SASH!	2	2000
ADIA SARAH McLACHLAN	18	1998
A.D.I.D.A.S. [A] KORN	22	1997
A.D.I.D.A.S. [B] KILLER MIKE FEATURING BIG BOI	22	2003
ADIDAS WORLD EDWYN COLLINS	71	1997
ADIEMUS ADIEMUS	48	1995
ADIOS AMIGO JIM REEVES	23	1962
ADORATION WALTZ DAVID WHITFIELD	9	1957
ADORATIONS KILLING JOKE	42	1986
ADORE JOE ROBERTS	45	1994
ADORED AND EXPLORED MARC ALMOND	25	1995
ADRENALIN (EP) N-JOI	23	1991
ADRIENNE CALLING	18	2002
ADRIFT (CAST YOUR MIND) ANTARCTICA	72	2000
ADULT EDUCATION DARYL HALL & JOHN OATES	63	1984
ADVENTURE [A] BE YOUR OWN PET	36	2006
THE ADVENTURE [B] ANGELS AND AIRWAVES	20	2006
THE ADVENTURES OF THE LOVE CRUSADER SARAH BRIGHTMAN & THE STARSHIP TROOPERS	53	1979
ADVERTISING SPACE ROBBIE WILLIAMS	8	2005
ADVICE FOR THE YOUNG AT HEART TEARS FOR FEARS	36	1990
AERODYNAMIK KRAFTWERK	33	2004
AEROPLANE RED HOT CHILI PEPPERS	11	1996
THE AEROPLANE SONG STRAW	37	1999
AFFAIR CHERRELLE	67	1989
AFFIRMATION SAVAGE GARDEN	8	2000
AFRAID MOTLEY CRUE	58	1997
AFRICA TOTO	3	1983
AFRICA UNITE BOB MARLEY & THE WAILERS	49	2005
AFRICAN AND WHITE CHINA CRISIS	45	1982
AFRICAN DREAM WASIS DIOP FEATURING LENA FIAGBE	44	1996
AFRICAN HORIZON MYSTICA	59	1998
AFRICAN REIGN DEEP C	75	1991
AFRICAN WALTZ JOHNNY DANKWORTH	9	1961
AFRIKA HISTORY FEATURING Q-TEE	42	1990
AFRIKA SHOX LEFTFIELD/BAMBAATAA	7	1999
AFRO DIZZI ACT CRY SISCO!	42	1989
AFRO KING EMF	51	1995
AFRO PUFFS LADY OF RAGE	72	1994
AFRO SLEEZE ROACH MOTEL	73	1993
AFRODISIAC [A] POWDER	72	1995
AFRODISIAC [B] BRANDY	11	2004
THE AFRO-LEFT EP LEFTFIELD FEATURING DJUM DJUM	22	1995
AFTER A FASHION MIDGE URE & MICK KARN	39	1983
AFTER ALL [A] FRANK & WALTERS	11	1993
AFTER ALL [B] DELERIUM FEATURING JAEL	46	2003
AFTER ALL THESE YEARS FOSTER & ALLEN	43	1986
AFTER ALL THIS TIME SIMON WEBBE	16	2006
AFTER DARK LE TIGRE	63	2005
AFTER HOURS [A] BLUETONES	26	2002
AFTER HOURS [B] WE ARE SCIENTISTS	15	2008
AFTER LOVE BLANK & JONES	57	2000
AFTER THE FIRE ROGER DALTREY	50	1985
AFTER THE GOLDRUSH PRELUDE	21	1974
AFTER THE LOVE JESUS LOVES YOU	68	1989
AFTER THE LOVE HAS GONE [A] EARTH, WIND & FIRE	4	1979
AFTER THE LOVE HAS GONE [A] DAMAGE	42	2001
AFTER THE LOVE HAS GONE [B] PRINCESS	28	1985
AFTER THE LOVE HAS GONE [C] STEPS	5	1999
AFTER THE RAIN TITIYO	60	1990
AFTER THE RAIN HAS FALLEN STING	31	2000
AFTER THE WAR GARY MOORE	37	1989
AFTER THE WATERSHED CARTER THE UNSTOPPABLE SEX MACHINE	11	1991
AFTER YOU'RE GONE ONE TRUE VOICE	2	2002
AFTER YOU'VE GONE ALICE BABS	43	1963
AFTERGLOW MISSION	53	1994
AFTERGLOW OF YOUR LOVE SMALL FACES	36	1969
AFTERMATH [A] NIGHTMARES ON WAX	38	1990
AFTERMATH [B] TRICKY	69	1994
AFTERMATH [C] R.E.M.	41	2004
AFTERNOON DELIGHT STARLAND VOCAL BAND	18	1976
AFTERNOON OF THE RHINO MIKE POST COALITION	47	1975
(AFTERNOON) SOAPS ARAB STRAP	74	1998
AFTERNOONS & COFFEESPOONS CRASH TEST DUMMIES	23	1994
AGADOO BLACK LACE	2	1984
AGAIN [A] JIMMY TARBUCK	68	1985
AGAIN [B] JANET JACKSON	6	1993
AGAIN [C] JULIET ROBERTS	33	1994
AGAIN [D] FAITH EVANS	12	2005
AGAIN AND AGAIN STATUS QUO	13	1978
AGAINST ALL ODDS STEVE BROOKSTEIN	1	2005
AGAINST ALL ODDS (TAKE A LOOK AT ME NOW) PHIL COLLINS	2	1984
AGAINST ALL ODDS (TAKE A LOOK AT ME NOW) MARIAH CAREY FEATURING WESTLIFE	1	2000
AGAINST THE WIND MAIRE BRENNAN	64	1992
AGE AIN'T NOTHING BUT A NUMBER AALIYAH	32	1995
AGE OF LONELINESS ENIGMA	21	1994
AGE OF LOVE AGE OF LOVE	38	1997
AGE OF PANIC SENSER	52	1994
AGENT DAN AGENT PROVOCATEUR	49	1997
AGNES QUEEN OF SORROW BONNIE PRINCE BILLY	69	2004
AHORA ES (NOW IS THE TIME) 2 IN A ROOM	43	1995
AI NO CORRIDA UNITING NATIONS FEATURING LAURA MORE	18	2005
AI NO CORRIDA (I-NO-KO-REE-DA) QUINCY JONES FEATURING DUNE	14	1981
AIKEA-GUINEA COCTEAU TWINS	41	1985
AIN'T COMPLAINING STATUS QUO	19	1988
AIN'T DOIN' NOTHIN' JET BRONX & THE FORBIDDEN	49	1977
AIN'T GOIN' TO GOA ALABAMA 3	40	1998
AIN'T GOING DOWN (TILL THE SUN COMES UP) GARTH BROOKS	13	1994
AIN'T GONNA BE THAT WAY MARV JOHNSON	50	1960

Title / Artist	Peak Position	Year of Entry
AIN'T GONNA BUMP NO MORE (WITH NO BIG FAT WOMAN) JOE TEX	2	1977
AIN'T GONNA CRY AGAIN PETER COX	37	1997
AIN'T GONNA WASH FOR A WEEK BROOK BROTHERS	13	1961
AIN'T GOT A CLUE LURKERS	45	1978
AIN'T GOT NO-I GOT LIFE NINA SIMONE	2	1968
AIN'T IT FUN GUNS N' ROSES	9	1993
AIN'T IT FUNNY JENNIFER LOPEZ	2	2001
AIN'T LOVE A BITCH ROD STEWART	11	1979
AIN'T MISBEHAVIN' JOHNNIE RAY	17	1956
AIN'T MISBEHAVIN' TOMMY BRUCE & THE BRUISERS	3	1960
AIN'T MY BEATING HEART TEN SHARP	1	1992
AIN'T NO CASANOVA SINCLAIR	28	1993
AIN'T NO DOUBT JIMMY NAIL	1	1992
AIN'T NO EASY WAY BLACK REBEL MOTORCYCLE CLUB	21	2005
AIN'T NO LOVE (AIN'T NO USE) SUB SUB FEATURING MELANIE WILLIAMS	3	1993
AIN'T NO LOVE (AIN'T NO USE) SODA CLUB FEATURING ASHLEY JADE	40	2004
AIN'T NO LOVE IN THE HEART OF THE CITY WHITESNAKE	51	1980
AIN'T NO MAN DINA CARROLL	16	1992
AIN'T NO MOUNTAIN HIGH ENOUGH DIANA ROSS	6	1970
AIN'T NO MOUNTAIN HIGH ENOUGH JOCELYN BROWN	35	1998
AIN'T NO MOUNTAIN HIGH ENOUGH WHITEHOUSE	60	1998
AIN'T NO MOUNTAIN HIGH ENOUGH - REMEMBER ME (MEDLEY) BOYSTOWN GANG	46	1981
AIN'T NO NEED TO HIDE SANDY B	60	1997
AIN'T NO OTHER MAN CHRISTINA AGUILERA	2	2006
AIN'T NO PARTY ORSON	21	2007
AIN'T NO PLAYA JAY-Z FEATURING FOXY BROWN	31	1997
AIN'T NO PLEASING YOU CHAS & DAVE	2	1982
AIN'T NO STOPPIN US DJ LUCK & MC NEAT FEATURING JJ	8	2000
AIN'T NO STOPPIN' US NOW [A] McFADDEN & WHITEHEAD	5	1979
AIN'T NO STOPPING [A] ENIGMA	11	1981
AIN'T NO STOPPIN' US NOW [B] BIG DADDY KANE	44	1990
AIN'T NO STOPPING US NOW [A] LUTHER VANDROSS	22	1995
AIN'T NO STOPPING US NOW [A] MOBO ALLSTARS	47	1998
AIN'T NO STOPPING US NOW (PARTY FOR THE WORLD) STEVE WALSH	44	1988
AIN'T NO SUNSHINE MICHAEL JACKSON	8	1972
AIN'T NO SUNSHINE SIVUCA	56	1984
AIN'T NO SUNSHINE LADYSMITH BLACK MAMBAZO FEATURING DES'REE	42	1999
AIN'T NOBODY RUFUS & CHAKA KHAN	6	1984
AIN'T NOBODY JAKI GRAHAM	44	1994
AIN'T NOBODY DIANA KING	13	1995
AIN'T NOBODY COURSE	8	1997
AIN'T NOBODY LL COOL J	1	1997
AIN'T NOBODY BETTER INNER CITY	10	1989
AIN'T NOBODY (LOVES ME BETTER) KWS & GWEN DICKEY	21	1994
AIN'T NOTHIN' LIKE IT MICHAEL LOVESMITH	75	1985
AIN'T NOTHING BUT A HOUSEPARTY SHOWSTOPPERS	11	1968
AIN'T NOTHING BUT A HOUSEPARTY PHIL FEARON	60	1986
AIN'T NOTHING GOIN' ON BUT THE RENT GWEN GUTHRIE	5	1986
AIN'T NOTHING GONNA KEEP ME FROM YOU TERI DE SARIO	52	1978
AIN'T NOTHING LIKE THE REAL THING MARVIN GAYE & TAMMI TERRELL	34	1968
AIN'T NOTHING LIKE THE REAL THING MARCELLA DETROIT & ELTON JOHN	24	1994
AIN'T NOTHING WRONG HOUSTON	33	2005
AIN'T SHE SWEET BEATLES	29	1964
AIN'T TALKIN' 'BOUT DUB APOLLO 440	7	1997
AIN'T THAT A LOT OF LOVE SIMPLY RED	14	1999
AIN'T THAT A SHAME PAT BOONE	7	1955
AIN'T THAT A SHAME FATS DOMINO	23	1957
AIN'T THAT A SHAME FOUR SEASONS	38	1963
AIN'T THAT ENOUGH TEENAGE FANCLUB	17	1997
AIN'T THAT ENOUGH FOR YOU JOHN DAVIS & THE MONSTER ORCHESTRA	70	1979
AIN'T THAT FUNNY JIMMY JUSTICE	8	1962
(AIN'T THAT) JUST LIKE ME HOLLIES	25	1963
AIN'T THAT JUST THE WAY LUTRICIA McNEAL	6	1997
AIN'T THAT LOVIN' YOU BABY ELVIS PRESLEY	15	1964
AIN'T THAT THE TRUTH FRANKIE KELLY	65	1985
AIN'T TOO PROUD TO BEG TEMPTATIONS	21	1966
AIN'T 2 PROUD 2 BEG TLC	13	1992
AIN'T WE FUNKIN' NOW BROTHERS JOHNSON	43	1978
AIN'T WHAT YOU DO BIG BROVAZ	15	2003
AIR GUITAR TOWERS OF LONDON	32	2006
AIR HOSTESS BUSTED	2	2004
THE AIR I BREATHE SIMPLY RED	6	1998
THE AIR THAT I BREATHE HOLLIES	2	1974
AIR TRAFFIC THREE DRIVES	75	2004
AIR 2000 ALBION	59	2000
AIR WE BREATHE ALISHA'S ATTIC	12	1997
THE AIR YOU BREATHE BOMB THE BASS	52	1991
AIRHEAD [A] THOMAS DOLBY	53	1988
AIRHEAD [B] GIRLS @ PLAY	18	2001
AIRPLANE GARDENS FAMILY CAT	69	1993
AIRPORT MOTORS	4	1978
AIRWAVE RANK 1	10	2000
AISHA DEATH IN VEGAS	9	2000
AISY WAISY CARTOONS	16	1999
AJARE WAY OUT WEST	36	1994
AL CAPONE PRINCE BUSTER	18	1967
AL DI LA EMILIO PERICOLI	30	1962
ALA KABOO SOUND 5	69	1999
ALABAMA BLUES (REVISITED) ST GERMAIN	50	1996
ALABAMA JUBILEE FERKO STRING BAND	20	1955
ALABAMA SONG DAVID BOWIE	23	1980
ALAN BEAN HEFNER	58	2001
ALANE WES	11	1998
ALARM CALL BJORK	33	1998
ALARM CLOCK RUMBLE STRIPS	41	2007
ALARMA 666	58	1998
ALAS AGNES MYSTERY JETS	34	2005
ALBATROSS FLEETWOOD MAC	1	1968
ALBINONI VS STAR WARS SIGUE SIGUE SPUTNIK	75	1989
ALBION BABYSHAMBLES	8	2005
ALCOHOLIC STARSAILOR	10	2001
ALEXANDER GRAHAM BELL SWEET	33	1971
ALFIE [A] CILLA BLACK	9	1966
ALFIE [B] LILY ALLEN	15	2007
ALIBI DAVID GRAY	71	2006
ALICE I WANT YOU JUST FOR ME FULL FORCE	9	1985
ALICE WHAT'S THE MATTER TERRORVISION	24	1994
ALICE (WHO THE X IS ALICE?) (LIVING NEXT DOOR TO ALICE) GOMPIE	17	1995
ALISHA RULES THE WORLD ALISHA'S ATTIC	12	1996
ALISON LINDA RONSTADT	66	1979
ALISON'S ROOM 60FT DOLLS	61	1998
ALIVE [A] PEARL JAM	16	1992
ALIVE [B] HELIOTROPIC FEATURING VERNA V	33	1999
ALIVE [C] BEASTIE BOYS	28	1999
ALIVE [D] P.O.D.	19	2002
ALIVE [E] ALIVE FEATURING D D KLEIN	49	2002
ALIVE [F] S CLUB	5	2002
ALIVE [G] SONIQUE	70	2003
ALIVE AND AMPLIFIED MOONEY SUZUKI	38	2005
ALIVE AND KICKING SIMPLE MINDS	6	1985
ALIVE AND KICKING EAST SIDE BEAT	26	1992
ALKALINE SCARFO	61	1997
ALL ABLAZE IAN BROWN	20	2005
ALL ABOUT EVE MARXMAN	28	1993
ALL ABOUT LOVIN' YOU BON JOVI	9	2003
ALL ABOUT SOUL BILLY JOEL	32	1993
ALL ABOUT US [A] PETER ANDRE	3	1997
ALL ABOUT US [B] tATu	8	2005
ALL ABOUT YOU McFLY	1	2005
ALL ALONE AM I BRENDA LEE	7	1963
ALL ALONE ON CHRISTMAS DARLENE LOVE	31	1992
ALL ALONG THE WATCHTOWER JIMI HENDRIX EXPERIENCE	5	1968
ALL ALONG THE WATCHTOWER (EP) JIMI HENDRIX	52	1990
ALL AMERICAN BOY BILL PARSONS	22	1959
ALL AMERICAN GIRLS SISTER SLEDGE	41	1981
ALL AND ALL JOYCE SIMS	16	1986
ALL APOLOGIES NIRVANA	32	1993
ALL AROUND MY HAT STEELEYE SPAN	5	1975
ALL AROUND MY HAT STATUS QUO	47	1996
ALL AROUND THE WORLD [A] JAM	13	1977
ALL AROUND THE WORLD [B] LISA STANSFIELD	1	1989
ALL AROUND THE WORLD [C] JASON DONOVAN	41	1993
ALL AROUND THE WORLD [D] OASIS	1	1998
ALL AROUND THE WORLD [E] NORTHERN LINE	27	2000
ALL BECAUSE OF YOU [A] GEORDIE	6	1973
ALL BECAUSE OF YOU [B] U2	4	2005
ALL 'BOUT THE MONEY MEJA	12	1998
ALL BY MYSELF ERIC CARMEN	12	1976
ALL BY MYSELF CELINE DION	6	1996
ALL CRIED OUT [A] ALISON MOYET	8	1984
ALL CRIED OUT [B] MELANIE WILLIAMS	60	1994
ALL CRIED OUT [C] ALLURE FEATURING 112	12	1998
ALL DAY ALL NIGHT STEPHANIE MILLS	68	1993
ALL DAY AND ALL OF THE NIGHT KINKS	2	1964
ALL DAY AND ALL OF THE NIGHT STRANGLERS	7	1988
ALL DOWNHILL FROM HERE NEW FOUND GLORY	58	2004
ALL EXHALE LUKE SLATER	74	2000
ALL EYES CHIKINKI	74	2004
ALL FALL DOWN [A] LINDISFARNE	34	1972
ALL FALL DOWN [B] FIVE STAR	15	1985
ALL FALL DOWN [C] ULTRAVOX	30	1986
ALL FALL DOWN [D] MIDGET	57	1998
ALL FALLS DOWN KANYE WEST FEATURING SYLEENA JOHNSON	10	2004
ALL FIRED UP PAT BENATAR	19	1988
ALL FOR LEYNA BILLY JOEL	40	1980
ALL FOR LOVE BRYAN ADAMS, ROD STEWART & STING	2	1994
ALL FOR YOU JANET JACKSON	3	2001
ALL 4 LOVE COLOR ME BADD	5	1991
ALL 4 LOVE (BREAK 4 LOVE 1990) RAZE FEATURING LADY J & SECRETARY OF ENTERTAINMENT	30	1990
ALL FUNKED UP MOTHER	34	1993
ALL GOD'S CHILDREN BELINDA CARLISLE	66	1999
ALL GONE AWAY JOYRIDER	54	1996
ALL GOOD DE LA SOUL FEATURING CHAKA KHAN	33	2000
ALL GOOD THINGS (COME TO AN END) NELLY FURTADO	4	2006

Title / Artist	Peak Position	Year of Entry
ALL HOOKED UP ALL SAINTS	7	2001
ALL I AM (IS LOVING YOU) BLUEBELLS	58	1985
ALL I ASK RAE & CHRISTIAN FEATURING VEBA	67	1999
ALL I ASK OF MYSELF IS THAT I HOLD TOGETHER NED'S ATOMIC DUSTBIN	33	1995
ALL I ASK OF YOU CLIFF RICHARD & SARAH BRIGHTMAN	3	1986
ALL I DO CLEPTOMANIACS FEATURING BRYAN CHAMBERS	23	2001
ALL I EVER NEED IS YOU SONNY & CHER	8	1972
ALL I EVER WANTED [A] SANTANA	57	1980
ALL I EVER WANTED [B] HUMAN LEAGUE	47	2001
ALL I EVER WANTED (DEVOTION) MYSTERY	57	2002
ALL I GAVE WORLD PARTY	37	1993
ALL I GOT NEWTON FAULKNER	59	2007
ALL I HAVE JENNIFER LOPEZ FEATURING LL COOL J	2	2003
ALL I HAVE TO DO IS DREAM EVERLY BROTHERS	1	1958
ALL I HAVE TO DO IS DREAM BOBBIE GENTRY & GLEN CAMPBELL	3	1969
ALL I HAVE TO DO IS DREAM PHIL EVERLY & CLIFF RICHARD	14	1994
ALL I HAVE TO GIVE BACKSTREET BOYS	2	1998
(ALL I KNOW) FEELS LIKE FOREVER JOE COCKER	25	1992
ALL I NEED AIR	29	1998
ALL I NEED IS A MIRACLE MIKE + THE MECHANICS	27	1986
ALL I NEED IS EVERYTHING AZTEC CAMERA	34	1984
ALL I NEED IS YOUR SWEET LOVIN' GLORIA GAYNOR	44	1975
ALL I NEED TO KNOW EMMA BUNTON	60	2007
ALL I REALLY WANT ALANIS MORISSETTE	59	1996
ALL I REALLY WANT TO DO BYRDS	4	1965
ALL I REALLY WANT TO DO CHER	9	1965
ALL I SEE IS YOU DUSTY SPRINGFIELD	9	1966
ALL I THINK ABOUT IS YOU NILSSON	43	1977
ALL I WANNA DO [A] SHERYL CROW	4	1994
ALL I WANNA DO [A] JOANNE FARRELL	40	1995
ALL I WANNA DO [A] AMY STUDT	21	2004
ALL I WANNA DO [B] TIN TIN OUT	31	1997
ALL I WANNA DO [C] DANNII	4	1997
ALL I WANNA DO IS MAKE LOVE TO YOU HEART	8	1990
ALL I WANT [A] HOWARD JONES	35	1986
ALL I WANT [B] THOSE 2 GIRLS	36	1995
ALL I WANT [C] SKUNK ANANSIE	14	1996
ALL I WANT [D] SUSANNA HOFFS	32	1996
ALL I WANT [E] OFFSPRING	31	1997
ALL I WANT [F] PURESSENCE	39	1998
ALL I WANT [G] REEF	51	2001
ALL I WANT [H] MIS-TEEQ	2	2001
ALL I WANT [I] WET WET WET	14	2004
ALL I WANT FOR CHRISTMAS IS A BEATLE DORA BRYAN	20	1963
ALL I WANT FOR CHRISTMAS IS YOU MARIAH CAREY	2	1994
ALL I WANT FROM YOU TEMPTATIONS	71	1989
ALL I WANT IS EVERYTHING DEF LEPPARD	38	1996
ALL I WANT IS YOU [A] ROXY MUSIC	12	1974
ALL I WANT IS YOU [B] U2	4	1989
ALL I WANT IS YOU [B] BELLEFIRE	18	2002
ALL I WANT IS YOU [C] BRYAN ADAMS	22	1992
ALL I WANT IS YOU [D] 911	4	1998
ALL I WANT TO DO UB40	41	1986
ALL I WANT TO DO IS ROCK TRAVIS	39	1997
ALL I WANTED IN TUA NUA	69	1988
ALL IN MY HEAD KOSHEEN	7	2003
ALL IN YOUR HANDS LAMB	71	1999
ALL IS FULL OF LOVE BJORK	24	1999
ALL JOIN HANDS SLADE	15	1984
ALL KINDS OF EVERYTHING DANA	1	1970
ALL MAPPED OUT DEPARTURE	30	2004
ALL MINE PORTISHEAD	8	1997
ALL MY BEST FRIENDS ARE METALHEADS LESS THAN JAKE	51	2000
ALL MY FRIENDS LCD SOUNDSYSTEM	41	2007
ALL MY LIFE [A] MAJOR HARRIS	61	1983
ALL MY LIFE [B] K-CI & JOJO	8	1998
ALL MY LIFE [C] FOO FIGHTERS	5	2002
ALL MY LOVE [A] CLIFF RICHARD	6	1967
ALL MY LOVE [B] HERNANDEZ	58	1989
ALL MY LOVE [C] QUEEN PEN FEATURING ERIC WILLIAMS	11	1998
ALL MY LOVE (ASK NOTHING) SPEAR OF DESTINY	61	1985
ALL MY LOVING DOWLANDS	33	1964
ALL MY TIME PAID + LIVE FEATURING LAURYN HILL	57	1997
ALL MY TRIALS PAUL McCARTNEY	35	1990
ALL 'N' ALL 187 LOCKDOWN (FEATURING D'EMPRESS)	43	1999
ALL N MY GRILL MISSY 'MISDEMEANOR' ELLIOTT FEATURING MC SOLAAR	20	1999
ALL NIGHT ALL RIGHT PETER ANDRE FEATURING WARREN G	16	1998
ALL NIGHT DISCO PARTY BRAKES	67	2005
ALL NIGHT HOLIDAY RUSS ABBOT	20	1985
ALL NIGHT LONG [A] DEXTER WANSELL	59	1978
ALL NIGHT LONG [B] RAINBOW	5	1980
ALL NIGHT LONG [C] CLOUD	72	1981
ALL NIGHT LONG [D] MARY JANE GIRLS	13	1983
ALL NIGHT LONG [D] JAY MONDI & THE LIVING BASS	63	1990
ALL NIGHT LONG [E] GANT	67	1997
ALL NIGHT LONG [F] FAITH EVANS FEATURING PUFF DADDY	23	1999
ALL NIGHT LONG [G] BLAZIN' SQUAD	54	2006
ALL NIGHT LONG (ALL NIGHT) LIONEL RICHIE	2	1983
ALL NITE (DON'T STOP) JANET JACKSON	19	2004
(ALL OF A SUDDEN) MY HEART SINGS PAUL ANKA	10	1959
ALL OF ME SABRINA	25	1988
ALL OF ME FOR ALL OF YOU 9.9	53	1985
ALL OF ME LOVES ALL OF YOU BAY CITY ROLLERS	4	1974
ALL OF MY HEART ABC	5	1982
ALL OF MY LIFE DIANA ROSS	9	1974
ALL OF THE GIRLS (ALL AI-DI-GIRL DEM) CARNIVAL FEATURING RIP VS RED RAT	51	1998
ALL OF YOU [A] SAMMY DAVIS Jr.	28	1956
ALL OF YOU [B] JULIO IGLESIAS & DIANA ROSS	43	1984
ALL OF YOUR DAYS WILL BE BLESSED ED HARCOURT	35	2003
ALL ON BLACK ALKALINE TRIO	60	2003
ALL OR NOTHING [A] SMALL FACES	1	1966
ALL OR NOTHING [A] DOGS D'AMOUR	53	1993
ALL OR NOTHING [B] MILLI VANILLI	74	1990
ALL OR NOTHING [C] JOE	56	1994
ALL OR NOTHING [D] CHER	12	1999
ALL OR NOTHING [E] O-TOWN	4	2001
ALL OUT OF LOVE [A] AIR SUPPLY	11	1980
ALL OUT OF LOVE [A] OTT	11	1997
ALL OUT OF LOVE [A] FOUNDATION FEATURING NATALIE ROSSI	40	2003
ALL OUT OF LOVE [B] H & CLAIRE	10	2002
ALL OUT TO GET YOU BEAT	22	1981
ALL OVER LISA MAFFIA	2	2003
ALL OVER AGAIN RONAN KEATING & KATE RUSBY	6	2006
ALL OVER ME [A] SUZI CARR	45	1994
ALL OVER ME [B] GRAHAM COXON	19	2004
ALL OVER THE WORLD [A] FRANCOISE HARDY	16	1965
ALL OVER THE WORLD [B] ELECTRIC LIGHT ORCHESTRA	11	1980
ALL OVER THE WORLD [C] JUNIOR GISCOMBE	74	1992
ALL OVER THIS TOWN UPPER ROOM	38	2006
ALL OVER YOU [A] LEVEL 42	26	1994
ALL OVER YOU [B] LIVE	48	1995
ALL POSSIBILITIES BADLY DRAWN BOY	24	2003
ALL RIGHT CHRISTOPHER CROSS	51	1983
ALL RIGHT NOW FREE	2	1970
ALL RIGHT NOW PEPSI & SHIRLIE	50	1987
ALL RIGHT NOW LEMONESCENT	37	2004
ALL RISE BLUE	4	2001
ALL SHE WANTS IS DURAN DURAN	9	1989
ALL SHE WROTE ROSS COPPERMAN	39	2007
ALL SHOOK UP ELVIS PRESLEY	1	1957
ALL SHOOK UP BILLY JOEL	27	1992
ALL SPARKS EDITORS	21	2006
ALL STAND UP (NEVER SAY NEVER) STATUS QUO	51	2002
ALL STAR SMASH MOUTH	24	1999
ALL STAR HIT PARADE VARIOUS ARTISTS	2	1956
ALL STAR HIT PARADE NO. 2 VARIOUS ARTISTS	15	1957
ALL STOOD STILL ULTRAVOX	8	1981
ALL SUSSED OUT ALMIGHTY	28	1996
ALL SYSTEMS GO DONNA SUMMER	54	1988
ALL THAT COUNTS IS LOVE STATUS QUO	29	2005
ALL THAT GLITTERS GARY GLITTER	48	1981
ALL THAT I AM [A] ELVIS PRESLEY	18	1966
ALL THAT I AM [B] JOE	52	1998
ALL THAT I CAN SAY MARY J BLIGE	29	1999
ALL THAT I GOT IS YOU GHOSTFACE KILLAH	11	1997
ALL THAT I NEED BOYZONE	1	1998
ALL THAT I'M ALLOWED (I'M THANKFUL) ELTON JOHN	20	2004
ALL THAT MATTERED (LOVE YOU DOWN) DE NUIT	38	2002
ALL THAT MATTERS LOUISE	11	1998
ALL THAT MATTERS TO ME ALEXANDER O'NEAL	67	1993
ALL THAT MONEY WANTS PSYCHEDELIC FURS	75	1988
ALL THAT SHE WANTS ACE OF BASE	1	1993
ALL THAT'S LEFT THRICE	69	2003
ALL THE LOVE IN THE WORLD [A] CONSORTIUM	22	1969
ALL THE LOVE IN THE WORLD [B] DIONNE WARWICK	10	1982
ALL THE LOVER I NEED KINANE	59	1996
ALL THE MAN THAT I NEED [A] WHITNEY HOUSTON	13	1990
ALL THE MAN THAT I NEED [B] SHERNETTE MAY	50	1998
ALL THE MONEY'S GONE BABYLON ZOO	46	1999
ALL THE MYTHS ON SUNDAY DIESEL PARK WEST	66	1989
ALL THE SMALL THINGS BLINK 182	2	2000
ALL THE THINGS DILLINJA	71	2004
ALL THE THINGS SHE SAID [A] SIMPLE MINDS	9	1986
ALL THE THINGS SHE SAID [B] tATu	1	2003
ALL THE THINGS (YOUR MAN WON'T DO) JOE	34	1996
ALL THE TIME AND EVERYWHERE DICKIE VALENTINE	9	1953
ALL THE WAY [A] FRANK SINATRA	3	1957
ALL THE WAY [B] ENGLAND FOOTBALL TEAM & THE SOUND OF STOCK, AITKEN & WATERMAN	64	1988
ALL THE WAY [C] CRAIG DAVID	3	2005
ALL THE WAY FROM AMERICA JOAN ARMATRADING	54	1980
ALL THE WAY FROM MEMPHIS MOTT THE HOOPLE	10	1973

Title / Artist	Peak Position	Year of Entry
ALL THE WAY FROM MEMPHIS CONTRABAND	65	1991
ALL THE WAY TO RENO R.E.M.	24	2001
ALL THE WORLD LOVES LOVERS PREFAB SPROUT	61	1992
ALL THE YOUNG DUDES MOTT THE HOOPLE	3	1972
ALL THE YOUNG DUDES BRUCE DICKINSON	23	1990
ALL THESE THINGS I HATE BULLET FOR MY VALENTINE	29	2006
ALL THESE THINGS THAT I'VE DONE KILLERS	18	2004
ALL THIS LOVE SIMILOU	20	2006
ALL THIS LOVE I'M GIVING GWEN McCRAE	63	1988
ALL THIS LOVE I'M GIVING MUSIC & MYSTERY FEATURING GWEN McCRAE	36	1993
ALL THIS TIME [A] TIFFANY	47	1989
ALL THIS TIME [B] STING	22	1991
ALL THIS TIME [C] MICHELLE	1	2003
ALL THOSE YEARS AGO GEORGE HARRISON	13	1981
ALL THROUGH THE NIGHT CYNDI LAUPER	64	1984
ALL THRU THE NITE P.O.V. FEATURING JADE	32	1994
ALL TIME HIGH RITA COOLIDGE	75	1983
ALL TIME LOVE WILL YOUNG	3	2006
ALL TOGETHER NOW FARM	4	1990
ALL TOGETHER NOW EVERTON FC	24	1995
ALL TOMORROW'S PARTIES JAPAN	38	1983
ALL TOO HUMAN RAKES	22	2006
ALL TRUE MAN ALEXANDER O'NEAL	18	1991
ALL WOMAN LISA STANSFIELD	20	1991
ALL YOU EVER DO VIOLENT DELIGHT	38	2003
ALL YOU GOOD GOOD PEOPLE EP EMBRACE	8	1997
ALL YOU NEED IS HATE DELGADOS	72	2003
ALL YOU NEED IS LOVE BEATLES	1	1967
ALL YOU NEED IS LOVE TOM JONES	19	1993
ALL YOU PRETTY GIRLS XTC	55	1984
ALL YOU WANTED MICHELLE BRANCH	33	2002
ALLEY CAT SONG DAVID THORNE	21	1963
ALLEY OOP HOLLYWOOD ARGYLES	24	1960
ALLY'S TARTAN ARMY ANDY CAMERON	6	1978
ALMA MATTERS MORRISSEY	16	1997
ALMAZ RANDY CRAWFORD	4	1987
ALMOST DOESN'T COUNT BRANDY	15	1999
ALMOST EASY AVENGED SEVENFOLD	67	2007
ALMOST GOLD JESUS & MARY CHAIN	41	1992
ALMOST HEAR YOU SIGH ROLLING STONES	31	1990
ALMOST HERE BRIAN McFADDEN & DELTA GOODREM	3	2005
ALMOST SATURDAY NIGHT DAVE EDMUNDS	58	1981
ALMOST SEE YOU (SOMEWHERE) CHINA BLACK	31	1995
ALMOST THERE ANDY WILLIAMS	2	1965
ALMOST UNREAL ROXETTE	7	1993
ALONE [A] PETULA CLARK	8	1957
ALONE [A] SHEPHERD SISTERS	14	1957
ALONE [A] SOUTHLANDERS	17	1957
ALONE [A] KAYE SISTERS	27	1958
ALONE [B] HEART	3	1987
ALONE [C] BIG COUNTRY	24	1993
ALONE [D] BEE GEES	5	1997
ALONE [E] LASGO	7	2002
ALONE AGAIN IN THE LAP OF LUXURY MARILLION	53	1994
ALONE AGAIN (NATURALLY) GILBERT O'SULLIVAN	3	1972
ALONE AGAIN OR DAMNED	27	1987
ALONE AT LAST JACKIE WILSON	50	1960
ALONE WITH YOU TEXAS	32	1992
ALONE WITHOUT YOU [A] KING	8	1985
ALONE WITHOUT YOU [B] MARK OWEN	26	2003
ALONG CAME CAROLINE MICHAEL COX	41	1960
ALPHA BETA GAGA AIR	44	2004
ALPHABET STREET PRINCE	9	1988
ALRIGHT [A] JANET JACKSON	20	1990
ALRIGHT [B] URBAN SOUL	43	1991
ALRIGHT [C] KRIS KROSS	47	1993
ALRIGHT [D] CAST	13	1995
ALRIGHT [E] SUPERGRASS	2	1995
ALRIGHT [F] JAMIROQUAI	6	1997
ALRIGHT [G] CLUB 69 FEATURING SUZANNE PALMER	70	1998
ALRIGHT [H] RED CARPET	58	2004
ALRIGHT [I] BEAT UP	58	2005
ALRIGHT ALRIGHT ALRIGHT MUNGO JERRY	3	1973
ALRIGHT BABY STEVENSON'S ROCKET	37	1975
ALSATIAN WHITE ROSE MOVEMENT	54	2005
ALSO SPRACH ZARATHUSTRA (2001) DEODATO	7	1973
ALTERNATE TITLE MONKEES	2	1967
ALWAYS [A] SAMMY TURNER	26	1959
ALWAYS [B] ATLANTIC STARR	3	1987
ALWAYS [C] URBAN SOUL	41	1992
ALWAYS [D] ERASURE	4	1994
ALWAYS [E] BON JOVI	2	1994
ALWAYS [F] MK FEATURING ALANA	69	1995
ALWAYS [G] SALIVA	47	2003
ALWAYS [H] BLINK 182	36	2005
ALWAYS A PERMANENT STATE DAVID JAMES	60	2001
ALWAYS AND EVER JOHNNY KIDD & THE PIRATES	46	1964
ALWAYS AND FOREVER [A] HEATWAVE	9	1978
ALWAYS AND FOREVER [A] LUTHER VANDROSS	20	1995
ALWAYS AND FOREVER [B] JJ72	43	2003
ALWAYS AND FOREVER [C] CHOCOLATE PUMA	43	2006
ALWAYS BE JIMMY EAT WORLD	37	2008
ALWAYS BE MY BABY MARIAH CAREY	3	1996
ALWAYS BREAKING MY HEART BELINDA CARLISLE	8	1996
ALWAYS COME BACK TO YOUR LOVE SAMANTHA MUMBA	3	2001
ALWAYS FIND A WAY NINE YARDS	50	1999
ALWAYS HAVE, ALWAYS WILL ACE OF BASE	12	1998
ALWAYS LOOK ON THE BRIGHT SIDE OF LIFE MONTY PYTHON	3	1991
ALWAYS LOOK ON THE BRIGHT SIDE OF LIFE CORONATION STREET CAST FEATURING BILL WADDINGTON	35	1995
ALWAYS MUSIC WESTBAM/KOON + STEPHENSON	51	1996
ALWAYS ON MY MIND ELVIS PRESLEY	9	1972
ALWAYS ON MY MIND WILLIE NELSON	49	1982
ALWAYS ON MY MIND PET SHOP BOYS	1	1987
ALWAYS ON THE RUN LENNY KRAVITZ	41	1991
ALWAYS ON TIME JA RULE FEATURING ASHANTI	6	2002
ALWAYS REMEMBER TO RESPECT AND HONOUR YOUR MOTHER DUSTED	31	2001
ALWAYS SOMETHING THERE TO REMIND ME NAKED EYES	59	1983
ALWAYS SOMETHING THERE TO REMIND ME TIN TIN OUT FEATURING ESPIRITU	14	1995
ALWAYS THE LAST TO KNOW DEL AMITRI	13	1992
ALWAYS THE LONELY ONE ALAN DREW	48	1963
ALWAYS THE SAME NEIL'S CHILDREN	56	2005
ALWAYS THE SUN STRANGLERS	29	1986
ALWAYS THERE [A] MARTI WEBB & THE SIMON MAY ORCHESTRA	13	1986
ALWAYS THERE [B] INCOGNITO FEATURING JOCELYN BROWN	6	1991
ALWAYS THERE [C] UB40	53	1997
ALWAYS TOMORROW GLORIA ESTEFAN	24	1992
ALWAYS YOU AND ME RUSS CONWAY	33	1962
ALWAYS YOUR WAY MY VITRIOL	31	2001
ALWAYS YOURS GARY GLITTER	1	1974
ALWAYZ INTO SOMETHIN' NWA	60	1991
AM I A TOY OR A TREASURE KAY STARR	17	1954
AM I ON YOUR MIND OXYGEN FEATURING ANDREA BRITTON	30	2002
AM I RIGHT (EP) ERASURE	15	1991
AM I THAT EASY TO FORGET ENGELBERT HUMPERDINCK	3	1968
AM I THE SAME GIRL DUSTY SPRINGFIELD	43	1969
AM I THE SAME GIRL SWING OUT SISTER	21	1992
AM I WASTING MY TIME ON YOU FRANKIE VAUGHAN	25	1958
AM I WRONG [A] ETIENNE DE CRECY	44	2001
AM I WRONG [B] MULL HISTORICAL SOCIETY	51	2003
AM I WRY NO MEW	47	2003
AM TO PM CHRISTINA MILIAN	3	2002
AMANDA [A] STUART GILLIES	13	1973
AMANDA [B] CRAIG McLACHLAN & CHECK 1-2	19	1990
AMARANTINE ENYA	53	2005
AMATEUR HOUR SPARKS	7	1974
AMAZED LONESTAR	21	2000
AMAZING [A] AEROSMITH	57	1993
AMAZING [B] GEORGE MICHAEL	4	2004
AMAZING [C] WESTLIFE	4	2006
AMAZING [D] SEAL	74	2007
AMAZING GRACE JUDY COLLINS	5	1970
AMAZING GRACE THE PIPES & DRUMS & MILITARY BAND OF THE ROYAL SCOTS DRAGOON GUARDS	1	1972
THE AMAZING SPIDER MAN MC SPY-D + FRIENDS	37	1995
AMAZON CHANT AIRSCAPE	46	1998
AMBUSH OUTLAWS	43	1961
AMEN (DON'T BE AFRAID) FLASH BROTHERS	75	2004
AMERICA [A] NICE	21	1968
AMERICA [A] KING KURT	73	1986
AMERICA [B] SIMON & GARFUNKEL	25	1972
AMERICA [C] DAVID ESSEX	32	1974
AMERICA [D] GARY NUMAN	49	1988
AMERICA [E] RAZORLIGHT	1	2006
AMERICA (I LOVE AMERICA) FULL INTENTION	32	1996
AMERICA THE BEAUTIFUL ELVIS PRESLEY	69	2001
AMERICA: WHAT TIME IS LOVE KLF	4	1992
AMERICA - WORLD CUP THEME 1994 LEONARD BERNSTEIN, ORCHESTRA & CHORUS	44	1994
THE AMERICAN SIMPLE MINDS	59	1981
AMERICAN BAD ASS KID ROCK	25	2000
AMERICAN BOY ESTELLE FEATURING KANYE WEST	1	2008
AMERICAN DREAM [A] CROSBY, STILLS, NASH & YOUNG	55	1989
AMERICAN DREAM [B] POWER OF DREAMS	74	1991
AMERICAN DREAM [C] JAKATTA	3	2001
AMERICAN ENGLISH IDLEWILD	15	2002
AMERICAN GENERATION RITCHIE FAMILY	49	1979
AMERICAN GIRL TOM PETTY & THE HEARTBREAKERS	40	1977
AMERICAN GIRLS COUNTING CROWS	33	2002
AMERICAN HEARTS BILLY OCEAN	54	1977
AMERICAN IDIOT GREEN DAY	3	2004
AMERICAN IN AMSTERDAM WHEATUS	59	2003
AMERICAN LIFE MADONNA	2	2003
AMERICAN PIE DON McLEAN	2	1972
AMERICAN PIE CHUPITO	54	1995
AMERICAN PIE JUST LUIS	31	1995
AMERICAN PIE MADONNA	1	2000
AMERICAN TRILOGY [A] ELVIS PRESLEY	8	1972
AMERICAN TRILOGY [A] MICKEY NEWBURY	42	1972
AMERICAN TRILOGY [B] DELGADOS	61	2000
AMERICAN TV TERRORVISION	63	1993
AMERICAN WOMAN GUESS WHO	19	1970
AMERICANOS HOLLY JOHNSON	4	1989
AMERIKA RAMMSTEIN	38	2004

Title / Artist	Peak Position	Year of Entry
AMIGO BLACK SLATE	9	1980
AMIGOS PARA SIEMPRE (FRIENDS FOR LIFE) JOSE CARRERAS & SARAH BRIGHTMAN	11	1992
AMITYVILLE (THE HOUSE ON THE HILL) LOVEBUG STARSKI	12	1986
AMNESIA [A] SHALAMAR	61	1984
AMNESIA [B] CHUMBAWAMBA	10	1998
AMONG MY SOUVENIRS CONNIE FRANCIS	11	1959
AMOR JULIO IGLESIAS	32	1982
AMOR AMOR BEN E. KING	38	1961
AMOUR AMOUR MOBILES	45	1982
AMOUR (C'MON) PORN KINGS	17	1997
AMOUREUSE KIKI DEE	13	1973
THE AMSTERDAM EP SIMPLE MINDS	18	1989
AN ACCIDENT IN PARADISE SVEN VATH	57	1993
AN AFFAIR TO REMEMBER VIC DAMONE	29	1957
AN ANGEL KELLY FAMILY	69	1995
AN EASIER AFFAIR GEORGE MICHAEL	13	2006
AN ENGLISH GENTLEMAN JAMES DEAN BRADFIELD	31	2006
AN EVERLASTING LOVE ANDY GIBB	10	1978
AN HONEST MISTAKE BRAVERY	7	2005
AN INNOCENT MAN BILLY JOEL	8	1984
AN OLYMPIC RECORD BARRON KNIGHTS	35	1968
AN OPEN LETTER TO NYC BEASTIE BOYS	38	2004
AN UBHAL AS AIRDE (THE HIGHEST APPLE) RUNRIG	18	1995
ANALOGUE (ALL IWANT) A-HA	10	2006
ANARCHY IN THE U.K. SEX PISTOLS	33	1976
ANARCHY IN THE UK MEGADETH	45	1988
ANARCHY IN THE UK GREEN JELLY	27	1993
ANA'S SONG SILVERCHAIR	45	1999
ANASTHASIA T99	14	1991
ANCHOR CAVE IN	53	2003
ANCHORAGE MICHELLE SHOCKED	60	1988
AND A BANG ON THE EAR WATERBOYS	51	1989
AND DA DRUM MACHINE PHATT B	58	2000
AND I LOVE YOU SO PERRY COMO	3	1973
AND I WISH DOOLEYS	52	1981
AND I'M TELLING YOU I'M NOT GOING JENNIFER HOLLIDAY	32	1982
AND I'M TELLING YOU I'M NOT GOING DONNA GILES	27	1994
AND IT FEELS LIKE LeANN RIMES	22	2006
AND IT HURTS DAYEENE	63	1999
AND IT WASN'T A DREAM RUTHLESS RAP ASSASSINS	75	1990
(AND NOW - THE WALTZ) C'EST LA VIE SLADE	50	1982
AND SHE WAS TALKING HEADS	17	1986
AND SO I WILL WAIT FOR YOU DEE FREDRIX	56	1993
AND SO IS LOVE KATE BUSH	26	1994
...AND STONES BLUE AEROPLANES	63	1990
...AND THAT'S BEFORE ME TEA! MR FOOD	62	1990
...(AND THAT'S NO LIE) HEAVEN 17	52	1985
AND THE BAND PLAYED ON (DOWN AMONG THE DEAD MEN) FLASH & THE PAN	54	1978
AND THE BANDS PLAYED ON SAXON	12	1981
AND THE BEAT GOES ON WHISPERS	2	1980
AND THE HEAVENS CRIED ANTHONY NEWLEY	6	1961
AND THE LEADER ROCKS ON GARY GLITTER	58	1992
(AND THE) PICTURES IN THE SKY MEDICINE HEAD	22	1971
AND THE SUN WILL SHINE JOSE FELICIANO	25	1969
AND THEN SHE KISSED ME GARY GLITTER	39	1981
AND THEN SHE SMILES MOCK TURTLES	44	1991
AND THEN THE RAIN FALLS BLUE AMAZON	53	1997
AND THEY OBEY KINESIS	63	2003
AND YOU SMILED MATT MONRO	28	1973
ANDRES L7	34	1994
ANDROGYNY GARBAGE	24	2001
ANFIELD RAP (RED MACHINE IN FULL EFFECT) LIVERPOOL FC	3	1988
ANGEL [A] ROD STEWART	4	1972
ANGEL [B] ARETHA FRANKLIN	37	1973
ANGEL [B] SIMPLY RED	4	1996
ANGEL [C] MADONNA	5	1985
ANGEL [D] AEROSMITH	69	1988
ANGEL [E] EURYTHMICS	23	1990
ANGEL [F] JON SECADA	23	1993
ANGEL [G] A-HA	41	1993
ANGEL [H] GOLDIE	41	1995
ANGEL [I] MASSIVE ATTACK	30	1998
ANGEL [J] TINA COUSINS	46	1999
ANGEL [K] RALPH FRIDGE	20	2000
ANGEL [L] LIONEL RICHIE	18	2000
ANGEL [M] SHAGGY FEATURING RAYVON	1	2001
ANGEL [N] SARAH McLACHLAN	36	2002
ANGEL [O] CORRS	16	2004
ANGEL [P] PHARRELL WILLIAMS	15	2006
THE ANGEL AND THE GAMBLER IRON MAIDEN	18	1998
ANGEL EYES [A] ROXY MUSIC	4	1979
ANGEL EYES [B] RAGHAV	7	2005
ANGEL EYES (HOME AND AWAY) WET WET WET	5	1987
ANGEL FACE GLITTER BAND	4	1974
ANGEL FINGERS WIZZARD	1	1973
ANGEL IN BLUE J GEILS BAND	55	1982
ANGEL INTERCEPTOR ASH	14	1995
ANGEL (LADADI O-HEYO) JAM & SPOON	26	1995
ANGEL LOOKING THROUGH STAGECOACH FEATURING PENNY FOSTER	59	2003
ANGEL OF HARLEM U2	9	1988
ANGEL OF MINE ETERNAL	4	1997
ANGEL OF MINE MONICA	55	1999
ANGEL OF THE MORNING PP ARNOLD	29	1968
ANGEL OF THE MORNING JUICE NEWTON	43	1981
ANGEL OF THE MORNING - ANY WAY THAT YOU WANT ME (MEDLEY) MARY MASON	27	1977
ANGEL ON MY SHOULDER GARETH GATES	22	2007
ANGEL STREET M PEOPLE	8	1998
ANGELA JONES MICHAEL COX	7	1960
ANGELEYES ABBA	3	1979
ANGELIA RICHARD MARX	45	1989
ANGELO BROTHERHOOD OF MAN	1	1977
ANGELS ROBBIE WILLIAMS	4	1997
ANGELS ALL ANGELS	48	2006
THE ANGELS & SHADOWS PROJECT OMNI TRIO	44	2001
ANGELS DON'T LIE JIM REEVES	32	1970
ANGELS GO BALD: TOO HOWIE B	36	1997
ANGEL'S HEAP FINN	41	1995
ANGELS OF THE SILENCES COUNTING CROWS	41	1996
ANGEL'S SYMPHONY RAF	73	1996
ANGELS WITH DIRTY FACES [A] SHAM 69	19	1978
ANGELS WITH DIRTY FACES [B] SUGABABES	7	2002
ANGIE ROLLING STONES	5	1973
ANGIE BABY HELEN REDDY	5	1975
ANGRY AT THE BIG OAK TREE FRANK IFIELD	25	1964
ANGRY CHAIR ALICE IN CHAINS	33	1993
THE ANGRY MOB KAISER CHIEFS	20	2007
ANGRY SKIES MARIA NAYLER	42	2000
ANIMAL [A] DEF LEPPARD	6	1987
ANIMAL [B] LOST IT.COM	70	2001
ANIMAL [C] R.E.M.	33	2003
ANIMAL [D] DUELS	47	2006
ANIMAL ARMY BABYLON ZOO	17	1996
ANIMAL CANNABUS MULL HISTORICAL SOCIETY	53	2001
ANIMAL INSTINCT [A] COMMODORES	74	1985
ANIMAL INSTINCT [B] CRANBERRIES	54	1999
ANIMAL NITRATE SUEDE	7	1993
THE ANIMAL SONG SAVAGE GARDEN	16	1999
ANIMATION SKIDS	56	1980
ANITINA (THE FIRST TIME I SEE SHE DANCE) M/A/R/R/S	1	1987
ANNABELLA JOHN WALKER	24	1967
ANNIE GET YOUR GUN SQUEEZE	43	1982
ANNIE I'M NOT YOUR DADDY KID CREOLE & THE COCONUTS	2	1982
ANNIE LET'S NOT WAIT GUILLEMOTS	27	2007
ANNIE'S SONG JAMES GALWAY	3	1974
ANNIE'S SONG JOHN DENVER	1	1978
ANNIVERSARY WALTZ ANITA HARRIS	21	1968
ANNIVERSARY WALTZ - PART 1 STATUS QUO	2	1990
ANNIVERSARY WALTZ - PART 2 STATUS QUO	16	1990
ANOMALY - CALLING YOUR NAME LIBRA PRESENTS TAYLOR	43	1996
ANONYMOUS BOBBY VALENTINO FEATURING TIMBALAND	25	2007
ANOTHER BLOOMING CHRISTMAS MEL SMITH	59	1991
ANOTHER BODY MURDERED FAITH NO MORE & BOO-YAA T.R.I.B.E.	26	1993
ANOTHER BRICK IN THE WALL (PART 2) PINK FLOYD	1	1979
ANOTHER CHANCE ROGER SANCHEZ	1	2001
ANOTHER CUP OF COFFEE MIKE + THE MECHANICS	51	1995
ANOTHER DAY [A] PAUL McCARTNEY	2	1971
ANOTHER DAY [B] WHIGFIELD	7	1994
ANOTHER DAY [C] BUCKSHOT LEFONQUE	65	1997
ANOTHER DAY [D] SKIP RAIDERS FEATURING JADA	46	2000
ANOTHER DAY [D] LEMAR	9	2004
ANOTHER DAY (ANOTHER GIRL) LAMBRETTAS	49	1980
ANOTHER DAY IN PARADISE PHIL COLLINS	2	1989
ANOTHER DAY IN PARADISE JAM TRONIK	19	1990
ANOTHER DAY IN PARADISE BRANDY & RAY J	5	2001
ANOTHER FINE MESS CHESNEY HAWKES	48	2005
ANOTHER FUNNY HONEYMOON DAVID DUNDAS	29	1977
ANOTHER GIRL - ANOTHER PLANET ONLY ONES	57	1992
ANOTHER HEARTACHE ROD STEWART	54	1986
ANOTHER KIND OF LOVE HUGH CORNWELL	71	1988
ANOTHER LONELY NIGHT IN NEW YORK ROBIN GIBB	71	1984
ANOTHER LOVER DANE	9	2001
ANOTHER MAN BARBARA MASON	45	1984
ANOTHER MONSTERJAM SIMON HARRIS FEATURING EINSTEIN	65	1989
ANOTHER MORNING STONER ...AND YOU WILL KNOW US BY THE TRAIL OF THE DEAD	54	2002
ANOTHER NAIL IN MY HEART SQUEEZE	17	1980
ANOTHER NIGHT [A] ARETHA FRANKLIN	54	1986
ANOTHER NIGHT [B] JASON DONOVAN	18	1990
ANOTHER NIGHT [C] (MC SAR &) THE REAL McCOY	2	1993
ANOTHER NIGHT IN STRANGELOVE	46	1998
ANOTHER ONE BITES THE DUST QUEEN	7	1980
ANOTHER ONE BITES THE DUST QUEEN WITH WYCLEF JEAN FEATURING PRAS MICHEL/FREE	5	1998
ANOTHER ONE BITES THE DUST QUEEN VS THE MIAMI PROJECT	31	2006
ANOTHER PART OF ME MICHAEL JACKSON	15	1988
ANOTHER PEARL BADLY DRAWN BOY	41	2000
ANOTHER PIECE OF MEAT SCORPIONS	39	1979
ANOTHER PLACE TO FALL KT TUNSTALL	52	2006
ANOTHER PLANET PENDULUM	46	2004
ANOTHER ROCK AND ROLL CHRISTMAS GARY GLITTER	7	1984
ANOTHER SAD LOVE SONG TONI BRAXTON	15	1993
ANOTHER SATURDAY NIGHT SAM COOKE	23	1963
ANOTHER SATURDAY NIGHT CAT STEVENS	19	1974

Title / Artist	Peak Position	Year of Entry
ANOTHER SILENT DAY ADVENTURES	71	1984
ANOTHER SLEEPLESS NIGHT [A] JIMMY CLANTON	50	1960
ANOTHER SLEEPLESS NIGHT [B] MIKE 'HITMAN' WILSON	74	1990
ANOTHER SLEEPLESS NIGHT [B] SHAWN CHRISTOPHER	50	1991
ANOTHER STAR STEVIE WONDER	29	1977
ANOTHER STAR KATHY SLEDGE	54	1995
ANOTHER STEP CLOSER TO YOU KIM WILDE & JUNIOR	6	1987
ANOTHER SUITCASE IN ANOTHER HALL BARBARA DICKSON	18	1977
ANOTHER SUITCASE IN ANOTHER HALL MADONNA	7	1997
ANOTHER TEAR FALLS WALKER BROTHERS	12	1966
ANOTHER TIME ANOTHER PLACE ENGELBERT HUMPERDINCK	13	1971
ANOTHER WAY PAUL VAN DYK	13	1999
ANOTHER WEEKEND FIVE STAR	18	1988
ANOTHERLOVERHOLENYOHEAD PRINCE	36	1986
ANSWER ME DAVID WHITFIELD	1	1953
ANSWER ME FRANKIE LAINE	1	1953
ANSWER ME RAY PETERSON	47	1960
ANSWER ME BARBARA DICKSON	9	1976
THE ANSWER TO WHY I HATE YOU SYMPOSIUM	32	1997
ANSWERING BELL RYAN ADAMS	39	2002
ANSWERS TO NOTHING MIDGE URE	49	1988
ANT RAP ADAM & THE ANTS	3	1981
ANTE UP M.O.P. FEATURING BUSTA RHYMES	7	2001
ANTHEM [A] N-JOI	8	1990
ANTHEM [B] WILDHEARTS	21	1997
THE ANTHEM [C] GOOD CHARLOTTE	10	2003
ANTHEM [D] FILO & PERI FEATURING ERIC LUMIERE	39	2007
ANTHEM (ONE DAY IN EVERY WEEK) NEW SEEKERS	21	1978
ANTHEM (WE ARE THE FIRE) TRIVIUM	40	2006
ANTI-SOCIAL ANTHRAX	44	1989
ANTMUSIC ADAM & THE ANTS	2	1980
THE ANTMUSIC EP (THE B-SIDES) ADAM & THE ANTS	46	1982
ANY DREAM WILL DO JASON DONOVAN	1	1991
ANY DREAM WILL DO LEE MEAD	2	2007
ANY LOVE LUTHER VANDROSS	31	1988
ANY MINUTE NOW SOULWAX	34	2004
ANY OLD IRON PETER SELLERS	17	1957
ANY OLD TIME FOUNDATIONS	48	1968
ANY ROAD GEORGE HARRISON	37	2003
ANY TIME ANY PLACE JANET JACKSON	13	1994
ANY WAY YOU LOOK NORTHERN UPROAR	36	1997
ANY WAY YOU WANT ME TROGGS	8	1966
ANYBODY SEEN MY BABY? ROLLING STONES	22	1997
ANYMORE SARAH CRACKNELL	39	1996
ANYONE CAN FALL IN LOVE ANITA DOBSON FEATURING THE SIMON MAY ORCHESTRA	4	1986
ANYONE CAN PLAY GUITAR RADIOHEAD	32	1993
ANYONE FOR TENNIS (THE SAVAGE SEVEN THEME) CREAM	40	1968
ANYONE OF US (STUPID MISTAKE) GARETH GATES	1	2002
ANYONE WHO HAD A HEART CILLA BLACK	1	1964
ANYONE WHO HAD A HEART DIONNE WARWICK	42	1964
ANYONE WHO HAD A HEART MARY MAY	49	1964
ANYSOUND VINES	63	2006
ANYTHING [A] DIRECT DRIVE	67	1985
ANYTHING [B] DAMNED	32	1986
ANYTHING [C] SYDNEY YOUNGBLOOD	48	1993
ANYTHING [D] CULTURE BEAT	5	1994
ANYTHING [E] SWV	24	1994
ANYTHING [F] 3T	2	1996
ANYTHING [G] DAMAGE	68	1996
ANYTHING [H] JAY-Z	18	2000
ANYTHING [I] JOJO	21	2007
ANYTHING BUT DOWN SHERYL CROW	19	1999
ANYTHING CAN HAPPEN WAS (NOT WAS)	67	1988
ANYTHING CAN HAPPEN IN THE NEXT HALF HOUR ENTER SHIKARI	27	2007
ANYTHING FOR YOU [A] GLORIA ESTEFAN & MIAMI SOUND MACHINE	10	1988
ANYTHING FOR YOU [B] STAMFORD AMP	33	2002
ANYTHING GOES HARPERS BIZARRE	33	1967
ANYTHING IS POSSIBLE [A] DEBBIE GIBSON	51	1991
ANYTHING IS POSSIBLE [B] WILL YOUNG	1	2002
ANYTHING THAT'S ROCK 'N' ROLL TOM PETTY & THE HEARTBREAKERS	36	1977
ANYTHING YOU WANT JODIE	47	1995
ANYTHING YOU WANT (I'VE GOT IT) ULTIMATE KAOS	52	1999
ANYTIME [A] NU-BIRTH	41	1997
ANYTIME [B] BRIAN McKNIGHT	48	1998
ANYTIME YOU NEED A FRIEND MARIAH CAREY	8	1994
ANYWAY HONEYCRACK	67	1996
ANYWAY ANYHOW ANYWHERE WHO	10	1965
ANYWAY THAT YOU WANT ME SPIRITUALIZED	75	1990
ANYWAY YOU DO IT LIQUID GOLD	41	1978
ANYWAY YOU WANT IT DAVE CLARK FIVE	25	1964
ANYWHERE [A] DUBSTAR	37	1995
ANYWHERE [B] BETH ORTON	55	2002
ANYWHERE FOR YOU BACKSTREET BOYS	4	1997
ANYWHERE IS ENYA	7	1995
APACHE [A] BERT WEEDON	24	1960
APACHE [A] SHADOWS	1	1960
APACHE [B] STARFIGHTER	31	2000
APACHE DROPOUT EDGAR BROUGHTON BAND	33	1971
APEMAN KINKS	5	1970
APHRODITE PARIS & SHARP	61	2001
APOCALYPSO MEW	75	2005
APOLLO 9 ADAM ANT	13	1984
APOLOGIES TO INSECT LIFE BRITISH SEA POWER	36	2003
APOLOGIZE TIMBALAND PRESENTS ONE REPUBLIC	3	2007
APPARENTLY NOTHIN' YOUNG DISCIPLES	13	1991
APPARENTLY NOTHING BRAND NEW HEAVIES	32	2000
THE APPLE EP VARIOUS ARTISTS (EP'S & LPS)	60	1991
APPLE GREEN MILLTOWN BROTHERS	43	1991
APPLE OF MY EYE ED HARCOURT	61	2002
THE APPLE STRETCHING GRACE JONES	50	1982
APPLE TREE ERYKAH BADU	47	1997
APPLEJACK JET HARRIS & TONY MEEHAN	4	1963
APPLY SOME PRESSURE MAXIMO PARK	17	2005
APPRENTICE OF THE UNIVERSE PURE REASON REVOLUTION	74	2004
APRIL LOVE PAT BOONE	7	1957
APRIL SKIES JESUS & MARY CHAIN	8	1987
AQUARIUS PAUL JONES	45	1969
AQUARIUS/LET THE SUNSHINE IN (MEDLEY) FIFTH DIMENSION	11	1969
ARABIAN KNIGHTS SIOUXSIE & THE BANSHEES	32	1981
ARE EVERYTHING BUZZCOCKS	61	1980
ARE 'FRIENDS' ELECTRIC? TUBEWAY ARMY	1	1979
ARE WE HERE ORBITAL	33	1994
ARE YOU BEING SERVED GRACE BROTHERS	51	1996
ARE YOU BEING SERVED SIR JOHN INMAN	39	1975
ARE YOU BLUE OR ARE YOU BLIND? BLUETONES	31	1995
ARE YOU DREAMING TWENTY 4 SEVEN FEATURING CAPTAIN HOLLYWOOD	17	1990
ARE YOU GETTING ENOUGH OF WHAT MAKES YOU HAPPY HOT CHOCOLATE	17	1980
ARE YOU GONNA BE MY GIRL? JET	16	2003
ARE YOU GONNA BE THERE? UP YER RONSON FEATURING MARY PEARCE	27	1996
ARE YOU GONNA GO MY WAY LENNY KRAVITZ	4	1993
ARE YOU GROWING TIRED OF MY LOVE STATUS QUO	46	1969
ARE YOU HAPPY NOW? MICHELLE BRANCH	31	2003
ARE YOU HEARING (WHAT I HEAR)? LEVEL 42	49	1982
ARE YOU IN INCUBUS	34	2002
ARE YOU JIMMY RAY? JIMMY RAY	13	1997
ARE YOU LONESOME TONIGHT ELVIS PRESLEY	1	1961
ARE YOU LOOKIN' AT ME RICKY TOMLINSON	28	2001
ARE YOU MAN ENOUGH UNO CLIO FEATURING MARTINE McCUTCHEON	62	1995
ARE YOU MINE BROS	12	1991
ARE YOU MY BABY WENDY & LISA	70	1989
ARE YOU OUT THERE CRESCENDO	20	1995
ARE YOU READY [A] BILLY OCEAN	42	1980
ARE YOU READY? [B] BREAK MACHINE	27	1984
ARE YOU READY [C] AC/DC	34	1991
ARE YOU READY [D] GYRES	71	1996
(ARE YOU READY) DO THE BUS STOP FATBACK BAND	18	1975
ARE YOU READY FOR LOVE [A] ELTON JOHN	1	1979
ARE YOU READY FOR LOVE [B] ULTRA HIGH	45	1996
ARE YOU READY FOR SOME MORE? REEL 2 REAL	24	1996
ARE YOU READY TO BE HEARTBROKEN SANDIE SHAW	68	1986
ARE YOU READY TO FLY ROZALLA	14	1992
ARE YOU READY TO PARTY SHRINK	39	2000
ARE YOU READY TO ROCK WIZZARD	8	1975
ARE YOU SATISFIED? (FUNKA NOVA) RAH BAND	70	1985
ARE YOU STILL HAVING FUN? EAGLE-EYE CHERRY	21	2000
ARE YOU SURE [A] ALLISONS	2	1961
ARE YOU SURE [B] SO	62	1988
ARE YOU THAT SOMEBODY? AALIYAH	11	1998
(ARE YOU) THE ONE THAT I'VE BEEN... NICK CAVE & THE BAD SEEDS	67	1997
ARE YOU TRYING TO BE LONELY ANDY LEWIS & PAUL WELLER	31	2007
AREA FUTUREHEADS	18	2005
AREA CODES LUDACRIS FEATURING NATE DOGG	25	2001
ARGENTINA JEREMY HEALY & AMOS	30	1997
ARGENTINE MELODY (CANCION DE ARGENTINA) SAN JOSE FEATURING RODRIGUEZ ARGENTINA	14	1978
ARIA ACKER BILK, HIS CLARINET & STRINGS	5	1976
ARIANA STARDUST	42	1977
ARIELS SYSTEM OF A DOWN	34	2002
ARIENNE TASMIN ARCHER	30	1993
ARIZONA SKY CHINA CRISIS	47	1986
ARMAGEDDON DAYS ARE HERE (AGAIN) THE THE	70	1989
ARMAGEDDON IT DEF LEPPARD	20	1988
ARMCHAIR ANARCHIST KINGMAKER	47	1992
ARMED AND EXTREMELY DANGEROUS FIRST CHOICE	16	1973
ARMED AND READY MICHAEL SCHENKER GROUP	53	1980
ARMS ALOFT JOE STRUMMER & THE MESCALEROS	46	2003
ARMS AROUND THE WORLD LOUISE	4	1997
ARMS OF LOREN E'VOKE	25	1996
ARMS OF MARY SUTHERLAND BROTHERS & QUIVER	5	1976
THE ARMS OF THE ONE WHO LOVES YOU XSCAPE	46	1998

Title / Artist	Peak Position	Year of Entry
THE ARMS OF ORION PRINCE WITH SHEENA EASTON	27	1989
ARMS OF SOLITUDE OUI 3	54	1993
ARMY BEN FOLDS FIVE	28	1999
ARMY DREAMERS KATE BUSH	16	1980
ARMY OF LOVERS LEE RYAN	3	2005
ARMY OF ME BJORK	10	1995
ARMY OF TWO DUM DUMS	27	2001
ARNOLD LAYNE PINK FLOYD	20	1967
ARNOLD LAYNE DAVID GILMOUR	19	2007
AROUND MY BRAIN PROGRESS FUNK	73	1997
AROUND THE WAY GIRL LL COOL J	36	1990
AROUND THE WORLD [A] BING CROSBY	5	1957
AROUND THE WORLD [A] GRACIE FIELDS	8	1957
AROUND THE WORLD [A] MANTOVANI	20	1957
AROUND THE WORLD [A] RONNIE HILTON	4	1957
AROUND THE WORLD [B] EAST 17	3	1994
AROUND THE WORLD [C] DAFT PUNK	5	1997
AROUND THE WORLD [D] RED HOT CHILI PEPPERS	35	1999
AROUND THE WORLD [E] AQUA	26	2000
AROUND THE WORLD [F] ATC	15	2002
ARRANGED MARRIAGE APACHE INDIAN	16	1993
ARRESTED BY YOU DUSTY SPRINGFIELD	70	1990
ARRIVEDERCI DARLING ANNE SHELTON	17	1955
ARRIVEDERCI DARLING EDNA SAVAGE	19	1956
ARSENAL NUMBER ONE ARSENAL FC	46	2000
ART FOR ART'S SAKE 10 C.C.	5	1975
THE ART OF DRIVING BLACK BOX RECORDER	53	2000
THE ART OF LOSING AMERICAN HI-FI	75	2003
ART OF LOVE ART OF NOISE	67	1990
THE ART OF MOVING BUTTS SHUT UP & DANCE FEATURING ERIN	69	1992
THE ART OF PARTIES JAPAN	48	1981
ARTHUR DALEY ('E'S ALRIGHT) FIRM	14	1982
ARTHUR'S THEME (BEST THAT YOU CAN DO) CHRISTOPHER CROSS	7	1981
AS GEORGE MICHAEL & MARY J BLIGE	4	1999
AS ALWAYS FARLEY 'JACKMASTER' FUNK FEATURING RICKY DILLARD	49	1989
AS ALWAYS SECRET LIFE	45	1992
AS GOOD AS IT GETS GENE	23	1999
AS I AM SOUND OF ONE FEATURING GLADEZZ	65	1993
AS I LAY ME DOWN SOPHIE B. HAWKINS	24	1995
AS I LOVE YOU SHIRLEY BASSEY	1	1958
AS I SAT SADLY BY HER SIDE NICK CAVE & THE BAD SEEDS	42	2001
AS IF WE NEVER SAID GOODBYE (FROM SUNSET BOULEVARD) BARBRA STREISAND	20	1994
AS LONG AS HE NEEDS ME SHIRLEY BASSEY	2	1960
AS LONG AS THE PRICE IS RIGHT DR FEELGOOD	40	1979
AS LONG AS YOU FOLLOW FLEETWOOD MAC	66	1988
AS LONG AS YOU LOVE ME BACKSTREET BOYS	3	1997
AS LONG AS YOU'RE GOOD TO ME JUDY CHEEKS	30	1995
AS TEARS GO BY MARIANNE FAITHFULL	9	1964
AS THE RUSH COMES MOTORCYCLE	11	2003
AS THE TIME GOES BY FUNKAPOLITAN	41	1981
AS TIME GOES BY RICHARD ALLAN	43	1960
AS TIME GOES BY DOOLEY WILSON	15	1977
AS TIME GOES BY JASON DONOVAN	26	1992
AS (UNTIL THE DAY) KNOWLEDGE	70	1997
AS USUAL BRENDA LEE	5	1964
AS WE DO DJ ZINC	72	2002
AS YOU LIKE IT ADAM FAITH	5	1962
ASCEND NITZER EBB	62	1992
ASCENSION NO ONE'S GONNA LOVE YOU, SO DON'T EVER WONDER MAXWELL	28	1996
ASHES EMBRACE	11	2004
ASHES AND DIAMONDS ZAINE GRIFF	68	1980
ASHES TO ASHES [A] MINDBENDERS	14	1966
ASHES TO ASHES [B] DAVID BOWIE	1	1980
ASHES TO ASHES [C] FAITH NO MORE	15	1997
ASIA MINOR KOKOMO	35	1961
ASK SMITHS	14	1986
ASK THE LORD HIPSWAY	50	1985
ASLEEP IN THE BACK ELBOW	19	2002
ASS LIKE THAT EMINEM	4	2005
ASSASSIN ORB	12	1992
ASSASSINATOR 13 CHIKINKI	72	2003
ASSASSING MARILLION	22	1984
ASSESSMENT BETA BAND	31	2004
ASSHOLE DENIS LEARY	58	1996
ASSOCIATION INTERNATIONAL AIRPORT/ TEENAGE FANCLUB	75	2004
ASTOUNDED BRAN VAN 3000 FEATURING CURTIS MAYFIELD	40	2001
ASTRAL AMERICA APOLLO 440	36	1994
ASYLUM ORB	20	1997
ASYLUMS IN JERUSALEM SCRITTI POLITTI	43	1982
AT HOME HE'S A TOURIST GANG OF FOUR	58	1979
AT MIDNIGHT T-CONNECTION	53	1979
AT MY MOST BEAUTIFUL R.E.M.	10	1999
AT NIGHT SHAKEDOWN	6	2002
AT THE CLUB DRIFTERS	3	1965
AT THE EDGE STIFF LITTLE FINGERS	15	1980
AT THE END IIO	20	2003
AT THE HOP DANNY & THE JUNIORS	3	1958
AT THE MOVIES RONI SIZE	67	2003
AT THE PALACE (PARTS 1 & 2) WILFRID BRAMBELL & HARRY H. CORBETT	25	1963
AT THE RIVER GROOVE ARMADA	19	1999
AT THE TOP OF THE STAIRS FORMATIONS	28	1971
AT THIS TIME OF YEAR CRAIG	14	2000
(AT YOUR BEST) YOU ARE LOVE AALIYAH	27	1994
ATHEAMA NEBULA II	55	1992
ATHENA WHO	40	1982
ATLANTIS [A] SHADOWS	2	1963
ATLANTIS [B] DONOVAN	23	1968
ATLANTIS [C] SECTION-X	42	1997
ATLANTIS IS CALLING (S.O.S. FOR LOVE) MODERN TALKING	55	1986
ATMOSPHERE [A] RUSS ABBOT	7	1984
ATMOSPHERE [B] JOY DIVISION	34	1988
ATMOSPHERE [C] KAYESTONE	55	2000
ATMOSPHERIC ROAD FAMILY CAT	69	1993
ATOM BOMB FLUKE	20	1996
ATOM POWERED ACTION (EP) BIS	54	1996
ATOMIC BLONDIE	1	1980
ATOMIC CITY HOLLY JOHNSON	18	1989
ATTACK [A] TOYS	36	1966
ATTACK [B] EXPLOITED	50	1982
ATTACK ME WITH YOUR LOVE CAMEO	65	1985
ATTACK OF THE GHOSTRIDERS RAVEONETTES	73	2002
ATTENTION! COMMANDER TOM	23	2005
ATTENTION TO ME NOLANS	9	1981
ATTITUDE [A] SEPULTURA	46	1996
ATTITUDE [B] ALIEN ANT FARM	66	2002
ATTITUDE [C] SUEDE	14	2003
AUBERGE CHRIS REA	16	1991
AUDIO VIDEO NEWS	52	1981
AUDITION WITNESS	71	1999
AUF WIEDERSEHEN SWEETHEART VERA LYNN	10	1952
AUGUST OCTOBER ROBIN GIBB	45	1970
AULD LANG SYNE WEEKEND	47	1985
AUSLANDER LIVING COLOUR	53	1993
AUSTRALIA [A] MANIC STREET PREACHERS	7	1996
AUSTRALIA [B] SHINS	62	2007
AUTHORITY CONFRONTATION SELFISH CUNT	66	2004
AUTO DRIVE HERBIE HANCOCK	33	1983
AUTOBAHN KRAFTWERK	11	1975
AUTOBAHN 66 PRIMAL SCREAM	44	2002
AUTOBIOGRAPHY OF A CRACKHEAD SHUT UP & DANCE	43	1992
AUTOMATIC [A] POINTER SISTERS	2	1984
AUTOMATIC [B] MILLIE SCOTT	56	1986
AUTOMATIC [C] FLOORPLAY	50	1996
AUTOMATIC [D] SARAH WHATMORE	11	2003
AUTOMATIC HIGH S CLUB JUNIORS	2	2002
AUTOMATIC LOVER [A] DEE D. JACKSON	4	1978
AUTOMATIC LOVER [B] VIBRATORS	35	1978
AUTOMATIC LOVER (CALL FOR LOVE) REAL McCOY	58	1995
AUTOMATICALLY SUNSHINE SUPREMES	10	1972
AUTOMATIK BEAT RENEGADES	73	2001
AUTOPHILIA BLUETONES	18	2000
AUTUMN RONI SIZE	70	2004
AUTUMN ALMANAC KINKS	3	1967
AUTUMN CONCERTO GEORGE MELACHRINO ORCHESTRA	18	1956
AUTUMN LEAVES COLDCUT	50	1994
AUTUMN LOVE ELECTRA	51	1989
AUTUMN TACTICS CHICANE	44	2000
AUTUMNSONG MANIC STREET PREACHERS	10	2007
AVA ADORE SMASHING PUMPKINS	11	1998
AVALON [A] ROXY MUSIC	13	1982
AVALON [B] JULIET	24	2005
AVE MARIA SHIRLEY BASSEY	31	1962
AVE MARIA LESLEY GARRETT & AMANDA THOMPSON	16	1993
AVE MARIA ANDREA BOCELLI	65	1999
AVENGING ANGELS SPACE	6	1998
AVENUE [A] SAINT ETIENNE	40	1992
AVENUE [B] PAUL VAN DYK	13	1999
THE AVENUE [C] ROLL DEEP	11	2005
AVENUES AND ALLEYWAYS TONY CHRISTIE	26	1973
AVERAGE MAN [A] SYMPOSIUM	45	1998
AVERAGE MAN [B] TURIN BRAKES	35	2003
THE AVERAGE MAN [C] SIMPLE KID	72	2003
THE AWAKENING YORK	11	1999
AWAY FROM HERE ENEMY	8	2007
AWAY FROM HOME DR ALBAN	42	1994
AWAY FROM ME PUDDLE OF MUDD	55	2003
AWFUL HOLE	42	1999
AXEL F HAROLD FALTERMEYER	2	1985
AXEL F CLOCK	7	1995
AXEL F SPACECORN	74	2001
AXEL F CRAZY FROG	1	2005
AXLE GRINDER PENDULUM	62	2007
AY AY AY AY MOOSEY MODERN ROMANCE	10	1981
AYLA AYLA	22	1999
AYO TECHNOLOGY 50 CENT & JUSTIN TIMBERLAKE	2	2007
AZTEC GOLD SILSOE	48	1986
AZTEC LIGHTNING (THEME FROM BBC WORLD CUP GRANDSTAND) HEADS	45	1986

B

Title / Artist	Peak Position	Year of Entry
B 2 GETHER ORIGINAL	29	1995
B BOY BABY MUTYA BUENA	73	2008
B GOOD 2 ME RONNI SIMON	73	1994
B LINE LAMB	52	1999
B WITH ME MIS-TEEQ	5	2002
B WITH U JUNIOR SANCHEZ FEATURING DAJAE	31	1999
BAA BAA BLACK SHEEP SINGING SHEEP	42	1982
BAAL'S HYMN (EP) DAVID BOWIE	29	1982
BA-BA-BANKROBBERY (ENGLISH VERSION) EAV	63	1986
BABARABATIN GYPSYMEN	32	2001
BABE [A] STYX	6	1980
BABE [B] TAKE THAT	1	1993

Title / Artist	Peak Position	Year of Entry
BABES IN THE WOOD MATCHBOX	46	1981
BABETTE TOMMY BRUCE	50	1962
BABIES ASHFORD & SIMPSON	56	1985
BABOOSHKA KATE BUSH	5	1980
B-A-B-Y RACHEL SWEET	35	1978
THE BABY [A] HOLLIES	26	1972
BABY [B] HALO JAMES	43	1990
BABY [C] ROZALLA	26	1995
BABY [D] FABOLOUS FEATURING MIKE SHOREY	41	2005
BABY BABY [A] FRANKIE LYMON & THE TEENAGERS	4	1957
BABY BABY [B] EIGHTH WONDER	65	1988
BABY BABY [C] AMY GRANT	2	1991
BABY BABY [D] CORONA	5	1995
BABY BABY [D] SUNBLOCK FEATURING SANDY	16	2007
BABY-BABY-BABY TLC	55	1992
BABY BABY BYE BYE JERRY LEE LEWIS	47	1960
BABY BABY MY LOVE'S ALL FOR YOU DENIECE WILLIAMS	32	1977
BABY BE MINE BLACKstreet FEATURING TEDDY RILEY	37	1993
BABY BLUE DUSTY SPRINGFIELD	61	1979
BABY BOY [A] BIG BROVAZ	4	2003
BABY BOY [B] BEYONCE FEATURING SEAN PAUL	2	2003
BABY BRITAIN ELLIOTT SMITH	55	1999
BABY, CAN I GET YOUR NUMBER OBI PROJECT FEATURING HARRY, ASHER D & DJ WHAT?	75	2001
BABY CAN I HOLD YOU BOYZONE	2	1997
BABY COME BACK [A] EQUALS	1	1968
BABY COME BACK [A] PATO BANTON	1	1994
BABY COME BACK [B] PLAYER	32	1978
BABY COME ON SPACEMAID	70	1997
BABY COME ON OVER SAMANTHA MUMBA	5	2001
BABY COME TO ME PATTI AUSTIN & JAMES INGRAM	11	1983
BABY COME TO ME ALEXANDER O'NEAL FEATURING CHERRELLE	56	1997
BABY DID A BAD BAD THING CHRIS ISAAK	44	1999
BABY DON'T CHANGE YOUR MIND GLADYS KNIGHT & THE PIPS	4	1977
BABY DON'T CRY [A] LALAH HATHAWAY	54	1991
BABY DON'T CRY [B] INXS	20	1992
BABY DON'T FORGET MY NUMBER MILLI VANILLI	16	1989
BABY DON'T GET HOOKED ON ME MAC DAVIS	29	1972
BABY DON'T GO [A] SONNY & CHER	11	1965
BABY DON'T GO [B] 4MANDU	47	1996
BABY FACE LITTLE RICHARD	2	1959
BABY FACE BOBBY DARIN	40	1962
BABY FACE WING & A PRAYER FIFE & DRUM CORPS	12	1976
BABY FRATELLI FRATELLIS	24	2007
BABY GET HIGHER DAVID SNEDDON	38	2003
BABY GOODBYE FRIDAY HILL	5	2005
BABY GOT BACK SIR MIX-A-LOT	56	1992
BABY I DON'T CARE [A] BUDDY HOLLY	12	1961
BABY I DON'T CARE [A] ELVIS PRESLEY	61	1983
BABY I DON'T CARE [B] TRANSVISION VAMP	3	1989
BABY I DON'T CARE [B] JENNIFER ELLISON	6	2003
BABY I KNOW RUBETTES	10	1977
BABY I LOVE YOU [A] RONETTES	11	1964
BABY I LOVE YOU [A] DAVE EDMUNDS	8	1973
BABY I LOVE YOU [A] RAMONES	8	1980
BABY I LOVE YOU [A] TSD	64	1996
BABY I LOVE YOU [B] ARETHA FRANKLIN	39	1967
BABY I LOVE U [C] JENNIFER LOPEZ	3	2004
BABY I LOVE YOU OK KENNY	12	1975
BABY I LOVE YOUR WAY PETER FRAMPTON	43	1976
BABY I LOVE YOUR WAY BIG MOUNTAIN	2	1994
BABY I LOVE YOUR WAY - FREEBIRD WILL TO POWER	6	1989
BABY I NEED YOUR LOVIN' FOURMOST	24	1964
BABY I WON'T LET YOU DOWN PICKETTYWITCH	27	1970
BABY I'M A-WANT YOU BREAD	14	1972
BABY I'M SCARED OF YOU WOMACK & WOMACK	72	1984
BABY I'M YOURS PETER & GORDON	19	1965
BABY I'M YOURS LINDA LEWIS	33	1976
BABY, IT'S COLD OUTSIDE TOM JONES & CERYS MATTHEWS	17	1999
BABY IT'S TRUE MARI WILSON	42	1982
BABY IT'S YOU [A] DAVE BERRY	24	1964
BABY IT'S YOU [A] BEATLES	7	1995
BABY IT'S YOU [B] SILK	44	1993
BABY IT'S YOU [C] MN8	22	1995
BABY IT'S YOU [D] JOJO FEATURING BOW WOW	8	2004
BABY JANE ROD STEWART	1	1983
BABY JUMP MUNGO JERRY	1	1971
BABY LAY DOWN RUBY WINTERS	43	1979
BABY LEE JOHN LEE HOOKER WITH ROBERT CRAY	65	1996
BABY LET ME TAKE YOU HOME ANIMALS	21	1964
BABY LOVE [A] SUPREMES	1	1964
BABY LOVE [A] HONEY BANE	58	1981
BABY LOVE [B] REGINA	50	1986
BABY LOVE [B] DANNII MINOGUE	14	1991
BABY LOVE [C] NICOLE SCHERZINGER FEATURING WILL.I.AM	14	2007
BABY LOVER PETULA CLARK	12	1958
BABY MAKE IT SOON MARMALADE	9	1969
BABY MY HEART CRICKETS	33	1960
BABY NEVER SAY GOODBYE UNIT FOUR PLUS TWO	49	1966
BABY NOW I DAN REED NETWORK	65	1991
BABY NOW THAT I'VE FOUND YOU FOUNDATIONS	1	1967
BABY NOW THAT I'VE FOUND YOU LAUREN WATERWORTH	24	2002
BABY OF MINE ALAN PRICE	32	1979
BABY (OFF THE WALL) SIRENS	49	2004
BABY ONE MORE TIME BRITNEY SPEARS	1	1999
BABY PHAT DE LA SOUL	55	2002
BABY PLAYS AROUND (EP) ELVIS COSTELLO	65	1989
BABY PLEASE DON'T GO THEM	10	1965
BABY ROO CONNIE FRANCIS	5	1961
BABY SITTIN' BOBBY ANGELO & THE TUXEDOS	30	1961
BABY SITTIN' BOOGIE BUZZ CLIFFORD	17	1961
BABY STOP CRYING BOB DYLAN	13	1978
BABY TAKE A BOW ADAM FAITH	22	1962
BABY TALK ALISHA	67	1986
BABY U LEFT ME (IN THE COLD) MARILYN	70	1985
BABY UNIVERSAL TIN MACHINE	48	1991
BABY WANTS TO RIDE HANI	70	2000
BABY, WE BETTER TRY TO GET IT TOGETHER BARRY WHITE	15	1976
BABY WE CAN'T GO WRONG CILLA BLACK	36	1974
BABY WHAT A BIG SURPRISE CHICAGO	41	1977
BABY WHAT I MEAN DRIFTERS	49	1965
BABY WHEN THE LIGHT DAVID GUETTA FEATURING COZI	50	2007
(BABY) YOU DON'T HAVE TO TELL ME WALKER BROTHERS	13	1966
BABY YOU SHOULD KNOW JOY ZIPPER	59	2004
BABY YOU'RE DYNAMITE CLIFF RICHARD	27	1984
BABYCAKES 3 OF A KIND	1	2004
BABYLON [A] BLACK DOG FEATURING OFRA HAZA	65	1999
BABYLON [B] DAVID GRAY	5	2000
BABYLON A.D. (SO GLAD FOR THE MADNESS) CRADLE OF FILTH	35	2003
BABYLON'S BURNING RUTS	7	1979
BABY'S COMING BACK [A] JELLYFISH	51	1991
BABY'S COMING BACK [B] McFLY	1	2007
BABY'S FIRST CHRISTMAS CONNIE FRANCIS	30	1961
BABY'S GOT A TEMPER PRODIGY	5	2002
BABY'S REQUEST WINGS	60	1979
BABYSHAMBLES PETE DOHERTY	32	2004
BACHELOR BOY CLIFF RICHARD & THE SHADOWS	1	1962
BACHELORETTE BJORK	21	1997
BACK AGAIN BOY KILL BOY	26	2006
BACK AND FORTH [A] CAMEO	11	1987
BACK AND FORTH [B] AALIYAH	16	1994
BACK AROUND ELEVATOR SUITE	71	2000
BACK BY DOPE DEMAND KING BEE	61	1991
BACK FOR GOOD REAL EMOTION	67	1995
BACK FOR GOOD TAKE THAT	1	1995
BACK FOR ME CANDEE JAY	23	2004
BACK FROM THE EDGE BRUCE DICKINSON	68	1996
BACK HERE BBMAK	5	1999
BACK HOME ENGLAND WORLD CUP SQUAD	1	1970
BACK IN LOVE AGAIN DONNA SUMMER	29	1978
BACK IN MY ARMS CHRIS PAUL	74	1987
BACK IN MY ARMS AGAIN SUPREMES	40	1965
BACK IN MY ARMS (ONCE AGAIN) HAZELL DEAN	41	1984
BACK IN MY LIFE [A] JOE ROBERTS	39	1993
BACK IN MY LIFE [B] ALICE DEEJAY	4	1999
BACK IN POWER GLITTERATI	62	2005
BACK IN THE DAY [A] AHMAD	64	1994
BACK IN THE DAY [B] ASHER D	43	2002
BACK IN THE HIGH LIFE AGAIN STEVE WINWOOD	53	1987
BACK IN THE UK SCOOTER	18	1996
BACK IN THE U.S.S.R. BEATLES	19	1976
BACK IT UP ROBIN S	43	1994
BACK LIKE THAT GHOSTFACE KILLAH FEATURING NE-YO	46	2006
THE BACK OF LOVE ECHO & THE BUNNYMEN	19	1982
BACK OF MY HAND JAGS	17	1979
BACK OFF BOOGALOO RINGO STARR	2	1972
BACK ON MY FEET AGAIN FOUNDATIONS	18	1968
BACK ON THE CHAIN GANG PRETENDERS	17	1982
BACK ON THE RADIO HISS	65	2003
BACK ON THE ROAD [A] MARMALADE	35	1971
BACK ON THE ROAD [B] EARTH, WIND & FIRE	63	1980
BACK ON THE STREETS SAXON	75	1985
BACK ON TOP VAN MORRISON	69	1999
BACK SEAT OF MY CAR PAUL & LINDA McCARTNEY	39	1971
BACK STABBERS O'JAYS	14	1972
BACK STREET LUV CURVED AIR	4	1971
BACK THEN MORE FIRE CREW	45	2003
BACK TO BASICS SHAPESHIFTERS	10	2005
BACK TO BLACK AMY WINEHOUSE	25	2007
BACK TO CALI MAURO PICOTTO	42	2002
BACK TO EARTH YVES DERUYTER	56	2001
BACK TO FRONT [A] STIFF LITTLE FINGERS	49	1980
BACK TO FRONT [B] ADAMSKI	63	1992
BACK TO LIFE (HOWEVER DO YOU WANT ME) SOUL II SOUL FEATURING CARON WHEELER	1	1989
BACK TO LOVE [A] EVELYN KING	40	1982
BACK TO LOVE [B] BRAND NEW HEAVIES FEATURING N'DEA DAVENPORT	23	1994
BACK TO LOVE [C] E-Z ROLLERS	61	2003
BACK TO MY ROOTS RuPAUL	40	1993
BACK TO REALITY INTELLIGENT HOODLUM	55	1990
BACK TO SCHOOL AGAIN FOUR TOPS	62	1982
BACK TO THE LIGHT BRIAN MAY	19	1992
BACK TO THE OLD SCHOOL BASSHEADS	12	1992
BACK TO THE SIXTIES TIGHT FIT	4	1981

	Peak Position	Year of Entry
BACK TO THE SIXTIES PART 2 TIGHT FIT	33	1981
BACK TO YOU BRYAN ADAMS	18	1997
BACK TOGETHER [A] BABYBIRD	22	1999
BACK TOGETHER [B] HARDSOUL FEATURING RON CARROLL	60	2004
BACK TOGETHER AGAIN ROBERTA FLACK & DONNY HATHAWAY	3	1980
BACK TOGETHER AGAIN INNER CITY	49	1993
BACK UP (TO ME) WOOKIE FEATURING LAIN	38	2001
BACK WHEN ALLSTARS	19	2002
BACK WITH THE BOYS AGAIN JOE FAGIN	53	1986
BACK WITH THE KILLER AGAIN AUTEURS	45	1996
BACKCHAT QUEEN	40	1982
BACKFIELD IN MOTION JB'S ALL STARS	48	1984
BACKFIRE AT THE DISCO WOMBATS	67	2007
BACKFIRED [A] DEBBIE HARRY	32	1981
BACKFIRED [B] MASTERS AT WORK FEATURING INDIA	62	2002
BACKS TO THE WALL SAXON	64	1980
BACKSEAT EDUCATION ZODIAC MINDWARP & THE LOVE REACTION	49	1987
BACKSTABBERS MARK MORRISON	48	2004
BACKSTAGE GENE PITNEY	4	1966
BACKSTREET SYMPHONY THUNDER	25	1990
BACKSTROKIN' FATBACK	41	1980
BAD MICHAEL JACKSON	3	1987
BAD ACTRESS TERRORVISION	10	1996
BAD AMBASSADOR DIVINE COMEDY	34	2001
BAD ASS STRIPPA JENTINA	22	2004
BAD BABYSITTER PRINCESS SUPERSTAR	11	2002
BAD BAD BOY NAZARETH	10	1973
BAD BLOOD SUPERGRASS	73	2008
BAD BOY [A] MARTY WILDE	7	1959
BAD BOY [B] ADICTS	75	1983
BAD BOY [C] MIAMI SOUND MACHINE	16	1986
BAD BOY [D] WILDCHILD FEATURING JOMALSKI	38	1998
BAD BOY FOR LIFE P DIDDY FEATURING BLACK ROB & MARK CURRY	13	2001
BAD BOYS [A] WHAM!	2	1983
BAD BOYS [B] INNER CIRCLE	52	1993
BAD BOYS HOLLER BOO 5050	73	2002
BAD CASE OF LOVIN' YOU (DOCTOR DOCTOR) ROBERT PALMER	61	1979
BAD COVER VERSION PULP	27	2002
BAD DAY [A] CARMEL	15	1983
BAD DAY [B] R.E.M.	8	2003
BAD DAY [C] DANIEL POWTER	2	2005
THE BAD DAYS EP SPACE	20	1998
A BAD DREAM KEANE	23	2007
BAD FEELINGS BEATINGS	68	2002
BAD GIRL [A] MADONNA	10	1993
BAD GIRL [B] SCARLET	54	1996
BAD GIRL [C] DJ RAP	32	1998
BAD GIRL (AT NIGHT) DAVE SPOON FEATURING LISA MAFFIA	36	2007
BAD GIRLS DONNA SUMMER	14	1979
BAD GIRLS JULIET ROBERTS	17	1999
BAD HABIT A.T.F.C. PRESENTS ONEPHATDEEVA FEATURING LISA MILLETT	17	2000
BAD HABITS JENNY BURTON	68	1985
BAD INTENTIONS DR DRE FEATURING KNOC-TURN'AL	4	2002
BAD LIFE PUBLIC IMAGE LTD.	71	1984
BAD LOVE ERIC CLAPTON	25	1990
BAD LUCK FM	54	1989
BAD MEDICINE BON JOVI	17	1988
BAD MOON RISING CREEDENCE CLEARWATER REVIVAL	1	1969
A BAD NIGHT CAT STEVENS	20	1967
BAD OLD DAYS CO-CO	13	1978
BAD OLD MAN BABYBIRD	31	1998
BAD PENNY BLUES HUMPHREY LYTTELTON BAND	19	1956
THE BAD PHOTOGRAPHER SAINT ETIENNE	27	1998
BAD THING CRY OF LOVE	60	1994
BAD THINGS N-JOI	57	1995
BAD TIME JAYHAWKS	70	1995
BAD TO ME BILLY J. KRAMER & THE DAKOTAS	1	1963
THE BAD TOUCH BLOODHOUND GANG	4	2000
A BAD TOWN BIG SOUND AUTHORITY	54	1985
BAD WEATHER SUPREMES	37	1973
BAD YOUNG BROTHER DEREK B	16	1988
BADABOOM B2K FEATURING FABOLOUS	26	2004
BADDER BADDER SCHWING FREDDY FRESH FEATURING FATBOY SLIM	34	1999
BADDEST RUFFEST BACKYARD DOG	15	2001
BADGE CREAM	18	1969
BADMAN [A] COCKNEY REJECTS	65	1980
BADMAN [B] SISTER BLISS	51	1996
THE BADMAN IS ROBBIN' HIJACK	56	1990
BAG IT UP GERI HALLIWELL	1	2000
BAGGY TROUSERS MADNESS	3	1980
THE BAGUIO TRACK LUZON	67	2001
BAILAMOS [A] ENRIQUE IGLESIAS	4	1999
BAILAMOS [B] M3	40	1999
BAILANDO CON LOBOS CABANA	65	1995
BAKER STREET GERRY RAFFERTY	3	1978
BAKER STREET UNDERCOVER	2	1992
BAKERMAN LAID BACK	44	1990
BALL AND CHAIN XTC	58	1982
BALL OF CONFUSION TEMPTATIONS	7	1970
BALL PARK INCIDENT WIZZARD	6	1972
BALLA BABY CHINGY	34	2004
BALLAD OF A LANDLORD TERRY HALL	50	1997
BALLAD OF BONNIE AND CLYDE GEORGIE FAME	1	1967
THE BALLAD OF CHASEY LAIN BLOODHOUND GANG	15	2000
BALLAD OF DAVY CROCKETT BILL HAYES	2	1956
BALLAD OF DAVY CROCKETT DICK JAMES	18	1956
BALLAD OF DAVY CROCKETT MAX BYGRAVES	20	1956
THE BALLAD OF DAVY CROCKETT TENNESSEE ERNIE FORD	6	1956
THE BALLAD OF JAYNE L.A. GUNS	53	1991
THE BALLAD OF JOHN AND YOKO BEATLES	1	1969
THE BALLAD OF LUCY JORDAN MARIANNE FAITHFULL	48	1979
BALLAD OF PALADIN DUANE EDDY	10	1962
THE BALLAD OF PAUL K McFLY	9	2005
THE BALLAD OF PETER PUMPKINHEAD XTC	71	1992
THE BALLAD OF PETER PUMPKINHEAD CRASH TEST DUMMIES	30	1995
THE BALLAD OF SPOTTY MULDOON PETER COOK	34	1965
BALLAD OF THE GREEN BERETS STAFF SERGEANT BARRY SADLER	24	1966
THE BALLAD OF TOM JONES SPACE WITH CERYS OF CATATONIA	4	1998
BALLAD OF YOUTH RICHIE SAMBORA	59	1991
BALLERINA GIRL LIONEL RICHIE	17	1986
BALLERINA (PRIMA DONNA) STEVE HARLEY	51	1983
BALLOON CATHERINE WHEEL	59	1992
BALLOONS FOALS	39	2007
THE BALLROOM BLITZ SWEET	2	1973
BALLROOM BLITZ TIA CARRERE	26	1992
THE BALLROOM OF ROMANCE CHRIS DE BURGH	40	1986
BALMES IAN POOLEY FEATURING ESTHERO	65	2001
BAM BAM BAM WESTBAM	57	1994
BAMA BOOGIE WOOGIE CLEVELAND EATON	35	1978
BAMA LAMA BAMA LOO LITTLE RICHARD	20	1964
BAMBAATA 2012 SHY FX	60	1999
BAMBAKITA RONI SIZE	60	2004
BAMBINO SPRINGFIELDS	16	1961
BAMBOO HOUSES SYLVIAN SAKAMOTO	30	1982
BAMBOOGIE BAMBOO	2	1998
BANANA BANANA KING KURT	54	1984
BANANA BOAT SONG HARRY BELAFONTE	2	1957
BANANA BOAT SONG SHIRLEY BASSEY	8	1957
BANANA BOAT SONG TARRIERS	15	1957
BANANA REPUBLIC BOOMTOWN RATS	3	1980
BANANA ROCK WOMBLES	9	1974
THE BANANA SONG GSP	38	1992
BANANA SPLITS (TRA LA LA SONG) DICKIES	7	1979
BA-NA-NA-BAM-BOO WESTWORLD	37	1987
BANANA-NA-NA (DUMB DI DUMB) TECHNOHEAD	64	1996
BAND OF GOLD [A] DON CHERRY	6	1956
BAND OF GOLD [B] FREDA PAYNE	1	1970
BAND OF GOLD [B] SYLVESTER	67	1983
BAND ON THE RUN PAUL McCARTNEY & WINGS	3	1974
THE BAND PLAYED THE BOOGIE C.C.S.	36	1973
BANDAGES HOT HOT HEAT	25	2003
BANDWAGON BLUES TWISTED INDIVIDUAL	51	2003
BANG [A] BLUR	24	1991
BANG [B] ROBBIE RIVERA PRESENTS RHYTHM BANGERS	13	2000
BANG AND BLAME R.E.M.	15	1994
BANG BANG [A] SQUEEZE	49	1978
BANG BANG [B] B.A. ROBERTSON	2	1979
BANG BANG (MY BABY SHOT ME DOWN) CHER	3	1966
BANG BANG YOU'RE DEAD DIRTY PRETTY THINGS	5	2006
BANG ON! PROPELLERHEADS	53	1998
BANG ZOOM (LET'S GO GO) REAL ROXANNE WITH HITMAN HOWIE TEE	11	1986
BANGERS AND MASH PETER SELLERS & SOPHIA LOREN	22	1961
BANGIN' BASS DA TECHNO BOHEMIAN	63	1997
THE BANGIN' MAN SLADE	3	1974
BANGLA DESH GEORGE HARRISON	10	1971
BANJO BOY GEORGE FORMBY	40	1960
BANJO BOY JAN & KJELD	36	1960
BANJO'S BACK IN TOWN ALMA COGAN	17	1955
BANKROBBER CLASH	12	1980
BANKROBBER AUDIOWEB	19	1997
BANKS OF THE OHIO OLIVIA NEWTON-JOHN	6	1971
THE BANNER MAN BLUE MINK	3	1971
BANQUET BLOC PARTY	13	2004
BARBADOS TYPICALLY TROPICAL	1	1975
BARBARA ANN BEACH BOYS	3	1966
BARBARELLA ALISHA'S ATTIC	34	1999
BARBER'S ADAGIO FOR STRINGS WILLIAM ORBIT	4	1999
BARBIE GIRL AQUA	1	1997
BARBIE GIRL SAMANDA	26	2007
BARCELONA [A] FREDDIE MERCURY & MONTSERRAT CABALLE	2	1987
BARCELONA [B] D KAY & EPSILON FEATURING STAMINA MC	14	2003
BARCELONA (FRIENDS UNTIL THE END) RUSSELL WATSON & SHAUN RYDER	68	2000
BARE NECESSITIES MEGAMIX U.K. MIXMASTERS	14	1991
BAREFOOT (EP) ULTRAMARINE	61	1994
BAREFOOT IN THE HEAD A MAN CALLED ADAM	60	1990
BAREFOOTIN' ROBERT PARKER	24	1966
BARK AT THE MOON OZZY OSBOURNE	21	1983
BARMY LONDON ARMY CHARLIE HARPER	68	1980
BARNEY (...& ME) BOO RADLEYS	48	1994
BARREL OF A GUN DEPECHE MODE	4	1997
BARRIERS SOFT CELL	25	1983

	Peak Position	Year of Entry
THE BARTENDER AND THE THIEF STEREOPHONICS	3	1998
BASEMENT TRACK HIGH CONTRAST	65	2003
BASKET CASE GREEN DAY	7	1995
BASKET CASE FREEFALLER	36	2005
THE BASS EP FERGIE	47	2002
BASS (HOW LOW CAN YOU GO) SIMON HARRIS	12	1988
BASS SHAKE URBAN SHAKEDOWN FEATURING MICKY FINN	59	1992
BASSCAD AUTECHRE	56	1994
BASSFLY TILLMAN + REIS	70	2000
BASSLICK SECOND PROTOCOL	58	2000
BASSLINE MANTRONIX	34	1986
BASTARDO CHARLOTTE HATHERLEY	31	2005
BAT OUT OF HELL MEAT LOAF	8	1979
BATDANCE PRINCE	2	1989
BATHTIME TINDERSTICKS	38	1997
BATHWATER NO DOUBT	17	2004
BATMAN THEME NEAL HEFTI	55	1988
BATTER UP NELLY & ST LUNATICS	28	2001
BATTLE WOOKIE FEATURING LAIN	10	2000
THE BATTLE OF NEW ORLEANS JOHNNY HORTON	16	1959
THE BATTLE OF NEW ORLEANS LONNIE DONEGAN	2	1959
BATTLE OF THE HEROES - STAR WARS JOHN WILLIAMS & THE LSO	25	2005
BATTLE OF THE SEXES FAITH, HOPE & CHARITY	53	1990
BATTLE OF WHO COULD CARE LESS BEN FOLDS FIVE	26	1997
BATTLEFLAG LO FIDELITY ALLSTARS FEATURING PIGEONHED	36	1999
THE BATTLE'S O'ER ANDY STEWART	28	1961
BATTLESHIP CHAINS GEORGIA SATELLITES	44	1987
BAUBLES, BANGLES AND BEADS GEORGE SHEARING	49	1962
BAWITDABA KID ROCK	41	2001
BBC WORLD CUP GRANDSTAND ROYAL PHILHARMONIC ORCHESTRA	61	1982
B-BOY HUMP OLD SKOOL ORCHESTRA	55	1999
B-BOY STANCE FREESTYLERS FEATURING TENOR FLY	23	1998
BE AGGRESSIVE FAITH NO MORE	3	1993
BE ALL YOU WANT ME TO BE MORNING RUNNER	44	2005
BE ALONE NO MORE ANOTHER LEVEL FEATURING JAY-Z	6	1998
BE ANGLED JAM & SPOON FEATURING REA	31	2002
BE AS ONE SASHA & MARIA	17	1996
BE BOP A LULA GENE VINCENT	16	1956
BE CAREFUL SPARKLE FEATURING R KELLY	7	1998
BE COOL PAFFENDORF	7	2002
BE FAITHFUL FATMAN SCOOP FEATURING THE CROOKLYN CLAN	1	2003
BE FREE LIVE ELEMENT	26	2002
BE FREE WITH YOUR LOVE SPANDAU BALLET	42	1989
BE GENTLE WITH ME BOY LEAST LIKELY TO	62	2006
BE GOOD TO YOURSELF FRANKIE MILLER	27	1977
BE HAPPY MARY J BLIGE	30	1994
BE LOUD BE PROUD (BE HEARD) TOYAH	30	1982
BE MINE [A] LANCE FORTUNE	4	1960
BE MINE [B] TREMELOES	39	1967
BE MINE [C] CHARLOTTE	59	1998
BE MINE [D] DAVID GRAY	23	2003
BE MINE [E] ROBYN	10	2008
BE MINE TONIGHT JAMMERS	65	1983
BE MY BABY [A] RONETTES	4	1963
BE MY BABY [B] VANESSA PARADIS	6	1992
BE MY BABY [C] CAPPELLA	53	1997
BE MY DOWNFALL DEL AMITRI	30	1992
BE MY ENEMY DEPARTURE	41	2004
BE MY FRIEND SOUL U*NIQUE	53	2000
BE MY GIRL [A] JIM DALE	2	1957
BE MY GIRL [B] DENNISONS	46	1963
BE MY GUEST FATS DOMINO	11	1959
BE MY LIGHT BE MY GUIDE GENE	54	1994
BE MY LOVER LA BOUCHE	25	1995
BE MY NUMBER TWO JOE JACKSON	70	1984
BE MY TWIN BROTHER BEYOND	14	1989
BE NEAR ME ABC	26	1985
BE QUICK OR BE DEAD IRON MAIDEN	2	1992
BE QUIET AND DRIVE (FAR AWAY) DEFTONES	50	1998
BE STIFF DEVO	71	1978
BE TENDER WITH ME BABY TINA TURNER	28	1990
BE THANKFUL FOR WHAT YOU'VE GOT WILLIAM DE VAUGHN	31	1974
BE THE FIRST TO BELIEVE A1	6	1999
BE THERE [A] TALL PAUL	45	1999
BE THERE [B] UNKLE FEATURING IAN BROWN	8	1999
BE WITH ME ALWAYS CLIFF RICHARD	52	1997
BE WITH YOU [A] BANGLES	23	1989
BE WITH YOU [B] ATOMIC KITTEN	2	2002
BE WITHOUT YOU [A] MARY J BLIGE	32	2006
BE WITHOUT YOU [B] WIFI FEATURING MELANIE M	42	2007
BE YOUNG BE FOOLISH BE HAPPY TAMS	32	1970
BE YOUNG BE FOOLISH BE HAPPY SONIA	22	1991
BE YOURSELF [A] CELEDA	61	1999
BE YOURSELF [B] AUDIOSLAVE	40	2005
BEACH BABY FIRST CLASS	13	1974
BEACH BOYS MEDLEY BEACH BOYS	47	1981
BEACH BUMP BABY FORD	68	1990
BEACH OF THE WAR GODDESS CARON WHEELER	75	1993
BEACHBALL NALIN & KANE	17	1997
BEACHBOY GOLD GIDEA PARK	11	1981
BEACHED ORBITAL & ANGELO BADALAMENTI	36	2000
BEACON LIGHT WEEN	20	1998
BEAR CAGE STRANGLERS	36	1980
BEAST AND THE HARLOT AVENGED SEVENFOLD	47	2006
A BEAT CALLED LOVE GRID	64	1990
BEAT DIS BOMB THE BASS	2	1988
BEAT FOR BEATNIKS JOHN BARRY ORCHESTRA	40	1960
THE BEAT GOES ON [A] SONNY & CHER	29	1967
BEAT GOES ON [A] ALL SEEING I	11	1998
THE BEAT GOES ON [B] BOB SINCLAR	33	2003
THE BEAT IS ROCKIN' ERICKE	25	2007
BEAT IT MICHAEL JACKSON	3	1983
BEAT MAMA CAST	9	1999
BEAT STREET BREAKDOWN GRANDMASTER MELLE MEL & THE FURIOUS FIVE	42	1984
BEAT SURRENDER JAM	1	1982
BEAT THE BEAT MARI WILSON	59	1982
BEAT THE CLOCK SPARKS	10	1979
BEAT YOUR HEART OUT DISTILLERS	74	2004
THE BEAT(EN) GENERATION THE THE	18	1989
BEATIN' THE HEAT JACK 'N' CHILL	42	1988
BEATING HEART BABY HEAD AUTOMATICA	44	2005
BEATLES AND THE STONES HOUSE OF LOVE	36	1990
BEATLES MOVIE MEDLEY BEATLES	10	1982
BEATNIK FLY JOHNNY & THE HURRICANES	8	1960
BEATNIK GIRL SNUG	55	1998
BEATSTIME SONIC SOLUTION	59	1992
BEAUTIFUL [A] MARILLION	29	1995
BEAUTIFUL [B] MATT DAREY'S MASH UP PRESENTS MARCELLA WOODS	10	2000
BEAUTIFUL [C] BIGFELLA FEATURING NOEL McCALLA	52	2002
BEAUTIFUL [D] LEMONESCENT	70	2002
BEAUTIFUL [E] ATHLETE	41	2002
BEAUTIFUL [F] CHRISTINA AGUILERA	1	2003
BEAUTIFUL [G] SNOOP DOGG	23	2003
BEAUTIFUL [H] DAMIAN "JR GONG" MARLEY	39	2006
BEAUTIFUL ALONE STRANGELOVE	35	1996
BEAUTIFUL CHILD (A DEEPER LOVE) MADELYNE	63	2002
BEAUTIFUL DAY [A] 3 COLOURS RED	11	1999
BEAUTIFUL DAY [B] U2	1	2000
BEAUTIFUL DREAM WORLD PARTY	31	1997
THE BEAUTIFUL EXPERIENCE PRINCE	18	1994
BEAUTIFUL GIRL [A] INXS	23	1993
BEAUTIFUL GIRL [B] SEAN KINGSTON	1	2007
BEAUTIFUL IMBALANCE THRASHING DOVES	50	1987
BEAUTIFUL IN MY EYES JOSHUA KADISON	37	1994
BEAUTIFUL INSIDE LOUISE	13	2000
BEAUTIFUL LIAR BEYONCÉ & SHAKIRA	1	2007
BEAUTIFUL LIFE ACE OF BASE	15	1996
BEAUTIFUL LOVE [A] ADEVA	57	1989
BEAUTIFUL LOVE [B] JULIAN COPE	32	1991
BEAUTIFUL LOVER BROTHERHOOD OF MAN	15	1978
BEAUTIFUL NIGHT PAUL McCARTNEY	25	1997
BEAUTIFUL NOISE NEIL DIAMOND	13	1976
THE BEAUTIFUL OCCUPATION TRAVIS	48	2003
BEAUTIFUL ONES [A] SUEDE	8	1996
BEAUTIFUL ONES [B] BILLIAM	32	2007
BEAUTIFUL PEOPLE [A] STRESS	74	1990
BEAUTIFUL PEOPLE [B] BIG COUNTRY	72	1991
BEAUTIFUL PEOPLE [C] BARBARA TUCKER	23	1994
THE BEAUTIFUL PEOPLE [D] MARILYN MANSON	18	1997
BEAUTIFUL SON HOLE	54	1993
BEAUTIFUL SOUL JESSE McCARTNEY	16	2006
BEAUTIFUL STRANGER MADONNA	2	1999
BEAUTIFUL SUNDAY DANIEL BOONE	21	1972
BEAUTIFUL YOU NEIL SEDAKA	43	1972
BEAUTY AND THE BEAST [A] DAVID BOWIE	39	1978
BEAUTY AND THE BEAST [B] CELINE DION & PEABO BRYSON	9	1992
BEAUTY DIES YOUNG LOWGOLD	40	2000
BEAUTY IS ONLY SKIN DEEP TEMPTATIONS	18	1966
THE BEAUTY OF SILENCE SVENSON & GIELEN	41	2001
BEAUTY OF THE RIDE SEBADOH	74	1996
BEAUTY ON THE FIRE NATALIE IMBRUGLIA	26	2002
BEAUTY'S ONLY SKIN DEEP ASWAD	31	1989
BECAUSE [A] DEMIS ROUSSOS	39	1977
BECAUSE [B] JULIAN LENNON	40	1985
BECAUSE [C] JUSTICE	48	2007
BECAUSE I GOT HIGH AFROMAN	1	2001
BECAUSE I GOT IT LIKE THAT JUNGLE BROTHERS	32	1998
BECAUSE I LOVE YOU [A] GEORGIE FAME	15	1967
BECAUSE I LOVE YOU [B] SHAKIN' STEVENS	14	1986
BECAUSE I LOVE YOU (THE POSTMAN SONG) STEVIE B	6	1991
BECAUSE I WANT YOU PLACEBO	13	2006
BECAUSE OF LOVE [A] BILLY FURY	18	1962
BECAUSE OF LOVE [B] JANET JACKSON	19	1994
BECAUSE OF YOU [A] DEXY'S MIDNIGHT RUNNERS	13	1986
BECAUSE OF YOU [B] GABRIELLE	24	1994
BECAUSE OF YOU [C] 98°	36	1999
BECAUSE OF YOU [D] SCANTY SANDWICH	3	2000
BECAUSE OF YOU [E] MARQUES HOUSTON	51	2004
BECAUSE OF YOU [F] KELLY CLARKSON	7	2005
BECAUSE OF YOU [G] NE-YO	4	2007
BECAUSE THE NIGHT PATTI SMITH GROUP	5	1978
BECAUSE THE NIGHT CO-RO FEATURING TARLISA	61	1992
BECAUSE THE NIGHT 10,000 MANIACS	65	1993
BECAUSE THE NIGHT JAN WAYNE	14	2002
BECAUSE THEY'RE YOUNG DUANE EDDY & THE REBELS	2	1960
BECAUSE THEY'RE YOUNG JAMES DARREN	29	1960
BECAUSE WE WANT TO BILLIE	1	1998

Title / Artist	Peak Position	Year of Entry
BECAUSE YOU COSMIC ROUGH RIDERS	34	2003
BECAUSE YOU LOVED ME (THEME FROM UP CLOSE AND PERSONAL) CELINE DION	5	1996
BECAUSE YOU'RE MINE MARIO LANZA	3	1952
BECAUSE YOU'RE MINE NAT 'KING' COLE	6	1952
BECAUSE YOU'RE YOUNG CLASSIX NOUVEAUX	43	1982
BECOMING MORE LIKE ALFIE DIVINE COMEDY	27	1996
BECOMING MORE LIKE GOD JAH WOBBLE'S INVADERS OF THE HEART	36	1994
BED J HOLIDAY	32	2007
BED OF NAILS ALICE COOPER	38	1989
BED OF ROSES BON JOVI	13	1993
BED SITTER SOFT CELL	4	1981
BEDS ARE BURNING MIDNIGHT OIL	6	1988
THE BED'S TOO BIG WITHOUT YOU SHEILA HYLTON	35	1981
BEDSHAPED KEANE	10	2004
BEDTIME STORY MADONNA	4	1995
THE BEE SCIENTIST	47	1990
BEE BOM ANTHONY NEWLEY	12	1961
BEE STING CAMOUFLAGE FEATURING MYSTI	48	1977
BEEF GARY CLAIL	64	1990
BEEN A LONG TIME FOG	27	1994
BEEN AROUND THE WORLD [A] PUFF DADDY & THE FAMILY	20	1997
BEEN AROUND THE WORLD [B] ZENA FEATURING VYBZ KARTEL	44	2004
BEEN CAUGHT STEALING JANE'S ADDICTION	34	1991
BEEN IT CARDIGANS	56	1996
BEEN THERE DONE THAT SMOKE 2 SEVEN	26	2002
BEEN THINKING ABOUT YOU MARTINE GIRAULT	63	1995
BEEN TRAINING DOGS COOPER TEMPLE CLAUSE	20	2002
BEEP PUSSYCAT DOLLS FEATURING WILL.I.AM	2	2006
BEEP ME 911 MISSY 'MISDEMEANOR' ELLIOTT	14	1998
BEER DRINKERS AND HELL RAISERS MOTORHEAD	43	1980
BEETHOVEN (I LOVE TO LISTEN TO) EURYTHMICS	25	1987
BEETLEBUM BLUR	1	1997
BEFORE PET SHOP BOYS	7	1996
BEFORE I FALL TO PIECES RAZORLIGHT	17	2006
BEFORE I FORGET SLIPKNOT	35	2005
BEFORE TODAY EVERYTHING BUT THE GIRL	25	1997
BEFORE YOU LEAVE PEPE DELUXE	20	2001
BEFORE YOU LOVE ME ALSOU	27	2001
BEFORE YOU WALK OUT OF MY LIFE MONICA	22	1996
BEG, STEAL OR BORROW NEW SEEKERS	2	1972
A BEGGAR ON A BEACH OF GOLD MIKE + THE MECHANICS	33	1995
BEGGIN' TIMEBOX	38	1968
BEGGIN' FRANKIE VALLI & THE FOUR SEASONS	32	2007
BEGGIN' TO BE WRITTEN WORLDS APART	29	1994
BEGGING YOU STONE ROSES	15	1995
BEGIN AGAIN SPACE	21	1998
BEGIN THE BEGUINE (VOLVER A EMPEZAR) JULIO IGLESIAS	1	1981
THE BEGINNING SEAL	24	1991
BEGINNING OF THE END STATUS QUO	48	2007
THE BEGINNING OF THE TWIST FUTUREHEADS	20	2008
BEHIND A PAINTED SMILE ISLEY BROTHERS	5	1969
BEHIND BLUE EYES LIMP BIZKIT	18	2003
BEHIND CLOSED DOORS CHARLIE RICH	16	1974
BEHIND THE COUNTER FALL	75	1993
BEHIND THE GROOVE TEENA MARIE	6	1980
BEHIND THE MASK ERIC CLAPTON	15	1987
BEHIND THE WHEEL DEPECHE MODE	21	1988
BEHIND THESE HAZEL EYES KELLY CLARKSON	9	2005
BEIN' AROUND LEMONHEADS	19	1992
BEING A GIRL (PART ONE) EP MANSUN	13	1998
BEING BOILED HUMAN LEAGUE	6	1982
BEING BORING PET SHOP BOYS	20	1990
BEING BRAVE MENSWEAR	10	1996
BEING NOBODY RICHARD X VS LIBERTY X	3	2003
BEING WITH YOU SMOKEY ROBINSON	1	1981
BEL AMOUR BEL AMOUR	23	2001
BELARUSE LEVELLERS	12	1993
BELFAST [A] BONEY M	8	1977
BELFAST [B] BARNBRACK	45	1985
BELFAST [C] ENERGY ORCHARD	52	1990
BELFAST [D] ORBITAL	53	1995
BELFAST BOY DON FARDON	32	1970
BELFAST CHILD SIMPLE MINDS	1	1989
BELFAST TRANCE JOHN 'OO' FLEMING & SIMPLE MINDS	74	2002
BELIEVE [A] LENNY KRAVITZ	30	1993
BELIEVE [B] Q-TEX	41	1994
BELIEVE [C] ELTON JOHN	15	1995
BELIEVE [D] GOLDIE	36	1998
BELIEVE [E] CHER	1	1998
BELIEVE [F] MINISTERS DE LA FUNK FEATURING JOCELYN BROWN	42	2000
BELIEVE [G] IAN VAN DAHL	27	2004
BELIEVE [H] CHEMICAL BROTHERS	18	2005
BELIEVE IN ME [A] UTAH SAINTS	8	1993
BELIEVE IN ME [B] QUIVVER	56	1995
BELIEVE IN ME [C] MANKEY	74	1996
BELIEVE IN ME [D] RAW STYLUS	66	1996
BELIEVE IN THE BEAT CAROL LYNN TOWNES	56	1985
BELIEVE IN THE BOOGIE MARK OWEN	57	2005
BELIEVE WHAT YOU'RE SAYING SUGAR	73	1994
BELIEVER REAL PEOPLE	38	1992
BELIEVERS BAZ	36	2001
THE BELL MIKE OLDFIELD	50	1993
BELL BOTTOM BLUES ALMA COGAN	4	1954
BELL BOTTOMED TEAR BEAUTIFUL SOUTH	16	1992
THE BELLE OF ST MARK SHEILA E	18	1985
BELLISSIMA DJ QUICKSILVER	4	1997
BELLS OF AVIGNON MAX BYGRAVES	36	1961
BELLS OF NY SLO-MOSHUN	29	1994
BELLY DANCER (BANANZA) AKON	5	2005
BELO HORIZONTI HEARTISTS	40	1997
BEN MICHAEL JACKSON	7	1972
BEN MARTI WEBB	5	1985
BEN TONI WARNE	50	1987
BEND IT DAVE DEE, DOZY, BEAKY, MICK & TICH	2	1966
BEND ME SHAPE ME AMEN CORNER	3	1968
BEND ME SHAPE ME AMERICAN BREED	24	1968
BENEDICTUS BRAINBUG	24	1997
BENJAMIN VERUCA SALT	75	1997
BENNIE AND THE JETS ELTON JOHN	37	1976
BENNY'S THEME PAUL HENRY & MAYSON GLEN ORCHESTRA	39	1978
BENTLEY'S GONNA SORT YOU OUT! BENTLEY RHYTHM ACE	17	1997
BENZIN RAMMSTEIN	58	2005
BERMUDA TRIANGLE BARRY MANILOW	15	1981
BERNADETTE FOUR TOPS	8	1967
BERRY TC 1991	73	1992
BERSERKER GARY NUMAN	32	1984
BESAME MUCHO JET HARRIS	22	1962
BESIDE YOU IGGY POP	47	1994
THE BEST TINA TURNER	5	1989
BEST BIT EP BETH ORTON FEATURING TERRY CALLIER	36	1997
THE BEST CHRISTMAS OF THEM ALL SHAKIN' STEVENS	19	1990
BEST DAYS JUICE	28	1998
THE BEST DAYS OF OUR LIVES LISBON LIONS FEATURING MARTIN O'NEILL	17	2002
THE BEST DISCO IN TOWN RITCHIE FAMILY	10	1976
BEST FRIEND [A] BEAT	22	1980
BEST FRIEND [B] MARK MORRISON & CONNOR REEVES	23	1999
BEST FRIEND [C] PUFF DADDY FEATURING MARIO WINANS	24	1999
BEST FRIENDS [A] TOY - BOX	41	1999
BEST FRIENDS [B] ALLSTARS	20	2001
BEST FRIENDS FOREVER TWEENIES	12	2001
BEST FRIEND'S GIRL ELECTRASY	41	1998
BEST I CAN QUEENSRYCHE	36	1991
BEST IN ME LET LOOSE	8	1995
THE BEST IS YET TO COME SCOOCH	12	2000
BEST KEPT SECRET CHINA CRISIS	36	1987
BEST LOVE COURSE	51	1997
THE BEST OF BOTH WORLDS HANNAH MONTANA	43	2007
THE BEST OF EVERYTHING JOHNNY MATHIS	30	1959
THE BEST OF LOVE MICHAEL BOLTON	14	1997
THE BEST OF ME [A] CLIFF RICHARD	2	1989
THE BEST OF ME [B] BRYAN ADAMS	47	1999
BEST OF MY LOVE [A] EMOTIONS	4	1977
BEST OF MY LOVE [A] LOVESTATION	73	1993
BEST OF MY LOVE [A] C.J. LEWIS	13	1994
BEST OF MY LOVE [B] DEE LEWIS	47	1988
BEST OF MY LOVE [C] JAVINE	18	2004
BEST OF ORDER DAVID SNEDDON	19	2003
THE BEST OF TIMES STYX	42	1981
BEST OF YOU [A] KENNY THOMAS	11	1991
BEST OF YOU [B] FOO FIGHTERS	4	2005
(THE BEST PART OF) BREAKING UP RONETTES	43	1964
BEST PART OF BREAKING UP SYMBOLS	25	1968
(THE BEST PART OF) BREAKING UP RONI GRIFFITH	63	1984
BEST REGRETS GENEVA	38	1997
BEST THING [A] ADAM RICKITT	25	2000
THE BEST THING [B] SAVAGE GARDEN	35	2001
BEST THING IN THE WORLD OPTIMYSTIC	70	1995
BEST THING THAT EVER HAPPENED TO ME GLADYS KNIGHT & THE PIPS	7	1975
THE BEST THINGS IN LIFE ARE FREE LUTHER VANDROSS & JANET JACKSON WITH SPECIAL GUESTS BBD & RALPH TRESVANT	2	1992
BEST WISHES ULTRASOUND	68	1998
THE BEST YEARS OF MY LIFE DIANA ROSS	28	1994
BEST YEARS OF OUR LIVES MODERN ROMANCE	4	1982
BET ON IT TROY	65	2007
BET YER LIFE I DO HERMAN'S HERMITS	22	1970
BETA EMPIRION	75	1997
BETCHA BY GOLLY WOW STYLISTICS	13	1972
BETCHA BY GOLLY WOW! THE ARTIST	11	1996
BETCHA CAN'T LOSE (WITH MY LOVE) MAGIC LADY	58	1988
BETCHA CAN'T WAIT E-17	12	1999
BETCHA' WOULDN'T HURT ME QUINCY JONES	52	1981
BETTE DAVIS' EYES KIM CARNES	10	1981
BETTER TOM BAXTER	67	2007
BETTER BE GOOD TO ME TINA TURNER	45	1984
BETTER BELIEVE IT (CHILDREN IN NEED) SID OWEN & PATSY PALMER	60	1995
BETTER BEST FORGOTTEN STEPS	2	1999
BETTER DAY OCEAN COLOUR SCENE	9	1997
BETTER DAYS [A] GUN	33	1989
BETTER DAYS [B] BRUCE SPRINGSTEEN	34	1992
BETTER DAYS [C] TQ	32	1999
BETTER DAYS AHEAD TYRREL CORPORATION	29	1995
BETTER DO BETTER HARD-FI	14	2006
BETTER DO IT SALSA GIBSON BROTHERS	12	1980

	Peak Position	Year of Entry
BETTER GET READY LULU	59	2000
BETTER IN TIME LEONA LEWIS	2	2008
A BETTER LOVE LONDONBEAT	23	1990
BETTER LOVE NEXT TIME DR HOOK	8	1980
BETTER MADE HEADSWIM	42	1998
A BETTER MAN [A] THUNDER	18	1993
A BETTER MAN [B] BRIAN KENNEDY	28	1996
BETTER OFF ALONE DJ JURGEN PRESENTS ALICE DEEJAY	2	1999
BETTER OFF WITH HIM A	52	2005
BETTER OFF WITHOUT YOU HAZELL DEAN	72	1991
BETTER TAKE TIME SECOND IMAGE	67	1983
BETTER THAN LIFE ULTRABEAT	23	2004
BETTER THE DEVIL YOU KNOW [A] KYLIE MINOGUE	2	1990
BETTER THE DEVIL YOU KNOW [A] SONIA	15	1993
BETTER THE DEVIL YOU KNOW [B] STEPS	4	1999
BETTER THINGS KINKS	46	1981
BETTER TOGETHER JACK JOHNSON	24	2006
BETTER USE YOUR HEAD LITTLE ANTHONY & THE IMPERIALS	42	1976
BETTER WATCH OUT ANT & DEC	10	1996
BETTER WORLD REBEL MC	20	1990
BETTY BETTY BETTY LONNIE DONEGAN	11	1958
(BETWEEN A) ROCK AND A HARD PLACE CUTTING CREW	66	1989
BETWEEN ANGELS AND INSECTS PAPA ROACH	17	2001
BETWEEN ME AND YOU JA RULE FEATURING CHRISTINA MILIAN	26	2001
BETWEEN THE SHEETS ISLEY BROTHERS	52	1983
BETWEEN THE WARS (EP) BILLY BRAGG	15	1985
BEVERLY HILLS WEEZER	9	2005
BEWARE VIVIENNE McKONE	69	1992
(BEWARE) BOYFRIEND MARI WILSON	51	1982
BEWARE OF THE BOYS PANJABI MC FEATURING JAY-Z	25	2003
BEWARE OF THE DOG JAMELIA	10	2006
BEYOND THE INVISIBLE ENIGMA	26	1997
BEYOND THE PALE MISSION	32	1988
BEYOND THE REEF ELVIS PRESLEY	3	1980
BEYOND THE SEA (LA MER) GEORGE BENSON	60	1985
BEYOND THE STARS DAVID WHITFIELD	8	1955
BEYOND TIME BLANK & JONES	53	2001
BEYOND YOUR WILDEST DREAMS LONNIE GORDON	48	1990
BEYOND YOUR WILDEST DREAMS SYBIL	41	1993
THE BHOYS ARE BACK IN TOWN DANCE TO TIPPERARY	44	2003
BICYCLE RACE QUEEN	11	1978
BIG APPLE KAJAGOOGOO	8	1983
BIG AREA THEN JERICO	13	1989
BIG BAD EP LITTLE ANGELS	74	1989
BIG BAD JOHN JIMMY DEAN	2	1961
BIG BAD MAMMA FOXY BROWN FEATURING DRU HILL	12	1997
THE BIG BEAN PIGBAG	40	1982
THE BIG BEAT [A] FATS DOMINO	20	1958
BIG BEAT [B] CAPPELLA	16	1994
BIG BEAT BOOGIE BERT WEEDON	37	1960
BIG BIG WORLD EMILIA	5	1998
BIG BOSS GROOVE STYLE COUNCIL	5	1984
BIG BOYS DON'T CRY LOLLY	10	1999
***BIG BROTHER* UK TV THEME** ELEMENT FOUR	4	2000
BIG BUBBLES, NO TROUBLES ELLIS, BEGGS & HOWARD	41	1988
BIG CITY DANDY LIVINGSTONE	26	1973
BIG CITY LIFE MATTAFIX	15	2005
BIG DEAL BOBBY G	46	1984
BIG DECISION THAT PETROL EMOTION	43	1987
BIG DICK MAN SEX CLUB FEATURING BROWN SUGAR	67	1995
BIG EIGHT JUDGE DREAD	14	1973
BIG FUN [A] KOOL & THE GANG	14	1982
BIG FUN [B] GAP BAND	4	1986
BIG FUN [C] INNER CITY FEATURING KEVIN SAUNDERSON	8	1988
BIG GAY HEART LEMONHEADS	55	1994
BIG GIRL PRECOCIOUS BRATS/KEVIN & PERRY	16	2000
BIG GIRL (YOU ARE BEAUTIFUL) MIKA	9	2007
BIG GIRLS DON'T CRY FOUR SEASONS	13	1963
BIG GIRLS DON'T CRY (PERSONAL) FERGIE	2	2007
BIG GREEN CAR POLECATS	35	1981
BIG GUN AC/DC	23	1993
A BIG HUNK O' LOVE ELVIS PRESLEY	4	1959
THE BIG HURT MAUREEN EVANS	26	1960
THE BIG HURT TONI FISHER	30	1960
BIG IN AMERICA STRANGLERS	48	1986
BIG IN JAPAN ALPHAVILLE	8	1984
BIG IRON MARTY ROBBINS	48	1960
THE BIG L ROXETTE	21	1991
BIG LOG ROBERT PLANT	11	1983
BIG LOVE [A] FLEETWOOD MAC	9	1987
BIG LOVE [B] PETE HELLER	12	1999
BIG LOVE [C] FRESH	58	2003
BIG MAN FOUR PREPS	2	1958
THE BIG MAN AND THE SCREAM TEAM MEET THE BARMY ARMY UPTOWN PRIMAL SCREAM, IRVINE WELSH & ON U-SOUND	17	1996
BIG MAN IN A BIG HOUSE LEROY VAN DYKE	34	1962
BIG ME FOO FIGHTERS	19	1996
BIG MISTAKE NATALIE IMBRUGLIA	2	1998
THE BIG MONEY RUSH	46	1985
BIG MOUTH STRIKES AGAIN SMITHS	26	1986
BIG N BASHY FALLACY FEATURING TUBBY T	45	2003
BIG NEW PRINZ FALL	59	1988
BIG NIGHT OUT FUN LOVIN' CRIMINALS	29	1998
THE BIG ONE BLACK	54	1988
THE BIG ONES GET AWAY BUFFY SAINTE-MARIE	39	1992
BIG PANTY WOMAN BAREFOOT MAN	21	1998
BIG PIMPIN' JAY-Z	29	2000
BIG POPPA NOTORIOUS B.I.G.	63	1995
BIG PUNK JUDGE DREAD	49	1978
BIG RIVER JIMMY NAIL	18	1995
BIG SCARY ANIMAL BELINDA CARLISLE	12	1972
BIG SEVEN JUDGE DREAD	8	1993
BIG SHIP CLIFF RICHARD	8	1972
BIG SIX JUDGE DREAD	11	1969
THE BIG SKY KATE BUSH	37	1986
BIG SKY NEW LIGHT MARTIN STEPHENSON & THE DAINTEES	71	1992
BIG SPENDER SHIRLEY BASSEY	21	1967
BIG SUR THRILLS	17	2003
BIG TEASER SAXON	66	1980
BIG TEN JUDGE DREAD	14	1975
BIG THING COMING STRANGLERS	31	2004
BIG TIME [A] RICK JAMES	41	1980
BIG TIME [B] PETER GABRIEL	13	1987
BIG TIME [C] WHIGFIELD	21	1995
BIG TIME OPERATOR ZOOT MONEY & THE BIG ROLL BAND	25	1966
BIG TIME SENSUALITY BJORK	17	1993
BIG WEDGE FISH	25	1990
BIG WHEELS LLAMA FARMERS	67	1999
BIG YELLOW TAXI JONI MITCHELL	11	1970
BIG YELLOW TAXI AMY GRANT	20	1995
BIG YELLOW TAXI COUNTING CROWS FEATURING VANESSA CARLTON	16	2003
BIGAMY AT CHRISTMAS TONY FERRINO	42	1996
BIGBOY MINUTEMAN	45	2002
BIGGER BETTER DEAL DESERT EAGLE DISCS FEATURING KEISHA	67	2003
BIGGER THAN BIG SUPER MAL FEATURING LUCIANA	19	2007
BIGGER THAN MY BODY JOHN MAYER	72	2004
BIGGEST HORIZON CLINT BOON EXPERIENCE	70	2000
BIGGEST MISTAKE ROLLING STONES	51	2006
BIKINI GIRLS WITH MACHINE GUNS CRAMPS	35	1990
BIKO PETER GABRIEL	38	1980
BILJO CLODAGH RODGERS	22	1969
BILL BAILEY BOBBY DARIN	34	1960
BILL MCCAI CORAL	23	2003
BILLIE JEAN MICHAEL JACKSON	1	1983
BILLIE JEAN BATES	67	1996
BILLIE JEAN SOUND BLUNTZ	32	2002
BILLS, BILLS, BILLS DESTINY'S CHILD	6	1999
BILLS 2 PAY GLAMMA KID	17	2000
BILLY BOY DICK CHARLESWORTH & HIS CITY GENTS	43	1961
BILLY, DON'T BE A HERO PAPER LACE	1	1974
BIMBO RUBY WRIGHT	7	1954
BING BANG (TIME TO DANCE) LAZY TOWN	4	2006
BINGO CATCH	23	1997
BINGO BANGO BASEMENT JAXX	13	2000
BIOLOGY GIRLS ALOUD	4	2005
BIONIC KING ADORA	30	2001
BIONIC SANTA CHRIS HILL	10	1976
BIRD DOG EVERLY BROTHERS	2	1958
BIRD OF PARADISE SNOWY WHITE	6	1984
BIRD ON A WIRE NEVILLE BROTHERS	72	1990
BIRD SONG LENE LOVICH	39	1979
BIRDHOUSE IN YOUR SOUL THEY MIGHT BE GIANTS	6	1990
THE BIRDIE SONG (BIRDIE DANCE) TWEETS	2	1981
BIRDMAN RIDE	38	1994
THE BIRDS AND THE BEES ALMA COGAN	25	1956
THE BIRDS AND THE BEES JEWEL AKENS	29	1965
BIRDS AND BEES WARM SOUNDS	27	1967
BIRDS FLY (WHISPER TO A SCREAM) ICICLE WORKS	53	1984
BIRDS OF A FEATHER KILLING JOKE	64	1982
BIRTH PEDDLERS	17	1969
BIRTHDAY [A] SUGARCUBES	64	1987
BIRTHDAY [B] PAUL McCARTNEY	29	1990
BIS VS THE DIY CORPS (EP) BIS	45	1996
THE BIT GOES ON SNAKEBITE	25	1997
A BIT OF U2 KISS AMC	58	1989
BITCH [A] ROLLING STONES	2	1971
THE BITCH [B] OLYMPIC RUNNERS	37	1979
BITCH [C] MEREDITH BROOKS	6	1997
B*TCH [D] DAVE McCULLEN	54	2005
THE BITCH IS BACK ELTON JOHN	15	1974
BITCH SCHOOL SPINAL TAP	35	1992
BITCH WITH A PERM TIM DOG	49	1994
BITCHES BREW INSPIRAL CARPETS	36	1992
BITE YOUR LIP (GET UP AND DANCE) ELTON JOHN	28	1977
BITES DA DUST PLANET PERFECTO	52	2001
BITS AND PIECES [A] DAVE CLARK FIVE	2	1964
BITS + PIECES [B] ARTEMESIA	46	1995
BITS OF KIDS STIFF LITTLE FINGERS	73	1982
BITTER END PLACEBO	12	2003
BITTER FRUIT LITTLE STEVEN	66	1987
BITTER SWEET MARC ALMOND	40	1988
BITTER SWEET SYMPHONY VERVE	2	1997
BITTER TEARS INXS	30	1991
THE BITTEREST PILL (I EVER HAD TO SWALLOW) JAM	2	1982
BITTERSWEET BILLY OCEAN	44	1986
BITTERSWEET BUNDLE OF MAN GRAHAM COXON	22	2004
BITTERSWEET ME R.E.M.	19	1996
BIZARRE LOVE TRIANGLE NEW ORDER	56	1986
BIZZI'S PARTY BIZZI	62	1997
BJANGO LUCKY MONKEYS	50	1996
BLACK & GOLD SAM SPARRO	23	2008
BLACK AND WHITE [A] GREYHOUND	6	1971

	Peak Position	Year of Entry
BLACK AND WHITE [B] STATIC-X	65	2001
BLACK AND WHITE [C] UPPER ROOM	22	2006
BLACK & WHITE ARMY BLACK & WHITE ARMY	26	1998
BLACK AND WHITE TOWN DOVES	6	2005
BLACK ANGEL MICA PARIS	72	1998
BLACK BEAR FRANK CORDELL	44	1961
BLACK BETTY RAM JAM	7	1977
BLACK BETTY TOM JONES	50	2003
BLACK BOOK E.Y.C.	13	1994
BLACK CAT JANET JACKSON	15	1990
BLACK CHERRY GOLDFRAPP	28	2004
BLACK COFFEE ALL SAINTS	1	2000
BLACK COFFEE IN BED SQUEEZE	51	1982
BLACK EYED BOY TEXAS	5	1997
THE BLACK EYED BOYS PAPER LACE	11	1974
BLACK GIRL FOUR PENNIES	20	1964
BLACK GOLD SOUL ASYLUM	26	1994
BLACK HEART MARC & THE MAMBAS	49	1983
BLACK HILLS OF DAKOTA DORIS DAY	7	1954
BLACK HISTORY MONTH DEATH FROM ABOVE 1979	48	2005
BLACK HOLE SUN SOUNDGARDEN	12	1994
BLACK HORSE AND THE CHERRY TREE KT TUNSTALL	28	2005
BLACK IS BLACK [A] LOS BRAVOS	2	1966
BLACK IS BLACK [A] LA BELLE EPOQUE	2	1977
BLACK IS BLACK [B] JUNGLE BROTHERS	72	1989
BLACK JESUS EVERLAST	37	2001
BLACK LODGE ANTHRAX	53	1993
BLACK MAGIC WOMAN FLEETWOOD MAC	37	1968
BLACK MAN RAY CHINA CRISIS	14	1985
BLACK MEANING GOOD REBEL MC	73	1991
BLACK METALLIC (EP) CATHERINE WHEEL	68	1991
BLACK NIGHT DEEP PURPLE	2	1970
BLACK NITE CRASH RIDE	67	1996
BLACK OR WHITE MICHAEL JACKSON	1	1991
BLACK ORCHID STEVIE WONDER	63	1980
BLACK PEARL HORACE FAITH	13	1970
BLACK PUDDING BERTHA (THE QUEEN OF NORTHERN SOUL) GOODIES	19	1975
BLACK SABBATH MAGOO : MOGWAI	60	1998
BLACK SKIN BLUE EYED BOYS EQUALS	9	1971
BLACK STATIONS WHITE STATIONS M + M	46	1984
BLACK STEEL TRICKY	28	1995
BLACK STOCKINGS JOHN BARRY SEVEN	27	1960
BLACK SUITS COMIN' (NOD YA HEAD) WILL SMITH FEATURING TRA-KNOX	3	2002
BLACK SUPERMAN (MUHAMMAD ALI) JOHNNY WAKELIN & THE KINSHASA BAND	7	1975
BLACK SWEAT PRINCE	43	2006
BLACK TIE WHITE NOISE DAVID BOWIE FEATURING AL B. SURE!	36	1993
BLACK VELVET ALANNAH MYLES	2	1990
BLACK VELVET BAND DUBLINERS	15	1967
BLACK WHITE ASIAN DUB FOUNDATION	52	1998
BLACKBERRY WAY MOVE	1	1969
BLACKBIRD ON THE WIRE BEAUTIFUL SOUTH	23	1997
BLACKBOARD JUMBLE BARRON KNIGHTS	52	1981
BLACKEN MY THUMB DATSUNS	48	2004
BLACKENED BLUE EYES CHARLATANS	28	2006
BLACKER THAN BLACK GOODBYE MR MACKENZIE	61	1990
BLACKERTHREETRACKER EP CURVE	39	1993
BLACKWATER [A] RAIN TREE CROW	62	1991
BLACKWATER [B] OCTAVE ONE FEATURING ANN SAUNDERSON	47	2002
BLAG STEAL & BORROW KOOPA	31	2007
BLAH HELTAH SKELTAH & ORIGINOO GUNN CLAPPAZ AS THE FABULOUS FIVE	60	1996
BLAME IT ON ME D:REAM	25	1994
BLAME IT ON THE BASSLINE NORMAN COOK FEATURING MC WILDSKI	1	1989
BLAME IT ON THE BOOGIE JACKSONS	8	1978
BLAME IT ON THE BOOGIE MICK JACKSON	15	1978
BLAME IT ON THE BOOGIE BIG FUN	4	1989
BLAME IT ON THE BOOGIE CLOCK	16	1998
BLAME IT ON THE BOSSA NOVA EYDIE GORME	32	1963
(BLAME IT) ON THE PONY EXPRESS JOHNNY JOHNSON & THE BANDWAGON	7	1970
BLAME IT ON THE RAIN MILLI VANILLI	52	1989
BLAME IT ON THE WEATHERMAN B*WITCHED	1	1999
BLANKET URBAN SPECIES FEATURING IMOGEN HEAP	56	1999
BLANKET ON THE GROUND BILLIE JO SPEARS	6	1975
BLASPHEMOUS RUMOURS DEPECHE MODE	16	1984
BLAST THE SPEAKERS WARP BROTHERS	40	2002
BLAZE OF GLORY JON BON JOVI	13	1990
BLAZIN' TALI	42	2004
BLAZING SADDLES YELLO	47	1989
BLEACH EASYWORLD	67	2002
BLEED CATATONIA	46	1996
BLEED IT LINKIN PARK	29	2007
BLEED ME WHITE EAT	73	1993
BLEEDING LOVE LEONA LEWIS	1	2007
BLESS YOU [A] TONY ORLANDO	5	1961
BLESS YOU [B] MARTHA REEVES & THE VANDELLAS	33	1972
BLIND [A] TALKING HEADS	59	1988
BLIND [B] BAD COMPANY	59	2002
BLIND [C] HERCULES & LOVE AFFAIR	40	2008
BLIND AMONG THE FLOWERS TOURISTS	52	1979
BLIND MAN AEROSMITH	23	1994
BLIND PILOTS COOPER TEMPLE CLAUSE	37	2003
BLIND VISION BLANCMANGE	10	1983
BLINDED BY THE LIGHT MANFRED MANN'S EARTH BAND	6	1976
BLINDED BY THE LIGHTS STREETS	10	2004
BLINDED BY THE SUN SEAHORSES	7	1997
BLINDFOLD MORCHEEBA	56	1998
THE BLINDFOLD (EP) CURVE	68	1991
BLINK ROSIE RIBBONS	12	2002
BLISS [A] MUSE	22	2001
BLISS [B] SYNTAX	69	2004
THE BLOCK PARTY LISA LEFT EYE LOPES	16	2001
BLOCK ROCKIN' BEATS CHEMICAL BROTHERS	1	1997
BLOCKBUSTER SWEET	1	1973
BLONDE HAIR BLUE JEANS CHRIS DE BURGH	51	1994
BLONDES (HAVE MORE FUN) ROD STEWART	63	1979
BLOOD EDITORS	18	2005
BLOOD IS PUMPIN' VOODOO & SERANO	19	2001
BLOOD MAKES NOISE SUZANNE VEGA	60	1992
BLOOD MUSIC (EP) EARTHLING	69	1996
BLOOD OF EDEN PETER GABRIEL	43	1993
BLOOD ON OUR HANDS DEATH FROM ABOVE 1979	33	2005
BLOOD ON THE DANCE FLOOR MICHAEL JACKSON	1	1997
BLOOD SUGAR PENDULUM	62	2007
BLOOD SWEAT & TEARS V	6	2004
THE BLOOD THAT MOVES THE BODY A-HA	25	1988
BLOODNOK'S ROCK 'N' ROLL CALL GOONS	3	1956
BLOODSHOT EYES MILLIE	48	1965
BLOODSPORTS FOR ALL CARTER-THE UNSTOPPABLE SEX MACHINE	48	1991
BLOODY LUXURY WHITESNAKE	34	1982
A BLOSSOM FELL DICKIE VALENTINE	9	1955
A BLOSSOM FELL NAT 'KING' COLE	3	1955
A BLOSSOM FELL RONNIE HILTON	10	1955
BLOSSOMS FALLING OOBERMAN	39	1999
BLOW AWAY GEORGE HARRISON	51	1979
BLOW THE HOUSE DOWN [A] LIVING IN A BOX	10	1989
BLOW THE HOUSE DOWN [B] WEE PAPA GIRL RAPPERS	65	1989
BLOW UP THE OUTSIDE WORLD SOUNDGARDEN	40	1996
BLOW YA MIND LOCK 'N' LOAD	6	2000
BLOW YOUR HORNY HORNS PERFECT PHASE	75	2004
BLOW YOUR MIND JAMIROQUAI	12	1993
BLOW YOUR MIND (I AM THE WOMAN) LISA PIN-UP	60	2002
BLOW YOUR WHISTLE DJ DUKE	15	1994
THE BLOWER'S DAUGHTER DAMIEN RICE	27	2005
BLOWIN' IN THE WIND STEVIE WONDER	36	1966
BLOWIN' ME UP JC CHASEZ	13	2004
BLOWING IN THE WIND PETER, PAUL & MARY	13	1963
BLOWING WILD FRANKIE LAINE	2	1954
BLUE [A] FINE YOUNG CANNIBALS	41	1985
BLUE [B] VERVE	69	1993
BLUE [C] WAY OUT WEST	41	1997
BLUE [D] SYMPOSIUM	48	1998
BLUE [E] LeANN RIMES	23	1998
BLUE ANGEL [A] ROY ORBISON	11	1960
BLUE ANGEL [B] GENE PITNEY	39	1974
BLUE ANGELS PRAS	6	1998
BLUE BAYOU ROY ORBISON	3	1963
BLUE BAYOU LINDA RONSTADT	35	1978
BLUE BLUE HEARTACHES JOHNNY DUNCAN & THE BLUE GRASS BOYS	27	1957
BLUE CHRISTMAS ELVIS PRESLEY	11	1964
BLUE (DA BA DEE) EIFFEL 65	1	1999
BLUE DAY SUGGS & CO FEATURING CHELSEA TEAM	22	1997
BLUE EMOTION FIAT LUX	59	1984
BLUE-EYED BOY AL SAXON	39	1960
BLUE EYES [A] DON PARTRIDGE	3	1968
BLUE EYES [B] ELTON JOHN	8	1982
BLUE EYES [C] WEDDING PRESENT	26	1992
BLUE FEAR ARMIN	45	1998
BLUE FLOWERS DR OCTAGON	66	1996
BLUE FOR YOU WET WET WET	38	1993
BLUE GIRL BRUISERS	31	1963
BLUE GUITAR JUSTIN HAYWARD & JOHN LODGE	8	1975
BLUE HAT FOR A BLUE DAY NICK HEYWARD	14	1983
BLUE HOTEL CHRIS ISAAK	17	1991
BLUE IS THE COLOUR CHELSEA F.C.	5	1972
BLUE JEAN DAVID BOWIE	6	1984
BLUE JEAN BOP GENE VINCENT	16	1956
BLUE JEANS LADYTRON	43	2003
BLUE LIGHT RED LIGHT (SOMEONE'S THERE) HARRY CONNICK Jr.	54	1991
BLUE LOVE (CALL MY NAME) DNA FEATURING JOE NYE	66	1992
BLUE MONDAY [A] FATS DOMINO	23	1957
BLUE MONDAY [B] NEW ORDER	3	1983
BLUE MOON ELVIS PRESLEY	9	1956
BLUE MOON MARCELS	1	1961
BLUE MOON SHOWADDYWADDY	32	1980
BLUE MOON JOHN ALFORD	9	1996
BLUE MORNING BLUE DAY FOREIGNER	45	1979
BLUE NOTE HARRISONS	69	2006
BLUE ORCHID WHITE STRIPES	9	2005
BLUE PETER MIKE OLDFIELD	19	1979
BLUE RIVER ELVIS PRESLEY	22	1966
BLUE ROOM ORB	8	1992
THE BLUE ROOM T-EMPO	71	1996
BLUE SAVANNAH ERASURE	3	1990
BLUE SKIES [A] JOHN DUMMER & HELEN APRIL	54	1982
BLUE SKIES [B] JETS	53	1983
BLUE SKIES [C] BT FEATURING TORI AMOS	26	1996
BLUE SKIES [D] LONGPIGS	21	1999
BLUE SKY MINE MIDNIGHT OIL	66	1990
BLUE SONG MINT ROYALE	35	2003
BLUE STAR (THE MEDIC THEME) CHARLIE APPLEWHITE	20	1955

	Peak Position	Year of Entry
BLUE STAR (THE MEDIC THEME) CYRIL STAPLETON ORCHESTRA FEATURING JULIE DAWN	2	1955
BLUE STAR (THE MEDIC THEME) RON GOODWIN	20	1955
BLUE SUEDE SHOES CARL PERKINS	10	1956
BLUE SUEDE SHOES ELVIS PRESLEY	9	1956
BLUE TANGO RAY MARTIN	8	1952
BLUE TOMORROW CHELSEA FOOTBALL CLUB	22	2000
BLUE TURNS TO GREY CLIFF RICHARD & THE SHADOWS	15	1966
BLUE VELVET BOBBY VINTON	2	1990
BLUE WATER [A] FIELDS OF THE NEPHILIM	75	1987
BLUE WATER [B] BLACK ROCK FEATURING DEBRA ANDREW	36	2005
BLUE WEEKEND KARL DENVER	33	1962
BLUE WORLD MOODY BLUES	35	1983
BLUEBEARD COCTEAU TWINS	33	1994
BLUEBELL POLKA JIMMY SHAND	20	1955
BLUEBERRY HILL FATS DOMINO	6	1956
BLUEBERRY HILL JOHN BARRY ORCHESTRA	34	1960
BLUEBIRDS OVER THE MOUNTAIN BEACH BOYS	33	1969
BLUEBOTTLE POB FEATURING DJ PATRICK REID	74	1999
BLUEBOTTLE BLUES GOONS	4	1956
BLUER THAN BLUE ROLF HARRIS	30	1969
THE BLUES ARE STILL BLUE BELLE & SEBASTIAN	25	2006
BLUES BAND (EP) BLUES BAND	68	1980
BLUES FROM A GUN JESUS & MARY CHAIN	32	1989
BLUES SKIES SPECIAL NEEDS	56	2005
BLUETONIC BLUETONES	19	1995
BLURRED PIANOMAN	6	1996
BLURRY PUDDLE OF MUDD	8	2002
BO DIDDLEY BUDDY HOLLY	4	1963
BOA VS PYTHON TEST ICICLES	46	2005
THE BOAT THAT I ROW LULU	6	1967
BOAT TO BOLIVIA MARTIN STEPHENSON & THE DAINTEES	70	1986
B.O.B. (BOMBS OVER BAGHDAD) OUTKAST	61	2000
BOBBY TOMORROW BOBBY VEE	21	1963
BOBBY'S GIRL SUSAN MAUGHAN	3	1962
BODIES DROWNING POOL	34	2002
BODY FUNKY GREEN DOGS	46	1999
BODY AND SOUL [A] SISTERS OF MERCY	46	1984
BODY AND SOUL [B] MAI TAI	9	1985
BODY AND SOUL [C] ANITA BAKER	48	1994
BODY BUMPIN' (YIPPIE-YI-YO) PUBLIC ANNOUNCEMENT	38	1998
THE BODY ELECTRIC RUSH	56	1984
BODY GROOVE ARCHITECHS FEATURING NANA	3	2000
BODY HEAT JAMES BROWN	36	1977
BODY IN MOTION ATLANTIC OCEAN	15	1994
BODY LANGUAGE [A] DETROIT SPINNERS	40	1980
BODY LANGUAGE [B] DOOLEYS	46	1980
BODY LANGUAGE [C] QUEEN	25	1982
BODY LANGUAGE [D] ADVENTURES OF STEVIE V	29	1990
BODY MOVIN' [A] BEASTIE BOYS	15	1998
BODY MOVIN [D] DRUMSOUND/SIMON BASSLINE SMITH	66	2004
BODY MUSIC STRIKERS	45	1981
BODY ROCK [A] MARIA VIDAL	11	1985
BODY ROCK [B] SHIMON & ANDY C	28	2001
BODY ROCKIN' ERROL BROWN	51	1987
THE BODY SHINE (EP) BILLY HENDRIX	55	1998
BODY TALK IMAGINATION	4	1981
BODY II BODY SAMANTHA MUMBA	5	2000
BODY WORK HOT STREAK	19	1983
BODYROCK [A] MOBY	38	1999
BODYROCK [B] TYMES 4	23	2001
BODYSHAKIN' 911	3	1997
BOG EYED JOG RAY MOORE	61	1987
BOHEMIAN LIKE YOU DANDY WARHOLS	5	2000
BOHEMIAN RHAPSODY QUEEN	1	1975
BOHEMIAN RHAPSODY BAD NEWS	44	1987
BOHEMIAN RHAPSODY BRAIDS	21	1996
BOHEMIAN RHAPSODY ROLF HARRIS	50	1996
BOHEMIAN RHAPSODY G4	9	2005
THE BOILER [A] RHODA WITH THE SPECIAL A.K.A.	35	1982
BOILER [B] LIMP BIZKIT	18	2001
BOING! WEDDING PRESENT	19	1992
BOLL WEEVIL SONG BROOK BENTON	30	1961
BOM DIGI BOM (THINK ABOUT THE WAY) ICE MC	38	1996
THE BOMB [A] LOVE CONNECTION	53	2000
THE BOMB [B] NEW YOUNG PONY CLUB	47	2007
BOMB DIGGY ANOTHER LEVEL	6	1999
THE BOMB! (THESE SOUNDS FALL INTO MY MIND) BUCKETHEADS	5	1995
BOMBADIN 808 STATE	67	1994
BOMBER MOTORHEAD	34	1979
BOMBS FAITHLESS FEATURING HARRY COLLIER	26	2006
BOMBSCARE 2 BAD MICE	46	1996
BOMBTRACK RAGE AGAINST THE MACHINE	37	1993
BON BON VIE TS MONK	63	1981
BOND 808 STATE	57	1996
BONE DRIVEN BUSH	49	1997
BONES KILLERS	15	2006
BONEY M MEGAMIX BONEY M	7	1988
BONEYARD LITTLE ANGELS	33	1991
BONITA APPLEBUM A TRIBE CALLED QUEST	47	1990
BONITA MANANA ESPIRITU	50	1994
BONNIE CAME BACK DUANE EDDY & THE REBELS	12	1960
BONY MORONIE LARRY WILLIAMS	11	1958
BOO! FOREVER BOO RADLEYS	67	1992
BOOGALOO PARTY FLAMINGOS	26	1969
BOOGIE [A] DIVE	35	1998
BOOGIE [B] BRAND NEW HEAVIES FEATURING NICOLE	66	2004
BOOGIE AT RUSSIAN HILL JOHN LEE HOOKER	53	1993
BOOGIE DOWN [A] EDDIE KENDRICKS	39	1974
BOOGIE DOWN [B] AL JARREAU	63	1983
BOOGIE DOWN (BRONX) MAN PARISH	56	1985
BOOGIE DOWN (GET FUNKY NOW) REAL THING	33	1979
BOOGIE MAN MATCH	48	1979
BOOGIE NIGHTS HEATWAVE	2	1977
BOOGIE NIGHTS LA FLEUR	51	1983
BOOGIE NIGHTS SONIA	30	1992
BOOGIE ON REGGAE WOMAN STEVIE WONDER	12	1975
BOOGIE ON UP ROKOTTO	40	1977
BOOGIE OOGIE OOGIE A TASTE OF HONEY	3	1978
BOOGIE SHOES KC & THE SUNSHINE BAND	34	1978
BOOGIE 2NITE BOOTY LUV	3	2006
BOOGIE TOWN F.L.B.	46	1979
BOOGIE WONDERLAND EARTH, WIND & FIRE WITH THE EMOTIONS	4	1979
BOOGIE WOOGIE BUGLE BOY (DON'T STOP) 2 IN A TANK	48	1995
THE BOOK DAVID WHITFIELD	5	1954
BOOK OF DAYS ENYA	10	1992
BOOK OF DREAMS SUZANNE VEGA	66	1990
BOOK OF LOVE MUDLARKS	8	1958
BOOKS BELLE & SEBASTIAN	20	2004
BOOKS FROM BOXES MAXIMO PARK	16	2007
BOOM BANG-A-BANG LULU	2	1969
BOOM BLAST FREESTYLERS FEATURING MILLION DAN	75	2005
BOOM BOOM [A] BLACK SLATE	51	1980
BOOM BOOM [B] JOHN LEE HOOKER	16	1992
BOOM BOOM [C] DEFINITION OF SOUND	59	1995
BOOM BOOM [D] N-TYCE	18	1998
BOOM BOOM [E] BASIL BRUSH FEATURING INDIA BEAU	44	2003
BOOM BOOM BOOM OUTHERE BROTHERS	1	1995
BOOM BOOM BOOM BOOM!! VENGABOYS	1	1999
BOOM BOOM (LET'S GO BACK TO MY ROOM) PAUL LEKAKIS	60	1987
THE BOOM BOOM ROOM NATASHA	44	1982
BOOM LIKE THAT MARK KNOPFLER	34	2004
BOOM ROCK SOUL BENZ	62	1995
BOOM SELECTION GENIUS CRU	12	2001
BOOM! SHAKE THE ROOM JAZZY JEFF & THE FRESH PRINCE	1	1993
BOOM! THERE SHE WAS SCRITTI POLITTI FEATURING ROGER	55	1988
BOOMBASTIC SHAGGY	1	1995
BOOO STICKY FEATURING MS DYNAMITE	12	2001
BOOPS (HERE TO GO) SLY & ROBBIE	12	1987
BOOTI CALL BLACKstreet	56	1994
BOOTIE CALL ALL SAINTS	1	1998
BOOTY LA LA BUGZ IN THE ATTIC	44	2005
BOOTYLICIOUS DESTINY'S CHILD	2	2001
BOOTZILLA BOOTSY'S RUBBER BAND	43	1978
BOP BOP BABY WESTLIFE	5	2002
BOP GUN (ONE NATION) ICE CUBE FEATURING GEORGE CLINTON	22	1994
BORA BORA DA HOOL	35	1998
BORDERLINE [A] MADONNA	2	1984
BORDERLINE [B] MICHAEL GRAY FEATURING SHELLEY POOLE	12	2006
BORDERS SUNSHINE UNDERGROUND	56	2007
BORN A WOMAN SANDY POSEY	24	1966
BORN AGAIN [A] CHRISTIANS	25	1988
BORN AGAIN [B] BADLY DRAWN BOY	16	2002
BORN AGAIN [C] STARSAILOR	40	2003
BORN DEAD BODY COUNT	28	1994
BORN FREE VIC REEVES & THE ROMAN NUMERALS	6	1991
BORN IN ENGLAND TWISTED X	9	2004
BORN IN 69 ROCKET FROM THE CRYPT	68	1996
BORN IN THE GHETTO FUNKY POETS	72	1994
BORN IN THE 70'S ED HARCOURT	61	2004
BORN IN THE USA BRUCE SPRINGSTEEN	5	1985
BORN OF FRUSTRATION JAMES	13	1992
BORN ON THE 5TH OF NOVEMBER CARTER-THE UNSTOPPABLE SEX MACHINE	35	1995
BORN SLIPPY UNDERWORLD	2	1995
BORN SLIPPY NUXX UNDERWORLD	27	2003
BORN THIS WAY (LET'S DANCE) COOKIE CREW	23	1989
BORN TO BE ALIVE [A] PATRICK HERNANDEZ	10	1979
BORN TO BE ALIVE [B] ADAMSKI FEATURING SOHO	51	1991
BORN TO BE MY BABY BON JOVI	22	1988
BORN TO BE SOLD TRANSVISION VAMP	22	1989
BORN TO BE WILD STEPPENWOLF	18	1969
BORN TO BE WITH YOU CHORDETTES	8	1956
BORN TO BE WITH YOU DAVE EDMUNDS	5	1973
BORN TO LIVE AND BORN TO DIE FOUNDATIONS	46	1969
BORN TO LOSE KING ADORA	68	2003
BORN TO MAKE YOU HAPPY BRITNEY SPEARS	1	2000
BORN TO RAISE HELL MOTORHEAD/ICE-T/WHITFIELD CRANE	47	1994
BORN TO RUN BRUCE SPRINGSTEEN	16	1987
BORN TO TRY DELTA GOODREM	3	2003
BORN TOO LATE PONI-TAILS	5	1958
BORN 2 B.R.E.E.D. MONIE LOVE	18	1993
BORN WITH A SMILE ON MY FACE STEPHANIE DE SYKES WITH RAIN	2	1974

	Peak Position	Year of Entry
BORNE ON THE WIND ROY ORBISON	15	1964
BORROWED LOVE S.O.S. BAND	50	1986
BORROWED TIME JOHN LENNON	32	1984
BORSALINO BOBBY CRUSH	37	1972
THE BOSS DIANA ROSS	40	1979
THE BOSS BRAXTONS	31	1997
BOSS DRUM SHAMEN	4	1992
BOSS GUITAR DUANE EDDY & THE REBELETTES	27	1963
BOSS OF ME THEY MIGHT BE GIANTS	21	2001
BOSSA NOVA BABY ELVIS PRESLEY	13	1963
BOSSY KELIS FEATURING TOO SHORT	22	2006
BOSTICH YELLO	55	1992
THE BOSTON TEA PARTY SENSATIONAL ALEX HARVEY BAND	13	1976
BOTH ENDS BURNING ROXY MUSIC	25	1975
BOTH SIDES NOW JUDY COLLINS	14	1970
BOTH SIDES NOW VIOLA WILLS	35	1986
BOTH SIDES NOW CLANNAD & PAUL YOUNG	74	1991
BOTH SIDES OF THE STORY PHIL COLLINS	7	1993
BOTHER STONE SOUR	28	2003
THE BOTTLE [A] TYRREL CORPORATION	71	1992
THE BOTTLE [B] CHRISTIANS	39	1993
THE BOTTLE [B] PAUL WELLER	13	2004
BOTTLE LIVING DAVE GAHAN	36	2003
BOTTLE ROCKET THE GO! TEAM	64	2005
BOULEVARD OF BROKEN DREAMS [A] BEATMASTERS	62	1991
BOULEVARD OF BROKEN DREAMS [B] GREEN DAY	5	2004
BOUNCE SARAH CONNOR	14	2004
BOUNCE ALONG WAYNE WONDER	19	2003
BOUNCE, ROCK, SKATE, ROLL BABY DC FEATURING IMAJIN	45	1999
BOUNCE SHAKE MOVE STOP MVP	22	2006
BOUNCE WITH THE MASSIVE TZANT	39	1998
THE BOUNCER KICKS LIKE A MULE	7	1992
BOUNCIN' BACK MYSTIKAL	45	2002
BOUNCING FLOW K2 FAMILY	27	2001
BOUNCY BALL LADYFUZZ	52	2006
BOUND 4 DA RELOAD (CASUALTY) OXIDE & NEUTRINO	1	2000
BOUNDARIES LEENA CONQUEST & HIP HOP FINGER	67	1994
BOURGIE BOURGIE GLADYS KNIGHT & THE PIPS	32	1980
BOUT JAMELIA FEATURING RAH DIGGA	37	2003
BOW DOWN MISTER JESUS LOVES YOU	27	1991
BOW WOW (THAT'S MY NAME) LIL BOW WOW	6	2001
BOW WOW WOW FUNKDOOBIEST	34	1994
THE BOX ORBITAL	11	1996
BOX SET GO HIGH	28	1991
THE BOXER [A] SIMON & GARFUNKEL	6	1969
THE BOXER [B] CHEMICAL BROTHERS	41	2005
BOXER BEAT JO BOXERS	3	1983
BOXERS MORRISSEY	23	1995
BOY LULU	15	1968
THE BOY DONE GOOD BILLY BRAGG	55	1997
BOY FROM NEW YORK CITY DARTS	2	1978
BOY FROM NEW YORK CITY ALISON JORDAN	23	1992
A BOY FROM NOWHERE TOM JONES	2	1987
BOY FROM SCHOOL HOT CHIP	40	2006
BOY I GOTTA HAVE YOU RIO & MARS	43	1995
BOY (I NEED YOU) MARIAH CAREY FEATURING CAM'RON	17	2003
THE BOY IN THE BUBBLE PAUL SIMON	26	1986
BOY IS CRYING SAINT ETIENNE	34	2001
THE BOY IS MINE BRANDY & MONICA	2	1998
A BOY NAMED SUE JOHNNY CASH	4	1969
BOY NEXT DOOR JAMELIA	42	2000
BOY OH BOY RACEY	22	1979
BOY ON TOP OF THE NEWS DIESEL PARK WEST	58	1992
BOY OR A GIRL IMPERIAL DRAG	54	1996
THE BOY RACER MORRISSEY	36	1995
THE BOY WHO CAME BACK MARC ALMOND	52	1984
THE BOY WHO RAN AWAY MYSTERY JETS	23	2006
THE BOY WITH THE THORN IN HIS SIDE SMITHS	23	1985
THE BOY WITH X-RAY EYES BABYLON ZOO	32	1996
BOY WONDER SPEEDY	56	1996
BOY YOU KNOCK ME OUT TATYANA ALI FEATURING WILL SMITH	3	1999
BOYFRIEND ASHLEE SIMPSON	12	2006
BOYS [A] KIM WILDE	11	1981
BOYS [B] MARY JANE GIRLS	74	1983
BOYS [C] B.O.N.	15	2001
BOYS [D] BRITNEY SPEARS FEAUTRING PHARRELL WILLIAMS	7	2002
BOYS AND GIRLS [A] HUMAN LEAGUE	48	1981
BOYS AND GIRLS [B] CHEEKY GIRLS	50	2004
THE BOYS ARE BACK IN TOWN THIN LIZZY	8	1976
THE BOYS ARE BACK IN TOWN GLADIATORS	70	1996
THE BOYS ARE BACK IN TOWN HAPPY MONDAYS	24	1999
BOYS BETTER DANDY WARHOLS	36	1998
BOYS CRY EDEN KANE	8	1964
BOYS DON'T CRY CURE	22	1986
THE BOYS IN THE OLD BRIGHTON BLUE BRIGHTON & HOVE ALBION FC	65	1983
BOYS KEEP SWINGIN' DAVID BOWIE	7	1979
THE BOYS OF SUMMER DON HENLEY	12	1985
THE BOYS OF SUMMER ATARIS	49	2003
THE BOYS OF SUMMER DJ SAMMY	2	2003
BOYS (SUMMERTIME LOVE) SABRINA	3	1988
BOYS WILL BE BOYS [A] OSMOND BOYS	65	1991
BOYS WILL BE BOYS [B] ORDINARY BOYS	3	2005
BOZOS LEVELLERS	44	1998
BRACKISH KITTIE	46	2000
BRAIN JUNGLE BROTHERS	52	1997
BRAIN STEW GREEN DAY	28	1996
BRAINS NUT	64	1996
BRAINSTORM ARCTIC MONKEYS	2	2007
BRAINWASHED (CALL YOU) TOMCRAFT	43	2003
BRAND NEW [A] FINITRIBE	69	1994
BRAND NEW [B] RHYMEFEST FEATURING KANYE WEST	32	2006
BRAND NEW DAY [A] DARKMAN	74	1995
BRAND NEW DAY [B] MINDS OF MEN	41	1996
BRAND NEW DAY [C] STING	13	1999
BRAND NEW FRIEND LLOYD COLE & THE COMMOTIONS	19	1985
BRAND NEW KEY MELANIE	4	1972
BRAND NEW LOVER DEAD OR ALIVE	31	1986
BRAND NEW START PAUL WELLER	16	1998
BRANDY [A] SCOTT ENGLISH	12	1971
BRANDY [B] O'JAYS	21	1978
BRAS ON 45 (FAMILY VERSION) IVOR BIGGUN & THE D CUPS	50	1981
BRASS IN POCKET PRETENDERS	1	1979
BRASS, LET THERE BE HOUSE PARTY FAITHFUL	54	1995
BRASSNECK WEDDING PRESENT	24	1990
BRAVE NEW WORLD [A] DAVID ESSEX	55	1978
BRAVE NEW WORLD [B] TOYAH	21	1982
BRAVE NEW WORLD [C] NEW MODEL ARMY	57	1985
BRAZEN 'WEEP' SKUNK ANANSIE	11	1997
BRAZIL CRISPY & COMPANY	26	1975
BRAZIL RITCHIE FAMILY	41	1975
BRAZILIAN DAWN SHAKATAK	48	1981
BRAZILIAN LOVE AFFAIR GEORGE DUKE	36	1980
BRAZILIAN LOVE SONG NAT 'KING' COLE	34	1962
BREACH THE PEACE (EP) SPIRAL TRIBE	66	1992
BREAD AND BUTTER NEWBEATS	15	1964
BREAK AWAY BEACH BOYS	6	1969
BREAK DANCIN' - ELECTRIC BOOGIE WEST STREET MOB	64	1983
BREAK DOWN THE DOORS MORILLO FEATURING THE AUDIOBULLYS	44	2004
BREAK EVERY RULE TINA TURNER	43	1987
BREAK 4 LOVE RAZE	28	1989
BREAK FROM THE OLD ROUTINE OUI 3	17	1993
BREAK IT DOWN AGAIN TEARS FOR FEARS	20	1993
BREAK IT TO ME GENTLY BRENDA LEE	46	1962
BREAK MY HEART SLOWLY NICKY WIRE	74	2006
BREAK MY STRIDE MATTHEW WILDER	4	1984
BREAK MY WORLD DARK GLOBE FEATURING AMANDA GHOST	52	2004
BREAK OF DAWN RHYTHM ON THE LOOSE	36	1995
BREAK OF DAWN 2008 OUT OF OFFICE	41	2008
BREAK ON THROUGH DOORS	64	1991
BREAK THE CHAIN [A] MOTIV 8	31	1995
BREAK THE CHAIN [B] ELKIE BROOKS	55	1987
BREAK THE NIGHT WITH COLOUR RICHARD ASHCROFT	3	2006
BREAK THE RULES STATUS QUO	8	1974
BREAK UP KIM SOZZI	23	2007
BREAK UP TO MAKE UP STYLISTICS	34	1973
BREAK UPS 2 MAKE UPS METHOD MAN FEATURING D'ANGELO	33	1999
BREAK YA NECK BUSTA RHYMES	11	2002
BREAKADAWN DE LA SOUL	39	1993
BREAKAWAY [A] SPRINGFIELDS	31	1961
BREAKAWAY [B] GALLAGHER & LYLE	35	1976
BREAKAWAY [C] TRACEY ULLMAN	4	1983
BREAKAWAY [D] DONNA SUMMER	49	1991
BREAKAWAY [E] KIM APPLEBY	56	1993
BREAKAWAY [F] ZZ TOP	60	1994
BREAKAWAY [G] KELLY CLARKSON	22	2006
BREAKBEAT ERA BREAKBEAT ERA	38	1998
BREAKDANCE PARTY BREAK MACHINE	9	1984
BREAKDOWN [A] ONE DOVE	24	1993
BREAKDOWN [B] DOUBLE SIX	59	1999
BREAKDOWN [C] JACK JOHNSON	73	2005
BREAKFAST ASSOCIATES	49	1985
BREAKFAST AT TIFFANY'S DEEP BLUE SOMETHING	1	1996
BREAKFAST IN AMERICA SUPERTRAMP	9	1979
BREAKFAST IN BED SHEILA HYLTON	57	1979
BREAKFAST IN BED UB40 FEATURING CHRISSIE HYNDE	6	1988
BREAKFAST ON PLUTO DON PARTRIDGE	26	1969
BREAKIN' MUSIC	20	2005
BREAKIN' AWAY KIM WILDE	43	1995
BREAKIN' DOWN SKID ROW	48	1995
BREAKIN' DOWN (SUGAR SAMBA) JULIA & COMPANY	15	1984
BREAKIN' DOWN THE WALLS OF HEARTACHE BANDWAGON	4	1968
BREAKIN' IN A BRAND NEW BROKEN HEART CONNIE FRANCIS	12	1961
BREAKIN'...THERE'S NO STOPPING US OLLIE & JERRY	5	1984
BREAKIN' UP WILD WEEKEND	74	1989
BREAKIN' UP IS BREAKIN' MY HEART ROY ORBISON	22	1966
BREAKING AWAY JAKI GRAHAM	16	1986
BREAKING FREE CAST OF HIGH SCHOOL MUSICAL	9	2006
BREAKING GLASS (EP) DAVID BOWIE	54	1978
BREAKING HEARTS (AIN'T WHAT IT USED TO BE) ELTON JOHN	59	1985
BREAKING POINT BOURGIE BOURGIE	48	1984
BREAKING THE GIRL RED HOT CHILI PEPPERS	41	1992
BREAKING THE HABIT LINKIN PARK	39	2004
BREAKING THE LAW JUDAS PRIEST	12	1980
BREAKING UP IS HARD TO DO NEIL SEDAKA	7	1962

	Peak Position	Year of Entry
BREAKING UP IS HARD TO DO PARTRIDGE FAMILY STARRING SHIRLEY JONES FEATURING DAVID CASSIDY	3	1972
BREAKING UP MY HEART SHAKIN' STEVENS	14	1985
BREAKING UP THE GIRL GARBAGE	27	2002
BREAKING US IN TWO JOE JACKSON	59	1983
BREAKOUT [A] SWING OUT SISTER	4	1986
BREAKOUT [B] FOO FIGHTERS	29	2000
THE BREAKS KURTIS BLOW	47	1980
BREAKS YOU OFF ROOTS FEATURING MUSIQ	59	2003
BREAKTHRU' QUEEN	7	1989
BREATH OF LIFE ERASURE	8	1992
BREATHE [A] MARIA McKEE	59	1991
BREATHE [B] MIDGE URE	70	1996
BREATHE [C] PRODIGY	1	1996
BREATHE [D] KYLIE MINOGUE	14	1998
BREATHE [E] BLUE AMAZON	73	2000
BREATHE [F] FAITH HILL	33	2000
BREATHE [G] SCIENCE DEPT FEATURING ERIRE	64	2001
BREATHE [H] TELEPOPMUSIK	42	2002
BREATHE [I] BLU CANTRELL FEATURING SEAN PAUL	1	2003
BREATHE [J] FABOLOUS	28	2004
BREATHE [K] ERASURE	4	2005
BREATHE (A LITTLE DEEPER) BLAMELESS	27	1996
BREATHE A SIGH DEF LEPPARD	43	1996
BREATHE AGAIN TONI BRAXTON	2	1994
BREATHE AND STOP Q-TIP	12	2000
BREATHE DON'T STOP MR ON VS THE JUNGLE BROTHERS	21	2004
BREATHE EASY BLUE	4	2004
BREATHE IN [A] FROU FROU	44	2002
BREATHE IN [B] LUCIE SILVAS	6	2005
BREATHE LIFE INTO ME MICA PARIS	26	1988
BREATHE ME SIA	71	2004
BREATHE STRETCH SHAKE MASE	29	2004
BREATHING [A] KATE BUSH	16	1980
BREATHING [B] NORTH & SOUTH	27	1997
BREATHING IS E-ZEE E-ZEE POSSEE FEATURING TARA NEWLEY	72	1991
BREATHLESS [A] JERRY LEE LEWIS	8	1958
BREATHLESS [B] CORRS	1	2000
BREATHLESS [C] NICK CAVE & THE BAD SEEDS	45	2004
BREATHLESS [D] SHAYNE WARD	6	2007
THE BREEZE AND I CATERINA VALENTE	5	1955
THE BREEZE AND I FENTONES	48	1962
BREEZE ON BY DONNY OSMOND	8	2004
BRIAN WILSON BARENAKED LADIES	73	1999
BRICK BEN FOLDS FIVE	26	1998
BRICK HOUSE COMMODORES	32	1977
THE BRICK TRACK VERSUS GITTY UP SALTNPEPA	22	1999
BRIDESHEAD THEME GEOFFREY BURGON	48	1981
BRIDGE [A] ORANGE JUICE	67	1984
THE BRIDGE [B] CACTUS WORLD NEWS	74	1986
BRIDGE [C] QUEENSRYCHE	40	1995
BRIDGE OF SIGHS DAVID WHITFIELD	9	1953
BRIDGE OVER TROUBLED WATER SIMON & GARFUNKEL	1	1970
BRIDGE OVER TROUBLED WATER LINDA CLIFFORD	28	1979
BRIDGE OVER TROUBLED WATER PJB FEATURING HANNAH & HER SISTERS	21	1991
BRIDGE TO YOUR HEART WAX	12	1987
BRIDGET THE MIDGET (THE QUEEN OF THE BLUES) RAY STEVENS	2	1971
BRIDGING THE GAP NAS	18	2004
THE BRIGHT AMBASSADORS OF MORNING PURE REASON REVOLUTION	68	2005
BRIGHT EYES ART GARFUNKEL	1	1979
BRIGHT EYES STEPHEN GATELY	3	2000
BRIGHT IDEA ORSON	11	2006
THE BRIGHT LIGHT TANYA DONELLY	64	1997
BRIGHT LIGHTS SPECIAL A.K.A.	60	1983
BRIGHT SIDE OF LIFE TENOR FLY	16	1995
BRIGHT SIDE OF THE ROAD VAN MORRISON	63	1979
BRIGHT YELLOW GUN THROWING MUSES	51	1994
BRIGHTER DAY KELLY LLORENNA	43	1996
BRIGHTER THAN SUNSHINE AQUALUNG	37	2003
BRIGHTEST STAR DRIZABONE	45	1994
BRILLIANT DISGUISE BRUCE SPRINGSTEEN	20	1987
BRILLIANT FEELING FULL MONTY ALLSTARS FEATURING TJ DAVIS	72	1996
BRILLIANT MIND FURNITURE	21	1986
BRIMFUL OF ASHA CORNERSHOP	1	1997
BRING A LITTLE WATER SYLVIE LONNIE DONEGAN	7	1956
BRING 'EM ALL IN MIKE SCOTT	56	1995
BRING EM OUT TI	59	2005
BRING FORTH THE GUILLOTINE SILVER BULLET	45	1989
BRING IT ALL BACK S CLUB 7	1	1999
BRING IT ALL HOME GERRY RAFFERTY	54	1980
BRING IT BACK McALMONT & BUTLER	36	2002
BRING IT BACK AGAIN [A] STRAY CATS	64	1989
BRING IT BACK AGAIN [B] EARLIES	61	2005
BRING IT BACK 2 LUV PROJECT FEATURING GERIDEAU	65	1994
BRING IT DOWN (THIS INSANE THING) REDSKINS	33	1985
BRING IT ON [A] N'DEA DAVENPORT	52	1998
BRING IT ON [B] GOMEZ	21	1999
BRING IT ON [C] NICK CAVE & THE BAD SEEDS	58	2003
BRING IT ON [D] ALISTAIR GRIFFIN	5	2004
BRING IT ON BACK JET	51	2006
BRING IT ON...BRING IT ON JAMES BROWN	45	1983
BRING IT ON DOWN JESUS JONES	46	1989
BRING IT ON HOME URBAN COOKIE COLLECTIVE	56	1994
BRING IT ON HOME TO ME ANIMALS	7	1965
BRING IT ON TO MY LOVE DE NADA	24	2002
BRING ME CLOSER ALTERED IMAGES	29	1983
BRING ME EDELWEISS EDELWEISS	5	1989
BRING ME LOVE ANDREA MENDEZ	44	1996
BRING ME TO LIFE EVANESCENCE	1	2003
BRING ME YOUR CUP UB40	24	1993
BRING MY FAMILY BACK FAITHLESS	14	1999
BRING ON THE DANCING HORSES ECHO & THE BUNNYMEN	21	1985
BRING THE FAMILY BACK BILLY PAUL	51	1979
BRING THE NOISE PUBLIC ENEMY	32	1988
BRING THE NOISE ANTHRAX FEATURING CHUCK D	14	1991
BRING UP THE MIC SOME MORE RAGGA TWINS	65	1992
BRING YOUR DAUGHTER...TO THE SLAUGHTER IRON MAIDEN	1	1991
BRINGING BACK THOSE MEMORIES MARK JOSEPH	34	2004
BRINGING ON BACK THE GOOD TIMES LOVE AFFAIR	9	1969
BRISTOL STOMP LATE SHOW	40	1979
BRITANNIA RAG WINIFRED ATWELL	5	1952
BRITE SIDE DEBORAH HARRY	59	1989
BRITISH HUSTLE HI TENSION	8	1978
THE BRITISH WAY OF LIFE CHORDS	54	1980
THE BRITS 1990 VARIOUS ARTISTS (MONTAGES)	2	1990
BROKE [A] BETA BAND	30	2001
BROKE [B] CASSIUS HENRY	31	2002
BROKE [C] CAPTAIN	34	2006
BROKE AWAY WET WET WET	19	1989
BROKEN ARROW [A] WATERFRONT	63	1989
BROKEN ARROW [B] ROD STEWART	41	1991
BROKEN BONES LOVE INC	8	2003
BROKEN BOY SOLDIER RACONTEURS	22	2006
BROKEN DOLL TOMMY BRUCE & THE BRUISERS	36	1960
BROKEN DOWN ANGEL NAZARETH	9	1973
BROKEN ENGLISH SUNSCREEM	13	1993
A BROKEN HEART CAN MEND ALEXANDER O'NEAL	53	1986
BROKEN HEART (THIRTEEN VALLEYS) BIG COUNTRY	47	1988
BROKEN HEARTED KEN DODD	15	1970
BROKEN HEARTED MELODY SARAH VAUGHAN	7	1959
BROKEN HOMES TRICKY	25	1998
BROKEN LAND ADVENTURES	20	1988
BROKEN NOSE CATHERINE WHEEL	48	1998
BROKEN SILENCE SO SOLID CREW	9	2003
BROKEN STONES PAUL WELLER	20	1995
BROKEN WINGS [A] ART & DOTTY TODD	6	1953
BROKEN WINGS [A] DICKIE VALENTINE	12	1953
BROKEN WINGS [A] STARGAZERS	1	1953
BROKEN WINGS [B] MR MISTER	4	1986
BROKEN WINGS [B] NETWORK	46	1992
THE BROKEN YEARS HIPSWAY	72	1985
BRONTOSAURUS MOVE	7	1970
BROOKLYN BEATS SCOTTI DEEP	67	1997
BROOKLYN-QUEENS 3RD BASS	61	1990
BROTHA PART II ANGIE STONE FEATURING ALICIA KEYS & EVE	37	2002
BROTHER [A] C.C.S.	25	1972
BROTHER [B] URBAN SPECIES	40	1994
BROTHER BRIGHT CA VA CA VA	65	1983
BROTHER LOUIE [A] HOT CHOCOLATE	7	1973
BROTHER LOUIE [B] QUIREBOYS	32	1993
BROTHER LOUIE [C] MODERN TALKING	4	1986
BROTHER OF MINE ANDERSON BRUFORD WAKEMAN HOWE	63	1989
BROTHERS AND SISTERS 2 FUNKY 2 FEATURING KATHRYN DION	36	1993
BROTHERS GONNA WORK IT OUT PUBLIC ENEMY	46	1990
BROTHERS IN ARMS DIRE STRAITS	16	1985
BROWN-EYED HANDSOME MAN BUDDY HOLLY	3	1963
BROWN EYED HANDSOME MAN PAUL McCARTNEY	42	1999
BROWN GIRL IN THE RING BONEY M	1	1978
BROWN PAPER BAG RONI SIZE REPRAZENT	20	1997
BROWN SKIN INDIA.ARIE	29	2001
BROWN SUGAR [A] ROLLING STONES	2	1971
BROWN SUGAR [B] D'ANGELO	24	1995
BRUISE PRISTINE PLACEBO	14	1997
BRUSHED PAUL WELLER	14	1997
BRUTAL-8-E ALTERN 8	43	1992
BUBBLE FLUKE	37	1994
BUBBLIN' BLUE	9	2004
BUBBLING HOT PATO BANTON WITH RANKING ROGER	15	1995
BUBBLY COLBIE CAILLAT	72	2007
BUCCI BAG ANDREA DORIA	57	2003
BUCK ROGERS FEEDER	5	2001
THE BUCKET KINGS OF LEON	16	2004
THE BUCKET OF WATER SONG FOUR BUCKETEERS	26	1980
BUDDHA OF SUBURBIA DAVID BOWIE FEATURING LENNY KRAVITZ	35	1993
BUDDY DE LA SOUL	7	1989
BUDDY HOLLY WEEZER	12	1995
BUDDY X NENEH CHERRY	35	1993
BUDDY X 99 DREEM TEEM Vs NENEH CHERRY	15	1999
BUFFALO BILL'S LAST SCRATCH BARRON KNIGHTS	49	1983

	Peak Position	Year of Entry
BUFFALO GALS STAMPEDE MALCOLM McLAREN & THE WORLD'S FAMOUS SUPREME TEAM PLUS RAKIM & ROGER SANCHEZ	65	1998
BUFFALO GALS MALCOLM McLAREN & THE WORLD'S FAMOUS SUPREME TEAM	9	1982
BUFFALO SOLDIER BOB MARLEY & THE WAILERS	4	1983
BUFFALO STANCE NENEH CHERRY	3	1988
THE BUG DIRE STRAITS	67	1992
BUG A BOO DESTINY'S CHILD	9	1999
BUG IN THE BASSBIN INNERZONE ORCHESTRA	68	1996
BUG POWDER DUST BOMB THE BASS FEATURING JUSTIN WARFIELD	24	1994
BUGGIN' TRUE STEPPERS FEATURING DANE BOWERS	6	2000
BUGS HEPBURN	14	1999
BUILD [A] HOUSEMARTINS	15	1987
BUILD [B] INNOCENCE	72	1992
BUILD ME UP BUTTERCUP FOUNDATIONS	2	1968
BUILD ME UP BUTTERCUP 2003 PARTY BOYS	44	2004
BUILD YOUR LOVE (ON A STRONG FOUNDATION) JOHNNIE RAY	17	1957
BUILDING THE CITY OF LIGHT MIKE SCOTT	60	1995
BULGARIAN TRAVEL	67	1999
BULL IN THE HEATHER SONIC YOUTH	24	1994
BULLDOG NATION KEVIN KENNEDY	70	2000
BULLET FLUKE	23	1995
BULLET COMES CHARLATANS	32	1995
BULLET IN THE GUN PLANET PERFECTO	7	1999
BULLET IN THE HEAD RAGE AGAINST THE MACHINE	16	1993
BULLET WITH BUTTERFLY WINGS SMASHING PUMPKINS	20	1995
BULLETPROOF! POP WILL EAT ITSELF	24	1992
BULLETS EDITORS	27	2005
BULLFROG GTO	72	1991
BULLITPROOF BREAKBEAT ERA	65	2000
BULLITT LALO SCHIFRIN	36	1997
BULLS ON PARADE RAGE AGAINST THE MACHINE	8	1996
BULLY BOY SHED SEVEN	22	1996
BULLY FOR YOU TOM ROBINSON BAND	68	1979
THE BUMP KENNY	3	1974
BUMP BUMP BUMP B2K FEATURING P DIDDY	11	2003
BUMP N' GRIND R KELLY	8	1995
BUMP N GRIND (I AM FEELING HOT TONIGHT) M DUBS FEATURING LADY SAW	59	2000
BUMP/RUN DADDY RUN FUN LOVIN' CRIMINALS	50	2001
BUMPED RIGHT SAID FRED	32	1993
A BUNCH OF THYME FOSTER & ALLEN	18	1982
BUNSEN BURNER JOHN OTWAY	9	2002
BUONA SERA LOUIS PRIMA	25	1958
BUONA SERA MR ACKER BILK & HIS PARAMOUNT JAZZ BAND	7	1960
BUONA SERA BAD MANNERS	34	1981
BUOY MICK KARN FEATURING DAVID SYLVIAN	63	1987
BURDEN IN MY HAND SOUNDGARDEN	33	1996
BURIAL LEVITICUS	66	1995
BURIED ALIVE BY LOVE H.I.M.	30	2003
BURLESQUE FAMILY	13	1972
BURN [A] DOCTOR & THE MEDICS	29	1986
BURN [B] TINA ARENA	47	1999
BURN [C] USHER	1	2004
BURN [D] ALKALINE TRIO	34	2006
BURN BABY BURN [A] HUDSON- FORD	15	1974
BURN BABY BURN [B] ASH	13	2001
BURN BURN LOSTPROPHETS	17	2003
BURN FASTER NINE BLACK ALPS	42	2007
BURN IT UP BEATMASTERS WITH P.P. ARNOLD	14	1988

	Peak Position	Year of Entry
BURN RUBBER ON ME (WHY YOU WANNA HURT ME) GAP BAND	22	1981
BURN YOUR YOUTH JOHNNY PANIC	69	2004
BURNED WITH DESIRE ARMIN VAN BUUREN FEATURING JUSTINE SUISSA	45	2004
BURNIN' [A] DAFT PUNK	30	1997
BURNIN' [B] K-KLASS	45	1998
BURNIN' [C] MIRRORBALL	47	2000
BURNIN' HOT JERMAINE JACKSON	32	1980
BURNIN' LOVE CON FUNK SHUN	68	1986
BURNING [A] MK	44	1995
BURNING [B] BABY BUMPS	17	1998
BURNING BENCHES MORNING RUNNER	19	2006
BURNING BRIDGES JACK SCOTT	32	1960
BURNING BRIDGES (ON AND OFF AND ON AGAIN) STATUS QUO	5	1988
BURNING CAR JOHN FOXX	35	1980
BURNING DOWN ONE SIDE ROBERT PLANT	73	1982
BURNING DOWN THE HOUSE TOM JONES & THE CARDIGANS	7	1999
BURNING HEART SURVIVOR	5	1986
BURNING LOVE ELVIS PRESLEY	7	1972
BURNING OF THE MIDNIGHT LAMP JIMI HENDRIX EXPERIENCE	18	1967
BURNING THE GROUND DURAN DURAN	31	1989
BURNING UP [A] TONY DE VIT	25	1995
BURNING UP [B] BINI & MARTINI	65	2001
BURNING WHEEL PRIMAL SCREAM	17	1997
BURST DARLING BUDS	50	1988
BURUCHACCA MUKKAA	74	1993
BURUNDI BLACK BURUNDI STEIPHENSON BLACK	31	1971
BURUNDI BLUES BEATS INTERNATIONAL	51	1990
BURY YOU SYMPOSIUM	41	1998
BUS STOP HOLLIES	5	1966
BUSHEL AND A PECK VIVIAN BLAINE	12	1953
BUSHES MARKUS NIKOLAI	74	2001
THE BUSINESS [A] BRIAN MAY	51	1998
BUSINESS [B] EMINEM	6	2003
BUST A MOVE YOUNG MC	73	1989
BUST THIS HOUSE DOWN PENTHOUSE 4	56	1988
BUSTED RAY CHARLES	21	1963
BUSY BEE UGLY KID JOE	39	1993
BUSY DOING NOTHING DAVE STEWART WITH BARBARA GASKIN	49	1983
BUT I DO LOVE YOU LeANN RIMES	20	2002
BUT I FEEL GOOD GROOVE ARMADA	50	2003
BUT IT'S BETTER IF YOU DO PANIC! AT THE DISCO	23	2006
BUT NOT FOR ME ELLA FITZGERALD	25	1959
BUT NOT FOR ME KETTY LESTER	45	1962
BUT YOU LOVE ME DADDY JIM REEVES	15	1969
BUT YOU'RE MINE SONNY & CHER	17	1965
BUTCHER BABY PLASMATICS	55	1980
BUTTERCUP CARL ANDERSON	49	1985
BUTTERFINGERS TOMMY STEELE & THE STEELMEN	8	1957
BUTTERFLIES AND HURRICANES MUSE	14	2004
BUTTERFLY [A] ANDY WILLIAMS	1	1957
BUTTERFLY [A] CHARLIE GRACIE	12	1957
BUTTERFLY [B] DANYEL GERARD	11	1971
BUTTERFLY [C] MARIAH CAREY	22	1997
BUTTERFLY [D] TILT FEATURING ZEE	41	1998
BUTTERFLY [E] CRAZY TOWN	3	2001
BUTTERFLY KISSES BOB CARLISLE	56	1997
BUTTERFLY ON A WHEEL MISSION	12	1990
BUTTONS PUSSYCAT DOLLS FEATURING SNOOP DOGG	3	2006
BUY IT IN BOTTLES RICHARD ASHCROFT	26	2003
BUZZ BUZZ A DIDDLE IT MATCHBOX	22	1980
BUZZIN' ASIAN DUB FOUNDATION	31	1998
BY MY SIDE INXS	42	1991
BY THE DEVIL (I WAS TEMPTED) BLUE MINK	26	1973

	Peak Position	Year of Entry
BY THE FOUNTAINS OF ROME DAVID HUGHES	27	1956
BY THE FOUNTAINS OF ROME EDMUND HOCKRIDGE	17	1956
BY THE LIGHT OF THE SILVERY MOON LITTLE RICHARD	17	1959
BY THE TIME THIS NIGHT IS OVER KENNY G WITH PEABO BRYSON	56	1993
BY THE WAY [A] BIG THREE	22	1963
BY THE WAY [B] TREMELOES	35	1970
BY THE WAY [C] RED HOT CHILI PEPPERS	2	2002
BY YOUR SIDE [A] PETERS & LEE	39	1973
BY YOUR SIDE [B] JIMMY SOMERVILLE	41	1995
BY YOUR SIDE [C] SADE	17	2000
BYE BABY RUBY TURNER	52	1986
BYE BYE BABY [A] JOHNNY OTIS SHOW, VOCALS BY MARIE ADAMS & JOHNNY OTIS	20	1958
BYE BYE BABY [B] SYMBOLS	44	1967
BYE BYE BABY [B] BAY CITY ROLLERS	1	1975
BYE BYE BABY [C] TONY JACKSON & THE VIBRATIONS	38	1964
BYE BYE BABY [D] TQ	7	1999
BYE BYE BLUES BERT KAEMPFERT	24	1966
BYE BYE BOY JENNIFER ELLISON	13	2004
BYE BYE BYE N SYNC	3	2000
BYE BYE LOVE EVERLY BROTHERS	6	1957
B.Y.O.F. (BRING YOUR OWN FUNK) FANTASTIC FOUR	62	1979
BYRDS TURN TO STONE SHACK	63	2003

C

	Peak Position	Year of Entry
C-C (YOU SET THE FIRE IN ME) TOM VEK	60	2005
C I AM 15 KING BISCUIT TIME	67	2005
C MOON WINGS	5	1972
C U WHEN U GET THERE COOLIO FEATURING 40 THEVZ	3	1997
C30, C60, C90, GO BOW WOW WOW	34	1980
CA PLANE POUR MOI PLASTIC BERTRAND	8	1978
CA PLANE POUR MOI LEILA K	69	1993
CABARET [A] LOUIS ARMSTRONG	1	1968
THE CABARET [B] TIME UK	63	1983
CACHARPAYA (ANDES PUMPSA DAESI) INCANTATION	12	1982
CAFÉ DEL MAR ENERGY 52	12	1997
CAFFEINE BOMB WILDHEARTS	31	1994
CALEDONIA FRANKIE MILLER	45	1992
CALENDAR GIRL [A] NEIL SEDAKA	8	1961
CALENDAR GIRL [B] NOISE NEXT DOOR	11	2005
THE CALENDAR SONG (JANUARY, FEBRUARY, MARCH, APRIL, MAY) TRINIDAD OIL COMPANY	34	1977
CALIBRE CUTS VARIOUS ARTISTS (MONTAGES)	75	1980
CALIFORNIA [A] WEDDING PRESENT	16	1992
CALIFORNIA [B] BELINDA CARLISLE	31	1997
CALIFORNIA [C] LENNY KRAVITZ	62	2004
CALIFORNIA [D] LOW	57	2005
CALIFORNIA [E] PHANTOM PLANET	9	2005
CALIFORNIA DREAMIN' MAMAS & THE PAPAS	9	1966
CALIFORNIA DREAMIN' COLORADO	45	1978
CALIFORNIA DREAMIN' RIVER CITY PEOPLE	13	1990
CALIFORNIA DREAMIN' BOBBY WOMACK	59	2004
CALIFORNIA DREAMIN' ROYAL GIGOLOS	44	2004
CALIFORNIA GIRLS BEACH BOYS	26	1965
CALIFORNIA GIRLS DAVID LEE ROTH	68	1985
CALIFORNIA HERE I COME [A] FREDDY CANNON	25	1960
CALIFORNIA HERE I COME [B] SOPHIE B. HAWKINS	53	1992
CALIFORNIA LOVE 2PAC FEATURING DR DRE	6	1996
CALIFORNIA MAN MOVE	7	1972

	Peak Position	Year of Entry
CALIFORNIA SAGA-CALIFORNIA BEACH BOYS	37	1973
CALIFORNIA SCREAMIN' CARRIE	55	1998
CALIFORNIA SOUL RIOT ACT	59	2005
CALIFORNIA WAITING KINGS OF LEON	61	2004
CALIFORNIA'S BLEEDING AMEN	52	2004
CALIFORNICATION RED HOT CHILI PEPPERS	16	2000
CALINDA RITMO-DYNAMIC	68	2003
THE CALL BACKSTREET BOYS	8	2001
CALL AND ANSWER BARENAKED LADIES	52	1999
CALL HER YOUR SWEETHEART FRANK IFIELD	24	1967
CALL IT FATE RICHIE DAN	34	2000
CALL IT LOVE DEUCE	11	1995
CALL IT ROCK 'N' ROLL GREAT WHITE	67	1991
CALL IT WHAT YOU WANT [A] NEW KIDS ON THE BLOCK	12	1991
CALL IT WHAT YOU WANT [B] CREDIT TO THE NATION	57	1993
CALL ME [A] BLONDIE	1	1980
CALL ME [B] GO WEST	12	1985
CALL ME [C] SPAGNA	2	1987
CALL ME [D] LE CLICK	38	1997
CALL ME [E] JAMELIA	11	2000
CALL ME [F] TWEET	35	2002
(CALL ME) NUMBER ONE TREMELOES	2	1969
CALL ME ROUND PILOT	34	1975
CALL ME WHEN YOU'RE SOBER EVANESCENCE	4	2006
CALL MY NAME [A] ORCHESTRAL MANOEUVRES IN THE DARK	50	1991
CALL MY NAME [B] CHARLOTTE CHURCH	10	2005
CALL OF THE WILD [A] MIDGE URE	27	1986
CALL OF THE WILD [B] GUS GUS	75	2003
CALL OFF THE SEARCH KATIE MELUA	19	2004
CALL ON ME [A] ERIC PRYDZ	1	2004
CALL ON ME [B] JANET & NELLY	18	2006
CALL OUT THE DOGS GARY NUMAN	49	1985
CALL ROSIE ON THE PHONE GUY MITCHELL	17	1957
CALL THE MAN CELINE DION	11	1997
CALL THE SHOTS GIRLS ALOUD	3	2007
CALL U SEXY VS	11	2004
THE CALL UP CLASH	40	1980
CALL UP THE GROUPS BARRON KNIGHTS WITH DUKE D'MOND	3	1964
CALLING GERI HALLIWELL	7	2001
CALLING ALL GIRLS ATL	12	2004
CALLING ALL THE HEROES IT BITES	6	1986
CALLING AMERICA ELECTRIC LIGHT ORCHESTRA	28	1986
CALLING ELVIS DIRE STRAITS	21	1991
CALLING OCCUPANTS OF INTERPLANETARY CRAFT (THE RECOGNISED ANTHEM OF WORLD CONTACT DAY) CARPENTERS	9	1977
CALLING OUT YOUR NAME JIMMY NAIL	65	1995
CALLING YOU PAUL YOUNG	57	1991
CALLING YOUR NAME MARILYN	4	1983
CALLS THE TUNE HAZEL O'CONNOR	60	1982
CALM DOWN (BASS KEEPS PUMPIN') CHRIS & JAMES	74	1994
CALM DOWN DEAREST JAMIE T	9	2007
CALYPSO CRAZY BILLY OCEAN	35	1988
CAMBODIA KIM WILDE	12	1981
CAMDEN TOWN SUGGS	14	1995
CAMEL BOBSLED RACE DJ SHADOW	62	1997
CAMELS SANTOS	9	2001
CAMOUFLAGE STAN RIDGWAY	4	1986
CAMPIONE 2000 E-TYPE	58	2000
CAN CAN BAD MANNERS	3	1981
CAN CAN 62 PETER JAY & THE JAYWALKERS	31	1962
CAN CAN YOU PARTY JIVE BUNNY & THE MASTERMIXERS	8	1990
CAN I CASHMERE	29	1985
CAN I GET A... JAY-Z FEATURING AMIL & JA RULE	24	1999
CAN I GET A WITNESS SAM BROWN	15	1989
CAN I GET OVER DEFINITION OF SOUND	61	1992
CAN I HAVE IT LIKE THAT PHARRELL FEATURING GWEN STEFANI	3	2005
CAN I KICK IT A TRIBE CALLED QUEST	15	1991
CAN I PLAY WITH MADNESS IRON MAIDEN	3	1988
CAN I TAKE YOU HOME LITTLE GIRL DRIFTERS	10	1975
CAN I TOUCH YOU...THERE? MICHAEL BOLTON	6	1995
CAN I TRUST YOU BACHELORS	26	1966
CAN THE CAN SUZI QUATRO	1	1973
CAN THIS BE LOVE MATT MONRO	24	1961
CAN U DANCE KENNY 'JAMMIN' JASON & DJ 'FAST' EDDIE SMITH	71	1987
CAN U DIG IT [A] POP WILL EAT ITSELF	38	1989
CAN U DIG IT [B] JAMX & DELEON	40	2002
CAN U FEEL IT DEEP CREED '94	59	1994
CAN WE SWV	18	1997
CAN WE CHILL NE-YO	62	2007
CAN WE FIX IT BOB THE BUILDER	1	2000
CAN WE START AGAIN? TINDERSTICKS	54	1999
CAN WE TALK... CODE RED	29	1997
CAN YOU DIG IT MOCK TURTLES	19	1991
CAN YOU DO IT GEORDIE	13	1973
CAN YOU FEEL IT [A] JACKSONS	6	1981
CAN YOU FEEL IT [A] V	5	2004
CAN YOU FEEL IT [B] ELEVATION	62	1992
CAN YOU FEEL IT [C] REEL 2 REAL FEATURING THE MAD STUNTMAN	13	1994
CAN YOU FEEL IT [D] CLS	46	1998
CAN YOU FEEL IT (ROCK DA HOUSE) NYCC	68	1998
CAN YOU FEEL IT/CAN YOU FEEL IT RAZE/ CHAMPIONSHIP LEGEND	62	1990
CAN YOU FEEL THE FORCE REAL THING	5	1979
CAN YOU FEEL THE LOVE TONIGHT ELTON JOHN	14	1994
(CAN YOU) FEEL THE PASSION BLUE PEARL	14	1992
CAN YOU FEEL (WHAT I'M GOING THROUGH) SHOLAN	47	2003
CAN YOU FORGIVE HER PET SHOP BOYS	7	1993
CAN YOU FORGIVE ME KARL DENVER	32	1963
CAN YOU HANDLE IT SHARON REDD	31	1981
CAN YOU HANDLE IT DNA FEATURING SHARON REDD	17	1992
CAN YOU KEEP A SECRET BROTHER BEYOND	22	1988
CAN YOU PARTY ROYAL HOUSE	14	1988
CAN YOU PLEASE CRAWL OUT YOUR WINDOW BOB DYLAN	17	1966
CAN YOUR PUSSY DO THE DOG? CRAMPS	68	1985
CANCER FOR THE CURE EELS	60	2000
CANDIDA DAWN	9	1971
CANDIDATE FOR LOVE TS MONK	58	1981
CANDLE IN THE WIND ELTON JOHN	1	1974
CANDLEFIRE DAWN OF THE REPLICANTS	52	1998
CANDLELAND (THE SECOND COMING) IAN McCULLOCH FEATURING ELIZABETH FRASER	75	1990
CANDLELIGHT SIX BY SEVEN	70	1998
CANDLES ALEX REECE	33	1996
CANDY [A] CAMEO	27	1986
CANDY [B] IGGY POP	67	1990
CANDY [C] MANDY MOORE	6	2000
CANDY [D] ASH	20	2001
CANDY EVERYBODY WANTS 10,000 MANIACS	47	1993
CANDY GIRL [A] NEW EDITION	1	1983
CANDY GIRL [B] BABYBIRD	14	1997
CANDY MAN [A] BRIAN POOLE & THE TREMELOES	6	1964
CANDY MAN [B] MARY JANE GIRLS	60	1983
CANDY RAIN SOUL FOR REAL	23	1995
CANDY SHOP 50 CENT	4	2005
CANDYBAR EXPRESS LOVE & MONEY	56	1986
CANDYMAN [A] SIOUXSIE & THE BANSHEES	34	1986
CANDYMAN [B] CHRISTINA AGUILERA	17	2007
CANNED HEAT JAMIROQUAI	4	1999
CANNIBALS MARK KNOPFLER	42	1996
CANNONBALL [A] DUANE EDDY & THE REBELS	22	1959
CANNONBALL [B] DAMIEN RICE	19	2003
CANNONBALL (EP) BREEDERS	40	1993
CAN'T BE SURE SUNDAYS	45	1989
CAN'T BE WITH YOU TONIGHT JUDY BOUCHER	2	1987
CAN'T BUY ME LOVE BEATLES	1	1964
CAN'T BUY ME LOVE ELLA FITZGERALD	34	1964
CAN'T CATCH TOMORROW LOSTPROPHETS	35	2006
CAN'T CHANGE ME CHRIS CORNELL	62	1999
CAN'T CONTAIN ME TAZ	46	2004
CAN'T CRY ANYMORE SHERYL CROW	33	1995
CAN'T DO A THING (TO STOP ME) CHRIS ISAAK	36	1993
CAN'T DO NUTTIN' FOR YA MAN PUBLIC ENEMY	53	1990
CAN'T DO RIGHT FOR DOING WRONG ERIN ROCHA	36	2003
CAN'T EXPLAIN LONGVIEW	51	2003
CAN'T FAKE THE FEELING GERALDINE HUNT	44	1980
CAN'T FIGHT THE MOONLIGHT LeANN RIMES	1	2000
CAN'T FIGHT THIS FEELING REO SPEEDWAGON	16	1985
CAN'T FORGET YOU SONIA	17	1989
CAN'T GET ALONG WITHOUT YOU [A] FRANKIE VAUGHAN	11	1958
CAN'T GET ALONG (WITHOUT YOU) [B] HARD-FI	45	2007
CAN'T GET ANY HARDER JAMES BROWN	59	1993
CAN'T GET AWAY MOOD II SWING	45	2004
CAN'T GET BY SLAMM	47	1995
CAN'T GET BY WITHOUT YOU REAL THING	2	1976
CAN'T GET ENOUGH [A] BAD COMPANY	15	1974
CAN'T GET ENOUGH [B] SOULSEARCHER	8	1999
CAN'T GET ENOUGH [C] SUEDE	23	1999
CAN'T GET ENOUGH [D] RAGHAV	10	2004
CAN'T GET ENOUGH [E] INFADELS	43	2006
CAN'T GET ENOUGH OF YOU EDDY GRANT	13	1981
CAN'T GET ENOUGH OF YOUR LOVE [A] DARTS	43	1979
CAN'T GET ENOUGH OF YOUR LOVE [B] KWS	71	1993
CAN'T GET ENOUGH OF YOUR LOVE [B] TAYLOR DAYNE	14	1993
CAN'T GET ENOUGH OF YOUR LOVE BABE [B] BARRY WHITE	8	1974
CAN'T GET IT BACK MIS-TEEQ	8	2003
(CAN'T GET MY) HEAD AROUND YOU OFFSPRING	48	2004
CAN'T GET OUT OF BED CHARLATANS	24	1994
CAN'T GET THE BEST OF ME CYPRESS HILL	35	2000
CAN'T GET USED TO LOSING YOU ANDY WILLIAMS	2	1963
CAN'T GET USED TO LOSING YOU BEAT	3	1983
CAN'T GET USED TO LOSING YOU COLOUR GIRL	31	2000
CAN'T GET YOU OFF MY MIND LENNY KRAVITZ	54	1996
CAN'T GET YOU OUT OF MY HEAD KYLIE MINOGUE	1	2001
CAN'T GET YOU OUT OF MY THOUGHTS DUM DUMS	18	2000
CAN'T GIVE ME NOW PEPSI & SHIRLIE	58	1987
CAN'T GIVE YOU ANYTHING (BUT MY LOVE) STYLISTICS	1	1975
CAN'T GIVE YOU MORE STATUS QUO	37	1991
CAN'T HAPPEN HERE RAINBOW	20	1981
CAN'T HAVE YOU LYTE FUNKIE ONES	54	1999

	Peak Position	Year of Entry
CAN'T HELP FALLING IN LOVE ELVIS PRESLEY	1	1962
CAN'T HELP FALLING IN LOVE ANDY WILLIAMS	3	1970
CAN'T HELP FALLING IN LOVE STYLISTICS	4	1976
CAN'T HELP FALLING IN LOVE LICK THE TINS	42	1986
CAN'T HELP FALLING IN LOVE RUSSELL WATSON	69	2006
CAN'T HELP IT HAPPY CLAPPERS	18	1996
CAN'T HELP MYSELF LINX	55	1981
CAN'T HOLD US DOWN CHRISTINA AGUILERA FEATURING LIL' KIM	6	2003
CAN'T I? NAT 'KING' COLE	6	1953
CAN'T KEEP IT IN CAT STEVENS	13	1972
CAN'T KEEP LIVING THIS WAY ROOTJOOSE	73	1997
CAN'T KEEP ME SILENT ANGELIC	12	2001
CAN'T KEEP THIS FEELING IN CLIFF RICHARD	10	1998
CAN'T KNOCK THE HUSTLE JAY-Z FEATURING MARY J BLIGE	30	1997
CAN'T LET GO [A] EARTH, WIND & FIRE	46	1979
CAN'T LET GO [B] MARIAH CAREY	20	1992
CAN'T LET HER GO BOYZ II MEN	23	1998
CAN'T LET YOU GO [A] BARRY RYAN	32	1972
CAN'T LET YOU GO [B] RAINBOW	43	1983
CAN'T LET YOU GO [C] FABOLOUS	14	2003
CAN'T LIVE WITH YOU (CAN'T LIVE WITHOUT YOU) MINDBENDERS	28	1966
CAN'T LIVE WITHOUT YOU SCORPIONS	63	1982
(CAN'T LIVE WITHOUT YOUR) LOVE AND AFFECTION NELSON	54	1990
CAN'T MAKE MY MIND UP SONIQUE	17	2003
CAN'T NOBODY KELLY ROWLAND	5	2003
CAN'T NOBODY HOLD ME DOWN PUFF DADDY FEATURING MASE	19	1997
CAN'T RESIST TEXAS	13	2005
CAN'T SAY 'BYE STONEFREE	73	1987
CAN'T SAY GOODBYE POP!	26	2004
CAN'T SAY HOW MUCH I LOVE YOU DEMIS ROUSSOS	35	1976
CAN'T SEE ME IAN BROWN	21	1998
CAN'T SET THE RULES ABOUT LOVE ADAM ANT	47	1990
CAN'T SHAKE LOOSE AGNETHA FALTSKOG	63	1983
CAN'T SHAKE THE FEELING BIG FUN	8	1989
CAN'T SMILE VEX RED	45	2002
CAN'T SMILE WITHOUT YOU BARRY MANILOW	43	1978
CAN'T SMILE WITHOUT YOU JAMES BULLER	51	1999
CAN'T SPEAK FRENCH GIRLS ALOUD	9	2008
CAN'T STAND IT WILCO	67	1999
CAN'T STAND LOSING YOU POLICE	2	1978
CAN'T STAND ME NOW LIBERTINES	2	2004
CAN'T STAY AWAY FROM YOU GLORIA ESTEFAN & MIAMI SOUND MACHINE	7	1989
CAN'T STOP [A] AFTER 7	54	1990
CAN'T STOP [B] RED HOT CHILI PEPPERS	22	2003
CAN'T STOP A RIVER DUNCAN JAMES	59	2006
CAN'T STOP LOVING YOU [A] VAN HALEN	33	1995
CAN'T STOP LOVING YOU [B] PHIL COLLINS	28	2002
CAN'T STOP RUNNING SPACE MONKEY	53	1983
CAN'T STOP THE MUSIC VILLAGE PEOPLE	11	1980
CAN'T STOP THESE THINGS CHINA DRUM	65	1996
CAN'T STOP THIS FEELING RHYHTM-N-BASS	59	1993
CAN'T STOP THIS THING WE STARTED BRYAN ADAMS	12	1991
CAN'T TAKE MY EYES OFF YOU ANDY WILLIAMS	5	1968
CAN'T TAKE MY EYES OFF YOU BOYSTOWN GANG	4	1982
CAN'T TAKE MY EYES OFF YOU ANDY WILLIAMS & DENISE VAN OUTEN	23	2002
CAN'T TAKE NO FOR AN ANSWER SOUP DRAGONS	65	1987
CAN'T TAKE YOUR LOVE PAULINE HENRY	30	1994
CAN'T TRUSS IT PUBLIC ENEMY	22	1991
CAN'T TURN BACK SPEEDWAY	12	2004
CAN'T WAIT ANOTHER MINUTE FIVE STAR	7	1986
CAN'T WAIT TO BE WITH YOU JAZZY JEFF & THE FRESH PRINCE	29	1994
CAN'T YOU HEAR MY HEART DANNY RIVERS	36	1961
CAN'T YOU HEAR MY HEART BEAT? GOLDIE & THE GINGERBREADS	25	1965
CAN'T YOU HEAR THE BEAT OF A BROKEN HEART IAIN GREGORY	39	1962
CAN'T YOU SEE TOTAL FEATURING THE NOTORIOUS B.I.G.	43	1995
CAN'T YOU SEE THAT SHE'S MINE DAVE CLARK FIVE	10	1964
(CAN'T YOU) TRIP LIKE I DO FILTER & THE CRYSTAL METHOD	39	1997
CANTALOOP US3 FEATURING KOBIE POWELL & RAHSAAN	23	1993
CANTGETAMAN CANTGETAJOB (LIFE'S A BITCH) SISTER BLISS WITH COLETTE	31	1994
CANTO DELLA TERRA ANDREA BOCELLI	24	1999
CANTON (LIVE) JAPAN	42	1983
CANTONESE BOY JAPAN	24	1982
CAPOIERA INFARED VS GIL FELIX	67	2003
CAPSTICK COMES HOME TONY CAPSTICK & THE CARLTON MAIN/FRICKLEY COLLIERY BAND	3	1981
CAPTAIN BEAKY KEITH MICHELL	5	1980
CAPTAIN DREAD DREADZONE	49	1995
CAPTAIN KREMMEN (RETRIBUTION) KENNY EVERETT & MIKE VICKERS	32	1977
THE CAPTAIN OF HER HEART DOUBLE	8	1986
CAPTAIN OF YOUR SHIP REPARATA & THE DELRONS	13	1968
CAPTAIN SCARLET THEME BARRY GRAY ORCHESTRA WITH PETER BECKETT - KEYBOARDS	53	1986
CAPTURE THE FLAG FRESH	70	2005
CAPTURE THE HEART (EP) RUNRIG	49	1990
CAR 67 DRIVER 67	7	1979
CAR BOOT SALE BILL	73	1993
CAR SONG MADDER ROSE	68	1994
CAR WASH ROSE ROYCE	9	1977
CAR WASH GWEN DICKEY	72	1990
CAR WASH CHRISTINA AGUILERA & MISSY ELLIOTT	4	2004
CARA MIA DAVID WHITFIELD WITH CHORUS & MANTOVANI & HIS ORCHESTRA	1	1954
CARAMEL CITY HIGH FEATURING EVE	9	2002
CARAVAN [A] DUANE EDDY	42	1961
CARAVAN [B] INSPIRAL CARPETS	30	1991
CARAVAN OF LOVE ISLEY JASPER ISLEY	52	1985
CARAVAN OF LOVE HOUSEMARTINS	1	1986
CARAVAN SONG BARBARA DICKSON	41	1980
CARBON KID ALPINESTARS FEATURING BRIAN MOLKO	63	2002
CARDBOY KING SALAD	65	1997
CARDIAC ARREST MADNESS	14	1982
CAREFUL (STRESS) HORSE	44	1990
CARELESS HANDS DES O'CONNOR	6	1967
CARELESS LOVE SWIMMING WITH SHARKS	63	1988
CARELESS MEMORIES DURAN DURAN	37	1981
CARELESS WHISPER GEORGE MICHAEL	1	1984
CARELESS WHISPER SARAH WASHINGTON	45	1993
CARELESS WHISPER 2PLAY FEATURING THOMAS JULES & JUCXI D	29	2004
CARIBBEAN BLUE ENYA	13	1991
THE CARIBBEAN DISCO SHOW LOBO	8	1981
CARIBBEAN HONEYMOON FRANK WEIR	42	1960
CARIBBEAN QUEEN (NO MORE LOVE ON THE RUN) BILLY OCEAN	6	1984
CARMEN QUEASY MAXIM	33	2000
CARNATION LIAM GALLAGHER & STEVE CRADDOCK	6	1999
CARNAVAL DE PARIS DARIO G	5	1998
CARNIVAL [A] LIONROCK	34	1993
CARNIVAL [B] CARDIGANS	35	1995
CARNIVAL GIRL TEXAS FEATURING KARDINAL OFFISHALL	9	2003
CARNIVAL IN HEAVEN MALANDRA BURROWS	49	1997
THE CARNIVAL IS OVER SEEKERS	1	1965
CAROLINA MOON CONNIE FRANCIS	1	1958
CAROLINE [A] STATUS QUO	5	1973
CAROLINE [B] KIRSTY MacCOLL	58	1995
CAROLYNA MELANIE C	49	2007
CAROUSEL- ORIGINAL SOUNDTRACK (LP) VARIOUS ARTISTS (EP'S & LPS)	26	1956
CAROUSEL WALTZ RAY MARTIN	24	1956
CARRERA 2 THREE DRIVES	57	2003
CARRIE [A] CLIFF RICHARD	4	1980
CARRIE [B] EUROPE	22	1987
CARRIE-ANNE HOLLIES	3	1967
CARRION BRITISH SEA POWER	36	2003
CARROT ROPE PAVEMENT	27	1999
CARRY ME HOME GLOWORM	9	1994
CARRY ON [A] MARTHA WASH	49	1992
CARRY ON [B] SPACEHOG	43	1998
CARRY ON [C] DONNA SUMMER & GIORGIO MORODER	65	1998
CARRY ON WAYWARD SON KANSAS	51	1978
CARRY THAT WEIGHT TRASH	35	1969
CARRY THE BLAME RIVER CITY PEOPLE	13	1990
CARRY YOU HOME JAMES BLUNT	65	2008
CARRYING A TORCH TOM JONES	57	1991
CARS [A] GARY NUMAN	1	1979
CARS [B] FEAR FACTORY	57	1999
CARS AND GIRLS PREFAB SPROUT	44	1986
CARTE BLANCHE VERACOCHA	22	1999
CARTOON HEROES AQUA	7	2000
CARTROUBLE ADAM & THE ANTS	33	1981
CASABLANCA KENNY BALL & HIS JAZZMEN	21	1963
CASANOVA [A] PETULA CLARK	39	1963
CASANOVA [B] COFFEE	13	1980
CASANOVA [B] BABY D	67	1994
CASANOVA [C] LEVERT	9	1987
CASANOVA [C] ULTIMATE KAOS	24	1997
CASCADE FUTURE SOUND OF LONDON	27	1993
CASE OF THE EX (WHATCHA GONNA DO) MYA	3	2001
CASH MACHINE HARD-FI	14	2006
CASINO ROYALE [A] HERB ALPERT & THE TIJUANA BRASS	27	1967
CASINO ROYALE [B] DJ ZINC	58	2001
CASSIUS FOALS	26	2008
CASSIUS 1999 CASSIUS	7	1999
CAST YOUR FATE TO THE WIND SOUNDS ORCHESTRAL	5	1964
CASTLE ROCK BLUETONES	7	1996
CASTLES IN SPAIN ARMOURY SHOW	69	1984
CASTLES IN THE AIR [A] DON McLEAN	47	1982
CASTLES IN THE AIR [B] COLOUR FIELD	51	1985
CASTLES IN THE SAND THUNDER	30	1995
CASTLES IN THE SKY IAN VAN DAHL	3	2001
CASUAL SUB (BURNING SPEAR) ETA	28	1997
CAT AMONG THE PIGEONS BROS	2	1988
THE CAT CAME BACK SONNY JAMES	30	1956
THE CAT CREPT IN MUD	2	1974
CAT PEOPLE (PUTTING OUT THE FIRE) DAVID BOWIE	26	1982
CATALAN TOUR DE FORCE	71	1998
CATALYST OCEANSIZE	73	2004
CATCH [A] CURE	27	1987
CATCH [B] SUNSCREEM	55	1997
CATCH [C] KOSHEEN	15	2001
CATCH A FALLING STAR PERRY COMO	9	1958

	Peak Position	Year of Entry
CATCH A FIRE HADDAWAY	39	1995
CATCH ME ABSOLUTE	69	1998
CATCH ME UP GOMEZ	36	2004
CATCH MY FALL BILLY IDOL	63	1988
CATCH THE BREEZE SLOWDIVE	52	1991
CATCH THE FIRE DRIZABONE	54	1991
CATCH THE LIGHT MARTHA WASH	45	1998
CATCH THE SUN DOVES	32	2000
CATCH THE WIND DONOVAN	4	1965
CATCH UP TO MY STEP JUNKIE XL FEATURING SOLOMON BURKE	63	2003
CATCH US IF YOU CAN DAVE CLARK FIVE	5	1965
CATCH YOU SOPHIE ELLIS-BEXTOR	8	2007
CATERINA PERRY COMO	37	1962
THE CATERPILLAR CURE	14	1984
CATH BLUEBELLS	38	1983
CATHEDRAL PARK DUBSTAR	41	1997
CATHEDRAL SONG TANITA TIKARAM	48	1989
CATHY'S CLOWN EVERLY BROTHERS	1	1960
CAT'S IN THE CRADLE UGLY KID JOE	7	1993
CAT'S IN THE CRADLE JASON DOWNS FEATURING MILK	65	2001
CAUGHT A LITE SNEEZE TORI AMOS	20	1996
CAUGHT BY THE FUZZ SUPERGRASS	43	1994
CAUGHT BY THE RIVER DOVES	29	2002
CAUGHT IN A MOMENT SUGABABES	8	2004
CAUGHT IN MY SHADOW WONDER STUFF	18	1991
CAUGHT IN THE MIDDLE [A] JULIET ROBERTS	14	1993
CAUGHT IN THE MIDDLE [B] A1	2	2002
CAUGHT IN THE MIDDLE [C] CERYS MATTHEWS	47	2003
CAUGHT OUT THERE KELIS	4	2000
CAUGHT UP [A] USHER	9	2005
CAUGHT UP [B] JA RULE FEATURING LLOYD	20	2005
CAUGHT UP IN MY HEART OPTIMYSTIC	49	1994
CAUGHT UP IN THE RAPTURE ANITA BAKER	51	1987
CAUSING A COMMOTION MADONNA	4	1987
CAVATINA JOHN WILLIAMS	13	1979
CAVE MUSE	52	1999
CCCAN'T YOU SEE VICIOUS PINK	67	1984
CECILIA SUGGS FEATURING LOUCHIE LOU & MICHIE ONE	4	1996
THE CEDAR ROOM DOVES	33	2000
CELEBRATE [A] AN EMOTIONAL FISH	46	1990
CELEBRATE [B] HORSE	49	1994
CELEBRATE [C] LEVELLERS	28	1997
CELEBRATE OUR LOVE ALICE DEEJAY	17	2001
(CELEBRATE) THE DAY AFTER YOU BLOW MONKEYS WITH CURTIS MAYFIELD	52	1987
CELEBRATE THE WORLD WOMACK & WOMACK	19	1989
CELEBRATE YOUR MOTHER EIGHTIES MATCHBOX B-LINE DISASTER	66	2002
CELEBRATION [A] KOOL & THE GANG	7	1980
CELEBRATION [A] KYLIE MINOGUE	20	1992
A CELEBRATION [B] U2	47	1982
CELEBRATION GENERATION WESTBAM	48	1994
CELEBRATION OF LIFE TRUCE	51	1996
CELEBRITY HIT LIST TERRORVISION	20	1996
CELEBRITY SKIN HOLE	19	1998
CELL 151 STEVE HACKETT	66	1983
THE CELTIC SOUL BROTHERS KEVIN ROWLAND & DEXY'S MIDNIGHT RUNNERS	20	1982
THE CELTS ENYA	29	1992
CEMENT FEEDER	53	1997
CEMENTED SHOES MY VITRIOL	65	2000
CENTERFOLD J GEILS BAND	3	1982
CENTERFOLD ADAM AUSTIN	41	1999
CENTRAL PARK ARREST THUNDERTHIGHS	30	1974
CENTRAL RESERVATION BETH ORTON	37	1999
CENTRE CITY FAT LARRY'S BAND	31	1977
CENTURY INTASTELLA	70	1991
CEREMONY NEW ORDER	34	1981
CERTAIN PEOPLE I KNOW MORRISSEY	35	1992
A CERTAIN SMILE JOHNNY MATHIS	4	1958
THE CERTAINTY OF CHANCE DIVINE COMEDY	49	1998
C'EST LA VIE [A] ROBBIE NEVIL	3	1987
C'EST LA VIE [B] UB40	37	1994
C'EST LA VIE [C] B*WITCHED	1	1998
C'EST LA VIE [D] JEAN-MICHEL JARRE FEATURING NATACHA	40	2000
C'EST SI BON CONWAY TWITTY	40	1961
CH-CHECK IT OUT BEASTIE BOYS	8	2004
CHA CHA CHA FLIPMODE SQUAD	54	1998
CHA CHA HEELS EARTHA KITT & BRONSKI BEAT	32	1989
CHA CHA SLIDE DJ CASPER	1	2004
CHA CHA SLIDE MC JIG	33	2004
CHA CHA TWIST DETROIT COBRAS	59	2004
CHACARRON EL CHOMBO	20	2006
CHAIN GANG [A] JIMMY YOUNG	9	1956
CHAIN GANG [B] SAM COOKE	9	1960
CHAIN HANG LOW JIBBS	63	2007
CHAIN OF FOOLS ARETHA FRANKLIN	43	1967
CHAIN REACTION [A] DIANA ROSS	1	1986
CHAIN REACTION [A] STEPS	2	2001
CHAIN REACTION [B] HURRICANE #1	30	1997
CHAIN-GANG SMILE BROTHER BEYOND	57	1987
CHAINS [A] COOKIES	50	1963
CHAINS [B] RIVER DETECTIVES	51	1989
CHAINS [C] TINA ARENA	6	1995
CHAINS AROUND MY HEART RICHARD MARX	29	1992
CHAINS OF LOVE ERASURE	11	1988
CHAINSAW CHARLIE (MURDERS IN THE NEW MORGUE) W.A.S.P.	17	1992
CHAIRMAN OF THE BOARD CHAIRMEN OF THE BOARD	48	1971
CHALK DUST-THE UMPIRE STRIKES BACK BRAT	19	1982
THE CHAMP MOHAWKS	58	1987
CHAMPAGNE SALT-N-PEPA	23	1996
CHAMPAGNE DANCE PAY AS U GO	13	2002
CHAMPAGNE HIGHWAY SKANDAL	53	2000
THE CHAMPION WILLIE MITCHELL	47	1976
CHANCE BIG COUNTRY	9	1983
CHANCES HOT CHOCOLATE	32	1982
CHANGE [A] TEARS FOR FEARS	4	1983
CHANGE [B] DAVID GRANT	55	1987
CHANGE [C] LISA STANSFIELD	10	1991
CHANGE [D] INCOGNITO	52	1992
CHANGE [E] BLIND MELON	35	1994
CHANGE [F] LIGHTNING SEEDS	13	1995
CHANGE [G] DAPHNE	71	1995
CHANGE [H] PHATS & SMALL	45	2001
CHANGE [I] SUGABABES	13	2007
CHANGE CLOTHES JAY-Z	32	2003
CHANGE HIS WAYS ROBERT PALMER	28	1989
CHANGE (IN THE HOUSE OF FLIES) DEFTONES	53	2000
CHANGE ME JOCASTA	60	1997
CHANGE MY MIND BLUESKINS	56	2004
CHANGE OF HEART [A] CHANGE	17	1984
CHANGE OF HEART [B] CYNDI LAUPER	67	1986
A CHANGE OF HEART [C] BERNARD BUTLER	45	1998
CHANGE THE WORLD [A] ERIC CLAPTON	18	1996
CHANGE THE WORLD [B] DINO LENNY VS THE HOUSEMARTINS	51	2003
CHANGE WITH THE TIMES VAN McCOY	36	1975
A CHANGE WOULD DO YOU GOOD SHERYL CROW	8	1997
CHANGE YOUR MIND [A] SHARPE & NUMAN	17	1985
CHANGE YOUR MIND [B] UPSIDE DOWN	11	1996
CHANGES [A] CRISPIAN ST. PETERS	47	1966
CHANGES [B] IMAGINATION	31	1983
CHANGES [C] ALAN PRICE	54	1988
CHANGES [D] 2PAC	3	1999
CHANGES [E] SANDY RIVERA FEATURING HAZE	48	2002
CHANGES [F] OZZY & KELLY OSBOURNE	1	2003
CHANGES [G] CHRIS LAKE FEATURING LAURA V	27	2006
CHANGES [H] GARETH GATES	14	2007
CHANGES ARE NO GOOD STILLS	51	2004
CHANGING FOR YOU CHI-LITES	61	1983
CHANGING PARTNERS BING CROSBY	9	1954
CHANGING PARTNERS KAY STARR	4	1954
THE CHANGINGMAN PAUL WELLER	7	1995
CHANNEL Z B-52's	61	1990
CHANSON D'AMOUR MANHATTAN TRANSFER	1	1977
THE CHANT HAS BEGUN LEVEL 42	41	1984
THE CHANT HAS JUST BEGUN ALARM	48	1984
CHANT NO. 1 (I DON'T NEED THIS PRESSURE ON) SPANDAU BALLET	3	1981
THE CHANT (WE R)/RIP PRODUCTIONS RIP PRODUCTIONS	50	1997
CHANTILLY LACE BIG BOPPER	12	1958
CHANTILLY LACE JERRY LEE LEWIS	33	1972
CHAPEL OF LOVE [A] DIXIE CUPS	22	1964
CHAPEL OF LOVE [B] LONDON BOYS	75	1990
CHAPEL OF THE ROSES MALCOLM VAUGHAN	13	1957
CHAPTER FIVE RAM TRILOGY	62	2002
CHAPTER FOUR RAM TRILOGY	71	2002
CHAPTER SIX RAM TRILOGY	60	2002
CHARADE SKIDS	31	1979
CHARIOT [A] RHET STOLLER	26	1961
CHARIOT [B] PETULA CLARK	39	1963
CHARIOTS OF FIRE - TITLES VANGELIS	12	1981
CHARITY SKUNK ANANSIE	20	1995
CHARLESTON TEMPERANCE SEVEN	22	1961
CHARLIE BIG POTATO SKUNK ANANSIE	17	1999
CHARLIE BROWN COASTERS	6	1959
CHARLIE'S ANGELS 2000 APOLLO FOUR FORTY	29	2000
CHARLOTTE [A] KITTIE	60	2000
CHARLOTTE [B] AIR TRAFFIC	33	2007
CHARLOTTE ANNE JULIAN COPE	35	1988
CHARLOTTE SOMETIMES CURE	44	1981
CHARLTON HESTON STUMP	72	1988
CHARLY PRODIGY	3	1991
CHARMAINE BACHELORS	6	1963
CHARMING BILLY JOHNNY PRESTON	34	1960
CHARMING DEMONS SENSER	42	1996
CHARMLESS MAN BLUR	5	1996
CHASE GIORGIO MORODER	48	1979
CHASE MIDI XPRESS	73	1996
THE CHASE DJ EMPIRE PRESENTS GIORGIO MORODER	46	2000
CHASE THE SUN PLANET FUNK	5	2001
CHASING CARS SNOW PATROL	6	2006
CHASING FOR THE BREEZE ASWAD	51	1984
CHASING PAVEMENTS ADELE	2	2008
CHASING RAINBOWS SHED SEVEN	17	1996
CHEAP THRILLS PLANET PATROL	64	1983
CHEATED PRAYING MANTIS	69	1981
CHECK IT OUT (EVERYBODY) BMR FEATURING FELICIA	29	1999
CHECK ON IT BEYONCE FEATURING SLIM THUG	3	2006
CHECK OUT THE GROOVE BOBBY THURSTON	10	1980
CHECK THE MEANING RICHARD ASHCROFT	11	2002
CHECK THIS OUT L.A. MIX	6	1988
CHECK YO SELF ICE CUBE FEATURING DAS EFX	36	1993
CHECKIN' IT OUT LIL' CHRIS	3	2006
CHEEKAH BOW WOW (THAT COMPUTER SONG) VENGABOYS	19	2000
CHEEKY BONIFACE	25	2002

	Peak Position	Year of Entry
CHEEKY ARMADA ILLICIT FEATURING GRAM'MA FUNK	72	2000
CHEEKY FLAMENCO CHEEKY GIRLS	29	2004
CHEEKY SONG (TOUCH MY BUM) CHEEKY GIRLS	2	2002
CHEERS THEN BANANARAMA	45	1982
CHELSEA STAMFORD BRIDGE	47	1970
CHELSEA DAGGER FRATELLIS	5	2006
CHEMICAL #1 JESUS JONES	71	1997
CHEMICAL WORLD BLUR	28	1993
THE CHEMICALS BETWEEN US BUSH	46	1999
CHEMISTRY [A] NOLANS	15	1981
CHEMISTRY [B] SEMISONIC	35	2001
CHEQUE ONE-TWO SUNSHIP FEATURING M.C.R.B.	75	2000
CHEQUERED LOVE KIM WILDE	4	1981
CHERI BABE HOT CHOCOLATE	31	1974
CHERISH [A] DAVID CASSIDY	2	1972
CHERISH [A] JODECI	56	1993
CHERISH [B] KOOL & THE GANG	4	1985
CHERISH [B] PAPPA BEAR FEATURING VAN DER TOORN	47	1998
CHERISH [C] MADONNA	3	1989
CHERISH THE DAY SADE	53	1993
CHERISH THE DAY PLUMMET	35	2004
CHERISH WHAT IS DEAR TO YOU FREDA PAYNE	46	1971
CHERRY LIPS (DER ERDBEERMUND) CULTURE BEAT	55	1990
CHERRY LIPS (GO BABY GO) GARBAGE	22	2002
CHERRY OH BABY UB40	12	1984
CHERRY PIE [A] JESS CONRAD	39	1960
CHERRY PIE [B] WARRANT	35	1990
CHERRY PINK AND APPLE BLOSSOM WHITE EDDIE CALVERT	1	1955
CHERRY PINK AND APPLE BLOSSOM WHITE PEREZ 'PREZ' PRADO & HIS ORCHESTRA, THE KING OF THE MAMBO	1	1955
CHERRY PINK AND APPLE BLOSSOM WHITE MODERN ROMANCE FEATURING JOHN DU PREZ	15	1982
CHERUB ROCK SMASHING PUMPKINS	31	1993
CHERYL'S GOIN' HOME ADAM FAITH	46	1966
CHESHIRE CAT SMILE MILBURN	32	2006
CHESTNUT MARE BYRDS	19	1971
CHEWING GUM ANNIE	25	2004
CHI MAI (THEME FROM THE TV SERIES *THE LIFE AND TIMES OF DAVID LLOYD GEORGE*) ENNIO MORRICONE	2	1981
CHIC MYSTIQUE CHIC	48	1992
CHICAGO [A] FRANK SINATRA	21	1957
CHICAGO [B] KIKI DEE	28	1977
CHICK-A-BOOM (DON'T YA JES LOVE IT) 53RD & A 3RD FEATURING THE SOUND OF SHAG	36	1975
CHICK CHICK CHICKEN NATALIE CASEY	72	1984
CHICKA BOOM GUY MITCHELL	4	1953
CHICKEN EIGHTIES MATCHBOX B-LINE DISASTER	30	2003
CHICKEN PAYBACK BEES	28	2005
THE CHICKEN SONG SPITTING IMAGE	1	1986
THE CHIEF TONI SCOTT	48	1989
CHIEF INSPECTOR WALLY BADAROU	46	1985
CHIHUAHUA [A] BOW WOW WOW	51	1981
CHIHUAHUA [B] DARE	45	2003
CHIHUAHUA [B] DJ BOBO	36	2003
CHIKKI CHIKKI AHH AHH BABY FORD	54	1988
CHILD [A] DEFINITION OF SOUND	48	1996
CHILD [B] MARK OWEN	3	1996
CHILD COME AWAY KIM WILDE	43	1982
CHILD OF LOVE LEMON TREES	55	1993
CHILD OF THE UNIVERSE DJ TAUCHER	74	1999
CHILD STAR MARC ALMOND	41	1995
CHILDREN [A] EMF	19	1991
CHILDREN [B] ROBERT MILES	2	1996
CHILDREN [B] TILT	51	1999
CHILDREN [B] 4 CLUBBERS	45	2002
CHILDREN [C] BATTLE	60	2006
CHILDREN OF PARADISE BONEY M	66	1981
CHILDREN OF THE NIGHT [A] RICHARD MARX	54	1990
CHILDREN OF THE NIGHT [B] NAKATOMI	31	1998
CHILDREN OF THE REVOLUTION T REX	2	1972
CHILDREN OF THE REVOLUTION BABY FORD	53	1989
CHILDREN OF THE REVOLUTION UNITONE ROCKERS FEATURING STEEL	60	1993
CHILDREN OF THE WORLD ANA ANN & THE LONDON COMMUNITY CHOIR	44	2004
CHILDREN SAY LEVEL 42	22	1987
CHILDREN'S CHILDREN AGENT BLUE	62	2005
A CHILD'S PRAYER HOT CHOCOLATE	7	1975
CHILI BOM BOM TEMPERANCE SEVEN	28	1961
CHILL OUT (THINGS GONNA CHANGE) JOHN LEE HOOKER	45	1995
CHILL TO THE PANIC DEEP C	73	1991
CHILLIN' MODJO	12	2001
CHILLIN' OUT CURTIS HAIRSTON	57	1986
CHIME ORBITAL	17	1990
CHINA TORI AMOS	51	1992
CHINA DOLL [A] SLIM WHITMAN	15	1955
CHINA DOLL [B] JULIAN COPE	53	1989
CHINA GIRL DAVID BOWIE	2	1983
CHINA IN YOUR HAND T'PAU	1	1987
CHINA TEA RUSS CONWAY	5	1959
CHINATOWN [A] MOVE	23	1971
CHINATOWN [B] THIN LIZZY	21	1980
CHINESE BAKERY AUTEURS	42	1994
CHINESE BURN HEAVY STEREO	45	1996
THE CHINESE WAY LEVEL 42	24	1983
CHING CHING (LOVIN' YOU STILL) TERRI WALKER	38	2003
CHIQUITITA ABBA	2	1979
CHIRPY CHIRPY CHEEP CHEEP MAC & KATIE KISSOON	41	1971
CHIRPY CHIRPY CHEEP CHEEP MIDDLE OF THE ROAD	1	1971
CHIRPY CHIRPY CHEEP CHEEP MICHAEL COURTNEY	64	2002
THE CHISELERS FALL	60	1996
CHOC ICE LONG & THE SHORT	40	1964
CHOCOLATE [A] Y?N-VEE	65	1994
CHOCOLATE [B] SNOW PATROL	24	2004
CHOCOLATE [C] KYLIE MINOGUE	6	2004
CHOCOLATE BOX BROS	9	1989
CHOCOLATE CAKE CROWDED HOUSE	69	1991
CHOCOLATE (CHOCO CHOCO) SOUL CONTROL	25	2004
CHOCOLATE GIRL DEACON BLUE	43	1988
CHOCOLATE SALTY BALLS (PS I LOVE YOU) CHEF	1	1998
CHOCOLATE SENSATION LENNY FONTANA & DJ SHORTY	39	2000
CHOICE? BLOW MONKEYS FEATURING SYLVIA TELLA	22	1989
CHOK THERE APACHE INDIAN	30	1993
CHOLI KE PEECHE BALLY SAGOO	45	1995
CHOOSE COLOR ME BADD	65	1994
CHOOSE LIFE PF PROJECT FEATURING EWAN McGREGOR	6	1997
CHOOSE ME (RESCUE ME) LOOSE ENDS	59	1984
CHOOZA LOOZA MARIA WILLSON	29	2003
CHOP SUEY SYSTEM OF A DOWN	17	2001
CHORUS ERASURE	3	1991
THE CHOSEN FEW DOOLEYS	7	1979
CHOSEN ONE CONCRETES	54	2006
CHRISTIAN CHINA CRISIS	12	1983
CHRISTIANSANDS TRICKY	36	1996
CHRISTINE [A] MISS X	37	1963
CHRISTINE [B] SIOUXSIE & THE BANSHEES	22	1980
CHRISTINE KEELER SENSELESS THINGS	56	1994
CHRISTMAS ALPHABET DICKIE VALENTINE	1	1955
CHRISTMAS AND YOU DAVE KING	23	1956
CHRISTMAS COUNTDOWN FRANK KELLY	26	1983
CHRISTMAS IN BLOBBYLAND MR BLOBBY	36	1995
CHRISTMAS IN DREADLAND JUDGE DREAD	14	1975
CHRISTMAS IN HOLLIS RUN D.M.C.	56	1987
CHRISTMAS IN SMURFLAND FATHER ABRAHAM & THE SMURFS	19	1978
CHRISTMAS IS ALL AROUND BILLY MACK	26	2003
CHRISTMAS ISLAND DICKIE VALENTINE	8	1956
A CHRISTMAS KISS DANIEL O'DONNELL	20	1999
CHRISTMAS MEDLEY WEEKEND	47	1985
CHRISTMAS MY A*SE RICKY TOMLINSON	25	2006
CHRISTMAS ON 45 HOLLY & THE IVYS	40	1981
CHRISTMAS RAPPIN' KURTIS BLOW	30	1979
CHRISTMAS RAPPING DIZZY HEIGHTS	49	1982
CHRISTMAS SLIDE BASIL BRUSH FEATURING INDIA BEAU	44	2003
CHRISTMAS SONG (CHESTNUTS ROASTING ON AN OPEN FIRE) [A] ALEXANDER O'NEAL	30	1988
THE CHRISTMAS SONG [A] NAT 'KING' COLE	51	1991
CHRISTMAS SONG [B] GILBERT O'SULLIVAN	12	1974
CHRISTMAS SPECTRE JINGLE BELLES	37	1983
CHRISTMAS THROUGH YOUR EYES GLORIA ESTEFAN	8	1992
CHRISTMAS TIME BRYAN ADAMS	55	1985
CHRISTMAS TIME (DON'T LET THE BELLS END) DARKNESS	2	2003
CHRISTMAS WILL BE JUST ANOTHER LONELY DAY BRENDA LEE	25	1964
CHRISTMAS WRAPPING WAITRESSES	45	1982
THE CHRONICLES OF A BOHEMIAN TEENAGER GET CAPE WEAR CAPE FLY	38	2006
THE CHRONICLES OF LIFE AND DEATH GOOD CHARLOTTE	30	2005
CHRONOLOGIE PART 4 JEAN-MICHEL JARRE	55	1993
CHUCK E.'S IN LOVE RICKIE LEE JONES	18	1979
CHUNG KUO (REVISITED) ADDAMS & GEE	72	1991
CHURA LIYA BALLY SAGOO	64	1994
CHURCH T-PAIN FEATURING TEDDY VERSETI	42	2008
CHURCH OF FREEDOM AMOS	54	1995
THE CHURCH OF THE HOLY SPOOK SHANE MacGOWAN & THE POPES	74	1994
CHURCH OF NOISE THERAPY?	29	1998
CHURCH OF THE POISON MIND CULTURE CLUB	20	1983
CHURCH OF YOUR HEART ROXETTE	21	1992
CIAO CIAO BAMBINA DOMENICO MODUGNO	29	1959
CIAO CIAO BAMBINA MARINO MARINI & HIS QUARTET	24	1959
CIGARETTES AND ALCOHOL OASIS	7	1994
CINDERELLA LEMONESCENT	31	2003
CINDERELLA ROCKEFELLA ESTHER & ABI OFARIM	1	1968
CINDY INCIDENTALLY FACES	2	1973
CINDY OH CINDY EDDIE FISHER	5	1956
CINDY OH CINDY TONY BRENT	16	1956
CINDY OH CINDY VINCE MARTIN & THE TARRIERS	26	1956
CINDY'S BIRTHDAY SHANE FENTON & THE FENTONES	19	1962
CINNAMON GIRL PRINCE	43	2004
CIRCLE [A] EDIE BRICKELL & THE NEW BOHEMIANS	74	1989
THE CIRCLE [B] OCEAN COLOUR SCENE	6	1996
CIRCLE IN THE SAND BELINDA CARLISLE	4	1988
CIRCLE OF LIFE ELTON JOHN	11	1994

Title / Artist	Peak Position	Year of Entry
CIRCLE OF ONE OLETA ADAMS	73	1991
CIRCLE SQUARE TRIANGLE TEST ICICLES	25	2005
CIRCLES [A] NEW SEEKERS	4	1972
CIRCLES [B] SAFFRON	60	1993
CIRCLES [C] ADAM F	20	1997
CIRCLESQUARE WONDER STUFF	20	1990
CIRCUS [A] LENNY KRAVITZ	54	1995
CIRCUS [B] ERIC CLAPTON	39	1998
THE CIRCUS [C] ERASURE	6	1987
CIRCUS GAMES SKIDS	32	1980
CITIES IN DUST SIOUXSIE & THE BANSHEES	21	1985
THE CITY IS AT STANDSTILL LIAM FROST & SLOWDOWN FAMILY	74	2006
THE CITY IS MINE JAY-Z FEATURING BLACKstreet	38	1998
CITY LIGHTS DAVID ESSEX	24	1976
CITY OF BLINDING LIGHTS U2	2	2005
CITYSONG LUSCIOUS JACKSON	69	1995
CIVIL SIN BOY KILL BOY	44	2006
THE CIVIL WAR EP GUNS N' ROSES	11	1993
CLAIR GILBERT O'SULLIVAN	1	1972
CLAIRE PAUL & BARRY RYAN	47	1967
THE CLAIRVOYANT IRON MAIDEN	6	1988
CLAP BACK JA RULE	9	2003
THE CLAP CLAP SOUND KLAXONS	45	1983
CLAP YOUR HANDS [A] ROCKY SHARPE & THE REPLAYS	54	1982
CLAP YOUR HANDS [B] CAMISRA	34	1999
THE CLAPPING SONG SHIRLEY ELLIS	6	1965
THE CLAPPING SONG BELLE STARS	11	1982
CLARE FAIRGROUND ATTRACTION	49	1989
CLASH CITY ROCKERS CLASH	35	1978
CLASSIC ADRIAN GURVITZ	8	1982
CLASSIC GIRL JANE'S ADDICTION	60	1991
CLASSICAL GAS MASON WILLIAMS	9	1968
CLASSICAL GAS VANESSA-MAE	41	1995
CLASSICAL MUDDLEY PORTSMOUTH SINFONIA	38	1981
CLAUDETTE EVERLY BROTHERS	1	1958
CLEAN CLEAN BUGGLES	38	1980
CLEAN UP YOUR EYES DYKEENIES	53	2007
CLEAN UP YOUR OWN BACK YARD ELVIS PRESLEY	21	1969
CLEANIN' OUT MY CLOSET EMINEM	4	2002
CLEAR BLUE WATER OCEANLAB FEATURING JUSTINE SUISSA	48	2002
CLEMENTINE [A] BOBBY DARIN	8	1960
CLEMENTINE [B] MARK OWEN	3	1997
CLEOPATRA'S CAT SPIN DOCTORS	29	1994
CLEOPATRA'S THEME CLEOPATRA	3	1998
CLEVER KICKS HISS	49	2003
THE CLICHES ARE TRUE MANCHILD FEATURING KELLY JONES	60	2000
CLIMB EV'RY MOUNTAIN SHIRLEY BASSEY	1	1961
CLINT EASTWOOD GORILLAZ	4	2001
CLIPPED CURVE	36	1991
CLOAKING SEAFOOD	71	2001
CLOCKS COLDPLAY	9	2003
CLOG DANCE VIOLINSKI	17	1979
CLOSE...BUT ECHOBELLY	59	1994
CLOSE BUT NO CIGAR THOMAS DOLBY	22	1992
CLOSE COVER MINIMALISTIX	12	2002
CLOSE EVERY DOOR PHILIP SCOFIELD	27	1992
CLOSE MY EYES OPEN	46	2004
CLOSE MY EYES FOREVER LITA FORD DUET WITH OZZY OSBOURNE	47	1989
CLOSE THE DOOR [A] STARGAZERS	6	1955
CLOSE THE DOOR [B] TEDDY PENDERGRASS	41	1978
CLOSE TO ME CURE	13	1985
CLOSE TO PERFECTION MIQUEL BROWN	63	1985
CLOSE (TO THE EDIT) ART OF NOISE	8	1985
CLOSE TO YOU [A] MAXI PRIEST	7	1990
CLOSE TO YOU [B] BRAND NEW HEAVIES FEATURING N'DEA DAVENPORT	38	1995
CLOSE TO YOU [C] WHIGFIELD	13	1995
CLOSE TO YOU [D] MARTI PELLOW	9	2001
CLOSE TO YOUR HEART JX	18	1997
CLOSE YOUR EYES TONY BENNETT	18	1955
CLOSED FOR BUSINESS MANSUN	10	1997
CLOSER [A] MR FINGERS	50	1992
CLOSER [B] NINE INCH NAILS	25	1994
CLOSER [C] LIQUID	47	1995
CLOSER [D] NYLON	64	2006
CLOSER [E] TRAVIS	10	2007
THE CLOSER I GET TO YOU ROBERTA FLACK & DONNY HATHAWAY	42	1978
CLOSER THAN CLOSE ROSIE GAINES	4	1997
CLOSER THAN MOST BEAUTIFUL SOUTH	22	2000
CLOSER TO ALL YOUR DREAMS RHYTHM QUEST	45	1992
CLOSER TO ME FIVE	4	2001
CLOSER TO THE HEART RUSH	36	1978
THE CLOSEST THING TO CRAZY KATIE MELUA	10	2003
CLOSEST THING TO HEAVEN [A] KANE GANG	12	1984
CLOSEST THING TO HEAVEN [B] LIONEL RICHIE	26	1998
CLOSEST THING TO HEAVEN [C] TEARS FOR FEARS	40	2005
CLOSING TIME [A] DEACON BLUE	42	1991
CLOSING TIME [B] SEMISONIC	25	1999
CLOTHES OFF GYM CLASS HEROES	5	2007
CLOUD 8 FRAZIER CHORUS	52	1990
CLOUD 99 ST. ANDREWS CHORALE	31	1976
CLOUD LUCKY SEVEN GUY MITCHELL	2	1953
CLOUD NINE TEMPTATIONS	15	1969
CLOUD NUMBER 9 BRYAN ADAMS	6	1999
CLOUDBURST [A] DON LANG & THE MAIRANTS-LANGHORN BIG SIX	16	1955
CLOUDBURST [B] NIAGRA	65	1997
CLOUDBUSTING KATE BUSH	20	1985
CLOUDS SOURCE	38	1997
CLOUDS ACROSS THE MOON RAH BAND	6	1985
THE CLOUDS WILL SOON ROLL BY TONY BRENT	20	1958
CLOWN SHOES JOHNNY BURNETTE	35	1962
CLUB AT THE END OF THE STREET ELTON JOHN	47	1990
CLUB BIZARRE U96	70	1996
CLUB COUNTRY ASSOCIATES	13	1982
CLUB FANTASTIC MEGAMIX WHAM!	15	1983
CLUB FOOT KASABIAN	19	2004
CLUB FOR LIFE '98 CHRIS & JAMES	66	1998
CLUB LONELY GROOVE CONNEKTION 2	54	1998
CLUB TROPICANA WHAM!	4	1983
CLUBBED TO DEATH ROB DOUGAN	24	2002
CLUBBIN' MARQUES HOUSTON	15	2004
CLUBLAND ELVIS COSTELLO & THE ATTRACTIONS	60	1980
CLUMSY FERGIE	62	2007
CLUNK CLICK LAUREL & HARDY	65	1983
CLUTCH SHEA SEGER	47	2001
C'MERE INTERPOL	19	2005
C'MON [A] MILLIONAIRE HIPPIES	59	1994
C'MON [B] MARIO	28	2003
C'MON AND GET MY LOVE D MOB WITH CATHY DENNIS	15	1989
C'MON BILLY PJ HARVEY	29	1995
C'MON CHAMELEON RESEARCH	63	2005
C'MON CINCINNATI DELAKOTA FEATURING ROSE SMITH	55	1998
C'MON C'MON VON BONDIES	21	2004
C'MON EVERY BEATBOX BIG AUDIO DYNAMITE	51	1986
C'MON EVERYBODY EDDIE COCHRAN	6	1959
C'MON EVERYBODY SEX PISTOLS	3	1979
C'MON GET IT ON STUDIO B	28	2006
C'MON KIDS BOO RADLEYS	18	1996
C'MON LET'S GO GIRLSCHOOL	42	1981
C'MON MARIANNE GRAPEFRUIT	31	1968
C'MON PEOPLE PAUL McCARTNEY	41	1993
C'MON PEOPLE (WE'RE MAKING IT NOW) RICHARD ASHCROFT	21	2000
COAST IS CLEAR CURVE	34	1991
COCHISE AUDIOSLAVE	24	2003
COCK A DOODLE DO IT EGGS ON LEGS	42	1995
COCKNEY TRANSLATION SMILEY CULTURE	71	1985
CO-CO SWEET	2	1971
COCO JAMBOO MR PRESIDENT	8	1997
COCOA CLIPZ	71	2004
COCOMOTION EL COCO	31	1978
COCONUT NILSSON	42	1972
COCOON BJORK	35	2002
CODE OF LOVE MIKE SARNE	29	1963
CODE RED [A] CONQUERING LION	53	1994
CODE RED [B] BOXER REBELLION	61	2004
CODED LANGUAGE KRUST FEATURING SAUL WILLIAMS	66	1999
COFFEE SUPERSISTER	16	2000
COFFEE + TEA BLUR	11	1999
THE COFFEE SONG FRANK SINATRA	39	1961
COGNOSCENTI VERSUS THE INTELLIGENTSIA CUBAN BOYS	4	1999
COLD [A] ANNIE LENNOX	26	1992
COLD [B] TEARS FOR FEARS	72	1993
COLD AS CHRISTMAS ELTON JOHN	33	1983
COLD AS ICE FOREIGNER	24	1978
COLD AS ICE M.O.P.	4	2001
COLD COLD HEART [A] MIDGE URE	17	1991
COLD COLD HEART [B] WET WET WET	20	1994
COLD DAY IN HELL GARY MOORE	24	1992
COLD DAY IN THE SUN FOO FIGHTERS	64	2006
COLD HARD BITCH JET	34	2004
COLD HEARTED PAULA ABDUL	46	1990
COLD LIGHT OF DAY HALO	49	2002
COLD LOVE DONNA SUMMER	44	1981
COLD ROCK A PARTY MC LYTE	15	1997
COLD SHOULDER CULTURE CLUB	2	1999
COLD SWEAT [A] THIN LIZZY	27	1983
COLD SWEAT [B] SUGARCUBES	56	1988
COLD TURKEY PLASTIC ONO BAND	14	1969
COLD WIND ARCADE FIRE	52	2005
COLD WORLD GENIUS/GZA FEATURING D'ANGELO	40	1996
COLDCUT'S CHRISTMAS BREAK COLDCUT	67	1989
COLETTE BILLY FURY	9	1960
COLOR OF MY SKIN SWING 52	60	1995
COLOSSAL INSIGHT ROOTS MANUVA	33	2005
COLOSSUS FRESH BC	74	2004
THE COLOUR FIELD COLOUR FIELD	43	1984
COLOUR MY LIFE M PEOPLE	35	1992
THE COLOUR OF LOVE [A] BILLY OCEAN	65	1988
THE COLOUR OF LOVE [B] SNAP	54	1991
THE COLOUR OF LOVE [C] REESE PROJECT	52	1992
COLOUR OF MY LOVE JEFFERSON	22	1969
COLOUR THE WORLD SASH!	15	1999
COLOURBLIND DARIUS	1	2002
COLOURED KISSES MARTIKA	41	1992
COLOURS [A] DONOVAN	4	1965
THE COLOURS [B] MEN THEY COULDN'T HANG	61	1988
COLOURS FADED FRANCESCA BERLIN	60	2006
COLOURS FLY AWAY TEARDROP EXPLODES	54	1981
COLOURS IN WAVES SOUTH	60	2004
COLOURS OF THE WIND VANESSA WILLIAMS	21	1995
COMA AROMA INAURA	57	1996
COMA GIRL JOE STRUMMER & THE MESCALEROS	33	2003

	Peak Position	Year of Entry
THE COMANCHEROS LONNIE DONEGAN	14	1962
COMBINE HARVESTER (BRAND NEW KEY) WURZELS	1	1976
COME MARTHA WASH	64	1999
COME AGAIN TRUMAN & WOLFF FEATURING STEEL HORSES	57	1998
COME ALONG PLEASE BOB WALLIS & HIS STORYVILLE JAZZ BAND	33	1962
COME AND GET IT BADFINGER	4	1970
COME AND GET ME CLEOPATRA	29	2000
COME AND GET SOME COOKIE CREW	42	1989
COME AND GET WITH ME KEITH SWEAT FEATURING SNOOP DOGG	58	1998
COME AND GET YOUR LOVE REAL McCOY	19	1995
COME AND STAY WITH ME MARIANNE FAITHFULL	4	1965
COME AS YOU ARE [A] NIRVANA	9	1992
COME AS YOU ARE [B] BEVERLEY KNIGHT	9	2004
COME AWAY MELINDA BARRY ST JOHN	47	1965
COME BABY COME K7	3	1993
COME BACK [A] MIGHTY WAH	20	1984
COME BACK [B] SPEAR OF DESTINY	55	1985
COME BACK [C] LUTHER VANDROSS	53	1989
COME BACK [D] LONDONBEAT	69	1995
COME BACK [E] JESSICA GARLICK	13	2002
COME BACK AND FINISH WHAT YOU STARTED GLADYS KNIGHT & THE PIPS	15	1978
COME BACK AND SHAKE ME CLODAGH RODGERS	3	1969
COME BACK AND STAY PAUL YOUNG	4	1983
COME BACK AROUND FEEDER	14	2002
COME BACK BABY DAN REED NETWORK	51	1990
COME BACK BRIGHTER REEF	8	1997
COME BACK DARLING UB40	10	1998
COME BACK (FOR REAL LOVE) ALISON LIMERICK	53	1991
COME BACK JONEE DEVO	60	1978
COME BACK MY LOVE DARTS	2	1978
COME BACK TO ME [A] JANET JACKSON	20	1990
COME BACK TO ME [B] ANGELHEART FEATURING ROCHELLE HARRIS	68	1996
COME BACK TO WHAT YOU KNOW EMBRACE	6	1998
COME BACK TOMORROW INSPIRAL CARPETS	43	2003
COME CLEAN HILARY DUFF	18	2004
COME DANCE WITH ME (LP) FRANK SINATRA	30	1959
COME DANCING [A] NO DICE	65	1979
COME DANCING [B] KINKS	12	1983
COME DIG IT MACHEL	56	1996
COME GET MY LOVIN' DIONNE	69	1989
COME GET SOME ROOSTER	7	2004
COME GIVE ME YOUR LOVE RICHIE STEPHENS	62	1997
COME HELL OR WATERS HIGH DEE C. LEE	46	1986
COME HOME [A] DAVE CLARK FIVE	16	1965
COME HOME [B] JAMES	32	1990
COME HOME [C] LIL' DEVIOUS	55	2001
COME HOME BILLY BIRD DIVINE COMEDY	25	2004
COME HOME WITH ME BABY DEAD OR ALIVE	62	1989
COME IN OUT OF THE RAIN WENDY MOTEN	8	1994
COME INSIDE THOMPSON TWINS	56	1991
COME INTO MY LIFE [A] JOYCE SIMS	7	1988
COME INTO MY LIFE [B] GALA	38	1998
COME INTO MY ROOM NATHAN	37	2005
COME INTO MY WORLD KYLIE MINOGUE	8	2002
COME LIVE WITH ME HEAVEN 17	5	1983
COME NEXT SPRING TONY BENNETT	29	1956
COME ON [A] ROLLING STONES	21	1963
COME ON! [B] SOLO	63	1992
COME ON [C] DJ SEDUCTION	37	1992
COME ON [D] JESUS & MARY CHAIN	52	1994
COME ON [E] NEW POWER GENERATION	65	1998
COME ON [F] LEVELLERS	44	2002
COME ON [G] D4	50	2002
COME ON (AND DO IT) FPI PROJECT	59	1993
COME ON, COME ON BRONSKI BEAT	20	1986
COME ON DANCE DANCE SATURDAY NIGHT BAND	16	1978
COME ON EILEEN DEXY'S MIDNIGHT RUNNERS WITH THE EMERALD EXPRESS	1	1982
COME ON ENGLAND! [A] ENGLAND'S BARMY ARMY	45	1999
COME ON ENGLAND [B] FOUR FOUR TWO	2	2004
COME ON EVERYBODY (GET DOWN) URGE OVERKILL	37	1997
COME ON GIRL TAIO CRUZ FEATURING LUCIANA	5	2008
COME ON HOME [A] SPRINGFIELDS	31	1963
COME ON HOME [B] WAYNE FONTANA	16	1966
COME ON HOME [C] EVERYTHING BUT THE GIRL	44	1986
COME ON HOME [D] CYNDI LAUPER	39	1995
COME ON, LET'S GO [A] TOMMY STEELE	10	1958
COME ON, LET'S GO [A] LOS LOBOS	18	1987
COME ON/LET'S GO [B] PAUL WELLER	15	2005
COME ON OVER [A] JOHN SILVER	35	2003
COME ON OVER [B] KYM MARSH	10	2003
COME ON OVER BABY (ALL I WANT IS YOU) CHRISTINA AGUILERA	8	2000
COME ON OVER TO MY PLACE DRIFTERS	9	1965
COME ON YALL RHYTHM MASTERS	49	1997
COME ON YOU REDS MANCHESTER UNITED FOOTBALL CLUB	1	1994
COME OUTSIDE MIKE SARNE WITH WENDY RICHARD	1	1962
COME OUTSIDE JUDGE DREAD	14	1975
COME PLAY WITH ME WEDDING PRESENT	10	1992
COME PRIMA MARINO MARINI & HIS QUARTET	2	1958
(COME 'ROUND HERE) I'M THE ONE YOU NEED SMOKEY ROBINSON & THE MIRACLES	13	1966
COME SEE ABOUT ME SUPREMES	27	1965
COME SEE ABOUT ME SHAKIN' STEVENS	24	1987
COME SEE ME PRETTY THINGS	43	1966
COME SOFTLY TO ME FLEETWOODS	6	1959
COME SOFTLY TO ME FRANKIE VAUGHAN & THE KAYE SISTERS	9	1959
COME SOFTLY TO ME NEW SEEKERS FEATURING MARTY KRISTIAN	20	1972
COME TO DADDY APHEX TWIN	36	1997
COME TO ME [A] JULIE GRANT	31	1964
COME TO ME [B] RUBY WINTERS	11	1978
COME TO ME [C] ATEED	56	2003
COME TO ME [D] P DIDDY FEATURING NICOLE SCHERZINGER	4	2006
COME TO ME (I AM WOMAN) SU POLLARD	71	1985
COME TO MILTON KEYNES STYLE COUNCIL	23	1985
COME TO MY AID SIMPLY RED	66	1985
COME TO MY PARTY KEITH HARRIS & ORVILLE WITH DIPPY	44	1983
COME TO THE DANCE BARRON KNIGHTS WITH DUKE D'MOND	42	1964
COME TOGETHER [A] BEATLES	4	1969
COME TOGETHER [A] MICHAEL JACKSON	3	1992
COME TOGETHER (WAR CHILD) [A] SMOKIN' MOJO FILTERS	19	1995
COME TOGETHER [B] PRIMAL SCREAM	26	1990
COME TOGETHER [C] M FACTOR	46	2003
COME TOGETHER AS ONE WILL DOWNING	48	1990
COME TOMORROW MANFRED MANN	4	1965
COME UNDONE [A] DURAN DURAN	13	1993
COME UNDONE [B] ROBBIE WILLIAMS	4	2003
COME WHAT MAY [A] VICKY LEANDROS	2	1972
COME WHAT MAY [B] NICOLE KIDMAN & EWAN McGREGOR	27	2001
COME WITH ME [A] JESSE GREEN	29	1977
COME WITH ME [B] RONNY JORDAN	63	1994
COME WITH ME [C] QATTARA	31	1997
COME WITH ME [D] PUFF DADDY FEATURING JIMMY PAGE	2	1998
COME WITH ME [E] SPECIAL D	6	2004
COME WITH US CHEMICAL BROTHERS	14	2002
THE COMEBACK SHOUT OUT LOUDS	63	2005
COMEDY SHACK	44	1999
COMES A-LONG A-LOVE KAY STARR	1	1952
COMEUPPANCE THOUSAND YARD STARE	37	1992
COMFORTABLY NUMB SCISSOR SISTERS	10	2004
COMFORTING SOUNDS MEW	48	2003
COMIN' BACK CRYSTAL METHOD	73	1998
COMIN' HOME [A] DELANEY & BONNIE & FRIENDS FEATURING ERIC CLAPTON	16	1969
COMIN' HOME [B] DANGER DANGER	75	1992
COMIN' IN AND OUT OF YOUR LIFE BARBRA STREISAND	66	1982
COMIN' ON STRONG [A] BROKEN ENGLISH	18	1987
COMIN' ON STRONG [B] DESIYA FEATURING MELISSA YIANNAKOU	74	1992
COMIN' RIGHT UP BRUCE WILLIS	73	1988
COMING AROUND TRAVIS	5	2000
COMING AROUND AGAIN [A] CARLY SIMON	10	1987
COMING AROUND AGAIN [B] SIMON WEBBE	12	2006
COMING BACK DJ DADO	63	1998
COMING BACK FOR MORE [A] L.A. MIX	50	1990
COMING BACK FOR MORE [B] JELLYBEAN FEATURING RICHARD DARBYSHIRE	41	1988
COMING DOWN [A] CULT	50	1994
COMING DOWN [B] LONGVIEW	32	2005
COMING HOME [A] DAVID ESSEX	24	1976
COMING HOME [B] MARSHALL HAIN	39	1978
COMING HOME [C] K WARREN FEATURING LEE O	32	2001
COMING HOME [D] JJ72	52	2005
COMING HOME BABY MEL TORME	13	1963
COMING HOME NOW BOYZONE	4	1996
COMING ON STRONG SIGNUM FEATURING SCOTT MAC	66	1999
COMING OUT OF THE DARK GLORIA ESTEFAN	25	1991
COMING UNDONE KORN	63	2006
COMING UP PAUL McCARTNEY	2	1980
COMING UP ROSES CURVE	51	1998
COMMENT TE DIRE ADIEU JIMMY SOMERVILLE FEATURING JUNE MILES-KINGSTON	14	1989
COMMERCIAL BREAKDOWN SUNSHINE UNDERGROUND	46	2006
COMMITMENT LeANN RIMES	38	1998
COMMON PEOPLE PULP	2	1995
COMMUNICATION [A] DAVID McCALLUM	32	1966
COMMUNICATION [B] SPANDAU BALLET	12	1983
COMMUNICATION [C] POWER STATION	75	1985
COMMUNICATION [D] ARMIN	18	2000
COMMUNICATION BREAKDOWN JUNIOR	57	1983
COMMUNICATION (SOMEBODY ANSWER THE PHONE) MARIO PIU	5	1999
THE COMPASS DAVE CLARKE	46	2001
COMPLETE JAIMESON	4	2003
COMPLETE CONTROL CLASH	28	1977
THE COMPLETE DOMINATOR HUMAN RESOURCE	18	1991
THE COMPLETE STELLA (REMIX) JAM & SPOON	66	1992
COMPLEX GARY NUMAN	6	1979
COMPLICATED AVRIL LAVIGNE	3	2002
COMPLIMENTS ON YOUR KISS RED DRAGON WITH BRIAN & TONY GOLD	2	1994
COMPUTER GAME (THEME FROM 'THE INVADERS') YELLOW MAGIC ORCHESTRA	17	1980
COMPUTER LOVE [A] KRAFTWERK	1	1981

	Peak Position	Year of Entry
COMPUTER LOVE (PART 1) [B] ZAPP	64	1986
COMPUTER LOVE [C] SUPERCAR FEATURING MIKAELA	67	1999
CON LOS ANOS QUE ME QUEDIN GLORIA ESTEFAN	40	1993
CON TE PARTIRO ANDREA BOCELLI	69	2007
CONCEIVED BETH ORTON	44	2006
THE CONCEPT TEENAGE FANCLUB	51	1991
CONCRETE AND CLAY UNIT FOUR PLUS TWO	1	1965
CONCRETE AND CLAY RANDY EDELMAN	11	1976
CONCRETE SCHOOLYARD JURASSIC 5	35	1998
CONDEMNATION DEPECHE MODE	9	1993
CONFESSIN' (THAT I LOVE YOU) FRANK IFIELD	1	1963
CONFESSIONS OF A BOUNCER JUDGE DREAD	27	1976
CONFESSIONS PART II USHER	5	2004
CONFETTI LEMONHEADS	44	1993
CONFIDE IN ME KYLIE MINOGUE	2	1994
CONFUSION [A] LEE DORSEY	38	1966
CONFUSION [B] ELECTRIC LIGHT ORCHESTRA	8	1979
CONFUSION [C] NEW ORDER	12	1983
CONFUSION [C] ARTHUR BAKER VS NEW ORDER	64	2002
CONFUSION [D] ZUTONS	37	2005
CONFUSION (HITS US EVERY TIME) TRUTH	22	1983
CONGO [A] BOSS	54	1994
CONGO [B] GENESIS	29	1997
CONGO SQUARE GREAT WHITE	62	1991
CONGRATULATIONS CLIFF RICHARD	1	1968
CONNECTED [A] STEREO MC'S	18	1992
CONNECTED [B] PAUL VAN DYK FEATURING VEGA 4	28	2003
CONNECTION ELASTICA	17	1994
CONQUEST WHITE STRIPES	30	2008
CONQUEST OF PARADISE VANGELIS	60	1992
CONQUISTADOR [A] PROCOL HARUM	22	1972
CONQUISTADOR [B] ESPIRITU	47	1993
CONSCIENCE JAMES DARREN	30	1962
CONSCIOUS MAN JOLLY BROTHERS	46	1979
CONSIDER YOURSELF MAX BYGRAVES	50	1960
CONSIDERATION REEF	13	1997
A CONSPIRACY BLACK CROWES	45	1995
CONSTANT CRAVING k.d. lang	15	1992
CONSTANTLY CLIFF RICHARD	4	1964
CONSTANTLY WAITING PAULINE TAYLOR	51	1996
CONTACT [A] EDWIN STARR	6	1979
CONTACT... [B] EAT STATIC	67	1998
CONTAGIOUS WHISPERS	56	1985
THE CONTINENTAL MAUREEN McGOVERN	16	1976
CONTRARY MARY THEE UNSTRUNG	59	2004
CONTRIBUTION MICA PARIS	33	1990
CONTROL [A] JANET JACKSON	42	1986
CONTROL [B] TIME OF THE MUMPH	69	1995
CONTROL [C] PUDDLE OF MUDD	15	2002
CONTROL MYSELF LL COOL J FEATURING JENNIFER LOPEZ	2	2006
CONTROLLING ME OCEANIC	14	1992
CONTROVERSY PRINCE	5	1993
CONVERSATION INTERCOM SOULWAX	50	2000
CONVERSATIONS CILLA BLACK	7	1969
CONVOY CW McCALL	2	1976
CONVOY G.B. LAURIE LINGO & THE DIPSTICKS	4	1976
CONWAY REEL 2 REAL FEATURING THE MAD STUNTMAN	27	1995
COOCHY COO EN-CORE FEATURING STEPHEN EMMANUEL & ESKA	32	2000
COOKIN' UP YAH BRAIN 4 HERO	59	1992
COOL GWEN STEFANI	11	2005
COOL BABY CHARLIE GRACIE	26	1958
COOL FOR CATS SQUEEZE	2	1979
COOL JERK GO-GOS	60	1991
COOL MEDITATION THIRD WORLD	17	1979
COOL OUT TONIGHT DAVID ESSEX	23	1977
COOL RUNNING TIK & TOK	69	1983
COOL WATER FRANKIE LAINE	2	1955
COP THAT SHIT TIMBALAND/MAGOO/MISSY ELLIOTT	22	2004
COPACABANA (AT THE COPA) BARRY MANILOW	22	1978
COPPER GIRL 3 COLOURS RED	30	1997
COPPERHEAD ROAD STEVE EARLE	45	1988
CORNER OF THE EARTH JAMIROQUAI	31	2002
CORNERSHOP BABYBIRD	37	1997
CORNFLAKE GIRL TORI AMOS	4	1994
CORONATION RAG WINIFRED ATWELL	5	1953
CORPSES IAN BROWN	14	1998
CORRINE, CORRINA RAY PETERSON	41	1961
COSMIC GIRL JAMIROQUAI	6	1996
COSMONAUT NO. 7 SCARFO	67	1997
THE COST OF LIVING EP CLASH	22	1979
COSTAFINE TOWN SPLINTER	17	1974
COSY PRISONS A-HA	39	2006
COTTON EYE JOE REDNEX	1	1994
COTTONFIELDS BEACH BOYS	5	1970
COULD HAVE TOLD YOU SO HALO JAMES	6	1990
COULD HEAVEN EVER BE LIKE THIS IDRIS MUHAMMAD	42	1977
COULD I HAVE THIS KISS FOREVER WHITNEY HOUSTON & ENRIQUE IGLESIAS	7	2000
COULD IT BE JAHEIM	33	2001
COULD IT BE FOREVER DAVID CASSIDY	2	1972
COULD IT BE FOREVER GEMINI	38	1996
COULD IT BE I'M FALLING IN LOVE DETROIT SPINNERS	11	1973
COULD IT BE I'M FALLING IN LOVE DAVID GRANT & JAKI GRAHAM	5	1985
COULD IT BE I'M FALLING IN LOVE WORLDS APART	15	1994
COULD IT BE I'M FALLING IN LOVE EP DETROIT SPINNERS	32	1977
COULD IT BE MAGIC DONNA SUMMER	40	1976
COULD IT BE MAGIC BARRY MANILOW	25	1979
COULD IT BE MAGIC TAKE THAT	3	1992
COULD WELL BE IN STREETS	30	2004
COULD YOU BE LOVED BOB MARLEY & THE WAILERS	5	1980
COULDN'T GET IT RIGHT CLIMAX BLUES BAND	10	1976
COULDN'T HAVE SAID IT BETTER MEAT LOAF	31	2003
COULDN'T SAY GOODBYE TOM JONES	51	1991
COULD'VE BEEN TIFFANY	4	1988
COULD'VE BEEN ME BILLY RAY CYRUS	24	1992
COULD'VE BEEN YOU CHER	31	1992
COUNT ON ME [A] JULIE GRANT	24	1963
COUNT ON ME [B] WHITNEY HOUSTON	12	1996
COUNT YOUR BLESSINGS BING CROSBY	11	1955
COUNTDOWN RUSH	36	1983
COUNTERFEIT LOWGOLD	52	2001
COUNTING BACKWARDS THROWING MUSES	70	1991
COUNTING DOWN THE DAYS [A] NATALIE IMBRUGLIA	23	2005
COUNTING DOWN THE DAYS [B] SUNFREAKZ FEATURING ANDREA BRITTON	37	2007
COUNTING EVERY MINUTE SONIA	16	1990
COUNTING SHEEP AIRHEAD	35	1991
COUNTING TEARDROPS EMILE FORD & THE CHECKMATES	4	1960
COUNTING THE DAYS ABI	44	1998
COUNTRY BOY [A] FATS DOMINO	19	1960
COUNTRY BOY [B] HEINZ	26	1963
COUNTRY BOY [C] JIMMY NAIL	25	1996
COUNTRY GIRL PRIMAL SCREAM	5	2006
COUNTRY HOUSE BLUR	1	1995
THE COUNTRY OF THE BLIND FAITH BROTHERS	63	1985
COUNTRY ROADS HERMES HOUSE BAND	7	2001
COURSE BRUV GENIUS CRU	39	2001
COUSIN NORMAN MARMALADE	6	1971
COVER FROM THE SKY DEACON BLUE	31	1991
COVER GIRL NEW KIDS ON THE BLOCK	4	1990
COVER ME BRUCE SPRINGSTEEN	16	1984
COVER MY EYES (PAIN AND HEAVEN) MARILLION	34	1991
(COVER PLUS) WE'RE ALL GROWN UP HAZEL O'CONNOR	41	1981
COVER UP UB40	54	2002
COVERED IN PUNK PORTOBELLA	54	2004
COVERS EP EVERYTHING BUT THE GIRL	13	1992
COWARD OF THE COUNTY KENNY ROGERS	1	1980
COWBOY [A] KID ROCK	36	1999
COWBOY [B] CHIPZ	44	2007
COWBOY DREAMS JIMMY NAIL	13	1995
COWBOY JIMMY JOE ALMA COGAN	37	1961
COWBOYS AND ANGELS GEORGE MICHAEL	45	1991
COWBOYS AND INDIANS CROSS	74	1987
COWBOYS & KISSES ANASTACIA	28	2001
COWGIRL UNDERWORLD	24	2000
COWPUNCHER'S CANTATA MAX BYGRAVES	6	1952
COWPUNK MEDLUM SPLODGENESSABOUNDS	69	1981
COZ I LUV YOU SLADE	1	1971
CRACKERS INTERNATIONAL EP ERASURE	2	1988
CRACKIN' UP [A] TOMMY HUNT	39	1975
CRACKIN' UP [B] NICK LOWE	34	1979
CRACKING UP [C] JESUS & MARY CHAIN	35	1998
CRACKLIN' ROSIE NEIL DIAMOND	3	1970
CRADLE ATOMIC KITTEN	10	2005
CRADLE OF LOVE [A] JOHNNY PRESTON	2	1960
CRADLE OF LOVE [B] BILLY IDOL	34	1990
CRANK CATHERINE WHEEL	66	1993
CRANK THAT (SOULJA BOY) SOULJA BOY TELL 'EM	2	2007
CRASH [A] PRIMITIVES	5	1988
CRASH [B] FEEDER	48	1997
CRASH [C] MATT WILLIS	31	2007
THE CRASH [D] KOOPA	16	2007
CRASH AND BURN SAVAGE GARDEN	14	2000
CRASH! BOOM! BANG! ROXETTE	26	1994
CRASH LANDING ROUTE ONE FEATURING JENNY FROST	47	2005
CRASHED THE WEDDING BUSTED	1	2003
CRASHIN' A PARTY LUMIDEE FEATURING NORE	55	2003
CRASHIN' IN CHARLATANS	31	1995
CRAWL HEADSWIM	64	1995
CRAWL HOME DESERT SESSIONS	41	2003
CRAWLIN' BACK ROY ORBISON	19	1965
CRAWLING LINKIN PARK	16	2001
CRAWLING FROM THE WRECKAGE DAVE EDMUNDS	59	1979
CRAWLING IN THE DARK HOOBASTANK	47	2002
CRAWLING UP A HILL KATIE MELUA	46	2004
CRAYZY MAN BLAST FEATURING VDC	22	1994
CRAZIER GARY NUMAN VS RICO	13	2003
CRAZY [A] MUD	12	1973
CRAZY [B] MANHATTANS	63	1983
CRAZY [C] ICEHOUSE	38	1987
CRAZY [D] BOYS	57	1990
CRAZY [E] PATSY CLINE	14	1990
CRAZY [E] JULIO IGLESIAS	43	1994
CRAZY [E] LeANN RIMES	36	1999
CRAZY [F] SEAL	2	1990
CRAZY [F] ALANIS MORISSETTE	65	2005
CRAZY [G] BOB GELDOF	65	1994
CRAZY [H] AEROSMITH	23	1994
CRAZY [I] ETERNAL	15	1994
CRAZY [J] MARK MORRISON	6	1995
CRAZY [K] NUT	56	1996

Title / Artist	Peak Position	Year of Entry
CRAZY [L] AWESOME	63	1998
CRAZY [M] MOFFATTS	16	1999
CRAZY [N] LUCID	14	1999
CRAZY [O] TOMCAT	48	2000
CRAZY [P] K-CI & JOJO	35	2001
CRAZY [Q] ANDY BELL	35	2005
CRAZY [R] GNARLS BARKLEY	1	2006
CRAZY [S] LUMIDEE	74	2007
CRAZY BEAT BLUR	18	2003
CRAZY CHANCE KAVANA	16	1996
CRAZY CHICK CHARLOTTE CHURCH	2	2005
CRAZY CRAZY NIGHTS KISS	4	1987
CRAZY CUTS GRANDMIXER DST	71	1983
CRAZY DREAM JIM DALE	24	1958
CRAZY (FOR ME) FREDDIE JACKSON	41	1988
CRAZY FOR YOU [A] MADONNA	2	1985
CRAZY FOR YOU [B] SYBIL	71	1990
CRAZY FOR YOU [C] INCOGNITO FEATURING CHYNA	59	1991
CRAZY FOR YOU [D] LET LOOSE	2	1993
CRAZY HORSES OSMONDS	2	1972
CRAZY IN LOVE BEYONCÉ	1	2003
CRAZY LITTLE PARTY GIRL AARON CARTER	7	1998
CRAZY LITTLE THING CALLED LOVE QUEEN	2	1979
CRAZY LITTLE THING CALLED LOVE DWIGHT YOAKAM	43	1999
CRAZY LOVE [A] PAUL ANKA	26	1958
CRAZY LOVE [B] MAXI PRIEST	67	1986
CRAZY LOVE [C] CE CE PENISTON	44	1992
CRAZY LOVE [D] MJ COLE	10	2000
CRAZY LOWDOWN WAYS OCEAN COLOUR SCENE	64	2001
CRAZY OTTO RAG STARGAZERS	18	1955
THE CRAZY PARTY MIXES JIVE BUNNY & THE MASTERMIXERS	13	1990
CRAZY RAP AFROMAN	10	2002
CRAZY SEXY MARVELLOUS PAFFENDORF	52	2003
CRAZY TRAIN OZZY OSBOURNE'S BLIZZARD OF OZ	49	1980
CRAZY WATER ELTON JOHN	27	1977
CRAZY WORDS CRAZY TUNE DOROTHY PROVINE	45	1962
CRAZY YOU GUN	21	1997
CREAM [A] PRINCE & THE NEW POWER GENERATION	15	1991
CREAM [B] BLANK & JONES	24	1999
CREAM (ALWAYS RISES TO THE TOP) GREGG DIAMOND BIONIC BOOGIE	61	1979
CREATION STEREO MC'S	19	1993
CREATURES OF THE NIGHT KISS	34	1983
CREDO FISH	38	1992
THE CREEP [A] KEN MACKINTOSH	10	1954
CREEP [B] RADIOHEAD	7	1993
CREEP [C] TLC	6	1995
THE CREEPS CAMILLE JONES & FEDDE LE GRAND	7	2007
THE CREEPS (YOU'RE GIVING ME) FREAKS	9	2007
CREEQUE ALLEY MAMAS & THE PAPAS	9	1967
CREOLE JAZZ MR ACKER BILK & HIS PARAMOUNT JAZZ BAND	22	1961
CRESCENT MOON LYNDEN DAVID HALL	45	1998
CRICKETS SING FOR ANAMARIA EMMA	15	2004
CRIME OF PASSION MIKE OLDFIELD FEATURING MAGGIE REILLY	61	1984
CRIMINALLY INSANE SLAYER	64	1987
CRIMSON AND CLOVER JOAN JETT & THE BLACKHEARTS	60	1982
CRISPY BACON LAURENT GARNIER	60	1997
CRITICAL (IF ONLY YOU KNEW) WALL OF SOUND FEATURING GERALD LETHAN	73	1993
CRITICIZE ALEXANDER O'NEAL	4	1987
CROCKETT'S THEME JAN HAMMER	2	1987
CROCODILE ROCK ELTON JOHN	5	1972
CROCODILE SHOES JIMMY NAIL	4	1994
CROOKED TEETH DEATH CAB FOR CUTIE	69	2006
CROSS MY BROKEN HEART SINITTA	6	1988
CROSS MY HEART EIGHTH WONDER	13	1988
CROSS THAT BRIDGE WARD BROTHERS	32	1987
CROSS THE TRACK (WE BETTER GO BACK) MACEO & THE MACKS	54	1987
THE CROSSFIRE STARSAILOR	22	2005
CROSSROADS [A] TRACY CHAPMAN	61	1989
CROSSROADS [B] BLAZIN' SQUAD	1	2002
CROSSTOWN TRAFFIC JIMI HENDRIX EXPERIENCE	37	1969
THE CROWD ROY ORBISON	40	1962
THE CROWN GARY BYRD & THE GB EXPERIENCE	6	1983
CROWS MODEY LEMON	75	2004
CRUCIAL NEW EDITION	70	1989
CRUCIFIED ARMY OF LOVERS	31	1991
CRUCIFY TORI AMOS	15	1992
CRUEL PUBLIC IMAGE LTD.	49	1992
THE CRUEL SEA DAKOTAS	18	1963
CRUEL SUMMER BANANARAMA	8	1983
CRUEL SUMMER ACE OF BASE	8	1998
CRUEL TO BE KIND NICK LOWE	12	1979
CRUISE INTO CHRISTMAS MEDLEY JANE McDONALD	10	1998
CRUISIN' D'ANGELO	31	1996
CRUISING SINITTA	2	1986
THE CRUNCH RAH BAND	6	1977
CRUSH [A] ZHANE	44	1997
CRUSH [B] JENNIFER PAIGE	4	1998
CRUSH [C] DARREN HAYES	19	2003
CRUSH [D] PAUL VAN DYK FEATURING SECOND SUN	42	2004
CRUSH CRUSH CRUSH PARAMORE	61	2007
CRUSH ME HOUSE OF LOVE	67	1992
CRUSH ON YOU [A] JETS	5	1987
CRUSH ON YOU [A] AARON CARTER	9	1997
CRUSH ON YOU [A] DANIEL O'DONNELL	21	2006
CRUSH ON YOU [B] LIL' KIM	23	1997
CRUSH TONIGHT FAT JOE FEATURING GINUWINE	42	2002
CRUSH WITH EYELINER R.E.M.	23	1995
CRUSHED BY THE WHEELS OF INDUSTRY HEAVEN 17	17	1983
CRUSHED LIKE FRUIT INME	25	2002
CRY [A] GERRY MONROE	38	1970
CRY [B] GODLEY & CREME	19	1985
CRY [C] WATERFRONT	17	1989
CRY [D] SUNDAYS	43	1997
CRY [E] SYSTEM F	19	2000
CRY [F] MICHAEL JACKSON	25	2001
CRY [G] SIMPLE MINDS	47	2002
CRY [H] FAITH HILL	25	2002
CRY [I] KYM MARSH	2	2003
CRY [J] ALEX PARKS	13	2004
CRY AND BE FREE MARILYN	31	1984
CRY BABY [A] SPILLER	40	2002
CRY BABY [B] JEMINI	15	2003
CRY BABY CRY SANTANA FEATURING SEAN PAUL & JOSS STONE	71	2006
CRY BOY CRY BLUE ZOO	13	1982
CRY DIGNITY DUB WAR	59	1996
CRY FOR HELP [A] RICK ASTLEY	7	1991
CRY FOR HELP [B] SHED SEVEN	30	2001
CRY FOR ME ROACHFORD	46	1994
CRY FOR THE NATIONS MICHAEL SCHENKER GROUP	56	1980
CRY FOR YOU JODECI	20	1993
CRY FREEDOM [A] GEORGE FENTON & JONAS GWANGWA	75	1988
CRY FREEDOM [B] MOMBASSA	63	1997
CRY INDIA UMBOZA	19	1995
CRY JUST A LITTLE BIT SHAKIN' STEVENS	3	1983
CRY LIKE A BABY BOX TOPS	15	1968
CRY LITTLE SISTER (I NEED U NOW) LOST BROTHERS FEATURING G TOM MAC	21	2003
CRY ME A RIVER [A] JULIE LONDON	22	1957
CRY ME A RIVER [A] MARI WILSON	27	1983
CRY ME A RIVER [A] DENISE WELCH	23	1995
CRY ME A RIVER [B] JUSTIN TIMBERLAKE	2	2003
CRY MY HEART DAVID WHITFIELD	22	1958
CRY MYSELF TO SLEEP DEL SHANNON	29	1962
CRY OVER ME MEAT LOAF	47	2007
CRY TO BE FOUND DEL AMITRI	40	1998
CRY TO HEAVEN ELTON JOHN	47	1986
CRY TO ME PRETTY THINGS	28	1965
CRY WOLF A-HA	5	1986
CRYIN' [A] ROY ORBISON	25	1961
CRYIN' [B] VIXEN	27	1989
CRYIN' [C] AEROSMITH	17	1993
CRYIN' MY HEART OUT FOR YOU DIANA ROSS	58	1981
CRYIN' TIME RAY CHARLES	50	1966
CRYING DON McLEAN	1	1980
CRYING ROY ORBISON (DUET WITH k d lang)	13	1992
CRYING AT THE DISCOTEQUE ALCAZAR	13	2001
THE CRYING GAME DAVE BERRY	5	1964
THE CRYING GAME BOY GEORGE	22	1992
CRYING IN THE CHAPEL LEE LAWRENCE WITH RAY MARTIN & HIS ORCHESTRA	7	1953
CRYING IN THE CHAPEL ELVIS PRESLEY	1	1965
CRYIN' IN THE RAIN [A] EVERLY BROTHERS	6	1962
CRYING IN THE RAIN [A] A-HA	13	1990
CRYING IN THE RAIN [B] CULTURE BEAT	29	1996
CRYING LAUGHING LOVING LYING LABI SIFFRE	11	1972
CRYING OVER YOU KEN BOOTHE	11	1975
THE CRYING SCENE AZTEC CAMERA	70	1990
CRYPTIK SOULS CREW LEN	28	2000
CRYSTAL NEW ORDER	8	2001
CRYSTAL CLEAR GRID	27	1993
THE CRYSTAL LAKE GRANDADDY	38	2001
CRYSTALL BALL KEANE	20	2006
CUBA GIBSON BROTHERS	41	1979
CUBA EL MARIACHI	38	1996
CUBAN PETE JIM CARREY	31	1995
CUBIK 808 STATE	10	1990
CUDDLY TOY ROACHFORD	4	1988
CUFF OF MY SHIRT GUY MITCHELL	9	1954
CULT OF PERSONALITY LIVING COLOUR	67	1991
CULT OF SNAP HI POWER	73	1990
CULT OF SNAP SNAP	8	1990
CUM ON FEEL THE NOIZE SLADE	1	1973
CUM ON FEEL THE NOIZE QUIET RIOT	45	1983
CUMBERLAND GAP LONNIE DONEGAN	1	1957
CUMBERLAND GAP VIPERS SKIFFLE GROUP	10	1957
THE CUP OF LIFE RICKY MARTIN	29	1998
CUPBOARD LOVE JOHN LEYTON	22	1963
CUPID [A] SAM COOKE	7	1961
CUPID [A] JOHNNY NASH	6	1969
CUPID [B] JC 001	56	1993
CUPID-I'VE LOVED YOU FOR A LONG TIME (MEDLEY) DETROIT SPINNERS	4	1980
CUPID'S CHOKEHOLD/BREAKFAST IN AMERICA GYM CLASS HEROES	3	2007
THE CURE & THE CAUSE FISH GO DEEP FEATURING TRACEY K	23	2006
CURIOSITY JETS	41	1987
CURIOUS LEVERT SWEAT GILL	23	1998
CURLY MOVE	12	1969
THE CURSE OF VOODOO RAY LISA MAY	64	1996
CURTAIN FALLS BLUE	4	2004
CURVY COLA BOTTLE BODY CHICO	45	2007
CUT CHEMIST SUITE OZOMATLI	58	1999

Title / Artist	Peak Position	Year of Entry
CUT HERE CURE	54	2001
CUT ME DOWN LLOYD COLE & THE COMMOTIONS	38	1986
CUT SOME RUG BLUETONES	7	1996
CUT THE CAKE AVERAGE WHITE BAND	31	1975
CUT YOUR HAIR PAVEMENT	52	1994
A CUTE SWEET LOVE ADDICTION JOHNNY GILL	46	1994
CUTS ACROSS THE LAND DUKE SPIRIT	45	2004
CUTS BOTH WAYS GLORIA ESTEFAN	49	1990
CUTT OFF KASABIAN	8	2005
THE CUTTER ECHO & THE BUNNYMEN	8	1983
CUTTY SARK JOHN BARRY SEVEN	35	1962
CYANIDE LURKERS	72	1979
CYBELE'S REVERIE STEREOLAB	62	1996
CYCLONE DUB PISTOLS	63	1998
THE CYPHER: PART 3 FRANKIE CUTLASS	59	1997

D

Title / Artist	Peak Position	Year of Entry
D-DARLING ANTHONY NEWLEY	25	1962
D-DAYS HAZEL O'CONNOR	10	1981
D-FUNKTIONAL MEKON FEATURING AFRIKA BAMBAATAA	72	2004
DA ANTIDOTE STANTON WARRIORS	69	2001
DA DA DA TRIO	2	1982
DA DOO RON RON CRYSTALS	5	1963
DA-FORCE BEDLAM	68	1999
DA FUNK DAFT PUNK	7	1997
DA GOODNESS REDMAN	52	1999
DA HYPE JUNIOR JACK FEATURING ROBERT SMITH	25	2004
DA LICKS DJ FRESH	60	2003
DA YA THINK I'M SEXY ROD STEWART	1	1978
DA YA THINK I'M SEXY REVOLTING COCKS	61	1993
DA YA THINK I'M SEXY? N-TRANCE FEATURING ROD STEWART	7	1997
DA YA THINK I'M SEXY? GIRLS OF FHM	10	2004
D-A-A-ANCE LAMBRETTAS	12	1980
DADDY COOL [A] BONEY M	6	1976
DADDY COOL [B] DARTS	6	1977
DADDY DON'T YOU WALK SO FAST DANIEL BOONE	17	1971
DADDY'S HOME CLIFF RICHARD	2	1981
DADDY'S LITTLE GIRL NIKKI D	75	1991
DAFT PUNK IS PLAYING AT MY HOUSE LCD SOUNDSYSTEM	29	2005
DAGENHAM DAVE MORRISSEY	26	1995
DAILY TQ	14	2000
DAKOTA STEREOPHONICS	1	2005
DALLIANCE WEDDING PRESENT	29	1991
DAMAGED PLUMMET	12	2003
THE DAMBUSTERS MARCH THE CENTRAL BAND OF THE ROYAL AIR FORCE, CONDUCTOR W/CDR A.E. SIMS O.B.E.	18	1955
DAMN DAMN LEASH BE YOUR OWN PET	68	2005
DAMN GOOD DAVID LEE ROTH	72	1988
DAMN I WISH I WAS YOUR LOVER SOPHIE B. HAWKINS	14	1992
DAMNED DON'T CRY VISAGE	11	1982
DAMNED ON 45 CAPTAIN SENSIBLE	6	1984
DANCANDO LAMBADA KAOMA	62	1990
DANCE [A] THAT PETROL EMOTION	64	1987
THE DANCE [B] GARTH BROOKS	36	1995
DANCE A LITTLE BIT CLOSER CHARO & THE SALSOUL ORCHESTRA	44	1978
DANCE AND SHOUT SHAGGY	19	2001
DANCE AWAY ROXY MUSIC	2	1979
DANCE COMMANDER ELECTRIC SIX	40	2003
DANCE DANCE [A] DESKEE	74	1990
DANCE DANCE [B] FALL OUT BOY	8	2006
DANCE DANCE DANCE BEACH BOYS	24	1965
DANCE DANCE DANCE (YOWSAH YOWSAH YOWSAH) CHIC	6	1977
DANCE (DISCO HEAT) SYLVESTER	29	1978
DANCE FOR ME [A] SISQO	6	2001
DANCE FOR ME [B] MARY J BLIGE FEATURING COMMON	13	2002
DANCE, GET DOWN (FEEL THE GROOVE) AL HUDSON	57	1978
DANCE HALL DAYS WANG CHUNG	21	1984
DANCE INTO THE LIGHT PHIL COLLINS	9	1996
DANCE LADY DANCE CROWN HEIGHTS AFFAIR	44	1979
DANCE LITTLE LADY DANCE TINA CHARLES	6	1976
DANCE LITTLE SISTER (PART ONE) TERENCE TRENT D'ARBY	20	1987
DANCE ME IN SONS & DAUGHTERS	40	2005
DANCE ME UP GARY GLITTER	25	1984
DANCE NO MORE E-LUSTRIOUS FEATURING DEBORAH FRENCH	58	1992
DANCE OF THE CUCKOOS (THE LAUREL AND HARDY THEME) BAND OF THE BLACK WATCH	37	1975
DANCE OF THE MAD POP WILL EAT ITSELF	32	1990
DANCE ON! [A] SHADOWS	1	1962
DANCE ON [A] KATHY KIRBY	11	1963
DANCE ON [B] MOJO	70	1981
DANCE OUT OF MY HEAD PIA	65	1988
DANCE STANCE DEXY'S MIDNIGHT RUNNERS	40	1980
DANCE SUCKER SET THE TONE	62	1983
DANCE THE BODY MUSIC OSIBISA	31	1976
DANCE THE KUNG FU CARL DOUGLAS	35	1974
DANCE THE NIGHT AWAY MAVERICKS	4	1998
DANCE TO THE MUSIC SLY & THE FAMILY STONE	7	1968
DANCE TO THE MUSIC HUSTLERS CONVENTION FEATURING DAVE LAUDAT & ONDRERA DUVERNY	71	1995
DANCE TO THE RHYTHM BULLETPROOF	62	2001
DANCE TONIGHT [A] LUCY PEARL	36	2000
DANCE TONIGHT [B] PAUL McCARTNEY	26	2007
DANCE WIT ME RICK JAMES	53	1982
DANCE WITH ME [A] DRIFTERS	17	1960
DANCE WITH ME [B] PETER BROWN	57	1978
DANCE WITH ME [C] CONTROL	17	1991
DANCE WITH ME [D] TIN TIN OUT FEATURING TONY HADLEY	35	1997
DANCE WITH ME [E] DEBELAH MORGAN	10	2001
DANCE WITH MY FATHER LUTHER VANDROSS	21	2004
DANCE WITH THE DEVIL COZY POWELL	3	1973
DANCE WITH THE GUITAR MAN DUANE EDDY & THE REBELETTES	4	1962
DANCE (WITH U) LEMAR	2	2003
DANCE WITH YOU CARRIE LUCAS	40	1979
DANCE WITH YOU (NACHNA TERE NAAL) RISHI RICH PROJECT FEATURING JAY SEAN	12	2003
DANCE YOURSELF DIZZY LIQUID GOLD	2	1980
DANCE4LIFE TIESTO FEATURING MAXI JAZZ	67	2006
DANCEFLOOR HOLLOWAYS	41	2007
DANCEHALL MOOD ASWAD	48	1993
DANCEHALL QUEEN CHEVELLE FRANKLYN/ BEENIE MAN	70	1997
DANCER [A] GINO SOCCIO	46	1979
DANCER [B] MICHAEL SCHENKER GROUP	52	1982
DANCERAMA SIGUE SIGUE SPUTNIK	50	1989
DANCIN' AARON SMITH FEATURING LUVLI	20	2005
DANCIN' EASY DANNY WILLIAMS	30	1977
DANCIN' IN THE KEY OF LIFE STEVE ARRINGTON	21	1985
DANCIN' IN THE MOONLIGHT (IT'S CAUGHT ME IN THE SPOTLIGHT) THIN LIZZY	14	1977
DANCIN' ON A WIRE SURFACE NOISE	59	1980
DANCIN' PARTY CHUBBY CHECKER	19	1962
DANCIN' PARTY SHOWADDYWADDY	4	1977
DANCIN' THE NIGHT AWAY VOGGUE	39	1981
DANCIN' TONIGHT STEREOPOL FEATURING NEVADA	36	2003
DANCING BABY (OOGA-CHAKA) TRUBBLE	21	1998
DANCING GIRLS NIK KERSHAW	13	1984
DANCING IN OUTER SPACE ATMOSFEAR	46	1979
DANCING IN THE CITY MARSHALL HAIN	3	1978
DANCING IN THE DARK [A] KIM WILDE	67	1983
DANCING IN THE DARK [B] BRUCE SPRINGSTEEN	4	1984
DANCING IN THE DARK [C] 4 TUNE 500	75	2003
DANCING IN THE DARK [D] MICKEY MODELLE V JESSY	10	2006
DANCING IN THE DARK EP BIG DADDY	21	1985
DANCING IN THE MOONLIGHT TOPLOADER	7	2000
DANCING IN THE SHEETS SHALAMAR	41	1984
DANCING IN THE STREET [A] MARTHA REEVES & THE VANDELLAS	4	1964
DANCING IN THE STREET [A] DAVID BOWIE & MICK JAGGER	1	1985
DANCING IN THE STREET [B] MATT BIANCO	64	1986
DANCING LASHA TUMBAI (UKRAINE) VERKA SERDUCHKA	28	2007
(DANCING) ON A SATURDAY NIGHT BARRY BLUE	2	1973
DANCING ON THE CEILING LIONEL RICHIE	7	1986
DANCING ON THE FLOOR (HOOKED ON LOVE) THIRD WORLD	10	1981
DANCING ON THE JAGGED EDGE SISTER SLEDGE	50	1985
DANCING QUEEN ABBA	1	1976
DANCING QUEEN ABBACADABRA	57	1992
DANCING THE NIGHT AWAY MOTORS	42	1977
DANCING TIGHT GALAXY FEATURING PHIL FEARON	4	1983
DANCING WITH MYSELF GEN X	62	1980
DANCING WITH MYSELF (EP) GENERATION X	60	1981
DANCING WITH TEARS IN MY EYES ULTRAVOX	3	1984
DANCING WITH THE CAPTAIN PAUL NICHOLAS	8	1976
DANDELION ROLLING STONES	8	1967
DANGER [A] AC/DC	48	1985
DANGER [B] BLAHZAY BLAHZAY	56	1996
DANGER (BEEN SO LONG) MYSTIKAL FEATURING NIVEA	28	2001
DANGER GAMES PINKEES	8	1982
DANGER HIGH VOLTAGE ELECTRIC SIX	2	2002
THE DANGER OF A STRANGER STELLA PARTON	35	1977
DANGER ZONE KENNY LOGGINS	45	1986
DANGEROUS [A] PENNYE FORD	43	1985
DANGEROUS [B] ROXETTE	6	1990
DANGEROUS [C] BUSTA RHYMES	32	1997
DANGEROUS MINDS EP AARON HALL:DE VANTE:SISTA FEATURING CRAIG MACK	35	1996
DANGEROUS SEX TACK HEAD	48	1990
DANI CALIFORNIA RED HOT CHILI PEPPERS	2	2006
DANIEL ELTON JOHN	4	1973
DARE GORILLAZ	1	2005
DARE ME POINTER SISTERS	17	1985
DARE ME (STUPIDISCO) JUNIOR JACK FEATURING SHENA	20	2007
DARE TO DREAM VIOLA WILLS	35	1986
DARK ALAN (AILEIN DUNN) CAPERCAILLIE	65	1995
DARK AND LONG UNDERWORLD	57	1994
DARK CLOUDS SPACE	14	1997
DARK IS LIGHT ENOUGH DUKE SPIRIT	55	2004
THE DARK IS RISING MERCURY REV	16	2002
DARK IS THE NIGHT [A] SHAKATAK	15	1983
DARK IS THE NIGHT [B] A-HA	19	1993
DARK LADY CHER	36	1974

Title / Artist	Peak Position	Year of Entry
DARK MOON TONY BRENT	17	1957
DARK NIGHT GORKY'S ZYGOTIC MYNCI	49	1997
DARK ROAD ANNIE LENNOX	58	2007
DARK SCIENCE (EP) TILT	55	2000
DARK SIDE OF THE MOON ERNESTO VS BASTIAN	48	2005
DARK SKY JIMMY SOMERVILLE	66	1997
DARK THERAPY ECHOBELLY	20	1996
DARKHEART BOMB THE BASS FEATURING SPIKEY TEE	35	1994
DARKLANDS JESUS & MARY CHAIN	33	1987
DARKTOWN STRUTTERS BALL JOE BROWN & THE BRUVVERS	34	1960
DARLIN' [A] BEACH BOYS	11	1968
DARLIN' [A] DAVID CASSIDY	16	1975
DARLIN' [B] FRANKIE MILLER	6	1978
DARLIN' [C] BOB SINCLAR FEATURING JAMES WILLIAMS	46	2001
DARLIN' DARLIN' BABY (SWEET, TENDER, LOVE) O'JAYS	24	1977
DARLING BE HOME SOON LOVIN' SPOONFUL	44	1967
DARLING BE HOME SOON LET LOOSE	65	1996
DARLING PRETTY MARK KNOPFLER	33	1996
DARTS OF PLEASURE FRANZ FERDINAND	44	2003
DAS BOOT U96	18	1992
DAS GLOCKENSPIEL SCHILLER	17	2001
DAT PLUTO SHERVINGTON	6	1976
DATE WITH THE NIGHT YEAH YEAH YEAH	16	2003
DAUGHTER PEARL JAM	18	1994
DAUGHTER OF DARKNESS TOM JONES	5	1970
DAVID GUS GUS	52	2003
DAVID WATTS JAM	25	1978
DAVID'S SONG (MAIN THEME FROM *KIDNAPPED*) VLADIMIR COSMA	64	1979
DAVY'S ON THE ROAD AGAIN MANFRED MANN'S EARTH BAND	6	1978
DAWN [A] FLINTLOCK	30	1976
DAWN [B] TONY DE VIT	56	2000
DAY AFTER DAY [A] BADFINGER	10	1972
DAY AFTER DAY [B] PRETENDERS	45	1981
DAY AFTER DAY [C] JULIAN LENNON	66	1998
DAY & NIGHT BILLIE PIPER	1	2000
THE DAY BEFORE YESTERDAY'S MAN SUPERNATURALS	25	1997
THE DAY BEFORE YOU CAME ABBA	32	1982
THE DAY BEFORE YOU CAME BLANCMANGE	22	1984
DAY BY DAY [A] HOLLY SHERWOOD	29	1972
DAY BY DAY [B] SHAKATAK FEATURING AL JARREAU	53	1985
DAY BY DAY [C] SERAFIN	49	2003
THE DAY THE EARTH CAUGHT FIRE CITY BOY	67	1979
THE DAY I FALL IN LOVE DOLLY PARTON & JAMES INGRAM	64	1994
THE DAY I MET MARIE CLIFF RICHARD	10	1967
THE DAY I TRIED TO LIVE SOUNDGARDEN	42	1994
DAY-IN DAY-OUT [A] DAVID BOWIE	17	1987
DAY IN DAY OUT [B] FEEDER	31	1999
A DAY IN THE LIFE [A] BLACK RIOT	68	1988
A DAY IN THE LIFE [B] LARRIKIN LOVE	31	2007
A DAY IN THE LIFE OF VINCE PRINCE RUSS ABBOT	61	1982
THE DAY IS ENDED THE PIPES & DRUMS & MILITARY BAND OF THE ROYAL SCOTS DRAGOON GUARDS	30	1972
THE DAY IT RAINED FOREVER AURORA	29	2002
THE DAY THE RAINS CAME JANE MORGAN	1	1958
THE DAY THAT CURLY BILLY SHOT DOWN CRAZY SAM MCGHEE HOLLIES	24	1973
DAY TIME 4 STRINGS	48	2000
DAY TRIP TO BANGOR (DIDN'T WE HAVE A LOVELY TIME) FIDDLER'S DRAM	3	1979
DAY TRIPPER BEATLES	1	1965
DAY TRIPPER OTIS REDDING	43	1967
THE DAY WE CAUGHT THE TRAIN OCEAN COLOUR SCENE	4	1996
THE DAY WE FIND LOVE 911	4	1997
THE DAY WILL COME QUAKE FEATURING MARCIA RAE	53	1998
A DAY WITHOUT LOVE LOVE AFFAIR	6	1968
THE DAY THE WORLD TURNED DAY-GLO X-RAY SPEX	23	1978
DAYDREAM [A] LOVIN' SPOONFUL	2	1966
DAYDREAM [A] RIGHT SAID FRED	29	1992
DAYDREAM [B] BACK TO THE PLANET	52	1993
DAYDREAM BELIEVER MONKEES	5	1967
DAYDREAM BELIEVER ANNE MURRAY	61	1980
DAYDREAM BELIEVER (CHEER UP PETER REID) SIMPLY RED & WHITE	41	1996
DAYDREAM IN BLUE I MONSTER	20	2001
DAYDREAMER [A] DAVID CASSIDY	1	1973
DAYDREAMER [B] MENSWEAR	14	1995
DAYDREAMIN' [A] TATYANA ALI	6	1998
DAYDREAMIN' [B] LUPE FIASCO FEATURING JILL SCOTT	25	2006
DAYDREAMING PENNY FORD	43	1993
DAYLIGHT FADING COUNTING CROWS	54	1997
DAYLIGHT KATY GORDON LIGHTFOOT	41	1978
DAYS KINKS	12	1968
DAYS KIRSTY MacCOLL	12	1989
DAYS ARE O.K. MOTELS	41	1981
THE DAYS EP KINKS	35	1997
DAYS GO BY DIRTY VEGAS	16	2001
DAYS LIKE THESE BILLY BRAGG	43	1985
DAYS LIKE THIS [A] SHEENA EASTON	43	1989
DAYS LIKE THIS [B] VAN MORRISON	65	1995
DAYS LIKE THIS [C] SHAUN ESCOFFERY	53	2002
DAYS OF NO TRUST MAGNUM	32	1988
DAYS OF OUR LIVEZ BONE THUGS-N-HARMONY	37	1997
THE DAYS OF PEARLY SPENCER MARC ALMOND	4	1992
DAYS OF YOUTH LAURNEA	36	1997
DAYSLEEPER R.E.M.	6	1998
DAYTIME FRIENDS KENNY ROGERS	39	1977
DAYTONA DEMON SUZI QUATRO	14	1973
DAYZ LIKE THAT FIERCE	11	1999
DAZZ BRICK	36	1977
DAZZLE SIOUXSIE & THE BANSHEES	33	1984
DE DAH DAH (SPICE OF LIFE) KEITH MAC PROJECT	66	1994
DE DO DO DO, DE DA DA DA POLICE	5	1980
DE NIRO DISCO EVANGELISTS	59	1993
DEAD A'S DJ HYPE	58	2001
DEAD BATTERY PITCHSHIFTER	71	2000
DEAD CITIES EXPLOITED	31	1981
DEAD END STREET KINKS	5	1966
DEAD FROM THE WAIST DOWN CATATONIA	7	1999
DEAD GIVEAWAY SHALAMAR	8	1983
THE DEAD HEART MIDNIGHT OIL	62	1988
DEAD HUSBAND DEEJAY PUNK-ROC	71	1998
DEAD IN HOLLYWOOD MURDERDOLLS	54	2002
DEAD LEAVES AND THE DIRTY GROUND WHITE STRIPES	25	2002
DEAD MAN WALKING DAVID BOWIE	32	1997
DEAD OR ALIVE LONNIE DONEGAN	7	1956
DEAD POP STARS ALTERED IMAGES	67	1981
DEAD RINGER FOR LOVE MEAT LOAF	5	1981
DEAD STAR MUSE	13	2002
DEADLIER THAN THE MALE WALKER BROTHERS	32	1966
DEADLINE DUTCH FORCE	35	2000
DEADLINE USA SHALAMAR	52	1984
DEADWEIGHT BECK	23	1997
DEADWOOD DIRTY PRETTY THINGS	20	2006
DEAF FOREVER MOTORHEAD	67	1986
THE DEAL PAT CAMPBELL	31	1969
THE DEAN AND I 10 C.C.	10	1973
DEAR ADDY KID CREOLE & THE COCONUTS	29	1982
DEAR BOOPSIE PAM HALL	54	1986
DEAR DELILAH GRAPEFRUIT	21	1968
DEAR ELAINE ROY WOOD	18	1973
DEAR GOD MIDGE URE	55	1988
DEAR JESSIE MADONNA	5	1989
DEAR JESSIE ROLLERGIRL	22	2000
DEAR JOHN [A] STATUS QUO	10	1982
DEAR JOHN [B] EDDI READER	48	1994
DEAR LIE TLC	31	1999
DEAR LONELY HEARTS NAT 'KING' COLE	37	1962
DEAR MAMA 2PAC	27	1999
DEAR MISS LONELY HEARTS PHILIP LYNOTT	32	1980
DEAR MRS. APPLEBEE DAVID GARRICK	22	1966
DEAR PRUDENCE SIOUXSIE & THE BANSHEES	3	1983
DEATH DISCO (PARTS 1 & 2) PUBLIC IMAGE LTD.	20	1979
DEATH OF A CLOWN DAVE DAVIES	3	1967
DEBASER PIXIES	23	1997
DEBORA TYRANNOSAURUS REX	7	1968
A DECADE UNDER THE INFLUENCE TAKING BACK SUNDAY	70	2004
DECADENCE DANCE EXTREME	36	1991
DECADENT & DESPERATE MORTIIS	49	2005
THE DECEIVER ALARM	51	1984
DECEMBER ALL ABOUT EVE	34	1989
DECEMBER BRINGS ME BACK TO YOU ANDY ABRAHAM & MICHAEL UNDERWOOD	18	2006
DECEMBER '63 (OH WHAT A NIGHT) FOUR SEASONS	1	1976
DECEMBER WILL BE MAGIC AGAIN KATE BUSH	29	1980
DECENT DAYS AND NIGHTS FUTUREHEADS	26	2004
DECEPTION FERGIE	47	2000
THE DECISION YOUNG KNIVES	60	2006
DECK OF CARDS WINK MARTINDALE	5	1959
DECK OF CARDS MAX BYGRAVES	13	1973
DEDICATED FOLLOWER OF FASHION KINKS	4	1966
DEDICATED TO THE ONE I LOVE MAMAS & THE PAPAS	2	1967
DEDICATED TO THE ONE I LOVE BITTY McLEAN	6	1994
DEDICATION THIN LIZZY	35	1991
DEEE-LITE THEME DEEE-LITE	25	1990
DEEP EAST 17	5	1993
THE DEEP GLOBAL COMMUNICATION	51	1997
DEEP AND MEANINGLESS ROOSTER	29	2005
DEEP AND WIDE AND TALL AZTEC CAMERA	55	1988
DEEP DEEP DOWN HEPBURN	16	2000
DEEP DEEP TROUBLE SIMPSONS FEATURING BART & HOMER	7	1991
DEEP DOWN AND DIRTY STEREO MC'S	17	2001
DEEP FEELING MIKE SAGAR	44	1960
DEEP FOREST DEEP FOREST	20	1994
DEEP HEAT '89 VARIOUS ARTISTS (MONTAGES)	12	1989
DEEP (I'M FALLING DEEPER) ARIEL	47	1997
DEEP IN MY HEART CLUBHOUSE	55	1991
DEEP IN THE HEART OF TEXAS DUANE EDDY	19	1962
DEEP IN YOU LIVIN' JOY	17	1997
DEEP INSIDE MARY J BLIGE	42	1999
DEEP MENACE (SPANK) D'MENACE	20	1998
DEEP PURPLE BILLY WARD	30	1957
DEEP PURPLE NINO TEMPO & APRIL STEVENS	17	1963
DEEP PURPLE DONNY & MARIE OSMOND	25	1976
DEEP RIVER WOMAN LIONEL RICHIE	17	1986
DEEP SEA AQUANUTS	75	2002
DEEP SHAG LUSCIOUS JACKSON	69	1995
DEEPER [A] ESCRIMA	27	1995
DEEPER [B] DELIRIOUS?	20	1997
DEEPER [C] SERIOUS DANGER	40	1997

	Peak Position	Year of Entry
DEEPER AND DEEPER [A] FREDA PAYNE	33	1970
DEEPER AND DEEPER [B] MADONNA	6	1992
A DEEPER LOVE [A] CLIVILLES & COLE	15	1992
A DEEPER LOVE [A] ARETHA FRANKLIN	5	1994
DEEPER LOVE [A] RUFF DRIVERZ	19	1998
DEEPER LOVE (SYMPHONIC PARADISE) [B] BBE	19	1998
DEEPER SHADE OF BLUE STEPS	4	2000
DEEPER THAN THE NIGHT OLIVIA NEWTON-JOHN	64	1979
THE DEEPER THE LOVE WHITESNAKE	35	1990
DEEPER UNDERGROUND JAMIROQUAI	1	1998
DEEPEST BLUE DEEPEST BLUE	7	2003
DEEPLY DIPPY RIGHT SAID FRED	1	1992
DEF CON ONE POP WILL EAT ITSELF	63	1988
DEFINITE DOOR POSIES	67	1994
DEFINITION OF HOUSE MINIMAL FUNK	63	2002
DÉJÀ VU [A] E-SMOOVE FEATURING LATANZA WATERS	63	1998
DÉJÀ VU [B] BEYONCE FEATURING JAY-Z	1	2006
DEJA VU (UPTOWN BABY) LORD TARIQ & PETER GUNZ	21	1998
DELAWARE PERRY COMO	3	1960
DELICATE TERENCE TRENT D'ARBY FEATURING DES'REE	14	1993
DELICIOUS [A] SLEEPER	75	1994
DELICIOUS [B] SHAMPOO	21	1995
DELICIOUS [C] CATHERINE WHEEL	53	1997
DELICIOUS [D] DENI HINES FEATURING DON-E	52	1998
DELICIOUS [E] KULAY	73	1998
DELICIOUS [F] PURE SUGAR	70	1998
DELILAH TOM JONES	2	1968
DELILAH SENSATIONAL ALEX HARVEY BAND	7	1975
DELILAH JONES McGUIRE SISTERS	24	1956
DELIVER ME SISTER BLISS FEATURING JOHN MARTYN	31	2001
DELIVERANCE [A] MISSION	27	1990
DELIVERANCE [B] BUBBA SPARXXX	55	2004
DELIVERING THE GOODS SKID ROW	22	1992
DELIVERY BABYSHAMBLES	6	2007
DELLA AND THE DEALER HOYT AXTON	48	1980
DELTA LADY JOE COCKER	10	1969
DELTA SUN BOTTLENECK STOMP MERCURY REV	26	1999
DEM GIRLZ (I DON'T KNOW WHY) OXIDE & NEUTRINO FEATURING KOWDEAN	10	2002
DEMOCRACY KILLING JOKE	39	1996
DEMOLITION MAN STING	21	1993
DEMONS [A] SUPER FURRY ANIMALS	27	1997
DEMONS [B] FATBOY SLIM FEATURING MACY GRAY	16	2001
DEMONS [C] BRIAN McFADDEN	28	2005
DENIAL SUGABABES	15	2008
THE DENIAL TWIST WHITE STRIPES	10	2005
DENIS BLONDIE	2	1978
DENISE FOUNTAINS OF WAYNE	57	1999
DER KOMMISSAR AFTER THE FIRE	47	1983
DER SCHIEBER TIMO MAAS	50	2000
DESAFINADO ELLA FITZGERALD	38	1962
DESAFINADO STAN GETZ & CHARLIE BYRD	11	1962
DESECRATION SMILE RED HOT CHILI PEPPERS	27	2007
DESERT DROUGHT CAST	45	2001
DESERT SONG STING FEATURING CHEB MAMI	15	2000
DESIDERATA LES CRANE	7	1972
A DESIGN FOR LIFE MANIC STREET PREACHERS	2	1996
DESIRE [A] U2	1	1988
DESIRE [B] NU COLOURS	31	1996
DESIRE [C] BBE	19	1998
DESIRE [D] DJ ERIC	67	2000
DESIRE [E] ULTRA NATE	40	2000
DESIRE [F] GERI HALLIWELL	22	2005
DESIRE LINES LUSH	60	1994
DESIRE ME DOLL	28	1979
DESIREE NEIL DIAMOND	39	1977
DESPERATE BUT NOT SERIOUS ADAM ANT	33	1982
DESPERATE DAN LIEUTENANT PIGEON	17	1972
THE DESPERATE HOURS MARC ALMOND	45	1990
DESTINATION DT8 FEATURING ROXANNE WILDE	23	2003
DESTINATION CALABRIA ALEX GAUDINO FEATURING CRYSTAL WATERS	4	2007
DESTINATION ESCHATON SHAMEN	15	1995
DESTINATION SUNSHINE BALEARIC BILL	36	1999
DESTINATION VENUS REZILLOS	43	1978
DESTINATION ZULULAND KING KURT	36	1983
DESTINY [A] ANNE MURRAY	41	1972
DESTINY [B] CANDI STATON	41	1976
DESTINY [C] JACKSONS	39	1979
DESTINY [C] N-TRANCE	37	2003
DESTINY [D] BABY D	69	1993
DESTINY [E] KENNY THOMAS	59	1994
DESTINY [F] DEM 2	58	1998
DESTINY [G] ZERO 7 FEATURING SIA & SOPHIE	30	2001
DESTINY CALLING JAMES	17	1998
DESTROY EVERYTHING YOU TOUCH LADYTRON	42	2005
DESTROY ROCK AND ROLL MYLO	15	2005
DETROIT WHITEOUT	73	1994
DETROIT CITY TOM JONES	8	1967
DEUS SUGARCUBES	51	1988
DEUTSCHER GIRLS ADAM & THE ANTS	13	1982
DEVIL [A] 666	18	2000
DEVIL [B] STEREOPHONICS	11	2005
DEVIL GATE DRIVE SUZI QUATRO	1	1974
DEVIL IN A MIDNIGHT MASS BILLY TALENT	66	2006
DEVIL IN YOUR SHOES (WALKING ALL OVER) SHED SEVEN	37	1998
DEVIL INSIDE INXS	47	1988
THE DEVIL MADE ME DO IT THUNDER	40	2006
DEVIL OR ANGEL BILLY FURY	58	1982
THE DEVIL WENT DOWN TO GEORGIA CHARLIE DANIELS BAND	14	1979
DEVIL WOMAN [A] MARTY ROBBINS	5	1962
DEVIL WOMAN [B] CLIFF RICHARD	9	1976
THE DEVIL YOU KNOW JESUS JONES	10	1993
THE DEVIL'S ANSWER ATOMIC ROOSTER	4	1971
DEVIL'S BALL DOUBLE	71	1987
DEVIL'S GUN C.J. & CO	43	1977
DEVILS HAIRCUT BECK	22	1996
DEVIL'S NIGHTMARE OXIDE & NEUTRINO	16	2001
DEVIL'S THRILL VANESSA-MAE	53	1998
DEVIL'S TOY ALMIGHTY	36	1991
DEVOTED TO YOU CACIQUE	69	1985
DEVOTION [A] TEN CITY	29	1989
DEVOTION [B] KICKING BACK WITH TAXMAN	47	1990
DEVOTION [C] DAVE HOLMES	66	2001
DIABLA FUNK D'VOID	70	2001
DIABLO GRID	32	1995
DIAL MY HEART BOYS	61	1988
DIAMANTE ZUCCHERO WITH RANDY CRAWFORD	44	1992
DIAMOND BACK MEKKA	67	2001
DIAMOND DEW GORKY'S ZYGOTIC MYNCI	42	1997
DIAMOND DOGS DAVID BOWIE	21	1974
DIAMOND GIRL PETE WYLIE	57	1986
DIAMOND LIFE LOUIE VEGA & JAY 'SINISTER' SEALEE STARRING JULIE McKNIGHT	52	2002
DIAMOND LIGHTS GLENN & CHRIS	12	1987
DIAMOND SMILES BOOMTOWN RATS	13	1979
DIAMONDS [A] JET HARRIS & TONY MEEHAN	1	1963
DIAMONDS [B] CHRIS REA	44	1979
DIAMONDS [C] HERB ALPERT	27	1987
DIAMONDS AND GUNS TRANSPLANTS	27	2003
DIAMONDS AND PEARLS PRINCE & THE NEW POWER GENERATION	25	1991
DIAMONDS ARE FOREVER SHIRLEY BASSEY	38	1972
DIAMONDS ARE FOREVER DAVID McALMONT & DAVID ARNOLD	39	1997
DIAMONDS FROM SIERRA LEONE KANYE WEST	8	2005
DIAMONDS IN THE DARK EP MYSTERY JETS	47	2006
DIANA PAUL ANKA	1	1957
DIANE [A] BACHELORS	1	1964
DIANE [B] THERAPY?	26	1995
DIARY OF A WIMP SPACE	49	2000
THE DIARY OF HORACE WIMP ELECTRIC LIGHT ORCHESTRA	8	1979
DICK-A-DUM-DUM (KING'S ROAD) DES O'CONNOR	14	1969
DID I DREAM (SONG TO THE SIREN) LOST WITNESS	28	2002
DID I TELL YOU SPINTO BAND	55	2006
DID IT AGAIN KYLIE MINOGUE	14	1997
DID MY TIME KORN	15	2003
DID YOU EVER NANCY SINATRA & LEE HAZLEWOOD	2	1971
DID YOU EVER REALLY LOVE ME NICKI FRENCH	55	1995
DID YOU EVER THINK R KELLY	20	1999
DID YOU HAVE TO LOVE ME LIKE YOU DID COCONUTS	60	1983
DIDDY P DIDDY FEATURING THE NEPTUNES	19	2002
DIDN'T I BLOW YOUR MIND NEW KIDS ON THE BLOCK	8	1990
DIDN'T I (BLOW YOUR MIND THIS TIME) DELFONICS	22	1971
DIDN'T I TELL YOU TRUE THOMAS JULES-STOCK	59	1998
DIDN'T WE ALMOST HAVE IT ALL WHITNEY HOUSTON	14	1987
DIE ANOTHER DAY MADONNA	3	2002
DIE LAUGHING THERAPY?	29	1994
DIE YOUNG BLACK SABBATH	41	1980
DIFFERENCES GUYVER	72	2003
DIFFERENT AIR LIVING IN A BOX	57	1989
A DIFFERENT BEAT BOYZONE	1	1996
A DIFFERENT CORNER GEORGE MICHAEL	1	1986
DIFFERENT STORY BOWA FEATURING MALA	64	1991
DIFFERENT STROKES ISOTONIK	12	1992
DIFFERENT TIME DIFFERENT PLACE JULIA FORDHAM	41	1994
DIFFERENT WORLD IRON MAIDEN	3	2007
DIG FOR FIRE PIXIES	62	1990
DIG, LAZARUS, DIG NICK CAVE & THE BAD SEEDS	66	2008
DIGERIDOO APHEX TWIN	55	1992
DIGGI LOO-DIGGI LEY HERREYS	46	1984
DIGGIN' MY POTATOES HEINZ & THE WILD BOYS	49	1965
DIGGIN' ON YOU TLC	18	1995
DIGGING THE DIRT PETER GABRIEL	24	1992
DIGGING THE GRAVE FAITH NO MORE	16	1995
DIGGING YOUR SCENE BLOW MONKEYS	12	1986
DIGITAL GOLDIE FEATURING KRS ONE	13	1997
DIGITAL LOVE DAFT PUNK	14	2001
DIGNITY [A] DEACON BLUE	20	1988
DIGNITY [B] BOB DYLAN	33	1995
DIL CHEEZ (MY HEART...) BALLY SAGOO	12	1996
DILEMMA NELLY FEATURING KELLY ROWLAND	1	2002
DIM ALL THE LIGHTS DONNA SUMMER	29	1979
DIME AND A DOLLAR GUY MITCHELL	8	1954
DIMENSION [A] SALT TANK	52	1999
DIMENSION [B] WOLFMOTHER	49	2006
DIMPLES JOHN LEE HOOKER	23	1964
DIN DA DA KEVIN AVIANCE	65	1998

Title / Artist	Peak Position	Year of Entry
DINAH BLACKNUSS	56	1997
DING DONG GEORGE HARRISON	38	1975
DING DONG SONG GUNTHER & THE SUNSHINE GIRLS	14	2004
DING-A-DONG TEACH-IN	13	1975
DINNER WITH DELORES ARTIST FORMERLY KNOWN AS PRINCE (AFKAP)	36	1996
DINNER WITH GERSHWIN DONNA SUMMER	13	1987
DINOSAUR ADVENTURE 3D UNDERWORLD	34	2003
DIP IT LOW CHRISTINA MILIAN	2	2004
DIPPETY DAY FATHER ABRAHAM & THE SMURFS	13	1978
DIRECT-ME REESE PROJECT	44	1995
DIRGE DEATH IN VEGAS	24	2000
DIRRTY CHRISTINA AGUILERA FEATURING REDMAN	1	2002
DIRT DEATH IN VEGAS	61	1997
DIRT OFF YOUR SHOULDER JAY-Z	12	2004
DIRTY BEATS RONI SIZE REPRAZENT	32	2001
DIRTY CASH ADVENTURES OF STEVIE V	2	1990
DIRTY DAWG NKOTB	27	1994
DIRTY DEEDS JOAN JETT	69	1990
DIRTY DEEDS DONE DIRT CHEAP AC/DC	47	1993
DIRTY DIANA MICHAEL JACKSON	4	1988
DIRTY HARRY GORILLAZ	6	2005
DIRTY HARRY'S REVENGE ADAM F FEATURING BEENIE MAN	50	2002
DIRTY LAUNDRY DON HENLEY	59	1983
DIRTY LITTLE SECRET ALL-AMERICAN REJECTS	18	2006
DIRTY LOOKS DIANA ROSS	49	1987
DIRTY LOVE THUNDER	32	1990
DIRTY MIND [A] SHAKESPEARS SISTER	71	1990
DIRTY MIND [B] PIPETTES	63	2005
DIRTY MONEY DEE FREDRIX	74	1993
DIRTY MOTHA QWILO & FELIX DA HOUSECAT	66	1997
DIRTY OLD TOWN POGUES	62	1985
DIRTY OLD TOWN BHOYS OF PARADISE	46	2004
DIRTY STICKY FLOORS DAVE GAHAN	18	2003
DIRTY WATER MADE IN LONDON	15	2000
DISAPPEAR INXS	21	1990
DISAPPEARING ACT SHALAMAR	18	1983
DISAPPOINTED [A] PUBLIC IMAGE LTD.	38	1989
DISAPPOINTED [B] ELECTRONIC	6	1992
THE DISAPPOINTED [C] XTC	33	1992
DISARM SMASHING PUMPKINS	11	1994
DISCIPLINE OF LOVE ROBERT PALMER	68	1986
D.I.S.C.O. OTTAWAN	2	1980
D.I.S.C.O. N-TRANCE	11	1997
DISCO JO JINGLES	44	2005
DISCO CHICO	24	2006
DISCO 2000 PULP	7	1995
DISCO BABES FROM OUTER SPACE BABE INSTINCT	21	1999
DISCO BEATLEMANIA DBM	45	1977
DISCO CONNECTION ISAAC HAYES MOVEMENT	10	1976
DISCO COP BLUE ADONIS FEATURING LIL' MISS MAX	27	1998
DISCO DOWN [A] SHED SEVEN	13	1999
DISCO DOWN [B] HOUSE OF GLASS	72	2001
DISCO DUCK (PART ONE) RICK DEES & HIS CAST OF IDIOTS	6	1976
DISCO INFERNO TRAMMPS	16	1977
DISCO INFERNO TINA TURNER	12	1993
DISCO INFILTRATOR LCD SOUNDSYSTEM	49	2005
DISCO' LA PASSIONE CHRIS REA & SHIRLEY BASSEY	41	1996
DISCO LADY JOHNNIE TAYLOR	25	1976
DISCO MACHINE GUN LO FIDELITY ALLSTARS	50	1997
DISCO MUSIC (I LIKE IT) J.A.L.N. BAND	21	1976
DISCO NIGHTS (ROCK FREAK) GQ	42	1979
DISCO QUEEN HOT CHOCOLATE	11	1975
DISCO SCIENCE MIRWAIS	68	2000
DISCO STOMP HAMILTON BOHANNON	6	1975
DISCOBUG '97 FREAKYMAN	68	1997
DISCOHOPPING KLUBHEADS	35	1997
DISCOLAND FLIP & FILL FEATURING KAREN PARRY	11	2004
DISCONNECTED ROLLINS BAND	27	1994
DISCO'S REVENGE GUSTO	9	1996
DISCOTHEQUE U2	1	1997
DISCRETION GROVE STEPHEN MALKMUS	60	2001
DISEASE MATCHBOX 20	50	2003
DISENCHANTED COMMUNARDS	29	1986
DISILLUSION BADLY DRAWN BOY	26	2000
DIS-INFECTED EP THE THE	17	1994
DISPOSABLE TEENS MARILYN MANSON	12	2000
DISREMEMBRANCE DANNII	21	1998
DISSIDENT PEARL JAM	14	1994
THE DISTANCE CAKE	22	1997
DISTANT DRUMS JIM REEVES	1	1966
DISTANT STAR ANTHONY HOPKINS	75	1986
DISTANT SUN CROWDED HOUSE	19	1993
DISTORTION WILT	66	2002
DISTRACTIONS ZERO 7	45	2002
DIVA DANA INTERNATIONAL	11	1998
DIVA LADY DIVINE COMEDY	52	2006
DIVE! DIVE! DIVE! BRUCE DICKINSON	45	1990
DIVE IN CATCH	44	1998
DIVE TO PARADISE EUROGROOVE	31	1995
DIVEBOMB NUMBER ONE CUP	61	1996
DIVINE EMOTIONS NARADA	8	1988
DIVINE HAMMER BREEDERS	59	1993
DIVINE THING SOUP DRAGONS	53	1992
DIVING 4 STRINGS	38	2002
DIVING FACES LIQUID CHILD	25	1999
D.I.V.O.R.C.E. BILLY CONNOLLY	1	1975
D.I.V.O.R.C.E. TAMMY WYNETTE	12	1975
DIXIE-NARCO EP PRIMAL SCREAM	11	1992
DIZZY TOMMY ROE	1	1969
DIZZY VIC REEVES & THE WONDER STUFF	1	1991
D.J. [A] DAVID BOWIE	29	1979
DJ [B] RESONANCE FEATURING THE BURRELLS	67	2001
DJ [C] H & CLAIRE	3	2002
DJ [D] JAMELIA	9	2004
DJ CULTURE PET SHOP BOYS	13	1991
DJ DJ TRANSPLANTS	49	2003
DJ NATION NUKLEUZ DJ'S	40	2002
DJ NATION - HARDER EDITION NUKLEUZ DJs	48	2003
DJ SPINNIN' PUNK CHIC	69	2001
DJS FANS AND FREAKS BLANK & JONES	45	2002
DJS TAKE CONTROL SL2	11	1991
DK 50-80 OTWAY & BARRETT	45	1980
DO AND DON'T FOR LOVE KIOKI	66	2002
DO ANYTHING NATURAL SELECTION	69	1991
DO ANYTHING YOU WANT TO THIN LIZZY	14	1979
DO ANYTHING YOU WANT TO DO RODS	9	1977
DO EVERYTHING I TAUGHT YOU ALTERKICKS	71	2005
DO FOR LOVE 2PAC FEATURING ERIC WILLIAMS	12	1998
DO FRIES GO WITH THAT SHAKE GEORGE CLINTON	57	1986
DO I GIFTED	60	1997
DO I DO STEVIE WONDER	10	1982
DO I HAVE TO SAY THE WORDS BRYAN ADAMS	30	1992
DO I LOVE YOU RONETTES	35	1964
DO I QUALIFY? LYNDEN DAVID HALL	26	1998
DO IT [A] TONY DI BART	21	1994
DO IT [B] NELLY FURTADO	75	2007
DO IT AGAIN [A] BEACH BOYS	1	1968
DO IT AGAIN [B] STEELY DAN	39	1975
DO IT AGAIN [C] COOKIE	52	2005
DO IT AGAIN [D] CHEMICAL BROTHERS	12	2007
DO IT AGAIN-BILLIE JEAN (MEDLEY) CLUBHOUSE	11	1983
DO IT ALL OVER AGAIN SPIRITUALIZED	31	2002
DO IT ANY WAY YOU WANNA PEOPLE'S CHOICE	36	1975
DO IT DO IT AGAIN RAFFAELLA CARRA	9	1978
DO IT FOR LOVE [A] DANNI'ELLE GAHA	52	1993
DO IT FOR LOVE [B] SUBTERRANIA FEATURING ANN CONSUELO	68	1993
DO IT FOR LOVE [C] 4MANDU	45	1996
DO IT LIKE YOU LIKE STANDS	28	2005
DO IT NOW BRAINBASHERS	64	2000
DO IT PROPERLY ('NO WAY BACK')/NO WAY BACK ADONIS FEATURING 2 PUERTO RICANS, A BLACK MAN & A DOMINICAN	47	1987
DO IT TO IT CHERISH FEATURING SEAN PAUL	30	2006
DO IT TO ME LIONEL RICHIE	33	1992
DO IT TO ME AGAIN SOULSEARCHER	32	2000
DO IT TO THE CROWD TWIN HYPE	65	1989
DO IT TO THE MUSIC RAW SILK	18	1982
DO IT 2 ME CUSHH	31	2007
DO IT WELL JENNIFER LOPEZ	11	2007
DO IT WITH MADONNA ANDROIDS	15	2003
DO IT YOURSELF (GO OUT AND GET IT) UNITING NATIONS	64	2007
DO ME BELL BIV DEVOE	56	1990
DO ME RIGHT INNER CITY	47	1996
DO ME WRONG MEL BLATT	18	2003
DO MY THING BUSTA RHYMES	39	1997
DO NO WRONG THIRTEEN SENSES	38	2004
DO NOT DISTURB BANANARAMA	31	1985
DO NOT PASS ME BY HAMMER	14	1992
DO NOTHING SPECIALS	4	1980
DO OR DIE SUPER FURRY ANIMALS	20	2000
DO RE ME SO FAR SO GOOD CARTER-THE UNSTOPPABLE SEX MACHINE	22	1992
DO SOMETHING [A] MACY GRAY	51	1999
DO SOMETHIN' [B] BRITNEY SPEARS	6	2005
DO THAT THANG MASAI	42	2003
DO THAT TO ME LISA MARIE EXPERIENCE	33	1996
DO THAT TO ME ONE MORE TIME CAPTAIN & TENNILLE	7	1980
DO THE BARTMAN SIMPSONS	1	1991
DO THE BIRD DEE DEE SHARP	46	1963
DO THE BIRD VERNONS GIRLS	44	1963
DO THE CAN CAN SKANDI GIRLS	38	2005
DO THE CLAM ELVIS PRESLEY	19	1965
DO THE CONGA BLACK LACE	10	1984
DO THE FUNKY CHICKEN RUFUS THOMAS	18	1970
(DO) THE HUCKLEBUCK COAST TO COAST	5	1981
DO THE LOLLIPOP TWEENIES	17	2001
DO THE RIGHT THING [A] REDHEAD KINGPIN & THE FBI	13	1989
DO THE RIGHT THING [B] IAN WRIGHT	43	1993
(DO THE) SPANISH HUSTLE FATBACK BAND	10	1976
DO THEY KNOW IT'S CHRISTMAS? BAND AID	1	1984
DO THEY KNOW IT'S CHRISTMAS? BAND AID II	1	1989
DO THEY KNOW IT'S CHRISTMAS? BAND AID 20	1	2004
DO THIS! DO THAT! FREEFALLER	8	2005
DO THIS MY WAY KID 'N' PLAY	48	1988
DO U FEEL 4 ME EDEN	51	1993
DO U KNOW WHERE YOU'RE COMING FROM M-BEAT FEATURING JAMIROQUAI	12	1996
DO U STILL? EAST 17	7	1996
DO U WANNA FUNK SPACE 2000	50	1995
DO WAH DIDDY DJ OTZI	9	2001
DO WAH DIDDY DIDDY MANFRED MANN	1	1964
DO WAH DIDDY DIDDY BLUE MELONS	70	1996
DO WATCHA DO HYPER GO GO & ADEVA	54	1996
DO WE ROCK POINT BREAK	29	1999
DO WHAT WE WOULD ACZESS	65	2001
DO WHAT YOU DO [A] JERMAINE JACKSON	6	1985
DO WHAT YOU DO [B] ANNABELLA LWIN	61	1995

Title / Artist	Peak Position	Year of Entry
DO WHAT YOU DO (EARWORM SONG) CLINT BOON EXPERIENCE	63	2000
DO WHAT YOU DO WELL NED MILLER	48	1965
DO WHAT YOU FEEL [A] JOEY NEGRO	36	1991
DO WHAT YOU FEEL [B] JOHNNA	43	1996
DO WHAT YOU GOTTA DO NINA SIMONE	2	1968
DO WHAT YOU GOTTA DO FOUR TOPS	11	1969
DO WHAT YOU WANNA DO T-CONNECTION	11	1977
DO WHAT'S GOOD FOR ME 2 UNLIMITED	16	1995
DO WITHOUT MY LOVE NATHAN	44	2007
DO YA INNER CITY	44	1994
DO YA DO YA (WANNA PLEASE ME) SAMANTHA FOX	10	1986
DO YA WANNA GET FUNKY WITH ME PETER BROWN	43	1978
DO YOU BELIEVE IN LOVE [A] HUEY LEWIS & THE NEWS	9	1986
DO YOU BELIEVE IN LOVE [B] UNATION	75	1993
DO YOU BELIEVE IN LOVE [C] ULTRA-SONIC	47	1996
DO YOU BELIEVE IN MIRACLES SLADE	54	1985
DO YOU BELIEVE IN SHAME DURAN DURAN	30	1989
DO YOU BELIEVE IN THE WESTWORLD THEATRE OF HATE	40	1982
DO YOU BELIEVE IN THE WONDER JEANIE TRACY	57	1994
DO YOU BELIEVE IN US JON SECADA	30	1992
DO YOU DREAM IN COLOUR? BILL NELSON	52	1980
DO YOU EVER THINK OF ME? ANTONY COSTA	19	2006
DO YOU FEEL LIKE I FEEL BELINDA CARLISLE	29	1991
DO YOU FEEL LIKE WE DO PETER FRAMPTON	39	1976
DO YOU FEEL ME? (...FREAK YOU) MEN OF VIZION	36	1999
DO YOU FEEL MY LOVE EDDY GRANT	8	1980
DO YOU KNOW [A] SECRET AFFAIR	57	1981
DO YOU KNOW [B] MICHELLE GAYLE	6	1997
DO YOU KNOW (I GO CRAZY) ANGEL CITY	8	2004
DO YOU KNOW (THE PING PONG SONG) ENRIQUE IGLESIAS	3	2007
DO YOU KNOW THE WAY TO SAN JOSE DIONNE WARWICK	8	1968
DO YOU KNOW (WHAT IT TAKES) ROBYN	26	1997
DO YOU LIKE IT KINGDOM COME	73	1989
DO YOU LOVE ME [A] BRIAN POOLE & THE TREMELOES	1	1963
DO YOU LOVE ME [A] DAVE CLARK FIVE	30	1963
DO YOU LOVE ME [A] DEEP FEELING	34	1970
DO YOU LOVE ME [A] DUKE BAYSEE	46	1995
DO YOU LOVE ME [A] MADEMOISELLE	56	2001
DO YOU LOVE ME [B] NICK CAVE & THE BAD SEEDS	68	1994
DO YOU LOVE ME BOY? KERRI-ANN	58	1998
DO YOU LOVE ME LIKE YOU SAY TERENCE TRENT D'ARBY	14	1993
DO YOU LOVE WHAT YOU FEEL INNER CITY	16	1989
DO YOU MIND ANTHONY NEWLEY	1	1960
DO YOU REALISE FLAMING LIPS	32	2002
DO YOU REALLY LIKE IT DJ PIED PIPER & THE MASTERS OF CEREMONIES	1	2001
(DO YOU REALLY LOVE ME) TELL ME LOVE MICHAEL WYCOFF	60	1983
DO YOU REALLY LOVE ME TOO BILLY FURY	13	1964
DO YOU REALLY WANT ME [A] JON SECADA	30	1993
DO YOU REALLY WANT ME [B] ROBYN	20	1998
DO YOU REALLY (WANT MY LOVE) JUNIOR	47	1985
DO YOU REALLY WANT TO HURT ME CULTURE CLUB	43	1982
DO YOU REMEMBER SCAFFOLD	34	1968
DO YOU REMEMBER HOUSE BLAZE FEATURING PALMER BROWN	55	2002
DO YOU REMEMBER (LIVE) PHIL COLLINS	57	1990
DO YOU REMEMBER ROCK 'N' ROLL RADIO RAMONES	54	1980
DO YOU REMEMBER THE FIRST TIME PULP	33	1994
DO YOU SEE WARREN G	29	1995
DO YOU SEE THE LIGHT SNAP VS PLAYTHING	14	2002
DO YOU SEE THE LIGHT (LOOKING FOR) SNAP FEATURING NIKI HARIS	10	1993
DO YOU SLEEP? LISA LOEB & NINE STORIES	45	1995
DO YOU THINK ABOUT US TOTAL	49	1997
DO YOU THINK YOU'RE SPECIAL? NIO	52	2003
DO YOU UNDERSTAND ALMIGHTY	38	1996
DO YOU WANNA DANCE [A] CLIFF RICHARD & THE SHADOWS	2	1962
DO YOU WANNA DANCE [B] BARRY BLUE	7	1973
DO YOU WANNA FUNK SYLVESTER WITH PATRICK COWLEY	32	1982
DO YOU WANNA GET FUNKY C & C MUSIC FACTORY	27	1994
DO YOU WANNA GO OUR WAY??? PUBLIC ENEMY	66	1999
DO YOU WANNA HOLD ME? BOW WOW WOW	47	1983
DO YOU WANNA PARTY DJ SCOTT FEATURING LORNA B	36	1995
DO YOU WANNA TOUCH ME (OH YEAH!) GARY GLITTER	2	1973
DO YOU WANT IT RIGHT NOW DEGREES OF MOTION FEATURING BITI	26	1992
DO YOU WANT ME [A] SALT-N-PEPA	5	1991
DO YOU WANT ME [B] Q-TEX	48	1996
DO YOU WANT ME? [C] LEILANI	40	1999
DO YOU WANT ME TO FOUR PENNIES	47	1964
DO YOU WANT TO FRANZ FERDINAND	4	2005
DO YOU WANT TO KNOW A SECRET? BILLY J. KRAMER & THE DAKOTAS	2	1963
DO YOUR DANCE ROSE ROYCE	30	1977
DO YOUR THING BASEMENT JAXX	32	2005
DOA FOO FIGHTERS	25	2005
THE DOCTOR DOOBIE BROTHERS	73	1989
DR BEAT MIAMI SOUND MACHINE	6	1984
DOCTOR DOCTOR [A] UFO	35	1979
DOCTOR DOCTOR [B] THOMPSON TWINS	3	1984
DR FEELGOOD MOTLEY CRUE	50	1989
DR FINLAY ANDY STEWART	43	1965
DR GREENTHUMB CYPRESS HILL	34	1999
DR HECKYLL AND MR. JIVE MEN AT WORK	31	1983
DR JACKYLL AND MISTER FUNK JACKIE McLEAN	53	1979
DOCTOR JEEP SISTERS OF MERCY	37	1990
DOCTOR JONES AQUA	1	1998
DR KISS KISS 5000 VOLTS	8	1976
DR LOVE TINA CHARLES	4	1976
DR MABUSE PROPAGANDA	27	1984
DOCTOR MY EYES JACKSON 5	9	1973
DOCTOR PRESSURE MYLO VS MIAMI SOUND MACHINE	3	2005
DR STEIN HELLOWEEN	57	1988
DR WHO MANKIND	25	1978
DOCTORIN' THE HOUSE COLDCUT FEATURING YAZZ & THE PLASTIC POPULATION	6	1988
DOCTORIN' THE TARDIS TIMELORDS	1	1988
DOCTOR'S ORDERS SUNNY	7	1974
DOES HE LOVE YOU REBA McENTIRE	62	1999
DOES IT FEEL GOOD B.T. EXPRESS	52	1980
DOES IT FEEL GOOD TO YOU DJ CARL COX	35	1992
DOES SHE HAVE A FRIEND GENE CHANDLER	28	1980
DOES THAT RING A BELL DYNASTY	53	1983
DOES THIS HURT BOO RADLEYS	67	1992
DOES THIS TRAIN STOP ON MERSEYSIDE AMSTERDAM	53	2005
DOES YOUR CHEWING GUM LOSE IT'S FLAVOUR LONNIE DONEGAN	3	1959
DOES YOUR HEART GO BOOM HELEN LOVE	71	1997
DOES YOUR MOTHER KNOW ABBA	4	1979
DOESN'T ANYBODY KNOW MY NAME? VINCE HILL	50	1969
DOESN'T REALLY MATTER JANET JACKSON	5	2000
DOG DADA	71	1993
DOG EAT DOG ADAM & THE ANTS	4	1980
DOG ON WHEELS BELLE & SEBASTIAN	59	1997
DOG TRAIN LEVELLERS	24	1997
DOGGY DOGG WORLD SNOOP DOGGY DOGG	32	1994
DOGMAN GO WOOF UNDERWORLD	63	1993
DOGMONAUT 2000 (IS THERE ANYONE OUT THERE) FRIJID VINEGAR	53	1999
DOGS WHO	25	1968
DOGS OF LUST THE THE	25	1993
DOGS OF WAR EXPLOITED	63	1981
DOGS WITH NO TAILS PALE	51	1992
DOGZ N SLEDGEZ MILLION DAN	66	2003
DOIN' IT [A] LL COOL J	15	1996
DOIN' IT [B] LIBERTY	14	2001
DOIN' IT IN A HAUNTED HOUSE YVONNE GAGE	45	1984
DOIN' OUR OWN DANG JUNGLE BROTHERS	33	1990
DOIN' OUR THING PHOEBE ONE	59	1998
DOIN' THE DO BETTY BOO	7	1990
DOING ALRIGHT WITH THE BOYS GARY GLITTER	6	1975
DOING IT RIGHT THE GO! TEAM	55	2007
DOLCE VITA RYAN PARIS	5	1983
DOLL HOUSE KING BROTHERS	21	1961
DOLL PARTS HOLE	16	1995
DOLLAR BILL SCREAMING TREES	52	1993
DOLLAR IN THE TEETH UPSETTERS	5	1969
DOLLARS C.J. LEWIS	34	1994
DOLLARS IN THE HEAVENS GENEVA	59	1999
DOLLS PRIMAL SCREAM	40	2006
DOLLY MY LOVE MOMENTS	10	1975
DOLPHIN SHED SEVEN	28	1994
THE DOLPHINS CRY LIVE	62	2000
DOLPHINS MAKE ME CRY MARTYN JOSEPH	34	1992
DOLPHINS WERE MONKEYS IAN BROWN	5	2000
DOMINATION WAY OUT WEST	38	1996
DOMINATOR HUMAN RESOURCE	36	1991
DOMINION SISTERS OF MERCY	13	1988
DOMINIQUE SINGING NUN	7	1963
DOMINO DANCING PET SHOP BOYS	7	1988
DOMINOES ROBBIE NEVIL	26	1987
DOMINOID MOLOKO	65	1996
THE DON 187 LOCKDOWN	29	1998
THE DON THE VIEW	33	2007
DON GARGON COMIN' PROJECT 1	64	1992
DON JUAN DAVE DEE, DOZY, BEAKY, MICK & TICH	23	1969
DON QUIXOTE NIK KERSHAW	10	1985
DONALD WHERE'S YOUR TROOSERS ANDY STEWART	4	1960
DONKEY CART FRANK CHACKSFIELD	26	1956
DONNA [A] MARTY WILDE	3	1959
DONNA [A] RITCHIE VALENS	29	1959
DONNA [B] 10 C.C.	2	1972
DON'T [A] ELVIS PRESLEY	2	1958
DON'T [B] SHANIA TWAIN	30	2005
DON'T ANSWER ME [A] CILLA BLACK	6	1966
DON'T ANSWER ME [B] ALAN PARSONS PROJECT	58	1984
DON'T ARGUE CABARET VOLTAIRE	69	1987
DON'T ASK ME PUBLIC IMAGE LTD.	22	1990
DON'T ASK ME WHY EURYTHMICS	25	1989
DON'T BE A DUMMY JOHN DU CANN	33	1979
DON'T BE A FOOL LOOSE ENDS	13	1990
DON'T BE A STRANGER DINA CARROLL	3	1993
DON'T BE AFRAID [A] AARON HALL	56	1992
DON'T BE AFRAID [B] MOONMAN	41	1997
DON'T BE CRUEL [A] BILL BLACK'S COMBO	32	1960

	Peak Position	Year of Entry
DON'T BE CRUEL [A] BILLY SWAN	42	1975
DON'T BE CRUEL [A] ELVIS PRESLEY	24	1978
DON'T BE CRUEL [B] BOBBY BROWN	13	1988
DON'T BE STUPID (YOU KNOW I LOVE YOU) SHANIA TWAIN	5	2000
DON'T BELIEVE A WORD THIN LIZZY	12	1977
DON'T BELIEVE THE HYPE MISTA E	41	1988
DON'T BELIEVE THE HYPE PUBLIC ENEMY	18	1988
DON'T BET MONEY HONEY LINDA SCOTT	50	1961
DON'T BLAME IT ON LOVE SHAKATAK	55	1984
DON'T BLAME IT ON THAT GIRL MATT BIANCO	11	1988
DON'T BLAME ME EVERLY BROTHERS	20	1961
DON'T BLAME ME FRANK IFIELD	8	1964
DON'T BOTHER SHAKIRA	9	2006
DON'T BREAK MY HEART UB40	3	1985
DON'T BREAK MY HEART AGAIN WHITESNAKE	17	1981
DON'T BREAK THE HEART THAT LOVES YOU CONNIE FRANCIS	39	1962
DON'T BRING HARRY (EP) STRANGLERS	41	1979
DON'T BRING LULU DOROTHY PROVINE	17	1961
DON'T BRING ME DOWN [A] PRETTY THINGS	10	1964
DON'T BRING ME DOWN [B] ANIMALS	6	1966
DON'T BRING ME DOWN [C] ELECTRIC LIGHT ORCHESTRA	3	1979
DON'T BRING ME DOWN [D] SPIRITS	31	1994
DON'T BRING ME YOUR HEARTACHES PAUL & BARRY RYAN	13	1965
DON'T CALL ME BABY [A] VOICE OF THE BEEHIVE	15	1988
DON'T CALL ME BABY [B] MADISON AVENUE	1	1999
DON'T CARE [A] KLARK KENT	48	1978
DON'T CARE [B] ANGELS REVERSE	71	2002
DON'T CARE [C] RICKY MARTIN	11	2005
DON'T CARE WHO KNOWS KEISHA WHITE	29	2005
DON'T CHA PUSSYCAT DOLLS FEATURING BUSTA RHYMES	1	2005
DON'T CHA WANNA RIDE JOSS STONE	20	2005
DON'T COME AROUND HERE NO MORE TOM PETTY & THE HEARTBREAKERS	50	1985
DON'T COME CLOSE RAMONES	39	1978
DON'T COME HOME TOO SOON DEL AMITRI	15	1998
DON'T COME TO STAY HOT HOUSE	70	1987
DON'T CRY [A] ASIA	33	1983
DON'T CRY [B] BOY GEORGE	60	1988
DON'T CRY [C] GUNS N' ROSES	8	1991
DON'T CRY [D] SEAL	51	1995
DON'T CRY DADDY ELVIS PRESLEY	8	1970
DON'T CRY FOR ME ARGENTINA JULIE COVINGTON	1	1976
DON'T CRY FOR ME ARGENTINA SHADOWS	5	1979
DON'T CRY FOR ME ARGENTINA SINEAD O'CONNOR	53	1992
DON'T CRY FOR ME ARGENTINA MADONNA	3	1996
DON'T CRY FOR ME ARGENTINA MIKE FLOWERS POPS	30	1996
DON'T CRY OUT LOUD ELKIE BROOKS	12	1978
DON'T DANCE MIDAS	59	2007
DON'T DIE JUST YET DAVID HOLMES	33	1998
DON'T DO IT BABY MAC & KATIE KISSOON	9	1975
DON'T DO THAT [A] GEORDIE	32	1972
DON'T DO THAT [B] YOUNG & MOODY BAND	63	1981
DON'T DON'T TELL ME NO SOPHIE B. HAWKINS	36	1994
DON'T DREAM DOVE	37	1999
DON'T DREAM IT'S OVER CROWDED HOUSE	25	1987
DON'T DREAM IT'S OVER PAUL YOUNG	20	1991
DON'T DRIVE DRUNK STEVIE WONDER	62	1984
DON'T DRIVE MY CAR STATUS QUO	11	1980
DON'T DROP BOMBS LIZA MINNELLI	46	1989
DON'T EVER CHANGE CRICKETS	5	1962
DON'T EVER THINK (TOO MUCH) ZUTONS	15	2004
DON'T FALL IN LOVE (I SAID) TOYAH	22	1985
DON'T FALTER MINT ROYALE FEATURING LAUREN LAVERNE	15	2000
(DON'T FEAR) THE REAPER BLUE OYSTER CULT	16	1978
(DON'T FEAR) THE REAPER APOLLO 440	35	1995
DON'T FIGHT IT WILSON PICKETT	29	1965
DON'T FIGHT IT FEEL IT PRIMAL SCREAM FEATURING DENISE JOHNSON	41	1991
DON'T FORBID ME PAT BOONE	2	1957
DON'T FORGET ABOUT US MARIAH CAREY	11	2005
DON'T FORGET ME (WHEN I'M GONE) GLASS TIGER	29	1986
DON'T FORGET TO CATCH ME CLIFF RICHARD	21	1968
DON'T FORGET TO DANCE KINKS	58	1983
DON'T FORGET TO REMEMBER BEE GEES	2	1968
DON'T GET ME WRONG PRETENDERS	10	1986
(DON'T) GIVE HATE A CHANCE JAMIROQUAI	27	2005
DON'T GIVE IT UP [A] SONIC SURFERS	54	1994
DON'T GIVE IT UP [B] LEMAR	21	2005
DON'T GIVE IT UP [C] SIOBHAN DONAGHY	45	2007
DON'T GIVE ME UP HAROLD MELVIN & THE BLUENOTES	59	1984
DON'T GIVE ME YOUR LIFE ALEX PARTY	2	1995
DON'T GIVE UP [A] PETER GABRIEL & KATE BUSH	9	1986
DON'T GIVE UP [B] MICHELLE WEEKS	28	1997
DON'T GIVE UP [C] CHICANE FEATURING BRYAN ADAMS	1	2000
DON'T GIVE UP [D] NOISETTES	73	2006
DON'T GIVE UP ON US BABY DAVID SOUL	1	1976
DON'T GO [A] JUDAS PRIEST	51	1981
DON'T GO [B] YAZOO	3	1982
DON'T GO [B] LIZZY MACK	52	1995
DON'T GO [C] HOTHOUSE FLOWERS	11	1988
DON'T GO [D] AWESOME 3 FEATURING JULIE McDERMOTT	27	1992
DON'T GO [D] THIRD DIMENSION FEATURING JULIE McDERMOTT	34	1996
DON'T GO [E] DUALERS	61	2006
DON'T GO BREAKING MY HEART ELTON JOHN & KIKI DEE	1	1976
DON'T GO BREAKING MY HEART ELTON JOHN WITH RuPAUL	7	1994
DON'T GO MESSIN' WITH MY HEART MANTRONIX	22	1991
DON'T HANG UP ORLONS	39	1963
DON'T HOLD BACK CHANSON	33	1979
DON'T HURT YOURSELF MARILLION	16	2004
DON'T IT MAKE MY BROWN EYES BLUE CRYSTAL GAYLE	5	1977
DON'T IT MAKE YOU FEEL GOOD STEFAN DENNIS	16	1989
DON'T JUMP OFF THE ROOF DAD TOMMY COOPER	40	1961
DON'T KILL IT CAROL MANFRED MANN'S EARTH BAND	45	1979
DON'T KILL THE WHALE YES	36	1978
DON'T KNOCK IT (UNTIL YOU TRY IT) BOBBY NUNN	65	1984
DON'T KNOCK THE ROCK BILL HALEY & HIS COMETS	7	1957
DON'T KNOW MUCH LINDA RONSTADT & AARON NEVILLE	2	1989
DON'T KNOW WHAT TO TELL YA AALIYAH	22	2003
DON'T KNOW WHAT YOU GOT CINDERELLA	54	1989
DON'T KNOW WHY NORAH JONES	59	2002
DON'T LAUGH WINX	38	1995
DON'T LAUGH AT ME NORMAN WISDOM	3	1954
DON'T LEAVE FAITHLESS	21	1996
DON'T LEAVE HOME DIDO	25	2004
DON'T LEAVE ME [A] BLACKstreet	6	1997
DON'T LEAVE ME [B] MALANDRA BURROWS	54	1998
DON'T LEAVE ME BEHIND EVERYTHING BUT THE GIRL	72	1986
DON'T LEAVE ME THIS WAY HAROLD MELVIN & THE BLUENOTES	5	1977
DON'T LEAVE ME THIS WAY THELMA HOUSTON	13	1977
DON'T LEAVE ME THIS WAY COMMUNARDS WITH SARAH-JANE MORRIS	1	1986
DON'T LET 'EM GRIND YOU DOWN EXPLOITED & ANTI-PASTI	70	1981
DON'T LET GO [A] MANHATTAN TRANSFER	32	1977
DON'T LET GO [B] DAVID SNEDDON	3	2003
DON'T LET GO (LOVE) EN VOGUE	5	1997
DON'T LET GO THE COAT WHO	47	1981
DON'T LET HIM STEAL YOUR HEART AWAY PHIL COLLINS	45	1983
DON'T LET HIM TOUCH YOU ANGELETTES	35	1972
DON'T LET HIM WASTE YOUR TIME JARVIS COCKER	36	2007
DON'T LET IT DIE HURRICANE SMITH	2	1971
DON'T LET IT END STYX	56	1983
DON'T LET IT FADE AWAY DARTS	18	1978
DON'T LET IT GET YOU DOWN ECHO & THE BUNNYMEN	50	1997
DON'T LET IT GO TO WASTE MATT WILLIS	19	2006
DON'T LET IT GO TO YOUR HEAD BRAND NEW HEAVIES FEATURING N'DEA DAVENPORT	24	1992
DON'T LET IT PASS YOU BY UB40	16	1981
DON'T LET IT SHOW ON YOUR FACE ADEVA	34	1992
DON'T LET LOVE GET YOU DOWN ARCHIE BELL & THE DRELLS	49	1986
DON'T LET ME BE MISUNDERSTOOD ANIMALS	3	1965
DON'T LET ME BE MISUNDERSTOOD SANTA ESMERALDA & LEROY GOMEZ	41	1977
DON'T LET ME BE MISUNDERSTOOD COSTELLO SHOW FEATURING THE CONFEDERATES	33	1986
DON'T LET ME BE MISUNDERSTOOD JOE COCKER	53	1996
DON'T LET ME BE THE LAST TO KNOW BRITNEY SPEARS	12	2001
DON'T LET ME DOWN [A] FARM	36	1991
DON'T LET ME DOWN [B] WILL YOUNG	2	2002
DON'T LET ME DOWN GENTLY WONDER STUFF	19	1989
DON'T LET ME GET ME P!NK	6	2002
DON'T LET NOBODY HOLD YOU DOWN LJ REYNOLDS	53	1984
DON'T LET THE FEELING GO NIGHTCRAWLERS	13	1995
DON'T LET THE MORNING COME SOUL AVENGERZ FEATURING JAVINE	49	2006
DON'T LET THE RAIN COME DOWN RONNIE HILTON	21	1964
DON'T LET THE STARS GET IN YOUR EYES PERRY COMO WITH THE RAMBLERS	1	1953
DON'T LET THE SUN CATCH YOU CRYING GERRY & THE PACEMAKERS	6	1964
DON'T LET THE SUN GO DOWN ON ME ELTON JOHN	16	1974
DON'T LET THE SUN GO DOWN ON ME GEORGE MICHAEL & ELTON JOHN	1	1991
DON'T LET THE SUN GO DOWN ON ME OLETA ADAMS	33	1991
DON'T LET THEM ASHANTI	38	2005
DON'T LET THIS MOMENT END GLORIA ESTEFAN	28	1999
DON'T LIE [A] SINCLAIR	70	1994
DON'T LIE [B] BLACK EYED PEAS	6	2005
DON'T LISTEN TO THE RADIO VINES	66	2006

Title / Artist	Peak Position	Year of Entry
DON'T LOOK ANY FURTHER DENNIS EDWARDS FEATURING SIEDAH GARRETT	45	1984
DON'T LOOK ANY FURTHER KANE GANG	52	1988
DON'T LOOK ANY FURTHER M PEOPLE	9	1993
DON'T LOOK AT ME THAT WAY CHAKA KHAN	73	1993
DON'T LOOK BACK [A] BOSTON	43	1978
DON'T LOOK BACK [B] FINE YOUNG CANNIBALS	34	1989
DON'T LOOK BACK [C] LLOYD COLE	59	1990
DON'T LOOK BACK [D] LUCIE SILVAS	34	2005
DON'T LOOK BACK IN ANGER OASIS	1	1996
DON'T LOOK BACK IN ANGER WURZELS	59	2002
DON'T LOOK BACK INTO THE SUN LIBERTINES	11	2003
DON'T LOOK DOWN [A] PLANETS	16	1980
DON'T LOOK DOWN [B] MICK RONSON WITH JOE ELLIOTT	55	1994
DON'T LOOK DOWN - THE SEQUEL GO WEST	13	1985
DON'T LOSE THE MAGIC SHAWN CHRISTOPHER	30	1992
DON'T LOSE YOUR TEMPER XTC	32	1980
DON'T LOVE ME TOO HARD NOLANS	14	1982
DON'T LOVE YOU NO MORE CRAIG DAVID	4	2005
DON'T MAKE ME (FALL IN LOVE WITH YOU) BABBITY BLUE	48	1965
DON'T MAKE ME OVER [A] SWINGING BLUE JEANS	31	1966
DON'T MAKE ME OVER [B] SYBIL	19	1989
DON'T MAKE ME WAIT [A] PEECH BOYS	49	1982
DON'T MAKE ME WAIT [B] BOMB THE BASS FEATURING LORRAINE	6	1988
DON'T MAKE ME WAIT [C] LOVELAND FEATURING RACHEL McFARLANE	22	1995
DON'T MAKE ME WAIT [D] 911	10	1996
DON'T MAKE ME WAIT TOO LONG [A] BARRY WHITE	17	1976
DON'T MAKE ME WAIT TOO LONG [B] ROBERTA FLACK	44	1980
DON'T MAKE MY BABY BLUE SHADOWS	10	1965
DON'T MAKE WAVES NOLANS	12	1980
DON'T MARRY HER BEAUTIFUL SOUTH	8	1996
DON'T MATTER AKON	3	2007
DON'T MESS WITH DOCTOR DREAM THOMPSON TWINS	15	1985
DON'T MESS WITH MY MAN [A] LUCY PEARL	20	2000
DON'T MESS WITH MY MAN [B] NIVEA FEATURING BRIAN & BRANDON CASEY	41	2002
DON'T MESS WITH MY MAN [C] BOOTY LUV	11	2007
DON'T MESS WITH THE RADIO NIVEA	75	2002
DON'T MISS THE PARTY LINE BIZZ NIZZ	7	1990
DON'T MISTAKE ME KEISHA WHITE	48	2006
DON'T MUG YOURSELF STREETS	21	2002
DON'T NEED A GUN BILLY IDOL	26	1987
DON'T NEED THE SUN TO SHINE (TO MAKE ME SMILE) GABRIELLE	9	2001
DON'T PANIC [A] LIQUID GOLD	42	1981
DON'T PANIC [B] LOGO FEATURING DAWN JOSEPH	42	2001
DON'T PAY THE FERRYMAN CHRIS DE BURGH	48	1982
DON'T PHUNK WITH MY HEART BLACK EYED PEAS	3	2005
DON'T PLAY NICE VERBALICIOUS	11	2005
DON'T PLAY THAT SONG ARETHA FRANKLIN	13	1970
DON'T PLAY THAT SONG AGAIN NICKI FRENCH	34	2000
DON'T PLAY WITH ME ROZALLA	50	1993
DON'T PLAY YOUR ROCK 'N' ROLL TO ME SMOKEY	8	1975
DON'T PULL YOUR LOVE SEAN MAGUIRE	14	1996
DON'T PUSH IT RUTH JOY	66	1989
DON'T PUSH IT, DON'T FORCE IT LEON HAYWOOD	12	1980
DON'T PUT YOUR SPELL ON ME IAN McNABB	72	1996
DON'T QUIT CARON WHEELER	53	1991
DON'T RUSH (TAKE LOVE SLOWLY) K-CI & JOJO	16	1998
DON'T SAY GOODBYE PAULINA RUBIO	68	2002
DON'T SAY I TOLD YOU SO TOURISTS	40	1980
DON'T SAY IT'S LOVE JOHNNY HATES JAZZ	48	1988
DON'T SAY IT'S OVER GUN	19	1994
DON'T SAY THAT'S JUST FOR WHITE BOYS WAY OF THE WEST	54	1981
DON'T SAY YOU LOVE ME [A] M2M	16	2000
DON'T SAY YOU LOVE ME [B] ERASURE	15	2005
DON'T SAY YOUR LOVE IS KILLING ME ERASURE	23	1997
DON'T SET ME FREE RAY CHARLES	37	1963
DON'T SHED A TEAR PAUL CARRACK	60	1989
DON'T SHOOT ME SANTA KILLERS	34	2007
DON'T SING PREFAB SPROUT	62	1984
DON'T SLEEP IN THE SUBWAY PETULA CLARK	12	1967
DON'T SLOW DOWN UB40	16	1981
DON'T SPEAK CLUELESS	61	1997
DON'T SPEAK NO DOUBT	1	1997
DON'T STAND SO CLOSE TO ME POLICE	1	1980
DON'T STAY AWAY TOO LONG PETERS & LEE	3	1974
DON'T STEAL OUR SUN THRILLS	45	2003
DON'T STOP [A] FLEETWOOD MAC	32	1977
DON'T STOP [A] STATUS QUO	35	1996
DON'T STOP [B] K.I.D.	49	1981
DON'T STOP [C] MOOD	59	1982
DON'T STOP [D] JEFFREY OSBORNE	61	1984
DON'T STOP [E] K-KLASS	32	1992
DON'T STOP [F] HAMMER	72	1994
DON'T STOP [G] RUFF DRIVERZ	30	1998
DON'T STOP [H] NO AUTHORITY	54	1998
DON'T STOP [I] ATB	3	1999
DON'T STOP [J] ROLLING STONES	36	2002
DON'T STOP BELIEVIN' JOURNEY	62	1982
DON'T STOP FUNKIN' 4 JAMAICA MARIAH CAREY	32	2002
DON'T STOP IT NOW HOT CHOCOLATE	11	1976
DON'T STOP (JAMMIN') L.A. MIX	47	1987
DON'T STOP LOVIN' ME BABY PINKERTON'S ASSORTED COLOURS	50	1966
DON'T STOP ME NOW [A] QUEEN	9	1979
DON'T STOP ME NOW [B] McFLY	1	2006
DON'T STOP MOVIN' [A] LIVIN' JOY	5	1996
DON'T STOP MOVIN' [B] S CLUB 7	1	2001
DON'T STOP NOW [A] GENE FARROW & G.F. BAND	71	1978
DON'T STOP NOW [B] CROWDED HOUSE	41	2007
DON'T STOP THAT CRAZY RHYTHM MODERN ROMANCE	14	1983
DON'T STOP THE CARNIVAL ALAN PRICE SET	13	1968
DON'T STOP THE DANCE BRYAN FERRY	21	1985
DON'T STOP THE FEELING ROY AYERS	56	1980
DON'T STOP THE MUSIC [A] YARBOROUGH & PEOPLES	7	1981
DON'T STOP THE MUSIC [B] LIONEL RICHIE	34	2000
DON'T STOP THE MUSIC [C] RIHANNA	4	2007
DON'T STOP 'TIL YOU GET ENOUGH MICHAEL JACKSON	3	1979
DON'T STOP TWIST FRANKIE VAUGHAN	22	1962
DON'T STOP (WIGGLE WIGGLE) OUTHERE BROTHERS	1	1995
DON'T TAKE AWAY THE MUSIC TAVARES	4	1976
DON'T TAKE IT LYIN' DOWN DOOLEYS	60	1978
DON'T TAKE IT PERSONAL JERMAINE JACKSON	69	1989
DON'T TAKE IT PERSONAL (JUST ONE OF DEM DAYS) MONICA	32	1995
DON'T TAKE MY KINDNESS FOR WEAKNESS HEADS WITH SHAUN RYDER	60	1996
DON'T TAKE MY MIND ON A TRIP BOY GEORGE	68	1989
DON'T TAKE NO FOR AN ANSWER TOM ROBINSON BAND	18	1978
DON'T TALK [A] HANK MARVIN	49	1982
DON'T TALK [B] JON B	29	2001
DON'T TALK ABOUT LOVE BAD BOYS INC	19	1993
DON'T TALK DIRTY TO ME JERMAINE STEWART	61	1988
DON'T TALK JUST KISS RIGHT SAID FRED. GUEST VOCALS: JOCELYN BROWN	3	1991
DON'T TALK TO HIM CLIFF RICHARD & THE SHADOWS	2	1963
DON'T TALK TO ME ABOUT LOVE ALTERED IMAGES	7	1983
DON'T TELL ME [A] CENTRAL LINE	55	1982
DON'T TELL ME [B] BLANCMANGE	8	1984
DON'T TELL ME [C] VAN HALEN	27	1995
DON'T TELL ME [D] MADONNA	4	2000
DON'T TELL ME [E] AVRIL LAVIGNE	5	2004
DON'T TELL ME LIES BREATHE	45	1989
DON'T TELL ME YOU'RE SORRY S CLUB 8	11	2004
DON'T TEST JUNIOR TUCKER	54	1990
DON'T THAT BEAT ALL ADAM FAITH	8	1962
DON'T THINK I'M NOT KANDI	9	2000
DON'T THINK IT (FEEL IT) LANGE FEATURING LEAH	59	2003
DON'T THINK THE WAY THEY DO SPAN	52	2004
DON'T THINK YOU'RE THE FIRST CORAL	10	2003
DON'T THROW AWAY ALL THOSE TEARDROPS FRANKIE AVALON	37	1960
DON'T THROW IT ALL AWAY GARY BENSON	20	1975
DON'T THROW YOUR LOVE AWAY SEARCHERS	1	1964
DON'T TREAT ME BAD FIREHOUSE	71	1991
DON'T TREAT ME LIKE A CHILD HELEN SHAPIRO	3	1961
DON'T TRY TO CHANGE ME CRICKETS	37	1963
DON'T TRY TO STOP IT ROMAN HOLIDAY	14	1983
DON'T TURN AROUND [A] MERSEYBEATS	13	1964
DON'T TURN AROUND [B] ASWAD	1	1988
DON'T TURN AROUND [B] ACE OF BASE	5	1994
DON'T WAIT DASHBOARD CONFESSIONAL	68	2006
DON'T WAIT UP THUNDER	27	1997
DON'T WALK BIG SUPREME	58	1986
DON'T WALK AWAY [A] ELECTRIC LIGHT ORCHESTRA	21	1980
DON'T WALK AWAY [B] FOUR TOPS	16	1981
DON'T WALK AWAY [C] PAT BENATAR	42	1988
DON'T WALK AWAY [D] TONI CHILDS	53	1989
DON'T WALK AWAY [E] JADE	7	1993
DON'T WALK AWAY [E] JAVINE	16	2004
DON'T WALK AWAY TILL I TOUCH YOU ELAINE PAIGE	46	1978
DON'T WANNA BE A PLAYER JOE	16	1997
DON'T WANNA BE ALONE TRICIA PENROSE	44	2000
DON'T WANNA FALL IN LOVE JANE CHILD	22	1990
DON'T WANNA KNOW SHY FX/T POWER/DI & SKIBADEE	19	2002
DON'T WANNA LET YOU GO FIVE	9	2000
DON'T WANNA LOSE THIS FEELING DANNII MINOGUE	5	2003
DON'T WANNA LOSE YOU [A] GLORIA ESTEFAN	6	1989
DON'T WANNA LOSE YOU [B] LIONEL RICHIE	17	1996
DON'T WANNA SAY GOODNIGHT KANDIDATE	47	1978
DON'T WANT TO FORGIVE ME NOW WET WET WET	7	1995
DON'T WANT TO WAIT ANYMORE TUBES	60	1981
DON'T WANT YOU BACK ELLIE CAMPBELL	50	2001
DON'T WASTE MY TIME PAUL HARDCASTLE FEATURING CAROL KENYON	8	1986

	Peak Position	Year of Entry
DON'T WASTE YOUR TIME YARBOROUGH & PEOPLES	60	1984
DON'T WORRY [A] JOHNNY BRANDON	18	1955
DON'T WORRY [B] BILLY FURY WITH THE FOUR KESTRELS	40	1961
DON'T WORRY [C] KIM APPLEBY	2	1990
DON'T WORRY [D] NEWTON	61	1997
DON'T WORRY [E] APPLETON	5	2003
DON'T WORRY BABY LOS LOBOS	57	1985
DON'T WORRY BE HAPPY BOBBY McFERRIN	2	1988
DON'T YOU SECOND IMAGE	68	1983
DON'T YOU FORGET ABOUT ME SIMPLE MINDS	7	1985
DON'T YOU FORGET ABOUT ME BEST COMPANY	65	1993
DON'T YOU GET SO MAD JEFFREY OSBORNE	54	1983
DON'T YOU JUST KNOW IT AMAZULU	15	1985
DON'T YOU KNOW BUTTERSCOTCH	17	1970
DON'T YOU KNOW IT ADAM FAITH	12	1961
DON'T YOU LOVE ME [A] 49ERS	12	1990
DON'T YOU LOVE ME [B] ETERNAL	3	1997
DON'T YOU ROCK ME DADDY-O LONNIE DONEGAN	4	1957
DON'T YOU ROCK ME DADDY-O VIPERS SKIFFLE GROUP	10	1957
DON'T YOU THINK IT'S TIME MIKE BERRY WITH THE OUTLAWS	6	1963
DON'T YOU WANNA BE RELEVANT? CRIBS	39	2007
DON'T YOU WANT ME [A] HUMAN LEAGUE	1	1981
DON'T YOU WANT ME BABY [A] MANDY SMITH	59	1989
DON'T YOU WANT ME [A] FARM	18	1992
DON'T YOU WANT ME [B] JODY WATLEY	55	1987
DON'T YOU WANT ME [C] FELIX	6	1992
DON'T YOU WORRY MADASUN	14	2000
DON'T YOU WORRY 'BOUT A THING INCOGNITO	19	1992
DOO WOP (THAT THING) LAURYN HILL	3	1998
DOOBEDOOD'NDOOBE DOOBEDOOD'NDOOBE DIANA ROSS	12	1972
DOODAH CARTOONS	7	1999
DOOMS NIGHT AZZIDO DA BASS	8	2000
DOOMSDAY EVELYN THOMAS	41	1976
DOOP DOOP	1	1994
THE DOOR TURIN BRAKES	67	2001
THE DOOR IS STILL OPEN TO MY HEART DEAN MARTIN	42	1964
DOOR #1 LEVERT SWEAT GILL	45	1998
DOORS OF YOUR HEART BEAT	33	1981
DOOT DOOT FREUR	59	1983
THE DOPE SHOW MARILYN MANSON	12	1998
DOPES TO INFINITY MONSTER MAGNET	58	1995
DOUBLE BARREL DAVE & ANSIL COLLINS	1	1971
DOUBLE DOUBLE DUTCH DOPE SMUGGLAZ	15	1999
DOUBLE DROP FIERCE GIRL	74	2004
DOUBLE DUTCH [A] FATBACK BAND	31	1977
DOUBLE DUTCH [B] MALCOLM McLAREN	3	1983
DOUBLE TROUBLE LYNYRD SKYNYRD	21	1976
DOUBLEBACK ZZ TOP	29	1990
DOVE (I'LL BE LOVING YOU) MOONY	9	2002
DOV'E L'AMORE CHER	21	1999
DOWN BLINK 182	24	2004
DOWN AND UNDER (TOGETHER) KID CRÈME FEATURING MC SHURAKANO	55	2003
DOWN AT THE DOCTOR'S DR FEELGOOD	48	1978
DOWN BOY HOLLY VALANCE	2	2002
DOWN BY THE LAZY RIVER OSMONDS	40	1972
DOWN BY THE WATER PJ HARVEY	38	1995
DOWN DEEP INSIDE (THEME FROM *THE DEEP*) DONNA SUMMER	5	1977
DOWN DOWN STATUS QUO	1	1974
DOWN DOWN DOWN GAMBAFREAKS	57	2000
DOWN FOR THE ONE BEVERLEY KNIGHT	55	1995
DOWN 4 U IRV GOTTI FEATURING ASHANTI, CHARLI BALTIMORE & VITA	4	2002
DOWN 4 WHATEVA NUTTIN' NYCE	62	1995
DOWN IN A HOLE ALICE IN CHAINS	36	1993
DOWN IN THE BOONDOCKS BILLY JOE ROYAL	38	1965
DOWN IN THE SUBWAY SOFT CELL	24	1984
DOWN IN THE TUBE STATION AT MIDNIGHT JAM	15	1978
DOWN LOW (NOBODY HAS TO KNOW) R KELLY FEATURING RONALD ISLEY	23	1996
DOWN ON THE BEACH TONIGHT DRIFTERS	7	1974
DOWN ON THE CORNER CREEDENCE CLEARWATER REVIVAL	31	1970
DOWN ON THE STREET SHAKATAK	9	1984
DOWN SO LONG JEWEL	38	1999
DOWN THAT ROAD SHARA NELSON	19	1993
DOWN THE DRAIN STAKKA BO	64	1993
DOWN THE DUSTPIPE STATUS QUO	12	1970
DOWN THE HALL FOUR SEASONS	34	1977
DOWN THE RIVER NILE JOHN LEYTON	42	1962
DOWN THE WIRE ASAP	67	1990
DOWN TO EARTH [A] CURIOSITY KILLED THE CAT	3	1987
DOWN TO EARTH [B] MONIE LOVE	31	1990
DOWN TO EARTH [C] GRACE	20	1996
DOWN TO THE SEA TIM BOOTH	68	2004
DOWN TO THE WIRE GHOST DANCE	66	1989
DOWN UNDER MEN AT WORK	1	1983
DOWN WITH THE CLIQUE AALIYAH	33	1995
DOWN WITH THE KING RUN D.M.C.	69	1993
DOWN YONDER JOHNNY & THE HURRICANES	8	1960
DOWNHEARTED EDDIE FISHER	3	1953
DOWNING STREET KINDLING LARRIKIN LOVE	35	2006
DOWNLOAD IT CLEA	21	2003
DOWNTOWN EMMA BUNTON	3	2006
DOWNTOWN PEACHES	50	2006
DOWNTOWN [A] PETULA CLARK	2	1964
DOWNTOWN [B] ONE 2 MANY	43	1988
DOWNTOWN [C] SWV	19	1994
THE DOWNTOWN LIGHTS BLUE NILE	67	1989
DOWNTOWN TRAIN ROD STEWART	10	1990
DOWNTOWN VENUS PM DAWN	58	1995
DRACULA'S TANGO TOTO COELO	54	1982
DRAG ME DOWN BOOMTOWN RATS	50	1984
DRAGGING ME DOWN INSPIRAL CARPETS	12	1992
DRAGNET RAY ANTHONY	7	1953
DRAGNET TED HEATH	9	1953
DRAGNET ART OF NOISE	60	1987
DRAGON POWER JKD BAND	58	1978
DRAGONFLY TORNADOS	41	1963
DRAGOSTEA DIN TEI O-ZONE	3	2004
DRAGULA ROB ZOMBIE	44	1998
DRAIN THE BLOOD DISTILLERS	51	2003
DRAMA! ERASURE	4	1989
DRAMA QUEEN SWITCHES	61	2007
DRAW OF THE CARDS KIM CARNES	49	1981
(DRAWING) RINGS AROUND THE WORLD SUPER FURRY ANIMALS	28	2001
DRAWING SHAPES MORNING RUNNER	70	2005
DRE DAY DR DRE	59	1994
DREADLOCK HOLIDAY 10 C.C.	1	1978
THE DREAM [A] DREAM FREQUENCY	67	1994
DREAM [B] DIZZEE RASCAL	14	2004
DREAM A LIE UB40	10	1980
DREAM A LITTLE DREAM OF ME ANITA HARRIS	33	1968
DREAM A LITTLE DREAM OF ME MAMA CASS	11	1968
DREAM ABOUT YOU D'BORA	75	1991
DREAM ANOTHER DREAM RIALTO	39	1998
DREAM BABY ROY ORBISON	2	1962
DREAM BABY GLEN CAMPBELL	39	1971
DREAM CATCH ME NEWTON FAULKNER	7	2007
DREAM COME TRUE BRAND NEW HEAVIES FEATURING N'DEA DAVENPORT	24	1992
DREAM GIRL MARK WYNTER	27	1961
DREAM KITCHEN FRAZIER CHORUS	57	1989
DREAM LOVER BOBBY DARIN	1	1959
DREAM OF ME (BASED ON LOVE'S THEME) ORCHESTRAL MANOEUVRES IN THE DARK	24	1993
DREAM OF OLWEN SECOND CITY SOUND	43	1969
DREAM ON DEPECHE MODE	6	2001
DREAM ON DREAMER BRAND NEW HEAVIES FEATURING N'DEA DAVENPORT	15	1994
DREAM ON (IS THIS A DREAM) LOVE DECADE	52	1991
DREAM SEQUENCE (ONE) PAULINE MURRAY & THE INVISIBLE GIRLS	67	1980
DREAM SOME PARADISE INTASTELLA	69	1991
DREAM SWEET DREAMS AZTEC CAMERA	67	1993
DREAM TALK ALMA COGAN	48	1960
DREAM TO ME DARIO G	9	2001
DREAM TO SLEEP H20	17	1983
DREAM UNIVERSE DJ GARRY	36	2002
DREAMBOAT [A] ALMA COGAN	1	1955
DREAMBOAT [B] LIMMIE & THE FAMILY COOKIN'	31	1973
DREAMER [A] SUPERTRAMP	13	1975
DREAMER [A] CK & SUPREME DREAM TEAM	23	2002
DREAMER [B] JACKSONS	22	1977
THE DREAMER ALL ABOUT EVE	41	1991
DREAMER [D] COLDCUT	54	1993
DREAMER [E] LIVIN' JOY	1	1994
DREAMER [F] OZZY OSBOURNE	18	2002
DREAMIN' [A] JOHNNY BURNETTE	5	1960
DREAMIN' [B] LIVERPOOL EXPRESS	40	1977
DREAMIN' [C] CLIFF RICHARD	8	1980
DREAMIN' [D] STATUS QUO	15	1986
DREAMIN' [E] VANESSA WILLIAMS	74	1989
DREAMIN' [F] LOLEATTA HOLLOWAY	59	2000
DREAMIN' [G] AMP FIDDLER	71	2004
DREAMING [A] BLONDIE	2	1979
THE DREAMING [B] KATE BUSH	48	1982
DREAMING [C] ORCHESTRAL MANOEUVRES IN THE DARK	50	1988
DREAMING [D] GLEN GOLDSMITH	12	1988
DREAMING [E] MN8	21	1996
DREAMING [F] RUFF DRIVERZ PRESENTS ARROLA	10	1998
DREAMING [G] M PEOPLE	13	1999
DREAMING [H] BT FEATURING KIRSTY HAWKSHAW	38	2000
DREAMING [I] AURORA	24	2002
DREAMING [J] I DREAM FEATURING FRANKIE & CALVIN	19	2004
DREAMING OF ME DEPECHE MODE	57	1981
DREAMING OF YOU [A] THRILLSEEKERS	48	2002
DREAMING OF YOU [B] CORAL	13	2002
DREAMLOVER MARIAH CAREY	9	1993
DREAMS [A] FLEETWOOD MAC	24	1977
DREAMS [A] WILD COLOUR	25	1995
DREAMS [A] CORRS	6	1998
DREAMS [A] DEEP DISH FEATURING STEVIE NICKS	14	2006
DREAMS [B] GRACE SLICK	50	1980
DREAMS [C] VAN HALEN	62	1986
DREAMS [D] GABRIELLE	1	1993
DREAMS [E] CRANBERRIES	27	1994
DREAMS [F] SMOKIN' BEATS FEATURING LYN EDEN	23	1998
DREAMS [G] QUENCH	75	1996
DREAMS [H] MISS SHIVA	30	2001
DREAMS [I] KINGS OF TOMORROW	69	2003
DREAMS [K] GAME	8	2005

Title / Artist	Peak Position	Year of Entry
DREAMS CAN TELL A LIE NAT 'KING' COLE	10	1956
A DREAM'S A DREAM SOUL II SOUL	6	1990
THE DREAMS I DREAM SHADOWS	42	1966
DREAMS OF CHILDREN JAM	1	1980
DREAMS OF HEAVEN GROUND LEVEL	54	1993
DREAMS OF YOU RALPH McTELL	36	1976
DREAMS TO REMEMBER ROBERT PALMER	68	1991
DREAMSCAPE '94 TIME FREQUENCY	32	1994
DREAMTIME [A] DARYL HALL	28	1986
DREAMTIME [B] ZEE	31	1996
DREAMY DAYS ROOTS MANUVA	53	2001
DREAMY LADY T REX DISCO PARTY	30	1975
DRED BASS DEAD DRED	60	1994
DRESS YOU UP MADONNA	5	1985
DRESSED FOR SUCCESS ROXETTE	18	1989
DRIFT AWAY MICHAEL BOLTON	18	1992
DRIFTING [A] SHEILA WALSH & CLIFF RICHARD	64	1983
DRIFTING [B] MOJOLATORS FEATURING CAMILLA	52	2001
DRIFTING AWAY LANGE FEATURING SKYE	9	2002
DRIFTWOOD TRAVIS	13	1999
THE DRILL DIRT DEVILS	15	2002
DRINK THE ELIXIR SALAD	66	1995
DRINK UP THY ZIDER ADGE CUTLER & THE WURZELS	45	1967
DRINKING IN LA BRAN VAN 3000	3	1998
DRINKING SONG MARIO LANZA	13	1955
DRIP FED FRED MADNESS FEATURING IAN DURY	55	2000
DRIVE [A] CARS	4	1984
DRIVE [B] R.E.M.	11	1992
DRIVE [C] GEOFFREY WILLIAMS	52	1997
DRIVE [D] INCUBUS	40	2001
DRIVE ME CRAZY PARTIZAN	36	1997
DRIVE ON BROTHER BEYOND	39	1989
DRIVE SAFELY DARLIN' TONY CHRISTIE	35	1976
DRIVE-IN SATURDAY DAVID BOWIE	3	1973
DRIVEN BY YOU BRIAN MAY	6	1991
DRIVER'S SEAT SNIFF 'N' THE TEARS	42	1979
DRIVIN' HOME DUANE EDDY & THE REBELS	30	1961
DRIVIN' ME WILD COMMON FEATURING LILY ALLEN	56	2007
DRIVING EVERYTHING BUT THE GIRL	36	1990
DRIVING AWAY FROM HOME (JIM'S TUNE) IT'S IMMATERIAL	18	1986
DRIVING HOME FOR CHRISTMAS CHRIS REA	33	2007
DRIVING HOME FOR CHRISTMAS (EP) CHRIS REA	53	1988
DRIVING IN MY CAR MADNESS	4	1982
DRIVING IN MY CAR MAUREEN REES	49	1997
DRIVING WITH THE BRAKES ON DEL AMITRI	18	1995
DROP DEAD GORGEOUS REPUBLICA	7	1997
DROP DOWN TO EARTH PURESSENCE	56	2007
DROP IT LIKE IT'S HOT SNOOP DOGG FEATURING PHARRELL	10	2004
DROP SOME DRUMS (LOVE) TATTOO	58	2001
DROP THE BOY BROS	2	1988
DROP THE PILOT JOAN ARMATRADING	11	1983
DROP THE PRESSURE MYLO	19	2004
DROP THE ROCK (EP) D-TEK	70	1993
DROPS OF JUPITER (TELL ME) TRAIN	10	2001
DROWNED WORLD (SUBSTITUTE FOR LOVE) MADONNA	10	1998
THE DROWNERS SUEDE	49	1992
DROWNING [A] BEAT	22	1981
DROWNING [B] BACKSTREET BOYS	4	2002
DROWNING [C] CRAZY TOWN	50	2002
DROWNING IN BERLIN MOBILES	9	1982
DROWNING THE THE SEA OF LOVE ADVENTURES	44	1988
DROWSY WITH HOPE SHAKEDOWN	46	2003
THE DRUGS DON'T WORK VERVE	1	1997
DRUMBEATS SL2	26	1992
DRUMMER MAN TONIGHT	14	1978
DRUMMIN' UP A STORM SANDY NELSON	39	1962
DRUMS ARE MY BEAT SANDY NELSON	30	1962
THE DRUMSTRUCK (EP) N-JOI	33	1993
DRUNK ON LOVE BASIA	41	1995
DRUNKARD LOGIC FAT LADY SINGS	56	1993
DRUNKEN FOOL BURN	54	2003
DRUNKEN STARS MAMPI SWIFT	72	2004
DRY COUNTY [A] BLACKFOOT	43	1982
DRY COUNTY [B] BON JOVI	9	1994
DRY LAND MARILLION	34	1991
DRY RISER KERBDOG	60	1994
DRY YOUR EYES STREETS	1	2004
DU THE DUDEK TROPHY BOYZ	49	2005
DUALITY SLIPKNOT	15	2004
DUB BE GOOD TO ME BEATS INTERNATIONAL FEATURING LINDY LAYTON	1	1990
DUB WAR DANCE CONSPIRACY	72	1992
DUBPLATE CULTURE SOUNDSCAPE	48	1998
DUCHESS [A] STRANGLERS	14	1979
DUCHESS [A] MY LIFE STORY	39	1997
DUCHESS [B] GENESIS	46	1980
DUCK FOR THE OYSTER MALCOLM McLAREN	54	1983
DUCK TOY HAMPENBERG	30	2002
DUDE BEENIE MAN FEATURING MS THING	7	2004
DUDE DESCENDING A STAIRCASE APOLLO FOUR FORTY FEATURING THE BEATNUTS	58	2003
DUDE (LOOKS LIKE A LADY) AEROSMITH	20	1987
DUEL [A] PROPAGANDA	21	1985
DUEL [B] SWERVEDRIVER	60	1993
DUELLING BANJOS 'DELIVERANCE' SOUNDTRACK	17	1973
DUI HAR MAR SUPERSTAR	46	2004
DUKE OF EARL DARTS	6	1979
DUM DUM BRENDA LEE	22	1961
DUM DUM GIRL TALK TALK	74	1984
DUMB [A] BEAUTIFUL SOUTH	16	1998
DUMB [B] 411	3	2004
DUMB WAITERS PSYCHEDELIC FURS	59	1981
DUMMY CRUSHER KERBDOG	37	1994
DUNE BUGGY PRESIDENTS OF THE UNITED STATES OF AMERICA	15	1996
DUNE SEA UNBELIEVABLE TRUTH	46	1998
DUNNO WHAT IT IS (ABOUT YOU) BEATMASTERS FEATURING ELAINE VASSELL	43	1992
DURHAM TOWN (THE LEAVIN') ROGER WHITTAKER	12	1969
DUSK TIL DAWN DANNY HOWELLS & DICK TREVOR	37	2004
DUSTED LEFTFIELD/ROOTS MANUVA	28	1999
D. W. WASHBURN MONKEES	17	1968
D'YA WANNA GO FASTER TERRORVISION	28	2001
DYNA-MITE MUD	4	1973
DYNAMITE [A] CLIFF RICHARD & THE SHADOWS	16	1959
DYNAMITE [B] STACY LATTISHAW	51	1980
DY-NA-MI-TEE MS DYNAMITE	5	2002
DYNOMITE (PART 1) TONY CAMILLO'S BAZUKA	28	1975
D'YOU KNOW WHAT I MEAN? OASIS	1	1997

E–H

KEY TO INDEX ENTRIES

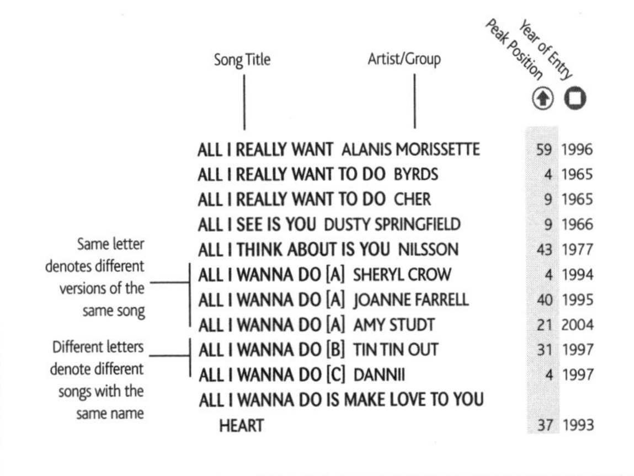

		Peak Position	Year of Entry
E	DRUNKENMUNKY	41	2003
E = MC2	BIG AUDIO DYNAMITE	11	1986
E - BOW THE LETTER	R.E.M.	4	1996
E SAMBA	JUNIOR JACK	34	2003
E TALKING	SOULWAX	27	2005
EACH AND EVERYONE	EVERYTHING BUT THE GIRL	28	1984
EACH TIME	E-17	2	1998
EACH TIME YOU BREAK MY HEART	NICK KAMEN	5	1986
EANIE MEANY	JIM NOIR	67	2006
EARDRUM BUZZ	WIRE	68	1989
EARLY IN THE MORNING [A]	BUDDY HOLLY	17	1958
EARLY IN THE MORNING [B]	VANITY FARE	8	1969
EARLY IN THE MORNING [C]	GAP BAND	55	1982
EARLY MORNING RAIN	PAUL WELLER	40	2005
EARLY TO BED	PONI-TAILS	26	1959
EARTH ANGEL [A]	CREW CUTS	4	1955
EARTH ANGEL [B]	DREADZONE	51	1997
THE EARTH DIES SCREAMING	UB40	10	1980
EARTH SONG	MICHAEL JACKSON	1	1995
EARTHBOUND	CONNOR REEVES	14	1997
THE EARTHSHAKER	PAUL MASTERSON PRESENTS SUSHI	35	2002
EASE MY MIND	ARRESTED DEVELOPMENT	33	1994
EASE ON BY	BASS-O-MATIC	61	1990
EASE ON DOWN THE ROAD	DIANA ROSS & MICHAEL JACKSON	45	1978
EASE THE PRESSURE [A]	2WO THIRD3	45	1994
EASE THE PRESSURE [B]	BELOVED	43	1996
EASE YOUR MIND	GALLIANO	45	1996
EASIER SAID THAN DONE [A]	ESSEX	41	1963
EASIER SAID THAN DONE [B]	SHAKATAK	12	1982
EASIER SAID THAN DONE [C]	STARGATE	55	2002
EASIER TO LIE	AQUALUNG	60	2004
EASIER TO WALK AWAY	ELTON JOHN	63	1990
EAST COAST/WEST COAST KILLAS	GROUP THERAPY	51	1996
EAST EASY RIDER	JULIAN COPE	51	1991
EAST OF EDEN	BIG COUNTRY	17	1984
EAST RIVER	BRECKER BROTHERS	34	1978
EAST WEST	HERMAN'S HERMITS	33	1966
EASTER	MARILLION	34	1990
EASY [A]	COMMODORES	9	1977
EASY [B]	LOUD	67	1992
EASY [C]	TERRORVISION	12	1997
EASY [D]	EMILIANA TORRINI	63	2000
EASY [E]	GROOVE ARMADA	31	2003
EASY [F]	SUGABABES	8	2006
EASY COME EASY GO	SUTHERLAND BROTHERS	50	1979
EASY EASY	SCOTLAND WORLD CUP SQUAD	20	1974
EASY GOING ME	ADAM FAITH	12	1961
EASY LADY	SPAGNA	62	1987
EASY LIFE [A]	BODYSNATCHERS	50	1980
EASY LIFE [B]	CABARET VOLTAIRE	61	1990
EASY LIVIN'	FASTWAY	74	1983
EASY LOVER	PHILIP BAILEY (DUET WITH PHIL COLLINS)	1	1985
EASY/LUCKY/FREE	BRIGHT EYES	42	2005
EASY RIDER	RAIN BAND	63	2003
EASY TO SMILE	SENSELESS THINGS	18	1992
EAT IT	WEIRD AL YANKOVIC	36	1984
EAT ME DRINK ME LOVE ME	POP WILL EAT ITSELF	17	1992
EAT MY GOAL	COLLAPSED LUNG	18	1996
EAT THE RICH	AEROSMITH	34	1993
EAT YOU ALIVE	LIMP BIZKIT	10	2003
EAT YOUR HEART OUT	PAUL HARDCASTLE	59	1984
EAT YOURSELF WHOLE	KINGMAKER	15	1992
EATEN ALIVE	DIANA ROSS	71	1985
EATING ME ALIVE	DIANA BROWN & BARRIE K. SHARPE	53	1992
EBB TIDE	FRANK CHACKSFIELD	9	1954
EBB TIDE	RIGHTEOUS BROTHERS	3	1966
EBENEEZER GOODE	SHAMEN	1	1992
EBONY AND IVORY	PAUL McCARTNEY & STEVIE WONDER	1	1982
EBONY EYES	EVERLY BROTHERS	1	1961
ECHO BEACH [A]	MARTHA & THE MUFFINS	10	1980
ECHO BEACH [B]	TOYAH	54	1987
ECHO CHAMBER	BEATS INTERNATIONAL	60	1991
ECHO MY HEART	LINDY LAYTON	42	1991
ECHO ON MY MIND PART II	EARTHLING	61	1995
ECHOES IN A SHALLOW BAY (EP)	COCTEAU TWINS	65	1985
ECUADOR	SASH! FEATURING RODRIGUEZ	2	1997
EDDIE'S GUN	KOOKS	35	2005
EDDIE'S SONG	SON OF DORK	10	2006
EDDY VORTEX	STEVE GIBBONS BAND	56	1978
EDELWEISS	VINCE HILL	2	1967
EDEN	SARAH BRIGHTMAN	68	1999
EDGE OF A BROKEN HEART	VIXEN	51	1988
EDGE OF DARKNESS	ERIC CLAPTON FEATURING MICHAEL KAMEN	65	1986
THE EDGE OF HEAVEN	WHAM!	1	1986
EDIBLE FLOWERS	FINN BROTHERS	32	2005
EDIE (CIAO BABY)	CULT	32	1989
ED'S FUNKY DINER (FRIDAY NIGHT, SATURDAY MORNING)	IT'S IMMATERIAL	65	1986
EDWOULD	LARRIKIN LOVE	49	2006
EENY MEENY	SHOWSTOPPERS	33	1968
EGG RUSH	FLOWERED UP	54	1991
EGO	ELTON JOHN	34	1978
EGYPTIAN REGGAE	JONATHAN RICHMAN & THE MODERN LOVERS	5	1977
EI	NELLY	11	2001
EIGHT BY TEN	KEN DODD	22	1964
8 DAYS A WEEK	SWEET FEMALE ATTITUDE	43	2000
EIGHT MILES HIGH	BYRDS	24	1966
808	BLAQUE IVORY	31	1999
EIGHTEEN	FORWARD, RUSSIA!	44	2006
18 AND LIFE	SKID ROW	12	1990
18 CARAT LOVE AFFAIR	ASSOCIATES	21	1982
EIGHTEEN STRINGS	TINMAN	9	1994
18 TIL I DIE	BRYAN ADAMS	22	1997
EIGHTEEN WITH A BULLET	PETE WINGFIELD	7	1975
EIGHTEEN YELLOW ROSES	BOBBY DARIN	37	1963
EIGHTH DAY	HAZEL O'CONNOR	5	1980
8TH WORLD WONDER	KIMBERLEY LOCKE	49	2004
EIGHTIES	KILLING JOKE	60	1984
80S ROMANCE	BELLE STARS	71	1984
86'D	SUBCIRCUS	56	1997
EINSTEIN A GO-GO	LANDSCAPE	5	1981
EITHER WAY	TWANG	8	2007
EL BIMBO	BIMBO JET	12	1975
EL CAMINOS IN THE WEST	GRANDADDY	48	2003
EL CAPITAN [A]	OPM	20	2002
EL CAPITAN [B]	IDLEWILD	39	2005
EL LUTE	BONEY M	12	1979
EL MANANA	GORILLAZ	27	2006
EL NINO	AGNELLI & NELSON	21	1998
EL PARAISO RICO	DEETAH	39	1999
EL PASO	MARTY ROBBINS	19	1960
EL PRESIDENT	DRUGSTORE	20	1998
EL SALVADOR	ATHLETE	31	2003
EL SCORCHO	WEEZER	50	1996
EL TRAGO (THE DRINK)	2 IN A ROOM	34	1994
EL VINO COLLAPSO	BLACK LACE	42	1985
ELDORADO	DRUM THEATRE	44	1987
ELEANOR PUT YOUR BOOTS ON	FRANZ FERDINAND	30	2006
ELEANOR RIGBY	BEATLES	1	1966
ELEANOR RIGBY	RAY CHARLES	36	1968
ELECTED	ALICE COOPER	4	1972
ELECTION DAY	ARCADIA	7	1985
ELECTRIC	LISA SCOTT-LEE	13	2005
ELECTRIC AVENUE	EDDY GRANT	2	1983
ELECTRIC BARBARELLA	DURAN DURAN	23	1999
ELECTRIC BLUE	ICEHOUSE	53	1988
ELECTRIC BOOGALOO	OLLIE & JERRY	57	1985
ELECTRIC GUITAR	FLUKE	58	1993
ELECTRIC GUITARS	PREFAB SPROUT	53	1997
ELECTRIC HEAD PART 2 (THE ECSTASY)	WHITE ZOMBIE	31	1996
ELECTRIC LADY	GEORDIE	32	1973
ELECTRIC MAINLINE	SPIRITUALIZED	49	1993
ELECTRIC MAN	MANSUN	23	2000
ELECTRIC TRAINS	SQUEEZE	44	1995
ELECTRIC YOUTH	DEBBIE GIBSON	14	1989
ELECTRICAL STORM	U2	5	2002
ELECTRICITY [A]	SPIRITUALIZED	32	1997
ELECTRICITY [B]	SUEDE	5	1999
ELECTRICITY [C]	ELTON JOHN	4	2005
ELECTROLITE	R.E.M.	29	1996
ELECTRON BLUE	R.E.M.	26	2005
ELECTRONIC PLEASURE	N-TRANCE	11	1996
ELEGANTLY AMERICAN: ONE NIGHT IN HEAVEN	M PEOPLE	31	1994
ELEGANTLY WASTED	INXS	20	1997
ELEKTRO	OUTWORK FEATURING MR GEE	49	2006
ELEKTROBANK	CHEMICAL BROTHERS	17	1997
ELEMENTS	NEO CORTEX	67	2004
ELENI	TOL & TOL	73	1990
ELENORE	TURTLES	7	1968
ELEPHANT PAW (GET DOWN TO THE FUNK)	PAN POSITION	55	1994
ELEPHANT STONE	STONE ROSES	8	1990
ELEPHANT TANGO	CYRIL STAPLETON	19	1955
THE ELEPHANT'S GRAVEYARD (GUILTY)	BOOMTOWN RATS	26	1981
ELEVATE MY MIND	STEREO MC'S	74	1990
ELEVATION [A]	XPANSIONS	49	1990
ELEVATION [B]	GTO	59	1992
ELEVATION [C]	U2	3	2001
ELEVATION [D]	OPEN	54	2004
ELEVATOR SONG	DUBSTAR	25	1996
ELEVEN TO FLY	TIN TIN OUT FEATURING WENDY PAGE	26	1999
ELISABETH SERENADE	GUNTER KALLMAN CHOIR	39	1964
ELIZABETHAN REGGAE	BORIS GARDINER	14	1970
ELLE	DJ GREGORY	73	2003
ELMO JAMES	CHAIRMEN OF THE BOARD	21	1972
ELO EP	ELECTRIC LIGHT ORCHESTRA	34	1978
ELOISE	BARRY RYAN	2	1968
ELOISE	DAMNED	3	1986
ELSTREE	BUGGLES	55	1980
ELUSIVE	SCOTT MATTHEWS	56	2006
ELUSIVE BUTTERFLY	BOB LIND	5	1966
ELUSIVE BUTTERFLY	VAL DOONICAN	5	1966
ELVIS AIN'T DEAD	SCOUTING FOR GIRLS	8	2007
THE ELVIS MEDLEY	ELVIS PRESLEY	51	1985
ELYSIUM (I GO CRAZY)	ULTRABEAT VERSUS SCOTT BROWN	35	2006
EMBARRASSMENT	MADNESS	4	1980
EMBRACE	AGNELLI & NELSON	35	2000
EMBRACING THE SUNSHINE	BT	34	1995
EMERALD CITY	SEEKERS	50	1967
EMERGE	FISCHERSPOONER	25	2002
EMERGENCY	KOOL & THE GANG	50	1985
EMERGENCY 72	TURIN BRAKES	41	2001
EMERGENCY (DIAL 999)	LOOSE ENDS	41	1984
EMERGENCY ON PLANET EARTH	JAMIROQUAI	32	1993
EMILY [A]	BOWLING FOR SOUP	67	2002
EMILY [B]	ADAM GREEN	53	2005
EMILY [C]	STEPHEN FRETWELL	42	2005
EMILY KANE	ART BRUT	41	2005

Title / Artist	Peak Position	Year of Entry
EMMA HOT CHOCOLATE	3	1974
EMOTION SAMANTHA SANG	11	1978
EMOTION DESTINY'S CHILD	3	2001
EMOTIONAL CONTENT FUNK D'VOID	74	2004
EMOTIONAL RESCUE ROLLING STONES	9	1980
EMOTIONAL TIME HOTHOUSE FLOWERS	38	1993
EMOTIONS [A] BRENDA LEE	45	1961
EMOTIONS [B] MARIAH CAREY	17	1991
THE EMPEROR'S NEW CLOTHES SINEAD O'CONNOR	31	1990
EMPIRE [A] QUEENSRYCHE	61	1990
EMPIRE [B] KASABIAN	9	2006
EMPIRE LINE MY LIFE STORY	58	1999
EMPIRE SONG KILLING JOKE	43	1982
EMPIRE STATE HUMAN HUMAN LEAGUE	62	1980
EMPTY AT THE END ELECTRIC SOFT PARADE	39	2001
EMPTY GARDEN ELTON JOHN	51	1982
EMPTY ROOMS GARY MOORE	23	1984
EMPTY SKIES KOSHEEN	73	2000
EMPTY SOULS MANIC STREET PREACHERS	2	2005
EMPTY WORLD DOGS D'AMOUR	61	1990
ENCHANTED LADY PASADENAS	31	1988
ENCORE CHERYL LYNN	68	1984
ENCORE TONGUE 'N' CHEEK	37	1989
ENCORE UNE FOIS SASH!	2	1997
ENCORES EP DIRE STRAITS	31	1993
THE END HAS A START EDITORS	27	2007
THE END HAS NO END STROKES	27	2004
THE END IS THE BEGINNING IS THE END SMASHING PUMPKINS	10	1997
END OF A CENTURY BLUR	19	1994
THE END OF THE INNOCENCE DON HENLEY	48	1992
END OF THE LINE [A] TRAVELING WILBURYS	52	1989
END OF THE LINE [B] HONEYZ	5	1998
END OF THE LINE [C] MOHAIR	52	2005
END OF THE ROAD BOYZ II MEN	1	1992
END OF THE WORLD [A] SKEETER DAVIS	18	1963
END OF THE WORLD [A] SONIA	18	1990
THE END OF THE WORLD [B] CURE	25	2004
END OF THE WORLD [C] ASH	62	2007
THE END...OR THE BEGINNING CLASSIX NOUVEAUX	60	1982
ENDLESS DICKIE VALENTINE	19	1954
ENDLESS ART A HOUSE	46	1992
ENDLESS LOVE DIANA ROSS & LIONEL RICHIE	7	1981
ENDLESS LOVE LUTHER VANDROSS & MARIAH CAREY	3	1994
ENDLESS SLEEP MARTY WILDE	4	1958
ENDLESS SLEEP JODY REYNOLDS	66	1979
ENDLESS SUMMER NIGHTS RICHARD MARX	50	1988
ENDLESSLY [A] BROOK BENTON	28	1959
ENDLESSLY [B] JOHN FOXX	66	1983
ENDS EVERLAST	47	1999
ENEMIES FRIENDS HOPE OF THE STATES	25	2003
ENEMY MAKER DUB WAR	41	1996
THE ENEMY WITHIN THIRST	61	1991
ENERGIZE SLAMM	57	1993
THE ENERGY (FEEL THE VIBE) ASTRO TRAX	74	1998
ENERGY FLASH (EP) BELTRAM	52	1991
ENERGY IS EUROBEAT MAN TO MAN	43	1987
ENERVATE TRANSA	42	1998
ENGINE ENGINE NO. 9 ROGER MILLER	33	1965
ENGINE NO 9 MIDNIGHT STAR	64	1987
ENGLAND CRAZY RIDER & TERRY VENABLES	46	2002
ENGLAND SWINGS ROGER MILLER	13	1966
ENGLAND WE'LL FLY THE FLAG ENGLAND WORLD CUP SQUAD	2	1982
ENGLAND'S IRIE BLACK GRAPE FEATURING JOE STRUMMER & KEITH ALLEN	6	1996
ENGLISH CIVIL WAR (JOHNNY COMES MARCHING HOME) CLASH	25	1979
ENGLISH COUNTRY GARDEN [A] JIMMIE RODGERS	5	1962
ENGLISH COUNTRY GARDEN [B] DANDYS	57	1998
ENGLISH SUMMER RAIN PLACEBO	23	2004
ENGLISHMAN IN NEW YORK STING	15	1988
ENJOY THE SILENCE DEPECHE MODE	6	1990
ENJOY THE SILENCE LACUNA COIL	41	2006
ENJOY YOURSELF [A] JACKSONS	42	1977
ENJOY YOURSELF [B] A+	5	1999
ENOLA GAY ORCHESTRAL MANOEUVRES IN THE DARK	8	1980
ENOUGH CRYIN' MARY J BLIGE FEATURING BROOK-LYNN	46	2006
ENOUGH IS ENOUGH [A] CHUMBAWAMBA & CREDIT TO THE NATION	56	1993
ENOUGH IS ENOUGH [B] Y-TRIBE FEATURING ELISABETH TROY	49	1999
ENTER SANDMAN METALLICA	5	1991
ENTER THE SCENE DJ SUPREME VS THE RHYTHM MASTERS	49	1997
ENTER YOUR FANTASY EP JOEY NEGRO	35	1992
THE ENTERTAINER MARVIN HAMLISCH	25	1974
ENTOURAGE OMARION	58	2007
ENTRY OF THE GLADIATORS NERO & THE GLADIATORS	37	1961
ENVY ASH	21	2002
THE EP ZERO B	32	1992
EP THREE HUNDRED REASONS	37	2001
EP TWO HUNDRED REASONS	47	2001
EPIC FAITH NO MORE	25	1990
EPLE ROYKSOPP	16	2003
E-PRO BECK	38	2005
EQUINOXE PART 5 JEAN-MICHEL JARRE	45	1979
EQUINOXE (PART V) SHADOWS	50	1980
ERASE/REWIND CARDIGANS	7	1999
ERASURE-ISH (A LITTLE RESPECT/STOP!) BJORN AGAIN	25	1992
ERECTION (TAKE IT TO THE TOP) CORTINA FEATURING BK & MADAM FRICTION	48	2002
ERNIE (THE FASTEST MILKMAN IN THE WEST) BENNY HILL	1	1971
EROTICA MADONNA	3	1992
ESCAPADE JANET JACKSON	17	1990
ESCAPE [A] GARY CLAIL ON-U SOUND SYSTEM	44	1991
ESCAPE [B] ENRIQUE IGLESIAS	3	2002
ESCAPE ARTISTS NEVER DIE FUNERAL FOR A FRIEND	19	2004
ESCAPE (THE PINA COLADA SONG) RUPERT HOLMES	23	1980
ESCAPING [A] ASIA BLUE	50	1992
ESCAPING [B] DINA CARROLL	3	1996
E.S.P. BEE GEES	51	1987
ESPECIALLY FOR YOU KYLIE MINOGUE & JASON DONOVAN	1	1988
ESPECIALLY FOR YOU DENISE & JOHNNY	3	1998
THE ESSENTIAL WALLY PARTY MEDLEY GAY GORDON & THE MINCE PIES	60	1986
ET LES OISEAUX CHANTAIENT (AND THE BIRDS WERE SINGING) SWEET PEOPLE	4	1980
ET MEME FRANCOISE HARDY	31	1965
ETERNAL FLAME BANGLES	1	1989
ETERNAL FLAME ATOMIC KITTEN	1	2001
ETERNAL LOVE PJ & DUNCAN	12	1994
ETERNALLY JIMMY YOUNG	8	1953
ETERNITY [A] ORION	38	2000
ETERNITY [B] ROBBIE WILLIAMS	1	2001
ETHER RADIO CHIKINKI	50	2004
ETHNIC PRAYER HAVANA	71	1993
THE ETON RIFLES JAM	3	1979
EUGINA SALT TANK	40	1996
EURODISCO BIS	37	1998
EUROPA AND THE PIRATE TWINS THOMAS DOLBY	48	1981
EUROPE (AFTER THE RAIN) JOHN FOXX	40	1981
EUROPEAN FEMALE STRANGLERS	9	1983
EUROPEAN SON JAPAN	31	1982
EVANGELINE [A] ICICLE WORKS	53	1987
EVANGELINE [B] COCTEAU TWINS	34	1993
EVAPOR 8 ALTERN 8	6	1992
EVE OF DESTRUCTION BARRY McGUIRE	3	1965
THE EVE OF THE WAR JEFF WAYNE'S WAR OF THE WORLDS	3	1978
EVE THE APPLE OF MY EYE BELL X1	65	2004
EVEN AFTER ALL FINLEY QUAYE	10	1997
EVEN BETTER THAN THE REAL THING U2	8	1992
EVEN FLOW PEARL JAM	27	1992
EVEN GOD CAN'T CHANGE THE PAST CHARLOTTE CHURCH	17	2005
EVEN MORE PARTY POPS RUSS CONWAY	27	1960
EVEN NOW BOB SEGER & THE SILVER BULLET BAND	73	1983
EVEN THE BAD TIMES ARE GOOD TREMELOES	4	1967
EVEN THE NIGHTS ARE BETTER AIR SUPPLY	44	1982
EVEN THOUGH YOU BROKE MY HEART GEMINI	40	1995
EVEN THOUGH YOU'VE GONE JACKSONS	31	1978
EVENING FALLS... ENYA	20	1988
EVENING STARS JUDAS PRIEST	53	1979
EVER BLAZIN' SEAN PAUL	12	2005
EVER FALLEN IN LOVE FINE YOUNG CANNIBALS	9	1987
EVER FALLEN IN LOVE (WITH SOMEONE YOU SHOULDN'T'VE) BUZZCOCKS	12	1978
EVER FALLEN IN LOVE (WITH SOMEONE YOU SHOULDN'T'VE) VARIOUS ARTISTS (EP'S & LPS)	28	2005
EVER REST MYSTICA	62	1998
EVER SINCE YOU SAID GOODBYE MARTY WILDE	31	1962
EVER SO LONELY MONSOON	12	1982
EVEREST SUPERNATURALS	52	1999
EVERGLADE L7	27	1992
EVERGREEN [A] HAZELL DEAN	63	1984
EVERGREEN [B] LAWRENCE BELLE	73	2002
EVERGREEN [B] WILL YOUNG	1	2002
EVERLASTING [A] NATALIE COLE	28	1988
THE EVERLASTING [B] MANIC STREET PREACHERS	11	1998
EVERLASTING LOVE [A] LOVE AFFAIR	1	1968
EVERLASTING LOVE [A] ROBERT KNIGHT	19	1969
EVERLASTING LOVE [A] REX SMITH & RACHEL SWEET	35	1981
EVERLASTING LOVE [A] SANDRA	45	1988
EVERLASTING LOVE [A] WORLDS APART	20	1993
EVERLASTING LOVE [A] GLORIA ESTEFAN	19	1995
EVERLASTING LOVE [A] CAST OF CASUALTY	5	1998
EVERLASTING LOVE [A] JAMIE CULLUM	20	2004
EVERLASTING LOVE [B] HOWARD JONES	62	1989
EVERLONG FOO FIGHTERS	18	1997
EVERLOVIN' RICK NELSON	23	1961
EVERMORE RUBY MURRAY	3	1955
EVERY ANGEL ALL ABOUT EVE	30	1988
EVERY BEAT OF MY HEART ROD STEWART	2	1986
EVERY BEAT OF THE HEART RAILWAY CHILDREN	24	1990
EVERY BREATH OF THE WAY MELANIE	70	1983
EVERY BREATH YOU TAKE POLICE	1	1983
EVERY DAY ANTICAPPELLA	45	1992
EVERY DAY HURTS SAD CAFE	3	1979
EVERY DAY I FALL APART SUPERSTAR	66	1998
EVERY DAY I LOVE YOU BOYZONE	3	1999
EVERY DAY (I LOVE YOU MORE) JASON DONOVAN	2	1989
EVERY DAY OF MY LIFE MALCOLM VAUGHAN	5	1955
EVERY DAY OF THE WEEK JADE	19	1995

Title / Artist	Peak Position	Year of Entry
EVERY DAY SHOULD BE A HOLIDAY DANDY WARHOLS	29	1998
EVERY GIRL AND BOY SPAGNA	23	1988
EVERY HEARTBEAT AMY GRANT	25	1991
EVERY KINDA PEOPLE ROBERT PALMER	43	1978
EVERY KINDA PEOPLE MINT JULEPS	58	1987
EVERY KINDA PEOPLE CHAKA DEMUS & PLIERS	47	1996
EVERY LITTLE BIT HURTS SPENCER DAVIS GROUP	41	1965
EVERY LITTLE STEP BOBBY BROWN	6	1989
EVERY LITTLE TEARDROP GALLAGHER & LYLE	32	1977
EVERY LITTLE THING JEFF LYNNE	59	1990
EVERY LITTLE THING HE DOES IS MAGIC SHAWN COLVIN	65	1994
EVERY LITTLE THING I DO SOUL FOR REAL	31	1996
EVERY LITTLE THING SHE DOES IS MAGIC POLICE	1	1981
EVERY LITTLE THING SHE DOES IS MAGIC CHAKA DEMUS & PLIERS	51	1997
EVERY LITTLE TIME POPPERS PRESENTS AURA	44	1997
EVERY LITTLE TIME ONYX FEATURING GEMMA J	66	2004
EVERY LOSER WINS NICK BERRY	1	1986
EVERY MAN MUST HAVE A DREAM LIVERPOOL EXPRESS	17	1976
EVERY MORNING SUGAR RAY	10	1999
EVERY NIGHT PHOEBE SNOW	37	1979
EVERY NITE'S A SATURDAY NIGHT WITH YOU DRIFTERS	29	1976
EVERY 1'S A WINNER HOT CHOCOLATE	12	1978
EVERY OTHER TIME LYTE FUNKIE ONES	24	2002
EVERY ROSE HAS ITS THORN POISON	13	1989
EVERY SINGLE DAY DODGY	32	1998
EVERY TIME JANET JACKSON	46	1998
EVERY TIME I FALL GINA G	52	1997
EVERY TIME I FALL IN LOVE UPSIDE DOWN	18	1996
EVERY TIME IT RAINS ACE OF BASE	22	1999
EVERY TIME YOU GO AWAY PAUL YOUNG	4	1985
EVERY TIME YOU TOUCH ME MOBY	28	1995
EVERY WAY THAT I CAN SERTAB	72	2003
EVERY WHICH WAY BUT LOOSE EDDIE RABBITT	41	1979
EVERY WOMAN KNOWS LULU	44	1994
EVERY WOMAN NEEDS LOVE STELLA BROWNE	55	2000
EVERY YEAR EVERY CHRISTMAS LUTHER VANDROSS	43	1995
EVERY YOU EVERY ME PLACEBO	11	1999
EVERYBODY [A] TOMMY ROE	9	1963
EVERYBODY [B] CAPPELLA	66	1991
EVERYBODY [C] ALTERN 8	58	1993
EVERYBODY [D] DJ BOBO	47	1994
EVERYBODY [E] CLOCK	6	1995
EVERYBODY [F] KINKY	71	1996
EVERYBODY [G] PROGRESS PRESENTS THE BOY WUNDA	7	1999
EVERYBODY [H] HEAR'SAY	4	2001
EVERYBODY [I] MARTIN SOLVEIG	22	2005
EVERYBODY (ALL OVER THE WORLD) FPI PROJECT	65	1991
EVERYBODY (BACKSTREET'S BACK) BACKSTREET BOYS	3	1997
EVERYBODY BE SOMEBODY RUFFNECK FEATURING YAVAHN	13	1995
EVERYBODY COME DOWN DELGADOS	67	2004
EVERYBODY COME ON (CAN U FEEL IT) MR REDZ VS DJ SKRIBBLE	13	2003
EVERYBODY CRIES LIBERTY X	13	2004
EVERYBODY DANCE CHIC	9	1978
EVERYBODY DANCE EVOLUTION	19	1993
EVERYBODY DANCE (THE HORN SONG) BARBARA TUCKER	28	1998

Title / Artist	Peak Position	Year of Entry
EVERYBODY EVERYBODY BLACK BOX	16	1990
(EVERYBODY) GET DANCIN' BOMBERS	37	1979
EVERYBODY GET TOGETHER DAVE CLARK FIVE	8	1970
EVERYBODY GET UP [A] FIVE	2	1998
EVERYBODY GET UP [B] CAPRICCIO	44	1999
EVERYBODY GETS A SECOND CHANCE MIKE + THE MECHANICS	56	1992
EVERYBODY GO HOME THE PARTY'S OVER CLODAGH RODGERS	47	1970
EVERYBODY GONFI-GON TWO COWBOYS	7	1994
EVERYBODY HAVE A GOOD TIME ARCHIE BELL & THE DRELLS	43	1977
EVERYBODY HERE WANTS YOU JEFF BUCKLEY	43	1998
EVERYBODY HURTS R.E.M.	7	1993
EVERYBODY IN THE PLACE (EP) PRODIGY	2	1992
EVERYBODY IS A STAR POINTER SISTERS	61	1979
EVERYBODY KNOWS [A] DAVE CLARK FIVE	37	1965
EVERYBODY KNOWS [B] DAVE CLARK FIVE	2	1967
EVERYBODY KNOWS [C] FREE ASSOCIATION	74	2003
EVERYBODY KNOWS (EXCEPT YOU) DIVINE COMEDY	14	1997
EVERYBODY LETS SOMEBODY LOVE FRANK K FEATURING WISTON OFFICE	61	1991
EVERYBODY LOVES A LOVER DORIS DAY	25	1958
EVERYBODY LOVES SOMEBODY DEAN MARTIN	11	1964
EVERYBODY MOVE CATHY DENNIS	25	1991
EVERYBODY (MOVE YOUR BODY) DIVA	44	1996
EVERYBODY MUST PARTY GEORGIE PORGIE	61	1995
EVERYBODY NEEDS A 303 FATBOY SLIM	34	1997
EVERYBODY NEEDS SOMEBODY [A] BIRDLAND	44	1991
EVERYBODY NEEDS SOMEBODY [B] NICK HOWARD	64	1995
EVERYBODY NEEDS SOMEBODY TO LOVE BLUES BROTHERS	12	1990
EVERYBODY ON THE FLOOR (PUMP IT) TOKYO GHETTO PUSSY	26	1995
EVERYBODY PUMP DJ POWER	46	1992
EVERYBODY (RAP) CRIMINAL ELEMENT ORCHESTRA & WENDELL WILLIAMS	30	1990
EVERYBODY SALSA MODERN ROMANCE	12	1981
EVERYBODY SAY EVERYBODY DO LET LOOSE	29	1995
EVERYBODY THINKS THEY'RE GOING TO GET THEIRS BIS	64	1997
EVERYBODY UP! GLAM METAL DETECTIVES	29	1995
EVERYBODY WANTS HER THUNDER	36	1992
EVERYBODY WANTS TO RULE THE WORLD TEARS FOR FEARS	2	1985
EVERYBODY WANTS TO RUN THE WORLD TEARS FOR FEARS	5	1986
EVERYBODY'S A ROCK STAR TALL PAUL	60	2002
EVERYBODY'S CHANGING KEANE	4	2004
EVERYBODY'S FOOL EVANESCENCE	24	2004
EVERYBODY'S FREE (TO FEEL GOOD) ROZALLA	6	1991
EVERYBODY'S FREE (TO WEAR SUNSCREEN) BAZ LUHRMANN	1	1999
EVERYBODY'S GONE SENSELESS THINGS	73	1991
EVERYBODY'S GONE TO WAR NERINA PALLOT	14	2006
EVERYBODY'S GONNA BE HAPPY KINKS	17	1965
EVERYBODY'S GOT SUMMER ATLANTIC STARR	36	1994
EVERYBODY'S GOT TO LEARN SOMETIME KORGIS	5	1980
EVERYBODY'S GOT TO LEARN SOMETIME YAZZ	56	1994
(EVERYBODY'S GOT TO LEARN SOMETIME) I NEED YOUR LOVING BABY D	3	1995
EVERYBODY'S GOTTA LEARN SOMETIME CANTAMUS GIRLS CHOIR	73	2005

Title / Artist	Peak Position	Year of Entry
EVERYBODY'S HAPPY NOWADAYS BUZZCOCKS	29	1979
EVERYBODY'S LAUGHING PHIL FEARON & GALAXY	10	1984
EVERYBODY'S SOMEBODY'S FOOL CONNIE FRANCIS	5	1960
EVERYBODY'S SOMEONE LeANN RIMES & BRIAN McFADDEN	48	2006
EVERYBODY'S TALKIN' NILSSON	23	1969
EVERYBODY'S TALKIN' BEAUTIFUL SOUTH	12	1994
EVERYBODY'S TALKIN' 'BOUT LOVE SILVER CONVENTION	25	1977
EVERYBODY'S TWISTING FRANK SINATRA	22	1962
EVERYDAY [A] MOODY BLUES	44	1965
EVERYDAY [B] DON McLEAN	38	1973
EVERYDAY [C] SLADE	3	1974
EVERYDAY [D] JAM MACHINE	68	1989
EVERYDAY [E] ORCHESTRAL MANOEUVRES IN THE DARK	59	1993
EVERYDAY [F] PHIL COLLINS	15	1994
EVERYDAY [G] INCOGNITO	23	1995
EVERYDAY [H] CRAIG McLACHLAN & THE CULPRITS	65	1995
EVERYDAY [I] AGNELLI & NELSON	17	1999
EVERYDAY [J] BON JOVI	5	2002
EVERYDAY [K] SHY FX & T POWER FEATURING TOP CAT	75	2006
EVERYDAY [L] CAST OF HIGH SCHOOL MUSICAL 2	59	2007
EVERYDAY GIRL DJ RAP	47	1999
EVERYDAY I LOVE YOU LESS AND LESS KAISER CHIEFS	10	2005
EVERYDAY I WRITE THE BOOK ELVIS COSTELLO & THE ATTRACTIONS	28	1983
EVERYDAY IS A WINDING ROAD SHERYL CROW	12	1996
EVERYDAY IS LIKE SUNDAY MORRISSEY	9	1988
EVERYDAY LIVING WOODENTOPS	72	1986
EVERYDAY NOW TEXAS	44	1989
EVERYDAY OF MY LIFE HOUSE TRAFFIC	24	1997
EVERYDAY PEOPLE SLY & THE FAMILY STONE	36	1969
EVERYDAY PEOPLE ARETHA FRANKLIN	69	1991
EVERYDAY SUNSHINE FISHBONE	60	1992
EVERYDAY THANG MELANIE WILLIAMS	38	1994
EVERYONE I MEET IS FROM CALIFORNIA AMERICA	3	1972
EVERYONE SAYS 'HI' DAVID BOWIE	20	2002
EVERYONE SAYS I'M PARANOID APARTMENT	67	2005
EVERYONE SAYS YOU'RE SO FRAGILE IDLEWILD	47	1998
EVERYONE'S GONE TO THE MOON JONATHAN KING	4	1965
EVERYTHING [A] JODY WATLEY	74	1990
EVERYTHING [B] KICKING BACK WITH TAXMAN	54	1990
EVERYTHING [C] UHF	46	1991
EVERYTHING [D] HYSTERIX	65	1995
EVERYTHING [E] SARAH WASHINGTON	30	1996
EVERYTHING [F] INXS	71	1997
EVERYTHING [G] MARY J BLIGE	6	1997
EVERYTHING [H] DUM DUMS	21	2000
EVERYTHING [I] FEFE DOBSON	42	2004
EVERYTHING [J] ALANIS MORISSETTE	22	2004
EVERYTHING [K] MICHAEL BUBLE	38	2007
EVERYTHING A MAN COULD EVER NEED GLEN CAMPBELL	32	1970
EVERYTHING ABOUT YOU UGLY KID JOE	3	1992
EVERYTHING CHANGES TAKE THAT	1	1994
EVERYTHING COUNTS DEPECHE MODE	6	1983
EVERYTHING EVENTUALLY APPLETON	38	2003
EVERYTHING GOOD IS BAD WESTWORLD	72	1988
EVERYTHING I AM PLASTIC PENNY	6	1968

Title / Artist	Peak Position	Year of Entry
(EVERYTHING I DO) I DO IT FOR YOU BRYAN ADAMS	1	1991
(EVERYTHING I DO) I DO IT FOR YOU FATIMA MANSIONS	7	1992
(EVERYTHING I DO) I DO IT FOR YOU Q FEATURING TONY JACKSON	47	1994
EVERYTHING I HAVE IS YOURS EDDIE FISHER	8	1953
EVERYTHING I OWN BREAD	32	1972
EVERYTHING I OWN KEN BOOTHE	1	1974
EVERYTHING I OWN BOY GEORGE	1	1987
EVERYTHING I WANTED DANNII	15	1997
EVERYTHING IS ALRIGHT (UPTIGHT) C.J. LEWIS	10	1994
EVERYTHING IS AVERAGE NOWADAYS KAISER CHIEFS	19	2007
EVERYTHING IS BEAUTIFUL RAY STEVENS	6	1970
EVERYTHING IS EVERYTHING [A] LAURYN HILL	19	1999
EVERYTHING IS EVERYTHING [B] PHOENIX	74	2004
EVERYTHING IS GONNA BE ALRIGHT SOUNDS OF BLACKNESS	29	1994
EVERYTHING IS GREAT INNER CIRCLE	37	1979
EVERYTHING I'VE GOT IN MY POCKET MINNIE DRIVER	34	2004
EVERYTHING MUST CHANGE PAUL YOUNG	9	1984
EVERYTHING MUST GO MANIC STREET PREACHERS	5	1996
EVERYTHING MY HEART DESIRES ADAM RICKITT	15	1999
EVERYTHING SHE WANTS WHAM!	2	1984
EVERYTHING STARTS WITH AN 'E' E-ZEE POSSEE	15	1989
EVERYTHING TO EVERYONE EVERCLEAR	41	1998
EVERYTHING WILL FLOW SUEDE	24	1999
EVERYTHING YOU NEED MADISON AVENUE	33	2001
EVERYTHING YOU WANT VERTICAL HORIZONS	42	2000
EVERYTHING'L TURN OUT FINE STEALERS WHEEL	33	1973
EVERYTHING'S ALRIGHT MOJOS	9	1964
EVERYTHING'S COOL POP WILL EAT ITSELF	23	1994
EVERYTHING'S GONE GREEN NEW ORDER	38	1981
EVERYTHING'S GONNA BE ALRIGHT SWEETBOX	5	1998
EVERYTHING'S NOT YOU STONEPROOF	68	1999
EVERYTHING'S RUINED FAITH NO MORE	28	1992
EVERYTHING'S TUESDAY CHAIRMEN OF THE BOARD	12	1971
EVERYTIME [A] LUSTRAL	30	1997
EVERYTIME [B] TATYANA ALI	20	1999
EVERYTIME [C] A1	3	1999
EVERYTIME [D] BRITNEY SPEARS	1	2004
EVERYTIME I CLOSE MY EYES BABYFACE	13	1997
EVERYTIME I SEE HER (SOUND OF EDEN) ANOTHER CHANCE	62	2007
EVERYTIME I THINK OF YOU FM	73	1990
EVERYTIME WE TOUCH CASCADA	2	2006
EVERYTIME YOU NEED ME FRAGMA FEATURING MARIA RUBIA	3	2001
EVERYTIME YOU SLEEP DEACON BLUE	64	2001
EVERYTIME YOU TOUCH ME QFX	22	1996
EVERYWHERE [A] FLEETWOOD MAC	4	1988
EVERYWHERE [A] LNM PROJEKT FEATURING BONNIE BAILEY	38	2005
EVERYWHERE [B] MICHELLE BRANCH	18	2002
EVERYWHERE I GO [A] ISOTONIK	25	1992
EVERYWHERE I GO [B] JACKSON BROWNE	67	1994
EVERYWHERE I LOOK DARYL HALL & JOHN OATES	74	1991
EVE'S VOLCANO (COVERED IN SIN) JULIAN COPE	41	1987
EVIDENCE FAITH NO MORE	32	1995
EVIL [A] LADYTRON	44	2003
EVIL [B] INTERPOL	18	2005
EVIL HEARTED YOU YARDBIRDS	3	1965
EVIL MAN FATIMA MANSIONS	59	1992
THE EVIL THAT MEN DO IRON MAIDEN	5	1988
EVIL TWIN LOVE/HATE	59	1991
EVIL WOMAN ELECTRIC LIGHT ORCHESTRA	10	1976
EVOLUTIONDANCE PART ONE (EP) EVOLUTION	52	1994
EV'RY LITTLE BIT MILLIE SCOTT	63	1987
EV'RY TIME WE SAY GOODBYE SIMPLY RED	11	1987
EV'RYWHERE DAVID WHITFIELD	3	1955
THE EX BILLY TALENT	61	2004
EXCEEDER MASON VS PRINCESS SUPERSTAR	3	2007
EXCERPT FROM A TEENAGE OPERA KEITH WEST	2	1967
EXCITABLE AMAZULU	12	1985
EXCITED M PEOPLE	29	1992
EXCLUSIVE APOLLO PRESENTS HOUSE OF VIRGINISM	67	1996
EXCLUSIVELY YOURS MARK WYNTER	32	1961
EXCUSE SOULWAX	35	2005
EXCUSE ME BABY MAGIC LANTERNS	44	1966
EXCUSE ME MISS JAY-Z	17	2003
EXCUSE MY BROTHER MITCHELL BROTHERS	58	2005
EX-FACTOR LAURYN HILL	4	1999
EX-GIRLFRIEND NO DOUBT	23	2000
EXHALE (SHOOP SHOOP) WHITNEY HOUSTON	11	1995
EXODUS [A] BOB MARLEY & THE WAILERS	14	1977
EXODUS [B] SUNSCREEM	40	1995
EXODUS - LIVE LEVELLERS	24	1996
THE EXORCIST [A] SCIENTIST	46	1990
EXORCIST [B] SHADES OF RHYTHM	53	1991
EXPANDER FUTURE SOUND OF LONDON	72	1994
EXPANSIONS SCOTT GROOVES FEATURING ROY AYERS	68	1998
EXPANSIONS '86 (EXPAND YOUR MIND) CHRIS PAUL FEATURING DAVID JOSEPH	58	1986
EXPERIENCE DIANA ROSS	47	1986
EXPERIMENT IV KATE BUSH	23	1986
EXPERIMENTS WITH MICE JOHNNY DANKWORTH	7	1956
EXPLAIN THE REASONS FIRST LIGHT	65	1983
EXPLORATION OF SPACE COSMIC GATE	29	2002
EXPO 2000 KRAFTWERK	27	2000
EXPRESS [A] B.T. EXPRESS	34	1975
EXPRESS [B] DINA CARROLL	12	1993
EXPRESS YOUR FREEDOM ANTICAPPELLA	31	1995
EXPRESS YOURSELF [A] MADONNA	5	1989
EXPRESS YOURSELF [B] NWA	26	1989
EXPRESS YOURSELF [C] JIMI POLO	59	1992
EXPRESSION SALT-N-PEPA	23	1990
EXPRESSLY (EP) EDWYN COLLINS	42	1994
EXPRESSO BONGO EP CLIFF RICHARD & THE SHADOWS	14	1960
EXTACY SHADES OF RHYTHM	16	1991
EXTENDED PLAY EP BRYAN FERRY	7	1976
THE EXTENDED PLEASURE OF DANCE (EP) 808 STATE	56	1990
EXTERMINATE! SNAP FEATURING NIKI HARIS	2	1993
EXTRAVAGANZA JAMIE FOXX	43	2006
EXTREME WAYS MOBY	39	2002
EXTREMIS HAL FEATURING GILLIAN ANDERSON	23	1997
EYE BEE M COMMANDER TOM	75	2000
EYE FOR AN EYE UNKLE	31	2003
EYE HATE U ARTIST FORMERLY KNOWN AS PRINCE (AFKAP)	20	1995
EYE KNOW DE LA SOUL	14	1989
EYE LEVEL SIMON PARK ORCHESTRA	1	1972
EYE OF THE TIGER SURVIVOR	1	1982
EYE OF THE TIGER FRANK BRUNO	28	1995
EYE TALK FASHION	69	1984
EYE TO EYE CHAKA KHAN	16	1985
EYE WONDER APPLES	75	1991
EYEBALL (EYEBALL PAUL'S THEME) SUNBURST	48	2000
EYES DON'T LIE TRUCE	20	1998
THE EYES HAVE IT KAREL FIALKA	52	1980
EYES OF A STRANGER QUEENSRYCHE	59	1989
EYES OF BLUE PAUL CARRACK	40	1996
EYES OF SORROW A GUY CALLED GERALD	52	1989
THE EYES OF TRUTH ENIGMA	21	1994
EYES ON YOU JAY SEAN FEATURING RISHI RICH PROJECT	6	2004
EYES THAT SEE IN THE DARK KENNY ROGERS	61	1983
EYES WITHOUT A FACE BILLY IDOL	18	1984
EZ PASS HAR MAR SUPERSTAR	59	2003
EZY WOLFSBANE	68	1991

F

Title / Artist	Peak Position	Year of Entry
FA FA FA FA FA (SAD SONG) OTIS REDDING	23	1966
FABLE ROBERT MILES	7	1996
FABRICATED LUNACY TERRIS	62	2001
FABULOUS [A] CHARLIE GRACIE	8	1957
FABULOUS [B] JAHEIM	41	2003
FABULOUS [C] SHARPAY	64	2007
THE FACE AND WHY NOT?	13	1990
FACE FOR THE RADIO THE VIEW	69	2007
FACE THE STRANGE EP THERAPY?	18	1993
FACE TO FACE SIOUXSIE & THE BANSHEES	21	1992
FACES 2 UNLIMITED	8	1993
THE FACES (EP) FACES	41	1977
FACT OF LIFE [A] OUI 3	38	1994
FACTS + FIGURES HUGH CORNWELL	61	1987
THE FACTS OF LIFE [A] DANNY MADDEN	72	1990
THE FACTS OF LIFE [B] BLACK BOX RECORDER	20	2000
FACTS OF LOVE CLIMIE FISHER	50	1989
FADE [A] PARIS ANGELS	70	1991
FADE [B] SOLU MUSIC FEATURING KIMBLEE	18	2006
FADE INTO YOU MAZZY STAR	48	1994
FADE TO GREY VISAGE	8	1981
FADED BEN HARPER	54	1998
FADER DRUGSTORE	72	1995
FADING LIKE A FLOWER ROXETTE	12	1991
FADING LIKE A FLOWER DANCING DJS VS ROXETTE	18	2005
FAILURE [A] SKINNY	31	1998
FAILURE [B] KINGS OF CONVENIENCE	63	2001
FAILURE'S NOT FLATTERING NEW FOUND GLORY	67	2004
FAINT LINKIN PARK	15	2003
A FAIR AFFAIR (JE T'AIME) MISTY OLDLAND	49	1994
FAIR BLOWS THE WIND FOR FRANCE PELE	62	1992
FAIR FIGHT DJ ZINC	72	2002
FAIRGROUND SIMPLY RED	1	1995
FAIRPLAY SOUL II SOUL FEATURING ROSE WINDROSS	63	1988
FAIRWEATHER FRIEND SYMPOSIUM	25	1997
FAIRYTALE DANA	13	1976
FAIRYTALE OF NEW YORK POGUES FEATURING KIRSTY MacCOLL	5	1987
FAIT ACCOMPLI CURVE	22	1992
FAITH [A] GEORGE MICHAEL	2	1987
FAITH [B] WEE PAPA GIRL RAPPERS	60	1988
FAITH CAN MOVE MOUNTAINS JOHNNIE RAY & THE FOUR LADS	7	1952
FAITH CAN MOVE MOUNTAINS JIMMY YOUNG	11	1953
FAITH CAN MOVE MOUNTAINS NAT 'KING' COLE	10	1953
FAITH HEALER RECOIL	60	1992
FAITH IN PEOPLE HONEYMOON MACHINE	64	2005
FAITH (IN THE POWER OF LOVE) ROZALLA	11	1991

Title / Artist	Peak Position	Year of Entry
FAITH OF THE HEART ROD STEWART	60	1999
FAITHFUL GO WEST	13	1992
THE FAITHFUL HUSSAR LOUIS ARMSTRONG WITH HIS ALL-STARS	27	1956
THE FAITHFUL HUSSAR TED HEATH	18	1956
THE FAITHFUL HUSSAR (DON'T CRY MY LOVE) VERA LYNN	29	1957
FAITHFULNESS SKIN	64	2003
FAITHLESS SCRITTI POLITTI	56	1982
FAKE [A] ALEXANDER O'NEAL	16	1987
FAKE [B] SIMPLY RED	21	2003
FAKE FUR URUSEI YATSURA	40	1997
FAKE PLASTIC TREES RADIOHEAD	20	1995
THE FAKE SOUND OF PROGRESS LOSTPROPHETS	21	2002
FAKER AUDIOWEB	70	1997
FALCON RAH BAND	35	1980
FALIING IN LOVE AGAIN TECHNO TWINS	70	1982
THE FALL [A] MINISTRY	53	1996
THE FALL [B] WAY OUT WEST	61	2000
FALL AT YOUR FEET CROWDED HOUSE	17	1991
FALL AT YOUR FEET CM2 FEATURING LISA LAW	66	2002
FALL BACK DOWN RANCID	42	2003
FALL BEHIND ME DONNAS	55	2004
FALL DOWN (SPIRIT OF LOVE) TRAMAINE	60	1985
FALL EP RIDE	34	1990
FALL FROM GRACE ESKIMOS & EGYPT	51	1993
FALL IN LOVE WITH ME [A] EARTH, WIND & FIRE	47	1983
FALL IN LOVE WITH ME [B] BOOTH & THE BAD ANGEL	57	1998
FALL IN LOVE WITH YOU CLIFF RICHARD	2	1960
FALL OUT POLICE	47	1979
FALL TO LOVE DIESEL PARK WEST	48	1992
FALL TO PIECES VELVET REVOLVER	32	2004
THE FALL VS 2003 FALL	64	2002
FALLEN SARAH McLACHLAN	50	2004
THE FALLEN FRANZ FERDINAND	14	2006
FALLEN ANGEL [A] FRANKIE VALLI	11	1976
FALLEN ANGEL [B] POISON	59	1988
FALLEN ANGEL [C] TRACI LORDS	72	1995
FALLEN ANGEL [D] ELBOW	19	2003
FALLEN ANGELS BUFFY SAINTE-MARIE	57	1992
FALLIN' [A] CONNIE FRANCIS	20	1958
FALLIN' [B] TEENAGE FANCLUB & DE LA SOUL	59	1994
FALLIN' [C] ALICIA KEYS	3	2001
FALLIN' [D] UN-CUT	63	2003
FALLIN' [E] SADIE AMA	68	2007
FALLIN' IN LOVE HAMILTON, JOE FRANK & REYNOLDS	33	1975
FALLING [A] ROY ORBISON	9	1963
FALLING [B] JULEE CRUISE	7	1990
FALLING [C] CATHY DENNIS	32	1993
FALLING [D] ALISON MOYET	42	1993
FALLING [E] ANT & DEC	14	1997
FALLING [F] BOOM!	11	2001
FALLING [G] LIQUID STATE FEATURING MARCELLA WOODS	60	2002
FALLING [H] McALMONT & BUTLER	23	2002
FALLING ANGELS RIDING (MUTINY) DAVID ESSEX	29	1985
FALLING APART AT THE SEAMS MARMALADE	9	1976
FALLING AWAY FROM ME KORN	24	2000
FALLING DOWN DURAN DURAN	52	2007
FALLING IN AND OUT OF LOVE FEMME FATALE	69	1989
FALLING IN LOVE [A] SURFACE	67	1983
FALLING IN LOVE [B] SYBIL	68	1986
FALLING IN LOVE [C] LA BOUCHE	43	1995
FALLING IN LOVE AGAIN [A] LONDONBEAT	60	1989
FALLING IN LOVE AGAIN [B] EAGLE-EYE CHERRY	8	1998
FALLING IN LOVE (IS HARD ON THE KNEES) AEROSMITH	22	1997
FALLING INTO YOU CELINE DION	10	1996
FALLING STARS SUNSET STRIPPERS	3	2005
FALLING TO PIECES FAITH NO MORE	41	1990
FALSE ALARM BRONX	73	2004
FALTER HUNDRED REASONS	38	2002
FAME [A] DAVID BOWIE	17	1975
FAME [B] IRENE CARA	1	1982
FAMILIAR FEELING MOLOKO	10	2003
FAMILIUS HORRIBILUS POP WILL EAT ITSELF	27	1993
FAMILY AFFAIR [A] SLY & THE FAMILY STONE	15	1972
FAMILY AFFAIR [A] B.E.F. FEATURING LALAH HATHAWAY	37	1991
FAMILY AFFAIR [A] SHABBA RANKS FEATURING PATRA & TERRY & MONICA	18	1993
FAMILY AFFAIR [B] MARY J BLIGE	8	2001
FAMILY MAN [A] MIKE OLDFIELD FEATURING MAGGIE REILLY	45	1982
FAMILY MAN [A] DARYL HALL & JOHN OATES	15	1983
FAMILY MAN [B] FLEETWOOD MAC	54	1987
FAMILY MAN [C] ROACHFORD	25	1989
FAMILY OF MAN FARM	58	1990
FAMILY PORTRAIT P!NK	11	2002
FAMINE SINEAD O'CONNOR	51	1995
FAMOUS LAST WORDS MY CHEMICAL ROMANCE	8	2007
FAN MAIL DICKIES	57	1980
FAN THE FLAME BARBARA PENNINGTON	62	1985
FANCY PANTS KENNY	4	1975
FAN'DABI'DOZI KRANKIES	46	1981
FANFARE FOR THE COMMON MAN EMERSON, LAKE & PALMER	2	1977
FANLIGHT FANNY CLINTON FORD	22	1962
FANS KINGS OF LEON	13	2007
FANTASTIC DAY HAIRCUT 100	9	1982
FANTASTIC VOYAGE COOLIO	41	1994
FANTASY [A] EARTH, WIND & FIRE	14	1978
FANTASY [A] BLACK BOX	5	1990
FANTASY [B] GERARD KENNY	34	1980
FANTASY [C] FANTASY UFO	56	1990
FANTASY [D] TEN CITY	45	1993
FANTASY [E] MARIAH CAREY	4	1995
FANTASY [F] LEVELLERS	16	1995
FANTASY [G] APPLETON	2	2002
FANTASY ISLAND [A] TIGHT FIT	5	1982
FANTASY ISLAND [B] M PEOPLE	33	1997
FANTASY REAL GALAXY FEATURING PHIL FEARON	41	1983
FAR LONGPIGS	37	1996
FAR ABOVE THE CLOUDS MIKE OLDFIELD	53	1999
FAR AND AWAY AIDA	58	2000
FAR AWAY [A] SHIRLEY BASSEY	24	1962
FAR AWAY [B] NICKELBACK	40	2006
FAR AWAY EYES ROLLING STONES	3	1978
FAR FAR AWAY SLADE	2	1974
FAR FROM HOME [A] LEVELLERS	71	1991
(FAR FROM) HOME [B] TIGA	65	2006
FAR FROM OVER FRANK STALLONE	68	1983
FAR GONE AND OUT JESUS & MARY CHAIN	23	1992
FAR OUT [A] SON'Z OF A LOOP DA LOOP ERA	36	1992
FAR OUT [B] DEEJAY PUNK-ROC	43	1998
FARAWAY PLACES BACHELORS	36	1963
FAREWELL ANGELINA JOAN BAEZ	35	1966
FAREWELL - BRING IT ON HOME TO ME ROD STEWART	7	1974
FAREWELL IS A LONELY SOUND JIMMY RUFFIN	8	1970
FAREWELL MR SORROW ALL ABOUT EVE	36	1991
FAREWELL MY SUMMER LOVE MICHAEL JACKSON	7	1984
FAREWELL MY SUMMER LOVE CHAOS	55	1992
FAREWELL TO THE MOON YORK	37	2000
FAREWELL TO TWILIGHT SYMPOSIUM	25	1997
FARMER BILL'S COWMAN (I WAS KAISER BILL'S BATMAN) WURZELS	32	1977
FARON YOUNG PREFAB SPROUT	74	1985
FAR-OUT SON OF LUNG & THE RAMBLINGS OF A MADMAN FUTURE SOUND OF LONDON	22	1995
FASCINATED [A] LISA B	35	1993
FASCINATED [B] RAVEN MAIZE	37	2002
FASCINATING RHYTHM BASS-O-MATIC	9	1990
FASCINATION ALPHABEAT	6	2008
FASHION DAVID BOWIE	5	1980
FASHION '98 GLAMMA KID	49	1998
FASHION CRISIS HITS NEW YORK FRANK & WALTERS	42	1993
FASSY HOLE RONI SIZE	60	2004
FAST AS YOU CAN FIONA APPLE	33	2000
FAST BOY BLUETONES	25	2003
FAST CAR [A] TRACY CHAPMAN	5	1988
FAST CAR [B] DILLINJA	56	2003
FAST FOOD SONG FAST FOOD ROCKERS	2	2003
FASTEN YOUR SEATBELT PENDULUM & FRESH FEATURING SPYDA	60	2005
FASTER MANIC STREET PREACHERS	16	1994
FASTER KILL PUSSYCAT PAUL OAKENFOLD FEATURING BRITTANY MURPHY	7	2006
FASTER THAN THE SPEED OF NIGHT BONNIE TYLER	43	1983
FASTER THE CHASE INME	31	2004
FASTLOVE GEORGE MICHAEL	1	1996
FAT BASTARD (EP) MEDWAY	69	2000
FAT BLACK HEART PELE	75	1993
FAT BOTTOMED GIRLS QUEEN	11	1978
FAT LIP SUM 41	8	2001
FAT NECK BLACK GRAPE	10	1996
FATAL HESITATION CHRIS DE BURGH	44	1986
FATHER [A] CHRISTIANS	55	1992
FATHER [B] LL COOL J	10	1998
FATHER AND DAUGHTER PAUL SIMON	31	2006
FATHER AND SON BOYZONE	2	1995
FATHER AND SON RONAN KEATING & YUSUF	2	2005
FATHER CHRISTMAS DO NOT TOUCH ME GOODIES	7	1974
FATHER FIGURE GEORGE MICHAEL	11	1988
FATTIE BUM BUM CARL MALCOLM	8	1975
FATTIE BUM BUM DIVERSIONS	34	1975
FAVOURITE SHIRTS (BOY MEETS GIRL) HAIRCUT 100	4	1981
FAVOURITE THINGS BIG BROVAZ	2	2003
FBI SHADOWS	6	1961
FE' REAL MAXI PRIEST FEATURING APACHE INDIAN	33	1992
F.E.A.R. IAN BROWN	13	2001
FEAR LOVES THIS PLACE JULIAN COPE	42	1992
FEAR OF THE DARK [A] GORDON GILTRAP BAND	58	1979
FEAR OF THE DARK (LIVE) [B] IRON MAIDEN	8	1993
FEAR SATAN MOGWAI	57	1998
FEAR, THE MINDKILLER EON	63	1991
FEARLESS BRAVERY	43	2005
FED UP HOUSE OF PAIN	68	1996
FEDORA (I'LL BE YOUR DAWG) CARAMBA	56	1983
FEE FI FO FUM CANDY GIRLS FEATURING SWEET PUSSY PAULINE	23	1995
FEED MY FRANKENSTEIN ALICE COOPER	27	1992
FEED THE FEELING PERCEPTION	58	1992
FEED THE TREE BELLY	32	1993
FEED YOUR ADDICTION EASTERN LANE	72	2003
FEEDING TIME LOOK	50	1981
FEEL [A] RUTH JOY	67	1992
FEEL [B] HOUSE OF LOVE	45	1992
FEEL [C] ROBBIE WILLIAMS	4	2002
FEEL EVERY BEAT ELECTRONIC	39	1991

Title / Artist	Peak Position	Year of Entry
FEEL FREE SOUL II SOUL FEATURING DO'REEN	64	1988
FEEL GOOD [A] PHATS & SMALL	7	1999
FEEL GOOD [B] MADASUN	29	2000
FEEL GOOD INC GORILLAZ	2	2005
FEEL GOOD TIME P!NK FEATURING WILLIAM ORBIT	3	2003
FEEL IT [A] HI-LUX	41	1995
FEEL IT [B] CAROL BAILEY	41	1995
FEEL IT [C] NENEH CHERRY	68	1997
FEEL IT [D] TAMPERER FEATURING MAYA	1	1998
FEEL IT [E] INAYA DAY	51	2000
FEEL IT BOY BEENIE MAN FEATURING JANET JACKSON	9	2002
FEEL IT WITH ME ULTRABEAT	57	2005
FEEL LIKE CALLING HOME MR BIG	35	1977
FEEL LIKE CHANGE BLACK	56	1991
FEEL LIKE MAKING LOVE [A] ROBERTA FLACK	34	1974
FEEL LIKE MAKIN' LOVE [A] GEORGE BENSON	28	1983
FEEL LIKE MAKIN' LOVE [B] BAD COMPANY	20	1975
FEEL LIKE MAKING LOVE [B] PAULINE HENRY	12	1993
FEEL LIKE SINGIN' [A] SANDY B	60	1993
FEEL LIKE SINGING [B] TAK TIX	33	1996
FEEL ME BLANCMANGE	46	1982
FEEL ME FLOW NAUGHTY BY NATURE	23	1995
FEEL MY BODY FRANK'O MOIRAGHI FEATURING AMNESIA	39	1996
FEEL NO PAIN SADE	56	1992
FEEL SO FINE JOHNNY PRESTON	18	1960
FEEL SO GOOD [A] MASE	10	1997
FEEL SO GOOD [B] JON THE DENTIST VS OLLIE JAYE	72	2000
FEEL SO HIGH DES'REE	13	1991
FEEL SO REAL [A] STEVE ARRINGTON	5	1985
FEEL SO REAL [B] DREAM FREQUENCY FEATURING DEBBIE SHARP	23	1992
FEEL SURREAL FREEFALL FEATURING PSYCHOTROPIC	63	1991
FEEL THA VIBE THAT KID CHRIS	52	1997
FEEL THE BEAT [A] CAMISRA	32	1998
FEEL THE BEAT [B] DARUDE	5	2000
FEEL THE DRUM (EP) PARKS & WILSON	71	2000
FEEL THE DRUMS NATIVE	46	2001
FEEL THE HEAT RONI SIZE	55	2002
FEEL THE MUSIC GURU	34	1995
FEEL THE NEED [A] LEIF GARRETT	38	1979
FEEL THE NEED [A] G NATION FEATURING ROSIE	58	1997
FEEL THE NEED [B] JT TAYLOR	57	1991
FEEL THE NEED [C] WEIRD SCIENCE	62	2000
FEEL THE NEED IN ME DETROIT EMERALDS	4	1973
FEEL THE NEED IN ME FORREST	17	1983
FEEL THE NEED IN ME SHAKIN' STEVENS	26	1988
FEEL THE PAIN DINOSAUR Jr.	25	1994
FEEL THE RAINDROPS ADVENTURES	58	1985
FEEL THE REAL DAVID BENDETH	44	1979
FEEL THE RHYTHM [A] JAZZI P	51	1990
FEEL THE RHYTHM [B] TERRORIZE	69	1992
FEEL THE RHYTHM [C] JINNY	74	1993
FEEL THE SAME TRIPLE X	32	1999
FEEL THE SUNSHINE ALEX REECE	26	1995
FEEL THE VIBE (TIL THE MORNING COMES) AXWELL	16	2005
FEEL TOGETHER BEN MACKLIN FEATURING TIGER LILY	71	2007
FEEL WHAT YOU WANT KRISTINE W	33	1994
FEELIN' LA'S	43	1991
FEELIN' ALRIGHT E.Y.C.	16	1993
THE FEELIN (CLAP YOUR HANDS) RHYTHMATIC JUNKIES	67	1999
FEELIN' FINE ULTRABEAT	12	2003
FEELIN' INSIDE BOBBY BROWN	40	1997
FEELIN' ME THERESE	61	2007
FEELIN' SO GOOD JENNIFER LOPEZ FEATURING BIG PUN & FAT JOE	15	2000
FEELIN' THE SAME WAY NORAH JONES	72	2002
FEELIN' U SHY FX & T-POWER FEATURING KELE LE ROC	34	2003
FEELIN' WAY TOO DAMN GOOD NICKELBACK	39	2004
FEELIN' YOU ALI	63	1998
THE FEELING [A] URBAN HYPE	67	1992
THE FEELING [B] TIN TIN OUT FEATURING SWEET TEE	32	1994
FEELING A MOMENT FEEDER	13	2005
FEELING FOR YOU CASSIUS	16	1999
FEELING GOOD NINA SIMONE	40	1994
FEELING GOOD HUFF & HERB	31	1997
FEELING GOOD MUSE	24	2001
FEELING IT TOO 3 JAYS	17	1999
FEELING SO REAL MOBY	30	1994
FEELING THE LOVE REACTOR	56	2004
FEELING THIS BLINK 182	15	2003
FEELING THIS WAY CONDUCTOR & THE COWBOY	35	2000
FEELINGS MORRIS ALBERT	4	1975
FEELINGS OF FOREVER TIFFANY	52	1988
FEELS GOOD (DON'T WORRY BOUT A THING) NAUGHTY BY NATURE FEATURING 3LW	44	2002
FEELS JUST LIKE IT SHOULD JAMIROQUAI	8	2005
(FEELS LIKE) HEAVEN [A] FICTION FACTORY	6	1984
FEELS LIKE HEAVEN [B] URBAN COOKIE COLLECTIVE	5	1993
FEELS LIKE HOME MECK FEATURING DINO	39	2007
FEELS LIKE I'M IN LOVE KELLY MARIE	1	1980
FEELS LIKE THE FIRST TIME [A] FOREIGNER	39	1978
FEELS LIKE THE FIRST TIME [B] SINITTA	45	1986
FEELS LIKE THE RIGHT TIME SHAKATAK	41	1980
FEELS SO GOOD [A] VAN HALEN	63	1989
FEELS SO GOOD [B] XSCAPE	34	1995
FEELS SO GOOD [C] ZERO VU FEATURING LORNA B	69	1997
FEELS SO GOOD [D] MELANIE B	5	2001
FEELS SO REAL (WON'T LET GO) PATRICE RUSHEN	51	1984
FEELS SO RIGHT VICTOR SIMONELLI PRESENTS SOLUTION	63	1996
FEENIN' JODECI	18	1994
FEET UP GUY MITCHELL	2	1952
FELICITY ORANGE JUICE	63	1982
FELL IN LOVE WITH A BOY JOSS STONE	18	2004
FELL IN LOVE WITH A GIRL WHITE STRIPES	21	2002
FELL ON BLACK DAYS SOUNDGARDEN	24	1995
FEMALE INTUITION MAI TAI	54	1986
FEMALE OF THE SPECIES SPACE	14	1996
FERGUS SINGS THE BLUES DEACON BLUE	14	1989
FERNANDO ABBA	1	1976
FERRIS WHEEL EVERLY BROTHERS	22	1964
FERRY ACROSS THE MERSEY GERRY & THE PACEMAKERS	8	1964
FERRY 'CROSS THE MERSEY CHRISTIANS, HOLLY JOHNSON, PAUL McCARTNEY, GERRY MARSDEN & STOCK AITKEN WATERMAN	1	1989
FESTIVAL TIME SAN REMO STRINGS	39	1971
FEUER FREI RAMMSTEIN	35	2002
FEVA LAS VEGAS N-DUBZ	57	2007
FEVER [A] PEGGY LEE	5	1958
FEVER [A] HELEN SHAPIRO	38	1964
FEVER [A] McCOYS	44	1965
FEVER [A] MADONNA	6	1993
FEVER [B] S-J	46	1997
FEVER [C] STARSAILOR	18	2001
FEVER CALLED LOVE RHC	65	1992
FEVER FOR THE FLAVA HOT ACTION COP	41	2003
FEVER PITCH THE EP PRETENDERS, LA'S, ORLANDO, NICK HORNBY	65	1997
FICTION OF LIFE CHINA DRUM	65	1997
FIDELITY REGINA SPEKTOR	45	2007
FIELD OF DREAMS FLIP & FILL FEATURING JO JAMES	28	2003
FIELDS OF FIRE (400 MILES) BIG COUNTRY	10	1983
FIELDS OF GOLD STING	16	1993
THE FIELDS OF LOVE ATB FEATURING YORK	16	2001
FIESTA [A] POGUES	24	1988
FIESTA [B] R KELLY FEATURING JAY-Z	23	2001
!FIESTA FATAL! B-TRIBE	64	1993
FIFTEEN FEET OF PURE WHITE SNOW NICK CAVE & THE BAD SEEDS	52	2001
15 MINUTES OF FAME SHEEP ON DRUGS	44	1993
15 STEPS (EP) MONKEY MAFIA	67	1997
15 WAYS FALL	65	1994
15 YEARS (EP) LEVELLERS	11	1992
5TH ANNIVERSARY EP JUDGE DREAD	31	1977
A FIFTH OF BEETHOVEN WALTER MURPHY & THE BIG APPLE BAND	28	1976
50:50 LEMAR	5	2003
51ST STATE NEW MODEL ARMY	71	1986
50FT QUEENIE PJ HARVEY	27	1993
54-66 (WAS MY NUMBER) ASWAD	70	1984
FIFTY GRAND FOR CHRISTMAS PAUL HOLT	35	2004
59TH STREET BRIDGE SONG (FEELING GROOVY) HARPERS BIZARRE	34	1967
57 BIFFY CLYRO	61	2002
57 CHANNELS (AND NOTHIN' ON) BRUCE SPRINGSTEEN	32	1992
50 TO A POUND PADDINGTONS	32	2005
50 WAYS TO LEAVE YOUR LOVER PAUL SIMON	23	1976
FIFTY-FOUR SEA LEVEL	63	1979
FIGARO BROTHERHOOD OF MAN	1	1978
THE FIGHT MARTY WILDE	47	1960
FIGHT McKOY	54	1993
FIGHT FOR OURSELVES SPANDAU BALLET	15	1986
FIGHT FOR YOUR RIGHT (TO PARTY) NYCC	14	1998
FIGHT MUSIC D12	11	2001
THE FIGHT SONG MARILYN MANSON	24	2001
FIGHT TEST FLAMING LIPS	28	2003
FIGHT THE POWER PUBLIC ENEMY	29	1989
FIGHT THE YOUTH FISHBONE	60	1992
FIGHTER CHRISTINA AGUILERA	3	2003
FIGHTING FIT GENE	22	1996
FIGURE IT OUT LIL' CHRIS	57	2007
FIGURE OF 8 GRID	50	1992
FIGURE OF EIGHT PAUL McCARTNEY	42	1989
FIJI ATLANTIS VS AVATAR	52	2000
FILL HER UP GENE	36	1999
FILL ME IN CRAIG DAVID	1	2000
FILL MY LITTLE WORLD THE FEELING	10	2006
FILLING UP WITH HEAVEN HUMAN LEAGUE	36	1995
A FILM FOR THE FUTURE IDLEWILD	53	1998
FILM MAKER COOPER TEMPLE CLAUSE	20	2002
FILMSTAR SUEDE	9	1997
FILTHY SAINT ETIENNE	39	1991
FILTHY/GORGEOUS SCISSOR SISTERS	5	2005
THE FINAL ARREARS MULL HISTORICAL SOCIETY	32	2003
THE FINAL COUNTDOWN EUROPE	1	1986
FINALLY [A] CE CE PENISTON	2	1991
FINALLY [B] KINGS OF TOMORROW FEATURING JULIE McKNIGHT	24	2001
FINALLY FOUND HONEYZ	4	1998
FINCHLEY CENTRAL NEW VAUDEVILLE BAND	11	1967
FIND A WAY [A] COLDCUT FEATURING QUEEN LATIFAH	52	1990
FIND A WAY [B] A TRIBE CALLED QUEST	41	1998
FIND 'EM, FOOL 'EM, FORGET 'EM S-EXPRESS	43	1992
FIND ME (ODYSSEY TO ANYOONA) JAM & SPOON FEATURING PLAVKA	22	1994

Title / Artist	Peak Position	Year of Entry
FIND MY LOVE FAIRGROUND ATTRACTION	7	1988
FIND MY WAY BACK HOME NASHVILLE TEENS	34	1965
FIND THE ANSWER WITHIN BOO RADLEYS	37	1995
FIND THE COLOUR FEEDER	24	2003
FIND THE RIVER R.E.M.	54	1993
FIND THE TIME [A] FIVE STAR	7	1986
FIND THE TIME (PART ONE) [B] QUADROPHONIA	41	1991
FIND THE TIME [C] GET CAPE WEAR CAPE FLY	33	2008
FINDERS KEEPERS CHAIRMEN OF THE BOARD	21	1973
FINDING OUT TRUE LOVE IS BLIND LOUIS XIV	57	2005
FINE DAY [A] ROLF HARRIS	24	2000
FINE DAY [B] KIRSTY HAWKSHAW	62	2002
FINE LINE PAUL McCARTNEY	20	2005
FINE TIME [A] NEW ORDER	11	1988
FINE TIME [B] YAZZ	9	1989
FINER NIGHTMARES ON WAX	63	1999
FINER FEELINGS KYLIE MINOGUE	11	1992
THE FINEST S.O.S. BAND	17	1986
THE FINEST TRUCE	54	1995
FINEST DREAMS RICHARD X FEATURING KELIS	8	2003
FINEST WORKSONG R.E.M.	50	1988
FINETIME CAST	17	1995
FINGER OF SUSPICION DICKIE VALENTINE WITH THE STARGAZERS	1	1954
FINGERS AND THUMBS (COLD SUMMER'S DAY) ERASURE	20	1995
FINGERS OF LOVE CROWDED HOUSE	25	1994
FINGS AIN'T WOT THEY USED T'BE MAX BYGRAVES	5	1960
FINGS AIN'T WOT THEY USED TO BE RUSS CONWAY	47	1960
FINISHED SYMPHONY HYBRID	58	1999
FIRE [A] CRAZY WORLD OF ARTHUR BROWN	1	1968
FIRE [B] POINTER SISTERS	34	1979
FIRE [B] BRUCE SPRINGSTEEN	54	1987
FIRE [C] U2	35	1981
FIRE [D] SLY & ROBBIE	60	1987
FIRE [E] PRODIGY	11	1992
FIRE [F] PRIZNA FEATURING DEMOLITION MAN	33	1995
FIRE [G] SCOOTER	45	1997
FIRE [H] BUSTA RHYMES	60	2000
FIRE [I] MOUSSE T FEATURING EMMA LANFORD	58	2002
FIRE [J] LETHAL BIZZLE	34	2005
FIRE [K] FERRY CORSTEN	40	2006
FIRE AND RAIN JAMES TAYLOR	42	1970
FIRE BRIGADE MOVE	3	1968
FIRE DEPARTMENT BE YOUR OWN PET	59	2005
FIRE DOWN BELOW JERI SOUTHERN	22	1957
FIRE DOWN BELOW SHIRLEY BASSEY	30	1957
FIRE IN MY HEART SUPER FURRY ANIMALS	25	1999
FIRE ISLAND FIRE ISLAND	66	1992
FIRE OF LOVE JUNGLE HIGH WITH BLUE PEARL	71	1993
FIRE UP THE SHOESAW LIONROCK	43	1996
FIRE WOMAN CULT	15	1989
FIRE WORKS SIOUXSIE & THE BANSHEES	22	1982
FIREBALL [A] DON SPENCER	32	1963
FIREBALL [B] DEEP PURPLE	15	1971
FIRED UP [A] ELEVATORMAN	44	1995
FIRED UP! [B] FUNKY GREEN DOGS	17	1997
FIREFLY INME	43	2002
FIREPILE (EP) THROWING MUSES	46	1992
FIRES BURNING RUN TINGS	58	1992
FIRESTARTER PRODIGY	1	1996
FIREWIRE COSMIC GATE	9	2001
FIREWORKS ROXETTE	30	1994
FIREWORKS EP EMBRACE	34	1997
FIRM BIZZ FIRM FEATURING DAWN ROBINSON	18	1997
FIRST ATHEIST TABERNACLE CHOIR SPITTING IMAGE	22	1986
FIRST BOY IN THIS TOWN (LOVE SICK) SCRITTI POLITTI	63	1988
FIRST CUT IS THE DEEPEST PP ARNOLD	18	1967
FIRST CUT IS THE DEEPEST ROD STEWART	1	1977
FIRST CUT IS THE DEEPEST SHERYL CROW	37	2003
FIRST DATE BLINK 182	31	2001
FIRST DAY FUTUREHEADS	58	2003
THE FIRST DAY (HORIZON) MAN WITH NO NAME	72	1998
FIRST DAY OF MY LIFE [A] RASMUS	50	2004
FIRST DAY OF MY LIFE [B] BRIGHT EYES	37	2005
FIRST IMPRESSIONS IMPRESSIONS	16	1975
FIRST IT GIVETH QUEENS OF THE STONE AGE	33	2003
THE FIRST THE LAST THE ETERNITY SNAP FEATURING SUMMER	15	1995
FIRST LOVE MACCABEES	40	2006
1ST MAN IN SPACE ALL SEEING I	28	1999
THE FIRST MAN YOU REMEMBER MICHAEL BALL & DIANA MORRISON	68	1989
THE FIRST NIGHT MONICA	6	1998
FIRST OF MAY BEE GEES	6	1969
1ST OF THA MONTH BONE THUGS-N-HARMONY	32	1995
FIRST OF THE GANG TO DIE MORRISSEY	6	2004
THE FIRST PICTURE OF YOU LOTUS EATERS	15	1983
FIRST TASTE OF LOVE BEN E. KING	27	1961
FIRST THING IN THE MORNING KIKI DEE	32	1977
THE FIRST TIME [A] ADAM FAITH & THE ROULETTES	5	1963
THE FIRST TIME [B] ROBIN BECK	1	1988
THE FIRST TIME [C] SURFACE	60	1991
FIRST TIME [D] SUNBLOCK	9	2006
FIRST TIME EVER JOANNA LAW	67	1990
THE FIRST TIME EVER I SAW YOUR FACE ROBERTA FLACK	14	1972
THE FIRST TIME EVER I SAW YOUR FACE CELINE DION	19	2000
THE FIRST TIME EVER I SAW YOUR FACE LEONA LEWIS	73	2007
FIRST WE TAKE MANHATTAN JENNIFER WARNES	74	1987
FISH OUT OF WATER ONE MINUTE SILENCE	56	2001
FISHERMAN'S BLUES WATERBOYS	32	1989
FISHING FOR A DREAM TURIN BRAKES	32	2005
FIT BUT YOU KNOW IT STREETS	4	2004
FIVE COLOURS IN HER HAIR McFLY	1	2004
THE $5.98 EP - GARAGE DAYS REVISITED METALLICA	27	1987
FIVE FATHOMS EVERYTHING BUT THE GIRL	27	1999
5.15 WHO	20	1973
555 DELAKOTA	42	1999
555 FOR FILMSTARS DIVE DIVE	48	2005
5-4-3-2-1 MANFRED MANN	5	1964
FIVE GET OVER EXCITED HOUSEMARTINS	11	1987
505 ARCTIC MONKEYS	74	2007
500 (SHAKE BABY SHAKE) LUSH	21	1996
FIVE LITTLE FINGERS FRANKIE McBRIDE	19	1967
FIVE LIVE EP GEORGE MICHAEL & QUEEN WITH LISA STANSFIELD	1	1993
5 MILE (THESE ARE THE DAYS) TURIN BRAKES	31	2003
FIVE MILES OUT MIKE OLDFIELD FEATURING MAGGIE REILLY	43	1982
5 MILES TO EMPTY BROWNSTONE	12	1997
FIVE MINUTES [A] STRANGLERS	11	1978
5 MINUTES [B] LIL' MO FEATURING MISSY 'MISDEMEANOR' ELLIOTT	72	1998
5 O'CLOCK NONCHALANT	44	1996
5 O'CLOCK WORLD JULIAN COPE	42	1989
5-7-0-5 CITY BOY	8	1978
5, 6, 7, 8 STEPS	14	1997
5 STEPS DRU HILL	22	1997
5000 MINUTES OF PAIN MINUTEMAN	75	2002
FIX BLACKstreet	7	1997
FIX MY SINK DJ SNEAK FEATURING BEAR WHO	26	2003
FIX UP LOOK SHARP DIZZEE RASCAL	17	2003
FIX YOU COLDPLAY	4	2005
FIXATION ANDY LING	55	2000
FIXER VENT 414	71	1996
FLAGPOLE SITTA HARVEY DANGER	57	1998
FLAMBOYANT PET SHOP BOYS	12	2004
THE FLAME [A] ARCADIA	58	1986
FLAME [A] SEBADOH	30	1999
THE FLAME [B] FINE YOUNG CANNIBALS	17	1996
FLAME [B] BELL X1	65	2006
THE FLAME STILL BURNS JIMMY NAIL WITH STRANGE FRUIT	47	1998
THE FLAME TREES OF THIKA VIDEO SYMPHONIC	42	1981
FLAMES OF PARADISE JENNIFER RUSH & ELTON JOHN	59	1987
FLAMING JUNE BT	19	1997
FLAMING SWORD CARE	48	1983
FLAP YOUR WINGS NELLY	1	2004
FLASH [A] QUEEN	10	1980
FLASH [A] QUEEN & VANGUARD	15	2003
FLASH [B] BBE	5	1997
FLASH [C] BK & NICK SENTIENCE	67	2001
FLASH [D] GRIFTERS	63	1999
FLASHBACK IMAGINATION	16	1981
FLASHBACK JACK ADAMSKI	46	1990
FLASHDANCE DEEP DISH	3	2004
FLASHDANCE...WHAT A FEELING IRENE CARA	2	1983
FLASHDANCE...WHAT A FEELING BJORN AGAIN	65	1993
THE FLASHER MISTURA FEATURING LLOYD MICHELS	23	1976
FLAT BEAT MR OIZO	1	1999
FLATHEAD FRATELLIS	67	2007
FLATLINERS NEBULA II	54	1992
FLAVA [A] PETER ANDRE	1	1996
FLAVA [B] IMAJIN	64	2000
FLAVA IN YOUR EAR CRAIG MACK	57	1994
FLAVOR OF THE WEAK AMERICAN HI-FI	31	2001
FLAVOUR OF THE OLD SCHOOL BEVERLEY KNIGHT	33	1995
FLAWLESS ONES	7	2001
FLAWLESS (GO TO THE CITY) GEORGE MICHAEL	8	2004
FLEE FLY FLO FE-M@IL	46	2000
FLESH A SPLIT SECOND	68	1991
FLESH JAN JOHNSTON	36	2001
FLESH FOR FANTASY BILLY IDOL	54	1984
FLESH OF MY FLESH ORANGE JUICE	41	1983
FLETCH THEME HAROLD FALTERMEYER	74	1985
FLEX DIZZEE RASCAL	23	2007
FLIGHT OF ICARUS IRON MAIDEN	11	1983
FLIGHT 643 DJ TIESTO	56	2001
FLIP JESSE GREEN	26	1977
FLIP REVERSE BLAZIN' SQUAD	2	2003
THE FLIPSIDE MOLOKO	53	1998
FLIRT JONATHAN KING	22	1972
FLIRTATION WALTZ WINIFRED ATWELL	10	1953
F.L.M. MEL & KIM	7	1987
FLOAT ON [A] FLOATERS	1	1977
FLOAT ON [B] MODEST MOUSE	46	2004
FLOATATION GRID	60	1990
FLOATING TERRA FIRMA	64	1996
FLOATING IN THE WIND HUDSON-FORD	35	1974
FLOBBADANCE BILL & BEN	23	2002
FLOETIC FLOETRY	73	2003

Title / Artist	Peak Position	Year of Entry
FLOODLIT WORLD ULTRASOUND	39	1999
THE FLOOR JOHNNY GILL	53	1993
FLOOR SPACE OUR HOUSE	52	1996
FLOOR-ESSENCE MAN WITH NO NAME	68	1995
THE FLORAL DANCE BRIGHOUSE & RASTRICK BRASS BAND	2	1977
FLORAL DANCE TERRY WOGAN	21	1978
FLORIBUNDA MOTHER'S PRIDE	42	1998
FLOWER DUET JONATHAN PETERS PRESENTS LUMINAIRE	75	1999
FLOWER DUET (FROM LAKME) MADY MESPLE & DANIELLE MILLET WITH THE PARIS OPERACOMIQUE ORCHESTRA CONDUCTED BY ALAIN LOMBARD	47	1985
FLOWER OF SCOTLAND SCOTTISH RUGBY TEAM WITH RONNIE BROWNE	73	1990
FLOWER OF THE WEST RUNRIG	43	1991
FLOWERS [A] TITIYO	71	1990
FLOWERS [B] SWEET FEMALE ATTITUDE	2	2000
FLOWERS IN DECEMBER MAZZY STAR	40	1996
FLOWERS IN THE RAIN MOVE	2	1967
FLOWERS IN THE WINDOW TRAVIS	18	2002
FLOWERS OF ROMANCE PUBLIC IMAGE LTD.	24	1981
FLOWERS ON THE WALL STATLER BROTHERS	38	1966
FLOWERZ ARMAND VAN HELDEN FEATURING ROLAND CLARK	18	1999
FLOWTATION VINCENT DE MOOR	54	1997
FLOY JOY SUPREMES	9	1972
FLUORESCENT ADOLESCENT ARCTIC MONKEYS	5	2007
FLUX BLOC PARTY	8	2007
THE FLY [A] U2	1	1991
FLY [B] SUGAR RAY	58	1998
FLY [C] POB FEATURING DJ PATRICK REID	74	1999
FLY [D] MARK JOSEPH	28	2003
FLY [E] MATT GOSS	31	2004
FLY [F] HILARY DUFF	20	2006
FLY AWAY [A] HADDAWAY	20	1995
FLY AWAY [B] LENNY KRAVITZ	1	1999
FLY AWAY [C] VINCENT DE MOOR	30	2001
FLY AWAY (BYE BYE) EYES CREAM	53	1999
FLY BI TEEBONE FEATURING MC KIE & MC SPARKS	43	2000
FLY BY II BLUE	6	2002
FLY GIRL QUEEN LATIFAH	67	1991
FLY LIFE BASEMENT JAXX	19	1997
FLY LIKE AN EAGLE SEAL	13	1997
FLY ME AWAY GOLDFRAPP	26	2006
FLY ON THE WINGS OF LOVE XTM & DJ CHUCKY PRESENTS ANNIA	8	2003
FLY ROBIN FLY SILVER CONVENTION	28	1975
FLY TO THE ANGELS SLAUGHTER	55	1991
FLY TOO HIGH JANIS IAN	44	1979
FLY WITH ME COLOURSOUND	49	2002
FLYING [A] CAST	4	1996
FLYING [B] BRYAN ADAMS	39	2004
FLYING ELVIS LEILANI	73	2000
FLYING HIGH [A] COMMODORES	37	1978
FLYING HIGH [B] FREEEZ	35	1981
FLYING HIGH [C] CAPTAIN HOLLYWOOD PROJECT	58	1995
FLYING MACHINE CLIFF RICHARD	37	1971
FLYING SAUCER WEDDING PRESENT	22	1992
THE FLYING SONG PQM FEATURING CICA	68	2000
FLYING THE FLAG (FOR YOU) SCOOCH	5	2007
FLYING WITHOUT WINGS WESTLIFE	1	1999
FLYSWATER EELS	55	2000
FM (NO STATIC AT ALL) STEELY DAN	49	1978
FOE-DEE-O-DEE RUBETTES	15	1975
FOG ON THE TYNE (REVISITED) GAZZA & LINDISFARNE	2	1990
FOGGY MOUNTAIN BREAKDOWN LESTER FLATT & EARL SCRUGGS	39	1967
FOGHORN A	63	1998
FOLDING STARS BIFFY CLYRO	18	2007
THE FOLK SINGER TOMMY ROE	4	1963
FOLLOW DA LEADER NIGEL & MARVIN	5	2002
FOLLOW ME [A] JT TAYLOR	59	1992
FOLLOW ME [B] ALY-US	43	1992
FOLLOW ME [C] ATOMIC KITTEN	20	2000
FOLLOW ME [D] UNCLE KRACKER	3	2001
FOLLOW ME HOME SUGABABES	32	2006
FOLLOW THAT DREAM EP ELVIS PRESLEY	34	1962
FOLLOW THE LEADER ERIC B & RAKIM	21	1988
FOLLOW THE LEADERS KILLING JOKE	55	1981
FOLLOW THE RULES LIVIN' JOY	9	1996
FOLLOW YOU DOWN GIN BLOSSOMS	30	1996
FOLLOW YOU FOLLOW ME GENESIS	7	1978
FOLLOW YOU FOLLOW ME SONNY JONES FEATURING TARA CHASE	42	2000
FOLLOWED THE WAVES AUF DER MAUR	35	2004
FOLLOWING BANGLES	55	1987
THE FOOD CHRISTMAS EP VARIOUS ARTISTS (EP'S & LPS)	63	1989
FOOD FOR THOUGHT [A] BARRON KNIGHTS	46	1979
FOOD FOR THOUGHT [B] UB40	4	1980
FOOL [A] ELVIS PRESLEY	15	1973
FOOL [B] AL MATTHEWS	16	1975
FOOL [C] MANSUN	28	2001
FOOL AGAIN WESTLIFE	1	2000
A FOOL AM I CILLA BLACK	13	1966
FOOL FOR LOVE RUSSELL	52	2000
FOOL FOR YOUR LOVING WHITESNAKE	13	1980
FOOL (IF YOU THINK IT'S OVER) CHRIS REA	30	1978
FOOL IF YOU THINK IT'S OVER ELKIE BROOKS	17	1982
A FOOL NEVER LEARNS ANDY WILLIAMS	40	1964
FOOL NO MORE S CLUB 8	4	2003
FOOL NUMBER ONE BRENDA LEE	38	1961
THE FOOL ON THE HILL SHIRLEY BASSEY	48	1971
A FOOL SUCH AS I ELVIS PRESLEY	1	1959
FOOL TO CRY ROLLING STONES	6	1976
FOOLED AROUND AND FELL IN LOVE ELVIN BISHOP	34	1976
FOOLED BY A SMILE SWING OUT SISTER	43	1987
FOOLIN' YOURSELF PAUL HARDCASTLE	51	1986
FOOLISH [A] ASHANTI	4	2002
FOOLISH [B] TYLER JAMES	16	2005
FOOLISH BEAT DEBBIE GIBSON	9	1988
FOOLISH LITTLE GIRL SHIRELLES	38	1963
FOOL'S GOLD STONE ROSES	8	1989
FOOL'S PARADISE MELI'SA MORGAN	41	1986
FOOLS RUSH IN BROOK BENTON	50	1961
FOOLS RUSH IN RICK NELSON	12	1963
FOOT STOMPIN' MUSIC HAMILTON BOHANNON	23	1975
FOOT TAPPER SHADOWS	1	1963
FOOTLOOSE KENNY LOGGINS	6	1984
FOOTPRINT DISCO CITIZENS	34	1997
FOOTPRINTS IN THE SAND LEONA LEWIS	2	2007
FOOTPRINTS IN THE SNOW JOHNNY DUNCAN & THE BLUE GRASS BOYS	27	1957
FOOTSEE WIGAN'S CHOSEN FEW	9	1975
FOOTSTEPS [A] RONNIE CARROLL	36	1960
FOOTSTEPS [A] STEVE LAWRENCE	4	1960
FOOTSTEPS [A] SHOWADDYWADDY	31	1981
FOOTSTEPS [B] STILTSKIN	34	1994
FOOTSTEPS [C] DANIEL O'DONNELL	25	1996
FOOTSTEPS FOLLOWING ME FRANCES NERO	17	1991
FOR A FEW DOLLARS MORE SMOKIE	17	1978
FOR A FRIEND COMMUNARDS	28	1988
FOR A LIFETIME ASCENSION FEATURING ERIN LORDAN	45	2002
FOR A PENNY PAT BOONE	19	1959
FOR ALL THAT YOU WANT GARY BARLOW	24	1999
FOR ALL THE COWS FOO FIGHTERS	28	1995
FOR ALL TIME CATHERINE ZETA JONES	36	1992
FOR ALL WE KNOW CARPENTERS	18	1971
FOR ALL WE KNOW SHIRLEY BASSEY	6	1971
FOR ALL WE KNOW NICKI FRENCH	42	1995
FOR AMERICA RED BOX	10	1986
FOR AN ANGEL PAUL VAN DYK	28	1998
FOR BRITAIN ONLY ALICE COOPER	66	1982
(FOR GOD'S SAKE) GIVE MORE POWER TO THE PEOPLE CHI-LITES	32	1971
FOR HER LIGHT FIELDS OF THE NEPHILIM	54	1990
FOR LOVE (EP) LUSH	35	1992
FOR LOVERS WOLFMAN FEATURING PETE DOHERTY	7	2004
FOR MAMA MATT MONRO	23	1964
FOR OLD TIME'S SAKE MILLICAN & NESBITT	38	1974
FOR ONCE IN MY LIFE STEVIE WONDER	3	1968
FOR ONCE IN MY LIFE DOROTHY SQUIRES	24	1969
FOR REAL TRICKY	45	1999
FOR REASONS UNKNOWN KILLERS	53	2007
FOR SPACIOUS LIES NORMAN COOK FEATURING LESTER	48	1989
FOR SURE SCOOCH	15	2000
FOR THE DEAD GENE	14	1996
FOR THE GOOD TIMES PERRY COMO	7	1973
FOR THOSE ABOUT TO ROCK (WE SALUTE YOU) AC/DC	15	1982
FOR TOMORROW BLUR	28	1993
FOR WHAT IT'S WORTH [A] OUI 3	26	1993
FOR WHAT IT'S WORTH [B] CARDIGANS	31	2003
FOR WHAT YOU DREAM OF BEDROCK FEATURING KYO	25	1996
FOR WHOM THE BELL TOLLS [A] SIMON DUPREE & THE BIG SOUND	43	1968
FOR WHOM THE BELL TOLLS [B] BEE GEES	4	1993
FOR YOU [A] RICK NELSON	14	1964
FOR YOU [B] FARMERS BOYS	66	1983
FOR YOU [C] SNOWY WHITE	65	1985
FOR YOU [D] ELECTRONIC	16	1996
FOR YOU [E] STAIND	55	2002
FOR YOU FOR LOVE AVERAGE WHITE BAND	46	1980
FOR YOU I WILL MONICA	27	1997
FOR YOUR BABIES SIMPLY RED	9	1992
FOR YOUR BLUE EYES ONLY TONY HADLEY	67	1992
FOR YOUR EYES ONLY SHEENA EASTON	8	1981
FOR YOUR LOVE [A] YARDBIRDS	3	1965
FOR YOUR LOVE [B] STEVIE WONDER	23	1995
FORBIDDEN CITY ELECTRONIC	14	1996
FORBIDDEN COLOURS DAVID SYLVIAN & RYUICHI SAKAMOTO	16	1983
FORBIDDEN FRUIT PAUL VAN DYK	69	1997
FORBIDDEN ZONE BEDROCK	71	1997
FORCA NELLY FURTADO	40	2004
THE FORCE BEHIND THE POWER DIANA ROSS	27	1992
FOREIGN SAND ROGER TAYLOR & YOSHIKI	26	1994
FORERUNNER NATURAL BORN GROOVES	64	1996
A FOREST CURE	31	1980
FOREST FIRE LLOYD COLE & THE COMMOTIONS	41	1984
FOREVER [A] ROY WOOD	8	1973
FOREVER [B] KISS	65	1990
FOREVER [C] DAMAGE	6	1996
FOREVER [D] CHARLATANS	12	1999
FOREVER [E] TINA COUSINS	45	1999
FOREVER [F] DEE DEE	12	2002
FOREVER [G] N-TRANCE	6	2002
FOREVER [H] TRINITY-X	19	2002
FOREVER AND A DAY [A] BROTHERS IN RHYTHM PRESENT CHARVONI	51	1994
FOREVER AND A DAY [B] STATE ONE	62	2003
FOREVER AND EVER SLIK	1	1976
FOREVER AND EVER, AMEN RANDY TRAVIS	55	1988
FOREVER AND FOR ALWAYS SHANIA TWAIN	6	2003
FOREVER AS ONE VENGABOYS	28	2001

Title / Artist	Peak Position	Year of Entry
FOREVER AUTUMN JUSTIN HAYWARD	5	1978
FOREVER CAME TODAY DIANA ROSS & THE SUPREMES	25	1968
FOREVER FAILURE PARADISE LOST	66	1995
FOREVER FREE W.A.S.P.	25	1989
FOREVER GIRL OTT	24	1997
FOREVER IN BLUE JEANS NEIL DIAMOND	16	1979
FOREVER IN LOVE KENNY G	47	1993
FOREVER J TERRY HALL	67	1994
A FOREVER KIND OF LOVE BOBBY VEE	13	1962
(FOREVER) LIVE AND DIE ORCHESTRAL MANOEUVRES IN THE DARK	11	1986
FOREVER LOST MAGIC NUMBERS	15	2005
FOREVER LOVE GARY BARLOW	1	1996
FOREVER MAN ERIC CLAPTON	51	1985
FOREVER MAN (HOW MANY TIMES) BEATCHUGGERS FEATURING ERIC CLAPTON	26	2000
FOREVER MORE [A] PUFF JOHNSON	29	1997
FOREVER MORE [B] MOLOKO	17	2003
FOREVER NOW LEVEL 42	19	1994
FOREVER REELING KINESIS	65	2003
FOREVER TOGETHER RAVEN MAIZE	67	1989
FOREVER YOUNG [A] ROD STEWART	57	1988
FOREVER YOUNG [B] INTERACTIVE	28	1996
FOREVER YOUNG [C] 4 VINI FEATURING ELIZABETH TROY	75	2002
FOREVER YOUR GIRL PAULA ABDUL	24	1989
FOREVERGREEN FINITRIBE	51	1992
FORGET ABOUT THE WORLD GABRIELLE	23	1996
FORGET ABOUT TOMORROW FEEDER	12	2003
FORGET ABOUT YOU MOTORS	13	1978
FORGET HIM BOBBY RYDELL	13	1963
FORGET HIM BILLY FURY	59	1983
FORGET I WAS A G WHITEHEAD BROTHERS	40	1995
FORGET ME KNOTS RONI SIZE	61	2003
FORGET-ME-NOT [A] VERA LYNN	5	1952
FORGET ME NOT [B] EDEN KANE	3	1962
FORGET ME NOT [C] MARTHA REEVES & THE VANDELLAS	11	1971
FORGET ME NOTS PATRICE RUSHEN	8	1982
FORGET ME NOTS TONGUE 'N' CHEEK	26	1991
FORGET MYSELF ELBOW	22	2005
FORGIVE ME LYNDEN DAVID HALL	30	2000
FORGIVEN (I FEEL YOUR LOVE) SPACE BROTHERS	27	1997
FORGIVENESS [A] ENGINEERS	48	2005
FORGIVENESS [B] LEONA LEWIS	46	2007
FORGOT ABOUT DRE DR DRE FEATURING EMINEM	7	2000
FORGOTTEN DREAMS CYRIL STAPLETON	27	1957
FORGOTTEN DREAMS LEROY ANDERSON & HIS POPS CONCERT ORCHESTRA	24	1957
FORGOTTEN TOWN CHRISTIANS	22	1987
FORMED A BAND ART BRUT	52	2004
FORMULAE JJ72	28	2002
FORSAKEN DREAMS DILLINJA	71	2004
FORT WORTH JAIL LONNIE DONEGAN	14	1959
FORTRESS AROUND YOUR HEART STING	49	1985
FORTRESS EUROPE ASIAN DUB FOUNDATION	57	2003
FORTUNE FADED RED HOT CHILI PEPPERS	11	2003
FORTUNES OF WAR FISH	67	1994
48 CRASH SUZI QUATRO	3	1973
45 RPM POPPYFIELDS	28	2004
40 MILES CONGRESS	26	1991
FORTY MILES OF BAD ROAD DUANE EDDY & THE REBELS	11	1959
49 PERCENT ROYKSOPP	55	2005
40 YEARS PAUL HARDCASTLE	53	1988
FORWARD THE REVOLUTION SPIRAL TRIBE	70	1992
FOUND A CURE ULTRA NATE	6	1998
FOUND LOVE DOUBLE DEE FEATURING DANY	33	1990
FOUND OUT ABOUT YOU GIN BLOSSOMS	40	1994
FOUND OUT TOO LATE 999	69	1979
FOUND THAT SOUL MANIC STREET PREACHERS	9	2001
FOUND YOU [A] DODGY	19	1997
FOUND YOU [B] ROSS COPPERMAN	68	2007
FOUNDATION BEENIE MAN AND THE TAXI GANG	69	1998
FOUNDATIONS KATE NASH	2	2007
FOUNTAIN O' YOUTH CANDYLAND	72	1991
4 AM FOREVER LOSTPROPHETS	34	2007
FOUR BACHARACH AND DAVID SONGS EP DEACON BLUE	2	1990
FOUR BIG SPEAKERS WHALE FEATURING BUS 75	69	1998
FOUR FROM TOYAH EP TOYAH	4	1981
4 IN THE MORNING GWEN STEFANI	22	2007
FOUR KICKS KINGS OF LEON	24	2005
FOUR LETTER WORD KIM WILDE	6	1988
FOUR LITTLE HEELS AVONS	45	1960
FOUR LITTLE HEELS BRIAN HYLAND	29	1960
FOUR MINUTE WARNING MARK OWEN	4	2003
4 MINUTES MADONNA FEATURING JUSTIN TIMBERLAKE	7	2008
4 MORE DE LA SOUL FEATURING ZHANE	52	1997
FOUR MORE FROM TOYAH EP TOYAH	14	1981
4 MY PEOPLE MISSY ELLIOTT	5	2002
4 PAGE LETTER AALIYAH	24	1997
THE 4 PLAYS EPS R KELLY	23	1995
FOUR SEASONS IN ONE DAY CROWDED HOUSE	26	1992
4 SEASONS OF LONELINESS BOYZ II MEN	10	1997
FOUR STRONG WINDS NEIL YOUNG	57	1979
FOUR TO THE FLOOR STARSAILOR	24	2004
FOUR WINDS BRIGHT EYES	57	2007
4 WORDS (TO CHOKE UPON) BULLET FOR MY VALENTINE	40	2005
FOURPLAY (EP) VARIOUS ARTISTS (EP'S & LPS)	45	1992
FOURTEEN FORWARD, RUSSIA!	74	2005
14 HOURS TO SAVE THE EARTH TOMSKI	42	1998
FOURTH RENDEZ-VOUS JEAN-MICHEL JARRE	65	1986
FOX FORCE FIVE CHRIS & JAMES	71	1995
FOX ON THE RUN [A] MANFRED MANN	5	1969
FOX ON THE RUN [B] SWEET	2	1975
FOXHOLE TELEVISION	36	1978
FOXTROT UNIFORM CHARLIE KILO BLOODHOUND GANG	47	2005
FOXY FOXY MOTT THE HOOPLE	33	1974
FRAGGLE ROCK THEME FRAGGLES	33	1984
FRAGILE STING	70	1988
FRAGILE JULIO IGLESIAS	53	1994
FRAGILE THING BIG COUNTRY FEATURING EDDI READER	69	1999
FRANCESCA - THE MADDENING GLARE SPECIAL NEEDS	69	2004
THE FRANK SONATA LONGPIGS	57	1999
FRANKENSTEIN EDGAR WINTER GROUP	18	1973
FRANKIE SISTER SLEDGE	1	1985
FRANKIE AND JOHNNY MR ACKER BILK & HIS PARAMOUNT JAZZ BAND	42	1962
FRANKIE AND JOHNNY SAM COOKE	30	1963
FRANKIE AND JOHNNY ELVIS PRESLEY	21	1966
FRANTIC METALLICA	16	2003
FREAK [A] BRUCE FOXTON	23	1983
FREAK [B] SILVERCHAIR	34	1997
FREAK [C] STRANGELOVE	43	1997
FREAK IT! STUDIO 45	36	1999
FREAK LIKE ME ADINA HOWARD	33	1995
FREAK LIKE ME TRU FAITH & DUB CONSPIRACY	12	2000
FREAK LIKE ME SUGABABES	1	2002
FREAK ME SILK	46	1993
FREAK ME ANOTHER LEVEL	1	1998
FREAK MODE REELISTS	16	2002
FREAK ON STONEBRIDGE VS ULTRA NATE	37	2005
FREAK ON A LEASH KORN	24	1999
FREAKIN' IT WILL SMITH	15	2000
FREAKIN' OUT GRAHAM COXON	37	2004
FREAKIN' YOU JUNGLE BROTHERS	70	2000
FREAKS LIVE	60	1997
THE FREAKS COME OUT CEVIN FISHER'S BIG BREAK	34	1998
FREAKS (LIVE) MARILLION	24	1988
FREAKY BE BEAUTIFUL MOIST	47	1995
FREAKYTIME POINT BREAK	13	2000
THE FRED EP VARIOUS ARTISTS (EP'S & LPS)	26	1992
FREDDY KREUGER REUBEN	53	2004
FREDERICK PATTI SMITH GROUP	63	1979
FREE [A] DENIECE WILLIAMS	1	1977
FREE [B] CURIOSITY KILLED THE CAT	56	1987
FREE [C] WILL DOWNING	58	1988
FREE [D] STEVIE WONDER	49	1989
FREE [E] DJ QUICKSILVER	7	1997
FREE [F] ULTRA NATE	4	1997
FREE [G] JOHN 'OO' FLEMING	61	2000
FREE [H] VAST	55	2000
FREE [I] CLAIRE FREELAND	44	2001
FREE [J] MYA	11	2001
FREE [K] ESTELLE	15	2004
FREE AS A BIRD BEATLES	2	1995
FREE AT LAST SIMON	36	2001
FREE BIRD LYNYRD SKYNYRD	21	1976
FREE (C'MON) CATCH	70	1990
FREE ELECTRIC BAND ALBERT HAMMOND	19	1973
FREE EP FREE	11	1978
FREE FALLIN' TOM PETTY	64	1989
FREE, GAY AND HAPPY COMING OUT CREW	50	1995
FREE HUEY BOO RADLEYS	54	1998
FREE (LET IT BE) STUART	41	2003
FREE LOVE JULIET ROBERTS	25	1993
FREE ME [A] ROGER DALTREY	39	1980
FREE ME [B] CAST	7	1997
FREE ME [C] EMMA BUNTON	5	2003
FREE MY NAME OCEAN COLOUR SCENE	23	2005
FREE 'N' EASY ALMIGHTY	35	1991
FREE RANGE FALL	40	1992
FREE SALUTE LITTLE BARRIE	73	2005
FREE SATPAL RAM ASIAN DUB FOUNDATION	56	1998
FREE SPIRIT KIM APPLEBY	51	1994
THE FREE STYLE MEGA-MIX BOBBY BROWN	14	1990
FREE TO DECIDE CRANBERRIES	33	1996
FREE TO FALL DEBBIE HARRY	46	1987
FREE TO LOVE AGAIN SUZETTE CHARLES	58	1993
FREE WORLD KIRSTY MacCOLL	43	1989
FREE YOUR BODY PRAGA KHAN FEATURING JADE 4 U	39	1992
FREE YOUR MIND [A] EN VOGUE	16	1992
FREE YOUR MIND [B] SPACE BABY	55	1995
FREE YOURSELF UNTOUCHABLES	26	1985
FREE/SAIL ON CHANTE MOORE	69	1995
FREEBASE TALL PAUL	43	2000
FREED FROM DESIRE GALA	2	1997
FREEDOM [A] WHAM!	1	1984
FREEDOM [B] ALICE COOPER	50	1988
FREEDOM [C] GEORGE MICHAEL	28	1990
FREEDOM [C] ROBBIE WILLIAMS	2	1996
FREEDOM [D] A HOMEBOY, A HIPPIE & A FUNKI DREDD	68	1990
FREEDOM [E] LONDON BOYS	54	1991
FREEDOM [F] MICHELLE GAYLE	16	1995
FREEDOM [G] SHIVA	18	1995
FREEDOM [H] ROBERT MILES FEATURING KATHY SLEDGE	15	1997
FREEDOM [I] ERASURE	27	2000
FREEDOM [J] QFX	36	2003
FREEDOM COME FREEDOM GO FORTUNES	6	1971
FREEDOM (EP) QFX	41	1995

Title / Artist	Peak Position	Year of Entry
FREEDOM FIGHTERS MUSIC	15	2004
FREEDOM GOT AN A.K. DA LENCH MOB	51	1993
FREEDOM (MAKE IT FUNKY) BLACK MAGIC	41	1996
FREEDOM OVERSPILL STEVE WINWOOD	69	1986
FREEDOM'S PRISONER STEVE HARLEY	58	1979
FREEEK! GEORGE MICHAEL	7	2002
FREEFLOATING GARY CLARK	50	1993
FREEK 'N YOU JODECI	17	1995
FREEK U BON GARCON	42	2005
FREELOADER DRIFTWOOD	32	2003
FREELOVE DEPECHE MODE	19	2001
FREESTYLER BOMFUNK MC'S	2	2000
FREET TATA BOX INHIBITORS	67	2001
FREEWAY OF LOVE ARETHA FRANKLIN	51	1985
FREEWHEEL BURNIN' JUDAS PRIEST	42	1984
THE FREEZE SPANDAU BALLET	17	1981
FREEZE THE ATLANTIC CABLE	44	1997
FREEZE-FRAME J GEILS BAND	27	1982
FREIGHT TRAIN CHARLES McDEVITT SKIFFLE GROUP FEATURING NANCY WHISKEY	5	1957
FRENCH DISCO STEREOLAB	75	1994
FRENCH FOREIGN LEGION FRANK SINATRA	18	1959
FRENCH KISS LIL' LOUIS	2	1989
FRENCH KISSES JENTINA	20	2004
FRENCH KISSIN' IN THE USA DEBBIE HARRY	8	1986
FREQUENCY ALTERN 8	41	1992
FRESH [A] KOOL & THE GANG	11	1984
FRESH! [B] GINA G	6	1997
FRIDAY DANIEL BEDINGFIELD	28	2003
FRIDAY 13TH (EP) DAMNED	50	1981
FRIDAY I'M IN LOVE CURE	6	1992
FRIDAY NIGHT McFLY	3	2006
FRIDAY NIGHT (LIVE VERSION) KIDS FROM 'FAME'	13	1983
FRIDAY ON MY MIND EASYBEATS	6	1966
FRIDAY ON MY MIND GARY MOORE	26	1987
FRIDAY STREET PAUL WELLER	21	1997
FRIDAY'S ANGELS GENERATION X	62	1979
FRIDAY'S CHILD WILL YOUNG	4	2004
FRIED MY LITTLE BRAINS KILLS	55	2003
A FRIEND KRS ONE	66	1997
FRIEND OF MINE KELLY PRICE	25	1998
FRIEND OF THE NIGHT MOGWAI	38	2006
FRIEND OR FOE [A] ADAM ANT	9	1982
FRIEND OR FOE [B] tATu	48	2006
FRIENDLY PERSUASION PAT BOONE	3	1956
FRIENDLY PERSUASION FOUR ACES FEATURING AL ALBERTS	29	1957
FRIENDLY PRESSURE JHELISA	75	1995
FRIENDS [A] BEACH BOYS	25	1968
FRIENDS [B] ARRIVAL	8	1970
FRIENDS [C] SHALAMAR	12	1982
FRIENDS [D] AMII STEWART	12	1985
FRIENDS [E] JODY WATLEY WITH ERIC B & RAKIM	21	1989
FRIENDS [F] TIGER	72	1998
THE FRIENDS AGAIN EP FRIENDS AGAIN	59	1984
FRIENDS AND NEIGHBOURS BILLY COTTON & HIS BAND, VOCALS BY THE BANDITS	3	1954
FRIENDS FOREVER THUNDERBUGS	5	1999
FRIENDS IN LOW PLACES GARTH BROOKS	36	1995
FRIENDS WILL BE FRIENDS QUEEN	14	1986
FRIENDSHIP SABRINA JOHNSTON	58	1991
FRIGGIN' IN THE RIGGIN' SEX PISTOLS	3	1979
FRIGHTENED CITY SHADOWS	3	1961
THE FROG PRINCESS DIVINE COMEDY	15	1996
FROGGY MIX JAMES BROWN	50	1985
FROGGY STYLE NUTTIN' NYCE	68	1995
FROM A DISTANCE BETTE MIDLER	6	1990
FROM A DISTANCE CLIFF RICHARD	11	1990
FROM A JACK TO A KING NED MILLER	2	1963
FROM A LOVER TO A FRIEND PAUL McCARTNEY	45	2001
FROM A TO H AND BACK AGAIN SHEEP ON DRUGS	40	1993
FROM A WINDOW [A] BILLY J. KRAMER & THE DAKOTAS	10	1964
FROM A WINDOW [B] NORTHERN UPROAR	17	1996
FROM DESPAIR TO WHERE MANIC STREET PREACHERS	25	1993
FROM EAST TO WEST VOYAGE	13	1978
FROM HEAD TO TOE ELVIS COSTELLO	43	1982
FROM HERE TO ETERNITY [A] GIORGIO	16	1977
FROM HERE TO ETERNITY [B] IRON MAIDEN	21	1992
FROM HERE TO ETERNITY [C] MICHAEL BALL	36	1994
FROM HERE TO THERE TO YOU HANK LOCKLIN	44	1962
FROM ME TO YOU BEATLES	1	1963
FROM NEW YORK TO L.A. PATSY GALLANT	6	1977
FROM NOW ON JAKI GRAHAM	73	1989
FROM OUT OF NOWHERE FAITH NO MORE	23	1990
FROM PARIS TO BERLIN INFERNAL	2	2006
FROM RUSH HOUR WITH LOVE REPUBLICA	20	1998
FROM RUSSIA WITH LOVE [A] JOHN BARRY ORCHESTRA	39	1963
FROM RUSSIA WITH LOVE [A] MATT MONRO	20	1963
FROM RUSSIA WITH LOVE [B] MATT DAREY PRESENTS DSP	40	2000
FROM THA CHUUUCH TO DA PALACE SNOOP DOGG	27	2002
FROM THE BEGINNING NEW RHODES	64	2005
FROM THE BENCH AT BELVIDERE BOO RADLEYS	24	1995
FROM THE BOTTOM OF MY HEART MOODY BLUES	22	1965
FROM THE FIRE FIELDS OF THE NEPHILIM	62	2002
FROM THE FLOORBOARDS UP PAUL WELLER	6	2005
FROM THE GHETTO DREAD FLIMSTONE & THE NEW TONE AGE FAMILY	66	1991
FROM THE HEART ANOTHER LEVEL	6	1999
FROM THE HIP (EP) LLOYD COLE & THE COMMOTIONS	59	1988
FROM THE UNDERWORLD HERD	6	1967
FROM THIS DAY MACHINE HEAD	74	1999
FROM THIS MOMENT ON SHANIA TWAIN	9	1998
FROM YESTERDAY 30 SECONDS TO MARS	37	2008
FRONTIER PSYCHIATRIST AVALANCHES	18	2001
FRONTIN' PHARRELL WILLIAMS FEATURING JAY-Z	6	2003
FRONTIN' JAMIE CULLUM	12	2004
FRONTLINE CAPTAIN	62	2006
FROSTY THE SNOWMAN COCTEAU TWINS	58	1993
FROZEN MADONNA	1	1998
FROZEN HEART FM	64	1987
FROZEN METAL HEAD (EP) BEASTIE BOYS	55	1992
FROZEN ORANGE JUICE PETER SARSTEDT	10	1969
FRQUENCY RHYTHMATIC	62	1990
FUCK FOREVER BABYSHAMBLES	4	2005
FK IT (I DON'T WANT YOU BACK)** EAMON	1	2004
FUCK IT UP TOWERS OF LONDON	46	2005
*****K THE MILLENNIUM** 2K	28	1997
FUEL METALLICA	31	1998
FU-GEE-LA FUGEES	21	1996
FUGITIVE MOTEL ELBOW	44	2003
FULL METAL JACKET (I WANNA BE YOUR DRILL INSTRUCTOR) ABIGAIL MEAD & NIGEL GOULDING	2	1987
THE FULL MONTY-MONSTER MIX VARIOUS ARTISTS (EP'S & LPS)	62	1998
FULL MOON BRANDY	15	2002
FULL OF LIFE (HAPPY NOW) WONDER STUFF	28	1993
FULL TERM LOVE MONIE LOVE	34	1992
FULL TIME JOB DORIS DAY & JOHNNIE RAY	11	1953
FUN DA MOB FEATURING JOCELYN BROWN	33	1998
FUN DAY STEVIE WONDER	63	1991
FUN FOR ME MOLOKO	36	1996
FUN FUN FUN STATUS QUO WITH THE BEACH BOYS	24	1996
THE FUN LOVIN' CRIMINAL FUN LOVIN' CRIMINALS	26	1996
THE FUNERAL OF HEARTS H.I.M.	15	2004
FUNERAL PYRE JAM	4	1981
THE FUNERAL (SEPTEMBER 25TH, 1977) THULI DUMAKUDE	75	1988
FUNGI MAMA (BEBOPAFUNKADISCOLYPSO) TOM BROWNE	58	1982
FUNK & DRIVE ELEVATORMAN	37	1995
FUNK DAT SAGAT	25	1993
FUNK ON AH ROLL JAMES BROWN	40	1999
THE FUNK PHENOMENA ARMAND VAN HELDEN	38	1997
FUNK THEORY ROKOTTO	49	1978
FUNKATARIUM JUMP	56	1997
FUNKDAFIED DA BRAT	65	1994
FUNKIN' FOR JAMAICA (N.Y.) TOM BROWNE	10	1980
FUNKY BROADWAY WILSON PICKETT	43	1967
FUNKY COLD MEDINA TONE LOC	13	1989
FUNKY DORY RACHEL STEVENS	26	2003
FUNKY GIBBON GOODIES	4	1975
FUNKY GUITAR TC 1992	40	1992
FUNKY JAM PRIMAL SCREAM	7	1994
FUNKY LOVE KAVANA	32	1998
FUNKY LOVE VIBRATIONS BASS-O-MATIC	71	1991
FUNKY MOPED JASPER CARROTT	5	1975
FUNKY MUSIC UTAH SAINTS	23	2000
FUNKY NASSAU BEGINNING OF THE END	31	1974
FUNKY SENSATION LADIES CHOICE	41	1986
FUNKY STREET ARTHUR CONLEY	46	1968
FUNKY TOWN LIPPS INC	2	1980
FUNKY TOWN PSEUDO ECHO	8	1987
FUNKY WEEKEND STYLISTICS	10	1976
FUNNY ALL OVER VERNONS GIRLS	31	1963
FUNNY BREAK (ONE IS ENOUGH) ORBITAL	21	2001
FUNNY FAMILIAR FORGOTTEN FEELINGS TOM JONES	7	1967
FUNNY FUNNY SWEET	13	1971
FUNNY HOW AIRHEAD	57	1991
FUNNY HOW LOVE CAN BE IVY LEAGUE	8	1965
FUNNY HOW LOVE IS FINE YOUNG CANNIBALS	58	1986
FUNNY HOW TIME FLIES (WHEN YOU'RE HAVING FUN) JANET JACKSON	59	1987
FUNNY HOW TIME SLIPS AWAY DOROTHY MOORE	38	1976
FUNNY LITTLE FROG BELLE & SEBASTIAN	13	2006
FUNNY WAY OF LAUGHIN' BURL IVES	29	1962
FUNTIME BOY GEORGE	45	1995
F.U.R.B. (F U RIGHT BACK) FRANKEE	1	2004
FURIOUS ANGELS ROB DOUGAN	42	1998
FURNITURE FUGAZI	61	2001
FURNITURE MUSIC BILL NELSON'S RED NOISE	59	1979
FURTHER LONGVIEW	24	2003
THE FURTHER ADVENTURES OF THE NORTH VARIOUS ARTISTS (EP'S & LPS)	64	1990
FURY PRINCE	60	2006
FUTURE HALO VARGAS	67	2000
FUTURE LOVE PRESENCE	66	1999
FUTURE LOVE EP SEAL	12	1991
FUTURE MANAGEMENT ROGER TAYLOR	49	1981
THE FUTURE MUSIC (EP) LIQUID	59	1992
THE FUTURE OF THE FUTURE (STAY GOLD) DEEP DISH WITH EBTG	31	1998
FUTURE SHOCK HERBIE HANCOCK	54	1984
FUTURE SOUND (EP) PHUTURE ASSASSINS	64	1992
THE FUTURE'S SO BRIGHT I GOTTA WEAR SHADES TIMBUK 3	21	1987
FUZION PESHAY FEATURING CO-ORDINATE	41	2002
THE F-WORD BABYBIRD	35	2000
FX A GUY CALLED GERALD	52	1989

G

Title / Artist	Peak Position	Year of Entry
GABRIEL ROY DAVIS Jr FEATURING PEVEN EVERETT	22	1997
GAINESVILLE ROCK CITY LESS THAN JAKE	57	2001
GAL WINE CHAKA DEMUS & PLIERS	20	1994
GAL WITH THE YALLER SHOES MICHAEL HOLLIDAY	13	1956
GALAXIA MOONMAN FEATURING CHANTAL	50	2000
GALAXIE BLIND MELON	37	1995
GALAXY WAR	14	1978
GALAXY OF LOVE CROWN HEIGHTS AFFAIR	24	1978
GALLOPING HOME LONDON STRING CHORALE	31	1974
GALLOWS POLE JIMMY PAGE & ROBERT PLANT	35	1994
GALVANIZE CHEMICAL BROTHERS	3	2005
GALVESTON GLEN CAMPBELL	14	1969
GALVESTON BAY LONNIE HILL	51	1986
GAMBLER [A] MADONNA	4	1985
THE GAMBLER [B] KENNY ROGERS	22	2007
GAMBLIN' BAR ROOM BLUES SENSATIONAL ALEX HARVEY BAND	38	1975
GAMBLIN' MAN LONNIE DONEGAN	1	1957
THE GAME [A] ECHO & THE BUNNYMEN	28	1987
THE GAME [B] NICHOLA HOLT	72	2000
GAME BOY KWS	1	1992
THE GAME IS WON LUCIE SILVAS	38	2005
GAME OF LOVE [A] WAYNE FONTANA & THE MINDBENDERS	2	1965
GAME OF LOVE [B] TONY HADLEY	72	1993
THE GAME OF LOVE [C] SANTANA FEATURING MICHELLE BRANCH	16	2002
GAME ON CATATONIA	33	1998
GAME OVER SCARFACE	34	1997
GAMEMASTER LOST TRIBE	24	1999
GAMES NEW KIDS ON THE BLOCK	14	1991
GAMES PEOPLE PLAY JOE SOUTH	6	1969
GAMES PEOPLE PLAY INNER CIRCLE	67	1994
GAMES THAT LOVERS PLAY DONALD PEERS	46	1966
THE GAMES WE PLAY ANDREAS JOHNSON	41	2000
GAMES WITHOUT FRONTIERS PETER GABRIEL	4	1980
GANGSTA, GANGSTA NWA	70	1990
GANGSTA LOVIN' EVE FEATURING ALICIA KEYS	6	2002
GANGSTA WALK COOLIO FEATURING SNOOP DOGG	67	2006
GANGSTA'S PARADISE COOLIO FEATURING LV	1	1995
GANGSTA'S PARADISE LV	24	1995
GANGSTER OF THE GROOVE HEATWAVE	19	1981
GANGSTER TRIPPIN FATBOY SLIM	3	1998
GANGSTERS SPECIAL A.K.A.	6	1979
GANGSTERS AND THUGS TRANSPLANTS	35	2005
GARAGE CORRUPTED CRU FEATURING MC NEAT	59	2002
GARAGE GIRLS LONYO FEATURING MC ONYX STONE	39	2001
GARDEN OF DELIGHT MISSION	49	1986
GARDEN OF EDEN DICK JAMES	14	1957
GARDEN OF EDEN GARY MILLER	14	1957
THE GARDEN OF EDEN FRANKIE VAUGHAN	1	1957
THE GARDEN OF EDEN JOE VALINO	23	1957
GARDEN PARTY RICK NELSON	41	1972
GARDEN PARTY [A] MEZZOFORTE	17	1983
GARDEN PARTY [B] MARILLION	16	1983
GARY GILMORE'S EYES ADVERTS	18	1977
GARY GLITTER (EP) GARY GLITTER	57	1980
THE GAS FACE 3RD BASS	71	1990
GASOLINA DADDY YANKEE	5	2005
GASOLINE ALLEY ELKIE BROOKS	52	1983
GASOLINE ALLEY BRED HOLLIES	14	1970
GATECRASHING LIVING IN A BOX	36	1989
GATHER IN THE MUSHROOMS BENNY HILL	12	1961
GAUDETE STEELEYE SPAN	14	1973
GAY BAR ELECTRIC SIX	5	2003
GAY BOYFRIEND HAZZARDS	67	2003
THE GAY CAVALIEROS (THE STORY SO FAR) STEVE WRIGHT	61	1984
GAYE CLIFFORD T WARD	8	1973
GBI TOWA TEI FEATURING KYLIE MINOGUE	63	1998
GEE BABY PETER SHELLEY	4	1974
GEE BUT IT'S LONELY PAT BOONE	30	1958
GEE WHIZ IT'S YOU CLIFF RICHARD	4	1961
GEEK STINK BREATH GREEN DAY	16	1995
GENERAL PUBLIC GENERAL PUBLIC	60	1984
GENERALS AND MAJORS XTC	32	1980
GENERATION SEX DIVINE COMEDY	19	1998
GENERATIONS INSPIRAL CARPETS	28	1992
GENERATIONS OF LOVE JESUS LOVES YOU	35	1991
GENERATOR HOLLOWAYS	14	2006
GENETIC ENGINEERING ORCHESTRAL MANOEUVRES IN THE DARK	20	1983
GENIE BROOKLYN BRONX & QUEENS	40	1985
GENIE IN A BOTTLE CHRISTINA AGUILERA	1	1999
GENIE IN A BOTTLE SPEEDWAY	10	2003
GENIE WITH THE LIGHT BROWN LAMP SHADOWS	17	1964
GENIUS PITCHSHIFTER	71	1998
GENIUS MOVE THAT PETROL EMOTION	65	1987
GENIUS OF LOVER TOM TOM CLUB	65	1981
GENO DEXY'S MIDNIGHT RUNNERS	1	1980
THE GENTLE ART OF CHOKING MY VITRIOL	39	2002
GENTLE ON MY MIND DEAN MARTIN	2	1969
GENTLEMAN WHO FELL MILLA	65	1994
A GENTLEMAN'S EXCUSE ME FISH	30	1990
GENTLEMEN TAKE POLAROIDS JAPAN	60	1980
GEORDIE BOYS (GAZZA RAP) GAZZA	31	1990
GEORDIE IN WONDERLAND WILDHEARTS	31	1995
GEORGE BEST - A TRIBUTE BRIAN KENNEDY & PETER CORRY	4	2006
GEORGIA ON MY MIND RAY CHARLES	24	1960
GEORGINA BAILEY NOOSHA FOX	31	1977
GEORGY GIRL SEEKERS	3	1967
GEORGY PORGY [A] CHARME	68	1984
GEORGY PORGY [B] ERIC BENET FEATURING FAITH EVANS	28	1999
GEPETTO BELLY	49	1993
GERM FREE ADOLESCENCE X-RAY SPEX	19	1978
GERONIMO SHADOWS	11	1963
GERTCHA CHAS & DAVE	20	1979
GESUNDHEIT HYSTERICS	44	1981
(GET A) GRIP (ON YOURSELF) STRANGLERS	33	1977
GET A LIFE [A] SOUL II SOUL	3	1989
GET A LIFE [B] JULIAN LENNON	56	1992
GET A LIFE [C] FREESTYLERS	66	2004
GET A LITTLE FREAKY WITH ME AARON HALL	66	1993
GET ALONG WITH YOU KELIS	51	2000
GET ANOTHER LOVE CHANTAL CURTIS	51	1979
GET AWAY GEORGIE FAME & THE BLUE FLAMES	1	1966
GET BACK [A] BEATLES WITH BILLY PRESTON	1	1969
GET BACK [A] ROD STEWART	11	1976
GET BACK [B] MOTHER	73	1994
GET BUSY [A] MR LEE	41	1989
GET BUSY [B] SEAN PAUL	4	2003
GET CARTER ROY BUDD	68	1999
GET DANCING DISCO TEX & THE SEX-O-LETTES	8	1974
GET DOWN [A] GILBERT O'SULLIVAN	1	1973
GET DOWN [B] GENE CHANDLER	11	1979
GET DOWN [C] M-D-EMM	55	1992
GET DOWN [D] CRAIG MACK	54	1995
GET DOWN [E] JUNGLE BROTHERS	52	1999
GET DOWN [F] FLEET	71	2005
GET DOWN [G] GROOVE ARMADA FEATURING STUSH	9	2007
GET DOWN AND GET WITH IT SLADE	16	1971
GET DOWN ON IT KOOL & THE GANG	3	1981
GET DOWN ON IT LOUCHIE LOU & MICHIE ONE	58	1995
GET DOWN SATURDAY NIGHT OLIVER CHEATHAM	38	1983
GET DOWN TONIGHT KC & THE SUNSHINE BAND	21	1975
GET DOWN (YOU'RE THE ONE FOR ME) BACKSTREET BOYS	14	1996
GET 'EM OFF TOKYO DRAGONS	75	2004
GET FREE VINES	24	2002
GET GET DOWN PAUL JOHNSON	5	1999
GET HERE OLETA ADAMS	4	1991
GET HERE Q FEATURING TRACY ACKERMAN	37	1993
GET HIGHER BLACK GRAPE	24	1997
GET IN THE SWING SPARKS	27	1975
GET INTO IT TONY SCOTT	63	1990
GET INTO THE MUSIC DJ'S RULE FEATURING KAREN BROWN	65	1996
GET INTO YOU DANNII MINOGUE	36	1994
GET INVOLVED RAPHAEL SAADIQ & Q-TIP	36	1999
GET IT [A] DARTS	10	1979
GET IT [B] STEVIE WONDER & MICHAEL JACKSON	37	1988
GET IT ON [A] T REX	1	1971
GET IT ON [A] POWER STATION	22	1985
GET IT ON [A] BUS STOP FEATURING T REX	59	2000
GET IT ON [B] KINGDOM COME	75	1988
GET IT ON [C] INTENSO PROJECT/LISA SCOTT-LEE	23	2004
GET IT ON THE FLOOR DMX FEATURING SWIZZ BEATZ	34	2004
GET IT ON TONITE MONTELL JORDAN	15	2000
GET IT POPPIN' FAT JOE FEATURING NELLY	34	2005
GET IT RIGHT [A] ARETHA FRANKLIN	74	1983
GET IT RIGHT [B] JOE FAGIN	53	1986
GET IT RIGHT NEXT TIME GERRY RAFFERTY	30	1979
GET IT SHAWTY LLOYD	72	2007
GET IT TOGETHER [A] CRISPY & COMPANY	21	1975
GET IT TOGETHER [B] BEASTIE BOYS	19	1994
GET IT TOGETHER [C] SEAL	25	2003
GET IT UP RM PROJECT	49	1999
GET IT UP FOR LOVE DAVID CASSIDY	11	1975
GET IT UP FOR LOVE TATA VEGA	52	1979
GET IT UP FOR LOVE LUCIANA	55	1994
GET IT UP (THE FEELING) ULTRA NATE	51	2001
GET IT WHILE IT'S HOT NODESHA	55	2003
GET IT WHILE YOU CAN OLYMPIC RUNNERS	35	1978
GET LOOSE [A] EVELYN 'CHAMPAGNE' KING	45	1983
GET LOOSE [B] L.A. MIX PERFORMED BY JAZZI P	25	1989
GET LOOSE [C] D4	64	2002
GET LOST EDEN KANE	10	1961
GET LOW LIL JON & THE EAST SIDE BOYZ	10	2005
GET LUCKY JERMAINE STEWART	13	1988
GET ME DINOSAUR Jr.	44	1992
GET ME HOME FOXY BROWN FEATURING BLACKstreet	11	1997
GET ME OFF BASEMENT JAXX	22	2002
GET ME OUT NEW MODEL ARMY	34	1990
GET ME OUTTA HERE JET	37	2005
GET ME TO THE WORLD ON TIME ELECTRIC PRUNES	42	1967
GET MYSELF ARRESTED GOMEZ	45	1998
GET MYSELF INTO IT RAPTURE	36	2006
GET NO BETTER CASSIDY FEATURING MASHONDA	24	2004
GET OFF DANDY WARHOLS	34	2000
GET OFF OF MY CLOUD ROLLING STONES	1	1965
GET OFF THIS CRACKER	41	1994
GET OFF YOUR HIGH HORSE ROLLO GOES CAMPING	43	1994

Title / Artist	Peak Position	Year of Entry
GET ON IT PHOEBE ONE	38	1999
GET ON THE BUS DESTINY'S CHILD FEATURING TIMBALAND	15	1999
GET ON THE DANCE FLOOR ROB BASE & DJ E-Z ROCK	14	1989
GET ON THE FUNK TRAIN MUNICH MACHINE	41	1977
GET ON UP [A] JAZZY DEE	53	1983
GET ON UP [B] JODECI	20	1996
GET ON UP, GET ON DOWN ROY AYERS	41	1978
GET ON YOUR FEET GLORIA ESTEFAN	23	1989
GET OUT [A] HAROLD MELVIN & THE BLUENOTES	35	1975
GET OUT [B] BUSTA RHYMES	57	2000
GET OUT [C] FELON	31	2002
GET OUT OF MY LIFE WOMAN LEE DORSEY	22	1966
GET OUT OF MYSELF REDD KROSS	63	1997
GET OUT OF THIS HOUSE SHAWN COLVIN	70	1997
GET OUT YOUR LAZY BED MATT BIANCO	15	1984
GET OUTTA MY DREAMS GET INTO MY CAR BILLY OCEAN	3	1988
GET OVER IT [A] OK GO	21	2003
GET OVER IT [B] GUILLEMOTS	20	2008
GET OVER YOU [A] UNDERTONES	57	1979
GET OVER YOU [B] SOPHIE ELLIS-BEXTOR	3	2002
GET READY [A] TEMPTATIONS	10	1969
GET READY [A] CAROL HITCHCOCK	56	1987
GET READY! [B] ROACHFORD	22	1991
GET READY [C] MASE FEATURING BLACKstreet	32	1999
GET READY FOR LOVE NICK CAVE & THE BAD SEEDS	62	2005
GET READY FOR THIS 2 UNLIMITED	2	1991
GET REAL PAUL RUTHERFORD	47	1988
GET RIGHT JENNIFER LOPEZ	1	2005
GET SOME THERAPY STEVE WRIGHT & THE SISTERS OF SOUL	75	1983
GET THAT LOVE THOMPSON TWINS	66	1987
GET THE BALANCE RIGHT DEPECHE MODE	13	1983
GET THE FUNK OUT EXTREME	19	1991
GET THE GIRL! KILL THE BADDIES! POP WILL EAT ITSELF	9	1993
GET THE KEYS AND GO LLAMA FARMERS	74	1999
GET THE MESSAGE ELECTRONIC	8	1991
GET THE PARTY STARTED P!NK	2	2002
GET THE PARTY STARTED SHIRLEY BASSEY	47	2007
GET THROUGH MARK JOSEPH	38	2003
GET TOGETHER [A] WONDER STUFF	33	1989
GET TOGETHER [B] MADONNA	7	2006
GET TOUGH KLEEER	49	1981
GET UP [A] J.A.L.N. BAND	53	1978
GET UP [B] BLACKOUT	67	2001
GET UP [C] BEVERLEY KNIGHT	17	2001
GET UP AND BOOGIE [A] SILVER CONVENTION	7	1976
GET UP AND BOOGIE [B] FREDDIE JAMES	54	1979
GET UP AND MOVE HARVEY	24	2002
GET UP (BEFORE THE NIGHT IS OVER) TECHNOTRONIC FEATURING YA KID K	2	1990
GET UP (EVERYBODY) BYRON STINGILY	14	1997
GET UP! GET INSANE! STRETCH 'N' VERN PRESENTS MADDOG	6	1997
GET UP I FEEL LIKE BEING A SEX MACHINE JAMES BROWN	32	1970
GET UP OFFA THAT THING JAMES BROWN	22	1976
GET UP STAND UP [A] PHUNKY PHANTOM	27	1998
GET UP STAND UP [B] STELLAR PROJECT FEATURING BRANDI EMMA	14	2004
GET UP SUNSHINE SREET BIZARRE INC	45	1996
GET UR FREAK ON MISSY ELLIOTT	4	2001
GET WILD NEW POWER GENERATION	19	1995
GET YOUR BODY ADAMSKI FEATURING NINA HAGEN	68	1992
GET YOUR FEET OUT OF MY SHOES BOOTHILL FOOT-TAPPERS	64	1984
GET YOUR HANDS OFF MY MAN! JUNIOR VASQUEZ	22	1995
GET YOUR HANDS OFF MY WOMAN DARKNESS	43	2003
GET YOUR LOVE BACK THREE DEGREES	34	1974
GET YOUR NUMBER MARIAH CAREY	9	2005
GET YOUR WAY JAMIE CULLUM	44	2005
GET YOURSELF TOGETHER YOUNG DISCIPLES	65	1990
GET-A-WAY [A] MAXX	4	1994
GETAWAY [B] MUSIC	26	2002
GETAWAY [C] TEXAS	6	2005
GETO HEAVEN COMMON FEATURING MACY GRAY	48	2001
GETS ME THROUGH OZZY OSBOURNE	18	2002
GETT OFF PRINCE & THE NEW POWER GENERATION	4	1991
GETTIN' IN THE WAY JILL SCOTT	30	2000
GETTIN' JIGGY WIT IT WILL SMITH	3	1998
GETTIN' READY FOR LOVE DIANA ROSS	23	1977
GETTING A DRAG LYNSEY DE PAUL	18	1972
GETTING AWAY WITH IT [A] ELECTRONIC	12	1989
GETTING AWAY WITH IT [B] EGG	58	1999
GETTING AWAY WITH IT (ALL MESSED UP) JAMES	22	2001
GETTING AWAY WITH MURDER PAPA ROACH	45	2004
GETTING BETTER SHED SEVEN	14	1996
GETTING CLOSER [A] WINGS	60	1979
GETTING CLOSER [B] HAYWOODE	67	1985
GETTING' ENOUGH LIL' CHRIS	17	2006
GETTING INTO SOMETHING ALISON MOYET	51	1994
GETTING' INTO U W.O.S.P.	48	2001
GETTING' IT RIGHT ALISON LIMERICK	57	1992
GETTING MIGHTY CROWDED BETTY EVERETT	29	1965
GETTING' MONEY JUNIOR M.A.F.I.A.	63	1996
GETTING OVER YOU ANDY WILLIAMS	35	1974
GETTING UP PIGBAG	61	1982
GETTO JAM DOMINO	33	1994
GHANDARA GODIEGO	56	1980
GHETTO RHYTHM MASTERS FEATURING JOE WATSON	71	2002
GHETTO CHILD DETROIT SPINNERS	7	1973
GHETTO DAY CRYSTAL WATERS	40	1994
GHETTO GIRL SIMPLY RED	34	1998
GHETTO GOSPEL 2PAC FEATURING ELTON JOHN	1	2005
GHETTO HEAVEN FAMILY STAND	10	1990
GHETTO MUSICK OUTKAST	55	2003
GHETTO ROMANCE DAMAGE	7	2000
GHETTO STORY CHAM	62	2006
GHETTO SUPERSTAR (THAT IS WHAT YOU ARE) PRAS MICHEL FEATURING ODB & MYA	2	1998
G.H.E.T.T.O.U.T. CHANGING FACES	10	1997
THE GHOST AT NUMBER ONE JELLYFISH	43	1993
GHOST DANCER ADDRISI BROTHERS	57	1979
GHOST HOUSE HOUSE ENGINEERS	69	1987
GHOST IN YOU PSYCHEDELIC FURS	68	1984
THE GHOST OF LOVE [A] TAVARES	29	1978
GHOST OF LOVE [B] FICTION FACTORY	64	1984
THE GHOST OF TOM JOAD BRUCE SPRINGSTEEN	26	1996
THE GHOST OF YOU MY CHEMICAL ROMANCE	27	2005
GHOST TOWN SPECIALS	1	1981
GHOSTBUSTERS [A] RAY PARKER Jr.	2	1984
GHOSTBUSTERS [B] RUN D.M.C.	65	1989
GHOSTDANCING SIMPLE MINDS	13	1986
GHOSTFACED KILLER DEAD 60'S	25	2005
GHOSTS [A] JAPAN	5	1982
GHOSTS [B] MICHAEL JACKSON	5	1997
GHOSTS [C] TENTH PLANET	59	2001
GHOSTS [D] DIRTY VEGAS	31	2002
GIA DESPINA VANDI	63	2004
GIDDY STRATOSPHERES LONG BLONDES	37	2007
GIDDY-UP 2 IN A ROOM	74	1996
GIDDY-UP-A-DING-DONG FREDDIE BELL & THE BELLBOYS	4	1956
THE GIFT [A] INXS	11	1993
THE GIFT [B] DANIEL O'DONNELL	46	1994
THE GIFT [C] WAY OUT WEST/MISS JOANNA LAW	15	1996
THE GIFT OF CHRISTMAS CHILDLINERS	9	1995
GIGANTOR DICKIES	72	1980
GIGI BILLY ECKSTINE	8	1959
GIGOLO DAMNED	29	1987
GILLY GILLY OSSENFEFFER KATZENELLEN BOGEN BY THE SEA MAX BYGRAVES	7	1954
GIMME ALL YOUR LOVIN' ZZ TOP	10	1983
GIMME ALL YOUR LOVIN' KYM MAZELLE & JOCELYN BROWN	22	1994
GIMME DAT BANANA BLACK GORILLA	29	1977
GIMME DAT DING PIPKINS	6	1970
GIMME GIMME GIMME (A MAN AFTER MIDNIGHT) ABBA	3	1979
GIMME GIMME GOOD LOVIN' CRAZY ELEPHANT	12	1969
GIMME HOPE JO'ANNA EDDY GRANT	7	1988
GIMME LITTLE SIGN BRENTON WOOD	8	1967
GIMME LITTLE SIGN DANIELLE BRISEBOIS	75	1995
GIMME LOVE ALEXIA	17	1998
GIMME LUV (EENIE MEENIE MINY MO) DAVID MORALES & THE BAD YARD CLUB	37	1993
GIMME MORE BRITNEY SPEARS	3	2007
GIMME SHELTER (EP) VARIOUS ARTISTS (EP'S & LPS)	23	1993
GIMME SOME BRENDON	14	1977
GIMME SOME PAT & MICK	53	1991
GIMME SOME LOVE GINA G	25	1997
GIMME SOME LOVIN' THUNDER	36	1990
GIMME SOME LOVING SPENCER DAVIS GROUP	2	1966
GIMME SOME MORE BUSTA RHYMES	5	1999
GIMME THAT BODY Q-TEE	40	1996
GIMME THAT REMIX CHRIS BROWN FEATURING LIL' WAYNE	23	2006
GIMME THE LIGHT SEAN PAUL	5	2002
GIMME THE SUNSHINE CURIOSITY	73	1993
GIMME YOUR LOVIN' ATLANTIC STARR	66	1978
GIMMIX! PLAY LOUD JOHN COOPER CLARKE	39	1979
GIN AND JUICE SNOOP DOGGY DOGG	39	1994
GIN GAN GOOLIE SCAFFOLD	38	1969
GIN HOUSE BLUES AMEN CORNER	12	1967
GIN SOAKED BOY DIVINE COMEDY	38	1999
GINCHY BERT WEEDON	35	1961
GINGER DAVID DEVANT & HIS SPIRIT WIFE	54	1997
GINGERBREAD FRANKIE AVALON	30	1958
GINNY COME LATELY BRIAN HYLAND	5	1962
GIRL [A] ST. LOUIS UNION	11	1966
GIRL [A] TRUTH	27	1966
GIRL [B] DESTINY'S CHILD	6	2005
GIRL [C] BECK	45	2005
GIRL ALL THE BAD GUYS WANT BOWLING FOR SOUP	8	2002
THE GIRL CAN'T HELP IT LITTLE RICHARD	9	1957
THE GIRL CAN'T HELP IT DARTS	6	1977
GIRL CRAZY HOT CHOCOLATE	7	1982
GIRL DON'T COME SANDIE SHAW	3	1964
THE GIRL FROM IPANEMA STAN GETZ & JOAO GILBERTO	29	1964
THE GIRL FROM IPANEMA ASTRUD GILBERTO	55	1984
GIRL FROM MARS ASH	11	1995
A GIRL I ONCE KNEW NORTHERN UPROAR	63	1997
THE GIRL I USED TO KNOW BROTHER BEYOND	48	1991
GIRL I'M GONNA MISS YOU MILLI VANILLI	2	1989
GIRL IN THE MOON DARIUS	21	2003
GIRL IN THE WOOD FRANKIE LAINE	11	1953

		Peak Position	Year of Entry
THE GIRL IS MINE	MICHAEL JACKSON & PAUL McCARTNEY	8	1982
GIRL IS ON MY MIND	BLACK KEYS	62	2004
GIRL (IT'S ALL I HAVE)	SHY	60	1980
GIRL I'VE BEEN HURT	SNOW	48	1993
A GIRL LIKE YOU [A]	CLIFF RICHARD & THE SHADOWS	3	1961
A GIRL LIKE YOU [B]	YOUNG RASCALS	37	1967
A GIRL LIKE YOU [C]	EDWYN COLLINS	4	1995
GIRL OF MY BEST FRIEND	ELVIS PRESLEY	9	1976
GIRL OF MY BEST FRIEND	BRYAN FERRY	57	1993
GIRL OF MY DREAMS	TONY BRENT	16	1958
GIRL OF MY DREAMS	GERRY MONROE	43	1972
GIRL ON TV	LYTE FUNKIE ONES	6	2000
GIRL POWER	SHAMPOO	25	1996
THE GIRL SANG THE BLUES	EVERLY BROTHERS	25	1963
GIRL TALK	TLC	30	2002
GIRL TO GIRL	49ERS	31	1990
GIRL TONITE	TWISTA FEATURING TREY SONGZ	47	2005
GIRL U FOR ME	SILK	67	1993
GIRL U WANT	ROBERT PALMER	57	1994
THE GIRL WITH THE LONELIEST EYES	HOUSE OF LOVE	58	1991
GIRL YOU KNOW IT'S TRUE	MILLI VANILLI	3	1988
GIRL YOU KNOW IT'S TRUE	KEITH 'N' SHANE	36	2000
GIRL, YOU'LL BE A WOMAN SOON	URGE OVERKILL	61	1994
GIRL YOU'RE SO TOGETHER	MICHAEL JACKSON	33	1984
GIRL/BOY (EP)	APHEX TWIN	64	1996
GIRLFIGHT	BROOKE VALENTINE	35	2005
GIRLFRIEND [A]	MICHAEL JACKSON	41	1980
GIRLFRIEND [B]	PEBBLES	8	1988
GIRLFRIEND [C]	BILLIE	1	1998
GIRLFRIEND [D]	N SYNC FEATURING NELLY	2	2002
GIRLFRIEND [E]	ALICIA KEYS	24	2002
GIRLFRIEND [F]	B2K	10	2003
GIRLFRIEND [G]	DARKNESS	39	2006
GIRLFRIEND [H]	AVRIL LAVIGNE	2	2007
GIRLFRIEND IN A COMA	SMITHS	13	1987
GIRLFRIEND/BOYFRIEND	BLACKstreet FEATURING JANET	11	1999
GIRLFRIEND'S STORY	GEMMA FOX FEATURING MC LYTE	38	2004
GIRLIE	PEDDLERS	34	1970
GIRLIE GIRLIE	SOPHIA GEORGE	7	1985
GIRLS [A]	JOHNNY BURNETTE	37	1961
GIRLS [B]	MOMENTS & WHATNAUTS	3	1975
GIRLS [B]	POWERCUT FEATURING NUBIAN PRINZ	50	1991
GIRLS [C]	BEASTIE BOYS	34	1987
GIRLS [D]	PRODIGY	19	2004
GIRLS [E]	CAM'RON FEATURING MONA LISA	25	2005
GIRLS [F]	BEENIE FEATURING AKON	47	2006
THE GIRLS [G]	CALVIN HARRIS	3	2007
THE GIRL'S A FREAK	DJ TOUCHE	65	2004
GIRLS AIN'T NOTHING BUT TROUBLE	DJ JAZZY JEFF & THE FRESH PRINCE	21	1986
GIRLS AND BOYS [A]	PRINCE & THE REVOLUTION	11	1986
GIRLS AND BOYS [B]	BLUR	5	1994
GIRLS + BOYS [C]	HED BOYS	21	1994
GIRLS AND BOYS [D]	GOOD CHARLOTTE	6	2003
GIRLS AND BOYS IN LOVE	RUMBLE STRIPS	64	2007
GIRLS ARE MORE FUN	RAY PARKER Jr.	46	1986
GIRLS ARE OUT TO GET YOU	FASCINATIONS	32	1971
GIRLS BEST FRIEND	DATSUNS	71	2004
GIRLS CAN GET IT	DR HOOK	40	1980
GIRLS DEM SUGAR	BEENIE MAN FEATURING MYA	13	2001
GIRLS GIRLS GIRLS [A]	STEVE LAWRENCE	49	1960
GIRLS GIRLS GIRLS [B]	FOURMOST	33	1966
GIRLS GIRLS GIRLS [C]	SAILOR	7	1976
GIRLS GIRLS GIRLS [D]	KANDIDATE	34	1979
GIRLS GIRLS GIRLS [E]	MOTLEY CRUE	26	1987
GIRLS GIRLS GIRLS [F]	JAY-Z	11	2002
GIRLS JUST WANNA HAVE FUN	LOLLY	14	2000
GIRLS JUST WANT TO HAVE FUN	CYNDI LAUPER	2	1984
GIRL'S LIFE	GIRLFRIEND	68	1993
GIRLS LIKE US	B-15 PROJECT FEATURING CHRISSY D	7	2000
GIRLS NIGHT OUT	ALDA	20	1998
GIRL'S NOT GREY	AFI	22	2003
THE GIRLS OF SUMMER (EP)	ARAB STRAP	74	1997
GIRLS ON FILM	DURAN DURAN	5	1981
GIRLS ON MY MIND	FATBACK	69	1985
GIRLS ON TOP	GIRL THING	25	2000
GIRLS' SCHOOL	WINGS	1	1977
GIRLS TALK	DAVE EDMUNDS	4	1979
GIRLS WHO PLAY GUITARS	MAXIMO PARK	31	2007
GIRLSHAPEDLOVEDRUG	GOMEZ	66	2006
GIT DOWN	CENOGINERZ	75	2002
GIT DOWN (SHAKE YOUR THANG)	GAYE BYKERS ON ACID	54	1987
GIT ON UP	DJ 'FAST' EDDIE FEATURING SUNDANCE	49	1989
GITTIN' FUNKY	KID 'N' PLAY	55	1988
GIV ME LUV	ALCATRAZZ	12	1996
GIVE A LITTLE BIT	SUPERTRAMP	29	1977
GIVE A LITTLE LOVE [A]	BAY CITY ROLLERS	1	1975
GIVE A LITTLE LOVE [B]	ASWAD	11	1988
GIVE A LITTLE LOVE [C]	DANIEL O'DONNELL	7	1998
GIVE A LITTLE LOVE [D]	INVISIBLE MAN	48	1999
GIVE A LITTLE LOVE BACK TO THE WORLD	EMMA	33	1990
GIVE AND TAKE [A]	PIONEERS	35	1972
GIVE AND TAKE [B]	BRASS CONSTRUCTION	62	1985
GIVE GIVE GIVE	TOMMY STEELE	28	1959
GIVE GIVE GIVE ME MORE MORE MORE	WONDER STUFF	72	1988
GIVE HER MY LOVE	JOHNSTON BROTHERS	27	1957
GIVE HER WHAT SHE WANTS	FRANKIE OLIVER	58	1997
GIVE IN TO ME	MICHAEL JACKSON	2	1993
GIVE IRELAND BACK TO THE IRISH	WINGS	16	1972
GIVE IT	X-PRESS 2 FEATURING KURT WAGNER	33	2005
GIVE IT ALL AWAY	WORLD PARTY	43	1993
GIVE IT AWAY [A]	RED HOT CHILI PEPPERS	9	1994
GIVE IT AWAY [B]	DEEPEST BLUE	9	2004
GIVE IT SOME EMOTION	TRACIE	24	1983
GIVE IT TO ME [A]	TROGGS	12	1967
GIVE IT TO ME [B]	BAM BAM	65	1988
GIVE IT TO ME [C]	TIMBALAND FEATURING NELLY FURTADO & JUSTIN TIMBERLAKE	1	2007
GIVE IT TO ME BABY	RICK JAMES	47	1981
GIVE IT TO ME NOW	KENNY	38	1973
GIVE IT TO YOU [A]	MARTHA WASH	37	1993
GIVE IT TO YOU [B]	JORDAN KNIGHT	5	1999
GIVE IT UP [A]	KC & THE SUNSHINE BAND	1	1983
GIVE IT UP [A]	CUT 'N' MOVE	61	1993
GIVE IT UP [B]	TALK TALK	59	1986
GIVE IT UP [C]	HOTHOUSE FLOWERS	30	1990
GIVE IT UP [D]	WILSON PHILLIPS	36	1992
GIVE IT UP [E]	GOODMEN	5	1993
GIVE IT UP [F]	PUBLIC ENEMY	18	1994
GIVE IT UP [G]	SELENA VS X MEN	61	2001
GIVE IT UP TURN IT LOOSE	EN VOGUE	22	1993
GIVE ME A LITTLE MORE TIME	GABRIELLE	5	1996
GIVE ME A REASON [A]	CORRS	27	2001
GIVE ME A REASON [B]	TONY DE VIT FEATURING NIKI MAK	53	2003
GIVE ME A REASON [C]	TRIPLE EIGHT	9	2003
GIVE ME ALL YOUR LOVE [A]	WHITESNAKE	18	1988
GIVE ME ALL YOUR LOVE [B]	MAGIC AFFAIR	30	1994
GIVE ME AN INCH	HAZEL O'CONNOR	41	1980
GIVE ME BACK ME BRAIN	DUFFO	60	1979
GIVE ME BACK MY HEART	DOLLAR	4	1982
GIVE ME BACK MY MAN	B-52's	61	1980
GIVE ME FIRE	GBH	69	1982
GIVE ME JUST A LITTLE MORE TIME	CHAIRMEN OF THE BOARD	3	1970
GIVE ME JUST A LITTLE MORE TIME	KYLIE MINOGUE	2	1992
GIVE ME JUST ONE MORE NIGHT (UNA NOCHE)	98o	61	2000
GIVE ME LIFE	MR V	40	1994
GIVE ME LOVE [A]	DIDDY	23	1994
GIVE ME LOVE [B]	DJ DADO VS MICHELLE WEEKS	59	1998
GIVE ME LOVE (GIVE ME PEACE ON EARTH)	GEORGE HARRISON	8	1973
GIVE ME MORE TIME [A]	NICOLE	75	1982
GIVE ME MORE TIME [B]	WHITESNAKE	29	1984
GIVE ME ONE MORE CHANCE [A]	DONALD PEERS	36	1972
GIVE ME ONE MORE CHANCE [B]	LUKE GOSS & THE BAND OF THIEVES	68	1993
GIVE ME RHYTHM	BLACK CONNECTION	32	1998
GIVE ME SOME KINDA MAGIC	DOLLAR	34	1982
GIVE ME SOME MORE	DJ GERT	50	2001
GIVE ME STRENGTH	JON OF THE PLEASED WIMMIN	30	1996
GIVE ME THE NIGHT	GEORGE BENSON	7	1980
GIVE ME THE NIGHT	MIRAGE FEATURING ROY GAYLE	49	1984
GIVE ME THE NIGHT	RANDY CRAWFORD	60	1997
GIVE ME THE NIGHT	XAVIER	65	2005
GIVE ME THE REASON	LUTHER VANDROSS	26	1986
GIVE ME TIME	DUSTY SPRINGFIELD	24	1967
GIVE ME TONIGHT	SHANNON	24	1984
GIVE ME YOU	MARY J BLIGE	19	2000
GIVE ME YOUR BODY	CHIPPENDALES	28	1992
GIVE ME YOUR HEART TONIGHT	SHAKIN' STEVENS	11	1982
GIVE ME YOUR LOVE [A]	REEF	44	2003
GIVE ME YOUR LOVE [B]	XTM & DJ CHUCKY PRESENTS ANNIA	28	2005
GIVE ME YOUR WORD	TENNESSEE ERNIE FORD	6	1953
GIVE ME YOUR WORD	BILLY FURY	27	1966
GIVE MYSELF TO LOVE	FRANCIS ROSSI OF STATUS QUO	42	1996
GIVE PEACE A CHANCE	PLASTIC ONO BAND	2	1969
GIVE U ONE 4 CHRISTMAS	HOT PANTZ	64	2005
GIVE UP THE FUNK (LET'S DANCE)	B.T. EXPRESS	52	1980
GIVE YOU	DJAIMIN	45	1992
GIVE YOU ALL THE LOVE	MISHKA	34	1999
GIVEN TO FLY	PEARL JAM	12	1998
GIVEN UP	MIRRORBALL	12	1999
GIVIN' IT UP	INCOGNITO	43	1993
GIVIN' UP GIVIN' IN	THREE DEGREES	12	1978
GIVING HIM SOMETHING HE CAN FEEL	EN VOGUE	16	1992
GIVING IN	ADEMA	62	2002
GIVING IT ALL AWAY	ROGER DALTREY	5	1973
GIVING IT BACK	PHIL HURTT	36	1978
GIVING UP GIVING IN	SHEENA EASTON	54	2000
GIVING YOU THE BENEFIT	PEBBLES	73	1990
GIVING YOU THE BEST THAT I GOT	ANITA BAKER	55	1988
GIVING YOU UP	KYLIE MINOGUE	6	2005
G.L.A.D.	KIM APPLEBY	10	1991
GLAD ALL OVER	DAVE CLARK FIVE	1	1963
GLAD ALL OVER	CRYSTAL PALACE	50	1990
GLAD IT'S ALL OVER	CAPTAIN SENSIBLE	6	1984

Title / Artist	Peak Position	Year of Entry
GLAM LISA B	49	1993
GLAM RAID SPACE RAIDERS	68	1998
GLAM ROCK COPS CARTER-THE UNSTOPPABLE SEX MACHINE	24	1994
GLAM SLAM PRINCE	29	1988
GLAMOROUS FERGIE FEATURING LUDACRIS	6	2007
GLASGOW RANGERS (NINE IN A ROW) RANGERS FC	54	1997
A GLASS OF CHAMPAGNE SAILOR	2	1975
GLASTONBURY SONG WATERBOYS	29	1993
GLENDORA GLEN MASON	28	1956
GLENDORA PERRY COMO	18	1956
GLENN MILLER MEDLEY JOHN ANDERSON BIG BAND	61	1985
GLITTER AND TRAUMA BIFFY CLYRO	21	2004
GLITTERBALL [A] SIMPLE MINDS	18	1998
GLITTERBALL [B] FC KAHUNA	64	2002
GLITTERING PRIZE SIMPLE MINDS	16	1982
GLOBAL LOVE HIGH CONTRAST	68	2002
GLOBETROTTER TORNADOS	5	1963
GLORIA [A] JONATHAN KING	65	1979
GLORIA [A] LAURA BRANIGAN	6	1983
GLORIA [B] U2	55	1981
GLORIA [C] VAN MORRISON & JOHN LEE HOOKER	31	1993
GLORIOUS [A] ANDREAS JOHNSON	4	2000
GLORIOUS [B] CAPTAIN	30	2006
GLORIOUS [C] NATALIE IMBRUGLIA	23	2007
A GLORIOUS DAY EMBRACE	28	2005
GLORY BOX PORTISHEAD	13	1995
GLORY DAYS [A] BRUCE SPRINGSTEEN	17	1985
GLORY DAYS [B] JUST JACK	32	2007
GLORY GLORY MAN. UNITED MANCHESTER UNITED FOOTBALL CLUB	13	1983
GLORY OF LOVE PETER CETERA	3	1986
GLORY OF THE 80'S TORI AMOS	46	1999
GLORYLAND DARYL HALL & THE SOUNDS OF BLACKNESS	36	1994
GLOVES HORRORS	34	2007
GLOW SPANDAU BALLET	10	1981
GLOW OF LOVE CHANGE	14	1980
GLOW WORM MILLS BROTHERS	10	1953
GO [A] SCOTT FITZGERALD	52	1988
GO [B] MOBY	10	1991
GO [C] JOCASTA	50	1997
GO [D] HANSON	44	2007
GO AWAY [A] GLORIA ESTEFAN	13	1993
GO AWAY [B] HONEYCRACK	41	1996
GO AWAY LITTLE GIRL MARK WYNTER	6	1962
GO (BEFORE YOU BREAK MY HEART) GIGLIOLA CINQUETTI	8	1974
GO BUDDY GO STRANGLERS	8	1977
GO CUT CREATOR GO LL COOL J	66	1987
GO DEEP JANET JACKSON	13	1998
GO DEH YAKA (GO TO THE TOP) MONYAKA	14	1983
GO ENGLAND ENGLAND BOYS	26	2002
GO FOR IT! COVENTRY CITY CUP FINAL SQUAD	61	1987
GO FOR IT (HEART AND SOUL) ROCKY V FEATURING JOEY B. ELLIS & TYNETTA HARE	20	1991
GO FOR THE HEART SOX	47	1995
GO GO GO CHUCK BERRY	38	1963
GO GONE ESTELLE	32	2005
GO HOME STEVIE WONDER	67	1985
GO INTO THE LIGHT IAN McNABB	66	1994
GO LET IT OUT OASIS	1	2000
GO MR SUNSHINE REMI NICOLE	57	2007
GO NORTH RICHARD BARNES	38	1970
GO NOW MOODY BLUES	1	1964
GO ON BY ALMA COGAN	16	1955
GO ON GIRL ROXANNE SHANTE	55	1988
GO ON MOVE REEL 2 REAL FEATURING THE MAD STUNTMAN	7	1994
GO TECHNO 2 HOUSE	65	1992
GO THE DISTANCE MICHAEL BOLTON	14	1997
GO TO SLEEP RADIOHEAD	12	2003
GO WEST VILLAGE PEOPLE	15	1979
GO WEST PET SHOP BOYS	2	1993
GO WILD IN THE COUNTRY BOW WOW WOW	7	1982
GO WITH THE FLOW [A] LOOP DA LOOP	47	1997
GO WITH THE FLOW [B] QUEENS OF THE STONE AGE	21	2003
GO YOUR OWN WAY FLEETWOOD MAC	38	1977
GOD TORI AMOS	44	1994
GOD GAVE ROCK AND ROLL TO YOU ARGENT	18	1973
GOD GAVE ROCK AND ROLL TO YOU II KISS	4	1992
GOD IS A DJ [A] FAITHLESS	6	1998
GOD IS A DJ [B] P!NK	11	2004
GOD KILLED THE QUEEN LOUIS XIV	68	2005
GOD KNOWS MANDO DIAO	64	2005
GOD LEAD YOUR SOUL SLEEPY JACKSON	69	2006
GOD OF ABRAHAM MNO	66	1991
GOD ONLY KNOWS BEACH BOYS	2	1966
GOD ONLY KNOWS DIESEL PARK WEST	57	1992
GOD PUT A SMILE ON YOUR FACE RONSON FEATURING DAPTONE HORNS	63	2007
GOD SAVE THE QUEEN SEX PISTOLS	2	1977
GOD! SHOW ME MAGIC SUPER FURRY ANIMALS	33	1996
GOD THANK YOU WOMAN CULTURE CLUB	1	1986
GODDESS ON A HIWAY MERCURY REV	26	1998
GODHEAD NITZER EBB	52	1992
GODHOPPING DOGS DIE IN HOT CARS	24	2004
GODLESS DANDY WARHOLS	66	2001
GOD'S CHILD BIG BANG THEORY	51	2002
GOD'S GONNA PUNISH YOU TYMES	41	1976
GOD'S GREAT BANANA SKIN CHRIS REA	31	1992
GOD'S HOME MOVIE HORSE	56	1993
GOD'S KITCHEN BLANCMANGE	65	1982
GOD'S MISTAKE TEARS FOR FEARS	61	1996
GODSPEED BT	54	1998
GODSTAR PSYCHIC TV	67	1986
GODZILLA CREATURES	53	2003
GO-GO DANCER WEDDING PRESENT	20	1992
GOIN' DOWN MELANIE C	4	1999
GOIN' PLACES JACKSONS	26	1977
GOIN' TO THE BANK COMMODORES	43	1986
GOIN' TO VEGAS JIMMY RAY	49	1998
GOING ALL THE WAY ALLSTARS	19	2002
GOING BACK DUSTY SPRINGFIELD	10	1966
GOING BACK TO CALI LL COOL J	37	1988
GOING BACK TO MY HOME TOWN HAL PAIGE & THE WHALERS	50	1960
GOING BACK TO MY ROOTS ODYSSEY	4	1981
GOING BACK TO MY ROOTS FPI PROJECT	9	1989
GOING DOWN THE ROAD ROY WOOD	13	1974
GOING DOWN TO LIVERPOOL BANGLES	56	1986
GOING DOWN TOWN TONIGHT STATUS QUO	20	1984
GOING FOR GOLD SHED SEVEN	8	1996
GOING FOR THE ONE YES	24	1977
GOING HOME [A] OSMONDS	4	1973
GOING HOME [B] TYRREL CORPORATION	58	1992
GOING HOME (THEME OF 'LOCAL HERO') MARK KNOPFLER	56	1983
GOING IN WITH MY EYES OPEN DAVID SOUL	2	1977
GOING LEFT RIGHT DEPARTMENT S	55	1981
GOING MISSING MAXIMO PARK	20	2005
GOING NOWHERE GABRIELLE	9	1993
GOING OUT SUPERGRASS	5	1996
GOING OUT OF MY HEAD [A] DODIE WEST	39	1965
GOING OUT OF MY HEAD [B] FATBOY SLIM	57	1997
GOING OUT WITH GOD KINKY MACHINE	74	1993
GOING ROUND D'BORA	40	1995
GOING THROUGH THE MOTIONS HOT CHOCOLATE	53	1979
GOING TO A GO-GO MIRACLES	44	1966
GOING TO A GO-GO SHARONETTES	46	1975
GOING TO A GO GO ROLLING STONES	26	1982
GOING TO A TOWN RUFUS WAINWRIGHT	54	2007
GOING UNDER EVANESCENCE	8	2003
GOING UNDERGROUND JAM	1	1980
GOING UNDERGROUND BUFFALO TOM	6	1999
GOING UP THE COUNTRY CANNED HEAT	19	1969
GOLD [A] JOHN STEWART	43	1979
GOLD [B] SPANDAU BALLET	2	1983
GOLD [C] EAST 17	28	1992
GOLD [D] ARTIST FORMERLY KNOWN AS PRINCE (AFKAP)	10	1995
GOLD [E] BEVERLEY KNIGHT	27	2002
GOLD DIGGER KANYE WEST FEATURING JAMIE FOXX	2	2005
GOLD LION YEAH YEAH YEAHS	53	2006
GOLDEN JILL SCOTT	59	2004
GOLDEN AGE OF ROCK AND ROLL MOTT THE HOOPLE	16	1974
GOLDEN BROWN STRANGLERS	2	1982
GOLDEN BROWN KALEEF	22	1996
GOLDEN BROWN OMAR	37	1997
GOLDEN DAYS BUCKS FIZZ	42	1984
GOLDEN GATE BRIDGE OCEAN COLOUR SCENE	40	2004
GOLDEN GAZE IAN BROWN	29	2000
GOLDEN GREEN WONDER STUFF	33	1989
GOLDEN GUN SUEDE	14	2003
THE GOLDEN LADY THREE DEGREES	56	1979
GOLDEN LIGHTS TWINKLE	21	1965
THE GOLDEN PATH CHEMICAL BROTHERS FEATURING THE FLAMING LIPS	17	2003
GOLDEN RETRIEVER SUPER FURRY ANIMALS	13	2003
GOLDEN SKANS KLAXONS	7	2007
GOLDEN SKIN SILVER SUN	32	1997
GOLDEN SLUMBERS TRASH	35	1969
GOLDEN TOUCH [A] LOOSE ENDS	59	1985
GOLDEN TOUCH [B] RAZORLIGHT	9	2004
GOLDEN YEARS DAVID BOWIE	8	1975
THE GOLDEN YEARS EP MOTORHEAD	8	1980
GOLDENBALLS (MR BECKHAM TO YOU) BELL & SPURLING	25	2002
GOLDENBOOK FAMILY CAT	42	1994
GOLDENEYE TINA TURNER	10	1995
GOLDFINGER [A] SHIRLEY BASSEY	21	1964
GOLDFINGER [B] ASH	5	1996
GOLDRUSH YELLO	54	1986
GONE [A] SHIRLEY BASSEY	36	1964
GONE [B] DAVID HOLMES	75	1996
GONE [C] CURE	60	1996
GONE [D] N SYNC	24	2001
GONE AWAY OFFSPRING	42	1997
GONE DEAD TRAIN NAZARETH	49	1978
GONE GONE GONE [A] EVERLY BROTHERS	36	1964
GONE GONE GONE [B] JOHNNY MATHIS	15	1979
GONE TILL NOVEMBER WYCLEF JEAN	3	1998
GONE TOO SOON MICHAEL JACKSON	33	1993
GONE UP IN FLAMES MORNING RUNNER	39	2005
GONNA BE MINE ADDICTIVE FEATURING T2	47	2008
GONNA BUILD A MOUNTAIN MATT MONRO	44	1961
GONNA BUILD A MOUNTAIN SAMMY DAVIS Jr.	26	1962
GONNA CAPTURE YOUR HEART BLUE	18	1977
GONNA CATCH YOU LONNIE GORDON	32	1991
GONNA CATCH YOU BARKIN BROTHERS FEATURING JOHNNIE FIORI	51	2000
GONNA FLY NOW (THEME FROM *ROCKY*) BILL CONTI	52	2007
GONNA GET ALONG WITHOUT YA NOW PATIENCE & PRUDENCE	22	1957

Title / Artist	Peak Position	Year of Entry
GONNA GET ALONG WITHOUT YA NOW TRINI LOPEZ	41	1967
GONNA GET ALONG WITHOUT YOU NOW VIOLA WILLS	8	1979
GONNA GIVE HER ALL THE LOVE I'VE GOT JIMMY RUFFIN	26	1967
GONNA MAKE YOU A STAR DAVID ESSEX	1	1974
GONNA MAKE YOU AN OFFER YOU CAN'T REFUSE JIMMY HELMS	8	1973
GONNA MAKE YOU BLUSH PAPERDOLLS	65	1998
GONNA MAKE YOU SWEAT (EVERYBODY DANCE NOW) C & C MUSIC FACTORY (FEATURING FREEDOM WILLIAMS)	3	1990
GONNA WORK IT OUT HI-GATE	25	2001
GOO GOO BARABAJAGAL (LOVE IS HOT) DONOVAN WITH THE JEFF BECK GROUP	12	1969
GOOD AS GOLD BEAUTIFUL SOUTH	23	1994
THE GOOD THE BAD THE UGLY HUGO MONTENEGRO	1	1968
GOOD BEAT DEEE-LITE	53	1991
GOOD BOYS BLONDIE	12	2003
GOOD DANCERS SLEEPY JACKSON	71	2003
GOOD DAY SEAN MAGUIRE	12	1996
GOOD ENOUGH [A] BOBBY BROWN	41	1992
GOOD ENOUGH [B] DODGY	4	1996
GOOD ENOUGH FOR YOU FREEFALLER	21	2005
GOOD ENOUGH (LA VACHE) MILK INC	23	1998
GOOD EVENING FRIENDS FRANKIE LAINE & JOHNNIE RAY	25	1957
GOOD EVENING PHILADELPHIA RICKY ROSS	58	1996
GOOD FEELING REEF	24	1995
GOOD FOR ME AMY GRANT	60	1992
GOOD FORTUNE PJ HARVEY	41	2000
GOOD FRIEND PARIS RED	61	1992
GOOD FRUIT HEFNER	50	2000
GOOD GIRLS JOE	29	1998
GOOD GIRLS DON'T KNACK	66	1979
GOOD GOD [A] KORN	25	1997
GOOD GOD [B] JFK	71	2001
GOOD GOLLY MISS MOLLY LITTLE RICHARD	8	1958
GOOD GOLLY MISS MOLLY JERRY LEE LEWIS	31	1963
GOOD GOLLY MISS MOLLY SWINGING BLUE JEANS	11	1964
GOOD GOOD FEELING ERIC & THE GOOD GOOD FEELING	73	1989
GOOD GRIEF CHRISTINA CHICORY TIP	17	1973
A GOOD HEART FEARGAL SHARKEY	1	1985
A GOOD IDEA SUGAR	65	1992
GOOD IS GOOD SHERYL CROW	75	2005
THE GOOD LIFE [A] TONY BENNETT	27	1963
GOOD LIFE [B] INNER CITY	4	1988
GOOD LIFE [C] E.V.E.	39	1995
THE GOOD LIFE [D] NEW POWER GENERATION	15	1995
GOOD LIFE [E] KANYE WEST FEATURING T-PAIN	23	2007
GOOD LOVE MELI'SA MORGAN	59	1988
GOOD LOVE CAN NEVER DIE ALVIN STARDUST	11	1975
GOOD LOVE REAL LOVE D'BORA	58	1996
GOOD LOVER D-INFLUENCE	46	1992
GOOD LOVIN' REGINA BELLE	73	1989
GOOD LOVIN' AIN'T EASY TO COME BY MARVIN GAYE & TAMMI TERRELL	26	1969
GOOD LOVIN' GONE BAD BAD COMPANY	31	1975
GOOD LUCK BASEMENT JAXX FEATURING LISA KEKAULA	12	2003
GOOD LUCK CHARM ELVIS PRESLEY	1	1962
GOOD MORNING LEAPY LEE	29	1970
GOOD MORNING BRITAIN AZTEC CAMERA & MICK JONES	19	1990
GOOD MORNING FREEDOM BLUE MINK	10	1970
GOOD MORNING JUDGE 10 C.C.	5	1977
GOOD MORNING LITTLE SCHOOLGIRL YARDBIRDS	44	1964
GOOD MORNING STARSHINE OLIVER	6	1969
GOOD MORNING SUNSHINE AQUA	18	1998
GOOD OLD ARSENAL ARSENAL F.C. FIRST TEAM SQUAD	16	1971
GOOD OLD ROCK 'N ROLL DAVE CLARK FIVE	7	1969
THE GOOD ONES KILLS	23	2005
GOOD PEOPLE JACK JOHNSON	50	2005
GOOD REASON SEAFOOD	65	2004
GOOD RHYMES DA CLICK	14	1999
GOOD ROCKIN' TONIGHT MONTROSE	71	1980
GOOD SIGN EMILIA	54	1999
GOOD SONG BLUR	22	2003
GOOD SOULS STARSAILOR	12	2001
GOOD STUFF [A] B-52's	21	1992
GOOD STUFF [B] KELIS	19	2000
GOOD STUFF [C] CLOR	50	2005
GOOD SWEET LOVIN' LOUCHIE LOU & MICHIE ONE	34	1996
A GOOD THING SAINT ETIENNE	70	2005
GOOD THING [A] FINE YOUNG CANNIBALS	7	1989
GOOD THING [B] ETERNAL	8	1996
GOOD THING GOING YAZZ	53	1996
GOOD THING GOING SID OWEN	14	2000
GOOD THING GOING (WE'VE GOT A GOOD THING GOING) SUGAR MINOTT	4	1981
GOOD THINGS RIVAL SCHOOLS	74	2002
GOOD TIME [A] PERAN	37	2002
GOOD TIME [B] A	23	2003
GOOD TIME BABY BOBBY RYDELL	42	1961
GOOD TIMES [A] ERIC BURDON & THE ANIMALS	20	1967
GOOD TIMES [B] CHIC	5	1979
GOOD TIMES [C] MATT BIANCO	55	1988
GOOD TIMES [D] REID	55	1989
GOOD TIMES [E] JIMMY BARNES & INXS	18	1991
GOOD TIMES [F] EDIE BRICKELL	40	1994
GOOD TIMES [G] ED CASE & SKIN	49	2002
GOOD TIMES [H] DREAM FREQUENCY	67	1994
GOOD TIMES (BETTER TIMES) CLIFF RICHARD	12	1969
GOOD TIMES GONNA COME AQUALUNG	71	2002
GOOD TIMIN' JIMMY JONES	1	1960
GOOD TO BE ALIVE DJ RAP	36	1998
GOOD TO GO LOVER GWEN GUTHRIE	37	1987
GOOD TRADITION TANITA TIKARAM	10	1988
GOOD 2 GO TRIPLE EIGHT	42	2005
GOOD VIBRATIONS [A] BEACH BOYS	1	1966
GOOD VIBRATIONS [A] PSYCHIC TV	65	1986
GOOD VIBRATIONS [A] BRIAN WILSON	30	2004
GOOD VIBRATIONS [B] MARKY MARK & THE FUNKY BUNCH FEATURING LOLEATTA HOLLOWAY	14	1991
GOOD VIBRATIONS [C] BROTHERS LIKE OUTLAW FEATURING ALISON EVELYN	74	1993
GOOD WEEKEND ART BRUT	56	2005
A GOOD YEAR FOR THE ROSES ELVIS COSTELLO & THE ATTRACTIONS	6	1981
GOODBYE [A] MARY HOPKIN	2	1969
A GOODBYE [B] CAMEO	65	1986
GOODBYE [C] SUNDAYS	27	1992
GOODBYE [D] AIR SUPPLY	66	1993
GOODBYE [E] SPICE GIRLS	1	1998
GOODBYE [F] DEF LEPPARD	54	1999
GOODBYE [G] CORAL	21	2002
GOODBYE BABY AND AMEN LULU	40	1994
GOODBYE BLUEBIRD WAYNE FONTANA	49	1966
GOODBYE CIVILIAN SKIDS	52	1980
GOODBYE CRUEL WORLD [A] JAMES DARREN	28	1961
GOODBYE CRUEL WORLD [B] SHAKESPEARS SISTER	32	1991
GOODBYE GIRL [A] SQUEEZE	63	1978
GOODBYE GIRL [B] GO WEST	25	1985
GOODBYE HEARTBREAK LIGHTHOUSE FAMILY	14	1996
GOODBYE IS JUST ANOTHER WORD NEW SEEKERS	36	1973
GOODBYE JIMMY GOODBYE RUBY MURRAY	10	1959
GOODBYE MR A HOOSIERS	4	2007
GOODBYE MR MACKENZIE GOODBYE MR MACKENZIE	62	1988
GOODBYE MY LOVE [A] SEARCHERS	4	1965
GOODBYE MY LOVE [B] GLITTER BAND	2	1975
GOODBYE MY LOVER JAMES BLUNT	9	2006
GOODBYE NOTHING TO SAY JAVELLS FEATURING NOSMO KING	26	1974
GOODBYE SAM HELLO SAMANTHA CLIFF RICHARD	6	1970
GOODBYE STRANGER [A] SUPERTRAMP	57	1979
GOODBYE STRANGER [B] PEPSI & SHIRLIE	9	1987
GOODBYE TO LOVE CARPENTERS	9	1972
GOODBYE TO LOVE AGAIN MAXI PRIEST	57	1988
GOODBYE TONIGHT LOSTPROPHETS	42	2004
GOODBYE YELLOW BRICK ROAD ELTON JOHN	6	1973
GOODBYE-EE [A] PETER COOK & DUDLEY MOORE	18	1965
GOODBYE-EE [B] 14-18	33	1975
GOODBYE'S (THE SADDEST WORD) CELINE DION	38	2002
GOODGROOVE DEREK B	16	1988
GOODIES CIARA FEATURING PETEY PABLO	1	2005
GOODNESS GRACIOUS ME PETER SELLERS & SOPHIA LOREN	4	1960
GOODNIGHT [A] ROY ORBISON	14	1965
GOODNIGHT [B] BABYBIRD	28	1996
GOODNIGHT AND GO IMOGEN HEAP	56	2006
GOODNIGHT GIRL WET WET WET	1	1992
GOODNIGHT GOODNIGHT HOT HOT HEAT	36	2005
GOODNIGHT MIDNIGHT CLODAGH RODGERS	4	1969
GOODNIGHT MRS. FLINTSTONE PILTDOWN MEN	18	1961
GOODNIGHT MOON SHIVAREE	63	2001
GOODNIGHT SAIGON BILLY JOEL	29	1984
GOODNIGHT SWEET PRINCE MR ACKER BILK & HIS PARAMOUNT JAZZ BAND	50	1960
GOODNIGHT TONIGHT WINGS	5	1979
GOODWILL CITY GOODBYE MR MACKENZIE	49	1989
GOODY GOODY FRANKIE LYMON & THE TEENAGERS	24	1957
GOODY TWO SHOES ADAM ANT	1	1982
GOODYBYE BAD TIMES GIORGIO MORODER & PHIL OAKEY	44	1985
GOOGLE EYE NASHVILLE TEENS	10	1964
GORECKI LAMB	30	1997
GORGEOUS GENE LOVES JEZEBEL	68	1987
GOSP LWS	65	1994
GOSPEL OAK EP SINEAD O'CONNOR	28	1997
GOSSIP CALYPSO BERNARD CRIBBINS	25	1962
GOSSIP FOLKS MISSY ELLIOTT FEATURING LUDACRIS	9	2003
GOT 'TIL IT'S GONE JANET FEATURING Q-TIP & JONI	6	1997
GOT A FEELING PATRICK JUVET	34	1978
GOT A GIRL FOUR PREPS	28	1960
GOT A LITTLE HEARTACHE ALVIN STARDUST	55	1985
GOT A LOT O' LIVIN' TO DO ELVIS PRESLEY	17	1957
GOT A LOVE FOR YOU JOMANDA	43	1991
GOT A MATCH RUSS CONWAY	30	1958
GOT FUNK FUNK JUNKEEZ	57	1998
GOT IT AT THE DELMAR SENSELESS THINGS	50	1991
GOT LOVE TO KILL JULIETTE & THE LICKS	56	2005
GOT ME A FEELING MISTY OLDLAND	59	1993
GOT MY MIND MADE UP INSTANT FUNK	46	1979

Title / Artist	Peak Position	Year of Entry
GOT MY MIND SET ON YOU GEORGE HARRISON	2	1987
GOT MY MOJO WORKING JIMMY SMITH	48	1966
GOT MYSELF TOGETHER BUCKETHEADS	12	1996
GOT NO BRAINS BAD MANNERS	44	1982
GOT NONE ROBERT POST	42	2005
GOT SOME TEETH OBIE TRICE	8	2003
GOT THE FEELIN' FIVE	3	1998
GOT THE LIFE KORN	23	1998
GOT THE TIME ANTHRAX	16	1991
GOT TO BE CERTAIN KYLIE MINOGUE	2	1988
GOT TO BE REAL ERIK	42	1994
GOT TO BE THERE MICHAEL JACKSON	5	1972
GOT TO GET ROB 'N' RAZ FEATURING LEILA K	8	1989
GOT TO GET IT [A] CULTURE BEAT	4	1993
GOT TO GET IT [B] SISQO	14	2000
GOT TO GET UP AFRIKA BAMBAATAA	22	1998
GOT TO GET YOU BACK KYM MAZELLE	29	1989
GOT TO GET YOU INTO MY LIFE CLIFF BENNETT & THE REBEL ROUSERS	6	1966
GOT TO GET YOU INTO MY LIFE EARTH, WIND & FIRE	33	1978
GOT TO GIVE IT UP MARVIN GAYE	7	1977
GOT TO GIVE IT UP AALIYAH	37	1996
GOT TO GIVE ME LOVE DANA DAWSON	27	1995
GOT TO HAVE YOUR LOVE MANTRONIX FEATURING WONDRESS	4	1990
GOT TO HAVE YOUR LOVE LIBERTY X	2	2002
GOT TO KEEP ON COOKIE CREW	17	1989
GOT TO LOVE SOMEBODY SISTER SLEDGE	34	1980
GOT TO RELEASE SATURATED SOUL FEATURING MISS BUNTY	56	2004
GOT UR SELF A NAS	30	2002
GOT YOU PHAROAHE MONCH	27	2001
GOT YOU ON MY MIND TONY BRENT	12	1953
GOT YOUR MONEY OL' DIRTY BASTARD FEATURING KELIS	11	2000
GOTHAM CITY R KELLY	9	1997
GOTTA BE A SIN ADAM ANT	48	1995
GOTTA BE YOU 3T: RAP BY HERBIE	10	1997
GOTTA CATCH 'EM ALL 50 GRIND FEATURING POKEMON ALLSTARS	57	2001
GOTTA GET A DATE FRANK IFIELD	49	1960
GOTTA GET AWAY OFFSPRING	43	1995
GOTTA GET IT RIGHT LENA FIAGBE	20	1993
GOTTA GET LOOSE MR & MRS SMITH	70	1996
GOTTA GET THRU THIS DANIEL BEDINGFIELD	1	2001
GOTTA GET YOU HOME TONIGHT EUGENE WILDE	18	1984
GOTTA GETCHA JERMAINE DUPRI	54	2005
GOTTA GO HOME BONEY M	12	1979
GOTTA GO MY OWN WAY GABRIELLA & TROY	40	2007
GOTTA HAVE HOPE BLACKOUT	46	1999
GOTTA HAVE RAIN MAX BYGRAVES	28	1958
GOTTA HAVE SOMETHING IN THE BANK FRANK FRANKIE VAUGHAN & THE KAYE SISTERS	8	1957
GOTTA KEEP PUSHIN' Z FACTOR	47	1998
GOTTA KNOW (YOUR NAME) MALAIKA	68	1993
GOTTA LOTTA LOVE ICE-T	24	1994
GOTTA...MOVIN' ON UP PM DAWN FEATURING KY-MANI	68	1998
GOTTA PULL MYSELF TOGETHER NOLANS	9	1980
GOTTA SEE BABY TONIGHT MR ACKER BILK & HIS PARAMOUNT JAZZ BAND	24	1962
GOTTA SEE JANE R. DEAN TAYLOR	17	1968
GOTTA TELL YOU SAMANTHA MUMBA	2	2000
GOTTA WORK AMERIE	21	2007
GOURYELLA GOURYELLA	15	1999
GOVINDA [A] RADHA KRISHNA TEMPLE	23	1970
GOVINDA [B] KULA SHAKER	7	1996
GRACE [A] BAND AKA	41	1982
GRACE [B] SUPERGRASS	13	2002
GRACE [C] SIMON WEBBE	36	2007
GRACE KELLY MIKA	1	2007
GRACEADELICA DARK STAR	25	2000
GRACELAND BIBLE	51	1989
GRAFFITI MAXIMO PARK	15	2005
GRANADA FRANKIE LAINE	9	1954
GRANADA FRANK SINATRA	15	1961
GRAND COOLIE DAM LONNIE DONEGAN	6	1958
GRAND PIANO MIXMASTER	9	1989
GRAND UNIFICATION (PART 1) FIGHTSTAR	20	2005
GRANDAD CLIVE DUNN	1	1970
GRANDMA'S PARTY PAUL NICHOLAS	9	1976
GRANDPA'S PARTY MONIE LOVE	16	1989
GRANITE PENDULUM	29	2007
GRANITE STATUE SALAD	50	1995
GRAPEVYNE BROWNSTONE	16	1995
GRATEFUL WHEN YOU'RE DEAD - JERRY WAS THERE KULA SHAKER	35	1996
THE GRAVE AND THE CONSTANT FUN LOVIN' CRIMINALS	72	1996
GRAVEL PIT WU-TANG CLAN	6	2000
GRAVITATE TO ME THE THE	63	1989
GRAVITY [A] JAMES BROWN	65	1986
GRAVITY [B] EMBRACE	7	2004
GRAVITY'S RAINBOW KLAXONS	35	2007
GREASE FRANKIE VALLI	3	1978
GREASE CRAIG McLACHLAN	44	1993
GREASE MEGAMIX FRANKIE VALLI, JOHN TRAVOLTA & OLIVIA NEWTON-JOHN	47	1990
GREASED LIGHTNIN' JOHN TRAVOLTA	11	1978
GREAT BALLS OF FIRE JERRY LEE LEWIS	1	1957
GREAT BALLS OF FIRE TINY TIM	45	1969
THE GREAT BEYOND R.E.M.	3	2000
THE GREAT ESCAPE [A] ENGLAND SUPPORTERS' BAND	26	1998
THE GREAT ESCAPE [B] WE ARE SCIENTISTS	37	2005
THE GREAT ESCAPE [C] MORNING RUNNER	56	2006
GREAT GOSH A'MIGHTY (IT'S A MATTER OF TIME) LITTLE RICHARD	62	1986
THE GREAT PRETENDER JIMMY PARKINSON	9	1956
THE GREAT PRETENDER PLATTERS	5	1956
THE GREAT PRETENDER FREDDIE MERCURY	4	1987
THE GREAT ROCK 'N' ROLL SWINDLE SEX PISTOLS	21	1979
THE GREAT SNOWMAN BOB LUMAN	49	1961
THE GREAT SONG OF INDIFFERENCE BOB GELDOF	15	1990
THE GREAT TEST HUNDRED REASONS	29	2003
GREAT THINGS ECHOBELLY	13	1995
THE GREAT TRAIN ROBBERY BLACK UHURU	62	1986
GREATER LOVE SOUNDMAN & DON LLOYDIE WITH ELISABETH TROY	49	1995
THE GREATEST COCKNEY RIPOFF COCKNEY REJECTS	21	1980
GREATEST DAY BEVERLEY KNIGHT	14	1999
THE GREATEST FLAME RUNRIG	30	1993
THE GREATEST HIGH HURRICANE #1	43	1999
THE GREATEST LOVE OF ALL GEORGE BENSON	27	1977
GREATEST LOVE OF ALL WHITNEY HOUSTON	8	1986
THE GREATEST LOVE YOU'LL NEVER KNOW LUTRICIA McNEAL	17	1998
THE GREATEST ROMANCE EVER SOLD THE ARTIST	65	2000
THE GREATEST SHOW ON EARTH STRANGELOVE	36	1997
THE GREATNESS AND PERFECTION OF LOVE JULIAN COPE	52	1984
GREECE THREE DRIVES	12	1999
GREECE 2000 THREE DRIVES	12	1998
GREED LAURENT GARNIER	36	2000
GREEDY FLY BUSH	22	1997
THE GREEDY UGLY PEOPLE HEFNER	64	2000
GREEN AND GREY NEW MODEL ARMY	37	1989
GREEN DOOR GLEN MASON	24	1956
THE GREEN DOOR FRANKIE VAUGHAN	2	1956
THE GREEN DOOR JIM LOWE	8	1956
GREEN DOOR SHAKIN' STEVENS	1	1981
GREEN FIELDS [A] BEVERLEY SISTERS	29	1960
GREEN FIELDS [A] UNIT FOUR PLUS TWO	48	1964
GREEN FIELDS [B] THE GOOD THE BAD & THE QUEEN	51	2007
GREEN GREEN GRASS OF HOME TOM JONES	1	1966
GREEN GREEN GRASS OF HOME ELVIS PRESLEY	29	1975
GREEN GREEN GRASS OF HOME KATHERINE JENKINS	62	2006
GREEN JEANS FLEE-REKKERS	23	1960
THE GREEN LEAVES OF SUMMER KENNY BALL & HIS JAZZMEN	7	1962
GREEN LIGHT CLIFF RICHARD	57	1979
GREEN LIGHT FREEMASONS EP BEYONCÉ	12	2007
THE GREEN MAN SHUT UP & DANCE	43	1992
THE GREEN MANALISHI (WITH THE TWO-PRONG CROWN) FLEETWOOD MAC	10	1970
GREEN ONIONS BOOKER T. & THE M.G.'s	7	1979
GREEN RIVER CREEDENCE CLEARWATER REVIVAL	19	1969
GREEN SHIRT ELVIS COSTELLO	68	1985
GREEN STREET GREEN NEW VAUDEVILLE BAND	37	1967
GREEN TAMBOURINE LEMON PIPERS	7	1968
GREEN TAMBOURINE SUNDRAGON	50	1968
GREEN TINTED SIXTIES MIND MR BIG	72	1992
GREENBACK DOLLAR CHARLES McDEVITT SKIFFLE GROUP FEATURING NANCY WHISKEY	28	1957
GREENBANK DRIVE CHRISTIANS	63	1990
GREENFIELDS BROTHERS FOUR	40	1960
GREETINGS TO THE NEW BRUNETTE BILLY BRAGG WITH JOHNNY MARR & KIRSTY MacCOLL	58	1986
GREY DAY MADNESS	4	1981
GRIEF NEVER GROWS OLD ONE WORLD PROJECT	4	2005
GRILLZ NELLY FEATURING PAUL WALL, ALI & GIPP	24	2006
GRIMLY FIENDISH DAMNED	21	1985
GRIND ALICE IN CHAINS	23	1995
GRIND WITH ME PRETTY RICKY	26	2005
GRIP LIKE A VICE THE GO! TEAM	57	2007
GRITTY SHAKER DAVID HOLMES	53	1997
THE GROOVE RODNEY FRANKLIN	7	1980
GROOVE BABY GROOVE (EP) STARGAZERS	56	1982
GROOVE IS IN THE HEART DEEE-LITE	2	1990
THE GROOVE LINE HEATWAVE	12	1978
GROOVE MACHINE MARVIN & TAMARA	11	1999
GROOVE OF LOVE E.V.E.	30	1994
GROOVE THANG ZHANE	34	1994
GROOVE TO MOVE CHANNEL X	67	1991
GROOVEBIRD NATURAL BORN GROOVES	21	1997
GROOVEJET (IF THIS AIN'T LOVE) SPILLER	1	2000
GROOVELINE BLOCKSTER	18	1999
THE GROOVER T REX	4	1973
GROOVIN' [A] YOUNG RASCALS	8	1967
GROOVIN' [A] PATO BANTON & THE REGGAE REVOLUTION	14	1996
GROOVIN' [B] WAR	43	1985
GROOVIN' IN THE MIDNIGHT MAXI PRIEST	50	1992
GROOVIN' (THAT'S WHAT WE'RE DOIN') S.O.S. BAND	72	1983
GROOVIN' WITH MR. BLOE MR BLOE	2	1970
GROOVIN' (YOU'RE THE BEST THING STYLE COUNCIL	5	1984
GROOVY BABY MICROBE	29	1969
GROOVY BEAT D.O.P.	54	1996

Title / Artist	Peak Position	Year of Entry
GROOVY FEELING FLUKE	45	1993
A GROOVY KIND OF LOVE MINDBENDERS	2	1966
A GROOVY KIND OF LOVE LES GRAY	32	1977
A GROOVY KIND OF LOVE PHIL COLLINS	1	1988
THE GROOVY THANG MINIMAL FUNK 2	65	1998
GROOVY TRAIN FARM	6	1990
GROUND LEVEL STEREO MC'S	19	1993
THE GROUNDBREAKER FALLACY & FUSION	47	2002
GROUNDED MY VITRIOL	29	2001
GROUNDS FOR DIVORCE ELBOW	19	2008
GROUPIE GIRL TONY JOE WHITE	22	1970
GROW KUBB	18	2006
GROWING ON ME DARKNESS	11	2003
GROWN AND SEXY CHAMILLIONAIRE	35	2006
THE GRUDGE MORTIIS	51	2004
G.T.O. SINITTA	15	1987
GUAGLIONE PEREZ 'PREZ' PRADO & HIS ORCHESTRA	2	1994
GUANTANAMERA SANDPIPERS	7	1966
GUANTANAMERA WYCLEF JEAN & THE REFUGEE ALLSTARS	25	1997
GUANTANAMO OUTLANDISH	31	2003
GUARANTEED LEVEL 42	17	1991
GUARDIAN ANGEL NINO DE ANGELO	57	1984
GUARDIANS OF THE LAND GEORGE BOWYER	33	1998
GUDBUY T' JANE SLADE	2	1972
GUDVIBE TINMAN	49	1995
GUERRILLA FUNK PARIS	38	1995
GUERRILLA RADIO RAGE AGAINST THE MACHINE	32	1999
GUESS I WAS A FOOL ANOTHER LEVEL	5	1998
GUESS WHO'S BACK RAKIM	32	1997
GUESS YOU DIDN'T LOVE ME TERRI WALKER	60	2003
GUIDING STAR CAST	9	1997
GUILTY [A] JIM REEVES	29	1963
GUILTY [B] PEARLS	10	1974
GUILTY [C] MIKE OLDFIELD	22	1979
GUILTY [D] BARBRA STREISAND & BARRY GIBB	34	1981
GUILTY [E] CLASSIX NOUVEAUX	43	1981
GUILTY [F] PAUL HARDCASTLE	55	1984
GUILTY [G] YARBOROUGH & PEOPLES	53	1986
GUILTY [H] BLUE	2	2003
GUILTY [I] RASMUS	15	2004
GUILTY [J] DE SOUZA FEATURING SHENA	46	2007
GUILTY CONSCIENCE EMINEM FEATURING DR DRE	5	1999
GUILTY OF LOVE WHITESNAKE	31	1983
GUITAR BOOGIE SHUFFLE BERT WEEDON	10	1959
GUITAR MAN [A] ELVIS PRESLEY	19	1968
THE GUITAR MAN [B] BREAD	16	1972
GUITAR TANGO SHADOWS	4	1962
GUITARRA G BANDA SONORA	50	2001
GUN-LAW KANE GANG	53	1985
GUNMAN 187 LOCKDOWN	16	1997
GUNS AT DAWN DJ BARON FEATURING PENDULUM	71	2005
GUNS DON'T KILL PEOPLE RAPPERS DO GOLDIE LOOKIN CHAIN	3	2004
GUNS FOR HIRE AC/DC	37	1983
GUNS OF NAVARONE SKATALITES	36	1967
GUNSLINGER FRANKIE LAINE	50	1961
GUNZ AND PIANOZ BASS BOYZ	74	1996
GURNEY SLADE MAX HARRIS	11	1960
THE GUSH RAGING SPEEDHORN	47	2001
GYM AND TONIC SPACEDUST	1	1998
GYPSY FLEETWOOD MAC	46	1982
GYPSY BEAT PACKABEATS	49	1961
GYPSY BOY, GYPSY GIRL SHARADA HOUSE GANG	52	1997
GYPSY EYES JIMI HENDRIX EXPERIENCE	35	1971
GYPSY ROAD CINDERELLA	54	1988
GYPSY ROAD HOG SLADE	48	1977
GYPSY ROVER HIGHWAYMEN	41	1961
GYPSY WOMAN BRIAN HYLAND	42	1971
GYPSY WOMAN (LA DA DEE) CRYSTAL WATERS	2	1991
GYPSYS TRAMPS AND THIEVES CHER	4	1971

H

Title / Artist	Peak Position	Year of Entry
HA CHA CHA (FUNKTION) BRASS CONSTRUCTION	37	1977
HA HA SAID THE CLOWN MANFRED MANN	4	1967
HAD ENOUGH ENEMY	4	2007
HAD TO BE CLIFF RICHARD & OLIVIA NEWTON-JOHN	22	1995
HAIL CAESAR AC/DC	56	1996
HAIL HAIL ROCK 'N' ROLL GARLAND JEFFREYS	72	1992
HAIL MARY MAKAVELI	43	1998
HAITIAN DIVORCE STEELY DAN	17	1976
HALE BOPP DER DRITTE RAUM	75	1999
HALEY'S GOLDEN MEDLEY BILL HALEY & HIS COMETS	50	1981
HALF A BOY HALF A MAN NICK LOWE	53	1984
HALF A HEART H & CLAIRE	8	2002
HALF A MINUTE MATT BIANCO	23	1984
HALF AS MUCH ROSEMARY CLOONEY	3	1952
HALF LIGHT ATHLETE	16	2005
HALF MAN HALF MACHINE GOLDIE LOOKIN CHAIN	32	2004
HALF OF MY HEART EMILE FORD	42	1961
HALF ON A BABY R KELLY	16	1998
HALF THE DAY'S GONE AND WE HAVEN'T EARNT A PENNY KENNY LYNCH	50	1983
HALF THE MAN JAMIROQUAI	15	1994
HALF THE WORLD BELINDA CARLISLE	35	1992
HALFWAY AROUND THE WORLD A*TEENS	30	2001
HALFWAY DOWN THE STAIRS MUPPETS	7	1977
HALFWAY HOTEL VOYAGER	33	1979
HALFWAY TO HEAVEN EUROPE	42	1992
HALFWAY TO PARADISE BILLY FURY	3	1961
HALFWAY UP HALFWAY DOWN DENNIS BROWN	56	1982
HALLELUIAH MAN LOVE & MONEY	63	1988
HALLELUJAH [A] MILK & HONEY FEATURING GALI ATARI	5	1979
HALLELUJAH [B] JEFF BUCKLEY	65	2007
HALLELUJAH '92 INNER CITY	22	1992
HALLELUJAH DAY JACKSON 5	20	1973
HALLELUJAH FREEDOM JUNIOR CAMPBELL	10	1972
HALLELUJAH I LOVE HER SO DICK JORDAN	47	1960
HALLELUJAH I LOVE HER SO EDDIE COCHRAN	22	1960
HALLO SPACEBOY DAVID BOWIE	12	1996
HALLOWED BE THY NAME (LIVE) IRON MAIDEN	9	1993
HALLS OF ILLUSION INSANE CLOWN POSSE	56	1998
HALO [A] TEXAS	10	1997
HALO [B] SOIL	74	2002
(HAMMER HAMMER) THEY PUT ME IN THE MIX MC HAMMER	20	1991
HAMMER HORROR KATE BUSH	44	1978
HAMMER TO FALL QUEEN	13	1984
HAMMER TO THE HEART TAMPERER FEATURING MAYA	6	2000
HAND A HANDKERCHIEF TO HELEN SUSAN MAUGHAN	41	1963
HAND HELD IN BLACK AND WHITE DOLLAR	19	1981
HAND IN GLOVE SANDIE SHAW	27	1984
HAND IN HAND GRACE	38	1997
HAND IN MY POCKET ALANIS MORISSETTE	26	1995
HAND IN YOUR HEAD MONEY MARK	40	1998
HAND OF THE DEAD BODY SCARFACE FEATURING ICE CUBE	41	1995

Title / Artist	Peak Position	Year of Entry
HAND ON MY HEART SHRIEKBACK	52	1984
HAND ON YOUR HEART KYLIE MINOGUE	1	1989
HAND ON YOUR HEART JOSE GONZALEZ	29	2006
THE HAND THAT FEEDS NINE INCH NAILS	7	2005
HANDBAGS AND GLADRAGS CHRIS FARLOWE	33	1967
HANDBAGS AND GLADRAGS STEREOPHONICS	4	2001
HANDFUL OF PROMISES BIG FUN	21	1990
HANDFUL OF SONGS TOMMY STEELE & THE STEELMEN	5	1957
HANDLE ME ROBYN	17	2007
HANDLE WITH CARE TRAVELING WILBURYS	21	1988
HANDS [A] JEWEL	41	1998
HANDS [B] RACONTEURS	29	2006
HANDS ACROSS THE OCEAN MISSION	28	1990
HANDS AROUND MY THROAT DEATH IN VEGAS	36	2002
HANDS CLEAN ALANIS MORISSETTE	12	2002
HANDS DOWN DASHBOARD CONFESSIONAL	60	2003
HANDS OFF - SHE'S MINE BEAT	9	1980
HANDS TO HEAVEN BREATHE	4	1988
HANDS UP [A] CLUBZONE	50	1994
HANDS UP [B] TREVOR & SIMON	12	2000
HANDS UP [C] LLOYD BANKS FEATURING 50 CENT	43	2006
HANDS UP [D] OUT OF OFFICE	52	2007
HANDS UP (4 LOVERS) RIGHT SAID FRED	60	1993
HANDS UP (GIVE ME YOUR HEART) OTTAWAN	3	1981
HANDS UP! HANDS UP! ZIG & ZAG	21	1995
HANDY MAN JIMMY JONES	3	1960
HANDY MAN DEL SHANNON	36	1964
HANG 'EM HIGH HUGO MONTENEGRO	50	1969
HANG IN LONG ENOUGH PHIL COLLINS	34	1990
HANG ME UP TO DRY COLD WAR KIDS	57	2007
HANG MYSELF ON YOU CANDYSKINS	65	1997
HANG ON IN THERE BABY JOHNNY BRISTOL	3	1974
HANG ON IN THERE BABY CURIOSITY	3	1992
HANG ON NOW KAJAGOOGOO	13	1983
HANG ON SLOOPY McCOYS	5	1965
HANG ON SLOOPY SANDPIPERS	32	1976
HANG ON TO A DREAM TIM HARDIN	50	1967
HANG ON TO YOUR LOVE JASON DONOVAN	8	1990
HANG TOGETHER ODYSSEY	36	1981
HANG UP ANDY ABRAHAM	63	2006
HANG YOUR HEAD DEACON BLUE	21	1993
HANGAR 18 MEGADETH	26	1991
HANGIN' CHIC	64	1983
HANGIN' AROUND BIG BROVAZ	57	2006
HANGIN' ON A STRING (CONTEMPLATING) LOOSE ENDS	13	1985
HANGIN' OUT KOOL & THE GANG	52	1980
HANGIN' TOUGH NEW KIDS ON THE BLOCK	1	1989
HANGING AROUND [A] HAZEL O'CONNOR	45	1981
HANGING AROUND [B] ME ME ME	19	1996
HANGING AROUND [C] CARDIGANS	17	1999
HANGING AROUND [D] GEMMA HAYES	62	2002
HANGING AROUND [E] POLYPHONIC SPREE	39	2002
HANGING AROUND WITH THE BIG BOYS BLOOMSBURY SET	56	1983
HANGING BY A MOMENT LIFEHOUSE	25	2001
HANGING GARDEN CURE	34	1982
HANGING ON THE TELEPHONE BLONDIE	5	1978
HANGINAROUND COUNTING CROWS	46	1999
HANGOVER BETTY BOO	50	1993
HANKY PANKY [A] TOMMY JAMES & THE SHONDELLS	38	1966
HANKY PANKY [B] MADONNA	2	1990
HANNA HANNA CHINA CRISIS	44	1984
HANNAH WE KNOW TINY DANCERS	33	2007
HAPPENIN' ALL OVER AGAIN LONNIE GORDON	4	1990

Title / Artist	Peak Position	Year of Entry
HAPPENIN' ALL OVER AGAIN TRACY SHAW	46	1998
THE HAPPENING SUPREMES	6	1967
HAPPENINGS TEN YEARS TIME AGO YARDBIRDS	43	1966
HAPPINESS [A] KEN DODD	31	1964
HAPPINESS [B] SERIOUS ROPE PRESENTS SHARON DEE CLARK	54	1993
HAPPINESS [C] ROGER TAYLOR	32	1994
HAPPINESS [D] PIZZAMAN	19	1995
HAPPINESS [E] KAMASUTRA FEATURING JOCELYN BROWN	45	1997
HAPPINESS [F] SOUND DE-ZIGN	19	2001
HAPPINESS [G] ORSON	27	2006
HAPPINESS HAPPENING LOST WITNESS	18	1999
HAPPINESS IS JUST AROUND THE BEND CUBA GOODING	72	1983
HAPPINESS IS ME AND YOU GILBERT O'SULLIVAN	19	1974
HAPPINESS (MY VISION IS CLEAR) BINI & MARTINI	53	2000
HAPPY [A] SURFACE	56	1987
HAPPY [A] MN8	8	1995
HAPPY [A] PAULINE HENRY	46	1996
HAPPY [B] NED'S ATOMIC DUSTBIN	16	1991
HAPPY [C] TRAVIS	38	1997
HAPPY [D] LIGHTHOUSE FAMILY	51	2002
HAPPY [E] ASHANTI	13	2002
HAPPY [F] MAX SEDGLEY	30	2004
HAPPY ANNIVERSARY [A] JOAN REGAN	29	1960
HAPPY ANNIVERSARY [B] SLIM WHITMAN	14	1974
HAPPY AS ANNIE LARRIKIN LOVE	32	2006
HAPPY BIRTHDAY [A] STEVIE WONDER	2	1981
HAPPY BIRTHDAY [B] ALTERED IMAGES	2	1981
HAPPY BIRTHDAY [C] TECHNOHEAD	18	1996
HAPPY BIRTHDAY REVOLUTION LEVELLERS	57	2000
HAPPY BIRTHDAY SWEET SIXTEEN NEIL SEDAKA	3	1961
HAPPY BIZZNESS ROACH MOTEL	75	1994
HAPPY BUSMAN FRANK & WALTERS	49	1992
HAPPY DAY BLINK	57	1994
HAPPY DAYS [A] PRATT & McCLAIN WITH BROTHERLOVE	31	1977
HAPPY DAYS [B] SWEET MERCY FEATURING JOE ROBERTS	63	1996
HAPPY DAYS [C] PJ	57	1997
HAPPY DAYS AND LONELY NIGHTS FRANKIE VAUGHAN	12	1955
HAPPY DAYS AND LONELY NIGHTS RUBY MURRAY	6	1955
HAPPY DAYS AND LONELY NIGHTS SUZI MILLER & THE JOHNSTON BROTHERS	14	1955
HAPPY ENDING [A] JOE JACKSON	58	1984
HAPPY ENDING [B] MIKA	7	2007
HAPPY ENDINGS (GIVE YOURSELF A PINCH) LIONEL BART	68	1989
HAPPY EVER AFTER JULIA FORDHAM	27	1988
HAPPY FEELING HAMILTON BOHANNON	49	1975
HAPPY GO LUCKY ME GEORGE FORMBY	40	1960
HAPPY GUITAR TOMMY STEELE	20	1958
HAPPY HEART ANDY WILLIAMS	19	1969
HAPPY HOME 2PAC	17	1998
HAPPY HOUR HOUSEMARTINS	3	1986
HAPPY HOUSE SIOUXSIE & THE BANSHEES	17	1980
HAPPY JACK WHO	3	1966
HAPPY JUST TO BE WITH YOU MICHELLE GAYLE	11	1995
HAPPY (LOVE THEME FROM *LADY SINGS THE BLUES*) MICHAEL JACKSON	52	1983
THE HAPPY MAN THOMAS LANG	67	1988
HAPPY NATION ACE OF BASE	40	1993
HAPPY PEOPLE [A] STATIC REVENGER	23	2001
HAPPY PEOPLE [B] R KELLY	6	2004
H.A.P.P.Y. RADIO EDWIN STARR	9	1979
H-A-P-P-Y RADIO MICHAELA	62	1989
HAPPY SHOPPER 60FT DOLLS	38	1996
THE HAPPY SONG OTIS REDDING	24	1968
HAPPY TALK CAPTAIN SENSIBLE	1	1982
HAPPY TO BE ON AN ISLAND IN THE SUN DEMIS ROUSSOS	5	1975
HAPPY TO MAKE YOUR ACQUAINTANCE SAMMY DAVIS Jr. & CARMEN McRAE	46	1960
HAPPY TOGETHER TURTLES	12	1967
HAPPY TOGETHER JASON DONOVAN	10	1991
HAPPY WANDERER OBERKIRCHEN CHILDREN'S CHOIR	2	1954
HAPPY WANDERER STARGAZERS	12	1954
HAPPY WHEN IT RAINS JESUS & MARY CHAIN	25	1987
THE HAPPY WHISTLER CYRIL STAPLETON ORCHESTRA FEATURING DESMOND LANE, PENNY WHISTLE	22	1956
THE HAPPY WHISTLER DON ROBERTSON	8	1956
HAPPY XMAS (WAR IS OVER) JOHN & YOKO & THE PLASTIC ONO BAND WITH THE HARLEM COMMUNITY CHOIR	2	1972
HAPPY XMAS (WAR IS OVER) IDOLS	5	2003
HARBOUR LIGHTS PLATTERS	11	1960
HARD AS A ROCK AC/DC	33	1995
HARD BEAT EP 19 VARIOUS ARTISTS (EP'S & LPS)	71	2001
A HARD DAY'S NIGHT BEATLES	1	1964
A HARD DAY'S NIGHT PETER SELLERS	14	1965
HARD HABIT TO BREAK CHICAGO	8	1984
HARD HEADED WOMAN ELVIS PRESLEY	2	1958
HARD HEARTED HANNAH TEMPERANCE SEVEN	28	1961
HARD HOUSE MUSIC MELT FEATURING LITTLE MS MARCIE	59	2000
HARD KNOCK LIFE (GHETTO ANTHEM) JAY-Z	2	1998
A HARD RAIN'S GONNA FALL BRYAN FERRY	10	1973
HARD ROAD BLACK SABBATH	33	1978
HARD ROCK HALLELUJAH LORDI	25	2006
THE HARD TIMES RESEARCH	73	2006
HARD TIMES COME EASY RICHIE SAMBORA	37	1998
HARD TO BEAT HARD-FI	9	2005
HARD TO EXPLAIN STROKES	16	2001
HARD TO HANDLE OTIS REDDING	15	1968
HARD TO HANDLE BLACK CROWES	39	1990
HARD TO MAKE A STAND SHERYL CROW	22	1997
HARD TO SAY I'M SORRY CHICAGO	4	1982
HARD TO SAY I'M SORRY AZ YET FEATURING PETER CETERA	7	1997
HARD TO SAY I'M SORRY AQUAGEN	33	2003
HARD UP AWESOME 3	55	1990
THE HARD WAY NASHVILLE TEENS	45	1966
THE HARDCORE EP HYPNOTIST	68	1991
HARDCORE HEAVEN DJ SEDUCTION	26	1992
HARDCORE HIP HOUSE TYREE	70	1989
HARDCORE - THE FINAL CONFLICT HARDCORE RHYTHM TEAM	69	1992
HARDCORE UPROAR TOGETHER	12	1990
HARDCORE WILL NEVER DIE Q-BASS	64	1992
HARDEN MY HEART QUATERFLASH	49	1982
HARDER KOSHEEN	53	2002
HARDER BETTER FASTER STRONGER DAFT PUNK	25	2001
THE HARDER I TRY BROTHER BEYOND	2	1988
THE HARDER THEY COME [A] ROCKER'S REVENGE	30	1983
THE HARDER THEY COME [A] MADNESS	44	1992
THE HARDER THEY COME [B] PAUL OAKENFOLD	38	2003
HARDER TO BREATHE MAROON 5	13	2004
THE HARDEST BUTTON TO BUTTON WHITE STRIPES	23	2003
HARDEST PART IS THE NIGHT BON JOVI	68	1985
THE HARDEST THING 98o	29	2000
HARDROCK HERBIE HANCOCK	65	1984
HARDTRANCE ACPERIENCE HARDFLOOR	56	1992
HARE KRISHNA MANTRA RADHA KRISHNA TEMPLE	12	1969
HARLEM DESIRE LONDON BOYS	17	1989
HARLEM SHUFFLE BOB & EARL	7	1969
HARLEM SHUFFLE ROLLING STONES	13	1986
HARLEQUIN - THE BEAUTY AND THE BEAST SVEN VATH	72	1994
HARMONIC GENERATOR DATSUNS	33	2003
HARMONICA MAN BRAVADO	37	1994
HARMONY TC 1993	51	1993
HARMONY IN MY HEAD BUZZCOCKS	32	1979
HARMOUR LOVE SYREETA	32	1975
HARPER VALLEY P.T.A. JEANNIE C. RILEY	12	1968
HARROWDOWN HILL THOM YORKE	23	2006
HARVEST FOR THE WORLD ISLEY BROTHERS	10	1976
HARVEST FOR THE WORLD CHRISTIANS	8	1988
HARVEST FOR THE WORLD TERRY HUNTER	48	1997
HARVEST MOON NEIL YOUNG	36	1993
HARVEST OF LOVE BENNY HILL	20	1963
HARVESTER OF SORROW METALLICA	20	1988
HARVEY NICKS MITCHELL BROTHERS FEATURING SWAY	62	2005
HAS IT COME TO THIS STREETS	18	2001
HASH PIPE WEEZER	21	2001
HASTA LA VISTA SYLVIA	38	1975
HATE (I REALLY DON'T LIKE YOU) PLAIN WHITE T'S	53	2008
HATE IT OR LOVE IT GAME FEATURING 50 CENT	4	2005
HATE ME NOW NAS FEATURING PUFF DADDY	14	1999
THE HATE SONG RAGING SPEEDHORN	69	2002
HATE THAT I LOVE YOU RIHANNA FEATURING NE-YO	15	2007
HATE TO SAY I TOLD YOU SO HIVES	23	2002
HATERS SO SOLID CREW PRESENTS MR SHABZ	8	2002
HATS OFF TO LARRY DEL SHANNON	6	1961
HAUNTED POGUES	42	1986
HAUNTED SHANE MacGOWAN & SINEAD O'CONNOR	30	1995
HAUNTED BY YOU GENE	32	1995
HAVA NAGILA SPOTNICKS	13	1963
HAVE A CHEEKY CHRISTMAS CHEEKY GIRLS	10	2003
HAVE A DRINK ON ME LONNIE DONEGAN	8	1961
HAVE A GOOD FOREVER COOLNOTES	73	1985
HAVE A LITTLE FAITH JOE COCKER	67	1995
HAVE A NICE DAY [A] ROXANNE SHANTE	58	1987
HAVE A NICE DAY [B] STEREOPHONICS	5	2001
HAVE A NICE DAY [C] BON JOVI	6	2005
HAVE FUN, GO MAD! BLAIR	37	1995
HAVE FUN GO MAD TWEENIES	20	2002
HAVE I BEEN A FOOL JACK PENATE	73	2007
HAVE I STAYED TOO LONG SONNY & CHER	42	1966
HAVE I THE RIGHT HONEYCOMBS	1	1964
HAVE I THE RIGHT DEAD END KIDS	6	1977
HAVE I TOLD YOU LATELY VAN MORRISON	74	1989
HAVE I TOLD YOU LATELY ROD STEWART	5	1993
HAVE I TOLD YOU LATELY THAT I LOVE YOU CHIEFTAINS WITH VAN MORRISON	71	1995
HAVE IT ALL FOO FIGHTERS	37	2003
HAVE LOST IT (EP) TEENAGE FANCLUB	53	1995
HAVE LOVE WILL TRAVEL (EP) CRAZYHEAD	68	1989
HAVE MERCY YAZZ	42	1994
HAVE PITY ON THE BOY PAUL & BARRY RYAN	18	1966
HAVE YOU EVER? [A] BRANDY	13	1998
HAVE YOU EVER [B] S CLUB 7	1	2001
HAVE YOU EVER BEEN IN LOVE LEO SAYER	10	1982
HAVE YOU EVER BEEN MELLOW (EP) PARTY ANIMALS	43	1996
HAVE YOU EVER HAD IT BLUE STYLE COUNCIL	14	1986

Title / Artist	Peak Position	Year of Entry
HAVE YOU EVER LOVED SOMEBODY [A] PAUL & BARRY RYAN	49	1966
HAVE YOU EVER LOVED SOMEBODY [A] SEARCHERS	48	1966
HAVE YOU EVER LOVED SOMEBODY [B] FREDDIE JACKSON	33	1987
HAVE YOU EVER NEEDED SOMEONE SO BAD DEF LEPPARD	16	1992
HAVE YOU EVER REALLY LOVED A WOMAN? BRYAN ADAMS	4	1995
HAVE YOU EVER SEEN THE RAIN CREEDENCE CLEARWATER REVIVAL	36	1971
HAVE YOU EVER SEEN THE RAIN BONNIE TYLER	47	1983
HAVE YOU EVER SEEN THE RAIN? JEEVAS	70	2004
HAVE YOU SEEN HER CHI-LITES	3	1972
HAVE YOU SEEN HER MC HAMMER	8	1990
HAVE YOU SEEN YOUR MOTHER BABY STANDING IN THE SHADOW ROLLING STONES	5	1966
HAVEN'T SEEN YOU PERFUME	71	1996
HAVEN'T STOPPED DANCING YET GONZALEZ	15	1979
HAVEN'T YOU HEARD PATRICE RUSHEN	62	1980
HAVIN' A GOOD TIME SOUVERNANCE	63	2002
HAVING A PARTY OSMONDS	28	1975
HAWAII TATTOO WAIKIKIS	41	1965
HAWAIIAN WEDDING SONG JULIE ROGERS	31	1965
HAWKEYE FRANKIE LAINE	7	1955
HAYFEVER TRASH CAN SINATRAS	61	1993
HAYLING FC KAHUNA	49	2003
HAZARD RICHARD MARX	3	1992
HAZEL LOOP DA LOOP	20	1999
HAZELL MAGGIE BELL	37	1978
HAZIN' & PHAZIN' CHOO CHOO PROJECT	21	2000
HAZY EYES FIGHTSTAR	47	2006
HAZY SHADE OF WINTER BANGLES	11	1988
A HAZY SHADE OF WINTER SIMON & GARFUNKEL	30	1991
HE AIN'T HEAVY, HE'S MY BROTHER HOLLIES	1	1969
HE AIN'T HEAVY, HE'S MY BROTHER BILL MEDLEY	25	1988
HE AIN'T NO COMPETITION BROTHER BEYOND	6	1988
HE DOESN'T LOVE YOU LIKE I DO NICK HEYWARD	58	1993
HE DON'T LOVE YOU HUMAN NATURE	18	2001
HE GOT GAME PUBLIC ENEMY FEATURING STEPHEN STILLS	16	1998
HE GOT WHAT HE WANTED (BUT HE LOST WHAT HE HAD) LITTLE RICHARD	38	1962
HE IS SAILING JON & VANGELIS	61	1983
HE KNOWS YOU KNOW MARILLION	35	1983
HE LOVES U NOT DREAM	17	2001
HE REMINDS ME RANDY CRAWFORD	65	1983
HE SAID HE LOVED ME REVEREND & THE MAKERS	16	2007
HE THINKS HE'LL KEEP HER MARY CHAPIN CARPENTER	71	1993
HE WAS BEAUTIFUL (CAVATINA) (THE THEME FROM *THE DEER HUNTER*) IRIS WILLIAMS	18	1979
HE WASN'T AVRIL LAVIGNE	23	2005
HE WASN'T MAN ENOUGH TONI BRAXTON	5	2000
HEAD JULIAN COPE	57	1991
HEAD ABOVE WATER CLIVE GRIFFIN	60	1989
HEAD LIKE A HOLE NINE INCH NAILS	45	1991
HEAD ON JESUS & MARY CHAIN	57	1989
HEAD ON COLLISION NEW FOUND GLORY	64	2002
HEAD OVER FEET ALANIS MORISSETTE	7	1996
HEAD OVER HEELS [A] ABBA	25	1982
HEAD OVER HEELS [B] TEARS FOR FEARS	12	1985
HEAD OVER HEELS [C] NIC HAVERSON	48	1993
HEAD OVER HEELS [D] ALLURE FEATURING NAS	18	1997
HEAD OVER HEELS IN LOVE KEVIN KEEGAN	31	1979
HEAD TO TOE (EP) BREEDERS	68	1994
HEADACHE FRANK BLACK	53	1994
HEADING FOR A BREAKDOWN THE SOUNDTRACK OF OUR LIVES	70	2005
HEADING WEST CYNDI LAUPER	68	1989
HEADLESS CROSS BLACK SABBATH	62	1989
HEADLIGHTS ON PARADE BLUE NILE	72	1990
HEADLINE NEWS EDWIN STARR	39	1966
HEADLINE NEWS WILLIAM BELL	70	1986
HEADLINES MIDNIGHT STAR	16	1986
HEADLINES (FRIENDSHIP NEVER ENDS) SPICE GIRLS	11	2007
HEADLOCK IMOGEN HEAP	74	2006
HEADLONG QUEEN	14	1991
HEADS DOWN NO NONSENSE MINDLESS BOOGIE ALBERTO Y LOS TRIOS PARANOIAS	47	1978
HEADS HIGH MR VEGAS	16	1998
HEADSPRUNG LL COOL J	25	2004
HEAL THE PAIN GEORGE MICHAEL	31	1991
HEAL (THE SEPARATION) SHAMEN	31	1996
HEAL THE WORLD MICHAEL JACKSON	2	1992
THE HEALING GAME VAN MORRISON	46	1997
HEALING HANDS ELTON JOHN	45	1989
HEALING LOVE CLIFF RICHARD	19	1993
HEAR ME CALLING 2WO THIRD3	48	1994
HEAR MY CALL ALISON LIMERICK	73	1992
HEAR MY NAME ARMAND VAN HELDEN	34	2004
HEAR THE DRUMMER (GET WICKED) CHAD JACKSON	3	1990
HEAR YOU CALLING AURORA	17	1999
HEARD 'EM SAY KANYE WEST FEATURING ADAM LEVINE	22	2005
HEARD IT ALL BEFORE SUNSHINE ANDERSON	9	2001
HEARSAY '89 ALEXANDER O'NEAL	56	1989
HEART [A] JOHNSTON BROTHERS	23	1957
HEART [A] MAX BYGRAVES	14	1957
HEART [B] RITA PAVONE	27	1967
HEART [C] PET SHOP BOYS	1	1988
HEART [D] GARY NUMAN	43	1991
HEART [E] SERAPHIM SUITE	45	2004
HEART AND SOUL [A] JAN & DEAN	24	1961
HEART AND SOUL [B] EXILE	54	1981
HEART AND SOUL [C] T'PAU	4	1987
HEART AND SOUL [D] NO SWEAT	64	1990
HEART AND SOUL [E] CILLA BLACK WITH DUSTY SPRINGFIELD	75	1993
HEART AND SOUL [F] TSD	69	1996
HEART AND SOUL (EP) HUEY LEWIS & THE NEWS	61	1985
THE HEART ASKS PLEASURE FIRST MICHAEL NYMAN	60	1994
HEART ATTACK OLIVIA NEWTON-JOHN	46	1982
HEART ATTACK AND VINE SREAMIN' JAY HAWKINS	42	1993
HEART (DON'T CHANGE MY MIND) DIANA ROSS	31	1993
HEART FAILED (IN THE BACK OF A TAXI) SAINT ETIENNE	50	2000
HEART FULL OF SOUL YARDBIRDS	2	1965
HEART GO BOOM APOLLO FOUR FORTY	57	1999
HEART IN A CAGE STROKES	25	2006
HEART LIKE A WHEEL [A] HUMAN LEAGUE	29	1990
HEART LIKE A WHEEL [B] CORRS	68	2005
THE HEART NEVER LIES McFLY	3	2007
THE HEART OF A MAN FRANKIE VAUGHAN	5	1959
HEART OF A SINGLE GIRL GEORGE CHAKIRIS	49	1960
THE HEART OF A TEENAGE GIRL CRAIG DOUGLAS	10	1960
HEART OF ASIA WATERGATE	3	2000
HEART OF GLASS BLONDIE	1	1979
HEART OF GLASS ASSOCIATES	56	1988
HEART OF GOLD [A] NEIL YOUNG	10	1972
HEART OF GOLD [B] JOHNNY HATES JAZZ	19	1988
HEART OF GOLD [C] FORCE & STYLES FEATURING KELLY LLORENNA	55	1998
HEART OF GOLD [C] KELLY LLORENNA	19	2002
HEART OF LOTHIAN MARILLION	29	1985
HEART OF MY HEART MAX BYGRAVES	7	1954
THE HEART OF ROCK AND ROLL HUEY LEWIS & THE NEWS	49	1986
HEART OF SOUL CULT	51	1992
HEART OF STONE [A] KENNY	11	1973
HEART OF STONE [B] SUZI QUATRO	60	1982
HEART OF STONE [C] BUCKS FIZZ	50	1988
HEART OF STONE [C] CHER	43	1990
HEART OF STONE [D] DAVE STEWART	36	1994
HEART OF THE SUN RED BOX	71	1987
HEART OF THE WORLD BIG COUNTRY	50	1990
HEART ON MY SLEEVE GALLAGHER & LYLE	6	1976
HEART OVER MIND KIM WILDE	34	1992
HEART (STOP BEATING IN TIME) LEO SAYER	22	1982
HEART USER CLIFF RICHARD	46	1985
HEARTACHE [A] ROY ORBISON	44	1968
HEARTACHE [B] GENE LOVES JEZEBEL	71	1986
HEARTACHE [C] PEPSI & SHIRLIE	2	1987
HEARTACHE ALL OVER THE WORLD ELTON JOHN	45	1986
HEARTACHE AVENUE MAISONETTES	7	1982
HEARTACHE TONIGHT EAGLES	40	1979
HEARTACHES PATSY CLINE	31	1962
HEARTACHES VINCE HILL	28	1966
HEARTACHES BY THE NUMBER GUY MITCHELL	5	1959
HEARTBEAT [A] RUBY MURRAY	3	1954
HEARTBEAT [B] BUDDY HOLLY	30	1959
HEARTBEAT [B] ENGLAND SISTERS	33	1960
HEARTBEAT [B] SHOWADDYWADDY	7	1975
HEARTBEAT [B] NICK BERRY	2	1992
HEARTBEAT [B] HEARTBEAT COUNTRY	75	1994
HEARTBEAT [C] SAMMY HAGAR	67	1980
HEARTBEAT [D] TIPPA IRIE	59	1986
HEARTBEAT [E] DON JOHNSON	46	1986
HEARTBEAT [F] SEDUCTION	75	1990
HEARTBEAT [G] GRID	72	1992
HEARTBEAT [H] JIMMY SOMERVILLE	24	1995
HEARTBEAT [I] KRS ONE	66	1997
HEARTBEAT [J] STEPS	1	1998
HEARTBEAT [K] ANNIE	50	2005
HEARTBEAT [L] SCOUTING FOR GIRLS	64	2008
A HEARTBEAT AWAY McGANNS	42	1999
HEARTBEAT (TAINAI KAIKI II) RETURNING TO THE WOMB DAVID SYLVIAN/RYUICHI SAKAMOTO FEATURING INGRID CHAVEZ	58	1992
HEARTBEATS JOSE GONZALEZ	9	2006
HEARTBEATZ STYLES & BREEZE FEATURING KAREN DANZIG	16	2005
HEARTBREAK MRS WOOD FEATURING EVE GALLAGHER	44	1996
HEARTBREAK HOTEL [A] ELVIS PRESLEY	2	1956
HEARTBREAK HOTEL [A] STAN FREBERG & HIS SKIFFLE GROUP	24	1956
HEARTBREAK HOTEL [B] JACKSONS	44	1980
HEARTBREAK HOTEL [C] WHITNEY HOUSTON FEATURING FAITH EVANS & KELLY PRICE	26	2000
HEARTBREAK RADIO ROY ORBISON	36	1992
HEARTBREAK STATION CINDERELLA	63	1991
HEARTBREAK STROLL RAVEONETTES	49	2003
HEARTBREAKER [A] DIONNE WARWICK	2	1982
HEARTBREAKER [B] MUSICAL YOUTH	44	1983
HEARTBREAKER [C] COLOR ME BADD	58	1992

Title / Artist	Peak Position	Year of Entry
HEARTBREAKER [D] MARIAH CAREY FEATURING JAY-Z	5	1999
HEARTBREAKER [E] GLITTERATI	45	2005
HEARTBREAKER [F] WILL.I.AM	74	2008
HEARTBROKE AND BUSTED MAGNUM	49	1990
HEARTBROKEN T2 & JODIE	2	2007
HEARTHAMMER (EP) RUNRIG	25	1991
HEARTLAND THE THE	29	1986
THE HEARTLESS CREW THEME HEARTLESS CREW	21	2002
HEARTLIGHT NEIL DIAMOND	47	1982
HEARTLINE ROBIN GEORGE	68	1985
THE HEART'S FILTHY LESSON DAVID BOWIE	35	1995
THE HEART'S LONE DESIRE MATTHEW MARSDEN	13	1998
HEARTS ON FIRE [A] SAM HARRIS	67	1985
HEARTS ON FIRE [B] BRYAN ADAMS	57	1987
HEART-SHAPED BOX NIRVANA	5	1993
HEART-SHAPED GLASSES MARILYN MANSON	19	2007
HEARTSONG GORDON GILTRAP	21	1978
HEARTSPARK DOLLARSIGN EVERCLEAR	48	1996
THE HEAT IS ON [A] AGNETHA FALTSKOG	35	1983
THE HEAT IS ON [B] GLENN FREY	12	1985
HEAT IT UP WEE PAPA GIRL RAPPERS FEATURING TWO MEN & A DRUM MACHINE	21	1988
HEAT OF THE BEAT ROY AYERS & WAYNE HENDERSON	43	1979
HEAT OF THE MOMENT ASIA	46	1982
HEAT OF THE NIGHT BRYAN ADAMS	50	1987
HEATER SAMIM	12	2007
HEATHER HONEY TOMMY ROE	24	1969
HEATSEEKER AC/DC	12	1988
HEAVEN [A] PSYCHEDELIC FURS	29	1984
HEAVEN [B] BRYAN ADAMS	38	1985
HEAVEN [B] DJ SAMMY & YANOU FEATURING DO	1	2002
HEAVEN [C] TWO PEOPLE	63	1987
HEAVEN [D] CHIMES	24	1989
HEAVEN [E] CHRIS REA	57	1991
HEAVEN [F] TIGERTAILZ	71	1991
HEAVEN [G] WHYCLIFFE	56	1993
HEAVEN [H] FITS OF GLOOM	47	1994
HEAVEN [I] SOLO (US)	35	1996
HEAVEN [J] SARAH WASHINGTON	28	1996
HEAVEN [K] KINANE	49	1998
HEAVEN & EARTH [A] RED	41	2001
HEAVEN AND EARTH [B] POP!	14	2004
HEAVEN AND HELL, THIRD MOVEMENT (THEME FROM THE BBC-TV SERIES *THE COSMOS*) VANGELIS	48	1981
HEAVEN BESIDE YOU ALICE IN CHAINS	35	1996
HEAVEN CAN WAIT PAUL YOUNG	71	1990
HEAVEN FOR EVERYONE QUEEN	2	1995
HEAVEN GIVE ME WORDS PROPAGANDA	36	1990
HEAVEN HELP LENNY KRAVITZ	20	1993
HEAVEN HELP ME DEON ESTUS	41	1989
HEAVEN HELP MY HEART TINA ARENA	25	1995
HEAVEN HELP US ALL STEVIE WONDER	29	1970
THE HEAVEN I NEED THREE DEGREES	42	1985
HEAVEN IN MY HANDS LEVEL 42	12	1988
HEAVEN IS DEF LEPPARD	13	1993
HEAVEN IS A HALFPIPE OPM	4	2001
HEAVEN IS A PLACE ON EARTH BELINDA CARLISLE	1	1987
HEAVEN IS A PLACE ON EARTH SODA CLUB FEATURING HANNAH ALETHA	13	2003
HEAVEN IS CLOSER (FEELS LIKE HEAVEN) DARIO G	39	2003
HEAVEN IS HERE JULIE FELIX	22	1970
HEAVEN IS IN THE BACK SEAT OF MY CADILLAC HOT CHOCOLATE	25	1976
HEAVEN IS MY WOMAN'S LOVE VAL DOONICAN	34	1973
HEAVEN IS WAITING DANSE SOCIETY	60	1983
HEAVEN KNOWS [A] DONNA SUMMER	34	1979
HEAVEN KNOWS [B] JAKI GRAHAM	59	1985
HEAVEN KNOWS [B] LALAH HATHAWAY	66	1990
HEAVEN KNOWS [C] ROBERT PLANT	33	1988
HEAVEN KNOWS [D] COOL DOWN ZONE	52	1990
HEAVEN KNOWS [E] LUTHER VANDROSS	34	1993
HEAVEN KNOWS [F] SQUEEZE	27	1996
HEAVEN KNOWS - DEEP DEEP DOWN ANGEL MORAES	72	1996
HEAVEN KNOWS I'M MISERABLE NOW SMITHS	10	1984
HEAVEN MUST BE MISSING AN ANGEL TAVARES	4	1976
HEAVEN MUST BE MISSING AN ANGEL WORLDS APART	29	1993
HEAVEN MUST HAVE SENT YOU ELGINS	3	1971
HEAVEN MUST HAVE SENT YOU BACK CICERO	70	1992
HEAVEN ON EARTH SPELLBOUND	73	1997
HEAVEN ON THE 7TH FLOOR PAUL NICHOLAS	40	1977
HEAVEN OR HELL STRANGLERS	46	1992
HEAVEN SCENT BEDROCK	35	1999
HEAVEN SENT [A] PAUL HAIG	74	1983
HEAVEN SENT [B] INXS	31	1992
HEAVEN SENT [C] M1	72	2003
HEAVEN WILL COME SPACE BROTHERS	25	1999
HEAVENLY SHOWADDYWADDY	34	1975
HEAVEN'S EARTH DELERIUM	44	2000
HEAVEN'S HERE HOLLY JOHNSON	62	1989
HEAVEN'S ON FIRE KISS	43	1984
HEAVEN'S WHAT I FEEL GLORIA ESTEFAN	17	1998
HEAVY FUEL DIRE STRAITS	55	1991
HEAVY MAKES YOU HAPPY BOBBY BLOOM	31	1971
HEAVY ON MY HEART ANASTACIA	21	2005
HEAVY VIBES MONTANA SEXTET	59	1983
HEAVYWEIGHT CHAMPION OF THE WORLD REVEREND & THE MAKERS	8	2007
HEDONISM (JUST BECAUSE YOU FEEL GOOD) SKUNK ANANSIE	13	1997
THE HEINRICH MANEUVER INTERPOL	31	2007
HELEN WHEELS PAUL McCARTNEY & WINGS	12	1973
HELENA MY CHEMICAL ROMANCE	20	2005
HELICOPTER BLOC PARTY	26	2004
HELICOPTER TUNE DEEP BLUE	68	1994
HELIOPOLIS BY NIGHT ABERFELDY	66	2004
HELIUM DALLAS SUPERSTARS	64	2003
THE HELL EP TRICKY VS THE GRAVEDIGGAZ	12	1995
HELL HATH NO FURY FRANKIE LAINE	28	1956
HE'LL HAVE TO GO JIM REEVES	12	1960
HE'LL HAVE TO GO BRYAN FERRY	63	1989
HE'LL HAVE TO STAY JEANNE BLACK	41	1960
HELL RAISER SWEET	2	1973
THE HELL SONG SUM 41	35	2003
HELL YEAH GINUWINE	27	2003
HELLA GOOD NO DOUBT	12	2002
HELLBOUND TYGERS OF PAN TANG	48	1981
HELLO [A] LIONEL RICHIE	1	1984
HELLO [A] JHAY PALMER FEATURING MC IMAGE	69	2002
HELLO [B] BELOVED	19	1990
HELLO AGAIN NEIL DIAMOND	51	1981
HELLO AMERICA DEF LEPPARD	45	1980
HELLO BUDDY TREMELOES	32	1971
HELLO DARLIN' [A] FUZZ TOWNSHEND	51	1997
HELLO DARLING [B] TIPPA IRIE	22	1986
HELLO DOLLY FRANK SINATRA WITH COUNT BASIE	47	1964
HELLO DOLLY FRANKIE VAUGHAN	18	1964
HELLO DOLLY KENNY BALL & HIS JAZZMEN	30	1964
HELLO DOLLY LOUIS ARMSTRONG	4	1964
HELLO DOLLY BACHELORS	38	1966
HELLO GOODBYE BEATLES	1	1967
HELLO HAPPINESS DRIFTERS	12	1976
HELLO HEARTACHE GOODBYE LOVE LITTLE PEGGY MARCH	29	1963
HELLO! HELLO! I'M BACK AGAIN GARY GLITTER	2	1973
HELLO HONKY TONKS (ROCK YOUR BODY) PIZZAMAN	41	1996
HELLO HOW ARE YOU EASYBEATS	20	1968
HELLO HURRAY ALICE COOPER	6	1973
HELLO I AM YOUR HEART BETTE BRIGHT	50	1980
HELLO I LOVE YOU DOORS	15	1968
HELLO JOSEPHINE WAYNE FONTANA & THE MINDBENDERS	46	1963
HELLO LITTLE GIRL FOURMOST	9	1963
HELLO MARY LOU (GOODBYE HEART) RICKY NELSON	2	1961
HELLO MUDDAH HELLO FADDAH ALLAN SHERMAN	14	1963
HELLO STRANGER YVONNE ELLIMAN	26	1977
HELLO SUMMERTIME BOBBY GOLDSBORO	14	1974
HELLO SUNSHINE SUPER FURRY ANIMALS	31	2003
HELLO SUZIE AMEN CORNER	4	1969
HELLO THIS IS JOANNIE (THE TELEPHONE ANSWERING MACHINE SONG) PAUL EVANS	6	1978
HELLO TIGER URUSEI YATSURA	63	1998
HELLO (TURN YOUR RADIO ON) SHAKESPEARS SISTER	14	1992
HELLO WORLD [A] TREMELOES	14	1969
HELLO WORLD [B] SEA FRUIT	59	1999
HELLO YOUNG LOVERS PAUL ANKA	44	1960
HELLO? IS THIS THING ON? !!!	74	2004
HELLRAISER ANNE SAVAGE	74	2003
HELL'S PARTY GLAM	42	1993
HELP! BEATLES	1	1965
HELP TINA TURNER	40	1984
HELP! BANANARAMA/LA NA NEE NEE NOO NOO	3	1989
HELP (EP) VARIOUS ARTISTS (EP'S & LPS)	51	1995
HELP, GET ME SOME HELP! OTTAWAN	49	1981
HELP I'M A FISH LITTLE TREES	11	2001
HELP IT ALONG CLIFF RICHARD	29	1973
HELP ME [A] TIMO MAAS FEATURING KELIS	65	2002
HELP ME [B] NICK CARTER	17	2002
HELP ME FIND A WAY TO YOUR HEART DARYL HALL	70	1994
HELP ME GIRL ERIC BURDON & THE ANIMALS	14	1966
HELP ME MAKE IT HUFF & PUFF	31	1996
HELP ME MAKE IT THROUGH THE NIGHT GLADYS KNIGHT & THE PIPS	11	1972
HELP ME MAKE IT THROUGH THE NIGHT JOHN HOLT	6	1974
HELP ME MAMA LEMONESCENT	36	2003
HELP ME RHONDA BEACH BOYS	27	1965
HELP MY FRIEND SLO-MOSHUN	52	1994
HELP THE AGED PULP	8	1997
HELP YOURSELF [A] TOM JONES	5	1968
HELP YOURSELF [A] TONY FERRINO	42	1996
HELP YOURSELF [B] JULIAN LENNON	53	1991
HELP YOURSELF [C] AMY WINEHOUSE	46	2004
HELPLESS TRACEY ULLMAN	61	1984
HELULE HELULE TREMELOES	14	1968
HELYOM HALIB CAPPELLA	11	1989
HENRIETTA FRATELLIS	19	2006
HENRY LEE NICK CAVE & THE BAD SEEDS & PJ HARVEY	36	1996
HENRY VIII SUITE (EP) EARLY MUSIC CONSORT DIRECTED BY DAVID MUNROW	49	1971
HER GUY	58	1991
HER ROYAL MAJESTY JAMES DARREN	36	1962
HERCULEAN THE GOOD THE BAD & THE QUEEN	22	2006

	Peak Position	Year of Entry
HERCULES FRANKIE VAUGHAN	42	1962
HERE LUSCIOUS JACKSON	59	1995
HERE AND NOW [A] LUTHER VANDROSS	43	1990
HERE AND NOW [B] DEL AMITRI	21	1995
HERE AND NOW [C] STEPS	4	2001
HERE COME THE GIRLS ERNIE K-DOE	43	2007
HERE COME THE GOOD TIMES A HOUSE	37	1994
HERE COME THE NICE SMALL FACES	12	1967
HERE COMES MY BABY TREMELOES	4	1967
HERE COMES SUMMER JERRY KELLER	1	1959
HERE COMES SUMMER DAVE CLARK FIVE	44	1970
HERE COMES THAT FEELING BRENDA LEE	5	1962
HERE COMES THAT SOUND SIMON HARRIS	38	1988
HERE COMES THE BIG RUSH ECHOBELLY	56	1997
HERE COMES THE HAMMER MC HAMMER	15	1991
HERE COMES THE HOTSTEPPER INI KAMOZE	4	1995
HERE COMES THE JUDGE [A] SHORTY LONG	30	1968
HERE COMES THE JUDGE [B] PIGMEAT MARKHAM	19	1968
HERE COMES THE MAN BOOM BOOM BOOM	74	1986
HERE COMES THE NIGHT [A] LULU	50	1964
HERE COMES THE NIGHT [A] THEM	2	1965
HERE COMES THE NIGHT [B] BEACH BOYS	37	1979
HERE COMES THE PAIN LEE HASLAM	71	2004
HERE COMES THE RAIN AGAIN EURYTHMICS	8	1984
HERE COMES THE RUMOUR MILL YOUNG KNIVES	36	2006
HERE COMES THE STAR HERMAN'S HERMITS	33	1969
HERE COMES THE SUMMER UNDERTONES	34	1979
HERE COMES THE SUN STEVE HARLEY	10	1976
HERE COMES THE WAR NEW MODEL ARMY	25	1993
HERE COMES YOUR MAN PIXIES	54	1989
HERE 4 ONE BLAZIN' SQUAD	6	2004
HERE I AM [A] BRYAN ADAMS	5	2002
HERE I AM [B] EXPLOSION	75	2005
HERE I AM (COME AND TAKE ME) UB40	46	1990
HERE I COME BARRINGTON LEVY	41	1985
HERE I COME (SING DJ) TALISMAN P MEETS BARRINGTON LEVY	37	2001
HERE I GO 2 UNLIMITED	22	1995
HERE I GO AGAIN [A] HOLLIES	4	1964
HERE I GO AGAIN [B] ARCHIE BELL & THE DRELLS	11	1972
HERE I GO AGAIN [C] GUYS & DOLLS	33	1975
HERE I GO AGAIN [D] TWIGGY	17	1976
HERE I GO AGAIN [E] WHITESNAKE	9	1982
HERE I GO AGAIN [E] FRASH	69	1995
HERE I GO AGAIN [F] MARIO	11	2005
HERE I GO IMPOSSIBLE AGAIN ERASURE	25	2005
HERE I STAND [A] MILLTOWN BROTHERS	41	1991
HERE I STAND [B] BITTY McLEAN	10	1994
HERE IN MY HEART AL MARTINO	1	1952
HERE (IN YOUR ARMS) HELLOGOOODBYE	4	2007
HERE IS THE NEWS ELECTRIC LIGHT ORCHESTRA	24	1982
HERE IT COMES DOVES	73	1999
HERE IT COMES AGAIN [A] FORTUNES	4	1965
HERE IT COMES AGAIN [B] BLACK	70	1991
HERE IT COMES AGAIN [C] MELANIE C	7	2003
HERE IT GOES AGAIN OK GO	36	2006
HERE SHE COMES AGAIN STANDS	25	2004
HERE THERE AND EVERYWHERE EMMYLOU HARRIS	30	1976
HERE TO STAY [A] NEW ORDER	15	2002
HERE TO STAY [B] KORN	12	2002
HERE WE ARE GLORIA ESTEFAN	23	1990
HERE WE COME TIMBALAND/MISSY ELLIOTT & MAGOO	43	1999
HERE WE GO [A] EVERTON FC	14	1985
HERE WE GO [B] C & C MUSIC FACTORY (FEATURING FREEDOM WILLIAMS)	20	1991
HERE WE GO [C] STAKKA BO	13	1993
HERE WE GO [D] ARAB STRAP	48	1998
HERE WE GO [E] FREESTYLERS	45	1999
HERE WE GO [F] TRINA FEATURING KELLY ROWLAND	15	2006
HERE WE GO AGAIN [A] RAY CHARLES	38	1967
HERE WE GO AGAIN [B] PORTRAIT	37	1993
HERE WE GO AGAIN [C] A HOMEBOY, A HIPPIE & A FUNKI DREDD	57	1994
HERE WE GO AGAIN [D] ARETHA FRANKLIN	68	1998
HERE WE GO ROCK 'N' ROLL SPIDER	57	1984
HERE WE GO ROUND THE MULBERRY BUSH TRAFFIC	8	1967
HERE WITH ME DIDO	4	2001
HERE YOU COME AGAIN DOLLY PARTON	75	1984
HERE'S MY A RAPINATION FEATURING CAROL KENYON	69	1993
HERE'S THE GOOD NEWS PAUL WELLER	21	2005
HERE'S TO LOVE (AULD LANG SYNE) JOHN CHRISTIE	24	1977
HERE'S WHERE THE STORY ENDS TIN TIN OUT FEATURING SHELLEY NELSON	7	1998
HERMANN LOVES PAULINE SUPER FURRY ANIMALS	26	1997
HERNANDO'S HIDEAWAY JOHNNIE RAY	11	1955
HERNANDO'S HIDEAWAY JOHNSTON BROTHERS	1	1955
HERO [A] DAVID CROSBY FEATURING PHIL COLLINS	56	1993
HERO [B] MARIAH CAREY	7	1993
HERO [C] ENRIQUE IGLESIAS	1	2002
HERO [D] CHAD KROEGER FEATURING JOSEY SCOTT	4	2002
HERO OF THE DAY METALLICA	17	1996
HEROES [A] DAVID BOWIE	24	1977
HEROES [B] RONI SIZE REPRAZENT	31	1997
THE HEROES [C] SHED SEVEN	18	1998
HEROES AND VILLAINS BEACH BOYS	8	1967
HERSHAM BOYS SHAM 69	6	1979
HE'S A PIRATE KLAUS BADELT	40	2006
HE'S A REBEL CRYSTALS	19	1962
HE'S A SAINT, HE'S A SINNER MIQUEL BROWN	68	1984
HE'S BACK (THE MAN BEHIND THE MASK) ALICE COOPER	61	1986
HE'S FIT LOVE BITES	48	2006
HE'S GONNA STEP ON YOU AGAIN JOHN KONGOS	4	1971
HE'S GOT NO LOVE SEARCHERS	12	1965
HE'S GOT THE WHOLE WORLD IN HIS HANDS LAURIE LONDON	12	1957
HE'S IN TOWN ROCKIN' BERRIES	3	1964
HE'S MINE MOKENSTEF	70	1995
HE'S MISSTRA KNOW IT ALL STEVIE WONDER	10	1974
HE'S OLD ENOUGH TO KNOW BETTER BROOK BROTHERS	37	1962
HE'S ON THE PHONE SAINT ETIENNE FEATURING ETIENNE DAHO	11	1995
HE'S SO FINE CHIFFONS	16	1963
HE'S THE GREATEST DANCER SISTER SLEDGE	6	1979
HE'S THE ONE BILLIE DAVIS	40	1963
HEWLETT'S DAUGHTER GRANDADDY	71	2000
HEXAGRAM DEFTONES	68	2003
HEY! JULIO IGLESIAS	31	1983
HEY AMERICA JAMES BROWN	47	1971
HEY! BABY [A] BRUCE CHANNEL	2	1962
HEY BABY [A] DJ OTZI	1	2001
HEY BABY [B] NO DOUBT	2	2002
HEY BOY HEY GIRL CHEMICAL BROTHERS	3	1999
HEY CHILD EAST 17	3	1997
HEY DJ [A] WORLD'S FAMOUS SUPREME TEAM	52	1984
HEY DJ [B] LIGHTER SHADE OF BROWN	33	1994
HEY DJ I CAN'T DANCE TO THAT MUSIC YOU'RE PLAYING BEATMASTERS FEATURING BETTY BOO	7	1989
HEY DJ! (PLAY THAT SONG) N-TYCE	20	1997
HEY DUDE KULA SHAKER	2	1996
HEY GIRL [A] SMALL FACES	10	1966
HEY GIRL [B] EXPRESSOS	60	1980
HEY GIRL [C] DELAYS	40	2003
HEY GIRL DON'T BOTHER ME TAMS	1	1971
HEY GOD BON JOVI	13	1996
HEY GOOD LOOKIN' BO DIDDLEY	39	1965
HEY GOOD LOOKING TOMMY ZANG	45	1961
HEY JEALOUSY GIN BLOSSOMS	24	1994
HEY JOE [A] FRANKIE LAINE	1	1953
HEY JOE [B] JIMI HENDRIX	6	1967
HEY JUDE BEATLES	1	1968
HEY JUDE WILSON PICKETT	16	1969
HEY JULIE FOUNTAINS OF WAYNE	57	2004
HEY JUPITER TORI AMOS	20	1996
HEY KID MATT WILLIS	11	2006
HEY LITTLE GIRL [A] DEL SHANNON	2	1962
HEY LITTLE GIRL [B] ICEHOUSE	17	1983
HEY LITTLE GIRL [C] MATHIAS WARE FEATURING ROB TAYLOR	42	2002
HEY LORD DON'T ASK ME QUESTIONS GRAHAM PARKER	32	1978
HEY LOVE KING SUN-D'MOET	66	1987
HEY LOVER LL COOL J FEATURING BOYZ II MEN	17	1996
HEY! LUCIANI FALL	59	1986
HEY MA CAM'RON FEATURING JUELZ SANTANA	8	2003
HEY MAMA [A] FRANKIE VAUGHAN	21	1963
HEY MAMA [B] JOE BROWN	33	1973
HEY MAMA [C] BLACK EYED PEAS	6	2004
HEY MAN (NOW YOU'RE REALLY LIVING) EELS	45	2005
HEY MANHATTAN PREFAB SPROUT	72	1988
HEY MATTHEW KAREL FIALKA	9	1987
HEY MISS PAYNE CHEQUERS	32	1976
HEY MR. CHRISTMAS SHOWADDYWADDY	13	1974
HEY MR. DJ [A] ZHANE	26	1993
HEY MR DJ [B] OPEN ARMS FEATURING ROWETTA	62	1996
HEY MR DJ [C] VAN MORRISON	58	2002
HEY MR. DREAM MAKER CLIFF RICHARD	31	1976
HEY MISTER HEARTACHE KIM WILDE	31	1988
HEY MR. MUSIC MAN PETERS & LEE	16	1976
HEY MUSIC LOVER S-EXPRESS	6	1989
HEY NOW (GIRLS JUST WANT TO HAVE FUN) CYNDI LAUPER	4	1994
HEY NOW (MEAN MUGGIN') XZIBIT	9	2005
HEY NOW NOW SWIRL 360	61	1998
HEY PAPA! ALEX CARTANA	34	2004
HEY! PARADISE FLICKMAN	69	2001
HEY PAULA PAUL & PAULA	8	1963
HEY ROCK AND ROLL SHOWADDYWADDY	2	1974
HEY SCENESTERS! CRIBS	27	2005
HEY SENORITA WAR	40	1978
HEY SEXY LADY SHAGGY FEATURING BRIAN AND TONY GOLD	10	2002
HEY STOOPID ALICE COOPER	21	1991
HEY THERE JOHNNIE RAY	5	1955
HEY THERE LITA ROZA	17	1955
HEY THERE ROSEMARY CLOONEY	4	1955
HEY THERE SAMMY DAVIS Jr.	19	1955
HEY THERE DELILAH PLAIN WHITE T'S	2	2007
(HEY THERE) LONELY GIRL EDDIE HOLMAN	4	1974
HEY THERE LONELY GIRL BIG FUN	62	1990
HEY VENUS THAT PETROL EMOTION	49	1990
HEY WHATEVER WESTLIFE	4	2003
HEY! WHAT'S YOUR NAME BABY JUNE	75	1992
HEY WILLY HOLLIES	22	1971

	Peak Position	Year of Entry
HEY YA! OUTKAST	3	2003
HEY YOU [A] TOMMY STEELE	28	1957
HEY YOU [B] QUIREBOYS	14	1990
(HEY YOU) THE ROCKSTEADY CREW ROCKSTEADY CREW	6	1983
HEYKENS SERANADE THE PIPES & DRUMS & MILITARY BAND OF THE ROYAL SCOTS DRAGOON GUARDS	30	1972
HI DE HI, HI DE HO KOOL & THE GANG	29	1982
HI DE HI (HOLIDAY ROCK) PAUL SHANE & THE YELLOWCOATS	36	1981
HI DE HO K7 & THE SWING KIDS	17	1994
HI FIDELITY [A] ELVIS COSTELLO & THE ATTRACTIONS	30	1980
HI-FIDELITY [B] KIDS FROM FAME FEATURING VALERIE LANDSBERG	5	1982
HI HI HAZEL GENO WASHINGTON & THE RAM JAM BAND	45	1966
HI HI HAZEL TROGGS	42	1967
HI HI HI WINGS	5	1972
HI HO SILVER JIM DIAMOND	5	1986
HI! HOW YA DOIN'? KENNY G	70	1984
HI LILI HI LO ALAN PRICE SET	11	1966
HI TENSION HI TENSION	13	1978
HIBERNACULUM MIKE OLDFIELD	47	1994
HIDDEN AGENDA CRAIG DAVID	10	2003
HIDDEN PLACE BJORK	21	2001
HIDE TWEN2Y 4 SE7EN	42	2004
HIDE AND SEEK [A] MARTY WILDE	47	1961
HIDE AND SEEK [B] HOWARD JONES	12	1984
HIDE U KOSHEEN	6	2000
HIDE YOUR HEART KISS	59	1989
HIDE-A-WAY NU SOUL FEATURING KELI RICH	27	1996
HIDEAWAY [A] DAVE DEE, DOZY, BEAKY, MICK & TICH	10	1966
HIDEAWAY [B] DE'LACY	9	1995
HIDEAWAY [C] DELAYS	35	2006
HIGH [A] CURE	8	1992
HIGH [B] HYPER GO GO	30	1992
HIGH [C] FEEDER	24	1997
HIGH [D] PROPHETS OF SOUND	73	1998
HIGH [E] LIGHTHOUSE FAMILY	4	1998
HIGH [F] JAMES BLUNT	16	2005
HIGH AGAIN (HIGH ON EMOTION) THOMAS FALKE	55	2005
HIGH & DRY RADIOHEAD	17	1995
HIGH AS A KITE ONE TRIBE FEATURING ROGER	55	1995
HIGH CLASS BABY CLIFF RICHARD & THE DRIFTERS	7	1958
HIGH ENERGY EVELYN THOMAS	5	1984
HIGH 5 PALLADIUM	44	2007
HIGH FLY JOHN MILES	17	1975
HIGH HEAD BLUES BLACK CROWES	25	1995
HIGH HOPES [A] FRANK SINATRA	6	1959
HIGH HOPES [B] PINK FLOYD	26	1994
HIGH HORSE EVELYN KING	55	1986
HIGH IN THE SKY AMEN CORNER	6	1968
HIGH LIFE MODERN ROMANCE	8	1983
HIGH NOON [A] FRANKIE LAINE	7	1952
HIGH NOON [B] DJ SHADOW	22	1997
HIGH NOON [C] SERIOUS DANGER	54	1998
HIGH ON A HAPPY VIBE URBAN COOKIE COLLECTIVE	31	1994
HIGH ON EMOTION CHRIS DE BURGH	44	1984
HIGH ROLLERS ICE-T	63	1989
HIGH SCHOOL CONFIDENTIAL JERRY LEE LEWIS	12	1959
HIGH SCHOOL NEVER ENDS BOWLING FOR SOUP	40	2007
HIGH TIME PAUL JONES	4	1966
HIGH TIMES JAMIROQUAI	20	1997
HIGH VOLTAGE JOHNNY & THE HURRICANES	24	1961
HIGH VOLTAGE (LIVE VERSION) AC/DC	48	1980
HIGH VOLTAGE/POINTS OF AUTHORITY LINKIN PARK	9	2002
HIGHER [A] CREED	47	2000
HIGHER [B] DAVID MORALES & ALBERT CABRERA PRESENT MOCA FEATURING DEANNA	41	2000
HIGHER AND HIGHER UNATION	42	1993
HIGHER (FEEL IT) ERICK 'MORE' MORILLO PRESENTS RAW	74	1995
HIGHER GROUND [A] STEVIE WONDER	29	1973
HIGHER GROUND [A] RED HOT CHILI PEPPERS	54	1990
HIGHER GROUND [B] GUN	48	1992
HIGHER GROUND [C] UB40	8	1993
HIGHER GROUND [D] SASHA WITH SAM MOLLISON	19	1994
HIGHER LOVE STEVE WINWOOD	13	1986
A HIGHER PLACE PEYTON	68	2004
HIGHER STATE OF CONSCIOUSNESS '96 REMIXES WINK	7	1996
HIGHER THAN HEAVEN [A] AGE OF CHANCE	53	1990
HIGHER THAN HEAVEN [B] KELLE BRYAN	14	1999
HIGHER THAN REASON UNBELIEVABLE TRUTH	38	1998
HIGHER THAN THE SUN PRIMAL SCREAM	40	1991
HIGHLIFE CYPRESS HILL	35	2000
HIGHLY EVOLVED VINES	32	2002
HIGHLY INFLAMMABLE X-RAY SPEX	45	1979
HIGHLY STRUNG SPANDAU BALLET	15	1984
HIGHNESS ENVY & OTHER SINS	65	2008
HIGHRISE TOWN LANTERNS	50	1999
HIGHWAY 5 BLESSING	30	1991
HIGHWAY CODE MASTER SINGERS	25	1966
THE HIGHWAY SONG NANCY SINATRA	21	1969
HIGHWAY TO HELL (LIVE) AC/DC	56	1979
HIGHWAYS OF MY LIFE ISLEY BROTHERS	25	1974
HIGHWIRE [A] LINDA CARR & THE LOVE SQUAD	15	1975
HIGHWIRE [B] ROLLING STONES	29	1991
HI-HEEL SNEAKERS TOMMY TUCKER	23	1964
HI-HO SILVER LINING JEFF BECK	14	1967
HI-LILI HI-LO RICHARD CHAMBERLAIN	20	1963
HILLBILLY ROCK HILLBILLY ROLL WOOLPACKERS	5	1996
HIM [A] RUPERT HOLMES	31	1980
HIM [B] SARAH BRIGHTMAN & THE LONDON PHILHARMONIC	55	1983
THE HINDU TIMES OASIS	1	2002
HIP HOP DEAD PREZ	41	2000
HIP HOP, BE BOP (DON'T STOP) MAN PARISH	41	1983
HIP HOP DON'T YA DROP HONKY	70	1996
HIP HOP HOORAY NAUGHTY BY NATURE	20	1993
HIP HOP IS DEAD NAS FEATURING WILL I AM	35	2007
HIP HOP POLICE CHAMILLIONAIRE FEATURING SLICK RICK	50	2007
HIP HOUSE DJ 'FAST' EDDIE	47	1989
HIP HOUSIN' X-PRESS 2 FEATURING LO-PRO	55	1994
HIP TO BE SQUARE HUEY LEWIS & THE NEWS	41	1986
HIP TO HIP V	5	2004
HIP TODAY EXTREME	44	1995
HIPPY CHICK SOHO	8	1990
HIPPY HIPPY SHAKE SWINGING BLUE JEANS	2	1963
HIPPY HIPPY SHAKE GEORGIA SATELLITES	63	1989
HIPS DON'T LIE SHAKIRA FEATURING WYCLEF JEAN	1	2006
HIS GIRL GUESS WHO	45	1967
HISTORY [A] MAI TAI	8	1985
HISTORY [B] VERVE	24	1995
HISTORY [C] MICHAEL JACKSON	5	1997
HISTORY [D] FUNERAL FOR A FRIEND	21	2005
HISTORY NEVER REPEATS SPLIT ENZ	63	1981
HISTORY OF THE WORLD (PART 1) DAMNED	51	1980
HISTORY REPEATING PROPELLERHEADS & SHIRLEY BASSEY	19	1997
HIT [A] SUGARCUBES	17	1992
HIT [B] WANNADIES	20	1997
HIT 'EM HIGH (THE MONSTARS' ANTHEM) B REAL/BUSTA RHYMES/COOLIO/LL COOL J/METHOD MAN	8	1997
HIT 'EM WIT DA HEE MISSY 'MISDEMEANOR' ELLIOTT	25	1998
HIT AND MISS JOHN BARRY SEVEN	10	1960
HIT AND RUN [A] GIRLSCHOOL	32	1981
HIT AND RUN [B] TOTAL CONTRAST	41	1985
HIT BY LOVE CE CE PENISTON	33	1994
HIT 'EM UP STYLE (OOPS) BLU CANTRELL	12	2001
HIT IT BEAT	70	1981
HIT ME OFF NEW EDITION	20	1996
HIT ME WITH YOUR RHYTHM STICK IAN & THE BLOCKHEADS	1	1978
HIT OR MISS (WAITED TOO LONG) NEW FOUND GLORY	58	2001
HIT THAT OFFSPRING	11	2004
HIT THAT PERFECT BEAT BRONSKI BEAT	3	1985
HIT THE FREEWAY TONI BRAXTON FEATURING LOON	29	2003
HIT THE GROUND DARLING BUDS	27	1989
HIT THE GROUND RUNNING TIM FINN	50	1993
HIT THE NORTH FALL	57	1987
HIT THE ROAD JACK RAY CHARLES	6	1961
HITCHIN' A RIDE [A] VANITY FARE	16	1969
HITCHIN' A RIDE [A] SINITTA	24	1990
HITCHIN' A RIDE [B] GREEN DAY	25	1997
HI-TEK MAMPI SWIFT	72	2004
HITMIX (OFFICIAL BOOTLEG MEGA-MIX) ALEXANDER O'NEAL	19	1989
HITS MEDLEY GIPSY KINGS	53	1994
HITSVILLE UK CLASH	56	1981
HOBART PAVING SAINT ETIENNE	23	1993
HOBO HUMPIN' SLOBO BABE WHALE	15	1994
HOCUS POCUS FOCUS	20	1973
HOGWASH FARM (THE DIESEL HANDS EP) DAWN OF THE REPLICANTS	65	1998
HOKEY COKEY JUDGE DREAD	64	1978
HOKEY COKEY SNOWMEN	18	1981
HOKEY COKEY BLACK LACE	31	1985
THE HOKEY COKEY CAPTAIN SENSIBLE	71	1994
HOKOYO ORANGE JUICE	60	1982
HOKUS POKUS INSANE CLOWN POSSE	53	1998
HOLD BACK THE NIGHT TRAMMPS	5	1975
HOLD BACK THE NIGHT KWS FEATURES GUEST VOCAL FROM THE TRAMMPS	30	1992
HOLD BACK THE RIVER WET WET WET	31	1990
HOLD BACK TOMORROW MIKI & GRIFF	26	1959
HOLD IT STEPHEN 'TIN TIN' DUFFY	55	1983
HOLD IT, DON'T DROP IT JENNIFER LOPEZ	72	2008
HOLD IT DOWN [A] SENSELESS THINGS	19	1992
HOLD IT DOWN [B] 2 BAD MICE	48	1992
HOLD ME [A] TEDDY PENDERGRASS & WHITNEY HOUSTON	44	1986
HOLD ME [B] P.J. PROBY	3	1964
HOLD ME [B] B.A. ROBERTSON & MAGGIE BELL	11	1981
HOLD ME [C] SAVAGE GARDEN	16	2000
HOLD ME CLOSE DAVID ESSEX	1	1975
HOLD ME IN YOUR ARMS RICK ASTLEY	10	1989
HOLD ME NOW [A] THOMPSON TWINS	4	1983
HOLD ME NOW [B] JOHNNY LOGAN	2	1987
HOLD ME NOW [C] POLYPHONIC SPREE	72	2004
HOLD ME THRILL ME KISS ME MURIEL SMITH	3	1953
HOLD ME THRILL ME KISS ME GLORIA ESTEFAN	11	1994
HOLD ME, THRILL ME, KISS ME, KILL ME U2	2	1995
HOLD ME TIGHT JOHNNY NASH	5	1968

	Peak Position	Year of Entry
HOLD ME TIGHTER IN THE RAIN BILLY GRIFFIN	17	1983
HOLD MY BODY TIGHT EAST 17	12	1995
HOLD MY HAND [A] DON CORNELL	1	1954
HOLD MY HAND [B] KEN DODD	44	1981
HOLD MY HAND [C] HOOTIE & THE BLOWFISH	50	1995
HOLD ON [A] STREETBAND	18	1978
HOLD ON [B] EN VOGUE	5	1990
HOLD ON [C] WILSON PHILLIPS	6	1990
HOLD ON [D] C.B. MILTON	62	1995
HOLD ON [E] HAPPY CLAPPERS	27	1995
HOLD ON [F] JOSE NUNEZ FEATURING OCTAHVIA	44	1999
HOLD ON [G] GOOD CHARLOTTE	34	2003
HOLD ON [H] KT TUNSTALL	21	2007
HOLD ON (EP) ANN NESBY	75	1997
HOLD ON ME PHIXX	10	2003
HOLD ON MY HEART GENESIS	16	1992
HOLD ON TIGHT [A] ELECTRIC LIGHT ORCHESTRA	4	1981
HOLD ON TIGHT [B] SAMANTHA FOX	26	1986
HOLD ON TO LOVE [A] PETER SKELLERN	14	1975
HOLD ON TO LOVE [B] GARY MOORE	65	1984
HOLD ON TO ME MJ COLE FEATURING ELISABETH TROY	35	2000
HOLD ON TO MY LOVE JIMMY RUFFIN	7	1980
HOLD ON TO OUR LOVE JAMES FOX	13	2004
HOLD ON TO THE NIGHTS RICHARD MARX	60	1990
HOLD ON TO WHAT YOU'VE GOT EVELYN KING	47	1988
HOLD ON TO YOUR FRIENDS MORRISSEY	47	1994
HOLD THAT SUCKER DOWN OT QUARTET	24	1994
HOLD THE HEART BIG COUNTRY	55	1986
HOLD THE LINE TOTO	14	1979
HOLD TIGHT [A] DAVE DEE, DOZY, BEAKY, MICK & TICH	4	1966
HOLD TIGHT [B] LIVERPOOL EXPRESS	46	1976
HOLD YOU DOWN JENNIFER LOPEZ FEATURING FAT JOE	6	2005
HOLD YOU TIGHT TARA KEMP	69	1991
HOLD YOUR HEAD UP ARGENT	5	1972
HOLD YOUR HEAD UP HIGH BORIS DLUGOSCH PRESENTS BOOM	23	1997
HOLD YOUR HORSES BABE CELI BEE & THE BUZZY BUNCH	72	1978
HOLDIN' ON TONY RALLO & THE MIDNIGHT BAND	34	1980
HOLDING BACK THE YEARS SIMPLY RED	2	1985
HOLDING ON [A] BEVERLEY CRAVEN	32	1991
HOLDING ON [B] CLOCK	66	1993
HOLDING ON [C] DJ MANTA	47	1999
HOLDING ON [D] HEATHER SMALL	58	2000
HOLDING ON FOR YOU LIBERTY X	5	2002
HOLDING ON 4 U CLOCK	27	1996
HOLDING ON TO NOTHING AGNELLI & NELSON FEATURING AUREUS	41	2004
HOLDING ON TO YOU TERENCE TRENT D'ARBY	20	1995
HOLDING ON (WHEN LOVE IS GONE) LTD	70	1978
HOLDING OUT FOR A HERO BONNIE TYLER	2	1985
HOLE HEARTED EXTREME	12	1991
HOLE IN MY SHOE TRAFFIC	2	1967
HOLE IN MY SHOE neil	2	1984
HOLE IN MY SOUL AEROSMITH	29	1997
HOLE IN THE BUCKET [A] HARRY BELAFONTE & ODETTA	32	1961
HOLE IN THE BUCKET [B] SPEARHEAD	55	1995
HOLE IN THE EARTH DEFTONES	69	2006
HOLE IN THE GROUND BERNARD CRIBBINS	9	1962
HOLE IN THE HEAD SUGABABES	1	2003
HOLE IN THE ICE NEIL FINN	43	2001
HOLE IN THE WORLD EAGLES	69	2003
HOLIDAE INN CHINGY	35	2004
HOLIDAY [A] MADONNA	2	1984
HOLIDAY [A] MADHOUSE	24	2002
HOLIDAY [B] GREEN DAY	11	2005
HOLIDAY 80 (DOUBLE SINGLE) HUMAN LEAGUE	46	1980
HOLIDAY RAP MC MIKER 'G' & DEEJAY SVEN	6	1986
HOLIDAYS IN THE SUN SEX PISTOLS	8	1977
HOLLABACK GIRL GWEN STEFANI	8	2005
HOLLER [A] GINUWINE	13	1998
HOLLER [B] SPICE GIRLS	1	2000
HOLLIEDAZE (MEDLEY) HOLLIES	28	1981
THE HOLLOW A PERFECT CIRCLE	72	2000
HOLLOW HEART BIRDLAND	70	1989
THE HOLLOW MAN MARILLION	30	1994
HOLLY HOLY UB40	31	1998
HOLLYWOOD [A] BOZ SCAGGS	33	1977
HOLLYWOOD [B] MADONNA	2	2003
HOLLYWOOD (DOWN ON YOUR LUCK) THIN LIZZY	53	1982
HOLLYWOOD NIGHTS BOB SEGER & THE SILVER BULLET BAND	42	1978
HOLLYWOOD TEASE GIRL	50	1980
THE HOLY CITY MOIRA ANDERSON	43	1969
HOLY COW LEE DORSEY	6	1966
HOLY DAYS ZOE	72	1992
HOLY DIVER DIO	72	1983
HOLY JOE HAYSI FANTAYZEE	51	1982
THE HOLY RIVER PRINCE	19	1997
HOLY ROLLER NAZARETH	36	1975
HOLY ROLLER NOVACAINE KINGS OF LEON	53	2003
HOLY SMOKE IRON MAIDEN	3	1990
HOLY WARS...THE PUNISHMENT DUE MEGADETH	24	1990
HOMBURG PROCOL HARUM	6	1967
HOME [A] PUBLIC IMAGE LTD.	75	1986
HOME [B] GOD MACHINE	65	1993
HOME [C] DEPECHE MODE	23	1997
HOME [F] COAST 2 COAST FEATURING DISCOVERY	44	2001
HOME [D] CHAKRA	46	1997
HOME [E] SHERYL CROW	25	1997
HOME [D] JULIE McKNIGHT	61	2002
HOME [H] BONE THUGS-N-HARMONY FEATURING PHIL COLLINS	19	2003
HOME [I] SIMPLY RED	40	2004
HOME [J] MICHAEL BUBLE	31	2005
HOME [K] SIMPLE MINDS	41	2005
HOME [L] ROOSTER	33	2006
HOME [M] WESTLIFE	3	2007
HOME ALONE R KELLY FEATURING KEITH MURRAY	17	1998
HOME AND AWAY KAREN BODINGTON & MARK WILLIAMS	73	1989
HOME AND DRY PET SHOP BOYS	14	2002
HOME FOR CHRISTMAS DAY RED CAR AND THE BLUE CAR	44	1991
HOME IS WHERE THE HEART IS GLADYS KNIGHT & THE PIPS	35	1977
HOME LOVIN' MAN ANDY WILLIAMS	7	1970
HOME OF THE BRAVE JODY MILLER	49	1965
HOME SWEET HOME MOTLEY CRUE	37	1986
HOMECOMING KANYE WEST FEATURING CHRIS MARTIN	9	2008
HOMELY GIRL CHI-LITES	5	1974
HOMELY GIRL UB40	6	1989
HOMETOWN GLORY ADELE	32	2008
HOMETOWN UNICORN SUPER FURRY ANIMALS	47	1996
HOMEWARD BOUND QUIET FIVE	44	1966
HOMEWARD BOUND SIMON & GARFUNKEL	9	1966
HOMICIDE [A] 999	40	1978
HOMICIDE [B] SHADES OF RHYTHM	53	1991
HOMING WALTZ VERA LYNN	9	1952
HOMO SAPIENS COOPER TEMPLE CLAUSE	36	2006
HOMOPHOBIC ASSHOLE SENSELESS THINGS	52	1992
HONALOOCHIE BOOGIE MOTT THE HOOPLE	12	1973
HONDY (NO ACCESS) HONDY	26	1997
HONEST I DO DANNY STORM	42	1962
HONEST I DO LOVE YOU CANDI STATON	48	1978
HONEST MEN ELECTRIC LIGHT ORCHESTRA PART 2	60	1991
HONESTLY ZWAN	28	2003
HONESTY ALEX PARKS	56	2006
HONEY [A] BOBBY GOLDSBORO	2	1968
HONEY [B] MARIAH CAREY	3	1997
HONEY [C] MOBY	33	1998
HONEY [D] BILLIE RAY MARTIN	54	1999
HONEY [E] R KELLY & JAY-Z	35	2002
HONEY BE GOOD BIBLE	54	1989
HONEY CHILE [A] FATS DOMINO	29	1957
HONEY CHILE [B] MARTHA REEVES & THE VANDELLAS	30	1968
HONEY COME BACK GLEN CAMPBELL	4	1970
HONEY HONEY SWEET DREAMS	10	1974
HONEY I GEORGE McCRAE	33	1976
HONEY I NEED PRETTY THINGS	13	1965
HONEY I'M LOST DOOLEYS	24	1979
HONEY TO THE BEE BILLIE	3	1999
HONEYCOMB JIMMIE RODGERS	30	1957
THE HONEYDRIPPER JETS	58	1982
THE HONEYMOON SONG MANUEL & HIS MUSIC OF THE MOUNTAINS	22	1959
THE HONEYTHIEF HIPSWAY	17	1986
HONG KONG GARDEN SIOUXSIE & THE BANSHEES	7	1978
HONKY CAT ELTON JOHN	31	1972
THE HONKY DOODLE DAY EP HONKY	61	1993
HONKY TONK TRAIN BLUES KEITH EMERSON	21	1976
HONKY TONK WOMEN ROLLING STONES	1	1969
HONKY TONK WOMEN POGUES	56	1992
HOOCHIE BOOTY ULTIMATE KAOS	17	1995
HOODED FRESH BC	74	2004
HOODIE LADY SOVEREIGN	44	2005
HOOKED 99TH FLOOR ELEVATORS FEATURING TONY DE VIT	28	1995
HOOKED ON A FEELING JONATHAN KING	23	1971
HOOKED ON CAN-CAN ROYAL PHILHARMONIC ORCHESTRA ARRANGED & CONDUCTED BY LOUIS CLARK	47	1981
HOOKED ON CLASSICS ROYAL PHILHARMONIC ORCHESTRA ARRANGED & CONDUCTED BY LOUIS CLARK	2	1981
HOOKED ON LOVE DEAD OR ALIVE	69	1987
HOOKED ON YOU [A] SYDNEY YOUNGBLOOD	72	1991
HOOKED ON YOU [B] VOLATILE AGENTS FEATURING SIMONE BENN	54	2001
HOOKS IN YOU MARILLION	30	1989
HOOLIGAN EMBRACE	18	1999
HOOLIGAN 69 RAGGA TWINS	56	1991
HOOLIGAN'S HOLIDAY MOTLEY CRUE	36	1994
HOORAY HOORAY (IT'S A CHEEKY HOLIDAY) CHEEKY GIRLS	3	2003
HOORAY HOORAY IT'S A HOLI-HOLIDAY BONEY M	3	1979
HOOTIN' NIGEL GEE	57	2001
HOOTS MON LORD ROCKINGHAM'S XI	1	1958
HOOVERS & HORNS FERGIE & BK	57	2000
HOOVERVILLE (THEY PROMISED US THE WORLD) CHRISTIANS	21	1987
THE HOP THEATRE OF HATE	70	1982
HOPE [A] SHAGGY	19	2001
HOPE [B] TWISTA FEATURING FAITH EVANS	25	2005
HOPE AND WAIT ORION TOO	46	2002
HOPE (I WISH YOU'D BELIEVE ME) WAH!	37	1983

Title / Artist	Peak Position	Year of Entry
HOPE IN A HOPELESS WORLD PAUL YOUNG	42	1993
HOPE (NEVER GIVE UP) LOVELAND FEATURING RACHEL McFARLANE	37	1994
HOPE OF DELIVERANCE PAUL McCARTNEY	18	1993
HOPE ST LEVELLERS	12	1995
HOPE THERE'S SOMEONE ANTONY & THE JOHNSONS	44	2005
HOPELESS DIONNE FARRIS	42	1997
HOPELESSLY RICK ASTLEY	33	1993
HOPELESSLY DEVOTED TO YOU OLIVIA NEWTON-JOHN	2	1978
HOPELESSLY DEVOTED TO YOU SONIA	61	1994
HOPPIPOLLA SIGUR ROS	24	2005
THE HORN TRACK EGYPTIAN EMPIRE	61	1992
HORNY [A] MARK MORRISON	5	1996
HORNY [B] MOUSSE T VERSUS HOT 'N' JUICY	2	1998
HORNY AS A DANDY MOUSSE T VS DANDY WARHOLS	17	2006
HORNY AS FUNK SOAPY	35	1996
HORNY HORNS PERFECT PHASE	21	1999
HORROR HEAD (EP) CURVE	31	1992
HORSE SPLODGENESSABOUNDS	26	1980
HORSE AND CARRIAGE CAM'RON FEATURING MASE	12	1998
HORSE WITH NO NAME AMERICA	3	1972
HORSEMEN BEES	41	2004
HORSEPOWER RAVESIGNAL III	61	1991
HOSANNAS FROM THE BASEMENTS OF HELL KILLING JOKE	72	2006
HOSPITAL FOOD DAVID GRAY	34	2005
HOSTAGE IN A FROCK CECIL	68	1997
HOT [A] IDEAL	49	1994
HOT [B] AVRIL LAVIGNE	30	2007
HOT & WET (BELIEVE IT) TZANT	36	1996
HOT BLOODED FOREIGNER	42	1978
HOT BOYZ MISSY MISDEMEANOR ELLIOTT FEATURING NAS, EVE & Q-TIP	18	2000
HOT DIGGITY MICHAEL HOLLIDAY	14	1956
HOT DIGGITY PERRY COMO	4	1956
HOT DIGGITY STARGAZERS	28	1956
HOT DOG SHAKIN' STEVENS	24	1980
HOT FUN 7TH HEAVEN	47	1985
HOT HOT HOT [A] ARROW	38	1984
HOT HOT HOT [A] PAT & MICK	47	1993
HOT HOT HOT!!! [B] CURE	45	1988
HOT IN HERRE NELLY	4	2002
HOT IN HERRE TIGA	46	2003
HOT IN THE CITY BILLY IDOL	13	1982
HOT KISS JULIETTE & THE LICKS	50	2006
HOT LIKE FIRE [A] AALIYAH	30	1997
HOT LIKE FIRE [B] DJ AMS & KHIZA FEATURING BINNS & TAFARI	72	2005
HOT LOVE [A] T REX	1	1971
HOT LOVE [B] DAVID ESSEX	57	1980
HOT LOVE [C] KELLY MARIE	22	1981
HOT LOVE [D] FIVE STAR	68	1990
HOT LOVE NOW WONDER STUFF	19	1994
HOT PEPPER FLOYD CRAMER	46	1962
HOT ROCKIN' JUDAS PRIEST	60	1981
(HOT S**T) COUNTRY GRAMMAR NELLY	7	2000
HOT SHOT [A] BARRY BLUE	23	1974
HOT SHOT [B] KAREN YOUNG	34	1978
HOT SHOT [C] CLIFF RICHARD	46	1979
HOT SHOT TOTTENHAM TOTTENHAM HOTSPUR F.A. CUP FINAL SQUAD	18	1987
HOT SPOT FOXY BROWN	31	1999
HOT STUFF [A] DONNA SUMMER	11	1979
HOT STUFF [A] ARSENAL FC	9	1998
HOT STUFF [B] CRAIG DAVID	7	2007
HOT SUMMER SALSA JIVE BUNNY & THE MASTERMIXERS	43	1991
HOT TODDY TED HEATH	6	1953
HOT TRACKS EP NAZARETH	15	1977
HOT VALVES EP BE BOP DELUXE	36	1976
HOT WATER LEVEL 42	18	1984
HOTEL CASSIDY FEATURING R KELLY	3	2004
HOTEL CALIFORNIA EAGLES	8	1977
HOTEL CALIFORNIA JAM ON THE MUTHA	62	1990
HOTEL ILLNESS BLACK CROWES	47	1992
HOTEL LOUNGE (BE THE DEATH OF ME) dEUS	55	1995
HOTEL ROOM RICHARD HAWLEY	64	2006
HOTEL YORBA WHITE STRIPES	26	2001
HOTLEGS ROD STEWART	5	1978
HOTLINE TO HEAVEN BANANARAMA	58	1984
HOTNESS DYNAMITE MC & ORIGIN UNKNOWN	66	2003
HOUND DOG ELVIS PRESLEY	2	1956
HOUND DOG MAN FABIAN	46	1960
HOUNDS OF LOVE KATE BUSH	18	1986
HOUNDS OF LOVE FUTUREHEADS	8	2005
HOURGLASS SQUEEZE	16	1987
HOUSE ARREST KRUSH	3	1987
HOUSE ENGERY REVENGE CAPPELLA	73	1989
HOUSE FLY TRICKY DISCO	55	1991
A HOUSE IN THE COUNTRY PRETTY THINGS	50	1966
THE HOUSE IS HAUNTED (BY THE ECHO OF YOUR LAST GOODBYE) MARC ALMOND	55	1986
THE HOUSE IS MINE HYPNOTIST	65	1991
HOUSE IS NOT A HOME CHARLES & EDDIE	29	1993
HOUSE MUSIC EDDIE AMADOR	37	1998
HOUSE NATION HOUSEMASTER BOYZ & THE RUDE BOY OF HOUSE	8	1987
HOUSE OF BROKEN LOVE GREAT WHITE	44	1990
HOUSE OF FIRE ALICE COOPER	65	1989
HOUSE OF FUN MADNESS	1	1982
HOUSE OF GOD DHS	72	2002
HOUSE OF JEALOUS LOVERS RAPTURE	27	2003
HOUSE OF JOY VICKI SUE ROBINSON	48	1997
HOUSE OF LOVE [A] EAST 17	10	1992
HOUSE OF LOVE [B] RuPAUL	40	1993
HOUSE OF LOVE [C] SKIN	45	1994
HOUSE OF LOVE [D] AMY GRANT WITH VINCE GILL	46	1995
HOUSE OF LOVE (IN MY HOUSE) SMOOTH TOUCH	58	1994
HOUSE OF THE BLUE DANUBE MALCOLM McLAREN & THE BOOTZILLA ORCHESTRA	73	1989
HOUSE OF THE RISING SUN ANIMALS	1	1964
HOUSE OF THE RISING SUN FRIJID PINK	4	1970
HOUSE OF THE RISING SUN RAGE	41	1993
HOUSE ON FIRE [A] BOOMTOWN RATS	24	1982
HOUSE ON FIRE [B] ARKARNA	33	1997
HOUSE PARTY AT BOOTHY'S LITTLE MAN TATE	29	2006
HOUSE SOME MORE LOCK 'N' LOAD	45	2001
THE HOUSE THAT JACK BUILT [A] ALAN PRICE SET	4	1967
THE HOUSE THAT JACK BUILT [B] TRACIE	9	1983
A HOUSE WITH LOVE IN IT VERA LYNN	17	1956
HOUSECALL SHABBA RANKS FEATURING MAXI PRIEST	8	1991
HOUSES IN MOTION TALKING HEADS	50	1981
HOW ABOUT THAT ADAM FAITH	4	1960
HOW AM I SUPPOSED TO LIVE WITHOUT YOU MICHAEL BOLTON	3	1990
HOW BIZARRE OMC	5	1996
HOW 'BOUT I LOVE YOU MORE MULL HISTORICAL SOCIETY	37	2004
HOW 'BOUT US CHAMPAIGN	5	1981
HOW 'BOUT US LULU	46	1993
HOW CAN I BE SURE DUSTY SPRINGFIELD	36	1970
HOW CAN I BE SURE DAVID CASSIDY	1	1972
HOW CAN I BE SURE? DARREN DAY	71	1998
HOW CAN I FALL BREATHE	48	1988
HOW CAN I FORGET YOU ELISA FIORILLO	50	1988
HOW CAN I KEEP FROM SINGING ENYA	32	1991
HOW CAN I LOVE YOU MORE M PEOPLE	8	1991
HOW CAN I MEET HER EVERLY BROTHERS	12	1962
HOW CAN I TELL HER FOURMOST	33	1964
HOW CAN THIS BE LOVE ANDREW GOLD	19	1978
HOW CAN WE BE LOVERS MICHAEL BOLTON	10	1990
HOW CAN WE EASE THE PAIN MAXI PRIEST FEATURING BERES HAMMOND	41	1988
HOW CAN YOU EXPECT ME TO BE TAKEN SERIOUSLY PET SHOP BOYS	4	1991
HOW CAN YOU TELL SANDIE SHAW	21	1965
HOW CAN YOU TELL ME IT'S OVER LORRAINE CATO	46	1993
HOW COME? [A] RONNIE LANE & SLIM CHANCE	11	1974
HOW COME [B] YOUSSOU N'DOUR & CANIBUS	52	1998
HOW COME [C] D12	4	2004
HOW COME, HOW LONG BABYFACE FEATURING STEVIE WONDER	10	1997
HOW COME IT NEVER RAINS DOGS D'AMOUR	44	1989
HOW COME YOU DON'T CALL ME ALICIA KEYS	26	2002
HOW COULD AN ANGEL BREAK MY HEART TONI BRAXTON WITH KENNY G	22	1997
HOW COULD I? (INSECURITY) ROACHFORD	34	1998
HOW COULD THIS GO WRONG EXILE	67	1979
HOW COULD WE DARE TO BE WRONG COLIN BLUNSTONE	45	1973
(HOW COULD YOU) BRING HIM HOME EAMON	61	2007
HOW DEEP IS YOUR LOVE PORTRAIT	41	1995
HOW DEEP IS YOUR LOVE [A] BEE GEES	3	1977
HOW DEEP IS YOUR LOVE [A] TAKE THAT	1	1996
HOW DEEP IS YOUR LOVE [B] DRU HILL FEATURING REDMAN	9	1998
HOW DID IT EVER COME TO THIS? EASYWORLD	50	2004
HOW DID YOU KNOW KURTIS MANTRONIK PRESENTS CHAMONIX	16	2003
HOW DO I BREATHE MARIO	21	2007
HOW DO I KNOW? MARLO	56	1999
HOW DO I LIVE TRISHA YEARWOOD	66	1997
HOW DO I LIVE LeANN RIMES	7	1998
HOW DO I SAY GOODBYE D-RAIL	63	2005
HOW DO YOU DO [A] AL HUDSON	57	1978
HOW DO YOU DO! [B] ROXETTE	13	1992
HOW DO YOU DO IT? GERRY & THE PACEMAKERS	1	1963
HOW DO YOU KNOW IT'S LOVE TERESA BREWER	21	1960
HOW DO YOU LIKE IT KEITH SWEAT	71	1994
HOW DO YOU SAY...LOVE DEEE-LITE	52	1991
HOW DO YOU SPEAK TO AN ANGEL DEAN MARTIN	15	1954
HOW DO YOU WANT IT? 2PAC FEATURING K-CI & JOJO	17	1996
HOW DO YOU WANT ME TO LOVE YOU? 911	10	1998
HOW DOES IT FEEL [A] SLADE	15	1975
HOW DOES IT FEEL [B] ELECTROSET	27	1992
HOW DOES IT FEEL [C] WANNADIES	53	1996
(HOW DOES IT FEEL TO BE) ON TOP OF THE WORLD ENGLAND UNITED	9	1998
HOW DOES IT FEEL TO FEEL RIDE	58	1994
HOW DOES THAT GRAB YOU DARLIN' NANCY SINATRA	19	1966
HOW GEE BLACK MACHINE	17	1994
HOW HIGH CHARLATANS	6	1997
HOW HIGH THE MOON ELLA FITZGERALD	46	1960
HOW HIGH THE MOON GLORIA GAYNOR	33	1976
HOW HOW YELLO	59	1994
HOW I WANNA BE LOVED DANA DAWSON	42	1996

	Peak Position	Year of Entry
HOW I'M COMIN' LL COOL J	37	1993
HOW IT IS BIOHAZARD	62	1994
HOW IT SHOULD BE INSPIRAL CARPETS	49	1993
HOW LONG ACE	20	1974
HOW LONG ROD STEWART	41	1982
HOW LONG YAZZ & ASWAD	31	1993
HOW LONG? PAUL CARRACK	32	1996
HOW LONG DO I GET RAISSA	47	2000
HOW LONG HAS IT BEEN JIM REEVES	45	1965
HOW LONG'S A TEAR TAKE TO DRY? BEAUTIFUL SOUTH	12	1999
HOW LUCKY YOU ARE SKIN	32	1996
HOW MANY LIES SPANDAU BALLET	34	1987
HOW MANY TEARS BOBBY VEE	10	1961
HOW MANY TEARS CAN YOU HIDE SHAKIN' STEVENS	47	1988
HOW MANY TIMES BROTHER BEYOND	62	1987
HOW MEN ARE AZTEC CAMERA	25	1988
HOW MUCH I FEEL ALIBI	58	1998
(HOW MUCH IS) THAT DOGGIE IN THE WINDOW LITA ROZA	1	1953
(HOW MUCH IS) THAT DOGGIE IN THE WINDOW PATTI PAGE	9	1953
HOW MUCH LOVE [A] LEO SAYER	10	1977
HOW MUCH LOVE [B] VIXEN	35	1990
HOW MUSIC CAME ABOUT (BOP B DA B DA DA) GAP BAND	61	1987
HOW RUDE SHE WAS TOWERS OF LONDON	30	2005
HOW SHE THREW IT ALL AWAY (EP) STYLE COUNCIL	41	1988
HOW SOON HENRY MANCINI	10	1964
HOW SOON IS NOW SMITHS	16	1985
HOW SOON IS NOW INNER SANCTUM	75	1998
HOW SOON IS NOW HUNDRED REASONS	47	2004
HOW SOON WE FORGET COLONEL ABRAMS	75	1987
HOW SWEET IT IS MARVIN GAYE	49	1964
HOW SWEET IT IS JUNIOR WALKER & THE ALL-STARS	22	1966
HOW THE HEART BEHAVES WAS (NOT WAS)	53	1990
HOW TO BE A MILLIONAIRE ABC	49	1984
HOW TO BE DEAD SNOW PATROL	39	2004
HOW TO FALL IN LOVE PART 1 BEE GEES	30	1994
HOW TO SAVE A LIFE THE FRAY	4	2007
HOW TO WIN YOUR LOVE ENGELBERT HUMPERDINCK	59	2000
HOW U LIKE BASS NORMAN BASS	17	2001
HOW WAS IT FOR YOU JAMES	32	1990
HOW WE DO GAME FEATURING 50 CENT	5	2005
HOW WILL I KNOW WHITNEY HOUSTON	5	1986
HOW WILL I KNOW (WHO YOU ARE) JESSICA	47	1999
HOW WONDERFUL TO KNOW PEARL CARR & TEDDY JOHNSON	23	1961
HOW WONDERFUL YOU ARE GORDON HASKELL	2	2002
HOW WOULD U FEEL DAVID MORALES FEATURING LEA LORIEN	71	2004
HOW YOU GONNA ACT LIKE THAT TYRESE	30	2003
HOW YOU GONNA SEE ME NOW ALICE COOPER	61	1978
HOW YOU REMIND ME NICKELBACK	4	2002
HOWARD'S WAY SIMON MAY ORCHESTRA	21	1985
HOW'D I DO DAT BENTLEY RHYTHM ACE	57	2000
HOW'S IT GOING TO BE THIRD EYE BLIND	51	1998
HOW'S YOUR EVENING SO FAR JOSH WINK & LIL LOUIS	23	2000
HOWZAT SHERBET	4	1976
HUBBLE BUBBLE TOIL AND TROUBLE MANFRED MANN	11	1964
HUDSON STREET AGNELLI & NELSON	29	2000
HUG MY SOUL SAINT ETIENNE	32	1994
HUMAN [A] HUMAN LEAGUE	8	1986
HUMAN [B] PRETENDERS	33	1999
HUMAN BEHAVIOUR BJORK	36	1993
HUMAN BEING BETA BAND	57	2001
HUMAN BEINGS SEAL	50	1998
HUMAN NATURE [A] GARY CLAIL ON-U SOUND SYSTEM	10	1991
HUMAN NATURE [B] MADONNA	8	1995
HUMAN RACING NIK KERSHAW	19	1984
HUMAN TOUCH [A] RICK SPRINGFIELD	23	1984
HUMAN TOUCH [B] BRUCE SPRINGSTEEN	11	1992
HUMAN WORK OF ART MAXI PRIEST	71	1990
HUMAN WORK OF ART CLIFF RICHARD	24	1993
HUMANISTIC KAWALA	68	2000
HUMANITY REBEL MC FEATURING LINCOLM THOMPSON	62	1992
HUMMING BIRD FRANKIE LAINE	16	1955
HUMP DE BUMP RED HOT CHILI PEPPERS	41	2007
HUMPIN' GAP BAND	36	1981
HUMPIN' AROUND BOBBY BROWN	8	1992
101 DAM-NATIONS SCARLET PARTY	44	1982
HUNDRED MILE HIGH CITY OCEAN COLOUR SCENE	4	1997
100MPH EL PRESIDENTE	37	2005
A HUNDRED POUNDS OF CLAY CRAIG DOUGLAS	9	1961
HUNG UP [A] PAUL WELLER	11	1994
HUNG UP [B] MADONNA	1	2005
HUNGAH KARYN WHITE	69	1994
THE HUNGER DISTILLERS	48	2004
HUNGER STRIKE TEMPLE OF THE DOG	51	1992
HUNGRY KOSHEEN	13	2002
HUNGRY EYES EYEOPENER	16	2004
HUNGRY FOR HEAVEN DIO	56	1985
HUNGRY FOR LOVE JOHNNY KIDD & THE PIRATES	20	1963
HUNGRY HEART BRUCE SPRINGSTEEN	28	1980
HUNGRY LIKE THE WOLF DURAN DURAN	5	1982
HUNT BARRY RYAN	34	1969
HUNTER [A] BJORK	44	1998
HUNTER [B] DIDO	17	2001
HUNTING FOR WITCHES BLOC PARTY	22	2007
HUNTING HIGH AND LOW A-HA	5	1988
HURDY GURDY MAN DONOVAN	4	1968
HURRICANE [A] BOB DYLAN	43	1976
HURRICANE [B] WARM JETS	34	1998
HURRICANE [C] ATHLETE	31	2007
HURRY HOME WAVELENGTH	17	1982
HURRY UP AND WAIT STEREOPHONICS	11	1999
HURRY UP ENGLAND - THE PEOPLE'S ANTHEM SHAM 69 & THE SPECIAL ASSEMBLY	10	2006
HURRY UP HARRY SHAM 69	10	1978
HURT [A] ELVIS PRESLEY	37	1976
HURT [A] MANHATTANS	4	1976
HURT [B] JOHNNY CASH	42	2003
HURT [C] CHRISTINA AGUILERA	11	2006
HURT BY LOVE INEZ FOXX	40	1964
HURT ME SO BAD LULU	42	1999
HURT SO GOOD SUSAN CADOGAN	4	1975
HURT SO GOOD JIMMY SOMERVILLE	15	1995
HURTING KIND (I'VE GOT MY EYES ON YOU) ROBERT PLANT	45	1990
HUSAN BHANGRA KNIGHTS VS HUSAN	7	2003
HUSBAND FLUFFY	58	1996
HUSH [A] DEEP PURPLE	62	1988
HUSH [A] KULA SHAKER	2	1997
HUSH [B] LL COOL J FEATURING 7 AURELIUS	3	2005
HUSH BOY BASEMENT JAXX	27	2006
HUSH NOT A WORD TO MARY JOHN ROWLES	12	1968
THE HUSTLE VAN McCOY WITH THE SOUL CITY SYMPHONY	3	1975
HUSTLE! (TO THE MUSIC...) FUNKY WORM	13	1988
HUSTLER'S AMBITION 50 CENT	13	2006
HYBRID EAT STATIC	41	1997
HYMN [A] ULTRAVOX	11	1982
HYMN [B] MOBY	31	1994
HYMN [C] ULTRAMARINE FEATURING DAVID McALMONT	65	1996
HYMN TO HER PRETENDERS	8	1986
HYMNE A L'AMOUR ELAINE PAIGE	68	1995
HYPE! HYPE! SLK	22	2005
HYPER MUSIC MUSE	24	2001
HYPERACTIVE THOMAS DOLBY	17	1984
HYPERBALLAD BJORK	8	1996
HYPERREAL SHAMEN	29	1991
HYPNOSIS MUD	16	1973
HYPNOTIC ST-8 ALTERN 8	16	1992
HYPNOTIC TANGO MASTER BLASTER	64	2004
HYPNOTISED [A] CABARET VOLTAIRE	66	1989
HYPNOTISED [B] SIMPLE MINDS	18	1995
HYPNOTISED [C] PAUL OAKENFOLD	57	2003
HYPNOTISING KID CRÈME FEATURING CHARLISE	31	2003
HYPNOTIZE [A] SCRITTI POLITTI	68	1984
HYPNOTIZE [B] D-INFLUENCE	33	1997
HYPNOTIZE [C] NOTORIOUS B.I.G.	10	1997
HYPNOTIZE [D] SYSTEM OF A DOWN	48	2005
HYPNOTIZIN' WINX	35	1996
HYPOCRITE [A] LUSH	52	1994
HYPOCRITE [B] SPECIALS	66	1996
HYSTERIA [A] DEF LEPPARD	26	1987
HYSTERIA [B] MUSE	17	2003

I–L

KEY TO INDEX ENTRIES
Song Title
Artist/Group
Peak Position
Year of Entry
ALL I REALLY WANT ALANIS MORISSETTE 59 1996
ALL I REALLY WANT TO DO BYRDS 4 1965
ALL I REALLY WANT TO DO CHER 9 1965
ALL I SEE IS YOU DUSTY SPRINGFIELD 9 1966
ALL I THINK ABOUT IS YOU NILSSON 43 1977
ALL I WANNA DO [A] SHERYL CROW 4 1994
ALL I WANNA DO [A] JOANNE FARRELL 40 1995
ALL I WANNA DO [A] AMY STUDT 21 2004
ALL I WANNA DO [B] TIN TIN OUT 31 1997
ALL I WANNA DO [C] DANNII 4 1997
ALL I WANNA DO IS MAKE LOVE TO YOU HEART 37 1993
Same letter denotes different versions of the same song
Different letters denote different songs with the same name

	Peak Position	Year of Entry
I [A] PETEY PABLO	51	2002
I [B] JOY ZIPPER	73	2005
I ADORE MI AMOR COLOR ME BADD	44	1991
I ADORE YOU CARON WHEELER	59	1992
I AIN'T GOIN' OUT LIKE THAT CYPRESS HILL	15	1993
I AIN'T GONNA CRY LITTLE ANGELS	26	1991
I AIN'T GONNA STAND FOR IT STEVIE WONDER	10	1981
I AIN'T GOT TIME ANYMORE CLIFF RICHARD	21	1970
I AIN'T LOSING ANY SLEEP SUNSHINE UNDERGROUND	47	2006
I AIN'T LYIN' GEORGE McCRAE	12	1975
I AIN'T MAD AT CHA 2PAC FEATURING K-CI & JOJO	13	1996
I AIN'T NEW TA THIS ICE-T	62	1993
I AIN'T SAYING MY GOODBYES TOM VEK	45	2005
I ALMOST FELT LIKE CRYING CRAIG McLACHLAN & CHECK 1-2	50	1990
I ALMOST LOST MY MIND PAT BOONE	14	1956
I ALONE LIVE	48	1995
I AM [A] CHAKRA	24	1997
I AM [B] SUGGS	38	1998
I AM A CIDER DRINKER 2007 WURZELS FEATURING TONY BLACKBURN	57	2007
I AM A CIDER DRINKER (PALOMA BLANCA) WURZELS	3	1976
I AM A ROCK SIMON & GARFUNKEL	17	1966
I AM BLESSED ETERNAL	7	1995
I AM DOWN SALT-N-PEPA	41	1988
I AM I QUEENSRYCHE	40	1995
I AM, I FEEL ALISHA'S ATTIC	14	1996
I AM (I'M ME) TWISTED SISTER	18	1983
I AM IN LOVE WITH THE WORLD CHICKEN SHED THEATRE	15	1997
I AM LV LV	64	1996
I AM MINE PEARL JAM	26	2002
I AM NOT MY HAIR INDIA.ARIE	65	2006
I AM ONE [A] SMASHING PUMPKINS	73	1992
I AM ONE [B] W.A.S.P.	56	1992
I AM THE BEAT LOOK	6	1981
I AM THE BLACK GOLD OF THE SUN NUYORICAN SOUL FEATURING JOCELYN BROWN	31	1997
I AM THE LAW ANTHRAX	32	1987
I AM THE MOB CATATONIA	40	1997
I AM THE MUSIC HEAR ME! MILLIONAIRE HIPPIES	52	1993
I AM THE MUSIC MAN BLACK LACE	52	1989
I AM THE NEWS OCEAN COLOUR SCENE	31	2000
I AM THE ONE CRACKOUT	72	2002
I AM THE RESURRECTION STONE ROSES	33	1992
I AM THE SUN DARK STAR	31	2000
I AM WHAT I AM [A] GREYHOUND	20	1972
I AM WHAT I AM [B] GLORIA GAYNOR	13	1984
I AM WHAT I AM [C] MARK OWEN	29	1997
I AM...I SAID NEIL DIAMOND	4	1971
I AN'T MOVIN' DES'REE	44	1994
I APOLOGISE P.J. PROBY	11	1965
I BE THE PROPHET STARVING SOULS	66	1995
I BEG YOUR PARDON KON KAN	5	1989
I BEGIN TO WONDER DANNII MINOGUE	2	2003
I BELIEVE [A] FRANKIE LAINE	1	1953
I BELIEVE [A] DAVID WHITFIELD	49	1960
I BELIEVE [A] BACHELORS	2	1964
I BELIEVE [A] ROBSON GREEN & JEROME FLYNN	1	1995
I BELIEVE [B] EMF	6	1991
I BELIEVE [C] REESE PROJECT	74	1992
I BELIEVE [D] BON JOVI	11	1993
I BELIEVE [E] ROBERT PLANT	64	1993
I BELIEVE [F] MARCELLA DETROIT	11	1994
I BELIEVE [G] SOUNDS OF BLACKNESS	17	1994
I BELIEVE [H] BLESSID UNION OF SOULS	29	1995
I BELIEVE [I] HAPPY CLAPPERS	7	1995
I BELIEVE [J] BOOTH & THE BAD ANGEL	25	1996
I BELIEVE [K] ABSOLUTE FEATURING SUZANNE PALMER	38	1997
I BELIEVE [L] LANGE FEATURING SARAH DWYER	68	1999
I BELIEVE [M] JAMESTOWN FEATURING JOCELYN BROWN	62	1999
I BELIEVE [N] STEPHEN GATELY	11	2000
I BELIEVE (A SOULFUL RECORDING) TEARS FOR FEARS	23	1985
I BELIEVE I CAN FLY R KELLY	1	1997
I BELIEVE I'M GONNA LOVE YOU FRANK SINATRA	34	1975
I BELIEVE IN A THING CALLED LOVE DARKNESS	2	2003
I BELIEVE IN CHRISTMAS TWEENIES	9	2001
I BELIEVE IN FATHER CHRISTMAS GREG LAKE	2	1975
I BELIEVE (IN LOVE) [A] HOT CHOCOLATE	8	1971
I BELIEVE IN LOVE [B] COOPER	50	2002
I BELIEVE IN MIRACLES JACKSON SISTERS	72	1987
I BELIEVE IN MIRACLES PASADENAS	34	1992
I BELIEVE IN THE SPIRIT TIM BURGESS	44	2003
I BELIEVE IN YOU [A] OUR TRIBE	42	1993
I BELIEVE IN YOU [A] AMP FIDDLER	72	2004
I BELIEVE IN YOU [B] KYLIE MINOGUE	2	2004
I BELIEVE IN YOU AND ME WHITNEY HOUSTON	16	1997
I BELIEVE MY HEART DUNCAN JAMES & KEEDIE	2	2004
I BELIEVE YOU DOROTHY MOORE	20	1977
I BELONG KATHY KIRBY	36	1965
I BELONG TO YOU [A] WHITNEY HOUSTON	54	1991
I BELONG TO YOU [B] GINA G	6	1996
I BELONG TO YOU [C] LENNY KRAVITZ	75	1998
I BET YOU LOOK GOOD ON THE DANCEFLOOR ARCTIC MONKEYS	1	2005
I BREATHE AGAIN ADAM RICKITT	5	1999
I BRUISE EASILY NATASHA BEDINGFIELD	12	2005
I CALL IT LOVE LIONEL RICHIE	45	2006
I CALL YOUR NAME A-HA	44	1990
I CALLED U LIL' LOUIS	16	1990
I CAN NAS	19	2003
I CAN BUY YOU A CAMP	46	2001
I CAN CALL YOU PORTRAIT	61	1995
I CAN CAST A SPELL DISCO TEX PRESENTS CLOUDBURST	35	2001
I CAN CLIMB MOUNTAINS HELL IS FOR HEROES	41	2002
I CAN DANCE [A] BRIAN POOLE & THE TREMELOES	21	1963
I CAN DANCE [B] DJ 'FAST' EDDIE	47	1989
I CAN DO IT RUBETTES	7	1975
I CAN DO THIS MONIE LOVE	37	1989
I CAN DREAM SKUNK ANANSIE	41	1995
I CAN DREAM ABOUT YOU DAN HARTMAN	12	1985
I CAN DRIVE SHAKESPEARS SISTER	30	1996
I CAN FEEL IT SILENCERS	62	1993
I CAN HEAR MUSIC BEACH BOYS	10	1969
I CAN HEAR THE GRASS GROW MOVE	5	1967
I CAN HEAR VOICES/CANED AND UNABLE HI-GATE	12	2000
I CAN HEAR YOUR HEARTBEAT CHRIS REA	60	1983
I CAN HELP BILLY SWAN	6	1974
I CAN HELP ELVIS PRESLEY	30	1983
I CAN LOVE YOU LIKE THAT ALL-4-ONE	33	1995
I CAN MAKE IT BETTER [A] WHISPERS	44	1981
I CAN MAKE IT BETTER [B] LUTHER VANDROSS	44	1996
I CAN MAKE YOU FEEL GOOD SHALAMAR	7	1982
I CAN MAKE YOU FEEL GOOD KAVANA	8	1997
I CAN MAKE YOU FEEL LIKE MAXX	56	1995
I CAN ONLY DISAPPOINT U MANSUN	8	2000
I CAN PROVE IT TONY ETORIA	21	1977
I CAN PROVE IT PHIL FEARON	8	1986
I CAN SEE CLEARLY NOW [A] JOHNNY NASH	5	1972
I CAN SEE CLEARLY NOW [A] HOTHOUSE FLOWERS	23	1990
I CAN SEE CLEARLY NOW [A] JIMMY CLIFF	23	1994
I CAN SEE CLEARLY NOW [B] DEBORAH HARRY	23	1993
I CAN SEE FOR MILES WHO	10	1967
I CAN SEE HER NOW DRAMATIS	57	1982
I CAN SEE IT BLANCMANGE	71	1986
I CAN SING A RAINBOW - LOVE IS BLUE (MEDLEY) DELLS	15	1969
I CAN TAKE OR LEAVE YOUR LOVING HERMAN'S HERMITS	11	1968
I CANNOT GIVE YOU MY LOVE CLIFF RICHARD	13	2005
I CAN'T ASK FOR ANY MORE THAN YOU CLIFF RICHARD	17	1976
I CAN'T BE WITH YOU CRANBERRIES	23	1995
I CAN'T BELIEVE YOU'RE GONE WEBB BROTHERS	69	2001
I CAN'T BREAK DOWN SINEAD QUINN	2	2003
I CAN'T COME DOWN EMBRACE	54	2006
I CAN'T CONTROL MYSELF TROGGS	2	1966
I CAN'T DANCE GENESIS	7	1992
I CAN'T DECIDE SCISSOR SISTERS	64	2007
I CAN'T DENY IT ROD STEWART	26	2001
I CAN'T EXPLAIN WHO	8	1965
I CAN'T FACE THE WORLD LEMON TREES	52	1993
(I CAN'T GET ME NO) SATISFACTION DEVO	41	1978
I CAN'T GET NEXT TO YOU TEMPTATIONS	13	1970
(I CAN'T GET NO) SATISFACTION ROLLING STONES	1	1965
(I CAN'T GET NO) SATISFACTION BUBBLEROCK	29	1974
I CAN'T GET NO SLEEP MASTERS AT WORK PRESENT INDIA	44	1995
I CAN'T GET YOU OUT OF MY MIND YVONNE ELLIMAN	17	1977
I CAN'T GO FOR THAT (NO CAN DO) DARYL HALL & JOHN OATES	8	1982
(I CAN'T HELP) FALLING IN LOVE WITH YOU UB40	1	1993
I CAN'T HELP IT [A] JOHNNY TILLOTSON	41	1962
I CAN'T HELP IT [B] JUNIOR	53	1982
I CAN'T HELP IT [C] BANANARAMA	20	1988
I CAN'T HELP MYSELF [A] FOUR TOPS	10	1965
I CAN'T HELP MYSELF [A] DONNIE ELBERT	11	1972
I CAN'T HELP MYSELF [B] ORANGE JUICE	42	1982
I CAN'T HELP MYSELF [C] JOEY LAWRENCE	27	1993
I CAN'T HELP MYSELF [D] JULIA FORDHAM	62	1994
I CAN'T HELP MYSELF [E] LUCID	7	1998
I CAN'T IMAGINE THE WORLD WITHOUT ME ECHOBELLY	39	1994
I CAN'T LEAVE YOU ALONE GEORGE McCRAE	9	1974
I CAN'T LEAVE YOU ALONE TRACIE YOUNG	60	1985
I CAN'T LET GO [A] HOLLIES	2	1966
I CAN'T LET GO [B] MARTI WEBB	65	1987
I CAN'T LET MAGGIE GO HONEYBUS	8	1968
I CAN'T LET YOU GO [D] IAN VAN DAHL	20	2003
I CAN'T LET YOU GO [A] HAYWOODE	50	1984
I CAN'T LET YOU GO [B] 52ND STREET	57	1986
I CAN'T LET YOU GO [C] MACK VIBE FEATURING JACQUELINE	53	1995
I CAN'T LIVE A DREAM OSMONDS	37	1976
I CAN'T MAKE A MISTAKE MC LYTE	46	1998
I CAN'T MAKE IT SMALL FACES	26	1967
I CAN'T MAKE IT ALONE P.J. PROBY	37	1966
I CAN'T MAKE IT ALONE MARIA McKEE	74	1993
I CAN'T MAKE YOU LOVE ME [A] BONNIE RAITT	50	1991
I CAN'T MAKE YOU LOVE ME [B] GEORGE MICHAEL	3	1997

	Peak Position	Year of Entry
I CAN'T READ DAVID BOWIE	73	1998
I CAN'T READ YOU DANIEL BEDINGFIELD	6	2003
I CAN'T SAY GOODBYE KIM WILDE	51	1990
I CAN'T SAY GOODBYE TO YOU HELEN REDDY	43	1981
I CAN'T SEE NICOLE RAY	55	1998
I CAN'T SLEEP BABY (IF I) R KELLY	1	2000
I CAN'T STAND IT [A] SPENCER DAVIS GROUP	47	1964
I CAN'T STAND IT [B] TWENTY 4 SEVEN FEATURING CAPTAIN HOLLYWOOD	7	1990
I CAN'T STAND MY BABY REZILLOS	71	1979
I CAN'T STAND THE RAIN ANN PEEBLES	41	1974
I CAN'T STAND THE RAIN ERUPTION FEATURING PRECIOUS WILSON	5	1978
I CAN'T STAND THE RAIN TINA TURNER	57	1985
I CAN'T STAND UP FOR FALLING DOWN ELVIS COSTELLO & THE ATTRACTIONS	4	1980
I CAN'T STOP [A] OSMONDS	12	1974
I CAN'T STOP [B] GARY NUMAN	27	1986
I CAN'T STOP [C] SANDY RIVERA	58	2003
I CAN'T STOP LOVIN' YOU (THOUGH I TRY) LEO SAYER	6	1978
I CAN'T STOP LOVING YOU RAY CHARLES	1	1962
I CAN'T STOP THIS FEELING I'VE GOT RAZORLIGHT	44	2007
I CAN'T TAKE THE POWER OFF-SHORE	7	1991
I CAN'T TELL A WALTZ FROM A TANGO ALMA COGAN	6	1954
I CAN'T TELL THE BOTTOM FROM THE TOP HOLLIES	7	1970
I CAN'T TELL YOU WHY BROWNSTONE	27	1995
I CAN'T TURN AROUND JM SILK	62	1986
I CAN'T TURN AWAY SAVANNA	61	1981
I CAN'T TURN YOU LOOSE OTIS REDDING	29	1966
I CAN'T WAIT [A] STEVIE NICKS	47	1986
I CAN'T WAIT [B] NU SHOOZ	2	1986
I CAN'T WAIT [B] LADIES FIRST	19	2002
I CAN'T WAIT ANYMORE SAXON	71	1988
I CARE SOUL II SOUL	17	1995
I CAUGHT YOU OUT REBECCA DE RUVO	72	1994
I CHANGED MY MIND KEYSHIA COLE	48	2006
I CHOOSE LIFE KEISHA WHITE	63	2006
I CLOSE MY EYES AND COUNT TO TEN DUSTY SPRINGFIELD	4	1968
I COME FROM ANOTHER PLANET, BABY JULIAN COPE	34	1996
I CONFESS BEAT	54	1982
I COULD BE AN ANGLE EIGHTIES MATCHBOX B-LINE DISASTER	35	2004
I COULD BE HAPPY ALTERED IMAGES	7	1981
I COULD BE SO GOOD FOR YOU DENNIS WATERMAN WITH THE DENNIS WATERMAN BAND	3	1980
I COULD BE THE ONE STACIE ORRICO	34	2004
I COULD EASILY FALL CLIFF RICHARD & THE SHADOWS	6	1964
I COULD FALL IN LOVE WITH YOU ERASURE	21	2007
I COULD HAVE BEEN A DREAMER DIO	69	1987
I COULD NEVER LOVE ANOTHER TEMPTATIONS	47	1968
I COULD NEVER MISS YOU (MORE THAN I DO) LULU	62	1981
I COULD NEVER TAKE THE PLACE OF YOUR MAN PRINCE	29	1987
I COULD NOT LOVE YOU MORE BEE GEES	14	1997
I COULD SING OF YOUR LOVE FOREVER DELIRIOUS?	40	2001
I COULDN'T LIVE WITHOUT YOUR LOVE PETULA CLARK	6	1966
I COUNT THE TEARS DRIFTERS	28	1961
I CRIED FOR YOU [A] RICKY STEVENS	34	1961
I CRIED FOR YOU [B] KATIE MELUA	35	2005
I DID WHAT I DID FOR MARIA TONY CHRISTIE	2	1971
I DIDN'T KNOW I LOVED YOU (TILL I SAW YOU ROCK 'N' ROLL) GARY GLITTER	4	1972
I DIDN'T KNOW I LOVED YOU (TILL I SAW YOU ROCK 'N' ROLL) ROCK GODDESS	57	1984
I DIDN'T KNOW I WAS LOOKING FOR LOVE (EP) EVERYTHING BUT THE GIRL	72	1993
I DIDN'T MEAN IT STATUS QUO	21	1994
I DIDN'T MEAN TO HURT YOU ROCKIN' BERRIES	43	1964
I DIDN'T MEAN TO TURN YOU ON ROBERT PALMER	9	1986
I DIDN'T WANT TO NEED YOU HEART	47	1990
I DIE: YOU DIE GARY NUMAN	6	1980
I DIG YOU BABY MARVIN RAINWATER	19	1958
I DISAPPEAR METALLICA	35	2000
I DO JAMELIA	36	1999
I DO I DO I DO I DO I DO ABBA	38	1975
I DO WHAT I DO...THEME FOR *9½ WEEKS* JOHN TAYLOR	42	1986
I DON'T BELIEVE IN 'IF' ANYMORE ROGER WHITTAKER	8	1970
I DON'T BELIEVE IN MIRACLES [A] COLIN BLUNSTONE	31	1972
I DON'T BELIEVE IN MIRACLES [B] SINITTA	22	1988
I DON'T BLAME YOU AT ALL SMOKEY ROBINSON & THE MIRACLES	11	1971
I DON'T CARE [A] LIBERACE	28	1956
I DON'T CARE [B] LOS BRAVOS	16	1966
I DON'T CARE [C] SHAKESPEARS SISTER	7	1992
I DON'T CARE [D] TONY DE VIT	65	2002
I DON'T CARE IF THE SUN DON'T SHINE ELVIS PRESLEY	23	1956
I DON'T DANCE CHAD & RYAN	57	2007
I DON'T EVEN KNOW IF I SHOULD CALL YOU BABY SOUL FAMILY SENSATION	49	1991
I DON'T EVER WANT TO SEE YOU AGAIN UNCLE SAM	30	1998
I DON'T FEEL LIKE DANCIN' SCISSOR SISTERS	1	2006
I DON'T KNOW [A] RUTH	66	1997
I DON'T KNOW [B] HONEYZ	28	2001
I DON'T KNOW ANYBODY ELSE BLACK BOX	4	1990
I DON'T KNOW HOW TO LOVE HIM PETULA CLARK	47	1972
I DON'T KNOW HOW TO LOVE HIM YVONNE ELLIMAN	47	1972
I DON'T KNOW IF IT'S RIGHT EVELYN 'CHAMPAGNE' KING	67	1979
I DON'T KNOW WHAT IT IS RUFUS WAINWRIGHT	74	2004
I DON'T KNOW WHAT IT IS BUT I LOVE IT CHRIS REA	65	1984
I DON'T KNOW WHAT YOU WANT BUT I CAN'T GIVE IT TO YOU PET SHOP BOYS	15	1999
I DON'T KNOW WHERE IT COMES FROM RIDE	46	1994
I DON'T KNOW WHY [A] EDEN KANE	7	1962
I DON'T KNOW WHY [B] SHAWN COLVIN	52	1993
I DON'T KNOW WHY [C] ANDY & DAVID WILLIAMS	37	1973
(I DON'T KNOW WHY) BUT I DO CLARENCE 'FROGMAN' HENRY	3	1961
I DON'T KNOW WHY (I LOVE YOU) [A] STEVIE WONDER	14	1969
I DON'T KNOW WHY I LOVE YOU [B] HOUSE OF LOVE	41	1989
I DON'T LIKE MONDAYS BOOMTOWN RATS	1	1979
I DON'T LOVE YOU MY CHEMICAL ROMANCE	13	2007
I DON'T LOVE YOU ANYMORE QUIREBOYS	24	1990
I DON'T LOVE YOU BUT I THINK I LIKE YOU GILBERT O'SULLIVAN	14	1975
I DON'T MIND BUZZCOCKS	55	1978
I DON'T MIND AT ALL BOURGEOIS TAGG	35	1988
I DON'T NEED A MAN PUSSYCAT DOLLS	7	2006
I DON'T NEED ANYTHING SANDIE SHAW	50	1967
I DON'T NEED NO DOCTOR (LIVE) W.A.S.P.	31	1987
I DON'T NEED TO TELL HER LURKERS	49	1978
I DON'T REALLY CARE K-GEE	22	2000
I DON'T REMEMBER PETER GABRIEL	62	1983
I DON'T SMOKE DJ DEE KLINE	11	2000
I DON'T THINK SO DINOSAUR Jr.	67	1995
I DON'T THINK THAT MAN SHOULD SLEEP ALONE RAY PARKER Jr.	13	1987
I DON'T WANNA BE A STAR CORONA	22	1995
I DON'T WANNA DANCE EDDY GRANT	1	1982
I DON'T WANNA FIGHT TINA TURNER	7	1993
I DON'T WANNA GET HURT DONNA SUMMER	7	1989
I DON'T WANNA GO ON WITH YOU LIKE THAT ELTON JOHN	30	1988
(I DON'T WANNA GO TO) CHELSEA ELVIS COSTELLO & THE ATTRACTIONS	16	1978
I DON'T WANNA KNOW [A] MARIO WINANS FEATURING ENYA & P DIDDY	1	2004
I DON'T WANNA KNOW [B] NEW FOUND GLORY	48	2005
I DON'T WANNA LOSE AT LOVE TANITA TIKARAM	73	1998
I DON'T WANNA LOSE YOU [A] KANDIDATE	11	1979
I DON'T WANNA LOSE YOU [B] TINA TURNER	8	1989
I DON'T WANNA PLAY HOUSE TAMMY WYNETTE	37	1976
I DON'T WANNA TAKE THIS PAIN DANNII MINOGUE	40	1992
I DON'T WANNA TO LOSE YOUR LOVE EMOTIONS	40	1977
I DON'T WANT A LOVER TEXAS	8	1989
I DON'T WANT CONTROL OF YOU TEENAGE FANCLUB	43	1997
I DON'T WANT NOBODY (TELLIN' ME WHAT TO DO) CHERIE AMORE	33	2000
I DON'T WANT OUR LOVING TO DIE HERD	5	1968
I DON'T WANT TO TONI BRAXTON	9	1997
I DON'T WANT TO BE GAVIN DEGRAW	38	2005
I DON'T WANT TO BE A FREAK (BUT I CAN'T HELP MYSELF) DYNASTY	20	1979
I DON'T WANT TO BE A HERO JOHNNY HATES JAZZ	11	1987
I DON'T WANT TO GO ON WITHOUT YOU MOODY BLUES	33	1965
I DON'T WANT TO HURT YOU (EVERY SINGLE TIME) FRANK BLACK	63	1996
I DON'T WANT TO KNOW DONNAS	55	2005
I DON'T WANT TO LOSE MY WAY DREAMCATCHER	14	2002
I DON'T WANT TO MISS A THING AEROSMITH	4	1998
I DON'T WANT TO PUT A HOLD ON YOU BERNIE FLINT	3	1977
I DON'T WANT TO TALK ABOUT IT ROD STEWART	1	1977
I DON'T WANT TO TALK ABOUT IT EVERYTHING BUT THE GIRL	3	1988
I DON'T WANT TO WAIT PAULA COLE	43	1998
I DON'T WANT YOUR LOVE DURAN DURAN	14	1988
I DREAM TILT	69	1995
I DREAMED BEVERLEY SISTERS	24	1957
I DROVE ALL NIGHT CYNDI LAUPER	7	1989
I DROVE ALL NIGHT ROY ORBISON	7	1992
I EAT CANNIBALS PART 1 TOTO COELO	8	1982
I ENJOY BEING A GIRL PAT SUZUKI	49	1960
I FEEL A CRY COMING ON HANK LOCKLIN	29	1966
I FEEL DIVINE S-J	30	1998
I FEEL FINE BEATLES	1	1964
I FEEL FINE WET WET WET	30	1990
I FEEL FOR YOU [A] CHAKA KHAN	1	1984

	Peak Position	Year of Entry
I FEEL FOR YOU [B] BOB SINCLAR	9	2000
I FEEL FREE CREAM	11	1966
I FEEL GOOD THINGS FOR YOU DADDY'S FAVOURITE	44	1998
I FEEL IT [A] MOBY	38	1993
I FEEL IT [B] LORRAINE	29	2006
I FEEL JUST LIKE A CHILD DEVENDRA BANHART	68	2005
I FEEL LIKE BUDDY HOLLY ALVIN STARDUST	7	1984
I FEEL LIKE WALKIN' IN THE RAIN MILLIE JACKSON	55	1984
I FEEL LOVE [A] DONNA SUMMER	1	1977
I FEEL LOVE [A] MESSIAH FEATURING PRECIOUS WILSON	19	1992
I FEEL LOVE [A] VANESSA-MAE	41	1997
I FEEL LOVE [B] CRW	15	2000
I FEEL LOVE COMIN' ON FELICE TAYLOR	11	1967
I FEEL LOVE COMIN' ON DANA	66	1982
I FEEL LOVE (MEDLEY) BRONSKI BEAT & MARC ALMOND	3	1985
I FEEL LOVED DEPECHE MODE	12	2001
I FEEL SO BOX CAR RACER	41	2002
I FEEL SO BAD ELVIS PRESLEY	4	1961
I FEEL SO FINE KMC FEATURING DAHNY	33	2002
I FEEL SOMETHING IN THE AIR CHER	43	1966
I FEEL STEREO DINO LENNY	60	2002
I FEEL THE EARTH MOVE MARTIKA	7	1989
I FEEL YOU [A] LOVE DECADE	34	1992
I FEEL YOU [B] DEPECHE MODE	8	1993
I FEEL YOU [C] PETER ANDRE	1	1996
I FINALLY FOUND SOMEONE BARBRA STREISAND & BRYAN ADAMS	10	1997
I FORGOT [A] COOLNOTES	63	1984
I FORGOT [B] LIONEL RICHIE	34	2001
I FOUGHT THE LAW BOBBY FULLER FOUR	33	1966
I FOUGHT THE LAW CLASH	29	1988
I FOUGHT THE LLOYDS OYSTAR	25	2008
I FOUND HEAVEN TAKE THAT	15	1992
I FOUND LOVE [A] DARLENE DAVIS	55	1987
I FOUND LOVE [B] LONE JUSTICE	45	1987
I FOUND LOVE [C] C & C MUSIC FACTORY FEATURING ZELMA DAVIS	26	1995
I FOUND LOVIN' FATBACK	7	1984
I FOUND LOVIN' STEVE WALSH	9	1987
I FOUND OUT [A] CHRISTIANS	56	1990
I FOUND OUT [B] PIGEON DETECTIVES	39	2006
I FOUND OUT THE HARD WAY FOUR PENNIES	14	1964
I FOUND SOMEONE [A] CHER	5	1987
I FOUND SOMEONE [B] BILLY & SARAH GAINES	48	1997
I FOUND SUNSHINE CHI-LITES	35	1974
I FOUND U AXWELL FEATURING MAX C	6	2007
I (FRIDAY NIGHT) DUBSTAR	37	2000
I GAVE IT UP (WHEN I FELL IN LOVE) LUTHER VANDROSS	28	1988
I GAVE MY EYES TO STEVIE WONDER MILLION DEAD	72	2004
I GAVE YOU EVERYTHING CODE RED	50	1996
I GAVE YOU MY HEART (DIDN'T I) HOT CHOCOLATE	13	1984
I GET A KICK OUT OF YOU GARY SHEARSTON	7	1974
I GET A LITTLE SENTIMENTAL OVER YOU NEW SEEKERS	5	1974
I GET ALONG PET SHOP BOYS	18	2002
I GET AROUND BEACH BOYS	7	1964
I GET LIFTED BARBARA TUCKER	33	1994
I GET LONELY JANET JACKSON	5	1998
I GET SO EXCITED EQUALS	44	1968
I GET THE SWEETEST FEELING JACKIE WILSON	3	1972
I GET THE SWEETEST FEELING LIZ McCLARNON	5	2006
I GET WEAK BELINDA CARLISLE	10	1988
I GIVE TAKE 5	70	1998
I GIVE IT ALL TO YOU MARY KIANI	35	1995
I GIVE YOU MY HEART MR PRESIDENT	52	1997
I GO APE NEIL SEDAKA	9	1959
I GO TO EXTREMES BILLY JOEL	70	1990
I GO TO PIECES (EVERYTIME) GERRI GRANGER	50	1978
I GO TO SLEEP PRETENDERS	7	1981
I GO WILD ROLLING STONES	29	1995
I GOT 5 ON IT LUNIZ	3	1996
I GOT A FEELING RICKY NELSON	27	1958
I GOT A GIRL LOU BEGA	55	1999
I GOT A LITTLE SONG OFF-SHORE	64	1991
I GOT A MAN POSITIVE K	43	1993
I GOT DA FEELIN' SWEET TEE	31	1988
I GOT IT FROM MY MAMA WILL.I.AM	38	2007
I GOT IT GOIN' ON [A] TONE LOC	55	1989
I GOT IT GOIN' ON [B] US3 FEATURING KOBIE POWELL & RAHSAAN	52	1994
I GOT MINE MOTORHEAD	46	1983
I GOT MY EDUCATION UNCANNY ALLIANCE	39	1992
I GOT RHYTHM HAPPENINGS	28	1967
I GOT SOMEBODY ELSE CHANGING FACES	42	1997
I GOT STUNG ELVIS PRESLEY	1	1959
I GOT THE MUSIC IN ME KIKI DEE BAND	19	1974
I GOT THE VIBRATION/A POSITIVE VIBRATION BLACK BOX	21	1996
I GOT THIS FEELING BABY BUMPS	22	2000
I GOT TO SING J.A.L.N. BAND	40	1977
I GOT YOU SPLIT ENZ	12	1980
I GOT YOU BABE SONNY & CHER	1	1965
I GOT YOU BABE UB40 FEATURING CHRISSIE HYNDE	1	1985
I GOT YOU BABE CHER WITH BEAVIS & BUTT-HEAD	35	1994
I GOT YOU BABE AVID MERRION/DAVINA McCALL/PATSY KENSIT	5	2005
I GOT YOU (I FEEL GOOD) JAMES BROWN & THE FAMOUS FLAMES	29	1966
I GUESS I'LL ALWAYS LOVE YOU ISLEY BROTHERS	45	1966
I GUESS THAT'S WHY THEY CALL IT THE BLUES ELTON JOHN	5	1983
I HAD TOO MUCH TO DREAM LAST NIGHT ELECTRIC PRUNES	49	1967
I HATE MYSELF FOR LOVING YOU JOAN JETT & THE BLACKHEARTS	46	1988
I HATE...PEOPLE ANTI-NOWHERE LEAGUE	46	1982
I HATE ROCK 'N' ROLL JESUS & MARY CHAIN	61	1995
I HAVE A DREAM ABBA	2	1979
I HAVE A DREAM WESTLIFE	1	1999
I HAVE FORGIVEN JESUS MORRISSEY	10	2005
I HAVE NOTHING WHITNEY HOUSTON	3	1993
I HAVE PEACE STRIKE	17	1997
I HAVEN'T STOPPED DANCING YET PAT & MICK	9	1989
I HEAR A SYMPHONY SUPREMES	39	1966
I HEAR TALK BUCKS FIZZ	34	1985
I HEAR YOU KNOCKING DAVE EDMUNDS' ROCKPILE	1	1970
I HEAR YOU NOW JON & VANGELIS	8	1980
I HEAR YOUR NAME INCOGNITO	42	1995
I HEARD A HEART BREAK LAST NIGHT JIM REEVES	38	1967
I HEARD A RUMOUR BANANARAMA	14	1987
I HEARD IT THROUGH THE GRAPEVINE GLADYS KNIGHT & THE PIPS	47	1967
I HEARD IT THROUGH THE GRAPEVINE MARVIN GAYE	1	1969
I HEARD IT THROUGH THE GRAPEVINE SLITS	60	1979
I HONESTLY LOVE YOU OLIVIA NEWTON-JOHN	22	1974
I HOPE YOU DANCE LEE ANN WOMACK	40	2001
I HOPE YOU DANCE RONAN KEATING	2	2004
I IMAGINE MARY KIANI	35	1995
I JUST CALLED TO SAY I LOVE YOU STEVIE WONDER	1	1984
I JUST CAN'T BE HAPPY TODAY DAMNED	46	1979
I JUST CAN'T (FORGIVE AND FORGET) BLUE ZOO	60	1983
I JUST CAN'T GET ENOUGH HERD & FITZ FEATURING ABIGAIL BAILEY	11	2005
I JUST CAN'T HELP BELIEVING ELVIS PRESLEY	6	1971
I JUST CAN'T STOP LOVING YOU MICHAEL JACKSON	1	1987
(I JUST) DIED IN YOUR ARMS CUTTING CREW	4	1986
I JUST DIED IN YOUR ARMS RESOURCE	42	2003
I JUST DON'T HAVE THE HEART CLIFF RICHARD	3	1989
I JUST DON'T KNOW WHAT TO DO WITH MYSELF DUSTY SPRINGFIELD	3	1964
I JUST DON'T KNOW WHAT TO DO WITH MYSELF WHITE STRIPES	13	2003
I JUST FALL IN LOVE AGAIN ANNE MURRAY	58	1979
I JUST GO FOR YOU JIMMY JONES	35	1960
I JUST HAD TO HEAR YOUR VOICE OLETA ADAMS	42	1993
I JUST KEEP THINKING ABOUT YOU BABY TATA VEGA	52	1979
I JUST NEED MYSELF OCEAN COLOUR SCENE	13	2003
(I JUST WANNA) B WITH U TRANSVISION VAMP	30	1991
I JUST WANNA BE LOVED CULTURE CLUB	31	1998
I JUST WANNA BE YOUR EVERYTHING ANDY GIBB	26	1977
I JUST WANNA KNOW TAIO CRUZ	29	2006
I JUST WANNA LIVE GOOD CHARLOTTE	9	2005
I JUST WANNA LOVE U (GIVE IT TO ME) JAY-Z	17	2000
I JUST WANNA (SPEND SOME TIME WITH YOU) ALTON EDWARDS	20	1982
I JUST WANT TO DANCE WITH YOU DANIEL O'DONNELL	20	1992
I JUST WANT TO MAKE LOVE TO YOU ETTA JAMES	5	1996
I JUST WANT TO SEE THE BOY HAPPY MORRISSEY	16	2006
I JUST WANT YOU OZZY OSBOURNE	43	1996
I KEEP FORGETTIN' MICHAEL McDONALD	43	1986
I KEEP RINGING MY BABY SOUL BROTHERS	43	1965
I KISS YOUR LIPS TOKYO GHETTO PUSSY	43	1996
I KNEW I LOVED YOU SAVAGE GARDEN	10	1999
I KNEW THE BRIDE DAVE EDMUNDS	26	1977
I KNEW YOU WERE WAITIN' FOR ME ARETHA FRANKLIN & GEORGE MICHAEL	1	1987
I KNOW [A] PERRY COMO	13	1959
I KNOW [B] PAUL KING	59	1987
I KNOW [C] BLUR	48	1990
I KNOW [D] NEW ATLANTIC	12	1992
I KNOW [E] DIONNE FARRIS	41	1995
I KNOW A PLACE [A] PETULA CLARK	17	1965
I KNOW A PLACE [B] KIM ENGLISH	52	1995
I KNOW ENOUGH (I DON'T GET ENOUGH) THEAUDIENCE	25	1998
I KNOW HIM SO WELL ELAINE PAIGE & BARBARA DICKSON	1	1985
I KNOW HIM SO WELL STEPS	5	2001
(I KNOW) I'M LOSING YOU TEMPTATIONS	19	1966
I KNOW MY LOVE CHIEFTAINS FEATURING THE CORRS	37	1999
I KNOW THE LORD TABERNACLE	55	1995
I KNOW THERE'S SOMETHING GOING ON FRIDA	43	1982
I KNOW WHAT BOYS LIKE SHAMPOO	42	1996
I KNOW WHAT I LIKE (IN YOUR WARDROBE) GENESIS	21	1974
I KNOW WHAT I'M HERE FOR JAMES	22	1999

Peak Position | Year of Entry

I KNOW WHAT YOU WANT BUSTA RHYMES & MARIAH CAREY 3 2003
I KNOW WHERE I'M GOING GEORGE HAMILTON IV 23 1958
I KNOW WHERE I'M GOING COUNTRYMEN 45 1962
I KNOW WHERE IT'S AT ALL SAINTS 4 1997
I KNOW YOU DON'T LOVE ME ROACHFORD 42 1995
I KNOW YOU GOT SOUL ERIC B & RAKIM 13 1988
I KNOW YOU'RE OUT THERE SOMEWHERE MOODY BLUES 52 1988
I LEARNED FROM THE BEST WHITNEY HOUSTON 19 1999
I LEFT MY HEART IN SAN FRANCISCO TONY BENNETT 25 1965
I LIFT MY CUP GLOWORM 20 1993
I LIKE [A] SHANICE 49 1994
I LIKE [B] KUT KLOSE 72 1995
I LIKE [C] MONTELL JORDAN FEATURING SLICK RICK 24 1996
I LIKE [D] JULIET ROBERTS 17 1999
I LIKE GIRLS HOUND DOGS 26 2006
I LIKE IT [A] GERRY & THE PACEMAKERS 1 1963
I LIKE IT [B] DJH FEATURING STEFY 16 1991
I LIKE IT [C] OVERWEIGHT POOCH FEATURING CE CE PENISTON 58 1992
I LIKE IT [D] D:REAM 26 1993
I LIKE IT [E] JOMANDA 67 1993
I LIKE IT [F] ANGEL MORAES 70 1997
I LIKE IT [G] NARCOTIC THRUST 9 2004
I LIKE LOVE (I LOVE LOVE) SOLITAIRE 57 2003
I LIKE THAT HOUSTON 11 2004
I LIKE THE WAY [A] DENI HINES 37 1997
I LIKE THE WAY [B] BODYROCKERS 3 2005
I LIKE THE WAY (THE KISSING GAME) HI-FIVE 43 1991
I LIKE THE WAY (THE KISSING GAME) KALEEF 58 1997
I LIKE TO MOVE IT REEL 2 REAL FEATURING THE MAD STUNTMAN 5 1994
I LIKE TO ROCK APRIL WINE 41 1980
I LIKE (WHAT YOU'RE DOING TO ME) YOUNG & COMPANY 20 1980
I LIKE YOUR KIND OF LOVE ANDY WILLIAMS 16 1957
I LIVE FOR SPEED STAR SPANGLES 60 2003
I LIVE FOR THE SUN VANITY FARE 20 1968
I LIVE FOR THE WEEKEND TRIUMPH 59 1980
I LIVE FOR YOUR LOVE NATALIE COLE 23 1988
I LOST MY HEART TO A STARSHIP TROOPER SARAH BRIGHTMAN & HOT GOSSIP 6 1978
I LOVE A MAN IN UNIFORM GANG OF FOUR 65 1982
I LOVE A RAINY NIGHT EDDIE RABBITT 53 1981
I LOVE AMERICA PATRICK JUVET 12 1978
I LOVE BEING IN LOVE WITH YOU ADAM FAITH & THE ROULETTES 33 1964
I LOVE CHRISTMAS FAST FOOD ROCKERS 25 2003
I LOVE FOOTBALL WES 75 1998
I LOVE HER PAUL & BARRY RYAN 17 1966
I LOVE HOW YOU LOVE ME JIMMY CRAWFORD 18 1961
I LOVE HOW YOU LOVE ME MAUREEN EVANS 34 1964
I LOVE HOW YOU LOVE ME PAUL & BARRY RYAN 21 1966
I LOVE I HATE NEIL ARTHUR 50 1994
I LOVE IT WHEN WE DO RONAN KEATING 5 2002
I LOVE LAKE TAHOE A 59 1999
I LOVE MEN EARTHA KITT 50 1984
I LOVE MUSIC [A] O'JAYS 13 1976
I LOVE MUSIC [B] ENIGMA 25 1981
I LOVE MUSIC [A] ROZALLA 18 1994
I LOVE MY CHICK BUSTA RHYMES 8 2006
I LOVE MY DOG CAT STEVENS 28 1966
I LOVE MY RADIO (MY DEE JAY'S RADIO) TAFFY 6 1987
I LOVE ROCK 'N' ROLL JOAN JETT & THE BLACKHEARTS 4 1982
I LOVE ROCK 'N' ROLL BRITNEY SPEARS 13 2002
I LOVE SATURDAY ERASURE 20 1994
I LOVE THE NIGHTLIFE (DISCO ROUND) ALICIA BRIDGES 32 1978
I LOVE THE SOUND OF BREAKING GLASS NICK LOWE 7 1978
I LOVE THE WAY YOU LOVE MARV JOHNSON 35 1960
I LOVE THE WAY YOU LOVE ME BOYZONE 2 1998
I LOVE TO BOOGIE T REX 13 1976
I LOVE TO LOVE (BUT MY BABY LOVES TO DANCE) TINA CHARLES 1 1976
I LOVE YOU [A] CLIFF RICHARD & THE SHADOWS 1 1960
I LOVE YOU [B] DONNA SUMMER 10 1977
I LOVE YOU [C] YELLO 41 1983
I LOVE YOU [D] VANILLA ICE 45 1991
I LOVE YOU [E] FLESH & BONES 70 2002
I LOVE YOU ALWAYS FOREVER DONNA LEWIS 5 1996
I LOVE YOU BABY PAUL ANKA 3 1957
I LOVE YOU BABY FREDDIE & THE DREAMERS 16 1964
I LOVE YOU BECAUSE AL MARTINO 48 1963
I LOVE YOU BECAUSE JIM REEVES 5 1964
I LOVE YOU BUT RESEARCH 63 2005
I LOVE YOU 'CAUSE I HAVE TO DOGS DIE IN HOT CARS 32 2004
I LOVE YOU GOODBYE THOMAS DOLBY 36 1992
I LOVE YOU LOVE ME LOVE GARY GLITTER 1 1973
I LOVE YOU MORE THAN ROCK N ROLL THUNDER 27 2004
I LOVE YOU SO MUCH IT HURTS CHARLIE GRACIE 14 1957
(I LOVE YOU) WHEN YOU SLEEP TRACIE 59 1984
I LOVE YOU, YES I DO MERSEYBEATS 22 1965
I LOVE YOU, YES I LOVE YOU EDDY GRANT 37 1981
I LOVE YOUR SMILE SHANICE 2 1991
I LOVE YOU...STOP! RED 5 11 1997
I LUV U [A] SHUT UP & DANCE FEATURING RICHIE DAVIS & PROFESSOR T 68 1995
I LUV U [B] DIZZEE RASCAL 29 2003
I LUV U [C] ORDINARY BOYS 7 2007
I LUV U BABY ORIGINAL 2 1995
I MADE IT THROUGH THE RAIN BARRY MANILOW 37 1981
I MAY NEVER PASS THIS WAY AGAIN PERRY COMO 15 1958
I MAY NEVER PASS THIS WAY AGAIN ROBERT EARL 14 1958
I MAY NEVER PASS THIS WAY AGAIN RONNIE HILTON WITH THE MICHAEL SAMMES SINGERS 27 1958
I MET A GIRL SHADOWS 22 1966
I MIGHT SHAKIN' STEVENS 18 1990
I MIGHT BE CRYING TANITA TIKARAM 64 1995
I MIGHT BE LYING EDDIE & THE HOT RODS 44 1977
I MISS YOU [A] HADDAWAY 9 1993
I MISS YOU [B] 4 OF US 62 1993
I MISS YOU [C] BJORK 36 1997
I MISS YOU [D] DARREN HAYES 20 2002
I MISS YOU [E] BLINK 182 8 2004
I MISS YOU BABY MARV JOHNSON 25 1969
I MISSED AGAIN PHIL COLLINS 14 1981
I MISSED THE BUS KRIS KROSS 57 1992
I MUST BE IN LOVE RUTLES 39 1978
I MUST BE SEEING THINGS GENE PITNEY 6 1965
I MUST STAND ICE-T 23 1996
I NEED MEREDITH BROOKS 28 1997
I NEED A GIRL GROUNDED 43 2005
I NEED A GIRL (PART ONE) P DIDDY FEATURING USHER & LOON 4 2002
I NEED A MAN [A] MAN TO MAN 43 1987
I NEED A MAN [B] EURYTHMICS 26 1988
I NEED A MAN [C] LI KWAN 51 1994
I NEED A MIRACLE [A] COCO 39 1997
I NEED A MIRACLE [B] CASCADA 8 2007
I NEED ANOTHER (EP) DODGY 67 1993
I NEED DIRECTION TEENAGE FANCLUB 48 2000
I NEED IT JOHNNY 'GUITAR' WATSON 35 1976
I NEED LOVE [A] LL COOL J 8 1987
I NEED LOVE [B] OLIVIA NEWTON-JOHN 75 1992
I NEED SOME FINE WINE AND YOU, YOU NEED TO BE NICER CARDIGANS 59 2005
I NEED SOMEBODY LOVELAND FEATURING RACHEL McFARLANE 21 1995
I NEED THE KEY MINIMAL CHIC FEATURING MATT GOSS 54 2004
I NEED TO BE IN LOVE CARPENTERS 36 1976
I NEED TO KNOW MARC ANTHONY 28 1999
I NEED YOU [A] JOE DOLAN 43 1977
I NEED YOU [B] POINTER SISTERS 25 1984
I NEED YOU [C] B.V.S.M.P. 3 1988
I NEED YOU [D] DEUCE 10 1995
I NEED YOU [E] NIKITA WARREN 48 1996
I NEED YOU [F] 3T 3 1996
I NEED YOU [G] WIRELESS 68 1997
I NEED YOU [H] LEANN RIMES 13 2001
I NEED YOU [I] DAVE GAHAN 27 2003
I NEED YOU [J] STANDS 39 2003
I NEED YOU NOW [A] EDDIE FISHER 13 1954
I NEED YOU NOW [B] SINNAMON 70 1996
I NEED YOU TONIGHT JUNIOR M.A.F.I.A. FEATURING AALIYAH 66 1996
I NEED YOUR LOVE TONIGHT ELVIS PRESLEY 1 1959
I NEED YOUR LOVIN' [A] TEENA MARIE 28 1980
I NEED YOUR LOVIN' [A] CURIOSITY 47 1992
I NEED YOUR LOVIN' [B] ALYSON WILLIAMS 8 1989
I NEED YOUR LOVIN' (LIKE THE SUNSHINE) MARC ET CLAUDE 12 2000
I NEED YOUR LOVING HUMAN LEAGUE 72 1986
I NEVER FELT LIKE THIS BEFORE MICA PARIS 15 1993
I NEVER GO OUT IN THE RAIN HIGH SOCIETY 53 1980
I NEVER KNEW ROGER SANCHEZ 24 2000
I NEVER LOVED YOU ANYWAY CORRS 43 1997
I NEVER WANT AN EASY LIFE IF ME AND HE WERE EVER TO GET THERE CHARLATANS 38 1994
I ONLY HAVE EYES FOR YOU ART GARFUNKEL 1 1975
I ONLY LIVE TO LOVE YOU CILLA BLACK 26 1967
I ONLY WANNA BE WITH YOU [A] BAY CITY ROLLERS 4 1976
I ONLY WANNA BE WITH YOU [A] SAMANTHA FOX 16 1989
I ONLY WANT TO BE WITH YOU [A] DUSTY SPRINGFIELD 4 1963
I ONLY WANT TO BE WITH YOU [A] TOURISTS 4 1979
I ONLY WANT TO BE WITH YOU [B] BARRY WHITE 36 1995
I OWE YOU NOTHING BROS 1 1988
I OWE YOU ONE SHALAMAR 13 1980
I PREDICT A RIOT KAISER CHIEFS 9 2004
I PRETEND DES O'CONNOR 1 1968
I PROMISE STACIE ORRICO 22 2004
I PROMISE YOU (GET READY) SAMANTHA FOX 58 1987
I PROMISED MYSELF NICK KAMEN 50 1990
I PRONOUNCE YOU THE MADNESS 44 1988
I PUT A SPELL ON YOU NINA SIMONE 28 1965
I PUT A SPELL ON YOU ALAN PRICE SET 9 1966
I PUT A SPELL ON YOU BRYAN FERRY 18 1993
I PUT A SPELL ON YOU SONIQUE 8 1998
I QUIT [A] BROS 4 1988
I QUIT [B] HEPBURN 8 1999
I RAN A FLOCK OF SEAGULLS 43 1982
I REALLY DIDN'T MEAN IT LUTHER VANDROSS 16 1987
I RECALL A GYPSY WOMAN DON WILLIAMS 13 1976
I REFUSE HUE & CRY 47 1988
I REFUSE (WHAT YOU WANT) SOMORE FEATURING DAMON TRUEITT 21 1998

	Peak Position	Year of Entry
I REMEMBER COOLIO	73	1994
I REMEMBER ELVIS PRESLEY (THE KING IS DEAD) DANNY MIRROR	4	1977
I REMEMBER YESTERDAY DONNA SUMMER	14	1977
I REMEMBER YOU [A] FRANK IFIELD	1	1962
I REMEMBER YOU [B] SKID ROW	36	1990
I ROCK TOM NOVY	55	2000
I SAID I LOVE YOU RAUL MALO	57	2002
I SAID NEVER AGAIN (BUT HERE WE ARE) RACHEL STEVENS	12	2005
I SAID PIG ON FRIDAY EASTERN LANE	65	2004
I SAVED THE WORLD TODAY EURYTHMICS	11	1999
I SAW HER AGAIN MAMAS & THE PAPAS	11	1966
I SAW HER STANDING THERE ELTON JOHN BAND FEATURING JOHN LENNON & THE MUSCLE SHOALS HORNS	40	1981
I SAW HIM STANDING THERE TIFFANY	8	1988
I SAW LINDA YESTERDAY DOUG SHELDON	36	1963
I SAW MOMMY KISSING SANTA CLAUS BEVERLEY SISTERS	6	1953
I SAW MOMMY KISSING SANTA CLAUS BILLY COTTON & HIS BAND, VOCALS BY THE MILL GIRLS & THE BANDITS	11	1953
I SAW MOMMY KISSING SANTA CLAUS JIMMY BOYD	3	1953
I SAW THE LIGHT [A] TODD RUNDGREN	36	1973
I SAW THE LIGHT [B] THE THE	31	1995
I SAY A LITTLE PRAYER DIANA KING	17	1997
I SAY A LITTLE PRAYER FOR YOU ARETHA FRANKLIN	4	1968
I SAY NOTHING VOICE OF THE BEEHIVE	22	1987
I SAY YEAH SECCHI FEATURING ORLANDO JOHNSON	46	1991
I SCARE MYSELF THOMAS DOLBY	46	1984
I SECOND THAT EMOTION SMOKEY ROBINSON & THE MIRACLES	27	1968
I SECOND THAT EMOTION DIANA ROSS & THE SUPREMES & THE TEMPTATIONS	18	1969
I SECOND THAT EMOTION JAPAN	9	1982
I SECOND THAT EMOTION ALYSON WILLIAMS WITH CHUCK STANLEY	44	1989
I SEE A STAR MOUTH & MACNEAL	8	1974
I SEE GIRLS (CRAZY) STUDIO B/ROMEO & HARRY BROOKS	12	2003
I SEE ONLY YOU NOOTROPIC	42	1996
I SEE THE MOON STARGAZERS	1	1954
I SEE YOU BABY GROOVE ARMADA FEATURING GRAM'MA FUNK	11	1999
I SEE YOU YOU SEE ME MAGIC NUMBERS	20	2006
I SEE YOUR SMILE GLORIA ESTEFAN	48	1993
I SEEN A MAN DIE SCARFACE	55	1995
I SHALL BE RELEASED TREMELOES	29	1968
I SHALL BE THERE B*WITCHED FEATURING LADYSMITH BLACK MAMBAZO	13	1999
I SHALL OVERCOME HARD-FI	36	2008
I SHOT THE SHERIFF ERIC CLAPTON	9	1974
I SHOT THE SHERIFF LIGHT OF THE WORLD	40	1981
I SHOT THE SHERIFF WARREN G	2	1997
I SHOT THE SHERIFF BOB MARLEY & THE WAILERS	67	2005
I SHOULD BE SO LUCKY KYLIE MINOGUE	1	1988
I SHOULD CARE FRANK IFIELD	33	1964
I SHOULD HAVE CHEATED KEYSHIA COLE	48	2006
I SHOULD HAVE KNOWN BETTER [A] NATURALS	24	1964
I SHOULD HAVE KNOWN BETTER [B] JIM DIAMOND	1	1984
I SHOULDA LOVED YA NARADA MICHAEL WALDEN	8	1980
I SHOULD'VE KNOWN AIMEE MANN	45	1993
I SINGS MARY MARY	32	2000
I SLEEP ALONE AT NIGHT JIM DIAMOND	72	1985
I SPEAKA DA LINGO BLACK LACE	49	1985
I SPECIALIZE IN LOVE SHARON BROWN	38	1982
I SPECIALIZE IN LOVE ARIZONA FEATURING ZEITIA	74	1994
I SPY GET CAPE WEAR CAPE FLY	37	2007
I SPY FOR THE FBI JAMO THOMAS	44	1969
I SPY FOR THE FBI UNTOUCHABLES	59	1985
I STAND ACCUSED MERSEYBEATS	38	1966
I STAND ALONE E-MOTION	60	1996
I STARTED A JOKE FAITH NO MORE	49	1998
I STARTED SOMETHING I COULDN'T FINISH SMITHS	23	1987
I STILL BELIEVE [A] RONNIE HILTON	3	1954
I STILL BELIEVE [B] MARIAH CAREY	16	1999
I STILL BELIEVE IN YOU CLIFF RICHARD	7	1992
I STILL HAVEN'T FOUND WHAT I'M LOOKING FOR U2	6	1987
I STILL LOVE YOU ALL KENNY BALL & HIS JAZZMEN	24	1961
I STILL REMEMBER GARY NUMAN	74	1986
I STILL REMEMBER BLOC PARTY	20	2007
I STILL THINK ABOUT YOU DANGER DANGER	46	1992
I STILL THINK OF YOU UTAH SAINTS	32	1994
I SURRENDER [A] RAINBOW	3	1981
I SURRENDER [B] ROSIE GAINES	39	1997
I SURRENDER [C] DAVID SYLVIAN	40	1999
I SURRENDER (TO THE SPIRIT OF THE NIGHT) SAMANTHA FOX	25	1987
I SURRENDER TO YOUR LOVE BY ALL MEANS	65	1988
I SWEAR ALL-4-ONE	2	1994
I TALK TO THE TREES CLINT EASTWOOD	18	1970
I TALK TO THE WIND OPUS III	52	1992
I THANK YOU [A] SAM & DAVE	34	1968
I THANK YOU [B] ADEVA	17	1989
I THINK I LOVE YOU PARTRIDGE FAMILY STARRING SHIRLEY JONES FEATURING DAVID CASSIDY	18	1971
I THINK I LOVE YOU VOICE OF THE BEEHIVE	25	1991
I THINK I LOVE YOU KACI	10	2002
I THINK I WANT TO DANCE WITH YOU RUMPLE-STILTS-SKIN	51	1983
I THINK I'M IN LOVE SPIRITUALIZED	27	1998
I THINK I'M IN LOVE WITH YOU JESSICA SIMPSON	15	2000
I THINK I'M PARANOID GARBAGE	9	1998
I THINK IT'S GOING TO RAIN UB40	6	1980
I THINK OF YOU [A] MERSEYBEATS	5	1964
I THINK OF YOU [B] PERRY COMO	14	1971
I THINK OF YOU [C] DETROIT EMERALDS	27	1973
I THINK OF YOU [D] BRYAN POWELL	61	1993
I THINK THEY LIKE ME DEM FRANCHIZE BOYZ	66	2006
I THINK WE'RE ALONE NOW TIFFANY	1	1988
I THINK WE'RE ALONE NOW PASCAL FEATURING KAREN PARRY	23	2002
I THINK WE'RE ALONE NOW GIRLS ALOUD	4	2006
I THOUGHT I MEANT THE WORLD TO YOU ALYSHA WARREN	40	1995
I THOUGHT IT TOOK A LITTLE TIME DIANA ROSS	32	1976
I THOUGHT IT WAS OVER THE FEELING	9	2008
I THOUGHT IT WAS YOU [A] HERBIE HANCOCK	15	1978
I THOUGHT IT WAS YOU [A] SEX-O-SONIQUE	32	1997
I THOUGHT IT WAS YOU [B] JULIA FORDHAM	45	1991
I THREW IT ALL AWAY BOB DYLAN	30	1969
I TOLD YOU SO [A] JIMMY JONES	33	1961
I TOLD YOU SO [B] OCEAN COLOUR SCENE	34	2007
I TOUCH MYSELF DIVINYLS	10	1991
I TOUCH MYSELF FHM HIGH STREET HONEYS	34	2007
I TRIED BONE THUGS-N-HARMONY FEATURING AKON	69	2007
I TRY [A] MACY GRAY	6	1999
I TRY [B] TALIB KWELI FEATURING MARY J BLIGE	59	2004
I TURN TO YOU [A] CHRISTINA AGUILERA	19	2000
I TURN TO YOU [B] MELANIE C	1	2000
I UNDERSTAND G-CLEFS	17	1961
I UNDERSTAND FREDDIE & THE DREAMERS	5	1964
I UNDERSTAND IT IDLEWILD	32	2005
I WALK THE EARTH VOICE OF THE BEEHIVE	42	1988
I WANNA BE A FLINTSTONE SCREAMING BLUE MESSIAHS	28	1988
I WANNA BE A HIPPY TECHNOHEAD	6	1996
I WANNA BE A WINNER BROWN SAUCE	15	1981
I WANNA BE ADORED STONE ROSES	20	1991
I WANNA BE DOWN BRANDY	36	1994
I WANNA BE FREE MINTY	67	1999
I WANNA BE FREE (TO BE WITH HIM) SCARLET	21	1995
I WANNA BE IN LOVE AGAIN BEIJING SPRING	43	1993
I WANNA BE LOVED [A] RICKY NELSON	30	1960
I WANNA BE LOVED [B] ELVIS COSTELLO	25	1984
I WANNA BE THE ONLY ONE ETERNAL FEATURING BEBE WINANS	1	1997
I WANNA BE U CHOCOLATE PUMA	6	2001
I WANNA BE WITH YOU MANDY MOORE	21	2000
I WANNA BE WITH YOU [A] COFFEE	57	1980
I WANNA BE WITH YOU [B] MAZE FEATURING FRANKIE BEVERLY	55	1986
I WANNA BE YOUR LADY HINDA HICKS	14	1998
I WANNA BE YOUR LOVER PRINCE	41	1980
I WANNA BE YOUR MAN [A] ROLLING STONES	12	1963
I WANNA BE YOUR MAN [A] REZILLOS	71	1979
I WANNA BE YOUR MAN [B] CHAKA DEMUS & PLIERS	19	1994
I WANNA DANCE WIT CHOO DISCO TEX & THE SEX-O-LETTES FEATURING SIR MONTI ROCK III	6	1975
I WANNA DANCE WITH SOMEBODY FLIP & FILL	13	2002
I WANNA DANCE WITH SOMEBODY (WHO LOVES ME) WHITNEY HOUSTON	1	1987
I WANNA DO IT WITH YOU BARRY MANILOW	8	1982
I WANNA GET NEXT TO YOU ROSE ROYCE	14	1977
(I WANNA GIVE YOU) DEVOTION NOMAD FEATURING MC MIKEE FREEDOM	2	1991
I WANNA GO BACK NEW SEEKERS	25	1977
I WANNA GO HOME LONNIE DONEGAN	5	1960
I WANNA GO WHERE THE PEOPLE GO WILDHEARTS	16	1995
I WANNA HAVE SOME FUN SAMANTHA FOX	63	1989
I WANNA HAVE YOUR BABIES NATASHA BEDINGFIELD	7	2007
I WANNA HOLD ON TO YOU MICA PARIS	27	1993
I WANNA HOLD YOU McFLY	3	2005
I WANNA HOLD YOUR HAND DOLLAR	9	1979
I WANNA KNOW [A] STACCATO	65	1996
I WANNA KNOW [B] JOE	37	2001
I WANNA KNOW [C] BLUESKINS	56	2004
(I WANNA KNOW) WHY SINCLAIR	58	1994
(I WANNA) LOVE MY LIFE AWAY GENE PITNEY	26	1961
I WANNA LOVE YOU AKON FEATURING SNOOP DOGGY DOGG	3	2007
I WANNA LOVE YOU [A] JADE	13	1993
I WANNA LOVE YOU [B] SOLID HARMONIE	20	1998
I WANNA LOVE YOU FOREVER JESSICA SIMPSON	7	2000
I WANNA MAKE YOU FEEL GOOD SYSTEM	73	1984
I WANNA 1-2-1 WITH YOU SOLID GOLD CHARTBUSTERS	62	1999
I WANNA SEX YOU UP COLOR ME BADD	1	1991
I WANNA SING SABRINA JOHNSTON	46	1992
I WANNA STAY HERE MIKI & GRIFF	23	1963
I WANNA STAY HOME JELLYFISH	59	1991
I WANNA STAY WITH YOU GALLAGHER & LYLE	6	1976
I WANNA STAY WITH YOU UNDERCOVER	28	1993

	Peak Position	Year of Entry
I WANNA THANK YOU ANGIE STONE FEATURING SNOOP DOGG	31	2004
I WANT AN ALIEN FOR CHRISTMAS FOUNTAINS OF WAYNE	36	1997
I WANT CANDY BRIAN POOLE & THE TREMELOES	25	1965
I WANT CANDY BOW WOW WOW	9	1982
I WANT CANDY CANDY GIRLS FEATURING VALERIE MALCOLM	30	1996
I WANT CANDY AARON CARTER	31	2000
I WANT CANDY MELANIE C	24	2007
I WANT HER KEITH SWEAT	26	1988
I WANT IT ALL QUEEN	3	1989
I WANT IT THAT WAY BACKSTREET BOYS	1	1999
I WANT LOVE ELTON JOHN	9	2001
I WANT MORE [A] CAN	26	1976
I WANT MORE [B] FAITHLESS	22	2004
I WANT OUT HELLOWEEN	69	1988
I WANT OUT (I CAN'T BELIEVE) HARRY CHOO CHOO ROMERO	51	2001
I WANT THAT MAN DEBORAH HARRY	13	1989
I WANT THE WORLD 2WO THIRD3	20	1994
I WANT TO BE ALONE 2WO THIRD3	29	1994
(I WANT TO BE) ELECTED MR BEAN & SMEAR CAMPAIGN FEATURING BRUCE DICKINSON	9	1992
I WANT TO BE FREE TOYAH	8	1981
I WANT TO BE STRAIGHT IAN DURY & THE BLOCKHEADS	22	1980
I WANT TO BE THERE WHEN YOU COME ECHO & THE BUNNYMEN	30	1997
I WANT TO BE WANTED BRENDA LEE	31	1960
I WANT TO BE YOUR MAN ROGER	61	1987
I WANT TO BE YOUR PROPERTY BLUE MERCEDES	23	1987
I WANT TO BREAK FREE QUEEN	3	1984
I WANT TO GIVE PERRY COMO	31	1974
I WANT TO GO WITH YOU EDDY ARNOLD	46	1966
I WANT TO HEAR IT FROM YOU GO WEST	43	1987
I WANT TO HOLD YOUR HAND BEATLES	1	1963
(I WANT TO) KILL SOMEBODY S*M*A*S*H	26	1994
I WANT TO KNOW WHAT LOVE IS FOREIGNER	1	1984
I WANT TO KNOW WHAT LOVE IS TERRI SYMON	54	1995
I WANT TO LIVE GRACE	30	1995
I WANT TO STAY HERE STEVE (Lawrence) & EYDIE (Gorme)	3	1963
I WANT TO THANK YOU ROBIN S	48	1994
I WANT TO TOUCH YOU CATHERINE WHEEL	35	1992
I WANT TO WAKE UP WITH YOU BORIS GARDINER	1	1986
I WANT TO WALK YOU HOME FATS DOMINO	14	1959
I WANT U ROSIE GAINES	70	1995
I WANT YOU [A] BOB DYLAN	16	1966
I WANT YOU [A] SOPHIE B. HAWKINS	49	1993
I WANT YOU [B] GARY LOW	52	1983
I WANT YOU [C] UTAH SAINTS	25	1993
I WANT YOU [D] JULIET ROBERTS	28	1994
I WANT YOU [E] SECRET LIFE	70	1994
I WANT YOU [F] SALAD	60	1996
I WANT YOU [G] INSPIRAL CARPETS FEATURING MARK E SMITH	18	1994
I WANT YOU [H] SAVAGE GARDEN	11	1997
I WANT YOU [I] Z2 VOCAL BY ALISON RIVERS	61	2000
I WANT YOU [J] CZR FEATURING DELANO	57	2000
I WANT YOU [K] JANET JACKSON	14	2004
I WANT YOU (ALL TONIGHT) CURTIS HAIRSTON	44	1983
I WANT YOU BACK [A] JACKSON 5	2	1970
I WANT YOU BACK [A] CLEOPATRA	4	1998
I WANT YOU BACK [B] BANANARAMA	5	1988
I WANT YOU BACK [C] MELANIE B FEATURING MISSY 'MISDEMEANOR' ELLIOTT	1	1998
I WANT YOU BACK [D] N SYNC	5	1997
I WANT YOU BACK [E] X-PRESS 2	50	2002
I WANT YOU FOR MYSELF ANOTHER LEVEL/ GHOSTFACE KILLAH	2	1999
I WANT YOU (FOREVER) DJ CARL COX	23	1991
I WANT YOU I NEED YOU I LOVE YOU ELVIS PRESLEY	14	1956
I WANT YOU NEAR ME TINA TURNER	22	1992
I WANT YOU SO HARD (BOY'S BAD NEWS) EAGLES OF DEATH METAL	73	2006
I WANT YOU TO BE MY BABY BILLIE DAVIS	33	1968
I WANT YOU TO STAY MAXIMO PARK	21	2006
I WANT YOU TO WANT ME [A] CHEAP TRICK	29	1979
I WANT YOU TO WANT ME [B] SOLID HARMONIE	16	1998
I WANT YOUR LOVE [A] CHIC	4	1979
I WANT YOUR LOVE [A] ROGER SANCHEZ PRESENTS TWILIGHT	31	1999
I WANT YOUR LOVE [B] TRANSVISION VAMP	5	1988
I WANT YOUR LOVE [C] ATOMIC KITTEN	10	2000
I WANT YOUR LOVIN' (JUST A LITTLE BIT) CURTIS HAIRSTON	13	1985
I WANT YOUR SEX GEORGE MICHAEL	3	1987
I WANT YOUR SOUL ARMAND VAN HELDEN	19	2007
I WAS A KING EDDIE MURPHY FEATURING SHABBA RANKS	64	1993
I WAS BORN ON CHRISTMAS DAY SAINT ETIENNE CO STARRING TIM BURGESS	37	1993
I WAS BORN TO BE ME TOM JONES	61	1988
I WAS BORN TO LOVE YOU FREDDIE MERCURY	11	1985
I WAS BROUGHT TO MY SENSES STING	31	1996
I WAS KAISER BILL'S BATMAN WHISTLING JACK SMITH	5	1967
I WAS MADE FOR DANCIN' LEIF GARRETT	4	1979
I WAS MADE FOR LOVIN' YOU KISS	50	1979
I WAS MADE TO LOVE HER STEVIE WONDER	5	1967
I WAS MADE TO LOVE YOU LORRAINE CATO	41	1996
I WAS ONLY JOKING ROD STEWART	5	1978
I WAS RIGHT AND YOU WERE WRONG DEACON BLUE	32	1994
I WAS THE ONE ELVIS PRESLEY	45	1996
I WAS TIRED OF BEING ALONE PATRICE RUSHEN	39	1982
I WASN'T BUILT TO GET UP SUPERNATURALS	25	1998
I WEAR MY SKIN ONE MINUTE SILENCE	44	2003
I (WHO HAVE NOTHING) SHIRLEY BASSEY	6	1963
I (WHO HAVE NOTHING) TOM JONES	16	1970
I (WHO HAVE NOTHING) SYLVESTER	46	1979
I WILL BILLY FURY	14	1964
I WILL RUBY WINTERS	4	1977
I WILL ALWAYS LOVE YOU WHITNEY HOUSTON	1	1992
I WILL ALWAYS LOVE YOU SARAH WASHINGTON	12	1993
I WILL ALWAYS LOVE YOU RIK WALLER	6	2002
I WILL BE RELEASED UP YER RONSON FEATURING MARY PEARCE	32	1997
I WILL BE WITH YOU T'PAU	14	1988
I WILL BE YOUR GIRLFRIEND DUBSTAR	28	1998
I WILL COME TO YOU HANSON	5	1997
I WILL DRINK THE WINE FRANK SINATRA	16	1971
I WILL FOLLOW UNO MAS	55	2002
I WILL FOLLOW YOU INTO THE DARK DEATH CAB FOR CUTIE	66	2006
I WILL GO WITH YOU (CON TE PARTIRO) DONNA SUMMER	44	1999
I WILL LOVE AGAIN LARA FABIAN	63	2000
I WILL LOVE YOU ALL MY LIFE FOSTER & ALLEN	49	1983
I WILL LOVE YOU (EV'RY TIME WHEN WE ARE GONE) FUREYS	54	1982
I WILL REMEMBER TOTO	64	1995
I WILL RETURN SPRINGWATER	5	1971
I WILL SURVIVE [A] ARRIVAL	16	1970
I WILL SURVIVE [B] BILLIE JO SPEARS	47	1979
I WILL SURVIVE [B] GLORIA GAYNOR	1	1979
I WILL SURVIVE [B] CHANTAY SAVAGE	12	1996
I WILL SURVIVE [B] DIANA ROSS	14	1996
I WILL SURVIVE [B] CAKE	29	1997
I WILL WAIT HOOTIE & THE BLOWFISH	57	1998
I WILL WAIT FOR YOU TINY DANCERS	36	2007
I WISH [A] STEVIE WONDER	5	1976
I WISH [B] GABRIELLE	26	1993
I WISH [C] SKEE-LO	15	1995
I WISH [D] R KELLY	12	2000
I WISH HE DIDN'T TRUST ME SO MUCH BOBBY WOMACK	64	1985
I WISH I COULD SHIMMY LIKE MY SISTER KATE OLYMPICS	40	1961
I WISH I KNEW HOW IT WOULD FEEL SHARLENE HECTOR	28	2004
(I WISH I KNEW HOW IT WOULD FEEL TO BE) FREE/ONE LIGHTHOUSE FAMILY	6	2001
I WISH I WAS A GIRL VIOLENT DELIGHT	25	2003
I WISH I WAS A PUNK ROCKER SANDI THOM	1	2005
I WISH I WAS YOU NEW RHODES	63	2004
I WISH IT COULD BE A WOMBLING CHRISTMAS WOMBLES FEATURING ROY WOOD	22	2000
I WISH IT COULD BE CHRISTMAS EVERY DAY WIZZARD	4	1973
I WISH IT COULD BE CHRISTMAS EVERYDAY ROY WOOD BIG BAND	59	1995
I WISH IT WASN'T TRUE SUPATONIC	69	2004
I WISH IT WOULD RAIN TEMPTATIONS	45	1968
I WISH IT WOULD RAIN FACES	8	1973
I WISH IT WOULD RAIN DOWN PHIL COLLINS	7	1990
I WISH U HEAVEN PRINCE	24	1988
I WISH YOU LOVE PAUL YOUNG	33	1997
I WISH YOU WOULD JOCELYN BROWN	51	1984
I WONDER [A] DICKIE VALENTINE	4	1955
I WONDER [A] JANE FROMAN	14	1955
I WONDER [B] BRENDA LEE	14	1963
I WONDER [C] CRYSTALS	36	1964
I WONDER HOW SHINING	58	2002
I WONDER IF HEAVEN GOT A GHETTO 2PAC	21	1998
I WONDER IF I TAKE YOU HOME LISA LISA & CULT JAM WITH FULL FORCE	12	1985
I WONDER WHO'S KISSING HER NOW EMILE FORD	43	1962
I WONDER WHY [A] SHOWADDYWADDY	2	1978
I WONDER WHY [B] CURTIS STIGERS	5	1992
I WONDER WHY HE'S THE GREATEST DJ TONY TOUCH FEATURING TOTAL	68	2000
I WON'T BACK DOWN TOM PETTY	28	1989
I WON'T BLEED FOR YOU CLIMIE FISHER	35	1988
I WON'T CHANGE YOU SOPHIE ELLIS-BEXTOR	9	2004
I WON'T CLOSE MY EYES UB40	32	1982
I WON'T COME IN WHILE HE'S THERE JIM REEVES	12	1967
I WON'T CRY GLEN GOLDSMITH	34	1987
I WON'T FEEL BAD SIMPLY RED	68	1988
I WON'T FORGET YOU JIM REEVES	3	1964
I WON'T HOLD YOU BACK TOTO	37	1983
I WON'T LAST A DAY WITHOUT YOU CARPENTERS	9	1972
I WON'T LET THE SUN GO DOWN ON ME NIK KERSHAW	2	1983
I WON'T LET YOU DOWN PhD	3	1982
I WON'T LET YOU DOWN W.I.P. FEATURING EMMIE	53	2002
I WON'T MENTION IT AGAIN RUBY WINTERS	45	1978
I WON'T RUN AWAY ALVIN STARDUST	7	1984
I WOULD DIE 4 U PRINCE & THE REVOLUTION	58	1984

	Peak Position	Year of Entry
I WOULD DIE 4 U SPACE COWBOY	55	2002
I WOULD DO FOR YOU UB40	45	1989
I WOULD FIX YOU KENICKIE	36	1998
I WOULD NEVER BLUE NILE	52	2004
I WOULDN'T BELIEVE YOUR RADIO STEREOPHONICS	11	1999
I WOULDN'T LIE YARBOROUGH & PEOPLES	61	1986
I WOULDN'T NORMALLY DO THIS KIND OF THING PET SHOP BOYS	13	1993
I WOULDN'T TRADE YOU FOR THE WORLD BACHELORS	4	1964
I WOULDN'T WANNA HAPPEN TO YOU EMBRACE	23	2000
I WRITE SINS NOT TRAGEDIES PANIC! AT THE DISCO	25	2006
I WRITE THE SONGS DAVID CASSIDY	11	1975
I WROTE YOU A SONG MISTY OLDLAND	73	1994
IBIZA MAXIMA FEATURING LILY	55	1993
ICE BOX OMARION	14	2007
ICE CREAM NEW YOUNG PONY CLUB	40	2007
ICE CREAM GUERILLA WOLFMAN	60	2005
THE ICE CREAM MAN TORNADOS	18	1963
ICE HOCKEY HAIR SUPER FURRY ANIMALS	12	1998
ICE ICE BABY VANILLA ICE	1	1990
ICE IN THE SUN STATUS QUO	8	1968
ICE RAIN ALEX WHITCOMBE & BIG C	44	1998
ICEBLINK LUCK COCTEAU TWINS	38	1990
ICH BIN EIN AUSLANDER POP WILL EAT ITSELF	28	1994
ICH WILL RAMMSTEIN	30	2002
ICING ON THE CAKE STEPHEN 'TIN TIN' DUFFY	14	1985
ICKY THUMP WHITE STRIPES	2	2007
I'D BE SURPRISINGLY GOOD FOR YOU LINDA LEWIS	40	1979
I'D DIE WITHOUT YOU PM DAWN	30	1992
I'D DO ANYTHING MIKE PRESTON	23	1960
I'D DO ANYTHING FOR LOVE (BUT I WON'T DO THAT) MEAT LOAF	1	1993
I'D LIE FOR YOU (AND THAT'S THE TRUTH) MEAT LOAF	2	1995
I'D LIKE TO TEACH THE WORLD TO SING NO WAY SIS	27	1996
I'D LIKE TO TEACH THE WORLD TO SING DEMI HOLBORN	27	2002
I'D LIKE TO TEACH THE WORLD TO SING (IN PERFECT HARMONY) NEW SEEKERS	1	1971
I'D LOVE YOU TO WANT ME LOBO	5	1974
I'D NEVER FIND ANOTHER YOU BILLY FURY	5	1961
I'D RATHER DANCE WITH YOU KINGS OF CONVENIENCE	60	2004
I'D RATHER GO BLIND CHICKEN SHACK	14	1969
I'D RATHER GO BLIND RUBY TURNER	24	1987
I'D RATHER GO BLIND SYDNEY YOUNGBLOOD	44	1990
I'D RATHER JACK REYNOLDS GIRLS	8	1989
I'D REALLY LOVE TO SEE YOU TONIGHT ENGLAND DAN & JOHN FORD COLEY	26	1976
I'D WAIT FOR LIFE TAKE THAT	17	2007
THE IDEAL HEIGHT BIFFY CLYRO	46	2003
IDEAL WORLD CHRISTIANS	14	1987
IDENTITY X-RAY SPEX	24	1978
IDIOTS AT THE WHEEL EP. KINGMAKER	30	1992
IDLE GOSSIP PERRY COMO	3	1954
IDLE ON PARADE EP ANTHONY NEWLEY	13	1959
IDOL [C] AMANDA GHOST	63	2000
THE IDOL [A] W.A.S.P.	41	1992
THE IDOL [B] MARC ALMOND	44	1995
IEYA TOYAH	48	1982
IF [A] TELLY SAVALAS	1	1975
IF [A] YIN & YAN	25	1975
IF [A] JOHN ALFORD	24	1996
IF [A] DOLLY PARTON	73	2002
IF [B] JANET JACKSON	14	1993
IF... [C] BLUETONES	13	1998
IF A MAN ANSWERS BOBBY DARIN	24	1962
IF ANYONE FINDS THIS I LOVE YOU RUBY MURRAY WITH ANNE WARREN	4	1955
IF DREAMS CAME TRUE PAT BOONE	16	1958
IF EVER 3RD STOREE	53	1999
IF EVERY DAY WAS LIKE CHRISTMAS ELVIS PRESLEY	9	1966
IF EVERYBODY LOOKED THE SAME GROOVE ARMADA	25	1999
IF EYE LOVE U 2 NIGHT MAYTE	67	1995
IF GOD WILL SEND HIS ANGELS U2	12	1997
IF HE TELLS YOU ADAM FAITH & THE ROULETTES	25	1964
IF I AIN'T GOT YOU ALICIA KEYS	18	2004
IF I CAN DREAM ELVIS PRESLEY	11	1969
IF I CAN DREAM (EP) MICHAEL BALL	51	1992
IF I CAN'T 50 CENT/G-UNIT	10	2004
IF I CAN'T CHANGE YOUR MIND SUGAR	30	1993
IF I CAN'T HAVE YOU YVONNE ELLIMAN	4	1978
IF I CAN'T HAVE YOU KIM WILDE	12	1993
IF I COULD [A] DAVID ESSEX	13	1975
IF I COULD [B] HUNDRED REASONS	19	2002
IF I COULD BUILD MY WHOLE WORLD AROUND YOU MARVIN GAYE & TAMMI TERRELL	41	1968
IF I COULD (EL CONDOR PASA) JULIE FELIX	19	1970
IF I COULD FLY GRACE	29	1996
IF I COULD GIVE YOU ALL MY LOVE COUNTING CROWS	50	2003
IF I COULD GO ANGIE MARTINEZ FEATURING LIL MO	61	2003
IF I COULD ONLY MAKE YOU CARE MIKE BERRY	37	1980
IF I COULD ONLY SAY GOODBYE DAVID HASSELHOFF	35	1993
IF I COULD TALK I'D TELL YOU LEMONHEADS	39	1996
IF I COULD TURN BACK THE HANDS OF TIME R KELLY	2	1999
IF I COULD TURN BACK TIME CHER	6	1989
IF I DIDN'T CARE DAVID CASSIDY	9	1974
IF I DIE TOMORROW MOTLEY CRUE	63	2005
IF I EVER FALL IN LOVE SHAI	36	1993
IF I EVER FEEL BETTER PHOENIX	65	2001
IF I EVER LOSE MY FAITH IN YOU STING	14	1993
IF I FALL ALICE MARTINEAU	45	2002
IF I GIVE MY HEART TO YOU DORIS DAY	4	1954
IF I GIVE MY HEART TO YOU JOAN REGAN	3	1954
IF I GIVE YOU MY NUMBER PJ & DUNCAN	15	1994
IF I HAD A HAMMER TRINI LOPEZ	4	1963
IF I HAD EYES JACK JOHNSON	60	2008
IF I HAD NO LOOT TONY TONI TONE	44	1993
IF I HAD WORDS SCOTT FITZGERALD & YVONNE KEELEY & THE ST THOMAS MORE SCHOOL CHOIR	3	1978
IF I HAD YOU KORGIS	13	1979
IF I HAVE TO GO AWAY JIGSAW	36	1977
IF I HAVE TO STAND ALONE LONNIE GORDON	68	1990
IF I KNEW THEN WHAT I KNOW NOW VAL DOONICAN	14	1968
IF I LET YOU GO WESTLIFE	1	1999
IF I LOVE U 2 NITE MICA PARIS	43	1991
IF I LOVE YA THEN I NEED YA IF I NEED YA THEN I WANT YOU AROUND EARTHA KITT	43	1994
IF I LOVED YOU RICHARD ANTHONY	18	1964
IF I NEEDED SOMEONE HOLLIES	20	1965
IF I NEVER KNEW YOU (LOVE THEME FROM *POCAHONTAS*) JON SECADA & SHANICE	51	1995
IF I NEVER SEE YOU AGAIN WET WET WET	3	1997
IF I ONLY HAD TIME JOHN ROWLES	3	1968
IF I ONLY KNEW TOM JONES	11	1994
IF I REMEMBER BENZ	59	1997
IF I RULED THE WORLD [A] HARRY SECOMBE	18	1963
IF I RULED THE WORLD [A] TONY BENNETT	40	1965
IF I RULED THE WORLD [B] KURTIS BLOW	24	1986
IF I RULED THE WORLD [B] NAS	12	1996
IF I SAID YOU HAD A BEAUTIFUL BODY WOULD YOU HOLD IT AGAINST ME BELLAMY BROTHERS	3	1979
IF I SAY YES FIVE STAR	15	1986
IF I SHOULD FALL FROM GRACE WITH GOD POGUES	58	1988
IF I SHOULD LOVE AGAIN BARRY MANILOW	66	1982
IF I SURVIVE HYBRID FEATURING JULEE CRUISE	52	1999
IF I THOUGHT YOU'D EVER CHANGE YOUR MIND CILLA BLACK	20	1969
IF I THOUGHT YOU'D EVER CHANGE YOUR MIND AGNETHA FALTSKOG	11	2004
IF I TOLD YOU THAT WHITNEY HOUSTON & GEORGE MICHAEL	9	2000
IF I WAS [A] MIDGE URE	1	1985
IF I WAS [B] ASWAD	58	1995
IF I WAS A RIVER TINA ARENA	43	1998
IF I WAS YOUR GIRLFRIEND PRINCE	20	1987
IF I WERE A CARPENTER BOBBY DARIN	9	1966
IF I WERE A CARPENTER FOUR TOPS	7	1968
IF I WERE A CARPENTER ROBERT PLANT	63	1993
IF I WERE A RICH MAN TOPOL	9	1967
IF I WERE YOU [A] k.d. lang	53	1995
IF I WERE YOU [B] CANDEE JAY	14	2004
IF I'M NOT YOUR LOVER AL B SURE! FEATURING SLICK RICK	54	1989
IF IT DON'T FIT DON'T FORCE IT KELLEE PATTERSON	44	1978
IF IT HAPPENS AGAIN UB40	9	1984
IF IT MAKES YOU HAPPY SHERYL CROW	9	1996
IF IT WASN'T FOR THE REASON THAT I LOVE YOU MIKI ANTHONY	27	1973
IF IT'S ALRIGHT WITH YOU BABY KORGIS	56	1980
IF IT'S LOVE THAT YOU WANT DONNY OSMOND	70	1988
IF IT'S LOVIN' THAT YOU WANT RIHANNA	11	2005
IF LEAVING ME IS EASY PHIL COLLINS	17	1981
IF LIFE IS LIKE A LOVE BANK I WANT AN OVERDRAFT WILDHEARTS	31	1995
IF LOOKS COULD KILL TRANSVISION VAMP	41	1991
IF LOVE WAS A TRAIN MICHELLE SHOCKED	63	1989
IF LOVE WAS LIKE GUITARS IAN McNABB	67	1993
IF LOVING YOU IS WRONG (I DON'T WANT TO BE RIGHT) ROD STEWART	23	1980
IF MADONNA CALLS JUNIOR VASQUEZ	24	1996
IF MY FRIENDS COULD SEE ME NOW LINDA CLIFFORD	50	1978
IF NOT FOR YOU OLIVIA NEWTON-JOHN	7	1971
IF NOT YOU DR HOOK	5	1976
IF ONLY [A] HANSON	15	2000
IF ONLY [B] KT TUNSTALL	45	2008
IF ONLY I COULD SYDNEY YOUNGBLOOD	3	1989
IF ONLY I COULD LIVE MY LIFE AGAIN JANE MORGAN	27	1959
IF ONLY TOMORROW RONNIE CARROLL	33	1962
(IF PARADISE IS) HALF AS NICE AMEN CORNER	1	1969
IF - READ TO FAURE'S 'PAVANE' DES LYNAM FEATURING WIMBLEDON CHORAL SOCIETY	45	1998
IF SHE KNEW WHAT SHE WANTS BANGLES	31	1986
IF SHE SHOULD COME TO YOU ANTHONY NEWLEY	4	1960
IF 60S WERE 90S BEAUTIFUL PEOPLE	74	1994
IF THAT WERE ME MELANIE C	18	2000
IF THAT'S OK WITH YOU SHAYNE WARD	2	2007
IF THAT'S YOUR BOYFIEND (HE WASN'T LAST NIGHT) ME'SHELL NDEGEOCELLO	74	1994

	Peak Position	Year of Entry
IF THE KIDS ARE UNITED SHAM 69	9	1978
IF THE RIVER CAN BEND ELTON JOHN	32	1998
IF THE WHOLE WORLD STOPPED LOVING VAL DOONICAN	3	1967
IF THERE WAS A MAN PRETENDERS FOR 007	49	1987
IF THERE'S ANY JUSTICE LEMAR	3	2004
IF THIS IS IT HUEY LEWIS & THE NEWS	39	1984
IF THIS IS LOVE [A] JJ	55	1991
IF THIS IS LOVE [B] JEANIE TRACY	73	1994
IF TOMORROW NEVER COMES RONAN KEATING	1	2002
IF U WANT ME MICHAEL WOODS FEATURING IMOGEN BAILEY	46	2003
IF WE FALL IN LOVE TONIGHT ROD STEWART	58	1996
IF WE HOLD ON TOGETHER DIANA ROSS	11	1992
IF WE TRY KAREN RAMIREZ	23	1998
IF WE WERE LOVERS GLORIA ESTEFAN	40	1993
IF YA GETTING' DOWN FIVE	2	1999
IF YOU ASKED ME TO CELINE DION	57	1992
IF YOU BELIEVE JOHNNIE RAY	7	1955
IF YOU BUY THIS RECORD YOU LIFE WILL BE BETTER TAMPERER FEATURING MAYA	3	1998
IF YOU C JORDAN SOMETHING CORPORATE	68	2003
IF YOU CAN WANT SMOKEY ROBINSON & THE MIRACLES	50	1968
IF YOU CAN'T DO IT WHEN YOU'RE YOUNG, WHEN CAN YOU DO IT? THEAUDIENCE	48	1998
IF YOU CAN'T GIVE ME LOVE SUZI QUATRO	4	1978
IF YOU CAN'T SAY NO LENNY KRAVITZ	48	1998
IF YOU CAN'T STAND THE HEAT BUCKS FIZZ	10	1982
IF YOU CARED KIM APPLEBY	44	1991
IF YOU COME BACK BLUE	1	2001
IF YOU COME TO ME ATOMIC KITTEN	3	2003
IF YOU COULD READ MY MIND GORDON LIGHTFOOT	30	1971
IF YOU COULD READ MY MIND STARS ON 54	23	1998
IF YOU COULD SEE ME NOW SHAKATAK	49	1983
IF YOU DON'T KNOW ME BY NOW HAROLD MELVIN & THE BLUENOTES	9	1973
IF YOU DON'T KNOW ME BY NOW SIMPLY RED	2	1989
IF YOU DON'T LOVE ME PREFAB SPROUT	33	1992
IF YOU DON'T WANT ME TO DESTROY YOU SUPER FURRY ANIMALS	18	1996
IF YOU DON'T WANT MY LOVE ROBERT JOHN	42	1968
IF YOU EVER EAST 17 FEATURING GABRIELLE	2	1996
IF YOU EVER LEAVE ME BARBRA STREISAND/ VINCE GILL	26	1999
IF YOU FEEL IT THELMA HOUSTON	48	1981
IF YOU GO JON SECADA	39	1994
IF YOU GO AWAY [A] TERRY JACKS	8	1974
IF YOU GO AWAY [B] NEW KIDS ON THE BLOCK	9	1991
IF YOU GOT THE MONEY JAMIE T	13	2006
IF YOU GOTTA GO GO NOW MANFRED MANN	2	1965
IF YOU GOTTA MAKE A FOOL OF SOMEBODY FREDDIE & THE DREAMERS	3	1963
IF YOU HAD MY LOVE JENNIFER LOPEZ	4	1999
IF YOU HAVE TO GO GENEVA	69	2000
IF YOU KNEW SOUSA (AND FRIENDS) ROYAL PHILHARMONIC ORCHESTRA ARRANGED & CONDUCTED BY LOUIS CLARK	71	1982
IF YOU KNOW WHAT I MEAN NEIL DIAMOND	35	1976
IF YOU LEAVE ORCHESTRAL MANOEUVRES IN THE DARK	48	1986
IF YOU LEAVE ME NOW CHICAGO	1	1976
IF YOU LEAVE ME NOW UPSIDE DOWN	27	1996
IF YOU LEAVE ME NOW SYSTEM PRESENTS KERRI B	55	2003
IF YOU LET ME STAY TERENCE TRENT D'ARBY	7	1987
IF YOU LOVE HER DICK EMERY	32	1969
IF YOU LOVE ME [A] MARY HOPKIN	32	1976
IF YOU LOVE ME [B] BROWNSTONE	8	1995
IF YOU LOVE SOMEBODY SET THEM FREE STING	26	1985
IF YOU ONLY LET ME IN MN8	6	1995
IF YOU REALLY CARED GABRIELLE	15	1996
IF YOU REALLY LOVE ME STEVIE WONDER	20	1972
IF YOU REALLY WANNA KNOW MARC DORSEY	58	1999
IF YOU REALLY WANT TO MEAT LOAF	59	1983
IF YOU REMEMBER ME CHRIS THOMPSON	42	1979
IF YOU SHOULD NEED A FRIEND FIRE ISLAND FEATURING MARK ANTHONI	51	1995
IF YOU TALK IN YOUR SLEEP ELVIS PRESLEY	40	1974
IF YOU THINK YOU KNOW HOW TO LOVE ME SMOKEY	3	1975
(IF YOU THINK YOU'RE) GROOVY PP ARNOLD	41	1968
IF YOU TOLERATE THIS YOUR CHILDREN WILL BE NEXT MANIC STREET PREACHERS	1	1998
IF YOU WALK AWAY PETER COX	24	1997
IF YOU WANNA BE HAPPY JIMMY SOUL	39	1963
IF YOU WANNA BE HAPPY ROCKY SHARPE & THE REPLAYS	46	1983
IF YOU WANNA PARTY MOLELLA FEATURING THE OUTHERE BROTHERS	9	1995
IF YOU WANT LUCIANA	47	1994
IF YOU WANT ME HINDA HICKS	25	1998
IF YOU WANT MY LOVE CHEAP TRICK	57	1982
IF YOU WANT MY LOVIN' EVELYN KING	43	1981
IF YOU WERE A SAILBOAT KATIE MELUA	23	2007
IF YOU WERE HERE TONIGHT ALEXANDER O'NEAL	13	1986
IF YOU WERE HERE TONIGHT MATT GOSS	23	1996
IF YOU WERE MINE MARCOS HERNANDEZ	41	2006
IF YOU WERE MINE MARY EDDY ARNOLD	49	1966
IF YOU WERE THE ONLY BOY IN THE WORLD STEVIE MARSH	24	1959
IF YOU WERE WITH ME NOW KYLIE MINOGUE & KEITH WASHINGTON	4	1991
IF YOU'LL BE MINE BABYBIRD	28	1998
IF YOUR GIRL ONLY KNEW AALIYAH	15	1996
IF YOUR HEART ISN'T IN IT ATLANTIC STARR	48	1986
IF YOU'RE GONE MATCHBOX 20	50	2001
IF YOU'RE LOOKING FOR A WAY OUT ODYSSEY	6	1980
IF YOU'RE NOT THE ONE DANIEL BEDINGFIELD	1	2002
IF YOU'RE READY (COME GO WITH ME) STAPLE SINGERS	34	1974
IF YOU'RE READY (COME GO WITH ME) RUBY TURNER FEATURING JONATHAN BUTLER	30	1986
IF YOU'RE THINKING OF ME DODGY	11	1996
IGGIN' ME CHICO DeBARGE	50	1998
IGNITION R KELLY	1	2003
IGNORANCE OCEANIC FEATURING SIOBHAN MAHER	72	1992
IGUANA MAURO PICOTTO	33	2000
III WISHES TERRORVISION	42	1999
IKO IKO DIXIE CUPS	23	1965
IKO IKO BELLE STARS	35	1982
IKO IKO NATASHA	10	1982
IL ADORE BOY GEORGE	50	1995
IL EST NE LE DIVIN ENFANT SIOUXSIE & THE BANSHEES	49	1982
IL NOSTRO CONCERTO UMBERTO BINDI	47	1960
IL SILENZIO NINI ROSSO	8	1965
I'LL ALWAYS BE AROUND C & C MUSIC FACTORY	42	1995
I'LL ALWAYS BE IN LOVE WITH YOU MICHAEL HOLLIDAY	27	1958
I'LL ALWAYS LOVE MY MAMA INTRUDERS	32	1974
I'LL ALWAYS LOVE YOU TAYLOR DAYNE	41	1988
I'LL BE FOXY BROWN FEATURING JAY-Z	9	1997
(I'LL BE A) FREAK FOR YOU ROYALLE DELITE	45	1985
I'LL BE AROUND TERRI WELLS	17	1984
I'LL BE AROUND RAPPIN' 4-TAY FEATURING THE SPINNERS	30	1995
I'LL BE BACK ARNEE & THE TERMINATORS	5	1991
I'LL BE GOOD RENE & ANGELA	22	1985
I'LL BE GOOD TO YOU QUINCY JONES FEATURING RAY CHARLES & CHAKA KHAN	21	1990
I'LL BE HOME PAT BOONE	1	1956
I'LL BE HOME THIS CHRISTMAS SHAKIN' STEVENS	34	1991
I'LL BE LOVING YOU (FOREVER) NEW KIDS ON THE BLOCK	5	1990
I'LL BE MISSING YOU PUFF DADDY & FAITH EVANS	1	1997
I'LL BE OK McFLY	1	2005
I'LL BE READY SUNBLOCK	4	2006
I'LL BE SATISFIED SHAKIN' STEVENS	10	1982
I'LL BE THERE [A] GERRY & THE PACEMAKERS	15	1965
I'LL BE THERE [B] JACKIE TRENT	38	1969
I'LL BE THERE [C] JACKSON 5	4	1970
I'LL BE THERE [C] MARIAH CAREY	2	1992
I'LL BE THERE [D] INNOCENCE	26	1992
I'LL BE THERE [E] 99TH FLOOR ELEVATORS FEATURING TONY DE VIT	37	1996
I'LL BE THERE [F] EMMA	7	2004
I'LL BE THERE FOR YOU [A] BON JOVI	18	1989
I'LL BE THERE FOR YOU [B] REMBRANDTS	3	1995
I'LL BE THERE FOR YOU [C] SOLID HARMONIE	18	1998
I'LL BE THERE FOR YOU (DOYA DODODO DOYA) HOUSE OF VIRGINISM	29	1993
I'LL BE THERE FOR YOU-YOU'RE ALL I NEED TO GET BY METHOD MAN/MARY J BLIGE	10	1995
I'LL BE WAITING [A] CLIVE GRIFFIN	56	1991
I'LL BE WAITING [B] FULL INTENTION PRESENTS SHENA	44	2001
I'LL BE WITH YOU IN APPLE BLOSSOM TIME ROSEMARY JUNE	14	1959
I'LL BE YOUR ANGEL KIRA	9	2003
I'LL BE YOUR BABY TONIGHT ROBERT PALMER & UB40	6	1990
I'LL BE YOUR BABY TONIGHT NORAH JONES	67	2003
I'LL BE YOUR EVERYTHING TOMMY PAGE	53	1990
I'LL BE YOUR FRIEND ROBERT OWENS	25	1991
I'LL BE YOUR SHELTER TAYLOR DAYNE	43	1990
I'LL COME RUNNIN' JUICE	48	1998
I'LL COME RUNNING CLIFF RICHARD	26	1967
I'LL COME WHEN YOU CALL RUBY MURRAY	6	1955
I'LL CRY FOR YOU EUROPE	28	1992
I'LL CUT YOUR TAIL OFF JOHN LEYTON	36	1963
I'LL DO ANYTHING - TO MAKE YOU MINE HOLLOWAY & CO	58	1999
I'LL DO ANYTHING YOU WANT ME TO BARRY WHITE	20	1975
I'LL DO YA WHALE	53	1995
I'LL FIND MY WAY HOME JON & VANGELIS	6	1981
I'LL FIND YOU [A] DAVID WHITFIELD	27	1957
I'LL FIND YOU [B] MICHELLE GAYLE	26	1994
I'LL FLY FOR YOU SPANDAU BALLET	9	1984
I'LL GET BY CONNIE FRANCIS	19	1958
I'LL GET BY SHIRLEY BASSEY	10	1961
I'LL GIVE YOU THE EARTH (TOUS LES BATEAUX, TOUS LES OISEAUX) KEITH MICHELL	30	1971
I'LL GO ON HOPING DES O'CONNOR	30	1970
I'LL GO WHERE YOUR MUSIC TAKES ME JIMMY JAMES & THE VAGABONDS	23	1976
I'LL GO WHERE YOUR MUSIC TAKES ME TINA CHARLES	27	1978
I'LL HOUSE YOU RICHIE RICH MEETS THE JUNGLE BROTHERS	22	1988
I'LL KEEP ON LOVING YOU PRINCESS	16	1986
I'LL KEEP YOU SATISFIED BILLY J. KRAMER & THE DAKOTAS	4	1963

Title / Artist	Peak Position	Year of Entry
I'LL KEEP YOUR DREAMS ALIVE GEORGE BENSON & PATTI AUSTIN	68	1992
I'LL LOVE YOU FOREVER TODAY CLIFF RICHARD	27	1968
I'LL MAKE LOVE TO YOU BOYZ II MEN	5	1994
I'LL MANAGE SOMEHOW MENSWEAR	49	1995
I'LL MEET YOU AT MIDNIGHT SMOKIE	11	1976
I'LL NEVER BREAK YOUR HEART BACKSTREET BOYS	8	1995
I'LL NEVER FALL IN LOVE AGAIN [A] JOHNNIE RAY	26	1959
I'LL NEVER FALL IN LOVE AGAIN [B] TOM JONES	2	1967
I'LL NEVER FALL IN LOVE AGAIN [C] BOBBIE GENTRY	1	1969
I'LL NEVER FIND ANOTHER YOU SEEKERS	1	1965
I'LL NEVER GET OVER YOU [A] JOHNNY KIDD & THE PIRATES	4	1963
I'LL NEVER GET OVER YOU [B] EVERLY BROTHERS	35	1965
I'LL NEVER GET OVER YOU (GETTING OVER ME) EXPOSE	75	1993
I'LL NEVER LOVE THIS WAY AGAIN DIONNE WARWICK	62	1983
I'LL NEVER QUITE GET OVER YOU BILLY FURY	35	1966
I'LL NEVER STOP N SYNC	13	2000
I'LL NEVER STOP LOVING YOU DORIS DAY	17	1955
I'LL PICK A ROSE FOR MY ROSE MARV JOHNSON	10	1969
I'LL PUT YOU TOGETHER AGAIN HOT CHOCOLATE	13	1978
I'LL REMEMBER MADONNA	7	1994
I'LL REMEMBER TONIGHT PAT BOONE	18	1959
I'LL SAIL THIS SHIP ALONE BEAUTIFUL SOUTH	31	1989
I'LL SAY FOREVER MY LOVE JIMMY RUFFIN	7	1970
I'LL SEE IT THROUGH TEXAS	40	2003
I'LL SEE YOU ALONG THE WAY RICK CLARKE	63	1988
I'LL SEE YOU AROUND SILVER SUN	26	1998
I'LL SEE YOU IN MY DREAMS PAT BOONE	27	1962
I'LL SET YOU FREE BANGLES	74	1989
I'LL SLEEP WHEN I'M DEAD BON JOVI	17	1993
I'LL STAND BY YOU PRETENDERS	10	1994
I'LL STAND BY YOU GIRLS ALOUD	1	2004
I'LL STAY BY YOU KENNY LYNCH	29	1965
I'LL STAY SINGLE JERRY LORDAN	26	1960
I'LL STEP DOWN GARRY MILLS	39	1961
I'LL STICK AROUND FOO FIGHTERS	18	1995
I'LL STOP AT NOTHING SANDIE SHAW	4	1965
I'LL TAKE THE RAIN R.E.M.	44	2001
I'LL TAKE YOU HOME DRIFTERS	37	1963
I'LL TAKE YOU HOME CLIFF BENNETT & THE REBEL ROUSERS	42	1965
I'LL TAKE YOU HOME AGAIN KATHLEEN SLIM WHITMAN	7	1957
I'LL TAKE YOU THERE STAPLE SINGERS	30	1972
I'LL TAKE YOU THERE GENERAL PUBLIC	73	1994
I'LL TRY ANYTHING DUSTY SPRINGFIELD	13	1967
I'LL WAIT TAYLOR DAYNE	29	1994
I'LL WALK WITH GOD MARIO LANZA	18	1955
ILLEGAL SHAKIRA FEATURING CARLOS SANTANA	34	2006
ILLEGAL ALIEN GENESIS	46	1984
ILLEGAL ATTACKS IAN BROWN FEATURING SINEAD O'CONNOR	16	2007
ILLEGAL GUNSHOT RAGGA TWINS	51	1990
ILLUMINATIONS SWANS WAY	57	1984
ILLUSIONS CYPRESS HILL	23	1996
ILOVEROCKNROLL JESUS & MARY CHAIN	38	1998
I'M A BELIEVER MONKEES	1	1967
I'M A BELIEVER ROBERT WYATT	29	1974
I'M A BELIEVER EMF/REEVES & MORTIMER	3	1995
I'M A BETTER MAN (FOR HAVING LOVED YOU) ENGELBERT HUMPERDINCK	15	1969
I'M A BITCH OLGA	68	1994
I'M A BOY WHO	2	1966
I'M A CLOWN DAVID CASSIDY	3	1973
I'M A CUCKOO BELLE & SEBASTIAN	14	2004
I'M A DISCO DANCER CHRISTOPHER JUST	69	1997
I'M A DOUN FOR LACK O' JOHNNIE (A LITTLE SCOTTISH FANTASY) VANESSA-MAE	28	1996
(I'M A) DREAMER B B & Q BAND	35	1986
I'M A FLIRT R KELLY FEATURING TI & T-PAIN	18	2007
I'M A FOOL SLIM WHITMAN	16	1956
I'M A FOOL TO CARE JOE BARRY	49	1961
I'M A GOOD MAN MARTIN SOLVEIG	57	2004
I'M A LITTLE CHRISTMAS CRACKER BOUNCING CZECKS	72	1984
I'M A MAN SPENCER DAVIS GROUP	9	1967
I'M A MAN CHICAGO	8	1970
I'M A MAN NOT A BOY [A] CHESNEY HAWKES	27	1991
I'M A MAN NOT A BOY [B] NORTH & SOUTH	7	1997
I'M A MAN – YE KE YE KE (MEDLEY) CLUBHOUSE	69	1989
I'M A MESSAGE IDLEWILD	41	1998
I'M A MIDNIGHT MOVER WILSON PICKETT	38	1968
I'M A MOODY GUY SHANE FENTON & THE FENTONES	22	1961
I'M A RAT TOWERS OF LONDON	46	2007
(I'M A) ROAD RUNNER JUNIOR WALKER & THE ALL-STARS	12	1969
I'M A SLAVE 4 U BRITNEY SPEARS	4	2001
I'M A SUCKER FOR YOUR LOVE TEENA MARIE, CO-LEAD VOCALS RICK JAMES	43	1979
I'M A TIGER LULU	9	1968
I'M A WONDERFUL THING, BABY KID CREOLE & THE COCONUTS	4	1982
I'M ALIVE [A] HOLLIES	1	1965
I'M ALIVE [B] ELECTRIC LIGHT ORCHESTRA	20	1980
I'M ALIVE [C] CUT 'N' MOVE	49	1995
I'M ALIVE [D] SEAL	4	1994
I'M ALIVE [E] STRETCH 'N' VERN PRESENT MADDOG	17	1996
I'M ALIVE [F] CELINE DION	17	2002
I'M ALL ABOUT YOU DJ LUCK & MC NEAT FEATURING ARI GOLD	18	2001
I'M ALL YOU NEED SAMANTHA FOX	41	1986
I'M ALREADY THERE WESTLIFE	62	2007
I'M ALRIGHT [A] YOUNG STEVE & THE AFTERNOON BOYS	40	1982
I'M ALRIGHT [B] KATHERINE E	41	1991
(I'M ALWAYS TOUCHED BY YOUR) PRESENCE DEAR BLONDIE	10	1978
I'M AN UPSTART ANGELIC UPSTARTS	31	1979
I'M BACK FOR MORE LULU & BOBBY WOMACK	27	1993
I'M BAD LL COOL J	71	1987
I'M BLUE 5,6,7,8'S	71	2004
I'M BORN AGAIN BONEY M	35	1979
I'M BROKEN PANTERA	19	1994
I'M CHILLIN' KURTIS BLOW	64	1986
I'M COMIN' HARDCORE M.A.N.I.C.	60	1992
I'M COMING HOME TOM JONES	2	1967
I'M COMING HOME CINDY TRINI LOPEZ	28	1966
I'M COMING OUT DIANA ROSS	13	1980
I'M COMING WITH YA MATT GOSS	22	2003
I'M COUNTING ON YOU PETULA CLARK	41	1962
I'M CRYING ANIMALS	8	1964
I'M DOIN' FINE DAY ONE	68	1999
I'M DOING FINE JASON DONOVAN	22	1990
I'M DOING FINE NOW NEW YORK CITY	20	1973
I'M DOING FINE NOW PASADENAS	4	1992
I'M EASY FAITH NO MORE	3	1993
I'M EVERY WOMAN CHAKA KHAN	8	1978
I'M EVERY WOMAN WHITNEY HOUSTON	4	1993
I'M FALLING BLUEBELLS	62	1984
I'M FOR REAL NIGHTMARES ON WAX	38	1990
I'M FOREVER BLOWING BUBBLES WEST HAM UNITED CUP SQUAD	31	1975
I'M FOREVER BLOWING BUBBLES COCKNEY REJECTS	35	1980
I'M FREE [A] ROGER DALTREY	13	1973
I'M FREE [B] SOUP DRAGONS FEATURING JUNIOR REID	5	1990
I'M FREE [C] JON SECADA	50	1993
I'M FROM FURTHER NORTH THAN YOU WEDDING PRESENT	34	2005
I'M GLAD JENNIFER LOPEZ	11	2003
I'M GOIN' DOWN MARY J BLIGE	12	1995
I'M GOING ALL THE WAY SOUNDS OF BLACKNESS	14	1993
I'M GOING HOME (TO SEE MY BABY) GENE VINCENT	36	1961
I'M GOING SLIGHTLY MAD QUEEN	22	1991
I'M GONE DIANA ROSS	36	1995
I'M GONNA BE (500 MILES) PROCLAIMERS	11	1988
I'M GONNA BE (500 MILES) PROCLAIMERS FEATURING BRIAN POTTER & ANDY PIPKIN	1	2007
I'M GONNA BE A COUNTRY GIRL AGAIN BUFFY SAINTE-MARIE	34	1972
I'M GONNA BE ALRIGHT JENNIFER LOPEZ FEATURING NAS	3	2002
I'M GONNA BE STRONG GENE PITNEY	2	1964
I'M GONNA BE STRONG CYNDI LAUPER	37	1995
I'M GONNA BE WARM THIS WINTER CONNIE FRANCIS	48	1962
I'M GONNA CHANGE EVERYTHING JIM REEVES	42	1962
(I'M GONNA) CRY MYSELF BLIND PRIMAL SCREAM	49	1994
I'M GONNA GET MARRIED LLOYD PRICE	23	1959
I'M GONNA GET ME A GUN CAT STEVENS	6	1967
I'M GONNA GET THERE SOMEHOW VAL DOONICAN	25	1965
I'M GONNA GET YA BABY BLACK CONNECTION	62	1998
I'M GONNA GET YOU BIZARRE INC FEATURING ANGIE BROWN	3	1992
I'M GONNA GET YOU SUCKA GAP BAND	63	1989
I'M GONNA GETCHA GOOD! SHANIA TWAIN	4	2002
I'M GONNA KNOCK ON YOUR DOOR EDDIE HODGES	37	1961
I'M GONNA KNOCK ON YOUR DOOR LITTLE JIMMY OSMOND	11	1974
I'M GONNA LOVE HER FOR BOTH OF US MEAT LOAF	62	1981
I'M GONNA LOVE YOU FOREVER CROWN HEIGHTS AFFAIR	47	1978
I'M GONNA LOVE YOU JUST A LITTLE BIT MORE BABY BARRY WHITE	23	1973
I'M GONNA MAKE YOU LOVE ME DIANA ROSS & THE SUPREMES & THE TEMPTATIONS	3	1969
I'M GONNA MAKE YOU MINE [A] LOU CHRISTIE	2	1969
I'M GONNA MAKE YOU MINE [B] TANYA BLOUNT	69	1994
I'M GONNA MISS YOU FOREVER AARON CARTER	24	1998
I'M GONNA RUN AWAY FROM YOU TAMI LYNN	4	1971
I'M GONNA SIT RIGHT DOWN AND WRITE MYSELF A LETTER BARRY MANILOW	36	1982
I'M GONNA SIT RIGHT DOWN AND WRITE MYSELF A LETTER BILLY WILLIAMS	22	1957
I'M GONNA SOOTHE YOU MARIA McKEE	35	1993
I'M GONNA TEAR YOUR PLAYHOUSE DOWN PAUL YOUNG	9	1984

	Peak Position	Year of Entry
I'M IN A DIFFERENT WORLD FOUR TOPS	27	1968
I'M IN A PHILLY MOOD DARYL HALL	52	1993
I'M IN FAVOUR OF FRIENDSHIP FIVE SMITH BROTHERS	20	1955
I'M IN HEAVEN [A] JASON NEVINS PRESENTS UKNY FEATURING HOLLY JAMES	9	2003
I'M IN HEAVEN [B] N-TRANCE	46	2004
I'M IN IT FOR LOVE DONNY OSMOND	70	1987
I'M IN LOVE [A] FOURMOST	17	1964
I'M IN LOVE [B] EVELYN KING	27	1981
I'M IN LOVE [C] RUBY TURNER	57	1986
I'M IN LOVE [D] LILLO THOMAS	54	1987
I'M IN LOVE [E] STARPARTY	26	2000
I'M IN LOVE [F] AUDIO BULLYS	27	2005
I'M IN LOVE AGAIN [A] FATS DOMINO	12	1956
I'M IN LOVE AGAIN [B] SAD CAFE	40	1981
I'M IN LOVE (AND I LOVE THE FEELING) ROSE ROYCE	51	1979
I'M IN LOVE WITH A GERMAN FILM STAR PASSIONS	25	1981
I'M IN LOVE WITH THE GIRL ON A CERTAIN MANCHESTER VIRGIN MEGASTORE CHECKOUT DESK FRESHIES	54	1981
I'M IN LUV JOE	22	1994
I'M IN THE MOOD CE CE PENISTON	16	1994
I'M IN THE MOOD FOR DANCING NOLANS	3	1980
I'M IN THE MOOD FOR LOVE LORD TANAMO	58	1990
I'M IN THE MOOD FOR LOVE JOOLS HOLLAND & JAMIROQUAI	29	2001
I'M IN YOU PETER FRAMPTON	41	1977
I'M INTO SOMETHING GOOD HERMAN'S HERMITS	1	1964
I'M JUST A BABY LOUISE CORDET	13	1962
I'M JUST A SINGER (IN A ROCK 'N' ROLL BAND) MOODY BLUES	36	1973
I'M JUST YOUR PUPPET ON A ... (STRING) LONDONBEAT	55	1995
I'M LEAVIN' [A] ELVIS PRESLEY	23	1971
I'M LEAVING [B] LODGER	40	1998
I'M LEAVIN' [C] OUTSIDAZ FEATURING RAH DIGGA	41	2002
I'M LEAVING IT (ALL) UP TO YOU DONNY & MARIE OSMOND	2	1974
I'M LEAVING IT UP TO YOU DALE & GRACE	42	1964
I'M LEFT YOU'RE RIGHT SHE'S GONE ELVIS PRESLEY	21	1958
I'M LIKE A BIRD NELLY FURTADO	5	2001
I'M LIVING IN SHAME DIANA ROSS & THE SUPREMES	14	1969
I'M LONELY HOLLIS P MONROE	51	1999
I'M LOOKING FOR THE ONE (TO BE WITH ME) JAZZY JEFF & THE FRESH PRINCE	24	1993
I'M LOOKING OUT THE WINDOW CLIFF RICHARD & THE SHADOWS	2	1962
I'M LOST WITHOUT YOU BILLY FURY	16	1965
I'M LUCKY JOAN ARMATRADING	46	1981
I'M MANDY FLY ME 10 C.C.	6	1976
I'M NEVER GIVING UP SWEET DREAMS	21	1983
IM NIN'ALU OFRA HAZA	15	1988
I'M NO ANGEL MARCELLA DETROIT	33	1994
I'M NO REBEL VIEW FROM THE HILL	59	1987
I'M NOT A FOOL COCKNEY REJECTS	65	1979
I'M NOT A GIRL NOT YET A WOMAN BRITNEY SPEARS	2	2002
I'M NOT A TEENAGE DELINQUENT FRANKIE LYMON & THE TEENAGERS	12	1957
I'M NOT ANYBODY'S GIRL KACI	55	2003
I'M NOT ASHAMED BIG COUNTRY	69	1995
I'M NOT FEELING YOU YVETTE MICHELLE	36	1997
I'M NOT GIVING YOU UP GLORIA ESTEFAN	28	1996
I'M NOT GONNA LET YOU (GET THE BEST OF ME) COLONEL ABRAMS	24	1986
I'M NOT IN LOVE 10 C.C.	1	1975
I'M NOT IN LOVE JOHNNY LOGAN	51	1987
I'M NOT IN LOVE WILL TO POWER	29	1991
I'M NOT IN LOVE FUN LOVIN' CRIMINALS	12	1997
I'M NOT MISSING YOU STACIE ORRICO	22	2006
I'M NOT OKAY (I PROMISE) MY CHEMICAL ROMANCE	19	2005
I'M NOT PERFECT (BUT I'M PERFECT FOR YOU) GRACE JONES	56	1986
I'M NOT READY KEITH SWEAT	53	1999
I'M NOT SATISFIED FINE YOUNG CANNIBALS	46	1990
I'M NOT SCARED EIGHTH WONDER	7	1988
I'M NOT SHY FRANK	40	2006
I'M NOT SORRY PIGEON DETECTIVES	12	2007
I'M NOT THE MAN I USED TO BE FINE YOUNG CANNIBALS	20	1989
I'M NOT TO BLAME ALIBI	51	1997
(I'M NOT YOUR) STEPPING STONE SEX PISTOLS	21	1980
I'M ON AUTOMATIC SHARPE & NUMAN	44	1989
I'M ON FIRE [A] 5000 VOLTS	4	1975
I'M ON FIRE [B] BRUCE SPRINGSTEEN	5	1985
I'M ON MY WAY [A] DEAN PARRISH	38	1975
I'M ON MY WAY [B] PROCLAIMERS	43	1989
I'M ON MY WAY [C] BETTY BOO	44	1992
I'M ON MY WAY TO A BETTER PLACE CHAIRMEN OF THE BOARD	30	1972
I'M ONLY SLEEPING SUGGS	7	1995
I'M OUT OF YOUR LIFE ARNIE'S LOVE	67	1983
I'M OUTSTANDING SHAQUILLE O'NEAL	70	1994
I'M OUTTA LOVE ANASTACIA	6	2000
I'M OVER YOU MARTINE McCUTCHEON	2	2000
I'M QUALIFIED TO SATISFY BARRY WHITE	37	1977
I'M RAVING SCOOTER	33	1996
I'M READY [A] CAVEMAN	65	1991
I'M READY [B] SIZE 9	52	1995
I'M READY [C] BRYAN ADAMS	20	1998
I'M READY FOR LOVE MARTHA REEVES & THE VANDELLAS	22	1966
I'M REAL [A] JAMES BROWN FEATURING FULL FORCE	31	1988
I'M REAL [B] JENNIFER LOPEZ FEATURING JA RULE	4	2001
I'M REALLY HOT MISSY ELLIOTT	22	2004
I'M RIFFIN (ENGLISH RASTA) MC DUKE	75	1989
I'M RIGHT HERE SAMANTHA MUMBA	5	2002
I'M RUSHING BUMP	45	1992
I'M SHAKIN' ROONEY	73	2004
I'M SHY MARY ELLEN (I'M SHY) BOB WALLIS & HIS STORYVILLE JAZZ BAND	44	1961
I'M SICK OF YOU GOODBYE MR MACKENZIE	49	1989
I'M SO BEAUTIFUL DIVINE	52	1984
I'M SO CRAZY [A] KC & THE SUNSHINE BAND	34	1975
I'M SO CRAZY [B] PAR-T-ONE VS INXS	19	2001
I'M SO EXCITED POINTER SISTERS	11	1984
I'M SO GLAD I'M STANDING HERE TODAY CRUSADERS, FEATURED VOCALIST JOE COCKER	61	1981
I'M SO HAPPY [A] LIGHT OF THE WORLD	35	1981
I'M SO HAPPY [B] JULIA & COMPANY	56	1985
I'M SO HAPPY [C] WALTER BEASLEY	70	1988
I'M SO HAPPY I CAN'T STOP CRYING STING	54	1996
I'M SO IN LOVE ALYSHA WARREN	61	1994
I'M SO INTO YOU SWV	17	1993
I'M SO LONELY CAST	14	1997
I'M SORRY [A] PLATTERS	18	1957
I'M SORRY [B] BRENDA LEE	12	1960
I'M SORRY [C] HOTHOUSE FLOWERS	53	1988
I'M SORRY I MADE YOU CRY CONNIE FRANCIS	11	1958
I'M SPRUNG T-PAIN	30	2006
I'M STANDING (HIGHER) X-STATIC	41	1995
I'M STARTING TO GO STEADY JOHNNY PRESTON	49	1960
I'M STILL GONNA NEED YOU OSMONDS	32	1975
I'M STILL IN LOVE WITH YOU [A] AL GREEN	35	1972
I'M STILL IN LOVE WITH YOU [B] SEAN PAUL FEATURING SASHA	6	2003
I'M STILL STANDING ELTON JOHN	4	1983
I'M STILL WAITING DIANA ROSS	1	1971
I'M STILL WAITING COURTNEY PINE FEATURING CARROLL THOMPSON	66	1990
I'M STILL WAITING ANGELHEART FEATURING ALETIA BOURNE	74	1997
I'M STONE IN LOVE WITH YOU STYLISTICS	9	1972
I'M STONE IN LOVE WITH YOU JOHNNY MATHIS	10	1975
I'M TELLIN' YOU CHUBBY CHUNKS FEATURING KIM RUFFIN	61	1999
I'M TELLING YOU NOW FREDDIE & THE DREAMERS	2	1963
I'M THAT TYPE OF GUY LL COOL J	43	1989
I'M THE FACE HIGH NUMBERS	49	1980
I'M THE LEADER OF THE GANG HULK HOGAN WITH GREEN JELLY	25	1993
I'M THE LEADER OF THE GANG (I AM) GARY GLITTER	1	1973
I'M THE LONELY ONE CLIFF RICHARD & THE SHADOWS	8	1964
I'M THE MAN ANTHRAX	20	1987
I'M THE ONE GERRY & THE PACEMAKERS	2	1964
I'M THE ONE FOR YOU ADEVA	51	1992
I'M THE ONE YOU NEED JODY WATLEY	50	1992
I'M THE URBAN SPACEMAN BONZO DOG DOO-DAH BAND	5	1968
I'M TIRED OF GETTING PUSHED AROUND TWO MEN, A DRUM MACHINE & A TRUMPET	18	1988
I'M TOO SCARED STEVEN DANTE	34	1988
I'M TOO SEXY RIGHT SAID FRED	2	1991
I'M WAKING UP TO US BELLE & SEBASTIAN	39	2001
I'M WALKIN' FATS DOMINO	19	1957
I'M WALKING BACKWARDS FOR CHRISTMAS GOONS	4	1956
I'M WALKING BEHIND YOU DOROTHY SQUIRES	12	1953
I'M WALKING BEHIND YOU EDDIE FISHER WITH SALLY SWEETLAND (SOPRANO)	1	1953
I'M WITH STUPID PET SHOP BOYS	8	2006
I'M WITH YOU AVRIL LAVIGNE	7	2003
I'M WONDERING STEVIE WONDER	22	1967
I'M YOUR ANGEL CELINE DION & R KELLY	3	1998
I'M YOUR BABY TONIGHT WHITNEY HOUSTON	5	1990
I'M YOUR BOOGIE MAN KC & THE SUNSHINE BAND	41	1977
I'M YOUR MAN [A] BLUE ZOO	55	1982
I'M YOUR MAN [B] WHAM!	1	1985
I'M YOUR MAN [B] LISA MOORISH	24	1995
I'M YOUR MAN [B] SHANE RICHIE	2	2003
I'M YOUR PUPPET JAMES & BOBBY PURIFY	12	1976
I'M YOUR TOY ELVIS COSTELLO & THE ATTRACTIONS WITH THE ROYAL PHILHARMONIC ORCHESTRA	51	1982
IMAGE HANK LEVINE	45	1961
IMAGE OF A GIRL MARK WYNTER	11	1960
IMAGE OF A GIRL NELSON KEENE	37	1960
IMAGE OF YOU RED SNAPPER	60	1998
IMAGINATION [A] ROCKY SHARPE & THE REPLAYS	39	1979
IMAGINATION [B] BELOUIS SOME	17	1985
IMAGINATION [C] JON THE DENTIST VS OLLIE JAYE	72	1999
IMAGINE [A] JOHN LENNON	1	1975
IMAGINE [A] RANDY CRAWFORD	60	1982
IMAGINE [B] SHOLA AMA	24	2000

Title / Artist	Peak Position	Year of Entry
IMAGINE ME IMAGINE YOU FOX	15	1975
IMITATION OF LIFE [A] BILLIE RAY MARTIN	29	1996
IMITATION OF LIFE [B] R.E.M.	6	2001
IMMACULATE FOOLS IMMACULATE FOOLS	51	1985
IMMORTALITY CELINE DION WITH THE BEE GEES	5	1998
IMPERIAL WIZARD DAVID ESSEX	32	1979
THE IMPORTANCE OF BEING IDLE OASIS	1	2005
IMPORTANCE OF YOUR LOVE VINCE HILL	32	1968
IMPOSSIBLE [A] CAPTAIN HOLLYWOOD PROJECT	29	1994
IMPOSSIBLE [B] CHARLATANS	15	2000
THE IMPOSSIBLE DREAM CARTER-THE UNSTOPPABLE SEX MACHINE	21	1992
IMPOSSIBLE LOVE UB40	47	1990
THE IMPRESSION THAT I GET MIGHTY MIGHTY BOSSTONES	12	1998
THE IMPRESSIONS EP SOLAR STONE	75	1998
IMPULSIVE WILSON PHILLIPS	42	1990
IN 4 CHOONS LATER ROZALLA	50	1992
IN A BIG COUNTRY BIG COUNTRY	17	1983
IN A BROKEN DREAM PYTHON LEE JACKSON	3	1972
IN A BROKEN DREAM THUNDER	26	1995
IN A CAGE (ON PROZAC) MY RED CELL	61	2004
IN A DARK PLACE GARY NUMAN	63	2006
IN A DREAM LONGVIEW	38	2004
IN A FUNNY WAY MERCURY REV	28	2005
IN A GOLDEN COACH BILLY COTTON & HIS BAND, VOCALS BY DOREEN STEPHENS	3	1953
IN A GOLDEN COACH DICKIE VALENTINE	7	1953
IN A LIFETIME CLANNAD FEATURING BONO	17	1985
IN A LITTLE SPANISH TOWN BING CROSBY	22	1956
IN A PERSIAN MARKET SAMMY DAVIS Jr.	28	1956
IN A ROOM DODGY	12	1996
IN A STATE [A] 2 FOR JOY	61	1990
IN A STATE [B] UNKLE	44	2003
IN A WORD OR 2 MONIE LOVE	33	1993
IN ALL THE RIGHT PLACES LISA STANSFIELD	8	1993
IN AND OUT [A] WILLIE HUTCH	51	1982
IN AND OUT [B] 3RD EDGE	15	2002
IN AND OUT [C] SPEEDWAY	31	2004
IN AND OUT OF LOVE [A] DIANA ROSS & THE SUPREMES	13	1967
IN AND OUT OF LOVE [B] IMAGINATION	16	1981
IN AND OUT OF MY LIFE [A] TONJA DANTZLER	66	1994
IN AND OUT OF MY LIFE [B] A.T.F.C. PRESENTS ONEPHATDEEVA	11	1999
IN BETWEEN DAYS CURE	15	1985
THE IN BETWEENIES GOODIES	7	1974
IN BLOOM NIRVANA	28	1992
THE IN CROWD DOBIE GRAY	25	1965
THE IN CROWD BRYAN FERRY	13	1974
IN DA CLUB 50 CENT	3	2003
IN DE GHETTO DAVID MORALES & THE BAD YARD CLUB FEATURING CRYSTAL WATERS & DELTA	35	1996
IN DEMAND TEXAS	6	2000
IN DREAMS ROY ORBISON	6	1963
IN DULCE DECORUM DAMNED	72	1987
IN DULCE JUBILO MIKE OLDFIELD	4	1975
IN FOR A PENNY SLADE	11	1975
IN GOD'S COUNTRY (IMPORT) U2	48	1987
IN IT FOR LOVE RICHIE SAMBORA	58	1998
IN IT FOR THE MONEY CLIENT	51	2004
IN LIVERPOOL SUZANNE VEGA	52	1992
IN LOVE [A] MICHAEL HOLLIDAY	26	1958
IN LOVE [B] DATSUNS	25	2002
IN LOVE [C] LISA MAFFIA	13	2003
IN LOVE WITH LOVE DEBBIE HARRY	45	1987
IN LOVE WITH THE FAMILIAR WIRELESS	69	1998
IN MY ARMS [A] ERASURE	13	1997
IN MY ARMS [B] MYLO	13	2005
IN MY BED [A] DRU HILL	16	1997
IN MY BED [B] AMY WINEHOUSE	60	2004
IN MY CHAIR STATUS QUO	21	1970
IN MY DEFENCE FREDDIE MERCURY	8	1992
IN MY DREAMS [A] WILL DOWNING	34	1988
IN MY DREAMS [B] JOHNNA	66	1996
IN MY EYES MILK INC	9	2002
IN MY HEAD QUEENS OF THE STONE AGE	44	2005
IN MY HEART [A] TEXAS	74	1991
IN MY HEART [B] ETHAN	49	2005
IN MY LIFE [A] SOULED OUT	75	1992
IN MY LIFE [B] KIM WILDE	54	1993
IN MY LIFE [C] JOSE NUNEZ FEATURING OCTAHVIA	56	1998
IN MY LIFE [D] RYZE	46	2002
IN MY LIFE [E] OZZY OSBOURNE	63	2005
IN MY MIND MILKY	48	2002
IN MY OWN TIME FAMILY	4	1971
IN MY PLACE COLDPLAY	2	2002
IN MY STREET CHORDS	50	1980
IN MY WORLD ANTHRAX	29	1990
IN OLD LISBON FRANK CHACKSFIELD	15	1956
IN OUR LIFETIME TEXAS	4	1999
IN PRIVATE DUSTY SPRINGFIELD	14	1989
IN PUBLIC KELIS FEATURING NAS	17	2005
IN PURSUIT BOXER REBELLION	57	2004
IN SPIRIT DILEMMA	42	1996
IN SUMMER BILLY FURY	5	1963
IN THE AIR TONIGHT PHIL COLLINS	2	1981
IN THE AIR TONIGHT LIL' KIM FEATURING PHIL COLLINS	26	2001
IN THE ARMS OF LOVE [A] ANDY WILLIAMS	33	1966
IN THE ARMS OF LOVE [B] CATHERINE ZETA JONES	72	1995
IN THE ARMY NOW STATUS QUO	2	1986
IN THE BACK OF MY MIND FLEETWOOD MAC	58	1990
IN THE BAD BAD OLD DAYS FOUNDATIONS	8	1969
IN THE BEGINNING [A] FRANKIE LAINE	20	1955
IN THE BEGINNING [B] E.Y.C.	41	1995
IN THE BEGINNING [C] ROGER GOODE FEATURING TASHA BAXTER	33	2002
IN THE BELLY OF A SHARK GALLOWS	56	2007
IN THE BEST POSSIBLE TASTE (PART 2) KINGMAKER	41	1995
IN THE BLEAK MID WINTER NEVADA	71	1983
IN THE BOTTLE C.O.D.	54	1983
IN THE BROWNIES BILLY CONNOLLY	38	1979
IN THE BUSH MUSIQUE	16	1978
IN THE CAULDRON OF LOVE ICICLE WORKS	53	1984
IN THE CHAPEL IN THE MOONLIGHT BACHELORS	27	1965
IN THE CITY [A] JAM	21	1977
IN THE CITY [B] LAHAYNA	33	2007
IN THE CLOSET MICHAEL JACKSON	8	1992
IN THE CLOUDS ALL ABOUT EVE	47	1987
(IN THE) COLD LIGHT OF DAY GENE PITNEY	38	1967
IN THE COUNTRY CLIFF RICHARD	6	1966
IN THE COUNTRY FARMERS BOYS	44	1984
IN THE END LINKIN PARK	8	2001
IN THE EVENING SHERYL LEE RALPH	64	1985
IN THE FOREST BABY O	46	1980
IN THE FUTURE WHEN ALL'S WELL MORRISSEY	17	2006
IN THE GHETTO ELVIS PRESLEY	2	1969
IN THE GHETTO BEATS INTERNATIONAL	44	1991
IN THE GRIND DILLINJA	71	2004
IN THE HALL OF THE MOUNTAIN KING NERO & THE GLADIATORS	48	1961
IN THE HEAT OF A PASSIONATE MOMENT PRINCESS	74	1986
IN THE HEAT OF THE NIGHT [A] DIAMOND HEAD	67	1982
IN THE HEAT OF THE NIGHT [B] IMAGINATION	22	1982
IN THE HOUSE CLOCK	23	1995
IN THE MEANTIME [A] GEORGIE FAME & THE BLUE FLAMES	22	1965
IN THE MEANTIME [B] SPACEHOG	29	1996
IN THE MIDDLE [A] ALEXANDER O'NEAL	32	1993
IN THE MIDDLE [B] SUGABABES	8	2004
IN THE MIDDLE OF A DARK DARK NIGHT GUY MITCHELL	25	1957
IN THE MIDDLE OF AN ISLAND KING BROTHERS	19	1957
IN THE MIDDLE OF NOWHERE DUSTY SPRINGFIELD	8	1965
IN THE MIDDLE OF THE HOUSE ALMA COGAN	20	1956
IN THE MIDDLE OF THE HOUSE JIMMY PARKINSON	26	1956
IN THE MIDDLE OF THE HOUSE JOHNSTON BROTHERS	27	1956
IN THE MIDDLE OF THE NIGHT MAGIC AFFAIR	38	1994
IN THE MIDNIGHT HOUR WILSON PICKETT	12	1965
IN THE MOOD ERNIE FIELDS	13	1959
IN THE MOOD GLENN MILLER	12	1976
IN THE MOOD SOUND 9418	46	1976
IN THE MOOD RAY STEVENS	31	1977
IN THE MORNING [A] CORAL	6	2005
IN THE MORNING [B] RAZORLIGHT	3	2006
IN THE NAME OF LOVE [A] SHARON REDD	31	1983
IN THE NAME OF LOVE [B] SWAN LAKE	53	1988
IN THE NAME OF LOVE '88 THOMPSON TWINS	46	1988
IN THE NAME OF THE FATHER [A] BONO & GAVIN FRIDAY	46	1994
IN THE NAME OF THE FATHER [B] BLACK GRAPE	8	1995
IN THE NAVY VILLAGE PEOPLE	2	1979
IN THE NIGHT BARBARA DICKSON	48	1980
IN THE ONES YOU LOVE DIANA ROSS	34	1996
IN THE REALM OF THE SENSES BASS-O-MATIC	66	1990
IN THE SHADOWS RASMUS	3	2004
IN THE SHAPE OF A HEART JACKSON BROWNE	66	1986
IN THE SPRINGTIME MAXI PRIEST	54	1986
IN THE STILL OF THE NITE (I'LL REMEMBER) BOYZ II MEN	27	1993
IN THE STONE EARTH, WIND & FIRE	53	1980
IN THE SUMMERTIME MUNGO JERRY	1	1970
IN THE SUMMERTIME SHAGGY FEATURING RAYVON	5	1995
IN THE SUMMERTIME JUNGLE BOYS	72	2004
IN THE THICK OF IT BRENDA RUSSELL	51	1980
IN THE VALLEY MIDNIGHT OIL	60	1993
IN THE WAITING LINE ZERO 7	47	2001
IN THE YEAR 2525 (EXORDIUM AND TERMINUS) ZAGER & EVANS	1	1969
IN THESE ARMS BON JOVI	9	1993
IN THIS HOME ON ICE CLAP YOUR HANDS SAY YEAH	68	2006
IN THIS WORLD MOBY	35	2002
IN THOUGHTS OF YOU BILLY FURY	9	1965
IN TOO DEEP [A] DEAD OR ALIVE	14	1985
IN TOO DEEP [B] GENESIS	19	1986
IN TOO DEEP [C] BELINDA CARLISLE	6	1996
IN TOO DEEP [D] SUM 41	13	2001
IN WALKED LOVE LOUISE	17	1996
IN YER FACE 808 STATE	9	1991
IN YOUR ARMS (RESCUE ME) NU GENERATION	8	2000
IN YOUR BONES FIRE ISLAND	66	1992
IN YOUR CAR [A] COOLNOTES	13	1985

Title / Artist	Peak Position	Year of Entry
IN YOUR CAR [B] KENICKIE	24	1997
IN YOUR CARE TASMIN ARCHER	16	1993
IN YOUR DANCE E-LUSTRIOUS	69	1994
IN YOUR EYES [A] GEORGE BENSON	7	1983
IN YOUR EYES [B] NIAMH KAVANAGH	24	1993
IN YOUR EYES [C] KYLIE MINOGUE	3	2002
IN YOUR HANDS REDD SQUARE FEATURING TIFF LACEY	64	2002
IN YOUR ROOM [A] BANGLES	35	1988
IN YOUR ROOM [B] DEPECHE MODE	8	1994
IN YOUR WILDEST DREAMS TINA TURNER FEATURING BARRY WHITE	32	1996
IN YOUR WORLD MUSE	13	2002
IN ZAIRE [A] JOHNNY WAKELIN	4	1976
IN ZAIRE [B] AFRICAN BUSINESS	73	1990
INBETWEENER SLEEPER	16	1995
THE INCIDENTALS ALISHA'S ATTIC	13	1998
INCOMMUNICADO MARILLION	6	1987
INCOMPLETE [A] SISQO	13	2000
INCOMPLETE [B] BACKSTREET BOYS	8	2005
INCONSOLABLE BACKSTREET BOYS	24	2007
INCREDIBLE [A] M-BEAT FEATURING GENERAL LEVY	8	1994
INCREDIBLE [B] KEITH MURRAY FEATURING LL COOL J	52	1998
INCREDIBLE [C] SHAPESHIFTERS	12	2006
INCREDIBLE (WHAT I MEANT TO SAY) DARIUS	9	2003
INDEPENDENCE LULU	11	1993
INDEPENDENCE DAY COMSAT ANGELS	71	1984
INDEPENDENT LOVE SONG SCARLET	12	1995
INDEPENDENT WOMEN PART 1 DESTINY'S CHILD	1	2000
INDESCRIBABLY BLUE ELVIS PRESLEY	21	1967
INDESTRUCTIBLE [A] FOUR TOPS FEATURING SMOKEY ROBINSON	30	1989
INDESTRUCTIBLE [B] ALISHA'S ATTIC	12	1997
INDIAN LOVE CALL SLIM WHITMAN	7	1955
INDIAN LOVE CALL KARL DENVER	32	1963
INDIAN LOVE CALL RAY STEVENS	34	1975
INDIAN RESERVATION DON FARDON	3	1970
INDIAN RESERVATION 999	51	1981
INDIAN ROPE CHARLATANS	57	1991
INDIAN SUMMER [A] BELLE STARS	52	1983
INDIAN SUMMER [B] MANIC STREET PREACHERS	22	2007
INDIANA FREDDY CANNON	42	1960
INDIANA WANTS ME R. DEAN TAYLOR	2	1971
INDIANS ANTHRAX	44	1987
INDICA MOVIN' MELODIES	62	1996
INDIE-YARN TRICKBABY	47	1996
INDIGO MOLOKO	51	2000
INDUSTRIAL STRENGTH (EP) KROKUS	62	1981
INERTIATIC ESP MARS VOLTA	42	2003
INFATUATION ROD STEWART	27	1984
INFECTED [A] THE THE	48	1986
INFECTED [B] BARTHEZZ	25	2002
INFERNO SOUVLAKI	24	1997
INFIDELITY SIMPLY RED	31	1987
INFILTRATE 202 ALTERN 8	28	1991
INFINITE DREAMS IRON MAIDEN	6	1989
INFINITY GURU JOSH	5	1990
INFO-FREAKO JESUS JONES	42	1989
INFORMER SNOW	2	1993
INFRA-RED PLACEBO	42	2006
INHALE STONE SOUR	63	2003
INHERIT THE WIND WILTON FELDER	39	1980
INJECTED WITH A POISON PRAGA KHAN FEATURING JADE 4 U	39	1992
THE INK IN THE WELL DAVID SYLVIAN	36	1984
INKANYEZI NEZAZI (THE STAR AND THE WISEMAN) LADYSMITH BLACK MAMBAZO	33	1997
INNA CITY MAMMA NENEH CHERRY	31	1989
INNAMORATA DEAN MARTIN	21	1956
INNER CITY LIFE GOLDIE PRESENTS METALHEADS	39	1994
INNER LIFE DECOY AND ROY	45	2003
INNER SMILE TEXAS	6	2001
INNOCENT ADDIS BLACK WIDOW	42	1996
INNOCENT EYES DELTA GOODREM	9	2003
INNOCENT MAN MARK MORRISON FEATURING DMX	46	2006
INNOCENT X THERAPY?	53	1995
INNOCENTE (FALLING IN LOVE) DELERIUM FEATURING LEIGH NASH	32	2001
INNUENDO QUEEN	1	1991
INSANE [A] TEXAS FEATURING THE WU TANG CLAN	4	1998
INSANE [B] DARK MONKS	62	2002
INSANE IN THE BRAIN CYPRESS HILL	21	1993
INSANE IN THE BRAIN JASON NEVINS VERSUS CYPRESS HILL	19	1999
INSANIA PETER ANDRE	3	2004
INSANITY OCEANIC	3	1991
INSATIABLE [A] DARREN HAYES	8	2002
INSATIABLE [B] THICK D	35	2002
INSENSITIVE JANN ARDEN	40	1996
INSIDE STILTSKIN	1	1994
INSIDE A DREAM JANE WIEDLIN	64	1988
INSIDE AMERICA JUGGY JONES	39	1976
INSIDE - LOOKING OUT ANIMALS	12	1966
INSIDE LOOKING OUT GRAND FUNK RAILROAD	40	1971
INSIDE LOVE (SO PERSONAL) GEORGE BENSON	57	1983
INSIDE OF LOVE NADA SURF	73	2003
INSIDE OUT [A] ODYSSEY	3	1982
INSIDE OUT [B] MIGHTY LEMON DROPS	74	1988
INSIDE OUT [C] GUN	57	1989
INSIDE OUT [D] SHARA NELSON	34	1994
INSIDE OUT [E] CULTURE BEAT	32	1996
INSIDE OUTSIDE CLASSIX NOUVEAUX	45	1981
INSIDE THAT I CRIED CE CE PENISTON	42	1992
INSIDE YOUR DREAMS U96	44	1994
INSOMNIA [A] FAITHLESS	3	1995
INSOMNIA [B] FEEDER	22	1999
INSOMNIAC ECHOBELLY	47	1994
INSPECTOR GADGET KARTOON KREW	58	1985
***INSPECTOR MORSE* THEME** BARRINGTON PHELOUNG	61	1993
INSPIRATION STRIKE	27	1996
INSSOMNIAK DJPC	62	1991
INSTANT KARMA LENNON, ONO & THE PLASTIC ONO BAND	5	1970
INSTANT REPLAY DAN HARTMAN	8	1978
INSTANT REPLAY YELL!	10	1990
INSTANT REPLAY GAMBAFREAKS FEATURING PACO RIVAZ	57	1998
INSTANT STREET dEUS	49	1997
INSTINCT CROWDED HOUSE	12	1996
INSTINCTION SPANDAU BALLET	10	1982
INSTINCTUAL IMAGINATION	62	1988
INSTRUMENTS OF DARKNESS (ALL OF US ARE ONE PEOPLE) ART OF NOISE	45	1992
INTACT NED'S ATOMIC DUSTBIN	36	1992
INTENSIFY WAY OUT WEST	46	2001
INTERCEPTOR EAT STATIC	44	1997
INTERESTING DRUG MORRISSEY	9	1989
INTERGALACTIC BEASTIE BOYS	5	1998
INTERLUDE MORRISSEY & SIOUXSIE	25	1994
INTERNAL EXILE FISH	37	1991
INTERNATIONAL BRASS CONSTRUCTION	70	1984
INTERNATIONAL BRIGHT YOUNG THING JESUS JONES	7	1991
INTERNATIONAL JET SET SPECIALS	6	1980
THE INTERNATIONAL LANGUAGE OF SCREAMING SUPER FURRY ANIMALS	24	1997
INTERNATIONAL RESCUE FUZZBOX	11	1989
INTERSTATE 5 WEDDING PRESENT	62	2004
INTERSTATE LOVE SONG STONE TEMPLE PILOTS	53	1994
INTERVENTION LAVINE HUDSON	57	1988
INTO A SWAN SIOUXSIE	59	2007
INTO MY ARMS NICK CAVE & THE BAD SEEDS	53	1997
INTO MY WORLD AUDIOWEB	42	1996
INTO OBLIVION (REUNION) FUNERAL FOR A FRIEND	16	2007
INTO SPACE PLAYTHING	48	2001
INTO THE BLUE [A] MISSION	32	1990
INTO THE BLUE [B] MOBY	34	1995
INTO THE BLUE [C] GENEVA	26	1997
INTO THE FIRE THIRTEEN SENSES	35	2004
INTO THE FUTURE NEW ATLANTIC FEATURING LINDA WRIGHT	70	1992
INTO THE GROOVE MADONNA	1	1985
INTO THE MOTION COOLNOTES	66	1986
INTO THE NIGHT LOVE INC	39	2004
INTO THE SUN WEEKEND PLAYERS	42	2002
INTO THE VALLEY SKIDS	10	1979
INTO TOMORROW PAUL WELLER MOVEMENT	36	1991
INTO YOU FABOLOUS FEATURING TAMIA	18	2003
INTO YOUR ARMS LEMONHEADS	14	1993
INTO YOUR EYES ARMAND VAN HELDEN	48	2005
INTO YOUR HEAD HONEYMOON MACHINE	66	2005
INTO YOUR HEART 6 BY SIX	51	1996
INTOXICATION REACT 2 RHYTHM	73	1997
INTRO ALAN BRAXE & FRED FALKE	35	2000
INTUITION [A] LINX	7	1981
INTUITION [B] JEWEL	52	2003
INVALID LITTER DEPT AT THE DRIVE-IN	50	2001
INVINCIBLE MUSE	21	2007
INVINCIBLE (THEME FROM *THE LEGEND OF BILLIE JEAN*) PAT BENATAR	53	1985
INVISIBLE [A] ALISON MOYET	21	1984
INVISIBLE [B] PUBLIC DEMAND	41	1997
INVISIBLE [C] TILT	20	1999
INVISIBLE [D] D-SIDE	7	2003
INVISIBLE BALLOON MIDGET	66	1998
INVISIBLE GIRL MINNIE DRIVER	68	2005
THE INVISIBLE MAN [A] QUEEN	12	1989
INVISIBLE MAN [B] 98°	66	1997
INVISIBLE SUN POLICE	2	1981
INVISIBLE TOUCH GENESIS	7	1986
INVITATIONS SHAKATAK	24	1982
I.O.I.O. BEE GEES	49	1970
I.O.U. [A] JANE KENNAWAY & STRANGE BEHAVIOUR	65	1981
I.O.U. [B] FREEEZ	2	1983
IOU [C] BILL TARMEY	55	1994
IOU LOVE SIX BY SEVEN	48	2002
IRE FEELINGS (SKANGA) RUPIE EDWARDS	9	1974
IRENE PHOTOS	56	1980
IRIE LUCK & NEAT	31	2002
IRIS GOO GOO DOLLS	26	1998
IRIS RONAN KEATING	15	2006
IRISH BLOOD ENGLISH HEART MORRISSEY	3	2004
IRISH BLUE FLIP & FILL FEATURING JUNIOR	20	2003
THE IRISH KEEP GATE-CRASHING THRILLS	48	2005
THE IRISH ROVER POGUES & THE DUBLINERS	8	1987
IRISH SON BRIAN McFADDEN	6	2004
IRON MEGA CITY FOUR	48	1993
IRON FIST MOTORHEAD	29	1982
IRON HORSE CHRISTIE	47	1972
IRON LION ZION BOB MARLEY & THE WAILERS	5	1992
IRONIC ALANIS MORISSETTE	11	1996
IRREPLACEABLE BEYONCÉ	4	2006
IRRESISTIBLE [A] CATHY DENNIS	24	1992

Title / Artist	Peak Position	Year of Entry
IRRESISTIBLE [B] CORRS	20	2000
IRRESISTIBLE [C] JESSICA SIMPSON	11	2001
IS SMALLER	55	1997
IS A BLUE BIRD BLUE CONWAY TWITTY	43	1960
IS IT A CRIME SADE	49	1986
IS IT A DREAM [A] CLASSIX NOUVEAUX	11	1982
IS IT A DREAM [B] DAMNED	34	1985
IS IT A SIN? DEEPEST BLUE	24	2004
IS IT ANY WONDER KEANE	3	2006
IS IT BECAUSE HONEYCOMBS	38	1964
IS IT COS I'M COOL? MOUSSE T FEATURING EMMA LANFORD	9	2004
IS IT GOOD TO YOU HEAVY D. & THE BOYZ	46	1991
IS IT GOOD TO YOU TEDDY RILEY FEATURING TAMMY LUCAS	53	1992
IS IT JUST ME? DARKNESS	8	2006
IS IT LIKE TODAY WORLD PARTY	19	1993
IS IT LOVE BASEMENT BOYS PRESENT ULTRA NATE	71	1991
IS IT LOVE YOU'RE AFTER ROSE ROYCE	13	1979
IS IT LOVE? CHILI HI FLY	37	2000
IS IT REALLY OVER JIM REEVES	17	1965
IS IT TRUE BRENDA LEE	17	1964
IS NOTHING SACRED MEAT LOAF FEATURING PATTI RUSSO	15	1999
IS SHE REALLY GOING OUT WITH HIM? JOE JACKSON	13	1979
IS THAT LOVE SQUEEZE	35	1981
IS THAT YOUR FINAL ANSWER? (WHO WANTS TO BE A MILLIONAIRE - THE SINGLE) AMOURE	33	2000
IS THERE ANY LOVE IN YOUR HEART LENNY KRAVITZ	52	1993
IS THERE ANYBODY OUT THERE BASSHEADS	5	1991
IS THERE ANYBODY THERE SCORPIONS	39	1979
IS THERE SOMEONE OUT THERE? CODE RED	34	1997
IS THERE SOMETHING I SHOULD KNOW DURAN DURAN	1	1983
IS THERE SOMETHING I SHOULD KNOW ALLSTARS	12	2001
IS THIS A DREAM? LOVE DECADE	39	1996
IS THIS A LOVE THING RAYDIO	27	1978
IS THIS LOVE [A] BOB MARLEY & THE WAILERS	9	1978
IS THIS LOVE [C] WHITESNAKE	9	1987
IS THIS LOVE [D] CLAP YOUR HANDS SAY YEAH	74	2005
IS THIS LOVE? [B] ALISON MOYET	3	1986
IS THIS THE WAY TO AMARILLO TONY CHRISTIE	18	1971
IS THIS THE WAY TO AMARILLO (SANTA'S) SANTA	30	2006
(IS THIS THE WAY TO) AMARILLO? TONY CHRISTIE FEATURING PETER KAY	1	2005
(IS THIS THE WAY TO) THE WORLD CUP? TONY CHRISTIE	8	2006
IS THIS WHAT I GET FOR LOVING YOU MARIANNE FAITHFULL	43	1967
IS VIC THERE? DEPARTMENT S	22	1981
IS YOUR LOVE IN VAIN BOB DYLAN	56	1978
IS YOUR LOVE STRONG ENOUGH BRYAN FERRY	22	1986
ISLAND GIRL ELTON JOHN	14	1975
ISLAND HEAD EP INSPIRAL CARPETS	21	1990
ISLAND IN THE SUN [A] HARRY BELAFONTE	3	1957
ISLAND IN THE SUN [A] RIGHTEOUS BROTHERS	24	1966
ISLAND IN THE SUN [B] WEEZER	31	2001
ISLAND OF DREAMS SPRINGFIELDS	5	1962
ISLAND OF LOST SOULS BLONDIE	11	1982
ISLANDS IN THE STREAM KENNY ROGERS & DOLLY PARTON	7	1983
ISLE OF INNISFREE BING CROSBY	3	1952
ISMS DOG EAT DOG	43	1996
ISN'T IT A WONDER BOYZONE	2	1997
ISN'T IT AMAZING HOTHOUSE FLOWERS	46	1993
ISN'T IT MIDNIGHT FLEETWOOD MAC	60	1988
ISN'T IT TIME BABYS	45	1978
ISN'T LIFE STRANGE MOODY BLUES	13	1972
ISN'T SHE LOVELY DAVID PARTON	4	1977
ISOBEL BJORK	23	1995
ISRAEL SIOUXSIE & THE BANSHEES	41	1980
THE ISRAELITES DESMOND DEKKER & THE ACES	1	1969
ISTANBUL FRANKIE VAUGHAN WITH THE PETER KNIGHT SINGERS	11	1954
ISTANBUL (NOT CONSTANTINOPLE) THEY MIGHT BE GIANTS	61	1990
IT AIN'T A CRIME HOUSE OF PAIN	37	1994
IT AIN'T ENOUGH DREEM TEEM VERSUS ARTFUL DODGER	20	2001
IT AIN'T FAIR EDWIN STARR	56	1985
IT AIN'T GONNA BE ME C.J. BOLLAND	35	1999
IT AIN'T HARD TO TELL NAS	64	1994
IT AIN'T ME, BABE JOHNNY CASH	28	1965
IT AIN'T NECESSARILY SO BRONSKI BEAT	16	1984
IT AIN'T OVER TIL IT'S OVER LENNY KRAVITZ	11	1991
IT AIN'T WHAT YOU DO IT'S THE WAY THAT YOU DO IT FUN BOY THREE & BANANARAMA	4	1982
IT BEGAN IN AFRICA URBAN ALL STARS	64	1988
IT BEGAN IN AFRIKA CHEMICAL BROTHERS	8	2001
IT CAN'T BE RIGHT 2PLAY FEATURING RAGHAV & NAILA BOSS	8	2004
IT COULD HAPPEN TO YOU ROBERT PALMER	71	1989
IT DIDN'T MATTER STYLE COUNCIL	9	1987
IT DOESN'T HAVE TO BE ERASURE	12	1987
IT DOESN'T HAVE TO BE THIS WAY BLOW MONKEYS	5	1987
IT DOESN'T MATTER WYCLEF JEAN FEATURING THE ROCK & MELKY SEDECK	3	2000
IT DOESN'T MATTER ANYMORE [A] BUDDY HOLLY	1	1959
IT DOESN'T MATTER ANYMORE [B] PURESSENCE	47	1998
IT DOESN'T REALLY MATTER ZAPP	57	1986
IT DON'T COME EASY RINGO STARR	4	1971
IT ENDED ON AN OILY STAGE BRITISH SEA POWER	18	2005
IT ENDS TONIGHT ALL-AMERICAN REJECTS	66	2006
IT FE DONE SUPERCAT	66	1992
IT FEELS SO GOOD SONIQUE	1	1998
IT HAD TO BE YOU HARRY CONNICK Jr.	32	1991
IT HURTS ANGELS AND AIRWAVES	59	2006
IT HURTS SO MUCH JIM REEVES	8	1965
IT HURTS TO BE IN LOVE GENE PITNEY	36	1964
IT IS JAZZ TINGO TANGO	68	1990
IT IS TIME TO GET FUNKY D MOB FEATURING LRS	9	1989
IT ISN'T, IT WASN'T, IT AIN'T NEVER GONNA BE ARETHA FRANKLIN & WHITNEY HOUSTON	29	1989
IT ISN'T RIGHT PLATTERS	23	1957
IT JUST WON'T DO TIM DELUXE FEATURING SAM OBERNIK	14	2002
IT KEEPS RAININ FATS DOMINO	49	1961
IT KEEP'S RAININ' (TEARS FROM MY EYES) BITTY McLEAN	2	1993
IT KEEPS RIGHT ON A HURTIN' JOHNNY TILLOTSON	31	1962
IT LOOKS LIKE YOU EVAN DANDO	68	2003
IT MAKES ME WONDER BRUCE FOXTON	74	1984
IT MAKES YOU FEEL LIKE DANCIN' ROSE ROYCE	16	1978
IT MAY BE WINTER OUTSIDE (BUT IN MY HEART IT'S SPRING) LOVE UNLIMITED	11	1975
IT MEANS NOTHING STEREOPHONICS	12	2007
IT MEK DESMOND DEKKER	7	1969
IT MIGHT AS WELL RAIN UNTIL SEPTEMBER CAROLE KING	3	1962
IT MUST BE HIM (SEUL SUR SON ETOILE) VIKKI CARR	2	1967
IT MUST BE LOVE [A] LABI SIFFRE	14	1971
IT MUST BE LOVE [A] MADNESS	4	1981
IT MUST BE LOVE [B] ROBIN S	37	1997
IT MUST BE LOVE [C] MERO	33	2000
IT MUST BE SANTA JOAN REGAN	42	1961
IT MUST HAVE BEEN LOVE [A] MAGNUM	33	1988
IT MUST HAVE BEEN LOVE [B] ROXETTE	3	1990
IT NEVER RAINS (IN SOUTHERN CALIFORNIA) TONY! TONI! TONE!	69	1991
IT ONLY TAKES A MINUTE ONE HUNDRED TON & A FEATHER	9	1976
IT ONLY TAKES A MINUTE TAVARES	46	1986
IT ONLY TAKES A MINUTE TAKE THAT	7	1992
IT ONLY TOOK A MINUTE JOE BROWN & THE BRUVVERS	6	1962
IT OUGHTA SELL A MILLION LYN PAUL	37	1975
IT SEEMS TO HANG ON ASHFORD & SIMPSON	48	1978
IT SEEMS TO HANG ON KWS	58	1994
IT SHOULD HAVE BEEN ME YVONNE FAIR	5	1976
IT SHOULD'VE BEEN ME ADEVA	48	1991
IT STARTED ALL OVER AGAIN BRENDA LEE	15	1962
IT STARTED WITH A KISS HOT CHOCOLATE	5	1982
IT SURE BRINGS OUT THE LOVE IN YOUR EYES DAVID SOUL	12	1978
IT TAKES ALL NIGHT LONG GARY GLITTER	25	1977
IT TAKES MORE MS DYNAMITE	7	2002
IT TAKES SCOOP FATMAN SCOOP FEATURING THE CROOKLYN CLAN	9	2004
IT TAKES TWO [A] MARVIN GAYE & KIM WESTON	16	1967
IT TAKES TWO [A] ROD STEWART & TINA TURNER	5	1990
IT TAKES TWO [B] ROB BASE & DJ E-Z ROCK	24	1988
IT TAKES TWO BABY LIZ KERSHAW, BRUNO BROOKES, JIVE BUNNY & LONDONBEAT	53	1989
IT TAKES TWO TO TANGO RICHARD MYHILL	17	1978
IT WAS A GOOD DAY ICE CUBE	27	1993
IT WAS EASIER TO HURT HER WAYNE FONTANA	36	1965
IT WASN'T ME SHAGGY	1	2001
IT WILL BE ALRIGHT ODYSSEY	43	1981
IT WILL BE YOU PAUL YOUNG	34	1994
IT WILL COME IN TIME BILLY PRESTON & SYREETA	47	1980
IT WILL MAKE ME CRAZY FELIX	11	1992
IT WON'T BE LONG ALISON MOYET	50	1991
IT WON'T SEEM LIKE CHRISTMAS (WITHOUT YOU) ELVIS PRESLEY	13	1979
THE ITALIAN THEME CYRIL STAPLETON	18	1956
ITALO HOUSE MIX ROCOCO	54	1989
ITCHYCOO PARK SMALL FACES	3	1967
ITCHYCOO PARK M PEOPLE	11	1995
IT'LL BE ME CLIFF RICHARD & THE SHADOWS	2	1962
IT'S A BEAUTIFUL THING OCEAN COLOUR SCENE	12	1998
IT'S A BETTER THAN GOOD TIME GLADYS KNIGHT & THE PIPS	59	1978
IT'S A DISCO NIGHT (ROCK DON'T STOP) ISLEY BROTHERS	14	1979
IT'S A FINE DAY OPUS III	5	1992
IT'S A FINE DAY MISS JANE	62	1999
IT'S A GAME BAY CITY ROLLERS	16	1977
IT'S A GAS WEDDING PRESENT	71	1994
IT'S A GIRL THING MY LIFE STORY	37	1999
IT'S A GOOD LIFE CEVIN FISHER FEATURING RAMONA KELLY	54	2001
IT'S A HARD LIFE QUEEN	6	1984

Title / Artist	Peak Position	Year of Entry
IT'S A HEARTACHE BONNIE TYLER	4	1977
IT'S A HIT WE ARE SCIENTISTS	29	2006
IT'S A LONG WAY TO THE TOP (IF YOU WANNA ROCK 'N' ROLL) AC/DC	55	1980
IT'S A LOVE THING WHISPERS	9	1981
IT'S A LOVING THING C.B. MILTON	34	1994
IT'S A MAN'S MAN'S MAN'S WORLD JAMES BROWN & THE FAMOUS FLAMES	13	1966
IT'S A MAN'S MAN'S MAN'S WORLD BRILLIANT	58	1985
IT'S A MAN'S MAN'S MAN'S WORLD JEANIE TRACY & BOBBY WOMACK	73	1995
IT'S A MIRACLE CULTURE CLUB	4	1984
IT'S A MISTAKE MEN AT WORK	33	1983
IT'S A PARTY [A] BUSTA RHYMES FEATURING ZHANE	23	1996
IT'S A PARTY [B] BOUNTY KILLER	65	1999
IT'S A RAGGY WALTZ DAVE BRUBECK QUARTET	36	1962
IT'S A RAINBOW RAINBOW (GEORGE & ZIPPY)	15	2002
IT'S A RAINY DAY ICE MC	73	1995
IT'S A SHAME [A] MOTOWN SPINNERS	20	1970
IT'S A SHAME [B] KRIS KROSS	31	1992
IT'S A SHAME ABOUT RAY LEMONHEADS	31	1992
IT'S A SHAME (MY SISTER) MONIE LOVE FEATURING TRUE IMAGE	12	1990
IT'S A SIN PET SHOP BOYS	1	1987
IT'S A SIN TO TELL A LIE GERRY MONROE	13	1971
IT'S A TRIP (TUNE IN, TURN ON, DROP OUT) CHILDREN OF THE NIGHT	52	1988
IT'S ABOUT TIME LEMONHEADS	57	1993
IT'S ABOUT TIME YOU WERE MINE THUNDERBUGS	43	1999
IT'S ALL ABOUT THE BENJAMINS PUFF DADDY & THE FAMILY	18	1998
IT'S ALL ABOUT U [A] SWV	36	1996
IT'S ALL ABOUT YOU [B] JUSTIN	34	1999
IT'S ALL ABOUT YOU (NOT ABOUT ME) TRACIE SPENCER	65	1999
IT'S ALL BEEN DONE BEFORE BARENAKED LADIES	28	1999
IT'S ALL COMING BACK TO ME NOW PANDORA'S BOX	51	1989
IT'S ALL COMING BACK TO ME NOW CELINE DION	3	1996
IT'S ALL COMING BACK TO ME NOW MEAT LOAF FEATURING MARION RAVEN	6	2006
IT'S ALL GONE CHRIS REA	69	1986
IT'S ALL GOOD [A] HAMMER	52	1994
IT'S ALL GOOD [B] DA MOB FEATURING JOCELYN BROWN	54	1999
IT'S ALL GRAVY ROMEO FEATURING CHRISTINA MILIAN	9	2002
IT'S ALL IN THE GAME TOMMY EDWARDS	1	1958
IT'S ALL IN THE GAME CLIFF RICHARD	2	1963
IT'S ALL IN THE GAME FOUR TOPS	5	1970
IT'S ALL OVER CLIFF RICHARD	9	1967
IT'S ALL OVER NOW [A] SHANE FENTON & THE FENTONES	29	1962
IT'S ALL OVER NOW [B] ROLLING STONES	1	1964
IT'S ALL OVER NOW BABY BLUE JOAN BAEZ	22	1965
IT'S ALL OVER NOW BABY BLUE MILLTOWN BROTHERS	48	1993
IT'S ALL RIGHT STERLING VOID	53	1989
IT'S ALL THE WAY LIVE (NOW) COOLIO	34	1996
IT'S ALL TRUE [A] LEMONHEADS	61	1996
IT'S ALL TRUE [B] TRACEY THORN	75	2007
IT'S ALL UP TO YOU JIM CAPALDI	27	1974
IT'S ALL VAIN MAGNOLIA	55	2004
IT'S ALL YOURS MC LYTE FEATURING GINA THOMPSON	36	1998
IT'S ALMOST TOMORROW DREAMWEAVERS	1	1956
IT'S ALMOST TOMORROW MARK WYNTER	12	1963
IT'S ALRIGHT [A] SHO NUFF	53	1980
IT'S ALRIGHT [B] PET SHOP BOYS	5	1989
IT'S ALRIGHT [B] HYPER GO GO	49	1994
IT'S ALRIGHT [C] EAST 17	3	1993
IT'S ALRIGHT [D] BRYAN POWELL	73	1993
IT'S ALRIGHT [E] DENI HINES	35	1997
IT'S ALRIGHT [F] ECHO & THE BUNNYMEN	41	2001
IT'S ALRIGHT (BABY'S COMING BACK) EURYTHMICS	12	1986
IT'S ALRIGHT, I FEEL IT! NUYORICAN SOUL FEATURING JOCELYN BROWN	26	1997
IT'S ALRIGHT NOW BELOVED	48	1990
IT'S AN OPEN SECRET JOY STRINGS	32	1964
IT'S BEEN A WHILE STAIND	15	2001
IT'S BEEN NICE EVERLY BROTHERS	26	1963
IT'S BEEN SO LONG GEORGE McCRAE	4	1975
IT'S BEGINNING TO LOOK A LOT LIKE CHRISTMAS PERRY COMO	49	2007
IT'S BETTER TO HAVE (AND DON'T NEED) DON COVAY	29	1974
IT'S CALLED A HEART DEPECHE MODE	18	1985
IT'S CHICO TIME CHICO	1	2006
IT'S DIFFERENT FOR GIRLS JOE JACKSON	5	1980
IT'S ECSTASY WHEN YOU LAY DOWN NEXT TO ME BARRY WHITE	40	1977
IT'S FOR YOU CILLA BLACK	7	1964
IT'S FOUR IN THE MORNING FARON YOUNG	3	1972
IT'S GETTING BETTER MAMA CASS	8	1969
IT'S GOING DOWN X-ECUTIONERS	7	2002
IT'S GOING TO HAPPEN! UNDERTONES	18	1981
IT'S GONNA BE A COLD COLD CHRISTMAS DANA	4	1975
IT'S GONNA BE A LOVELY DAY S.O.U.L. S.Y.S.T.E.M. INTRODUCING MICHELLE VISAGE	17	1993
IT'S GONNA BE (A LOVELY DAY) BRANCACCIO & AISHER	40	2002
IT'S GONNA BE ALL RIGHT GERRY & THE PACEMAKERS	24	1964
IT'S GONNA BE ALRIGHT [A] RUBY TURNER	57	1990
IT'S GONNA BE ALRIGHT [B] PUSSY 2000	70	2001
IT'S GONNA BE ME N SYNC	9	2000
IT'S GONNA BE MY WAY PRECIOUS	27	2000
IT'S GOOD NEWS WEEK HEDGEHOPPERS ANONYMOUS	5	1965
IT'S GREAT WHEN WE'RE TOGETHER FINLEY QUAYE	29	1997
IT'S GRIM UP NORTH JUSTIFIED ANCIENTS OF MU MU	10	1991
IT'S GROWING TEMPTATIONS	45	1965
IT'S HAPPENIN' PLUS ONE FEATURING SIRRON	40	1990
IT'S HARD SOMETIMES FRANKIE KNUCKLES	67	1991
IT'S HARD TO BE HUMBLE MAC DAVIS	27	1980
IT'S HERE KIM WILDE	42	1990
IT'S IMPOSSIBLE PERRY COMO	4	1971
IT'S IN EVERY ONE OF US CLIFF RICHARD	45	1985
IT'S IN HIS KISS BETTY EVERETT	34	1968
IT'S IN HIS KISS LINDA LEWIS	6	1975
IT'S IN OUR HANDS BJORK	37	2002
IT'S IN YOUR EYES PHIL COLLINS	30	1996
IT'S JURASSIC SOUL CITY ORCHESTRA	70	1993
IT'S JUST A FEELING TERRORIZE	47	1992
IT'S JUST PORN MUM TRUCKS	35	2002
(IT'S JUST) THE WAY THAT YOU LOVE ME PAULA ABDUL	74	1989
IT'S LATE RICKY NELSON	3	1959
IT'S LATE SHAKIN' STEVENS	11	1983
(IT'S LIKE A) SAD OLD KINDA MOVIE PICKETTYWITCH	16	1970
IT'S LIKE THAT [A] RUN DMC VERSUS JASON NEVINS	1	1998
IT'S LIKE THAT [B] MARIAH CAREY	4	2005
IT'S LIKE THAT Y'ALL SWEET TEE	31	1988
IT'S LOVE KEN DODD	36	1966
IT'S LOVE THAT REALLY COUNTS MERSEYBEATS	24	1963
IT'S LOVE (TRIPPIN') GOLDTRIX PRESENTS ANDREA BROWN	6	2002
IT'S LULU BOO RADLEYS	25	1995
IT'S ME ALICE COOPER	34	1994
IT'S MY HOUSE DIANA ROSS	32	1979
IT'S MY HOUSE STORM	36	1979
IT'S MY LIFE [A] ANIMALS	7	1965
IT'S MY LIFE [B] TALK TALK	13	1984
IT'S MY LIFE [B] LIQUID PEOPLE VS TALK TALK	64	2003
IT'S MY LIFE [B] NO DOUBT	17	2003
IT'S MY LIFE [C] DR ALBAN	2	1992
IT'S MY LIFE [D] BON JOVI	3	2000
IT'S MY PARTY [A] LESLEY GORE	9	1963
IT'S MY PARTY [A] DAVE STEWART WITH BARBARA GASKIN	1	1981
IT'S MY PARTY [B] CHAKA KHAN	71	1989
IT'S MY TIME EVERLY BROTHERS	39	1968
IT'S MY TURN [A] DIANA ROSS	16	1981
IT'S MY TURN [B] ANGELIC	11	2000
IT'S NATURE'S WAY (NO PROBLEM) DOLLAR	58	1988
IT'S NEVER TOO LATE DIANA ROSS	41	1982
IT'S NICE TO GO TRAV'LING FRANK SINATRA	48	1960
IT'S NO GOOD DEPECHE MODE	5	1997
IT'S NOT A LOVE THING GEOFFREY WILLIAMS	63	1992
IT'S NOT ABOUT YOU SCOUTING FOR GIRLS	31	2007
IT'S NOT OVER YET KLAXONS	13	2007
IT'S NOT RIGHT BUT IT'S OKAY WHITNEY HOUSTON	3	1999
IT'S NOT THAT EASY LEMAR	7	2006
IT'S NOT THE END OF THE WORLD? SUPER FURRY ANIMALS	30	2002
IT'S NOT UNUSUAL TOM JONES	1	1965
IT'S NOW OR NEVER ELVIS PRESLEY	1	1960
IT'S OH SO QUIET BJORK	4	1995
IT'S OK [A] DELIRIOUS?	18	2000
IT'S OK [B] ATOMIC KITTEN	3	2002
IT'S OKAY [A] DES'REE	69	2003
IT'S OKAY [B] GAME FEATURING JUNIOR REID	26	2006
IT'S ON [A] FLOWERED UP	38	1990
IT'S ON [B] NAUGHTY BY NATURE	48	1993
IT'S ON YOU (SCAN ME) EUROGROOVE	25	1995
IT'S ONE OF THOSE NIGHTS (YES LOVE) PARTRIDGE FAMILY STARRING SHIRLEY JONES FEATURING DAVID CASSIDY	11	1972
IT'S ONLY LOVE [A] TONY BLACKBURN	40	1969
IT'S ONLY LOVE [A] ELVIS PRESLEY	3	1980
IT'S ONLY LOVE [B] GARY U.S. BONDS	43	1981
IT'S ONLY LOVE [C] BRYAN ADAMS & TINA TURNER	29	1985
IT'S ONLY LOVE [D] SIMPLY RED	13	1989
IT'S ONLY MAKE BELIEVE CONWAY TWITTY	1	1958
IT'S ONLY MAKE BELIEVE BILLY FURY	10	1964
IT'S ONLY MAKE BELIEVE GLEN CAMPBELL	4	1970
IT'S ONLY MAKE BELIEVE CHILD	10	1978
IT'S ONLY NATURAL CROWDED HOUSE	24	1992
IT'S ONLY PAIN KATIE MELUA	41	2006
IT'S ONLY ROCK 'N' ROLL VARIOUS ARTISTS (EP'S & LPS)	19	1999
IT'S ONLY ROCK AND ROLL ROLLING STONES	10	1974
IT'S ONLY US ROBBIE WILLIAMS	1	1999
IT'S ONLY YOU (MEIN SCHMERZ LENE LOVICH	68	1982
IT'S 'ORRIBLE BEING IN LOVE (WHEN YOU'RE 8_) CLAIRE & FRIENDS	13	1986
IT'S OVER [A] ROY ORBISON	1	1964
IT'S OVER [B] FUNK MASTERS	8	1983
IT'S OVER [B] CLOCK	10	1997
IT'S OVER [C] LEVEL 42	10	1987

Title / Artist	Peak Position	Year of Entry
IT'S OVER [D] RIMES FEATURING SHAILA PROSPERE	51	1999
IT'S OVER [E] KURUPT	21	2001
IT'S OVER (DISTORTION) PIANOHEADZ	39	1998
IT'S OVER LOVE TODD TERRY PRESENTS SHANNON	16	1997
IT'S OVER NOW [A] ULTRA NATE	62	1989
IT'S OVER NOW [B] DEBORAH COX	49	1999
IT'S OVER NOW [B] BIG ANG FEATURING SIOBHAN	29	2005
IT'S OVER NOW [C] 112	22	2001
IT'S PARTY TIME AGAIN GEORGE VAN DUSEN	43	1988
IT'S PROBABLY ME STING WITH ERIC CLAPTON	30	1992
IT'S RAINING [A] DARTS	2	1978
IT'S RAINING [B] SHAKIN' STEVENS	10	1981
IT'S RAINING AGAIN SUPERTRAMP FEATURING VOCALS BY ROGER HODGSON	26	1982
IT'S RAINING MEN WEATHER GIRLS	2	1983
IT'S RAINING MEN MARTHA WASH	56	2000
IT'S RAINING MEN GERI HALLIWELL	1	2001
IT'S RAINING MEN...THE SEQUEL MARTHA WASH FEATURING RuPAUL	21	1998
IT'S SO EASY ANDY WILLIAMS	13	1970
IT'S SO HIGH MATT FRETTON	50	1983
IT'S SO NICE (TO HAVE YOU HOME) NEW SEEKERS	44	1976
IT'S STILL ROCK AND ROLL TO ME BILLY JOEL	14	1980
IT'S STILL YOU MICHAEL BALL	58	1991
IT'S SUMMERTIME (LET IT GET INTO YOU) SMOOTH	46	1995
IT'S TEMPTATION SHEER ELEGANCE	41	1976
IT'S THE END OF THE WORLD AS WE KNOW IT R.E.M.	39	1991
IT'S THE LITTLE THINGS WE DO ZUTONS	47	2006
IT'S THE MOST WONDERFUL TIME OF THE YEAR ANDY WILLIAMS	21	2007
IT'S THE SAME OLD SONG FOUR TOPS	34	1965
IT'S THE SAME OLD SONG WEATHERMEN	19	1971
IT'S THE SAME OLD SONG KC & THE SUNSHINE BAND	47	1978
IT'S THE WAY YOU MAKE ME FEEL STEPS	2	2001
IT'S TIME [A] ELVIS COSTELLO & THE ATTRACTIONS	58	1996
IT'S TIME [B] FERRY CORSTEN	51	2004
IT'S TIME FOR LOVE CHI-LITES	5	1975
IT'S TIME TO CRY PAUL ANKA	28	1960
IT'S TOO LATE [A] CAROLE KING	6	1971
IT'S TOO LATE [A] QUARTZ INTRODUCING DINA CARROLL	8	1991
IT'S TOO LATE [B] LUCIE SILVAS	62	2000
IT'S TOO LATE NOW [A] SWINGING BLUE JEANS	30	1963
IT'S TOO LATE NOW [B] LONG JOHN BALDRY	21	1969
IT'S TOO SOON TO KNOW PAT BOONE	7	1958
IT'S TRICKY RUN D.M.C.	16	1987
IT'S TRICKY 2003 RUN DMC FEATURING JACKNIFE LEE	20	2003
IT'S TRUE QUEEN PEN	24	1998
IT'S UP TO YOU RICK NELSON	22	1963
IT'S UP TO YOU PETULA EDISON LIGHTHOUSE	49	1971
IT'S UP TO YOU (SHINING THROUGH) LAYO & BUSHWACKA	25	2003
IT'S WHAT WE'RE ALL ABOUT SUM 41	32	2002
IT'S WHAT'S UPFRONT THAT COUNTS YOSH PRESENTS LOVEDEEJAY AKEMI	31	1995
IT'S WONDERFUL (TO BE LOVED BY YOU) JIMMY RUFFIN	6	1970
IT'S WRITTEN IN THE STARS PAUL WELLER	7	2002
IT'S WRITTEN ON YOUR BODY RONNIE BOND	52	1980

Title / Artist	Peak Position	Year of Entry
IT'S YER MONEY I'M AFTER BABY WONDER STUFF	40	1988
IT'S YOU [A] FREDDIE STARR	9	1974
IT'S YOU [B] MANHATTANS	43	1977
IT'S YOU [C] EMF	23	1992
IT'S YOUR DAY TODAY P.J. PROBY	32	1968
IT'S YOUR DESTINY ELECTRA	51	1989
IT'S YOUR LIFE SMOKIE	5	1977
IT'S YOUR THING ISLEY BROTHERS	30	1969
IT'S YOUR TIME ARTHUR BAKER FEATURING SHIRLEY LEWIS	64	1989
IT'S YOURS JON CUTLER FEATURING E-MAN	38	2002
IT'S...IT'S...THE SWEET MIX SWEET	45	1985
ITSY BITSY TEENY WEENY YELLOW POLKA DOT BIKINI BRIAN HYLAND	8	1960
ITSY BITSY TEENY WEENY YELLOW POLKA DOT BIKINI BOMBALURINA FEATURING TIMMY MALLETT	1	1990
ITZA TRUMPET THING MONTANO VS THE TRUMPET MAN	46	1999
I'VE BEEN A BAD BAD BOY PAUL JONES	5	1967
I'VE BEEN AROUND THE WORLD MARTI PELLOW	28	2001
I'VE BEEN DRINKING JEFF BECK & ROD STEWART	27	1973
I'VE BEEN HURT GUY DARRELL	12	1973
I'VE BEEN IN LOVE BEFORE CUTTING CREW	24	1986
I'VE BEEN LONELY FOR SO LONG FREDERICK KNIGHT	22	1972
I'VE BEEN LOSING YOU A-HA	8	1986
I'VE BEEN THINKING ABOUT YOU LONDONBEAT	2	1990
I'VE BEEN TO A MARVELOUS PARTY DIVINE COMEDY	28	1998
I'VE BEEN WAITING STEREO NATION	53	1996
I'VE BEEN WATCHIN' JOE PUBLIC	75	1992
I'VE BEEN WRONG BEFORE CILLA BLACK	17	1965
I'VE DONE EVERYTHING FOR YOU SAMMY HAGAR	36	1980
I'VE FOUND LOVE AGAIN RICHARD CARTRIDGE	50	2004
I'VE GOT A LIFE EURYTHMICS	14	2005
I'VE GOT A LITTLE PUPPY SMURFS	4	1996
I'VE GOT A LITTLE SOMETHING FOR YOU MN8	2	1995
I'VE GOT A THING ABOUT YOU BABY ELVIS PRESLEY	33	1974
I'VE GOT MINE UB40	45	1983
I'VE GOT NEWS FOR YOU FEARGAL SHARKEY	12	1991
I'VE GOT SOMETHING TO SAY REEF	15	1999
I'VE GOT THIS FEELING MAVERICKS	27	1998
I'VE GOT TO LEARN TO SAY NO RICHARD 'DIMPLES' FIELDS	56	1982
I'VE GOT TO MOVE CALVIN RICHARDSON	74	2004
I'VE GOT YOU MARTINE McCUTCHEON	6	1999
I'VE GOT YOU ON MY MIND DORIAN GRAY	36	1968
I'VE GOT YOU ON MY MIND WHITE PLAINS	17	1970
I'VE GOT YOU UNDER MY SKIN FOUR SEASONS WITH FRANKIE VALLI	12	1966
I'VE GOT YOU UNDER MY SKIN NENEH CHERRY	25	1990
I'VE GOT YOU UNDER MY SKIN FRANK SINATRA WITH BONO	4	1993
(I'VE GOT YOUR) PLEASURE CONTROL SIMON HARRIS FEATURING LONNIE GORDON	60	1989
I'VE GOTTA GET A MESSAGE TO YOU BEE GEES	1	1968
I'VE HAD ENOUGH [A] WINGS	42	1978
I'VE HAD ENOUGH [A] IVAN MATAIS	69	1996
I'VE HAD ENOUGH [B] EARTH, WIND & FIRE	29	1982
I'VE HAD ENOUGH [C] HILLMAN MINX	72	1998

Title / Artist	Peak Position	Year of Entry
(I'VE HAD) THE TIME OF MY LIFE BILL MEDLEY & JENNIFER WARNES	6	1987
I'VE JUST BEGUN TO LOVE YOU DYNASTY	51	1980
I'VE LOST YOU ELVIS PRESLEY	9	1970
I'VE NEVER BEEN IN LOVE SUZI QUATRO	56	1980
I'VE NEVER BEEN TO ME CHARLENE	1	1982
I'VE PASSED THIS WAY BEFORE JIMMY RUFFIN	29	1967
I'VE SEEN THE WORD BLANCMANGE	65	1982
I'VE TOLD EVERY LITTLE STAR LINDA SCOTT	7	1961
I'VE WAITED SO LONG ANTHONY NEWLEY	3	1959
IVORY SKIN UP	48	1991
IVORY TOWER THREE KAYES	20	1956
IZ U NELLY	36	2003
IZZO (H.O.V.A.) JAY-Z	21	2001

J

Title / Artist	Peak Position	Year of Entry
JACK AND DIANE JOHN COUGAR	25	1982
JACK AND JILL RAYDIO	11	1978
JACK AND JILL PARTY PETE BURNS	75	2004
JACK IN THE BOX [A] CLODAGH RODGERS	4	1971
JACK IN THE BOX [B] MOMENTS	7	1977
JACK LE FREAK CHIC	19	1987
JACK MIX II MIRAGE	4	1987
JACK MIX III MIRAGE	4	1987
JACK MIX IV MIRAGE	8	1987
JACK MIX VII MIRAGE	50	1988
JACK O' DIAMONDS LONNIE DONEGAN	14	1957
JACK TALKING DAVE STEWART & THE SPIRITUAL COWBOYS	69	1990
THE JACK THAT HOUSE BUILT JACK 'N' CHILL	6	1987
JACK THE GROOVE RAZE	20	1987
JACK THE RIPPER [A] LL COOL J	37	1988
JACK THE RIPPER [B] NICK CAVE & THE BAD SEEDS	68	1992
JACK TO THE SOUND OF THE UNDERGROUND HITHOUSE	14	1988
JACK YOUR BODY STEVE 'SILK' HURLEY	1	1987
JACKET HANGS BLUE AEROPLANES	72	1990
JACKIE SCOTT WALKER	22	1967
JACKIE WILSON SAID KEVIN ROWLAND & DEXY'S MIDNIGHT RUNNERS	5	1982
JACKIE'S RACING WHITEOUT	72	1995
JACK'S HEROES POGUES & THE DUBLINERS	63	1990
JACKSON NANCY SINATRA & LEE HAZLEWOOD	11	1967
JACKY MARC ALMOND	17	1991
JACQUELINE [A] BOBBY HELMS WITH THE ANITA KERR SINGERS	20	1958
JACQUELINE [B] CORAL	44	2007
JACQUES DERRIDA SCRITTI POLITTI	43	1982
JACQUES YOUR BODY (MAKE ME SWEAT) LES RYTHMES DIGITALES	9	1999
JA-DA JOHNNY & THE HURRICANES	14	1961
JADED [A] GREEN DAY	28	1996
JADED [B] AEROSMITH	13	2001
JAGGED EDGE MICHAEL COURTNEY	64	2002
JAGUAR DJ ROLANDO AKA AZTEC MYSTIC	43	2000
JAIL HOUSE RAP FAT BOYS	63	1985
JAILBIRD PRIMAL SCREAM	29	1994
JAILBREAK [A] THIN LIZZY	31	1976
JAILBREAK [B] PARADOX	66	1990
JAILHOUSE ROCK ELVIS PRESLEY	1	1958
JAILHOUSE ROCK EP ELVIS PRESLEY	18	1958
JAM MICHAEL JACKSON	13	1992
THE JAM EP A TRIBE CALLED QUEST	61	1997
JAM IT JAM SHE ROCKERS	58	1990
JAM J JAMES	24	1994
JAM JAM JAM PEOPLE'S CHOICE	40	1978
JAM ON REVENGE (THE WIKKI WIKKI SONG) NEWCLEUS	44	1983

Title / Artist	Peak Position	Year of Entry
JAM SIDE DOWN STATUS QUO	17	2002
JAMAICAN IN NEW YORK SHINEHEAD	30	1993
JAMBALAYA JO STAFFORD	11	1952
JAMBALAYA FATS DOMINO	41	1962
JAMBALAYA (ON THE BAYOU) CARPENTERS	12	1974
JAMBOREE NAUGHTY BY NATURE FEATURING ZHANE	51	1999
THE JAMES BOND THEME JOHN BARRY ORCHESTRA	13	1962
JAMES BOND THEME MOBY	8	1997
JAMES DEAN (I WANNA KNOW) DANIEL BEDINGFIELD	4	2002
JAMES HAS KITTENS BLU PETER	70	1998
JAMMIN' BOB MARLEY FEATURING MC LYTE	42	2000
JAMMIN' IN AMERICA GAP BAND	64	1984
JAMMING BOB MARLEY & THE WAILERS	9	1977
JANA KILLING JOKE	54	1995
JANE [A] JEFFERSON STARSHIP	21	1980
JANE [B] PERFECT DAY	68	1989
JANE FALLS DOWN MODERN	35	2005
JANEIRO SOLID SESSIONS	47	2002
JANIE, DON'T TAKE YOUR LOVE TO TOWN JON BON JOVI	13	1997
JANIE JONES (STRUMMERVILLE) BABYSHAMBLES & FRIENDS	17	2006
JANUARY PILOT	1	1975
JANUARY FEBRUARY BARBARA DICKSON	11	1980
JAPANESE BOY ANEKA	1	1981
JARROW SONG ALAN PRICE	6	1974
JAWS LALO SCHIFRIN	14	1976
JAYOU JURASSIC 5	56	1998
JAZZ CARNIVAL AZYMUTH	19	1980
JAZZ IT UP REEL 2 REAL	7	1996
JAZZ RAP KIM CARNEGIE	73	1991
JAZZ THING GANG STARR	66	1990
JAZZIN' THE WAY YOU KNOW JAZZY M	47	2000
JCB SONG NIZLOPI	1	2005
JE NE SAIS PAS POURQUOI KYLIE MINOGUE	2	1988
JE SUIS MUSIC CERRONE	39	1979
JE T'AIME (ALLO ALLO) RENE & YVETTE	57	1986
JE T'AIME (MOI NON PLUS) JUDGE DREAD	9	1975
JE T'AIME...MOI NON PLUS JANE BIRKIN & SERGE GAINSBOURG	1	1969
JE VOULAIS TE DIRE (QUE JE T'ATTENDS) MANHATTAN TRANSFER	40	1978
JEALOUS AGAIN BLACK CROWES	70	1991
JEALOUS GUY ROXY MUSIC	1	1981
JEALOUS GUY JOHN LENNON	65	1985
JEALOUS HEART CADETS WITH EILEEN READ	42	1965
JEALOUS HEART CONNIE FRANCIS	44	1966
JEALOUS LOVE [A] JO BOXERS	72	1983
JEALOUS LOVE [B] HAZELL DEAN	63	1984
JEALOUS MIND ALVIN STARDUST	1	1974
JEALOUSY [A] BILLY FURY	2	1961
JEALOUSY [B] AMII STEWART	58	1979
JEALOUSY [C] ADVENTURES OF STEVIE V	58	1991
JEALOUSY [D] PET SHOP BOYS	12	1991
JEALOUSY [E] OCTOPUS	59	1996
JEALOUSY [F] MARTIN SOLVEIG	62	2006
THE JEAN GENIE DAVID BOWIE	2	1972
JEAN THE BIRDMAN DAVID SYLVIAN & ROBERT FRIPP	68	1993
JEANETTE BEAT	45	1982
JEANNIE DANNY WILLIAMS	14	1962
JEANNIE, JEANNIE, JEANNIE EDDIE COCHRAN	31	1961
JEANNY FALCO	68	1986
JEANS ON DAVID DUNDAS	3	1976
JEDI WANNABE BELLATRIX	65	2000
JEEPSTER T REX	2	1971
JEEPSTER POLECATS	53	1981
JELLYHEAD CRUSH	50	1996
JENNIFER ECCLES HOLLIES	7	1968
JENNIFER JUNIPER DONOVAN	5	1968
JENNIFER JUNIPER SINGING CORNER MEETS DONOVAN	68	1990
JENNIFER SHE SAID LLOYD COLE & THE COMMOTIONS	31	1988
JENNY STELLASTARR*	46	2003
JENNY DON'T BE HASTY PAOLO NUTINI	20	2006
JENNY FROM THE BLOCK JENNIFER LOPEZ	3	2002
JENNY JENNY LITTLE RICHARD	11	1957
JENNY ONDIOLINE STEREOLAB	75	1994
JENNY TAKE A RIDE MITCH RYDER & THE DETROIT WHEELS	33	1966
JENNY WREN PAUL McCARTNEY	22	2005
JEOPARDY GREG KIHN BAND	63	1983
JEREMY PEARL JAM	15	1992
JERICHO [A] SIMPLY RED	53	1986
JERICHO [B] PRODIGY	11	1992
JERK IT OUT CAESARS	8	2003
JERUSALEM [A] FALL	69	1988
JERUSALEM [A] FAT LES 2000	10	2000
JERUSALEM [A] KEEDIE & THE ENGLAND CRICKET TEAM	19	2005
JERUSALEM [B] HERB ALPERT & THE TIJUANA BRASS	42	1970
JESAMINE CASUALS	2	1968
JESSE HOLD ON B*WITCHED	4	1999
JESSICA [A] JOSHUA KADISON	15	1994
JESSICA [B] ADAM GREEN	63	2004
JESSICA [C] ELLIOT MINOR	19	2007
JESSIE'S GIRL RICK SPRINGFIELD	43	1984
JESUS CLIFF RICHARD	35	1972
JESUS CHRIST LONGPIGS	61	1995
JESUS CHRIST POSE SOUNDGARDEN	30	1992
JESUS HAIRDO CHARLATANS	48	1994
JESUS HE KNOWS ME GENESIS	20	1992
JESUS OF SUBURBIA GREEN DAY	17	2005
JESUS SAYS ASH	15	1998
JESUS TO A CHILD GEORGE MICHAEL	1	1996
JESUS WALKS KANYE WEST	16	2004
JET PAUL McCARTNEY & WINGS	7	1974
JET CITY WOMAN QUEENSRYCHE	39	1991
JET-STAR TEKNOO TOO	56	1991
JETSTREAM NEW ORDER FEATURING ANA MANTRONIC	20	2005
JEWEL CRANES	29	1993
JEZEBEL MARTY WILDE	19	1962
JEZEBEL SHAKIN' STEVENS	58	1989
JIBARO ELECTRA	54	1988
JIG A JIG EAST OF EDEN	7	1971
JIGGA JIGGA SCOOTER	48	2004
JIGGY CLIPZ	71	2004
JIGSAW FALLING INTO PLACE RADIOHEAD	30	2008
JILTED JOHN JILTED JOHN	4	1978
JIMMIE JONES VAPORS	44	1981
JIMMY [A] PURPLE HEARTS	60	1980
JIMMY [B] MIA	66	2007
JIMMY JIMMY UNDERTONES	16	1979
JIMMY LEE ARETHA FRANKLIN	46	1987
JIMMY MACK MARTHA REEVES & THE VANDELLAS	21	1967
JIMMY OLSEN'S BLUES SPIN DOCTORS	40	1993
JIMMY UNKNOWN LITA ROZA	15	1956
JIMMY'S GIRL JOHNNY TILLOTSON	43	1961
JINGLE BELL ROCK MAX BYGRAVES	7	1959
JINGLE BELL ROCK CHUBBY CHECKER & BOBBY RYDELL	40	1962
JINGLE BELLS JUDGE DREAD	64	1978
JINGLE BELLS CRAZY FROG	5	2005
JINGLE BELLS LAUGHING ALL THE WAY HYSTERICS	44	1981
JINGO CANDIDO	55	1981
JINGO JELLYBEAN	12	1987
JINGO F.K.W.	30	1994
JITTERBUGGIN' HEATWAVE	34	1981
JIVE TALKIN' BEE GEES	5	1975
JIVE TALKIN' BOOGIE BOX HIGH	7	1987
JJ TRIBUTE ASHA	38	1995
JOAN OF ARC ORCHESTRAL MANOEUVRES IN THE DARK	5	1981
JOANNA [A] SCOTT WALKER	7	1968
JOANNA [B] KOOL & THE GANG	2	1984
JOANNA [C] MRS WOOD	34	1995
JOCELYN SQUARE LOVE & MONEY	51	1989
JOCK MIX 1 MAD JOCKS FEATURING JOCKMASTER B.A.	46	1987
JOCKO HOMO DEVO	62	1978
JODY JERMAINE STEWART	50	1986
JOE INSPIRAL CARPETS	37	1995
JOE LE TAXI VANESSA PARADIS	3	1988
JOE LOUIS JOHN SQUIRE	43	2002
***JOE 90* (THEME)** BARRY GRAY ORCHESTRA WITH PETER BECKETT - KEYBOARDS	53	1986
JOGI PANJABI MC FEATURING JAY-Z	25	2003
JOHN AND JULIE EDDIE CALVERT	6	1955
JOHN I'M ONLY DANCING DAVID BOWIE	12	1972
JOHN I'M ONLY DANCING POLECATS	35	1981
JOHN KETLEY (IS A WEATHERMAN) TRIBE OF TOFFS	21	1988
JOHN THE REVELATOR DEPECHE MODE	18	2006
JOHN WAYNE IS BIG LEGGY HAYSI FANTAYZEE	11	1982
JOHNNY AND MARY ROBERT PALMER	44	1980
JOHNNY ANGEL PATTI LYNN	37	1962
JOHNNY ANGEL SHELLEY FABARES	41	1962
JOHNNY B. GOODE JIMI HENDRIX	35	1972
JOHNNY B GOODE PETE TOSH	48	1983
JOHNNY B. GOODE JUDAS PRIEST	64	1988
JOHNNY CASH SONS & DAUGHTERS	68	2004
JOHNNY COME HOME FINE YOUNG CANNIBALS	8	1985
JOHNNY COME LATELY STEVE EARLE	75	1988
JOHNNY DAY ROLF HARRIS	44	1963
JOHNNY FRIENDLY JO BOXERS	31	1983
JOHNNY GET ANGRY CAROL DEENE	32	1962
JOHNNY JOHNNY PREFAB SPROUT	64	1986
JOHNNY MATHIS' FEET AMERICAN MUSIC CLUB	58	1993
JOHNNY PANIC AND THE BIBLE OF DREAMS JOHNNY PANIC & THE BIBLE OF DREAMS	70	1991
JOHNNY REGGAE PIGLETS	3	1971
JOHNNY REMEMBER ME JOHN LEYTON	1	1961
JOHNNY REMEMBER ME METEORS	66	1983
JOHNNY ROCCO MARTY WILDE	30	1960
JOHNNY THE HORSE MADNESS	44	1999
JOHNNY WILL PAT BOONE	4	1961
JOIN IN AND SING AGAIN JOHNSTON BROTHERS	9	1955
JOIN IN AND SING (NO. 3) JOHNSTON BROTHERS	24	1956
JOIN ME LIGHTFORCE	53	2000
JOIN OUR CLUB SAINT ETIENNE	21	1992
JOIN THE PARTY HONKY	28	1977
JOIN TOGETHER WHO	9	1972
JOINING YOU ALANIS MORISSETTE	28	1999
JOINTS & JAMS BLACK EYED PEAS	53	1998
JOJO ACTION MR PRESIDENT	73	1998
JOKE (I'M LAUGHING) EDDI READER	42	1994
THE JOKE ISN'T FUNNY ANYMORE SMITHS	49	1985
THE JOKER STEVE MILLER BAND	1	1990
THE JOKER FATBOY SLIM	32	2005
JOKER & THE THIEF WOLFMOTHER	64	2006
THE JOKER (THE WIGAN JOKER) ALLNIGHT BAND	50	1979
JOLE BLON GARY U.S. BONDS	51	1981
JOLENE DOLLY PARTON	7	1976
JOLENE STRAWBERRY SWITCHBLADE	53	1985

Title / Artist	Peak Position	Year of Entry
JOLENE - LIVE UNDER BLACKPOOL LIGHTS WHITE STRIPES	16	2004
JONAH BREATHE	60	1988
JONATHAN DAVID BELLE & SEBASTIAN	31	2001
THE JONES' TEMPTATIONS	69	1992
JONES VS JONES KOOL & THE GANG	17	1981
JONESTOWN MIND ALMIGHTY	26	1995
JONNY SNIPER ENTER SHIKARI	75	2007
JOOK GAL ELEPHANT MAN	41	2004
JORDAN: THE EP PREFAB SPROUT	35	1991
JOSE AND HIS AMAZING TECHNICOLOR OVERCOAT MARIO ROSENSTOCK	45	2006
JOSEPH MEGA REMIX JASON DONOVAN & ORIGINAL LONDON CAST FEATURING LINZI HATELY, DAVID EASTER & JOHNNY AMOBI	13	1991
JOSEPHINE [A] CHRIS REA	67	1985
JOSEPHINE [B] TERRORVISION	23	1998
JOSEY DEEP BLUE SOMETHING	27	1996
JOURNEY [A] DUNCAN BROWNE	23	1972
THE JOURNEY [A] CITIZEN CANED	41	2001
THE JOURNEY [B] 911	3	1997
THE JOURNEY [C] AMSTERDAM	32	2005
THE JOURNEY CONTINUES MARK BROWN FEATURING SARAH CRACKNELL	11	2008
JOURNEY TO THE MOON BIDDU ORCHESTRA	41	1978
JOURNEY TO THE PAST AALIYAH	22	1998
JOY [A] BAND AKA	24	1983
JOY [B] TEDDY PENDERGRASS	58	1988
JOY [C] SOUL II SOUL	4	1992
JOY [D] STAXX FEATURING CAROL LEEMING	14	1993
JOY [E] 7669	60	1994
JOY [F] BLACKstreet	56	1995
JOY [G] DENI HINES	47	1998
JOY [H] KATHY BROWN	63	1999
JOY! [I] GAY DAD	22	1999
JOY [J] MARK RYDER	34	2001
JOY AND HAPPINESS STABBS	65	1994
JOY AND HEARTBREAK MOVEMENT 98 FEATURING CARROLL THOMPSON	27	1990
JOY AND PAIN [A] DONNA ALLEN	10	1989
JOY AND PAIN [A] MAZE	57	1989
JOY AND PAIN [A] ROB BASE & DJ E-Z ROCK	47	1989
JOY AND PAIN [B] ANGELLE	43	2002
(JOY) I KNOW IT ODYSSEY	51	1985
JOY OF LIVING [A] CLIFF (Richard) & HANK (Marvin)	25	1970
JOY OF LIVING [B] OUI 3	55	1995
JOY TO THE WORLD THREE DOG NIGHT	24	1971
JOYBRINGER MANFRED MANN'S EARTH BAND	9	1973
JOYENERGIZER JOY KITIKONTI	57	2001
JOYRIDE ROXETTE	4	1991
JOYRIDER (YOU'RE PLAYING WITH FIRE) COLOUR GIRL	51	2000
JOYS OF CHRISTMAS CHRIS REA	67	1987
JOYS OF LIFE DAVID JOSEPH	61	1984
JUDGE FUDGE HAPPY MONDAYS	24	1991
JUDGEMENT DAY MS DYNAMITE	25	2005
THE JUDGEMENT IS THE MIRROR DALI'S CAR	66	1984
JUDY PIPETTES	46	2006
JUDY IN DISGUISE (WITH GLASSES) JOHN FRED & THE PLAYBOY BAND	3	1968
JUDY OVER THE RAINBOW ORANGE	73	1994
JUDY SAYS (KNOCK YOU IN THE HEAD) VIBRATORS	70	1978
JUDY TEEN COCKNEY REBEL	5	1974
JUGGLING RAGGA TWINS	71	1991
JUICEBOX STROKES	5	2005
JUICY WRECKS-N-EFFECT	29	1990
JUICY NOTORIOUS B.I.G.	72	1994
JUICY FRUIT MTUME	34	1983
A JUICY RED APPLE SKIN UP	32	1992
JUKE BOX BABY PERRY COMO	22	1956
JUKE BOX GYPSY LINDISFARNE	56	1978
JUKE BOX HERO FOREIGNER	48	1981
JUKE BOX JIVE RUBETTES	3	1974
JULIA [A] EURYTHMICS	44	1985
JULIA [B] CHRIS REA	18	1993
JULIA [C] SILVER SUN	51	1997
JULIA SAYS WET WET WET	3	1995
JULIE ANN KENNY	10	1975
JULIE DO YA LOVE ME BOBBY SHERMAN	28	1970
JULIE DO YA LOVE ME WHITE PLAINS	8	1970
JULIE (EP) LEVELLERS	17	1994
JULIE OCEAN UNDERTONES	41	1981
JULIET FOUR PENNIES	1	1964
JULIET (KEEP THAT IN MIND) THEA GILMORE	35	2003
JULY OCEAN COLOUR SCENE	31	2000
JUMBO [A] BEE GEES	25	1968
JUMBO [B] UNDERWORLD	21	1999
JUMP [A] VAN HALEN	7	1984
JUMP [A] BUS STOP	23	1999
JUMP [B] AZTEC CAMERA	34	1984
JUMP [C] KRIS KROSS	2	1992
JUMP! [D] MOVEMENT	57	1992
JUMP [E] GIRLS ALOUD	2	2003
JUMP [F] FADERS	21	2005
JUMP [G] FUN DMENTAL 03	44	2006
JUMP [H] MADONNA	9	2006
JUMP AROUND HOUSE OF PAIN	8	1992
JUMP BACK (SET ME FREE) DHAR BRAXTON	32	1986
JUMP DOWN B*WITCHED	16	2000
JUMP (FOR MY LOVE) POINTER SISTERS	6	1984
JUMP IN MY CAR DAVID HASSELHOFF	3	2006
JUMP JIVE AN' WAIL BRIAN SETZER ORCHESTRA	34	1999
JUMP N' SHOUT BASEMENT JAXX	12	1999
THE JUMP OFF LIL' KIM FEATURING MR CHEEKS	16	2003
JUMP ON DEMAND SPUNGE	39	2002
JUMP START NATALIE COLE	36	1987
JUMP THE GUN THREE DEGREES	48	1979
JUMP THEY SAY DAVID BOWIE	9	1993
JUMP TO IT ARETHA FRANKLIN	42	1982
JUMP TO MY BEAT WILDCHILD	30	1996
JUMP TO MY LOVE INCOGNITO	29	1996
JUMP TO THE BEAT STACY LATTISHAW	3	1980
JUMP TO THE BEAT DANNII MINOGUE	8	1991
JUMP UP JUST 4 JOKES FEATURING MC RB	67	2002
JUMPIN' LIBERTY X	6	2003
JUMPIN' JACK FLASH ARETHA FRANKLIN	58	1986
JUMPIN' JIVE JOE JACKSON'S JUMPIN' JIVE	43	1981
JUMPIN' JUMPIN' DESTINY'S CHILD	5	2000
JUMPING JACK FLASH ROLLING STONES	1	1968
JUNE AFTERNOON ROXETTE	52	1996
JUNE JULY APARTMENT	67	2005
JUNEAU FUNERAL FOR A FRIEND	19	2003
JUNGLE BILL YELLO	61	1992
THE JUNGLE BOOK GROOVE JUNGLE BOOK	14	1993
JUNGLE BROTHER JUNGLE BROTHERS	18	1997
JUNGLE FEVER CHAKACHAS	29	1972
JUNGLE HIGH JUNO REACTOR	45	1997
JUNGLE ROCK HANK MIZELL	3	1976
JUNGLE ROCK JUNGLE BOYS	30	2004
JUNGLIST DRUMSOUND/SIMON BASSLINE SMITH	67	2003
JUNIOR'S FARM PAUL McCARTNEY & WINGS	16	1974
JUNKIES EASYWORLD	40	2003
JUPITER EARTH, WIND & FIRE	41	1978
JUS 1 KISS BASEMENT JAXX	23	2001
JUS' A RASCAL DIZZEE RASCAL	30	2003
JUS' COME COOL JACK	44	1996
JUS' REACH (RECYCLED) GALLIANO	66	1992
JUST [A] RADIOHEAD	19	1995
JUST [A] MARK RONSON FEATURING ALEX GREENWALD	36	2006
JUST [B] JAMIE SCOTT	29	2004
JUST A DAY FEEDER	12	2001
JUST A DAY AWAY BARCLAY JAMES HARVEST	68	1983
JUST A DREAM [A] NENA	70	1984
JUST A DREAM [B] DONNA DE LORY	71	1993
JUST A FEELING BAD MANNERS	13	1981
JUST A FEW THINGS THAT I AIN'T BEAUTIFUL SOUTH	30	2003
JUST A FRIEND [A] BIZ MARKIE	55	1990
JUST A FRIEND [B] MARIO	18	2003
JUST A GIRL NO DOUBT	3	1996
JUST A GROOVE NOMAD	16	1991
JUST A LIL BIT 50 CENT	10	2005
JUST A LITTLE LIBERTY X	1	2002
JUST A LITTLE BIT [A] UNDERTAKERS	49	1964
JUST A LITTLE BIT [B] MUTYA BUENA	65	2007
JUST A LITTLE BIT BETTER HERMAN'S HERMITS	15	1965
JUST A LITTLE BIT OF LOVE REBEKAH RYAN	51	1996
JUST A LITTLE BIT TOO LATE WAYNE FONTANA & THE MINDBENDERS	20	1965
JUST A LITTLE GIRL AMY STUDT	14	2002
JUST A LITTLE MISUNDERSTANDING CONTOURS	31	1970
JUST A LITTLE MORE DELUXE	74	1989
JUST A LITTLE MORE LOVE DAVID GUETTA FEATURING CHRIS WILLIS	19	2003
JUST A LITTLE TOO MUCH RICKY NELSON	11	1959
JUST A LITTLE WHILE JANET JACKSON	15	2004
JUST A MAN MARK MORRISON	48	2004
JUST A MIRAGE JELLYBEAN FEATURING ADELE BERTEI	13	1988
JUST A RIDE JEM	16	2005
JUST A SHADOW BIG COUNTRY	26	1985
JUST A SMILE PILOT	31	1975
JUST A STEP FROM HEAVEN ETERNAL	8	1994
JUST A TOUCH KEITH SWEAT	35	1996
JUST A TOUCH OF LOVE SLAVE	64	1980
JUST A TOUCH OF LOVE EVERYDAY C & C MUSIC FACTORY FEATURING ZELMA DAVIS	31	1991
JUST AN ILLUSION IMAGINATION	2	1982
JUST ANOTHER BROKEN HEART SHEENA EASTON	33	1981
JUST ANOTHER DAY [A] JON SECADA	5	1992
JUST ANOTHER DAY [B] JONATHAN WILKES	24	2001
JUST ANOTHER DREAM CATHY DENNIS	13	1991
JUST ANOTHER GROOVE MIGHTY DUB KATZ	43	1996
JUST ANOTHER ILLUSION HURRICANE #1	35	1997
JUST ANOTHER NIGHT MICK JAGGER	32	1985
JUST AROUND THE HILL SASH!	8	2000
JUST AS LONG AS YOU ARE THERE VANESSA PARADIS	57	1993
JUST AS MUCH AS EVER NAT 'KING' COLE	18	1960
JUST BE TIESTO FEATURING KIRSTY HAWKSHAW	43	2004
JUST BE DUB TO ME REVELATION	36	2003
JUST BE GOOD TO ME S.O.S. BAND	13	1984
JUST BE TONIGHT BBG	45	1997
JUST BECAUSE JANE'S ADDICTION	14	2003
JUST BEFORE YOU LEAVE DEL AMITRI	37	2002
JUST BETWEEN YOU AND ME APRIL WINE	52	1981
JUST BORN JIM DALE	27	1958
JUST CALL SHERRICK	23	1987
JUST CALL ME GOOD GIRLS	75	1993
JUST CAN'T GET ENOUGH [A] DEPECHE MODE	8	1981
JUST CAN'T GET ENOUGH [B] TRANSFORMER 2	45	1996
JUST CAN'T GET ENOUGH [C] HARRY 'CHOO CHOO' ROMERO PRESENTS INAYA DAY	39	1999
JUST CAN'T GET ENOUGH (NO NO NO NO) EYE TO EYE FEATURING TAKA BOOM	36	2001
JUST CAN'T GIVE YOU UP MYSTIC MERLIN	20	1980

	Peak Position	Year of Entry
JUST CAN'T STAND IT MATT BIANCO	66	1986
JUST CAN'T WAIT (SATURDAY) 100% FEATURING JENNIFER JOHN	28	2005
JUST CHECKIN' BEAUTIFUL SOUTH	59	2000
JUST CRUISIN' WILL SMITH	23	1997
JUST DON'T WANT TO BE LONELY MAIN INGREDIENT	27	1974
JUST DON'T WANT TO BE LONELY FREDDIE McGREGOR	9	1987
JUST FADE AWAY STIFF LITTLE FINGERS	47	1981
JUST FINE MARY J BLIGE	16	2008
JUST FOR KICKS MIKE SARNE	22	1963
JUST FOR MONEY PAUL HARDCASTLE	19	1985
JUST FOR OLD TIME'S SAKE FOSTER & ALLEN	47	1984
JUST FOR ONE DAY (HEROES) DAVID GUETTA VS DAVID BOWIE	73	2003
JUST FOR TONIGHT ONE NIGHT ONLY	9	2008
JUST FOR YOU [A] FREDDIE & THE DREAMERS	41	1964
JUST FOR YOU [B] GLITTER BAND	10	1974
JUST FOR YOU [C] ALAN PRICE	32	1978
JUST FOR YOU [D] M PEOPLE	8	1997
JUST FOR YOU [E] LIONEL RICHIE	20	2004
JUST FRIENDS NINE BLACK ALPS	52	2005
JUST FUCK TOM NEVILLE	60	2004
JUST GET UP AND DANCE AFRIKA BAMBAATAA	45	1991
JUST GETS BETTER TJR FEATURING XAVIER	28	1987
JUST GIVE THE DJ A BREAK DYNAMIX II FEATURING TOO TOUGH TEE	50	1987
JUST GOOD FRIENDS FISH FEATURING SAM BROWN	63	1995
JUST GOT LUCKY JO BOXERS	7	1983
JUST GOT PAID JOHNNY KEMP	68	1988
JUST HOLD ON TOPLOADER	20	2000
JUST IN CASE JAHEIM	34	2001
JUST IN LUST WILDHEARTS	28	1995
JUST IN TIME RAW SILK	49	1983
JUST KEEP IT UP DEE CLARK	26	1959
JUST KEEP ME MOVING k.d. lang	59	1993
JUST KEEP ROCKIN' DOUBLE TROUBLE & THE REBEL MC	11	1989
JUST KICK COHEN VS DELUXE	70	2004
JUST KICKIN' IT XSCAPE	49	1993
JUST LET ME DO MY THING SINE	33	1978
JUST LIKE A MAN DEL AMITRI	25	1992
JUST LIKE A PILL P!NK	1	2002
JUST LIKE A WOMAN MANFRED MANN	10	1966
JUST LIKE ANYONE SOUL ASYLUM	52	1995
JUST LIKE BRUCE LEE KILLCITY	63	2004
JUST LIKE EDDIE HEINZ	5	1963
JUST LIKE FRED ASTAIRE JAMES	17	1999
JUST LIKE HEAVEN CURE	29	1987
JUST LIKE HEAVEN KATIE MELUA	35	2005
JUST LIKE HONEY JESUS & MARY CHAIN	45	1985
JUST LIKE JESSE JAMES CHER	11	1990
JUST LIKE PARADISE DAVID LEE ROTH	27	1988
(JUST LIKE) STARTING OVER JOHN LENNON	1	1980
JUST LISTEN TO MY HEART SPOTNICKS	36	1963
JUST LOOKIN' [A] CHARLATANS	32	1995
JUST LOOKING [B] STEREOPHONICS	4	1999
JUST LOSE IT EMINEM	1	2004
JUST LOVING YOU ANITA HARRIS	6	1967
(JUST) ME AND YOU NEW VISION	23	2000
JUST MELLOW RUTHLESS RAP ASSASSINS	75	1990
JUST MY IMAGINATION McGANNS	59	1998
JUST MY IMAGINATION (RUNNING AWAY WITH ME) TEMPTATIONS	8	1971
JUST MY SOUL RESPONDING SMOKEY ROBINSON	35	1974
JUST ONE LOOK [A] HOLLIES	2	1964
JUST ONE LOOK [B] FAITH, HOPE & CHARITY	38	1976
JUST ONE MORE KISS RENEE & RENATO	48	1983
JUST ONE MORE NIGHT YELLOW DOG	8	1978
JUST ONE SMILE GENE PITNEY	8	1966
JUST OUT OF REACH (OF MY TWO EMPTY ARMS) KEN DODD	29	1972
JUST OUTSIDE OF HEAVEN H20	38	1983
JUST PLAY MUSIC BIG AUDIO DYNAMITE	51	1988
JUST PLAYIN' JT PLAYAZ	30	1997
JUST PUT YOUR HAND IN MINE SPACE COWBOY	71	2003
JUST RIGHT SOUL II SOUL	38	1992
JUST ROUND A VERY GOOD FRIEND OF MINE	55	1999
JUST SAY NO GRANGE HILL CAST	5	1986
JUST SAY YOU LOVE ME MALACHI CUSH	49	2003
JUST SEVEN NUMBERS (CAN STRAIGHTEN OUT MY LIFE) FOUR TOPS	36	1971
JUST SHOW ME HOW TO LOVE YOU SARAH BRIGHTMAN & THE LSO FEATURING JOSE CURA	54	1997
JUST SO YOU KNOW AMERICAN HEAD CHARGE	52	2002
JUST TAH LET U KNOW EAZY-E	30	1996
JUST TAKE MY HEART MR BIG	26	1992
JUST THE ONE LEVELLERS, SPECIAL GUEST JOE STRUMMER	12	1995
JUST THE TWO OF US GROVER WASHINGTON Jr.	34	1981
JUST THE TWO OF US WILL SMITH	2	1998
JUST THE WAY ALFONZO HUNTER	38	1997
JUST THE WAY I'M FEELING FEEDER	10	2003
JUST THE WAY IT IS LISA MOORISH	42	1995
JUST THE WAY YOU ARE [A] BARRY WHITE	12	1978
JUST THE WAY YOU ARE [A] BILLY JOEL	19	1978
JUST THE WAY YOU ARE [B] MILKY	8	2002
JUST THE WAY YOU LIKE IT S.O.S. BAND	32	1984
JUST THIRTEEN LURKERS	66	1979
JUST THIS SIDE OF LOVE MALANDRA BURROWS	11	1990
JUST TO BE CLOSE TO YOU COMMODORES	62	1978
JUST TO SEE HER SMOKEY ROBINSON	52	1987
JUST WALK IN MY SHOES GLADYS KNIGHT & THE PIPS	35	1972
JUST WALKIN' IN THE RAIN JOHNNIE RAY	1	1956
JUST WANNA KNOW MAXI PRIEST	33	1992
JUST WANNA TOUCH ME FIDELFATTI FEATURING RONETTE	65	1990
JUST WANT TO LIVE OPEN	52	2004
JUST WANT YOU TO KNOW BACKSTREET BOYS	8	2005
JUST WAVE HELLO CHARLOTTE CHURCH	34	1999
JUST WHAT I ALWAYS WANTED MARI WILSON	8	1982
JUST WHAT I NEEDED CARS	17	1979
JUST WHEN I NEEDED YOU MOST RANDY VANWARMER	8	1979
JUST WHEN I NEEDED YOU MOST BARBARA JONES	31	1981
JUST WHEN YOU'RE THINKING THINGS OVER CHARLATANS	12	1995
JUST WHO IS THE FIVE O'CLOCK HERO JAM	8	1982
JUSTIFIED AND ANCIENT KLF, GUEST VOCALS TAMMY WYNETTE	2	1991
JUSTIFY MY LOVE MADONNA	2	1990
JUSTIFY THE RAIN COSMIC ROUGH RIDERS	39	2003
JUXTAPOZED WITH U SUPER FURRY ANIMALS	14	2001

K

	Peak Position	Year of Entry
KA-CHING SHANIA TWAIN	8	2003
KALEIDOSCOPE SKIES JAM & SPOON FEATURING PLAVKA	48	1997
KAMICHI HELL IS FOR HEROES	72	2004
KAMIKAZE KING ADORA	68	2003
KANSAS CITY LITTLE RICHARD	26	1959
KANSAS CITY TRINI LOPEZ	35	1963
KANSAS CITY STAR ROGER MILLER	48	1965
KARA KARA NEW WORLD	17	1971
KARAOKE QUEEN CATATONIA	36	1999
KARAOKE SOUL TOM McRAE	48	2003
KARMA CHAMELEON CULTURE CLUB	4	1983
KARMA HOTEL SPOOKS	15	2001
KARMA POLICE RADIOHEAD	8	1997
KARMACOMA MASSIVE ATTACK	28	1995
KARMADROME POP WILL EAT ITSELF	17	1992
KATE BEN FOLDS FIVE	39	1997
KATE BUSH ON STAGE EP KATE BUSH	10	1979
KATHLEEN ROACHFORD	43	1989
KATHLEEN (EP) TINDERSTICKS	61	1994
KAYLEIGH MARILLION	2	1985
KEEEP YOUR BODY WORKING KLEEER	51	1979
KEEP A KNOCKIN' LITTLE RICHARD	21	1957
KEEP AWAY FROM OTHER GIRLS HELEN SHAPIRO	40	1962
KEEP COMING BACK RICHARD MARX	55	1991
KEEP CONTROL SONO	66	2001
KEEP DOIN' IT SHOWDOWN	41	1977
KEEP EACH OTHER WARM BUCKS FIZZ	45	1986
(KEEP FEELING) FASCINATION HUMAN LEAGUE	2	1983
KEEP FISHIN' WEEZER	29	2002
KEEP GIVIN' ME YOUR LOVE CE CE PENISTON	36	1994
KEEP GIVING ME LOVE [A] D TRAIN	65	1983
KEEP GIVING ME LOVE [B] BOMB THE BASS	62	1992
KEEP HOPE ALIVE [A] SERIAL DIVA	57	1997
KEEP HOPE ALIVE [B] CRYSTAL METHOD	71	1998
KEEP IN TOUCH FREEEZ	49	1980
KEEP IN TOUCH (BODY TO BODY) SHADES OF LOVE	64	1995
KEEP IT COMIN' (DANCE TILL YOU CAN'T DANCE NO MORE) C & C MUSIC FACTORY FEATURING UNIQUE & DEBORAH COOPER	34	1992
KEEP IT COMIN' LOVE KC & THE SUNSHINE BAND	31	1976
KEEP IT DARK GENESIS	33	1981
KEEP IT ON HANNAH JONES	67	1993
KEEP IT OUT OF SIGHT PAUL & BARRY RYAN	30	1967
KEEP IT TO YOURSELF REUBEN	62	2005
KEEP IT TOGETHER DAVID GRANT	56	1990
KEEP IT UP SHARADA HOUSE GANG	36	1995
KEEP LOVE NEW BETTY WRIGHT	71	1989
KEEP LOVE TOGETHER LOVE TO INFINITY	38	1995
KEEP LOVE TOGETHER SODA CLUB FEATURING ANDREA ANATOLA	31	2003
KEEP ME A SECRET AINSLIE HENDERSON	5	2003
KEEP ME FROM THE COLD CURTIS STIGERS	57	1995
KEEP ME IN MIND BOY GEORGE	29	1987
KEEP ON [A] BRUCE CHANNEL	12	1968
KEEP ON [B] CABARET VOLTAIRE	55	1990
KEEP ON BELIEVING GRAND PRIX	75	1982
KEEP ON BURNING EDWYN COLLINS	45	1996
KEEP ON DANCIN' GARY'S GANG	8	1979
KEEP ON DANCIN' (LET'S GO) PERPETUAL MOTION	12	1998
KEEP ON DANCING BAY CITY ROLLERS	9	1971
KEEP ON JAMMIN' WILLIE HUTCH	73	1985
KEEP ON JUMPIN' LISA MARIE EXPERIENCE	7	1996
KEEP ON JUMPIN' TODD TERRY FEATURING MARTHA WASH & JOCELYN BROWN	8	1996
KEEP ON JUMPIN' CORENELL & LISA MARIE EXPERIENCE	37	2007
KEEP ON KEEPIN' ON [A] REDSKINS	43	1984
KEEP ON LOVING YOU REO SPEEDWAGON	7	1981
KEEP ON MOVIN' [A] SOUL II SOUL FEATURING CARON WHEELER	5	1989
KEEP ON MOVIN' [C] FIVE	1	1999
KEEP ON MOVING [B] BOB MARLEY & THE WAILERS	17	1995

Title / Artist	Peak Position	Year of Entry
KEEP ON PUMPIN' IT VISIONMASTERS WITH TONY KING & KYLIE MINOGUE	49	1991
KEEP ON PUSHING OUR LOVE NIGHTCRAWLERS FEATURING JOHN REID & ALYSHA WARREN	30	1996
KEEP ON RUNNIN' (TILL YOU BURN) U.K. SUBS	41	1981
KEEP ON RUNNING SPENCER DAVIS GROUP	1	1965
KEEP ON RUNNING JOHN ALFORD	24	1996
(KEEP ON) SHINING LOVELAND FEATURING RACHEL McFARLANE	37	1994
KEEP ON TRUCKIN' EDDIE KENDRICKS	18	1973
KEEP ON WALKIN' CE CE PENISTON	10	1992
KEEP ON, KEEPIN' ON [B] MC LYTE FEATURING XSCAPE	27	1996
KEEP PUSHIN' [A] CLOCK	7	1995
KEEP PUSHIN' [B] BORIS DLUGOSCH PRESENTS BOOOM!	41	1996
KEEP PUSHIN' ON YETI	57	2005
KEEP REACHING OUT FOR LOVE LINER	49	1979
KEEP SEARCHIN' (WE'LL FOLLOW THE SUN) DEL SHANNON	3	1965
KEEP STEPPIN' OMAR	57	1994
KEEP TALKING PINK FLOYD	26	1994
KEEP THE CAR RUNNING ARCADE FIRE	56	2007
KEEP THE CUSTOMER SATISFIED MARSHA HUNT	41	1970
KEEP THE FAITH BON JOVI	5	1992
KEEP THE FIRE BURNIN' DAN HARTMAN STARRING LOLEATTA HOLLOWAY	49	1995
KEEP THE FIRES BURNING CLOCK	36	1994
KEEP THE HOME FIRES BURNING BLUETONES	13	2000
KEEP THE MUSIC STRONG BIZARRE INC	33	1996
KEEP THEIR HEADS RINGIN' DR DRE	25	1995
KEEP THIS FIRE BURNING BEVERLEY KNIGHT	16	2005
KEEP THIS FREQUENCY CLEAR DTI	73	1988
KEEP US TOGETHER STARSAILOR	47	2006
KEEP WARM JINNY	11	1991
KEEP WHAT YA GOT IAN BROWN	18	2004
KEEP YOUR EYE ON ME HERB ALPERT	19	1987
KEEP YOUR HANDS OFF MY BABY LITTLE EVA	30	1963
KEEP YOUR HANDS OFF MY GIRL GOOD CHARLOTTE	23	2007
KEEP YOUR HANDS TO YOURSELF GEORGIA SATELLITES	69	1987
KEEP YOUR LOVE PARTIZAN FEATURING NATALIE ROBB	53	1997
KEEP YOUR WORRIES GURU'S JAZZAMATAZZ FEATURING ANGIE STONE	57	2000
KEEPER OF THE CASTLE FOUR TOPS	18	1972
KEEPIN' LOVE NEW HOWARD JOHNSON	45	1982
KEEPIN' THE FAITH DE LA SOUL	50	1991
KEEPING A RENDEZVIUS BUDGIE	71	1981
KEEPING SECRETS SWITCH	61	1984
KEEPING THE DREAM ALIVE FREIHEIT	14	1988
KEEPS IN ME IN WONDERLAND STEVE MILLER BAND	52	1982
KEINE LUST RAMMSTEIN	35	2005
KELLY WAYNE GIBSON	48	1964
KELLY WATCH THE STARS AIR	18	1998
KELLY'S HEROES BLACK GRAPE	17	1995
KENNEDY WEDDING PRESENT	33	1989
KENTUCKY RAIN ELVIS PRESLEY	21	1970
KERNKRAFT 400 ZOMBIE NATION	2	2000
KERRY KERRY CINERAMA	71	1998
THE KETCHUP SONG (ASEREJE) LAS KETCHUP	1	2002
KEVIN CARTER MANIC STREET PREACHERS	9	1996
KEWPIE DOLL FRANKIE VAUGHAN	10	1958
KEWPIE DOLL PERRY COMO	9	1958
THE KEY [A] SENSER	47	1993
THE KEY [B] MATT GOSS	40	1995
KEY LARGO BERTIE HIGGINS	60	1982
THE KEY THE SECRET URBAN COOKIE COLLECTIVE	2	1993
KEY TO MY LIFE BOYZONE	3	1995
A KICK I N THE MOUTH REUBEN	58	2005
KICK IN THE EYE BAUHAUS	59	1981
KICK IN THE EYE (EP) BAUHAUS	45	1982
KICK IT [A] NITZER EBB	56	1995
KICK IT [B] REGGAE BOYZ	59	1998
KICK IT [C] PEACHES FEATURING IGGY POP	39	2003
KICK IT IN SIMPLE MINDS	15	1989
KICK PUSH LUPE FIASCO	27	2006
KICKIN' HARD KLUBHEADS	36	1998
KICKIN' IN THE BEAT PAMELA FERNANDEZ	43	1994
KICKING MY HEART AROUND BLACK CROWES	55	1998
KICKING UP DUST LITTLE ANGELS	46	1990
KICKING UP THE LEAVES MARK WYNTER	24	1960
KID PRETENDERS	33	1979
KID 2000 HYBRID FEATURING CHRISSIE HYNDE	32	2000
KIDDIO BROOK BENTON	41	1960
KIDS ROBBIE WILLIAMS & KYLIE MINOGUE	2	2000
THE KIDS ARE ALRIGHT WHO	41	1966
THE KIDS ARE BACK TWISTED SISTER	32	1983
THE KIDS AREN'T ALRIGHT OFFSPRING	11	1999
KIDS IN AMERICA KIM WILDE	2	1981
THE KID'S LAST FIGHT FRANKIE LAINE	3	1954
KIDS OF THE CENTURY HELLOWEEN	56	1991
KIDS ON THE STREET ANGELIC UPSTARTS	57	1981
KIDS WITH GUNS GORILLAZ	27	2006
KIKI RIRI BOOM SHAFT	62	2001
THE KILL 30 SECONDS TO MARS	28	2007
KILL ALL HIPPIES PRIMAL SCREAM	24	2000
KILL 100 X-PRESS 2	59	2006
KILL THE DIRECTOR WOMBATS	35	2007
KILL THE KING RAINBOW	41	1977
KILL THE POOR DEAD KENNEDYS	49	1980
KILL YOUR OWN HUNDRED REASONS	48	2006
KILL YOUR TELEVISION NED'S ATOMIC DUSTBIN	53	1990
KILLAMANGIRO BABYSHAMBLES	8	2004
KILLED BY DEATH MOTORHEAD	51	1984
KILLER ADAMSKI	1	1990
KILLER ATB	4	2000
KILLER (EP) SEAL	8	1991
KILLER ON THE LOOSE THIN LIZZY	10	1980
KILLER QUEEN QUEEN	2	1974
KILLERS LIVE EP THIN LIZZY	19	1981
KILLIN' TIME TINA COUSINS	15	1999
KILLING IN THE NAME RAGE AGAINST THE MACHINE	25	1993
THE KILLING JAR SIOUXSIE & THE BANSHEES	41	1988
KILLING LONELINESS H.I.M.	26	2006
KILLING ME SOFTLY FUGEES	1	1996
KILLING ME SOFTLY WITH HIS SONG ROBERTA FLACK	6	1973
THE KILLING MOON ECHO & THE BUNNYMEN	9	1984
THE KILLING OF GEORGIE ROD STEWART	2	1976
A KIND OF CHRISTMAS CARD MORTEN HARKET	53	1995
A KIND OF MAGIC QUEEN	3	1986
KINDA LOVE DARIUS	8	2004
KINDA NEW SPEKTRUM	70	2004
KINETIC GOLDEN GIRLS	38	1998
KING UB40	4	1980
THE KING AND QUEEN OF AMERICA EURYTHMICS	29	1990
KING CREOLE ELVIS PRESLEY	2	1958
KING FOR A DAY [A] THOMPSON TWINS	22	1985
KING FOR A DAY [B] JAMIROQUAI	20	1999
KING IN A CATHOLIC STYLE (WAKE UP) CHINA CRISIS	19	1985
THE KING IS DEAD GO WEST	67	1987
THE KING IS HALF UNDRESSED JELLYFISH	39	1991
THE KING IS HERE/THE 900 NUMBER 45 KING	60	1989
KING KONG TERRY LIGHTFOOT & HIS NEW ORLEANS JAZZMEN	29	1961
KING MIDAS IN REVERSE HOLLIES	18	1967
KING OF CLOWNS NEIL SEDAKA	23	1962
KING OF DREAMS DEEP PURPLE	70	1990
KING OF EMOTION BIG COUNTRY	16	1988
KING OF KINGS EZZ RECO & THE LAUNCHERS WITH BOSIE GRANT	44	1964
THE KING OF KISSINGDOM MY LIFE STORY	35	1997
KING OF LOVE DAVE EDMUNDS	68	1990
KING OF MISERY HONEYCRACK	32	1996
KING OF MY CASTLE WAMDUE PROJECT	1	1999
KING OF NEW YORK FUN LOVIN' CRIMINALS	28	1997
KING OF PAIN POLICE	17	1984
THE KING OF ROCK 'N' ROLL PREFAB SPROUT	7	1988
KING OF SNAKE UNDERWORLD	17	1999
KING OF SORROW SADE	59	2001
KING OF THE COPS BILLY HOWARD	6	1975
KING OF THE DANCEHALL BEENIE MAN	14	2004
KING OF THE KERB ECHOBELLY	25	1995
KING OF THE MOUNTAIN KATE BUSH	4	2005
KING OF THE NEW YORK STREET DION	74	1989
KING OF THE ROAD ROGER MILLER	1	1965
KING OF THE ROAD (EP) PROCLAIMERS	9	1990
KING OF THE RODEO KINGS OF LEON	41	2005
KING OF THE RUMBLING SPIRES TYRANNOSAURUS REX	44	1969
THE KING OF WISHFUL THINKING GO WEST	18	1990
KING ROCKER GENERATION X	11	1979
KING WITHOUT A CROWN ABC	44	1987
KINGDOM ULTRAMARINE	46	1993
KINGDOM DAVE GAHAN	44	2007
KINGDOM OF DOOM THE GOOD THE BAD & THE QUEEN	20	2007
KINGS AND QUEENS KILLING JOKE	58	1985
KING'S CALL PHIL LYNOTT	35	1980
KINGS OF THE WILD FRONTIER ADAM & THE ANTS	2	1980
KINGSTON TOWN UB40	4	1990
KINKY AFRO HAPPY MONDAYS	5	1990
KINKY BOOTS PATRICK MACNEE & HONOR BLACKMAN	5	1990
KINKY LOVE PALE SAINTS	72	1991
KISS [A] DEAN MARTIN	5	1953
KISS [B] PRINCE & THE REVOLUTION	6	1986
KISS [B] AGE OF CHANCE	50	1987
KISS [B] ART OF NOISE FEATURING TOM JONES	5	1988
KISS AND SAY GOODBYE MANHATTANS	4	1976
KISS AND SAY GOODBYE UB40	19	2005
KISS AND TELL [A] BRYAN FERRY	41	1988
KISS AND TELL [B] BROWNSTONE	21	1997
KISS FROM A ROSE SEAL	4	1994
KISS KISS [A] HOLLY VALENCE	1	2002
KISS KISS [B] CHRIS BROWN FEATURING T-PAIN	38	2007
KISS LIKE ETHER CLAUDIA BRUCKEN	63	1991
KISS ME [A] STEPHEN 'TIN TIN' DUFFY	4	1985
KISS ME [B] SIXPENCE NONE THE RICHER	4	1999
KISS ME ANOTHER GEORGIA GIBBS	24	1956
KISS ME DEADLY LITA FORD	75	1988
KISS ME GOODBYE PETULA CLARK	50	1968
KISS ME HONEY HONEY KISS ME SHIRLEY BASSEY	3	1958
KISS ME QUICK ELVIS PRESLEY	14	1963
KISS MY EYES BOB SINCLAR	67	2003

Title / Artist	Peak Position	Year of Entry
THE KISS OF DAWN H.I.M.	59	2007
KISS OF LIFE [A] SADE	44	1993
KISS OF LIFE [B] SUPERGRASS	23	2004
KISS ON MY LIST DARYL HALL & JOHN OATES	33	1980
KISS ON THE LIPS DUALERS	21	2004
KISS THAT FROG PETER GABRIEL	46	1993
KISS THE BRIDE ELTON JOHN	20	1983
KISS THE DIRT (FALLING DOWN THE MOUNTAIN) INXS	54	1986
KISS THE GIRL PETER ANDRE	9	1998
KISS THE RAIN BILLIE MYERS	4	1998
KISS THEM FOR ME SIOUXSIE & THE BANSHEES	32	1991
KISS THIS THING GOODBYE DEL AMITRI	43	1989
KISS (WHEN THE SUN DON'T SHINE) VENGABOYS	3	1999
KISS YOU ALL OVER EXILE	6	1978
KISS YOU ALL OVER NO MERCY	16	1997
KISS YOU OFF SCISSOR SISTERS	43	2007
KISSES IN THE MOONLIGHT GEORGE BENSON	60	1986
KISSES ON THE WIND NENEH CHERRY	20	1989
KISSES SWEETER THAN WINE FRANKIE VAUGHAN	8	1957
KISSES SWEETER THAN WINE JIMMIE RODGERS	7	1957
KISSIN' COUSINS ELVIS PRESLEY	10	1964
KISSIN' IN THE BACK ROW OF THE MOVIES DRIFTERS	2	1974
KISSIN' YOU TOTAL	29	1996
KISSING A FOOL GEORGE MICHAEL	18	1988
KISSING GATE SAM BROWN	23	1990
KISSING WITH CONFIDENCE WILL POWERS	17	1983
KITE NICK HEYWARD	44	1993
KITES SIMON DUPREE & THE BIG SOUND	9	1967
KITSCH BARRY RYAN	37	1970
KITTY CAT STEVENS	47	1967
KLACTOVEESEDSTEIN BLUE RONDO A LA TURK	50	1982
KLUB KOLLABORATIONS BK	43	2003
KLUBHOPPING KLUBHEADS	10	1996
KNEE DEEP AND DOWN RAIN BAND	56	2003
KNEE DEEP IN THE BLUES GUY MITCHELL	3	1957
KNEE DEEP IN THE BLUES TOMMY STEELE & THE STEELMEN	15	1957
KNIFE EDGE ALARM	43	1986
KNIGHTS OF CYDONIA MUSE	10	2006
KNIVES OUT RADIOHEAD	13	2001
KNOCK KNOCK WHO'S THERE MARY HOPKIN	2	1970
KNOCK ME OUT GARY'S GANG	45	1982
KNOCK ON WOOD EDDIE FLOYD	19	1967
KNOCK ON WOOD OTIS REDDING & CARLA THOMAS	35	1967
KNOCK ON WOOD DAVID BOWIE	10	1974
KNOCK ON WOOD AMII STEWART	6	1979
KNOCK OUT TRIPLE EIGHT	8	2003
KNOCK THREE TIMES DAWN	1	1971
KNOCKDOWN ALESHA	45	2006
KNOCKED IT OFF B.A. ROBERTSON	8	1979
KNOCKED OUT PAULA ABDUL	21	1990
KNOCKIN' ON HEAVEN'S DOOR BOB DYLAN	14	1973
KNOCKIN' ON HEAVEN'S DOOR ERIC CLAPTON	38	1975
KNOCKIN' ON HEAVEN'S DOOR GUNS N' ROSES	2	1992
KNOCKIN' ON HEAVEN'S DOOR DUNBLANE	1	1996
KNOCKING AT YOUR BACK DOOR DEEP PURPLE	68	1985
KNOCKS ME OFF MY FEET DONELL JONES	58	1997
KNOW BY NOW ROBERT PALMER	25	1994
KNOW YOU WANNA 3RD EDGE	17	2003
KNOW YOUR RIGHTS CLASH	43	1982
KNOWING ME KNOWING YOU ABBA	1	1977
KO SMUJJI	43	2004
KOKOMO [A] BEACH BOYS	25	1988
KOKOMO [B] ADAM GREEN	63	2004
KOMMOTION DUANE EDDY & THE REBELS	13	1960
KOMODO (SAVE A SOUL) MAURO PICOTTO	13	2001
KON-TIKI SHADOWS	1	1961
KOOCHIE RYDER FREAKY REALISTIC	52	1993
KOOCHY ARMAND VAN HELDEN	4	2000
KOOKIE KOOKIE (LEND ME YOUR COMB) EDWARD BYRNES & CONNIE STEVENS	27	1960
KOOKIE LITTLE PARADISE FRANKIE VAUGHAN	31	1960
KOOL IN THE KAFTAN B.A. ROBERTSON	17	1980
KOOTCHI NENEH CHERRY	38	1996
KOREAN BODEGA FUN LOVIN' CRIMINALS	15	1999
KOWALSKI PRIMAL SCREAM	8	1997
KRAFTY NEW ORDER	8	2005
KRUPA APOLLO 440	23	1996
KU KLUX KHAN STEEL PULSE	41	1978
KUMBAYA SANDPIPERS	38	1969
KUNG FU ASH	57	1995
KUNG FU FIGHTING CARL DOUGLAS	1	1974
KUNG FU FIGHTING BUS STOP FEATURING CARL DOUGLAS	8	1998
KUNG-FU 187 LOCKDOWN	9	1998
KUT IT RED EYE	62	1994
KYRIE MR MISTER	11	1986
KYRILA (EP) DEMIS ROUSSOS	33	1977

L

Title / Artist	Peak Position	Year of Entry
L WELLS FRANZ FERDINAND	14	2006
LA [A] MARC ET CLAUDE	28	1998
LA [B] AMY MacDONALD	48	2007
LA BAMBA LOS LOBOS	1	1987
LA BAMBA RITCHIE VALENS	49	1987
LA BOOGA ROOGA SURPRISE SISTERS	38	1976
LA BREEZE SIMIAN	55	2003
LA CAMISA NEGRA JUANES	32	2006
L.A. CONNECTION RAINBOW	40	1978
LA DEE DAH JACKIE DENNIS	4	1958
LA DERNIERE VALSE MIREILLE MATHIEU	26	1967
LA DONNA E MOBILE JOSE CARRERAS, PLACIDO DOMINGO & LUCIANO PAVAROTTI	21	1994
LA FEMME ACCIDENT ORCHESTRAL MANOEUVRES IN THE DARK	42	1985
LA FOLIE STRANGLERS	47	1982
LA ISLA BONITA MADONNA	1	1987
LA LA LA [A] MASSIEL	35	1968
LA LA LA [B] NAILA BOSS	65	2004
LA LA LA HEY HEY OUTHERE BROTHERS	7	1995
LA LA LAND GREEN VELVET	29	2002
LA LA (MEANS I LOVE YOU) SWING OUT SISTER	37	1994
LA LUNA [A] BELINDA CARLISLE	38	1989
LA LUNA [B] MOVIN' MELODIES PRODUCTION	64	1994
LA MER (BEYOND THE SEA) BOBBY DARIN	8	1960
LA MOUCHE CASSIUS	53	1999
LA MUSICA RUFF DRIVERZ PRESENTS ARROLA	14	1999
LA PLUME DE MA TANTE HUGO & LUIGI	29	1959
LA PRIMAVERA SASH!	3	1998
LA RITOURNELLE SEBASTIEN TELLIER	66	2005
THE L.A. RUN CARVELLS	31	1977
LA SERENISSIMA DNA	34	1990
LA SERENISSIMA (THEME FROM 'VENICE IN PERIL') RONDO VENEZIANO	58	1983
LA TODAY ALEX GOLD FEATURING PHILIP OAKEY	68	2003
LA TRISTESSE DURERA (SCREAM TO A SIGH) MANIC STREET PREACHERS	22	1993
A LA VIE, A L'AMOUR JAKIE QUARTZ	55	1989
LA VIE EN ROSE GRACE JONES	12	1986
L.A. WOMAN BILLY IDOL	70	1990
LA YENKA JOHNNY & CHARLEY	49	1965
LABELLED WITH LOVE SQUEEZE	4	1981
LABOUR OF LOVE HUE & CRY	6	1987
THE LABYRINTH MOOGWAI	68	2001
LACKEY OTHERS	21	2005
LA-DI-DA SAD CAFE	41	1980
LADIES MANTRONIX	55	1986
THE LADIES' BRAS JONNY TRUNK & WISBEY	27	2007
LADIES MAN D4	41	2003
LADIES NIGHT KOOL & THE GANG	9	1979
LADIES NIGHT ATOMIC KITTEN FEATURING KOOL & THE GANG	8	2003
LADY [A] WHISPERS	55	1980
LADY [B] KENNY ROGERS	12	1980
LADY [C] D'ANGELO	21	1996
LADY BARBARA PETER NOONE & HERMAN'S HERMITS	13	1970
LADY D'ARBANVILLE CAT STEVENS	8	1970
LADY ELEANOR LINDISFARNE	3	1972
LADY GODIVA PETER & GORDON	16	1966
LADY (HEAR ME TONIGHT) MODJO	1	2000
THE LADY IN RED CHRIS DE BURGH	1	1986
LADY IS A TRAMP BUDDY GRECO	26	1960
LADY JANE DAVID GARRICK	28	1966
LADY JANE TONY MERRICK	49	1966
LADY LADY MARK JOSEPH	36	2005
LADY LET IT LIE FISH	46	1994
LADY LINE PAINTER JANE BELLE & SEBASTIAN	41	1997
LADY LOVE BUG CLODAGH RODGERS	28	1971
LADY LOVE ME (ONE MORE TIME) GEORGE BENSON	11	1983
LADY LUCK [A] LLOYD PRICE	45	1960
LADY LUCK [B] ROD STEWART	56	1995
LADY LYNDA BEACH BOYS	6	1979
LADY MADONNA BEATLES	1	1968
LADY MARMALADE ALL SAINTS	1	1998
LADY MARMALADE CHRISTINA AGUILERA/LIL' KIM/MYA/PINK	1	2001
LADY MARMALADE (VOULEZ-VOUS COUCHER AVEC MOI CE SOIR) LABELLE	17	1975
LADY OF THE SEA (HEAR HER CALLING) SETH LAKEMAN	52	2006
LADY ROSE MUNGO JERRY	5	1971
LADY SHINE (SHINE ON) THS - THE HORN SECTION	54	1984
LADY WILLPOWER UNION GAP FEATURING GARY PUCKETT	5	1968
LADY WRITER DIRE STRAITS	51	1979
LADY (YOU BRING ME UP) COMMODORES	56	1980
LADY (YOU BRING ME UP) SIMPLY SMOOTH	70	1998
LADYBIRD NANCY SINATRA & LEE HAZLEWOOD	47	1967
THE LADYBOY IS MINE STUNTMASTERZ	10	2001
LADYFINGERS LUSCIOUS JACKSON	43	1999
LADYFLASH THE GO! TEAM	26	2004
LADYKILLERS LUSH	22	1996
LADYSHAVE GUS GUS	64	1999
LAFFY TAFFY D4L	29	2006
LAGARTIJA NICK BAUHAUS	44	1983
LAID JAMES	25	1993
LAID SO LOW (TEARS ROLL DOWN) TEARS FOR FEARS	17	1992
LAILA TAZ & STEREO NATION	44	2001
LAKINI'S JUICE LIVE	29	1997
LALA ASHLEE SIMPSON	11	2005
LA-LA MEANS I LOVE YOU DELFONICS	19	1971
LAMBADA KAOMA	4	1989
LAMBORGHINI SHUT UP & DANCE	55	1990
LAMENT ULTRAVOX	22	1984
LAMPLIGHT DAVID ESSEX	7	1973

Title / Artist	Peak Position	Year of Entry
LANA ROY ORBISON	15	1966
LAND OF 1000 DANCES WILSON PICKETT	22	1966
LAND OF A MILLION DRUMS OUTKAST FEATURING KILLER MIKE & S BROWN	46	2002
LAND OF A THOUSAND WORDS SCISSOR SISTERS	19	2006
LAND OF CONFUSION GENESIS	14	1986
LAND OF HOPE AND GLORY EX PISTOLS	69	1985
THE LAND OF MAKE BELIEVE BUCKS FIZZ	1	1981
THE LAND OF MAKE BELIEVE ALLSTARS	9	2002
THE LAND OF RING DANG DO KING KURT	67	1987
LAND OF THE LIVING [A] KRISTINE W	57	1996
LAND OF THE LIVING [B] MILK INC	18	2002
LANDSLIDE [A] OLIVIA NEWTON-JOHN	18	1982
LANDSLIDE [B] HARMONIX	28	1996
LANDSLIDE [C] SPIN CITY	30	2000
LANDSLIDE [D] DIXIE CHICKS	55	2003
LANDSLIDE OF LOVE TRANSVISION VAMP	14	1989
THE LANE ICE-T	18	1996
THE LANGUAGE OF LOVE JOHN D. LOUDERMILK	13	1962
LANGUAGE OF VIOLENCE DISPOSABLE HEROES OF HIPHOPRISY	68	1992
LAP OF LUXURY JETHRO TULL	70	1984
LAPDANCE N*E*R*D FEATURING LEE HARVEY & VITA	20	2001
LARGER THAN LIFE BACKSTREET BOYS	5	1999
LAS PALABRAS DE AMOR QUEEN	17	1982
LAS VEGAS TONY CHRISTIE	21	1971
LASER LOVE [A] T REX	41	1976
LASER LOVE [B] AFTER THE FIRE	62	1979
THE LAST BEAT OF MY HEART SIOUXSIE & THE BANSHEES	44	1988
LAST CHANCE CHINA DRUM	60	1996
LAST CHRISTMAS WHAM!	2	1984
LAST CHRISTMAS WHIGFIELD	21	1995
LAST CHRISTMAS ALIEN VOICES FEATURING THE THREE DEGREES	54	1998
LAST CHRISTMAS CRAZY FROG	16	2006
LAST CUP OF SORROW FAITH NO MORE	51	1997
LAST DANCE DONNA SUMMER	51	1978
LAST DAY SILVER SUN	48	1997
LAST DROP KEVIN LYTTLE	22	2004
THE LAST FAREWELL ROGER WHITTAKER	2	1975
THE LAST FAREWELL SHIP'S COMPANY & ROYAL MARINE BAND OF HMS ARK ROYAL	46	1978
THE LAST FAREWELL ELVIS PRESLEY	48	1984
LAST FILM KISSING THE PINK	19	1983
LAST GOODBYE [A] JEFF BUCKLEY	54	1995
LAST GOODBYE [B] ATOMIC KITTEN	2	2002
LAST HORIZON BRIAN MAY	51	1993
THE LAST KISS [A] DAVID CASSIDY	6	1985
LAST KISS [B] PEARL JAM	42	1999
LAST NIGHT P DIDDY FEATURING KEYSHIA COLE	14	2007
LAST NIGHT [A] MERSEYBEATS	40	1964
LAST NIGHT [B] KID 'N' PLAY	71	1987
LAST NIGHT [C] AZ YET	21	1997
LAST NIGHT [C] STROKES	14	2001
LAST NIGHT [D] GLORIA GAYNOR	67	2000
LAST NIGHT A DJ BLEW MY MIND FAB FOR FEATURING ROBERT OWENS	34	2003
LAST NIGHT A DJ SAVED MY LIFE INDEEP	13	1983
LAST NIGHT A DJ SAVED MY LIFE COLD JAM FEATURING GRACE	64	1990
LAST NIGHT A DJ SAVED MY LIFE SYLK 130	33	1998
LAST NIGHT A DJ SAVED MY LIFE (BIG LOVE) SEAMUS HAJI	13	2004
LAST NIGHT ANOTHER SOLDIER ANGELIC UPSTARTS	51	1980
LAST NIGHT AT DANCELAND RANDY CRAWFORD	61	1980
LAST NIGHT I DREAMT THAT SOMEBODY LOVED ME SMITHS	30	1987
LAST NIGHT IN SOHO DAVE DEE, DOZY, BEAKY, MICK & TICH	8	1968
LAST NIGHT ON EARTH U2	10	1997
LAST NIGHT ON THE BACK PORCH ALMA COGAN	27	1959
LAST NIGHT WAS MADE FOR LOVE BILLY FURY	4	1962
LAST NITE VITAMIN C	70	2003
LAST OF THE FAMOUS INTERNATIONAL PLAYBOYS MORRISSEY	6	1989
LAST ONE STANDING GIRL THING	8	2000
LAST PLANE (ONE WAY TICKET) CLINT EASTWOOD & GENERAL SAINT	51	1984
LAST REQUEST PAOLO NUTINI	5	2006
LAST RESORT [A] PAPA ROACH	3	2001
THE LAST RESORT [B] DEAD 60'S	24	2005
LAST RHYTHM LAST RHYTHM	62	1996
THE LAST SONG [A] ELTON JOHN	21	1992
THE LAST SONG [B] ALL-AMERICAN REJECTS	69	2003
LAST STOP THIS TOWN EELS	23	1998
LAST SUMMER LOSTPROPHETS	13	2004
LAST THING ON MY MIND [A] BANANARAMA	71	1992
LAST THING ON MY MIND [A] STEPS	6	1998
LAST THING ON MY MIND [B] RONAN KEATING & LeANN RIMES	5	2004
THE LAST TIME [A] ROLLING STONES	1	1965
THE LAST TIME [A] WHO	44	1967
THE LAST TIME [B] PARADISE LOST	60	1995
LAST TIME FOREVER SQUEEZE	45	1985
LAST TIME I SAW HIM DIANA ROSS	35	1974
LAST TO KNOW P!NK	21	2004
LAST TRAIN HOME LOSTPROPHETS	8	2004
LAST TRAIN TO CLARKSVILLE MONKEES	23	1967
LAST TRAIN TO LONDON ELECTRIC LIGHT ORCHESTRA	8	1979
LAST TRAIN TO SAN FERNANDO JOHNNY DUNCAN & THE BLUE GRASS BOYS	2	1957
LAST TRAIN TO TRANCENTRAL KLF FEATURING THE CHILDREN OF THE REVOLUTION	2	1991
THE LAST WALTZ ENGELBERT HUMPERDINCK	1	1967
LATE AT NIGHT FUTURESHOCK	73	2003
LATE IN THE DAY SUPERGRASS	18	1997
LATE IN THE EVENING PAUL SIMON	58	1980
LATELY [A] RUDY GRANT	58	1981
LATELY [A] STEVIE WONDER	3	1981
LATELY [B] SKUNK ANANSIE	33	1999
LATELY [C] DIVINE	52	1999
LATELY [C] SAMANTHA MUMBA	6	2001
LATELY [D] LISA SCOTT-LEE	6	2003
LATELY [E] JON B	68	2005
THE LATIN THEME CARL COX	52	1998
LATIN THING LATIN THING	41	1996
LATINO HOUSE MIRAGE	70	1989
LAUGH AT ME SONNY	9	1965
THE LAUGHING GNOME DAVID BOWIE	6	1973
LAUGHTER IN THE RAIN NEIL SEDAKA	15	1974
THE LAUNCH DJ JEAN	2	1999
LAUNDROMAT NIVEA	33	2003
LAURA [A] NICK HEYWARD	45	1985
LAURA [B] JIMMY NAIL	58	1992
LAURA [C] NEK	59	1998
LAURA [D] SCISSOR SISTERS	12	2003
LAUREL AND HARDY EQUALS	35	1968
LAVA SILVER SUN	35	1996
LAVENDER MARILLION	5	1985
LAW OF THE LAND TEMPTATIONS	41	1973
LAW UNTO MYSELF KONKRETE	60	2001
LAWDY MISS CLAWDY ELVIS PRESLEY	15	1957
LAWNCHAIRS OUR DAUGHTER'S WEDDING	49	1981
LAY ALL YOUR LOVE ON ME ABBA	7	1981
LAY BACK IN THE ARMS OF SOMEONE SMOKIE	12	1977
LAY DOWN STRAWBS	12	1972
LAY DOWN SALLY ERIC CLAPTON	39	1978
LAY DOWN THE LAW SWITCHES	51	2007
LAY DOWN YOUR ARMS [A] ANNE SHELTON	1	1956
LAY DOWN YOUR ARMS [B] BELINDA CARLISLE	27	1993
LAY LADY LAY BOB DYLAN	5	1969
LAY LOVE ON YOU LUISA FERNANDEZ	31	1978
LAY YOUR HANDS SIMON WEBBE	4	2005
LAY YOUR HANDS ON ME [A] THOMPSON TWINS	13	1984
LAY YOUR HANDS ON ME [B] BON JOVI	18	1989
LAY YOUR LOVE ON ME [A] RACEY	3	1978
LAY YOUR LOVE ON ME [B] ROACHFORD	36	1994
LAYLA DEREK & THE DOMINOES	4	1972
LAYLA (ACOUSTIC) ERIC CLAPTON	45	1992
LAZARUS BOO RADLEYS	50	1994
LAZER BEAM SUPER FURRY ANIMALS	28	2005
LAZY [A] SUEDE	9	1997
LAZY [B] X-PRESS 2	2	2002
LAZY BONES JONATHAN KING	23	1971
LAZY DAYS ROBBIE WILLIAMS	8	1997
LAZY LOVER SUPERNATURALS	34	1996
LAZY RIVER BOBBY DARIN	2	1961
LAZY SUNDAY SMALL FACES	2	1968
LAZYITIS - ONE ARMED BOXER HAPPY MONDAYS & KARL DENVER	46	1990
LDN LILY ALLEN	6	2006
LE DISC JOCKEY ENCORE	12	1998
LE FREAK CHIC	7	1978
LE VOIE LE SOLEIL SUBLIMINAL CUTS	23	1994
LEADER OF THE PACK SHANGRI-LAS	3	1965
LEADER OF THE PACK TWISTED SISTER	47	1986
LEADER OF THE PACK JOAN COLLINS FAN CLUB	60	1988
LEADERS OF THE FREE WORLD ELBOW	53	2005
LEAFY MYSTERIES PAUL WELLER	23	2002
LEAN BACK TERROR SQUAD FEATURING FAT JOE & REMY	24	2004
LEAN ON ME BILL WITHERS	18	1972
LEAN ON ME MUD	7	1976
LEAN ON ME CLUB NOUVEAU	3	1987
LEAN ON ME MICHAEL BOLTON	14	1994
LEAN ON ME (AH-LI-AYO) RED BOX	3	1985
LEAN ON ME I WON'T FALL OVER CARTER-THE UNSTOPPABLE SEX MACHINE	16	1993
LEAN ON ME (WITH THE FAMILY) 2-4 FAMILY	69	1999
LEAN ON YOU CLIFF RICHARD	17	1989
LEAN PERIOD ORANGE JUICE	74	1984
LEAP OF FAITH BRUCE SPRINGSTEEN	46	1992
LEAP UP AND DOWN (WAVE YOUR KNICKERS IN THE AIR) ST. CECILIA	12	1971
LEARN CHINESE JIN	59	2005
LEARN TO FLY FOO FIGHTERS	21	1999
LEARNIN' THE BLUES FRANK SINATRA	2	1955
LEARNIN' THE GAME BUDDY HOLLY	36	1960
LEARNING TO BREATHE NERINA PALLOT	70	2007
LEARNING TO FLY [A] TOM PETTY & THE HEARTBREAKERS	46	1991
LEARNING TO FLY [B] MOTHER'S PRIDE	54	1999
THE LEATHER SEA GARY NUMAN VS ADE FENTON	72	2007
LEAVE A LIGHT ON BELINDA CARLISLE	4	1989
LEAVE A LITTLE LOVE LULU	8	1965
LEAVE A TENDER MOMENT ALONE BILLY JOEL	29	1984
LEAVE BEFORE THE LIGHTS COME ON ARCTIC MONKEYS	4	2006

Title / Artist	Peak Position	Year of Entry
LEAVE 'EM SOMETHING TO DESIRE SPRINKLER	45	1998
LEAVE (GET OUT) JOJO	2	2004
LEAVE HOME CHEMICAL BROTHERS	17	1995
LEAVE IN SILENCE DEPECHE MODE	18	1982
LEAVE IT [A] MIKE McGEAR	36	1974
LEAVE IT [B] YES	56	1984
LEAVE IT ALONE LIVING COLOUR	34	1993
LEAVE IT UP TO ME AARON CARTER	22	2002
LEAVE ME ALONE MICHAEL JACKSON	2	1989
LEAVE ME ALONE (I'M LONELY) P!NK	34	2007
LEAVE RIGHT NOW WILL YOUNG	1	2003
LEAVE THEM ALL BEHIND RIDE	9	1992
LEAVIN' [A] TONY RICH PROJECT	52	1996
LEAVIN' [B] SHELBY LYNNE	73	2000
LEAVIN' ON A JET PLANE PETER, PAUL & MARY	2	1970
LEAVING HERE BIRDS	45	1965
LEAVING LAS VEGAS SHERYL CROW	66	1994
LEAVING ME NOW LEVEL 42	15	1985
LEAVING NEW YORK R.E.M.	5	2004
LEAVING ON A JET PLANE CHANTAL KREVIAZUK	59	1999
LEAVING ON THE MIDNIGHT TRAIN NICK STRAKER BAND	61	1980
THE LEAVING SONG PART 2 AFI	43	2003
THE LEBANON HUMAN LEAGUE	11	1984
LEEDS LEEDS LEEDS LEEDS UNITED F.C.	54	1992
LEEDS UNITED LEEDS UNITED F.C.	10	1972
LEFT HOPE OF THE STATES	63	2006
LEFT BANK WINIFRED ATWELL	14	1956
LEFT BEHIND SLIPKNOT	24	2001
LEFT OF CENTER SUZANNE VEGA FEATURING JOE JACKSON	32	1986
LEFT OUTSIDE ALONE ANASTACIA	3	2004
LEFT TO MY OWN DEVICES PET SHOP BOYS	4	1988
LEGACY [A] MAD COBRA FEATURING RICHIE STEPHENS	64	1993
THE LEGACY [B] PUSH	22	2001
LEGACY EP MANSUN	7	1998
LEGACY (SHOW ME LOVE) SPACE BROTHERS	31	1999
LEGAL MAN BELLE & SEBASTIAN	15	2000
A LEGAL MATTER WHO	32	1966
LEGEND OF A COWGIRL IMANI COPPOLA	32	1998
LEGEND OF THE GOLDEN SNAKE DEPTH CHARGE	75	1995
THE LEGEND OF XANADU DAVE DEE, DOZY, BEAKY, MICK & TICH	1	1968
LEGENDS OF THE DARK BLACK - PART 2 WILDCHILD	34	1995
LEGO SKANGA RUPIE EDWARDS	32	1975
LEGS [A] ART OF NOISE	69	1985
LEGS [B] ZZ TOP	16	1985
LEMMINGS SFX	51	1993
LEMON TREE FOOL'S GARDEN	26	1996
LENINGRAD BILLY JOEL	53	1989
LENNY SUPERGRASS	10	1995
LENNY AND TERENCE CARTER-THE UNSTOPPABLE SEX MACHINE	40	1993
LENNY VALENTINO AUTEURS	41	1993
LEONARD NIMOY FREAKY REALISTIC	71	1993
LEROY WHEATUS	22	2002
LES BICYCLETTES DE BELSIZE ENGELBERT HUMPERDINCK	5	1968
LES FLEUR 4 HERO	53	2001
L'ESPERANZA [A] SVEN VATH	63	1993
L'ESPERANZA [B] AIRSCAPE	33	1999
LESS TALK MORE ACTION TIM DELUXE	45	2003
LESSON ONE RUSS CONWAY	21	1962
LESSONS IN LOVE [A] ALLISONS	30	1962
LESSONS IN LOVE [B] LEVEL 42	3	1986
LESSONS LEARNT FROM ROCK I TO ROCKY III CORNERSHOP	37	2002
LET A BOY CRY GALA	11	1997
LET A GOOD THING GO GEMMA HAYES	54	2002
LET 'EM IN WINGS	2	1976
LET 'EM IN BILLY PAUL	26	1977
LET 'EM IN SHINEHEAD	70	1993
LET FOREVER BE CHEMICAL BROTHERS	9	1999
LET GO WITH THE FLOW BEAUTIFUL SOUTH	47	2003
LET HER CRY HOOTIE & THE BLOWFISH	75	1995
LET HER DOWN EASY TERENCE TRENT D'ARBY	18	1993
LET HER FALL THEN JERICO	65	1987
LET HER FEEL IT SIMPLICIOUS	34	1984
LET HER GO STRAWBERRY SWITCHBLADE	59	1985
LET IT ALL BLOW DAZZ BAND	12	1984
LET IT ALL HANG OUT JONATHAN KING	26	1970
LET IT BE BEATLES	2	1970
LET IT BE FERRY AID	1	1987
LET IT BE ME EVERLY BROTHERS	13	1960
LET IT BE ME JUSTIN	15	2000
LET IT BE WITH YOU BELOUIS SOME	53	1987
LET IT FLOW SPIRITUALIZED ELECTRIC MAINLINE	30	1995
LET IT LAST CARLEEN ANDERSON	16	1995
LET IT LIVE HAVEN	72	2001
LET IT LOOSE LEMON TREES	55	1993
LET IT RAIN [A] UFO	62	1982
LET IT RAIN [B] EAST 17	10	1995
LET IT RAIN [C] 4 STRINGS	49	2003
LET IT REIGN INNER CITY	51	1991
LET IT RIDE TODD TERRY PROJECT	58	1999
LET IT ROCK CHUCK BERRY	6	1963
LET IT ROCK ROLLING STONES	2	1971
LET IT ROLL RAZE PRESENTS DOUG LAZY	27	1989
LET IT SLIDE [A] MUDHONEY	60	1991
LET IT SLIDE [B] ARIEL	57	1993
LET IT SWING BOBBYSOCKS	44	1985
LET LOVE BE THE LEADER FM	71	1987
LET LOVE BE YOUR ENERGY ROBBIE WILLIAMS	10	2001
LET LOVE LEAD THE WAY SPICE GIRLS	1	2000
LET LOVE RULE LENNY KRAVITZ	39	1990
LET LOVE SHINE AMOS	31	1995
LET LOVE SPEAK UP ITSELF BEAUTIFUL SOUTH	51	1991
LET ME BE BLACK DIAMOND	56	1994
LET ME BE THE NUMBER 1 (LOVE OF YOUR LIFE) DOOLEY SILVERSPOON	44	1976
LET ME BE THE ONE [A] SHADOWS	12	1975
LET ME BE THE ONE [B] FIVE STAR	18	1985
LET ME BE THE ONE [C] BLESSID UNION OF SOULS	74	1996
LET ME BE THE ONE [D] MINT CONDITION	63	1997
LET ME BE THE ONE [E] CLIFF RICHARD	29	2002
LET ME BE YOUR FANTASY BABY D	1	1994
(LET ME BE YOUR) TEDDY BEAR ELVIS PRESLEY	3	1957
LET ME BE YOUR UNDERWEAR CLUB 69	33	1992
LET ME BE YOUR WINGS BARRY MANILOW & DEBRA BYRD	73	1994
LET ME BE YOURS FIVE STAR	51	1988
LET ME BLOW YA MIND EVE FEATURING GWEN STEFANI	4	2001
LET ME CLEAR MY THROAT DJ KOOL	8	1997
LET ME COME ON HOME OTIS REDDING	48	1967
LET ME CRY ON YOUR SHOULDER KEN DODD	11	1967
LET ME DOWN EASY STRANGLERS	48	1985
LET ME ENTERTAIN YOU ROBBIE WILLIAMS	3	1998
LET ME FLY DARREN STYLES/MARK BREEZE	59	2003
LET ME GO HEAVEN 17	41	1982
LET ME GO HOME ALL ABOUT EVE	52	2004
LET ME GO LOVER DEAN MARTIN	3	1955
LET ME GO LOVER JOAN WEBER	16	1955
LET ME GO LOVER RUBY MURRAY	5	1955
LET ME GO LOVER TERESA BREWER WITH THE LANCERS	9	1955
LET ME GO LOVER KATHY KIRBY	10	1964
LET ME HEAR YOU SAY 'OLE OLE' OUTHERE BROTHERS	18	1997
LET ME HOLD YOU BOW WOW FEATURING OMARION	27	2005
LET ME IN [A] OSMONDS	2	1973
LET ME IN [A] OTT	12	1997
LET ME IN [B] YOUNG BUCK	62	2004
LET ME INTRODUCE YOU TO THE FAMILY STRANGLERS	42	1981
LET ME KISS YOU MORRISSEY	8	2004
LET ME KISS YOU NANCY SINATRA	46	2004
LET ME KNOW [A] JUNIOR	53	1982
LET ME KNOW [B] MAXI PRIEST	49	1987
LET ME KNOW [C] ROISIN MURPHY	28	2007
LET ME KNOW (I HAVE THE RIGHT) GLORIA GAYNOR	32	1979
LET ME LET GO FAITH HILL	72	1999
LET ME LIVE QUEEN	9	1996
LET ME LOVE YOU MARIO	2	2005
LET ME LOVE YOU FOR TONIGHT KARIYA	44	1989
LET ME MOVE ON GENE	69	2005
LET ME OUT BEN'S BROTHER	38	2007
LET ME RIDE DR DRE	31	1994
LET ME ROCK YOU KANDIDATE	58	1980
LET ME SEE MORCHEEBA	46	1998
LET ME SHOW YOU [A] K-KLASS	13	1993
LET ME SHOW YOU [B] CAMISRA	5	1998
LET ME SHOW YOU [C] TONY MOMRELLE	67	1998
LET ME TAKE YOU THERE BETTY BOO	12	1992
LET ME TALK EARTH, WIND & FIRE	29	1980
LET ME THINK ABOUT IT IDA CORR & FEDDE LE GRANDE	2	2007
LET ME TRY AGAIN TAMMY JONES	5	1975
LET ME WAKE UP IN YOUR ARMS LULU	51	1993
LET MY LOVE OPEN YOUR DOOR PETE TOWNSHEND	46	1980
LET MY NAME BE SORROW MARY HOPKIN	46	1971
LET MY PEOPLE GO (PART 1) WINANS	71	1985
LET MY PEOPLE GO-GO RAINMAKERS	18	1987
LET ROBESON SING MANIC STREET PREACHERS	19	2001
LET SOMEBODY LOVE YOU KENI BURKE	59	1981
LET THE BASS KICK 2 FOR JOY	67	1991
LET THE BEAT CONTROL YOUR BODY 2 UNLIMITED	6	1994
LET THE BEAT HIT 'EM LISA LISA & CULT JAM	17	1991
LET THE BEAT HIT 'EM SHENA	28	1997
LET THE BEAT HIT 'EM PART 2 LISA LISA & CULT JAM	49	1991
LET THE BEATS ROLL TIM DELUXE FEATURING SIMON FRANKS	71	2007
LET THE DAY BEGIN CALL	42	1989
LET THE DRUMS SPEAK MIGHTY DUB KATZ	73	2002
LET THE FLAME BURN BRIGHTER GRAHAM KENDRICK	55	1989
LET THE FREAK BIG RON	57	2000
LET THE GOOD TIMES ROLL SHEEP ON DRUGS	56	1994
LET THE HAPPINESS IN DAVID SYLVIAN	66	1987
LET THE HEALING BEGIN JOE COCKER	32	1994
LET THE HEARTACHES BEGIN LONG JOHN BALDRY	1	1967
LET THE LITTLE GIRL DANCE BILLY BLAND	15	1960
LET THE LOVE Q-TEX	30	1996
LET THE MUSIC HEAL YOUR SOUL BRAVO ALL STARS	36	1998
LET THE MUSIC (LIFT YOU UP) LOVELAND FEATURING RACHEL McFARLANE Vs DARLENE LEWIS	16	1994

Title / Artist	Peak Position	Year of Entry
LET THE MUSIC MOVE U RAZE	57	1987
LET THE MUSIC PLAY [A] BARRY WHITE	9	1976
LET THE MUSIC PLAY [B] CHARLES EARLAND	46	1978
LET THE MUSIC PLAY [C] SHANNON	14	1984
LET THE MUSIC PLAY [C] BBG FEATURING ERIN	46	1996
LET THE MUSIC PLAY [C] MARY KIANI	19	1996
LET THE MUSIC TAKE CONTROL JM SILK	47	1987
LET THE MUSIC USE YOU NIGHTWRITERS	51	1992
LET THE PEOPLE KNOW TOPLOADER	52	1999
LET THE RHYTHM MOVE YOU SHARADA HOUSE GANG	50	1996
LET THE RHYTHM PUMP DOUG LAZY	45	1989
LET THE SUNSHINE IN PEDDLERS	50	1965
LET THE SUNSHINE IN MILK & SUGAR FEATURING LIZZY PATTINSON	18	2003
LET THE WATER RUN DOWN P.J. PROBY	19	1965
LET THE YOUNG GIRL DO WHAT SHE WANTS TO IAN McNABB	38	2005
LET THEM ALL TALK ELVIS COSTELLO	59	1983
LET THERE BE DRUMS SANDY NELSON	3	1961
LET THERE BE HOUSE DESKEE	52	1990
LET THERE BE LIGHT MIKE OLDFIELD	51	1995
LET THERE BE LOVE [A] NAT 'KING' COLE WITH GEORGE SHEARING	11	1962
LET THERE BE LOVE [B] SIMPLE MINDS	6	1991
LET THERE BE LOVE [C] OASIS	2	2005
LET THERE BE PEACE ON EARTH (LET IT BEGIN WITH ME) MICHAEL WARD	15	1973
LET THERE BE ROCK ONSLAUGHT	50	1989
LET THIS BE A PRAYER ROLLO GOES SPIRITUAL WITH PAULINE TAYLOR	26	1996
LET THIS FEELING SIMONE ANGEL	60	1993
LET TRUE LOVE BEGIN NAT 'KING' COLE	29	1961
LET U GO ATB	34	2001
LET YOUR BODY GO TOM WILSON	60	1996
LET YOUR BODY GO DOWNTOWN MARTYN FORD	38	1977
LET YOUR HEAD GO VICTORIA BECKHAM	3	2004
LET YOUR HEART DANCE SECRET AFFAIR	32	1979
LET YOUR LOVE FLOW BELLAMY BROTHERS	7	1976
LET YOUR SOUL BE YOUR PILOT STING	15	1996
LET YOUR YEAH BE YEAH PIONEERS	5	1971
LET YOUR YEAH BE YEAH ALI CAMPBELL	25	1995
LET YOURSELF GO [A] T-CONNECTION	52	1978
LET YOURSELF GO [B] SYBIL	32	1987
LETHAL INDUSTRY DJ TIESTO	25	2002
LETITGO PRINCE	30	1994
LET'S SARAH VAUGHAN	37	1961
LET'S ALL CHANT MICHAEL ZAGER BAND	8	1978
LET'S ALL CHANT PAT & MICK	11	1988
LET'S ALL CHANT GUSTO	21	1996
(LET'S ALL GO BACK) DISCO NIGHTS JAZZ & THE BROTHERS GRIMM	57	1988
LET'S ALL (GO TO THE FIRE DANCES) KILLING JOKE	51	1983
LET'S ALL GO TOGETHER MARION	37	1995
LET'S ALL SING LIKE THE BIRDIES SING TWEETS	44	1981
LET'S BE FRIENDS JOHNNY NASH	42	1975
LET'S BE LOVERS TONIGHT SHERRICK	63	1987
LET'S CALL IT LOVE LISA STANSFIELD	48	2001
LET'S CALL IT QUITS SLADE	11	1976
LET'S CELEBRATE NEW YORK SKYY	67	1982
LET'S CLEAN UP THE GHETTO PHILADELPHIA INTERNATIONAL ALL-STARS	34	1977
LET'S DANCE [A] CHRIS MONTEZ	2	1962
LET'S DANCE [A] BRUNO & LIZ & THE RADIO 1 POSSE	54	1990
LET'S DANCE [B] BOMBERS	58	1979
LET'S DANCE [C] DAVID BOWIE	1	1983
LET'S DANCE [C] HI-TACK	38	2007
LET'S DANCE [D] CHRIS REA	12	1987
LET'S DANCE [D] MIDDLESBROUGH FC FEATURING BOB MORTIMER & CHRIS REA	44	1997
LET'S DANCE [E] FIVE	1	2001
LET'S DANCE TO JOY DIVISION WOMBATS	15	2007
LET'S DO IT AGAIN [A] GEORGE BENSON	56	1988
LET'S DO IT AGAIN [B] LYNDEN DAVID HALL	69	2000
LET'S DO ROCK STEADY BODYSNATCHERS	22	1980
LET'S DO THE LATIN HUSTLE EDDIE DRENNON & B.B.S. UNLIMITED	20	1976
LET'S DO THE LATIN HUSTLE M & O BAND	16	1976
LET'S FACE THE MUSIC AND DANCE NAT 'KING' COLE	30	1994
LET'S FLY AWAY VOYAGE	38	1979
LET'S FUNK TONIGHT BLUE FEATHERS	50	1982
LET'S GET BACK TO BED...BOY SARAH CONNOR FEATURING TQ	16	2001
LET'S GET BLOWN SNOOP DOGG FEATURING PHARRELL	13	2005
LET'S GET BRUTAL NITRO DELUXE	24	1988
LET'S GET DOWN [A] ISOTONIK	25	1992
LET'S GET DOWN [B] MARK MORRISON	39	1995
LET'S GET DOWN [C] TONY TONI TONE FEATURING DJ QUIK	33	1997
LET'S GET DOWN [D] JT PLAYAZ	64	1998
LET'S GET DOWN [E] SPACEDUST	20	1999
LET'S GET DOWN [F] SUPAFLY VS FISHBOWL	22	2005
LET'S GET FUNKTIFIED BOILING POINT	41	1978
LET'S GET HAPPY MASS ORDER	45	1992
LET'S GET ILL P DIDDY FEATURING KELIS	25	2003
LET'S GET IT ON [A] MARVIN GAYE	31	1973
LET'S GET IT ON [B] SHABBA RANKS	22	1995
LET'S GET IT ON [C] BIG BOSS STYLUS PRESENTS RED VENOM	72	1999
LET'S GET IT STARTED BLACK EYED PEAS	11	2004
LET'S GET IT UP AC/DC	13	1982
LET'S GET MARRIED PROCLAIMERS	21	1994
LET'S GET READY TO RHUMBLE PJ & DUNCAN	9	1994
LET'S GET ROCKED DEF LEPPARD	2	1992
LET'S GET SANDY BE YOUR OWN PET	51	2006
LET'S GET SERIOUS JERMAINE JACKSON	8	1980
LET'S GET TATTOOS CARTER-THE UNSTOPPABLE SEX MACHINE	30	1994
LET'S GET THIS PARTY STARTED ZENA	69	2003
LET'S GET THIS STRAIGHT (FROM THE START) KEVIN ROWLAND & DEXY'S MIDNIGHT RUNNERS	17	1982
LET'S GET TOGETHER [A] HAYLEY MILLS	17	1961
LET'S GET TOGETHER [B] ALEXANDER O'NEAL	38	1996
LET'S GET TOGETHER AGAIN [A] BIG BEN BANJO BAND	18	1955
LET'S GET TOGETHER AGAIN [B] GLITTER BAND	8	1974
LET'S GET TOGETHER (IN OUR MINDS) GORKY'S ZYGOTIC MYNCI	43	1998
LET'S GET TOGETHER NO. 1 BIG BEN BANJO BAND	6	1954
LET'S GET TOGETHER (SO GROOVY NOW) KRUSH PERSPECTIVE	61	1993
LET'S GET TOGETHER (TONITE) STEVE WALSH	74	1987
LET'S GO [A] ROUTERS	32	1963
LET'S GO [B] CARS	51	1979
LET'S GO [C] VARDIS	59	1980
LET'S GO [D] TRICK DADDY FEATURING TWISTA & LIL' JON	26	2005
LET'S GO ALL THE WAY SLY FOX	3	1986
LET'S GO CRAZY PRINCE & THE REVOLUTION	7	1985
LET'S GO DISCO REAL THING	39	1978
LET'S GO ROUND AGAIN LOUISE	10	1997
LET'S GO ROUND AGAIN PART 1 AVERAGE WHITE BAND	12	1980
LET'S GO ROUND THERE DARLING BUDS	49	1989
LET'S GO STEADY AGAIN NEIL SEDAKA	42	1963
LET'S GO TO BED CURE	44	1982
LET'S GO TO SAN FRANCISCO FLOWERPOT MEN	4	1967
LET'S GO TOGETHER CHANGE	37	1985
LET'S GROOVE [A] EARTH, WIND & FIRE	3	1981
LET'S GROOVE [A] PHAT 'N' PHUNKY	61	1997
LET'S GROOVE [B] GEORGE MOREL FEATURING HEATHER WILDMAN	42	1996
LET'S HANG ON FOUR SEASONS WITH THE SOUND OF FRANKIE VALLI	4	1965
LET'S HANG ON BANDWAGON	36	1969
LET'S HANG ON DARTS	11	1980
LET'S HANG ON BARRY MANILOW	12	1981
LET'S HANG ON SHOOTING PARTY	66	1990
LET'S HAVE A BALL WINIFRED ATWELL	4	1957
LET'S HAVE A DING DONG WINIFRED ATWELL	3	1955
LET'S HAVE A PARTY [A] WINIFRED ATWELL	2	1953
LET'S HAVE A PARTY [B] WANDA JACKSON	32	1960
LET'S HAVE A QUIET NIGHT IN DAVID SOUL	8	1977
LET'S HAVE ANOTHER PARTY WINIFRED ATWELL	1	1954
LET'S HEAR IT FOR THE BOY DENIECE WILLIAMS	2	1984
LET'S JUMP THE BROOMSTICK BRENDA LEE	12	1961
LET'S JUMP THE BROOMSTICK COAST TO COAST	28	1981
LET'S KILL MUSIC COOPER TEMPLE CLAUSE	41	2001
LET'S LIVE IT UP (NITE PEOPLE) DAVID JOSEPH	26	1983
LET'S LOVE DANCE TONIGHT GARY'S GANG	49	1979
LET'S MAKE A BABY BILLY PAUL	30	1976
LET'S MAKE A NIGHT TO REMEMBER BRYAN ADAMS	10	1996
LET'S MAKE LOVE AND LISTEN TO DEATH FROM ABOVE CSS	39	2007
LET'S PARTY JIVE BUNNY & THE MASTERMIXERS	1	1989
LET'S PLAY HOUSE KRAZE	71	1989
LET'S PRETEND LULU	11	1967
LET'S PUSH IT [A] INNOCENCE	25	1990
LET'S PUSH IT [B] NIGHTCRAWLERS FEATURING JOHN REID	23	1996
LET'S PUSH THINGS FORWARD STREETS	30	2002
LET'S PUT IT ALL TOGETHER STYLISTICS	9	1974
LET'S RIDE [A] MONTELL JORDAN FEATURING MASTER P & SILKK THE SHOCKER	25	1998
LET'S RIDE [B] GAME	42	2007
LET'S ROCK E-TRAX	60	2001
LET'S ROCK 'N' ROLL WINIFRED ATWELL	24	1957
LET'S SEE ACTION WHO	16	1971
LET'S SLIP AWAY CLEO LAINE	42	1960
LET'S SPEND THE NIGHT TOGETHER ROLLING STONES	3	1967
LET'S SPEND THE NIGHT TOGETHER MASH!	66	1995
LET'S START OVER PAMELA FERNANDEZ	59	1995
LET'S START THE DANCE HAMILTON BOHANNON	56	1978
LET'S START TO DANCE AGAIN HAMILTON BOHANNON	49	1982
LET'S STAY HOME TONIGHT JOE	29	2002
LET'S STAY TOGETHER AL GREEN	7	1972
LET'S STAY TOGETHER BOBBY M FEATURING JEAN CARN	53	1983
LET'S STAY TOGETHER TINA TURNER	6	1983
LET'S STAY TOGETHER PASADENAS	22	1992
LET'S STICK TOGETHER BRYAN FERRY	4	1976
LET'S SWING AGAIN JIVE BUNNY & THE MASTERMIXERS	19	1990
LET'S TALK ABOUT LOVE HELEN SHAPIRO	23	1962
LET'S TALK ABOUT SEX SALT-N-PEPA FEATURING PSYCHOTROPIC	2	1991
LET'S TALK ABOUT SHHH ONE WAY FEATURING AL HUDSON	64	1985

	Peak Position	Year of Entry
LET'S THINK ABOUT LIVING BOB LUMAN	6	1960
LET'S TRY AGAIN NEW KIDS ON THE BLOCK	8	1990
LET'S TURKEY TROT LITTLE EVA	13	1963
LET'S TWIST AGAIN CHUBBY CHECKER	2	1961
LET'S TWIST AGAIN JOHN ASHER	14	1975
LET'S WAIT AWHILE JANET JACKSON	3	1987
LET'S WALK THATA-WAY DORIS DAY & JOHNNIE RAY	4	1953
LET'S WHIP IT UP (YOU GO GIRL) SLEAZESISTERS WITH VIKKI SHEPARD	46	1996
LET'S WOMBLE TO THE PARTY TONIGHT WOMBLES	34	1975
LET'S WORK MICK JAGGER	31	1987
LET'S WORK IT OUT RAGHAV FEATURING JAHAZIEL	15	2004
LET'S WORK TOGETHER CANNED HEAT	2	1970
THE LETTER [A] LONG & THE SHORT	35	1964
THE LETTER [B] BOX TOPS	5	1967
THE LETTER [B] MINDBENDERS	42	1967
THE LETTER [B] JOE COCKER	39	1970
THE LETTER [B] AMII STEWART	39	1980
THE LETTER [C] PJ HARVEY	28	2004
LETTER FROM AMERICA PROCLAIMERS	3	1987
LETTER FULL OF TEARS BILLY FURY	32	1962
LETTER TO A SOLDIER BARBARA LYON	27	1956
A LETTER TO ELSIE CURE	28	1992
LETTER TO LUCILLE TOM JONES	31	1973
A LETTER TO YOU SHAKIN' STEVENS	10	1984
LETTER 2 MY UNBORN 2PAC	21	2001
LETTERS TO YOU FINCH	39	2003
LETTIN' YA MIND GO DESERT	74	2001
LETTING GO WINGS	41	1975
LETTING THE CABLES SLEEP BUSH	51	2000
LEVI STUBBS TEARS BILLY BRAGG	29	1986
LFO LFO	12	1990
LIAR [A] GRAHAM BONNET	51	1981
LIAR [B] ROLLINS BAND	27	1994
LIAR LIAR CREDIT TO THE NATION	60	1995
LIARS' BAR BEAUTIFUL SOUTH	43	1997
LIBERATE LEE HASLAM	71	2004
LIBERATION [A] LIBERATION	28	1992
LIBERATION [B] PET SHOP BOYS	14	1994
LIBERATION [C] LIPPY LOU	57	1995
LIBERATION (TEMPTATION – FLY LIKE AN EAGLE) MATT DAREY PRESENTS MASH UP	19	1999
LIBERATOR SPEAR OF DESTINY	67	1984
LIBERIAN GIRL MICHAEL JACKSON	13	1989
THE LIBERTINE PATRICK WOLF	67	2005
LIBERTY TOWN PERFECT DAY	58	1989
LIBIAMO JOSE CARRERAS, PLACIDO DOMINGO & LUCIANO PAVAROTTI	21	1994
LICENCE TO KILL GLADYS KNIGHT	6	1989
LICK A SHOT CYPRESS HILL	20	1994
LICK A SMURP FOR CHRISTMAS (ALL FALL DOWN) FATHER ABRAPHART & THE SMURPS	58	1978
LICK IT 20 FINGERS FEATURING ROULA	48	1995
LICK IT UP KISS	31	1983
LIDO SHUFFLE BOZ SCAGGS	13	1977
LIE TO ME BON JOVI	10	1995
LIES [A] STATUS QUO	11	1980
LIES [B] THOMPSON TWINS	67	1982
LIES [C] JONATHAN BUTLER	18	1987
LIES [D] EN VOGUE	44	1990
LIES [E] EMF	28	1991
LIES IN YOUR EYES SWEET	35	1976
LIFE [A] HADDAWAY	6	1993
LIFE [B] BLAIR	44	1996
LIFE [C] DES'REE	8	1998
THE LIFE [D] STYLES & PHAROAHE MONCH	50	2002
LIFE AIN'T EASY CLEOPATRA	4	1998
LIFE AT A TOP PEOPLE'S HEALTH FARM STYLE COUNCIL	28	1988
LIFE BECOMING A LANDSLIDE MANIC STREET PREACHERS	36	1994
LIFE BEGINS AT THE HOP XTC	54	1979
LIFE FOR RENT DIDO	8	2003
LIFE GOES ON [A] GEORGIE PORGIE	54	2000
LIFE GOES ON [B] LeANN RIMES	11	2002
LIFE GOT COLD GIRLS ALOUD	3	2003
LIFE IN A DAY [A] SIMPLE MINDS	62	1979
LIFE IN A DAY [B] I AM KLOOT	43	2003
LIFE IN A NORTHERN TOWN DREAM ACADEMY	15	1985
LIFE IN MONO MONO	60	1998
LIFE IN ONE DAY HOWARD JONES	14	1985
LIFE IN TOKYO JAPAN	28	1982
LIFE IS A FLOWER ACE OF BASE	5	1998
LIFE IS A HIGHWAY TOM COCHRANE	62	1992
LIFE IS A LONG SONG JETHRO TULL	11	1971
LIFE IS A MINESTRONE 10 C.C.	7	1975
LIFE IS A ROCK (BUT THE RADIO ROLLED ME) REUNION	33	1974
LIFE IS A ROLLERCOASTER RONAN KEATING	1	2000
LIFE IS FOR LIVING BARCLAY JAMES HARVEST	61	1980
LIFE IS SWEET CHEMICAL BROTHERS	25	1995
LIFE IS TOO SHORT GIRL SHEER ELEGANCE	9	1976
A LIFE LESS ORDINARY ASH	10	1997
LIFE, LOVE AND HAPPINESS BRIAN KENNEDY	27	1996
LIFE LOVE AND UNITY DREADZONE	56	1996
THE LIFE OF RILEY LIGHTNING SEEDS	28	1992
LIFE OF SURPRISES PREFAB SPROUT	24	1993
LIFE ON MARS DAVID BOWIE	3	1973
LIFE ON YOUR OWN HUMAN LEAGUE	16	1984
LIFE STORY ANGIE STONE	22	2000
LIFE SUPPORTING MACHINE THESE ANIMAL MEN	62	1997
LIFE WILL BE THE DEATH OF ME ORDINARY BOYS	50	2005
LIFE WITH YOU PROCLAIMERS	58	2007
LIFEBOAT TERRY NEASON	72	1994
THE LIFEBOAT PARTY KID CREOLE & THE COCONUTS	49	1983
LIFEFORMS FUTURE SOUND OF LONDON	14	1994
LIFELINE SPANDAU BALLET	7	1982
LIFE'S A CINCH MUNDY	75	1996
LIFE'S A TREAT SHAUN THE SHEEP	20	2007
LIFE'S BEEN GOOD JOE WALSH	14	1978
LIFE'S JUST A BALLGAME WOMACK & WOMACK	32	1988
LIFE'S TOO SHORT [A] HOLE IN ONE	36	1997
LIFE'S TOO SHORT [B] LIGHTNING SEEDS	27	1999
LIFE'S WHAT YOU MAKE IT TALK TALK	16	1986
LIFESAVER GURU	61	1996
LIFESTYLES OF THE RICH AND FAMOUS GOOD CHARLOTTE	8	2003
LIFETIME LOVE JOYCE SIMS	34	1987
LIFETIME PILING UP TALKING HEADS	50	1992
LIFETIMES SLAM FEATURING TYRONE PALMER	61	2001
LIFT 808 STATE	38	1991
LIFT EVERY VOICE (TAKE ME AWAY) MASS ORDER	35	1992
LIFT IT HIGH (ALL ABOUT BELIEF) 1999 MANCHESTER UNITED SQUAD	11	1999
LIFT ME UP [A] HOWARD JONES	52	1992
LIFT ME UP [B] RED 5	26	1997
LIFT ME UP [C] GERI HALLIWELL	1	1999
LIFT ME UP [C] REEL	39	2001
LIFT ME UP [D] MOBY	18	2005
LIFTED LIGHTHOUSE FAMILY	4	1995
LIFTING ME HIGHER GEMS FOR JEM	28	1995
THE LIGHT [A] COMMON	56	2000
LIGHT [B] PHAROAHE MONCH	72	2000
THE LIGHT [C] MICHELLE WEEKS	69	2003
LIGHT A CANDLE DANIEL O'DONNELL	23	2000
LIGHT A RAINBOW TUKAN	38	2001
LIGHT AIRCRAFT ON FIRE AUTEURS	58	1996
LIGHT AND DAY POLYPHONIC SPREE	40	2003
THE LIGHT COMES FROM WITHIN LINDA McCARTNEY	56	1999
LIGHT EMITTING ELECTRICAL WAVE THESE ANIMAL MEN	72	1997
LIGHT FLIGHT PENTANGLE	43	1970
LIGHT IN YOUR EYES SHERYL CROW	73	2004
LIGHT MY FIRE [A] DOORS	7	1968
LIGHT MY FIRE [A] JOSE FELICIANO	6	1968
LIGHT MY FIRE [A] MIKE FLOWERS POPS	39	1996
LIGHT MY FIRE [A] UB40	63	2000
LIGHT MY FIRE [A] WILL YOUNG	1	2002
LIGHT MY FIRE [B] CLUBHOUSE FEATURING CARL	7	1993
LIGHT MY FIRE/137 DISCO HEAVEN (MEDLEY) AMII STEWART	7	1979
(LIGHT OF EXPERIENCE) DOINA DE JALE GHEORGHE ZAMFIR	4	1976
LIGHT OF LOVE T REX	22	1974
LIGHT OF MY LIFE LOUISE	8	1995
LIGHT OF THE WORLD KIM APPLEBY	41	1993
LIGHT UP THE FIRE PARCHMENT	31	1972
LIGHT UP THE NIGHT BROTHERS JOHNSON	47	1980
LIGHT UP THE WORLD FOR CHRISTMAS LAMPIES	48	2001
LIGHT YEARS PEARL JAM	52	2000
LIGHT YOUR ASS ON FIRE BUSTA RHYMES FEATURING PHARRELL	62	2003
THE LIGHTER DJ SS	63	2002
LIGHTERS UP LIL' KIM	12	2005
LIGHTNIN' STRIKES LOU CHRISTIE	11	1966
LIGHTNING ZOE	37	1991
LIGHTNING BLUE EYES SECRET MACHINES	57	2006
LIGHTNING CRASHES LIVE	33	1996
LIGHTNING FLASH BROTHERHOOD OF MAN	67	1982
LIGHTNING STRIKES OZZY OSBOURNE	72	1986
THE LIGHTNING TREE SETTLERS	36	1971
LIGHTS AND SOUNDS YELLOWCARD	59	2006
LIGHTS OF CINCINNATI SCOTT WALKER	13	1969
LIGHTS OUT LISA MARIE PRESLEY	16	2003
LIKE A BABY LEN BARRY	10	1966
LIKE A BOY CIARA	16	2007
LIKE A BUTTERFLY MAC & KATIE KISSOON	18	1975
LIKE A CAT CRW FEATURING VERONIKA	57	2002
LIKE A CHILD JULIE ROGERS	20	1964
LIKE A CHILD AGAIN MISSION	30	1992
LIKE A FEATHER NIKKA COSTA	53	2001
LIKE A HURRICANE MISSION	49	1986
LIKE A MOTORWAY SAINT ETIENNE	47	1994
LIKE A PLAYA LA GANZ	75	1996
LIKE A PRAYER MADONNA	1	1989
LIKE A PRAYER MADHOUSE	3	2002
LIKE A ROLLING STONE BOB DYLAN	4	1965
LIKE A ROLLING STONE ROLLING STONES	12	1995
LIKE A ROSE A1	6	2000
LIKE A SATELLITE (EP) THUNDER	28	1993
LIKE A STAR CORINNE BAILEY RAE	32	2005
LIKE A VIRGIN MADONNA	3	1984
LIKE A WOMAN TONY RICH PROJECT	27	1996
LIKE A YO-YO SABRINA	72	1989
LIKE AN ANIMAL GLOVE	52	1983
LIKE AN OLD TIME MOVIE THE VOICE OF SCOTT McKENZIE	50	1967
LIKE CLOCKWORK BOOMTOWN RATS	6	1978
LIKE DREAMERS DO [A] APPLEJACKS	20	1964
LIKE DREAMERS DO [B] MICA PARIS FEATURING COURTNEY PINE	26	1988
LIKE FLAMES BERLIN	47	1987
LIKE GLUE SEAN PAUL	3	2003
LIKE I DO [A] MAUREEN EVANS	3	1962
LIKE I DO [B] FOR REAL	45	1997
LIKE I LIKE IT AURRA	43	1985

	Peak Position	Year of Entry
LIKE I LOVE YOU JUSTIN TIMBERLAKE	2	2002
LIKE IT OR LEAVE IT CHIKINKI	65	2004
LIKE I'VE NEVER BEEN GONE BILLY FURY	3	1963
LIKE LOVERS DO LLOYD COLE	24	1995
LIKE MARVIN GAYE SAID (WHAT'S GOING ON) SPEECH	35	1996
LIKE PRINCES DO DIESEL PARK WEST	58	1989
LIKE SISTER AND BROTHER DRIFTERS	7	1973
LIKE STRANGERS EVERLY BROTHERS	11	1960
LIKE THE SUN RYANDAN	69	2007
LIKE THIS KELLY ROWLAND FEATURING EVE	4	2007
LIKE THIS AND LIKE THAT [A] MONICA	33	1996
LIKE THIS AND LIKE THAT [B] LaKIESHA BERRI	54	1997
LIKE THIS LIKE THAT [A] MAURO PICOTTO	21	2001
LIKE THIS LIKE THAT [B] SE:SA FEATURING SHARON PHILIPS	63	2007
LIKE TO GET TO KNOW YOU WELL HOWARD JONES	4	1984
LIKE TOY SOLDIERS EMINEM	1	2005
LIKE WE USED TO BE GEORGIE FAME & THE BLUE FLAMES	33	1965
LIKE WHAT TOMMI	12	2003
LIKE YOU BOW WOW FEATURING CIARA	17	2006
LIKE YOU'LL NEVER SEE ME AGAIN ALICIA KEYS	53	2008
A LIL' AIN'T ENOUGH DAVID LEE ROTH	32	1991
LIL' BIG MAN OMERO MUMBA	42	2002
LIL' DEVIL CULT	11	1987
LIL' DUB CHEFIN' SPACE MONKEY VS GORILLAZ	73	2002
LIL' RED RIDING HOOD SAM THE SHAM & THE PHARAOHS	46	1966
LIL' RED RIDING HOOD 999	59	1981
LIL STAR KELIS FEATURING CEE LO	3	2007
LILAC WINE ELKIE BROOKS	16	1978
LILIAN DEPECHE MODE	18	2006
LILY THE PINK SCAFFOLD	1	1968
LILY WAS HERE DAVID A STEWART FEATURING CANDY DULFER	6	1990
LIMBO ROCK CHUBBY CHECKER	32	1962
LINDA LU JOHNNY KIDD & THE PIRATES	47	1961
THE LINE LISA STANSFIELD	64	1997
LINE DANCE PARTY WOOLPACKERS	25	1997
LINE UP ELASTICA	20	1994
LINES PLANETS	36	1979
LINGER CRANBERRIES	14	1993
LION RIP DUKE SPIRIT	25	2005
THE LION SLEEPS TONIGHT (WIMOWEH) TOKENS	11	1961
THE LION SLEEPS TONIGHT DAVE NEWMAN	34	1972
THE LION SLEEPS TONIGHT TIGHT FIT	1	1982
LIONROCK LIONROCK	63	1992
THE LION'S MOUTH KAJAGOOGOO	25	1984
LIP GLOSS PULP	50	1993
LIP SERVICE (EP) WET WET WET	15	1992
LIP UP FATTY BAD MANNERS	15	1980
LIPS LIKE SUGAR ECHO & THE BUNNYMEN	36	1987
LIPSMACKIN' ROCK 'N' ROLLIN' PETER BLAKE	40	1977
LIPSTICK [A] ROCKET FROM THE CRYPT	64	1998
LIPSTICK [B] ALESHA	14	2006
LIPSTICK ON YOUR COLLAR CONNIE FRANCIS	3	1959
LIPSTICK POWDER AND PAINT SHAKIN' STEVENS	11	1985
LIQUID COOL APOLLO 440	35	1994
LIQUID DREAMS O-TOWN	3	2001
LIQUID LIPS BLUETONES	25	2003
LIQUID LIVES HADOUKEN	36	2007
THE LIQUIDATOR HARRY J. ALL STARS	9	1969
LISTEN [A] URBAN SPECIES FEATURING MC SOLAAR	47	1994
LISTEN [B] BEYONCÉ	16	2007
LISTEN EP STIFF LITTLE FINGERS	33	1982
LISTEN LIKE THIEVES INXS	46	1986
LISTEN LIKE THIEVES WAS (NOT WAS)	58	1992
LISTEN LITTLE GIRL KEITH KELLY	47	1960
LISTEN TO ME [A] BUDDY HOLLY	16	1958
LISTEN TO ME [B] HOLLIES	11	1968
LISTEN TO THE MUSIC DOOBIE BROTHERS	29	1974
LISTEN TO THE OCEAN NINA & FREDERICK	46	1960
LISTEN TO THE RADIO: ATMOSPHERICS TOM ROBINSON	39	1983
LISTEN TO THE RHYTHM K3M	71	1992
LISTEN TO THE RHYTHM FLOW GTO	72	1991
LISTEN TO WHAT THE MAN SAID WINGS	6	1975
LISTEN TO YOUR FATHER FEARGAL SHARKEY	23	1984
LISTEN TO YOUR HEART [A] ROXETTE	6	1989
LISTEN TO YOUR HEART [A] DHT FEATURING EDMEE	7	2005
LISTEN TO YOUR HEART [B] SONIA	10	1989
LISTEN UP GOSSIP	39	2007
LITHIUM NIRVANA	11	1992
LITHIUM EVANESCENCE	32	2007
LITTLE ARITHMETICS dEUS	44	1996
LITTLE ARROWS LEAPY LEE	2	1968
LITTLE BABY NOTHING MANIC STREET PREACHERS	29	1992
LITTLE BAND OF GOLD JAMES GILREATH	29	1963
LITTLE BERNADETTE HARRY BELAFONTE	16	1958
LITTLE BIRD ANNIE LENNOX	3	1993
A LITTLE BIT ROSIE RIBBONS	19	2003
A LITTLE BIT FURTHER AWAY KOKOMO	45	1982
A LITTLE BIT ME A LITTLE BIT YOU MONKEES	3	1967
A LITTLE BIT MORE [A] DR HOOK	2	1976
A LITTLE BIT MORE [A] 911	1	1999
A LITTLE BIT MORE [B] KYM SIMS	30	1992
A LITTLE BIT OF ACTION NADIA	27	2004
LITTLE BIT OF HEAVEN LISA STANSFIELD	32	1993
LITTLE BIT OF LOVE FREE	13	1972
LITTLE BIT OF LOVIN' KELE LE ROC	8	1998
A LITTLE BIT OF LUCK DJ LUCK & MC NEAT	9	1999
A LITTLE BIT OF SNOW HOWARD JONES	70	1987
A LITTLE BIT OF SOAP SHOWADDYWADDY	5	1978
A LITTLE BITTY TEAR BURL IVES	9	1962
LITTLE BITTY TEAR MIKI & GRIFF	16	1962
LITTLE BLACK BOOK [A] JIMMY DEAN	33	1962
LITTLE BLACK BOOK [B] BELINDA CARLISLE	28	1992
LITTLE BLUE BIRD VINCE HILL	42	1969
A LITTLE BOOGIE WOOGIE IN THE BACK OF MY MIND GARY GLITTER	31	1977
A LITTLE BOOGIE WOOGIE (IN THE BACK OF MY MIND) SHAKIN' STEVENS	12	1987
LITTLE BOY LOST MICHAEL HOLLIDAY	50	1960
LITTLE BOY SAD JOHNNY BURNETTE	12	1961
LITTLE BRITAIN DREADZONE	20	1996
LITTLE BROTHER BLUE PEARL	31	1990
LITTLE BROWN JUG GLENN MILLER	12	1976
LITTLE BY LITTLE [A] DUSTY SPRINGFIELD	17	1966
LITTLE BY LITTLE [B] OASIS	2	2002
LITTLE CHILD DES'REE	69	1994
LITTLE CHILDREN BILLY J. KRAMER & THE DAKOTAS	1	1964
LITTLE CHRISTINE DICK JORDAN	39	1960
LITTLE DARLIN' [A] DIAMONDS	3	1957
LITTLE DARLIN' [B] MARVIN GAYE	50	1966
LITTLE DARLING [C] RUBETTES	30	1975
LITTLE DEREK SWAY	38	2006
LITTLE DEVIL NEIL SEDAKA	9	1961
LITTLE DISCOURAGE IDLEWILD	24	1999
LITTLE DOES SHE KNOW KURSAAL FLYERS	14	1976
LITTLE DONKEY BEVERLEY SISTERS	14	1959
LITTLE DONKEY GRACIE FIELDS	21	1959
LITTLE DONKEY NINA & FREDERICK	3	1960
LITTLE DROPS OF SILVER GERRY MONROE	37	1971
LITTLE DRUMMER BOY BEVERLEY SISTERS	6	1959
LITTLE DRUMMER BOY HARRY SIMEONE CHORALE	13	1959
LITTLE DRUMMER BOY MICHAEL FLANDERS	20	1959
LITTLE DRUMMER BOY THE PIPES & DRUMS & MILITARY BAND OF THE ROYAL SCOTS DRAGOON GUARDS	13	1972
LITTLE DRUMMER BOY (REMIX) RuPAUL	61	1994
LITTLE 15 (IMPORT) DEPECHE MODE	60	1988
LITTLE FLUFFY CLOUDS ORB	10	1993
LITTLE GIRL [A] MARTY WILDE	16	1960
LITTLE GIRL [B] TROGGS	37	1968
LITTLE GIRL [C] BANNED	36	1977
LITTLE GIRL LOST ICICLE WORKS	59	1988
LITTLE GREEN APPLES ROGER MILLER	19	1968
LITTLE HOUSE OF SAVAGES WALKMEN	72	2004
A LITTLE IN LOVE CLIFF RICHARD	15	1981
LITTLE JEANNIE ELTON JOHN	33	1980
LITTLE L JAMIROQUAI	5	2001
LITTLE LADY ANEKA	50	1981
A LITTLE LESS CONVERSATION ELVIS VS JXL	1	2002
A LITTLE LESS 16 CANDLES, A LITTLE MORE "TOUCH ME" FALL OUT BOY	38	2006
LITTLE LIES FLEETWOOD MAC	5	1987
LITTLE LOST SOMETIMES ALMIGHTY	42	1991
LITTLE LOVE LIL' LOVE	34	2005
A LITTLE LOVE AND UNDERSTANDING GILBERT BECAUD	10	1975
A LITTLE LOVE A LITTLE KISS KARL DENVER	19	1962
A LITTLE LOVIN' [A] NEIL SEDAKA	34	1974
A LITTLE LOVING [B] FOURMOST	6	1964
LITTLE MAN SONNY & CHER	4	1966
LITTLE MIRACLES (HAPPEN EVERY DAY) LUTHER VANDROSS	28	1993
LITTLE MISS CAN'T BE WRONG SPIN DOCTORS	23	1993
LITTLE MISS LONELY HELEN SHAPIRO	8	1962
LITTLE MISS PERFECT SUMMER MATTHEWS	32	2004
A LITTLE MORE LOVE OLIVIA NEWTON-JOHN	4	1978
A LITTLE PEACE NICOLE	1	1982
LITTLE PIECE OF LEATHER DONNIE ELBERT	27	1972
LITTLE PINK STARS RADISH	32	1997
LITTLE RED CORVETTE PRINCE & THE REVOLUTION	2	1983
LITTLE RED MONKEY FRANK CHACKSFIELD'S TUNESMITHS, FEATURING JACK JORDAN - CLAVIOLINE	10	1953
LITTLE RED ROOSTER ROLLING STONES	1	1964
A LITTLE RESPECT ERASURE	4	1988
A LITTLE RESPECT WHEATUS	3	2001
LITTLE RHYMES MERCURY REV	51	2002
A LITTLE SAMBA UGLY DUCKLING	70	2001
LITTLE SERENADE EDDIE CALVERT	28	1958
THE LITTLE SHOEMAKER PETULA CLARK	7	1954
LITTLE SISTER [A] ELVIS PRESLEY	1	1961
LITTLE SISTER [B] QUEENS OF THE STONE AGE	18	2005
A LITTLE SOUL PULP	22	1998
LITTLE STAR [A] ELEGANTS	25	1958
LITTLE STAR [B] MADONNA	6	1998
LITTLE THINGS [A] DAVE BERRY	5	1965
LITTLE THINGS [B] INDIA.ARIE	62	2003
LITTLE THINGS MEAN A LOT ALMA COGAN	11	1954
LITTLE THINGS MEAN A LOT KITTY KALLEN	1	1954
LITTLE THOUGHT BLOC PARTY	38	2004
A LITTLE TIME BEAUTIFUL SOUTH	1	1990
LITTLE TOWN CLIFF RICHARD	11	1982
LITTLE TOWN FLIRT DEL SHANNON	4	1963
LITTLE TRAIN MAX BYGRAVES	28	1958
LITTLE WHITE BERRY ROY CASTLE	40	1960
LITTLE WHITE BULL TOMMY STEELE	6	1959
LITTLE WHITE LIES STATUS QUO	47	1999
LITTLE WILLY SWEET	4	1972
LITTLE WONDER DAVID BOWIE	14	1997

	Peak Position	Year of Entry
A LITTLE YOU FREDDIE & THE DREAMERS	26	1965
LITTLEST THINGS LILY ALLEN	21	2006
LIVE AND LEARN JOE PUBLIC	43	1992
LIVE AND LET DIE WINGS	9	1973
LIVE AND LET DIE GUNS N' ROSES	5	1991
LIVE ANIMAL (F**K LIKE A BEAST) W.A.S.P.	61	1988
LIVE ANOTHER LIFE PLASTIC BOY FEATURING ROZALLA	55	2003
LIVE AT TFI FRIDAY EP STING	53	1996
LIVE AT THE MARQUEE (EP) EDDIE & THE HOT RODS	43	1976
LIVE (EP) BARCLAY JAMES HARVEST	49	1977
THE LIVE EP GARY NUMAN	27	1985
LIVE FOR LOVING YOU GLORIA ESTEFAN	33	1991
LIVE FOR THE ONE I LOVE TINA ARENA	63	2000
LIVE FOREVER OASIS	10	1994
LIVE IN A HIDING PLACE IDLEWILD	26	2002
LIVE IN MANCHESTER (PARTS 1 + 2) N-JOI	12	1992
LIVE IN THE SKY DAVE CLARK FIVE	39	1968
LIVE IN TROUBLE BARRON KNIGHTS	7	1977
LIVE IS LIFE OPUS	6	1985
LIVE IS LIFE HERMES HOUSE BAND & DJ OTZI	50	2002
LIVE IT UP MENTAL AS ANYTHING	3	1987
LIVE LIKE HORSES ELTON JOHN & LUCIANO PAVAROTTI	9	1996
LIVE MY LIFE BOY GEORGE	62	1988
LIVE OR DIE DILLINJA	53	2002
LIVE THE DREAM CAST	7	1997
LIVE TO TELL MADONNA	2	1986
LIVE TOGETHER LISA STANSFIELD	10	1990
LIVE TWICE DARIUS	7	2005
LIVE WITH ME MASSIVE ATTACK	17	2006
LIVE YOUR LIFE BE FREE BELINDA CARLISLE	12	1991
LIVELY LONNIE DONEGAN	13	1960
LIVERPOOL (ANTHEM) LIVERPOOL FC	54	1983
LIVERPOOL LOU SCAFFOLD	7	1974
LIVERPOOL (WE'RE NEVER GONNA...) LIVERPOOL FC	54	1983
LIVIN' IN THE LIGHT CARON WHEELER	14	1990
LIVIN' IN THIS WORLD GURU	61	1996
LIVIN' IT UP [A] NORTHERN UPROAR	24	1996
LIVIN' IT UP [B] JA RULE FEATURING CASE	5	2001
LIVIN' IT UP (FRIDAY NIGHT) BELL & JAMES	59	1979
LIVIN' LA VIDA LOCA RICKY MARTIN	1	1999
LIVIN' LOVIN' DOLL CLIFF RICHARD	20	1959
LIVIN' ON A PRAYER BON JOVI	4	1986
LIVIN' ON THE EDGE AEROSMITH	19	1993
LIVIN' ON THE EDGE OF THE NIGHT IGGY POP	51	1990
LIVIN' THING ELECTRIC LIGHT ORCHESTRA	4	1976
LIVIN' THING BEAUTIFUL SOUTH	24	2004
LIVING AFTER MIDNIGHT JUDAS PRIEST	12	1980
LIVING BY NUMBERS NEW MUSIK	13	1980
THE LIVING DAYLIGHTS A-HA	5	1987
LIVING DOLL CLIFF RICHARD & THE SHADOWS	1	1959
LIVING DOLL CLIFF RICHARD & THE YOUNG ONES FEATURING HANK B MARVIN	1	1986
THE LIVING DREAM SUNDANCE	56	1999
LIVING FOR THE CITY STEVIE WONDER	15	1974
LIVING FOR THE CITY GILLAN	50	1982
LIVING FOR THE WEEKEND HARD-FI	15	2005
LIVING FOR YOU SONNY & CHER	44	1966
LIVING IN A BOX BOBBY WOMACK	70	1987
LIVING IN A BOX LIVING IN A BOX	5	1987
LIVING IN A FANTASY URBAN HYPE	57	1993
LIVING IN A WORLD (TURNED UPSIDE DOWN) PRIVATE LIVES	53	1984
LIVING IN AMERICA JAMES BROWN	5	1986
LIVING IN ANOTHER WORLD TALK TALK	48	1986
LIVING IN DANGER ACE OF BASE	18	1995
LIVING IN HARMONY CLIFF RICHARD	12	1972
LIVING IN SIN BON JOVI	35	1989
LIVING IN THE PAST [A] JETHRO TULL	3	1969
LIVING IN THE PAST [B] DRUM THEATRE	67	1986
LIVING IN THE ROSE (THE BALLADS EP) NEW MODEL ARMY	51	1993
LIVING IN THE (SLIGHTLY MORE RECENT) PAST JETHRO TULL	32	1993
LIVING IN THE SUNSHINE CLUBHOUSE FEATURING CARL	21	1994
LIVING IN THE UK SHAKATAK	52	1981
LIVING IS A PROBLEM BECAUSE EVERYTHING DIES BIFFY CLYRO	19	2007
LIVING NEXT DOOR TO ALICE SMOKIE	5	1976
LIVING NEXT DOOR TO ALICE (WHO THE F**K IS ALICE) SMOKIE FEATURING ROY CHUBBY BROWN	3	1995
LIVING ON AN ISLAND STATUS QUO	16	1979
LIVING ON MY OWN FREDDIE MERCURY	1	1985
LIVING ON THE CEILING BLANCMANGE	7	1982
LIVING ON THE FRONT LINE EDDY GRANT	11	1979
LIVING ON VIDEO TRANS-X	9	1985
LIVING THE DREAM MILLION DEAD	60	2005
THE LIVING TREE SHIRLEY BASSEY	37	2007
LIVING WITH THE HUMAN MACHINES STRANGELOVE	53	1996
THE LIVING YEARS MIKE + THE MECHANICS	2	1989
LIZARD (GONNA GET YOU) MAURO PICOTTO	27	1999
LK (CAROLINA CAROL BELA) DJ MARKY & XRS FEATURING STAMINA MC	17	2002
L-L-LUCY MUD	10	1975
LO MISMO QUE YO (IF ONLY) ALEX CUBA BAND FEATURING RON SEXSMITH	52	2004
LOADED [A] PRIMAL SCREAM	16	1990
LOADED [B] RICKY MARTIN	19	2001
LOADED GUN DEAD 60'S	28	2005
LOADSAMONEY (DOIN' UP THE HOUSE) HARRY ENFIELD	4	1988
LOBSTER & SCRIMP TIMBALAND FEATURING JAY-Z	48	1999
LOCAL BOY RIFLES	36	2005
LOCAL BOY IN THE PHOTOGRAPH STEREOPHONICS	14	1997
LOC'ED AFTER DARK TONE LOC	21	1989
LOCH LOMOND RUNRIG & THE TARTAN ARMY	9	2007
LOCK AND LOAD BOB SEGER & THE SILVER BULLET BAND	57	1996
LOCK UP YA DAUGHTERS NOISE NEXT DOOR	12	2004
LOCK UP YOUR DAUGHTERS SLADE	29	1981
LOCKED OUT CROWDED HOUSE	12	1994
LOCKED UP AKON	5	2004
LOCO FUN LOVIN' CRIMINALS	5	2001
LOCO IN ACAPULCO FOUR TOPS	7	1988
LOCO-MOTION [A] VERNONS GIRLS	47	1962
THE LOCO-MOTION [A] LITTLE EVA	2	1962
THE LOCOMOTION [A] DAVE STEWART WITH BARBARA GASKIN	70	1986
THE LOCO-MOTION [A] KYLIE MINOGUE	2	1988
LOCOMOTION [B] ORCHESTRAL MANOEUVRES IN THE DARK	5	1984
L.O.D. (LOVE ON DELIVERY) BILLY OCEAN	19	1976
THE LODGERS STYLE COUNCIL	13	1985
THE LOGICAL SONG SUPERTRAMP	7	1979
THE LOGICAL SONG SCOOTER	2	2002
L'OISEAU ET L'ENFANT MARIE MYRIAM	42	1977
LOLA KINKS	2	1970
LOLA ANDY TAYLOR	60	1990
LOLA STARS AND STRIPES STILLS	39	2004
LOLA'S THEME SHAPESHIFTERS	1	2004
LOLLIPOP [A] CHORDETTES	6	1958
LOLLIPOP [A] MUDLARKS	2	1958
LOLLIPOP [B] DADA FEATURING SANDY RIVERA & TRIX	18	2007
LOLLIPOP [C] MIKA	59	2007
LOLLY LOLLY WENDY & LISA	64	1989
LONDINIUM CATATONIA	20	1999
LONDON BOYS T REX	40	1976
LONDON BRIDGE FERGIE	3	2006
LONDON CALLING CLASH	11	1979
LONDON GIRLS CHAS & DAVE	63	1983
LONDON KID JEAN-MICHEL JARRE FEATURING HANK MARVIN	52	1989
LONDON NIGHTS LONDON BOYS	2	1989
A LONDON THING SCOTT GARCIA FEATURING MC STYLES	29	1997
LONDON TIMES RADIO HEART FEATURING GARY NUMAN	48	1987
LONDON TONIGHT COLLAPSED LUNG	31	1996
LONDON TOWN [A] WINGS	60	1978
LONDON TOWN [B] LIGHT OF THE WORLD	41	1980
LONDON TOWN [C] BUCKS FIZZ	34	1983
LONDON TOWN [D] JDS	49	1998
LONDON X-PRESS X-PRESS 2	59	1993
LONDON'S BRILLIANT WENDY JAMES	62	1993
LONDON'S BRILLIANT PARADE ELVIS COSTELLO & THE ATTRACTIONS	48	1994
LONDRES STRUTT SMELLS LIKE HEAVEN	57	1993
THE LONE RANGER QUANTUM JUMP	5	1979
LONE RIDER JOHN LEYTON	40	1962
THE LONELIEST MAN IN THE WORLD TOURISTS	32	1979
LONELINESS [A] DES O'CONNOR	18	1969
LONELINESS [B] TOMCRAFT	1	2003
LONELINESS [C] ED HARCOURT	59	2005
LONELINESS IS GONE NINE YARDS	70	1998
LONELY [A] EDDIE COCHRAN	41	1960
LONELY [B] MR ACKER BILK WITH THE LEON YOUNG STRING CHORALE	14	1962
LONELY [C] PETER ANDRE	6	1997
LONELY [D] AKON	1	2005
LONELY AT THE TOP ORDINARY BOYS	10	2006
LONELY BALLERINA MANTOVANI	16	1955
LONELY BOY [A] PAUL ANKA	3	1959
LONELY BOY [B] ANDREW GOLD	11	1977
LONELY BOY LONELY GUITAR DUANE EDDY & THE REBELETTES	35	1963
THE LONELY BULL TIJUANA BRASS	22	1963
LONELY BUOY JOE LEAN & THE JING JANG JONG	43	2008
LONELY CITY JOHN LEYTON	14	1962
LONELY, CRYIN', ONLY THERAPY?	32	1998
LONELY DAYS BEE GEES	33	1970
LONELY DAYS, LONELY NIGHTS DON DOWNING	32	1973
LONELY (HAVE WE LOST OUR LOVE) LANCE ELLINGTON	57	1993
LONELY HEART UFO	41	1981
LONELY HEARTS STILL BEAT THE SAME RESEARCH	50	2006
LONELY MAN THEME CLIFF ADAMS	39	1960
LONELY NIGHT MAGNUM	70	1986
LONELY NO MORE ROB THOMAS	11	2005
THE LONELY ONE ALICE DEEJAY	16	2000
LONELY PUP (IN A CHRISTMAS SHOP) ADAM FAITH	4	1960
LONELY STREET CLARENCE 'FROGMAN' HENRY	42	1961
LONELY SYMPHONY FRANCES RUFFELLE	25	1994
LONELY TEENAGER DION	47	1961
LONELY THIS CHRISTMAS MUD	1	1974
LONELY TOGETHER BARRY MANILOW	21	1980
THE LONER GARY MOORE	53	1987
LONESOME ADAM FAITH	12	1962
LONESOME DAY BRUCE SPRINGSTEEN	39	2002
LONESOME NUMBER ONE DON GIBSON	47	1962
LONESOME (SI TU VOIS MA MERE) CHRIS BARBER FEATURING MONTY SUNSHINE	27	1959

Title / Artist	Peak Position	Year of Entry
LONESOME TRAVELLER LONNIE DONEGAN	28	1958
LONG AFTER TONIGHT IS ALL OVER JIMMY RADLCIFFE	40	1965
LONG AND LASTING LOVE (ONCE IN A LIFETIME) GLENN MEDEIROS	42	1988
THE LONG AND WINDING ROAD RAY MORGAN	32	1970
THE LONG AND WINDING ROAD WILL YOUNG & GARETH GATES	1	2002
LONG AS I CAN SEE THE LIGHT CREEDENCE CLEARWATER REVIVAL	20	1970
LONG AS I CAN SEE THE LIGHT MONKEY MAFIA	51	1998
LONG BLACK VEIL STRANGLERS	51	2004
LONG COOL WOMAN IN A BLACK DRESS HOLLIES	32	1972
A LONG DECEMBER COUNTING CROWS	62	1996
LONG DISTANCE TURIN BRAKES	22	2002
THE LONG GOODBYE RONAN KEATING	3	2003
LONG HAIRED LOVER FROM LIVERPOOL LITTLE JIMMY OSMOND	1	1972
LONG HOT SUMMER [A] STYLE COUNCIL	3	1983
LONG HOT SUMMER [B] GIRLS ALOUD	7	2005
LONG HOT SUMMER NIGHT JT TAYLOR	63	1991
LONG LEGGED GIRL (WITH THE SHORT DRESS ON) ELVIS PRESLEY	49	1967
LONG LEGGED WOMAN DRESSED IN BLACK MUNGO JERRY	13	1974
LONG LIVE LOVE [A] SANDIE SHAW	1	1965
LONG LIVE LOVE [A] NICK BERRY	47	1992
LONG LIVE LOVE [B] OLIVIA NEWTON-JOHN	11	1974
LONG LIVE ROCK WHO	48	1979
LONG LIVE ROCK 'N' ROLL RAINBOW	33	1978
LONG LIVE THE UK MUSIC SCENE HELEN LOVE	65	1998
LONG LONG WAY TO GO DEF LEPPARD	40	2003
LONG LOST LOVER THREE DEGREES	40	1975
LONG MAY YOU RUN (LIVE) NEIL YOUNG	71	1993
LONG NIGHT CORRS	31	2004
LONG ROAD TO RUIN FOO FIGHTERS	35	2007
THE LONG RUN EAGLES	66	1979
LONG SHOT KICK DE BUCKET PIONEERS	21	1969
LONG TALL GLASSES LEO SAYER	4	1974
LONG TALL SALLY PAT BOONE	18	1956
LONG TALL SALLY LITTLE RICHARD	3	1957
LONG TERM LOVERS OF PAIN (EP) HUE & CRY	48	1991
LONG TIME ARROW	30	1985
LONG TIME COMING [A] BUMP & FLEX	73	1998
LONG TIME COMING [B] DELAYS	16	2004
LONG TIME GONE GALLIANO	15	1994
LONG TRAIN RUNNIN' DOOBIE BROTHERS	7	1993
LONG TRAIN RUNNING BANANARAMA	30	1991
A LONG WALK JILL SCOTT	54	2001
LONG WAY ROOTJOOSE	68	1997
LONG WAY AROUND EAGLE-EYE CHERRY FEATURING NENEH CHERRY	48	2000
LONG WAY FROM HOME WHITESNAKE	55	1979
LONG WAY SOUTH JJ72	68	2000
LONG WAY TO GO STEVIE NICKS	60	1989
LONG WAY 2 GO CASSIE	12	2006
LONG WHITE CAR HIPSWAY	55	1986
LONGER DAN FOGELBERG	59	1980
THE LONGEST DAY 24	56	2005
THE LONGEST TIME BILLY JOEL	25	1984
LONGTIME BOY NINA & FREDERICK	43	1961
LONGVIEW GREEN DAY	30	1995
LONNIE DONEGAN SHOWCASE (LP) LONNIE DONEGAN	26	1956
LONNIE'S SKIFFLE PARTY LONNIE DONEGAN	23	1958
LOO-BE-LOO CHUCKS	22	1963
THE LOOK ROXETTE	7	1989
LOOK AROUND VINCE HILL	12	1971
LOOK AT ME GERI HALLIWELL	2	1999
LOOK AT ME (I'M IN LOVE) MOMENTS	42	1975
LOOK AT ME NOW JESSY	29	2003
LOOK AT THAT GIRL GUY MITCHELL	1	1953
LOOK AT US NORTHERN HEIGHTZ	29	2004
LOOK AT YOURSELF DAVID McALMONT	40	1997
LOOK AWAY BIG COUNTRY	7	1986
LOOK BEFORE YOU LEAP DAVE CLARK FIVE	50	1966
LOOK BUT DON'T TOUCH (EP) SKIN	33	1994
LOOK FOR A STAR GARRY MILLS	7	1960
LOOK HOMEWARD ANGEL JOHNNIE RAY	7	1957
LOOK INTO MY EYES BONE THUGS-N-HARMONY	16	1997
LOOK MAMA HOWARD JONES	10	1985
LOOK ME IN THE HEART TINA TURNER	31	1990
LOOK OF LOVE [A] GLADYS KNIGHT & THE PIPS	21	1973
THE LOOK OF LOVE [A] T-EMPO	71	1996
THE LOOK OF LOVE [B] ABC	4	1982
THE LOOK OF LOVE [C] MADONNA	9	1987
LOOK ON THE FLOOR (HYPNOTIC TANGO) BANANARAMA	26	2005
LOOK THROUGH ANY WINDOW HOLLIES	4	1965
LOOK THROUGH MY EYES PHIL COLLINS	61	2003
LOOK UP TO THE LIGHT EVOLUTION	55	1995
LOOK WHAT YOU DONE FOR ME AL GREEN	44	1972
LOOK WHAT YOU STARTED TEMPTATIONS	63	1988
LOOK WHAT YOU'VE DONE JET	28	2004
LOOK WHO IT IS HELEN SHAPIRO	47	1963
LOOK WHO'S DANCING ZIGGY MARLEY & THE MELODY MAKERS	65	1989
LOOK WHO'S PERFECT NOW TRANSISTER	56	1998
LOOK WHO'S TALKING DR ALBAN	55	1994
LOOK WOT YOU DUN SLADE	4	1972
LOOKIN' AT YOU WARREN G FEATURING TOI	60	2002
LOOKIN' THROUGH THE WINDOWS JACKSON 5	9	1972
LOOKING AFTER NO. 1 BOOMTOWN RATS	11	1977
LOOKING AS YOU ARE EMBRACE	11	2005
LOOKING AT MIDNIGHT IMAGINATION	29	1983
LOOKING FOR A LOVE JOYCE SIMS	39	1989
LOOKING FOR A NEW LOVE JODY WATLEY	13	1987
LOOKING FOR A PLACE MANIA	29	2004
LOOKING FOR A SONG BIG AUDIO	68	1994
LOOKING FOR ATLANTIS PREFAB SPROUT	51	1990
LOOKING FOR CLUES ROBERT PALMER	33	1980
LOOKING FOR LEWIS AND CLARK LONG RYDERS	59	1985
LOOKING FOR LINDA HUE & CRY	15	1989
LOOKING FOR LOVE KAREN RAMIREZ	8	1998
LOOKING FOR LOVE TONIGHT FAT LARRY'S BAND	46	1979
LOOKING FOR THE SUMMER CHRIS REA	49	1991
LOOKING HIGH HIGH HIGH BRYAN JOHNSON	20	1960
LOOKING THROUGH PATIENT EYES PM DAWN	11	1993
LOOKING THROUGH THE EYES OF LOVE GENE PITNEY	3	1965
LOOKING THROUGH THE EYES OF LOVE PARTRIDGE FAMILY STARRING DAVID CASSIDY	9	1973
LOOKING THROUGH YOUR EYES LeANN RIMES	38	1998
LOOKING UP MICHELLE GAYLE	11	1993
LOOKS LIKE I'M IN LOVE AGAIN KEY WEST FEATURING ERIK	46	1993
LOOKS LOOKS LOOKS SPARKS	26	1975
LOOP DI LOVE SHAG	4	1972
LOOP-DE-LOOP FRANKIE VAUGHAN	5	1963
LOOPS OF FURY EP CHEMICAL BROTHERS	13	1996
LOOPS OF INFINITY COSMIC BABY	70	1994
LOOPZILLA GEORGE CLINTON	57	1982
LOOSE THERAPY?	25	1995
LOOSE CANNON KILLING JOKE	25	2003
LOOSE FIT HAPPY MONDAYS	17	1991
LOOSEN YOUR HOLD SOUTH	73	2003
LOPEZ 808 STATE	20	1997
LORD DON'T SLOW ME DOWN OASIS	10	2007
LORDS OF THE NEW CHURCH TASMIN ARCHER	26	1993
LORELEI LONNIE DONEGAN	10	1960
LORRAINE BAD MANNERS	21	1980
LOS AMERICANOS ESPIRITU	45	1993
LOS ANGELES IS BURNING BAD RELIGION	67	2004
LOSE CONTROL [A] JAMES	38	1990
LOSE CONTROL [B] MISSY ELLIOTT	7	2005
LOSE IT SUPERGRASS	75	1995
LOSE MY BREATH DESTINY'S CHILD	2	2004
LOSE YOURSELF EMINEM	1	2002
LOSER [A] BECK	15	1994
LOSER [B] THUNDER	48	2003
LOSING A FRIEND NYLON	29	2006
LOSING GRIP AVRIL LAVIGNE	22	2003
LOSING MY GRIP SAMSON	63	1982
LOSING MY MIND LIZA MINNELLI	6	1989
LOSING MY RELIGION R.E.M.	19	1991
LOSING YOU [A] BRENDA LEE	10	1963
LOSING YOU [B] DUSTY SPRINGFIELD	9	1964
LOST MICHAEL BUBLE	19	2007
LOST AGAIN YELLO	73	1983
LOST AND FOUND [A] D*NOTE	59	1997
LOST & FOUND [B] FEEDER	12	2006
THE LOST ART OF KEEPING A SECRET QUEENS OF THE STONE AGE	31	2000
LOST CAT CATATONIA	41	1996
LOST FOR WORDS RONAN KEATING	9	2003
LOST IN A MELODY DELAYS	28	2004
LOST IN AMERICA ALICE COOPER	22	1994
LOST IN EMOTION [A] LISA LISA & CULT JAM	58	1987
LOST IN EMOTION [B] JOHN 'OO' FLEMING	74	1999
LOST IN FRANCE BONNIE TYLER	9	1976
LOST IN LOVE [A] UP YER RONSON FEATURING MARY PEARCE	27	1995
LOST IN LOVE [B] LEGEND B	45	1997
LOST IN MUSIC [A] SISTER SLEDGE	4	1979
LOST IN MUSIC [B] STEREO MC'S	46	1991
LOST IN SPACE [A] APOLLO FOUR FORTY	4	1998
LOST IN SPACE [B] ELECTRASY	60	1998
LOST IN SPACE [C] LIGHTHOUSE FAMILY	6	1998
LOST IN THE PLOT DEARS	49	2004
LOST IN THE TRANSLATION PACIFICA	54	1999
LOST IN YOU [A] ROD STEWART	21	1988
LOST IN YOU [B] GARTH BROOKS	70	1999
LOST IN YOUR EYES DEBBIE GIBSON	34	1989
LOST IN YOUR LOVE TONY HADLEY	42	1992
LOST JOHN LONNIE DONEGAN	2	1956
LOST MYSELF LONGPIGS	22	1996
LOST WEEKEND LLOYD COLE & THE COMMOTIONS	17	1985
LOST WITHOUT EACH OTHER HANSON	39	2005
LOST WITHOUT U ROBIN THICKE	11	2007
LOST WITHOUT YOU [A] JAYN HANNA	44	1997
LOST WITHOUT YOU [B] DELTA GOODREM	4	2003
LOST WITHOUT YOUR LOVE BREAD	27	1977
LOST YOU SOMEWHERE CHICANE	35	1997
A LOT OF LOVE MARTI PELLOW	59	2003
LOTTERY WINNERS ON ACID CRIMEA	31	2006
LOTUS R.E.M.	26	1998
LOUIE LOUIE KINGSMEN	26	1964
LOUIE LOUIE MOTORHEAD	68	1978
LOUIE LOUIE FAT BOYS	46	1988
LOUIE LOUIE THREE AMIGOS	15	1999
LOUIS QUATORZE BOW WOW WOW	66	1982
LOUISE [A] PHIL EVERLY	47	1982
LOUISE [B] HUMAN LEAGUE	13	1984

	Peak Position	Year of Entry
LOUNGER DOGS DIE IN HOT CARS	43	2004
LOUNGIN LL COOL J	7	1996
L.O.V.E. AL GREEN	24	1975
LOVE JOHN LENNON	41	1982
LOVE JIMMY NAIL	33	1995
LOVE ACTION (I BELIEVE IN LOVE) HUMAN LEAGUE	3	1981
LOVE AIN'T GONNA WAIT FOR YOU S CLUB	2	2003
LOVE AIN'T HERE ANYMORE TAKE THAT	3	1994
LOVE AIN'T NO STRANGER WHITESNAKE	44	1985
LOVE ALL DAY NICK HEYWARD	31	1984
LOVE ALL THE HURT AWAY ARETHA FRANKLIN & GEORGE BENSON	49	1981
LOVE AND AFFECTION JOAN ARMATRADING	10	1976
LOVE AND AFFECTION SINITTA	62	1990
LOVE AND AFFECTION MR PINK PRESENTS THE PROGRAM	22	2002
LOVE AND ANGER KATE BUSH	38	1990
LOVE AND DESIRE (PART 1) ARPEGGIO	63	1979
LOVE & DEVOTION (MC SAR &) THE REAL McCOY	11	1995
LOVE AND HAPPINESS (YEMAYA Y OCHUN) RIVER OCEAN FEATURING INDIA	50	1994
LOVE AND KISSES DANNII MINOGUE	8	1991
LOVE AND LONELINESS MOTORS	58	1980
LOVE AND MARRIAGE FRANK SINATRA	3	1956
LOVE AND MONEY LOVE & MONEY	68	1987
LOVE AND PAIN [A] CARLTON	56	1991
LOVE & PAIN [B] CLOR	48	2005
LOVE AND PRIDE KING	2	1985
LOVE AND REGRET DEACON BLUE	28	1989
LOVE AND TEARS NAOMI CAMPBELL	40	1994
LOVE AND UNDERSTANDING CHER	10	1991
LOVE ANYWAY MIKE SCOTT	50	1997
LOVE AT FIRST SIGHT [A] KYLIE MINOGUE	2	2002
LOVE @ 1ST SIGHT [B] MARY J BLIGE FEATURING METHOD MAN	18	2003
LOVE AT FIRST SIGHT (JE T'AIME...MOI NON PLUS) SOUNDS NICE	18	1969
LOVE ATTACK SHAKIN' STEVENS	28	1989
LOVE BALLAD GEORGE BENSON	29	1979
LOVE BE MY LOVER (PLAYA SOL) NOVACANE VS NO ONE DRIVING	69	2002
LOVE BITES DEF LEPPARD	11	1988
LOVE BLONDE KIM WILDE	23	1983
LOVE BOMB BABY TIGERTAILZ	75	1989
LOVE BREAKDOWN ROZALLA	65	1992
LOVE BUG RAMSEY & FEN FEATURING LYNSEY MOORE	75	2000
LOVE BUG - SWEETS FOR MY SWEET (MEDLEY) TINA CHARLES	26	1977
LOVE BURNS BLACK REBEL MOTORCYCLE CLUB	37	2002
LOVE CAN BUILD A BRIDGE CHILDREN FOR RWANDA	57	1994
LOVE CAN BUILD A BRIDGE CHER, CHRISSIE HYNDE & NENEH CHERRY WITH ERIC CLAPTON	1	1995
LOVE CAN MOVE MOUNTAINS CELINE DION	46	1992
LOVE CAN'T TURN AROUND FARLEY 'JACKMASTER' FUNK	10	1986
LOVE CAN'T TURN AROUND HEAVY WEATHER	56	1996
THE LOVE CATS CURE	7	1983
LOVE CHANGES EVERYTHING [A] CLIMIE FISHER	2	1987
LOVE CHANGES EVERYTHING [B] MICHAEL BALL	2	1989
LOVE CHILD [A] DIANA ROSS & THE SUPREMES	15	1968
LOVE CHILD [B] GOODBYE MR MACKENZIE	52	1990
LOVE CITY GROOVE LOVE CITY GROOVE	7	1995
LOVE COME DOWN [A] EVELYN KING	7	1982
LOVE COME DOWN [A] ALISON LIMERICK	36	1994
LOVE COME DOWN [B] EVE GALLAGHER	57	1990
LOVE COME HOME OUR TRIBE WITH FRANKE PHAROAH & KRISTINE W	73	1994
LOVE COME RESCUE ME LOVESTATION	42	1995
LOVE COMES AGAIN TIESTO FEATURING BT	30	2004
LOVE COMES QUICKLY PET SHOP BOYS	19	1986
LOVE COMES TO MIND CHIMES	49	1990
LOVE COMMANDMENTS GISELE JACKSON	54	1997
LOVE CONQUERS ALL [A] DEEP PURPLE	57	1991
LOVE CONQUERS ALL [B] ABC	47	1991
LOVE DANCE VISION	74	1983
LOVE DETECTIVE ARAB STRAP	66	2001
LOVE DISCO STYLE EROTIC DRUM BAND	47	1979
LOVE DOESN'T HAVE TO HURT ATOMIC KITTEN	4	2003
LOVE DON'T COME EASY ALARM	48	1990
LOVE DON'T COST A THING JENNIFER LOPEZ	1	2001
LOVE DON'T LET ME GO DAVID GUETTA FEATURING CHRIS WILLIS	46	2002
LOVE DON'T LET ME GO (WALKING AWAY) DAVID GUETTA VS THE EGG	3	2006
LOVE DON'T LIVE URBAN BLUES PROJECT PRESENTS MICHAEL PROCTER	55	1996
LOVE DON'T LIVE HERE ANYMORE ROSE ROYCE	2	1978
LOVE DON'T LIVE HERE ANYMORE JIMMY NAIL	3	1985
LOVE DON'T LIVE HERE ANYMORE DOUBLE TROUBLE FEATURING JANETTE SEWELL & CARL BROWN	21	1990
LOVE DON'T LOVE YOU EN VOGUE	64	1993
LOVE ENOUGH FOR TWO PRIMA DONNA	48	1980
LOVE ENUFF SOUL II SOUL	12	1995
LOVE EVICTION QUARTZ LOCK FEATURING LONNIE GORDON	32	1995
LOVE FOOLOSOPHY JAMIROQUAI	14	2002
LOVE FOR LIFE LISA MOORISH	37	1996
THE LOVE GAME MUDLARKS	30	1959
LOVE GAMES [A] DRIFTERS	33	1975
LOVE GAMES [B] LEVEL 42	38	1981
LOVE GAMES [C] BELLE & THE DEVOTIONS	11	1984
LOVE GENERATION BOB SINCLAR FEATURING GARY NESTA PINE	12	2005
LOVE GLOVE VISAGE	54	1984
LOVE GROOVE (GROOVE WITH YOU) SMOOTH	46	1996
LOVE GROWS (WHERE MY ROSEMARY GOES) EDISON LIGHTHOUSE	1	1970
LOVE GUARANTEED DAMAGE	7	1997
LOVE HANGOVER [A] DIANA ROSS	10	1976
LOVE HANGOVER [A] ASSOCIATES	21	1982
LOVE HANGOVER [A] PAULINE HENRY	37	1995
LOVE HANGOVER [B] SCARLET	54	1995
LOVE HAS COME AGAIN HUMAN MOVEMENT FEATURING SOPHIE MOLET	53	2001
LOVE HAS COME AROUND DONALD BYRD	41	1981
LOVE HAS FOUND ITS WAY DENNIS BROWN	47	1982
LOVE HAS GONE DAVE ARMSTRONG & REDROCHE FEATURING H-BOOGIE	43	2008
LOVE HAS PASSED AWAY SUPERNATURALS	38	1997
LOVE HER WALKER BROTHERS	20	1965
LOVE HERE I COME BAD BOYS INC	26	1994
LOVE HIT ME MAXINE NIGHTINGALE	11	1977
LOVE HOUSE SAMANTHA FOX	32	1988
LOVE HOW YOU FEEL SHARON REDD	39	1983
LOVE HURTS [A] JIM CAPALDI	4	1975
LOVE HURTS [A] CHER	43	1991
LOVE HURTS [B] PETER POLYCARPOU	26	1993
THE LOVE I LOST HAROLD MELVIN & THE BLUENOTES	21	1974
THE LOVE I LOST WEST END FEATURING SYBIL	3	1993
LOVE IN A PEACEFUL WORLD LEVEL 42	31	1994
LOVE IN A TRASHCAN RAVEONETTES	26	2005
LOVE IN AN ELEVATOR AEROSMITH	13	1989
LOVE IN ANGER ARMOURY SHOW	63	1987
LOVE IN C MINOR CERRONE	31	1977
LOVE IN ITSELF.2 DEPECHE MODE	21	1983
LOVE IN THE FIRST DEGREE BANANARAMA	3	1987
LOVE IN THE KEY OF C BELINDA CARLISLE	20	1996
LOVE IN THE NATURAL WAY KIM WILDE	32	1989
LOVE IN THE SUN GLITTER BAND	15	1975
THE LOVE IN YOUR EYES VICKY LEANDROS	40	1973
THE LOVE IN YOUR EYES DANIEL O'DONNELL	47	1993
LOVE INFINITY SILVER CITY	62	1993
LOVE INJECTION TRUSSEL	43	1980
LOVE INSIDE SHARON FORRESTER	50	1995
LOVE IS...[A] VIKKI	49	1985
LOVE IS [B] ALANNAH MYLES	61	1990
LOVE IS A BATTLEFIELD PAT BENATAR	17	1984
LOVE IS A BEAUTIFUL THING AL GREEN	56	1993
LOVE IS A DESERTER KILLS	44	2005
LOVE IS A GOLDEN RING FRANKIE LAINE	19	1957
LOVE IS A KILLER VIXEN	41	1990
LOVE IS A LOSING GAME AMY WINEHOUSE	46	2007
LOVE IS A MANY SPLENDOURED THING FOUR ACES FEATURING AL ALBERTS	2	1955
LOVE IS A STRANGER EURYTHMICS	6	1982
LOVE IS A WONDERFUL COLOUR ICICLE WORKS	15	1984
LOVE IS A WONDERFUL THING MICHAEL BOLTON	23	1991
LOVE IS ALL [A] MALCOLM ROBERTS	12	1969
LOVE IS ALL [A] ENGELBERT HUMPERDINCK	44	1973
LOVE IS ALL [B] RAPTURE	38	2004
LOVE IS ALL AROUND [A] TROGGS	5	1967
LOVE IS ALL AROUND [A] WET WET WET	1	1994
LOVE IS ALL AROUND [B] DJ BOBO	49	1995
LOVE IS ALL IS ALRIGHT UB40	29	1982
LOVE IS ALL THAT MATTERS HUMAN LEAGUE	41	1988
LOVE IS ALL WE NEED MARY J BLIGE	15	1997
LOVE IS AN ARROW ABERFELDY	60	2005
LOVE IS AN UNFAMILIAR NAME DUKE SPIRIT	33	2005
LOVE IS BLUE [A] JEFF BECK	23	1968
LOVE IS BLUE [B] EDWARD BALL	59	1997
LOVE IS BLUE (L'AMOUR EST BLEU) [A] PAUL MAURIAT	12	1968
LOVE IS CONTAGIOUS TAJA SEVELLE	7	1988
LOVE IS DEAD BRETT ANDERSON	42	2007
LOVE IS EVERYWHERE CICERO	19	1992
LOVE IS FOREVER BILLY OCEAN	34	1987
LOVE IS GONE DAVID GUETTA	9	2007
LOVE IS HERE AND NOW YOU'RE GONE SUPREMES	17	1967
LOVE IS HOLY KIM WILDE	16	1992
LOVE IS IN CONTROL (FINGER ON THE TRIGGER) DONNA SUMMER	18	1982
LOVE IS IN THE AIR JOHN PAUL YOUNG	5	1978
LOVE IS IN THE AIR MILK & SUGAR/JOHN PAUL YOUNG	25	2002
LOVE IS IN YOUR EYES LEMON TREES	75	1992
LOVE IS JUST THE GREAT PRETENDER ANIMAL NIGHTLIFE	28	1985
LOVE IS LIFE HOT CHOCOLATE	6	1970
LOVE IS LIKE A VIOLIN KEN DODD	8	1960
LOVE IS LIKE OXYGEN SWEET	9	1978
LOVE IS LOVE BARRY RYAN	25	1969
LOVE IS NOT A GAME J MAJIK FEATURING KATHY BROWN	34	2001
LOVE IS ON THE ONE XAVIER	53	1982
LOVE IS ON THE WAY LUTHER VANDROSS	38	1993
LOVE IS ONLY A FEELING DARKNESS	5	2004
LOVE IS SO EASY STARGARD	45	1978
LOVE IS SO NICE URBAN SOUL	75	1998
LOVE IS STRANGE EVERLY BROTHERS	11	1965
LOVE IS STRONG ROLLING STONES	14	1994

	Peak Position	Year of Entry
LOVE IS STRONGER THAN DEATH THE THE	39	1993
LOVE IS STRONGER THAN PRIDE SADE	44	1988
LOVE IS THE ANSWER ENGLAND DAN & JOHN FORD COLEY	45	1979
LOVE IS THE ART LIVING IN A BOX	45	1988
LOVE IS THE DRUG ROXY MUSIC	2	1975
LOVE IS THE DRUG GRACE JONES	35	1986
LOVE IS THE GOD MARIA NAYLER	65	1998
LOVE IS THE GUN BLUE MERCEDES	46	1988
LOVE IS THE ICON BARRY WHITE	20	1995
LOVE IS THE KEY CHARLATANS	16	2001
LOVE IS THE LAW SEAHORSES	3	1997
LOVE IS THE MESSAGE LOVE INCORPORATED FEATURING MC NOISE	59	1991
LOVE IS THE SEVENTH WAVE STING	41	1985
LOVE IS THE SLUG WE'VE GOT A FUZZBOX & WE'RE GONNA USE IT	31	1986
LOVE IS THE SWEETEST THING PETER SKELLERN FEATURING GRIMETHORPE COLLIERY BAND	60	1978
(LOVE IS) THE TENDER TRAP FRANK SINATRA	2	1956
LOVE IS WAR BRILLIANT	64	1986
LOVE IT WHEN YOU CALL THE FEELING	18	2006
LOVE IZ ERICK SERMON	72	2003
LOVE KILLS [A] FREDDIE MERCURY	10	1984
LOVE KILLS [B] JOE STRUMMER	69	1986
LOVE KISSES AND HEARTACHES MAUREEN EVANS	44	1960
LOVE LADY DAMAGE	33	1997
LOVE LETTER MARC ALMOND	68	1985
LOVE LETTERS [A] KETTY LESTER	4	1962
LOVE LETTERS [A] ELVIS PRESLEY	6	1966
LOVE LETTERS [A] ALISON MOYET	4	1987
LOVE LETTERS [B] ALI	63	1998
LOVE LETTERS IN THE SAND PAT BOONE	2	1957
LOVE LETTERS IN THE SAND VINCE HILL	23	1967
LOVE LIES LOST HELEN TERRY	34	1984
LOVE LIGHT IN FLIGHT STEVIE WONDER	44	1984
LOVE LIKE A FOUNTAIN IAN BROWN	23	1999
LOVE LIKE A MAN TEN YEARS AFTER	3	1970
LOVE LIKE A RIVER CLIMIE FISHER	22	1989
LOVE LIKE A ROCKET BOB GELDOF	61	1987
LOVE LIKE BLOOD KILLING JOKE	16	1985
LOVE LIKE THIS [A] FAITH EVANS	24	1998
LOVE LIKE THIS [B] NATASHA BEDINGFIELD FEATURING SEAN KINGSTON	27	2008
LOVE LIKE YOU AND ME GARY GLITTER	10	1975
A LOVE LIKE YOURS IKE & TINA TURNER	16	1966
L.O.V.E...LOVE ORANGE JUICE	65	1981
LOVE LOVE LOVE BOBBY HEBB	32	1972
LOVE, LOVE, LOVE - HERE I COME ROLLO GOES MYSTIC	32	1995
LOVE LOVES TO LOVE LOVE LULU	32	1967
LOVE MACHINE [A] ELVIS PRESLEY	38	1967
LOVE MACHINE (PART 1) [B] MIRACLES	3	1976
LOVE MACHINE [C] GIRLS ALOUD	2	2004
LOVE MADE ME VIXEN	36	1989
LOVE MAKES NO SENSE ALEXANDER O'NEAL	26	1993
LOVE MAKES THE WORLD GO ROUND [A] PERRY COMO	6	1958
LOVE MAKES THE WORLD GO ROUND [A] JETS	21	1982
LOVE MAKES THE WORLD GO ROUND [B] DON-E	18	1992
LOVE MAN OTIS REDDING	43	1969
LOVE ME [A] DIANA ROSS	38	1974
LOVE ME [B] YVONNE ELLIMAN	6	1976
LOVE ME [B] MARTINE McCUTCHEON	6	1999
LOVE ME [C] PATRIC	54	1994
LOVE ME AND LEAVE ME SEAHORSES	16	1997
LOVE ME AS THOUGH THERE WERE NO TOMORROW NAT 'KING' COLE	11	1956
LOVE ME BABY SUSAN CADOGAN	22	1975
LOVE ME DO BEATLES	4	1962
LOVE ME FOR A REASON OSMONDS	1	1974
LOVE ME FOR A REASON BOYZONE	2	1994
LOVE ME FOREVER EYDIE GORME	21	1958
LOVE ME FOREVER FOUR ESQUIRES	23	1958
LOVE ME FOREVER MARION RYAN	5	1958
LOVE ME LIKE A LOVER TINA CHARLES	31	1976
LOVE ME LIKE I LOVE YOU BAY CITY ROLLERS	4	1976
LOVE ME LIKE THIS REAL TO REEL	68	1984
LOVE ME LIKE YOU MAGIC NUMBERS	12	2005
LOVE ME LOVE MY DOG PETER SHELLEY	3	1975
LOVE ME NOW [A] BRIANA CORRIGAN	48	1996
LOVE ME NOW [B] SECRET KNOWLEDGE	66	1996
LOVE ME OR HATE ME LADY SOVEREIGN	26	2007
LOVE ME OR LEAVE ME DORIS DAY	20	1955
LOVE ME OR LEAVE ME SAMMY DAVIS Jr.	8	1955
LOVE ME RIGHT NOW ROSE ROYCE	60	1985
LOVE ME RIGHT (OH SHEILA) ANGEL CITY FEATURING LARA McALLEN	11	2003
LOVE ME TENDER ELVIS PRESLEY	11	1956
LOVE ME TENDER RICHARD CHAMBERLAIN	15	1962
LOVE ME TENDER ROLAND RAT SUPERSTAR	32	1984
LOVE ME THE RIGHT WAY RAPINATION & KYM MAZELLE	22	1993
LOVE ME TO SLEEP HOT CHOCOLATE	50	1980
LOVE ME TONIGHT [A] TOM JONES	9	1969
LOVE ME TONIGHT [B] TREVOR WALTERS	27	1981
LOVE ME WARM AND TENDER PAUL ANKA	19	1962
LOVE ME WITH ALL YOUR HEART KARL DENVER	37	1964
LOVE MEETING LOVE LEVEL 42	61	1980
LOVE MISSILE F1-11 SIGUE SIGUE SPUTNIK	3	1986
LOVE MOVES IN MYSTERIOUS WAYS JULIA FORDHAM	19	1992
LOVE MY WAY PSYCHEDELIC FURS	42	1982
LOVE NEEDS NO DISGUISE GARY NUMAN & DRAMATIS	33	1981
LOVE NEVER DIES... BELINDA CARLISLE	54	1988
LOVE OF A LIFETIME [A] CHAKA KHAN	52	1986
LOVE OF A LIFETIME [B] HONEYZ	9	1999
LOVE OF MY LIFE [A] DOOLEYS	9	1977
LOVE OF MY LIFE [B] QUEEN	63	1979
THE LOVE OF RICHARD NIXON MANIC STREET PREACHERS	2	2004
LOVE OF THE COMMON PEOPLE NICKY THOMAS	9	1970
LOVE OF THE COMMON PEOPLE PAUL YOUNG	2	1983
LOVE OF THE LOVED CILLA BLACK	35	1963
LOVE OH LOVE LIONEL RICHIE	52	1992
LOVE ON A FARMBOY'S WAGES XTC	50	1983
LOVE ON A MOUNTAIN TOP ROBERT KNIGHT	10	1973
LOVE ON A MOUNTAIN TOP SINITTA	20	1989
LOVE ON A SUMMER NIGHT McCRARYS	52	1982
LOVE ON LOVE E-ZEE POSSEE	59	1990
LOVE ON LOVE CANDI STATON	27	1999
LOVE ON MY MIND FREEMASONS FEATURING AMANDA WILSON	11	2005
LOVE ON THE LINE [A] BARCLAY JAMES HARVEST	63	1980
LOVE ON THE LINE [B] BLAZIN' SQUAD	6	2002
LOVE ON THE NORTHERN LINE NORTHERN LINE	15	2000
LOVE ON THE ROCKS NEIL DIAMOND	17	1980
LOVE ON THE RUN CHICANE FEATURING PETER CUNNAH	33	2003
LOVE ON THE SIDE BROKEN ENGLISH	69	1987
LOVE ON YOUR SIDE THOMPSON TWINS	9	1983
LOVE OR MONEY [A] BLACKWELLS	46	1961
LOVE OR MONEY [A] JIMMY CRAWFORD	49	1961
LOVE OR MONEY [A] BILLY FURY	57	1982
LOVE OR MONEY [B] SAMMY HAGAR	67	1980
LOVE OR NOTHING DIANA BROWN & BARRIE K. SHARPE	71	1991
LOVE OVER GOLD (LIVE) DIRE STRAITS	50	1984
LOVE OVERBOARD GLADYS KNIGHT & THE PIPS	42	1988
LOVE PAINS HAZELL DEAN	48	1989
LOVE PAINS LIZA MINNELLI	41	1990
THE LOVE PARADE DREAM ACADEMY	68	1985
LOVE PATROL DOOLEYS	29	1980
LOVE, PEACE & GREASE BT	41	1997
LOVE, PEACE & HAPPINESS LOST BOYZ	57	1997
LOVE PEACE AND UNDERSTANDING DREAM FREQUENCY	71	1991
LOVE PLUS ONE HAIRCUT 100	3	1982
LOVE POTION NO. 9 TYGERS OF PAN TANG	45	1982
LOVE POWER DIONNE WARWICK & JEFFREY OSBORNE	63	1987
LOVE PROFUSION MADONNA	11	2003
LOVE REACTION DIVINE	65	1983
LOVE REALLY HURTS WITHOUT YOU BILLY OCEAN	2	1976
LOVE REARS ITS UGLY HEAD LIVING COLOUR	12	1991
LOVE REMOVAL MACHINE CULT	18	1987
LOVE RENDEZVOUS M PEOPLE	32	1995
LOVE RESURRECTION ALISON MOYET	10	1984
LOVE RESURRECTION D'LUX	58	1996
LOVE REVOLUTION PHIXX	13	2004
LOVE ROLLERCOASTER RED HOT CHILI PEPPERS	7	1997
LOVE RULES WEST END	44	1995
THE LOVE SCENE JOE	22	1997
LOVE SCENES BEVERLEY CRAVEN	34	1993
LOVE SEE NO COLOUR FARM	35	1991
LOVE SENSATION 911	21	1996
LOVE SENSATION '06 LOLEATTA HOLLOWAY	37	2006
LOVE SENSATION 2006 EDDIE THONEICK & KURD MAVERICK	39	2006
LOVE SHACK B-52's	2	1990
LOVE SHADOW FASHION	51	1982
LOVE SHINE RHYTHM SOURCE	74	1995
LOVE SHINE A LIGHT KATRINA & THE WAVES	3	1997
LOVE SHINES THROUGH CHAKRA	67	1999
LOVE SHOULD BE A CRIME O-TOWN	38	2002
LOVE SHOULDA BROUGHT YOU HOME TONI BRAXTON	33	1994
LOVE SHY KRISTINE BLOND	22	1998
LOVE SICK BOB DYLAN	64	1998
LOVE SITUATION MARK FISHER FEATURING DOTTY GREEN	59	1985
LOVE SLAVE WEDDING PRESENT	17	1992
LOVE SNEAKIN' UP ON YOU BONNIE RAITT	69	1994
A LOVE SO BEAUTIFUL MICHAEL BOLTON	27	1995
LOVE SO BRIGHT MARK SHAW	54	1990
LOVE SO RIGHT BEE GEES	41	1976
LOVE SO STRONG SECRET LIFE	37	1993
LOVE SONG [A] DAMNED	20	1979
LOVE SONG [B] SIMPLE MINDS	6	1981
LOVE SONG [C] UTAH SAINTS	37	2000
LOVE SONG FOR A VAMPIRE ANNIE LENNOX	3	1993
LOVE SONGS ARE BACK AGAIN (MEDLEY) BAND OF GOLD	24	1984
THE LOVE SONGS EP DANIEL O'DONNELL	27	1997
LOVE SPREADS STONE ROSES	2	1994
LOVE STEALS US FROM LONELINESS IDLEWILD	16	2005
LOVE STIMULATION HUMATE	18	1999
LOVE STORY [A] JETHRO TULL	29	1969
LOVE STORY [B] LAYO & BUSHWACKA	8	2002
LOVE STRAIN KYM MAZELLE	52	1989
A LOVE SUPREME WILL DOWNING	14	1988
LOVE TAKE OVER FIVE STAR	25	1985
LOVE TAKES TIME MARIAH CAREY	37	1990
LOVE THE LIFE JTQ WITH NOEL McKOY	34	1993

Title / Artist	Peak Position	Year of Entry
LOVE THE ONE YOU'RE WITH STEPHEN STILLS	37	1971
LOVE THE ONE YOU'RE WITH BUCKS FIZZ	47	1986
LOVE THE ONE YOU'RE WITH LUTHER VANDROSS	31	1994
LOVE THEM EAMON FEATURING GHOSTFACE	27	2004
LOVE THEME FROM *A STAR IS BORN* (EVERGREEN) BARBRA STREISAND	3	1977
LOVE THEME FROM *SPARTACUS* TERRY CALLIER	57	1998
LOVE THEME FROM *THE GODFATHER* ANDY WILLIAMS	42	1972
LOVE THEME FROM *THE THORN BIRDS* JUAN MARTIN	10	1984
LOVE THING [A] PASADENAS	22	1990
LOVE THING [B] TINA TURNER	29	1992
LOVE THING [C] EVOLUTION	32	1993
LOVE...THY WILL BE DONE MARTIKA	9	1991
LOVE TIMES LOVE HEAVY PETTIN'	69	1984
LOVE TO HATE YOU ERASURE	4	1991
LOVE II LOVE DAMAGE	12	1996
LOVE TO LOVE YOU CORRS	62	1997
LOVE TO LOVE YOU BABY DONNA SUMMER	4	1976
LOVE TO SEE YOU CRY ENRIQUE IGLESIAS	12	2002
LOVE TO STAY ALTERED IMAGES	46	1983
LOVE TODAY MIKA	6	2007
LOVE TOGETHER L.A. MIX FEATURING KEVIN HENRY	66	1989
LOVE TOUCH ROD STEWART	27	1986
LOVE TOWN BOOKER NEWBURY III	6	1983
LOVE TRAIN [A] O'JAYS	9	1973
LOVE TRAIN [B] HOLLY JOHNSON	4	1989
LOVE TRAIN [C] WOLFMOTHER	62	2006
LOVE TRIAL KELLY MARIE	51	1981
LOVE, TRUTH AND HONESTY BANANARAMA	23	1988
LOVE U 4 LIFE JODECI	23	1995
LOVE U MORE SUNSCREEM	23	1992
LOVE UNLIMITED FUN LOVIN' CRIMINALS	18	1998
LOVE WALKED IN THUNDER	21	1991
LOVE WARS WOMACK & WOMACK	14	1984
LOVE WASHES OVER ART OF TRANCE	60	2002
LOVE WHAT YOU DO DIVINE COMEDY	26	2001
LOVE WILL COME TOMSKI FEATURING JAN JOHNSTON	31	2000
LOVE WILL COME THROUGH TRAVIS	28	2004
LOVE WILL CONQUER ALL LIONEL RICHIE	45	1986
LOVE WILL FIND A WAY [A] DAVID GRANT	24	1983
LOVE WILL FIND A WAY [B] YES	73	1987
LOVE WILL KEEP US ALIVE EAGLES	52	1996
LOVE WILL KEEP US TOGETHER CAPTAIN & TENNILLE	32	1975
LOVE WILL KEEP US TOGETHER JTQ FEATURING ALISON LIMERICK	63	1995
LOVE WILL LEAD YOU BACK TAYLOR DAYNE	69	1990
LOVE WILL MAKE YOU FAIL IN SCHOOL ROCKY SHARPE & THE REPLAYS FEATURING THE TOP LINERS	60	1979
LOVE WILL NEVER DO (WITHOUT YOU) JANET JACKSON	34	1990
LOVE WILL SAVE THE DAY WHITNEY HOUSTON	10	1988
LOVE WILL SET YOU FREE (JAMBE MYTH) STARCHASER	24	2002
LOVE WILL TEAR US APART JOY DIVISION	13	1980
LOVE WILL TEAR US APART HONEYROOT	70	2005
LOVE WON'T LET ME WAIT MAJOR HARRIS	37	1975
LOVE WON'T WAIT GARY BARLOW	1	1997
LOVE WORTH DYING FOR THUNDER	60	1997
A LOVE WORTH WAITING FOR SHAKIN' STEVENS	2	1984
LOVE X LOVE GEORGE BENSON	10	1980
LOVE YA UNKLEJAM	54	2007
LOVE YOU ALL MY LIFETIME CHAKA KHAN	49	1992
LOVE YOU ANYWAY DE NADA	15	2001
LOVE YOU DOWN READY FOR THE WORLD	60	1987
LOVE YOU INSIDE OUT BEE GEES	13	1979
LOVE YOU LIKE MAD VS	7	2004
LOVE YOU MORE BUZZCOCKS	34	1978
THE LOVE YOU SAVE JACKSON 5	7	1970
LOVE YOU SOME MORE CEVIN FISHER FEATURING SHEILA SMITH	60	2001
LOVE YOU TOO MUCH HOUSE OF LOVE	73	2005
LOVE YOUR MONEY DAISY CHAINSAW	26	1992
LOVE YOUR SEXY...!! BYKER GROOOVE!	48	1994
LOVE ZONE BILLY OCEAN	49	1986
LOVEBIRDS DODGY	65	1993
LOVEDRIVE SCORPIONS	69	1979
LOVEFOOL CARDIGANS	2	1996
LOVELIGHT ROBBIE WILLIAMS	8	2006
LOVELIGHT (RIDE ON A LOVE TRAIN) JAYN HANNA	42	1996
LOVELY BUBBA SPARXXX	24	2002
LOVELY DAUGHTER MERZ	60	1999
LOVELY DAY BILL WITHERS	4	1978
LOVELY DAZE JAZZY JEFF & FRESH PRINCE	37	1998
LOVELY MONEY DAMNED	42	1982
LOVELY ONE JACKSONS	29	1980
LOVELY THING REGGAE PHILHARMONIC ORCHESTRA	71	1990
LOVENEST WEDDING PRESENT	58	1991
LOVER [A] JOE ROBERTS	22	1994
LOVER [B] DAN REED NETWORK	45	1990
LOVER [C] RACHEL McFARLANE	36	1998
LOVER COME BACK TO ME DEAD OR ALIVE	11	1985
THE LOVER IN ME SHEENA EASTON	15	1989
THE LOVER IN YOU SUGARHILL GANG	54	1982
LOVER LOVER LOVER IAN McCULLOCH	47	1992
LOVER PLEASE VERNONS GIRLS	16	1962
A LOVER SPURNED MARC ALMOND	29	1990
THE LOVER THAT YOU ARE PULSE FEATURING ANTOINETTE ROBERTSON	22	1996
LOVERBOY [A] BILLY OCEAN	15	1985
LOVERBOY [B] CHAIRMEN OF THE BOARD FEATURING GENERAL JOHNSON	56	1986
LOVERBOY [C] MARIAH CAREY	12	2001
LOVERIDE NUANCE FEATURING VIKKI LOVE	59	1985
THE LOVERS [A] ALEXANDER O'NEAL	28	1988
LOVERS [B] TEARS	24	2005
LOVERS & FRIENDS LIL JON & THE EAST SIDE BOYZ	10	2005
A LOVER'S CONCERTO TOYS	5	1965
A LOVERS HOLIDAY CHANGE	14	1980
LOVER'S LANE GEORGIO	54	1988
LOVERS OF THE WORLD UNITE DAVID & JONATHAN	7	1966
THE LOVERS WE WERE MICHAEL BALL	63	1994
LOVE'S A GAME MAGIC NUMBERS	24	2005
LOVE'S A LOADED GUN ALICE COOPER	38	1991
LOVE'S A PRIMA DONNA STEVE HARLEY	41	1976
LOVE'S ABOUT TO CHANGE MY HEART DONNA SUMMER	20	1989
LOVE'S BEEN GOOD TO ME FRANK SINATRA	8	1969
LOVE'S COMIN' AT YA MELBA MOORE	15	1982
LOVE'S CRASHING WAVES DIFFORD & TILBROOK	57	1984
LOVE'S DIVINE SEAL	68	2003
LOVE'S EASY TEARS COCTEAU TWINS	53	1986
LOVE'S GONNA GET YOU [A] UK PLAYERS	52	1983
LOVE'S GONNA GET YOU [B] JOCELYN BROWN	70	1986
LOVE'S GOT A HOLD ON MY HEART STEPS	2	1999
LOVE'S GOT ME LOOSE ENDS	40	1990
LOVE'S GOT ME ON A TRIP SO HIGH LONI CLARK	59	1994
LOVE'S GOTTA HOLD ON ME [A] DOLLAR	4	1979
LOVE'S GOTTA HOLD ON ME [B] ZOO EXPERIENCE FEATURING DESTRY	66	1992
LOVE'S GREAT ADVENTURE ULTRAVOX	12	1984
LOVE'S JUST A BROKEN HEART CILLA BLACK	5	1966
LOVE'S MADE A FOOL OF YOU CRICKETS	26	1959
LOVE'S MADE A FOOL OF YOU BUDDY HOLLY	39	1964
LOVE'S MADE A FOOL OF YOU MATCHBOX	63	1981
LOVES ME LIKE A ROCK PAUL SIMON	39	1973
LOVE'S ON EVERY CORNER DANNII MINOGUE	44	1992
LOVE'S SUCH A WONDERFUL THING REAL THING	33	1977
LOVE'S SWEET EXILE MANIC STREET PREACHERS	26	1991
LOVE'S TAKEN OVER CHANTE MOORE	54	1993
LOVE'S THEME LOVE UNLIMITED ORCHESTRA	10	1974
LOVE'S UNKIND DONNA SUMMER	3	1977
LOVE'S UNKIND SOPHIE LAWRENCE	21	1991
LOVESICK [A] GANG STARR	50	1991
LOVESICK [B] UNDERCOVER FEATURING JOHN MATTHEWS	62	1993
LOVESICK BLUES FRANK IFIELD	1	1962
LOVESONG CURE	18	1989
LOVESTONED I THINK SHE KNOWS JUSTIN TIMBERLAKE	11	2007
LOVESTRUCK MADNESS	10	1999
LOVETOWN PETER GABRIEL	49	1994
LOVEY DOVEY TONY TERRY	44	1988
LOVIN' CRW	49	2000
LOVIN' EACH DAY RONAN KEATING	2	2001
LOVIN' IS EASY HEAR'SAY	6	2002
LOVIN' (LET ME LOVE YOU) APACHE INDIAN	53	1997
LOVIN' LIVIN' AND GIVIN' DIANA ROSS	54	1978
LOVIN' ON THE SIDE REID	71	1989
LOVIN' THINGS MARMALADE	6	1968
LOVIN' UP A STORM JERRY LEE LEWIS	28	1959
LOVIN' YOU [A] SHANICE	54	1992
LOVIN' YOU [A] UBM	46	1998
LOVIN' YOU [B] POKER PETS FEATURING NATE JAMES	43	2005
LOVIN' YOU MORE STEVE MAC/STEVE SMITH	73	2005
LOVIN' YOU YOU SPARKLE	65	1999
LOVING AND FREE KIKI DEE	13	1976
LOVING ARMS ELVIS PRESLEY	47	1981
LOVING EVERY MINUTE LIGHTHOUSE FAMILY	20	1996
LOVING JUST FOR FUN KELLY MARIE	21	1980
LOVING ON THE LOSING SIDE TOMMY HUNT	28	1976
LOVING THE ALIEN DAVID BOWIE	19	1985
LOVING THE ALIEN SCUMFROG VS BOWIE	41	2002
LOVING YOU [A] ELVIS PRESLEY	24	1957
LOVING YOU [B] MINNIE RIPERTON	2	1975
LOVING YOU [B] MASSIVO FEATURING TRACY	25	1990
LOVING YOU '03 [B] MARC ET CLAUDE	37	2003
LOVING YOU [C] DONALD BYRD	41	1983
LOVING YOU [D] CHRIS REA	65	1982
LOVING YOU [E] FEARGAL SHARKEY	26	1985
LOVING YOU AGAIN CHRIS REA	47	1987
LOVING YOU AIN'T EASY PAGLIARO	31	1972
LOVING YOU HAS MADE ME BANANAS GUY MARKS	25	1978
LOVING YOU IS SWEETER THAN EVER FOUR TOPS	21	1966
LOVING YOU IS SWEETER THAN EVER NICK KAMEN	16	1987
LOVING YOU MORE BT FEATURING VINCENT COVELLO	14	1995
LOVING YOU (OLE OLE OLE) BRIAN HARVEY & THE REFUGEE CREW	20	2001
LOVING YOU'S A DIRTY JOB BUT SOMEBODY'S GOTTA DO IT BONNIE TYLER, GUEST VOALS TODD RUNDGREN	73	1985
LOW [A] CRACKER	43	1994
LOW [B] FOO FIGHTERS	21	2003
LOW [C] KELLY CLARKSON	35	2003

	Peak Position	Year of Entry
LOW [D] FLO-RIDA FEATURING T-PAIN	6	2008
LOW C SUPERGRASS	52	2005
LOW FIVE SNEAKER PIMPS	39	1999
LOW LIFE IN HIGH PLACES THUNDER	22	1992
LOW RIDER WAR	12	1976
LOWDOWN [A] BOZ SCAGGS	28	1976
LOWDOWN [A] HINDSIGHT	62	1987
LOWDOWN [B] ELECTRAFIXION	54	1995
LOWRIDER CYPRESS HILL	33	2001
THE LOYALISER FATIMA MANSIONS	58	1994
LSD (EP) KAOTIC CHEMISTRY	68	1992
LSF KASABIAN	10	2004
LSI SHAMEN	6	1992
LUCAS WITH THE LID OFF LUCAS	37	1994
LUCHINI AKA (THIS IS IT) CAMP LO	74	1997
LUCILLE [A] LITTLE RICHARD	10	1957
LUCILLE [A] EVERLY BROTHERS	4	1960
LUCILLE [B] KENNY ROGERS	1	1977
LUCKY BRITNEY SPEARS	5	2000
LUCKY 7 MEGAMIX U.K. MIXMASTERS	43	1991
LUCKY DEVIL CARL DOBKINS	44	1960
LUCKY DEVIL FRANK IFIELD	22	1960
LUCKY FIVE RUSS CONWAY	14	1960
LUCKY LIKE THAT CLEA	55	2006
LUCKY LIPS CLIFF RICHARD	4	1963
LUCKY LOVE ACE OF BASE	20	1995
LUCKY LUCKY ME MARVIN GAYE	67	1994
LUCKY MAN VERVE	7	1997
LUCKY NUMBER LENE LOVICH	3	1979
THE LUCKY ONE [A] LAURA BRANIGAN	56	1984
LUCKY ONE [B] AMY GRANT	60	1994
LUCKY PRESSURE RONI SIZE REPRAZENT	58	2001
LUCKY STAR [A] MADONNA	14	1984
LUCKY STAR [B] SUPERFUNK FEATURING RON CARROLL	42	2000
LUCKY STAR [C] BASEMENT JAXX FEATURING DIZZEE RASCAL	23	2002
LUCKY STARS DEAN FRIEDMAN	3	1978
LUCKY TOWN (LIVE) BRUCE SPRINGSTEEN	48	1993
LUCKY YOU LIGHTNING SEEDS	15	1994
LUCRETIA MY REFLECTION SISTERS OF MERCY	20	1988
LUCY [A] HABIT	56	1988
LUCY [B] JEALOUSY	30	2006
LUCY IN THE SKY WITH DIAMONDS ELTON JOHN	10	1974
LUDI DREAM WARRIORS	39	1991
LUKA SUZANNE VEGA	23	1987
LULLABY [A] CURE	5	1989
LULLABY [B] SHAWN MULLINS	9	1999
LULLABY [C] MELANIE B	13	2001
LULLABY [D] STARSAILOR	36	2001
LULLABY [E] LEMAR	5	2003
LULLABY OF BROADWAY WINIFRED SHAW	42	1976
LULLABY OF THE LEAVES VENTURES	43	1961
LUMBERED LONNIE DONEGAN	6	1961
LUMP PRESIDENTS OF THE UNITED STATES OF AMERICA	15	1996
LUMP IN MY THROAT DEPARTURE	30	2005
THE LUNATICS (HAVE TAKEN OVER THE ASYLUM) FUN BOY THREE	20	1981
LUNCH OR DINNER SUNSHINE ANDERSON	57	2001
LUSH ORBITAL	43	1993
LUST FOR LIFE IGGY POP	26	1996
LUTON AIRPORT CATS U.K.	22	1979
LUV DA SUNSHINE INTENSO PROJECT	22	2002
LUV DUP HIGH FIDELITY	70	1998
LUV 4 LUV ROBIN S	11	1993
LUV IS COOL SYSTEM OF LIFE	63	2004
LUV ME LUV ME SHAGGY	5	2001
LUV U BETTER LL COOL J	7	2002
LUV'D UP CRUSH	45	1996
LUVSTRUCK SOUTHSIDE SPINNERS	9	2000
LUVSTUFF SAGAT	71	1994
LUXURIOUS GWEN STEFANI	44	2005
L'VIA L'VIAQUEZ MARS VOLTA	53	2005
LYDIA DEAN FRIEDMAN	31	1978
LYIN' EYES EAGLES	23	1975
LYING IS THE MOST FUN A GIRL CAN HAVE PANIC! AT THE DISCO	39	2006
LYLA OASIS	1	2005
LYRIC ZWAN	44	2003
LYRIC ON MY LIP TALI	39	2002

M–P

KEY TO INDEX ENTRIES

Song Title | Artist/Group | Peak Position | Year of Entry

	Song Title / Artist/Group	Peak Position	Year of Entry
	ALL I REALLY WANT ALANIS MORISSETTE	59	1996
	ALL I REALLY WANT TO DO BYRDS	4	1965
	ALL I REALLY WANT TO DO CHER	9	1965
	ALL I SEE IS YOU DUSTY SPRINGFIELD	9	1966
	ALL I THINK ABOUT IS YOU NILSSON	43	1977
Same letter denotes different versions of the same song	ALL I WANNA DO [A] SHERYL CROW	4	1994
	ALL I WANNA DO [A] JOANNE FARRELL	40	1995
	ALL I WANNA DO [A] AMY STUDT	21	2004
Different letters denote different songs with the same name	ALL I WANNA DO [B] TIN TIN OUT	31	1997
	ALL I WANNA DO [C] DANNII	4	1997
	ALL I WANNA DO IS MAKE LOVE TO YOU HEART	37	1993

	Peak Position	Year of Entry
MA BAKER BONEY M	2	1977
MA HE'S MAKING EYES AT ME JOHNNY OTIS & HIS ORCHESTRA WITH MARIE ADAMS & THE THREE TONS OF JOY	2	1957
MA HE'S MAKING EYES AT ME LENA ZAVARONI	10	1974
MA I DON'T LOVE HER CLIPSE FEATURING FAITH EVANS	38	2003
MA SAYS PA SAYS DORIS DAY & JOHNNIE RAY	12	1953
MA SOLITUDA CATHERINE WHEEL	53	1998
MACARENA LOS DEL CHIPMUNKS	65	1996
MACARENA LOS DEL MAR FEATURING WIL VELOZ	43	1996
MACARENA LOS DEL RIO	2	1996
MACARTHUR PARK RICHARD HARRIS	4	1968
MACARTHUR PARK DONNA SUMMER	5	1978
MACDONALD'S CAVE PILTDOWN MEN	14	1960
MACH 5 PRESIDENTS OF THE UNITED STATES OF AMERICA	29	1996
MACHINE YEAH YEAH YEAH	18	2002
MACHINE + SOUL GARY NUMAN	72	1992
MACHINE GUN COMMODORES	20	1974
MACHINE SAYS YES FC KAHUNA	58	2002
MACHINEHEAD BUSH	48	1996
MACHINERY SHEENA EASTON	38	1982
MACHINES BIFFY CLYRO	29	2007
MACK THE KNIFE BOBBY DARIN	1	1959
MACK THE KNIFE LOUIS ARMSTRONG WITH HIS ALL-STARS	24	1959
MACK THE KNIFE ELLA FITZGERALD	19	1960
MACK THE KNIFE KING KURT	55	1984
MACUSHLA BERNIE NOLAN	38	2004
MAD ABOUT THE BOY DINAH WASHINGTON	41	1992
MAD ABOUT YOU [A] BRUCE RUFFIN	9	1972
MAD ABOUT YOU [B] BELINDA CARLISLE	67	1988
MAD ABOUT YOU [C] STING	56	1991
MAD DOG ELASTICA	44	2000
MAD EYED SCREAMER CREATURES	24	1981
MAD IF YA DON'T GAYLE & GILLIAN	75	1993
MAD LOVE (EP) LUSH	55	1990
MAD PASSIONATE LOVE BERNARD BRESSLAW	6	1958
MAD WORLD TEARS FOR FEARS	3	1982
MAD WORLD MICHAEL ANDREWS FEATURING GARY JULES	1	2003
MADAGASCAR ART OF TRANCE	41	1998
MADAM BUTTERFLY (UN BEL DI VEDREMO) MALCOLM McLAREN	13	1984
MADAME HELGA STEREOPHONICS	4	2003
MADCHESTER RAVE ON EP HAPPY MONDAYS	19	1989
MADE FOR LOVIN' YOU ANASTACIA	27	2001
MADE IN ENGLAND ELTON JOHN	18	1995
MADE IN HEAVEN FREDDIE MERCURY	57	1985
MADE IN TWO MINUTES BUG KAN & PLASTIC JAM FEATURING PATTI LOW & DOOGIE	64	1991
MADE IT BACK BEVERLEY KNIGHT FEATURING REDMAN	19	1998
MADE IT LAST HIGH CONTRAST	74	2004
MADE OF STONE STONE ROSES	20	1990
MADE TO LOVE (GIRLS GIRLS GIRLS) EDDIE HODGES	37	1962
MADE YOU ADAM FAITH	5	1960
MADE YOU LOOK NAS	27	2003
MADE-UP LOVE SONG #43 GUILLEMOTS	23	2006
THE MADISON RAY ELLINGTON	36	1962
MADLY IN LOVE BROS	14	1990
MADNESS (IS ALL IN THE MIND) MADNESS	8	1983
MADNESS THING LEILANI	19	1999
MAGGIE FOSTER & ALLEN	27	1983
MAGGIE MAY ROD STEWART	1	1971
MAGGIE'S FARM BOB DYLAN	22	1965
MAGGIE'S FARM SPECIALS	4	1980
MAGGIE'S FARM (LIVE) TIN MACHINE	48	1989
MAGGIE'S LAST PARTY V.I.M.	68	1991
MAGIC [A] PILOT	11	1974
MAGIC [B] OLIVIA NEWTON-JOHN	32	1980
MAGIC [C] SASHA WITH SAM MOLLISON	32	1994
MAGIC [D] D-INFLUENCE	45	1997
MAGIC [E] NICK DRAKE	32	2004
MAGIC BUS WHO	26	1968
MAGIC CARPET RIDE MIGHTY DUB KATZ	24	1997
MAGIC FLY SPACE	2	1977
MAGIC FLY MINIMALISTIX	36	2003
THE MAGIC FRIEND 2 UNLIMITED	11	1992
MAGIC HOUR [A] HALO JAMES	59	1990
MAGIC HOUR [B] CAST	28	1999
THE MAGIC IS THERE DANIEL O'DONNELL	16	1998
MAGIC MANDRAKE SARR BAND	68	1978
MAGIC MIND EARTH, WIND & FIRE	54	1978
MAGIC MOMENTS PERRY COMO	1	1958
MAGIC MOMENTS RONNIE HILTON	22	1958
THE MAGIC NUMBER DE LA SOUL	7	1989
THE MAGIC PIPER (OF LOVE) EDWYN COLLINS	32	1997
THE MAGIC POSITION PATRICK WOLF	69	2007
MAGIC ROUNDABOUT JASPER CARROTT	5	1975
MAGIC SMILE ROSIE VELA	27	1987
MAGIC STYLE BADMAN	61	1991
MAGIC TOUCH [A] ODYSSEY	41	1982
MAGIC TOUCH [B] ROSE ROYCE	43	1984
MAGIC TOUCH [C] LOOSE ENDS	16	1985
MAGICAL BUCKS FIZZ	57	1985
MAGICAL MYSTERY TOUR (DOUBLE EP) BEATLES	2	1967
MAGICAL SPIEL BARRY RYAN	49	1970
MAGICK KLAXONS	29	2006
MAGIC'S BACK (THEME FROM *THE GHOSTS OF OXFORD STREET*) MALCOLM McLAREN FEATURING ALISON LIMERICK	42	1991
MAGIC'S WAND WHODINI	47	1982
MAGIC'S WAND (THE WHODINI ELECTRIC EP) WHODINI	63	1984
THE MAGNIFICENT AGENT OO	65	1998
THE MAGNIFICENT SEVEN [A] AL CAIOLA	34	1961
THE MAGNIFICENT SEVEN [A] JOHN BARRY SEVEN	45	1961
THE MAGNIFICENT SEVEN [B] CLASH	34	1981
THE MAGNIFICENT 7 [B] SCOOBIE	58	2001
MAGNUM (DOUBLE SINGLE) MAGNUM	47	1980
MAH NA MAH NA PIERO UMILIANI	8	1977
MAID OF ORLEANS (THE WALTZ JOAN OF ARC) ORCHESTRAL MANOEUVRES IN THE DARK	4	1982
MAIDEN JAPAN IRON MAIDEN	43	1981
MAIDS WHEN YOU'RE YOUNG NEVER WED AN OLD MAN DUBLINERS	43	1967
THE MAIGRET THEME JOE LOSS ORCHESTRA	20	1962
THE MAIN ATTRACTION PAT BOONE	12	1962
MAIN OFFENDER HIVES	24	2002
MAIN THEME FROM *THE THORNBIRDS* HENRY MANCINI	23	1984
MAIN TITLE THEME FROM *MAN WITH THE GOLDEN ARM* BILLY MAY	9	1956
MAIN TITLE THEME FROM *MAN WITH THE GOLDEN ARM* JET HARRIS	12	1962
MAINSTREAM THEA GILMORE	50	2003
MAIS OUI KING BROTHERS	16	1960
THE MAJESTY OF ROCK SPINAL TAP	61	1992
MAJOR TOM (COMING HOME) PETER SCHILLING	42	1984
MAJORCA PETULA CLARK	12	1955
MAKE A DAFT NOISE FOR CHRISTMAS GOODIES	20	1975
MAKE A FAMILY GARY CLARK	70	1993
MAKE A MOVE ON ME [A] OLIVIA NEWTON-JOHN	43	1982
MAKE A MOVE ON ME [B] JOEY NEGRO	11	2006
MAKE BELIEVE IT'S YOUR FIRST TIME CARPENTERS	60	1983
MAKE HER MINE NAT 'KING' COLE	11	1954
MAKE IT A PARTY WINIFRED ATWELL	7	1956
MAKE IT CLAP BUSTA RHYMES FEATURING SPLIFF STAR	16	2003
MAKE IT EASY SHYSTIE	59	2004
MAKE IT EASY ON YOURSELF WALKER BROTHERS	1	1965
MAKE IT GOOD A1	11	2002
MAKE IT HAPPEN MARIAH CAREY	17	1992
MAKE IT HOT [A] NICOLE FEATURING MISSY 'MISDEMEANOR' ELLIOTT	22	1998
MAKE IT HOT [B] VS	29	2004
MAKE IT LAST [A] SKIPWORTH & TURNER	60	1989
MAKE IT LAST [B] EMBRACE	35	2001
MAKE IT MINE SHAMEN	42	1990
MAKE IT ON MY OWN ALISON LIMERICK	16	1992
MAKE IT REAL SCORPIONS	72	1980
MAKE IT RIGHT CHRISTIAN FALK FEATURING DEMETREUS	22	2000
MAKE IT SOON TONY BRENT	9	1953
MAKE IT TONIGHT WET WET WET	37	1991
MAKE IT UP WITH LOVE ATL	21	2004
MAKE IT WITH YOU [A] BREAD	5	1970
MAKE IT WITH YOU [A] PASADENAS	20	1992
MAKE IT WITH YOU [A] LET LOOSE	7	1996
MAKE IT WITH YOU [B] UNIVERSAL	33	1997
MAKE LOVE EASY FREDDIE JACKSON	70	1994
MAKE LOVE LIKE A MAN DEF LEPPARD	12	1992
MAKE LOVE TO ME [A] JO STAFFORD	8	1954
MAKE LOVE TO ME [A] JOHN LEYTON & THE LeROYS	49	1964
MAKE LOVE TO ME [B] JILL FRANCIS	70	1993
MAKE LUV ROOM 5 FEATURING OLIVER CHEATHAM	1	2003
MAKE ME AN ISLAND JOE DOLAN	3	1969
MAKE ME BAD KORN	25	2000
MAKE ME LAUGH ANTHRAX	26	1988
MAKE ME SMILE (COME UP AND SEE ME) STEVE HARLEY & COCKNEY REBEL	1	1975
MAKE ME SMILE (COME UP AND SEE ME) ERASURE	14	2003
MAKE ME WANNA SCREAM BLU CANTRELL	24	2003
MAKE MY BODY ROCK JOMANDA	44	1989
MAKE MY DAY BUJU BANTON	72	1993
MAKE MY HEART FLY PROCLAIMERS	63	1988
MAKE MY LOVE SHAWN CHRISTOPHER	57	1994
MAKE SOMEONE HAPPY JIMMY DURANTE	69	1996
MAKE THAT MOVE SHALAMAR	30	1981
MAKE THE DEAL OCEAN COLOUR SCENE	35	2003
MAKE THE WORLD GO AWAY EDDY ARNOLD	8	1966
MAKE THE WORLD GO AWAY DONNY & MARIE OSMOND	18	1975
MAKE THE WORLD GO ROUND SANDY B	20	1996
MAKE THINGS RIGHT LEMON JELLY	33	2005
MAKE UP YOUR MIND BASS JUMPERS	44	1999
MAKE WAY FOR NODDY NODDY	29	2003
MAKE WAY FOR THE INDIAN APACHE INDIAN & TIM DOG	29	1995
MAKE YOU HAPPY LEVELLERS	38	2005
MAKE YOURS A HAPPY HOME GLADYS KNIGHT & THE PIPS	35	1976
MAKEDAMN SURE TAKING BACK SUNDAY	36	2006
MAKES ME LOVE YOU ECLIPSE	25	1999
MAKES ME WANNA DIE TRICKY	29	1997
MAKES ME WONDER MAROON 5	2	2007
MAKIN' HAPPY CRYSTAL WATERS	18	1991
MAKIN' IT DAVID NAUGHTON	44	1979
MAKIN' LOVE FLOYD ROBINSON	9	1959
MAKIN' OUT MARK OWEN	30	2004
MAKIN' WHOOPEE RAY CHARLES	42	1965

	Peak Position	Year of Entry
MAKING LOVE (OUT OF NOTHING AT ALL) BONNIE TYLER	45	1996
MAKING PLANS FOR NIGEL XTC	17	1979
MAKING THE MOST OF DODGY WITH THE KICK HORNS	22	1995
MAKING TIME CREATION	49	1966
MAKING UP AGAIN GOLDIE	7	1978
MAKING YOUR MIND UP BUCKS FIZZ	1	1981
MALE STRIPPER MAN 2 MAN MEET MAN PARRISH	4	1986
MALIBU HOLE	22	1999
MALT AND BARLEY BLUES McGUINNESS FLINT	5	1971
MAMA [A] DAVID WHITFIELD	12	1955
MAMA [A] CONNIE FRANCIS	2	1960
MAMA [B] DAVE BERRY	5	1966
MAMA [C] GENESIS	4	1983
MAMA [D] KIM APPLEBY	19	1991
MAMA [E] SPICE GIRLS	1	1997
MAMA AFRICA AKON	47	2007
MAMA GAVE BIRTH TO THE SOUL CHILDREN QUEEN LATIFAH + DE LA SOUL	14	1991
MAMA I'M COMING HOME OZZY OSBOURNE	46	1991
MAMA (LOVES A CRACKHEAD) PLAN B	41	2006
MAMA NEVER TOLD ME SISTER SLEDGE	20	1975
MAMA SAID [A] CARLEEN ANDERSON	26	1994
MAMA SAID [B] METALLICA	19	1996
MAMA SAID KNOCK YOU OUT LL COOL J	41	1990
MAMA TOLD ME NOT TO COME THREE DOG NIGHT	3	1970
MAMA TOLD ME NOT TO COME TOM JONES & STEREOPHONICS	4	2000
MAMA USED TO SAY JUNIOR	7	1982
MAMA USED TO SAY AZURE	56	1998
MAMA WEER ALL CRAZEE NOW SLADE	1	1972
MAMA - WHO DA MAN? RICHARD BLACKWOOD	3	2000
MA-MA-MA-BELLE ELECTRIC LIGHT ORCHESTRA	22	1974
MAMA'S BOY SUZI QUATRO	34	1980
MAMA'S PEARL JACKSON 5	25	1971
MAMBO ITALIANO ROSEMARY CLOONEY WITH THE MELLOMEN	1	1954
MAMBO ITALIANO DEAN MARTIN	14	1955
MAMBO ITALIANO SHAFT	12	2000
MAMBO NO 5 (A LITTLE BIT OF...) LOU BEGA	1	1999
MAMBO NO 5 BOB THE BUILDER	1	2001
MAMBO ROCK BILL HALEY & HIS COMETS	14	1955
MAMMA MIA ABBA	1	1975
MAMMA MIA A*TEENS	12	1999
MAMMOTH INTERPOL	44	2007
MAMMY BLUE ROGER WHITTAKER	31	1971
MAMOUNA BRYAN FERRY	57	1995
MAMY BLUE LOS POP TOPS	35	1971
MAN ROSEMARY CLOONEY	7	1954
MAN BEHIND THE MUSIC QUEEN PEN	38	1998
THE MAN DON'T GIVE A FUCK SUPER FURRY ANIMALS	16	1996
THE MAN FROM LARAMIE AL MARTINO	19	1955
THE MAN FROM LARAMIE JIMMY YOUNG	1	1955
MAN FROM MADRID TONY OSBORNE SOUND FEATURING JOANNE BROWN	50	1961
MAN FROM NAZARETH JOHN PAUL JOANS	25	1971
MAN! I FEEL LIKE A WOMAN SHANIA TWAIN	3	1999
MAN I HATE YOUR BAND LITTLE MAN TATE	26	2006
THE MAN I LOVE KATE BUSH & LARRY ADLER	27	1994
THE MAN IN BLACK COZY POWELL	18	1974
MAN IN THE MIRROR MICHAEL JACKSON	21	1988
MAN IN THE MOON CSILLA	69	1996
MAN LIKE ME NO REASON	53	2004
A MAN NEEDS TO BE TOLD CHARLATANS	31	2001
MAN OF MYSTERY SHADOWS	5	1960
MAN OF STEEL MEAT LOAF	21	2003
MAN OF THE WORLD FLEETWOOD MAC	2	1969
MAN ON FIRE [A] FRANKIE VAUGHAN	6	1957
MAN ON FIRE [B] ROGER TAYLOR	66	1984
MAN ON THE CORNER GENESIS	41	1982
MAN ON THE EDGE IRON MAIDEN	10	1995
MAN ON THE MOON R.E.M.	18	1992
MAN OUT OF TIME ELVIS COSTELLO	58	1982
MAN SHORTAGE LOVINDEER	69	1986
THE MAN THAT GOT AWAY JUDY GARLAND	18	1955
MAN TO MAN HOT CHOCOLATE	14	1976
THE MAN WHO PLAYS THE MANDOLINO DEAN MARTIN	21	1957
THE MAN WHO SOLD THE WORLD LULU	3	1974
THE MAN WHO SOLD THE WORLD (LIVE) DAVID BOWIE	39	1995
THE MAN WHO TOLD EVERYTHING DOVES	32	2000
MAN WITH THE CHILD IN HIS EYES KATE BUSH	6	1978
MAN WITH THE RED FACE LAURENT GARNIER	36	2000
A MAN WITHOUT LOVE KENNETH McKELLAR	30	1966
A MAN WITHOUT LOVE ENGELBERT HUMPERDINCK	2	1968
MANCHESTER BEAUTIFUL SOUTH	41	2006
MANCHESTER UNITED MANCHESTER UNITED FOOTBALL CLUB	50	1976
MANCHILD NENEH CHERRY	5	1989
MANDINKA SINEAD O'CONNOR	17	1988
MANDOLIN RAIN BRUCE HORNSBY & THE RANGE	70	1987
MANDOLINS IN THE MOONLIGHT PERRY COMO	13	1958
MANDY [A] EDDIE CALVERT	9	1958
MANDY [B] BARRY MANILOW	11	1975
MANDY [B] WESTLIFE	1	2003
MANEATER [A] DARYL HALL & JOHN OATES	6	1982
MANEATER [B] NELLY FURTADO	1	2006
MANGOS ROSEMARY CLOONEY	17	1957
MANHATTAN SKYLINE A-HA	13	1987
MANHATTAN SPIRITUAL REG OWEN	20	1959
MANIAC MICHAEL SEMBELLO	43	1983
MANIC MINDS MANIX	63	1991
MANIC MONDAY BANGLES	2	1986
MANILA SEELENLUFT FEATURING MICHAEL SMITH	70	2003
MANN GEGEN MANN RAMMSTEIN	59	2006
MANNEQUIN KIDS FROM FAME FEATURING GENE ANTHONY RAY	50	1982
MANNISH BOY MUDDY WATERS	51	1988
MAN-SIZE PJ HARVEY	42	1993
MANSIZE ROOSTER SUPERGRASS	20	1995
MANTRA FOR A STATE MIND S-EXPRESS	21	1989
MANY RIVERS TO CROSS UB40	16	1983
MANY RIVERS TO CROSS CHER	37	1993
MANY TEARS AGO CONNIE FRANCIS	12	1961
MANY TOO MANY GENESIS	43	1978
MANY WEATHERS APART MERZ	48	1999
MAP OF THE PROBLEMATIQUE MUSE	18	2007
MAPS YEAH YEAH YEAH	37	2003
MARBLE BREAKS IRON BENDS PETER FENTON	46	1966
MARBLEHEAD JOHNSON BLUETONES	7	1996
MARBLES BLACK GRAPE	46	1998
MARCH OF THE MODS JOE LOSS ORCHESTRA	31	1964
MARCH OF THE PIGS NINE INCH NAILS	45	1994
MARCH OF THE SIAMESE CHILDREN KENNY BALL & HIS JAZZMEN	4	1962
MARCHETA KARL DENVER	8	1961
MARGATE CHAS & DAVE	46	1982
MARGIE FATS DOMINO	18	1959
MARGO BILLY FURY	28	1959
MARGUERITA TIME STATUS QUO	3	1983
MARIA [A] P.J. PROBY	8	1965
MARIA [B] US5	38	2006
MARIA [C] BLONDIE	1	1999
MARIA ELENA [A] LOS INDIOS TABAJARAS	5	1963
MARIA ELENA [B] GENE PITNEY	25	1969
MARIA (I LIKE IT LOUD) SCOOTER VS MARC ACARDIPANE & DICK RULES	16	2003
MARIA MARIA SANTANA FEATURING THE PRODUCT G&B	6	2000
MARIANA GIBSON BROTHERS	11	1980
MARIANNE [A] HILLTOPPERS	20	1957
MARIANNE [B] CLIFF RICHARD	22	1968
MARIE BACHELORS	9	1965
MARIE CELESTE POLECATS	53	1981
MARIE MARIE SHAKIN' STEVENS	19	1980
(MARIE'S THE NAME) HIS LATEST FLAME ELVIS PRESLEY	1	1961
MARJORINE JOE COCKER	48	1968
MARKET SQUARE HEROES MARILLION	53	1982
MARLENE ON THE WALL SUZANNE VEGA	21	1986
MAROC 7 SHADOWS	24	1967
MARQUEE MOON TELEVISION	30	1977
MARQUIS LINOLEUM	73	1997
MARRAKESH EXPRESS CROSBY STILLS & NASH	17	1969
MARRIED MEN BONNIE TYLER	35	1979
MARRY ME MIKE PRESTON	14	1961
MARTA BACHELORS	20	1967
MARTA'S SONG DEEP FOREST	26	1995
MARTELL CRIBS	39	2005
MARTHA'S HARBOUR ALL ABOUT EVE	10	1988
MARTIAN HOP ROCKY SHARPE & THE REPLAYS	55	1980
MARTIKA'S KITCHEN MARTIKA	17	1991
MARTYR DEPECHE MODE	13	2006
MARVELLOUS LIGHTNING SEEDS	24	1995
MARVIN MARVIN THE PARANOID ANDROID	53	1981
MARY [A] SUPERGRASS	36	1999
MARY [B] SCISSOR SISTERS	14	2004
MARY ANN BLACK LACE	42	1979
MARY ANNE SHADOWS	17	1965
MARY HAD A LITTLE BOY SNAP	8	1990
MARY HAD A LITTLE LAMB WINGS	9	1972
MARY JANE [A] DEL SHANNON	35	1964
MARY JANE [B] MEGADETH	46	1988
MARY JANE [C] SPIN DOCTORS	55	1994
MARY JANE (ALL NIGHT LONG) MARY J BLIGE	17	1995
MARY JANE'S LAST DANCE TOM PETTY	52	1994
MARY OF THE FOURTH FORM BOOMTOWN RATS	15	1977
MARY'S BOY CHILD HARRY BELAFONTE	1	1957
MARY'S BOY CHILD NINA & FREDERICK	26	1959
MARY'S BOY CHILD - OH MY LORD BONEY M	1	1978
MARY'S PRAYER DANNY WILSON	3	1987
MAS QUE MANCADA RONALDO'S REVENGE	37	1998
MAS QUE NADA ECHOBEATZ	10	1998
MAS QUE NADA TAMBA TRIO	34	1998
MAS QUE NADA COLOUR GIRL FEATURING PSG	57	2001
MAS QUE NADA SERGIO MENDES & THE BLACK EYED PEAS	6	2006
MASH IT UP MDM	66	2001
MASQUERADE [A] SKIDS	14	1979
MASQUERADE [B] EVELYN THOMAS	60	1984
MASQUERADE [C] FALL	69	1998
MASQUERADE [D] GERIDEAU	63	1998
MASS DESTRUCTION FAITHLESS	7	2004
MASSACHUSETTS BEE GEES	1	1967
THE MASSES AGAINST THE CLASSES MANIC STREET PREACHERS	1	2000
MASSIVE ATTACK EP MASSIVE ATTACK	27	1992
MASTER AND SERVANT DEPECHE MODE	9	1984

	Peak Position	Year of Entry
THE MASTER HAS COME BACK DAMIAN "JR GONG" MARLEY	74	2005
MASTERBLASTER 2000 DJ LUCK & MC NEAT FEATURING JJ	5	2000
MASTERBLASTER (JAMMIN') STEVIE WONDER	2	1980
THE MASTERPLAN DIANA BROWN & BARRIE K. SHARPE	39	1990
MATADOR JEFF WAYNE	57	1982
MATCHSTALK MEN AND MATCHSTALK CATS AND DOGS BRIAN & MICHAEL	1	1978
MATED DAVID GRANT & JAKI GRAHAM	20	1985
MATERIAL GIRL MADONNA	3	1985
MATHAR INDIAN VIBES	52	1994
MATHEMATICS CHERRY GHOST	57	2007
MATINEE FRANZ FERDINAND	8	2004
A MATTER OF FACT INNOCENCE	37	1990
MATTER OF TIME NINE YARDS	59	1999
A MATTER OF TRUST BILLY JOEL	52	1986
MATTHEW AND SON CAT STEVENS	2	1967
MATT'S MOOD BREEKOUT KREW	51	1984
MATT'S MOOD MATT BIANCO	44	1984
MAX DON'T HAVE SEX WITH YOUR EX E-ROTIC	45	1995
THE MAXI PRIEST EP MAXI PRIEST	62	1991
MAXIMUM (EP) DREADZONE	56	1995
MAXIMUM OVERDRIVE 2 UNLIMITED	15	1993
MAY EACH DAY ANDY WILLIAMS	19	1966
MAY I HAVE THE NEXT DREAM WITH YOU MALCOLM ROBERTS	8	1968
MAY IT BE ENYA	50	2002
MAY THE SUN SHINE NAZARETH	22	1979
MAY YOU ALWAYS JOAN REGAN	9	1959
MAY YOU ALWAYS McGUIRE SISTERS	15	1959
MAYBE [A] THOM PACE	14	1979
MAYBE [B] ENRIQUE IGLESIAS	12	2002
MAYBE [C] EMMA	6	2003
MAYBE [D] N*E*R*D	25	2004
MAYBE BABY CRICKETS	4	1958
MAYBE I KNOW LESLEY GORE	20	1964
MAYBE I KNOW SEASHELLS	32	1972
MAYBE I'M AMAZED WINGS	28	1977
MAYBE I'M AMAZED CARLEEN ANDERSON	24	1998
MAYBE I'M DEAD MONEY MARK	45	1998
MAYBE LOVE STEVIE NICKS	42	1994
MAYBE THAT'S WHAT IT TAKES ALEX PARKS	3	2003
MAYBE TOMORROW [A] BILLY FURY	18	1959
MAYBE TOMORROW [B] CHORDS	40	1980
MAYBE TOMORROW [C] UB40	14	1987
MAYBE TOMORROW [D] STEREOPHONICS	3	2003
MAYBE (WE SHOULD CALL IT A DAY) HAZELL DEAN	15	1988
MAYOR OF SIMPLETON XTC	46	1989
ME AGAINST THE MUSIC BRITNEY SPEARS FEATURING MADONNA	2	2003
ME AND BABY BROTHER WAR	21	1976
ME AND JULIO DOWN BY THE SCHOOLYARD PAUL SIMON	15	1972
ME AND MRS JONES BILLY PAUL	12	1973
ME AND MRS JONES FREDDIE JACKSON	32	1992
ME AND MR SANCHEZ BLUE RONDO A LA TURK	40	1981
ME AND MY GIRL (NIGHT-CLUBBING) DAVID ESSEX	13	1982
ME AND MY IMAGINATION SOPHIE ELLIS-BEXTOR	23	2007
ME AND MY LIFE TREMELOES	4	1970
ME AND MY SHADOW FRANK SINATRA & SAMMY DAVIS JR	20	1962
ME AND THE FARMER HOUSEMARTINS	15	1987
ME & U CASSIE	6	2006
ME AND YOU AND A DOG NAMED BOO LOBO	4	1971
ME AND YOU VERSUS THE WORLD SPACE	9	1996
ME. IN TIME CHARLATANS	28	1991
ME ISRAELITES CHOPS-EMC + EXTENSIVE	60	1992
ME JULIE ALI G & SHAGGY	2	2002
ME LOVE SEAN KINGSTON	32	2007
ME MYSELF AND I [A] DE LA SOUL	22	1989
ME, MYSELF & I [B] BEYONCÉ	11	2004
ME MYSELF AND I [B] DARREN HAYES	59	2007
ME MYSELF I JOAN ARMATRADING	21	1980
ME NO POP I KID CREOLE & THE COCONUTS PRESENTS COATI MUNDI	32	1981
ME OR YOU? KILLING JOKE	57	1983
ME PLUS ONE KASABIAN	22	2007
ME THE PEACEFUL HEART LULU	9	1968
MEA CULPA PART II ENIGMA	55	1991
MEAN GIRL STATUS QUO	20	1973
MEAN MAN W.A.S.P.	21	1989
MEAN MEAN MAN WANDA JACKSON	40	1961
MEAN STREAK [A] CLIFF RICHARD	10	1959
MEAN STREAK [B] Y&T	41	1983
MEAN TO ME SHAYE COGAN	40	1960
MEAN WOMAN BLUES ROY ORBISON	3	1963
THE MEANING OF CHRISTMAS BORIS GARDINER	69	1986
THE MEANING OF LOVE [A] DEPECHE MODE	12	1982
THE MEANING OF LOVE [B] MICHELLE	16	2004
MEANT TO LIVE SWITCHFOOT	29	2004
MEANTIME FUTUREHEADS	49	2004
MEASURE OF A MAN SAM & MARK	19	2004
MEAT PIE SAUSAGE ROLL GRANDAD ROBERTS & HIS SON ELVIS	67	1998
MECCA CHEETAHS	36	1964
MECHANICAL WONDER OCEAN COLOUR SCENE	49	2001
THE MEDAL SONG CULTURE CLUB	32	1984
MEDICATION SPIRITUALIZED	55	1992
MEDICINE SHOW BIG AUDIO DYNAMITE	29	1986
THE MEDICINE SONG STEPHANIE MILLS	29	1984
MEDS PLACEBO FEATURING ALISON MOSSHART	35	2006
MEET EL PRESIDENTE DURAN DURAN	24	1987
MEET HER AT THE LOVE PARADE DA HOOL	11	1998
MEET ME ON THE CORNER [A] MAX BYGRAVES	2	1955
MEET ME ON THE CORNER [B] LINDISFARNE	5	1972
(MEET) THE FLINTSTONES BC-52's	3	1994
MEGABLAST BOMB THE BASS FEATURING MERLIN & ANTONIA	6	1988
MEGACHIC - CHIC MEDLEY CHIC	58	1990
MEGALOMANIA PELE	73	1992
MEGAMIX [A] TECHNOTRONIC	6	1990
MEGAMIX [B] CRYSTAL WATERS	39	1992
MEGAMIX [C] CORONA	36	1997
MEGAREX MARC BOLAN & T REX	72	1985
MEGLOMANIAC INCUBUS	23	2004
MEIN TEIL (IMPORT) RAMMSTEIN	61	2004
MEISO DJ KRUSH	52	1996
MELANCHOLY ROSE MARC ALMOND	71	1987
MELLOW DOUBT TEENAGE FANCLUB	34	1995
MELLOW MELLOW RIGHT ON LOWRELL	37	1979
MELLOW YELLOW DONOVAN	8	1967
THE MELOD-EP DODGY	53	1994
MELODY OF LOVE INK SPOTS	10	1955
MELODY OF LOVE (WANNA BE LOVED) DONNA SUMMER	21	1994
MELT [A] SIOUXSIE & THE BANSHEES	49	1982
MELT [B] MELANIE C	27	2003
THE MELTING MOON VHS OR BETA	63	2005
MELTING POT BLUE MINK	3	1969
MEMO FROM TURNER MICK JAGGER	32	1970
MEMORIES [A] PUBLIC IMAGE LTD.	60	1979
MEMORIES [B] MIKE BERRY	55	1981
MEMORIES [C] BEVERLEY CRAVEN	68	1991
MEMORIES ARE MADE OF THIS DAVE KING FEATURING THE KEYNOTES	5	1956
MEMORIES ARE MADE OF THIS DEAN MARTIN	1	1956
MEMORIES ARE MADE OF THIS VAL DOONICAN	11	1967
MEMORY ELAINE PAIGE	6	1981
MEMORY BARBRA STREISAND	34	1982
MEMORY LANE CHOONG FAMILY	57	2006
THE MEMORY REMAINS METALLICA	13	1997
MEMORY: THEME FROM THE MUSICAL 'CATS' ALED JONES	42	1985
MEMPHIS LONNIE MACK	47	1979
MEMPHIS TENNESSEE CHUCK BERRY	6	1963
MEMPHIS TENNESSEE DAVE BERRY & THE CRUISERS	19	1963
MEN IN BLACK [A] FRANK BLACK	37	1996
MEN IN BLACK [B] WILL SMITH	1	1997
MEN'S NEEDS CRIBS	17	2007
MENTAL MANIC MC's FEATURING SARA CARLSON	30	1989
MENTAL PICTURE JON SECADA	44	1995
MENTASM SECOND PHASE	48	1991
MERCEDES BOY PEBBLES	42	1988
MERCI CHERI VINCE HILL	36	1966
MERCURY LOWGOLD	48	2001
MERCURY AND SOLACE BT	38	1999
MERCY DUFFY	1	2008
MERCY ME ALKALINE TRIO	30	2005
MERCY MERCY ME - I WANT YOU ROBERT PALMER	9	1991
MERKINBALL EP PEARL JAM	25	1995
MERMAIDS PAUL WELLER	30	1997
MERRY CHRISTMAS DARLING CARPENTERS	25	1972
MERRY CHRISTMAS EVERYONE SHAKIN' STEVENS	1	1985
MERRY GENTLE POPS BARRON KNIGHTS WITH DUKE D'MOND	9	1965
A MERRY JINGLE GREEDIES	28	1980
THE MERRY PLOUGHBOY DERMOT O'BRIEN	46	1966
MERRY XMAS EVERYBODY SLADE	1	1973
MERRY XMAS EVERYBODY METAL GURUS	55	1990
MERRY XMAS EVERYBODY TONY CHRISTIE	49	2005
MERRY X-MESS ROTTERDAM TERMINATION SOURCE	73	1993
MERRYMAKING AT MY PLACE CALVIN HARRIS	43	2007
MERSEYBEAT IAN McNABB	74	1996
MESCALITO SOURMASH	73	2000
MESMERISE CHAPTERHOUSE	60	1991
MESMERIZE JA RULE FEATURING ASHANTI	12	2003
MESMERIZED FAITH EVANS	48	2005
A MESS OF BLUES ELVIS PRESLEY	2	1960
A MESS OF THE BLUES STATUS QUO	15	1983
THE MESSAGE [A] GRANDMASTER FLASH & THE FURIOUS FIVE	8	1982
THE MESSAGE [B] 49ERS	68	1992
MESSAGE IN A BOTTLE POLICE	1	1979
MESSAGE IN A BOTTLE DANCE FLOOR VIRUS	49	1995
MESSAGE IN A BOTTLE T FACTORY	51	2002
MESSAGE IN THE BOX WORLD PARTY	39	1990
THE MESSAGE IS LOVE ARTHUR BAKER & THE BACKSTREET DISCIPLES FEATURING AL GREEN	38	1989
MESSAGE OF LOVE [A] PRETENDERS	11	1981
MESSAGE OF LOVE [B] LOVEHAPPY	37	1995
MESSAGE TO MARTHA LOU JOHNSON	36	1964
MESSAGE TO MARTHA (KENTUCKY BLUEBIRD) ADAM FAITH	12	1964
A MESSAGE TO YOU RUDY SPECIALS (FEATURING RICO)	10	1979
A MESSAGE TO YOUR HEART SAMANTHA JANUS	30	1991

	Peak Position	Year of Entry
MESSAGE II (SURVIVAL) MELLE MEL & DUKE BOOTEE	74	1983
MESSAGE UNDERSTOOD SANDIE SHAW	6	1965
MESSAGES ORCHESTRAL MANOEUVRES IN THE DARK	13	1980
MESSAGES FROM THE STARS RAH BAND	42	1983
MESSED UP BEAT UP	62	2004
MESSIN' LADIES FIRST	30	2001
METAFORCE ART OF NOISE	53	1999
METAL GURU T REX	1	1972
METAL HEALTH QUIET RIOT	45	1983
METAL MICKEY SUEDE	17	1992
METEOR MAN DEE D. JACKSON	48	1978
METHOD OF MODERN LOVE DARYL HALL & JOHN OATES	21	1985
METROPOLIS OLIVER LIEB	72	2000
METROSOUND ADAM F & J MAJIK	54	2002
MEXICALI ROSE KARL DENVER	8	1961
THE MEXICAN FENTONES	41	1962
MEXICAN GIRL SMOKIE	19	1978
MEXICAN RADIO WALL OF VOODOO	64	1983
MEXICAN WAVE KERBDOG	49	1997
MEXICO LONG JOHN BALDRY	15	1968
MF FROM HELL DATSUNS	55	2003
MFEO KAVANA	8	1997
MI CHICO LATINO GERI HALLIWELL	1	1999
MI TIERRA GLORIA ESTEFAN	36	1993
MIAMI WILL SMITH	3	1998
MIAMI HIT MIX GLORIA ESTEFAN	8	1992
MIAMI VICE THEME JAN HAMMER	5	1985
MICHAEL [A] HIGHWAYMEN	1	1961
MICHAEL [A] GENO WASHINGTON & THE RAM JAM BAND	39	1967
MICHAEL [B] FRANZ FERDINAND	17	2004
MICHAEL AND THE SLIPPER TREE EQUALS	24	1969
MICHAEL CAINE MADNESS	11	1984
MICHAEL JACKSON MITCHELL BROTHERS	65	2007
MICHAEL JACKSON MEDLEY ASHAYE	45	1983
MICHAEL ROW THE BOAT LONNIE DONEGAN	6	1961
MICHELLE DAVID & JONATHAN	11	1966
MICHELLE OVERLANDERS	1	1966
MICHIKO SULTANS OF PING	43	1993
MICKEY TONI BASIL	2	1982
MICKEY LOLLY	4	1999
MICRO KID LEVEL 42	37	1983
THE MICROPHONE FIEND ERIC B & RAKIM	74	1988
MICROWAVED PITCHSHIFTER	54	1998
MIDAS TOUCH MIDNIGHT STAR	8	1986
THE MIDDLE JIMMY EAT WORLD	26	2002
MIDDLE OF NOWHERE HOT HOT HEAT	47	2005
MIDDLE OF THE NIGHT BROTHERHOOD OF MAN	41	1978
MIDDLEMAN TERRORVISION	25	1994
MIDLIFE CRISIS FAITH NO MORE	10	1992
MIDNIGHT [A] PAUL ANKA	26	1958
MIDNIGHT [B] UN-CUT	26	2003
MIDNIGHT AT THE LOST AND FOUND MEAT LOAF	17	1983
MIDNIGHT AT THE OASIS MARIA MULDAUR	21	1974
MIDNIGHT AT THE OASIS BRAND NEW HEAVIES FEATURING N'DEA DAVENPORT	13	1994
MIDNIGHT BLUE LOUISE TUCKER	59	1983
MIDNIGHT COWBOY MIDNIGHT COWBOY SOUNDTRACK	47	1980
MIDNIGHT FLYER NAT 'KING' COLE	23	1959
MIDNIGHT GROOVIN' LIGHT OF THE WORLD	72	1979
MIDNIGHT IN A PERFECT WORLD DJ SHADOW	54	1996
MIDNIGHT IN CHELSEA JON BON JOVI	4	1997
MIDNIGHT IN MOSCOW KENNY BALL & HIS JAZZMEN	2	1961
MIDNIGHT RIDER PAUL DAVIDSON	10	1976
MIDNIGHT SHIFT BUDDY HOLLY	26	1959
MIDNIGHT SUMMER DREAM STRANGLERS	35	1983
MIDNIGHT TO SIX MAN PRETTY THINGS	46	1966
MIDNIGHT TRAIN TO GEORGIA GLADYS KNIGHT & THE PIPS	10	1976
MIDNITE D-INFLUENCE	58	1995
MIDNITE DYNAMOS MATCHBOX	14	1980
MIDNITE SPECIAL PAUL EVANS	41	1960
MIDSUMMER MADNESS (EP) RHYTHM SECTION	66	1992
MIG29 MIG29	62	1992
MIGHT BE STARS WANNADIES	51	1995
THE MIGHTY HIGH REVIVAL 3000	47	1997
MIGHTY JOE SHOCKING BLUE	43	1970
MIGHTY POWER OF LOVE TAVARES	25	1977
MIGHTY QUINN MANFRED MANN	1	1968
MIKE OLDFIELD'S SINGLE (THEME FROM TUBULAR BELLS) MIKE OLDFIELD	31	1974
MILES AWAY [A] JOHN FOXX	51	1980
MILES AWAY [B] WINGER	56	1991
MILES FROM HOME PESHAY	75	1998
MILK GARBAGE FEATURING TRICKY	10	1996
MILK AND ALCOHOL DR FEELGOOD	9	1979
MILKMAN'S SON UGLY KID JOE	39	1995
MILKSHAKE KELIS	2	2003
MILKY WAY SHEER ELEGANCE	18	1976
THE MILL HILL SELF HATE CLUB EDWARD BALL	57	1996
MILLENNIUM [A] KILLING JOKE	34	1994
MILLENNIUM [B] ROBBIE WILLIAMS	1	1998
MILLENNIUM CHIMES BIG BEN	53	2000
THE MILLENNIUM PRAYER CLIFF RICHARD	1	1999
MILLION DOLLAR LOVE DUB WAR	73	1997
MILLION DRUMS TONY SHEVETON	49	1964
A MILLION LOVE SONGS TAKE THAT	7	1992
MILLION MILES AWAY OFFSPRING	21	2001
MILLION SUNS OOBERMAN	43	1999
A MILLION WAYS OK GO	43	2006
MILLIONAIRE KELIS FEATURING ANDRE 3000	3	2004
MILLIONAIRE SWEEPER KENICKIE	60	1996
MILLIONS LIKE US PURPLE HEARTS	57	1979
MILLY MOLLY MANDY GLYN POOLE	35	1973
MILORD EDITH PIAF	24	1960
MILORD FRANKIE VAUGHAN	34	1960
MIND FARM	31	1991
MIND ADVENTURES DES'REE	43	1992
MIND BLOWIN' SMOOTH	36	1995
MIND BLOWING DECISIONS HEATWAVE	9	1978
MIND BODY SOUL FANTASY UFO FEATURING JAY GROOVE	50	1991
MIND GAMES JOHN LENNON	26	1973
MIND OF A TOY VISAGE	13	1981
A MIND OF ITS OWN VICTORIA BECKHAM	6	2002
THE MIND OF LOVE k.d. lang	72	1993
THE MIND OF THE MACHINE N-TRANCE	15	1997
MIND OVER MONEY TURIN BRAKES	31	2001
MIND TRICK JAMIE CULLUM	32	2005
MIND UP TONIGHT MELBA MOORE	22	1983
MINDCIRCUS WAY OUT WEST FEATURING TRICIA LEE	39	2002
MINDLESS BOOGIE HOT CHOCOLATE	46	1979
MINDSTREAM MEAT BEAT MANIFESTO	55	1993
MINE EVERYTHING BUT THE GIRL	58	1984
MINE ALL MINE CA$HFLOW	15	1986
MINE TO GIVE PHOTEK FEATURING ROBERT OWENS	44	2001
MINEFIELD I-LEVEL	52	1983
MINERVA DEFTONES	15	2003
MINIMAL PET SHOP BOYS	19	2006
MINISTRY OF LOVE HYSTERIC EGO	39	1997
MINISTRY OF MAYHEM NOISE NEXT DOOR	12	2004
MINNIE THE MOOCHER REGGAE PHILHARMONIC ORCHESTRA	35	1988
MINORITY GREEN DAY	18	2000
MINORITY OF ONE JOHNNY PANIC	60	2005
MINT CAR CURE	31	1996
MINUETTO ALLEGRETTO WOMBLES	16	1974
MINUTE BY MINUTE DOOBIE BROTHERS	47	1979
A MINUTE OF YOUR TIME TOM JONES	14	1968
THE MINUTE YOU'RE GONE CLIFF RICHARD	1	1965
THE MIRACLE [A] QUEEN	21	1989
MIRACLE [B] JON BON JOVI	29	1990
MIRACLE [C] OLIVE	41	1997
THE MIRACLE [D] CLIFF RICHARD	23	1999
A MIRACLE [E] HIDDEN CAMERAS	70	2003
MIRACLE GOODNIGHT DAVID BOWIE	40	1993
THE MIRACLE OF LOVE EURYTHMICS	23	1986
THE MIRACLE OF YOU DANNY WILLIAMS	41	1961
MIRACLES [A] GARY NUMAN	49	1985
MIRACLES [B] PET SHOP BOYS	10	2003
MIRROR IN THE BATHROOM BEAT	4	1980
MIRROR KISSERS CRIBS	27	2005
MIRROR MAN HUMAN LEAGUE	2	1982
MIRROR MIRROR [A] PINKERTON'S ASSORTED COLOURS	9	1966
MIRROR MIRROR [B] DIANA ROSS	36	1982
MIRROR MIRROR (MON AMOUR) DOLLAR	4	1981
MIRRORS SALLY OLDFIELD	19	1978
MISERERE ZUCCHERO WITH LUCIANO PAVAROTTI	15	1992
MISERY [A] SOUL ASYLUM	30	1995
MISERY [B] MOFFATTS	47	1999
MISERY BUSINESS PARAMORE	17	2007
MISFIT [A] CURIOSITY KILLED THE CAT	7	1987
MISFIT [B] AMY STUDT	6	2003
MISGUIDED DYVERSE	71	2004
MISIRLOU (THE THEME TO THE MOTION PICTURE *PULP FICTION*) SPAGHETTI SURFERS	55	1995
MISLED [A] KOOL & THE GANG	28	1985
MISLED [B] QUIREBOYS	37	1990
MISLED [C] CELINE DION	15	1995
MISS AMERICA BIG DISH	37	1991
MISS CALIFORNIA DANTE THOMAS FEATURING PRAS	25	2001
MISS CHATELAINE k.d. lang	68	1993
MISS FAT BOOTY - PART II MOS DEF FEATURING GHOSTFACE KILLAH	64	2000
MISS HIT AND RUN BARRY BLUE	26	1974
MISS INDEPENDENT KELLY CLARKSON	6	2003
MISS LUCIFER PRIMAL SCREAM	25	2002
MISS MODULAR STEREOLAB	60	1997
MISS MURDER AFI	44	2006
MISS PARKER [A] BENZ	35	1996
MISS PARKER [B] MORGAN	74	1999
MISS PERFECT ABS FEATURING NODESHA	5	2003
MISS SARAJEVO PASSENGERS	6	1995
MISS THE GIRL CREATURES	21	1983
MISS WORLD HOLE	64	1994
MISS YOU [A] JIMMY YOUNG	15	1963
MISS YOU [B] ROLLING STONES	3	1978
MISS YOU LIKE CRAZY NATALIE COLE	2	1989
MISS YOU MUCH JANET JACKSON	22	1989
MISS YOU NIGHTS CLIFF RICHARD	15	1976
MISS YOU NIGHTS WESTLIFE	3	2003
MIS-SHAPES PULP	2	1995
MISSING [A] TERRY HALL	75	1989
MISSING [B] EVERYTHING BUT THE GIRL	3	1994
MISSING WORDS SELECTER	23	1980
MISSING YOU [A] CHRIS DE BURGH	3	1988
MISSING YOU [B] JOHN WAITE	9	1984
MISSING YOU [B] TINA TURNER	12	1996
MISSING YOU [C] SOUL II SOUL FEATURING KYM MAZELLE	22	1990
MISSING YOU [D] MARY J BLIGE	19	1997
MISSING YOU [E] LUCY CARR	28	2003

	Peak Position	Year of Entry
MISSING YOU NOW MICHAEL BOLTON FEATURING KENNY G	28	1992
MISSION OF LOVE JASON DONOVAN	26	1992
MISSIONARY MAN EURYTHMICS	31	1987
MISSISSIPPI PUSSYCAT	1	1976
MRS HOOVER CANDYSKINS	65	1996
MRS MILLS' MEDLEY MRS MILLS	18	1961
MRS MILLS PARTY MEDLEY MRS MILLS	50	1964
MRS. ROBINSON SIMON & GARFUNKEL	4	1968
MRS ROBINSON LEMONHEADS	19	1992
MRS. ROBINSON (EP) SIMON & GARFUNKEL	9	1969
MRS WASHINGTON GIGOLO AUNTS	74	1994
MISSY MISSY PAUL & BARRY RYAN	43	1966
MISTAKE STEPHANIE McINTOSH	47	2007
MISTAKES AND REGRETS ...AND YOU WILL KNOW US BY THE TRAIL OF THE DEAD	69	2000
MR ALIBI MARIA WILLSON	43	2003
MR BACHELOR LOOSE ENDS	50	1988
MR BASS MAN JOHNNY CYMBAL	24	1963
MR BIG STUFF HEAVY D. & THE BOYZ	61	1986
MR BIG STUFF QUEEN LATIFAH, SHADES & FREE	31	1997
MR BLOBBY MR BLOBBY	1	1993
MR BLUE DAVID MacBETH	18	1959
MR BLUE MIKE PRESTON	12	1959
MR BLUE SKY ELECTRIC LIGHT ORCHESTRA	6	1978
MR BRIGHTSIDE KILLERS	10	2004
MR CABDRIVER LENNY KRAVITZ	58	1990
MR CROWLEY OZZY OSBOURNE'S BLIZZARD OF OZ	46	1980
MR CUSTER CHARLIE DRAKE	12	1960
MR DEVIL BIG TIME CHARLIE FEATURING SOOZY Q	39	2000
MR DJ [A] CONCEPT	27	1985
MR DJ [B] BLACKOUT	19	2001
MR DJ [C] CHARLEAN DANCE	51	2007
MR E'S BEAUTIFUL BLUES EELS	11	2000
MR FIXIT ROOTJOOSE	54	1997
MR FRIDAY NIGHT LISA MOORISH	24	1996
MR GUDER CARPENTERS	12	1974
MR GUITAR BERT WEEDON	47	1961
MR HANKEY THE CHRISTMAS POO MR HANKEY	4	1999
MISTER JONES [A] OUT OF MY HAIR	73	1995
MR JONES [B] COUNTING CROWS	28	1994
MR KIRK'S NIGHTMARE 4 HERO	73	1990
MR LEE DIANA ROSS	58	1988
MR LOVERMAN SHABBA RANKS	3	1992
MR MANIC AND SISTER COOL SHAKATAK	56	1987
MISTER MENTAL EIGHTIES MATCHBOX B-LINE DISASTER	25	2004
MR PHARMACIST FALL	75	1986
MISTER PORTER MICKIE MOST	45	1963
MR PRESIDENT D, B, M & T	33	1970
MR RAFFLES (MAN IT WAS MEAN) STEVE HARLEY & COCKNEY REBEL	13	1975
MR ROCK & ROLL AMY MacDONALD	12	2007
MR SANDMAN CHORDETTES	11	1954
MR SANDMAN DICKIE VALENTINE	5	1954
MR SANDMAN FOUR ACES FEATURING AL ALBERTS	9	1955
MR SANDMAN MAX BYGRAVES	16	1955
MR SECOND CLASS SPENCER DAVIS GROUP	35	1968
MR SLEAZE STOCK AITKEN WATERMAN	3	1987
MR SOFT COCKNEY REBEL	8	1974
MR SOLITAIRE ANIMAL NIGHTLIFE	25	1984
MR SUCCESS FRANK SINATRA	25	1958
MR TAMBOURINE MAN BYRDS	1	1965
MR TELEPHONE MAN NEW EDITION	19	1985
MR VAIN CULTURE BEAT	1	1993
MR WENDAL ARRESTED DEVELOPMENT	4	1993
MR WONDERFUL PEGGY LEE	5	1957
MR WRITER STEREOPHONICS	5	2001
MR ZERO KEITH RELF	50	1966
MISTI BLU AMILLIONSONS	39	2002
MISTLETOE AND WINE CLIFF RICHARD	1	1988
MISTY JOHNNY MATHIS	12	1960
MISTY RAY STEVENS	2	1975
MISTY BLUE DOROTHY MOORE	5	1976
MISTY MORNING, ALBERT BRIDGE POGUES	41	1989
MISUNDERSTANDING GENESIS	42	1980
MISUNDERSTOOD [A] BON JOVI	21	2002
MISUNDERSTOOD [B] ROBBIE WILLIAMS	8	2004
MISUNDERSTOOD MAN CLIFF RICHARD	19	1995
MITCH BISCUIT BOY	75	2001
MITTAGEISEN (METAL POSTCARD) SIOUXSIE & THE BANSHEES	47	1979
MIX IT UP DAN REED NETWORK	49	1991
MIXED BIZNESS BECK	34	2000
MIXED EMOTIONS ROLLING STONES	36	1989
MIXED TRUTH RAGGA TWINS	65	1992
MIXED UP WORLD SOPHIE ELLIS-BEXTOR	7	2003
MIYAKO HIEAWAY MARION	45	1998
MJB DA MVP MARY J BLIGE	33	2006
M'LADY SLY & THE FAMILY STONE	32	1968
MMM MMM MMM MMM CRASH TEST DUMMIES	2	1994
MMMBOP HANSON	1	1997
MO' FIRE BAD COMPANY UK/RAWHILL CRU	24	2003
MO MONEY MO PROBLEMS NOTORIOUS B.I.G. FEATURING PUFF DADDY & MASE	10	1997
MOAN AND GROAN MARK MORRISON	7	1997
MOANIN' CHRIS FARLOWE	46	1967
MOB RULES BLACK SABBATH	46	1981
MOBILE RAY BURNS	4	1955
MOBSCENE MARILYN MANSON	13	2003
MOCKIN' BIRD HILL MIGIL FIVE	10	1964
MOCKINGBIRD [A] INEZ & CHARLIE FOXX	33	1969
MOCKINGBIRD [A] CARLY SIMON & JAMES TAYLOR	34	1974
MOCKINGBIRD [A] BELLE STARS	51	1982
MOCKINGBIRD [B] EMINEM	4	2005
THE MODEL KRAFTWERK	1	1981
MODEL LIFE CHOCOLATE MONDAY	61	2005
MODELS FOR THE PROGRAMME HELL IS FOR HEROES	56	2005
MODERN AGE STROKES	68	2001
MODERN ART ART BRUT	49	2004
MODERN FEELING IKARA COLT	61	2004
MODERN GIRL [A] SHEENA EASTON	8	1980
MODERN GIRL [B] MEAT LOAF	17	1984
MODERN LOVE DAVID BOWIE	2	1983
MODERN ROMANCE (I WANT TO FALL IN LOVE AGAIN) FRANCIS ROSSI & BERNARD FROST	54	1985
MODERN WAY KAISER CHIEFS	11	2005
A MODERN WAY OF LETTING GO IDLEWILD	28	2003
THE MODERN WORLD JAM	36	1977
MODUS OPERANDI PHOTEK	66	1998
MOI...LOLITA ALIZEE	9	2002
MOIRA JANE'S CAFE DEFINITION OF SOUND	34	1992
MOLLIE'S SONG BEVERLEY CRAVEN	61	1993
MOLLY CARRIE	56	1998
MOLLY'S CHAMBERS KINGS OF LEON	23	2003
A MOMENT LIKE THIS LEONA LEWIS	1	2006
MOMENT OF MY LIFE BOBBY D'AMBROSIO FEATURING MICHELLE WEEKS	23	1997
MOMENTS IN LOVE/BEAT BOX ART OF NOISE	51	1985
MOMENTS IN SOUL JT & THE BIG FAMILY	7	1990
MOMENTS OF PLEASURE KATE BUSH	26	1993
MON AMI GIRESSE	61	2001
MON AMOUR TOKYO PIZZICATO FIVE	72	1997
MONA CRAIG McLACHLAN & CHECK 1-2	2	1990
MONA LISA CONWAY TWITTY	5	1959
MONDAY MONDAY MAMAS & THE PAPAS	3	1966
MONDAY MORNING CANDYSKINS	34	1997
MONDAY MORNING 5:19 RIALTO	37	1997
MONEY [A] BERN ELLIOTT & THE FENMEN	14	1963
MONEY [A] FLYING LIZARDS	5	1979
MONEY [A] BACKBEAT BAND	48	1994
MONEY [B] SKIN	18	1994
MONEY [C] CHARLI BALTIMORE	12	1998
MONEY [D] DAN REED NETWORK	45	1990
MONEY [E] JAMELIA FEATURING BEENIE MAN	5	2000
(MONEY CAN'T) BUY ME LOVE BLACKstreet	18	1997
MONEY DON'T MATTER 2 NIGHT PRINCE & THE NEW POWER GENERATION	19	1992
MONEY (EVERYBODY LOVES HER) GUN	73	1989
MONEY FOR NOTHING DIRE STRAITS	4	1985
MONEY GO ROUND (PART 1) STYLE COUNCIL	11	1983
MONEY GREED TRICKY	25	1998
MONEY HONEY BAY CITY ROLLERS	3	1975
MONEY IN MY POCKET DENNIS BROWN	14	1979
MONEY LOVE NENEH CHERRY	23	1992
MONEY MONEY MONEY ABBA	3	1976
MONEY THAT'S YOUR PROBLEM TONIGHT	66	1978
MONEY TO BURN RICHARD ASHCROFT	17	2000
MONEY'S TOO TIGHT TO MENTION VALENTINE BROTHERS	73	1983
MONEY'S TOO TIGHT TO MENTION SIMPLY RED	13	1985
MONEYTALKS AC/DC	36	1990
MONIE IN THE MIDDLE MONIE LOVE	46	1990
THE MONKEES RAMPAGE	51	1995
THE MONKEES EP MONKEES	33	1980
MONKEY [A] GEORGE MICHAEL	13	1988
MONKEY [B] SHAFT	61	1992
MONKEY BUSINESS [A] SKID ROW	19	1991
MONKEY BUSINESS [B] DANGER DANGER	42	1992
MONKEY CHOP DAN-I	30	1979
MONKEY GONE TO HEAVEN PIXIES	60	1989
MONKEY MAN MAYTALS	47	1970
MONKEY MAN GENERAL LEVY	75	1993
MONKEY SPANNER DAVE & ANSIL COLLINS	7	1971
MONKEY WAH RADICAL ROB	67	1992
MONKEY WRENCH FOO FIGHTERS	12	1997
MONO COURTNEY LOVE	41	2004
MONOCULTURE SOFT CELL	52	2002
MONSIEUR DUPONT SANDIE SHAW	6	1969
MONSTER [A] L7	33	1992
MONSTER [B] LIQUID PEOPLE VS SIMPLE MINDS	67	2002
MONSTER [C] AUTOMATIC	4	2006
MONSTER HOSPITAL METRIC	55	2006
MONSTER MASH BOBBY 'BORIS' PICKETT & THE CRYPT-KICKERS	3	1973
MONSTERS FUNERAL FOR A FRIEND	36	2005
MONSTERS AND ANGELS VOICE OF THE BEEHIVE	17	1991
MONTEGO BAY BOBBY BLOOM	3	1970
MONTEGO BAY FREDDIE NOTE & THE RUDIES	45	1970
MONTEGO BAY SUGAR CANE	54	1978
MONTEGO BAY AMAZULU	16	1986
MONTREAL WEDDING PRESENT	40	1997
MONTREUX EP SIMPLY RED	11	1992
MONTUNO GLORIA ESTEFAN	55	1993
MONY MONY TOMMY JAMES & THE SHONDELLS	1	1968
MONY MONY AMAZULU	38	1987
MONY MONY BILLY IDOL	7	1987
MONY MONY STATUS QUO	48	2000
THE MOOD CLUB FIRSTBORN	69	1999
MOODSWINGS MY VITRIOL	39	2002
MOODSWINGS (TO COME AT ME LIKE THAT) CHARLOTTE CHURCH	14	2006
MOODY BLUE ELVIS PRESLEY	6	1977
MOODY PLACES NORTHSIDE	32	1990
MOODY RIVER PAT BOONE	18	1961

	Peak Position	Year of Entry
MOOG ERUPTION DIGITAL ORGASM	62	1992
MOON VIRUS	36	1997
MOON HOP DERRICK MORGAN	49	1970
MOON OVER BOURBON STREET STING	44	1986
MOON RIVER DANNY WILLIAMS	1	1961
MOON RIVER HENRY MANCINI	44	1961
MOON RIVER GREYHOUND	12	1972
MOON SHADOW CAT STEVENS	22	1971
MOON TALK PERRY COMO	17	1958
MOONCHILD FIELDS OF THE NEPHILIM	28	1988
MOONGLOW MORRIS STOLOFF	7	1956
MOONGLOW SOUNDS ORCHESTRAL	43	1965
MOONLIGHT AND MUZAK M	33	1979
MOONLIGHT & ROSES JIM REEVES	34	1971
MOONLIGHT GAMBLER FRANKIE LAINE	13	1956
MOONLIGHT SERENADE GLENN MILLER	12	1954
MOONLIGHT SHADOW MIKE OLDFIELD FEATURING MAGGIE REILLY	4	1983
MOONLIGHTING LEO SAYER	2	1975
MOONLIGHTING THEME AL JARREAU	8	1987
MOONSHINE SALLY MUD	10	1975
MOR BLUR	15	1997
MORE [A] JIMMY YOUNG	4	1956
MORE [A] PERRY COMO	10	1956
MORE [B] SISTERS OF MERCY	14	1990
MORE... [C] HIGH	67	1991
MORE AND MORE [A] ANDY WILLIAMS	45	1967
MORE AND MORE [B] CAPTAIN HOLLYWOOD PROJECT	23	1993
MORE & MORE [C] SPOILED & ZIGO	31	2000
MORE & MORE [D] JOE FEATURING G UNIT	12	2004
MORE AND MORE PARTY POPS RUSS CONWAY	5	1959
MORE BEATS & PIECES COLDCUT	37	1997
MORE GOOD OLD ROCK 'N ROLL DAVE CLARK FIVE	34	1970
MORE HUMAN THAN HUMAN WHITE ZOMBIE	51	1995
THE MORE I GET THE MORE I WANT KWS FEATURING TEDDY PENDERGRASS	35	1994
THE MORE I SEE (THE LESS I BELIEVE) FUN BOY THREE	68	1983
THE MORE I SEE YOU CHRIS MONTEZ	3	1966
THE MORE I SEE YOU JOY MARSHALL	34	1966
THE MORE I SEE YOU BARBARA WINDSOR & MIKE REID	46	1999
MORE LIFE IN A TRAMP'S VEST STEREOPHONICS	33	1997
MORE LIKE THE MOVIES DR HOOK	14	1978
MORE LOVE [A] FEARGAL SHARKEY	44	1988
MORE LOVE [B] NEXT OF KIN	33	1999
MORE MONEY FOR YOU AND ME (MEDLEY) FOUR PREPS	39	1961
MORE MORE MORE [A] ANDREA TRUE CONNECTION	5	1976
MORE MORE MORE [A] BANANARAMA	24	1993
MORE MORE MORE [A] RACHEL STEVENS	3	2004
MORE, MORE, MORE [B] CARMEL	23	1984
MORE PARTY POPS RUSS CONWAY	10	1958
MORE THAN A FEELING BOSTON	22	1977
MORE THAN A LOVER BONNIE TYLER	27	1977
MORE THAN A WOMAN [A] TAVARES	7	1978
MORE THAN A WOMAN [A] 911	2	1998
MORE THAN A WOMAN [B] AALIYAH	1	2002
MORE THAN EVER (COME PRIMA) MALCOLM VAUGHAN WITH THE MICHAEL SAMMES SINGERS	5	1958
MORE THAN EVER (COME PRIMA) ROBERT EARL	26	1958
MORE THAN I CAN BEAR MATT BIANCO	50	1985
MORE THAN I CAN SAY CRICKETS	42	1960
MORE THAN I CAN SAY BOBBY VEE	4	1961
MORE THAN I CAN SAY LEO SAYER	2	1980
MORE THAN I NEEDED TO KNOW SCOOCH	5	2000
MORE THAN IN LOVE KATE ROBBINS & BEYOND	2	1981
MORE THAN LIKELY PM DAWN FEATURING BOY GEORGE	40	1993
MORE THAN LOVE [A] KEN DODD	14	1966
MORE THAN LOVE [B] WET WET WET	19	1992
MORE THAN ONE KIND OF LOVE JOAN ARMATRADING	75	1990
MORE THAN PHYSICAL BANANARAMA	41	1986
MORE THAN THAT BACKSTREET BOYS	12	2001
MORE THAN THIS [A] ROXY MUSIC	6	1982
MORE THAN THIS [A] EMMIE	5	1999
MORE THAN THIS [B] PETER GABRIEL	47	2002
MORE THAN US EP TRAVIS	16	1998
MORE THAN WORDS EXTREME	2	1991
MORE THAN YOU KNOW MARTIKA	15	1990
THE MORE THEY KNOCK, THE MORE I LOVE YOU GLORIA D BROWN	57	1985
MORE TO LIFE CLIFF RICHARD	23	1991
MORE TO LOVE VOLCANO	32	1994
MORE TO THIS WORLD BAD BOYS INC	8	1994
THE MORE YOU IGNORE ME THE CLOSER I GET MORRISSEY	8	1994
THE MORE YOU LIVE, THE MORE YOU LOVE A FLOCK OF SEAGULLS	26	1984
MORGEN IVO ROBIC	23	1959
MORNIN' AL JARREAU	28	1983
MORNING [A] VAL DOONICAN	12	1971
MORNING [B] WET WET WET	16	1996
THE MORNING AFTER (FREE AT LAST) STRIKE	38	1995
MORNING AFTERGLOW ELECTRASY	19	1998
MORNING ALWAYS COMES TOO SOON BRAD CARTER	48	2004
MORNING DANCE SPYRO GYRA	17	1979
MORNING GLORY JAMES & BOBBY PURIFY	27	1976
MORNING HAS BROKEN CAT STEVENS	9	1972
MORNING HAS BROKEN NEIL DIAMOND	36	1992
MORNING HAS BROKEN DANIEL O'DONNELL	32	2000
MORNING OF OUR LIVES MODERN LOVERS	29	1978
THE MORNING PAPERS PRINCE & THE NEW POWER GENERATION	52	1993
MORNING SIDE OF THE MOUNTAIN DONNY & MARIE OSMOND	5	1975
MORNING WONDER EARLIES	67	2004
MORNINGLIGHT TEAM DEEP	42	1997
MORNINGTOWN RIDE SEEKERS	2	1966
MORRIS BROWN OUTKAST	43	2006
THE MOST BEAUTIFUL GIRL CHARLIE RICH	2	1974
THE MOST BEAUTIFUL GIRL IN THE WORLD PRINCE	1	1994
MOST GIRLS P!NK	5	2000
MOST HIGH PAGE & PLANT	26	1998
MOST LIKELY YOU GO YOUR OWN WAY BOB DYLAN	51	2007
MOST PRECIOUS LOVE BLAZE PRESENTS UDA FEATURING BARBARA TUCKER	17	2005
THE MOST TIRING DAY CECIL	69	1998
MOTHER [A] DANZIG	62	1994
MOTHER [B] M FACTOR	18	2002
MOTHER AND CHILD REUNION PAUL SIMON	5	1972
MOTHER DAWN BLUE PEARL	50	1992
MOTHER FIXATION MINUTEMAN	45	2003
MOTHER NATURE AND FATHER TIME NAT 'KING' COLE	7	1953
MOTHER OF MINE NEIL REID	2	1972
MOTHER UNIVERSE SOUP DRAGONS	26	1990
MOTHER-IN-LAW ERNIE K-DOE	29	1961
MOTHERLAND-A-FRI-CA TRIBAL HOUSE	57	1990
MOTHERLESS CHILD ERIC CLAPTON	63	1994
MOTHER'S TALK TEARS FOR FEARS	14	1984
MOTHERSHIP RECONNECTION SCOTT GROOVES FEATURING PARLIAMENT/ FUNKADELIC	55	1998
THE MOTION OF LOVE GENE LOVES JEZEBEL	56	1987
MOTIVATION SUM 41	21	2002
THE MOTIVE (LIVING WITHOUT YOU) THEN JERICO	18	1987
MOTIVELESS CRIME SOUTH	72	2004
MOTOR BIKING CHRIS SPEDDING	14	1975
MOTORBIKE BEAT REVILLOS	45	1980
MOTORBIKE TO HEAVEN SALAD	42	1995
MOTORCYCLE RUMBLE STRIPS	46	2007
MOTORCYCLE EMPTINESS MANIC STREET PREACHERS	17	1992
MOTORCYCLE MICHAEL JO ANN CAMPBELL	41	1961
MOTORCYCLE RIDER ICICLE WORKS	73	1990
MOTORHEAD LIVE MOTORHEAD	6	1981
MOTORMANIA ROMAN HOLIDAY	40	1983
MOTORTOWN KANE GANG	45	1987
THE MOTOWN SONG ROD STEWART	10	1991
MOTOWNPHILLY BOYZ II MEN	23	1992
MOULDY OLD DOUGH LIEUTENANT PIGEON	1	1972
MOUNTAIN GREENERY MEL TORME	4	1956
MOUNTAIN OF LOVE KENNY LYNCH	33	1960
MOUNTAINS PRINCE & THE REVOLUTION	45	1986
THE MOUNTAIN'S HIGH DICK & DEEDEE	37	1961
MOUSE IN A HOLE HEAVY STEREO	53	1996
MOUTH MERRIL BAINBRIDGE	51	1996
MOUTH FOR WAR PANTERA	73	1992
MOUTHWASH KATE NASH	23	2007
MOVE [A] INSPIRAL CARPETS	49	1989
MOVE [B] MOBY	21	1993
MOVE ALONG ALL-AMERICAN REJECTS	42	2006
MOVE ANY MOUNTAIN SHAMEN	4	1991
MOVE AWAY CULTURE CLUB	1	1986
MOVE AWAY JIMMY BLUE DEL AMITRI	36	1990
MOVE BABY MOVE SARTORELLO	56	1996
MOVE CLOSER PHYLLIS NELSON	1	1985
MOVE CLOSER TOM JONES	49	1989
MOVE IN A LITTLE CLOSER HARMONY GRASS	24	1969
MOVE IN MY DIRECTION BANANARAMA	14	2005
MOVE IN STEREO (LIV ULLMAN ON DRUMS) DO ME BAD THINGS	49	2005
MOVE IT CLIFF RICHARD & THE DRIFTERS	2	1958
MOVE IT BABY SIMON SCOTT	37	1964
MOVE IT LIKE THIS BAHA MEN	16	2002
MOVE IT UP CAPPELLA	16	1994
MOVE MANIA SASH! FEATURING SHANNON	8	1998
MOVE ME NO MOUNTAIN SOUL II SOUL, LEAD VOCALS KOFI	31	1992
MOVE MOVE MOVE (THE RED TRIBE) MANCHESTER UNITED FOOTBALL CLUB	6	1996
MOVE NOW MARK B FEATURING TOMMY EVANS	61	2004
MOVE ON BABY CAPPELLA	7	1994
MOVE ON UP CURTIS MAYFIELD	12	1971
MOVE ON UP SUE CHALONER	64	1993
MOVE ON UP TRICKSTER	19	1998
MOVE OVER DARLING DORIS DAY	8	1964
MOVE OVER DARLING TRACEY ULLMAN	8	1983
MOVE RIGHT OUT RICK ASTLEY	58	1991
MOVE THAT BODY [A] TECHNOTRONIC FEATURING REGGIE	12	1991
MOVE THAT BODY [B] NUSH	46	1995
MOVE THE CROWD ERIC B & RAKIM	53	1988
MOVE THIS MOUNTAIN SOPHIE ELLIS-BEXTOR	3	2002
MOVE TO MEMPHIS A-HA	47	1991
MOVE YA BODY NINA SKY	6	2004
MOVE YOUR ASS SCOOTER	23	1995
MOVE YOUR BODY [A] GENE FARROW & G.F. BAND	33	1978
MOVE YOUR BODY [B] TYREE FEATURING JMD	72	1989
MOVE YOUR BODY [C] XPANSIONS	7	1991
MOVE YOUR BODY [D] ANTICAPPELLA FEATURING MC FIXX IT	21	1994

	Peak Position	Year of Entry
MOVE YOUR BODY [E] EUROGROOVE	29	1995
MOVE YOUR BODY [F] RUFFNECK FEATURING YAVAHN	60	1996
MOVE YOUR BODY [G] EIFFEL 65	3	2000
MOVE YOUR FEET [A] M-D-EMM	67	1992
MOVE YOUR FEET [B] JUNIOR SENIOR	3	2003
MOVE YOUR FEET TO THE RHYTHM OF THE BEAT HITHOUSE	69	1989
MOVE YOUR LOVE DJH FEATURING STEFY	73	1991
MOVEMENT LCD SOUNDSYSTEM	52	2004
MOVIE STAR HARPO	24	1976
MOVIES [A] HOTHOUSE FLOWERS	68	1990
MOVIES [B] ALIEN ANT FARM	5	2001
MOVIESTAR STEREOPHONICS	5	2004
MOVIN' [A] BRASS CONSTRUCTION	23	1976
MOVIN' [A] 400 BLOWS	54	1985
MOVIN' [B] MARATHON	36	1992
MOVIN' [C] MONE	48	1996
MOVIN' ON [A] BANANARAMA	24	1992
MOVIN' ON [B] APACHE INDIAN	48	1993
MOVIN' ON [C] DEBBIE PENDER	41	1998
MOVIN' ON [D] PROSPECT PARK/CAROLYN HARDING	55	1998
MOVIN' OUT (ANTHONY'S SONG) BILLY JOEL	35	1978
MOVIN' THRU YOUR SYSTEM JARK PRONGO	58	1999
MOVIN TOO FAST ARTFUL DODGER & ROMINA JOHNSON	2	2000
MOVING SUPERGRASS	9	1999
MOVING IN THE RIGHT DIRECTION PASADENAS	49	1992
MOVING ON [A] DREADZONE	58	1997
MOVING ON [B] TAIO CRUZ	26	2007
MOVING ON UP M PEOPLE	2	1993
MOVING ON UP (ON THE RIGHT SIDE) BEVERLEY KNIGHT	42	1996
MOVING PICTURES CRIBS	38	2007
MOVING TO BLACKWATER REUBEN	59	2004
MOVING TO CALIFORNIA STRAW	50	1999
MOVING TO NEW YORK WOMBATS	13	2008
MOVING TOO FAST SUPAFLY INC	23	2006
MOVING UP MOVING ON MOZAIC	62	1996
MOZART 40 SOVEREIGN COLLECTION	27	1971
MOZART SYMPHONY NO. 40 IN G MINOR K550 1ST MOVEMENT (ALLEGRO MOLTO) WALDO DE LOS RIOS	5	1971
MS GRACE TYMES	1	1974
MS JACKSON OUTKAST	2	2001
MUCH AGAINST EVERYONE'S ADVICE SOULWAX	56	2000
MUCH LOVE SHOLA AMA	17	1998
MUCHO MACHO TOTO COELO	8	1982
(MUCHO MAMBO) SWAY SHAFT	2	1999
MUCK IT OUT FARMERS BOYS	48	1983
MUDDY WATER BLUES PAUL RODGERS	45	1994
MUHAMMAD ALI FAITHLESS	29	2001
MULDER AND SCULLY CATATONIA	3	1998
MULE (CHANT NO. 2) BEGGAR & CO	37	1981
MULE SKINNER BLUES FENDERMEN	32	1960
MULE SKINNER BLUES RUSTY DRAPER	39	1960
MULE TRAIN FRANK IFIELD	22	1963
MULL OF KINTYRE WINGS	1	1977
MULTIPLICATION BOBBY DARIN	5	1961
MULTIPLICATION SHOWADDYWADDY	39	1981
MULTIPLY XZIBIT	39	2002
MUM'S GONE TO ICELAND BENNETT	34	1997
MUNDAYA (THE BOY) TIM DELUXE FEATURING SHAHIN BADAR	61	2004
MUNDIAN TO BACH KE PANJABI MC	5	2003
MUNICH EDITORS	10	2005
THE MUPPET SHOW MUSIC HALL EP MUPPETS	19	1977
MURDER ON THE DANCEFLOOR SOPHIE ELLIS-BEXTOR	2	2001
MURDER SHE WROTE [A] TAIRRIE B	71	1990
MURDER SHE WROTE [B] CHAKA DEMUS & PLIERS	27	1994
MURDERATION EBONY DUBSTERS	59	2004
MURPHY AND THE BRICKS NOEL MURPHY	57	1987
MURPHY'S LAW CHERI	13	1982
MUSAK TRISCO	28	2001
MUSCLE CAR MYLO FEATURING FREEFORM FIVE	38	2006
MUSCLE DEEP THEN JERICO	48	1987
MUSCLE MUSEUM MUSE	25	1999
MUSCLEBOUND SPANDAU BALLET	10	1981
MUSCLES DIANA ROSS	15	1982
MUSIC [A] JOHN MILES	3	1976
MUSIC [A] FARGETTA & ANNE-MARIE SMITH	34	1993
MUSIC [B] ONE WAY FEATURING AL HUDSON	56	1979
MUSIC [C] F.R. DAVID	71	1983
MUSIC PART 1 [D] D TRAIN	23	1983
MUSIC [E] OMAR	53	1992
MUSIC [F] MADONNA	1	2000
MUSIC [G] ERICK SERMON FEATURING MARVIN GAYE	36	2001
MUSIC AND LIGHTS IMAGINATION	5	1982
MUSIC AND YOU [A] SAL SOLO WITH THE LONDON COMMUNITY GOSPEL CHOIR	52	1985
MUSIC AND YOU [B] ROOM 5 FEATURING OLIVER CHEATHAM	38	2003
MUSIC FOR CHAMELEONS GARY NUMAN	19	1982
MUSIC GETS THE BEST OF ME SOPHIE ELLIS-BEXTOR	14	2002
THE MUSIC I LIKE ALEXIA	31	1998
MUSIC IN MY MIND ADAM F	27	1998
THE MUSIC IN YOU MONOBOY FEATURING DELORES	50	2001
MUSIC IS A PASSION ATLANTIC OCEAN	59	1994
MUSIC IS LIFE DIRT DEVILS	53	2003
THE MUSIC IS MOVING FARGETTA	74	1996
MUSIC IS MOVING CORTINA	42	2001
MUSIC IS MY RADAR BLUR	10	2000
MUSIC IS POWER RICHARD ASHCROFT	20	2006
MUSIC IS THE ANSWER (DANCING' & PRANCIN') DANNY TENAGLIA & CELEDA	36	1998
MUSIC MAKES ME HIGH LOST BOYZ	42	1996
MUSIC MAKES YOU FEEL LIKE DANCING BRASS CONSTRUCTION	39	1980
MUSIC MAKES YOU LOSE CONTROL LES RYTHMES DIGITALES	69	1998
MUSIC MATTERS FAITHLESS FEATURING CASS FOX	38	2007
THE MUSIC OF GOODBYE (LOVE THEME FROM *OUT OF AFRICA*) AL JARREAU	75	1986
MUSIC OF MY HEART N SYNC & GLORIA ESTEFAN	34	2000
THE MUSIC OF THE NIGHT MICHAEL CRAWFORD	7	1987
THE MUSIC OF THE NIGHT BARBRA STREISAND (DUET WITH MICHAEL CRAWFORD)	54	1994
THE MUSIC OF TORVILL AND DEAN EP RICHARD HARTLEY/MICHAEL REED ORCHESTRA	9	1984
MUSIC POWER PORNO	72	2006
MUSIC REVOLUTION SCUMFROG	46	2003
MUSIC SAVED MY LIFE CEVIN FISHER	67	1999
MUSIC SOUNDS BETTER WITH YOU STARDUST	2	1998
MUSIC STOP RAILWAY CHILDREN	66	1990
MUSIC TAKES YOU BLAME	48	1992
THE MUSIC THAT WE HEAR (MOOG ISLAND) MORCHEEBA	47	1997
MUSIC TO WATCH GIRLS BY ANDY WILLIAMS	9	1967
MUSICAL FREEDOM (MOVING ON UP) PAUL SIMPSON FEATURING ADEVA	22	1989
MUSICAL MELODY UNIQUE 3	29	1990
THE MUSIC'S GOT ME BASS BUMPERS	25	1994
THE MUSIC'S GOT ME BROOKLYN BOUNCE	67	1998
THE MUSIC'S NO GOOD WITHOUT YOU CHER	8	2001
MUSIQUE DAFT PUNK	7	1997
MUSKRAT EVERLY BROTHERS	20	1961
MUSKRAT RAMBLE FREDDY CANNON	32	1961
MUST BE LOVE FYA FEATURING SMUJJI	13	2004
MUST BE MADISON JOE LOSS ORCHESTRA	20	1962
MUST BE SANTA TOMMY STEELE	40	1960
MUST BE THE MUSIC [A] HYSTERIX	40	1994
MUST BE THE MUSIC [B] JOEY NEGRO FEATURING TAKA BOOM	8	2000
MUST BEE THE MUSIC KING BEE FEATURING MICHELE	44	1991
MUST GET OUT MAROON 5	39	2005
A MUST TO AVOID HERMAN'S HERMITS	6	1965
MUSTAFA CHA CHA CHA STAIFFI & HIS MUSTAFAS	43	1964
MUSTANG SALLY WILSON PICKETT	28	1966
MUSTANG SALLY COMMITMENTS	63	1991
MUSTAPHA BOB AZZAM	23	1960
MUTANTS IN MEGA CITY ONE FINK BROTHERS	50	1985
MUTATIONS EP ORBITAL	24	1992
MUTUAL ATTRACTION CHANGE	60	1985
MUTUALLY ASSURED DESTRUCTION GILLAN	32	1981
MUZIKIZUM X-PRESS 2	52	2001
MY 16TH APOLOGY (EP) SHAKESPEARS SISTER	61	1993
MY ADIDAS RUN D.M.C.	62	1986
MY AFFAIR KIRSTY MacCOLL	56	1991
MY ALL MARIAH CAREY	4	1998
MY ANGEL ROCK GODDESS	64	1983
MY ARMS KEEP MISSING YOU RICK ASTLEY	2	1987
MY BABY LIL' ROMEO	67	2001
MY BABY JUST CARES FOR ME NINA SIMONE	5	1987
MY BABY LEFT ME DAVE BERRY & THE CRUISERS	37	1964
MY BABY LEFT ME ELVIS PRESLEY	18	2007
MY BABY LEFT ME - THAT'S ALL RIGHT (MEDLEY) SLADE	32	1977
MY BABY LOVES LOVIN' WHITE PLAINS	9	1970
MY BAG LLOYD COLE & THE COMMOTIONS	46	1987
MY BAND D12	2	2004
MY BEAT BLAZE FEATURING PALMER BROWN	53	2001
MY BEATBOX DEEJAY PUNK-ROC	43	1998
MY BEAUTIFUL FRIEND CHARLATANS	31	1999
MY BEST FRIEND'S GIRL CARS	3	1978
MY BLUE HEAVEN FRANK SINATRA	33	1961
MY BODY LEVERT SWEAT GILL	21	1998
MY BONNIE TONY SHERIDAN & THE BEATLES	48	1963
MY BOO USHER	5	2004
MY BOOK BEAUTIFUL SOUTH	43	1990
MY BOOMERANG WON'T COME BACK CHARLIE DRAKE	14	1961
MY BOY ELVIS PRESLEY	5	1974
MY BOY FLAT TOP FRANKIE VAUGHAN	20	1956
MY BOY LOLLIPOP MILLIE	2	1964
MY BOYFRIEND'S BACK ANGELS	50	1963
MY BRAVE FACE PAUL McCARTNEY	18	1989
MY BROTHER JAKE FREE	4	1971
MY CAMERA NEVER LIES BUCKS FIZZ	1	1982
MY CHERIE AMOUR STEVIE WONDER	4	1969
MY CHILD CONNIE FRANCIS	26	1965
MY COCO STELLASTARR*	73	2004
MY COO-CO-CHOO ALVIN STARDUST	2	1973
MY COUNTRY MIDNIGHT OIL	66	1993
MY CULTURE 1 GIANT LEAP FEATURING MAXI JAZZ & ROBBIE WILLIAMS	9	2002
MY CUTIE CUTIE SHAKIN' STEVENS	75	1990

	Peak Position	Year of Entry
MY DEFINITION OF A BOOMBASTIC JAZZ STYLE DREAM WARRIORS	13	1990
MY DESIRE AMIRA	20	1997
MY DESTINY [A] LIONEL RICHIE	7	1992
MY DESTINY [B] DELINQUENT FEATURING K-CAT	19	2008
MY DING-A-LING CHUCK BERRY	1	1972
MY DIXIE DARLING LONNIE DONEGAN	10	1957
MY DJ (PUMP IT UP SOME) RICHIE RICH	74	1988
MY DOCS KISS AMC	66	1990
MY DOORBELL WHITE STRIPES	10	2005
MY DRUG CHERRYFALLS	71	2005
MY DRUG BUDDY LEMONHEADS	44	1993
MY DYING MACHINE GARY NUMAN	66	1984
MY EGYPTIAN LOVER SPACE COWBOY FEATURING NADIA OH	45	2007
MY EVER CHANGING MOODS STYLE COUNCIL	5	1984
MY EYES TRAVIS	60	2007
MY EYES ADORED YOU FRANKIE VALLI	5	1975
MY FAMILY DEPENDS ON ME SIMONE	75	1991
MY FATHER'S EYES ERIC CLAPTON	33	1998
MY FATHER'S SHOES LEVEL 42	55	1992
MY FATHER'S SON CONNOR REEVES	12	1997
MY FAVORITE MISTAKE SHERYL CROW	9	1998
MY FAVOURITE GAME CARDIGANS	14	1998
MY FAVOURITE WASTE OF TIME OWEN PAUL	3	1986
MY FEELING JUNIOR JACK	31	2000
MY FEET KEEP DANCING CHIC	21	1979
MY FIRST NIGHT WITHOUT YOU CYNDI LAUPER	53	1989
MY FOOLISH FRIEND TALK TALK	57	1983
MY FORBIDDEN LOVER CHIC	15	1979
MY FORBIDDEN LOVER ROMINA JOHNSON FEATURING LUCI MARTIN & NORMA JEAN	59	2000
MY FREND STAN SLADE	2	1973
MY FRIEND [A] FRANKIE LAINE	3	1954
MY FRIEND [B] ROY ORBISON	35	1969
MY FRIEND [C] GROOVE ARMADA	36	2001
MY FRIEND JACK SMOKE	45	1967
MY FRIEND JACK BONEY M	57	1980
MY FRIEND THE SEA PETULA CLARK	7	1961
MY FRIENDS [A] RED HOT CHILI PEPPERS	29	1995
MY FRIENDS [B] STEREOPHONICS	32	2007
MY FRIENDS OVER YOU NEW FOUND GLORY	30	2002
MY GENERATION [A] WHO	2	1965
MY GENERATION [A] ZIMMERS	26	2007
MY GENERATION [B] LIMP BIZKIT	15	2000
MY GETAWAY TIONNE 'T-BOZ' WATKINS	44	2001
MY GIRL [A] OTIS REDDING	11	1965
MY GIRL [A] TEMPTATIONS	2	1965
MY GIRL [A] WHISPERS	26	1980
MY GIRL [B] MADNESS	3	1980
MY GIRL [C] ROD STEWART	32	1981
MY GIRL BILL JIM STAFFORD	20	1974
MY GIRL JOSEPHINE FATS DOMINO	32	1961
MY GIRL JOSEPHINE SUPERCAT FEATURING JACK RADICS	22	1995
MY GIRL LOLLIPOP (MY BOY LOLLIPOP) BAD MANNERS	9	1982
MY GIRL LOVES ME SHALAMAR	45	1985
MY GIRL MY GIRL WARREN STACEY	26	2002
MY GUY [A] MARY WELLS	5	1964
MY GUY [B] TRACEY ULLMAN	23	1984
MY GUY - MY GIRL (MEDLEY) AMII STEWART & JOHNNY BRISTOL	39	1980
MY GUY - MY GIRL (MEDLEY) AMII STEWART & DEON ESTUS	63	1986
MY HAND OVER MY HEART MARC ALMOND	33	1992
MY HAPPINESS CONNIE FRANCIS	4	1959
MY HAPPY ENDING AVRIL LAVIGNE	5	2004
MY HEAD'S IN MISSISSIPPI ZZ TOP	37	1991
MY HEART GENE VINCENT	16	1960
MY HEART CAN'T TELL YOU NO ROD STEWART	49	1989
MY HEART GOES BANG (GET ME TO THE DOCTOR) DEAD OR ALIVE	23	1985
MY HEART GOES BOOM FRENCH AFFAIR	44	2000
MY HEART HAS A MIND OF ITS OWN CONNIE FRANCIS	3	1960
MY HEART THE BEAT D-SHAKE	42	1991
MY HEART WILL GO ON CELINE DION	1	1998
MY HEART'S BEATING WILD (TIC TAC TIC TAC) GIBSON BROTHERS	56	1983
MY HEART'S SYMPHONY GARY LEWIS & THE PLAYBOYS	36	1975
MY HERO FOO FIGHTERS	21	1998
MY HOMETOWN BRUCE SPRINGSTEEN	9	1985
MY HOUSE TERRORVISION	29	1994
MY HOUSE IS YOUR HOUSE MAXTREME	66	2002
MY HUMPS BLACK EYED PEAS	3	2005
MY IMMORTAL EVANESCENCE	7	2003
MY IRON LUNG RADIOHEAD	24	1994
MY JAMAICAN GUY GRACE JONES	56	1983
MY KIND OF GIRL MATT MONRO	5	1961
MY KIND OF GIRL FRANK SINATRA WITH COUNT BASIE	35	1963
MY KINDA LIFE CLIFF RICHARD	15	1977
MY KINGDOM FUTURE SOUND OF LONDON	13	1996
MY LAST NIGHT WITH YOU ARROWS	25	1975
MY LIFE [A] BILLY JOEL	12	1978
MY LIFE [B] CHANEL	39	2006
MY LIFE IS IN YOUR HANDS MELTDOWN	44	1996
MY LITTLE BABY MIKE BERRY WITH THE OUTLAWS	34	1963
MY LITTLE BROTHER ART BRUT	49	2004
MY LITTLE CORNER OF THE WORLD ANITA BRYANT	48	1960
MY LITTLE GIRL [A] CRICKETS	17	1963
MY LITTLE GIRL [B] AUTUMN	37	1971
MY LITTLE LADY TREMELOES	6	1968
MY LITTLE ONE MARMALADE	15	1971
MY LOVE [A] PETULA CLARK	4	1966
MY LOVE [B] PAUL McCARTNEY & WINGS	9	1973
MY LOVE [C] LIONEL RICHIE	70	1983
MY LOVE [D] JULIO IGLESIAS FEATURING STEVIE WONDER	5	1988
MY LOVE [E] LONDON BOYS	46	1989
MY LOVE [F] MARY J BLIGE	29	1994
MY LOVE [G] KELE LE ROC	8	1999
MY LOVE [H] WESTLIFE	1	2000
MY LOVE [I] KLUSTER FEATURING RON CARROLL	73	2001
MY LOVE [J] JUSTIN TIMBERLAKE FEATURING TI	2	2006
MY LOVE AND DEVOTION DORIS DAY	10	1952
MY LOVE AND DEVOTION MATT MONRO	29	1962
MY LOVE FOR YOU JOHNNY MATHIS	9	1960
MY LOVE IS A FIRE DONNY OSMOND	64	1991
MY LOVE IS ALWAYS SAFFRON HILL FEATURING BEN ONONO	28	2003
MY LOVE IS DEEP SARA PARKER	22	1997
MY LOVE IS FOR REAL PAULA ABDUL FEATURING OFFRA HAZA	28	1995
MY LOVE IS FOR REAL STRIKE	35	1996
MY LOVE IS GUARANTEED SYBIL	42	1987
MY LOVE IS LIKE...WO! MYA	33	2003
MY LOVE IS MAGIC BAS NOIR	73	1989
MY LOVE IS SO RAW ALYSON WILLIAMS FEATURING NIKKI D	34	1989
MY LOVE IS THE SHHH! SOMETHIN' FOR THE PEOPLE FEATURING TRINA & TAMARA	64	1998
MY LOVE IS WAITING MARVIN GAYE	34	1983
MY LOVE IS YOUR LOVE WHITNEY HOUSTON	2	1999
MY LOVE LIFE MORRISSEY	29	1991
MY LOVER'S PRAYER OTIS REDDING	37	1966
MY LOVER'S PRAYER ALISTAIR GRIFFIN	5	2004
MY LOVIN' EN VOGUE	4	1992
MY MAGIC MAN ROCHELLE	27	1986
MY MAMMY HAPPENINGS	34	1967
MY MAN A SWEET MAN MILLIE JACKSON	50	1972
MY MAN AND ME LYNSEY DE PAUL	40	1975
MY MARIE ENGELBERT HUMPERDINCK	31	1970
MY MATE PAUL DAVID HOLMES	39	1998
MY MELANCHOLY BABY TOMMY EDWARDS	29	1959
MY MELANCHOLY BABY CHAS & DAVE	51	1983
MY MIND'S EYE SMALL FACES	4	1966
MY MUM IS ONE IN A MILLION THE CHILDREN OF TANSLEY SCHOOL	27	1981
MY MY MY ARMAND VAN HELDEN	15	2004
MY NAME IS EMINEM	2	1999
MY NAME IS JACK MANFRED MANN	8	1968
MY NAME IS NOT SUSAN WHITNEY HOUSTON	29	1991
MY NAME IS PRINCE PRINCE & THE NEW POWER GENERATION	7	1992
MY NECK MY BACK (LICK IT) KHIA	4	2004
MY NEIGHBOUR'S HOUSE BLUETONES	68	2006
MY OH MY [A] SAD CAFE	14	1980
MY OH MY [B] SLADE	2	1983
MY OH MY [C] AQUA	6	1998
MY OLD MAN'S A DUSTMAN LONNIE DONEGAN	1	1960
MY OLD PIANO DIANA ROSS	5	1980
MY ONE SIN NAT 'KING' COLE	17	1955
MY ONE TEMPTATION MICA PARIS	7	1988
MY ONE TRUE FRIEND BETTE MIDLER	58	1998
MY ONLY LOVE BOB SINCLAR FEATURING LEE A GENESIS	56	1999
MY OWN SUMMER (SHOVE IT) DEFTONES	29	1998
MY OWN TRUE LOVE DANNY WILLIAMS	45	1963
MY OWN WAY DURAN DURAN	14	1981
MY OWN WORST ENEMY LIT	16	1999
MY PATCH JIM NOIR	65	2006
MY PEACE OF HEAVEN TEN CITY	63	1992
MY PERFECT COUSIN UNDERTONES	9	1980
MY PERSONAL POSSESSION NAT 'KING' COLE & THE FOUR KNIGHTS	21	1957
MY PHILOSOPHY BOOGIE DOWN PRODUCTIONS	69	1988
MY PLACE NELLY	1	2004
MY PLAGUE SLIPKNOT	43	2002
MY PRAYER PLATTERS	4	1956
MY PRAYER GERRY MONROE	9	1970
MY PREROGATIVE BOBBY BROWN	6	1988
MY PREROGATIVE BRITNEY SPEARS	3	2004
MY PRETTY ONE CLIFF RICHARD	6	1987
MY PUPPET PAL TIGER	62	1996
MY RECOVERY INJECTION BIFFY CLYRO	24	2004
MY REMEDY HINDA HICKS	61	2000
MY RESISTANCE IS LOW ROBIN SARSTEDT	3	1976
MY RISING STAR NORTHSIDE	50	1990
MY SACRIFICE CREED	18	2002
MY SALT HEART HUE & CRY	47	1991
MY SENTIMENTAL FRIEND HERMAN'S HERMITS	2	1969
MY SEPTEMBER LOVE DAVID WHITFIELD	3	1956
MY SHARONA KNACK	6	1979
MY SHIP IS COMING IN WALKER BROTHERS	3	1965
MY SIDE OF THE BED SUSANNA HOFFS	44	1991
MY SIMPLE HEART THREE DEGREES	9	1979
MY SISTER JULIANA HATFIELD THREE	71	1993
MY SON JOHN DAVID WHITFIELD	22	1956
MY SON MY SON VERA LYNN WITH FRANK WEIR, HIS SAXOPHONE, HIS ORCHESTRA & CHORUS	1	1954
MY SOUL PLEADS FOR YOU SIMON WEBBE	45	2007
MY SPECIAL ANGEL BOBBY HELMS WITH THE ANITA KERR SINGERS	22	1957
MY SPECIAL ANGEL MALCOLM VAUGHAN	3	1957

	Peak Position	Year of Entry
MY SPECIAL CHILD SINEAD O'CONNOR	42	1991
MY SPECIAL DREAM SHIRLEY BASSEY	32	1964
MY SPIRIT TILT	61	1997
MY STAR IAN BROWN	5	1998
MY SUNDAY BABY DALE SISTERS	36	1961
MY SUPERSTAR DIMESTARS	72	2001
MY SWEET JANE G.U.N.	51	1997
MY SWEET LORD GEORGE HARRISON	1	1971
MY SWEET ROSALIE BROTHERHOOD OF MAN	30	1976
MY TELEPHONE COLDCUT	52	1989
MY TIME [A] SOUVLAKI	63	1998
MY TIME [B] DUTCH FEATURING CRYSTAL WATERS	22	2003
MY TOOT TOOT DENISE LA SALLE	6	1985
MY TOWN GLASS TIGER	33	1991
MY TRUE LOVE JACK SCOTT	9	1958
MY UKELELE MAX BYGRAVES	19	1959
MY UNFINISHED SYMPHONY DAVID WHITFIELD	29	1956
MY UNKNOWN LOVE COUNT INDIGO	59	1996
MY VISION JAKATTA FEATURING SEAL	6	2002
MY WAY [A] EDDIE COCHRAN	23	1963
MY WAY [B] FRANK SINATRA	5	1969
MY WAY [B] DOROTHY SQUIRES	25	1970
MY WAY [B] ELVIS PRESLEY	9	1977
MY WAY [B] SEX PISTOLS	7	1978
MY WAY [B] SHANE MacGOWAN	29	1996
MY WAY [C] LIMP BIZKIT	6	2001
MY WAY OF GIVING IN CHRIS FARLOWE	48	1967
MY WAY OF THINKING UB40	6	1980
MY WEAKNESS IS NONE OF YOUR BUSINESS EMBRACE	9	1998
MY WHITE BICYCLE NAZARETH	14	1975
MY WOMAN'S MAN DAVE DEE	42	1970
MY WORLD [A] CUPID'S INSPIRATION	33	1968
MY WORLD [B] BEE GEES	16	1972
MY WORLD [C] SECRET AFFAIR	16	1980
MY WORLD OF BLUE KARL DENVER	29	1964
MYFANWY DAVID ESSEX	41	1987
MYMYMY ARMAND VAN HELDEN FEATURING TARA	12	2006
MYSTERIES OF LOVE L.A. MIX	46	1991
MYSTERIES OF THE WORLD MFSB	41	1981
MYSTERIOUS GIRL PETER ANDRE FEATURING BUBBLER RANX	1	1995
MYSTERIOUS TIMES SASH! FEATURING TINA COUSINS	2	1998
MYSTERIOUS WAYS U2	13	1991
MYSTERY [A] DIO	34	1984
MYSTERY [B] MYSTERY	56	2001
THE MYSTERY [C] DOUG WALKER	36	2008
MYSTERY GIRL [A] JESS CONRAD	18	1961
MYSTERY GIRL [B] DUKES	47	1981
MYSTERY LADY BILLY OCEAN	49	1985
MYSTERY LAND Y-TRAXX FEATURING NEVE	70	2003
MYSTERY LAND (EP) Y-TRAXX	63	1997
MYSTERY SONG STATUS QUO	11	1976
MYSTERY TRAIN ELVIS PRESLEY	25	1957
MYSTICAL MACHINE GUN KULA SHAKER	14	1999
MYSTIFY INXS	14	1989
MYZSTERIOUS MIZSTER JONES SLADE	50	1985
N		
N DEY SAY NELLY	6	2005
NA NA HEY HEY KISS HIM GOODBYE STEAM	9	1970
NA NA HEY HEY KISS HIM GOODBYE BANANARAMA	5	1983
NA NA IS THE SADDEST WORD STYLISTICS	5	1975
NA NA NA COZY POWELL	10	1974
NADINE (IS IT YOU) CHUCK BERRY	27	1964
NAGASAKI BADGER DISCO CITIZENS	56	1998
NAILS IN MY FEET CROWDED HOUSE	22	1993
NAIROBI TOMMY STEELE	3	1958
NAIVE KOOKS	5	2006
NAIVE SONG MIRWAIS	50	2000
NAKASAKI EP (I NEED A LOVER TONIGHT) KEN DOH	7	1996
NAKED [A] REEF	11	1995
NAKED [B] LOUISE	5	1996
NAKED AND SACRED CHYNNA PHILLIPS	62	1996
NAKED AND SACRED MARIA NAYLER	32	1998
NAKED EYE LUSCIOUS JACKSON	25	1997
NAKED IN THE RAIN BLUE PEARL	4	1990
NAKED LOVE (JUST SAY YOU WANT ME) QUARTZ & DINA CARROLL	39	1991
NAKED WITHOUT YOU ROACHFORD	53	1998
NAME AND NUMBER CURIOSITY	14	1989
THE NAME OF THE GAME ABBA	1	1977
THE NAMELESS ONE WENDY JAMES	34	1993
NANCY BOY PLACEBO	4	1997
A NANNY IN MANHATTAN LILYS	16	1998
NAPOLEON WOLFMAN	44	2004
NAPPY LOVE GOODIES	21	1975
NARCO TOURISTS SLAM VS UNKLE	66	2001
NARCOTIC INFLUENCE EMPIRION	64	1996
NASHVILLE BOOGIE BERT WEEDON	29	1959
NASHVILLE CATS LOVIN' SPOONFUL	26	1967
NASTRADAMUS NAS	24	2000
NASTY JANET JACKSON	19	1986
NASTY BREAKS CLIPZ	72	2005
NASTY GIRL [A] INAYA DAY	9	2005
NASTY GIRL [B] NOTORIOUS B.I.G. FEATURING DIDDY, NELLY, JAGGED EDGE AND AVERY STORM	1	2006
NASTY GIRLS T.W.A.	51	1995
NATALIE'S PARTY SHACK	63	1999
NATHAN JONES SUPREMES	5	1971
NATHAN JONES BANANARAMA	15	1988
NATIONAL EXPRESS DIVINE COMEDY	8	1999
NATIVE BOY (UPTOWN) ANIMAL NIGHTLIFE	60	1983
NATIVE LAND EVERYTHING BUT THE GIRL	73	1984
NATIVE NEW YORKER ODYSSEY	5	1978
NATIVE NEW YORKER BLACK BOX	46	1997
NATURAL [A] BRYAN POWELL	73	1993
NATURAL [B] PETER ANDRE	6	1997
NATURAL [C] S CLUB 7	3	2000
NATURAL BLUES MOBY	11	2000
NATURAL BORN BUGIE HUMBLE PIE	4	1969
NATURAL BORN KILLAZ DR DRE & ICE CUBE	45	1995
NATURAL HIGH [A] BLOODSTONE	40	1973
NATURAL HIGH [B] BITTY McLEAN	63	1996
NATURAL LIFE NATURAL LIFE	47	1992
NATURAL ONE FOLK IMPLOSION	45	1996
NATURAL SINNER FAIR WEATHER	6	1970
NATURAL THING INNOCENCE	16	1990
NATURAL WORLD RODEO JONES	75	1993
NATURE BOY [A] BOBBY DARIN	24	1961
NATURE BOY [A] GEORGE BENSON	26	1977
NATURE BOY [A] CENTRAL LINE	21	1983
NATURE BOY [B] NICK CAVE & THE BAD SEEDS	37	2004
NATURE OF LOVE WATERFRONT	63	1989
NATURE'S LAW EMBRACE	2	2006
NATURE'S TIME FOR LOVE JOE BROWN & THE BRUVVERS	26	1963
NAUGHTY CHRISTMAS (GOBLIN IN THE OFFICE) FAT LES	21	1998
NAUGHTY GIRL [A] HOLLY VALANCE	16	2002
NAUGHTY GIRL [B] BEYONCÉ	10	2004
NAUGHTY GIRLS SAMANTHA FOX FEATURING FULL FORCE	31	1988
NAUGHTY LADY OF SHADY LANE AMES BROTHERS	6	1955
NAUGHTY LADY OF SHADY LANE DEAN MARTIN	5	1955
NAUGHTY NAUGHTY JOHN PARR	58	1986
NAUGHTY NAUGHTY NAUGHTY JOY SARNEY	26	1977
THE NAUGHTY NORTH & THE SEXY SOUTH E-MOTION	17	1996
NAZIS ROGER TAYLOR	22	1994
NEANDERTHAL MAN HOTLEGS	2	1970
NEAR TO ME TEENAGE FANCLUB & JAD FAIR	68	2002
NEAR WILD HEAVEN R.E.M.	27	1991
NEAR YOU MIGIL FIVE	31	1964
NEARER THAN HEAVEN DELAYS	21	2004
NEARLY LOST YOU SCREAMING TREES	50	1993
NECESSARY EVIL BODY COUNT	45	1994
NEED GOOD LOVE TUFF JAM	44	1998
NEED TO FEEL LOVED REFLEKT FEATURING DELLINE BASS	14	2005
NEED YOU TONIGHT INXS	2	1987
NEED YOUR LOVE SO BAD FLEETWOOD MAC	31	1968
NEED YOUR LOVE SO BAD GARY MOORE	48	1995
NEEDIN' U DAVID MORALES PRESENTS THE FACE	8	1998
NEEDIN' YOU II DAVID MORALES PRESENTS THE FACE FEATURING JULIET ROBERTS	11	2001
THE NEEDLE AND THE DAMAGE DONE NEIL YOUNG	75	1993
NEEDLES AND PINS SEARCHERS	1	1964
NEEDLES AND PINS SMOKIE	10	1977
NEGASONIC TEENAGE WARHEAD MONSTER MAGNET	49	1995
NEGATIVE MANSUN	27	1998
NEGOTIATE WITH LOVE RACHEL STEVENS	10	2005
NEHEMIAH HOPE OF THE STATES	30	2004
NEIGHBOUR UGLY KID JOE	28	1992
NEIGHBOURHOOD #2 (LAIKA) ARCADE FIRE	30	2005
NEIGHBOURHOOD [A] SPACE	11	1996
NEIGHBOURHOOD [B] ZED BIAS	25	2000
NEIL JUNG TEENAGE FANCLUB	62	1995
NEITHER ONE OF US GLADYS KNIGHT & THE PIPS	31	1973
NELLIE THE ELEPHANT TOY DOLLS	4	1984
NELSON MANDELA SPECIAL A.K.A.	9	1984
NE-NE-NA-NA-NA-NA-NU-NU BAD MANNERS	28	1980
NEON KNIGHTS BLACK SABBATH	22	1980
NEON LIGHTS KRAFTWERK	53	1978
NEPTUNE INME	46	2003
NERVOUS MATT BIANCO	59	1989
NERVOUS BREAKDOWN [A] CARLEEN ANDERSON	27	1994
NERVOUS BREAKDOWN [B] SHRINK	42	1998
NERVOUS SHAKEDOWN AC/DC	35	1984
NERVOUS WRECK RADIO STARS	39	1978
NESSAJA SCOOTER	4	2002
NESSUN DORMA LUCIANNO PAVAROTTI	2	1990
NESSUN DORMA FROM 'TURANDOT' LUIS COBOS FEATURING PLACIDO DOMINGO	59	1990
NETHERWORLD LSG	63	1997
NEUROTICA CUD	37	1994
NEUTRON DANCE POINTER SISTERS	31	1985
NEVER [A] HEART	8	1988
NEVER [B] HOUSE OF LOVE	41	1989
NEVER [C] JOMANDA	40	1993
NEVER [D] ELECTRAFIXION	58	1995
NEVER 'AD NOTHIN' ANGELIC UPSTARTS	52	1979
NEVER AGAIN KELLY CLARKSON	9	2007
NEVER AGAIN [A] DISCHARGE	64	1981
NEVER AGAIN [B] MISSION	34	1992
NEVER AGAIN [C] JC 001	67	1993
NEVER AGAIN [D] HAPPY CLAPPERS	49	1996
NEVER AGAIN [E] NICKELBACK	30	2002
NEVER AGAIN (THE DAYS TIME ERASED) CLASSIX NOUVEAUX	44	1981
NEVER BE ANYONE ELSE BUT YOU RICKY NELSON	14	1959
NEVER BE LONELY THE FEELING	9	2006

Title / Artist	Peak Position	Year of Entry
NEVER BE THE SAME AGAIN MELANIE C & LISA LEFT EYE LOPES	1	2000
NEVER BEFORE DEEP PURPLE	35	1972
NEVER CAN SAY GOODBYE JACKSON 5	33	1971
NEVER CAN SAY GOODBYE GLORIA GAYNOR	2	1974
NEVER CAN SAY GOODBYE COMMUNARDS	4	1987
NEVER CAN SAY GOODBYE YAZZ	61	1997
NEVER CAN TELL I KAMANCHI	69	2003
NEVER DO A TANGO WITH AN ESKIMO ALMA COGAN	6	1955
NEVER DO YOU WRONG STEPHANIE MILLS	57	1993
NEVER DONE NOTHING LIKE THAT BEFORE SUPERGRASS	75	2002
NEVER ENDING HALO	56	2002
NEVER ENDING DREAM CASCADA	46	2007
NEVER ENDING SONG OF LOVE NEW SEEKERS	2	1971
NEVER ENDING STORY LIMAHL	4	1984
NEVER ENOUGH [A] JESUS JONES	42	1989
NEVER ENOUGH [B] CURE	13	1990
NEVER ENOUGH [C] BORIS DLUGOSCH FEATURING ROISIN MURPHY	16	2001
NEVER ENOUGH [D] OPEN	53	2004
NEVER EVER ALL SAINTS	1	1997
NEVER FELT LIKE THIS BEFORE SHAZNAY LEWIS	8	2004
NEVER FELT THIS WAY HI-LUX	58	1995
NEVER FORGET TAKE THAT	1	1995
NEVER FOUND A LOVE LIKE THIS BEFORE UPSIDE DOWN	19	1996
NEVER GIVE UP MONIE LOVE	41	1993
NEVER GIVE UP ON A GOOD THING GEORGE BENSON	14	1982
NEVER GIVE YOU UP SHARON REDD	20	1982
NEVER GOIN' DOWN ADAMSKI FEATURING JIMI POLO	51	1991
NEVER GOING NOWHERE BLUETONES	40	2003
NEVER GONNA BE THE SAME [A] DANNY WILSON	69	1989
NEVER GONNA BE THE SAME [B] SEAN PAUL	22	2006
NEVER GONNA CHANGE MY MIND JOEY LAWRENCE	49	1998
NEVER GONNA COME BACK DOWN BT	51	2001
NEVER GONNA CRY AGAIN EURYTHMICS	63	1981
NEVER GONNA FALL IN LOVE AGAIN DANA	31	1976
NEVER GONNA GIVE YOU UP [A] MUSICAL YOUTH	6	1983
NEVER GONNA GIVE YOU UP [B] RICK ASTLEY	1	1987
NEVER GONNA (GIVE YOU UP) [B] F.K.W.	48	1993
NEVER GONNA GIVE YOU UP (WON'T LET YOU BE) PATRICE RUSHEN	66	1981
NEVER GONNA LEAVE YOUR SIDE DANIEL BEDINGFIELD	1	2003
NEVER GONNA LET YOU GO [A] SERGIO MENDES	45	1983
NEVER GONNA LET YOU GO [B] TINA MOORE	7	1997
NEVER GOODBYE KARL DENVER	9	1962
NEVER HAD A DREAM COME TRUE [A] STEVIE WONDER	6	1970
NEVER HAD A DREAM COME TRUE [B] S CLUB 7	1	2000
NEVER HAD IT SO GOOD TAKE 5	34	1999
NEVER IN A MILLION YEARS BOOMTOWN RATS	62	1981
NEVER KNEW LOVE [A] RICK ASTLEY	70	1991
NEVER KNEW LOVE [B] OLETA ADAMS	22	1995
NEVER KNEW LOVE [C] NIGHTCRAWLERS	59	1999
NEVER KNEW LOVE [D] STELLA BROWNE	42	2002
NEVER KNEW LOVE LIKE THIS ALEXANDER O'NEAL FEATURING CHERRELLE	26	1988
NEVER KNEW LOVE LIKE THIS PAULINE HENRY FEATURING WAYNE MARSHALL	40	1996
NEVER KNEW LOVE LIKE THIS BEFORE STEPHANIE MILLS	4	1980
NEVER LEAVE YOU (UH OOOH UH OOOH) LUMIDEE	2	2003
NEVER LET GO [A] JOHN BARRY ORCHESTRA	49	1960
NEVER LET GO [B] HYPER GO GO	45	1993
NEVER LET GO [C] CLIFF RICHARD	32	1993
NEVER LET HER SLIP AWAY ANDREW GOLD	5	1978
NEVER LET HER SLIP AWAY TREVOR WALTERS	73	1984
NEVER LET HER SLIP AWAY UNDERCOVER	5	1992
NEVER LET ME DOWN DAVID BOWIE	34	1987
NEVER LET ME DOWN AGAIN DEPECHE MODE	22	1987
NEVER LET YOU DOWN HONEYZ	7	1999
NEVER LET YOU GO NKOTB	42	1994
NEVER LOOK BACK DUMONDE	36	2001
NEVER LOSE YOUR SENSE OF WONDER YETI	36	2005
NEVER LOST HIS HARDCORE NRG	59	1997
NEVER LOST THAT FEELING SWERVEDRIVER	62	1992
NEVER MEANT TO HURT YOU GOOD SHOES	34	2007
NEVER MIND CLIFF RICHARD	21	1959
NEVER MIND THE PRESENTS BARRON KNIGHTS	17	1980
NEVER MISS THE WATER CHAKA KHAN FEATURING ME'SHELL NDEGEOCELLO	59	1997
NEVER MY LOVE SUGAR MINOTT	52	1981
NEVER NEVER [A] ASSEMBLY	4	1983
NEVER NEVER [B] WARM JETS	37	1998
NEVER NEVER GONNA GIVE YA UP BARRY WHITE	14	1974
NEVER NEVER GONNA GIVE YOU UP LISA STANSFIELD	25	1997
NEVER NEVER LOVE SIMPLY RED	18	1996
NEVER NEVER NEVER SHIRLEY BASSEY	8	1973
NEVER ON SUNDAY CHAQUITO	50	1960
NEVER ON SUNDAY DON COSTA	27	1960
NEVER ON SUNDAY LYNN CORNELL	30	1960
NEVER ON SUNDAY MAKADOPOULOS & HIS GREEK SERENADERS	36	1960
NEVER ON SUNDAY MANUEL & HIS MUSIC OF THE MOUNTAINS	29	1960
NEVER (PAST TENSE) ROC PROFECT FEATURING TINA ARENA	42	2003
NEVER REALLY WAS MARIO WINANS FEATURING LIL' FLIP	44	2004
NEVER SAW A MIRACLE CURTIS STIGERS	34	1992
NEVER SAY DIE BLACK SABBATH	21	1978
NEVER SAY DIE (GIVE A LITTLE BIT MORE) CLIFF RICHARD	15	1983
NEVER SAY GOODBYE BON JOVI	21	1987
NEVER STOP [A] ECHO & THE BUNNYMEN	15	1983
NEVER STOP [B] BRAND NEW HEAVIES FEATURING N'DEA DAVENPORT	43	1991
NEVER SURRENDER SAXON	18	1981
NEVER TAKE ME ALIVE SPEAR OF DESTINY	14	1987
NEVER TEAR US APART INXS	24	1988
NEVER THERE CAKE	66	1999
NEVER TOO FAR MARIAH CAREY FEATURING MYSTIKAL	32	2002
NEVER TOO LATE KYLIE MINOGUE	4	1989
NEVER TOO MUCH LUTHER VANDROSS	13	1983
NEVER TRUST A STRANGER KIM WILDE	7	1988
NEVER TURN AWAY ORCHESTRAL MANOEUVRES IN THE DARK	70	1984
NEVER TURN YOUR BACK ON MOTHER EARTH SPARKS	13	1974
NEVER UNDERSTAND JESUS & MARY CHAIN	47	1985
NEVER WANNA SAY SOUNDBWOY ENT	18	2006
NEVER WENT TO CHURCH STREETS	20	2006
NEVER WIN FISCHERSPOONER	55	2005
NEVERTHELESS FRANKIE VAUGHAN	29	1968
NEVERTHELESS EVE GRAHAM & THE NEW SEEKERS	34	1973
NEW NO DOUBT	30	1999
NEW AMSTERDAM ELVIS COSTELLO & THE ATTRACTIONS	36	1980
NEW ANGER GARY NUMAN	46	1988
NEW BEGINNING [A] STEPHEN GATELY	3	2000
NEW BEGINNING [B] PRECIOUS	50	2000
NEW BEGINNING (MAMBA SEYRA) BUCKS FIZZ	8	1986
NEW BIRD REEF	73	1999
NEW BORN MUSE	12	2001
NEW DAWN PROPHETS OF SOUND	51	2002
A NEW DAY [A] KILLING JOKE	56	1984
NEW DAY [B] WYCLEF JEAN FEATURING BONO	23	1999
NEW DAY [C] SHAPESHIFTERS	72	2007
A NEW DAY HAS COME CELINE DION	7	2002
NEW DIMENSIONS IMAGINATION	56	1983
NEW DIRECTION [A] FREAKPOWER	60	1996
NEW DIRECTION [B] S CLUB JUNIORS	2	2002
NEW EMOTION TIME FREQUENCY	36	1993
A NEW ENGLAND KIRSTY MacCOLL	7	1985
A NEW FASHION BILL WYMAN	37	1982
A NEW FLAME SIMPLY RED	17	1989
NEW GENERATION SUEDE	21	1995
NEW GRANGE CLANNAD	65	1983
NEW GUITAR IN TOWN LURKERS	72	1979
NEW HOME NEW LIFE ALARM	45	2004
NEW HORIZON JOHN PARR VERSUS TOMMYKNOCKERS	43	2006
NEW IDEAS DYKEENIES	54	2007
NEW KICKS JOHANN	54	1996
NEW KID IN TOWN EAGLES	20	1977
NEW KIND OF MEDICINE ULTRA NATE	14	1998
NEW LIFE DEPECHE MODE	11	1981
NEW LIVE AND RARE EP DEEP PURPLE	31	1977
NEW LIVE AND RARE II (EP) DEEP PURPLE	45	1978
NEW LIVE AND RARE VOLUME 3 EP DEEP PURPLE	48	1980
NEW MISTAKE JELLYFISH	55	1993
NEW MOON ON MONDAY DURAN DURAN	9	1984
NEW ORLEANS U.S. BONDS	16	1961
NEW ORLEANS BERN ELLIOTT & THE FENMEN	24	1964
NEW ORLEANS HARLEY QUINNE	19	1972
NEW ORLEANS GILLAN	17	1981
NEW POLICY ONE TERRORVISION	42	1993
THE NEW POLLUTION BECK	14	1997
NEW POWER GENERATION PRINCE	26	1990
NEW SENSATION INXS	25	1988
NEW SHOES PAOLO NUTINI	21	2007
NEW SONG HOWARD JONES	3	1983
NEW SOUL YAEL NAIM	36	2008
A NEW SOUTH WALES ALARM FEATURING THE MORRISTON ORPHEUS MALE VOICE CHOIR	31	1989
NEW THING FROM LONDON TOWN SHARPE & NUMAN	52	1986
NEW TOY LENE LOVICH	53	1981
NEW WAY, NEW LIFE ASIAN DUB FOUNDATION	49	2000
NEW WORLD IN THE MORNING ROGER WHITTAKER	17	1970
NEW WORLD MAN RUSH	36	1982
NEW YEAR SUGABABES	12	2000
NEW YEARS DAY U2	10	1983
NEW YEARS DUB MUSIQUE VS U2	15	2001
NEW YORK AFTERNOON MONDO KANE	70	1986
NEW YORK CITY T REX	15	1975
NEW YORK CITY BOY PET SHOP BOYS	14	1999
NEW YORK CITY COPS STROKES	16	2001
NEW YORK EYES NICOLE WITH TIMMY THOMAS	41	1985
NEW YORK GROOVE HELLO	9	1975

	Peak Position	Year of Entry
NEW YORK MINING DISASTER 1941 BEE GEES	12	1967
NEW YORK, NEW YORK GERARD KENNY	43	1996
NEW YORK NEW YORK [B] RYAN ADAMS	53	2001
NEW YORK NEW YORK [C] MOBY FEATURING DEBBIE HARRY	43	2006
NEW YORK UNDERCOVER 4-TRACK EP VARIOUS ARTISTS (EP'S & LPS)	39	1978
NEWBORN ELBOW	42	2001
NEWBORN FRIEND SEAL	45	1994
THE NEWS CARBON/SILICON	59	2007
NEWS AT TEN VAPORS	44	1980
NEWS OF THE WORLD JAM	27	1978
NEXT BEST SUPERSTAR MELANIE C	10	2005
THE NEXT BIG THING JESUS JONES	49	1997
NEXT DOOR TO AN ANGEL NEIL SEDAKA	29	1962
THE NEXT EPISODE DR DRE FEATURING SNOOP DOGGY DOGG	3	2001
NEXT LEVEL ILS	75	2002
NEXT LIFETIME ERYKAH BADU	30	1997
THE NEXT TIME CLIFF RICHARD & THE SHADOWS	1	1962
NEXT TIME YOU FALL IN LOVE REVA RICE & GREG ELLIS	59	1993
NEXT TO YOU ASWAD	24	1990
NEXT YEAR FOO FIGHTERS	42	2000
NHS (EP) DJ DOC SCOTT	64	1992
NIALL QUINN'S DISCO PANTS A LOVE SUPREME	59	1999
NICE AND SLOW [A] JESSE GREEN	17	1976
NICE AND SLOW [B] USHER	24	1998
NICE GUY EDDIE SLEEPER	10	1996
NICE IN NICE STRANGLERS	30	1986
NICE LEGS SHAME ABOUT HER FACE MONKS	19	1979
NICE 'N' EASY FRANK SINATRA	15	1960
NICE 'N' SLEAZY STRANGLERS	18	1978
NICE 'N' SLOW FREDDIE JACKSON	56	1988
NICE ONE CYRIL COCKEREL CHORUS	14	1973
NICE WEATHER FOR DUCKS LEMON JELLY	16	2003
THE NIGHT [A] FRANKIE VALLI & THE FOUR SEASONS	7	1975
THE NIGHT [A] INTASTELLA	60	1995
THE NIGHT [A] SOFT CELL	39	2003
THE NIGHT [B] SCOOTER	16	2003
A NIGHT AT DADDY GEE'S SHOWADDYWADDY	39	1979
A NIGHT AT THE APOLLO LIVE! DARYL HALL & JOHN OATES FEATURING DAVID RUFFIN & EDDIE KENDRICK	58	1985
NIGHT BIRDS SHAKATAK	9	1982
NIGHT BOAT TO CAIRO MADNESS	56	1993
THE NIGHT CHICAGO DIED PAPER LACE	3	1974
NIGHT CRAWLER JUDAS PRIEST	63	1993
NIGHT DANCING JOE FARRELL	57	1978
THE NIGHT THE EARTH CRIED GRAVEDIGGAZ	44	1998
NIGHT FEVER [A] FATBACK BAND	38	1976
NIGHT FEVER [B] BEE GEES	1	1978
NIGHT FEVER [B] CAROL DOUGLAS	66	1978
NIGHT FEVER [B] ADAM GARCIA	15	1998
THE NIGHT FEVER MEGAMIX U.K. MIXMASTERS	23	1991
NIGHT GAMES GRAHAM BONNET	6	1981
THE NIGHT HAS A THOUSAND EYES BOBBY VEE	3	1963
NIGHT IN MOTION CUBIC 22	15	1991
NIGHT IN MY VEINS PRETENDERS	25	1994
A NIGHT IN NEW YORK ELBOW BONES & THE RACKETEERS	33	1984
THE NIGHT IS YOUNG GARY MILLER	29	1961
NIGHT LADIES CRUSADERS	55	1984
NIGHT LIFE DAVID LEE ROTH	72	1994
NIGHT LINE RANDY CRAWFORD	51	1983
NIGHT MOVES BOB SEGER & THE SILVER BULLET BAND	45	1995
NIGHT NURSE SLY & ROBBIE FEATURING SIMPLY RED	14	1997
NIGHT OF FEAR MOVE	2	1967
NIGHT OF THE LIVING BASEHEADS PUBLIC ENEMY	63	1988
NIGHT OF THE LONG GRASS TROGGS	17	1967
NIGHT OF THE VAMPIRE MOONTREKKERS	50	1961
NIGHT ON FIRE VHS OR BETA	69	2005
NIGHT OWL GERRY RAFFERTY	5	1979
NIGHT PORTER JAPAN	29	1982
THE NIGHT THEY DROVE OLD DIXIE DOWN JOAN BAEZ	6	1971
A NIGHT TO REMEMBER SHALAMAR	5	1982
NIGHT TO REMEMBER 911	38	1996
A NIGHT TO REMEMBER LIBERTY X	6	2005
NIGHT TRAIN [A] BUDDY MORROW	12	1953
NIGHT TRAIN [B] VISAGE	12	1982
NIGHT VISION HELL IS FOR HEROES	38	2002
THE NIGHT THE WINE THE ROSES LIQUID GOLD	32	1980
THE NIGHT YOU MURDERED LOVE ABC	31	1987
NIGHTBIRD CONVERT	39	1992
THE NIGHTFLY BLANK & JONES	55	2000
NIGHTLIFE KENICKIE	27	1997
NIGHTMARE [A] GILLAN	36	1981
NIGHTMARE [B] SAXON	50	1983
NIGHTMARE [C] KID UNKNOWN	64	1992
NIGHTMARE [D] BRAINBUG	11	1997
NIGHTMARES A FLOCK OF SEAGULLS	53	1983
NIGHTRAIN GUNS N' ROSES	17	1988
NIGHTS IN WHITE SATIN MOODY BLUES	9	1969
NIGHTS IN WHITE SATIN DICKIES	39	1979
NIGHTS IN WHITE SATIN ELKIE BROOKS	33	1982
NIGHTS OF PLEASURE LOOSE ENDS	42	1986
NIGHTS ON BROADWAY CANDI STATON	6	1977
NIGHTS OVER EGYPT INCOGNITO	56	1999
NIGHTSHIFT COMMODORES	3	1985
NIGHTSWIMMING R.E.M.	27	1993
NIGHTTRAIN [A] PUBLIC ENEMY	55	1992
THE NIGHTTRAIN [B] KADOC	14	1996
NIKITA ELTON JOHN	3	1985
NIKKE DOES IT BETTER NIKKE? NICOLE!	73	1991
NIMBUS 808 STATE	59	1992
NINE FORWARD, RUSSIA!	40	2006
9 A.M. (THE COMFORT ZONE) LONDONBEAT	19	1988
9 CRIMES DAMIEN RICE	29	2006
911 WYCLEF FEATURING MARY J BLIGE	9	2000
911 IS A JOKE PUBLIC ENEMY	41	1990
900 DEGREES IAN POOLEY	57	2001
NINE IN THE AFTERNOON PANIC! AT THE DISCO	13	2008
NINE MILLION BICYCLES KATIE MELUA	5	2005
9PM (TILL I COME) ATB	1	1999
977 PRETENDERS	66	1994
NINE TIMES OUT OF TEN CLIFF RICHARD & THE SHADOWS	3	1960
9 TO 5 [A] SHEENA EASTON	3	1980
9 TO 5 [B] DOLLY PARTON	47	1981
9 TO 5 [C] LADY SOVEREIGN	33	2005
NINE 2FIVE [D] ORDINARY BOYS FEATURING LADY SOVEREIGN	6	2006
NINE WAYS JDS	47	1997
19 [A] PAUL HARDCASTLE	1	1985
NINETEEN [B] FORWARD, RUSSIA!	67	2006
1985 BOWLING FOR SOUP	35	2004
1980 ESTELLE	14	2004
1999 [A] PRINCE & THE REVOLUTION	2	1983
1999 [B] BINARY FINARY	11	1998
1979 SMASHING PUMPKINS	16	1996
1973 JAMES BLUNT	4	2007
NINETEEN63 NEW ORDER	21	1995
1962 GRASS-SHOW	53	1997
19/2000 GORILLAZ	6	2001
NINETEENTH NERVOUS BREAKDOWN ROLLING STONES	2	1966
90S GIRL BLACKGIRL	23	1994
98.6 BYSTANDERS	45	1967
98.6 KEITH	24	1967
95 - NASTY W.A.S.P.	70	1986
99.5 CAROL LYNN TOWNES	47	1984
99.9O F SUZANNE VEGA	46	1992
99 PROBLEMS JAY-Z	12	2004
99 RED BALLOONS NENA	1	1984
96 TEARS ? (QUESTION MARK) & THE MYSTERIANS	37	1966
96 TEARS STRANGLERS	17	1990
92 DEGREES POP WILL EAT ITSELF	23	1990
92 TOUR (EP) MOTORHEAD	63	1992
NINETY-NINE WAYS TAB HUNTER	5	1957
NIPPLE TO THE BOTTLE GRACE JONES	50	1982
NITE AND DAY AL B SURE!	44	1988
NITE AND FOG MERCURY REV	47	2001
NITE CLUB SPECIALS (FEATURING RICO)	10	1979
NITE LIFE KIM ENGLISH	35	1994
NITE NITE KANO FEATURING MIKE SKINNER & LEO THE LION	25	2005
NI-TEN-ICHI-RYU (TWO SWORDS TECHNIQUE) PHOTEK	37	1997
NITRO PALE X	74	2001
N-N-NINETEEN NOT OUT COMMENTATORS	13	1985
NO CHUCK D	55	1996
NO ALIBIS ERIC CLAPTON	53	1990
NO ARMS CAN EVER HOLD YOU BACHELORS	7	1964
NO BIG DEAL OVERCAST & BECKY MEASURES	67	2007
NO BLUE SKIES LLOYD COLE	42	1990
NO CHANCE (NO CHARGE) BILLY CONNOLLY	24	1976
NO CHARGE J.J. BARRIE	1	1976
NO CHEAP THRILL SUZANNE VEGA	40	1997
NO CHRISTMAS WEDDING PRESENT	25	1992
NO CLASS MOTORHEAD	61	1979
NO CLAUSE 28 BOY GEORGE	57	1988
NO CONVERSATION VIEW FROM THE HILL	58	1986
NO DIGGITY BLACKstreet FEATURING DR DRE	9	1996
NO DISTANCE LEFT TO RUN BLUR	14	1999
NO DOUBT [A] 702	59	1997
NO DOUBT [B] IMAJIN	42	1999
NO DOUBT ABOUT IT HOT CHOCOLATE	2	1980
NO DREAM IMPOSSIBLE LINDSAY	32	2001
NO EDUCATION NO FUTURE (F**K THE CURFEW) MOGWAI	68	1998
NO EMOTION IDLEWILD	36	2007
NO ESCAPIN' THIS BEATNUTS	47	2001
NO FACE, NO NAME, NO NUMBER TRAFFIC	40	1968
NO FEAR RASMUS	43	2005
NO FLOW LISA ROXANNE	18	2001
NO FOOL (FOR LOVE) HAZELL DEAN	41	1985
NO FRONTS DOG EAT DOG	9	1995
NO GETTING OVER YOU PARIS	49	1982
NO GOOD DA FOOL	38	1999
NO GOOD ADVICE GIRLS ALOUD	2	2003
NO GOOD FOR ME [A] BRUCE WAYNE	70	1998
NO GOOD 4 ME [B] OXIDE & NEUTRINO FEATURING MEGAMAN	6	2000
NO GOOD (START THE DANCE) PRODIGY	4	1994
NO GOODBYES [A] CURTIS MAYFIELD	65	1978
NO GOODBYES [B] SUBWAYS	27	2005
NO GOVERNMENT NICOLETTE	67	1995
NO HIDING PLACE KEN MACKINTOSH	45	1960
NO HONESTLY LYNSEY DE PAUL	7	1974
NO LAUGHING IN HEAVEN GILLAN	31	1981
NO LETTING GO WAYNE WONDER	3	2003
NO LIES S.O.S. BAND	64	1987
NO LIMIT 2 UNLIMITED	1	1993
NO LIMITS BAKSHELF DOG	51	2002

Title / Artist	Peak Position	Year of Entry
NO LOVE JOAN ARMATRADING	50	1982
NO MAN'S LAND [A] GERARD KENNY	56	1985
NO MAN'S LAND [B] BILLY JOEL	50	1994
NO MAN'S LAND [C] BEVERLEY KNIGHT	43	2007
(NO MATTER HOW HIGH I GET) I'LL STILL BE LOOKIN' UP TO YOU WILTON FELDER FEATURING BOBBY WOMACK & INTRODUCING ALLTRINA GRAYSON	63	1985
NO MATTER HOW I TRY GILBERT O'SULLIVAN	5	1971
NO MATTER WHAT [A] BADFINGER	5	1971
NO MATTER WHAT [B] BOYZONE	1	1998
NO MATTER WHAT I DO WILL MELLOR	23	1998
NO MATTER WHAT SIGN YOU ARE DIANA ROSS & THE SUPREMES	37	1969
NO MATTER WHAT THEY SAY LIL' KIM	35	2000
NO MATTER WHAT YOU DO BENNY BENASSI PRESENTS THE BIZ	40	2004
NO MEMORY SCARLET FANTASTIC	24	1987
NO MERCY STRANGLERS	37	1984
NO MILK TODAY HERMAN'S HERMITS	7	1966
NO MORE [A] McGUIRE SISTERS	20	1955
NO MORE [B] UNIQUE 3	74	1991
NO MORE [C] RUFF ENDZ	11	2000
NO MORE [D] A1	6	2001
NO MORE [E] RONI SIZE FEATURING BEVERLEY KNIGHT	26	2005
NO MORE [F] JAMELIA	43	2007
NO MORE AFFAIRS TINDERSTICKS	58	1995
NO MORE ALCOHOL SUGGS FEATURING LOUCHIE LOU & MICHIE ONE	24	1996
NO MORE (BABY I'MA DO RIGHT) 3LW	6	2001
NO MORE DRAMA MARY J BLIGE	9	2002
NO MORE HEROES STRANGLERS	8	1977
NO MORE (I CAN'T STAND IT) MAXX	8	1994
NO MORE 'I LOVE YOU'S LOVER SPEAKS	58	1986
NO MORE 'I LOVE YOUS' ANNIE LENNOX	2	1995
NO MORE LIES SHARPE & NUMAN	34	1988
NO MORE LONELY NIGHTS (BALLAD) PAUL McCARTNEY	2	1984
(NO MORE) LOVE AT YOUR CONVENIENCE ALICE COOPER	44	1977
NO MORE MR. NICE GUY ALICE COOPER	10	1973
NO MORE MR. NICE GUY MEGADETH	13	1990
NO MORE RAINY DAYS FREE SPIRIT	68	1995
NO MORE RUNNING AWAY AIR TRAFFIC	45	2007
NO MORE TALK DUBSTAR	20	1997
NO MORE TEARS [A] HOLLYWOOD BEYOND	47	1986
NO MORE TEARS [B] JAKI GRAHAM	60	1988
NO MORE TEARS [C] OZZY OSBOURNE	32	1991
NO MORE TEARS (ENOUGH IS ENOUGH) DONNA SUMMER & BARBRA STREISAND	3	1979
NO MORE TEARS (ENOUGH IS ENOUGH) KYM MAZELLE & JOCELYN BROWN	13	1994
NO MORE THE FOOL ELKIE BROOKS	5	1986
NO MORE TOMORROWS PAUL JOHNSON	67	1989
NO MORE TURNING BACK GITTA	54	2000
NO MULE'S FOOL FAMILY	29	1969
NO NEED ALFIE	66	2004
NO NO JOE SILVER CONVENTION	41	1976
NO NO NO [A] NANCY NOVA	63	1982
NO NO NO [B] DESTINY'S CHILD FEATURING WYCLEF JEAN	5	1998
NO NO NO [C] MANIJAMA FEATURING MUKUPA & LIL'T	66	2003
NO, NOT NOW HOT HOT HEAT	38	2003
NO ONE [A] RAY CHARLES	35	1963
NO ONE [B] 2 UNLIMITED	17	1994
NO ONE [C] ALICIA KEYS	6	2007
NO ONE BUT YOU BILLY ECKSTINE	3	1954
NO ONE CAN MARILLION	26	1991
NO ONE CAN BREAK A HEART LIKE YOU DAVE CLARK FIVE	28	1968
NO ONE CAN LOVE YOU MORE THAN ME KYM MAZELLE	62	1991
NO ONE CAN MAKE MY SUNSHINE SMILE EVERLY BROTHERS	11	1962
NO ONE CAN STOP US NOW CHELSEA F.C.	23	1994
NO ONE ELSE COMES CLOSE JOE	41	1998
NO ONE GETS THE PRIZE DIANA ROSS	59	1979
NO ONE IS INNOCENT SEX PISTOLS, PUNK PRAYER BY RONALD BIGGS	7	1978
NO ONE IS TO BLAME HOWARD JONES	16	1986
NO ONE KNOWS QUEENS OF THE STONE AGE	15	2002
NO ONE KNOWS MARK RONSON	66	2007
NO ONE LIKE YOU SCORPIONS	64	1982
NO ONE SPEAKS GENEVA	32	1996
NO ONE TO CRY TO RAY CHARLES	38	1964
NO ONE WILL EVER KNOW FRANK IFIELD	25	1966
NO ONE'S DRIVING DAVE CLARKE	37	1996
NO ORDINARY LOVE SADE	14	1992
NO ORDINARY MORNING/HALCYON CHICANE	28	2000
NO OTHER BABY BOBBY HELMS	30	1958
NO OTHER BABY PAUL McCARTNEY	42	1999
NO OTHER LOVE EDMUND HOCKRIDGE	24	1956
NO OTHER LOVE JOHNSTON BROTHERS	22	1956
NO OTHER LOVE RONNIE HILTON	1	1956
NO PANTIES TRINA	45	2002
NO PARTICULAR PLACE TO GO CHUCK BERRY	3	1964
NO PIGEONS SPORTY THIEVZ	21	1999
NO PLACE TO HIDE KORN	26	1996
NO PROMISES [A] ICEHOUSE	72	1986
NO PROMISES [B] SHAYNE WARD	2	2006
NO PUSSY BLUES GRINDERMAN	64	2007
NO RAIN BLIND MELON	17	1993
NO REGRETS [A] SHIRLEY BASSEY	39	1965
NO REGRETS [B] WALKER BROTHERS	7	1976
NO REGRETS [B] MIDGE URE	9	1982
NO REGRETS [C] ROBBIE WILLIAMS	4	1998
NO RELIGION VAN MORRISON	54	1995
NO REST NEW MODEL ARMY	28	1985
NO SCRUBS TLC	3	1999
NO SELF CONTROL PETER GABRIEL	33	1980
NO SELL OUT MALCOLM X	60	1984
NO SLEEP NO NEED EP VAULTS	70	2004
NO SLEEP TO BROOKLYN BEASTIE BOYS	14	1987
NO SLEEP TONIGHT FADERS	13	2005
NO SON OF MINE GENESIS	6	1991
NO STONE UNTURNED TRUTH	66	1984
NO STRESS CYCLEFLY	68	2002
NO SUCH THING JOHN MAYER	42	2003
NO SURPRISES RADIOHEAD	4	1998
NO SURRENDER DEUCE	29	1996
NO SURVIVORS GBH	63	1982
NO SWEAT '98 NORTH & SOUTH	29	1998
NO TENGO DINERO LOS UMERELLOS	33	1998
NO TIME LIL' KIM FEATURING PUFF DADDY	45	1997
NO TIME TO BE 21 ADVERTS	34	1978
NO TIME TO CRY SISTERS OF MERCY	63	1985
NO TIME TO PLAY GURU FEATURING D C LEE	25	1993
NO TOMORROW ORSON	1	2006
NO TREND KOOPA	71	2005
NO U HANG UP/IF THAT'S OKAY WITH YOU SHAYNE WARD	2	2007
NO WAY FREAKPOWER	29	1998
NO WAY BACK FOO FIGHTERS	64	2006
NO WAY NO WAY VANILLA	14	1997
NO WAY OUT FRANCESCO ZAPPALA	69	1992
NO WOMAN NO CRY BOB MARLEY & THE WAILERS	8	1975
NO WOMAN NO CRY LONDONBEAT	64	1991
NO WOMAN NO CRY FUGEES	2	1996
NO WORRIES SIMON WEBBE	4	2005
NO WOW KILLS	53	2005
THE NOBODIES MARILYN MANSON	34	2001
NOBODY [A] TONI BASIL	52	1982
NOBODY [B] TONGUE 'N' CHEEK	59	1990
NOBODY [C] SHARA NELSON	49	1994
NOBODY [D] KEITH SWEAT FEATURING ATHENA CAGE	30	1997
NOBODY BETTER TINA MOORE	20	1998
NOBODY BUT YOU GLADYS KNIGHT & THE PIPS	34	1977
NOBODY (CAN LOVE ME) TONGUE IN CHEEK	41	1988
NOBODY DOES IT BETTER CARLY SIMON	7	1977
NOBODY ELSE [A] NICK KAMEN	47	1987
NOBODY ELSE [B] TYRESE	59	1999
NOBODY I KNOW PETER & GORDON	10	1964
NOBODY KNOWS [A] NIK KERSHAW	44	1986
NOBODY KNOWS [B] TONY RICH PROJECT	4	1996
NOBODY KNOWS [C] P!NK	27	2006
NOBODY MADE ME RANDY EDELMAN	60	1982
NOBODY MOVE NOBODY GET HURT WE ARE SCIENTISTS	21	2005
NOBODY NEEDS YOUR LOVE GENE PITNEY	2	1966
NOBODY TOLD ME JOHN LENNON	6	1984
NOBODY WANTS TO BE LONELY RICKY MARTIN WITH CHRISTINA AGUILERA	4	2001
NOBODY WINS ELTON JOHN	42	1981
NOBODY'S BUSINESS [A] H20 FEATURING BILLIE	19	1996
NOBODY'S BUSINESS [B] PEACE BY PIECE	50	1998
NOBODY'S CHILD KAREN YOUNG	6	1969
NOBODY'S CHILD TRAVELING WILBURYS	44	1990
NOBODY'S DARLIN' BUT MINE FRANK IFIELD	4	1963
NOBODY'S DIARY YAZOO	3	1983
NOBODY'S FOOL [A] JIM REEVES	32	1970
NOBODY'S FOOL [B] HAIRCUT 100	9	1982
NOBODY'S HERO STIFF LITTLE FINGERS	36	1980
NOBODY'S HOME AVRIL LAVIGNE	24	2004
NOBODY'S SUPPOSED TO BE HERE DEBORAH COX	55	1999
NOBODY'S TWISTING YOUR ARM WEDDING PRESENT	46	1988
NOCTURNE T99	33	1991
NOMANSLAND (DAVID'S SONG) DJ SAKIN & FRIENDS	14	1999
NOMZAMO (ONE PEOPLE ONE CAUSE) LATIN QUARTER	73	1987
NON HO L'ETA PER AMARTI GIGLIOLA CINQUETTI	17	1964
NON STOP WHITEY	67	2005
NONE OF YOUR BUSINESS SALT-N-PEPA	19	1994
(NONSTOPOPERATION) DUST JUNKYS	47	1997
NOOKIE JAMESY P	14	2005
NO-ONE BUT YOU [B] QUEEN	13	1998
NO-ONE DRIVING (DOUBLE SINGLE) JOHN FOXX	32	1980
NORA MALONE TERESA BREWER	26	1957
NORMAN CAROL DEENE	24	1962
NORMAN BATES LANDSCAPE	40	1981
NORMAN 3 TEENAGE FANCLUB	50	1993
NORTH AMERICAN SCUM LCD SOUNDSYSTEM	40	2007
NORTH COUNTRY BOY CHARLATANS	4	1997
NORTH, SOUTH, EAST, WEST MARVIN & TAMARA	38	2000
NORTH TO ALASKA JOHNNY HORTON	23	1961
NORTHERN LIGHTS [A] RENAISSANCE	10	1978
NORTHERN LITES [B] SUPER FURRY ANIMALS	11	1999
NORTHERN STAR MELANIE C	4	1999
NOT A DRY EYE IN THE HOUSE MEAT LOAF	7	1996
NOT A JOB ELBOW	26	2004
NOT A MINUTE TOO SOON VIXEN	37	1991
NOT ABOUT US GENESIS	66	1998
NOT ALONE BERNARD BUTLER	27	1998
NOT ANYONE BLACK BOX	31	1995

	Peak Position	Year of Entry
NOT AS A STRANGER FRANK SINATRA	18	1955
NOT AT ALL STATUS QUO	50	1989
NOT ENOUGH MELANIE WILLIAMS	65	1994
NOT ENOUGH LOVE IN THE WORLD CHER	31	1996
NOT EVEN GONNA TRIP HONEYZ	24	2000
NOT EVERYONE NINE BLACK ALPS	31	2005
NOT FADE AWAY ROLLING STONES	3	1964
NOT FOR ALL THE LOVE IN THE WORLD THRILLS	39	2004
NOT FOR YOU PEARL JAM	34	1995
NOT GON' CRY MARY J BLIGE	39	1996
NOT GONNA GET US tATu	7	2003
NOT IF YOU WERE THE LAST JUNKIE ON EARTH DANDY WARHOLS	13	1998
NOT IN LOVE ENRIQUE FEATURING KELIS	5	2004
NOT ME NOT I DELTA GOODREM	18	2003
NOT NOW BLINK 182	30	2005
NOT NOW JOHN PINK FLOYD	30	1983
NOT OVER YET GRACE	6	1995
NOT OVER YOU YET DIANA ROSS	9	1999
NOT READY TO MAKE NICE DIXIE CHICKS	70	2006
NOT RESPONSIBLE TOM JONES	18	1966
NOT SLEEPING AROUND NED'S ATOMIC DUSTBIN	19	1992
NOT SO MANIC NOW DUBSTAR	18	1996
NOT SUCH AN INNOCENT GIRL VICTORIA BECKHAM	6	2001
NOT THAT KIND ANASTACIA	11	2001
NOT THE GIRL YOU THINK YOU ARE CROWDED HOUSE	20	1996
(NOT THE) GREATEST RAPPER 1000 CLOWNS	23	1999
NOT TODAY MARY J BLIGE FEATURING EVE	40	2003
NOT TONIGHT LIL' KIM	11	1997
NOT TOO LATE FOR LOVE BEVERLEY KNIGHT	31	2004
NOT TOO LITTLE NOT TOO MUCH CHRIS SANDFORD	17	1963
NOT UNTIL NEXT TIME JIM REEVES	13	1965
NOT WHERE IT'S AT DEL AMITRI	21	1997
NOTGONNACHANGE SWING OUT SISTER	49	1992
NOTHIN' NORE	11	2002
NOTHIN' AT ALL HEART	38	1988
NOTHIN' BETTER TO DO LeANN RIMES	48	2007
NOTHIN' BUT A GOOD TIME POISON	35	1988
NOTHIN' BUT A PARTY TRUCE	71	1997
NOTHIN' MY LOVE CAN'T FIX JOEY LAWRENCE	13	1993
NOTHIN' PERSONAL DUST JUNKYS	62	1998
(NOTHIN' SERIOUS) JUST BUGGIN' WHISTLE	7	1986
NOTHIN' (THAT COMPARES 2 U) JACKSONS	33	1989
NOTHIN' TO DO MICHAEL HOLLIDAY	20	1956
NOTHING [A] FRAZIER CHORUS	51	1990
NOTHING [B] FLUFFY	52	1996
NOTHING [C] A	9	2002
NOTHING [D] HOLDEN & THOMPSON	51	2003
NOTHING AS IT SEEMS PEARL JAM	22	2000
NOTHING AT ALL LUKE SLATER	70	2002
NOTHING 'BOUT ME STING	32	1994
NOTHING BUT GREEN LIGHTS TOM VEK	59	2005
NOTHING BUT LOVE OPTIMYSTIC	37	1994
NOTHING BUT YOU PAUL VAN DYK FEATURING HEMSTOCK	14	2003
NOTHING CAN CHANGE THIS LOVE BITTY McLEAN	55	1995
NOTHING CAN DIVIDE US JASON DONOVAN	5	1988
NOTHING CAN STOP ME GENE CHANDLER	41	1968
NOTHING CAN STOP US SAINT ETIENNE	54	1991
NOTHING CHANGES AROUND HERE THRILLS	40	2007
NOTHING COMES EASY SANDIE SHAW	14	1966
NOTHING COMPARES 2 U MXM	68	1990
NOTHING COMPARES 2 U SINEAD O'CONNOR	1	1990
NOTHING ELSE MATTERS METALLICA	6	1992
NOTHING EVER HAPPENS DEL AMITRI	11	1990
NOTHING FAILS MADONNA	11	2003
NOTHING HAS BEEN PROVED DUSTY SPRINGFIELD	16	1989
NOTHING HAS BEEN PROVED STRINGS OF LOVE	59	1990
NOTHING HURTS LIKE LOVE DANIEL BEDINGFIELD	3	2004
NOTHING IN MY WAY KEANE	19	2006
NOTHING IN PARTICULAR BROTHERHOOD	55	1996
NOTHING IN THIS WORLD PARIS HILTON	55	2006
NOTHING IS FOREVER ULTRACYNIC	47	1992
NOTHING IS REAL BUT THE GIRL BLONDIE	26	1999
NOTHING LASTS FOREVER ECHO & THE BUNNYMEN	8	1997
NOTHING LEFT ORBITAL	32	1999
NOTHING LEFT TOULOUSE SAD CAFE	62	1980
NOTHING LESS THAN BRILLIANT SANDIE SHAW	66	1994
NOTHING NATURAL LUSH	43	1991
NOTHING REALLY MATTERS MADONNA	7	1999
NOTHING RHYMED GILBERT O'SULLIVAN	8	1970
NOTHING SACRED - A SONG FOR KIRSTY RUSSELL WATSON	17	2002
NOTHING TO DECLARE LAPTOP	74	1999
NOTHING TO FEAR CHRIS REA	16	1992
NOTHING TO LOSE [A] UK	67	1979
NOTHING TO LOSE [B] S-EXPRESS	32	1990
NOTHING WITHOUT ME MANCHILD	40	2001
NOTHING WRONG WITH YOU FINN BROTHERS	31	2004
NOTHING'S GONNA CHANGE MY LOVE FOR YOU GLENN MEDEIROS	1	1988
NOTHING'S GONNA CHANGE YOUR MIND BADLY DRAWN BOY	38	2006
NOTHING'S GONNA STOP ME NOW SAMANTHA FOX	8	1987
NOTHING'S GONNA STOP US NOW STARSHIP	1	1987
NOTHIN'S GONNA CHANGE LABI SIFFRE	52	1987
NOTORIOUS DURAN DURAN	7	1986
NOTORIOUS B.I.G. NOTORIOUS B.I.G. FEATURING PUFF DADDY	16	2000
NOVELTY WAVES BIOSPHERE	51	1995
NOVEMBER RAIN GUNS N' ROSES	4	1992
NOVEMBER SPAWNED A MONSTER MORRISSEY	12	1990
NOVOCAINE FOR THE SOUL EELS	10	1997
NOW [A] AL MARTINO	3	1953
NOW [B] VAL DOONICAN	43	1968
NOW [C] DEF LEPPARD	23	2002
NOW ALWAYS AND FOREVER GAY DAD	41	2001
NOW AND FOREVER RICHARD MARX	13	1994
NOW I KNOW WHAT MADE OTIS BLUE PAUL YOUNG	14	1993
NOW I'M HERE QUEEN	11	1975
NOW IS THE TIME JIMMY JAMES & THE VAGABONDS	5	1976
NOW IS TOMORROW DEFINITION OF SOUND	46	1991
NOW IT'S GONE CHORDS	63	1979
NOW IT'S ON GRANDADDY	23	2003
NOW I'VE FOUND YOU SEAN MAGUIRE	22	1995
NOW OR NEVER TOM NOVY FEATURING LIMA	64	2001
NOW THAT I OWN THE BBC SPARKS	60	1996
NOW THAT THE MAGIC HAS GONE JOE COCKER	28	1992
NOW THAT WE FOUND LOVE HEAVY D. & THE BOYZ	2	1991
NOW THAT WE'VE FOUND LOVE THIRD WORLD	10	1978
NOW THAT YOU GOT IT GWEN STEFANI	59	2007
NOW THAT YOU LOVE ME ALICE BAND	44	2002
NOW THAT YOU'VE GONE MIKE + THE MECHANICS	35	1999
NOW THEY'LL SLEEP BELLY	28	1995
NOW THOSE DAYS ARE GONE BUCKS FIZZ	8	1982
NOW WE ARE FREE GLADIATOR FEATURING IZZY	19	2004
NOW WE'RE THRU POETS	31	1964
NOW YOU'RE GONE [A] BLACK	66	1989
NOW YOU'RE GONE [B] WHITESNAKE	31	1990
NOW YOU'RE GONE [C] BASSHUNTER FEATURING DJ MENTAL THEOS	1	2008
NOW YOU'RE IN HEAVEN JULIAN LENNON	59	1989
NOWHERE [A] THERAPY?	18	1994
NOWHERE [B] LONGVIEW	72	2003
NOWHERE AGAIN SECRET MACHINES	49	2004
NOWHERE FAST MEAT LOAF	67	1984
NOWHERE GIRL B-MOVIE	67	1982
NOWHERE LAND CLUBHOUSE FEATURING CARL	56	1995
NOWHERE MAN THREE GOOD REASONS	47	1966
NOWHERE TO RUN MARTHA REEVES & THE VANDELLAS	26	1962
NOWHERE TO RUN 2000 NU GENERATION	66	2000
N-R-G ADAMSKI	12	1990
NU FLOW BIG BROVAZ	3	2002
NUCLEAR RYAN ADAMS	37	2002
NUCLEAR DEVICE (THE WIZARD OF AUS) STRANGLERS	36	1979
NUCLEAR HOLIDAY 3 COLOURS RED	22	1997
NUFF VIBES EP APACHE INDIAN	5	1993
NUMB [A] LINKIN PARK	14	2003
NUMB [B] PET SHOP BOYS	23	2006
NUMB/ENCORE JAY-Z VS LINKIN PARK	14	2004
#9 DREAM JOHN LENNON	23	1975
THE NUMBER OF THE BEAST IRON MAIDEN	3	1982
NUMBER ONE [A] E.Y.C.	27	1994
NUMBER ONE [B] A	47	1998
NUMBER 1 [C] TWEENIES	5	2000
NUMBER ONE [D] PLAYGROUP	66	2001
NUMBER 1 [E] EBONY DUBSTERS	58	2004
NUMBER ONE [F] JOHN LEGEND	62	2005
NUMBER 1 [G] GOLDFRAPP	9	2005
NUMBER ONE [H] PHARRELL FEATURING KANYE WEST	31	2006
NUMBER ONE BLIND VERUCA SALT	68	1995
NUMBER ONE DEE JAY GOODY GOODY	55	1978
NUMBER ONE DOMINATOR TOP	67	1991
NO. 1 RAT FAN ROLAND RAT SUPERSTAR	72	1985
THE NUMBER ONE SONG IN HEAVEN SPARKS	14	1979
NUMBER ONE SPOT LUDACRIS	30	2005
NUMBERS SOFT CELL	25	1983
NUMERO UNO STARLIGHT	9	1989
NUNC DIMITTIS PAUL PHEONIX	56	1979
NURSERY RHYMES ICEBERG SLIMM	37	2000
NURTURE LFO	47	1991
NUT ROCKER B. BUMBLE & THE STINGERS	1	1962
NUTBUSH CITY LIMITS IKE & TINA TURNER	4	1973
NUTBUSH CITY LIMITS TINA TURNER	23	1991
NUTHIN' BUT A 'G' THANG DR DRE	31	1994
NW5 MADNESS	24	2008
N.WO MINISTRY	49	1992
NYC BEAT ARMAND VAN HELDEN	22	2007
N.Y.C. (CAN YOU BELIEVE THIS CITY) CHARLES & EDDIE	33	1993
NYC (THERE'S NO NEED TO STOP) CHARLATANS	53	2006

O

	Peak Position	Year of Entry
O OMARION	47	2005
O BABY SIOUXSIE & THE BANSHEES	34	1995

	Peak Position	Year of Entry
O L'AMOUR DOLLAR	7	1988
O' MY FATHER HAD A RABBIT RAY MOORE	24	1986
O SUPERMAN LAURIE ANDERSON	2	1981
03 BONNIE AND CLYDE JAY-Z FEATURING BEYONCE KNOWLES	2	2003
OAKLAND STROKE TONY! TONI! TONE!	50	1990
OBJECT OF MY DESIRE DANA RAYNE	7	2005
OBJECTION (TANGO) SHAKIRA	17	2002
OBJECTS IN THE REAR VIEW MIRROR MAY APPEAR CLOSER THAN THEY ARE MEAT LOAF	26	1994
OB-LA-DI OB-LA-DA BEDROCKS	20	1968
OB-LA-DI OB-LA-DA MARMALADE	1	1968
OBLIVION TERRORVISION	21	1994
OBLIVION (HEAD IN THE CLOUDS) (EP) MANIX	43	1992
OBLIVIOUS AZTEC CAMERA	18	1983
THE OBOE SONG CLERGY	50	2002
OBSESSED 999	71	1981
OBSESSION [A] REG OWEN	43	1960
OBSESSION [B] ANIMOTION	5	1985
OBSESSION [C] ARMY OF LOVERS	67	1991
OBSESSION [D] ULTRA-SONIC	75	1994
OBSESSION [E] TIESTO & JUNKIE XL	56	2002
OBSESSION (NO ES AMOR) FRANKIE J	38	2005
OBSESSION (SI ES AMOR) 3RD WISH	15	2004
OBSESSIONS SUEDE	29	2002
OBSTACLE 1 INTERPOL	41	2002
OBVIOUS WESTLIFE	3	2004
THE OBVIOUS CHILD PAUL SIMON	15	1990
OBVIOUSLY McFLY	1	2004
OCEAN AVENUE YELLOWCARD	65	2004
OCEAN BLUE ABC	51	1986
OCEAN DEEP CLIFF RICHARD	27	1984
OCEAN DRIVE LIGHTHOUSE FAMILY	11	1995
OCEAN OF ETERNITY FUTURE BREEZE	46	2002
OCEAN PIE SHED SEVEN	33	1994
OCEAN SPRAY MANIC STREET PREACHERS	15	2001
OCTOBER SWIMMER JJ72	29	2000
ODE TO BILLY JOE BOBBIE GENTRY	13	1967
ODE TO BOY ALISON MOYET	59	1994
ODE TO JOY (FROM BEETHOVEN'S SYMPHONY NO 9) BBC CONCERT ORCHESTRA/BBC SYMPHONY CHORUS/ STEPHEN JACKSON	36	1996
ODE TO MY FAMILY CRANBERRIES	26	1994
THE ODYSSEY DRUMSOUND/SIMON BASSLINE SMITH	66	2004
OF COURSE I'M LYING YELLO	23	1989
OF COURSE YOU CAN SPEARHEAD	74	1994
OFF ON HOLIDAY SUGGS	7	1995
OFF ON YOUR OWN (GIRL) AL B SURE!	70	1988
OFF THE HOOK [A] JODY WATLEY	51	1998
OFF THE HOOK [B] CSS	43	2007
OFF THE WALL MICHAEL JACKSON	7	1979
OFF THE WALL WISDOME	33	2000
OFF 2 WORK DIZZEE RASCAL	44	2005
OFFICE BOY BONDE DO ROLE	75	2007
OFFICIAL SECRETS M	64	1980
OFFSHORE CHICANE	14	1996
OFFSHORE BANKING BUSINESS MEMBERS	31	1979
OH CIARA FEATURING LUDACRIS	4	2005
OH BABE WHAT WOULD YOU SAY? HURRICANE SMITH	4	1972
OH BABY RHIANNA	18	2002
OH BABY I... ETERNAL	4	1994
(OH BABY MINE) I GET SO LONELY FOUR KNIGHTS	5	1954
OH BOY [A] CRICKETS	3	1957
OH BOY [A] MUD	1	1975
OH BOY [A] FABULOUS BAKER BOYS	34	1997
OH BOY [B] CAM'RON FEATURING JUELZ SANTANA	13	2002
OH BOY (THE MOOD I'M IN) BROTHERHOOD OF MAN	8	1977
OH CAROL [A] NEIL SEDAKA	3	1959
OH CAROL! [A] CLINT EASTWOOD & GENERAL SAINT	54	1994
OH CAROL [B] SMOKIE	5	1978
OH CAROLINA SHAGGY	1	1993
OH DIANE FLEETWOOD MAC	9	1983
OH FATHER MADONNA	16	1996
OH GIRL CHI-LITES	5	1972
OH GIRL PAUL YOUNG	25	1990
OH HAPPY DAY [A] JOHNSTON BROTHERS	4	1953
OH HAPPY DAY [B] EDWIN HAWKINS SINGERS FEATURING DOROTHY COMBS MORRISON	2	1969
OH HOW I MISS YOU BACHELORS	30	1967
OH JIM GAY DAD	47	1999
OH JULIE SHAKIN' STEVENS	1	1982
OH LA LA LA 2 EIVISSA	13	1997
OH L'AMOUR ERASURE	13	2003
OH LONESOME ME CRAIG DOUGLAS	15	1962
OH LORI ALESSI	8	1977
OH LOUISE JUNIOR	74	1985
OH MANDY SPINTO BAND	54	2006
OH ME OH MY (I'M A FOOL FOR YOU BABY) LULU	47	1969
OH MEIN PAPA EDDIE CALVERT	1	1953
OH MILLWALL MILLWALL FC	41	2004
OH MY GOD [A] A TRIBE CALLED QUEST	68	1994
OH MY GOD [B] KAISER CHIEFS	6	2004
OH MY GOD [B] MARK RONSON FEATURING LILY ALLEN	8	2007
OH MY GOSH BASEMENT JAXX	8	2005
OH MY PAPA EDDIE FISHER	9	1954
OH NO [A] COMMODORES	44	1981
OH NO [B] MOS DEF/NATE DOGG/PHAROAHE MONCH	24	2001
OH NO NOT MY BABY MANFRED MANN	11	1965
OH NO NOT MY BABY ROD STEWART	6	1973
OH NO NOT MY BABY CHER	33	1992
OH NO WON'T DO CUD	49	1991
OH OH, I'M FALLING IN LOVE AGAIN JIMMIE RODGERS	18	1958
OH PATTI (DON'T FEEL SORRY FOR LOVERBOY) SCRITTI POLITTI	13	1988
OH, PEOPLE PATTI LABELLE	26	1986
OH PRETTY WOMAN ROY ORBISON	1	1964
OH PRETTY WOMAN GARY MOORE FEATURING ALBERT KING	48	1990
OH ROMEO MINDY McCREADY	41	1998
OH SHEILA READY FOR THE WORLD	50	1985
OH STACEY (LOOK WHAT YOU'VE DONE!) ZUTONS	24	2006
OH THE GUILT NIRVANA	12	1993
OH WELL FLEETWOOD MAC	2	1969
OH WELL OH WELL	28	1989
OH WHAT A CIRCUS DAVID ESSEX	3	1978
OH! WHAT A DAY CRAIG DOUGLAS	43	1960
OH WHAT A FEELING CHANGE	56	1985
OH! WHAT A GIRL! SIMPLY RED	57	2006
OH WHAT A NIGHT CLOCK	13	1996
OH WHAT A SHAME ROY WOOD	13	1975
OH! WHAT A WORLD SISTER BLISS WITH COLETTE	40	1995
OH WORLD PAUL RUTHERFORD	61	1989
OH YEAH! [A] BILL WITHERS	60	1985
OH YEAH [B] ASH	6	1996
OH YEAH [C] CAPRICE	24	1999
OH YEAH [D] FOXY BROWN	27	2001
OH YEAH [E] SUBWAYS	25	2005
OH YEAH, BABY DWEEB	70	1997
OH YEAH (ON THE RADIO) ROXY MUSIC	5	1980
OH YES! YOU'RE BEAUTIFUL GARY GLITTER	2	1974
OH YOU PRETTY THING PETER NOONE	12	1971
OH YOU WANT MORE TY FEATURING ROOTS MANUVA	65	2004
OHIO UTAH SAINTS	42	1995
OI PLATINUM 45 FEATURING MORE FIRE CREW	8	2002
OK BIG BROVAZ	7	2003
O.K. FRED ERROLL DUNKLEY	11	1979
O.K.? JULIE COVINGTON, RULA LENSKA, CHARLOTTE CORNWELL & SUE JONES-DAVIES	10	1977
OKAY! DAVE DEE, DOZY, BEAKY, MICK & TICH	4	1967
OL' MACDONALD FRANK SINATRA	11	1960
OL' RAG BLUES STATUS QUO	9	1983
OLD [A] KEVIN ROWLAND & DEXY'S MIDNIGHT RUNNERS	17	1982
OLD [B] MACHINE HEAD	43	1995
OLD AND WISE ALAN PARSONS PROJECT	74	1983
OLD BEFORE I DIE ROBBIE WILLIAMS	2	1997
THE OLD FASHIONED WAY CHARLES AZNAVOUR	38	1973
OLD FLAMES FOSTER & ALLEN	51	1982
OLD FOLKS A	54	1999
OLD HABITS DIE HARD MICK JAGGER & DAVE STEWART	45	2004
THE OLD MAN AND THE ANGEL IT BITES	72	1987
OLD MAN AND ME (WHEN I GET TO HEAVEN) HOOTIE & THE BLOWFISH	57	1996
OLD OAKEN BUCKET TOMMY SANDS	25	1960
THE OLD PAYOLA ROLL BLUES STAN FREBERG WITH JESSIE WHITE	40	1960
OLD PIANO RAG DICKIE VALENTINE	15	1955
OLD POP IN AN OAK REDNEX	12	1995
OLD RED EYES IS BACK BEAUTIFUL SOUTH	22	1992
OLD RIVERS WALTER BRENNAN	38	1962
THE OLD RUGGED CROSS ETHNA CAMPBELL	33	1976
OLD SHEP CLINTON FORD	27	1959
OLD SIAM SIR WINGS	35	1979
OLD SMOKEY JOHNNY & THE HURRICANES	24	1961
THE OLD SONGS BARRY MANILOW	48	1981
OLD TOWN CORRS	68	2005
OLDER GEORGE MICHAEL	3	1997
OLDEST SWINGER IN TOWN FRED WEDLOCK	6	1981
OLE OLA (MULHER BRASILEIRA) ROD STEWART FEATURING THE SCOTTISH WORLD CUP FOOTBALL SQUAD	4	1978
OLIVE TREE JUDITH DURHAM	33	1967
OLIVER'S ARMY ELVIS COSTELLO & THE ATTRACTIONS	2	1979
OLYMPIAN GENE	18	1995
OLYMPIC 808 STATE	10	1990
THE OMD REMIXES ORCHESTRAL MANOEUVRES IN THE DARK	56	1998
OMEN [A] ORBITAL	46	1990
THE OMEN [B] PROGRAM 2 BELTRAM	53	1991
OMEN III MAGIC AFFAIR	17	1994
ON APHEX TWIN	32	1993
ON A CAROUSEL HOLLIES	4	1967
ON A CROWDED STREET BARBARA PENNINGTON	57	1985
ON A DAY LIKE TODAY BRYAN ADAMS	13	1998
ON A GOOD THING C-SIXTY FOUR	54	2005
ON A LITTLE STREET IN SINGAPORE MANHATTAN TRANSFER	20	1978
ON A MISSION ALOOF	64	1992
ON A NIGHT LIKE THIS KYLIE MINOGUE	2	2000
ON A NOOSE TOWERS OF LONDON	32	2005
ON A RAGGA TIP SL2	2	1992
ON A ROPE ROCKET FROM THE CRYPT	12	1996
ON A SATURDAY NIGHT TERRY DACTYL & THE DINOSAURS	45	1973
ON A SLOW BOAT TO CHINA EMILE FORD & THE CHECKMATES	3	1960
ON A SUNDAY [A] NICK HEYWARD	52	1983

	Peak Position	Year of Entry
ON A SUN-DAY [B] BENZ	73	1997
ON AND ON [A] ASWAD	25	1989
ON AND ON [B] LONGPIGS	16	1996
ON & ON [C] ERYKAH BADU	12	1997
ON BENDED KNEE BOYZ II MEN	20	1994
ON CALL KINGS OF LEON	18	2007
ON EVERY STREET DIRE STRAITS	42	1992
ON FIRE [A] T-CONNECTION	16	1978
ON FIRE [B] TONE LOC	13	1989
ON FIRE [C] LLOYD BANKS	19	2004
ON HER MAJESTY'S SECRET SERVICE PROPELLERHEADS & DAVID ARNOLD	7	1997
ON HORSEBACK MIKE OLDFIELD	4	1975
ON MOTHER KELLY'S DOORSTEP DANNY LA RUE	33	1968
ON MY KNEES 411 FEATURING GHOSTFACE KILLAH	4	2004
ON MY MIND FUTURESHOCK FEATURING BEN ONONO	51	2003
ON MY OWN [A] PATTI LABELLE & MICHAEL McDONALD	2	1986
ON MY OWN [B] CRAIG McLACHLAN	59	1992
ON MY OWN [C] PEACH	69	1998
ON MY RADIO SELECTER	8	1979
ON MY WAY [A] MR FINGERS	71	1992
ON MY WAY [B] MIKE KOGLIN FEATURING BEATRICE	28	1999
ON MY WAY HOME ENYA	26	1996
ON MY WORD CLIFF RICHARD	12	1965
ON OUR OWN (FROM GHOSTBUSTERS II) BOBBY BROWN	4	1989
ON POINT HOUSE OF PAIN	19	1994
ON SILENT WINGS TINA TURNER	13	1996
ON STANDBY SHED SEVEN	12	1996
ON THE BEACH [A] CLIFF RICHARD & THE SHADOWS	7	1964
ON THE BEACH [B] CHRIS REA	12	1986
ON THE BEACH [B] YORK	4	2000
ON THE BEAT B B & Q BAND	41	1981
ON THE BIBLE DEUCE	13	1995
ON THE DANCEFLOOR DJ DISCIPLE	67	1994
ON THE HORIZON MELANIE C	14	2003
ON THE INSIDE (THEME FROM *PRISONER CELL BLOCK H*) LYNNE HAMILTON	3	1989
ON THE LEVEL YOMANDA	28	2000
ON THE MOVE BARTHEZZ	18	2001
ON THE NIGHT PAT & MICK	11	1988
ON THE ONE LUKK FEATURING FELICIA COLLINS	72	1985
ON THE RADIO DONNA SUMMER	32	1980
ON THE RADIO MARTINE McCUTCHEON	7	2001
ON THE RADIO REGINA SPEKTOR	60	2006
...ON THE RADIO (REMEMBER THE DAYS) NELLY FURTADO	18	2002
ON THE REBOUND FLOYD CRAMER	1	1961
ON THE ROAD AGAIN CANNED HEAT	8	1968
ON THE ROPES (EP) WONDER STUFF	10	1993
ON THE ROSE TIGER	57	1997
ON THE RUN [A] DE BOS	51	1997
ON THE RUN [B] OMC	56	1997
ON THE RUN [C] BIG TIME CHARLIE	22	1999
ON THE RUN [D] TILLMANN UHRMACHER	16	2002
ON THE RUN [E] CRESCENT	49	2002
ON THE STREET WHERE YOU LIVE DAVID WHITFIELD	16	1958
ON THE STREET WHERE YOU LIVE VIC DAMONE	1	1958
ON THE TOP OF THE WORLD DIVA SURPRISE FEATURING GEORGIA JONES	29	1998
ON THE TRAIL PRIME MOVERS	74	1986
ON THE TURNING AWAY PINK FLOYD	55	1987
ON THE VERGE OF SOMETHING WONDERFUL DARREN HAYES	20	2007
ON THE WINGS OF A NIGHTINGALE EVERLY BROTHERS	41	1984
ON THE WINGS OF LOVE JEFFREY OSBORNE	11	1984
ON WITH THE MOTLEY HARRY SECOMBE	16	1955
ON YA WAY HELICOPTER	32	1994
ON YOUR OWN [A] VERVE	28	1995
ON YOUR OWN [B] BLUR	5	1997
ONCE GENEVIEVE	43	1966
ONCE AGAIN [A] CUD	45	1992
1NCE AGAIN [B] A TRIBE CALLED QUEST	34	1996
ONCE AND NEVER AGAIN LONG BLONDES	30	2006
ONCE AROUND THE BLOCK BADLY DRAWN BOY	27	1999
ONCE AROUND THE SUN CAPRICE	24	2001
ONCE BITTEN TWICE SHY [A] IAN HUNTER	14	1975
ONCE BITTEN TWICE SHY [B] VESTA WILLIAMS	14	1987
ONCE I HAD A SWEETHEART PENTANGLE	46	1969
ONCE IN A LIFETIME TALKING HEADS	14	1981
ONCE IN A WHILE BLACK VELVETS	75	2005
ONCE IN EVERY LIFETIME KEN DODD	28	1961
ONCE MORE ORB	38	2001
ONCE THERE WAS A TIME TOM JONES	18	1966
ONCE UPON A DREAM BILLY FURY	7	1962
ONCE UPON A LONG AGO PAUL McCARTNEY	10	1987
ONCE UPON A TIME [A] MARVIN GAYE & MARY WELLS	50	1964
ONCE UPON A TIME [B] TOM JONES	32	1965
ONCE UPON A TIME [C] POGUES	66	1994
ONCE UPON A TIME IN AMERICA JEEVAS	61	2003
ONCE YOU'VE TASTED LOVE TAKE THAT	47	1992
ONE [A] METALLICA	13	1989
ONE [B] BEE GEES	71	1989
ONE [C] U2	7	1992
ONE [C] MICA PARIS	29	1995
ONE [C] MARY J BLIGE & U2	2	2006
THE ONE [D] ELTON JOHN	10	1992
ONE [E] BUSTA RHYMES FEATURING ERYKAH BADU	23	1998
THE ONE [F] BACKSTREET BOYS	8	2000
THE ONE [G] DEE DEE	28	2003
THE ONE [H] CASSIUS HENRY FEATURING FREEWAY	56	2004
THE ONE [I] UPPER STREET	35	2006
ONE & ONE ROBERT MILES FEATURING MARIA NAYLER	3	1996
ONE AND ONE IS ONE MEDICINE HEAD	3	1973
THE ONE AND ONLY [A] GLADYS KNIGHT & THE PIPS	32	1978
THE ONE AND ONLY [B] CHESNEY HAWKES	1	1991
ONE ARMED SCISSOR AT THE DRIVE-IN	64	2000
ONE BETTER DAY MADNESS	17	1984
ONE BETTER WORLD ABC	32	1989
ONE BIG FAMILY EP EMBRACE	21	1997
ONE BROKEN HEART FOR SALE ELVIS PRESLEY	12	1963
ONE BY ONE CHER	7	1996
ONE CALL AWAY CHINGY FEATURING J WEAV	26	2004
ONE COOL REMOVE SHAWN COLVIN WITH MARY CHAPIN CARPENTER	40	1995
ONE DANCE WON'T DO AUDREY HALL	20	1986
ONE DAY [A] TYRREL CORPORATION	59	1992
ONE DAY [B] D MOB	41	1994
ONE DAY AT A TIME [A] LENA MARTELL	1	1979
ONE DAY AT A TIME [B] ALICE BAND	52	2001
ONE DAY I'LL FLY AWAY RANDY CRAWFORD	2	1980
ONE DAY IN YOUR LIFE [A] MICHAEL JACKSON	1	1981
ONE DAY IN YOUR LIFE [B] ANASTACIA	11	2002
ONE DRINK TOO MANY SAILOR	35	1977
ONE EP MANSUN	37	1996
ONE FINE DAY [A] CHIFFONS	29	1963
ONE FINE DAY [B] OPERABABES	54	2002
ONE FINE DAY [C] JAKATTA	39	2003
ONE FINE MORNING TOMMY HUNT	44	1976
ONE FOOT IN THE GRAVE ERIC IDLE FEATURING RICHARD WILSON	50	1994
THE ONE FOR ME JOE	34	1994
ONE FOR SORROW STEPS	2	1998
ONE FOR THE BRISTOL CITY BRISTOL CITY & THE WURZELS	66	2007
ONE FOR THE MOCKINGBIRD CUTTING CREW	52	1987
ONE FOR THE MONEY HORACE BROWN	12	1996
ONE FOR YOU ONE FOR ME JONATHAN KING	29	1978
ONE FOR YOU ONE FOR ME LA BIONDA	54	1978
ONE GIANT LOVE CUD	52	1994
ONE GIFT OF LOVE DEAR JON	68	1995
ONE GOODBYE IN TEN SHARA NELSON	21	1993
ONE GREAT THING BIG COUNTRY	19	1986
ONE HEADLIGHT WALLFLOWERS	54	1997
ONE HEART CELINE DION	27	2003
ONE HEART BETWEEN TWO DAVE BERRY	41	1964
ONE HELLO RANDY CRAWFORD	48	1982
ONE HORSE TOWN THRILLS	18	2003
101 SHEENA EASTON	54	1989
100 MILES AND RUNNIN' NWA	38	1990
100% [A] SONIC YOUTH	28	1992
100% [B] MARY KIANI	23	1997
100% PURE LOVE CRYSTAL WATERS	15	1994
THE ONE I GAVE MY HEART TO AALIYAH	30	1997
THE ONE I LOVE [A] R.E.M.	16	1987
THE ONE I LOVE [B] DAVID GRAY	8	2005
ONE IN A MILLION AALIYAH	15	1997
ONE IN TEN UB40	7	1981
ONE IN TEN 808 STATE Vs UB40	17	1992
ONE INCH ROCK TYRANNOSAURUS REX	7	1968
ONE KISS FROM HEAVEN LOUISE	9	1996
ONE LAST BREATH/BULLETS CREED	47	2002
ONE LAST KISS J GEILS BAND	74	1979
ONE LAST LOVE SONG BEAUTIFUL SOUTH	14	1994
ONE LOVE [A] ATLANTIC STARR	58	1985
ONE LOVE [B] PAT BENATAR	59	1989
ONE LOVE [C] STONE ROSES	4	1990
ONE LOVE [D] DR ALBAN	45	1992
ONE LOVE [E] PRODIGY	8	1993
ONE LOVE [F] BLUE	3	2002
ONE LOVE FAMILY LIQUID	14	1995
ONE LOVE IN MY LIFETIME INNOCENCE	40	1992
ONE LOVE - PEOPLE GET READY BOB MARLEY & THE WAILERS	5	1984
ONE LOVER AT A TIME ATLANTIC STARR	57	1987
ONE LOVER (DON'T STOP THE SHOW) FORREST	67	1983
ONE MAN CHANELLE	16	1989
ONE MAN ARMY OUR LADY PEACE	70	2000
ONE MAN BAND LEO SAYER	6	1974
ONE MAN IN MY HEART HUMAN LEAGUE	13	1995
ONE MAN WOMAN SHEENA EASTON	14	1980
ONE MAN'S BITCH PHOEBE ONE	59	1998
ONE MIND, TWO HEARTS PARADISE	42	1983
ONE MINUTE MAN MISSY ELLIOTT FEATURING LUDACRIS	10	2001
ONE MIRROR TO MANY BLACK CROWES	51	1996
ONE MOMENT IN TIME WHITNEY HOUSTON	1	1988
ONE MORE HAZIZA	75	2001
ONE MORE CHANCE [A] DIANA ROSS	49	1981
ONE MORE CHANCE [B] MAXI PRIEST	40	1993
ONE MORE CHANCE [C] E.Y.C.	25	1994
ONE MORE CHANCE [D] MADONNA	11	1995
ONE MORE CHANCE [E] THE ONE	31	1997
ONE MORE CHANCE [F] MICHAEL JACKSON	5	2003
ONE MORE CHANCE/STAY WITH ME NOTORIOUS B.I.G.	34	1997
ONE MORE DANCE ESTHER & ABI OFARIM	13	1968

	Peak Position	Year of Entry
ONE MORE GOOD NIGHT WITH THE BOYS TASMIN ARCHER	45	1996
ONE MORE NIGHT PHIL COLLINS	4	1985
ONE MORE NIGHT ALONE FRIDAY HILL	13	2006
ONE MORE RIVER LUCIANA	67	1994
ONE MORE SATURDAY NIGHT MATCHBOX	63	1982
ONE MORE SUNRISE (MORGEN) DICKIE VALENTINE	14	1959
ONE MORE TIME [A] WHYCLIFFE	72	1994
ONE MORE TIME [B] DAFT PUNK	2	2000
ONE MORE TRY [A] GEORGE MICHAEL	8	1988
ONE MORE TRY [B] KRISTINE W	41	1996
ONE NATION MASQUERADE	54	1986
ONE NATION UNDER A GROOVE (PART 1) FUNKADELIC	9	1978
ONE NIGHT ELVIS PRESLEY	1	1959
ONE NIGHT MUD	32	1975
ONE NIGHT IN BANGKOK MURRAY HEAD	12	1984
ONE NIGHT IN HEAVEN M PEOPLE	6	1993
ONE NIGHT STAND [A] LET LOOSE	12	1995
ONE NIGHT STAND [B] ALOOF	30	1996
ONE NIGHT STAND [C] MIS-TEEQ	5	2001
ONE NINE FOR SANTA FOGWELL FLAX & THE ANKLEBITERS FROM FREHOLD JUNIOR SCHOOL	68	1981
10538 OVERTURE ELECTRIC LIGHT ORCHESTRA	9	1972
ONE OF THE LIVING TINA TURNER	55	1985
ONE OF THE LUCKY ONES JOAN REGAN	47	1960
ONE OF THE PEOPLE ADAMSKI'S THING	56	1998
ONE OF THESE DAYS AMBASSADOR	67	2000
ONE OF THESE NIGHTS EAGLES	23	1975
ONE OF THOSE NIGHTS BUCKS FIZZ	20	1981
ONE OF US [A] ABBA	3	1981
ONE OF US [B] JOAN OSBORNE	6	1996
ONE OF US [C] HELL IS FOR HEROES	71	2004
ONE OF US MUST KNOW (SOONER OR LATER) BOB DYLAN	33	1966
ONE ON ONE DARYL HALL & JOHN OATES	63	1983
ONE PERFECT SUNRISE ORBITAL	29	2004
ONE PIECE AT A TIME JOHNNY CASH WITH THE TENNESSEE THREE	32	1976
ONE REASON WHY CRAIG McLACHLAN	29	1992
ONE ROAD LOVE AFFAIR	16	1969
ONE RULE FOR YOU AFTER THE FIRE	40	1979
ONE SHINING MOMENT DIANA ROSS	10	1992
ONE SHOT BROTHERHOOD	55	1996
ONE SLIP PINK FLOYD	50	1988
ONE SMALL DAY ULTRAVOX	27	1984
ONE STEP KILLAH PRIEST	45	1998
ONE STEP AHEAD NIK KERSHAW	55	1989
ONE STEP AWAY TAVARES	16	1977
ONE STEP BEYOND MADNESS	7	1979
ONE STEP CLOSER [A] LINKIN PARK	24	2001
ONE STEP CLOSER [B] S CLUB JUNIORS	2	2002
ONE STEP CLOSER (TO LOVE) GEORGE McCRAE	57	1984
ONE STEP FURTHER BARDO	2	1982
ONE STEP OUT OF TIME MICHAEL BALL	20	1992
ONE STEP TOO FAR FAITHLESS FEATURING DIDO	6	2002
ONE SWEET DAY MARIAH CAREY & BOYZ II MEN	6	1995
1 THING AMERIE	4	2005
1000% FATIMA MANSIONS	61	1992
1000 YEARS (JUST LEAVE ME NOW) JUPITER ACE FEATURING SHEENA	51	2005
138 TREK DJ ZINC	27	2000
ONE TO ANOTHER CHARLATANS	3	1996
THE ONE TO CRY ESCORTS	49	1964
1 TO 1 RELIGION BOMB THE BASS FEATURING CARLTON	53	1995
THE ONE TO SING THE BLUES MOTORHEAD	45	1991
ONE TONGUE HOTHOUSE FLOWERS	45	1993
ONE TOUCH 365	60	2006
ONE TRUE WOMAN YAZZ	60	1992
1 2 STEP CIARA FEATURING MISSY ELLIOTT	3	2005
1-2-3 [A] LEN BARRY	3	1965
1-2-3 [B] PROFESSIONALS	43	1980
1-2-3 [C] GLORIA ESTEFAN & MIAMI SOUND MACHINE	9	1988
1-2-3 [D] CHIMES	60	1989
ONE, TWO, THREE [E] DINA CARROLL	16	1998
1234 [A] MRS WOOD	54	1998
1234 [B] FEIST	8	2007
1-2-3-4 GET WITH THE WICKED RICHARD BLACKWOOD	10	2000
1,2,3,4 (SUMPIN' NEW) COOLIO	13	1996
1-2-3 O'LEARY DES O'CONNOR	4	1968
ONE VISION QUEEN	7	1985
ONE VOICE BILL TARMEY	16	1993
ONE WAY LEVELLERS	33	1991
ONE WAY LOVE CLIFF BENNETT & THE REBEL ROUSERS	9	1964
ONE WAY MIRROR KINESIS	71	2003
ONE WAY OUT REID	66	1988
ONE WAY TICKET [A] ERUPTION	9	1979
ONE WAY TICKET [B] DARKNESS	8	2005
ONE WEEK BARENAKED LADIES	5	1999
ONE WILD NIGHT BON JOVI	10	2001
ONE WISH [A] SHYSTIE	40	2004
ONE WISH [B] RAY J	13	2005
ONE WOMAN JADE	22	1993
ONE WORD KELLY OSBOURNE	9	2005
THE ONE-OFF SONG FOR THE SUMMER KOOPA	21	2007
THE ONES YOU LOVE RICK ASTLEY	48	1993
ONION SONG MARVIN GAYE & TAMMI TERRELL	9	1969
ONLY [A] ANTHRAX	36	1993
ONLY [B] NINE INCH NAILS	20	2005
ONLY A BOY TIM BURGESS	54	2003
ONLY CRYING KEITH MARSHALL	12	1981
THE ONLY FLAME IN TOWN ELVIS COSTELLO	71	1984
ONLY FOOLS (NEVER FALL IN LOVE) SONIA	10	1991
ONLY FOR A WHILE TOPLOADER	19	2001
ONLY FOR LOVE LIMAHL	16	1983
ONLY HAPPY WHEN IT RAINS GARBAGE	29	1995
ONLY HUMAN DINA CARROLL	33	1996
ONLY IF... ENYA	43	1997
ONLY IN MY DREAMS DEBBIE GIBSON	11	1987
THE ONLY LIVING BOY IN NEW CROSS CARTER-THE UNSTOPPABLE SEX MACHINE	7	1992
THE ONLY LIVING BOY IN NEW YORK (EP) EVERYTHING BUT THE GIRL	42	1993
ONLY LOVE NANA MOUSKOURI	2	1986
ONLY LOVE CAN BREAK YOUR HEART ELKIE BROOKS	43	1978
ONLY LOVE CAN BREAK YOUR HEART MINT JULEPS	62	1986
ONLY LOVE CAN BREAK YOUR HEART SAINT ETIENNE	39	1991
ONLY LOVE REMAINS PAUL McCARTNEY	34	1986
ONLY LOVING DOES IT GUYS & DOLLS	42	1978
THE ONLY MAN ON THE ISLAND TOMMY STEELE	16	1958
THE ONLY MAN ON THE ISLAND VIC DAMONE	24	1958
ONLY ME HYPERLOGIC	35	1995
THE ONLY ONE [A] TRANSVISION VAMP	15	1989
THE ONLY ONE [B] GUN	29	1995
ONLY ONE [C] PETER ANDRE	16	1996
THE ONLY ONE [D] THUNDER	31	1998
THE ONLY ONE I KNOW CHARLATANS	9	1990
ONLY ONE ROAD CELINE DION	8	1995
ONLY ONE WOMAN MARBLES	5	1968
ONLY ONE WORD PROPAGANDA	71	1990
ONLY ONE WORD COMES TO MIND BIFFY CLYRO	27	2005
THE ONLY RHYME THAT BITES MC TUNES VERSUS 808 STATE	10	1990
ONLY SAW TODAY - INSTANT KARMA AMOS	48	1994
ONLY SIXTEEN AL SAXON	24	1959
ONLY SIXTEEN CRAIG DOUGLAS	1	1959
ONLY SIXTEEN SAM COOKE	23	1959
ONLY TENDER LOVE DEACON BLUE	22	1993
ONLY THE HEARTACHES HOUSTON WELLS	22	1963
ONLY THE LONELY [A] ROY ORBISON	1	1960
ONLY THE LONELY [A] PRELUDE	55	1982
ONLY THE LONELY [B] T'PAU	28	1989
ONLY THE LOOT CAN MAKE ME HAPPY R KELLY	24	2000
ONLY THE MOMENT MARC ALMOND	45	1989
ONLY THE ONES WE LOVE TANITA TIKARAM	69	1991
ONLY THE STRONG SURVIVE BILLY PAUL	33	1977
ONLY THE STRONG SURVIVE DJ KRUSH	71	1996
ONLY THE STRONGEST WILL SURVIVE HURRICANE #1	19	1998
ONLY THE WOMEN KNOW SIX CHIX	72	2000
THE ONLY THING THAT LOOKS GOOD ON ME IS YOU BRYAN ADAMS	6	1996
ONLY THIS MOMENT ROYKSOPP	33	2005
ONLY TIME ENYA	32	2000
ONLY TIME WILL TELL [A] ASIA	54	1982
ONLY TIME WILL TELL [B] TEN CITY	63	1992
ONLY TO BE WITH YOU ROACHFORD	21	1994
ONLY U ASHANTI	2	2005
ONLY WANNA KNOW U COS URE FAMOUS OXIDE & NEUTRINO	12	2001
THE ONLY WAY IS UP YAZZ & THE PLASTIC POPULATION	1	1988
THE ONLY WAY OUT CLIFF RICHARD	10	1982
ONLY WHEN I LOSE MYSELF DEPECHE MODE	17	1998
ONLY WHEN I SLEEP CORRS	58	1997
ONLY WHEN YOU LEAVE SPANDAU BALLET	3	1984
ONLY WITH YOU CAPTAIN HOLLYWOOD PROJECT	61	1993
ONLY WOMEN BLEED JULIE COVINGTON	12	1977
ONLY YESTERDAY CARPENTERS	7	1975
ONLY YOU [A] HILLTOPPERS	3	1956
ONLY YOU [A] PLATTERS	5	1956
ONLY YOU [A] MARK WYNTER	38	1964
ONLY YOU [A] JEFF COLLINS	40	1972
ONLY YOU [A] RINGO STARR	28	1974
ONLY YOU (AND YOU ALONE) [A] CHILD	33	1979
ONLY YOU [A] JOHN ALFORD	9	1996
ONLY YOU [B] TEDDY PENDERGRASS	41	1978
ONLY YOU [C] YAZOO	2	1982
ONLY YOU [C] FLYING PICKETS	1	1983
ONLY YOU [D] PRAISE	4	1991
ONLY YOU [E] PORTISHEAD	35	1998
ONLY YOU [F] CASINO	72	1999
ONLY YOU CAN FOX	3	1975
ONLY YOU CAN ROCK ME UFO	50	1978
ONLY YOUR LOVE BANANARAMA	27	1990
ONWARD CHRISTIAN SOLDIERS HARRY SIMEONE CHORALE	35	1960
OO...AH...CANTONA OO LA LA	64	1992
007 MUSICAL YOUTH	26	1983
007 (SHANTY TOWN) DESMOND DEKKER & THE ACES	14	1967
OOCHIE WALLY QB FINEST FEATURING NAS & BRAVEHEARTS	30	2001
OOCHY KOOCHY (F.U. BABY YEAH YEAH) BABY FORD	58	1988
OO-EEH BABY STONEBRIDGE McGUINNESS	54	1979
OOH! AAH! CANTONA 1300 DRUMS FEATURING THE UNJUSTIFIED ANCIENTS OF MU	11	1996

	Peak Position	Year of Entry
OOH AAH (G-SPOT) WAYNE MARSHALL	29	1994
OOH AAH...JUST A LITTLE BIT GINA G	1	1996
OOH-AH-AA (I FEEL IT) E.Y.C.	33	1995
OOH BABY GILBERT O'SULLIVAN	18	1973
OOH BOY ROSE ROYCE	46	1980
OOH I DO LYNSEY DE PAUL	25	1974
OOH I LIKE IT JONNY L	73	1993
OOH LA KOOKS	20	2006
OOH! LA! LA! [A] JOE 'MR PIANO' HENDERSON	44	1960
OOH LA LA [B] COOLIO	14	1997
OOH LA LA [C] ROD STEWART	16	1998
OOH LA LA [D] WISEGUYS	2	1998
OOH LA LA [E] GOLDFRAPP	4	2005
OOH LA LA LA RED RAW FEATURING 007	59	1995
OOH LA LA LA (LET'S GO DANCIN') KOOL & THE GANG	6	1982
OOH MY SOUL LITTLE RICHARD	22	1958
OOH STICK YOU! DAPHNE & CELESTE	8	2000
OOH TO BE AH KAJAGOOGOO	7	1983
OOH-WAKKA-DOO-WAKKA-DAY GILBERT O'SULLIVAN	8	1972
OOH WEE MARK RONSON	15	2003
OOH! WHAT A LIFE GIBSON BROTHERS	10	1979
OOHHH BABY VIDA SIMPSON	70	1995
O-O-O ADRENALIN M.O.D.	49	1988
OOO LA LA LA TEENA MARIE	74	1988
OOOH DE LA SOUL FEATURING REDMAN	29	2000
OOOIE, OOOIE, OOOIE PRICKLY HEAT	57	1998
OOOPS 808 STATE FEATURING BJORK	42	1991
OOOPS UP SNAP	5	1990
OOPS!...I DID IT AGAIN BRITNEY SPEARS	1	2000
OOPS (OH MY) TWEET	5	2002
OOPS UPSIDE YOUR HEAD GAP BAND	6	1980
OOPS UPSIDE YOUR HEAD DJ CASPER FEATURING THE GAP BAND	16	2004
OPAL MANTRA THERAPY?	13	1993
OPEN ARMS [A] MARIAH CAREY	4	1996
OPEN ARMS [B] WILT	59	2000
OPEN ARMS [C] TINA TURNER	25	2004
OPEN HEART ZOO MARTIN GRECH	68	2002
OPEN ROAD [A] GARY BARLOW	7	1997
OPEN ROAD [B] BRYAN ADAMS	21	2004
OPEN ROADS CERYS MATTHEWS	53	2006
OPEN SESAME LEILA K	23	1993
OPEN UP [A] MUNGO JERRY	21	1972
OPEN UP [B] LEFTFIELD LYDON	13	1993
OPEN UP THE RED BOX SIMPLY RED	61	1986
OPEN UP YOUR HEART JOAN & RUSTY REGAN	19	1955
OPEN YOUR EYES [A] BLACK BOX	48	1991
OPEN YOUR EYES [B] GOLDFINGER	75	2002
OPEN YOUR EYES [C] SNOW PATROL	26	2007
OPEN YOUR HEART [A] HUMAN LEAGUE	6	1981
OPEN YOUR HEART [B] M PEOPLE	9	1995
OPEN YOUR HEART [C] MADONNA	4	1986
OPEN YOUR MIND [A] 808 STATE	38	1991
OPEN YOUR MIND [B] USURA	7	1993
OPEN YOUR MIND (LET ME IN) REAL PEOPLE	70	1991
OPEN YOUR WINDOW REVEREND & THE MAKERS	65	2007
THE OPERA HOUSE JACK E MAKOSSA	48	1987
THE OPERA SONG (BRAVE NEW WORLD) JURGEN VRIES FEATURING CMC	3	2003
OPERAA HOUSE WORLD'S FAMOUS SUPREME TEAM SHOW	75	1990
OPERATION BLADE (BASS IN THE PLACE) PUBLIC DOMAIN FEATURING CHUCK D	5	2000
OPERATOR [A] MIDNIGHT STAR	66	1985
OPERATOR [B] LITTLE RICHARD	67	1986
OPIUM SCUMBAGZ OLAV BASOSKI	56	2000
O.P.P. NAUGHTY BY NATURE	35	1991
OPPORTUNITIES (LET'S MAKE LOTS OF MONEY) PET SHOP BOYS	11	1986
OPPOSITES ATTRACT PAULA ABDUL & THE WILD PAIR	2	1990
OPTIMISTIC SOUNDS OF BLACKNESS	28	1992
OPUS 40 MERCURY REV	31	1999
OPUS 17 (DON'T YOU WORRY 'BOUT ME) FOUR SEASONS WITH FRANKIE VALLI	20	1966
ORANGE BLOSSOM SPECIAL SPOTNICKS	29	1962
ORANGE CRUSH R.E.M.	28	1989
THE ORANGE THEME CYGNUS X	43	2000
ORCHARD ROAD LEO SAYER	16	1983
ORCHESTRAL MANOEUVRES IN THE DARKNESS EP DIFF'RENT DARKNESS	66	2003
ORDINARY ANGEL HUE & CRY	42	1988
ORDINARY DAY [A] CURIOSITY KILLED THE CAT	11	1987
ORDINARY DAY [B] VANESSA CARLTON	53	2002
ORDINARY GIRL ALISON MOYET	43	1987
ORDINARY LIVES BEE GEES	54	1989
ORDINARY PEOPLE JOHN LEGEND	27	2005
ORDINARY WORLD DURAN DURAN	6	1993
ORDINARY WORLD AURORA FEATURING NAIMEE COLEMAN	5	2000
ORIGINAL LEFTFIELD FEATURING TONI HALLIDAY	18	1995
ORIGINAL BIRD DANCE ELECTRONICAS	22	1981
ORIGINAL NUTTAH U.K. APACHI WITH SHY FX	39	1994
ORIGINAL PRANKSTER OFFSPRING	6	2000
ORIGINAL SIN ELTON JOHN	39	2002
ORIGINAL SIN (THEME FROM *THE SHADOW*) TAYLOR DAYNE	63	1995
ORINOCO FLOW ENYA	1	1988
ORLANDO DAWN LIQUID	53	2000
ORPHEUS ASH	13	2004
ORVILLE'S SONG KEITH HARRIS & ORVILLE	4	1982
OSCAR SHACK	67	2000
OSSIE'S DREAM (SPURS ARE ON THEIR WAY TO WEMBLEY) TOTTENHAM HOTSPUR F.A. CUP FINAL SQUAD	5	1981
THE OTHER MAN'S GRASS PETULA CLARK	20	1967
THE OTHER SIDE [A] AEROSMITH	46	1990
THE OTHER SIDE [B] DAVID GRAY	35	2002
THE OTHER SIDE [C] PAUL VAN DYK FEATURING WAYNE JACKSON	58	2005
THE OTHER SIDE OF LOVE YAZOO	13	1982
THE OTHER SIDE OF ME ANDY WILLIAMS	42	1976
THE OTHER SIDE OF SUMMER ELVIS COSTELLO	43	1991
THE OTHER SIDE OF THE SUN JANIS IAN	44	1980
OTHER SIDE OF THE WORLD KT TUNSTALL	13	2005
THE OTHER SIDE OF YOU MIGHTY LEMON DROPS	67	1986
THE OTHER WOMAN, THE OTHER MAN GERARD KENNY	69	1984
OTHERNESS (EP) COCTEAU TWINS	59	1995
OTHERSIDE [A] RED HOT CHILI PEPPERS	33	2000
THE OTHERSIDE [B] BREAKS CO-OP	43	2006
OTHERWISE MORCHEEBA	64	2002
OUIJA BOARD OUIJA BOARD MORRISSEY	18	1989
OUR DAY WILL COME RUBY & THE ROMANTICS	38	1963
OUR FAVOURITE MELODIES CRAIG DOUGLAS	9	1962
OUR FRANK MORRISSEY	26	1991
OUR GOAL ARSENAL FC	46	2000
OUR HOUSE MADNESS	5	1982
OUR KIND OF LOVE HANNAH	41	2000
OUR LAST SONG TOGETHER NEIL SEDAKA	31	1973
OUR LIPS ARE SEALED GO-GOS	47	1982
OUR LIPS ARE SEALED FUN BOY THREE	7	1983
OUR LIVES CALLING	13	2004
OUR LOVE ELKIE BROOKS	43	1982
(OUR LOVE) DON'T THROW IT ALL AWAY ANDY GIBB	32	1979
OUR RADIO ROCKS PJ & DUNCAN	15	1995
OUR TRUTH LACUNA COIL	40	2006
OUR VELOCITY MAXIMO PARK	9	2007
OUR WORLD BLUE MINK	17	1970
OUT COME THE FREAKS WAS (NOT WAS)	41	1984
OUT COME THE FREAKS (AGAIN) WAS (NOT WAS)	44	1988
OUT DEMONS OUT EDGAR BROUGHTON BAND	39	1970
OUT HERE ON MY OWN IRENE CARA	58	1982
OUT IN THE DARK LURKERS	72	1979
OUT IN THE FIELDS GARY MOORE & PHIL LYNOTT	5	1985
OUT IS THROUGH ALANIS MORISSETTE	56	2004
OUT OF BREATH RONI SIZE FEATURING RAHZEL	44	2004
OUT OF CONTROL [A] ANGELIC UPSTARTS	58	1980
OUT OF CONTROL [B] ROLLING STONES	51	1998
OUT OF CONTROL [C] CHEMICAL BROTHERS	21	1999
OUT OF CONTROL (BACK FOR MORE) DARUDE	13	2001
OUT OF HAND MIGHTY LEMON DROPS	66	1987
OUT OF MY HEAD MARRADONA	38	1994
OUT OF MY HEART BBMAK	36	2002
OUT OF MY MIND [A] JOHNNY TILLOTSON	34	1963
OUT OF MY MIND [B] DURAN DURAN	21	1997
OUT OF OUR MINDS CRACKOUT	63	2003
OUT OF REACH [A] VICE SQUAD	68	1982
OUT OF REACH [B] PRIMITIVES	25	1988
OUT OF REACH [C] GABRIELLE	4	2001
OUT OF SEASON ALMIGHTY	41	1993
OUT OF SIGHT [A] BABYBIRD	58	2000
OUT OF SIGHT [B] SPIRITUALIZED	65	2001
OUT OF SIGHT, OUT OF MIND LEVEL 42	41	1983
OUT OF SPACE PRODIGY	5	1992
OUT OF TEARS ROLLING STONES	36	1994
OUT OF THE BLUE [A] DEBBIE GIBSON	19	1988
OUT OF THE BLUE [B] SYSTEM F	14	1999
OUT OF THE BLUE [C] DELTA GOODREM	9	2004
OUT OF THE QUESTION MUMM RA	45	2006
OUT OF THE SILENT PLANET IRON MAIDEN	20	2000
OUT OF THE SINKING PAUL WELLER	16	1994
OUT OF THE STORM INCOGNITO	57	1996
OUT OF THE VOID GRASS-SHOW	75	1997
OUT OF THIS WORLD TONY HATCH	50	1962
OUT OF TIME [A] CHRIS FARLOWE	1	1966
OUT OF TIME [A] DAN McCAFFERTY	41	1975
OUT OF TIME [A] ROLLING STONES	45	1975
OUT OF TIME [B] BLUR	5	2003
OUT OF TOUCH DARYL HALL & JOHN OATES	48	1984
OUT OF TOUCH UNITING NATIONS	7	2004
OUT OF TOWN MAX BYGRAVES	18	1956
OUT OF YOUR MIND TRUE STEPPERS & DANE BOWERS FEATURING VICTORIA BECKHAM	2	2000
OUT ON THE FLOOR DOBIE GRAY	42	1975
OUT THERE [A] DINOSAUR Jr.	44	1993
OUT THERE [B] FRIENDS OF MATTHEW	61	1999
OUT THERE [C] PENDULUM	34	2005
OUT WITH HER BLOW MONKEYS	30	1987
OUTA SPACE BILLY PRESTON	44	1972
OUTDOOR MINER WIRE	51	1979
OUTERSPACE GIRL BELOVED	38	1993
OUTLAW OLIVE	14	1997
OUTLINES CLOR	43	2005
OUTRAGEOUS STIX 'N' STONED	39	1996
OUTSHINED SOUNDGARDEN	50	1992
OUTSIDE [A] OMAR	43	1994
OUTSIDE [B] GEORGE MICHAEL	2	1998
OUTSIDE [C] STAIND	33	2001
OUT-SIDE [D] BETA BAND	54	2004
OUTSIDE IN THE RAIN GWEN GUTHRIE	37	1987

	Peak Position	Year of Entry
OUTSIDE MY WINDOW STEVIE WONDER	52	1980
OUTSIDE OF HEAVEN EDDIE FISHER	1	1953
OUTSIDE YOUR DOOR STANDS	49	2004
OUTSIDE YOUR ROOM (EP) SLOWDIVE	69	1993
OUTSPOKEN - PART 1 BEN WATT FEAT. ESTELLE & BABY BLAK	74	2005
OUTSTANDING GAP BAND	68	1983
OUTSTANDING KENNY THOMAS	12	1991
OUTSTANDING ANDY COLE	68	1999
OUTTA CONTROL 50 CENT FEATURING MOBB DEEP	7	2005
OUTTA SPACE MELLOW TRAX	41	2000
OUTTATHAWAY VINES	20	2002
OVER [A] PORTISHEAD	25	1997
OVER [B] LINDSAY LOHAN	27	2005
OVER AND OVER [A] DAVE CLARK FIVE	45	1965
OVER AND OVER [B] JAMES BOYS	39	1973
OVER AND OVER [C] SHALAMAR	23	1983
OVER & OVER [D] PLUX FEATURING GEORGIA JONES	33	1996
OVER AND OVER [E] PUFF JOHNSON	20	1997
OVER AND OVER [F] NELLY FEATURING TIM McGRAW	1	2005
OVER AND OVER [G] TURIN BRAKES	62	2005
OVER AND OVER [H] HOT CHIP	27	2006
OVER MY HEAD LIT	37	2000
OVER MY HEAD (CABLE CAR) THE FRAY	19	2007
OVER MY SHOULDER [A] MIKE + THE MECHANICS	12	1995
OVER MY SHOULDER [B] I AM KLOOT	38	2005
OVER RISING CHARLATANS	15	1991
OVER THE BARRICADE MESH 29	35	2007
OVER THE EDGE ALMIGHTY	38	1993
OVER THE HILLS AND FAR AWAY GARY MOORE	20	1986
OVER THE RAINBOW SAM HARRIS	67	1985
OVER THE RAINBOW EVA CASSIDY	42	2001
OVER THE RAINBOW - YOU BELONG TO ME (MEDLEY) MATCHBOX	15	1980
OVER THE RIVER BITTY McLEAN	27	1995
OVER THE SEA JESSE RAE	65	1985
OVER THE WEEKEND NICK HEYWARD	43	1986
OVER THERE BABE TEAM	45	2002
OVER THERE (I DON'T CARE) HOUSE OF PAIN	20	1995
OVER TO YOU JOHN (HERE WE GO AGAIN) JIVE BUNNY & THE MASTERMIXERS	28	1991
OVER UNDER SIDEWAYS DOWN YARDBIRDS	10	1966
OVER YOU [A] FREDDIE & THE DREAMERS	13	1964
OVER YOU [B] ROXY MUSIC	5	1980
OVER YOU [C] RAY PARKER Jr.	65	1988
OVER YOU [D] JUSTIN	11	1999
OVER YOU [E] WARREN CLARKE FEATURING KATHY BROWN	42	2001
OVER YOU [F] MICKEY MODELLE V JESSY	35	2006
OVERCOME TRICKY	34	1995
OVERDRIVE DJ SANDY VS HOUSETRAP	32	2000
OVERJOYED STEVIE WONDER	17	1986
OVERKILL [A] MOTORHEAD	39	1979
OVERKILL [B] MEN AT WORK	21	1983
OVERLOAD [A] SUGABABES	6	2000
OVERLOAD [B] VOODOO & SERANO	30	2003
OVERNIGHT CELEBRITY TWISTA	16	2004
OVERPROTECTED BRITNEY SPEARS	4	2002
OVERRATED SIOBHAN DONAGHY	19	2003
OVERRATED (EVERYTHING IS) LESS THAN JAKE	61	2006
OVERTHROWN LIBIDO	53	1998
OVERTIME LEVEL 42	62	1991
OWNER OF A LONELY HEART YES	28	1983
OWNER OF A LONELY HEART MAX GRAHAM VS YES	9	2005
OXBOW LAKES ORB	38	1995
OXYGEN [A] BLAGGERS I.T.A.	51	1993
OXYGEN [B] JJ72	23	2000
OXYGEN [C] WILLY MASON	23	2005
OXYGENE 8 JEAN-MICHEL JARRE	17	1997
OXYGENE PART IV JEAN-MICHEL JARRE	4	1977
OXYGENE 10 JEAN-MICHEL JARRE	21	1997
OYE GLORIA ESTEFAN	33	1998
OYE COMO VA TITO PUENTE Jr & THE LATIN RHYTHM FEATURING TITO PUENTE, INDIA & CALI ALEMAN	36	1996
OYE MI CANTO (HEAR MY VOICE) GLORIA ESTEFAN	16	1989

P

	Peak Position	Year of Entry
P MACHINERY PROPAGANDA	50	1985
PABLO RUSS CONWAY	45	1961
PACIFIC 808 STATE	10	1989
PACIFIC MELODY AIRSCAPE	27	1997
PACK OF WOLVES NIGHTBREED	45	2004
PACK UP YOUR SORROWS JOAN BAEZ	50	1966
PACKET OF PEACE LIONROCK	32	1993
PACKJAMMED (WITH THE PARTY POSSE) STOCK AITKEN WATERMAN	41	1987
PAC-MAN [A] POWERPILL	43	1992
PACMAN [B] ED RUSH & OPTICAL/UNIVERSAL	61	2002
PAC'S LIFE 2PAC FEATURING TI & ASHANTI	21	2007
THE PADDLE DJ TOUCHE	65	2004
PAGAN POETRY BJORK	38	2001
PAID IN FULL ERIC B & RAKIM	15	1987
PAID MY DUES ANASTACIA	14	2001
PAIN [A] BETTY WRIGHT	42	1986
PAIN [B] JIMMY EAT WORLD	38	2004
THE PAIN INSIDE COSMIC ROUGH RIDERS	36	2001
PAIN KILLER TURIN BRAKES	5	2003
A PAIN THAT I'M USED TO DEPECHE MODE	15	2005
PAINKILLER JUDAS PRIEST	74	1990
PAINT A PICTURE MAN WITH NO NAME FEATURING HANNAH	42	1996
PAINT IT, BLACK ROLLING STONES	1	1966
PAINT IT BLACK MODETTES	42	1980
PAINT ME DOWN SPANDAU BALLET	30	1981
PAINT THE SILENCE SOUTH	69	2001
PAINT THE TOWN RED DELIRIOUS?	56	2005
PAINT YOUR TARGET FIGHTSTAR	9	2005
PAINTED MOON SILENCERS	57	1988
PAINTER MAN CREATION	36	1966
PAINTER MAN BONEY M	10	1979
A PAIR OF BROWN EYES POGUES	72	1985
PAISLEY PARK PRINCE & THE REVOLUTION	18	1985
PAL OF MY CRADLE DAYS ANN BREEN	69	1983
PALE BLUE EYES PAUL QUINN & EDWYYN COLLINS	72	1984
PALE MOVIE SAINT ETIENNE	28	1994
PALE RED JERRY BURNS	64	1992
PALE SHELTER TEARS FOR FEARS	5	1983
PALISADES PARK FREDDY CANNON	20	1962
PALOMA BLANCA GEORGE BAKER SELECTION	10	1975
PAMELA PAMELA WAYNE FONTANA	11	1966
PANAMA VAN HALEN	61	1984
THE PANDEMONIUM SINGLE KILLING JOKE	28	1994
PANDORA'S BOX [A] PROCOL HARUM	16	1975
PANDORA'S BOX [B] ORCHESTRAL MANOEUVRES IN THE DARK	7	1991
PANDORA'S KISS LOUISE	5	2003
PANIC SMITHS	11	1986
PANIC ATTACK PADDINGTONS	25	2005
PANIC ON MADDER ROSE	65	1994
PANINARO '95 PET SHOP BOYS	15	1995
PANIS ANGELICUS ANTHONY WAY	55	1995
PANTHER PARTY MAD MOSES	50	1997
PAPA DON'T PREACH MADONNA	1	1986
PAPA DON'T PREACH KELLY OSBOURNE	3	2002
PAPA LOVES MAMA JOAN REGAN	29	1960
PAPA LOVES MAMBO PERRY COMO	16	1954
PAPA OOM MOW MOW GARY GLITTER	38	1975
PAPA OOM MOW MOW SHARONETTES	26	1975
PAPA WAS A ROLLIN' STONE TEMPTATIONS	14	1973
PAPA WAS A ROLLING STONE WAS (NOT WAS)	12	1990
PAPA'S GOT A BRAND NEW BAG JAMES BROWN & THE FAMOUS FLAMES	25	1965
PAPA'S GOT A BRAND NEW PIGBAG PIGBAG	3	1982
PAPA'S GOT A BRAND NEW PIGBAG SILENT UNDERDOG	73	1985
PAPER DOLL [A] WINDSOR DAVIES & DON ESTELLE	41	1975
PAPER DOLL [B] PM DAWN	49	1991
PAPER HOUSE FOOLPROOF	53	2004
PAPER PLANE STATUS QUO	8	1973
PAPER ROSES ANITA BRYANT	24	1960
PAPER ROSES KAYE SISTERS	7	1960
PAPER ROSES MAUREEN EVANS	40	1960
PAPER ROSES MARIE OSMOND	2	1973
PAPER SUN TRAFFIC	5	1967
PAPER TIGER SUE THOMPSON	30	1965
PAPERBACK WRITER BEATLES	1	1966
PAPERCUT LINKIN PARK	14	2001
PAPERFACES FEEDER	41	1999
PAPILLON N-JOI	70	1994
PAPUA NEW GUINEA FUTURE SOUND OF LONDON	22	1992
PARA MI MOTIVATION	71	2001
PARADE WHITE & TORCH	54	1982
PARADISE [A] FRANK IFIELD	26	1965
PARADISE [B] STRANGLERS	48	1983
PARADISE [C] BLACK	38	1988
PARADISE [D] SADE	29	1988
PARADISE [E] BIRDLAND	70	1989
PARADISE [F] DIANA ROSS	61	1989
PARADISE [G] RALPH FRIDGE	68	1999
PARADISE [H] KACI	11	2001
PARADISE [I] LL COOL J FEATURING AMERIE	18	2003
PARADISE BIRD AMII STEWART	39	1980
PARADISE CITY GUNS N' ROSES	6	1989
PARADISE CITY N-TRANCE	28	1998
PARADISE LOST HERD	15	1968
PARADISE SKIES MAX WEBSTER	43	1979
PARALYSED ELVIS PRESLEY	8	1957
PARANOID BLACK SABBATH	4	1970
PARANOID DICKIES	45	1979
PARANOID ANDROID RADIOHEAD	3	1997
PARANOIMIA ART OF NOISE FEATURING MAX HEADROOM	12	1986
PARDON ME INCUBUS	61	2000
PARIS BY AIR TYGERS OF PAN TANG	63	1982
PARIS IS ONE DAY AWAY MOOD	42	1982
PARIS MATCH STYLE COUNCIL	3	1983
PARISIENNE GIRL INCOGNITO	73	1980
PARISIENNE WALKWAYS GARY MOORE	8	1979
PARKLIFE BLUR	10	1994
PART OF THE PROCESS MORCHEEBA	38	1998
PART OF THE UNION STRAWBS	2	1973
PART TIME LOVE [A] GLADYS KNIGHT & THE PIPS	30	1975
PART TIME LOVE [B] ELTON JOHN	15	1978
PARTAY FEELING B-CREW	45	1997
PART-TIME LOVER STEVIE WONDER	3	1985
PARTY [A] ELVIS PRESLEY	2	1957
THE PARTY [B] KRAZE	29	1988
THE PARTY AIN'T OVER YET STATUS QUO	11	2005
PARTY ALL NIGHT [A] KREUZ	75	1995
PARTY ALL NIGHT [B] MYTOWN	22	1999
PARTY CRASHERS RADIO 4	75	2004
PARTY DOLL BUDDY KNOX	29	1957
PARTY DOLL JETS	72	1984

	Peak Position	Year of Entry
PARTY FEARS TWO ASSOCIATES	9	1982
PARTY FOR TWO SHANIA TWAIN & MARK McGRATH	10	2004
PARTY FOUR (EP) MAD JOCKS FEATURING JOCKMASTER B.A.	57	1993
PARTY FREAK CA$HFLOW	15	1986
PARTY HARD [A] PULP	29	1998
PARTY HARD [B] ANDREW WK	19	2001
PARTY IN PARIS U.K. SUBS	37	1980
PARTY LIGHTS GAP BAND	30	1980
PARTY PARTY ELVIS COSTELLO & THE ATTRACTIONS WITH THE ROYAL HORN GUARDS	48	1982
PARTY PEOPLE (LIVE YOUR LIFE BE FREE) PIANOMAN	43	1997
PARTY PEOPLE...FRIDAY NIGHT 911	5	1997
PARTY POPS RUSS CONWAY	24	1957
PARTY STARTER WILL SMITH	19	2005
PARTY TIME FATBACK BAND	41	1976
PARTY TIME (THE GO-GO EDIT) KURTIS BLOW	67	1985
PARTY UP THE WORLD D:REAM	20	1995
PARTY ZONE DAFFY DUCK FEATURING THE GROOVE GANG	58	1991
PARTYLINE BRASS CONSTRUCTION	56	1984
PARTYMAN PRINCE	14	1989
THE PARTY'S JUST BEGUN CHEETAH GIRLS	53	2007
THE PARTY'S OVER LONNIE DONEGAN	9	1962
PASADENA TEMPERANCE SEVEN	4	1961
PASILDA AFRO MEDUSA	31	2000
PASS & MOVE (IT'S THE LIVERPOOL GROOVE) LIVERPOOL FC & THE BOOT ROOM BOYS	4	1996
PASS IT ON [A] BITTY McLEAN	35	1993
PASS IT ON [B] CORAL	5	2003
PASS THAT DUTCH MISSY ELLIOTT	10	2003
PASS THE COURVOISIER - PART II BUSTA RHYMES, P DIDDY & PHARRELL	16	2002
PASS THE DUTCHIE MUSICAL YOUTH	1	1982
PASS THE MIC BEASTIE BOYS	47	1992
PASS THE VIBES DEFINITION OF SOUND	23	1995
A PASSAGE TO BANGKOK RUSH	41	1981
PASSCHENDAELE GOODBOOKS	73	2007
THE PASSENGER SIOUXSIE & THE BANSHEES	41	1987
THE PASSENGER IGGY POP	22	1998
PASSENGERS ELTON JOHN	5	1984
PASSIN' ME BY PHARCYDE	55	1993
PASSING BREEZE RUSS CONWAY	16	1960
PASSING STRANGERS [A] BILLY ECKSTINE & SARAH VAUGHAN	20	1957
PASSING STRANGERS [A] JOE LONGTHORNE & LIZ DAWN	34	1994
PASSING STRANGERS [B] ULTRAVOX	57	1980
P.A.S.S.I.O.N. RHYTHM SYNDICATE	58	1991
PASSION [A] ROD STEWART	17	1980
PASSION [B] GAT DECOR	6	1992
PASSION [C] JON OF THE PLEASED WIMMIN	27	1995
PASSION [D] AMEN! UK	15	1997
PASSION IN DARK ROOMS MOOD	74	1982
PASSION KILLER ONE THE JUGGLER	71	1983
THE PASSION OF LOVERS BAUHAUS	56	1981
PASSION RULES THE GAME SCORPIONS	74	1989
PASSIONATE FRIEND TEARDROP EXPLODES	25	1981
PAST, PRESENT AND FUTURE CINDY & THE SAFFRONS	56	1983
PAST THE MISSION TORI AMOS	31	1994
PATCHES CLARENCE CARTER	2	1970
PATHS ROBERT MILES FEATURING NINA MIRANDA	74	2001
PATHS OF PARADISE JOHNNIE RAY	20	1955
PATHWAY TO THE MOON MN8	25	1996
PATIENCE [A] GUNS N' ROSES	10	1989
PATIENCE [B] NERINA PALLOT	61	2001
PATIENCE [C] TAKE THAT	1	2006
PATIENCE OF ANGELS EDDI READER	33	1994
PATIO SONG GORKY'S ZYGOTIC MYNCI	41	1996
PATRICIA PEREZ 'PREZ' PRADO & HIS ORCHESTRA	8	1958
PATT (PARTY ALL THE TIME) SHARAM	8	2006
THE PAY OFF (AMOI DE PAYER) KENNY BALL & HIS JAZZMEN	23	1962
PAY TO THE PIPER CHAIRMEN OF THE BOARD	34	1971
THE PAYBACK MIX JAMES BROWN	12	1988
PAYBACK TIME DYSFUNCTIONAL PSYCHEDELIC WALTONS	48	2003
PAYING THE PRICE OF LOVE BEE GEES	23	1993
PCP MANIC STREET PREACHERS	16	1994
PE 2000 PUFF DADDY FEATURING HURRICANE G	13	1999
PEACE SABRINA JOHNSTON	8	1991
PEACE AND JOY SOUNDSTATION	62	1995
PEACE & QUIET RIFLES	48	2006
PEACE IN OUR TIME [A] IMPOSTER	48	1984
PEACE IN OUR TIME [B] BIG COUNTRY	39	1989
PEACE IN OUR TIME [C] CLIFF RICHARD	8	1993
PEACE IN THE WORLD DON-E	41	1992
PEACE ON EARTH HI TENSION	8	1978
PEACE ON EARTH - LITTLE DRUMMER BOY DAVID BOWIE & BING CROSBY	3	1982
PEACE + LOVEISM SON'Z OF A LOOP DA LOOP ERA	60	1992
PEACE THROUGHOUT THE WORLD MAXI PRIEST FEATURING JAZZIE B	41	1990
PEACEFUL GEORGIE FAME	16	1969
PEACH PRINCE	14	1993
PEACHES [A] STRANGLERS	8	1977
PEACHES [B] DARTS	66	1980
PEACHES [C] PRESIDENTS OF THE UNITED STATES OF AMERICA	8	1996
PEACHES [D] PINK GREASE	44	2005
PEACHES AND CREAM 112	32	2001
PEACOCK SUIT PAUL WELLER	5	1996
PEAKIN' BLEACHIN'	32	2000
PEARL CHAPTERHOUSE	67	1991
PEARL IN THE SHELL HOWARD JONES	7	1984
PEARL RIVER THREE 'N' ONE PRESENTS JOHNNY SHAKER FEATURING SERIAL DIVA	32	1999
PEARL'S A SINGER ELKIE BROOKS	8	1977
PEARL'S GIRL UNDERWORLD	22	1996
PEARLY-DEWDROPS' DROPS COCTEAU TWINS	29	1984
PEEK-A-BOO [A] NEW VAUDEVILLE BAND FEATURING TRISTRAM	7	1967
PEEK-A-BOO [B] STYLISTICS	35	1973
PEEK-A-BOO [C] SIOUXSIE & THE BANSHEES	16	1988
THE PEEL SESSIONS (1ST JUNE 1982) NEW ORDER	54	1986
PEGGY SUE BUDDY HOLLY	6	1957
PEGGY SUE GOT MARRIED BUDDY HOLLY	13	1959
PENNIES FROM HEAVEN INNER CITY	24	1992
PENNY AND ME HANSON	10	2005
PENNY ARCADE ROY ORBISON	27	1969
PENNY LANE BEATLES	2	1967
PENNY LOVER LIONEL RICHIE	18	1984
PENTHOUSE AND PAVEMENT HEAVEN 17	54	1981
PEOPLE [A] TYMES	16	1969
PEOPLE [B] INTASTELLA	74	1991
PEOPLE [C] ALFIE	53	2003
PEOPLE ARE PEOPLE DEPECHE MODE	4	1984
PEOPLE ARE STILL HAVING SEX LaTOUR	15	1991
PEOPLE ARE STRANGE ECHO & THE BUNNYMEN	29	1988
PEOPLE EVERYDAY ARRESTED DEVELOPMENT	2	1992
PEOPLE GET READY JEFF BECK & ROD STEWART	49	1992
PEOPLE GET READY ROD STEWART	45	1993
PEOPLE GET REAL SAINT ETIENNE	21	1992
PEOPLE HELP THE PEOPLE CHERRY GHOST	27	2007
PEOPLE HOLD ON COLDCUT FEATURING LISA STANSFIELD	11	1989
PEOPLE HOLD ON LISA STANSFIELD Vs THE DIRTY ROTTEN SCOUNDRELS	4	1997
PEOPLE IN THA MIDDLE SPEARHEAD	49	1995
PEOPLE LIKE YOU PEOPLE LIKE ME GLITTER BAND	5	1976
PEOPLE OF LOVE AMEN! UK	36	1997
PEOPLE OF THE SUN RAGE AGAINST THE MACHINE	26	1996
PEPE DUANE EDDY & THE REBELS	2	1961
PEPE RUSS CONWAY	19	1961
PEPPER BUTTHOLE SURFERS	59	1996
PEPPER BOX PEPPERS	6	1974
PEPPERMINT TWIST DANNY PEPPERMINT & THE JUMPING JACKS	26	1962
PEPPERMINT TWIST JOEY DEE & THE STARLITERS	33	1962
PER SEMPRE AMORE (FOREVER IN LOVE) LOLLY	11	2000
PERFECT [A] FAIRGROUND ATTRACTION	1	1988
PERFECT [B] LIGHTNING SEEDS	18	1995
PERFECT [C] PJ & DUNCAN	16	1995
PERFECT [D] SMASHING PUMPKINS	24	1998
PERFECT BLISS BELLEFIRE	18	2001
PERFECT DAY [A] EMF	27	1995
PERFECT DAY [B] DURAN DURAN	28	1995
PERFECT DAY [B] KIRSTY MacCOLL & EVAN DANDO	75	1995
PERFECT DAY [B] VARIOUS ARTISTS (EP'S & LPS)	1	1997
PERFECT DAY [C] SKIN	33	1996
A PERFECT DAY ELISE PJ HARVEY	25	1998
THE PERFECT DRUG NINE INCH NAILS	43	1997
PERFECT GENTLEMAN WYCLEF JEAN	4	2001
THE PERFECT KISS NEW ORDER	46	1985
PERFECT LOVE SIMPLY RED	30	2005
PERFECT LOVESONG DIVINE COMEDY	42	2001
PERFECT MOMENT MARTINE McCUTCHEON	1	1999
PERFECT MOTION SUNSCREEM	18	1992
PERFECT PLACE VOICE OF THE BEEHIVE	37	1992
PERFECT SKIN LLOYD COLE & THE COMMOTIONS	26	1984
PERFECT STRANGERS DEEP PURPLE	48	1985
PERFECT 10 BEAUTIFUL SOUTH	2	1998
PERFECT TIMING KIKI DEE	66	1981
PERFECT WAY SCRITTI POLITTI	48	1985
PERFECT WORLD HUEY LEWIS & THE NEWS	48	1988
THE PERFECT YEAR DINA CARROLL	5	1993
PERFECTION DANNII MINOGUE & SOUL SEEKERZ	11	2005
PERFIDIA VENTURES	4	1960
PERFUME PARIS ANGELS	55	1991
PERFUMED GARDEN RAH BAND	45	1982
PERHAPS LOVE PLACIDO DOMINGO WITH JOHN DENVER	46	1981
PERMANENT YEARS EAGLE-EYE CHERRY	43	1999
PERPETUAL DAWN ORB	18	1991
PERRY MASON OZZY OSBOURNE	23	1995
PERSEVERANCE TERRORVISION	5	1996
PERSONAL FEELING AUDIOWEB	65	1998
PERSONAL JESUS DEPECHE MODE	13	1989
PERSONAL JESUS JOHNNY CASH	42	2003
PERSONAL JESUS MARILYN MANSON	13	2004
PERSONAL TOUCH ERROL BROWN	25	1987
PERSONALITY [A] ANTHONY NEWLEY	6	1959
PERSONALITY [A] LLOYD PRICE	9	1959
PERSONALITY [A] LENA ZAVARONI	33	1974
PERSONALITY [B] EUGENE WILDE	34	1985
PER-SO-NAL-LY WIGAN'S OVATION	38	1975
PERSUASION TIM FINN	43	1993

	Peak Position	Year of Entry
A PESSIMIST IS NEVER DISAPPOINTED THEAUDIENCE	27	1998
PETAL WUBBLE-U	55	1998
PETER AND THE WOLF CLYDE VALLEY STOMPERS	25	1962
PETER GUNN ART OF NOISE FEATURING DUANE EDDY	8	1986
PETER GUNN THEME DUANE EDDY & THE REBELS	6	1959
PETER PIPER RUN D.M.C.	62	1986
PETITE FLEUR CHRIS BARBER'S JAZZ BAND	3	1959
PETS PORNO FOR PYROS	53	1993
PHANTOM LIMB SHINS	42	2007
THE PHANTOM OF THE OPERA SARAH BRIGHTMAN & STEVE HARLEY	7	1986
PHASED (EP) ALL ABOUT EVE	38	1992
PHAT BEACH (I'LL BE READY) NAUGHTY BOY	36	2006
PHAT GIRLS IGNORANTS	59	1993
PHATT BASS WARP BROTHERS VERSUS AQUAGEN	9	2000
PHENOMENON LL COOL J	9	1997
PHEW WOW FARMERS BOYS	59	1984
PHILADELPHIA NEIL YOUNG	62	1994
PHILADELPHIA FREEDOM ELTON JOHN BAND	12	1975
PHOBIA FLOWERED UP	75	1990
PHONE HOME JONNY CHINGAS	43	1983
PHOREVER PEOPLE SHAMEN	5	1992
PHOTOGRAPH [A] RINGO STARR	8	1973
PHOTOGRAPH [B] DEF LEPPARD	66	1983
PHOTOGRAPH [C] NICKELBACK	29	2005
PHOTOGRAPH OF MARY TREY LORENZ	38	1993
THE PHOTOS ON MY WALL GOOD SHOES	48	2007
PHUTURE 2000 CARL COX	40	1999
PHYSICAL OLIVIA NEWTON-JOHN	7	1981
PIANISSIMO KEN DODD	21	1962
PIANO IN THE DARK BRENDA RUSSELL	23	1988
PIANO LOCO DJ LUCK & MC NEAT	12	2001
PIANO MEDLEY NO. 114 CHARLIE KUNZ	16	1954
PIANO PARTY WINIFRED ATWELL	10	1959
PICCADILLY PALARE MORRISSEY	18	1990
PICK A BALE OF COTTON LONNIE DONEGAN	11	1962
PICK A PART THAT'S NEW STEREOPHONICS	4	1999
PICK ME UP I'LL DANCE MELBA MOORE	48	1979
PICK UP THE PIECES [A] HUDSON-FORD	8	1973
PICK UP THE PIECES [B] AVERAGE WHITE BAND	6	1975
PICKIN' A CHICKEN EVE BOSWELL	9	1955
PICKNEY GAL DESMOND DEKKER & THE ACES	42	1970
PICNIC IN THE SUMMERTIME DEEE-LITE	43	1994
A PICTURE OF YOU [A] JOE BROWN & THE BRUVVERS	2	1962
PICTURE OF YOU [B] BOYZONE	2	1997
PICTURE THIS BLONDIE	12	1978
PICTURES IN THE DARK MIKE OLDFIELD FEATURING ALED JONES, ANITA HEGERLAND & BARRY PALMER	50	1985
PICTURES OF LILY WHO	4	1967
PICTURES OF MATCHSTICK MEN STATUS QUO	7	1968
PICTURES OF YOU CURE	24	1990
PIE JESU SARAH BRIGHTMAN & PAUL MILES-KINGSTON	3	1985
PIECE BY PIECE KENNY THOMAS	36	1993
PIECE OF ME BRITNEY SPEARS	2	2007
PIECE OF MY HEART SAMMY HAGAR	67	1982
PIECE OF MY HEART SHAGGY FEATURING MARSHA	7	1997
PIECE OF MY HEART BEVERLEY KNIGHT	16	2006
PIECE OF THE ACTION [A] BUCKS FIZZ	12	1981
PIECE OF THE ACTION [B] MEAT LOAF	47	1985
PIECES MY VITRIOL	56	2000
THE PIECES DON'T FIT ANYMORE JAMES MORRISON	30	2006
PIECES OF A DREAM [A] INCOGNITO	35	1994
PIECES OF A DREAM [B] ANASTACIA	48	2005
PIECES OF ICE DIANA ROSS	46	1983
PIECES OF ME ASHLEE SIMPSON	4	2004
PIED PIPER CRISPIAN ST. PETERS	5	1966
PIED PIPER BOB & MARCIA	11	1971
PIED PIPER (THE BEEJE) STEVE RACE	29	1963
PIES WILEY	45	2004
PIHA IAN POOLEY & MAGIK J	53	2002
PILGRIMAGE SOURMASH	73	2000
PILLOW TALK SYLVIA	14	1973
PILLS AND SOAP IMPOSTER	16	1983
PILOT OF THE AIRWAVES CHARLIE DORE	66	1979
PILOTS GOLDFRAPP	68	2001
PILTDOWN RIDES AGAIN PILTDOWN MEN	14	1961
PIMP 50 CENT	5	2003
PIN YEAH YEAH YEAH	26	2003
PINBALL BRIAN PROTHEROE	22	1974
PINBALL WIZARD WHO	4	1969
PINBALL WIZARD ELTON JOHN	7	1976
PINBALL WIZARD - SEE ME FEEL ME (MEDLEY) NEW SEEKERS	16	1973
PINCUSHION ZZ TOP	15	1994
PINEAPPLE HEAD CROWDED HOUSE	27	1994
PING PONG STEREOLAB	45	1994
PINK AEROSMITH	13	1997
PINK CADILLAC NATALIE COLE	5	1988
PINK CHAMPAGNE [A] SHAKIN' STEVENS	59	1990
PINK CHAMPAGNE [B] RHYTHM ETERNITY	72	1992
PINK FLOWER DAISY CHAINSAW	65	1992
THE PINK GREASE PINK GREASE	75	2004
THE PINK PARKER EP GRAHAM PARKER & THE RUMOUR	24	1977
PINK SQUARES IWASACUBSCOUT	71	2008
PINK SUNSHINE FUZZBOX	14	1989
PINKY BLUE ALTERED IMAGES	35	1982
THE PIONEERS BLOC PARTY	18	2005
PIPELINE CHANTAYS	16	1963
PIPELINE BRUCE JOHNSTON	33	1977
PIPES OF PEACE PAUL McCARTNEY	1	1983
PIRANHA TRIPPING DAISY	72	1996
PISSING IN THE WIND BADLY DRAWN BOY	22	2001
PISTOL PACKIN' MAMA GENE VINCENT	15	1960
PISTOL WHIP JOSHUA RYAN	29	2001
PITCHIN' (IN EVERY DIRECTION) HI-GATE	6	2000
A PLACE CALLED HOME PJ HARVEY	43	2001
A PLACE IN THE SUN [A] SHADOWS	24	1966
A PLACE IN THE SUN [B] STEVIE WONDER	20	1967
PLACE IN YOUR HEART NAZARETH	70	1978
PLACE YOUR HANDS REEF	6	1996
PLACES TILT	64	1997
PLACES THAT BELONG TO YOU BARBRA STREISAND	17	1992
PLAN A DANDY WARHOLS	66	2003
PLAN B DEXY'S MIDNIGHT RUNNERS	58	1981
PLAN 9 808 STATE	50	1993
PLAN OF MY OWN DEEYAH	37	2005
PLANET CARAVAN PANTERA	26	1994
PLANET CLAIRE B-52's	12	1986
THE PLANET DANCE (MOVE YA BODY) LIQUID OXYGEN	56	1990
PLANET E K.C. FLIGHTT	48	1989
PLANET EARTH DURAN DURAN	12	1981
PLANET GIRL ZODIAC MINDWARP & THE LOVE REACTION	63	1988
PLANET LOVE DJ QUICKSILVER	12	1998
THE PLANET OF LOVE CARL COX	44	1993
PLANET OF SOUND PIXIES	27	1991
PLANET ROCK AFRIKA BAMBAATAA & THE SONIC SOUL FORCE	53	1982
PLANET ROCK PAUL OAKENFOLD PRESENTS AFRIKA BAMBAATAA	47	2001
PLANET ROCK/FUNKY PLANET POWERS THAT BE	63	2003
PLANET TELEX RADIOHEAD	17	1995
PLANET VIOLET NALIN I.N.C.	51	1998
PLANETARY SIT-IN (EVERY GIRL HAS YOUR NAME) JULIAN COPE	34	1996
THE PLASTIC AGE BUGGLES	16	1980
PLASTIC DREAMS JAYDEE	18	1997
PLASTIC MAN KINKS	31	1969
PLATINUM BLONDE PRELUDE	45	1980
PLATINUM POP THIS YEAR'S BLONDE	46	1981
PLAY JENNIFER LOPEZ	3	2001
PLAY DEAD BJORK & DAVID ARNOLD	12	1993
PLAY EP RIDE	32	1990
PLAY IT COOL SUPER FURRY ANIMALS	27	1997
PLAY ME LIKE YOU PLAY YOUR GUITAR DUANE EDDY & THE REBELETTES	9	1975
PLAY THAT FUNKY MUSIC WILD CHERRY	7	1976
PLAY THAT FUNKY MUSIC THUNDER	39	1991
PLAY THAT FUNKY MUSIC VANILLA ICE	10	1998
PLAY THE GAME QUEEN	14	1980
PLAY THE HITS HAL	38	2005
PLAY TO WIN HEAVEN 17	46	1981
PLAYA HATA LUNIZ	20	1996
PLAYA NO MO' LINA	46	2001
PLAYAS GON' PLAY 3LW	21	2001
PLAYA'S ONLY R KELLY FEATURING GAME	33	2005
PLAYAZ CLUB RAPPIN' 4-TAY	63	1995
PLAYED A LIVE (THE BONGO SONG) SAFRI DUO	6	2001
PLAYGROUND [A] ANITA HARRIS	46	1967
PLAYGROUND [B] FUN DMENTAL 03	44	2006
PLAYGROUND LOVE AIR	25	2000
PLAYGROUND SUPERSTAR HAPPY MONDAYS	51	2005
PLAYGROUND TWIST SIOUXSIE & THE BANSHEES	28	1979
PLAYING WITH KNIVES BIZARRE INC	4	1991
PLAYING WITH THE BOY TECHNICIAN 2	70	1992
PLAYTHING LINX	48	1982
PLAYTIME RONI SIZE	53	2002
PLEASANT VALLEY SUNDAY MONKEES	11	1967
PLEASE [A] ELTON JOHN	33	1996
PLEASE [B] U2	7	1997
PLEASE [C] ROBIN GIBB	23	2003
PLEASE BE CRUEL INSPIRAL CARPETS	50	1991
PLEASE COME HOME FOR CHRISTMAS EAGLES	30	1978
PLEASE COME HOME FOR CHRISTMAS BON JOVI	7	1994
PLEASE DON'T ASK ABOUT BARBARA BOBBY VEE	29	1962
PLEASE DON'T BE SCARED BARRY MANILOW	35	1989
PLEASE DON'T FALL IN LOVE CLIFF RICHARD	7	1983
PLEASE DON'T GO [A] DONALD PEERS	3	1968
PLEASE DON'T GO [B] KC & THE SUNSHINE BAND	3	1979
PLEASE DON'T GO [B] DOUBLE YOU?	41	1992
PLEASE DON'T GO [B] KWS	1	1992
PLEASE DON'T GO [C] NO MERCY	4	1997
PLEASE DON'T MAKE ME CRY UB40	10	1983
PLEASE DON'T TEASE CLIFF RICHARD & THE SHADOWS	1	1960
PLEASE DON'T TOUCH JOHNNY KIDD	25	1959
PLEASE DON'T TURN ME ON ARTFUL DODGER FEATURING LIFFORD	4	2000
PLEASE FORGIVE ME [A] BRYAN ADAMS	2	1993
PLEASE FORGIVE ME [B] DAVID GRAY	18	1999
PLEASE HELP ME I'M FALLING HANK LOCKLIN	9	1960
PLEASE MR. POSTMAN CARPENTERS	2	1975
PLEASE MR POSTMAN BACKBEAT BAND	69	1994

	Peak Position	Year of Entry
PLEASE, PLEASE McFLY	1	2006
PLEASE PLEASE ME BEATLES	2	1963
PLEASE PLEASE ME DAVID CASSIDY	16	1974
PLEASE PLEASE PLEASE SHOUT OUT LOUDS	53	2006
PLEASE RELEASE ME MIKE FLOWERS POPS	39	1996
PLEASE SAVE ME SUNSCREEM VS PUSH	36	2001
PLEASE SIRE MARTYN JOSEPH	45	1993
PLEASE STAND UP BRITISH SEA POWER	34	2005
PLEASE STAY [A] CRYIN' SHAMES	26	1966
PLEASE STAY [B] KYLIE MINOGUE	10	2000
PLEASE TELL HIM I SAID HELLO DANA	8	1975
PLEASE (YOU GOT THAT...) INXS	50	1993
PLEASE YOURSELF BIG SUPREME	64	1987
PLEASURE BOYS VISAGE	44	1982
PLEASURE DOME SOUL II SOUL	51	1997
PLEASURE FROM THE BASS TIGA	57	2004
PLEASURE LOVE DE FUNK FEATURING F45	49	1999
PLEASURE PRINCIPLE JANET JACKSON	24	1987
PLENTY GOOD LOVIN' CONNIE FRANCIS	18	1959
PLOWED SPONGE	74	1995
PLUG IN BABY MUSE	11	2001
PLUG IT IN BASEMENT JAXX FEATURING JC CHASEZ	22	2004
PLUG ME IN (TO THE CENTRAL LOVE LINE) SCARLET FANTASTIC	67	1988
PLUG MYSELF IN D.O.S.E. FEATURING MARK E SMITH	50	1996
PLUS ECHELON	57	2004
PLUSH STONE TEMPLE PILOTS	23	1993
THE POACHER RONNIE LANE & SLIM CHANCE	36	1974
POCKET CALCULATOR KRAFTWERK	39	1981
POD TENACIOUS D	51	2006
POEMS NEARLY GOD	28	1996
POETRY IN MOTION JOHNNY TILLOTSON	1	1960
POGUETRY IN MOTION EP POGUES	29	1986
POING ROTTERDAM TERMINATION SOURCE	27	1992
POINT OF NO RETURN [A] NU SHOOZ	48	1986
POINT OF NO RETURN [B] CENTORY	67	1994
POINT OF VIEW [A] MATUMBI	35	1979
POINT OF VIEW [B] DB BOULEVARD	3	2002
POISON [A] ALICE COOPER	2	1989
POISON [B] BELL BIV DEVOE	19	1990
POISON [C] PRODIGY	15	1995
POISON [D] BARDOT	45	2001
POISON [E] GROOVE COVERAGE	32	2005
POISON ARROW ABC	6	1982
POISON HEART RAMONES	69	1992
POISON IVY COASTERS	15	1959
POISON IVY PARAMOUNTS	35	1964
POISON IVY LAMBRETTAS	7	1980
POISON STREET NEW MODEL ARMY	64	1987
POLARIS ASH	32	2007
POLICE AND THIEVES JUNIOR MURVIN	23	1980
POLICE OFFICER SMILEY CULTURE	12	1984
POLICE ON MY BACK LETHAL BIZZLE	37	2007
POLICE STATE T-POWER	63	1996
POLICEMAN SKANK...(THE STORY OF MY LIFE) AUDIOWEB	21	1998
POLICY OF TRUTH DEPECHE MODE	16	1990
THE POLITICS OF DANCING RE-FLEX	28	1984
POLK SALAD ANNIE ELVIS PRESLEY	23	1973
POLYESTERDAY GUS GUS	55	1998
PON DE REPLAY RIHANNA	2	2005
PON DE RIVER, PON DE BANK ELEPHANT MAN	29	2003
PONY GINUWINE	16	1997
PONY TIME CHUBBY CHECKER	27	1961
POODLE ROCKIN' GORKY'S ZYGOTIC MYNCI	52	2000
POOL HALL RICHARD FACES	8	1973
POOR JENNY EVERLY BROTHERS	14	1959
POOR LENO ROYKSOPP	38	2001
POOR LITTLE FOOL RICKY NELSON	4	1958
POOR MAN'S SON ROCKIN' BERRIES	5	1965
POOR ME ADAM FAITH	1	1960
POOR MISGUIDED FOOL STARSAILOR	23	2002
POOR PEOPLE OF PARIS WINIFRED ATWELL	1	1956
POP N SYNC	9	2001
POP COP GYRES	71	1996
POP GO THE WORKERS BARRON KNIGHTS WITH DUKE D'MOND	5	1965
POP GOES MY LOVE FREEEZ	26	1983
POP GOES THE WEASEL [A] ANTHONY NEWLEY	12	1961
POP GOES THE WEASEL [B] 3RD BASS	64	1991
POP IS DEAD RADIOHEAD	42	1993
POP LIFE PRINCE & THE REVOLUTION	60	1985
POP MUZIK M	2	1979
POP MUZIK ALL SYSTEMS GO	63	1988
THE POP SINGER'S FEAR OF THE POLLEN COUNT DIVINE COMEDY	17	1999
POP THAT BOOTY MARQUES HOUSTON FEATURING JERMAINE	23	2004
POP YA COLLAR USHER	2	2001
POPCORN HOT BUTTER	5	1972
POPCORN CRAZY FROG	12	2005
POPCORN LOVE NEW EDITION	43	1983
POPPA JOE SWEET	11	1972
POPPA PICCOLINO DIANA DECKER	2	1953
POPPED! FOOL BOONA	52	1999
POPS WE LOVE YOU DIANA ROSS, MARVIN GAYE, SMOKEY ROBINSON & STEVIE WONDER	66	1979
POPSCENE BLUR	32	1992
POP!ULAR DARREN HAYES	12	2004
PORCELAIN MOBY	5	2000
PORNOGRAPHY CLIENT	22	2005
PORT AU PRINCE WINIFRED ATWELL & FRANK CHACKSFIELD	18	1956
PORTRAIT OF MY LOVE MATT MONRO	3	1960
PORTSMOUTH MIKE OLDFIELD	3	1976
PORTUGUESE WASHERWOMAN JOE 'FINGERS' CARR	20	1956
POSITIVE BLEEDING URGE OVERKILL	67	1993
POSITIVE EDUCATION SLAM	44	2001
POSITIVE TENSION BLOC PARTY	5	2005
POSITIVELY FOURTH STREET BOB DYLAN	8	1965
POSITIVITY [A] SUEDE	16	2002
POSITIVITY [B] STEVIE WONDER FEATURING AISHA MORRIS	54	2005
POSSE (I NEED YOU ON THE FLOOR) SCOOTER	15	2002
POSSESSED VEGAS	32	1992
POSSESSION TRANSFER	54	2001
POSSIBLY MAYBE BJORK	13	1996
POST MODERN SLEAZE SNEAKER PIMPS	22	1997
POSTCARD FROM HEAVEN LIGHTHOUSE FAMILY	24	1999
POSTMAN PAT KEN BARRIE	44	1982
POTENTIAL BREAK UP SONG ALY & AJ	22	2007
POUNDCAKE VAN HALEN	74	1991
POUNDING DOVES	21	2002
POUR LE MONDE CROWDED HOUSE	51	2007
POUR SOME SUGAR ON ME DEF LEPPARD	18	1987
POW (FORWARD) LETHAL BIZZLE	11	2005
POW WOW WOW FONTANA FEATURING DARRYL D'BONNEAU	62	2001
POWDER BLUE ELBOW	41	2001
THE POWER [A] SNAP	1	1990
POWER [B] NU COLOURS	40	1992
THE POWER [C] MONIE LOVE	33	1993
POWER AND THE GLORY SAXON	32	1983
THE POWER IS YOURS REDSKINS	59	1986
POWER OF A WOMAN ETERNAL	5	1995
THE POWER (OF ALL THE LOVE IN THE WORLD) D:REAM	40	1995
P.OWER OF A.MERICAN N.ATIVES DANCE 2 TRANCE	25	1993
THE POWER (OF BHANGRA) SNAP VS MOTIVO	34	2003
THE POWER OF GOODBYE MADONNA	6	1998
THE POWER OF LOVE [A] FRANKIE GOES TO HOLLYWOOD	1	1984
THE POWER OF LOVE [B] JENNIFER RUSH	1	1985
THE POWER OF LOVE [B] CELINE DION	4	1994
THE POWER OF LOVE [B] FITS OF GLOOM FEATURING LIZZY MACK	49	1994
THE POWER OF LOVE [C] HUEY LEWIS & THE NEWS	9	1985
POWER OF LOVE [D] DEEE-LITE	25	1990
THE POWER OF LOVE [E] Q-TEX	49	1994
THE POWER OF LOVE [F] HOLLY JOHNSON	56	1999
POWER OF LOVE-LOVE POWER LUTHER VANDROSS	31	1991
POWER OUT ARCADE FIRE	26	2005
POWER RANGERS MIGHTY MORPH'N POWER RANGERS	3	1994
POWER TO ALL OUR FRIENDS CLIFF RICHARD	4	1973
POWER TO THE PEOPLE JOHN LENNON & THE PLASTIC ONO BAND	7	1971
THE POWER ZONE TIME FREQUENCY	17	1993
POWERLESS (SAY WHAT YOU WANT) NELLY FURTADO	13	2003
POWERSIGN (ONLY YOUR LOVE) PKA	70	1992
POWERTRIP MONSTER MAGNET	39	1999
PRACTICE WHAT YOU PREACH BARRY WHITE	20	1995
PRAISE INNER CITY	59	1992
PRAISE YOU FATBOY SLIM	1	1999
PRANCE ON EDDIE HENDERSON	44	1978
PRANGIN' OUT STREETS FEATURING PETE DOHERTY	25	2006
PRAY [A] MC HAMMER	8	1990
PRAY [B] TAKE THAT	1	1993
PRAY [C] TINA COUSINS	20	1998
PRAY [D] LASGO	17	2002
PRAY [E] SYNTAX	28	2003
PRAY FOR LOVE LOVE TO INFINITY	69	1996
PRAYER [A] DISTURBED	31	2002
THE PRAYER [B] BLOC PARTY	4	2007
PRAYER FOR THE DYING SEAL	14	1994
PRAYER FOR YOU TEXAS	73	1989
A PRAYER TO THE MUSIC MARCO POLO	65	1995
PRAYER TOWER PARADISE ORGANISATION	70	1993
PRAYING FOR TIME GEORGE MICHAEL	6	1990
PREACHER MAN BANANARAMA	20	1991
PREACHER PREACHER ANIMAL NIGHTLIFE	67	1985
PRECIOUS [A] JAM	1	1982
PRECIOUS [B] ANNIE LENNOX	23	1992
PRECIOUS [C] DEPECHE MODE	4	2005
PRECIOUS HEART TALL PAUL VS INXS	14	2001
PRECIOUS ILLUSIONS ALANIS MORISSETTE	53	2002
PRECIOUS LIFE CRW PRESENTS VERONIKA	57	2002
PRECIOUS TIME VAN MORRISON	36	1999
PRECIOUS TIME MACCABEES	49	2007
PREDICTABLE GOOD CHARLOTTE	12	2004
PREGNANT FOR THE LAST TIME MORRISSEY	25	1991
PREPARE TO LAND SUPERNATURALS	48	1997
PRESENCE OF LOVE (LAUGHERNE) ALARM	44	1988
PRESS PAUL McCARTNEY	25	1986
PRESSURE [A] SUNSCREEM	60	1992
PRESSURE [B] BILLY OCEAN	55	1993
PRESSURE [C] DRIZABONE	33	1994
PRESSURE COOKER G CLUB PRESENTS BANDA SONORA	46	2002
PRESSURE DROP IZZY STADLIN'	45	1992
PRESSURE ON ROGER TAYLOR	45	1998
THE PRESSURE PART 1 SOUNDS OF BLACKNESS	46	1991

	Peak Position	Year of Entry
PRESSURE POINT ZUTONS	19	2004
PRESSURE US SUNSCREEM	19	1993
PRETEND NAT 'KING' COLE	2	1953
PRETEND ALVIN STARDUST	4	1981
PRETEND BEST FRIEND TERRORVISION	25	1994
PRETEND WE'RE DEAD L7	21	1992
THE PRETENDER FOO FIGHTERS	8	2007
PRETENDER GOT MY HEART ALISHA'S ATTIC	43	2001
PRETENDERS TO THE THRONE BEAUTIFUL SOUTH	18	1995
PRETTIEST EYES BEAUTIFUL SOUTH	37	1994
PRETTY BLUE EYES CRAIG DOUGLAS	4	1960
PRETTY BROWN EYES JIM REEVES	33	1968
PRETTY DEEP TANYA DONELLY	55	1997
PRETTY FLAMINGO MANFRED MANN	1	1966
PRETTY FLY (FOR A WHITE GUY) OFFSPRING	1	1999
PRETTY GOOD YEAR TORI AMOS	7	1994
PRETTY GREEN EYES ULTRABEAT	2	2003
PRETTY IN PINK PSYCHEDELIC FURS	18	1981
PRETTY JENNY JESS CONRAD	50	1962
PRETTY LADY SAVANA	48	2004
PRETTY LITTLE ANGEL EYES CURTIS LEE	47	1961
PRETTY LITTLE ANGEL EYES SHOWADDYWADDY	5	1978
PRETTY LITTLE BLACK EYED SUSIE GUY MITCHELL	2	1953
PRETTY NOOSE SOUNDGARDEN	14	1996
PRETTY PAPER ROY ORBISON	6	1964
PRETTY THING BO DIDDLEY	34	1963
PRETTY VACANT SEX PISTOLS	6	1977
PRETTY WOMAN JUICY LUCY	44	1970
THE PRICE OF LOVE EVERLY BROTHERS	2	1965
THE PRICE OF LOVE (REMIX) BRYAN FERRY	49	1989
PRICE TO PAY STAIND	36	2003
PRICE YOU PAY QUESTIONS	56	1983
PRIDE (IN THE NAME OF LOVE) U2	3	1984
PRIDE (IN THE NAME OF LOVE) CLIVILLES & COLE	15	1992
PRIDE'S PARANOIA FUTURESHOCK	60	2003
PRIMAL SCREAM MOTLEY CRUE	32	1991
PRIMARY CURE	43	1981
PRIMARY INSTINCT SENSELESS THINGS	41	1993
PRIMARY RHYMING MC TUNES	67	1990
PRIME MOVER [A] ZODIAC MINDWARP & THE LOVE REACTION	18	1987
PRIME MOVER [B] RUSH	43	1988
PRIME TIME [A] TUBES	34	1979
PRIME TIME [B] HAIRCUT 100	46	1983
PRIME TIME [C] MTUME	57	1984
PRIMITIVE (THE WAY I TREAT YOU) AMBULANCE LTD	72	2005
PRIMROSE LANE DICKIE PRIDE	28	1959
THE PRINCE MADNESS	16	1979
A PRINCE AMONG ISLANDS EP CAPERCAILLIE	39	1992
PRINCE CHARMING ADAM & THE ANTS	1	1981
PRINCE HARRY SOHO DOLLS	57	2004
PRINCE IGOR RHAPSODY FEATURING WARREN G & SISSEL	15	1998
PRINCE OF DARKNESS BOW WOW WOW	58	1981
PRINCE OF PEACE GALLIANO	47	1992
PRINCES OF THE NIGHT BLAST FEATURING VDC	40	1994
PRINCESS IN RAGS GENE PITNEY	9	1965
PRINCESS OF THE NIGHT SAXON	57	1981
PRINCIPAL'S OFFICE YOUNG MC	54	1990
PRINCIPLES OF LUST ENIGMA	59	1991
THE PRISONER FAB FEATURING MC NUMBER 6	56	1990
PRISONER ALL BLUE	73	1999
PRISONER OF LOVE MILLIE SCOTT	52	1986
PRISONER OF LOVER SPEAR OF DESTINY	59	1984
A PRISONER OF THE PAST PREFAB SPROUT	30	1997
PRIVATE DANCER TINA TURNER	26	1984
PRIVATE EMOTION RICKY MARTIN FEATURING MEJA	9	2000
PRIVATE EYE ALKALINE TRIO	51	2002
PRIVATE EYES DARYL HALL & JOHN OATES	32	1982
PRIVATE INVESTIGATIONS DIRE STRAITS	2	1982
PRIVATE LIFE GRACE JONES	17	1980
PRIVATE NUMBER JUDY CLAY & WILLIAM BELL	8	1968
PRIVATE NUMBER 911	3	1999
PRIVATE PARTY WALLY JUMP Jr. & THE CRIMINAL ELEMENT ORCHESTRA	57	1988
PRIVILEGE (SET ME FREE) PATTI SMITH GROUP	72	1978
PRIX CHOC REMIXES ETIENNE DE CRECY	60	1998
PRIZE OF GOLD JOAN REGAN	6	1955
PROBABLY A ROBBERY RENEGADE SOUNDWAVE	38	1990
PROBLEM IS DUB PISTOLS FEATURING TERRY HALL	66	2003
PROBLEMS EVERLY BROTHERS	6	1959
PROCESS OF ELMINATION ERIC GABLE	63	1994
PROCESSED BEATS KASABIAN	17	2004
PROCESSION NEW ORDER	38	1981
PRODIGAL BLUES BILLY IDOL	47	1990
PRODIGAL SON STEEL PULSE	35	1978
PRODUCT OF THE WORKING CLASS LITTLE ANGELS	40	1991
PROFESSIONAL WIDOW (IT'S GOT TO BE BIG) TORI AMOS	1	1996
PROFIT IN PEACE OCEAN COLOUR SCENE	13	1999
PROFOUNDLY IN LOVE WITH PANDORA IAN & THE BLOCKHEADS	45	1985
PROFOUNDLY YOURS HUE & CRY	74	1992
PRO-GEN SHAMEN	4	1990
THE PROGRAM DAVID MORALES	66	1993
PROMISCUOUS NELLY FURTADO FEATURING TIMBALAND	3	2006
A PROMISE ECHO & THE BUNNYMEN	49	1981
PROMISE DELIRIOUS?	20	1997
THE PROMISE [A] ARCADIA	37	1986
THE PROMISE [B] WHEN IN ROME	58	1989
THE PROMISE [C] MICHAEL NYMAN	60	1994
THE PROMISE [D] ESSENCE	27	1998
PROMISE ME BEVERLEY CRAVEN	3	1991
THE PROMISE OF A NEW DAY PAULA ABDUL	52	1991
THE PROMISE YOU MADE COCK ROBIN	28	1986
PROMISED LAND [A] CHUCK BERRY	26	1965
PROMISED LAND [A] ELVIS PRESLEY	9	1975
PROMISED LAND [B] JOE SMOOTH	56	1989
PROMISED LAND [B] STYLE COUNCIL	27	1989
PROMISED YOU A MIRACLE SIMPLE MINDS	13	1982
PROMISES [A] KEN DODD	6	1966
PROMISES [B] ERIC CLAPTON	37	1978
PROMISES [C] BUZZCOCKS	20	1978
PROMISES [D] BASIA	48	1988
PROMISES [E] TAKE THAT	38	1991
PROMISES [F] PARIS RED	59	1993
PROMISES [G] DEF LEPPARD	41	1999
PROMISES [H] CRANBERRIES	13	1999
PROMISES PROMISES COOPER TEMPLE CLAUSE	19	2003
PROPER CRIMBO BO SELECTA	4	2003
PROPER EDUCATION ERIC PRYDZ VS FLOYD	2	2007
PROPHASE TRANSA	65	1997
THE PROPHET C.J. BOLLAND	19	1997
PROTECT YOUR MIND (FOR THE LOVE OF A PRINCESS) DJ SAKIN & FRIENDS	4	1999
PROTECTION MASSIVE ATTACK FEATURING TRACEY THORN	14	1995
PROUD HEATHER SMALL	16	2000
PROUD MARY CHECKMATES LTD.	30	1969
PROUD MARY CREEDENCE CLEARWATER REVIVAL	8	1969
THE PROUD ONE OSMONDS	5	1975
PROUD TO FALL IAN McCULLOCH	51	1989
PROVE IT TELEVISION	25	1977
PROVE YOUR LOVE TAYLOR DAYNE	8	1988
PROVIDER N*E*R*D	20	2003
PSYCHE ROCK PIERRE HENRY	58	1997
PSYCHEDELIC SHACK TEMPTATIONS	33	1970
PSYCHO THEE UNSTRUNG	41	2005
PSYCHO BASE SHADES OF RHYTHM	57	1997
PSYCHONAUT FIELDS OF THE NEPHILIM	35	1989
PSYCHOSIS SAFARI EIGHTIES MATCHBOX B-LINE DISASTER	26	2002
PSYKO FUNK BOO-YAA T.R.I.B.E.	43	1990
A PUB WITH NO BEER SLIM DUSTY	3	1959
A PUBLIC AFFAIR JESSICA SIMPSON	20	2007
PUBLIC ENEMY NO 1 HYPO PSYCHO	53	2004
PUBLIC IMAGE PUBLIC IMAGE LTD.	9	1978
PUCKWUDGIE CHARLIE DRAKE	47	1972
PUFF KENNY LYNCH	33	1962
PULL SHAPES PIPETTES	26	2006
PULL THE WIRES FROM THE WALL DELGADOS	69	1998
PULL UP TO THE BUMPER GRACE JONES	12	1981
PULL UP TO THE BUMPER PATRA	50	1995
PULLIN' ME BACK CHINGY FEATURING TYRESE	44	2006
PULLING MUSSELS (FROM THE SHELL) SQUEEZE	44	1980
PULLING PUNCHES DAVID SYLVIAN	56	1984
PULSAR 2002 MAURO PICOTTO	35	2002
PULS(T)AR BEN LIEBRAND	68	1990
PULVERTURM NIELS VAN GOGH	75	1999
PUMP IT BLACK EYED PEAS	3	2006
PUMP IT UP [A] ELVIS COSTELLO & THE ATTRACTIONS	24	1978
PUMP IT UP [B] JOE BUDDEN	13	2003
PUMP IT UP [C] DANZEL	11	2004
PUMP ME UP GRANDMASTER MELLE MEL & THE FURIOUS FIVE	45	1985
PUMP UP LONDON MR LEE	64	1988
PUMP UP THE BITTER STARTURN ON 45 (PINTS)	12	1988
PUMP UP THE JAM TECHNOTRONIC FEATURING FELLY	2	1989
PUMP UP THE JAM DONS FEATURING TECHNOTRONIC	22	2005
PUMP UP THE VOLUME M/A/R/R/S	1	1987
PUMP UP THE VOLUME GREED FEATURING RICARDO DA FORCE	51	1995
PUMPIN' NOVY VERSUS ENIAC	19	2000
PUMPING ON YOUR STEREO SUPERGRASS	11	1999
PUMPKIN TRICKY	26	1995
PUMPKIN SOUP KATE NASH	23	2007
PUMPS AMY WINEHOUSE	69	2004
PUNCH AND JUDY MARILLION	29	1984
PUNK [A] FERRY CORSTEN	29	2002
A PUNK [B] VAMPIRE WEEKEND	55	2008
PUNK ROCK 101 BOWLING FOR SOUP	43	2003
PUNK ROCK PRINCESS SOMETHING CORPORATE	33	2003
PUNKA KENICKIE	38	1996
PUNKY REGGAE PARTY BOB MARLEY & THE WAILERS	9	1977
PUPPET MAN TOM JONES	49	1971
PUPPET ON A STRING SANDIE SHAW	1	1967
PUPPY LOVE PAUL ANKA	33	1960
PUPPY LOVE DONNY OSMOND	1	1972
PUPPY LOVE S CLUB JUNIORS	6	2002
THE PUPPY SONG DAVID CASSIDY	1	1973
PURE [A] LIGHTNING SEEDS	16	1989
PURE [B] GTO	57	1990
PURE [C] 3 COLOURS RED	28	1997
PURE AND SIMPLE HEAR'SAY	1	2001

	Peak Position	Year of Entry
PURE MASSACRE SILVERCHAIR	71	1995
PURE MORNING PLACEBO	4	1998
PURE PLEASURE DIGITAL EXCITATION	37	1992
PURE PLEASURE SEEKER MOLOKO	21	2000
PURE SHORES ALL SAINTS	1	2000
PURELY BY COINCIDENCE SWEET SENSATION	11	1975
PURGATORY IRON MAIDEN	52	1981
PURITY NEW MODEL ARMY	61	1990
PURPLE HAZE [A] JIMI HENDRIX EXPERIENCE	3	1967
PURPLE HAZE [B] GROOVE ARMADA	36	2002
PURPLE HEATHER ROD STEWART WITH THE SCOTTISH EURO '96 SQUAD	16	1996
PURPLE LOVE BALLOON CUD	27	1992
PURPLE MEDLEY PRINCE	33	1995
PURPLE PEOPLE EATER JACKIE DENNIS	29	1958
PURPLE PEOPLE EATER SHEB WOOLEY	12	1958
PURPLE PILLS D12	2	2001
PURPLE RAIN PRINCE & THE REVOLUTION	8	1984
PUSH [A] MOIST	20	1994
PUSH [B] MATCHBOX 20	38	1998
PUSH [C] GHOSTFACE FEATURING MISSY ELLIOTT	34	2004
THE PUSH (FAR FROM HERE) PAUL JACKSON & STEVE SMITH	51	2004
PUSH IT [A] SALT-N-PEPA	2	1988
PUSH IT [B] GARBAGE	9	1998
PUSH IT ALL ASIDE ALISHA'S ATTIC	24	2001
PUSH THE BEAT MIRAGE	67	1988
PUSH THE BEAT/BAUHAUS CAPPELLA	60	1988
PUSH THE BUTTON SUGABABES	1	2005
PUSH THE FEELING ON NIGHTCRAWLERS	3	1994
PUSH THE GHOST TWANG	63	2007
PUSH UP FREESTYLERS	22	2004
PUSH UPSTAIRS UNDERWORLD	12	1999
THE PUSHBIKE SONG MIXTURES	2	1971
PUSHER SHAPESHIFTERS	56	2007
PUSHIN' ME OUT D-SIDE	21	2004
PUSHING THE SENSES FEEDER	30	2005
PUSS JESUS LIZARD	12	1993
PUSS 'N' BOOTS ADAM ANT	5	1983
PUSSYCAT MULU	50	1997
PUSSYOLE (OLD SKOOL) DIZZEE RASCAL	22	2007
PUT A LIGHT IN THE WINDOW KING BROTHERS	25	1958
PUT A LITTLE LOVE IN YOUR HEART DAVE CLARK FIVE	31	1969
PUT A LITTLE LOVE IN YOUR HEART ANNIE LENNOX & AL GREEN	28	1988
PUT EM HIGH STONEBRIDGE	6	2004
PUT EM' IN THEIR PLACE MOBB DEEP	75	2006
PUT HIM OUT MS DYNAMITE	19	2002
PUT HIM OUT OF YOUR MIND DR FEELGOOD	73	1979
PUT IT THERE PAUL McCARTNEY	32	1990
PUT MY ARMS AROUND YOU KEVIN KITCHEN	64	1985
PUT OUR HEADS TOGETHER O'JAYS	45	1983
PUT THE LIGHT ON WET WET WET	56	1991
PUT THE MESSAGE IN THE BOX BRIAN KENNEDY	37	1997
PUT THE NEEDLE ON IT DANNII MINOGUE	7	2002
PUT THE NEEDLE TO THE RECORD CRIMINAL ELEMENT ORCHESTRA	63	1987
PUT THE SUN BACK CORAL	64	2008
PUT YOU IN YOUR PLACE SUNSHINE UNDERGROUND	39	2006
PUT YOU ON THE GAME GAME	46	2005
PUT YOUR ARMS AROUND ME [A] TEXAS	10	1997
PUT YOUR ARMS AROUND ME [B] NATURAL	32	2002
PUT YOUR FAITH IN ME ALISON LIMERICK	42	1997
PUT YOUR HANDS TOGETHER D MOB FEATURING NUFF JUICE	7	1990
PUT YOUR HANDS UP REFLEX FEATURING MC VIPER	72	2001
PUT YOUR HANDS UP FOR DETROIT FEDDE LE GRAND	1	2006
PUT YOUR HANDS WHERE MY EYES COULD SEE BUSTA RHYMES	16	1997
PUT YOUR HANDZ UP WHOOLIGANZ	53	1994
PUT YOUR HEAD ON MY SHOULDER PAUL ANKA	7	1959
PUT YOUR LOVE IN ME HOT CHOCOLATE	10	1977
PUT YOUR MONEY WHERE YOUR MOUTH IS ROSE ROYCE	44	1977
PUT YOUR MONEY WHERE YOUR MOUTH IS JET	23	2006
PUT YOUR RECORDS ON CORINNE BAILEY RAE	2	2006
PUT YOURSELF IN MY PLACE [A] ISLEY BROTHERS	13	1969
PUT YOURSELF IN MY PLACE [A] ELGINS	28	1971
PUT YOURSELF IN MY PLACE [B] KYLIE MINOGUE	11	1994
PUTTING ON THE STYLE LONNIE DONEGAN	1	1957
PYJAMARAMA ROXY MUSIC	10	1973
PYRAMID SONG RADIOHEAD	5	2001
P.Y.T. (PRETTY YOUNG THING) MICHAEL JACKSON	11	1984

Q–T

Q–T

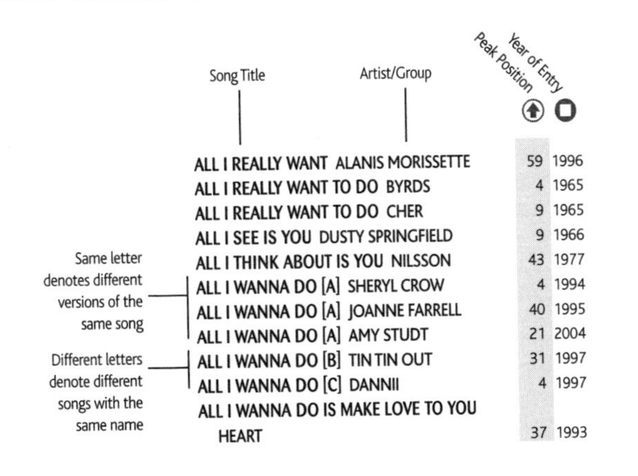
KEY TO INDEX ENTRIES

	Peak Position	Year of Entry
QUADROPHONIA QUADROPHONIA	14	1991
QUANDO M'INNAMORO (A MAN WITHOUT LOVE) SANDPIPERS	33	1968
QUANDO QUANDO QUANDO PAT BOONE	41	1962
QUANDO QUANDO QUANDO ENGELBERT HUMPERDINCK	40	1999
THE QUARTER MOON V.I.P.'S	55	1980
QUARTER TO THREE U.S. BONDS	7	1961
QUE SERA CHRIS REA	73	1988
QUE SERA MI VIDA (IF YOU SHOULD GO) GIBSON BROTHERS	5	1979
QUE SERA SERA GENO WASHINGTON & THE RAM JAM BAND	43	1966
QUE SERA SERA HERMES HOUSE BAND	53	2002
QUE TAL AMERICA TWO MAN SOUND	46	1979
QUEEN FOR TONIGHT HELEN SHAPIRO	33	1963
QUEEN JANE KINGMAKER	29	1993
QUEEN OF CLUBS KC & THE SUNSHINE BAND	7	1974
QUEEN OF HEARTS [A] DAVE EDMUNDS	11	1979
QUEEN OF HEARTS [B] CHARLOTTE	54	1994
QUEEN OF MY HEART WESTLIFE	1	2001
QUEEN OF MY SOUL AVERAGE WHITE BAND	23	1976
QUEEN OF NEW ORLEANS JON BON JOVI	10	1997
THE QUEEN OF 1964 NEIL SEDAKA	35	1975
THE QUEEN OF OUTER SPACE WEDDING PRESENT	23	1992
QUEEN OF RAIN ROXETTE	28	1992
QUEEN OF THE HOP BOBBY DARIN	24	1959
QUEEN OF THE NEW YEAR DEACON BLUE	21	1990
QUEEN OF THE NIGHT WHITNEY HOUSTON	14	1993
QUEEN OF THE RAPPING SCENE (NOTHING EVER GOES THE WAY YOU PLAN) MODERN ROMANCE	37	1982
THE QUEEN'S BIRTHDAY SONG ST. JOHN'S COLLEGE SCHOOL CHOIR & THE BAND OF THE GRENADIER GUARDS	40	1986
QUEEN'S FIRST EP QUEEN	17	1977
QUEER GARBAGE	13	1995
QUESTION [A] MOODY BLUES	2	1970
THE QUESTION [B] SEVEN GRAND HOUSING AUTHORITY	70	1993
QUESTION [C] SYSTEM OF A DOWN	41	2005
QUESTION OF FAITH LIGHTHOUSE FAMILY	21	1998
A QUESTION OF LUST DEPECHE MODE	28	1986
A QUESTION OF TIME DEPECHE MODE	17	1986
QUESTIONS AND ANSWERS [A] SHAM 69	18	1979
QUESTIONS AND ANSWERS [B] BIFFY CLYRO	26	2003
QUESTIONS I CAN'T ANSWER HEINZ	39	1964
QUESTIONS (MUST BE ASKED) DAVID FORBES	57	2001
QUICK JOEY SMALL (RUN JOEY RUN) KASENETZ-KATZ SINGING ORCHESTRAL CIRCUS	19	1968
QUIEREME MUCHO (YOURS) JULIO IGLESIAS	3	1982
QUIET LIFE JAPAN	19	1981
THE QUIET THINGS THAT NO ONE EVER KNOWS BRAND NEW	39	2004
QUIT PLAYING GAMES (WITH MY HEART) BACKSTREET BOYS	2	1997
QUIT THIS TOWN EDDIE & THE HOT RODS	36	1978
QUITE A PARTY FIREBALLS	29	1961
QUITE RIGHTLY SO PROCOL HARUM	50	1968
QUOTE GOODBYE QUOTE CAROLYNE MAS	71	1980
QUOTH POLYGON WINDOW	49	1993

R

	Peak Position	Year of Entry
R 'N' B GOLDIE LOOKIN CHAIN	26	2005
R TO THE A C.J. LEWIS	34	1995
R U READY SALT-N-PEPA	24	1997
R U SLEEPING INDO	31	1998
RABBIT CHAS & DAVE	8	1980
THE RACE [A] YELLO	7	1988
RACE [B] TIGER	37	1996
RACE [C] LEAVES	66	2002
RACE FOR THE PRIZE FLAMING LIPS	39	1999
THE RACE IS ON [A] SUZI QUATRO	43	1978
THE RACE IS ON [B] DAVE EDMUNDS & THE STRAY CATS	34	1981
RACE WITH THE DEVIL [A] GENE VINCENT	28	1956
RACE WITH THE DEVIL [B] GUN	8	1968
RACE WITH THE DEVIL [B] GIRLSCHOOL	49	1980
RACHEL AL MARTINO	10	1953
RACHMANINOFF'S 18TH VARIATION ON A THEME BY PAGANINI (THE STORY OF THREE LOVES) WINIFRED ATWELL	9	1954
RACING GREEN HIGH CONTRAST	73	2004
THE RACING RATS EDITORS	26	2007
RACIST FRIEND SPECIAL A.K.A.	60	1983
RADANCER MARMALADE	6	1972
RADAR LOVE GOLDEN EARRING	7	1973
RADAR LOVE OH WELL	65	1990
RADIATION VIBE FOUNTAINS OF WAYNE	32	1997
RADICAL YOUR LOVER LITTLE ANGELS FEATURING THE BIG BAD HORNS	34	1990
RADICCIO EP ORBITAL	37	1992
RADIO [A] SHAKY FEATURING ROGER TAYLOR	37	1992
RADIO [B] TEENAGE FANCLUB	31	1993
RADIO [C] CORRS	18	1999
RADIO [D] CLIENT	68	2004
RADIO [E] ROBBIE WILLIAMS	1	2004
RADIO [F] LUDES	68	2004
RADIO AFRICA LATIN QUARTER	19	1986
RADIO DISCO WILT	56	2000
RADIO 4 UK THEME ROYAL BALLET SINFONIA & GAVIN SUTHERLAND	29	2006
RADIO GA GA QUEEN	2	1984
RADIO GAGA ELECTRIC SIX	21	2005
RADIO HEAD TALKING HEADS	52	1987
RADIO HEART RADIO HEART FEATURING GARY NUMAN	35	1987
RADIO MUSICOLA NIK KERSHAW	43	1986
RADIO NO 1 AIR	31	2001
RADIO ON RICKY ROSS	35	1996
RADIO RADIO ELVIS COSTELLO & THE ATTRACTIONS	29	1978
RADIO ROMANCE TIFFANY	13	1988
RADIO SONG R.E.M.	28	1991
RADIO WALL OF SOUND SLADE	21	1991
RADIO WAVES ROGER WATERS	74	1987
RADIOACTIVE GENE SIMMONS	41	1979
RADIOACTIVITY KRAFTWERK	43	1991
RAG DOLL [A] FOUR SEASONS WITH THE SOUND OF FRANKIE VALLI	2	1964
RAG DOLL [B] AEROSMITH	42	1990
RAG MAMA RAG BAND	16	1970
RAGAMUFFIN MAN MANFRED MANN	8	1969
RAGE HARD FRANKIE GOES TO HOLLYWOOD	4	1986
RAGE TO LOVE KIM WILDE	19	1985
RAGGA HOUSE (ALL NIGHT LONG) SIMON HARRIS FEATURING DADDY FREDDY	56	1990
RAGGAMUFFIN GIRL APACHE INDIAN FEATURING FRANKIE PAUL	31	1995
RAGING COSMIC GATE	48	2003
RAGING EP BEYOND	68	1991
RAGS TO RICHES DAVID WHITFIELD	3	1953
RAGS TO RICHES ELVIS PRESLEY	9	1971
RAGTIME COWBOY JOE DAVID SEVILLE & THE CHIPMUNKS	11	1959
RAIN [A] BRUCE RUFFIN	19	1971
RAIN [B] STATUS QUO	7	1976
RAIN [C] CULT	17	1985
THE RAIN [D] ORAN 'JUICE' JONES	4	1986
RAIN [E] MADONNA	7	1993
RAIN [F] GROOVE CORPORATION	71	1994
RAIN AND TEARS APHRODITE'S CHILD	29	1968
RAIN DOWN LOVE FREEMASONS FEATURING SIEDAH GARRETT	12	2007
RAIN DOWN ON ME KANE	38	2004
RAIN FALL DOWN ROLLING STONES	33	2005
RAIN FALLS FRANKIE KNUCKLES FEATURING LISA MICHAELIS	48	1992
RAIN FOREST [A] BIDDU ORCHESTRA	39	1976
RAIN FOREST [B] PAUL HARDCASTLE	41	1984
RAIN IN THE SUMMERTIME ALARM	18	1987
RAIN KING COUNTING CROWS	49	1994
RAIN ON ME ASHANTI	19	2003
RAIN OR SHINE FIVE STAR	2	1986
RAIN RAIN RAIN FRANKIE LAINE & THE FOUR LADS	8	1954
RAIN SHOWERS SIZZLA	51	1999
THE RAIN (SUPA DUPA FLY) MISSY 'MISDEMEANOR' ELLIOTT	16	1997
RAINBOW [A] MARMALADE	3	1970
RAINBOW [B] PETERS & LEE	17	1974
RAINBOW CHASER NIRVANA	34	1968
RAINBOW CHILD DAN REED NETWORK	60	1990
RAINBOW COUNTRY BOB MARLEY VERSUS FUNKSTAR DELUXE	11	2000
RAINBOW IN THE DARK DIO	46	1983
RAINBOW LAKE WENDY & LISA	70	1990
RAINBOW PEOPLE MANIX	57	1992
RAINBOW (SAMPLE FREE) SOLO	59	1991
RAINBOW THEME SAXON	66	1980
RAINBOW VALLEY LOVE AFFAIR	5	1968
RAINBOWS (EP) TERRY HALL	62	1995
RAINBOWS OF COLOUR GROOVERIDER	40	1998
RAINCLOUD LIGHTHOUSE FAMILY	6	1997
THE RAINDANCE DARE	62	1989
RAINDROPS STUNT	51	2006
RAINDROPS KEEP FALLIN' ON MY HEAD BOBBIE GENTRY	40	1970
RAINDROPS KEEP FALLING ON MY HEAD B.J. THOMAS	38	1970
RAINDROPS KEEP FALLING ON MY HEAD SACHA DISTEL	10	1970
RAININ' THROUGH MY SUNSHINE REAL THING	40	1978
RAINING ALL OVER THE WORLD ADVENTURES	68	1992
RAINING IN MY HEART LEO SAYER	21	1978
RAINMAKER [A] SPARKLEHORSE	61	1996
RAINMAKER [B] IRON MAIDEN	13	2003
RAINY DAY WOMEN NOS. 12 & 35 BOB DYLAN	7	1966
RAINY DAYS AND MONDAYS CARPENTERS	63	1993
RAINY DAYZ MARY J BLIGE FEATURING JA RULE	17	2002
RAINY NIGHT IN GEORGIA RANDY CRAWFORD	18	1981
A RAINY NIGHT IN SOHO POGUES	67	1991
RAISE HYPER GO GO	36	1994
RAISE YOUR HAND EDDIE FLOYD	42	1967
RAISE YOUR HANDS [A] REEL 2 REAL FEATURING THE MAD STUNTMAN	14	1994
RAISE YOUR HANDS [B] BIG ROOM GIRL FEATURING DARRYL PANDY	40	1999
RAISED ON ROCK ELVIS PRESLEY	36	1973
RAM GOAT LIVER PLUTO SHERVINGTON	43	1976
RAMA LAMA DING DONG ROCKY SHARPE & THE REPLAYS	17	1979
RAMBLIN' ROSE NAT 'KING' COLE	5	1962
RAM-BUNK-SHUSH VENTURES	45	1961
RAME SNAP FEATURING RUKMANI	50	1996
RAMONA BACHELORS	4	1964
RANDOM LADY SOVEREIGN	73	2005
RANDY BLUE MINK	9	1973
RANKING FULL STOP BEAT	6	1979

	Peak Position	Year of Entry
RAOUL AUTOMATIC	30	2006
RAOUL AND THE KINGS OF SPAIN TEARS FOR FEARS	31	1995
RAP DIS OXIDE & NEUTRINO	12	2001
RAP SCHOLAR DAS EFX FEATURING REDMAN	42	1998
RAP SUMMARY BIG DADDY KANE	52	1989
RAP SUPERSTAR/ROCK SUPERSTAR CYPRESS HILL	13	2000
RAP YOUR LOVE SET THE TONE	67	1983
RAPE ME NIRVANA	32	1993
RAPID HOPE LOSS DASHBOARD CONFESSIONAL	75	2004
RAPP PAYBACK (WHERE IZ MOSES?) JAMES BROWN	39	1981
RAPPAZ R N DAINJA KRS ONE	47	1996
RAPPER'S DELIGHT SUGARHILL GANG	3	1979
RAPTURE [A] BLONDIE	5	1981
RAPTURE [B] IIO	2	2001
RARE, PRECIOUS AND GONE MIKE SCOTT	74	1998
THE RASCAL KING MIGHTY MIGHTY BOSSTONES	63	1998
RASPBERRY BERET PRINCE & THE REVOLUTION	25	1985
RASPUTIN BONEY M	2	1978
THE RAT WALKMEN	45	2004
RAT IN MI KITCHEN UB40	12	1987
RAT RACE SPECIALS	5	1980
RAT RAPPING ROLAND RAT SUPERSTAR	14	1983
RAT TRAP BOOMTOWN RATS	1	1978
RATAMAHATTA SEPULTURA	23	1996
THE RATTLER GOODBYE MR MACKENZIE	37	1989
RATTLESNAKES LLOYD COLE & THE COMMOTIONS	65	1984
RAUNCHY BILL JUSTIS	11	1958
RAUNCHY KEN MACKINTOSH	19	1958
RAVE ALERT PRAGA KHAN	52	1992
THE RAVE DIGGER MC LETHAL	66	1992
RAVE GENERATOR TOXIC TWO	13	1992
RAVE ON BUDDY HOLLY	5	1958
RAVEL'S PAVANE POUR UNE INFANTE DEFUNTE WILLIAM ORBIT	31	2000
RAVING I'M RAVING SHUT UP & DANCE FEATURING PETER BOUNCER	2	1992
RAW [A] SPANDAU BALLET	47	1988
RAW [B] ALARM	51	1991
RAW [C] MELKY SEDECK	50	1999
RAW POWER APOLLO FOUR FORTY	32	1997
RAWHIDE FRANKIE LAINE	6	1959
RAY OF LIGHT MADONNA	2	1998
RAYS OF THE RISING SUN DENISE JOHNSON	45	1994
RAYS OF THE RISING SUN MOZAIC	32	1996
RAZOR'S EDGE MEAT LOAF	41	1984
RAZZAMATAZZ QUINCY JONES FEATURING PATTI AUSTIN	11	1981
RAZZLE DAZZLE [A] BILL HALEY & HIS COMETS	13	1956
RAZZLE DAZZLE [B] HEATWAVE	43	1979
RE:EVOLUTION SHAMEN WITH TERENCE McKENNA	18	1993
REACH [A] JUDY CHEEKS	17	1994
REACH [B] LIL MO'YIN YANG	28	1996
REACH [C] GLORIA ESTEFAN	15	1996
REACH [D] S CLUB 7	2	2000
REACH 4 THE MELODY VICTORIA WILSON JAMES	72	1997
REACH FOR THE STARS SHIRLEY BASSEY	1	1961
REACH OUT MIDFIELD GENERAL FEATURING LINDA LEWIS	61	2000
REACH OUT AND TOUCH DIANA ROSS	33	1970
REACH OUT FOR ME DIONNE WARWICK	23	1964
REACH OUT I'LL BE THERE FOUR TOPS	1	1966
REACH OUT I'LL BE THERE GLORIA GAYNOR	14	1975
REACH OUT I'LL BE THERE MICHAEL BOLTON	37	1993
REACH UP TONEY LEE	64	1983
(REACH UP FOR THE) SUNRISE DURAN DURAN	5	2004
REACH UP (PAPA'S GOT A BRAND NEW PIG BAG) PERFECTO ALLSTARZ	6	1995
REACHIN' [A] PHASE II	70	1989
REACHIN' [B] HOUSE OF VIRGINISM	35	1994
REACHING FOR THE BEST EXCITERS	31	1975
REACHING FOR THE WORLD HAROLD MELVIN & THE BLUENOTES	48	1977
REACHOUT DJ ZINC	73	2002
REACT ERICK SERMON FEATURING REDMAN	14	2002
REACTOR PARTY SHITDISCO	73	2006
READ 'EM AND WEEP BARRY MANILOW	17	1983
READ MY LIPS [A] DSK	46	1991
READ MY LIPS [B] ALEX PARTY	28	1996
READ MY LIPS (ENOUGH IS ENOUGH) JIMMY SOMERVILLE	26	1990
READ MY MIND CONNOR REEVES	19	1998
READ MY MIND KILLERS	15	2007
READY BRUCE WAYNE	44	1997
READY AN' WILLING (SWEET SATISFACTION) WHITESNAKE	43	1980
READY FOR A NEW DAY TODD TERRY FEATURING MARTHA WASH	20	1998
READY FOR LOVE [A] JIMMY JONES	46	1960
READY FOR LOVE [B] GARY MOORE	56	1989
READY FOR THE FLOOR HOT CHIP	6	2008
READY OR NOT [A] LIGHTNING SEEDS	20	1996
READY OR NOT [B] FUGEES	1	1996
READY OR NOT [B] COURSE	5	1997
READY OR NOT [C] DJ DADO & SIMONE JAY	51	1999
READY OR NOT [D] A1	3	1999
READY OR NOT HERE I COME DELFONICS	41	1971
READY STEADY GO [A] GENERATION X	47	1978
READY STEADY GO [B] PAUL OAKENFOLD	16	2002
READY STEADY WHO (EP) WHO	58	1983
READY TO GO REPUBLICA	13	1996
READY TO RECEIVE ANIMALHOUSE	61	2000
READY TO RUN DIXIE CHICKS	53	1999
READY WILLING AND ABLE DORIS DAY	7	1955
READY2WEAR FELIX DA HOUSECAT	62	2005
REAL [A] DONNA ALLEN	34	1995
REAL [B] PLUMB	41	2004
REAL A LIE AUF DER MAUR	33	2004
REAL COOL WORLD DAVID BOWIE	53	1992
REAL EMOTION REID	65	1989
REAL FASHION REGGAE STYLE CAREY JOHNSON	19	1987
REAL GIRL MUTYA BUENA	2	2007
REAL GONE KID DEACON BLUE	8	1988
REAL GOOD DOUBLE SIX	66	1998
REAL GOOD TIME ALDA	7	1998
REAL GREAT BRITAIN ASIAN DUB FOUNDATION	41	2000
REAL LIFE [A] SIMPLE MINDS	34	1991
REAL LIFE [B] BON JOVI	21	1999
THE REAL LIFE [C] RAVEN MAIZE	12	2001
REAL LOVE [A] RUBY MURRAY	18	1958
REAL LOVE [B] JODY WATLEY	31	1989
REAL LOVE [C] DRIZABONE	16	1991
REAL LOVE [D] DARE	67	1991
REAL LOVE [D] TIME FREQUENCY	8	1992
REAL LOVE [E] MARY J BLIGE	26	1992
REAL LOVE [F] BEATLES	4	1996
THE REAL ME W.A.S.P.	23	1989
A REAL MOTHER FOR YA JOHNNY 'GUITAR' WATSON	44	1977
REAL PEOPLE APACHE INDIAN	66	1997
REAL REAL REAL JESUS JONES	19	1990
THE REAL SLIM SHADY EMINEM	1	2000
THE REAL THING [A] JELLYBEAN FEATURING STEVEN DANTE	13	1987
THE REAL THING [B] BROTHERS JOHNSON	50	1981
THE REAL THING [C] ABC	68	1989
THE REAL THING [D] TONY DI BART	1	1994
THE REAL THING [E] LISA STANSFIELD	9	1997
THE REAL THING [F] 2 UNLIMITED	6	1994
REAL THINGS JAVINE	4	2003
REAL TO ME BRIAN McFADDEN	1	2004
REAL VIBRATION EXPRESS OF SOUND	45	1996
REAL WILD CHILD (WILD ONE) IGGY POP	10	1987
THE REAL WILD HOUSE RAUL ORELLANA	29	1989
REAL WORLD D-SIDE	9	2003
REALITY USED TO BE A GOOD FRIEND OF MINE PM DAWN	29	1992
REALLY DOE ICE CUBE	66	1993
REALLY FREE JOHN OTWAY & WILD WILLY BARRETT	27	1977
REALLY SAYING SOMETHING BANANARAMA WITH FUN BOY THREE	5	1982
REAP THE WILD WIND ULTRAVOX	12	1982
REASON IAN VAN DAHL	8	2002
THE REASON [A] CELINE DION	11	1997
THE REASON [B] HOOBASTANK	12	2004
REASON FOR LIVING RODDY FRAME	45	1998
REASON TO BELIEVE ROD STEWART	1	1971
REASON TO LIVE KISS	33	1987
REASONS [A] KLESHAY	33	1998
REASONS [B] UB40/HUNTERZ/DHOL BLASTERS	75	2005
REASONS TO BE CHEERFUL (PART 3) IAN DURY & THE BLOCKHEADS	3	1979
REBEL MUSIC REBEL MC	53	1990
REBEL NEVER GETS OLD DAVID BOWIE	47	2004
REBEL REBEL DAVID BOWIE	5	1974
REBEL ROUSER DUANE EDDY & THE REBELS	19	1958
REBEL RUN TOYAH	24	1983
REBEL WITHOUT A PAUSE PUBLIC ENEMY	37	1987
REBEL WOMAN DNA FEATURING JAZZI P	42	1991
REBEL YELL BILLY IDOL	6	1984
REBEL YELL SCOOTER	30	1996
REBELLION (LIES) ARCADE FIRE	19	2005
REBIRTH OF SLICK (COOL LIKE DAT) DIGABLE PLANETS	67	1993
RECIPE FOR LOVE HARRY CONNICK Jr.	32	1991
RECKLESS AFRIKA BAMBAATAA FEATURING UB40 & FAMILY	17	1988
RECKLESS GIRL BEGINERZ	28	2002
RECONNECTION (EP) ZERO B	54	1993
RECOVER AUTOMATIC	25	2006
RECOVER YOUR SOUL ELTON JOHN	16	1998
RECOVERY FONTELLA BASS	32	1966
RED ELBOW	36	2001
RED ALERT BASEMENT JAXX	5	1999
RED BALLOON DAVE CLARK FIVE	7	1968
RED BLOODED WOMAN KYLIE MINOGUE	5	2004
RED DRESS [A] ALVIN STARDUST	7	1974
RED DRESS [B] SUGABABES	4	2006
RED FLAG BILLY TALENT	49	2006
RED FRAME WHITE LIGHT ORCHESTRAL MANOEUVRES IN THE DARK	67	1980
RED GUITAR DAVID SYLVIAN	17	1984
RED HOT [A] PRINCESS	58	1987
RED HOT [B] VANESSA-MAE	37	1995
RED LETTER DAY PET SHOP BOYS	9	1997
RED LIGHT GREEN LIGHT MITCHELL TOROK	29	1957
RED LIGHT GREEN LIGHT EP WILDHEARTS	30	1996
RED LIGHT SPECIAL TLC	18	1995
RED LIGHT SPELLS DANGER BILLY OCEAN	2	1977
RED RAIN PETER GABRIEL	46	1987
RED RED WINE JIMMY JAMES & THE VAGABONDS	36	1968
RED RED WINE TONY TRIBE	46	1969
RED RED WINE UB40	1	1983

	Peak Position	Year of Entry
RED RIVER ROCK JOHNNY & THE HURRICANES	3	1959
RED SAILS IN THE SUNSET FATS DOMINO	34	1963
THE RED SHOES KATE BUSH	21	1994
RED SKIES [A] FIXX	57	1982
RED SKIES [B] SAMSON	65	1983
RED SKY STATUS QUO	19	1986
THE RED STROKES GARTH BROOKS	13	1994
RED SUN RISING LOST WITNESS	22	1999
RED THREE, THUNDER/STORM DAVE CLARKE	45	1995
THE RED, THE WHITE, THE BLUE HOPE OF THE STATES	15	2004
REDEFINE SOIL	68	2004
REDEMPTION SONG JOE STRUMMER & THE MESCALEROS	46	2003
REDNECK WOMAN GRETCHEN WILSON	42	2004
REDONDO BEACH MORRISSEY	11	2005
REDUNDANT GREEN DAY	27	1998
REELIN' AND ROCKIN' DAVE CLARK FIVE	24	1965
REELIN' AND ROCKIN' CHUCK BERRY	18	1973
REELING PASADENAS	75	1990
REET PETITE (THE SWEETEST GIRL IN TOWN) JACKIE WILSON	1	1957
REET PETITE DARTS	51	1979
REET PETITE PINKY & PERKY	47	1993
REFLECT THREE 'N' ONE	66	1997
REFLECTION VANESSA-MAE	53	1998
REFLECTIONS DIANA ROSS & THE SUPREMES	5	1967
REFLECTIONS OF MY LIFE MARMALADE	3	1969
THE REFLEX DURAN DURAN	1	1984
REFUGEES TEARS	9	2005
REFUSE-RESIST SEPULTURA	51	1994
REGGAE FOR IT NOW BILL LOVELADY	12	1979
REGGAE LIKE IT USED TO BE PAUL NICHOLAS	17	1976
REGGAE MUSIC UB40	28	1994
REGGAE TUNE ANDY FAIRWEATHER-LOW	10	1974
REGINA SUGARCUBES	55	1989
REGRET NEW ORDER	4	1993
REGULATE WARREN G & NATE DOGG	5	1994
REHAB AMY WINEHOUSE	7	2006
REIGN UNKLE FEATURING IAN BROWN	40	2004
REIGNS JA RULE	9	2003
REILLY OLYMPIC ORCHESTRA	26	1983
RELAX [A] FRANKIE GOES TO HOLLYWOOD	1	1984
RELAX [B] CRYSTAL WATERS	37	1995
RELAX [C] DEETAH	11	1998
RELAX TAKE IT EASY MIKA	18	2007
RELAY WHO	21	1973
RELEASE [A] AFRO CELT SOUND SYSTEM	71	2000
RELEASE [B] MEDWAY	67	2001
RELEASE ME [A] ENGELBERT HUMPERDINCK	1	1967
RELEASE ME [B] WILSON PHILLIPS	36	1990
RELEASE ME [C] LAURA	47	2007
RELEASE THE PRESSURE LEFTFIELD	13	1996
RELEASE YO' SELF [A] METHOD MAN	46	1995
RELEASE YO SELF [B] TRANSATLANTIC SOUL	43	1997
RELIGHT MY FIRE TAKE THAT FEATURING LULU	1	1993
RELIGION FRONT 242	46	1993
RELOAD PPK	39	2002
REMAIN KUBB	45	2005
REMEDY BLACK CROWES	24	1992
REMEMBER [A] ROCK CANDY	32	1971
REMEMBER [B] JIMI HENDRIX EXPERIENCE	35	1971
REMEMBER [C] BT	27	1998
REMEMBER [D] DISTURBED	56	2002
REMEMBER I LOVE YOU JIM DIAMOND	42	1985
REMEMBER ME [A] DIANA ROSS	7	1971
REMEMBER ME [B] CLIFF RICHARD	35	1987
REMEMBER ME [C] BLUE BOY	8	1997
REMEMBER ME [D] JORIO	54	2001
REMEMBER ME [E] BRITISH SEA POWER	30	2003
REMEMBER ME [F] ZUTONS	39	2004
REMEMBER ME [G] KANO	71	2005
REMEMBER ME THIS WAY GARY GLITTER	3	1974
REMEMBER ME WITH LOVE GLORIA ESTEFAN	22	1991
REMEMBER (SHA-LA-LA) BAY CITY ROLLERS	6	1974
REMEMBER THE DAY INNOCENCE	56	1991
(REMEMBER THE DAYS OF THE) OLD SCHOOL YARD CAT STEVENS	44	1977
REMEMBER THE RAIN BOB LIND	46	1966
REMEMBER THE TIME MICHAEL JACKSON	3	1992
REMEMBER THEN SHOWADDYWADDY	17	1979
REMEMBER (WALKIN' IN THE SAND) SHANGRI-LAS	14	1964
REMEMBER WHEN PLATTERS	25	1959
REMEMBER YESTERDAY JOHN MILES	32	1976
REMEMBER YOU'RE A WOMBLE WOMBLES	3	1974
REMEMBER YOU'RE MINE PAT BOONE	5	1957
REMEMBERANCE DAY B-MOVIE	61	1981
REMEMBERESE STILLS	75	2003
REMEMBERING CHRISTMAS EXETER BRAMDEAN BOYS' CHOIR	46	1993
REMEMBERING THE FIRST TIME SIMPLY RED	22	1995
REMIND ME ROYKSOPP	21	2002
REMINDING ME (OF SEF) COMMON FEATURING CHANTAY SAVAGE	59	1997
REMINISCE [A] MARY J BLIGE	31	1993
REMINISCE [B] BLAZIN' SQUAD	8	2003
REMINISCING BUDDY HOLLY	17	1962
REMIXES - VOLUME 2 ED RUSH & OPTICAL	69	2004
REMOTE CONTROL BEASTIE BOYS	21	1999
RENAISSANCE M PEOPLE	5	1994
RENDEZVOUS [A] TINA CHARLES	27	1977
RENDEZVOUS [B] TYGERS OF PAN TANG	49	1982
RENDEZVOUS [C] CRAIG DAVID	8	2001
RENDEZ-VOUS 98 JEAN-MICHEL JARRE & APOLLO 440	12	1998
RENDEZ-VU BASEMENT JAXX	4	1999
RENE DMC (DEVASTATING MACHO CHARISMA) RENE & YVETTE	57	1986
RENEGADE CAVALCADE ASH	33	2004
RENEGADE MASTER WILDCHILD	3	1995
RENEGADE SNARES OMNI TRIO	61	2003
RENEGADE SOUNDWAVE RENEGADE SOUNDWAVE	64	1994
RENEGADES OF FUNK AFRIKA BAMBAATAA & THE SONIC SOUL FORCE	30	1984
RENT PET SHOP BOYS	8	1987
RENTA SANTA CHRIS HILL	10	1975
RENTED ROOMS TINDERSTICKS	56	1997
RE-OFFENDER TRAVIS	7	2003
REPEAT MANIC STREET PREACHERS	26	1991
REPEATED LOVE ATGOC	38	1998
REPEATED OFFENDER RIFLES	26	2006
REPORT TO THE DANCEFLOOR ENERGISE	69	1991
REPRESENT SOUL II SOUL	39	1997
REPTILLA STROKES	17	2004
REPUBLICAN PARTY REPTILE (EP) BIG COUNTRY	37	1991
REPUTATION DUSTY SPRINGFIELD	38	1990
REPUTATIONS (JUST BE GOOD TO ME) ANDREA GRANT	75	1998
REQUEST & LINE BLACK EYED PEAS FEATURING MACY GRAY	31	2001
REQUEST LINE ZHANE	22	1997
REQUIEM [A] SLIK	24	1976
REQUIEM [B] LONDON BOYS	4	1988
RE-REWIND THE CROWD SAY BO SELECTA ARTFUL DODGER FEATURING CRAIG DAVID	2	1999
RESCUE ECHO & THE BUNNYMEN	62	1980
RESCUE ME [A] FONTELLA BASS	11	1965
RESCUE ME [B] ALARM	48	1987
RESCUE ME [C] MADONNA	3	1991
RESCUE ME [D] BELL BOOK & CANDLE	63	1998
RESCUE ME [E] SUNKIDS FEATURING CHANCE	50	1999
RESCUE ME [F] ULTRA	8	1999
RESOLVE FOO FIGHTERS	32	2005
RESPECT [A] ARETHA FRANKLIN	10	1967
RESPECT [A] REAL ROXANNE	71	1988
RESPECT [A] ADEVA	17	1989
RESPECT [B] SUB SUB	49	1994
RESPECT [C] JUDY CHEEKS	23	1995
RESPECT YOURSELF KANE GANG	21	1984
RESPECT YOURSELF BRUCE WILLIS	7	1987
RESPECT YOURSELF ROBERT PALMER	45	1995
RESPECTABLE [A] ROLLING STONES	23	1978
RESPECTABLE [B] MEL & KIM	1	1987
RESPECTABLE [B] GIRLS @ PLAY	29	2001
REST AND PLAY EP ORBITAL	33	2002
REST IN PEACE EXTREME	13	1992
REST OF MY LOVE URBAN COOKIE COLLECTIVE	67	1995
REST OF THE NIGHT NATALIE COLE	56	1989
RESTLESS [A] JOHNNY KIDD & THE PIRATES	22	1960
RESTLESS [B] GILLAN	25	1982
RESTLESS [C] STATUS QUO	39	1994
RESTLESS [D] JX	22	2004
RESTLESS DAYS (SHE CRIES OUT LOUD) AND WHY NOT?	38	1989
RESTLESS (I KNOW YOU KNOW) NEJA	47	1998
RESURRECTION [A] BRIAN MAY WITH COZY POWELL	23	1993
RESURRECTION [B] PPK	3	2001
RESURRECTION JOE CULT	74	1984
RESURRECTION SHUFFLE ASHTON, GARDNER & DYKE	3	1971
RETOX FATBOY SLIM	73	2002
RETREAT [A] HELL IS FOR HEROES	39	2003
RETREAT [B] RAKES	24	2005
RETURN OF DJANGO UPSETTERS	5	1969
THE RETURN OF EVIL BILL CLINIC	70	2000
THE RETURN OF NOTHING SANDSTORM	54	2000
THE RETURN OF PAN WATERBOYS	24	1993
RETURN OF THE ELECTRIC WARRIOR (EP) MARC BOLAN & T REX	50	1981
RETURN OF THE LOS PALMAS SEVEN MADNESS	7	1981
RETURN OF THE MACK MARK MORRISON	1	1996
RETURN OF THE RED BARON ROYAL GUARDSMEN	37	1967
THE RETURN (TIME TO SAY GOODBYE) DJ VISAGE FEATURING CLARISSA	58	2000
RETURN TO BRIXTON CLASH	57	1990
RETURN TO INNOCENCE ENIGMA	3	1994
RETURN TO ME DEAN MARTIN	2	1958
RETURN TO REALITY ANTARCTICA	53	2000
RETURN TO SENDER ELVIS PRESLEY	1	1962
REUNITED PEACHES & HERB	4	1979
REVEILLE ROCK JOHNNY & THE HURRICANES	14	1959
REVELATION ELECTRIQUE BOUTIQUE	37	2000
REVERENCE [A] JESUS & MARY CHAIN	10	1992
REVERENCE [B] FAITHLESS	10	1997
REVEREND BLACK GRAPE BLACK GRAPE	9	1995
REVIVAL [A] CHRIS BARBER'S JAZZ BAND	43	1962
REVIVAL [B] EURYTHMICS	26	1989
REVIVAL [C] MARTINE GIRAULT	37	1992
REVOL MANIC STREET PREACHERS	22	1994
REVOLT IN STYLE BILL NELSON'S RED NOISE	69	1979
REVOLUTION [A] CULT	30	1985
REVOLUTION [B] THOMPSON TWINS	56	1985
REVOLUTION [C] ARRESTED DEVELOPMENT	4	1993
REVOLUTION [D] COLDCUT	67	2001
REVOLUTION [E] BK	42	2002
REVOLUTION BABY TRANSVISION VAMP	30	1988
REVOLUTION (IN THE SUMMERTIME) COSMIC ROUGH RIDERS	35	2001
REVOLUTION 909 DAFT PUNK	47	1998
REVOLUTION OVER THE PHONE MARDOUS	74	2005

	Peak Position	Year of Entry
REVOLUTIONS JEAN-MICHEL JARRE	52	1988
REVOLUTIONS (EP) SHARKEY	53	1997
REVOLVING DOOR CRAZY TOWN	23	2001
REWARD TEARDROP EXPLODES	6	1981
REWIND [A] CELETIA	29	1998
REWIND [B] PRECIOUS	11	2000
REWIND [C] STEREOPHONICS	17	2005
REWIND [D] PAOLO NUTINI	27	2006
REWIND (FIND A WAY) BEVERLEY KNIGHT	40	1998
RHAPSODY FOUR SEASONS	37	1977
RHAPSODY IN THE RAIN LOU CHRISTIE	37	1966
RHIANNON FLEETWOOD MAC	46	1978
RHINESTONE COWBOY GLEN CAMPBELL	4	1975
RHINESTONE COWBOY (GIDDY UP GIDDY UP) RIKKI & DAZ FEATURING GLEN CAMPBELL	12	2002
THE RHYME KEITH MURRAY	59	1996
THE RHYTHM CLOCK	28	1994
RHYTHM & BLUES ALIBI GOMEZ	18	1999
RHYTHM AND GREENS SHADOWS	22	1964
RHYTHM BANDITS JUNIOR SENIOR	22	2003
THE RHYTHM DIVINE [A] YELLO FEATURING SHIRLEY BASSEY	54	1987
RHYTHM DIVINE [B] ENRIQUE IGLESIAS	45	1999
RHYTHM IS A DANCER SNAP	1	1992
RHYTHM IS A MYSTERY K-KLASS	3	1991
RHYTHM IS GONNA GET YOU GLORIA ESTEFAN & MIAMI SOUND MACHINE	16	1988
RHYTHM NATION JANET JACKSON	23	1989
RHYTHM OF LIFE OLETA ADAMS	38	1990
RHYTHM OF LOVE SCORPIONS	59	1988
RHYTHM OF MY HEART ROD STEWART	3	1991
RHYTHM OF MY HEART RUNRIG	24	1996
RHYTHM OF THE BEAST NICKO McBRAIN	72	1991
RHYTHM OF THE JUNGLE QUICK	41	1982
RHYTHM OF THE NIGHT [A] DeBARGE	4	1985
THE RHYTHM OF THE NIGHT [B] CORONA	2	1994
RHYTHM OF THE NIGHT [C] POWERHOUSE	38	1997
RHYTHM OF THE RAIN CASCADES	5	1963
RHYTHM OF THE RAIN JASON DONOVAN	9	1990
RHYTHM TAKES CONTROL UNIQUE 3 FEATURING KARIN	41	1990
RHYTHM TALK JOCKO	56	1980
RIBBON IN THE SKY STEVIE WONDER	45	1982
RICE IS NICE LEMON PIPERS	41	1968
RICH AH GETTING RICHER REBEL MC INTRODUCING LITTLE T	48	1992
RICH AND STRANGE CUD	24	1992
RICH GIRL GWEN STEFANI FEATURING EVE	4	2005
RICH IN PARADISE FPI PROJECT	9	1989
RICH KIDS RICH KIDS	24	1978
RICH MAN POOR MAN JIMMY YOUNG	25	1956
RICHARD III SUPERGRASS	2	1997
RICOCHET [A] JOAN REGAN & THE SQUADRONAIRES	8	1953
RICOCHET [B] B B & Q BAND	71	1987
RICOCHET [C] FAITH NO MORE	27	1995
RIDDIM US3 FEATURING TUKKA YOOT	34	1993
THE RIDDLE [A] NIK KERSHAW	3	1984
RIDDLE [B] EN VOGUE	33	2000
RIDDLE ME UB40	59	1984
RIDE [A] ANA ANN	24	2002
RIDE [B] VINES	25	2004
RIDE [C] DYNAMITE MC	54	2004
RIDE A ROCKET LITHIUM & SONYA MADAN	40	1997
RIDE A WHITE HORSE [B] GOLDFRAPP	15	2006
RIDE A WHITE SWAN T REX	2	1970
RIDE A WILD HORSE [A] DEE CLARK	16	1975
RIDE AWAY ROY ORBISON	34	1965
RIDE (EP) RIDE	71	1990
RIDE IT [A] GERI HALLIWELL	4	2004
RIDE IT [B] JAY SEAN	11	2008
RIDE LIKE THE WIND CHRISTOPHER CROSS	69	1980
RIDE LIKE THE WIND SAXON	52	1988
RIDE LIKE THE WIND EAST SIDE BEAT	3	1991
RIDE MY SEE-SAW MOODY BLUES	42	1968
RIDE ON BABY CHRIS FARLOWE	31	1966
RIDE ON THE RHYTHM LITTLE LOUIE & MARC ANTHONY	36	1991
RIDE ON TIME BLACK BOX	1	1989
RIDE THE BULLET ARMY OF LOVERS	67	1992
RIDE THE GROOVE PLAYERS ASSOCIATION	42	1979
RIDE THE LOVE TRAIN LIGHT OF THE WORLD	49	1981
RIDE THE RHYTHM Z FACTOR	52	2001
RIDE THE STORM [A] AKABU FEATURING LINDA CLIFFORD	69	2001
RIDE THE STORM [B] SIMON WEBBE	36	2007
RIDE THE TIGER BOO RADLEYS	38	1997
RIDE WID US SO SOLID CREW	19	2002
RIDE WIT ME NELLY FEATURING CITY SPUD	3	2001
RIDE WIT U JOE FEATURING G UNIT	12	2004
RIDE-O-ROCKET BROTHERS JOHNSON	50	1978
RIDERS IN THE SKY RAMRODS	8	1961
RIDERS IN THE SKY SHADOWS	12	1980
RIDERS ON THE STORM DOORS	22	1971
RIDERS ON THE STORM ANNABEL LAMB	27	1983
RIDICULOUS THOUGHTS CRANBERRIES	20	1995
RIDIN' CHAMILLIONAIRE FEATURING KRAYZIE BONE	2	2006
RIDING ON A TRAIN PASADENAS	13	1988
RIDING ON THE WINGS MOTIV 8	44	2005
RIDING WITH THE ANGELS SAMSON	55	1981
RIGHT ABOUT NOW MOUSSE T FEATURING EMMA LANFORD	28	2004
RIGHT AND EXACT CHRISSY WARD	59	1995
RIGHT BACK WHERE WE STARTED FROM MAXINE NIGHTINGALE	8	1975
RIGHT BACK WHERE WE STARTED FROM SINITTA	4	1989
RIGHT BEFORE MY EYES PATTI DAY	69	1989
RIGHT BEFORE MY EYES N + G FEATURING KALLAGHAN & MC NEAT	12	2000
RIGHT BESIDE YOU SOPHIE B. HAWKINS	13	1994
RIGHT BETWEEN THE EYES WAX	60	1986
RIGHT BY YOUR SIDE EURYTHMICS	10	1983
THE RIGHT COMBINATION SEIKO & DONNIE WAHLBERG	44	1990
THE RIGHT DECISION JESUS JONES	36	1993
RIGHT HERE [A] SWV	3	1993
RIGHT HERE [B] ULTIMATE KAOS	18	1995
RIGHT HERE RIGHT NOW [A] JESUS JONES	31	1990
RIGHT HERE RIGHT NOW [B] DISCO CITIZENS	40	1995
RIGHT HERE RIGHT NOW [C] FIERCE	25	1999
RIGHT HERE RIGHT NOW [D] FATBOY SLIM	2	1999
RIGHT HERE WAITING RICHARD MARX	2	1989
RIGHT IN THE NIGHT (FALL IN LOVE WITH MUSIC) JAM & SPOON FEATURING PLAVKA	10	1994
RIGHT IN THE SOCKET SHALAMAR	44	1980
THE RIGHT KINDA LOVER PATTI LABELLE	50	1994
RIGHT NEXT DOOR (BECAUSE OF ME) ROBERT CRAY BAND	50	1987
RIGHT NOW [A] CREATURES	14	1983
RIGHT NOW [B] AIRHEAD	50	1992
RIGHT NOW [C] ATOMIC KITTEN	10	1999
RIGHT ON SILICONE SOUL	15	2001
RIGHT ON TRACK BREAKFAST CLUB	54	1987
RIGHT SAID FRED BERNARD CRIBBINS	10	1962
THE RIGHT STUFF [A] BRYAN FERRY	37	1987
THE RIGHT STUFF [B] VANESSA WILLIAMS	62	1988
RIGHT STUFF [C] LC ANDERSON VS PSYCHO RADIO	45	2003
THE RIGHT THING SIMPLY RED	11	1987
THE RIGHT THING TO DO CARLY SIMON	17	1973
THE RIGHT THING TO SAY NAT 'KING' COLE	42	1962
RIGHT THURR CHINGY	17	2003
THE RIGHT TIME ULTRA	28	1998
RIGHT TO BE WRONG JOSS STONE	29	2004
THE RIGHT TO LOVE DAVID WHITFIELD	30	1958
THE RIGHT WAY PETER ANDRE	14	2004
RIGHT WHERE YOU WANT ME JESSE McCARTNEY	54	2006
RIKKI DON'T LOSE THAT NUMBER STEELY DAN	58	1979
RIKKI DON'T LOSE THAT NUMBER TOM ROBINSON	58	1984
RING ALEXIA	48	2003
RING A DING GIRL RONNIE CARROLL	46	1962
RING DING DING [A] PONDLIFE	11	2005
RING DING DING [B] LOC	58	2005
RING MY BELL [A] ANITA WARD	1	1979
RING MY BELL [A] DJ JAZZY JEFF & THE FRESH PRINCE	37	1991
RING MY BELL [B] MONIE LOVE Vs ADEVA	20	1991
RING OF BRIGHT WATER VAL DOONICAN	48	1969
RING OF FIRE [A] DUANE EDDY & THE REBELS	17	1961
RING OF FIRE [B] ERIC BURDON & THE ANIMALS	35	1969
RING OF ICE JENNIFER RUSH	14	1985
RING OUT SOLSTICE BELLS (EP) JETHRO TULL	28	1976
RING RING [A] ABBA	32	1974
RING RING [B] DOLLAR	61	1982
RING RING RING AARON SOUL	14	2001
RING RING RING (HA HA HEY) DE LA SOUL	10	1991
RING THE BELLS JAMES	37	1992
RINGO LORNE GREENE	22	1964
RIO [A] MICHAEL NESMITH	28	1977
RIO [B] DURAN DURAN	9	1982
RIOT RADIO DEAD 60'S	30	2004
RIP GARY NUMAN	29	2002
RIP IT UP [A] BILL HALEY & HIS COMETS	4	1956
RIP IT UP [A] LITTLE RICHARD	30	1956
RIP IT UP [A] ELVIS PRESLEY	27	1957
RIP IT UP [B] ORANGE JUICE	8	1983
RIP IT UP [C] RAZORLIGHT	20	2003
RIPGROOVE DOUBLE 99	14	1997
RIPPED IN 2 MINUTES A VS B	49	1998
RIPPIN KITTIN GOLDEN BOY WITH MISS KITTIN	67	2002
RISE [A] HERB ALPERT	13	1979
RISE [B] PUBLIC IMAGE LTD.	11	1986
RISE [C] ZION TRAIN	61	1996
RISE [D] EDDIE AMADOR	19	2000
RISE [E] GABRIELLE	1	2000
RISE [F] SOUL PROVIDERS FEATURING MICHELLE SHELLERS	59	2001
RISE & FALL CRAIG DAVID & STING	2	2003
THE RISE AND FALL OF FLINGEL BUNT SHADOWS	5	1964
RISE AND SHINE CARDIGANS	29	1996
RISE 'IN STEVE LAWLER	50	2000
RISE OF THE EAGLES EIGHTIES MATCHBOX B-LINE DISASTER	40	2004
RISE TO THE OCCASION CLIMIE FISHER	10	1987
RISE UP [A] JAMAICA UNITED	54	1998
RISE UP [B] YVES LAROCK	13	2007
RISIN' TO THE TOP KENI BURKE	70	1992
RISING SIGN HURRICANE #1	47	1998
RISING SUN [A] MEDICINE HEAD	11	1973
RISING SUN [B] FARM	48	1992
RISINGSON MASSIVE ATTACK	11	1997
THE RITUAL EBONY DUBSTERS	58	2004
THE RIVER [A] BRUCE SPRINGSTEEN	35	1981
THE RIVER [B] KING TRIGGER	57	1982
THE RIVER [C] TOTAL CONTRAST	44	1986
THE RIVER [D] BEAUTIFUL SOUTH	59	2000
THE RIVER [E] BREED 77	39	2004
RIVER BELOW BILLY TALENT	70	2004

	Peak Position	Year of Entry
RIVER DEEP MOUNTAIN HIGH IKE & TINA TURNER	3	1966
RIVER DEEP MOUNTAIN HIGH SUPREMES & THE FOUR TOPS	11	1971
THE RIVER (LE COLLINE SONO IN FIORO) KEN DODD	3	1965
RIVER MAN NICK DRAKE	48	2004
THE RIVER OF DREAMS BILLY JOEL	3	1993
RIVER OF PAIN THUNDER	31	1995
RIVER STAY 'WAY FROM MY DOOR FRANK SINATRA	18	1960
THE RIVERBOAT SONG OCEAN COLOUR SCENE	15	1996
RIVERDANCE BILL WHELAN FEATURING ANUNA & THE RTE CONCERT ORCHESTRA	9	1994
RIVERS OF BABYLON BONEY M	1	1978
THE RIVERS OF BELIEF ENIGMA	68	1992
THE RIVER'S RUN DRY VINCE HILL	41	1962
ROACHES TRANCESETTERS	55	2000
THE ROAD LEADS WHERE IT'S LED SECRET MACHINES	56	2005
ROAD RAGE CATATONIA	5	1998
THE ROAD TO HELL (PART 2) CHRIS REA	10	1989
THE ROAD TO MANDALAY ROBBIE WILLIAMS	1	2001
ROAD TO NOWHERE TALKING HEADS	6	1985
ROAD TO OUR DREAM T'PAU	42	1988
THE ROAD TO PARADISE BHOYS OF PARADISE	46	2004
ROAD TO YOUR SOUL ALL ABOUT EVE	37	1989
ROAD TRIPPIN' RED HOT CHILI PEPPERS	30	2001
ROADBLOCK STOCK AITKEN WATERMAN	13	1987
ROADHOUSE MEDLEY (ANNIVERSARY WALTZ PART 25) STATUS QUO	21	1992
ROADRUNNER JONATHAN RICHMAN & THE MODERN LOVERS	11	1977
ROAM B-52's	17	1990
ROBERT DE NIRO'S WAITING BANANARAMA	3	1984
ROBIN HOOD DICK JAMES	29	1956
ROBIN HOOD GARY MILLER	10	1956
ROBIN (THE HOODED MAN) CLANNAD	42	1984
ROBIN'S RETURN NEVILLE DICKIE	33	1969
ROBOT TORNADOS	17	1963
ROBOT MAN CONNIE FRANCIS	2	1960
ROBOT ROCK DAFT PUNK	32	2005
ROBOT WARS (ANDROID LOVE) SIR KILLALOT VS ROBO BABE	51	2000
THE ROBOTS KRAFTWERK	20	1991
ROC YA BODY (MIC CHECK 1 2) MVP	5	2005
ROCCO DEATH IN VEGAS	51	1997
ROCHDALE COWBOY MIKE HARDING	22	1975
ROC-IN-IT DEEJAY PUNK-ROC VS ONYX	59	1999
THE ROCK [A] ALARM FEATURING THE MORRISTON ORPHEUS MALE VOICE CHOIR	31	1989
THE ROCK [B] DELAKOTA	60	1998
THE ROCK [C] PUNX	59	2002
ROCK A HULA BABY ELVIS PRESLEY	1	1962
ROCK AND A HARD PLACE ROLLING STONES	63	1989
ROCK AND ROLL DREAMS COME THROUGH MEAT LOAF	11	1994
ROCK AND ROLL IS DEAD LENNY KRAVITZ	22	1995
ROCK AND ROLL (IS GONNA SET THE NIGHT ON FIRE) PRETTY BOY FLOYD	75	1990
ROCK AND ROLL MUSIC BEACH BOYS	36	1976
ROCK AND ROLL (PARTS 1 & 2) GARY GLITTER	2	1972
ROCK & ROLL QUEEN SUBWAYS	22	2005
ROCK AND ROLL SUICIDE DAVID BOWIE	22	1974
ROCK AND ROLL WALTZ KAY STARR	1	1956
ROCK AROUND THE CLOCK BILL HALEY & HIS COMETS	1	1955
ROCK AROUND THE CLOCK TELEX	34	1979
ROCK AROUND THE CLOCK TEN POLE TUDOR	63	1979
ROCK BOTTOM [A] LYNSEY DE PAUL & MIKE MORAN	19	1977
ROCK BOTTOM [B] BABYFACE	50	1994
ROCK DA FUNKY BEATS PUBLIC DOMAIN FEATURING CHUCK D	19	2001
ROCK DA HOUSE TALL PAUL	12	1997
ROCK DJ ROBBIE WILLIAMS	1	2000
ROCK HARD SUZI QUATRO	68	1980
R.O.C.K. IN THE USA JOHN COUGAR MELLENCAMP	67	1986
ROCK IS DEAD MARILYN MANSON	23	1999
ROCK ISLAND LINE LONNIE DONEGAN	8	1956
ROCK ISLAND LINE STAN FREBERG & HIS SKIFFLE GROUP	24	1956
ROCK LOBSTER B-52's	12	1979
ROCK ME AMADEUS FALCO	1	1986
ROCK ME BABY [A] DAVID CASSIDY	11	1972
ROCK ME BABY [B] JOHNNY NASH	47	1985
ROCK ME BABY [C] BABY ROOTS	71	1992
ROCK ME GENTLY ANDY KIM	2	1974
ROCK ME GOOD UNIVERSAL	19	1997
ROCK ME STEADY DJ PROFESSOR	49	1992
ROCK ME TONIGHT (FOR OLD TIME'S SAKE) FREDDIE JACKSON	18	1986
ROCK MY HEART HADDAWAY	9	1994
ROCK MY WORLD FIVE STAR	28	1988
ROCK 'N ME STEVE MILLER BAND	11	1976
ROCK 'N' ROLL [A] STATUS QUO	8	1981
ROCK 'N' ROLL [B] JOHN McENROE & PAT CASH WITH THE FULL METAL RACKETS	66	1991
ROCK 'N' ROLL AIN'T NOISE POLLUTION AC/DC	15	1980
ROCK 'N' ROLL CHILDREN DIO	26	1985
ROCK 'N' ROLL DAMNATION AC/DC	24	1978
ROCK 'N' ROLL DANCE PARTY JIVE BUNNY & THE MASTERMIXERS	48	1991
ROCK 'N' ROLL (DOLE) J PAC	51	1995
ROCK 'N' ROLL DREAMS COME THROUGH JIM STEINMAN,VOCALS BY RORY DODD	52	1981
ROCK 'N' ROLL GYPSY SAXON	72	1986
ROCK 'N' ROLL HIGH SCHOOL RAMONES	67	1979
ROCK 'N ROLL (I GAVE YOU THE BEST YEARS OF MY LIFE) KEVIN JOHNSON	23	1975
ROCK 'N' ROLL IS KING ELECTRIC LIGHT ORCHESTRA	13	1983
ROCK 'N' ROLL LADY SHOWADDYWADDY	15	1974
ROCK 'N' ROLL LIES RAZORLIGHT	56	2003
ROCK 'N' ROLL MERCENARIES MEAT LOAF FEATURING JOHN PARR	31	1986
ROCK 'N' ROLL NIGGER BIRDLAND	47	1990
ROCK 'N' ROLL OUTLAW ROSE TATTOO	60	1981
ROCK 'N' ROLL STAGE SHOW (LP) BILL HALEY & HIS COMETS	30	1956
ROCK 'N' ROLL WINTER WIZZARD	6	1974
ROCK OF AGES DEF LEPPARD	41	1983
ROCK ON DAVID ESSEX	3	1973
ROCK ON BROTHER CHEQUERS	21	1975
THE ROCK SHOW BLINK 182	14	2001
ROCK STAR N*E*R*D	15	2002
ROCK STEADY [A] WHISPERS	38	1987
ROCK STEADY [B] BONNIE RAITT & BRYAN ADAMS	50	1995
ROCK STEADY [C] ALL SAINTS	3	2006
ROCK THE BELLS KADOC	34	1997
ROCK THE BOAT [A] HUES CORPORATION	6	1974
ROCK THE BOAT [A] FORREST	4	1983
ROCK THE BOAT [A] DELAGE	63	1990
ROCK THE BOAT [B] AALIYAH	12	2002
ROCK THE CASBAH CLASH	15	1982
ROCK THE DISCOTEK RAMP	49	1996
ROCK THE FUNKY BEAT NATURAL BORN CHILLERS	30	1997
ROCK THE HOUSE [A] SOURCE FEATURING NICOLE	63	1992
ROCK THE HOUSE [B] GORILLAZ	18	2001
ROCK THE JOINT BILL HALEY & HIS COMETS	20	1957
ROCK THE MIDNIGHT DAVID GRANT	46	1983
ROCK THE NIGHT EUROPE	12	1987
ROCK THIS PARTY (EVERYBODY DANCE NOW) BOB SINCLAR & CUTEE B	3	2006
ROCK THIS TOWN STRAY CATS	9	1981
ROCK 'TIL YOU DROP STATUS QUO	38	1992
ROCK 2 HOUSE X-PRESS 2 FEATURING LO-PRO	55	1994
ROCK WIT U (AWWW BABY) ASHANTI	7	2003
ROCK WIT'CHA BOBBY BROWN	33	1989
ROCK WITH THE CAVEMAN TOMMY STEELE & THE STEELMEN	13	1956
ROCK WITH YOU MICHAEL JACKSON	7	1980
ROCK WITH YOU D-INFLUENCE	30	1998
ROCK YOUR BABY GEORGE McCRAE	1	1974
ROCK YOUR BABY KWS	8	1992
ROCK YOUR BODY [A] CLOCK	30	1998
ROCK YOUR BODY [B] JUSTIN TIMBERLAKE	2	2003
ROCK YOUR BODY ROCK FERRY CORSTEN	11	2004
ROCK-A-BEATIN' BOOGIE BILL HALEY & HIS COMETS	4	1955
ROCK-A-BILLY GUY MITCHELL	1	1957
ROCKABILLY BOB COLUMBO FEATURING OOE	59	1999
ROCKABILLY GUY POLECATS	35	1981
ROCKABILLY REBEL MATCHBOX	18	1979
ROCK-A-BYE YOUR BABY (WITH A DIXIE MELODY) JERRY LEWIS	12	1957
ROCK-A-DOODLE-DOO LINDA LEWIS	15	1973
THE ROCKAFELLER SKANK FATBOY SLIM	6	1998
ROCKALL MEZZOFORTE	75	1983
ROCKARIA! ELECTRIC LIGHT ORCHESTRA	9	1977
ROCKER ALTER EGO	32	2004
ROCKET [A] MUD	6	1974
ROCKET [B] DEF LEPPARD	15	1989
ROCKET [C] EL PRESIDENTE	48	2005
ROCKET (A NATURAL GAMBLER) BRAUND REYNOLDS	27	2005
ROCKET MAN [A] SPOTNICKS	38	1962
ROCKET MAN [B] ELTON JOHN	2	1972
ROCKET MAN (I THINK IT'S GOING TO BE A LONG LONG TIME) [B] KATE BUSH	12	1991
ROCKET RIDE FELIX DA HOUSECAT	55	2004
ROCKET 2 U JETS	69	1988
ROCKFERRY DUFFY	45	2008
ROCKIN' ALL OVER THE WORLD STATUS QUO	3	1977
ROCKIN' ALONE MIKI & GRIFF	44	1960
ROCKIN' AROUND THE CHRISTMAS TREE BRENDA LEE	6	1962
ROCKIN' AROUND THE CHRISTMAS TREE JETS	62	1983
ROCKIN' AROUND THE CHRISTMAS TREE MEL & KIM	3	1987
ROCKIN' BACK INSIDE MY HEART JULEE CRUISE	66	1991
ROCKIN' CHAIR MAGNUM	27	1990
ROCKIN' FOR MYSELF MOTIV 8	18	1993
ROCKIN' GOOD CHRISTMAS ROY 'CHUBBY' BROWN	51	1996
A ROCKIN' GOOD WAY SHAKY & BONNIE	5	1984
ROCKIN' ME PROFESSOR	56	1994
ROCKIN' MY BODY 49ERS FEATURING ANN-MARIE SMITH	31	1995
ROCKIN' OVER THE BEAT TECHNOTRONIC FEATURING YA KID K	9	1990
ROCKIN' RED WING SAMMY MASTERS	36	1960
ROCKIN' ROBIN BOBBY DAY	29	1958
ROCKIN' ROBIN MICHAEL JACKSON	3	1972

	Peak Position	Year of Entry
ROCKIN' ROBIN LOLLY	10	1999
ROCKIN' ROLL BABY STYLISTICS	6	1974
ROCKIN' SOUL HUES CORPORATION	24	1974
ROCKIN' THE SUBURBS BEN FOLDS	53	2001
ROCKIN' THROUGH THE RYE BILL HALEY & HIS COMETS	3	1956
ROCKIN' TO THE MUSIC BLACK BOX	39	1993
ROCKIN' TO THE RHYTHM CONVERT	42	1993
ROCKIN' WITH RITA (HEAD TO TOE) VINDALOO SUMMER SPECIAL	56	1986
ROCKING GOOSE JOHNNY & THE HURRICANES	3	1960
ROCKING MUSIC MARTIN SOLVEIG	35	2004
ROCKIT HERBIE HANCOCK	8	1983
ROCKS PRIMAL SCREAM	7	1994
ROCKS ROD STEWART	55	1998
ROCKS ON THE ROAD JETHRO TULL	47	1992
ROCKSTAR [A] BIZARRE	17	2005
ROCKSTAR [B] NICKELBACK	2	2007
ROCKY AUSTIN ROBERTS	22	1975
ROCKY MOUNTAIN EP JOE WALSH	39	1977
THE RODEO SONG GARRY LEE & SHOWDOWN	44	1993
RODRIGO'S GUITAR CONCERTO DE ARANJUEZ (THEME FROM 2ND MOVEMENT) MANUEL & HIS MUSIC OF THE MOUNTAINS	3	1976
ROFO'S THEME ROFO	44	1992
ROK DA HOUSE [A] BEATMASTERS FEATURING THE COOKIE CREW	5	1988
ROK DA HOUSE [B] VINYLGROOVER & THE RED HED	72	2001
ROK THE NATION ROB 'N' RAZ FEATURING LEILA K	41	1990
ROLL AWAY DUSTY SPRINGFIELD	68	1995
ROLL AWAY THE STONE MOTT THE HOOPLE	8	1973
ROLL CALL LIL JON & THE EAST SIDE BOYZ	38	2005
ROLL ON MIS-TEEQ	7	2002
ROLL ON DOWN THE HIGHWAY BACHMAN-TURNER OVERDRIVE	22	1975
ROLL OVER BEETHOVEN ELECTRIC LIGHT ORCHESTRA	6	1973
ROLL OVER LAY DOWN STATUS QUO	9	1975
ROLL THE BONES RUSH	49	1992
ROLL TO ME DEL AMITRI	22	1995
ROLL WID US AKALA	72	2005
ROLL WITH IT [A] STEVE WINWOOD	53	1988
ROLL WITH IT [B] OASIS	2	1995
A ROLLER SKATING JAM NAMED 'SATURDAYS' DE LA SOUL	22	1991
ROLLERBLADE [A] NICK HEYWARD	37	1996
ROLLERBLADE [B] MOVIN' MELODIES	71	1997
ROLLERCOASTER [A] GRID	19	1994
ROLLERCOASTER [B] NORTHERN UPROAR	41	1995
ROLLERCOASTER [C] B*WITCHED	1	1998
ROLLERCOASTER (EP) JESUS & MARY CHAIN	46	1990
ROLLERCOASTER (EP) EVERYTHING BUT THE GIRL	65	1994
ROLLIN' LIMP BIZKIT	1	2001
ROLLIN' HOME STATUS QUO	9	1986
ROLLIN' IN MY 5.0 VANILLA ICE	27	1991
ROLLIN' ON CIRRUS	62	1978
ROLLIN' STONE DAVID ESSEX	5	1975
ROLLOUT (MY BUSINESS) LUDACRIS	20	2002
ROLLOVER DJ JET	34	2003
ROLODEX PROPAGANDA AT THE DRIVE-IN	54	2000
ROMAN P PSYCHIC TV	65	1986
ROMANCE (LET YOUR HEART GO) DAVID CASSIDY	54	1985
ROMANCING THE STONE EDDY GRANT	52	1984
ROMANTIC KARYN WHITE	23	1991
ROMANTIC RIGHTS DEATH FROM ABOVE 1979	57	2004
ROMANTIC TYPE PIGEON DETECTIVES	19	2007
ROMANTICA JANE MORGAN	39	1960
ROME WASN'T BUILT IN A DAY MORCHEEBA	34	2000
ROMEO [A] PETULA CLARK	3	1961
ROMEO [B] MR BIG	4	1977
ROMEO [C] BASEMENT JAXX	6	2001
ROMEO AND JULIET DIRE STRAITS	8	1981
ROMEO DUNN ROMEO	3	2002
ROMEO ME SLEEPER	39	1997
ROMEO WHERE'S JULIET COLLAGE	46	1985
RONDO KENNY BALL & HIS JAZZMEN	24	1963
RONI BOBBY BROWN	21	1989
ROOBARB AND CUSTARD SHAFT	7	1991
ROOF IS ON FIRE WESTBAM	58	1998
ROOF TOP SINGING NEW WORLD	50	1973
ROOFTOPS (A LIBERATION BROADCAST) LOSTPROPHETS	8	2006
ROOM AT THE TOP ADAM ANT	13	1990
ROOM ELEVEN DAISY CHAINSAW	65	1992
ROOM IN BROOKLYN JOHN SQUIRE	44	2004
ROOM IN YOUR HEART LIVING IN A BOX	5	1989
ROOM ON THE 3RD FLOOR McFLY	5	2004
ROOMS ON FIRE STEVIE NICKS	16	1989
THE ROOT OF ALL EVIL BEAUTIFUL SOUTH	50	2001
ROOTLESS TREE DAMIEN RICE	50	2007
ROOTS SPUNGE	52	2002
ROOTS BLOODY ROOTS SEPULTURA	19	1996
ROSALIE - COWGIRLS' SONG (MEDLEY) THIN LIZZY	20	1978
ROSALYN PRETTY THINGS	41	1964
ROSANNA TOTO	12	1983
THE ROSE [A] MICHAEL BALL	42	1995
THE ROSE [A] HEATHER PEACE	56	2000
THE ROSE [A] WESTLIFE	1	2006
ROSE [B] THE FEELING	38	2007
ROSE GARDEN LYNN ANDERSON	3	1971
ROSE GARDEN NEW WORLD	15	1971
A ROSE HAS TO DIE DOOLEYS	11	1978
A ROSE IS STILL A ROSE ARETHA FRANKLIN	22	1998
ROSE MARIE SLIM WHITMAN	1	1955
ROSE ROUGE ST GERMAIN	54	2001
ROSEABILITY IDLEWILD	38	2000
ROSES [A] HAYWOODE	11	1985
ROSES [A] RHYTHM-N-BASS	56	1992
ROSES [B] dEUS	56	1997
ROSES [C] OUTKAST	4	2004
ROSES ARE RED [A] RONNIE CARROLL	3	1962
ROSES ARE RED [B] MAC BAND FEATURING THE McCAMPBELL BROTHERS	8	1988
ROSES ARE RED (MY LOVE) BOBBY VINTON	15	1962
ROSES FOR THE DEAD FUNERAL FOR A FRIEND	39	2006
ROSES IN THE HOSPITAL MANIC STREET PREACHERS	15	1993
ROSES OF PICARDY VINCE HILL	13	1967
ROSETTA FAME & PRICE TOGETHER	11	1971
ROSIE [A] DON PARTRIDGE	4	1968
ROSIE [B] JOAN ARMATRADING	49	1980
ROTATION HERB ALPERT	46	1980
ROTTERDAM BEAUTIFUL SOUTH	6	1996
ROUGH BOY ZZ TOP	23	1986
ROUGH BOYS [A] PETE TOWNSHEND	39	1980
ROUGH BOYS [B] NORTHERN UPROAR	41	1995
ROUGH JUSTICE [A] BANANARAMA	23	1984
ROUGH JUSTICE [B] ROLLING STONES	15	2005
ROUGH WITH THE SMOOTH SHARA NELSON	30	1995
ROUGHNECK (EP) PROJECT 1	49	1992
ROULETTE RUSS CONWAY	1	1959
ROUND AND ROUND [A] JIMMY YOUNG	30	1957
ROUND AND ROUND [B] SPANDAU BALLET	18	1984
ROUND AND ROUND [C] JAKI GRAHAM	9	1985
ROUND AND ROUND [D] NEW ORDER	21	1989
ROUND & ROUND [E] HI-TEK FEATURING JONELL	73	2001
ROUND EVERY CORNER PETULA CLARK	43	1965
ROUND HERE [A] COUNTING CROWS	70	1994
ROUND HERE [B] GEORGE MICHAEL	32	2004
ROUND OF BLUES SHAWN COLVIN	73	1994
ROUND ROUND SUGABABES	1	2002
THE ROUSSOS PHENOMENON EP DEMIS ROUSSOS	1	1976
ROUTINE CHECK THE MITCHELL BROTHERS/ KANO/THE STREETS	42	2005
ROXANNE POLICE	12	1979
ROYAL EVENT RUSS CONWAY	15	1959
ROYAL MILE GERRY RAFFERTY	67	1980
ROY'S KEEN MORRISSEY	42	1997
R.R. EXPRESS ROSE ROYCE	52	1981
RSVP [A] FIVE STAR	45	1985
RSVP [B] JASON DONOVAN	17	1991
RSVP [C] POP WILL EAT ITSELF	27	1993
RUB A DUB DUB EQUALS	34	1970
RUB-A-DUB DOUBLE TROUBLE	66	1991
RUBBER BALL AVONS	30	1961
RUBBER BALL BOBBY VEE	4	1961
RUBBER BALL MARTY WILDE	9	1961
RUBBER BULLETS 10 C.C.	1	1973
RUBBERBAND GIRL KATE BUSH	12	1993
THE RUBBERBAND MAN DETROIT SPINNERS	16	1976
RUBBERBANDMAN YELLO	58	1991
RUBBERNECKIN' ELVIS PRESLEY	5	2003
RUBBISH CARTER-THE UNSTOPPABLE SEX MACHINE	14	1992
THE RUBETTES AUTEURS	66	1999
RUBY KAISER CHIEFS	1	2007
RUBY ANN MARTY ROBBINS	24	1963
RUBY DON'T TAKE YOUR LOVE TO TOWN KENNY ROGERS & THE FIRST EDITION	2	1969
RUBY RED [A] SLADE	51	1982
RUBY RED [B] MARC ALMOND	47	1986
RUBY TUESDAY ROLLING STONES	3	1967
RUBY TUESDAY MELANIE	9	1970
RUBY TUESDAY ROD STEWART	11	1993
RUDD IKARA COLT	72	2002
RUDE BOY ROCK LIONROCK	20	1998
RUDE BUOYS OUTA JAIL SPECIALS	5	1980
RUDEBOX ROBBIE WILLIAMS	4	2006
RUDI GOT MARRIED LAUREL AITKEN & THE UNITONE	60	1980
RUDI'S IN LOVE LOCOMOTIVE	25	1968
RUDY'S ROCK BILL HALEY & HIS COMETS	26	1956
RUFF IN THE JUNGLE BIZNESS PRODIGY	5	1992
RUFF MIX WONDER DOGS	31	1982
RUFFNECK MC LYTE	67	1994
RUGGED AND MEAN, BUTCH AND ON SCREEN PEE BEE SQUAD	52	1985
RUINED IN A DAY NEW ORDER	22	1993
RULE THE WORLD TAKE THAT	2	2007
RULES AND REGULATIONS WE'VE GOT A FUZZBOX & WE'RE GONNA USE IT	41	1986
RULES OF THE GAME BUCKS FIZZ	57	1983
RUMBLE IN THE JUNGLE FUGEES	3	1997
RUMORS TIMEX SOCIAL CLUB	13	1986
RUMOUR HAS IT DONNA SUMMER	19	1978
RUMOURS [A] HOT CHOCOLATE	44	1973
RUMOURS [B] AWESOME	58	1997
RUMOURS [C] DAMAGE	22	2000
RUMP SHAKER WRECKS-N-EFFECT	24	1992
RUN [A] SANDIE SHAW	32	1966
RUN [B] SPIRITUALIZED	59	1991
RUN [C] LIGHTHOUSE FAMILY	30	2002
RUN [D] SNOW PATROL	5	2004
RUN [E] GNARLS BARKLEY	32	2008
RUN [F] AMY MacDONALD	75	2008
RUN AWAY [A] 10 C.C.	50	1982

	Peak Position	Year of Entry
RUN AWAY [B] (MC SAR &) THE REAL McCOY	6	1995
RUN AWAY (I WANNA BE WITH U) NIVEA	48	2002
RUN BABY RUN [A] NEWBEATS	10	1971
RUN, BABY, RUN [B] SHERYL CROW	24	1995
RUN BACK CARL DOUGLAS	25	1977
RUN FOR COVER SUGABABES	13	2001
RUN FOR HOME LINDISFARNE	10	1978
RUN FOR YOUR LIFE [A] BUCKS FIZZ	14	1983
RUN FOR YOUR LIFE [B] NORTHERN LINE	18	1999
RUN FROM LOVE JIMMY SOMERVILLE	52	1991
RUN IT! CHRIS BROWN FEATURING JUELZ SANTANA	2	2006
RUN ON MOBY	33	1999
RUN RUDOLPH RUN CHUCK BERRY	36	1963
RUN RUN AWAY SLADE	7	1984
RUN RUN RUN [A] JO JO GUNNE	6	1972
RUN RUN RUN [B] PHOENIX	66	2004
RUN SILENT SHAKESPEARS SISTER	54	1989
RUN TO HIM BOBBY VEE	6	1961
RUN TO ME BEE GEES	9	1972
RUN TO MY LOVIN' ARMS BILLY FURY	25	1965
RUN TO THE DOOR CLINTON FORD	25	1967
RUN TO THE HILLS IRON MAIDEN	7	1982
RUN TO THE SUN ERASURE	6	1994
RUN TO YOU [A] BRYAN ADAMS	11	1985
RUN TO YOU [A] RAGE	3	1992
RUN TO YOU [B] WHITNEY HOUSTON	15	1993
RUN TO YOU [C] ROXETTE	27	1994
RUN 2 NEW ORDER	49	1989
RUNAGROUND JAMES	29	1998
RUNAROUND MARTHA WASH	49	1993
RUNAROUND SUE DION	11	1961
RUNAROUND SUE DOUG SHELDON	36	1961
RUNAROUND SUE RACEY	13	1980
RUNAWAY [A] DEL SHANNON	1	1961
THE RUNAWAY [B] ELKIE BROOKS	50	1979
RUNAWAY [C] DEEE-LITE	45	1992
RUNAWAY [D] JANET JACKSON	6	1995
RUNAWAY [E] CORRS	2	1996
RUNAWAY [F] E'VOKE	30	1995
RUNAWAY [G] NUYORICAN SOUL FEATURING INDIA	24	1997
RUNAWAY [H] JAMIROQUAI	18	2006
RUNAWAY BOYS STRAY CATS	9	1980
RUNAWAY GIRL STERLING VOID	53	1989
RUNAWAY HORSES BELINDA CARLISLE	40	1990
RUNAWAY LOVE EN VOGUE	36	1993
RUNAWAY LOVE LUDACRIS FEATURING MARY J. BLIGE	52	2007
RUNAWAY SKIES CELETIA	66	1998
RUNAWAY TRAIN [A] ELTON JOHN & ERIC CLAPTON	31	1992
RUNAWAY TRAIN [B] SOUL ASYLUM	7	1993
THE RUNNER THREE DEGREES	10	1979
RUNNIN [A] BASSTOY	62	2000
RUNNIN' [B] BASS BUMPERS	68	1993
RUNNIN' [C] 2PAC & THE NOTORIOUS B.I.G.	15	1998
RUNNIN' [D] PHARCYDE	36	1996
RUNNIN' [E] MARK PICCHIOTTI PRESENTS BASSTOY	13	2002
RUNNIN' AWAY SLY & THE FAMILY STONE	17	1972
RUNNIN' AWAY NICOLE	69	1996
RUNNIN' DOWN A DREAM TOM PETTY	55	1989
RUNNIN' (DYIN' TO LIVE) 2PAC & THE NOTORIOUS B.I.G.	17	2004
RUNNIN' FOR THE RED LIGHT (I GOTTA LIFE) MEAT LOAF	21	1996
RUNNIN' WITH THE DEVIL VAN HALEN	52	1980
RUNNING ALL OVER THE WORLD STATUS QUO	17	1988
RUNNING AROUND TOWN BILLIE RAY MARTIN	29	1995
RUNNING BEAR JOHNNY PRESTON	1	1960

	Peak Position	Year of Entry
RUNNING FREE IRON MAIDEN	19	1980
RUNNING FROM PARADISE DARYL HALL & JOHN OATES	41	1980
RUNNING IN THE FAMILY LEVEL 42	6	1987
RUNNING OUT OF TIME DIGITAL ORGASM	16	1991
RUNNING SCARED ROY ORBISON	9	1961
RUNNING UP THAT HILL KATE BUSH	3	1985
RUNNING UP THAT HILL PLACEBO	66	2007
RUNNING WITH THE NIGHT LIONEL RICHIE	9	1984
RUN'S HOUSE RUN D.M.C.	37	1988
RUPERT JACKIE LEE	14	1971
THE RUSH [A] LUTHER VANDROSS	53	1992
RUSH [B] FREAKPOWER	62	1994
RUSH [C] KLESHAY	19	1999
RUSH HOUR [A] JANE WIEDLIN	12	1988
RUSH HOUR [A] JOYRIDER	22	1996
RUSH HOUR [B] BAD COMPANY	59	2002
RUSH RUSH PAULA ABDUL	6	1989
RUSH SONG A	35	2005
RUSHES DARIUS	5	2002
RUSHING LONI CLARK	37	1993
RUSSIANS STING	12	1985
RUST ECHO & THE BUNNYMEN	22	1999
RUSTY CAGE SOUNDGARDEN	41	1992

S

	Peak Position	Year of Entry
S CLUB PARTY S CLUB 7	2	1999
SABOTAGE BEASTIE BOYS	19	1994
SABRE DANCE LOVE SCULPTURE	5	1968
SACRAMENTO MIDDLE OF THE ROAD	23	1972
SACRED CYCLES PETER LAZONBY	49	2000
SACRED TRUST ONE TRUE VOICE	2	2002
THE SACREMENT H.I.M.	23	2003
SACRIFICE ELTON JOHN	1	1989
SAD AND LONELY SECRET MACHINES	38	2005
SAD BUT TRUE METALLICA	20	1993
SAD EYES ROBERT JOHN	31	1979
SAD MOVIES (MAKE ME CRY) CAROL DEENE	44	1961
SAD MOVIES (MAKE ME CRY) SUE THOMPSON	46	1965
SAD SONGS (SAY SO MUCH) ELTON JOHN	7	1984
SAD SWEET DREAMER SWEET SENSATION	1	1974
SADDLE UP DAVID CHRISTIE	9	1982
SADIE'S SHAWL FRANK CORDELL	29	1956
SADNESS PART 1 ENIGMA	1	1990
SAFARI (EP) BREEDERS	69	1992
SAFE FROM HARM [A] MASSIVE ATTACK	25	1991
SAFE FROM HARM [B] NARCOTIC THRUST	24	2002
THE SAFETY DANCE MEN WITHOUT HATS	6	1983
SAFFRON EASTERN LANE	55	2004
SAID I LOVED YOU BUT I LIED MICHAEL BOLTON	15	1993
SAID SHE WAS A DANCER JETHRO TULL	55	1988
SAIL AWAY [A] LITTLE ANGELS	45	1993
SAIL AWAY [B] URBAN COOKIE COLLECTIVE	18	1994
SAIL AWAY [C] DAVID GRAY	26	2001
SAIL ON COMMODORES	8	1979
SAILING [A] ROD STEWART	1	1975
SAILING [B] CHRISTOPHER CROSS	48	1981
SAILING OFF THE EDGE OF THE WORLD STRAW	52	2001
SAILING ON THE SEVEN SEAS ORCHESTRAL MANOEUVRES IN THE DARK	3	1991
SAILOR ANNE SHELTON	10	1961
SAILOR PETULA CLARK	1	1961
SAILORTOWN ENERGY ORCHARD	73	1990
THE SAINT [A] THOMPSON TWINS	53	1992
THE SAINT [B] ORBITAL	3	1997
ST ANGER METALLICA	9	2003
ST ELMO'S FIRE (MAN IN MOTION) JOHN PARR	6	1985
SAINT OF ME ROLLING STONES	26	1998
ST PETERSBURG SUPERGRASS	22	2005
ST TERESA JOAN OSBORNE	33	1996
ST. THERESE OF THE ROSES MALCOLM VAUGHAN	3	1956
ST VALENTINE'S DAY MASSACRE EP MOTORHEAD & GIRLSCHOOL	5	1981
THE SAINTS ARE COMING SKIDS	48	1978
THE SAINTS ARE COMING U2 & GREEN DAY	2	2006
THE SAINTS ROCK 'N' ROLL BILL HALEY & HIS COMETS	5	1956
SALE OF THE CENTURY SLEEPER	10	1996
SALLY [A] GERRY MONROE	4	1970
SALLY [B] CARMEL	60	1986
SALLY [C] KERBDOG	69	1996
SALLY ANN JOE BROWN & THE BRUVVERS	28	1963
SALLY CINNAMON STONE ROSES	46	1990
SALLY DON'T YOU GRIEVE LONNIE DONEGAN	11	1958
SALLY MACLENNANE POGUES	51	1985
SALMON DANCE CHEMICAL BROTHERS	27	2007
SAL'S GOT A SUGAR LIP LONNIE DONEGAN	13	1959
SALSA HOUSE RICHIE RICH	50	1989
SALSOUL NUGGET (IF U WANNA) M&S PRESENTS GIRL NEXT DOOR	6	2001
SALT IN THE WOUND CARPET BOMBERS FOR PEACE	67	2003
SALT SWEAT SUGAR JIMMY EAT WORLD	60	2001
THE SALT WOUND ROUTINE THIRTEEN SENSES	45	2005
SALTWATER [A] JULIAN LENNON	6	1991
SALTWATER [B] CHICANE FEATURING MAIRE BRENNAN OF CLANNAD	6	1999
SALTY DYLAN RHYMES FEATURING K ELLIS	70	2005
SALTY DOG PROCOL HARUM	44	1969
SALVA MEA (SAVE ME) FAITHLESS	9	1995
SALVATION CRANBERRIES	13	1996
SAM [A] KEITH WEST	38	1967
SAM [B] OLIVIA NEWTON-JOHN	6	1977
SAMANTHA KENNY BALL & HIS JAZZMEN	13	1961
SAMBA DE JANIERO BELLINI	8	1997
SAMBA MAGIC SUMMER DAZE	61	1996
SAMBA PA TI SANTANA	27	1974
SAMBUCA WIDEBOYS FEATURING DENNIS G	15	2001
SAME GIRL R KELLY & USHER	26	2007
SAME JEANS THE VIEW	3	2007
SAME MAN TILL WEST & DJ DELICIOUS	36	2006
SAME MISTAKE JAMES BLUNT	57	2007
SAME OLD BRAND NEW YOU A1	1	2000
THE SAME OLD SCENE ROXY MUSIC	12	1980
SAME OLD STORY ULTRAVOX	31	1986
SAME PICTURE GOLDRUSH	64	2002
SAME SONG DIGITAL UNDERGROUND	52	1991
SAME TEMPO CHANGING FACES	53	1998
SAME THING IN REVERSE BOY GEORGE	56	1995
SAMSON AND DELILAH [A] MIDDLE OF THE ROAD	26	1972
SAMSON AND DELILAH [B] BAD MANNERS	58	1982
SAN ANTONIO ROSE FLOYD CRAMER	36	1961
SAN BERNADINO CHRISTIE	7	1970
SAN DAMIANO (HEART AND SOUL) SAL SOLO	15	1985
SAN FRANCISCAN NIGHTS ERIC BURDON & THE ANIMALS	7	1967
SAN FRANCISCO (BE SURE TO WEAR SOME FLOWERS IN YOUR HAIR) SCOTT McKENZIE	1	1967
SAN FRANCISCO DAYS CHRIS ISAAK	62	1993
SAN FRANCISCO (YOU'VE GOT ME) VILLAGE PEOPLE	45	1977
SAN MIGUEL KINGSTON TRIO	29	1959
SAN MIGUEL LONNIE DONEGAN	19	1959
SANCTIFIED LADY MARVIN GAYE	51	1985

	Peak Position	Year of Entry
SANCTIFY YOURSELF SIMPLE MINDS	10	1986
SANCTIMONIOUS HALO	44	2002
SANCTUARY [A] IRON MAIDEN	29	1980
SANCTUARY [B] NEW MUSIK	31	1980
SANCTUARY [C] DEJURE	62	2003
SANCTUS (MISSA LUBA) TROUBADOURS DU ROI BAUDOUIN	28	1969
SAND IN MY SHOES DIDO	29	2004
SANDBLASTED (EP) SWERVEDRIVER	67	1991
SANDCASTLES BOMB THE BASS FEATURING BERNARD FOWLER	54	1995
SANDMAN BLUE BOY	25	1997
SANDS OF TIME KALEEF	26	1998
SANDSTORM [A] CAST	8	1996
SANDSTORM [B] DARUDE	3	2000
SANDWICHES DETROIT GRAND PU BAHS	29	2000
SANDY JOHN TRAVOLTA	2	1978
SANITY KILLING JOKE	70	1986
SANTA BRING MY BABY BACK TO ME ELVIS PRESLEY	7	1957
SANTA CLAUS IS BACK IN TOWN ELVIS PRESLEY	41	1980
SANTA CLAUS IS COMIN' TO TOWN CARPENTERS	37	1975
SANTA CLAUS IS COMIN' TO TOWN BRUCE SPRINGSTEEN	9	1985
SANTA CLAUS IS COMING TO TOWN JACKSON 5	43	1972
SANTA CLAUS IS COMING TO TOWN BJORN AGAIN	55	1992
SANTA CLAUS IS ON THE DOLE SPITTING IMAGE	22	1986
SANTA CRUZ (YOU'RE NOT THAT FAR) THRILLS	33	2003
SANTA MARIA TATJANA	40	1996
SANTA MARIA DJ MILANO FEATURING SAMANTHA FOX	31	1998
SANTA MONICA (WATCH THE WORLD DIE) EVERCLEAR	40	1996
SANTA'S LIST CLIFF RICHARD	5	2003
SANTO NATALE DAVID WHITFIELD	2	1954
SARA [A] FLEETWOOD MAC	37	1980
SARA [B] STARSHIP	66	1986
SARAH THIN LIZZY	24	1979
SARTORIAL ELOQUENCE ELTON JOHN	44	1980
SAT IN YOUR LAP KATE BUSH	11	1981
SATAN ORBITAL	3	1991
SATAN REJECTED MY SOUL MORRISSEY	39	1998
THE SATCH EP JOE SATRIANI	53	1993
SATELLITE [A] HOOTERS	22	1987
SATELLITE [B] BELOVED	19	1996
SATELLITE [C] OCEANLAB	19	2004
SATELLITE KID DOGS D'AMOUR	26	1989
SATELLITE OF LOVE 04 LOU REED	10	2004
SATIN SHEETS BELLAMY BROTHERS	43	1976
SATISFACTION [A] OTIS REDDING	33	1966
SATISFACTION [A] ARETHA FRANKLIN	37	1967
SATISFACTION [A] VANILLA ICE	22	1991
SATISFACTION [B] WENDY & LISA	27	1989
SATISFACTION [C] EVE	20	2003
SATISFACTION [D] BENNY BENASSI PRESENTS THE BIZ	2	2003
SATISFACTION GUARANTEED (OR TAKE YOUR LOVE BACK) HAROLD MELVIN & THE BLUENOTES	32	1974
SATISFIED RICHARD MARX	52	1989
SATISFIED (TAKE ME HIGHER) H20	66	1997
SATISFY MY LOVE [A] EXOTERIX	62	1994
SATISFY MY LOVE [B] SABRINA JOHNSTON	62	1994
SATISFY MY LOVE [C] PESHAY VERSUS FLYTRONIX	67	2002
SATISFY MY SOUL BOB MARLEY & THE WAILERS	21	1978
SATISFY YOU PUFF DADDY FEATURING R KELLY	8	2000
SATURDAY [A] JOEY NEGRO FEATURING TAKA BOOM	41	2000
SATURDAY [B] OMAR	43	1994
SATURDAY [C] EAST 57TH STREET FEATURING DONNA ALLEN	29	1997
SATURDAY GIGS MOTT THE HOOPLE	41	1974
SATURDAY LOVE CHERRELLE WITH ALEXANDER O'NEAL	6	1985
SATURDAY LOVE ILLEGAL MOTION FEATURING SIMONE CHAPMAN	67	1993
SATURDAY NIGHT [A] T-CONNECTION	41	1979
SATURDAY NIGHT [B] BLUE NILE	50	1991
SATURDAY NIGHT [C] WHIGFIELD	1	1994
SATURDAY NIGHT [C] SINDY	70	1996
SATURDAY NIGHT [D] SUEDE	6	1997
SATURDAY NIGHT [E] UD PROJECT	19	2004
SATURDAY NIGHT AT THE MOVIES DRIFTERS	3	1972
SATURDAY NIGHT AT THE MOVIES ROBSON & JEROME	1	1996
SATURDAY NIGHT (BENEATH THE PLASTIC PALM TREES) LEYTON BUZZARDS	53	1979
SATURDAY NIGHT PARTY (READ MY LIPS) ALEX PARTY	29	1993
SATURDAY NIGHT SUNDAY MORNING T-EMPO	19	1994
SATURDAY NIGHT'S ALRIGHT FOR FIGHTING ELTON JOHN	7	1973
SATURDAY NITE [A] EARTH, WIND & FIRE	17	1977
SATURDAY NITE [B] BRAND NEW HEAVIES	35	1999
SATURDAY NITE AT THE DUCK POND COUGARS	33	1963
SATURDAY (OOOH OOOH) LUDACRIS	31	2002
SATURDAY SUPERHOUSE BIFFY CLYRO	13	2007
SATURDAY'S NOT WHAT IT USED TO BE KINGMAKER	63	1993
SATURN 5 INSPIRAL CARPETS	20	1994
THE SAVAGE SHADOWS	10	1961
SAVANNA DANCE DEEP FOREST	28	1994
SAVE A LITTLE BIT GLEN GOLDSMITH	73	1988
SAVE A PRAYER DURAN DURAN	2	1982
SAVE A PRAYER 56K FEATURING BEJAY	46	2003
SAVE IT FOR LATER BEAT	47	1982
SAVE IT 'TIL THE MOURNING AFTER SHUT UP & DANCE	25	1995
SAVE ME [A] DAVE DEE, DOZY, BEAKY, MICK & TICH	3	1966
SAVE ME [B] SILVER CONVENTION	30	1975
SAVE ME [C] QUEEN	11	1980
SAVE ME [D] FLEETWOOD MAC	53	1990
SAVE ME [E] BIG COUNTRY	41	1990
SAVE ME [F] EMBRACE	29	2000
SAVE ME [G] MEEKER	60	2000
SAVE ME [H] REMY ZERO	55	2002
SAVE ME [I] DARREN STYLES	70	2007
SAVE MYSELF WILLY MASON	42	2007
SAVE OUR LOVE ETERNAL	8	1994
SAVE THE BEST FOR LAST VANESSA WILLIAMS	3	1992
SAVE THE CHILDREN MARVIN GAYE	41	1971
SAVE THE LAST DANCE FOR ME DRIFTERS	2	1960
SAVE THE LAST DANCE FOR ME BEN E. KING	69	1987
SAVE THE LAST DANCE FOR ME GENERAL SAINT FEATURING DON CAMPBELL	75	1994
SAVE TONIGHT EAGLE-EYE CHERRY	6	1998
SAVE UP ALL YOUR TEARS CHER	37	1991
SAVE US [A] PHILIP JAP	53	1982
SAVE US [B] FEEDER	34	2006
SAVE YOUR KISSES FOR ME BROTHERHOOD OF MAN	1	1976
SAVE YOUR LOVE RENEE & RENATO	1	1982
SAVE YOUR LOVE (FOR NUMBER 1) RENE & ANGELA FEATURING KURTIS BLOW	66	1985
SAVE YOURSELF SPEEDWAY	10	2003
SAVED [A] MR ROY	24	1995
SAVED [B] OCTOPUS	40	1996
SAVED BY THE BELL ROBIN GIBB	2	1969
SAVED MY LIFE LIL' LOUIS & THE WORLD	74	1992
SAVING ALL MY LOVE FOR YOU WHITNEY HOUSTON	1	1985
SAVING FOREVER FOR YOU SHANICE	42	1993
SAVING MY FACE KT TUNSTALL	50	2007
SAVIOUR'S DAY CLIFF RICHARD	1	1990
SAXUALITY CANDY DULFER	60	1990
SAXY LADY QUIVVER	56	1994
SAY CREATURES	72	1999
SAY A LITTLE PRAYER BOMB THE BASS FEATURING MAUREEN	10	1988
SAY A PRAYER TAYLOR DAYNE	58	1995
SAY CHEESE (SMILE PLEASE) FAST FOOD ROCKERS	10	2003
SAY GOODBYE S CLUB	2	2003
SAY, HAS ANYBODY SEEN MY SWEET GYPSY ROSE DAWN FEATURING TONY ORLANDO	12	1973
SAY HELLO DEEP DISH	14	2005
SAY HELLO TO THE ANGELS INTERPOL	65	2003
SAY HELLO WAVE GOODBYE SOFT CELL	3	1982
SAY HELLO WAVE GOODBYE DAVID GRAY	26	2002
SAY HOW I FEEL RHIAN BENSON	27	2004
SAY I CHRISTINA MILIAN FEATURING YOUNG JEEZY	4	2006
SAY I WON'T BE THERE SPRINGFIELDS	5	1963
SAY...IF YOU FEEL ALRIGHT CRYSTAL WATERS	45	1997
SAY I'M YOUR NO. 1 PRINCESS	7	1985
SAY IT [A] ABC	42	1992
SAY IT [B] MARIA RUBIA	40	2001
SAY IT AGAIN [A] JERMAINE STEWART	7	1988
SAY IT AGAIN [B] PRECIOUS	6	1999
SAY IT AIN'T SO WEEZER	37	1995
SAY IT ISN'T SO [A] DARYL HALL & JOHN OATES	69	1983
SAY IT ISN'T SO [B] BON JOVI	10	2000
SAY IT ISN'T SO [C] GARETH GATES	4	2003
SAY IT ONCE ULTRA	16	1998
SAY IT RIGHT NELLY FURTADO	10	2007
SAY IT WITH FLOWERS DOROTHY SQUIRES & RUSS CONWAY	23	1961
SAY IT WITH PRIDE SCOTLAND WORLD CUP SQUAD	45	1990
SAY JUST WORDS PARADISE LOST	53	1997
SAY MY NAME [A] ZEE	36	1997
SAY MY NAME [B] DESTINY'S CHILD	3	2000
SAY NO GO DE LA SOUL	18	1989
SAY NOTHIN' OMAR	29	1997
SAY SAY SAY PAUL McCARTNEY & MICHAEL JACKSON	2	1983
SAY SAY SAY (WAITING 4 U) HI-TACK	4	2006
SAY SOMETHIN' MARIAH CAREY	27	2006
SAY SOMETHING [A] JAMES	24	1994
SAY SOMETHING [B] HAVEN	24	2002
SAY SOMETHING ANYWAY BELLEFIRE	26	2004
SAY THAT YOU'RE HERE FRAGMA	25	2001
SAY WHAT! X-PRESS 2	32	1993
SAY WHAT YOU WANT TEXAS	3	1997
SAY WHEN LENE LOVICH	19	1979
SAY WONDERFUL THINGS RONNIE CARROLL	6	1963
SAY YEAH [A] LIMIT	17	1985
SAY YEAH [B] BULLETPROOF	40	2001
SAY YES BLOOD ARM	52	2005
SAY YOU DO ULTRA	11	1998
SAY YOU DON'T MIND COLIN BLUNSTONE	15	1972
SAY YOU LOVE ME [A] FLEETWOOD MAC	40	1976
SAY YOU LOVE ME [B] SIMPLY RED	7	1998
SAY YOU LOVE ME [C] JOHNSON	56	1999

	Peak Position	Year of Entry
SAY YOU REALLY WANT ME KIM WILDE	29	1987
SAY YOU, SAY ME LIONEL RICHIE	8	1985
SAY YOU WILL FOREIGNER	71	1987
SAY YOU'LL BE MINE [A] AMY GRANT	41	1994
SAY YOU'LL BE MINE [B] STEPS	4	1999
SAY YOU'LL BE MINE [C] QFX	34	1999
SAY YOU'LL BE THERE SPICE GIRLS	1	1996
SAY YOU'LL STAY UNTIL TOMORROW TOM JONES	40	1977
SAY YOU'RE MINE AGAIN JUNE HUTTON & AXEL STORDAHL & THE BOYS NEXT DOOR	6	1953
(SAY) YOU'RE MY GIRL ROY ORBISON	23	1965
SAY YOU'RE WRONG JULIAN LENNON	75	1985
SCALES OF JUSTICE LIVING IN A BOX	30	1987
SCANDAL QUEEN	25	1989
SCANDALOUS [A] CLICK	54	1996
SCANDALOUS [B] MIS-TEEQ	2	2003
SCAR TISSUE RED HOT CHILI PEPPERS	15	1999
SCARECROW SUB FOCUS	60	2005
SCARED SLACKER	36	1997
SCARLET ALL ABOUT EVE	34	1990
SCARLET RIBBONS HARRY BELAFONTE	18	1957
SCARLETT O'HARA JET HARRIS & TONY MEEHAN	2	1963
SCARS WITNESS	71	1999
SCARY MONSTERS (AND SUPER CREEPS) DAVID BOWIE	20	1981
SCARY MOVIES BAD MEETS EVIL FEATURING EMINEM & ROYCE DA 5'9"	63	2001
THE SCARY-GO-ROUND EP JELLYFISH	49	1991
SCATMAN (SKI-BA-BOP-BA-DOP-BOP) SCATMAN JOHN	3	1995
SCATMAN'S WORLD SCATMAN JOHN	10	1995
SCATTER & SWING LIONROCK	54	1998
SCATTERLINGS OF AFRICA JULUKA	44	1983
SCATTERLINGS OF AFRICA JOHNNY CLEGG & SAVUKA	75	1987
SCHEMING MAXIM	53	2000
SCHMOO SPOOKY	72	1993
SCHNAPPI SCHNAPPI	32	2005
SCHONEBERG MARMIO	53	1996
SCHOOL DAY CHUCK BERRY	24	1957
SCHOOL DAY (RING! RING! GOES THE BELL) DON LANG & HIS FRANTIC FIVE	26	1957
SCHOOL LOVE BARRY BLUE	11	1974
SCHOOL OF ROCK SCHOOL OF ROCK	51	2004
SCHOOL'S OUT ALICE COOPER	1	1972
SCHOOL'S OUT DAPHNE & CELESTE	12	2000
SCHOOLTIME CHRONICLE SMILEY CULTURE	59	1986
SCHTEEVE YOURCODENAMEIS:MILO	58	2004
SCIENCE OF SILENCE RICHARD ASHCROFT	14	2002
THE SCIENTIST COLDPLAY	10	2002
SCOOBY DOO [A] DWEEB	63	1997
SCOOBY DOO [B] J MAJIK & WICKAMAN	67	2004
SCOOBY SNACKS FUN LOVIN' CRIMINALS	22	1996
SCOPE PARIS ANGELS	75	1990
SCORCHIO SASHA/EMERSON	23	2000
SCORPIO RISING DEATH IN VEGAS FEATURING LIAM GALLAGHER	14	2002
SCOTCH ON THE ROCKS BAND OF THE BLACK WATCH	8	1975
SCOTLAND BE GOOD TARTAN ARMY	54	1998
SCOTLAND FOREVER SIDNEY DEVINE	48	1978
SCOTLAND SCOTLAND JASON SCOTLAND TRINIDAD & TOBAGO TARTAN ARMY	30	2006
SCOTS MACHINE VOYAGE	13	1978
SCOTTISH RAIN SILENCERS	71	1989
A SCOTTISH SOLDIER ANDY STEWART	19	1961
SCRAMBLED EGGS RONI SIZE	57	2002
THE SCRATCH SURFACE NOISE	26	1980
SCREAM [A] DISCO ANTHEM	47	1994
SCREAM [B] MICHAEL JACKSON & JANET JACKSON	3	1995
SCREAM [C] NUT	43	1997
SCREAM [D] TIMBALAND FEATURING KERI HILSON & NICOLE SCHERZINGER	12	2008
SCREAM AIM FIRE BULLET FOR MY VALENTINE	34	2008
SCREAM IF YOU WANNA GO FASTER GERI HALLIWELL	8	2001
SCREAM (PRIMAL SCREAM) MANTRONIX	46	1987
SCREAM UNTIL YOU LIKE IT W.A.S.P.	32	1987
THE SCREAMER YOSH PRESENTS LOVEDEEJAY AKEMI	38	1996
SCULLERY CLIFFORD T WARD	37	1974
SE A VIDA E (THAT'S THE WAY LIFE IS) PET SHOP BOYS	8	1996
SEA OF BLUE TECHNATION	56	2001
SEA OF HEARTBREAK DON GIBSON	14	1961
SEA OF LOVE MARTY WILDE	3	1959
SEA OF LOVE HONEYDRIPPERS	56	1985
SEA OF TROUBLE CORD	50	2006
SEAGULL RAINBOW COTTAGE	33	1976
THE SEAGULL'S NAME WAS NELSON PETER E BENNETT WITH THE CO-OPERATION CHOIR	45	1970
SEAL MY FATE BELLY	35	1995
SEAL OUR FATE GLORIA ESTEFAN	24	1991
SEALED WITH A KISS BRIAN HYLAND	3	1962
SEALED WITH A KISS JASON DONOVAN	1	1989
SÉANCE NEBULA II	55	1992
SEARCH AND DESTORY DICTATORS	49	1977
SEARCH FOR THE HERO M PEOPLE	9	1995
SEARCHIN' COASTERS	30	1957
SEARCHIN' HOLLIES	12	1963
SEARCHIN' FOR MY RIZLA RATPACK	58	1992
SEARCHIN' (I GOTTA FIND A MAN) HAZELL DEAN	6	1984
SEARCHIN' MY SOUL VONDA SHEPARD	10	1998
SEARCHING [A] CHANGE	11	1980
SEARCHING [B] CHINA BLACK	4	1994
SEARCHING [C] JAMIE SCOTT	33	2005
SEARCHING FOR A SOUL CONNOR REEVES	28	1998
SEARCHING FOR THE GOLDEN EYE MOTIV 8 & KYM MAZELLE	40	1995
SEASIDE ORDINARY BOYS	27	2004
SEASIDE SHUFFLE TERRY DACTYL & THE DINOSAURS	2	1972
SEASON NO. 5 BEDLAM AGO GO	57	1998
SEASONS IN THE ABYSS SLAYER	51	1991
SEASONS IN THE SUN TERRY JACKS	1	1974
SEASONS IN THE SUN WESTLIFE	1	1999
SEASONS OF GOLD GIDEA PARK	28	1981
SEASONSTREAM (EP) THOUSAND YARD STARE	65	1991
SEATTLE PUBLIC IMAGE LTD.	47	1987
2ND AMENDMENT EASYWORLD	42	2003
SECOND CHANCE PHILLIP LEO	57	1994
SECOND HAND ROSE BARBRA STREISAND	14	1966
THE SECOND LINE CLINIC	56	2000
SECOND, MINUTE OR HOUR JACK PENATE	17	2007
SECOND NATURE [A] DAN HARTMAN	66	1985
SECOND NATURE [B] ELECTRONIC	35	1997
SECOND ROUND KO CANIBUS	35	1998
THE SECOND SUMMER OF LOVE DANNY WILSON	23	1989
THE SECOND TIME KIM WILDE	29	1984
THE SECOND TIME AROUND SHALAMAR	45	1979
THE SECOND TIME (THEME FROM 'BILITIS') ELAINE PAIGE	69	1987
SECRET [A] ORCHESTRAL MANOEUVRES IN THE DARK	34	1985
SECRET [B] MADONNA	5	1994
SECRET AGENT MAN - JAMES BOND IS BACK BRUCE WILLIS	43	1987
SECRET COMBINATION RANDY CRAWFORD	48	1981
SECRET GARDEN [A] T'PAU	18	1988
SECRET GARDEN [B] QUINCY JONES FEATURING AL B SURE!, JAMES INGRAM, EL DeBARGE & BARRY WHITE	67	1990
SECRET GARDEN [C] BRUCE SPRINGSTEEN	17	1995
SECRET HEART TIGHT FIT	41	1982
SECRET KISS CORAL	25	2003
SECRET LOVE [A] DORIS DAY	1	1954
SECRET LOVE [A] KATHY KIRBY	4	1963
SECRET LOVE [A] DANIEL O'DONNELL & MARY DUFF	28	1995
SECRET LOVE [B] BEE GEES	5	1991
SECRET LOVE [C] DANNI'ELLE GAHA	41	1993
SECRET LOVE [D] SHAH	69	1998
SECRET LOVE [E] KELLY PRICE	26	1999
SECRET LOVERS ATLANTIC STARR	10	1986
SECRET MESSAGES ELECTRIC LIGHT ORCHESTRA	48	1983
SECRET RENDEZVOUS [A] RENE & ANGELA	54	1985
SECRET RENDEZVOUS [B] KARYN WHITE	22	1989
SECRET SMILE SEMISONIC	13	1999
SECRET STAR HOUSE OF ZEKKARIYAS AKA WOMACK & WOMACK	46	1994
SECRET SUNDAY LOVER ALI LOVE	45	2007
THE SECRET VAMPIRE SOUNDTRACK EP BIS	25	1996
SECRETLY SKUNK ANANSIE	16	1999
SECRETS [A] SUTHERLAND BROTHERS & QUIVER	35	1976
SECRETS [B] FIAT LUX	65	1984
SECRETS [C] PRIMITIVES	49	1989
SECRETS [D] SUNSCREEM	36	1996
SECRETS [E] ETERNAL	9	1996
SECRETS [F] MUTINY UK	47	2001
SECRETS IN THE STREET NILS LOFGREN	53	1985
SECRETS (OF SUCCESS) COOKIE CREW FEATURING DANNY D	53	1991
SECRETS OF THE HEART CHESNEY HAWKES	57	1991
THE SECRETS THAT YOU KEEP MUD	3	1975
THE SEDUCTION (LOVE THEME) JAMES LAST BAND	48	1980
SEE A BRIGHTER DAY JTQ WITH NOEL McKOY	49	1993
SEE EMILY PLAY PINK FLOYD	6	1967
SEE IT IN A BOY'S EYES JAMELIA	5	2004
SEE IT LIKE A BABY MARILLION	45	2007
SEE JUNGLE (JUNGLE BOY) BOW WOW WOW	45	1982
SEE LINE WOMAN '99 SONGSTRESS	64	1999
SEE ME LUTHER VANDROSS	60	1987
SEE MY BABY JIVE WIZZARD	1	1973
SEE MY FRIEND KINKS	10	1965
SEE THAT GLOW THIS ISLAND EARTH	47	1985
SEE THE DAY DEE C. LEE	3	1985
SEE THE DAY GIRLS ALOUD	9	2006
SEE THE LIGHT PARADISE	73	2005
SEE THE LIGHTS SIMPLE MINDS	20	1991
SEE THE STAR DELIRIOUS?	16	1999
SEE THOSE EYES ALTERED IMAGES	11	1982
SEE THRU IT APHRODITE FEATURING WILDFLOWER	68	2002
SEE WANT MUST HAVE BLUE MERCEDES	57	1988
SEE YA ATOMIC KITTEN	6	2000
SEE YOU DEPECHE MODE	6	1982
SEE YOU LATER REGENTS	55	1980
SEE YOU LATER ALLIGATOR BILL HALEY & HIS COMETS	7	1956
THE SEED (2.0) ROOTS FEATURING CODY CHESTNUTT	33	2003
SEEING THINGS BLACK CROWES	72	1991
THE SEEKER WHO	19	1970
SEEMS FINE CONCRETES	52	2004
SEEN THE LIGHT SUPERGRASS	22	2003
SEETHER VERUCA SALT	61	1994
SEIZE THE DAY F.K.W.	45	1993
SELA LIONEL RICHIE	43	1987

		Peak Position	Year of Entry
SELECTA (URBAN HEROES)	JAMESON & VIPER	51	2002
SELF!	FUZZBOX	24	1989
SELF CONTROL	LAURA BRANIGAN	5	1984
SELF CONTROL	INFERNAL	18	2006
SELF DESTRUCTION	STOP THE VIOLENCE	75	1989
SELF ESTEEM	OFFSPRING	37	1995
SELF SUICIDE	GOLDIE LOOKIN CHAIN	32	2004
SELFISH	OTHER TWO	46	1993
SELFISH JEAN	TRAVIS	30	2007
SELFISH WAYS	DOGS	45	2005
SELLING JESUS	SKUNK ANANSIE	46	1995
SELLING THE DRAMA	LIVE	30	1995
SEMI-CHARMED LIFE	THIRD EYE BLIND	33	1997
SEMI-DETACHED SUBURBAN MR. JAMES	MANFRED MANN	2	1966
SEND HIS LOVE TO ME	PJ HARVEY	34	1995
SEND IN THE BOYS	MILBURN	22	2006
SEND IN THE CLOWNS	JUDY COLLINS	6	1975
SEND ME AN ANGEL [A]	BLACKFOOT	66	1983
SEND ME AN ANGEL [B]	SCORPIONS	27	1991
SEND ME THE PILLOW YOU DREAM ON	JOHNNY TILLOTSON	21	1962
SEND MY HEART	ADVENTURES	62	1984
SEND ONE YOUR LOVE	STEVIE WONDER	52	1979
SEND YOUR LOVE	STING	30	2003
SENDING OUT AN S.O.S.	RETTA YOUNG	28	1975
SENORITA	JUSTIN TIMBERLAKE	13	2003
SENSATION	ELECTROSET	69	1995
SENSATIONAL	MICHELLE GAYLE	14	1997
SENSE	LIGHTNING SEEDS	31	1992
SENSE	TERRY HALL	54	1994
SENSE OF DANGER	PRESENCE FEATURING SHARA NELSON	61	1998
SENSES WORKING OVERTIME	XTC	10	1982
SENSITIVITY [A]	RALPH TRESVANT	18	1991
SENSITIVITY [B]	SHAPESHIFTERS & CHIC	40	2006
SENSITIZE	THAT PETROL EMOTION	55	1991
SENSUAL SOPHIS-TI-CAT/THE PLAYER	CARL COX	25	1996
THE SENSUAL WORLD	KATE BUSH	12	1989
SENSUALITY	LOVESTATION	16	1998
SENTIMENTAL [A]	ALEXANDER O'NEAL	53	1992
SENTIMENTAL [B]	DEBORAH COX	34	1995
SENTIMENTAL [C]	KYM MARSH	35	2003
SENTIMENTAL FOOL	LLOYD COLE	73	1995
SENTINEL	MIKE OLDFIELD	10	1992
SENZA UNA DONNA (WITHOUT A WOMAN)	ZUCCHERO & PAUL YOUNG	4	1991
SEPARATE LIVES	PHIL COLLINS & MARILYN MARTIN	4	1985
SEPARATE TABLES	CHRIS DE BURGH	30	1992
SEPARATE WAYS	GARY MOORE	59	1992
SEPTEMBER	EARTH, WIND & FIRE	3	1978
SEPTEMBER IN THE RAIN	DINAH WASHINGTON	35	1961
SEPTEMBER SONG	IAN McCULLOCH	51	1984
SERENADE [A]	MARIO LANZA	15	1955
SERENADE [B]	MARIO LANZA	25	1956
SERENADE [B]	SLIM WHITMAN	8	1956
SERENADE [C]	SHADES	75	1997
SERENATA	SARAH VAUGHAN	37	1961
SERENITY	ARMIN VAN BUUREN	72	2005
SERENITY IN MURDER	SLAYER	50	1995
SERIOUS [A]	BILLY GRIFFIN	64	1984
SERIOUS [B]	SERIOUS INTENTION	51	1986
SERIOUS [C]	DEJA	75	1987
SERIOUS [D]	DONNA ALLEN	8	1987
SERIOUS [E]	DURAN DURAN	48	1990
SERIOUS [F]	MAXWELL D	38	2001
SERIOUS [G]	POP!	16	2005
SERIOUS MIX	MIRAGE	42	1987
SERPENTS KISS	MISSION	70	1986
SESAME'S TREET	SMART E'S	2	1992
SET ADRIFT ON A MEMORY BLISS	PM DAWN	3	1991
SET FIRE TO ME	WILLIE COLON	41	1986
SET IN STONE	BEDROCK	71	1997
SET IT OFF [A]	HARLEQUIN 4S/BUNKER KRU	55	1988
SET IT OFF [B]	PEACHES	36	2002
SET ME FREE [A]	KINKS	9	1965
SET ME FREE [B]	JAKI GRAHAM	7	1986
SET ME FREE [C]	BRIT PACK	41	2000
SET ME FREE [C]	LORENZ	35	2006
SET THE FIRE TO THE THIRD BAR	SNOW PATROL FEATURING MARTHA WAINWRIGHT	18	2006
SET THE RECORD STRAIGHT	REEF	19	2000
SET THE TONE	NATE JAMES	69	2005
SET THEM FREE	ASWAD	70	1988
THE SET UP (YOU DON'T KNOW)	OBIE TRICE FEATURING NATE DOGG	32	2004
SET YOU FREE	N-TRANCE FEATURING KELLY LLORENNA	2	1994
SET YOUR LOVING FREE	LISA STANSFIELD	28	1992
SETTING SUN	CHEMICAL BROTHERS	1	1996
SETTLE DOWN [A]	LILLO THOMAS	66	1985
SETTLE DOWN [B]	UNBELIEVABLE TRUTH	46	1998
7 [A]	PRINCE & THE NEW POWER GENERATION	27	1992
SEVEN [B]	DAVID BOWIE	32	2000
SEVEN AND SEVEN IS (LIVE)	ALICE COOPER	62	1982
SEVEN CITIES	SOLAR STONE	39	1999
7 COLOURS	LOST WITNESS	28	2000
SEVEN DAFFODILS	CHEROKEES	33	1964
SEVEN DAFFODILS	MOJOS	30	1964
SEVEN DAYS [A]	ANNE SHELTON	20	1956
SEVEN DAYS [B]	STING	25	1993
SEVEN DAYS [C]	MARY J BLIGE FEATURING GEORGE BENSON	22	1998
7 DAYS [D]	CRAIG DAVID	1	2000
SEVEN DAYS AND ONE WEEK	BBE	3	1996
SEVEN DAYS IN SUNNY JUNE	JAMIROQUAI	14	2005
SEVEN DAYS IN THE SUN	FEEDER	14	2001
SEVEN DRUNKEN NIGHTS	DUBLINERS	7	1967
SEVEN (EP)	JAMES	46	1992
747	KENT	61	1999
747 (STRANGERS IN THE NIGHT)	SAXON	13	1980
SEVEN LITTLE GIRLS SITTING IN THE BACK SEAT	AVONS	3	1959
SEVEN LITTLE GIRLS SITTING IN THE BACK SEAT	PAUL EVANS & THE CURLS	25	1959
SEVEN LITTLE GIRLS SITTING IN THE BACKSEAT	BOMBALURINA	18	1990
SEVEN LONELY DAYS	GISELE MacKENZIE	6	1953
7 NATION ARMY	WHITE STRIPES	7	2003
7 O'CLOCK	QUIREBOYS	36	1989
SEVEN O'CLOCK NEWS	SIMON & GARFUNKEL	30	1991
SEVEN ROOMS OF GLOOM	FOUR TOPS	12	1967
SEVEN SEAS	ECHO & THE BUNNYMEN	16	1984
SEVEN SEAS OF RHYE	QUEEN	10	1974
7 SECONDS	YOUSSOU N'DOUR (FEATURING NENEH CHERRY)	3	1994
7:7 EXPANSION	SYSTEM 7	39	1993
7-6-5-4-3-2-1 (BLOW YOUR WHISTLE)	RIMSHOTS	26	1975
SEVEN TEARS	GOOMBAY DANCE BAND	1	1982
7000 DOLLARS AND YOU	STYLISTICS	24	1977
7 WAYS TO LOVE	COLA BOY	8	1991
7 WEEKS	INME	36	2005
SEVEN WONDERS	FLEETWOOD MAC	56	1987
7 YEAR BITCH	SLADE	60	1985
SEVEN YEARS IN TIBET	DAVID BOWIE	61	1997
7TEEN	REGENTS	11	1980
17	YOURCODENAMEIS:MILO	65	2005
SEVENTEEN [A]	BOYD BENNETT & HIS ROCKETS	16	1955
SEVENTEEN [A]	FRANKIE VAUGHAN	18	1955
SEVENTEEN [B]	LET LOOSE	11	1994
SEVENTEEN [C]	LADYTRON	68	2002
17 AGAIN	EURYTHMICS	27	2000
SEVENTH SON	GEORGIE FAME	25	1969
78 STONE WOBBLE	GOMEZ	44	1998
74-'75	CONNELLS	14	1995
77 STRINGS	KURTIS MANTRONIK PRESENTS CHAMONIX	71	2002
76 TROMBONES	KING BROTHERS	19	1961
SEVERINA	MISSION	25	1987
SEWN	THE FEELING	7	2006
SEX [A]	SLEAZESISTERS WITH VIKKI SHEPARD	53	1995
SEX [B]	ROBBIE RIVERA FEATURING BILLY PAUL	55	2002
SEX [C]	GA GAS	71	2005
SEX AND CANDY	MARCY PLAYGROUND	29	1998
SEX AS A WEAPON	PAT BENATAR	67	1986
SEX BOMB	TOM JONES & MOUSSE T	3	2000
SEX DRUGS AND ROCKS THROUGH YOUR WINDOW	AGENT BLUE	71	2004
SEX IS NOT THE ENEMY	GARBAGE	24	2005
SEX LIFE	GEOFFREY WILLIAMS	71	1997
SEX ME	R KELLY & PUBLIC ANNOUNCEMENT	75	1993
THE SEX OF IT	KID CREOLE & THE COCONUTS	29	1990
SEX ON THE BEACH	T-SPOON	2	1998
SEX ON THE STREETS	PIZZAMAN	23	1995
SEX OVER THE PHONE	VILLAGE PEOPLE	59	1985
SEX TALK (LIVE)	T'PAU	23	1988
SEX TYPE THING	STONE TEMPLE PILOTS	55	1993
SEXCRIME (NINETEEN EIGHTY FOUR)	EURYTHMICS	4	1984
SEXED UP	ROBBIE WILLIAMS	10	2003
SEXIEST MAN IN JAMAICA	MINT ROYALE	20	2002
SEXOMATIC	BAR-KAYS	51	1985
SEXUAL [A]	MARIA ROWE	67	1995
SEXUAL [B]	AMBER	34	2000
SEXUAL GUARANTEE	ALCAZAR	30	2002
(SEXUAL) HEALING	MARVIN GAYE	4	1982
SEXUAL HEALING	ALIBI VS ROCKEFELLER	34	2007
SEXUAL REVOLUTION	MACY GRAY	45	2001
SEXUALITY	BILLY BRAGG	27	1991
SEXX LAWS	BECK	27	1999
SEXY	MFSB	37	1975
SEXY BOY	AIR	13	1998
SEXY CINDERELLA	LYNDEN DAVID HALL	17	1997
SEXY CREAM	SLICK	47	1979
SEXY EYES	DR HOOK	4	1980
SEXY EYES - REMIXES	WHIGFIELD	68	1998
SEXY GIRL	LILLO THOMAS	23	1987
SEXY IN LATIN	LITTLE MAN TATE	20	2007
SEXY LOVE	NE-YO	5	2006
SEXY MF	PRINCE & THE NEW POWER GENERATION	4	1992
SEXY! NO NO NO	GIRLS ALOUD	5	2007
SEXYBACK	JUSTIN TIMBERLAKE	1	2006
SGT PEPPER'S LONELY HEARTS CLUB BAND - WITH A LITTLE HELP FROM MY FRIENDS	BEATLES	63	1978
SGT ROCK (IS GOING TO HELP ME)	XTC	16	1981
SHA LA LA	MANFRED MANN	3	1964
SHA LA LA LA LEE	SMALL FACES	3	1966
SHA LA LA LA LEE	PLASTIC BERTRAND	39	1978
SHA LA LA MEANS I LOVE YOU	BARRY WHITE	55	1979
SHACKLES (PRAISE YOU)	MARY MARY	5	2000
SHADDAP YOU FACE	JOE DOLCE MUSIC THEATRE	1	1981
SHADES OF BLUE (EP)	THE THE	54	1991
SHADES OF GREEN	MISSION	49	1992
SHADES OF PARANOIMIA	ART OF NOISE	53	1992
SHADES OF SUMMER	RODEO JONES	59	1993
SHADES (THEME FROM THE CROWN PAINT TELEVISION COMMERCIAL)	UNITED KINGDOM SYMPHONY	68	1985

	Peak Position	Year of Entry
SHADOW DANCING ANDY GIBB	42	1978
THE SHADOW OF LOVE DAMNED	25	1985
SHADOW OF THE DAY LINKIN PARK	46	2007
SHADOWS BREED 77	42	2005
SHADOWS OF THE NIGHT PAT BENATAR	50	1985
SHADOWTIME SIOUXSIE & THE BANSHEES	57	1991
SHADY LADY GENE PITNEY	29	1970
SHADY LANE PAVEMENT	40	1997
SHAFT VAN TWIST	57	1985
SHAKABOOM! HUNTER FEATURING RUBY TURNER	64	1995
SHAKALAKA BABY PREEYA KALIDAS	38	2002
SHAKE [A] OTIS REDDING	28	1967
SHAKE [B] ANDREW RIDGELEY	58	1990
SHAKE [C] YING YANG TWINS FEATURING PITBULL	49	2006
SHAKE A LEG ROLL DEEP	24	2005
SHAKE! (HOW ABOUT A SAMPLING GENE) GENE AND JIM ARE INTO SHAKES	68	1988
SHAKE IT BABY DJD PRESENTS HYDRAULIC DOGS	56	2002
SHAKE IT DOWN MUD	12	1976
SHAKE IT (MOVE A LITTLE CLOSER) LEE CABRERA FEATURING ALEX CARTANA	16	2003
SHAKE IT (NO TE MUEVAS TANTO) LEE-CABRERA	58	2003
SHAKE IT OFF MARIAH CAREY	9	2005
SHAKE ME I RATTLE KAYE SISTERS	27	1958
SHAKE RATTLE AND ROLL BILL HALEY & HIS COMETS	4	1954
(SHAKE SHAKE SHAKE) SHAKE YOUR BOOTY KC & THE SUNSHINE BAND	22	1976
SHAKE THE DISEASE DEPECHE MODE	18	1985
SHAKE THIS MOUNTAIN HORSE	52	1993
SHAKE UR BODY SHY FX & T POWER FEATURING DI	7	2002
SHAKE (WHAT YA MAMA GAVE YA) GENERAL LEVY VS ZEUS	51	2004
SHAKE YA ASS MYSTIKAL	30	2000
SHAKE YA BODY N-TRANCE	37	2000
SHAKE YA SHIMMY PORN KINGS VERSUS FLIP & FILL	28	2003
SHAKE YA TAILFEATHER NELLY, P DIDDY & MURPHY LEE	10	2003
SHAKE YOU DOWN GREGORY ABBOTT	6	1986
SHAKE YOUR BODY (DOWN TO THE GROUND) JACKSONS	4	1979
SHAKE YOUR BODY (DOWN TO THE GROUND) FULL INTENTION	34	1997
SHAKE YOUR BON-BON RICKY MARTIN	12	1999
SHAKE YOUR FOUNDATIONS AC/DC	24	1986
SHAKE YOUR GROOVE THING PEACHES & HERB	26	1979
SHAKE YOUR HEAD WAS (NOT WAS)	4	1992
SHAKE YOUR LOVE DEBBIE GIBSON	7	1988
SHAKE YOUR RUMP TO THE FUNK BAR-KAYS	41	1977
SHAKE YOUR THANG (IT'S YOUR THING) SALT-N-PEPA FEATURING E.U.	22	1988
SHAKERMAKER OASIS	11	1994
SHAKESPEARE'S SISTER SMITHS	26	1985
SHAKESPEARE'S WAY WITH WORDS ONE TRUE VOICE	10	2003
SHAKIN' ALL OVER JOHNNY KIDD & THE PIRATES	1	1960
SHAKIN' LIKE A LEAF STRANGLERS	58	1987
THE SHAKIN' STEVENS EP SHAKIN' STEVENS	2	1982
SHAKING THE TREE YOUSSOU N'DOUR & PETER GABRIEL	57	1989
SHAKING THE TREE PETER GABRIEL	57	1990
SHAKTI (THE MEANING OF WITHIN) MONSOON	41	1982
SHALALA LALA VENGABOYS	5	2000
SHA-LA-LA (MAKES ME HAPPY) AL GREEN	20	1974
SHALL WE TAKE A TRIP NORTHSIDE	50	1990
SHAME [A] ALAN PRICE SET	45	1967
SHAME [B] EVELYN 'CHAMPAGNE' KING	39	1978
SHAME [B] ALTERN 8 VS EVELYN KING	74	1992
SHAME [B] ZHANE	66	1995
SHAME [B] RUFF DRIVERZ	51	1998
SHAME [C] ORCHESTRAL MANOEUVRES IN THE DARK	52	1987
SHAME [D] EURYTHMICS	41	1987
SHAME [E] PJ HARVEY	45	2004
SHAME & SCANDAL MADNESS	38	2005
SHAME AND SCANDAL IN THE FAMILY LANCE PERCIVAL	37	1965
SHAME ON ME ALEXANDER O'NEAL	71	1991
SHAME ON YOU GUN	33	1990
SHAME SHAME SHAME [A] JIMMY REED	45	1964
SHAME SHAME SHAME [B] SHIRLEY & COMPANY	6	1975
SHAME SHAME SHAME [B] SINITTA	28	1992
SHAMELESS GARTH BROOKS	71	1992
SHAMROCKS AND SHENIGANS HOUSE OF PAIN	23	1993
SHANG-A-LANG BAY CITY ROLLERS	2	1974
SHANGHAI'D IN SHANGHAI NAZARETH	41	1974
SHANGRI-LA RUTLES	68	1996
SHANNON HENRY GROSS	32	1976
SHANTE MASS PRODUCTION	59	1980
SHAPE SUGABABES	11	2003
SHAPE OF MY HEART [A] STING	57	1993
SHAPE OF MY HEART [B] BACKSTREET BOYS	4	2000
THE SHAPE OF THINGS TO COME HEADBOYS	45	1979
THE SHAPE YOU'RE IN ERIC CLAPTON	75	1983
SHAPES OF THINGS YARDBIRDS	3	1966
SHAPES THAT GO TOGETHER A-HA	27	1994
SHARE MY LIFE INNER CITY	62	1994
SHARE THE FALL RONI SIZE REPRAZENT	37	1997
SHARE THE NIGHT WORLD PREMIERE	64	1984
SHARE YOUR LOVE (NO DIGGITY) PASSION	62	1997
SHARING THE NIGHT TOGETHER DR HOOK	43	1980
SHARING YOU BOBBY VEE	10	1962
SHARK THROWING MUSES	53	1996
SHARP AS A KNIFE BRANDON COOKE FEATURING ROXANNE SHANTE	45	1988
SHARP DRESSED MAN ZZ TOP	22	1983
SHATTER FEEDER	11	2005
SHATTERED DREAMS JOHNNY HATES JAZZ	5	1987
SHATTERED GLASS DTOX	75	1992
SHAZAM! DUANE EDDY & THE REBELS	4	1960
SH-BOOM CREW CUTS	12	1954
SH-BOOM STAN FREBERG WITH THE TOADS	15	1954
SH-BOOM (LIFE COULD BE A DREAM) DARTS	48	1980
SHE [A] CHARLES AZNAVOUR	1	1974
SHE [A] ELVIS COSTELLO	19	1999
SHE [B] VEGAS	43	1992
SHE AIN'T WORTH IT GLENN MEDEIROS FEATURING BOBBY BROWN	12	1990
SHE BANGS RICKY MARTIN	3	2000
SHE BANGS THE DRUMS STONE ROSES	34	1989
SHE BELIEVES IN ME [A] KENNY ROGERS	42	1979
SHE BELIEVES (IN ME) [B] RONAN KEATING	2	2004
SHE BLINDED ME WITH SCIENCE THOMAS DOLBY	49	1982
SHE BOP CYNDI LAUPER	46	1984
SHE CAME HOME FOR CHRISTMAS MEW	55	2003
SHE CAN ROCK IT POWER STATION	63	1996
SHE COMES FROM THE RAIN WEATHER PROPHETS	62	1987
SHE COMES IN THE FALL INSPIRAL CARPETS	27	1990
SHE CRIES YOUR NAME BETH ORTON	40	1997
SHE DON'T FOOL ME STATUS QUO	36	1982
SHE DON'T LET NOBODY CHAKA DEMUS & PLIERS	4	1993
SHE DRIVES ME CRAZY FINE YOUNG CANNIBALS	5	1989
SHE DROVE ME TO DAYTIME TELEVISION FUNERAL FOR A FRIEND	20	2003
SHE GOT GAME TYMES 4	40	2001
SHE GOT ME ON PAUL JOHNSON	70	2005
SHE HATES ME PUDDLE OF MUDD	14	2002
SHE HITS ME 4 OF US	35	1993
SHE HOLDS THE KEY SECRET LIFE	63	1994
SHE IS BEAUTIFUL ANDREW WK	55	2002
SHE IS LOVE OASIS	2	2002
SHE IS SUFFERING MANIC STREET PREACHERS	25	1994
SHE KISSED ME TERENCE TRENT D'ARBY	16	1993
SHE KISSED ME (IT FELT LIKE A HIT) SPIRITUALIZED	38	2003
SHE KNOWS BALAAM AND THE ANGEL	70	1986
SHE LEFT ME ON FRIDAY SHED SEVEN	11	1998
SHE LOVED LIKE DIAMOND SPANDAU BALLET	49	1982
SHE LOVES ME NOT PAPA ROACH	14	2002
SHE LOVES YOU BEATLES	1	1963
SHE MAKES MY DAY ROBERT PALMER	6	1988
SHE MAKES MY NOSE BLEED MANSUN	9	1997
SHE MEANS NOTHING TO ME PHIL EVERLY & CLIFF RICHARD	9	1983
SHE MIGHT NOISE NEXT DOOR	27	2005
SHE MOVES IN HER OWN WAY KOOKS	7	2006
SHE MOVES (LALALA) KARAJA	42	2002
SHE NEEDS LOVE WAYNE FONTANA & THE MINDBENDERS	32	1965
SHE SAID [A] LONGPIGS	16	1995
SHE SAID [B] PHARCYDE	51	1996
SHE SAID [C] JON SPENCER BLUES EXPLOSION	58	2002
SHE SELLS BANDERAS	41	1991
SHE SELLS SANCTUARY CULT	15	1985
SHE SHE LITTLE SHEILA GENE VINCENT	22	1961
SHE SOLD ME MAGIC LOU CHRISTIE	25	1969
SHE TALKS TO ANGELS BLACK CROWES	70	1991
SHE USED TO BE MINE SPIN DOCTORS	55	1996
SHE WAITS FOR ME PROTOCOL	65	2005
SHE WANTS TO DANCE WITH ME RICK ASTLEY	6	1988
SHE WANTS TO MOVE NERD	12	2004
SHE WANTS YOU BILLIE	3	1998
SHE WAS HOT ROLLING STONES	42	1984
SHE WEARS MY RING SOLOMON KING	3	1968
SHE WEARS RED FEATHERS GUY MITCHELL	1	1953
SHE WILL BE LOVED MAROON 5	4	2004
SHE WILL HAVE HER WAY NEIL FINN	26	1998
SHE WON'T TALK TO ME LUTHER VANDROSS	34	1989
SHE WORKS HARD FOR THE MONEY DONNA SUMMER	25	1983
SHED A TEAR WET WET WET	22	1993
SHED MY SKIN D NOTE	73	2002
SHE'D RATHER BE WITH ME TURTLES	4	1967
SHEELA-NA-GIG PJ HARVEY	69	1992
SHEENA IS A PUNK ROCKER RAMONES	22	1977
SHEEP HOUSEMARTINS	56	1986
THE SHEFFIELD GRINDER TONY CAPSTICK & THE CARLTON MAIN/FRICKLEY COLLIERY BAND	3	1981
SHEFFIELD SONG SUPERNATURALS	45	1998
SHEILA [A] TOMMY ROE	3	1962
SHEILA [B] JAMIE T	15	2006
SHEILA TAKE A BOW SMITHS	10	1987
SHELLSHOCK NEW ORDER	28	1986
SHELTER BRAND NEW HEAVIES	31	1998
SHELTER ME [A] CINDERELLA	55	1990
SHELTER ME [B] CIRCUIT	44	1991
THE SHEPHERD'S SONG TONY OSBORNE SOUND	46	1973

		Peak Position	Year of Entry
SHERIFF FATMAN	CARTER-THE UNSTOPPABLE SEX MACHINE	23	1991
SHERRI DON'T FAIL ME NOW	STATUS QUO	38	1994
SHERRY	FOUR SEASONS	8	1962
SHERRY	ADRIAN BAKER	10	1975
SHE'S A BAD MAMA JAMA (SHE'S BUILT, SHE'S STACKED)	CARL CARLTON	34	1981
SHE'S A GIRL AND I'M A MAN	LLOYD COLE	55	1991
SHE'S A GOOD GIRL	SLEEPER	28	1997
SHE'S A GROOVY FREAK	REAL THING	52	1980
SHE'S A LADY	TOM JONES	13	1971
SHE'S A LITTLE ANGEL	LITTLE ANGELS	21	1990
SHE'S A MYSTERY TO ME	ROY ORBISON	27	1989
SHE'S A RAINBOW	WORLD OF TWIST	62	1992
SHE'S A RIVER	SIMPLE MINDS	9	1995
SHE'S A STAR	JAMES	9	1997
SHE'S A SUPERSTAR	VERVE	66	1992
SHE'S A VISION	ALL EYES	65	2004
SHE'S A WIND UP	DR FEELGOOD	34	1977
SHE'S A WOMAN	SCRITTI POLITTI FEATURING SHABBA RANKS	20	1991
SHE'S ABOUT A MOVER	SIR DOUGLAS QUINTET	15	1965
SHE'S ALL ON MY MIND	WET WET WET	17	1995
SHE'S ALRIGHT	BITTY McLEAN	53	1996
SHE'S ALWAYS A WOMAN	BILLY JOEL	53	1986
SHE'S ATTRACTED TO	YOUNG KNIVES	38	2006
SHE'S CRAFTY	BEASTIE BOYS	34	1987
SHE'S EVERY WOMAN	GARTH BROOKS	55	1996
SHE'S GONE [A]	BUDDY KNOX	45	1962
SHE'S GONE [B]	DARYL HALL & JOHN OATES	42	1976
SHE'S GONE [B]	MATTHEW MARSDEN FEATURING DESTINY'S CHILD	24	1998
SHE'S GONNA BREAK SOON	LESS THAN JAKE	39	2003
SHE'S GONNA WIN	BILBO	42	1978
SHE'S GOT A REASON	DOGS	36	2005
SHE'S GOT CLAWS	GARY NUMAN	6	1981
SHE'S GOT ISSUES	OFFSPRING	41	1999
SHE'S GOT IT	LITTLE RICHARD	15	1957
SHE'S GOT ME GOING CRAZY	2 IN A ROOM	54	1991
SHE'S GOT SOUL	JAMESTOWN FEATURING JOCELYN BROWN	57	1991
SHE'S GOT STANDARDS	RIFLES	32	2006
SHE'S GOT THAT VIBE	R KELLY	3	1992
SHE'S GOT YOU	PATSY CLINE	43	1962
SHE'S GOT YOU HIGH	MUMM RA	41	2007
SHE'S IN FASHION	SUEDE	13	1999
SHE'S IN LOVE WITH YOU	SUZI QUATRO	11	1979
SHE'S IN PARTIES	BAUHAUS	26	1983
SHE'S LEAVING HOME	BILLY BRAGG WITH CARA TIVEY	1	1988
SHE'S LIKE THE WIND	PATRICK SWAYZE FEATURING WENDY FRASER	17	1988
SHE'S LOST YOU	ZEPHYRS	48	1965
SHE'S MADONNA	ROBBIE WILLIAMS & PET SHOP BOYS	16	2007
SHE'S MINE	CAMEO	35	1987
SHE'S MY EVERYTHING	FREEFALLER	36	2005
SHE'S MY MACHINE	DAVID LEE ROTH	64	1994
SHE'S MY MAN	SCISSOR SISTERS	29	2007
SHE'S NEW TO YOU	SUSAN MAUGHAN	45	1963
SHE'S NOT LEAVING	RESEARCH	73	2004
SHE'S NOT THERE	ZOMBIES	12	1964
SHE'S NOT THERE	NEIL MacARTHUR	34	1969
SHE'S NOT THERE	SANTANA	11	1977
SHE'S NOT THERE/KICKS EP	U.K. SUBS	36	1979
SHE'S NOT YOU	ELVIS PRESLEY	1	1962
SHE'S ON FIRE [A]	TRAIN	49	2002
SHE'S ON FIRE [B]	CUBAN HEELS	72	2005
SHE'S ON IT	BEASTIE BOYS	10	1987
SHE'S OUT OF MY LIFE	MICHAEL JACKSON	3	1980
SHE'S PLAYING HARD TO GET	HI-FIVE	55	1992
(SHE'S) SEXY AND 17	STRAY CATS	29	1983
SHE'S SO BEAUTIFUL	CLIFF RICHARD	17	1985
SHE'S SO COLD	ROLLING STONES	33	1980
SHE'S SO FINE	THUNDER	34	1990
SHE'S SO HIGH [A]	BLUR	48	1990
SHE'S SO HIGH [B]	TAL BACHMAN	30	1999
SHE'S SO HIGH [B]	KURT NILSEN	25	2004
SHE'S SO LOVELY	SCOUTING FOR GIRLS	7	2007
SHE'S SO MODERN	BOOMTOWN RATS	12	1978
SHE'S STRANGE	CAMEO	22	1984
SHE'S THE MASTER OF THE GAME	RICHARD JON SMITH	63	1983
SHE'S THE ONE [A]	JAMES BROWN	45	1988
SHE'S THE ONE [B]	ROBBIE WILLIAMS	1	1999
SHIFTER	TIMO MAAS FEATURING MC CHICKABOO	38	2002
SHIFTING WHISPERING SANDS	BILLY VAUGHN ORCHESTRA & CHORUS, NARRATION BY KEN NORDENE	20	1956
SHIFTING WHISPERING SANDS (PARTS 1 & 2)	EAMONN ANDREWS WITH RON GOODWIN & HIS ORCHESTRA	18	1956
SHIMMY SHAKE	740 BOYZ	54	1995
SHINDIG	SHADOWS	6	1963
SHINE [A]	JOE BROWN	33	1961
SHINE [B]	MOTORHEAD	59	1983
SHINE [C]	SLOWDIVE	52	1991
SHINE [D]	ASWAD	5	1994
SHINE [E]	MOLLY HALF HEAD	73	1995
SHINE [F]	SPACE BROTHERS	18	1997
SHINE [G]	MONTROSE AVENUE	58	1998
SHINE [H]	LOVEFREEKZ	6	2005
SHINE [I]	LUTHER VANDROSS	50	2006
SHINE [I]	BOOTY LUV	10	2007
SHINE [J]	TAKE THAT	1	2007
SHINE A LITTLE LOVE	ELECTRIC LIGHT ORCHESTRA	6	1979
SHINE EYE	RAGGA TWINS FEATURING JUNIOR REID	63	1992
SHINE EYE GAL	SHABBA RANKS (FEATURING MYKAL ROSE)	46	1995
SHINE IT ALL AROUND	ROBERT PLANT & THE STRANGE SENSATION	32	2005
SHINE LIKE A STAR	BERRI	20	1995
SHINE ON [A]	HOUSE OF LOVE	20	1990
SHINE ON [B]	DEGREES OF MOTION FEATURING BITI	8	1992
SHINE ON [C]	SCOTT & LEON	34	2001
SHINE ON ME	LOVESTATION FEATURING LISA HUNT	71	1993
SHINE ON SILVER SUN	STRAWBS	34	1973
SHINE SO HARD (EP)	ECHO & THE BUNNYMEN	37	1981
SHINE (SOMEONE WHO NEEDS ME)	MONACO	55	1997
SHINED ON ME	PRAISE CATS FEATURING ANDREA LOVE	24	2002
SHINING [A]	DOUBLE DEE	58	2003
SHINING [B]	KRISTIAN LEONTIOU	13	2004
SHINING LIGHT	ASH	8	2001
SHINING ROAD	CRANES	57	1994
SHINING STAR	MANHATTANS	45	1980
SHINING STAR (EP)	INXS	27	1991
SHINOBI VS DRAGON NINJA	LOSTPROPHETS	41	2001
SHINY DISCO BALLS	WHO DA FUNK FEATURING JESSICA EVE	15	2002
SHINY HAPPY PEOPLE	R.E.M.	6	1991
SHINY SHINY	HAYSI FANTAYZEE	16	1983
SHIP AHOY	MARXMAN	64	1993
SHIP OF FOOLS [A]	WORLD PARTY	42	1987
SHIP OF FOOLS [B]	ERASURE	6	1988
SHIPBUILDING	ROBERT WYATT	35	1983
SHIPBUILDING	TASMIN ARCHER	40	1994
SHIPS IN THE NIGHT	BE BOP DELUXE	23	1976
SHIPS (WHERE WERE YOU)	BIG COUNTRY	29	1993
SHIPWRECKED	GENESIS	54	1997
SHIRALEE	TOMMY STEELE	11	1957
SHIRLEY	SHAKIN' STEVENS	6	1982
SHIT ON YOU	D12	10	2001
SHIVER [A]	GEORGE BENSON	19	1986
SHIVER [B]	S-J	59	1998
SHIVER [C]	COLDPLAY	35	2000
SHIVER [D]	NATALIE IMBRUGLIA	8	2005
SHIVERING SAND	MEGA CITY FOUR	35	1992
SHIVERS	ARMIN VAN BUUREN	72	2005
SHO' YOU RIGHT	BARRY WHITE	14	1987
SHOCK THE MONKEY	PETER GABRIEL	58	1982
SHOCK TO THE SYSTEM	BILLY IDOL	30	1993
SHOCK YOUR MAMA	DEBBIE GIBSON	74	1993
SHOCKAHOLIC	KINKY MACHINE	70	1993
SHOCKED	KYLIE MINOGUE	6	1991
SHOES	REPARATA	43	1975
SHOO BE DOO BE DOO DA DAY	STEVIE WONDER	46	1968
SHOO DOO FU FU OOH	LENNY WILLIAMS	38	1977
SHOOP	SALT-N-PEPA	13	1993
THE SHOOP SHOOP SONG (IT'S IN HIS KISS)	CHER	1	1991
SHOORAH SHOORAH	BETTY WRIGHT	27	1975
SHOOT ALL THE CLOWNS	BRUCE DICKINSON	37	1994
SHOOT ME DOWN	BOY KILL BOY	63	2006
SHOOT ME (WITH YOUR LOVE) [A]	TASHA THOMAS	59	1979
SHOOT ME WITH YOUR LOVE [B]	D:REAM	7	1995
SHOOT SHOOT	UFO	48	1979
SHOOT THE DOG	GEORGE MICHAEL	12	2002
SHOOT THE RUNNER	KASABIAN	17	2006
SHOOT YOUR GUN	22-20'S	30	2004
SHOOTING FROM MY HEART	BIG BAM BOO	61	1989
SHOOTING FROM THE HEART	CLIFF RICHARD	51	1984
SHOOTING STAR [A]	DOLLAR	14	1978
SHOOTING STAR [A]	BOYZONE	2	1997
SHOOTING STAR [B]	FLIP & FILL	3	2002
SHOOTING STAR [C]	DEEPEST BLUE	57	2004
SHOOTING STAR [D]	AIR TRAFFIC	30	2007
SHOPLIFTERS OF THE WORLD UNITE	SMITHS	12	1987
SHOPPING	SUPERSISTER	36	2001
SHORLEY WALL	OOBERMAN	47	2000
SHORT CUT TO SOMEWHERE	FISH & TONY BANKS	75	1986
SHORT DICK MAN	20 FINGERS FEATURING GILLETTE	21	1994
SHORT FAT FANNY	LARRY WILLIAMS	21	1957
SHORT SHORT MAN	20 FINGERS FEATURING GILLETTE	11	1995
SHORT SKIRT LONG JACKET	CAKE	63	2001
SHORT'NIN' BREAD	TONY CROMBIE & HIS ROCKETS	25	1956
SHORT'NIN' BREAD	VISCOUNTS	16	1960
SHORTSHARPSHOCK EP	THERAPY?	9	1993
SHORTY	WANNADIES	41	1997
SHORTY (GOT HER EYES ON ME)	DONELL JONES	19	2000
SHORTY (YOU KEEP PLAYIN' WITH MY MIND)	IMAJIN FEATURING KEITH MURRAY	22	1998
SHOT BY BOTH SIDES	MAGAZINE	41	1978
SHOT DOWN	NINE BLACK ALPS	25	2005
SHOT DOWN IN THE NIGHT	HAWKWIND	59	1980
SHOT IN THE DARK [A]	OZZY OSBOURNE	20	1986
SHOT IN THE DARK [B]	DJ HYPE	63	1993
SHOT OF POISON	LITA FORD	63	1992
SHOT OF RHYTHM AND BLUES	JOHNNY KIDD & THE PIRATES	48	1963
SHOT SHOT	GOMEZ	28	2002
SHOT YOU DOWN	AUDIO BULLYS FEATURING NANCY SINATRA	3	2005

	Peak Position	Year of Entry
SHOTGUN WEDDING ROY C	6	1966
SHOTGUN WEDDING ROD STEWART	21	1993
SHOULD I DO IT? POINTER SISTERS	50	1981
SHOULD I EVER (FALL IN LOVE) NIGHTCRAWLERS	34	1996
SHOULD I STAY GABRIELLE	13	2000
SHOULD I STAY OR SHOULD I GO CLASH	1	1982
SHOULDA WOULDA COULDA BEVERLEY KNIGHT	10	2002
SHOULDER HOLSTER MORCHEEBA	53	1997
SHOULDN'T DO THAT KAJA	63	1985
SHOULDN'T LET THE SIDE DOWN HOGGBOY	74	2002
SHOULD'VE KNOWN BETTER RICHARD MARX	50	1988
SHOUT [A] LULU & THE LUVVERS	7	1964
SHOUT (IT OUT) [A] LOUCHIE LOU & MICHIE ONE	7	1993
SHOUT [B] TEARS FOR FEARS	4	1984
SHOUT [C] ANT & DEC	10	1997
SHOUT SHOUT (KNOCK YOURSELF OUT) ROCKY SHARPE & THE REPLAYS	19	1982
SHOUT TO THE TOP STYLE COUNCIL	7	1984
SHOUT TO THE TOP FIRE ISLAND FEATURING LOLEATTA HOLLOWAY	23	1998
SHOUTING FOR THE GUNNERS ARSENAL FA CUP SQUAD FEATURING TIPPA IRIE & PETER HUNNIGALE	34	1993
THE SHOUTY TRACK LEMON JELLY	21	2005
THE SHOW [A] DOUG E. FRESH & THE GET FRESH CREW	7	1985
THE SHOW [B] GIRLS ALOUD	2	2004
SHOW A LITTLE LOVE ULTIMATE KAOS	23	1995
SHOW ME [A] DEXY'S MIDNIGHT RUNNERS	16	1981
SHOW ME [B] LINDY LAYTON	47	1993
SHOW ME [C] ULTRA NATE	62	1994
SHOW ME [D] DANA DAWSON	28	1996
SHOW ME A SIGN KONTAKT	19	2003
SHOW ME GIRL HERMAN'S HERMITS	19	1964
SHOW ME HEAVEN MARIA McKEE	1	1990
SHOW ME HEAVEN TINA ARENA	29	1995
SHOW ME HEAVEN CHIMIRA	70	1997
SHOW ME HEAVEN SAINT FEATURING SUZANNA DEE	36	2003
SHOW ME LOVE [A] ROBIN S	6	1993
SHOW ME LOVE [B] ROBYN	8	1998
SHOW ME LOVE [C] INDIEN	69	2003
SHOW ME MARY CATHERINE WHEEL	62	1993
SHOW ME THE MEANING OF BEING LONELY BACKSTREET BOYS	3	2000
SHOW ME THE MONEY ARCHITECHS	20	2001
SHOW ME THE WAY [A] PETER FRAMPTON	10	1976
SHOW ME THE WAY [B] OSMOND BOYS	60	1992
SHOW ME WHAT YOU GOT JAY-Z	38	2006
SHOW ME YOUR MONKEY PERCY FILTH	72	2003
SHOW ME YOUR SOUL P DIDDY, LENNY KRAVITZ, PHARRELL WILLIAMS & LOON	35	2004
SHOW ME YOU'RE A WOMAN MUD	8	1975
THE SHOW MUST GO ON [A] LEO SAYER	2	1973
THE SHOW MUST GO ON [B] QUEEN	16	1991
THE SHOW (THEME FROM *CONNIE*) REBECCA STORM	22	1985
SHOW YOU THE WAY TO GO JACKSONS	1	1977
SHOW YOU THE WAY TO GO DANNII MINOGUE	30	1992
SHOW YOUR HAND SUPER FURRY ANIMALS	46	2007
SHOWDOWN [A] ELECTRIC LIGHT ORCHESTRA	12	1973
SHOWDOWN [B] JODY LEI	34	2003
SHOWER YOUR LOVE KULA SHAKER	14	1999
SHOWING OUT (GET FRESH AT THE WEEKEND) MEL & KIM	3	1986
SHOWROOM DUMMIES KRAFTWERK	25	1982
THE SHUFFLE VAN McCOY	4	1977
SHUGGIE LOVE MONKEY BARS/GABRIELLE WIDMAN	61	2004
SHUT 'EM DOWN PUBLIC ENEMY	21	1992
SHUT UP [A] MADNESS	7	1981
SHUT UP [B] KELLY OSBOURNE	12	2003
SHUT UP [C] BLACK EYED PEAS	2	2003
SHUT UP [D] SIMPLE PLAN	44	2005
SHUT UP AND DANCE AEROSMITH	24	1994
SHUT UP AND DRIVE RIHANNA	5	2007
SHUT UP AND FORGET ABOUT IT DANE	9	2001
SHUT UP AND KISS ME MARY CHAPIN CARPENTER	35	1995
SHUT UP (AND SLEEP WITH ME) SIN WITH SEBASTIAN	44	1995
SHUT YOUR MOUTH [A] MADE IN LONDON	74	2000
SHUT YOUR MOUTH [B] GARBAGE	20	2002
SHUTDOWN PITCHSHIFTER	66	2002
SHY BOY BANANARAMA	4	1982
SHY GIRL MARK WYNTER	28	1963
SHY GUY DIANA KING	2	1995
SHY GUY ASWAD	62	2002
(SI SI) JE SUIS UN ROCK STAR BILL WYMAN	14	1981
SI TU DOIS PARTIR FAIRPORT CONVENTION	21	1969
SIC TRANSIT GLORIA GLORY FADES BRAND NEW	37	2004
SICK AND TIRED [A] FATS DOMINO	26	1958
SICK & TIRED [B] CARDIGANS	34	1995
SICK AND TIRED [C] ANASTACIA	4	2004
SICK MAN BLUES GOODIES	4	1975
SICK OF DRUGS WILDHEARTS	14	1996
SICK OF GOODBYES SPARKLEHORSE	57	1998
SICK OF IT PRIMITIVES	24	1989
SIDE TRAVIS	14	2001
SIDE BY SIDE KAY STARR	7	1953
SIDE SADDLE RUSS CONWAY	1	1959
SIDE SHOW [A] CHANTER SISTERS	43	1976
SIDE SHOW [B] WENDY & LISA	49	1988
SIDE STREETS SAINT ETIENNE	36	2005
THE SIDEBOARD SONG (GOT MY BEER IN THE SIDEBOARD HERE) CHAS & DAVE	55	1979
SIDESHOW BARRY BIGGS	3	1976
SIDEWALK TALK JELLYBEAN FEATURING CATHERINE BUCHANAN	47	1986
SIDEWALKING JESUS & MARY CHAIN	30	1988
THE SIDEWINDER SLEEPS TONITE R.E.M.	17	1993
SIGHT FOR SORE EYES M PEOPLE	6	1994
THE SIGN ACE OF BASE	2	1994
SIGN O' THE TIMES PRINCE	10	1987
A SIGN OF THE TIMES [A] PETULA CLARK	49	1966
SIGN OF THE TIMES [B] BRYAN FERRY	37	1978
SIGN OF THE TIMES [C] BELLE STARS	3	1983
SIGN OF THE TIMES [D] GRANDMASTER FLASH	72	1985
SIGN YOUR NAME TERENCE TRENT D'ARBY	2	1988
SIGNAL [A] JD AKA DREADY	64	2003
SIGNAL [B] FRESH	58	2003
SIGNAL FIRE SNOW PATROL	4	2007
SIGNALS OVER THE AIR THURSDAY	62	2003
THE SIGNATURE TUNE OF 'THE ARMY GAME' MICHAEL MEDWIN, BERNARD BRESSLAW, ALFIE BASS & LESLIE FYSON	5	1958
SIGNED SEALED DELIVERED I'M YOURS STEVIE WONDER	15	1970
SIGNED SEALED DELIVERED (I'M YOURS) BOYSTOWN GANG	50	1982
SIGNED SEALED DELIVERED I'M YOURS BLUE FEATURING STEVIE WONDER & ANGIE STONE	11	2003
SIGNS [A] TESLA	70	1991
SIGNS...[B] BLAMELESS	49	1996
SIGNS [C] DJ BADMARSH & SHRI FEATURING UK APACHE	63	2001
SIGNS [D] SNOOP DOGG FEATURING CHARLIE WILSON & JUSTIN TIMBERLAKE	2	2005
THE SILENCE [A] MIKE KOGLIN	20	1998
SILENCE [B] DELERIUM FEATURING SARAH McLACHLAN	3	1999
SILENCE [C] TAIKO	72	2002
SILENCE [D] GOMEZ	41	2004
SILENCE IS EASY STARSAILOR	9	2003
SILENCE IS GOLDEN TREMELOES	1	1967
SILENCE WHEN YOU'RE BURNING HAPPYLIFE	73	2004
SILENT ALL THESE YEARS TORI AMOS	26	1991
SILENT LUCIDITY QUEENSRYCHE	18	1991
SILENT NIGHT BING CROSBY	8	1952
SILENT NIGHT DICKIES	47	1978
SILENT NIGHT BROS	2	1988
SILENT NIGHT SIMON & GARFUNKEL	30	1991
SILENT NIGHT SINEAD O'CONNOR	60	1991
SILENT RUNNING (ON DANGEROUS GROUND) MIKE + THE MECHANICS	21	1986
SILENT SCREAM RICHARD MARX	32	1994
SILENT SIGH BADLY DRAWN BOY	16	2002
SILENT TO THE DARK II ELECTRIC SOFT PARADE	23	2002
SILENT VOICE INNOCENCE	37	1990
SILENT WORDS JAN JOHNSTON	57	2001
SILENTLY BAD MINDED PRESSURE DROP	53	1998
SILHOUETTES HERMAN'S HERMITS	3	1965
SILHOUETTES CLIFF RICHARD	10	1990
SILK PYJAMAS THOMAS DOLBY	62	1992
SILLY GAMES JANET KAY	2	1979
SILLY GAMES LINDY LAYTON FEATURING JANET KAY	22	1990
SILLY LOVE 10 C.C.	24	1974
SILLY LOVE SONGS WINGS	2	1976
SILLY THING SEX PISTOLS	6	1979
SILVER [A] ECHO & THE BUNNYMEN	30	1984
SILVER [B] MOIST	50	1995
SILVER [C] HUNDRED REASONS	15	2002
SILVER AND GOLD ASAP	60	1989
SILVER DREAM MACHINE (PART 1) DAVID ESSEX	4	1980
SILVER LADY DAVID SOUL	1	1977
SILVER LINING STIFF LITTLE FINGERS	68	1981
SILVER MACHINE HAWKWIND	3	1972
SILVER SCREEN SHOWER SCENE FELIX DA HOUSECAT	39	2001
SILVER SHADOW ATLANTIC STARR	41	1985
SILVER SHORTS WEDDING PRESENT	14	1992
SILVER STAR FOUR SEASONS	3	1976
SILVER THUNDERBIRD MARC COHN	54	1991
SILVERMAC WESTWORLD	42	1987
SILVERY RAIN CLIFF RICHARD	27	1971
SIMBA GROOVE HI POWER	73	1990
SIMON SAYS [A] 1910 FRUITGUM CO.	2	1968
SIMON SAYS [B] PHAROAHE MONCH	24	2000
SIMON SMITH AND HIS AMAZING DANCING BEAR ALAN PRICE SET	4	1967
SIMON TEMPLAR SPLODGENESSABOUNDS	7	1980
SIMPLE AS THAT HUEY LEWIS & THE NEWS	47	1987
SIMPLE GAME FOUR TOPS	3	1971
SIMPLE KIND OF LIFE NO DOUBT	69	2000
SIMPLE LIFE ELTON JOHN	44	1993
SIMPLE SIMON (YOU GOTTA REGARD) MANTRONIX	72	1988
SIMPLE SINCERITY RADISH	50	1997
THE SIMPLE THINGS [A] JOE COCKER	17	1994
SIMPLE THINGS [B] SAW DOCTORS	56	1997
THE SIMPLE TRUTH (A CHILD IS BORN) CHRIS DE BURGH	36	1987
SIMPLY IRRESISTABLE ROBERT PALMER	44	1988
THE SIMPSONS THEME GREEN DAY	19	2007
SIN NINE INCH NAILS	35	1991
SIN SIN SIN ROBBIE WILLIAMS	22	2006

	Peak Position	Year of Entry
SINBAD QUEST SYSTEM 7	74	1993
SINCE DAY ONE TEENA MARIE	69	1990
SINCE I DON'T HAVE YOU ART GARFUNKEL	38	1979
SINCE I DON'T HAVE YOU GUNS N' ROSES	10	1994
SINCE I LEFT YOU AVALANCHES	16	2001
SINCE I MET YOU BABY GARY MOORE & BB KING	59	1992
SINCE I MET YOU LADY UB40 FEATURING LADY SAW	40	2001
SINCE I TOLD YOU IT'S OVER STEREOPHONICS	16	2003
SINCE U BEEN GONE KELLY CLARKSON	5	2005
SINCE YESTERDAY STRAWBERRY SWITCHBLADE	5	1985
SINCE YOU'RE GONE CARS	37	1982
SINCE YOU'VE BEEN GONE [A] ARETHA FRANKLIN	47	1968
SINCE YOU'VE BEEN GONE [B] RAINBOW	6	1979
SINCERE MJ COLE	13	1998
SINCERELY McGUIRE SISTERS	14	1955
SINFUL PETE WYLIE	13	1986
SING TRAVIS	3	2001
SING A HAPPY SONG [A] GEORGE McCRAE	38	1975
SING A HAPPY SONG [B] O'JAYS	39	1979
SING A LITTLE SONG DESMOND DEKKER & THE ACES	16	1975
SING-A-LONG [A] A	57	1998
SING A LONG [B] SHANKS & BIGFOOT	12	2000
SING A SONG BYRON STINGILY	38	1997
SING A SONG (BREAK IT DOWN) MANTRONIX	61	1988
SING A SONG OF FREEDOM CLIFF RICHARD	13	1971
SING AND SHOUT SECOND IMAGE	53	1984
SING BABY SING STYLISTICS	3	1975
SING DON'T SPEAK BLACKFOOT SUE	36	1973
SING FOR ABSOLUTION MUSE	16	2004
SING FOR EVER ST PHILIPS CHOIR	49	1987
SING FOR THE MOMENT EMINEM	6	2003
SING HALLELUJAH! DR ALBAN	16	1993
SING IT AGAIN WITH JOE JOE 'MR PIANO' HENDERSON	18	1955
SING IT BACK MOLOKO	4	1999
SING IT FOR ENGLAND YOUNG STANLEY	58	2006
SING IT OUT HOPE OF THE STATES	39	2006
SING IT (THE HALLELUJAH SONG) MOZAIC	14	1995
SING IT TO YOU (DEE-DOOB-DEE-DOO) LAVINIA JONES	45	1995
SING IT WITH JOE JOE 'MR PIANO' HENDERSON	14	1955
SING LIKE AN ANGEL JERRY LORDAN	36	1960
SING LITTLE BIRDIE PEARL CARR & TEDDY JOHNSON	12	1959
SING ME BROTHERS	8	1977
SING ME AN OLD FASHIONED SONG BILLIE JO SPEARS	34	1976
SING (OOH-EE-OOH) VIVIENNE McKONE	47	1992
SING OUR OWN SONG UB40	5	1986
SING SING GAZ	60	1979
SING UP FOR THE CHAMPIONS REDS UNITED	12	1997
SING YOUR LIFE MORRISSEY	33	1991
SINGALONG-A-SANTA SANTA CLAUS & THE CHRISTMAS TREES	19	1982
SINGALONG-A-SANTA AGAIN SANTA CLAUS & THE CHRISTMAS TREES	39	1983
THE SINGER SANG HIS SONG BEE GEES	25	1968
SINGIN' IN THE RAIN MINT ROYALE	20	2005
SINGIN' IN THE RAIN PART 1 SHEILA B. DEVOTION	11	1978
THE SINGING DOGS (MEDLEY) DON CHARLES PRESENTS THE SINGING DOGS	13	1955
SINGING IN MY SLEEP SEMISONIC	39	2000
SINGING THE BLUES GUY MITCHELL	1	1956
SINGING THE BLUES TOMMY STEELE & THE STEELMEN	1	1956
SINGING THE BLUES DAVE EDMUNDS	28	1980
SINGING THE BLUES DANIEL O'DONNELL	23	1994
THE SINGLE [A] RISE	70	1994
SINGLE [B] EVERYTHING BUT THE GIRL	20	1996
SINGLE [C] PET SHOP BOYS	14	1996
SINGLE [D] NATASHA BEDINGFIELD	3	2004
SINGLE AGAIN FIERY FURNACES	49	2004
SINGLE GIRL [A] SANDY POSEY	15	1967
SINGLE GIRL [B] LUSH	21	1996
SINGLE LIFE CAMEO	15	1985
THE SINGLES 1981-83 BAUHAUS	52	1983
SINK A SHIP KAISER CHIEFS	9	2005
SINK THE BISMARK DON LANG	43	1960
SINK TO THE BOTTOM FOUNTAINS OF WAYNE	42	1997
SINNER NEIL FINN	39	1998
SINS OF THE FAMILY P.F. SLOAN	38	1965
SIPPIN' SODA GUY MITCHELL	11	1954
SIR DANCEALOT OLYMPIC RUNNERS	35	1979
SIR DUKE STEVIE WONDER	2	1977
SIREN SOUNDS RONI SIZE	67	2003
SIRENS DIZZEE RASCAL	20	2007
SISSYNECK BECK	30	1997
SISTA SISTA BEVERLEY KNIGHT	31	1999
SISTER [A] BROS	10	1989
SISTER [B] SISTER 2 SISTER	18	2000
SISTER DEW dEUS	62	1999
SISTER FRICTION HAYSI FANTAYZEE	62	1983
SISTER HAVANA URGE OVERKILL	58	1993
SISTER JANE NEW WORLD	9	1972
SISTER MOON TRANSVISION VAMP	41	1988
SISTER OF MERCY THOMPSON TWINS	11	1984
SISTER PAIN ELECTRAFIXION	27	1996
SISTER ROSETTA (CAPTURE THE SPIRIT) NOISETTES	63	2007
SISTER SAVIOUR RAPTURE	51	2003
SISTER SISTER SISTER BLISS	34	2000
SISTER SURPRISE GARY NUMAN	32	1983
SISTERS ARE DOING IT FOR THEMSELVES EURYTHMICS & ARETHA FRANKLIN	9	1985
THE SISTERS EP PULP	19	1994
SIT AND WAIT SYDNEY YOUNGBLOOD	16	1989
SIT DOWN JAMES	2	1991
SIT DOWN AND CRY ERROLL DUNKLEY	52	1980
THE SIT SONG BARRON KNIGHTS	44	1980
SITTIN' ON A FENCE TWICE AS MUCH	25	1966
(SITTIN' ON) THE DOCK OF THE BAY OTIS REDDING	3	1968
SITTIN' UP IN MY ROOM BRANDY	30	1996
SITTING AT HOME HONEYCRACK	32	1995
SITTING DOWN HERE LENE MARLIN	5	2000
SITTING IN THE PARK GEORGIE FAME & THE BLUE FLAMES	12	1967
SITTING ON TOP OF THE WORLD LIVERPOOL FC	50	1986
SITTING, WAITING, WISHING JACK JOHNSON	65	2006
SITUATION YAZOO	14	1990
SIX MANSUN	16	1999
SIX DAYS DJ SHADOW	28	2002
SIX FEET DEEP (EP) GRAVEDIGGAZ	64	1995
643 (LOVE'S ON FIRE) DJ TIESTO FEATURING SUZANNE PALMER	36	2002
SIX MILLION STEPS (WEST RUNS SOUTH) RAHNI HARRIS & F.L.O.	43	1978
6 OF 1 THING CRAIG DAVID	39	2008
SIX PACK POLICE	17	1980
THE SIX TEENS SWEET	9	1974
634-5789 WILSON PICKETT	36	1966
6 UNDERGROUND SNEAKER PIMPS	9	1996
SIXTEEN MUSICAL YOUTH	23	1984
16 BARS STYLISTICS	7	1976
SIXTEEN REASONS CONNIE STEVENS	9	1960
SIXTEEN TONS FRANKIE LAINE	10	1956
SIXTEEN TONS TENNESSEE ERNIE FORD	49	1956
THE SIXTH SENSE VARIOUS ARTISTS (MONTAGES)	49	1990
THE 6TH SENSE COMMON	56	2000
68 GUNS ALARM	17	1983
SIXTY MILE SMILE 3 COLOURS RED	20	1997
60 MILES AND HOUR NEW ORDER	29	2001
SIXTY MINUTE MAN TRAMMPS	40	1975
69 POLICE DAVID HOLMES	53	2000
THE SIZE OF A COW WONDER STUFF	5	1991
SK8ER BOI AVRIL LAVIGNE	8	2002
SKA DJ ZINC	54	2004
SKA TRAIN BEATMASTERS FEATURING BETTY BOO	7	1989
SKAT STRUT MC SKAT KAT & THE STRAY MOB	64	1991
SKATEAWAY DIRE STRAITS	37	1981
SKELETONS STEVIE WONDER	59	1987
SKIFFLE SESSION EP LONNIE DONEGAN	20	1956
SKIING IN THE SNOW WIGAN'S OVATION	12	1975
SKIN CHARLOTTE	56	1999
SKIN DEEP [A] DUKE ELLINGTON	7	1954
SKIN DEEP [A] TED HEATH	9	1954
SKIN DEEP [B] STRANGLERS	15	1984
SKIN DEEP [C] NATASHA THOMAS	54	2006
THE SKIN GAME GARY NUMAN	68	1992
SKIN O' MY TEETH MEGADETH	13	1992
SKIN ON SKIN GRACE	21	1996
SKIN TRADE DURAN DURAN	22	1987
THE SKIN UP (EP) SKIN	67	1993
SKINHEAD MOONSTOMP SYMARIP	54	1980
SKINNY LO-RIDER FEATURING CUMBERBATCH	44	2006
SKIP A BEAT BARRATT WAUGH	56	2003
SKIP TO MY LU LISA LISA	34	1994
SKIP TO THE END FUTUREHEADS	24	2006
SKUNK FUNK GALLIANO	41	1992
SKWEEZE ME PLEEZE ME SLADE	1	1973
SKY SONIQUE	2	2000
A SKY BLUE SHIRT AND A RAINBOW TIE NORMAN BROOKS	17	1954
SKY HIGH JIGSAW	9	1975
SKY HIGH NEWTON	56	1995
SKY PILOT ERIC BURDON & THE ANIMALS	40	1968
SKY PLUS NYLON MOON	43	1996
SKY STARTS FALLING DOVES	45	2005
SKYDIVE (I FEEL WONDERFUL) FREEFALL FEATURING JAN JOHNSTON	35	1998
THE SKYE BOAT SONG ROGER WHITTAKER & DES O'CONNOR	10	1986
SKYLARK MICHAEL HOLLIDAY	39	1960
SKY'S THE LIMIT NOTORIOUS B.I.G. FEATURING 112	35	1998
SKYWRITER JACKSON 5	25	1973
SLADE LIVE AT READING '80 (EP) SLADE	44	1980
SLAIN BY ELF URUSEI YATSURA	64	1998
SLAIN THE TRUTH (AT THE ROADHOUSE) BASEMENT	48	2003
SLAM [A] HUMANOID	54	1989
SLAM [B] ONYX	31	1993
SLAM [C] PENDULUM	34	2005
SLAM DUNK (DA FUNK) FIVE	10	1997
SLAM JAM WWF SUPERSTARS	4	1992
SLANG DEF LEPPARD	17	1996
SLAP AND TICKLE SQUEEZE	24	1979
SLASH DOT DASH FATBOY SLIM	12	2004
SLASH 'N' BURN MANIC STREET PREACHERS	20	1992
SLAVE NEW WORLD SEPULTURA	46	1994
SLAVE TO LOVE BRYAN FERRY	10	1985
SLAVE TO THE GRIND SKID ROW	43	1991
SLAVE TO THE RHYTHM GRACE JONES	12	1985
SLAVE TO THE VIBE AFTERSHOCK	11	1993
SLAVE TO THE WAGE PLACEBO	19	2000

		Peak Position	Year of Entry
SLAVES NO MORE	BLOW MONKEYS FEATURING SYLVIA TELLA	73	1989
SLEAZY BED TRACK	BLUETONES	35	1998
SLEDGEHAMMER	PETER GABRIEL	4	1986
SLEDGER	PORN KINGS	71	2001
SLEEP [A]	MARION	17	1995
SLEEP [B]	CONJURE ONE	42	2003
SLEEP [C]	TEXAS	6	2006
SLEEP ALONE	WONDER STUFF	43	1991
SLEEP FREAK	HEAVY STEREO	46	1995
SLEEP NOW IN THE FIRE	RAGE AGAINST THE MACHINE	43	2000
SLEEP ON THE LEFT SIDE	CORNERSHOP	23	1998
SLEEP TALK [A]	ALYSON WILLIAMS	17	1989
SLEEP TALK [B]	A.T.F.C. FEATURING LISA MILLETT	33	2002
SLEEP WALK	SANTO & JOHNNY	22	1959
SLEEP WELL TONIGHT	GENE	36	1994
SLEEP WITH ME	BIRDLAND	32	1990
SLEEPER	AUDIOWEB	50	1995
SLEEPIN' ON THE JOB	GILLAN	55	1980
SLEEPING AWAKE	P.O.D.	42	2003
SLEEPING BAG	ZZ TOP	27	1985
SLEEPING IN	MENSWEAR	24	1995
SLEEPING IN MY CAR	ROXETTE	14	1994
SLEEPING SATELLITE	TASMIN ARCHER	1	1992
SLEEPING WITH THE LIGHT ON	BUSTED	3	2003
SLEEPING WITH THE LIGHTS ON	CURTIS STIGERS	53	1992
SLEEPING WITH VICTOR	LYNDEN DAVID HALL	49	2000
SLEEPWALK	ULTRAVOX	29	1980
SLEEPWALKERS	MODEY LEMON	71	2005
SLEEPWALKING	MARIA LAWSON	20	2006
SLEEPY JOE	HERMAN'S HERMITS	12	1968
SLEEPY SHORES	JOHNNY PEARSON	8	1971
SLEIGH RIDE	S CLUB JUNIORS	6	2002
SLICE OF DA PIE	MONIE LOVE	29	2000
SLID	FLUKE	59	1993
SLIDE [A]	RAH BAND	50	1981
SLIDE [B]	GOO GOO DOLLS	43	1999
SLIDE ALONG SIDE	SHIFTY	29	2004
SLIDLING	IAN McCULLOCH	61	2003
SLIGHT RETURN	BLUETONES	2	1996
THE SLIGHTEST TOUCH	FIVE STAR	4	1987
SLIP AND DIP	COFFEE	57	1980
SLIP AND SLIDE	MEDICINE HEAD	22	1974
(SLIP & SLIDE) SUICIDE	KOSHEEN	50	2001
SLIP SLIDIN' AWAY	PAUL SIMON	36	1977
SLIP YOUR DISC TO THIS	HEATWAVE	15	1977
SLIPPERY PEOPLE	TALKING HEADS	68	1984
SLIPPERY SLOPES	CLIPZ	72	2005
SLIPPIN'	DMX	30	1999
SLIPPING AWAY [A]	DAVE EDMUNDS	60	1983
SLIPPING AWAY [B]	MANSUN	55	2004
SLIPPING AWAY [C]	MOBY	53	2006
SLITHER	VELVET REVOLVER	35	2004
SLOGANS	BOB MARLEY & THE WAILERS	45	2005
SLOOP JOHN B	BEACH BOYS	2	1966
SLOPPY HEART	FRAZIER CHORUS	73	1989
SLOW	KYLIE MINOGUE	1	2003
SLOW AND SEXY	SHABBA RANKS FEATURING JOHNNY GILL	17	1992
SLOW DOWN [A]	JOHN MILES	10	1977
SLOW DOWN [B]	LOOSE ENDS	27	1986
SLOW DOWN [C]	BOBBY VALENTINO	4	2005
SLOW EMOTION REPLAY	THE THE	35	1993
SLOW FLOW	BRAXTONS	26	1997
SLOW HANDS	INTERPOL	36	2004
SLOW IT DOWN	EAST 17	13	1993
SLOW JAMZ	TWISTA	3	2004
SLOW MOTION	ULTRAVOX	33	1981
SLOW RIVERS	ELTON JOHN & CLIFF RICHARD	44	1986
SLOW TRAIN TO DAWN	THE THE	64	1987
SLOW TRAIN TO PARADISE	TAVARES	62	1978
SLOW TWISTIN'	CHUBBY CHECKER	23	1962
SLOWDIVE	SIOUXSIE & THE BANSHEES	41	1982
SLOWHAND	POINTER SISTERS	10	1981
SLY	MASSIVE ATTACK	24	1994
SMACK MY BITCH UP	PRODIGY	8	1997
SMACK THAT	AKON FEATURING EMINEM	1	2006
SMALL ADS	SMALL ADS	63	1981
SMALL BIT OF LOVE	SAW DOCTORS	24	1994
SMALL BLUE THING	SUZANNE VEGA	65	1986
SMALL SAD SAM	PHIL McLEAN	34	1962
SMALL TOWN	JOHN COUGAR MELLENCAMP	53	1986
SMALL TOWN BOY	UK	74	1996
A SMALL VICTORY	FAITH NO MORE	29	1992
SMALLTOWN BOY	BRONSKI BEAT	3	1984
SMALLTOWN CREED	KANE GANG	60	1984
SMARTY PANTS	FIRST CHOICE	9	1973
SMASH IT UP	DAMNED	35	1979
SMASH SUMTHIN'	ADAM F FEATURING REDMAN	47	2001
S.M.D.U.	BROCK LANDARS	49	1998
SMELLS LIKE NIRVANA	WEIRD AL YANKOVIC	58	1992
SMELLS LIKE TEEN SPIRIT	NIRVANA	7	1991
SMELLS LIKE TEEN SPIRIT	ABIGAIL	29	1994
SMILE [A]	NAT 'KING' COLE	2	1954
SMILE [A]	ROBERT DOWNEY JR	68	1993
SMILE [B]	PUSSYCAT	24	1977
THE SMILE [C]	DAVID ESSEX	52	1983
SMILE [D]	AUDREY HALL	14	1986
SMILE [E]	ASWAD FEATURING SWEETIE IRIE	53	1990
SMILE [F]	SUPERNATURALS	23	1997
SMILE [G]	LONESTAR	55	2000
SMILE [H]	FUTURE BREEZE	67	2001
SMILE [I]	MONROE	60	2004
SMILE [J]	DAVID GILMOUR	72	2006
SMILE [K]	LILY ALLEN	1	2006
A SMILE IN A WHISPER	FAIRGROUND ATTRACTION	75	1988
SMILE LIKE YOU MEAN IT	KILLERS	11	2005
SMILE TO SHINE	BAZ	58	2002
SMILER	HEAVY STEREO	46	1995
SMILEY FACES	GNARLS BARKLEY	10	2006
THE SMILING FACE	BURN	72	2002
SMOKE	NATALIE IMBRUGLIA	5	1998
SMOKE GETS IN YOUR EYES	PLATTERS	1	1959
SMOKE GETS IN YOUR EYES	BLUE HAZE	32	1972
SMOKE GETS IN YOUR EYES	BRYAN FERRY	17	1974
SMOKE GETS IN YOUR EYES	JOHN ALFORD	13	1996
SMOKE IT	DANDY WARHOLS	59	2005
SMOKE MACHINE	X-PRESS 2	43	2001
SMOKE ON THE WATER	DEEP PURPLE	21	1977
SMOKE ON THE WATER	ROCK AID ARMENIA	39	1989
SMOKEBELCH II	SABRES OF PARADISE	55	1993
SMOKERS OUTSIDE THE HOSPITAL DOORS	EDITORS	7	2007
SMOKESTACK LIGHTNIN'	HOWLIN' WOLF	42	1964
SMOKEY BLUES AWAY	A NEW GENERATION	38	1968
SMOKIN' IN THE BOYS ROOM	MOTLEY CRUE	51	1985
SMOKIN' IN THE BOYS' ROOM	BROWNSVILLE STATION	27	1974
SMOKIN' ME OUT	WARREN G FEATURING RONALD ISLEY	14	1997
SMOOTH	SANTANA FEATURING ROB THOMAS	3	1999
SMOOTH CRIMINAL	MICHAEL JACKSON	8	1988
SMOOTH CRIMINAL	ALIEN ANT FARM	3	2001
SMOOTH OPERATOR	SADE	19	1984
SMOOTHER OPERATOR	BIG DADDY KANE	65	1989
SMOOTHIN' GROOVIN'	INGRAM	56	1983
SMOULDER	KING ADORA	62	2000
SMUGGLER'S BLUES	GLENN FREY	22	1985
THE SMURF	TYRONE BRUNSON	52	1982
THE SMURF SONG	FATHER ABRAHAM & THE SMURFS	2	1978
THE SNAKE [A]	AL WILSON	41	1975
SNAKE [B]	R KELLY FEATURING BIG TIGGER	10	2003
SNAKE BITE (EP)	DAVID COVERDALE'S WHITESNAKE	61	1978
SNAKE IN THE GRASS	DAVE DEE, DOZY, BEAKY, MICK & TICH	23	1969
SNAP MEGAMIX	SNAP	10	1991
SNAP YOUR FINGAZ	KUMARA	70	2000
SNAPPED IT	KRUST	58	2002
SNAPPINESS	BBG FEATURING DINA TAYLOR	28	1990
SNAPSHOT 3	RONI SIZE	61	2003
SNEAKIN' SUSPICION	DR FEELGOOD	47	1977
SNEAKING OUT THE BACK DOOR	MATT BIANCO	44	1984
SNITCH	OBIE TRICE FEATURING AKON	44	2006
SNOBBERY AND DECAY	ACT	60	1987
SNOOKER LOOPY	MATCHROOM MOB WITH CHAS & DAVE	6	1986
SNOOP DOGG	SNOOP DOGG	13	2001
SNOOP'S UPSIDE YA HEAD	SNOOP DOGGY DOGG FEATURING CHARLIE WILSON	12	1996
SNOOPY VS. THE RED BARON	ROYAL GUARDSMEN	8	1967
SNOOPY VS. THE RED BARON	HOTSHOTS	4	1973
SNOT RAP	KENNY EVERETT	9	1983
SNOW [A]	ORN	61	1997
SNOW [B]	JJ72	21	2001
SNOW COACH	RUSS CONWAY	7	1959
SNOW (HEY HO)	RED HOT CHILI PEPPERS	16	2006
SNOWBIRD	ANNE MURRAY	23	1970
SNOWBOUND FOR CHRISTMAS	DICKIE VALENTINE	28	1957
SNOWDEN	DOVES	17	2005
THE SNOWS OF NEW YORK	CHRIS DE BURGH	60	1995
SO ALIVE	RYAN ADAMS	21	2004
SO AMAZING	LUTHER VANDROSS	33	1987
SO BEAUTIFUL [A]	URBAN COOKIE COLLECTIVE	68	1995
SO BEAUTIFUL [B]	CHRIS DE BURGH	29	1997
SO BEAUTIFUL [C]	DJ INNOCENCE FEATURING ALEX CHARLES	51	2002
SO BEAUTIFUL [D]	DARREN HAYES	15	2005
SO CALLED FRIEND	TEXAS	30	1993
SO CLOSE [A]	DIANA ROSS	43	1983
SO CLOSE [B]	HALL & OATES	69	1990
SO CLOSE [C]	DINA CARROLL	20	1992
SO CLOSE TO LOVE	WENDY MOTEN	35	1994
SO COLD THE NIGHT	COMMUNARDS	8	1986
SO CONFUSED	2PLAY FEATURING RAGHAV & JUCXI	6	2004
SO DAMN BEAUTIFUL	POLOROID	28	2003
SO DAMN COOL	UGLY KID JOE	44	1992
SO DEEP	REESE PROJECT	54	1993
SO DEEP IS THE NIGHT	KEN DODD	31	1964
SO DO I	KENNY BALL & HIS JAZZMEN	14	1962
SO EASY	ROYKSOPP	21	2002
SO EMOTIONAL	WHITNEY HOUSTON	5	1987
SO FAR AWAY	DIRE STRAITS	20	1985
SO FINE [A]	HOWARD JOHNSON	45	1982
SO FINE [B]	KINANE	63	1998
SO FRESH SO CLEAN	OUTKAST	16	2001
SO GOOD [A]	ROY ORBISON	32	1967
SO GOOD [B]	ETERNAL	13	1994
SO GOOD [C]	BOYZONE	3	1995
SO GOOD [D]	JULIET ROBERTS	15	1998
SO GOOD [E]	RACHEL STEVENS	10	2005
SO GOOD [F]	BRATZ ROCK ANGELZ	23	2005
SO GOOD SO RIGHT	BRENDA RUSSELL	51	1980
SO GOOD TO BE BACK HOME AGAIN	TOURISTS	8	1980
SO GOOD (TO COME HOME TO)	IVAN MATAIS	69	1996
SO GRIMEY	SO SOLID CREW	62	2004

	Peak Position	Year of Entry
SO GROOVY WENDELL WILLIAMS	74	1991
SO HARD PET SHOP BOYS	4	1990
SO HELP ME GIRL GARY BARLOW	11	1997
SO HERE I AM UB40	25	1982
SO HERE WE ARE BLOC PARTY	5	2005
SO HOT JC	74	1998
SO I BEGIN GALLEON	36	2002
SO IN LOVE ORCHESTRAL MANOEUVRES IN THE DARK	27	1985
SO IN LOVE (THE REAL DEAL) JUDY CHEEKS	27	1993
SO IN LOVE WITH YOU [A] FREDDY BRECK	44	1974
SO IN LOVE WITH YOU [B] SPEAR OF DESTINY	36	1988
SO IN LOVE WITH YOU [C] TEXAS	28	1994
SO IN LOVE WITH YOU [D] DUKE	22	1996
SO INTO YOU [A] MICHAEL WATFORD	53	1994
SO INTO YOU [B] WILDHEARTS	22	2003
SO IT WILL ALWAYS BE EVERLY BROTHERS	23	1963
SO LITTLE TIME ARKARNA	46	1997
SO LONELY [A] POLICE	6	1980
SO LONELY [B] JAKATTA	8	2002
SO LONG [A] FISCHER-Z	72	1980
SO LONG [B] FIERCE	15	1999
SO LONG [C] WILLY MASON	45	2005
SO LONG BABY DEL SHANNON	10	1961
SO LOW OCEAN COLOUR SCENE	34	1999
SO MACHO SINITTA	2	1986
SO MANY TIMES GADJO FEATURING ALEXANDRA PRINCE	22	2005
SO MANY WAYS [A] BRAXTONS	32	1997
SO MANY WAYS [B] ELLIE CAMPBELL	26	1999
SO MUCH IN LOVE [A] TYMES	21	1963
SO MUCH IN LOVE [A] ALL-4-ONE	49	1994
SO MUCH IN LOVE [B] MIGHTY AVENGERS	46	1964
SO MUCH LOVE TONY BLACKBURN	31	1968
SO MUCH LOVE TO GIVE [A] THOMAS BANGALTER & DJ FALCON	71	2003
SO MUCH LOVE TO GIVE [B] FREELOADERS FEATURING THE REAL THING	9	2005
SO MUCH TROUBLE IN THE WORLD BOB MARLEY & THE WAILERS	56	1979
SO NATURAL LISA STANSFIELD	15	1993
SO NEAR TO CHRISTMAS ALVIN STARDUST	29	1984
SO NOT OVER YOU SIMPLY RED	34	2007
SO PURE [A] BABY D	3	1996
SO PURE [B] ALANIS MORISSETTE	38	1999
SO REAL [A] LOVE DECADE	14	1991
SO REAL [B] HARRY	53	2002
SO RIGHT [A] RAILWAY CHILDREN	68	1990
SO RIGHT [B] K-KLASS	20	1992
SO ROTTEN BLAK TWANG FEATURING JAHMALI	48	2002
SO SAD THE SONG GLADYS KNIGHT & THE PIPS	20	1976
SO SAD (TO WATCH GOOD LOVE GO BAD) EVERLY BROTHERS	4	1960
SO SAYS I SHINS	73	2004
SO SEDUCTIVE TONY YAYO FEATURING 50 CENT	28	2005
SO SEXY TWISTA FEATURING R KELLY	28	2004
SO SICK NE-YO	1	2006
SO SORRY I SAID LIZA MINNELLI	62	1989
SO STRONG BEN SHAW FEATURING ADELE HOLNESS	72	2001
SO TELL ME WHY POISON	25	1991
SO THE STORY GOES LIVING IN A BOX FEATURING BOBBY WOMACK	34	1987
SO THIS IS ROMANCE LINX	15	1981
SO TIRED [A] FRANKIE VAUGHAN	21	1967
SO TIRED [B] OZZY OSBOURNE	20	1984
SO TIRED OF BEING ALONE SYBIL	53	1996
SO UNDER PRESSURE DANNII MINOGUE	20	2006
SO WATCHA GONNA DO NOW PUBLIC ENEMY	50	1995
SO WHAT [A] GILBERT O'SULLIVAN	70	1990
SO WHAT! [B] RONNY JORDAN	32	1992
SO WHAT [C] FIELD MOB FEATURING CIARA	56	2006
SO WHAT IF I DAMAGE	12	2001
SO WHAT THE FUSS STEVIE WONDER	19	2005
SO WHY SO SAD MANIC STREET PREACHERS	8	2001
SO YESTERDAY HILARY DUFF	9	2003
SO YOU KNOW INME	33	2005
SO YOU WIN AGAIN HOT CHOCOLATE	1	1977
SO YOU'D LIKE TO SAVE THE WORLD LLOYD COLE	72	1993
SO YOUNG [A] SUEDE	22	1993
SO YOUNG [B] CORRS	6	1998
SOAK UP THE SUN SHERYL CROW	16	2002
SOAPBOX LITTLE ANGELS	33	1993
SOBER [A] DRUGSTORE	68	1998
SOBER [B] JENNIFER PAIGE	68	1999
SOC IT TO ME BADFELLAS FEATURING CK	55	2003
SOCK IT 2 ME MISSY 'MISDEMEANOR' ELLIOTT	33	1997
SODA POP AVID MERRION/DAVINA McCALL/ PATSY KENSIT	5	2005
SOFA SONG KOOKS	28	2005
SOFT AS YOUR FACE SOUP DRAGONS	66	1987
SOFT LIKE ME SAINT ETIENNE	40	2003
SOFT TOP HARD SHOULDER CHRIS REA	53	1993
SOFTLY AS I LEAVE YOU MATT MONRO	10	1962
SOFTLY SOFTLY [A] RUBY MURRAY	1	1955
SOFTLY SOFTLY [B] EQUALS	48	1968
SOFTLY WHISPERING I LOVE YOU CONGREGATION	4	1971
SOFTLY WHISPERING I LOVE YOU PAUL YOUNG	21	1990
SOLACE OF YOU LIVING COLOUR	33	1991
SOLD BOY GEORGE	24	1987
SOLD ME DOWN THE RIVER ALARM	43	1989
SOLD MY ROCK 'N' ROLL (GAVE IT FOR FUNKY SOUL) LINDA & THE FUNKY BOYS	36	1976
SOLD OUT EP REEL BIG FISH	62	2002
SOLDIER DESTINY'S CHILD FEATURING TI & LIL' WAYNE	4	2005
SOLDIER BLUE BUFFY SAINTE-MARIE	7	1971
SOLDIER BOY SHIRELLES	23	1962
SOLDIER BOY CHEETAHS	39	1965
SOLDIER GIRL POLYPHONIC SPREE	26	2003
SOLDIER OF LOVE DONNY OSMOND	29	1988
SOLDIER'S SONG HOLLIES	58	1980
SOLEX (CLOSE TO THE EDGE) MICHAEL WOODS	52	2003
SOLEY SOLEY MIDDLE OF THE ROAD	5	1971
SOLID ASHFORD & SIMPSON	3	1985
SOLID BOND IN YOUR HEART STYLE COUNCIL	11	1983
SOLID GOLD EASY ACTION T REX	2	1972
SOLID ROCK (LIVE) DIRE STRAITS	50	1984
SOLID WOOD ALISON MOYET	44	1995
SOLITAIRE ANDY WILLIAMS	4	1974
SOLITAIRE CARPENTERS	32	1975
SOLITARY MAN H.I.M.	9	2004
SOLOMON BITES THE WORM BLUETONES	10	1998
SOLSBURY HILL PETER GABRIEL	13	1977
SOLSBURY HILL ERASURE	10	2002
(SOLUTION TO) THE PROBLEM MASQUERADE	64	1986
SOLVED UNBELIEVABLE TRUTH	39	1998
SOME BEAUTIFUL JACK WILD	46	1970
SOME CANDY TALKING JESUS & MARY CHAIN	13	1986
SOME FANTASTIC PLACE SQUEEZE	73	1993
SOME FINER DAY ALL ABOUT EVE	57	1992
SOME GIRLS [A] RACEY	2	1979
SOME GIRLS [B] ULTIMATE KAOS	9	1994
SOME GIRLS [C] JC CHASEZ	13	2004
SOME GIRLS [D] RACHEL STEVENS	2	2004
SOME GUYS HAVE ALL THE LUCK ROBERT PALMER	16	1982
SOME GUYS HAVE ALL THE LUCK ROD STEWART	15	1984
SOME GUYS HAVE ALL THE LUCK MAXI PRIEST	12	1987
SOME JUSTICE URBAN SHAKEDOWN FEATURING MICKY FINN	23	1992
SOME KIND OF A SUMMER DAVID CASSIDY	3	1973
SOME KIND OF BLISS KYLIE MINOGUE	22	1997
SOME KIND OF FRIEND BARRY MANILOW	48	1983
SOME KIND OF HEAVEN BBG	65	1990
SOME KIND OF WONDERFUL BLOW MONKEYS	67	1987
SOME KINDA EARTHQUAKE DUANE EDDY & THE REBELS	12	1959
SOME KINDA FUN CHRIS MONTEZ	10	1963
SOME KINDA RUSH BOOTY LUV	19	2007
SOME LIE 4 LOVE L.A. GUNS	61	1991
SOME LIKE IT HOT POWER STATION	14	1985
SOME MIGHT SAY OASIS	1	1995
SOME MIGHT SAY DE-CODE FEATURING BEVERLI SKEETE	69	1996
SOME MIGHT SAY SUPERNOVA	55	1996
SOME OF YOUR LOVIN' DUSTY SPRINGFIELD	8	1965
SOME OLD GIRL PADDINGTONS	47	2004
SOME OTHER GUY BIG THREE	37	1963
SOME OTHER SUCKER'S PARADE DEL AMITRI	46	1997
SOME PEOPLE [A] CAROL DEENE	25	1962
SOME PEOPLE [B] BELOUIS SOME	33	1986
SOME PEOPLE [C] PAUL YOUNG	56	1986
SOME PEOPLE [D] CLIFF RICHARD	3	1987
SOME PEOPLE SAY TERRORVISION	22	1995
SOME SAY KRISTIAN LEONTIOU	54	2004
SOME THINGS YOU NEVER GET USED TO DIANA ROSS & THE SUPREMES	34	1968
SOME VELVET MORING PRIMAL SCREAM	44	2003
SOMEBODY [A] STARGAZERS	20	1955
SOMEBODY [B] JUNIOR	64	1984
SOMEBODY [C] DEPECHE MODE	16	1984
SOMEBODY [D] BRYAN ADAMS	35	1985
SOMEBODY [E] BRILLIANT	67	1986
SOMEBODY [F] SHORTIE VS BLACK LEGEND	37	2001
SOMEBODY ELSE'S GIRL BILLY FURY	18	1963
SOMEBODY ELSE'S GUY JOCELYN BROWN	13	1984
SOMEBODY ELSE'S GUY LOUCHIE LOU & MICHIE ONE	54	1993
SOMEBODY ELSE'S GUY CE CE PENISTON	13	1998
SOMEBODY HELP ME SPENCER DAVIS GROUP	1	1966
(SOMEBODY) HELP ME OUT BEGGAR & CO	15	1981
SOMEBODY IN THE HOUSE SAY YEAH! 2 IN A ROOM	66	1989
SOMEBODY LIKE YOU ELATE	38	1997
SOMEBODY LOVES YOU NIK KERSHAW	70	1999
SOMEBODY PUT SOMETHING IN MY DRINK RAMONES	69	1986
SOMEBODY STOLE MY GAL JOHNNIE RAY	6	1953
SOMEBODY TO LOVE [A] BRAD NEWMAN	47	1962
SOMEBODY TO LOVE [A] JETS	56	1982
SOMEBODY TO LOVE [B] QUEEN	2	1976
SOMEBODY TO LOVE [C] BOOGIE PIMPS	3	2003
SOMEBODY TO SHOVE SOUL ASYLUM	32	1993
SOMEBODY TOLD ME KILLERS	3	2004
SOMEBODY'S BABY PAT BENATAR	48	1993
SOMEBODY'S WATCHING ME ROCKWELL	6	1984
SOMEBODY'S WATCHING ME BEATFREAKZ	3	2006
SOMEDAY [A] RICKY NELSON	9	1958
SOMEDAY [B] GAP BAND	17	1984
SOMEDAY [C] GLASS TIGER	66	1987
SOMEDAY [D] MARIAH CAREY	38	1991
SOMEDAY [D] REZONANCE Q	29	2003
SOMEDAY [E] M PEOPLE WITH HEATHER SMALL	38	1992

	Peak Position	Year of Entry
SOMEDAY [F] EDDY	49	1994
SOMEDAY [G] LOVE TO INFINITY	75	1995
SOMEDAY [H] ETERNAL	4	1996
SOMEDAY [I] CHARLOTTE	74	1999
SOMEDAY [J] STROKES	27	2002
SOMEDAY [K] NICKELBACK	6	2003
SOMEDAY I'LL BE SATURDAY NIGHT BON JOVI	7	1995
SOMEDAY I'LL FIND YOU SHOLA AMA & CRAIG ARMSTRONG	28	1998
SOMEDAY (I'M COMING BACK) LISA STANSFIELD	10	1992
SOMEDAY MAN MONKEES	47	1969
SOMEDAY ONE DAY SEEKERS	11	1966
SOMEDAY WE'LL BE TOGETHER DIANA ROSS & THE SUPREMES	13	1969
SOMEDAY WE'LL KNOW NEW RADICALS	48	1999
SOMEDAY WE'RE GONNA LOVE AGAIN SEARCHERS	11	1964
SOMEDAY (YOU'LL BE SORRY) KENNY BALL & HIS JAZZMEN	28	1961
SOMEDAY (YOU'LL COME RUNNING) FM	64	1989
SOMEDAY (YOU'LL WANT ME TO WANT YOU) JODIE SANDS	14	1958
SOMEHOW SOMEWHERE DEEP SENSATION	74	2004
SOMEONE [A] JOHNNY MATHIS	6	1959
SOMEONE [B] ASCENSION	43	1997
SOMEONE [C] SWV FEATURING PUFF DADDY	34	1997
SOMEONE ALWAYS GETS THERE FIRST BENNETT	69	1997
SOMEONE BELONGING TO SOMEONE BEE GEES	49	1983
SOMEONE ELSE NOT ME DURAN DURAN	53	2000
SOMEONE ELSE'S BABY ADAM FAITH	2	1960
SOMEONE ELSE'S ROSES JOAN REGAN	5	1954
SOMEONE LIKE ME ATOMIC KITTEN	8	2004
SOMEONE LIKE YOU [A] DINA CARROLL	38	2001
SOMEONE LIKE YOU [B] RUSSELL WATSON & FAYE TOZER	10	2002
SOMEONE LOVES YOU HONEY LUTRICIA McNEAL	9	1998
SOMEONE MUST HAVE HURT YOU A LOT FRANKIE VAUGHAN	46	1965
SOMEONE ON YOUR MIND JIMMY YOUNG	13	1955
SOMEONE SAVED MY LIFE TONIGHT ELTON JOHN	22	1975
SOMEONE SHOULD TELL HER MAVERICKS	45	1999
SOMEONE SHOULD TELL YOU LEMAR	21	2006
SOMEONE SOMEONE BRIAN POOLE & THE TREMELOES	2	1964
SOMEONE SOMEWHERE WANNADIES	38	1996
SOMEONE SOMEWHERE (IN SUMMERTIME) SIMPLE MINDS	36	1982
SOMEONE THERE FOR ME RICHARD BLACKWOOD	23	2000
SOMEONE TO CALL MY LOVER JANET JACKSON	11	2001
SOMEONE TO HOLD TREY LORENZ	65	1992
SOMEONE TO LOVE [A] SEAN MAGUIRE	14	1994
SOMEONE TO LOVE [B] EAST 17	16	1996
SOMEONE TO SOMEBODY FEARGAL SHARKEY	64	1986
SOMEONE'S DAUGHTER BETH ORTON	49	1997
SOMEONE'S LOOKING AT YOU BOOMTOWN RATS	4	1980
SOMEONE'S TAKEN MARIA AWAY ADAM FAITH	34	1965
SOMERSAULT ZERO 7 FEATURING SIA	56	2004
SOMETHIN' ELSE EDDIE COCHRAN	22	1959
SOMETHIN' 4 DA HONEYZ MONTELL JORDAN	15	1995
SOMETHIN' IS GOIN' ON CLIFF RICHARD	9	2004
SOMETHIN' STUPID NANCY SINATRA & FRANK SINATRA	1	1967
SOMETHIN' STUPID ALI & KIBIBI CAMPBELL	30	1995
SOMETHIN' STUPID ROBBIE WILLIAMS & NICOLE KIDMAN	1	2001
SOMETHING [A] GEORGIE FAME & THE BLUE FLAMES	23	1965
SOMETHING [B] BEATLES	4	1969
SOMETHING [B] SHIRLEY BASSEY	4	1970
SOMETHING [C] LASGO	4	2002
SOMETHING ABOUT THE MUSIC DA SLAMMIN' PHROGZ	53	2000
SOMETHING ABOUT THE WAY YOU LOOK TONIGHT ELTON JOHN	1	1997
SOMETHING ABOUT YOU [A] LEVEL 42	6	1985
SOMETHING ABOUT YOU [B] MR ROY	49	1994
SOMETHING ABOUT YOU [C] NEW EDITION	16	1997
SOMETHING ABOUT YOU [D] JAMELIA	9	2006
SOMETHING BEAUTIFUL ROBBIE WILLIAMS	3	2003
SOMETHING BEAUTIFUL REMAINS TINA TURNER	27	1996
SOMETHING BETTER BEGINNING HONEYCOMBS	39	1965
SOMETHING BETTER CHANGE STRANGLERS	9	1977
SOMETHING 'BOUT YOU BABY I LIKE TOM JONES	36	1974
SOMETHING 'BOUT YOU BABY I LIKE STATUS QUO	9	1981
SOMETHING CHANGED PULP	10	1996
SOMETHING DEEP INSIDE BILLIE PIPER	4	2000
SOMETHING DIFFERENT SHAGGY FEATURING WAYNE WONDER	21	1996
SOMETHING ELSE [A] SEX PISTOLS	3	1979
SOMETHING ELSE [B] AGENT BLUE	59	2004
SOMETHING FOR THE GIRL WITH EVERYTHING SPARKS	17	1975
SOMETHING FOR THE PAIN BON JOVI	8	1995
SOMETHING FOR THE WEEKEND [A] DIVINE COMEDY	14	1996
SOMETHING 4 THE WEEKEND [B] SUPER FURRY ANIMALS	18	1996
SOMETHING FOR THE WEEKEND [C] FRED & ROXY	36	2000
SOMETHING GOIN' ON TODD TERRY FEATURING MARTHA WASH & JOCELYN BROWN	5	1997
SOMETHING GOOD UTAH SAINTS	4	1992
SOMETHING GOT ME STARTED SIMPLY RED	11	1991
SOMETHING HAPPENED ON THE WAY TO HEAVEN PHIL COLLINS	15	1990
SOMETHING HERE IN MY HEART (KEEPS A-TELLIN' ME NO) PAPER DOLLS	11	1968
SOMETHING IN COMMON BOBBY BROWN & WHITNEY HOUSTON	16	1994
SOMETHING IN MY HOUSE DEAD OR ALIVE	12	1987
SOMETHING IN THE AIR THUNDERCLAP NEWMAN	1	1969
SOMETHING IN THE AIR FISH	51	1992
SOMETHING IN THE AIR TOM PETTY	53	1993
SOMETHING IN THE AIR HAYLEY SANDERSON	61	2006
SOMETHING IN YOUR EYES [A] BELL BIV DEVOE	60	1993
SOMETHING IN YOUR EYES [B] ED CASE	38	2000
SOMETHING INSIDE OF ME CORAL	41	2005
(SOMETHING INSIDE) SO STRONG LABI SIFFRE	4	1987
SOMETHING INSIDE SO STRONG MICHAEL BALL	40	1996
SOMETHING INSIDE (SO STRONG) RIK WALLER	25	2002
SOMETHING JUST AIN'T RIGHT KEITH SWEAT	55	1988
SOMETHING KINDA OOOOH GIRLS ALOUD	3	2006
SOMETHING MISSING PETULA CLARK	44	1961
SOMETHING OLD, SOMETHING NEW FANTASTICS	9	1971
SOMETHING ON MY MIND CHRIS ANDREWS	41	1966
SOMETHING ON YOUR MIND MYNC PROJECT FEATURING ABIGAIL BAILEY	71	2006
SOMETHING OUTA NOTHING LETITIA DEAN & PAUL MEDFORD	12	1986
SOMETHING SO GOOD RAILWAY CHILDREN	57	1991
SOMETHING SO REAL (CHINHEADS THEME) LOVE DECREE	61	1989
SOMETHING SO RIGHT ANNIE LENNOX FEATURING PAUL SIMON	44	1995
SOMETHING SPECIAL [A] STEVE HARVEY	46	1983
SOMETHING SPECIAL [B] NOMAD	73	1991
SOMETHING STUPID CORONATION STREET CAST: AMANDA BARRIE & JOHNNIE BRIGGS	35	1995
SOMETHING TELLS ME (SOMETHING IS GONNA HAPPEN TONIGHT) CILLA BLACK	3	1971
SOMETHING THAT I SAID RUTS	29	1979
SOMETHING THAT YOU SAID BANGLES	38	2003
SOMETHING TO BELIEVE IN [A] POISON	35	1990
SOMETHING TO BELIEVE IN [B] RAMONES	69	1986
SOMETHING TO DO DEPECHE MODE	75	2004
SOMETHING TO MISS SENSELESS THINGS	57	1995
SOMETHING TO TALK ABOUT BADLY DRAWN BOY	28	2002
SOMETHING WILD RARE	57	1996
SOMETHING WORTHWHILE GUN	39	1995
SOMETHING YOU GOT AND WHY NOT?	39	1990
SOMETHING'S BEEN MAKING ME BLUE SMOKIE	17	1976
SOMETHING'S BURNING KENNY ROGERS & THE FIRST EDITION	8	1970
SOMETHING'S COOKIN' IN THE KITCHEN DANA	44	1979
SOMETHING'S GOIN' ON [A] MYSTIC 3	63	2000
SOMETHING'S GOING ON [B] A	51	2002
SOMETHING'S GOTTA GIVE SAMMY DAVIS Jr.	11	1955
SOMETHING'S GOTTEN HOLD OF MY HEART GENE PITNEY	5	1967
SOMETHING'S GOTTEN HOLD OF MY HEART MARC ALMOND FEATURING SPECIAL GUEST STAR GENE PITNEY	1	1989
SOMETHING'S HAPPENING HERMAN'S HERMITS	6	1968
SOMETHING'S JUMPIN' IN YOUR SHIRT MALCOLM McLAREN & THE BOOTZILLA ORCHESTRA FEATURING LISA MARIE	29	1989
SOMETHING'S MISSING CHORDS	55	1980
SOMETIMES [A] ERASURE	2	1986
SOMETIMES [B] MAX Q	53	1990
SOMETIMES [C] JAMES	18	1993
SOMETIMES [D] BRAND NEW HEAVIES	11	1997
SOMETIMES [E] TIN TIN OUT FEATURING SHELLEY NELSON	20	1998
SOMETIMES [F] LES RYTHMES DIGITALES FEATURING NIK KERHSAW	56	1999
SOMETIMES [G] BRITNEY SPEARS	3	1999
SOMETIMES [H] ASH	21	2001
SOMETIMES ALWAYS JESUS & MARY CHAIN	22	1994
SOMETIMES I MISS YOU SO MUCH PM DAWN	58	1996
SOMETIMES IT HURTS TINDERSTICKS	60	2003
SOMETIMES (IT SNOWS IN APRIL) AMAR	48	2000
SOMETIMES IT'S A BITCH STEVIE NICKS	40	1991
SOMETIMES LOVE JUST AIN'T ENOUGH PATTY SMYTH WITH DON HENLEY	22	1992
SOMETIMES (THEME FROM *CHAMPIONS*) ELAINE PAIGE	72	1984
SOMETIMES WHEN WE TOUCH DAN HILL	13	1978
SOMETIMES WHEN WE TOUCH NEWTON	32	1997

	Peak Position	Year of Entry
SOMETIMES YOU CAN'T MAKE IT ON YOUR OWN U2	1	2005
SOMEWHERE [A] P.J. PROBY	6	1964
SOMEWHERE [A] PET SHOP BOYS	9	1997
SOMEWHERE [B] EFUA	42	1993
SOMEWHERE ACROSS FOREVER STELLASTARR	61	2003
SOMEWHERE ALONG THE WAY NAT 'KING' COLE	3	1952
SOMEWHERE DOWN THE CRAZY RIVER ROBBIE ROBERTSON	15	1988
SOMEWHERE ELSE [A] CHINA DRUM	74	1997
SOMEWHERE ELSE [B] RAZORLIGHT	2	2005
SOMEWHERE I BELONG LINKIN PARK	10	2003
SOMEWHERE IN AMERICA (THERE'S A STREET NAMED AFTER MY DAD) WAS (NOT WAS)	57	1992
SOMEWHERE IN MY HEART AZTEC CAMERA	3	1988
SOMEWHERE IN THE COUNTRY GENE PITNEY	19	1968
SOMEWHERE IN THE NIGHT BARRY MANILOW	42	1978
SOMEWHERE MY LOVE MANUEL & HIS MUSIC OF THE MOUNTAINS	42	1966
SOMEWHERE MY LOVE MIKE SAMMES SINGERS	14	1966
SOMEWHERE ONLY WE KNOW KEANE	3	2004
SOMEWHERE OUT THERE LINDA RONSTADT & JAMES INGRAM	8	1987
SOMEWHERE OVER THE RAINBOW CLIFF RICHARD	11	2001
SOMEWHERE OVER THE RAINBOW ISRAEL KAMAKAWIWO'OLE	68	2007
SOMEWHERE SOMEBODY FIVE STAR	23	1987
SOMEWHERE SOMEHOW WET WET WET	7	1995
SON OF A GUN JX	6	1994
SON OF A GUN (BETCHA THINK THIS SONG IS ABOUT YOU) JANET JACKSON FEATURING CARLY SIMON	13	2001
SON OF A PREACHER MAN DUSTY SPRINGFIELD	9	1968
SON OF HICKORY HOLLER'S TRAMP O.C. SMITH	2	1968
SON OF MARY HARRY BELAFONTE	18	1958
SON OF MY FATHER CHICORY TIP	1	1972
SON OF SAM ELLIOTT SMITH	55	2000
SON OF THREE BREEDERS	72	2002
SON THIS IS SHE JOHN LEYTON	15	1962
SONG 4 MUTYA (OUT OF CONTROL) GROOVE ARMADA	8	2007
(SONG FOR A) FUTURE GENERATION B-52's	63	1983
SONG FOR GUY ELTON JOHN	4	1978
SONG FOR LOVE EXTREME	12	1992
A SONG FOR LOVERS [A] RICHARD ASHCROFT	3	2000
SONG 4 LOVERS [B] LIBERTY X	5	2005
A SONG FOR MAMA BOYZ II MEN	34	1997
A SONG FOR SHELTER FATBOY SLIM	30	2001
SONG FOR WHOEVER BEAUTIFUL SOUTH	2	1989
SONG FOR YOU MICHAEL BUBLE	45	2005
THE SONG FROM MOULIN ROUGE MANTOVANI	1	1953
SONG FROM THE EDGE OF THE WORLD SIOUXSIE & THE BANSHEES	59	1987
SONG OF DREAMS BECKY TAYLOR	60	2001
SONG OF JOY MIGUEL RIOS	16	1970
SONG OF LIFE LEFTFIELD	59	1992
SONG OF MEXICO TONY MEEHAN COMBO	39	1964
THE SONG OF MY LIFE PETULA CLARK	32	1971
SONG OF THE DREAMER JOHNNIE RAY	10	1955
SONG SUNG BLUE NEIL DIAMOND	14	1972
THE SONG THAT I SING (THEME FROM 'WE'LL MEET AGAIN') STUTZ BEARCATS & THE DENIS KING ORCHESTRA	36	1982
SONG TO THE SIREN THIS MORTAL COIL	66	1983
SONG 2 BLUR	2	1997
SONGBIRD [A] KENNY G	22	1987
SONGBIRD [B] OASIS	3	2003
SONGS FOR CHRISTMAS '87 EP MINI POPS	39	1988
SONGS FOR SWINGING LOVERS (LP) FRANK SINATRA	12	1956
SONIC BOOM BOY WESTWORLD	11	1987
SONIC BOOM (LIFE'S TOO SHORT) QUO VADIS	49	2000
SONIC EMPIRE MEMBERS OF MAYDAY	59	2002
SONNET (IMPORT) VERVE	74	1998
SONS AND DAUGHTERS' THEME KERRI & MICK	68	1984
SONS OF THE STAGE WORLD OF TWIST	47	1991
SOON MY BLOODY VALENTINE	41	1990
SOON BE DONE SHAGGY	46	1993
SOONER OR LATER [A] LARRY GRAHAM	54	1982
SOONER OR LATER [B] DUNCAN JAMES	35	2006
SOOPA HOOPZ SOOPA HOOPZ FEATURING QPR MASSIVE	54	2004
SOOTHE ME SAM & DAVE	35	1967
SOPHIA NERINA PALLOT	32	2006
SORRENTO MOON (I REMEMBER) TINA ARENA	22	1996
SORROW [A] MERSEYS	4	1966
SORROW [B] DAVID BOWIE	3	1973
SORRY [A] BEN ADAMS	18	2005
SORRY [B] PADDINGTONS	41	2005
SORRY [C] MADONNA	1	2006
SORRY [D] MADNESS	23	2007
SORRY BLAME IT ON ME AKON	22	2007
SORRY BUT I'M GONNA HAVE TO PASS COASTERS	41	1994
SORRY DOESN'T ALWAYS MAKE IT RIGHT DIANA ROSS	23	1975
SORRY FOR YOU RONI SIZE	61	2003
SORRY (I DIDN'T KNOW) MONSTA BOY FEATURING DENZIE	25	2000
SORRY (I RAN ALL THE WAY HOME) IMPALAS	28	1959
SORRY I'M A LADY BACCARA	8	1978
SORRY ROBBIE BERT WEEDON	28	1960
SORRY SEEMS TO BE THE HARDEST WORD ELTON JOHN	11	1976
SORRY SEEMS TO BE THE HARDEST WORD BLUE FEATURING ELTON JOHN	1	2002
THE SORRY SUITOR DIVE DIVE	54	2005
SORRY SUZANNE HOLLIES	3	1969
SORRY'S NOT GOOD ENOUGH McFLY	3	2006
SORTED FOR ES & WIZZ PULP	2	1995
A SORTA FAIRYTALE TORI AMOS	41	2002
S.O.S. [A] ABBA	6	1975
S.O.S. [B] ABC	39	1984
SOS [C] RIHANNA	2	2006
SOS [D] A-STUDIO FEATURING POLINA	64	2006
THE SOS EP SHAMEN	14	1993
SOS (MESSAGE IN A BOTTLE) FILTERFUNK	60	2006
SOUL BEAT CALLING I KAMANCHI	69	2003
SOUL BOSSA NOVA COOL, THE FAB & THE GROOVY PRESENT QUINCY JONES	47	1998
THE SOUL CAGES STING	57	1991
SOUL CHA CHA VAN McCOY	34	1977
SOUL CITY WALK ARCHIE BELL & THE DRELLS	13	1976
SOUL CLAP '69 BOOKER T. & THE M.G.'s	35	1969
SOUL COAXING RAYMOND LEFEVRE	46	1968
SOUL DEEP BOX TOPS	22	1969
SOUL DEEP GARY U.S. BONDS	59	1982
SOUL DEEP (PART 1) COUNCIL COLLECTIVE	24	1984
SOUL DRACULA HOT BLOOD	32	1976
SOUL FINGER BAR-KAYS	33	1967
SOUL FREEDOM - FREE YOUR SOUL DEGREES OF MOTION FEATURING BITI	64	1992
SOUL HEAVEN GOODFELLAS FEATURING LISA MILLETT	27	2001
SOUL INSIDE SOFT CELL	16	1983
SOUL INSPIRATION SIMON CLIMIE	60	1992
SOUL LIMBO BOOKER T. & THE M.G.'s	30	1969
SOUL LOVE BLESSING	73	1994
SOUL LOVE - SOUL MAN WOMACK & WOMACK	58	1986
SOUL MAN SAM & DAVE	24	1967
SOUL MAN SAM MOORE & LOU REED	30	1987
SOUL OF MY SOUL MICHAEL BOLTON	32	1994
THE SOUL OF MY SUIT T REX	42	1977
SOUL PASSING THROUGH SOUL TOYAH	57	1985
SOUL PROVIDER MICHAEL BOLTON	35	1996
SOUL SEARCHIN' TIME TRAMMPS	42	1976
SOUL SERENADE WILLIE MITCHELL	43	1968
SOUL SISTER BROWN SUGAR SAM & DAVE	15	1969
SOUL SOUND SUGABABES	30	2001
SOUL SURVIVOR YOUNG JEEZY FEATURING AKON	16	2006
SOUL TRAIN SWANS WAY	20	1984
SOULJACKER PART 1 EELS	30	2001
SOULMATE [A] WEE PAPA GIRL RAPPERS	45	1988
SOULMATE [B] NATASHA BEDINGFIELD	7	2007
SOULS RICK SPRINGFIELD	23	1984
SOUL'S ON FIRE TRACIE	73	1984
THE SOULSHAKER MAX LINEN	55	2001
SOUND [A] JAMES	9	1991
THE SOUND [B] X-PRESS 2	38	1996
SOUND ADVICE RONI SIZE	61	2002
SOUND AND VISION DAVID BOWIE	3	1977
SOUND BWOY BURIAL GANT	67	1997
SOUND CLASH (CHAMPION SOUND) KICK SQUAD	59	1990
THE SOUND OF BAMBOO FLICKMAN	11	2000
THE SOUND OF BLUE JFK	55	2002
SOUND OF CONFUSION SECRET AFFAIR	45	1980
THE SOUND OF THE CROWD HUMAN LEAGUE	12	1981
THE SOUND OF CRYING PREFAB SPROUT	23	1992
SOUND OF DRUMS KULA SHAKER	3	1998
THE SOUND OF EDEN SHADES OF RHYTHM	35	1991
SOUND OF EDEN CASINO	52	1997
SOUND OF FREEDOM BOB SINCLAR, CUTEE B & DOLLARMAN	14	2007
THE SOUND OF MUSIC DAYTON	75	1983
THE SOUND OF MUSIK FALCO	61	1986
THE SOUND OF OH YEAH TOMBA VIRA	51	2001
THE SOUND OF SILENCE BACHELORS	3	1966
SOUND OF SOUNDS/PING ONE DOWN GOMEZ	48	2002
SOUND OF SPEED (EP) JESUS & MARY CHAIN	30	1993
THE SOUND OF THE SUBURBS MEMBERS	12	1979
SOUND OF THE UNDERGROUND GIRLS ALOUD	1	2002
THE SOUND OF VIOLENCE CASSIUS	49	2002
THE SOUND OF YOUR CRY ELVIS PRESLEY	59	1982
SOUND SYSTEM [A] STEEL PULSE	71	1979
SOUND SYSTEM [B] DRUM CLUB	62	1993
SOUND YOUR FUNKY HORN KC & THE SUNSHINE BAND	17	1974
SOUNDS OF EDEN (EVERYTIME I SEE THE) DEEP COVER	63	2002
SOUNDS OF WICKEDNESS TZANT	11	1998
SOUR TIMES PORTISHEAD	13	1994
SOUTH AFRICAN MAN HAMILTON BOHANNON	22	1975
SOUTH MANZ DILLINJA	53	2002
SOUTH OF THE BORDER ROBBIE WILLIAMS	14	1997
SOUTH OF THE RIVER MICA PARIS	50	1990
SOUTH PACIFIC DJ ZINC	62	2004
SOUTHAMPTON BOYS RED 'N' WHITE MACHINES	16	2003

	Peak Position	Year of Entry
SOUTHERN COMFORT BERNIE FLINT	48	1977
SOUTHERN FREEEZ FREEEZ	8	1981
SOUTHERN NIGHTS GLEN CAMPBELL	28	1977
SOUTHERN SUN PAUL OAKENFOLD	16	2002
SOUTHSIDE DAVE CLARKE	34	1996
SOUVENIR ORCHESTRAL MANOEUVRES IN THE DARK	3	1981
SOUVENIRS VOYAGE	56	1978
SOWETO [A] MALCOLM McLAREN & THE McLARENETTES	32	1983
SOWETO [B] JEFFREY OSBORNE	44	1986
SOWING THE SEEDS OF HATRED CREDIT TO THE NATION	72	1994
SOWING THE SEEDS OF LOVE TEARS FOR FEARS	5	1989
SPACE [A] NEW MODEL ARMY	39	1991
SPACE [B] SLIPMATT	41	2003
SPACE AGE LOVE SONG A FLOCK OF SEAGULLS	34	1982
SPACE BASS SLICK	16	1979
THE SPACE BETWEEN DAVE MATTHEWS BAND	35	2001
SPACE COWBOY JAMIROQUAI	17	1994
SPACE JAM QUAD CITY DJS	57	1997
THE SPACE JUNGLE ADAMSKI	7	1990
SPACE LORD MONSTER MAGNET	45	1999
SPACE OASIS BILLIE RAY MARTIN	66	1996
SPACE ODDITY DAVID BOWIE	1	1969
SPACE RIDER SHAUN ESCOFFERY	52	2001
SPACE STATION NO. 5 SAMMY HAGAR	52	1979
SPACE STATION NO. 5 MONTROSE	71	1980
SPACE WALK LEMON JELLY	36	2002
SPACED INVADER HATIRAS FEATURING SLARTA JOHN	14	2001
SPACEHOPPER BAD COMPANY	56	2002
SPACEMAN [A] 4 NON BLONDES	53	1993
SPACEMAN [B] BABYLON ZOO	1	1996
A SPACEMAN CAME TRAVELLING CHRIS DE BURGH	40	1986
SPACER SHEILA & B. DEVOTION	18	1979
SPANISH CRAIG DAVID	8	2003
SPANISH DANCE TROUPE GORKY'S ZYGOTIC MYNCI	47	1999
SPANISH EYES AL MARTINO	5	1970
SPANISH FLEA HERB ALPERT & THE TIJUANA BRASS	3	1965
SPANISH HARLEM JIMMY JUSTICE	20	1962
SPANISH HARLEM SOUNDS INCORPORATED	35	1964
SPANISH HARLEM ARETHA FRANKLIN	14	1971
SPANISH HORSES AZTEC CAMERA	52	1992
SPANISH STROLL MINK DE VILLE	20	1977
SPANISH WINE CHRIS WHITE	37	1976
SPARE PARTS BRUCE SPRINGSTEEN	32	1988
SPARK TORI AMOS	16	1998
SPARKLE MY LIFE STORY	34	1996
SPARKLE OF MY EYES UB40	40	2001
SPARKS ROYKSOPP	41	2003
SPARKY'S DREAM TEENAGE FANCLUB	40	1995
THE SPARROW RAMBLERS (FROM THE ABBEY HEY JUNIOR SCHOOL)	11	1979
THE SPARTANS SOUNDS INCORPORATED	30	1964
SPEAK LIKE A CHILD STYLE COUNCIL	4	1983
SPEAK TO ME PRETTY BRENDA LEE	3	1962
SPEAK TO ME SOMEONE GENE	30	1997
SPEAKEASY SHED SEVEN	24	1994
SPECIAL [A] GARBAGE	15	1998
SPECIAL [B] MEW	46	2005
THE SPECIAL A.K.A. LIVE! EP SPECIAL A.K.A.	1	1980
SPECIAL BREW BAD MANNERS	3	1980
SPECIAL CASES MASSIVE ATTACK	15	2003
SPECIAL F/X WHISPERS	69	1987
SPECIAL KIND OF LOVE DINA CARROLL	16	1992
SPECIAL KIND OF LOVER NU COLOURS	38	1996
SPECIAL KIND OF SOMETHING KAVANA	13	1998
SPECIAL NEEDS PLACEBO	27	2003
SPECIAL 2003 LEE-CABRERA	45	2003
SPECIAL WAY RIVER CITY PEOPLE	44	1991
THE SPECIAL YEARS VAL DOONICAN	7	1965
SPECTACULAR GRAHAM COXON	32	2004
THE SPECTRE OF LOVE STRANGLERS	57	2006
SPEECHLESS [A] D-SIDE	9	2003
SPEECHLESS [B] MISH MASH	16	2006
SPEED BILLY IDOL	47	1994
SPEED AT THE SOUND OF LONELINESS ALABAMA 3	72	1997
SPEED (CAN YOU FEEL IT?) AZZIDO DA BASS FEATURING ROLAND CLARK	68	2002
SPEED OF SOUND COLDPLAY	2	2005
SPEED YOUR LOVE TO ME SIMPLE MINDS	20	1984
SPEEDWELL SAINT ETIENNE	54	1991
SPEEDY GONZALES PAT BOONE	2	1962
THE SPELL! FUNKY WORM	61	1988
SPELLBOUND SIOUXSIE & THE BANSHEES	22	1981
SPEND SOME TIME BRAND NEW HEAVIES FEATURING N'DEA DAVENPORT	26	1994
SPEND THE DAY URBAN COOKIE COLLECTIVE	59	1995
SPEND THE NIGHT [A] COOLNOTES	11	1985
SPEND THE NIGHT [B] DANNY J LEWIS	29	1998
SPENDING MY TIME ROXETTE	22	1991
SPICE OF LIFE MANHATTAN TRANSFER	19	1984
SPICE UP YOUR LIFE SPICE GIRLS	1	1997
SPIDER PIG SIMPSONS	23	2007
SPIDERS MOBY	50	2005
SPIDERS AND SNAKES JIM STAFFORD	14	1974
SPIDER'S WEB KATIE MELUA	52	2006
SPIDERWEBS NO DOUBT	16	1997
SPIES LIKE US PAUL McCARTNEY	13	1985
SPIKEE UNDERWORLD	63	1993
SPILLER FROM RIO (DO IT EASY) LAGUNA	40	1997
SPIN SPIN SUGAR SNEAKER PIMPS	21	1997
SPIN THAT WHEEL (TURTLES GET REAL) HI-TEK 3 FEATURING YA KID K	15	1990
SPIN THE BLACK CIRCLE PEARL JAM	10	1994
SPIN THE WHEEL BELLEFIRE	67	2004
SPINDRIFT (EP) THOUSAND YARD STARE	58	1992
SPINNIN' AND SPINNIN' SYREETA	49	1974
SPINNIN' WHEELS CRESCENT	61	2002
SPINNING CLARKSVILLE	72	2004
SPINNING AROUND KYLIE MINOGUE	1	2000
SPINNING ROCK BOOGIE HANK C. BURNETTE	21	1976
SPINNING THE WHEEL GEORGE MICHAEL	2	1996
SPIRAL SCRATCH EP BUZZCOCKS	31	1979
SPIRAL SYMPHONY SCIENTIST	74	1991
SPIRIT [A] BAUHAUS	42	1982
SPIRIT [B] WAYNE MARSHALL	58	1995
SPIRIT [C] SOUNDS OF BLACKNESS FEATURING CRAIG MACK	35	1997
SPIRIT BODY AND SOUL NOLAN SISTERS	34	1979
SPIRIT IN THE SKY NORMAN GREENBAUM	34	1970
SPIRIT IN THE SKY DOCTOR & THE MEDICS	1	1986
SPIRIT IN THE SKY GARETH GATES FEATURING THE KUMARS	1	2003
SPIRIT INSIDE SPIRITS	39	1995
THE SPIRIT IS WILLING PETER STRAKER & THE HANDS OF DR TELENY	40	1972
SPIRIT OF RADIO RUSH	13	1980
SPIRIT OF '76 ALARM	22	1986
SPIRITS (HAVING FLOWN) BEE GEES	16	1980
SPIRITS IN THE MATERIAL WORLD POLICE	12	1981
SPIRITS IN THE MATERIAL WORLD PATO BANTON WITH STING	36	1996
SPIRITUAL HIGH (STATE OF INDEPENDENCE) MOODSWINGS FEATURING CHRISSIE HYNDE	66	1991
SPIRITUAL LOVE URBAN SPECIES	35	1994
SPIRITUAL THANG ERIC BENET	62	1997
SPIRITUALIZED FINLEY QUAYE	26	2000
SPIT IN THE RAIN DEL AMITRI	21	1990
SPIT IT OUT [A] SLIPKNOT	28	2000
SPIT IT OUT [B] BRENDAN BENSON	75	2005
SPIT YOUR GAME NOTORIOUS B.I.G.	64	2006
SPITTING GAMES SNOW PATROL	23	2003
SPLIFFHEAD RAGGA TWINS	51	1990
SPLISH SPLASH BOBBY DARIN	18	1958
SPLISH SPLASH CHARLIE DRAKE	7	1958
SPOILED JOSS STONE	32	2005
SPOOKY [A] CLASSICS IV	46	1968
SPOOKY [A] ATLANTA RHYTHM SECTION	48	1979
SPOOKY [B] NEW ORDER	22	1993
SPOONMAN SOUNDGARDEN	20	1994
SPOT THE PIGEON EP GENESIS	14	1977
SPREAD A LITTLE HAPPINESS STING	16	1982
SPREAD LOVE FIGHT CLUB FEATURING LAURENT KONRAD	70	2004
SPREAD YOUR LOVE BLACK REBEL MOTORCYCLE CLUB	27	2002
SPREAD YOUR WINGS QUEEN	34	1978
SPRING IN MY STEP NU MATIC	58	1992
SPRINGTIME FOR THE WORLD BLOW MONKEYS	69	1990
SPUTNIK STYLUS TROUBLE	63	2001
SPY IN THE HOUSE OF LOVE WAS (NOT WAS)	21	1987
SPYBREAK! PROPELLERHEADS	40	1997
SPYCATCHER J MAJIK & WICKAMAN	67	2004
SQUARES BETA BAND	42	2002
SQUEEZE BOX WHO	10	1976
SQUIRT FLUKE	46	1997
SS PAPARAZZI STOCK AITKEN WATERMAN	68	1988
S-S-S-SINGLE BED FOX	4	1976
SSSST (LISTEN) JONAH	25	2000
STABBED IN THE BACK MIND OF KANE	64	1991
STACCATO'S THEME ELMER BERNSTEIN	4	1959
STACY'S MUM FOUNTAINS OF WAYNE	11	2004
STAGE ONE SPACE MANOEUVRES	25	2000
STAGES ZZ TOP	43	1986
STAGGER LEE LLOYD PRICE	7	1959
STAINSBY GIRLS CHRIS REA	26	1985
THE STAIRCASE (MYSTERY) SIOUXSIE & THE BANSHEES	24	1979
STAIRWAY OF LOVE MICHAEL HOLLIDAY	3	1958
STAIRWAY OF LOVE TERRY DENE	16	1958
STAIRWAY TO HEAVEN [A] NEIL SEDAKA	8	1960
STAIRWAY TO HEAVEN [B] FAR CORPORATION	8	1985
STAIRWAY TO HEAVEN [B] DREAD ZEPPELIN	62	1991
STAIRWAY TO HEAVEN [B] ROLF HARRIS	7	1993
STAIRWAY TO HEAVEN [B] LED ZEPPELIN	37	2007
STAKES IS HIGH DE LA SOUL	55	1996
STAKKER HUMANOID HUMANOID	17	1988
STALEMATE MAC BAND FEATURING THE McCAMPBELL BROTHERS	40	1988
STAMP! JEREMY HEALY & AMOS	11	1996
STAN EMINEM	1	2000
STAN BOWLES OTHERS	36	2004
STAND [A] R.E.M.	48	1989
STAND [B] POISON	25	1993
STAND ABOVE ME ORCHESTRAL MANOEUVRES IN THE DARK	21	1993
STAND AND DELIVER ADAM & THE ANTS	1	1981
STAND AND FIGHT PACK FEATURING NIGEL BENN	61	1990
STAND BACK LINUS LOVES FEATURING SAM OBERNIK	31	2003
STAND BY ROMAN HOLIDAY	61	1983
STAND BY LOVE SIMPLE MINDS	13	1991
STAND BY ME [A] BEN E. KING	1	1961
STAND BY ME [A] KENNY LYNCH	39	1964
STAND BY ME [A] JOHN LENNON	30	1975
STAND BY ME [A] 4 THE CAUSE	12	1998

	Peak Position	Year of Entry
STAND BY ME [B] OASIS	2	1997
STAND BY ME [C] SHAYNE WARD	14	2006
STAND BY MY WOMAN LENNY KRAVITZ	55	1991
STAND BY YOUR MAN TAMMY WYNETTE	1	1975
STAND CLEAR ADAM F FEATURING M.O.P.	43	2001
STAND DOWN MARGARET (DUB) BEAT	22	1980
STAND INSIDE YOUR LOVE SMASHING PUMPKINS	23	2000
STAND OR FALL FIXX	54	1982
STAND TOUGH POINT BREAK	7	2000
STAND UP [A] DAVID LEE ROTH	72	1988
STAND UP [B] LOLEATTA HOLLOWAY	68	1994
STAND UP [C] THUNDER	23	1995
STAND UP [D] LOVE TRIBE	23	1996
STAND UP [E] LUDACRIS	14	2003
STAND UP [F] DEAD 60'S	54	2007
STAND UP FOR YOUR LOVE RIGHTS YAZZ	2	1988
STAND UP JAMROCK BOB MARLEY & THE WAILERS	56	2005
STAND UP TALL DIZZEE RASCAL	10	2004
STANDING SILVIO ECOMO	70	2000
STANDING HERE CREATURES	53	1989
STANDING HERE ALL ALONE MICHELLE	69	1996
STANDING IN THE NEED OF LOVE RIVER CITY PEOPLE	36	1992
STANDING IN THE ROAD BLACKFOOT SUE	4	1972
STANDING IN THE SHADOW WHITESNAKE	62	1984
STANDING IN THE SHADOWS OF LOVE FOUR TOPS	6	1967
STANDING IN THE WAY OF CONTROL GOSSIP	7	2006
STANDING ON MY OWN AGAIN GRAHAM COXON	20	2006
STANDING ON THE CORNER FOUR LADS	34	1960
STANDING ON THE CORNER KING BROTHERS	4	1960
STANDING ON THE INSIDE NEIL SEDAKA	26	1973
STANDING ON THE TOP (PART 1) TEMPTATIONS FEATURING RICK JAMES	53	1982
STANDING ON THE VERGE (OF GETTING IT ON) PLATINUM HOOK	72	1978
STANDING OUTSIDE A BROKEN PHONE BOOTH WITH MONEY IN MY HAND PRIMITIVE RADIO GODS	74	1996
STANDING OUTSIDE THE FIRE GARTH BROOKS	28	1994
STANDING TOGETHER - WORLD CUP 2006 SIGNAL 1 & SIGNAL 2	67	2006
STANDING WATCHING CHERRYFALLS	64	2004
STANLEY (HERE I AM) AIRHEADZ	36	2001
STAN'S WORLD CUP SONG STAN BOARDMAN	15	2006
STAR [A] STEALERS WHEEL	25	1974
STAR [B] EARTH, WIND & FIRE	16	1979
STAR [C] NAZARETH	54	1979
STAR [D] KIKI DEE	13	1981
STAR [E] SECOND IMAGE	60	1982
STAR [F] ERASURE	11	1990
STAR [G] D:REAM	26	1993
STAR [H] CULT	65	1995
STAR [I] BRYAN ADAMS	13	1996
STAR [J] PRIMAL SCREAM	16	1997
THE STAR AND THE WISEMAN LADYSMITH BLACK MAMBAZO	63	1998
STAR CATCHING GIRL BROTHER BROWN FEATURING FRANK'EE	51	2001
STAR CHASERS 4 HERO	41	1998
STAR FLEET BRIAN MAY & FRIENDS	65	1983
STAR GIRL McFLY	1	2006
STAR GUITAR CHEMICAL BROTHERS	8	2002
STAR ON A TV SHOW STYLISTICS	12	1975
STAR PEOPLE '97 GEORGE MICHAEL	2	1997
STAR SIGN TEENAGE FANCLUB	44	1991
STAR 69 FATBOY SLIM	10	2001
STAR TO FALL CABIN CREW	4	2005
STAR TREKKIN' FIRM	1	1987
STAR WARS THEME - CANTINA BAND MECO	7	1977
STARBRIGHT JOHNNY MATHIS	47	1960
STARBUCKS A	20	2002
STARCHILD LEVEL 42	47	1981
STARCROSSED ASH	22	2004
STARDATE 1990 DAN REED NETWORK	39	1990
STARDUST [A] BILLY WARD	13	1957
STARDUST [A] NAT 'KING' COLE	24	1957
STARDUST [B] DAVID ESSEX	7	1974
STARDUST [B] MARTIN L GORE	44	2003
STARDUST [C] MENSWEAR	16	1995
STARGAZER SIOUXSIE & THE BANSHEES	64	1995
STARING AT THE RUDE BOIS GALLOWS	31	2007
STARING AT THE RUDE BOYS RUTS	22	1980
STARING AT THE SUN [A] U2	3	1997
STARING AT THE SUN [B] ROOSTER	5	2005
STARLIGHT MUSE	13	2006
STARLIGHT [A] DESIDERIO	57	2000
STARLIGHT [B] SUPERMEN LOVERS FEATURING MANI HOFFMAN	2	2001
STARLITE YOUNG HEART ATTACK	69	2004
STARLOVERS GUS GUS	62	1999
STARMAKER KIDS FROM 'FAME'	3	1982
STARMAN DAVID BOWIE	10	1972
STARMAN CULTURE CLUB	7	1999
STARRY EYED MICHAEL HOLLIDAY	1	1960
STARRY EYED SURPRISE PAUL OAKENFOLD	6	2002
A STARRY NIGHT JOY STRINGS	35	1964
STARS [A] SYLVESTER	47	1979
STARS [A] FELIX	29	1993
STARS [B] HEAR 'N AID	26	1986
STARS [C] SIMPLY RED	8	1991
STARS [D] CHINA BLACK	19	1994
STARS [E] DUBSTAR	15	1995
STARS [F] ROXETTE	56	1999
STARS [G] MORJAC FEATURING RAZ CONWAY	38	2003
STARS AND STRIPES FOREVER MR ACKER BILK & HIS PARAMOUNT JAZZ BAND	22	1961
STARS ARE BLIND PARIS	5	2006
STARS ON 45 STARSOUND	2	1981
STARS ON 45 VOLUME 2 STARSOUND	2	1981
STARS ON 45 VOLUME 3 STARSOUND	17	1981
STARS ON STEVIE STARSOUND	14	1982
STARS OVER 45 CHAS & DAVE	21	1981
STARS OVER CLOUGHANOVER SAW DOCTORS	69	2005
STARS SHINE IN YOUR EYES RONNIE HILTON	13	1955
STARSHIP ICEBERG SLIMM FEATURING COREE	73	2004
STARSHIP TROOPERS UNITED CITIZEN FEDERATION FEATURING SARAH BRIGHTMAN	58	1998
STARSKY & HUTCH – THE THEME ANDY G'S STARSKY & HUTCH ALL STARS	51	1998
START JAM	1	1980
START A BRAND NEW LIFE (SAVE ME) BASSHEADS	49	1993
START AGAIN [A] TEENAGE FANCLUB	54	1997
START AGAIN [B] MONTROSE AVENUE	59	1998
START CHOPPIN DINOSAUR Jr.	20	1993
START ME UP [A] ROLLING STONES	7	1981
START ME UP [B] SALT-N-PEPA	39	1992
START MOVIN' SAL MINEO	16	1957
START MOVIN' TERRY DENE	15	1957
START TALKING LOVE MAGNUM	22	1988
START THE COMMOTION WISEGUYS	47	1998
STARTING AGAIN SECOND IMAGE	65	1985
STARTING OVER AGAIN NATALIE COLE	56	1989
STARTING TOGETHER SU POLLARD	2	1986
STARTOUCHERS DIGITAL ORGASM	31	1992
STARTRAX CLUB DISCO STARTRAX	18	1981
STARTURN ON 45 (PINTS) STARTURN ON 45 (PINTS)	45	1981
STARVATION STARVATION	33	1985
STARZ IN THEIR EYES JUST JACK	2	2007
STATE OF INDEPENDENCE DONNA SUMMER	14	1982
STATE OF INDEPENDENCE JON & VANGELIS	67	1984
STATE OF LOVE IMAGINATION	67	1984
STATE OF MIND [A] FISH	32	1989
STATE OF MIND [B] HOLLY VALANCE	8	2003
STATE OF SHOCK JACKSONS, LEAD VOCALS MICK JAGGER & MICHAEL JACKSON	14	1984
STATE OF THE NATION NEW ORDER	30	1986
STATUESQUE SLEEPER	17	1996
STATUS ROCK HEADBANGERS	60	1981
STAY [A] MAURICE WILLIAMS & THE ZODIACS	14	1961
STAY [A] HOLLIES	8	1963
STAY [A] JACKSON BROWNE	12	1978
STAY [A] DREAMHOUSE	62	1995
STAY [B] BARRY MANILOW FEATURING KEVIN DiSIMONE & JAMES JOLIS	23	1982
STAY [C] SHAKESPEARS SISTER	1	1992
STAY [D] KENNY THOMAS	22	1993
STAY [E] ETERNAL	4	1993
STAY [F] 60FT DOLLS	48	1996
STAY [G] 18 WHEELER	59	1997
STAY [H] SASH! FEATURING LA TREC	2	1997
STAY [I] BERNARD BUTLER	12	1998
STAY [J] MICA PARIS	40	1998
STAY [K] STEPHEN GATELY	13	2001
STAY [L] ROB TISSERA & VINYLGROOVER	61	2004
STAY [M] SIMPLY RED	36	2007
STAY A LITTLE WHILE, CHILD LOOSE ENDS	52	1986
STAY A WHILE RAKIM	53	1998
STAY ANOTHER DAY EAST 17	1	1994
STAY AWAY BABY JANE CHESNEY HAWKES	74	2002
STAY AWAY FROM ME STAR SPANGLES	52	2003
STAY AWHILE DUSTY SPRINGFIELD	13	1964
STAY BEAUTIFUL MANIC STREET PREACHERS	40	1991
STAY (FARAWAY, SO CLOSE) U2	4	1993
STAY FLY THREE 6 MAFIA	33	2006
STAY FOREVER JOEY LAWRENCE	41	1993
STAY GOLD DEEP DISH	41	1996
STAY (I MISSED YOU) LISA LOEB & NINE STORIES	6	1994
STAY IN THE SUN KENICKIE	43	1998
STAY ON THESE ROADS A-HA	5	1988
STAY OUT OF MY LIFE FIVE STAR	9	1987
STAY RIGHT HERE AKIN	60	1997
STAY THE NIGHT GHOSTS	25	2007
STAY THE SAME [A] BENT	59	2003
STAY THE SAME [B] GABRIELLE	20	2004
STAY THIS WAY BRAND NEW HEAVIES FEATURING N'DEA DAVENPORT	40	1992
STAY TOGETHER [A] SUEDE	3	1994
STAY TOGETHER [B] BARBARA TUCKER	46	1995
STAY (TONIGHT) ISHA-D	28	1995
STAY WHERE YOU ARE AMBULANCE LTD	67	2005
STAY WITH ME [A] FACES	6	1972
STAY WITH ME [B] BLUE MINK	11	1972
STAY WITH ME [C] EIGHTH WONDER	65	1985
STAY WITH ME [D] MISSION	30	1986
STAY WITH ME [E] JOHN O'KANE	41	1992
STAY WITH ME [F] ERASURE	15	1995
STAY WITH ME [G] ULTRA HIGH	36	1995
STAY WITH ME [H] RICHIE RICH & ESERA TUAOLO	58	1997
STAY WITH ME [I] ANGELIC	36	2001
STAY WITH ME BABY WALKER BROTHERS	26	1967
STAY WITH ME BABY DAVID ESSEX	45	1978
STAY WITH ME BABY RUBY TURNER	39	1994
STAY WITH ME (BABY) REBECCA WHEATLEY	10	2000
STAY WITH ME HEARTACHE WET WET WET	30	1990
STAY WITH ME TILL DAWN JUDIE TZUKE	16	1979

	Peak Position	Year of Entry
STAY WITH ME TILL DAWN LUCID	25	1999
STAY WITH ME TONIGHT [A] JEFFREY OSBORNE	18	1984
STAY WITH ME TONIGHT [B] HUMAN LEAGUE	40	1996
STAY WITH YOU [A] LEMON JELLY	31	2004
STAY WITH YOU [B] GOO GOO DOLLS	39	2006
STAY YOUNG ULTRASOUND	30	1998
STAYIN' ALIVE BEE GEES	4	1978
STAYIN' ALIVE RICHARD ACE	66	1978
STAYIN' ALIVE N-TRANCE FEATURING RICARDO DA FORCE	2	1995
STAYING ALIVE 95 FEVER FEATURING TIPPA IRIE	48	1995
STAYING FAT BLOC PARTY	51	2004
STAYING IN BOBBY VEE	4	1961
STAYING OUT FOR THE SUMMER DODGY	19	1994
STAYING TOGETHER DEBBIE GIBSON	53	1988
STEADY AS SHE GOES RACONTEURS	4	2006
STEAL MY SUNSHINE LEN	8	1999
STEAL YOUR FIRE GUN	24	1992
STEAL YOUR LOVE AWAY GEMINI	37	1996
STEALTH WAY OUT WEST FEATURING KIRSTY HAWKSHAW	67	2002
STEAM [A] PETER GABRIEL	10	1993
STEAM [B] EAST 17	7	1994
STEAMY WINDOWS TINA TURNER	13	1990
STEEL BARS MICHAEL BOLTON	17	1992
A STEEL GUITAR AND A GLASS OF WINE PAUL ANKA	41	1962
STEELO 702	41	1996
STEM DJ SHADOW	74	1996
STEP BACK IN TIME KYLIE MINOGUE	4	1990
STEP BY STEP [A] STEVE PERRY	41	1960
STEP BY STEP [B] JOE SIMON	14	1973
STEP BY STEP [C] TAFFY	59	1987
STEP BY STEP [D] NEW KIDS ON THE BLOCK	2	1990
STEP BY STEP [E] WHITNEY HOUSTON	13	1996
STEP IN THE NAME OF LOVE R KELLY	14	2003
A STEP IN THE RIGHT DIRECTION TRUTH	32	1983
STEP INSIDE LOVE CILLA BLACK	8	1968
STEP INTO A DREAM WHITE PLAINS	21	1973
STEP INTO A WORLD (RAPTURE'S DELIGHT) KRS ONE	24	1997
STEP INTO CHRISTMAS ELTON JOHN	24	1973
STEP INTO MY OFFICE BABY BELLE & SEBASTIAN	32	2003
STEP INTO MY WORLD HURRICANE #1	19	1997
STEP INTO THE BREEZE SPIRITUALIZED	75	1990
STEP IT UP STEREO MC'S	12	1992
STEP OFF JUNIOR GISCOMBE	63	1990
STEP OFF (PART 1) GRANDMASTER MELLE MEL & THE FURIOUS FIVE	8	1984
STEP ON HAPPY MONDAYS	5	1990
STEP ON MY OLD SIZE NINES STEREOPHONICS	16	2001
STEP RIGHT UP JAKI GRAHAM	15	1986
STEP TO ME (DO ME) MANTRONIX	59	1991
STEPPIN' OUT [A] KOOL & THE GANG	12	1981
STEPPIN' OUT [B] JOE JACKSON	6	1983
STEPPIN STONES DJ ZINC	62	2004
STEPPING STONE FARM	58	1990
STEPPING STONE PJ & DUNCAN	11	1996
STEP-TWO-THREE-FOUR STRICT INSTRUCTOR	49	1998
STEREO PAVEMENT	48	1997
STEREOTYPE SPECIALS	6	1980
STEREOTYPES BLUR	7	1996
STEVE MCQUEEN SHERYL CROW	44	2002
STEWBALL LONNIE DONEGAN	27	1956
STICK IT OUT RIGHT SAID FRED & FRIENDS	4	1993
STICK TO THE STATUS QUO CAST OF HIGH SCHOOL MUSICAL	74	2007
STICKS AND STONES CUD	68	1994
STICKWITU PUSSYCAT DOLLS	1	2005
STICKY WEDDING PRESENT	17	1992
STIFF UPPER LIP AC/DC	65	2000
STILL [A] KARL DENVER	13	1963
STILL [A] KEN DODD	35	1963
STILL [B] COMMODORES	4	1979
STILL [C] MACY GRAY	18	2000
STILL A FRIEND OF MINE INCOGNITO	47	1993
STILL A THRILL SYBIL	55	1997
STILL BE LOVIN' YOU DAMAGE	11	2001
STILL BELIEVE SHOLA AMA	26	1999
STILL DRE DR DRE FEATURING SNOOP DOGGY DOGG	6	2000
STILL FEEL THE RAIN STEX	63	1991
STILL FIGURING OUT ELLIOT MINOR	17	2008
STILL GOT THE BLUES (FOR YOU) GARY MOORE	31	1990
STILL HAVEN'T FOUND WHAT I'M LOOKING FOR CHIMES	6	1990
STILL I'M SAD YARDBIRDS	3	1965
STILL IN LOVE [A] GO WEST	43	1993
STILL IN LOVE [B] LIONEL RICHIE	66	1996
STILL IN LOVE SONG STILLS	45	2004
A STILL LIFE LESS THAN JAKE	61	2006
STILL OF THE NIGHT WHITESNAKE	16	1987
STILL ON YOUR SIDE BBMAK	8	2001
STILL THE SAME SLADE	73	1987
STILL TOO YOUNG TO REMEMBER IT BITES	60	1989
STILL WAITING SUM 41	16	2002
STILL WATER (LOVE) FOUR TOPS	10	1970
STILL WATERS (RUN DEEP) BEE GEES	18	1997
STILLNESS IN TIME JAMIROQUAI	9	1995
STILLNESS OF HEART LENNY KRAVITZ	44	2002
THE STING RAGTIMERS	31	1974
STING ME BLACK CROWES	42	1992
STING ME RED (YOU THINK YOU'RE SO) WHO DA FUNK FEATURING TERRA DEVA	32	2003
STINGRAY SHADOWS	19	1965
THE STINGRAY MEGAMIX FAB FEATURING AQUA MARINA	66	1990
STINKIN THINKIN HAPPY MONDAYS	31	1992
STIR IT UP JOHNNY NASH	13	1972
STITCHES DYKEENIES	61	2007
STOLE KELLY ROWLAND	2	2002
STOLEN JAY SEAN	4	2004
STOLEN CAR BETH ORTON	34	1999
STOLEN CAR (TAKE ME DANCING) STING	60	2004
STOMP [A] BROTHERS JOHNSON	6	1980
STOMP [A] QUINCY JONES FEATURING MELLE MEL, COOLIO, YO-YO, SHAQUILLE O'NEAL & THE LUNIZ	28	1996
STOMP [B] GOD'S PROPERTY	60	1997
STOMP [C] STEPS	1	2000
STONE BY STONE CATATONIA	19	2001
STONE COLD RAINBOW	34	1982
STONE LOVE KOOL & THE GANG	45	1987
STONED IN LOVE CHICANE FEATURING TOM JONES	7	2006
STONED LOVE SUPREMES	3	1971
STONEY END BARBRA STREISAND	27	1971
STONEY GROUND GUYS & DOLLS	38	1976
THE STONK HALE & PACE & THE STONKERS	1	1991
STOOD ON GOLD GORKY'S ZYGOTIC MYNCI	65	2001
STOOD UP RICKY NELSON	27	1958
STOOL PIGEON KID CREOLE & THE COCONUTS	7	1982
STOP [A] SAM BROWN	4	1988
STOP [B] SPICE GIRLS	2	1998
STOP [C] BLACK REBEL MOTORCYCLE CLUB	19	2003
STOP [D] JAMELIA	9	2004
STOP AND GO DAVID GRANT	19	1983
STOP AND STARE ONE REPUBLIC	4	2008
STOP BAJON...PRIMAVERA TULLIO DE PISCOPO	58	1987
STOP BREAKING MY HEART INNER CIRCLE	50	1979
STOP BY RAHSAAN PATTERSON	50	1997
STOP CRYING YOUR HEART OUT OASIS	2	2002
STOP DRAGGIN' MY HEART AROUND STEVIE NICKS WITH TOM PETTY & THE HEARTBREAKERS	50	1981
STOP (EP) MEGA CITY FOUR	36	1992
STOP FEELING SORRY FOR YOURSELF ADAM FAITH	23	1965
STOP HER ON SIGHT (SOS) EDWIN STARR	11	1966
STOP IN THE NAME OF LOVE SUPREMES	7	1965
STOP KNOCKING THE WALLS DOWN RICKY	32	2005
STOP LISTENING TANITA TIKARAM	67	1998
STOP LIVING THE LIE DAVID SNEDDON	1	2003
STOP LOOK AND LISTEN [A] WAYNE FONTANA & THE MINDBENDERS	37	1964
STOP LOOK AND LISTEN [B] DONNA SUMMER	57	1984
STOP LOOK LISTEN (TO YOUR HEART) DIANA ROSS & MARVIN GAYE	25	1974
STOP LOVING ME LOVING YOU DARYL HALL	30	1994
STOP ME MARK RONSON FEATURING DANIEL MERRIWEATHER	2	2007
STOP ME (IF YOU'VE HEARD IT ALL BEFORE) BILLY OCEAN	12	1976
STOP MY HEAD EVAN DANDO	38	2003
STOP PLAYING WITH MY MIND BARBARA TUCKER FEATURING DARYL D'BONNEAU	17	2000
STOP SIGN ABS	10	2003
STOP STARTING TO START STOPPING (EP) D.O.P.	58	1996
STOP STOP STOP HOLLIES	2	1966
STOP THAT GIRL CHRIS ANDREWS	36	1966
STOP THE CAVALRY JONA LEWIE	3	1980
STOP THE ROCK APOLLO FOUR FORTY	10	1999
STOP THE VIOLENCE BOOGIE DOWN PRODUCTIONS	69	1988
STOP THE WAR NOW EDWIN STARR	33	1971
STOP THE WORLD EXTREME	22	1992
STOP THIS CRAZY THING COLDCUT FEATURING JUNIOR REID & THE AHEAD OF OUR TIME ORCHESTRA	21	1988
STOP TO LOVE LUTHER VANDROSS	24	1987
STOP YOUR CRYING SPIRITUALIZED	18	2001
STOP YOUR SOBBING PRETENDERS	34	1979
STORIES [A] IZIT	52	1989
STORIES [B] THERAPY?	14	1995
STORIES [C] HOLIDAY PLAN	58	2004
STORIES OF JOHNNY MARC ALMOND	23	1985
THE STORM [A] WORLD OF TWIST	42	1990
STORM [B] SPACE KITTENS	58	1996
STORM [C] VANESSA-MAE	54	1997
STORM [D] STORM	32	1998
STORM ANIMAL STORM	21	2000
STORM IN A TEACUP FORTUNES	7	1972
THE STORM IS OVER R KELLY	18	2001
STORMS IN AFRICA (PART II) ENYA	41	1989
STORMTROOPER IN DRAG PAUL GARDINER	49	1981
STORMY IN THE NORTHA KARMA IN THE SOUTH WILDHEARTS	17	2003
STORMY WEATHER ECHO & THE BUNNYMEN	55	2005
THE STORY OF THE BLUES [A] WAH!	3	1983
THE STORY OF THE BLUES [B] GARY MOORE	40	1992
THE STORY OF LOVE OTT	11	1998
STORY OF MY LIFE [A] GARY MILLER	14	1958
THE STORY OF MY LIFE [A] ALMA COGAN	25	1958
THE STORY OF MY LIFE [A] DAVE KING	20	1958
THE STORY OF MY LIFE [A] MICHAEL HOLLIDAY	1	1958
THE STORY OF MY LIFE [B] KRISTIAN LEONTIOU	9	2004
STORY OF MY LOVE CONWAY TWITTY	30	1959
STORY OF TINA RONNIE HARRIS	12	1954

	Peak Position	Year of Entry
THE STORY OF TINA AL MARTINO	10	1954
STOWAWAY BARBARA LYON	12	1955
STRAIGHT AHEAD [A] KOOL & THE GANG	15	1983
STRAIGHT AHEAD [B] TUBE & BERGER FEATURING CHRISSIE HYNDE	29	2004
STRAIGHT AT YER HEAD LIONROCK	33	1996
STRAIGHT FROM THE HEART [A] BRYAN ADAMS	51	1986
STRAIGHT FROM THE HEART [B] DOOLALLY	9	1998
STRAIGHT LINES NEW MUSIK	53	1979
STRAIGHT OUT OF THE JUNGLE JUNGLE BROTHERS	72	1989
STRAIGHT TO HELL CLASH	17	1982
STRAIGHT TO MY FEET HAMMER FEATURING DEION SAUNDERS	57	1995
STRAIGHT TO THE HEART REAL THING	71	1986
STRAIGHT TO YOU NICK CAVE & THE BAD SEEDS	68	1992
STRAIGHT UP [A] PAULA ABDUL	3	1989
STRAIGHT UP [B] CHANTE MOORE	11	2001
STRAIGHT UP NO BENDS BRIAN HARVEY	26	2001
STRAIGHTEN OUT STRANGLERS	9	1977
STRANDED [A] HEART	60	1990
STRANDED [B] DEEP DISH	60	1997
STRANDED [C] LUTRICIA McNEAL	3	1998
STRANGE WET WET WET	13	1997
STRANGE AND BEAUTIFUL AQUALUNG	7	2002
STRANGE BAND FAMILY	11	1970
STRANGE BREW CREAM	17	1967
STRANGE CURRENCIES R.E.M.	9	1995
STRANGE GLUE CATATONIA	11	1998
STRANGE KIND OF LOVE LOVE & MONEY	45	1989
STRANGE KIND OF WOMAN DEEP PURPLE	8	1971
STRANGE LADY IN TOWN FRANKIE LAINE	6	1955
STRANGE LITTLE GIRL [A] SAD CAFE	32	1980
STRANGE LITTLE GIRL [B] STRANGLERS	7	1982
STRANGE LOVE PHIXX	19	2005
STRANGE MAGIC ELECTRIC LIGHT ORCHESTRA	38	1976
STRANGE RELATIONSHIP DARREN HAYES	15	2002
STRANGE TOWN JAM	15	1979
STRANGE WAY ALL ABOUT EVE	51	1991
STRANGE WORLD [A] KE	73	1996
STRANGE WORLD [B] PUSH	21	2001
STRANGELOVE DEPECHE MODE	16	1987
THE STRANGER [A] SHADOWS	5	1960
STRANGER [B] SHAKATAK	43	1982
STRANGER IN A STRANGE LAND IRON MAIDEN	22	1986
STRANGER IN MOSCOW MICHAEL JACKSON	4	1996
STRANGER IN PARADISE BING CROSBY	17	1955
STRANGER IN PARADISE DON CORNELL	19	1955
STRANGER IN PARADISE EDDIE CALVERT	14	1955
STRANGER IN PARADISE FOUR ACES	6	1955
STRANGER IN PARADISE TONY BENNETT	1	1955
STRANGER IN PARADISE TONY MARTIN	6	1955
STRANGER IN TOWN DEL SHANNON	40	1965
A STRANGER ON HOME GROUND FAITH BROTHERS	69	1985
STRANGER ON THE SHORE MR ACKER BILK WITH THE LEON YOUNG STRING CHORALE	2	1961
STRANGER ON THE SHORE ANDY WILLIAMS	30	1962
STRANGER ON THE SHORE OF LOVE STEVIE WONDER	55	1987
STRANGER THINGS ABC	57	1997
STRANGERS IN OUR TOWN SPEAR OF DESTINY	49	1987
STRANGERS IN THE NIGHT FRANK SINATRA	1	1966
STRANGERS WHEN WE MEET DAVID BOWIE	39	1995
THE STRANGEST PARTY (THESE ARE THE TIMES) INXS	15	1994
THE STRANGEST THING '97 GEORGE MICHAEL	2	1997
STRANGLEHOLD U.K. SUBS	26	1979
STRASBOURG RAKES	57	2004
STRATEGIC HAMLETS URUSEI YATSURA	38	1997
STRAW DOGS STIFF LITTLE FINGERS	44	1979
STRAWBERRY NICOLA RENEE	55	1998
STRAWBERRY BLONDE (THE BAND PLAYED ON) FRANK D'RONE	24	1960
STRAWBERRY FAIR ANTHONY NEWLEY	3	1960
STRAWBERRY FIELDS FOREVER BEATLES	32	1967
STRAWBERRY FIELDS FOREVER CANDY FLIP	3	1990
STRAWBERRY KISSES NIKKI WEBSTER	64	2002
STRAWBERRY LETTER 23 BROTHERS JOHNSON	35	1977
STRAY CAT STRUT STRAY CATS	11	1981
THE STREAK RAY STEVENS	1	1974
STREAMLINE TRAIN VIPERS SKIFFLE GROUP	23	1957
STREET CAFÉ ICEHOUSE	62	1983
A STREET CALLED HOPE GENE PITNEY	37	1970
STREET DANCE BREAK MACHINE	3	1984
STREET DREAMS NAS	12	1997
STREET FIGHTER II WORLD WARRIOR	70	1994
STREET FIGHTING MAN ROLLING STONES	21	1971
STREET GANG A.R.E. WEAPONS	72	2001
STREET LIFE [A] ROXY MUSIC	9	1973
STREET LIFE [B] CRUSADERS	5	1979
STREET LIFE [C] BEENIE MAN	13	2003
STREET OF DREAMS RAINBOW	52	1983
STREET SPIRIT (FADE OUT) RADIOHEAD	5	1996
STREET TUFF DOUBLE TROUBLE & THE REBEL MC	3	1989
STREETCAR FUNERAL FOR A FRIEND	15	2005
STREETPLAYER (MECHANIK) FASHION	46	1982
THE STREETS WC FEATURING SNOOP DOGG & NATE DOGG	48	2003
STREETS OF LONDON RALPH McTELL	2	1974
STREETS OF LONDON ANTI-NOWHERE LEAGUE	48	1982
STREETS OF LOVE ROLLING STONES	15	2005
STREETS OF PHILADELPHIA BRUCE SPRINGSTEEN	2	1994
STREETWALKIN' SHAKATAK	38	1982
STRENGTH ALARM	40	1985
STRENGTH TO STRENGTH HUE & CRY	46	1987
STRESS BLAGGERS I.T.A.	56	1993
STRESSED OUT A TRIBE CALLED QUEST FEATURING FAITH EVANS & RAPHAEL SAADIQ	33	1996
STRETCHIN' OUT GAYLE ADAMS	64	1980
STRICT MACHINE GOLDFRAPP	20	2003
STRICTLY BUSINESS MANTRONIK VS EPMD	43	1998
STRICTLY ELVIS EP ELVIS PRESLEY	26	1960
STRICTLY HARDCORE GOLD BLADE	64	1997
STRICTLY SOCIAL RONI SIZE	70	2004
STRIKE IT DUB WAR	70	1995
STRIKE IT UP BLACK BOX	16	1991
STRIKE ME PINK DEBORAH HARRY	46	1993
STRINGS KRISTIN HERSH	60	1994
STRINGS FOR YASMIN TIN TIN OUT	31	1997
STRINGS OF LIFE RHYTHIM IS RHYTHIM	74	1989
STRINGS OF LIFE PLANK 15	60	2002
STRINGS OF LIFE (STRONGER ON MY OWN) SOUL CENTRAL FEATURING KATHY BROWN	6	2005
STRIP [A] ADAM ANT	41	1983
STRIP [B] PINK GREASE	36	2005
STRIPPED DEPECHE MODE	15	1986
THE STROKE BILLY SQUIER	52	1981
STROKE YOU UP CHANGING FACES	43	1994
STROLLIN' PRINCE & THE NEW POWER GENERATION	4	1992
STROLLIN' ON MAXI PRIEST	32	1986
STRONG [A] LIQUID	15	1998
STRONG [B] ROBBIE WILLIAMS	4	1999
STRONG ARM OF THE LAW SAXON	63	1980
STRONG AS STEEL FIVE STAR	16	1987
STRONG ENOUGH [A] SHERYL CROW	33	1995
STRONG ENOUGH [B] CHER	5	1999
STRONG IN LOVE CHICANE FEATURING MASON	32	1998
STRONG LOVE SPENCER DAVIS GROUP	44	1965
STRONGER KANYE WEST	1	2007
STRONGER [A] GARY BARLOW	16	1999
STRONGER [B] BRITNEY SPEARS	7	2000
STRONGER [C] SUGABABES	7	2002
STRONGER THAN ME AMY WINEHOUSE	71	2003
STRONGER THAN THAT CLIFF RICHARD	14	1990
STRONGER TOGETHER [A] SHANNON	46	1985
STRONGER TOGETHER [B] SYBIL	41	1993
STRUMMIN' CHAS & DAVE WITH ROCKNEY	52	1978
STRUMPET MY LIFE STORY	27	1997
STRUNG OUT [A] WENDY & LISA	44	1990
STRUNG OUT [B] DOT ALLISON	67	2002
STRUT YOUR FUNKY STUFF FRANTIQUE	10	1979
THE STRUTT BAMBOO	36	1998
STUCK [A] NED'S ATOMIC DUSTBIN	64	1995
STUCK [B] STACIE ORRICO	9	2003
STUCK IN A GROOVE PURETONE	26	2003
STUCK IN A MOMENT YOU CAN'T GET OUT OF U2	2	2001
STUCK IN THE MIDDLE [A] DANNI'ELLE GAHA	68	1992
STUCK IN THE MIDDLE [B] CLEA	23	2004
STUCK IN THE MIDDLE WITH YOU STEALERS WHEEL	8	1973
STUCK IN THE MIDDLE WITH YOU LOUISE	4	2001
STUCK ON U [A] PJ & DUNCAN	12	1995
STUCK ON YOU [B] ELVIS PRESLEY	3	1960
STUCK ON YOU [C] LIONEL RICHIE	12	1984
STUCK ON YOU [C] TREVOR WALTERS	9	1984
STUCK WITH ME GREEN DAY	24	1996
STUCK WITH YOU HUEY LEWIS & THE NEWS	12	1986
STUFF LIKE THAT QUINCY JONES	34	1978
STUMBLE AND FALL RAZORLIGHT	27	2004
STUMBLIN' IN SUZI QUATRO & CHRIS NORMAN	41	1978
STUNT 101 G UNIT	25	2003
STUNTMAN ALFIE	51	2003
STUPID CUPID CONNIE FRANCIS	1	1958
STUPID GIRL GARBAGE	4	1996
STUPID GIRLS P!NK	4	2006
STUPID KID [A] SULTANS OF PING FC	67	1992
STUPID KID [B] ALKALINE TRIO	53	2002
THE STUPID ONES BLUESKINS	61	2004
STUPID QUESTION NEW MODEL ARMY	31	1989
STUPID THING AIMEE MANN	47	1993
STUPIDISCO JUNIOR JACK	26	2004
STUTTER JOE FEATURING MYSTIKAL	7	2001
STUTTER RAP (NO SLEEP 'TIL BEDTIME) MORRIS MINOR & THE MAJORS	4	1988
STYLE [A] ORBITAL	13	1999
STYLE [B] MIS-TEEQ	13	2003
SUB-CULTURE NEW ORDER	63	1985
SUBDIVISIONS RUSH	53	1982
SUBHUMAN GARBAGE	50	1995
SUBMARINES DJ FRESH	73	2004
SUBPLATES VOLUME 1 (EP) VARIOUS ARTISTS (EP'S & LPS)	69	1993
SUBSTITUTE [A] WHO	5	1966
SUBSTITUTE [B] CLOUT	2	1978
SUBSTITUTE [C] LIQUID GOLD	8	1980
SUBTERRANEAN HOMESICK BLUES BOB DYLAN	9	1965
SUBURBAN KNIGHTS HARD-FI	7	2007
SUBURBAN ROCK 'N' ROLL SPACE	67	2004
SUBURBIA PET SHOP BOYS	8	1986
SUCCESS [A] SIGUE SIGUE SPUTNIK	31	1988
SUCCESS [B] DANNII MINOGUE	11	1991

	Peak Position	Year of Entry
SUCCESS HAS MADE A FAILURE OF OUR HOME SINEAD O'CONNOR	18	1992
SUCH A FEELING BIZARRE INC	13	1991
SUCH A FOOL 22-20'S	29	2005
SUCH A GOOD FEELIN' MISS BEHAVIN'	62	2002
SUCH A GOOD FEELING BROTHERS IN RHYTHM	64	1991
SUCH A NIGHT JOHNNIE RAY	1	1954
SUCH A NIGHT ELVIS PRESLEY	13	1964
SUCH A PHANTASY TIME FREQUENCY	25	1994
SUCH A SHAME TALK TALK	49	1984
SUCK YOU DRY MUDHONEY	65	1992
SUCKER DJ DIMPLES D	17	1990
SUCKERPUNCH WILDHEARTS	38	1994
SUCU SUCU JOE LOSS ORCHESTRA	48	1961
SUCU SUCU LAURIE JOHNSON ORCHESTRA	9	1961
SUCU SUCU NINA & FREDERICK	23	1961
SUCU SUCU PING PING & AL VERLANE	41	1961
SUCU SUCU TED HEATH	36	1961
SUDDENLY [A] OLIVIA NEWTON-JOHN & CLIFF RICHARD	15	1980
SUDDENLY [B] BILLY OCEAN	4	1985
SUDDENLY [C] ANGRY ANDERSON	3	1988
SUDDENLY [D] SEAN MAGUIRE	18	1995
SUDDENLY [E] LeANN RIMES	47	2003
SUDDENLY I SEE KT TUNSTALL	12	2005
SUDDENLY THERE'S A VALLEY JO STAFFORD	12	1955
SUDDENLY THERE'S A VALLEY LEE LAWRENCE WITH RAY MARTIN & HIS ORCHESTRA	14	1955
SUDDENLY THERE'S A VALLEY PETULA CLARK	7	1955
SUDDENLY YOU LOVE ME TREMELOES	6	1968
SUEDEHEAD MORRISSEY	5	1988
SUENO LATINO SUENO LATINO FEATURING CAROLINA DAMAS	47	2000
SUE'S GOTTA BE MINE DEL SHANNON	21	1963
SUFFER NEVER FINN	29	1995
SUFFER THE CHILDREN TEARS FOR FEARS	52	1985
SUFFER WELL DEPECHE MODE	12	2006
THE SUFFERING COHEED AND CAMBRIA	60	2006
SUFFOCATE [A] FEEDER	37	1998
SUFFOCATE [B] KING ADORA	39	2001
SUFFOCATING UNDER WORDS OF SORROW BULLET FOR MY VALENTINE	37	2005
SUGAH RUBY AMANFU	32	2003
SUGAR LADYTRON	45	2005
SUGAR AND SPICE SEARCHERS	2	1963
SUGAR BABY LOVE RUBETTES	1	1974
SUGAR BEE CANNED HEAT	49	1970
SUGAR BOX THEN JERICO	22	1989
SUGAR BRIDGE (IT WILL STAND) BLUEBELLS	11	1983
SUGAR CANDY KISSES MAC & KATIE KISSOON	3	1975
SUGAR COATED ICEBERG LIGHTNING SEEDS	12	1997
SUGAR DADDY SECRET KNOWLEDGE	75	1996
SUGAR DOLL JETS	55	1981
SUGAR FOR THE SOUL STEVE BALSAMO	32	2002
SUGAR FREE JUICY	45	1986
SUGAR FREE PAULINE HENRY	57	1995
SUGAR (GIMME SOME) TRICK DADDY	61	2005
SUGAR HONEY ICE TEA GOODFELLAZ	25	1997
SUGAR IS SWEETER C J BOLLAND	11	1996
SUGAR KANE SONIC YOUTH	26	1993
SUGAR ME LYNSEY DE PAUL	5	1972
SUGAR MICE MARILLION	22	1987
SUGAR MOON PAT BOONE	6	1958
SUGAR RUSH MAN WITH NO NAME	55	1996
SUGAR SHACK [A] JIMMY GILMER & THE FIREBALLS	45	1963
SUGAR SHACK [B] SEB	61	1995
SUGAR SUGAR ARCHIES	1	1969
SUGAR SUGAR SAKKARIN	12	1971
SUGAR SUGAR DUKE BAYSEE	30	1994
SUGAR TOWN NANCY SINATRA	8	1967
SUGAR WE'RE GOIN' DOWN FALL OUT BOY	8	2006
SUGARBUSH DORIS DAY & FRANKIE LAINE	8	1952
SUGARHILL AZ	67	1996
SUGARMAN FREE ASSOCIATION	53	2003
SUGARTIME ALMA COGAN	16	1958
SUGARTIME JIM DALE	25	1958
SUGARTIME McGUIRE SISTERS	14	1958
SUICIDE BLONDE INXS	11	1990
SUKIYAKI KENNY BALL & HIS JAZZMEN	10	1963
SUKIYAKI KYU SAKAMOTO	6	1963
SULKY GIRL ELVIS COSTELLO & THE ATTRACTIONS	22	1994
SULTANA TITANIC	5	1971
SULTANS OF SWING DIRE STRAITS	8	1979
SUMAHAMA BEACH BOYS	45	1979
SUMATRAN ELECTRIC SOFT PARADE	65	2001
SUMERLAND (DREAMED) FIELDS OF THE NEPHILIM	37	1990
SUMMER CHARLOTTE HATHERLEY	31	2004
SUMMER BREEZE ISLEY BROTHERS	16	1974
SUMMER BREEZE GEOFFREY WILLIAMS	56	1992
SUMMER BUNNIES R KELLY	23	1994
SUMMER EDITION NUKLEUZ DJs	59	2003
SUMMER '89 CALIFORNIA SUNSHINE	56	1997
SUMMER FUN BARRACUDAS	37	1980
SUMMER GIRLS LYTE FUNKIE ONES	16	1999
SUMMER GONNA COME AGAIN SUPERSISTER	51	2001
SUMMER HOLIDAY CLIFF RICHARD & THE SHADOWS	1	1963
SUMMER HOLIDAY KEVIN THE GERBIL	50	1984
SUMMER HOLIDAY (EP) ZZ TOP	51	1985
SUMMER HOLIDAY MEDLEY DARREN DAY	17	1996
SUMMER IN SIAM POGUES	64	1990
SUMMER IN SPACE COSMOS	49	1999
SUMMER IN THE CITY LOVIN' SPOONFUL	8	1966
THE SUMMER IS MAGIC EXOTICA FEATURING ITSY FOSTER	68	1995
SUMMER IS OVER FRANK IFIELD	25	1964
SUMMER JAM UD PROJECT	14	2003
SUMMER MADNESS KOOL & THE GANG	17	1981
SUMMER MOVED ON A-HA	33	2000
SUMMER NIGHT CITY ABBA	5	1978
SUMMER NIGHTS [A] MARIANNE FAITHFULL	10	1965
SUMMER NIGHTS [B] JOHN TRAVOLTA & OLIVIA NEWTON-JOHN	1	1978
SUMMER OF '42 BIDDU ORCHESTRA	14	1975
SUMMER OF 69 BRYAN ADAMS	42	1985
SUMMER OF LOVE (COMME CI COMME CA) [A] LONYO - COMME CI COMME CA	8	2000
SUMMER OF LOVE [B] STEPS	5	2000
SUMMER OF MY LIFE SIMON MAY	7	1976
THE SUMMER OF SEVENTEENTH DOLL WINIFRED ATWELL	24	1959
SUMMER ON THE UNDERGROUND A	72	1998
SUMMER RAIN BELINDA CARLISLE	23	1991
SUMMER SET MR ACKER BILK & HIS PARAMOUNT JAZZ BAND	5	1960
SUMMER SON TEXAS	5	1999
SUMMER SONG BEDAZZLED	73	1992
SUMMER SUNSHINE CORRS	6	2004
SUMMER (THE FIRST TIME) BOBBY GOLDSBORO	9	1973
SUMMER WIND FRANK SINATRA	36	1966
SUMMERLANDS BEIJING SPRING	53	1993
SUMMERLOVE SENSATION BAY CITY ROLLERS	3	1974
SUMMER'S MAGIC MARK SUMMERS	27	1991
SUMMER'S OVER RIALTO	60	1998
SUMMERSAULT TASTE XPERIENCE FEATURING NATASHA PEARL	66	1999
SUMMERTIME [A] AL MARTINO	49	1960
SUMMERTIME [A] MARCELS	46	1961
SUMMERTIME [A] BILLY STEWART	39	1966
SUMMERTIME [A] FUN BOY THREE	18	1982
SUMMERTIME [B] DJ JAZZY JEFF & THE FRESH PRINCE	8	1991
SUMMERTIME [C] SUNDAYS	15	1997
SUMMERTIME [D] ANOTHER LEVEL FEATURING TQ	7	1999
SUMMERTIME BLUES EDDIE COCHRAN	18	1958
SUMMERTIME BLUES WHO	38	1970
SUMMERTIME CITY MIKE BATT WITH THE NEW EDITION	4	1975
SUMMERTIME HEALING EUSEBE	32	1995
SUMMERTIME OF OUR LIVES A1	5	1999
SUMTHIN' SUMTHIN' THE MANTRA MAXWELL	27	1997
SUN [A] VIRUS	62	1995
SUN [B] JOHN LYDON	42	1997
SUN [C] SLUSNIK LUNA	40	2001
THE SUN AIN'T GONNA SHINE ANYMORE WALKER BROTHERS	1	1966
THE SUN AIN'T GONNA SHINE ANYMORE CHER	26	1996
THE SUN ALWAYS SHINES ON TV A-HA	1	1985
THE SUN ALWAYS SHINES ON TV DIVA	53	1995
THE SUN AND THE RAIN MADNESS	5	1983
SUN ARISE ROLF HARRIS	3	1962
SUN CITY ARTISTS UNITED AGAINST APARTHEID	21	1985
THE SUN DOES RISE JAH WOBBLE'S INVADERS OF THE HEART	41	1994
THE SUN DOESN'T SHINE BEATS INTERNATIONAL	66	1991
THE SUN GOES DOWN [A] THIN LIZZY	52	1983
SUN GOES DOWN [B] DAVID JORDAN	4	2008
THE SUN GOES DOWN (LIVING IT UP) LEVEL 42	10	1983
THE SUN HAS COME YOUR WAY SAM & MARK	1	2004
SUN HITS THE SKY SUPERGRASS	10	1997
SUN IS SHINING [A] TECHNIQUE	64	1999
SUN IS SHINING [B] BOB MARLEY VERSUS FUNKSTAR DE LUXE	3	1999
THE SUN IS SHINING (DOWN ON ME) DT8 PROJECT	17	2004
SUN KING CULT	39	1989
THE SUN MACHINE E-ZEE POSSEE	62	1990
SUN OF JAMAICA GOOMBAY DANCE BAND	50	1982
THE SUN RISING BELOVED	26	1989
SUN SHINING DOWN CIRCA FEATURING DESTRY	70	1999
SUN STREET KATRINA & THE WAVES	22	1986
SUN WORSHIPPERS (POSITIVE THINKING) DIANA BROWN & BARRIE K. SHARPE	61	1990
SUNBURN [A] GRAHAM GOULDMAN	52	1979
SUNBURN [B] MICHELLE COLLINS	28	1999
SUNBURN [C] MUSE	22	2000
SUNCHYME DARIO G	2	1997
SUNDANCE SUNDANCE	33	1997
SUNDAY [A] BUSTER	49	1976
SUNDAY [B] SONIC YOUTH	72	1998
SUNDAY GIRL [A] BLONDIE	1	1979
SUNDAY GIRL [B] ERASURE	33	2007
SUNDAY MORNING [A] NO DOUBT	50	1997
SUNDAY MORNING [B] MAROON 5	27	2004
SUNDAY MORNING CALL OASIS	4	2000
SUNDAY MORNINGS VANESSA PARADIS	49	1993
SUNDAY SHINING FINLEY QUAYE	16	1997
SUNDAY SHOUTIN' JOHNNY CORPORATE	45	2000
SUNDAY SUNDAY BLUR	26	1993
SUNDOWN [A] GORDON LIGHTFOOT	33	1974
SUNDOWN [A] ELWOOD	72	2000
SUNDOWN [B] S CLUB 8	4	2003

	Peak Position	Year of Entry
SUNFLOWER PAUL WELLER	16	1993
SUNGLASSES TRACEY ULLMAN	18	1984
SUNGLASSES AT NIGHT TIGA & ZYNTHERIUS	25	2002
SUNLIGHT DJ SAMMY	8	2003
SUNMACHINE DARIO G	17	1998
SUNNY [A] BOBBY HEBB	12	1966
SUNNY [A] CHER	32	1966
SUNNY [A] GEORGIE FAME	13	1966
SUNNY [A] BONEY M	3	1976
SUNNY [A] BOOGIE PIMPS	10	2004
SUNNY [B] MORRISSEY	42	1995
SUNNY AFTERNOON KINKS	1	1966
SUNNY CAME HOME SHAWN COLVIN	29	1998
SUNNY DAY PIGBAG	53	1981
SUNNY HONEY GIRL CLIFF RICHARD	19	1971
SUNRISE [A] MOVEMENT 98 FEATURING CARROLL THOMPSON	58	1990
SUNRISE [B] GOLDENSCAN	52	2000
SUNRISE [C] PULP	23	2001
SUNRISE [D] SIMPLY RED	7	2003
SUNRISE [E] NORAH JONES	30	2004
SUNRISE [F] ANGEL CITY	9	2005
SUNRISE (HERE I AM) RATTY	51	2001
SUNSET NITIN SAWHNEY FEATURING ESKA	65	2001
SUNSET AND BABYLON W.A.S.P.	38	1993
SUNSET (BIRD OF PREY) FATBOY SLIM	9	2000
SUNSET BOULEVARD MICHAEL BALL	72	1993
SUNSET NOW HEAVEN 17	24	1984
SUNSET ON IBIZA THREE DRIVES ON A VINYL	44	2001
SUNSET PEOPLE DONNA SUMMER	46	1980
SUNSHINE [A] WARREN MILLS	74	1985
SUNSHINE [B] UMBOZA	14	1996
SUNSHINE [C] JAY-Z FEATURING BABYFACE & FOXY	25	1997
SUNSHINE [D] GABRIELLE	9	1999
SUNSHINE [E] ALEXANDER O'NEAL	72	1989
SUNSHINE [F] YOMANDA	16	2000
SUNSHINE [G] GARETH GATES	3	2003
SUNSHINE [H] HOLIDAY PLAN	58	2004
SUNSHINE [I] TWISTA	3	2004
SUNSHINE [J] LIL' FLIP	14	2004
THE SUNSHINE AFTER THE RAIN NEW ATLANTIC/U4EA FEATURING BERRI	26	1994
THE SUNSHINE AFTER THE RAIN BERRI	4	1995
SUNSHINE AFTER THE RAIN ELKIE BROOKS	10	1977
SUNSHINE & HAPPINESS DARRYL PANDY/NERIO'S DUBWORK	68	1999
SUNSHINE AND LOVE HAPPY MONDAYS	62	1992
SUNSHINE DAY OSIBISA	17	1976
SUNSHINE DAY CLOCK	58	1999
SUNSHINE GIRL HERMAN'S HERMITS	8	1968
SUNSHINE IN THE RAIN BWO	69	2008
THE SUNSHINE OF LOVE LOUIS ARMSTRONG	41	1968
SUNSHINE OF YOUR LOVE CREAM	25	1968
THE SUNSHINE OF YOUR SMILE MIKE BERRY	9	1980
SUNSHINE ON A RAINY DAY ZOE	4	1990
SUNSHINE ON A RAINY DAY REAL & RICHARDSON FEATURING JOBABE	69	2003
SUNSHINE ON LEITH PROCLAIMERS	41	1988
SUNSHINE PLAYROOM JULIAN COPE	64	1983
SUNSHINE SUPERMAN DONOVAN	2	1966
SUNSTORM HURLEY & TODD	38	2000
SUNSTROKE CHICANE	21	1997
SUNTAN STAN	40	1993
SUPER BOWL SUNDAE OZOMATLI	68	1999
SUPER DUPER LOVE (ARE YOU DIGGIN ON ME) JOSS STONE	18	2004
SUPER GRAN BILLY CONNOLLY	32	1985
SUPER LOVE WIGAN'S OVATION	41	1975
SUPER MASSIVE BLACK HOLE MUSE	4	2006
SUPER POPOID GROOVE WIN	63	1987
SUPER TROUPER ABBA	1	1980
SUPER TROUPER A*TEENS	21	1999
SUPER WOMBLE WOMBLES	20	1975
SUPERBAD SUPERSLICK REDHEAD KINGPIN & THE FBI	68	1989
SUPERCHANNEL ALARM MMVI	24	2006
SUPERFLY 1990 CURTIS MAYFIELD & ICE-T	48	1990
SUPERFLY GUY S-EXPRESS	5	1988
SUPERFREAK BEATFREAKZ	7	2006
SUPERFREAKON MISSY ELLIOTT	72	2001
SUPERGIRL GRAHAM BONNEY	19	1966
SUPERHERO REEF	55	2000
SUPERMAN STEREOPHONICS	13	2005
SUPERMAN (GIOCA JOUER) BLACK LACE	9	1983
SUPERMAN (IT'S NOT EASY) FIVE FOR FIGHTING	48	2002
SUPERMAN'S BIG SISTER IAN DURY & THE BLOCKHEADS	51	1980
SUPERMARIOLAND AMBASSADORS OF FUNK FEATURING MC MARIO	8	1992
SUPERMARKET SWEEP (WILL YOU DANCE WITH ME) BAR CODES FEATURING ALISON BROWN	72	1994
SUPERMODEL (YOU BETTER WORK) RuPAUL	39	1993
SUPERNATURAL KIM ENGLISH	50	1997
SUPERNATURAL GIVER KINKY MACHINE	70	1993
SUPERNATURAL SUPERSERIOUS R.E.M.	54	2008
SUPERNATURAL THING FREELAND	65	2004
SUPERNATURE [A] CERRONE	8	1978
SUPERNATURE [B] BARON & FRESH	59	2005
SUPERNOVA FIVE THIRTY	75	1991
SUPERSHIP GEORGE 'BAD' BENSON	30	1975
SUPERSONIC [A] HWA FEATURING SONIC THE HEDGEHOG	33	1992
SUPERSONIC [B] OASIS	31	1994
SUPERSONIC [C] JAMIROQUAI	22	1999
SUPERSONIC ROCKET SHIP KINKS	16	1972
SUPERSTAR [A] CARPENTERS	18	1971
SUPERSTAR [A] SONIC YOUTH	45	1994
SUPERSTAR [B] MURRAY HEAD	47	1972
SUPERSTAR [C] LYDIA MURDOCK	14	1983
SUPERSTAR [D] NOVY VERSUS ENIAC	32	1998
SUPERSTAR [E] SUPERSTAR	49	1998
SUPERSTAR [F] ONES	45	2003
SUPERSTAR [G] JAMELIA	3	2003
SUPERSTAR [H] LUPE FIASCO FEATURING MATTHEW SANTOS	4	2008
SUPERSTAR (REMEMBER HOW YOU GOT WHERE YOU ARE) TEMPTATIONS	32	1972
SUPERSTAR TRADESMAN THE VIEW	15	2006
SUPERSTITION STEVIE WONDER	11	1973
SUPERSTITION - GOOD TIMES (MEDLEY) CLUBHOUSE	59	1983
SUPERSTITIOUS EUROPE	34	1988
SUPERSTRING CYGNUS X	33	2001
SUPERSTYLIN' GROOVE ARMADA	12	2001
SUPERWOMAN KARYN WHITE	11	1989
SUPPORT THE TOON - IT'S YOUR DUTY (EP) MUNGO JERRY & TOON TRAVELLERS	57	1999
SUPREME ROBBIE WILLIAMS	4	2000
THE SUPREME EP SINITTA	49	1993
SURE TAKE THAT	1	1994
SURE FEELS GOOD ULTRABEAT VERSUS DARREN STYLES	52	2007
SURE SHOT BEASTIE BOYS	27	1994
SURE THING DARLING BUDS	71	1992
SURF CITY JAN & DEAN	26	1963
SURFIN' USA BEACH BOYS	34	1963
SURFIN' USA AARON CARTER	18	1998
SURPRISE BIZARRE INC	21	1996
SURPRISE SURPRISE CENTRAL LINE	48	1983
SURRENDER [A] ELVIS PRESLEY	1	1961
SURRENDER [B] DIANA ROSS	10	1971
SURRENDER [C] SWING OUT SISTER	7	1987
SURRENDER [D] ROGER TAYLOR	38	1999
SURRENDER [E] LASGO	24	2004
SURRENDER YOUR LOVE [A] NIGHTCRAWLERS	7	1995
SURRENDER (YOUR LOVE) [B] JAVINE	15	2003
SURROUND YOURSELF WITH SORROW CILLA BLACK	3	1969
SURVIVAL CAR FOUNTAINS OF WAYNE	53	1997
SURVIVALISM NINE INCH NAILS	29	2007
SURVIVE DAVID BOWIE	28	2000
SURVIVOR DESTINY'S CHILD	1	2001
SUSANNA ART COMPANY	12	1984
SUSANNAH'S STILL ALIVE DAVE DAVIES	20	1967
SUSAN'S HOUSE EELS	9	1997
SUSIE DARLIN' ROBIN LUKE	23	1958
SUSIE DARLIN' TOMMY ROE	37	1962
SUSPICION TERRY STAFFORD	31	1964
SUSPICION ELVIS PRESLEY	9	1977
SUSPICIOUS CHARACTER BLOOD ARM	62	2006
SUSPICIOUS MINDS ELVIS PRESLEY	2	1969
SUSPICIOUS MINDS CANDI STATON	31	1982
SUSPICIOUS MINDS FINE YOUNG CANNIBALS	8	1986
SUSPICIOUS MINDS GARETH GATES	1	2002
SUSSUDIO PHIL COLLINS	12	1985
SUZANNE BEWARE OF THE DEVIL DANDY LIVINGSTONE	14	1972
SUZIE BOY KILL BOY	17	2006
SVEN SVEN SVEN BELL & SPURLING	7	2001
SW LIVE EP PETER GABRIEL	39	1994
SWALLOW MY PRIDE RAMONES	49	1977
SWALLOWED BUSH	7	1997
SWAMP THING GRID	3	1994
SWAN LAKE CATS	48	1979
SWASTIKA EYES PRIMAL SCREAM	22	1999
SWAY [A] DEAN MARTIN	6	1954
SWAY [A] BOBBY RYDELL	12	1960
SWAY [B] STRANGELOVE	47	1996
SWEAR IT AGAIN WESTLIFE	1	1999
SWEARIN' TO GOD FRANKIE VALLI	31	1975
SWEAT USURA	29	1993
SWEAT (A LA LA LA LA LONG) INNER CIRCLE	3	1992
SWEAT IN A BULLET SIMPLE MINDS	52	1981
SWEATING BULLETS MEGADETH	26	1993
SWEDISH RHAPSODY MANTOVANI	2	1953
SWEDISH RHAPSODY RAY MARTIN	4	1953
SWEET ABOUT ME GABRIELLA CILMI	38	2008
SWEET AND LOW DEBORAH HARRY	57	1990
SWEET BABY MACY GRAY FEATURING ERYKAH BADU	23	2001
SWEET BIRD OF TRUTH THE THE	55	1987
SWEET CAROLINE NEIL DIAMOND	8	1971
SWEET CATATONIA CATATONIA	61	1996
SWEET CHEATIN' RITA ALVIN STARDUST	37	1975
SWEET CHILD O' MINE GUNS N' ROSES	6	1988
SWEET CHILD O' MINE SHERYL CROW	30	1999
SWEET DANGER ANGELWITCH	75	1980
SWEET DREAM JETHRO TULL	7	1969
SWEET DREAMS [A] DAVE SAMPSON	29	1960
SWEET DREAMS [B] DJ SCOTT FEATURING LORNA B	37	1995
SWEET DREAMS [B] SWING FEATURING DR ALBAN	59	1995
SWEET DREAMS [C] TOMMY McLAIN	49	1966
SWEET DREAMS [C] ROY BUCHANAN	40	1973
SWEET DREAMS [C] ELVIS COSTELLO	42	1981
SWEET DREAMS [D] LA BOUCHE	44	1994
SWEET DREAMS (ARE MADE OF THIS) EURYTHMICS	2	1983
SWEET DREAMS MY LA EX RACHEL STEVENS	2	2003
SWEET EMOTION AEROSMITH	74	1994
THE SWEET ESCAPE GWEN STEFANI FEATURING AKON	2	2007
SWEET FREEDOM [A] MICHAEL McDONALD	12	1986

	Peak Position	Year of Entry
SWEET FREEDOM [A] SAFRI DUO FEATURING MICHAEL McDONALD	54	2002
SWEET FREEDOM [B] POSITIVE GANG	34	1993
SWEET FREEDOM PART 2 POSITIVE GANG	67	1993
SWEET HARMONY [A] LIQUID	14	1992
SWEET HARMONY [B] BELOVED	8	1993
SWEET HEART CONTRACT MAGAZINE	54	1980
SWEET HITCH-HIKER CREEDENCE CLEARWATER REVIVAL	36	1971
SWEET HOME ALABAMA LYNYRD SKYNYRD	21	1976
SWEET ILLUSION JUNIOR CAMPBELL	15	1973
SWEET IMPOSSIBLE YOU BRENDA LEE	28	1963
SWEET INSPIRATION JOHNNY JOHNSON & THE BANDWAGON	10	1970
SWEET INVISIBILITY HUE & CRY	55	1989
SWEET JOHNNY GORKY'S ZYGOTIC MYNCI	60	1998
SWEET LADY TYRESE	55	1999
SWEET LADY LUCK WHITESNAKE	25	1994
SWEET LEAF MAGOO : MOGWAI	60	1998
SWEET LIES [A] ROBERT PALMER	58	1988
SWEET LIES [B] ELLIE CAMPBELL	42	1999
SWEET LIKE CHOCOLATE SHANKS & BIGFOOT	1	1999
SWEET LIPS MONACO	18	1997
SWEET LITTLE MYSTERY WET WET WET	5	1987
SWEET LITTLE ROCK 'N' ROLLER SHOWADDYWADDY	15	1979
SWEET LITTLE SIXTEEN CHUCK BERRY	16	1958
SWEET LITTLE SIXTEEN JERRY LEE LEWIS	38	1962
SWEET LOVE [A] COMMODORES	32	1977
SWEET LOVE [B] ANITA BAKER	13	1986
SWEET LOVE [B] M-BEAT FEATURING NAZLYN	18	1994
SWEET LOVE 2K [B] FIERCE	3	2000
SWEET LUI-LOUISE IRONHORSE	64	1979
SWEET LULLABY DEEP FOREST	10	1994
SWEET MEMORY BELLE STARS	22	1983
SWEET MUSIC SHOWADDYWADDY	14	1975
SWEET N SOUR JON SPENCER BLUES EXPLOSION	66	2002
SWEET NOTHINS SEARCHERS	48	1963
SWEET NOTHIN'S BRENDA LEE	4	1960
SWEET OLD-FASHIONED GIRL TERESA BREWER	3	1956
SWEET PEA MANFRED MANN	36	1967
SWEET PEA, MY SWEET PEA PAUL WELLER	44	2000
SWEET POTATO PIE DOMINO	42	1994
SWEET REVENGE SPOOKS	67	2001
SWEET REVIVAL (KEEP IT COMIN') SHADES OF RHYTHM	61	1993
SWEET SENSATION [A] MELODIANS	41	1970
SWEET SENSATION [B] SHADES OF RHYTHM	54	1991
SWEET SENSATION [C] SHABOOM	64	1999
SWEET SENSUAL LOVE BIG MOUNTAIN	51	1994
SWEET SHOP AVENGERZ BIS	46	1997
SWEET SISTER PEACE BY PIECE	46	1996
SWEET SIXTEEN BILLY IDOL	17	1987
SWEET SMELL OF SUCCESS STRANGLERS	65	1990
SWEET SOMEBODY SHANNON	25	1984
SWEET SOUL MUSIC ARTHUR CONLEY	7	1967
SWEET SOUL SENSATIONS LIGHTNING SEEDS	67	2000
SWEET SOUL SISTER CULT	42	1990
SWEET STUFF GUY MITCHELL	25	1957
SWEET SUBURBIA SKIDS	70	1978
SWEET SURRENDER [A] ROD STEWART	23	1983
SWEET SURRENDER [B] WET WET WET	6	1989
SWEET SWEET SMILE CARPENTERS	40	1978
SWEET TALKIN' GUY CHIFFONS	4	1966
SWEET TALKIN' WOMAN ELECTRIC LIGHT ORCHESTRA	6	1978
SWEET THANG JONESTOWN	49	1998
SWEET THING MICK JAGGER	24	1993
SWEET TOXIC LOVE JESUS LOVES YOU	65	1992
SWEET UNDERSTANDING LOVE FOUR TOPS	29	1973
SWEET WILLIAM MILLIE	30	1964
SWEETER THAN THE MIDNIGHT RAIN LUKE GOSS & THE BAND OF THIEVES	52	1993
SWEETER THAN WINE DIONNE RAKEEM	46	2001
SWEETER THAN YOU RICKY NELSON	19	1959
SWEETEST CHILD MARIA McKEE	45	1992
SWEETEST DAY OF MAY JOE T VANNELLI PROJECT	45	1995
THE SWEETEST DAYS VANESSA WILLIAMS	41	1995
THE SWEETEST GIRL SCRITTI POLITTI	64	1981
SWEETEST GIRL MADNESS	35	1986
SWEETEST GIRL (DOLLAR BILL) WYCLEF JEAN FEATURING AKON, LIL WAYNE & NIIA	66	2007
SWEETEST SMILE BLACK	8	1987
THE SWEETEST SURRENDER FACTORY OF UNLIMITED RHYTHM	59	1996
SWEETEST SWEETEST JERMAINE JACKSON	52	1984
THE SWEETEST TABOO SADE	31	1985
SWEETEST THING [A] GENE LOVES JEZEBEL	75	1986
THE SWEETEST THING [B] REFUGEE ALLSTARS FEATURING LAURYN HILL	18	1997
SWEETEST THING [C] U2	3	1998
SWEETHEART ENGELBERT HUMPERDINCK	22	1970
SWEETIE PIE EDDIE COCHRAN	38	1960
SWEETNESS [A] MICHELLE GAYLE	4	1994
SWEETNESS [B] XSTASIA	65	2001
SWEETNESS [C] JIMMY EAT WORLD	38	2002
SWEETNESS AND LIGHT LUSH	47	1990
SWEETS WORLD OF TWIST	58	1991
SWEETS FOR MY SWEET SEARCHERS	1	1963
SWEETS FOR MY SWEET C.J. LEWIS	3	1994
SWEETSMOKE MR SCRUFF	75	2002
SWEETY REEF	46	1999
SWIM FISHBONE	54	1993
SWIMMING HORSES SIOUXSIE & THE BANSHEES	28	1984
SWING LOW UB40 FEATURING UNITED COLOURS OF SOUND	15	2003
SWING LOW '99 RUSSELL WATSON	38	1999
SWING LOW (RUN WITH THE BALL) UNION FEATURING THE ENGLAND WORLD CUP SQUAD	16	1991
SWING LOW SWEET CHARIOT ERIC CLAPTON	19	1975
SWING LOW SWEET CHARIOT LADYSMITH BLACK MAMBAZO FEATURING CHINA BLACK	15	1995
SWING MY HIPS (SEX DANCE) LEMONESCENT	48	2002
SWING MY WAY KP & ENVYI	14	1998
SWING SWING ALL-AMERICAN REJECTS	13	2003
SWING THAT HAMMER MIKE COTTON'S JAZZMEN	36	1963
SWING THE MOOD JIVE BUNNY & THE MASTERMIXERS	1	1989
SWING YOUR DADDY JIM GILSTRAP	4	1975
SWINGIN' LIGHT OF THE WORLD	45	1979
SWINGIN' LOW OUTLAWS	46	1961
SWINGIN' SHEPHERD BLUES ELLA FITZGERALD	15	1958
SWINGIN' SHEPHERD BLUES MOE KOFFMAN QUARTETTE	23	1958
SWINGIN' SHEPHERD BLUES TED HEATH	3	1958
SWINGING IN THE RAIN NORMAN VAUGHAN	34	1962
SWINGING ON A STAR BIG DEE IRWIN	7	1963
SWINGING SCHOOL BOBBY RYDELL	44	1960
SWINGS & ROUNDABOUTS RONI SIZE	57	2002
SWISS MAID DEL SHANNON	2	1962
SWITCH [A] BENELUX & NANCY DEE	52	1979
SWITCH [B] SENSER	39	1994
SWITCH [C] HOWIE B	62	1997
SWITCH [D] PESHAY	59	1999
THE SWITCH [E] PLANET FUNK	52	2003
SWITCH [F] WILL SMITH	4	2005
SWITCH IT ON WILL YOUNG	5	2005
SWITCHED ON SWING KINGS OF SWING ORCHESTRA	48	1982
SWOON MISSION	73	1995
SWORDS OF A THOUSAND MEN TEN POLE TUDOR	10	1981
SYLVIA FOCUS	4	1973
SYLVIA'S MOTHER DR HOOK & THE MEDICINE SHOW	2	1972
SYLVIE SAINT ETIENNE	12	1998
SYMMETRY C BRAINCHILD	31	1999
SYMPATHY [A] RARE BIRD	27	1970
SYMPATHY [B] MARILLION	17	1992
SYMPATHY FOR THE DEVIL GUNS N' ROSES	9	1995
SYMPATHY FOR THE DEVIL ROLLING STONES	14	2003
SYMPHONY DONELL RUSH	66	1992
SYMPHONY OF DESTRUCTION MEGADETH	15	1992
SYNAESTHESIA (FLY AWAY) THRILLSEEKERS FEATURING SHERYL DEANE	28	2001
SYNCHRONICITY II POLICE	17	1983
SYNERGY TRANCESETTERS	72	2001
SYNTH & STRINGS YOMANDA	8	1999
SYSTEM ADDICT FIVE STAR	3	1986
SYSTEM CHECK BROCKIE/ED SOLO	68	2004
SYSTEM OF SURVIVAL EARTH, WIND & FIRE	54	1987
SZIGET (WE GET WRECKED) HAMFATTER	54	2007

T

	Peak Position	Year of Entry
T-10/THE TENTH PLANET DISTORTED MINDS	43	2003
THE TABLE BEAUTIFUL SOUTH	47	1999
TABOO GLAMMA KID FEATURING SHOLA AMA	10	1999
TACKY LOVE SONG CREDIT TO THE NATION	60	1998
TAHITI DAVID ESSEX	8	1983
TAINTED LOVE SOFT CELL	1	1981
TAINTED LOVE IMPEDANCE	54	1989
TAINTED LOVE ICON	51	1996
TAINTED LOVE MARILYN MANSON	5	2002
TAINTED LOVE RICHARD GREY	52	2007
TAKE COLOUR FIELD	70	1984
TAKE A BOW MADONNA	16	1994
TAKE A CHANCE MAGIC NUMBERS	16	2006
TAKE A CHANCE ON ME ABBA	1	1978
TAKE A CHANCE WITH ME ROXY MUSIC	26	1982
TAKE A FREE FALL DANCE 2 TRANCE	36	1993
TAKE A HEART SORROWS	21	1965
(TAKE A LITTLE) PIECE OF MY HEART ERMA FRANKLIN	9	1992
TAKE A LITTLE TIME (DOUBLE SINGLE) GARY MOORE	75	1987
TAKE A LOOK LEVEL 42	32	1988
TAKE A LOOK AROUND [A] TEMPTATIONS	13	1972
TAKE A LOOK AROUND [B] LIMP BIZKIT	3	2000
TAKE A LOOK AT YOURSELF COVERDALE PAGE	43	1993
TAKE A MESSAGE TO MARY EVERLY BROTHERS	20	1959
TAKE A PICTURE FILTER	25	2000
TAKE A REST GANG STARR	63	1991
TAKE A RUN AT THE SUN DINOSAUR Jr.	53	1997
TAKE A TOKE C & C MUSIC FACTORY FEATURING MARTHA WASH	26	1995
TAKE CALIFORNIA PROPELLERHEADS	69	1996
TAKE CARE OF YOURSELF LEVEL 42	39	1989
TAKE CONTROL AMERIE	10	2007
TAKE CONTROL [A] STATE OF MIND	46	1998
TAKE CONTROL [B] JAIMESON FEATURING ANGEL BLU & CK	16	2004
TAKE CONTROL OF THE PARTY BG THE PRINCE OF RAP	71	1992

Title	Artist	Peak Position	Year of Entry
TAKE DOWN THE UNION JACK	BILLY BRAGG & THE BLOKES	22	2002
TAKE FIVE [A]	DAVE BRUBECK QUARTET	6	1961
TAKE 5 [B]	NORTHSIDE	40	1991
TAKE 4 (EP)	MIKE OLDFIELD	72	1978
TAKE GOOD CARE OF HER	ADAM WADE	38	1961
TAKE GOOD CARE OF MY BABY	BOBBY VEE	3	1961
TAKE GOOD CARE OF MY BABY	SMOKIE	34	1980
TAKE GOOD CARE OF MY HEART	MICHAELA	66	1990
TAKE GOOD CARE OF YOURSELF	THREE DEGREES	9	1975
TAKE HER BACK	PIGEON DETECTIVES	20	2007
TAKE IT	FLOWERED UP	34	1991
TAKE IT AND RUN	BANDITS	32	2003
TAKE IT AWAY [A]	PAUL McCARTNEY	15	1982
TAKE IT AWAY [B]	USED	44	2005
TAKE IT BACK	PINK FLOYD	23	1994
TAKE IT (CLOSING TIME)	TOM NOVY & LIMA	31	2006
TAKE IT EASY [A]	LET LOOSE	25	1996
TAKE IT EASY [B]	MINT ROYALE	66	2000
TAKE IT EASY [C]	3SL	11	2002
TAKE IT EASY ON ME	A HOUSE	55	1992
TAKE IT FROM ME [A]	ROGER CHRISTIAN	63	1989
TAKE IT FROM ME [B]	GIRLFRIEND	47	1993
TAKE IT OFF	DONNAS	38	2003
TAKE IT ON THE RUN	REO SPEEDWAGON	19	1981
TAKE IT OR LEAVE IT	SEARCHERS	31	1966
TAKE IT SATCH EP	LOUIS ARMSTRONG WITH HIS ALL-STARS	29	1956
TAKE IT TO THE LIMIT	EAGLES	12	1976
TAKE IT TO THE STREETS	RAMPAGE FEATURING BILLY LAWRENCE	58	1997
TAKE IT TO THE TOP [A]	KOOL & THE GANG	15	1981
TAKE IT TO THE TOP [B]	CLOUD	72	1981
TAKE ME	DREAM FREQUENCY	39	1992
TAKE ME AWAY [A]	TRUE FAITH WITH FINAL CUT	51	1991
TAKE ME AWAY [A]	CAPPELLA FEATURING LOLEATTA HOLLOWAY	25	1992
TAKE ME AWAY [B]	D:REAM	18	1994
TAKE ME AWAY [C]	CULTURE BEAT	51	1996
TAKE ME AWAY [D]	STONEBRIDGE FEATURING THERESE	9	2005
TAKE ME AWAY [E]	HAJI & EMANUEL	73	2006
TAKE ME AWAY (I'LL FOLLOW YOU)	BAD BOYS INC	15	1994
TAKE ME AWAY INTO THE NIGHT	4 STRINGS	15	2002
TAKE ME AWAY (PARADISE)	MIX FACTORY	51	1993
TAKE ME BACK	RHYTHMATIC	71	1990
TAKE ME BACK TO LOVE AGAIN	KATHY SLEDGE	62	1992
TAKE ME BACK TO YOUR HOUSE	BASEMENT JAXX	42	2006
TAKE ME BAK 'OME	SLADE	1	1972
TAKE ME BY THE HAND	SUBMERGE FEATURING JAN JOHNSTON	28	1997
TAKE ME DOWN TO THE RIVER	SKIN	26	1995
TAKE ME FOR A LITTLE WHILE	COVERDALE PAGE	29	1993
TAKE ME FOR WHAT I'M WORTH	SEARCHERS	20	1965
TAKE ME GIRL I'M READY	JUNIOR WALKER & THE ALL-STARS	16	1973
TAKE ME HIGH	CLIFF RICHARD	27	1973
TAKE ME HIGHER [A]	RAF	59	1994
TAKE ME HIGHER [B]	DIANA ROSS	32	1995
TAKE ME HIGHER [C]	GEORGIE PORGIE	61	1996
TAKE ME HOME [A]	PHIL COLLINS	19	1985
TAKE ME HOME [B]	JOE COCKER FEATURING BEKKA BRAMLETT	41	1994
TAKE ME HOME COUNTRY ROADS	OLIVIA NEWTON-JOHN	15	1973
TAKE ME HOME - MUTINY	SOPHIE ELLIS-BEXTOR	2	2001
TAKE ME HOME (WOMBLE 'TIL I DIE)	EVERSTRONG	73	2005
TAKE ME I'M YOURS	SQUEEZE	19	1978
TAKE ME IN YOUR ARMS	DOOBIE BROTHERS	29	1975
TAKE ME IN YOUR ARMS AND LOVE ME	GLADYS KNIGHT & THE PIPS	13	1967
TAKE ME IN YOUR ARMS AND LOVE ME	SCRITTI POLITTI & SWEETIE IRIE	47	1991
TAKE ME NOW	TAMMY PAYNE	55	1991
TAKE ME OUT	FRANZ FERDINAND	3	2004
TAKE ME OVER	McKAY	65	2003
TAKE ME THERE	BLACKstreet & MYA FEATURING MASE & BLINKY BLINK	7	1998
TAKE ME TO HEAVEN	BABY D	15	1996
TAKE ME TO THE CLOUDS ABOVE	LMC VS U2	1	2004
TAKE ME TO THE MARDI GRAS	PAUL SIMON	7	1973
TAKE ME TO THE NEXT PHASE	ISLEY BROTHERS	50	1978
TAKE ME TO YOUR HEART	RICK ASTLEY	8	1988
TAKE ME TO YOUR HEART AGAIN	VINCE HILL	13	1966
TAKE ME TO YOUR HEAVEN	CHARLOTTE NILSSON	20	1999
TAKE ME UP [A]	SOUNDSOURCE	61	1992
TAKE ME UP [B]	SONIC SURFERS FEATURING JOCELYN BROWN	61	1993
TAKE ME WITH YOU [A]	PRINCE & THE REVOLUTION	7	1985
TAKE ME WITH YOU [B]	COSMOS	32	2002
TAKE MY ADVICE	KYM SIMS	13	1992
TAKE MY BREATH AWAY (LOVE THEME FROM *TOP GUN*) [A]	BERLIN	1	1986
TAKE MY BREATH AWAY [A]	SODA CLUB FEATURING HANNAH ALETHA	16	2002
TAKE MY BREATH AWAY [B]	EMMA BUNTON	5	2001
TAKE MY HAND	JURGEN VRIES FEATURING ANDREA BRITTON	23	2004
TAKE MY HEART	AL MARTINO	9	1952
TAKE MY HEART (YOU CAN HAVE IT IF YOU WANT IT)	KOOL & THE GANG	29	1982
TAKE MY SCARS	MACHINE HEAD	73	1997
TAKE MY TIME	SHEENA EASTON	44	1981
TAKE OFF SOME TIME	NEW ATLANTIC	64	1993
TAKE ON ME	A-HA	2	1985
TAKE ON ME	A1	1	2000
TAKE ON THE WORLD	JUDAS PRIEST	14	1979
THE TAKE OVER THE BREAKS OVER	FALL OUT BOY	48	2007
TAKE THAT LOOK OFF YOUR FACE	MARTI WEBB	3	1980
TAKE THAT SITUATION	NICK HEYWARD	11	1983
TAKE THAT TO THE BANK	SHALAMAR	20	1979
TAKE THE BOX	AMY WINEHOUSE	57	2004
TAKE THE LONG ROAD AND WALK IT	MUSIC	14	2002
TAKE THE LONG WAY HOME	FAITHLESS	15	1998
TAKE THESE CHAINS FROM MY HEART	RAY CHARLES	5	1963
TAKE THIS HEART	RICHARD MARX	13	1992
TAKE THIS TIME	SEAN MAGUIRE	27	1994
TAKE TO THE MOUNTAINS	RICHARD BARNES	35	1970
TAKE YOU OUT	LUTHER VANDROSS	59	2001
TAKE YOU THERE [A]	RONNI SIMON	58	1995
TAKE YOU THERE [B]	SEAN KINGSTON	47	2008
TAKE YOUR MAMA	SCISSOR SISTERS	17	2004
TAKE YOUR MAMA FOR A RIDE	LULU	37	1975
TAKE YOUR PARTNER BY THE HAND	HOWIE B FEATURING ROBBIE ROBERTSON	74	1998
TAKE YOUR SHOES OFF	CHEEKY GIRLS	3	2003
TAKE YOUR TIME [A]	HIGH	56	1990
TAKE YOUR TIME [B]	MANTRONIX FEATURING WONDRESS	10	1990
TAKE YOUR TIME [C]	LOVE BITE	56	2000
TAKE YOUR TIME (DO IT RIGHT) PART 1	S.O.S. BAND	51	1980
TAKEN FOR GRANTED	SIA	10	2000
TAKES A LITTLE TIME	TOTAL CONTRAST	17	1985
TAKES TWO TO TANGO	LOUIS ARMSTRONG	6	1952
TAKIN' A CHANCE ON YOU	DOLLAR	62	1980
TAKIN' HOLD	SAM LA MORE	70	2003
TAKING CHANCES	CELINE DION	40	2007
TAKING OFF	CURE	39	2004
TAKING ON THE WORLD	GUN	50	1990
TAKING THE VEIL	DAVID SYLVIAN	53	1986
TALES FROM A DANCEOGRAPHIC OCEAN (EP)	JAM & SPOON	49	1992
TALES FROM THE HARD SIDE	BIOHAZARD	47	1994
TALES OF THE HOOD	TUBBY T	47	2002
TALK	COLDPLAY	10	2006
TALK ABOUT IT IN THE MORNING	MARTYN JOSEPH	43	1995
TALK ABOUT OUR LOVE	BRANDY FEATURING KANYE WEST	6	2004
TALK BACK	DOUBLE TROUBLE FEATURING JANETTE SEWELL	71	1990
TALK DIRTY TO ME	POISON	67	1987
TALK OF THE TOWN	PRETENDERS	8	1980
TALK SHOWS ON MUTE	INCUBUS	43	2004
TALK TALK	TALK TALK	23	1982
TALK TALK TALK	ORDINARY BOYS	17	2004
TALK TO ME [A]	THIRD WORLD	56	1979
TALK TO ME [B]	STEVIE NICKS	68	1986
TALK TO ME [C]	ANITA BAKER	68	1990
TALK TO ME [D]	60FT DOLLS	37	1996
TALKIN' ALL THAT JAZZ	STETSASONIC	54	1988
TALKING IN YOUR SLEEP [A]	CRYSTAL GAYLE	11	1978
TALKING IN YOUR SLEEP [A]	MARTINE McCUTCHEON	6	1999
TALKING IN YOUR SLEEP [B]	BUCKS FIZZ	15	1984
TALKING LOUD AND CLEAR	ORCHESTRAL MANOEUVRES IN THE DARK	11	1984
TALKING OF LOVE	ANITA DOBSON	43	1987
TALKING WITH MYSELF	ELECTRIBE 101	23	1990
TALL DARK STRANGER	ROSE BRENNAN	31	1961
TALL 'N' HANDSOME	OUTRAGE	51	1995
TALLAHASSEE LASSIE	FREDDY CANNON	17	1959
TALLAHASSEE LASSIE	TOMMY STEELE	16	1959
TALLYMAN	JEFF BECK	30	1967
TALULA	TORI AMOS	22	1996
TAMBOURINE	EVE	19	2007
TAMMY	DEBBIE REYNOLDS	2	1957
TAM-TAM POUR L'ETHIOPE	STARVATION	33	1985
TANGERINE	FEEDER	60	1997
TANGO IN MONO	EXPRESSOS	70	1981
TANSY	ALEX WELSH	45	1961
TANTALISE (WO WO EE YEH YEH)	JIMMY THE HOOVER	18	1983
TAP THE BOTTLE	YOUNG BLACK TEENAGERS	39	1994
TAP TURNS ON THE WATER	C.C.S.	5	1971
TAPE LOOP	MORCHEEBA	42	1996
TARANTINO'S NEW STAR	NORTH & SOUTH	18	1997
TARANTULA [A]	FAITHLESS	29	2002
TARANTULA [B]	PENDULUM & FRESH FEATURING SPYDA	60	2005
TARANTULA [C]	SMASHING PUMPKINS	59	2007
TARA'S THEME	SPIRO & WIX	29	1996
TARA'S THEME FROM *GONE WITH THE WIND*	ROSE OF ROMANCE ORCHESTRA	71	1982
TARGET	EMBRACE	29	2006
TARRED & FEATHERED (WHAT A BAD BOY)	DOGS	64	2005
TARZAN BOY	BALTIMORA	3	1985
TASTE IN MEN	PLACEBO	16	2000
TASTE IT	INXS	21	1992
A TASTE OF AGGRO	BARRON KNIGHTS	3	1978
TASTE OF BITTER LOVE	GLADYS KNIGHT & THE PIPS	35	1980

	Peak Position	Year of Entry
A TASTE OF HONEY MR ACKER BILK WITH THE LEON YOUNG STRING CHORALE	16	1963
THE TASTE OF INK USED	52	2003
THE TASTE OF YOUR TEARS KING	11	1985
TASTE THE LAST GIRL SONS & DAUGHTERS	75	2005
TASTE THE PAIN RED HOT CHILI PEPPERS	29	1990
TASTE YOU AUF DER MAUR	51	2004
TASTE YOUR LOVE HORACE BROWN	58	1995
TASTY FISH OTHER TWO	41	1991
TASTY LOVE FREDDIE JACKSON	73	1986
TATTOO MIKE OLDFIELD	33	1992
TATTOOED MILLIONAIRE BRUCE DICKINSON	18	1990
TATTVA KULA SHAKER	4	1996
TAVERN IN THE TOWN TERRY LIGHTFOOT & HIS NEW ORLEANS JAZZMEN	49	1962
TAXI J BLACKFOOT	48	1984
TAXLOSS MANSUN	15	1997
TCHAIKOVSKY ONE SECOND CITY SOUND	22	1966
TE AMO SULTANA	57	1994
TEA FOR TWO CHA CHA TOMMY DORSEY ORCHESTRA STARRING WARREN COVINGTON	3	1958
TEACH ME TO TWIST CHUBBY CHECKER & BOBBY RYDELL	45	1962
TEACH ME TONIGHT DE CASTRO SISTERS	20	1955
TEACH YOU TO ROCK TONY CROMBIE & HIS ROCKETS	25	1956
TEACHER [A] JETHRO TULL	4	1970
TEACHER [B] I-LEVEL	56	1983
THE TEACHER [C] BIG COUNTRY	28	1986
TEACHER TEACHER JOHNNY MATHIS	27	1958
TEAR AWAY DROWNING POOL	65	2002
TEAR DOWN THE WALLS NO SWEAT	61	1991
A TEAR FELL TERESA BREWER	2	1956
TEAR ME APART SUZI QUATRO	27	1977
TEAR OFF YOUR OWN HEAD ELVIS COSTELLO	58	2002
TEAR SOUP QUESTIONS	66	1983
TEARDROP [A] SANTO & JOHNNY	50	1960
TEARDROP [B] MASSIVE ATTACK	10	1998
TEARDROP [B] NEWTON FAULKNER	57	2007
TEARDROP CITY MONKEES	44	1969
TEARDROPS [A] SHAKIN' STEVENS	5	1984
TEARDROPS [B] WOMACK & WOMACK	3	1988
TEARDROPS [B] LOVESTATION	14	1998
TEARDROPS [C] 411	23	2004
TEARIN' UP MY HEART N SYNC	9	1997
TEARING ROLLINS BAND	54	1992
TEARING US APART ERIC CLAPTON & TINA TURNER	56	1987
TEARS [A] DANNY WILLIAMS	22	1962
TEARS [B] KEN DODD	1	1965
TEARS [C] FRANKIE KNUCKLES PRESENTS SATOSHI TOMIIE	50	1989
TEARS [C] NU COLOURS	55	1992
TEARS ARE FALLING KISS	57	1985
TEARS ARE NOT ENOUGH ABC	19	1981
TEARS DON'T FALL BULLET FOR MY VALENTINE	37	2006
TEARS DON'T LIE MARK' OH	24	1995
TEARS DRY ON THEIR OWN AMY WINEHOUSE	16	2007
TEARS FROM A WILLOW OOBERMAN	63	1999
TEARS FROM HEAVEN HEARTBEAT	32	1987
TEARS FROM THE MOON CONJURE ONE	42	2003
THE TEARS I CRIED GLITTER BAND	8	1975
TEARS IN HEAVEN ERIC CLAPTON	5	1992
TEARS IN HEAVEN CHOIRBOYS	22	2005
TEARS IN THE RAIN N-TRANCE	53	1998
TEARS IN THE WIND CHICKEN SHACK	29	1969
TEARS OF A CLOWN SMOKEY ROBINSON & THE MIRACLES	1	1970
TEARS OF A CLOWN BEAT	6	1979
TEARS OF THE DRAGON BRUCE DICKINSON	28	1994
TEARS ON MY PILLOW [A] JOHNNY NASH	1	1975
TEARS ON MY PILLOW [B] KYLIE MINOGUE	1	1990
TEARS ON THE TELEPHONE [A] CLAUDE FRANCOIS	35	1976
TEARS ON THE TELEPHONE [B] HOT CHOCOLATE	37	1983
TEARS RUN RINGS MARC ALMOND	26	1988
TEARS WON'T WASH AWAY MY HEARTACHE KEN DODD	22	1969
TEARY EYED MISSY ELLIOTT	47	2005
TEASE ME [A] KEITH KELLY	27	1960
TEASE ME [B] CHAKA DEMUS & PLIERS	3	1993
TEASER GEORGE BENSON	45	1987
TECHNARCHY CYBERSONIK	73	1990
TECHNO FUNK LOST	75	1991
TECHNO TRANCE D-SHAKE	20	1990
TECHNOCAT TECHNOCAT FEATURING TOM WILSON	33	1995
TECHNOLOGIC DAFT PUNK	40	2005
TEDDY BEAR [A] RED SOVINE	4	1981
TEDDY BEAR [B] BOOKER NEWBURY III	44	1983
TEDDY BEAR'S LAST RIDE DIANA WILLIAMS	54	1981
TEDDY PICKER ARCTIC MONKEYS	20	2007
TEEN ANGEL MARK DINNING	37	1960
TEEN BEAT SANDY NELSON	9	1959
TEENAGE U.K. SUBS	32	1980
TEENAGE ANGST PLACEBO	30	1996
TEENAGE DEPRESSION EDDIE & THE HOT RODS	35	1976
TEENAGE DIRTBAG WHEATUS	2	2001
TEENAGE DREAM MARC BOLAN & T REX	13	1974
TEENAGE IDOL RICK NELSON	39	1962
TEENAGE KICKS UNDERTONES	31	1978
TEENAGE LAMENT '74 ALICE COOPER	12	1974
TEENAGE LIFE DAZ SAMPSON	8	2006
TEENAGE PUNKS SULTANS OF PING	49	1993
TEENAGE RAMPAGE SWEET	2	1974
TEENAGE SCREAMERS TOKYO DRAGONS	61	2004
TEENAGE SENSATION CREDIT TO THE NATION	24	1994
TEENAGE TURTLES BACK TO THE PLANET	52	1993
TEENAGE WARNING ANGELIC UPSTARTS	29	1979
A TEENAGER IN LOVE CRAIG DOUGLAS	13	1959
A TEENAGER IN LOVE DION & THE BELMONTS	28	1959
A TEENAGER IN LOVE MARTY WILDE	2	1959
TEENAGERS MY CHEMICAL ROMANCE	9	2007
TEENSVILLE CHET ATKINS	46	1960
TEETHGRINDER THERAPY?	30	1992
TELEFUNKIN' N-TYCE	16	1998
TELEGRAM SAM T REX	1	1972
TELEGRAPH ORCHESTRAL MANOEUVRES IN THE DARK	42	1983
THE TELEPHONE ALWAYS RINGS FUN BOY THREE	17	1982
TELEPHONE LINE ELECTRIC LIGHT ORCHESTRA	8	1977
TELEPHONE MAN MERI WILSON	6	1977
TELEPHONE OPERATOR PETE SHELLEY	66	1983
TELEPHONE THING FALL	58	1990
TELEPORT MAN WITH NO NAME	55	1996
TELETUBBIES SAY EH-OH! TELETUBBIES	1	1997
TELEVATORS MARS VOLTA	41	2004
TELEVISION THE DRUG OF THE NATION DISPOSABLE HEROES OF HIPHOPRISY	44	1992
TELL HER ABOUT IT BILLY JOEL	4	1983
TELL HER I'M NOT HOME IKE & TINA TURNER	48	1966
TELL HER NO ZOMBIES	42	1965
TELL HER THIS DEL AMITRI	32	1995
TELL HIM [A] BILLIE DAVIS	10	1963
TELL HIM [A] EXCITERS	46	1963
TELL HIM [A] HELLO	6	1974
TELL HIM [A] QUENTIN & ASH	25	1996
TELL HIM [B] BARBRA STREISAND & CELINE DION	3	1997
TELL IT LIKE IT T-I-IS B-52's	61	1992
TELL IT ON THE MOUNTAIN PETER, PAUL & MARY	33	1964
TELL IT TO MY FACE KEITH	50	1967
TELL IT TO MY HEART TAYLOR DAYNE	3	1988
TELL IT TO MY HEART Q-CLUB	28	1996
TELL IT TO MY HEART KELLY LLORENNA	9	2002
TELL IT TO THE RAIN FOUR SEASONS WITH FRANKIE VALLI	37	1967
TELL LAURA I LOVE HER RICKY VALENCE	1	1960
TELL ME [A] NICK KAMEN	40	1988
TELL ME [B] GROOVE THEORY	31	1995
TELL ME [C] DRU HILL	30	1997
TELL ME [D] BILLIE MYERS	28	1998
TELL ME [E] MELANIE B	4	2000
TELL ME [F] P DIDDY FEATURING CHRISTINA AGUILERA	8	2006
TELL ME A STORY FRANKIE LAINE & JIMMY BOYD	5	1953
TELL ME BABY RED HOT CHILI PEPPERS	16	2006
TELL ME 'BOUT IT JOSS STONE	28	2007
TELL ME DO U WANNA GINUWINE	16	1997
TELL ME (HOW IT FEELS) 52ND STREET	54	1985
TELL ME I'M NOT DREAMING TITIYO	45	1994
TELL ME IS IT TRUE UB40	14	1997
TELL ME IT'S REAL K-CI & JOJO	16	1999
TELL ME MA SHAM ROCK	13	1998
TELL ME ON A SUNDAY MARTI WEBB	67	1980
TELL ME THAT YOU LOVE ME PAUL ANKA	25	1957
TELL ME THE WAY CAPPELLA	17	1995
TELL ME THERE'S A HEAVEN CHRIS REA	24	1990
TELL ME TOMORROW [A] SMOKEY ROBINSON	51	1982
TELL ME TOMORROW [B] PRINCESS	34	1986
TELL ME WHAT HE SAID HELEN SHAPIRO	2	1962
TELL ME WHAT IT'S WORTH LIGHTSPEED CHAMPION	72	2008
TELL ME WHAT YOU SEE VON BONDIES	43	2004
TELL ME WHAT YOU WANT [A] JIMMY RUFFIN	39	1974
TELL ME WHAT YOU WANT [B] LOOSE ENDS	74	1984
TELL ME WHAT YOU WANT [C] BLU PETER	70	1998
TELL ME WHAT YOU WANT ME TO DO TEVIN CAMPBELL	63	1992
TELL ME WHEN [A] APPLEJACKS	7	1964
TELL ME WHEN [B] HUMAN LEAGUE	6	1995
TELL ME WHEN THE FEVER ENDED ELECTRIBE 101	32	1989
TELL ME WHERE IT HURTS GARBAGE	50	2007
TELL ME WHERE YOU'RE GOING SILJE	55	1990
TELL ME WHY [A] ELVIS PRESLEY	15	1965
TELL ME WHY [B] ALVIN STARDUST	16	1974
TELL ME WHY [C] MUSICAL YOUTH	33	1983
TELL ME WHY [D] BOBBY WOMACK	60	1984
TELL ME WHY [E] THIS WAY UP	72	1987
TELL ME WHY [F] GENESIS	40	1993
TELL ME WHY [G] DECLAN FEATURING THE YOUNG VOICES CHOIR	29	2002
TELL ME WHY [H] SUPERMODE	13	2006
TELL ME WHY (THE RIDDLE) PAUL VAN DYK FEATURING SAINT ETIENNE	7	2000
TELL ME WHY BOBBY VALENTINO	38	2005
TELL THAT GIRL TO SHUT UP TRANSVISION VAMP	45	1988
TELL THE CHILDREN SHAM 69	45	1980
TELLIN' STORIES CHARLATANS	16	1997
TELSTAR TORNADOS	1	1962
TEMMA HARBOUR MARY HOPKIN	6	1970
TEMPERATURE SEAN PAUL	11	2006
TEMPERATURE RISING PKA	68	1991
TEMPERAMENTAL EVERYTHING BUT THE GIRL	72	2000
TEMPERTEMPER GOLDIE	13	1998

	Peak Position	Year of Entry
TEMPLE OF DOOM DJ FRESH	60	2003
TEMPLE OF DREAMS [A] MESSIAH	20	1992
TEMPLE OF DREAMS [B] FUTURE BREEZE	21	2002
TEMPLE OF LOVE SISTERS OF MERCY	3	1992
TEMPO FIESTA (PARTY TIME) ITTY BITTY BOOZY WOOZY	34	1995
TEMPORARY BEAUTY GRAHAM PARKER & THE RUMOUR	50	1982
TEMPTATION [A] EVERLY BROTHERS	1	1961
TEMPTATION [B] NEW ORDER	29	1982
TEMPTATION [C] HEAVEN 17	2	1983
TEMPTATION [D] JOAN ARMATRADING	65	1985
TEMPTATION [E] WET WET WET	12	1988
TEMPTED SQUEEZE	41	1981
TEMPTED TO TOUCH RUPEE	44	2004
10AM AUTOMATIC BLACK KEYS	66	2004
10 IN 01 MEMBERS OF MAYDAY	31	2001
TEN MILES HIGH LITTLE ANGELS	18	1994
10 SECOND BIONIC MAN KINKY MACHINE	66	1994
TEN STOREY LOVE SONG STONE ROSES	11	1995
TEN THOUSAND MILES MICHAEL HOLLIDAY	24	1956
10 X 10 808 STATE	67	1993
TEN TO TWENTY SNEAKER PIMPS	56	1999
10 YEARS ASLEEP KINGMAKER	15	1993
TEN YEARS TIME GABRIELLE	43	2004
TENDENCY BATTLE	37	2006
TENDER [A] BLUR	2	1999
TENDER [B] FEEDER	11	2005
TENDER HANDS CHRIS DE BURGH	43	1989
TENDER HEART LIONEL RICHIE	29	2001
TENDER LOVE FORCE MDs	23	1986
TENDER LOVE KENNY THOMAS	26	1991
TENDERLY NAT 'KING' COLE	10	1954
TENDERNESS DIANA ROSS	73	1982
TENNESSEE ARRESTED DEVELOPMENT	18	1992
TENNESSEE WIG WALK BONNIE LOU	4	1954
TENSHI GOURYELLA	45	2000
TEQUILA [A] CHAMPS	5	1958
TEQUILA [A] TED HEATH	21	1958
TEQUILA [A] NO WAY JOSE	47	1985
TEQUILA [B] TERRORVISION	2	1999
TEQUILA SUNRISE CYPRESS HILL	23	1998
TERESA JOE DOLAN	20	1969
TERRA FIRMA YOUNG KNIVES	43	2007
TERRITORY SEPULTURA	66	1993
TERRY TWINKLE	4	1964
TERRY'S THEME FROM *LIMELIGHT* FRANK CHACKSFIELD	2	1953
TERRY'S THEME FROM *LIMELIGHT* RON GOODWIN	3	1953
TESLA GIRLS ORCHESTRAL MANOEUVRES IN THE DARK	21	1984
THE TEST CHEMICAL BROTHERS	14	2002
TEST OF TIME [A] WILL DOWNING	67	1989
TEST OF TIME [B] CRESCENT	60	2002
TEST THE THEORY AUDIOWEB	56	1999
TESTAMENT 4 CHUBBY CHUNKS VOLUME II	52	1994
TESTIFY [A] M PEOPLE	12	1998
TESTIFY [B] BYRON STINGILY	48	1998
TETRIS DOCTOR SPIN	6	1992
TEXAS CHRIS REA	69	1990
TEXAS COWBOYS GRID	17	1993
THA CROSSROADS BONE THUGS-N-HARMONY	8	1996
THA DOGGFATHER SNOOP DOGGY DOGG	36	1998
THA HORNS OF JERICHO DJ SUPREME	29	1998
THA WILD STYLE DJ SUPREME	24	1996
THANK ABBA FOR THE MUSIC STEPS, TINA COUSINS, CLEOPATRA, B*WITCHED, BILLIE	4	1999
THANK GOD I FOUND YOU MARIAH CAREY FEATURING JOE & 98°	10	2000
THANK GOD IT'S CHRISTMAS QUEEN	21	1984
THANK GOD IT'S FRIDAY R KELLY	14	1996
THANK U ALANIS MORISSETTE	5	1998
THANK U VERY MUCH SCAFFOLD	4	1967
THANK YOU [A] PALE FOUNTAINS	48	1982
THANK YOU [B] BOYZ II MEN	26	1995
THANK YOU [C] DIDO	3	2001
THANK YOU [D] JAMELIA	2	2004
THANK YOU BABY! SHANIA TWAIN	11	2003
THANK YOU FOR A GOOD YEAR ALEXANDER O'NEAL	30	1988
THANK YOU FOR BEING A FRIEND ANDREW GOLD	42	1978
THANK YOU FOR HEARING ME SINEAD O'CONNOR	13	1994
THANK YOU FOR LOVING ME BON JOVI	12	2000
THANK YOU FOR THE MUSIC ABBA	33	1983
THANK YOU FOR THE PARTY DUKES	53	1982
THANK YOU FOR THE VENOM MY CHEMICAL ROMANCE	71	2005
THANK YOU MY LOVE IMAGINATION	22	1985
THANK YOU WORLD WORLD PARTY	68	1991
THANKS A LOT BRENDA LEE	41	1965
THANKS FOR MY CHILD CHERYL PEPSII RILEY	75	1989
THANKS FOR SAVING MY LIFE BILLY PAUL	33	1974
THANKS FOR THE MEMORY (WHAM BAM THANK YOU MAM) SLADE	7	1975
THANKS FOR THE NIGHT DAMNED	43	1984
THANKYOU WHOEVER YOU ARE MARILLION	15	2007
THAT CERTAIN SMILE MIDGE URE	28	1985
THAT DAY NATALIE IMBRUGLIA	11	2001
THAT DON'T IMPRESS ME MUCH SHANIA TWAIN	3	1999
THAT EXTRA MILE RICKY	50	2004
THAT FEELING DJ CHUS PRESENTS GROOVE FOUNDATION	65	2002
THAT GIRL [A] STEVIE WONDER	39	1982
THAT GIRL [B] MAXI PRIEST/SHAGGY	15	1996
THAT GIRL [C] McFLY	3	2004
THAT GIRL BELONGS TO YESTERDAY GENE PITNEY	7	1964
THAT GIRL (GROOVY SITUATION) FREDDIE McGREGOR	47	1987
THAT GREAT LOVE SOUND RAVEONETTES	34	2003
THAT LADY ISLEY BROTHERS	14	1973
THAT LOOK DE'LACY	19	1996
THAT LOOK IN YOUR EYE ALI CAMPBELL	5	1995
THAT LOVING FEELING CICERO	46	1992
THAT LUCKY OLD SUN VELVETS	46	1961
THAT MAN (HE'S ALL MINE) INNER CITY	42	1990
THAT MAN WILL NOT HANG McLUSKY	71	2004
THAT MEANS A LOT P.J. PROBY	30	1965
THAT NOISE ANTHONY NEWLEY	34	1962
THAT OLD BLACK MAGIC SAMMY DAVIS Jr.	16	1955
THAT OLD PAIR OF JEANS FATBOY SLIM	39	2006
THAT OLE DEVIL CALLED LOVE ALISON MOYET	2	1985
THAT SAME OLD FEELING PICKETTYWITCH	5	1970
THAT SOUND MICHAEL MOOG	32	1999
THAT SOUNDS GOOD TO ME JIVE BUNNY & THE MASTERMIXERS	4	1990
THAT THING YOU DO! WONDERS	22	1997
THAT WAS MY VEIL JOHN PARISH & POLLY JEAN HARVEY	75	1996
THAT WAS THEN BUT THIS IS NOW ABC	18	1983
THAT WAS THEN, THIS IS NOW MONKEES	68	1986
THAT WAS YESTERDAY FOREIGNER	28	1985
THAT WOMAN'S GOT ME DRINKING SHANE MacGOWAN & THE POPES	34	1994
THAT ZIPPER TRACK DJ DAN PRESENTS NEEDLE DAMAGE	53	2001
THAT'LL BE THE DAY CRICKETS	1	1957
THAT'LL BE THE DAY EVERLY BROTHERS	30	1965
THAT'LL DO NICELY BAD MANNERS	49	1983
THAT'S ALL GENESIS	16	1983
THAT'S ALL RIGHT ELVIS PRESLEY	3	2004
THAT'S AMORE DEAN MARTIN	2	1954
THAT'S ENTERTAINMENT JAM	21	1981
THAT'S HOW A LOVE SONG WAS BORN RAY BURNS WITH THE CORONETS	14	1955
THAT'S HOW GOOD YOUR LOVE IS IL PADRINOS FEATURING JOCELYN BROWN	54	2002
THAT'S HOW I FEEL ABOUT YOU LONDONBEAT	69	1992
THAT'S HOW I'M LIVIN' ICE-T	21	1993
THAT'S HOW I'M LIVING TONI SCOTT	48	1989
THAT'S HOW PEOPLE GROW UP MORRISSEY	14	2008
THAT'S HOW STRONG MY LOVE IS IN CROWD	48	1965
THAT'S JUST THE WAY IT IS PHIL COLLINS	26	1990
THAT'S LIFE FRANK SINATRA	44	1966
THAT'S LIVIN' ALRIGHT JOE FAGIN	3	1984
THAT'S LOVE BILLY FURY WITH THE FOUR JAYS	19	1960
THAT'S LOVE, THAT IS BLANCMANGE	33	1983
THAT'S MORE LIKE IT SKYLARK	62	2004
THAT'S MY DOLL FRANKIE VAUGHAN	28	1959
THAT'S MY GOAL SHAYNE WARD	1	2006
THAT'S MY HOME MR ACKER BILK & HIS PARAMOUNT JAZZ BAND	7	1961
THAT'S NICE NEIL CHRISTIAN	14	1966
THAT'S NO WAY TO TELL A LIE JAMES DEAN BRADFIELD	18	2006
THAT'S RIGHT DEEP RIVER BOYS	29	1956
THAT'S THAT S**** SNOOP DOGG FEATURING R KELLY	38	2006
THAT'S THE WAY HONEYCOMBS	12	1965
THAT'S THE WAY GOD PLANNED IT BILLY PRESTON	11	1969
THAT'S THE WAY (I LIKE IT) KC & THE SUNSHINE BAND	4	1975
THAT'S THE WAY (I LIKE IT) DEAD OR ALIVE	22	1984
THAT'S THE WAY (I LIKE IT) CLOCK	11	1998
THAT'S THE WAY I WANNA ROCK 'N' ROLL AC/DC	22	1988
THAT'S THE WAY IT FEELS TWO NATIONS	74	1987
THAT'S THE WAY IT IS [A] MEL & KIM	10	1988
THAT'S THE WAY IT IS [B] CELINE DION	12	1999
THAT'S THE WAY LOVE GOES [A] CHARLES DICKENS	37	1965
THAT'S THE WAY LOVE GOES [B] YOUNG MC	65	1991
THAT'S THE WAY LOVE GOES [C] JANET JACKSON	2	1993
THAT'S THE WAY LOVE IS [A] TEN CITY	8	1989
THAT'S THE WAY LOVE IS [A] VOLCANO WITH SAM CARTWRIGHT	72	1995
THAT'S THE WAY LOVE IS [A] BYRON STINGILY	32	2000
THAT'S THE WAY LOVE IS [B] BOBBY BROWN	56	1993
THAT'S THE WAY OF THE WORLD D MOB WITH CATHY DENNIS	48	1990
THAT'S THE WAY THE MONEY GOES M	45	1980
THAT'S THE WAY YOU DO IT PURPLE KINGS	26	1994
THAT'S WHAT FRIENDS ARE FOR [A] DENIECE WILLIAMS	8	1977
THAT'S WHAT FRIENDS ARE FOR [B] DIONNE WARWICK & FRIENDS FEATURING ELTON JOHN, STEVIE WONDER & GLADYS KNIGHT	16	1985
THAT'S WHAT I LIKE JIVE BUNNY & THE MASTERMIXERS	1	1989
THAT'S WHAT I THINK CYNDI LAUPER	31	1993
THAT'S WHAT I WANT MARAUDERS	43	1963
THAT'S WHAT I WANT TO BE NEIL REID	45	1972
THAT'S WHAT LIFE IS ALL ABOUT BING CROSBY	41	1975
THAT'S WHAT LOVE CAN DO TOUTES LES FILLES	44	1999
THAT'S WHAT LOVE IS FOR AMY GRANT	60	1991

	Peak Position	Year of Entry
THAT'S WHAT LOVE WILL DO JOE BROWN & THE BRUVVERS	3	1963
THAT'S WHEN I REACH FOR MY REVOLVER MOBY	50	1996
THAT'S WHEN I THINK OF YOU 1927	46	1989
THAT'S WHEN THE MUSIC TAKES ME NEIL SEDAKA	18	1973
THAT'S WHERE MY MIND GOES SLAMM	68	1994
THAT'S WHERE THE HAPPY PEOPLE GO TRAMMPS	35	1976
THAT'S WHY I LIE RAY J	71	1998
THAT'S WHY I'M CRYING IVY LEAGUE	22	1965
THAT'S WHY WE LOSE CONTROL YOUNG OFFENDERS	60	1998
THAT'S YOU NAT 'KING' COLE	10	1960
THEIR WAY LITTL'ANS FEATURING PETER DOHERTY	22	2005
THEM BONES ALICE IN CHAINS	26	1993
THEM GIRLS THEM GIRLS ZIG & ZAG	5	1994
THEM THANGS 50 CENT/G-UNIT	10	2004
THEM THERE EYES EMILE FORD	18	1960
THE THEME [A] UNIQUE 3	61	1989
THEME [B] SABRES OF PARADISE	56	1994
THE THEME [C] DREEM TEEM	34	1997
THE THEME [D] TRACEY LEE	51	1997
THE THEME [E] JURGEN VRIES	13	2002
THEME FOR A DREAM CLIFF RICHARD	3	1961
THEME FOR YOUNG LOVERS SHADOWS	12	1964
THEME FROM *A SUMMER PLACE* NORRIE PARAMOUR	36	1960
THEME FROM *A SUMMER PLACE* PERCY FAITH	2	1960
THEME FROM *CADE'S COUNTY* HENRY MANCINI	42	1972
THEME FROM *CHEERS* GARY PORTNOY	58	1984
THEME FROM *COME SEPTEMBER* BOBBY DARIN ORCHESTRA	50	1961
THEME FROM DIXIE DUANE EDDY & THE REBELS	7	1961
THEME FROM *DR. KILDARE* JOHNNIE SPENCE	15	1962
THEME FROM *DR. KILDARE* (THREE STARS WILL SHINE TONIGHT) RICHARD CHAMBERLAIN	12	1962
THEME FROM *E.T. (THE EXTRA-TERRESTRIAL)* JOHN WILLIAMS	17	1982
THEME FROM *EXODUS* FERRANTE & TEICHER	6	1961
THEME FROM *EXODUS* SEMPRINI	25	1961
THEME FROM GUTBUSTER BENTLEY RHYTHM ACE	29	2000
THEME FROM *HARRY'S GAME* CLANNAD	5	1982
THEME FROM *HILL STREET BLUES* MIKE POST FEATURING LARRY CARLTON	25	1982
THEME FROM *JURASSIC PARK* JOHN WILLIAMS	45	1993
THEME FROM *M*A*S*H* (SUICIDE IS PAINLESS) MASH	1	1980
THEME FROM *M.A.S.H.* (SUICIDE IS PAINLESS) MANIC STREET PREACHERS	7	1992
THEME FROM *MAHOGANY* (DO YOU KNOW WHERE YOU'RE GOING TO) DIANA ROSS	5	1976
THEME FROM *MISSION: IMPOSSIBLE* ADAM CLAYTON & LARRY MULLEN	7	1996
THEME FROM *NEW YORK, NEW YORK* FRANK SINATRA	4	1980
THEME FROM *PICNIC* MORRIS STOLOFF	7	1956
THEME FROM P.O.P. PERFECTLY ORDINARY PEOPLE	61	1988
THEME FROM *RANDALL & HOPKIRK (DECEASED)* NINA PERSSON & DAVID ARNOLD	49	2000
THEME FROM S-EXPRESS S-EXPRESS	1	1988
THEME FROM *SHAFT* ISAAC HAYES	4	1971
THE THEME FROM *SHAFT* EDDY & THE SOUL BAND	13	1985
THEME FROM SPARTA FC FALL	66	2004
THEME FROM *SUPERMAN* (MAIN TITLE) LONDON SYMPHONY ORCHESTRA	32	1979
THEME FROM *THE APARTMENT* FERRANTE & TEICHER	44	1960
THEME FROM *THE DEER HUNTER* (CAVATINA) SHADOWS	9	1979
THEME FROM THE FILM *THE LEGION'S LAST PATROL* KEN THORNE	4	1963
THEME FROM *THE HONG KONG BEAT* RICHARD DENTON & MARTIN COOK	25	1978
THEME FROM *THE ONEDIN LINE* VIENNA PHILHARMONIC ORCHESTRA	15	1971
THE THEME FROM *THE PERSUADERS* JOHN BARRY ORCHESTRA	13	1971
THEME FROM *THE PROFESSIONALS* LAURIE JOHNSON'S LONDON BIG BAND	36	1997
THEME FROM *THE THREEPENNY OPERA* LOUIS ARMSTRONG WITH HIS ALL-STARS	8	1956
THEME FROM *THE THREEPENNY OPERA* DICK HYMAN TRIO	9	1956
THEME FROM *THE THREEPENNY OPERA* BILLY VAUGHN	12	1956
THEME FROM *THE TRAVELLING MAN* DUNCAN BROWNE	68	1984
THEME FROM TURNPIKE (EP) dEUS	68	1996
THEME FROM *VIETNAM* (CANON IN D) ORCHESTRE DE CHAMBRE JEAN-FRANCOIS PAILLARD	61	1988
THEME FROM *WHICH WAY IS UP* STARGARD	19	1978
THEME FROM *Z CARS* NORRIE PARAMOUR	33	1962
THEME FROM *Z-CARS* JOHNNY KEATING	8	1962
THEME ONE COZY POWELL	62	1979
THEME TO *ST TRINIAN'S* GIRLS ALOUD	51	2008
THEN CHARLATANS	12	1990
THEN CAME YOU DIONNE WARWICK & THE DETROIT SPINNERS	29	1974
THEN CAME YOU JUNIOR GISCOMBE	32	1992
THEN HE KISSED ME CRYSTALS	2	1963
THEN I FEEL GOOD KATHERINE E	56	1992
THEN I KISSED HER BEACH BOYS	4	1967
THEN YOU CAN TELL ME GOODBYE CASINOS	28	1967
THEN YOU TURN AWAY ORCHESTRAL MANOEUVRES IN THE DARK	50	1991
THERE AIN'T NOTHIN' LIKE THE LOVE MONTAGE	64	1997
THERE AIN'T NOTHING LIKE SHAGGIN' TAMS	21	1987
THERE ARE MORE QUESTIONS THAN ANSWERS JOHNNY NASH	9	1972
THERE ARE MORE SNAKES THAN LADDERS CAPTAIN SENSIBLE	57	1984
THERE BUT FOR FORTUNE JOAN BAEZ	8	1965
THERE BUT FOR THE GRACE OF GOD FIRE ISLAND FEATURING LOVE NELSON	32	1994
THERE BY THE GRACE OF GOD MANIC STREET PREACHERS	6	2002
THERE GOES MY EVERYTHING ENGELBERT HUMPERDINCK	2	1967
THERE GOES MY EVERYTHING ELVIS PRESLEY	6	1971
THERE GOES MY FIRST LOVE DRIFTERS	3	1975
THERE GOES THAT SONG AGAIN GARY MILLER	29	1961
THERE GOES THE FEAR DOVES	3	2002
THERE GOES THE NEIGHBORHOOD SHERYL CROW	19	1998
THERE I GO VIKKI CARR	50	1967
THERE I GO AGAIN POWER OF DREAMS	65	1992
THERE IS A LIGHT THAT NEVER GOES OUT SMITHS	25	1992
THERE IS A LIGHT THAT NEVER GOES OUT MORRISSEY	11	2005
THERE IS A MOUNTAIN DONOVAN	8	1967
THERE IS A STAR PHARAO	43	1995
THERE IS ALWAYS SOMETHING THERE TO REMIND ME HOUSEMARTINS	35	1988
THERE IS NO LOVE BETWEEN US ANYMORE POP WILL EAT ITSELF	66	1988
THERE IT GO (THE WHISTLE SONG) JUELZ SANTANA	47	2006
THERE IT IS SHALAMAR	5	1982
THERE I'VE SAID IT AGAIN AL SAXON	48	1961
THERE I'VE SAID IT AGAIN BOBBY VINTON	34	1964
THERE MUST BE A REASON FRANKIE LAINE	9	1954
THERE MUST BE A WAY JONI JAMES	24	1959
THERE MUST BE A WAY FRANKIE VAUGHAN	7	1967
THERE MUST BE AN ANGEL (PLAYING WITH MY HEART) EURYTHMICS	1	1985
THERE MUST BE THOUSANDS QUADS	66	1979
THERE SHE GOES [A] LA'S	13	1989
THERE SHE GOES [B] SIXPENCE NONE THE RICHER	14	1999
THERE SHE GOES AGAIN QUIREBOYS	37	1990
THERE SHE GOES MY BEAUTIFUL WORLD NICK CAVE & THE BAD SEEDS	45	2004
THERE THERE RADIOHEAD	4	2003
THERE THERE MY DEAR DEXY'S MIDNIGHT RUNNERS	7	1980
THERE WILL NEVER BE ANOTHER TONIGHT BRYAN ADAMS	32	1991
THERE WILL NEVER BE ANOTHER YOU [A] CHRIS MONTEZ	37	1966
THERE WILL NEVER BE ANOTHER YOU [B] JIMMY RUFFIN	68	1985
THERE WON'T BE MANY COMING HOME ROY ORBISON	12	1966
THERE YOU GO P!NK	6	2000
THERE YOU'LL BE FAITH HILL	3	2001
(THERE'LL BE BLUEBIRDS OVER) WHITE CLIFFS OF DOVER ROBSON GREEN & JEROME FLYNN	1	1995
THERE'LL BE SAD SONGS (TO MAKE YOU CRY) BILLY OCEAN	12	1986
THERE'S A BRAND NEW WORLD FIVE STAR	61	1988
THERE'S A GHOST IN MY HOUSE R. DEAN TAYLOR	3	1974
THERE'S A GHOST IN MY HOUSE FALL	30	1987
THERE'S A GOLDMINE IN THE SKY PAT BOONE	5	1957
THERE'S A GUY WORKS DOWN THE CHIPSHOP SWEARS HE'S ELVIS KIRSTY MacCOLL	14	1981
THERE'S A HEARTACHE FOLLOWING ME JIM REEVES	6	1964
THERE'S A KIND OF HUSH HERMAN'S HERMITS	7	1967
THERE'S A KIND OF HUSH (ALL OVER THE WORLD) CARPENTERS	22	1976
THERE'S A SILENCE ELECTRIC SOFT PARADE	52	2001
THERE'S A STAR ASH	13	2002
THERE'S A WHOLE LOT OF LOVING GUYS & DOLLS	2	1975
THERE'S ALWAYS ROOM ON THE BROOM LIARS	74	2004
(THERE'S) ALWAYS SOMETHING THERE TO REMIND ME SANDIE SHAW	1	1964
THERE'S GONNA BE A SHOWDOWN ARCHIE BELL & THE DRELLS	36	1973
THERE'S GOT TO BE A WAY MARIAH CAREY	54	1991
THERE'S GOTTA BE MORE TO LIFE STACIE ORRICO	12	2003
THERE'S MORE TO LOVE COMMUNARDS	20	1988

	Peak Position	Year of Entry
THERE'S NO LIVING WITHOUT YOU WILL DOWNING	67	1993
THERE'S NO ONE QUITE LIKE GRANDMA ST WINIFRED'S SCHOOL CHOIR	1	1980
THERE'S NO OTHER WAY BLUR	8	1991
THERE'S NOTHING BETTER THAN LOVE LUTHER VANDROSS, DUET WITH GREGORY HINES	72	1988
THERE'S NOTHING I WON'T DO JX	4	1996
THERE'S NOTHING LIKE THIS OMAR	14	1991
THERE'S SOMETHING WRONG IN PARADISE KID CREOLE & THE COCONUTS	35	1983
THERE'S THE GIRL HEART	34	1987
THERE'S YOUR TROUBLE DIXIE CHICKS	26	1999
THESE ARE DAYS 10,000 MANIACS	58	1992
THESE ARE THE DAYS [A] O-TOWN	36	2003
THESE ARE THE DAYS [B] JAMIE CULLUM	12	2004
THESE ARE THE DAYS OF OUR LIVES QUEEN	1	1991
THESE ARE THE TIMES DRU HILL	4	1999
THESE ARMS OF MINE PROCLAIMERS	51	1994
THESE BOOTS ARE MADE FOR WALKIN' NANCY SINATRA	1	1966
THESE BOOTS ARE MADE FOR WALKIN' BILLY RAY CYRUS	63	1992
THESE BOOTS ARE MADE FOR WALKIN' JESSICA SIMPSON	4	2005
THESE DAYS BON JOVI	7	1996
THESE DREAMS HEART	8	1986
THESE EARLY DAYS EVERYTHING BUT THE GIRL	75	1988
THESE THINGS ARE WORTH FIGHTING FOR GARY CLAIL ON-U SOUND SYSTEM	45	1993
THESE THINGS WILL KEEP ME LOVING YOU VELVELETTES	34	1971
THESE WOODEN IDEAS IDLEWILD	32	2000
THESE WORDS NATASHA BEDINGFIELD	1	2004
THEY JEM	6	2005
THEY ALL LAUGHED FRANK SINATRA	41	1999
(THEY CALL HER) LA BAMBA CRICKETS	21	1964
THEY DON'T CARE ABOUT US MICHAEL JACKSON	4	1996
THEY DON'T KNOW [A] TRACEY ULLMAN	2	1983
THEY DON'T KNOW [B] JON B	32	1998
THEY DON'T KNOW [C] SO SOLID CREW	3	2001
THEY GLUED YOUR HEAD ON UPSIDE DOWN BELLRAYS	75	2002
(THEY LONG TO BE) CLOSE TO YOU CARPENTERS	6	1970
(THEY LONG TO BE) CLOSE TO YOU GWEN GUTHRIE	25	1986
THEY SAY IT'S GONNA RAIN HAZELL DEAN	58	1985
THEY SHOOT HORSES DON'T THEY RACING CARS	14	1977
THEY WILL KILL US ALL (WITHOUT MERCY) BRONX	65	2004
THEY'RE COMING TO TAKE ME AWAY HA-HAAA! NAPOLEON XIV	4	1966
THEY'RE HERE EMF	29	1992
THIEVES IN THE TEMPLE PRINCE	7	1990
THIEVES LIKE US NEW ORDER	18	1984
THIGHS HIGH (GRIP YOUR HIPS AND MOVE) TOM BROWNE	45	1980
THIN LINE BETWEEN LOVE AND HATE PRETENDERS	49	1984
THE THIN WALL ULTRAVOX	14	1981
A THING CALLED LOVE JOHNNY CASH WITH THE EVANGEL TEMPLE CHOIR	4	1972
THE THING I LIKE AALIYAH	33	1995
THINGS [A] BOBBY DARIN	2	1962
THE THINGS [B] AUDIOBULLYS	22	2003
THINGS CAN ONLY GET BETTER [A] HOWARD JONES	6	1985
THINGS CAN ONLY GET BETTER [B] D:REAM	1	1993
THINGS FALL APART SERAFIN	49	2003
THINGS GET BETTER EDDIE FLOYD	31	1967
THINGS HAVE CHANGED BOB DYLAN	58	2000
THINGS I'VE SEEN SPOOKS	6	2001
THE THINGS THE LONELY DO AMAZULU	43	1986
THINGS THAT ARE RUNRIG	40	1995
THINGS THAT GO BUMP IN THE NIGHT ALLSTARS	12	2001
THINGS THAT MAKE YOU GO HMMM C & C MUSIC FACTORY (FEATURING FREEDOM WILLIAMS)	4	1991
THINGS WE DO FOR LOVE [A] 10 C.C.	6	1976
THINGS WE DO FOR LOVE [B] HORACE BROWN	27	1996
THINGS WILL GO MY WAY CALLING	34	2004
THINK [A] CHRIS FARLOWE	37	1966
THINK [B] BRENDA LEE	26	1964
THINK [C] ARETHA FRANKLIN	26	1968
THINK ABOUT... DJH FEATURING STEFY	22	1991
THINK ABOUT ME ARTFUL DODGER FEATURING MICHELLE ESCOFFERY	11	2001
THINK ABOUT THAT DANDY LIVINGSTONE	26	1973
THINK ABOUT THE WAY (BOM DIGI DIGI BOM...) ICE MC	42	1994
THINK ABOUT YOUR CHILDREN MARY HOPKIN	19	1970
THINK FOR A MINUTE HOUSEMARTINS	18	1986
THINK I'M GONNA FALL IN LOVE WITH YOU DOOLEYS	13	1977
THINK IT ALL OVER SANDIE SHAW	42	1969
THINK IT OVER CRICKETS	11	1958
(THINK OF ME) WHEREVER YOU ARE KEN DODD	21	1975
THINK OF YOU [A] USHER	70	1995
THINK OF YOU [B] WHIGFIELD	7	1995
THINK SOMETIMES ABOUT ME SANDIE SHAW	32	1966
THINK TWICE CELINE DION	1	1994
THINKIN' ABOUT YOUR BODY BOBBY McFERRIN	46	1988
THINKIN' AIN'T FOR ME PAUL JONES	32	1967
THINKING ABOUT TOMORROW BETH ORTON	57	2003
THINKING ABOUT YOUR BODY 2 MAD	43	1991
THINKING ABOUT YOUR LOVE [A] SKIPWORTH & TURNER	24	1985
THINKING ABOUT YOUR LOVE [A] PHILLIP LEO	64	1995
THINKING ABOUT YOUR LOVE [B] KENNY THOMAS	4	1991
THINKING IT OVER LIBERTY	5	2001
THINKING OF YOU [A] SISTER SLEDGE	11	1984
THINKING OF YOU [A] MAUREEN	11	1990
THINKING OF YOU [A] CURTIS LYNCH JR FEATURING KELE LE ROC & RED RAT	70	2000
THINKING OF YOU [A] PAUL WELLER	18	2004
THINKING OF YOU [B] COLOUR FIELD	12	1985
THINKING OF YOU [C] HANSON	23	1998
THINKING OF YOU [D] STATUS QUO	21	2004
THINKING OF YOU BABY DAVE CLARK FIVE	26	1964
THINKING OVER DANA GLOVER	38	2003
THIRD FINGER, LEFT HAND PEARLS	31	1972
THE THIRD MAN SHADOWS	44	1981
THIRD RAIL SQUEEZE	39	1993
THIRTEEN FORWARD, RUSSIA!	74	2005
13 STEPS LEAD DOWN ELVIS COSTELLO & THE ATTRACTIONS	59	1994
THE 13TH CURE	15	1996
13TH DISCIPLE FIVE THIRTY	67	1991
30TH CENTURY MAN CATHERINE WHEEL	47	1993
36D BEAUTIFUL SOUTH	46	1992
THIRTY THREE SMASHING PUMPKINS	21	1996
THIS AIN'T A LOVE SONG BON JOVI	6	1995
THIS AIN'T A SCENE IT'S AN ARMS RACE FALL OUT BOY	2	2007
THIS AND THAT TOM JONES	44	1966
THIS BEAT IS MINE VICKY D	42	1982
THIS BEAT IS TECHNOTRONIC TECHNOTRONIC FEATURING MC ERIC	14	1990
THIS BOY [A] JUSTIN	34	1998
THIS BOY [B] TOM BAXTER	65	2004
THIS BRUTAL HOUSE NITRO DELUXE	47	1987
THIS CAN BE REAL CANDY FLIP	60	1990
THIS CHARMING MAN SMITHS	8	1983
THIS CORROSION SISTERS OF MERCY	7	1987
THIS COWBOY SONG STING FEATURING PATO BANTON	15	1995
THIS DAY SHOULD LAST FOREVER OCEAN COLOUR SCENE	53	2005
THIS DJ WARREN G	12	1994
THIS DOOR SWINGS BOTH WAYS HERMAN'S HERMITS	18	1966
THIS FEELIN' [A] FRANK HOOKER & POSITIVE PEOPLE	48	1980
THIS FEELING [B] PURESSENCE	33	1998
THIS FLIGHT TONIGHT NAZARETH	11	1973
THIS GARDEN LEVELLERS	12	1993
THIS GENERATION ROACHFORD	38	1994
THIS GOLDEN RING FORTUNES	15	1966
THIS GROOVE VICTORIA BECKHAM	3	2004
THIS GUY'S IN LOVE WITH YOU HERB ALPERT	3	1968
THIS HERE GIRAFFE FLAMING LIPS	72	1996
THIS HOUSE [A] TRACIE SPENCER	65	1991
THIS HOUSE [B] ALISON MOYET	40	1991
THIS HOUSE IS NOT A HOME REMBRANDTS	58	1996
THIS HOUSE (IS WHERE YOUR LOVE STANDS) BIG SOUND AUTHORITY	21	1985
THIS I PROMISE YOU N SYNC	21	2000
THIS I SWEAR [A] RICHARD DARBYSHIRE	50	1993
THIS I SWEAR [B] KIM WILDE	46	1996
THIS IS A CALL FOO FIGHTERS	5	1995
THIS IS A REBEL SONG SINEAD O'CONNOR	60	1997
THIS IS A SONG MAGIC NUMBERS	36	2007
THIS IS A WARNING/SUPER DJ DILLINJA	47	2003
THIS IS ENGLAND CLASH	24	1985
THIS IS FOR REAL DAVID DEVANT & HIS SPIRIT WIFE	61	1997
THIS IS FOR THE LOVER IN YOU BABYFACE	12	1996
THIS IS FOR THE POOR OTHERS	42	2004
THIS IS GOODBYE LUCY CARR	41	2003
THIS IS HARDCORE PULP	12	1998
THIS IS HOW A HEART BREAKS ROB THOMAS	67	2005
THIS IS HOW IT FEELS INSPIRAL CARPETS	14	1990
THIS IS HOW WE DO IT MONTELL JORDAN	11	1995
THIS IS HOW WE DO IT MIS-TEEQ	7	2002
THIS IS HOW WE PARTY S.O.A.P.	36	1998
THIS IS IT! [A] ADAM FAITH	5	1961
THIS IS IT [B] MELBA MOORE	9	1976
THIS IS IT [B] DANNII MINOGUE	10	1993
THIS IS IT [C] DAN HARTMAN	17	1979
THIS IS IT [D] 4MANDU	45	1995
THIS IS IT [E] STATE OF MIND	30	1998
THIS IS IT (YOUR SOUL) HOTHOUSE FLOWERS	67	1993
THIS IS LOVE [A] GARY NUMAN	28	1986
THIS IS LOVE [B] GEORGE HARRISON	55	1988
THIS IS LOVE [C] PJ HARVEY	41	2001
THIS IS ME [A] CLIMIE FISHER	22	1988
THIS IS ME [B] SAW DOCTORS	31	2002
THIS IS MINE HEAVEN 17	23	1984
THIS IS MUSIC VERVE	35	1995
THIS IS MY HOLLYWOOD 3 COLOURS RED	48	1997
THIS IS MY LIFE EARTHA KITT	73	1986
THIS IS MY NIGHT CHAKA KHAN	14	1985
THIS IS MY SONG HARRY SECOMBE	2	1967
THIS IS MY SONG PETULA CLARK	1	1967

	Peak Position	Year of Entry
THIS IS MY SOUND DJ SHOG	40	2002
THIS IS MY TIME 3 COLOURS RED	36	1999
THIS IS NOT A LOVE SONG PUBLIC IMAGE LTD.	5	1983
THIS IS NOT A SONG FRANK & WALTERS	46	1992
THIS IS NOT AMERICA DAVID BOWIE & THE PAT METHENY GROUP	14	1985
THIS IS NOT REAL LOVE GEORGE MICHAEL & MUTYA	15	2006
THIS IS OUR SONG CODE RED	59	1996
THIS IS RADIO CLASH CLASH	47	1981
THIS IS SKA LONGSY D'S HOUSE SOUND	56	1989
THIS IS THE DAY THE THE	71	1983
THIS IS THE GIRL KANO FEATURING CRAIG DAVID	18	2007
THIS IS THE LAST TIME KEANE	18	2004
THIS IS THE LIFE AMY MacDONALD	28	2007
THIS IS THE NEW SHIT MARILYN MANSON	29	2003
THIS IS THE PLACE ZEITIA MASSIAH	62	1994
THIS IS THE RIGHT TIME LISA STANSFIELD	13	1989
THIS IS THE SOUND OF YOUTH THESE ANIMAL MEN	72	1994
THIS IS THE STORY OF MY LIFE (BABY) WIZZARD	34	1974
THIS IS THE WAY [A] BRUCE FOXTON	56	1983
THIS IS THE WAY [B] DANNII MINOGUE	27	1993
THIS IS THE WAY [C] F.K.W.	63	1994
THIS IS THE WAY [D] E-TYPE	53	1995
THIS IS THE WORLD CALLING BOB GELDOF	25	1986
THIS IS THE WORLD WE LIVE IN ALCAZAR	15	2004
THIS IS TOMORROW BRYAN FERRY	9	1977
THIS IS WHAT WE DO CRACKOUT	65	2004
THIS IS WHERE I CAME IN BEE GEES	18	2001
THIS IS WHY I'M HOT MIMS	18	2007
THIS IS YOUR LAND SIMPLE MINDS	13	1989
THIS IS YOUR LIFE [A] BLOW MONKEYS	32	1988
THIS IS YOUR LIFE [B] BANDERAS	16	1991
THIS IS YOUR LIFE [C] DUST BROTHERS	60	1999
THIS IS YOUR NIGHT [A] HEAVY D. & THE BOYZ	30	1994
THIS IS YOUR NIGHT [B] ANOTHERSIDE	41	2003
THIS IZ REAL SHYEIM	61	1996
THIS KIND OF LOVE PHIL FEARON & GALAXY	70	1985
THIS KISS FAITH HILL	13	1998
THIS LITTLE BIRD MARIANNE FAITHFULL	6	1965
THIS LITTLE BIRD NASHVILLE TEENS	38	1965
THIS LITTLE GIRL GARY U.S. BONDS	43	1981
THIS LOVE [A] LeANN RIMES	54	2004
THIS LOVE [B] MAROON 5	3	2004
THIS LOVE AFFAIR STEFAN DENNIS	67	1989
THIS LOVE I HAVE FOR YOU LANCE FORTUNE	26	1960
THIS MONDAY MORNING FEELING TITO SIMON	45	1975
THIS MORNING NORTHERN UPROAR	17	1996
THIS MUST BE LOVE LITTLE MAN TATE	33	2007
THIS MUST BE THE PLACE TALKING HEADS	51	1984
THIS NEW YEAR CLIFF RICHARD	30	1992
THIS OLD HEART OF MINE ISLEY BROTHERS	3	1966
THIS OLD HEART OF MINE ROD STEWART	4	1975
THIS OLD SKIN BEAUTIFUL SOUTH	43	2004
THIS OLD TOWN PAUL WELLER & GRAHAM COXON	39	2007
THIS OLE HOUSE BILLIE ANTHONY	4	1954
THIS OLE HOUSE ROSEMARY CLOONEY	1	1954
THIS OLE HOUSE SHAKIN' STEVENS	1	1981
THIS ONE PAUL McCARTNEY	18	1989
THIS ONE'S FOR THE CHILDREN NEW KIDS ON THE BLOCK	9	1990
THIS ONE'S FOR YOU ED HARCOURT	41	2004
THIS PARTY SUCKS! FUSED	64	1999
THIS PERFECT DAY SAINTS	34	1977
THIS PICTURE PLACEBO	23	2003
THIS PLANET'S ON FIRE SAMMY HAGAR	52	1979
THIS SONG IS ABOUT YOU ENEMY	41	2008
THIS STRANGE EFFECT DAVE BERRY	37	1965
THIS SUMMER SQUEEZE	32	1995
THIS TIME [A] TROY SHONDELL	22	1961
THIS TIME [B] BRYAN ADAMS	41	1986
THIS TIME [C] DINA CARROLL	23	1993
THIS TIME [D] MICHELLE SWEENEY	57	1994
THIS TIME [E] JUDY CHEEKS	23	1995
THIS TIME [F] CURTIS STIGERS	28	1995
THIS TIME [G] STARSAILOR	24	2006
THIS TIME AROUND PHATS & SMALL	15	2001
THIS TIME BABY JACKIE MOORE	49	1979
THIS TIME I FOUND LOVE ROZALLA	33	1994
THIS TIME I KNOW IT'S FOR REAL DONNA SUMMER	3	1989
THIS TIME I KNOW IT'S FOR REAL KELLY LLORENNA	14	2004
THIS TIME (I'M GONNA TRY IT MY WAY) DJ SHADOW	54	2007
THIS TIME (LIVE) WET WET WET	38	1993
THIS TIME OF YEAR RUNRIG	38	1995
THIS TIME (WE'LL GET IT RIGHT) ENGLAND WORLD CUP SQUAD	2	1982
THIS TOWN AIN'T BIG ENOUGH FOR BOTH OF US SPARKS	2	1974
THIS TOWN AIN'T BIG ENOUGH FOR BOTH OF US BRITISH WHALE	6	2005
THIS TRAIN DON'T STOP THERE ANYMORE ELTON JOHN	24	2002
THIS USED TO BE MY PLAYGROUND MADONNA	3	1992
THIS WAITING HEART CHRIS DE BURGH	59	1989
THIS WAY DILATED PEOPLES	35	2004
THIS WHEEL'S ON FIRE [A] JULIE DRISCOLL, BRIAN AUGER & THE TRINITY	5	1968
THIS WHEEL'S ON FIRE [B] SIOUXSIE & THE BANSHEES	14	1987
THIS WILL BE NATALIE COLE	32	1975
THIS WILL BE OUR YEAR BEAUTIFUL SOUTH	36	2005
THIS WOMAN'S WORK KATE BUSH	25	1989
THIS WORLD IS NOT MY HOME JIM REEVES	22	1965
THIS WORLD OF WATER NEW MUSIK	31	1980
THIS WRECKAGE GARY NUMAN	20	1980
THIS YEAR'S LOVE DAVID GRAY	20	2001
THNKS FR TH MMRS FALL OUT BOY	12	2007
THOIA THONG R KELLY	14	2003
THONG SONG SISQO	3	2000
THE THORN EP SIOUXSIE & THE BANSHEES	47	1984
THORN IN MY SIDE EURYTHMICS	5	1986
THOSE FIRST IMPRESSIONS ASSOCIATES	43	1984
THOSE SIMPLE THINGS RIGHT SAID FRED	29	1992
THOSE WERE THE DAYS MARY HOPKIN	1	1968
THOU SHALT ALWAYS KILL DAN LE SAC VS SCROOBIUS PIP	34	2007
THOU SHALT NOT STEAL FREDDIE & THE DREAMERS	44	1965
THOUGHT I'D DIED AND GONE TO HEAVEN BRYAN ADAMS	8	1992
THE THOUGHT OF IT LOUIE LOUIE	34	1992
THOUGHT U WERE THE ONE FOR ME JOEY B ELLIS	58	1991
THOUGHTLESS KORN	37	2002
A THOUSAND MILES VANESSA CARLTON	6	2002
A THOUSAND STARS BILLY FURY	14	1961
A THOUSAND TREES STEREOPHONICS	22	1997
THREE WEDDING PRESENT	14	1992
3AM [A] MATCHBOX 20	64	1998
3AM [B] BOBBY BLANCO & MIKKI MOTO	70	2004
3AM [C] BUSTED	1	2004
3AM ETERNAL KLF FEATURING THE CHILDREN OF THE REVOLUTION	1	1991
THREE BABIES SINEAD O'CONNOR	42	1990
THE THREE BELLS BROWNS	6	1959
THREE BELLS BRIAN POOLE & THE TREMELOES	17	1965
THE THREE BELLS DANIEL O'DONNELL	71	1993
THE THREE BELLS (THE JIMMY BROWN SONG) COMPAGNONS DE LA CHANSON	21	1959
THREE COINS IN THE FOUNTAIN FOUR ACES FEATURING AL ALBERTS	5	1954
THREE COINS IN THE FOUNTAIN FRANK SINATRA	1	1954
THREE EP MANSUN	19	1996
3 FEET TALL I AM KLOOT	46	2003
3 IS FAMILY DANA DAWSON	9	1995
3 LIBRAS A PERFECT CIRCLE	49	2001
THREE LIONS (THE OFFICIAL SONG OF THE ENGLAND FOOTBALL TEAM) BADDIEL & SKINNER & LIGHTNING SEEDS	1	1996
THREE LITTLE BIRDS BOB MARLEY & THE WAILERS	17	1980
THREE LITTLE PIGS GREEN JELLY	5	1993
THREE LITTLE WORDS (I LOVE YOU) APPLEJACKS	23	1964
3 MCS AND 1 DJ BEASTIE BOYS	21	1999
THREE MINUTE HERO SELECTER	16	1980
THREE NIGHTS A WEEK FATS DOMINO	45	1960
THREE RING CIRCUS BARRY BIGGS	22	1977
3..6..9 SECONDS OF LIGHT BELLE & SEBASTIAN	32	1997
3 SONGS EP WEDDING PRESENT	25	1990
THREE STARS RUBY WRIGHT	19	1959
THREE STEPS TO HEAVEN EDDIE COCHRAN	1	1960
THREE STEPS TO HEAVEN SHOWADDYWADDY	2	1975
3345 BLACK VELVETS	34	2005
THREE TIMES A LADY COMMODORES	1	1978
THREE TIMES A MAYBE K CREATIVE	58	1992
3 X 3 EP GENESIS	10	1982
3'S & 7'S QUEENS OF THE STONE AGE	19	2007
THREESOME FENIX TX	66	2002
3IL (THRILL) SOUL U*NIQUE	66	2000
THRILL HAS GONE TEXAS	60	1989
THRILL ME [A] SIMPLY RED	33	1992
THRILL ME [B] JUNIOR JACK	29	2002
THRILLER MICHAEL JACKSON	10	1983
THROUGH KINGS OF TOMORROW	74	2003
THROUGH THE BARRICADES SPANDAU BALLET	6	1986
THROUGH THE GATE ARTIFICIAL INTELLIGENCE	73	2004
THROUGH THE PAIN (SHE TOLD ME) P DIDDY FEATURING MARIO WINANS	50	2007
THROUGH THE RAIN MARIAH CAREY	8	2002
THROUGH THE ROOF CUD	44	1992
THROUGH THE STORM ARETHA FRANKLIN & ELTON JOHN	41	1989
THROUGH THE WIRE KANYE WEST	9	2004
THROUGH THE YEARS [A] GARY GLITTER	49	1992
THROUGH THE YEARS [B] CILLA BLACK	54	1993
THROW AWAY THE KEY LINX	21	1981
THROW DOWN A LINE CLIFF RICHARD & HANK MARVIN	7	1969
THROW THESE GUNS AWAY DUNBLANE	1	1996
THROW YA GUNZ ONYX	34	1993
THROW YOUR HANDS UP LV	24	1995
THROW YOUR SET IN THE AIR CYPRESS HILL	15	1995
THROWING IT ALL AWAY GENESIS	22	1987
THROWING MY BABY OUT WITH BATHWATER TEN POLE TUDOR	10	1981
THROWN AWAY STRANGLERS	42	1981
THRU KINGS OF TOMORROW FEATURING HAZE	55	2005
THRU THE GLASS THIRTEEN SENSES	18	2005
THRU' THESE WALLS PHIL COLLINS	56	1982

	Peak Position	Year of Entry
THUG LOVIN' JA RULE FEATURING BOBBY BROWN	15	2002
THUGZ MANSION 2PAC	24	2003
THUNDER [A] PRINCE & THE NEW POWER GENERATION	28	1992
THUNDER [B] EAST 17	4	1995
THUNDER AND LIGHTNING THIN LIZZY	39	1983
THUNDER IN MY HEART LEO SAYER	22	1977
THUNDER IN MY HEART AGAIN MECK FEATURING LEO SAYER	1	2006
THUNDER IN THE MOUNTAINS TOYAH	4	1981
THUNDERBALL TOM JONES	35	1966
THUNDERBIRDS [A] BARRY GRAY ORCHESTRA	61	1981
THUNDERBIRDS [B] BUSTED	1	2004
THUNDERBIRDS ARE GO FAB FEATURING MC PARKER	5	1990
THUNDERDOME MESSIAH	29	1993
THUNDERSTRUCK AC/DC	13	1990
THURSDAY'S CHILD DAVID BOWIE	16	1999
THUS SPAKE ZARATHUSTRA PHILHARMONIA ORCHESTRA, CONDUCTOR LORIN MAAZEL	33	1969
TI AMO GINA G	11	1997
TIC, TIC TAC CHILLI FEATURING CARRAPICHO	59	1997
TIC TOC KLEA	61	2002
TICK TICK BOOM HIVES	41	2007
TICK TOCK LEMAR	45	2007
TICKET OUTTA LOSERVILLE SON OF DORK	3	2005
TICKET TO RIDE BEATLES	1	1965
TICKET TO THE MOON ELECTRIC LIGHT ORCHESTRA	24	1982
THE TIDE IS HIGH BLONDIE	1	1980
THE TIDE IS HIGH (GET THE FEELING) ATOMIC KITTEN	1	2002
THE TIDE IS TURNING (AFTER LIVE AID) ROGER WATERS	54	1987
THE TIDE THAT LEFT AND NEVER CAME BACK VEILS	63	2004
TIE A YELLOW RIBBON ROUND THE OLD OAK TREE DAWN FEATURING TONY ORLANDO	1	1973
TIE ME KANGAROO DOWN SPORT ROLF HARRIS	9	1960
TIE YOUR MOTHER DOWN QUEEN	13	1977
TIED TO THE 90'S TRAVIS	30	1997
TIED UP YELLO	60	1988
TIED UP TOO TIGHT HARD-FI	15	2005
TIGER BABY SILVER CONVENTION	41	1976
TIGER FEET MUD	1	1974
TIGHTEN UP - I JUST CAN'T STOP DANCING WALLY JUMP Jr. & THE CRIMINAL ELEMENT ORCHESTRA	24	1987
TIJUANA TAXI HERB ALPERT & THE TIJUANA BRASS	37	1966
TIL I HEAR IT FROM YOU GIN BLOSSOMS	39	1996
('TIL) I KISSED YOU EVERLY BROTHERS	2	1959
...TIL THE COPS COME KNOCKIN' MAXWELL	63	1996
TIL THE DAY EASYWORLD	27	2004
TIL THE END HAVEN	28	2002
TILL TONY BENNETT	35	1961
TILL DOROTHY SQUIRES	25	1970
TILL TOM JONES	2	1971
TILL I CAN'T TAKE LOVE NO MORE EDDY GRANT	42	1983
TILL I GET MY WAY BLACK KEYS	62	2004
TILL I LOVED YOU PLACIDO DOMINGO & JENNIFER RUSH	24	1989
TILL I LOVED YOU (LOVE THEME FROM 'GOYA') BARBRA STREISAND & DON JOHNSON	16	1988
TILL TEARS DO US PART HEAVENS CRY	68	2001
TILL THE END OF THE DAY KINKS	8	1965
TILL THERE WAS YOU PEGGY LEE	30	1961
TILL WE MEET AGAIN [A] INNER CITY	47	1991
TILL WE MEET AGAIN [B] PUSH	46	2000
TILL YOU COME BACK TO ME LEO SAYER	51	1983
TILT YA HEAD BACK NELLY & CHRISTINA AGUILERA	5	2004
TILTED SUGAR	48	1993
TIME [A] CRAIG DOUGLAS	9	1961
TIME [B] LIGHT OF THE WORLD	35	1981
TIME [C] FRIDA & BA ROBERTSON	45	1983
TIME [D] FREDDIE MERCURY	32	1986
TIME [E] KIM WILDE	71	1990
TIME [F] SUPERGRASS	2	1995
TIME [G] MARION	29	1996
TIME AFTER TIME [A] CYNDI LAUPER	3	1984
TIME AFTER TIME [A] HYPERSTATE	71	1993
TIME AFTER TIME [A] CHANGING FACES	35	1998
TIME AFTER TIME [A] DISTANT SOUNDZ	20	2002
TIME AFTER TIME [A] NOVASPACE	29	2003
TIME AFTER TIME [B] BELOVED	46	1990
TIME ALONE WILL TELL MALCOLM ROBERTS	45	1967
TIME AND CHANCE COLOR ME BADD	62	1993
A TIME AND PLACE MIKE + THE MECHANICS	58	1991
TIME AND THE RIVER NAT 'KING' COLE	23	1960
TIME AND TIDE BASIA	61	1988
TIME AND TIME AGAIN PAPA ROACH	54	2002
TIME BOMB [A] 808 STATE	59	1992
TIME BOMB [B] RANCID	56	1995
TIME (CLOCK OF THE HEART) CULTURE CLUB	3	1982
TIME DRAGS BY CLIFF RICHARD	10	1966
TIME FOR ACTION SECRET AFFAIR	13	1979
TIME FOR DELIVERANCE DO ME BAD THINGS	57	2004
TIME FOR HEROES LIBERTINES	20	2003
TIME FOR LIVING ASSOCIATION	23	1968
TIME FOR LOVE KIM ENGLISH	48	1995
TIME FOR THE REVOLUTION 10 REVOLUTIONS	59	2003
THE TIME HAS COME ADAM FAITH	4	1961
THE TIME HAS COME PP ARNOLD	47	1967
TIME HAS TAKEN ITS TOLL ON YOU CRAZYHEAD	65	1988
THE TIME IN BETWEEN CLIFF RICHARD & THE SHADOWS	22	1965
TIME IS MY EVERYTHING IAN BROWN	15	2005
THE TIME IS NOW MOLOKO	2	2000
TIME IS ON MY SIDE ROLLING STONES	62	1982
TIME IS RUNNING OUT MUSE	8	2003
TIME IS TIGHT BOOKER T. & THE M.G.'s	4	1969
A TIME LIKE THIS HAYWOODE	48	1983
TIME LOVE AND TENDERNESS MICHAEL BOLTON	28	1991
TIME OF MY LIFE TOPLOADER	18	2002
TIME OF OUR LIVES ALISON LIMERICK	36	1994
TIME OF YOUR LIFE (GOOD RIDDANCE) GREEN DAY	11	1998
TIME SELLER SPENCER DAVIS GROUP	30	1967
TIME STAND STILL RUSH WITH AIMEE MANN	42	1987
TIME TO BURN STORM	3	2000
TIME TO GET BACK HYSTERIC EGO	50	1999
TIME TO GET UP LIQUID	46	1993
TIME TO GROW LEMAR	9	2005
TIME TO MAKE THE FLOOR BURN VARIOUS ARTISTS (MONTAGES)	16	1990
TIME TO MAKE YOU MINE LISA STANSFIELD	14	1992
TIME TO MOVE ON SPARKLE	40	1998
TIME TO PRETEND MGMT	49	2008
TIME TO SAY GOODBYE SARAH BRIGHTMAN/ ANDREA BOCELLI	2	1997
TIME TO WASTE ALKALINE TRIO	32	2005
THE TIME WARP 2 DAMIAN	7	1987
TIME WILL CRAWL DAVID BOWIE	33	1987
TIMEBOMB CHUMBAWAMBA	59	1993
TIMELESS DANIEL O'DONNELL & MARY DUFF	32	1996
TIMELESS (KEEP ON MOVIN') RON VAN DEN BEUKEN	65	2004
TIMELESS MELODY LA'S	57	1990
TIMES LIKE THESE FOO FIGHTERS	12	2002
TIMES OF OUR LIVES PAUL VAN DYK FEATURING VEGA 4	28	2003
THE TIMES THEY ARE A-CHANGIN' PETER, PAUL & MARY	44	1964
THE TIMES THEY ARE A-CHANGIN' IAN CAMPBELL FOLK GROUP	42	1965
TIMES THEY ARE A-CHANGIN' BOB DYLAN	9	1965
THE TIMEWARP CAST OF THE NEW ROCKY HORROR SHOW	57	1998
TIN MACHINE TIN MACHINE	48	1989
TIN SOLDIER SMALL FACES	9	1967
TIN SOLDIERS STIFF LITTLE FINGERS	36	1980
TINA MARIE PERRY COMO	24	1955
TINGLE THAT PETROL EMOTION	49	1991
TINSEL TOWN RONNY JORDAN	64	1994
TINSELTOWN TO THE BOOGIEDOWN SCRITTI POLITTI	46	1999
TINY CHILDREN TEARDROP EXPLODES	44	1982
TINY DANCER MARCO DEMARK FEATURING CASEY BARNES	54	2008
TINY DYNAMITE (EP) COCTEAU TWINS	52	1985
TINY MACHINE DARLING BUDS	60	1990
TIPP CITY AMPS	61	1995
THE TIPS OF MY FINGERS DES O'CONNOR	15	1970
TIPSY J-KWON	4	2004
TIRED OF BEING ALONE AL GREEN	4	1971
TIRED OF BEING ALONE TEXAS	19	1992
TIRED OF BEING SORRY ENRIQUE IGLESIAS	20	2007
TIRED OF TOEIN' THE LINE ROCKY BURNETTE	58	1979
TIRED OF WAITING FOR YOU KINKS	1	1965
TISHBITE COCTEAU TWINS	34	1996
TKO LE TIGRE	50	2005
TNT FOR THE BRAIN ENIGMA	60	1997
TO A BRIGHTER DAY (O' HAPPY DAY) BEAT SYSTEM	70	1993
TO ALL THE GIRLS I'VE LOVED BEFORE JULIO IGLESIAS & WILLIE NELSON	17	1984
TO BE A LOVER BILLY IDOL	22	1986
TO BE FREE EMILIANA TORRINI	44	2001
TO BE IN LOVE MAW PRESENTS INDIA	23	1999
TO BE LOVED JACKIE WILSON	23	1958
TO BE LOVED MALCOLM VAUGHAN WITH THE MICHAEL SAMMES SINGERS	14	1958
TO BE OR NOT TO BE B.A. ROBERTSON	9	1980
TO BE OR NOT TO BE (THE HITLER RAP) MEL BROOKS	12	1984
TO BE REBORN BOY GEORGE	13	1987
TO BE WITH YOU MR BIG	3	1992
TO BE WITH YOU AGAIN LEVEL 42	10	1987
TO CUT A LONG STORY SHORT SPANDAU BALLET	5	1980
TO DIE A VIRGIN DIVINE COMEDY	67	2006
TO DIE FOR LUKE GALLIANA	42	2001
TO EARTH WITH LOVE GAY DAD	10	1999
TO FRANCE MIKE OLDFIELD FEATURING MAGGIE REILLY	48	1984
TO GET DOWN (ROCK THING) TIMO MAAS	14	2002
TO HAVE AND TO HOLD CATHERINE STOCK	17	1986
TO HERE KNOWS WHEN MY BLOODY VALENTINE	29	1991
TO KNOW HIM IS TO LOVE HIM TEDDY BEARS	2	1958
TO KNOW SOMEONE DEEPLY IS TO KNOW SOMEONE SOFTLY TERENCE TRENT D'ARBY	55	1990
TO KNOW YOU IS TO LOVE YOU PETER & GORDON	5	1965
TO LIVE AND DIE IN LA MAKAVELI	10	1997
TO LOVE A WOMAN LIONEL RICHIE FEATURING ENRIQUE IGLESIAS	19	2003

	Peak Position	Year of Entry
TO LOVE ONCE AGAIN SOLID HARMONIE	55	1998
TO LOVE SOMEBODY BEE GEES	41	1967
TO LOVE SOMEBODY NINA SIMONE	5	1969
TO LOVE SOMEBODY JIMMY SOMERVILLE	8	1990
TO LOVE SOMEBODY MICHAEL BOLTON	16	1992
TO MAKE A BIG MAN CRY P.J. PROBY	34	1966
TO THE BEAT OF THE DRUM (LA LUNA) ETHICS	13	1995
TO THE BIRDS SUEDE	49	1992
TO THE CLUB SPANKOX	69	2004
TO THE END BLUR	16	1994
TO THE LIMIT TONY DE VIT	44	1995
TO THE MOON AND BACK SAVAGE GARDEN	3	1997
TO THE WORLD O.R.G.A.N.	33	1998
TO WHOM IT CONCERNS CHRIS ANDREWS	13	1965
TO WIN JUST ONCE SAW DOCTORS	14	1996
TO YOU I BELONG B*WITCHED	1	1998
TO YOU I BESTOW MUNDY	60	1996
TOAST STREETBAND	18	1978
TOAST OF LOVE THREE DEGREES	36	1976
TOBACCO ROAD NASHVILLE TEENS	6	1964
TOCA ME FRAGMA	11	1999
TOCA'S MIRACLE FRAGMA	1	2000
TOCCATA SKY	5	1980
TOCCATA & FUGUE VANESSA-MAE	16	1995
TODAY [A] SANDIE SHAW	27	1968
TODAY [B] TALK TALK	14	1982
TODAY [C] SMASHING PUMPKINS	44	1993
TODAY [D] MELANIE BROWN	41	2005
TODAY FOREVER RIDE	14	1990
TODAY THE SUN'S ON US SOPHIE ELLIS-BEXTOR	64	2007
TODAY'S THE DAY SEAN MAGUIRE	27	1997
TODAY'S YOUR LUCKY DAY HAROLD MELVIN & THE BLUENOTES FEATURING NIKKO	66	1984
TOGETHER [A] CONNIE FRANCIS	6	1961
TOGETHER [A] P.J. PROBY	8	1964
TOGETHER [B] O.C. SMITH	25	1977
TOGETHER [C] DANNY CAMPBELL & SASHA	57	1993
TOGETHER [D] ARTIFICIAL FUNK FEATURING NELLIE ETTISON	40	2003
TOGETHER AGAIN [A] RAY CHARLES	48	1966
TOGETHER AGAIN [B] JANET JACKSON	4	1997
TOGETHER FOREVER RICK ASTLEY	2	1988
TOGETHER IN ELECTRIC DREAMS GIORGIO MORODER & PHIL OAKEY	3	1984
TOGETHER WE ARE BEAUTIFUL STEVE ALLAN	67	1979
TOGETHER WE ARE BEAUTIFUL FERN KINNEY	1	1980
TOGETHERNESS MIKE PRESTON	41	1960
TOKOLOSHE MAN JOHN KONGOS	4	1971
TOKYO CLASSIX NOUVEAUX	67	1981
TOKYO JOE BRYAN FERRY	15	1977
TOKYO MELODY HELMUT ZACHARIAS	9	1964
TOKYO STEALTH FIGHTER DAVE ANGEL	58	1997
TOKYO STORM WARNING ELVIS COSTELLO	73	1986
TOLEDO ELVIS COSTELLO/BURT BACHARACH	72	1999
TOM DOOLEY KINGSTON TRIO	5	1958
TOM DOOLEY LONNIE DONEGAN	3	1958
TOM HARK ELIAS & HIS ZIGZAG JIVE FLUTES	2	1958
TOM HARK TED HEATH	24	1958
TOM HARK PIRANHAS	6	1980
TOM HARK (WE WANT FALMER) SEAGULLS SKA	17	2005
TOM JONES INTERNATIONAL TOM JONES	31	2002
TOM PILLIBI JACQUELINE BOYER	33	1960
TOM SAWYER RUSH	25	1981
TOM THE MODEL BETH GIBBONS AND RUSTIN MAN	70	2003
TOM THE PEEPER ACT ONE	40	1974
TOM TRAUBERT'S BLUES (WALTZING MATILDA) ROD STEWART	6	1992
TOMB OF MEMORIES PAUL YOUNG	16	1985
TOMBOY PERRY COMO	10	1959
TOMMY GUN CLASH	19	1978
TOMMY SHOTS YOUNG HEART ATTACK	54	2004
TOMORROW [A] JOHNNY BRANDON & THE PHANTOMS	8	1955
TOMORROW [B] SANDIE SHAW	9	1966
TOMORROW [C] COMMUNARDS	23	1987
TOMORROW [D] TONGUE 'N' CHEEK	20	1990
TOMORROW [E] SILVERCHAIR	59	1995
TOMORROW [F] JAMES	12	1997
TOMORROW [G] DUMONDE	60	2001
TOMORROW COMES TODAY GORILLAZ	33	2002
TOMORROW NEVER DIES SHERYL CROW	12	1997
TOMORROW NIGHT ATOMIC ROOSTER	11	1971
TOMORROW PEOPLE ZIGGY MARLEY & THE MELODY MAKERS	22	1988
TOMORROW RISING CLIFF RICHARD	29	1973
TOMORROW ROBINS WILL SING STEVIE WONDER	71	1995
TOMORROW TOMORROW BEE GEES	23	1969
TOMORROW'S CLOWN MARTY WILDE	33	1961
TOMORROW'S GIRLS [A] U.K. SUBS	28	1979
TOMORROW'S GIRLS [B] DONALD FAGEN	46	1993
TOMORROW'S (JUST ANOTHER DAY) MADNESS	8	1983
TOM'S DINER SUZANNE VEGA	58	1987
TOM'S DINER DNA FEATURING SUZANNE VEGA	2	1990
TOM'S PARTY T-SPOON	27	1999
TOM-TOM TURNAROUND NEW WORLD	6	1971
TONES OF HOME BLIND MELON	62	1993
TONGUE R.E.M.	13	1995
TONGUE TIED CAT	17	1993
TONIGHT [A] SHIRLEY BASSEY	21	1962
TONIGHT [B] MOVE	11	1971
TONIGHT [C] RUBETTES	12	1974
TONIGHT [D] ZAINE GRIFF	54	1980
TONIGHT [E] MODETTES	68	1981
TONIGHT [F] STEVE HARVEY	63	1983
TONIGHT [G] KOOL & THE GANG	2	1984
TONIGHT [H] BOOMTOWN RATS	73	1984
TONIGHT [I] DAVID BOWIE	53	1984
TONIGHT [J] NEW KIDS ON THE BLOCK	3	1990
TONIGHT [K] DEF LEPPARD	34	1993
TONIGHT [L] BAD COMPANY	56	2002
TONIGHT [M] WESTLIFE	3	2003
TONIGHT (COULD BE THE NIGHT) VELVETS	50	1961
TONIGHT I CELEBRATE MY LOVE PEABO BRYSON & ROBERTA FLACK	2	1983
TONIGHT I'M ALL RIGHT NARADA MICHAEL WALDEN	34	1980
TONIGHT I'M FREE PJ & DUNCAN	62	1993
TONIGHT I'M GONNA LET GO SYLEENA JOHNSON	38	2002
TONIGHT I'M GONNA LOVE YOU ALL OVER FOUR TOPS	43	1982
TONIGHT I'M YOURS (DON'T HURT ME) ROD STEWART	8	1981
TONIGHT IN TOKYO SANDIE SHAW	21	1967
TONIGHT IS WHAT IT MEANS TO BE YOUNG JIM STEINMAN & FIRE INC	67	1984
TONIGHT THE STREETS ARE OURS RICHARD HAWLEY	40	2007
TONIGHT TONIGHT SMASHING PUMPKINS	7	1996
TONIGHT TONIGHT TONIGHT GENESIS	18	1987
TONIGHT YOU BELONG TO ME PATIENCE & PRUDENCE	28	1956
TONIGHT'S THE NIGHT [A] ROD STEWART	5	1976
TONIGHT'S THE NIGHT [B] GINA G	57	2006
TONITE [A] SUPERCAR	15	1999
TONITE [B] PHATS & SMALL	11	1999
TOO BAD NICKELBACK	9	2002
TOO BEAUTIFUL TO LAST ENGELBERT HUMPERDINCK	14	1972
TOO BIG SUZI QUATRO	14	1974
TOO BLIND TO SEE IT KYM SIMS	5	1991
TOO BUSY THINKING ABOUT MY BABY MARVIN GAYE	5	1969
TOO BUSY THINKING 'BOUT MY BABY MARDI GRAS	19	1972
TOO BUSY THINKING ABOUT MY BABY STEPS	2	2001
TOO CLOSE NEXT	24	1998
TOO CLOSE BLUE	1	2001
TOO COLD ROOTS MANUVA	39	2005
TOO DRUNK TO FUCK DEAD KENNEDYS	36	1981
TOO FAR GONE LISA SCOTT-LEE	11	2003
TOO GONE, TOO LONG EN VOGUE	20	1997
TOO GOOD LITTLE TONY	19	1960
TOO GOOD TO BE FORGOTTEN CHI-LITES	10	1974
TOO GOOD TO BE FORGOTTEN AMAZULU	5	1986
TOO GOOD TO BE TRUE TOM PETTY & THE HEARTBREAKERS	34	1992
TOO HARD TO BE FREE AMEN	72	2001
TOO HOT [A] KOOL & THE GANG	23	1980
TOO HOT [A] COOLIO	9	1996
TOO HOT [B] FUN LOVIN' CRIMINALS	61	2003
TOO HOT [C] FYA	49	2004
TOO HOT TO HANDLE HEATWAVE	15	1977
TOO HOT TO TROT COMMODORES	38	1978
TOO LATE JUNIOR	20	1982
TOO LATE FOR GOODBYES JULIAN LENNON	6	1984
TOO LATE TO SAY GOODBYE RICHARD MARX	38	1990
TOO LATE TOO LATE MR HUDSON & THE LIBRARY	53	2007
TOO LATE, TOO SOON JON SECADA	43	1997
TOO LITTLE TOO LATE JOJO	4	2007
TOO LOST IN YOU SUGABABES	10	2003
TOO MANY BEAUTIFUL GIRLS CLINTON FORD	48	1961
TOO MANY BROKEN HEARTS JASON DONOVAN	1	1989
TOO MANY DJ'S SOULWAX	40	2000
TOO MANY FISH FRANKIE KNUCKLES FEATURING ADEVA	34	1995
TOO MANY GAMES MAZE FEATURING FRANKIE BEVERLY	36	1985
TOO MANY MC'S/LET ME CLEAR MY THROAT PUBLIC DOMAIN	34	2002
TOO MANY PEOPLE [A] PAULINE HENRY	38	1993
TOO MANY PEOPLE [B] WET WET WET	46	2007
TOO MANY RIVERS BRENDA LEE	22	1965
TOO MANY TEARS DAVID COVERDALE & WHITESNAKE	46	1997
TOO MANY WALLS CATHY DENNIS	17	1991
TOO MUCH [A] ELVIS PRESLEY	6	1957
TOO MUCH [B] BROS	2	1989
TOO MUCH [C] SPICE GIRLS	1	1997
TOO MUCH FOR ONE HEART MICHAEL BARRYMORE	25	1995
TOO MUCH HEAVEN BEE GEES	3	1978
TOO MUCH INFORMATION DURAN DURAN	35	1993
TOO MUCH KISSING SENSELESS THINGS	69	1993
TOO MUCH LOVE WILL KILL YOU BRIAN MAY	5	1992
TOO MUCH LOVE WILL KILL YOU QUEEN	15	1996
TOO MUCH TEQUILA CHAMPS	49	1960
TOO MUCH TOO LITTLE TOO LATE JOHNNY MATHIS & DENIECE WILLIAMS	3	1978
TOO MUCH TOO LITTLE TOO LATE SILVER SUN	20	1998
TOO MUCH TOO YOUNG LITTLE ANGELS	22	1992
TOO MUCH TROUBLE LIMAHL	64	1984
TOO NICE TO TALK TO BEAT	7	1980
TOO REAL LEVELLERS	46	1998
TOO RIGHT TO BE WRONG CARTER TWINS	61	1997
TOO RISKY JIM DAVIDSON	52	1980
TOO SHY KAJAGOOGOO	1	1983

	Peak Position	Year of Entry
TOO SOON TO KNOW ROY ORBISON	3	1966
TOO TIRED GARY MOORE	71	1990
TOO WICKED (EP) ASWAD	61	1991
TOO YOUNG BILL FORBES	29	1960
TOO YOUNG DONNY OSMOND	5	1972
TOO YOUNG TO DIE JAMIROQUAI	10	1993
TOO YOUNG TO GO STEADY NAT 'KING' COLE	8	1956
TOOFUNKY GEORGE MICHAEL	4	1992
TOOK MY LOVE BIZARRE INC FEATURING ANGIE BROWN	19	1993
TOOK THE LAST TRAIN DAVID GATES	50	1978
TOOTHPASTE KISSES MACCABEES	70	2008
TOP O' THE MORNING TO YA HOUSE OF PAIN	8	1993
TOP OF THE POPS REZILLOS	17	1978
TOP OF THE STAIRS SKEE-LO	38	1996
TOP OF THE WORLD [A] CARPENTERS	5	1973
TOP OF THE WORLD [B] VAN HALEN	63	1991
TOP OF THE WORLD [C] BRANDY FEATURING MASE	2	1998
TOP OF THE WORLD [D] WILDHEARTS	26	2003
TOP OF THE WORLD (OLÉ OLÉ OLÉ) CHUMBAWAMBA	21	1998
TOP TEEN BABY GARRY MILLS	24	1960
TOPKNOT CORNERSHOP	53	2004
TOPSY (PARTS 1 AND 2) COZY COLE	29	1958
TORCH SOFT CELL	2	1982
TORERO JULIUS LAROSA	15	1958
TORERO - CHA CHA CHA RENATO CAROSONE & HIS SEXTET	25	1958
TORN [A] NATALIE IMBRUGLIA	2	1997
TORN [B] LeTOYA	35	2006
TORN BETWEEN TWO LOVERS MARY MacGREGOR	4	1977
TORN ON THE PLATFORM JACK PENATE	7	2007
TORTURE [A] JACKSONS	26	1984
TORTURE [B] KING	23	1986
TOSH FLUKE	32	1995
TOSS IT UP MAKAVELI	15	1997
TOSSING AND TURNING [A] IVY LEAGUE	3	1965
TOSSING AND TURNING [B] WINDJAMMER	18	1984
TOSSING AND TURNING [C] CHAKKA BOOM BANG	57	1996
TOTAL CONFUSION A HOMEBOY, A HIPPIE & A FUNKI DREDD	56	1990
TOTAL ECLIPSE OF THE HEART BONNIE TYLER	1	1983
TOTAL ECLIPSE OF THE HEART NICKI FRENCH	5	1994
TOTAL ECLIPSE OF THE HEART JAN WAYNE	28	2003
TOTAL ERASURE PHILIP JAP	41	1982
THE TOTAL MIX BLACK BOX	12	1990
TOTTENHAM TOTTENHAM TOTTENHAM HOTSPUR F.A. CUP FINAL SQUAD	19	1982
TOUCH [A] LORI & THE CHAMELEONS	70	1979
THE TOUCH [B] KIM WILDE	56	1984
TOUCH [C] AMERIE	19	2005
TOUCH BY TOUCH DIANA ROSS	47	1984
TOUCH IT [A] MONIFAH	29	1999
TOUCH IT [B] BUSTA RHYMES	6	2006
TOUCH ME CASS FOX	52	2006
TOUCH ME [A] 49ERS	3	1989
TOUCH ME [B] RUI DA SILVA FEATURING CASSANDRA	1	2001
TOUCH ME [C] ANGEL CITY	18	2004
TOUCH ME (ALL NIGHT LONG) CATHY DENNIS	5	1991
TOUCH ME (I WANT YOUR BODY) SAMANTHA FOX	3	1986
TOUCH ME IN THE MORNING DIANA ROSS	9	1973
TOUCH ME LIKE THAT DANNII MINOGUE VS JASON NEVINS	48	2007
TOUCH ME TEASE ME [A] CASE FEATURING FOXY BROWN	26	1996
TOUCH ME TEASE ME [B] 3SL	16	2002
TOUCH ME TOUCH ME DAVE DEE, DOZY, BEAKY, MICK & TICH	13	1967
TOUCH ME WITH YOUR LOVE BETH ORTON	60	1997
TOUCH MY FIRE JAVINE	18	2005
TOUCH MYSELF T-BOZ	48	1996
A TOUCH OF EVIL JUDAS PRIEST	58	1991
A TOUCH OF LOVE CLEOPATRA	24	1999
A TOUCH OF VELVET A STING OF BRASS RON GRAINER ORCHESTRA	60	1978
TOUCH THE SKY [A] 29 PALMS	51	2002
TOUCH THE SKY [B] KANYE WEST FEATURING LUPE FIASCO	6	2006
A TOUCH TOO MUCH [A] ARROWS	8	1974
TOUCH TOO MUCH [B] AC/DC	29	1980
TOUCH YOU KATOI	70	2003
TOUCHED BY GOD KATCHA	57	1999
TOUCHED BY THE HAND OF CICCIOLINA POP WILL EAT ITSELF	28	1990
TOUCHED BY THE HAND OF GOD NEW ORDER	20	1987
TOUCHY! A-HA	11	1988
TOUGHER THAN THE REST BRUCE SPRINGSTEEN	13	1988
TOUR DE FRANCE KRAFTWERK	20	1983
TOURIST ATHLETE	43	2005
TOURNIQUET [A] MARILYN MANSON	28	1997
TOURNIQUET [B] HEADSWIM	30	1998
TOUS LES GARCONS ET LES FILLES FRANCOISE HARDY	36	1964
TOWER OF STRENGTH [A] FRANKIE VAUGHAN	1	1961
TOWER OF STRENGTH [A] GENE McDANIELS	49	1961
TOWER OF STRENGTH [B] MISSION	12	1988
TOWER OF STRENGTH [C] SKIN	19	1994
TOWERS OF LONDON XTC	31	1980
TOWN NORTHERN UPROAR	48	1996
A TOWN CALLED HYPOCRISY LOSTPROPHETS	23	2006
A TOWN CALLED MALICE JAM	1	1982
TOWN CLOWNS BLAMELESS	56	1995
TOWN CRIER CRAIG DOUGLAS	36	1963
TOWN OF PLENTY ELTON JOHN	74	1988
TOWN TO TOWN MICRODISNEY	55	1987
TOWN WITHOUT PITY GENE PITNEY	32	1962
TOWN WITHOUT PITY EDDI READER	26	1996
TOXIC BRITNEY SPEARS	1	2004
TOXIC GIRL KINGS OF CONVENIENCE	44	2001
TOXICITY SYSTEM OF A DOWN	25	2002
TOXYGENE ORB	4	1997
TOY CASUALS	30	1968
TOY BALLOONS RUSS CONWAY	7	1961
TOY BOY SINITTA	4	1987
TOY SOLDIERS MARTIKA	5	1989
TOYS FOR BOYS MARION	57	1995
TRACEY IN MY ROOM EBTG VERSUS SOUL VISION	34	2001
TRACIE LEVEL 42	25	1989
TRACKIN' BILLY CRAWFORD	32	2003
TRACKS OF MY TEARS SMOKEY ROBINSON & THE MIRACLES	9	1969
TRACKS OF MY TEARS LINDA RONSTADT	42	1976
TRACKS OF MY TEARS COLIN BLUNSTONE	60	1982
TRACKS OF MY TEARS GO WEST	16	1993
TRACY CUFF LINKS	4	1969
TRADE (EP) (DISC 2) VARIOUS ARTISTS (EP'S & LPS)	75	1998
TRAFFIC [A] STEREOPHONICS	20	1997
TRAFFIC [B] TIESTO	48	2003
TRAGEDY [A] ARGENT	34	1972
TRAGEDY [B] BEE GEES	1	1979
TRAGEDY [B] STEPS	1	1998
TRAGEDY AND MYSTERY CHINA CRISIS	46	1983
TRAGIC COMIC EXTREME	15	1993
THE TRAIL OF THE LONESOME PINE LAUREL & HARDY WITH THE AVALON BOYS FEATURING CHILL WILLS	2	1975
TRAIL OF TEARS DOGS D'AMOUR	47	1989
TRAILER LOAD A GIRLS SHABBA RANKS	63	1991
TRAIN [A] SISTERS OF MERCY	46	1984
TRAIN [B] GOLDFRAPP	23	2003
THE TRAIN IS COMING SHAGGY FEATURING WAYNE WONDER	21	1996
THE TRAIN IS COMING UB40	30	1999
TRAIN OF CONSEQUENCES MEGADETH	22	1995
TRAIN OF LOVE ALMA COGAN	27	1960
TRAIN OF THOUGHT [A] A-HA	8	1986
TRAIN OF THOUGHT [B] ESCRIMA	36	1995
TRAIN ON A TRACK KELLY ROWLAND	20	2003
TRAIN TO SKAVILLE ETHIOPIANS	40	1967
TRAIN TOUR TO RAINBOW CITY PYRAMIDS	35	1967
TRAINS AND BOATS AND PLANES BILLY J. KRAMER & THE DAKOTAS	12	1965
TRAINS AND BOATS AND PLANES BURT BACHARACH	4	1965
TRAINS TO BRAZIL GUILLEMOTS	36	2006
TRAMBONE KREW-KATS	33	1961
TRAMP [A] OTIS REDDING & CARLA THOMAS	18	1967
TRAMP [B] SALT-N-PEPA	2	1988
TRAMPOLENE JULIAN COPE	31	1987
TRAMPS AND THIEVES QUIREBOYS	41	1992
TRANCESCRIPT HARDFLOOR	72	1993
TRANQUILIZE KILLERS	13	2007
TRANQUILLIZER GENEVA	24	1997
TRANSAMAZONIA SHAMEN	28	1995
TRANSATLANTIC ROACH MOTEL	73	1993
TRANSFER AFFECTION A FLOCK OF SEAGULLS	38	1983
TRANSISTOR RADIO BENNY HILL	24	1961
TRANSMISSION [A] GAY DAD	58	2001
TRANSMISSION [B] VIOLENT DELIGHT	64	2003
TRANSONIC WIRED	73	1999
TRANSYLVANIA McFLY	1	2007
TRANZ EURO XPRESS X-PRESS 2	45	1996
TRANZY STATE OF MIND PUSH	31	2002
TRAPPED [A] COLONEL ABRAMS	3	1985
TRAPPED [B] GUYVER	72	2003
TRASH [A] ROXY MUSIC	40	1979
TRASH [B] SUEDE	3	1996
TRASHED SKIN	30	2003
THE TRAVELLER SPEAR OF DESTINY	44	1987
TRAVELLERS TUNE OCEAN COLOUR SCENE	5	1997
TRAVELLIN' BAND CREEDENCE CLEARWATER REVIVAL	8	1970
TRAVELLIN' HOME VERA LYNN	20	1957
TRAVELLIN' LIGHT CLIFF RICHARD & THE SHADOWS	1	1959
TRAVELLIN' MAN RICKY NELSON	2	1961
TRAVELLING LIGHT TINDERSTICKS	51	1995
TRAVELLING MAN STUDIO 2	40	1998
TREASON (IT'S JUST A STORY) TEARDROP EXPLODES	18	1981
TREASURE OF LOVE CLYDE McPHATTER	27	1956
TREAT 'EM RIGHT CHUBB ROCK	67	1991
TREAT HER LIKE A LADY [A] TEMPTATIONS	12	1984
TREAT HER LIKE A LADY [B] CELINE DION	29	1999
TREAT HER LIKE A LADY [C] JOE	60	2000
TREAT HER RIGHT ROY HEAD	30	1965
TREAT INFAMY REST ASSURED	14	1998
TREAT ME GOOD YAZZ	20	1990
TREAT ME LIKE A LADY [A] FIVE STAR	54	1990
TREAT ME LIKE A LADY [B] ZOE BIRKETT	12	2003
TREAT ME RIGHT ADEVA	62	1990
TREATY YOTHU YINDI	72	1992
TREBLE CHANCE JOE 'MR PIANO' HENDERSON	28	1959
TREE FROG HOPE A.D.	73	1994

	Peak Position	Year of Entry
THE TREES PULP	23	2001
TREMBLE MARC ET CLAUDE	29	2002
TREMELO SONG (EP) CHARLATANS	44	1992
THE TRIAL OF HISSING SID KEITH MICHELL, CAPTAIN BEAKY & HIS BAND	53	1980
TRIALS OF LIFE KALEEF	75	1997
TRIBAL BASE REBEL MC FEATURING TENOR FLY & BARRINGTON LEVY	20	1991
TRIBAL DANCE 2 UNLIMITED	4	1993
TRIBULATIONS LCD SOUNDSYSTEM	59	2005
TRIBUTE (RIGHT ON) PASADENAS	5	1988
TRIBUTE TO A KING WILLIAM BELL	31	1968
TRIBUTE TO BUDDY HOLLY MIKE BERRY WITH THE OUTLAWS	24	1961
TRIBUTE TO JIM REEVES LARRY CUNNINGHAM & THE MIGHTY AVONS	40	1965
TRIBUTE TO JINKY JIMMY JOHNSTONE, JIM KERR, SIMPLE MINDS & LAURA MCGHEE	28	2006
TRIBUTE TO OUR ANCESTORS RUBBADUBB	56	1998
TRICK ME KELIS	2	2004
A TRICK OF THE LIGHT TRIFFIDS	73	1988
TRICK OF THE NIGHT BANANARAMA	32	1987
TRICKY DISCO TRICKY DISCO	14	1990
TRICKY KID TRICKY	28	1997
TRIGGER HIPPIE MORCHEEBA	40	1996
TRIGGER INSIDE THERAPY?	22	1994
TRINI TRAX TRINI LOPEZ	59	1981
TRIP II THE MOON ACEN	38	1992
A TRIP TO TRUMPTON URBAN HYPE	6	1992
TRIPLE TROUBLE BEASTIE BOYS	37	2004
TRIPPIN' [A] MARK MORRISON	8	1996
TRIPPIN' [B] ORIS JAY PRESENTS DELSENA	42	2002
TRIPPIN' ON SUNSHINE PIZZAMAN	18	1994
TRIPPIN' ON YOUR LOVE [A] A WAY OF LIFE	55	1990
TRIPPIN' ON YOUR LOVE [B] KENNY THOMAS	17	1993
TRIPPING ROBBIE WILLIAMS	2	2005
TRIPPY ARAB STRAP	48	1998
TRIPWIRE LIONROCK	44	1994
TRIUMPH [A] WU-TANG CLAN FEATURING CAPPADONNA	46	1997
TRIUMPH [B] HISS	53	2003
TRIUMPH OF A HEART BJORK	31	2005
TRIXSTAR BLAK TWANG FEATURING ESTELLE	54	2002
TROCADERO SHOWADDYWADDY	32	1976
THE TROOPER IRON MAIDEN	5	1983
TROPIC ISLAND HUM PAUL McCARTNEY	21	2004
TROPICAL ICE-LAND FIERY FURNACES	52	2004
TROPICAL SOUNDCLASH DJ GREGORY	59	2002
TROPICALIA BECK	39	1998
T.R.O.U.B.L.E. ELVIS PRESLEY	31	1975
TROUBLE [A] GILLAN	14	1980
TROUBLE [B] LINDSEY BUCKINGHAM	31	1982
TROUBLE [C] HEAVEN 17	51	1987
TROUBLE [D] SHAMPOO	11	1994
TROUBLE [E] COLDPLAY	10	2000
TROUBLE [F] CYPRESS HILL	33	2001
TROUBLE [G] P!NK	7	2003
TROUBLE [G] SHAKIN' STEVENS	20	2005
TROUBLE [H] RAY LAMONTAGNE	25	2006
TROUBLE BOYS THIN LIZZY	53	1981
TROUBLE IN PARADISE AL JARREAU	36	1983
TROUBLE IS MY MIDDLE NAME BROOK BROTHERS	38	1963
TROUBLE IS MY MIDDLE NAME FOUR PENNIES	32	1966
TROUBLE SLEEPING CORINNE BAILEY RAE	40	2006
TROUBLE TOWN MARTIN STEPHENSON & THE DAINTEES	58	1987
THE TROUBLE WITH HARRY ALFI & HARRY	15	1956
THE TROUBLE WITH LOVE IS KELLY CLARKSON	35	2003
TROUBLED GIRL KAREN RAMIREZ	50	1998
TROY (THE PHOENIX FROM THE FLAME) SINEAD O'CONNOR	48	2002
TRUCK ON SIMPLE KID	38	2004
TRUCK ON (TYKE) T REX	12	1973
TRUDIE JOE 'MR PIANO' HENDERSON	14	1958
TRUE [A] SPANDAU BALLET	1	1983
TRUE [B] JAIMESON FEATURING ANGEL BLU	4	2003
TRUE BLUE MADONNA	1	1986
TRUE COLORS [A] CYNDI LAUPER	12	1986
TRUE COLOURS [A] PHIL COLLINS	26	1998
TRUE COLOURS [B] GO WEST	48	1986
TRUE DEVOTION SAMANTHA FOX	62	1987
TRUE FAITH NEW ORDER	4	1987
TRUE LOVE [A] TERRY LIGHTFOOT & HIS NEW ORLEANS JAZZMEN	33	1961
TRUE LOVE [A] RICHARD CHAMBERLAIN	30	1963
TRUE LOVE [A] BING CROSBY & GRACE KELLY	4	1983
TRUE LOVE [A] SHAKIN' STEVENS	23	1988
TRUE LOVE [A] ELTON JOHN & KIKI DEE	2	1993
TRUE LOVE [B] CHIMES	48	1990
TRUE LOVE FOR EVER MORE BACHELORS	34	1965
TRUE LOVE NEVER DIES FLIP AND FULL FEATURING KELLY LLORENNA	7	2001
TRUE LOVE WAYS BUDDY HOLLY	25	1960
TRUE LOVE WAYS PETER & GORDON	2	1965
TRUE LOVE WAYS CLIFF RICHARD WITH THE LONDON PHILHARMONIC ORCHESTRA	8	1983
TRUE LOVE WAYS DAVID ESSEX & CATHERINE ZETA JONES	38	1994
TRUE LOVE WILL FIND YOU IN THE END SPECTRUM	70	1992
TRUE NATURE JANE'S ADDICTION	41	2003
TRUE SKOOL COLDCUT FEATURING ROOTS MANUVA	61	2006
TRUE SPIRIT CARLEEN ANDERSON	24	1994
TRUE STEP TONIGHT TRUE STEPPERS FEATURING BRIAN HARVEY	25	2000
TRUE (THE FAGGOT IS YOU) MOREL	64	2000
TRUE TO FORM HYBRID FEATURING PETER HOOK	59	2003
TRUE TO US VANILLA	36	1998
TRUE TO YOUR HEART 98o FEATURING STEVIE WONDER	51	1998
TRUGANINI MIDNIGHT OIL	29	1993
TRULY [A] LIONEL RICHIE	6	1982
TRULY [A] STEVEN HOUGHTON	23	1998
TRULY [B] HINDA HICKS	31	1998
TRULY [C] PESHAY FEATURING KYM MAZELLE	55	2000
TRULY [D] DELERIUM	54	2004
TRULY MADLY DEEPLY [A] SAVAGE GARDEN	4	1998
TRULY MADLY DEEPLY [A] CASCADA	4	2006
TRULY MADLY DEEPLY [B] DUALERS	23	2005
TRULY ONE ORIGIN UNKNOWN	53	2002
TRUST [A] BROTHER BEYOND	53	1990
TRUST [B] NED'S ATOMIC DUSTBIN	21	1991
TRUST ME GURU FEATURING N'DEA DAVENPORT	34	1993
TRUST ME TO OPEN MY MOUTH SQUEEZE	72	1987
THE TRUTH [A] COLONEL ABRAMS	53	1985
THE TRUTH [B] REAL PEOPLE	41	1991
THE TRUTH IS NO WORDS MUSIC	18	2003
TRUTH OR DARE SHIRLEY MURDOCK	60	1986
TRY [A] BROS	27	1991
TRY [B] IAN VAN DAHL	15	2002
TRY [C] NELLY FURTADO	15	2004
TRY A LITTLE KINDNESS GLEN CAMPBELL	45	1970
TRY A LITTLE TENDERNESS OTIS REDDING	46	1967
TRY AGAIN AALIYAH	5	2000
TRY AGAIN TODAY CHARLATANS	24	2004
TRY HONESTY BILLY TALENT	68	2003
TRY JAH LOVE THIRD WORLD	47	1982
TRY ME OUT CORONA	6	1995
TRY MY WORLD GEORGIE FAME	37	1967
TRY TO UNDERSTAND LULU	25	1965
TRY TRY TRY [A] JULIAN COPE	24	1995
TRY TRY TRY [B] SMASHING PUMPKINS	73	2000
TRYIN' HILLTOPPERS	30	1956
TRYIN' TO GET THE FEELING AGAIN CARPENTERS	44	1994
TRYING TO FORGET JIM REEVES	33	1967
TRYING TO GET TO YOU ELVIS PRESLEY	16	1957
TRYOUTS FOR THE HUMAN RACE SPARKS	45	1979
TSOP (THE SOUND OF PHILADELPHIA) MFSB FEATURING THE THREE DEGREES	22	1974
TSUNAMI MANIC STREET PREACHERS	11	1999
TU AMOR KACI	24	2001
TU M'AIMES ENCORE (TO LOVE ME AGAIN) CELINE DION	7	1995
TUBTHUMPING CHUMBAWAMBA	2	1997
TUBULAR BELLS CHAMPS BOYS	41	1976
TUCH ME FONDA RAE	49	1984
TUESDAY AFTERNOON JENNIFER BROWN	57	1999
TUESDAY MORNING POGUES	18	1993
TUESDAY SUNSHINE QUESTIONS	46	1984
TUFF ACT TO FOLLOW MN8	15	1996
TUG OF WAR PAUL McCARTNEY	53	1982
TULANE STEVE GIBBONS BAND	12	1977
TULIPS BLOC PARTY	38	2004
TULIPS FROM AMSTERDAM MAX BYGRAVES	3	1958
TUM BIN JIYA BALLY SAGOO	21	1997
TUMBLE AND FALL FEEDER	5	2005
TUMBLING DICE ROLLING STONES	5	1972
TUMBLING TUMBLEWEEDS SLIM WHITMAN	19	1956
THE TUNE SUGGS	33	1995
TUNED TO A DIFFERENT STATION DOGS	29	2005
TUNES SPLITS THE ATOM MC TUNES VERSUS 808 STATE	18	1990
TUNNEL OF LOVE [A] DIRE STRAITS	54	1981
TUNNEL OF LOVE [B] FUN BOY THREE	10	1983
TUNNEL OF LOVE [C] BRUCE SPRINGSTEEN	45	1987
TURN [A] TRAVIS	8	1999
TURN [B] FEEDER	27	2001
TURN AROUND [A] FAB!	59	1998
TURN AROUND [B] PHATS & SMALL	2	1999
TURN AROUND AND COUNT 2 TEN DEAD OR ALIVE	70	1988
TURN BACK THE CLOCK JOHNNY HATES JAZZ	12	1987
TURN BACK TIME AQUA	1	1998
TURN DA LIGHTS OFF TWEET FEATURING MISSY ELLIOTT	29	2005
TURN INTO YEAH YEAH YEAHS	54	2006
TURN IT AROUND ALENA	14	1999
TURN IT AROUND 4 STRINGS	50	2004
TURN IT DOWN SWEET	41	1974
TURN IT INTO LOVE HAZELL DEAN	21	1988
TURN IT ON LEVEL 42	57	1981
TURN IT ON AGAIN GENESIS	8	1980
TURN IT UP [A] CONWAY BROTHERS	11	1985
TURN IT UP [B] RICHIE RICH	48	1988
TURN IT UP [C] TECHNOTRONIC FEATURING MELISSA & EINSTEIN	42	1990
TURN IT UP [D] PETER ANDRE	64	1995
TURN IT UP [E] RAJA NEE	42	1995
TURN IT UP (SAY YEAH) DJ DUKE	31	1994
TURN IT UP/FIRE IT UP BUSTA RHYMES	2	1998
TURN ME LOOSE WALLY JUMP Jr. & THE CRIMINAL ELEMENT ORCHESTRA	60	1987
TURN ME ON RMXCRW FEATURING EBON-E PLUS AMBUSH	52	2003
TURN ME ON [A] DANNY TENAGLIA FEATURING LIZ TORRES	53	1999
TURN ME ON [B] KEVIN LYTTLE	2	2003
TURN ME ON TURN ME OFF HONEY BANE	37	1981
TURN ME OUT (TURN TO SUGAR) PRAXIS FEATURING KATHY BROWN	35	1995
TURN OFF MILLTOWN BROTHERS	55	1993
TURN OFF THE LIGHT NELLY FURTADO	4	2001

	Peak Position	Year of Entry
TURN ON THE NIGHT KISS	41	1988
TURN ON, TUNE IN, COP OUT FREAKPOWER	3	1993
TURN THE BEAT AROUND GLORIA ESTEFAN	21	1994
TURN THE LIGHTS OUT WHEN YOU LEAVE ELTON JOHN	32	2005
TURN THE MUSIC UP PLAYERS ASSOCIATION	8	1979
TURN THE MUSIC UP CHRIS PAUL	73	1988
TURN THE TIDE SYLVER	56	2002
TURN THIS THING AROUND EL PRESIDENTE	39	2006
TURN TO GOLD DAVID AUSTIN	68	1984
TURN TO STONE ELECTRIC LIGHT ORCHESTRA	18	1977
TURN! TURN! TURN! (TO EVERYTHING THERE IS A SEASON) BYRDS	26	1965
TURN UP THE BASS TYREE FEATURING KOOL ROCK STEADY	12	1989
TURN UP THE NIGHT BLACK SABBATH	37	1982
TURN UP THE POWER N-TRANCE	23	1994
TURN UP THE SOUND LISA PIN-UP	60	2002
TURN YOUR BACK ON ME KAJAGOOGOO	47	1984
TURN YOUR CAR AROUND LEE RYAN	12	2005
TURN YOUR LIGHTS DOWN LOW BOB MARLEY FEATURING LAURYN HILL	15	1999
TURN YOUR LOVE AROUND GEORGE BENSON	29	1981
TURN YOUR LOVE AROUND TONY DI BART	66	1996
TURN YOUR RADIO ON RAY STEVENS	33	1972
TURNED AWAY AUDIOBULLYS	22	2003
TURNING AWAY SHAKIN' STEVENS	15	1986
TURNING JAPANESE VAPORS	3	1980
TURNING THE TOWN RED ELVIS COSTELLO	25	1984
TURQUOISE [A] DONOVAN	30	1965
TURQUOISE [B] CIRCULATION	64	2001
TURTLE POWER PARTNERS IN KRYME	1	1990
TURTLE RHAPSODY ORCHESTRA ON THE HALF SHELL	36	1990
TUSK FLEETWOOD MAC	6	1979
TUTTI FRUTTI LITTLE RICHARD	29	1957
TUXEDO JUNCTION MANHATTAN TRANSFER	24	1976
TV FLYING LIZARDS	43	1980
TV CRIMES BLACK SABBATH	33	1992
TV DINNERS ZZ TOP	67	1984
TV SAVAGE BOW WOW WOW	45	1982
TV TAN WILDHEARTS	53	1993
TVC 15 DAVID BOWIE	33	1976
TWANGLING THREE FINGERS IN A BOX MIKE	40	1994
TWEEDLE DEE FRANKIE VAUGHAN	17	1955
TWEEDLE DEE GEORGIA GIBBS	20	1955
TWEEDLE DEE LITTLE JIMMY OSMOND	4	1973
TWEEDLE DEE TWEEDLE DUM MIDDLE OF THE ROAD	2	1971
THE TWELFTH OF NEVER CLIFF RICHARD	8	1964
THE TWELFTH OF NEVER DONNY OSMOND	1	1973
THE TWELFTH OF NEVER ELVIS PRESLEY	21	1995
THE TWELFTH OF NEVER CARTER TWINS	61	1997
TWELFTH STREET RAG BERT WEEDON	47	1960
TWELVE FORWARD, RUSSIA!	36	2006
12:51 STROKES	7	2003
12 REASONS WHY I LOVE HER MY LIFE STORY	32	1996
TWELVE STEPS TO LOVE BRIAN POOLE & THE TREMELOES	32	1964
20TH CENTURY BRAD	64	1993
20TH CENTURY BOY T REX	3	1973
20 DEGREES JONNY L	66	1998
21ST CENTURY WEEKEND PLAYERS	22	2001
21ST CENTURY CHRISTMAS CLIFF RICHARD	2	2006
21ST CENTURY (DIGITAL BOY) BAD RELIGION	41	1995
21ST CENTURY GIRLS 21ST CENTURY GIRLS	16	1999
25 MILES EDWIN STARR	36	1969
25 MILES 2001 THREE AMIGOS	30	2001
25 OR 6 TO 4 CHICAGO	7	1970
TWENTY FOREPLAY JANET JACKSON	22	1996
24 HOURS [A] BETTY BOO	25	1990
24 HOURS [B] AGENT SUMO	44	2001
TWENTY FOUR HOURS [C] ATHLETE	42	2005
24 HOURS A DAY NOMAD	61	1992
TWENTY FOUR HOURS FROM TULSA GENE PITNEY	5	1963
24 HOURS FROM YOU NEXT OF KIN	13	1999
24/7 [A] 3T	11	1996
24/7 [B] FIXATE	42	2001
24-7-365 CHARLES & EDDIE	38	1995
24 SYCAMORE GENE PITNEY	34	1973
20 HZ (NEW FREQUENCIES) CAPRICORN	73	1997
29 PALMS ROBERT PLANT	21	1993
21 PADDINGTONS	47	2004
21 QUESTIONS 50 CENT FEATURING NATE DOGG	6	2003
21 SECONDS SO SOLID CREW	1	2001
£20 TO GET IN SHUT UP & DANCE	56	1990
20 SECONDS TO COMPLY SILVER BULLET	11	1989
TWENTY TINY FINGERS ALMA COGAN	17	1955
TWENTY TINY FINGERS CORONETS	20	1955
TWENTY TINY FINGERS STARGAZERS	4	1955
20/20 GEORGE BENSON	29	1985
22 DAYS 22-20'S	34	2004
22 GRAND JOB RAKES	39	2005
22 - THE DEATH OF ALL THE ROMANCE DEARS	53	2005
TWENTY WILD HORSES STATUS QUO	53	1999
TWENTY YEARS PLACEBO	18	2004
TWENTY-FIRST CENTURY BOY SIGUE SIGUE SPUTNIK	20	1986
TWENTYFOURSEVEN [C] ARTFUL DODGER FEATURING MELANIE BLATT	6	2001
TWENTY-TWENTY SURGERY TAKING BACK SUNDAY	60	2006
TWICE AS HARD BLACK CROWES	47	1991
TWILIGHT ELECTRIC LIGHT ORCHESTRA	30	1981
TWILIGHT CAFE SUSAN FASSBENDER	21	1981
TWILIGHT TIME PLATTERS	3	1958
TWILIGHT WORLD SWING OUT SISTER	32	1987
TWILIGHT ZONE [A] IRON MAIDEN	31	1981
TWILIGHT ZONE [B] 2 UNLIMITED	2	1992
TWILIGHT ZONE - TWILIGHT TONE (MEDLEY) MANHATTAN TRANSFER	25	1980
TWILIGHTS LAST GLEAMING HIGH CONTRAST	74	2004
TWIN EARTH MONSTER MAGNET	67	1993
TWINKIE LEE GARY WALKER	26	1966
TWINKLE WHIPPING BOY	55	1996
TWINKLE TOES ROY ORBISON	29	1966
TWINKLE TWINKLE (I'M NOT A STAR) JAZZY JEFF & THE FRESH PRINCE	62	1994
TWINLIGHTS (EP) COCTEAU TWINS	59	1995
THE TWIST [A] CHUBBY CHECKER	2	1960
TWIST [B] GOLDFRAPP	31	2003
TWIST AND SHOUT [A] BRIAN POOLE & THE TREMELOES	4	1963
TWIST AND SHOUT [A] ISLEY BROTHERS	42	1963
TWIST AND SHOUT [A] SALT-N-PEPA	4	1988
TWIST AND SHOUT [A] CHAKA DEMUS & PLIERS FEATURING JACK RADICS & TAXI GANG	1	1993
TWIST AND SHOUT [B] DEACON BLUE	10	1991
TWIST 'EM OUT DILLINJA FEATURING SKIBADEE	35	2002
TWIST IN MY SOBRIETY TANITA TIKARAM	22	1988
TWIST OF FATE [A] OLIVIA NEWTON-JOHN	57	1983
TWIST OF FATE [B] SIOBHAN DONAGHY	52	2003
TWIST (ROUND 'N' ROUND) CHILL FAC-TORR	37	1983
TWIST TWIST CHAKACHAS	48	1962
THE TWIST (YO, TWIST) FAT BOYS & CHUBBY CHECKER	2	1988
TWISTED KEITH SWEAT	39	1996
TWISTED (EVERYDAY HURTS) SKUNK ANANSIE	26	1996
TWISTED TRANSISTOR KORN	27	2005
THE TWISTER VIPER	55	1998
TWISTERELLA RIDE	36	1992
TWISTIN' THE NIGHT AWAY SAM COOKE	6	1962
TWISTIN' THE NIGHT AWAY DIVINE	47	1985
TWISTING BY THE POOL DIRE STRAITS	14	1983
'TWIXT TWELVE AND TWENTY PAT BOONE	18	1959
2 BECOME 1 SPICE GIRLS	1	1996
TWO CAN PLAY THAT GAME BOBBY BROWN	3	1994
2 DEEP GANG STARR	67	1992
TWO DIFFERENT WORLDS RONNIE HILTON	13	1956
TWO EP MANSUN	32	1996
2 FACED LOUISE	3	2000
TWO FATT GUITARS (REVISITED) DIRECKT	36	1994
2-4-6-8 MOTORWAY TOM ROBINSON BAND	5	1977
TWO HEARTS [A] CLIFF RICHARD	34	1988
TWO HEARTS [B] PHIL COLLINS	6	1988
TWO HEARTS [C] STEPHANIE MILLS FEATURING TEDDY PENDERGRASS	49	1981
2 HEARTS [D] KYLIE MINOGUE	4	2007
TWO HEARTS BEAT AS ONE U2	18	1983
TWO HEARTS TOGETHER ORANGE JUICE	60	1982
TWO IN A MILLION [A] MICA PARIS	51	1993
TWO IN A MILLION [B] S CLUB 7	2	1999
TWO KINDS OF TEARDROPS DEL SHANNON	5	1963
TWO LEFT FEET HOLLOWAYS	33	2006
2 LEGIT 2 QUIT HAMMER	60	1991
TWO LITTLE BOYS ROLF HARRIS	1	1969
TWO LITTLE BOYS SPLODGENESSABOUNDS	26	1980
2 LITTLE BOYS/NEVER SAY DIE 2005 MONKEY HANGERZ	24	2005
TWO LOVERS TWANG	34	2007
2 MINUTES TO MIDNIGHT IRON MAIDEN	11	1984
TWO MONTHS OFF UNDERWORLD	12	2002
TWO MORE YEARS BLOC PARTY	7	2005
THE TWO OF US MAC & KATIE KISSOON	46	1976
TWO OUT OF THREE AIN'T BAD MEAT LOAF	32	1978
TWO PAINTINGS AND A DRUM CARL COX	24	1996
TWO PEOPLE [A] TINA TURNER	43	1986
2 PEOPLE [B] JEAN JACQUES SMOOTHIE	12	2001
TWO PINTS OF LAGER AND A PACKET OF CRISPS PLEASE SPLODGENESSABOUNDS	7	1980
2 + 2 = 5 RADIOHEAD	15	2003
TWO PRINCES SPIN DOCTORS	3	1993
2 REMIXES BY AFX AFX	69	2001
TWO SILHOUETTES DEL SHANNON	23	1963
2 STEP ROCK BANDITS	35	2003
TWO STEPS BEHIND DEF LEPPARD	32	1993
TWO STREETS VAL DOONICAN	39	1967
2 THE RHYTHM SOUND FACTORY	72	1993
2000 MILES PRETENDERS	15	1983
2, 3, GO WEDDING PRESENT	67	1996
2 TIMES ANN LEE	2	1999
TWO TIMING TOUCH AND BROKEN BONES HIVES	44	2004
THE TWO TONE EP VARIOUS ARTISTS (EP'S & LPS)	30	1993
TWO TRIBES FRANKIE GOES TO HOLLYWOOD	1	1984
$2\sqrt{231}$ ANTICAPPELLA	24	1991
2-WAY RAYVON	67	2002
2 WAY STREET MISSJONES	49	1998
TWO WORLDS COLLIDE INSPIRAL CARPETS	32	1992
TWO WRONGS (DON'T MAKE A RIGHT) WYCLEF JEAN FEATURING CLAUDETTE ORTIZ	14	2002
TWYFORD DOWN GALLIANO	37	1994
TYPE LIVING COLOUR	75	1990
TYPICAL! FRAZIER CHORUS	53	1989
TYPICAL AMERICAN GOATS	53	1993
TYPICAL GIRLS SLITS	60	1979
TYPICAL MALE TINA TURNER	33	1986
TYPICAL ME KANO	22	2005

U–X

KEY TO INDEX ENTRIES

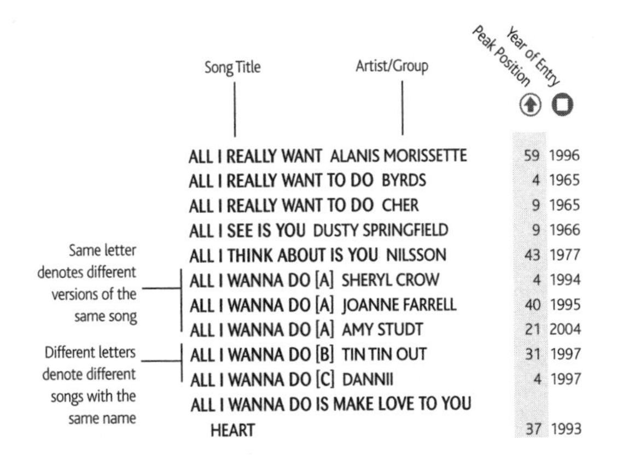

	Peak Position	Year of Entry
U LONI CLARK	28	1994
U & ME CAPPELLA	10	1994
U & UR HAND P!NK	10	2006
U BLOW MY MIND BLACKstreet	39	1995
U CAN'T TOUCH THIS MC HAMMER	3	1990
U CAN'T TOUCH THIS CRAZY FROG	5	2005
U DON'T HAVE TO SAY U LOVE ME MASH!	37	1994
U DON'T KNOW ME BASEMENT JAXX FEATURING LISA KEKAULA	26	2005
U FOUND OUT HANDBAGGERS	55	1996
U GIRLS (LOOK SO SEXY) NUSH	15	1994
U GOT 2 KNOW CAPPELLA	6	1993
U GOT 2 LET THE MUSIC CAPPELLA	2	1993
U GOT IT BAD USHER	5	2001
U GOT ME PARA BEATS FEATURING CARMEN REECE	59	2005
U GOT THE LOOK PRINCE	11	1987
U (I GOT THE FEELING) DJ SCOT PROJECT	66	1996
U KNOW WHAT'S UP DONELL JONES	2	2000
U KNOW Y MOGUAI	62	2003
U KRAZY KATZ PJ & DUNCAN	15	1995
U MAKE ME WANNA BLUE	4	2003
U + ME = LOVE FUNKY WORM	46	1989
U R THE BEST THING D:REAM	4	1992
U REMIND ME USHER	3	2001
U SEXY THING CLOCK	11	1997
U SHINE ON MATT DAREY & MARCELLA WOODS	34	2002
U16 GIRLS TRAVIS	40	1997
U SURE DO STRIKE	4	1994
U TURN USHER	16	2002
U WILL KNOW BMU	23	1995
UBIK TIMO MAAS FEATURING MARTIN BETTINGHAUS	33	2000
UGLY [A] DAPHNE & CELESTE	18	2000
UGLY [B] BUBBA SPARXXX	7	2001
UGLY [C] SUGABABES	3	2005
UGLY DUCKLING MIKE REID	10	1975
UH HUH B2K	31	2002
UH HUH OH YEH PAUL WELLER	18	1992
UH LA LA LA ALEXIA	10	1998
UH OH (I'M BACK) LETHAL BIZZLE	47	2005
UH UH NO NO CASUAL SEX CARRIE McDOWELL	68	1987
UHF UHF	46	1991
UHH IN YOU SNOW	67	1993
UH-UH OOH OOH LOOK OUT (HERE IT COMES) ROBERTA FLACK	72	1989
UK BLAK CARON WHEELER	40	1990
UK-USA ESKIMOS & EGYPT	52	1993
'ULLO JOHN GOT A NEW MOTOR? ALEXEI SAYLE	15	1984
THE ULTIMATE FUNKY CHOAD FEATURING NICK SKITZ	51	1998
THE ULTIMATE HIGH TIME FREQUENCY	17	1993
THE ULTIMATE SIN OZZY OSBOURNE	72	1986
ULTIMATE TRUNK FUNK EP BRAND NEW HEAVIES FEATURING N'DEA DAVENPORT	19	1992
ULTRA FLAVA HELLER & FARLEY PROJECT	22	1996
ULTRA STIMULATION FINLEY QUAYE	51	1998
ULTRAFUNKULA ARMAND VAN HELDEN	46	1997
ULTRA-OBSCENE BREAKBEAT ERA	48	1999
ULTRAVIOLET McFLY	9	2005
UM UM UM UM UM UM MAJOR LANCE	40	1964
UM UM UM UM UM UM WAYNE FONTANA & THE MINDBENDERS	5	1964
UMBRELLA RIHANNA FEATURING JAY-Z	1	2007
UMBRELLA MANIC STREET PREACHERS	47	2008
UMI SAYS MOS DEF	60	2000
UN BANC, UN ABRE, UNE RUE SEVERINE	9	1971
(UN, DOS, TRES) MARIA RICKY MARTIN	6	1997
UNA PALOMA BLANCA JONATHAN KING	5	1975
UNBEARABLE WONDER STUFF	16	1994

	Peak Position	Year of Entry
UNBELIEVABLE [A] EMF	3	1990
UNBELIEVABLE [B] SKIN	18	1994
UNBELIEVABLE [C] LISA LASHES	63	2000
UNBELIEVABLE [D] CRAIG DAVID	18	2006
UN-BREAK MY HEART TONI BRAXTON	2	1996
UNBREAKABLE WESTLIFE	1	2002
UNCERTAIN SMILE THE THE	68	1982
UNCHAIN MY HEART JOE COCKER	46	1987
UNCHAINED MELODY AL HIBBLER	2	1955
UNCHAINED MELODY JIMMY YOUNG	1	1955
UNCHAINED MELODY LES BAXTER	10	1955
UNCHAINED MELODY LIBERACE	20	1955
UNCHAINED MELODY JIMMY YOUNG WITH THE MICHAEL SAMMES SINGERS	43	1964
UNCHAINED MELODY RIGHTEOUS BROTHERS	1	1965
UNCHAINED MELODY LEO SAYER	54	1986
UNCHAINED MELODY ROBSON GREEN & JEROME FLYNN	1	1995
UNCHAINED MELODY GARETH GATES	1	2002
UNCLE JOHN FROM JAMAICA VENGABOYS	6	2000
UNCLE SAM MADNESS	21	1985
UNCONDITIONAL BRAVERY	49	2005
UNCONDITIONAL LOVE [A] DONNA SUMMER	14	1983
UNCONDITIONAL LOVE [B] SUSANNA HOFFS	65	1991
UNDECIDED YOUSSOU N'DOUR	53	1995
UNDER A RAGING MOON ROGER DALTREY	43	1986
UNDER ATTACK ABBA	26	1982
(UNDER HER) SPELL HUGH CORNWALL	62	2005
UNDER MY THUMB WHO	44	1967
UNDER MY THUMB WAYNE GIBSON	17	1974
UNDER MY WHEELS ALICE COOPER	66	1982
UNDER NEW MANAGEMENT BARRON KNIGHTS WITH DUKE D'MOND	15	1966
UNDER ONE ROOF RUBETTES	40	1976
UNDER PRESSURE QUEEN & DAVID BOWIE	1	1981
UNDER THE BOARDWALK DRIFTERS	45	1964
UNDER THE BOARDWALK TOM TOM CLUB	22	1982
UNDER THE BOARDWALK BRUCE WILLIS	2	1987
UNDER THE BRIDGE RED HOT CHILI PEPPERS	13	1992
UNDER THE BRIDGE ALL SAINTS	1	1998
UNDER THE BRIDGES OF PARIS DEAN MARTIN	6	1955
UNDER THE BRIDGES OF PARIS EARTHA KITT	7	1955
UNDER THE COVERS EP HARRY	43	2003
UNDER THE GOD TIN MACHINE	51	1989
UNDER THE GUN SISTERS OF MERCY	19	1993
UNDER THE MOON OF LOVE SHOWADDYWADDY	1	1976
UNDER THE THUMB AMY STUDT	10	2003
UNDER THE TREE WATER BABIES	27	2005
UNDER THE WATER BROTHER BROWN FEATURING FRANK'EE	18	1999
UNDER THE WEATHER KT TUNSTALL	39	2005
UNDER YOUR SPELL RONNY JORDAN	72	1993
UNDER YOUR THUMB GODLEY & CREME	3	1981
UNDERCOVER GEMMA HAYES	63	2006
UNDERCOVER ANARCHIST SILVER BULLET	33	1991
UNDERCOVER ANGEL ALAN O'DAY	43	1977
UNDERCOVER LOVER SMOOTH	41	1996
UNDERCOVER OF THE NIGHT ROLLING STONES	11	1983
UNDERDOG (SAVE ME) TURIN BRAKES	39	2001
UNDERDOSE INME	66	2002
UNDERGROUND [A] DAVID BOWIE	21	1986
UNDERGROUND [B] BEN FOLDS FIVE	37	1996
UNDERGROUND [C] RHYTHM MASTERS	50	2001
UNDERLOVE MELBA MOORE	60	1983
UNDERNEATH IT ALL NO DOUBT	18	2002
UNDERNEATH THE BLANKET GO GILBERT O'SULLIVAN	40	1971
UNDERNEATH YOUR CLOTHES SHAKIRA	3	2002
UNDERPASS JOHN FOXX	31	1980
UNDERSTAND THIS GROOVE FRANKE	60	1992

	Peak Position	Year of Entry
UNDERSTANDING JANE ICICLE WORKS	52	1986
UNDERWATER [A] HARRY THUMANN	41	1981
UNDERWATER [B] DELERIUM FEATURING RANI	33	2001
UNDERWATER LOVE SMOKE CITY	4	1997
UNDERWEAR GOES INSIDE THE PANTS LAZY-B	30	2006
UNDISCOVERED JAMES MORRISON	63	2007
UNDIVIDED LOVE LOUISE	5	1996
UNDONE - THE SWEATER SONG WEEZER	35	1995
UNDRESSED WHITE TOWN	57	1997
UNEMPLOYED IN SUMMERTIME EMILIANA TORRINI	63	2000
UNEXPLAINED GRAVEDIGGAZ	48	1998
UNEXPLAINED EP EMF	18	1992
UNFAITHFUL RIHANNA	2	2006
UNFINISHED SYMPATHY MASSIVE	13	1991
UNFORGETTABLE NATALIE COLE WITH NAT 'KING' COLE	19	1991
THE UNFORGETTABLE FIRE U2	6	1985
UNFORGIVABLE SINNER LENE MARLIN	13	2000
THE UNFORGIVEN [A] METALLICA	15	1991
UNFORGIVEN [B] D:REAM	29	1993
THE UNFORGIVEN II METALLICA	15	1998
UNHOLY KISS	26	1992
UNIFORM INSPIRAL CARPETS	51	1994
UNIFORMS (CORPS D'ESPRIT) PETE TOWNSHEND	48	1982
UNINTENDED MUSE	20	2000
UNINVITED FREEMASONS FEATURING BAILEY TZUKE	8	2007
UNINVITED GUEST MARILLION	53	1989
UNION CITY BLUES BLONDIE	13	1979
UNION OF THE SNAKE DURAN DURAN	3	1983
UNITED JUDAS PRIEST	26	1980
UNITED CALYPSO '98 REDS UNITED	33	1998
UNITED COLOURS BEST SHOT	64	1994
UNITED NATIONS OF HOUSE - VOLUME 1 VARIOUS ARTISTS (EP'S & LPS)	71	2005
UNITED STATES OF WHATEVER LIAM LYNCH	10	2002
UNITED (WE LOVE YOU) MANCHESTER UNITED & THE CHAMPIONS	37	1993
UNITED WE STAND BROTHERHOOD OF MAN	10	1970
UNITY UNITY	64	1991
U.N.I.T.Y. QUEEN LATIFAH	74	1994
UNITY (PART 1 - THE THIRD COMING) AFRIKA BAMBAATAA & JAMES BROWN	49	1984
UNIVERSAL NATE JAMES	72	2005
UNIVERSAL [A] SMALL FACES	16	1968
UNIVERSAL [B] ORCHESTRAL MANOEUVRES IN THE DARK	55	1996
THE UNIVERSAL [C] BLUR	5	1995
UNIVERSAL HEART-BEAT JULIANA HATFIELD	65	1995
UNIVERSAL MUSIC METEOR SEVEN	71	2002
UNIVERSAL NATION PUSH	35	1999
UNIVERSALLY SPEAKING RED HOT CHILI PEPPERS	27	2003
THE UNKNOWN MARK B & BLADE	49	2001
UNLEASH THE DRAGON SISQO	6	2000
UNLOCK THE FUNK LOCKSMITH	42	1980
THE UNNAMED FEELING METALLICA	42	2004
UNO MUSE	73	1999
UNO MAS DANIEL O'DONNELL	25	1999
UNPLAYED PIANO DAMIEN RICE & LISA HANNIGAN	24	2005
UNPREDICTABLE JAMIE FOXX FEATURING LUDACRIS	16	2006
UNPRETTY TLC	6	1999
UNSAFE BUILDING 1990 ALARM	54	1990
UNSATISFIED NINE BLACK ALPS	30	2005
UNSKINNY BOP POISON	15	1990
UNSQUARE DANCE DAVE BRUBECK QUARTET	14	1962
UNSTABLE ADEMA	46	2003

	Peak Position	Year of Entry
THE UNSUNG HEROES OF HIP HOP SUBSONIC	63	1991
UNTIL IT SLEEPS METALLICA	5	1996
UNTIL IT'S TIME FOR YOU TO GO FOUR PENNIES	19	1965
UNTIL IT'S TIME FOR YOU TO GO ELVIS PRESLEY	5	1972
UNTIL MY DYING DAY UB40	15	1995
UNTIL THE DAY FUNKY GREEN DOGS	75	1998
UNTIL THE DAY I DIE STORY OF THE YEAR	62	2004
UNTIL THE END OF TIME 2PAC	4	2001
UNTIL THE NIGHT BILLY JOEL	50	1979
UNTIL THE TIME IS THROUGH FIVE	2	1998
UNTIL YOU COME BACK (THAT'S WHAT I'M GONNA DO) MIKI HOWARD	67	1990
UNTIL YOU COME BACK TO ME ADEVA	45	1992
UNTIL YOU COME BACK TO ME (THAT'S WHAT I'M GONNA DO) ARETHA FRANKLIN	26	1974
UNTIL YOU FIND OUT NED'S ATOMIC DUSTBIN	51	1990
UNTIL YOU LOVED ME MOFFATTS	36	1999
UNTIL YOU SUFFER SOME (FIRE AND ICE) POISON	32	1993
UNTOUCHABLE RIALTO	20	1998
UNWRITTEN NATASHA BEDINGFIELD	6	2004
UP! SHANIA TWAIN	21	2003
UP ABOVE MY HEAD I HEAR MUSIC IN THE AIR FRANKIE LAINE & JOHNNIE RAY	25	1957
UP AGAINST THE WALL TOM ROBINSON BAND	33	1978
UP ALL NIGHT [A] SLAUGHTER	62	1990
UP ALL NIGHT [B] MATT WILLIS	7	2006
UP ALL NIGHT [C] YOUNG KNIVES	45	2008
UP ALL NIGHT/TAKE CONTROL JOHN B	58	2002
UP AND DOWN [A] HIGH	53	1990
UP AND DOWN [B] VENGABOYS	4	1998
UP AND DOWN [C] BOYSTEROUS	53	2003
UP AND DOWN [D] SCENT	23	2004
UP AROUND THE BEND CREEDENCE CLEARWATER REVIVAL	3	1970
UP AROUND THE BEND HANOI ROCKS	61	1984
UP AT THE LAKE CHARLATANS	23	2004
UP IN A PUFF OF SMOKE POLLY BROWN	43	1974
UP MIDDLE FINGER OXIDE & NEUTRINO	7	2001
UP ON THE CATWALK SIMPLE MINDS	27	1984
UP ON THE DOWN SIDE OCEAN COLOUR SCENE	19	2001
UP ON THE ROOF KENNY LYNCH	10	1962
UP ON THE ROOF JULIE GRANT	33	1963
UP ON THE ROOF ROBSON GREEN & JEROME FLYNN	1	1995
UP ROCKING BEATS BOMFUNK MC'S	11	2000
UP TEMPO TRONIKHOUSE	68	1992
UP THE BRACKET LIBERTINES	29	2002
UP THE HILL BACKWARDS DAVID BOWIE	32	1981
UP THE JUNCTION SQUEEZE	2	1979
UP THE LADDER TO THE ROOF SUPREMES	6	1970
UP THE POOL JETHRO TULL	11	1971
UP TO NO GOOD PORN KINGS	28	1996
UP TO THE WILDSTYLE PORN KINGS VERSUS DJ SUPREME	10	1999
UP TOWN TOP RANKING ALTHIA & DONNA	1	1977
UP, UP AND AWAY JOHNNY MANN SINGERS	6	1967
UP WHERE WE BELONG JOE COCKER & JENNIFER WARNES	7	1983
UP WITH THE COCK JUDGE DREAD	49	1978
UP WITH THE PEOPLE LAMBCHOP	66	2000
UPFIELD BILLY BRAGG	46	1996
UPRISING ARTIFICIAL INTELLIGENCE	73	2004
UPROCK ROCKSTEADY CREW	64	1984
UPS AND DOWN SNOOP DOGG	36	2005
UPSIDE DOWN [A] DIANA ROSS	2	1980
UPSIDE DOWN [B] A*TEENS	10	2001
UPSIDE DOWN [C] JACK JOHNSON	30	2006
UPTIGHT [A] STEVIE WONDER	14	1966
UPTIGHT [B] SHARA NELSON	19	1994
UPTOWN DOWNTOWN FULL INTENTION	61	1996
UPTOWN FESTIVAL SHALAMAR	30	1977
UPTOWN GIRL BILLY JOEL	1	1983
UPTOWN GIRL WESTLIFE	1	2001
UPTOWN TOP RANKING ALI & FRAZIER	33	1993
UPTOWN UPTEMPO WOMAN RANDY EDELMAN	25	1976
URBAN CITY GIRL BENZ	31	1996
URBAN GUERRILLA HAWKWIND	39	1973
URBAN PRESSURE GRIM NORTHERN SOCIAL	60	2003
URBAN TRAIN DJ TIESTO	22	2001
THE URGE [A] FREDDY CANNON	18	1960
URGE [B] WILDHEARTS	26	1997
URGENT FOREIGNER	45	1981
URGENTLY IN LOVE BILLY CRAWFORD	48	1998
US AGAINST THE WORLD WESTLIFE	8	2008
U.S. MALE ELVIS PRESLEY	15	1968
USA WWF SUPERSTARS FEATURING HACKSAW JIM DUGGAN	71	1993
USE IT UP AND WEAR IT OUT ODYSSEY	1	1980
USE IT UP AND WEAR IT OUT PAT & MICK	22	1990
USED FOR GLUE RIVAL SCHOOLS	42	2002
USED TA BE MY GIRL O'JAYS	12	1978
USED TO LOVE U JOHN LEGEND	29	2005
USELESS DEPECHE MODE	28	1997
USELESS (I DON'T NEED YOU NOW) KYM MAZELLE	48	1988
UTOPIA GOLDFRAPP	62	2001
UTOPIA (WHERE I WANT TO BE) STEREO STAR FEATURING MIA J	66	2005

V

	Peak Position	Year of Entry
V THIRTEEN BIG AUDIO DYNAMITE	49	1987
VACATION CONNIE FRANCIS	10	1962
VADO VIA DRUPI	17	1973
VAGABONDS NEW MODEL ARMY	37	1989
VALENTINE [A] T'PAU	9	1988
VALENTINE [B] DELAYS	23	2006
VALENTINO CONNIE FRANCIS	27	1960
VALERIE [A] STEVE WINWOOD	19	1982
VALERIE [B] ZUTONS	9	2006
VALERIE [B] AMY WINEHOUSE	37	2007
VALERIE [B] MARK RONSON FEATURING AMY WINEHOUSE	2	2007
VALLERI MONKEES	12	1968
VALLEY OF TEARS FATS DOMINO	25	1957
VALLEY OF TEARS BUDDY HOLLY	12	1961
VALLEY OF THE DOLLS DIONNE WARWICK	28	1968
VALLEY OF THE DOLLS GENERATION X	23	1979
VALLEY OF THE SHADOWS ORIGIN UNKNOWN	60	1996
THE VALLEY ROAD BRUCE HORNSBY & THE RANGE	44	1988
VALOTTE JULIAN LENNON	55	1984
VAMOS A LA PLAYA RIGHEIRA	53	1983
VAMP OUTLANDER	51	1991
VAMPIRE RACECOURSE SLEEPY JACKSON	50	2003
VANESSA TED HEATH	11	1953
VANILLA RADIO WILDHEARTS	26	2002
VANITY KILLS ABC	70	1985
VAPORIZER LUPINE HOWL	68	2000
VAPORS SNOOP DOGGY DOGG	18	1997
VASOLINE STONE TEMPLE PILOTS	48	1994
VAVOOM! MAN WITH NO NAME	43	1998
VAYA CON DIOS LES PAUL & MARY FORD	7	1953
VAYA CON DOS MILLICAN & NESBITT	20	1973
VEGAS [A] SLEEPER	33	1995
VEGAS [B] AGNELLI & NELSON	48	2001
VEGAS TWO TIMES STEREOPHONICS	23	2002
VEHICLE IDES OF MARCH	31	1970
VELCRO FLY ZZ TOP	54	1986
VELOURIA PIXIES	28	1990
VELVET MOODS JOHAN GIELEN PRESENTS ABNEA	74	2001
VENCEREMOS - WE WILL WIN WORKING WEEK	64	1984
VENI VIDI VICI RONNIE HILTON	12	1954
VENTOLIN APHEX TWIN	49	1995
VENTURA HIGHWAY AMERICA	43	1972
VENUS [A] DICKIE VALENTINE	20	1959
VENUS [A] FRANKIE AVALON	16	1959
VENUS [B] SHOCKING BLUE	8	1970
VENUS [B] BANANARAMA	8	1986
VENUS [B] DON PABLO'S ANIMALS	4	1990
VENUS AND MARS JO BREEZER	27	2001
VENUS AS A BOY BJORK	29	1993
VENUS IN BLUE JEANS MARK WYNTER	4	1962
VENUS IN FURS (LIVE) VELVET UNDERGROUND	71	1994
VERDI MAURO PICOTTO	74	2001
VERMILION SLIPKNOT	31	2004
VERNON'S WONDERLAND VERNON'S WONDERLAND	59	1996
VERONICA [A] ELVIS COSTELLO	31	1989
VERONICA [B] SULTANS OF PING FC	69	1992
VERSION OF ME THOUSAND YARD STARE	57	1993
VERTIGO U2	1	2004
VERY BEST FRIEND PROUD MARY	75	2001
VERY METAL NOISE POLLUTION (EP) POP WILL EAT ITSELF	45	1989
A VERY PRECIOUS LOVE DORIS DAY	16	1958
THE VERY THOUGHT OF YOU TONY BENNETT	21	1965
THE VERY THOUGHT OF YOU NATALIE COLE	71	1992
VESSEL ED RUSH & OPTICAL/UNIVERSAL	61	2002
VIBE ZHANE	67	1994
VIBEOLOGY PAULA ABDUL	19	1992
VIBRATOR TERENCE TRENT D'ARBY	57	1995
VICE RAZORLIGHT	18	2004
VICIOUS CIRCLES POLTERGEIST	32	1996
VICIOUS CIRCLES VICIOUS CIRCLES	68	2000
VICTIM OF LOVE [A] ERASURE	7	1987
VICTIM OF LOVE [B] BRYAN ADAMS	68	1987
VICTIMS CULTURE CLUB	3	1983
VICTIMS OF SUCCESS DOGS D'AMOUR	36	1990
VICTORIA KINKS	33	1970
VICTORIA FALL	35	1988
VICTORY KOOL & THE GANG	30	1987
VIDEO INDIA.ARIE	32	2001
VIDEO KILLED THE RADIO STAR BUGGLES	1	1979
VIDEO KILLED THE RADIO STAR PRESIDENTS OF THE UNITED STATES OF AMERICA	52	1998
VIDEO KILLED THE RADIO STAR DRAGONHEART	74	2004
VIDEOTHEQUE DOLLAR	17	1982
VIENNA ULTRAVOX	2	1981
VIENNA CALLING FALCO	10	1986
VIETNAM JIMMY CLIFF	46	1970
VIEW FROM A BRIDGE KIM WILDE	16	1982
A VIEW TO A KILL DURAN DURAN	2	1985
VILLAGE OF ST. BERNADETTE ANNE SHELTON	27	1959
VINCENT DON McLEAN	1	1972
VINDALOO FAT LES	2	1998
VIOLA MOOGWAI	55	2000
VIOLAINE COCTEAU TWINS	56	1996
VIOLENCE OF SUMMER (LOVE'S TAKING OVER) DURAN DURAN	20	1990
VIOLENTLY (EP) HUE & CRY	21	1989
VIOLENTLY HAPPY BJORK	13	1994
VIOLET [A] SEAL	39	1992
VIOLET [B] HOLE	17	1995

		Peak Position	Year of Entry
VIP	JUNGLE BROTHERS	33	1999
VIRGIN MARY	LONNIE DONEGAN	27	1960
VIRGINIA PLAIN	ROXY MUSIC	4	1972
VIRGINIA PLAIN	SLAMM	60	1993
VIRTUAL INSANITY	JAMIROQUAI	3	1996
VIRTUALITY	V-BIRDS	21	2003
VIRUS [A]	IRON MAIDEN	16	1996
VIRUS [B]	MUTINY UK	42	2001
VISAGE	VISAGE	21	1981
THE VISION	MARIO PIU PRESENTS DJ ARABESQUE	16	2001
VISION INCISION	LO FIDELITY ALLSTARS	30	1998
VISION OF LOVE	MARIAH CAREY	9	1990
VISION OF YOU	BELINDA CARLISLE	41	1990
VISIONARY	REDD KROSS	75	1994
VISIONS [A]	CLIFF RICHARD	7	1966
VISIONS [B]	LENA FIAGBE	48	1994
VISIONS IN BLUE	ULTRAVOX	15	1983
VISIONS OF CHINA	JAPAN	32	1981
VISIONS OF PARADISE	MICK JAGGER	43	2002
VISIONS OF YOU	JAH WOBBLE'S INVADERS OF THE HEART	35	1992
VITAL SIGNS	RUSH	41	1981
VITO SATAN	CAMPAG VELOCET	75	2000
VIVA BOBBY JOE	EQUALS	6	1969
VIVA EL FULHAM	TONY REES & THE COTTAGERS	46	1975
VIVA ENGLAND	UNDERCOVER	49	2004
VIVA FOREVER	SPICE GIRLS	1	1998
VIVA LA MEGABABES	SHAMPOO	27	1994
VIVA LA RADIO	LOLLY	6	1999
VIVA LAS VEGAS	ELVIS PRESLEY	15	1964
VIVA LAS VEGAS	ZZ TOP	10	1992
VIVE LE ROCK	ADAM ANT	50	1985
VIVID	ELECTRONIC	17	1999
VIVRANT THING	Q-TIP	39	2000
VOGUE	MADONNA	1	1990
THE VOICE [A]	ULTRAVOX	16	1981
THE VOICE [B]	EIMEAR QUINN	40	1996
VOICE IN THE WILDERNESS	CLIFF RICHARD	2	1960
VOICE OF FREEDOM	FREEDOM WILLIAMS	62	1993
VOICE OF THE SIREN	IRRITANT	70	2007
THE VOICE WITHIN	CHRISTINA AGUILERA	9	2003
VOICES [A]	ANN LEE	27	2000
VOICES [B]	DARIO G	37	2000
VOICES [C]	BEDROCK	44	2000
VOICES [D]	DISTURBED	52	2001
VOICES [E]	K.C. FLIGHTT VS FUNKY JUNCTION	59	2001
VOICES IN THE SKY	MOODY BLUES	27	1968
VOID	EXOTERIX	58	1993
VOLARE	CHARLIE DRAKE	28	1958
VOLARE	DEAN MARTIN	2	1958
VOLARE	DOMENICO MODUGNO	10	1958
VOLARE	MARINO MARINI & HIS QUARTET	13	1958
VOLARE	BOBBY RYDELL	22	1960
VOLCANO	DAMIEN RICE	29	2005
VOLCANO GIRLS	VERUCA SALT	56	1997
VOLUME 1 (WHAT YOU WANT WHAT YOU NEED)	INDUSTRY STANDARD	34	1998
VOODOO	WARRIOR	37	2001
VOODOO CHILD	ROGUE TRADERS	3	2006
VOODOO CHILE	JIMI HENDRIX EXPERIENCE	1	1970
VOODOO LOVE	LEE-CABRERA	58	2004
VOODOO PEOPLE	PRODIGY	13	1994
VOODOO RAY	A GUY CALLED GERALD	12	1989
VOODOO VOODOO	DEN HEGARTY	73	1979
VOULEZ-VOUS	ABBA	3	1979
THE VOW	TOYAH	50	1983
VOYAGE VOYAGE	DESIRELESS	5	1987
VOYAGER	PENDULUM	46	2004
VOYEUR	KIM CARNES	68	1982
VULNERABLE	ROXETTE	44	1995

W

		Peak Position	Year of Entry
WACK ASS MF	RHYTHMKILLAZ	32	2001
WADE IN THE WATER	RAMSEY LEWIS	31	1972
WAGES DAY	DEACON BLUE	18	1989
THE WAGON	DINOSAUR Jr.	49	1991
WAIL	JON SPENCER BLUES EXPLOSION	66	1997
WAIT	ROBERT HOWARD & KYM MAZELLE	7	1989
WAIT A MINUTE	RAY J FEATURING LIL' KIM	54	2001
WAIT AND BLEED	SLIPKNOT	27	2000
WAIT FOR ME	MALCOLM VAUGHAN	13	1959
WAIT FOR ME DARLING	JOAN REGAN & THE JOHNSTON BROTHERS	18	1954
WAIT FOR ME MARIANNE	MARMALADE	30	1968
WAIT (THE WHISPER SONG)	YING YANG TWINS	47	2005
WAIT UNTIL MIDNIGHT	YELLOW DOG	54	1978
WAIT UNTIL TONIGHT (MY LOVE)	GALAXY FEATURING PHIL FEARON	20	1983
WAITIN' FOR A SUPERMAN	FLAMING LIPS	73	1999
WAITING [A]	STYLE COUNCIL	52	1987
WAITING [B]	GREEN DAY	34	2001
THE WAITING 18	AMEN	61	2001
WAITING FOR A GIRL LIKE YOU	FOREIGNER	8	1981
WAITING FOR A STAR TO FALL	BOY MEETS GIRL	9	1988
WAITING FOR A TRAIN	FLASH & THE PAN	7	1983
WAITING FOR AN ALIBI	THIN LIZZY	9	1979
WAITING FOR THAT DAY	GEORGE MICHAEL	23	1990
(WAITING FOR) THE GHOST TRAIN	MADNESS	18	1986
WAITING FOR THE GREAT LEAP FORWARDS	BILLY BRAGG	52	1988
WAITING FOR THE LOVEBOAT	ASSOCIATES	53	1984
WAITING FOR THE NIGHT	SAXON	66	1986
WAITING FOR THE SIRENS' CALL	NEW ORDER	21	2005
WAITING FOR THE SUMMER	DELIRIOUS?	26	2001
WAITING FOR THE SUN	RUFF DRIVERZ	37	1999
WAITING FOR TONIGHT	JENNIFER LOPEZ	5	1999
WAITING 4	PETER GELDERBLOM	29	2007
WAITING GAME	COOPER TEMPLE CLAUSE	41	2007
WAITING HOPEFULLY	D*NOTE	46	1997
WAITING IN VAIN	BOB MARLEY & THE WAILERS	27	1977
WAITING IN VAIN	LEE RITENOUR & MAXI PRIEST	65	1993
WAITING IN VAIN	ANNIE LENNOX	31	1995
WAITING ON A FRIEND	ROLLING STONES	50	1981
WAKE IN THE CITY	IKARA COLT	55	2004
WAKE ME UP	GIRLS ALOUD	4	2005
WAKE ME UP BEFORE YOU GO GO	WHAM!	1	1984
WAKE ME UP WHEN SEPTEMBER ENDS	GREEN DAY	8	2005
WAKE UP [A]	DANSE SOCIETY	61	1983
WAKE UP [B]	LOSTPROPHETS	18	2004
WAKE UP [C]	HILARY DUFF	7	2005
WAKE UP [D]	ARCADE FIRE	29	2005
WAKE UP AND SCRATCH ME	SULTANS OF PING	50	1994
WAKE UP BOO!	BOO RADLEYS	9	1995
WAKE UP CALL	MAROON 5	33	2007
WAKE UP DEAD	MEGADETH	65	1987
WAKE UP EVERYBODY	HAROLD MELVIN & THE BLUENOTES	23	1976
WAKE UP LITTLE SUSIE	EVERLY BROTHERS	2	1957
WAKE UP LITTLE SUSIE	KING BROTHERS	22	1957
WAKE UP SUSAN	DETROIT SPINNERS	29	1977
WAKING UP	ELASTICA	13	1995
WAKING WITH A STRANGER	TYRREL CORPORATION	59	1992
WALHALLA	GOURYELLA	27	1999
THE WALK [A]	INMATES	36	1980
THE WALK [B]	CURE	12	1983
WALK [C]	PANTERA	35	1993
WALK AWAY [A]	SHANE FENTON & THE FENTONES	38	1962
WALK AWAY [B]	MATT MONRO	4	1964
WALK AWAY [C]	SISTERS OF MERCY	45	1984
WALK AWAY [D]	JOYCE SIMS	24	1988
WALK AWAY [F]	FRANZ FERDINAND	13	2005
WALK AWAY [G]	KELLY CLARKSON	21	2006
WALK AWAY [H]	FUNERAL FOR A FRIEND	40	2007
WALK AWAY FROM LOVE	DAVID RUFFIN	10	1976
WALK AWAY RENEE	FOUR TOPS	3	1967
WALK DON'T RUN	JOHN BARRY SEVEN	11	1960
WALK DON'T RUN	VENTURES	8	1960
WALK/DON'T WALK	MY LIFE STORY	48	2000
WALK HAND IN HAND	JIMMY PARKINSON	26	1956
WALK HAND IN HAND	RONNIE CARROLL	13	1956
WALK HAND IN HAND	TONY MARTIN	2	1956
WALK HAND IN HAND	GERRY & THE PACEMAKERS	29	1965
WALK IDIOT WALK	HIVES	13	2004
WALK IN LOVE	MANHATTAN TRANSFER	12	1978
A WALK IN THE BLACK FOREST	HORST JANKOWSKI	3	1965
A WALK IN THE DARK	WHITEY	67	2005
WALK IN THE NIGHT	JUNIOR WALKER & THE ALL-STARS	16	1972
WALK IN THE NIGHT	PAUL HARDCASTLE	54	1988
A WALK IN THE PARK	NICK STRAKER BAND	20	1980
WALK INTO THE SUN	DIRTY VEGAS	54	2004
WALK INTO THE WIND	VEGAS	65	1993
WALK LIKE A CHAMPION	KALIPHZ FEATURING PRINCE NASEEM	23	1996
WALK LIKE A MAN	FOUR SEASONS	12	1963
WALK LIKE A MAN	DIVINE	23	1985
WALK LIKE A PANTHER '98	ALL SEEING I FEATURING TONY CHRISTIE	10	1999
WALK LIKE AN EGYPTIAN	BANGLES	3	1986
WALK OF LIFE [A]	DIRE STRAITS	2	1986
WALK OF LIFE [B]	BILLIE PIPER	25	2000
WALK ON [A]	ROY ORBISON	39	1968
WALK ON [B]	U2	5	2001
WALK ON AIR	T'PAU	62	1991
WALK ON BY [A]	LEROY VAN DYKE	5	1962
WALK ON BY [B]	DIONNE WARWICK	9	1964
WALK ON BY [B]	STRANGLERS	21	1978
WALK ON BY [B]	AVERAGE WHITE BAND	46	1979
WALK ON BY [B]	D TRAIN	44	1982
WALK ON BY [B]	SYBIL	6	1990
WALK ON BY [B]	GABRIELLE	7	1997
WALK ON GILDED SPLINTERS	MARSHA HUNT	46	1969
WALK ON THE WILD SIDE	LOU REED	10	1973
WALK ON THE WILD SIDE	BEAT SYSTEM	63	1990
WALK ON THE WILD SIDE	JAMIE J. MORGAN	27	1990
WALK ON WATER	MILK INC	10	2002
WALK OUT TO WINTER	AZTEC CAMERA	64	1983
WALK RIGHT BACK	EVERLY BROTHERS	1	1961
WALK RIGHT BACK	PERRY COMO	33	1973
WALK RIGHT IN	ROOFTOP SINGERS	10	1963
WALK RIGHT NOW	JACKSONS	7	1981
WALK TALL	VAL DOONICAN	3	1964
WALK THE DINOSAUR	WAS (NOT WAS)	10	1987
WALK...(THE DOG) LIKE AN EGYPTIAN	JODE FEATURING YO-HANS	48	1998
WALK THIS LAND	E-Z ROLLERS	18	1999
WALK THIS WAY	RUN D.M.C.	8	1986
WALK THIS WAY	SUGABABES VS GIRLS ALOUD	1	2007
WALK THIS WORLD	HEATHER NOVA	69	1995
WALK THROUGH THE FIRE	PETER GABRIEL	69	1984
WALK THROUGH THE WORLD	MARC COHN	37	1993
WALK WITH FAITH IN YOUR HEART	BACHELORS	21	1966
WALK WITH ME	SEEKERS	10	1966

	Peak Position	Year of Entry
WALK WITH ME MY ANGEL DON CHARLES	39	1962
WALK WITH ME TALK WITH ME DARLING FOUR TOPS	32	1972
WALKAWAY CAST	9	1996
WALKED OUTTA HEAVEN JAGGED EDGE	21	2004
WALKIE TALKIE MAN STERIOGRAM	19	2004
WALKIN' C.C.S.	7	1971
WALKIN' BACK TO HAPPINESS HELEN SHAPIRO	1	1961
WALKIN' IN THE RAIN WITH THE ONE I LOVE LOVE UNLIMITED	14	1972
A WALKIN' MIRACLE LIMMIE & THE FAMILY COOKIN'	6	1974
WALKIN' ON SHEER BRONZE FEATURING LISA MILLETT	63	1994
WALKIN' ON THE SUN SMASH MOUTH	19	1997
WALKIN' ON UP DJ PROF-X-OR	64	1997
WALKIN' TALL [A] FRANKIE VAUGHAN	28	1959
WALKIN' TALL [B] ADAM FAITH	23	1963
WALKIN' THE DOG DENNISONS	36	1964
WALKIN' THE LINE BRASS CONSTRUCTION	47	1983
WALKIN' TO MISSOURI TONY BRENT	7	1952
WALKING AFTER YOU FOO FIGHTERS	20	1998
WALKING ALONE RICHARD ANTHONY	37	1963
WALKING AWAY [A] CRAIG DAVID	3	2000
WALKING AWAY [B] THE EGG VERSUS DAVID GUETTA	56	2006
WALKING BY MYSELF GARY MOORE	48	1990
WALKING DEAD PURESSENCE	40	2002
WALKING DOWN MADISON KIRSTY MacCOLL	23	1991
WALKING DOWN YOUR STREET BANGLES	16	1987
WALKING IN MEMPHIS MARC COHN	22	1991
WALKING IN MEMPHIS CHER	11	1995
WALKING IN MY SHOES DEPECHE MODE	14	1993
WALKING IN MY SLEEP ROGER DALTREY	56	1984
WALKING IN RHYTHM BLACKBYRDS	23	1975
WALKING IN THE AIR ALED JONES	5	1985
WALKING IN THE AIR PETER AUTY & THE SINFONIA OF LONDON	37	1985
WALKING IN THE AIR DIGITAL DREAM BABY	49	1991
WALKING IN THE NAME FUNKSTAR DE LUXE VS TERRY MAXX	42	2000
WALKING IN THE RAIN [A] WALKER BROTHERS	26	1967
WALKING IN THE RAIN [A] PARTRIDGE FAMILY STARRING DAVID CASSIDY	10	1973
WALKING IN THE RAIN [B] MODERN ROMANCE	7	1983
WALKING IN THE SUN TRAVIS	20	2004
WALKING IN THE SUNSHINE BAD MANNERS	10	1981
WALKING INTO SUNSHINE CENTRAL LINE	42	1981
WALKING MY BABY BACK HOME JOHNNIE RAY	12	1952
WALKING MY CAT NAMED DOG NORMA TANEGA	22	1966
WALKING ON AIR [A] FRAZIER CHORUS	60	1991
WALKING ON AIR [B] BAD BOYS INC	24	1993
WALKING ON BROKEN GLASS ANNIE LENNOX	8	1992
WALKING ON ICE RIVER CITY PEOPLE	62	1990
WALKING ON SUNSHINE [A] ROCKER'S REVENGE FEATURING DONNIE CALVIN	4	1982
WALKING ON SUNSHINE [A] EDDY GRANT	57	1989
WALKING ON SUNSHINE [A] KRUSH	71	1992
WALKING ON SUNSHINE [B] KATRINA & THE WAVES	8	1985
WALKING ON THE CHINESE WALL PHILIP BAILEY	34	1985
WALKING ON THE MILKY WAY ORCHESTRAL MANOEUVRES IN THE DARK	17	1996
WALKING ON THE MOON POLICE	1	1979
WALKING ON THIN ICE YOKO ONO	35	1981
WALKING ON WATER MADASUN	14	2000
WALKING SHADE BILLY CORGAN	74	2005
WALKING THE FLOOR OVER YOU PAT BOONE	39	1960
WALKING TO NEW ORLEANS FATS DOMINO	19	1960
WALKING WITH THEE CLINIC	65	2002
WALKING WOUNDED EVERYTHING BUT THE GIRL	6	1996
WALL STREET SHUFFLE 10 C.C.	10	1974
WALL TO WALL CHRIS BROWN	75	2007
WALLFLOWER MEGA CITY FOUR	69	1993
WALLS COME TUMBLING DOWN! STYLE COUNCIL	6	1985
THE WALLS FELL DOWN MARBLES	28	1969
WALTZ #2 (XO) ELLIOTT SMITH	52	1998
WALTZ AWAY DREAMING TOBY BOURKE/ GEORGE MICHAEL	10	1997
WALTZ DARLING MALCOLM McLAREN & THE BOOTZILLA ORCHESTRA	31	1989
WALTZING ALONG JAMES	23	1997
WAM BAM [A] HANDLEY FAMILY	30	1973
WAM BAM [B] NT GANG	71	1988
THE WAND FLAMING LIPS	41	2006
THE WANDERER [A] DION	10	1962
THE WANDERER [A] STATUS QUO	7	1984
THE WANDERER [B] DONNA SUMMER	48	1980
WANDERIN' EYES CHARLIE GRACIE	6	1957
WANDERIN' EYES FRANKIE VAUGHAN	6	1957
THE WANDERING DRAGON SHADES OF RHYTHM	55	1994
WANDERLUST [A] DELAYS	28	2004
WANDERLUST [B] R.E.M.	27	2005
WAND'RIN' STAR LEE MARVIN	1	1970
WANNA BE STARTIN' SOMETHING MICHAEL JACKSON	8	1983
WANNA BE THAT WAY IKARA COLT	49	2004
WANNA BE WITH YOU JINNY	30	1995
WANNA BE YOUR LOVER GAYLE & GILLIAN	62	1994
WANNA DROP A HOUSE (ON THAT BITCH) URBAN DISCHARGE FEATURING SHE	51	1996
WANNA GET TO KNOW YA G UNIT	27	2004
WANNA GET UP 2 UNLIMITED	38	1998
WANNA MAKE YOU GO...UUH! THOSE 2 GIRLS	74	1994
WANNABE SPICE GIRLS	1	1996
WANNABE GANGSTER WHEATUS	22	2002
WANT LOVE HYSTERIC EGO	28	1996
WANT YOU BAD OFFSPRING	15	2001
WANTED [A] AL MARTINO	4	1954
WANTED [A] PERRY COMO	4	1954
WANTED [B] DOOLEYS	3	1979
WANTED [C] STYLE COUNCIL	20	1987
WANTED [D] HALO JAMES	45	1989
WANTED [E] PRINCESS IVORI	69	1990
WANTED DEAD OR ALIVE [A] BON JOVI	13	1987
WANTED DEAD OR ALIVE [B] 2PAC & SNOOP DOGGY DOGG	16	1997
WANTED IT ALL CLAYTOWN TROUPE	74	1992
WAP-BAM-BOOGIE MATT BIANCO	11	1988
WAR [A] EDWIN STARR	3	1970
WAR [A] BRUCE SPRINGSTEEN	18	1986
WAR [B] UGLY RUMOURS	21	2007
WAR BABIES SIMPLE MINDS	43	1998
WAR BABY TOM ROBINSON	6	1983
WAR CHILD BLONDIE	39	1982
WAR LORD SHADOWS	18	1965
WAR OF NERVES ALL SAINTS	7	1998
WAR OF THE WORLDS GET CAPE WEAR CAPE FLY	39	2006
WAR PARTY EDDY GRANT	42	1983
THE WAR SONG CULTURE CLUB	2	1984
WAR STORIES STARJETS	51	1979
WARFAIR CLAWFINGER	54	1994
WARHEAD U.K. SUBS	30	1980
WARLOCK BLACK RIOT	68	1988
WARM AND TENDER LOVE PERCY SLEDGE	34	1966
WARM IT UP KRIS KROSS	16	1992
WARM LOVE BEATMASTERS FEATURING CLAUDIA FONTAINE	51	1989
WARM MACHINE BUSH	45	2000
WARM SUMMER DAZE VYBE	60	1995
WARM WET CIRCLES MARILLION	22	1987
WARMED OVER KISSES BRIAN HYLAND	28	1962
WARNING [A] ADEVA	17	1989
WARNING [B] AKA	43	1996
WARNING [C] FREESTYLERS FEATURING NAVIGATOR	68	1998
WARNING [D] GREEN DAY	27	2000
WARNING SIGN NICK HEYWARD	25	1984
WARPAINT BROOK BROTHERS	5	1961
WARPED RED HOT CHILI PEPPERS	31	1995
WARRIOR [A] MC WILDSKI	49	1990
WARRIOR [B] DANCE 2 TRANCE	56	1995
WARRIOR [C] WARRIOR	19	2000
WARRIOR GROOVE DSM	68	1985
WARRIOR SOUND PRESSURE DROP	72	2001
WARRIORS [A] GARY NUMAN	20	1983
WARRIORS [B] ASWAD	33	1994
WARRIORS (OF THE WASTELAND) FRANKIE GOES TO HOLLYWOOD	19	1986
WAS IT WORTH IT PET SHOP BOYS	24	1991
WAS THAT ALL IT WAS KYM MAZELLE	33	1990
WAS THAT YOU SPEAR OF DESTINY	55	1987
WASH IN THE RAIN BEES	31	2004
WASH YOUR FACE IN MY SINK DREAM WARRIORS	16	1990
WASHOUT FALLOUT TRUST	75	2006
WASSUUP DA MUTTZ	11	2000
WASTE A MOMENT FIGHTSTAR	29	2006
WASTED SMALLER	72	1996
WASTED IN AMERICA LOVE/HATE	38	1992
WASTED LITTLE DJS THE VIEW	15	2006
WASTED TIME [A] SKID ROW	20	1991
WASTED TIME [B] KINGS OF LEON	51	2003
WASTED YEARS IRON MAIDEN	18	1986
WASTELAND MISSION	11	1987
WASTELANDS MIDGE URE	46	1986
WASTER REEF	56	2003
WASTES DEF LEPPARD	61	1979
WASTING MY TIME [A] DEFAULT	73	2003
WASTING MY TIME [B] KOSHEEN	49	2003
WATCH ME LABI SIFFRE	29	1972
WATCH OUT [A] BRANDI WELLS	74	1982
WATCH OUT [B] FERRY CORSTEN	57	2006
WATCH THE MIRACLE START PAULINE HENRY	54	1994
WATCH THE SUNRISE AXWELL FEATURING STEVE EDWARDS	70	2006
WATCH WHAT YOU SAY GURU FEATURING CHAKA KHAN	28	1995
WATCHA GONNA DO KEISHA WHITE	53	2004
WATCHA GONNA DO WITH MY LOVIN' INNER CITY	12	1989
WATCHDOGS UB40	39	1987
A WATCHER'S POINT OF VIEW PM DAWN	36	1991
WATCHIN' FREEMASONS FEATURING AMANDA WILSON	19	2006
WATCHING THOMPSON TWINS	33	1983
WATCHING CARS GO BY FELIX DA HOUSECAT	49	2004
WATCHING THE DETECTIVES ELVIS COSTELLO	15	1977
WATCHING THE RIVER FLOW BOB DYLAN	24	1971
WATCHING THE WHEELS JOHN LENNON	30	1981
WATCHING THE WILDLIFE FRANKIE GOES TO HOLLYWOOD	28	1987
WATCHING THE WORLD GO BY MAXI PRIEST	36	1996
WATCHING WINDOWS RONI SIZE REPRAZENT	28	1998
WATCHING XANADU MULL HISTORICAL SOCIETY	36	2002
WATCHING YOU [A] ETHER	74	1998

	Peak Position	Year of Entry
WATCHING YOU [B] ROGUE TRADERS	33	2006
WATCHING YOU WATCHING ME DAVID GRANT	10	1983
WATER [A] GENO WASHINGTON & THE RAM JAM BAND	39	1966
WATER [B] MARTIKA	59	1990
WATER FROM A VINE LEAF WILLIAM ORBIT	59	1993
THE WATER IS OVER MY HEAD ROCKIN' BERRIES	43	1996
THE WATER MARGIN GODIEGO	37	1977
THE WATER MARGIN PETE MAC JR	37	1977
WATER ON GLASS KIM WILDE	11	1981
WATER RUNS DRY BOYZ II MEN	24	1995
WATER WATER TOMMY STEELE & THE STEELMEN	5	1957
WATER WAVE MARK VAN DALE WITH ENRICO	71	1998
WATERFALL [A] WENDY & LISA	66	1987
WATERFALL [B] STONE ROSES	27	1992
WATERFALL [C] ATLANTIC OCEAN	21	1994
WATERFALLS [A] PAUL McCARTNEY	9	1980
WATERFALLS [B] TLC	4	1995
WATERFRONT SIMPLE MINDS	13	1983
WATERLOO [A] STONEWALL JACKSON	24	1959
WATERLOO [B] ABBA	1	1974
WATERLOO [B] DOCTOR & THE MEDICS FEATURING ROY WOOD	45	1986
WATERLOO SUNSET KINKS	2	1967
WATERLOO SUNSET CATHY DENNIS	11	1997
WATERMAN OLAV BASOSKI FEATURING MICHIE ONE	45	2005
WATERY, DOMESTIC (EP) PAVEMENT	58	1992
THE WAVE COSMIC GATE	48	2003
THE WAVE OF THE FUTURE QUADROPHONIA	40	1991
WAVES BLANCMANGE	19	1983
WAVING FLAGS BRITISH SEA POWER	31	2008
WAVY GRAVY SASHA	64	2002
WAX THE VAN LOLA	65	1987
THE WAY [A] FUNKY GREEN DOGS	43	1997
THE WAY [B] GLOBAL COMMUNICATION	51	1997
THE WAY [C] FASTBALL	21	1998
THE WAY [D] DANIEL BEDINGFIELD	41	2005
WAY AWAY YELLOWCARD	63	2004
WAY BACK HOME JUNIOR WALKER & THE ALL-STARS	35	1973
WAY BEHIND ME PRIMITIVES	36	1988
WAY DOWN ELVIS PRESLEY	1	1977
WAY DOWN NOW WORLD PARTY	66	1990
WAY DOWN YONDER IN NEW ORLEANS FREDDY CANNON	3	1960
THE WAY DREAMS ARE DANIEL O'DONNELL	18	1999
THE WAY I AM EMINEM	8	2000
THE WAY I ARE TIMBALAND FEATURING DOE & KERI HILSON	1	2007
THE WAY I FEEL [A] LEMON TREES	62	1992
THE WAY I FEEL [B] ROACHFORD	20	1997
THE WAY I FEEL ABOUT YOU KARYN WHITE	65	1992
THE WAY I WALK JACK SCOTT	30	1959
THE WAY I WANT TO TOUCH YOU CAPTAIN & TENNILLE	28	1976
WAY IN MY BRAIN SL2	26	1991
THE WAY IT GOES STATUS QUO	39	1999
THE WAY IT IS BRUCE HORNSBY & THE RANGE	15	1986
THE WAY IT IS CHAMELEON	34	1996
THE WAY IT USED TO BE ENGELBERT HUMPERDINCK	3	1969
THE WAY IT WAS/REDHEAD BARON	71	2004
THE WAY IT'S GOIN' DOWN (T.W.I.S.M. FOR LIFE) SHAQUILLE O'NEAL	62	1998
A WAY OF LIFE [A] FAMILY DOGG	6	1969
WAY OF LIFE [B] DAVE CLARKE	59	2003
WAY OF THE WORLD [A] CHEAP TRICK	73	1980
WAY OF THE WORLD [B] TINA TURNER	13	1991
THE WAY (PUT YOUR HAND IN MY HAND) DIVINE INSPIRATION	5	2002
THE WAY SHE LOVES ME RICHARD MARX	38	1994
THE WAY THAT YOU FEEL ADEVA	54	1997
THE WAY THAT YOU LOVE ME VANESSA WILLIAMS	52	1995
THE WAY TO YOUR LOVE HEAR'SAY	1	2001
THE WAY WE WERE BARBRA STREISAND	31	1974
THE WAY WE WERE - TRY TO REMEMBER GLADYS KNIGHT & THE PIPS	4	1975
THE WAY YOU ARE TEARS FOR FEARS	24	1983
THE WAY YOU DO THE THINGS YOU DO UB40	49	1991
THE WAY YOU LIKE IT ADEMA	61	2002
THE WAY YOU LOOK TONIGHT LETTERMEN	36	1961
THE WAY YOU LOOK TONIGHT DENNY SEYTON & THE SABRES	48	1964
THE WAY YOU LOOK TONIGHT EDWARD WOODWARD	42	1971
THE WAY YOU LOVE ME [A] KARYN WHITE	42	1988
THE WAY YOU LOVE ME [B] FAITH HILL	15	2001
THE WAY YOU MAKE ME FEEL [A] MICHAEL JACKSON	3	1987
THE WAY YOU MAKE ME FEEL [B] RONAN KEATING	6	2000
THE WAY YOU MOVE OUTKAST FEATURING SLEEPY BROWN	7	2004
THE WAY YOU USED TO SMILE RESEARCH	66	2005
THE WAY YOU WORK IT E.Y.C.	14	1994
WAYDOWN CATHERINE WHEEL	67	1995
WAYS OF LOVE CLAYTOWN TROUPE	57	1990
WAYUH (PEOPLE DON'T DANCE NO MORE) RAPTURE	65	2006
WAYWARD WIND GOGI GRANT	9	1956
WAYWARD WIND JIMMY YOUNG	27	1956
WAYWARD WIND TEX RITTER	8	1956
THE WAYWARD WIND FRANK IFIELD	1	1963
WE ALL FOLLOW MAN. UNITED MANCHESTER UNITED FOOTBALL CLUB	10	1985
WE ALL SLEEP ALONE CHER	47	1988
WE ALL STAND TOGETHER PAUL McCARTNEY & THE FROG CHORUS	3	1984
WE ALMOST GOT IT TOGETHER TANITA TIKARAM	52	1990
WE APOLOGISE FOR NOTHING FIGHTSTAR	63	2007
WE ARE ANA JOHNSSON	8	2004
WE ARE ALIVE PAUL VAN DYK	15	2000
WE ARE ALL MADE OF STARS MOBY	11	2002
WE ARE ALL ON DRUGS WEEZER	47	2005
WE ARE BACK LFO	47	1991
WE ARE DA CLICK DA CLICK	38	1999
WE ARE DETECTIVE THOMPSON TWINS	7	1983
WE ARE EACH OTHER BEAUTIFUL SOUTH	30	1992
WE ARE E-MALE E-MALE	44	1998
WE ARE ENGLAND RICKY	54	2006
WE ARE FAMILY SISTER SLEDGE	5	1979
WE ARE GLASS GARY NUMAN	5	1980
WE ARE GOING ON DOWN DEADLY SINS	45	1994
WE ARE I. E. LENNIE DE ICE	61	1999
WE ARE IN LOVE [A] ADAM FAITH & THE ROULETTES	11	1963
WE ARE IN LOVE [B] HARRY CONNICK Jr.	62	1991
WE ARE LOVE DJ ERIC	37	1999
WE ARE NOT ALONE FRANKIE VAUGHAN	11	1958
WE ARE RAVING - THE ANTHEM SLIPSTREEM	18	1992
WE ARE THE BAND MORE	59	1981
WE ARE THE CHAMPIONS QUEEN	2	1977
WE ARE THE CHAMPIONS HANK MARVIN FEATURING BRIAN MAY	66	1992
WE ARE THE CHAMPIONS CRAZY FROG	11	2006
WE ARE THE FIRM COCKNEY REJECTS	54	1980
WE ARE THE PIGS SUEDE	18	1994
WE ARE THE WORLD USA FOR AFRICA	1	1985
WE ARE YOUR FRIENDS JUSTICE VERSUS SIMIAN	20	2006
WE BE BURNIN' SEAN PAUL	2	2005
WE BELONG PAT BENATAR	22	1985
WE BELONG IN THIS WORLD TOGETHER STEREO MC'S	59	2001
WE BELONG TOGETHER MARIAH CAREY	2	2005
WE BUILT THIS CITY STARSHIP	12	1985
WE CALL IT ACIEED D MOB FEATURING GARY HAISMAN	3	1988
WE CAME TO DANCE ULTRAVOX	18	1983
WE CAN LeANN RIMES	27	2003
WE CAN BE BRAVE AGAIN ARMOURY SHOW	66	1985
WE CAN BE STRONG WILLY MASON	52	2007
WE CAN DO ANYTHING COCKNEY REJECTS	65	1980
WE CAN DO IT (EP) LIVERPOOL FC	15	1977
WE CAN GET DOWN MYRON	74	1997
WE CAN MAKE IT MONE	64	1995
WE CAN MAKE IT HAPPEN PRINCE CHARLES & THE CITY BEAT BAND	56	1986
WE CAN WORK IT OUT [A] BEATLES	1	1965
WE CAN WORK IT OUT [A] STEVIE WONDER	27	1971
WE CAN WORK IT OUT [A] FOUR SEASONS	34	1976
WE CAN WORK IT OUT [B] BRASS CONSTRUCTION	70	1983
WE CARE A LOT FAITH NO MORE	53	1988
WE CLOSE OUR EYES GO WEST	5	1985
WE CLOSE OUR EYES GROOVE CUTTERS	33	2005
WE COME 1 FAITHLESS	3	2001
WE COME TO PARTY N-TYCE	12	1997
WE COULD BE KINGS GENE	17	1997
WE COULD BE TOGETHER DEBBIE GIBSON	22	1989
WE DANCED TOGETHER RAKES	38	2007
WE DIDN'T START THE FIRE BILLY JOEL	7	1989
WE DO IT R & J STONE	5	1976
WE DON'T CARE AUDIOBULLYS	15	2002
WE DON'T HAVE TO... JERMAINE STEWART	2	1986
WE DON'T HAVE TO TAKE OUR CLOTHES OFF DA PLAYAZ VS CLEA	35	2005
WE DON'T HAVE TO TAKE OUR CLOTHES OFF LIL' CHRIS	63	2007
WE DON'T NEED A REASON DARE	52	1991
WE DON'T NEED ANOTHER HERO (THUNDERDOME) TINA TURNER	3	1985
WE DON'T NEED NOBODY ELSE WHIPPING BOY	51	1995
(WE DON'T NEED THIS) FASCIST GROOVE THANG HEAVEN 17	40	1981
WE DON'T TALK ANYMORE CLIFF RICHARD	1	1979
WE DON'T WORK FOR FREE GRANDMASTER MELLE MEL & THE FURIOUS FIVE	45	1984
WE FIT TOGETHER O-TOWN	20	2001
WE GOT A LOVE THANG CE CE PENISTON	6	1992
WE GOT IT IMMATURE FEATURING SMOOTH	26	1996
WE GOT LOVE ALMA COGAN	26	1959
WE GOT OUR OWN THANG HEAVY D. & THE BOYZ	69	1989
WE GOT THE FUNK POSITIVE FORCE	18	1980
WE GOT THE GROOVE PLAYERS ASSOCIATION	61	1980
WE GOT THE LOVE [A] TOUCH OF SOUL	46	1990
WE GOT THE LOVE [B] LINDY LAYTON	38	1993
WE GOT THE LOVE [B] ERIK	55	1994
WE GOT THE LOVE [C] TRI	61	1995
WE GOTTA DO IT DJ PROFESSOR FEATURING FRANCESCO ZAPPALA	57	1991
WE GOTTA GET OUT OF THIS PLACE ANIMALS	2	1965
WE GOTTA GET OUT OF THIS PLACE ANGELIC UPSTARTS	65	1980
WE GOTTA LOVE KYM SIMS	58	1996
WE HATE IT WHEN OUR FRIENDS BECOME SUCCESSFUL MORRISSEY	17	1992

	Peak Position	Year of Entry
WE HAVE A DREAM SCOTLAND WORLD CUP SQUAD	5	1982
WE HAVE ALL THE TIME IN THE WORLD LOUIS ARMSTRONG	3	1994
WE HAVE EXPLOSIVE FUTURE SOUND OF LONDON	12	1997
WE HAVEN'T TURNED AROUND GOMEZ	38	1999
WE JUST BE DREAMIN' BLAZIN' SQUAD	3	2003
WE JUST WANNA PARTY WITH YOU SNOOP DOGGY DOGG FEATURING JD	21	1997
WE KILL THE WORLD (DON'T KILL THE WORLD) BONEY M	39	1981
WE KNOW SOMETHING YOU DON'T KNOW DJ FORMAT FEATURING CHARLI 2NA & AKIL	73	2003
WE LAUGHED ROSETTA LIFE FEATURING BILLY BRAGG	11	2005
WE LET THE STARS GO PREFAB SPROUT	50	1990
WE LIKE TO PARTY (THE VENGABUS) VENGABOYS	3	1999
WE LOVE EACH OTHER CHARLIE RICH	37	1975
WE LOVE YOU [A] ROLLING STONES	8	1967
WE LOVE YOU [B] ORCHESTRAL MANOEUVRES IN THE DARK	54	1986
WE LOVE YOU [C] MENSWEAR	22	1996
WE LUV U GRAND THEFT AUDIO	70	2001
WE NEED A RESOLUTION AALIYAH FEATURING TIMBALAND	20	2001
WE NEED LOVE CASHMERE	52	1985
WE RIDE RIHANNA	17	2006
WE ROCK DIO	42	1984
WE RUN THIS MISSY ELLIOTT	38	2006
WE SAIL ON THE STORMY WATERS GARY CLARK	34	1993
WE SHALL OVERCOME JOAN BAEZ	26	1965
WE SHOULD BE TOGETHER CLIFF RICHARD	10	1991
WE SHOULDN'T HOLD HANDS IN THE DARK L.A. MIX	69	1991
WE TAKE MYSTERY (TO BED) GARY NUMAN	9	1982
WE THUGGIN' FAT JOE	48	2002
WE TRYING TO STAY ALIVE WYCLEF JEAN & THE REFUGEE ALLSTARS	13	1997
WE USED TO BE FRIENDS DANDY WARHOLS	18	2003
WE WAIT AND WE WONDER PHIL COLLINS	45	1994
WE WALKED IN LOVE DOLLAR	61	1986
WE WANNA THANK YOU (THE THINGS YOU DO) BIG BROVAZ	17	2004
(WE WANT) THE SAME THING BELINDA CARLISLE	6	1990
WE WANT YOUR SOUL FREELAND	35	2003
WE WILL GILBERT O'SULLIVAN	16	1971
WE WILL MAKE LOVE RUSS HAMILTON	2	1957
WE WILL MEET AGAIN OLETA ADAMS	51	1996
WE WILL NEVER BE THIS YOUNG AGAIN DANNY WILLIAMS	44	1961
WE WILL ROCK YOU FIVE & QUEEN	1	2000
WE WILL SURVIVE WARP BROTHERS	19	2001
WEAK [A] SWV	33	1993
WEAK [B] SKUNK ANANSIE	20	1996
WEAK BECOME HEROES STREETS	27	2002
WEAK IN THE PRESENCE OF BEAUTY ALISON MOYET	6	1987
WEAK SPOT EVELYN THOMAS	26	1976
THE WEAKNESS IN ME KEISHA WHITE	17	2006
WEAPON OF CHOICE BLACK REBEL MOTORCYCLE CLUB	35	2007
WEAR MY HAT PHIL COLLINS	43	1997
WEAR MY RING AROUND YOUR NECK ELVIS PRESLEY	3	1958
WEAR YOU TO THE BALL UB40	35	1990
WEAR YOUR LOVE LIKE HEAVEN DEFINITION OF SOUND	17	1991
WEATHER FORECAST MASTER SINGERS	45	1966
WEATHER WITH YOU CROWDED HOUSE	7	1992
WEAVE YOUR SPELL LEVEL 42	43	1982
THE WEAVER (EP) PAUL WELLER	18	1993
THE WEDDING [A] JULIE ROGERS	3	1964
THE WEDDING [B] CLIFF RICHARD FEATURING HELEN HOBSON	40	1996
WEDDING BELL BLUES FIFTH DIMENSION	16	1970
WEDDING BELLS [A] EDDIE FISHER	5	1955
WEDDING BELLS [B] GODLEY & CREME	7	1981
WEDDING RING RUSS HAMILTON	20	1957
WEDNESDAY WEEK UNDERTONES	11	1980
WEE RULE WEE PAPA GIRL RAPPERS	6	1988
WEE TOM LORD ROCKINGHAM'S XI	16	1959
WEEK IN WEEK OUT ORDINARY BOYS	36	2004
WEEKEND [A] EDDIE COCHRAN	15	1961
WEEKEND [B] MICK JACKSON	38	1979
WEEKEND [C] CLASS ACTION FEATURING CHRIS WILTSHIRE	49	1983
WEEKEND [C] TODD TERRY PROJECT	28	1988
WEEKEND [D] BAD HABIT BOYS	41	2000
WEEKEND [E] SCOOTER	12	2003
THE WEEKEND [F] MICHAEL GRAY	7	2004
WEEKEND GIRL S.O.S. BAND	51	1984
THE WEEKEND HAS LANDED MINKY	70	1999
WEEKEND WITHOUT MAKEUP LONG BLONDES	28	2006
WEEKENDER FLOWERED UP	20	1992
WEEKENDS AND BLEAK DAYS (HOT SUMMER) YOUNG KNIVES	35	2006
THE WEIGHT BAND	21	1968
WEIGHT FOR THE BASS UNIQUE 3	29	1990
WEIGHT OF THE WORLD RINGO STARR	74	1992
WEIGHTLESS WET WET WET	10	2008
WEIRD [A] REEF	19	1995
WEIRD [B] HANSON	19	1998
WEIRDO CHARLATANS	19	1992
WELCOME GINO LATINO	17	1990
WELCOME BACK MASE	29	2004
WELCOME HOME PETERS & LEE	1	1973
WELCOME HOME BABY BROOK BROTHERS	33	1962
WELCOME TO CHICAGO EP GENE FARRIS	74	2003
WELCOME TO JAMROCK DAMIAN "JR GONG" MARLEY	13	2005
WELCOME TO MY LIFE SIMPLE PLAN	49	2005
WELCOME TO MY TRUTH ANASTACIA	25	2004
WELCOME TO MY WORLD JIM REEVES	6	1963
WELCOME TO OUR WORLD (OF MERRY MUSIC) MASS PRODUCTION	44	1977
WELCOME TO PARADISE GREEN DAY	20	1994
WELCOME TO THE BLACK PARADE MY CHEMICAL ROMANCE	1	2006
WELCOME TO THE CHEAP SEATS (EP) WONDER STUFF	8	1992
(WELCOME) TO THE DANCE DES MITCHELL	5	2000
WELCOME TO THE FUTURE SHIMMON & WOOLFSON	69	1998
WELCOME TO THE JUNGLE GUNS N' ROSES	24	1987
WELCOME TO THE PLEASURE DOME FRANKIE GOES TO HOLLYWOOD	2	1985
WELCOME TO THE REAL WORLD GUN	43	1992
WELCOME TO THE TERRORDOME PUBLIC ENEMY	18	1990
WELCOME TO TOMORROW SNAP FEATURING SUMMER	6	1994
WELCOME TO WHEREVER YOU ARE BON JOVI	19	2006
WELL ALL RIGHT SANTANA	53	1978
WE'LL BE RIGHT BACK STEINSKI & MASS MEDIA	63	1987
WE'LL BE TOGETHER STING	41	1987
WE'LL BE WITH YOU POTTERS	34	1972
WE'LL BRING THE HOUSE DOWN SLADE	10	1981
WELL DID YOU EVAH! DEBORAH HARRY & IGGY POP	42	1991
WE'LL FIND OUR DAY STEPHANIE DE SYKES	17	1975
WE'LL GATHER LILACES - ALL MY LOVING (MEDLEY) SIMON MAY	49	1977
WELL I ASK YOU EDEN KANE	1	1961
WE'LL LIVE AND DIE IN THESE TOWNS ENEMY	21	2007
WE'LL SING IN THE SUNSHINE LANCASTRIANS	44	1964
WE'RE ALL ALONE RITA COOLIDGE	6	1977
WE'RE ALL GOING TO DIE MALCOLM MIDDLETON	31	2007
WE'RE ALL IN LOVE BLACK REBEL MOTORCYCLE CLUB	45	2003
WE'RE ALL IN THIS TOGETHER CAST OF HIGH SCHOOL MUSICAL	40	2006
WE'RE ALMOST THERE MICHAEL JACKSON	46	1981
WE'RE COMIN' AT YA QUARTZ FEATURING STEPZ	65	1990
WE'RE COMING OVER MR SMASH & FRIENDS	67	2002
WE'RE ENGLAND (TOM HARK) TALKSPORT ALLSTARS	37	2006
WE'RE GOING OUT YOUNGER YOUNGER 28'S	61	1999
WE'RE GOING TO IBIZA! VENGABOYS	1	1999
WE'RE GOING TO MISS YOU JAMES	48	1999
WE'RE GONNA DO IT AGAIN MANCHESTER UNITED FEATURING STRYKER	6	1995
WE'RE GONNA GO FISHIN' HANK LOCKLIN	18	1962
WE'RE IN THIS LOVE TOGETHER AL JARREAU	55	1981
WE'RE IN THIS TOGETHER [A] SIMPLY RED	11	1996
WE'RE IN THIS TOGETHER [B] NINE INCH NAILS	39	1999
WE'RE NOT ALONE HHC	44	1997
WE'RE NOT GONNA SLEEP TONIGHT EMMA BUNTON	20	2001
WE'RE NOT GONNA TAKE IT TWISTED SISTER	58	1984
WE'RE ON THE BALL ANT & DEC	3	2002
WE'RE ONLY YOUNG ONCE AVONS	45	1960
WE'RE REALLY SAYING SOMETHING BUFFALO G	17	2000
WE'RE THROUGH HOLLIES	7	1964
WEST END GIRLS PET SHOP BOYS	1	1985
WEST END GIRLS EAST 17	11	1993
WEST END PAD CATHY DENNIS	25	1996
WEST OF ZANZIBAR ANTHONY STEEL & THE RADIO REVELLERS	11	1954
WEST ONE (SHINE ON ME) RUTS	43	1980
WESTERN MOVIES OLYMPICS	12	1958
WESTSIDE [A] TQ	4	1999
WESTSIDE [B] ATHLETE	42	2003
WET DREAM MAX ROMEO	10	1969
WET MY WHISTLE MIDNIGHT STAR	60	1987
WE'VE GOT IT GOIN' ON BACKSTREET BOYS	3	1995
WE'VE GOT THE JUICE DEREK B	56	1988
WE'VE GOT THE WHOLE WORLD AT OUR FEET ENGLAND WORLD CUP SQUAD	66	1986
WE'VE GOT THE WHOLE WORLD IN OUR HANDS NOTTINGHAM FOREST FC & PAPER LACE	24	1978
WE'VE GOT TO LIVE TOGETHER RAF	34	1992
WE'VE GOT TO WORK IT OUT BEL CANTO	65	1995
WE'VE GOT TONIGHT BOB SEGER & THE SILVER BULLET BAND	22	1979
WE'VE GOT TONIGHT KENNY ROGERS & SHEENA EASTON	28	1983
WE'VE GOT TONIGHT ELKIE BROOKS	69	1987
WE'VE GOT TONIGHT RONAN KEATING FEATURING LULU	4	2002
WE'VE HAD ENOUGH ALKALINE TRIO	50	2003
WE'VE ONLY JUST BEGUN CARPENTERS	28	1971
WE'VE ONLY JUST BEGUN BITTY McLEAN	23	1995
WFL HAPPY MONDAYS	68	1989
WHADDA U WANT (FROM ME) FRANKIE KNUCKLES FEATURING ADEVA	36	1995

	Peak Position	Year of Entry
WHADDA WE LIKE? ROUND SOUND PRESENTS ONYX STONE & MC MALIBU	69	2002
WHAM BAM CANDY GIRLS FEATURING SWEET PUSSY PAULINE	20	1996
WHAM RAP WHAM!	8	1983
WHAT SOFT CELL	3	1982
WHAT A BEAUTIFUL DAY LEVELLERS	13	1997
WHAT A CRAZY WORLD WE'RE LIVING IN JOE BROWN & THE BRUVVERS	37	1962
WHAT A DIFFERENCE A DAY MAKES ESTHER PHILLIPS	6	1975
WHAT A FOOL BELIEVES DOOBIE BROTHERS	31	1979
WHAT A FOOL BELIEVES ARETHA FRANKLIN	46	1980
WHAT A FOOL BELIEVES PETER COX	39	1998
WHAT A GIRL WANTS CHRISTINA AGUILERA	3	2000
WHAT A LOVELY DANCE HAL	36	2005
WHAT A MOUTH TOMMY STEELE	5	1960
WHAT A NIGHT CITY BOY	39	1978
WHAT A PARTY FATS DOMINO	43	1961
WHAT A WASTE IAN DURY & THE BLOCKHEADS	9	1978
WHAT A WASTER LIBERTINES	37	2002
WHAT A WOMAN IN LOVE WON'T DO SANDY POSEY	48	1967
WHAT A WONDERFUL WORLD [A] LOUIS ARMSTRONG	1	1968
WHAT A WONDERFUL WORLD [A] NICK CAVE & SHANE McGOWAN	72	1992
WHAT A WONDERFUL WORLD [A] CLIFF RICHARD	11	2001
WHAT A WONDERFUL WORLD [A] EVA CASSIDY & KATIE MELUA	1	2007
(WHAT A) WONDERFUL WORLD [B] JOHNNY NASH	25	1976
WHAT ABOUT LOVE HEART	14	1988
WHAT ABOUT ME CRIBS	75	2004
WHAT ABOUT THIS LOVE MR FINGERS	74	1990
WHAT ABOUT US [A] POINT BREAK	24	2000
WHAT ABOUT US [B] BRANDY	4	2002
WHAT ABOUT YOUR FRIENDS TLC	59	1992
WHAT AM I FIGHTING FOR UNKLEJAM	16	2007
WHAT AM I GONNA DO [A] EMILE FORD & THE CHECKMATES	33	1961
WHAT AM I GONNA DO [B] ROD STEWART	3	1983
WHAT AM I GONNA DO WITH YOU BARRY WHITE	5	1975
WHAT AM I TO YOU KENNY LYNCH	37	1964
WHAT ARE WE GONNA DO ABOUT IT? MERCY MERCY	59	1985
WHAT ARE WE GONNA GET 'ER INDOORS DENNIS WATERMAN & GEORGE COLE	21	1983
WHAT ARE YOU DOING SUNDAY DAWN FEATURING TONY ORLANDO	3	1971
WHAT ARE YOU UNDER DEFINITION OF SOUND	68	1992
WHAT BECAME OF THE LIKELY LADS LIBERTINES	9	2004
WHAT BECOMES OF THE BROKENHEARTED JIMMY RUFFIN	4	1966
WHAT BECOMES OF THE BROKENHEARTED DAVE STEWART. GUEST VOCALS: COLIN BLUNSTONE	13	1981
WHAT BECOMES OF THE BROKENHEARTED ROBSON GREEN & JEROME FLYNN	1	1996
WHAT CAN I DO CORRS	3	1998
WHAT CAN I SAY BOZ SCAGGS	10	1977
(WHAT CAN I SAY) TO MAKE YOU LOVE ME ALEXANDER O'NEAL	27	1988
WHAT CAN YOU DO FOR ME [A] UTAH SAINTS	10	1991
WHAT CAN YOU DO 4 ME? [B] LISA LASHES	52	2003
WHAT CAR CLIFF RICHARD	12	2005
WHAT DID I DO TO YOU (EP) LISA STANSFIELD	25	1990
WHAT DIFFERENCE DOES IT MAKE SMITHS	12	1984
WHAT DO I DO PHIL FEARON & GALAXY	5	1984
WHAT DO I DO NOW? SLEEPER	14	1995
WHAT DO I GET BUZZCOCKS	37	1978
WHAT DO I HAVE TO DO KYLIE MINOGUE	6	1991
WHAT DO YA SAY CHUBBY CHECKER	37	1963
WHAT DO YOU WANT [A] ADAM FAITH	1	1959
WHAT DO YOU WANT? [B] MORILLO FEATURING TERRA DEVA	61	2005
WHAT DO YOU WANT FROM ME? MONACO	11	1997
WHAT DO YOU WANT TO MAKE THOSE EYES AT ME FOR EMILE FORD & THE CHECKMATES	1	1959
WHAT DO YOU WANT TO MAKE THOSE EYES AT ME FOR SHAKIN' STEVENS	5	1987
WHAT DOES IT FEEL LIKE? FELIX DA HOUSECAT	66	2002
WHAT DOES IT TAKE THEN JERICO	33	1989
WHAT DOES IT TAKE (TO WIN YOUR LOVE) JUNIOR WALKER & THE ALL-STARS	13	1969
WHAT DOES IT TAKE (TO WIN YOUR LOVE) KENNY G	64	1986
WHAT DOES YOUR SOUL LOOK LIKE (PART 1) DJ SHADOW	54	1995
WHAT ELSE IS THERE? ROYKSOPP	32	2005
WHAT EVER HAPPENED TO OLD FASHIONED LOVE DANIEL O'DONNELL	21	1993
WHAT GOD WANTS PART 1 ROGER WATERS	35	1992
WHAT GOES AROUND [A] BITTY McLEAN	36	1994
WHAT GOES AROUND [B] LUCIANA	67	1994
WHAT GOES AROUND COMES AROUND [A] BOB MARLEY & THE WAILERS	42	1996
WHAT GOES AROUND COMES AROUND [B] JUSTIN TIMBERLAKE	4	2007
WHAT GOES ON BRYAN FERRY	67	1978
WHAT GOOD AM I CILLA BLACK	24	1967
WHAT HAPPENED TO THE MUSIC JOEY NEGRO	51	1993
WHAT HAPPENS TOMORROW DURAN DURAN	11	2005
WHAT HAVE I DONE TO DESERVE THIS PET SHOP BOYS & DUSTY SPRINGFIELD	2	1987
WHAT HAVE THEY DONE TO MY SONG MA NEW SEEKERS	44	1970
WHAT HAVE THEY DONE TO MY SONG MA MELANIE	39	1971
WHAT HAVE THEY DONE TO THE RAIN SEARCHERS	13	1964
WHAT HAVE YOU DONE FOR ME LATELY JANET JACKSON	3	1986
WHAT HAVE YOU DONE (IS THIS ALL) ONE TRIBE FEATURING GEM	52	1992
WHAT HOPE HAVE I SPHINX	43	1995
WHAT HURTS THE MOST [A] JO O'MEARA	13	2005
WHAT HURTS THE MOST [B] CASCADA	10	2007
WHAT I AM EDIE BRICKELL & THE NEW BOHEMIANS	31	1989
WHAT I AM TIN TIN OUT FEATURING EMMA BUNTON	2	1999
WHAT I CAN DO FOR YOU SHERYL CROW	43	1995
WHAT I DO BEST ROBIN S	43	1993
WHAT I GO TO SCHOOL FOR BUSTED	3	2002
WHAT I GOT SUBLIME	71	1997
WHAT I GOT IS WHAT YOU NEED UNIQUE	27	1983
WHAT I LIKE MOST ABOUT YOU IS YOUR GIRLFRIEND SPECIAL A.K.A.	51	1984
WHAT I MEAN MODJO	59	2001
WHAT I MISS THE MOST ALOOF	70	1998
WHAT I REALLY WANT FOR CHRISTMAS BRIAN WILSON	66	2005
WHAT I SAW KINGS OF LEON	22	2003
WHAT IF... [A] LIGHTNING SEEDS	14	1996
WHAT IF [B] KATE WINSLET	6	2001
WHAT IF A WOMAN JOE	53	2002
WHAT IF I'M RIGHT SANDI THOM	22	2006
WHAT IN THE WORLD NU COLOURS	57	1993
WHAT IN THE WORLD'S COME OVER YOU JACK SCOTT	11	1960
WHAT IN THE WORLD'S COME OVER YOU ROCKIN' BERRIES	23	1965
WHAT IN THE WORLD'S COME OVER YOU TAM WHITE	36	1975
WHAT IS A MAN FOUR TOPS	16	1969
WHAT IS HOUSE (EP) LFO	62	1992
WHAT IS LIFE [A] OLIVIA NEWTON-JOHN	16	1972
WHAT IS LIFE [A] SHAWN MULLINS	62	1999
WHAT IS LIFE? [B] BLACK UHURU	56	1984
WHAT IS LOVE [A] HOWARD JONES	2	1983
WHAT IS LOVE [B] DEEE-LITE	2	1990
WHAT IS LOVE [C] HADDAWAY	2	1993
WHAT IS THE PROBLEM? GRAFITI	37	2003
WHAT IS THIS THING CALLED LOVE ALEXANDER O'NEAL	53	1991
WHAT IS TRUTH JOHNNY CASH	21	1970
WHAT IT FEELS LIKE FOR A GIRL MADONNA	7	2001
WHAT IT IS [A] GARNET MIMMS & TRUCKIN' CO	44	1977
WHAT IT IS [B] FREDDY FRESH	63	1999
WHAT IT'S LIKE EVERLAST	34	1999
WHAT I'VE DONE LINKIN PARK	6	2007
WHAT I'VE GOT IN MIND BILLIE JO SPEARS	4	1976
WHAT KIND OF FOOL ALL ABOUT EVE	29	1988
WHAT KIND OF FOOL AM I? ANTHONY NEWLEY	36	1961
WHAT KIND OF FOOL AM I? SAMMY DAVIS Jr.	26	1962
WHAT KIND OF FOOL AM I? SHIRLEY BASSEY	47	1963
WHAT KIND OF FOOL (HEARD IT ALL BEFORE) KYLIE MINOGUE	14	1992
WHAT KIND OF MAN WOULD I BE MINT CONDITION	38	1997
WHAT KINDA BOY YOU LOOKING FOR (GIRL) HOT CHOCOLATE	10	1983
WHAT MADE MILWAUKEE FAMOUS (HAS MADE A LOSER OUT OF ME) ROD STEWART	4	1972
WHAT MAKES A GIRL FIERCE FIERCE GIRL	52	2005
WHAT MAKES A MAN WESTLIFE	2	2000
WHAT MAKES A MAN A MAN (LIVE) MARC ALMOND	60	1993
WHAT MAKES YOU CRY PROCLAIMERS	38	1994
WHAT MORE DO YOU WANT FRANKIE VAUGHAN	25	1960
WHAT MY HEART WANTS TO SAY GARETH GATES	5	2002
WHAT NOW ADAM FAITH WITH JOHNNY KEATING & HIS ORCHESTRA	31	1963
WHAT NOW MY LOVE SHIRLEY BASSEY	5	1962
WHAT NOW MY LOVE SONNY & CHER	13	1966
WHAT PLANET YOU ON BODYROX FEATURING LUCIANA	54	2008
WHAT PRESENCE? ORANGE JUICE	47	1984
WHAT THE HELL TOKYO DRAGONS	59	2005
WHAT THE WORLD IS WAITING FOR STONE ROSES	8	1989
WHAT THEY DO ROOTS	49	1997
WHAT TIME IS IT [A] SPIN DOCTORS	56	1993
WHAT TIME IS IT? [A] DUST JUNKYS	39	1998
WHAT TIME IS IT [B] CAST OF HIGH SCHOOL MUSICAL 2	20	2007
WHAT TIME IS LOVE (LIVE AT TRANCENTRAL) KLF FEATURING THE CHILDREN OF THE REVOLUTION	5	1990
WHAT TO DO BUDDY HOLLY	27	1961

	Peak Position	Year of Entry
WHAT TOOK YOU SO LONG [A] EMMA BUNTON	1	2001
WHAT TOOK YOU SO LONG [B] COURTEENERS	20	2008
WHAT U DO COLOURS FEATURING EMMANUEL & ESKA	51	1999
WHAT U GON' DO LIL JON & THE EAST SIDE BOYZ	38	2005
WHAT 'U' WAITIN' '4' JUNGLE BROTHERS	35	1990
WHAT WAS HER NAME DAVE CLARKE FEATURING CHICKS ON SPEED	50	2004
WHAT WE DO KRAY TWINZ FEATURING TWISTA & LETHAL B	23	2005
WHAT? WHAT YOU GOT? LITTLE MAN TATE	40	2006
WHAT WILL BE WILL BE (DESTINY) DIVINE INSPIRATION	55	2003
WHAT WILL I DO WITHOUT YOU LENE LOVICH	58	1980
WHAT WILL MARY SAY JOHNNY MATHIS	49	1963
WHAT WILL YOU DO (WHEN THE MONEY GOES) MILBURN	44	2007
WHAT WOULD HAPPEN MEREDITH BROOKS	49	1998
WHAT WOULD I BE VAL DOONICAN	2	1966
WHAT WOULD STEVE DO MUMM RA	40	2007
WHAT WOULD WE DO DSK	46	1991
WHAT WOULD YOU DO CITY HIGH	3	2001
WHAT WOULD YOU DO IF...? CODE RED	55	1998
WHAT YA GOT 4 ME SIGNUM	70	1998
WHAT YA LOOKIN' AT CROW	60	2001
WHAT YOU COULD'VE WON MILBURN	66	2006
WHAT YOU DO BIG BASS VS MICHELLE NARINE	67	2000
WHAT YOU DO (PLAYING WITH STONES) BIG BASS VS MICHELLE NARINE	27	2007
WHAT YOU DO TO ME (EP) TEENAGE FANCLUB	31	1992
WHAT YOU GET HUNDRED REASONS	30	2004
WHAT YOU GET IS WHAT YOU SEE TINA TURNER	30	1987
WHAT YOU GONNA DO ABOUT IT TOTAL CONTRAST	63	1986
WHAT YOU GOT ABS	4	2002
WHAT YOU NEED [A] INXS	51	1986
WHAT YOU NEED [B] POWERHOUSE FEATURING DUANE HARDEN	13	1999
WHAT YOU NEED IS SINEAD QUINN	19	2003
WHAT YOU NEED (TONIGHT) NU CIRCLES FEATURING EMMA B	46	2003
WHAT YOU SAY LIGHTNING SEEDS	41	1997
WHAT YOU SEE IS WHAT YOU GET GLEN GOLDSMITH	33	1988
WHAT YOU THINK OF THAT MEMPHIS BLEEK FEATURING JAY-Z	58	1999
WHAT YOU WAITING FOR [A] STARGARD	39	1978
WHAT YOU WAITING FOR [B] GWEN STEFANI	4	2004
WHAT YOU WANT [A] XPANSIONS FEATURING DALE JOYNER	55	1991
WHAT YOU WANT [B] FUTURE FORCE	47	1996
WHAT YOU WANT [C] MASE FEATURING TOTAL	15	1998
WHAT YOU WON'T DO FOR LOVE GO WEST	15	1993
WHAT YOU'RE MADE OF LUCIE SILVAS	7	2004
WHAT YOU'RE MISSING K-KLASS	24	1994
WHAT YOU'RE PROPOSING STATUS QUO	2	1980
WHATCHA GONE DO? LINK	48	1998
WHAT'CHA GONNA DO [A] SHABBA RANKS FEATURING QUEEN LATIFAH	21	1993
WHAT'CHA GONNA DO [B] ETERNAL	16	1999
WHATCHA GONNA DO ABOUT IT DORIS TROY	37	1964
WHATCHA GONNA DO ABOUT IT SMALL FACES	14	1965
WHATCHA GONNA DO NOW CHRIS ANDREWS	40	1966
WHATCHULOOKINAT WHITNEY HOUSTON	13	2002
WHAT'D I SAY JERRY LEE LEWIS	10	1961
WHAT'D YOU COME HERE FOR? TRINA & TAMARA	46	1999
WHATEVER [A] OASIS	3	1994
WHATEVER [B] EN VOGUE	14	1997
WHATEVER [C] IDEAL US FEATURING LIL' MO	31	2000
WHATEVER GETS YOU THROUGH THE NIGHT JOHN LENNON WITH THE PLASTIC ONO NUCLEAR BAND	36	1974
WHATEVER HAPPENED TO COREY HAIM? THRILLS	22	2004
WHATEVER HAPPENED TO MY ROCK AND ROLL BLACK REBEL MOTORCYCLE CLUB	46	2002
WHATEVER HAPPENED TO YOU (*LIKELY LADS* THEME) HIGHLY LIKELY	35	1973
WHATEVER I DO (WHEREVER I GO) HAZELL DEAN	4	1984
WHATEVER IT TAKES [A] OLYMPIC RUNNERS	61	1978
WHATEVER IT TAKES [B] LEONA LEWIS	61	2007
WHATEVER LOLA WANTS ALMA COGAN	26	1957
WHATEVER MAKES YOU HAPPY TEN CITY	60	1990
WHATEVER U WANT CHRISTINA MILIAN FEATURING JOE BUDDEN	9	2004
WHATEVER WILL BE WILL BE DORIS DAY	1	1956
WHATEVER YOU NEED TINA TURNER	27	2000
WHATEVER YOU WANT [A] STATUS QUO	4	1979
WHATEVER YOU WANT [B] TINA TURNER	23	1996
WHAT'LL I DO JANET JACKSON	9	1995
WHAT'S A GIRL TO DO SISTER 2 SISTER	61	2000
WHAT'S ANOTHER YEAR JOHNNY LOGAN	1	1980
WHAT'S GOIN' DOWN HONKY	49	1996
WHAT'S GOING ON [A] MEKON FEATURING ROXANNE SHANTE	43	2000
WHAT'S GOING ON [B] CYNDI LAUPER	57	1987
WHAT'S GOING ON [B] MUSIC RELIEF '94	70	1994
WHAT'S GOING ON [B] ARTISTS AGAINST AIDS WORLDWIDE	6	2001
WHAT'S GOING ON [C] WOOKIE	45	2000
WHAT'S HAPPENIN' METHOD MAN FEATURING BUSTA RHYMES	17	2004
WHAT'S HIDEOUS DO ME BAD THINGS	33	2005
WHAT'S IN A KISS? GILBERT O'SULLIVAN	19	1980
WHAT'S IN A WORD CHRISTIANS	33	1992
WHAT'S IN THE BOX? (SEE WHATCHA GOT) BOO RADLEYS	25	1996
WHAT'S IT ALL ABOUT RUN D.M.C.	48	1990
WHAT'S IT GONNA BE?! [A] BUSTA RHYMES FEATURING JANET	6	1999
WHAT'S IT GONNA BE [B] H TWO O FEATURING PLATINUM	2	2008
WHAT'S IT LIKE TO BE BEAUTIFUL LENA FIAGBE	52	1994
WHAT'S LEFT OF ME NICK LACHEY	47	2007
WHAT'S LOVE GOT TO DO WITH IT TINA TURNER	3	1984
WHAT'S LOVE GOT TO DO WITH IT WARREN G FEATURING ADINA HOWARD	2	1996
WHAT'S LUV FAT JOE FEATURING ASHANTI	4	2002
WHAT'S MY AGE AGAIN? BLINK 182	17	1999
WHAT'S MY NAME? SNOOP DOGGY DOGG	20	1993
WHAT'S NEW PUSSYCAT TOM JONES	11	1965
WHAT'S ON YOUR MIND GEORGE BENSON	45	1981
WHAT'S SO DIFFERENT? GINUWINE	10	1999
WHAT'S THAT TUNE (DOO-DOO-DOO-DOO-DOO-DOO-DOO-DOO-DOO-DOO) DOROTHY	31	1995
WHAT'S THE COLOUR OF MONEY? HOLLYWOOD BEYOND	7	1986
WHAT'S THE FREQUENCY, KENNETH R.E.M.	9	1994
WHAT'S THE POINT WE'VE GOT A FUZZBOX & WE'RE GONNA USE IT	51	1987
WHAT'S UP 4 NON BLONDES	2	1993
WHAT'S UP DJ MIKO	6	1994
WHAT'S UP WITH THAT ZZ TOP	58	1996
(WHAT'S WRONG WITH) DREAMING RIVER CITY PEOPLE	40	1989
WHAT'S WRONG WITH THIS PICTURE CHESNEY HAWKES	63	1993
WHAT'S YOUR DAMAGE? TEST ICICLES	31	2006
WHAT'S YOUR FANTASY LUDACRIS	19	2001
WHAT'S YOUR FLAVA CRAIG DAVID	8	2002
WHAT'S YOUR NAME [A] CHICORY TIP	13	1972
WHAT'S YOUR NAME WHAT'S YOUR NUMBER ANDREA TRUE CONNECTION	34	1978
WHAT'S YOUR NAME? [B] ANGEL LEE	39	2000
WHAT'S YOUR NUMBER? CYPRESS HILL	44	2004
WHAT'S YOUR PROBLEM? BLANCMANGE	40	1985
WHAT'S YOUR SIGN DES'REE	19	1998
WHAT'S YOUR SIGN GIRL BARRY BIGGS	55	1979
WHATTA MAN SALT-N-PEPA WITH EN VOGUE	7	1994
WHAZZUP TRUE PARTY	13	2000
THE WHEEL SPEAR OF DESTINY	59	1983
WHEEL OF FORTUNE ACE OF BASE	20	1993
WHEELS STRING-A-LONGS	8	1961
WHEELS AIN'T COMING DOWN SLADE	60	1981
WHEELS CHA CHA JOE LOSS ORCHESTRA	21	1961
WHEELS OF STEEL SAXON	20	1980
THE WHEELS ON THE BUS MAD DONNA	17	2002
WHEN [A] KALIN TWINS	1	1958
WHEN [A] SHOWADDYWADDY	3	1977
WHEN [B] SUNSCREEM	47	1995
WHEN [C] SHANIA TWAIN	18	1998
WHEN A CHILD IS BORN (SOLEADO) JOHNNY MATHIS	1	1976
WHEN A CHILD IS BORN JOHNNY MATHIS & GLADYS KNIGHT	74	1981
WHEN A HEART BEATS NIK KERSHAW	27	1985
WHEN A MAN LOVES A WOMAN [A] PERCY SLEDGE	2	1966
WHEN A MAN LOVES A WOMAN [A] MICHAEL BOLTON	8	1991
WHEN A MAN LOVES A WOMAN [B] JODY WATLEY	33	1994
WHEN A WOMAN GABRIELLE	6	2000
WHEN A WOMAN'S FED UP R KELLY	24	2000
WHEN AM I GONNA MAKE A LIVING SADE	36	1984
WHEN BOUZOUKIS PLAYED VICKY LEANDROS	44	1973
WHEN BOYS TALK INDEEP	67	1983
WHEN CAN I SEE YOU BABYFACE	35	1994
WHEN CHILDREN RULE THE WORLD RED HILL CHILDREN	40	1996
WHEN DID YOUR HEART GO MISSING? ROONEY	45	2007
WHEN DO I GET TO SING 'MY WAY' SPARKS	32	1994
WHEN DOVES CRY PRINCE	4	1984
WHEN DOVES CRY GINUWINE	10	1997
WHEN DREAMS TURN TO DUST CATHY DENNIS	43	1997
WHEN FOREVER HAS GONE DEMIS ROUSSOS	2	1976
WHEN HE SHINES SHEENA EASTON	12	1981
WHEN HEROES GO DOWN SUZANNE VEGA	58	1993
WHEN I ARGUE I SEE SHAPES IDLEWILD	19	1999
WHEN I CALL YOUR NAME MARY KIANI	18	1995
WHEN I COME AROUND GREEN DAY	27	1995
WHEN I COME HOME SPENCER DAVIS GROUP	12	1966
WHEN I DREAM [A] TEARDROP EXPLODES	47	1980
WHEN I DREAM [B] CAROL KIDD FEATURING TERRY WAITE	58	1992
WHEN I FALL IN LOVE [A] NAT 'KING' COLE	2	1957
WHEN I FALL IN LOVE [A] DONNY OSMOND	4	1973
WHEN I FALL IN LOVE [A] RICK ASTLEY	2	1987

	Peak Position	Year of Entry
WHEN I FALL IN LOVE [B] ANT & DEC	12	1996
WHEN I GET HOME SEARCHERS	35	1965
WHEN I GROW UP [A] MICHELLE SHOCKED	67	1989
WHEN I GROW UP [B] GARBAGE	9	1999
WHEN I GROW UP TO BE A MAN BEACH BOYS	27	1964
WHEN I KISS YOU (I HEAR CHARLIE PARKER PLAYING) SPARKS	36	1995
WHEN I LEAVE THE WORLD BEHIND ROSE MARIE	63	1983
WHEN I LOOK INTO YOUR EYES [A] FIREHOUSE	65	1992
WHEN I LOOK INTO YOUR EYES [B] MAXEE	55	2001
WHEN I LOST YOU SARAH WHATMORE	6	2002
WHEN I NEED YOU LEO SAYER	1	1977
WHEN I NEED YOU WILL MELLOR	5	1998
WHEN I NEED YOU CLIFF RICHARD	38	2007
WHEN I SAID GOODBYE STEPS	5	2000
WHEN I SEE YOU MACY GRAY	26	2003
WHEN I SEE YOU SMILE BAD ENGLISH	61	1989
WHEN I THINK OF YOU [A] JANET JACKSON	10	1986
WHEN I THINK OF YOU [B] KENNY THOMAS	27	1995
WHEN I THINK OF YOU [C] CHRIS DE BURGH	59	1999
WHEN I THINK OF YOU [D] LEE RYAN	15	2006
WHEN I WAS YOUNG [A] ERIC BURDON & THE ANIMALS	45	1967
WHEN I WAS YOUNG [B] RIVER CITY PEOPLE	62	1991
WHEN I'M ALONE RIFLES	64	2005
WHEN I'M AWAY FROM YOU FRANKIE MILLER	42	1979
WHEN I'M BACK ON MY FEET AGAIN MICHAEL BOLTON	44	1990
WHEN I'M CLEANING WINDOWS (TURNED OUT NICE AGAIN) 2 IN A TENT	25	1994
WHEN I'M DEAD AND GONE McGUINNESS FLINT	2	1970
WHEN I'M GONE [A] EMINEM	5	2006
WHEN I'M GONE [B] SIMPLE PLAN	26	2008
WHEN I'M GOOD AND READY SYBIL	5	1993
WHEN I'M SIXTY FOUR KENNY BALL & HIS JAZZMEN	43	1967
WHEN IT'S LOVE VAN HALEN	28	1988
WHEN IT'S OVER SUGAR RAY	32	2001
WHEN IT'S TIME TO ROCK UFO	70	1983
WHEN JOHNNY COMES MARCHING HOME ADAM FAITH	5	1960
WHEN JULIE COMES AROUND CUFF LINKS	10	1970
WHEN LOVE & HATE COLLIDE DEF LEPPARD	2	1995
WHEN LOVE BREAKS DOWN PREFAB SPROUT	25	1985
WHEN LOVE COMES ALONG MATT MONRO	46	1962
WHEN LOVE COMES CALLING PAUL JOHNSON	52	1987
WHEN LOVE COMES ROUND AGAIN (L'ARCA DI NOE) KEN DODD	19	1971
WHEN LOVE COMES TO TOWN U2 FEATURING BB KING	6	1989
WHEN LOVE TAKES OVER YOU DONNA SUMMER	72	1989
WHEN MEXICO GAVE UP THE RHUMBA MITCHELL TOROK	6	1956
WHEN MY BABY SCOOCH	29	1999
WHEN MY LITTLE GIRL IS SMILING CRAIG DOUGLAS	9	1962
WHEN MY LITTLE GIRL IS SMILING DRIFTERS	31	1962
WHEN MY LITTLE GIRL IS SMILING JIMMY JUSTICE	9	1962
WHEN ONLY LOVE WILL DO RICHARD DARBYSHIRE	54	1994
WHEN ROCK 'N ROLL CAME TO TRINIDAD NAT 'KING' COLE	28	1957
WHEN SHE WAS MY GIRL FOUR TOPS	3	1981
WHEN SMOKEY SINGS ABC	11	1987
WHEN THE BOYS TALK ABOUT THE GIRLS VALERIE CARR	29	1958
WHEN THE DAWN BREAKS NARCOTIC THRUST	28	2005
WHEN THE FINGERS POINT CHRISTIANS	34	1987
WHEN THE GIRL IN YOUR ARMS IS THE GIRL IN YOUR HEART CLIFF RICHARD	3	1961
WHEN THE GOING GETS TOUGH BOYZONE	1	1999
WHEN THE GOING GETS TOUGH, THE TOUGH GET GOING BILLY OCEAN	1	1986
WHEN THE HEARTACHE IS OVER TINA TURNER	10	1999
WHEN THE HOODOO COMES DIESEL PARK WEST	62	1989
WHEN THE LAST TIME CLIPSE	41	2003
WHEN THE LIGHTS GO DOWN ARMAND VAN HELDEN	70	2005
WHEN THE LIGHTS GO OUT FIVE	4	1998
WHEN THE MORNING COMES LOVE DECADE	69	1993
WHEN THE MORNING SUN DRIES THE DEW QUIET FIVE	45	1965
WHEN THE NIGHT COMES JOE COCKER	61	1990
WHEN THE NIGHT FEELS MY SONG BEDOUIN SOUNDCLASH	24	2005
WHEN THE RAIN BEGINS TO FALL JERMAINE JACKSON & PIA ZADORA	68	1984
WHEN THE SH.. GOES DOWN CYPRESS HILL	19	1993
WHEN THE SUMMERTIME IS OVER JACKIE TRENT	39	1965
WHEN THE SUN COMES SHINING THRU' LONG JOHN BALDRY	29	1968
WHEN THE SUN GOES DOWN [A] DJ FRESH FEATURING ADAM F	68	2004
WHEN THE SUN GOES DOWN [B] ARCTIC MONKEYS	1	2006
WHEN THE TIGERS BROKE FREE PINK FLOYD	39	1982
WHEN THE WIND BLOWS DAVID BOWIE	44	1986
WHEN THE WORLD IS RUNNING DOWN DIFFERENT GEAR VERSUS THE POLICE	28	2000
WHEN THE YEAR ENDS IN 1 TOTTENHAM HOTSPUR F.A. CUP FINAL SQUAD	44	1991
WHEN THIS RIVER ROLLS OVER YOU STANDS	32	2003
WHEN TOMORROW COMES EURYTHMICS	30	1986
WHEN TWO WORLDS COLLIDE JIM REEVES	17	1969
WHEN TWO WORLDS DRIFT APART CLIFF RICHARD	46	1977
WHEN WE ARE FAR FROM HOME ENGLAND WORLD CUP SQUAD	66	1986
WHEN WE ARE GONE FALLOUT TRUST	73	2005
WHEN WE ARE TOGETHER TEXAS	12	1999
WHEN WE DANCE STING	9	1994
WHEN WE WAS FAB GEORGE HARRISON	25	1988
WHEN WE WERE YOUNG [A] SOLOMON KING	21	1968
WHEN WE WERE YOUNG [B] BUCKS FIZZ	10	1983
WHEN WE WERE YOUNG [C] WHIPPING BOY	46	1996
WHEN WE WERE YOUNG [D] HUMAN NATURE	43	2001
WHEN WILL I BE FAMOUS BROS	2	1988
WHEN WILL I BE LOVED EVERLY BROTHERS	4	1960
WHEN WILL I SEE YOU AGAIN THREE DEGREES	1	1974
WHEN WILL I SEE YOU AGAIN BROTHER BEYOND	43	1989
WHEN WILL I SEE YOU AGAIN SHEILA FERGUSON	60	1994
WHEN WILL I SEE YOUR FACE AGAIN JAMIE SCOTT & THE TOWN	41	2007
WHEN WILL THE GOOD APPLES FALL SEEKERS	11	1967
WHEN WILL YOU BE MINE AVERAGE WHITE BAND	49	1979
WHEN WILL YOU MAKE MY TELEPHONE RING DEACON BLUE	34	1988
WHEN WILL YOU SAY I LOVE YOU BILLY FURY	3	1963
WHEN YOU ARE A KING WHITE PLAINS	13	1971
WHEN YOU ASK ABOUT LOVE CRICKETS	27	1960
WHEN YOU ASK ABOUT LOVE MATCHBOX	4	1980
WHEN YOU BELIEVE MARIAH CAREY & WHITNEY HOUSTON	4	1998
WHEN YOU BELIEVE LEON JACKSON	1	2007
WHEN YOU COME BACK TO ME JASON DONOVAN	2	1989
WHEN YOU GET RIGHT DOWN TO IT RONNIE DYSON	34	1971
(WHEN YOU GONNA) GIVE IT UP TO ME SEAN PAUL FEATURING KEYSHIA COLE	31	2006
WHEN YOU GONNA LEARN JAMIROQUAI	28	1992
WHEN YOU KISS ME SHANIA TWAIN	21	2003
WHEN YOU LOOK AT ME CHRISTINA MILIAN	3	2002
WHEN YOU LOSE THE ONE YOU LOVE DAVID WHITFIELD WITH CHORUS & MANTOVANI & HIS ORCHESTRA	7	1955
WHEN YOU MADE THE MOUNTAIN OPUS III	71	1994
WHEN YOU SAY NOTHING AT ALL RONAN KEATING	1	1999
(WHEN YOU SAY YOU LOVE SOMEBODY) IN THE HEART KOOL & THE GANG	7	1984
WHEN YOU SLEEP LONGVIEW	74	2002
WHEN YOU TELL ME THAT YOU LOVE ME DIANA ROSS	2	1991
WHEN YOU TELL ME THAT YOU LOVE ME WESTLIFE FEATURING DIANA ROSS	2	2005
WHEN YOU WALK IN THE ROOM SEARCHERS	3	1964
WHEN YOU WALK IN THE ROOM CHILD	38	1978
WHEN YOU WALK IN THE ROOM PAUL CARRACK	48	1987
WHEN YOU WALK IN THE ROOM STATUS QUO	34	1995
WHEN YOU WALK IN THE ROOM AGNETHA FALTSKOG	34	2004
WHEN YOU WASN'T FAMOUS STREETS	8	2006
WHEN YOU WERE SWEET SIXTEEN FUREYS WITH DAVEY ARTHUR	14	1981
WHEN YOU WERE YOUNG [A] DEL AMITRI	20	1993
WHEN YOU WERE YOUNG [B] KILLERS	2	2006
WHEN YOUR 'EX' WANTS YOU BACK SURFACE	52	1984
WHEN YOUR HEART STOPS BEATING PLUS 44	47	2007
WHEN YOUR OLD WEDDING RING WAS NEW JIMMY ROSELLI	51	1983
WHEN YOU'RE GONE [A] BRYAN ADAMS FEATURING MELANIE C	3	1998
WHEN YOU'RE GONE [B] SORAYA VIVIAN	59	2002
WHEN YOU'RE GONE [C] AVRIL LAVIGNE	3	2007
WHEN YOU'RE IN LOVE WITH A BEAUTIFUL WOMAN DR HOOK	1	1979
WHEN YOU'RE NUMBER 1 GENE CHANDLER	43	1979
WHEN YOU'RE YOUNG JAM	17	1979
WHEN YOU'RE YOUNG AND IN LOVE MARVELETTES	13	1967
WHEN YOU'RE YOUNG AND IN LOVE FLYING PICKETS	7	1984
WHENEVER GOD SHINES HIS LIGHT VAN MORRISON WITH CLIFF RICHARD	20	1989
WHENEVER I SAY YOUR NAME STING & MARY J BLIGE	60	2003
WHENEVER I STOP MIKE + THE MECHANICS	73	1999
WHENEVER WHEREVER SHAKIRA	2	2002
WHENEVER YOU NEED ME T'PAU	16	1991
WHENEVER YOU NEED SOMEBODY RICK ASTLEY	3	1987
WHENEVER YOU NEED SOMEONE BAD BOYS INC	26	1993
WHENEVER YOU WANT MY LOVE REAL THING	18	1978
WHENEVER YOU'RE NEAR CHER	72	1993
WHENEVER YOU'RE READY FIVE STAR	11	1987

	Peak Position	Year of Entry
WHERE ARE THEY NOW? GENE	22	1997
WHERE ARE YOU [A] KAVANA	26	1996
WHERE ARE YOU [B] IMAANI	15	1998
WHERE ARE YOU BABY BETTY BOO	3	1990
WHERE ARE YOU GOING TO MY LOVE BROTHERHOOD OF MAN	22	1970
WHERE ARE YOU NOW (MY LOVE) JACKIE TRENT	1	1965
WHERE ARE YOU NOW? GENERATOR	60	1999
WHERE CAN I FIND LOVE LIVIN' JOY	12	1997
WHERE DID ALL THE GOOD TIMES GO DONNY OSMOND	18	1974
WHERE DID I GO WRONG UB40	26	1988
WHERE DID OUR LOVE GO SUPREMES	3	1964
WHERE DID OUR LOVE GO DONNIE ELBERT	8	1972
WHERE DID OUR LOVE GO MANHATTAN TRANSFER	40	1978
WHERE DID OUR LOVE GO TRICIA PENROSE	71	1996
WHERE DID WE GO WRONG LIQUID GOLD	56	1982
WHERE DID YOUR HEART GO WHAM!	1	1986
WHERE DO BROKEN HEARTS GO WHITNEY HOUSTON	14	1988
(WHERE DO I BEGIN) LOVE STORY ANDY WILLIAMS	4	1971
(WHERE DO I BEGIN) LOVE STORY SHIRLEY BASSEY	34	1971
WHERE DO I STAND? MONTROSE AVENUE	38	1998
WHERE DO U WANT ME TO PUT IT SOLO (US)	45	1996
WHERE DO WE GO TEN CITY	60	1989
WHERE DO WE GO FROM HERE CLIFF RICHARD	60	1982
WHERE DO YOU GO NO MERCY	2	1997
WHERE DO YOU GO TO MY LOVELY PETER SARSTEDT	1	1969
WHERE DOES MY HEART BEAT NOW CELINE DION	72	1993
WHERE DOES TIME GO JULIA FORDHAM	41	1989
WHERE EAGLES FLY CRYSTAL PALACE	50	1990
WHERE HAS ALL THE LOVE GONE YAZZ	16	1989
WHERE HAS ALL THE LOVE GONE MAUREEN	51	1991
WHERE HAS LOVE GONE HOLLY JOHNSON	73	1990
WHERE HAVE ALL THE COWBOYS GONE? PAULA COLE	15	1997
WHERE HAVE YOU BEEN TONIGHT? SHED SEVEN	23	1995
WHERE I FIND MY HEAVEN GIGOLO AUNTS	29	1995
WHERE I WANNA BE SHADE SHEIST FEATURING NATE DOGG & KURUPT	14	2001
WHERE I'M HEADED LENE MARLIN	31	2001
WHERE IN THE WORLD [A] SWING OUT SISTER	47	1989
WHERE IN THE WORLD [B] BBM	57	1994
WHERE IS MY MAN EARTHA KITT	36	1984
WHERE IS THE FEELING? KYLIE MINOGUE	16	1995
WHERE IS THE LOVE [A] ROBERTA FLACK & DONNY HATHAWAY	29	1972
WHERE IS THE LOVE [A] MICA PARIS & WILL DOWNING	19	1989
WHERE IS THE LOVE [B] BETTY WRIGHT	25	1975
WHERE IS THE LOVE [C] ADEVA	54	1997
WHERE IS THE LOVE [D] BLACK EYED PEAS	1	2003
WHERE IS THE LOVE (WE USED TO KNOW) DELEGATION	22	1977
WHERE IS TOMORROW CILLA BLACK	39	1968
WHERE IT'S AT BECK	35	1996
WHERE LOVE LIVES ALISON LIMERICK	9	1991
WHERE MY GIRLS AT? 702	22	1999
WHERE THE ACTION IS WESTWORLD	54	1987
WHERE THE BOYS ARE CONNIE FRANCIS	5	1961
WHERE THE HEART IS SOFT CELL	21	1982
WHERE THE HOOD AT? DMX	16	2003
WHERE THE POOR BOYS DANCE LULU	24	2000
WHERE THE ROSE IS SOWN BIG COUNTRY	29	1984
WHERE THE STORY ENDS BLAZIN' SQUAD	8	2003
WHERE THE STREETS HAVE NO NAME U2	4	1987
WHERE THE STREETS HAVE NO NAME - CAN'T TAKE MY EYES OFF YOU PET SHOP BOYS	4	1991
WHERE THE WILD ROSES GROW NICK CAVE + KYLIE MINOGUE	11	1995
WHERE THE WINDS BLOW FRANKIE LAINE	2	1953
WHERE WERE YOU ADULT NET	66	1989
WHERE WERE YOU HIDING WHEN THE STORM BROKE ALARM	22	1984
WHERE WERE YOU (ON OUR WEDDING DAY)? LLOYD PRICE	15	1959
WHERE WILL THE BABY'S DIMPLE BE ROSEMARY CLOONEY WITH THE MELLOMEN	6	1955
WHERE WILL YOU BE SUE NICHOLLS	17	1968
WHERE YOU ARE RAHSAAN PATTERSON	55	1998
WHERE YOU GONNA BE TONIGHT? WILLIE COLLINS	46	1986
WHERE'S JACK THE RIPPER GROOVERIDER	61	1999
WHERE'S ME JUMPER SULTANS OF PING FC	67	1992
WHERE'S MY ADAM F FEATURING LIL' MO	37	2002
WHERE'S ROMEO CA VA CA VA	49	1982
WHERE'S THE LOVE HANSON	4	1997
WHERE'S THE PARTY AT JAGGED EDGE FEATURING NELLY	25	2001
WHERE'S THE PLEASURE PROTOCOL	27	2006
WHERE'S YOUR HEAD AT BASEMENT JAXX	9	2001
WHERE'S YOUR LOVE BEEN HELIOCENTRIC WORLD	71	1995
WHEREVER I LAY MY HAT (THAT'S MY HOME) PAUL YOUNG	1	1983
WHEREVER I MAY ROAM METALLICA	25	1992
WHEREVER WOULD I BE DUSTY SPRINGFIELD & DARYL HALL	44	1995
WHEREVER YOU ARE NEIL FINN	32	2001
WHEREVER YOU WILL GO CALLING	3	2002
WHICH WAY SHOULD I JUMP MILLTOWN BROTHERS	38	1991
WHICH WAY YOU GOIN' BILLY POPPY FAMILY	7	1970
WHIGGLE IN LINE BLACK DUCK	33	1994
WHILE I LIVE KENNY DAMON	48	1966
WHILE YOU SEE A CHANCE STEVE WINWOOD	45	1981
WHINE AND GRINE PRINCE BUSTER	21	1998
WHIP IT DEVO	51	1980
WHIPLASH JFK	47	2002
WHIPPIN' PICCADILLY GOMEZ	35	1998
WHISKEY IN THE JAR THIN LIZZY	6	1973
WHISKEY IN THE JAR POGUES & THE DUBLINERS	63	1990
WHISKEY IN THE JAR METALLICA	29	1999
THE WHISPER SELECTER	36	1980
WHISPER A PRAYER MICA PARIS	65	1993
WHISPER YOUR NAME HUMAN NATURE	53	1997
WHISPERING BACHELORS	18	1963
WHISPERING NINO TEMPO & APRIL STEVENS	20	1964
WHISPERING GRASS WINDSOR DAVIES & DON ESTELLE	1	1975
WHISPERING HOPE JIM REEVES	50	1961
WHISPERING YOUR NAME ALISON MOYET	18	1994
WHISPERS [A] ELTON JOHN	47	1990
WHISPERS [B] IAN BROWN	33	2002
WHISTLE DOWN THE WIND NICK HEYWARD	13	1983
WHISTLE DOWN THE WIND TINA ARENA	24	1998
WHISTLE FOR THE CHOIR FRATELLIS	9	2006
THE WHISTLE SONG FRANKIE KNUCKLES	17	1991
THE WHISTLE SONG (BLOW MY WHISTLE BITCH) DJ ALIGATOR PROJECT	5	2000
THE WHISTLER HONKY	41	1994
WHITE BIRD VANESSA-MAE	66	2001
WHITE BOY WITH A FEATHER JASON DOWNS FEATURING MILK	19	2001
WHITE BOYS AND HEROES GARY NUMAN	20	1982
WHITE CHRISTMAS MANTOVANI	6	1952
WHITE CHRISTMAS PAT BOONE	29	1957
WHITE CHRISTMAS FREDDIE STARR	41	1975
WHITE CHRISTMAS BING CROSBY	5	1977
WHITE CHRISTMAS DARTS	48	1980
WHITE CHRISTMAS JIM DAVIDSON	52	1980
WHITE CHRISTMAS KEITH HARRIS & ORVILLE	40	1986
WHITE CHRISTMAS MAX BYGRAVES	71	1989
WHITE CLIFFS OF DOVER MR ACKER BILK & HIS PARAMOUNT JAZZ BAND	30	1960
WHITE CLIFFS OF DOVER RIGHTEOUS BROTHERS	21	1966
WHITE COATS (EP) NEW MODEL ARMY	50	1987
THE WHITE COLLAR BOY BELLE & SEBASTIAN	45	2006
WHITE FLAG DIDO	2	2003
THE WHITE HARE SETH LAKEMAN	47	2006
WHITE HORSES JACKY	10	1968
WHITE LIE FOREIGNER	58	1994
WHITE LIGHT, WHITE HEAT DAVID BOWIE	46	1983
WHITE LIGHTNING FALL	56	1990
WHITE LINES (DON'T DO IT) DURAN DURAN FEATURING MELLE MEL & GRANDMASTER FLASH & THE FURIOUS FIVE	17	1995
WHITE LINES (DON'T DON'T DO IT) GRANDMASTER FLASH & MELLE MEL	7	1984
WHITE LOVE ONE DOVE	43	1993
(WHITE MAN) IN HAMMERSMITH PALAIS CLASH	32	1978
WHITE NO SUGAR CLINT BOON EXPERIENCE	61	1999
WHITE ONE IS EVIL ELLIOT MINOR	27	2007
WHITE PUNKS ON DOPE TUBES	28	1977
WHITE RIBBON DAY DELIRIOUS?	41	1997
WHITE RIOT CLASH	38	1977
WHITE ROOM CREAM	28	1969
WHITE RUSSIAN GALAXY CRIMEA	51	2006
WHITE SILVER SANDS BILL BLACK'S COMBO	50	1960
WHITE SKIES SUNSCREEM	25	1996
A WHITE SPORT COAT TERRY DENE	18	1957
A WHITE SPORT COAT (AND A PINK CARNATION) KING BROTHERS	6	1957
WHITE WEDDING BILLY IDOL	6	1985
WHITE WEDDING MURDERDOLLS	24	2003
A WHITER SHADE OF PALE PROCOL HARUM	1	1967
A WHITER SHADE OF PALE MUNICH MACHINE INTRODUCING CHRIS BENNETT	42	1978
A WHITER SHADE OF PALE ANNIE LENNOX	16	1995
WHO? ED CASE & SWEETIE IRIE	29	2001
WHO AM I [A] ADAM FAITH	5	1961
WHO AM I [B] BEENIE MAN	10	1998
WHO AM I [C] WILL YOUNG	11	2006
WHO ARE WE RONNIE HILTON	6	1956
WHO ARE WE VERA LYNN	30	1956
WHO ARE YOU WHO	18	1978
WHO CAN I RUN TO XSCAPE	31	1996
WHO CAN IT BE NOW? MEN AT WORK	45	1982
WHO CAN MAKE ME FEEL GOOD BASSHEADS	38	1992
WHO CARES GNARLS BARKLEY	60	2006
WHO COMES TO BOOGIE LITTLE BENNY & THE MASTERS	33	1985
WHO COULD BE BLUER JERRY LORDAN	16	1960
WHO DO U LOVE DEBORAH COX	31	1996
WHO DO YOU LOVE [A] JUICY LUCY	14	1970
WHO DO YOU LOVE? [B] INTRUDERS	65	1984
WHO DO YOU LOVE [C] JOSE PADILLA FEATURING ANGELA JOHN	59	1998
WHO DO YOU LOVE NOW (STRINGER) RIVA FEATURING DANNII MINOGUE	3	2001
WHO DO YOU THINK YOU ARE [A] CANDLEWICK GREEN	21	1974

		Peak Position	Year of Entry
WHO DO YOU THINK YOU ARE [B]	KIM WILDE	49	1992
WHO DO YOU THINK YOU ARE [C]	SAINT ETIENNE	23	1993
WHO DO YOU THINK YOU ARE [D]	SPICE GIRLS	1	1997
WHO DO YOU THINK YOU ARE KIDDING JURGEN KLINSMANN	TONEDEF ALLSTARS	13	2006
WHO DO YOU WANT FOR YOUR LOVE	ICICLE WORKS	54	1986
WHO FEELS LOVE?	OASIS	4	2000
WHO FOUND WHO	JELLYBEAN FEATURING ELISA FIORILLO	10	1987
WHO GETS THE LOVE	STATUS QUO	34	1988
WHO INVITED YOU	DONNAS	61	2003
WHO IS IT [A]	MANTRONIX	40	1987
WHO IS IT [B]	MICHAEL JACKSON	10	1992
WHO IS IT [C]	BJORK	26	2004
WHO IS SHE 2 U	BRANDY	50	2005
WHO KEEPS CHANGING YOUR MIND	SOUTH ST. PLAYER	49	2000
WHO KILLED BAMBI	TEN POLE TUDOR	24	1979
WHO KNEW	P!NK	5	2006
WHO LET IN THE RAIN	CYNDI LAUPER	32	1994
WHO LET THE DOGS OUT	BAHA MEN	2	2000
WHO LOVES YOU	FOUR SEASONS	6	1975
WHO MADE WHO	AC/DC	16	1986
WHO NEEDS ENEMIES	COOPER TEMPLE CLAUSE	22	2002
WHO NEEDS LOVE LIKE THAT	ERASURE	10	1985
WHO PAYS THE FERRYMAN	YANNIS MARKOPOULOS	11	1977
WHO PAYS THE PIPER	GARY CLAIL ON-U SOUND SYSTEM	31	1992
WHO PUT THE BOMP	VISCOUNTS	21	1961
WHO PUT THE BOMP (IN THE BOMP-A-BOMP-A-BOMP)	SHOWADDYWADDY	37	1982
WHO PUT THE LIGHTS OUT	DANA	14	1971
WHO SAID (STUCK IN THE UK)	PLANET FUNK	36	2003
WHO SAYS YOU CAN'T GO HOME	BON JOVI	5	2006
WHO THE HELL ARE YOU	MADISON AVENUE	10	2000
WHO TOLD YOU	RONI SIZE REPRAZENT	17	2000
WHO WANTS THE WORLD	STRANGLERS	39	1980
WHO WANTS TO BE THE DISCO KING	WONDER STUFF	28	1989
WHO WANTS TO LIVE FOREVER	QUEEN	24	1986
WHO WANTS TO LIVE FOREVER	SARAH BRIGHTMAN	45	1997
WHO WAS IT	HURRICANE SMITH	23	1972
WHO WE BE	DMX	34	2001
WHO WEARS THESE SHOES	ELTON JOHN	50	1984
WHO WERE YOU WITH IN THE MOONLIGHT	DOLLAR	14	1979
WHO WHAT WHEN WHERE WHY	MANHATTAN TRANSFER	49	1978
WHO WHERE WHY	JESUS JONES	21	1991
WHO WILL SAVE YOUR SOUL	JEWEL	52	1997
WHO WILL YOU RUN TO	HEART	30	1987
WHO YOU ARE	PEARL JAM	18	1996
WHO YOU LOOKING AT	SALFORD JETS	72	1980
WHO YOU WIT	JAY-Z	65	1997
WHOA [A]	BLACK ROB	44	2000
WHOA [B]	LIL' KIM	43	2006
WHO'D SHE COO	OHIO PLAYERS	43	1976
WHODUNNIT	TAVARES	5	1977
WHOLE AGAIN	ATOMIC KITTEN	1	2001
WHOLE LOTTA HISTORY	GIRLS ALOUD	6	2006
WHOLE LOTTA LOVE	C.C.S.	13	1970
WHOLE LOTTA LOVE	GOLDBUG	3	1996
WHOLE LOTTA LOVE	LED ZEPPELIN	21	1997
WHOLE LOTTA ROSIE	AC/DC	36	1980
WHOLE LOTTA SHAKIN' GOIN' ON	JERRY LEE LEWIS	8	1957
WHOLE LOTTA TROUBLE	STEVIE NICKS	62	1989
WHOLE LOTTA WOMAN	MARVIN RAINWATER	1	1958
WHOLE NEW WORLD [A]	IT BITES	54	1986
A WHOLE NEW WORLD (ALADDIN'S THEME) [B]	PEABO BRYSON & REGINA BELLE	12	1993
A WHOLE NEW WORLD [B]	KATIE PRICE & PETER ANDRE	12	2006
THE WHOLE OF THE MOON	WATERBOYS	3	1985
THE WHOLE OF THE MOON	LITTLE CAESAR	68	1990
THE WHOLE TOWN'S LAUGHING AT ME	TEDDY PENDERGRASS	44	1977
THE WHOLE WORLD	OUTKAST FEATURING KILLER MIKE	19	2002
THE WHOLE WORLD LOST ITS HEAD	GO-GOS	29	1995
WHOOMP! (THERE IT IS)	TAG TEAM	34	1994
WHOOMP THERE IT IS	BM DUBS PRESENT MR RUMBLE	32	2001
WHOOMPH! (THERE IT IS)	CLOCK	4	1995
WHOOPS NOW	JANET JACKSON	9	1995
WHOOPSIE DAISY	TERRI WALKER	41	2005
WHOOSH	WHOOSH	72	1997
WHO'S AFRAID OF THE BIG BAD LOVE	WILD WEEKEND	70	1990
WHO'S AFRAID OF THE BIG BAD NOISE?	AGE OF CHANCE	65	1987
WHO'S COMING ROUND	5050	54	2001
WHO'S CRYING NOW	JOURNEY	46	1982
WHO'S DAVID	BUSTED	1	2004
WHO'S GONNA FIND ME	CORAL	25	2007
WHO'S GONNA LOVE ME	IMPERIALS	17	1978
WHO'S GONNA RIDE YOUR WILD HORSES	U2	14	1992
WHO'S GONNA ROCK YOU	NOLANS	12	1980
WHO'S GOT A MATCH	BIFFY CLYRO	27	2008
WHO'S IN THE HOUSE	BEATMASTERS FEATURING MERLIN	8	1989
WHO'S IN THE STRAWBERRY PATCH WITH SALLY	TONY ORLAND & DAWN	37	1974
WHO'S JOHNNY (*SHORT CIRCUIT* THEME)	EL DeBARGE	60	1986
WHO'S LEAVING WHO	HAZELL DEAN	4	1988
WHO'S LOVING MY BABY	SHOLA AMA	13	1997
WHO'S SORRY NOW	JOHNNIE RAY	17	1956
WHO'S SORRY NOW	CONNIE FRANCIS	1	1958
WHO'S THAT GIRL? [A]	EURYTHMICS	3	1983
WHO'S THAT GIRL [B]	FLYING PICKETS	71	1984
WHO'S THAT GIRL [C]	MADONNA	1	1987
WHO'S THAT GIRL [D]	EVE	6	2001
WHO'S THAT GIRL (SHE'S GOT IT)	A FLOCK OF SEAGULLS	66	1985
WHO'S THAT MIX	THIS YEAR'S BLONDE	62	1987
WHO'S THE BAD MAN	DEE PATTEN	42	1999
WHO'S THE DADDY	LOVEBUG	35	2003
WHO'S THE DARKMAN	DARKMAN	46	1994
WHO'S THE MACK	MARK MORRISON	13	1997
WHO'S THE MAN	HOUSE OF PAIN	23	1993
WHO'S ZOOMIN' WHO	ARETHA FRANKLIN	11	1986
WHOSE FIST IS THIS ANYWAY EP	PRONG	58	1992
WHOSE LAW (IS IT ANYWAY)	GURU JOSH	26	1990
WHOSE PROBLEM?	MOTELS	42	1980
WHY [A]	ANTHONY NEWLEY	1	1960
WHY [A]	FRANKIE AVALON	20	1960
WHY [A]	DONNY OSMOND	3	1972
WHY [B]	ROGER WHITTAKER	47	1971
WHY [C]	CARLY SIMON	10	1982
WHY [C]	GLAMMA KID	10	1999
WHY? [D]	BRONSKI BEAT	6	1984
WHY [E]	ANNIE LENNOX	5	1992
WHY [E]	DJ SAMMY	7	2005
WHY [F]	D MOB WITH CATHY DENNIS	23	1994
WHY [G]	RICARDO DA FORCE	58	1996
WHY [H]	3T FEATURING MICHAEL JACKSON	2	1996
WHY [I]	MIS-TEEQ	8	2001
WHY [J]	AGENT SUMO	40	2002
WHY [K]	GABRIELLE	42	2007
WHY ARE PEOPLE GRUDGEFUL	FALL	43	1993
WHY ARE YOU BEING SO REASONABLE NOW	WEDDING PRESENT	42	1988
WHY ARE YOU LOOKING GRAVE?	MEW	53	2006
WHY BABY WHY	PAT BOONE	17	1957
WHY BELIEVE IN YOU	TEXAS	66	1991
WHY CAN'T I BE YOU [A]	CURE	21	1987
WHY CAN'T I BE YOU? [B]	SHED SEVEN	23	2003
WHY CAN'T I WAKE UP WITH YOU	TAKE THAT	2	1993
WHY CAN'T THIS BE LOVE	VAN HALEN	8	1986
WHY CAN'T WE BE LOVERS	HOLLAND-DOZIER FEATURING LAMONT DOZIER	29	1972
WHY CAN'T WE LIVE TOGETHER	TIMMY THOMAS	12	1973
WHY CAN'T YOU	CLARENCE 'FROGMAN' HENRY	42	1961
WHY CAN'T YOU FREE SOME TIME	ARMAND VAN HELDEN	34	2001
WHY DID YA	TONY DI BART	46	1995
WHY DID YOU DO IT	STRETCH	16	1975
WHY DIDN'T YOU CALL ME	MACY GRAY	38	2000
WHY DO FOOLS FALL IN LOVE	ALMA COGAN	22	1956
WHY DO FOOLS FALL IN LOVE	TEENAGERS FEATURING FRANKIE LYMON	1	1956
WHY DO FOOLS FALL IN LOVE	DIANA ROSS	4	1981
WHY DO I ALWAYS GET IT WRONG	LIVE REPORT	73	1989
WHY DO I DO	TYLER JAMES	25	2004
WHY DO LOVERS BREAK EACH OTHER'S HEARTS	SHOWADDYWADDY	22	1980
WHY DO YOU KEEP ON RUNNING BOY	STINX	49	2001
WHY DO YOU LOVE ME	GARBAGE	7	2005
WHY DOES A MAN HAVE TO BE STRONG	PAUL YOUNG	63	1987
WHY DOES IT ALWAYS RAIN ON ME	TRAVIS	10	1999
WHY DOES MY HEART FEEL SO BAD	MOBY	16	1999
WHY DON'T THEY UNDERSTAND	GEORGE HAMILTON IV	22	1958
WHY DON'T WE FALL IN LOVE	AMERIE FEATURING LUDACRIS	40	2002
WHY DON'T WE TRY AGAIN	BRIAN MAY	44	1998
WHY DON'T YOU	RAGE	44	1993
WHY DON'T YOU BELIEVE ME	JONI JAMES	11	1953
WHY DON'T YOU DANCE WITH ME	FUTURE BREEZE	50	1997
WHY DON'T YOU DO IT FOR ME	22-20'S	41	2004
WHY DON'T YOU GET A JOB	OFFSPRING	2	1999
WHY DON'T YOU TAKE ME	ONE DOVE	30	1994
WHY D'YA LIE TO ME	SPIDER	65	1983
WHY GO?	FAITHLESS FEATURING ESTELLE	49	2005
WHY (LOOKING BACK)	HEARTLESS CREW	50	2003
WHY ME [A]	LINDA MARTIN	59	1992
WHY ME [B]	A HOUSE	52	1994
WHY ME [C]	PJ & DUNCAN	27	1994
WHY ME [D]	ASHER D	43	2002
WHY (MUST WE FALL IN LOVE)	DIANA ROSS & THE SUPREMES & THE TEMPTATIONS	31	1970
WHY MUST WE WAIT UNTIL TONIGHT	TINA TURNER	16	1993
WHY NOT NOW	MATT MONRO	24	1961
WHY NOT TONIGHT	MOJOS	25	1964
WHY OH WHY	SPEARHEAD	45	1997
WHY OH WHY OH WHY	GILBERT O'SULLIVAN	6	1973
WHY SHE'S A GIRL FROM THE CHAINSTORE	BUZZCOCKS	61	1980
WHY SHOULD I	BOB MARLEY & THE WAILERS	42	1992
WHY SHOULD I BE LONELY	TONY BRENT	24	1959
WHY SHOULD I CRY	NONA HENDRYX	60	1987
WHY SHOULD I LOVE YOU	DES'REE	44	1992
WHY WHY BYE BYE	BOB LUMAN	46	1960

	Peak Position	Year of Entry
WHY WHY WHY DÉJÀ VU	57	1994
WHY WON'T YOU GIVE ME YOUR LOVE ZUTONS	9	2006
WHY YOU FOLLOW ME ERIC BENET	48	2000
WHY YOU TREAT ME SO BAD SHAGGY FEATURING GRAND PUBA	11	1996
WHY YOU WANNA TI	22	2006
WHY'D YOU LIE TO ME ANASTACIA	25	2002
WHY'S EVERYBODY ALWAYS PICKIN' ON ME? BLOODHOUND GANG	56	1997
WIBBLING RIVALRY (INTERVIEWS WITH NOEL AND LIAM GALLAGHER) OAS*S	52	1995
WICHITA LINEMAN GLEN CAMPBELL	7	1969
WICKED ICE CUBE	62	1993
WICKED GAME CHRIS ISAAK	10	1990
WICKED LOVE OCEANIC	25	1991
WICKED SOUL KUBB	25	2005
WICKED WAYS BLOW MONKEYS	60	1986
WICKEDEST SOUND REBEL MC FEATURING TENOR FLY	43	1991
THE WICKER MAN IRON MAIDEN	9	2000
WICKY WACKY HOUSE PARTY TEAM	55	1985
WIDE AWAKE TWANG	15	2007
WIDE AWAKE IN A DREAM BARRY BIGGS	44	1981
WIDE BOY NIK KERSHAW	9	1985
WIDE EYED AND LEGLESS ANDY FAIRWEATHER-LOW	6	1975
WIDE EYED ANGEL ORIGIN	73	2000
WIDE OPEN SKY GOLDRUSH	70	2002
WIDE OPEN SPACE MANSUN	15	1996
WIDE PRAIRIE LINDA McCARTNEY	74	1998
THE WIDOW MARS VOLTA	20	2005
WIFEY NEXT	19	2000
WIG WAM BAM BLACK LACE	63	1986
WIG WAM BAM DAMIAN	49	1989
WIGGLE IT 2 IN A ROOM	3	1991
WIGGLY WORLD MR JACK	32	1997
WIGWAM WIGWAM	60	2006
WIG-WAM BAM SWEET	4	1972
WIKKA WRAP EVASIONS	20	1981
WILD 2NITE SHAGGY	61	2005
THE WILD AMERICA (EP) IGGY POP	63	1993
WILD AND WONDERFUL ALMIGHTY	50	1990
WILD AS ANGELS EP LEVELLERS	34	2002
WILD BLUE YONDER PAUL WELLER	22	2006
WILD BOYS DURAN DURAN	2	1984
WILD BOYS PHIXX	12	2004
WILD CAT GENE VINCENT	21	1956
WILD CHILD [A] W.A.S.P.	71	1986
WILD CHILD [B] ENYA	72	2001
WILD DANCES RUSLANA	47	2004
WILD FLOWER CULT	24	1987
WILD FRONTIER GARY MOORE	35	1987
WILD HEARTED SON CULT	40	1991
WILD HEARTED WOMAN ALL ABOUT EVE	33	1988
WILD HONEY BEACH BOYS	29	1967
WILD IN THE COUNTRY ELVIS PRESLEY	4	1961
WILD IS THE WIND DAVID BOWIE	24	1981
WILD LOVE MUNGO JERRY	32	1973
WILD LUV ROACH MOTEL	75	1994
WILD 'N FREE REDNEX	55	1995
WILD NIGHT JOHN MELLENCAMP FEATURING ME'SHELL NDEGEOCELLO	34	1994
WILD ONE [A] BOBBY RYDELL	7	1960
THE WILD ONE [B] SUZI QUATRO	7	1974
THE WILD ONES SUEDE	18	1994
WILD SIDE MOTLEY CRUE	23	1988
WILD SIDE OF LIFE TOMMY QUICKLY & THE REMO FOUR	33	1964
WILD SIDE OF LIFE STATUS QUO	9	1976
THE WILD SON VEILS	74	2004
WILD SURF ASH	31	1998
WILD THING [A] TROGGS	2	1966
WILD THING [A] GOODIES	21	1975
WILD THING [B] TONE LOC	21	1989
WILD WEST HERO ELECTRIC LIGHT ORCHESTRA	6	1978
WILD WILD LIFE TALKING HEADS	43	1986
WILD WILD WEST [A] WILL SMITH FEATURING DRU HILL	2	1999
WILD WILD WEST [B] GET READY	65	1995
WILD WIND JOHN LEYTON	2	1961
WILD WOMEN DO NATALIE COLE	16	1990
WILD WOOD PAUL WELLER	14	1993
WILD WORLD JIMMY CLIFF	8	1970
WILD WORLD MAXI PRIEST	5	1988
WILD WORLD MR BIG	59	1993
WILD WORLD CAT STEVENS	52	2007
WILDERNESS JURGEN VRIES FEATURING SHENA	20	2003
WILDEST DREAMS IRON MAIDEN	6	2003
WILDLIFE (EP) GIRLSCHOOL	58	1982
WILDSIDE MARKY MARK & THE FUNKY BUNCH	42	1991
WILFRED THE WEASEL KEITH MICHELL	5	1980
WILL I EVER ALICE DEEJAY	7	2000
WILL I WHAT MIKE SARNE WITH BILLIE DAVIS	18	1962
WILL I? IAN VAN DAHL	5	2001
WILL SHE ALWAYS BE WAITING BLUEBELLS	72	1983
WILL THE WOLF SURVIVE LOS LOBOS	57	1985
WILL 2K WILL SMITH	2	1999
WILL WE BE LOVERS DEACON BLUE	31	1993
WILL YOU [A] HAZEL O'CONNOR	8	1981
WILL YOU [B] P.O.D.	68	2004
WILL YOU BE MY BABY INFINITI FEATURING GRAND PUBA	53	1996
WILL YOU BE THERE MICHAEL JACKSON	9	1993
WILL YOU BE THERE (IN THE MORNING) HEART	19	1993
WILL YOU BE WITH ME MARIA NAYLER	65	1998
WILL YOU LOVE ME TOMORROW SHIRELLES	4	1961
WILL YOU LOVE ME TOMORROW MELANIE	37	1974
WILL YOU LOVE ME TOMORROW BRYAN FERRY	23	1993
WILL YOU MARRY ME PAULA ABDUL	73	1992
WILL YOU SATISFY? CHERRELLE	57	1986
WILL YOU WAIT FOR ME KAVANA	29	1999
WILLIAM OTHERS	29	2005
WILLIAM, IT WAS REALLY NOTHING SMITHS	17	1984
WILLIE CAN ALMA COGAN WITH DESMOND LANE - PENNY WHISTLE	13	1956
WILLIE CAN BEVERLEY SISTERS	23	1956
WILLING TO FORGIVE ARETHA FRANKLIN	17	1994
WILLINGLY MALCOLM VAUGHAN	13	1959
WILLOW TREE IVY LEAGUE	50	1966
WILMOT SABRES OF PARADISE	36	1994
WIMMIN' ASHLEY HAMILTON	27	2003
WIMOWEH KARL DENVER	4	1962
(WIN PLACE OR SHOW) SHE'S A WINNER INTRUDERS	14	1974
WINCHESTER CATHEDRAL NEW VAUDEVILLE BAND	4	1966
THE WIND PJ HARVEY	29	1999
THE WIND BENEATH MY WINGS LEE GREENWOOD	49	1984
WIND BENEATH MY WINGS BETTE MIDLER	5	1989
WIND BENEATH MY WINGS BILL TARMEY	40	1994
WIND BENEATH MY WINGS STEVEN HOUGHTON	3	1997
THE WIND CRIES MARY JIMI HENDRIX EXPERIENCE	6	1967
WIND IT UP GWEN STEFANI	3	2006
WIND IT UP (REWOUND) PRODIGY	11	1993
WIND ME UP (LET ME GO) CLIFF RICHARD	2	1965
WIND OF CHANGE SCORPIONS	2	1991
WIND THE BOBBIN UP JO JINGLES	21	2004
A WINDMILL IN OLD AMSTERDAM RONNIE HILTON	23	1965
WINDMILLS OF YOUR MIND NOEL HARRISON	8	1969
WINDOW IN THE SKIES U2	4	2007
WINDOW PANE (EP) REAL PEOPLE	60	1991
WINDOW SHOPPER 50 CENT	11	2005
WINDOW SHOPPING R. DEAN TAYLOR	36	1974
WINDOWLICKER APHEX TWIN	16	1999
WINDOWS '98 SIL	58	1998
WINDPOWER THOMAS DOLBY	31	1982
THE WINDSOR WALTZ VERA LYNN	11	1953
WINDSWEPT BRYAN FERRY	46	1985
WINGDINGS SUGACOMA	57	2002
WINGS OF A BUTTERFLY H.I.M.	10	2005
WINGS OF A DOVE MADNESS	2	1983
WINGS OF LOVE BONE	55	1994
WINKER'S SONG (MISPRINT) IVOR BIGGUN & THE RED NOSE BURGLARS	22	1978
THE WINKLE MAN JUDGE DREAD	35	1976
THE WINNER [A] HEARTBEAT	70	1988
THE WINNER [B] COOLIO	53	1997
THE WINNER TAKES IT ALL ABBA	1	1980
WINNING DAYS VINES	42	2004
WINTER [A] LOVE & MONEY	52	1991
WINTER [B] TORI AMOS	25	1992
WINTER [C] SPECIAL NEEDS	69	2004
WINTER [D] DT8 PROJECT FEATURING ANDREA BRITTON	35	2005
WINTER [E] CORD	34	2006
WINTER CEREMONY (TOR-CHENEY-NAHANA) SACRED SPIRIT	45	1996
WINTER IN JULY BOMB THE BASS	7	1991
WINTER MELODY DONNA SUMMER	27	1977
WINTER SONG CHRIS REA	27	1991
A WINTER STORY ALED JONES	51	1986
WINTER WONDERLAND JOHNNY MATHIS	17	1958
WINTER WONDERLAND COCTEAU TWINS	58	1993
WINTER WORLD OF LOVE ENGELBERT HUMPERDINCK	7	1969
A WINTER'S TALE [A] DAVID ESSEX	2	1982
A WINTER'S TALE [B] QUEEN	6	1995
WIPE OUT SURFARIS	5	1963
WIPEOUT FAT BOYS & THE BEACH BOYS	2	1987
WIPE OUT ANIMAL	38	1994
WIPE THE NEEDLE RAGGA TWINS	71	1991
WIRED FOR SOUND CLIFF RICHARD	4	1981
WIRES ATHLETE	4	2005
THE WISDOM OF A FOOL RONNIE CARROLL	20	1957
WISDOM OF A FOOL NORMAN WISDOM	13	1957
WISE UP! SUCKER POP WILL EAT ITSELF	41	1989
WISEMEN JAMES BLUNT	23	2005
WISER TIME BLACK CROWES	34	1995
WISH SOUL II SOUL	24	1993
A WISH AWAY WONDER STUFF	43	1988
WISH I JEM	24	2005
WISH I COULD FLY ROXETTE	11	1999
WISH I DIDN'T MISS YOU ANGIE STONE	30	2002
WISH I HAD AN ANGEL NIGHTWISH	60	2004
WISH I WAS SKINNY BOO RADLEYS	75	1993
WISH I WERE YOU ALISHA'S ATTIC	29	1999
WISH THE WORLD AWAY AMERICAN MUSIC CLUB	46	1994
WISH YOU WERE HERE [A] EDDIE FISHER	8	1953
WISH YOU WERE HERE [B] FIRST LIGHT	71	1984
WISH YOU WERE HERE [C] ALOOF	43	1996
WISH YOU WERE HERE [D] WYCLEF JEAN	28	2001
WISH YOU WERE HERE [E] INCUBUS	27	2002
WISHES HUMAN NATURE	44	1997
WISHFUL THINKING CHINA CRISIS	9	1984
WISHIN' AND HOPIN' MERSEYBEATS	13	1964
WISHING BUDDY HOLLY	10	1963
WISHING I WAS HERE NATALIE IMBRUGLIA	19	1998

	Peak Position	Year of Entry
WISHING I WAS LUCKY WET WET WET	6	1987
WISHING (IF I HAD A PHOTOGRAPH OF YOU) A FLOCK OF SEAGULLS	10	1982
WISHING ON A STAR ROSE ROYCE	3	1978
WISHING ON A STAR FRESH 4 FEATURING LIZZ E	10	1989
WISHING ON A STAR COVER GIRLS	38	1992
WISHING ON A STAR 88.3 FEATURING LISA MAY	61	1995
WISHING ON A STAR JAY-Z FEATURING GWEN DICKEY	13	1998
WISHING ON A STAR PAUL WELLER	11	2004
WISHING WELL [A] FREE	7	1973
WISHING WELL [B] TERENCE TRENT D'ARBY	4	1987
THE WISHING WELL [C] G.O.S.H.	22	1988
WISHING YOU WERE HERE ALISON MOYET	72	1991
WISHING YOU WERE SOMEHOW HERE AGAIN SARAH BRIGHTMAN	7	1987
WISHLIST PEARL JAM	30	1998
THE WITCH RATTLES	8	1970
WITCH DOCTOR DAVID SEVILLE	11	1958
WITCH DOCTOR DON LANG & HIS FRANTIC FIVE	5	1958
WITCH DOCTOR CARTOONS	2	1999
THE WITCH QUEEN OF NEW ORLEANS REDBONE	2	1971
WITCHCRAFT FRANK SINATRA	12	1958
WITCHCRAFT ROBERT PALMER	50	1992
WITCHES' BREW JANIE JONES	46	1966
THE WITCH'S PROMISE JETHRO TULL	4	1970
WITH A GIRL LIKE YOU TROGGS	1	1966
WITH A LITTLE HELP FROM MY FRIENDS JOE BROWN	32	1967
WITH A LITTLE HELP FROM MY FRIENDS YOUNG IDEA	10	1967
WITH A LITTLE HELP FROM MY FRIENDS JOE COCKER	1	1968
WITH A LITTLE HELP FROM MY FRIENDS WET WET WET	1	1988
WITH A LITTLE HELP FROM MY FRIENDS SAM & MARK	1	2004
WITH A LITTLE LOVE SAM BROWN	44	1990
WITH A LITTLE LUCK WINGS	5	1978
WITH ALL MY HEART PETULA CLARK	4	1957
WITH ARMS WIDE OPEN CREED	13	2001
WITH EVERY BEAT OF MY HEART TAYLOR DAYNE	53	1989
WITH EVERY HEARTBEAT [A] FIVE STAR	49	1989
WITH EVERY HEARTBEAT [B] ROBYN WITH KLEERUP	1	2007
WITH GOD ON OUR SIDE NEVILLE BROTHERS	47	1989
WITH LOVE HILARY DUFF	29	2007
WITH ME DESTINY'S CHILD	19	1998
WITH MY OWN EYES SASH!	10	2000
WITH ONE LOOK BARBRA STREISAND	30	1993
WITH OR WITHOUT YOU U2	4	1987
WITH OR WITHOUT YOU MARY KIANI	46	1997
WITH PEN IN HAND VIKKI CARR	39	1969
WITH THE EYES OF A CHILD CLIFF RICHARD	20	1969
WITH THE WIND AND THE RAIN IN YOUR HAIR PAT BOONE	21	1959
WITH THESE HANDS SHIRLEY BASSEY	38	1960
WITH THESE HANDS TOM JONES	13	1965
WITH YOU [A] JESSICA SIMPSON	7	2004
WITH YOU [B] SUBWAYS	29	2005
WITH YOU [C] CHRIS BROWN	14	2008
WITH YOU I'M BORN AGAIN BILLY PRESTON & SYREETA	2	1980
WITH YOUR LOVE MALCOLM VAUGHAN	18	1956
WITHOUT A DOUBT BLACK SHEEP	60	1994
WITHOUT HER HERB ALPERT & THE TIJUANA BRASS	36	1969
WITHOUT LOVE [A] DONNA LEWIS	39	1997
WITHOUT LOVE [B] DINA CARROLL	13	1999
WITHOUT LOVE (THERE IS NOTHING) TOM JONES	10	1969
WITHOUT ME EMINEM	1	2002
WITHOUT YOU [A] MATT MONRO	37	1965
WITHOUT YOU [B] NILSSON	1	1972
WITHOUT YOU [B] MARIAH CAREY	1	1994
WITHOUT YOU [C] MOTLEY CRUE	39	1990
WITHOUT YOU [D] LUCY PEARL	51	2001
WITHOUT YOU [E] EL PRESIDENTE	30	2005
WITHOUT YOU (ONE AND ONE) LINDY LAYTON	71	1991
WITHOUT YOUR LOVE ROGER DALTREY	55	1980
WITNESS (1 HOPE) ROOTS MANUVA	45	2001
WITNESS (EP) ANN NESBY	42	1996
WITNESS FOR THE WORLD CRY BEFORE DAWN	67	1989
THE WIZARD PAUL HARDCASTLE	15	1986
WIZARDS OF THE SONIC WESTBAM	32	1995
WIZZY WOW BLACKstreet	37	2003
WOE IS ME HELEN SHAPIRO	35	1963
W.O.L.D. HARRY CHAPIN	34	1974
WOLF [A] SHY FX	60	2002
THE WOLF [B] DAVE CLARKE	66	2002
WOMAN [A] JOSE FERRER	7	1954
WOMAN [B] PETER & GORDON	28	1966
WOMAN [C] JOHN LENNON	1	1981
WOMAN [D] ANTI-NOWHERE LEAGUE	72	1982
WOMAN [E] NENEH CHERRY	9	1996
WOMAN [F] WOLFMOTHER	31	2006
WOMAN FROM LIBERIA JIMMIE RODGERS	18	1958
THE WOMAN I LOVE HOLLIES	42	1993
WOMAN IN CHAINS TEARS FOR FEARS	26	1989
WOMAN IN CHAINS TEARS FOR FEARS FEATURING OLETA ADAMS	57	1992
A WOMAN IN LOVE [A] FRANKIE LAINE	1	1956
WOMAN IN LOVE [A] FOUR ACES FEATURING AL ALBERTS	19	1956
WOMAN IN LOVE [A] RONNIE HILTON	30	1956
WOMAN IN LOVE [B] THREE DEGREES	3	1979
WOMAN IN LOVE [C] BARBRA STREISAND	1	1980
WOMAN IN LOVE [C] LIZ McCLARNON	5	2006
WOMAN IN LOVE [D] REBEKAH RYAN	64	1997
THE WOMAN IN ME [A] DONNA SUMMER	62	1983
THE WOMAN IN ME [B] KINANE	73	1996
WOMAN IN ME [C] CARLEEN ANDERSON	74	1998
WOMAN IN WINTER SKIDS	49	1980
WOMAN OF MINE DEAN FRIEDMAN	52	1978
WOMAN OF PRINCIPLE TROUBLE FUNK	65	1987
WOMAN TO WOMAN BEVERLEY CRAVEN	40	1991
WOMAN TROUBLE ARTFUL DODGER FEATURING ROBBIE CRAIG & CRAIG DAVID	6	2000
WOMAN WOMAN GARY PUCKETT AND THE UNION GAP	48	1968
WOMANKIND LITTLE ANGELS	12	1993
A WOMAN'S PLACE GILBERT O'SULLIVAN	42	1974
A WOMAN'S STORY MARC ALMOND & THE WILLING SINNERS	41	1986
WOMAN'S WORLD JAGS	75	1980
A WOMAN'S WORTH ALICIA KEYS	18	2002
WOMBLING MERRY CHRISTMAS WOMBLES	2	1974
THE WOMBLING SONG WOMBLES	4	1974
WOMBLING WHITE TIE AND TAILS WOMBLES	22	1975
WOMEN BEAT THEIR MEN JUNIOR CARTIER	70	1999
WOMEN IN UNIFORM SKYHOOKS	73	1979
WOMEN IN UNIFORM IRON MAIDEN	35	1980
WOMEN OF IRELAND MIKE OLDFIELD	70	1997
WON BETA BAND	30	2001
WONDER EMBRACE	14	2001
THE WONDER OF LOVE LOVELAND FEATURING RACHEL McFARLANE	53	1995
THE WONDER OF YOU RAY PETERSON	23	1959
THE WONDER OF YOU RONNIE HILTON	22	1959
THE WONDER OF YOU ELVIS PRESLEY	1	1970
WONDERBOY [A] KINKS	36	1968
WONDERBOY [B] TENACIOUS D	21	2002
WONDERFUL [A] MARI WILSON	47	1983
WONDERFUL [B] RUNRIG	29	1993
WONDERFUL [C] ADAM ANT	32	1995
WONDERFUL [D] EVERCLEAR	36	2000
WONDERFUL [E] BRIAN WILSON	29	2004
WONDERFUL [F] JA RULE FEATURING R KELLY & ASHANTI	1	2004
WONDERFUL CHRISTMASTIME PAUL McCARTNEY	6	1979
WONDERFUL COPENHAGEN DANNY KAYE	5	1953
WONDERFUL DREAM ANNE-MARIE DAVID	13	1973
WONDERFUL EXCUSE FAMILY CAT	48	1994
WONDERFUL LAND SHADOWS	1	1962
WONDERFUL LIFE BLACK	8	1986
WONDERFUL LIFE TJ DAVIS	42	2001
WONDERFUL LIFE TINA COUSINS	58	2005
WONDERFUL NIGHT FATBOY SLIM	51	2004
WONDERFUL SECRET LOVE ROBERT EARL	17	1959
WONDERFUL THINGS FRANKIE VAUGHAN	22	1958
A WONDERFUL TIME UP THERE PAT BOONE	2	1958
A WONDERFUL TIME UP THERE ALVIN STARDUST	56	1981
WONDERFUL TONIGHT DAMAGE	3	1997
WONDERFUL TONIGHT (LIVE) ERIC CLAPTON	30	1991
WONDERFUL WONDERFUL GARY MILLER	29	1957
WONDERFUL WONDERFUL RONNIE HILTON	27	1957
WONDERFUL WORLD [A] SAM COOKE	2	1960
WONDERFUL WORLD [A] HERMAN'S HERMITS	7	1965
WONDERFUL WORLD [B] WORLDS APART	51	1993
WONDERFUL WORLD [C] JAMES MORRISON	8	2006
WONDERFUL WORLD BEAUTIFUL PEOPLE JIMMY CLIFF	6	1969
WONDERFUL WORLD OF THE YOUNG DANNY WILLIAMS	8	1962
WONDERING DIRTY PRETTY THINGS	34	2006
WONDERING WHY MJ COLE	30	2003
WONDERLAND [A] COMMODORES	40	1980
WONDERLAND [B] BIG COUNTRY	8	1984
WONDERLAND [C] PAUL YOUNG	24	1986
WONDERLAND [D] 911	13	1999
WONDERLAND [E] THE PSYCHEDLIC WALTONS FEATURING ROISIN MURPHY	37	2002
WONDERMAN RIGHT SAID FRED	55	1994
WONDEROUS STORIES YES	7	1977
WONDERWALL MIKE FLOWERS POPS	2	1995
WONDERWALL OASIS	2	1995
WONDERWALL DE-CODE FEATURING BEVERLI SKEETE	69	1996
WONDERWALL RYAN ADAMS	27	2004
WONDROUS PLACE BILLY FURY	25	1960
WON'T GET FOOLED AGAIN WHO	9	1971
WON'T GIVE IN FINN BROTHERS	26	2004
WON'T GO HOME WITHOUT YOU MAROON 5	44	2007
WON'T LET THIS FEELING GO SUNDANCE	40	2000
WON'T SOMEBODY DANCE WITH ME LYNSEY DE PAUL	14	1973
WON'T STOP LOVING YOU A CERTAIN RATIO	55	1990
WON'T TAKE IT LYING DOWN HONEYZ	7	2000
WON'T TALK ABOUT IT NORMAN COOK FEATURING BILLY BRAGG	29	1989
WON'T TALK ABOUT IT BEATS INTERNATIONAL	9	1990
WON'T YOU HOLD MY HAND NOW KING	24	1985
WON'T YOU SAY CHRISTIAN FRY	48	1999
WOO HOO 5,6,7,8'S	28	2004
WOOD BEEZ (PRAY LIKE ARETHA FRANKLIN) SCRITTI POLITTI	10	1984
WOODEN HEART ELVIS PRESLEY	1	1961
WOODPECKERS FROM SPACE VIDEO KIDS	72	1985

		Peak Position	Year of Entry
WOODSTOCK	MATTHEWS' SOUTHERN COMFORT	1	1970
WOO-HAH!! GOT YOU ALL IN CHECK	BUSTA RHYMES	8	1996
WOOLY BULLY	SAM THE SHAM & THE PHARAOHS	11	1965
WOPBABALUBOP	FUNKDOOBIEST	37	1993
THE WORD	DOPE SMUGGLAZ	62	1998
THE WORD GIRL	SCRITTI POLITTI FEATURING RANKING ANN	6	1985
A WORD IN YOUR EAR	ALFIE	66	2002
THE WORD IS LOVE (SAY THE WORD)	VOICES OF LIFE	26	1998
WORD IS OUT	KYLIE MINOGUE	16	1991
WORD LOVE	RHIANNA	41	2002
WORD OF MOUTH	MIKE + THE MECHANICS	13	1991
WORD PERFECT	KRS ONE	70	1997
WORD UP	CAMEO	3	1986
WORD UP	GUN	8	1994
WORD UP	MELANIE G	14	1999
WORDS [A]	ALLISONS	34	1961
WORDS [B]	BEE GEES	8	1968
WORDS [B]	RITA COOLIDGE	25	1978
WORDS [B]	BOYZONE	1	1996
WORDS [C]	F.R. DAVID	2	1983
WORDS [D]	CHRISTIANS	18	1989
WORDS [E]	PAUL VAN DYK FEATURING TONI HALLIDAY	54	1997
WORDS ARE NOT ENOUGH	STEPS	5	2001
WORDS JUST GET IN THE WAY	RICHARD ASHCROFT	40	2006
WORDS OF LOVE	MAMAS & THE PAPAS	47	1967
WORDS THAT SAY	MEGA CITY FOUR	66	1991
WORDS WITH THE SHAMEN	DAVID SYLVIAN	72	1985
WORDY RAPPINGHOOD	TOM TOM CLUB	7	1981
WORDY RAPPINGHOOD	CHICKS ON SPEED	66	2004
WORK [A]	TECHNOTRONIC FEATURING REGGIE	40	1991
WORK [B]	BARRINGTON LEVY	65	1994
WORK [C]	JIMMY EAT WORLD	49	2005
WORK [D]	KELLY ROWLAND	4	2008
WORK ALL DAY	BARRY BIGGS	38	1976
WORK IT [A]	MISSY ELLIOTT	6	2002
WORK IT [B]	NELLY FEATURING JUSTIN TIMBERLAKE	7	2003
WORK IT OUT [A]	SHIVA	36	1995
WORK IT OUT [B]	DEF LEPPARD	22	1996
WORK IT OUT [C]	BEYONCÉ	7	2002
WORK IT TO THE BONE	LNR	64	1989
WORK IT UP	SLEAZE SISTERS	74	1998
WORK MI BODY	MONKEY MAFIA FEATURING PATRA	75	1996
W.O.R.K. (N.O. NAH NO NO MY DADDY DON'T)	BOW WOW WOW	62	1981
WORK REST AND PLAY (EP)	MADNESS	6	1980
WORK THAT BODY	DIANA ROSS	7	1982
WORK THAT MAGIC	DONNA SUMMER	74	1991
WORK THAT SUCKER TO DEATH	XAVIER	53	1982
WORK WORK WORK (PUB CLUB SLEEP)	RAKES	28	2005
WORKAHOLIC	2 UNLIMITED	4	1992
THE WORKER	FISCHER-Z	53	1979
WORKIN' FOR THE MAN	ROY ORBISON	50	1962
WORKIN' OVERTIME	DIANA ROSS	32	1989
WORKIN' UP A SWEAT	FULL CIRCLE	41	1987
WORKING FOR THE YANKEE DOLLAR	SKIDS	20	1979
WORKING IN A GOLDMINE	AZTEC CAMERA	31	1988
WORKING IN THE COALMINE	LEE DORSEY	8	1966
WORKING MAN	RITA MacNEIL	11	1990
WORKING MOTHER	MARTYN JOSEPH	65	1992
WORKING MY WAY BACK TO YOU	FOUR SEASONS WITH FRANKIE VALLI	50	1966
WORKING MY WAY BACK TO YOU - FORGIVE ME GIRL (MEDLEY)	DETROIT SPINNERS	1	1980
WORKING ON A BUILDING OF LOVE	CHAIRMEN OF THE BOARD	20	1972
WORKING ON IT	CHRIS REA	53	1989
WORKING WITH FIRE AND STEEL	CHINA CRISIS	48	1983
WORLD	BEE GEES	9	1967
THE WORLD	NICK HEYWARD	47	1995
WORLD AT YOUR FEET	EMBRACE	3	2006
WORLD CUP '98 - PAVANE	WIMBLEDON CHORAL SOCIETY	26	1998
WORLD DESTRUCTION	TIME ZONE	44	1985
WORLD FILLED WITH LOVE	CRAIG DAVID	15	2003
WORLD, HOLD ON (CHILDREN OF THE SKY)	BOB SINCLAR FEATURING STEVE EDWARDS	9	2006
WORLD IN MOTION	ENGLANDNEWORDER	1	1990
THE WORLD IN MY ARMS	NAT 'KING' COLE	36	1961
WORLD IN MY EYES	DEPECHE MODE	17	1990
THE WORLD IN MY HANDS	SNAP FEATURING SUMMER	44	1995
WORLD IN UNION	KIRI TE KANAWA	4	1991
WORLD IN UNION	SHIRLEY BASSEY/BRYN TERFEL	35	1999
WORLD IN UNION '95	LADYSMITH BLACK MAMBAZO FEATURING PJ POWERS	47	1995
WORLD IN YOUR HANDS	CULTURE BEAT	52	1994
THE WORLD IS A GHETTO	GETO BOYS FEATURING FLAJ	49	1996
THE WORLD IS FLAT	ECHOBELLY	31	1997
THE WORLD IS MINE [A]	MALCOLM VAUGHAN	29	1957
THE WORLD IS MINE [B]	ICE CUBE	60	1997
THE WORLD IS MINE [C]	DAVID GUETTA FEATURING JD DAVIS	49	2005
THE WORLD IS NOT ENOUGH	GARBAGE	11	1999
THE WORLD IS OUTSIDE	GHOSTS	35	2007
THE WORLD IS STONE	CYNDI LAUPER	15	1992
THE WORLD IS WHAT YOU MAKE IT	PAUL BRADY	67	1996
WORLD LOOKING IN	MORCHEEBA	48	2001
WORLD OF BROKEN HEARTS	AMEN CORNER	24	1967
WORLD OF GOOD	SAW DOCTORS	15	1996
A WORLD OF OUR OWN [A]	SEEKERS	3	1965
WORLD OF OUR OWN [B]	WESTLIFE	1	2002
WORLD ON FIRE	SARAH McLACHLAN	72	2004
THE WORLD OUTSIDE	FOUR ACES	18	1959
THE WORLD OUTSIDE	RONNIE HILTON WITH THE MICHAEL SAMMES SINGERS	18	1959
THE WORLD OUTSIDE	RUSS CONWAY	24	1959
WORLD OUTSIDE YOUR WINDOW	TANITA TIKARAM	58	1989
THE WORLD SHE KNOWS	DMAC	33	2002
WORLD SHUT YOUR MOUTH	JULIAN COPE	19	1986
WORLD (THE PRICE OF LOVE)	NEW ORDER	13	1993
THE WORLD TONIGHT	PAUL McCARTNEY	23	1997
THE WORLD WE KNEW	FRANK SINATRA	33	1967
A WORLD WITHOUT HEROES	KISS	55	1982
A WORLD WITHOUT LOVE	PETER & GORDON	1	1964
WORLD WITHOUT YOU	BELINDA CARLISLE	34	1988
WORLDS APART	CACTUS WORLD NEWS	58	1986
THE WORLD'S GREATEST	R KELLY	4	2002
WORLD'S ON FIRE	BREED 77	43	2004
WORRIED ABOUT RAY	HOOSIERS	5	2007
WORRY ABOUT IT LATER	FUTUREHEADS	52	2006
WORRY ABOUT THE WIND	HAL	53	2004
WORST COMES TO WORST	DILATED PEOPLES	29	2002
WORZEL SONG	JON PERTWEE	33	1980
WOT	CAPTAIN SENSIBLE	26	1982
WOT DO U CALL IT?	WILEY	31	2004
WOT'S IT TO YA	ROBBIE NEVIL	43	1987
WOULD	ALICE IN CHAINS	19	1993
WOULD I LIE TO YOU [A]	WHITESNAKE	37	1981
WOULD I LIE TO YOU? [B]	EURYTHMICS	17	1985
WOULD I LIE TO YOU [C]	CHARLES & EDDIE	1	1992
WOULD YOU BE HAPPIER	CORRS	14	2001
WOULD YOU...?	TOUCH & GO	3	1998
WOULDN'T CHANGE A THING [A]	KYLIE MINOGUE	2	1989
WOULDN'T CHANGE A THING [B]	HAVEN	57	2004
WOULDN'T IT BE GOOD	NIK KERSHAW	4	1984
WOULDN'T IT BE NICE	BEACH BOYS	58	1990
WOULDN'T YOU LOVE TO LOVE ME	TAJA SEVELLE	59	1988
WOW [A]	KATE BUSH	14	1979
WOW [B]	KYLIE MINOGUE	5	2007
WOW AND FLUTTER	STEREOLAB	70	1994
WOW WOW - NA NA	GRAND PLAZ	41	1990
WOZ NOT WOZ	ERIC PRYDZ & STEVE ANGELLO	55	2004
WRAP HER UP	ELTON JOHN	12	1985
WRAP ME UP	ALEX PARTY	17	1995
WRAP MY BODY TIGHT	JOHNNY GILL	57	1991
WRAP MY WORDS AROUND YOU	DANIEL BEDINGFIELD	12	2005
WRAP YOUR ARMS AROUND ME	AGNETHA FALTSKOG	44	1983
WRAPPED AROUND HER	JOAN ARMATRADING	56	1992
WRAPPED AROUND YOUR FINGER	POLICE	7	1983
WRAPPING PAPER	CREAM	34	1966
WRATH CHILD	IRON MAIDEN	31	1981
WRATH OF KANE	BIG DADDY KANE	52	1989
THE WRECK OF THE EDMUND FITZGERALD	GORDON LIGHTFOOT	40	1977
WRECK OF THE ANTOINETTE	DAVE DEE, DOZY, BEAKY, MICK & TICH	14	1968
THE WRECKONING	BOOMKAT	37	2003
WRECKX SHOP	WRECKX-N-EFFECT FEATURING APACHE INDIAN	26	1994
WRENCH	ALMIGHTY	26	1994
WRESTLEMANIA	WWF SUPERSTARS	14	1993
WRITER'S BLOCK	JUST JACK	74	2007
WRITING ON THE WALL	TOMMY STEELE	30	1961
WRITING TO REACH YOU	TRAVIS	14	1999
WRITTEN IN THE STARS	ELTON JOHN & LeANN RIMES	10	1999
WRITTEN ON THE WIND	ROGER DALTREY	46	1977
WRONG	EVERYTHING BUT THE GIRL	8	1996
WRONG IMPRESSION	NATALIE IMBRUGLIA	10	2002
WRONG NUMBER	CURE	62	1997
WRONG OR RIGHT	SABRE FEATURING PREZIDENT BROWN	71	1995
WUNDERBAR	TEN POLE TUDOR	34	1981
WUTHERING HEIGHTS	KATE BUSH	1	1978

X

		Peak Position	Year of Entry
X [A]	XZIBIT FEATURING SNOOP DOGG	14	2001
X [B]	WARRIOR	64	2003
X [C]	LIBERTY X	47	2006
THE X FILES	MARK SNOW	2	1996
X GON GIVE IT TO YA	DMX	6	2003
X-RATED	DJ NATION	52	2004
X RAY FOLLOW ME	SPACE FROG	70	2002
X Y & ZEE	POP WILL EAT ITSELF	15	1991
XANADU	OLIVIA NEWTON-JOHN & ELECTRIC LIGHT ORCHESTRA	1	1980
X-FILES	DJ DADO	8	1996
XMAS PARTY	SNOWMEN	44	1982
X-MAS TIME	DJ OTZI	51	2001
XPAND YA MIND (EXPANSIONS)	WAG YA TAIL	49	1992
XPRESS YOURSELF	FAMILY FOUNDATION	42	1992
X-RAY	SUB FOCUS	60	2005
XX SEX	WE'VE GOT A FUZZBOX & WE'RE GONNA USE IT	41	1986

Y–Z

KEY TO INDEX ENTRIES

Song Title — Artist/Group — Peak Position — Year of Entry

Note	Entry	Peak Position	Year of Entry
	ALL I REALLY WANT ALANIS MORISSETTE	59	1996
	ALL I REALLY WANT TO DO BYRDS	4	1965
	ALL I REALLY WANT TO DO CHER	9	1965
	ALL I SEE IS YOU DUSTY SPRINGFIELD	9	1966
	ALL I THINK ABOUT IS YOU NILSSON	43	1977
Same letter denotes different versions of the same song	ALL I WANNA DO [A] SHERYL CROW	4	1994
	ALL I WANNA DO [A] JOANNE FARRELL	40	1995
	ALL I WANNA DO [A] AMY STUDT	21	2004
Different letters denote different songs with the same name	ALL I WANNA DO [B] TIN TIN OUT	31	1997
	ALL I WANNA DO [C] DANNII	4	1997
	ALL I WANNA DO IS MAKE LOVE TO YOU HEART	37	1993

	Peak Position	Year of Entry
Y CONTROL YEAH YEAH YEAH	29	2004
Y (HOW DEEP IS YOUR LOVE) DJ SCOT PROJECT	57	1998
Y VIVA ESPANA SYLVIA	4	1974
Y VIVA SUSPENDERS JUDGE DREAD	27	1976
YA DON'T SEE THE SIGNS MARK B & BLADE	23	2001
YA MAMA FATBOY SLIM	30	2001
YA PLAYIN YASELF JERU THE DAMAJA	67	1996
YA YA TWIST PETULA CLARK	14	1962
YAAH D-SHAKE	20	1990
YABBA DABBA DOO DARKMAN	37	1994
YAH MO B THERE JAMES INGRAM WITH MICHAEL McDONALD	12	1984
YAKETY YAK COASTERS	12	1958
YEAH [A] AUDIOWEB	73	1996
YEAH [B] WANNADIES	56	2000
YEAH [C] USHER FEATURING LIL' JON & LUDACRIS	1	2004
YEAH! BUDDY ROYAL HOUSE	35	1989
YEAH YEAH BODYROX FEATURING LUCIANA	2	2006
THE YEAH YEAH YEAH SONG FLAMING LIPS	16	2006
YEAH YEAH YEAH YEAH YEAH [A] POGUES	43	1988
YEAH YEAH YEAH YEAH YEAH [B] WEDDING PRESENT	51	1994
YEAR OF DECISION THREE DEGREES	13	1974
YEAR OF THE CAT AL STEWART	31	1977
YEAR OF THE RAT BADLY DRAWN BOY	38	2004
YEAR 3000 BUSTED	2	2003
YEARNING FOR YOUR LOVE GAP BAND	47	1981
YEARS FROM NOW DR HOOK	47	1980
YEARS GO BY STAN CAMPBELL	65	1987
YEARS LATER CACTUS WORLD NEWS	59	1986
YEARS MAY COME, YEARS MAY GO HERMAN'S HERMITS	7	1970
YEBO ART OF NOISE	63	1989
YEH YEH GEORGIE FAME & THE BLUE FLAMES	1	1964
YEH YEH MATT BIANCO	13	1985
YEH YEH YEH MELANIE C	27	2003
YEHA-NOHA (WISHES OF HAPPINESS AND PROSPERITY) SACRED SPIRIT	37	1995
YEKE YEKE MORY KANTE	25	1988
YELLOW COLDPLAY	4	2000
YELLOW PEARL PHILIP LYNOTT	14	1981
YELLOW RIVER CHRISTIE	1	1970
YELLOW ROSE OF TEXAS GARY MILLER	13	1955
YELLOW ROSE OF TEXAS MITCH MILLER	2	1955
YELLOW ROSE OF TEXAS RONNIE HILTON	15	1955
YELLOW SUBMARINE BEATLES	1	1966
YEOVIL TRUE YEOVIL TOWN FC	36	2004
YEP DUANE EDDY & THE REBELS	17	1959
YER OLD REEF	21	1997
YES [A] MERRY CLAYTON	70	1988
YES [B] McALMONT & BUTLER	8	1995
YES I DO SHAKIN' STEVENS	60	1990
YES I WILL HOLLIES	9	1965
YES MY DARLING DAUGHTER EYDIE GORME	10	1962
YES SIR I CAN BOOGIE BACCARA	1	1977
YES TONIGHT JOSEPHINE JOHNNIE RAY	1	1957
YES TONIGHT JOSEPHINE JETS	25	1981
YESTERDAY MARIANNE FAITHFULL	36	1965
YESTERDAY MATT MONRO	8	1965
YESTERDAY RAY CHARLES	44	1967
YESTERDAY BEATLES	8	1976
YESTERDAY WET WET WET	4	1997
YESTERDAY HAS GONE CUPID'S INSPIRATION	4	1968
YESTERDAY HAS GONE PJ PROBY & MARC ALMOND FEATURING THE MY LIFE STORY ORCHESTRA	58	1996
YESTERDAY MAN CHRIS ANDREWS	3	1965
YESTERDAY ONCE MORE CARPENTERS	2	1973
YESTERDAY ONCE MORE REDD KROSS	45	1994
YESTERDAY TODAY OCEAN COLOUR SCENE	49	1991
YESTERDAY WENT TOO SOON FEEDER	20	1999
YESTERDAY WHEN I WAS MAD PET SHOP BOYS	13	1994
YESTERDAYS GUNS N' ROSES	8	1992
YESTERDAY'S DREAMS FOUR TOPS	23	1968
YESTERDAY'S GONE CHAD STUART & JEREMY CLYDE	37	1963
YESTERDAY'S MEN MADNESS	18	1985
YESTER-ME YESTER-YOU YESTERDAY STEVIE WONDER	2	1969
YET ANOTHER DAY ARMIN VAN BUUREN FEATURING RAY WILSON	70	2003
YIM JEZ & CHOOPIE	36	1998
YING TONG SONG GOONS	3	1956
YIPPIE I OH BARNDANCE BOYS	32	2003
Y.M.C.A. VILLAGE PEOPLE	1	1978
YO! (EXCUSE ME MISS) CHRIS BROWN	13	2006
YO! SWEETNESS MC HAMMER	16	1991
YO YO GET FUNKY DJ 'FAST' EDDIE	54	1989
THE YODELLING SONG FRANK IFIELD FEATURING THE BACKROOM BOYS	40	1991
YOSHIMI BATTLES THE PINK ROBOTS PART 1 FLAMING LIPS	18	2003
YOU [A] BANDWAGON	34	1969
YOU [B] GEORGE HARRISON	38	1975
YOU [C] RANDY EDELMAN	49	1977
YOU [D] TEN SHARP	1	1992
YOU [E] BONNIE RAITT	31	1994
YOU [F] STAXX FEATURING CAROL LEEMING	50	1995
YOU [G] POINT BREAK	14	2000
YOU [H] S CLUB 7	2	2002
YOU [I] SHAZNAY LEWIS	56	2004
YOU [J] THEE UNSTRUNG	59	2004
YOU [K] LLOYD FEATURING LIL WAYNE	45	2007
YOU (EP) FIVE THIRTY	72	1991
YOU AIN'T GOIN' NOWHERE BYRDS	45	1968
YOU AIN'T LIVIN' TILL YOU'RE LOVIN' MARVIN GAYE & TAMMI TERRELL	21	1969
YOU AIN'T REALLY DOWN STATUS IV	56	1983
YOU AIN'T SEEN NOTHIN' YET BACHMAN-TURNER OVERDRIVE	2	1974
YOU AIN'T SEEN NOTHIN' YET BUS STOP FEATURING RANDY BACHMAN	22	1998
YOU ALL DAT BAHA MEN: GUEST VOCAL IMANI COPPOLA	14	2001
YOU ALWAYS HURT THE ONE YOU LOVE CONNIE FRANCIS	13	1958
YOU ALWAYS HURT THE ONE YOU LOVE CLARENCE 'FROGMAN' HENRY	6	1961
YOU AND I [A] RICK JAMES	46	1978
YOU AND I [B] WILL YOUNG	2	2002
YOU & I [C] GRAHAM COXON	39	2006
YOU AND I WILL NEVER SEE THINGS EYE TO EYE KINGMAKER	33	1995
YOU AND ME [A] LINER	44	1979
YOU AND ME [B] DJ SEDUCTION	26	1992
YOU AND ME [C] LISA B	39	1994
YOU AND ME [D] EASYWORLD	57	2002
YOU AND ME [E] UNITING NATIONS	15	2005
YOU AND ME [F] ONE NIGHT ONLY	46	2007
YOU & ME SONG WANNADIES	18	1996
YOU AND ME TONIGHT [A] AURRA	12	1986
YOU AND ME (TONIGHT) [B] ALISTAIR GRIFFIN	18	2004
YOU AND YOUR HEART SO BLUE BUCKS FIZZ	43	1985
YOU ANGEL YOU MANFRED MANN'S EARTH BAND	54	1979
YOU ARE LIONEL RICHIE	43	1983
YOU ARE ALIVE FRAGMA	4	2001
YOU ARE AWFUL DICK EMERY	43	1973
YOU ARE BEAUTIFUL JOHNNY MATHIS	38	1960
YOU ARE EVERYTHING PEARLS	41	1973
YOU ARE EVERYTHING DIANA ROSS & MARVIN GAYE	5	1974
YOU ARE EVERYTHING MELANIE WILLIAMS & JOE ROBERTS	28	1995
YOU ARE IN MY SYSTEM ROBERT PALMER	53	1983
YOU ARE MY DESTINY PAUL ANKA	6	1958
YOU ARE MY FIRST LOVE RUBY MURRAY	16	1956
YOU ARE MY HIGH DEMON VS HEARTBREAKER	70	2001
YOU ARE MY LADY FREDDIE JACKSON	49	1985
YOU ARE MY LOVE LIVERPOOL EXPRESS	11	1976
YOU ARE MY MELODY CHANGE	48	1984
YOU ARE MY SISTER ANTONY & THE JOHNSONS	39	2005
YOU ARE MY WORLD COMMUNARDS	21	1985
YOU ARE NOT ALONE MICHAEL JACKSON	1	1995
YOU ARE SOMEBODY FULL INTENTION	75	1998
YOU ARE THE GENERATION THAT BOUGHT MORE SHOES AND YOU GET WHAT YOU DESERVE JOHNNY BOY	50	2004
YOU ARE THE MUSIC IN ME CAST OF HIGH SCHOOL MUSICAL 2	26	2007
YOU ARE THE ONE A-HA	13	1988
YOU ARE THE SUNSHINE OF MY LIFE STEVIE WONDER	7	1973
YOU ARE THE UNIVERSE BRAND NEW HEAVIES	21	1997
YOU ARE THE WAY PRIMITIVES	58	1991
YOU ARE THE WEAKEST LINK ECHOBASS	53	2001
YOU BE ILLIN' RUN D.M.C.	42	1987
YOU BELONG IN ROCK 'N' ROLL TIN MACHINE	33	1991
YOU BELONG TO ME [A] JO STAFFORD	1	1952
YOU BELONG TO ME [B] GARY GLITTER	40	1976
YOU BELONG TO ME [C] JX	17	1995
YOU BELONG TO ME [D] MICHAEL MOOG	62	2001
YOU BET YOUR LOVE HERBIE HANCOCK	18	1979
YOU BETTER MOUNT RUSHMORE PRESENTS THE KNACK	53	1999
YOU BETTER COME HOME PETULA CLARK	44	1965
YOU BETTER NOT WASTE MY TIME N-DUBZ	26	2007
YOU BETTER YOU BET WHO	9	1981
YOU BLOW ME AWAY ROBERT PALMER	38	1994
YOU BRING ME DOWN BLOOD RED SHOES	64	2008
YOU BRING ME JOY [A] MEECHIE	74	1995
YOU BRING ME JOY [B] RHYTHM FACTOR	53	1995
YOU BRING ME UP K-CI & JOJO	21	1997
YOU BRING ON THE SUN LONDONBEAT	32	1992
YOU BROKE MY HEART LOVE BITES	13	2005
YOU CAME KIM WILDE	3	1988
YOU CAME YOU SAW YOU CONQUERED PEARLS	32	1972
YOU CAN CALL ME AL PAUL SIMON	4	1986
YOU CAN COUNT ON ME JAKI GRAHAM	62	1995
YOU CAN DANCE (IF YOU WANT TO) GO GO LORENZO & THE DAVIS PINCKNEY PROJECT	46	1986
YOU CAN DO IT [A] AL HUDSON & THE PARTNERS	15	1979
YOU CAN DO IT [B] ICE CUBE FEATURING MACK 10 & MS TOI	2	2004
YOU CAN DO MAGIC [A] LIMMIE & THE FAMILY COOKIN'	3	1973
YOU CAN DO MAGIC [B] AMERICA	59	1982
YOU CAN GET IT MAXX	21	1994
YOU CAN GET IT IF YOU REALLY WANT DESMOND DEKKER	2	1970
YOU CAN GO YOUR OWN WAY CHRIS REA	28	1994
YOU CAN HAVE HIM DIONNE WARWICK	37	1965
YOU CAN HAVE IT ALL [A] GEORGE McCRAE	23	1975
YOU CAN HAVE IT ALL [B] EVE GALLAGHER	43	1995
YOU CAN HAVE IT (TAKE MY HEART) ROBERT PALMER	66	1983
YOU CAN LEAVE ME NOW HOTHOUSE FLOWERS	65	1998

	Peak Position	Year of Entry
YOU CAN MAKE ME DANCE SING OR ANYTHING (EVEN TAKE THE DOG FOR A WALK, MEND A FUSE, FOLD AWAY THE IRONING BOARD, OR ANY OTHER DOMESTIC SHORTCOMINGS) ROD STEWART & THE FACES	12	1974
YOU CAN NEVER STOP ME LOVING YOU KENNY LYNCH	10	1963
YOU CAN TALK TO ME SEAHORSES	15	1997
YOU CAN WIN IF YOU WANT MODERN TALKING	70	1985
YOU CAN'T BE TRUE TO TWO DAVE KING FEATURING THE KEYNOTES	11	1956
YOU CAN'T BLAME LOVE THOMAS & TAYLOR	53	1986
YOU CAN'T CHANGE ME ROGER SANCHEZ FEATURING ARMAND VAN HELDEN AND N'DEA DAVENPORT	25	2001
YOU CAN'T FOOL ME DENNIS MYSTERY JETS	41	2005
YOU CAN'T GO HOME AGAIN DJ SHADOW	30	2002
YOU CAN'T HAVE IT ALL ASH	16	2007
YOU CAN'T HIDE (YOUR LOVE FROM ME) DAVID JOSEPH	13	1983
YOU CAN'T HURRY LOVE [A] SUPREMES	3	1966
YOU CAN'T HURRY LOVE [A] PHIL COLLINS	1	1982
YOU CAN'T HURRY LOVE [B] CONCRETES	55	2004
YOU CAN'T RUN FROM LOVE MAXINE SINGLETON	57	1983
YOU CAN'T SIT DOWN PHIL UPCHURCH COMBO	39	1966
YOU CAN'T STEAL MY LOVE MANDO DIAO	73	2005
YOU CAN'T STOP ROCK 'N' ROLL TWISTED SISTER	43	1983
YOU CANT STOP THE BEAT (HAIRSPRAY) NIKKI BLONSKY, ZAC EFRON & AMANDA BYNES	71	2007
YOU CAN'T STOP THE REIGN SHAQUILLE O'NEAL	40	1997
YOU CAUGHT MY EYE JUDY BOUCHER	18	1987
YOU COME FROM EARTH LENA	69	1993
YOU COME THROUGH PJ HARVEY	41	2004
YOU COULD BE MINE GUNS N' ROSES	3	1991
YOU COULD BE MY EVERYTHING MIKEY GRAHAM	62	2001
YOU COULD HAVE BEEN A LADY HOT CHOCOLATE	22	1971
YOU COULD HAVE BEEN WITH ME SHEENA EASTON	54	1981
YOU DID CUT ME CHINA CRISIS	54	1985
YOU DIDN'T EXPECT THAT BILLY CRAWFORD	35	2003
YOU DISAPPEAR FROM VIEW TEARDROP EXPLODES	41	1983
YOU DO McALMONT & BUTLER	17	1995
YOU DO SOMETHING TO ME [A] PAUL WELLER	9	1995
YOU DO SOMETHING TO ME [B] DUM DUMS	27	2000
YOU DON'T BELIEVE ME STRAY CATS	57	1981
YOU DON'T BRING ME FLOWERS BARBRA (Streisand) & NEIL (Diamond)	5	1978
YOU DON'T CARE ABOUT US PLACEBO	5	1998
YOU DON'T FOOL ME - THE REMIXES QUEEN	17	1996
YOU DON'T HAVE TO BE A BABY TO CRY CARAVELLES	6	1963
YOU DON'T HAVE TO BE A STAR (TO BE IN MY SHOW) MARILYN McCOO & BILLY DAVIS Jr.	7	1977
YOU DON'T HAVE TO BE IN THE ARMY TO FIGHT IN THE WAR MUNGO JERRY	13	1971
YOU DON'T HAVE TO GO CHI-LITES	3	1976
YOU DON'T HAVE TO SAY YOU LOVE ME DUSTY SPRINGFIELD	1	1966
YOU DON'T HAVE TO SAY YOU LOVE ME ELVIS PRESLEY	9	1971
YOU DON'T HAVE TO SAY YOU LOVE ME GUYS & DOLLS	5	1976
YOU DON'T HAVE TO SAY YOU LOVE ME DENISE WELCH	23	1995
YOU DON'T HAVE TO WORRY MARY J BLIGE	36	1993
YOU DON'T KNOW [A] HELEN SHAPIRO	1	1961
YOU DON'T KNOW [B] BERLIN	39	1987
YOU DON'T KNOW [C] CYNDI LAUPER	27	1997
YOU DON'T KNOW [D] MASS SYNDICATE FEATURING SU SU BOBIEN	71	1998
YOU DON'T KNOW [E] 702	36	1999
YOU DON'T KNOW [F] 50 CENT	32	2007
(YOU DON'T KNOW) HOW GLAD I AM KIKI DEE BAND	33	1975
YOU DON'T KNOW ME [A] RAY CHARLES	9	1962
YOU DON'T KNOW ME [B] ARMAND VAN HELDEN FEATURING DUANE HARDEN	1	1999
YOU DON'T KNOW MY NAME ALICIA KEYS	19	2003
YOU DON'T KNOW NOTHIN' FOR REAL	54	1995
YOU DON'T KNOW (OH-OH-OH) SERIOUS INTENTION	75	1985
YOU DON'T KNOW WHAT LOVE IS WHITE STRIPES	18	2007
YOU DON'T KNOW WHAT YOU'VE GOT RAL DONNER	25	1961
YOU DON'T LOVE ME [A] GARY WALKER	26	1966
YOU DON'T LOVE ME [B] MARILYN	40	1984
YOU DON'T LOVE ME [C] JAGGED EDGE	66	1990
YOU DON'T LOVE ME [D] KOOKS	12	2006
YOU DON'T LOVE ME (NO NO NO) DAWN PENN	3	1994
YOU DON'T MISS YOUR WATER CRAIG DAVID	43	2004
YOU DON'T NEED A REASON PHIL FEARON & GALAXY	42	1985
YOU DON'T NEED SOMEONE NEW LOTUS EATERS	53	1983
YOU DON'T OWE ME A THING JOHNNIE RAY	12	1957
YOU DON'T UNDERSTAND HOUSE OF LOVE	46	1992
YOU DON'T UNDERSTAND ME ROXETTE	42	1996
YOU DREAMER BIG COUNTRY	68	1995
YOU DRIVE ME CRAZY [A] SHAKIN' STEVENS	2	1981
(YOU DRIVE ME) CRAZY [B] BRITNEY SPEARS	5	1999
YOU DRIVE ME CRAZY [B] SUGACOMA	57	2002
YOU DROVE ME TO IT HELL IS FOR HEROES	28	2002
YOU GAVE ME LOVE CROWN HEIGHTS AFFAIR	10	1980
YOU GAVE ME SOMEBODY TO LOVE MANFRED MANN	36	1966
YOU GET THE BEST FROM ME (SAY SAY SAY) ALICIA MYERS	58	1984
YOU GET WHAT YOU GIVE NEW RADICALS	5	1999
YOU GET WHAT YOU GIVE LMC FEATURING RACHEL McFARLANE	30	2006
YOU GIVE LOVE A BAD NAME BON JOVI	14	1986
YOU GIVE ME SOMETHING JAMIROQUAI	16	2001
YOU GIVE ME SOMETHING JAMES MORRISON	5	2006
YOU GO TO MY HEAD BRYAN FERRY	33	1975
YOU GONNA WANT ME TIGA	64	2005
YOU GOT IT ROY ORBISON	3	1989
YOU GOT IT (THE RIGHT STUFF) NEW KIDS ON THE BLOCK	1	1989
YOU GOT ME [A] CHRISTIAN FRY	45	1998
YOU GOT ME [B] ROOTS FEATURING ERYKAH BADU	31	1999
YOU GOT ME BURNING [A] LENNY WILLIAMS	67	1978
YOU GOT ME BURNING [B] PESHAY FEATURING CO-ORDINATE	41	2002
(YOU GOT ME) BURNING UP CEVIN FISHER FEATURING LOLEATTA HOLLOWAY	14	1999
YOU GOT ME ROCKING ROLLING STONES	23	1994
YOU GOT NOTHING ON ME GLITTERATI	36	2005
YOU GOT SOUL JOHNNY NASH	6	1969
YOU GOT THE FLOOR ARTHUR ADAMS	38	1981
YOU GOT THE LOVE [A] SOURCE FEATURING CANDI STATON	4	1991
YOU GOT THE LOVE [A] SOLITAIRE	63	2005
YOU GOT THE LOVE [B] T2 FEATURING ROBIN S	62	1997
YOU GOT THE POWER [A] WAR	58	1982
YOU GOT THE POWER [B] QFX	33	1996
YOU GOT THE STYLE ATHLETE	37	2002
YOU GOT TO BE THERE KADOC	45	1996
YOU GOT WHAT IT TAKES JOHNNY KIDD & THE PIRATES	25	1960
YOU GOT WHAT IT TAKES MARV JOHNSON	7	1960
YOU GOT WHAT IT TAKES DAVE CLARK FIVE	28	1967
YOU GOT WHAT IT TAKES SHOWADDYWADDY	2	1977
YOU GOTTA BE DES'REE	10	1994
YOU GOTTA BE A HUSTLER IF YOU WANNA GET ON SUE WILKINSON	25	1980
YOU GOTTA BELIEVE MARKY MARK & THE FUNKY BUNCH	54	1992
(YOU GOTTA) FIGHT FOR YOUR RIGHT TO PARTY BEASTIE BOYS	11	1987
YOU GOTTA HAVE LOVE IN YOUR HEART SUPREMES & THE FOUR TOPS	25	1971
YOU GOTTA LOVE SOMEONE ELTON JOHN	33	1990
YOU GOTTA STOP ELVIS PRESLEY	38	1967
(YOU GOTTA WALK) DON'T LOOK BACK PETE TOSH	43	1978
YOU HAD ME JOSS STONE	9	2004
YOU HAVE MARC ALMOND	57	1984
YOU HAVE BEEN LOVED GEORGE MICHAEL	2	1997
YOU HAVE KILLED ME MORRISSEY	3	2006
YOU HAVE PLACED A CHILL IN MY HEART EURYTHMICS	16	1988
YOU HAVEN'T DONE NOTHIN' STEVIE WONDER	30	1974
YOU HELD THE WORLD IN YOUR ARMS IDLEWILD	9	2002
YOU JUST MIGHT SEE ME CRY OUR KID	2	1976
YOU KEEP IT ALL IN BEAUTIFUL SOUTH	8	1989
YOU KEEP ME HANGIN' ON [A] SUPREMES	8	1966
YOU KEEP ME HANGIN' ON [A] VANILLA FUDGE	18	1967
YOU KEEP ME HANGIN' ON [A] KIM WILDE	2	1986
(YOU KEEP ME) HANGIN' ON [B] CLIFF RICHARD	13	1974
YOU KEEP ME HANGIN' ON - STOP IN THE NAME OF LOVE (MEDLEY) RONI HILL	36	1977
YOU KEEP RUNNING AWAY FOUR TOPS	26	1967
YOU KNOW HOW TO LOVE ME PHYLLIS HYMAN	47	1980
YOU KNOW HOW WE DO IT ICE CUBE	41	1994
YOU KNOW I LOVE YOU...DON'T YOU HOWARD JONES	43	1986
YOU KNOW I'M NO GOOD AMY WINEHOUSE	18	2007
YOU KNOW MY NAME CHRIS CORNELL	7	2006
YOU KNOW THAT I LOVE YOU DONELL JONES	41	2002
YOU KNOW WHAT I MEAN VERNONS GIRLS	16	1962
(YOU KNOW) YOU CAN DO IT CENTRAL LINE	67	1981
YOU KNOWS I LOVES YOU GOLDIE LOOKIN CHAIN	22	2005
YOU LAY SO EASY ON MY MIND ANDY WILLIAMS	32	1975
YOU LEARN ALANIS MORISSETTE	24	1996
YOU LET YOUR HEART GO TOO FAST SPIN DOCTORS	66	1994
YOU LIED TO ME CATHY DENNIS	34	1992
YOU LIFT ME UP REBEKAH RYAN	26	1996
YOU LIGHT MY FIRE SHEILA B. DEVOTION	44	1978
YOU LIGHT UP MY LIFE DEBBY BOONE	48	1977
YOU LIKE ME DON'T YOU JERMAINE JACKSON	41	1981
YOU LITTLE FOOL ELVIS COSTELLO	52	1982

	Peak Position	Year of Entry
YOU LITTLE THIEF FEARGAL SHARKEY	5	1986
YOU LITTLE TRUSTMAKER TYMES	18	1974
YOU LOOK SO FINE GARBAGE	19	1999
YOU LOVE US MANIC STREET PREACHERS	16	1991
YOU LOVE YOU SUBCIRCUS	61	1997
YOU MADE ME BELIEVE IN MAGIC BAY CITY ROLLERS	34	1977
YOU MADE ME LOVE YOU NAT 'KING' COLE	22	1959
YOU MADE ME THE THIEF OF YOUR HEART SINEAD O'CONNOR	42	1994
YOU MAKE IT HEAVEN TERRI WELLS	53	1983
YOU MAKE IT MOVE DAVE DEE, DOZY, BEAKY, MICK & TICH	26	1966
YOU MAKE LOVING FUN FLEETWOOD MAC	45	1977
YOU MAKE ME FEEL BRAND NEW STYLISTICS	2	1974
YOU MAKE ME FEEL BRAND NEW SIMPLY RED	7	2003
(YOU MAKE ME FEEL LIKE A) NATURAL WOMAN MARY J BLIGE	23	1995
YOU MAKE ME FEEL LIKE DANCING LEO SAYER	2	1976
YOU MAKE ME FEEL LIKE DANCING GROOVE GENERATION FEATURING LEO SAYER	32	1998
YOU MAKE ME FEEL (MIGHTY REAL) SYLVESTER	8	1978
YOU MAKE ME FEEL (MIGHTY REAL) JIMMY SOMERVILLE	5	1990
YOU MAKE ME FEEL MIGHTY REAL DREAM FREQUENCY	65	1994
YOU MAKE ME FEEL (MIGHTY REAL) BYRON STINGILY	13	1998
YOU MAKE ME GO OOH KRISTINE BLOND	35	2002
YOU MAKE ME SICK P!NK	9	2001
YOU MAKE ME WANNA... USHER	1	1998
YOU MAKE ME WANT TO SCREAM DANDYS	71	1998
YOU MAKE ME WORK CAMEO	74	1988
YOU MAKE NO BONES ALFIE	61	2001
YOU ME AND US ALMA COGAN	18	1957
YOU MEAN EVERYTHING TO ME NEIL SEDAKA	45	1960
YOU MEAN THE WORLD TO ME TONI BRAXTON	30	1994
YOU MIGHT NEED SOMEBODY RANDY CRAWFORD	11	1981
YOU MIGHT NEED SOMEBODY SHOLA AMA	4	1997
YOU MUST BE PREPARED TO DREAM IAN McNABB	54	1994
YOU MUST GO ON BERNARD BUTLER	44	1999
YOU MUST HAVE BEEN A BEAUTIFUL BABY BOBBY DARIN	10	1961
YOU MUST LOVE ME MADONNA	10	1996
YOU MY LOVE FRANK SINATRA	13	1955
YOU NEED HANDS MAX BYGRAVES	3	1958
YOU NEED LOVE LIKE I DO TOM JONES & HEATHER SMALL	24	2000
YOU NEED WHEELS MERTON PARKAS	40	1979
YOU NEEDED ME ANNE MURRAY	22	1979
YOU NEEDED ME BOYZONE	1	1999
YOU NEVER CAN TELL CHUCK BERRY	23	1964
YOU NEVER DONE IT LIKE THAT CAPTAIN & TENNILLE	63	1978
YOU NEVER KNOW MARLY	23	2004
YOU NEVER KNOW WHAT YOU'VE GOT ME & YOU FEATURING WE THE PEOPLE BAND	31	1979
YOU NEVER LOVE THE SAME WAY TWICE ROZALLA	16	1994
YOU ON MY MIND SWING OUT SISTER	28	1989
YOU ONLY LIVE TWICE NANCY SINATRA	11	1967
YOU ONLY TELL ME YOU LOVE ME WHEN YOU'RE DRUNK PET SHOP BOYS	8	2000
YOU ONLY YOU RITA PAVONE	21	1967
YOU OUGHTA KNOW ALANIS MORISSETTE	22	1995
YOU OWE IT ALL TO ME TEXAS	39	1993
YOU PLAYED YOURSELF ICE-T	64	1990
YOU + ME TECHNIQUE	56	1999
YOU + ME = LOVE UNDISPUTED TRUTH	43	1977
YOU PUT ME IN HEAVEN WITH YOUR TOUCH RHYTHM OF LIFE	24	2000
YOU RAISE ME UP DANIEL O'DONNELL	22	2003
YOU RAISE ME UP WESTLIFE	1	2005
YOU RAISE ME UP JOSH GROBAN	74	2007
YOU REALLY GOT ME KINKS	1	1964
YOU REMIND ME MARY J BLIGE	48	1993
YOU REMIND ME OF SOMETHING R KELLY	24	1995
YOU ROCK MY WORLD MICHAEL JACKSON	2	2001
YOU SAID NO BUSTED	1	2003
(YOU SAID) YOU'D GIMME SOME MORE KC & THE SUNSHINE BAND	41	1983
YOU SCARE ME TO DEATH MARC BOLAN & T REX	51	1981
YOU SEE THE TROUBLE WITH ME BARRY WHITE	2	1976
YOU SEE THE TROUBLE WITH ME BLACK LEGEND	1	2000
YOU SEND ME SAM COOKE	29	1958
YOU SEND ME ROD STEWART	7	1974
YOU SENT ME FLYING AMY WINEHOUSE	60	2004
YOU SEXY DANCER ROCKFORD FILES	34	1995
YOU SEXY SUGAR PLUM (BUT I LIKE IT) RODGER COLLINS	22	1976
YOU SEXY THING HOT CHOCOLATE	2	1975
YOU SEXY THING T-SHIRT	63	1997
YOU SHOOK ME ALL NIGHT LONG AC/DC	38	1980
YOU SHOULD BE... BLOCKSTER	3	1999
YOU SHOULD BE DANCING BEE GEES	5	1976
YOU SHOULD BE MINE BRIAN McKNIGHT FEATURING MASE	36	1998
YOU SHOULD HAVE KNOWN BETTER TC CURTIS	50	1985
YOU SHOULD READILY KNOW PIRATES FEATURING ENYA, SHOLA AMA, NAILA BOSS & ISHANI	8	2004
YOU SHOWED ME SALT-N-PEPA	15	1991
YOU SHOWED ME LIGHTNING SEEDS	8	1997
YOU SPIN ME ROUND (LIKE A RECORD) DEAD OR ALIVE	1	1985
YOU STILL TOUCH ME STING	27	1996
YOU STOLE THE SUN FROM MY HEART MANIC STREET PREACHERS	5	1999
YOU STOOD UP V	12	2004
YOU SURE LOOK GOOD TO ME PHYLLIS HYMAN	56	1981
YOU SURROUND ME ERASURE	15	1989
YOU TAKE ME AWAY REEL	31	2002
YOU TAKE ME UP THOMPSON TWINS	2	1984
YOU TAKE MY BREATH AWAY [A] SUREAL	15	2000
YOU TAKE MY BREATH AWAY [B] EVA CASSIDY	54	2003
YOU TAKE MY HEART AWAY DE ETTA LITTLE & NELSON PIGFORD	35	1977
YOU TALK BABYSHAMBLES	54	2007
YOU TALK TOO MUCH SULTANS OF PING FC	26	1993
YOU THINK YOU OWN ME HINDA HICKS	19	1998
YOU THINK YOU'RE A MAN DIVINE	16	1984
YOU TO ME ARE EVERYTHING REAL THING	1	1976
YOU TO ME ARE EVERYTHING SONIA	13	1991
YOU TO ME ARE EVERYTHING SEAN MAGUIRE	16	1995
YOU TOOK THE WORDS RIGHT OUT OF MY MOUTH MEAT LOAF	33	1978
YOU TRIP ME UP JESUS & MARY CHAIN	55	1985
YOU USED TO HOLD ME SCOTT & LEON	19	2000
YOU USED TO HOLD ME SO TIGHT THELMA HOUSTON	49	1984
YOU USED TO LOVE ME FAITH EVANS	42	1995
YOU USED TO SALSA RICHIE RICH FEATURING RALPHI ROSARIO	52	1991
YOU WANNA KNOW THUNDER	49	1999
YOU WANT IT YOU GOT IT DETROIT EMERALDS	12	1973
YOU WANT THIS JANET JACKSON	14	1994
(YOU WANT TO) MAKE A MEMORY BON JOVI	33	2007
YOU WEAR IT WELL [A] ROD STEWART	1	1972
YOU WEAR IT WELL [B] EL DeBARGE WITH DeBARGE	54	1985
YOU WERE ALWAYS THE ONE CRIBS	66	2004
(YOU WERE MADE FOR) ALL MY LOVE JACKIE WILSON	33	1960
YOU WERE MADE FOR ME FREDDIE & THE DREAMERS	3	1963
YOU WERE MEANT FOR ME JEWEL	32	1997
YOU WERE ON MY MIND CRISPIAN ST. PETERS	2	1966
YOU WERE RIGHT BADLY DRAWN BOY	9	2002
YOU WERE THE LAST LAUGH DANDY WARHOLS	34	2003
YOU WERE THERE HEINZ	26	1964
YOU WEREN'T IN LOVE WITH ME BILLY FIELD	67	1982
YOU WEREN'T THERE LENE MARLIN	59	2003
YOU WILL RISE SWEETBACK	64	1997
YOU WILL YOU WON'T ZUTONS	22	2004
YOU WIN AGAIN BEE GEES	1	1987
YOU WOKE UP MY NEIGHBOURHOOD BILLY BRAGG	54	1991
YOU WON'T BE LEAVING HERMAN'S HERMITS	20	1966
YOU WON'T FIND ANOTHER FOOL LIKE ME NEW SEEKERS	1	1973
YOU WON'T FORGET ABOUT ME DANNII MINOGUE VS FLOWER POWER	7	2004
YOU WON'T SEE ME CRY WILSON PHILLIPS	18	1992
YOU WOULDN'T KNOW LOVE CHER	55	1990
YOU YOU ROMEO SHIRLEY BASSEY	29	1957
YOU YOU YOU ALVIN STARDUST	6	1974
YOU'LL ALWAYS BE A FRIEND HOT CHOCOLATE	23	1972
YOU'LL ALWAYS FIND ME IN THE KITCHEN AT PARTIES JONA LEWIE	16	1980
YOU'LL ANSWER TO ME CLEO LAINE	5	1961
YOU'LL BE IN MY HEART PHIL COLLINS	17	1999
YOU'LL BE MINE (PARTY TIME) GLORIA ESTEFAN	18	1996
YOU'LL BE SORRY STEPS	4	2001
YOU'LL COME 'ROUND STATUS QUO	14	2004
YOU'LL NEVER BE ALONE ANASTACIA	31	2002
YOU'LL NEVER BE SO WRONG HOT CHOCOLATE	52	1981
YOU'LL NEVER FIND ANOTHER LOVE LIKE MINE LOU RAWLS	10	1976
YOU'LL NEVER GET TO HEAVEN DIONNE WARWICK	20	1964
YOU'LL NEVER GET TO HEAVEN EP STYLISTICS	24	1976
YOU'LL NEVER KNOW [A] SHIRLEY BASSEY	6	1961
YOU'LL NEVER KNOW [B] HI GLOSS	12	1981
YOU'LL NEVER KNOW WHAT YOU'RE MISSING REAL THING	16	1977
YOU'LL NEVER KNOW WHAT YOU'RE MISSING ('TIL YOU TRY) EMILE FORD & THE CHECKMATES	12	1960
YOU'LL NEVER NEVER KNOW PLATTERS	23	1957
YOU'LL NEVER STOP ME LOVING YOU SONIA	1	1989
YOU'LL NEVER WALK ALONE GERRY & THE PACEMAKERS	1	1963
YOU'LL NEVER WALK ALONE ELVIS PRESLEY	44	1968
YOU'LL NEVER WALK ALONE CROWD	1	1985
YOU'LL NEVER WALK ALONE ROBSON & JEROME	1	1996
YOU'LL NEVER WALK ALONE CARRERAS/DOMINGO/PAVAROTTI WITH MEHTA	35	1998
YOU'LL SEE MADONNA	5	1995
YOUNG AGAIN SHINING	52	2002
YOUNG AMERICANS DAVID BOWIE	18	1975

	Peak Position	Year of Entry
YOUNG AMERICANS TALKING DAVID VAN DAY	43	1983
YOUNG AND FOOLISH RONNIE HILTON	17	1955
YOUNG AND FOOLISH DEAN MARTIN	20	1956
YOUNG AND FOOLISH EDMUND HOCKRIDGE	10	1956
THE YOUNG AND THE HOPELESS GOOD CHARLOTTE	34	2003
YOUNG AT HEART [A] FRANK SINATRA	12	1954
YOUNG AT HEART [B] BLUEBELLS	1	1984
YOUNG BLOOD UFO	36	1980
YOUNG BOY PAUL McCARTNEY	19	1997
YOUNG DISCIPLES (EP) YOUNG DISCIPLES	48	1992
YOUNG EMOTIONS RICKY NELSON	48	1960
YOUNG FOLKS PETER BJORN & JOHN FEATURING VICTORIA BERGSMAN	13	2006
YOUNG, FREE AND SINGLE SUNFIRE	20	1983
YOUNG FREE AND SINGLE URBNRI	34	2008
YOUNG FRESH N' NEW KELIS	32	2001
YOUNG GIFTED AND BLACK BOB & MARCIA	5	1970
YOUNG GIRL UNION GAP FEATURING GARY PUCKETT	1	1968
YOUNG GIRL DARREN DAY	42	1994
YOUNG GIRL JOE LONGTHORNE	61	1994
YOUNG GIRLS & HAPPY ENDINGS GORKY'S ZYGOTIC MYNCI	49	1997
YOUNG GODS LITTLE ANGELS	34	1991
YOUNG GUNS (GO FOR IT) WHAM!	3	1982
YOUNG HEARTS KINGS OF TOMORROW	45	2002
YOUNG HEARTS KUJAY DADA	41	2003
YOUNG HEARTS RUN FREE CANDI STATON	2	1976
YOUNG HEARTS RUN FREE KYM MAZELLE	20	1997
YOUNG LIVERS ROCKET FROM THE CRYPT	67	1996
YOUNG LOVE [A] SONNY JAMES	11	1957
YOUNG LOVE [A] TAB HUNTER	1	1957
YOUNG LOVE [A] DONNY OSMOND	1	1973
YOUNG LOVE [B] MYSTERY JETS	34	2008
YOUNG LOVERS PAUL & PAULA	9	1963
THE YOUNG MC SUPERFUNK	62	2000
THE YOUNG NEW MEXICAN PUPPETEER TOM JONES	6	1972
THE YOUNG OFFENDER'S MUM CARTER-THE UNSTOPPABLE SEX MACHINE	34	1995
THE YOUNG ONES CLIFF RICHARD & THE SHADOWS	1	1962
YOUNG PARISIANS ADAM & THE ANTS	9	1981
YOUNG SOUL REBELS MICA PARIS	61	1991
YOUNG TURKS ROD STEWART	11	1981
YOUNG WORLD RICKY NELSON	19	1962
YOUNGER GIRL CRITTERS	38	1966
THE YOUNGEST WAS THE MOST LOVED MORRISSEY	14	2006
YOUR BABY AIN'T YOUR BABY ANYMORE PAUL DA VINCI	20	1974
YOUR BABY'S GONE SURFIN' DUANE EDDY & THE REBELETTES	49	1963
YOUR BODY [A] TOM NOVY FEATURING MICHAEL MARSHALL	10	2005
YOUR BODY [B] PRETTY RICKY	37	2006
YOUR BODY'S CALLIN' R KELLY	19	1994
YOUR CARESS (ALL I NEED) DJ FLAVOURS	19	1997
YOUR CASSETTE PET BOW WOW WOW	58	1980
YOUR CHEATING HEART RAY CHARLES	13	1962
YOUR CHRISTMAS WISH SMURFS	8	1996
YOUR DREAM ADRIAN GURVITZ	61	1982
YOUR DRESS JOHN FOXX	61	1983
YOUR EARS SHOULD BE BURNING NOW MARTI WEBB	61	1980
YOUR EYES [A] SIMPLY RED	26	2000
YOUR EYES [B] RIK ROK FEATURING SHAGGY	57	2004
YOUR FACE SLACKER	33	1997
YOUR FASCINATION GARY NUMAN	46	1985
YOUR FAVOURITE THING SUGAR	40	1994
YOUR GAME WILL YOUNG	3	2004
YOUR GENERATION GENERATION X	36	1977
YOUR GHOST KRISTIN HERSH	45	1994
YOUR HONOUR PLUTO	19	1982
YOUR HURTIN' KIND OF LOVE DUSTY SPRINGFIELD	37	1965
YOUR KISS IS SWEET SYREETA	12	1975
YOUR KISSES ARE CHARITY CULTURE CLUB	25	1999
YOUR KISSES ARE WASTED ON ME PIPETTES	35	2006
YOUR LATEST TRICK DIRE STRAITS	26	1986
YOUR LOSS MY GAIN OMAR	47	1992
YOUR LOVE [A] HIPSWAY	66	1989
YOUR LOVE [B] FRANKIE KNUCKLES	59	1989
YOUR LOVE [C] DIANA ROSS	14	1993
YOUR LOVE [D] INNER CITY	28	1996
YOUR LOVE ALONE IS NOT ENOUGH MANIC STREET PREACHERS	2	2007
YOUR LOVE GETS SWEETER FINLEY QUAYE	16	1998
(YOUR LOVE HAS LIFTED ME) HIGHER AND HIGHER RITA COOLIDGE	48	1977
YOUR LOVE IS A 187 WHITEHEAD BROTHERS	32	1995
YOUR LOVE IS CALLING EVOLUTION	60	1996
YOUR LOVE IS KING SADE	6	1984
YOUR LOVE IS LIFTING ME NOMAD	60	1992
(YOUR LOVE KEEPS LIFTING ME) HIGHER AND HIGHER JACKIE WILSON	11	1969
YOUR LOVE TAKES ME HIGHER BELOVED	39	1990
YOUR LOVING ARMS BILLIE RAY MARTIN	6	1994
YOUR LUCKY DAY IN HELL EELS	35	1997
YOUR MA SAID YOU CRIED IN YOUR SLEEP LAST NIGHT DOUG SHELDON	29	1962
YOUR MAGIC PUT A SPELL ON ME L.J. JOHNSON	27	1976
YOUR MAMA DON'T DANCE POISON	13	1989
YOUR MAMA WON'T LIKE ME SUZI QUATRO	31	1975
YOUR MIRROR SIMPLY RED	17	1992
YOUR MISSUS IS A NUTTER GOLDIE LOOKIN CHAIN	14	2005
YOUR MOTHER'S GOT A PENIS GOLDIE LOOKIN CHAIN	14	2004
YOUR MUSIC INTENSO PROJECT FEATURING LAURA JAYE	32	2003
YOUR NEW CUCKOO CARDIGANS	35	1997
YOUR OWN RELIGION ALFIE	61	2005
YOUR OWN SPECIAL WAY GENESIS	43	1977
YOUR PAINTED SMILE BRYAN FERRY	52	1994
YOUR PERSONAL TOUCH EVELYN KING	37	1985
YOUR PLACE OR MINE CHOCOLATE MONDAY	49	2005
YOUR SECRET LOVE LUTHER VANDROSS	14	1996
YOUR SMILE OCTOPUS	42	1996
YOUR SONG ELTON JOHN	7	1971
YOUR SONG BILLY PAUL	37	1977
YOUR SONG ROD STEWART	41	1992
YOUR SONG ELTON JOHN & ALESSANDRO SAFINA	4	2002
YOUR SWAYING ARMS DEACON BLUE	23	1991
YOUR TENDER LOOK JOE BROWN & THE BRUVVERS	31	1962
YOUR TIME HASN'T COME YET BABY ELVIS PRESLEY	22	1968
YOUR TIME IS GONNA COME DREAD ZEPPELIN	59	1990
YOUR TOWN DEACON BLUE	14	1992
YOUR WOMAN WHITE TOWN	1	1997
YOUR WOMAN TYLER JAMES	60	2005
YOU'RE A BETTER MAN THAN I SHAM 69	49	1979
YOU'RE A LADY PETER SKELLERN	3	1972
YOU'RE A STAR AQUARIAN DREAM	67	1979
YOU'RE A SUPERSTAR LOVE INC	7	2002
YOU'RE ALL I HAVE SNOW PATROL	7	2006
YOU'RE ALL I NEED MOTLEY CRUE	23	1988
YOU'RE ALL I NEED TO GET BY MARVIN GAYE & TAMMI TERRELL	19	1968
YOU'RE ALL I NEED TO GET BY JOHNNY MATHIS & DENIECE WILLIAMS	45	1978
YOU'RE ALL THAT MATTERS TO ME CURTIS STIGERS	6	1992
YOU'RE BEAUTIFUL JAMES BLUNT	1	2005
YOU'RE BREAKIN' MY HEART KEELY SMITH	14	1965
YOU'RE DRIVING ME CRAZY TEMPERANCE SEVEN	1	1961
YOU'RE EVERYTHING TO ME BORIS GARDINER	11	1986
(YOU'RE) FABULOUS BABE KENNY WILLIAMS	35	1977
YOU'RE FREE YOMANDA	22	2003
YOU'RE FREE TO GO JIM REEVES	48	1972
YOU'RE GONE MARILLION	7	2004
YOU'RE GONNA GET NEXT TO ME BO KIRKLAND & RUTH DAVIS	12	1977
YOU'RE GONNA LOSE US CRIBS	30	2005
YOU'RE GONNA MISS ME TURNTABLE ORCHESTRA	52	1989
YOU'RE GORGEOUS BABYBIRD	3	1996
(YOU'RE) HAVING MY BABY PAUL ANKA FEATURING ODIA COATES	6	1974
YOU'RE HISTORY SHAKESPEARS SISTER	7	1989
YOU'RE IN A BAD WAY SAINT ETIENNE	12	1993
YOU'RE IN LOVE WILSON PHILLIPS	29	1991
YOU'RE IN MY HEART [A] ROD STEWART	3	1977
YOU'RE IN MY HEART [B] DAVID ESSEX	59	1983
YOU'RE INVITED (BUT YOUR FRIEND CAN'T COME) VINCE NEIL	63	1992
YOU'RE LOOKING HOT TONIGHT BARRY MANILOW	47	1983
YOU'RE LYING LINX	15	1980
YOU'RE MAKIN ME HIGH TONI BRAXTON	7	1996
YOU'RE MORE THAN A NUMBER IN MY LITTLE RED BOOK DRIFTERS	5	1976
YOU'RE MOVING OUT TODAY CAROLE BAYER SAGER	6	1977
YOU'RE MY ANGEL MIKEY GRAHAM	13	2000
YOU'RE MY BEST FRIEND [A] QUEEN	7	1976
YOU'RE MY BEST FRIEND [B] DON WILLIAMS	35	1976
YOU'RE MY EVERYTHING [A] TEMPTATIONS	26	1967
YOU'RE MY EVERYTHING [B] MAX BYGRAVES	34	1969
YOU'RE MY EVERYTHING [C] LEE GARRETT	15	1976
YOU'RE MY EVERYTHING [C] EAST SIDE BEAT	65	1993
YOU'RE MY GIRL ROCKIN' BERRIES	40	1965
YOU'RE MY HEART, YOU'RE MY SOUL MODERN TALKING	56	1985
YOU'RE MY LAST CHANCE 52ND STREET	49	1986
YOU'RE MY LIFE BARRY BIGGS	36	1977
YOU'RE MY MATE RIGHT SAID FRED	18	2001
YOU'RE MY NUMBER ONE S CLUB 7	2	1999
(YOU'RE MY ONE AND ONLY) TRUE LOVE ANN-MARIE SMITH	46	1995
(YOU'RE MY) SOUL AND INSPIRATION RIGHTEOUS BROTHERS	15	1966
YOU'RE MY WORLD [A] CILLA BLACK	1	1964
YOU'RE MY WORLD [B] NICK HEYWARD	67	1988
YOU'RE NEVER TOO YOUNG COOLNOTES	42	1984
YOU'RE NO GOOD SWINGING BLUE JEANS	3	1964
YOU'RE NO GOOD ASWAD	35	1995
YOU'RE NOT ALONE ENEMY	18	2007
YOU'RE NOT ALONE [A] OLIVE	1	1997
YOU'RE NOT ALONE [B] EMBRACE	14	2000
YOU'RE NOT HERE TYRREL CORPORATION	42	1994
YOU'RE OK [A] OTTAWAN	56	1980
YOU'RE OK [B] k.d. lang	44	1996
YOU'RE ONE IMPERIAL TEEN	69	1996
(YOU'RE PUTTIN') A RUSH ON ME STEPHANIE MILLS	62	1987
YOU'RE READY NOW FRANKIE VALLI	11	1971
YOU'RE SHINING STYLES & BREEZE	19	2004
YOU'RE SINGING OUR LOVE SONG TO SOMEBODY ELSE JERRY WALLACE	46	1960

	Peak Position	Year of Entry
YOU'RE SIXTEEN JOHNNY BURNETTE	3	1961
YOU'RE SIXTEEN RINGO STARR	4	1974
YOU'RE SO PRETTY WE'RE SO PRETTY CHARLATANS	56	2006
YOU'RE SO RIGHT FOR ME [A] EASTSIDE CONNECTION	44	1978
YOU'RE SO RIGHT FOR ME [B] ROOSTER	14	2005
YOU'RE SO VAIN CARLY SIMON	3	1972
YOU'RE SPEAKING MY LANGUAGE JULIETTE & THE LICKS	35	2005
YOU'RE STILL THE ONE SHANIA TWAIN	10	1998
YOU'RE SUCH A GOOD LOOKING WOMAN JOE DOLAN	17	1970
(YOU'RE THE) DEVIL IN DISGUISE ELVIS PRESLEY	1	1963
YOU'RE THE FIRST THE LAST MY EVERYTHING BARRY WHITE	1	1974
YOU'RE THE FIRST THE LAST MY EVERYTHING HOWARD BROWN	13	2005
YOU'RE THE GREATEST LOVER JONATHAN KING	67	1979
YOU'RE THE INSPIRATION CHICAGO	14	1985
YOU'RE THE ONE [A] KATHY KIRBY	17	1964
YOU'RE THE ONE [B] PETULA CLARK	23	1965
YOU'RE THE ONE [C] BANG	74	1989
YOU'RE THE ONE [D] SWV	13	1996
YOU'RE THE ONE FOR ME D TRAIN	15	1982
YOU'RE THE ONE FOR ME - DAYBREAK - AM PAUL HARDCASTLE	41	1984
YOU'RE THE ONE FOR ME, FATTY MORRISSEY	19	1992
YOU'RE THE ONE I LOVE SHOLA AMA	3	1997
YOU'RE THE ONE THAT I WANT HYLDA BAKER & ARTHUR MULLARD	22	1978
YOU'RE THE ONE THAT I WANT JOHN TRAVOLTA & OLIVIA NEWTON-JOHN	1	1978
YOU'RE THE ONE THAT I WANT CRAIG McLACHLAN & DEBBIE GIBSON	13	1993
YOU'RE THE ONLY GOOD THING JIM REEVES	17	1961
YOU'RE THE ONLY ONE VAL DOONICAN	37	1968
YOU'RE THE REASON WAMDUE PROJECT	39	2000
YOU'RE THE REASON WHY RUBETTES	28	1976
YOU'RE THE STAR ROD STEWART	19	1995
YOU'RE THE STORM CARDIGANS	74	2003
YOU'RE THE STORY OF MY LIFE JUDY CHEEKS	30	1995
YOU'RE THE TOP CHA AL SAXON	17	1959
YOU'RE THE VOICE JOHN FARNHAM	6	1987
YOU'RE THE VOICE HEART	56	1991
YOU'RE THE WORLD TO ME DAVID GRAY	53	2007
YOU'RE WALKING ELECTRIBE 101	50	1990
YOURS DIONNE WARWICK	66	1983
YOURS FATALLY BIG BROVAZ	15	2004
YOURS UNTIL TOMORROW GENE PITNEY	34	1968
YOUTH AGAINST FASCISM SONIC YOUTH	52	1992
YOUTH GONE WILD SKID ROW	22	1989
YOUTH OF NATION ON FIRE BILL NELSON	73	1981
YOUTH OF THE NATION P.O.D.	36	2002
YOUTH OF TODAY MUSICAL YOUTH	13	1982
YOU'VE BEEN DOING ME WRONG DELEGATION	49	1977
YOU'VE BEEN GONE CROWN HEIGHTS AFFAIR	44	1980
YOU'VE COME BACK P.J. PROBY	25	1966
YOU'VE GIVEN ME SOMETHING THAT I CAN'T GIVE BACK NEW RHODES	38	2005
YOU'VE GOT A FRIEND JAMES TAYLOR	4	1971
YOU'VE GOT A FRIEND BIG FUN & SONIA FEATURING GARY BARNACLE	14	1990
YOU'VE GOT A FRIEND BRAND NEW HEAVIES	9	1997
YOU'VE GOT A FRIEND McFLY	1	2005
YOU'VE GOT A LOT TO ANSWER FOR CATATONIA	35	1996
YOU'VE GOT ANOTHER THING COMIN' JUDAS PRIEST	66	1982
YOU'VE GOT IT SIMPLY RED	46	1989
YOU'VE GOT IT BAD OCEAN COLOUR SCENE	7	1996
YOU'VE GOT LOVE BUDDY HOLLY & THE CRICKETS	40	1964
YOU'VE GOT ME DANGLING ON A STRING CHAIRMEN OF THE BOARD	5	1970
YOU'VE GOT ME THINKING BELOVED	23	1993
YOU'VE GOT MY NUMBER (WHY DON'T YOU USE IT) UNDERTONES	32	1979
YOU'VE GOT THAT SOMETHIN' ROBYN	54	1996
YOU'VE GOT TO CHOOSE DARLING BUDS	45	1989
YOU'VE GOT TO GIVE ME ROOM OLETA ADAMS	49	1991
YOU'VE GOT TO HIDE YOUR LOVE AWAY SILKIE	28	1965
YOU'VE GOT YOUR TROUBLES FORTUNES	2	1965
YOU'VE LOST THAT LOVIN' FEELIN' CILLA BLACK	2	1965
YOU'VE LOST THAT LOVIN' FEELIN' RIGHTEOUS BROTHERS	1	1965
YOU'VE LOST THAT LOVIN' FEELIN' TELLY SAVALAS	47	1975
YOU'VE LOST THAT LOVIN' FEELIN' DARYL HALL & JOHN OATES	55	1980
YOU'VE MADE ME SO VERY HAPPY BLOOD SWEAT & TEARS	35	1969
YOU'VE NEVER BEEN IN LOVE LIKE THIS BEFORE UNIT FOUR PLUS TWO	14	1965
YOU'VE NOT CHANGED SANDIE SHAW	18	1967
YOU'VE SAID ENOUGH CENTRAL LINE	58	1982
YOYO BOY ALBERTA	48	1998
YUM YUM (GIMME SOME) FATBACK BAND	40	1975
YUMMY YUMMY YUMMY OHIO EXPRESS	5	1968

Z

	Peak Position	Year of Entry
ZABADAK! DAVE DEE, DOZY, BEAKY, MICK & TICH	3	1967
ZAMBESI EDDIE CALVERT	13	1956
ZAMBESI LOU BUSCH	2	1956
ZAMBESI PIRANHAS FEATURING BORING BOB GROVER	17	1982
ZEPHYR ELECTRAFIXION	47	1994
THE ZEPHYR SONG RED HOT CHILI PEPPERS	11	2002
ZEROES AND ONES JESUS JONES	30	1993
ZEROTONINE JUNKIE XL	63	2000
ZEROX ADAM & THE ANTS	45	1981
ZEROXED ZERO ZERO	71	1991
ZIGGY STARDUST BAUHAUS	15	1982
ZING A LITTLE ZONG BING CROSBY & JANE WYMAN	10	1952
ZING WENT THE STRINGS OF MY HEART TRAMMPS	29	1974
ZION YOUTH DREADZONE	49	1995
ZIP GUN BOOGIE T REX	41	1974
ZIP - LOCK LIT	60	1999
ZIP-A-DEE-DOO-DAH BOB B SOXX & THE BLUE JEANS	45	1963
ZODIACS ROBERTA KELLY	44	1978
ZOE PAGANINI TRAXX	47	1997
ZOMBIE CRANBERRIES	14	1994
ZOMBIE A.D.A.M. FEATURING AMY	16	1995
THE ZOO SCORPIONS	75	1980
THE ZOO (THE HUMAN ZOO) COMMODORES	44	1974
ZOOM [A] COMMODORES	38	1978
ZOOM [B] FAT LARRY'S BAND	2	1982
ZOOM [B] SCOTT BRADLEY	61	1994
ZOOM [C] DR DRE & LL COOL J	15	1998
ZORBA'S DANCE MARCELLO MINERBI	6	1965
ZORBA'S DANCE LCD	20	1998
ZUNGA ZENG K7 & THE SWING KIDS	63	1994